HANDBOOK OF
BUSINESS ADMINISTRATION

HANDBOOK OF
BUSINESS ADMINISTRATION

H. B. MAYNARD *Editor-in-Chief*

President, Maynard Research Council Incorporated
Pittsburgh, Pennsylvania

McGRAW-HILL BOOK COMPANY

New York   St. Louis   San Francisco   Düsseldorf   Johannesburg
Kuala Lumpur   London   Mexico   Montreal   New Delhi
Panama   Rio de Janeiro   Singapore   Sydney   Toronto

HANDBOOK OF BUSINESS ADMINISTRATION

SECOND PRINTING, 1970

07-041090-9

678910112KPKP79876543

To Managers at all levels who, by striving continually to perfect their skill and competence in the practice of management, help to provide ever higher standards of living for the society which they serve.

CONTRIBUTORS

HERMAN A. AFFEL, JR. *President, Standard Computers, Inc., Philadelphia, Pennsylvania*

WILLIAM M. AIKEN *Vice President, H. B. Maynard and Company, Incorporated, Pittsburgh, Pennsylvania*

DR. R. S. ALEXANDER *Professor Emeritus, Columbia University, Hightstown, New Jersey*

DR. H. I. ANSOFF *Professor of Industrial Administration, Graduate School of Industrial Administration, Carnegie Institute of Technology, Pittsburgh, Pennsylvania*

WILLIAM ANTIS *Technical Director, Maynard Research Council, Inc., Pittsburgh, Pennsylvania*

ANDERSON ASHBURN *Editor,* American Machinist, *McGraw-Hill, Inc., New York, New York*

SAUL D. ASTOR *President, Management Safeguards, Inc., New York, New York*

J. P. BARGER *President, Dynatech Corporation, Cambridge, Massachusetts*

DR. LAWRENCE W. BASS *Consultant, formerly Vice President of Arthur D. Little, Inc., New York, New York*

JOHN STANLEY BAUMGARTNER *Center for Management Sciences, Los Angeles, California; Lecturer, R & D Management, Graduate School of Business, University of Southern California, Los Angeles, California*

MISS ESTHER R. BECKER *Editorial Director,* Management Information, *Elliott Service Company, Inc., Mount Vernon, New York*

DR. L. J. BENNINGER *Professor, College of Business Administration, University of Florida, Gainesville, Florida*

DR. CONRAD BERENSON *Associate Professor of Marketing, Graduate Division, Bernard M. Baruch School of Business and Public Administration, The City College, New York, New York; Executive Director, Research Foundation of the City University of New York, New York, New York*

GEORGE M. BETTERLEY *Partner, Betterley Associates, Worcester, Massachusetts*

OSCAR M. BEVERIDGE *Beveridge Organization, Inc., Chicago, Illinois*

MAURICE O. BEVERLEY *General Production Manager, Moore Business Forms, Inc., Niagara Falls, New York*

PROFESSOR HAROLD BIERMAN, JR. *Professor of Accounting and Managerial Economics, Graduate School of Business and Public Administration, Cornell University, Ithaca, New York*

LESTER R. BITTEL *Editor-in-Chief, Factory, McGraw-Hill, Inc., New York, New York*

WILLIAM H. BOKUM *Partner, Cresap, McCormick and Paget, New York, New York*

ROBERT W. BOSLER *Senior Consultant, H. B. Maynard and Company, Incorporated, Pittsburgh, Pennsylvania*

DR. HUGH M. BOWEN *Managing Scientist, Laboratory Director, Dunlap and Associates, Inc., Darien, Connecticut*

JAMES E. BOYCE *Associates for International Research, Inc., Cambridge, Massachusetts*

PHILIP BOYER *Philip Boyer Organization, Inc., New York, New York*

DR. R. G. BRANDENBURG *Assistant Dean and Assistant Professor of Industrial Administration, Graduate School of Industrial Administration, Carnegie Institute of Technology, Pittsburgh, Pennsylvania*

SIDNEY BRUNELL *Vice President, Smithcraft Corporation, Chelsea, Massachusetts*

VICTOR P. BUELL *Vice President, American Radiator & Standard Sanitary Corporation, New York, New York*

SAMUEL L. H. BURK *Boyden Associates, Inc., New York, New York*

C. A. CAMERON *Partner, Leahy—Cameron Associates, New York, New York*

GRAY L. CARPENTER *President, Gray L. Carpenter & Associates, Pocono Manor, Pennsylvania*

PHIL CARROLL *Professional Engineer, Maplewood, New Jersey*

GEORGE L. CHAMBERLIN *Controller, Scott Paper Company, Philadelphia, Pennsylvania*

WILLIAM GUY CHATER *Bronxville, New York*

EARLE A. CHILES *President, Fred Meyer, Inc., Portland, Oregon*

DR. KALMAN J. COHEN *Professor of Economics and Industrial Administration, Graduate School of Industrial Administration, Carnegie Institute of Technology, Pittsburgh, Pennsylvania*

RICHARD R. CONARROE *Conarroe Associates, Inc., New York, New York*

DR. ARNOLD CORBIN *Professor of Marketing, Graduate School of Business Administration, New York University, New York, New York*

PROFESSOR ROBERT N. CORLEY *Associate Professor of Business Law, Department of Industrial Administration, University of Illinois, Urbana, Illinois*

JOHN F. CROSBY *Principal Associate, Cresap, McCormick and Paget, New York, New York*

JOHN R. CROWLEY *Manager, Administrative Services, International Bank for Reconstruction and Development, Washington, D.C.*

FRANK M. CUSHMAN *Frank M. Cushman Associates, Sharon, Massachusetts*

DR. JOEL DEAN *President, Joel Dean Associates, Inc., New York, New York; Professor of Business Economics, Graduate School of Business, Columbia University, New York, New York*

DR. DONALD D. DEMING *Professor, School of Management, Rensselaer Polytechnic Institute, Troy, New York*

RUSSELL DeREAMER *International Business Machines Corporation, Armonk, New York*

HOWARD M. DIRKS *Vice President—Personnel, Harris-Intertype Corporation, Cleveland, Ohio*

RANDOLPH S. DRIVER *Manager of Industrial Relations, Atlantic Richfield Company, Philadelphia, Pennsylvania*

WALLACE H. EGBERT *Mead Johnson & Company, Evansville, Indiana*

DR. ERNEST J. ENRIGHT *Director of Research, International Marketing Institute, Cambridge, Massachusetts*

C. SPENCER EVERHARDT *Controller, Administrative Management Society, Willow Grove, Pennsylvania*

JOSEPH J. FAMULARO *Vice President, Personnel Relations, McGraw-Hill, Inc., New York, New York*

SAMUEL C. FARMER *President & Treasurer, Farmer Electrical Supply Division, Seaboard Electrical Supply Co., Inc., Hanover, New Jersey*

COLONEL DONALD E. FARR (deceased) *President, H. B. Maynard and Company, Incorporated, Pittsburgh, Pennsylvania*

MITCHELL FEIN *Professional Engineer, Hillsdale, New Jersey*

DR. J. S. FELTON *Professor of Occupational Health, School of Medicine, University of California, Los Angeles, California*

FRANK E. FISCHER *Cresap, McCormick and Paget, New York, New York*

RICHARD L. FORSTER *Vice President and Director of Planning, Frederic R. Harris, Inc., New York, New York*

ROY A. FOULKE *formerly Vice President and Director, Dun & Bradstreet, Inc., Bronxville, New York*

DUANE C. GEITGEY *Director of Training Program Development, Maynard Research Council, Inc., Pittsburgh, Pennsylvania*

DR. RICHARD S. GILLMER *Resident Manager, Humber, Mundie & McClary, Minneapolis, Minnesota*

HENRY GOLIGHTLY *President, International Management Services, Henry Golightly & Company, Inc., New York, New York*

THEODORE GOODMAN *Associate, Martin & Tucker, Little Neck, New York*

CHARLES H. GRANGER *Partner, William E. Hill & Company, Inc., New York, New York*

S. GEORGE GREENSPAN *Partner, Adler, Faunce & Leonard, New York, New York*

E. A. GRUNWALD *Editor-in-Chief, Purchasing Week, McGraw-Hill, Inc., New York, New York*

S. J. GUADAGNA *Secretary-Treasurer, Pandick Press, Inc., New York, New York*

DR. ROBERT H. GUEST *Professor of Organization and Administration, The Amos Tuck School of Business Administration, Dartmouth College, Hanover, New Hampshire*

HENRY J. GUMPEL *Price Waterhouse & Co., New York, New York*

JOHN W. HANNON *Executive Vice President, Maynard Research Council, Inc., Pittsburgh, Pennsylvania*

CARL HEYEL *Management Counsel, Manhasset, New York*

LEE H. HILL *President, Lee H. Hill Consultants, West Palm Beach, Florida; Chairman, Rogers, Slade and Hill, Inc., New York, New York*

WILLIAM E. HILL *Managing Partner, William E. Hill & Company, Inc., New York, New York*

ROBERT HILLE *Senior Operations Research Analyst, Management Services, Celanese Corporation of America, New York, New York*

WILLIAM K. HODSON *President, H. B. Maynard and Company, Incorporated, Pittsburgh, Pennsylvania*

D. C. HOOPER *Director, Marketing Customer Services, Westinghouse Electric Corporation, Pittsburgh, Pennsylvania*

FREDERICK W. HORNBRUCH, JR. *Vice President, Calumet & Hecla, Inc.; General Manager, Flexonics Division, Bartlett, Illinois*

JOHN HORST *Senior Consultant, International Management Services, Henry Golightly & Company, Inc., New York, New York*

DR. W. J. HUMBER *Partner, Humber, Mundie & McClary, Milwaukee, Wisconsin*

JOHN W. HUNT *Lecturer in Business Administration, University of New South Wales, Sydney, Australia*

J. J. JEHRING *Director, Center for the Study of Productivity Motivation, Graduate School of Business, University of Wisconsin, Madison, Wisconsin*

FRANK J. JOHNSON *Manager, Value Engineering Department, Lockheed-Georgia Company, Division of Lockheed Aircraft Corporation, Marietta, Georgia*

JAMES KAHN *President, Pension Planning Company, Inc., New York, New York*

SYLVAN L. KAPNER *Manager, Western Division, H. B. Maynard and Company, Incorporated, Los Angeles, California*

DR. JOHN C. R. KELLY, JR. *General Manager, Advanced Reactors Division, Westinghouse Electric Corporation, Pittsburgh, Pennsylvania*

JOHN P. KELSEY *Price Waterhouse & Co., Philadelphia, Pennsylvania*

DONALD KIRCHHOFFER *Manager, Wage and Salary Administration, Radio Corporation of America, Camden, New Jersey*

WALTER A. KLEINSCHROD *Editor,* Administrative Management; *Vice President and Editorial Director, Geyer—McAllister Publications, New York, New York*

FRANK M. KNOX *President, Frank M. Knox Company, Inc., New York, New York*

DR. HAROLD KOONTZ *Mead Johnson Professor of Management, Graduate School of Business Administration, University of California, Los Angeles, California*

WILLIAM V. KREWATCH *E. I. du Pont de Nemours & Company, Wilmington, Delaware*

ALBERT KUSHNER *Partner, Cresap, McCormick and Paget, New York, New York*

STEPHEN LANDEKICH *Editor,* Management Accounting, *National Association of Accountants, New York, New York*

EUGENE M. LANG *President, Resources and Facilities Corporation, New York, New York*

DR. THEOS A. LANGLIE *President, Langlie, Goodwillie & Moore, Inc., Stamford, Connecticut*

H. B. LAWSON *Principal, H. B. Maynard and Company, Incorporated, Charlotte, North Carolina*

BRUCE A. LENTZ *Chief Engineer, Century Furniture Company, Century Chair Company, Hickory, North Carolina*

ROBERT E. LEVINSON *Vice President and General Manager, The Steelcraft Manufacturing Company, Cincinnati, Ohio*

JOHN F. LEWIS *Controller, H. B. Maynard and Company, Incorporated, Pittsburgh, Pennsylvania*

LEONARD M. LEWIS *Director of Communications, Edward N. Hay & Associates, Philadelphia, Pennsylvania*

J. KEITH LOUDEN *Chairman of the Board, The Presidents Association; Vice President and Director, American Management Association, New York, New York*

DR. PAUL J. LOVEWELL *President, Management & Economics Research Incorporated, Palo Alto, California*

E. NOBLES LOWE *Vice President and General Counsel, West Virginia Pulp and Paper Company, New York, New York*

EDMUND J. McCORMICK *President, McCormick & Company, Yonkers, New York*

DR. WALTER R. MAHLER *President, Mahler Associates, Inc., Wyckoff, New Jersey*

SYLVESTER F. MAJESTIC *Vice President, Chemical Bank New York Trust Company, New York, New York*

WALTER P. MARGULIES *President, Lippincott & Margulies, Inc., New York, New York*

ALLEN D. MARSHALL *President and Chief Executive, United Student Aid Funds, Inc., New York, New York*

JOHN E. MARTIN *Arthur Andersen & Co., Chicago, Illinois*

EDWIN C. MEAD *Partner, Mead—Ross Associates, Hanover, New Hampshire*

H. DWIGHT MEADER *Manager, Business Effectiveness Consulting Service, General Electric Company, New York, New York*

L. I. MEDLOCK *Director of Reliability Control, General Dynamics, Convair Division, San Diego, California*

DR. FRANK MEISSNER *Marketing Manager, Latin American Group, W. R. Grace & Co., New York, New York*

WILLARD V. MERRIHUE *General Electric Company, New York, New York*

RICHARD J. MEYERS *General Sales Manager, Moore Business Forms, Inc., Niagara Falls, New York*

ROBERT W. MILLER *Vice President, United Research, Inc., Washington, D.C.*

FRANCIS S. MOLLOY *Vice President—Operations & Treasurer, United Medical Service, Inc., New York, New York*

DR. ROBERT G. MURDICK *Professor, State University of New York at Albany, Albany, New York*

RICHARD MUTHER *Executive Director, Richard Muther & Associates, Inc., Kansas City, Missouri*

ROBERT NEWCOMB *Partner, Newcomb & Sammons, Chicago, Illinois*

CHARLES H. NEWMAN *Independent Marketing Consultant, Chicago, Illinois*

LOUIS E. NEWMAN *President, Smithcraft Corporation, Chelsea, Massachusetts*

PROFESSOR BENJAMIN W. NIEBEL *Head, Department of Industrial Engineering, The Pennsylvania State University, University Park, Pennsylvania*

RICHARD M. PAGET *Senior Partner, Cresap, McCormick and Paget, New York, New York*

BERNARD T. PARKER *President, Tax Research Institute of America, Inc., New York, New York*

JAMES A. PARSONS *Management Science Services Group Leader, Lederle Laboratories, Division of American Cyanamid Company, Pearl River, New York*

ARTHUR W. PEARCE *Director of Public Relations, The Warner Brothers Company, Bridgeport, Connecticut*

ALVIN PEDERSON, CPA *Partner, Arthur Andersen & Co., Philadelphia, Pennsylvania*

GEORGE PETITPAS *Cresap, McCormick and Paget, New York, New York*

MELVIN POSIN *Manager, Industry Sales, Electronic Data Processing Division, Radio Corporation of America, Camden, New Jersey*

THOMAS J. PURCELL *Attorney, Pittsburgh, Pennsylvania*

HARRISON M. RAINIE, JR. *President, Stewart, Dougall & Associates, Inc., New York, New York*

DONALD RAPPAPORT *Price Waterhouse & Co., Philadelphia, Pennsylvania*

RICHARD J. REBELLINO *Supervisor, Employee Suggestion Plan, The Timken Roller Bearing Company, Canton, Ohio*

JOSEPH H. REDDING   *H. B. Maynard and Company, Incorporated, Pittsburgh, Pennsylvania*

RAYMOND I. REUL   *FMC Corporation, New York, New York*

J. WILLIAM ROBINSON   *Secretary and Assistant General Counsel, West Virginia Pulp and Paper Company, New York, New York*

PATRICK J. ROBINSON   *Marketing Science Institute, Philadelphia, Pennsylvania*

DR. MILTON L. ROCK   *Managing Partner, Edward N. Hay & Associates, Philadelphia, Pennsylvania*

ROBERT T. ROSS   *Partner, Mead—Ross Associates, Hanover, New Hampshire*

GEORGE P. RUDERMAN   *Consultant, Exempt Employee Compensation, General Electric Company, New York, New York*

MARG SAMMONS   *Partner, Newcomb & Sammons, Chicago, Illinois*

ROBERT C. SAMPSON   *Sampson Associates, Chicago, Illinois*

JOHN R. SARGENT   *Partner, Cresap, McCormick and Paget, New York, New York*

LAUREN F. SARGENT   *H. B. Maynard and Company, Incorporated, Pittsburgh, Pennsylvania*

DAVID V. SAVIDGE   *UNIVAC Division of Sperry Rand Corporation, Blue Bell, Pennsylvania*

DR. J. S. SCHIFF   *Dean, Graduate School of Business Administration, Pace College, New York, New York*

DR. BRIAN W. SCOTT   *Manager, Economic & Market Research Division, W. D. Scott & Co. Pty. Ltd., North Sydney, N.S.W., Australia*

WILSON SENEY   *President, Wilson Seney, Inc., New York, New York*

DR. PHILIP W. SHAY   *Executive Director, Association of Consulting Management Engineers, Inc., New York, New York*

ROBERT A. SHIFF   *President, Naremco Services, Inc., New York, New York; Chairman of the Board, National Records Management Council, New York, New York*

ROBERT E. SIBSON   *President, Sibson & Company, Inc., New York, New York*

LEONARD S. SILK   *Vice Chairman and Economist, Business Week, McGraw-Hill, Inc., New York, New York*

HOKE S. SIMPSON   *Director, Executive Programs, Graduate School of Business, Columbia University, New York, New York*

E. RALPH SIMS, JR.   *Professional Engineer, Principal, E. Ralph Sims, Jr. & Associates, Lancaster, Ohio*

DR. WICKHAM SKINNER   *Associate Professor of Business Administration, Graduate School of Business Administration, Harvard University, Boston, Massachusetts*

DR. REUBEN E. SLESINGER   *Professor, Department of Economics, University of Pittsburgh, Pittsburgh, Pennsylvania*

HAROLD F. SMIDDY   *Vice President (retired), General Electric Company, New York, New York*

PROFESSOR DAVID B. SMITH *Professor of Electrical Engineering, The Moore School, University of Pennsylvania, Philadelphia, Pennsylvania*

DR. EZRA SOLOMON *Dean Witter Professor of Finance, Graduate School of Business, Stanford University, Stanford, California*

ALEXANDER O. STANLEY *Associate Director, International Marketing Institute, Cambridge, Massachusetts*

NORMAN STATLAND *Director of Systems Development, Automatic Data Processing, Inc., New York, New York*

CHARLES E. TOWNSEND *Manager of Management Development, International Business Machines Corporation, Kingston, New York*

SPENCER A. TUCKER *Partner, Martin & Tucker, Little Neck, New York*

STANLEY TULCHIN *Stanley Tulchin Associates, New York, New York*

C. W. UFFORD *Vice President—Industrial Relations, The Warner & Swasey Company, Cleveland, Ohio*

COLONEL L. F. URWICK *Honorary President, Urwick, Orr & Partners, Ltd., Longueville, Australia*

DR. PHILIP W. VAN VLACK *Vice President and Dean of Academy of Christian Thought and Service, Tarkio College, Tarkio, Missouri*

DR. STANLEY C. VANCE *Head, Personnel and Industrial Management Departments, University of Oregon, Eugene, Oregon*

LUIS J. A. VILLALON *President, Communications Associates, Inc., Westport, Connecticut*

DR. RAYMOND VILLERS *Professor, Graduate School of Business Administration, Pace College, New York, New York; Consultant in Industrial Management, Rautenstrauch and Villers, New York, New York*

JAMES L. VINCENT *Secretary and Treasurer, Anaconda Wire and Cable Company, New York, New York*

WILLIAM R. VOGEL *Chief, Management Research Division, Directorate of Management Systems and Data Automation, Headquarters, United States Army Materiel Command, Washington, D.C.*

WALTER WEIR *President, West, Weir and Bartel, Inc., New York, New York*

DR. J. FRED WESTON *Professor and Chairman of Finance Department, Graduate School of Business Administration, University of California, Los Angeles, California*

DOUGLAS WILLIAMS *Chairman, Douglas Williams Associates, Inc., New York, New York*

LEONARD C. YASEEN *Chairman, The Fantus Company, New York, New York*

S. BLAKE YATES *Director of Corporate Licensing, Armour and Company, Chicago, Illinois*

DR. W. C. ZINCK *Vice President, Operations, Arbogast & Bastian, Inc., Allentown, Pennsylvania*

DR. STANLEY ZIONTS *Program Specialist to the Ministry of Steel and Mines, Government of India, The Ford Foundation, Calcutta, India*

PREFACE

The task of business administration, or managing, is quite difficult to define clearly. In developing the initial outline for this Handbook, many recognized authorities in the field of management were consulted. It was evident from the start that each of them viewed the task of managing slightly differently, perhaps because of the different environmental situation in which he had personally worked and perhaps because of his own temperamental characteristics which had led him to develop certain methods of managing which, for him, had proved to be effective. In any case, the identification of the component parts of the task of managing to be discussed in this *Handbook of Business Administration* proved to be a difficult task indeed. The final outline, in the form of Section and Chapter titles which became the framework on which the Handbook was eventually built, was the result of many hours of serious discussion on the part of many sincere people with long experience in the field of management who stated their convictions honestly and forcefully. It represents a compromise among many different viewpoints. When it was finally evolved, however, it won the unanimous endorsement of those who had contributed to its development.

Part of the difficulty was undoubtedly due to the fact that the art and science of managing has been undergoing considerable change since midcentury. Mathematical and statistical concepts, the computer, and the developing behavioral sciences, to name a few, have had a tremendous impact on concepts and methods of managing. Those who have been in the forefront in these developments have tended to see in them the answers to many, if not most, of management's problems. Others, equally sincere, who have successfully practiced management for many years using older concepts which unquestionably gave good results, if not actually fearing the to them new and often not clearly understood techniques, were by no means willing to discard their older, time-tested practices. This conflict of viewpoint, which exists widely among practicing managers at the present time, undoubtedly had its influence on the planners of this Handbook. It resulted in a decision to present the best of the time-tested, older management practices together with a number of chapters which discuss the newer techniques and procedures. Now that the Handbook is completed, this appears to have been a wise decision. The composite picture of the task of managing, which the total Handbook presents, melds together the best of the old with the best of the new to form a practical concept of the task of managing which many people will undoubtedly find to be quite acceptable.

But if there are differences of opinion on the methods by which the task of managing may best be carried out, there is one point on which everyone, planners and authors alike, is in complete agreement. That is the fact that managing is a very complex function. Author after author comments on this as he discusses the application of the specific procedure he is dealing with to the successful managing of an enterprise.

And indeed, as one leafs through the pages of the Handbook, he cannot help but be impressed with the number and variety of the problems which must be dealt with by managers. Their very number appears at first to make it impossible for any one manager to master the art and science of managing sufficiently well to do his work effectively. As one reads on, however, he presently also becomes impressed by the limitless creativity and ingenuity which managers as a group have brought to bear in developing solutions to the problems they have had to face. For every problem, a workable solution has been developed. Although no one would claim that methods of managing have been perfected and that no further improvement is possible, the reader will nevertheless find workable solutions to most of his current problems set forth in the pages of the Handbook.

Not that there are any simple formulas or pat answers. Managing is much too complex a task for that. But if the reader will study what is said about whatever problem concerns him at the moment and then read as well the peripheral discussions of related problems, which he can locate with the help of the index, he will unquestionably gain insights which will help him manage more effectively than ever before.

And that, of course, is just what the planners had in mind when they developed the framework for the Handbook. The need for the Handbook was first recognized by the McGraw-Hill Book Company as the result of a number of comments made by practical managers and teachers of management. Nowhere within the covers of one volume was there to be found an authoritative discussion of the myriad problems faced by managers which could be referred to for guidance in time of perplexity. The company decided, therefore, to publish such a book.

After selecting an Editor-in-Chief, the next step was to set up an Advisory Planning Committee to assist with the planning of the Handbook. This committee was constituted of the following members:

DR. H. IGOR ANSOFF
PROFESSOR OF INDUSTRIAL ADMINISTRATION
GRADUATE SCHOOL OF INDUSTRIAL ADMINISTRATION
CARNEGIE INSTITUTE OF TECHNOLOGY

RICHARD R. CONARROE
CONARROE ASSOCIATES, INC.

M. JOSEPH DOOHER, EDITOR
INDUSTRIAL AND BUSINESS BOOKS
MCGRAW-HILL BOOK COMPANY

KENNETH KRAMER, EXECUTIVE EDITOR
Business Week

LOUIS E. NEWMAN, PRESIDENT
SMITHCRAFT CORPORATION

RICHARD M. PAGET
CRESAP, McCORMICK AND PAGET

JAMES O. RICE
JAMES O. RICE ASSOCIATES

PHILIP W. SHAY, EXECUTIVE DIRECTOR
ASSOCIATION OF CONSULTING MANAGEMENT ENGINEERS

HAROLD F. SMIDDY, VICE PRESIDENT (retired)
GENERAL ELECTRIC COMPANY

DEAN JOSEPH H. TAGGART
GRADUATE SCHOOL OF BUSINESS ADMINISTRATION
NEW YORK UNIVERSITY

The committee met together on several occasions for general discussion. Individual members assisted further by correspondence as the Editor-in-Chief referred various matters to them for their opinion. In addition, during the planning stage, a number of other people, as individuals, contributed valuable ideas which found their way into the final outline. This group included Professor Harold Koontz, Carl Heyel, Donald E. Farr, John Sargent, Alexander Stanley, and several anonymous reviewers of the plans as they developed, brought into the project by McGraw-Hill.

The planning stage consumed nearly a year, but when it was finished, those that had worked on it felt that a sound practical framework for a discussion of the many facets of the task of managing had been developed.

The Handbook has been designed to serve the needs of two groups of people:

1. *Top management to middle management, inclusive.* This group includes directors, top managers, activity area managers, functional managers, and managers of the more important subfunctions.

2. *Students of management.* This group includes managers and aspiring managers or supervisors on the way to greater responsibilities, management consultants, teachers of management, and university students taking business administration or related courses.

The Handbook provides comprehensive and authoritative information on the practice of management. It gives insights into the nature of general management and each management function. When a Handbook user finds himself confronted with a management problem he is uncertain of how to handle, he can reach for the Handbook and find an answer, or at least guidance toward an answer, in its pages. The Handbook is replete with practical how-to-do-it information, as any Handbook should be.

But in addition, most of the authors have not limited themselves to the pure "cookbook" approach, but have included observations embracing the philosophy and background of their subjects, spiced with comments that give a feel for the practical application of what they are discussing in the real world of business and industry. Thus, the individual who is seriously interested in improving the breadth of his management knowledge will find it advantageous to read systematically through the Handbook. By reading a chapter a day, he can go through the Handbook in a little under six months. At the end of that time, he will have a comprehension of the practice of management far greater than he is likely to acquire in any other way. Thus the Handbook provides an invaluable means for management self-development.

There will be occasions, of course, where the reader will wish to know more about a specific subject than is set forth in the Handbook. Although it is obvious that a complete book could easily be written on any of the subjects dealt with in a chapter, the authors were held to strict space limitations to keep the Handbook to a manageable size. To compensate for this, most authors have included a brief bibliography at the end of their chapters so that the reader who is truly interested in a subject will be directed to further sources of authoritative information.   Again because of space limitations, the bibliographies are not extensive, but they do list a few books or articles which the author believes will be helpful in acquiring a deeper understanding of his subject.

The Handbook is the work of many people.   The authors were selected because of the knowledge they were known to possess of the subjects assigned to them.   As a group, they form a good cross section of management practitioners, including as they do, practicing general or functional managers, management consultants, teachers of management, and men from other professional fields having a close relationship to business and industry.

To all of the authors, whose work will be helpful to managers and future managers throughout the world, the Editor-in-Chief expresses his deep appreciation.   Especial appreciation is extended to the authors who were instrumental in obtaining other authors in their areas of competence.   In addition to those who also served on the Advisory Planning Committee, this group includes Lester R. Bittel, Carl Heyel, Richard Brandenburg, John Sargent, John Kelsey, Dwight Meader, Samuel Burk, Willard Merrihue, and Alexander Stanley.

Great credit for the successful conclusion of the Handbook project must be given to Rita Carlson, who was tireless in editing and styling chapters and in handling the voluminous correspondence which a Handbook of this magnitude involves.   In addition, she ably handled proofreading and the complexities of scheduling the Handbook through to a successful conclusion.

Grateful acknowledgment is also extended to Barbara Hattemer, who prepared the Handbook index with such meticulous care.

Without the devoted efforts of the entire team—advisors, authors, and editorial assistants—this Handbook would not have been possible.

H. B. MAYNARD
Editor-in-Chief

CONTENTS

Section Eight   MARKETING MANAGEMENT

Section Nine   FINANCIAL MANAGEMENT

HANDBOOK OF
BUSINESS ADMINISTRATION

INTRODUCTION TO BUSINESS ADMINISTRATION

CHAPTER ONE

The Managing Process

J. P. BARGER   *President, Dynatech Corporation, Cambridge, Massachusetts*

Because rewards to managers usually follow the results they produce, most management people are interested in becoming more skillful managers, developing and using better management methods and learning how to handle ever-increasing amounts of responsibility.

Although the manager's vocational experience and a thorough knowledge of the business being managed form prerequisites for management success, managers must also possess a thorough understanding of the process of managing itself to manage the key asset of the business: its people.

EVOLUTION OF A THEORY OF MANAGING

Recognizing the need for a unifying philosophy to describe the process of managing, management philosophers have devoted their considerable energies to developing a more general theory. This development has progressed at a remarkable rate since World War II began. Following this has been a much fuller understanding of the managing process as it is most effectively carried out.

One of the ways in which a "profession" emerges is through development of an underlying fundamental or theoretical understanding of its common activities. As the knowledge and skills developed become more describable, each generation may teach the next. A body of literature develops; centers of education spring up to prepare novitiates; and standards of performance, conduct, and ethics appear. The profession becomes more "professional."

All through the development of a profession, philosophers of the profession attempt to catch the essence of its activities, describing them for improved understanding and communication. The reduction of common elements in the managing process to a simple theory forms an example of what happens when a profession becomes more professional.

Some decades ago, an early theory of managing grew around the "scientific management" approach of the early management philosophers, Taylor and Gilbreth. Although the activities of these men were chiefly concerned with organization, efficiency, and production, they gave managers an initial start toward professionalism by proposing rational or "scientific" theories or principles for describing the process of managing.

Later, management philosophers lent further enrichment to the concepts of managing by contributing theories for the basic purposes of managing and by describing the principles, activities, skills, and tools of management. This continuing work led to the development of a large number of not always complementary views of managing as a professional activity. One of the reasons for this fragmentation of description is the diverse professional training of the contributors. Coming from different backgrounds, including the law, the physical and biological sciences, the social and behavioral sciences, the arts, and engineering, these people see management in many different lights.

Another reason for the diversity of description is that *not all managers who write about managing are "well-rounded" managers;* that is, they do not place the proper relative emphasis on all the requirements of their job. In short, they do not engage in the whole process of managing. Further, in describing the process of managing to others, they tend to overemphasize their "favorite" activity at the expense of other vital management activities, in effect presenting an unbalanced and partial view of the managing process.

A third reason is the relative newness of the subject. Intensive analysis of the managing process has been going on for a few decades only, because the need for complex management structures relates chiefly to the emergence of large industrial corporations.

The end result of all the thousands of articles and books is a chaos of description. All those in management who care to study the subject find a vast management literature containing a tremendous number of randomly created, often conflicting views of management activity. Because most writers begin from different vantage points, use different premises, and end up with results that do not fit together with those of other writers, the managing process is presently caricatured by different authors as embodying from one to literally dozens of management "functions."[1] Worse, all of these myriad functions seem to be rated at the same high level of importance by different authors. Anyone who reads a portion of the advice given managers by management activity specialists in the hundreds of articles which appear each year, each article featuring one "particularly vital" function to be paid more attention, knows the impossibility of becoming an expert in all the different management functions so far promulgated.

Another problem is that the names given the functions have misleading connotations because of peculiarities of our language and usage (for example, if your company calls shipments "sales," does your "sales manager" head up the shipping department?). Still another difficulty is that the functions described by different philosophers are not each unique, lying in a contiguous relationship to each other. Duties included in one function by one management philosopher are often found included in another function under a different label by another management philosopher.

[1] For example: administrating, allocating, analyzing, appraising, arbitrating, authoring, building, communicating, conceptualizing, controlling, deciding, describing, developing, directing, establishing, evaluating, executing, financing, hiring, judging, leading, listening, manufacturing, marketing, motivating, organizing, participating, planning, producing, purchasing, rationalizing, reading, reporting, reviewing, selecting, selling, speaking, staffing, substituting, teaching, thinking, training, traveling, and writing.

Diversity in thinking, like the synthetic process in creativity, is healthy in putting forward the greatest number of ideas. But it is highly desirable to put the pieces back together in a rational way. The task will not be easy; we shall have to work with the conflicting views of the most important management functions, gathering together only the most useful concepts. We shall have to resolve the innumerable conflicts in the theory, sidestep the unfortunate connotations of many management words, develop a concise, unredundant vocabulary of management words, and reconcile our views to practice as it is and should be. Moreover, our emerging theory should be accurate, simple, and concise if it is to have value to practicing managers.

The purpose of this chapter, then, is to make a beginning toward a simpler view of the management functions, evolving a sequential, if certainly cyclically reoccurring, set of activities which are clear, yet meaningful enough to practice simply, and which fit together in a logical, orderly fashion. Most important, the pattern evolved must be simple enough to be retained easily in the mind, because only the simplest concepts will be useful to large numbers of managers. A key element in simplicity is number: we must reduce the number of chief, or top-rated, management functions to a useful, easily remembered minimum.

THE THREE BASIC FUNCTIONS OF MANAGEMENT

Management functions have already been separated into more important and less important categories by a relatively few expert management philosophers. The smallest number of distinct, first-ranking management functions in the present management literature is five, with one exception. In H. B. Maynard's first chapter, "Management and Managing," in McGraw-Hill's *Top Management Handbook* (1960), Maynard categorized eleven secondary functions within three of first rank, thus making a significant step forward in developing a simpler management philosophy. The description of management functions presented here differs not markedly from Maynard's in approach, but rather significantly in detail. Both Maynard and the writer have proposed that there are only three basic activities or functions which a manager must accomplish:

A manager must *plan*.
A manager must *execute*.
A manager must *review*.

Everyone knows that to "plan" means to think ahead or carry out a conceptual activity and to relate the possibilities of the future to the actualities of the present and the past. Almost everyone can see, too, that to "execute" is to carry out a plan or put it into practice. But "review" in this chapter is given a new connotation: it means the total activity of the manager in dealing with the plans and executions of his immediate subordinates. Very few managers use the word "review" for their interactions with their subordinates. Moreover, most managers have trouble recognizing the true nature of their planning and execution functions in relation to the review of their immediate superiors.

The first basic management function, *planning*, encompasses the conceptual relation of the uncertainties and possibilities of tomorrow and beyond to the facts of today and yesterday, in attempting to cope with or, in part, to determine the future. The second basic function, *execution*, is a collection of activities by which a manager puts into being his own plans for his own job. The third basic function is *review*, by which a manager interacts with his subordinates

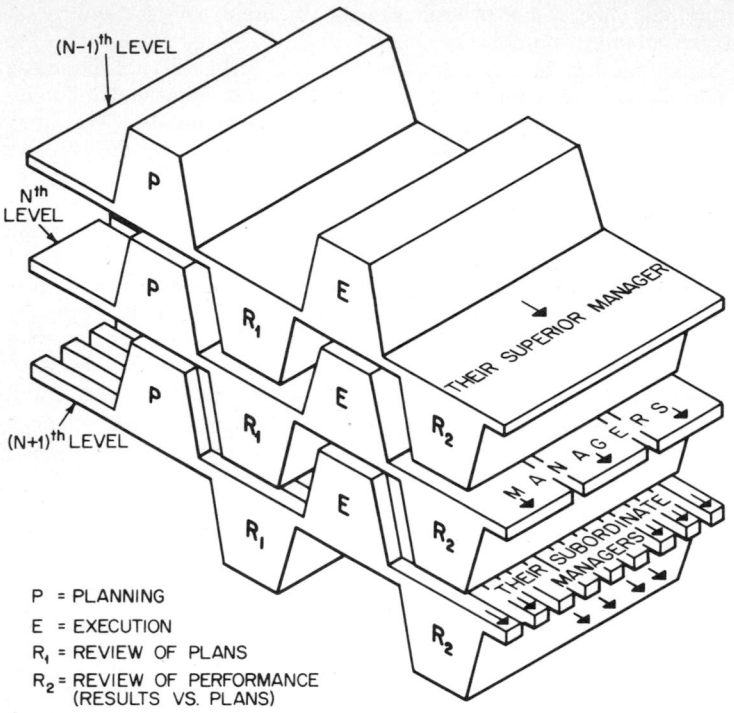

$(N-1)^{th}$ LEVEL

N^{th} LEVEL

$(N+1)^{th}$ LEVEL

THEIR SUPERIOR MANAGER

MANAGERS

THEIR SUBORDINATE MANAGERS

P = PLANNING
E = EXECUTION
R_1 = REVIEW OF PLANS
R_2 = REVIEW OF PERFORMANCE
    (RESULTS VS. PLANS)

FIG. 1-1.   *The managing process.*

during their planning stages and helps them keep score on their performance against their plans.

Of the three functions, planning and review have been the ones to which managers have not usually devoted enough time and care. Time spent on execution has usually usurped time which might more properly be devoted to the other two, so necessary, functions.

The diagram in Figure 1-1 gives a pictorial view of the interrelationship of the three management functions as applied by three managers all on the same nth level of management, their superior on the $(n-1)$st level, and their subordinate managers on the $(n+1)$st level. Each of the three horizontal webs in the diagram represents the center of the manager's job, an arbitrary division between his interactions with his superior and those with his subordinates. The lugs on the top of the web represent review constraints on the manager, causing him to plan and to execute his job in harmony with his superior's reviews. The lugs on the bottom of the web show the manager reviewing the planning and execution of his subordinate managers.

At this point, note that every manager is in the same functional relationship to his superior and to his subordinates as every other in the n-level organization. There are, however, two common misconceptions about this structure, one at the top and one at the bottom.

The first misconception concerns the chief executive officer's role. At the top of the structure is a chief executive officer who supposedly, in the layman's view, does not report to any one. Facts show the contrary: almost all chief executives report to reasonably effective boards of directors. Many chief executives of smaller, privately owned companies, who have not set up competent legal boards, have obtained the services of professional adviser boards. Almost all chief executives recognize the need to obtain some conscience or authority to interact with them to enhance the quality of their plans and performance.

At the bottom of the management structure is the level of management next to the direct workers. Most direct workers have a very small role in planning their own jobs. Thus, the manager usually reviews the workers' performance against plans which probably resulted chiefly from his *own* planning process, rather than from that of the workers. Failures in this area over the last century have probably resulted in more trouble for the management of business enterprises than failures in any other area. Studies of human motivational behavior reveal this practice as the key villain in causing lowered worker morale and productivity. For it is in this area—the classical failure of management to include the workers' knowledge of their own jobs and their thoughts for improving their own efficiency in the planning of their own jobs—that the main seed of discontent arises in the minds of workers. Changing this method of supervising workers stands as one of management's greatest challenges.

Planning. Accepting, for the moment, that every manager *must plan his own activity*, let us examine planning first as a concept.

Two views of the purpose of planning currently exist. The first view concerns the need to "foresee" or "predict" the future to determine as exactly as possible what the future will bring. The second view is to "make" the future—insofar as possible—by previously deciding what objectives to be accomplished in the future are worthwhile and then laying sound plans to make them come true. The "soundness" of the plans is in proportion to the parallel paths or countermeasures designed into the plan to offset possible negative influences on the success of the plan.

The proponents of the first, or predictive, view take accurate prediction as the precondition for any planning process. The approach is passive in that the planning process usually stops short of determining in advance the exact positive steps to be taken in the future to offset the changing conditions of the future.

The proponents of the second, or active, view state that because we can never predict the future with great certainty anyway, the future can be made to happen with more certainty than it can be predicted.

Putting planning before execution—concentrating part-time attention on future activities instead of on today's activities—is a function not all people are suited for, either temperamentally or by training. Possession of a high degree of conceptual skill—the ability to see things in an abstract way and to see future happenings as they might or will be, especially if they are forced by future human endeavor—is not common to all human beings. But let us make no mistake. Every manager must have conceptual skill in some reasonable degree if he is to plan at all. If he cannot plan, he cannot be an effective manager. In comparison with other managers who could make a much greater conceptual contribution to his job if they had it, a manager with little planning skill will suffer.

We are told by experts in human motivational behavior that all individuals possess a need to participate in planning their own future. If all individuals have this need, is it in proportion to their conceptual ability? Unfortunately, it is not. But clearly, real managers must have the skill. We know they have the need at least to participate in the planning process.

Planning, then, is an ability to visualize a future process and its results. The skill is both conceptual and organizational. The manager must conceive of concepts, drawing them from the vast storehouse of facts already in his brain.

Then he must synthesize these facts with perhaps a brand-new arrangement, or possibly not, and "store" the plan for later evaluation by writing it down or by remembering it. Pulling out facts or scanning for information, and then synthesizing or combining these facts into all possible relevant combinations, forms the first part of the planning process. The second part of the planning process is completely different, consisting of analysis of all relevant plans and selection of the best one or ones.

Most managers generally accept the premise that intelligent and detailed planning in advance of any business activity pays handsome rewards in improved results. The days of intuitive management, "seat of the pants" operation, and the attendant difficulties in getting organizations to perform to the manager's plans are, hopefully, on the way out. But beside the rational approach in planning—leading to improved business results at the end of the ensuing activity—there are three other, more important and far-reaching, effects of the planning process on the management structure. First, it forms the only method of achieving the level and quality of communications among managers for the blending of individual with organizational goals, so important to the needs of the managers and thus the enterprise itself. Second, the formulation of formal plans in advance by the same managers responsible for execution of the plans achieves commitment to accomplishment of the plans. Finally, the human need of all individuals to participate in planning their own personal future is not bypassed.

Subfunctions of Planning. Planning experts have generally agreed that there are four subfunctions which must be carried out in the planning activity:

1. Establishing situation descriptions
2. Setting objectives
3. Setting goals
4. Programming

The four subfunctions produce the following written documents:

1. *Situation descriptions:* Descriptions of the key factors in the present and possible future situation, both outside and inside a company

2. *Objectives:* Basic, qualitative directions in which a company should move

3. *Goals:* Sets of quantitative values for key result parameters when objectives have been satisfied (how far to go in the direction of the objectives within the time selected for the planning period)

4. *Programs:* Detailed descriptions of the paths to be taken, methods and resources to be used or acquired, and functional interrelations of all factors required for successful accomplishment of the goals

Establishing Situation Descriptions. Creating a situation description involves a thorough, searching, synthetic, and analytic look at both the external business environment and the internal resources of a company which may be used to capitalize on the external situation. Beginning his planning, the manager examines the status and rate of change of all pertinent *external* factors. He must not miss key factors; he must use a penetrating synthetic approach to locate all possible factors in order not to miss any important ones. He must "scope" the possible values of these factors, that is, determine their best and worst, least and greatest, values. He must then analyze the factors to separate out only the key ones for further analysis. Finally, the manager determines the relationship of these factors to the present or potential business enterprise.

The *internal resources*—men, money, and materials—must then be analyzed to determine carefully the "taking-off" place for the next assault toward achieving the next objectives.

What is really needed for a competent description of internal resources is an objective, comparative analysis of the firm's capabilities versus those of the competition. This is not easy to obtain. In a highly competitive market situation, recitation of statistics about the firm, involving numbers of people, floor space, money in the bank, and so forth, is particularly useless in an internal-resource description. Clearly, most managements are not objective when it comes to an evaluation of their own company's talents versus those of other competitive teams. Because people rationalize when describing their own talents and their own results, no really effective way has been found to get them to put objectivity into this evaluation themselves. An unbiased superior authority is not usually present to perform the analysis. Management consultants are usually prevented from making truly effective comparisons of relative worth versus other competing companies by the ethics of their own profession and by their inability to serve competitors at the same time.

The end purpose of the situation description is to decide what need of what market the business is serving, and how well; and every effort should be made to develop an honest, objective situation description.

Objectives. When a comprehensive analysis of the state of the business has been made, it becomes time to decide what objectives should next be pursued. Are previously written objectives, if clearly stated, still valid? Or must they be changed to take advantage of a changed external environment or a change in internal resources?

Stating objectives only in qualitative terms is an intellectual exercise designed to tax the best minds. Because amazing clarifications of managers' thinking always result when the process of setting objectives is carried forward properly, great immediate value to a business enterprise can result from focusing diverse human energies and tendencies on the most rewarding objectives. Further, opportunities for achieving personal commitment of large groups of managers and employees present themselves. Determining all reasonably promising objectives comes first; then the tentative selection of the most rewarding objectives can follow.

Those objectives which do not prove workable later, when firm quantitative goals or programs cannot really be set up for them, will have to be changed before the planning process is continued. The feedback loop thus created, wherein the objectives, goals, and programs must be continually reworked until a satisfactory relationship is established among them, is typical of all planning activity which does not flow perfectly from objectives to programs without a hitch. Fortunately, in the planning process, the capable, conceptually skilled mind can leap forward and backward over the whole process to "see" blocks as planning progresses.

Goals. To be sure, putting down on paper quantitative goals for results to be obtained causes traumatic "moments of truth" for everyone in a planning process. Everyone involved must calculate his ability to produce in advance, adding up all positive factors, subtracting negative ones, and rating his chance of success against the goal. But only when firm quantitative goals are primarily personally set by an individual can true commitment of that individual to a plan really be obtained.

Programs. Because of the human tendency toward impatience, causing one to want to start to execute a plan before it is finished—to jump directly from establishing goals to achieving them to save time—programming is perhaps the most difficult subfunction for which to find time in planning.

In the programming area, the time invested to conceptualize the exact route by which an objective and goal may be met may save untold difficulty later. The key problem is to separate the important from the unimportant facts, to pull apart the important few from the trivial many. The difficulty is to decide in advance which are which. "For the want of a nail, the shoe was lost, the horse was lost, the rider fell . . . the battle was lost" expresses the fear that only one seemingly unimportant detail missed in the plan can later cause untold trouble, perhaps even complete failure. Yet the manager, in his planning, must be concerned with the importance of all details in deciding what level of detail his programs will include.

Fortunately, there are some ways to get around the necessity for putting down on paper *all* details in a plan, which is tantamount to executing the plan once on an actual trial basis instead of in a conceptual way. The attempt is, after all, to get "planning leverage" by planning in a short time what will require a large amount of time to accomplish. One of the ways is to reject all details which are rated as totally unimportant to the success of the plan. Another is to keep a list of those factors which *could* prevent the plan from working, the interference of which factors there is still time to prevent.

Perhaps the best way to program any plan is to use a logical planning method, which forces the planner to put down all steps in proper logical sequence about how the activity will flow from beginning to desired result. Such techniques— sophisticated and unsophisticated—are well developed and are ready for application by any manager who wants to learn their manipulation. These techniques include program evaluation and review technique (PERT), critical path management (CPM, or uncomputerized PERT), and decision tree methods, among many.

Execution. After a manager develops his plans and describes them to his superior, obtains approval of them, and psychologically commits himself to their accomplishment, he begins the phase of implementation. The word "execution" was chosen for this major function for several reasons, among which are:

1. "Execution" is a shorter word than "implementation" or "administration."

2. "Accomplishing" denotes more the finish of an activity.

Execution includes *all* those activities which a manager employs in carrying out his plans, including reporting his results to his superior and carrying out a list of other personal duties, but excluding those of direct interaction with his subordinates. This direct interaction with his subordinates is especially reserved for the third basic function, review.

The execution portion of all managers' jobs always includes the common duty of *reporting* facts concerning the rate of completion of results for which the managers are personally responsible, whether the duties are carried out personally or by subordinates.

In addition, each manager's job description usually includes a list of personal duties he has—ideally—personally developed or perhaps accepted from a prior description, but to which he has—again, ideally—fully committed himself. Depending on the level of the manager's job in the organization, some of these duties may be leftover vocational duties from his prior skills as a worker, some may represent accomplishment toward new challenges which can be most effectively started by the man himself, and still others may be concerned with the "staffing" function, that is, selecting, hiring, and organizing subordinates into a potentially effective structure. Another category of duties revolves around getting facts from all sources besides those used in reviewing the plans and performances of subordinates. Facts are acquired by properly curious managers from diverse sources—from answers to questions by people inside and outside the business, reading, lectures, courses, and discussions of topics germane to the operation of the business. Many other duties which may be personal to the manager are suggested by the list of functions previously given in the footnote.

There are other kinds of duties which managers classically and improperly have taken to themselves in the execution function. An example concerns over-stepping execution by performing planning[2] for subordinates. Many managers, after having planned in some detail the forthcoming activities of their subordinates, are amazed that they cannot seem to "get the cooperation" of the subordinates in carrying out the plans. The managers, not understanding that their methods violate the "participative planning" principle of letting each man plan his own job to the fullest extent possible, cannot understand the ensuing lack of cooperation, putting it down to stubbornness or other undesirable personality traits on the part of their subordinates. Because the subordinates have been cheated out of fulfilling their strong desire to participate in planning their own futures, they are, of course, merely exhibiting their resentment by failing to cooperate with the manager's plan beyond an amount made necessary by their desire to remain employed at the firm or their hesitation to move. If this desire is not strong, they may leave the employ of the firm if the manager does not mend his ways, or they may take out their resentment in other equally undesirable ways.

One might say that the execution function, in which a manager works primarily by himself and with himself, organizing his habits and his work and setting the management climate for the organization, is not properly a management function, because it does not heavily involve getting things done through other people. However, in this function, the manager does interact with others in several ways. In staffing and organizing, he interacts heavily with new or "re-arranged" subordinates. In his reporting relationship to his superior, he again interacts with the superior. Both are examples of interpersonal relationships in the execution function.

Review. Clearly the least understood of the major management functions, review is almost the most important, because in carrying out this function, a manager either seizes the opportunity to construct a management organization soundly conceived and carried out along practical social and motivational principles or, in failing this, creates for himself the seeds of his own destruction as a manager. It is in this area of relationships with subordinates that most managers succeed or fail as managers. Good management relationships with subordinates, causing the subordinates to excel at their work, naturally enhance the reputation of the manager and pushes him up through the ranks of any organization, because he becomes known as a man who can get results on an ever-broadening scale.

Motivational Methods. The late Douglas McGregor made a fine contribution to clarifying the basic attitudes of managers toward their subordinates. In his book *The Human Side of Enterprise,* published in 1960 by McGraw-Hill, McGregor clearly draws a line between two opposing views of the proper human

[2] Of course, planning activities do not belong in the execution function, either for a man's own job or for others. We might say, alternatively, that a manager oversteps his own planning function when he plans for his subordinates without consulting them. The intent here is to show the dire consequences of exceeding the proper bounds of one's own job. In the past, classical managers not only planned for everyone in their organizations, but carried out the plans, too. Their failure was in not effectively multiplying their own talents by organizing a management structure where other managers could be developed and where others could take responsibility for portions of the overall task. "One-man shows" resulted.

climate in business structures, calling these two views "Theory X" and "Theory Y." Perhaps it will be best to reiterate McGregor's words exactly.

Theory X uses as its premises:
1. The average human being has an inherent dislike of work and will avoid it if he can.
2. Because of this human characteristic of dislike of work, most people must be coerced, controlled, directed, threatened with punishment to get them to put forth adequate effort toward the achievement of organizational objectives.
3. The average human being prefers to be directed, wishes to avoid responsibility, has relatively little ambition, wants security above all.
On the other hand, Theory Y uses as its premises:
1. The expenditure of physical and mental effort in work is as natural as play or rest.
2. External control and the threat of punishment are not the only means for bringing about effort toward organizational objectives. Man will exercise self-direction and self-control in the service of the objectives to which he is committed.
3. Commitment to objectives is a function of the rewards associated with their achievement.
4. The average human being learns, under proper conditions, not only to accept but to seek responsibility.
5. The capacity to exercise a relatively high degree of imagination, ingenuity, and creativity in the solution of organizational problems is widely, not narrowly, distributed in the population.
6. Under the conditions of modern industrial life, the intellectual potentialities of the average human being are only partially utilized.

After the opposing points of view were stated so clearly by McGregor, more managers seemed to recognize the advantages of pursuing the premises of Theory Y. But there are holdouts. The reader will immediately recognize management friends and associates who seem to be following one course or the other.

Having looked at the premises concerning management's attitudes toward its subordinates, let us turn our attention now to the basic human needs of the subordinates, to see how these needs may be satisfied in the accomplishment of tasks in a business structure. Various social scientists have compiled lists of the most important human needs. There seems, however, not to be too great a diversity of ideas presented. Most of the lists are structured as a progression from basic unsophisticated needs to quite sophisticated ones.

One such list reads approximately as follows:
1. *Physiological needs*—the needs for food, shelter, clothing, air, and water
2. *Safety needs*—the needs to live, work, and play in a relatively safe environment, free from imminent termination of life or serious injury
3. *Social needs*—the needs to associate with other human beings for stimulation, mutual reinforcement, and intellectual challenge
4. *Ego needs*—the needs of respecting oneself and knowing that others respect one, also
5. *Self-development needs*—the needs for self-improvement, to increase physical and/or mental capacity, develop new and higher skills, and acquire new knowledge

In dealing with human beings in our normal business affairs, we are not usually preoccupied with discussions relating to the more basic needs, because most people already have satisfied these basic needs. This leads to the principle that "a satisfied need cannot furnish effective motivation." The kinds of people with whom managers normally interact in modern society have already satisfied most of their needs. Certainly the first two are satisfied almost everywhere in this country for managers, submanagers, and most direct-work-level people.

Most people who have not really achieved full satisfaction in the social and ego needs will respond to challenges leading toward greater self- and peer-respect. But the chief challenge to most management people stems from the large unfilled need for greater self-development. All of us can obviously make great strides in self-enrichment by effort in that direction. In dealing with subordinates and other business associates, it will be well to remember that we can achieve significant motivation of the individual concerned only when an unsatisfied need is in line to be satisfied.

To be more specific: Industrial psychologists keep coming up with the same answers to the question, "What are the chief desires of people *in business organizations?*" Ranked in order, these always seem to come out:

1. Desire to participate in planning one's own future
2. Knowledge that individual talent is being used to the highest degree of effectiveness by the organization
3. Knowledge that "rewards follow results," or that "the game is fair"

The first desire can only be satisfied by a management climate where participative planning is allowed or encouraged. The second desire can best be satisfied where the organization permits individuals a high degree of opportunity to move ahead in expansion of responsibility commensurate with the rate of expansion of their ability to accept responsibility. The third desire can only be satisfied where there is sound planning. Otherwise, no one knows clearly what the objectives and goals of the business are.

We can now proceed to build a management system which pays full respect to the sociological facts and principles just presented.

We have named the function of dealing with subordinates "review" because the word is sufficiently passive in connotation to give managers pause to consider that perhaps their subordinates would like primarily to do their own planning, execution, and review, and that perhaps managers should refrain from performing these duties for their subordinates or suffer the consequences of reassuming the duties supposedly delegated.

Review of Planning. The competent manager can simultaneously satisfy several of his subordinates' human desires when he asks them to perform planning, execution, and review in their jobs and limits his interaction with them to review. At the same time, he can satisfy several objectives of the organization such as the need to select intelligently and then develop management personnel.

1. First, the *desire of the subordinate for participation in planning his own future* is completely satisfied when planning is begun by the individual. If the manager has properly selected the subordinate for sufficient conceptual skill and has given him a chance to get enough facts, the subordinate may well do a far superior job when he initiates the plan than the manager would have done had he initiated it himself. There are at least two reasons:

a. Unless he is brand new on the job, the *subordinate usually has the facts surrounding his own job straighter than the manager does,* and thus does a better job in planning. The manager, on the other hand, has many people to supervise and many plans to write (one for each, if he is going to attempt to do them all). Clearly, the manager cannot have the same total detailed information about all his subordinates' jobs as they in totality have themselves. Nor has he as much time as his subordinates have in total.

b. Communications between manager and subordinate are greatly enhanced when the *manager reviews the subordinate's thinking.* The reverse process will not work at all. Subordinates will not normally criticize their superiors in a direct exchange. They would usually rather give grudging support to a poor plan than tell the superior how bad the plan is. The subordinate's human need for security appears at this point, preventing him from criticizing his superior's judgment.

2. Second, many managers worry a great deal about the "dire" results to the organization if their subordinates' plans are not optimum. They think they could do better themselves and then do not "get around" to reviewing the plans before the execution phase starts. Thus, no *communication of the plan between manager and subordinate* results. Trouble is bound to ensue when the manager starts to criticize the execution of a plan which he has tacitly accepted but has not contributed to and is therefore unfamiliar with.

Managers can get their thoughts into subordinates' planning easily. All they have to do is:

  a. Review their subordinates' plans on schedule
  b. Study the plans carefully and contribute their ideas

There may be important gaps in the subordinates' plans. The subordinate will usually be grateful to the manager for pointing out these gaps and for contributing his ideas for their solution. At this point, the manager must make decisions on points of disagreement. He may be sure that some element of the plan is wrong. If the cost to the organization is minimal, he may let the subordinate make his mistake and learn a lesson thereby. If the cost is very high, he may explain the situation to the subordinate and see if the subordinate would not like to change his plan.

Barring agreement after discussion, when the stakes are high, and as a last resort, the manager may have to go back to "Theory X" and instruct the subordinate to change the plan, deciding to accept the poor motivational consequences rather than risk a large loss to the business. In any event, because the whole communication process between the manager and the subordinate during the review has been excellent, they both know where they stand relative to each other and how the game should be played *before* the starting whistle.

3. That precious commodity, *commitment on the part of the subordinate to the accomplishment of his own plan,* can easily be obtained if he writes his own plan; it can be obtained only rarely and with great difficulty for someone else's plan.

4. How many times have we heard managers say, "I don't know about giving that employee more responsibility; he's untried"? One of the basic purposes of getting all managers to plan, execute, and perform review on their own jobs is to *test, in advance, their skills on these tasks.* Following the principle that the best way to evaluate a man is to evaluate him "on the job," the manager needs as many chances to test the skills of his subordinates as he can devise. In reviewing subordinates' plans, he evaluates their conceptual ability to plan; in reviewing their performance after execution, he measures their ability to perform according to plan.

5. Many managers are astonished to learn, after participating with their subordinates in a few rounds of planning and performance reviews, that the subordinates are beginning to *set standards for themselves* and to accomplish results meeting these standards which are higher than the manager had previously been setting. Studies of "achievement motivation" in individuals by sociologists at Harvard Business School have shown that the degree of achievement motivation may be detected in individuals by the goals they set for themselves. High achievers usually initially select targets higher than they can accomplish, but then adjust goals downward and performance upward until the two are in agreement. Managers can thus identify potential high achievers early in the game.

6. Finally, all managers keep one eye on "Father Time." Because everyone becomes one year older every year, *the manager constantly must keep bringing*

younger men along, training them and developing them for accepting more responsibility. The best way to do this is to let them practice for greater responsibility by gradually permitting or encouraging them to increase the level and magnitude of their tasks, each step along the way representing a new test of their worth as managers. The manager can best satisfy the self-development desires of his subordinates by this process.

Review of Performance. Performance is relative. But relative to what? Management has fumbled this question for a long time and is only beginning to use *measures of performance acceptable to subordinates*—those measures which the employee has accepted and to which he has previously committed himself. The managers who were employees of corporations in the late forties and early fifties can remember a previous system of rating people partly or chiefly by personality factors. This system drove most of these managers to consider finding new employment. But fortunately, management is becoming more enlightened on this subject. We now have a system based on much sounder sociological and motivational premises. The system is known by different labels, and the basic functions of managers using this system vary somewhat, but the system is basically as depicted in this chapter.

If performance is to be relative to standards probably drafted by the individual whose performance will be measured against them, clearly the individual's manager has two responsibilities: review of plan (or standards) and review of performance (measured against the plan or standards). This means the manager must regularly devote enough time to his subordinates to stay on top of all their major plans and their performances against those plans. One way to solve the scheduling problem posed by this is to get the subordinates to accept the additional responsibility of soliciting review of plans or performance at appropriate intervals. After all, each one has only two per interval to remember, while the superior has two for each of his subordinates to remember.

Managers who confine their interactions with their subordinates to the review function find that morale is higher, personal conflict is reduced, the conflict of ideas is enhanced, and the performance of their organization is constantly rising.

CONCLUSION

In reducing the number of separate chief functions of managers, in organizing the many other functions into subcategories, in establishing a chronological or cyclical order for the chief functions, and in showing the correct interpersonal relationship for each function (up or down the structure), a simple and concise description for the entire managing process has been developed in this chapter. It is hoped that its presentation will be of some value to other managers.

BIBLIOGRAPHY

Barger, J. P., Materials from Management Course for Presidents, Presidents' Professional Association, New York, 1964.

Drucker, Peter F., *The Practice of Management,* Harper & Row, Publishers, Incorporated, New York, 1954.

McClelland, David C., "Achievement Motivation Can Be Developed," *Harvard Business Review,* vol. 42, November–December, 1965.

McGregor, Douglas, *The Human Side of Enterprise,* McGraw-Hill Book Company, New York, 1960.

Maynard, H. B. (ed.), *Top Management Handbook,* McGraw-Hill Book Company, New York, 1960.

CHAPTER TWO

Business Administration in the Modern Setting

HAROLD KOONTZ   *Mead Johnson Professor of Management, University of California, Los Angeles, California*

Business is truly one of the dominant forces of social existence. The survival, growth, and happiness of a society and the ability of a government to meet the needs of the public depend upon the efficiency and effectiveness of its business enterprises—whether farm or factory, department store or service station, bake shop or beauty salon, transportation company or construction company. These, in turn, depend very substantially on the quality and aggressiveness of their management.

Just as the business firm and its administration lie at the basis of social existence, through their ability to create and distribute the material things of life, so is every business enterprise, whether privately or publicly owned, interwoven in the fabric of society. Every business problem is clearly influenced by and contributes to a broad spectrum of society. Although the social responsibility of the business is essentially economic, it must always be recognized that the operation of any business takes place in a broad social setting. The existence of a business depends upon this recognition.

THE EVOLVING PATTERN OF BUSINESS ADMINISTRATION

The evolution of business generally, and its life-giving element—the manager—in particular, has been molded in the past century and a half, and especially since the 1930s, by certain major cultural developments. As one looks at business administration as it has evolved, he sees a pattern largely influenced by these developments. Although these developments are too numerous to recount in this chapter, a few of the major influences may be noted.

Impact of the Industrial Revolution. The Industrial Revolution, set in motion by the factory system and the invention of new machines at the beginnning of the nineteenth century, has often been regarded as a technical and social revolution. But one of its most important impacts has been on management.

Separation of the worker from control over his work and his change from a member of a family group to a member of a larger group of specialists have modified and complicated the job of management. The managing of a small group can be undertaken with the simple intuitions of leadership. Each member can be directed personally, organization can be so informal as hardly to exist, planning may be limited to the moment, and general guidance and overseeing may be all the control required. When a large number of persons are gathered together, however, and their activities coordinated toward the attainment of objectives of the larger group, the managerial problem becomes the key to success or failure of the group.

The problem of coordinating the activities of the larger group has been accentuated by another characteristic of the Industrial Revolution. Machines used and products made by members of the group are not ordinarily the members' property. Thus, workers in a group do not usually have the same objectives as owners. Although both may share a desire to better themselves through the business enterprise, their underlying motives are likely to be different. A worker wishes to gain money, status, or power for himself through enhancing his wage or position; an owner may have the same goals, but he accomplishes them through the successful operation of the business enterprise *as a whole*.

It is an interesting commentary on modern civilization and the myopia of man that, until the twentieth century, the central problem of administration, or management, was probably the most neglected phase of the Industrial Revolution. Although much attention was given to technical, human exploitation, division of labor, and other economic problems, the problem of establishing an environment for the effective and efficient performance of people working together as a group received little attention until after the Great Depression of the thirties and World War II.

Separation of Ownership and Management in the Modern Corporation. Further separation of ownership and management, wrought by the modern corporation, has been believed to be so fundamental a change as also to constitute a revolution.[1] Because of dispersion of ownership and the smaller share held by each owner as a corporation increases in size, the typical large company (and many fairly small ones) tend to be owned by a large number of shareholders who can neither take part in the management of the corporation nor do much to exercise control through their voting power as stockholders. Because of this and the fact that existing corporate top managers ordinarily control the proxy machinery of the company, the latter are typically able to perpetuate themselves in office and to name their successors.[2]

Separation of ownership and control has tended to give great emphasis to administrative leadership in the modern business enterprise. Although shareholders themselves may have little real, direct control over a company's management, demands of a competitive market place and needs for capital for expansion, as well as social pressures for success and various controls exerted by governmental agencies, have forced responsible managers to take steps toward assuring effective business administration.

The Effect of Government Controls. The pattern of business administration is materially influenced by the burgeoning number and extent of government con-

[1] James Burnham was one of the first to discern this "revolution." See his *Managerial Revolution*, The John Day Company, Inc., New York, 1941.

[2] R. A. Gordon found in 1945 that, out of a total of 176 corporations analyzed, management controlled with less than 1 percent of the stock in 63 cases and with less than 5 percent in 120 cases. See his *Business Leadership in the Large Corporation*, Brookings Institution, Washington, D.C., 1945.

trols. Such controls have not only complicated the tasks of the business manager but have also forced him to give government an ever greater share in policy determination. In fact, managers often understandably feel that the government sits in as a partner in the making of many decisions.

Government controls assume a number of forms. Under both Federal and state laws, controls exist to preserve the competitive system. There is also an ever-widening area of government control in which business economic decisions may be directly regulated. These include direct regulation of prices, the right to enter a business, the quality and quantity of services rendered, the means used to finance an enterprise, the character of accounting records kept, the wages paid, who may be hired, and many other business decisions. Until· approximately 1930, most direct economic regulation was limited to a class of business characterized as affected by the public interest, such as transportation companies and public utilities. This direct regulation of the economic incidents of business operation was justified on the grounds of unique dependence of the public on their services, the supposed "natural" tendencies toward monopoly, and the fact that most of these businesses received public aid, through either outright subsidies, use of public property, or power to utilize public rights of eminent domain.

With the events since 1930—depression, war, and defense—distinction between quasi-public and private businesses tended to disappear. On grounds of national emergency and with the ready willingness of the courts to approve expansion of the power of governments to act in the interests of the public welfare, morals, health, and safety, direct economic regulation tended to be applied, to a greater or lesser extent, to all types of businesses.

Although all aspects of government control affect the managing of a business, those applicable to labor have had an unusually marked effect. Among these are regulations designed to protect the position of labor—controls over minimum wages, maximum hours of work, safety conditions, and insurance against the hazards of accidents, health, unemployment, and old age. Another set of regulations has been designed to protect labor's rights to bargain collectively without interference and coercion. By encouraging and protecting the organization of labor, the government has been placed in the center of the traditional conflict between management and labor.

An intrusion into business operations occurs also when the government undertakes to subsidize private business or enter into business itself. It is not always easy to distinguish between government controls, government aids, and government ownership. The right to withhold, as well as to grant, subsidies on certain conditions can have a powerful regulatory force. When the government goes into business itself, its dealing with other businesses serves often to cause considerable control.

Perhaps one of the major areas of government control is that existing when the government is a buyer of service or hardware. Experience with military, space, and other contracting agencies shows that the government is a very demanding customer. Profit controls, accounting systems designed for regulation rather than for management, detailed performance and delivery specifications, prescribed planning and control systems, and various labor requirements are indicative of the kinds of areas over which the government, as a customer, exerts control.

Less direct, but nonetheless real, is the influence of the government in fiscal and taxation matters. The cost and availability of funds for expansion often fall under credit controls. The rate of business taxes, the kind and amount of depreciation allowances, and the myriad interpretations of basic tax laws have made the taxing power of both the state and Federal governments strong determinants of business operations.

A problem in government control, beyond the regulations themselves, is the energy expended by business in attempting to live lawfully under them. One gets the impression in certain closely regulated companies, such as railroads and public utilities, that the company is being run primarily to comply with a multitude of laws and commission regulations. In other types of businesses, there is often so much fear of running afoul of a law, such as a fair trade or price discrimination law, that the very competitive vigor which the law is intended to promote becomes dulled. Even though the objectives of most government controls of business are completely defensible as being in the public interest, the complexity of the laws and administrative regulations causes many serious interferences with business and goes far to mold the character of a business and its management.

The Impact of Trade Unions. One of the major influences on the manager is the trade union. Spawned by a long period when many managers gave inadequate attention to the human factor, accelerated by the unemployment ushered in with the Great Depression of the early thirties, and given governmental protection and encouragement by the Wagner Act of 1935, the labor union movement in the United States has developed great strength. Even though trade union membership in 1966 comprised only some one-fourth of the employed population of the country, its influence has been great in forcing such practices as seniority, grievance procedures, pension plans, favorable labor legislation, and wage levels and systems that effectively curtail the authority of managers in dealing with their subordinates.

Thus the manager has often had to look at his job not only as one of achieving coordination of enterprise objectives with his subordinates, but also as one of developing an identity of objective with a nonsubordinate leader of a labor union. Moreover, labor union contracts, with their requirement of careful administration, have tended to force the transfer of much of the traditional authority of operating managers to top managers where uniformity of policy in line with union agreements may be assured.

The impact of unionism, although general, has been particularly noticeable in certain industries where long traditions of union control, sometimes buttressed by legislation, have struck at the heart of the manager's function of assuring efficient operation of an enterprise. In the railroad industry, for example, the struggle to remove firemen from diesel locomotives long after they were clearly unneeded, the attempt to adopt organizational changes through consolidating operating districts, and the removal of obsolete rules which made efficient operations difficult are instances where union power has interfered with and molded the course of business administration.

Fortunately, restrictive practices so rife in most of the transportation industry are not completely typical, because many unions, such as those in the mining and automotive industries, have not stood in the way of technical progress. But the power of the union to control many of the economic aspects of a business, backed up by union power in the Federal and state legislatures, has often been a source of inflexibility, restricting the business manager who wishes to adopt flexible measures to meet changing environments.

Awakening to the Importance of the Human Element. A number of events of the 1930s served to focus special attention on the human element and its importance in business management. One of these was the unemployment and human suffering brought on by the Great Depression. Another was the famous Western Electric–Harvard Hawthorne experiments which showed that people wanted to be noticed and treated like people and that productivity resulted from effective human relations in industry as well as from machines, working conditions, and efficient methods.[3] Unquestionably one of the most forceful influences was the growth of a militant national unionism which required employers to give increasing attention to the human factor.

By giving labor the position of a semi-independent contractor, instead of a resource to be used in the production process, the modern trade union movement forced managers to reexamine their job. They had to realize that the principal task of management is to bring about coordination of human effort and that a manager must attain enterprise objectives through the cooperation of people. This awakening to the importance of the human element has taken extreme forms in the case of some managers who have regarded their task as one of making subordinates happy at any cost. But the enlightened manager has realized that his fundamental task is not happiness itself but creating an environment for effective and efficient performance of those for whom he is responsible.

Awakening to the Importance and Nature of Management. Perhaps no influence has been greater in the modern era of business administration than the awakening to the nature and importance of management itself. Too few businesses realized the importance of the managerial task in making effective and efficient cooperation of individuals possible. It is probably true, as many critics have pointed out, that, prior to the 1930s, many managers regarded the employee as an inert instrument to be used, controlled, and dealt with in an authoritarian way. It likewise appears to be true that many managers became so immersed in the techniques of time and motion study, determining the one best way of doing things, adopting labor-saving machinery, and developing procedures which control action but stultify thinking that the full capacities and abilities of human beings were not being utilized.

This has been blamed by many critics, who have not carefully studied the literature of management, on the so-called classical management theorists. One finds in many books the statement that these writers of the classical school regarded the employee as an inert instrument and took a completely mechanistic approach toward the task of managing. Careful study of the classicists shows this is not true. One finds ample evidence in the writings of Taylor,[4] Fayol,[5] Gantt,[6] Mary Parker Follett,[7] and Urwick,[8] among others, that the classicists deeply appreciated the human element, did not regard human beings as inert instruments, and understood well, particularly when one considers the embryonic

---

[3] The so-called Hawthorne experiments, carried on by Professors Elton Mayo, F. J. Roethlisberger, and W. Lloyd Warner of Harvard, and assisted by executives of the Western Electric Company, have been reported in a number of studies, the most complete of which is F. J. Roethlisberger and W. J. Dickson, *Management and the Worker,* Harvard University Press, Cambridge, Mass., 1939.

[4] See, for example, *Scientific Management,* Harper & Row, Publishers, Incorporated, New York, 1911, p. 29.

[5] See, for example, *General and Industrial Management,* Sir Isaac Pitman & Sons, Ltd., London, 1949 (originally published in the French in 1916), p. 40.

[6] See, for example, *Work, Wages, and Profits,* The Engineering Magazine Company, New York, 1913, pp. 47–48.

[7] Throughout her writings there is such evidence, but see especially *Freedom and Co-ordination,* Management Publications Trust, London, 1949 (lecture given in 1933), pp. 47–60.

[8] From his earliest writings, Urwick emphasized the human element and the importance of leadership. See, for example, his *Elements of Administration,* Harper & Row, Publishers, Incorporated, New York, 1943, pp. 49–50, 88–89, 118.

state of the behavioral sciences, how the manager who did so was courting disaster.

To be sure, many early managers did not heed their advice in this regard, and many of them can be criticized for being unduly concerned with mechanisms rather than people. But the period since World War II has been dominated by a concern for improvement in the quality and understanding of management. This concern has been particularly expressed in managerial development and training. And it has likewise been directed toward discovering, codifying, and developing underlying knowledge of management—a drive for scientific under-pinnings of practice—although admittedly this interest has as yet brought only limited results.

In addition, there has been the development and application of many new techniques and approaches which have unquestionably improved management effectiveness.

MODERN BUSINESS ADMINISTRATION AND THE MANAGER

The modern business administration setting is characterized by a great and expanding interest in the science underlying the art of managing and in improving this art. Yet, there are indications that a considerable amount of confusion exists in the field.[9] Much of this has apparently arisen from a lack of under-standing of what the task of the manager is and what the area of management knowledge encompasses.

The Task of the Manager. As is increasingly recognized, the basic task of the manager is to establish an internal enterprise environment for effective and efficient operation of individuals working together in groups. This environment is characterized primarily by a commonality of understood purpose, an intentional structure of roles, and managers who regard their obligation as one of removing obstacles to individual performance and creating motivation for performance. The manager, then, is an environment creator, and his job is to design and operate an environment where people, working together in groups, contribute, *as individuals,* toward the attainment of group purposes.

It is only in the sense of environment creation that the manager gets things done through people. Merely to say that the manager's job is to get things done through people is not enough—indeed it may even be dangerous, since it implies futile psychiatric manipulation by amateurs in a difficult field of medical practice.

To see the manager's task as one of designing an environment for performance is to see it as an engineer, a bridge designer, or a physician sees his task. All such artists attempt to use underlying knowledge to create an environment that yields optimum results, often through compromises in applying science in the light of the various realities and uncertainties faced.

All science is, to some extent, inexact—not everything in a field of knowledge is known and much "known" is not known for certain. The social sciences have perhaps the greatest areas of inexactness, and the field of management probably has the greatest amount of inexactness in the social sciences. Neverthe-less, this does not mean that the knowledge that is available should not be used by the practitioner.

---

[9] For an explanation of some of this confusion see Harold Koontz, "Management Theory Jungle," *Journal of the Academy of Management,* vol. 4, no. 3, December, 1961, pp. 174–188, and "Making Sense of Management Theory," *Harvard Business Review,* vol. 40, no. 4, July–August, 1962, pp. 24–48.

The Goals of the Manager. The goals of all managers in any kind of enterprise are in a very real sense economic. Their objective must be to obtain the maximum possible results, in terms of the goals of their company or department, with the least possible input of resources—time, effort, materials, or money. It should be pointed out that this objective is the same for government or for a university or for a golf club. This is not to say that every enterprise has a goal of making money. A moment's thought will discern that this is not the goal of a police department, a university, or a golf club. But whatever the goals of these nonbusiness enterprises are, those responsible for their administration have an obligation of seeing that they so manage the operation as to make possible an optimum "surplus" of results over inputs.

In business, the measure of surplus of outputs over inputs is profits, because it is the purpose of the business enterprise to show economic gain, in terms of outputs of marketable goods or services, over costs. Indeed, the business enterprise has an advantage over many other enterprises in that more progress has been made in business than elsewhere in obtaining fairly exact measurement (even with all the inexactness of accounting) of surplus attainment involved in operations.

Increasing Complexity of the Managerial Task. As needs for more effective management have been understood, as supercompetitive rivalry for markets, materials, men, money, and position spreads on a world-wide basis, and as new managerial knowledge and techniques are discovered, the job of managing, at every level of a business, has become more complex. In the first place, there is surely no more complex a phenomenon than interrelated human relationships in the typical business concern. Unpredictable human beings doing a variety of changing tasks and communicating in language that lacks crystal clarity are placed in horizontally and vertically coordinated arrangements of a complexity that makes nuclear structures seem simple by comparison.

In the second place, the manager must deal with not only an internal enterprise environment but an external one. The interfaces between the typical company and the market, political, social, educational, and other environments are many and complex. No business can operate in a vacuum, and virtually all businesses strive for continuity. The manager therefore deals constantly with a dynamic and intricate system of interweaving environments. To be socially responsive and responsible is merely to recognize the hard realities of business life. To do so is not an "extra," a state of "doing good," but rather a matter of self-preservation.

A third problem of the business manager is to handle economic problems of survival with change. Products, processes, costs, markets, and competition are almost invariably highly dynamic. And these changes are compounded by an acceleration of science and art in the physical and biological environments, by technological change that can obsolete a product or modify materially a market or process virtually overnight, and by consumer tastes which are not easily predicted or rationalized.

A fourth major factor affecting the complexity of business administration is the change in management knowledge and techniques themselves. Unless a manager is in the position to capitalize on this fast-developing knowledge, he will almost certainly find himself at the mercy of the manager who does.

THE CHANGING ENVIRONMENT FACING MODERN BUSINESS ADMINISTRATION

The changing environment of the modern business may be brought into sharper focus by noting some of the major needs and challenges facing the manager.

Management must be for reality. The successful business enterprise must deal with reality. But reality is a moving target. Reality is always tomorrow.

Need for Flexibility in Management. Because of the naturally high acceleration of change in society, and particularly because change has been quickened by the advent of two world wars and a long cold war since the turn of the century, a business must be geared to rapid change. But to be geared to change is to be flexible. This implies, in part, that those responsible for managing an enterprise must not only be aware of changes in the external environment, but move in time with the environment and be able to forecast the changes.

It also implies that the business must be able to change internally, in terms of organization, products, business methods and approaches, and human attitudes. It implies that the business manager must be able to understand that change does not come easily and that there are always resistances to change. Not the least of these is the well-known fact that human beings tend to resist change. The great scientist Edward Teller has said that the most inert material he has found in his scientific explorations is the human mind—with one exception, a group of human minds. And this is exactly what the manager must deal with.

In addition to human resistance to change, there are other serious inflexibilities which the manager must face. Some companies tend to look upon policies as written on stone instead of as guides to the thinking of people in their decision making which should change when necessary for effective planning.

There are also externally imposed inflexibilities. The most ubiquitous and dangerous are those involved in government and labor. These include the stubbornly inert network of government laws and administrative regulations, the intractable labor practices of seniority, automatic wage increases, and outmoded work rules and organizational jurisdictions—and the unwillingness of leaders to face up to the costs and dangers of these expensive restrictions to progress.

That handling these restraints to flexibility is essential to the modern business hardly need be noted. Handling them requires acute awareness, constant study, strong leadership, and forceful teaching of people, both inside and outside the business enterprise, on the need for change. Change must be dealt with in an enterprise as a way of life. One must remember that people affected by change will understand it best if they help make it and that change must be so introduced as to eliminate to the maximum extent possible its impact on those hurt by it.

Need for Understanding the Role of Formalized Management. A second area of challenge is that involved in misunderstanding the role of formalized management. With increased awareness of the human factor in administration, with extensive writings of behavioral scientists asking for more individual freedom and greater job satisfaction for people, and with growing concerns for individuality and creativity, formalized management structures have often come under fire. As dramatized by William Whyte in his famous book on the *Organization Man,* Simon and Schuster, Inc., New York, 1956, the picture often drawn is that of a formalized management situation where people are expected to be conformists, to practice intense "belongingness," and where the manager wields an authoritarian hand to suppress the needs, wants, and creativity of intelligent human beings.

One can grant the underlying thesis of Whyte and many management psychologists that people rarely think or create as groups, but rather as individuals. One can agree that the want satisfactions of people go far beyond the paycheck, without casting any necessarily damaging criticism on formalized management, particularly as exercised by intelligent practitioners in many of our outstanding business enterprises.

The question is not of conformity in organized life, but of the degree; no one can operate as a member of a group without some kind of conformity. Conformity is necessary in such things as speaking the same language, operating in the same quarters, filling out uniform accounting reports, and working common hours. The question is not whether there should be formalized organization and administration; no person can perform as a part of a group without a role to play, a task to do, a position to fill. The question is rather one of whether the role and the structure of roles give a clear task to be performed and make possible the exercise of creativity, initiative, and intelligence where they are required. The definition of a task need not imply undue restriction of the job to be done. And, by the same token, there can be no role, no task, without some curtailment of the freedom of an individual. Most individuals welcome this, particularly if it gives them a chance effectively to contribute to group accomplishment.

Increased Sophistication of Planning. A third challenge to modern business administration is the rapidly increasing sophistication of management planning—the task of setting actionable goals and ways of meeting them. This involves better and more comprehensive long-range forecasts, political, social, and technical, as well as economic; better spelling out of goals and giving them meaning so that their attainment can be verified; better and more formalized organization and procedure to induce planning; and better techniques by which planning can be developed in a systematic way.

Perhaps the most striking aspect of the newer approaches to planning has been the introduction of the logic and methodology of the physical sciences. Looking upon a business as a system—interconnected parts of a whole—and upon various elements as subsystems, attempts have been made to conceptualize systems, to use mathematical symbols to depict their variables and relationships, to arrange these relationships so as to give an "answer" in terms of specific goals, to develop data to replace the symbols, and thereby to arrive at logically based quantitative values for aiding in decision making. This approach, usually referred to as "operations research," has the advantage of forcing the decision maker to see the problem and the important variables involved. It requires him to give clear meaning to goals and measures of effectiveness in reaching them and to search for input data that can help him come to the best possible decision.

Other systemic approaches to planning may be found in such tools as variable budgeting, PERT (program review and evaluation technique), and information systems.[10] Variable budgeting regards budget making as a means of relating expense requirements to volume differences, thus giving the manager a tool for determining, in advance, what various levels of output volume *should* require in terms of manpower, money, or materials. PERT expands upon the Gantt chart by recognizing that almost every desired end event (such as the construction of a building or the design of an instrument) is preceded by a number of smaller, but determinable, events (such as the development of a sketch, the preliminary design of a needed circuit, or the completion of a "breadboard" model); that many of these contributing events are not completed in a linear way (that is, one after another) but in a network fashion (one event will be worked upon while another is being accomplished). PERT thus recognizes

[10] There are, of course, many other techniques besides those used here as examples. For a more complete analysis of these, the reader is referred to any of a large number of books on the subject, such as D. B. Hertz and R. T. Eddison, *Progress in Operations Research,* John Wiley & Sons, Inc., New York, 1964, and R. L. Martino, *Applied Operational Planning,* American Management Association, New York, 1964.

that any problem solution normally involves a system of interrelated events, related to each other in a network fashion. Out of this comes the possibility of determining which series (path) of events have the least slack time (or most cost) and therefore are most critical to the accomplishment of the final event. Information systems, likewise, are designed to look at information flows as interrelated and dynamic networks and therefore subject to clearer planning.

All these systemic approaches offer great possibilities to the manager for clarifying his thinking, forcing him to do planning, enabling him to see more critical or strategic factors in a problem, and developing information for more accurate and clearer analysis. Used in these approaches, the tools of mathematics are powerful primarily because business problems are complex. Also, the use of electronic data-processing machinery is important because of the sheer complexity of the models and the data being manipulated. But none of these means management by mathematics or computer. Instead, they mean assistance to the decision maker in dealing with complex phenomena and getting better analyzed information from which he can reach decisions.

Despite much hailing of the "computer age," practice has been slow in adopting the newer techniques of the physical sciences. This is partially because too many managers do not understand the newer techniques. Too many experts have inserted in their fields a mysticism and "mumbo jumbo" that makes understanding difficult. There is too much insistence on pure mathematics and too little on conceptualizing problem relationships, recognizing that a mathematical "model" is only a "black box," the inner workings and design of which the manager need not understand. Although it is important for experts in the field to expand the frontiers of knowledge by developing new techniques and approaches to planning, it is even more important for creative minds to find better ways of helping the practicing manager make existing knowledge operational.

Need for Improved Implementation of Plans. One must not forget that better planning is to no avail without better organizing, staffing, directing, and controlling. What is needed is an organization structure responsive to change and to the needs of plans; staffing of the structure based on knowledge of how to relate appraisal, selection, and training of people to enterprise requirements and to the need satisfactions of people; direction that will see that people are taught and led so as to assure their self-interest in performing organizational roles; and controls that objectively and understandably measure performance against goals so that deviations from plans can be corrected, preferably before they occur, by the person immediately responsible for the deviation.

There are numerous challenges for the modern manager in every area of plan implementation, but there is none more demanding than that involved in the improvement of control. To be effective, controls must be tailored. They must be tailored by being adapted individually to the needs of each plan and by being forward-looking so that deviations from plans can be detected and corrected before they are important. They should be tailored to the organization structure so that light can be cast on progress at a responsible point in it. They should be tailored also to the needs of the enterprise and to the man using them, by being understandable, verifiable, aimed at exceptions at strategic points, and economical.

New Vistas of Information. Perhaps the greatest challenge of control is that related to new vistas of information. It has been well said that "the reach of the executive is determined by the information system *at his command.*"[11]

---

[11] Stahrl Edmunds, "The Reach of an Executive," *Harvard Business Review,* vol. 37, no. 1, January–February, 1959, pp. 87–96.

This means information, preferably of a forecast nature, that is pertinent, measures performance against goals, and can be analyzed to determine what and where actions are missing goals.

The information problem is not data processing, storage, or retrieval. Hardware already developed can furnish more raw data than the business administrator can possibly digest and use. The problem is, instead, data indigestion. What is sometimes not realized is that data are unprocessed raw materials and require design and modification before they can become information. By simple definition, data are not information unless they inform. This requires specification of the information outputs desired and the design and definition of information inputs.

The quality of data, the widening of the spectrum to include social, technical, and political, as well as economic, data, and the need for digging deep into the organization structure for the right information present difficult problems to modern management. Managers, particularly in upper levels, cannot become lost in details, yet they must dredge up the information they need for decision making and the discharge of their job responsibilities. Managers cannot afford to spend excessive time and effort in keeping informed, for their task is to solve problems and see that decisions are implemented.

Need for Absorbing New Findings into Management Science and Practice. Attention has already been given to the need for absorbing new findings and techniques of the physical sciences into the area of business administration. But emphasis also should be placed on the need for absorbing new findings in other fields, particularly those in the behavioral sciences. Although some of these findings have been absorbed into management practice, the amount absorbed still appears to be relatively small.

There are many reasons for this, including difficulties of bridging the gap between the scientist and the practitioner, the natural tendency for managers to fear what they do not understand, and the regrettable fact that much of the research done by experts is not aimed at the realities of the management environment. But perhaps the greatest challenge lies in finding methods of integrating these new findings and approaches into the basic theory of an operational management science.

This seems particularly true with the outpouring of behavioral research which has appeared as yet to have little practical value for the practitioner. At times this has been because of the behavioralists' misunderstanding the nature and needs of practical management. For example, many behavioralists have mistakenly seemed to believe that practicing managers look upon the employee as an inert instrument, do not understand that people are motivated by a desire to accomplish, or establish organization structures to force subservience and limit decision making to the top.

There is much to be learned and absorbed from the researches of the behavioral scientists. In one of the most extensive inventories of empirically based scientific findings on human behavior, over a thousand separate findings are identified as supported by significant research.[12] Of these, many are not particularly significant to the manager. However, in the areas of motivation, face-to-face relations in small groups, organization, economic institutions, mass communications, and attitudes and beliefs, there are findings which are valuable.

The difficulty many business managers find with behavioral scientists is that many seem to "discover" what the manager has long "known." For example, such findings as "the larger the organization becomes, the more ranks of personnel

[12] See B. Berelson and G. A. Steiner, *Human Behavior*, Harcourt, Brace & World, Inc., New York, 1964.

there will tend to be within it,"[13] or "the closer the requirements of organizational membership are to the member's interests, training, ambition, or self-image generally, the better he likes the organization and the more likely he is to stay in it"[14] are not likely to surprise the experienced business manager.

On the other hand, a study of some of the findings of behavioralists will unquestionably open the eyes and improve the operation of managers. Particularly important are some of the findings on informal association and communication, motivation, the human desire to "belong" and "accomplish," the impacts of social stratification, union relations, and the interaction with management of such cultural institutions as private property. One of the shortcomings of the manager, understandably immersed in the problems of his department or company, is his inability to see himself and his subordinates as members and products of a cultural environment.

ASSURING THE QUALITY OF MANAGEMENT

When one looks at business administration in the modern setting, when he realizes the growing importance of management as the central force for efficiency and survival, and when he recognizes the challenges facing present management, he cannot help but be impressed with the overwhelming need for taking steps to assure the quality of those entrusted with managing. The most direct control of all is to assure management quality. Highly qualified managers not only make fewer mistakes, but are most likely to understand the impact of change and the future, to prepare for these, and to make sure that the enterprise takes advantage of its opportunities effectively and efficiently.

Despite tremendous advances in both management appraisal and training, the need for even better efforts is greater than ever before. To be sure, progress is being made. In the field of appraisal—which is the key to training—business and other enterprises have been moving toward the sensible system of appraising managerial performance by comparing actual results with verifiable quantitative and qualitative goals. If goals are properly developed and structured consistently with other goals of the enterprise, the system has the great merit of tying performance tightly into the operations of the enterprise. Likewise, as the system has developed, it has shown the way toward information needs and, by helping in information design, has helped in getting the right information to the right person, thereby hastening the day of control through self-control.

But as good as these performance appraisals are, they are not good enough. To remove elements of doubt or luck, and to get a better picture of probable *future* results, appraisal should be made of the quality of managing itself. How well does a person plan, organize, staff, direct, and control? It is entirely possible that fairly objective questions, based on existing principles of management, can be framed which can cast useful light on these subjects.

It is possible, also, that it will not be too many years before business firms will undertake a systematic and objective audit of the quality of management, aimed both at individual managers in a firm and toward the management group as an interlocking system of administrators. For the investor, the customer, the supplier, the banker, and the employee looking for a promising opportunity, this would seem to be the most important criterion by which trust could be placed in the enterprise. A balance sheet or income statement, if attractive, is powerful testimony to past performance. But there is nothing more persuasive than objectively determined and appraised management to give confidence in the future.

[13] *Ibid.*, p. 368.
[14] *Ibid.*, p. 378.

In fact, it could well be that, for publicly owned companies at least, a certified management audit may be a future requirement to supplement and give meaning to the certified accounting audit.

BIBLIOGRAPHY

Anshen, M., and G. L. Bach, *Management and Corporations, 1985,* McGraw-Hill Book Company, New York, 1960.

Berelson, B., and G. A. Steiner, *Human Behavior,* Harcourt, Brace & World, Inc., New York, 1964.

Drucker, P. F., *Landmarks of Tomorrow,* Harper & Row, Publishers, Incorporated, New York, 1959.

Eells, R., *The Government of Corporations,* The Free Press of Glencoe, New York, 1962.

Golembiewski, R. T., *Men, Management and Morality,* McGraw-Hill Book Company, New York, 1965.

Harbison, F., and C. A. Myers, *Management in the Industrial World,* McGraw-Hill Book Company, New York, 1959.

Hertz, D. B., and R. T. Eddison, *Progress in Operations Research,* John Wiley & Sons, Inc., New York, 1964.

Koontz, H. (ed.), *Toward a Unified Theory of Management,* McGraw-Hill Book Company, New York, 1964.

McGuire, J. W., *Business and Society,* McGraw-Hill Book Company, New York, 1963.

Roethlisberger, F. J., and W. J. Dickson, *Management and the Worker,* Harvard University Press, Cambridge, Mass., 1939.

CHAPTER THREE

The Emerging Discipline of Management

PHILIP W. SHAY *Executive Director, Association of Consulting Management Engineers, Inc., New York, New York*

The title of this chapter may sound somewhat cryptic and even esoteric in a handbook on business administration; yet the area of investigation that it designates is one of focal importance. To say that the modern mind is one that is characterized by its preoccupation with the managerial dimension of things is to emphasize the obvious and the often remarked. Long centuries of gradual awakening have led to an explosive realization of the importance of management in the twentieth century. The period since the end of World War II in particular has seen a rash of writing on the nature of management. Disconcertingly, this study of the nature of management has uncovered the fact that we do not know too clearly what management really is. Many questions have been raised to which no completely adequate answer has been given. Exactly what kind of knowledge is management? What is its object? Why have we had to wait until the twentieth century for the emergence of a discipline of management? What are the dimensions of the emerging body of managerial knowledge? What practical purpose will it serve? One cannot ignore these questions, nor can he reasonably abandon the search for their answers.

The purpose of this chapter, then, is to describe how and why a specific discipline of management began to emerge as a product of the twentieth century, and to try to shed additional light on its nature and characteristics, its purpose and function in economy and society.

MANAGEMENT THEORY: ITS GENESIS AND HISTORICAL DEVELOPMENT

Management is the process by which man attempts to give order, direction, and control to the various institutions of society to achieve certain purposes or objectives.[1] There has been this kind of direction of people in joint effort since the beginning of organized life. When one looks at the process of managing in historical perspective, he finds that what actually has gone on in management has differed over time and place throughout civilization. However, management has always had one common concern. The process of managing has always been a process of directing people in organized effort. In a primitive society, this may consist merely in having the young learn from association with their elders by assisting them in food-getting in the field or on the hunt or in other common efforts affecting the welfare of the clan or tribe. In more differentiated societies, it may be learned by passing through a period of apprenticeship. In modern, complex, industrial societies, it is no longer regarded as a wholly practical art requiring only common sense and experience. Rather, the managing process is beginning to be understood as a specific kind of intellectual work, a specific function in society, based on a growing body of theoretical knowledge. But in each case the goal has always been the same: to order, direct, and control the various institutions in a given society to achieve the common good. The basic insight resulting from reflection on the actual process of managing is that always and everywhere it is the process of ensuring the managerial and economic performance of the institutions of society.

It was not until the beginning of the twentieth century, however, that we began to understand that "managing" is a specific kind of work performed at several different levels in the various institutions of society, that the "manager" occupies a special role and performs a distinct function in society, and that it is possible to develop a unified discipline of management, a practical theory of the work of managing, which will incorporate its economic, moral, social, and technical aspects.

Although the practice of management is as old as civilization, the history of management properly began only toward the beginning of the twentieth century. Despite their important insights, nineteenth-century and earlier practitioners and thinkers in this field represent the prehistory of management, because they did not realize that they were dealing with a distinct and identifiable body of knowledge, practice, and function in society.

The Need for a Discipline of Management. In management, as in all arts and sciences, the effectiveness and efficiency of its practitioners depend upon the state of the underlying body of knowledge. It is no exaggeration to say that the most important index of the state of maturity of an art or science is the state of its systematic theory. This includes the character of the general conceptual scheme in use in the discipline, the kinds and degree of logical integration of the different elements which make it up, its methodology, and the ways in which it is actually used in research, teaching, and practice.

When we look at it in this way, we can clearly see that we do not have an organized, systematic body of knowledge or discipline of management that is formal yet practical and applicable. Since the first decade of the twentieth century, there has been an unprecedented increase in our knowledge of selected aspects of management. But there is, as yet, no fully developed discipline which helps make the tasks of the manager effective and rational, understandable and understood.

---

[1] These add up to the common good in a given society. The common good includes all the social goods, spiritual and moral as well as material, which man pursues here on earth in accord with the demands on his personal and social nature. The pursuit of the common good devolves upon society as a whole, on all its members, and on all its institutions, in accord with the principles of minimum intervention, legal justice, and distributive justice.

Every manager and student of management is confronted by the inescapable fact that the number and complexity of management problems far outpace the capacity of managers to deal with them on the basis of common sense, experience, general ability, and established practice. Although practitioners can never lose sight of immediate problems or tangible results, they must look to theory for new concepts, new approaches, and new techniques for help in the solution of these problems. There is no other recourse.

Theoretical knowledge does not replace practical judgment. Nor does the latter *necessarily* follow from the former. Nonetheless, theoretical knowledge makes practical judgment easier and more confident. Just as the work of day-to-day education cannot ignore the philosophy of education, and the practice of medicine cannot afford to forego the body of theoretical and practical knowledge developed and handed on in medical centers, so, too, managers cannot really be effective without an underlying theory of management.

In our highly complex civilization, it is no longer enough for managers to practice their art by means of a set of general abilities which they hold in common. They must become more and more active as students as well as practitioners of management knowledge. Managers must be able to look to theory for the foundation of good practice in managing. Management must become a rational, systematic, logical discipline in the practical order. It must enable managers to act on the basis of a definite hypothesis regarding the nature and structure of the principal institutions of society and of the environment in which they operate. This is increasingly becoming a central need of our economy and society.

Most Important Reasons. Thus there are urgent reasons for the early development of a fully integrated theory of management. Six of these reasons are particularly compelling.

First, it is virtually impossible to codify existing knowledge about management without some conceptual framework within which to do so. Theory is important for this purpose in any field of investigation. But it is crucially important in a practical art which must ultimately draw together contributions from many different knowledges, disciplines of knowledge, tools, and techniques. As a framework for the organization of information distilled from practice and research, a working theory is equally needed by the management consultant, the professionally conscious manager, the teacher, and the research worker.

Second, a comprehensive theory is needed as a guide to research. However tentative that theory may be in the beginning, it should help to discern gaps in both existing knowledge and ongoing research and thus to further the design of other research efforts. It will also provide working hypotheses as guides to individual research efforts and serve as a framework for the subsequent incorporation of research efforts into an organized body of thought.

Third, the absence of such a discipline makes it impossible to teach or learn it, and managers cannot use it as a guide to managerial behavior. All they have now are isolated parts of the total discipline to use in measuring their performance. Yet the need both for managers and for constant improvement of their knowledge and performance is so great, quantitatively as well as qualitatively, that we simply cannot depend on the natural development of a few outstanding managers.

Fourth, without an adequate theory of management, it is difficult, if not impossible, to understand modern business enterprise and other major institutions of society and their behavior. All we can do is accept what managers do on faith rather than on the basis of knowledge and understanding. Yet such understanding is needed for the success of the individual institutions of society as well as for the survival of industrial society and of the free enterprise system itself.

Fifth, the absence of an adequate theory of management also creates very real problems in the internal integration of the various institutions of our complex society in which there is growing specialization of work. Each specialist must be dedicated to his specialty. Yet each one must focus his specialized knowledge and contribution upon the whole institution as an operating entity that has tangible characteristics and qualities as opposed to its functional segmented parts. This kind of integrated effort is very difficult to achieve without a common understanding of the need to share a common vision and common goals and engage in a common effort. This can only come from a theory of management.

Sixth, the need for a systematic discipline of management is particularly important in the underdeveloped countries of the world. Their ability to develop themselves will depend, above all, on their ability to develop men capable of managing business enterprise and other institutions in their societies; that is, on the availability of a discipline that can be taught and learned. If these countries are to develop in freedom and with human dignity, management must serve as the central resource of development, and managers must act as the central catalyst of development. If all that is available to them is development through experience, they will almost inevitably be pushed toward some form of collectivism which economizes the managerial resource through concentration of entrepreneurial and managerial decisions in the hands of a few "planners" at the top.

For these and other important reasons, we must develop a unified discipline of management—a theory of the work of managing as social, technical, economic, and moral. It must incorporate what we have learned about managing so far from such fields of investigation, bodies of knowledge, and tools and techniques as scientific management, human relations, managerial economics, management science, management information systems, and systems engineering. And we must realize that it will have to draw upon a number of other knowledges and disciplines which can make useful contributions to it. These will have to be made one in theory as well as in practice. Without such a sound theoretical basis for managing, management decisions must be based largely on good fortune, brilliant strokes of strategy, hunches, hopes, and opinions. In view of the dependence of modern society on its institutions and their direction by managers, this is not sufficient.

Origins of Management Theory. The genesis and development of management theory appear to be related to the stage of social, economic, and technological advance and industrialization in society. There is considerable evidence to indicate there is a close relationship between the degree of industrial and technological development in society and the degree of interest in management theory. During the eighteenth and early nineteenth centuries, there were isolated contributions to management thought by a number of men in several different countries. Yet their contributions had little influence on the development of management during that time.

During the first 150 years of the Industrial Revolution, attention was focused on things and processes rather than on the ways people worked together in group effort. Emphasis was concentrated on knowledge of how to make steel, or clothing, or furniture. Men engaged in these callings gained their knowledge of how to manage the aggregates of money, plants, equipment, materials, and men by which these things were made, through apprenticeship or experience. Management was regarded primarily as a matter of common sense and general experience. Knowledge of a particular branch of business was the principal criterion of competence. There was no recognition of management as we are beginning to understand it.

There was little development or influence of management theory in society until society became highly industrialized. It was not until a factory system and large industrial organizations developed in society that there also developed an interest in and a need for an underlying theory of management for the conduct of business enterprise. Its need in the conduct of the other institutions of society gradually become apparent as they became more important and complex. Consequently, the systematic development of management theory began to occur in the highly industrialized twentieth century, with contributions to it coming mainly from theoreticians and practitioners in the United States, England, and several European countries.

Stages in the Development of Management Thought.[2] In the United States, management thought originated in response to the desire of pioneering industrial managers and engineers to separate waste and inefficiency from group endeavors in a growing industrial economy. In England and several European countries, management thought developed in response to the desire of top management industrialists and scholars to identify the vital functions of a business in economy and society and formulate some basic principles of management to serve as guides for more effective managerial performance in the conduct of the activities of business enterprises. During each stage of development, management thought has been influenced by the contributions of previously established disciplines such as economics, psychology, sociology, law, and engineering.

Progress in the development of management thought during the twentieth century has resulted in the convergence of these different concepts of management thought into similar conceptual frameworks for managers throughout the world. This has been facilitated by management education and research in colleges of engineering and commerce and business; graduate schools of business; professional management societies such as the Society for the Advancement of Management, the American Management Association, the British Institute of Management, and the Comité National de l'Organisation Francaise; and the International Management Congresses.

Stage 1—The Scientific Management Approach. The first identifiable stage of management thought in the United States was the *scientific management movement.* Scientific management was conceived by the pioneers in management thought as a philosophy or a mental attitude toward the intelligent use of human effort. The emphasis in scientific management was on maximum output with minimum effort through the separation of waste and inefficiency from human work at the operative level of performance. The approach to scientific management was: (1) experimenting; (2) setting work standards; (3) planning the work; and (4) maintaining by control devices the standards which were set. This conceptual approach to scientific management was modified during the 1920s to (1) management research; (2) management standards; (3) management control; and (4) cooperation of managers and workers.

By means of experimentation or research, proper tasks and standards were established. The tasks were the objectives; the standards pertained to personnel, conditions, equipment, procedures, and performance. Planning was separated from operative performance. This resulted in management responsibility for

[2] Parts of this discussion are adapted from Peter F. Drucker, "Fifty Years of Management—A Look Back and a Look Forward," *Fifty Years' Progress in Management,* ASME, 1960, and John F. Mee, *Management Thought In a Dynamic Economy,* New York University Press, New York, 1963.

the proper planning of the work and the employees' responsibility for the proper performance of work. An organizational framework was necessary for the specialization of the management functions and the work functions. Consequently, the functional type and the line-and-staff type of organization structures began to develop. Wage payment plans were devised to provide incentives for workers and to gain worker motivation and cooperation. The managerial function of control developed to assure actual performance in accordance with planned performance as established by the task and standards which were set.

The scientific management approach to the utilization of human effort in work assignments included emerging concepts of several functions of management, namely, a goal or objective, a managerial process for achieving the objective (now known as setting objectives, organizing, innovating, motivating, communicating, measuring, and developing people), and the use of people for the performance of work projects.

But by and large, the great body of industrial practice during this period dealt with the work of workers as presenting a separate design problem from the work of managers. Today, we believe it is impossible to maintain such a separation, for the design of the work of workers is one of the primary elements in the design of the manager's job—not only in terms of technology and similar productive competences, but also in terms of the design of intelligence and freedom into the total system.

Actually, the ten years between 1910 and 1920, the decade of World War I, was the period when the major themes underlying the discipline of management were largely developed. Much of the progress we have made since then, in theory as well as in practice, is only variation, extension, refinement, and better understanding of the attempts made during that decade to develop the conceptual framework underlying this discipline.

Taylor's *Principles and Methods of Scientific Management* appeared in 1911. Together with his famous testimony before the Congressional Committee a year later, this converted what had been a technique into an organized, systematic, teachable approach to the study of work and of its rational organization. This should not be equated with the art of management, even though Taylor was awarded the title of "father of scientific management" on his tombstone. Almost at the same time, Elihu Root, reorganizing the United States Army, and Henri Fayol, reorganizing a French mining company, established a counterpart to Taylor's study of the individual task within a work force. They established the systematic study of organization to determine what tasks have to be performed. And at roughly the same time, the Germans, especially Schmalenbach, developed the systematic study of the individual transactions which together make up the total economic results of an enterprise.

These three approaches look at enterprise and its management in isolation. But in the years after 1910, approaches that looked upon enterprise and management in society and the economy were also developed. In 1911, at the same time Taylor's *Principles and Methods of Scientific Management* appeared, Schumpeter in Austria published his *Theory of Economic Development,* which for the first time raised the question of the role of the manager in a modern expanding economy. Such recent "discoveries" as innovation, marketing, and long-range planning were all anticipated in this book. In the years before World War I, Walter Rathenau in Germany first concerned himself with the impact of large organizations on modern society and with the responsibility of management in a modern society. His concern was echoed in the United States, in the closing years of World War I, by Henry Gantt.

The question of the individual in the plant community and the industrial organization was the first of the management themes struck—it was Robert Owen's main concern in the eighteenth century. It was, however, the last one to be studied during this pre-World War I period. It was not raised again until World War I, most effectively perhaps by Elton Mayo, then still in Australia.

These major themes were developed independently. Although they have been further developed and refined since their inception, they have not been incorporated into a unified discipline of management to this day. Yet they have been part of the conceptual framework of management since their development. They are: (1) the systematic analysis of work; (2) the systematic study of the structure of work organization; (3) the systematic study of institutional efforts and results; (4) managerial and entrepreneurial economics; (5) the social position and responsibilities of management; and (6) the human relations of an industrial society and the place of the individual in it.

Stage 2—The Organizational Approach. During the 1930s, management thought was largely concerned with *organization* as the structure for managerial work. Administration and management were considered separate parts of managerial work.

Administration represented the ownership point of view. It involved the formulation of policies and the establishment of the organization. Then the organization became the mechanism of management for carrying out work assignments throughout the structure, which was conceived of as a network of routine operating and control procedures. The main function of management consisted of the exercise of executive control to assure the proper performance of work within the organization. The scientific management approach to work at the operative level continued in use for the purpose of separating waste and inefficiency from the operating procedures.

Although the principal concerns of administration were the general planning and organizing functions, it also performed a general control function. Management performed the functions of leadership, operative planning, and operative control within the organization. The concepts of administration and management were later modified by some authorities as administrative management and operative management. The former was concerned with the general management of the enterprise, and the latter with the management of specific projects or operative functions.

Basically, operative management was concerned with the division of labor and the assignment of responsibility as the primary organizational task. It was in this manner that the structural and juridical elements of the organization were brought into existence together.

For example, on the assumptions that everybody should have a boss, but no more than one (principle of unity of command), and that the number of people in relationship to whom one could be such a boss must be limited and on the small side, if the relationship be characterized by commanding and controlling (principle of span of control), there was developed inevitably the pyramidal shape or structure of organization, which is part of the classic language of the organization chart. The pyramid was forced to grow larger and higher, and intermediate levels of supervision or management were created as the enterprise itself expanded and grew.

At the same time, the lines on the organization chart expressed primarily juridical lines of force. They indicated, for example, the person over whom one has "authority," who is "responsible" for something, and who can be held "accountable" in case something goes wrong. Indeed, such a structure was more frequently a structure of internal positive law than a structure for doing the work of the business. In any event, the structure provided a way of visualizing the means by which a vast pool of authority at the top could be made to cascade over subsequent layers of management by something called "delegation" or "scalar process" and thus be divided among various managerial jobs.

To approach the design of an organization exclusively from the top down, to orient its process to the division of labor and the assignment of responsibility rather than to the mobilization of competences required by the design of the business and the needs of integrated tasks to be performed, and to think of a structure more in terms of juridical than of communication, decision-making, or action requirements—all these are characteristics of organizational practice prior to the 1950s.

Stage 3—Management by Objective. The general management approach to the attainment of desired objectives characterized the third stage in the development of management thought. During the 1940s, the conceptual framework for management developed into a *process of managing* that could be used as a general approach to the achievement of objectives for an enterprise as a whole or any functional part of it. Whereas management had previously been associated with production, personnel, and office functions, the concept of the managing process now became associated with such functions as marketing and finance as well as general management. This concept gave added importance to the functional areas of business and enabled scholars and practitioners in those fields to think in terms of objectives, functional processes, and guiding principles instead of descriptions of procedures and events.

During this period, management thought became oriented around the identification and refinement of the elements or functions in the managing process. The concept of "professional management" diminished the distinction between administration and management. Either or both were conceived of as a management or an administrative process. The governmental, institutional, and political pressures on professional management to justify the existence of private enterprise generated interest in the setting of socially justifiable, as well as economic, objectives for business. The experiences in the war economy and the subsequent period of reconstruction stimulated interest in the planning and decision-making functions. The growth of organizations in size and numbers of employees necessitated the use of divisionalized or decentralized types of organization to bring them under control and help people adjust to life within them.

The concept of managing as a process, which became highly developed during this period, consisted of definite and identifiable elements or functions: (1) setting goals, (2) formulating policies as guides to thought and action, (3) planning to achieve goals, (4) organizing to put plans into effect, (5) directing or motivating people in the organization to carry out the plans, and (6) controlling the activities in conformance with plans. The concepts which were inherent in the scientific management approach during the first stage and the organization framework of the second stage of management thought became sharply identified and were combined with the concept of managing as a process into an initial system or theory of management.

The concept of the managing process changed the concept of managing from that of a man or a group of men to a conceptual framework as the foundation for effective thinking and problem solving in the managing of business and other enterprises. The art or process of managing became a separate and identifiable activity that could be taught, learned, and practiced.

Stage 4—An Emerging General Theory of Management. A fourth stage of management thought is emerging. A number of the thought streams that emerged during the first half of the twentieth century have developed and converged to such an extent that they can be identified and integrated with the general concept of a generic managing process. We have reached a point where we can begin to construct a conceptual framework for a general theory of management as a synthesis of the management concepts that have been developed during the past sixty years by scholars and practitioners with diverse but related viewpoints about the actual process of managing the institutions of economy and society.

The trend toward a general theory of management promises a much broader perspective which will include its economic, moral, social, and technical aspects. Management has important allies in many different fields of investigation, fields of knowledge, disciplines, and tools and techniques which will help provide this total horizon. Thought streams and conceptual contributions from a number of these allies are beginning to be synthesized with the established concept of the managing process to form the body of knowledge which must be incorporated in the discipline of management.

Technology, in particular, is beginning to have far-reaching effects on the process of managing itself. It is becoming increasingly apparent that some basic management concepts which are part of this process will have to be reexamined in terms of the new tools and techniques for running an enterprise.

Advances in technology, which have been made in connection with large physical systems, particularly in the communications and computer area, are clearly and directly applicable to corporate organizations. A major transition of larger companies has been initiated by the explosive advances in communications and information technology.

The concepts and methodology which have been developed in connection with large systems engineering projects and military command management can also be used to advantage in the organization and management of companies. As the role of the manager evolves in this new environment, he will need to know more about systems engineering, and a significant part of his function will have a strong systems engineering flavor.

THE SEARCH FOR THE THEORY UNDERLYING MANAGEMENT

A study of the history of any discipline portrays the struggle that occurred before emergence and development eventually took place. The emerging discipline of management is no exception. First, there was the awareness of the need for a system of management thought because information remains a hodgepodge of fragments without an integrating structure. Unless it is organized, practical knowledge is a mere collection of observations, experiences, practices, and conflicting incidents. Second, there was investigation and experimentation designed to identify the principal elements of managing by means of analysis and induction. This analysis gradually resulted in a clear understanding of the generic process of managing. At the same time, various attempts to determine the theoretical framework of the discipline of management have produced both progress and confusion.

The systematic search for the structure or theory underlying management has taken place, with few exceptions, during the twentieth century and more especially since 1945. Until recent years, almost all of those who have attempted to analyze the process of management and develop theory to help the practice of management were perceptive practitioners of the art who based their thinking on many years of experience. The earliest meaningful attempts to order and unify the diverse manifestations of the total management job came from such experienced practitioners as Fayol, Mooney, Alvin Brown, Sheldon, Barnard, and Urwick.

During recent years, educators and scholars from many different fields have developed a considerable body of literature which offers many different and often conflicting points of view about the theory underlying management. The orderly analysis of management, which began to take place during the years 1910–1920 and later by some of the practitioners mentioned above, has been clouded and distorted to some extent by these newer approaches. There are the behaviorists, who see management as a complex of interpersonal relationships and consider the tenets of psychology and sociology the basis of management theory. A closely related group sees management as a system of institutional and cultural interrelationships. The significant orientation of this group is sociological. There are also those who feel that decision making is at the core of management and attempt to build the underlying theory around this concept. Still others consider management primarily as a logical process which can be expressed in terms of mathematical symbols and relationships. There are even those who regard the study of management as a study of one of a number of systems and subsystems, with an understandable tendency to include a larger and larger universe in the system.

It is possible to identify meaningful groupings of these management theorists, but because they may be classified in many different ways, there is no universally accepted listing. However, one logical way of ordering the various schools of management thought is to classify them in seven main groups as follows:

The management process school
The empirical school
The human behavior school
The social system school
The decision theory school
The mathematical school
The industrial dynamics school

Because these schools have been treated extensively in management literature (see the Bibliography at the end of this chapter), there is no point in analyzing and evaluating them here. Suffice it to say that these different approaches to the development of management theory have important insights to offer which can help give greater breadth and depth to the managing process and the emerging discipline itself. Management theorists will have to sift out and weave the valid contributions of these different schools of thought into a logical structure of management theory. At the present time, the theorists face such obstacles as semantic difficulties, lack of agreement on the definition of management as a body of knowledge, inability to understand that the ultimate test of accuracy of management theory must be practice, and mutual reluctance to understand each other.

However, a better appreciation of the insights and contributions of these schools of thought is developing. More educators and practitioners are aware that a study of human behavior or motivation, or of mathematical applications to problem solving, does not constitute the entire field of management. Also, there is an increasing understanding that many of the approaches are not really "schools of thought," but rather men with different training and specialties probing different aspects of the total management job.

Similarly, even though managerial terms are still being used in different ways and semantic differences exist, there is growing awareness that the words are being used differently. It is hoped that this awareness will lead to greater care in defining many simple management words in common use, such as authority, organization, decision making, and human behavior, in terms that can be clearly understood. This simple step, on which much needs to be done, is a requirement for communication as well as for the development of any discipline.

There is also a growing awareness that a discipline of management is emerging. There are considerable doubts as to what it is. Some see it as a synthetic art made up of bits and pieces of other disciplines. Others see it as a behavioral science in which the subject of study is the behavior of people and their managers in a group setting. Still others feel it is not possible to develop a generic discipline but only a series of isolated types of management. They seem to be saying that there is business management, hospital management, and school management; that there is military management, hotel management, and church management. A growing number of practitioners and theorists see it as a distinct discipline dealing with the specific process of managing in all types of institutions in society but drawing, as many other disciplines do, on the findings and theories of many other branches of knowledge.

Threefold Aspect of Nature and Characteristics of Management. *Managing* is a distinct kind of work, the *manager* is a distinct organ of and function in society, and *management* is an emerging discipline whose peculiar hallmark, in relation to other bodies of knowledge, is its focus on the managerial and economic performance of the institutions of society.

Initially, the theory of an art or science has no content of its own but reflects instead on content from elsewhere, formulating that content explicitly and theoretically. Thus philosophy begins with the attempt to understand understanding, and does so by reflecting on the actual act of understanding. The theory of education begins with the attempt to understand education, and does so by reflecting on the actual process of education. So, too, understanding of what management is results from an analysis of what happens when managing takes place. It does not begin with certain first principles from which the nature of management can be deduced. Rather, it looks to the actual process of managing. Thus, a theory of management, like theory in general, is a second-order knowledge, a reflexive explication of what is already given.

If anyone wishes to know what management is, then, he had better look at the concrete reality of what happens when managing takes place. This is not a question of what men have said it is or of what they have said it ought to be. It is a question of what, in fact, actually happens when managing takes place.

When one looks at the actual tasks involved in managing institutions of various kinds in economy and society, it is clear that they include guiding and directing the total design of the institution, setting the basic objectives, optimizing its resources, determining the main lines of strategy, planning and coordinating the means to achieve them, implementing the plans, managing human work and the relationships among people at work for joint performance, providing for its perpetuity, and keeping it relevant to the total environment in which it functions.

We are beginning to understand that there is such a thing as top management work with its own array of tasks and that such work cannot possibly be part of what managers do at other levels of the organization. Its specific concern is the net effect, the overall results of the total institution. It is becoming clear that this focus requires specific knowledge, specific information, and specific skills in addition to the knowledge of the process of managing.

Managers perform the complex tasks mentioned above at different levels and in different ways by means of the central and focal act of *decision making,* of which the concomitant, complementary, corrective, and regenerative act is *measurement.* Decision making looks to action and involves setting forces and people in action through a form of managerial action which is communication. Measurement is quantitative or qualitative appraisal of goal realization. There is a looseness and fluidity in the terms used to describe the specific work of managers throughout the literature on the subject. But these two central and focal managerial activities may be divided into the basic operations of setting objectives, organizing, innovating, motivating, communicating, measuring, and developing people. Every one of these categories can be divided and subdivided and discussed in great detail. The work of the manager, in other words, is complex. And every one of its basic operations requires different qualities and qualifications, knowledges, and tools. This work is the art or process, method or methodology, function or elements of managing.

These seven basic constituent operations constitute the work which every manager does, whatever his function or activity, rank or position, in the various institutions in economy and society. They describe the work which is common to all managers and peculiar to them. They can, therefore, be used by every manager to appraise his own skill and performance, and to work systematically in improving himself and his performance as a manager. The possession of an understanding of the work of managing constitutes the intellectual habit of managing. The development of the intellectual habit is the ultimate reason for the study of an art or science.[3]

The proper object of management is the managerial and economic performance of the institutions of economy and society by means of the process or act of managing—the specific work of managers. This is the formal object of the discipline of management. It forms the basis for explaining the nature and characteristics of management, for structuring the organized body of knowledge required for the total job of managing, and for making this knowledge available and understandable to its practitioners.

What holds management together and makes it a common possession of managers is the literature of management. The intellectual habit of management is control of managerial sources, familiarity with managerial knowledge, methods, tools, and techniques, and facility in managerial thinking which results in confidence in managerial practice. This habit of managing ought to be the professional skill of the manager, as a physician thinks medically and an attorney thinks legally without making any special effort to do so. Not all will possess this habit in the same degree, but each one should strive to become a better manager through study of the more significant literature and by using this acquired knowledge to improve his skill and performance in all categories of his work.

CONCLUSION

It has become clear that management is a distinct and identifiable body of knowledge about the managing process that lends itself to study, research, experimentation, understanding, teaching, and practice. It is a practical art, whose object is managerial and economic performance of the institutions of economy and society. This art is a special kind of intellectual work performed at several different levels of the institution. It is a specific function, distinct from super-

[3] Management should be primarily a vital quality and activity in the intellect of the manager, and not a collection or systematic organization of data either in print or in the memory. The purpose of teaching management should be first and foremost to develop in the student's mind a living habit of thinking managerially.

visory, functional, professional, technical, or any other kind of work.   It is emerging as a kind of general social dynamics for organizing, directing, and controlling the institutions of economy and society.   Managers have become a major leadership function in twentieth-century civilization, especially as the catalyst which makes rapid economic and social development possible.   This unique role of managers in modern society poses the need for the establishment of professional standards which will make the manager responsible to society for his use of its resources.   Moreover, management, like education or medicine, is tributary to many other knowledges, bodies of knowledge, tools, and techniques.   Undoubtedly, there will be a tendency for management to branch out into an increasing number of specialties, resulting in a continuously broadening scope of underlying knowledge.   Unless this tendency receives constant attention, management will be in danger of losing its identity as a formal body of knowledge.

Finally, management is not speculative or theoretical knowledge, but practical knowledge.   It is concerned with human activity to be guided and human tasks to be achieved.   This type of knowledge applies its conclusions to action.   These conclusions are stated in terms of what *is to be* done and are applied to singular actions here and now.

BIBLIOGRAPHY

Darr, John W., "The Management-as-a-Process Concept: A Consideration," *Industrial Management Review*, Massachusetts Institute of Technology, Cambridge, Fall, 1964.

Forrester, Jay W., "Structure Underlying Management Processes," The Academy of Management Meeting, Chicago, Dec. 30, 1964.

Koontz, Harold, "Making Sense of Management Theory," *Harvard Business Review*, July–August, 1962.

Koontz, Harold, "The Management Theory Jungle," *Journal of the Academy of Management*, December, 1961.

Koontz, Harold (ed.), *Toward a Unified Theory of Management*, McGraw-Hill Book Company, New York, 1964.

Mee, John F., *Management Thought in a Dynamic Economy*, New York University Press, New York, 1963.

Suojanen, Waino W., "Management Theory: Functional and Evolutionary," *Journal of the Academy of Management*, March, 1963.

Urwick, Lyndall F., "Management in Perspective: The Tactics of Jungle Warfare," *Journal of the Academy of Management*, December, 1963.

Urwick, Lyndall F., "The Problems of Management Semantics," *California Management Review*, Spring, 1960.

CHAPTER FOUR

Economics for the Manager

REUBEN E. SLESINGER *Professor, Department of Economics, and Associate Dean, Social Sciences, University of Pittsburgh, Pittsburgh, Pennsylvania*

The business manager must be aware of basic economic relationships, whether or not he has specialized in the tools and interpretations of economics as a separate discipline. Broadly conceived, economics is concerned with that facet of human behavior which seeks to explain how scarce resources are allocated among a wide variety of conflicting uses.

In the private-oriented, enterprise economies, these decisions are made in the market place as the forces of competition manifest themselves through the interplay of demand and supply. In other economies that are organized along totalitarian lines, the allocation decisions stem from the political policies of the group in power. In the former case, it is assumed that resources will be utilized where they will yield the greatest returns; in the latter, the planning group is supposed to be vested with some sort of knowledge that will keep its errors at a minimum.

Positive, Normative, and Applied Economics. The study of economics may be examined from three points of view: positive, normative, and applied. *Positive economics* seeks to discover the fundamental, all-pervasive laws of economics that are true under any circumstances and conditions. By and large these principles are related to physical features of the economy, such as the principle of diminishing returns.

Normative economics deals with value judgments and attempts to indicate what "should" or "should not" be. As such, these statements often reflect the attitude of the economist, and so must be treated in this light when they are used as the basis for public policy. Normative economics abounds everywhere—when one discusses, for example, whether a high tariff should be enacted, whether there should be minimum wages, whether the government should cut taxes, and the like.

Applied economics involves the attempt to relate economic principles and behavior to the solution of specific problems of an individual buyer or seller.

1–42

Thus, when a manager tries to assess the factors that should influence his pricing policies, he is dealing with applied economics. When the consumer studies whether he should purchase an automobile or save his funds, this is another instance of applied economics.

Micro- and Macroeconomics. In the study of economics, one may begin at one of two starting points. The more traditional approach, *microeconomics*, studies the nature of the decision-making process as demonstrated by individual components of the economy. Thus, it studies the behavior of individual firms and how they go about using resources or making their supplies available for the market. Microeconomics also is concerned with the manner in which individual consumers make their choices about which goods and services to buy.

Macroeconomics begins with the totality of the economy and describes the aggregate measures of the economy. It is concerned basically with why the level of economic activity is what it happens to be and what can be done about changing that level—usually to increase it. Thus, macroeconomics treats subjects such as the level of gross national product, the status of employment and unemployment, and the influence of the business cycle. The roles of the individual firm and consumer are then depicted as functioning within the structure of the aggregate economy.

Need for Clear Thinking about Economics. In this chapter, we will outline the processes of economics and discuss each briefly—in terms of a microeconomic approach. This will be followed by a review of the factors that determine the level of national economic activity—a macro-discussion. But, before these can be discussed, it is important to point out some of the pitfalls in thinking about economics so that economic thinking may be clear. There is one caution to be kept in mind constantly. The objective of this discussion is not to make an economist of the reader; rather, it is to familiarize him with certain basic economic tools and to explain how these are utilized in the process of making basic economic decisions. As a result, the reader should recognize that there are differences in approaches to national economic issues and that there may be several different policies suggested as a solution to the same problem. This chapter should help him in assessing what is basic economics and what is propaganda in these policy pronouncements.

There are several fallacies in economic thinking that have become so ingrained into popular discussions about economics that unfortunately they often are accepted as economic truths. One of the most common of these is the *fallacy of composition*. This is the fallacy of believing that what is true of the parts must necessarily be true of the whole. This type of reasoning is met when one begins to generalize after the examination of empirical data or when one attempts to describe group behavior as the summation of individual behavior. For example, it is argued that because individuals and business firms make up the nation, and because neither of these can go into debt indefinitely without bankruptcy, then the national government which consists of the summation of these parts also cannot run sustained budgetary deficits without bankruptcy. The fallacy, however, consists in failing to recognize that a national government has powers far different from those of its constituents, such as the power to create money and the ability to borrow on a wider base than can an individual firm.

Another fallacy is that of improper syllogistic reasoning, or more commonly, the *fallacy of the undistributed middle*. This type of erroneous reasoning sets forth a series of statements which in themselves are valid, but because they are unrelated, cannot be used to draw conclusions. For example, a major premise might be stated as: "Protective tariffs are necessary to provide essential skills for national defense." A minor premise then is asserted, such as: "Industry K is essential for national defense." The conclusion is that this industry should be the recipient of preferred tariff treatment. The fallacy, however, consists in (1) accepting that the particular industry is essential for national defense and (2) agreeing that there is any relationship between the major premise and what has been asserted as a minor premise. In other words, we have a *non sequitur*.

A third common fallacy in economic reasoning is that of the *post hoc ergo propter hoc* ("after this, therefore because of this") type of reasoning. This kind of reasoning assumes that a certain event will follow because another event has preceded it, because, in the past, this has been the pattern of behavior. Thus, it often is asserted that steel stock prices rise when the steel industry is on strike. Although this type of behavior has been observed on some occasions in the past, there are other instances where the opposite has been true. There is no causal connection between the two events; the relationship has been coincidental. Another similar illustration is the assertion that business will decline if one political party is in power and will improve if the other is in power. Closer examination of history will reveal that there are a multitude of forces in action and reaction and that a simple assertion such as the foregoing is erroneous because it overlooks a wide range of causes and effects.

THE PROCESSES OF MICROECONOMICS

The scope of economics may be appreciated if the study of economics is broken down into a series of processes. These are four in number.

Production. To begin with, economics studies the process of production. "Production" is defined as any activity that creates or imparts usefulness or utility into goods and services.

The normative question of the desirability of the production is not pertinent at this juncture. So long as anybody is willing to pay for the goods and services that are produced, production has taken place. One may contribute to the processes of production in several ways. He may change the form or shape of goods. He may store goods so that they are available when buyers desire them. He may transport goods to make them available where purchasers are located. Or he may facilitate the actual purchase and possession of the goods by rendering merchandising and financing services.

Exchange. Once goods and services are produced—for example, some $625 billion worth of national product in 1964—the problem immediately arises as to how these will be exchanged or sold by producer to buyer. This involves the process of exchange, or the determination of the value of the goods and services that have been produced. In simple societies, exchange may be conducted by means of barter where one individual who possesses an item seeks out another who has a commodity that the first person desires, and they trade their goods. This requires a double coincidence of exchange or the necessity for each of the persons involved to have exactly what the other desires.

In any complex society, such behavior becomes impossible. *Money* is introduced to facilitate trade. Now it becomes possible for the seller to state his asking price in terms of a common denominator, and the buyer likewise to express his offering price in the same medium. Money thus becomes a medium of exchange as well as a standard of value. In the process of exchange, attention is directed at how the eventual market price is reached and what guides the buyer in determining his bid price and the seller in setting his asking price.

Here, the principles of supply and demand are met. These will be described later in this chapter.

Distribution. In the process of production, the employer makes use of a combination of factors or agents of production. These include labor, or the human element; land, or the gifts of nature including natural resources; capital, or man-made goods that are used in further production; and entrepreneurial or managerial ability, or the services of the owner. The combination of these factors results in the national product, such as the $625 billion of 1964. The process of economics of distribution attempts to explain how each of the foregoing factors of production is evaluated in the marketplace and receives its share of the national product in the form of wages and salaries for labor, interest for capital, economic rent on land, and profits or losses for the entrepreneur.

Consumption. Once a factor of production has received its share in the distributive process and has paid the various taxes, that which remains is available to the factor to spend in a variety of types of consumption or to save. And so the final process of economics concerns itself with a study of consumption, or how the recipients of the national income use their funds.

DEMAND AND SUPPLY ANALYSIS

The heart of microeconomic analysis is found in the study of demand and supply. This approach begins with the assumption that economic activity essentially is concerned with the process of exchanging goods and services.

Before goods will be exchanged, the parties must see value in the things to be exchanged. The analysis of value takes the economist through the realm of economic theory concerned with the determination of the relative worth of goods or services. The "value" of a good or service in the economist's technical language may be defined as the power of that good or service to command other goods and/or services in exchange for itself.

Thus, if a fountain pen will trade for a wrist watch, for a pair of shoes, for an automobile tire, or for some advice from an attorney, we may say that the fountain pen is valued as one wrist watch, a pair of shoes, an automobile tire, or a specific amount of legal advice. This method of expressing the value of an object in terms of the multitude of goods and services for which it will exchange is cumbersome and inexact because of the limitations of divisibility possessed by most goods and services. Hence, qualitative measurement in terms of the many potential other goods is inadequate for market use. Other questions arise also, because of the vast amount of differentiation among products. What kind of watch, what brand, how many jewels? Or what is the relationship between the fountain pen and a suit of clothes? It would lead us nowhere to say that the fountain pen is worth one-eighth of a suit of clothes. Not only are there so many types of clothes, but of what value is one-eighth of a suit?

To resolve these difficulties, it has been found convenient to express value in terms of a common denominator—money. Thus, the value of a good or service expressed in terms of money is called its "price." Since each good or service finds its own value expressed in terms of this uniform common medium, it becomes easy to compare the relative worths of the goods and services to be exchanged.

Thus, if the fountain pen bears a price of $7 and the suit of clothes $56, the traders are enabled to measure the relative worths of their possessions and exchange them without the necessity of seeking a perfect balance in the value of each of the components.

We just assumed that one price was $7 and another was $56. But, this fails to answer why those particular two prices were chosen. Underlying the determination of relative prices are the forces of demand, representing the consumers, and supply, indicating the wishes of producers.

"Demand," to the economist, carries a special connotation. More often when the economist speaks of demand, he actually is referring to a "demand schedule." Thus, "demand" or "demand schedule" may be defined as an account indicating the various quantities of a good or service which will be taken by an individual or a group of individuals at respective prices. Underlying this schedule in determining the various price-quantity relationships is the principle of *marginal utility*.

Marginal Utility. "Marginal utility" refers to the subjective valuation or estimate of satisfaction placed by an individual on the next further unit of consumption. For example, if I have four oranges, what would the utility be to me of a fifth? My answer to this question would measure the marginal utility of oranges to me at that point.

A graphic illustration may serve to clarify the idea of utility. Let us assume some commodity, such as oranges. I now possess none, but am desirous of obtaining some for eating purposes. Conceivably, if I desired an orange strongly enough, I might pay a very high price for one. But, let us assume that $1.00 is as much as I would pay for the first orange. Having already consumed one, I might be willing to pay only ninety cents for the second. Having consumed five, I might be willing to pay only five cents for the sixth, and so on until after having consumed nine, I would pay nothing for a tenth. We may summarize my psychological attitude toward oranges as in Table 4-1.

This table tells me how much I would pay for an extra unit of the commodity in question. Thus, already possessing seven units, I would pay only two cents to gain the eighth. Hence, my subjective valuation for the eighth unit is two cents. Column *B* thus measures the marginal utilities. It is not that orange number four is any different from orange number two, but that it happens to be fourth in the series. Table 4-1 depicts the nature of marginal utility.

Marginal utility should be distinguished from total utility, which represents the summation of the individual marginal utilities. Thus, the total utility for all ten units is $2.92, although there was no marginal utility of that specific value.

Demand. Now that we have seen how utility fits into the picture of prices, we may return to the problem of demand. "Demand" has already been defined in the schedule sense as a listing of the quantities of a commodity which an individual will take at respective prices. Strictly speaking, we are then looking at demand from the individual reaction not only to a price, but to all reasonable

TABLE 4-1. The Nature of Marginal Utility

A Number Already Possessed	B Value of an Additional Unit
0	$1.00
1	.90
2	.60
3	.20
4	.10
5	.05
6	.04
7	.02
8	.01
9	.00

TABLE 4-2. Demand Schedule for Fountain Pens

Price per Unit	Quantity That Would Be Demanded
$10	0
8	1
6	2
4	3
3	4
2	5
1	6

prices. This concept of demand includes the usual implication that the individual is ready to buy, has decided to buy, and would be able to buy (purchasing power) the quantities listed.

There are several assumptions underlying demand analysis which must be understood and agreed upon before proceeding further.

1. We must consider the commodity as of a given time, place, and use. The idea is one of an instantaneous picture.

2. We must assume that all other things remain equal, save the individual's separate reactions to various prices.

3. All units of the commodity must be perfectly homogeneous and used for the same purpose.

The individual assumes an attitude, based upon his marginal utility, toward the prices of specific commodities. Let us assume that the commodity is fountain pens. There may be a range of prices at which a particular pen may be offered for sale. The individual subjectively calculates, on the basis of his marginal utility, how many he would take at the various reasonable prices and thus ends up with his demand or demand schedule. We might get the results shown in Table 4-2.

This table informs us that at a price of $10, the individual will take no pens. Evidently, the marginal utility of a fountain pen would not be great enough at that point to induce him to pay the quoted price of $10. But, as the price is lowered, he becomes a potential buyer, and at a price of $8, he is willing to take one pen. As the price declines, he indicates a willingness to take more pens, until at a price of $1 he would purchase six.

The tendency of buyers to take more of the same commodity as its price is lowered illustrates the *law of demand*, which tells us that under normal conditions, as the price declines the quantity that will be taken at the lower price will increase, and that as the price rises the quantity that will be taken at the higher prices will decrease. This is shown graphically by Figure 4-1, using the demand schedule of Table 4-2.

Figure 4-1 depicts the individual's subjective relationship between the various prices of the given commodity and the respective quantities. It becomes possible from such a graph by reading the approximate ordinates to make a rough estimate of the quantity that he would take at any price not specifically listed in the schedule but included within the range. Thus, at a price of $7, we find him taking one and a half units. When the unit of measurement is small, permitting small additions, such estimates are more important. The quantity of one and a half fountain pens is meaningless. Also, as the monetary unit of quotation becomes smaller, this estimation procedure becomes more important.

The discontinuity of individual demand curves tends to disappear when the many separate demand curves for each buyer are summated into market demand. Thus "market demand" refers to the composite demand which results

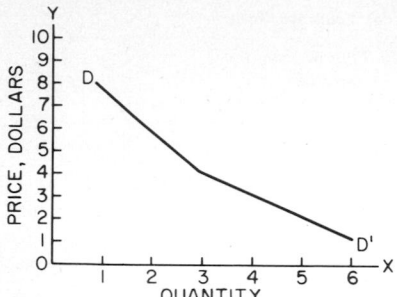

FIG. 4-1. *Graphic representation of the law of demand.*

when the various individual demands are compiled and added together. It is this resulting demand which interests the producer.

Because of a multitude of individual psychological reasons, buyers may increase or decrease their demand, and as a consequence, market demand may increase or decrease. Thus, demand is not a static concept. It changes. By a "change in demand" we mean that now, at the same given prices, the same buyers will be willing to take a different quantity of the commodity in question than formerly.

By an "increase in demand" we mean that at the same prices as formerly, the buyer is now willing to take greater quantities. By a "decrease in demand" we mean that now, at the same prices, the buyer is willing to take a smaller quantity than before.

The idea of changes in demand, including increases and decreases, is depicted in Table 4-3.

Whenever demand has increased, the new curve will lie to the right and above the original curve. When demand has decreased, the new curve will lie to the left and below the original curve. There need not be a change at every price, however. There may be areas when demand has increased, then decreased, or remained constant with reference to the same individual and commodity. Figure 4-2 presents the ideas involved in changing demands.

Given a demand curve DD^1, the quantity OQ will be taken at the price OA. When demand has increased as shown by the new demand curve DI, the increased quantity OQ^2 will be taken. When demand has decreased as shown by DL, the quantity taken at the old price of OA has diminished to $OQ.^1$

TABLE 4-3.   Quantity Taken as Demand Changes

Price	Quantity	Increased demand	Decreased demand
$10	0	1	0
8	1	3	0
6	2	4	1
4	3	5	2
3	4	7	3
2	5	8	4
1	6	9	5

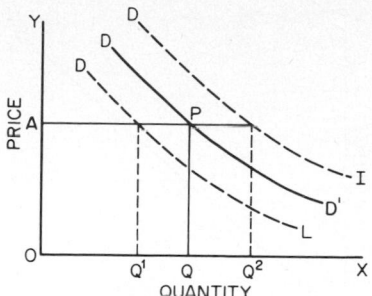

FIG. 4-2. *Graphic representation of changing demands.*

Demand Elasticity. Our next problem in the analysis of demand concerns itself with the concept of demand elasticity, or the nature of the responsiveness of the quantities demanded to changes in price. In general, demand is either relatively elastic or relatively inelastic, although conceptually there also is unitary elasticity, as well as perfect inelasticity and perfect elasticity.

By "unitary elasticity" we mean that the quantities which will be taken at various prices will change in such a way that the consumer always will spend the same amount for the item in question, regardless of the price. If he should spend more at higher than at lower prices, demand is called "relatively inelastic." If he should spend more at lower prices than at higher ones, the demand is described as "relatively elastic." In general, the demand for luxuries tends to exhibit relatively elastic tendencies, whereas the demand for necessities tends to be on the inelastic side.

Supply. Now that we have seen how the buyer side of market price behaves, let us turn to an analysis of supply to explain how sellers react.

"Supply," as understood by the economists, is conceived of in the schedule sense. Hence, we may look upon supply as a schedule listing the various amounts that sellers are willing to offer at respective prices, with the assumption that all other things remain the same, such as substitutes, time, and costs. Each supplier has his own supply schedules. These reflect his own reactions bearing in mind his opportunity costs, alternative uses, and reservation prices. These individual supply schedules are summated to give a market supply schedule.

The law of supply tells us that the quantities offered for sale increase as prices rise and decrease as prices decline. Thus, the quantity offered up for sale varies directly with prices. An example of an individual supply schedule illustrating the law of supply is shown in Table 4-4. This schedule shows that as we move from lower to higher prices, the quantities that are offered for sale increase. The typical supply schedule thus has a positive slope and moves upward when plotted on a curve as in Figure 4-3.

Given a particular supply schedule, supply is said to "change" when, at the

TABLE 4-4.   Supply Schedule Illustrating the Law of Supply

Price	Quantity Offered for Sale
$20	80
10	50
5	40
4	30
1	10

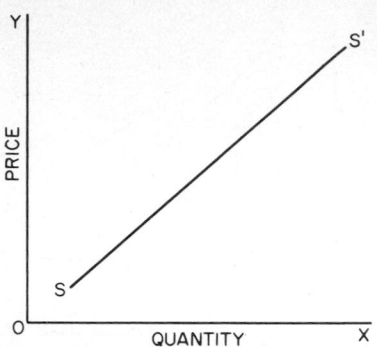

FIG. 4-3. *Graphic representation of a typical supply schedule.*

same prices as formerly, the suppliers are willing to offer different quantities than formerly. If they offer more at the same price, supply is said to have "increased." If less is offered at the same price, supply is said to have "decreased." Thus, a change in supply does not mean moving along on the same schedule to different price-quantity relationships; it implies an entirely new set of price and quantity relationships.

Supply Elasticity. Supply also exhibits the quality of elasticity. Supply is described as having "unitary elasticity" when the percentage change between two prices brings forth exactly the same percentage change in the quantity offered for sale. Should the percentage change in quantity offered for sale exceed the corresponding change in price, supply is said to be "relatively elastic"; if the percentage change in quantity is less than the corresponding percentage change in price, supply is described as "relatively inelastic."

COSTS

Underlying the supply curve is the cost situation of the producer. This may be compared with marginal utility in its relation to the demand curve.

The businessman looks upon supply as the result of his production. To him, it appears as tangible and physical. He considers the influence of price on supply as a varying factor depending on the length of time involved.

Although there is a serious danger of considering cost curves as supply curves, costs are most influential in determining the nature of the reactions of suppliers to prices. The supply schedule, it will be remembered, indicates how much the producer will offer at respective prices. The producer's costs throw light on why these quantities were selected for the particular prices, especially with reference to the longer-run situation.

There are many ways in which costs may be classified, each depending on the particular purpose of the classification. These classes include total fixed costs, average fixed costs, total variable costs, average variable costs, total costs, average total costs, and marginal costs.

Fixed Costs. Fixed costs are those costs which face the producer but do not vary in total amount with changes in the volume of production, within a given productive capacity. Hence, the unit (or average) fixed costs (total fixed costs divided by the number of units at a given stage of production) will decline as production increases. For example, if total fixed costs are $64.00 for a given range of production with a plant capacity of twenty-two units, the total fixed costs will be $64.00 whether one, ten, fifteen, or twenty-two units are produced. But the average fixed costs will decline from $64.00 to $6.40, to $4.27, and to $2.91, respectively.

The *average fixed* costs will tend to decline rapidly at first, because there are more units over which to spread the one lump cost. Then the rate of decline will decrease until the declines become small. So long as the given amount of plant capacity is unchanged, however, average fixed costs will show some sort of decline even though the actual amount of decline may be very small.

In practice, it is difficult to find examples of cost situations which are completely fixed. Most of the costs of business do have some sort of relation to the amount of output. However, for practical purposes those costs which do approximate the behavior outlined above are accepted as being fixed. These would include such costs as certain rents, interests, taxes, and other fixed charges, including some wage expenses. These will be present, technically, in an unvarying amount from the point of zero production to maximum production within the given capacity. Fixed costs are also known as "overhead," "burden," "indirect," and "supplementary" costs.

Variable Costs. Variable costs are those for which the total varies as the amount of production is changed. The rate of variation, when translated into terms of average variable costs, may be one which is declining, increasing, or constant. When total variable costs increase with production by a constant amount, the average variable costs will remain constant throughout; when total variable costs increase, but at a declining rate, the average variable costs will decline; and when total variable costs increase at an increasing rate, the average variable costs will decrease.

Variable costs include those costs which change with output, such as materials, labor, power, and transportation. These costs are also known as "direct" or "prime" costs.

The typical situation in most industries over the long run is for average variable costs to decline at first, because of internal economies of operation. These economies come about from such conditions as buying in bulk, more effective use of equipment, or better rates of purchase. Later, the average variable costs tend to level out until the stage of greatest economy is reached. Beyond that, average variable costs begin to rise once more as the producer begins to encounter various diseconomies of size.

The summation of fixed and variable costs at any point gives the total costs of operation for that quantity of output. Consequently, the nature of average total costs will be influenced directly by the nature of the average variable cost curve.

Marginal Costs. There is also another cost concept which is very useful and makes the actual determination of the optimum point of production easier to calculate (not considering the revenue side of the picture). This is the concept of marginal costs. Marginal costs are the addition to the total costs occasioned by the production of the next unit.

Table 4-5, depicting the hypothetical cost situation for a plant capable of producing twenty-two units of a given item, illustrates the reactions and interrelations among these various costs.

We may characterize the reactions of these various costs as follows:

Column *A* represents units of output. Because of the nature of the unit, represented by whole units, it is not possible to have the fine gradations called for under infinite changes.

TABLE 4-5.   Cost Situation for a Plant Capable of Producing Twenty-two Units

A Output	B Total fixed costs	C Average fixed costs	D Total variable costs	E Average variable costs	F Total costs	G Average total unit costs	H Marginal costs
1	$64.00	$64.00	$14.40	$14.40	$78.40	$78.40	$78.40
2	64.00	32.00	25.80	12.90	89.80	44.90	11.40
3	64.00	21.33	34.80	11.60	98.80	32.93	9.00
4	64.00	16.00	42.00	10.50	106.00	26.50	7.20
5	64.00	12.80	48.00	9.60	112.00	22.40	6.00
6	64.00	10.67	53.40	8.90	117.40	19.57	5.40
7	64.00	9.14	58.80	8.40	122.80	17.54	5.40
8	64.00	8.00	64.80	8.10	128.80	16.10	6.00
9	64.00	7.11	72.00	8.00	136.00	15.11	7.20
10	64.00	6.40	81.00	8.10	145.00	14.50	9.00
11	64.00	5.80	92.40	8.40	156.40	14.22	11.40
12	64.00	5.33	106.80	8.90	170.80	14.23	14.40
13	64.00	4.92	124.80	9.60	188.80	14.52	18.00
14	64.00	4.57	147.00	10.50	211.00	15.07	22.20
15	64.00	4.27	174.00	11.60	238.00	15.86	27.00
16	64.00	4.00	206.40	12.90	270.40	16.90	32.40
17	64.00	3.76	244.80	14.40	308.80	18.16	38.40
18	64.00	3.56	289.80	16.10	353.80	19.66	45.00
19	64.00	3.37	342.00	18.00	406.00	21.37	52.20
20	64.00	3.20	402.00	20.10	466.00	23.30	60.00
21	64.00	3.05	494.10	23.53	558.10	26.58	92.10
22	64.00	2.91	620.10	28.19	684.10	31.10	126.00

Column *B* remains constant throughout the capacity, because by definition this is the character of total fixed costs.

Column *C* declines, but at a declining rate, because a constant amount of fixed costs is being spread over an increasing number of units.

THE DETERMINATION OF VALUE AND PRICE UNDER PURE COMPETITION

Now that we have reviewed the fundamental forces behind the demand and supply sides of the valuation equation, let us direct our attention more explicitly to the determination of value itself and to price, the monetary expression of value. There may be many different solutions to this determination, each depending on the degree of competition present. This may range from the extremes of perfect and pure competition to those of perfect and pure monopoly, with duopoly, oligopoly, and monopolistic competition in between.

Pure competition (which is the type generally connoted when reference is made to competition) is the situation in which no one, two, or small group of producers acting as one are able through production control to affect price. In other words, a relatively *large number* of producers of a standardized and homogeneous product is required. Exactly how many will constitute a large number will vary under different circumstances. Nevertheless, the number must be large enough so that this number would not be in a position to control a portion of the market and, hence, affect price.

We already have indicated that value is the result of the interaction between the forces of demand and supply. These forces react to produce an equating quantity and an equilibrium price under conditions of pure competition. We may illustrate this behavior by means of the following example.

TABLE 4-6. Hypothetical Market Demand and Supply Schedule

P	Demand	Supply
$1	100	5
2	80	10
3	50	40
4	45	45
5	20	70
6	5	80
7	0	100

Assume the market demand and supply schedule for a given commodity shown by Table 4-6. Through the interaction of these supply and demand conditions, we find that supply and demand will be equated at a price of $4 a unit and that this will result in a quantity of forty-five being both the demand and supply quantities. At this price, there are no unsatisfied demanders or unsatisfied suppliers; at any other price there would be either more offered or more demanded. The price of $4 is then considered as the equilibrium and equating price. If, because of a temporary disturbance, price should be either higher or lower than $4, corrective forces will be set into motion which will restore the price to $4.

Figure 4-4 shows how a given demand and a given supply curve interact to determine the market price. Under conditions of competition (pure or perfect), it is quite easy to study the case of price determination and the action of the individual producer. The interaction of market demand and market supply determines the market price at a given time. The individual producer who forms a part of that market supply then faces that situation. By definition, under pure competition, the individual producer is not able to influence the price through manipulation of his production.

For example, suppose that suppliers and demanders of wheat have reacted to give a resultant market price of $2 a bushel for the equated quantity of

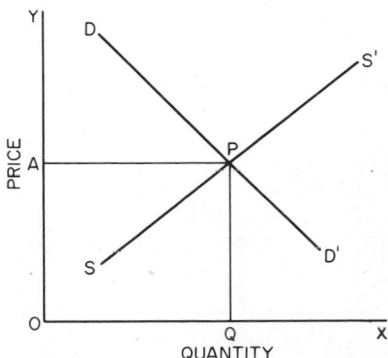

FIG. 4-4. *Interaction of demand curve DD¹ and supply curve SS¹ to determine market price OA.*

1,000,000,000 bushels. Any individual wheat producer, however, would have command over only a small portion of that supply. Assume that one producer commanded as much as 100,000 bushels. His share of the total output, however, is only 100,000/1,000,000,000 or 1/10,000. Hence, by withholding his production from the market, he would have but a minute effect in raising price. If he withheld his entire production, he might affect price by the amount $1/10,000 \times 2 = \$0.0002$. Under such circumstances, this farmer would seek to increase his income by producing more and selling this added amount at the going price rather than by curtailing production in search of a higher unit price to offset the reduction in quantity sold.

Thus the demand curve for the product of the individual producer under conditions of pure competition is *perfectly elastic* at the price which has equated the market supply and demand. Figure 4-5 shows this graphically.

Figure 4-5a represents the market equation under conditions of pure competition, the price and quantity being OB and OA. The individual producer now may sell all that he desires at the price OB. This same price is represented in Figure 4-5b by the line bp. There is no reason why the producer should take a price less than bp since OB ($= bp$) is the already-established market price. By definition, under pure competition, the individual producer is able to sell his entire output at the going price, because his percentage of total output is too small to be considered as important.

PRICE DETERMINATION UNDER OTHER CONDITIONS

Oligopoly. As the number of producers in an industry increases from the sole producer of monopoly to the many producers of competition, we have an in-between ground. In this case, the number of producers is more than two but less than the many necessary to result in pure competition. Thus, each producer does have an influence on the volume of output which, in turn, gives him some sort of influence over price.

Duopoly. This refers to a special case wherein the number of sellers is only two, each having an appreciable control over output, and hence affecting price by his own actions.

Monopoly. This is the situation wherein one producer is in control of the supply of the product. The degree of his monopoly will depend on the danger of potential substitutes for his product. Therefore, the pure monopolist would need a control not only over his product, but also over reasonable substitutes. Thus, although the American Tobacco Company controls all "Lucky Strikes," it is not a pure monopolist, because there are ready substitutes.

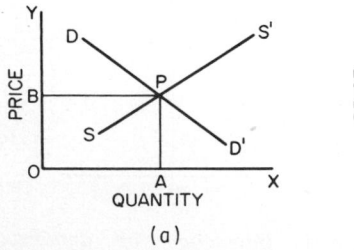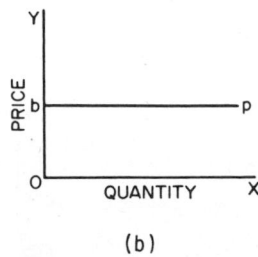

(a)   (b)

FIG. 4-5. *Demand, supply, and price curves under conditions of pure competition.*

Monopsony. In this situation, we have only one buyer. He may be coupled with one, two, a small number, or many sellers. His influence over price will vary in accordance with the number of sellers he meets.

Duopsony. In this case, there are two buyers coupled with one, two, several, or many sellers.

Oligopsony. This describes the situation wherein there are a small number of buyers accompanied by one, two, several, or many sellers.

Monopolistic Competition. This case covers the situation where there are several sellers of differentiated products all of which are close substitutes for each other.

MACROECONOMICS

A second basic approach to the study of economics is that described as the "macro-approach." This type of analysis begins with a review of the total national economy, and is concerned primarily with the aggregates of the economy, such as the level of national income, the volume of employment and unemployment, the structure of productivity, the shares of the national income earned by each productive factor, and the movement of general prices. Fundamentally, this approach premises that the economic health of each sector of the economy is uniquely linked with the status of the health of the economy as an aggregate body. Forecasting the future of the gross national product, for example, is a specific illustration of a macro-problem. Once such a forecast is made, then a given industry or firm within an industry is better able to predict its own future.

Measuring an Economy. The most commonly used measure of the performance of an economy is its *gross national product* (GNP), which is the market value of all the goods and services produced in the economy during a year, such as approximately $625 billion for the United States for 1964. To be included within the GNP, there must be current production as well as a market transaction. Thus, transfer payments such as the receipt of a pension, a social security payment, or a capital gain add to the income of an individual but are not included within the concept of GNP because they do not add to current production. Goods and services produced for one self also generally are not included, because these do not have a specific market value and their exact worth would be difficult to measure. There are a few exceptions, however, such as food grown by a farmer for his own use, the imputed value of the rent of an owner-occupied home, and goods produced for inventory.

Gross national product is adjusted further by subtracting the amount of the market price that represents the cost of capital consumption, such as depreciation. The result is known as "net national product" (NNP), and is a better measure of the annual contribution to national product than is GNP. Care must be exercised in calculating both of these measures to avoid double and multiple counting. For example, if a manufacturer buys $25 worth of raw materials and parts from a supplier, adds labor and entrepreneurial efforts to the item, and resells it for $40, his contribution to GNP would be $15 since the initial $25 would have been counted at the prior level of production. GNP and NNP thus may be calculated as either final prices or as a series of values added to production.

In the production process, the businessman uses a combination of factors of production—labor, land, capital, and entrepreneurial effort. We are interested also in finding out how much of the national product is earned by each of these factors. Because a part of the price of goods involves indirect business taxes, the amount of these is deducted from NNP and the resulting answer is *national income,* which then measures the returns for the various factors of production.

Next, we recognize that in the American economy factors may be owned by either natural persons (individuals) or artificial persons (corporations). Persons also may earn income as a result of transfer payments. At this stage, then, we add in the amount of transfer payments, but deduct the amount of corporate profits that are retained by corporations as well as the amount of their corporate income taxes. The result of these additions and subtractions yields *personal income.* Persons, themselves, are subjected to various types of personal taxes before they can exercise discretion over the use of their income. If we subtract these personal taxes from personal income, we end up with *disposable personal income,* which is the amount of income that persons have left for themselves, either to consume or to save. It is interesting to note that over the years, on the average, American consumers spend between 92 and 94 percent of their disposable personal income for consumption goods and save the remainder.

Another way of looking at the national income is to examine the types of buyers of the gross national product. These include consumers for their various types of consumption outlays, businesses for gross investment (replacement investment as well as new investment), the purchase of goods and services by the various units of government, and the excess of exports over imports.

Still another way of examining the national product is in terms of the income streams that have been generated. This involves a description of the various income recipients, including wages, salaries, and supplements thereto; rental income of persons; net interest; income of unincorporated ventures; and income of corporate ventures.

Influencing the Level of National Production. One of the characteristics of the American economy has been the recurring periods of business expansion and contraction or the phenomenon of industrial fluctuations, commonly called the "business cycle." Since the depression of the 1930s, attention has been focused on the ways that the national government may influence the level of national economic activity. Essentially, these are two in number: monetary policy and fiscal policy.

Monetary Policy. Monetary policy attempts to influence the level of national activity by making money "cheaper" to encourage business activity or "dearer" to act as a damper. Monetary policy basically is engineered through the banking system and attempts to increase or decrease the ability of the commercial banks to make loans. It does this by attempting to increase or decrease the size of bank reserves against which the banks in turn make their demand-deposit loans. Banks are in a crucial position to create money as they extend loans, so any actions that affect the level of bank reserves will likewise influence the ability of the banks to extend loans.

The Federal Reserve System is the key to monetary policy in that although only about 40 percent of all commercial banks belong to the system, these banks conduct about 80 percent of all commercial banking business. The Federal Reserve System has three basic direct tools by means of which it affects monetary policy. It may raise or lower reserve requirements, raise or lower rediscount and discount rates, or buy or sell in the open market.

Because commercial banks do not carry a 100 percent reserve backing against their demand deposits, raising the reserve requirement will mean that the banks must contract their loans. Lowering the requirement increases their potential to extend loans. By raising the discount or rediscount rates, the Federal Reserve banks make it more difficult for the member commercial banks to borrow from the Reserve banks. Similarly, by lowering the discount rate, member banks will find borrowing made easier.

The most significant monetary tool in recent years has been buying and selling on the open market by the Reserve System. When the Reserve banks buy on the open market, they pay the member banks for the securities (Federal government obligations) by increasing their reserve accounts, thus increasing the ability of the member banks to make more loans. When the Reserve System sells on the open market, it sops up reserves of the member banks and thereby makes it more difficult for the commercial banks to extend loans.

Thus, as inflationary techniques, the Reserve System will decrease reserve requirements, decrease rediscount and discount rates, and buy in the open market. To act in a retarding manner, the Reserve System will adopt the reverse policies, and raise reserve requirements, raise discount and rediscount rates, and sell in the open market.

Fiscal Policy. Fiscal policy involves the attempt by the national government to influence the level of national economic activity through manipulations in its budget. By an expansionary fiscal policy, we mean that the net influence on the economy of governmental action is of an inflationary type and involves an increase in governmental expenditures and/or a decrease in governmental taxation. A contracting type of fiscal policy involves a decline in governmental expenditures and/or an increase in taxation.

The American economy became an experimental ground for the full operation of fiscal policy in 1964, when the national government enacted a tax cut and did not reduce expenditures. The net result was an expansion in the economy, but at the cost of an increased deficit.

In the final analysis, it is necessary that monetary policy and fiscal policy be geared toward the same objective. If not, it is possible that the one might be expansionary and the other of a retarding nature, thus offsetting each other. To some extent, this was the case during part of 1965 when the Federal government definitely was pressing for an expansionary fiscal policy whereas the Federal Reserve System employed monetary policy in a more restrictive manner.

Applied Economics: Other Sectors of the Economy. In any discussion of the basics of the study of economics, one faces a series of applied problems concerned with the specific attempt to solve economic problems arising out of specific decisions relating to the allocation of resources, price policies, expansion of facilities, and the like. Among these are the problems of agriculture, industrial organization, industrial relations, insurance, business finance, marketing, government regulation of business, industrial mobilization and war economics, economic growth, economic development, public finance, comparative economic organization, small business, public utilities, transportation, and international economics.

SUMMARY

This review of the highlights in the field of economics has by no means been an all-inclusive treatment of the scope, nature, and method of economics. Such a task would require the approximately 1,000 pages of a standard principles-of-economics text. Instead, what has been attempted is to indicate some of the highlights in the task of an economist, point out some of his basic tools, depict some of the problem areas in which he works, and generate a series of questions for the business manager so that he may fit his problems into the total economic framework of the economy and better understand why certain economic decisions are made that have very direct effect and bearing on his own operations.

BIBLIOGRAPHY

American Assembly, John T. Dunlop (ed.), *Automation and Technological Change,* Prentice-Hall, Inc., Englewood Cliffs, N.J., 1962.

Bain, Joe S., *Industrial Organization,* John Wiley & Sons, Inc., New York, 1959.

Board of Governors of the Federal Reserve System, *The Federal Reserve System, Purposes and Functions,* 4th ed., Washington, D.C., 1961.

Chamberlin, Edward H., *The Economic Analysis of Labor Union Power,* American Enterprise Association, Washington, D.C., 1958.

Committee for Economic Development, *Economic Growth in the United States: Its Past and Future,* Research and Policy Committee of the Committee for Economic Development, New York, 1958.

Dillard, Dudley, *The Economics of John Maynard Keynes,* Prentice-Hall, Inc., Englewood Cliffs, N.J., 1948.

Galbraith, John K., *American Capitalism,* rev. ed., Houghton Mifflin Company, Boston, 1956.

Hague, Douglas C., and Alfred W. Stonier, *The Essentials of Economics,* Longmans, Green & Co., Ltd., London, 1955.

Hansen, Alvin H., *Economic Issues of the 1960's,* McGraw-Hill Book Company, New York, 1960.

Heilbroner, Robert, *The Making of Economic Society,* Prentice-Hall, Inc., Englewood Cliffs, N.J., 1962.

Isaacs, Asher, and Reuben E. Slesinger, *Business, Government and Public Policy,* D. Van Nostrand Company, Inc., Princeton, N.J., 1964.

Katona, George, *The Powerful Consumer,* McGraw-Hill Book Company, New York, 1960.

Kindleberger, Charles P., *Economic Development,* 2d ed., McGraw-Hill Book Company, New York, 1965.

Loucks, William N., *Comparative Economic Systems,* 6th ed., Harper & Row, Publishers, Incorporated, New York, 1961.

Rostow, W. W., *The Stages of Economic Growth,* Cambridge University Press, New York, 1960.

Slesinger, Reuben E., and Asher Isaacs, *Readings in Contemporary Economics,* Allyn and Bacon, Inc., Englewood Cliffs, N.J., 1963.

CHAPTER FIVE

The Management Sciences

PATRICK J. ROBINSON *Marketing Science Institute, Philadelphia, Pennsylvania*

Since the end of World War II, the professional management services called "management sciences" have experienced astonishing growth. By 1966, thousands of persons were engaged in applying scientific techniques to the problems of management. The growth of this new science has been so rapid that, despite the considerable interaction between some management scientists and a few managers, many line and staff executives have little idea of what the management sciences encompass and how management scientists can help them.

The purpose of this chapter is to describe the efforts being made to establish an effective management research activity—a research activity that will help progressive business administrators in whatever way seems profitable and appropriate. The management sciences may not appear to qualify as a science as we commonly understand it. In the management sciences, there are no test tubes and few research laboratories. There is also no long-standing reputation for solving problems in a scientific manner.

However, in the management sciences there is an approach as scientific as that used in the laboratory. The value of management research lies in its effectiveness in assisting operating and administrative people to make improved decisions by clearly defining problems, gathering evidence, and presenting objective evaluations of alternative courses of action.

MANAGEMENT SCIENCE ACTIVITIES

First, let us consider some more familiar research in business. Most of us have some idea of the work which can be done by groups such as marketing research, economics, planning, and industrial engineering. We probably recognize that the full potential of their work can be realized only when it is tailored to each application. Questions of the span of effective influence and level of a staff group's reporting and communication are problems faced by all service groups, and frequently their success or failure in solving problems depends on the "setting" and the "breaks." Each such technical or research group, however, tends to focus on a specialized approach. Its personnel may become homogeneous, its problems may tend toward a fairly uniform kind, and its techniques may become standardized. This is not so in the management sciences.

Management science activities involve variety, change, and even "maverick" personnel. Management scientists can make worthwhile contributions to business problem solving when identified primarily with one operating department or when sponsored by a key executive whose effective span of control provides a suitable umbrella under which to operate. There remains, however, a considerable untapped potential which is both a challenge and a stumbling block. Business problems and key decisions rarely fall neatly into just one formalized part of the organization. There are usually a number of related activities intimately involved, and these must be identified at the outset of each project if studies are to be realistic and worth top management attention and use.

The Management Scientist's Approach. "Scientific method" is the one all-inclusive description of a scientist's point of view or approach to problems. The management scientist starts with management's statement of a problem (frequently symptomatic in nature). The scientist may ask many questions about the problems and operations under study. Some of these questions may seem irreverent or suggest that the management scientist is uninformed. These questions, however, are entirely relevant and are essential to determine the underlying causes or relationships. From the information gathered, the management scientist may formulate some basic notions or hypotheses about what it is that requires study. He then evolves research objectives on which to design experiments or to plan observational studies to test and either support or set aside his ideas or hypotheses.

At the outset, the scientist must discuss the research plan with the manager to see whether the research objectives and anticipated results of the tested hypothesis will be worthwhile. This discussion is held before the research is undertaken. Business research cannot be purely academic in its problem-solving approach. It must be clear in advance of the scientific work that the outcome of the research will be almost certainly well aimed and that the results will be of importance as an effective basis for making decisions and taking action. The irreverent but vital question "so what?" should be asked at every opportunity by the manager and the researcher alike. Each must be satisfied with why the research is being done and how it may influence plans and operations. Even learning what not to do can be as important as finding new things to do or drastic changes to make.

The Scientific Method. The scientific method is a very special approach to defining and solving problems. In simple terms, the steps that define the scientific method are as follows:

1. Formulate one or more testable hypotheses or tentative theories with appropriate assumptions as to conditions.

2. Design an experiment (a very thorough and well-instrumented test) such that each hypothesis may be used to predict the expected outcome of the experiment before it is conducted.

3. Conduct one or more experiments under adequately controlled conditions, and measure the input factors and output results.

4. Compare experimental evidence with predictions, and then either set aside as false, or accept as apparently true, each hypothesis under test.

5. Proceed to use conclusions as operating guides or useful theories.

6. Continue to evolve and to test any further ideas by formulating new hypotheses for further experimentation.

Although this is not an elegant description of the scientific method, it is essentially complete. We are all apt to use something akin to the foregoing steps in our everyday work in trying to "figure things out." The true scientist, however, is more than a routine analyst. His mission is the quest for new knowledge. The scientist seeks truth and evidence to support his reasoning. He knows that through knowledge he achieves power—power to predict and to control; power to build and to change. Perhaps above all he gains the ability to shed light in dark places. This may lead in turn to other avenues which also invite illumination.

Judgment Based on Experience. The scientific method is the management scientist's chief *modus operandi.* Under certain circumstances, however, when time may prevent his use of the scientific method, there is at least one other approach. He should be prepared to offer a professional opinion based upon his own experience and special orientation, for a management scientist may be pressed for an immediate professional opinion without being given the opportunity for careful study, just as a doctor or a lawyer is often called on to express his informed views.

Management Sciences and the Manager. The practical business manager may ask why he needs to be concerned at all with this high-flown theoretical business research. What good can it be when it is so far removed from familiar operating practices? Some managers may even hope that it will all disappear if they only look the other way. It seems to be here to stay, however, and the only issue of merit is how to organize and exploit it effectively. A progressive manager will be anxious to learn more about the management sciences to discover how they may be utilized to help make better decisions.

The appropriate role of management science is difficult to define. The characteristic of mathematical complexity which appeals to the scientist has an unsettling impact on the businessman. There may be suspicion that the techniques will not accomplish all that is claimed for them. Unfortunately, this suspicion is often well founded—and the burden of proof must be on the scientist to demonstrate his potential. The burden on the manager should be to meet the scientist at least halfway. An indirect approach to the subject of what management scientists can do is to learn what they cannot do.

In making important decisions, it is not enough to know on purely intuitive or subjective grounds that such and such may happen. We need, and can get, sound qualitative and quantitative evaluations scientifically. With these, we may size up risks and compare alternatives better than ever before.

What is needed is acceptance of, and help from, trained observers and "professional thinkers" to "worry through" some of the practical ramifications of problems and possibly to introduce innovations and fresh viewpoints. These men can study systematically business decision-making problems and help focus on the probable consequences of alternative feasible courses of action.

THE ROLE OF THE MANAGEMENT SCIENTIST

The management scientist is a professionally trained researcher working on problems in management and business administration. It is his aim to aid industrial managers in their appraisal of complex problems to help them run their businesses most effectively.

When a manager is confronted with many alternative choices or decisions in a major problem area, he must rely on experience, judgment, and intuition. But sometimes even these may not be adequate to determine the best business tactics or strategy to follow. Whenever possible, it is desirable to reduce systematically the feasible alternatives to a manageable number for final review and action. This can be done through careful study and by weighing the odds and risks for each as objectively as possible. The executive must still make the decisions and assume responsibility, but he may be aided in this decision process by having the choices and risks narrowed to the most promising alternatives. He may then select from among these based on the precalculated chances for success, also weighing other factors of a more subjective nature which may be involved. Thus, the quantitative and qualitative considerations can be reviewed together to determine the best course of action for the organization as a whole.

Typical Problem Situation. A typical situation in which a manager can receive assistance from a management scientist is one in which the manager is responsible for directing certain limited resources and must use them to best advantage to achieve some desired objectives under conditions involving uncertainty or risk. The resources would probably include people, money, physical plant, products, and information. The objectives or measures of success might be maximum dollar profits, highest market position, desired percent return on capital employed, lowest-cost operation, or some more intangible aim such as best-possible public, government, or employee relations. Most often the so-called optimum or best performance to strive for is really an "optimum compromise" or blend of these and other considerations.

Clearly, it is not satisfactory to find a seemingly ideal solution to a problem, or to appraise the probable consequences of alternative courses of action based merely on what is best for one or another of many divisions or departments without regard for the general interest of the company as a whole.

A good example of the snowballing effect a management science study can generate is the problem of determining policies concerning the owning and operation of so-called supertankers. Initially, the problem centered on the question of selection of one of two sizes of ship for possible construction.

As the project got under way with a team of marine experts and management scientists, it took on new dimensions. For example, aspects which had seemed critical were displaced by others which had not even been considered at the definition stage. These new perspectives in turn evolved and changed under further examination so that the research led into some previously unquestioned areas of decision making. As progress was reported, it became apparent that these developments were logical and of great significance in assessing the proposed purchase. Many other related decisions concerning fleet operations and transportation and supply management strategy were also influenced.

The decision makers, at first surprised at these developments, quickly grasped their significance and proceeded to make a long series of decisions for which this new information and these novel insights provided unexpected assistance.

In this particular project, the scope of the study necessary to meet the initial request ended up encompassing a whole range of key problems.

This project in part illustrated rather dramatically that sometimes the payoff in management science lies in indicating what not to do, just as much as in what to do. Sometimes changes, no matter how desirable they appear on superficial analysis, do not stand up when adequately researched.

THE MODEL

A basic feature of the management sciences is the use of models. "Model" is just another name for a representation of the system being studied. A model can be manipulated or analyzed more easily than the real system and hence permits the scientist to carry on varied experimentation efficiently. The model represents those phases and/or properties of operations which are necessary for understanding.

We are not in business, however, solely for the purpose of constructing models. In management science and operations research, as in all branches of science, the purpose of a model is not merely to describe the system but rather to permit a determination of how one or more phases of the system may be changed to accomplish some well-defined objective better. The advantage of manipulating the model rather than the system itself is obvious, particularly where manipulation of the system is impossible or where manipulation is possible but excessively costly or risky.

Types of Models. The types of models usually employed by science are many, but generally fall into three classes. First, there is the pictorial type of model; thus, a relief map is a model of a certain section of the earth's topography. Second, there is the analog type of model, where the pertinent phases of the system are represented by "analogous" phases in the model, similar only in function, and not necessarily in appearance or physical structure (for example, a blotting paper and salt water representation of an oil reservoir on which electrical conductivity in the model reflects porosity in the oil-bearing formation). The third and most widely publicized is the symbolic, or mathematical, model. In it, the phases of the system are represented by symbols and are manipulated according to some set of logical mathematical rules. The three classes of model represent a progression in several respects:

1. The *pictorial model* is usually the simplest to conceive and the most concrete to visualize, but the most difficult to manipulate.

2. The *symbolic* (or mathematical) *model* is usually the most difficult to conceive and the most general and abstract, but the easiest to manipulate.

3. The *analog model* tends to fall between the other two in respect to both ease of conception and manipulation.

Simulation. Using simulation techniques, it is possible to pretest many alternative business plans in searching for the most advantageous business opportunities. It is neither desirable nor necessary to perform trial-and-error experiments on an actual operation or company in the search for better ways of doing things. If enough is known about the operations under study, one may construct models to use, like a wind tunnel for testing aircraft models through controlled experimentation. With the aid of electronic equipment and advanced computational procedures, simulation has become a powerful management aid—although it requires skill and patience in application.

In many cases, we would like to know something about the probable behavior of a business operation or competitive system before we actually start it. We cannot usually arrange to have an experiment conducted using an entire business operation, because it would take too long, be too costly, or be contrary to company policy, and so forth. About the only way that we can hope to predict the consequences of courses of action before committing ourselves is through intuitive business judgment, scientific study, or possibly sheer speculation. Probably the best approach is a blend of these. This is where we come to the possibility of simulation—particularly if we are dealing with a changing or dynamic situation of some complexity.

Simulation stems from the scientific method. Simulation studies require clear thinking and a methodical approach to gathering evidence. This is basic to all empirical research and is merely the outcome of trying to reason in a strictly logical fashion from initial hypotheses through various carefully designed experiments. What we try to do in simulating for research purposes is to develop first a crude idealized system or model. Then, through successive approximations and refinements, we strive to achieve a useful reflection of actuality.

PROFITABLE OPPORTUNITIES FOR APPLICATION OF MANAGEMENT SCIENCES

There are at least four business situations for which the management sciences can open up profitable opportunities. One is the integration of decisions in very complex situations. For example, a multirefinery oil company prepares an annual plan that shows the amounts of various crudes to be produced, purchased or traded, shipped to each of several plants, manufactured into a variety of products, and marketed in a number of locations. To do this, a complete understanding of the interactions and trade-offs between all of the operating decisions is crucial to determining a profitable plan. An integrated mathematical program allows management to request a company-wide analysis to suit its requirements at any time and yet to receive it in a matter of a few hours. Formerly, it would have been impractically expensive, time consuming, and too late to be of use.

Another success has been to help make order out of chaos. Advertising by a food manufacturer, for example, has significantly increased sales. Production facilities are limited, the supply of the foodstuff is seasonal, and the sales response is erratic. Consequently, the marketing divisions are poles apart in terms of objectives. Management scientists have helped provide a way to coordinate the marketing decisions within the limitations imposed on manufacturing capabilities, while giving full weight to the best overall company interests in long-range profits and short-range customer satisfaction.

Third, as profit margins become lower, continuous *executive supervision* over routine decisions becomes too costly. A scientific approach to management by exception has combined historical experience with modern statistical tools and has resulted in standard procedures for handling many routine activity reports. Thus, the executive is freed of masses of data to focus his attention on pressing matters. Exceptional circumstances, when they arise, receive much more concentrated and meaningful attention than was previously possible.

A final factor that leads to profitability lies in the superiority of the computer to man in the speed of performing certain arithmetic and logical operations, and in the extensive library of information and banks of data which can be efficiently stored, processed, and retrieved on demand.

Profitable business research, through the application of the management sciences, builds knowledge of the business structure, its markets, its resources, methods of control, and appraisal for use by executives. Good research gives a solid launching platform for making wise decisions based on competent professional work.

Decision Making and Forward Planning. There are a number of important ways in which the management sciences can be of assistance in making decisions and improving forward planning.

1. They can focus attention on the basic functions and characteristics of the business as a whole, clearly and concisely. Symbolic mathematical descriptions can emphasize key relationships crisply, free of redundancies or inconsistencies. Realistic symbolic models can provide comparatively simple pictures of the operations under study and can be manipulated realistically so that sound inferences may be drawn with respect to measurement, action, and control.

2. They help crystallize assumptions, objectives, and alternatives on which management must base decisions. Clearly, it is vital to know just what possible

range of control and influence management may exert and what realistic constraints exist in the business environment. A realistic framework permits various hypotheses and strategies to be tested and refined to help select the best course of action and also reveal the range of realistic alternatives prior to management's making final decisions or taking action.

3. They permit the evaluation of risks and the need for possible changes in policy or objectives or allocation of resources necessary for any plan of action.

4. They help determine appropriate measurements of key criteria and performance measures in the business operation, and indicate who should have what information available when for effective action and control. In addition, measures of significant trends or changes in performance and control limits are also provided.

The management scientist has a delicate tightrope to walk, because sometimes he will produce answers that are hard to accept. However, he cannot risk the stigma of being accused of working backward from the answer just to be more "socially acceptable." This would be neither a service to the manager nor a satisfaction to himself. Here indeed is a function in which a "yes man" could be dangerous. The competent researcher knows that by employing methods such as those mentioned above, he should be able to demonstrate his worth and place in the hands of the manager new tools, novel ideas, and sound advice which can be employed to good advantage in daily operations and in long-range planning. Mutual respect and trust is the key to success.

Evolution of the Scientific Manager. How can present-day managers go about borrowing from the management sciences so as to become gradually more scientific managers? First, a word of caution: They should not try too hard! It is perhaps best to begin with an "appreciation" sort of approach rather than to plunge directly into a sea of technical and scientific literature in a desperate attempt to catch up with all that has happened since the period of formal education ended.

Just as the production manager and engineering department head look to the R&D scientists in the laboratories for solutions to knotty problems, so should managers begin to turn to management scientists for assistance in formulating and solving problems.

Even here, however, there is danger of companies trying to move too fast. It is important to go slowly when seeking to understand and apply these research techniques to modern business operations.

The manager should recognize that, in a very real sense, his business is the management scientist's laboratory. In fact, the manager himself is "part of the problem"! If the scientist overlooks the human factors involved, he may produce sterile research or mechanistic solutions. As Sir Robert Watson Watt (who coined the name "operational research") said, the management scientist or operations research analyst should be a "licensed busybody."

The management scientist should be permitted to inquire, to ask seemingly irrelevant questions, and to suggest new ways of viewing and doing things. The management scientist can produce useful and significant findings only if he is given the complete confidence and cooperation of management, with adequate opportunities to identify important issues and to participate in relevant administrative and policy-level discussions. Although a researcher may be expected to remain in the background, he should be encouraged to suggest appropriate opportunities for research. Management cannot be expected to anticipate just where research fits into problems or how best to employ it. Only by being freely accepted by management people at all levels and in all areas can the management scientist hope to do an adequate job.

Of course, a management scientist's continued participation in high-level discussions cannot be a privilege extended to all. Entry should be earned and held as a consequence of satisfactory performance. So there is a proving period—but it must be fair and realistic. The management scientist, just as his physical scientist cousins in the laboratories, must justify his presence by demonstrating his professional skill and resourcefulness.

THE TEAM APPROACH TO MANAGEMENT RESEARCH

Effective management research is more often than not a group activity. What sort of scientists makes up a research group? In truth, there is virtually no set pattern. However, a blend of mathematical, physical, and behavioral scientists of Ph.D. caliber (plus experience) is generally desirable. Professor Russell L. Ackoff, Director of the Management Science Center, University of Pennsylvania, and Chairman, Department of Statistics and Operations Research, outlined a typically sound basic team of specialists as possibly consisting of the following men:

One company man
One scientist (physical)
One engineer
One mathematician and/or statistician
One scientist (behavioral; biology, psychology, or social science)
One logician or specialist in scientific methodology

Expansion beyond this should be designed to obtain as wide a representation of the fields of science and engineering as possible, consistent with the personality considerations associated with good teamwork.

Questions of where and when to formalize a business research activity naturally rest with senior management. However, successful groups usually are responsible to a level at which effective access to all departments involved in studies can be gained and with adequate authority to determine and implement action. It is probably better to start such an activity anywhere that is convenient and let it gravitate to its proper location as more familiarity with it and its relation to the organization is gained.

Unfortunately, trying management science for the first time often demands substantial intestinal fortitude on the part of the manager and the scientist, as well as a willingness to be tolerant of one another's point of view and to be patient in persuasion. Here, a concept of teamwork is a must. Lip service alone is not enough. Both the manager who on the surface tolerates (but privately scorns or fears) the scientist, and the scientist who is patronizing (and defiant or condescending) in his attitude toward the manager, are in for trouble.

To foster the concept of teamwork, it is generally the manager who must be willing to extend the initial hand of invitation, and in doing so, take the first step. Above all, he is the *decision maker;* the problems and decisions are *his.* Neither the problems nor the decisions can be delegated, nor should they be relegated to the management scientist whose role is merely that of *decision aider.*

Managing the Management Scientist. When he is contemplating the adoption of a management science study, perhaps the most vital question for a manager to settle is whether or not he is prepared to face up to the problems of "the care and feeding of Ph.D.s." One must consider such items as suitable working quarters, compensation and advancement, flexibility in regard to work habits, adequate financing of research, forms of internal recognition and status (for example, entry to the executive dining room), outside publishing privileges, and participation in professional societies (including trips and meetings).

A scientist is apt to be quite different from a technologist, analyst, or other college-trained staff worker. For example, the scientist may not be at all interested in getting into management. In fact, this may be one of the things that he is really concerned about avoiding. Although he may wish to establish himself in business, he might also entertain long-range ambitions such as private consulting or an academic post. In any event, he may be very emphatic about wanting to stay abreast of his field professionally. He may be anxious to become active in business research although wishing to avoid business administration.

The technically trained man is usually quite sensitive about what is "good" or "bad" from a professional standpoint. He prefers to work for a person who will recognize and respect this. Furthermore, he wants to work for someone who is willing to see him learn and develop professionally. The professional employee wants to perform tasks which will enable him to gain experience and insight in his profession while working on his assignments. He wants recognition for his ideas and often develops an interest in what is going on in other parts of the organization.

Also, good professional people like to be busy. Some things will be assigned and others will be innovations of their own. If the work is challenging, it offers opportunities for creative thinking. Recognition will result from competence at solving assigned tasks, plus resourcefulness in innovation.

Ideally, the supervisor of professionally trained personnel, even though he may have technical training superior to that of his subordinates, must be a stimulator and integrator rather than the initiator and developer of ideas. His job is to generate the environment in which *the ideas of others can grow.* He is not the proprietor of the shop, nor is he the one who gives the orders. He is a chairman, but not a boss, of his unit. And while encouraging all sorts of individual initiative and listening at times to all sorts of crazy ideas, he must find some way "to keep the boys on the reservation."

Supporting the Management Scientist. A management scientist needs adequate resources to carry through his assigned task. This includes staff services and research funds. It is also probable that he will require field services and outside consultants to gain the opinions of "thought leaders" from the academic community.

Just as lawyers flourish in bookcase-lined offices and require specialized secretaries, so management scientists require their professional journals and books, computer programmers, and even laboratories, along with specialized computation and charting assistants. As medical doctors require examination rooms, dispensaries, and laboratory technicians, so the scientist in business may require a private office equipped with blackboard, a project room for teamwork sessions, and other research associates and assistants for the most effective operation. These examples are intended only to illustrate a few representative needs that may set the management scientist apart from the routine business analyst. Although the latter may get by with a cubbyhole office, some sales and financial records, and possibly an adding machine, it is not likely that a highly qualified management scientist will produce good results or last very long under such conditions.

Going about the task of building up an adequate management science staff and accompanying facilities too slowly may prove disastrous. This might be equivalent to expecting a firm to build up gradually to owning an executive aircraft by starting with only one pilot and no airplane and letting him prove himself first by driving a company limousine to "show his stuff." As unlikely as this illustration may appear, its parallel is remarkably commonplace. Many of the reported research group failures in business stem from an inauspicious beginning. This represents failure to recognize and establish at least a minimum effort. This generally means securing two or three scientists plus one or two assistants and qualified secretarial and clerical personnel.

The know-how required to turn management science potentials into company profits is attained only over a long-term development period. The halfhearted "wait and see" approach to management science and operations research is a risky and expensive policy to follow.

Another common cause of failure arises from inadequate communications between the manager and the management scientists. If good men have been hired, they should be trusted at policy-level discussions. It should be possible for them to get a real feel for the business and its problems. They have to be present to help identify the areas, problems, and opportunities for which their special expertise is most apt to prove productive.

CONCLUSION

Just as an astronaut cannot guide his spacecraft using only a compass and a slide rule, neither can modern managers achieve their true potentials and retain their business footing in the shifting environment of modern times without the best blend of scientists and judgmental skills. It seems likely that the following formula is fast becoming a "must": modern managers + management scientists = the successful enterprise team.

BIBLIOGRAPHY

Ackoff, Russell L., and Patrick Rivett, *A Manager's Guide to Operations Research,* John Wiley & Sons, Inc., New York, 1963.

Alderson, Wroe, and Paul Green, *Planning and Problem Solving,* Richard D. Irwin, Inc., Homewood, Ill., 1964.

Alderson, Wroe, and Stanley J. Shapiro, *Marketing and the Computer,* Prentice-Hall, Inc., Englewood Cliffs, N.J., 1963.

Beer, Stafford, *Cybernetics and Management,* John Wiley & Sons, Inc., New York, 1959.

Bowman, E. K., and R. B. Fetter, *Analysis for Production Management,* Richard D. Irwin, Inc., Homewood, Ill., 1957.

Burck, Gilbert, and editors of *Fortune* magazine, *The Computer Age and Its Potential for Management,* Harper & Row, Publishers, Incorporated, New York, 1965.

Buzzel, Robert D., *Mathematical Models and Marketing Management,* Harvard University Press, Boston, 1964.

Forrester, Jay W., *Industrial Dynamics,* The M.I.T. Press, Cambridge, Mass., 1961.

Kibbee, Joel M., Clifford J. Kraft, and Burt Nanus, *Management Games,* Reinhold Publishing Corporation, New York, 1961.

Langhoff, Peter (ed.), *Models, Measurement and Marketing,* Prentice-Hall, Inc., Englewood Cliffs, N.J., 1965.

Miller, David W., and Martin K. Starr, *Executive Decisions and OR,* Prentice-Hall, Inc., Englewood Cliffs, N.J., 1960.

Simon, Herbert A., *The Shape of Automation: For Men and Management,* Harper & Row, Publishers, Incorporated, New York, 1965.

SECTION TWO

ORGANIZATION

CHAPTER ONE

Principles of Organization

HAROLD F. SMIDDY   *New York, New York*

"Principles" is a word of many meanings, but the meanings fall into two main classes: "principles" as settled rules or laws of action, and "principles" as essential characteristics or propositions inherent in the nature of the field covered.   The first category is conceptually mechanical, routine-focused, and often most apparent in connection with bureaucratic organization.   The second is also fundamentally causative, but in the sense of affording a source from which thoughtful and imaginative action can evolve, though not in precise or predetermined form.   The word "principles" is here used in this second context.

"Organization" is used fundamentally to connote the act of organizing, as distinct from the work structure or the personnel so established in a pattern of ordered—and hopefully, orderly—relationships.

THE BASIC NATURE OF ORGANIZATION

Organization always faces the historic dilemma of conflict between the freedom of the individual working alone and the restraints on that freedom which flow automatically when it is brought into systematic, continuing interlock with the corresponding personal freedoms of all the other individuals in the organized entity or working team.

The principles of organization which apply to a given situation are a function of the philosophy of organization—or more broadly of human relationships—which is to govern the design and operation of the organized entity, as expressed through the personalities of both the managers and nonmanagers, or functional individual contributors, of which it is composed.

Choice of Organizational Philosophy.   The available philosophies from which to choose are of innumerable variety in detailed differentiation.   In practice, they classify more simply into two basically contrasting systems of leader-follower relationships.

The first is that of "command and obey," in which "organization" becomes primarily the definition and ordering of authority.   The alternative is that of leadership of voluntary followers by inspiration or persuasion. Here, "organization" focuses primarily on identification, classification, and division of the work to be performed and of the responsibilities and accountabilities for that work in terms of personal work assignments and of teamwork or relationships, duties, and obligations, so that overall performance and individual contributions will be optimized.

From the followership vantage point, the opposing philosophies, as determinant of the purpose of organization, are similarly clear. In the first, obedience to authority is assumed as a specific or implied contractual obligation of the employee-employer relationship, and fundamentally tends to be limited to areas—of both work and teamwork—as specifically spelled out by the employer.

In the second, responsibility and accountability—again for both work and teamwork—are voluntarily accepted on the premise that the interests and purposes of both employer and employee have persuasive elements of commonality, with consequent tendency for flexibility rather than rigidity, or mere conformance to employer design, in scope of responsibility assumed.

Freedom and Teamwork. In either case, the mutual give and take required to adapt individual freedoms to team performance may be achieved. In the first approach, the employee in effect contractually limits his freedom to the prescribed degree. In the second, the concept of "freedom" is in terms of the old expression, "Freedom is the right to discipline myself so I don't have to be disciplined by others." The key word is "discipline," used in the sense of education to effectiveness, rather than of punishment or chastisement.

PURPOSE AS BASE OF PRINCIPLES OF ORGANIZATION

Recognition that the purpose of organization, and hence of choice of philosophies of relationships on which to base organization, is the primary factor fixing applicability of principles of organization is, perhaps, itself the first such principle.

This is because this deeply fundamental choice, whether to organize essentially in terms of division of authority or of specification of responsibility and accountability for voluntary personal contribution and performance, closely governs the selection and phrasing of the other principles needed and applicable.

Subgroupings of Principles. Further categorization of principles of organization, once such basic choice is clearly faced and taken, in turn falls into three broad groups.

The first deals with factors influencing organization which arise essentially out of its external relationships. An organized entity does not function in a vacuum, but is an element of wider systems, industries, or communities within which its own operations necessarily have either orderly and "organized" or else only casual, fortuitous, and too often chaotic relationships.

The second and third categories deal with organizational factors internal to the organized entity. One comprises the principles dealing with identification, classification, and division of the work to be performed; that is, with the nature and structure of the pattern of organization of the work.

The other class takes in those principles which apply to the doing of personal work within the organized pattern or framework and the defined objectives, and hence apply to team, or relationships, as well as purely individual work responsibilities. They deal, that is, with the progress and dynamics of personal work performance within the voluntarily assumed restraints inherent in the organizing process, to facilitate joint as well as individual performance and results.

The compensation for such voluntary limitation of personal freedoms goes beyond the monetary consideration which is, in fact, the major exchange measure under the command philosophy. It includes this monetary return but also added satisfaction from the opportunity to contribute and to share in accomplishments beyond those feasible if working entirely alone.

Again, the element of imaginative and creative flexibility is characteristic in such context; whereas bureaucratic rigidity and rather limited conformance to arbitrary routine is the normally predominant aspect in the "command" environment.

HISTORICAL IMPACTS ON ORGANIZATION

Historically, organization applied in communities where direction came from a rather small elite. Followership was the role of a lesser educated and motivated but much larger work force. It also applied when the work being organized was predominantly physical as to the energy and skills required.

It was probably natural, under such circumstances, that "authority" was the chief organizing factor, because capacity to carry more than limited, or even minimal, individual responsibility was considered relatively scarce, as to the work required, and was rather normally restricted as to the relationships, and so as to the teamwork, needed for organizational progress and success. "Principles of organization," as found in the managerial literature, accordingly tend to reflect—in both number and content—the predominance of these historic circumstances as to the actual or assumed capacity of the employees entrusted with work performance.

The applicability and usefulness of many of these principles—especially those in the first and third categories, where teamwork or relationships rather than direct personal work responsibilities constitute identifying elements—seem open to increasing question in today's and tomorrow's organized entities.

IMPACTS OF CHANGE ON MODERN SOCIETY

The prevalence of change, indeed of accelerating change, in all phases of our society and economy is even more widely sensed. Changes impinge in the technological sphere, as is dramatically evident to all. But parallel changes in the economic, social, and political aspects of our overall culture and civilization are probably of even greater organizational significance, although often less clearly visible.

The historic family, tribal, pastoral, and agricultural dominance in the local and national community give way progressively to prevalence of organizational elements which recognize increasingly technological, industrial, urban, and international characteristics.

A corollary distinguishing factor is the higher level of education—and so of knowledge and capacity to use it—of more and more individual members of the modern work community.

The instinctive will to human freedom and to creative application of personal mental and physical talents is presumably present before education, as such, takes place. But education, itself the systematic development and cultivation of natural powers, normally brings progressive increase in awareness of such instincts, talents, and potentials for their imaginative use in daily work and relationships.

A further corollary factor of modern change, and its impacts on all aspects of current and evolving culture, is a direct product of the greater ease of communication and transportation, and the automation of both physical and mental work, which have flowed from such change.

Teamwork in Complex Organizations. This latter factor takes form in the greater diversity, the more specialized content, and the more intricate interrelationships of resultant larger and more complex organizational entities.

A clear by-product is the progressive emergence of more, and of more complex, teamwork or relationship responsibilities in the combination of work and teamwork duties of individual jobs—both managerial and other, and both professional and nonprofessional.

Indeed, the day when the luxury of allowing dichotomies, or splits, to dictate job content—either "this" or "that," or, as often put, "this versus that"—could be indulged, has already passed in modern sizable and industrial organized entities, which function in urban rather than rural environments. It has to be "both," not "either-or."

The "no place to hide" aspect of modern living is visible in the shadow of globally destructive weapons. If perhaps less visible, it is no less dominant for most individuals today with respect to the social and political—the organizational as distinct from the individual—aspects of their lives both at home and at work. Community is a fact of modern life and community requires a choice, sooner or later, between anarchy (or chaos) and organization for mutual, but no less for personal, freedom.

The suggestion is pertinent here, therefore, that in judging or choosing between the essentially contrasting philosophies of organization—on the basis of authority or of responsibility and accountability, respectively—in today's real-life world, the historic prevalence of principles of organization geared primarily to the command and control approach is already undermined and is prospectively subject to progressive attrition and collapse. Education always has multiple consequences.

Organizing Educated Work Contributors. With increasingly educated, knowledgeable, and free individuals at all echelons of organized activities, the possibility that "command" can be imposed, or even that it will be contracted for, shrinks proportionately. The desire for "freedom" in organized efforts grows globally, whether in a follower or a leader post. It grows faster than understanding of its impacts and its implications for wisest choice of "principles of organization" on the part of leaders and followers simultaneously.

The preservation of "freedom" in the work community requires, as it did earlier in the civil or political community, the clearest of thought. Here, the historic examples of dictatorship, and its ultimate unacceptable human consequences and resultant practical unworkability, become as pertinent for the governing and the organizing of the new types of sizable complex work communities as for the older civil organizational units.

THE BASIC CONFLICT OF FREEDOM AND ORGANIZATION

Indeed, the first category of principles of organization dealing with external factors, including political as well as customer and other private relationships, only emphasizes the manager's mounting need to understand the essential conflict of freedom and organization and to develop competence to maximize personal freedoms in even the most complex organizational relationships. To do so calls for acute judgment in basing selection and use of "principles of organization" on the realities of today's and tomorrow's individuals and communities.

Thus the most basic nature of "organization," in the sense here used, is that it necessarily differentiates men working together to accomplish targeted common objectives from individuals working each for himself. The inevitable implications of such differentiation apply as much to the skilled "professional" worker, bringing chiefly mental skills to bear, as to the uneducated worker doing mainly manual work.

Human beings having the nature they do, this is a profound distinction. It is the nature of a man to be interested in himself to a high degree, to want and cherish the freedom to do things his own way, to try out his own ideas, and even to make—and hopefully to learn from—his own mistakes.

When that man is working entirely on his own, using his own time and capital and inner resources to satisfy his own purposes, the freedom to do so may be in proportion, limited only by the general statutory and community restrictions applicable and by the Golden Rule to do unto others as you would they do unto you.

But when a man agrees, for compensation and/or for the greater opportunity opened up, to work within an organized entity or group, although his desire for a similar measure of freedom may be unchanged, it clearly runs into new restraints required so that the parallel quests for personal freedom and creativity of all the others on the team may receive properly parallel recognition.

Restraints Inherent in Organization. The first and deepest nature of organization is thus that it brings restraints on individuals at the same time that it makes possible personal opportunities, challenges, and means for fulfilling them with personal satisfactions greater than those feasible or available when working alone. The identification and response to such restraints, on the part of leader and of follower alike, is a primary field for selection and application of principles of organization in the modern enterprise and community.

The root of most organizational problems, however unclear or difficult they later seem to get, is in this simple condition: namely, that organization for joint effort necessarily introduces restraints on purely personal freedom. And it also introduces, therefore, the basic issue of how best to sense, handle, and if necessary, enforce these essential restraints—and of how to do so in ways both humanly acceptable, on the one hand, and benign for greatest personal contributions and satisfactions, on the other hand.

The dilemma of organizational restrictions is, of course, inevitably personal to every individual in the organized enterprise. The more people in a particular entity, the greater is the need to face it in terms of mutually acceptable philosophy and principles—and acceptable to those specific persons and personalities—expressed and made known to all, rather than only by intuitive incident-by-incident approaches. Managerial second-guessing is properly cramped in such circumstances.

Managing as Leadership of Free Followers. A modern solution to the classic dilemma may be sought by defining "managing"—especially for organizing purposes—in the following terms:

Managing, as a distinct and professional kind of work, is *leading*, by inspiration and persuasion rather than by command . . . to secure balanced best results through the specific work of other people, who themselves are also acting with initiative, self-development, self-discipline, and competence in both their personal work and their voluntary teamwork and two-way communication.

Plainly, that definition is a broad philosophic base for preserving maximum personal freedom and yet achieving successful, timely, and profitable joint results. Because managing is practiced in a real-world organization of practical operating managers and other competent people, a "footnote" such as the following is perhaps also in order.

It is recognized that there may be emergency conditions or situations where persuasion has failed, and results of continued efforts at persuasion—in the judgment of the manager—would be worse than temporary use of "command" to get on with the job. In so doing, the manager is acknowledging temporary failure as a "professional" manager, and hence resorts to this course as an expedient only and takes requisite steps to identify and correct the root causes of the failure in order to prevent subsequent similar failures.

Voluntary Rather than Imposed Discipline. The above approach represents obviously strong dedication to the principle of organization that discipline should normally be voluntary rather than imposed. This concept is at odds with the principles of organization predominant in the past and most familiar to a great many pragmatic managers.

In essence, the root idea is that the degree to which managers are likely—in organizations of educated, reliant, thinking persons—to be continuingly successful and productive as leaders of fellow men is a fairly direct function of the attitudes and the values, no less than the managerial knowledge and skills, which they bring to their work. In the long run, it takes more than technical competence to lay out work for others and to lead and train them to get effective, economical, and enthusiastic continuity of performance in its doing. It takes ability to motivate so they will make the organizational goal their own and will voluntarily want to accomplish the tasks and timetables for which they are personally responsible, and in the context of the jobs and relationships of the others on the team.

In the United States, at least, taking and holding a job in an organized entity is voluntary. Anyone who does not care to discipline himself to adopt the organization's objectives, in addition to and in synchronism with his personal, professional, or other work aims—and thus to live harmoniously so that normal organizational restraints are most mutually effective and least chafing—can, and in due course he normally should, switch jobs to be able to operate in the context he most prefers.

The Rights of the Majority. A parallel principle of organization should be that any employee who is not of such mind, after due discussion and trial, should be removed. The organizational structure should not be unduly warped and varied to adapt to the idiosyncrasies of job holders whose incumbency is transient relative to the really long-run continuity of the organization and its dynamic teamwork requirements.

It is vital for the legitimacy of authority—and authority, in this sense, of both leaders and followers—to be clear, to be mutually recognized, and to be consistently exercised.

AUTHORITY OF KNOWLEDGE, NOT JUST COMMAND

Organized business and other efforts are carried on by increasingly educated people, many of them genuine "professionals" in their own work calling. In such an organizational world, a man's authority is really legitimatized, and accepted in the organization, by his authority of knowledge versus only of rank; by personal, visible competence in the specific situation; and, only as a last resort, by power to "boss" someone on the simple "do as I say" principle.

This does not mean that a manager, as such, should not have the power to decide and act, or that he should be a namby-pamby about using this power as good sense and good economics require and on time. It does not mean that, in trying fretfully to keep everybody happy, he should overlook personal failures or incompetence when, and for whatever reasons, the course of one threatens the aims and progress of all. The rights of the majority are not to be ignored, nor is the cooperation of the majority to be demotivated by tolerating noncooperative attitudes by the few.

Circuits of Authority. With highly skilled specialists, and even professionals, in nearly all functional work areas, it does mean that today's manager follows the principle of organization that he needs to acquire the skill to operate and perform effectively in what one European leader has called "circuits of authority"— not just "lines of authority" in the old-fashioned sense.

"Circuits" indicate flow, and the modern dynamics involved as the site of authority of knowledge for a particular situation shifts in real-life operations. "Lines" tend to imply the more static, and perhaps bureaucratic, aspects of the organization structure.

Channels of Contact. As a related principle of organization, the operational concept of "channels of contact" is similarly in point. This is the modern organizational practice that any two persons in an organization who have pertinent mutual, responsible interest in a situation or development should get in direct contact for information or ideas. The simple action of "go see the guy" will often save a bale of increasingly costly annd delaying memoranda.

There are limits, of course, and times to get back into formal organizational lines. This is specifically so where two persons in contact cannot agree, and therefore should refer the issue to their respective managers; where third parties are also involved; where the action considered would run counter to, or require amendment or waiver of, established policy; and where the direct responsibility of an upper-echelon manager is at stake. But by and large, one phone call will often save ten thousand words later.

Effective Use of Managerial Authority. The manager does have to exercise his authority, as a basic managerial skill, to move boldly from thought to action when the time is ripe. But throwing his weight around is more likely to develop experts in side-stepping its impact than in taking it on the chin.

Fundamentally in the modern enterprise, what is structured and organized is really responsibility, which then carries with it the appropriate authority to function, so as to be fairly accountable on a measurable basis. This inherent authority needs to be full and undiminished in each job so the individual incumbent can cope with its defined, and assigned, duties except only as most sparingly reserved, in writing and in advance, for particular kinds of organizational interests or recognizable operating situations.

Wise Delegation of Decision Responsibilities. Wise delegation to make a responsible organization workable involves more than decentralizing geographically or by readily identifiable products. Rather, it gets into delegating responsibility to make and to be accountable for particular kinds of purposefully riskful decisions. The aim of this decentralization is that resultant decentralized decisions will be made promptly and right the first time at the scene of the work and the job. In an internationally competitive world, it is not sensible, as an organizational alternative, to have the costs to do the work of deciding in duplicate or triplicate at two or three successive organizational levels, if only because these added costs would have to come out of hard-won net profits and could not be passed along in added prices to the customers.

Duplication of costs by excessive cushions of staff, audit, or so-called coordinating or control personnel—at any organizational echelon—causes competitively unfeasible delays, places emphasis on cure rather than prevention, and represents organizational clutter where streamlining is essential.

The attitude and skill of wise delegation is at the heart of profitability—that is, of the measure of value to customers above costs incurred—of the organized enterprise. It calls for delegating, really, to every human being in the enterprise the responsibility to make the timely decisions involved in carrying out his personal assigned work and teamwork duties within the established organization pattern.   The aim is to maximize the creative contribution of each individual in both his functional work and in the way he voluntarily gears that work in with the work of the others whom it affects.

Separation of Ineffective Workers.   A collateral requirement is that an employee who cannot or will not carry realistic responsibility needs either clarification or retraining on his job duties, or finally removal if, after fair trial, his continuing failures of either commission or omission threaten the effectiveness of the others and the profitability without which the jobs of all are at risk.

As the latter conclusion impinges, it is a basic organizational duty of the manager to see individual situations whole, to see individual men whole, and so to aid all concerned to develop the best pace, synchronized flow, timing, and turnover throughout all of the operations of the organized enterprise.

SPECIALIZATION IN THE ORGANIZED WORK COMMUNITY

Concentration on itsy-bitsy specialties alone is not enough.   If the cost of their performance is part of the costs of an organized entity, they have to be carried out responsibly and realistically in that context.   This is one price—but a fair one—for the privilege of functioning in the organization, with resources greater than the individual (even the highly dedicated professional) can have working by himself.

"Business" is truly an amalgam of "economics" and "politics" in the finest sense of both words: "economics" in the sense of being the base of the daily work satisfactions of most of our associates and fellow workers; "politics" in the sense of being the base of principles for the governing or managing of human affairs which truly rests on the consent of the governed, and with such consent by increasingly educated, creative, and reliant associates—volunteered and exercised with demanding self-discipline and personalized responsibility.

Organizing the Manager's Own Work.   As an organizational principle of sharp pertinence, only if the manager does seek, find, appoint, and wisely delegate responsibility to such associates is he safe to concentrate more of his own work in truly strategic fields.

He needs to do the latter so that he may better see and define overall goals, purposes, policies, and programs for attaining them—or alter their course in time as they advance or retard or shift.   But he does not need to spell out end elements or steps for accomplishing those goals, for he can be confident that his associates will do this better than he as their reciprocity for his confidence and motivation.

Unique Elements of the Organizing Process.   Viewed from this stance, the organizing process—for which persistent principles of organization are needed—comprises the following five unique components, here stated sequentially but carried on simultaneously and continuously in the dynamic real world.

1. *Determining and classifying work required* to accomplish plans and programs within the framework of designated objectives and policies; and dividing that total work into manageable components and jobs, in due combination with the facilities necessary for work performance, to provide best channels for coordinated application of available effort.

2. *Grouping components and jobs into an orderly organization structure;* grouping like and related work together in proper and most natural relationships to other work, to achieve best application of the combined human and material

resources of the enterprise, with appropriate parallel incentive and compensation for the organization structure so designed.

3. *Selecting individuals for designated positions and jobs,* with needed personal characteristics, skills, and knowledge and with personal values and character to perform the work of each job competently and in voluntarily integrated relationships to other jobs in the overall structure. The aim here is to man the organization structure to use the talents of each individual logically and effectively; finding and using what a man does well rather than what he does badly, to fit round pegs in round holes with sympathy and understanding—in turn removing, after fair appraisal against performance standards and after proper discussion with the man, any individual who is consistently inadequate either in performance or in compatibility.

4. *Formulating and defining methods and procedures for performing work to be done*—by seeking and describing the best and simplest way to do each task or kind of work, especially if repetitive, so that the aggregate work may be accomplished most imaginatively, quickly, easily, economically, systematically, understandably, and in good fit with perceived, or creatable, patterns of order in work and relationships, which will facilitate understanding, communication, and economy of money and energy in performing all necessary work (and no more) with greatest productivity rather than with greatest intensity of labor.

5. *Organizing the manager's own work and time* to allow focus on his specifically managerial responsibilities—especially to plan, organize, integrate, and measure to accomplish desired performance and results of the job, the component, and the enterprise as a whole.

Collateral Steps in Organizing. Pursuing most effectively the unique organizing work, comprised of the above five chief elements, calls also—as for other fundamental elements of managerial work—for three collateral steps on the part of the manager.

1. Making the designated organizational pattern, structure, and methods and procedures known to those in the organization, so that they and he can all perform as an effective, cooperative team.

2. Using results of regular and continuing measuring of all the work of organizing so as to facilitate its constant improvement, upgrading, expediting, and readjustment as practical experience and progressive observation and planning make possible.

3. Exercising judgment and making reasoned, objective, and timely decisions to effectuate the organizing work and progress; taking reasonable risks confidently, competitively, courageously, and on own responsibility, on the basis of facts and lore presently available; and choosing wisely from among possible alternatives as opportunity, responsibility, and need for each particular decision arise.

THREE CATEGORIES OF ORGANIZATIONAL PRINCIPLES

As indicated earlier, principles of organization within chosen organizational philosophy and structure fall into three broad categories: those dealing with relationships external to the particular organization, those internal to it, and those embracing the structuring of the work itself as distinct from elements or relationships arising out of its performance rather than its nature.

External Organizational Relationships. If the classic textbooks on organizing principles offer progressive weakness as aids in modern organizing efforts, a major reason is the multiplying complexity and impact of external relationships in today's world of work.

The classic categories of external groups whose interests have to be considered and balanced in organizing an enterprise are usually cited as customers, shareowners, suppliers, and the public, including government as the public's specific representative.

The complexity of relationships with all four of these groups (or five, looking on government in its own growing dimensions) grows apace, and this factor itself demands meticulous and progressive consideration of their respective, but also interlaced, interests in keeping the organization currently workable.

Before considering the four separately, a relatively new development of late years, with still undetermined consequences in impacts on organizing a competitive enterprise, deserves note.

External Aspects of Employee Relationships.   Relationships with and among employees—managers included (even when they also have some proprietary interests)—have long been classified as essentially internal to the organization.   For three major parallel reasons, employee relationships now, and on a forward-looking basis, have to be thought through as also having significant external aspects bearing on the corporate organizing process.

1. All employees to some degree have multiple interests and live multiple roles.   Work relationships are rarely even approximately coterminous with individual personal interests.

2. Unions, or organized bodies to represent groups of employees who make up their memberships, have growing practical and legal status in industrial nations.   In many vital operational areas, they actually supplant the individual employee to a high degree as a determining factor in managerial organizing potentials and processes.

3. Professional societies, or voluntary membership societies for individuals pursuing professional callings, make pertinent claims on the work choices and decision parameters of individual members even when the members are working as employees in organized enterprises rather than solely as personal professional practitioners.

As these combined internal-external relationship factors emerge and call for innovative managerial thought in keeping organization effective for future progress, the need for new research for identification, restatement, and new or revised application of pertinent principles of organization mounts proportionately.   Nor do principles for external relationships with the older recognized categories—customers, shareowners, suppliers, and the public (and its representative, government)—escape need for similar innovative research.

Customer Relationships.   Customers, in particular, are more affluent, more mobile, more educated, and more likely to have new wants (and the income to satisfy them) than ever before in history.

Competition consequently takes on bewildering new dimensions, with specific impacts on organizational principles.

The customer has new kinds of alternative wants beyond historic needs and also has available, from the fruits of technology, diverse avenues of fulfillment of particular wants.   Competition, which once was generally recognizably on a product-for-product basis, now takes in choices among greatly dissimilar devices for achieving a particular customer satisfaction.

Multiplicity of choices as a variable in customer decisions, and naturally in competitive thinking too, sets new norms.   They in turn hold stable for shorter time cycles.   Organizational principles and practices require anticipatory, or at least parallel, change and updating.

Shareowner Relationships. Among shareowners, a striking characteristic of modern society is that the proprietors or owners of the larger, usually pace-setting, enterprise and its managers or entrepreneurial decision makers increasingly are separate individuals.

As more businesses are conducted in the government-ownership sector of more nations, this dichotomy becomes even more striking. At the same time, managerial risks mount, and "professional" interests may seem to diverge substantially from those of management.

The legitimacy of managerial authority, divorced in a personal sense from that of proprietorship, calls for new foundations—hard to define and harder to communicate—so that public acceptance, with parallel scrapping of superseded traditions, keeps abreast of actual operational functioning. Here too, new "research" to discover, refine, and apply pertinent new or old organizational principles becomes ever more essential.

With people all over the world clamoring for improved local living standards, the business environment becomes more and more that of a savings-short, capital-short, and credit-short economy. Demands for venture, or shareowner, capital become cumulatively more intense. At the same time, political nationalism raises new barriers to free flow and supply of capital both at home and abroad. Resultant strains introduce wholly new aspects and factors in shareowner relationships, again with organizational as well as directly financial consequences.

Supplier Relationships. Suppliers of both materials and services also change in availability, scope, and interests, and external relationships of an organization are affected accordingly.

As technology and automation supplant variable direct labor or clerical costs with more fixed capital costs, with markets and customers still staying highly variable and dynamic, the enterprise moves toward rigor mortis unless old organizational principles are reappraised, reformulated, and remixed.

New kinds of make-or-buy decisions, especially on services rather than materials or product components, are called for. This is because specialized new kinds of vendors arise, and also because they may afford the only practical relief for painful or disruptive organizational cramps. Once more, "research" for continual modification and enhancement of useful principles of organization is demanded.

Public and Government Relationships. Public and government relations—because these groupings embrace the people in all the others—have, in a sense, multiple impacts on the organization, directly and indirectly through the others. With the public sector of the economy broadening at national and local levels, changes here have heavy influence on corporate operations and organization.

New uncertainties are created as governments tend to function in this period of rapid changes by having statutory law and regulations precede and form, rather than follow and codify, cultural customs in the business community.

Changes in all external relationships of organizations thus become constantly more intricate, uncertain, and bewildering. The general effect is to make anticipation of long-range organizational requirements more difficult and riskful, yet more necessary precisely due to the likelihood that past and current trends cannot be extrapolated safely far into the future years.

A peculiarly new and still unclear result is to create urgent needs for longer-range decisions. But these longer time cycles of decision responsibility increasingly tend to become shorter than those of normal tenure of an executive who has to make specific decisions currently. Normal present-day executive and managerial turnover consequently creates new needs for discriminating thought in measuring organizational performance against personal decision responsibilities. Inadequate, out-of-phase, or inapplicable managerial information has to be guarded against, lest it precipitate organizational changes of the wrong nature at the wrong time.

BUSINESS SYSTEMS RESEARCH

Under rapidly changing circumstances, from the standpoint of principles of organization, one new common denominator begins to appear widely as a current factor in corporate organization. However disguised in evolving nomenclature—often misguidedly clouded by thinking of "planning" as something of an end in itself—this new factor may be identified more sharply as the developing realization of, and recognition for, an additional primary work function in the organized enterprise, in parallel with such old standbys as research and engineering, manufacturing, marketing, financial and accounting, legal, and human relations work, and managerial work as such.

In its intrinsic aspects and characteristics, the new and evolving function perhaps may best be deemed "business systems research." Its work and purpose, broadly sensed, is to discover the patterns and relationships in the total situation of the organized enterprise, as well as of its responsible workers, whether as leaders or followers in particular respects, in order to facilitate wisest choices and risks in setting the enterprise's scope, goals, timetables, and overall operating efforts to reach optimum objectives successfully, profitably, and on time, both long and short range.

Organization Principles in Business Literature. Modern business literature comprises many thousands of volumes and articles on "principles of organization" applicable either for designing an organization structure or for staffing and operating an organization for effective human functioning. A competent business librarian can provide any interested manager with a reference list of such material of any desired scope, length, and depth.

But a warning and an indication of typical trends is in order to alert today's manager to the fact that organizational literature is still in the making. Indiscriminate application of so-called classic principles may fall far short of already foreseeable managerial needs.

INTERNAL ORGANIZATIONAL RELATIONSHIPS

In the sphere of internal relationships—the dynamics of operational human teamwork in the going concern—still-evolving factors have to be considered, such as the following:

1. Research into flow patterns or systems in operations, not alone into functioning in individual jobs or single organization components

2. The concept of "circuits of authority" earlier cited; perceiving the dynamics involved, or desirable, as the site of the "authority of knowledge" for a particular decision shifts in real-life situations, often at a pace making the conventional "lines of authority" concept economically hazardous

3. Perception and definition of the practical as well as the legalistic legitimacy of corporate managerial authority, with recognition that such legitimacy has to be humanly and practically acceptable in the organization, rather than only as statutorily applicable, where individual proprietary and organizational authority continue to diverge

4. Staffing to accommodate to multiplying needs to use specifically allotted work-time hours for long-range reeducation and retraining of all workers (managerial, professional, and others), to anticipate early obsolescence of current

work skills and greater mobility of personnel in specific jobs for both personal and work-connected reasons

5. Need for earliest feasible development of indigenous local work leadership, of requisite technical and cultural competence and responsibility, as decision responsibilities are progressively decentralized, not only within an organization but even internationally on an ever-faster scale

6. Realization and understanding that the advent of multiplying technology—especially by way of more rapid communication and transportation—creates human conditions where new organizational norms apply; where, on the one hand, change itself is a normal rather than a rare aspect of organizing, and where, on the other hand, multiple rather than narrowly channeled personal interests are also the normal dimension of human participation in organized work

7. Organizing functionally around continuing career work classifications, for synthesis and continuity of the work and results of individual persons as current problems and tasks or projects come and go

8. Helping present personnel and organization structure or relationships to develop and perform effectively, rather than impulsively trying needless changes which sacrifice critical competitive time, when a little more persistency and skill to get workers doing their best in relationships they already know can often get quicker results in work output and in satisfactions for all concerned

The above partial list of changing factors affecting internal relationships in the organization process is suggestive only of the scope of new concepts, varying emotional responses, diversifying interests, shifting motivations, evolving new man-machine interfaces, and reactions which necessitate the manager's attention and research to develop, define, and apply the currently most useful principles of organization for the changing work and people under his leadership, guidance, and inspiration.

ORGANIZATION STRUCTURING

In the area of organization structuring as such, new factors also arise or take on different emphasis almost continually as an aspect of normal operations. Again for example only, the sorts of new aspects impinging now embrace such items as:

1. Balancing the components of the organization structure so that due place is accorded for relatively stable and continuing functional work and also for essentially short-lived programs, projects, task forces, study teams, and so on; appreciating the high desirability of keeping the latter type of activities organized on essentially an incremental basis, so that upsets to established and familiar work contacts and relationships as projects rise and fade are effectively minimized

2. Achieving genuine decentralization and sincere acceptance of decision responsibilities and accountabilities

3. Putting long-range organizational emphasis on purposes and objectives rather than on detailed means and methods of subsequent individual performance

4. Making long-range plans for organizing in terms of the essential structures of the organization which are most subject to anticipatory guidance, such as the structures of the
   a. Product and market scopes
   b. Corporate financing
   c. Information and report system
   d. Facilities and material resources
   e. Human resources and their managerial leadership

f. Overall enterprise within the structure of the larger environment, industry, and communities of which it is but a component part

5. Minimizing so-called staff personnel external to the basic operating work functions and flow, with particular avoidance of duplication of staffs at each echelon of the organizational hierarchy so they become blockages rather than channels for decision flows and competitive, profitable work progress

6. Also minimizing the number of echelons of the organization structure, so that two-way interlevel communication is simplified and so that individual manager jobs have sufficient spans of responsibility to require full time on truly managerial work and to inhibit either kibitzing or, worse yet, second-guessing of the manager's own follower or leader associates

7. Understanding that conventional past accounting and report measurement periods increasingly may fail to give suitable information for measuring decision accountabilities of current incumbents of jobs with long-cycle decision requirements

8. Generally, re-researching accounting concepts and their operational applicability as the mix, in accounting statements, of ascertained current facts and of estimates (or guesses) for uncertain future impacts becomes evermore unstable and variable

9. Keeping operational information systems attuned to changes in the operating characteristics of the organization and its people and also to presently revolutionary changes in available computer-communication hardware and peripheral software for use in such systems

10. Sensing always that the imagination, the courage, and the ethical and spiritual values and beliefs of individuals will be the continuing basic source of creativity, change, and progress, with the technology of the physical sciences usefully employed but as tool, not master, for the men and women of the organization

Broadly, the need for enough stability of organization structure, and hence of attendant working relationships, to optimize individual creative performance and workable team results has progressively to be kept in good operational balance—both long and short range—with all the changing circumstances and interests which are normal in the ever-varying operating environment.

Keeping basic organization structure workably and recognizably steady and humanly comfortable, while still free of bureaucratic rigidities which cause the missing of opportunities to take advantage of new developments, taxes managerial skills and organizational principles heavily and constantly.

THE MANAGER'S SEARCH FOR PRINCIPLES OF ORGANIZATION

Faced with both the opportunities and the challenges of today's technological, industrial, heavily urbanized, international competitive trends, the modern manager's search for helpful and useful "principles of organization" has to center no less in his own head and heart than in his organization's library, or even in new managerial and organizational handbooks. Wisdom beyond mere knowledge, and beliefs beyond mere facts, are deeply essential for leadership.

Also essential is the ability to motivate increasingly educated followers by inspiration and persuasion beyond mere command authority. The continuity of the organized enterprise has to be apprehended, and comprehended, as an aim and purpose beyond current "problem solving" or projects.

The traditions and basic objectives of the organization, and its policies as their by-products, have to be made as clear and contributory as transient current work assignments or interests. Individuals oriented to the continuing work of the enterprise and willing and able to think and act to contribute to its effective performance for successful organizational continuity are always needed.

Imagination and continuing learning have to be consciously asked of all employees. Participation on their part as their personal work and teamwork responsibilities continue to become more complex and sophisticated has to extend to the organizational impacts no less than to the technological nature of the results of each man's thoughts and actions.

The manager's job, in turn, calls for ever-clear sensing that a fundamental purpose of formal organization is to fit the needed work and work relationships in the organization structure to patterns and trends which normally

Are longest lasting

Change most slowly

Facilitate continuing personal career development

Permit confinement of temporary project organizations to incremental functional activities

Offer a framework for teamwork least likely to require frequent upsets in working contacts, and in personal give and take, that at best take time to get flowing in a smooth groove with least wasteful friction

The responsibility to integrate as a specific personal commitment of work in organized enterprises is common and reciprocal to both the functional individual contributors (each reasoning and applying to contribute through his own work and teamwork) and the manager (planning and organizing to provide demanding yet inspiring leadership for such individuals).

The obligation and willingness to bring the combined power of wisdom and of empirical knowledge and skills to organized work is at once the governor and the flywheel for converting accelerating technological change into beneficial human progress.

Principles of organization are required which place that fundamental duty on both managers and their coworkers in good partnership in the modern work community.

CHAPTER TWO

Structuring the Organization

WALTER R. MAHLER *President, Mahler Associates, Inc., Wyckoff, New Jersey*

When a manager decides to change an organization structure, he usually begins by drawing boxes on a page. A new organization chart makes its appearance. As he does this, the manager may comment, "We are now changing from a functional organization to a product one." Or he may say, "We are going to become less decentralized from now on." If he needs to persuade himself or others about the value of the change, he will perhaps argue that this new organization chart is in the prevailing pattern in the industry.

This process is a far cry from effective organization planning. A change in organization structure should be viewed as a deliberate effort to make a change in the way the organization actually performs. At its best, the above process leads to a new chart. It is an accident, as often as not, if the behavior actually changes. Pushing "boxes" around on a chart has nothing in common with a process in which the change in structure is thought through in terms of the subsequent behavior that is expected to occur.

To avoid the "organizational chart pitfall," a process for thinking through a new organizational structure will be suggested. This process will facilitate the rather complex task of separating out those things which need to be taken into account so far as structure is concerned from the many other aspects of an organization which have an important bearing on the way it performs. It will also permit relating the decision on structure to the business objectives of the organization.

PROCESS FOR DESIGNING ORGANIZATION STRUCTURES

The process for designing the organization structure consists of five steps:
1. Establishing business objectives
2. Identifying major business obstacles
3. Considering several alternative structures

4. Testing the alternatives against behavioral benefits

5. Deciding on a structure which provides optimum benefits

Let us consider the reasons for each of these five steps. Changing the organization structure should be viewed as a deliberate attempt to change the behavior of an organization.

Step 1. The first step, establishing business objectives, pins down the nature of the behavior that is to be expected. Consider one example, the objective of growth. Some companies have set rather precise growth targets, others have not. The nature of the organization structure may be quite different if the objective is to double sales volume in the next five years rather than in the next ten years.

A manager usually changes an organization structure for one of two reasons. He wants to secure an improvement, or he wants to avoid some negative consequence. The suggestion to establish objectives as a first step in effect says: Be specific about the consequences and the results to be attained.

Often a clear statement of the objectives of an enterprise is lacking. Key executives will have quite different objectives. These differences are seldom recognized. If they are not brought to the surface, these unresolved differences in purpose will in all probability lead to quite different conclusions about structural alternatives. Having a set of business objectives as a reference will provide a basis for reconciling conflicting alternatives. It should minimize the possibility of "planning by analogy" or "following the leader."

It is quite possible that the process of first looking at objectives and obstacles may lead to a conclusion that a change in structure is not the solution.

A final value can be noted. Let us assume that the suggested design process has been followed and that the resultant structure is designed to overcome the obstacles and secure the objectives. Management has a clue as to when to change the structure again. The structure should not need to be changed unless a significant change occurs in either objectives or obstacles or both.

Step 2. The second step involves identifying major business obstacles. This step is recommended primarily to get managers to be more comprehensive in their analyses. A change in organization may be made to capitalize upon an opportunity or to overcome an important obstacle to achieving organizational objectives. A thorough review of obstacles may reveal many that do not have to do with organizational structure. It may be necessary to secure more adequate capital or to change the compensation system or to provide a change in advertising. Identifying specific obstacles often leads to the conclusion that there are important obstacles having nothing to do with organizational structure. This conclusion is useful. Only disappointment can result from changing an organization structure when a change is not really necessary.

Step 3. The third step recommends considering several alternative structures. Fortunately, the number of organization alternatives is limited. The importance of this step is a preventive one. It prevents the manager from jumping to a conclusion that there is one and only one solution. It overcomes the tendency to "oversell" oneself on the desirability of one organizational alternative. It also reveals that there is no "ideal" or "perfect" organization. Each alternative has its merits and demerits. The problem is to get the optimum possible benefits which can be expected from the most appropriate alternative. In addition, certain behavior tends to be associated with certain alternatives. Developing a "feel" for this pattern will be helpful to the manager in planning the change and in assessing the subsequent results.

Step 4. The fourth step involves testing the alternatives against certain benefits. Here again, it is fortunate that there are a limited number of benefits which can be derived from the structural aspects of an organization. These are the "behavioral" benefits. Putting a given structure in place increases the likelihood of getting certain behavior and certain types of performance results. The understanding and utilization of the behavioral benefits will be of assistance to the manager in thinking through to the desired behavior. Arguments for and against a given organizational alternative are difficult to resolve. The behavioral benefits provide a frame of reference against which differences of opinion can be resolved more objectively.

Step 5. The fifth step calls for a decision on a structure which provides optimum benefits. Stated another way, a decision needs to be made on the structure which will offer the most advantage in achieving the objectives of the business and in overcoming the obstacles. In a limited sense, the manager who pushes boxes around on an organizational chart carries out this fifth step— with this difference: he uses a one-step approach. The thinking involved in the first four steps either is bypassed altogether or is accomplished on an intuitive basis. It can be argued that this approach works out well on occasion—and so it does. However, it also fails on occasion. Skill and expertness in designing structures seldom grow and mature under the simple, one-step approach. It is similar to the "chopsticks" approach to learning to play the piano. The five-step approach represents a shifting from a simple, intuitive approach to a more complex and comprehensive one.

ESTABLISHING BUSINESS OBJECTIVES

"Objectives," as the term is used in this chapter, refers to the results an enterprise must secure year after year to be considered successful. For purposes of organization planning, it is helpful to use five-year business objectives. The choice of five years as a time span is deliberate—it forces longer-term thinking. A soundly conceived organization structure should last for at least five years. The basic structure of the General Motors organization was "jelled" in 1921 and still existed in 1966 with very minor modifications. It is, therefore, both possible and desirable to design an enduring structure. To do this, it is necessary to pin down the business results to be achieved year after year.

To be worthwhile, the objectives should be a reflection of the strongly held convictions of top management. The objectives should reflect what top management wants to see achieved over the next five years.

Suggestions for Preparation of Objectives. Before preparing objectives, it is necessary to identify the particular component of the organization for which the organization planning process is to be accomplished. It may be the president of the company. It may be the division general manager of a product group. It may be a functional organization such as the engineering department.

The objectives to be prepared should be the objectives of the manager who has overall responsibility for the organization to be changed. If, for example, a division general manager is the top manager, then the objectives should be his. Naturally, it is an advantage for the objectives of the division general manager to be "synchronized" with the objectives of the company, but this particular problem is outside the realm of this chapter. In effect, the objectives to be established should reflect the results which the top manager of the organization to be changed commits himself to achieve over the next five years.

Example of Objectives. The following objectives are for the XYZ Division of a large manufacturing organization. Its sales volume is over $150 million. The major objectives to be achieved within the next five years are:

1. Increase sales by 100 percent
2. Achieve a minimum of $50 million in sales by the introduction of new products for the division
3. Make a 10 percent return, after taxes, on total capital invested
4. Shift the responsibility for major engineering projects to corporate level, in line with corporate objectives
5. Reduce production costs, in terms of dollars per pound of product, each year over the previous year
6. Acquire a targeted number of technical personnel each year and retain them
7. Increase the effectiveness of relationships with unions
8. Demonstrate an interest and concern about the communities in which plants are located (specifically, improve the pollution problem in several locations)

IDENTIFY MAJOR BUSINESS OBSTACLES

A major business obstacle is any condition which is deemed to have an important adverse effect on the successful achievement of the business objectives. The effect can be either a current one or one that is anticipated. The condition can be either internal or external. Identifying major obstacles will help to avoid the pitfall of changing the structure to meet just one obstacle, often at the expense of other important results. The process also serves to identify action other than organization planning which may be needed.

Suggestions for Identifying Obstacles. "Brainstorm" as many obstacles as possible. In brainstorm fashion, do not get judicial initially. Avoid the tendency to identify only those obstacles which seem to have direct impact on organization planning. The main reason for doing this is that practically every obstacle of major consequence has an implication for organization planning. Proceed next to distill out the obstacles which are of major importance.

Obstacles can be identified in "arm chair" fashion or on the basis of intensive studies. The arm-chair approach can be accomplished by an individual or a group in a conference session. Intensive studies involve having a skilled interviewer consult with an appropriate sample of personnel. The intensive studies often help to identify internal obstacles which top management might overlook. The choice between arm-chair and intensive study is essentially a question of confidence in the data available. The greater the magnitude of the contemplated organization change, the more likely management is to want data in which it has a high degree of confidence.

Obstacles should be stated as precisely as possible.

Obstacles for the XYZ Division. The following list of obstacles of the XYZ Division mentioned above is presented to show examples of commonly encountered obstacles.

1. There is a serious lack of coordination among functional departments.
2. Price erosion has put and will continue to put a serious pressure on profits.
3. Competition of other industries is making important inroads.
4. There is an absence of systematic business planning, particularly long-range planning.
5. There is heavy pressure on the general manager to spend time "outside" the division and "upstairs" with headquarters.
6. Little attention has been given to acquiring new products from outside the division.
7. The engineering function has several critical problems (overrun on costs, meeting specifications).

8. Considerable duplication of effort exists among different departments (pricing, forecasts, and cost investigations).

9. Converting research efforts to commercial results has been difficult.

10. A large number of products are produced and distributed to a large number of different markets. Both products and markets will continue to increase in the future.

CONSIDER ORGANIZATION ALTERNATIVES

There are seven basic organizational groupings. Most of these have become commonplace in the management literature. The seven basic groupings are function, product, location, process, customer, time, and matrix. It is essential to develop a thorough understanding of these alternatives, particularly in terms of the behavioral aspects of each.

Grouping by Function. The distinguishing characteristic of a functional grouping is the nature of the work activities. Related activities aimed at a primary purpose are grouped together. The typical functional groups in a manufacturing company are manufacturing, engineering, marketing, finance, and personnel.

Most small organizations are of the functional type. From a behavioral viewpoint, the functional organization has certain rather predictable patterns. Each of the functions is primarily concerned about its own immediate objectives. Energy is concentrated on the function. Personnel become experienced with the function and develop increased capability to perform it. Conflict with other functional groups is frequent, because each group essentially wants to achieve its own purposes. Each function tends to become quite egocentric.

The functional organization develops difficulties as the number of products and the number of markets multiply. There is always a need to coordinate across functions such as engineering, production, and research. As the multiplicity of products and markets develops, the process of coordination becomes critical. At this stage in the evolution of a company, complaints can be heard about the number of meetings, the delay in decision making, and the difficulty of assigning responsibility. The president, upset about the lack of performance, asks that everybody involved with the problem appear in his office. Eventually a conference room is required, or even an auditorium to accommodate all those who have been involved. At this point, the president is inclined to consider his functional organization to be outmoded.

The top management of functional groups often finds that the various groups do not keep the interests of the total company in mind. "They do not seem to be concerned about the profitability of the company." This is predictable behavior. Each function is expected to make a contribution to the profit of the enterprise. However, no one function can be held entirely responsible for profit. The manufacturing function is primarily concerned with schedules, quality, and costs. Marketing is primarily concerned with sales, prices, and customer service. These quite different intermediate goals lead to egocentric action and friction. In summary, the primary benefit of the functional organization is in getting the specific functional work accomplished.

Grouping by Product. Activities directly associated with a product or group of products are grouped together in this alternative. A chemical company might have groups for organic, inorganic, and plastic products. An electrical company might have groups for large appliances, small appliances, large generators, and transformers.

Product grouping is most often found in larger companies, particularly those with a great variety of products and markets. The pressure on the functionally organized companies with diverse products is toward some type of grouping by product. Commonly, this has been known as "divisionalization."

A product grouping produces certain predictable behaviors. Energy and enthusiasm are concentrated on a given product or product line. Coordination is achieved more readily than in the case of the large functional organization. It is easier to "see" the business as a whole, thus lessening egocentricity.

It is true that one product group gives little consideration to other product groups in the company. Each concentrates on making its part of the business successful. It is therefore possible to hold the product group responsible, in large measure, for profits.

In summary, the primary benefit of the product alternative is that of getting business results for a given product. The enthusiasm for divisionalization leads many organizations to set up a multiplicity of small product divisions. Often, however, these organizations find that the administrative costs for each of the small divisions eat into the overall profitability of the enterprise.

Grouping by Geography. Geographical groups are distinguished by activities being carried on in a given locale. This is seen, particularly, in service industries. It is also frequently seen in selling organizations. As enterprises go global, they often set up regional arrangements.

A geographic grouping permits specializing in local conditions. It develops a responsiveness to the unique characteristics of a given region. The geographic grouping is intended to permit more timely coordination and more effective control within a region than is possible with a large central organization. It is interesting to contrast two large insurance companies, the Metropolitan and the Prudential. The former maintains a large central headquarters group, with field selling set up geographically. Prudential, on the other hand, has established regional headquarters, with all the work, except certain corporate matters, being done in the region.

As would be expected, personnel in the geographic regions become identified and concerned about their particular region, often to the exclusion of concern about the total enterprise. Energy is directed toward making the activities in the region as successful as possible. The primary benefit of geographic grouping is responsiveness to those conditions of importance in successfully achieving results.

Grouping by Process. In the process-type grouping, activities are grouped into a series of stages through which the work moves. Some industries are called "process industries." Aluminum and steel companies have groupings for discovery, extraction, processing, fabricating, and distribution. Oil companies have groupings for exploration, production, refining, and distribution.

Processes are most frequently found in manufacturing and in clerical-type activities. They can also be found in other functions. For example, setting up a long-range planning group is really setting up a process group.

The primary benefit of the process group is that individuals specialize by process. Again, energy and enthusiasm are concentrated upon the process with a minimum of concern about the next stage in the process.

Grouping by Customer. It is apparent that the characteristic of this grouping is the type of customer served. For example, in a tire company there may be one group concentrating on sales of tires to the original manufacturers and another to the retail store for second purchases. Chemical companies for many years have had divisions set up on a product basis. Many also set up customer groups. For example, one group sells to agricultural customers and another sells to the packaging industry. Insurance companies differentiate between components responsible for group sales and those responsible for individual sales. A personnel group may be organized to serve hourly, salaried, and managerial "customers."

In this grouping, individuals, essentially, specialize in the customer. They become knowledgeable about the customer, his needs, and his peculiarities. The primary benefit of grouping by customer is an appropriate responsiveness to the customer.

Grouping by Time.   Characteristic of time grouping are shifts performing much the same work at different time periods.   Such arrangements are found in selling, service, and manufacturing organizations.   In manufacturing, the purpose is, of course, to utilize physical resources fully.   Or the nature of the work, such as in the chemicals industries, may require a continuous process.

In selling and service companies, the purpose is to provide services to customers.   Department stores, for example, have found it necessary to maintain both a day and an evening schedule.   The primary benefit of the time grouping is an economic one.

The Matrix Grouping.   The term "matrix" is becoming more commonly used. This grouping has been in existence for years without the dignity of a special name.   The most usual matrix organization is a combination of function and product, as shown by Figure 2-1.   This arrangement is a compromise.   Rather than set up separate product groups, each with their own engineering, manufacturing, and marketing, these functions remain as they were.   However, a product group is set up and expected to coordinate only, or it may be given the power to instruct functions on what they will do with regard to their particular products.

The matrix arrangement can be found at many levels of the organization.   The Unilever organization, for example, has a product manager responsible for a major project, such as oleomargarine.   This manager reports directly to the chairman of the company.   In many marketing organizations, a product manager has been set up to ensure that the field sales force gives appropriate attention to his product.

The matrix organization is an effort to get the advantages of both the functional grouping and the product grouping without incurring the costly features of going entirely to a product grouping such as product divisions.   A multiplicity of products and markets pressures many organizations into some type of arrangement such as this.

It becomes apparent immediately that this is a tricky organization to manage. It poses some rather critical "power" questions.   A second benefit of this orga-

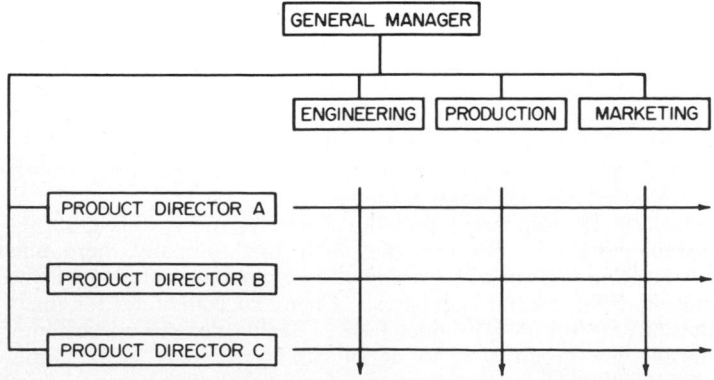

FIG. 2-1.   *A matrix-type organization for a manufacturing company.*

nization can be the deliberately built-in conflict. Properly managed, this can be helpful to the general manager.   Improperly managed, confusion reigns.

SELECTING ALTERNATIVE STRUCTURES

The third step in the process of deciding upon a structure is to consider several alternatives.   Seven basic organizational groupings have been described. The problem is to select from among the possibilities.   The following suggestions will assist in making this selection.

1. Work with one level at a time, starting with the level which reports directly to the top manager.

2. Consider at least two alternatives—the more diverse the better.   It is quite appropriate to have one of the alternatives be the present structure.

3. Plan the structure for at least two levels.   In some cases, it is advisable to plan for three levels or more.

4. It is helpful to use brief functional-type descriptions of the primary responsibilities for the positions at each level.

It will soon become apparent that any plan one develops will include three or more of the organizational alternatives.   The most crucial decision is the choice for the level reporting to the top manager.   This sets the overall "style" or "tone" for the rest of the organization.   The choice is essentially one of getting specialization, coordination, and control concentrated around quite different things.

A product grouping concentrates on the product.

A function grouping concentrates on the function.

A geographic grouping concentrates upon the locale.

A process grouping concentrates upon the process.

A customer grouping concentrates upon the customer.

A time grouping concentrates upon a shift or time period.

A matrix grouping concentrates upon both product and function at the same time.

Once several alternatives have been selected, it will be necessary to test the alternatives against the potential behavioral benefits.

TESTING THE ALTERNATIVES AGAINST BEHAVIORAL BENEFITS

The need for visualizing how the changed organization will actually perform was stressed earlier.   It would be possible to talk about "organizational criteria" or "organizational requirements."   We have chosen to use the words "behavioral benefits," because this is exactly what it is we are endeavoring to visualize.

An organization structure and the skeleton of a human being have a great deal in common.   The skeleton is not expected to move by itself.   However, it facilitates certain types of behavior, and it restricts or prevents other types of behavior.   Similarly, an organization, of itself, does not produce.   It takes leadership and many other things to get performance.   The structure can, however, make it easier for some things to happen—and make it difficult for other things to happen.   It can ensure that certain things will happen.

When talking about behavioral benefits, we must identify whom we want to benefit.   The organization structure is to serve the top man in achieving his established objectives.   Therefore, it is designed to benefit the top man.

We will consider six possible benefits, although it is possible that there are more. Achieving these benefits in an optimum manner is the challenge. Briefly, the six behavioral benefits have to do with specializing effort, facilitating control, aiding coordination, securing adequate managerial attention, achieving minimum costs, and facilitating the development and retention of managers.

Benefit of Specialized Effort. Specialization is a widely recognized characteristic of a modern enterprise. In fact, the explosion of knowledge and the increased complexity of current enterprises serve to accelerate specialization. If an individual or a group can concentrate upon one thing, several advantages occur. The time required to learn is shortened. The range of abilities or knowledge required is minimized. Energy and enthusiasm are focused. In all likelihood, the individual will complete the tasks readily, so a sense of achievement is secured. The main consequences are an individual or a group who is able to do a job and who is strongly motivated.

Because it is necessary that essential work be accomplished, specialization is usually given first consideration in setting up an organization. Notice that the organizational alternatives represent a type of specialization—function, product, geography, process, customer, and time.

The interaction of specialization and subsequent benefits is apparent. A great increase in specialization will detract from several other potential benefits. Costs are likely to increase, thus giving an adverse effect to the economy benefit. Securing an integrated effort is likely to become more difficult, thus giving an adverse effect to the coordination benefit. A potential gain is to be found in that the specialization will make for easier measurement, thus providing a gain on the facilitating control benefit. The eventual test is determining the structure which will yield the optimum benefits.

Benefit of Facilitating Control. One prime responsibility of the top manager is to maintain control. Numerous actions are taken to do this.

One advantage of one organization structure over another is that it may make it easier for the top manager to maintain control. It may mean that he has to devote less personal time to the challenge of maintaining control. This is the benefit of facilitating control. It is not to be confused with "systems" for maintaining control. The structure itself provides for improved or more effective control.

Typical ways by which this benefit is secured are:

Setting up a quality-control group independent of the group producing the product.

Establishing a traveling audit group.

Establishing parallel groups to provide comparisons. This might be product divisions to permit comparisons of factors such as return on investment, or geographic groups with comparable sales opportunities.

Reducing the number of levels to minimize the lag in response and the slippage and distortion of a long "line of command."

Setting the span of control to avoid either over- or under control.

Setting up a product director in a matrix grouping to have an individual or group concentrating on the business results of a given product line.

Establishing a "staff" group with the responsibility of ensuring compliance with policies or adherence to required processes.

The specialization benefit should increase the likelihood that work will be done. However, the control benefit, when achieved, means that the organization forces corrective action when required results are not forthcoming.

Benefit of Coordination. Specialization is designed to ensure that each organizational component accomplishes certain work. The final result of the total enterprise—profits—requires that the individual efforts of many units be synchronized. Timing becomes extremely important. Often this is a responsibility requiring the major portion of a top manager's time. It is possible to set up an organization that makes coordination difficult to achieve. The benefit of coordination is secured when business results are obtained with the minimum amount of time and energy devoted by key managers to coordination.

Numerous ways are utilized to get the benefit of coordination. Units may be set up so a minimum of coordination is needed, so that it occurs with the fewest possible people and at the lowest possible level and in as timely a manner as possible. The shift from a functional to a product type of organization usually takes place because the coordination benefit becomes crucial. As products and markets multiply, the old functional organization becomes more and more difficult to coordinate and to control. One of the usual benefits expected for a divisionalization move is that the division general manager can do the coordination without involving the top management of the enterprise.

The coordination benefit is sometimes secured by setting up a committee. The complexity of the oil industry has led most oil companies to have internal boards working full time and devoting most of their time to securing vitally needed coordination.

A device for getting the benefit of coordination is the product manager concept in the sales department, or the product coordinator–type position reporting to a general manager. The matrix alternative provides advantages both on the control benefit and on the coordination benefit.

The establishment of an executive vice president position is often done to secure more timely and effective coordination than the top officer can give.

When coordination is crucial to the success of the enterprise or is quite difficult to obtain, organizational arrangements are likely to be selected as one way of achieving the necessary results. Setting up special groups or special positions to secure this benefit, however, adversely affects the economy benefit.

The testing of the organizational alternatives requires asking such questions as:

How will the contemplated organization actually operate so far as coordination is concerned?

Will more or less time of the top manager be required to coordinate?

Will more or fewer people be involved?

Will coordination occur at a lower level than formerly?

Will obstacles arising from coordination be overcome?

Benefit of Adequate Manager Attention. This is a particularly interesting benefit. An organization has a multitude of objectives, each of which is important and must be achieved. Under pressure, however, managers are inclined to concentrate on limited objectives. For example, most managers will concentrate upon short-range objectives at the expense of long-range objectives. Many managers will devote more attention to the objectives they like or are enthusiastic about. Thus it is that a company president or a general manager has an interesting challenge. He must see that he gives adequate attention to all objectives. He must further see that managers at each level give appropriate attention to all major objectives. This problem often leads to the establishment of a special individual or group to ensure that managers give attention to one or more of their responsibilities. For example, the position of director of long-range planning may be established to ensure that managers at various levels give appropriate attention to long-range planning. Similarly, the position of director of executive development may be established to increase the time managers devote to this often-neglected responsibility.

In the case of these two positions, it appears at first also possible to set them up to get the benefit of specialization. The long-range planner would be expected to develop long-range plans, and the personnel development man would be expected to develop managers. Experience shows that these positions will not achieve results of this sort. The top manager is looking for the wrong benefit. It is necessary to think through when the specialist will be expected to provide the benefit of adequate management attention and when he is to do "operating" work on his own.

The term "staff" is often applied to positions set up to achieve the manager attention benefit. Among the more frequent positions are:

Director of public relations
Director of safety
Director of community relations
Director of planning
Director of executive development

The more important the top manager considers it to have managers give attention to a specific responsibility, the more likely it is that the corresponding staff position will report to the top manager.

This benefit adds costs and thus conflicts with the economy benefit. In effect, it contributes to the control benefit, and it increases the likelihood that the necessary work will be done. These positions have a tendency to multiply and create a coordination problem, however, thus conflicting with the coordination benefit.

The testing of organization alternatives requires asking such questions as the following:

1. Is this position absolutely necessary? Will an important objective go unrealized unless such a position is established?

2. Is the position located at the appropriate level?

3. Have we clearly differentiated between doing the job for managers and getting the managers to do the job?

Benefit of Minimum Costs. The cost of any organization is of critical importance. One of the most frequent reasons for changing an organization structure is to reduce costs. In some instances, this seems to be the only reason. Because an organization exists to accomplish certain results, the preceding benefits, particularly of specialization, should be given first consideration. However, in making choices between alternatives, the matter of minimum costs needs to be analyzed. Other things being equal, the least-expensive organizational structure should be selected.

Because most organization changes have to do with changing a current organization structure, it is possible to cost out the current structure. The cost of each alternative structure can then be compared. The least-expensive structure is not necessarily the best, but a more costly structure must have clear-cut performance advantages.

In discussing previous benefits, we called attention to the fact that increased specialization benefits are often costly. A gain in one benefit often results in a loss in another benefit. Adding individuals to get the benefit of management attention also costs money. Several suggestions for achieving minimum costs are in order.

The positions which are established should be full-time jobs. As Parkinson's law states, an individual will find work to fill the time available. It therefore behooves the designer of positions to be sure that work does fill the time.

The positions of "assistant" and "assistant to" are suspect when it comes to the cost benefit. They may be argued for on the grounds of some of the other benefits. If there is a full-time job, they may be worth considering. The next benefit to be discussed, that of developing general managers, is an important one. On balance, the benefits secured by "assistant" and "assistant to" positions may offset their costs.

Particular attention should be paid to the number of levels established. The more levels, the more costs. These costs are both payroll costs and the costs of coordination. It is essential that a position should have a unique reason for existing. Each layer of management must justify itself by performing some unique work which can be done only by individuals on that level.

Staff positions primarily serve to gain the specialization benefit and the management-attention benefit. If there is a real need for the specialization and increased management attention, then staff positions may more than justify their costs. But this has to be thought out.

When assessing the extent to which the benefit of minimum costs has been secured, review again the obstacles set up initially. These obstacles have to be overcome, and to do so will involve costs. Several kinds of questions need to be considered:

What will this particular structure cost in terms of the payroll?

If we were to eliminate this portion of the structure, what would we lose in the way of performance results?

How serious is this loss in light of our objectives?

Benefit of Manager Development and Retention. Many companies are concerned about developing and retaining managers who are broad "generalists." A functionally organized company, for example, has great difficulty in developing future presidents with a depth of knowledge of the entire business. There is no opportunity to give a high-potential manager a chance to manage a "little" business before giving him a "big" one to manage.

It is possible to set up an organizational arrangement to secure this benefit. Several organizational arrangements can facilitate development. Among these are "assistant" positions, and occasionally, "assistant to" positions. In the matrix-type organization, the product coordinator has an opportunity to become involved in all functions of the business. A divisionalized organization also has generalist positions.

APPLICATION OF PLANNING PROCESS

An example was given previously of the objectives of the XYZ Division of a manufacturing company. Obstacles were also identified. An analysis of the current structure of the division and an alternative structure will be presented to illustrate the process of testing current or contemplated structures against behavioral benefits.

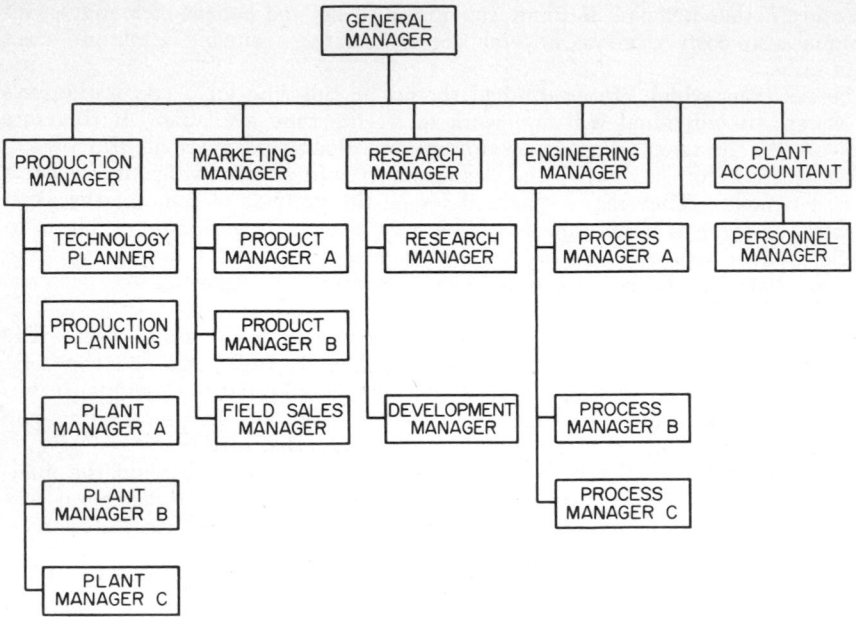

FIG. 2-2. *Current structure of the XYZ Division of a manufacturing company.*

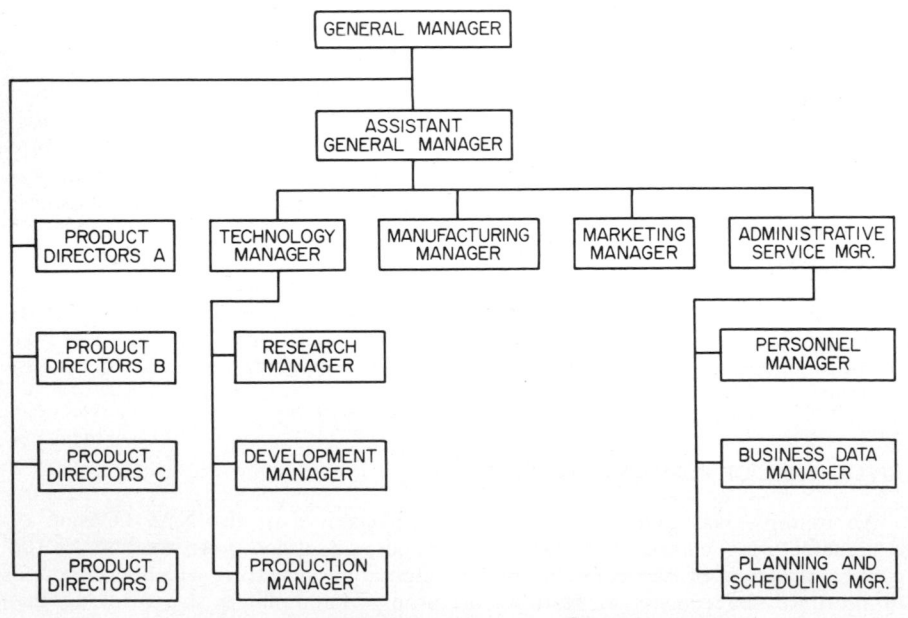

FIG. 2-3. *A matrix-type structure for the XYZ Division.*

The current structure is a traditional functional organization, with six functional managers reporting to the general manager of the division, as shown by Figure 2-2. Within marketing, there is a combination of geographic and product organizational alternatives. Engineering is strictly a process-type organization. Although not shown on the chart, research is a combination of product and process alternatives. Manufacturing is a combination of product, geographic, and process types.

Analysis of Current Organization

Behavioral benefit	Positive condition	Negative condition
Specialization	Major functions specialized Product specialization in marketing with product managers	No specialization by project in engineering No one specializing in acquisition of new companies or products No one specializing in business planning
Control	Both manufacturing and marketing managers have positions at headquarters to help them control plants and field sales respectively	General manager dependent entirely upon his functional managers for performance
Coordination	Planners in manufacturing aid coordination Product managers in marketing aid coordination Individuals at lower levels in research, marketing, and manufacturing coordinate by products	Coordination across functions difficult because of frequent absence of general manager Coordination of numerous projects in engineering done only by engineering manager
Management attention	Personnel group set up to stimulate managers to give attention to personnel responsibilities	No one available to focus attention on acquisitions, business planning, culling weak products, or the complexities of pricing
Mininum costs	No assistant managers or "assistant to" positions	"Staff" groups added within manufacturing and marketing are more costly than previous completely functional groups
Development and retention of managers	. . . .	No position to help functional managers to become "generalists" General manager does not have time to devote to developmental contacts

Analysis of a Matrix-type Alternative Organization. The organization reflected in Figure 2-3 is a matrix-type organization. The product directors have responsibilities for a given group of products. They are responsible for planning action on both current and future products to achieve overall divisional business objectives.

The directors do not have a staff of their own. With the shift of design work to a central engineering group, a new "technology" group is established. A new administrative services manager is created to provide supervision and coordination of a variety of "service" activities.

Behavioral benefit	Positive condition	Negative condition
Specialization	Both current and future plans for major product groups done by product directors Engineering function centralized for entire company; can secure much greater specialization and higher-caliber specialists	Some functions no longer report to general management
Control	Product directors give general managers a vehicle for control of both product and functions Administrative services will get closer supervision Plans and schedules placed under a "neutral" manager	Control over engineering effort will be more difficult with shift of design engineering to a central group
Coordination	Assistant general manager provides timely coordination of major functions Product directors can achieve much coordination across functions on their own Coordination within administrative services can be done more readily	Some coordination problems will exist with central engineering Some coordination problems will exist between product directors and functional managers
Management attention	Product directors focus management attention on both current and future product opportunities and problems Administrative services geared to aid managers in information systems approach	Outside acquisitions, to be done by product directors, may not receive needed attention
Minimum costs	Several positions are reduced in value Centralizing of engineering may eventually reduce engineering costs	Addition of four product director positions and administrative services manager position
Development and retention of managers	Product director positions aid both development and retention Centralizing of engineering should make some bigger positions which should make for retention of engineering talent	"Downgrading" of personnel and accounting from former status

BIBLIOGRAPHY

Allen, Louis A., *Management and Organization*, McGraw-Hill Book Company, New York, 1958.

Candler, Alfred D., *Strategy and Structure*, The M.I.T. Press, Cambridge, Mass., 1962.

Dale, Ernest, *Planning and Developing the Company Organization Structure*, American Management Association, New York, 1952.

Drucker, Peter F., *The Practice of Management*, Harper & Row, Publishers, Incorporated, New York, 1954.

Maynard, H. B. (ed.), *Top Management Handbook*, McGraw-Hill Book Company, New York, 1960.

Newman, William H., *Administrative Action*, Prentice-Hall, Inc., Englewood Cliffs, N.J., 1964.

Sloan, Alfred P., Jr., *My Years with General Motors*, Doubleday & Company, Inc., Garden City, N.Y., 1964.

CHAPTER THREE

Organization Planning

HENRY GOLIGHTLY *President, International Management Services, Henry Golightly & Company, Inc., New York, New York*

JOHN HORST *Senior Consultant, International Management Services, Henry Golightly & Company, Inc., New York, New York*

A sound organization plan is basic to business success regardless of the company or of the product that company offers. The plan must be practical and realistic; it must be flexible enough to accommodate change as the company grows and changes; it must not be filed away and forgotten, but must be made a living part of the company's operation.

The steps management should take in drawing up an effective organization plan are described in detail in this chapter. The chapter stresses the value and importance of establishing logical areas of responsibility for the key activities of the business and of allocating sufficient authority to permit these responsibilities to be properly discharged.

Definition of Organization Planning. Organization planning is the management process whereby company philosophy is translated into basic rules for directing manpower in a coordinated effort toward corporate objectives. These rules must take into consideration the company's structure, environment, potential, opportunities, and logical ambitions.

ORGANIZATION PLANNING PERSPECTIVE

Before launching into the details of organization planning, we should first establish broadly what we are trying to achieve with the plan and establish a frame of reference. The purpose of organizational planning is to achieve an organizational balance that emphasizes the important company elements, those functions that have the greatest influence upon the achievement of the company's objectives.

This statement implies that the company objectives can be defined in meaningful terms, and indeed they must be. For most companies, the overriding objective is to maximize return on investment. Out of this goal come many subordinate objectives dealing with the details of how to achieve this end.

It is the primary objective together with the subsidiary objectives that largely shapes the organization structure. For example, in the airline industry for many years, the primary problem and hence the primary objective was to transport passengers swiftly and safely. This concern was reflected in an organization which emphasized the operational aspects of the business—flight operations, aircraft maintenance, and ticket sales—and subordinated other activities such as marketing, finance, and engineering.

As time passes, corporate goals and philosophies change; therefore, the company's organization structure and policies must be synchronized with changing requirements. To return to the airline example, technology and operating efficiency have advanced to the point where the safe, swift transport of passengers is routine. Individual airlines are virtually indistinguishable to the public. As a result, each airline has found it necessary to increase its emphasis on factors that in the past it considered subordinate. Marketing, long-range planning, and sound administration have been added to safe, dependable flight as critical elements in airline management. Organization plans have been revamped to show the new importance of these activities.

This, then, is the perspective the organizational architect must have—a grasp of what the company is trying to achieve and the ability to identify those aspects of the business that bear heavily on it.

FUNCTIONS OF THE ORGANIZATION PLAN

The organization plan answers the basic organizational questions, who, what, and how. Through reporting relationships, titles, and work descriptions, organization charts and functional diagrams indicate *who* is responsible, *what* he is responsible for, and *how* his performance influences company affairs. Position descriptions establish what functions and duties are associated with each position and what authority resides there. Policy definitions provide the guidelines that tell the manager how to operate in accordance with company objectives.

The organization plan enables the company to cope with contingencies by establishing a consistent set of policies and rules that are the basis for day-to-day business operation.

The organization plan serves as a point of departure for planning corporate growth. By presenting the existing company structure, it indicates what organizational strengths and weaknesses to consider in long-range planning. It also indicates what organizational changes will be required for the alternative long-range plans that may be proposed.

Specific Functions. A complete organization plan must perform these specific functions.

1. Identify and state company objectives
2. State company policies regarding:
   a. Lines of communication
   b. Delegation of responsibility and authority
   c. Centralization/decentralization
   d. Administrative practices
   e. Use of committees
   f. Line and staff relationships and responsibilities
   g. Management planning and reporting requirements
3. Present the organization structure and management requirements through devices such as:

a. Organization charts
b. Functional diagrams
c. Position descriptions
4. Delineate department responsibilities and authorities

ELEMENTS OF THE ORGANIZATION PLAN

An organization plan should include a statement of company objectives, a statement of the company creed, organization charts, a listing of responsibilities common to all supervisory positions, carefully defined position descriptions, and functional assignments for organization units. Where necessary, it should also contain a glossary of standard terms and nomenclature for the organization.

In practice, the essential elements of the organization plan are usually embodied in a manual containing three sections:

Policy definition
Organization description
Position descriptions

The organization manual should spell out what the company's purpose really is and how the organizational framework, its personnel, and its spirit relate to each other to form the total company picture. The manual should further define company concepts concerning the relative importance of various functions.

Policy Definition. The policy definition section of an organization manual contains basic management information. It changes infrequently. At the minimum, it should include a statement of company objectives, an organization creed, specific policy statements for important functions within the corporation, and if necessary, a glossary of organization terms as they are defined and used in the company.

The general statement of objectives and the organization creed are closely related; hence, they are often combined into one short introductory section in the organization manual. Standard Oil Company of New Jersey covers them in its organization manual in this way: "To maintain a business climate favorable to reasonable profit making, management must impose upon itself a proper concern with many social responsibilities. No business exists in economic isolation. It is part of the economic and social environment of its time. Its policies and actions affect many segments of that environment and in turn are affected by them." Thus employees recognize that the company accepts, in addition to profit making, its obligation to the society in which it exists and that it will manifest this not only in policies and organization, but in employee attitudes and actions.

Policy statements should be keyed to specific functions. For example, policies relating to financial matters can be covered by four related but separate topics: financial planning, financial reporting, general accounting, and cost accounting. A fine example of a corporate policy statement follows.[1]

A Corporate Policy Statement
American Machine & Foundry Company and Subsidiaries
AMF Organization Concept

Basic Concept. The organization of AMF and its divisions and subsidiaries is based on the principle of centralized policy making and performance and fiscal review with decentralized responsibility for profit-making operations. A more specific treatment of AMF's concept of decentralized operations is contained in Policy Statement 1–3.

Corporate Management. The AMF board of directors, representing the owners of

[1] K. White, *Understanding the Company Organization Chart*, American Management Association, New York, 1964, pp. 210–212.

the business (the stockholders), provides top policy direction, elects officers, approves commitments and expenditures beyond certain limits (as defined in Policy Statement 1–4), and is responsible to the stockholders for the successful operation of the business and the custody of its physical assets.

The chairman of the board is the chief executive officer of the corporation and exercises general supervision over the business and affairs of the company.

The executive committee is appointed by the board of directors to act on its behalf between regular meetings. Unless specified otherwise by the board, the executive committee may exercise any power given to the board, but must report its actions to the board for ratification at its next meeting.

The executive office, from an organizational and operations standpoint, is considered to consist of the chief executive officer, the president, and the executive vice president.

Business Units. The basic profit-making entity is the "business unit," which may be either a subsidiary corporation or a division of the parent company. Except for legal considerations, no operating distinction is made between a subsidiary and a division.

The manager of each business unit is responsible for all operations affecting that unit's profits and profit-making capability. These include manufacturing, fiscal, engineering, and sales.

Groups. Each business unit, for purposes of administration, is normally assigned to a specific "group" headed by a group executive, who is directly responsible to the executive office. The group executive is responsible for the management and profitability of all the business units assigned to him. He exercises general administrative supervision and interprets and enforces corporate policy. He is the focal point for relationships between business units and corporate management or staff personnel. In the case of business units which are not assigned to a group executive, this administrative function will be exercised by the executive office.

One purpose of the group organization is to tie together business units whose products, markets, or method of operation are similar. Another purpose is to reduce the number of separate units reporting to the executive office. For this latter reason, it is desirable to limit the number of groups in being at any one time. There is no set minimum or maximum size for a group. A relatively small group might be established if the growth prospects looked good, while a very large group would not be split up merely because of its size.

Boards of Management. Each group normally has a board of management which exercises periodic review over and provides counsel to the managers of the business units within the group. In addition, boards of management provide approval authority for certain classes of expenditures, as covered in Policy Statement 1–4. Group boards will usually be made up of members of the executive office, other corporate officers, the group executive, and in some cases, heads of business units within the group and representation from other groups.

Business units which are subsidiary corporations will have legally elected boards of directors. The duties and rights of these subsidiary boards of directors are not superseded by the group board of management. In addition, the group executive may appoint divisional management committees or boards within his group. These may be staffed by group personnel only and will act purely in an advisory capacity.

If, for any reason, the establishment of a group board of management is not considered feasible, individual business unit boards of management will be designated to perform the same duties. In such cases and where the business unit is a subsidiary corporation, its boards of directors will usually serve as the business unit board of management.

A business unit not attached to a group will use the chairman's advisory group as its board of management, unless otherwise assigned.

Organization Description. The heart of the organization description is the organization chart. It is the "blueprint" that shows:

The command structure and associated responsibility delegation

The relationship between company units and their relative importance

Management's organizational philosophy
Formal communications channels

Through the command structure depicted in a chart, one can establish the levels of management, the span of management of each level, and the functional and administrative alignments. Organizational relationships indicate how line and staff functions are integrated, what relative importance is assigned to the various departments and divisions, and what role committees play within the company. Management's organizational philosophy is also apparent from the chart—whether it favors centralization or decentralization, product orientation or functional orientation. Primary communication channels for both supervisory and staff counsel are often indicated on the charts by solid and dotted lines.

Many different formats are used for organization charts. Those most commonly seen are line and box, concentric, and scalar. A sample of each is shown in Figure 3-1. By far the most familiar is the line-and-box system. The other

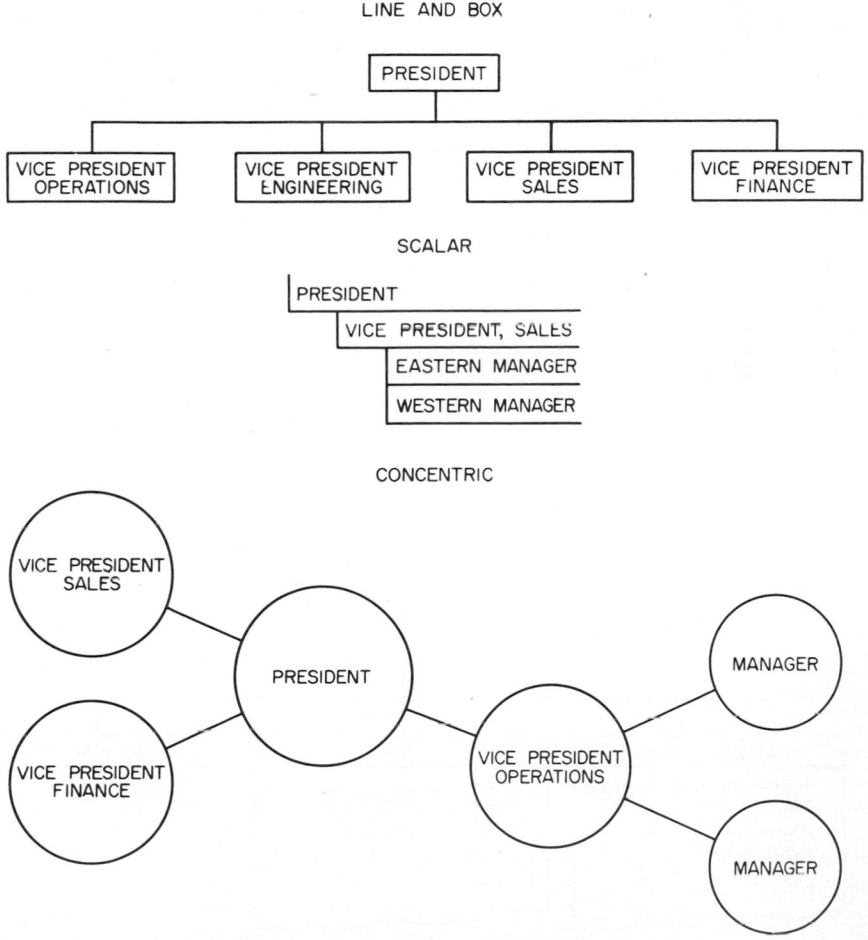

FIG. 3-1. *Organization chart formats.*

techniques are usually applied in special situations.   Many good books are available on this topic.

A reminder is in order at this point.   The chart is merely a device that portrays the organization.   Although it provides guidance, it does not assure conformity to the organization structure.

A second device that is used to depict an organization is the functional diagram.   It serves a purpose somewhat similar to that of the organization chart, but it concentrates on information flow and function delegation, whereas the organization chart emphasizes reporting relationships.   The functional diagram assures adequate coverage for all essential company activities and at the same

FUNCTIONAL BLOCK DIAGRAM

```
┌──────────────┐      ┌──────────────┐      ┌──────────────┐
│  MANAGEMENT  │──────│  EXECUTIVE   │──────│  BOARD OF    │
│  COMMITTEE   │      │  FUNCTIONS   │      │  DIRECTORS   │
└──────────────┘      └──────────────┘      └──────────────┘

    ┌──────────────────────┐      ┌──────────────────────┐
    │ OPERATING STAFF      │      │   SERVICE            │
    │ FUNCTIONS            │      │   FUNCTIONS          │
    │ ┌──────────────────┐ │      │ ┌──────────────────┐ │
    │ │ TOOL DESIGN      │ │------│ │ ADMINISTRATION   │ │
    │ ├──────────────────┤ │      │ ├──────────────────┤ │
    │ │ TOOL CONTROL     │ │      │ │ FINANCE          │ │
    │ └──────────────────┘ │      │ └──────────────────┘ │
    └──────────────────────┘      └──────────────────────┘

        ┌──────────────┐              ┌──────────────┐
        │  OPERATING   │              │  MARKETING   │
        │  MANAGEMENT  │              │  MANAGEMENT  │
        └──────────────┘              └──────────────┘

  ┌────────────────────────┐    ┌────────────────────────┐
  │ MANUFACTURING FUNCTIONS │    │  MARKETING FUNCTIONS    │
  │ ┌────────────────────┐  │    │ ┌────────────────────┐  │
  │ │INTERNATIONAL DIVISION│ │    │ │INTERNATIONAL DIVISION│ │
  │ ├────────────────────┤  │    │ ├────────────────────┤  │
  │ │ U. S. DIVISION     │  │    │ │ U. S. DIVISION     │  │
  │ └────────────────────┘  │    │ └────────────────────┘  │
  └────────────────────────┘    └────────────────────────┘
```

FUNCTIONAL DESCRIPTION CHART

```
┌────────────────────────────────────────────┐
│          OFFICE OF THE PRESIDENT            │
│ 1. GENERALLY DIRECT AND SUPERVISE           │
│    ALL COMPANY ACTIVITIES                   │
│ 2. PREPARE LONG-RANGE PLANS                 │
│ 3. ETC.                                     │
└────────────────────────────────────────────┘

┌──────────────────────┐ ┌──────────────────────┐ ┌──────────────────────┐
│    MANUFACTURING     │ │      FINANCE         │ │   INDUSTRIAL REL.    │
│ 1. SUPERVISE AND     │ │ 1. APPRAISE THE      │ │ 1. CONTROL HIRING    │
│    MONITOR           │ │    CORPORATE         │ │    POLICIES          │
│    PRODUCTION        │ │    FINANCIAL         │ │                      │
│ 2. CONTROL FACILITIES│ │    POSITION          │ │ 2. ADMINISTER        │
│    EXPANSION         │ │ 2. DEVELOP FINANCIAL │ │    PERSONNEL PROGRAMS │
│ 3. ETC.              │ │    PLANS             │ │ 3. ETC.              │
│                      │ │ 3. ETC.              │ │                      │
└──────────────────────┘ └──────────────────────┘ └──────────────────────┘
```

FIG. 3-2.   *Functional diagram formats.*

time minimizes duplication of effort and confusion regarding specific functions. Two sample formats for functional diagrams are presented in Figure 3-2.

Position Descriptions. Position descriptions are generally drawn up for each managerial position in the company. Serving several purposes, these descriptions:

Spell out what is expected of the individual executive

Are valuable aids for recruiting personnel

Provide an important foundation for executive compensation plans

Assure adequate coverage of all elements of company management

Assist in the executive appraisal process

At the top and middle management levels, individual descriptions are required for each position, because the unique aspects of each position must be described. At the lower management levels, it is often possible to write one description that will cover many individuals who hold similar positions. For example, all branch managers for a supermarket chain may be covered by a single position description.

The position description should define each person's position in the organization. It should describe the work to be performed, and as far as possible, the manner in which it is to be performed. No description, it must be remembered, can ever completely define what an executive does or the full scope of his authority.

Position descriptions vary from company to company, but almost all conform to the following general format:

1. General description of the importance of the position, its purpose, and its responsibilities

2. Specific duties, responsibilities, and authority

3. Reporting relationships

4. Administrative aspects (often incorporated in item 2)

An attempt to minimize the tendency to generalize which often creeps into position descriptions has resulted in the following form.[2]

POSITION DESCRIPTION FORM

1. *Core Function:* The heart and "guts" of the job to be accomplished—not the "petty" details and duties

2. *Authority:* The extent and limitations of authority—power over people, money, and physical assets, power to get the job done

3. *Accountability:* Communications upward for executive control—how this position reports to the immediate superior and how well the function is being performed

4. *Lateral Relationships:* The minimum basic cooperation and teamwork required; the relations with positions other than those shown as directly connected on the organization chart; the relationships that are necessary for the effective fulfillment of the indicated function

5. *Standard of Performance:* The part of the corporate objectives that must be achieved in that specific position; the measure of a job well done; the basis on which the performance of a man filling the position will be judged; the basis of remuneration

6. *Details of Functions:* An elaboration and expansion of the core function; specific statements about the exact duties the position should and does perform

7. *Man Specifications:* A factual description of a man at work—hopefully, a man who can and will achieve his part of the corporate goal; factual information of a historical nature dealing with the actual (or desired) age, education, experience, and personality of the man who fills (or is to be sought to fill) the position

[2] G. Fisch, *Organization for Profit,* McGraw-Hill Book Company, New York, 1964, p. 267.

RESPONSIBILITY FOR ORGANIZATION PLANNING

In large companies that recognize the importance of organization planning, a special staff reporting to the chief executive officer or one of his immediate subordinates is responsible for the function. This approach has been used at Ford, IBM, Jones and Laughlin Steel, and Creole Petroleum, to name a few.

In companies where no formal planning staff exists, several alternatives are open:

1. The organization planning function is considered a part of each executive's normal management responsibilities, and each executive changes his organization as the need arises. This relatively disorganized approach to planning is not recommended. Most experts in the organization planning field agree that it can cause serious inefficiencies, redundancies, and inconsistencies in the company organization structure.

2. A temporary committee acts as a planning staff for the chief executive. A representative cross section of the company executives is usually included on the committee to assure the development of a coordinated, balanced plan. The Carrier Corporation and Cluett-Peabody are two companies that have successfully used this approach.

3. The chief executive can handle the planning function on his own, relying on his subordinates for assistance and advice. Simple and effective though this method may appear, it can be dangerous in that the completed plan may overemphasize areas with which the president is personally familiar at the expense of those perhaps more critical to the successful operation of the business.

4. Outside consultants are often called in to assist in setting up or rearranging the organization plan. The consultant with an outsider's view, a knowledge of organization planning, plus professional experience can usually build a highly satisfactory plan even though he may lack intimate knowledge of the company and its management personalities. Young and Rubicam and Continental Airlines are two examples of the many companies who have used this approach.

Once the consultant has established a plan, however, the company must provide the means of keeping it up to date and responsive to changes.

STEPS IN DEVELOPING AN ORGANIZATION PLAN

A carefully thought-out, comprehensive approach to organization planning is necessary. The following approach has been applied many times and proved effective.

1. Establish the company objectives.
2. Establish the critical success factors that affect the attainment of those objectives.
3. Rank the company elements, such as departments, divisions, or functions, in order of their influence on the success factors.
4. Develop an ideal organization structure that will favor the activities related to the critical success factors.
5. Modify the ideal structure to achieve a satisfactory compromise between existing structure and ideal structure.
6. Prepare the documentation that fully describes the plan and will be used for implementation.

The timing of the initiation and completion of these steps can vary depending upon the urgency of the planning program and the resources available.

Company Objectives. Company objectives change with time, as business conditions, executive personnel, and company resources change. But even though these changes may be continuous, they are gradual, and a stable set of objectives can be established at any given point. When this set of objectives becomes clearly outdated, it is time to develop a new set and with it a new organization plan.

Setting objectives is the responsibility of the chief executive officer. He is in the best position to know the company's strengths and weaknesses and its potential and existing markets. Although he may look to his top and middle management for specific advice and data, the final setting of goals is his task.

The chief executive, or the planning staff, should prepare a checklist of possible objectives and priorities to ensure that the proper initial moves are taken in forming an organization plan. This can be an involved process, full of pitfalls for the uninitiated. Frequently, the personal objectives of an influential executive carry more weight than his activities justify. It is necessary for the chief executive to evaluate all activities and put them in proper perspective.

Long- and short-range objectives should be differentiated, because the time frame that is established for the achievement of each goal will influence the organization plan that is developed. For example, a long-term goal of continuing expansion through mergers and acquisitions may suggest the inclusion of a special acquisition department in the organization plan, whereas a short-term goal such as the acquisition of a specific firm or product line could perhaps be handled by a special task force.

Critical Success Factors. Once a company has established where it should be headed, the next step is to pinpoint the conditions and circumstances that will influence successful attainment of its goals. Some factors will be outside the company; others internal. Some factors may prove uncontrollable; others may be easily manipulated.

An excellent technique to employ here is to consider each goal independently, carefully noting any factor considered critical to its successful attainment. Once all factors have been determined, a chart can be developed showing the relative importance of the various factors and their relationship to essential company functions.

Such a chart can list vertically critical factors such as financial resources; engineering capabilities; marketing methods; production capacity, including tooling; personnel and facilities; material-control methods; inventory-control methods; patent position; advertising methods; and plant location. Laterally, across the top, objectives can be shown with column space to permit checkoff where objective and success factors coincide. Objectives may include product improvement, diversification, cost reduction, increased sales, and cash-flow improvement.

Once a relative ranking of objectives has been established, a weighting system for those critical factors that affect the more important objectives can be incorporated into the chart.

The Ideal Organization Structure. After the organization goals have been established and the critical success factors determined, the planner will see organizational alignments that naturally suggest themselves. From this information, he can develop an ideal organization structure disregarding, for the moment, the constraints that the existing organization may impose in terms of personalities, established relationships, and tradition.

The ideal organization should deal in realities just as the goals do. For example, average qualifications should be required in the positions that are established. It is unwise at this stage to plan an organization that requires exceptional talents. Certainly, special skills can be required, but an average ability in these skills should be planned for.

This ideal organization structure need not be developed in great detail. It should, however, be complete in its coverage of the functions that are critical to achieving established objectives.

The Optimum Organization Structure. It is assumed that the existing organization structure, together with the rationale that is the basis for its form and the characteristics of the personnel that operate within it, is known to the organization planner. If they are not known, then he must learn what they are before he can proceed effectively.

The next step is to modify the ideal organization he has outlined to form a realistic compromise between what exists and what would be ideal. The company should not compromise to the extent that the basic objectives are violated, and a timetable should be established and steps planned for reaching the ideal structure. Undoubtedly, some compromises will be made for people, but again caution must be exercised so that the most competent people are put in the most critical positions.

The philosophy usually applied in this optimization process has the following precepts:

1. Minimize as much as reasonably possible organizational realignments.
2. Use traditional organizational structures and relationships if feasible.
3. Minimize as much as reasonably possible personnel shifts, both vertical and lateral.
4. Plan to use currently employed personnel wherever possible in the new organization structure.

Organization Planning Documentation. In the organization planning steps, the planner has been establishing policy, allocating responsibilities, and generally making organizational decisions. To communicate his decisions, he must present them formally in a planning document. The organization manual discussed earlier is the device commonly used. In some cases, it is desirable to prepare auxiliary documents such as:

Salary structure plans

Procedure manuals

Implementation schedules

Organization Plan Implementation. Once the organization plan is complete and the installation timetable prepared, all that remains is to put the plan into effect, observe its functioning, and after a time adjust it in light of the experience gained while operating under it.

A series of "maxims" on the subject of implementation has been developed, and relevant extracts from it are summarized below.[3]

Complete the reorganization in twelve months or less except in very large companies.

Wait until a year after the reorganization is complete before attempting a meaningful appraisal.

Expect to make major personnel changes in a major reorganization.

Inform key personnel fully once a decision to reorganize is reached.

Plan changes in information flow to accompany the reorganization.

Expect hostility to the new organization plan. It takes courage and consistent leadership to reorganize successfully.

Use senior people to assist in evolving and implementing the organization plan.

[3] G. Fisch, *Organization for Profit,* McGraw-Hill Book Company, New York, 1964, pp. 302, 303, and 304.

Consider all the financial consequences of the reorganization before implementation.

Consider all tenable, alternative plans before implementation.

Expect to devote considerable personal time and energy to implementation.

Consider the organization spirit you hope to achieve and implement the organization plan accordingly.

Consider the organizational aspects such as status symbols, salaries, fringe benefits, and procedures that are related to the plan, but not a part of it before implementation.

Proceed with courage and confidence. The task is difficult, but the potential is great.

MAINTAINING THE ORGANIZATION PLAN

Once the organization plan has been developed and implemented, it should not be tampered with unless:

1. Operating experience indicates a serious flaw that must be corrected
2. The organization objectives or the critical success factors change significantly enough to require adjustments to the organization but not replanning

To maintain a balance between the need for a dependable, stable organization plan and the danger that the plan will become obsolete, a regular, periodic review should be undertaken. The review period should be brief. The objective should be to study any suggested changes and evaluate them in terms of profit improvement versus the cost of the change.

The review can be accomplished by either a special task force or the regular planning organization if the company has one.

CONCLUSION

Organization planning is the development of a coordinated, integrated management scheme that indicates what management tasks are to be performed, who will perform them, and what rules they will follow.

The minimal essentials of an organization plan are:

A definition of the company's objectives and operating philosophy

A description of the organization structure that will be used in attaining the objectives

An expression of the duties associated with the positions that appear in the organization structure

The responsibility for the planning function should reside at a high level in the organization structure. Otherwise, plans are uncoordinated and can even work at cross-purposes.

To develop an organization plan one must:

1. Establish objectives
2. Determine the factors that are critical to attaining those objectives
3. Determine the relative importance of the various company elements
4. Synthesize an optimum organization structure from the existing organization and the ideal organization, keeping in mind objectives and critical success factors
5. Prepare the supporting documentation for the organization structure

Once an organization plan is implemented, it should be left to operate unless significant flaws appear or significant changes occur in organization objectives or critical success factors. A properly prepared plan does not require frequent readjustment.

BIBLIOGRAPHY

Allen, Louis A., *Management and Organization*, McGraw-Hill Book Company, New York, 1958.

Anderson, Richard, *Management Practices*, McGraw-Hill Book Company, New York, 1960.

Bowman, D. M., and F. M. Fillerup, *Management: Organization and Planning*, McGraw-Hill Book Company, New York, 1964.

Dale, Ernest, *Planning and Developing the Company Organization Structure*, American Management Association, New York, 1959.

Dugdale, J. S., *Fundamentals of Modern Management*, James Brodie, Ltd., Bath, England, 1964.

Fish, Gerald, *Organization for Profit*, McGraw-Hill Book Company, New York, 1964.

Kaxmier, L. J., *Principles of Management*, McGraw-Hill Book Company, New York, 1964.

Longenecker, Justin, *Principles of Management and Organizational Behavior*, Charles E. Merrill Books, Inc., Columbus, Ohio, 1964.

Michael, S. R., *Appraising Management Practices and Performance*, Prentice-Hall, Inc., Englewood Cliffs, N.J., 1963.

Peterson, E., *Business Organization and Management*, 5th ed., Richard D. Irwin, Inc., Homewood, Ill., 1962.

White, K. K., *Understanding the Company Organization Chart*, American Management Association, New York, 1963.

CHAPTER FOUR

Growth and Organization

L. F. URWICK *Honorary President, Urwick Orr & Partners Ltd., Longueville, Australia*

JOHN W. HUNT *Lecturer in Business Administration, University of New South Wales, Sydney, Australia*

The word "organization," as used here, means the systematic arrangement of parts for a defined purpose. A "business" is any enterprise which makes, distributes, or provides any article or service which other members of the community need. Business transactions are normally measured in terms of money. These measurements must show a profit to the enterprise supplying the goods or services; otherwise it will be unable to remain in business. But money and profit are measuring devices, providing a common term in which to calculate business transactions. A measuring device is *not* a purpose. To realize a profit may be, and usually is, the purpose of some of the individuals who engage in business. But "the only valid definition of business purpose is *to create a customer*,"[1] that is, to provide goods or services which someone needs.

All the activities necessary to a wide range of businesses can be carried out by a single individual in series; there are, in fact, quite a large number of "one-man businesses." Here, the only parts which the individual can arrange systematically are his tools and materials and the different sections of his own time. When we talk of a "well-organized" bench or desk, we mean that all the implements and supplies which the user will need are conveniently stored and placed, so that any operation which he may have to carry out may be completed with the minimum of time and effort. Similarly, when we speak of a task or a day being "well-organized," we mean that the individual concerned can complete that task or the activities assigned to that period of time with the minimum of waste motion.

But in the majority of businesses, the total task to be performed is broken down into a number of parts, each of which is carried out by a different person

[1] Peter F. Drucker, *The Practice of Management*, Harper & Row, Publishers, Incorporated, New York, 1954, p. 37.

and each of which may consist of a cluster of activities of various kinds. Such a cluster of activities is usually described as a "position" or "job." It is to the systematic arrangement of such positions or jobs that the term "organization" is here applied. They are the parts which have to be arranged systematically if the business is to carry out its defined purpose with the minimum of effort or frictional loss.

ORGANIZATION AND PEOPLE

The concept of organization as consisting of a system of positions is, of course, abstract. An organization chart is no more than an architect's plan. It has little meaning, except to the architect, until the builders have been at work and have translated his "dream" into a concrete structure. Similarly, the organization chart is merely a sketch until the positions have been filled with people. Then, as the late Chester Barnard pointed out frequently and with emphasis, organization becomes of importance, because if people are to cooperate effectively, they must know who should communicate with whom about what. "The need of a definite system of communication creates the first task of the organizer and is the essential origin of executive organization."[2]

Business has been somewhat slow to recognize the necessity for formal organization for two main reasons.

1. Many businesses do not *start* with a formal organization. They start with an individual—an entrepreneur with an idea. In the beginning, he may carry out all the functions of his infant business personally. As it grows, he adds a helper for this and a helper for that. But in these early stages, communication among them and consequent cooperation are secured by the leadership of the founder and a network of "understandings." These are built up by constant association and commonsense acceptance of the requirements of the common task. Definition of channels of formal communication at first often disturbs the system of tacit understandings and relations between persons which underlies such spontaneous cooperation. People become afraid that formality will become the enemy of spontaneity.

2. People who are unaccustomed to formal communications, especially in writing, are intimidated by them. They feel that they do not understand what they are attempting to convey and are alarmed at the idea of having to communicate in writing. They may be complete masters of their craft, but their craft does not necessarily include the art of drafting clear and lucid statements in writing.

Some Basic Propositions. The propositions on which this chapter is based are the following:

1. A business is a group of people working cooperatively toward common ends. It can only develop, or even maintain, itself if it combines what the late Chester Barnard called *effectiveness*—being well designed to achieve those common ends—and *efficiency*—offering inducements to individuals which will maintain their cooperation and hence the equilibrium of the system.[3] It must recognize the multitude of individual differences, goals, needs, interests, and attitudes among those on whose cooperation it depends.

2. Reconciling individual differences and corporate purposes is not impossible, though the subject has received less attention than it deserves. If a business

[2] Chester I. Barnard, *The Functions of the Executive*, Harvard University Press, Cambridge, Mass., 1938, p. 217.
[3] *Ibid.*, p. 19.

has clarity of purpose and plan so that the right people are attracted to the right positions and if the positions are arranged in a way that will allow each individual to give his best to the common purpose of the undertaking, reconciliation of individual and corporate purposes is possible.

3. Where this reconciliation of purposes exists, it is the basis of cooperative effort, *but only at that moment in time.* If it is to endure, there must be sensitivity to change. Personal motives or needs and the cooperative system as a whole both change and develop.

4. No business can stifle individual development and growth. Human organisms develop or regress; there is no point of inertia. Because the units composing the cooperative system change, finding new needs and purposes, the business must also change if cooperation is to be maintained. The law of life is growth. If the business, regarded as an organism, does not provide an environment in which the cells can develop healthily, they will wither, exactly as the cells in any living body wither if their normal growth is interrupted.

5. A business must develop fast enough to enable those it employs to grow individually as fast and as far as their mental and emotional health will allow. Failure to recognize this need of the cells of the organism has one of two results, both often encountered in business.

   a. A number of employees, representing a valuable investment in training and experience, quit.

   b. Evidence develops of increasing frustration and low morale among a number of employees whose personal need of growth has found no outlet in the business. In an "affluent society," a high turnover of employees is usually evidence of an insensitivity on the part of managers to these needs of growth.

6. So important is this reconciliation of individual and corporate purpose that it is better to lose employees than to retain them if their personal growth is frustrated.

7. Many of the difficulties encountered in reconciling individual needs and corporate purpose arise from failure in communication. When employees are unaware of the corporate purpose or when it is misrepresented to them, the most powerful unifying force at the disposal of the manager is wasted. When this happens, the pressure of individual needs which cannot be satisfied within the framework of the business may lead to frustration; the employee has no definitive corporate purpose to set against them. Executives and others need to know the organization structure, the duties and authority of individuals, and the relations between them. People expect to know what they are meant to do and where their energies should be applied. More important, they want to know where the cooperative system of which they are a part is going. Breakdowns in communication lead to random behavior even when an honest attempt has been made to provide individual satisfactions. Man is a social animal.

8. Quite apart from these considerations of social coherence, a business that is not growing is almost certainly slipping backward. In a free economy, any individual who can see an opportunity of supplying goods or services at a lower cost to the consumer than the existing sources of supply is entitled to try to do so. Research is constantly uncovering new materials, new processes, alternative sources of supply, or new claims on the consumer's dollar. The business that does not have the margins, over and above its operating costs and a reasonable return on the capital invested, to be constantly alerted to and able to exploit such opportunities, is likely to be outdistanced by more aggressive or more wide-awake competitors. If it has the courage and the initiative and can command the capital to exploit them, it will probably grow.

BALANCE AND GROWTH

Whether a company is successful in growing or not will depend almost exclusively on whether it is able to maintain a correct balance between its objective requirements in personnel and the individuals available to meet those requirements. This balance is *never* static. It is an adjustment which is constantly moving between the requirements of the business in terms of skills and the development of the individuals whose services can be secured. The requirements are in a constant condition of evolution and so are the individuals employed.

In other words, the company's objective requirements in people are determined by the shape of its organization. What positions are involved? What skills, experience, and personal qualities are required to fill those positions adequately? Where are they to come from? These are the questions which every chief executive has constantly before him as he surveys the future of his business. If he is wise, he knows that his resources in people are the most critical of all his resources.

Years ago, F. W. Taylor quoted "one of the most successful manufacturers in this country." Asked by a group of financiers whether he thought that the difference between one style of organization and another amounted to much, this manufacturer replied, "If I had to choose now between abandoning my present organization and burning down all of my plants which have cost me millions, I should choose the latter. My plants could be rebuilt in a short while with borrowed money, but I could hardly replace my organization in a generation."[4] He was using the word "organization" in its popular context as covering both the positions and the people in them.

Pros and Cons of Promotion from Within. If a company has no person within the ranks of its existing employees competent to fill a position which organizational growth has made necessary, it can possibly hire a suitable individual from the outside. This is, however, a course of action which involves both a higher element of risk and certain specific disadvantages, as opposed to developing and training those required to fill higher responsibilities from existing employees. The risks involved are:

1. Despite advances in the use of psychological methods of testing unknown personalities, these methods are still far from foolproof. The candidate from within the company is well known. His faults as well as his virtues are seen clearly. The outside candidate may be astute in emphasizing his virtues and in pushing his weaknesses "under the rug." Shakespeare wrote, nearly four centuries ago, of the uncertainty that ". . . makes us rather bear those ills we have than fly to others that we know not of."[5] And a specialist in business efficiency expressed the same thought rather more colloquially in this century: "Far-off fields are green. But they are not nearly so green as you are if you put your good money in them."

2. The recruitment of an executive from outside to fill a position of trust within a corporation is almost invariably seen as a "vote of no confidence" by those already employed in the corporation who have ambitions for advancement and who may have been making serious efforts at self-development. It thus has a discouraging effect on executive morale. It may foster a cynical attitude toward the corporation's efforts at executive development as a whole.

[4] F. W. Taylor, "Shop Management," *Scientific Management,* Harper & Row, Publishers, Incorporated, New York, 1947, pp. 62–63.
[5] William Shakespeare, *Hamlet,* Act III, Scene 1.

Cynicism is the Achilles' heel of free enterprise. As Prof. Peter Drucker has observed, "Capitalism is being attacked not because it is inefficient or misgoverned but because it is cynical."[6]

On the other hand:

1. Where a corporation has started from small beginnings and is growing fast, it is almost inevitable that, in the early stages, it will need more "up and coming" executives than can be found among or developed from the comparatively small number of its early recruits. At the same time, it should never be forgotten that a young business tends to recruit young people, and young people *must* grow if they are to remain healthy. All human beings are inclined to give too much weight to their first impressions of others, to fail to see the adult man in the "nice boy" they recruited a few years ago.

2. Similar considerations apply at the opposite end of the business hierarchy. The more important the position to be filled and the greater the volume of initiative, experience, and skill required to fill it adequately, the less is it likely that an ideal candidate will be found within the comparatively limited field of choice presented by the relatively small number of individuals employed by a particular corporation. That is why boards of directors so frequently go outside the corporation in appointing a new president or a vice president who is to be "groomed for stardom."

3. Whatever the claims established by seniority and service of existing employees, no corporation should appoint any individual to a major post involving responsibility for the work, lives, and happiness of many others if there is serious doubt he possesses the requisite qualities of personality and, in particular, integrity. A younger man who is believed to possess such qualities, even if he lacks what is considered to be the requisite experience, should always be appointed in preference to a more senior candidate about whom there is doubt.

4. A certain amount of movement from corporation to corporation, especially among senior executives, promotes what is described as "the circulation of the elite." This is socially desirable and should not be restricted to safeguard the presumed interests or prejudices of the employees of a particular corporation.

NEED FOR CONTINUOUS REORGANIZATION

Because of the necessity for maintaining balance between its objective requirements and its developing personnel, the healthy corporation will treat reorganization as a continuous process.

The late Henry Sturgess Dennison of the Dennison Manufacturing Company was one of the first employers in the United States to appreciate the significance of the work of F. W. Taylor and the importance of the then new and unpopular idea of scientific management. Some of his words[7] on this subject are worth repeating; they are as true as when they were written many years ago.

The structure of organization which is best for a concern today will not be the best in all its details a month from today if the concern has grown as any live concern would wish to do. Reorganization has therefore to be carried along all the time, a continuous evolution. . . . To maintain too slow a rate of change in structure invites a real revolution, whatever name it may go by. Continuous reorganization can no more be left to chance or the "happening to think of it"—than can routine operation. Some kind of specific provision must be made for it or it will lag behind the needs.

[6] Drucker, *op. cit.*, p. 392.

[7] Henry S. Dennison, *Organization Engineering*, McGraw-Hill Book Company, New York, 1931, pp. 183–184.

Business has been somewhat slow in recognizing the need for this continuous study and readjustment of organization. A publication issued just before World War II noted that "very little attention seems to have been devoted to planning and designing the organization structure."[8] Another author has noted that the establishment of organization planning departments seems to have spread at a high rate in the late 1950s.[9] Of 639 of the "largest corporations in the U.S.A.," 436 replied to a questionnaire on the subject in 1962. Only 142, or 32.5 percent, gave answers which suggested that they had permanent machinery devoting continuous attention to organization planning.[10]

ORGANIZATIONAL BALANCE

Not only should balance be maintained between the organization and the growth of individuals, but the organization itself should be balanced. Here again, Dennison's wisdom[11] is wholly contemporary:

A special task of continuous reorganization is to see that the units of the organization are kept in balance—that there is a reasonable relative apportionment of strength among departments. It is literally true that one arm of any service may be at any moment too good, so that something in the nature of a salient may grow. Any provision, even for self-preservation, may become too much for the rest of the organization and defeat its own purpose. The classic example of over-preparedness is the armored dinosaur who was so well protected that he finally failed to earn a living.

DELEGATION

Organization becomes operational through delegation. To delegate is to assign to some other person the duty of carrying out some portion of the total task which is the responsibility of the assigner. "Responsibility" may be defined as accountability for the performance of duties. An individual, by assigning some portion of his total task to others, does not escape his accountability for the way the task is performed. The responsibility of a superior for the acts of his subordinates cannot be delegated.

Delegation is therefore an act of trust, an expression of confidence that the individual to whom duties are assigned will discharge them in a manner which satisfies the intention of the assigner. This also involves an assumption on the part of the assigner that the individual to whom duties are assigned possesses the necessary skill and strength to be *able* to discharge those duties, and that he possesses the requisite application and dedication to duty to be *willing* to discharge them.

Application and dedication to duty on the part of an individual to whom activities are assigned are not isolated phenomena. They are in part a reflection of the attitude of the assigner and of the reactions which that attitude produces in the mind and conduct of the assignee. They depend on interpersonal relations. As is often said, "confidence begets confidence." Or again, "an ounce

[8] Paul E. Holden, Lounsbury S. Fish, and Hubert L. Smith, *Top Management Organization and Control*, McGraw-Hill Book Company, New York, 1951; Stanford University Press, Stanford, Calif., 1941, p. 91.

[9] John M. Pfiffner and Frank P. Sherwood, *Administrative Organization*, Prentice-Hall, Inc., Englewood Cliffs, N.J., 1960, p. 225.

[10] Joseph K. Bailey, "Organization Planning: Whose Responsibility?" *The Academy of Management Journal*, vol. 7, no. 2, June, 1964, p. 99.

[11] Dennison, *op. cit.*, p. 185.

of example is worth a ton of precept." Where an individual who has to delegate duties to others possesses qualities which stimulate the application and dedication to duty of those others, we say that "in that situation, he is a good leader." If he lacks the necessary qualities, we say that "he is not, in that situation, a good leader."

Some personalities are literally quite unable to delegate. Some facet of their characters—usually to be traced to some psychological upset in infancy or early life—renders them literally incapable of trusting others. This inability to develop, and therefore to beget, confidence in other people is by no means incompatible with other qualities of initiative, imagination, foresight, and shrewdness which may equip an individual to be a most successful *entrepreneur*. But the minute the size of his business grows beyond the point at which it can be conducted successfully under his personal supervision, he would be wise either to limit its further growth or to find at least one other individual, *whom he can trust*, to undertake its executive management. Otherwise, it is likely to fold up for lack of leadership.

Although it is a subject on which objective evidence is hard to find, a considerable percentage of failures among small businesses can be traced to this lack of leadership. The infant business usually fails because its proprietor lacks the knowledge or the connections to provide adequate finance for expanding operations. But the failure of a small, expanding business which has done quite well over a period of years—and it is this type of failure which causes the most distress to the most people—usually arises from the fact that its proprietor, or his son, is no leader of other people, and lacks the insight to identify this weakness in himself.

Delegation, then, is not a single phenomenon. It is relationship between assigner and assignee which may vary very greatly both quantitatively and qualitatively. Quantitatively, it depends on the degree and frequency of supervision exercised by the superior. Qualitatively, it depends on the volume of skill, initiative, and independent decision expected of the subordinate in each particular situation. Both factors may vary from zero to near infinity, depending on the physical circumstances, the attitude and skill of the superior, and the attitude and skill of the subordinate.

The extremes may be illustrated by the following two cases.

1. *A craftsman with a single apprentice working at a bench alongside him.* Initially, the craftsman will expect virtually no skill from the apprentice. He will expect that the beginner will make a reasonable attempt to listen to what he says and to carry out instructions as to the elementary operations which he will entrust to him. Gradually, he will show him how to perform more complex operations. Ultimately, he will allow him to carry out *all* the operations involved in his "skill." Initially, he will watch and check *how* the apprentice goes about each element of the tasks assigned to him. Later, he will be satisfied with checking the completed task. Ultimately, when the apprentice is a sufficiently competent and conscientious craftsman to be entrusted with the tools and materials of his trade without involving his employer in unreasonable loss, he will complete his apprenticeship and become an independent craftsman.

2. *The trusted chief executive of a subsidiary company situated at the other end of the world from its parent corporation.* He is neither visited regularly nor recalled to headquarters, save in exceptional circumstances. He is trusted completely with the management of all the affairs of the subsidiary, and his corporate management is satisfied with his annual results. It merely keeps him informed of developments in other components of the corporation and meets his requests for assistance from its research or other headquarters' components

promptly. It has confidence that the personnel policy of the subsidiary is such that, should the chief executive suffer illness or accident, the corporation as a whole would not suffer. Others are being developed to take his place. The corporate management relies on him to advance such proposals for local development as are in the best interests of the corporation as a whole, and answers his requests for finances, compatible with its other commitments. If it cannot meet these requests, it is sympathetic to his suggestions for securing financing locally. In short, he enjoys all the independence he would find in conducting a business of his own, plus the advantage of belonging to a powerful group.

Major Levels of Delegation. Between these two extremes there is, of course, every possible permutation and combination of subordination and freedom of initiative. Certain main levels of delegation may conveniently be distinguished as follows.

I. Where what is delegated is merely liability for the performance of a given task by the subordinate, it may be described as "first-degree delegation." The degree of initiative allowed to the subordinate will vary greatly with:
   A. The frequency of supervision by the superior
   B. The degree of skill involved in the task:
      1. The subordinate is following standard practice,
      2. The subordinate is exercising a recognized skill under fairly precise instructions as to objectives and methods,
      3. The subordinate is following general instructions as to objectives but is left to his own devices as to methods, or
      4. The subordinate is admitted by the superior to know more about his specialized field than does the superior, who is satisfied with an occasional review of results.

II. Where what is delegated includes authority over others and the supervision of their work, it may be described as "second-degree delegation." The degree of initiative allowed usually follows on the factors listed above except for no. 4.

III. Where what is delegated includes authority over others, the supervision of their work, and general responsibility for the morale of the working group concerned, it may be described as "third-degree delegation." The degree of initiative allowed is usually as in II.

IV. Where what is delegated is full initiative for a major function of a business it may be described as "fourth-degree delegation." The degree of initiative allowed should include that listed in no. 4 above.

The distinction between levels II and III may be noted. It is that found in combat forces between officers and noncommissioned officers. The former are held directly responsible for the morale of those under their supervision; the latter are not. This distinction has not yet been generally recognized in business. It is the writers' opinion that it will be forced upon business by the size of the modern business corporation and the necessity of paying greater attention to social discipline which, in a free society, depends on morale. It is doubtful that an individual who is held responsible for daily discipline and technical details can, at the same time, be held responsible for morale. Much of the present confusion and argument about the position of the foreman in business can probably be traced to failure to make this distinction. Many so-called foremen are, in fact, discharging the functions of managers (officers); others are not. The title of "foreman" is used loosely and applied to a very wide span of duties and responsibilities; so is the title of "manager." Without greater precision in the use of titles which carry status implications, confusion about function is inevitable.

THE SUBDIVISION AND GROUPING OF ACTIVITIES

Three main methods of subdividing and grouping activities are found in almost all forms of human undertaking:

1. *The unitary method*, in which the limits of the task are defined with reference to persons, objects, areas, numbers, or periods
2. *The serial method*, in which the limits of the task are defined in accordance with the limits of processes which follow each other
3. *The functional method*, in which the limits of the task are fixed by subjects

The advantage of the functional method is that it facilitates specialization of task. It thus ensures a higher standard of skill *in that subject*. Its disadvantage is that it multiplies the number of opinions to be brought to bear on any course of action, thus increasing the burden of coordination. To secure unity of action among a large group of individuals, coordination of their opinions and actions is necessary. In securing coordination, communication is of primary importance. The underlying principles of organization are almost exclusively concerned with techniques of official communication.

The number of direct subordinates whose work a superior can supervise effectively is limited. The reason for this limitation is simple—he is supervising not only the work of each direct subordinate, but the relationships among the individuals. Although the addition of a sixth direct subordinate to five increases the superior's field of delegation by some 16.7 percent, it increases the complexity of the interpersonal relations with which he has to deal by more than 100 percent.[12]

On the other hand, authority to coordinate major functions cannot be delegated. The essence of the idea of specialization is that the specialist should have authority within the limits of his specialization, wherever that special knowledge or skill is used in the business. A superior, therefore, can secure relief from this increasing burden of coordination only by assigning some of the detailed work of coordination to subordinates who represent his authority ("assistants to" a superior). Because they have no authority, such assistants cannot relieve the superior's direct subordinates of any responsibility. They can only "represent" the authority of a common superior.

There has been considerable controversy in business circles in recent years over whether "assistants to" are a form of organization which is necessary or desirable in business situations. The writers' opinion is that the repeated experiments made with the form of organization show that the need for it is often present. The failures may be traced to lack of initiative in solving another problem. Business has often failed to distinguish between function and status. Status or rank within an undertaking is currently determined, therefore, by popular superstition and is attached to a large number of symbols, often physical objects. The appointment or behavior of an "assistant to" a high executive often infringes, quite unwillingly, on the unwritten code of status symbolism thus popularly established. Conflict is engendered. These conflicts, rather than any inherent ambiguity in such appointments, have brought the position of "assistant to" into question. Confusion on this issue has been compounded by the fact that, in the American Army, both specialist and "assistant to" positions are described as "staff."

[12] V. A. Graicunas, "Relationship in Organization," in Luther Gulick and L. Urwick (eds.), *Papers on the Science of Administration*, Columbia University Press, New York, 1937, pp. 183–187.

The three formal relationships commonly found in all types of organized human groups are:

Relationship	Authority	Responsibility
Line	Direct	General
Functional	Indirect	Specialized
(General) Staff	Representative	Advisory

Whatever the nature of his duties, every subordinate is in a line relationship to his immediate superior.

DEVELOPMENT OF A BUSINESS

To clarify these concepts of organization, we will outline the development of a hypothetical business from its first beginnings as an idea in the mind of a single individual.

A young engineer, whom we will call the "proprietor," has patented a new piece of equipment for automobiles. He has decided that he will manufacture and market it himself, and he has succeeded in raising sufficient capital to see him over the first year or two. He has bought a small plant with room for expansion, hired half-a-dozen workers, and set to work.

Stage 1. At this stage, the infant business is, as far as management is concerned, literally "a one-man business." The proprietor is his own production manager, chief accountant, development engineer, and sales manager. But, because he cannot be in two places at once and has to do much of his own selling, he must immediately face problems of delegation. Someone must be available to keep the little plant running and to deal with emergencies in his absence; someone, probably someone else because the two skills are not usually found in combination, must be available in his office to deal with correspondence, answer inquiries, and so on. The proprietor will certainly be involved in first-, and probably second-, degree delegation. If, as he hopes and believes, his little business is going to grow, and if he possesses foresight, he will realize that in making these appointments, he is creating a future problem for himself as to the balance between recruitment from within or without discussed earlier. Are the individuals he appoints to these first supervisory positions likely to grow into personalities competent to accept third- and fourth-degree delegation as quickly as the growth of the business will require? If the answer is in the negative, he has two alternatives:

1. He can consider whether action on his part will encourage and enable them so to grow. If so, he has a problem of executive development.

2. If the answer to 1 is in the negative, he must consider whether he will face the issue at this stage by recruiting an outsider with greater growth potential or by promoting the person available, on the ground that he is likely to be fitted for third-degree delegation, but unlikely to develop to fourth-degree level. There is a good deal to be said for allowing available personnel to go as far and as fast as they can to the extreme limit of their potential. On the other hand, the disappointment when they are passed over for further advancement is likely to be keener. Human social groups tend to place great emphasis on seniority as the basis for advancement. The individual in question is accumulating length of service, and if he is passed over in favor of an outsider at a later stage, there is likely to be a more adverse effect on general morale.

It is unusual for problems of executive development to be faced consciously and deliberately at this early stage in the growth of a business. More commonly, they are dealt with quasi-instinctively rather than analytically. They do exist, however, and the future success of many small businesses depends far more on the skill with which they are handled than on many other factors. The first syllable of "management" is "man."

Stage 2. The second stage arrives when the proprietor begins to specialize some of the functions which he has previously carried out personally. For instance, he may engage a salesman, or an accountant, or a production foreman. The group leader who looks after the plant in his absence has to fulfill many of the functions of a foreman, and this necessarily involves the proprietor in some third-degree delegation. He cannot be in the plant as much as before. The workers begin to look to the foreman for leadership.

Stage 3. The third stage sees the beginning of specialization within the production function. The proprietor appoints a second foreman as the number of employees increases. He also appoints an engineer in charge of maintenance. He adds two more salesmen and concentrates the control of work in the office in the hands of a senior clerk who is also something of an accountant. With the increasing number of personnel employed by the business, personnel records become something of a problem. For the time being, he asks his private secretary to take over this activity and to build up a separate set of files as the basis of a system of personnel records. He now has eight persons reporting directly to him, and he realizes that the burden of daily management of *all* the functions of the company is becoming too much for a single individual.

Stages 4, 5, and 6. The point has now been reached when the proprietor must begin to unload the actual *management* of one of the major functions of his business onto a subordinate. If he is to obtain the relief from details which are essential to growth and conserve his own energies for further expansion, he *must* pass to fourth-degree delegation. At this stage, he may, and probably will, know more about that particular function than the subordinate. But if that subordinate is to develop into the kind of executive who can handle production or marketing or control as the business develops, he must be expected to feel that the responsibility for *initiation with relation to that function* is his. He may well advance proposals or even take action with which the proprietor is in sharp disagreement, but he should never be "slapped down." He should, from this point forward, be guided. Unless the proprietor feels that some course of action on which the subordinate proposes to embark will involve the business in crippling losses, or unless his attitude to his subordinates is such that he is willing to risk the loss of valuable personnel, the proprietor should refrain from using authority.

In what order he decides to delegate the three major functions of production, marketing, and control to a genuine *executive* must depend on circumstances. Each of these changes is critical. Normally, they should not be undertaken simultaneously. Each of them will raise critical personnel issues as to the potential "horizon" of the individual concerned, of the same character as those discussed under stage 1. The new executive will need much personal help from the proprietor while he is "breaking in" on his new job. Organization resembles machinery in this: any new design needs "breaking in," and new parts need "breaking in." If the proprietor changes too much at one time, he may find that he lacks the time and energy to give to each of his "new parts" the attention they need.

On the other hand, because of the human difficulties involved in introducing changes in organization in any established institution, many young executives are tempted to dramatize the situation and to indulge in a complete reorganization. This sometimes enables them to offer an apparent "consolation prize" to subordinates who may be disappointed by someone else's promotion. It curtails the period of uncertainty and satisfies their own instinct for decisive action. But a complete reorganization is a revolution rather than an evolution, and as the quotation from the late Henry S. Dennison suggests, should be unnecessary.[13] Revolutions can be "bad medicine"; it is not always possible to "contain" them.

A special problem arises with the appointment of a controller. When the term was first introduced into business, it was "comptroller."[14] This was to distinguish it from the ordinary English use of the word "control," meaning to guide or dominate (to control or steer a boat, to keep a horse under control). The word was derived originally from the French words "contre roller," meaning to call over or check against a list; for example, to check results against budget. The simplification of the spelling has led to much misunderstanding and friction in business. Attention was called to the possible misunderstandings by the French industrialist Henri Fayol,[15] who wrote:

A further danger to avoid is infiltration of control into management and departmental running. This encroachment makes for duality of management in its most formidable aspect: on the one side there is irresponsible control, but capable at times of doing widespread harm; on the other there is the operating department, bereft of all but weak means of defense against hostile control. The tendency to encroach on the part of control is fairly common in large-scale affairs especially and may have the most serious consequences.

Because of the great importance attached in business to financial measurements, the person who makes and maintains such measurements may manage a large staff. In addition, he may have special opportunities of winning the confidence of a chief executive who relies on such measurements. These considerations do not alter the fact that although to his own staff the controller is an executive, to all other departments his duties are purely functional, *not* executive. These duties are limited to supplying and interpreting figures. As one distinguished American controller has written, "In fact, *interpretation is even a long way from advice.*"[16]

Stage 7. As the three executives in charge of the three major functions consolidate their responsibilities, they are likely to make demands for an effective machine for the management and control of each of these functions and also for the specialization of auxiliary functions calculated to make each function more effective.

Changes probable at this stage are:
1. Within the office:
   a. The breakdown of the original office into three parts, each servicing one of the major functions
2. Within the production division:
   a. Appointment of a general works manager, with his own production office

---

[13] Dennison, *op. cit.*
[14] Cf. J. P. Jordan, "The Comptroller" in W. J. Donald (ed.), *Handbook of Business Administration*, American Management Association and McGraw-Hill Book Company, New York, 1931, pp. 416–424.
[15] Henri Fayol, *General & Industrial Management* (translated by Constance Storrs), Sir Isaac Pitman & Sons, Ltd., London, 1949, p. 109. Original French *Administration Industrielle et Generale*, Dunod, Paris, 1916.
[16] Jordan, *op. cit.*, p. 419.

    b. Appointment of a superintendent of manufacturing, managing all production divisions and responsible to the general works manager

    c. Division of the engineering department into maintenance and development, and appointment of a development engineer responsible to the general works manager

3. Within the sales division:

    a. Division of the total national market into two or more divisions each under an assistant sales manager

    b. Appointment of an assistant to the sales manager, specializing in advertising

4. Within the controller's division:

    a. Specialization of purchasing under a purchasing agent

    b. Establishment of a central typing and duplicating service

    c. Appointment of an assistant to the controller, specializing in clerical methods

The proprietor, freed by these arrangements from some burden of daily executive management, is likely at this stage to turn his attention to those areas in which he feels that his functional organization requires completing. But it would be foolish to introduce newcomers on the same level with his principal functional managers, some of whom may have been with him almost since the beginning. He might at this point find two or three really well-qualified younger men and appoint them initially as assistants to himself for such subjects as:

1. Personnel, union questions, and employee services

2. Forward planning, economic analysis, market research, and development

As growth continues, the proprietor will probably discover sooner or later that the resources in capital with which he started are insufficient to carry his growing business and that bank loans are not intended for permanent financing. He will be wise to consider incorporation. But he will be wiser to secure the very best legal and financial advice before doing so and to be certain that it is strictly professional and independent. Otherwise, he may find that he has "sold his birthright for a mess of pottage."

The persons most likely to be disturbed by this development are his principal executives. The proprietor will be closely associated with all the negotiations leading up to this development and will understand the pros and cons of the course of action followed. Presuming that he remains president of the corporation, when he establishes a board of directors he merely gains the advice and assistance of a group of businessmen, some of whom have perhaps been known to him over a long period, in discussing the future policy of the company. The problem of the correct composition and working of a board of directors and its relations with the chief executive is, of course, a problem on which much has been written. But, providing the proprietor acts prudently in inviting individuals to become members of the board, he need not fear the outcome. Whether he invites some of his principal executives also to become directors is another question on which much ink has been spilled. He should remember that by such invitations, he is asking these individuals to "wear two hats." This is a feat which many people find difficult to achieve gracefully. There is a good deal to be said for the proposition that persons occupying executive positions in a business corporation, other than its chief executive, should not, *at the same time,* be directors.

If the proprietor does not invite any of his principal executives to become directors, from their point of view the leadership of an individual whom they have learned to know and trust has been exchanged for that of a group of unknown persons in whom they have no reason to feel confidence. The proprietor will therefore be wise to consider associating them more closely with the day-by-day executive management of the undertaking by forming what might be called a "management conference." It is not the purpose of such a conference to try to manage the undertaking by a committee. A committee, by its very constitution and procedure, is incapable of effective *executive* action.[17] The purpose of the conference is to ensure that, by associating his immediate colleagues in the thought processes leading up to the recommendations as to policy which he makes to the board, he does not find himself in the position of "trying to direct a formed society from without . . . a society that will evolve defense mechanisms and sentiments of antagonism if its social living appears to be in danger of interruption."[18]

Stage 8. At this point the proprietor, now the chief executive, may well start consolidating some of his other principal functions. The first of these should be the personnel function. The existence of a specialized personnel function does *not* mean that any responsibility for the effective handling of people is taken from their immediate "line" managers. The illusion that this is so accounts for much of the friction between "staff" and "line" and the tendency of some personnel departments to degenerate into "fire fighting"[19] which has been noted by some writers. The care and development of people must remain, as it has always been to those with understanding, one of the two *primary* responsibilities of every manager. Managing is "getting things done with, through, and for people." The manager must always try to concentrate on two objectives:

1. The most effective means of accomplishing work; that is, of doing the *things* which are assigned as his responsibility
2. The most effective way of winning the wholehearted cooperation of the *people* assigned to him to collaborate in doing that work

The case for a specialized personnel function is simply that in any but very small companies, there are certain services to the line manager which can be more effective if they are centralized. They include finding potential candidates for employment, hiring them, maintaining their individual records throughout their employment, inducting them, caring for their health and welfare (including feeding, transportation, housing, recreational, and other services that circumstances render necessary or desirable), arranging transfers from department to department, helping to develop them as people by providing or keeping in contact with facilities for further education and training and directing the attention of individuals to such facilities, and finally, pensioning them. The personnel function may also be held responsible for all union negotiations, although because of the legal aspects, this function is sometimes organized independently as industrial relations.

If the assistant to the proprietor, to whom some of these responsibilities were assigned at stage 7, has gained the confidence of his senior colleagues, the proprietor may well consider making him personnel manager with functional re-

[17] Cf. L. Urwick, *Committees in Organization* (3d ed.), issued as a pamphlet by the British Institute of Management, 1956. Originally published as two articles in *The British Management Review*.

[18] T. N. Whitehead, *Leadership in a Free Society*, Harvard University Press, Cambridge, Mass., and Oxford University Press, London, 1936, p. 79. Whitehead uses the sentences quoted in another context, but the two situations are parallel.

[19] Cf. Peter F. Drucker, "Is Personnel Management Bankrupt?" *op. cit.*, and L. Urwick, "Personnel Management—The Past" and "Personnel Management—The Future," in *Personnel Management*, vol. 3, no. 3, Institute of Personnel Management, Australia, July, 1965.

sponsibility for all such matters.   The personnel manager should be a member of the management conference.

Stage 9.   Once the personnel function is well established, the proprietor may well consider specializing the research and development function.   Perhaps he needs more special lines to sustain his expanding business, and technical development has become of key importance.   It should no longer be a subfunction responsible to the general works manager.   So he promotes the research and development engineer to full functional status responsible to himself.

Because, however, technical development is closely bound up with marketing and he does not consider that marketing should be divorced from the responsibility of the general sales manager ("after all, he has to sell the stuff and is likely to be the best judge of whether it will or will not sell"), he establishes a marketing conference to unify the thinking of all executives concerned with the development and introduction of new products.   At this stage, he also specializes purchasing.

Stage 10.   Still developing his policy of specializing *all* the major functions, the chief executive removes transport from the control of the different departments employing it and places it under the management of a traffic manager directly responsible to himself for all internal and external transportation and warehousing.   If there is no candidate within the undertaking specially competent in all phases of transportation, he recruits a specialist from the outside.

He also removes the clerical manager from the supervision of the controller and makes him directly responsible to himself for systems and methods and for all central office services.

Stage 11.   As a result of the moves outlined in stages 8, 9, and 10, the chief executive, although his senior executives (production, selling, and control) have relieved him of a great deal of the day-to-day management of the major functions of his business, has five more executives in charge of important functions reporting to him directly.   He is thus, once again, rather too preoccupied with administrative detail.   He has eight executives in charge of different functions reporting to him directly, and the task of keeping their views and actions coordinated absorbs too much of his time.   He wants more freedom for the reflection necessary to develop future policies for presentation to his fellow directors, and for guiding the future development of the business.

He considers that because the previous experiment of employing "assistants to" has worked out satisfactorily—they have become both important and trusted heads of important functions—he can safely attempt a further experiment in the same direction.

He therefore might appoint an assistant to himself for economic forecasting, long-range planning, general policy, and public relations (including all outside contacts) and a second assistant to himself for organization, internal publications, and internal administration.[20]

CONCLUSION

This brief sketch of the potential evolution of a hypothetical business from an idea in one man's mind to a substantial institution employing 2,000 to 3,000 people is necessarily the barest outline, designed to illustrate a few of the major

[20] Those who dislike the idea of "assistant to" arrangements always maintain that "they will not work" in business.   One such arrangement which worked admirably was at the American Enka Corporation in the 1950s.   See L. F. Urwick and Ernest Dale, *Profitably Using the General Staff Position in Business*, GM Series 165, American Management Association, New York, 1953.

problems of organization involved. A mass of detail on organizational refinements, personal attitudes, and the actual development of the business market-wise and product-wise is necessarily omitted. The items have been chosen merely as illustrations of the problems and principles discussed in the earlier part of the chapter.

At this stage in the development of this particular business, the chief executive and directors will have to consider very carefully whether they are wise to take growth much further as a single unit. There is an inertia in large-scale and unified institutions which is at odds with most of the virtues commonly claimed for free enterprise. A policy of decentralization and diversification, even at a higher comparative initial cost, might serve the long-term interests of this particular company better than greater expansion of the parent unit. The late Henry Dennison's analogy of "the armored dinosaur"[21] is not merely a pleasant quip. It points to one of the key problems facing business in the future.

BIBLIOGRAPHY

Brech, E. F. L., *Organization—The Framework of Management*, Longmans, Green & Co., Ltd., London, 1957.

Brown, Wilfred, *Exploration in Management*, William Heinemann, Ltd., London, 1960.

Dale, Ernest, *Planning and Developing the Company Organization Structure*, American Management Association, New York, 1952.

Follett, Mary Parker, *Dynamic Administration*, collected lectures edited by H. C. Metcalf and L. Urwick, Harper & Row, Publishers, Incorporated, New York, 1942.

Koontz, Harold, *Management—A Book of Readings*, McGraw-Hill Book Company, New York, 1964.

Koontz, Harold, and Cyril O'Donnell, *Principles of Management*, 2d ed., McGraw-Hill Book Company, New York, 1959.

Lilienthal, David E., *TVA—Democracy on the March*, Penguin Books, Baltimore, 1944.

Mayo, Elton, *The Human Problems of an Industrial Civilization*, The Macmillan Company, New York, 1933.

Mayo, Elton, *The Social Problems of an Industrial Civilization*, with an Appendix on "The Political Problem," Routledge & Kegan Paul, Ltd., London, 1949.

Mooney, James D., and Alan C. Reiley, *Onward Industry*, Harper & Row, Publishers, Incorporated, New York, 1931. A comparative study of organization in governments, armies, churches, and business. This is a much more useful book than later abbreviations.

Urwick, L., *Notes on the Theory of Organization*, American Management Association, New York, 1952.

[21] Dennison, *op. cit.*

CHAPTER FIVE

The Use of Consulting Specialists*

WILSON SENEY *President, Wilson Seney, Inc., New York, New York; Management Consultant, Seminars for Executives*

In facing the challenge of change since the turn of the century, companies have increasingly used the services of independent consulting specialists to supplement their own internal managerial resources.

The practice of using consultants is a reasonable response to the basic facts of business existence. To be successful, management should be prepared to meet and solve problems as they occur, no matter what. Ideally, to meet these requirements, every organization should have among its own members people who are experts in every field of knowledge. This ideal position, however, is neither attainable nor economic for the vast majority of companies. Therefore, it has become common practice for managers to expand the talents and know-how of the organization by employing outside consulting specialists as the occasion requires.

The scope of consulting is as broad as the problems of business. It is no exaggeration to say that consulting services are available in every function and subfunction described in this Handbook. Previous studies have indicated that consultants are used to help managers to deal with practically every kind of management problem, including problems in the field of management itself.

The problems in management's effective utilization of consulting services do not result from lack of such services. Rather, they lie in the areas of (1) understanding the respective roles of client and consultant; (2) defining the purpose, scope, and limits of the project on which consulting help is retained; (3) selecting a qualified consultant; (4) working productively with the consultant; and (5) taking action to obtain useful benefits from the consulting work.

* Adapted from *Effective Use of Business Consultants*, by Wilson Seney, published by Financial Executives Research Foundation, New York, 1963. Grateful acknowledgment is also made to the other sources listed in the Bibliography.

ROLES OF CLIENT AND CONSULTANT

Over the years, there has evolved a fairly clear definition of the consultant's basic role as one of stimulating, creating, and implementing change. In fulfilling this function, the consultant acts as staff to management. He assists in defining problems, spelling out and evaluating alternative courses of action, and recommending a chosen course of action. He may also assist in implementing recommendations.

The consultant performs his tasks as an independent party, not as an employee of the organization. He does not command or control the conduct of his client's business.

Management should remain in full charge of its own business. It should not surrender control either deliberately or by default to an outsider. This means that the manager who is responsible for retaining a consultant should, as part of his job, provide overall supervision of the consulting service and coordinate it with other company programs and operations.

At the same time, the manager should remember that his relationship with a consultant is fundamentally different from his relationships with his own associates. First, a consulting engagement is a joint venture undertaken by independent parties on the basis of a relatively formal agreement about the nature of the venture and who is to do what. The consultant is not subject to the normal command exercised over subordinates by a superior officer. Second, just because he is an independent outsider, the consultant cannot exercise any authority in his client's organization. To be effective, he is dependent on management backing to a marked degree.

DEFINITION OF THE PROBLEM

Problem definition is fundamental for the effective use of consulting services. Consultants work on a project basis. This holds true whether the project is limited in duration or whether it extends indefinitely in the nature of a retainer relationship. Therefore, good planning and control in this area rest on adequate definitions of the purpose, scope, and limits of the problem or problems on which the consultant is to work.

Problem definition should be approached with full recognition that it is usually accomplished in steps and that it usually extends over some period of time. It is not uniquely associated with consulting services, for management defines and solves problems as a matter of course in the discharge of its normal duties.

On occasion, in attempting to define or to solve a particular problem, management may explore the desirability of using consulting assistance. It is at this point that (1) the search for a consultant properly begins, and (2) the definition of the problem becomes a joint concern of the company and the consultant, to be worked out during negotiations.

Even after a consultant is retained, changes in the definition of purpose, scope, and limits of the project often occur. This is, of course, a relative matter depending on many factors, such as the complexity of the situation, the ease of communication between company personnel and consultant, the experience of the organization in working with consultants, and the background in the problem that the consultant brings to the situation.

Both before and after contact with a consultant, and regardless of whether a consultant is finally retained, management should try to answer the following questions about most problems with which it is faced.

What is the real purpose of the project? For example, is it really to assess marketing effectiveness, or is it to assess the engineering and product development represented in existing product lines? Or again, is it really to improve inventory control, or is it to review and revise product lines?

Does the project promote or conflict with long-range plans? Under ordinary circumstances, there is little use in developing refined management techniques to plan and control an operation that the company plans to discontinue.

What benefits are likely to occur if the project is accomplished? Are the possible benefits sufficient reward for undertaking the work? And, in terms of benefits, what is the priority of the project compared with other projects?

What is the work load of the project? Is the organization equipped to carry the burden of the proposed project in light of other ongoing work? In most companies, the organization is equipped to handle a limited number of special projects at any one time. Thus, selection becomes a matter of priority in terms of work as well as of benefits.

What is the receptivity of the organization to change? Bringing in a consultant may not work if managers take the attitude that they want change without any changes being made.

How would successful accomplishment of the project affect other areas of the business? If a survey is designed to uncover market opportunities, what must the company do to pursue those opportunities? If a new accounting system points the finger at excess costs, is the company prepared to do something about them?

What have other managements done about solving similar problems? Utilizing the experiences of others can be beneficial. Discussions with executives of other companies who have had experience with similar problems may aid in defining the dimensions of a contemplated program, the advantages which may be anticipated, and the costs, hazards, and work loads involved in achieving results.

Who can or should do the job? There should be specific reasons for considering the use of consulting services in any particular situation. These reasons vary widely and may include the need for special know-how, for an independent opinion, for development of an authoritative common language inside the company, or for concealing the identity of the company in searching for executive personnel or in investigating a new-product possibility. In any case, the reasons for retaining a consultant should be clear in the minds of management before he is retained.

SELECTION OF THE CONSULTANT

Sound selection of a consultant involves (1) developing confidence in the consultant by obtaining general information about him and by obtaining specific recommendations of his services; (2) developing confidence both in the consultant and in the validity of the project for which he is retained by conscientious conduct of a preliminary survey; and (3) following some general principles of negotiating a constructive basis for working together. The elements of selection may vary in sequence and importance depending on the situation. The following descriptions are general in nature.

Information and References. Informal checks on general reputation are a normal part of the preliminary search for consulting help. General information about consultants is available from a variety of sources. A common source is executives of other companies who have faced similar problems. In addition, company directors who are affiliated with other companies that have used consultants, and the company's normal banking, legal, and CPA contacts may be helpful.

The checking of pertinent references obtained from the consultant himself, however, is more useful. Two or three references investigated in depth may be more revealing than many references checked superficially.

Reference checks should be conducted by a person qualified by organizational level, and if possible by experience, to evaluate the quality of work done by the consultant in the previous situations and to assess the transferability of the consultant's skills to the particular situation.

A personal visit to references is the most effective procedure. Questions should be directed to more than one executive to find out how a consultant gets along with different levels of management and how he performs in areas of both technical and working relationships.

Basic questions to ask in reference checks include: What was the nature of the work done by the consultant? Were his findings accepted? Were his recommendations carried out? If he helped to implement the recommendations, how effective was he? Were his working relationships with client personnel pleasant or otherwise? Were real benefits obtained? If the client had to face the problem over again, would he be willing to engage the consultant again?

In general, the client may take the confidential nature of his relationship with the consultant for granted. Because the removal of mental reservations makes for better working relationships, however, the client executive may wish to investigate potential conflicts of interest. Any reputable consultant will discuss candidly the policies governing his practice on such matters as his directorships of competing companies, whether he serves competing clients, and whether he accepts fees or commissions from those whose equipment supplies or services he recommends.

The Preliminary Survey. One of the important features of negotiation is that it gives responsible executives the opportunity to review all those aspects of problem definition previously discussed, and thus assure themselves of the desirability of proceeding with the project before making a final decision to do so. This means that in many situations, negotiations with a consultant may include undertaking a preliminary survey to work out agreements about the purpose, scope, and limits of the project.

If such surveys involve more than one or two days of the consultant's time, they are conducted on a regular fee basis. The policy governing practice in this respect is summarized in the following statement:

If the problem is so complex that the method of solving it or the time required and potential results cannot be determined without gathering additional information, the consultant should recommend a preliminary survey. This preliminary survey will usually produce something of value to the client. It may be a clearer definition of the problem, the development of a method of solving the problem which the client may use himself without further assistance if he desires, or it may take the client part of the way toward solution of his problem. In such cases, it is entirely proper to charge normal fees for the time spent in making the survey and developing a report of the findings. Surveys made for a reduced fee for the purpose of gaining more opportunity for the selling of an assignment are unprofessional and are not used by ethical practitioners.[1]

It should be recognized that in complex situations there may be more than one stage in the consulting work, each stage requiring separate project definitions and separate estimates of time and fees. For example, there might be a diagnostic survey and recommendations, detailed surveys and recommendations in different areas, and installation assignments in certain of those areas.

[1] *Professional Practices in Management Consulting,* Association of Consulting Management Engineers, Inc., New York, 1959, p. 32.

Principles of Negotiation. In conducting negotiations, experience has shown the following precepts to be helpful.

The basic objective of negotiation is to arrive at a mutually advantageous agreement for working together. Attempts to drive a hard bargain may be self-defeating.

Begin in control of the situation. The executive who has arrived at a preliminary definition of the problem before meeting with consultants, and who looks on negotiations as a way of sharpening and evaluating that definition, is in a position of control. In contrast, the executive who begins thinking about a problem because a consultant tells him that he has one is starting with a handicap.

Do not see too many consultants. The time spent in negotiating with consultants increases rapidly as more consultants are introduced into the picture. If an executive talks with two consultants, he has one cross-comparison to make. If he talks with three consultants, he has three cross-comparisons to make; and if he talks with four consultants, he has six cross-comparisons to make.

Be candid with the consultant. Because the objectives of negotiation are to arrive at a firm estimate of the results to be achieved, and of the time, effort, and money required to achieve them, honest description of the situation is a must. Attempts to withhold information from the consultant or to gloss over problems can only hinder the achievement of a sound understanding of the work to be done.

Be sure to understand the consultant's proposal. Especially when the problem being discussed is relatively unfamiliar to the organization, really understanding the consultant's proposal may not be easy. A common weakness in such a situation is the human tendency to hear what is familiar and to skip over what is unfamiliar, because people tend to interpret new situations in terms of what they already know. One corrective of that tendency is to investigate thoroughly the experience of companies (either previous clients of the consultant or others) as they moved into the new area under consideration.

It is equally important to gage the consultant's ability to be what he is supposed to be: knowledgeable, articulate, and candid. If, after conscientious effort, company executives cannot understand the consultant's proposal, it may be risky to proceed with the project. Either the organization needs to add new skills before it can benefit from the consultant's services, or it needs to seek out a consultant who can communicate more clearly. At the very least, this approach should make it possible to avoid the glib character with a gleam in his eye who has read a book and wants to try it out on somebody.

Do not select a consultant on the basis of fee alone. In the first place, widely varying estimates from two consultants may mean that they are defining the situation differently. It is one thing to design and install a standard cost-accounting system that accepts existing factory operating standards, and it is another matter to include review and revision of those standards in the estimated work.

Even when it has been determined that the consultants are quoting on the same proposal, the executive should still consider which consultant he thinks will do the best job, and whether the low bidder is reacting wisely or unwisely to competitive pressures, before he makes his final decision.

Contingent fee arrangements are hazardous. If the consultant's fee is made contingent upon results such as increased sales, reduced costs, or similar factors, questions may be raised about achieving short-term results at the expense of more lasting benefits. For example, it is easy enough to improve profits by delaying necessary maintenance. There is also room for distressing differences of opinion about the quantitative measurement of results and who should receive credit for them.

Careful negotiations should result in reasonable estimates of time and fees. In normal situations when negotiations have been properly conducted, the consultant should be able to quote an estimate of elapsed time and fees for the accomplishment of the task. In such a case, estimated time is generally quoted in the maximum to minimum number of weeks or months, and fees are quoted on a bracket basis (minimum to maximum).

There are exceptions to every rule, but an open per diem arrangement is generally a reflection of the fact that the situation has not been completely defined.

Equally, it should be recognized that estimates of time and fees even under the best circumstances are somewhat tentative in nature. Errors in judgment may be made, or unexpected complications may arise.

Consider the personal aspects of prospective working relationships. In most consulting engagements, good results are fostered by cooperation of company and consultant personnel. Anticipation of friendly and productive relationships is an important factor in selection. Ideally, this applies not only at the top, but also down the line of both the client and consultant organizations.

WORKING WITH THE CONSULTANT

Although the detailed events of working with a consultant vary from situation to situation, certain general comments may be made about (1) the importance of an engagement plan; (2) the role of the liaison executive; (3) introducing the consultant to the organization; (4) exercising supervision of the consulting project; and (5) evaluating progress as the work proceeds.

The Engagement Plan. The engagement plan is an extension of the approach described in the letter of proposal. It is a double check on the mutual understanding of the objectives, scope, and nature of the project.

The plan may be developed by the consultant and reviewed with client personnel, or, as in many cases, it may be developed jointly by client and consultant. Sometimes, spelling out the plan in detail reveals points upon which more information may be needed to estimate work loads or to determine a sequence of steps.

The completed engagement plan covers the organization and staffing of the project. It includes a series of action steps and specifies logical checkpoints for review of status and progress during the course of the work.

The engagement plan should be regarded like any other plan—subject to revision to meet changing circumstances or new understandings, but a very necessary reference framework within which programmed steps are to be accomplished.

The Liaison Executive. The executive appointed as liaison with the consultant has an important role in helping to achieve good results. His responsibilities are to see that the work adheres to the defined objectives and scope of the project or that modifications are reviewed and accepted in the company's interest; that matters of policy are reviewed and confirmed or changed as required during the work; that company responsibilities for scheduling and accomplishing work are fulfilled; that roadblocks to the program are overcome; and that understanding of the project on the part of the company executives is facilitated.

The liaison executive provides the services of other company personnel as may be required. This may involve temporary transfers of duties, revisions of travel and vacation schedules, and the like. He also customarily provides any resources and facilities needed for the project other than those provided by the consultant. These include such things as office space, equipment, and secretarial services, if the consultant is to work on the premises; they may also include such items as temporary personnel, rented or purchased equipment, and outside services such as tabulating service bureaus.

Introducing the Consultant. Proper introduction of the consultant to the organization is important in getting the work off to a good start. Sensitivity to personnel attitudes in this area is important. First, the mere presence of a consultant may be taken as an implied criticism of the organization itself. Second, especially in companies that are not accustomed to using consulting services, the presence of a consultant may be interpreted as a threat to the freedom of executive decisions or even to job security.

Therefore, executives and supervisors should be informed of the objectives of the engagement, why these objectives are in the interests of the company, and why a consultant has been retained to work with the organization.

The consultant is introduced to the organization before he begins contacting executives other than those he met during negotiations. The introduction generally takes two forms: a written announcement given general circulation and a meeting or series of meetings.

The announcement, which is prepared jointly with the consultant, covers the purpose of the engagement and states that the consultant has been retained and that a given executive has been assigned liaison responsibility for the project. It requests that the consultant receive full cooperation in his requests for company time and effort on the project.

The meetings held following the announcement generally correspond with organizational lines. Each meeting is presided over by a company executive who describes his understanding of the study, introduces the consultant, and acts as chairman for any discussion of the project.

Supervising the Project. Working with a consultant, as previously discussed, is a situation in which the responsible executive both exercises supervision and cooperates with the consultant on a teamwork basis. From a practical point of view, however, organizational theory is less important in achieving good results than is accomplishing the following requirements.

Provide genuine management backing. Top management interest in a project should be evidenced by the caliber of executives appointed as liaison with the consultant and as members of the study and/or installation team. Also, if circumstances call for it, direct management intervention in the project in company with the consultant should be exercised. To be avoided at all costs is the attitude that the consultant should "sink or swim," while responsible executives stand by, not participating in the solution of practical problems. This posture may be appropriate under certain conditions in the field of executive development, but it has no place in relationships with a consultant.

Assign company personnel to work with the consultant on a clean-cut basis. If the engagement plan specifies staffing the study or installation team with company personnel, they should be assigned on a full-time or equivalent basis. Also, arrangements should be made to transfer their regular work to other members of the organization. It is not reasonable to expect people to work extensively with the consultant and at the same time perform their regular jobs.

Keep informed about project progress. Client management can properly discharge its responsibilities only if it keeps informed about what is going on. Much of this information will naturally come from the consultant. However, company personnel should also be reporting status through normal channels. Progress meetings are a major tool for keeping informed. The liaison executive and the consultant, using the engagement plan as a base, should work out meetings with appropriate personnel to keep them informed of progress, to get the benefit of their reactions, and to be aware of problems in any area of the project as they arise.

Keep subordinate executives informed. One hazard in the use of consulting services is that the responsible executive and the consultant may develop channels of communication that exclude other involved company executives. This sometimes happens because there is justification for considerable contact with the consultant, which takes some time away from the executive's normal contacts with his associates. Also, because the consultant is usually in a position to see the whole picture of the engagement better than many of the executive's associates, the executive comes to depend on the consultant. This may develop to the point where the executive is making decisions or taking actions based almost entirely on the consultant's recommendations. In so doing, the executive is short-circuiting his own associates. He is also exposing his comp y to the risk of acting on recommendations that have not been submitted for review by those who will have to make them work.

Evaluating Progress. Although evaluation on a total basis can be accomplished only after completion of an engagement, such evaluation is not the most useful sort.[2] Rather, evaluation should be inherent in the whole program from beginning to end. Checking results as the work proceeds is useful because corrective action can be taken in time to influence the program favorably. In contrast, evaluation after the end of the work cannot change what has already happened.

The engagement plan is the basic reference point in evaluating status and prospects. It is made up of action steps, which should spell out logical checkpoints at various stages of work completion and usually at approximate dates. In addition, the plan records the agreed objectives and scope of the work as further criteria.

At each periodic review, answers to the following questions should be helpful to keep the program on the track of achieving benefits.

Is the definition of the problem still valid? Do the objectives still seem desirable and attainable? If not, what are the changes that seem desirable, and what are the reasons for adopting such changes?

Is the program on the track toward the goals agreed on and is it within the scope and limits agreed on? Is there clear justification for the work being done?

Is the work being accomplished on time? Are there any roadblocks in terms of policy decisions, choices of technical alternatives, or work-load and staffing requirements?

Do client personnel understand the program? Are the right executives and supervisors participating in the program? Are responsible client executives reviewing, challenging, understanding, and accepting recommendations? Is the consultant devoting sufficient time and attention to the exposure of client personnel to recommendations and to indoctrination in their applications?

TAKING CONSTRUCTIVE ACTION

In most situations, the ultimate value of consulting work is measured by the achievement of constructive change in company direction and/or practices.

[2] For checklists for evaluation at completion of work, see Wilson Seney, *Effective Use of Business Consultants*, Financial Executives Research Foundation, New York, 1963, chap. 8, and *Professional Practices in Management Consulting*, Association of Consulting Management Engineers, Inc., New York, 1959, chap. 9.

This does not mean that the organization automatically follows the consultant's recommendations. In any given situation, there may be honest differences of opinion about interpretation of the facts, the need to take action, the times at which action should be taken, or the risks that should be incurred to obtain potential benefits.

The problem of taking action on recommendations occurs most frequently in the survey-type engagement that necessarily precedes action in complex situations. In action-type engagements, the problem is minimized by the very structure of the project. Therefore, the following comments are directed to the situation in which the company's management reviews recommendations prior to taking action. Reports sometimes "gather dust" instead of becoming useful tools, because executives may overlook one or more of the following guides to constructive review and evaluation of the consultant's findings.

Avoid the psychological hazard of feeling that the problem is solved because the consultant has submitted a report. Reports do not solve problems. People solve problems. These truisms are sometimes overlooked, especially when management is not accustomed to using the services of consultants. There is often the temptation to relax at the end of a long, hard study, and there is always the pressure of other business to serve as justification for delaying action on the study just completed.

Take a realistic attitude toward accomplishing the recommendations. It is highly desirable to adopt the mental sets that (1) sound understanding of the concepts and practices suggested in the report is required as a basis for action; (2) putting the recommendations into effect will take the time and attention of company executives; and (3) there will be a period of elapsed time between acceptance of the report in theory and the embodiment of that theory in company practices on an effective basis.

The report should be reviewed on a formal basis. There should be a decision on each recommendation submitted, even if it is only a decision not to take action at the time.

The report should be made available to all appropriate executives. Sound appraisal of the recommendations and full understanding of their implications may not be achieved if the report is withheld from those who will have to accomplish the program.

Accepting some recommendations and rejecting others on a unilateral basis is hazardous. Programs are generally developed to include those factors that, taken together, make for success. Elimination of any important factors might endanger the whole program. This means that each point of the report should be reviewed with the consultant before management decides to accept or reject the report either in whole or in part.

CONCLUSION

Management does not relieve itself of responsibility when it retains a consultant. The problem is management's problem before the consultant arrives and remains management's problem after the consultant leaves. Management should continue to manage. There are no magic shortcuts. Therefore, best results are obtained from the use of consulting services when management is convinced that the work is worthwhile and deserves backing and company effort. And that conviction in turn is best developed when management follows recognized sound practices of problem definition, exercises care in selection of consulting services, works on a practical basis with the consultant, and conscientiously discharges its duties of evaluating project progress and of acting decisively on recommendations.

BIBLIOGRAPHY

Books

Professional Practices in Management Consulting, Association of Consulting Management Engineers, Inc., New York, 1959.

Seney, Wilson, *Effective Use of Business Consultants,* Financial Executives Research Foundation, New York, 1963.

Articles and Reports

Axelson, Kenneth S., "Are Consulting and Auditing Compatible?" *The Journal of Accountancy,* April, 1963.

Bingham, J. R., "A Managing Director's Experience of Consultants," in *Does Business Need the Management Consultant?* Institute of Directors, London, 1959.

Bryson, Lyman, "Notes on a Theory of Advice," *Political Science Quarterly,* September, 1951.

"Can a Management Consultant Pay Off for You?" *Report to Management,* File 33, Research Institute of America, New York, Feb. 1, 1960.

"Employment of Experts and Consultants in the Executive Branch," a study prepared for the Subcommittee on General Government Matters of the House Committee on Appropriations, Bureau of the Budget, Washington, D.C., January, 1961.

Krentzman, Harvey C., and John M. Samaras, "Can Small Businesses Use Consultants?" *Harvard Business Review,* May–June, 1960.

Maynard, Harold B., "How to Select a Management Consultant," *Management Methods,* February, 1957.

Trueblood, Robert M., "The Management Service Function in Public Accounting," *Journal of Accountancy,* July, 1961.

"What Management Consultants Can Do," *Business Week,* Jan. 23, 1965.

CHAPTER SIX

The Use of Outside Services

CARL HEYEL *Management Counsel, Manhasset, New York*

In an increasingly complex world, outside management services will lengthen and strengthen the arm of the inside management team. These services, as here defined, mean specialized informational, advisory, and implementing aids available to anyone responsible for the conduct of an enterprise or important component of an enterprise, contracted and paid for or obtained without charge as an accommodation or extension of services related to the purchase of specified goods or services. That managements are making growing use of outside services is indicated by Department of Commerce figures which show that business and industry in 1958 spent $9.8 billion for such help, whereas in 1964 such expenditures amounted to over $15 billion—and this, of course, does not include services availed of without charge.

The reason for taking advantage of such aid is twofold. A company finds either that it cannot do a particular job as well as an outside specialist, or—even in the case of a large corporation—that it may not have enough continuing need for certain work to justify a full-time specialist on its payroll.

WHEN TO CONSIDER USING OUTSIDE SERVICES

Here are some typical situations where the use of outside services might well be considered.

Company A has for a number of years been toying with the idea of building a new plant and now realizes that this year it must take the plunge. Modern facilities are needed to meet increased volume demands and, more important, to stay competitive. Not only is the existing plant a high-cost producer; it is also poorly located for the markets now served. Who on the present management team should be "drafted" from his current responsibilities to head up the program? How can management be sure it is making the right decision on type of structure, location, and degree of automation? How finance the new facility? How best mesh it into operations? What personnel problems will be involved?

Company B has been a leader in its industry with a line of equipment known for its dependability and its ability to do a good "workhorse" job. But management has been highly conservative and perhaps even a bit complacent. The product line has not kept pace with innovations introduced by aggressive newcomers, and its share of the market has slipped badly. A new generation of the founding family has now taken over, and modernization of products and marketing methods is being planned. This will call for some stem-to-stern changes—in personnel, facilities, selling channels, and above all, in product design. How shall the company organize for forced-draft technological innovation? How adjust selling strategies to meet the strengthened competition? How develop a "new corporate look" of live-wire progressiveness and still retain the corporate image of steady dependability?

Company C, a long-established family enterprise, now sees tremendous advantages in "going public." What are its best moves as to timing, type of security offering, and safeguarding management control?

Company D has become aware of an attractive acquisition possibility. How shall it go about making an overture? What are the dangers of tipping its hand?

Company E is entering a new market. How best dislodge the entrenched competition? How minimize the gamble?

The above are typical of dramatic do-or-die challenges that lead managements to avail themselves of specialized professional services, either supplementing or entirely outside the competence of their existing organizations. But in addition to these non- or seldom-recurring situations are the more usual "pinching shoe" kind of problems calling for corrective action? Are upward-creeping costs eroding profits? Is the sales department plagued with customer rejects and late deliveries? Are there recurring production snafus? Nagging personnel problems? Inadequate and late management control reports? These may well justify management's going to outside specialists to introduce new methods and tighten operations.

Besides those that provide intermittent aids, there are countless service organizations which stand ready to take over routine operations in their entirety or for specified peak periods, leaving management free to concentrate on turning out the primary goods or services of the business. Thus, not for emergency situations, but rather for reasons of convenience or to avoid long-term personnel or money commitments, management may buy data-processing services, job out all of its processing or assembly, contract for peak office or production help rather than increase its own payroll, farm out its credit and collection problems, contract for its packing and shipping, take advantage of public warehousing, buy employee cafeteria services, and so on.

Buying Outside Services. Services are available in many more fields of activity than most managements realize. Many of these informational, advisory, and implementing aids may be had without charge as an accommodation or extension of services related to the purchase of specified goods or services. Others are obtainable through contractual arrangements, on either a retainer or a billed-for-services-rendered basis. Where paid for, the "standby" expenses are shared with hundreds of other users drawing upon the same pool.

The important thing, of course, is for management to know what it is getting—to have some basis upon which to evaluate results and judge the fairness of charges. Although not possessed of the specialist's background, the buyer of services should know enough, at least, to be able to ask the right kind of questions. Minimally, before making any extensive commitments, management should acquire clear-cut information on:

1. Definition of the service area
2. Extent and nature of the services available
3. Where and how the services are obtained
4. Normal mode of operation of those who provide the services
5. When charges are made, accepted order of magnitude of compensation, and the manner of arriving at it
6. Special advantages in using the service
7. How to select a specific service organization
8. Pitfalls to avoid

IMPORTANT OUTSIDE MANAGEMENT SERVICES

This chapter cannot, of course, cover the hundreds of management services available. However, it does attempt to provide a brief guide to those of most important concern to general management in seven major categories.[1] Because comprehensive coverage is not possible even for those included here, *information sources* are provided for each type of service discussed. They include, as appropriate, the names of important professional and trade associations active in each field and magazines which provide significant coverage of the subject. These sources will provide additional "live" information and will also usually furnish the names of leading commercial organizations offering the services indicated.

Administration

Management Consultants. Management consultants give counsel on basic economic, managerial, operating, and technical problems. There are approximately 2,500 management consulting firms in North America, the vast majority of these being small two- to five-man firms offering limited specialized services. Fewer than 100 consulting firms serve clients in a broad coverage of management problems. In addition, there are several thousand individual practitioners.

The range of consultants' services varies greatly. Some confine their work to one industry, such as textiles, metal working, or the like. Others serve clients in all industries on one or more technical or operating problems.

Reputable consultants will confer without obligation with an organization contemplating outside help, to explore the nature and scope of assistance required. (See Chapter 5 of Section 2.) This is followed by a letter of proposal or a letter confirming an oral agreement to go ahead. This letter generally covers definition of the problem; objectives, scope, and nature of the engagement; recommended program for accomplishing the work; general methods to be used; statement of who is to do the work (especially, the extent to which client personnel will be used); estimate of time required; and estimate of professional fees. There is usually an understanding that the client may terminate at any time. Fees are generally based on per diem rates for category of men assigned, plus out-of-pocket expenses.

There should be periodic meetings to explore progress, and informative interim reports should be requested. It is also important that management smooth the way by advanced indoctrination of all personnel involved, particularly middle management, which often feels most threatened by the presence of consultants. At the conclusion of the engagement, management should determine whether

[1] For a fuller treatment of the subject, see Carl Heyel, "Guide to Management Services," special supplement to the January, 1965, *Dun's Review & Modern Industry,* and its sequel, the special supplement to the January, 1966, issue of the same publication.

its organization can implement the consultant's recommendations or whether further consultant follow-up work is called for.

Information Sources: American Management Association, 135 West 50th Street, New York, publishes a *Directory of Consultant Members,* showing fields of special competence, addresses and descriptions of firms, and a geographical listing of firms with home or branch offices in areas other than the United States. The Association of Consulting Management Engineers, 347 Madison Avenue, New York, in addition to its *Directory of Membership and Services,* makes available special lists of management consulting firms (not restricted to its own membership). The Association of Management Consultants, Inc., 947 Old York Road, Abington, Pennsylvania, will provide names of members equipped to handle special assignments, as will the Society of Professional Management Consultants, 207 East 37th Street, New York, and the International Confederation of Independent Consultants to Management, 51 West 35th Street, New York. In Canada: Canadian Association of Management Consultants, 500 St. James Street, West, Montreal.

Management Science Services. Management science firms utilize logical and mathematical techniques developed since World War II to evaluate alternative operating programs. The term "mathematical programming" is applied to many of these techniques directed to solving the economic problems of allocation— assignment of scarce resources of money, men, and materials to attain specified goals as closely as possible, in the best way possible. Specific techniques include linear programming, critical path scheduling and other network controls, "Monte Carlo" simulation, queueing theory, game theory, and others. Many management consulting firms have specialists in these fields, and help may also be obtained from a college or university in the company's area. The past decade has seen the rise of numerous "problem solving" firms marshaling scientific talent ranging from a half dozen or so to hundreds of specialists, many at the Ph.D. level, with multidisciplined capabilities ranging from the physical sciences through mathematics and all fields of social sciences. Some of these firms operate computer services as well.

Information Sources: The Institute of Management Sciences, P.O. Box 626, Ann Arbor, Michigan; Operations Research Society of America, M.I.T., Cambridge 39, Massachusetts.

Public Relations Counselors. Management can get help from public relations experts in achieving optimum relations with its various "publics" for its organization, products, services, and objectives. These publics may include employees, customers, prospects, stockholders, the financial community, government at all levels, plant communities, suppliers, distributors, and educational institutions. Counseling firms may range from one-man operations to organizations employing as many as 250 persons and engaged in world-wide operations. Advanced public relations counseling is concerned not only with the projection of an "image" of the company as it exists, but also with the formulation of underlying policies. Public relations services deal with paid institutional advertising, publicity involving editorial use of information by media, and personal contacts and special exhibits and events. They do not usually include preparation of advertising copy or the purchase of space or time for product advertising.

There is no formula basis for compensation. Most large firms require contracts, usually of at least one year's duration, calling for a set fee that may or may not cover out-of-pocket costs.

A fruitful way of getting a lead to a public relations firm is the "one man tells another" referral—for example, by men who are on the boards of more than one company and who are aware of public relations programs that have been successfully carried on for one of them.

Information Sources: Public Relations Society of America, 845 Third Avenue, New York; *Public Relations News.* "The Public Relations Register," published by PRSA, is a comprehensive directory of public relations men. PRSA also publishes a roster of members of the counselors' section of PRSA.

Finance

Commercial Finance Companies and Factors. These are the "middlemen" of corporate finance. They borrow funds at "wholesale" interest rates and lend them out at "retail." Thus they bridge the financial gap for small- and medium-sized companies between the limits of normal unsecured bank credit and the needs of expanding sales or other requirements.

Factoring should be distinguished from commercial financing, although all of the large commercial finance companies do both. A factor will make outright purchase of accounts receivable, guarantee against credit losses, and assume collection expenses. For a fee he does the credit checking, bookkeeping, collecting, and in certain instances, mailing of invoices. On the maturity date of receivables, he will pay the amounts called for, and on request he will also make payments on receivables before their due date, charging interest at relatively low rates. Note that a factor purchases accounts receivable outright, without recourse. If a customer is unable to pay, the factor, who approved the credit, assumes the loss. For his basic services, the factor's fee usually averages ¾ to 2 percent of the net receivables purchased.

In *commercial financing*, advances are made on a revolving basis against the client's receivables. It involves solely the use of money, with no services. The client does his own credit checking and collecting, and repays the finance company when collections are made. The big difference between commercial financing and factoring is that the finance company has full recourse to the client in the event of credit collection losses. Commercial financing also advances funds through inventory loans, with basic raw materials or readily salable finished products as collateral, held through warehouse receipts, factors' liens, or other security instruments. Commercial finance interest rates were, in 1966, in the 11 to 15 percent range.

Commercial finance companies will purchase installment paper or leases from manufacturers and dealers emanating from the sale or lease of any type of income-producing equipment, with title retained by the purchaser or lessor.

A conscientious financing house will analyze the client's whole picture, cooperate in helping him obtain as much as possible of his financing needs through mortgages or other secured loans from primary sources, and assume the remainder, primarily against accounts receivable, but also possibly against inventory, perhaps together with chattel mortgages on equipment and a second mortgage on buildings. Some conduct continuing research into trends and opportunities in many industries and make the information available to clients at no cost.

Information Sources: *American Banker* each May publishes a list of the 100 largest, specialized finance companies, ranked in order of capital funds available for loans, together with a subsidiary list of companies below the top 100. National Commercial Finance Conference, Inc., 29 Broadway, New York.

Certified Public Accountants. The independent CPA operates under certification by the state, District of Columbia, or possessions, after having qualified by uniform examination graded by the American Institute of Certified Public Accountants.   The CPA in a town of 20,000 has the same professional standards and deals with problems of the same type as the CPA in a large-city firm.

Auditing is a unique function of the independent CPA.   The annual audit is a normal practice for any well-run business, and most corporations listed on the exchanges are required by law to have independent audits.   Here the CPA's opinion will follow one of five recognized forms: (1) an *unqualified* opinion, with no reservations; (2) a *qualified* opinion, stating where he disagrees with an accounting treatment; (3) an *adverse* opinion, if his exceptions are important; (4) a *disclaimer* if he has not done enough work to form an overall opinion; and (5) a notation, "*without an audit,*" on each page of the financial statement, where no report is submitted but his name appears on the statement.

Services of the CPA include representation of clients before the Internal Revenue Service on tax matters and advice as to tax consequences of specific transactions (but pointing out where legal counsel is required); advice and recommendations on systems; and general management counseling.

Fees are based on type of case, personnel assigned, and time spent on the account.   They may range from $10 per hour to as much as $50 or more per hour.   Special consulting services are estimated and negotiated, following the practices of management consultants.

Information Sources: American Institute of Certified Public Accountants, 666 5th Avenue, New York; *Journal of Accounting* and *Management Services,* both published by AICPA, in addition to numerous special publications and reports.

Credit Reporting Agencies.   These provide information needed to reach credit, sales, financial, and general management decisions.   As business has become more complex, sellers have found it quite expensive to make their own investigations, especially if the buyer is at a distant point and the account is relatively small.   There are a number of commercial credit reporting agencies, some operating on a national scale and many more working regionally or locally.   Their basic services are credit reports and credit rating books.

Credit reporters prepare reports on commercial enterprises in the industry or area their agencies cover, and often, in addition, on certain noncommercial enterprises.   A report to a subscriber will vary from one to five or six pages.   It typically includes a record of the ledger experience of suppliers, a balance sheet normally supplemented by profit and loss details and information on leases, insurance, and the like, together with comments by the reporter.   Normally included are details on what the firm does, how it operates, lines of merchandise sold or services rendered, price range, class of customers, selling terms, and so on, and the business history of the principals of the firm.

The agency assigns a rating which becomes part of its listing and represents an overall evaluation of the concern's credit standing.

Information Sources: National Association of Credit Management, 44 East 23d Street, New York (publishes *Credit and Financial Management*); Associated Credit Bureaus of America, Inc., 6707 Southwest Freeway, Houston; Central Credit Interchange Bureau, P.O. Box 1398, Central Station, St. Louis.

Equipment Leasing Companies.   These companies purchase specified fixed assets (machinery and office equipment) and install them at the lessee's place of business for use during the full term of the lease.   (See also Chapter 7 of Section 9.)   Advantages include conservation of working capital by the lessee, financing without diluting ownership, certain tax and depreciation-allowance advantages, and the use of the latest cost-saving equipment without waiting to accumulate the funds for it.   The lessee management selects the equipment and vendor and negotiates the best cash price.   It then arranges with the leasing company to purchase the equipment.   Lease payments are made monthly, quarterly, semi-annually, or as agreed to, usually with option to renew at greatly reduced rentals at the end of the lease.   Purchase options are available if desired.   (However, purchase at only nominal value, for example, $1 or 1 percent, will cause a lease to be disallowed by the Internal Revenue Service.)

A *sale leaseback* is a variant of the standard lease transaction.   Here all or part of a company's equipment is sold to a leasing company (usually at book value) and immediately leased back for a stated term.   This technique generates working capital and is also sometimes used to help in acquisition programs by selling the assets of the acquired company to a leasing company and using the cash generated for part of the payment.

Information Sources: Association of Equipment Lessors, 100 State Street, Boston, Massachusetts 02109.   Machinery and Allied Products Institute, 1200 18th Street, N.W., Washington, D.C.

Data-processing Centers.   In 1966 there were approximately one thousand data-processing centers of significant scope of operations in the United States and Canada.   These included independents and those run as departments or subsidiaries of computer manufacturers, counting separately each unit in multiple operations and including some centers with only large-scale tabulating equipment as distinguished from electronic computers which are normally associated with the concept of "data-processing centers."

Data processing in the business sense, as distinguished from scientific and engineering computation, includes inventory extensions; processing of payrolls, accounts receivable, and accounts payable; analysis of production, financial, and sales statistics; and the microfilming of records.   A job may include every type of punched card equipment or only the programming of a computer run. Typically the center will be called upon for a complete job, beginning with source data supplied by the client and ending with complete reports.   Significant entries into the business have been client operations of this sort set up by banks.   Most of the manufacturers of large-scale business computers operate centers.

Recent innovations are (1) various forms of "do it yourself" computer service centers, where customers may buy computer time by the hour and do programming and supervision with their own personnel; and (2) on-line "public utility" type of operations, where a customer, from terminal units on his own premises, can immediately connect into a large computer and secure answers based on a program held continuously in a portion of the computer memory allocated to him.

Center charges may be on a time and material basis; on fixed contract price; per unit, with a rate for a specified volume of work; or on a machine-hour basis.   Time on a large-scale computer can run to hundreds of dollars an hour. (See also Chapter 7 of Section 15.)

Information Sources: Association of Data Processing Service Organizations, Inc. (ADAPSO), 947 Old York Road, Abington, Pennsylvania, publishes an annual directory of service centers, with notations regarding their capabilities.   The annual September reference issue of *Business Automation* lists some 50 of the larger, multioffice service bureaus.

Manufacturing

Custom Manufacturers (Contract Manufacturers).   Contract manufacturers go beyond the making of parts, components, or products to strict customer specifications.   They may include the broader service of creative product and engineering design, the production of necessary tools and dies, and if desired, physical distribution and warehousing. Representatives of contract manufacturers will meet with prospective users of their services on a no-obligation basis to discuss product ideas and problems. Many manufacturers with surplus equipment time actively seek such business.

On the basis of the customer's preliminary sketches, custom manufacturers will develop an explicit proposal with firm price-volume quotations for the product itself, together with charges for tools, dies, special services, and the like. Normally the dies become the customer's property, held on the premises of the custom manufacturer. Although the manufacturers may have competing companies as customers, they will give guarantees against the use of tools, dies, and designs on work done for others. Often, however, arrangements are made for competing companies to share in most of the tools and dies and to schedule combined runs to take advantage of long-run economies.

Information Sources: Trade publication advertisements, trade associations, and the "yellow pages."

Contract Maintenance. This activity has reached sizable proportions, especially in the process industries, although it also occurs in other types of manufacturing. What is meant here is not the routine janitorial or building maintenance service or servicing of special equipment which has long been available from local contractors, but rather the maintenance of *all* equipment, sometimes including the function of maintenance management as well as the supplying of labor.

Advantages of contracting out for maintenance lie in the availability of forces for fluctuating demands or for totally unforeseeable demands (as in starting up a new plant), in the assumption by the contractor of all recruitment activity, fringe benefits, and the like, and in the use of equipment and facilities supplied by the contractor. There are also distinct labor-relations advantages, since the large contractors enter into separate national union agreements.

Plant maintenance contracts may be of four types: (1) skilled labor furnished as needed; (2) periodic turnaround or scheduled shutdown maintenance; (3) continuing supplemental maintenance force; or (4) complete maintenance management. Normal procedure is for the maintenance firm to investigate the scope of the job and special requirements, and to negotiate a contract based on estimated labor usage. A common arrangement is a sliding service percentage based on labor charges.

Information Sources: American Society of Mechanical Engineers, 345 East 47th Street, New York: *Factory Mazagine; Plant Engineering.*

Industrial Parks. An industrial park or district is a tract of land subdivided and promoted for industrial occupancy by a sponsoring managerial organization. Facilities will vary widely, but the basic concept calls for installation of streets, railroad sidings (in most cases), and utilities before the sites are sold or leased. In their most advanced form, industrial districts offer a full range of services: assistance in financing, designing, and constructing a plant; fire and police protection; public warehousing; centralized data processing; restaurants and clubrooms; and so on. Districts may be created by railroads, chambers of commerce, city or state bodies, or special industry groups. However, they are most frequently owned and operated by private enterprises for profit.

The typical occupant of an industrial district is a manufacturer or distributor requiring a small- to medium-sized structure, who would find intensive site investigation and his own construction uneconomical. There are, of course, some disadvantages. To "pay out," the developer may try for 50 percent land coverage, a ratio contrasting sharply with the requirements of many companies for expansion. Another disadvantage is the higher cost of land—not necessarily because of unreasonable inflation by the owners, but rather a tendency to overbuild in terms of utilities, interior roads, and the like. Finally, it may be difficult to establish wage patterns consistent with the needs of each individual company in an industrial district.

Information Sources: The Urban Land Institute, 1200 18th Street, N.W., Washington, D.C. Its *Industrial Districts, Principles in Practice,* Technical Bulletin no. 44, is a 200-page report, much of it devoted to detailed case studies of twenty-nine well-known developments. Conway Research, Inc., 2600 Apple Valley Road, Atlanta, Georgia 30319, publishes annually *Industrial Parks* listing industrial parks and districts throughout the United States and Canada.

Marketing[2]

Manufacturers' Representatives. A manufacturers' representative or agent is the independent sales representative for a group of manufacturers in a specific sales territory. The territory is defined geographically, by type of customer, or by other means. The representative's chief source of income is the commission paid by his principals, although he may receive a guaranteed income in special cases, as when the introduction of a product calls for unusual initial expenditures. Use of manufacturer's representatives has been particularly popular with small- and medium-sized manufacturers whose capital and potential sales volume may not support a full field sales force.

A manufacturer's representative can be one man or an organization of twenty or more salesmen, with nearly that many inside personnel. He may represent from two to as many as thirty principals. The products of all principals must be "related equipment," although, of course, the principals should not be in direct competition with one another. Commissions vary from a few percent of selling price to as high as 35 percent. Thus for electronic components sold principally to manufacturers for incorporation into their own products, average commissions have been about 5 percent. In the "engineered product" sale where the salesmen must be able to assist the customer to solve his problems, commissions may be as high as 25 percent. Some principals provide a higher commission when gross sales in a given territory exceed target, which may be set at 80 or 85 percent of quota.

The contract with a manufacturer's representative usually includes definition of relationship (for example, independent status of the representative), territory and coverage, products, sales policy, prices, credit responsibility, warranties, invoices and collections, cancellations, change orders, returns, commissions, servicing obligations, sales aids, and rights under termination.

Information Sources: Manufacturers' Agents National Association, Alhambra, California. Its monthly *The Agent and Representative* contains classified ads of representatives seeking principals, and principals seeking representatives. Electronic Representatives Association, 600 South Michigan Avenue, Chicago. Industrial Marketing Associates, 516 Pleasant Street, St. Joseph, Michigan.

Advertising Agencies. The advertising agency prepares and arranges for the placement of advertising in magazines, newspapers, radio, television, car cards,

[2] See also "Consulting Psychologists," on p. 2–83, with respect to marketing and survey research.

billboards, and elsewhere. Some agencies also provide direct mail, public relations, and marketing research services; design packages; prepare films; create sales and service literature; and help formulate and execute sales promotion programs. Agency services basically include: (1) study of competitive advantages and formulation of the advertising approach; (2) analysis of present and potential markets; (3) recommendations as to media; and (4) physical preparation of the advertising and its placement in the media authorized. Remuneration for placement of advertising generally consists of fixed percentages of the cost of the media purchased. For magazines, the commission is usually 15 percent. Fixed commissions are also charged for production costs of advertisements or commercials. Most other services are handled for a price agreed upon between client and agency. There is a trend toward a negotiated fee system for all services.

Some agencies are known to specialize or have special strengths in certain fields. An obvious check for selection is with others who have used their services, and most agencies will prepare suggested plans and programs. "Agency service standards" have been established by the American Association of Advertising Agencies, to which most established agencies belong, although some, of recognized competence, have not sought membership.

In evaluating results, a pitfall is the use of sales results alone as a yardstick. Obviously other forces are at work—the product itself, its availability, packaging, personal selling, promotion, and price. It is also important to remember the carry-over effect of advertising—today's advertising may pay off next week, next month, or several years from now.

Information Sources: American Association of Advertising Agencies, 420 Lexington Avenue, New York; Advertising Research Foundation, 3 East 54th Street, New York; Association of National Advertisers, 155 East 44th Street, New York; Bureau of Advertising, American Newspaper Publishers Association, 750 Third Avenue, New York; Magazine Advertising Bureau, 444 Madison Avenue, New York; Television Bureau of Advertising, 1 Rockefeller Center, New York. *Standard Advertising Register* lists some 3,800 agencies; see also directories of National Register Publishing Co., subsidiary of Standard Rate & Data Service, Inc., New York. *Advertising Age* publishes a special issue each February, giving "profiles" of leading agencies: billings, accounts, and other important information.

Freight Forwarders. A freight forwarder arranges transportation of freight, profiting from the spread between the carload rates he pays and the less-than-carload rates he charges his customers. In addition, he performs incidental services such as pickup and delivery, documentation, expediting and tracing, consolidation, and distribution. The two basic types are *surface freight* and *air freight* forwarders. REA Express (formerly Railway Express) and Air Express, owned jointly by a number of railroads, have many of the characteristics of freight forwarders. Freight forwarders using rail primarily are often referred to as "carloading companies." Forwarders are regulated by the Interstate Commerce Commission, Civil Aeronautics Board, or Federal Maritime Commission, depending upon their form of operations.

Freight forwarders generally offer direct transportation between major cities, consolidating shipments at origin and distributing them at destination. This offers advantages not only to the smaller shipper, but also to the larger shipper with numerous small shipments to a number of destinations in the same general area.

Since rates are regulated by law, the primary considerations in selection are the points served and the quality of service—that is, transit time, protection against loss and damage, and special services such as containerization. Some forwarders specialize in a certain item, such as garments. A number operate their own private wire communications system, thus greatly facilitating tracing and expediting.

A forwarder should be distinguished from a "shippers' association," which is a nonprofit organization performing forwarding solely for its members. A pitfall here is the unscrupulous operator, who, acting as a "manager" of such an organization, may be using it as a cover for illegal freight forwarding.

Information Sources: Freight Forwarders Institute, 1012 14th Street, N.W., Washington, D.C.; Air Freight Forwarders Association, 1200 18th Street, N.W., Washington, D.C.; National Customs Brokers & Forwarders Association of America, 8–10 Bridge Street, New York. *Traffic World; The Transportation Journal; Transportation & Distribution Management.*

Public Warehouses. Public warehouses are often an economical alternative to a company's buying or leasing a warehouse for operation by its own personnel, especially where spot stocks are required at strategic locations or where stock needs fluctuate seasonally or unpredictably. Storage charges are on a per package, per hundredweight, or other unit basis per month. Economies accrue to the user, because the warehouseman absorbs the fixed costs and his unit charges reflect cost of labor only as used, whereas a company facility may have to absorb significant idle time. Other cost advantages come from reduced capital investment, accurate distribution-cost prediction based on the warehouseman's tariff or quotation, and collateral services available. But perhaps the biggest advantage is the extreme flexibility provided. Other advantages include favorable purchase of raw materials and components, and holding them in a warehouse local to the factory, pending use; and delivery of subassemblies and components to the production line by the local warehouseman as needed.

The warehouseman keeps the goods of each customer separate, provides the individual care required by each commodity, and maintains exact stock records. "Branch office" services include supplying office and display space, clerical and telephone service, traffic information, pooled car and consolidated shipment handling, break-bulk operations, and COD collections.

Warehouse receipts, issued by responsible warehousemen, are acceptable collateral for loans. The term "bonded warehouses" does not refer to protection to the depositor of goods. The bond is to the Federal government against nonpayment of duties or taxes. In many states, warehousemen may be bonded or licensed under state regulations. Often this is little more than a revenue-producing measure, although it may mean that some degree of inspection is undertaken by state authorities.

Information Sources: American Warehousemen's Association, 222 West Adams Street, Chicago. *Distribution Age; Transportation & Distribution Management.*

Personnel

Private Employment Agencies. Some 4,000 private agencies in the United States perform recruiting and placement services for every class of industrial and commercial employment, including skilled and unskilled workers, technical and professional specialists, and executives and administrators. That the services are by no means confined to rank-and-file help is indicated by the fact that some agencies are known to fill positions in the $30,000 to $35,000 bracket. Some of the biggest corporations make use of employment agencies regularly, finding them more effective in time, cost per hire, and caliber of recruitment than having their own personnel departments advertise and initially screen for all openings.

Most agencies are small, perhaps one-man, operations. At the other end of the scale are heavily staffed, multioffice organizations. However, size is not particularly meaningful—a large, bustling agency may be recruiting for clerical and beginner jobs, and a small, quiet office may be specializing in highly technical or executive personnel. Some agents confine their efforts to particular industries or crafts.

In almost all states and possessions, there are laws regulating employment agencies. The laws vary widely, ranging from mere prohibition of misleading advertising to licensing and strict regulation, including the setting of maximum fees and stipulating the kind of references that must be obtained for certain classes of positions.

Normally the employee pays the fee upon successful placement. However, there has been a growing trend to fee-paid jobs. This has been found to gain access to a larger selection of good applicants. In many cases, paying the fee is the only way a company can compete for engineers, scientists, and other professional personnel.

Information Sources: National Employment Association, 2000 K Street, N.W., Washington, D.C. (publishes a directory of member agencies, keyed to types of services rendered); National Personnel Associates, 295 Madison Avenue, New York; U.S. Department of Labor, Bureau of Labor Standards (publishes up-to-date summaries of state laws regulating private employment agencies); U.S. Employment Service, Bureau of Employment Security, U.S. Department of Labor, Washington, D.C.

Executive Recruitment. The executive-recruiting consultant specializes in finding top-level talent. After a study of the position to be filled, he draws upon known qualified candidates and upon new ones he develops. He screens top candidates through extensive interviews (arranging for psychological testing as required), and through exhaustive inquiries among the candidate's associates, friends, and acquaintances. Executive recruiters are normally employed to fill positions in the range of $15,000 a year and over, for chief executives, other key management personnel, and many highly specialized individuals in accounting, engineering, marketing, planning, and the like. They tend to be more objective than members of management with respect to the positions in question. Moreover, because their searches are completely confidential, they can protect a client's identity while interviewing and investigating candidates.

Executive-recruiting firms are usually paid only by the companies employing them, as distinguished from employment agencies which normally receive all or part of their compensation from the person being placed. The charge is typically 20 to 25 percent of the first year's compensation of the executive employed, in addition to out-of-pocket expenses. They are usually engaged on a per search basis, but occasionally operate on an annual retainer. Three months is a normal duration of a search, although many are concluded in less time.

Responsible recruiting firms will not guarantee the people they turn up, but they will usually reopen the search at no additional fee should a recently recruited executive prove to be unsatisfactory. Firms which are members of the Association of Executive Recruiting Consultants must meet rigid professional and performance standards and are not permitted to accept fees from individual candidates.

Information Sources: Association of Executive Recruiting Consultants, Inc., 405 Lexington Avenue, New York. Many recruiting organizations are departments of management consulting firms. The Association of Consulting Management Engineers, 347 Madison

Avenue, New York, will supply a list of member firms which do recruiting. Most trade associations will render some assistance in executive search.

Temporary-help Contractors. There are several hundred temporary-help contractors in the United States, but a half-dozen big ones, operating nationally and sometimes internationally, account for over half the business. The personnel provided are paid by the service firm, and the user usually pays the firm 25 to 40 percent over the workers' normal rate of pay. However, when fringe benefits and other related employee costs are counted, the actual hourly cost can turn out to be significantly less than for permanent help.

Temporary-help contractors are not employment agencies, for no charge is made to employees for providing employment. The temporary-help firm is the employer, and in this respect is no different from a plumber who employs other plumbers and sends them to work on the premises of his customers, or the consulting firm whose engineers work for a short time at one firm, complete their assignment, and then move on to another location and another assignment. The temporary-help contractor, as the employer, is responsible for social security, workmen's compensation, unemployment insurance, bonding, and other insurance.

Temporary-help contractors do not limit themselves to office help, and especially not to the lower skills. Janitors and filing clerks will be supplied, but so will computer programmers, draftsmen, engineers, designers, and pharmacists. Auxiliary sales personnel will also be provided to handle new-product introduction, seasonal selling, and other temporary overloads.

Emphasis by the temporaries industry has moved away from the "emergency" concept toward that of "auxiliary" services: fitting their personnel into fluctuating production schedules, planned vacation periods, change-over to new processing techniques, scheduled opening of a new facility, and the like. The time to select a firm is when there is no emergency or panic. Management should check into how long the firm has been in business, what is behind its claims regarding training programs, whether it uses adequate hiring procedures, and its general reputation for service and quality of personnel supplied.

Information Sources: There is no national professional or trade association in this industry. The Association of Temporary Office Services, 99 Church Street, New York, covers New York State, but is also a source of information on general practices and opportunities.

Consulting Psychologists. Consulting psychologists serve in four major branches of their field: personnel research and administrative techniques; employee counseling; human engineering ("human factors engineering"); and marketing survey research.

Personnel research and administrative techniques include recruiting, selection, placement, and induction; performance evaluation, promotion, transfer, and job evaluation; training, management development, and supervisory techniques; employee communication, motivation, and attitude and morale studies; advisory work in accident prevention; and guidance in labor relations.

Employee counseling includes professional clinical evaluation of individuals and counseling on individual job adjustment, supervisor-subordinate relations, and problems of mental health.

Human engineering involves advice on the design of systems and equipment in terms of capabilities, limitations, and reactions of operators, covering such matters as instrument design, color coding, dial arrangement, and work space.

Marketing and survey research concerns external relationships with present and potential customers, competitors, suppliers, government, special-interest groups, specific communities, and the public at large. Included are the study of advertising effectiveness, employee and community attitude surveys, product-preference polls, and the like.

Information Sources: Names of qualified psychologists in any area can be secured from state psychological associations or by contacting the American Psychological Association, 1333 Sixteenth Street, N.W., Washington, D.C. (covers all fields), or the Board of Examiners in Professional Psychology, Southern Illinois University, Carbondale, Illinois. For information on available personnel tests: The Psychological Corporation, 304 East 45th Street, New York. A complete listing of tests is given in *Tests in Print*, Gryphon Press, Highland Park, New Jersey. Many of the large management consulting firms have professional psychologists on their staffs. The American Management Association's *Directory of Consultant Members* has a classification key for personnel management consultants. For employee counseling: American Personnel and Guidance Association, 1605 New Hampshire Avenue, N.W., Washington, D.C. Human engineering: Human Factors Society, P.O. Box 263, Arlington, Virginia. There are also professional groups in human factors in several technical societies, such as the Institute of Electrical and Electronic Engineers, 485 Lexington Avenue, New York, and the American Society of Mechanical Engineers, 345 East 47th Street, New York. On marketing and survey research, associations active in the science of human behavior are American Marketing Association, 27 East Monroe Street, Chicago; Advertising Research Foundation, 3 East 34th Street, New York; and Marketing Science Institute, 3401 Walnut Street, Philadelphia.

Research and Development

Outside Research.[3]   Available for research assignments are about 1,000 independent industrial laboratories, about a dozen research institutes, and about 300 academic institutions which will undertake research programs sponsored by industry. Supplementing these are thousands of individual consultants and consulting groups. There are also about 100 endowed foundations and institutes, technical service laboratories of suppliers, "captive" laboratories of some industrial companies, and trade association laboratories, and about 100 state and territory agricultural and engineering experiment stations.

There are an estimated 2,300-odd independent laboratories, but many of these do only testing, analysis, inspection, and sampling. Of the 100 or so research institutes in the United States, perhaps a dozen major ones whose principal activity is sponsored research are essentially independent of university connection. Universities have traditionally been a major source of basic and fundamental research. However, the pressures of World War II and postwar defense and space activities have made many shift their emphasis, thus creating a large number of applied research centers.

Many trade associations sponsor substantial programs of industrial research and development, with the results made generally available to their industry. Most trade associations, however, do not maintain laboratories of their own, but sponsor outside research, often in the laboratories of one member. "Captive" laboratories are those in which development work is done for a customer or group of customers by suppliers, where the potential for future business is great enough. Consultants normally do not conduct research themselves, but act in an advisory capacity.

Unless an outside research project is sizable, there is usually no need for a complicated legal document. Many outside laboratories will accept assignments of $1,000 or less on the basis of a simple letter of authorization. Subjects most frequently covered in contracts for outside research are scope, duration,

[3] This discussion draws heavily upon the chapter "Outside Research," by Murray Berdick, in Carl Heyel's *Handbook of Industrial Research Management*, Reinhold Publishing Corporation, New York, 1959.

cost (a maximum figure, requiring permission from the sponsor for exceeding), liaison, mode of reporting results, secrecy, exclusivity, and patent rights. Independent laboratories normally agree to assign all inventions to the client. Research institutes generally assign patent rights to sponsors, but often special provisions are involved. University patent policies vary widely. Most outside research groups arrive at charges by making accounting of all costs, direct and indirect. Some use a simplified method of computing charges by assigning standard billing rates to classes of personnel used on the project. (For a more detailed discussion of outside research, see Chapter 6 of Section 5.)

Information Sources: "Institutes, Foundations, and Research Units," Burns Compiling and Research Organization, Beloit, Wisconsin. National Academy of Sciences—National Research Council, 2101 Constitution Avenue, N.W., Washington, D.C. American Council of Independent Laboratories, Inc., 4302 East-West Highway, Washington, D.C., issues a directory of membership laboratories. Engineering College Research Council, New York University, New York, publishes *Engineering College Research Review.* Association of Consulting Chemists and Chemical Engineers, 50 East 41st Street, New York, publishes a directory, *Consulting Services.* Bowker Associates, Inc., 1677 Wisconsin Avenue, Chicago, publishes *Industrial Research Laboratories of the United States,* listing 5,200 industrial research laboratories and background of each, noting the independent laboratories.

International Operations

Export Sales Representatives. The combination export manager operates an independent business as export representative for a number of manufacturers. He does everything to sell products abroad that would be expected by a manufacturer of his own export manager. By sharing with others the CEM's expenses, the manufacturer can usually sell his product overseas at a lower cost than if he set up his own export department on a scale adequate to obtain the same value. Most CEMs are located in major trade centers such as New York, Boston, San Francisco, and Chicago.

Through the CEM, the manufacturer has access to well-selected connections with bankers, shippers, forwarders, and insurers whose close cooperation is vital to profitable exporting. A CEM can select, on the ground, the most suitable foreign distributor. His travel for this—a major expense in putting products into foreign markets—is financed by the sales of products of all the manufacturers he represents.

Form of compensation varies. Some CEMs work on a straight commission, typically 5 to 10 percent, depending upon how well known the product is, how easy it is to sell, and the like. Others will work on a retainer plus commission, or even on a straight purchase price plus their own markup.

Information Sources: Field offices of the U.S. Department of Commerce; Directory of Combination Export Managers, Foreign Operations Administration, Office of Small Business, Washington 25, D.C.; National Foreign Trade Council, Inc., 10 Rockefeller Plaza, New York; International Executives Association, 93 Worth Street, New York; *International Commerce* (published by the Department of Commerce); *International Trade Review.*

CONCLUSION

The foregoing represent major professional services. There are, of course, many specialized services not treated here. In addition, there are countless advisory services rendered by suppliers. To mention only a few of the latter: data-processing systems analyses and softwear aids by computer manufacturers;

systems helps by forms suppliers, paper houses, and manufacturers of office copying, printing, and duplicating equipment; plant relocation and site selection helps from public utilities, railroads, and other carriers, and local governmental bodies; transportation analyses by airlines (often with unexpected results as to economies possible with premium transportation); packaging advisory services by suppliers of paper, containers, and other packaging materials; recommendations on space utilization by interior designers; safety suggestions by insurance companies; and helps on pension planning and executive compensation by banks. All of these sources of information deserve careful investigation and use where applicable. To be sure, the thought is perhaps inescapable that self-interest may heighten the enthusiasm with which certain recommendations are advanced—but the seasoned analyst will find "safety in numbers" when he weighs information from diverse sources.

CHAPTER SEVEN

Use and Limitations of Committees

EARLE A. CHILES *President, Fred Meyer, Inc., Portland, Oregon*

Probably no other organizational device has been more maligned or made the butt of more jokes than committees. But the carping and ridicule are seldom focused properly, and accordingly are seldom justified. The difficulty is that the use of committees *looks* deceptively simple when, in fact, it necessitates dealing with enormously complex and dynamic human relationships. Effective, efficient committee work is very difficult, and therefore rather rare. Moreover, a committee is easy to abuse and easy to sabotage. It can be dominated, diverted, disrupted, defeated, or turned to private ends with regrettable ease by any one of its members—including, of course, its chairman. There is nothing wrong—and very much that is right—about committees per se. But there is often a lot wrong about *particular* committees. The issue is the caliber of the specific committee one is contemplating or dealing with.

Luckily, committees are *not* all alike. Moreover, even a given committee is not always the same throughout its life. Within moments, it can switch from an effective tool to a useless one—or worse. The mood of its members can change abruptly, providing the chairman with what is essentially an entirely different group of men. Nevertheless, committees have a vital role in business and not only can be, but are, effectively used. After all, few men are busier, more mature, and less given to unproductive, boring, or trivial activities than corporate directors. But virtually all boards of directors have set up permanent committees to save time, exploit special talents, and expedite important planning and action. It follows that they have found committees both effective and efficient tools.

NATURE OF COMMITTEES

A committee is a formal outgrowth of the universal urge of responsible men confronted with problems to "get together and talk things over." It is essentially a device for expediting or improving communications between a manager and his subordinates, his superiors, or his peers. A committee is usually formed to fill a need or function not adequately coped with by the normal organizational division of responsibilities. It is, therefore, supplemental in nature. Care must be taken that a committee does not duplicate or usurp functions more properly performed by an individual or a structural organization unit.

In this connection, it is important to note that an executive who appoints an advisory committee is still responsible for the actions he takes as a result (or in spite) of its deliberations. He does not have to take the advice or recommendations his committee offers, but as a practical matter, he usually does. He may well soften criticism of subsequent failure by following a committee's advice, but he cannot legitimately disclaim responsibility.

Committees can exist at any organizational level, and their nature, membership, and "charter" generally reflect the level on which they operate. For example, committees of the board of directors are normally permanent and are made up of top-stature members. They address themselves to major issues. Typical bodies include the policy, executive, and finance committees; but salary, trust, bonus, profit-sharing, pension, audit, and appropriations committees are also common. At lower levels, by contrast, one often finds committees set up to consider safety, recreation and other employee facilities, product quality, grievances, cost reduction, utility conservation, and the like.

Kinds of Committees. There are several ways of categorizing committees. For example, there are two kinds that differ in origin. *Corporate committees* are those authorized by the corporate charter. They are normally permanent and deal with matters of policy, finance, executive salaries, and so forth. *Administrative committees* are those authorized and created by specific managers to meet some need not recognized by (or appropriate in) the corporate charter. These may be permanent or temporary. *Ad hoc committees* are one form of administrative committees set up for one specific, discrete purpose. An *ad hoc* committee is expected to dissolve itself when its objective has been achieved.

Committees are often classified according to their organizational level, their form, or their duration. Subjects of concern, such as research, are also used to describe committees, and sometimes their constituency is used, as in the case of joint union-management committees. Perhaps the most useful form of classification is by objective. *Executive committees* are normally decision-making groups; their purpose is *to do* something (or get it done). *Advisory committees* offer guidance and counsel to the managers they were set up to serve. Their purpose is *to give* opinions or suggestions, to synthesize diverse viewpoints, or to distill the expertise of their members. *Educational committees* exist as vehicles for imparting information or notification. Their purpose is to *exchange* facts and knowledge. *Coordinating committees* seek harmony among functions. Their purpose is *to adjust* differences, to persuade and explain, and to win mutual confidence and commitment. *Investigative committees* exist *to probe* and explore; to study an idea, problem, or proposal thoroughly. Their purpose is to provide insight or background and to gather and assemble information. It is important to note that several of these objectives and purposes are often combined by a given committee. Committees may also shift their emphasis to suit the specific issues brought before them.

WHEN TO USE A COMMITTEE

Committees are fundamentally *communications media* brought into existence to deal with matters that cut across the normal lines of responsibility in an organization. Accordingly, they can be used to inform, to educate, to sell ideas or plans, to change attitudes, to marshall support, to explain and clarify policies, and so on.   They are effective for resolving conflict and improving coordination among organizational units.   Via committees, managers with similar responsibilities—such as sales managers—can exchange information and experiences related to problems common to all of them.

Top executives normally formulate policy in committees, and turn to them again when they seek guidance reflecting the collective expertise of various specialists.   This most common role of committees—advising executives—is helpful not only because special knowledge is brought to bear, but because an issue can be studied more thoroughly and be subjected to more critical discussion by a seasoned group than by an individual.   Moreover, the members of influential committees often can enlist further research and opinions from their staffs, thus increasing the likelihood of evolving a sound solution.

It should be noted in this connection that committees not only can tap the considered judgment of company specialists, but also are useful in combating the disintegrating influence of ever-increasing specialization.   This very real function of unifying support for management decisions and winning broad commitment to its objectives was underlined by a leading industrial editor[1] when he wrote:

While it has been increasingly popular to joke about committees, in many instances there is more than casual merit . . . in democratic decision making.   First of all, the integrated judgment of a qualified group of executives has a good chance of being superior to that of any one individual.   But even more important is the feeling that action arrived at by a majority is more likely to win the needed cooperation of that majority than action directed independently by one of the group's members.

There seems to be wide agreement that committees are best when called upon to discuss, suggest, or recommend courses of action.   They have also proved effective for planning and scheduling, for coordinating effort that bestrides several organizational units, and for investigation.   Committees generally do a good job of evaluating proposals and alternatives and reporting their findings, with or without recommendations.   But they are normally weak when called upon to probe and actually make decisions or take action on management problems.   This can be attributed largely to the political overtones of these assignments and the tendency of committees to arrive at decisions by compromise. (The standard quip is that a camel is a horse designed by a committee.)

Disadvantages of Committees.   The disadvantages of committees and the disappointments so commonly associated with them are not all inherent.   In fact, most of them result from inadequately conducting and controlling the committee. When poorly staffed, chaired, or handled, however, committees become notorious time wasters.   They arrive at conclusions reluctantly, and more often than not negotiate and compromise all vitality out of an idea or proposal before agreeing to recommend or accept it.   A few members often dominate a committee, so others—perhaps with valuable contributions to make—do not participate.   This not only deprives the organization of their ideas, but denies these members the opportunity to benefit and learn.   They therefore tend to lose interest and resent the time spent in meetings.

Committees are inherently slow and deliberate, and they broaden the risk of security leaks.   For reasons not fully understood, excellent, decisive men often do not think cogently or rationally in groups, and can fall into errors none would make alone.   Committees are prey to petty politics.   Membership tends to become a status symbol, leading men to contrive their way onto commit-

---

[1] Lester R. Bittel, *Management by Exception*, McGraw-Hill Book Company, New York, 1964, p. 156.

tees where they are wholly superfluous or unqualified, with disruptive and demoralizing results. With members pressed for time, higher-level committees, particularly, are prone to superficial consideration and premature conclusions. Some members, more eager to display than to contribute their knowledge, often lead the committee into irrelevant discussion. Others agree (or disagree) on trivial grounds, in an attempt to curry favor.

Effective and Ineffective Committees. Perhaps a contrast can best make the point that there is little *inherent* weakness in the use of committees. The problems are a function of poor management—or, more probably, of management deceived by the apparent simplicity of using committees.

On the one hand, we have a powerful, dependable, and efficient committee. Its members are seasoned managers, carefully selected for their specialized knowledge and skills and for their emotional and business maturity. Each is well informed, has good communication skills, is self-assured, and takes the time to study the topics on the agenda and to prepare himself to discuss them concisely. The purpose of the committee is well defined and clearly understood, and the specific objectives of each meeting are isolated at the outset. Ample work and thought go into the preparation of a realistic, well-focused agenda which is distributed well in advance of each meeting. The chairman is a skilled, sensitive discussion leader who keeps the meeting on schedule and makes specific follow-up assignments. Minutes are kept brief and distributed promptly.

On the other hand, there is the too familiar mediocre committee—over-large, lacking a specific purpose, sabotaged by men pursuing personal goals, and crippled by grossly unprepared members who either are indifferent or take obstinate positions in self-defense. The problem or issue before the committee is not clearly stated, nor are questions properly framed and timed to provoke thought or expedite agreement. The chairman is "too busy" to prepare an agenda—or himself, for that matter—in advance, so each meeting has unlimited scope. He arrives (late) with his mind made up as to what "the committee" should decide. This is an insensitive chairman—self-centered, and overly reliant on his authority. He is inept at mediating arguments that break out and does not know how to control aggressive participants or draw out the nonparticipants. Detailed minutes are meticulously kept—ponderous, dull, and unread. Finally, no clear provision is made for follow-up action at the conclusion of the meetings.

These extremes are both exaggerated for emphasis, of course, and to bring out common points of strength or weakness.

COMPOSITION OF COMMITTEES

The Committee Chairman. It is evident from the foregoing that the committee chairman can, and very frequently does, make the difference between an effective, productive committee and a poor one. Accordingly, he should be selected with great care, rather than appointed merely because he is senior or holds the highest corporate office. The committee, remember, is created largely to get around the limitations and parochialism of the formal organization. It is self-defeating to recreate the organizational unit, in miniature, within the committee. If, as normally happens, the ranking member of the committee is appointed chairman, he must consciously dissociate his role and function as chairman from his normal position of authority. He should be a catalyst and discussion leader via-à-vis the committee, not an autocratic lecturer or inquisitor. To encourage participation—without which a committee is unnecessary—the *situation,* not power or personality, should be the controlling factor.

Another important consideration is the chairman's work load. Properly chairing a committee is a challenging and time-consuming task. Hours of preparation and preliminary effort should go into each meeting before it convenes. At least some attention is necessary after it adjourns, or much of the potential benefit will be lost. It is important to recognize that a committee seldom produces results during its meetings. The action and accomplishment come after the meetings break up.

A committee chairman should be a good planner and a dogged follow-up man. He should also be skilled at mediating or at least distracting arguers. He will need a sense of humor and—perhaps more important—a sense of timing. The more sensitive and diplomatic he is, the better, for he must control overeager men without discouraging them, and recognize and draw out reluctant participants. He must, in short, familiarize himself with the human resources he has to work with. He must get to know their special strengths, interests, weaknesses, and biases. He should be articulate, prompt, and dependable. Especially if the committee has investigative or evaluating functions, the chairman should be an able delegator and administrator. He must be patient and mature; and, finally, he should be respected and fully accepted by the members of his committee.

His functions will vary as the objectives, mood, or nature of the committee change. He should strive to impersonalize the issues, and be at pains to detach ideas and opinions from the individuals offering them—especially when he himself is the individual. He should be adept at framing and phrasing questions, and in asking them in an orderly, productive sequence. If suggestions, guidance, or joint conclusions are sought, he must be careful to keep the issues—and his mind—open as long as appropriate.

Committee Members. Just as committees can and do exist at all organizational levels, committee membership may be drawn from one or from several levels. Moreover, membership, like committees themselves, may be permanent or temporary. Many companies prefer to rotate membership on selected committees deliberately, to broaden exposure and as a personnel development tool. Be that as it may, it is imperative to limit the size of committees scrupulously to the minimum possible for balanced deliberations. Moreover, each committee member must be able to add to the group's judgment and effectiveness. There should be *no* prestige or "automatic" appointments. Disinterested, superfluous, irrelevant, or unqualified members are an unnecessary impediment to the performance of any committee.

Another great disruptive influence is the member who is qualified, but comes to committee meetings unprepared. At minimum, a man asked to serve on a committee should agree to prepare himself and his material to the best of his ability and to coordinate his preparation with that of his colleagues on the committee. He should also fully accept his responsibility to participate actively in the meetings and other activities of the committee, but not to monopolize discussion. He should avoid consciously pursuing personal objectives via committee activities, but concentrate instead on sincerely helping the committee speedily achieve its objectives. He should agree to arrive on time and to complete his special assignments on time.

Personal Benefits Deriving from Committee Membership. What personal benefits can the committee member expect for all this extra effort and self-discipline? At least ten can be listed. (1) Committee membership will enable him to learn the reasons for the policies and actions of the organization. (2) He will gain insight into himself, his associates, and his industry. (3) He will broaden his understanding and appreciation of the problems and contributions of specialties other than his own. (4) He will enhance his objectivity and critical faculties. He will become a keener, more incisive manager. (5) He will learn to anticipate the larger and more remote impact of contemplated changes. (6) He will develop his human relation skills. (7) He will learn how to increase his cooperation with others, and how to win theirs. This should spill over into his day-to-day work relationships with them, which will improve his regular performance and effectiveness. (8) A series of "subcommittee of one" assignments will make him better informed and further increase his breadth and promotability. (9) He will have an opportunity to learn to be more persuasive and more successful in getting agreement and commitment without resort to authority—an indispensable executive skill. (10) His committee position will make him and his performance more visible to higher levels of management.

In short, committee membership affords a man excellent opportunities to serve, to learn and develop, to build self-confidence, and to expose his abilities more clearly.

BIBLIOGRAPHY

Auger, B. Y., *How to Run More Effective Business Meetings,* Grosset & Dunlap, Inc., New York, 1964.

Drucker, P. F., *The Practice of Management,* Harper & Row, Publishers, Incorporated, New York, 1954.

Gellerman, S. W., *People, Problems and Profits,* McGraw-Hill Book Company, New York, 1960.

Maynard, H. B., *Top Management Handbook,* McGraw-Hill Book Company, New York, 1960.

Moore, F. G., *Management, Organization and Practice,* Harper & Row, Publishers, Incorporated, New York, 1964.

Newman, W. H., *Administrative Action: The Techniques of Organization and Management,* 2d ed., Prentice-Hall, Inc., Englewood Cliffs, N.J., 1963.

Sayles, L. R., *Managerial Behavior,* McGraw-Hill Book Company, New York, 1964.

Scott, W. G., *Human Relations in Management,* Richard D. Irwin, Inc., Homewood, Ill., 1962.

Trecker, A. R., and B. Harleigh, *Committee Common Sense,* Association Press, New York, 1954.

Trecker, A. R., and B. Harleigh, *Focal Points for Improving Executive Meetings,* Young Presidents' Organization, New York.

GENERAL MANAGEMENT

CHAPTER ONE

Responsibilities of the Chief Executive

J. KEITH LOUDEN *Chairman of the Board, The Presidents Association; Vice President and Director, American Management Association*

It was Ralph Waldo Emerson who said that an organization is but the lengthening shadow of one man. At the time Emerson wrote this, industrial and business enterprises were quite small. Because of the size and diversity of modern enterprise, there are those who feel that Emerson's statement no longer holds true, and that the character of an organization is shaped by the shadows of many men. The actualities probably lie somewhere in between.

Regardless of size or complexity of an enterprise or the number of people involved in its management, the shadow of the chief executive still dominates. Knowingly or unknowingly, each member of an organization instinctively tends to reflect the character and thinking of the leader, the chief executive. Therefore, the chief executive should think through the image or identification model that he wants for himself and his company in all its relationships with members of management, with all employees, and with the customer, the vendor, the community, and the stockholder.

People make choices. Thus, it is the responsibility of the chief executive to decide what image he wants them to have and then to see that the business is conducted in all its areas so that the choice will be the desirable image which has been predetermined.

A CREED AND A PHILOSOPHY OF MANAGEMENT

One of the basic responsibilities of the chief executive is to develop, with the aid of his organization, a creed expressing a philosophy of management by which all members of the organization will live in conducting company affairs in every area of its influence and action.

The creed should be put in writing in the form of simple statements of intent. It should be discussed fully with everyone who can influence its implementation so that there will be not only understanding, but acceptance by those who will reflect the intent of the creed in their actions and work.

3–3

THE LEADERSHIP ROLE OF MANAGEMENT

In a rapidly changing, dynamic world, the nature of and need for leadership come under intensive study to determine the form it must take if we are to cope successfully with changing situations. All leadership groups determine the role they must play, and they also recognize the need for closer cooperation and understanding of the roles of one another. Whether it is the theologian, the academician, the career government head, or any other leader, there is increasing recognition of the fact that the primary leader in today's and tomorrow's world is the manager.

The theologian, for example, will state that, although he has a vital role to play in teaching the eternal truths and in laying a foundation for understanding and judgment of the moral and ethical laws by which man lives, his direct influence is limited by the relatively short time he is in contact with the members of his congregation. The academician prepares the young to understand the past, to think, and to have judgment. Through the educational process, he teaches them to analyze situations and make decisions on a sounder basis than otherwise would be possible, yet he breaks his formal contacts with his students in their early twenties, at the latest.

Therefore, whether or not people will achieve the recognition, the sense of purpose, the sense of accomplishment, and the sense of belonging they seek depends to a large extent upon the wisdom and ability of the manager of the enterprise in which they perform their life's work. He must be able to involve them in the processes of the enterprise to the point where they gain the fulfillment they seek for their lives under his leadership. He must be skilled in playing upon the natural desire of man to achieve, to be recognized as an individual, to find a worthwhile place for himself in life, and to realize the fulfillment which comes from knowing and proving he was not placed on earth to fail, but to make a contribution to society. This overwhelming desire to achieve, when led and guided to productive ends, is the hope of mankind. If this is not attained, it will become the destruction of mankind. Which it will be rests fully upon the shoulders of the manager and in each organization specifically upon the chief executive.

In considering this responsibility and opportunity, it must be recognized that managing is wherever it is found. When we speak of managing, we do not confine ourselves to business and industry, but include all situations where two or more people join together to accomplish a specific purpose where one becomes the leader.

THE CHANGING WORLD

We have but to look around us to recognize that we live in a changing world. This change is coming at an accelerating pace and is of two fundamental natures—technological and political, cultural, and social. Both kinds of change are explosive in their magnitude and speed. Managers in all walks of life and areas of influence must direct these elements of change to the good of mankind and not its destruction.

People instinctively resist change. Even though they might not like their current situation, they are used to it—if it is reasonably comfortable, there is a strong desire to leave it as it is. Therefore, in a time when change is inevitable, the manager must be fully aware of the logical and emotional aspects of change and be prepared to handle both. In an organization, resistance to change takes many forms.   Sometimes the problem is the chief executive's lack of a desire to change himself and to direct change in his organization.   He evidences a lack of willingness to think change through with his people so that the rewards to all may be seen and recognized.   And finally, the lack of persistence to see things through is often an important factor.

Master or Victim?   The successful manager is the master of change.   The unsuccessful manager is its victim.   Every manager in every organization must decide which he is to be.   Effective management creates a future; it does not wait for it.   It acts rather than reacts.   If a manager is to compete in a society that is undergoing massive change at an accelerating rate, he must take every step possible to make certain that he is in control of the destinies of his company.

The chief executive cannot leave the future of his company to chance.   He and his people must plan it, organize it to accomplish, and control it so that events conform to plan.

The chief executive cannot do all this alone.   He must do it through people.   To be successful in this concept, he must see that each member of his organization is placed in a position to perform with maximum effectiveness.

MANAGEMENT: A PROFESSION

If each member of an organization is to be placed so that he can perform at his maximum effectiveness, the chief executive must recognize the fact that management is an orderly process.   It is subject to a scientific approach to the solution of problems, using principles and practices that have been proved over the years.   Management has its recognized disciplines, and there is a pattern of action a manager follows.   Thus, management has many of the characteristics of a profession.   Everyone who engages in it is a professional.   The degree to which he is successful will be determined by his abilities and the time and effort he is willing to put into learning how to become more professional in his approach to the solution of the problems he faces.

The objective of the manager in this effort should be to enable his people to become more professional in their work by providing them with all the information essential to practice successfully the "three selfs": self-supervision, self-control, and self-appraisal.   Effective management is management by choice rather than by chance.   This means that the manager who manages effectively determines what he wants to have happen and then makes it happen, rather than letting things happen without plan or reason.   Therefore, if the manager wants his people to work with the sureness and confidence born of knowing where they want to go, what they must do to get there, and how they are achieving against their goals, he must place everyone in the organization in the position of knowing the following:

1. The business the company is in, the markets it serves, and its strengths and weaknesses

2. The company's objectives, including the businesses it should be in and the markets it should serve

3. The program established for achieving the objectives

4. The timetable for accomplishment

5. The assignment of responsibilities throughout the organization—who is going to do what

6. The resources needed and available

7. Whether or not the total capability exists for accomplishing the plan

This is the planning process which, coupled with confidence that what has been planned can be accomplished, leads to effective results.

In addition, each member of the organization should know:

1. The duties and responsibilities assigned to him
2. The authority given him to carry out the assignments
3. The results expected of him and the standards against which his performance will be measured
4. The help and guidance he may expect from his superior both on the presen⁺ job and in developing himself for further advancement

This is the organizing process which must be part of the manager's job.

Finally, the manager should provide members of the organization with necessary information in the form of controls of a "need to know" nature on a "fast feedback" basis so they can tell how they are doing and take corrective action when they get off course.

The chief executive should develop a uniform concept of management for his organization so that every member of it has the same understanding of what is meant by such terms as "planning," "organizing," and "controlling." This is essential, because joint human action is most effective when the mental image of the action to be taken is identical in the minds of all those involved. If the manager can get people to think together the way he wants them to think toward achieving agreed-upon objectives, he will less frequently have to tell them what to do.

If the manager is going to be the master of change and not its victim, he must place his people in a position to exercise the three selfs. Thereafter, he can devote less and less time to direct supervision and more and more time not only to mastering change but to creating it for the benefit of the organization and its customers.

THE NATURE AND ROLE OF PROFIT

The primary objective of every chief executive is to make a profit. This is not exclusively the responsibility of business and industry. Profit is the difference between the value of services rendered and the value of services consumed. Any organization—business, government, church, college, hospital, or labor union—must take in more than it pays out. The difference is profit. The source of the income does not change the profit-making responsibility. Whether the income is received from the sale of product or service, from taxes, or from donations, an organization still has to receive more money than it spends if it is to live.

The chief executive must understand and help his people understand that earning a profit is an honorable thing. Without profit, our whole way of life would grind to a halt. Profitable enterprise provides better products and services for the consumer, income for vendors, wages and benefits for employees, salaries and incentives for management, dividends for the stockholder, taxes for government, support for community services, charity for the needy, and retained earnings for the perpetuation of the business. Profit improves the standard of living and welfare of the people of the world, and the more profit there is, the more benefits there are for all.

Making a profit is difficult. Legislation, regulation, and social pressure have reduced the competitive advantages of one company over another, regardless of the industry or size or location of the company. Basic equipment, physical facilities, labor costs and practices, capital, current operating funds, and ethics have acquired a uniformity that is no respecter of the geography, nature, size, or status of a business. The only large area left for seeking competitive advantage is management competency. With all other factors becoming equal, survival is dependent upon the degree to which management is effective.

It is essential for the chief executive to recognize this and to live by this understanding. It will engender a determination to lead his people toward achieving greater management effectiveness and the development of their fullest potential. This is vital for the survival and success of the business.

THE ELEMENTS OF MANAGING

In the Management Course for Presidents conducted by The Presidents Association, an affiliate of the American Management Association, the elements of managing are divided and discussed in six categories: planning, organizing, controlling, decision managing, climate, and leadership. Any managing element or function that calls for getting things done through other people can be placed under one of these categories. If it cannot be so placed, it is probably an operating function or one that the individual performs himself.

The distinction between managing and operating is one that is not clear in the minds of many managers. In a successful organization, however, it is essential that the executive know the difference between managing and operating. The chief executive himself must be particularly clear in the distinction and, by example, help others arrive at the same clarity of understanding. To do this successfully calls for a uniform concept of managing accepted and understood at all levels of the management structure. The greater the degree of unanimity of understanding of what managing is and how it should be practiced, the greater likelihood there will be of successful performance.

The Chief Executive's Role. The chief executive, before he can really understand or spell out his responsibilities and role in the organization, must give considerable thought to the purpose of his position. Why does it exist? What is he supposed to provide or accomplish? The understanding of a position's purpose is often overlooked, and yet it is of great importance in gaining the breadth of understanding which makes possible a more definitive determination of exactly what the duties and responsibilities are together with the authority granted.

The purpose of the chief executive's position is to "provide leadership to the company's total activity of a quality and nature that will result in growth, profitability, and continuance; render a service to society; and provide an opportunity for the people engaged in the operation of the enterprise to develop to their fullest potential and gain a sense of accomplishment."

To fulfill this purpose, the chief executive must recognize and accept several fundamental truths that will not only govern his own actions as a manager, but set a pattern for the other managers in the organization to follow. The first is that he is a generalist and not a specialist. He may have entered management as a specialist, but as he moves toward the top of the organization, his knowledge and ability in his specialty become less important as his role becomes increasingly that of a coordinator of a group of specialists, leading them toward the effective achievement of common objectives.

One of the most difficult decisions the chief executive must reach is to refrain from becoming involved personally in the specialty he once headed. He must, instead, give his successor the opportunity to perform and develop. The manager, particularly the chief executive, must refrain from becoming involved in the execution of delegated responsibilities.

This leads to a second important principle, the philosophy of decentralization. Decentralization is the philosophy of managing which calls for the delegation of responsibility and authority to the lowest level in the organization where a decision can be made effectively and with full accountability. The essence of successful decentralization is definition, clear statement of policy, and controls of a fast feedback nature.

Delegation is not abdication, but assigning to a subordinate the responsibility and commensurate authority to accomplish an objective or specific result. True delegation exists only when the manager making the delegation confines himself to establishing the objectives and standards and measures of performance, reviewing the results, and coaching the subordinate in terms of the results and their variance from objectives and performance standards. A manager may delegate authority to others, but he may not delegate his responsibility and accountability for the end results.

In the light of these principles, then, let us consider the role of the chief executive in the performance of the six elements of managing.

Planning. It is the responsibility of the chief executive to develop, with the aid of his subordinates, a plan of action for the company, both short and long range, that will establish objectives, define strategies, and spell out in detail the operational actions that will lead to meeting the objectives.

There should be a plan of action for every level in the organization or for each team of managers. Every manager is on two teams, one of which he is a member—that is, his superior's team—and one of which he is the leader—the team composed of himself and his subordinates. Recognizing that the planning function is from the top down and not from the bottom up, it is important for the chief executive to see that there are corporate objectives established and that there is a strategy developed which will permit the sound development of operational planning at every level of the organization, the sum total of which will make possible the achievement of the corporate objectives.

The chief executive should see that every manager who has the responsibility for carrying out the plan develops his own program for participation with the aid of his subordinates and such staff assistance as may be needed. Thus, it becomes the manager's plan and one for which he can be held accountable.

Policies are an essential element of planning. At times, they are confused with planning, but they are rather the rules of the game or the guidelines or limits provided to serve the planning activity. The chief executive should lead in the development of policies for the corporate level that will define limits of action and provide guidelines for the planning activity. He should make sure that the approved corporate policies are properly interpreted and defined in writing for each area and level of the organization.

Policies should be clear statements of intent—not detailed, all-encompassing statements. Two of the three basic elements of planning are physical and fiscal, the third being manpower planning, which will be discussed below.

Organizing. The chief executive has the responsibility of developing a plan of organization, showing both structure and people, that is compatible with the physical and fiscal plans for the company's growth and development.

A long-range plan without a manpower and organization structure plan is incomplete. Manpower planning is increasingly important because of not only the impact of technological change on job knowledge and experience, but also the shortage of manpower which is increasingly evident. Accordingly, the chief executive must see that a manpower development program is prepared that will enable the company to meet its projected manpower needs. The program should be designed to encourage all executives both to improve their abilities in their current positions and to prepare themselves for positions of greater responsibility. Experience in lesser jobs no longer entirely qualifies a manager for promotion. He must take positive steps to prepare himself for promotion, because the demands of the times and the accelerating rate of change do not permit the time-honored approach of "learning on the job." The manager must strive to close the gap between his present ability and the demands of the position ahead as rapidly as possible.

Recognizing that definition is an essential element of good management, the chief executive must see that a plan of organization is developed that will show the current structure of the management organization together with position descriptions for each post. Position descriptions include purpose, scope, duties, responsibilities and authority granted, and working relationships. They usually include the organization chart for the unit involved and a man specification spelling out the "ideal" man for the position.

Controlling. Controls are a form of impersonal supervision, designed to inform the manager promptly whether or not events are conforming to plans. The essence of control is to set objectives for each level in the organization, spell out the duties and responsibilities assigned, decentralize authority, and review progress against plans. The chief executive should see that performance objectives, both short and long range, which will support the company plans are developed for each function of the business. These should be both quantitative and qualitative with the timetable for accomplishment clearly spelled out.

He must see that systems of informational controls of a fast feedback, need-to-know nature are developed to cover the total activities of the company and make it possible for each responsible person to measure his results quickly and accurately in relation to his predetermined objectives. These controls must be tailored to fit and of high quality if they are to be of real value.

Decision Managing. Believing in the philosophy of decentralization, the chief executive should see that there is developed within the limits of established policies and procedures an effective designation and operation of the philosophy of decentralized decision managing at every level in the organization.

Climate. The chief executive should create a working relationship pattern within the company that will maintain a high level of executive and employee morale. This is largely achieved through definition, proper structure, and carefully selected and well-trained people working with a unity of purpose.

He should see that people in all areas of the organization receive adequate advice, counsel, assistance, and service to aid them in attaining their objectives and developing to their maximum potential. His objective should be to get people to work hard and work well, because they want to work hard and well.

Leadership. The mere performance of his duties and responsibilities within the organization is not sufficient for success as a chief executive. Environmental factors external to the organization have great impact on the ability and right to manage the enterprise. These factors are social, economic, and political. The professional manager must recognize that he has an obligation to help shape the environment in which he performs his duties. He has a role to play as a citizen and as a participant in public affairs far beyond what he once believed necessary or even desirable. He must represent the company to the public, to industry, and to government so as to enhance the reputation of the company and gain recognition for its competency and its contribution. He will thus retain the right to manage in the public good as a member of a free society.

As a leader who has great influence over the people with whom he is associated, the chief executive's life is far from private. His actions have great impact on other people. Therefore, he must conduct himself in a manner that will reflect credit upon the company and the American system of free enterprise, and thus encourage others to do likewise.

Accepting the role of leadership, and accepting the impact on people of the company's philosophy, creeds, and practices, the chief executive has the responsibility for developing, maintaining, and disseminating throughout the company a basic corporate philosophy designed to ensure to all employees a maximum degree of personal satisfaction in the performance of their assigned tasks and the opportunity to develop to their fullest potential.

Of the six elements of managing, without in any way minimizing the importance of any one of them, planning and organizing are the two basic responsibilities of the chief executive. These cannot be delegated. He can utilize all the assistance he needs, but he must take the personal responsibility for seeing that these two elements are performed well. If he does, he will find he is at least two-thirds of the way toward doing an acceptable and successful job. If he does not do them well, he is in for a difficult time, regardless of his ability and brilliance in the other fields.

PERSONAL PLANNING

The chief executive is inclined to worry about lack of time to get things done. Perhaps the main cause of his lack of time is the failure to avoid becoming involved in delegated responsibilities. The professional approach to management is to employ the simplest way of doing everything that it is absolutely necessary to do. When there is a question as to whether a duty is necessary, that duty should be left out. It can. always be added, but it is difficult to remove once imbedded in the fabric of the organization.

A failing on the part of many managers, particularly chief executives, is in not helping people to develop an ability to manage decisions themselves. One approach is to permit no one to come with a problem to discuss without also bringing a suggested answer. It may not be the best answer, but it is one. This helps develop participative management and not dependency management.

CONCLUSION

To establish objectives and to have standards of performance are essential to the determination of how well the chief executive is doing. Many times, however, even though these objectives are being met, the thoughtful chief executive is concerned about whether he is truly measuring up to his opportunities and fulfilling his mission in life.

Some of the reflective questions that the chief executive can and should ask himself follow.

1. What is happening to my company because of the way it is being managed? Are we really professional managers? Are we managing in the simplest way we know how? Are we practicing decentralization? Do we really know where we are going, and why and how?

2. What kind of identification model do we want our vendors, customers, employees, and the public to have? People make choices. Are they making the decisions about us we want them to make?

3. Would I want my people to manage and think as I do? If so, I must recognize that I must lead in a manner they will want to follow.

4. What is happening to the people with whom I am associated because I am here? Are my people better or worse off this evening for knowing me and being associated with me today? Have I truly been a leader whom people want to follow?

On the answers to these questions rest the future and the hope of the world.

BIBLIOGRAPHY

Allen, Louis A., *The Management Profession,* McGraw-Hill Book Company, New York, 1964.
Appley, Lawrence A., "Management the Simple Way," *Management in Action,* American Management Association, New York, 1956.
Bennet, C. L., *Defining the Manager's Job,* Research Study, no. 33, American Management Association, New York, 1958.
Bittel, Lester R., *Management by Exception,* McGraw-Hill Book Company, New York, 1964.
Drucker, Peter F., *The Practice of Management,* Harper & Row, Publishers, Incorporated, New York, 1954.
Heyel, Carl, *Organizing Your Job in Management,* American Management Association, New York, 1960.
Maynard, H. B. (ed.), *Top Management Handbook,* McGraw-Hill Book Company, New York, 1960.
Merrihue, Willard V., *Managing by Communication,* McGraw-Hill Book Company, New York, 1960.
Merrill, Harwood F., and Elizabeth Marting (eds.), *Developing Executive Skills,* American Management Association, New York, 1958.
Scott, Brian W., *Long-range Planning in American Industry,* American Management Association, New York, 1965.
Simon, Herbert A., *The New Science of Management Decision,* Harper & Row, Publishers, Incorporated, New York, 1960.
Sloan, Alfred P., Jr., *My Years with General Motors,* Doubleday & Company, Inc., Garden City, N.Y., 1964.
White, K. K., *Understanding the Company Organization Chart,* Research Study, no. 56, American Management Association, New York, 1963.

CHAPTER TWO

The Board of Directors

RICHARD M. PAGET   *Senior Partner, Cresap, McCormick and Paget, New York, New York*

For all incorporated businesses, boards of directors are a legal requirement. In closely held or small concerns, the board may function only in token compliance with corporation law. A qualified, active board of directors, however, can be a powerful factor in the success of a business, and most chief executives seek ways to improve the composition and functioning of their boards.

In fact, a chief executive cannot perform his job of managing the affairs of his business unless he has sufficient standing with his directors to participate actively and effectively in all aspects of board organization and functioning. The imagination, attitude, energy, and leadership of the chief executive are the most important forces in securing constructive participation by individual directors and effective functioning by the board as a whole.

Accordingly, this chapter considers the board of directors primarily from the chief executive's point of view. After a brief discussion of why men are willing to become directors in the first place, it considers the "best" size and composition of a board, the problems of getting good directors, the role of the board and its organization, working with a board, and compensation and retirement of directors.

WHY DO MEN BECOME DIRECTORS?

There are well over one million incorporated businesses in America, which means several million persons sitting on governing boards. Some of these people, of course, are "inside" directors, executives of the corporations they serve. But why are people from the "outside" willing to serve? Being a director is time consuming, involves a man in problems not of his own making, requires occasional performance of unpleasant tasks, carries some risk of being a defendant in legal actions, and offers only minor direct financial inducements.

Undoubtedly, a man may be motivated to become a director by the prospect of indirect financial gain through the company on whose board he serves, or through his associations with the other directors. Most men, however, who have commented publicly and privately on the reasons for accepting directorates have indicated less ulterior motives. Many men receive considerable satisfaction from the status and prestige of being a director, factors which are helpful in developing a business reputation and in establishing a position in a community.

Men may serve as directors because of their ownership interests, because they feel they can broaden their own experience through exposure to new problems and situations, because of friendships with other directors, because of a desire to associate with the caliber of men already on a board, or because of a desire to make a social contribution.

Finally—and this is especially important for a chief executive to remember—competent men may be willing to serve as directors if they can have the satisfaction of feeling really useful to the enterprise in question. There is little attraction in serving on a board unless one is an active participant in decision making at the policy level or is called upon for advice and counsel.

SIZE AND COMPOSITION OF THE BOARD

How big should the board of directors be? Should it be an inside or an outside board? On these matters, there exists a body of well-documented experience. The National Industrial Conference Board has been making studies in this area since 1938; their reports are helpful and revealing.

Size. The legal minimum requirement is three directors. The trend, however, is toward boards of from ten to fifteen members. Usually, smaller companies may have seven to ten members, while larger enterprises tend to select ten to fifteen.

A board of three directors is normally too small to do much more than fulfill formal legal requirements. On the other hand, the large board of twenty or more directors frequently becomes ineffective because of the sheer difficulty of securing discussion of basic problems from so many individuals. On a large board, the work frequently is done in committees, and board action is a formality.

There is no best size for any board, but it should be small enough to secure free exchange of views and yet large enough to provide for a cross section of interests and to permit the necessary committee structure. As will be discussed later, most boards appoint an executive committee to act for the board between regular meetings; the board must be large enough not to be dominated by the executive committee. For many years, a large national corporation had a nine-man board and a seven-man executive committee—leaving small opportunity for independent board action!

Important factors influencing the size of boards are the number of lines of activity in which a company engages and its geographic dispersion. Insurance companies and some banks and trust companies frequently have large boards of directors, because of their need to have representation of their publics and to include a wide variety of outside interests.

The Inside, Outside, or Balanced Board. The National Industrial Conference Board reports a discernible trend toward boards in which a majority of the members are outside, or nonemployee, directors. Almost two-thirds of nearly 600 manufacturing companies cooperating in an NICB survey reported a majority of outside directors. Ninety-one percent of over 300 nonmanufacturing companies reported that outsiders constituted a majority of their boards.

This is a controversial subject, and some authorities argue strongly for the inside-dominated board. Although there is no way to prove the superiority of an inside or an outside board, there is a strong consensus, borne out by analysis of boards composition, to support the following conclusions:

1. A majority of the board members should be outsiders or nonemployees. Former employees seldom can qualify as objective outsiders.

2. The chief executive should be a regular member of the board.

3. A restrained leavening of important insiders is widely considered a sound way of bringing technical and company knowledge into board deliberations. It also exposes the outside board members to the thinking of key members of management. However, insiders cannot be expected to act independently of the chief executive, nor will they normally be independent in controversial matters.

4. A commercial banker and an investment banker, as well as a lawyer, are frequently included in the membership of corporate boards. When chosen for their personal abilities and when proper disclosure is made of their business dealings with the company, this kind of experienced outside director can frequently be of value.

GETTING GOOD DIRECTORS

The first problem confronting a chief executive who wants an effective board is to get good people. What are the legal qualifications a director must meet? Must he be a stockholder? What personal qualities are desirable?

Legal Qualifications. There are few onerous legal provisions governing the eligibility and qualifications of directors in industrial companies. Banks, insurance companies, investment organizations, public utilities, and transportation companies are regulated more specifically by the laws of some states regarding residence, stock ownership, voting procedures on declaration of dividends, and the like. Even here, the legal qualifications are not onerous.

A number of Federal statutes establish some qualification requirements for directors, most of which prohibit service of individuals in more than one corporation if the result would be any form of interlocking or other condition deemed not in the public interest. Broadly, the qualifications and restrictions of both state and Federal statutes are aimed at avoiding conflicts of interest and assuring the existence of free competition. In the long run, these requirements coincide with the best interests of industry. Legal qualifications for directors impose no unusual difficulties, but they must be known and observed, and legal counsel should be sought to pass on the qualifications of board candidates.

Stockholding Qualifications. In actual practice, very few companies require that directors own stock. Seventy-three percent of the 581 companies participating in an NICB survey require no ownership of stock by directors. Of all these companies, only 6 required that directors own more than 100 shares.

Board membership for large stockholders, however, is a frequent problem in corporate life. Where the representative of a large interest is qualified to act as a director, the combination of directoral ability and financial interest can be of real value. Because of differences in tax problems, income objectives, and investment goals, however, there are times when a large shareholder's views can be at substantial variance with the best interests of the corporation or its general body of smaller shareholders.

As a general principle, directors should be selected for their ability to serve as directors rather than for their financial interest in the company; substantial obligation to invest in a company's stock may be a serious added handicap in finding satisfactory directors. Although there is some validity in the belief that good stockholder relations are furthered by a director's ownership of at least modest amounts of stock, there is little truth to the popular view that a director's interest and contribution is in direct proportion to his stockholdings.

Furthermore, large shareholdings are not necessarily a reflection of the competence of the holder.

Desirable Personal Qualities.   A first and obvious requirement for a successful director is *the broadest possible business experience with general management problems.*   Except in unusual circumstances, most boards deal with financial and legal matters and the evaluation of risks.   Occasionally, university administrators, scientists, or public figures have made important contributions, but the selection of such individuals must be approached with great care.

High ethical standards are essential.   All directors are faced at times with situations which could tempt individuals to act with questionable integrity. Directors usually are well informed about company prospects and, subject to legal restrictions, can indulge in direct or indirect inside trading in stock.   Corporate managements have been known to propose actions of questionable honesty.   In the heat of the business battle, it is sometimes difficult to see ethical considerations with clarity.   Honesty and a reputation for fair dealing are indispensable qualities.

Another desirable quality is *a demonstrated willingness to take calculated business risks.*   Risk taking is at the root of success in business enterprise.   An overly cautious board of directors can be as serious a handicap to the results of the enterprise as a board composed exclusively of compulsive gamblers.

To function as effective directors, individuals must have *the energy and the inclination to do a reasonable amount of homework.*   No board can function effectively if all decisions are based only on data which can be exposed and considered during the formal meetings.   Occasionally, special situations require a good deal of directors' time outside of board meetings, and directors should be willing and able to make themselves reasonably available when needed.

Availability to attend meetings of the board and of committees is another qualification for board membership.   Here, place of residence may be an important factor.

The *courage* to face unpleasant tasks and decisions is an important characteristic of good directors.   Changing management, meeting the actions of competitors, protecting the corporation from unsound efforts to seize control, and taking large risks are matters which may require fortitude as well as judgment.   The legal risks of directors do not appear excessive, but they are nonetheless real, and acting in face of threats to the director's personal assets can call for a high order of courage.

Reasonable *physical stamina* is another quality to be sought.   Although a director's functions normally are not arduous, visits to company locations and attendance at various functions can be physically taxing.   Because boards usually include men in older age groups, physical problems should especially be avoided among board candidates.

Because the *ability to appraise people* is an important function of corporate boards, this quality should also be sought.   This is by no means a universal quality, and its lack can be a serious handicap.

Flexibility of mind is another important quality in a corporate director.   The continued existence of a corporation depends on its ability to adapt to changing conditions — in fact, some students consider that the essence of corporate vitality is the corporation's ability to act as an instrument of change.   Board members whose first reaction to a new course is negative can be serious problems for creative managers.

The *ability to ask discerning questions* is a quality possessed by only a minority of individuals available for service as directors.   This ability can be of such value that it is well worth the effort to find some board members possessing it.   Skill in identifying and opening up situations which the board should examine can make all the difference between a board that is mediocre and one that is effective.

Age Qualifications. A number of analyses of corporate boards have included studies of directors' ages, but none of the results seems conclusive except on one point.   A preponderance of elderly board members may be a sign of present or approaching difficulties.   Age and experience are companion phenomena, and many men retain their vigor and progressive outlook well beyond the threshold of sixty-five years.   Nevertheless, a board where the average age is high may well be overly conservative and less interested in long-range problems.   Also, because a good management group is likely to average in the forty-five to fifty-five age bracket, a board that is much older may not be able to relate smoothly to the younger management group.

In the selection of a board, the age mix of its members is a factor to consider, and some general policies governing this point should be agreed upon.

Finding Directors. It is not enough to define the qualities that make a director desirable; directors must be found.   This is never an easy task.

Turnover on corporate boards can be expected because of the relatively high average age of board members, conflicts of interest arising from the changing scope of corporate activities, and changes in the directors' own outlooks and interests.   Studies indicate that the average length of service of corporate directors may be as short as five years, and that at least one thousand vacancies on corporate boards exist at all times.

There are a few relatively simple steps which can be taken to improve a company's prospects for finding suitable directors when they are needed.

The first is to agree on a plan for the composition and continuity of the board.   A clear understanding of the various kinds of backgrounds desired on the board is a necessary prelude.   The proportion of inside and outside members, the kinds of skills or connections desired in outside members, the representation of important owners, and judgments on including or excluding bankers, lawyers, or other professional servants of the company are among the questions to be resolved.

Second, the company should agree on the mixture of personal qualifications to be sought.   The general qualities of courage, integrity, reputation, and the like are desirable in all directors.   However, such matters as age, involvement in active business, desired social compatibility, attitude toward nepotism, and similar qualifications will vary, and should be stated in terms against which candidates can be screened.

Finally, the development of sources of directors and actual candidates should be assigned as a specific responsibility.   Sometimes this is a principal function of the chairman of the board.   Frequently, it is a task for the chief executive when he is not also chairman.   There is a growing practice of setting up a standing committee of the board to find and screen candidates for board membership.

Sources can include the members of the board itself, recommendations from trusted professional advisers (lawyers, accountants, bankers, and management consultants), successful executives in noncompeting companies, public figures, and some individuals who regularly act as professional directors.

HOW SHOULD A BOARD BE SET UP?

Board organization usually is simple.   It involves the formal election of board members, actions of the board to "organize" itself and the company by the election of a chairman, the appointment of committees, and the election of corporation officers. The requirements and procedures for all of these actions are governed by statutes or provisions of the bylaws.

Election of Directors. Many students of corporate management have asserted that a typical board of directors is a self-perpetuating body. Although statutes and bylaws provide that a slate of directors shall be prepared for consideration by the shareholders, relatively few shareholders actually attend meetings at which directors are elected, and the election is accomplished through proxies.

One of the more interesting questions here is the technique of *cumulative* voting, whereby each shareholder is entitled to multiply the number of his voting shares times the number of board candidates on the slate and direct the resulting number of votes to one or more candidates. This is a method of voting believed by some to provide representation for minority stockholder groups, and mandatory or permissive provisions for it have been established in all but five states. In actual practice, cumulative voting is not widely used. By far the largest number of companies follow the practice of permitting one vote for each share of voting stock for each candidate.

The authority on cumulative voting, Dr. Charles M. Williams of Harvard, has concluded that management generally has little to fear from it. Managements, however, typically react against cumulative voting. Where cumulative voting is a problem, the usual remedies have been to reduce the size of the board or stagger the terms of directors. Both have the effect of reducing the number of candidates, which restricts the power of cumulative voters.

It is almost universal practice to elect directors annually and to have the entire board stand for election. Some notable exceptions are found among service businesses, such as banks, insurance companies, and railroads, where staggered two- and three-year terms are found with some frequency.

Board vacancies which occur between normal elections are dealt with in the manner prescribed in the bylaws.

Board Structure. Immediately following formal election, boards generally hold an organization meeting, elect a permanent chairman and corporate officers, and appoint standing committees. One question which frequently comes up is the extent to which nonmembers should be invited to sit with the board at its meetings. The secretary is usually not a member of the board, but his presence at meetings is essential. Where the legal counsel is not a board member, he may be invited to attend board meetings in his role as an adviser. With these exceptions, nonmembers rarely attend meetings except when invited to discuss special matters; the presence of nonmembers at board meetings can be a serious barrier to free discussion.

The number and kind of board committees vary. They usually include regular standing committees such as the executive, finance, and audit committees; special committees such as committees on officer-director compensation, salary and bonus committees, stock option committees, and committees on management development; and *ad hoc* committees appointed to study special problems such as an acquisition program or an important capital appropriation.

In the opinion of this writer, it is generally a mistake to include both an executive committee and a finance committee in the board structure of the average corporation, because it is extremely difficult to define the respective limits of the responsibilities of these two groups. An executive committee can hardly consider any management problems without taking into account the financial implications of proposed decisions. A finance committee has difficulty in confining its interest to the purely financial effects of corporate plans and programs. The overlapping of interest and responsibility between executive and finance committees almost always results in confusion and duplication unless, of course, one of the committees is content to be a rubber stamp. Although there are corporations with such sizable financial problems that a finance committee is needed to secure the necessary board specialization, any company will be well advised to think twice before including both finance and executive committees in the structure of its corporate board.

Again, experience indicates it is desirable to keep the number of board committees to a minimum. Special committees easily come to have "regular" committee status. Special committees dealing with the compensation of officer-directors or monitoring bonus or stock option plans and other forms of management compensation can be very useful, but special committees with responsibilities for such matters as insurance, long-range planning, corporate development programs, and the like tend to interfere with the operating responsibilities of full-time managers.

It seems far preferable to use *ad hoc* committees appointed by or with the consent of the board as a device for focusing board attention on specific problems, because *ad hoc* committees can be terminated when the job is done, and the risk of having committees usurp board and management prerogatives is minimized.

FUNCTIONS OF THE BOARD

There are two kinds of functions a board performs—its formal, legal functions, and special functions.

Formal Functions. In broad terms, the formal responsibilities of directors are defined by the laws of the state in which the business is incorporated and by the rules set forth in the certificate of incorporation and the corporate bylaws. Although there are wide variations in the detail in which these responsibilities and functions are defined, they fall broadly into two categories: (1) responsibilities for safeguarding and controlling the use of corporate assets and (2) duties involved in discharging legal obligations to manage the affairs of the business.

In carrying out these responsibilities, boards consider policy, select the corporate officers, provide for the continuity of management, measure management's performance, review budgets and long-range plans, declare dividends, and so on.

Special Functions. In addition to these formal obligations, a board has at least three important special functions—to give advice, to help in the selection of management talent, and to keep informed on the consequences of its decisions.

Advising the Chief Executive. Many chief executives consider the advisory function the most important of all the functions of a corporate board and individual directors. A good corporate board always includes individuals whose judgment on business problems can be of great value to a chief executive officer. Usually, such advice is best sought from individuals or small groups of directors on an informal basis. The chief executive should be especially careful not to present basic issues to his board without first seeking the private advice of respected board members.

The director, for his part, must expect to hold himself available to counsel with top management. Frequently, the most important contributions of directors are made in this fashion rather than in formal board meetings.

Selecting and Developing Management Talent. A principal duty of a board of directors is to assure itself that programs are being followed to develop successor management. A chief executive can benefit by securing the help of his directors in appraising management talent. Conscious efforts should therefore be made to expose potential talent to the board. Meetings in various company locations, presentations to the board by selected individuals, social affairs, and properly contrived personal interviews are all devices for exposing promising managers to board members.

Checking on Management Results. Managers frequently are sensitive about board efforts to check up on management results or to learn the actual effect on company fortunes of its policy decisions to build new plants, enter new markets, or acquire new products.

It must be recognized that a board of directors has an obligation to know whether it has contributed to corporate success or failure by picking good management or making wise decisions in policy areas. Any board which fails to check performance is derelict in its duty. A check on the accuracy of forecasts made in justification of a capital expenditure is no more an indication of lack of confidence in management than is an audit of the books.

Unless boards do check periodically on the results of their actions, there can be no assurance that their policies and instructions have been carried out. Also, boards make mistakes, and checks on results are necessary if they are to learn from these errors in judgment.

WORKING WITH A BOARD

How well a board functions can be greatly influenced by the quality of its leadership and the way in which it is kept informed.

Board Leadership as a Factor in Effective Board Performance. Boards of directors are instruments for group action, and the effectiveness of the group is greatly influenced by the caliber of its leadership. The leadership function is the responsibility of the presiding officer, who may be the chief executive, and his skill can make a great difference in the contribution of the board.

Leading a board does not mean dominating a board. A good presiding officer will insist on completed staff work on subjects to be considered by the board—if he is the chief executive, he will ensure that this staff work is forthcoming. He will keep in close touch with the directors and will seek their advice on ways to improve board meetings and to maintain proper communications between the board and management.

In conducting board meetings, the presiding officer should encourage free discussion. It is his responsibility to keep the discussion germane to the subject and to guide the board to decisive action. It is also part of his function to clarify the issues on which the board is to act and to see that all reasonable questions asked by board members are properly answered. Anyone who has served on a board with unskilled or uninterested leadership will recognize the importance of leadership in the effective functioning of a corporate board.

Keeping the Board Informed. The chief executive will be careful to keep his board happy by not shifting the regular meeting date, having too many long meetings (two or three hours should be the rule), or calling too many special meetings (which may indicate a lack of planning ability on his part). He will also see to it that the meetings are productive. A poor attendance record on the part of a director may be a reflection on the director, or it may indicate that meetings are dull and routine. Although it is the presiding officer's responsibility to see that meetings move along in an interesting way, it is the chief executive's responsibility to see that the proper matters come before his board and that it is kept informed and given the right materials to work with.

In a number of areas, it is difficult to define with precision the boundaries between board and management responsibilities and authorities. The wise chief executive will keep his board well informed concerning plans or actions of any important consequence, and will avoid the pitfalls inherent in the lack of clarity in this separation of responsibility.

Directors cannot act intelligently unless they are well informed. The snap decisions of otherwise competent men can be harmful. Too often, directors try to make decisions on company problems solely on the basis of their own experience. This kind of decision making can create serious problems.

Here is where the skill of a chief executive is called for. The following are eight ways in which managements can act to keep their boards informed but not overwhelmed by an avalanche of undigested statistics and reports.

1. Issue agenda in advance of board meetings, preferably a week or ten days in advance. Where necessary, items should be explained in a supplementary memorandum. Staff papers analyzing items on the agenda give directors an opportunity to study the facts and clarify the issues before discussion at the meeting.

2. Circulate the minutes of board and committee meetings. Minutes should be brief and should keep directors informed of matters on which action or ratification may be necessary later.

3. Provide directors with regular summary reports on financial changes and operating results, which highlight trends and deviations from plans. Brief written comments should point up important changes and explain results. These reports require a high level of staff competence in preparation, and directors should be asked to contribute suggestions regarding the material they wish to receive.

4. Give the board an opportunity to review the operating budget and the long-range forecast. Annually, the board should receive the operating budget and review it at a regular meeting. If major budget changes are required, these should be explained to the directors.

Many companies project their plans ahead for five or more years and compute the probable fiscal effects. Whenever these long-range plans are updated (usually annually), the board should receive these estimates, and the plans should be discussed at a board meeting.

5. Schedule periodic presentations on subjects of special interest. These presentations can be made by company personnel working in the areas concerned. Such reports not only inform the directors but can be a way of exposing company talent to the directors' appraisal. Subjects suitable for such treatment include a corporate acquisition program, research and development activities, an explanation of a corporate management development program, or special reports on large capital projects.

6. Include directors on the mailing list to receive all significant news releases, copies of house organs, important advertisements, and the like. This can be overdone, but when properly handled can be an important source of information for directors. At the very least, it can prevent directors from being scooped by their peers in matters appearing in the public press.

7. Make informal, as well as formal, efforts to keep directors informed through telephone calls, letters, and personal visits. Although these personal activities can be carried to extremes, in general more harm is done by failing to communicate with directors than by abusing this privilege.

8. Encourage directors to visit company plants and offices. These visits, arranged through the chief executive, give directors a better understanding of the business. A director visiting a company facility must, of course, be conscious of his obligation not to compromise the normal corporate chain of command by giving advice or expressing opinions which may be interpreted as decisions. It will be well for him to remember that as a director he has no authority. A board can exercise its powers by group action only.

COMPENSATION AND RETIREMENT

Finally come the questions of what should directors be paid and whether there should be an explicit understanding on retirement.

Compensation of Directors. It has already been suggested that most men who consent to serve as corporate directors find little motivation in the actual compensation received for their services. Legally, it is still presumed that directors serve gratuitously. The bylaws of most companies grant directors the authority to establish their own compensation, as well as the compensation of other executives.

Originally, most boards provided for a fixed fee, usually nominal, to be paid each director who attended a board meeting. In the latter part of the 1930s, a discernible trend developed toward greater use of annual retainers, either alone or in combination with meeting fees. Modern practices can be summarized as follows.

1. Per-meeting fees are a common method of paying directors, with $100 the single most usual fee. However, $200 has become an increasingly popular figure.

2. In 1964, as many companies paid directors a retainer (either with or without an additional meeting fee) as paid per-meeting fees. Annual retainers reported ranged from $350 to $10,000.

3. Most companies do not pay per-meeting fees to inside directors. Where fees are paid, however, the amount is usually the same as for outside directors.

4. Very few companies pay inside directors an annual retainer. (This observation does not apply, of course, to the compensation of inside directors for their services as full-time executives, or in those few companies where inside directors spend full time in their directoral capacities.)

5. The 1964 median per-meeting payment for all directors was $250, with a median of $150 for directors paid on a per-meeting basis and about $450 for directors receiving retainers or retainers plus per-meeting fees.

6. About 40 percent of companies paid some fee—most commonly, $100—for attendance at committee meetings. A growing number of companies include committee service in setting annual retainers.

Various fringe benefits are also used increasingly in compensating directors, such as:

Participation in group life insurance programs or coverage in employee travel accident insurance plans

Inclusion in corporate programs which provide for matching employees' gifts to educational institutions or to other charities

Plans to defer current compensation for service as a director until retirement—which has the effect of deferring the income tax on directors' compensation, thus increasing its value as retirement income

Special retirement plans, usually agreeing to pay nominal retirement incomes to directors who have met specified service requirements

A 1964 study by the American Management Association shows that most companies reimburse directors for actual living and traveling expenses when attending meetings of the board or committees or when traveling on company business; a few companies pay a flat fee.

There is a strong consensus that the compensation of directors should be nominal and that it should be linked at least in part to the service actually rendered the corporation. If compensation were to be set at meaningful levels, directors' views could be influenced by this additional factor of self-interest. Directors need to maintain their independence, and they cannot afford to be swayed unduly by the effect of independent action on their livelihood.

Retirement of Directors. The retirement of directors is a relatively new concept in corporate life. Many companies consider board membership a lifetime appointment and leave the matter of retirement to the individual judgment of directors. A number of corporations, however, have established formal retirement policies, and more are expected to follow.

Retirement for Age. Most companies require inside directors to retire from the board when they retire from active management, feeling that the tendency to criticize changes made by the new management team can create friction and resentment. If an inside director's advice is desired after his retirement, this service can be secured by paying him a fee as a consultant.

The mandatory retirement age for outside directors usually is set at seventy or seventy-two years. Some companies require that outside directors cease to serve on standing committees, such as the executive committee, after reaching normal retirement age for employees of the company. The theory here is that there should be a coincidence of age and presumably of outlook among members of key board committees and top management.

The transition to a retirement policy for directors frequently is eased by exempting all present directors from the policy or by postponing the application of the retirement policy until a future date. In actual practice, most directors will recognize the wisdom of a board retirement policy, and the embarrassments which might be expected in the first adoption of such a policy seldom materialize.

Retirement for Cause. The elimination of an unsatisfactory director is a delicate matter. If a director loses his value through publicly recognized wrongdoing, his elimination is less difficult. But when the problem arises from his physical or mental deterioration, his loss of interest, or his inability to work harmoniously with the other directors or the management, the problem of retirement can become a sticky issue.

Usually, the presiding officer or another director will have the task of polling board sentiment concerning the retention of the questionable director. If there is majority agreement on a change, it can frequently be arranged with the unwanted director to fail to stand for reelection. If the problem is more urgent, he can be asked for his resignation, but it is always desirable to avoid an open issue on a matter of this kind.

Boards usually hesitate to press for retirement of a director, feeling that a poorly qualified director can usually be ignored and that the damage he can do to the business is minimal.

SUMMARY

One of the difficulties of dealing with the board of directors as a general subject is that no two companies have the same types of board problems. Very large businesses, with sophisticated professional managers and competent corporate staffs, have very different problems of board selection and management than most medium- and small-sized industrial companies. Commercial enterprises such as banks and insurance companies sometimes must accommodate to special circumstances affecting the size, composition, and scope of activities of their boards of directors or trustees.

There are also those relatively few, but highly publicized, situations in which the board ceases to be an effective instrument for conducting normal custodial and managerial functions, but becomes instead an arena in which factions struggle for the control of the enterprise.   Board problems under these circumstances must be considered abnormal.

However, in any normal situation, in any size of company, the corporate board is recognized as a potentially invaluable adjunct to good management. The utilization and effectiveness of a corporate board is largely the result of the imagination, attitudes, energy, and leadership of the chief executive officer. By selecting his board carefully, by keeping it properly informed, and by making good use of its advice and wisdom, the chief executive can multiply his own effectiveness by taking into account the wider view of that community of which his own enterprise is but a part.

BIBLIOGRAPHY

Brown, Courtney, and E. Everett Smith, *The Director Looks at His Job,* Columbia University Press, New York, 1957.

Copeland, Melvin, *The Board of Directors and Business Management,* Harvard Graduate School of Business Administration, Boston, 1947.

Corporate Directorship Practices, Studies in Business Policy, no. 103, National Industrial Conference Board, New York, 1962.

Feuer, Mortimer, *Personal Liabilities of Corporate Officers and Directors,* Prentice-Hall, Inc., Englewood Cliffs, N.J., 1961.

Jackson, Percival, *Corporate Management: The Directors and Executives,* The Michie Company, Charlottesville, Va., 1955.

"Keeping Outside Directors Informed," *Conference Board Business Record,* March, 1961.

Mace, Myles L., *The Board of Directors in Small Corporations,* Harvard Graduate School of Business Administration, Boston, 1948.

CHAPTER THREE

Establishing Company Objectives

WILLIAM E. HILL *Managing Partner, William E. Hill & Company, Inc., New York, New York*

CHARLES H. GRANGER *Partner, William E. Hill & Company, Inc., New York, New York*

This chapter discusses the uses of objectives for a company and how they are set. After considering the somewhat specialized definition of the term "objectives" as it is commonly used by companies having formalized objectives, the practical importance and applications of objectives are examined. Particular emphasis is placed on strategic objectives, in contrast to operational objectives.

Nine types of objectives are classified, and their interrelationships are shown. Also discussed are five characteristics or tests of well-formulated objectives. The chapter then proceeds, with illustrations, to show a practical way by which many companies first establish formalized objectives, and how these initial efforts can be expanded upon to produce a well-rounded concept of strategic objectives for the enterprise.

As a concluding note, the emerging tendency to relate the objectives of the total enterprise to the objectives of individual positions is discussed.

"OBJECTIVES" DEFINED

In business use, there is widespread agreement that the term "objective" can be used synonymously with "aim or end of action," or "desired future state." There are, however, some further ramifications of the term. An objective may be not only "an aim or end of action"—for example, to be the leading producer of household paper products—but also *a guide to action*. Thus one frequently encounters in statements of objectives descriptions of policy as well as end points—for example, to conduct research for the development of superior household paper products. This is hardly a desired end point in itself.

A number of firms which have spent much time and thought in defining their objectives use the term "objective" to apply to the broader, ongoing type of goal, such as growth in earnings per common share. These firms specifically use the term "goal" or "target" or "standard" for the quantification or measurement of the objective, such as $5 earnings per common share by 1970. Although not uncommon, this terminology is far from universal. If it is a convenient device in any given case, it is probably quite suitable.

PRACTICAL IMPORTANCE OF HAVING STATED OBJECTIVES

The question is sometimes raised of the practical importance of having stated objectives. Here we are talking about objectives of the written type, communicated to those management people with the need to know. We are not necessarily referring to a particular piece of paper entitled "Our Objectives," and even less so to the plaque one so often sees on the reception room wall headed "Our Objectives." These written objectives may well be part of some other document—for example, part of the company long-range plan or the minutes of a planning conference. The important thing is that they exist in written form and that the various upper and middle management people know about them and understand them.

The question furthermore has to be looked at from two standpoints. The first is the probably more interesting question of the importance of strategic and longer-range objectives. The second, and less frequently debated point, is the importance of shorter-range or operational objectives.

The reasons for the importance of short-term objectives can be equated to the reasons for the importance of budgeting (see Chapter 4 of Section 10), and boil down to the fact that more desirable results can usually be achieved, especially in a complex organization, if there is some sort of control system which explicitly states desired standards of performance throughout the organization and has built-in measures against these standards so deviations can be promptly corrected. Whereas conventional budgeting emphasizes financial standards, some interesting results are being achieved in use of nonfinancial operational objectives as well (such as quality levels and service levels). One airline, for example, has an operational objective or standard that 90 percent of incoming telephone calls be answered within ten seconds.

The importance of strategic or longer-range objectives of the enterprise is based on somewhat different reasons. Fundamentally, the companies which use stated strategic objectives do so to accomplish results on a much broader and more successful scale than could ever be accomplished on year-to-year or month-to-month operational objectives. For example, one chemical company has had excellent overall results—but analysis shows that these overall results have been a combination of several exceptional acquisitions and joint ventures, whereas the six existing divisions have been producing a rather mediocre profit return. As a result, certain longer-range strategic objectives have now been set in the product groups representing the traditional divisions; these will involve upgrading and changing the nature of their businesses, and in some cases, discontinuation of the present lines. This upgrading will be a five-year process and can only be conceived, measured, and implemented in strategic terms rather than on a year-to-year basis.

A second reason underlying the importance of strategic objectives is often overlooked: A company has no choice in whether or not to set some types of strategic objectives—within limits, they are already set for a company willy-nilly. By way of illustration, in a public company, the stockholders (as represented by the sophisticated financial community which really makes the market in a stock) have certain expectations or strategic objectives for growth in earnings per share and dividends. If a company exceeds these externally set objectives, it will prosper at least in light of the price paid for the stock in the financial community—and, of course, vice versa. Furthermore, customers have strategic objectives or standards (it is amazing how many short-term disappointments customers will put up with) for a company's quality, service, prices, and new-product introduction. If a company exceeds these externally set standards or objectives, it will rise in the customers' eyes with increasing sales volume—and vice versa. Similarly, employees, who are also prone to put up with all sorts of short-term hardships, have set objectives for the company by way of advancement in pay, status, conditions, and other rewards. If a company does not meet these employee-set objectives, it will find it is losing its better people and is unable to attract new ones.

Because such strategic objectives (within limits) are already set for a company, the issue is not whether or not to have them. The issue is rather whether explicitly to recognize them in written and communicated form and to use these as control devices and stimulants to more effective action.

Without stated strategic objectives, it is much less likely that a company can capitalize on the opportunities available to it. For example, one company has a superior distribution system to the food retailing trade. Should it continue selling the existing product line, adding new products now and again as happenstance dictates, or should it set specific strategic objectives for new-products volume to capitalize on its position? There are, of course, pros and cons to such a question. After much study, specific objectives have been established for volume and earnings from new products which in results go far beyond what might have been achieved without strategic objectives in this area.

Similarly, many companies have used stated strategic objectives to overcome limitations or constraints in their existing businesses. For example, one medium-sized paper company had a high and quite profitable share of a particularly rapidly growing segment of the market. It could foresee new large-company competition coming in and driving down profit margins. It adopted, also after much study, certain strategic objectives of a quite specific nature as to amount and type for entry into certain classes of new products. The threatened change in the original business has now come about, but—because it set effective strategic objectives—the company continues to prosper.

Great leaders, from Alexander of Macedon to Theodore N. Vail, have proved that the stated strategic objective—especially if it has "stretch" built into it—can spur the organization to achieve otherwise unthinkable results. It can stimulate the organization into creative action that would rarely have taken place without the challenge of a sweeping strategic objective.

Needless to say, explicitly stated objectives can avoid much confusion in the ranks. One sometimes hears the comment, "We don't need to write down our objectives because all our management team fully understands them." This just is not so. It is a sadly amusing fact that, unless the management team has spent some time working specifically on a statement of objectives, there is probably considerable unrecognized disagreement and confusion on just what the main objectives and the priorities of the enterprise are. This has been confirmed time and again by having key management people independently write down or discuss in interviews their concepts of the principal company objectives and the priorities which should be attached thereto. The differences of opinion are remarkable.

A final important use of objectives, which is still in an emerging stage, is as a management development tool in relating the objectives of the enterprise to the objectives of the individual. This is discussed further below.

TYPES OF OBJECTIVES IN USE

There are a number of classes of objectives ("aims or ends of action," "guides to action") in common business use. In some companies, they overlap and interlock into what might be thought of as a "system" of objectives. It is useful to understand what these different classes of objectives are. However, experience has shown that it is not necessary for every firm to have most of these classes of objectives in explicit written form. In fact, as described below, it would be undesirable for a firm which was setting down its objectives for the first time to undertake establishing explicit directions in many of these categories at once.

Creeds. A creed is an ordered statement of beliefs. Creeds are probably the most sweeping (and least specific) of the commonly used objectives or guides to action. They are often, but not always, couched in self-righteous terms that perhaps have more value for public relations than actual decision-making purposes—for example, statements that the company will earn a fair return for its stockholders, provide superior products and service to its customers, and be good to its employees, vendors, the communities in which it operates, and to the public at large. The real test of the practicality of the creed type of objective is whether the company really lives by it even when it hurts. For example, one large and well-known company has continually espoused full employment in creed-type statements; it has passed up a number of short-term but attractive profit opportunities in military work because of its instability and inconsistency with full employment; when technical obsolescence has outdated some processes, it has spent very important sums of money in retraining its employees to new skills. This is an example of one of the minority of situations where the creed is not just a hollow statement.

Grand Design. Perhaps the next broadest class of objective is the grand-design type. This is a sweeping and usually visionary concept of the business. It too can be merely a public relations slogan, or it can be conscientiously pursued. In the latter category is the Bell System statement, "We will build a telephone system so that anybody, anywhere, can talk with anyone else, anywhere in the world, quickly, cheaply, and satisfactorily." Another is the Sears, Roebuck statement, "The company sees itself not so much as a catalog merchant or retailer, but as an organized system for efficient and economical distribution, dedicated to serving the public with a broad range of goods and services, and to meeting any change in demand."

Charters. Charters are the next most general class of objective. Some companies have what might be called "charter statements," but they are most commonly found spelling out the scope of division activities in multidivision companies—especially where it may be desirable to avoid overlap or conflict with other company activities. Thus a charter for a division of a chemical company might spell out the product scope of the division, possibly its geographical scope, markets to be served, and the like.

Long-range Plans. These constitute the next most specific type of objective, and usually embrace a great many subobjectives, such as share of markets served, volume and earnings objectives in present and new products, and objectives in each of the functional areas, such as marketing, manufacturing, technical, finance, and organization. Good long-range plans also spell out the action steps for achieving the objectives.

It is noteworthy that, as objectives become more specific, they are more prone to change with time. Creeds, if well stated, seldom change. Grand designs may change only with the coming of a new chief executive and not necessarily then.   Charters are necessarily adjusted from time to time.   Long-range plans, although they may not change radically from year to year, are usually updated annually.

Budgets.   These are also a set of objectives, expressed in financial terms.   Primary emphasis is often on cost control rather than broader strategy.

Additional Types of Objectives.   Several additional classes of objectives, although they are very real "ends of action" or "guides to action," do not fit neatly into an arrangement with the above categories, but rather cut across them.

Policies.   Policies are merely guidelines to action in certain recurring situations.   They nevertheless constitute very real objectives.

Key Result Areas.   One sometimes finds objectives, whether for a department, division, or a total company, couched in terms of the eight key result areas developed by Peter F. Drucker and General Electric.   In this approach, the main areas in which objectives and standards of performance are set are market standing, innovation, productivity, physical and financial resources, profitability, manager performance and development, worker performance and attitude, and public responsibility.   The idea is that continuing failure in any of these areas will result in failure of the enterprise.   Hence there should be objectives and performance standards in each.

Objectives Emphasizing Internal Opportunities and Challenges.   From time to time, one encounters objectives, which are quite real and quite appropriate, stressing to the exclusion of almost everything else certain internal opportunities or challenges.   A well-publicized example was Textron's making use of available tax credits.   There are other cases where a company's objectives have been overwhelmingly colored by other internal challenges, such as the need to capitalize on a research discovery while lead time over competition still exists, or the pressing need to obtain additional financing.   In such situations, other, more normal classes of objectives become quite secondary.

Objectives Emphasizing External Opportunities and Challenges.   These objectives are similar to those described in the preceding paragraph.   Presumably an overriding objective of the old Suez Canal Company was to take steps to protect itself against nationalization.   In other situations, changing competitive conditions may dictate seeking merger on favorable terms as the all-important objective—this happened to a number of independent shipping container manufacturers in the 1950s, when competitive shifts made integration necessary. When such situations exist, consideration of other types of objectives may become either quite secondary or altogether hypothetical.

THE DISTINGUISHING CHARACTERISTICS OF GOOD OBJECTIVES

Before proceeding to a discussion of how to set objectives in a particular case, it is well to consider the characteristics of objectives.   Some of these characteristics which objectives should have to be both effective and practical are as follows.

1. They should be a guide to action and explicit enough to suggest certain types of action.   Objectives should be helpful in decision making, not pious statements.   For example, "to carry on a profitable broad-line business in chemical specialties sold to the food industry" would seem to be a helpful objective in this respect.   A less explicit statement, such as "to make profits" or even "to make profits in the chemical business," would seem to be less helpful.

2. The objective should suggest tools to measure and control effectiveness. "To produce a growth in earnings per share and level of profit return comparable

to other companies in our field and to industry generally" would seem to do this. "To produce a fair return for the stockholders" is vague and less helpful. "To produce 5 percent annual earnings growth and 10 percent net profit on invested capital" is too inflexible. In good years, a company should do considerably better than such a fixed objective; in poor years, it may also be meaningless as there is no chance of meeting it.

3. Is the objective challenging? Frederick R. Kappel, Chairman of AT&T, suggests that in setting objectives which create vitality in a business, it is necessary to distinguish between the possible and the impossible, but to be willing to get very close to the latter.

4. The whole set of objectives should make sense. With rare exceptions, there is no single overriding objective. Profits are not the overriding objective, or more companies would be in organized gambling, bootlegging, and similar very profitable activities. Objectives have to be balanced in relation to one another. Very often, the first drafts have to be "recycled" to iron out inconsistencies.

5. Objectives, especially strategic objectives, must take into consideration external opportunities and constraints, and internal opportunities and constraints. Experience shows that it is not possible to sit down at one internal session, whether it is a week long or a year long, and write down a reasonably practical and specific set of objectives. It is necessary to study not only a company's internal challenges and opportunities, which can be done internally, but also its *external* opportunities and challenges, which can be done only by studying the trends in the company's business environment and selecting among these externally directed alternatives. For example, is it more desirable to set strategic objectives incorporating expanding in present lines domestically, expanding abroad, adding new forms of distribution, branching into related products for present markets, or similar alternatives? Any organization is faced with approximately ten such possibilities, and they require a certain amount of study of external conditions and trends ahead.

WHERE TO START IN SETTING COMPANY OBJECTIVES

Assume that a company has not heretofore given much attention to formalized or written objectives. Perhaps for some of the reasons outlined above, it now feels the need to do so.

The first principle to follow is to limit initial statements of objectives to questions which are quite recognizably of practical concern. The subject of objectives is too full of complexities and subtleties to be attacked comprehensively on the first undertaking. Even if a highly enthusiastic chief executive is spearheading the effort, he will find that if he attempts to work out with his people the first five or seven classes of objectives enumerated in the foregoing list, his people will soon become disillusioned with what to them seems to be a theoretical exercise. The more practical approach is to select a limited starting point, cover it well, and then branch out into other items on the list as the need to do so (which may indeed be very real) becomes recognized by the management group.

Objectives setting, to be most effective, calls for a certain degree of group participation. It is a well-recognized principle that people will work harder to achieve objectives which they have helped establish. On the other hand, the participation should be limited to that handful of people who really have primary responsibility for fulfilling the objectives. The chief executive and the group reporting to him would be adequate (or possibly more than adequate in some companies) for this purpose in setting overall corporate objectives. To have the next lower echelon as well would in many cases produce more of a training session than a working session.

On the other hand, in the last analysis, after all factors have been weighed, the chief executive is the one who must "call the shots." One can think of a number of outstandingly successful companies which have been strongly influenced and led by the chief executive. Their results would probably not be nearly so impressive if the chief executive established company objectives by a form of opinion polling among the top people.

Profit objectives make a very practical starting place. There are several advantages in beginning at this point: practically all managers, and directors as well, can see the desirability of profit objectives; they lead readily, when the time is ripe, into consideration of other types of objectives, such as strategic product objectives; they lend themselves readily to broadening comparisons of results in other companies.

The selection of the types of profit objectives is not as simple as might first appear. One could consider profit growth, or profit level (return on investment), or (especially in cyclical fields) profit stability. For publicly held companies, profit growth—as measured in growth in earnings per common share—is usually the aspect of profit to be emphasized. The attitude of sophisticated stockholders is determined by the opinion of the dozen or so leading security analysts, research directors, and portfolio managers of major brokerage houses, funds, and trust companies. Their attitude can often be expressed in seven words, "What have you done for me lately?" If earnings per share are going up, the stock price will go up, there is at least the potential for increased dividends, and the multiplier may also rise. If earnings per share are not increasing, no matter how glorious the return on investment or earnings stability may be, the pace-setting professional investors tend to lose interest.

Return on investment, especially if it can be made to increase, can be an important contributor to growth in earnings per share, and therefore cannot be altogether ignored. Also, return on investment may well be the profit factor to be emphasized at the division level.

The following form of analysis is helpful: Compare during the postwar period the record of your company, companies of a somewhat comparable nature as viewed by professional investors, and the composite record for all companies of your type (for example, Standard & Poor's 425 Industrials—this information is available from Standard & Poor's Corporation). In one analysis, compare growth in earnings per common share on semilog paper. In a second analysis, plot return on investment (earnings per share divided by book value per share happens to be convenient because data are available for stock groups).

This analysis will probably suggest profit objectives for consideration by the policy-forming group along the following lines. If earnings growth, the level of return on investment, and earnings stability have been less than those of comparable companies and the general company composite, it suggests minimum objectives of at least coming up to the trend in other companies. If the record is about comparable with those of other companies, this suggests a floor to be improved upon if possible. If the record is superior to those of other companies, this suggests at least maintaining this degree of superiority in the future. In the latter case, stockholders, and in a more general way employees and customers, have come to expect superior performance from your company and the accompanying conditions in employment opportunity, customer service, and the like.

Assume, for example, that as a result of this analysis a company is thinking in terms of a trend-line growth rate in earnings per common share of 7 percent annually and net profit on investment averaging slightly above the industry, or 15 percent per year. These objectives should normally have a little "stretch" or "reach" in them. The next step is to establish supporting objectives which will permit the attaining of these overall corporate profit objectives.

Similar analysis can be made for the individual divisions or product groups to see what objectives can be established for them for, say, the coming five-year period. This analysis should make heavy use of market forecasts and expected future trends in market, competitive, and technical conditions. When enlarged to include supporting action programs, this becomes division-level long-range planning (see Chapters 4 and 5 of Section 3).

Companies experienced in this aspect of objectives setting find it helpful to revise divisional long-range objectives each year by "adding a year and dropping a year." It usually takes several years' experience before divisional long-range planning of this type becomes reasonably reliable. Corporate overall financial objectives may also be revised periodically. As might be expected, there is frequently much back-and-forth discussion between the divisions and headquarters over what constitutes suitable objectives for a given division.

It frequently happens, if corporate objectives have some stimulation or stretch built into them, that the sum of the division objectives falls short of the objectives for the total corporation. What then? Filling the "gap" requires a refinement and expansion of thinking about objectives from the simpler profit types of objectives to company objectives of a truly strategic nature.

OBJECTIVES GOVERNING THE BUSINESS STRATEGY OF CORPORATE DEVELOPMENT

The foregoing types of objectives frequently involve an implied presupposition that the enterprise will pretty much adopt a future course which is not a radical departure from "keeping on doing what we have been doing"—perhaps doing it a little better. Partly because of the recognized need to fill the "gap" mentioned above, it is necessary to examine the question, "What should the enterprise *really* be doing in the future?"

Examining the various classes of objectives listed above, we see that grand designs, charters, objectives emphasizing internal opportunities and challenges, and objectives emphasizing external opportunities and challenges all have a bearing on this subject. How can they be attacked?

There are several underlying principles to be borne in mind. One is to capitalize on our strengths and opportunities. It is important to recognize that these are both internal, such as a certain type of manufacturing or technical skill, and external, such as a certain established market position or a new growth segment of the market opening up. A related principle is offsetting our limitations, both internal and external. Further principles relate to first establishing *criteria* for the future shape of the company and then screening all possibilities against these criteria.

Criteria for establishing strategic objectives for a company can be set up in the following categories.

1. *Profit opportunity*—growth, level, stability, and size of earnings.

2. *Compatibility and future development requirements*—capitalizing on our outstanding strengths and resources, and the concept of management under which the enterprise has prospered. This requires analysis of the products, markets, proprietary management functions, and business resources which make the company competitively unique and successful. Also, the opportunities that will capitalize on the pattern of corporate development and contribute new skills and resources should be considered.

3. *Feasibility*—any strategic objectives set through this pattern must be feasible in terms of financial resources, management resources, and the practical opportunity for actually carrying out the course indicated by the objective.

4. *Stockholder and management criteria*—in some companies, these have an important bearing on company objectives. In some companies, the stockholders might have a strong need to "go public," or to increase the liquidity of the shares, or to have liberal dividends, or to have sparse dividends. Management itself may also have particular requirements that are distinct and subject to consideration.

The above criteria do not, of course, make explicit objectives in themselves. To establish objectives of the charter or grand-design type, it is necessary to examine all practical alternatives in light of these criteria. These alternatives should be examined as business opportunities, for example, in the following categories.

1. In related businesses in the industry—for example, if a company now makes bearings, examination of opportunities in other types of bearings and mechanical power-transmission equipment

2. In businesses serving the same markets—for example, if a company is now in certain products for the educational market, examination of the range of other products serving the same market

3. In businesses based on similar technologies

4. Integration forward toward the market, or backward toward raw materials

5. Geographical expansion in this country and abroad

6. Business opportunities involving new forms of distribution to present markets—direct versus dealers, and the like

7. Expansion into a range of hard goods, soft goods, and service businesses

For comprehensiveness, many companies which have thoroughly studied their strategic objectives have also examined, in addition to the above categories, *all* business opportunities and *all* acquisition opportunities. This work is often assigned to a planning or corporate development group or to an outside consulting staff operating in a similar capacity.

The process leads to increasingly intense cycles of study, screening, and elimination. As the possibilities are further narrowed down, they are subjected to more and more study until finally a company can say: "These are our strategic objectives. Here is the strategic pattern we should pursue; here is our charter or our grand design; and here are the master steps in implementation."

Sears, Roebuck has evidenced an interesting strategic pattern involving various forms of retailing, a range of insurance services, operation of mutual funds, savings and loan, shopping-center operation, and expansion abroad. Some of the major oil companies have expanded into certain types of chemicals, services for the motoring public such as insurance or motels, and even real estate operation on a large scale. A more moderate-sized company, the McCall Corporation, as part of fulfilling its strategic objectives, has branched out into printing textbooks, telephone directories, and medium-run periodicals, and specialized commercial printing. There are many other examples including rather small companies where such a pattern has been based on conscientious pursuit of strategic objectives.

Such conditions can, of course, happen as a result of unthought-out opportunism. But in the examples cited above, as is the trend generally, strategic objectives have been arrived at in advance—by selecting the most promising from among the many opportunities available. In a dynamic organization, the process is never quite finished; it is subject to continuing refinement and evolution.

MANAGEMENT BY OBJECTIVES

There is little question that since the beginning of the 1950s the art or science of establishing company objectives, and supporting subobjectives for the component units of the business, has become rather highly developed. Now an interesting by-product of the process is beginning to emerge. But the by-product itself, often called "management by objectives" or some similar title, feeds back into company objectives by facilitating their attainment.

In management by objectives, some half-dozen specific and measurable objectives are established for each position. They are usually revised annually by the incumbent and his superior. They are over and above the customary "meet the budget" objective which is part of each person's job. They are closely related to and derived from the long-range plan type of objectives for the total company or the various component units.

Users of this approach have found several advantages which make it well worth the effort. For one thing, they have found that superior achievement is obtained when specific, measurable objectives—with a time limit for fulfillment—are set on each individual job. Another major advantage is as a management training device; perhaps the surest way to develop managerial skill and promotability to higher responsibility is to provide a means to help achieve superior results on the present job.

SUMMARY

The use of written and communicated objectives is now becoming quite common in business organizations. These company objectives relate closely to the planning process. Users find that by having objectives, especially of the broader, strategic type, they are able to achieve superior results and are able to consider alternatives more creatively than would otherwise be the case.

There are many types of objectives which tend to interlock and form a system of guidelines to action in any given case. However, to first establish company objectives, it is most effective to begin with simple, long-range profit objectives. The other types of objectives can then be developed as the need for them becomes apparent—for example, in laying out strategic new growth directions for a company.

Objectives for the total enterprise, and the supporting objectives for the individual component units of the enterprise, can also be broken down into interim specific objectives or individual positions. Use of this practice of "management by objectives" is an effective means of both developing managerial ability and achieving superior results in the undertaking.

BIBLIOGRAPHY

Drucker, Peter F., *Managing for Results,* Harper & Row, Publishers, Incorporated, New York, 1964.

Granger, Charles H., "The Hierarchy of Objectives," *Harvard Business Review,* May–June, 1964.

Hill, William E., "Planning for Profits," *California Management Review,* Spring, 1959.

Miller, Ernest C., *Management by Objectives and the Use of Performance Standards,* American Management Association, New York, 1965.

Thompson, Stewart, *How Companies Plan,* American Management Association, New York, 1962.

Wikstrom, Walter S., *Developing Managerial Competence,* National Industrial Conference Board, New York, 1964.

CHAPTER FOUR

Business Forecasting*

LEONARD S. SILK *Vice Chairman and Economist,* Business Week *Magazine, New York, New York*

Business forecasting is the analysis of statistical data and other economic, political, and market information for the purpose of reducing the risks involved in making business decisions and long-range plans.

The importance of business forecasting can scarcely be exaggerated: Correct forecasts can spell profits and growth; wrong forecasts can cause serious financial losses or failure. Growing awareness of the critical importance of forecasting to business and the economy generally has led to increasing concentration by economists upon the task of improving forecasting techniques. American corporations are increasingly drawing upon economic and statistical techniques of forecasting as a means of strengthening the basis for business decisions.

The Need for Business Forecasting. Management decisions in the areas of production, purchasing, finance, personnel, marketing, inventories, and capital spending depend upon the answers to questions such as these:

What will the general state of business be? What will be the demand for our products?

Will we be able to get the number and kinds of employees we will need? Or will we be laying off people? What is going to happen to wage rates?

What will be the effect on our sales if we change our prices? What are our competitors likely to do?

Where will the growing markets for our products be? What new industrial or regional developments are likely to create new opportunities for us?

What types of new products ought we to be developing?

Have we enough production capacity to meet probable future demand?

What outside financing will we require? What is it likely to cost us? Is this a good time to seek it, or should we wait?

* Adapted from *Forecasting Business Trends,* by Leonard S. Silk, published by McGraw-Hill Book Company, New York, 1963.

Should we be working down our inventories? Or are we likely to get caught short?

Questions like these go to the very heart of the managerial problem. The answers to all such questions necessitate forecasting. So the problem for business management is not whether to forecast, because it must—but how to forecast.

Approach to Business Forecasting. Although business forecasts cannot be expected to be as dependable and exact as predictions made in the physical sciences, business forecasts *can* be constructed in accordance with what we may call "scientific method"—that is, by attempting to collect all information relevant to the problem and by drawing logical inferences from this information.

Business forecasting requires time and work and, for the best results, economic skills of a high order. Business has grown so big and complex that managements of many companies find themselves confronted by tasks where decisions based on hunch or old rules of thumb are liable to large and costly mistakes. Under these circumstances, management is increasingly turning to professional economists for forecasting and other business research.

Many academic economists still regard business forecasting as a low, somewhat sporty pursuit, which social scientists are wise to avoid. Within the business world, however, the hazards of forecasting cannot be avoided; indeed, business forecasting is too important to be left to the business forecasters alone. Managers must reach their own conclusions about the outlook. And they must give direction and criticism to their staff technicians, encourage them to do the best possible work in this difficult field, and seek to extract from staff economic reports their maximum value.

Even if a company can afford to employ outstanding economic talent, high-level executives obviously cannot delegate to staff economists or outside consultants the responsibility for making final judgments about the business outlook and what it implies for their particular business. So management itself should seek always to improve its competence in this important field.

Managers should not expect too much of forecasting. Business will always remain to some extent a gamble. But a good gambler always tries to get the best odds he can. In business, the odds must improve when management acts on the basis of full and up-to-date information and careful analysis of the changing business picture.

STRATEGIES OF FORECASTING

Any logical approach to business forecasting is based on three assumptions:

1. Economic magnitudes—such as levels of production, income, prices, wages, interest rates, and consumer expenditures—are bound together in a system that has considerable stability over time.

2. Future changes in those magnitudes will result, to an appreciable extent, from presently operating causes, or may be deduced from presently observable symptoms.

3. The nature of those symptoms or causes, and their probable future consequences, may be discovered by studying past experience.

From these assumptions—which, incidentally, underlie not simply business forecasting but the whole of economic theory and statistics—we derive three basic strategies of forecasting: deterministic, symptomatic, and systematic strategies.

The deterministic strategy assumes that the present has a close causal relation to the future. This strategy would be used, for example, to predict construction expenditures by a knowledge of construction contract awards already made.

The symptomatic strategy assumes that present signs show how the future is developing; such signs do not "determine" the future, but reveal the process of change which is already taking place. This strategy calls for the spotting of "leading indicators"—time series whose movements foreshadow rises or declines in general business activity.

The systematic strategy assumes that, though changes in the real world may seem accidental or chaotic, careful analysis can reveal certain underlying regularities (sometimes called principles, theories, or laws). The way to find these regularities is to black out much of reality and hold only to the abstractions which make up a system, such as a solar system, a nuclear system, or an economic system.

Though the theories that result from this process of abstraction are "unreal," they may nevertheless possess the power to affect the real world—provided, of course, that the theories are sound. The test of the soundness of a theory is how it measures up when applied to reality; for example, an atomic explosion confirms Einstein's $E = mc^2$. Similarly, a price cut which leads to increased sales confirms the hypothetical demand curve that no man has ever seen outside an economics textbook. To be sure, economic "laws" do not have the consistency of those in the physical sciences. Nevertheless, economic relations or theories, derived from a study of the past, may be useful tools for prediction, within some acceptable range of probable error.

Advantages and Applicability of Basic Strategies. The great advantage of the simplest approach to forecasting, that which we have called the *deterministic* method, is its very simplicity. It would have been vain, in a period of defense buildup, such as World War II, for a business economist to have performed vast and complex analyses to predict the government's steel or copper requirements—if he could have examined the official document governing procurement requirements. Because of its emphasis upon the necessity of full, fast, and accurate reporting as part of the forecasting operation, and because, under many circumstances, it is the surest forecasting technique, the deterministic approach will never be made obsolete by more "sophisticated" methods.

Nevertheless, the accuracy of forecasts produced by the deterministic method varies greatly—and it varies inversely with the length of time to be covered by the forecast. Today's plans may not be changed tomorrow—but they may be changed next month, and will almost certainly be changed next year. It may be necessary, as in forecasting capital spending by business, to supplement the findings of capital spending surveys by economic analyses which try to weigh the effect of expected changes in general business activity upon announced capital spending plans. In such a case, the simplest and most direct solution to the forecasting problem simply may be inadequate. To deal with any extremely complicated forecasting problem—such as the course of the American economy for a year or more ahead—obviously there can be no "deterministic" solution.

The particular advantage of the *symptomatic* or "leading indicator" approach is its concentration upon one of the most important problems for the business forecaster in a free economy: the determination of a coming turning point in the business cycle. Some analysts prefer to consider the implications of a large number of indicators separately, without attempting to blend them into a combined index; others find it useful to synthesize a forecasting index out of the separate time series. But few, if any, analysts would put their trust solely in the movements of the leading indicators, whether taken singly or combined. The great majority of analysts would regard forecasting by the indicators alone as too mechanistic, and would seek further explanations of the likely future course of business through general economic analysis of the underlying forces affecting business.

The *systematic* approach to business forecasting is essential for the diagnosis of very complex problems in which the interaction of many factors must be analyzed. The forecaster using this approach may carefully define his assumptions and set up his analysis in strict mathematical formulas, derived from his measurement of past relationships of economic factors. This is the so-called econometric or model-building approach. Or the forecaster, though taking an essentially systematic approach, may prefer to deal with the available data less rigorously and to depend more upon his intuitions and common sense.

The great advantage of the less rigorous approach is that it enables the analyst to range freely over the whole terrain of factors which bear upon his problem and to employ his insights in reaching conclusions which could not be rigorously derived from the evidence, but which, nevertheless, may prove more nearly correct than the results of "correct" logic. Some economists feel that the trouble with the econometric approach is that it necessarily assumes a consistency of relationships among economic variables which the facts of the real world will not support.

Still the strict, econometric approach has many advantages:

It prevents the economist from "faking"—that is, pretending to have worked out an analysis of many factors when he has only stated what the factors are and has produced a conclusion that has slight, if any, relationship to the factors discussed.

It takes full advantage of the evidence of past economic relations and events, and does this in a way that can be checked.

It clearly casts into the discard obsolete or erroneous theories.

It can usefully be applied to many intricate business problems, such as the demand for particular products or future movements of costs.

For many business analysts, econometric model building of even a quite simple sort can be a useful start in the preparation of a forecast. It may give the first approximation of the forecast's structure, on which the analyst can continue to build.

In summary, in business forecasting, an approach which tries to take advantage of the best qualities of several techniques is necessary for three reasons:

1. The wide variety of types of forecasting problems calls for the use of quite different techniques.

2. The record of no single forecasting technique has been so unerring as to eliminate all other methods.

3. In a field where no technique can be depended upon always to yield accurate results, it is desirable to check the forecasts obtained by one method against those reached by other methods.

DETERMINISTIC TECHNIQUES OF FORECASTING

Deterministic techniques cover cases where a *close causal connection or a rough identity* is perceived between present and future. As we use the term "deterministic," however, we do not mean it to imply an absolutely fixed and irreversible relation between present and future. In the real economic world, completely fixed relationships do not exist.

Deterministic techniques may be used to forecast particular elements, such as capital spending, residential construction, or consumer expenditures, or they may be used, often in combination with other methods, to forecast general business conditions.

The principal deterministic techniques are the following.

Latest Information.   This technique, which is of great importance for short-run forecasting, is built on the assumption that economic magnitudes and relationships change slowly.   Hence, if one has the very latest information, one can generally assume that existing conditions or trends will continue for some time into the future.   For instance, one can do very well as a business forecaster (assuming that the very short run is all that one need worry about) by always predicting that next week's business will be the same as this week's, or that the current trend of business will last for a time.   All one misses this way are the turning points!

This technique is obviously naïve—but that does not make it any the less important to business for dealing with problems like setting weekly or even monthly production schedules, ordering merchandise, setting prices, and so on.

However complicated or sophisticated the forecasting operation may become, a business can never dispense with the necessity for fast reporting and analysis of all the significant facts about the changing business picture.

Knowledge of Programs or Limits.   A number of important factors bearing on the economic future are determined in advance and can be expected to remain virtually stable, or to change at a foreseeable rate, through the forecast period— such as budgeted government expenditures on goods and services, statutory tax provisions, capital budgets of business corporations, business contracts, population and labor force, wage rates determined by collective bargaining contracts or by minimum wage legislation, industrial capacity, the stock of houses or automobiles of some specified age, and so on.   These factors may be important in and of themselves, and they may also be used as elements which will affect, but not be significantly affected by, economic developments during the forecast period.   They may be the limiting factors on other, more variable types of economic activity.

For instance, a forecast of the production of durable consumer goods during a war emergency would depend essentially upon the availability of steel for civilian use after essential military programs had taken their share of the steel industry's total-capacity output.   (We assume that the general situation during the defense buildup will be one of full employment and high consumer demand.)

Spotting the Beginning of a Lengthy Process.   Certain presently available facts can be regarded either as causes or as early phases of future economic activities. Many such facts are available to the businessman.   For instance, contracts for residential and industrial building precede actual construction; the shipping of coal and iron ore precedes steel production; new orders or unfilled orders of manufacturers largely determine production; mortgage and installment debt contracted by consumers largely determine future repayments; approved company plans for investment in plant and equipment precede the execution of those plans.

In none of these cases is there a perfect causal connection between the initial and later stages of the process.   Construction work may be delayed or accelerated; contracts may be canceled; new orders may represent duplicate ordering for fear of shortages or strikes; floods, material, or manpower shortages may curtail production; consumers may default on debts or change their "propensities" to spend or save; businesses may delay or cancel capital spending and expansion plans.

Nevertheless, a close enough relation between initial and later stages of an economic process will usually exist to make forecasting on the basis of advance information feasible.

Diagnosing People's Expectations. The so-called expectational or psychological approach assumes that businessmen's and consumers' states of mind play a determining role in economic developments and that surveys of their expectations will have forecasting value.

Business observers should be curious about public states of mind and expectations, which often derive from a detailed knowledge of individuals' judgment of their own "objective condition," their financial status, employment prospects, and the like. In an economy like ours, the decisions of private individuals, as producers or consumers, cannot be predicted wholly on the basis of economic data. Hence, attempts to discover significant changes in public optimism or pessimism, which may imply greater or less willingness to spend or invest, may reveal information which an economist should attempt to relate to a broader analysis based upon more "objective" economic and financial information.

Some of the principal surveys of business or consumer expectations are as follows:

McGraw-Hill Department of Economics surveys of capital spending plans

Securities and Exchange Commission—Department of Commerce surveys of capital spending plans

National Industrial Conference Board—*Newsweek* surveys of capital appropriations

Survey Research Center of the University of Michigan consumer surveys

Department of Commerce, Bureau of Census consumer surveys

Dun & Bradstreet Surveys of Businessmen's Expectations

Monthly Business Survey of the National Association of Purchasing Agents

Railroad Shippers' Forecasts, conducted under auspices of the American Association of Railroads

Fortune magazine surveys, including surveys of business expectations and mood, retail sales, farm spending, homebuilding, inventories, and capital goods production

Manufacturers' Sales and Inventory Expectations of the U.S. Department of Commerce

Expectational surveys of this type are a broader application of one of the traditional business approaches to the forecasting problem: asking one's salesmen or dealers how much they expect to sell in a coming period.

The most serious weaknesses in such polls or surveys are that people may not know their own minds, may not plan very far ahead, may not be able to perceive the circumstances that will cause them to change their intentions, or may inaccurately report their intentions or expectations for a variety of reasons.

Nevertheless, expectational surveys may be the best way of catching a big switch in public attitudes which statistical evidence alone cannot explain. Surveys of consumer intentions to buy certain durable goods, such as automobiles, have shown a fair degree of reliability.

SYMPTOMATIC TECHNIQUES OF FORECASTING

The symptomatic approach to forecasting is based on the concept that, though the business cycle represents a highly complicated set of relationships among different economic variables, *the general sequence of events in a business cycle is sufficiently consistent to enable an analyst to forecast coming changes by watching the "leading indicators."*

The importance of the symptomatic approach to the business observer is its concentration upon the task of spotting *turning points* in business activity.

For many years, business analysts have been searching for a single indicator, or set of indicators, which would always lead general business developments. Some of the work which has been done in this area is described briefly below.

Indicators of the National Bureau of Economic Research. The National Bureau of Economic Research has been conducting detailed statistical analyses of business cycles for more than three decades and has done an exhaustive job of screening time series with forecasting value.

After World War II, the task of bringing prewar findings up to date was undertaken by Geoffrey H. Moore, who published the results of his findings in 1950.[1] Moore started with a collection of 801 series, of which he found 255 to be acceptable indicators, and 21 most reliable.

Moore concluded that:

1. Cyclical turning points of different series are rather widely dispersed in business cycles. Although peaks and troughs in each of 400 series, selected for the regularity of their behavior, tended to cluster around peaks and troughs in aggregate economic activity, each cluster was spread over one to three years.

2. A group of series can be selected whose turning points typically precede cyclical turns in business activity; another whose turns roughly coincide with aggregate turns; and a third whose turns characteristically lag behind turns in aggregate activity.

3. Series in all three timing groups are useful in anticipating and identifying cyclical revivals and recessions. The series collectively can be particularly helpful in facilitating prompt recognition of a development, once it occurs.

Nevertheless, Moore's study suggested that interpretation of the indicators would be subject to numerous difficulties and uncertainties—the chief ones being (1) to determine whether a change in a particular series, at the time it occurs, is only a temporary dip or rise, or really represents a reversal of trend, (2) to relate the significance of the changes in each series to changes in the others, as virtually all of the series are to some extent variable and erratic, and (3) to get the data for each series on a current basis.

Moore's leading series are of three general sorts: (1) "deterministic" series, such as new orders, residential building contracts, and commercial building contracts; (2) speculative or anticipatory series, such as the stock market index and the wholesale price index of basic commodities; and (3) sensitive measures of current change, such as business failures, new incorporations, and the average work week.

Each series in the leading group reaches its turning point from two to ten months before turns in the business cycle; each series in the lagging group follows turns in the business cycle by two to seven months. The variability of lead and lag times is obviously a hazard for the forecaster; allowing for the time until the data are actually received, the indicators may on occasion give little or no lead time.

Diffusion Indexes. To deal with one of the chief difficulties of interpreting the individual indicators—the problem of knowing whether change in any particular series is really forecasting a reversal in the general trend or is a more or less isolated development—Geoffrey Moore devised what he called the "diffusion index." This stemmed from his finding that business cycle movements "have invariably been preceded by a remarkably regular cycle in the proportion of industrial activities undergoing expansion or contraction," and that, with eco-

[1] Geoffrey H. Moore, *Statistical Indicators of Cyclical Revivals and Recessions*, Occasional Paper, no. 31, National Bureau of Economic Research, New York, 1950.

nomic time series as with human beings, "the individual is more variable than the group."[2]

To make his diffusion index, Moore first smoothed the individual series by means of moving averages, using longer moving averages for the more erratic series; he then combined the series in each of the leading, coincident, and lagging groups by counting the number of series in each group that were rising at a given time. That number he converted into a percentage of the number of indicators in the group. Thus, when the percentage was below 50, more indicators were contracting than expanding; when above 50, more were expanding than contracting.

Such diffusion indexes must be used with care. One must be very wary of "false signals" being given off by the leading indicators. They may be flashing only a slowdown in the rate of expansion or a lull rather than an actual downturn in the business cycle.

To distinguish the genuine from the abortive recession or revival, one must look at all three diffusion curves, not just one. A further test of whether a swing in the curves is signaling a change in general business is how much they rise or fall and how long they remain at an extreme level.

If regarded only as a simple and preliminary technique for relating the behavior of several different sorts of data to get a quick current picture of the economic trend, the diffusion index can be a useful device. When a diffusion index is dropping, it may be regarded as a blinking yellow light, signaling caution to the analyst. In a field so rife with uncertainties, such cautionary signals are not to be despised or ignored.

Other Statistical Indicators. Many business analysts have their own favorite statistical indicators for forecasting either general business activity or movements in certain other time series. For instance, Steven M. DuBrul, of the General Motors Corporation, considered changes in the total money supply (bank deposits and currency) plus marketable governments (interest-bearing government obligations held outside banks except savings bonds) to be a highly reliable forecaster of changes in the consumers' price index. DuBrul in effect accepted the quantity theory of money.

The late Leonard Ayres, of the Cleveland Trust Company, had high regard for bond price differentials (that is, the spread between low- and high-grade bonds) as a measure of business confidence. The rationale behind this index is the belief that sounder issues principally reflect long-term interest rates, whereas more speculative issues reflect investors' attitudes toward risk factors; hence, the differential in bond prices represents an evaluation of the risk premium over the nearly "pure" interest rate. The differential is therefore taken to represent investors' judgments of the types of activity most likely to add to the total level of activity.

The stock market is, of course, a similar sort of forecaster—though, obviously, not a wholly reliable one, since investors and speculators can hardly be expected always to have clear foresight, and "outside" factors, such as tax or credit measures, or margin requirements, may exert influences which distort the purely "expectational" evidence of stock market movements.

The Federal Reserve Board's Consultant Committee on General Business Expectations has suggested a number of additional leading series which it considers useful for forecasting cyclical changes,[3] including the spread between high-

[2] Geoffrey H. Moore, "Analyzing Business Cycles," *The American Statistician*, vol. 9, no. 3, April–May, 1954, p. 13.

[3] Report of Consultant Committee on General Business Expectations, Federal Reserve Board, U.S. Government Printing Office, Washington, D.C., 1955, pp. 119–148.

and low-grade bonds (mentioned above), unfilled orders, forward investment commitments, other contracts, budgeted expenditures, other price indexes, employee accessions in manufacturing establishments,[4] and money turnover.

Statistical indicators have many advantages over other types of information for business analysts. They are relatively objective and accurate, cover all areas of the economy, are more or less historically comparable for their behavior in different business cycles (and thus their reliability can be more adequately tested), and they are inexpensive (from the standpoint of the business user). They may also frequently constitute the very factors causing the changing expectations of businessmen and consumers, which "psychological" surveys are attempting to measure. But the statistical indicators may avoid certain difficulties involved in the expectational or "mood" surveys, such as the fact that respondents' answers "may be provided carelessly, by uninformed persons, and possibly somewhat inarticulately,"[5] or that direct surveys necessarily cover a relatively small sample of respondents.

Time-series data have the further advantage of being readily handled for forecasting purposes by modern statistical methods, such as the fitting and extrapolation of straight line or mathematical trends, cyclical or harmonic analysis of the residuals from trend, and simple or multiple correlation of different series.[6]

SYSTEMATIC TECHNIQUES OF FORECASTING

Systematic forecasting derives from the classic approach of economic theory—the discovery of cause-effect relations among different economic factors, which hold for past, present, or future.

The use of systematic methods for forecasting requires all the theoretical training, knowledge of institutional and statistical facts, technical skill, and social and political insight that an economist can command.

The economist who tackles the forecasting problem today has three great advantages over economists working a generation ago. One is the development of modern economic theory, which has made rapid progress since the Great Depression. The continuing development of economic theory in the past few decades has greatly advanced economists' understanding of how the major elements in a nation's economy are interrelated.

The second major advantage of economists today is the existence of several systems of national accounting, which present a comprehensive statistical picture of the national economy.

The third great advantage is the availability of high-speed electronic computers, which permit economists to handle far more data and far more complex interrelationships than was formerly possible.

By using modern economic theory and data from systems of national accounts as well as other data and information, economists are developing forecasting techniques of various degrees of rigor and complexity. The less rigorously mathematical (though not necessarily less complex) techniques leave more room for the judgments or "instincts" of the analyst and for the use of nonquantitative—even noneconomic—information. The more rigorous approach involves

---

[4] See also Geoffrey H. Moore, "Business Cycles and the Labor Market," *Monthly Labor Review*, vol. 78, no. 3, March, 1955, pp. 288–292.

[5] Report of Consultant Committee, *op. cit.*, p. 148.

[6] See Croxton and Cowden, *Applied General Statistics*, Prentice-Hall, Inc., Englewood Cliffs, N.J., 1948; Norbert Wiener, *The Extrapolation, Interpolation and Smoothing of Time Series*, Cambridge, 1942; M. G. Kendall, *The Theory of Advanced Statistics*, vol. II, London, 1948; H. Y. Davis, *The Analysis of Economic Time Series*, Bloomington, 1941.

the construction of econometric models, which may involve difficult mathematical and statistical procedures.

The model-building approach can be applied to short- and long-term general economic forecasting and to many more limited business problems, such as the future demand for particular products. Models need not, however, be forbiddingly difficult to be useful.

Systems of National Accounts. The first and most important of the three major systems of national accounts from the standpoint of the business analyst is that organized around the concept of the gross national product.

The GNP system regards the national output and income from three standpoints: as a receipts total, an expenditure total, and a total value of production. These three totals are identical, since every *expenditure* is simultaneously a *receipt;* and all the *goods and services produced,* if valued at their sales prices, also equal receipts or expenditures. The major components of GNP, as seen from the *expenditure* side, are personal consumption, private investment, and government spending. As seen from the *receipts* side, GNP equals wages, salaries, business earnings, rents, interest, corporate profits, and taxes. GNP thus measures the value of all goods and services produced in a year.

A second national accounting system, based upon so-called input-output analysis, has been developed by Prof. Wassily W. Leontief of Harvard University. Leontief's basic idea was to construct a table to show the way goods flow from one industry to another. The table thus describes the interrelations of all parts of the economy—and provides a basis for studying how disturbances to the system would be absorbed or aggravated by the various economic sectors.

An input-output table looks like a chart for a super game of tic-tac-toe—or the mileage table on a road map. Along the left side of the table are listed the separate industries or sectors of the economy to be covered, one industry or sector to one row. Across the top of the table, the same industries and sectors are repeated, each one heading a single column.

Every square or "cell" in the tic-tac-toe grid simultaneously stands for either an input or an output. From the standpoint of its position in the column, the number in a cell is an *input* to the industry named at the top of the column. From the standpoint of its position in a horizontal row, the same number represents an *output* of the industry named at the left of the row. The total inputs and outputs of each industry in the columns and rows will always be identical.

The point of this construction, then, is to show what every industry sells to every other industry to further its production. When the table is opened up to include government, consumers, and foreign countries, it presents a picture of the total flow of goods and services of the national economy.

Input-output tables for the American economy have now been extended to over 500 industrial and economic sectors. The job of handling the enormous amounts of data and the complex relations among the different sectors requires the use of large electronic computers.

Input-output analysis promises to continue to grow in this country and abroad, particularly because of its usefulness for studying individual industries in relationship to each other and to the national and international economies. The widespread availability of large electronic computers is making practical the use of input-output techniques for a wide range of business problems, including forecasting, marketing, and long-range planning.

A third system of national accounts is called the "flow-of-funds" system. The basic principle behind it is that the *transaction* is the ultimate unit of economic investigation, a transaction being defined as an exchange by two parties of rights over goods or services. Starting with the transaction as the basic unit, the

Federal Reserve has developed what can be called a "double-double-entry" system of national accounting, since every economic or financial transaction is recorded in the system in four places: (1) a purchase by the buyer, (2) a sale by the seller, (3) a reduction in cash for the buyer, and (4) an increase in cash for the seller. The latter two entries are designated the "financial" aspects; the former two entries are the "nonfinancial" aspects of the transaction.

The flow-of-funds system groups all transactions into twelve nonfinancial and nine financial classes. The nonfinancial are payroll, interest, rents and royalties, dividends, net withdrawals by proprietors, insurance premiums, insurance benefits, grants and donations, taxes, tax refunds, real estate transfers, and other goods and services. The financial are changes in currency and deposits, gold and other monetary reserves, bank loans other than mortgages, mortgages, Federal obligations, state and local obligations, corporate securities, trade credit, and miscellaneous financial assets and liabilities.

These transaction categories are carried through consistently under each of the ten sectors into which the economic system is divided. The ten sectors are the major decision-making groups that transact the national business: consumers, corporate business, farm business, the Federal government, state and local governments, the banking system, insurance companies, other institutional investors, and the rest of the world. The system also breaks a number of these major sectors into subsectors. For every sector and subsector, the flow-of-funds system presents a statement showing the sources and uses of funds. These separate accounts build up to a continuous record of our entire money economy in motion.

The three major systems of national accounts—GNP, input-output, and flow-of-funds—should not be conceived of as competitive with each other. They have different purposes and orientations. GNP focuses on the problem of measuring national output and income; input-output, on the productive and technological relations among different industries; flow-of-funds, on the role of money and credit in the productive process.

The Intuitive Approach. The approach to systematic forecasting which, although it makes use of economic theories, national accounting, and other statistical techniques, does not produce forecasts by exact mathematical techniques may be called the "intuitive" approach, though the analyst's conclusions obviously do not rest solely upon his intuitions.

In the case of general business forecasting, each component of the gross national product—consumption expenditures, domestic investment, foreign investment, and government expenditures—is regarded as a starting point. The analyst starts by noting where these variables were last reported by the Department of Commerce and the route they followed to get there.

But how the analyst answers the question of where each component of GNP will go from there, how deeply he probes beneath these vast aggregates to discover the cause of their behavior, how he handles the complex interrelations among them all (since none is independent of the others), how and to what extent he introduces political, psychological, or other factors which may affect the economy, will depend upon his skill, patience, insight, forecasting talent, and information.

A conscientious analyst will take apart each element in the economic system to get as detailed a picture as possible of its operation.

He will be working hard against time—not only because his report will be needed for early use but also because he will want to base his forecasts on the most recent information; if he takes too long, his facts will grow cold. The best procedure, most business economists have discovered, is to stay at the forecasting job continuously, constantly modifying the forecast on the basis of fresh information.

The test of whether an economist has done a good forecast is, of course, not its comprehensiveness, but how it comes out. Forecasts cannot be expected to come out with a highly consistent degree of accuracy. But, if done conscientiously, they should be a useful summarization of the main factors which management will want to take into consideration. A good forecast will give management a comprehensive view of the main elements in the business picture, together with the logical inferences about the data which a reasonable and economically well-trained man can draw.

The Econometric Approach. The more rigorous way of tackling the forecasting problem is to build an econometric model. The term "econometric" refers to an analytical technique which combines the disciplines of economics, mathematics, statistics, and accounting.

Every econometric model is based upon a theory or set of theories about what will determine general business activity or the specific industrial situation being forecast. Econometricians can invent or borrow their theories from the history of economic doctrine. When the econometrician has formulated the theory of his forecast, he must translate it into a set of mathematical equations; these equations will relate the things he wants to find out (the dependent variables) to the things he already knows or can estimate (the independent variables). And this set of equations is his model.

This description can best be clarified by presenting a very simple five-equation model of the national economy:

$$C = aY + b \tag{1}$$
$$I = cP_{-1} + d \tag{2}$$
$$T = eG \tag{3}$$
$$G = C + I + E \tag{4}$$
$$Y = G - T \tag{5}$$

where C stands for consumption; I, investment; T, taxes; G, gross national product; Y, national income; P_{-1}, previous year's profits; and E, government expenditures. The small letters, $a, \ldots, e$, are constants, which make the equations balance.

Let us spell out the meaning of each of the above equations. Equation (1) means that people's expenditures for consumer goods and services will depend on how much they earn—or, stated mathematically, consumption is a function of income.

Equation (2) means that next year's investment is a function of this year's profits.

Equation (3) means taxes will be a function of future gross national product (GNP).

Equation (4) is a definitional equation that simply means that GNP equals consumption plus investment plus government expenditures.

Equation (5) is another definitional equation, which says that national income equals GNP minus taxes.

All five equations, taken together, constitute our forecasting model. To prepare the model for use, you must first look up the statistics on consumption, national income, investment, profits, taxes, and gross national product over a series of years. From these records, you must calculate values for the constants a, b, c, d, and e that would make each of the first three functional equations come out about right in any given year.

Next you must find the values for the two independent variables in the forecasting equations—the current rate of corporation profits and the budget data covering next year's government spending. Let us assume that corporate profits *this year* are running at $60 billion and that Federal, state, and local government spending next year is budgeted to run at $130 billion.

Now put the profits and government-spending figures into the model, together with the value of the constants. The model will look as follows:

$$C = 0.7Y + 50 \qquad (1)$$
$$I = 0.9 \times 60 + 30 \qquad (2)$$
$$T = 0.2G \qquad (3)$$
$$G = C + I + 130 \qquad (4)$$
$$Y = G - T \qquad (5)$$

Now you must solve the above five equations. You want the values of C, I, T, G, and Y. Here are the results. Next year consumption will be $386 billion; investment will be $84 billion; tax receipts, $120 billion; gross national product, $600 billion; and national income, $480 billion.

The above model has of course been presented strictly for didactic purposes. It is based on the simple assumptions that next year's gross national product depends upon this year's profits and next year's government spending. No model can be better than the theory on which it is based.

Although theoretically and statistically more complex, actual econometric forecasting models are essentially the same in their structure as the simple model presented above.

The great advantage of econometric models is that they provide a superior means of organizing economics' complicated materials, of systematizing the whole forecasting process, of providing straightforward conclusions, and afterward, of discovering what may have gone wrong in a forecast and thereby of profiting from past mistakes.

Forecasting models can serve business. Some large corporations are starting to make serious use of them; their use promises to spread with the growth of modern computer technology.

Models are particularly valuable for doing one of the principal jobs for which American business is turning to economists: determining long-term projections of the national economy and of specific industries, which are needed for guidance to management in planning capital spending and expansion programs.

BIBLIOGRAPHY

Brennan, M. J., Jr., *Preface to Econometrics: An Introduction to Quantitative Methods in Economics*, McGraw-Hill Book Company, New York, 1960.

Butler, William F., and Robert A. Kavesh (eds.), *How Business Economists Forecast*, Prentice-Hall, Inc., Englewood Cliffs, N.J., 1965.

Duesenberry, James S., Otto Eckstein, and Gary Fromm, "A Simulation of the U.S. Economy in Recession," *Econometrica*, vol. 28, no. 4, October, 1960.

Friend, I., and R. Jones, "Short-run Forecasting Model Incorporating Anticipatory Data," *Models of Income Determination*, Studies in Income and Wealth, vol. 28, National Bureau of Economic Research, Princeton University Press, Princeton, N.J., 1964.

Klein, L. R., *An Introduction to Econometrics*, Prentice-Hall, Inc., Englewood Cliffs, N.J., 1962.

Lewis, John P., *Business Conditions Analysis*, McGraw-Hill Book Company, New York, 1959.

Liu, T. C., "An Exploratory Quarterly Econometric Model of Effective Demand in Postwar U.S. Economy," *Econometrica*, vol. 31, no. 3, July, 1963.

Maisel, Sherman J., *Fluctuations, Growth and Forecasting: The Principles of Dynamic Business Economics*, John Wiley & Sons, Inc., New York, 1957.

Okun, Arthur M., "The Predictive Value of Surveys of Business Intentions," *American Economic Review* (Papers and Proceedings), vol. 52, May, 1962, pp. 218–225.

Organisation for Economic Cooperation and Development, *Techniques of Economic Forecasting*, with an introduction by C. W. McMahon, Paris, 1965.

Silk, Leonard S., and M. Louise Curley, *Forecasting Business Trends*, McGraw-Hill Book Company, New York, 1963.

Suits, Daniel B., "Forecasting and Analysis with an Econometric Model," *American Economic Review*, vol. 52, March, 1962, pp. 104–132.

CHAPTER FIVE

Long-range Planning

BRIAN W. SCOTT   *W. D. Scott & Co. Pty. Ltd., North Sydney, Australia*

Of the many new management techniques and practices which have emerged
during the years since World War II, none has been of potentially greater
significance for the continued growth and vitality of a company than long-range
planning. Long-range planning is essentially a new development in management, for although there are many examples of successful and skillful long-range
planning scattered through each stage of industrial history, few companies in
the past have sought to develop long-range plans *in a systematic and formalized
manner.*

Long-range planning involves an attempt to anticipate, analyze, and make
decisions about basic problems and issues which have significance reaching well
beyond the present operating horizon of the company. Long-range planning
attempts to grapple with the question, "What must our company do today to
be ready for the uncertainties of tomorrow?" The critical influence on management of long-range planning stems not so much from the fact that it happens
to cover three years or five years or ten years ahead, but rather because of
the types of problems it encompasses and the kinds of decisions it involves.

Important concepts and techniques have been developed for application in
corporate long-range planning. These concepts and techniques are reviewed
in this chapter, and the managerial implications for policy formulation and organizational arrangements are discussed.

THE EMERGENCE OF LONG-RANGE PLANNING

Planning in business activities first became prominent during the late nineteenth and early twentieth centuries as a direct result of the scientific management movement. Its primary focus at that time was upon planning for better
factory performance and output, but the ensuing years have seen a steadily
widening range of managerial activities being planned. Furthermore, existing
planning techniques have become progressively more refined through continuing
experience and experiment. The present emphasis upon long-range planning

can, therefore, be seen as a continuation of these trends toward refinement and comprehensiveness.

In more specific terms, the central role held by long-range planning can be explained by the following several mainstreams of development and change.

Advances in Management Capabilities. Management has become a much more highly skilled practice than it was in the early years of this century. It has built upon the foundations of scientific management, the insights of human relations, the analytic skills of business mathematics, and the technological revolution of the computer. As a result, management has reached a stage where the concepts and techniques of long-range planning not only can be, but *need* to be, usefully employed.

Greater Company Size and Complexity. The typical company of the present is larger and more complex than its earlier counterpart. Characteristically it produces a much wider range of products; these products are distributed more widely (often internationally); and there are many more employees, particularly skilled employees, on the payroll. All these developments have emphasized the need for better communication and clearer policy formulation to provide guidance and order to company operations.

A Business Environment of Growing Complexity. The fact that the business environment is dynamic and fast-changing is so obvious that it needs little elaboration. A company must operate in a world in which the technological, social, economic, and political environment is fluid and subject to change, often at short notice. Long-range planning techniques offer ways of grappling with, and anticipating where possible, the developments of the future.

The growing attention to long-range planning by management has been a world-wide phenomenon. Important contributions toward long-range planning methodology have come from the United Kingdom and the Continent, and also from some Japanese companies. Noteworthy advances in long-range planning practice by some Australian organizations have also been achieved.

Nevertheless, it has been the United States which has led the way in corporate long-range planning activities. The extraordinary rise in attention to this subject is indicated by the following three survey reports.

1. In 1958, *Nation's Business* carried an article which observed that: "Management authorities say that more than 50 percent of today's businesses have some kind of long-range planning. Five years ago the figure was scarcely 20 percent."[1]

2. In 1959, a chemical industry survey gave these results: Sixty out of 240 chemical companies responded to a questionnaire on long-range planning; these 60 accounted for about 60 percent of the industry's dollar sales volume. The survey indicated that 93 percent of the responding companies had "definite long-range planning programs." Of these, 65 percent had initiated their present programs between 1954 and 1958, with about half of them giving 1956 as their starting date.[2]

3. In 1963, it was reported that ". . . . while less than two hundred corporations had formal long-range planning departments (one or more men assigned to the task) five years ago, over seven hundred companies have such departments operating today. In addition, a great many smaller companies have taken pains to make long-range planning a part-time assignment for one or more executives."[3]

[1] P. Gustafson, "Plan Tomorrow's Profits," *Nation's Business*, August, 1958, p. 29.

[2] B. Payne, "Long-range Planning: Special Report," *Chemical Week*, Jan. 9, 1960, p. 78.

[3] D. W. Ewing (ed.), *Long-range Planning for Management*, rev. ed., Harper & Row, Publishers, Incorporated, New York, 1964, p. ix.

There is every reason to believe that long-range planning will continue to grow as an influencing factor upon managements everywhere. The success of companies in years ahead will depend importantly upon the abilities of their executives to develop long-range plans which are creative and imaginative, and at the same time logical and sound.

DISTINGUISHING FEATURES OF LONG-RANGE PLANNING

The term "long-range planning" implies a classification in terms of the variable of time. The emphasis is not upon the point of time at which planning decisions are made, however, but rather upon the *futurity*, or future actualization, of such decisions. Long-range planning, like all other forms of planning, requires decisions in the *present* to prepare for the future.

How Long Is Long Range?   There is sometimes a great deal of discussion on the question of what constitutes "long range." Yet circumstances vary so widely among industries and among companies that it is unwise to try to impart a conformity and uniformity which does not really exist. Empirical observations show that the actual time period involved in long-range planning covers a very wide spread—a one-year period may be considered "long range" in a fashion company, whereas eighty years may be a timber company's concept of the term. Five-year plans are the most frequently encountered in practice.

The significance of the time variable becomes apparent only when associated with the scope and subject matter of the plans being contemplated. This becomes clear when it is realized that there are at least four different concepts of time measurement which can be relevant in long-range planning:

1. *Plan Preparation Time.*   This requires no elaboration except to note that the period involved may range from a few minutes to many months, depending upon the degree of complexity.

2. *Lead Time.*   This is a measure of the time which must elapse following one occurrence before a specified subsequent occurrence can take place.

3. *Direct-impact Time.*   This is the period of time during which the activity being planned will continue to operate or will continue to have direct influence on operations.

4. *Epochal Time.*   This concept does not strive to measure futurity in any precise manner, but it suggests the kinds of momentous changes which may take place in the business environment during coming decades, which need to be considered in the shaping of long-range plans.

Long-range Planning as a Process.   Long-range planning has evolved essentially from more traditional forms of business planning, and in this context it is important to see long-range planning as a *process*. It is composed of a series of conceptual phases, related to one another in an orderly fashion. Exact classifications of these phases, or elements, vary, but the following is typical:

1. Establishing objectives
2. Establishing planning assumptions
3. Seeking the facts regarding possible courses of action
4. Evaluating alternative courses of action
5. Selecting a course (or courses) of action

Several features in applying this process to long-range planning are particularly noteworthy. *First,* these phases or elements can be conceptually separated, but in long-range planning they must also be seen as interdependent and intertwined with other phases of the process. The objective of a long-range plan, for example, is often far from clear at the outset, and it is frequently necessary to work through an entire subordinate planning process which has the objective of determining or clarifying an appropriate basic objective. The objective of a long-range plan may emerge in its final form only after a great deal of analysis has taken place.

Second, the clarification of assumptions in long-range planning is of fundamental importance. One of the most dangerous pitfalls in this sort of planning is to assume uncritically that environmental factors will remain essentially the same. Such assumptions may hold up when planning involves only one or two years; but profound basic changes can take place over a five-, ten-, or twenty-year span, and this fact must be taken into account. There is, therefore, a special need to spell out assumptions for long-range plans *as explicitly as possible.* In particular, management frequently needs to be ruthless in following through an analysis of even the most unpleasant consequences of assumptions which may act against the long-term interests of its organization.

Third, the long-range planner needs to be as sure as he can be that he has cast wide enough in considering possible alternative courses of action. A proposed major capital investment often should be considered in terms of opportunity cost: what alternative projects are, in effect, being foregone to proceed with this choice. Moreover, in long-range planning, a major decision frequently has hidden time commitments. Once an organization commits itself to a particular line of action, it will often appear preferable to continue with it indefinitely rather than to sacrifice the portion already carried out.

Classifications of Long-range Plans. It is useful to distinguish at a very general level between two types of long-range planning—strategic and implementational.

Strategic planning is concerned with determining what, fundamentally, the firm wants to accomplish. It asks the question, *"Where are we going?"* It takes up questions of basic purpose and direction which will serve as an underlying and unifying guide for all the operational activities of the company. Strategic long-range planning often requires a fresh appraisal of the nature of the company itself and the assumptions which underlie its operations. The concepts which have been developed provide a means of dealing explicitly and systematically with matters of basic importance which in the past have usually been dealt with, if at all, only implicitly and nonsystematically.

Implementational planning is concerned with the details of accomplishment. It takes up the question, *"How do we get there?"* Implementational long-range planning seeks to spell out the details of the programs, policies, and procedures needed to accomplish the strategic plans in an effective manner. Implementational long-range plans span a wide number of subjects, including:

Product development
Market development
Capital budgeting
Facilities development
Resource development
Manager and employee development

STRATEGIC LONG-RANGE PLANNING[4]

The term "strategy" is derived from military usage, and the required assessments needed for strategic long-range planning in business parallel those required

[4] For a detailed discussion of strategic long-range planning, see Brian W. Scott, *Long-range Planning in American Industry,* American Management Association, New York, 1965.

for military strategy. There is, first, the need for an intensive self-appraisal of the company's own strengths and weaknesses. There is also the need to assess likely changes in the environment: economic, political, technological, and social. And, third, there is the need to assess competitor capabilities and probable competitor strategies.

Subject Areas. The essence of a strategy is that it encompasses the crucial or decisive elements in a situation, and therefore it is not possible to place limitations on the subject areas which might appropriately be covered. One strategy may plan for concentrated emphasis upon a certain area of research. Another strategy may state that wise selection of retail-store locations appears to be a controlling factor in the financial success of the company under review. In yet another circumstance, the strategic plan may focus upon the need for international expansion of plant operations.

Nevertheless, it can be said that the subjects of (1) finance and (2) product line are always involved to some extent in the development of strategic long-range plans. Financial analysis will indicate broadly what strategies are or are not feasible, and will furnish bench marks in judging possible alternative strategies. It has special relevance where the planning includes the possibility of merger and acquisition activities. Product line also has a major effect upon the unifying set of assumptions which a strategic long-range plan seeks to provide, because a company's operating characteristics are always greatly affected by the kinds of products which it chooses to produce and market.

A useful schematic presentation of the sorts of coverage of strategic planning in a company has been developed by Stanford Research Institute and is shown in Figure 5-1.

Conducting a Corporate Self-appraisal. One of the most striking features of strategic long-range planning is the importance given to intensive corporate self-appraisal. In company after company, efforts are being made to understand the nature of the organization's *present* business more clearly, in the belief that company executives will then be able to do a more effective job of charting the organization's *future* course.

It might seem that a corporate self-appraisal would normally be a simple matter, but this is not true. Actually, as Peter Drucker has rightly observed, the question, "What is our business?" is almost always a difficult one which can only be answered after hard thinking and study. In Drucker's view, *the most important single cause of business failure is that the question, "What is our business?" is so rarely asked and so rarely given adequate study and thought.*[5]

The following simple illustration will suggest the very basic implications which can stem from different self-appraisals.

The management of a luggage manufacturing company may decide through self-appraisal that the key resources of its organization involve *specializing in suitcases.* As a result, its long-range plans may be oriented toward developing a complete line of suitcases: high price and economy price; large size and small size; top quality and less expensive materials.

An alternative self-appraisal, however, may result in management seeing the company as having distinctive skills as *a leather-goods manufacturer.* In these circumstances, the long-range plans are likely to involve wider dispersion of company resources, with attention being given to new products in the leather industry and also to problems of distribution and marketing of these new products.

[5] P. F. Drucker, *The Practice of Management,* Harper & Row, Publishers, Incorporated, New York, 1954, pp. 49 and 50.

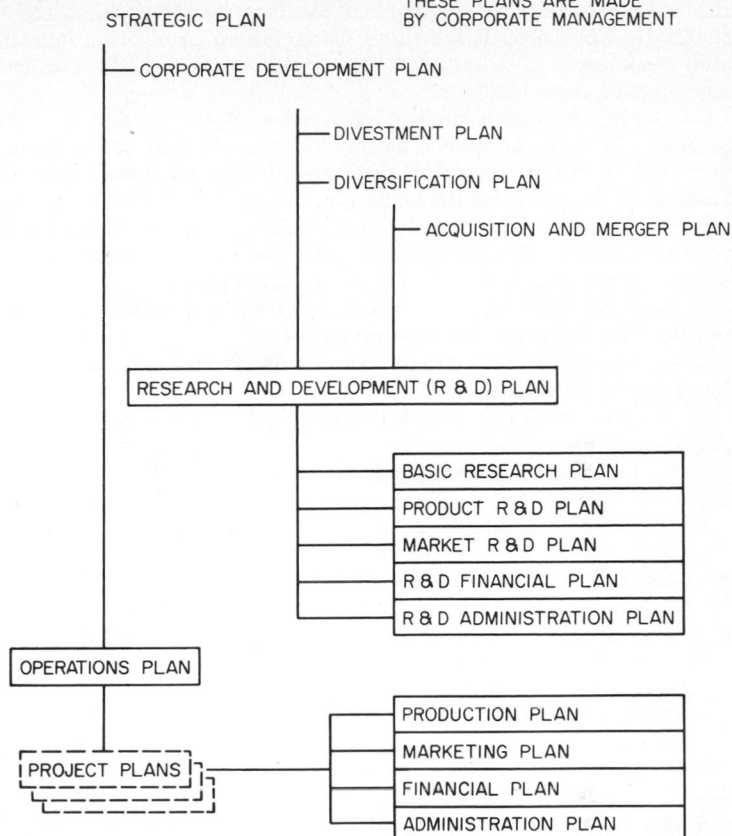

FIG. 5-1. *Coverage of strategic planning.* *As reproduced in* Business Week, *June 1, 1963, p. 54.*

A third possible self-appraisal may result in management perceiving the company's strengths to lie in the field of *travel accessories.* In this case, the dispersion of resources might be still wider than in the first two cases, for the management would presumably not limit its long-range expansion plans to leather or other closely associated materials.

When executives undertake a corporate self-appraisal, they make the presupposition that their company has some predominant characteristics which can be isolated. These characteristics may relate to products, processes, equipment, distribution, finance, manpower, and/or research, to name just some of the major possibilities. Thus it is assumed in many companies that the existing product line is not a conglomerate assortment of items, but that certain patterns of unification exist and that these suggest certain key strengths. One company describes this analysis as a search for "hard-core skills."

There are two major approaches to corporate self-appraisal, and they may be undertaken separately or in combination. One is to examine in turn each functional activity. This allows planning executives to draw some conclusions about the various strengths and weaknesses of their company, considering it as a composite of numerous parts. As a result, they can try to determine which strengths may best be exploited in planning for the long-range future. By the functional approach, a company's planners can provide an inventory of strengths and weaknesses in a systematic way, thus lessening the chance of overlooking any obvious considerations.

The other approach to corporate self-appraisal is that of "total entity." Its primary aim is to achieve a better understanding of the company as a cohesive unit and to determine what characteristics in its nature may prove of special value in laying plans for the long-range future.

When strategic planners attempt a self-appraisal of the total corporate entity, they frequently use a general industry classification as a starting point. Industry groupings are usually classified in one of three possible ways:

1. *A single product, product line, or group of products* (the automobile industry, the shoe industry, the furniture industry)

2. *A process or technology* (the chemical industry, the electronics industry, the printing industry)

3. *An end use* (the transportation industry, the communications industry, the defense industry)

Historically, most industry classifications have involved either method 1 or 2 above.

Although classifications of these kinds have proved useful for the purpose described above, it does not follow that they will *necessarily* provide insights into the best course of action a company should project for the long-range future. If a company is guided solely or even predominantly by an industry classification in terms of product or process, it may become bound so closely to existing products or processes that its ability to make changes in planning for the future is impaired.

The third type of classification—the end use—involves grouping a company's products in terms of performance characteristics rather than physical characteristics or production methods. This "product mission" approach brings the customer into the picture and can be very useful as a stimulus to further analysis.⁶ It is by no means a panacea, however. One difficulty, for example, is that most end-use methods of classification are very vague and very general. Thus the term "transportation" can be applied to automobiles, aircraft, railroads, various forms of public transit, and even bicycles.

The fact is that no sound corporate self-appraisal can be limited to a one-dimensional analysis of this kind.

The increased emphasis upon end use has an important effect, nevertheless—it underscores the significance of customer orientation in analyzing the basic nature of a firm. There are also other customer-oriented ways of looking at a firm, including:

1. *Basic wants.* A distinction is made here between a permanent need (light for the home) and the product which customers presently buy to satisfy that need (the electric lamp).

2. *A product system.* Whole families of products can be identified which have some relationship to the company's existing product line, to see if such relationships can be exploited and developed (the electrical industry).

3. *Product territory.* Identifying those market areas which surround the firm's existing product mission, as seen from the standpoint of the customer (water sprinklers and outdoor faucets).

Development of Corporate Objectives. Objectives are a most difficult aspect of strategic long-range planning, because management almost always finds it

⁶ See T. Levitt, *Innovations in Marketing*, McGraw-Hill Book Company, New York, 1962, for a spirited exposition of this viewpoint.

difficult to bridge the gap between lofty ideals and operationally useful targets. Frequently the establishment of clearly defined, long-term objectives is resisted because senior executives claim that they share a clear understanding of the company's aspirations and that they can proceed without delay to more tangible considerations. In one company, this viewpoint became shattered only after weeks of fruitless discussion, when the committee was challenged as follows: Each member was asked to write down independently what he believed should be the company's five-year goals. When these were read, there was no unanimity on even *one* objective. It took weeks to resolve these differences, and at times the ensuing meetings were "tough going." But once a general consensus was established, much more rapid progress was made in the development of the company's long-range plans.

Any company which is considering a systematized attempt to undertake long-range planning activities might well embark on a similar experiment, for it is particularly important to see if there is a real consensus about long-range objectives among the key men within one's own organization. If major conflicts exist, then it will be clear that these need to be discussed, analyzed, and ironed out.

Choosing a Strategy. Planning is fundamentally choosing, and there are problems of choice studded throughout the strategic planning process. Innumerable choices have to be made. Some are choices of technical method; some are choices of exclusion. Some are implicit choices which everyone accepts and which never come up for discussion; some are explicit choices which are made only after detailed analysis.

Among the explicit choices, there are basically four major types:

1. *Early choice concerning a strategic factor.* Sometimes a choice is made early (usually by the chief executive or top management) which, in effect, confines the mandate of the staff planners.

2. *Part-way choice concerning a strategic factor.* A second type is a choice which is made during the course of analysis, usually in the light of some preliminary findings.

3. *Choice of strategy alternatives.* This involves selection of major alternatives for consideration as the possible long-range strategy ultimately to be chosen. The selection of alternatives normally involves a paring down from a wide number of possibilities.

4. *Final choice of strategy from among alternatives.* Perhaps the most distinctive feature of choices in strategic long-range planning is their qualitative nature. They are qualitative because they necessarily are affected by a variety of judgmental and subjective considerations which impinge upon the strategic planning process at a number of different stages.

Flexibility and Planning. Flexibility concerns the ability to adjust or adapt to change. Three aspects of the future show the need for flexibility in long-range planning. First, the future itself is always clouded in uncertainty. Second, a large part of the environment of the future is not controllable by any individual company. And third, it is certain that the future—whatever its form—will differ in a great many ways from the present.

A distinction may be drawn between two different aspects of flexibility that are important in respect to problems of choice. One may be termed "built-in flexibility." Here, there is the notion of flexibility as a quality to be built into the choice made of a planning strategy. The other is called "deliberate-postponement flexibility." It involves delaying some choices until further information becomes available, while taking action on others.

Although the advantages of making choices which incorporate flexibility are clear, the desire for flexibility must be tempered by a need for decision making. There is such a thing as *too much* flexibility. Lip service to the need for flexibility can sometimes cover up a lack of courage or an indecisiveness on the part of top management. The costs of incorporating flexibility into a decision are sometimes uneconomic. An excessive preoccupation with flexibility can lead to a "revise" attitude all the time. For these reasons, the skillful planner has to make choices in which the advantages of flexibility are considered along with the alternative advantages of commitment or delay in a particular circumstance.

IMPLEMENTATIONAL LONG-RANGE PLANNING

Implementational long-range planning is concerned with the details of accomplishment. It is the side of long-range planning which is readily related to developments of traditional planning procedures.

Implementational long-range planning techniques have been progressively refined in the various areas of product development, market development, capital budgeting, facilities development, resource development, and manager and employee development. The techniques, of course, require special study in themselves and are well beyond the scope of this chapter. However, the interested reader will find within this Handbook chapters devoted specifically to all of these topics.

There are several observations which should be made about planning generally.

First of all, the pressure for more formalized implementational planning has increased as a result of increases in minimum lead times which apply in most industries, because of greater technological complexity and new-product competition. A five-year lead time is needed, for example, in the construction of a steel mill. Again, it is common for pharmaceutical and electronics firms to claim that more than 50 percent of current sales volume comes from products which were unknown five years ago.

Second, implementational long-range planning does not necessarily require detailed planning in many different areas. It is possible, sometimes even desirable, to confine the planning to one or two key elements. For example, one well-known retail chain concentrates its implementational long-range planning exclusively on store location. The result is that its stores are often too small; they often have insufficient parking areas; but they achieve high volume turnover because of the shrewd advance selections of locations.

Third, there have been several other factors aiding the development of implementational long-range planning since World War II. Firms have been able to work from more reliable statistics and have utilized better techniques of forecasting. There has also been growing attention to quantitative techniques, especially operations research and linear programming. Additionally, the great advances in computers and data-processing equipment generally have led to the provision of much more information than previously possible.

One major problem frequently observed in connection with this type of planning is the difficulty of achieving balance and consistency between long- and short-range plans. Often the contrast is best seen in companies which draw up one-year and five-year plans. On close examination, there often seems to be little, if anything, in the one-year plan which anticipates the changes and developments reflected in the five-year plan. The five-year plan all too often represents "a wishing list," whereas the one-year plan is concerned with short-range operating efficiency. It is interesting to note that some companies try to overcome this problem by bridging the gap with an intermediate-range two-year or three-year planning procedure.

Goal Setting. Goal setting represents another major problem in implementational long-range planning. The matter of relating goals to estimated capabilities is a problem for any sort of planning, and many of the goals established are rule-of-thumb projections—for example, "a 10 percent increase in sales volume each year."

The British economist Ely Devons has distinguished between two approaches to goal setting.[7] One he termed the "target" or "carrot" approach; the other the "realistic" approach. In the "target" or "carrot" approach, goals are set somewhat beyond the capabilities of the people to stimulate them to strive for this difficult-to-achieve target. It implies that people work at their best only when asked to do a little beyond their capacity. The "realistic" approach sets goals which represent the best estimate of what can in fact be achieved.

Between the two there is a whole range of interesting positions, and a common approach is to establish quantitative targets which are designed, in effect, to achieve a balance between the two extremes. In practice, there is often an oscillation first toward the one, then toward the other.

Overall, it can be said that implementational long-range planning techniques are relatively well established in many larger corporations. There is a growing use of more specialized and sophisticated techniques in such areas as those indicated above. However, the subject is more specific and more readily reducible to figures than its strategic counterpart, and as a result it has been better understood and more widely used.

ORGANIZING FOR LONG-RANGE PLANNING

Along with the general upsurge of interest in long-range planning, there has come a growing tendency toward more formalized organization of the activity.

The starting point in considering problems of organizing for long-range planning must always be *the place of the chief executive.* If long-range planning is to be taken seriously in a firm, then the chief executive must play a prominent role in promoting it. He must also be closely associated with the planning activity as it proceeds, and must continually give the subject his close attention. He needs to communicate enthusiasm, not just lukewarm support.

A simple but typical example will help explain this need for top-level support. Very often, a long-range planning project will involve the sacrifice of some current profits for future well-being. Sometimes, for example, a 5 percent return on sales will be much healthier than an 8 percent return, if additional funds have been devoted to long-range projects. Before undertaking such projects, however, subordinate managers will want to be sure that their performance is being measured in terms of long-term contribution, not merely current results.

Planning the Formal Organization. A basic problem in organizing involves deciding at what levels the various planning activities will be done. Usually, managers find that they have to balance out the relative advantages of centralization and decentralization. Centralized planning has the advantage of top-level expertise and coordination. Decentralized planning has the advantage of providing contact with "operational realities." This is perhaps the most persistent problem which managers must face as they seek to establish long-range planning activities in the going concern.

There are many different ways in which long-range planning activities are

[7] E. Devons, *Planning in Practice,* Cambridge University Press, New York, 1950, pp. 25ff.

organized. In the small business, the chief executive and some immediate sub-ordinates will often form a formal or informal committee to examine and discuss the company's planning activities. In the larger firm, a department or committee is frequently formed and given special responsibilities in this area. These groups may be composed of line officers, or they may include full-time staff specialists. In most cases, the department or committee will report directly to the chief executive.

The Staff Planning Department. The department or committee may be charged with responsibilities which will usually fit into one of the following five categories. Its members may act as *consultants on planning*, giving assistance, as requested, in planning activities throughout the organization. They may act as the *strategic long-range planning group*, charged with thinking through some of the fundamental problems and opportunities relating to the firm. They may be responsible for *statistical forecasts and projections*, providing bench marks for the firm's future activities. They may be assigned the function of *planning quality control*, making sure that the planning done throughout the organization is of satisfactory quality. They may have the role of *integrating plans*, of seeing that the various departmental plans, taken together, harmonize with one another and with the overall corporate objectives.

Characteristics of Planners. If long-range planning is to be done successfully, it is evident that the planners must demonstrate certain professional and personal qualities. Below are described five such qualities which are especially important.

Competence. Long-range planning clearly requires a high degree of technical competence. Astute understanding of trends in economics, finance, and technology (to name but three) is essential in making accurate assessments of the future. The skills involved may vary widely, but the competence and ingenuity of each man in his special field of endeavour are vital, and cannot be compromised.

Confidence. Coupled with this competence, the planners need a sense of confidence in themselves. Not confidence that they will always be right, but confidence in their ability to adapt the plans they have drawn; confidence that the company has better prospects for the future than would have been the case without their efforts.

The experience of the 1958 recession in America provides some evidence here. Some firms deserted their long-range plans at the first sign of adversity. Others, however, had thought through their plans so well that they saw no need to make radical adjustments. Those who stood by their plans are, in general, better off for having done so. The very existence of their plans probably gave them the bench marks from which they detected potential trouble earlier.

Flexibility. If it is desirable to build flexibility into long-range plans wherever possible, so also is it desirable for the planners themselves to display a flexibility of mind. In this case, a balance is needed between respect for tradition and respect for change. The successful planner will bring a lively, challenging mind to the job, with interest in appraising new ideas and different viewpoints. He will not, however, be unstable, or without the staying power to persevere with any one plan.

Resilience. Many environmental factors in long-range planning are uncontrollable, and therefore even the best of plans is likely to collapse sometimes. In such circumstances, the planner's job is not to panic, or even to complain. It is to pick up the pieces and start building again. The challenge to the planner is one of keeping a calm head and providing strong leadership in adversity. "The manager of the future," as former Dean Stanley F. Teele of the Harvard Business School once said, "will have to have the capacity to adjust when long-range plans don't work out."

Courage. Finally, although it is easy to give lip service to long-range planning, it is not so easy to follow through on it. It may require facing some uncomfortable questions and perhaps having to come to some even more uncomfortable decisions.

Managers frequently say that they are "too busy" to engage in long-range planning, desirable though it certainly would be. Studies indicate, however, that this is often a convenient excuse to stay with the more familiar daily routine. Long-range planning deals with the uncertainty and fogginess of the future, and it is often conveniently postponed. Yet a hallmark of the successful planner is his willingness to face today that which could conveniently, but unwisely, be left until tomorrow.

SUMMARY

Long-range planning focuses management attention upon such vitally important questions as these:

What business are we really in? What basic customer needs do we serve? What skills existing in our organization are distinctive, valuable, and/or unique?

What is the real nature of our existing markets? What image does our company have in the marketplace? What changes in this image do we consider desirable?

What major changes are likely: (1) In our present range of products? (2) In the technology of our industry within five years? Within ten years? (3) In the distribution methods of our industry within five years? Within ten years?

What basic objectives and aspirations do we have for our company in terms of five-year plans? Ten-year plans? In particular, what long-term profit objectives do we have, and at what rate do we want to grow?

What major capital expenditures are going to be necessary if we are to meet our objectives?

What steps do we need to take to develop an executive team which will be strong enough to meet the challenges of the long-term future?

As these questions suggest, the challenge for management in long-range planning is to direct the company in such a manner that it will both *adapt* to its environment and also *create* new needs and new markets within that environment.

Alfred North Whitehead observed many years ago, "The behavior of the community is largely dominated by the business mind," and he went on to say that "a great society is a society in which its men of business think greatly of their functions." As management becomes increasingly involved in long-range planning, it must seek to enlarge the points at which corporate interests and the interests of society coincide. Long-range planning therefore brings with it a special challenge to management to "think greatly" about its responsibilities.

BIBLIOGRAPHY

Ansoff, H. I., *Corporate Strategy*, McGraw-Hill Book Company, New York, 1965.
Chamberlain, N. W., *The Firm: Micro-economic Planning and Action*, McGraw-Hill Book Company, New York, 1962.
Devons, E., *Planning in Practice*, Cambridge University Press, New York, 1950.
Drucker, P. F., *Managing for Results*, Harper & Row, Publishers, Incorporated, New York, 1964.

Drucker, P. F., *The Practice of Management,* Harper & Row, Publishers, Incorporated, New York, 1954.

Ewing, D. W., *Long-range Planning for Management,* rev. ed., Harper & Row, Publishers, Incorporated, New York, 1964.

Payne, B., *Planning for Company Growth,* McGraw-Hill Book Company, New York, 1963.

Scott, B. W., *Long-range Planning in American Industry,* American Management Association, New York, 1965.

Steiner, G. A. (ed.), *Managerial Long-range Planning,* McGraw-Hill Book Company, New York, 1963.

Thompson, S., *How Companies Plan,* Research Study, no. 54, American Management Association, New York, 1962.

CHAPTER SIX

Growth through Acquisitions and Mergers

WILLIAM H. BOKUM *Partner, Cresap, McCormick and Paget, New York, New York*

In general, the success of a business enterprise is measured by its rate of growth and the elements that have produced the growth. Accepted standards of appraising growth are principally based upon an above-average annual increase in net income, net earnings per share, return on capital employed, or some similar measure of performance.

A lack of growth calls for a thorough examination and analysis of the business. Often, it is found to result from one or several rather common conditions or deficiencies. For example:

Market conditions which limit product demand—such as the limit imposed on the use of table salt by a stable rate of per capita consumption

Change in product demand, such as that which severely affected the piano industry when radio broadcasting was introduced and record players became increasingly popular

Supplantive competition, a good illustration of which is the displacement of soap by dry and liquid detergents for many household and commercial uses

Product obsolescence, which attacks the earning power of many companies when their mainstay products approach the end of their life cycles—for example, the steam locomotive building industry

Inadequacy of capital to conduct the business in a fully competitive manner— for example, too little capital to install branch plants to offset rising transportation costs on the company's products, with a resulting loss of a share of the market to competitors that have branch plants

The analysis should also endeavor to determine why the adverse conditions or deficiencies were not foreseen or recognized at an earlier date, for early recognition may be equally important in avoiding a similar situation in the future.

When it is further determined that the resources of the company are not sufficient for taking corrective action on the growth problem, or that it is necessary to "buy" growth in earnings quickly, the possibilities of an acquisition or merger should be investigated. It should be recognized at the outset, however, that acquisitions in themselves do not produce growth, but merely expansion. The expansion may provide an entrée to other markets, a new base of products, new competence in product development or management, and the like, and enable the combined companies through internal efforts to generate a rate of growth not feasible for the constituents separately.

In contemplating a program for acquisition or merger, a company should adopt a planned approach. It should establish the objectives to be achieved, and then go through a systematic process of selection of products and companies to obtain the desired result. Even though fortuitous circumstances may bring about a highly advantageous acquisition, a policy of querying various individuals and institutions to ascertain what companies are available is usually unproductive in finding an effective solution to a specific acquisition problem.

The process of establishing the acquisition objectives, formulating and implementing the program, and integrating the acquired company with the acquirer can be undertaken by the management group alone or with the assistance of professional consultants. Professionally qualified consultants can bring to the project an objective point of view, a background of experience, and the necessary time to perform the various tasks, which operating executives often lack.

ESTABLISHING OBJECTIVES

Before initiating an acquisition program, a company must establish specific corporate objectives defining the character of the business to be built through acquisition, the desired level of earning power, the return sought on the investment, share of the market, and the like. Defining the future direction of growth is the responsibility of the chief executive, whether he acts alone, leads the composite thinking of the top management group, or secures the aid of consultants.

The company may already have a set of basic objectives stating the long-term fundamental policies for the conduct of the business; here, the objectives of an acquisition constitute secondary or subsidiary definitions of targets and prescribed standards for courses of action. The procedure in establishing acquisition objectives consists in defining the strengths and weaknesses of the company, projecting the future course of existing product lines and earning power, and determining the requirements for generating growth. This process, whereby management thinks through where it desires the company to be five or ten years hence and how the company will get there, is a key element in the successful planning and implementation of an acquisition program.

Defining Strengths and Weaknesses. A realistic appraisal of the weaknesses—internal and external—of a company and its position in its industry, together with the causes of such weaknesses, is fundamental to determining the type and character of the enterprise to be acquired. Particular care should be given to defining the deficiencies which cannot be overcome by internal action and which thus are leading the company to resort to the acquisition process.

Of equal importance will be a realistic evaluation of the company's strengths, which are fundamental to the well-being of its existing business, conducive to managing the combination after the acquisition, and applicable to generating the desired growth.

Projecting Future Course of the Existing Business.   The sales volume and operating income of existing product lines should be projected, with full thought given to what can be accomplished by correcting internal weaknesses that constitute limiting factors, improving product lines and marketing strategy, and reducing manufacturing costs through improved processes or facilities.   This will establish the dimensions of the additional earning power that must be acquired and generated to provide above-average rate of growth.   Sometimes, the need for new technology, new manufacturing capacity, or integration forward toward the end-product user or backward to the source of raw materials becomes evident, and this need becomes an objective of the acquisition program.

In addition to sales volume and income, the balance sheets and cash flow must also be projected, to ascertain the company's financial resources available for any proposed acquisition.   The obvious purpose of this step is to avoid an overly ambitious acquisition program which will imperil the company's financial soundness or fail because it cannot be financed.

Determining Requirements for Growth.   Although each company's individual situation will be expressed in different objectives for the acquisition program, the following areas are more or less common to most corporate plans.

Earnings Objective.   The earnings objective is basic, for the simple reason that the company must produce satisfactory income on the investment of its stockholders.   Further, most companies must seek additional capital from time to time, either from their shareholders or through sale of securities to other investors, and thus compete with other investment opportunities in the capital market.

Invariably, the question will arise of how the earnings objective is to be established.   What is the "average" annual increase in earnings that constitutes the basic yardstick, and at how much above the "average" should the objective be set?   There is no recognized standard procedure even though the subject has been researched extensively by security analysts and others.   Consequently, each company must be judged separately against appropriate industry statistics. The following suggestions are given as typical approaches.

For a company in an industry characterized as a "growth industry," a composite index of the published results of publicly held companies can be used.   For example, in the chemical industry, Standard & Poor's compilation of eleven companies (excluding Du Pont) shows that aggregate net income increased from $406.8 million in 1957 to $561.1 million in 1963, or 38 percent in six years, which represents an average annual increase of 6.34 percent.

For a company in an industry characterized by a lack of growth, an index must be selected or constructed representing the performance of a broader classification of companies which could constitute alternative or competitive choices for investment funds.   Moody's index of fifty industrial companies may serve the purpose; or an index constructed from the data presented annually in the April issue of the *Monthly Economic Letter* of the First National City Bank (New York) may be more selective.   Further, an index can be constructed by compiling data on a group of individual companies generally regarded by security analysts to be well-managed, aggressive enterprises.   The base for such an index should be a "good" business year (avoiding either a "boom" or a "recession" year), or a period of three years which average out to the equivalent of a good year.

Comparison with such an index, no matter how carefully the index is selected, sometimes will be criticized on the grounds that "the other companies are in better segments of the market or have a broader range of products, and therefore our company should not be appraised against their performance."   Nevertheless, performance is the test applied by investors in retaining ownership in a company or investing additional funds in it. Further, it is just this better record of performance of others that motivates the company to initiate the acquisition program to accomplish what the others have accomplished through the exercise of foresight five, ten, or fifteen years ago.

Generally, the performance represented by a well-selected index is a supportable basis for establishing the earnings objective. The amount by which the objective is set above the trend line of the index will depend upon a realistic appraisal of the type of business, competitive conditions, and the estimated period required after acquisition to develop growth in the combined enterprise through internal action.

Product Line and Market Objectives. The appraisal of the company's strengths and weaknesses may produce a clear indication of the types of products that are to be sought through acquisition. However, it is generally necessary to use the broader approach of first establishing the company's market objectives.

These objectives should define in general terms the markets which are of interest to the company, the types of products which are suitable for manufacture in conjunction with existing product lines, the volume of sales and share of market, and where applicable, the desired channels of distribution. Also, any specific qualifications, such as patent protection, should be expressed in this objective to guide in the selection of products and companies.

In the definition of product line and market objectives for the acquisition program, advance thinking should be given to the capabilities already within the company, to avoid including among the selected companies those with products and markets which can be just as effectively developed internally as through acquisition, provided there is not too much urgency.

The broad objectives of product-line development are converted to a selection of specific products by establishing criteria for screening a comprehensive list of products. For example, to accomplish the objective of broadening the company's product base in the field of precision mechanical equipment, the criteria may specify:

Precision mechanical equipment used for packaging consumer products

Precision mechanical equipment for assembling small components

Precision mechanical, electromechanical, or pneumomechanical equipment for weighing, measuring, or proportioning dry materials in the process industries

The criteria will reflect the engineering, production, marketing, and servicing capabilities of the organization and the physical resources for production and distribution. A principal aim in the process is to ensure compatibility of the acquired business with that of the acquirer. Another principal aim should be to define kinds of products the full market potential of which can be developed by the acquirer's organization, laying the foundation for internal growth in the future.

When the criteria have been established, a comprehensive list of products is compiled from standard sources such as *Mechanical Engineering Catalog, Sweet's Services, Chemical Engineering Catalog,* advertisements appearing in trade magazines (such as *Product Engineering, Electro-Technology,* and *Chemical Engineering*), product literature gathered at trade shows, and any other sources applicable to the general field in which the company desires to gain an entrée. The new-products sections in some trade magazines also prove valuable in completing the list, and the U.S. Patent Office Register should not be overlooked if emphasis is to be placed on recently developed products.

Each product on the list is then screened through the criteria and either rejected or selected, with the selected products usually rated in three or four categories of suitability. Finally, estimates of market potential are developed to complete the selection process, the end result being several products or product lines identified as the objective of the acquisition program.

Financial Objectives. Financial objectives are of special importance. They include specific definition of such factors as:

1. The general dimensions of the company being sought, in terms of sales volume, current earnings, and financial condition.

2. The most desirable method of financing the acquisition—whether through payment in stock, obligations, or cash, or through any one of numerous variations, such as a substantial initial payment plus subsequent annual payments contingent upon earnings.

3. The form of ownership of the acquired company—closely held or publicly owned. The closely held company may be more easily acquired, but may bring into the stockholder group a new shareholder with an undesirably large proportion of the voting power. On the other hand, a closely held acquirer may find it advantageous to merge with a publicly held company and thereby automatically obtain marketability for the shares of its stockholders.

4. The limits to which the acquirer can go in the terms of acquisition without material or prolonged dilution of its earnings per share.

5. The policy (frequently encountered) that the acquiring company aims to avoid dilution of its stockholders' per share equity in net worth. This should be adopted as an objective only after careful consideration, for the acquirer's retained earnings may have been accumulated by refraining from development of products, processes, or markets in previous years, the very reason why it must now seek an acquisition.

FORMULATING THE ACQUISITION PROGRAM

After the objectives of acquisition have been established, the next procedure is to identify and select the candidate companies and rate them in the order of choice. The most effective method is to define the criteria by which the selection is to be made, assemble the key information on all independent manufacturers of the products classified as being within the scope of the product and market objectives, and then analyze this information and screen out the most suitable companies (making preferably a first, second, and third choice).

Setting Specific Criteria of Selection. Specific criteria will define more sharply the standards of company selection and will cover the following points.

Size of Company. Size establishes the minimum and maximum, in terms of earnings, sales volume, and assets, that are regarded as acceptable. Acquiring a small company (unless it possesses unique products or a process of unusual potential) can involve a disproportionate amount of the acquirer's time and effort. The upper limit on size must take into account either the acquirer's ability to finance the acquisition if it is to be for cash or an obligation (such as notes or debentures) or the acquirer's aim to retain control if acquisition is to be effected through an exchange of voting stock.

Potential Growth Rate. Because no two companies in an industry are alike, it is important to define the minimum rate of growth that will still accomplish the basic objective of the acquirer. This usually is expressed as the percentage of average annual increase in sales—either as demonstrated by results in recent years or in terms of potential, derived from market surveys, for new products or new market opportunities.

Also, even in some growth industries, there are companies with products reaching maturity or confronting supplantive competition; the criteria should be devised to identify such situations and products, and thus disqualify the producers.

Management and Personnel.   Criteria on management and personnel should reflect the needs of the acquirer for conducting the business after its acquisition by specifying such factors as age brackets of key executives to be retained, particular types of mechanical competence required to maintain product development activities or manage a complex manufacturing process, size of selling organization, and the like.

Coverage of the Market.   The aims of the acquirer in utilizing or supplementing its marketing operations and in avoiding the loss of a portion of the sales of the acquired company through changes in the channel of distribution must be defined.   Typical criteria in this area are:

1. Whether a company with regional distribution could be extended to a national basis through the acquirer's sales organization, assuming this is what the acquiring company desires

2. Whether the selling activities of a company selling through manufacturers' representatives (or food brokers for grocery store products) could be taken over by the acquirer's sales force

3. For products sold through wholesalers or distributors, the extent to which conflicts in representation would be incurred

Other Criteria.   Depending upon the circumstances, other criteria may be required to focus the selection process on certain objectives of the acquirer or to conform to some of the company's basic policies; for example, patent protection for principal products, minimum return on investment, minimum gross margin of profit, conformity with the acquirer's policy on plant unionization, location of plants to achieve economies in distribution (such as acquisition of an East Coast plant by an acquirer located on the West Coast), and the like.

Assembling Information on Possible Candidates.   In the next step, a list is compiled of all independent manufacturers (thus ruling out divisions or subsidiaries of large companies unless there is reason to suspect a particular one could be purchased) of the products selected to meet the objectives.   In the preparation of this list, such sources are drawn on as *Thomas Register of American Manufacturers,* advertisements in trade publications and listings in annual buyers' guide sections, and descriptions of new products carried by technical journals, such as *Mechanical Engineering* and *Product Engineering* in the mechanical arts.   Where these sources have already been reviewed in defining the product objectives, a notation of the manufacturers of the selected products will greatly simplify the selection process.

Financial information on the companies in the list is obtained from Standard & Poor's *Standard Corporation Descriptions, Moody's Industrial Manual,* prospectuses, Form 10-K reports to the Securities and Exchange Commission, and Dun & Bradstreet reports.   Dun & Bradstreet reports give information on such matters as the ages and previous affiliations of management personnel, methods of distribution, and number of salesmen or sales representatives.

Detailed product information is derived from catalogs and product brochures. Much helpful information can be obtained by inspecting products exhibited at any trade shows occurring during the period the program is in preparation.

Analyzing and Screening Further the Companies on the Preliminary List.   The most methodical approach to further screening is to tabulate the information for each of the companies under the various criteria that have been established. For some criteria, the data can be inserted—sales volume, net worth, location of plant.   Others will require an appraisal—a "yes" or "no," or an *A, B, C* rating.

Gross margins of profit, return on investment, and the like should be calculated and inserted.

As a result of this process, some companies can be eliminated quickly because of their failure to meet important criteria. Rating the remaining companies generally requires information beyond that available through published sources. If the companies are in the same or a related industry, the acquirer's sales personnel often have valuable knowledge; purchasing and engineering personnel frequently can elicit specified key information from salesmen of the companies being considered. Discreet inquiries among customers of these companies can be made regarding service, product quality, and performance—preferably through management consultants experienced in making surveys.

The assembled data are reviewed, and the first, second, and third choices among the companies are decided upon. Sometimes, one or more of the choices will be clearly evident, but often the decision will rest finally on judgment in weighing positive and negative factors. The perfect candidate for acquisition does not exist, and a compromise must be made on which criteria are of lesser importance in accomplishing the acquisition objective.

Submitting the Choices for the Approval of the Board of Directors. Irrespective of the latitude which the board of directors may grant management to initiate negotiations directed toward an acquisition or merger, it is important to inform the board and obtain approval of the chosen candidates, the key factors on which they were selected, and the projected results if the program goes through.

IMPLEMENTING THE ACQUISITION PROGRAM

There are seven key steps in carrying through an acquisition or merger, once the candidate company has been selected. They are: developing a strategy of approach, negotiation, preliminary agreement on terms, investigation of the company to be acquired, preparation of the agreement, approval by the boards of directors, and authorization by the stockholders.

Developing a Strategy of Approach. On the premise that the most desirable companies for acquisition or merger are not openly available, developing a strategy of approach is a critical step; success or failure may hinge on what is discussed during the first hour. The strategy is developed by assembling and reviewing all available information on the candidate company (that used in the selection process and whatever else can be found out about connections of directors and officers, banking connections, ownership of the controlling interest, estate problems, and so on), to define the vulnerable areas and to decide just how the approach is to be made. This will take time, but the time will be well spent.

The objective of the strategy is to convince the candidate company at the outset that it should be willing to explore the idea of affiliating with the acquirer and that it stands to gain from the affiliation. Questions should be anticipated and answers developed that will not short-circuit the discussion and terminate it prematurely.

The decision on who will make the approach is equally important. If the president of the acquirer is acquainted with a director or an officer of the other company, or an officer of its bank, he might logically initiate the proposition at a time and place selected to avoid creating rumors. Delegating the initial approach to his investment banker or to a consultant is another common tactic which has the added advantage that, should the proposal be rejected, the president of the acquirer remains free to make another attempt by changing the strategy to meet the reasons given for rejection.

In the event the candidate company previously was proposed to the acquirer by a business broker, the matter should be reviewed with legal counsel to ensure a full understanding of possible liability for payment of a commission, and the terms of the broker's authorization to act should be clarified in the initial discussion with the other company.

Undertaking Negotiations. The first few discussions usually are confined to generalities on why the two corporations should be combined, and their respective strengths, organizational structure and staffing, financial position, and outlook. Preliminary information exchanged will concern the areas where economies from the merger are anticipated, such as marketing, manufacturing, freight, and warehousing expense; it will also include the certificate of incorporation, the bylaws, copies of loan agreements, and frequently, the auditor's reports if these contain more information than presented in the annual reports and reports to the SEC. If a particular type of deal is sought by the seller—for example, a tax-free exchange of securities or a substantial portion of the acquisition price in the form of fixed-income securities to provide retirement income—this should be ascertained.

If the company to be acquired has an established market for its securities, on an exchange or over the counter, it is common practice for the terms to include a premium over market price to induce acceptance of the offer. If the acquisition is to be made through an exchange of stock, the acquirer will offer terms which avoid material or prolonged dilution of its own earnings, such as reduced earnings per share of common stock. A combination of preferred stock and common stock sometimes will meet the price requirements of the seller and enable the acquirer to avoid dilution of earnings.

The seller may demand an indication of price or terms before he is willing to continue the discussion seriously, and the acquirer should be prepared to submit proposed terms. Generally, the acquirer has limited information on which to propose terms, and the seller, with knowledge of the business, has more definite ideas regarding price. Thus, the acquirer should express terms which are preliminary and safely on the low side, with the condition that these terms could be improved if the seller demonstrates prospective earning power to support a higher price. On the other hand, the seller may demand that the terms be final if the investigation does not disclose any material misrepresentations or any adverse factors not previously disclosed. Failure to resolve divergent views on price (the number of shares of the acquirer's stock to be issued for the shares of the acquired company) frequently is overcome by authorizing a consulting firm to make a comprehensive examination of both companies and recommend an equitable combining ratio.

Although tax considerations may not be a factor in the decision to enter into a merger or acquisition, tax problems will nevertheless be encountered by both parties and may dictate the method of transaction and even have an important bearing on terms. For the most part, the tax problems stem from Subchapter C of the Internal Revenue Code. This is one of the Code's most complex areas, and both parties should retain competent tax counsel at an early stage. (See also Chapter 11 of Section 9.)

Reaching Preliminary Agreement. Upon reaching agreement, the negotiating officers of the two companies generally will draw up a simple memorandum stating the following information:

1. The basis of the agreement—that is, the terms of the merger or acquisition

2. The requirement that it be authorized by the shareholders of each corporation (in a cash purchase, the acquirer usually does not need shareholder authorization unless securities are to be issued and sold to provide the cash)

3. The right of the acquirer to have access to the business, properties, books, records, agreements, and operations of the company to be acquired and to examine them completely, with the proviso that the agreed-upon terms are contingent upon a favorable finding

4. The effective date of the merger or acquisition

5. The proviso that, in the interim, until stockholder action is taken, neither corporation will make any substantial change in its operations or enter into unusual commitments unless the other is informed and gives its approval beforehand

Conducting the Investigation. The investigation may precede or follow the signing of a detailed contract or agreement of merger; frequently, the contract is drafted during the period of investigation. The purposes of the investigation are threefold: to ensure the soundness of the enterprise as a going concern; to verify the asset values, stated and contingent liabilities, and the reported earning power; and to determine a fair value for the company being acquired, or in the event of merger, an equitable combining ratio. The report on the investigation supports the action of the board of directors of the acquirer in approving the acquisition or merger and its terms.

Also, during the investigation process, the information required to develop the plan for integration of the acquired company into the acquirer should be assembled.

Obviously, the investigation must be thoroughly and skillfully conducted, particularly to reveal any conditions or factors adverse to the combination of the two enterprises or to the proposed terms.

The public accountants for the acquirer should be delegated the task of examining the financial statements and the accounting policies and procedures of the company to be acquired. To meet the requirements for the financial statements to be contained in the proxy statements to shareholders, the accountants should also make the necessary examination of the books of the acquirer, assist in preparing its financial statements and in collaborating with the public accountants for the other company, and assist in preparing the *pro forma* combined balance sheet and statement of earnings.

Likewise, legal counsel for the acquirer should examine the articles of incorporation, titles to property, contracts, pending or threatened litigation, and matters such as antitrust implications.

Preparing the Agreement. The agreement to purchase or to merge is prepared by legal counsel for the acquirer in collaboration with counsel for the company to be acquired. It is a comprehensive document which defines precisely the terms and conditions of acquisition or merger, the representations of each company, the covenants by each company on specific actions, the closing date, and a provision to terminate the agreement if such action should become necessary.

Concurrently, counsel should prepare the amendment to the articles of incorporation, if required, and any other documents required at the closing, and should supervise the preparation of proxy statements to shareholders.

Securing Approval by the Boards of Directors. The agreement generally is executed by the president of each company and approved by formal action of their respective boards of directors. At this time, the boards issue the notices of meetings of stockholders to act upon the agreement and related matters.

Securing Authorization by Stockholders. Legal counsel advises both companies on the required action by their stockholders and the right of appraisal granted dissenting shareholders. Essentially, in the more common methods of combining two companies, stockholder action may be defined as follows.

Statutory Merger. Formal approval by the holders of each class of stock entitled to vote is required of each of the companies, approval usually being defined as two-thirds of the outstanding shares. Upon such approval, the merger becomes binding on all stockholders except those who exercise their right of appraisal.

Acquisition through Exchange of Stock. When a company makes an acquisition through an offer of its stock in a voluntary exchange for the stock of the other company, the stock offered must have voting rights, and at least 80 percent of all classes of stock of the other company must accept the transaction if it is to be nontaxable. Stockholders who decline the exchange offer do not have the right of appraisal, but retain their stock as minority stockholders in the acquired company, which is continued as a subsidiary of the acquiring company.

Acquisition of Assets. When the property and assets of a corporation are acquired, formal approval of the sale by the stockholders of the selling company generally requires the favorable vote of those holding two-thirds of the shares entitled to vote—although sometimes only a majority is required. Dissenting shareholders generally have the right of appraisal, but it is unlikely that the appraisal value of dissenting shares will exceed the pro rata distribution of the proceeds of sale if the transaction is arranged in good faith. Therefore, the right of appraisal becomes the right to receive cash in lieu of securities if the terms of acquisition provide for payment in securities of the acquiring company.

INTEGRATING THE ACQUISITION OR THE MERGED COMPANIES

Prompt and full realization of the benefits of an acquisition or merger requires a plan and a program for integrating the operations and organizations of the two enterprises rapidly and effectively. The planning should be initiated when the two boards of directors have approved the terms so as to implement the program as soon as possible after the closing date.

As of the closing date, there will be the routine procedures of transferring the acquired company's bank accounts, insurance coverage, titles to property, leases, contracts, and the like, and the obligations on short- and long-term indebtedness, if any.

The plan of integration should cover management functions, organization, accounting and controls, marketing operations, purchasing, economies in production, budgeting control of expenses and capital outlays, and any other aspects which were important in the initial decision to seek the acquisition or merger. Also, all salaried jobs should be studied promptly to eliminate inconsistencies in compensation, wherever possible, within the salary structure and policy of the acquirer. Fringe benefits (profit sharing, pensions, group insurance, vacations) should be examined with the idea of adjusting to a uniform basis.

In most acquisitions, a primary objective is to obtain competent managerial personnel experienced in the operation, to maintain continuity of the acquired business, and frequently, to increase the resources of management talent in the acquiring company also. It is extremely important to develop an organizational structure for the combined company and to confirm promptly to the personnel to be retained their roles in management, as a means of demonstrating the good faith of the executives of the acquirer. Compromise frequently must be reached on titles, and disparities in executive compensation must be adjusted to conform to the acquirer's compensation plan.

Major emphasis should be placed on planning the "growth from within" for which purpose the acquisition or merger is undertaken. For example:

If the combination is to provide a base for a broader line of products than the combined lines of the constituents, the product development group probably should be augmented and a new-product program prepared.

If the acquirer gains an entrée to new markets, its marketing activity should be reoriented to take full advantage of this fact.

If the market coverage is to be improved and economies realized through use of the production facilities of the company, steps should be taken to redistribute the manufacturing operations.

Usually, the integration can be planned effectively by setting up task forces comprised of key personnel of both companies to perform the various projects. A firm of consultants can be assigned the tasks of structuring the organization of the combined companies, evaluating the managerial and key personnel, and recommending the staffing of the positions from an objective point of view; also, it can be called upon to carry a part of the work load of the task forces.

The composition of the board of directors of the company after the acquisition or merger generally is determined during the course of the negotiations and usually announced in the proxy statement for the meetings of the stockholders.

An acquisition or merger and integration of the second company are complex undertakings. To be successful, they must be planned with infinite attention to completeness and detail.

BIBLIOGRAPHY

Bock, Betty, *Mergers and Markets: A Guide to Economic Analysis of Case Law,* 3d ed., National Industrial Conference Board, New York, 1964.

Business Combinations, Accounting Research Bulletin, no. 48, American Institute of Certified Public Accountants, New York, January, 1957.

Choka, Allen D., *Buying, Selling, and Merging Businesses,* Joint Committee on Continuing Legal Education, American Law Institute, Chicago, and American Bar Association, New York, 1958.

Corporate Mergers and Acquisitions: Basic Financial, Legal, and Policy Aspects, Report no. 4, American Management Association, New York, 1958.

McCarthy, George D., *Acquisitions and Mergers,* The Ronald Press Company, New York, 1963.

Mace, Myles L., and George G. Montgomery, Jr., *Management Problems of Corporate Acquisitions,* Harvard Graduate School of Business Administration, Boston, 1962.

Mergers and Acquisitions: Planning and Action, Financial Executives Research Foundation, Inc., New York, 1963.

Mergers and Markets: An Economic Analysis of the 1964 Supreme Court Merger Decisions, 4th ed., National Industrial Conference Board, New York, 1965.

Scharf, Charles A., *Techniques for Buying, Selling and Merging Businesses,* Prentice-Hall, Inc., Englewood Cliffs, N.J., 1964.

CHAPTER SEVEN

Evaluating Company Performance

J. FRED WESTON *Professor and Chairman of Finance Department, University of California, Los Angeles, California*

From a general management viewpoint, company performance may be evaluated with reference to three categories of decisions: (1) administrative performance, (2) operating performance, and (3) strategic performance.[1] Administrative performance is concerned with organization, the structuring of authority and responsibility relations, and information flows. Operating performance refers to the effectiveness with which the firm employs its resources.

The appraisal of the strategic performance of the firm is an evaluation of the firm's choice of its environment and the effectiveness of its adaptation to the environment or environments in which it has chosen to operate. This analysis of the evaluation of company performance will focus on operating performance and strategic performance.

THE RETURN ON INVESTMENT CONCEPT

Any discussion of the evaluation of company performance must begin with the central concept of return on investment. The return on investment measures the profitability with which a firm employs the economic resources, command over which is expressed in its total asset figure on its balance sheet. The return on investment is obtained by multiplying the turnover of total assets times the profit margin on sales.

$$\frac{\text{Sales}}{\text{Total assets}} \times \frac{\text{profit}}{\text{sales}} = \frac{\text{profit}}{\text{total assets}}$$

When turnover is multiplied by profit margin, the result is profit to total assets. Some firms measure total assets on a net basis as presented in the balance sheet. Other firms add back the reserve for depreciation to obtain

[1] See the discussion in H. Igor Ansoff, *Corporate Strategy*, McGraw-Hill Book Company, New York, 1965, pp. 3–11.

a gross asset figure. The argument for using a gross asset figure is that if the reserve for depreciation increases, the amount of net assets shown on the balance sheet may decline, while the amount of physical assets at the disposal of the firm or department remains the same. This may make for an inherent bias in the figures for reporting a higher return on investment because the denominator is decreasing.

The basis for using the total asset figure as reported on the balance sheet (net) is that it is an indication of the actual dollars invested in the resources being used by the firm.

Whether the net or gross total asset figure is used, the emphasis of the return on investment analysis is to focus on the factors which influence turnover and the factors which influence the profit margin on sales. When the analysis of the return on investment moves to this stage, it may properly be viewed as another form of conventional financial ratio analysis.

This chapter will not deal in detail with financial ratio analysis, because these ratios deal primarily with factors affecting performance. (See Chapter 5 of Section 9.) The subject of this chapter is the identification and explanation of the performance measures themselves. Therefore the following discussion of the traditional tests of enterprise operating performance will be provided in a summary fashion.

TRADITIONAL TESTS OF ENTERPRISE OPERATING PERFORMANCE

The traditional tests of enterprise performance have centered on financial ratio analysis. Although different authors have different approaches and concentrate on different ratios, there is beginning to be consensus on the use of three major types of ratios. These three major groupings of ratios are (1) liquidity, (2) leverage, and (3) activity.[2]

Description of Standard Financial Ratios. The first two groupings of ratios emphasize financial position. *Liquidity* measures the ability of the firm to meet its cash obligations as they mature. The standard ratio is the current ratio. This is obtained by dividing current assets by current liabilities. A widely accepted standard is the banker's rule of thumb of two to one.

Leverage refers to the extent to which the firm employs the funds of creditors. The fundamental measure is the ratio of debt to equity funds (creditors' to owners' funds). The norm is $0.50 of debt for $1.00 of equity. A measure of leverage which takes into account the earnings ability of the firm is the ratio of profits before taxes to all fixed financial charges comprised of fixed-interest obligations plus lease or rental obligations. A norm is six to seven times coverage.

Activity measures emphasize flows rather than financial position. They are more dynamic in their orientation. Activity ratios refer to the turnover of asset items into sales. The logic is that the fundamental orientation of the firm is to make sales and thereby achieve profits. The investment of assets must be utilized efficiently to achieve profitability.

The activity ratios can be expressed in their simplest form by dividing assets into sales individually or in groups. The result can be equally well expressed as a percentage of sales, a ratio of sales, the number of times divided into sales, or the number of days' sales embodied in the balance sheet item.

[2] For detailed analysis of the logic and use of these ratios see any standard textbook on financial management or financial ratio analysis, such as R. A. Foulke, *Practical Financial Statement Analysis,* Prentice-Hall, Inc., Englewood Cliffs, N.J., 1962, or J. Fred Weston, *Managerial Finance,* Holt, Rinehart and Winston, Inc., New York, 1962.

Each activity ratio will be expressed in its most meaningful form along with its characteristic magnitude for manufacturing firms generally. Cash is generally expressed as a percentage of sales and runs about 5 to 6 percent. The activity of receivables is most generally expressed as the average collection period (the number of days' sales in). The average collection period varies with the terms of sale, but is approximately thirty-six days for manufacturing firms as a group. Inventory activity is usually expressed as a turnover ratio. The turnover is eight times a year for all manufacturing. Fixed assets are also expressed as a turnover. It should run in the order of magnitude of four times. Total assets will turn over into sales about two times a year.

The foregoing is a brief summary of conventional financial ratio analysis. The ratios calculated are typically used in a comparative analysis. The data for the firm are compared with the standards provided by industry composites. Such industry composites are provided from numerous sources.[3] The performance of the firm is compared with the average for the industry. Another emphasis is time-trend analysis. In such an approach, the performance of the firm is compared over a period of time. Financial ratios are compiled for the firm. The behavior over time is charted and analyzed.[4]

PROFITABILITY MEASURES

We begin with a set of profitability ratios. Profitability ratios are subject to numerous pitfalls. For example, a firm may follow the policy of a small margin on sales with high volume. Or a firm may rent or lease a high proportion of its assets. This will make the return on asset measure misleading because renting or leasing involves both the use of resources and their financing as well. For these reasons, a minimum of at least three profitability ratios should be employed. One is the ratio of profit to total assets which measures the productivity of economic resources placed at the command of the firm. This is very similar to the return on investment concept. The average for all manufacturing industries is in the range of 10 to 12 percent. However, the return on total assets will be influenced by the turnover of assets into sales that is characteristic for the industry and the portion of assets employed by the firm represented by assets that are actually owned.

The second profit ratio is profit to sales, which indicates a margin by which the firm's prices may decline and still provide a margin of profit per unit of sales. A reference figure here is a 5 percent profit on sales after taxes.

The combination of turnover of assets, profit margin on sales, and the effectiveness and extent of the use of debt (leverage) determines the rate of return on net worth or ownership funds. In this sense, the return on net worth is a superior measure to the return on investment in that it reflects not only operating performance, but financial performance as well. Since leasing or renting involves a combination of operating and financial activity, a comparison between the performances of firms with different degrees of renting or leasing *must* be based on return on net worth or ownership funds rather than return on total assets.

[3] Sources include Dun & Bradstreet; Robert Morris Associates, *Statement Studies;* Federal Trade Commission–Securities and Exchange Commission reports; Accounting Corporation of America, *Barometer of Small Business;* First National Bank of Chicago; National Cash Register Co.; trade associations; and public accountants.

[4] This charting of financial ratios is supposed to be one of the valuable contributions of the Du Pont system of financial control. Increasingly, large firms are providing "chart rooms" in which the past and prospective performance of the firm is exhibited.

TABLE 7-1. The Influence of Turnover, Profit Margin, and Leverage on the Return on Investment and the Return on Net Worth

(Sales = $1,800)

	A	B	C	D	E
Turnover.........................	2	3	2	2	2
Profit margin on sales..............	5%	5%	5%	5%	8%
Debt to total assets................	⅓	⅓	½	½	⅓
Total assets.......................	$900	$600	$900	$900	$900
Return on total assets..............	10%	15%	10%	10%	16%
Return on net worth................	12.5%	20%	15%	10%	21.5%
Net operating income...............	90	90	90	90	144
Debt interest......................	15	10	22.5	45	15
Net income........................	75	80	67.5	45	129

Table 7-1 illustrates how turnover influences the return on net worth in five basic situations.[5] Situation A is characteristic of all manufacturing companies. With a turnover of two and a profit margin on sales of 5 percent and debt to total assets of ⅓, the return on total assets is 10 percent. With a debt to total assets ratio of ⅓ and cost of debt of 5 percent, the return on net worth is magnified to 12½ percent. (Because this example abstracts from taxes, the return on net worth is understated. The before-tax profit on sales would be about 10 percent.) In situation B, the turnover has increased to three times. Both the return on total assets and return on net worth are thereby increased substantially.

Situations C and D illustrate some aspects of leverage policy. When debt is increased to 50 percent of total assets, the return on total assets is unchanged from situation A. The return on net worth in situation C rises to 15 percent with the increased use of debt. In situation D, the return on net worth drops to 10 percent, because the cost of debt is as large as the return on total assets. In situation E, the profit margin on sales is increased with the other conditions the same as in situation A. The returns on both total assets and on net worth are increased.

These illustrations demonstrate how the use of leverage can increase the return on net worth if successfully employed. The critical relationship is the profitability of total assets compared with the cost of debt. Basically, the results depend upon how effectively the resources obtained through the use of debt are employed in comparison with the cost of debt.

FINANCIAL MARKET TESTS

Return on total assets or return on net worth may be an incomplete measure of performance. The financial markets may capitalize the earnings stream of companies differently when their capital structures differ. Different leverage and liquidity policies may result in different capitalization ratios.

Related to the four measures of profitability discussed in the preceding section are four financial market tests which are often employed. These are (1) growth in earnings per share, (2) growth in market price per share, (3) the price-earnings ratio, and (4) the ratio of market to book value.

[5] We exclude consideration of taxes at this stage to focus on the effects of the other variables.

The first two financial market tests are growth in earnings per share and growth in market price per share. Any growth figure, of course, is greatly influenced by the choice of base period. From the early 1950s to 1965, earnings per share for any stock index grew at about the same rate as the economy as a whole. Earnings per share grew 6 to 8 percent per annum.

The growth in the market price per share, however, was at a somewhat higher rate, in the range of 8 to 12 percent per annum. This higher growth rate in market price per share for any group of companies reflects a rise in the price-earnings ratio on common stocks since the early 1950s. For a long time, the normal price-range ratio was about ten times. This was its level in the 1950s. However, by the middle 1950s the standard price-earnings ratio moved up to about fourteen times. From the late 1950s to 1965, price-earnings ratios fluctuated in the 18 to 20 times range.

Finally we consider the ratio between the market price of stocks and their book values. Since book values reflect historical costs and earnings retention, they reflect in part the timing of asset purchases and earnings-retention policies. Although the ratios of market to book value fluctuate for different firms, a well-managed firm should expect a market value from 1½ to 2 times its book value per share.

For a growth firm, the performance measures would be higher. The growth in earnings per share could be expected to be over 10 percent per annum. The growth in market price per share might be 15 percent or more per annum. The price-earnings ratio would be twenty-five to thirty times or better. Finally, the ratio of market to book value for growth companies reaches as high as three times or more. These ratios for growth companies represent the upper ranges of financial market tests by which management may gage the performance of its own company.

MARKET POSITION TESTS

We now turn to an analysis of the firm's position in its own industry—market position tests. The relevant measures are (1) trends in share of market, (2) trends in quality of product, (3) productivity trends, (4) cost-reduction trends, and (5) trends in relative selling price.

One of the performance measures frequently employed is the firm's share of its industry. The firm's industry represents what the market potential for the firm may be. How well the firm exploits that opportunity is measured by its share of its total industry. Trends in the firm's share of its industry represent a significant measure of performance in comparison with its competitors.

The other market position tests help determine the firm's share of its industry. One of the important factors is the firm's reputation for leadership in quality and performance of its products. In the producer durable goods industries, reliability of performance and the availability of service are particularly important.

Productivity measures the efficiency with which the firm utilizes labor inputs and capital inputs. Productivity measures are output per unit of labor input, output per unit of capital input, and output per unit of total inputs. Over a long period of years, productivity in the American economy as a whole increased at approximately 3 percent per annum. In recent years, productivity increased over 3½ percent per annum. Although variation among individual industries occurs, a firm should aim at an increase in productivity of at least 3½ to 4 percent per annum if it is to compare favorably with the economy as a whole.

Related to productivity performance is cost reduction. Unit costs reflect the prices paid for labor and capital as well as their productivity. Characteristically, as an industry or a product line matures, many cost reductions are achieved. Hence, if a firm is to maintain its position in an industry or product line, cost reduction is necessary.

As an industry matures, the rise of new and increased competition can be expected to put increased pressure on prices. Thus, cost reduction is related to selling price. The performance of a product line or company is likely to be greatly influenced by the ability to reduce prices over time.

All of these five factors are a part of and reflect a firm's market position over time. These are critical measures of the firm's performance. They are significant indicators, or barometers, of what is likely to show up in the more quantitatively oriented ratios discussed in the preceding sections.

MEASURES OF STRATEGIC PERFORMANCE

Related to the measures of the firm's market position are measures of the strategic performance of the firm. The strategic performance measures discriminate between the causes of differential performance by the firm. Strategic planning emphasizes comparisons with individual close competitors rather than with industry standards. An industry is an average of a set of firms; some of these will be good, some poor. The aspiring firm seeks to compare itself with its close competitors.

The other important orientations of ratios for strategic production market planning are distinctive in two respects. First, the ratios are oriented to the future. Second, emphasis is on economic characteristics of the product-market environment rather than the internal performance measures of the firm. Conventional financial ratio analysis focuses on the internal operations of the firm. Financial ratios for evaluation of the strategic position of the firm emphasize characteristics of the firm's external environment, are oriented to the future, and emphasize proper modeling of the characteristics of the firm to survival and growth in its economic environment.

Economic Environment. The tests of the firm's strategic position emphasize the economic environment. The economic variables considered should include the following:

1. Industry demand
   a. Growth
   b. Stability
   c. Stage in life cycle
2. Competitive trends
   a. Entry
   b. Size structure
   c. Growth-to-capacity relationships
3. Impact of dynamic change
   a. Political
   b. Technological
   c. Economic
   d. Social

The third set of factors overlaps the first two. The distinction is that in going through the appraisal for the first two, we make our best probabilistic judgments about the future as we see it. In analyzing the third set of factors, we take into account the fact that the environment, as viewed under the first two sets of factors, is subject to forces of change whose general directions may be sketched, but whose specific manifestations cannot be described.

Goals versus Prospects. The strategic planning of the firm requires that the firm relate its characteristics to its future environment. Two exercises in this connection will be of great value. One is to look at the prospects for sales growth and stability, and profit growth and stability in the environment as the firm can best view it at the time. The difference between the firm's goals and what it is likely to achieve in its environment may be identified as the firm's strategic gap. Concretely, let us suppose that the firm has the following goals: growth rate in earnings per share of 8 percent per annum, return on investment after taxes of 15 percent, and a sales growth of 10 percent per annum. The difference between these goals and the firm's prospects may be used as indicators of the firm's strategic gap. The firm's executives must formulate plans, policies, and operations to achieve the firm's announced goals or change the goals.

The firm's strategic gap may also be expressed in qualitative terms by constructing a matrix. Along the top of the matrix is a list of items that are required for success in the environment at that stage of the firm's product-market life cycle. These are such items as ability to make an initial investment of $10 million, ability to spend $1 million per year on research and development, ability to carry out large-scale national advertising programs, and systems competence on advanced complex items. In different environments, these requirements exist in varying degrees.

On the left-hand side of the matrix, the firm analyzes its own capabilities. The difference between what it takes to succeed in the product-market environment

I. Financial ratios
   A. Liquidity ratios
      1. Current ratio... 2 times
      2. Quick ratio.. 1 time
   B. Leverage ratios
      1. Current debt to total assets............................... 25%
      2. Long-term debt to total assets............................ 10%
      3. Total debt to total assets................................. 35%
   C. Activity ratios
      1. Cash to sales... 6%
      2. Average collection period................................. 36 days
      3. Inventory turnover....................................... 8 times
      4. Fixed-asset turnover..................................... 4 times
      5. Total asset turnover...................................... 2 times
II. Profitability measures (after taxes)
   A. Return on investment....................................... 10%
   B. Profit margin on sales...................................... 5%
   C. Return on net worth.. 15%
   D. Margin over target ROI..................................... Plus
III. Financial market tests
   A. Growth in earnings per share............................... 6%
   B. Growth in market price per share........................... 6–8%
   C. Price-earnings ratio....................................... 18–20 times
   D. Market to book values..................................... 1.5–2.0 times
IV. Market position tests
   A. Market share.. Increasing
   B. Market quality leadership.................................. Improving
   C. Productivity.. 3–4% per year
   D. Cost reduction.. 1–2% per year
   E. Selling prices... 1–2% per year
V. Strategic performance tests
   A. Industry demand growth.................................... 6% per year
   B. Competitive trends.. Judgment
   C. Impact of dynamic change.................................. Judgment

FIG. 7-1. *Management performance measures.*

(with particular reference to the stage of the life cycle of the environment) and the capabilities which the firm possesses is another statement of the firm's strategic gap. One remedy for a strategic gap is found in diversification studies.[6]

SUMMARY

We may now bring together the large number of factors discussed earlier into a summary presented by Figure 7-1. It is clear that a broad list of considerations is involved in evaluating performance. For specific lines of business, some of the ratios are more important than others. No cookbook set of directions can be provided. The utilization of these performance measures must combine experience and judgment. This ultimately is the test of effective managerial performance.

BIBLIOGRAPHY

Ansoff, H. Igor, *Corporate Strategy*, McGraw-Hill Book Company, New York, 1965.
Davidson, Sidney, George H. Sorter, and Hemu Kalle, "Measuring the Defensive Position of a Firm," *Financial Analysts Journal*, vol. 20, January–February, 1964, pp. 23–29.
Gold, Bela, and Ralph M. Kraus, "Integrating Physical with Financial Measures for Managerial Controls," *Academy of Management Journal*, June, 1964, pp. 109–127.
Key Business Ratios, Dun & Bradstreet, Inc., New York.
Stryker, Perrin, "P&C for Profit," *Fortune*, vol. 45, April, 1952, p. 128.
Weston, J. Fred, *Managerial Finance*, Holt, Rinehart and Winston, Inc., New York, 1962.

[6] H. Igor Ansoff and J. Fred Weston, "Merger Objectives and Organization Structure," *The Quarterly Review of Economics and Business*, vol. 2, August, 1962, pp. 49–58.

CHAPTER EIGHT

Techniques for Evaluating Prospective Investments

RAYMOND I. REUL   *FMC Corporation, New York, New York*

The responsibilities of industrial managers are many in number and varied in nature, but it is possible to classify all of them into one of two basic categories:
1. *Custodial*—the audit and guidance of existing investments
2. *Entrepreneurial*—the planning, selecting, and implementation of new investments

Although both of these activities are addressed to the same ultimate objective—the continuance and expansion of the profitability of the enterprise—the tools, techniques, and philosophies employed are quite different.

CUSTODIAL FUNCTION

The custodial function requires the continuing measurement and control of the performance of past commitments to ensure the conservation of the committed assets and the optimization of their performance. The data required for this type of evaluation and guidance are provided by accounting techniques specifically devised for this purpose. They are designed to report performance promptly at frequent intervals so that corrective action can be timely and effective. A variety of logical but completely arbitrary assumptions are employed to achieve these results. There are three major tools:

The Balance Sheet. The balance sheet presents a comparison of the status of assets and liabilities of the entire enterprise at a given moment, the end of an accounting period. The length of accounting periods is completely arbitrary, but is usually one year or less. It provides a continuing check on the conservation of assets.

The Profit and Loss Statement. Prepared at the end of each accounting period, the profit and loss statement provides a measure of the performance of all existing assets of the entire enterprise during the just-completed accounting period. Completely arbitrary accruals of capital consumption and other non-period factors are required. It provides a continuing check on the productivity of committed assets.

The Return on Investment. Return on investment is the ratio of annual profits of the entire enterprise to the value of the assets in use. The choice of denominator varies, with book value, original investment, and current replacement cost being frequently used. It is an attempt to relate the magnitude of results to the magnitude of the commitment. Because of the many arbitrary assumptions used in its preparation, its usefulness is often questionable.

Thus, it should be clear that all these accounting techniques have three things in common. They record history, they are concerned with the enterprise as a whole, and they are designed to make frequent evaluations covering short periods of time.

ENTREPRENEURIAL FUNCTION

This function is concerned with the identification of new investment opportunities, the appraisal of the prospective profitability of each, and the selection of individual commitments which are anticipated to be both acceptably profitable and within the available financial and management resources of the enterprise. Consideration must be given to three aspects.

1. *Functional feasibility*—a measure of the technical and commercial soundness of the prospective project which examines market availability, product and facility suitability, and the extent to which qualified staffing and know-how are available or obtainable

2. *Financial acceptability*—a comparison of the magnitude of the probable reward and the probability of obtaining it with the cost of financing the required funds and with the possibility and extent of the consequences of failure

3. *Economic productivity*—a mathematical appraisal of the magnitude of the reward anticipated from an investment under consideration, expressed so that direct comparisons can be made with the cost of obtaining the required funds and the magnitude of rewards available from alternative investments, and so that the sensitivity of results to uncertainties in predictions can be tested

From the foregoing, it can be seen that the devising of an effective technique for the appraisal of economic productivity presents the following problems.

1. Although economic productivity is the only one of these three aspects susceptible to quantitative mathematical evaluation, this is no justification for ignoring the others. This means that the technique applied should be an evaluation procedure rather than a decision mechanism.

2. Because data on current business transactions are almost always expressed on an accounting basis, with all the built-in arbitrary assumptions of these techniques, care must be taken when evaluating individual projects to translate all input data to an actual cash-flow basis.

3. Because prospective productivity is dependent upon future events, its measurement must be based upon predictions and estimates. Because forecasts of future sales, costs, and technological developments can never be completely accurate, it has been quite widely argued that simple, approximate methods of economic evaluation are sufficiently accurate. Although there is some justification for this point of view, an informed and unprejudiced assessment of the facts indicates that such an attitude is more likely to represent an alibi for continuation of the enjoyment of making major decisions in a completely irresponsible manner without getting all of the available information and without devoting to such data the detailed and serious study they deserve. Decisions concerning prospective investments are by far the most important of management responsibilities. These decisions are almost always irrevocable, and the results

usually extend far into the future. Serious mistakes can be fatal. There is no excuse for not using the best available techniques for assisting judgment in this vitally important area of decision making.

Inadequacies of Traditional Methods of Evaluating Prospective Investments. There are three prime factors which must be considered in evaluating any prospective investment.

1. The size of the investment (total of net disbursements)
2. The amount of receipts (total over entire life)
3. The timing (time relationship between 1 and 2)

The simplest way of relating these factors is to ratio them against each other to get an overall performance ratio.

$$\text{Performance ratio} = \frac{\text{total receipts/total life}}{\text{total net disbursements}}$$

Multiplied by 100 and expressed in terms of dollars and years, this becomes the familiar percent annual return on original investment, or ROI.

$$\text{ROI} = \frac{\$ \text{ total receipts}}{\text{years of life} \times \$ \text{ total original investment}}$$

A more frequently used variation of this approach is the "payback" or "payout," which is merely the reciprocal of the ratio. This is the number of years required to return the original investment.

$$\text{Years to pay back} = \frac{\$ \text{ total original investment}}{\$ \text{ total receipts/years of life}}$$

Because of their simplicity and ease of computation, these yardsticks have had wide acceptance and use. This is unfortunate, for they can be inconclusive and can frequently give misleading evaluations. For instance, applied to the three prospective investments shown in Table 8-1, they fail to show any difference in economic desirability. It is obvious from mere observation that the alternatives vary widely in profitability, yet these practical yardsticks rate them as identical. The reason for their failure to give a valid indication is that although they take time into consideration in order to establish a rate of receipts per

TABLE 8-1

	Alt. *A*	Alt. *B*	Alt. *C*
Investment—start year 1	$10,000	$10,000	$10,000
Receipts—end year 1	3,000	3,000	3,000
end year 2	3,000	3,000	3,000
end year 3	3,000	3,000	3,000
end year 4	3,000	3,000	
end year 5	3,000	3,000	
end year 6	3,000		
end year 7	3,000		
end year 8	3,000		
end year 9	3,000		
end year 10	3,000		
Total	$30,000	$15,000	$ 9,000
ROI	30 %	30 %	30 %
Payout (years)	3⅓ %	3⅓ %	3⅓ %

TABLE 8-2

	Alt. D	Alt. E
Investment—start year 1	$10,000	$10,000
Receipts—end year 1	11,000	1,000
end year 2	1,000	1,000
end year 3	1,000	1,000
end year 4	1,000	1,000
end year 5	1,000	11,000
Total	$15,000	$15,000
Av. ret. on av. inv	20 %	20 %

unit of time, they neglect to take into consideration duration of time over which that rate is maintained.

The simplest way to incorporate duration into the above computation is to introduce a factor to cover amortization or recovery of the investment. This results in a new yardstick, which is called the "percentage average return on average investment."

$$\text{Av. ret. on av. inv.} = \frac{\$ \text{ total receipts} - \$ \text{ total investment}}{\text{years} \times \frac{1}{2} \$ \text{ total investment}} \times 100$$

Because the investment is completely recovered during its life, the average investment is just half of the original investment.

Applied to the three alternatives presented in Table 8-1, the following evaluation results.

$$\begin{array}{ll} \text{Alt. } A & 40\,\%^* \\ \text{Alt. } B & 20\,\% \\ \text{Alt. } C & 0\,\% \end{array}$$

Obviously, in this case, the average return on average investment does do a better job, but can it be depended upon to yield meaningful results when receipt patterns are not uniform? Will it yield valid comparisons among alterna-

* Sample calculation:

$$\frac{30,000 - 10,000}{10 \times \dfrac{10,000}{2}} \times 100 = 40\,\%$$

TABLE 8-3

	Alt. F	Alt. G
Investment—start year 1	$10,000	$10,000
Receipts—end year 1	3,000	3,000
end year 2	3,000	3,000
end year 3	3,000	3,000
end year 4	3,000	3,000
end year 5	3,000	3,000
end year 6	....	100
end year 7	....	100
end year 8	....	100
end year 9	....	100
end year 10	....	100
Total	$15,000	$15,500
Av. ret. on av. inv	20 %	11 %

tives? Will evaluations be an accurate representation of the true situation?

In Table 8-2, average return on average investment is applied to two prospective investments that differ only in respect to anticipated pattern of receipts. Alternative *D* is obviously much more profitable, but the average return on average investment gives no such indication.

Applied to the alternatives in Table 8-3, the results are most surprising. Alternative *G*, which yields exactly the same receipts in the same pattern as alternative *B*, plus additional receipts in later years, is reported by the average return on average investment as earning at a lower rate. Obviously, this is a false indication.

It is clear that the traditional methods, ROI payout and average return on average investment, are both inadequate and unreliable.

EVALUATIONS BASED UPON INTEREST CALCULATIONS

It has been fairly well established that interest-based computations can be depended upon to yield evaluations of profitability of prospective investments that will be both accurate and reliable. But there is a great deal of disagreement as to which of the many different promulgated methods is most appropriate. The source of these difficulties appears to be confusion as to just what should be measured and a failure to understand just what each of the promulgated methods actually measures.

All interest-based methods utilize the principle of equivalence. In all of these methods, the individual disbursements are converted to a common equivalent basis and compared. There are many of these methods, but all of the valid ones fall into one of three categories, each of which measures investment productivity from a different point of view. The nature of these differences will be carefully detailed and then illustrated by their application to the appraisal of the demonstration problem presented in Table 8-4. In these illustrations, annual compounding and instantaneous cash flows have been assumed in the interest of simplicity in demonstrating principles.

Net Equivalent Worth at a Specific Time. In this method, all cash flows are converted to their equivalent worth at a stated time with a stipulated interest rate and netted out. When the stated time is the time at which the investment is to be initiated, it is called the "net present worth method" (see Table 8-5). When the stated time is when the last receipt is expected to occur, it is called the "terminal value method" (see Table 8-6).

TABLE 8-4

Timing	Actual cash flows	
	Disbursements	Receipts
Start 1965.............	$1,000	
Start 1966.............	2,000	
End 1966.............	......	$ 800
End 1969.............	......	2,000
End 1970.............	......	3,904
Total.............	$3,000	$6,704

TABLE 8-5.   Net Present Worth with Interest at 10%

Timing	Actual cash flows	Present worth at 10%	
		Factors	Amounts
Start 1965................................	$-1,000	1.100	$-1,100
Start 1966................................	-2,000	1.000	-2,000
End 1966.................................	+ 800	0.909	+ 727
End 1969.................................	+2,000	0.683	+1,366
End 1970.................................	+3,904	0.621	+2,424
Net present worth at 10% (at the beginning of the first year of receipts)....			$+1,417

Note that the terminal value can be readily converted to the net present worth by multiplying it by the appropriate factor:

$$+\$2,281 \times 0.621 = +\$1,417$$

This method may be classified as a situation analysis. It measures what is accomplished by investing a stated amount of money for an established study period. It requires the stipulation of a specific reinvestment rate.

The answer may be defined as the difference between the results obtained by making the proposed investment with the proceeds assumed to be reinvested at the stipulated interest rate until the end of the project, and the results obtainable by investing a similar amount at the same stipulated interest rate for the same study period. This answer is the net difference, stated as the equivalent amount at some specified time.

This method is a decision technique suitable only for accept-reject conclusions. It is virtually impossible to derive a basis for comparing risk with yield, especially when comparing projects with different lives.

Net Level Annual Equivalent Worth. This method is also called the "equivalent annual cost method." All cash flows are converted to a level annual equivalent at a stipulated interest rate. This is accomplished in two steps. First, all cash flows are converted to their net equivalent worth at some point in time using this stipulated interest rate. Then this same interest rate is used again to convert this net equivalent worth to its level annual equivalent over a stipulated study period.

TABLE 8-6.   Net Terminal Value with Interest at 10%

Timing	Actual cash flows	Terminal value at 10%	
		Factors	Amounts
Start 1965................................	$-1,000	1.772	$-1,772
Start 1966................................	-2,000	1.611	-3,222
End 1966.................................	+ 800	1.464	+1,171
End 1969.................................	+2,000	1.100	+2,200
End 1970.................................	+3,904	1.000	+3,904
Net future worth at 10% at termination of project......................			$+2,281

TABLE 8-7

Timing	Deposits	Interest	Withdrawals	Balance
Start 1965............	$+1,000	......	....	$1,000
Start 1966............	+2,000	$+200	....	3,200
End 1966..............	....	+640	$− 800	3,040
End 1967..............	....	+608	....	3,648
End 1968..............	....	+730	....	4,378
End 1969.............	....	+876	−2,000	3,254
End 1970.............	....	+650	−3,904	0

Applying the second step of this procedure to the net present worth already obtained for this problem, we get

$$\text{Net level annual equiv.} = \frac{+\$1,417}{0.91 + 0.83 + 0.75 + 0.68 + 0.62} = +\$371$$

This method may also be classified as a situation analysis. It differs from the net equivalent worth evaluation, however, in one significant way. Because the answer is expressed as an annual equivalent, prospective investments with different lives may be directly compared. It should be understood, however, that when such comparisons are made, there is the built-in assumption that there will be infinite repetition of both alternatives.

If net level equivalent annual costs are divided by the interest rate used in their calculation, the result is the capitalized cost. This is the present worth of perpetual repetitions at the stipulated interest rate.

True Rate of Return. The word "true" is used here as a means of distinguishing this valid method from the many so-called rate of return approximations.

This method requires no stipulations whatsoever as to reference point in time, applicable interest rate, or study period. The answer obtained by this method may be defined as *the interest rate at which the proposed disbursements would have to be invested in an annuity fund for that fund to be able to make payments equal to and at the same time as the receipts anticipated from the project.* This is the equivalent average earning rate of the prospective project.

The true rate of return for the demonstration problem in Table 8-4 is 20 percent. The validity of this answer is demonstrated in Table 8-7 by simulating the investment of the prospective disbursements in an annuity fund from which withdrawals equal to the earnings of the project are simulated.

TABLE 8-8. Calculation with Zero Point at Start of 1966

Timing	Reference point	Actual cash flows	Present worth at 20 %	
			Factors	Amounts
Start 1965..............	−1	$−1,000	1.200	$−1,200
Start 1966..............	0	−2,000	1.000	−2,000
End 1966................	+1	+ 800	0.833	+ 666
End 1969................	+4	+2,000	0.482	+ 964
End 1970................	+5	+3,904	0.402	+1,570
Net present worth..				0

TABLE 8-9. Calculation with Zero Point at End of 1970

Timing	Reference point	Actual cash flows	Present worth at 20%	
			Factors	Amounts
Start 1965.............	−6	$−1,000	2.986	$−2,986
Start 1966.............	−5	−2,000	2.488	−4,976
End 1966..............	−4	+ 800	2.074	+1,658
End 1969..............	−1	+2,000	1.200	+2,400
End 1970..............	0	+3,904	1.000	+3,904
Net worth at end of 1970......................................				0

The method used to solve for this answer is to determine, by trial and error, the interest rate at which the sum of the present worths of receipts is equal to the sum of the present worths of disbursements.

The results of the successful trial calculations on the demonstration problem are illustrated in Table 8-8.

Table 8-9 demonstrates that a change in reference or zero point in no way changes the answer.

This method of solution is an algorithm. It is designed to handle the computation of the rate of return of prospective investments in which all net disbursements occur prior to all net receipts. *It should never be applied when net disbursements are predicted to occur after receipts.* Failure to observe this caution can result in false and sometimes multiple answers.

Simplified Computation of the True Rate of Return. The "profitability index" approach to the calculation of the true rate of return was first published in *Factory Management and Maintenance* in October 1955. It introduced the idea of using pretabulated work sheets and graphical interpolation as a means of reducing the time-consuming and often confusing trial and error computation of rate of return to a simple, routine clerical operation. The use of this technique to solve the demonstration problem in Table 8-4 is illustrated in Figure 8-1.

Description of the Work Sheet. The work sheet provides separate schedules for disbursements and receipts. Both, however, are oriented to the same zero point, which is identified by a heavy line with a diamond at the left. The form is designed to facilitate the assumption of the beginning of the first year in which receipts occur as the zero point. (With most problems this will result in minimum computational effort for specified accuracy of answer.) Single-payment compounding and discounting present worth factors for three different rates are provided. (On this demonstration form, the pretabulated present worth factors are based upon annual compounding and instantaneous cash flows. Conversion to the more frequently used convention of continuous compounding and during-the-year receipt is merely a matter of substituting different present worth factors. A blank form with such factors is illustrated in Figure 8-2.)

Directions for the Use of the Pretabulated Work Sheet. The first step in the use of this work sheet is to enter each of the anticipated disbursements and receipts at its scheduled time in the column headed "Trial 1 @ 0% Interest Rate." Note that by making this comparison of the totals of actual disbursements and receipts, we are literally making a trial at 0 percent interest rate. That is, because the sum of the actual receipts in this demonstration problem is greater than the sum of the actual disbursements, merely setting down the figures in this form demonstrates that the earning rate or rate of return of this project is greater than zero.

TIMING			TRIAL 1 0% INTEREST RATE		TRIAL 2 10% INTEREST RATE		TRIAL 3 25% INTEREST RATE		TRIAL 4 40% INTEREST RATE	
CAL. YEAR	PERIOD		ACTUAL AMOUNT OF DISBURSEMENTS	FACTOR	PRESENT WORTH	FACTOR	PRESENT WORTH	FACTOR	PRESENT WORTH	FACTOR	PRESENT WORTH
BEFORE / AFTER	1ST YR.	AT ST.	1,000	1.10	1,100	1.25	1,250	1.40	1,400		
		MIDDLE		1.05		1.13		1.20			
	1ST YR.	AT ST.	2,000	1.00	2,000	1.00	2,000	1.00	2,000		
		MIDDLE		0.95		0.91		0.83			
TOTALS (A)			3,000		3,100		3,250		3,400		
CAL. YEAR	PERIOD		ACTUAL AMOUNT OF RECEIPTS	FACTOR	PRESENT WORTH	FACTOR	PRESENT WORTH	FACTOR	PRESENT WORTH	FACTOR	PRESENT WORTH
BEFORE	1ST YEAR END		800	0.91	728	0.80	640	0.71	568		
AFTER ZERO POINT	2ND YEAR END			0.83		0.54		0.51			
	3RD YEAR END			0.75		0.51		0.36			
	4TH YEAR END		2,000	0.68	1,360	0.41	820	0.26	520		
	5TH YEAR END		3,904	0.62	2,420	0.33	1,288	0.19	742		
	6TH YEAR END			0.56		0.25		0.13			
	7TH YEAR END			0.51		0.21		0.09			
	8TH YEAR END			0.47		0.17		0.07			
	9TH YEAR END			0.42		0.13		0.05			
	10TH YEAR END			0.39		0.11		0.03			
	11TH YEAR END			0.35		0.09		0.02			
	12TH YEAR END			0.32		0.07		0.02			
	13TH YEAR END			0.29		0.06		0.01			
	14TH YEAR END			0.26		0.04		0.01			
	15TH YEAR END			0.24		0.04		0.01			
	16TH YEAR END			0.22		0.03					
	17TH YEAR END			0.20		0.02					
	18TH YEAR END			'0.18		0.02					
	19TH YEAR END			0.16		0.01					
	20TH YEAR END			0.15		0.01					
TOTALS (B)			6,704		4,508		2,748		1,830		
RATIO A/B			0.47		0.69		1.18		1.86		

INTERPOLATION CHART

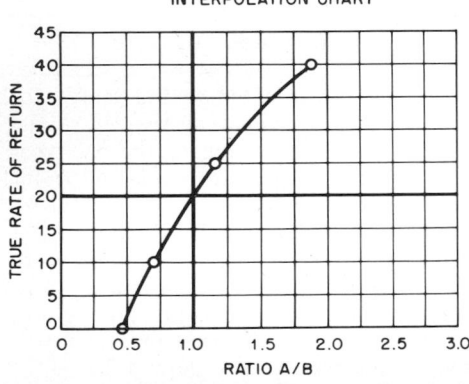

TRUE RATE OF RETURN, 20 %

FIG. 8-1. *Work sheet for computing true rate of return—annual compounding.*

The next trial, 2 at 10% interest rate, is made by multiplying each of the actual amounts of disbursements and receipts each year by the adjacent applicable present worth factor. The figures for trial 3 at 25% and 4 at 40% are calculated and entered in the same fashion. Then at each trial rate, the sum of the present worths of disbursements is divided by the sum of the present worths of receipts. The ratios thus obtained are entered in spaces labeled "A/B."

TIMING		PERIOD	TRIAL 1 0% INTEREST RATE — ACTUAL AMOUNT OF DISBURSEMENTS	TRIAL 2 10% FACTOR	TRIAL 2 PRESENT WORTH	TRIAL 3 15% FACTOR	TRIAL 3 PRESENT WORTH	TRIAL 4 25% FACTOR	TRIAL 4 PRESENT WORTH	TRIAL 5 40% FACTOR	TRIAL 5 PRESENT WORTH
SECTION A OUTFLOW / BEFORE ZERO	2	AT ST.		1.221		1.350		1.649		2.225	
		DURING		1.162		1.253		1.459		1.834	
	1	AT ST.		1.105		1.162		1.284		1.492	
		DURING		1.052		1.079		1.136		1.230	
AFTER ZERO	1	AT ST.		1.000		1.000		1.000		1.000	
		DURING		0.952		0.929		0.885		0.824	
		2. DURING		0.861		0.799		0.689		0.553	
		3. DURING		0.779		0.688		0.537		0.370	
		4. DURING		0.705		0.592		0.418		0.248	
		5. DURING		0.638		0.510		0.326		0.166	
TOTALS (A)											

			ACTUAL AMOUNT OF RECEIPTS	FACTOR	PRESENT WORTH	FACTOR	PRESENT WORTH	FACTOR	PRESENT WORTH	FACTOR	PRESENT WORTH
SECTION B CASH INFLOW AFTER ZERO		1. DURING		0.952		0.929		0.885		0.824	
		2. DURING		0.861		0.799		0.689		0.553	
		3. DURING		0.779		0.688		0.537		0.370	
		4. DURING		0.705		0.592		0.418		0.248	
		5. DURING		0.638		0.510		0.326		0.166	
		6. DURING		0.577		0.439		0.254		0.112	
		7. DURING		0.522		0.378		0.197		0.075	
		8. DURING		0.473		0.325		0.154		0.050	
		9. DURING		0.428		0.280		0.119		0.034	
		10. DURING		0.387		0.241		0.093		0.023	
		11. DURING		0.350		0.207		0.073		0.015	
		12. DURING		0.317		0.178		0.057		0.010	
TOTALS (B)											
RATIO A/B			0%	10%		15%		25%		40%	

INTERPOLATION CHART

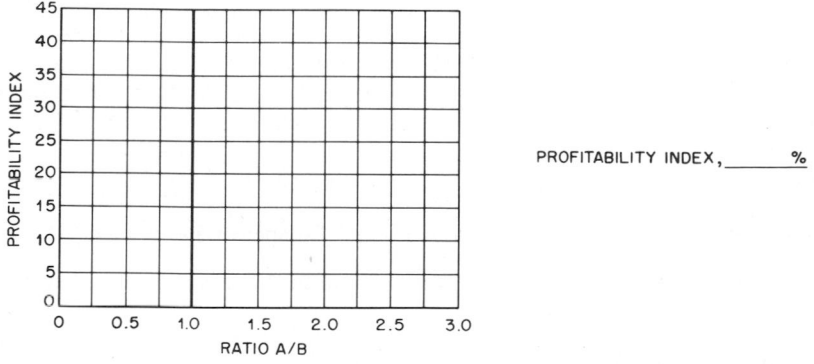

PROFITABILITY INDEX, _____ %

FIG. 8-2. *Alternative work sheet for computing true rate of return—continuous compounding.*

The solution is found by determining the interest rate at which this *A/B* ratio is equal to unity. This is done, using the chart provided, by plotting each of these ratios against the interest rate at which it was calculated (including the ratio at zero interest rate) and drawing a smooth curve through these points. A horizontal line drawn through the point at which this curve intersects the unity line indicates the answer on the vertical scale. This is the true earning rate or rate of return of the project.

The answer thus obtained by graphical interpolation is not approximately correct, but is as exact as the scale of the plotting chart will permit us to read. It is, to a certain extent, self-checking. If a smooth curve cannot be drawn through the four points plotted, it is positive evidence that a mistake has been made in the computations or plotting. Only three points are required to determine a curve. The fourth serves as a check on accuracy. In addition to simplicity, speed, and minimum possibility for errors, this method offers the maximum accuracy of answers with a given number of decimal places in the present worth factors. This is because the ratio at zero interest rate has maximum sensitivity to variations in cash flows regardless of their timing.

SUMMARY

Although all three of the appraisal methods described are quite valid and yield accurate evaluations, they answer different questions.

The *net equivalent worth* measures the results achieved by a given sum of money during a stated study period. The answer is expressed as a single number which is not directly related to the size of the investment or the life of the project. It evaluates the weighted average performance of both the project and the other uses to which the funds are applied.

The *net level annual equivalent worth* measures the continuing results that can be anticipated from perpetual repetition of the specified project. The answer is expressed as a single number which is not directly related to the size of the project, but is related to the life of the project in such a way that projects of unequal life can be directly compared.

The *true rate of return* measures the actual earning rate of funds in use. The answer is an interest rate which takes into consideration both the size of the investment and the life of the project. It yields a direct measurement of the economic productivity of the prospective investment itself.

The true rate of return is the only one of these yardsticks which gives an unequivocal answer to the question, "If I invest my money in this project, what will the project earn for me?" It gives an answer which is directly comparable with the cost of borrowing the required funds. It is the only one that yields a result which is an evaluation rather than a decision. For these reasons, it is recommended as the most suitable yardstick.

BIBLIOGRAPHY

Brickner, W. H., "The Dollars and Sense of Capital Equipment Justification," *TAPPI Journal,* February, 1960.

Dean, Joel, "Measuring the Productivity of Capital," *Harvard Business Review,* January–February, 1954.

Edge, C. G., *A Practical Manual on the Appraisal of Capital Expenditures,* Society of Industrial and Cost Accountants of Canada, Toronto, 1964.

Grant, Eugene L., and W. Grant Ireson, *Principles of Engineering Economy,* 4th ed., The Ronald Press Company, New York, 1960.

Martin, J. C., "How to Measure Project Profitability," *Petro/Chemical Engineering,* August, 1960.

Merrit, A. J., and Allen Sykes, *The Finance and Analysis of Capital Projects,* Longmans, Green & Co., Ltd., London, 1962.

Reul, Raymond I., "Algorithms vs. Concepts," *Management Accounting,* March, 1965.

Reul, Raymond I., "Newest Way to Figure Payoff," *Factory,* October, 1955.

Reul, Raymond I., "The Profitability Index," *Harvard Business Review,* July–August, 1957.

Reul, Raymond I., "Profitability Index for Machine Justification," *Automation,* March, 1965.

Weaver, J., and Robert Reilly, "Interest Rate of Return," *Chemical Engineering Progress,* October, 1956.

COMMON CONCERNS OF ALL MANAGERS

CHAPTER ONE

Establishing Policy

MAURICE O. BEVERLEY *General Production Manager, Moore Business Forms, Inc., Niagara Falls, New York*

Science and technology have placed many new and sophisticated tools at management's disposal. A basic management problem, however, is still the age-old one of human relations—helping people work effectively toward organizational goals. The large capital investment required for equipment has encouraged the development of larger plants and corporations which, in turn, involve much larger groupings of people than in the earlier stages of our industrial society. Effective direction of the activities of large organizations requires sound guidelines or basic reference information for decision making. Most successful companies provide this direction through soundly conceived and developed *policies*.

POLICY, OBJECTIVE, AND PROCEDURE DEFINED

Establishing policy may be described as "formalizing organizational attitudes toward specific types of repetitive problems as guides to decision making." The need for clearly defined and understood policies increases as an organization grows in size. Even a small owner-operated business, however, must have a framework of policies, written or understood, if it is to continue to function satisfactorily when the owner is absent.

It is important to differentiate between a *policy*, an *objective*, and a *procedure*. Policies form the basic framework of principles and rules to be used as reference information for decision making. They guide an organization's managers in a continuing and consistent pattern of decisions and direction of thought. Policies supplement each other. Over a period of years, policies form "a body of law" which expedites managerial decision making. Most importantly, they sharply diminish the hazard of conflicting verdicts and incompatible, ill-assorted ventures which result from inadequate information and guidance.

In contrast to a policy, an objective is a more or less specific goal or aim. The dictionary describes an objective as "that which any person or group is seeking ardently to achieve." An objective is something to achieve; a policy is a guide to its achievement.

A procedure is "the manner or way of performing anything, a process, method, or tactics." Well-defined procedures are important in any organization to direct employees in the performance of their duties. Because they tend to overlap, procedure is often confused with policy. A procedure essentially describes *how* to do something, whereas a policy is part of a framework of general principles, that is, the *why* behind decision making. Frequently, a written policy will include procedural information which describes how to implement a policy. A written procedure will sometimes include information on why certain procedures are necessary.

INFLUENCE OF POLICIES ON ORGANIZATIONAL EFFECTIVENESS

It is widely recognized in management that to achieve maximum success we must "out-manage" our competition. Comparatively speaking, money and first-class equipment are readily and broadly available. Therefore, management skill in "getting results through people" has increasingly become the key to a successful enterprise.

A group of people will function effectively as a team, however, only if they are properly organized, directed, and motivated. The team becomes a dynamic organization when authority for decision making is intelligently decentralized and delegated to the lowest appropriate supervisory level in the organization. The proper level should be that point where all the relevant and necessary information for the making of the decision comes together. Or, restated, every decision must be made at the lowest possible level where that particular decision can be made intelligently. Responsibility must be transferred when authority is delegated. The man next up the ladder in the organizational structure must avoid making decisions for his subordinate. The subordinate must make and live with his decisions; he must work his way through the results, be they good or bad.

An industrial organization may be described as an integrated and coordinated collection of small teams. Each "small team" consists of a group of workers and their leader. The leader may be a foreman, a section head, a corporal, a straw boss, or anyone else at the first level of management. He, in turn, is part of another "team," persons at the same level of authority who are responsible to the next level of management—supervisor, department head, shift boss, sergeant, or whatever. If the persons appointed to each supervisory level command the respect of their associates and subordinates, the organization can achieve maximum effectiveness. The relationships within each team must be those of mutual confidence and respect; there should be a freedom to discuss any member's problem based on the will to work together.

Organizational effectiveness largely depends on coordinated effort. Coordination will be achieved through well-defined and clearly understood policies, for policies play a central role in ensuring that the organization will make steady and consistent progress toward its goals.

A policy is essentially a "general decision," in the nature of an operating principle or standing rule, formulated by executives to enable them to delegate authority. At the same time, the executives retain control by reason of having established, through the statement of policy, the normal pattern for dealing with recurrent events.

Policies should be developed by thorough discussion so that all managers involved in related areas of responsibility are personally committed to the policies. Developed in this manner, policies will stand the test of fire; they will hold under stress. A set of policies may be compared to the rope holding mountain climbers together: being tied together, no climber can be lost; but they must coordinate their activities, or the rope will get in the way.

A gradually developed and thoroughly understood framework of policies can greatly simplify decision making throughout an organization. The pattern or framework of policies, as well as the policies themselves, help form guidelines for each member of the management team. Many repetitive problems can be resolved by the application of principles laid down in previously developed policies. This releases much management time and effort for new challenges and opportunities.

Each level of management, working within its own framework of well-developed, understood, and accepted policies, will make necessary day-to-day decisions more effectively. Higher levels of authority in the organization will be more able to make the broader, long-range decisions which help ensure the success of the enterprise. This is really an extension of the principle of "job breakdown" enunciated by Frederick W. Taylor and applied to the function of management.

POLICIES—INFORMAL VERSUS FORMAL

In many companies, clear policies exist even though they are not written. Through on-the-job training and supervisory practice and precedent, an employee learns the guideposts which channel his efforts toward desired ends. These guideposts may be called "informal policies." In fact, many firms do not get around to writing their policies and some that do, fail to keep them revised and up to date.

Many companies purposely do not write out many of their established policies. In some cases, such as certain confidential matters, unwritten policies may be more advisable. Some companies feel that policies in some areas are too difficult to state, or that they limit the complete freedom of the subordinate, or that the nature of the enterprise is too dynamic to set policies in certain areas, that is, they may become outmoded too soon.

A major problem with so-called informal policies is that control is lost too easily. Unwritten policies take on a folklore quality and are easily subject to reinterpretation to meet expediencies. In addition, the fast pace of today's world requires new members of a company to assimilate quickly the basic organizational values and philosophy. But there are only two ways to acquire a knowledge of informal policies: (1) spend a long time in an organization and gradually learn them or (2) spend a shorter but very intensive period of training with a knowledgeable member of the organization and hope that he covers every eventuality and that you can retain the knowledge thus imparted. Basically, policies are issued in response to the request, "Please tell us what you want us to do."

It is evident from the foregoing remarks that there are distinct advantages to written "formal" policies:

1. Those participating in the development and writing of a formal policy are forced to consider all factors, relevant and irrelevant, clearly and concisely.

2. Discrepancies, conflicting points of view, overlapping responsibilities, and inconsistent practices will be uncovered.

3. Written policies are not as subject to change by simple word of mouth.

4. Subordinates and new employees and appointees can review expectations with care. This is a real help for men assuming new responsibilities in management.

In the case of both informal and formal policies, however, application must be tempered with a liberal dose of judgment. In fact, although supervisors should be guided by company policies, the reason for any action should be explainable on its own merits. The trite expression, "Sorry, that's company policy," must be avoided as an explanation in its own right. It must be remembered that policies are broad guides—and only guides—which exist to channel the thinking of personnel charged with decision making. Flexibility in decision making is consciously implied in these guides. A subordinate manager must, however, intelligently apply policies to given circumstances in a consistent manner. Policies then, are not a set of inflexible rules; instead, they are the living precepts which guide an organization in a continuing and consistent pattern of behavior.

PRINCIPLES OF POLICY MAKING

Setting policies is a primary function of administration. As such, it should be accomplished with due regard to the following principles:

1. The statement of any policy should be definite, positive, clear, and understandable to everyone in the organization.

2. Policies should be translatable into the practices, terms, and peculiarities of every department or division of the enterprise.

3. Policies, regardless of how fundamental, should not be inflexible. They should, however, possess a high degree of permanency.

4. Stability of policies is essential; constantly changing policies are fatal to business success.

5. There should be as many policies as necessary to cover conditions that can be anticipated, but not so many policies as to become confusing or meaningless.

6. Policies should be predicated on organizational fact and sound judgment; they should not constitute merely personal reflections.

7. Policies should not prescribe detailed procedure except in rare instances.

8. Policies should recognize economic principles, be in conformity with Federal and other laws, and be compatible with the public interest.

Policy needs are developed at all levels of management. Existing policies should be periodically reexamined, because changed circumstances may introduce new factors which will modify previous thinking. Areas in which a company may wish to formalize its attitude through expressed policies include:

a. *Manufacturing*
   Inspection and quality control
   Purchasing of supplies and materials
   Size of inventories, rate of turnover, verification, and valuation
   Equipment replacement, additions, and improvements
   Plant maintenance and security
   Whether to manufacture or purchase components

b. *Finance*
   Capital structure—long-term sources of capital
   Dividends—stock and cash
   Extension of credit
   Collection of accounts
   Insurance—self or other
   Special funds
   Budgetary and cost control

   c. *Industrial Relations*
       Wage-payment scales, rates, and/or plans
       Stabilization of employment
       Employee training and development
       Retirement and pension plans
       Relocation of displaced employees
       Benefit programs: health, life, and accident insurance
       Recruiting and staffing
       Organizational planning
       Working conditions
   d. *Marketing*
       Product line—standardization, loss leaders, show items
       Channels of distribution
       Territorial expansion
       Customer relations
       Sales and quantity discounts—order size
       Incentive compensation—sales emphasis
       Advertising
       Sales training
   e. *General*
       Span of management control
       Salaries and bonuses
       Research and development
       Corporate organizational structure and personnel
       Replacement of top management personnel
       Plant construction and expansion
       Centralization or decentralization of facilities and management
       Executive pensions and retirement
   Every policy statement must be the result of a thorough knowledge of the operations and practices covered, and the effects of the policy on employees in all departments.

   Getting Policies Established.   Managing is a separate and distinct activity, quite different from the various functional activities, as well as the techniques and procedures, which are generally considered as belonging to the field of management.   A very important function of management is to guide and develop the thinking of subordinates toward the achievement of the objectives of the enterprise.

   Mechanics.   Identifying a problem area or situation in which decisions of a similar and repetitive nature are involved is the first step in the mechanics of establishing policy.   Repetitive problems may occur at any level in an organization, but it takes an alert executive with a keen "sixth sense" or "feel" for situations and conditions to recognize "a need" and translate this need into action.   This is really the essence of managing which, unfortunately, is only rarely found in men in management positions.   Many managers are so busy being salesmen, or technicians, or scrambling to do routine tasks, that they devote little time to thinking, reflecting, listening to, or questioning subordinates and associates.   Yet these are techniques by which a skillful manager recognizes or "senses" the problem areas.

   The executive who recognizes a need for a policy or set of policies will either prepare an outline draft himself or assign the task to a competent assistant.   This is not a job for an ivory-tower specialist—the person preparing the draft must be thoroughly familiar with the subject area from personal experience and involvement.   For example, the drafting of a personnel policy can usually best be done by a man who has had contact with situations the policy is intended to cover and the demands they place on the organization. A policy for the overhaul of equipment to be transferred to a new location might best be drafted by an engineer or supervisor who has had practical experience in this type of problem. The training value to the man assigned to draft a policy should not be overlooked. Good writing and clear thinking are closely allied; an executive becomes more effective and decisive as he learns to express himself more clearly.

After a policy draft has been prepared, the next step is to circulate copies to all managers who might be expected to operate under it. Their constructive criticism and suggestions should be genuinely solicited. Often, a free and open discussion with them will be fruitful. Following this, a second draft should be prepared and again circulated to make certain it is acceptable and workable. After clearing this hurdle, the policy statement can be cleared at the proper executive-group level and then promulgated throughout the organization.

Periodic Review. The wise executive, when a policy is issued, will set a date some months or a year or two ahead for reviewing, evaluating, and revising or canceling the policy. The time interval, of course, depends on the nature of the policy, the pace of activity in the area it covers, and similar considerations. Periodic review of policies is imperative if organizational complacency or managerial stagnation is to be avoided. It is part and parcel of the means of keeping an organization "vibrant" and "on its toes."

Policy revision is a sizable problem when applied to long-established policies. Over the years, everyone "knows the policy," so that when a change is publicized, there can be strong resistance to accepting the new version. If the change occurs without specific notice being drawn to it, it may be totally ignored; decisions will continue to be made according to the earlier version of the policy.

If there is not a clear need for the issuance of a policy, it should not be issued. Policies which cover unlikely eventualities will rarely fit the situation the few times they are referred to.

Severe difficulties may be experienced within an organization if an established policy is canceled or withdrawn and nothing is issued in its place. The canceled policy guided previous decision making, and its cancellation suggests that different thinking is required. Without a replacement, however, a guidepost has been removed from the paths along which management information flows. Without the guidepost, decisions may be delayed, information is likely to be misdirected or not communicated at all, and mismanagement may easily result. Because of the influence of official policies, then, they should be issued or withdrawn only with full consideration for the effects of such action.

The mechanics for review and evaluation of a revised policy should follow the same steps as those outlined above for its original establishment. It is good practice to reissue the updated policy with a revised date to keep management personnel aware of the policy and the changes made to it.

Policy Manuals. A policy manual is a collection of policy statements assembled in terms of their interrelationships. Each policy is numbered, and usually paragraphs are subnumbered for easy reference through a comprehensive index of all subjects on which policies have been issued. Policy manuals are essential in large organizations, particularly if activities are widely dispersed geographically. When there are a large number of policies included in a manual, policy amendment and revision is necessary on an almost continuous basis if the manuals are to be useful and practical as reference guides. Experience has shown that no far-flung, large sales organization, for instance, can operate effectively without a well-developed and up-to-date policy manual.

In a closely knit, compact manufacturing unit, however, there may be a danger in promulgating too many written policies. They can contribute to "red tape" and sluggishness. Writing policies is no substitute for "getting the job done." Writing policies must not be an end in itself, but only a means to an end.

External Influences. Every organization is an active part of the society in which it exists. The basic values of the society are inherent in the organization. Changing public opinion and the influence of community customs necessitate careful consideration of the acceptability of old, new, or revised policies. Well-established policies may have to be rewritten to reflect widespread changes in viewpoint on limitations and extensions of organizational responsibility. Thus, paternalistic policies have had decreasing acceptance over the years, and the social responsibilities of private enterprise have been given increasing emphasis. How an employee behaves off the job is no longer accepted as the rightful concern of a company to the degree that it was years ago. But the employee's problems off the job, such as illness or accident to himself or his family, have increasingly become included in the organization's responsibilities. Discriminatory employment practices, which were acceptable for hundreds of years, have become the object of critical scrutiny by the public eye. In response to these changes in public opinion, modification or alteration of company policies, written or not, formal or informal, must be made if the organization desires to avoid being spotlighted as rejecting the values of its society.

Community customs similarly come to bear on an organization. When, as in many communities, it is customary for organizations to participate actively in community-wide fund-raising campaigns for local charities, the organization which refuses to participate will be subjected to pressures from all parts of the community. If a community customarily observes certain holidays and not others, pressure will be brought to bear on an organization which deviates from the community pattern. Similarly, the industrial community will attempt to pressure a local industry to limit the compensation and benefits it gives its employees to no more than what is generally given in the area.

COMMON POLICY NEEDS

In addition to the policy needs described above, there are several kinds of policies that, sooner or later, are needed by practically every company. These policies are primarily related to organizational expectations, that is, what the company expects of its employees. A generalized listing of policies in accord with legitimate organizational expectations includes:

Hours of work
Attendance
Adherence to company rules
Demonstration of competency
Maintenance of equipment
Relations with superiors
Relations with coworkers
Safety habits and housekeeping
Overtime regulations
Job training and qualification
Self-development
Membership in outside organizations
Military service
Hiring practices and probation

Vacations and holidays
Leave of absence
Sick leave
Benefits programs and retirement
Wage and salary administration
Suspensions and dismissals
Promotions and transfers
Personal use of company facilities and equipment
Prohibited activities: gambling, imbibing, and soliciting on premises

Although model statements are available from personnel associations and consulting organizations, policy statements usually must be written to fit the needs and values of the specific company. What others have said, however, can be a useful guide to what is applicable to a particular organization. Policies should be clearly stated to avoid misinterpretation, but generalized to the extent that they fit all foreseeable eventualities of any significance to the organization. An example of a set of written personnel policies which has been found to be satisfactory over a period of time follows.

MOORE BUSINESS FORMS, INC.
Eastern Division

Summary of Personnel Policies

Name_____   Date of hire_____

Your department is_____   Your clock no. is_____

Your supervisor is_____

Your starting job assignment is_____

Your rate of pay is_____per_____

It is a pleasure to welcome you as a new employee to our organization.
This folder will acquaint you with the company policies pertaining to your employment.
If you have any questions regarding your employment or company policies, do not hesitate to ask your foreman or department head.
1. *Hiring Policy*
It is the policy of Moore to hire persons regardless of race, color, religion, age, or creed. Employment will be on the basis of qualification only.
2. *Probationary Period*
All new employees are on probation for the first 90 days of employment. During this period, they may be terminated without notice if, for any reason, their work is deemed unsatisfactory by management.
3. *Progress Review*
Progress will be reviewed at 30-, 60-, and 90-day intervals and thereafter on a semiannual or annual basis. Pay raises, based on established schedules for each job classification, are dependent on satisfactory performance.
4. *Hours of Work*
The normal work week consists of five 8-hour work days. Work-shift schedules are posted on bulletin boards. Schedules for service employees such as janitors and watchmen may not be the same as for other employees and will also be posted.
All employees are expected to be at their work place at the beginning of their assigned shift.
As a principle of operation, and in view of the heavy investment in each piece of major production equipment, it is important to eliminate or minimize breaks in production runs. For this reason, machine operators are expected to eat lunch at their machines whenever possible so that it will make it unnecessary to stop them.

Similarly, they are expected to be on the job at shift changes to avoid machine shutdowns.

It is a condition of employment that all employees be subject to second- or third-shift assignment, or rotating shift assignments, when conditions warrant.

5. *Absence and Tardiness*

Except as covered previously, an employee will be paid only for the hours he works. If an employee is late or absent, he will not be paid for the time lost.

6. *Wages*

Wage scales have been established for every job assignment. Employees will progress from minimum to maximum rates on a regular schedule, subject to satisfactory job performance. Each employee's supervisor will keep him informed of his progress.

A flat rate-per-hour shift premium will be paid to an employee assigned to the second or third shift.

Shift premium will not be paid to an employee assigned to the day shift who works overtime extending into hours normally worked by second- or third-shift employees.

7. *Overtime*

Overtime at the rate of time and a half will be paid for all hours in excess of 8 hours per day or 40 hours per week. In computing the hours over 40, paid holidays will be considered as having been worked if they fall within the normal work week. The overtime premium will be calculated on the rate including applicable shift premiums.

Overtime for service employees such as janitors and watchmen will be paid on the basis of those hours in excess of 40 hours per week.

Employees other than service employees will be paid double their normal hourly shift rate for hours worked on Sundays and holidays.

8. *Pay Day*

Employees will be paid each week for work performed during the previous week. Payment is by check to which is attached an itemized statement of gross wages and any deductions authorized by the employee or required by law.

9. *Job Transfers*

When an employee who has not attained the top rate on a job is permanently transferred to a higher-rated job, he will be placed on trainee status and paid in accordance with a trainee scale until his proficiency qualifies him to move to a step on the established rate schedule for the higher-rated job.

When an employee at the top rate on a job is permanently transferred to a higher-rated job, he will be given an increase to the minimum rate of the new job assignment if he is not already at that rate or above. If he is above the starting rate of the new job, he will be paid at his same rate until such time as his proficiency on the new job justifies a rate increase.

If an employee is permanently transferred from a higher-rated job to a lower-rated job, his new rate will be equivalent to the nearest step in grade of the lower-rated job.

Rate changes for temporary transfers will be at the discretion of the company.

10. *Promotions*

It is the company's policy to give full consideration to the advancement of its own people and to promote from within whenever the required talent and experience is available. Selections will be made on the basis of skills, aptitudes, experience, education, and length of service.

11. *Reduction in Staff*

If a reduction in staff becomes necessary, the company will give full consideration to length of service, skills, aptitudes, and past work records of employees affected in adjusting the work force to the proper level. Whenever practical, the company will attempt to retrain people for other jobs if they are displaced by changes in the workload or technology.

12. *Vacations*

Vacations will be granted to all employees according to service. The vacation year starts January 1 and ends December 31. As of January 1 each year, vacation entitlement for that year will be:

Service	Vacation
Less than 6 months	None
6 months	1 week
1 year	2 weeks
5 years	3 weeks
25 years	4 weeks

Every effort will be made to schedule vacations for the convenience of employees. However, the company reserves the right to limit the number of employees who may be absent on vacation from any one department at any one time. Where such limits must be imposed, employees with longest company service will be given precedence.

Vacation credit is not cumulative from year to year. Vacation pay is based on the straight-time day rate in effect one week prior to the actual vacation. If a paid holiday falls within the vacation period, an extra day's pay or an extra day's vacation will be granted at the discretion of the company.

13. *Paid Holidays*

The following eight (8) days have been set aside as paid holidays:

> New Year's Day
> Good Friday
> Memorial Day
> Independence Day
> Labor Day
> Thanksgiving Day
> Christmas Day
> One other day to be specified by management

The factory and office will be closed on these days. Holiday pay will be calculated at eight times the employee's normal hourly shift rate. To be paid for the holiday, the employee must work the day before, or the day after, the holiday.

If a holiday falls on a Saturday, the company will exercise the option of celebrating it on the preceding Friday, or on the following Monday, or of paying eight hours at the normal shift rate instead of providing a day off. If the holiday falls on a Sunday, it will be celebrated the following day.

14. *Jury Duty*

If an employee is required to serve on a jury, the company will protect his earnings at the normal shift rate for time actually lost in discharging his civic responsibilities. Employees are expected to report for work before and after jury duty each day when practical in order to give as much attention as possible to their regular job.

15. *Military Duty*

The company will grant a military leave of absence to any permanent employee who is inducted or enlists in the Armed Forces of the United States. Reemployment will be in accordance with Federal and state laws upon honorable discharge.

16. *Absence Due to Death in Family*

In the event of a death in the immediate family of an employee, time off with pay calculated at the employee's normal hourly shift rate will be allowed up to a maximum of three working days prior to and including the day of the funeral. The immediate family is considered to be husband, wife, children, father, mother, brother, sister, father-in-law, and mother-in-law.

17. *Tuition Refund*

Any employee with one or more years of service may apply for assistance in continuing his education. Approval of an application depends on the type of educational course and its value to the employee and the company. If approved, reimbursement will be made to the extent of 50 percent of tuition only, upon satisfactory completion of the course.

18. *Safety*

All employees are expected to conduct themselves in a manner which will contribute to their own and their fellow employees' safety.

19. *Pension, Health, Disability, and Life Insurance Programs*
These benefits are described in special booklets which are available at the time an employee becomes eligible for them. If you have questions about them, do not hesitate to ask your immediate supervisor.

BIBLIOGRAPHY

Alford, L. P., and J. R. Bangs, *Production Handbook*, The Ronald Press Company, New York, 1958.
Davis, R. C., *Industrial Organization and Management*, Harper & Row, Publishers, Incorporated, New York, 1956.
Haiman, T., *Professional Management*, Houghton Mifflin Company, Boston, 1962.
Lasser, J. K., *Business Management Handbook*, McGraw-Hill Book Company, New York, 1960.
Maynard, H. B. (ed.), *Top Management Handbook*, McGraw-Hill Book Company, New York, 1960.
Mitchell, D. G., "Assuming a Dynamic Organization" (lecture), Management Course, American Management Association, New York, 1965.
Newman, W. H., and J. P. Logan, *Business Policies and Management*, South-Western Publishing Company, Cincinnati, 1959.
Sloan, Alfred P., *My Years with General Motors*, Doubleday & Company, Inc., Garden City, N.Y., 1963.

CHAPTER TWO

Establishing Short-range Objectives and Directing and Controlling Their Attainment

LOUIS E. NEWMAN *President, Smithcraft Corporation, Chelsea, Massachusetts*

"Managing by objective and measurement" is a short way to describe a method of managing that is particularly useful in attaining short-range objectives. It requires the manager to set in advance the objectives that he intends to have accomplished and the measurements by which the degree of achievement of the objectives can be determined. It may be used for as finite a task as washing a window or as abstract a task as changing the attitude of a group of people. Our purpose will be to examine the work of the manager to see how he achieves objectives through the efforts of other people.

The work of the manager can be separated into these elements:

Setting objectives to be accomplished
Measuring progress toward objectives
Choosing who is to do the work
Directing, counseling, and controlling the work done
Communicating plans and progress to others

These elements fit together and overlap to the degree that it is difficult to distinguish lines of separation. But they will be separated here to establish the importance of each element.

SETTING SHORT-RANGE OBJECTIVES

A short-range objective is any objective that is planned to be accomplished within a year or less. Occasionally an objective that requires more than a year to attain can be classified as short range, but most objectives requiring more than a year to accomplish are better classified as intermediate- or long-range objectives.

4–14

Elements of a Short-range Objective. An adequate short-range objective is characterized by:

Simplicity of statement
Ease of understanding
Ability to measure with acceptable accuracy

In addition to these characteristics, the manager has a special concern that:

The objective be attainable
The objective be acceptable

There is the old "carrot and stick" theory of motivation that assumed that if you got a horse to follow a carrot held out in front of him on a stick, you could get men to strive harder for goals out of reach than for attainable goals. This theory is being followed, perhaps unconsciously, by the sales manager who justifies his overly high sales quotas by explaining that he "must give his men something to reach for."

The fact is that men quickly sense the carrot-on-the-stick approach and realize that the penalty for failing to get the carrot is not proportioned to the degree of failure.

A better approach is to set goals that men will accept as "hard to reach," but which they believe are attainable. It is human nature to want to be praised, and setting achievable goals tends to bring out better performance than otherwise.

Examples of Short-range Objectives. Good examples of short-range objectives are:

To reduce absenteeism
To increase sales
To make a profit

These examples have been simply stated but lack the element of measurement which is essential to understanding what is an acceptable level of attainment. If absenteeism, for example, were averaging 8 percent, reducing it to 7 percent would be an improvement, but it is unlikely that it would be an acceptable improvement. For these examples of short-range objectives to be sufficiently understood by the one responsible for attaining them, they should be stated in such a way as to establish what will be considered as adequate and acceptable measures of meeting the objectives. Each of these examples would be more precise if it were expressed more nearly in one of the following ways:

To reduce absenteeism from all causes from its present level of 8 percent in the group of employees working in Building A to less than 4 percent within the next six months
To increase sales this year by 10 percent over last year's sales at our current level of prices
To make a profit this year of 5 percent of sales after taxes

These last two examples are short-range objectives that might be set for the general manager. He will then have the task of breaking them down into separate, measurable objectives.

Breaking Major Objectives into Subobjectives. The manager has the special task of breaking major objectives into objectives that are attainable by the one assigned responsibility for attaining them. It does little good, for example, to assign the task of "making a better profit" to the entire organization. Instead, it must be broken into many subelements, each of which is assignable, acceptable, and measurable.

Examples of Subobjectives. "To make a profit this year of 5 percent of sales after taxes" is far too broad an objective to assign to anyone below the level of the manager responsible for all of the elements affecting profit. Normally, this would be the general manager.

The general manager would break down this objective into many separately assignable and measurable subobjectives. He could start with an initial breakdown into elements within the control of the manufacturing manager, and then separate elements within the control of the marketing manager, the engineering manager, and the financial manager. Each of these managers in turn would further subdivide the objectives assigned to him, always seeking to keep them simply stated, easily understood, and readily measurable. Examples of some of these final subdivisions of objectives might be:

For the shipping foreman: To cut out all overtime within thirty days

For the maintenance foreman: To reduce his work force by one man in the next three months

For the salesman: To bring in 10 percent more business from his territory in the coming year

For the engineer: To redesign a packing carton so that within six months complaints from breakage drop below 1 percent of all shipments

The manager must decide how far to go in subdividing elements of major objectives. Usually, the subdivision is not carried far enough rather than carried too far.

Using the Budget to Set Objectives. The budget is the usual financial tool to establish major objectives with all of their subobjectives. To set each objective and subobjective in a form to make understanding easy, it is necessary to provide bases for comparison. The usual bases are:

What was done last year?

What was planned to be done this year?

What is actually being done this year?

How does this year's performance compare with last year's performance and the planned performance for this year?

Example of a Budget Form. Figure 2-1 shows a budget form listing a few of the many expense account classifications for which subobjectives may be established. In each case of a subobjective, comparison for this year is easy with the performance for the same month last year, for the year-to-date last year, and with the planned performance. The last two columns can be expressed in percent or in dollars, whichever is most easily understood.

Using Other Means to Set Objectives. Nonfinancial objectives may be expressed in numbers or words and include a wide variety of simple and complex tasks. Financial objectives are easily recorded in the budget, but nonfinancial objectives should also be recorded.

The most common form for recording a nonfinancial objective is a simple memorandum outlining what is to be done. To avoid wasted effort and misunderstanding, special care should always be used to see that the results desired (the objectives) are clearly stated along with acceptable standards of performance (the measurements).

EXPENSE ACCOUNT CODE	LAST YEAR Actual		THIS YEAR Actual		THIS YEAR Budget		Variance (Negative)	
	Month	YTD	Month	YTD	Month	YTD	Month	YTD
01 Advertising								
02 Auto Expenses								
05 Bldg. Maint. & Repair								
06 Promotional Allow.								
07 Commissions – Agents								
08 Compensation Ins.								
10 Depreciation								
12 Dues, Subs. & Meetings								
15 Emp. Health & Welfare								
16 Emp. Relations Exp.								
17 Medical Supplies								
18 Safety Supplies								
20 Factory Exp. & Services								
21 Field Services								
24 Fuel								
26 Insurance								
30 Light & Power								
33 Maint. of Machy.								
37 Office Expenses								
38 Postage								
39 Payroll Taxes								
40 Professional Fees								
42 Rent								
43 Rental of Equip.								
44 Rearrange. & Alterations								
45 Royalties								
47 Selling Exp. – Hdqtrs.								
48 Production Supplies								
49 Office Supplies								
50 Samples								
51 Tel. & Tel.								
52 Travel								
53 Tools & Dies								
54 Trucking								
55 Taxes – Non Payroll								
56 Training								
57 Water								
60 Trade Shows, Reg. Meet.								
Indirect Labor								
86 Overtime Premium								
87 Vacation Pay								
88 Executive, Supervisory, Cler.								
89 Technical, Engineering								
Interest								
Outward Freight								
Direct Labor								
TOTAL								

Smithcraft CORPORATION

OVERHEAD BUDGET REPORT .... Date ....

FIG. 2-1. *Budget form used by one company to set objectives and measure progress.*

Better acceptance is usually achieved by placing emphasis on *what* is to be accomplished rather than *how* it is to be accomplished. Wherever possible, the objective should be stated numerically and a time given for its accomplishment.

Getting Acceptance of Objectives. The term "participative management" has evolved from managers' attempts to get acceptance for their leadership by giving those they manage a sense of participating in the objectives set and the methods for their attainment. In no sense does this imply management by committee or management by majority opinion. It means merely that most of us more willingly accept the leadership of another if we feel he has heard what we believe. The manager may choose to follow or not follow the opinions expressed by a group, but he makes it plain to them that he understands and has considered their views in choosing the course of action.

This does not mean that the manager can expect to get acceptance for his leadership if he decides in advance a course of action and then tries to brainwash the group into thinking that they formed his opinion. Nor does it mean that the manager need not have formed his opinion prior to discussion with his group. It means that he listens carefully and understandingly to the opinions expressed by the group he manages; lets them know that he does understand their views; and seeks to persuade them to follow the course he selects. He does not dilute his decision making—he merely counsels with others who will be affected by his decision and tries to get a high degree of acceptance. The interesting thing about this approach is that it sometimes elicits a comment like, "I disagree with the course we are taking, but I'll do my best to follow it." One cannot ask much more than this.

An Example of Participation. One president writes the following letter to each of his vice presidents a month ahead of the beginning of each year and asks that they in turn write similar letters to the managers reporting to them:

Memo to: Vice Presidents
From: President
To help us toward a better understanding of the objectives we hope to accomplish this year, will you please tell me:
1. What were the significant accomplishments in your area of responsibility for last year?
2. What are the significant accomplishments you plan for this year?
3. How shall these accomplishments be measured?
I would appreciate your replying to these questions in writing and being prepared to discuss them with me before the new year begins.

A letter of this form accomplishes several purposes. Among them are:

An increased feeling of participation by those being managed

A better understanding between the different levels of management of the relative importance of the work to be done

A valuable record for future appraisals of progress

MEASURING PROGRESS TOWARD OBJECTIVES

The purposes of a manager's measurements are to:

Recognize good performance, so that it can be continued

Recognize bad performance, so that it can be corrected

Recognize change in performance, good or bad, so that it can be evaluated

It is by using measurements in these ways that the manager is able to manage by objective and measurement.

Management by Exception. The term "managing by exception" means that the manager can watch a large mass of figures and feel neither the need to study nor any reason to act unless some of the figures move out of well-defined limits. These figures then stand out as warning flags that corrective action may be needed. In Chapter 7 of this section, managing by exception is treated in detail.

A good example of managing by exception is in the control of absenteeism. When absenteeism from all causes within each of several work groups stays under some set level, say 3 percent, there may be no need to draw attention to it.   It can be said to be in good control and meeting the objective, and it is better left alone than tampered with.

Its measurement, however, should be continued month after month even though this particular measure need not be watched.   If there should be an increase in absenteeism in any work group above the set level of 3 percent, it would be a warning signal to the manager.   It would indicate that inaction was no longer the best course—that corrective action should be considered.

Choosing What to Measure.   A good guide on choosing what to measure is to measure only those quantities for which it is worthwhile to set an objective and for which the measurement will have some influence on decisions affecting the work performed.   The ratio of male to female employees, for example, may be interesting but not significant to decision making.   The dollar output per employee per day on the assembly floor may be highly significant in one type of operation; in another, it may swing so widely because of product mix that some other, more meaningful, measure is needed.

To avoid needless extra effort and extra cost, it is a good idea to review all reports periodically to see if they are actually being used.   Regardless of how interesting a report may be, it is a needless cost to continue it if it is not being used to influence decisions.   It should be remembered, however, that certain measurements may be useful in telling *when not to act* as well as when to act.

Tests for Usefulness of a Measurement.   The basic tests for the retention or establishment of any measurement are: Does the measurement influence the quality of decisions?   Is the value of the measurement worth the cost of getting it?

There are other tests to be applied to measurements that are important, but none so vital as these two.   For example, it is of value to check the frequency of a measurement, the time lag in obtaining it, and its accuracy; but these do not answer the fundamental question of whether or not the measurement is needed at all.

Many measurements seem to "grow like weeds in the garden of management reports."   They were started to serve a purpose at one time, and then continued long after the need had disappeared.   Others took root because they were easy to obtain, or interesting to see, or commonly used by others.   But these are not of themselves sufficient reasons to continue a measurement.

The real test of any measurement is its use.   And this does not mean, "Is anyone interested in it?"   There are some reports and measurements that managers find interesting but do not use in influencing their decisions.   Reports are not worth the cost of preparation if they do not influence the quality of decisions.

Accuracy of Measurement.   Ease of measurement and speed in getting it are often more important than accuracy.   In fact, many of the measurements most important to the manager tell him only that he is gaining or losing in terms of progress toward his objective.   How exact the gain or loss is may not be important, but the fact that progress is being made or lost can be very important.

A good example of this is knowing if one is holding pace with competition.   In a falling market, sales can be dropping, but it is important to know whether the drop in sales is greater or less than the market drop.   It is a case of holding position in the market—maintaining the same position or improving the market penetration.

The exact level of market penetration is seldom of importance.   On the other hand, one cannot be content with an approximation of cash on hand, even though its exact value is not of importance in the day-to-day job of managing. It is readily capable of exact measurement. In contrast, good accounting procedures often provide for an approximation of inventory from one physical inventory to the next, and this may be adequate for the manager's needs.

Charting Measurements. The chart is a valuable tool for the manager. It gives a quick, visual picture of the way in which a measurement is varying and how it is varying relative to other measurements. It helps the manager understand the variations and their causes, and enables him to show others what he has learned.

In its simple forms, it may be a chart of sales billed, plotted each month as shown in Figure 2-2. In its more complex forms, it may plot several variables on the same chart so that the movement of one can be related to another. In Figure 2-3, for example, "orders received" has been added to the chart of "sales billed." A visual picture of the time lag between orders received and sales billed is now apparent, and the seasonality of both can be recognized.

Choosing the Proper Chart Paper. Manufacturers of chart paper have catalogs that offer the manager a wide choice of chart papers suitable for different kinds of data. The more usual of these are linear coordinates with special scales divided into days, weeks, months, or years. In addition to these, there is a wide selection of special scales.

One of the most useful of these special scales is the semilogarithmic scale. This type of chart paper has two especially useful properties: any quantity changing at a constant rate will plot as a straight line, and any line parallel to another line is changing at the same rate. These two properties reveal relationships to the manager that would otherwise be obscure.

Choosing the Proper Scales. Just as important as choosing the proper chart paper is choosing the proper scale. Two rules apply to all charting: always show the zero axis when you can, and only use scales of 1, 2, or 5.

When a chart, especially a business chart, is prepared without a zero axis, the manager may be misled by believing that variables are changing more rapidly than they are. And scales of other than 1, 2, or 5 are difficult to read at

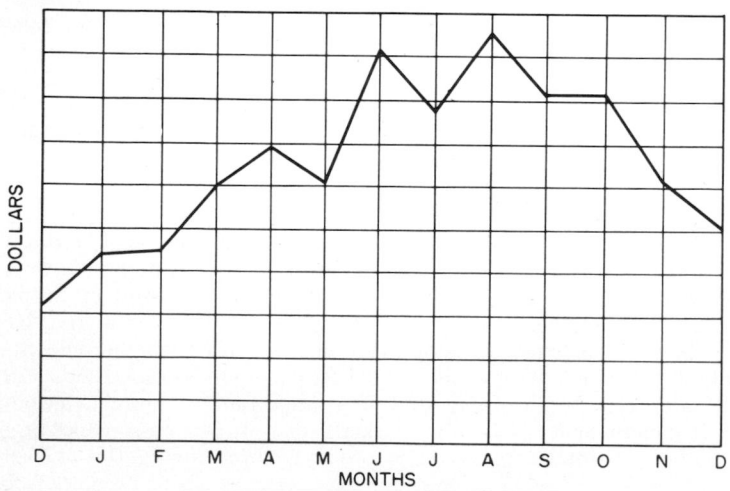

FIG. 2-2. *Chart of sales billed by months.*

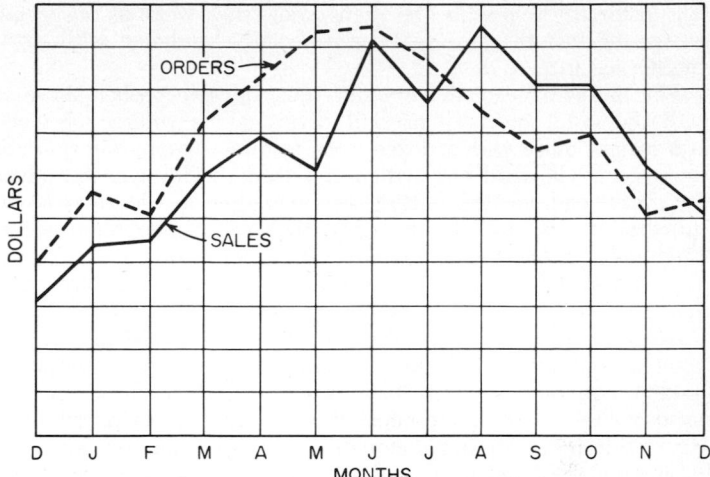

FIG. 2-3. *Chart of sales billed and orders received by months, shown on the same chart.*

in-between points. The scale of 4 should be especially avoided unless the quantity is expressed in "fours," such as quarters of a year or quarters of an inch.

Philosophy of Measurement. Measurement has the special purpose of serving as a guide to progress for the manager *and those he manages.* When measurements are not seen simultaneously by the manager and those whose progress is being measured, relationships can become strained.

The practice has been followed in some companies of first giving performance figures at top levels in the organization, and then letting each level in turn inform the one beneath it. This may be a proper procedure on an overall measurement such as the year-end net profit after taxes, but it can be a very poor procedure when a man is being held accountable for a result known last to him. It would be like putting the speedometer of a car in a place where the passenger could watch it, but not the driver. In such a case, the measurement would serve more as a guide for criticism than as a guide for progress. Wherever possible, a measurement that serves as a control should be seen by the one most directly guided by it as soon as it is seen by any other. This builds better relationships and encourages greater self-reliance.

CHOOSING AND DIRECTING WHO WILL DO THE WORK

An essential part of the manager's work is choosing those who are to do the work and then directing, controlling, or guiding them during the progress of the work. The traditional leader is often thought of as a man of impressive physical appearance and great force of personality, and there are many such leaders in business and other organizations. But a new kind of leader is emerging who sees his task as that of creating the climate that enables those he manages to be most productive. This is leadership by persuasion rather than command.

Principle of Automatic Selection. It is usually possible to organize the distribution of work so that "the work to be done selects who will do the work." This is taken for granted in the shop where there is one carpenter, one machinist, one accountant, one salesman, and one truck driver. The work to be done falls naturally to one of the men doing that work as a specialty, and the men accept the fact that one may be especially burdened with work at a time when another has little to do.

The problem becomes very different, however, when there are many workers with the same specialty or skill dividing the volume of work. For example, in a factory office with a dozen sales engineers preparing quotations, the manager can receive the mail and assign the work. This has the advantage of leveling the work load and permitting the manager to choose who will do each job. However, it has the disadvantage that some men may feel they "get all the tough jobs"; that they "do twice as much work as Jack"; or that "the boss plays favorites." These disadvantages sometimes so outweigh the advantages that it is worth organizing to avoid them.

Distribution of work can often be made automatic and impersonal by dividing it on a continuing basis into separable parts. For example, a group of men handling quotations could have the work divided on the basis of territorial responsibility, customer responsibility, or product responsibility. Such divisions may result in day-to-day inequality of work load, but this is more than offset by improved acceptance of the work assignments by each individual.

Principle of Selecting the One Least Qualified. The manager will get better results from a work group by striving to have work performed by the one just able to do it rather than seeking the one best able to do it. A common error in managing is to seek the person best qualified for each task with the result that certain employees are heavily overloaded and less able employees are lightly loaded. When, instead, the manager assigns work on the basis of using employees barely qualified for the task, the less skilled in the group are continuously being trained and upgraded, and the higher and more costly skills are used to better advantage.

An elemental example of this principle is the division of work in a large medical practice. The work could be divided vertically so that each doctor did every task from the most simple to the most complex. A better way would be to make horizontal divisions so that the top skills of the doctor would be used and not wasted while he performs less skilled work. This is illustrated in Figure 2-4. The square illustrates the total work to be done by four persons. Divided vertically, it would require four doctors. Divided horizontally, the work might be done by two doctors, a secretary, and a technician.

Creating the Proper Climate. There is a belief that happy workers are good workers and that groups with high morale out-produce groups with low morale. This generalization is highly questionable, and a manager believing it may seek

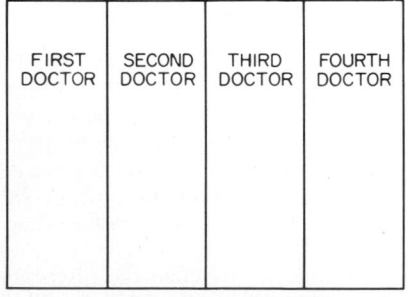
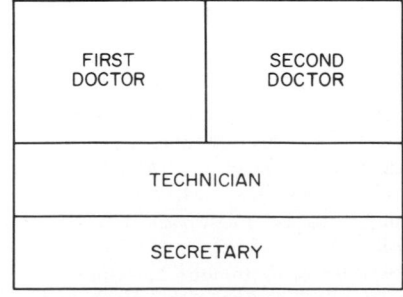

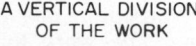

A VERTICAL DIVISION   A HORIZONTAL DIVISION
OF THE WORK   OF THE WORK

FIG. 2-4. *Comparison of vertical and horizontal divisions of the same work.*

to become popular with those he manages. Better results will be obtained from the work group if he manages by objective and measurement, sets high standards for the work group, insists on these standards being met, and develops a reputation for fairness in administering his responsibility.

Setting the Timetable. The most common ingredient of all work assignments is *when* is it to be completed. Usually it is not enough to set only the completion time for a complex task—intermediate checkpoints must also be established. For many years, the Gantt chart has been a basic planning tool for setting these checkpoints. This form of scheduling has evolved into "critical path" scheduling which focuses attention on the limiting factors.

Counseling during Progress of the Work. In a very real sense, the manager works for those he supervises rather than the converse. It is his job to make the work of others more effective; in doing this, he must be available to others for advice and guidance. Much of his work is that of a teacher rather than a disciplinarian. He is helped in maintaining the role of teacher and adviser by the degree to which he has been able to set objective measurements for the timeliness, quantity, and quality of the work performed.

Value of Long-range Planning. There is a need to relate the short-range plans to the long-range plans of an undertaking. In one company, for example, a group of twenty key executives meets annually for an entire day, reviewing and establishing the long-range plans of the enterprise. The result is that each understands the overall plans well enough to establish short-range objectives that will be consistent with the long-range objectives.

Need of Change to Get Improvement. The late Dr. Erwin Schell of the Massachusetts Institute of Technology often pointed out that "you can have change without improvement, but you cannot have improvement without change." This is a basic principle in the work of a manager. It is useful whether the improvement needed is in personnel, policy, or facilities. If improvement is needed, changes must be made. The most common example of the result of failure to use this principle is in the reluctance to replace or reassign an employee, or his manager, when the results have been below expectations for a long period of time.

COMMUNICATING PLANS AND PROGRESS TO OTHERS

The manager has the special responsibility of seeing that the organization's objectives, plans for achieving them, and progress toward them are known by those to whom such knowledge will be of value. He has the further responsibility of establishing a climate that provides easy and natural paths for communications within the organization and from the organization to others outside it.

Knowledge Builds Acceptance. It is important for a manager to have high ethical standards, but equally important that those he manages know that his standards are high. He should seek to achieve this good reputation by giving his organization information of interest to its members. He can establish his credibility when he tells employees on Thursday that ground will be broken Monday for a new building. He hurts his credibility when he forecasts steady employment in the next six months and then finds that a small layoff is necessary. He should follow the practice of making frequent disclosures of plans that are announced shortly before they will happen, that he knows will happen, and that the employees can easily check.

Organization Chart as a Means of Communication. The organization chart shows the paths of authority and is usually a poor diagram for paths of communication.

Certain communications necessarily follow the organization chart, but these are usually authoritative types such as approvals of pay raises and statements of policy. When other communication is forced to follow the organization chart, it may be an unnatural path. The manager should constantly endeavor to provide the broadest possible freedom of communication both within and outside the organization. He should encourage direct contact between persons with a common interest rather than have their interchange of information go through any third person. This speeds communication and improves the accuracy of transmission.

Meetings as a Means of Communication. The meeting of interested persons is the most common medium for communication. The manager should see that each person attending knows why he is there and what is expected of him. Is he supposed only to listen or to participate? Good practice calls for meetings to be started on time, to be held to a planned agenda, to be constituted of only those who need to attend, and to have suitable minutes distributed to those to whom they will be of importance.

Letters as a Means of Communication. The manager is apt to find that certain important communications between himself and others are best handled directly. The letter to all employees, or to sales representatives, customers, or stockholders, is an especially useful device when properly written. It should be cordial, concise, and clear. Rarely should it exceed one or two pages or cover more than a single subject. One company president makes a special point of using such letters at intervals far enough apart to make them seem important, but often enough to help build his credibility with employees, customers, stockholders, and the community.

CONCLUSION

The work of the manager in establishing short-range objectives and directing and controlling their attainment is a well-defined procedure capable of being taught and learned. It avoids approaches of an emotional, inspirational, or unstable type. It seeks to set clearly understood objectives; to measure progress toward these objectives; to have the work fairly assigned; to guide the execution of the work as needed; and to keep all interested persons informed about the work. It is a complex task demanding a high degree of skill.

BIBLIOGRAPHY

Bittel, Lester R., *Management by Exception,* McGraw-Hill Book Company, New York, 1965.
Carroll, Phil, *How to Chart Data,* McGraw-Hill Book Company, New York, 1960.
Drucker, Peter F., *Managing for Results,* Harper & Row, Publishers, Incorporated, New York, 1964.
Juran, J. M., *Managerial Breakthrough,* McGraw-Hill Book Company, New York, 1964.
McGregor, Douglas, *The Human Side of Enterprise,* McGraw-Hill Book Company, New York, 1960.
Maynard, H. B. (ed.), *Top Management Handbook,* McGraw-Hill Book Company, New York, 1960.
Scott, Brian W., *Long-range Planning in American Industry,* American Management Association, New York, 1965.

CHAPTER THREE

Providing for Two-way Communications

ESTHER R. BECKER *Editorial Director*, Management Information, *Elliott Service Company, Mount Vernon, New York*

It was Chester I. Barnard who established communications as the central theme of management, insisting that the executive was primarily a communications center.

"Communication" is a big word that means many things to many people. Some may think of letters, memos, reports, and booklets—the written word. Others may think of the devices of modern communication—telephone, radio, television, computers, and a host of adaptations. Still others may think of conferences, meetings, or talks.

All these tools and media of communication have one goal: the interchange of information, ideas, attitudes, thoughts, and opinions. Requisite to such interchange is *understanding*.

CHARACTERISTICS OF UNDERSTANDING

To achieve understanding, communication must have certain readily identifiable characteristics.

A Two-way Flow. Communication must be upward as well as downward. It must be information getting as well as information giving.

"All communication is two-way," says George R. Terry. "When communication moves freely in both directions, greater exchange of ideas and concepts are won and the way is open for greater understanding."

Sending and Receiving. When we send out facts and instructions or issue an order, either verbal or written, we may think we have communicated. But to transmit information effectively, the other person must also be "tuned in" to receive it and be ready to listen.

Thoreau said, "It takes two to speak the truth—one to speak and another to hear."

[1] George R. Terry, *Principles of Management*, Richard D. Irwin, Inc., Homewood, Ill., 1964.

Acceptable Code. The language of communication must have the same meaning to the other person as we intend to convey.

B. Balinsky and Ruth Berger say,[2] "'He speaks my language' seems to imply to most people, 'He is on my side.' Guard against the use of words which are outside the vocabulary of daily conversation. It may not be necessary to use the vernacular, but it is well to be certain that words you use are fully understood."

Deeds Match Words. Actions speak louder and are more believable than words. "The meanings of words are not in the words; they are in us," says S. I. Hayakawa.

Continuous Communication. A one-time message often falls on "deaf ears." Only by repetition does effective communication or learning of any type take place. The teachers of ancient Rome coined the phrase, "Repetition is the mother of learning."

Feedback. The communications circuit is not complete until we know that the other person understands. This does not mean that two parties have necessarily reached agreement. But they should thoroughly understand any areas of disagreement.

"After communicating information to an employee, we must do everything possible to encourage that person to indicate to us the degree of his understanding," say I. L. Heckmann, Jr., and S. G. Huneryager, both of the University of Illinois.[3] "It is imperative that we recognize that understanding can be determined only if we utilize the inherent two-way nature of the process of communication."

CHANNELS OF COMMUNICATION

Communication flows in three channels: downward, lateral, and upward.

Downward Communication. Top management to middle or supervisory management; middle management to employees; top management to employees.

Lateral Communication. Line management to line management; staff management to staff management; line to staff or vice versa; union to management or vice versa; employees to employees.

Upward Communication. Employees to middle (supervisory) management; middle management to top management; employees to top management.

Many communication channels cross each other or flow both upward and downward. But, regardless of what form communication takes or in what direction it goes, ultimately it is effective only if the circuit or loop is completed.

Robert N. McMurry warns:[4]

The top business manager is often lulled into a false sense of security regarding communication flows. His first and most egregious error is to assume that his supervisory hierarchy provides a clear channel of vertical communication, either upward or downward, and that lateral interdepartmental communication is equally reliable. Actually, most levels of supervision are less communication *centers* than communication *barriers.*

---

[2] B. Balinsky and Ruth Berger, *The Executive Interview,* Harper & Row, Publishers, Incorporated, New York, 1959.

[3] I. L. Heckmann, Jr., and S. G. Huneryager, *Human Relations in Management,* South-Western Publishing Co., Inc., Cincinnati, 1960.

[4] Robert N. McMurry, "Clear Communications for Chief Executives," *Harvard Business Review,* March–April, 1965.

ORAL COMMUNICATION

Oral communication is of two types:

1. *To individuals:* when specific instructions or coaching must be given; when a policy or decision affects individuals differently; when the individual's understanding must be doublechecked; when it is impractical or undesirable to bring a group together.

2. *To groups:* when speed is important; when it is essential for all people to get the same information at the same time; when group participation is desired or group reactions wanted; when the help of "key" employees is sought to help influence others; when the same instructions must be given to the entire group.

Listening. In all oral communication, the most critical factor is listening. Ralph G. Nichols and Leonard A. Stevens suggest listening habits to be avoided:[5]

1. Hop-skip-jump listening. Thinking time is 400 words per minute. Talking time is 275 words per minute. Thus we take excursions with our mind while the speaker is catching up with us.

2. We just listen for facts or figures.

3. We decide we are not interested or are bored and take a mental nap.

4. We just pretend to listen.

5. We yield to distractions—we listen with one ear to something else.

6. Pencil listening—we are so busy writing notes we do not really hear.

7. Emotional deafness—certain words excite us and we do not hear what follows.

8. We avoid difficult topics—we do not want to listen to anything that makes us think.

9. We do not listen "between the lines" for what a person is trying to convey.

10. We do not try to find something useful in what is being said.

WRITTEN COMMUNICATION

Written communication should be used when we want to:

1. Avoid mistakes—when messages are passed from person to person, between shifts, or when a number of people must be reached

2. Keep an essential record to serve as a reminder

3. Confirm agreements and decisions and record disciplinary action

4. Save time because memos and letters can be dictated in "off" hours

Readability. In all written communication, the most critical factor is to make certain that both words and style fit the language level and ability of the person to whom it is addressed. Two popular ways of measuring readability are as follows.

1. *The Flesch Formula.* Based on *The Art of Plain Talk* by Rudolf F. Flesch,[6] this formula counts the average sentence length and average number of syllables for each 100 words and grades them: easy, fairly easy, standard, fairly difficult, difficult, very difficult.

For *standard*, which should be read and understood by 83 percent of people, the average sentence length should be 15 to 17 words, with 140 to 147 syllables for every 100 words, and 6 personal references (you, me, man, woman, and so on) for every 100 words.

[5] Ralph G. Nichols and Leonard A. Stevens, *Are You Listening?* McGraw-Hill Book Company, New York, 1957.

[6] Rudolf F. Flesch, *The Art of Plain Talk,* Harper & Row, Publishers, Incorporated, New York, 1946.

2. *The Gunning Fog Index.* Based on *The Technique of Clear Writing* by Robert Gunning,[7] this formula consists in checking the average sentence length in some selected passage of 100 words and the number of "difficult" words in the same passage. A list of difficult words is supplied. The two figures are added and multiplied by 0.4. If the resulting score is 8, the material is of eighth-grade level; if 14, it is suitable for college students.

UPWARD COMMUNICATION

Briefly, the purposes of upward communication are (1) to encourage people to discuss fully the policies and plans of the company and (2) to provide a clear channel for funneling information, opinions, and attitudes up through the organization.

Earl G. Planty and William Machaver say:[8]

Upward communication reveals . . . the degree to which ideas passed down are accepted. In addition, it stimulates employees to participate in the operation of their department or unit, and, therefore, encourages them to defend the decisions and support the policies cooperatively developed with management. The opportunity for upward communication also encourages employees to contribute valuable ideas for improving departmental or company efficiency. Finally, it is through upward communication that executives and supervisors learn to avert the many explosive situations which arise daily in industry.

Barriers. A study by Opinion Research Corporation, Princeton, New Jersey, on "Employees' and Supervisors' Views on Upward Communication" found these obstacles to communication:

Fear that talking will get the employee "in dutch"

Belief that management is not interested in employee problems

Lack of training in communications skills

Feeling that upward communication is not a prime supervisory qualification

Belief that management will not respond to employee suggestions

Suggestion Systems. The purposes of most suggestions are to improve methods, equipment, and procedures; to make safer and better working conditions; to reduce the time or cost of an office, factory, or sales operation; and to minimize errors.

Usually, suggestions are placed in a locked box adjacent to which may be a bulletin board for displaying suggestion material and a receptacle for holding suggestion forms. The customary ratio is one box for every 25 to 50 employees, depending upon location factors.

A committee examines suggestions and sees that suggested improvements, if acceptable, are put into action. Awards are of two types: (1) merit and recognition awards and (2) cash or other tangible-value items that represent an actual payment for value received.

To be an effective tool of upward communication, all suggestions should be promptly investigated and the suggesters informed as to their disposal. When a suggestion is not practical, an explanation as to why should be given to the

---

[7] Robert Gunning, *The Technique of Clear Writing*, McGraw-Hill Book Company, New York, 1952.

[8] M. Joseph Dooher and Vivienne Marquis (eds.), *Effective Communication on the Job*, American Management Association, New York, 1956.

employee, who should be encouraged to "try again." (See also Chapter 9 of Section 11.)

Opinion Surveys. Opinion surveys are frequently in the form of questionnaires conducted through the cooperation of colleges and universities or through consultants. Standardized surveys are also available from publishers of industrial tests.

Opinion surveys are anonymous, giving employees a feeling of freedom in expressing themselves. These surveys seek reactions to working conditions, pay, employee benefits, cooperation of fellow employees, employee-supervisory relations, confidence in management, competence of supervision, effectiveness of administration, communication, job security, status, recognition, opportunity for growth and advancement, and identification with the company.

Opinion surveys may do more harm than good unless action is taken on dissatisfactions that are revealed. Most companies schedule supervisory meetings to map out a follow-up procedure. In Chapter 22 of Section 11 the subject is discussed more thoroughly.

Grievance Meetings. The grievance machinery provides an effective communications system for bringing an employee's complaints to management's attention or for management to register its complaints against the union or against individual employees. Most frequently, it is considered a means of giving an employee, either directly or through his union representative, the opportunity to present orally or in writing his particular complaint. It enables management, with the help of the union, to discover and correct the sore spots in working conditions and plant industrial relations before they are permitted to spread and cause real trouble. Machinery for handling grievances may also exist where there is no union, although usually in that case it is on a less formal basis.

Reports. Most formal reports are exchanged between top and middle management. Suggestions are:

1. Before passing on information, try to anticipate what facts will be needed. Supply only facts that apply to the situation.

2. Include recommendations and alternative plans of action as a basis for reaching a decision.

3. Supply background information which will help the person receiving the report to communicate, in turn, with his superior or subordinate.

4. Consider the purpose of the report to avoid giving too many—or too few—details.

Meetings. In the area of upward communication, meetings may discuss:

Facts and ideas upon which to base policies and decisions

Progress on plans and assignments, including status of long-run programs and completion of specific projects

Unsolved problems and possible problems which may arise

Out-of-line conditions

Goal setting

Ideas and suggestions for improvement

Employee attitudes and feelings toward work, associates, and company, and reactions to top management communications

In the area of downward communication, meetings often take the form of training sessions in such categories as:

Supervisory functions: job instruction, methods improvement, quality and waste control, safety

Case studies or role playing: human relations, employee motivation, problem solving

Managerial skills: reading faster and better, memo and report writing, effective speech, listening

Technical training: preparing for automation, new equipment and machines

"Hot Line" Telephones. These may be placed at strategic locations. Employees can pick up the phone and get a recorded message telling them what is going on around the plant. Often, a new tape is prepared every day dealing with a different subject—a safety message, company news, or information about company plans.

LATERAL COMMUNICATION

Research studies show that managers spend a greater part of their time in lateral relationships than in superior-subordinate contacts and that the amount of communication which takes place with those on the same level is on the increase.

Willard V. Merrihue says,[9] "Of great concern to the chief executive should be the misunderstandings, jealousies, jockeying, missed signals, lack of coordination, and wasteful internecine rivalries caused by faulty lateral communication." Temple Burling of Cornell University adds,[10] "People whose jobs are related must be able to work out their relationships between themselves and not depend exclusively on orders flowing from some central point above."

Lateral communication may take place through:

Project team or task force meetings

Planning sessions

Discussion of mutual problems

Barriers. No longer can it be said that line is line and staff is staff and never the twain shall meet. Complex business requires closer cooperation both intra- and inter-line and staff.

Management is also establishing a more favorable communications climate with union leaders.

The chief barriers with those on the same level are:

Lack of a "common language," particularly between line and staff, and among staff specialists themselves who have their own technical terminology; also between management and labor who may become enmeshed in legal semantics.

Jealousy among people who are anxious to guard their prerogatives and who resent those who may wish to give them advice, interfere, or dictate to them.

MANAGEMENT-UNION COMMUNICATION

Management-union communication may be viewed as a special form of lateral communication. In a study made by Princeton University,[11] four factors in successful communication are listed:

[9] Willard V. Merrihue, *Managing by Communication*, McGraw-Hill Book Company, New York, 1960.

[10] Temple Burling, "Aids and Bars to Internal Communication," *Hospitals*, vol. 28, p. 34, November, 1954.

[11] Helen Baker et al., *Transmitting Information through Management and Union Channels*, Princeton University Press, Princeton, N.J., 1949, pp. 124–133.

1. Clearly defined lines of authority and responsibility. Communication is closely allied with organization structure; therefore, formal and informal communication need to be closely coordinated. There should be no short circuiting. The staff should fulfill its important communication role.

2. A communication attitude. If past history has been anticommunication, then effort must first be devoted to getting people to know and believe the new procommunication policy. There must be listening as well as talking.

3. Recognition of the interrelation of management and union communication. The two are closely allied in a total framework. Management must accept the union's communication role, and the union must be willing to fulfill it. Each must recognize his common interest with the other.

4. Use of effective techniques. One medium is inadequate. There should be variety. The material should be readable and in terms of the personal interests of the employees who receive it.

Rumors. Rumors, or "the grapevine," are usually informal, employee-to-employee communication. They are not necessarily undesirable, but may give insight into employee attitudes and provide an outlet for employee emotions. Rumors can be used to spread useful information. Employee reaction to contemplated policies or changes can be tested by "planting" rumors.

Obviously, rumors can also do harm by spreading erroneous conceptions or by leaking information in advance of formal announcements.

To prevent destructive rumors:

Provide a natural outlet for employees' sentiments, hopes, and aspirations by feedback channels, personal discussions, and "minute meetings."

Try to keep employees informed in advance of changes that will affect them. Reduce unwarranted anxieties and suspicions.

DOWNWARD COMMUNICATION

The immediate, practical purpose of downward communication is to issue orders and to provide guidance and instruction. But the concept is much broader. Robert Newcomb and Marg Sammons say:[12]

In the company where employee communication is complete and consistent, the employee—convinced of the good intent of management—is inclined to accept the validity of what management says. He is disposed to resist attacks upon his company because, in his own experience and observation, the company has proved its sincerity.

Barriers. Dr. Leonard Sayles, of the Graduate School of Business, Columbia University, finds these barriers:[13]

The same words mean different things to different people.
The speaker and listener may differ in background and experience.
We may pass on information which the employee is not ready to grasp.
An employee may not believe his superior because what he hears may have been contradicted by previous actions.
An employee's emotional state of mind colors what he hears.
Stereotypes and beliefs influence what a man wants to hear.
A person may be dead set against a message because he suspects his superior's motivations.

[12] Robert Newcomb and Marg Sammons, *Employee Communications in Action*, Harper & Row, Publishers, Incorporated, New York, 1961.
[13] Leonard Sayles and George Strauss, *Human Behavior in Organization*, Prentice-Hall, Inc., Englewood Cliffs, N.J., 1966, pp. 237–257.

The group with which an employee identifies himself tends to shape his opinion on many matters and hence blocks communication.

An employee feels his superior does not grasp the meaning behind what the employee is trying to say and hence, in turn, is not receptive to what his superior is saying.

Communication may have a symbolic meaning to employees—fear sometimes makes them have strong reactions to mild statements.

House Organs. It is estimated that 10,000 employee publications enjoy a circulation of nearly 60 million a month. A good house organ can often drive home management's message more effectively than some other medium, because information is presented as a news story, combined with personal items.

A house organ generally has the following objectives:

Interprets company policies by giving employees prompt and accurate information on matters concerning their individual welfare

Informs about the company's products and services

Explains the company's place in the world

Gives recognition to employees

Bridges the gap between home and job

Promotes safety and health habits

Encourages ambition and ingenuity and promotes education

Serves as a liaison between management and labor, explaining the purpose of one to the other

A comprehensive discussion of employee publications will be found in Chapter 22 of Section 11.

Policy and Procedure Manuals. A well-planned policy and procedure manual usually has several hundred entries. In many companies, compilation of such a manual is a joint project in which various levels of management participate, either through joint meetings or through submitting written suggestions of what should be incorporated.

The National Industrial Conference Board, 845 Third Avenue, New York, New York 10022, has published several *Studies in Personnel Policy* dealing with policy and procedure manual content.

Company Creeds. To strengthen the corporate image, a number of companies formulate company creeds—an attempt to express the values, ideals, assumptions, and principles of the company for the guidance of those who work in it.

The creed may be a general statement, brief and abstract, or a detailed description of specific company goals and concrete objectives. It is usually embossed on heavy stock paper.

Posters. Attractive posters—usually printed in bright colors—are motivational devices. Usually, they deal with safety, quality and service, cost and waste, good housekeeping, and absenteeism. They should be placed at strategic points and changed frequently. Because poster making is an art, many companies purchase them from commercial concerns.

Company Libraries. Many company libraries confine their services to technical subjects. Others also offer general reading matter to all employees. Services performed include:

Circulating current periodicals

Abstracting articles and books

Maintaining company archives

Special researches on individual request

Translating reports, letters, and other documents from foreign languages

Handling newspaper clipping services

Exchanging material with other libraries or sources of information

Outside Services. Companies may also subscribe to outside services, newsletters, or bulletins which are regularly distributed to each member of management. The purpose is to keep managers "in the know" and to reinforce the company's own activities and policies by showing what others are doing.

Reading Racks. Also known as information racks, reading racks are used to distribute literature to employees on subjects that range from sports schedules, cooking, hobbies, housekeeping, home budgeting, retirement planning, health, taxation, economics, and free enterprise to information about the company itself. Information racks have a built-in check on their effectiveness. A count of what is picked up will show whether the plan meets overall employee approval, what booklets should go into the racks, and how much on each subject is wanted. Unlike many other forms of communication, reading racks do not carry the burden of requiring "captive audiences," because the system is completely voluntary. One of the largest suppliers of reading-rack material is Good Reading Rack Service, Inc., 505 Eighth Avenue, New York, New York.

Motion Picture Films. Business and industry spend $300 million a year for films to tell the "business story" to employees and to the general public. Some leading corporations have their own directors and producers. One suggested source of information is Education Films, Inc., 605 Third Avenue, New York, New York 10016.

Open House. The purpose of inviting the public to see the "insides" of an industrial plant, office, or computing center is twofold: to instill pride in employees in where they work and in what kind of work they do, and to improve the company's image in the eyes of the general public.

Loudspeakers. Loudspeaker or public-address systems afford a channel of direct communication from top management to employees. They are used for general orders or directions, such as announcing a fire drill; messages from management, particularly on such subjects as safety or quality; and bringing music to employees.

Closed-circuit TV. Closed-circuit TV is generally used at upper levels for meetings among men scattered over wide areas. At lower levels, it is increasingly adapted for giving instructions.

SUMMARY

Two-way communications are not just a function of management. They are vitally essential for the very conduct of business. Management must get across to employees:

The need for cutting costs and maintaining quality and service

Reasons why the company must install new methods and equipment to remain profitable

Employees want to know about:

Company plans that will affect their jobs—expansion, new products, automation, mergers

Promotion and growth opportunities

People on the same level must exchange:

Information of mutual interest and concern

Advice and specialized knowledge

Thus, communication is a most valuable tool in today's business world.

BIBLIOGRAPHY

Brown, Leland, *Communicating Facts and Ideas in Business,* Prentice-Hall, Inc., Englewood Cliffs, N.J., 1961.

Dooher, M. Joseph, and Vivienne Marquis, *Effective Communication on the Job,* American Management Association, New York, 1956.

Heron, Alexander R., *Sharing Information with Employees,* Stanford University Press, Stanford, 1942.

Merrihue, Willard V., *Managing by Communication,* McGraw-Hill Book Company, New York, 1960.

Newcomb, Robert, and Marg Sammons, *Employee Communications in Action,* Harper & Row, Publishers, Incorporated, New York, 1961.

Peters, Raymond W., *Communication within Industry,* Harper & Row, Publishers, Incorporated, New York, 1950.

Pigors, Paul, *Effective Communication in Industry,* National Association of Manufacturers, New York, 1949.

Redding, W. Charles, and George A. Sanborn, *Business and Industrial Communication,* Harper & Row, Publishers, Incorporated, New York, 1964.

Scholz, William, *Communication in the Business Organization,* Prentice-Hall, Inc., Englewood Cliffs, N.J., 1962.

Superior-Subordinate Communication in Management, American Management Association, New York, 1961.

Zelko, Harold P., and Harold J. O'Brien, *Management-Employee Communication in Action,* Howard Allen, Inc., Cleveland, 1957.

CHAPTER FOUR

Dealing with Change

ROBERT H. GUEST *Professor of Organization and Administration, The Amos Tuck School of Business Administration, Dartmouth College, Hanover, New Hampshire*

This chapter distills a large body of research and managerial experience in dealing effectively with change in complex organizations. Following the identification of both external and internal forces of change, certain questions about the change process are posed. An example of successful change is given to illustrate the "base-line" conditions necessary to achieve effective change.

From these conditions, some recommendations are given which serve as guideline principles in planning and implementing change programs. Also, guideline questions for dealing with individual resistance to change are put forward, followed by an outline for diagnosing and acting on problems of change. The balance of the chapter suggests programs and resources available to the manager in facilitating change in his organization.

THE DIMENSIONS OF CHANGE

In approaching the future, American management will have to find new ways of dealing with the accelerated rate of change. The individual enterprise will face a variety of forces which in large measure will determine its success and survival. Not only must it respond to the external changes, but it must find new ways of planning, organizing, and motivating its internal human resources.

The External Forces for Change. How organizations cope with change depends upon many external factors. Events on the world scene have a direct bearing on internal operations, even among companies not engaged in international trade. The continuing growth of the United States economy will force new readjustments within the organization. Shifts in market and consumer demands will increase. Management will have to adjust to the enlarged role of the Federal government and to the actions of regulatory bodies.

Internal Forces of Change. To survive, grow, and adjust to changes in the external environment, many internal changes can be expected. As enterprises be-

4–35

come more dependent upon research and development breakthroughs, new means must be found for stepping up the lead time between discovery and the ultimate production of goods and services. Automation of the factory and office is forcing new kinds of administrative relationships. Successful change will, to a large degree, depend upon improved methods of selecting and training managerial manpower. Traditional budgetary and other control systems will be revised. The trend toward decentralization may be reversed in the next generation with the onset of the "cybernetics revolution." The swift retrieval of information throughout the whole system of management may generate a trend toward greater centralized command and decision making.

All of the external and internal forces of change will find management seeking forms and structures of organization that may be radically different from past practice. Current research in organizations makes it quite apparent that any kind of change cannot be understood in simple cause-and-effect terms. Changes in any one segment of the organization are likely to have unanticipated consequences for the organization as a whole. The risks and consequences of any program of change to the total system of relationships must be understood if change is to be successful.

Basic Questions about the Change Process. Those responsible for initiating and implementing the change process need to ask certain basic questions:

Does the organization have internal mechanisms which are sensitive to new developments in the external environment?

Does it have planning policies and procedures for reacting to changing signals?

Are the action programs consistent with policy planning?

Has the organization developed stabilizing forces following action programs?

Does it have realistic and meaningful measurements for evaluating the results of change?

Is there feedback into the system to allow the organization to modify past policies and to make it sensitive to future changes?

AN EXAMPLE OF SUCCESSFUL CHANGE

Several common principles of successful change can be illustrated by the case of Plant Y. Plant Y was a sick organization. When compared with six other enterprises of comparable size and technology, its cost of operation was too high and the quality of the end product too low. It was sick in the human sense as well. Expressions of fear, mistrust, hostility, and dissatisfaction could be observed at all levels of the organization.

A new manager was installed, and three years later the same organization became an outstanding performer in every sense. The actions of the new manager not only explained the success of this particular organization, but they exemplified many of the findings emerging from research in many types of organizations.

The Manager Sets the Climate. The new manager openly declared that he did not intend to use threats of punishment as the primary vehicle for getting the job done. He was permitted considerable leeway by higher authorities to "run his own show." His first acts found him in the role of listener and not order giver. In initial meetings with his staff, he urged the upward flow of ideas and suggestions. There was a kind of "unfreezing" process in superior-subordinate relationships as well as among the lateral relationships between the various functional groups. The climate of fear disappeared in time. Supervisors were rewarded for a job well done without fear of reprisal. In time, the pattern of relationships and the attitudes of the members of those on top began to filter down to subordinate levels. Decisions that had previously been made only at the top of the organization were to an increasing extent made at appropriate levels below.

Getting Involved in the Decision Process. By the end of the first year, members of the various functional groups reached consensus as to what actions were needed to raise the general level of performance of the entire organization. As one of the supervisors put it, "Proposals were sound. We shared ideas freely without having to worry who next among us was going to get the axe." As the manager made final decisions to implement plans for improvement, those at lower levels felt a commitment to carry them out effectively. They had been involved in the decision process.

Action and Results. The planning phase led to concrete action programs. The most distinct feature of this stage was that stop-gap emergency measures for coping with new problems were virtually eliminated. The availability of planning time increased. Each action or new set of events made it increasingly possible for the organization to make internal adjustments to the external forces for change. Most important, performance indexes showed that the organization was slowly but steadily surpassing the performance of the six other comparable industrial plants.

The manager left the organization after three years, but the plant continued to improve. What happened in the change process basically was that the pattern of human relationships changed substantially, and this in turn led to a more efficient solution of technical problems. As the technical problems were solved, there was a disappearance of day-to-day crises. A reduction in the crises made possible still better planning.

BASE-LINE CONDITIONS FOR ASSURING SUCCESS

The above example serves to point up some of the findings from a growing number of studies of organizational change. For a management to change, for it to have a reasonable chance for success, certain underlying conditions and assumptions are necessary.

The Role of Top Management. The actions, behavior, and interest of those at the top are crucial. Formal authority to order change is meaningless when used solely to demonstrate power. The most rational kind of plan for change cannot be implemented without support at lower levels. This support, the studies show, comes when subordinates perceive the behavior of those on top to be in keeping with their own perception of what constitutes legitimate behavior at the top.

Assumptions about People. In motivating subordinates to carry out major changes, those at higher levels can adopt two different sets of assumptions. On one hand, they can assume that:

1. Subordinates are motivated to change only if there is some obvious economic gain to be realized.

2. Subordinates naturally resist change. Therefore, they must be stimulated through threats of punishment.

3. Most people are naturally lazy and must be kept in line.

On the other hand, a considerable body of research in the behavioral sciences as applied to the organizational setting challenges the above assumptions by stating:

1. Most people are self-motivated to go on to improve themselves in the organization, and they are not motivated solely on the basis of economic incentives and other controls superimposed by higher management.

2. People are not passive about change. With modest encouragement, they are capable of generating new ideas that will facilitate the change process.

3. Change in individual behavior comes primarily from involvement in meaningful tasks in a group situation. Granted the importance of the individual personality, management's efforts to implement change must come from a recognition that the individual is not an isolate but a member of one or more organizational groups. It is the group, not the individual, that facilitates the change process.

Realistic Goals. Studies in organizational change demonstrate that subordinate members of the organization must have a reasonably clear idea of what management expects of them in carrying out a program of change. They further suggest that although the goals can be difficult to reach, they nevertheless must be realistic and attainable.

Successful Change in the Past. It is generally agreed that the organization which has undergone successful changes in the past is in a better position to cope with present and future changes.

Avoid Multiple Simultaneous Changes. Although all organizations undergo many changes at the same time (new products, new technology, new personnel), a planned program for change has better chance of success when it is not being implemented at the same time that other major programs of change are under way.

The "Mopping-up" Operation. Several studies of computer installations, for example, have shown that too often organizations will make technical changes first, then later engage in a mopping-up operation with respect to the human consequences. Questions regarding displacement, skill training, transfer, and orientation are not adequately answered at the time of the initial plans for the technical innovation.

GUIDELINE PRINCIPLES FOR SUCCESSFUL CHANGE

No firm set of "scientific" principles can be applied to every type of organizational change. Yet research indicates that certain themes recur, and these are useful as guides for action.

Early Involvement. Studies of successful change repeatedly emphasize the value of early involvement in a change program by all parties concerned. Early participation is not only psychologically sound; it tends to eliminate unnecessary readjustment and replanning as plans are converted to action.

Maximum Involvement. Resistance to change is frequently found among those who will ultimately be affected by a change but who have not been allowed to participate in planning and action. Participation in programs of change tends to give the individual:

An opportunity to contribute ideas

An understanding of the relevant facets of the problem

A clearer definition of objectives and goals by higher management

A sense of responsibility for the success of the change program

A feeling of satisfaction as he sees the program bear fruit

Feedback of Information. As plans for change are acted upon, there is the need for constant feedback from subordinate levels to higher authorities (and in reverse) on the progress of the change program. Studies show that feedback in the form of written data and reports is not always adequate. Face-to-face interaction, especially among task groups, is desirable.

Problem Solving and Disagreements. It is expected that the implementation of a new program of change will result in certain disagreements. As long as the disagreement is focused on the substance of the problem at hand, a satisfactory resolution can be expected. Such disagreement can result in creative thinking and in the synthesis of new ideas. Often, however, disagreements generate interpersonal frictions. Such disagreements tend to cumulate and grow if not checked.

Leeway for Discretion. For those at higher levels to induce others to make changes, it is necessary that they give subordinates considerable leeway to make decisions. In the success story cited above, it was observed that top management allowed members of subordinate supervision to carry out many of the decisions for change without interference from above.

Enlarging the Scope of Understanding. When individuals have greater awareness about the relationship of other changes in the organization to changes in their own departments, there is greater likelihood of success. Limited information about the change or limited access to such information prevents the participants from seeing "the big picture." The chronic frictions between engineering, production, and sales departments, for example, often reflect a lack of interdepartmental understanding.

Lateral Communications in a Change Process. Traditional organization structures stress vertical lines of authority and communications. Because change involves a broader system of relationships, it is critical to ensure substantial interaction between representatives of functional groups laterally. A number of studies on industrial organization show that successful changes have been brought about through lateral communication between unit heads of research and development and their counterparts in development engineering, production, and marketing. This procedure avoids the time-consuming process of having reports and communications go up the line in each functional area for decisions before moving down to the next step in the information flow.

Group Participation. The formal organizational chart identifies one's position in the hierarchy. It reveals virtually nothing about the complex number of small groups that are necessary to make an organization function. Skilled managers know how to utilize committees and project groups effectively. Considerable knowledge about group behavior has developed from the behavioral sciences. In many companies, one finds specialists in the behavioral sciences advising managers in the effective use of group dynamics in planning and implementing changes.

THE INDIVIDUAL AND THE CHANGE PROCESS

Research in individual learning and motivation substantiates the fact that change is more likely to be accepted if the individual believes that the change is compatible with his own set of needs and expectations. These needs and expectations are deeply rooted in the individual. If an organizational change, an assignment to a new position, or a demand to operate in new ways is seen as a threat by the individual, then different degrees of resistance can be expected. Too often, those initiating the change process look at change exclusively in terms of the requirements of the organization. The sheer exercise of power from the top is likely to be ineffective without an understanding of the individual needs and expectations of subordinates.

The individual's reaction to a program of change is based upon:

1. What the change involves
2. The amount of control he feels over the events affecting him
3. The trust he has in those responsible for initiating the change

The process of acceptance can be stated in the following sequential questions:

How much *awareness* does the individual have of the need for change?
With this awareness, how much *knowledge* does he have about the program?
Does the knowledge about the change stimulate *interest* in the change?
Does interest then lead to a *commitment* to act in the desired direction?
Once the commitment is made, is there adequate opportunity for the individual to become *involved* in the planning and the implementation of the change?

GUIDELINES FOR DIAGNOSIS AND ACTION

In exploring problems leading to a program of change, certain guidelines for analysis are useful. These guidelines may be referred to as diagnosis, problem statement, and action.

The Diagnosis. Often, change programs are instituted in organizations without an adequate diagnosis of the present state of organizational relationships. Frequently, decisions are based upon a number of unsubstantiated speculations or assumptions. It is particularly important to identify the *facts* in a given situation and draw inferences from these facts. The facts include not only figures and numbers but the feelings of the members of the organization.

Diagnosis requires that the information under study be as concrete and complete as possible. The unimportant must be sifted from the important. Finally, as information is developed, it is necessary to keep in mind that a change in one part of the organization is likely to have consequences affecting the whole.

The process of diagnosis should avoid fixing personal blame on individuals. In diagnosis, one needs to understand the *perceptions* of others regardless of whether the superior making the diagnosis agrees or disagrees with the views of others. Moral judgment has no place in diagnosis. Nor should sympathy be a factor in judging a situation. The effective skill is the ability to use empathy—the ability to "get in the shoes of the other person."

Identifying the Problem. Once an impartial diagnosis of a situation is made, the next step is to identify the real problem to be solved. Statement of the problem should not be contaminated by action recommendations. Questions of how much time to act and of whose responsibility it is should be answered later.

Action Guidelines. Once the diagnosis has been made and the problem(s) identified, effective action begins. The action should consider both short-run and long-run strategies. In choosing alternative courses of action, the risk of each course should be appraised. The action decision should be put in the context of other problems which the organization faces. The action should also include getting more information or feedback as the change program is formulated and implemented.

PROGRAMS AND RESOURCES FOR EFFECTING CHANGE

Organizations have two types of resources for planning and implementing change. They can use the training and planning facilities already existing in their staffs.   They can call on the outside consultant or make use of a variety of university-sponsored manager development programs.

Internal Training.   Any kind of change program, whether it be an organizational realignment, a computer installation, or an effort to move into new areas of activity, will require a planned program of personnel orientation and training.

Shortcomings of Traditional Training.   Experience demonstrates certain shortcomings of traditional classroom methods of teaching.   The classroom is useful in imparting factual information with regard to the reasons behind a change and the general program to be adopted.   This is a unilateral approach that often overlooks some of the guideline principles stated earlier.   For the trainees, the mere exposure to factual information is not enough.   Take the installation of a new computer system, for example.   Facts about the type of computer, its data-processing capacity, and its projected cost savings are necessary.   Yet those being trained to use the computer system or those who will be affected by it are likely to resist if the program is seen as a threat.   Avoidance of individual or organized resistance is best accomplished when those involved feel they are part of the planning process itself.   The same can be said about major manager development programs and other efforts at organizational change. Traditional classroom procedures violate much of what is known about the influence process.

Planning Projects.   Another method of "training" is through the project method.   Individuals are assigned from various functions to head up a new project.   How such project groups are organized and led can determine the success or failure of the outcome.   Higher management must emphasize that ultimate success depends upon subordinating the desires of the separate functions for the good of the whole project.   When project groups are made up of persons representing various levels of the organization, there is often a tendency for those holding superior positions to dominate the course of the project groups' work.   The learning experience for those in subordinate positions can be lost and an entire program delayed if not destroyed.

Staff Meetings.   Perhaps the most common mechanism of change is through the use of staff meetings.   Through this vehicle, announcements of changes and plans for change are often made.   As in the case of classroom training, the regular staff meeting can be perceived by subordinates as a unilateral effort on the part of higher management "to jam a new idea down our throats."   The staff meeting can, with effective leadership, be a useful learning and motivating experience.   The free exchange of ideas from subordinates to the staff heads can result in modifications to the master plan for a change program.   With the subordinates a part of the planning process, there will be less resistance to change.

Utilizing External Resources.   Organizations frequently lack internal facilities for preparing their members for new programs.   This fact is reflected in part by the enormous proliferation of the use of outside consultants.   Business consultants vary in the types of services rendered and in the procedures used. Among the more effective consultants, one trend is noted.   The client is not given an elaborate list of recommendations following an audit or survey.   Effective consultants are coming to realize that action recommendations are not likely to work unless some assistance is given to the client on ways of bringing the changes about.   This kind of assistance by the consultant requires more than technical knowledge of the problem to be solved.   It requires a sophisticated sense of the client's "culture," of the internal political tugging and pulling in the organization, of the sense of readiness to act, and of the motivations and perceptions of those responsible for carrying out recommendations for change.

An effective consulting relationship is one in which the consultant helps the organization to develop its own course of action within the context of what its personnel are capable of doing.

Business organizations are making increasing use of the academic community. Professors and researchers are being called in to assist management in change programs. Also, almost all of the major business schools attached to universities have manager development programs. Companies use these programs both for exposing executives to new trends in professional management and for the further education of promising middle managers. Many of the programs deal explicitly with problems related to planned change.

Another device being used to an increasing extent by business and nonbusiness organizations is "sensitivity" training. Although considerably more research needs to be done on the effectiveness of sensitivity training programs, their enormous growth and popularity in both business and nonbusiness organizations attest to their effectiveness. One of the fundamental purposes of sensitivity training is to help individuals and groups understand and deal with the emotional roadblocks that frequently impair the change process in organizations. The theory of sensitivity training is founded on a variety of reasonably well-tested research experiments in individual and group behavior.

CONCLUSION

New developments in mathematics and behavioral science are being applied to problems of managerial change. Among the mathematical tools are linear programming, operations research, probability theory, computer simulation, Markov "chains," and a variety of mathematical models for testing out alternative choices for change. (See Section 17.)

The discipline of psychology has for many years provided testing tools for selection and placement purposes. (See Chapter 3 of Section 11.) Used judiciously, many of these tests have a high degree of predictive accuracy. Also, many companies are finding attitude, opinion, and morale surveys useful. (See Chapter 22 of Section 11.) These can be valuable when conducted prior to major programs of change. They are also sensitive measurement devices during change.

Many organizations have helped their personnel to adapt to changing conditions through the use of professional clinical counselors. Some of the most effective among this group are those who assist individuals to think about the implications of changes in their own lives and careers. In one large company, for example, the top company executives were convinced that a recent major change in the organization was facilitated largely through the efforts of a clinical counselor to the executives and middle managers.

The findings of sociology are to an increasing extent being applied by management as devices for facilitating change. (See Chapter 1 of Section 11.) Staff groups in organizations are finding places for specialists in small-group behavior. Dealing with role conflicts has been helped by more sophisticated knowledge of role behavior. Staff persons trained in the social sciences are able to take reasonably accurate measurements about the "climate" of interpersonal relationships and have been able to advise top management of the progress of various types of internal organization changes.

BIBLIOGRAPHY

Argyris, Chris, *Organization and Innovation,* Richard D. Irwin, Inc., Homewood, Ill. 1965.

Ginsberg, Eli, and Ewing W. Reilly, *Effecting Change in Large Organizations,* Columbia University Press, New York, 1957.

Gouldner, Alvin W., *Patterns of Industrial Bureaucracy,* The Free Press of Glencoe, New York, 1954.

Guest, Robert H., *Organizational Change: The Effect of Successful Leadership,* Richard D. Irwin, Inc., Homewood, Ill., 1962.

Likert, R., *New Patterns of Management,* McGraw-Hill Book Company, New York, 1961.

Lippitt, Ronald, Jeanne Watson, and Bruce Wesley, *The Dynamics of Planned Change,* Harcourt, Brace & World, Inc., New York, 1958.

Pelz, D., and F. M. Andrews, "Organizational Atmosphere, Motivation, and Research Contribution," *American Behavioral Scientist,* vol. 6, 1962, pp. 43–47.

Ronken, Harriet O., and Paul R. Lawrence, *Administering Changes: A Case Study of Human Relations in a Factory,* Harvard University Press, Cambridge, Mass., 1956.

CHAPTER FIVE

Selection of Management Personnel

CHARLES E. TOWNSEND   *Manager of Management Development, International Business Machines Corporation, Kingston, New York*

No one will deny the importance of selecting the best personnel available to manage in business and industry.   Nor will anyone deny that there appears to be a chronic shortage of properly qualified personnel.   This shortage has developed mainly because of the rapid expansion and the increased complexity of business and industry since World War II.

Because of these two factors, the importance of filling management positions at any level with the best people possible and the shortage of available qualified personnel, the selection process has become quite sophisticated.   It has also taken on all the aspects of a large-scale talent search.   Most of the selection procedures of the past are still in use, and many new selection techniques are being developed, tested, and used.

This chapter will first review traditional selection methods and show how they can be used successfully in a total selection program.   Then, some of the most commonly used selection techniques will be listed.   Following this, some of the newer techniques being tested to assess managerial potential will be described.

TRADITIONAL METHODS OF SELECTION

Obtaining the Candidates.   The most common method by which candidates for management positions are selected is nomination by their superiors.   It is typical for these nominations to be from an entire division or company, not just the area in which a vacancy exists.

Nominations by management are generally based on the following factors:

1. *Performance*—the level of performance on the present job as reported in appraisals.

2. *Potential*—an assessment of the employee's ability and desire to move ahead in the company.   This is usually based on the employee's educational record,

4–44

continued self-improvement activities, ability to work with others, and demonstrated leadership ability.

A number of companies have permitted self-nomination. This allows any employee who feels he is capable of managing to be considered. When equal consideration is given to those nominated by management and those who nominate themselves, the selection program becomes a morale booster in addition to being more comprehensive.

Evaluating the Candidates. It is in the evaluation of each individual nominee that the success of a management selection program ultimately depends. The evaluation can be based on a few or many different bases. The trend is toward the use of a number of methods of evaluation. The following are among the most commonly used methods.

1. An examination of past appraisals. These are either the periodic appraisals made of all employees or special appraisals required when an employee is being nominated for a management position.

2. A review of the nominee's past experience. This normally includes experience in prior places of employment.

3. An examination of past education, self-improvement activities, and participation in community and professional activities.

4. An analysis of performance on written tests. These are generally tests of learning ability, supervisory judgment or principles, interest inventories, personality inventories, and tests in certain technical knowledge and skill areas.

5. Interviews of the nominated candidates by some person involved in the selection process. The interviewer is normally skilled in interviewing and has a definite structure for each interview. It is common practice when interviews are used to have several people interview each candidate. In this way, a much more objective evaluation can be obtained, and a safeguard is inserted in the evaluation process.

A number of additional evaluation methods have recently been developed and researched. They will be discussed later on.

Choosing the Successful Candidates. After evaluation, final selections must be made. This is usually done by a committee made up of line managers and representatives of the personnel function. Candidates are ranked on the basis of the several ratings resulting from the evaluation process. In some cases, the committee may call for additional information. This might include discussions with the present managers of some of the nominees. After this final review, the most promising candidates are chosen for the management positions open or for the management pool if there are no current openings. Their appointment to management almost always requires the approval of the top manager.

TYPICAL MANAGEMENT SELECTION PROGRAM

The following is a step-by-step plan for manager selection which, if carefully followed, should uncover the best management material available at a given location.

1. Call for nominations from managers. Allow for self-nomination at this point, if desired.

2. Explain the selection program to all nominated candidates. This may be done individually or to the total group at once. If the explanation is given to the total group in one meeting, you are sure that they all have the same information.

3. Examine personnel records of the candidates, including their last two or three performance appraisals.

4. Examine existing test records of the candidates. Specify certain required tests and test any candidates who have not previously taken these tests.

5. At this point, reject any candidates who do not meet the minimum criteria. These rejected candidates should immediately be given career guidance. The reasons for their rejection should be made clear, and a program to help them overcome their shortcomings should be established where possible. No one should be rejected without an explanation that is as honest as possible.

6. Have a selection committee interview each candidate and each candidate's present manager. These interviews should be structured to seek certain information about attitudes, aspirations, and future plans. Again, after an analysis of the interview findings, reject any candidates found not ready for management. Once again, care should be taken to explain the reason for rejection and the steps that should be taken if the candidate is to be reconsidered in the future.

7. Narrow the group down to approximately the number of managerial candidates needed. This is a good time to give additional tests, both to aid in the final decision and to use for research into the total selection process.

8. Give those who must give the final approval for promotion or placement in a managerial pool the opportunity to interview each man still being considered. Have them also review the dossier prepared on each candidate.

9. Make final selections and arrange the promotions or the transfers to the management pool. Those not chosen should be the first to be considered for the next openings.

This program can be varied to fit specific situations and to take into consideration the personnel available to coordinate the program and do the interviewing and testing. It should yield good results even in an abbreviated form and excellent results in a more comprehensive form.

COMMONLY USED SELECTION TECHNIQUES

The chief reason for using an investigative technique in selecting managers is to get a prediction of future managerial effectiveness. The following techniques are all in widespread use for the selection of managers. Their value in predicting managerial effectiveness varies, but in almost all cases they have been found to have some degree of value when properly administered.

Performance Appraisals. Ratings of a person's performance in the actual job situation are almost universally used as a selection device. Their strong point is that they are usually made by a manager who has observed a person's performance over a long period of time. Their shortcoming is that they are subject to all the faults of subjective rating procedures.

Interviews. The interview is a popular assessment technique. It has not proved to be as valid as other selection devices, however, in comparisons made in some controlled studies.

If interviews are to be valid evaluations, the interviewers must be well trained. They must evaluate candidates against standards which are well formulated and specific. It is also important that the interviewer be friendly, self-confident, and intelligent.

Tests of Values and Interests. The values which guide a manager's behavior and the interests which motivate him are important characteristics to measure. They can be used to predict how a candidate will perform as a manager. Tests of values and interests do not correlate as highly with managerial effectiveness as intelligence and aptitude tests, however.

Some tests used to measure values and interests are the Kuder Preference Record (Personal), the Allport-Vernon Scale of Values, and the Strong Vocational Interest Inventory.

Personality Tests. Subjective and objective personality tests are often used in management selection. However, they have not always been found to exhibit good or consistent predictive power. Meyer and Bertotti[1] suggest that one reason why personality tests sometimes fail to be valid predictors is probably that personality "traits" are not always the same for any given individual. An individual might exhibit a certain trait in one situation but not exhibit it at all in another situation.

It is unfortunate that personality traits, which are so important in management, are the most difficult human characteristics to measure.

Some personality tests used in management selection are the Edwards Personal Preference Schedule, the Gordon Personal Inventory, the Gordon Personal Profile, the Thurstone Temperament Schedule, and the Bernreuter Personality Inventory.

Tests of Aptitude and Intelligence. A wide variety of tests are used to determine intelligence, aptitude, and knowledge in various technical and subject areas. Some have been found to be indicators of managerial effectiveness.

Intelligence tests have been found to be a valuable aid in predicting the success of managerial candidates. Some of the most widely used intelligence tests are the California Test of Mental Maturity, the Otis Self-Administering Test of Mental Ability, the Wechsler Adult Intelligence Scale—Vocabulary and General Information, and the Wonderlic Personnel Test.

Tests of aptitude and achievement can be found in almost any area. Among those often used in the assessment of potential are the General Clerical Test, the Minnesota Clerical Test, the How to Supervise Test, the Differential Ability Test—Language Usage, the Differential Ability Test—Verbal Reasoning, and the Watson-Glaser Critical Thinking Test. Many companies develop their own tests to seek out special aptitudes.

NEWER TECHNIQUES WHICH ASSESS MANAGERIAL POTENTIAL

Many companies have made serious and innovative attempts to identify their future top managers at an earlier age. They feel that, once located, these men can be quickly moved along to positions of greater influence. To do this, they have developed some new techniques for identifying this high level of management potential. As the title of an article in *Business Week*[2] suggests, they are trying to develop "Sharper Tools for the Talent Hunt."

This article points out that such companies as American Telephone and Telegraph Company, General Motors Corporation, International Business Machines Corporation, Sears, Roebuck and Company, and Standard Oil Company (New Jersey) have concentrated on the development of new tools to help spot potential managers.

A number of companies have experimented with personnel assessment centers. American Telephone and Telegraph Company appears to be the most heavily involved in this. *Business Week* reports that fourteen operating companies of the Bell System have set up fifty "assessment centers" and have run more than 15,000 employees through half-week testing sessions.[3]

The personnel assessment centers follow the same general pattern in most of the companies working with them. They include a number of relatively new techniques, at least new in their use, for the assessment of managerial potential.

[1] Herbert H. Meyer and Joseph Bertotti, "Uses and Misuses of Tests in Selecting Key Personnel," *Personnel*, vol. 33, no. 3, November, 1956, pp. 277–285.
[2] "Sharper Tools for the Talent Hunt," *Business Week*, vol. 1856, Mar. 27, 1965. p. 70.
[3] *Ibid.*

The central or main portion of these programs is a number of group exercises that simulate actual management situations. These exercises are usually of several different types. Among them are in-basket exercises, short business simulation exercises, leaderless group discussions, think-on-your-feet sessions, and conference leadership situations. In addition to these exercises, psychological tests, peer evaluations, interviews, and many other techniques that have been in use for years are used.

Groups being assessed are usually made up of from six to eight employees. An observer is generally assigned for each two group members. The observer group in most programs is made up of both psychologists and line managers. In the assessment of groups for middle and top management positions, a higher proportion of psychologists is normally used. The lengths of the programs vary from one day to two weeks.

The general consensus of employees going through these centers seems to be positive. This is especially true of nonmanagement personnel. D. L. Grant of American Telephone and Telegraph reports that at the craft level they tend to like the process as being far more objective than if the local manager makes the choice.[4]

Those assigned as observers in this type of assessment process are normally required to contribute twice as much time as the participants. This is because they must spend a great deal of time discussing and evaluating each participant's performance as well as observing all sessions.

A TYPICAL ONE-WEEK PROGRAM

The following is a typical one-week management potential assessment program. The staff and observers should have spent a few days in preparation prior to the program start.

Sunday Evening:
Participants arrive prior to dinner and are settled in their quarters. They have dinner with the center's staff and are introduced to each other. An orientation session, at which the week's program is outlined, is held following dinner.

Monday:
8 A.M. to noon. All participants are administered a battery of tests. These include intelligence, interest, values, aptitude, and personality tests.

1 to 3 P.M. In-basket exercise is conducted. Participants complete their in-baskets in the privacy of their rooms. All are turned in at a specified time.

3:15 to 5 P.M. Orientation to a management decision-making exercise is conducted and participants are divided into teams.

6:30 to 10 P.M. Teams meet and plan for the decision-making exercise and make their first decision.

Tuesday:
8 A.M. to 12:30 P.M. The decision-making exercise is conducted.

1:30 to 2:30 P.M. Teams give a critique of their own performances in the exercise.

2:45 to 3:45 P.M. All teams meet together for a critique of the total exercise. No structure or discussion leader is appointed. The Andlinger Business Game[5] is a good one for this.

[4] Donald L. Grant, "Situational Tests in the Assessment of Managers, Part II, Contributions to the Assessment Process," *Management Games in Selection and Development,* Educational Testing Service, Princeton, N.J., 1964, p. 135.

[5] G. R. Andlinger, "Business Games—Play One!" *Harvard Business Review,* vol. 36, no. 2, March–April, 1958, pp. 115–125.

4 to 5:30 P.M. A think-on-your-feet exercise is conducted with the total group. Each participant is given a topic. He is allowed thirty to sixty seconds to prepare a presentation on the topic. He then gives a three- to five-minute presentation.

Wednesday:

8 to 10 A.M. Observers give individual feedback on performance on the in-basket exercise.

10:45 A.M. to 12:30 P.M. Staff conducts thorough interviews with each participant. These can be interviews by a single member of the staff or group interviews by a panel of staff members.

1:30 to 3:30 P.M. Leaderless group discussions are conducted with groups of six to eight participants. In this exercise, it is important to pose a problem with a number of different solutions to which each member may become committed. They then have the problem of coming up with a joint solution.

3:45 to 5:30 P.M. A highly involving, short business game is conducted with the participants divided into two or three competing groups. Three-dimensional tic-tac-toe is such a game.

Thursday:

8 A.M. to noon. Conference leadership assignments are given, and each participant conducts a fifteen- to twenty-minute conference with the total group on his assigned topic.

1 to 5 P.M. Peer impression project. Each participant is given the task of rating each of the other participants in a very thorough manner. Part of this project is ranking the other participants. They are also asked to indicate how they think they will be rated by the group and by the observers.

Friday:

8 A.M. to noon. Individual feedback is given each participant by the observer assigned to him. This feedback includes the peer impression results.

Participants are dismissed in the afternoon to return to their locations. The observers spend almost the entire week following the program individually and jointly evaluating the candidates. They must take into consideration all test scores, interview results, performance data from the exercises, and peer evaluations, and recommend for promotion those they determine as possessors of good management potential.

BIBLIOGRAPHY

Assessing Managerial Potential, The Foundation for Research on Human Behavior, Ann Arbor, 1958.

Dooher, M. Joseph, and Elizabeth Marting, *Selection of Management Personnel,* vols. 1 and 2, American Management Association, New York, 1957.

Gordon, Leonard V., and Francis F. Medland, "The Cross-group Stability of Peer Ratings of Leadership Potential," *Personnel Psychology,* vol. 18, no. 2, Summer, 1965, pp. 173–177.

Identifying Management Talent: The Conference on Executive Study, December 7 and 8, 1961, Educational Testing Service, Princeton, N.J., 1962.

The In-basket Technique: The Conference on the Executive Study, November 30, December 1, 1960, Educational Testing Service, Princeton, N.J., 1961.

Mahoney, Thomas A., Thomas H. Jerdee, and Allen N. Nach, *The Identification of Management Potential,* William C. Brown Company, Publishers, Dubuque, Iowa, 1961.

Management Games in Selection and Development: The Executive Study Conference, May 5 and 6, 1964, Educational Testing Service, Princeton, N.J., 1964.

CHAPTER SIX

Manager Development

HOKE S. SIMPSON   *Director, Executive Programs, Graduate School of Business, Columbia University, New York, New York*

The growth and development of managers occurs in many ways. The most important factors contributing to executive growth are:
1. On-the-job training
2. Special task-force assignments
3. Seminars and conferences
4. Company executive programs
5. University-sponsored executive programs

By far the most important contribution to an individual's growth and development is experience on the job. This can be unplanned, haphazard, and left to chance, or it can be thought through and guided so that the experience is truly educational. In this chapter, we outline a step-by-step approach for ensuring that growth takes place to the full extent of each individual's capacity and ability.

ESTABLISHING THE CLIMATE FOR MANAGER DEVELOPMENT

The first requirement for a systematic plan of manager development is to establish a climate in which the executive can grow and flourish. Though it is easy to use the word "climate," it is very difficult to describe exactly the kind of climate that promotes manager development. Certainly one of the first things involved is to have proper organization and manpower planning. Organization planning is a basic management tool. Its usefulness is not limited to manager development, nor is a development program the sole reason for having an organization plan. But a sound organization plan is an absolute must for a program of manager development.

Organization Planning. The first step in organization planning is to set objectives and goals. It is essential for the people at the top of the company to know what kind of business they are involved in, where they are now, where they want to go, when they expect to get there, and how all of the resources of the company are going to be brought to bear to achieve these objectives.

Once there is a clear-cut plan of action communicated throughout the organization, the next step in organization planning is to determine what tasks must be performed, that is, what work must be done to achieve the objectives. Next, the work must be assigned to specific people. It is important for everyone on the payroll to know specifically what his duties are. Although many progressive companies still do not have written job and position descriptions, a failure to put job duties in writing often results in misunderstandings and either a duplication of effort or failure to perform some work necessary to the total task.

Clear-cut job descriptions, preferably in writing, for all supervisory personnel are indispensable to manager development. These job descriptions should show clearly the duties, the responsibilities, the freedom to act, and the working relationships of each person in each job with the rest of the organization. Similarly, job specifications or requirements must be thought through. What special skills, what previous experience, what management and leadership qualities are essential to the performance of the job as it exists today and as it may exist in the future? Without job descriptions and job specifications, it is almost impossible to establish meaningful individual development programs. After job descriptions and job specifications have been written and the jobs carefully assigned to specific individuals, it is desirable to prepare organization charts. Frequently, it is useful to chart the organization as it now exists and to prepare a second chart showing the organization required for the future objectives. This will help in future manpower planning.

Delegation. The next step in creating a proper climate is effective delegation. In essence, delegation means giving someone a task, a piece of work to accomplish, and then letting him do it without constant reference or instructions from his supervisor. Delegation is planned for in setting up the organization structure. The position description should spell out the degree of authority and the freedom of action which goes with each job. In any situation, there can be more or less delegation. For the purpose of manager development, the more delegation the better. When a man must think through on his own the possibilities of success or failure and the various courses of action which can be taken, and finally must make a risk-taking decision, he is at the same time developing a capacity for taking on responsibility and developing self-confidence to handle increasingly larger jobs.

Although delegation is provided for in the organization plan, whether one truly delegates or not is determined by the day-to-day work relationships. In one sense of the word, delegation is a state of mind. A supervisor who indulges in second guessing, in being ultracritical when mistakes are made, or in retaining rigid and detailed controls is defeating delegation. Delegation means freedom of action sufficient to get the task accomplished. It means freedom to make decisions, freedom to make mistakes, and freedom to use one's full abilities. This does not mean that the supervisor leaves the person on his own to sink or swim. Nor does it mean that he gives him a life preserver. It does mean that the supervisor assumes the role of a coach. To create the climate in which manager development can take place, each supervisor must counsel with subordinates to help them gain insights into their needs. In addition, each supervisor must coach each subordinate to accelerate acquisition of the necessary skills of behavior to get the job done. And finally, each supervisor must work with subordinates to make their on-the-job experience educational and meaningful.

Coaching. In the same manner as the famous athletic coaches of various sports, a successful supervisor must be readily available and must be the source of constructive guidance. Coaching is designed to change performance, to change skill, or to change behavior. There is a general notion that people resist change. The fact of the matter is that people do not necessarily resist change as such, but they often do resist the methods we use to try to get them to change. For a successful coaching job, certain things have to be done by the supervisor, certain things by the subordinate, and certain things by both of them.

The requirements on the part of the supervisor are:

1. A knowledge of what is expected on the job (not necessarily the "how")
2. Definite standards of performance
3. An intimate knowledge of the man, his capabilities, and his attitude
4. An interest in the man and his success
5. Determination to take the time to do it (and it is time consuming)

The requirements on the part of the subordinate are:

1. Knowledge of the company
2. Knowledge of the policies and procedures of the company
3. Knowledge of what is expected on the job
4. Confidence in the supervisor and his ability

How does the supervisor coach?

First, it is essential that the supervisor know what the real or basic need is.

Second, he must get the subordinate's interest in improving. If the desire for achievement is not there, no amount of coaching will in itself instill it.

Third, he shows or tells the subordinate what is expected and why.

Fourth, he has the individual walk through the skill which is to be improved. (In this first walk-through of the "play," it is important not to allow failures or mistakes.) The supervisor observes and corrects as the person walks through the play, and then has him walk through it again.

Fifth, during this part of the coaching operation, the coach watches performance, not results. He continues the process until the performance is letter-perfect. Then, when the person is performing the skill on his own, the results will be letter-perfect.

Counseling. As a part of a planned manager development program, it is necessary to make systematic appraisals of how well people are performing their jobs compared with what they are supposed to be doing, and to assess or make an estimate of how well they might perform in more responsible positions. These appraisals should be made on the basis of job performance and not on the basis of some ill-defined character traits that someone has decided are necessary for leadership. In most instances, people have a pretty good idea of how well they are performing the duties and responsibilities assigned to them. Almost everyone, however, regardless of position, wants to know how his supervisor assesses his work and wherein he and his supervisor agree or disagree on the priorities of his tasks.

All of us are constantly appraising the work of others—sometimes systematically, sometimes haphazardly. In a program of manager development, some systematic kind of appraisal should be arranged. This does not mean that good performance should be discussed with the individual at only periodic intervals. On the contrary, good performance should be commended when observed, and less than adequate performance should be corrected when observed. Planned manager development, however, calls for systematically reviewing the contents of the job, the results expected, and performance in comparison with the results expected. It is then important that this appraisal be discussed with the individual and a planned program of development scheduled.

In counseling with subordinates, bear in mind that the supervisor does not, in fact, develop anyone. All development is self-development. The best that you can do is to create the climate in which growth and development can take place. If you do your job badly, you can effectively stifle or block development. Therefore, in counseling a subordinate, you want to accomplish two main objectives. First, you want to find out how you have helped or hindered the effective performance of his job, and what you can do or refrain from doing in the future to make his performance more effective. Second, you want to help him gain insights on how to learn from experience—how to work at the development of his analytical and conceptual ability.

Making Experience Educational. "Experience is the best teacher" is an old adage, but it is only partially true. Experience is a slow teacher, and sometimes teaches the wrong things. For experience to be educational, each significant experience—each significant success or failure—must be analyzed after it has occurred. This analysis, or inquiry, is based on four questions: What happened and why? What do I need to know or be able to do, or what point of view should I have, to get desired results next time? What have I learned in this situation that can be applied to other situations even though different? What have I learned about how to learn from experience?

Unless each significant experience is subjected to this rigorous analysis, learning to manage on the job does not necessarily take place. There is a great difference between ten years of experience and one year's experience repeated ten times.

JOB ROTATION

Development for general management requires a broader breadth of experience and a broader perspective than can be obtained in one single managerial job or even in a single department. Methods of manager development at the general manager level, therefore, call for other means than regular on-the-job experience. These include job rotation, in-company courses, and university-sponsored out-company courses. Many companies have effectively used job rotation to help in the development of managers. It is necessary, however, to emphasize that a simple tour through other departments, spending one, two, or three months looking over someone's shoulder, is an extremely ineffective method of job rotation. Rather, job rotation should be on a selective basis for a particular individual at a particular stage in his career when it is indicated.

For example, in a large multidivisional consumer products company, the vice president of production of a major division of the company was appraised as a potential general manager and senior executive. In this consumer products company, it was felt that a knowledge of and skill in the marketing function was essential at the top management level. In the division in which this production man operated, there was a general sales manager, an advertising manager, and a director of market research. A new job, vice president of marketing, was created, and the production vice president was placed in this job. Initially, his subordinates—the general sales manager, the advertising manager, and the marketing research director—knew much more about the marketing function than did the new marketing vice president. It was the feeling of the senior executives in the company, however, that if this man was going to fail, the best place to fail was at this level and at this stage in his career when he could be returned to the production function, rather than at some later date and in the job of a division general manager. In this instance, the former production man learned fast, became an expert marketing man, and was eventually promoted to general manager of the division where he was completely successful.

Another type of different job experience is assignment to a special task force to study some part of the company's operation and come up with recommendations. Such assignments, if carefully planned, will enable a young manager to see the company as a total system, the enterprise as a complete entity, which is sometimes difficult or impossible from the narrow perspective of a single department.

IN-COMPANY COURSES

In considering manager development, it is important to consider the advisability of formalized courses for managers at a given level. These courses may be concerned with the specific policies of the company; they may be concerned with unique technical areas of the specific industry; or they may be more broadly based, such as courses in general management, motivation, or internal communications. There are advantages and disadvantages to in-company courses. One of the disadvantages is that often the managers who participate in company courses are looking for the "party line"—and frequently finding it. On the other hand, one of the big problems of managerial work in most enterprises is the difficulty of intermanager communications. Our language of business is not yet sufficiently precise to convey identical meanings to everyone. A company course attended by managers who work together, in addition to its other benefits, frequently evolves a common language which enables managers to work together more understandingly.

UNIVERSITY-SPONSORED COURSES

In the United States, over forty universities offer regular annual, formalized educational programs for managers. In addition, a number of professional and trade associations offer seminars, conferences, and programs. These have some advantages over in-company programs—they usually provide a more diverse and better-trained teaching faculty, and they bring together executives from different types of companies and different functions of business so that a broadening process takes place which is not possible with in-company courses. The disadvantage of university courses is that they cannot be tailored to a particular company. Therefore, when outside courses are used, it is necessary to determine what level of management the course is directed toward and what specific objectives the course is trying to accomplish. Then select the proper individual for the proper course.

One typical university program, a six-week program directed toward senior-level managers who are concerned with the general management function rather than a departmental function, has four specific objectives:

1. It is designed to broaden the horizons of the participants who attend and to make them more receptive to looking at new ideas.

2. It is designed to help them sharpen some particular general management skill, especially those of analytical ability, conceptual ability, interpersonal competence, and organizational planning.

3. It is designed to provide an educational setting where, in a spirit of objective inquiry, the participants can bring up to a conscious level their viewpoints, attitudes, beliefs, and assumptions. These can be explored and discussed, reviewed and analyzed, and either reaffirmed, modified, or changed.

4. And finally, this program, along with many similar programs, is designed to keep the managers who attend up to date in new management technologies.

A Typical University Program. The Executive Program in Business Administration, a concentrated six-week program conducted by the Graduate School of Business of Columbia University and held at Arden House, Harriman, New York, is representative of the kind of program for senior executives which includes the above four points in its overall objectives. This is an in-residence program and is conducted six days a week for six continuous weeks.

In 1966, the general format of this particular program was as follows:

First two weeks—internal administration of the business enterprise. This includes the range and scope of managerial problems, basic factors in organization structure, organizational planning, interpersonal relations, behavior of individuals in groups, and translating behavioral insights into effective action.

Second two weeks—making business relevant to a dynamic environment. This covers a study in some depth of the economic, political, cultural, and social forces, both domestic and international, which affect business.

Third two weeks—executives in action. This covers the establishment of company objectives and goals, long-range planning, effective decision making, building programs of action, and putting new programs into effect.

A typical day in this program, in addition to extensive reading of current management literature, would include:

In the morning, a lecture by a distinguished scholar on the concept and theory of the general management area under discussion

In the late morning or early afternoon, a case study in depth taken from an actual business situation

In the late afternoon, a lecture by a government official or business executive describing actual experience in the application of the concepts discussed in the morning

In the early evening, a round table discussion with other participants of the program on subjects of mutual interest

Selection of Programs. In selecting participants for programs such as the one described above, keep three things uppermost in your mind:

1. Although the general objectives may be the same, the programs differ in length, format, teaching methodology, and the general level of managers who participate. It is therefore highly desirable to know the details of the program you are considering and, where possible, to discuss your objectives with the program director.

2. Remember that these programs are not remedial. They are designed for managers who are successful, not for managers who are unsuccessful.

3. Such courses in themselves cannot develop managers. They are, however, indispensable in the total framework of manager development.

SUMMARY

Manager development consists of the following elements:
1. Experience on the job
    a. In the proper climate
    b. With appropriate coaching and counseling on the part of supervisors
    c. With carefully planned assignments to new jobs and new duties to round out necessary knowledge

2. Formal courses and programs within the company
    a. To teach company policy
    b. To teach technical knowledge
    c. To teach the internal administration of a specific enterprise
3. Formal programs in universities
    a. To broaden horizons
    b. To show the company as a total system
    c. To study the environment in which the company operates
    d. To sharpen general management skills
    e. To review an individual's viewpoints, beliefs, and assumptions
    f. To keep up to date on the newest management technologies

BIBLIOGRAPHY

Argyris, Chris, *Interpersonal Competence and Organizational Effectiveness,* Richard D. Irwin, Inc., Homewood, Ill., 1962.

Bradford, Leland P., Jack R. Gibb, and Kenneth D. Benne (eds.), *T-Group Theory and Laboratory Method,* John Wiley & Sons, Inc., New York, 1964.

DePhillips, Frank A., William M. Berliner, and James J. Cribbin, *Management of Training Programs,* Richard D. Irwin, Inc., Homewood, Ill., 1960.

Houston, George C., *Manager Development, Principles and Perspectives,* Richard D. Irwin, Inc., Homewood, Ill., 1961.

Marrow, Alfred J., *Behind the Executive Mask,* American Management Association, New York, 1964.

Newman, William, *Administrative Action,* 2d ed., Prentice-Hall, Inc., Englewood Cliffs, N.J., 1965, chaps. 18, 19, and 20.

Shartle, Carroll L., *Executive Performance and Leadership,* Prentice-Hall, Inc., Englewood Cliffs, N.J., 1956.

CHAPTER SEVEN

Business Gaming as an Aid to Manager Development

STANLEY C. VANCE   *Head, Personnel and Industrial Management Department, University of Oregon, Eugene, Oregon*

Management decision simulation, or as it is more familiarly called, business gaming, is an innovation in the field of executive training and development. The first full-scale business simulation model was presented publicly in May 1957. Twenty corporation presidents met at the Hotel Astor in New York City to participate in the American Management Association's Top Management Decision Simulation Seminar. The success of this and of subsequent AMA simulation seminars served as a strong stimulus in the development of many other management decision simulation models. Within the next four years, eighty-nine business simulation models or games were available for use in industry and in higher education.[1]   By 1965, there were approximately two hundred versions with about twenty new games being added to this list annually.

Proponents of management decision simulation consider it to be a major addition to the management development curriculum. There are some users who go so far as to claim that the simulation technique is one of the more significant breakthroughs in management training methods. Proponents point to the steadily expanding number and variety of games and to their increased usage as evidence of acceptance and worthwhileness.

Critics, on the other hand, sometimes disparage the technique by calling it a fad or a gimmick. They discount the almost immediate acceptance and continued growth in popularity of this innovation as just another instance of the cult of emulation. The detractors likewise point to the lack of measurable and verifiable positive benefits from application of the techniques. They say that all positive aspects, such as the claim that use of simulation models gives the participants a broader view of business, are supported only by subjective evidence. Critics of simulation also condemn the apparent lack of objective

---

[1] P. S. Greenlaw, L. W. Herron, and R. H. Rawdon, *Business Simulation in Industrial and University Education*, Prentice-Hall, Inc., Englewood Cliffs, N.J., 1962, p. 340.

or purpose that seems to be evidenced by the heterogeneity in models and even in the basic terminology. In particular, the terms "simulation" and "game playing" have negative connotations. Most dictionaries define simulation as implying deceit, falsehood, or pretense. Reference to business game playing brings to mind parlor games such as Monopoly.

BUSINESS GAMING CONCEPTS

The nature of business gaming is sometimes clouded by semantic confusions. Some of these can be minimized by a restatement of basic terms.

Simulation, in a relatively broad sense, means any attempt at system, process, or situation analysis through model structuring.

A *model* is a representation of reality. The basic reason for structuring a model of any kind is to facilitate analysis, experimentation, and comprehension. Models can be differentiated as to (1) structure, (2) function, or (3) scope.

From a structure or design point of view, models can be classified as physical, schematic, verbal, or mathematical. Considering the function or purpose, there are two basic categories: analytical models and training models. Finally, the representation of reality can be that of the entire system—a macro model—or that of only a specific component of the system—a micro model.

Perhaps the chief cause of semantic confusion is the indiscriminate use of the terms "simulation" and "business game." Much of the irritation can be avoided if it is recognized that business games are only one form of simulation. Although all business gaming is simulation, not all simulation is business gaming. With this reservation in mind, the terms "management decision simulation" and "business game" or "gaming" will be used interchangeably in the remainder of this discussion.

Characteristics of Management Decision Simulation Models. The nature of most business games can be understood by examining their structure, function, and scope.

Structure. For the most part, management decision simulation models or business games are mathematical in design. This does not mean that they must be mathematically complex. Invariably, however, they do require some sort of arithmetical or mathematical expressions.

Function. The prime purpose of practically all management decision simulation models is to help train present and prospective managers. In this capacity, business games are used to show, through a representation of reality, how the system or subsystem operates. This exposure to a facsimile of reality provides the trainee with opportunities to observe, to manipulate, and to learn.

Scope. Of all the simulation models in use, probably less than 20 percent could strictly be labeled as macro. On the other hand, it is this type of business game which has had by far the greatest usage. The macro models attempt to represent an economy, an industry, or even a company in a general or total-system fashion. Consequently, these models are particularly useful for university classrooms and for the broader management development programs. The micro models, although they tend to deal with more immediate and more concrete problems, have a much more limited usage. For example, a representation of an inventory control model in a specific company would tend to have less than universal appeal.

Types of Business Game Models. In addition to the three basic classifications as to structure, function, and scope, business games are also frequently differentiated according to the following norms:

1. Interactive or noninteractive
2. Deterministic or probabilistic
3. Dynamic or static
4. Team decision or individual decision
5. Manual or computer

Interactive or Noninteractive Models. Interaction is a characteristic of games where the decisions made by the individual participants generally have a causal impact upon the decisions and performance of all participants. Games of this type frequently try to focus attention upon the significance of competition as an all-pervading force. The players in the interaction-type game soon learn that no set of decisions is best in an absolute sense. All business decisions must be judged on a relative basis, that is, in terms of their effectiveness when matched against the competitors' decisions.

Noninteractive simulation has a very different objective. The decisions made by one group do not have a measurable impact upon the cause-effect sequences of the other players. In other words, while some courses of action lead to better results than do others, each course of action is independent of all others. Most of the micro models, particularly those concerned with a departmental activity or a single staff function, are of this type. Although the competitive characteristic is not entirely absent, it does play a very secondary role in the noninteractive-type game.

Deterministic or Probabilistic Models. Deterministic models are those where all the pertinent factors and forces are within the control of the game players. Because the element of chance is of no consequence in a deterministic-type model, a specific set of decisions will always yield the same result if the parameters are unchanged. A parameter in this instance is defined as a constant factor which serves as a constraint upon the simulation model. Examples of parameters in business games include factors such as price, capacity, demand, and capitalization.

Probabilistic, or as they quite frequently are called, stochastic, models incorporate the element of chance. One or more of the game components is considered as a variable factor so that its incidence is presumed to fall within a given probability pattern. There are a number of ways to simulate the stochastic model. Once the probability distributions are structured, the chance occurrence can be simulated by means of a roulette wheel, a roll of dice, the turn of a card, or by use of a random numbers sequence. Caution should be exercised when using probabilistic or stochastic models. There is a danger that the chance elements can appear to have a preponderant impact upon the game results. If the participants cannot see a meaningful cause-effect relationship between their decisions and the outcome, they will invariably become disinterested. The learning value in such a case is minimal.

Dynamic or Static Models. Dynamic or sequential simulation models involve periodic adjustment of selected strategies. The most popular games require a new set of decisions each quarter or three-month simulated time period. At the end of a period, the results of each selected strategy functioning within a given state of nature are set forth numerically. In a sense, the output of the preceding quarter becomes the input of the next quarter. In the second and subsequent decision-making rounds, the game players generally have an opportunity to change, within prescribed bounds, the values of most of the assignable variables such as the unit price to be charged or the number of units to be produced. Sequential simulation, consequently, provides a valuable teaching medium where mistakes can be rectified and sound decisions can be emulated.   In some games, the sequential characteristic is even applied to the succession of states of nature.   This situation presupposes a Markovian-type stability where the states of nature must change in some regular fashion.   However, the specific state of nature which exists at a given point in time is dependent on the state of nature which preceded.   For example, when an index is used to set total demand in a given simulated period, the index value invariably is very intimately dependent upon the index value of the immediately preceding period.

Static, discrete, or one-shot simulation is, as the term implies, a limited action. It is more in the nature of solving a specific problem.   Once the course of action has been determined, there is no reappraising or redoing.   This approach has particular significance in special-purpose functional-type games of micro dimensions.   By contrast, sequential simulation is particularly adaptable to analysis of total systems or macro models which continue to operate over a fairly long simulated time span.

Team or Individual-type Games.   Team games are by far the most common form of business decision simulation.   They have the advantage of creating an environment where the would-be decision maker must sell his ideas to his teammates or be sold upon their ideas.   This provides an excellent laboratory for testing interpersonal relations.   Much of the enthusiasm which characterizes most business game playing probably stems from this interaction of different personalities involved in selecting a single course of action.   Most games geared to team playing seem to have an optimal team size of between three and seven players.

Individual-type games obviously lack the benefits of learning through team action in decision making.   There are, however, compensating features.   Liability for poor playing and recognition for sound decision making can be more precisely pinpointed.   There is no opportunity, as there is in the team approach, for an individual to "goof off" without being readily spotted.

The team technique stresses the significance of discussion and deliberation by all concerned parties as a prerequisite to sound decision making.   The individual-type game puts emphasis on the role of the individual as the ultimate decision maker.   In this respect, the individual-type game is an excellent approximation of reality.   Even in the most democratic committee, after much talk and vote taking, it invariably remains one man's responsibility, generally the highest-ranking executive's, to make the decision authoritatively.

Manual or Computer Scoring.   Management decision simulation models range in format from relatively simple hand-scored exercises to rather complex computerized versions.   In between these extremes, there is a great variety, including some hybrids which incorporate both hand scoring and computer calculating.

Hand-scored or manual-type games have the advantage of simplicity, low cost, and flexibility.   If the prime objectives of the business game are to teach and to train prospective managers, then hand scoring serves a very useful purpose.   The participants are forced to observe how the pertinent variables interact.   Cause-effect relationships are better understood.   The consequences of a specific decision can be traced throughout the system.

Once the intricacies have been mastered, however, hand scoring can become a tedious operation.   This is particularly the case if the arithmetical calculations are lengthy and involved.   Consequently, computerized games serve a very useful purpose when they eliminate repetitive calculations.   The labor saving frequently means a reduction in cost.   There is also the positive aspect of sophistication.   Computerized games, however, are not effective if, in the game-playing process, the participants fail to recognize the reality the model is supposed to represent.   The real test of a business game's worth is its effectiveness as a training device.   This implies comprehension.

There are a number of business games which attempt to incorporate the good features of both hand scoring and computerizing.   In these compromises, the participants are first introduced to a hand-scored model.   After an adequate number of decision-making sessions, when it is assumed that the players have mastered the mechanism and understand the system, the computerized version is introduced.   In this joining of the two methods, the participants have an opportunity to get the maximum benefits of both the hand-scored and the computerized versions.

ILLUSTRATION OF A TYPICAL BUSINESS GAME

Because there are so many different kinds of business games in use, no single description can cover the entire field.   In addition to some very obvious reasons for selecting *Management Decision Simulation*[2] for illustration purposes, this model has been chosen because it has proved to be effective even after relatively long usage.   It was one of the very first games to be published.   From 1959 to 1965, it was played by more than eleven thousand students and management development personnel.   At the University of Oregon alone, about two thousand individuals had exposure to this simulation model.   In addition to the teaching-training goal, it is one of the very few models used for research and experimental purposes.   It fits the previously described simulation model characteristics in the following fashion:

Basic Characteristics.   Structure—mathematical, but not complex; function—teaching, training, and research; scope—macro or total enterprise.

Secondary Characteristics.   *Interactive.*   Three competing companies make comparable sets of decisions quarterly.   Each company's performance is affected by its competitors' decisions.

Stochastic and Probabilistic.   The ensuing states of nature are beyond the control of the participants.   In addition, there are some probabilistic elements in that demand forecasting can be ventured on an established probability pattern.   Labor negotiations are subject to given likelihoods of strikes under prescribed conditions.   If desired, an investment portfolio developed by each player can be subjected to selected probability patterns for both dividends and appreciation of the investment.

Dynamic.   Decisions and their consequences are sequentially related.   One quarter's results become the basis for making the next quarter's decisions.   This stress on the time element adds considerably to the game's approximation of reality.

Team or Individual.   Either approach can be used.   If training is the exclusive objective, then the team technique might be preferable.   If stress is placed upon individual appraisal, then the second approach is recommended.

Manual and Computer Programmed.   The original publication appeared in hand-scored form.   Subsequently, it was programmed for computer usage.   In its current form, it is a hybrid model.   It forces the players in the hand-scored approach to study the various interactions and to get some comprehension of their significance.   Once this objective is attained, the move to the computerized version permits concentration upon other facets.   For example, the group can attempt depth analysis of pertinent concepts such as inventory control, capital equipment policy, the nature of demand forecasting, and the like.

[2] Stanley Vance, *Management Decision Simulation*, McGraw-Hill Book Company, New York, 1960.

Other Features. In some respects, this is a zero-sum game. All gains or losses by one firm are shared by the other players. The size of the "pie" to be shared, however, does fluctuate according to a business index.

The simulated shares of the market are not equal. Although most games divide the market into *n* equal parts, this game structures Companies A, B, and C with 50, 30, and 20 percent respectively. In this feature, the game comes fairly close to reality. Most American industries—automobile, petroleum, and steel, for example—have a comparable inequality in scale of operation for the three leading firms.

Decision Matrix. Every quarter, each of the three companies makes a set of decisions including:

1. *Unit Price of the Product.* This is initially set at $10 and can be changed a maximum of $1 per quarter.

2. *Qualitative Factor.* This is a composite of all variables directly associated with quality. The initial qualitative cost of $2 per unit is subject to change according to a prescribed schedule as the qualitative factor is improved or lowered.

3. *Distribution Factor.* This is a composite of all variables directly associated with distributing the product. There is an initial $2 per unit charge for this factor which is subject to change according to a prescribed schedule when the distribution factor is modified.

4. *Capacity Factor.* At the beginning of the game, each company is presumed to be using 86 percent of its capacity. This capacity-utilization percentage is close to the preferred operating rate for most industries. The capacity factor can be improved or lowered at a specified cost for each unit of activated or shutdown capacity. Unit costs vary in curvilinear fashion with the percentage of capacity utilized.

5. *Periodic Decisions.* Provision is made for optional decisions which are, however, not essential to the game itself. These decisions include dividend payments, additional capacity, acquisition of an investment portfolio, and a collective bargaining sequence.

6. *State-of-nature Regulator.* The total industry sales volume per quarter is the prime state-of-nature element. The *Business Week* Index has been used very successfully as the barometer. However, since cyclical and seasonal patterns frequently give relatively prolonged upward or downward sequences in the *Business Week* Index, a barometer of this type has serious limitations. The game moderator can, at his discretion, substitute any of a large number of predetermined state-of-business patterns structured to include specific cyclical characteristics.

7. *The Basic Equation.* In the typical business situation, there are many variables which affect performance. Some of these variables are measurable, and some are not measurable; some are controllable, but many are beyond the manager's control. Any attempt at devising a business game which would reflect all or even most of these pertinent variables would result in an immensely complex model. The usefulness of such a model for training purposes would very likely be minimal.

The basic equation of the game illustration being discussed has, after considerable experimentation, been condensed to include only price factor (pf), qualitative factor (qf), and distribution factor (df). In the basic equation $(qf)(df)/pf$, the numerator represents all the forces which have a positive correlation with demand. In other words, improvements in quality and in distribution invariably tend to have a positive impact upon sales, particularly if price is kept constant.

The denominator represents all the variables which have an inverse relationship with demand.   Unit price is the best example.   In almost every typical situation, a price cut engenders more sales while a price hike tends to cut sales volume.

Manual Calculations.   After the participants have made their decisions, the calculations are worked out by each individual on work sheets similar to Figure 7-1.   The symbols are merely mnemonic abbreviations.   For example:

$$\begin{aligned}
\text{Smf} &= \text{Share of market factor} \\
\text{OSM} &= \text{Old share of market} \\
\text{NSM}' &= \text{New share of market, unadjusted} \\
\text{NSM} &= \text{New share of market, adjusted} \\
\text{S} &= \text{Total industry sales, per quarter} \\
\text{Up} &= \text{Unit price} \\
\text{R} &= \text{Revenue} \\
\text{C/S} &= \text{Cost of sales} \\
\text{NI} &= \text{Net income}
\end{aligned}$$

With these symbolic designations and an arithmetical procedure indicated by the various $+$, $-$, $\times$, $\div$, $/$, and $=$ signs, the participants can readily calculate the performance for teams A, B, and C.

Balance Sheet Analysis.   Because this is a sequential-type game, each quarter's results must be incorporated into the respective company's balance sheet.   Provision is made in the game playing for this tabulation by a second type of work sheet which is not included in this chapter.   In the final analysis, effective or poor performance is reflected in the relative balance sheet improvement made by the competing teams.

Performance Evaluation.   A serious flaw in many business games is their inability to measure results.   This is an area that needs improvement.   In the specific game just described, results are measured by a performance index and a learning curve.   The performance index is a composite of weighted values reflecting:

1. Changes in each team's share of the market
2. Profit or loss as a percentage of sales
3. Cash account level
4. Inventory level
5. Owners' equity
6. Dividend payment

The weighted relative values for these factors are summed for each team. This becomes a yardstick measuring game performance.   Inclusion of several norms of effective performance into a single index facilitates comparison.   Objections might be raised regarding the specific factors and their respective weights, but these objections can very easily be alleviated merely by adding to or subtracting from the list of success criteria.

One of the most common complaints against some sequential-type games is the disproportionate penalty imposed upon novices who do poorly in the first few rounds of play.   The learning curve is an attempt to correct this imperfection.   Each succeeding quarter's performance evaluation is multiplied by a progressively higher factor.   The multiplier can increase in simple arithmetic fashion (1.0, 1.1, 1.2, . . .) or in any other desired pattern.   This puts a premium upon improvement.

GAME-PLAYING RESULTS

The results of game playing are both positive and negative.   The following discussion covers the most commonly experienced results.

INCOME

	1	2	3	4	5	6	7	8	9	10	11	12
	$\dfrac{(qf)(df)}{pf}$	= Smf ×	OSM =	= NSM' +	>1< =	= NSM ×	ΣS =	S ×	Up =	R −	C/S =	NI
CO		=	=	=	=	=	=	=	=	−	=	=
A		×	=	+	=	×	=	×	=	−	=	=
B		×	=	+	=	×	=	×	=	−	=	=
C		×	=	+	=	×	=	×	=	−	=	=

COSTS

	13	14	15	16	17	18	19	20	21	22	23	24	25	26	27
	cf	qf	df	cc +	qc +	dc =	Uc ×	P =	C/P ±	C/ij =	C/GS +	C/cj +	C/ic +	C/in +	C/S
CO				=	+	+	=	×	=	=	+	+	+	−	=
A				+	+	+	×	=	±	=	+	+	+	+	=
B				+	+	+	×	=	±	=	+	+	+	+	=
C				+	+	+	×	=	±	=	+	+	+	+	=

INVENTORY

	28	29	30	31	32	33	34	35	36	37
	P −	S =	Ui ×	Uc =	C/ij	UiA ±	Ui =	UiZ	INV %	INV Uc
CO	P −	= S	=± Ui	× Uc	= C/ij	UiA ±	= Ui	= UiZ		
A	−	=±	=±	×	=	UiA ±	=±	=		
B	−	=±	=±	×	=	UiA ±	=±	=		
C	−	=±	=±	×	=	UiA ±	=±	=		

FIG. 7-1. *Work sheet for business game computations.*

Positive Results. *Interest Stimulation.* There seems to be incontestable evidence that games of this type are extremely effective in engendering the competitive spirit. In the post-game evaluation sessions for the model just described, the participants have overwhelmingly endorsed this technique, at least for its stated objectives. A summary of opinions from almost one thousand game players, who have also had experience in learning through the conventional case-method technique, provided the following breakdown:

	Extremely satisfactory	Moderately satisfactory	So-so	Not satisfactory
The game......................	40%	35%	20%	5%
Case-method experience...........	10%	40%	35%	15%

There are, of course, some serious questions as to the comparability of the two techniques. Nevertheless, from this compilation and from the commentary of practically all users of business games, this is an extremely effective interest arouser.

Group Dynamics. Probably the second most significant positive result is the realization by the participants that each and every functional activity is important for effective corporate performance. Overexposure to a single area of activity does very frequently lead to the equivalent of provincialism in tight-knit departmental organizations. Playing the game is an excellent device to show the significance and interaction of the several functional activities. Better comprehension and tolerance are by-products of this exercise in group dynamics.

Objectivity. Simulation models of this type force the contestants to quantify their decisions. This leads to precision in thinking. Cause and effect are graphically tied together. There is little latitude for the arbitrary-action type of decision, because consequences are spelled out precisely. Objectivity and the time dimension are especially emphasized in those games where feedback is integral.

Planning. If the participants are given at least some general indication of how the simulated business cycle will operate, each player can and should develop a specific course of action. Because each course of action should be defensible, this becomes an exercise in logic. There is ample evidence to show that poor planning or no planning almost always is directly correlated with poor game performance results.

Concept Comprehension. The apperceptive players have an excellent laboratory in games of this type. Concepts such as break-even analysis, economic lot size, elasticity of demand, leverage, and the like, can be tested in measurable terms. Very frequently, pet notions and academic arguments fall apart when the game players have a quantitative appraisal as to how this notion fits in reality.

Negative Results. *Fact Dissemination.* No game currently in use provides the players with more than a cursory introduction to what might be called the facts of business life. A few games, such as the illustration which has just been described, attempt to overcome this shortcoming. Once the game playing is progressing smoothly and the computer is doing the arithmetical chores, supplemental topics are studied in detail. These supplements can cover a vast area of topics such as depreciation policy, equipment replacement methods, business forecasting, inventory control, and linear programming.

Job Improvement. There is no conclusive evidence that, with a few exceptions, exposure to simulated decision making will improve actual decision making. Unfortunately, this situation exists because of an almost complete lack of follow-up. On the positive side, it can be stated that there is likewise no evidence that game playing does not contribute to improved individual performance.

Personnel Selection and Promotion. At the present time, it would be premature to state that any game can be used to select or promote personnel. This inadequacy stems from both simulation model design and our limitations in judging individuals. As yet there is no infallible norm, whether subjective appraisal, psychological test, or performance record, which can be recommended for this purpose.

Superficiality. Condensing the decision-making process into an incidental time interval certainly is not realistic. In every instance, the real decision—for example, raising prices—involves significantly more deliberation and evaluation than can be meaningfully structured into the simulation. This argument applies to general-purpose games far more than it does to the special, functional, problem-solving game. Actually, if the problem can be dissected into a minute segment, then reality can be miniaturized and approximated. Some critics contend the games put too much reliance on verisimilitude, that is, on subjective realism as opposed to objective realism.

Accountability. A frequently voiced objection to all games is their inability to simulate responsibility. In the sphere of business, decisions are invariably followed by consequences, good or bad. In the simulation approach, there is no comparable reward or failure. Without some sort of strict accountability, there is serious question that the simulated courses of action bear any resemblance to reality. This limitation has been accentuated in game playing involving top executives where it is not expedient for face-saving purposes to have any losers. In the classroom, this objection can be minimized if performance is reflected in recorded grades. Even when the game is merely an adjunct of a conventional course, allocating from 5 to 25 percent of the course grade to the game playing adds tremendously to the accountability factor.

THE FUTURE OF BUSINESS GAMING

As a Training Device. Even without any further improvements in model design and function, it seems appropriate to state that business gaming has excellent prospects as a training medium. This prediction is supported by the fact that new games are steadily being added to the roster. Even more significant is the caliber of users and innovators. Practically every major university and every dynamic corporation is involved to some extent in business simulation. With resources of this caliber being dedicated to testing, improving, and innovating, the probability is very high that the technique will be an even more important adjunct in training business leaders.

As an Analytical Device. The likelihood that simulation will prove its worth in this area is extremely low. Some special-purpose, functional, micro-type games come fairly close to meeting the minimum criteria for designation as analytical models. However, the multiplicity of variables in the business sphere makes meaningful analytical simulation very unlikely. Before real progress can be made in this regard, much more must be known about the forces and factors that are pertinent to business.

As a Research Device. Gaming as a research aid seems to have a great potential. To date, unfortunately, emphasis has been focused almost exclusively upon the training aspects.   As just a single, but authoritative, example of the research potential, there have been several very interesting experiments culminating in masters' theses and doctoral dissertations.[3]   Although caution should prevail at this stage, results of the fragmentary research endeavors are extremely encouraging.   For example, *Management Decision Simulation* has had both on-campus and off-campus testing.   On campus, nearly one thousand students, both undergraduate and graduate, have been closely studied, comparing game results and a long list of supposedly influencing factors such as grade-point average, age, risk-taking potential, competitiveness, and the like.   In addition, several hundred individuals in managerial capacities in industry have been subjected to similar analysis.   The industrial groups include both the heterogeneous and the homogeneous.   In the former category are several management development groups. In the latter classification are fairly large groups from a major retailing firm, a nationally known wood processing firm, and a leading aircraft builder.   Many of the experiments have yielded very inconclusive results.   However, the correlation in some instances is remarkable.   Probably the best results to date have been those linking good game players with tests for competitiveness and risk taking.   Fairly encouraging results have also been obtained for good game players and competency in business courses and, rather surprisingly, for expertise in vocabulary and communication.

Unfortunately, much more experimentation must be undertaken to confirm the research value of simulation as a decision-making aid.   This is not intended as an indictment.   Whereas the training potential has been perhaps 10 to 20 percent exploited, the research potential has not been utilized even a small fraction of 1 percent.   Even a minimal endeavor in this direction should yield disproportionately positive results.

SUMMARY

The business game is an exercise in decision making under uncertainty.   Although game playing was introduced only in 1957, it has proved to be a very useful training device.

Despite the great variety of business games, they can be differentiated on the basis of structure, function, and scope.   In addition, they can be categorized on norms such as interaction or noninteraction, deterministic or probabilistic, dynamic or static, team or individual, manual or computer calculated.

Critics condemn business games insofar as games cannot precisely duplicate reality.   This leads to charges of superficiality, lack of accountability, and a parlor-game level of performance.   Proponents counter with claims that simulation provides one of the best means for management development and research. They point to the benefits accruing from these exercises in model structuring and manipulation.   Among these benefits are the tremendous interest generated by games, the group dynamics aspects, the focusing of attention upon vital topics such as competition, the function of leadership, and the value of the heuristic approach.   The more ardent game players go so far as to claim that some games are an advancement over the case method of instruction.   Stress on feedback, verisimilitude, and decision making under uncertainty places these games in a special, advanced training technique category that might be termed "the dynamic case method."

Very obviously, more testing and evaluation are needed before simulation

[3] Clifford Gray, "A Comparison of Selected Personality Traits and Performance in a Total Enterprise Business Game," unpublished doctoral dissertation, University of Oregon, Eugene, Ore.

can be considered as a meaningful aid to management decision making. The prospects, however, are distinctly favorable.

BIBLIOGRAPHY

Dale, Alfred G., and Charles R. Klasson, *Business Gaming: A Survey of American Collegiate Schools of Business,* University of Texas Bureau of Business Research, Austin, 1964.

Fulmer, J. L., *Business Simulation Games,* South-Western Publishing Company, Cincinnati, 1963.

Greenlaw, Paul S., Lowell W. Herron, and Richard H. Rawdon, *Business Simulation in Industrial and University Education,* Prentice-Hall, Inc., Englewood Cliffs, N.J., 1962.

Kibbee, Joel M., Clifford J. Craft, and Burt Nanus, *Management Games: A New Technique for Executive Development,* Reinhold Publishing Corporation, New York, 1961.

Simulation and Gaming: A Symposium, AMA Management Report no. 55, American Management Association, New York, 1961.

Thorelli, H. B., and R. L. Graves, *International Operations Simulation,* The Macmillan Company, New York, 1964.

Vance, Stanley, *Management Decision Simulation,* McGraw-Hill Book Company, New York, 1960.

CHAPTER EIGHT

Motivating and Compensating Management Personnel

GEORGE PETITPAS *Cresap, McCormick and Paget, New York, New York*

This chapter reviews briefly developments in the theory of motivating managers, and then outlines various elements of the executive compensation program. It suggests certain specific areas requiring top management attention.

TRENDS IN MOTIVATIONAL THEORY AND PRACTICE

There are many theories regarding human motivation, and their popularity has fluctuated with the passage of time. There has been little conclusive evidence to support any of them.

Concern over the problem of motivating executives has developed with changing owner-manager relationships. Before the American Civil War, entrepreneurs usually managed their own businesses. These entrepreneurs were generally believed to be motivated by an inherent human desire to increase their personal wealth, presumably by guiding their enterprises toward larger profits. This theory of motivation, or belief in the "economic man," held great sway in the nineteenth century and still has a large, though less than universal, following.

Present acceptance of the "economic man" theory of motivation has been affected by two important circumstances.

1. Fewer managers are entrepreneurs. The larger capital requirements of bigger enterprises require broad-based capital markets. This requirement has diffused the ownership of companies among many stockholders, each of whom owns but a small part of the business. The companies are likely to be run by managerial employees (although these managers may also belong to the army of stockholders) and not by entrepreneurs in the classical sense of the term. Because the "economic man" theory is based largely on the performance of the managerial and entrepreneurial functions by one man, the embodiment of these functions in separate persons makes the theory less relevant.

2. The pursuit of wealth is no longer socially acceptable as the sole wellspring of human activity, not even of business activity. Society's disapproval of indi-

vidual wealth and economic power as man's proper goal is reflected in the graduated income tax and in such restrictive economic legislation as the antitrust laws and the Robinson-Patman Act. Thus, our society has sought to protect its young, old, unemployed, or underprivileged citizens from economic abuse at the hands of more powerful elements by limiting their powers. In the process, it has somewhat dulled the edge of financial incentives and, by allying itself against wealth per se, has rendered financial success less valuable in the eyes of society, as well as more difficult to attain.

The decline of potential wealth as an incentive, coupled with the proliferation of theories about human behavior and the sources of motivation, has led the social scientist (or behavioral scientist or psychologist) to replace the economist as the fountainhead of knowledge of human behavior in an industrial environment. Most of the research done by social scientists regarding work-oriented behavior has dealt primarily with nonexempt employees and not with management personnel. A great deal has been written, however, about the problem of executive motivation. Although there may be differences in detail or emphasis, all major contributions to the literature made since 1960 seem to agree that executives are most likely to attain maximum performance if they are personally *committed* to the objectives of the organization, are given the *opportunity to achieve*, and are *rewarded* on the basis of achievement attained.

Commitment. Commitment appears best attained when the executive knows and understands the goals of his organization and has participated in developing the objectives and standards for satisfactory performance of his own job. Recognition of the importance of securing commitment on the part of executives is reflected in the growth of "management by objectives" and "results-oriented performance appraisal" plans, which provide for agreement between a manager and his superiors on the manager's expected performance, with which his actual performance may later be compared. The comparison becomes the basis for appraisal.

Opportunity to Achieve. When an executive is given responsibility commensurate with his ability, and authority commensurate with his responsibility, opportunity to achieve exists. Opportunities to achieve are further enhanced by a generally supportive atmosphere of open communication and by encouragement of innovation and risk taking.

Rewards. Rewards mean, in part, compensation of one kind or another, which is the subject of the rest of this chapter.

The basic objectives of most executive compensation programs are to attract, retain, and motivate competent executives. To attain these objectives, the company's management compensation program should pay executives at levels comparable to those of the company's competitors and offer opportunities for rewards which are commensurate with performance. The individual elements of an executive compensation program are aimed at achieving these goals.

BASE SALARIES

Virtually all managers are paid base salaries which constitute the largest part of their total compensation. The base salary plan of an executive compensation program is normally the foundation of the entire program; in some companies, it is the entire program. It should, therefore, be designed and administered with great care.

A base salary plan typically includes an evaluation plan, a salary structure, and a set of procedures for administering the plan.

Evaluation Plan. In principle, the process of evaluating managerial positions is similar to that involved in evaluating nonmanagerial jobs. The basic purpose of an evaluation plan is to identify systematically the relative importance of management positions. This is normally accomplished by comparing positions with each other—either as a whole or on the basis of various elements (or evaluation factors) common to all of them. Some companies have found that one evaluation plan can be used to evaluate all of their management positions; others, particularly those with large numbers of scientific or technical employees, have found it necessary to develop more than one evaluation plan so that all positions can be evaluated on the basis of appropriate elements. Smaller companies frequently find that the management group is small enough to identify responsibility levels adequately by comparing the positions on an overall basis.

Evaluation factors, when used, typically number between three and five (fewer than for nonmanagerial jobs) and cover, as a minimum, position knowledge and skill requirements and the relative impact of the position on the overall results of the enterprise. Factors called "knowledge," "skills," "knowledge and skills," "education," or "experience" are examples of those included in position knowledge and skill requirements. Impact includes such factors as "profit responsibility," "accountability," and "profit impact." Some plans use additional factors to measure relative position complexity, supervisory responsibility, level of relationships, and even working conditions.

The type of plan used has less effect on the accuracy and usefulness of the evaluations than the accuracy and the completeness of the position information on which evaluations are based, the objectivity and thoroughness of the evaluators, and the attention devoted to maintaining the plan. The various types of evaluation plans and the relative merits of each type are discussed at length by Lanham (see the bibliography at the end of this chapter).

The evaluation process should result in a listing of positions in the order of their relative importance to the company. These positions are then typically grouped, so that positions involving about equal responsibility are placed together and separated from positions of clearly more or clearly less responsibility. These groups become one basis for developing a salary structure.

Salary Structure. The other basis for the salary structure is derived from salary levels paid to executives in similar positions in other companies. Information about competitive salary levels is normally obtained through compensation surveys. The best known of these surveys in the United States is the one published by the American Management Association's Executive Compensation Service. Many companies undertake their own surveys or utilize the services of consultants to make special surveys. The three most important characteristics of a good survey are the accuracy of the information obtained, a sampling large enough to ensure that survey results are representative of the market, and comparability of the content of the surveyed positions, regardless of position title.

The salary structure is usually developed on the basis of a trend line (sometimes called a line of best fit or line of least squares) relating evaluation points to surveyed salary levels for comparable positions, as illustrated in Figure 8-1. The midpoint of each grade can then be identified and the salary structure constructed by developing a salary range around each midpoint, as illustrated in Figure 8-2.

Another common approach, discussed in some detail by Patton (see the bibliography), consists in developing a trend line based on competitive total compensation levels and discounting that line to reflect average incentive payments. The discounted line then becomes the basis for the salary structure.

Most executive salary structures have range maximums that are about 40

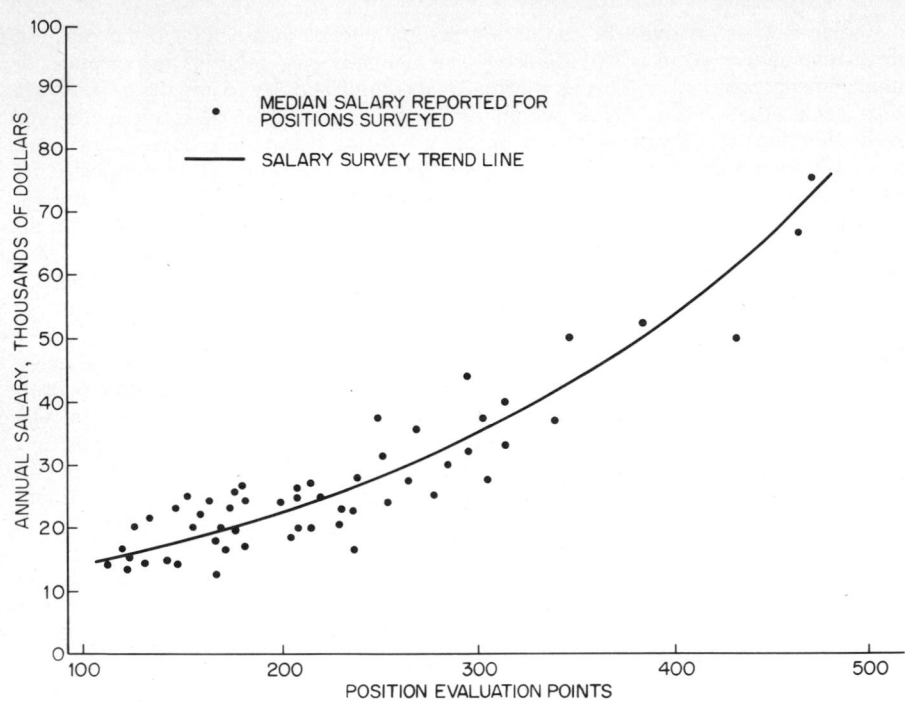

FIG. 8-1. *Industry salary survey data with salary survey trend line added.*

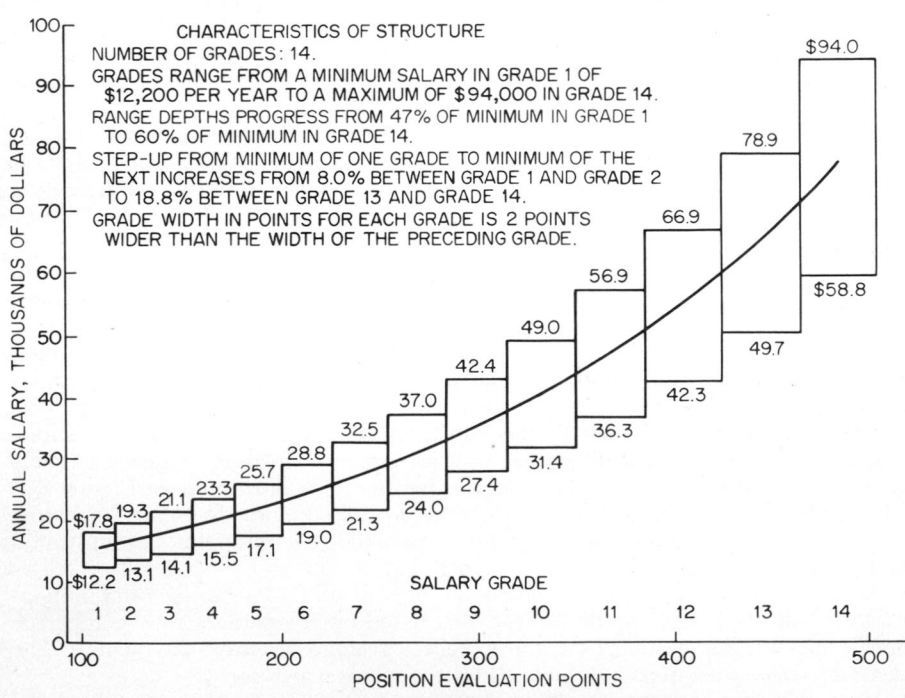

FIG. 8-2. *Typical management salary structure.*

Position in Salary Grade	Performance Level
Minimum to midpoint	Satisfactory performance. Incumbent's performance meets the essential requirements of the position.
Midpoint to three-quarter point	Superior performance. Incumbent fully meets position requirements and generally demonstrates performance above the satisfactory level.
Three-quarter point to maximum	Outstanding performance. Incumbent has consistently exceeded the satisfactory performance level over an extended period.

FIG. 8-3. *Guidelines for determining eligibility for merit increases.*

to 60 percent higher than range minimums, with spreads of between 10 and 20 percent from the midpoint of one salary grade to the midpoint of the next higher grade.

In the determination of the percent spread between the minimums and maximums of salary ranges, consideration should be given to the need for more merit increases within a salary range at the management level than is customary at the nonmanagement level. This is particularly important in those industries where cash compensation consists entirely of base salary or where growth is slow and hence opportunities for promotion are limited.

Administrative Procedures. The salary structure is a valuable guide in helping managers relate the pay of individual executives to that of other executives, both within the company (through the evaluation plan) and outside the company (through the application of survey data to the development of the structure). The heart of the base salary plan's ability to motivate managers, however, is in its administration. By relating pay to performance as suggested in Figure 8-3, and by providing for promotional increases and other changes as illustrated in Figure 8-4, a base salary plan can be used to encourage managers to improve their performance and to strive for advancement within the company.

Individual salaries should be reviewed periodically. A growing number of companies find that the best procedure is to have each manager review the salary of every subordinate once each year (particularly during the period of budget preparation) and schedule any appropriate increases at various times during the coming year. Although these plans can be changed if individual

HIRES

Category	Action
Applicants who satisfy minimum job requirements	Minimum of range
Applicants who exceed minimum job requirements	No more than one-fourth above range minimum
Applicants who do not meet minimum job requirements	Within 10 percent below range minimum

PROMOTIONS*

Present Salary Is:	Action
Lower than minimum of new grade	Receives new minimum
Substantially lower than (more than 15 percent below) minimum of new grade	Receives below minimum of new grade
At or above minimum of new grade	Receives above minimum of new grade

OTHER CHANGES IN STATUS

Change	Action
Transfers (lateral)	No change
Demotions	Salary within range based on qualifications for new position

* Promotional increases should not be less than 5 percent.

FIG. 8-4. *Policies for determining individual salaries for new hires or other changes in status.*

performance does not measure up to expectations or as changes in staffing occur, the preparation and approval of such plans greatly facilitate the planning, budgeting, and control of the administration of executive salaries.

Maintenance of the Plan. A base salary plan must be maintained properly if it is to operate effectively. Evaluations must be kept current. This is usually done by providing for changes in evaluations to be made as positions change and by having an overall review of all evaluations annually by a committee, or by staff executives, or both.

The structure must be kept competitive and equitable. This is normally accomplished by obtaining applicable survey data at least every two years and by adjusting the structure to compensate for changes in competitive compensation levels.

INCENTIVE COMPENSATION

Incentive compensation is defined as compensation over and above base salary, which can be awarded or withheld to encourage improved performance. Most incentive compensation plans can be described in summary by the following major characteristics: participation is limited to selected management positions; the total awards made in any year are related to company performance; the size of individual awards is related to individual performance; awards are normally paid out during a relatively short period following the period in which the award was earned; and the company has no legal obligation to make awards in a given year to any or to all management personnel. Thus, incentive compensation plans differ from profit-sharing plans in several important respects.

The lack of legal restrictions imposed on incentive compensation plans permits top management to use incentive compensation as a way of encouraging management personnel to improve their individual and company performance, to reward equitably the contribution of each participant in the plan, or to meet other objectives.

Although many companies have found incentive compensation plans to be an important means of improving managerial performance, this does not mean that an incentive plan is appropriate for every company. In fact, there are many companies in which an incentive plan is unlikely to be effective.

Any company considering adoption of an incentive plan should ask the following questions. Can the results of decisions be seen after a relatively short period of time? Do individual managers make decisions, and can they be held accountable for specific results? Are managers, including top management, willing to judge the performance of their subordinates? Does a generally competitive spirit exist in the company? The nearer to "yes" the answers to these questions are, the better will be the chances that an incentive plan will succeed.

Objectives of an Incentive Plan. Most incentive plans have as their primary objective the improvement of company performance through improved individual executive performance. Reward for contributions to corporate success is also a frequently stated objective.

The objectives of an incentive compensation plan should be established to meet the particular needs of the company. In addition, objectives should be as specific as possible to provide meaningful guidelines for all participants.

Eligibility for Participation. Most companies restrict participation in management incentive plans to a selected group of management employees who strongly influence the overall fortunes of the business. This group typically constitutes less than 3 percent of the total employee population, and may be as low as 0.1 to 1.0 percent. On the other hand, some large companies include as many as 10 to 15 percent of the employee group in their incentive compensation plans.

Decisions on the number of managers that should be eligible to participate should take into consideration the purposes of the plan, the company's compensation philosophy, practices of competitors, and the kind of business.

Common eligibility requirements include salary grade, salary, organization level, length of service, or a combination of these. The choice of appropriate criteria for eligibility should be based on how equitable the criteria are and how easily they can be administered.

Sources of Fund. Most incentive plans provide a fund to be drawn from overall company profits through the application of an incentive fund formula. In the typical formula, a stated percent of profits over a threshold is set aside for incentive compensation payments. Thus, a typical formula might state that 5 percent of net pretax earnings, after the deduction of an amount equal to 15 percent of net worth, could be paid in incentive awards. The fund formula normally determines the maximum amount that may be awarded; most plans give the board of directors (or a committee of the board) discretionary powers to pay out less than the maximum amount available in any year.

Formulas vary widely among companies and should be developed only after a careful analysis of the funds required to support the incentive plan, the company's financial and operating history and projections, practices within the industry, normal industry return on investment, and the specific objectives of the company's incentive plan. Of particular importance is the need to provide an adequate incentive fund in most years to allow the payment of awards large enough to be of significant incentive value. In addition, the fund formula should be developed in such a way that the size of the fund does not vary widely in response to relatively smaller variations in company performance.

Finally, some fund formulas provide for certain other stockholder safeguards, including a relationship between total incentive awards and dividends on common stock, and prohibitions on the carrying forward of unawarded portions of the fund for use in subsequent years.

Allocation of Fund. Funds are usually allocated among participants in the plan on the basis of division performance, individual position level, performance level, base salary, or a combination of these elements. *Division performance* is often used as a basis for allocation in large companies where each division is fairly autonomous and where, because of the large number of participants in the plan, coordination of incentive payments among divisions would become administratively onerous. However, unless considerable care is taken in the design of the plan, use of division performance can result in inequities among the participants in different divisions and can make transfers among divisions more difficult.

Position level is used as a basis for allocating incentive funds to reflect the fact that higher-level executives normally have a greater influence over company performance than is indicated by the relation of their salaries to those of lower-level managers. As a result, when this basis is used, higher-level executives normally receive incentive awards that are a larger percent of base salary than those received by lower-level executives, thus encouraging increased attention to company performance on the part of those executives most able to influence it.

The third and perhaps most important criterion for determining individual awards is *individual performance level*. This is also the most difficult from an administrative point of view, because individual executive performance is difficult to measure. Nevertheless, if an incentive plan is to provide motivation and reward, individual performance must be measured and considered in determining individual awards. Most companies that have incentive plans do, in fact, relate incentive payments to individual performance level, although there are considerable variations in the extent to which the measurement of performance or the application of performance level to incentive awards is formalized.

Significant differences should exist between the size of awards made for outstanding performance and those made for satisfactory performance, and no awards should be made to a participant whose performance fails to meet a minimum standard. Many companies make awards to outstanding performers in a range from one and one-half to four times the awards made to satisfactory performers at the same salary and same position level.

Minimum awards (other than no award) as a percent of base salary should generally not be less than 10 percent for lower-level executives and should increase as responsibility level increases.

Timing and Form of Award Payments. A majority of executive incentive compensation plans call for awards to be paid in cash as soon as practicable following determination of the amounts. Some plans, however, provide for spreading payments over a period of years following the award; two to five years is common. Other plans have provisions that enable executives to defer all or a part of their incentive awards until retirement. Such deferral privileges can result in substantial tax benefits, particularly for higher-paid executives who are approaching retirement age.

Although most companies provide for payment of awards in cash, some companies, particularly the larger and publicly held ones, make incentive awards partially or entirely in company stock to give recipients further incentive to improve company performance, thereby increasing the market price of the stock.

The timing and form of incentive award payments should be related to other company compensation plans. For example, a company having a deferred profit-sharing plan might decide to pay incentive compensation awards on a current basis. Similarly, payment of awards on a current basis in cash would be consistent with giving executives cash to exercise stock options.

Communications. If an incentive plan is actually to improve executive performance, effective communications are obviously necessary. Too often, however, a well-designed incentive plan bogs down because of a lack of communications and consequent misunderstanding and distrust on the part of managers.

As a minimum, eligible managers should be informed of the plan's objectives, its major formal provisions, and the way in which it is administered. Some companies also make it a practice to communicate information regarding the plan to managers *below* the eligible level to motivate these managers to advance to positions and salary levels that would permit participation.

Each participant should be informed of the amount of his individual award and the relation of this award to his performance. In most companies, awards are presented individually to managers by their immediate superior. Some companies also hold meetings, usually involving top management, in which incentive awards in general and company operating results for the past year are discussed, and in which participants are offered challenges to improve performance in the coming year.

STOCK OPTIONS

The objective of most stock option plans is to encourage executives to own stock in their company, thereby giving them a financial interest in the company's future success and in furthering that success.

Stock option plans may be either "qualified" or "unqualified." Under a qualified plan, an executive is granted an option to purchase shares of company stock at some future time, at a price equal to the market price as of the date that the option to purchase the shares was granted to him. Thus, an executive might be given an option today by the company to purchase stock at a price of $100 per share. When he actually purchases the stock (exercises the option), he will pay $100 per share even though the market price of the stock may then be higher than $100. When he sells the stock, any difference between his purchase price and the price at which he sells is taxed at capital gains rates. Options will normally be allowed to lapse if the per share market price does not rise above the price at the time of the grant.

If an executive is to realize these tax advantages, he first must have acquired the stock through a formal plan, certain provisions of which must have been approved by the company's stockholders. Second, the option must have been granted at no less than 100 percent of the market value on the date of the grant, and must be exercised within five years of the grant. Finally, the stock cannot be sold by the executive for three years following the date of purchase.

These restrictions have led some companies to adopt unqualified plans. The primary difference here is that, under an unqualified plan, the executive, upon selling his stock, must pay tax at ordinary income rates on any appreciation in market price over the option price.

Most companies typically include fewer executives in their stock option plans than in management incentive plans; the number of executives eligible to receive options is frequently less than 1 percent of the company's employee population. Practices of competitors, the type of company, and other elements in the management compensation program will influence the decision on how many executives to include.

The size of individual options granted varies widely among companies. Some evidence is emerging that options granted in amounts equal to between one and two times the recipient's annual cash compensation can afford substantial motivation and at the same time permit the executive not only to purchase but to retain his shares.

The design of a stock option plan is complex, as are the reporting requirements to stockholders and to the Securities and Exchange Commission. Furthermore, these requirements can vary from one state to the next. Any company seeking to develop a stock option plan should obtain qualified counsel before moving seriously into this area.

Other Elements of Compensation. Profit-sharing plans, fringe benefits (including accident, life, and health insurance and retirement plans), stock purchase plans, deferred compensation arrangements, and savings plans are among other elements used for executive compensation. Despite the fact that these elements have limited motivational value, they still constitute an important part of the total management compensation package.

MATTERS REQUIRING TOP MANAGEMENT ATTENTION

The various elements of an executive compensation program are normally developed by staff specialists or consultants, for such persons are usually best equipped to solve the technical problems involved. Certain matters, however, require top management attention even though the decisions made may be based upon recommendations developed by staff. Such matters generally involve overall executive compensation policy, the organization of the executive compensation function, and the extent to which the company's board of directors and stockholders should be involved in compensation matters.

Executive Compensation Policy. Top management must make a policy decision regarding whether the company wishes compensation in general to be below, at, or above the market. Not many companies deliberately elect to pay below the market, but some do tend to pay low, either to reflect unusually attractive working conditions or because of other special circumstances. On the other hand, some companies elect to pay above the market to help attract a higher-than-average caliber of executive. However, most companies have a policy (often unwritten) of paying at market for average performance and of providing opportunities for outstanding performers to earn considerably more than the average.

Another top management policy decision concerns the extent to which the company wishes to reward individual performance. If the company wishes to provide strong financial incentives to its managers, its specific salary and incentive compensation policies should reflect this desire by providing that substantially larger financial rewards be made to outstanding executives than to other executives.

Composition of the Executive Compensation Program. Top management should determine the elements that make up the company's management compensation package and the relative importance of each. These decisions should be based on the company's overall objectives and policies, its compensation philosophy, and the practices of competitors and of industry generally. The desire to provide strong financial motivation will lead a company to offer larger incentive opportunities, in relation to fixed compensation, through incentive compensation and stock options. Conversely, a company that desires to give its executives greater financial security and to limit managerial risk taking would pay relatively higher base salaries and would probably adopt a liberal attitude toward fringe benefits.

Competitive practices also influence the elements of the executive compensation program and their relative importance. For example, if the company's total compensation levels are competitive but its base salary levels are low, its compensation program may appear unattractive to outsiders. Thus the company may experience difficulty in attracting outstanding executives.

Organization of the Executive Compensation Function. Because of the need to coordinate the various elements of the executive compensation program, a growing number of companies are assigning responsibility for its administration to a single executive. This represents a departure from the approach, common during the years following World War II, of assigning responsibility to the personnel department for the base salary plan, to the treasurer's department for the incentive plan, and to the secretary's department for the stock plan, with the fringe benefit program administered by the controller's or treasurer's department. The need to consider executive compensation as a unified program and the concomitant need to coordinate the various elements in the program appear responsible for this trend.

The director or manager of executive compensation typically reports to the top personnel or industrial relations executive; or in very large companies, to an executive responsible for exempt or salaried employee relations.

Involvement of the Board of Directors and of Stockholders. Decisions on officer compensation are typically made by the board of directors, or by a committee of the board, upon recommendations made by the company's chief executive officer. The board, or board committee, also frequently makes incentive compensation and stock option decisions for positions below the officer level, where such positions are included in these plans. The board will also normally approve the adoption of, or changes in, an incentive compensation, profit-sharing, stock option, or other formal compensation plan.

Stockholder approval is required by law for qualified stock option plans but not for other executive compensation plans. However, many companies obtain stockholder approval of management incentive plans and of profit-sharing plans to preserve good stockholder relations.

SUMMARY

Executives seem to be most strongly motivated when they are committed to the goals of the organization, are given the opportunity to perform at their best, and are rewarded on the basis of their performance. The executive compensation program plays an important role in furnishing these rewards.

Typically, a sound program is composed of a number of elements. Although each has its special objectives, these elements, taken together, should constitute an integrated framework that can be used by top management to motivate executives to improve managerial performance.

The program can be developed and maintained by staff personnel, but it must be administered by line executives. Certain areas of administration require top management involvement, including executive compensation policy, composition of the executive compensation program, organization of the executive compensation function, and board and stockholder relations.

BIBLIOGRAPHY

Cresap, McCormick and Paget, *Management Incentive Plans,* New York, 1961.

Cresap, McCormick and Paget, *The Use and Effectiveness of Management Compensation Programs,* New York, 1963.

Ewing, David H., and Dan Fenn, *Incentives for Executives,* McGraw-Hill Book Company, New York, 1962.

Fox, Harland, *Top Executive Compensation,* National Industrial Conference Board, Studies in Personnel Policy, no. 193, New York, 1964.

Langsner, Adolph, and Herbert Zollitsch, "Compensating Executives," *Wage and Salary Administration,* South-Western Publishing Company, Cincinnati, 1961, pp. 654–683.

Lanham, Elizabeth, "Managerial Compensation," *Administration of Wages and Salaries,* Harper & Row, Publishers, Incorporated, New York, 1963, pp. 421–457.

McConkey, Dale D., *How to Manage by Results,* American Management Association, New York, 1965.

McGregor, Douglas, *The Human Side of Enterprise,* McGraw-Hill Book Company, New York, 1960.

Patton, Arch, *Men, Money and Motivation: Executive Compensation as an Instrument,* McGraw-Hill Book Company, New York, 1961.

Smyth, Richard C., *Financial Incentives for Management,* McGraw-Hill Book Company, New York, 1960.

Washington, G. T., and V. H. Rothschild, *Compensating the Corporate Executive,* The Ronald Press Company, New York, 1962.

Whyte, William F., *Money and Motivation,* Harper & Row, Publishers, Incorporated, New York, 1965.

CHAPTER NINE

Appraising Managerial Performance

MILTON L. ROCK *Managing Partner, Edward N. Hay & Associates, Philadelphia, Pennsylvania*

LEONARD M. LEWIS *Director of Communications, Edward N. Hay & Associates, Philadelphia, Pennsylvania*

Whether an organization accepts or denies the usefulness of performance appraisal, whether it adopts a formal appraisal system or not, top management is constantly appraising the performance of its subordinate managers. The latter are doing the same to their own subordinates. They are doing so because performance appraisal, formal or informal, lies at the heart of the art of managing. Good managers do it well; poor managers do it less satisfactorily; only bad managers do it not at all.

BACKGROUND OF MANAGERIAL PERFORMANCE APPRAISAL

Formal performance appraisal programs for managers have been introduced into many companies for a number of different reasons. These include the need to develop managers, identify promotable managers, motivate managers, improve managerial performance, and most frequently, determine annual salary increases ("merit rating").

Each of these reasons is directly related to some normal "managing" concern. The programs are intended to ensure that no manager can neglect his accountability for that concern, to raise the standards of performance to some uniformly high level throughout the organization, and to provide all subordinates with relatively equitable and just treatment. The weakness of many programs stems from their limited objectives—their emphasis on a single concern as if it were separate and distinct from the other elements of managing.

Managing is a dynamic process, concerned almost entirely with the present and the future, whereas performance appraisal, as generally used, has been a static rating of an employee related almost entirely with the past. But more recently, as some managements were recognizing that "rating" by itself had very limited utility, they began to appreciate that managing had evolved into an art. They saw that "management by hunch" could no longer be tolerated, and that measurements—no matter how vague—were essential to the further development of the art of managing.

The need for measurements gave birth to several "systems" of managing which attempted to apply measurements of various sorts to the different aspects and elements of the manager's job. A number of these systems leaned on the better performance appraisal methods for their measuring devices or at least for a starting point for measurement. In some instances, these systems expanded or broadened the meaning of performance appraisal from a mere rating to include the whole concept of management with all its elements.

For the purpose of this chapter, the different methods of performance appraisal are separated into two groups: the narrow interpretation (as a rating device only) and the broad interpretation (as an overall management concept).

THE NARROW INTERPRETATION OF PERFORMANCE APPRAISAL

In the narrow sense, performance appraisal is a post mortem by a supervisor of a subordinate's activities during a specified period of time—usually the past year. It is an attempt to assess the subordinate's performance in terms of selected criteria or according to some system of rating. The most common methods of performance appraisal which accept this narrow interpretation are as follows.

The Traits or Characteristics Rating Scale. The supervisor rates his subordinate according to such factors as the quality and quantity of his productivity; such abstractions as dependability, initiative, loyalty, and creativity; and various irrelevant factors such as punctuality and appearance. Using a scale ranging from high to low for each of the selected factors (which are sometimes weighted), the supervisor derives a numerical "measurement."

The Ranking Method. The supervisor merely ranks all of his people in a descending order according to his own estimate of their worth to his unit or department. Because, within any unit, certain jobs are more important and/or more difficult than others, the supervisor tends to rank jobs rather than the performance of individuals in those jobs. This tendency can only be overcome by setting criteria of performance for each job—something not usually done in the ranking method. In fact, ranking is inherently a most subjective procedure, because it lacks any real "rules of the game."

The Employee-comparison Method. This is merely a variation of the ranking method. The supervisor pairs each of his subordinates with every other of his subordinates, one at a time, and checks off which of the two is better in overall performance. The end result is a ranking of the entire group. If a supervisor has more than five subordinates to rate in this fashion, however, the task becomes monumental, and it is questionable if the end result will be sufficiently different from the straight ranking method to justify this extra effort.

The Forced-distribution Method. This method is based on the principle of the normal distribution curve. It requires the supervisor to rank each of his subordinates and then separate arbitrarily the group into three, four, or five percentage divisions. For example, those in the top 25 percent might be classified as very good performers, the middle 50 percent as satisfactory performers, and the bottom 25 percent as poor performers.

The Critical-incident Method. The supervisor rates his subordinates against a series or list of statements indicating critical incidents which have been judged to be of prime importance and essential to the carrying out of a manager's job. The selection of the statements is crucial to this mehod, which presumes that the substance of "managing" can be extracted into a relatively few sentences and that measurements can be made from them. This is a highly debatable presumption. Despite all that has been written about managing, no reputable writer has yet claimed that it has become a science. Consequently, any selected list of statements is subject to questioning and argument. Also, a single list of statements assumes that all management jobs are the same—which they are not. On the other hand, developing a list for each management job within the organization would undoubtedly require more time and effort than any company could justify.

Common Weaknesses. All of the above methods have common as well as individual weaknesses which make them inadequate as management tools for the rating of management performance. At best, they are all identical to, or slightly modified versions of, methods designed to rate clerical and low-level supervisory jobs. They fail to recognize that management jobs are considerably more complex and basically different from such jobs, not only in their accountabilities, but in the means of accomplishing those accountabilities. With the possible exception of the critical-incident method, each of them has little tie-in with what is expected from a manager in his particular job.

The very nature of these methods, which calls for one individual (the supervisor) to make judgments about other individuals (his subordinates) with respect to one another or with abstractions and generalities, virtually rules out the possibility that all such judgments can be made objectively. It is even more unlikely that all supervisors in an organization could administer any one of the methods in anything like a uniform manner or that any single supervisor would be consistent from one year to the next.

Subjective rather than objective judgments are fostered by these methods, because, lacking any meaningful standards, the supervisor can hardly avoid any of the unconscious biases, preferences, and special tolerances which are part of his own personality and psychological makeup. The "odd ball," no matter what his performance, will rarely get the same consideration from his supervisor as does the employee who is compatible with his supervisor in dress, habits, and personality. The most recent event—whether it is good or bad—is apt to influence a rating more than a man's year-long performance. Past records or future potential will be given attention in the appraisal even though they are irrelevant.

When judgments made under these conditions are given a "scientific" aura by assigning numerical "measurements" to them—measurements which sometimes are carried out to two decimal places—inestimable damage can be done to an individual's career and possibly, in the long run, to the organization. This is a considerable risk to run in view of the lack of significance that any such measurement reveals.

The problem of subjective judgments can be removed, to some extent, by the use of group appraisals where the subordinate is appraised by his superior and the latter's superior plus selected other managers who might have knowledge of the subordinate's work. By consensus, objectivity is enhanced, but the process can easily become both tiresome and cumbersome in its administration.

The ranking methods have additional special weaknesses. In a large organization, the men who are ranked as "poor" in a unit made up of men who are all exceptional might well rank very high in other units whose overall caliber is low; yet this fact can never be proved or brought to light. Also, the conscientious supervisor who is forced arbitrarily to rank one man above another when he can detect no noticeable difference in performance between them will probably work out some petty rationalization to justify his action; but he will suspect the whole procedure, particularly because he knows he may be a victim of the same circumstances when he is being appraised.

The weaknesses of the above methods are many, but perhaps the most striking is the uselessness of the actual face-to-face appraisal session between the supervisor and his subordinate when the results of the rating are discussed. Because the rating is based on subjective judgments, restricted only by vague and ill-defined guides, this session is inevitably an awkward and embarrassing meeting. It serves no purpose other than to conform with the generally accepted management principle that the results of an appraisal should be communicated to the subordinate.

The Performance-standard Method. Partially in response to the need, and partially as a result of the growing sophistication of other management techniques, a much more satisfactory and more meaningful method of evaluation than any of the above has evolved. It is based on preset performance standards against which the subordinate is appraised on a "go–no-go" basis.

In this method, the supervisor rates his subordinate according to whether or not he achieved specific standards which were set at the beginning of the appraisal period. The subordinate is fully aware of these standards—frequently he has been a party to setting them up—and he has accepted them as part of his "contract."

There are two requisites to this type of program which are indispensable for its success: corporate goals and objectives, both long and short range, must have been spelled out and communicated downward; and sophisticated job descriptions for every management position must be available. The job descriptions should be written and oriented around the end results for which each manager is accountable (answerable for both the action and the consequences of that action). These descriptions, instead of emphasizing *how* the job is done, stress *why* the job exists.

When these two requisites have been satisfied, the general procedure of this appraisal method can be reduced to the following three major steps.

Step 1. At the beginning of the appraisal period, the supervisor, either by himself or, preferably, with the subordinate, develops standards of performance for each accountability of the subordinate. A standard of performance may be defined as "a stipulated set of conditions that should exist when the desired end result is completed." Standards should be related to, and harmonious with, the achievement of some portion of the corporate goals.

For the most part, standards are short-range refinements of the accountability statements from the subordinate's job description, to which quantitative and sometimes qualitative measurements have been applied. They may also include elements of time and space.

Marketing positions—from the district sales manager up to the marketing vice president—might include standards based on desired gross sales volume, percentage increases to sales of selected product lines, increased share of market, or a reduced ratio of expenses to sales.

Manufacturing positions, depending on their level, would have standards based on increased productivity (by man, unit, or department), performance against standard costs, quality-control improvements, overtime reduction, accident reduction, and the like.

Financial positions, depending on their level, might have standards such as the cost versus the coverage of insurance programs; credit ratios relative to sales; the return on investment of temporary surplus funds; the timing, quality, and usefulness of regular and special reports; and so on.

Almost all management positions will include standards based on the selection, training, development, utilization, and organization of subordinates. They may also include standards for one-time objectives such as the introduction of a new sales-incentive program or new cost-accounting procedure, the selection of a new plant site or branch bank, or recommendations concerning the purchase of computer equipment.

These standards or statements can be written so that their achievement is considered "acceptable" performance and the failure to achieve them is considered "not acceptable." In almost every case, however, the evaluation of achievement can be further refined to provide for variations in performance below, above, and beyond mere "acceptability." Such a scale might be:

X—Unacceptable performance

C—Acceptable performance but below par

B—Par performance

A—Above par performance

Par performance must be clearly spelled out in terms of three criteria: (1) Is it realistic? (2) Is it measurable? and (3) Is it within the capacity of the subordinate to achieve it? Standards which are too easy to achieve will provide little motivation; those that are too difficult will be discouraging and therefore self-defeating.

It may be seen that this method begins to bridge the gap between the narrow interpretation and the broad interpretation of performance appraisal. Several of the basic elements of managing, including planning, review, and to a lesser degree, direction, begin to emerge as essential to carrying out the method. However, because the primary objective of this method is rating and not managing, it more nearly belongs with the narrow-interpretation group.

Step 2. At the conclusion of the appraisal period (usually one year, but sometimes sooner), the supervisor and subordinate meet together to review the latter's work in terms of the previously set standards. A common and worthwhile practice is for both of these men, separately and before the meeting, to rate the subordinate's performance against the standards. The meeting, then, is a conciliation of the two ratings. If the standards have been clearly stated in advance, there is little room for argument—either the subordinate met the standard or he did not meet it. In instances where the subordinate's performance was unacceptable or below par for a standard, the supervisor probes for the reasons and decides what corrective action is in order.

The supervisor then reviews all of the ratings, giving extra weight to the most important standards, and makes an overall rating using a scale similar to the one used for each standard.

Step 3. This step is a repeat of the first step. The subordinate and the supervisor establish new objectives and standards for the next period. There may be extensions or modifications of the old standards, or new standards based on changing corporate plans or the demonstrated capability of the subordinate.

Advantages and Disadvantages of Performance Standards. The advantages of this method over those described earlier are many. Although subjectivity of judgment can never be erased entirely from any appraisal method, it is reduced to a minimum by the use of standards. A subordinate is judged entirely on the results of his performance. His work habits, personality, and appearance are extraneous to the rating except as they may have affected a result. And because each of the standards has some definite meaning in terms of corporate objectives, each man is rewarded—or not rewarded—primarily in accordance with his contribution to their attainment.

The performance-standard method is an excellent communications device. The joint setting and review of the standards provides a common understanding by supervisor and subordinate alike of the latter's job, its major objectives and priorities, and what constitutes acceptable performance. The subordinate is provided with a way of answering the question which has always troubled subordinates, "How am I doing?" This appraisal method gives him the answer at the year-end appraisal session. In addition, because he knows the objectives and the measurements, he is able to appraise himself at any time during the year. This knowledge and the fact that he participated in setting the standards provide considerable stimulus and motivation for achievement.

Unquestionably, the most important advantage of this method over all others is that it naturally and logically fits in with the normal managing activities of planning (the setting of objectives upon which the standards are based) and review (the appraisal of performance according to those standards). It is a means of improving the supervisor's skills in both of these activities.

The performance-standard method satisfies most of the objectives of a merit-rating plan with the exception of identifying managerial potential. To the extent that performance in one's present job indicates managerial potential, this method is more adequate than any of the others mentioned thus far. But present performance is not the only guide—and sometimes it is the wrong one—for judging potential. An excellent field sales manager may make a poor marketing director; the opposite may also be true. An examination of the accountabilities of higher-level positions, and the determination of what combinations of experience, knowledge, skills, and personality are necessary to fulfill those accountabilities, can provide the factors for "measuring" a man for advancement and determining his development needs.

The weaknesses of this method stem primarily from its administration and execution rather than from the philosophy and principles on which it is founded. It is a more difficult and demanding method than any other. The setting of standards, in particular, is not an easy task, but the discipline it requires becomes a managing asset to every supervisor who acquires this ability.

Even when accepted and correctly practiced, this method has the weakness of a once-a-year project. Too many managers fail to appreciate that very small satisfaction is derived by a company that denies some employee his annual raise because his performance was "unacceptable." That unacceptable performance may have cost the company many times any possible salary increase, and it is too late at the time of the review date to do anything about it.

In addition, to a very great extent, reviewing performance only once a year may deprive a subordinate of the opportunity to succeed. Any subordinate has the right to expect guidance and direction from his superior, particularly when he is veering off course, while there is still time to achieve success. These are the primary dangers of viewing performance appraisal in its narrow interpretation, as a post mortem of actions completed. These are the reasons why such appraisals are more often resented than appreciated.

THE BROAD INTERPRETATION OF PERFORMANCE APPRAISAL

In recent years, programs have developed which interpret performance appraisal within a much broader context, but which use the performance-standard method as their base. They are variously titled ("accountability management," "management by objectives," "management by end results," or something similar) and they differ slightly in techniques and details, but they all utilize appraisal based on standards as their nerve center or at least as their information center.

More important, they all consider performance appraisal not as a backward look, but as a continuing and on-going process that links the past with the present and the future. They view performance appraisal as part and parcel of the entire managing process by extending their interpretation to include virtually all the basic elements of managing within it: organization, planning, delegation, control, review, motivation, development, and communications. The aim of these programs is to improve the whole managing process, as well as each individual manager, on a year-round rather than a year-end basis. Their success or failure hinges on how well and to what extent all of these elements are recognized and included in the formulation and administration of the plan.

The requisites of "accountability management" or "management by objectives" are the same as for the performance-standard method: clear-cut and well-enunciated corporate goals and results-oriented job descriptions. The accountability statements of the job descriptions coupled with a management audit provide the information for determining if the corporation is organized and staffed to make possible the achievement of its goals. They reveal the overlaps of accountability which must be eliminated as well as the voids which must be filled. They show the necessary relationships between jobs and between functions. And finally, they indicate where personnel gaps exist and whether they must be filled by recruitment or can be plugged by the development of present staff members.

When the organization is properly structured and staffed, the chief executive meets with his immediate subordinates to set the objectives—and the standards by which the accomplishment of the objectives will be measured—for each of those subordinates. These objectives are determined by the corporate goals and the accountabilities of each man. Their discussions will include a general determination of the means that will be used to accomplish the objectives; the backup in staff, material, and funds that will be required; the freedom to act that each subordinate will have; and the interrelationship among the different functions and men necessary to accomplish the individual objectives and the broader corporate goals.

Each of the subordinates then repeats this procedure with his own subordinates, breaking down the objectives into their component parts and assigning them according to the accountabilities and the competence of the individuals concerned. And so on, down to the lowest level of management.

The annual appraisal remains an important part of any of these programs. New objectives and standards are set and merit reviews for annual salary increases are made. The annual appraisal also serves as a general review of the subordinate's overall performance. But since the failure of any of his subordinates to meet an objective will affect the supervisor's ability to meet his own objectives, he cannot wait until the year's end to take corrective action. The supervisor learns that accountability means more than just being answerable for end results; it means that he is answerable for the actions that bring about the end results.

Thus, the supervisor must review his subordinates' work and progress toward the achievement of objectives regularly throughout the year and, when necessary, act. The subordinate must report to his supervisor any exceptional difficulties that might affect the achievement of an objective before they become insurmountable. Thus, on-the-job coaching becomes a vital part of the managing process as well as a management development technique.

This broader perspective of performance appraisal as a many-sided management tool can be expanded beyond the appraisal of managers to the appraisal of functions or units of the organization, to product lines, or to special cost programs of the manufacturing or accounting departments. As in the appraisal of managers, objectives and standards are established based on corporate goals and accountabilities against which performance of the function, unit, or product line is measured. The principle (emphasis on end results) is identical, the procedures are generally the same, and the results can be just as satisfactory.

Examples of Performance Standards. To illustrate more clearly what is meant by a performance standard, four standards for a hypothetical position, that of director of personnel administration, are shown below. The standards are appropriate ones, not only for those appraisal systems mentioned under "Broad Interpretation," but also for the performance-standard method included under "Narrow Interpretation." Performance standards, of course, are only one aspect of the broad-interpretation systems, whereas they are the prime feature of the performance-standard method.

To demonstrate the relationship between accountabilities and performance standards, the accountability statement from the job description from which the performance standard is derived is shown in each case.

1. Accountability statement: To establish the means of identifying the quantity and quality of the corporation's present human resources as well as its needs for both the present and the future; and to maintain the acquired information so that it is readily available, in a useful form, to top management.

   Specific performance standards for the year 1966:
   a. Complete a management audit of the corporation's headquarters staff by June 1966 and of the engineering and manufacturing divisions by October 1966.
   b. Train staff representatives from all other divisions and units of the corporation so that persons may begin management audits in their respective divisions and units. (These audits are to be completed by September 1967.)
   c. Code and process all collected data and information (see *a,* above) for the computer so that the management information retrieval system is operating by December 1966.

2. Accountability statement: To establish the procedures and programs for attracting, employing, and maintaining the numbers and kinds of personnel that will satisfy the corporation's present and future requirements.

   Specific performance standards for the year 1966:
   a. Increase the number of college graduates recruited in 1966, with no relaxation of standards, according to the following schedule:

      A.B. and B.S. degrees—up 15 percent from 1965
      M.A. and M.S. degrees—up 22 percent from 1965
      Ph.D. degrees—up 13 percent from 1965

   b. Prepare a report on the turnover rate of employees hired since 1961 under our college recruitment program. The report, which must be submitted to the vice president of personnel by May 30, 1966, should include an analysis of the causes of such turnover and recommendations for the improvement of the rate.

3. Accountability statement: To communicate to management and supervisory people throughout the corporation all pertinent and appropriate information concerning personnel (policies, programs, practices, and the like) that will assist them in achieving their department (or unit) objectives and in maintaining or improving employee morale.

Specific performance standards for the year 1966:

 a. Produce and distribute to all supervisory and management employees by September 1966 a booklet that explains the corporation's salary administration and job evaluation program in a concise and interesting manner.

 b. Produce and distribute to all supervisory personnel by April 1966 a booklet which will explain the new grievance procedures established in the new labor contracts, and which will emphasize the need and the means of cutting down the number of grievances filed.

 c. Conduct an employee attitude survey among all nonsupervisory employees throughout the corporation to be completed by August 1966. An analysis and report of the survey should be completed by October 1966.

4. Accountability statement: To install, administer, and supervise an effective and complete corporate benefit program.

 Specific performance standards for the year 1966:

 a. Prepare a report for presentation to top management in May 1966 which will offer one or more means of extending and enlarging our entire "fringe benefit" package so that it will be competitive in our industry.

 b. Ensure that all employees of the recently acquired ABC Company are included in the insurance and retirement programs offered by the corporation.

CONCLUSION

To a great degree, the essence of any program intended to evaluate performance, whether as a "rating" device or as a "managing" one, will be found in the freedom to act that is permitted an incumbent in a job. This freedom to act should be spelled out in the job description and must be understood and accepted by both the incumbent and his supervisor. In effect, this is the incumbent's "charter" to his job. How well he uses this charter is the measure of his performance.

BIBLIOGRAPHY

Drucker, Peter F., *The Practice of Management,* Harper & Row, Publishers, Incorporated, New York, 1954.

Enell, John W., and George H. Haas, *Setting Standards for Executive Performance,* AMA Research Study no. 42, American Management Association, New York, 1960.

Gluck, Harry R., "Appraising Managerial Performance," *Personnel Journal,* March, 1964.

Habbe, Stephen, "Personal Growth through Performance Appraisal," *Management Record* (NICB), July–August, 1962.

Harris, Chester R., and R. C. Heise, "Tasks, Not Traits—The Key to Better Performance Review," *Business Horizons,* Fall, 1964.

McConkey, Dale D., "Judging Managerial Performance," *Business Horizons,* Fall, 1964.

Meyer, Herbert H., Emanuel Kay, and John R. French, "Split Roles in Performance Appraisal," *Harvard Business Review,* January–February, 1965.

Richards, Kenneth E., "Performance Appraisal as a Supervisory Tool," *The Personnel Administrator,* vol. 10, no. 1, January–February, 1965, pp. 1, 2, 4–7, 12.

Rowland, Virgil K., *Management Performance Standards,* American Management Association, New York, 1960.

CHAPTER TEN

Management by Exception

LESTER R. BITTEL   *Editor-in-Chief,* Factory *Magazine, New York, New York*

Management by exception, in its simplest form, is a system of identification and communication that signals the manager when his attention is needed, and conversely, remains silent when his attention is not required. The primary purpose of such a system is to simplify the management process itself—to permit a manager to find the problems that need his action and avoid dealing with those that are better handled by his subordinates.

KEY ELEMENTS OF MANAGEMENT BY EXCEPTION

Management by exception has the following six key elements.

1. *Measurement* assigns values—often numerical—to past and present performances. Without measurement of some sort, it would be impossible to identify an exception.

2. *Projection* analyzes those measurements that are meaningful to business objectives and extends them into future expectations.

3. *Selection* pinpoints the criteria management will use to follow progress toward its objectives.

4. *Observation* is that phase of measurement that informs management of the current state of performance.

5. *Comparison* of actual performance with expected performance identifies the exceptions that require attention and reports the variances to management.

6. *Decision making* prescribes the action that must be taken to (1) bring performance back into control, or (2) adjust expectations to reflect changing conditions, or (3) exploit opportunity.

Advantages of Management by Exception. The practice of management by exception:

Saves personal time. You apply yourself to fewer problems—the ones that really count. Management by exception minimizes time-consuming work on trivia and details that others on your staff can handle.

Concentrates executive effort. Instead of spreading managerial talent thinly across all sorts of problems, you place your effort selectively only where and when it is needed.

Reduces distractions. The management-by-exception system flags attention to critical areas only. It remains silent on matters that are under control or that are delegated automatically to your subordinates.

Facilitates broader managerial coverage. Concentrated, more effective management effort enables you to increase the scope of your activities and your span of control. This frees you to tackle promising projects that otherwise might be left undone.

Lessens frequency of decision making. The system makes most of the minor decisions for you. You do not have to check every item under your supervision every day to see if it is okay. The system passes along to you only the few important problems for you to rule or act on. But these decisions are, of course, the more difficult ones.

Makes fuller use of knowledge of trends, history, and available business data. Management by exception, when applied systematically, forces you to review past history and to study related business data, because these are the foundations from which standards are derived and from which exceptions are noted.

More fully utilizes highly paid people on high-return work. Because delegation is planned, it more carefully relates and assigns the more complex problems to the more talented and highly paid people.

Identifies crises and critical problems. As much as anything, management by exception helps you to avoid uninformed, impulsive pushing of the panic button. Yet a crisis is almost always recognized, because seemingly unusual variations can be reliably and quickly compared with anticipated conditions.

Provides qualitative and quantitative yardsticks for judging situations and people. Management by exception takes much of the prejudice out of performance appraisals by making individual and organizational goals and measurements tangible and specific.

Enables inexperienced managers to handle new assignments with a minimum of related experience and training. A new man benefits from measurements and projections that have been established as standard for his function in the past. He can depend upon the system to alert him to problems rather than having to rely solely upon his own experience.

Alerts management to opportunities as well as difficulties. Managing by exception helps to counterbalance purely negative, control-minded management. Attention is directed to "breakthrough" variations as well as to omissions or shortcomings.

Encourages more comprehensive knowledge of all phases of business operations. You cannot practice management by exception systematically without continually gathering and updating real facts about your organization and its operation.

Stimulates communications between different segments of an organization. With its focus on results, management by exception seeks to relate causes, regardless of their place in the organization, with overall organizational results. As such, it encourages exchange of measurements between functions as well as between a function and the cost or profit center to which it reports.

Limitations.   Management by exception has pitfalls, of course.   Here are some:

It breeds "organization-man" thinking.

It is often dependent upon unreliable data.

It requires a comprehensive observing and reporting system.

It tends to proliferate paper work.

It often assumes an unnatural stability in business affairs.

In the absence of exceptions, it can give management a false sense of security.

It is silent about conditions predetermined not to be critical.

Standards of comparison tend to become obsolete (such as the ratio of indirect to direct labor).

Some critical business factors (such as human behavior) are difficult, if not impossible, to measure.

Finally, the process of management by exception cannot be a substitute for thinking—nor for decision making.   Its big advantage lies in the fact that much of the time-consuming process of thinking and decision making can be done *in advance.*   A progressive system of action can be prescribed beforehand, much as a troubleshooter's manual can give an instrument repairman step-by-step directions to isolate a fault.   As a result, only radical exceptions, either good or bad, need be interpreted and acted upon under pressure of time.

The executive's problem, therefore, is threefold.   First, he must convert his instinctive, unconscious approach to management by exception to a positive, systematic way of handling every kind of management problem—men, money, machines, and materials.   Second, he must guard against the conformity and false sense of security that systems of any kind tend to nourish.   Third, freed from the demands of routine work, he must fill his time with creative effort directed toward improving his plans, organization, staff, and decisions.

THE MEASUREMENT PHASE

The most successful executives build their management-by-exception decisions on the hard rock of accurately measured facts.   The scientific manager asks what is the *condition* of our financial resources; what is the *condition* of our materials and products; what is the *condition* of our equipment; what is the *condition* of our organization?   He asks these questions for good reason: management's task is to improve these conditions as time progresses.   Consequently, when we speak of measuring management's achievements in altering conditions of business today, we talk of measuring management's "performance"—its performance in changing conditions (1) with respect to time and (2) in accordance with predetermined objectives.   Management uses this concept to measure the performance of its whole range of inputs, such as:

People—hourly and clerical, skilled and unskilled, engineers and managers. We must know how well their efforts, physical and mental, contribute to the goals of the organization.

Money—its productivity, flow, liquidity, and conservation. Fundamentally, management wants to know how effectively its financial resources are being used to produce goods, services, and profits.

Materials—their condition, availability, convertibility, and waste.   The problem is to determine how economically materials are managed from their receipt, through processing and storage, to delivery.

Equipment—machine utilization, capability, and productivity. The specific objects of measurement, of course, are numbered in the thousands.

How to Measure. To list every means of measuring each of the four fundamental business inputs would be exhausting. However, some generalizations can be made.

Performance of individuals, for instance, can be measured with stopwatches or by predetermined estimates of the time it takes to make certain basic physical movements; it can be measured by psychological tests and by attitude surveys; it can be measured by the tangible results achieved—and by dozens of other techniques.

Management of capital can be measured by counting the money in the till at the end of the day or by making up a balance sheet at the year's end; it can be measured by tens of ratios, too (such as the ratio of current assets to current liabilities); it can be measured by its return of profit on investment —and in many other ways.

Materials management measurements range from simple inspections of finished products to complex comparisons of inventory accumulation to sales or current assets; consideration of the length of time materials are held in process or in storage, and so on.

Equipment performance is measured in terms of utilization or downtime; by its cost to operate and maintain; by simple counts of production; and by remote recording devices that detail a machine's every performance characteristic, such as temperature, vibration, and power consumption.

Kinds of Measurements. Generally speaking, measurements for industrial management purposes fall into the following three categories.

1. *Basic measurements* may be an element, a fragment of data, a point in space. Examples include the determination that a ⅛-inch bolt goes through a 0.126-inch gage and does not go through a 0.125-inch gage. Or that 75 percent of our research assistants have M.S. degrees. Or that it takes a workman 0.045 minute to solder a no. 12 wire to a terminal. Or that a sales call in Los Angeles costs $12.50. Generally, basic measurements show what has happened or what is happening at a certain point in time.

2. *Ratios* are comparisons of one or more elements of basic data with another one or more elements of basic data. For instance, a ratio of direct labor to indirect labor might be 2 to 1 or 200 percent. Or a ratio of net profits to net working capital might be 10.6 percent. Or a ratio of actual sales to bids issued might be 25 percent (or it could be expressed as a quotation mortality rate of 75 percent).

Measurement by ratio can also be more complex, such as comparing ratios with other ratios (for example, comparing the ratio of rejects to total output with the ratio of inspectors to assembly workers in order to seek a relationship between spoilage and quality control effort). Various other indexes, too, can be constructed empirically or statistically by combining ratios.

3. *Trends* measure the movement of basic data or ratios from one point in time to another. For instance, gross sales might be $2,000,000 in 1962 and $2,200,000 in 1963—a growth rate of 10 percent. Or indirect labor ten years ago might have been 30 percent of the manufacturing dollar; today it might be 40 percent—an increase of one-third in ten years. Or the trend of the ratio of sales to inventory (turnover rate) might move from 4.7 in August to 5.2 in December. Trends are always spoken of with reference to a time lapse.

Accuracy of Measurements. Most measurements available to and employed by management should be treated with caution. Some measurements that were accurate at the time they were made become obsolete—because of the introduction of new production methods, for instance. Other measurements, blithely taken at face value by management, are simply unreliable to begin with. Sometimes this inaccuracy may be due to statistical ignorance during sampling. More often, however, it is the result of either unintentional errors that creep into the observing process or deliberate falsification during observing, recording, or reporting. Still other measurements are accurate enough in themselves—that is, they do measure *something;* their unreliability emerges because of relationships to other factors which management assigned to them, although these relationships either no longer exist or never existed.

Unintentional Errors. These are often due to:

Simple mistakes in observation. A workman reads a counter and forgets to multiply the setting by a calibration factor.

Laziness. An accountant closes his books early every day and thus transfers late afternoon business to the following morning.

The "halo effect." An observer or reporter is impressed by only the high spots (or low points) in his data and throws out other readings as nonrepresentative.

Error during transcribing. Observations may be correct, but in the transfer and tabulation of data, errors creep in as figures pass from clerk to tab operator to clerk. For example, an accountant might accidentally add the March inventory figures twice into a year's total.

Misunderstanding of the system. A production control clerk reports as late only those deliveries one week overdue, when management is trying to identify *every* late shipment.

Deliberate Falsification. This takes place for a variety of reasons, for example:

To cover up for others. If the company president has insisted that salesmen increase their sales calls from five to six a day, the sales manager may report that the increase has taken place even though his salesmen may be reporting differently to him.

To imply progress. A plant superintendent holds back production from one week to the next in order to show an upward trend in output.

Measurements Out of Context. The fact is that measurements may be accurate in an absolute sense and still be misleading. Before judging the worth of measurements for use in managing by exception, an executive should consider a number of other factors that might influence their present and continuing representability. These factors include the following considerations: seasonal influences, equipment condition, extent of direct and supporting labor, operational methods in use, materials used, product specifications, nature of the organization and its staff, extent of competition, general economic conditions, growth rate of the company, state of employee morale, presence of a union or not, production rates, market conditions and growth rate, technological acceleration, product mix, company's financial position, company or plant size, and international harmony or discord, such as war, cold war, or peace.

Cost of Measurement. The cost of measuring and of measurements is a limiting factor in the practice of management by exception. Although ideally it would be desirable to have as many measurements to project from as possible, most organizations can afford only a relatively small number in each critical area of management. See Table 10-1.

TABLE 10-1.   Relative Costs of Measurements

Lower-cost Measurements	*Higher-cost Measurements*
Tangible Qualities: products made, machine performance, material usage, cash on hand, etc.	Intangible Qualities: attitudes, morale, loyalty, potential
Simple Tasks: assembly, clerical, unskilled, etc.	Complex Tasks: scientific work, troubleshooting, management, etc.
Routine Situations: mass production, volume sales, repetitive work, etc.	Variable Situations: small lots, special projects, engineered jobs, diversified products, etc.
Nearby Locations: centralized operations: concentrated areas, big plants, etc.	Remote Locations: field sales, branch plants, etc.

THE PROJECTION PHASE

In making projections and forecasts and converting them to goals, managers perform one of their most important functions. Planning targets, themselves, cover a wide spectrum. At the board level, objectives are likely to be abstract and involve projections of from one to five years or longer. At the operational level, plans are procedural and detailed, although these plans may extend up to five years also. Below that level, however, plans become predominantly short in duration and increasingly specific.

Goals at the Board Level. Initially, the president, his staff, and the board of directors may be called upon to set objectives that vary according to the state of development of the business. For instance, the first objectives might be any of these:

To set up a new company to produce an old or new product or service.

To expand an existing business by (1) securing a larger share of the existing market, (2) increasing the market, (3) adding products, (4) acquiring new companies, (5) improving quality or decreasing cost of present products or services, or (6) extending operations to new areas or to other countries.

To strengthen a slumping company by (1) rebuilding its organization, (2) defining new goals, (3) improving customer relations, or (4) creating better management-labor relations.

Goals at the Operational Level. Much of what happens in business that operational management must deal with occurs on a day-to-day basis. If nothing else, activities at the operational level are distractingly variable and dynamic. Long-range plans at that level may serve to keep management from becoming too expedient in its decisions, but that is about all they serve. On the other hand, short-term goals need to be specific. Figure 10-1 shows an example of well-planned objectives, very specific in content, for management at a rather high operational level.

Goals at the First Level of Management. The difference between goals at the first level of management and those at higher levels is in the degree of specificity. At the foreman level, especially, it is essential that goals be within reach and embrace only those targets over which the foreman has adequate control of ways and means for attaining them. See Figure 10-2 for an example.

Five-step Process for Making Projections. The plan-ahead process involves a series of steps, shown graphically by Figure 10-3.

First, we can take our measurements of past events and then, in relation to their time occurrence, project (extrapolate) them into the future.

Second, we must make a guess at what has not happened before, or recently,

Next year's goals for an operating division:

1. Strengthening of management staff by realignment of the organization to improve (*a*) communications, (*b*) controls, and (*c*) utilization of scarce skills
2. Raising of divisional profits to 17 percent before taxes
3. Extending markets to include the "Inner Seven" countries
4. Construction of new office building on leased land north of building no. 6; total cost not to exceed $675,000
5. Follow-through on a well-planned advertising and sales promotion program for product lines A and F
6. Negotiation of a labor contract with Local 137; settlements not to force price increases in our products
7. Completion of standard cost system to cover all products in our line
8. Consolidation of territorial sales personnel west of the Rockies into one work unit
9. Improvement of manufacturing methods and costs in small-lot area of our business, where 75 percent of orders now occur
10. Development of all personnel through existing training program; plant supervisors to attend forty hours of training in product quality control

FIG. 10-1.   *Example of operating goals.*

and try to forecast the chances of its happening in the future.   For our purposes in this chapter we shall draw a distinction between a projection and a forecast.

Third, we must figure out in what way these new happenings will change the projections we made in the first place.   These projections, modified by the forecasts, we can call "goals."

Fourth, we shift attention to our existing plans (which were set up sometime in the past to attain our previous goals) to determine whether they are now adequate.   Now we are aggressively looking for exceptions.   Whatever is in line, we let alone.   Whatever pops up as a weakness or a strength means we shall alter our plans.

Fifth, we are finally ready to do three things:

1. Alter existing policies and procedures to fit the projected goals.
2. Improve existing organization structure to serve the new goals and the new plans.
3. Check the adequacy of existing staff (and its assignments) for attaining the new goals and carrying on the new procedures within the new organizational structure.   Understaffed or weakly staffed positions will need to be taken care of; overstaffed positions and overqualified incumbents will need reassignment.

Area of measurement	Last year's record	Next year's goals
1. Ratio of jobs completed on schedule to total jobs worked	85% average, 92% highest, 65% lowest in June	90% average, minimum acceptable 75%
2. Percentage of job costs held within 3% of standard costs	91% average, 95% highest, 75% lowest in June	90% average, bring up low figure to 87% or better
3. Rejects and rework........	Less than 1% rejects. Rework averages 7%	Keep rejects to less than 1%, but cut rework to 3%
4. Labor stability...........	Two quits, one transfer	No quits of employees with over three years service
5. Absences, latenesses.......	5% absences, 7% latenesses	5% absences, 2% latenesses
6. Overtime................	Only on jobs OK'd by sales department	Only on jobs OK'd by sales department
7. Accidents................	No lost-time accidents. 37 calls to dispensary for minor ailments	No lost-time accidents. Reduce number of dispensary visits

FIG. 10-2.   *Example of objectives for first-line supervisor.*

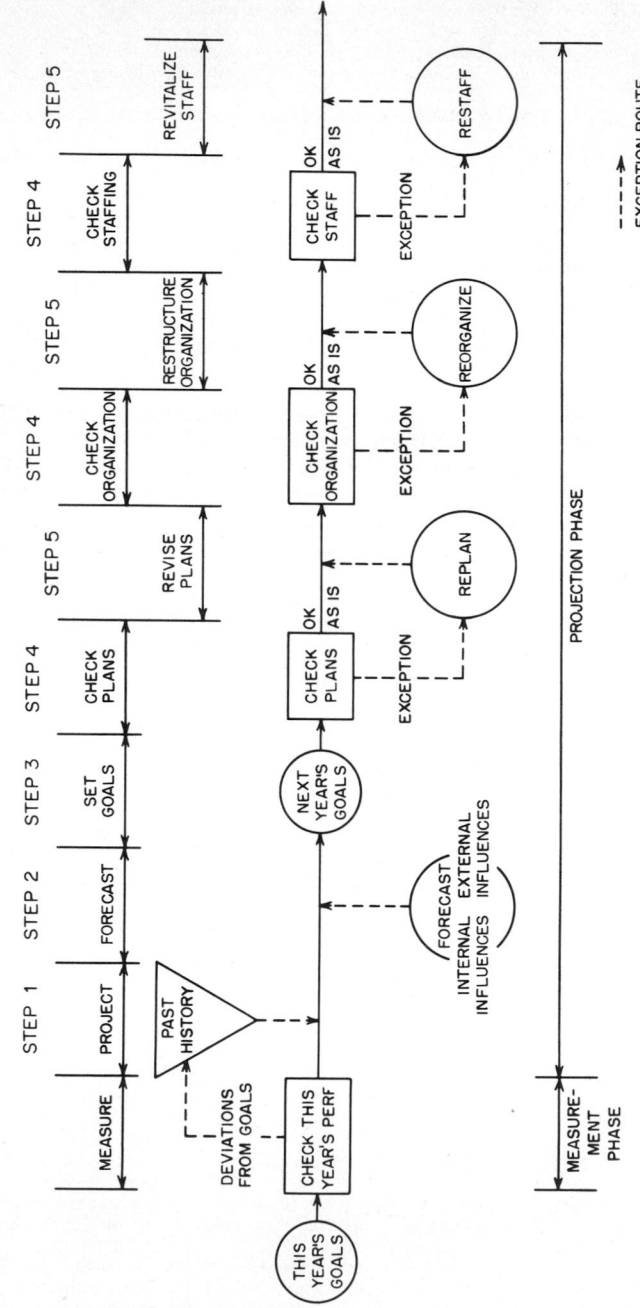

FIG. 10-3. *Diagram of five-step process for making projections.*

THE SELECTION PHASE

To minimize an empirical predetermination of our decisions, we must consciously try to cast our decisions way back in the planning stages of an activity. We do so by carefully selecting the criteria (or measurements) which will best enable us to control future actions.

Industry-wide Criteria. History has established many go–no-go gages for success or failure in any number of industries.

Functional Criteria. Similarly, specialists in almost every established field have come to agree on certain basic measurements as being reliable criteria for decision making regarding their particular specialties.

Personal Criteria. There are the hundreds of other "hunch" criteria which, while statistically difficult to verify, develop in an individual's mind through experience.

Regardless of whether the criteria have an industry, functional, or personal base, the fact is that in each area there are dozens of possible choices. It is because of the plethora of possible criteria that an executive must make his first critical decision if he is truly to practice management by exception. He must select those performance criteria, in advance, that (1) most directly relate to profit and loss in his business, (2) are available economically, (3) can be collected and assimilated promptly, (4) are acceptable to his associates and subordinates, and (5) are most easily understood and acted upon by the executive himself.

Setting Exception Indicators. For every projected goal (criteria of performance versus time), you must also establish limits of tolerance. A president predecides, for example, that he can—and will—tolerate for four weeks an inventory 5 percent over projected levels (specifically, in the spring, just before summer sales accelerate). An inventory-versus-time figure beyond this becomes an "exception indicator." When inventories exceed 5 percent for four consecutive weeks at that time, the president will automatically delegate corrective authority to his production control manager, for instance. If this corrective action is not effective within another predetermined time limit (or if inventories build, say, beyond 7 percent of expected) the president will again automatically place the problem in the hands of the executive vice president—who has also been given the necessary authority to correlate production cutbacks with intensified sales efforts. Finally, if the problem persists or intensifies—either in degree of variation from normal or in its time dimension—the president himself will step in. In other words, up to a certain preestablished tolerance threshold, no action is indicated. But from that level to the next preestablished tolerance level, the action responsibility will automatically fall into the hands of a preselected individual. In this manner, successive exception-indicator levels are chosen to match (1) the degree of tolerated variation from expected performance to (2) the capabilities of the executive from whom action will be expected.

Such preestablished exception indicators help a key executive to decide in advance of a crisis which problems may be delegated and which problems will require his personal attention. He can also decide beforehand to whom the problem will be delegated at each increasing step of difficulty. And, when a problem is anticipated to be of sufficient stature to warrant it, he can map out in advance various alternative plans of action.

So, in the selection-making phase of the practice of management by exception, there are four prime elements to be considered and planned for: (1) the degree of variation from projected performance, (2) the duration of the variation, (3) the level of authority and responsibility necessary to deal with the problem defined by observing the previous two, and (4) the predetermination of the course(s) of action to be taken, or reviewed, whenever an exception indicator lights up.

THE OBSERVATION PHASE

The mass of data that must be transformed to meaningful information is becoming increasingly unwieldy. Management must depend upon complex, ultrafast systems to collect, sift, and rationalize it. But on the other hand, management has long since come to the conclusion that the best system in the world must be supplemented by the keen perception and analytical mind of its key executives.

Automatic Observation.   The development of mechanical sensing devices (sensors) has broadened the scope of, and speeded up, the management-by-exception process.

More and more companies are using some sort of automatic reporting device to relay operating information from shop or plant to a data-gathering center.

An old standby for relaying information is the pneumatic tube. Other plants relay information by telephone, either directly to an operator or to a tape recorder. Some companies use two-way private-channel radio to transmit information from sales people, field repairmen, and truck operators. Others use closed-circuit television to monitor all kinds of operations, to serve as a substitute for watchmen, and to transmit data.

Managers as Observers.   When making use of electronic data processing, it is a temptation to rely too heavily on the infallibility of the system and to underrate the importance of the individual. When it comes to making observations in support of management by exception, each manager has the opportunity to be his own best friend. He can accept what the information-handling system delivers to him as being representative, or he can supplement the system by seeing for himself at first hand.

There are, for example, many ways to improve your observational powers:

Beware of the "halo bias."   This is the danger that arises from permitting your emotions to prevail over cold-headed logic. Literally, you see in a situation what you want to see.

Interview for facts.   Rare is the organization that can afford enough data on any single problem area. The best you can expect is that the information system will provide you with recognizable danger signals. As a result, digging up detailed facts will often be up to you.

Observe to fill in gaps.   Hard-to-measure qualities, such as the state of morale, rarely show up with any comprehensiveness on exception reports. Consequently, the executive who has set as an objective a favorable state of organizational morale will need to provide most of his own measurements. These are the measurements he will make with his own eyes and ears as he talks with all kinds of people—not just in his office or in the executive dining room, but also in the men's room, out on the production floor, and at recreational activities.

Try your own hand.   When an exception report shows that trouble is brewing, for example, in the production-scheduling department when too many orders are being shipped short, spend an hour or two actually working with the production expediter.

Sample routine paper work.   Too much objectivity can be a dangerous thing. That is, an overdependence upon reports prepared by your own staff would represent a naïveté on your part. Although a report occasionally will be constructed to mislead you deliberately, the real danger lies in abstract reports failing to give you the feel of the situation. From time to time it is good practice to look personally at original documents as they flow through your organization.

Make off-the-cuff inspections. Unless you frequently visit the work place of your subordinates, your office in mahogany row will be subtly cut off from the realities of the operations you are responsible for.

Sit in on group meetings at your own plant. If you have delegated a responsibility to a committee, you will not want to interfere with their prerogatives. But attending an occasional session will give you a chance to observe the trend of their thinking.

THE COMPARISON PHASE

The problem of identifying exceptions to performance standards is one of comparing actual performance with projected or predicted performance—and then determining which variations truly mean something.

The comparison stage of management by exception is the bridge between the measuring, planning, selection, and observing stages—and final decision making.

Fundamental Comparisons. Look briefly at the simpler part of comparison—detecting the variations. Most of the time, management deals with measures to which a numerical value has been assigned. In these cases, the comparison will be made either directly or in graphical form.

Direct numerical comparisons are of (1) one number and a standard number or (2) a table of numbers and a standard table of numbers. This is what accountants have done for centuries.

In graphical comparisons, the numbers are converted to proportionate lengths or shapes in order to make it easier for management to visualize variations and trends. The most common graphical measure is the bar chart. A trend chart, the most vital of management by exception's visual tools, is nothing more than a series of bars placed alongside each other chronologically upon a common footing. In making trend comparisons, one series of bars represents projected standards, the other series represents current performance.

Highlighting Variances. Deviations, when viewed either numerically or graphically, take a number of forms. When single numbers are compared, a particular variation is either above or below normal. This is illustrated by Figure 10-4.

When tables of numbers are compared, the sequence of variations (or the pattern they form) is as important as the fact that any of the variations are above or below standard.

When trends of numbers are compared graphically, current data may form a line or curve that (1) slopes parallel to the standard line or curve but is removed a distance above or below it, (2) converges with the standard curve at a slight or acute angle, (3) diverges from the standard curve at a slight or acute angle, (4) does any of these three—randomly or significantly—over a period of time.

Descriptive Comparisons. Many comparisons must take a narrative form or depend upon careful verbal qualification. Such standards are described with words, not numbers. Deviations must be expressed with adverbs and adjectives, not numbers.

VARIANCE REPORT*

		Department:	Sales Billing
Analysis of Performance		Month:	January

1. Earned standard hours.. 3151
2. Special assignments.. 28
3. Total hours of work earned.. 3179
4. Regular hours attended.. 3420
5. Overtime hours... 24
6. Total scheduled hours attended...................................... 3444
7. Scheduled hours (over) or under hours of work earned.................... (265)
8. Performance percentage.. 92 %
9. Unattended hours paid (vacation, holiday, illness, etc.)................. 40

Analysis of Dollar Cost Variance

A. Scheduled hours attended... 3444
B. Salaries paid for scheduled hours attended (exclusive of overtime premiums) $6888
C. Average hourly rate of pay.. $ 2.00
D. Salaries paid for scheduled hours attended (including overtime premiums)... $6912
E. Value of hours of work earned (C × 3)................................ $6358
F. Dollar cost (over) or under hours of work earned....................... ($ 554)

* Variations between actual performance figures (Items 6 and D) and standard performance figures (Items 3 and E) are reported in hours (Item 7) and dollars (Item F).

FIG. 10-4.   *Example of variance report for a single month.*

Visualizing Exceptions.   Three kinds of charts are commonly used for visualizing exceptions.   They are the Gantt chart, the break-even chart, and the action-demand chart.   All three demonstrate the principle of (1) showing the progress of work (or conditions) accomplished, (2) as compared with work (or conditions) scheduled (3) on the same chart, and (4) in relation to time.   Comparison and control depend in each instance upon planning done prior to current accomplishments.   And inherent in each are decisions made at the time plans are made—decisions about the significance to management of any variation from plans.

The Gantt Chart.   The Gantt chart is designed for management by exception because it brings to the attention of the executive the facts about his operation that are most urgent—and then holds his attention until he takes action and sees the results.   Although the Gantt chart resembles a bar chart in some ways, it differs from a bar chart or a trend-curve chart in that the latter two are used more frequently for historical analysis; the Gantt chart is used for relatively short-term planning and for controlling everyday operations.

In its simplest form, the Gantt chart consists of a sequence of horizontal boxes in which a notation appears of the amount of work to be done in the period of time indicated by the length of the space.   As work progresses, a light line is drawn from the left side toward the right of each box.   Its length, compared with the length of the box, represents the proportional amount of work actually done as compared with the total scheduled.   Thus for each time period the manager can tell at a glance whether the accomplishment is better or worse than predicted.   A heavier line is drawn continuously from the left-hand box toward the right, showing the cumulative amount of work done as compared with the cumulative scheduled work indicated by the total production-period space.

PERT, the critical path method, and other network or arrow diagraming techniques are, in the eyes of many, simply computer-oriented, 1960 versions of the Gantt chart.

The Break-even Chart.   This is a device that graphically shows management the relation between sales volume, costs, and profits.   For the average business, this relationship forms the single most important factor in planning profits. Chapter 5 in Section 10 discusses break-even charts in some detail.

Action-demand Chart. Devised by Gilbreth to relate performance variances from projected standards to the degree of action demanded from management, the action-demand chart is the single most valuable tool of management by exception.

A simplified version of the action-demand chart is shown in Figure 10-5. In this instance, the projected standard of performance for manufacturing costs, as measured by a percentage of sales income, is set at 60. But a vital ingredient has been added: *preplanned decisions on how far from standard present performance can stray before some sort of managerial action must be taken.* The decision in this example was that a variance of ¾ of 1 percent, either up or down, could be tolerated passively (action-demand zone no. 1). When the exception exceeds this tolerance (point A), action is needed. What kind of action—and by whom? That also is a preplanned decision. Typically, such action is initiated by the first level of supervision—for example, in the controller's office. And the action might be routine memo to the manufacturing department to cut out all overtime until the ratio returns to normal.

When the ratio measurement moves up another degree to point B in zone no. 3 (the emergency area), the responsibility shifts to a higher level of management. The controller himself would examine the situation and could take action without consultation, if he wished. Or together with the manufacturing vice president and the sales vice president, he could choose between a vigorous cost-reduction program or a step-up in sales activity.

If the action taken at point B brings performance back into line so sharply as to cause another exception in mid-April (point C), an exception in what appears to be a favorable direction (zone no. 2), it may be preplanned that the supervisor in the controller's office take action only if the tendency persists for more than a week. In this instance he would take no action.

When the ratio soars out of control into zone no. 4 (point D), the vitally disturbed area, planning would call for this condition to be brought to the immediate attention of the president, regardless of where he was or what he was doing. The president might call a meeting of his staff and line officers in order to assess the situation. The resulting decision could change any one of a number of operating practices, or it might result in a revision of performance objectives.

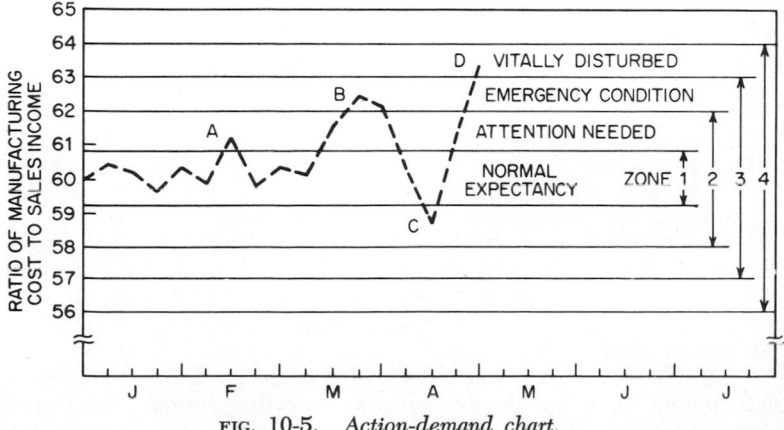

FIG. 10-5. *Action-demand chart.*

Note that as the variance becomes increasingly severe, the action demand passes into higher levels of management. And with each degree of variance, the extent to which action can be preplanned diminishes. In zone no. 1 (normal expectancy), only clerical attention—observing and plotting the measurements— is required. In zone no. 2 (management attention needed), the path of action is fairly routine and fixed. But in zone no. 3 (where conditions indicate an emergency), management action becomes more urgent. Often, complex and preplanned alternatives must be weighed before a decision can be made. Finally, in zone no. 4 (where the control is vitally disturbed), many functions of management become involved, and the decision is no longer confined to consideration of control action but also to modifications in the controls themselves.

Reporting Exceptions. Management by exception is based upon the principle that "no news is good news." Consequently, it is the exceptions rather than routine verifications of progress that need the ultrafast handling. Information on variances ought not to wait for a final polished report. They can be rushed to the action-demand executive in rough form by word of mouth, television, telegraph, or telephone. On the other hand, impulsiveness is to be guarded against. An exception must be seen in its context to be fully understood. So the information handlers need to work up supplementary data just as soon as it is feasible.

Form of the Report. There are three kinds of reports: tabular, visual, and narrative. A well-designed report should combine all three elements. Predominance of any one of the three elements should depend upon the information presented and the managers who will receive the reports.

Tabular reporting is most suitable when data are not profuse, when the report deals with relatively small sums of cash or with items of considerable value, and when detail is needed for analysis. Managers with a specific turn of mind, like foremen, often prefer tabular reports. Accountants and financial people also find it easier to work with figures.

Visual presentation, such as charting, is especially useful for condensing volumes of data, covering long periods of time, and providing the broad view. Charts speed up information transfer and are unusually good for presenting data to committees and larger groups.

Narrative presentation lends itself to the reporting of intangibles, to isolation of subtle deviations, or to pointing out variances that occur at lower levels, which are obscured in summary reports. Narrative, of course, is used to explain causes of exceptions, assess the severity of variances, and suggest corrective action.

Reporting Channels. As exception reports pass through the hands of successively higher-placed officials, they should contain more and more qualitative information. A variance report from a first-line supervisor to a department manager, for instance, should indicate what action has already been taken to alter current results. The department manager, in passing the report along to the general manager, ought to pin down the reason for the variance, make an estimate of how effective the corrective action will be, and indicate the need for changes in procedure requiring approval at the next upward level. As variance reports accumulate and flow upward through the channels of management to the various action levels, the reports should acquire more and more interpretation and advice that can be used at the higher levels in dealing with vitally disturbed conditions.

In the matter of exception reporting, each executive must use judgment in determining when to short-circuit the reporting format, the reporting period, or the reporting channel.

THE ACTION PHASE

Inexorably, there comes the time when planning, policy making, and procedure outlining can carry neither the individual nor the company further. A decision must be made. It is the moment of truth which each must face, in very small matters as well as in large. Probably it could best be described not as the moment but as the hour or day—sometimes month, or even year—of truth, for few business decisions must be made in a split second.

Analysis of Causes. When a deviation pops up, the basic question to ask is, "What caused it?" Is the deviation due to human error? Material deficiencies? Machine failure? Financial inadequacy? Market changes? Can the deviation be attributed to organizational weaknesses? Functional shortcomings? Are the measurements correct? Is the basic plan sound? Too much cannot be said about the need to localize the difficulty.

Variance Meetings. The best decisions will usually be made when based upon the diagnostic contributions of as many involved people as possible. Calling responsible managers together in a "variance meeting" to discuss causes and cures is a sound way for an executive to tap these resources.

Typically a well-run management-by-exception program holds four kinds of variance meetings:

1. Weekly meetings to review those short-term fluctuations that are deemed to be at critical variance from standard.

2. Monthly departmental meetings to analyze specific variations from monthly objectives.

3. Quarterly general meetings to discuss broad trends and to consider revision of either projections or action plans.

4. Emergency meetings when an urgent need for unusual high-level action is detected.

Outline of Options. In any exceptional condition, your final decision should be based upon a wide choice of action options. For example, you can:

1. Do nothing until you have checked for faults in your measurement-observation-reporting system.

2. Wait for a predetermined period of time to see if the condition is self-correcting.

3. Establish new performance standards.

4. Follow a series of preplanned corrective steps that are arranged in proportion to the degree of variations.

5. Seek expert, outside, and objective advice.

6. Move in an entirely new and unplanned direction—based upon a reassessment of the situation and followed by creative or intuitive thinking.

Exercising Control. Most of the texts, and the management language, emphasize decisions taken as the result of variances as "control" decisions. Actually, action options—in any kind of variance event—ought to embrace a spectrum which ranges from pure control of undesirable performance to outright exploitation of opportunity. Action at the control end of the spectrum is spoken of as "beating costs back into line." Variations at the sunny end of the spectrum can be viewed as "profit producing."

Where Drastic Action Is Needed. Occasionally, just exercising control is not enough to correct a deteriorating condition. Sometimes the executive has to decide whether to keep on fishing or to cut bait. Abandonment of a project into which time, money, effort, and enthusiasm have been poured is the most difficult kind of conclusion to reach.

Counterattack. Noted industrialist J. Paul Getty emphasizes the need to convert control action to positive gains. He observes that there "are those businessmen who are the real leaders. These are the imaginative, aggressive individuals who base their business philosophies on the ancient military axiom that attack—or at least, energetic counterattack—is invariably the best defense."

Balance. The best manager for management by exception is the one who is poised, ready to move in *either* direction.

Closing the Loop. After decisions are made, actions directed, controls exercised, and results obtained, management must see that its most recent experiences are considered in the development of each of the six phases of management by exception. This process is commonly referred to as "feedback." But feedback implies a clear-cut beginning and ending of a process. And up until this point in this text, we have been implying a simple, step-by-step process that might occur in a straight line. Unfortunately, like most of life's activities (and especially human ones), the management-by-exception path is more nearly circular.

What is needed now is a closed-loop concept in which (1) any of the six phases of management by exception might be either a beginning or an ending and (2) the relationship between any two of its links might be either cause or effect. Consequently, while many of management's activities are totaled up (like the profit and loss sheet) at the preestablished end of a period, there is value in thinking of the process as offering a chance to check results at *any* stage—and to feed these results back into the system.

Coordination of functions by management at each successive level is the true feedback that keeps an organization of people consistently on course. Oversystematizing this activity renders it inflexible and impairs its effectiveness. Ignore the need for continual coordination, and the organization will falter or fail.

It is at this coordinating stage—feedback adjustment and integration (closing the loop, if you will)—that characteristics of good management are tested. It is at this stage that management must reexamine its delegation practices and shuffle assignments upward and downward and laterally. It is here that managers and subordinates need coaching to see how they can better handle and prevent recurring situations. It is here that appraisals are made. Good results or good approaches (or both) are rewarded. Failures are counseled, remotivated, redirected, reassigned, or cut out of the organization altogether.

BIBLIOGRAPHY

Bittel, Lester R., *Management by Exception,* McGraw-Hill Book Company, New York, 1964.

Heyel, Carl, *Management for Modern Supervisors,* American Management Association, New York, 1962.

Payne, Bruce, *Planning for Corporate Growth,* McGraw-Hill Book Company, New York, 1957.

Rose, T. G., and Donald E. Farr, *Higher Management Control,* McGraw-Hill Book Company, New York, 1957.

Schleh, Edward C., *Management by Results,* McGraw-Hill Book Company, New York, 1961.

CHAPTER ELEVEN

Management Ethics*

PHILIP W. VAN VLACK *Vice President and Dean of Academy of Christian Thought and Service, Tarkio College, Tarkio, Missouri*

A business manager who is competent in the skills of ethical inquiry will be able to do the following five things:

1. Recognize the scope and nature of significant *moral problems* in business. This requires separating the significant from the insignificant moral issues, and knowing why certain issues are more significant.

2. Understand the strong and weak points of a number of widely held *moral standards.* The most important moral standards reported by American businessmen are the standards of obeying the law, preserving freedom, being responsible, being just, and being loving. The businessman should be able to adjust tensions, when they arise, between these moral standards.

3. Recognize, understand, and choose among various workaday *ethical viewpoints* available to business managers. Not only should business managers be able to do this; they should know *why* they are choosing those ethical viewpoints by which they guide their own business decisions.

4. Recognize various alternative ways to set a good moral example, to teach morals and ethics, and to enforce moral conduct.

5. Finally, understand the various methods of doing continued ethical reflection, day in and out, in the years ahead. Ethical inquiry must be a continuous process.

THE FIELD OF MANAGEMENT ETHICS

Management ethics is an applied field of study. *Ethics,* the parent discipline, is a systematic study of moral choices and of the moral standards by which right choices are made. *Management ethics* is a study of what is right and

* Parts of this chapter are adapted, with permission, from *Management Ethics Guide,* 2d ed., by Philip W. Van Vlack, published by the South Dakota State University Agr. Exp. Sta., Brookings, 1965. © South Dakota Agr. Exp. Sta. Also adapted from *Agri-Business Ethics,* by Philip W. Van Vlack, published by the South Dakota State University Agr. Exp. Sta., Brookings, 1965. Reprinted by permission.

This inventory, by no means complete, indicates some of the areas that various businessmen have indicated are of moral concern within the firm. You may or may not agree with these standards.

Check those items you believe apply to your business. Ignore those that do not, or revise the wording to make them applicable. With which of the standards would you personally disagree? Why?

In my business, these standards are:

Business standards	Held and almost always followed	Held but only sometimes followed	Held but almost never followed
1. Equal pay for equal work regardless of sex.........	( )	( )	( )
2. Equal pay for equal work regardless of race........	( )	( )	( )
3. Fair distribution of earnings among owners, managers, employees.....	( )	( )	( )
4. Stability of earnings for all who serve the firm......	( )	( )	( )
5. Job security for all who serve the firm.............	( )	( )	( )
6. *Freedom from* restraints on executives (unreasonable company policies, red tape, and so on)..........	( )	( )	( )
7. *Freedom to* try out new ideas and exercise initiative..	( )	( )	( )
8. Accurate and honest business records available to all authorized persons......................	( )	( )	( )
9. Accuracy in labeling and packaging................	( )	( )	( )
10. Truth in all advertising and sales contacts..........	( )	( )	( )
11. No "fringe" benefits given or received that are disguised as business expenses.....................	( )	( )	( )
12. No item of income unreported for purposes of avoiding income taxes............................	( )	( )	( )
13. Other:..	( )	( )	( )
14. Other:..	( )	( )	( )

Fig. 11-1. *Moral Problems Audit I: Inventory of moral problems within the firm.*

good in the moral decisions managers make. Ethics is the field of study, and morality is what is studied. *Morals* are the actual conduct, codes, customs, attitudes, and judgments of men.

What is moral may be opposed to what is either *immoral* or *nonmoral*. Actions are spoken of as immoral if they are wrong by reason of consequences or motives; as nonmoral if they have no moral significance.

Being able to analyze right and wrong, wanting to do right, and actually achieving good results are three different matters. Knowledge of principles of management ethics will not necessarily make a person want to do right.

This chapter does not attempt to prescribe detailed instructions on what to do to be moral in specific situations. There are two reasons for this: (1) Decision making is a complex process in which there are varying technical and social factors present. (2) Good managers do not "pass the buck" to someone else when a moral decision is at hand. Even when a manager directs a subordinate or asks a superior to take the responsibility of making some moral decision, he makes a moral decision that someone else will make the moral decision. The rest of this chapter, however, suggests five important processes for doing ethical inquiry.

IDENTIFYING MORAL PROBLEMS

A *moral problem* exists in business whenever there is a gap between moral standards and actual business practice. A moral problem is shown by the gap between the *ought* and the *is*.

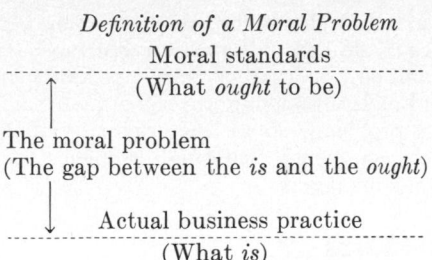

Definition of a Moral Problem

Moral standards

(What *ought* to be)

↑

The moral problem
(The gap between the *is* and the *ought*)

↓   Actual business practice

(What *is*)

Few thoughts or actions of a business executive are without moral significance. Some issues, however, are more significant than others.

To pinpoint significant moral problems, managers can use several kinds of moral problems audits, including some they might devise for themselves. Moral Problems Audits I and II (see Figures 11-1 and 11-2) contain several dozen moral standards in business. If the manager agrees with these standards, then a moral problem will exist if actual business practice deviates from the standards.

Note that moral problems in business are not always sensational problems. If someone has an unfair advantage, that is a moral problem. If a wage or a

Check the items you believe apply to your business. Ignore those that do not, or revise the wording to make them applicable. With which of the standards would you personally disagree? Why?

In my business, these standards are:

Business standards	Held and almost always followed	Held but only sometimes followed	Held but almost never followed
1. No price agreements in restraint of trade, except where authorized by law......................	( )	( )	( )
2. No price agreements in restraint of trade even if authorized by law...........................	( )	( )	( )
3. Free and open competition in all other ways........	( )	( )	( )
4. No secret kickbacks or payoffs to customers, suppliers, politicians, or others....................	( )	( )	( )
5. Compliance with just laws; and disobedience of unjust laws only if obeying them would mean disobedience of a higher law................................	( )	( )	( )
6. Refraining from acts which, though legal in themselves, might lead to controls by government of illegal acts by competitors......................	( )	( )	( )
7. Refraining from acts which, though legal in themselves, appear unfair in your own judgment or in the judgment of others........................	( )	( )	( )
8. Management of business duties such that time and energy are available to fulfill family responsibilities	( )	( )	( )
9. Management of duties so that time and energy are available to fulfill community responsibilities.....	( )	( )	( )
10. No business entertainment or inducement of customers designed to tempt a customer to be disloyal to his own company...........................	( )	( )	( )
11. Other:..	( )	( )	( )
12. Other:..	( )	( )	( )
13. Other:..	( )	( )	( )

FIG. 11-2. *Moral Problems Audit II: Inventory of moral problems outside the firm.*

price is not quite as fair as it should be, that is a moral problem. The sense of fair play and justice is strong in American life, and the sensational issues of call girls, price collusion, padded expense accounts, income tax cheating, and other types of fraud or law breaking are sometimes magnified out of proportion. There are moral problems about less dramatic things. It is a tribute to the American business conscience that small problems of fair play are treated seriously by many business managers.

APPRAISING MORAL STANDARDS

Identifying moral problems is merely the first step in moral and ethical analysis. Moral standards help decide what to do.

Moral standards are of three main types: (1) general moral principles, (2) moral policies (moral rules of thumb of a particular business), and (3) specific laws or regulations.

Moral Standards and the Law. Sometimes moral standards become *laws:* codified public law, unwritten common law, professional codes of conduct, company rules, or religious laws (such as the Ten Commandments). But not all moral standards are laws or rules imposed from without. Indeed, some businessmen who possess "high moral standards" are quite distrustful of relying primarily upon laws, or regulations, or rules of thumb, or even "moral principles." A crucial question in management ethics, as in religion, is whether some things are even more important than laws. An impossible-to-achieve ethical ideal, like that of sacrificial love, may be more significant than some moral rule which *can* be easily followed.

Social Responsibility as a Moral Standard. One commonly acknowledged moral standard in the business world is the standard of social responsibility. Managerial Responsibility Audits I, II, and III (see Figures 11-3, 11-4, and 11-5) help the business manager to pinpoint his own standards of *to whom* and *for what* he feels responsible.

Four statements are given below. Which statement best indicates the meaning of "responsibility" as applied to the businessman and his actions?

( ) 1. As a businessman, a man is sufficiently responsible if *he obeys the law and meets his obligations.*

( ) 2. As a businessman, a manager must not only obey the law and be honest in his transactions with other businessmen, *he must also adjust the claims of the many groups* (employees, stockholders, consumers, and the like) who have a sustained and serious interest in the existence and operation of the business firm.

( ) 3. In selecting a "responsible" man for the management of business, it is not enough to pick a man who strictly adheres to law and takes into account the competing demands of labor, stockholders, consumers, and the general public. For above all, "the responsible man" is a *man of prudence,* a man who by second nature acts in accord with his own principles of action, and who can be expected to deal effectively and judiciously with novel situations and unexpected difficulties. For this reason, the promotion of a man to a position of top management should turn on his "internal" habits of action as well as his popularity and uprightness in public life.

( ) 4. Only businessmen who rise to the exercise of "statesmanship" are truly responsible. Business freedom and responsibility are not opposed, for in the final analysis, it is the man who combines in himself both wisdom and power who is at once truly free and truly responsible. *Such men alone, who know what is good for the nurture of human nature, are fully qualified to be leaders of business institutions.*

FIG. 11-3. *Managerial Responsibility Audit I: The nature of social responsibility.**

* Dr. Charles D. England, formerly Assistant Professor of Philosophy and Economics at South Dakota State University and later at Wisconsin State University, Eau Claire, contributed the major ideas for this Managerial Responsibility Audit I. Prof. J. K. Hvistendahl contributed to this and to the other audits.

The practical day-to-day ethic of a businessman depends in a large part upon his loyalties and on his feelings of responsibility. Managers of businesses, like other people, have all sorts of responsibilities to all sorts of groups and persons. Some responsibilities conflict with other responsibilities.

This audit may give you some idea of how you distribute your responsibilities to various groups that depend upon you, and upon whom you depend. *Check the point on the line that seems to be about where your loyalties lie.* Rephrase or ignore items that seem to you inapplicable. Add others.

Great responsibility	Some responsibility	Little or no responsibility	Groups associated with your business to which responsibilities might be owed
			Owners (stockholders)
			Board members
			Company officers
			Employees
			Customers
			Suppliers, subcontractors
			Creditors
			Competitors
			Employee organizations
			Other:

FIG. 11.4. *Managerial Responsibility Audit II: How much responsibility do you owe to business groups?*

Other Moral Standards. Other moral standards frequently used by businessmen are those of obeying law, preserving freedom or liberty, being just, or being loving. Managerial Responsibility Audit IV (Figure 11-6) covers these.

Using these standards may be just so much sentimentalism unless businessmen precisely define what they mean by these standards.

A person in management is also expected to have various degrees of responsibility to social and political groups to which he belongs or with which he has relations. Responsibilities, of course, may change with circumstances. However, this audit may give you a general idea of the various degrees of responsibility you give to different political or social groups with which you have relations. *Check the point on the line that best indicates about where your responsibilities lie.*

Great responsibilities	Moderate responsibilities	Little or no responsibilities	Social or political groups to which responsibility is owed
			Businessman's family
			Social group
			Civic or service club
			Professional group
			Political party
			Race
			Government
			Mixed free enterprise (the "profit and loss system" which includes some economic activity by government)
			Other:
			Other:

FIG. 11-5. *Managerial Responsibility Audit III: How much responsibility to social and political groups?*

Compromise among Moral Standards. To some businessmen, any or all these moral standards, at the proper time or place, may seem reasonable. However, when certain moral standards are in tension with others, then choices must be made. Sometimes one cannot have both liberty (freedom *from*) and freedom *to*. Sometimes one kind of law is not in agreement with another kind of law. Sometimes laws are not fair or just; or one criterion of justice tells you to do something that another criterion would not tell you to do. Furthermore, some of the toughest questions a business manager may face ethically revolve around the dilemmas of being just versus being loving.

There are several solutions to the problem of conflicting moral standards. One solution is simply to decide that one standard always takes precedence over all others. For example, some businessmen conclude that any action which is legal, or even which is customary, is therefore moral. Another solution is to rank moral standards in some order of importance. One might distinguish between some standards which are easily followed rules of thumb and other standards which are frankly considered to be unattainable. The unattainable standard would serve as an ideal, and all lesser standards could be weighed in the light of the unattainable ideal. *Compromise* might be another solution. For some businessmen, compromise seems to suggest the abandonment of moral-

---

Following are four types of moral standards commonly acknowledged in the Judeo-Christian traditions. Check those moral standards which seem most significant to you.

Laws or customs as moral standards
( )   Codified public law
( )   Unwritten common law
( )   Professional codes of conduct
( )   Company or industry rules
( )   Religious laws (such as the Ten Commandments, the Great Commandment, the Golden Rule, or rules of abstinence)
( )   Business or community customs

Liberty or freedom as moral standards
( )   Liberty (freedom *from*)—means freedom from restraint, from restriction, from confinement, from interference
( )   Freedom *to* (opportunity for)—means freedom to decide, freedom to choose between several alternatives, freedom to act (freedom *to* depends upon freedom *from*, but sometimes certain liberties must be curbed so that other people may have freedom)

Justice as a moral standard
( )   Exchange justice—a standard which says to treat all parties to a business transaction *as if* they are equal
( )   Distributive justice—a standard which says to give to each according to his contribution to the community
( )   Redemptive justice—a standard which says to give to each according to his real need, because each person is a child of God
( )   Legal justice—a standard which reminds a person of his obligation to the organized community (e.g., to the state or an industrial organization)
( )   Contributive justice—a standard which reminds a person of his obligation (not required by law) to the unorganized or the disorganized community (e.g., a geographic area unorganized to cope with pollution problems, or a disorganized area of racial tension)

Love as a moral standard
( )   *Eros* love—the standard of desiring or self-regarding love
( )   *Philia* love—the standard of mutual or give-and-take love (a love which "counts the costs")
( )   *Agape* love—the moral ideal of self-giving or forgiving love (a love which is "a grateful response to someone else's earlier love" and which asks nothing in return)

FIG. 11-6. *Managerial Responsibility Audit IV: Laws, freedom, justice and love as moral standards.**

* These moral standards are described in Philip W. Van Vlack, *Management Ethics Guide,* 2d ed., South Dakota Agr. Exp. Sta., Brookings, 1965.

ity; for others, however, it has meant seeking the best moral solution but with the awareness that all solutions are less than perfect.

When a businessman considers how to compromise, or if he evaluates his own moral standards, he must carry his analysis one step further. He must analyze his own and others' workaday *ethical perspectives*.

RECOGNIZING ETHICAL PERSPECTIVES

Many of the most common ethical perspectives are associated with the names of world-famous philosophers. The *Ethical Perspectives Audit* (Figure 11-7) gives a thumbnail summary of some common ethical perspectives.

We shall now identify key ethical perspectives by certain ethical questions which businessmen ask. The ethical questions a business manager most frequently asks as he makes moral decisions are keys to that manager's basic ethical viewpoints. You can understand the ethical views of others and yourself better if you follow three steps of analyzing ethical perspectives:

1. Your first step is to recognize the actual workaday ethical viewpoints held by your colleagues in management, board members, employees, competitors, and customers. This requires knowing the key ethical questions which these persons are most likely to use as they make their own moral decisions.

2. Next, think again about the workaday ethical perspectives which you, yourself, use. In your own day-to-day ethical decisions, you also tend to ask one

With which philosophers do you agree? You may want to keep the right column covered until after you have checked the list.

Agree	Not sure	Disagree	Statement	Philosopher
( )	( )	( )	Wise action is that which is directed toward the ideal situation.	Plato
( )	( )	( )	Right actions avoid undesirable extremes.	Aristotle
( )	( )	( )	Wise action increases pleasure and avoids pain.	Epicurus
( )	( )	( )	Right action conforms to the common sentiments of mankind.	Hume
( )	( )	( )	Right action conforms to a rule that you would be willing to make the universal law.	Kant
( )	( )	( )	Wise action leads to the greatest possible happiness of the greatest number.	Bentham
( )	( )	( )	Scientifically determined action serves the interest of the class that is opposing outworn institutions.	Marx
( )	( )	( )	Right action fits into the historical trend of the evolving nation.	Hegel
( )	( )	( )	Right action conforms to laws or principles revealed by God or by nature.	Thomas Aquinas
( )	( )	( )	Moral actions are grateful responses to God's love—even if we know that we do wrong.	Tillich
( )	( )	( )	Intelligent action reduces the conflicts which impede social advance.	Dewey

FIG. 11-7. *Ethical Perspectives Audit: Thumbnail ethics.* *

* Parts of this audit are adapted from a description of ethical theories by Wayne A. R. Leys in *Bridging the Gap between Ethical Theory and Practical Decisions*, Informal Seminar in Operations Research, 1953–1954, Seminar Paper no. 4 (mimeographed), The Johns Hopkins University, Operations Research Office, Baltimore, Oct. 27, 1953. See also his *Ethics for Policy Decisions*, Prentice-Hall, Inc., Englewood Cliffs, N.J., 1952.

or more key ethical questions. These questions which you ask, consciously or unconsciously, reveal some of your basic views of life. You will need to recognize the basic ethical questions which *you* ask, if you are to know yourself and if you are to understand others.

3. Your next step might be to ask yourself (*a*) how consistent you are, (*b*) whether or not your day-to-day ethical viewpoints are in harmony with your fundamental convictions, and (*c*) whether or not some changes in your ethical perspectives would be wise.

Pleasure or Happiness as Guides. Consider the following questions which two business managers ask as they approach moral decisions in their businesses.

Manager A asks: *What are the alternatives before me, and what pleasures and happiness will I receive if I choose one or the other course of action?*

Manager B asks: *What alternative produces the greatest GOOD for the greatest number?*

The first viewpoint, called *egoistic hedonism,* is concerned with the pleasure or happiness of one person. The viewpoint assumes that because we *do* seek pleasure, it is therefore necessarily the best moral ideal. The second viewpoint, called *ideal utilitarianism,* is concerned with other kinds of good things besides pleasure, and the concern is for more than one person. Businessmen who hold either of these perspectives face difficult problems of measuring the things which they consider good.

Authority as a Guide. Consider the following questions:

Manager C: *What will people think? What is the custom?*

Manager D: *What does the law say?*

Manager E: *What do the authorities say is right?*

These managers all turn to authority as a guide in ethics. The authority may be God, the state, religious leaders, the public, or others. Basically there are two types of authority: heteronomy and autonomy. Heteronomy implies rule from without, by principles or forces imposed by persons or conditions beyond personal choice. Autonomy implies self-rule, subject to principles of individual choice. If the right to determine moral truths is claimed by someone else, but is not agreed to by those over whom it is asserted, then it is power rather than authority.

All ethical viewpoints are based upon some principle of authority. But just *what* authority, and whether it is imposed from without or self-imposed, makes a great deal of difference in judging how valid the viewpoint is.

Ideals as Guides. Manager F asks: *What is the ideal situation? If it is impossible to attain the ideal, toward what general ideals should our intentions be directed?*

Manager G asks: *Would I be willing to have the purpose behind my action held by everybody? Am I treating my employees, customers, and others as "ends" rather than merely as "means" to some end I have?*

Manager F would be a modern follower of Plato. He tells us we ought to keep our eyes on where we are going. Manager G has views similar to those of Immanuel Kant, who thought that people should act consistently and that the real test of the rightness of an action should be whether or not it is done with a good will.

Trends as Guides. Some people say that the right thing to do is determined primarily by the trends of the time. Some modern "business Darwinists" ask: *What are the evolutionary trends of nature and of our modern industrial society so that we can conform with those trends?* This viewpoint assumes that business institutions are getting better from a moral standpoint. If one seriously doubts that there is moral progress, he will question the validity of this viewpoint.

Other Questions Which Reveal Ethical Viewpoints. The views of John Dewey have influenced many businessmen who will ask: *What is the moral problem here? What is the conflict that is causing the trouble, and how can we reduce the tensions in the situation?* This viewpoint assumes that social harmony is desirable and that scientific methods are adequate for solving moral problems.

Some people ask a question associated with Aristotle: *What are the undesirable extremes that we should avoid?* Their assumption is that an extreme action is not likely to be morally right.

Other businessmen doubt that moral statements do really have meaning, and ask: *When we say something is "right" or "wrong," are we describing a provable fact, or are we merely satisfying our emotional needs?*

What One Trusts as a Guide—One's God. *What is the will of that person (or idea) which I ultimately trust?* This is the basic question of any ethical perspective. Few persons would think it right to go against that which they ultimately trust—whether it be a person, a principle, an idea, or a god. In fact, one's "god" can be defined as that which one *ultimately* trusts. Some persons trust themselves, or "humanity." Others trust the state, or their professional group, or money, or free enterprise. Any one of these objects of trust, if a person ultimately relies upon it, can be called a god.

To Sum Up. We have described a large number of ethical viewpoints. Surely the business manager cannot hold all of these views, for some are directly opposed to each other. How, then, are they useful?

In the first place, managers who recognize these viewpoints can better understand other people. Second, some of these viewpoints are not necessarily inconsistent with others. Some of these ethical questions are useful for particular kinds of moral decisions; others are helpful for other situations.

Third, a business manager who is really serious about doing right, and who analyzes all of these viewpoints, will be forced to recognize that some ethical perspectives are clearly more satisfactory and tenable for judging the most crucial problems of right and wrong. The conscientious business manager may not come to such a decision quickly, for ethical inquiry is a lifetime job. Study will be needed. (See the bibliography at the end of this chapter.)

STRATEGIES IN MANAGEMENT ETHICS

Thus far we have considered: (1) the process of ethical analysis, (2) identifying moral problems, (3) appraising moral standards, and (4) recognizing ethical perspectives. We turn, now, to problems of strategy: enforcing moral conduct, setting moral examples, and teaching morals and ethics.

Moral Sanctions. *Sanctions* refer to the ways by which moral conduct is rewarded, or moral misconduct is punished. Rewards and punishments can be by laws, professional codes, customs, religious traditions, or a man's own conscience. The business community is expressing a growing interest in enforcing moral standards by professional codes of ethics.

Codes of Ethics. Codes deal with the following types of problems: (1) competition among members of a profession; (2) conflicts among members; (3) relations between practitioners and clients, consumers, sources of supplies, or users of services; (4) relations of practitioners with superiors or executives; (5) relations between general practitioners and specialists in a profession.

There are three general types of codes: (1) codes combining general principles or precepts and specific rules for practice; (2) codes largely containing particular rules of moral practice; and (3) codes containing only the more general principles, leaving all matters of application to the individual business manager's interpretation and conscience (or permitting a committee of the profession to advise on what to do in specific situations).

Codes of ethics have certain advantages. They formulate the mature experience of a profession. They attempt to balance the public interest and private interest. They may offer guidance to young persons entering the profession. Codes may encourage discussion and even cause members of the profession to revise existing codes. And, in certain instances, codes can provide the bases of disciplinary action against offenders or provide a way of reconciling offenders with the standards of the profession.

Codes of ethics, however, have definite limitations. Some codes are written and adopted only to be ignored. Some are vaguely idealistic, with no practical application. Some codes are adopted and then seldom discussed, thus indicating that they are not significant aspects of professional organization. Some deal with old situations and not with the new, thus ignoring the effects of rapid change. Thus they are used to resist changes that portions of the members of a profession may deem necessary. Finally, some codes are regarded as so authoritative that they prevent discussion by members who fear discipline for dissenters.

Business managers who wish to explore further into what has been written on professional codes for business will find the collection of industry codes by the Business Ethics Advisory Service of the American Management Association valuable.

Moral Education. The use of professional codes or sanctions is not the only way to influence moral conduct. Education is another way. Self-study can be a place to start.

A business manager who takes ethics seriously will study management ethics. If he has not studied it in school, he will devote himself to nighttime and weekend study while on the job. He will attend management workshops or seminars, and he will insist that moral and ethical issues be covered by those seminars.

In short, if he says he is as interested in business ethics as he is in other phases of management, he will act accordingly.

BIBLIOGRAPHY

Business or Management Ethics

Baumhart, Raymond, S.J., *An Exploratory Study of Businessmen's Views on Ethics in Business* (D.B.A. dissertation), Graduate School of Business Administration, Harvard University, Boston, June, 1963.

Bowen, Howard, *Social Responsibilities of the Businessman*, Harper & Row, Publishers, Incorporated, New York, 1953.

Eells, Richard, and Clarence Walton, *Conceptual Foundations of Business*, Richard D. Irwin, Inc., Homewood, Ill., 1962.

Garrett, Thomas M., S.J., *Ethics in Business*, Sheed and Ward Ltd., London, 1963.

Greenwood, William T. (ed.), *Issues in Business and Society: Readings and Cases*, Houghton Mifflin Company, Boston, 1964.

Hall, Cameron P. (ed.), *On-the-Job Ethics: A Pioneering Analysis for Men Engaged in Six Major Occupations*, National Council of Churches, New York, 1963.

Johnson, Harold L., *The Christian as a Businessman*, Association Press, New York, 1964.

Johnston, Herbert, *Business Ethics*, 2d ed., Pitman Publishing Corporation, New York, 1956.

The National Council of the Churches of Christ in the U.S.A., *Ethics and Economics of Society* (a series), Harper & Row, Publishers, Incorporated, New York, 1953–1965.

Spurrier, William A., *Ethics and Business,* Charles Scribner's Sons, New York, 1962.
Van Vlack, Philip W., *Management Ethics Guide,* 2d ed., South Dakota State University Agr. Exp. Sta., Brookings, 1965.

Ethical Theory

Ewing, A. C., *Ethics,* Crowell-Collier Publishing Co., New York, 1962.
Frankena, W. D., *Ethics,* Prentice-Hall, Inc., Englewood Cliffs, N.J., 1963.
Leys, W. A. R., *Ethics for Policy Decisions: The Art of Asking Deliberative Questions,* Prentice-Hall, Inc., Englewood Cliffs, N.J., 1952.
Mothershead, John L., Jr., *Ethics: Modern Conceptions of the Right,* Holt, Rinehart and Winston, Inc., New York, 1955.

Related Readings in Economics and Ethics

Van Vlack, Philip W., et al., *Economic Ethics Bibliography,* South Dakota State University Agr. Exp. Sta., Brookings, 1964.

RESEARCH AND DEVELOPMENT MANAGEMENT

CHAPTER ONE

Organizing the Research and Development Function

CONRAD BERENSON *Associate Professor of Marketing, Graduate Division, Bernard M. Baruch School of Business and Public Administration, The City College, New York, New York; and Executive Director, Research Foundation of The City University of New York*

Research and development has become a major factor in influencing the economic growth of the nation as well as the success of individual firms and industries. Successful performance of the R&D function means technological change, increased national growth and productivity, maintenance of one's competitive position, profits, and above all, vigorous survival in the long run.

The cost of intensive activity in R&D totaled $21.5 billion for 1965; about 60 percent of this expenditure was paid for by Federal funds, although most of it (four-fifths of the federally supported work) was performed in nongovernmental organizations. This huge expenditure, requiring hundreds of thousands of men, thousands of laboratories, thousands of firms to provide supporting services, the development of new marketing channels, and an ability properly to transfer the research results to the firm's operations, must all be *organized* if it is to be carried out with any degree of success.

This chapter is devoted to an exploration of the *organization* of the research and development function so that the huge expenditures of money, personnel, material, opportunity, and technology can bear fruit. As such, it deals with the scope of research activities, methods of structuring research organizations, techniques for evaluating organizational effectiveness, and many other subjects important to the proper organization of R&D.

THE SCOPE OF R&D ACTIVITY

Some insight into the scope and importance of research and development can be obtained by looking at statistics on employment, expenditures, and the like.

Employment. In 1931, 70,000 people were employed in the United States in R&D work, 40,000 of whom were scientists and engineers. In 1965, 30

TABLE 1-1.　Number of R&D Scientists and Engineers in Industrial Organizations

Year	Number Employed
1957	229,400
1958	243,800
1959	268,400
1960	292,000
1961	312,100
1962	312,000
1963	329,100
1964	348,700

SOURCE: Adapted from *Reviews of Data on Science Resources*, National Science Foundation, vol. 1, no. 1, Washington, D.C., December, 1964, p. 3.

percent of all scientists and engineers in industry were involved in the performance of R&D, while another 5 percent were engaged in the management and administration of this work.　Table 1-1 presents data on the number of scientists and engineers employed in R&D tasks from 1957 to 1964 by *industrial* organizations.　For estimating the *total* number of scientists and engineers doing R&D work, including the Federal government, other government units, universities, and so on, Table 1-2 is useful.

The average yearly increase in the number of scientists and engineers engaged in industrial R&D over the period reported in Table 1-1 was more than 6 percent, although year-to-year changes varied from a slight decrease to an increase of 10 percent.

Nearly every industry shared in this growth of its R&D organization.　In particular, aircraft and missiles, electrical and communication equipment, and professional and scientific instruments had marked increases.　Table 1-3 presents a breakdown, by industry, of the totals for two selected years, 1957 and 1964.

Research Organizations.　The number of research laboratories grew along with the number of personnel engaged in R&D work.　In 1920, there were only 308 industrial laboratories; by 1940, there were close to 3,500; and by 1960, about 5,400.　These data do not reflect the very large body of research that is performed outside a formally organized or recognized laboratory.　In fact, the number of *firms* that performed research and development in 1961 was estimated by the National Science Foundation to be 11,800; of these, 10,300 were manufacturing companies and 1,500 nonmanufacturing.　In addition to these organizations, more thousands of laboratories exist in government agencies, universities, nonprofit institutions, and so on.

R&D Personnel Distribution.　What proportion of the firm's total number of scientists and engineers is employed in the laboratory?　How many technicians

TABLE 1-2.　Percentage Distribution of R&D Scientists and Engineers by Sector, 1960

Sector	Total	Research	Development
Industry..................	69.5	40.6	82.8
Government*.............	12.9	11.2	13.8
Colleges and universities....	12.9	37.0	1.7
Other†..................	4.7	11.2	1.7
Total.................	100.0	100.0	100.0

* Federal, state, and local.
† Includes nonprofit organizations.
SOURCE: *Manpower for Research and Development, Study Number II, Report of the Select Committee on Government Research*, House of Representatives, 88th Cong., 2d Sess., Sept. 29, 1964, p. 22.

TABLE 1-3   Number of R&D Scientists and Engineers, by Industry, 1957 and 1964

Industry	January 1964	January 1957
Total...	348,700	229,400
Food and kindred products..........................	5,700	3,800
Textiles and apparel....................................	*	700
Lumber, wood products, and furniture................	*	800
Paper and allied products............................	2,900	1,500
Chemicals and allied products.......................	38,800	29,400
Industrial chemicals................................	23,600	18,000
Drugs and medicines..............................	7,200	4,700
Other chemicals...................................	*	6,700
Petroleum refining and extraction....................	9,000	6,900
Rubber products......................................	5,700	4,700
Stone, clay, and glass products.......................	4,600	*
Primary metals.......................................	5,700	5,100
Primary ferrous products............................	2,900	2,900
Nonferrous and other metal products................	2,800	2,200
Fabricated metal products............................	7,300	8,400
Machinery..	32,300	24,900
Electrical equipment and communication..............	75,700	42,900
Communication equipment and electronic components.	42,100	19,200
Other electrical equipment.........................	33,600	23,700
Motor vehicles and other transportation equipment......	22,400	13,600
Aircraft and missiles.................................	105,900	58,700
Professional and scientific instruments................	17,200	10,200
Scientific and mechanical measuring instruments......	10,200	5,800
Optical, surgical, photographic, and other instruments.	7,000	4,400
Other industries†......................................	*	17,800

* Not separately available but included in total.

† Include the other manufacturing and nonmanufacturing industries for all years and the stone, clay, and glass products industry for 1957.

SOURCE: Adapted from *Reviews of Data on Science Resources*, National Science Foundation, vol. 1, no. 1, Washington, D.C., December, 1964, p. 3.

do these laboratory professionals usually have to assist them? Data such as this can provide those responsible for the organization of the R&D function with some guidelines to the necessary development of the human resources of the firm.

The Bureau of Labor Statistics of the U.S. Department of Labor has compiled statistics which shed a good deal of light on the subject of distribution of the work force.   Tables 1-4 and 1-5 present some of this information.

It can be seen that five industries employed at least half of their technical personnel in R&D assignments, and that most industries utilized between 5 and 10 percent of their engineers and scientists in the administration or management of the R&D function.   Few industries employed more technicians than scientists and engineers; the ratio of technicians to scientists and engineers was three to five in manufacturing industries compared with four to five in nonmanufacturing industries.

The charts reflect industry averages.   For any one firm, the proportion of R&D personnel to the total professional technical work force, or the ratio of technicians to scientists, may be different. Factors such as company philosophy, the life cycle of the firm, reactions to competition, company size, and profitability all affect the precise disposition of the total work force. Nevertheless, the data can be extremely useful in indicating to those responsible for the R&D organization what the normal range is; further reflection upon the specific problems and objectives of the enterprise will give valuable aid to these executives in showing them what their firm's R&D organization may have to provide in the way of human resources.

Education and Experience of the R&D Personnel. R&D managers have to make a great many decisions about staffing whatever units they organize. Among the questions which arise are some associated with the education of the work force, e.g., "How many Ph.D.'s should there be in relation to the total number of scientists and engineers?" "Does management's plan call for more or less Ph.D.'s than the industry average?" "Is this type of staffing consistent with the firm's objectives?" Table 1-6 can provide R&D management with some

TABLE 1-4.   Scientists and Engineers in R&D Activities as Percent of Total Scientists and Engineers, January 1962

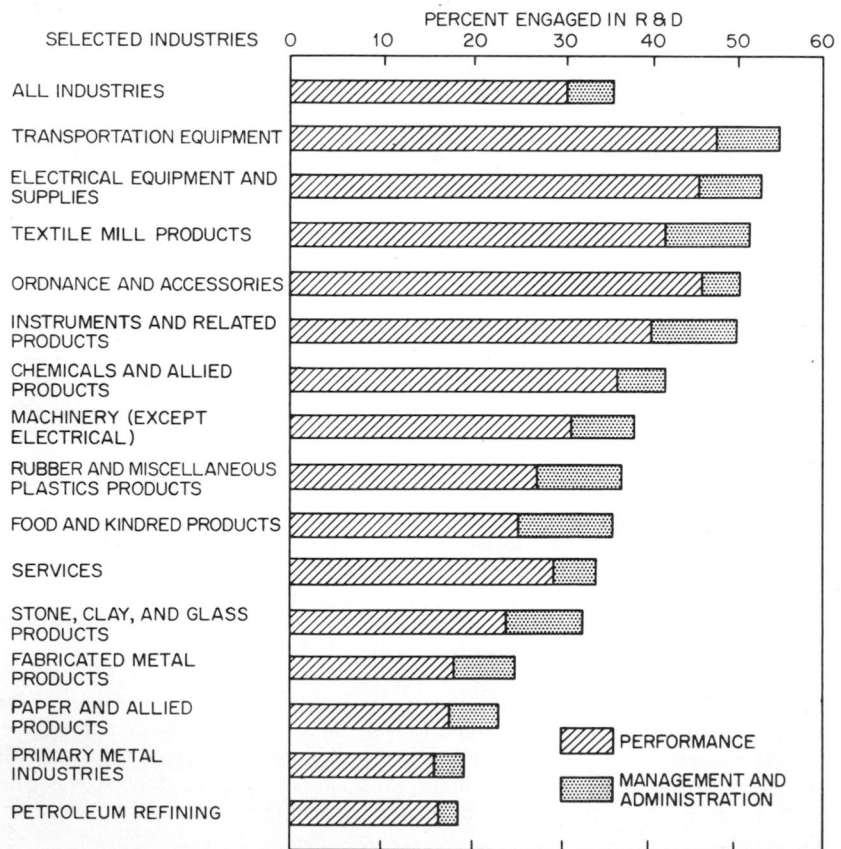

SOURCE: *Employment of Scientific and Technical Personnel in Industry, 1962*, U.S. Bureau of Labor Statistics, Bulletin 1418, June, 1964, p. 10.

TABLE 1-5. Average Number of Technicians per 100 Scientists and Engineers, January 1962

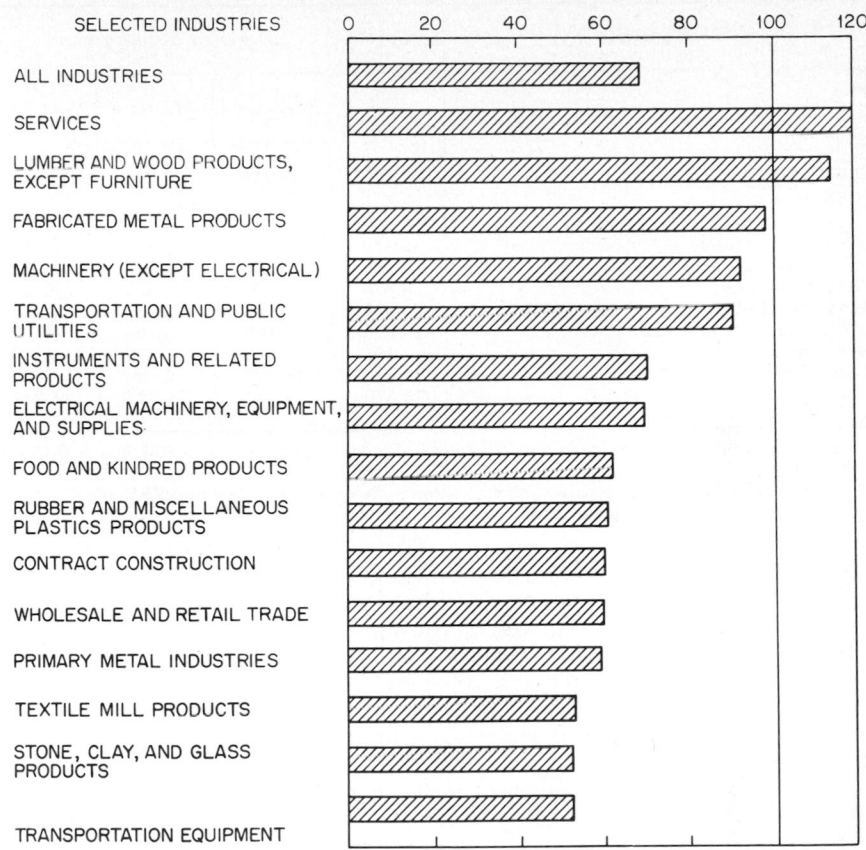

SELECTED INDUSTRIES	0	20	40	60	80	100	120
ALL INDUSTRIES							
SERVICES							
LUMBER AND WOOD PRODUCTS, EXCEPT FURNITURE							
FABRICATED METAL PRODUCTS							
MACHINERY (EXCEPT ELECTRICAL)							
TRANSPORTATION AND PUBLIC UTILITIES							
INSTRUMENTS AND RELATED PRODUCTS							
ELECTRICAL MACHINERY, EQUIPMENT, AND SUPPLIES							
FOOD AND KINDRED PRODUCTS							
RUBBER AND MISCELLANEOUS PLASTICS PRODUCTS							
CONTRACT CONSTRUCTION							
WHOLESALE AND RETAIL TRADE							
PRIMARY METAL INDUSTRIES							
TEXTILE MILL PRODUCTS							
STONE, CLAY, AND GLASS PRODUCTS							
TRANSPORTATION EQUIPMENT							

SOURCE: *Employment of Scientific and Technical Personnel in Industry, 1962*, U.S. Bureau of Labor Statistics, Bulletin 1418, June, 1964, p. 15.

insights into the distribution of degrees, by levels, in the performance and administration of research.

The experience of the work force is something that has to be considered along with education. To have an R&D staff which has an age-experience distribution that is extreme in one aspect or another can be quite risky and very expensive. With technological advances being introduced at an accelerated rate, it is necessary to feed new employees continuously into the R&D organization so that they can introduce the new technology. The unfortunate fact is that, for many reasons, older employees frequently do not utilize the latest technology in performing their R&D tasks. The younger employees have no background to rely upon except this recent technology—in the good schools, it is chiefly what they are taught. Older personnel are still extremely valuable, of course; they can provide a great deal of insight into the subtleties of their highly specialized fields. They can also provide the maturity of thought, the continuity, and the stability that are so necessary for a viable research unit.

Another important consideration in having a broad distribution of ages is that unless there is an occasional retirement due to age, or a promotion from

TABLE 1-6. Work Activity of Major Degree Groups Employed in Industry and Business, 1962

Work activity	Total	Major degree group		
		Bachelor's	Master's	Doctorate
All activities.............................	90,800*	45,718	22,244	18,972
Research, development, or design, total.....	32,419	13,731	8,834	9,854
Basic research.........................	6,728	1,501	1,253	3,974
Applied research.......................	16,383	6,308	4,895	5,180
Management or administration, total.......	26,301	12,700	6,361	7,240
Of research and development............	15,975	6,081	3,766	6,128
Teaching................................	191	69	82	40
Production and inspection.................	14,444	10,877	2,940	627
Other...................................	13,579	8,341	4,027	1,211

* Total includes 306 scientists with a professional medical degree, and 3,560 with less than a bachelor's degree or no report.

SOURCE: *Scientific Manpower Bulletin,* National Science Foundation, NSF 64-5, no. 20, Washington, D.C., March, 1964, p. 4.

the laboratory, there will be insufficient room in the R&D organization for providing rank and status incentives to deserving employees. The result of the lack of opportunity for advancement will be frustration, labor unrest, a marked decline in the effectiveness of the R&D function, and heavy turnover of key employees. Unfortunately, the best employees, those with the greatest drive and the most salable skills, will find it easiest to leave—and will do so. Eventually, only the poorest R&D professionals will remain in an organization in which the age and experience distributions are out of line.

A study of the age distribution of scientists and engineers conducted by the National Science Foundation is presented in Table 1-7. It can be seen that

TABLE 1-7. Age Profile of Scientists and Engineers, 1960

Age Group		Number of Persons in Each Age Group, in Thousands
Under 25	Scientists..........	30
	Engineers.........	45
25–29	Scientists..........	75
	Engineers.........	125
30–34	Scientists..........	90
	Engineers.........	160
35–39	Scientists..........	75
	Engineers.........	155
40–44	Scientists..........	55
	Engineers.........	120
45–49	Scientists..........	40
	Engineers.........	80
50–54	Scientists..........	30
	Engineers.........	60
55–59	Scientists..........	20
	Engineers.........	50
Over 59	Scientists..........	20
	Engineers.........	45
All scientists and engineers		1,275

SOURCE: *Profiles of Manpower in Science and Technology,* National Science Foundation, NSF 63-23, Washington, D.C., 1963, p. 26.

TABLE 1-8. Professional Experience of Scientists and Engineers

Years of Experience	Percent of Personnel
1 or less	3
2–4	15
5–9	20
10–14	21
15–19	10
20 or more	23
No report	8

SOURCE: *Scientific Manpower Bulletin*, National Science Foundation, NSF 64-5, no. 20, Washington, D.C., March, 1964, p. 1.

the population of scientists and engineers is made up largely of persons in the middle brackets of age.   More than one-half are over twenty-nine but under forty-five.

The professional experience of United States engineers and scientists is summarized in Table 1-8.   Although the data are for *all* such professionals, not just those employed in the research and development function, they are valuable for indicating to research executives the reservoir of experience that they can draw upon in staffing their R&D organizations.

Salaries.   Still another area which must be explored by the firm's management when organizing the research and development function is that of compensation.   So much salary data have been published by various governmental agencies professional associations, and consultants that it is unnecessary to do more than give an example of the type of information which is available.   Tables 1-9 and 1-10 illustrate such data.

Table 1-9 is self-explanatory.   In Table 1-10, salary data are given for just three types of jobs, but each job is divided further according to a system of job definitions established by the U.S. Department of Labor (Bureau of Labor Statistics).   Chemists I, for example, is for a trainee with a B.S. degree only; Chemists VIII is for a professional who has full responsibility over a very broad and highly complex and diversified chemical program, with several subordinates each directing large and important segments of the program.

TABLE 1-9. Salary Distribution of Scientists, by Field, 1964

Scientific and technical field	Lowest decile	Lowest quartile	Median	Highest quartile	Highest decile
All fields..............	$7,100	$8,600	$11,000	$14,000	$18,000
Chemistry.............	7,200	8,700	11,000	14,000	17,500
Earth sciences.........	7,100	8,500	10,300	13,000	17,000
Meteorology..........	7,800	9,000	10,600	12,900	15,500
Physics...............	7,400	9,000	12,000	15,000	18,700
Mathematics..........	7,000	8,600	11,000	14,700	18,500
Agricultural sciences....	6,200	7,500	9,200	11,400	14,000
Biological sciences......	6,500	8,300	10,700	14,500	19,000
Psychology...........	7,300	8,500	10,300	12,900	16,300
Statistics.............	8,000	9,500	12,000	14,900	17,200
Economics............	7,800	9,300	12,000	16,000	20,000
Sociology.............	7,300	8,500	10,100	13,000	16,000
Linguistics............	5,800	7,200	9,000	11,800	15,000
Other fields...........	7,000	8,600	11,100	15,000	18,500

SOURCE: *Reviews of Data on Science Resources*, National Science Foundation, vol. 1, no. 2, Washington, D.C., December, 1964, p. 2.

TABLE 1-10. Employment and Average Salaries for Selected Personnel in Private Industry, 1963

Occupation and class	Number of employees	Monthly salaries				Annual salaries				Percent increase in average salaries
		Mean	Median	Middle range		Mean	Median	Middle range		
				First quartile	Third quartile			First quartile	Third quartile	
Chemists I	1,348	532	537	492	582	6,384	6,444	5,904	6,984	4.3
Chemists II	3,722	599	590	546	646	7,188	7,080	6,552	7,752	4.0
Chemists III	6,512	691	680	621	754	8,292	8,160	7,452	9,048	4.2
Chemists IV	7,290	854	844	752	949	10,248	10,128	9,024	11,388	3.1
Chemists V	4,725	1,035	1,022	909	1,149	12,420	12,264	10,908	13,788	3.7
Chemists VI	2,544	1,176	1,159	1,034	1,303	14,112	13,908	12,408	15,636	4.8
Chemists VII	850	1,405	1,342	1,216	1,558	16,860	16,104	14,592	18,696	2.0
Chemists VIII	289	1,652	1,626	1,448	1,813	19,824	19,512	17,376	21,756	4.4
Engineers I	9,046	588	583	558	618	7,056	6,996	6,696	7,416	5.2
Engineers II	29,767	644	641	602	686	7,728	7,692	7,224	8,232	3.2
Engineers III	70,130	744	743	682	805	8,928	8,916	8,184	9,660	3.2
Engineers IV	80,867	894	885	806	974	10,728	10,620	9,672	11,688	4.7
Engineers V	47,034	1,045	1,033	924	1,152	12,540	12,396	11,088	13,824	5.6
Engineers VI	23,640	1,200	1,198	1,045	1,339	14,400	14,376	12,540	16,068	4.8
Engineers VII	7,368	1,438	1,426	1,278	1,572	17,256	17,112	15,336	18,864	3.9
Engineers VIII	1,758	1,666	1,640	1,461	1,841	19,992	19,680	17,532	22,092	2.1
Engineering technicians I	3,059	397	396	361	433	4,764	4,752	4,332	5,196	1.3
Engineering technicians II	9,272	465	464	426	506	5,580	5,568	5,112	6,072	2.2
Engineering technicians III	17,809	536	538	492	581	6,432	6,456	5,904	6,972	2.9
Engineering technicians IV	20,287	606	603	563	647	7,272	7,236	6,756	7,764	2.9
Engineering technicians V	8,763	688	679	635	737	8,256	8,148	7,620	8,844	4.1

SOURCE: Adapted from *National Survey of Professional, Administrative, Technical, and Clerical Pay*, U.S. Bureau of Labor Statistics, Bulletin 1387, October, 1963, p. 12.

TABLE 1-11. Funds for R&D Performance as Percent of Net Sales, in Manufacturing Companies Performing Research and Development, by Industry and Size of Company, 1961

Industry	Total	Companies with total employment of—		
		Less than 1,000	1,000 to 4,999	5,000 or more
Total..	4.4	2.0	2.2	5.2
Food and kindred products....................	0.3	*	0.3	0.4
Textiles and apparel..........................	0.6	*	0.5	0.5
Lumber, wood products, and furniture..........	0.5	1.8	0.6	0.3
Paper and allied products.....................	0.7	*	0.7	0.7
Chemicals and allied products.................	4.6	2.2	3.7	5.2
Industrial chemicals.......................	5.5	3.1	4.4	5.8
Drugs and medicines.......................	4.7	3.8	5.8	4.4
Other chemicals...........................	2.8	1.5	2.1	3.8
Petroleum refining and extraction..............	1.0	*	0.6	1.0
Rubber products.............................	2.2	0.8	0.9	2.6
Stone, clay, and glass products................	1.8	*	1.1	2.1
Primary metals..............................	0.8	*	0.9	0.8
Primary ferrous products...................	0.7	*	0.4	0.7
Nonferrous and other metal products.........	1.0	*	1.3	1.0
Fabricated metal products.....................	1.3	1.0	1.0	1.7
Machinery...................................	4.4	3.0	2.0	6.2
Electrical equipment and communication........	10.4	5.6	5.9	12.1
Communication equipment and electronic components.................................	12.4	10.1	10.7	12.9
Other electrical equipment..................	9.0	3.8	3.6	11.4
Motor vehicles and other transportation equipment......................................	2.9	*	1.3	3.5
Aircraft and missiles.........................	24.2	6.9	12.6	25.7
Professional and scientific instruments..........	7.3	4.8	4.3	9.6
Scientific and mechanical measuring instruments.....................................	9.2	7.4	2.8	13.8
Optical, surgical, photographic, and other instruments...............................	6.1	3.3	5.9	7.2
Other manufacturing industries................	1.4	*	1.6	1.9

* Not separately available but included in total.
SOURCE: *Research and Development in Industry, 1961*, National Science Foundation, NSF 64-9, Washington, D.C., 1964, p. 84.

Expenditures for R&D. How much should the laboratory budget be? Is the firm spending enough, too much, or too little?

Some insight into the subject of R&D budgets can be obtained by examining some recent data compiled by the National Science Foundation. These data are presented in Tables 1-11 and 1-12. Some caution must be used in applying the data to any one firm, because company size, corporate objectives, strategies, tactics, finances, and so on, all influence the optimum level of expenditure for a specific research and development organization. Nevertheless, the data do serve to provide management with a framework within which to analyze its budget.

The ratio of R&D funds to net sales, taken as a percentage, is undoubtedly the most widely used guide for R&D administrators in planning and budgeting expenditures. Table 1-11 data include research and development performed by manufacturing organizations for the Federal government, for themselves, and

TABLE 1-12. Median and Interquartile Range of R&D Performance Costs per R&D Scientist or Engineer, by Industry and Size of Company,* 1961

| Industry | Companies with total employment of— | | | | | |
| | 1,000 to 4,999 | | | 5,000 or more | | |
	Median	Lower quartile	Upper quartile	Median	Lower quartile	Upper quartile
Total.....................	$21,200	$14,200	$31,700	$26,100	$18,900	$37,300
Food and kindred products.......	15,800	10,700	27,600	19,800	16,300	29,900
Textiles and apparel.............	18,500	†	36,500	26,500	17,000	34,400
Lumber, wood products, and furniture......................	24,600	16,000	38,000	†	†	†
Paper and allied products........	19,700	12,600	27,200	23,600	19,000	33,400
Chemicals and allied products.....	20,800	16,400	29,200	30,200	25,900	34,800
Industrial chemicals...........	27,800	21,800	31,800	31,300	26,200	38,000
Drugs and medicines...........	22,600	19,200	26,700	27,400	25,200	33,400
Other chemicals...............	18,400	15,500	26,700	25,200	16,000	35,100
Petroleum refining and extraction..	19,200	17,100	23,500	30,600	28,200	36,800
Rubber products................	16,500	11,300	26,200	†	†	†
Stone, clay, and glass products....	24,800	13,400	30,200	23,300	20,600	29,200
Primary metals.................	21,200	16,900	39,800	29,000	24,400	41,200
Primary ferrous products.......	20,300	14,800	41,800	29,700	23,400	43,300
Nonferrous and other metal products..................	23,900	17,500	42,700	27,300	25,200	40,800
Fabricated metal products........	18,800	14,000	31,400	23,700	16,700	28,200
Machinery.....................	22,900	14,500	32,800	37,400	25,700	49,600
Electrical equipment and communication.................	21,000	17,100	33,600	25,300	19,300	35,700
Communication equipment and electronic components........	23,500	18,400	38,200	20,400	15,900	35,400
Other electrical equipment......	22,300	17,200	32,900	28,300	22,200	40,400
Motor vehicles and other transportation equipment..............	18,400	13,800	35,600	32,300	24,700	51,000
Aircraft and missiles.............	23,200	16,400	46,700	38,700	30,400	55,700
Professional and scientific instruments.....................	22,200	16,800	34,800	23,400	22,000	36,900
Scientific and mechanical measuring instruments...........	20,000	16,900	23,800	†	†	†
Optical, surgical, photographic, and other instruments.......	33,400	19,600	44,400	†	†	†
Other manufacturing industries...	19,700	14,100	29,500	23,800	16,200	36,200
Nonmanufacturing industries.....	18,500	10,300	26,600	16,800	12,500	28,400

* Data not available for companies with less than 1,000 employees.
† Not separately available but included in total.
SOURCE: *Research and Development in Industry, 1961*, National Science Foundation, NSF 64-9, Washington, D.C., 1964, p. 91.

for other firms—in short, *all* R&D performed, regardless of the sponsor or the object.   The data are presented only for those manufacturing organizations which perform R&D.   If the statistics of those firms without R&D programs were included, it would result in much lower ratios for various industries.   Net sales are defined as all sales and receipts for a company, excluding discounts, allowances, and intracompany transfers, and sales by foreign subsidiaries, but excluding transfers to these foreign subsidiaries.

During the four years preceding 1961, funds for R&D performance as a percent of net sales increased from 3.7 to 4.4 in 1960; the latter is the same as the figure for 1961. This apparent leveling off of R&D expenditure is not surprising, for R&D costs have already reached a point where the expense is causing many firms to examine seriously just what they are getting out of their R&D programs in an effort to conserve capital.

Table 1-12 provides data on R&D cost per scientist or engineer. Thus it provides a means by which one can compare the effectiveness of one's function with the average for its industry-size group. Because similar data are compiled annually, the comparison can also be made over a period of time, and thus a measure of response to organizational change is also available. In addition, these data can be used both to estimate the cost of projected R&D tasks and to determine the number of professionals that can be hired within a specific budget.

To a great extent, the salaries of the engineers and scientists are similar for men of equal education and experience, regardless of the industry in which they work. What accounts for most of the difference in cost per individual are the allocated shares of overhead expenses, testing equipment, supporting personnel, and whether the emphasis is on basic or applied research. Size of the firm is an important factor too—the larger the company, the greater is the likelihood that proportionately more supporting personnel, basic research, and other high-cost items will be budgeted. Table 1-13 reflects the influence of company size on R&D cost.

Character of Research and Development. The discussion thus far has been devoted to outlining the scope of R&D organization in the United States in terms of the number of scientists and engineers, their training, their rates of pay, cost to the firm, and the like. A key factor which remains before this R&D profile is completed is that of outlining the "character" of research and development activity which is carried out. Thus, we must determine how much of the company's budget is to be used for basic research, applied research, and development. Table 1-14 provides data on this aspect of organizing the R&D function.

In 1961, *industrial* firms devoted the great majority of their funds to applied research activities. For insight into how R&D funds were spent in that year by the Federal government, universities, and nonprofit institutions, Table 1-15 is valuable.

On a national basis, all organizations considered, development accounted for 68 percent of the total R&D expenditure, applied research for 22 percent, and basic research for 10 percent. These proportions were about the same as those for the 1959–1960 period. These data are not as accurate as the other data reported in this chapter, because many firms do not, when reporting to the government's surveys, differentiate between applied research and development. Also, company practices require that some firms classify certain work as "basic" when in actuality it has a definite commercial objective. However, these estimates are the best available and can serve as valuable guidelines to those responsible for organizing the R&D function in their firms.

TABLE 1-13. R&D Performance Cost per Scientist or Engineer, by Company Size, 1961

R&D Cost per Individual, $	Employees in Company
18,100	Below 1,000
26,100	1,000–4,999
38,200	5,000 or above
34,700	All companies

SOURCE: *Research and Development in Industry, 1961,* National Science Foundation, NSF 64 0, Washington, D.C., 1964, pp. 52–53.

The various raw materials of the R&D function—personnel, technology, time, money, and market position—must be integrated into an effective system for the fulfillment of the research objectives of the enterprise. An essential part of organizing the firm's R&D function is for management to make the necessary decisions on the character of its R&D. Shall it be defensive or offensive in design? How much effort should be devoted to applied research, basic research,

TABLE 1-14.   Percent Distribution of Funds for the Performance of Basic Research, Applied Research, and Development, by Industry and Size of Company, 1961*

(Dollar amounts in millions)

Industry and size of company	Total R&D funds	Percent distribution			
		Total	Basic research	Applied research	Development
Total...............................	$10,872	100	4	18	78
Distribution by industry:					
Food and kindred products..............	105	100	8	†	†
Textiles and apparel..................	33	100	†	†	†
Lumber, wood products, and furniture....	9	100	...	†	†
Paper and allied products..............	60	100	†	†	†
Chemicals and allied products...........	1,073	100	11	37	52
Industrial chemicals..................	693	100	12	38	50
Drugs and medicines.................	180	100	17	53	31
Other chemicals.....................	201	100	5	19	76
Petroleum refining and extraction........	294	100	16	42	42
Rubber products......................	126	100	7	20	73
Stone, clay, and glass products..........	103	100	5	36	58
Primary metals.......................	160	100	6	†	†
Primary ferrous products.............	94	100	8	†	†
Nonferrous and other metal products...	66	100	4	45	51
Fabricated metal products..............	118	100	2	30	69
Machinery............................	896	100	3	14	83
Electrical equipment and communication.	2,404	100	3	13	84
Communication equipment and electronic components..................	1,183	100	5	13	82
Other electrical equipment...........	1,221	100	2	13	86
Motor vehicles and other transportation equipment.........................	802	100	1	†	†
Aircraft and missiles..................	3,957	100	1	10	89
Professional and scientific instruments....	384	100	3	†	75
Scientific and mechanical measuring instruments.......................	190	100	2	16	82
Optical, surgical, photographic, and other instruments.....	194	100	†	†	†
Other manufacturing industries..........	168	100	3	13	84
Nonmanufacturing industries............	180	100	†	†	†
Distribution by size of company (based on number of employees):					
Less than 1,000......................	596	100	†	†	†
1,000 to 4,999.......................	935	100	4	28	68
5,000 or more.......................	9,341	100	4	17	80

* With regard to the estimates of relative amounts of applied research and development performance, the relatively high imputation rates characterizing the data for most industries should be taken into account.

† Not separately available but included in total.

SOURCE: *Research and Development in Industry, 1961*, National Science Foundation, NSF 64-9, Washington, D.C., 1964, p. 28.

TABLE 1-15. Funds Used in the Performance of Basic Research, Applied Research, and Development, 1961–1962

(Millions of dollars)

Sector	Amount			
	Total R&D	Basic research	Applied research	Development
Total.........................	$14,740	$1,488	$3,178	$10,074
Federal government..............	2,090	238	606	1,246
Industry......................	10,870	403	1,955	8,512
Colleges and universities.........	1,400	695	457	248
Other nonprofit institutions.......	380	152	160	68

SOURCE: *Reviews of Data on Research and Development*, National Science Foundation, NSF 63-40, no. 41, Washington, D.C., September, 1963, p. 3.

or development? The following discussion outlines the various categories of research and development effort which must be balanced, one against the other, and all against the other functions of the enterprise, to establish an optimum system for the firm.

Basic Research. This category includes all activities which are directed toward the advancement of scientific knowledge and which have no specific objective. These activities can, however, be directed at fields in which the company has a present commercial interest or is likely to have such an interest. Thus, it would be appropriate for a diversified chemical company, which does not yet manufacture plastics, to conduct basic research in the rheological properties of polymers.

Applied Research. This category covers those activities that are directed at obtaining new scientific knowledge which will have direct application to the commercial exploitation of products, processes, or concepts. The principal difference between basic and applied research, therefore, is that of the objectives of the firm with the research results.

Development. These activities are concerned with converting the results of the applied or basic research to products, processes, or services which can be profitably marketed.

The categories above may be stated to be definitions of the most fundamental characteristics of research effort. They are the categories used by the National Science Foundation and apply to nearly all of the data presented earlier in the chapter. Many industrial organizations, however, carry on a great deal of work which cannot be so explicitly defined or which they include in *their* concepts of research and development. Thus NSF's data would *exclude* activities such as product testing, technical service, market research, running the patent department, advertising research, psychological research, and so on; at the same time, many industrial organizations do not draw these distinctions. Half of the firms contacted in a survey by *Chemical & Engineering News* counted patent costs as part of the R&D costs, one out of five included some market research activities, and 40 percent included some technical service activities.

Even within any one company, accounting procedures can change and, consequently, so will the distribution of research costs. So a word of caution is necessary for those structuring R&D organizations and utilizing published data as a guideline. Before any organizational work is done, a clear concept of what the firm must do is absolutely essential.

OBJECTIVES OF RESEARCH AND DEVELOPMENT

Superimposed upon the confusion of research and development definitions are several other categories which are useful in analyzing the nature of the R&D function. These are listed below.

Defensive R&D. This is the research and development carried out in response to the demands of the market and to *catch up* with competitors. Customers, for example, may be able to get a polystyrene with higher impact resistance from one's competitors; unless this threat is countered by successful R&D, the *present* market will be lost to these competitors.

Offensive R&D. R&D of this class is carried out to *lead* competition, for example, to take away an existing market or to monopolize a new or developing market.

Long-term R&D. R&D carried out on a long-term basis is that which, if successful, cannot be immediately commercialized because the other units of the firm are not yet ready, markets are not prepared, financing is unavailable, the political or social situation may not permit it, and so on. The time required for commercialization of the research results might be greater than three years.

Short-term R&D. This classification applies to those efforts which, if successful, can be fed within a year or so into the firm's marketing divisions because marketing channels exist, money is available, the market demand is satisfactory, and there are no reasons why the results of these R&D operations cannot be commercialized.

Intermediate-term R&D. This category covers those R&D projects which, if technically successful, can be brought to commercial fruition in about one to three years. Thus, it applies to those projects whose results the firm wants to implement in the near term, but for which some preparatory activities must be undertaken, for example, plant construction, moderate market development, reduction of inventories of products to be de-emphasized or discontinued, and the like.

All of these research objectives are an outgrowth of the function of the R&D organization, which is to assist the *firm* in the attainment of the ultimate corporate objectives—survival and profitability in the long term. Generally, there is no single category of research effort that is implemented by the R&D organization. Instead, the management of the R&D department must carefully examine

TABLE 1-16. Factors Influencing R&D Organization

Corporate Objectives:
  Industry
  Size
  Image
  Profitability
  Public service
Capital Criteria:
  Sales
  Profits
  Return on investment
  Return on sales
  Cost of capital
  Investment opportunities
  Profit expectations of new research

Production Resources:
  Manpower
  Facilities
  Raw materials
  Power
  Patents
Marketing Factors:
  Skill
  Time
  Channels
  Competitor's strength
  Seasonal and cyclical effects
  Present and potential markets
  Product features
  Customers
  Personnel

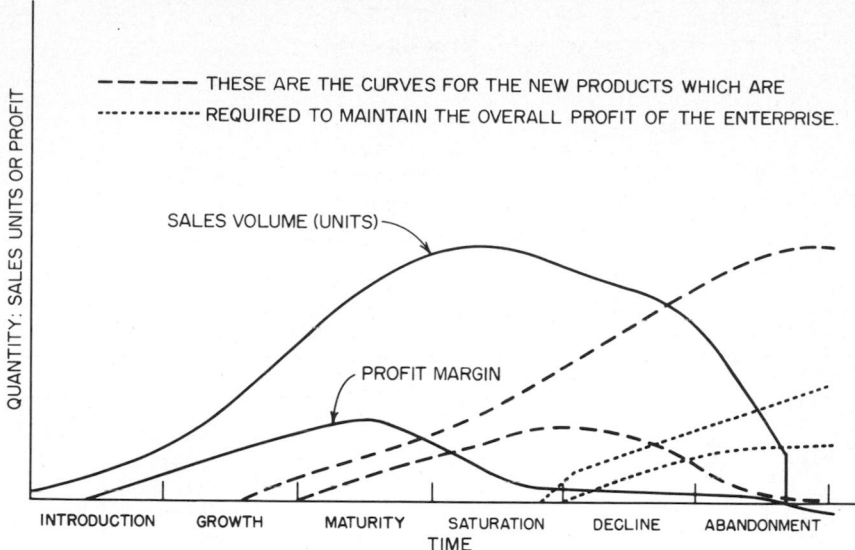

FIG. 1-1. *The product life cycle: general case.* (*Courtesy of Conrad Berenson, Administration of the Chemical Enterprise, John Wiley & Sons, Inc., New York, 1963, p. 26.*)

a number of factors and then allocate the total R&D effort among the several research objectives.

At times, the R&D effort might be primarily offensive in nature. This strategy would be appropriate when the enterprise was introducing a new product or was moving into an already established industry in competition with existing organizations. At other times, the best strategy to follow might be a short-term defensive strategy as, for example, when a product group or industry segment is firmly in the "decline" phase of its life cycle.

The selection of the optimum combination of research strategies depends upon many factors, the elucidation of which is beyond the scope of this chapter. It is sufficient to state at this point that organization of the research and development function is dependent upon the phase of the life cycle that the firm's product line is in (see Figure 1-1) and upon how a number of vitally important factors influencing the outcome of the R&D effort are rated by management. Table 1-16 indicates the nature of some of these factors.

STRUCTURING THE R&D ORGANIZATION

We have dealt thus far with the manpower utilized in R&D organizations, expenditures for R&D, the character and objectives of the R&D organizations, and so on. All of these aspects must be tied together into a structure which will act as the supporting element for the actual performance of the R&D function. There is no one structure that is equally good for all firms; nor is there one structure that is good for any one firm at all times. Rather, the organization structure must be a response of the organization to the firm's hierarchy of needs at any one time and to its ability to satisfy these needs. As the firm's life cycle progresses and as the factors influencing R&D organization structure change in their relative and absolute values (see Table 1-16), so must

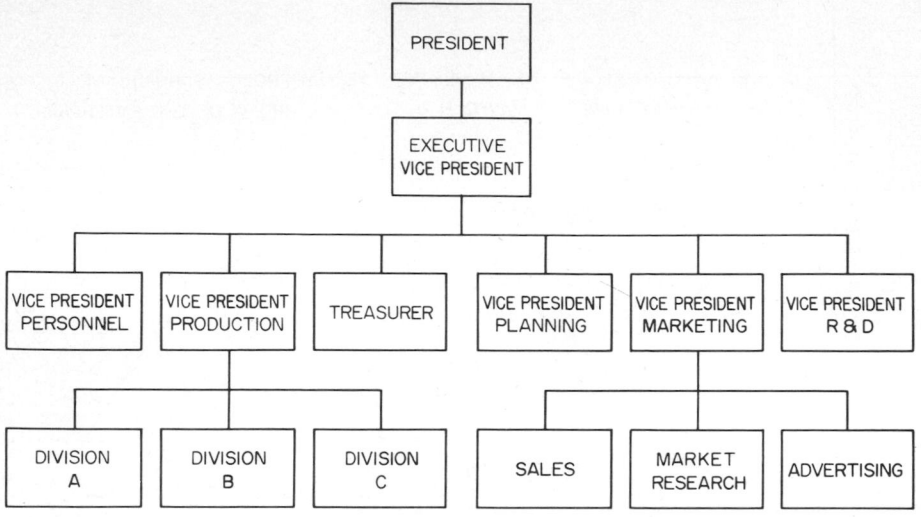

FIG. 1-2. *Centralized laboratory organization.*

the structure change, for structure is a response of the enterprise to a need, not the end in itself.

Another factor that must be borne in mind by those who make the decision as to the nature of the R&D effort is that the company can have several different R&D organization structures existent at the same time. In a decentralized or multi-product-line firm, there can be centralized and decentralized organization, there can be regional or divisional laboratories, and there can be units organized by customer, by product, or by process. Again, it is the duty of management to recognize the needs of the enterprise and to construct the best structure for the firm, whether it be a single type of organization or a combination of several. What counts is that the structure that is created should be able to do an efficient job; its form is of no consequence.

Several charts are presented here to illustrate one type of R&D organization decision—whether the R&D function should be centralized, decentralized, or a combination of these. (See Figures 1-2, 1-3, and 1-4.)

In a centralized R&D facility, the corporation has all of the research and development work performed at one location, that is, no R&D work will be performed at any of the firm's installations aside from the designated laboratory. This is shown in Figure 1-2.

In a decentralized R&D organization, there may be a number of R&D laboratories. Thus, if there are seven product divisions in a large organization, there may be seven R&D laboratories, one for each of the divisions. Figure 1-3 illustrates one type of such a decentralized unit.

Other decentralized systems can be used, for example, one in which each product division is headed by a vice president and which has within that division a number of operating and service departments such as production, planning, personnel, marketing, and R&D. In such an organization, all of the division or product vice presidents would report to an executive or corporate vice president. Some companies structured along these lines might even have a corporate R&D division in addition to those R&D units working under the divisional leaders. Figure 1-4 represents a system related to this, but different in that the

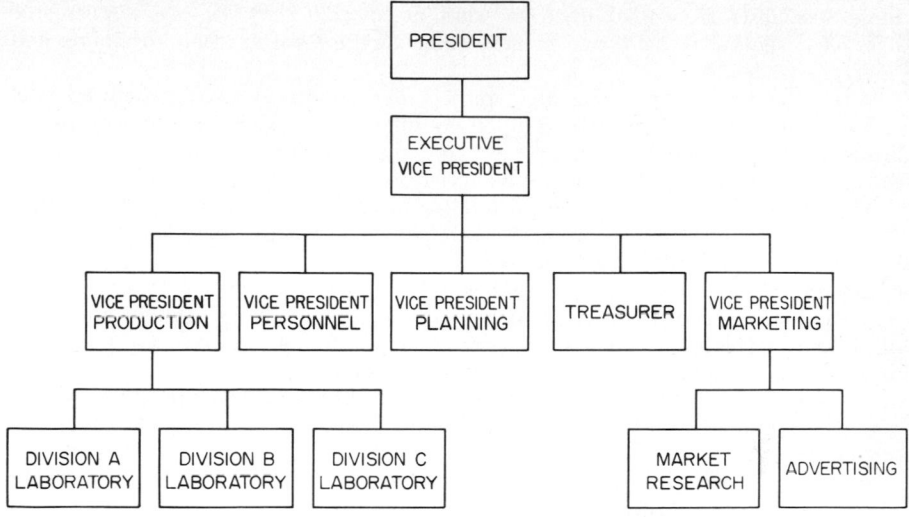

FIG. 1-3.   *Decentralized laboratory organization.*

product-division laboratories all are shown reporting to a single vice president in charge of production rather than to vice presidents in charge of the separate divisions.

Functional and Project Organizations. The previous paragraphs dealt with *where* in the company's organization the R&D function should be placed. Once this has been decided, a decision must be made as to *how* the R&D unit should be designed, that is, on a *functional* or on a *project* basis. The functional organization is one which maintains specialized subdivisions staffed by experts in a particular discipline, such as spectroscopy, reaction kinetics, or microwaves. As knowledge is required to achieve the ends of the firm's research program,

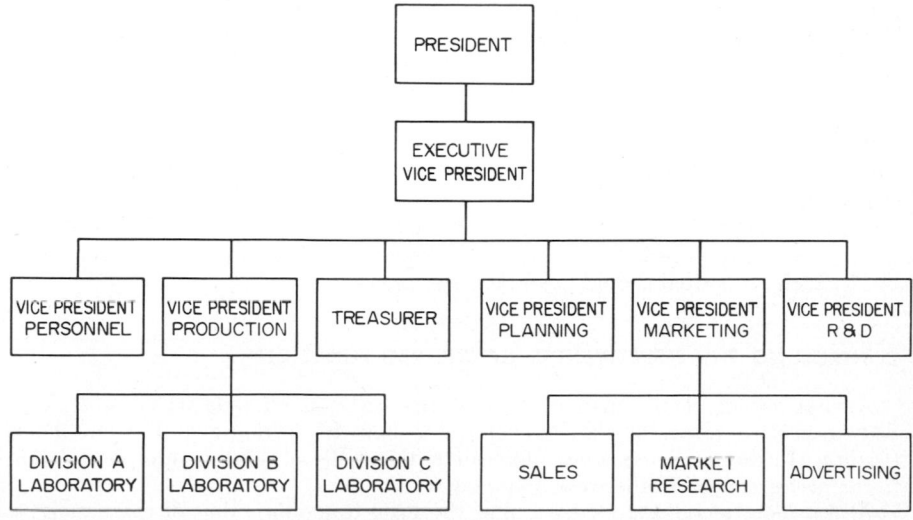

FIG. 1-4.   *Combination of centralized and decentralized laboratory organization.*

these specialists are called upon to work on specific projects. In essence, the functional specialists have two bosses—their superior within their discipline and their project leader.

When the firm is operating on a project basis, there is an unstructured pool of personnel who can be called upon to fill out a project's manpower roster. Assignments are made to the project for the duration of the project's need for the individual; there is only one boss, the project supervisor.

There are advantages and disadvantages to each of these two basic systems. In practice, a number of compromises are made with this theoretical framework to minimize organizational weaknesses.

Criteria for Selecting the Organization. Now that the several types of R&D organization have been discussed, the questions in the manager's mind are "How do I know which is best for my department? What criteria can I use for making or helping to make this organization decision?"

The following criteria may be used by the research and development manager, bearing in mind the advantages and disadvantages of the different systems of organization.

1. The structure of the R&D organization should be derived from the corporate objectives of the enterprise and, more applicable to the individual unit, from the function of the R&D unit in fulfilling these corporate objectives.

2. If interdepartmental cooperation is required, research and development laboratories should be structured in an independent position on the firm's organization chart.

3. The size of the firm must be considered, together with its physical form. Is it a regional, local, or national enterprise? Does it have one or many offices and plants?

4. The resources of the firm must be considered—resources of capital, personnel, technology, time, and market position.

5. The needs of the firm's customers must be strongly weighed, for unless the customers are satisfied, there is no lasting reason for the organization to exist.

6. The similarity of various functions that must be performed should be examined, and work which requires like skills should be grouped.

7. Long-range and day-to-day responsibilities should be separated when possible.

8. The span of managerial control should stimulate and challenge the R&D manager.

9. The structure of the R&D unit and its jobs should stimulate and challenge the unit's personnel and, to as great an extent as is possible, fulfill their personal objectives.

10. Decision making should be placed as close as possible to the "firing line."

11. Lines of responsibility should be clearly distinguishable.

12. Each individual should have just one supervisor.

CONTROLLING THE EFFECTIVENESS OF THE R&D FUNCTION

A vital aspect of the management of the R&D function is its control. The R&D executive must be able to determine how he is doing and where he is heading; furthermore, he must determine this both absolutely and in relation to the performance of other research groups.

An excellent technique for control of the R&D function is that of ratio analysis. This approach consists in measuring a number of variables, expressing them in the form of key ratios, and comparing the ratios with the same ratios of the R&D organization over a period of time. By relating the ratio changes over time to changes in the performance of R&D activities (for example, changes in scheduling, personnel, organization structure, area of research, and R&D results), the R&D manager can obtain an excellent perspective on the effect of his actions. In addition to these internal ratio comparisons, the R&D manager can compare key ratios with the ratios of other firms in the same industry which are of similar size and which have other characteristics that make such interfirm comparisons practicable.

Ratios can be computed for control of almost any aspect of the R&D function—cost ratios, productivity ratios, efficiency ratios, personnel ratios, and so on. Examples of some of the ratios that are useful in the control of the R&D function are:

Sales volume/number of R&D employees

Sales volume/number of R&D supervisors

Sales volume/number of R&D technicians

Number of R&D technicians/number of R&D scientists and engineers

Number of R&D professionals/number of R&D supervisors

Number of scientists and engineers leaving the R&D organization/total number of R&D professionals

Days lost due to absence/total number of days worked

R&D cost/number of engineers and scientists

R&D salaries/total R&D budget

R&D budget/sales volume

The data to compute such ratios are usually readily available for intrafirm comparisons. To compute these comparisons on an interfirm basis, so that the performance of the R&D function can be evaluated against the real world of competition, it is necessary to secure data from other R&D organizations. A great deal of these data are available from the National Science Foundation and the U.S. Department of Labor (many of the tables in this chapter can be used for such interfirm comparisons); additional data can be obtained with the assistance of trade associations, professional associations, consultants, and trade publications.

It is important, when control ratios are examined on an interfirm basis, that the nature and philosophy of the different organizations be taken into account. Merely because one organization may have a higher ratio of R&D scientists and engineers per $1 million of sales does not make that unit inefficient. Its competitors may be purchasing their technology from consultants, other firms, or elsewhere instead of creating their own. Or conversely, the competitors may have a higher ratio of these factors due to inefficiency which requires greater R&D spending, due to poor company sales which has the effect of increasing the ratio, and so on.

In any event, ratio analysis is an excellent control tool, one limited only by the imagination of its users. With this tool, the R&D manager can study his strengths and his weaknesses; he can then determine what actions he must take to effect the necessary results for higher R&D output, for example, to add or subtract technicians, to increase the working area, to reduce turnover, to raise salaries, or to bring in more experienced manpower.

In addition to these advantages, the ratio analysis technique works well for interdivisional comparisons when a firm has more than one R&D unit. Finally, ratio analysis provides the R&D executives with a strong incentive to establish uniform methods of control, budgeting, and reporting.

CONCLUSION

Research and development has become an essential part of the activities performed by organizations in every field. Measured in monetary terms, $21.5 *billion* was spent on this function in 1965 by businesses, governments, foundations, and others. Effective expenditure of this huge sum has a profound impact upon all segments of the nation's economic system. It is necessary, therefore, that the R&D function be treated in such a way that its importance is recognized and that its operation is effective.

In applying the principles, data, and techniques set forth in this chapter, it is vitally important to recognize that no single system of organization will satisfy the needs of the enterprise over a long period of time. Nor will a system that works well for one company necessarily be correct for another company. The system must be changed to keep pace with the changing needs of the firm. It is necessary, therefore, to review the R&D function constantly to make sure that it is organized in a way that fulfills the objectives of the entire organization.

BIBLIOGRAPHY

Berenson, Conrad, and Henry Ruhnke, *Job Descriptions of Production and Research Personnel in the Chemical Process Industries,* Corporate Publications, New York, 1964.

Employment of Scientific and Technical Personnel in Industry, 1962, U.S. Bureau of Labor Statistics, Bulletin 1418, June, 1964.

Federal Funds for Research, Development and Other Scientific Activities, National Science Foundation, NSF 64-11, vol. 12, Washington, D.C., 1964.

Industrial R&D Funds in Relation to Other Economic Variables, National Science Foundation, NSF 64-25, Washington, D.C., 1964.

Karger, Delmar, and Robert Murdick, *Managing Engineering and Research,* The Industrial Press, New York, 1963.

Rubenstein, Albert, "Organizational Factors Affecting Research and Development in Large Decentralized Companies," *Management Science,* vol. 10, no. 4, July, 1964, pp. 618–633.

Terleckyj, Nestor, *Research and Development: Its Growth and Composition,* Studies in Business Economics, no. 82, National Industrial Conference Board, New York, 1963.

CHAPTER TWO

Research and Development Planning

H. I. ANSOFF *Professor of Industrial Administration, Graduate School of Industrial Administration, Carnegie Institute of Technology, Pittsburgh, Pennsylvania*

R. G. BRANDENBURG *Assistant Dean and Assistant Professor of Industrial Administration, Graduate School of Industrial Administration, Carnegie Institute of Technology, Pittsburgh, Pennsylvania*

Industrial research and development is not only relatively new, but also distinctive and different from the traditional business functions of manufacturing, marketing, finance, and accounting. The distinctive features of the R&D process require distinctive management techniques, and these, in turn, call for special approaches to planning.

1. R&D is a major source of business change. Together with acquisition of other firms, internal R&D is the major instrument for change in the product-market position of a firm. The other business functions are concerned with exploiting the current position through maximizing current profitability, while R&D seeks new sources of profit.

2. R&D projects are not repeatable. While the other productive functions of the firm seek to maximize productivity by making operations repeatable and routine, productivity of R&D is measured by the novelty of its results.

3. Effectiveness of R&D is difficult to measure. Because it is the first in a chain of steps which lead to profitable sales, its effect on profits is obscured and delayed by the intervening steps of manufacturing, distribution, promotion, and sales.

4. R&D itself is a sequence of distinct and different steps. The chain from new knowledge and ideas to new marketable products is long in time and composed of different activities. Figure 2-1 presents a common breakdown of R&D into basic research, applied research, and engineering development. Each of these steps has a different objective and requires different talents, different resources, and different management practices.

Type	Output	Purpose
Basic research	Descriptions of phenomena Experimental results Postulates, theories, models	To discover and describe new phenomena To establish new relationships between phenomena To predict behavior
Applied research	Description of new devices and/or processes Results of bench tests, breadboards, mathematical proofs, market research studies, application studies, economic justification studies	To prove technological and economic feasibility of a new device or process
Engineering development	Pilot plants, engineering prototypes, drawings, and specifications	To design device or process

FIG. 2-1. *Phases of industrial R&D.*

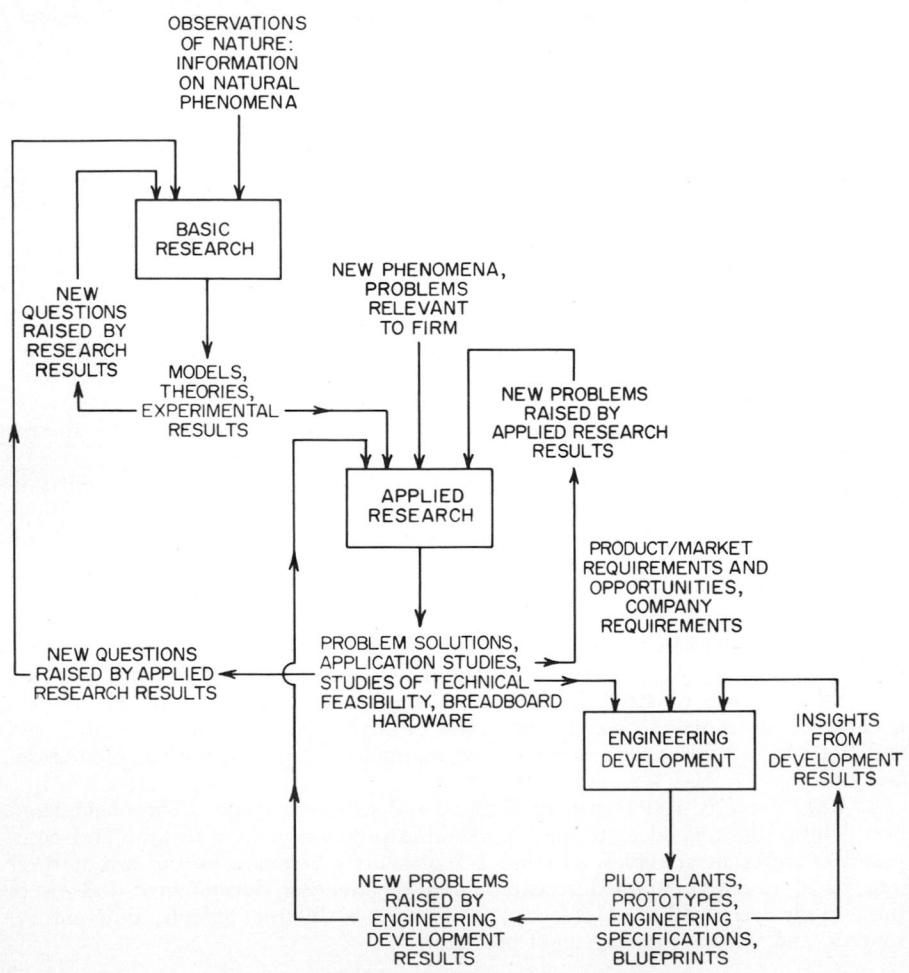

FIG. 2-2. *Information flows in the R&D process.*

5. The other principal processes of the firm seek to convert existing knowledge to profitable use. R&D, on the other hand, is a search for new knowledge. The search is not straightforward, but has many branches and byways. A basic research discovery will usually lead to a broad range of applied research projects and these, in turn, to a multiplicity of development projects. Conversely, both applied research and product development may stimulate work in earlier stages of the process.[1] The complex flow of information is illustrated in Figure 2-2.

SPECIAL PROBLEMS IN R&D PLANNING

By "planning" we shall mean a process of establishing guidelines and constraints for the firm. These are expressed in the form of objectives, strategies, policies, programs, budgets, and operating procedures. The distinctive characteristics of the R&D process raise special problems for R&D planning.

1. Establishment of objectives must be a continuous process. Unlike manufacturing, where an objective, such as a production quota, can be established and controlled to, generation of new knowledge in the course of an R&D project opens new vistas and makes possible new objectives. Therefore, customary separation of planning from control becomes difficult. As new knowledge develops, a decision has to be made on whether to control to earlier objectives or to establish new ones.

2. R&D strategies and policies must be clearly coupled to the strategies and policies of the firm. Other business functions concerned with exploitation of the firm's present product-market position can usually be expected to stay in the mainstream of the firm's business by force of inertia. R&D, which seeks to change the firm, will usually depart from past patterns. Therefore, it must be guided and oriented in directions which are desired by top management.

3. R&D programs and budgets must be flexible to new opportunities. Creation of new-product ideas and research ideas is a process which goes on throughout the firm 365 days a year. Therefore, at budgeting time, it is usually not possible to anticipate all good ideas for the next budget period. The programming and budgeting procedures must be receptive to change throughout the period.

4. Different approaches to planning are appropriate to different steps in the R&D sequence. Development usually lends itself to conventional planning and control techniques. Its objectives can be related directly to eventual profits. At the other extreme, basic research does not lend itself to formal programming and scheduling. Its planning must be largely indirect and less structured. Applied research falls in between.

When and How Much R&D Planning. Most managers, and all good managers, devote much attention to planning by setting guidelines and constraints for their areas of responsibility. Frequently such planning is *informal*, communicated verbally, and not a part of routine procedures. In this chapter, our concern is with *formal* planning in which regular planning and review procedures are established and written records are prepared and monitored.

Three kinds of formal planning are found in business firms.

1. *Operations planning* is concerned with programming and scheduling the activities of the firm. Two aspects of operations planning which have distinctive importance in R&D are (*a*) generation of project ideas and (*b*) evaluation

[1] R. R. Nelson, "The Link between Science and Invention: The Case of the Transistor," *The Rate and Direction of Inventive Activity,* Universities-National Bureau Committee for Economic Research, Special Conference Series, no. 13, Princeton University Press, Princeton, N.J., 1962, pp. 549–583.

and selection of projects. Two other important phases—project scheduling and resource budgeting—are in common with planning of other business functions.

2. *Administrative planning* is concerned with two problems: (*a*) establishing the firm's resource structure in the form of authority, responsibility, information flows, work flows, and the like, and (*b*) acquisition and development of resources needed for the firm's operations.

In R&D, two aspects of administrative planning are of special importance: (*a*) design of the information network[2] and (*b*) acquisition and development of competent research personnel.

3. *Strategic planning* is concerned with establishing objectives, strategy, major resource commitments, and criteria for project evaluation and selection. Because it sets the pattern for growth and change, strategic planning is of particular importance in R&D. It has a two-way relationship to the overall strategic plan of the firm. On one hand, the direction of R&D effort must conform with that of the firm's growth plan. On the other, R&D influences the growth plan by opening new technological opportunities.

The types of formal R&D planning appropriate in a firm depend on the nature of the firm's technological and product-market environment. If the technology is stable and products and markets change through gradual evolution (as, for example, in the automotive and food-processing industries), the focus can be placed on operations and on administrative R&D planning. If the technology and product markets are changing rapidly (as, for example, in the electronics and chemical industries), or if the firm is actively seeking to change its product-market position, strategic planning should be given major emphasis, backed up by vigorous operations and administrative planning.

The amount of formal planning in each of the categories should depend on the size of the firm and the relative size of R&D expenditures. A small firm with a small R&D organization and direct lines of communication can plan through informal procedures. A large firm with a substantial R&D budget needs well-structured formal R&D planning. R&D is an activity which takes the firm into new paths and byways. Unless these are well delineated, much wasted effort at cross-purposes may result.

Under any conditions, it is of extreme importance that operations planning be specific enough to subject research and development projects to the most stringent test possible of their ultimate contribution to the profitability of the firm. This aspect of planning is a basic factor which determines the success or failure of industrial R&D.

R&D Objectives. Objectives are goals or yardsticks by which the success of R&D can be measured. R&D objectives take their cue from the objectives of the firm as a whole. A firm will usually have multiple objectives; for example, a target return on investment, desired share of the market, growth rate of earnings, and stability of earnings. Because they are frequently antagonistic (pursuit of one precludes or even interferes with pursuit of others), the objectives of the firm should be assigned relative priorities. The overall objective of R&D is to support each one of these in the same order of priority.

But not all of R&D can be measured directly in terms of the objectives of the firm. Engineering development projects come closest to being measured in economic terms. Therefore, each major development project should be tested for the firm's objectives and assigned appropriate goals and priorities. This

---

[2] As will be discussed later, use of information for guidance of the organization replaces more structured planning procedures in the areas of basic and applied research.

will usually include a thorough evaluation of expected return on investment or a determination of the expected internal discount rate.

Major development projects are those which require a substantial commitment by the firm and are expected to produce a significant contribution. Many development projects are not large enough to warrant a full evaluation of the economic consequences. For these, "proxy objectives" which are related to the overall objectives should be used. These include payback period, contribution to profit, contribution to sales, savings in manufacturing, and manpower savings.

Because full-fledged evaluation of projects is costly and time consuming, the general rule should be to match the precision of project objectives to the size and potential importance of the project. Furthermore, determination of whether a project is meeting even these proxy economic objectives is frequently cumbersome, because it requires computation to convert the technical characteristics of the project into their economic consequences. Therefore, it is common to reserve evaluation against economic objectives for major reviews of the project. For day-to-day monitoring and control of projects, specific proxy objectives frequently are used which are even further removed from the overall objective, but can be more directly measured. For a development project, these usually include a target cost for the project, a set of technical performance specifications which the product (or process) must exhibit, a target price for the product, and a target date for completion.

Applied research objectives are more difficult to relate to the firm's overall objectives. Therefore the proxy objectives are even less precise. They may call for novelty in new-product or new-process ideas, contribution to the firm's technological competitive strength, enlargement of the firm's market position, and the like. However, each should be derived from and related to one or more of the overall objectives of the firm.

Basic research is furthest removed from ultimate profitability, because frequently it is not possible to foresee the consequences of basic research projects. Therefore, basic research objectives should be set along these dimensions: (1) the novelty and originality of projects, (2) quality of work in comparison with competition, (3) attainment of competence in the area specified by the research strategy (see below), and (4) the breadth of potential applicability—carry-over to adjacent technical fields relevant to the firm.

For convenience, we have discussed the different types of R&D objectives for individual projects. Each *area* of R&D (engineering development, applied research, basic research) should have objectives for the area as a whole from which the corresponding project objectives are derived. The respective objectives should be as specific as possible to permit measurements of accomplishment against them. For example, the engineering development branch may have the objective of "contributing x dollars of new sales per year" or of "reducing process costs by y dollars for process z by year-end." An applied research objective may be "to contribute m new technologically and economically feasible product ideas per year." Basic research may aim "to attain first-rate research competence by year-end in area A" (specified by strategy) or to "advance the state of the art in area B."

R&D Strategy. "Strategy" is the chosen means by which the objectives will be attained. A firm with stable growth prospects may not need an explicit strategy, since historical precedent and inertia can be expected to determine the means by which objectives are sought. On the other hand, a firm in a rapidly changing environment is in great need of a product-market strategy which specifies a set of guidelines and decision rules used to (1) guide the

Product-market strategy	Diversification	Product development	Market development	Market penetration
	New products, new markets	New products, current markets	Current products, new markets	Current products, current markets
New-product/process development..	X	X		
Product/process improvement....			X	X
Improvement of scientific and technological skills...........	X	X	X	X
Dimensions of R&D strategy	Offensive		Offensive-defensive	Defensive

FIG. 2-3. *Relation of product-market strategy to the firm's R&D strategy.*

firm's search for new product and market opportunities, (2) coordinate the growth and expansion efforts among the firm's organizational units, and (3) evaluate new opportunities for their fit with the desired growth directions.[3]

A complete strategy is a complex set of guidelines. One of its principal dimensions is a classification of growth into the four principal directions shown in Figure 2-3: increase of market share held by current products, called "market penetration"; penetration of new markets by current products, or "market development"; development of new products for current markets, or "product development"; and development of new products for new markets, or "diversification."

The R&D strategy of the firm serves the same purposes as the product-market strategy. One of its major uses is as a tool in allocation of the R&D budget and hence channeling effort into desired directions. The corresponding dimensions of strategy, as shown in Figure 2-3, are new-product and new-process development, product and process improvement, and maintenance and improvement of the scientific and technological capabilities of the firm.

The particular dimensions and priorities of the product-market strategy influence R&D priorities, as indicated by checks in Figure 2-3. Also shown is another commonly used classification of R&D strategy: "offensive" in support of new products and markets, "defensive" in support of present position, and "offensive-defensive" for penetration of new markets with the existing (possibly somewhat tailored to new-customer needs) product lines.

R&D as a Source of Strategy. The firm's product-market strategy is determined in part by the objectives and in part by *economic* trends, opportunities, and threats. As indicated above, these should be translated into corresponding dimensions of R&D strategy. At the same time, *technological* trends can and should serve as sources of opportunity for the product-market strategy. The responsibility for providing this input rests with the R&D manager.

This can be accomplished through an analysis of the technological foundations of the firm's product-market position—perceiving trends in technology and identifying *technological gaps* which, if closed, will lead to new product-market possi-

[3] For more detailed discussion of objectives and strategy see H. I. Ansoff, *Corporate Strategy*, McGraw-Hill Book Company, New York, 1965, chaps. 4, 5, and 6.

bilities.[4] These trends and gaps are then used to direct both economic and technological programs of the firm.   The analysis may be facilitated by setting up categories for technological progress.   The following categories are suggested:

New operating media
New rates
New spatial dimensions
New chemical, electrical, or mechanical properties
New physical properties
New magnitudes (macro or micro)
New measurement capabilities
New analytical capabilities

The R&D manager's responsibility for providing technological inputs to strategy places him in a special relationship to the top management of the firm.   He must be both a follower and a leader.   He must direct R&D activity in consonance with the strategy established by top management, but he must also analyze the strategy and make recommendations for changes and redirections as suggested by technological opportunities.   There is evidence that this rapport between top management and the R&D manager is not well developed in many firms.   There is room for much improvement.

The Make or Buy Decision.   Another major dimension of R&D strategy is the "make or buy" decision on whether desired results will be sought through in-house activities or through external sources such as acquiring products, licensing, or using research results published in the public domain.   A study of one large company[5] showed that outstandingly successful results were obtained through a combination of an intensive, wide-ranging, outside search with vigorous internal R&D.   Most smaller firms may not have the resources to do both.   General experience indicates that most firms engage in in-house product development as soon as they are large enough to afford it.   The solution with respect to applied and basic research is less clear.   The following criteria should be of use in making this part of the make or buy decision:

1. Will in-house research give the firm a strong proprietary advantage?
2. Can the firm afford to support applied and/or basic research?
3. Can the required knowledge be obtained from outside at lower cost than through in-house work?
4. Are the needs of the firm so specialized that required results can be obtained only through in-house effort?
5. Is basic research within the firm necessary to gain access to scientific results generated outside the firm which otherwise would not be available?

THE R&D BUDGET

An annual R&D budget is one of the most important plans in business firms, for the future of the firm depends on how the R&D money is programmed and spent.   At the same time, today's methods of preparing the budget are relatively unsophisticated.   There are several reasons for this: the relative new-

[4] See P. J. Klass, "New Approach Pinpoints Vital R&D Needs," *Aviation Week and Space Technology*, Dec. 28, 1964, pp. 56–59; and P. J. Klass, "Rating System Gives Planning Priorities," *Aviation Week and Space Technology*, Jan. 4, 1965, pp. 54–58.
[5] W. F. Mueller, "Origins of Basic Inventions Underlying DuPont's Major Product and Process Innovations: 1920 to 1950," in *The Rate and Direction of Inventive Activity*.

Industry	All companies	Employment greater than 1,000
Food and kindred products.............................	2.4	3.8
Lumber, wood products, and furniture..................	0.1	0.2
Paper and allied products.............................	0.4	0.6
Chemicals and allied products........................	3.6	4.5
Industrial chemicals...............................	5.0	5.3
Drugs and medicines...............................	4.6	5.9
Other chemicals...................................	1.4	1.9
Petroleum refining and extracting.....................	0.7	0.9
Rubber products......................................	1.3	2.0
Primary metals.......................................	0.5	0.6
Fabricated metal products............................	0.7	1.5
Machinery..	3.4	4.8
Electrical equipment and communications...............	9.1	11.2
Motor vehicles and other transportation equipment........	3.6	4.1
Aircraft and missiles..................................	17.3	18.3
Professional and scientific instruments..................	6.2	8.2
Scientific and mechanical measuring instruments........	8.4	11.1
Optical, surgical, photographic, and other instruments...	4.7	6.3
Other manufacturing industries........................	0.3	0.7

SOURCE: *Industrial R&D Funds in Relation to Other Economic Variables,* National Science Foundation Surveys of Science Resources Series, NSF 64-25, Washington, D.C., October, 1965, Table A-18, p. 66.

FIG. 2-4. *Funds for R&D performance as percent of net sales for all manufacturing companies in the 1958 census of manufactures.*

ness of formal R&D planning in business, lack of appropriate data, difficulties of relating R&D to the profit stream, and the internal complexity of the R&D process.

In many firms, the R&D budget is grouped into categories such as product development, market development, market penetration, and diversification. For each category, a ratio of sales to R&D expenditures is established on the basis of the firm's past experience. A firm which has no past record can use data for its industry and its competitors. A sample is shown in Figure 2-4. The tentative budget for the forthcoming year is established for each category by multiplying the respective ratios by the sales forecasted for the year.

This tentative budget may be adjusted through qualitative consideration of the following factors:

1. Changes in the firm's overall growth strategy. If, for example, emphasis is shifting to diversification, a greater proportion of sales will be devoted to offensive R&D. If the drive is to reduce costs or improve product quality, defensive R&D will be emphasized.

2. R&D budgets by successful competitors of the firm. If the firm has traditionally lagged behind others, the overall budget may be increased.

3. The opposite course may be indicated by the innovation strategy of the firm. If the firm has traditionally preferred the role of an R&D follower rather than a leader, it may keep its budget below that of the competitors.

4. The budget will also be influenced by technological trends in the respective product-market areas. Thus if the firm's traditional position is threatened with a new technology, a major increase in defensive R&D is indicated.

Even with all of these allowances, a major shortcoming of the procedure comes from basing the R&D budget on the sales forecasted for the following year, whereas in reality its major effect usually will be felt from three to ten years later. There is an urgent need for an analytical method which will establish a better relation between R&D dollars and the return on the firm's invested resources they eventually produce.[6]

Applications of an analytical method might proceed by the following steps. First, the firm's long-term sales forecast would be subdivided into the respective strategic categories: sales from diversification, from new products, from new markets, from current product markets. Next, a *product-life-cycle profile* would be established for typical products, tracing project history from the negative cash flows of the R&D and start-up phases through the positive cash flows of the successful product-exploitation period. Then the respective profiles would be applied to the categories of sales forecasts to generate the R&D budget for current and future years.

This more sophisticated method for generation of the R&D budget is more theory than reality. The analytic framework is not difficult to construct. Application is hampered primarily by lack of reliable data for constructing project profiles. Firms which are anxious to improve their R&D budgeting must start by revising their record keeping to produce the desired data.

Structure of the R&D Budget. The primary dimension used in setting the overall R&D budget is the product-market strategy of the firm. The budget is implemented by assigning it to projects within an administrative framework usually organized into basic research, applied research, and engineering development phases. Administratively, the R&D unit will frequently have subunits for development and for advanced research (including basic research and applied research). In large firms, the departments may be further specialized by product-market areas which are based on different technologies. As a result, the overall budget must be restructured from the strategy dimension to the administrative dimension.

In many firms, the state of the art for dividing the budget into basic, applied, and development components is at a stage comparable to setting the total budget. A usual procedure again is to use historical experience, modified by considerations of the same factors as above. The following additional factors may be applied:

1. Relative urgency of the firm's needs. If a near-term increase in sales is needed, product development will be given relative emphasis.

2. The ability of the firm to afford basic and applied research, as discussed above under the make or buy theory.

3. Depth of R&D appropriate to the size of the firm. A small firm will favor product development to the exclusion of the other activities.

There is yet another dimension of the budget which requires consideration—the need to balance expenditures among project generation, project planning and evaluation, and project implementation. This is another point at which R&D differs significantly from other business functions. In other functions, generation of action alternatives is usually a responsibility of managers, while implementation is carried out by their subordinates. In R&D, generation of new project ideas is everyone's responsibility. Furthermore, new ideas have a much greater relative importance.

[6] A limited method for petrochemical firms can be found in B. V. Dean and S. Sengupta, "Research Budgeting and Project Selection," *IRE Transactions in Engineering Management*, December, 1962, pp. 158–169. Further, E. Mansfield, in "Rates of Return from Industrial Research and Development," *American Economic Review*, May, 1965, pp. 310–322, reports preliminary findings on rates of return from total R&D expenditures of firms in different industries.

Similarly, evaluation and planning of projects in R&D is more demanding and time consuming. Adequate market research, application analysis, and commercial evaluation at the earliest possible stages are of utmost importance.

As a result, it is highly desirable to set separate budgets for project idea generation and exploration, for project planning and evaluation, and for project implementation.

In this case, past experience *is* the proper basis for allocation. The objective is a balanced budget which results in enough ideas to create a reserve of potentially attractive projects, and an adequate allocation to planning to assure commercial and technical evaluations which are commensurate with both the potential contribution and the cost of the proposed projects.

Thus, the R&D budget is seen to be three-dimensional, as illustrated in Figure 2-5. One dimension divides the budget among the categories of the product-market strategy, another among the phases of R&D activity, and the third among stages in inception and implementation of projects.

Coupling of R&D to Other Budgets. The cost of an R&D project is only one in a series of negative cash flows which will be incurred before the project shows profit. Engineering prototypes must be converted to manufacturing prototypes; tooling, jigs, and fixtures must be designed and procured, additions made to physical plant and equipment, inventories procured, distribution channels set up, and product introduction costs incurred. Thus, a dollar of R&D expenditure may require several additional dollars before it will yield a return. As a result, it is important that the R&D budget be reconciled with and reflected in other operating budgets of the firm. Furthermore, profit and loss forecasts should take account of the fact that acceleration of R&D, while promising future profitability, has a strong depressing effect on near-term earnings.

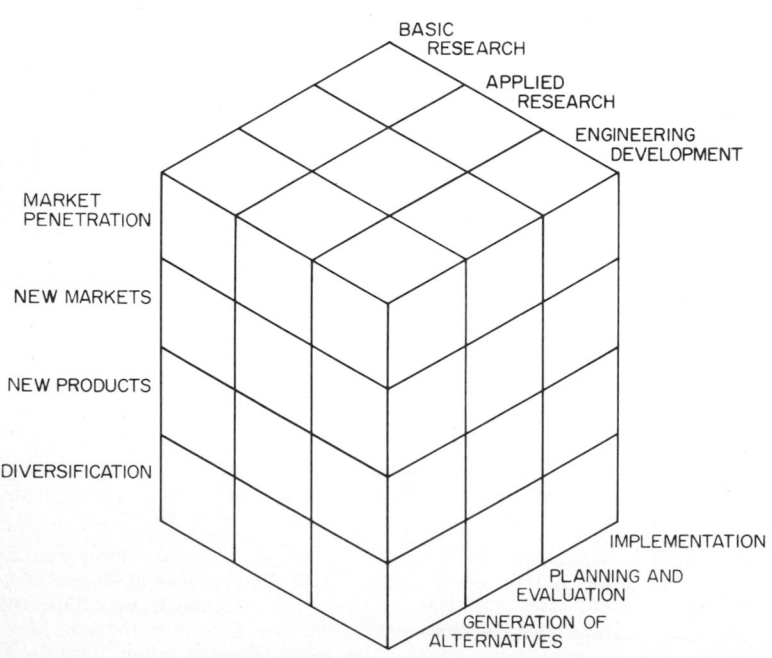

FIG. 2-5. *Structure of the R&D budget.*

SELECTION OF R&D PROJECTS

The preceding discussion demonstrates the role of objectives and strategy in setting budgets. Within these budgets, individual projects must be evaluated and selected. Objectives and strategy have a major role in this process.

The payoff expected from each project must be measured against the objectives to determine the *objectives fit,* that is, the contribution which will be made to the respective objectives. Similarly, the project must be evaluated for the *strategic fit* with the directions of the firm's growth to assure coordinated and orderly progress toward objectives.

Before final selection, each project must be subjected to two further tests. The first is to make sure that the project payoff is realistically estimated. This involves measuring the *capabilities fit* between the project and the firm—the availability of (or plans to acquire) the string of skills and facilities in R&D, manufacturing, marketing, and general management which are essential to making the project profitable. Finally, an evaluation must be made of the *portfolio fit* of the project with other active and potential projects of the firm.

Another way to classify methods for project selection is according to the evaluation technique. Among these are checklist or rating schemes, index number formulas, mathematical programming models, and portfolio analysis techniques.

Checklists for Individual Project Evaluation. Checklists are most appropriate to evaluation of basic and applied research projects, or of development projects when forecasting and measurement difficulties prohibit detailed cash flow projections. Expert judgments are applied to assess the merits of a project proposal with respect to each of a set of relevant factors. For example, the R&D department of an industrial chemical producer might consider the following characteristics of applied research and advanced development projects, and assign an excellent, satisfactory, or unsatisfactory rating to each:

R&D Capability Factors
  Research know-how
  Patent status
  R&D investment payback time
Production Capability Factors
  Required production capacity
  Raw materials
  Equipment requirements
  Process familiarity
  New fixed-capital payout time
Marketing Capability Factors
  Similarity to present product line
  Effect on present products
  Marketability to present customers
  Suitability to present sales force
  Promotional requirements
  Market development requirements
  Technical service requirements
Market Demand and Competitive Factors
  Product competition
  Product advantage
  Length of product life

Estimated annual sales
Time to reach estimated sales volume
Cyclical or seasonal demand
Market stability
Market trend

Objectives Factors
Contribution to profitability
Contribution to growth
Contribution to market share
Contribution to flexibility

Strategic Factors
Fit with firm's present product markets
Fit with firm's desired product-market position
Fit with desired R&D projects
Carry-over to other R&D projects
Unique advantages to the firm

Often, a numerical weight is assigned to each rating for each factor, and a total "score" for a proposal is obtained by adding up the results.[7]

Index Number Procedures. An index number or figure-of-merit approach is typified by ranking each project according to an index computed as

$$\Pi = \frac{r \times P_R \times P_I}{C_R + C_I}$$

where r = estimated profit
P_R = probability of R&D success
P_I = probability of successful implementation of R&D results
C_I = costs of introducing R&D results to operations
C_R = costs of R&D

As suggested earlier, index numbers may be used under one of two sets of conditions: (1) when the size and potential importance of a project do not merit the costs and time required for a more precise, thorough evaluation of return on investment, or (2) when the information for such evaluation is not available, as, for example, in applied research projects.[8]

Mathematical Programming Models. Mathematical programming techniques have been proposed for allocating resources among a set of development project alternatives so as to meet specified constraints on resources and maximize the profit obtainable from the results.[9] These models are conceptually useful to

---

[7] A typical checklist for evaluating basic research projects is found in L. B. Hitchcock, "Selection and Evaluation of R&D Projects," *Research Management*, May, 1963. See also C. Mottley and R. Newton, "The Selection of Projects for Industrial Research," *Operations Research*, December, 1959, pp. 740–751, for an example of another rating scheme, suited to applied research and development project evaluation.

[8] See J. B. Quinn, *Yardsticks for Industrial Research*, The Ronald Press Company, New York, 1959, for a compilation of such indexes, used in many companies for project evaluation.

[9] An example of a linear programming model is found in D. T. Asher, "A Linear Programming Model for the Allocation of R&D Efforts," *IRE Transactions on Engineering Management*, December, 1962, pp. 154–157. An integer programming formulation is given in R. J. Freeman, "A Stochastic Model for Determining the Size and Allocation of the Research Budget," *IRE Transactions on Engineering Management*, March, 1960, pp. 2–7.

the manager in organizing his approach to project selection decisions under circumstances when all alternatives are available for simultaneous review, and estimates of costs and payoffs can be made in dollar terms with high confidence. Several implementation problems should be recognized, however. First, the different types of research and development objectives and associated differences in project selection criteria are not taken into account. Second, all relevant project opportunities usually are not available for the manager to consider at any one time. Third, data to formulate reasonably valid estimates of the decision variables often are hard to obtain. Fourth, there may be difficulties encountered in implementing the results of a mathematical programming formulation because of resistance by R&D personnel to acceptance of the decision outputs from the model. Finally, various interdependencies among project alternatives are not reflected in many mathematical programming models.

Portfolio Selection. Each of the preceding methods fails to include one or more of the four phases of a complete project evaluation described previously. A portfolio selection approach aims at a comprehensive framework which does include all four. Understandably, such a framework is complex and complicated. This is illustrated in Figure 2-6, which calls for eighteen distinct evaluation steps.[10]

The four major phases are demonstrated in the figure as follows.

1. Steps 1 through 6 are concerned with the strategic fit. They assure that an opportunity is consistent with the firm's product-market, finance, and administrative strategies.

2. Steps 7 through 11 measure both the capabilities fit and the objectives fit. The former assesses the match between the project and the firm's capabilities, and the latter between the project and the objectives of the firm. Additionally, step 7 assures that the project, if successful, will be fully competitive in the marketplace.

3. Step 12 measures the portfolio fit of the project. Here, the project is examined against the current projects, projects being held in reserve, the current products and markets, and the planned projects.

4. In addition, steps 13 through 17 indicate an especially thorough evaluation of the project if it happens to be outstandingly promising, or requires a major departure from the firm's strategy, or requires major commitments and risks by the firm.

The portfolio selection approach is not a replacement for the previously described methods but rather an integrating framework. Thus, it is possible to use a checklist approach for steps 1 through 10, an index number procedure for step 11, and a mathematical programming approach for step 12.

GENERATION OF PROJECT IDEAS

As discussed previously, generation of project alternatives is of distinct importance in research and development. Ideas are generated both inside and outside the R&D department. Among outside sources are the customers, the marketing department, general management, information about changes in scientific and engineering knowledge, and problems encountered in other parts of the firm. Internally, unanticipated results from current R&D projects may trigger the formulation of project proposals. Or, results from basic research projects suggest

---

[10] A detailed discussion of this particular portfolio analysis technique is found in Ansoff, *op. cit.*, chap. 10.

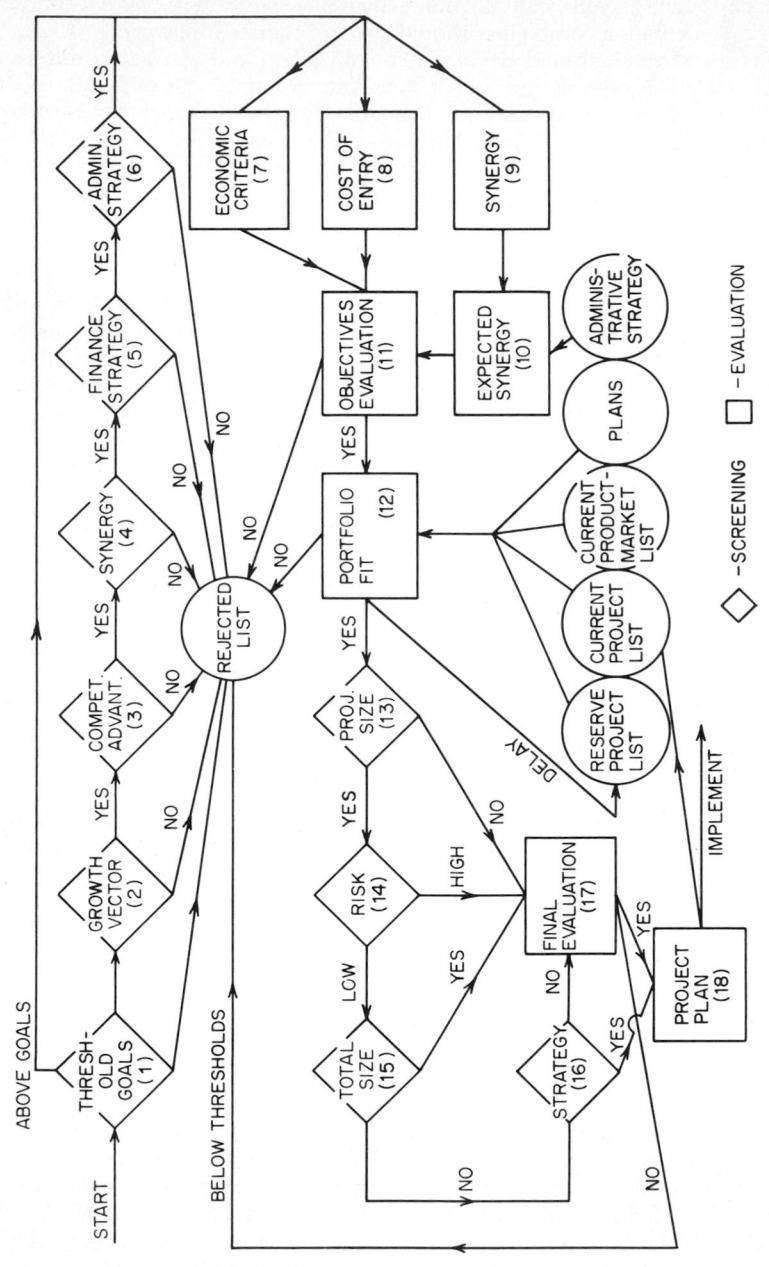

FIG. 2-6. *Portfolio selection flow diagram.*

◇ – SCREENING   ☐ – EVALUATION

applied research possibilities, while applied research results lead to engineering development project ideas.

In view of the multitude of sources, the R&D manager has a special responsibility for designing a responsive project idea generation and filter system. This system should tie the research and development laboratory to the rest of the firm, to present and potential customers, and to the technological environment on one hand, and to scientists and engineers responsible for preparing project proposals on the other. Further, as suggested earlier, a special idea-generation budget should be provided within the R&D laboratory to enable internal generation of project ideas.

Recognition of project generation as an important management tool and an R&D responsibility is not common today. It is very likely that major improvements in project selection within firms will come in the future from an increasing awareness that the generation of project ideas is an essential part of the total R&D planning problem.

CLOSE COUPLING OF PROJECT PLANNING AND IMPLEMENTATION

In contrast to other business activities, the implementation of R&D projects is closely related to planning the project portfolio. After some projects have been chosen for implementation, planning of their execution may be aided by using PERT network scheduling techniques.[11] In other cases, however, unanticipated problems and opportunities arising during project implementation may necessitate frequent major revisions of the project which require more flexible scheduling techniques. New insights developed during project implementation may indicate a major reorientation of the project or even a shift of resources to some different project. Waste can be avoided if such new information also is acquired by investing modest amounts of resources in preliminary investigations of alternatives during early stages of project implementation. By undertaking parallel exploratory studies at the beginning of a potentially major project, the R&D manager may be able to improve early estimates of expected costs and payoffs of several different approaches and thus tailor his plans and budgets to the increasing quality of information.[12] This opportunity and the need to learn by doing, which is characteristic of the R&D process, make it difficult to separate project implementation and control on one hand from generation and selection of projects on the other.

This places special requirements on planning and control forms in R&D. To be fully effective, a form should give a running historical perspective of the project. A quick examination should reveal where the project has been, where it is, what the anticipated outcome is, and very importantly, how the performance and the estimation of prospects have changed over time. The major items to be included are: (1) the budget, its history, and estimated total cost to commercialization of the project; (2) the objectives and their evolution; (3) the history of project reviews and approvals; (4) a record of planned versus

[11] See R. W. Miller, *Schedule, Cost, and Profit Control with PERT*, McGraw-Hill Book Company, New York, 1963, for an introduction to the basic ideas of PERT and PERT/cost, and for a comprehensive bibliography of the PERT literature.

[12] See R. R. Nelson, "Uncertainty, Learning, and the Economics of Parallel R&D Efforts," *Review of Economics and Statistics*, November, 1961, pp. 351–364; and B. H. Klein, "The Decision Making Problem in Development," *The Rate and Direction of Inventive Activity*, for further discussion of R&D implementation strategies designed to yield improved information prior to final commitment of resources to project execution.

PROJECT PLANNING AND CONTROL FORM

PROJECT TITLE AND DESCRIPTION	PROJECT NO.
	PLAN PREPARED BY _____ DATE _____
	PROJECT MANAGER _____ DATE _____
INITIAL OBJECTIVES	LITERATURE SEARCH BY ____ DATE _____
1.	
2.	
3.	

BUDGET REVIEWS

	SPENT TO DATE		THIS REQUEST				ESTIMATED COST TO COMPLETE			
	PERIOD	AMOUNT	FROM	TO	AMOUNT	APPR. BY	DATE	P & D	MFG.	MKG.	TOTAL
1											
2											
3											

SELECTION AND EVALUATION

	TECHNICAL			BUSINESS			PORTFOLIO				OVERALL			
	DATE	RATING	BY	DATE	RATING*	BY	DATE	RATING	PRIORITY	BY	DATE	RTG.	OBJ. CHANGE	BY
1														
2														
3														

*USE DCF OR ROI IF AVAILABLE

PROJECT PERFORMANCE MILESTONES

MILESTONES	MONTHS		1	2	3	4	5	6	7	8	9	10	11	12
1		PL.												
		ACT.												
2		PL.												
		ACT.												
3		PL.												
		ACT.												

PROJECT COSTS

		1	2	3	4	5	6	7	8	9	10	11	12
MANPOWER	PL.												
	ACT.												
PERIOD COSTS	PL.												
	ACT.												
CUM. COSTS	PL.												
	ACT.												
COST TO COMPLETE													

PERFORMANCE EVALUATION   INITIAL PROB. OF SUCCESS _____

PROB. OF SUCCESS												
PERCENT OF BUDGET COSTS												
PERCENT OF MILESTONE PERF.												
PERF. INDEX $= \dfrac{\text{PERCENT PERF.}}{\text{PERCENT COST}}$												
COST INDEX $= \dfrac{\text{ESTIMATED TOTAL COST}}{\text{BUDGET}}$												

FIG. 2-7.   *Project planning and control form.*

actual performance; (5) planned versus actual costs; and (6) an overall evaluation of performance versus costs. One such form is illustrated in Figure 2-7.

SPECIAL CHARACTERISTICS OF RESEARCH PLANNING

Most of the preceding discussion has been oriented to the "D" rather than the "R" end of the research and development spectrum. Planning in the areas of basic and applied research has distinctive characteristics, requiring emphasis on "planning for" rather than "planning of" research activities.

A key dimension of research planning is the design and maintenance of the information environment. Adequate budgeting for project alternative generation and its proper implementation is an especially important part of planning for research. Mechanisms must be maintained for surveillance of scientific and technological areas associated with current and future product-market problems and opportunities. Because alternative generation tends to be decentralized to the level of the individual scientist in research, channels for a two-way flow of information must be provided. Channels must be available for the upward flow of information on research proposals from research and development personnel to higher-level managers. Concurrently, channels must be provided for the downward flow from management to research personnel. The downward flow should provide guidelines and other data which will, on one hand, promote generation of proposals in directions desired by the firm and, on the other hand, assure evaluation of proposals on premises consistent with the firm's capabilities and competitive environment.

Another major tool of research planning is selecting, assigning, and motivating the individual professional scientist or engineer. The individual can have significant impact on proposal generation, project selection, and project execution in basic research. He often is in the best position to appraise the technical merits of his work and to guide management in assessing the relevance of a particular field to the firm. R&D personnel should participate in proposing what basic research should be done and in decisions affecting program implementation. Benefits of motivation and commitment which come from stable project assignments for the individual researcher must be balanced against benefits of flexibility to shift directions of R&D effort in response to new requirements of the business. Procedures for acquiring and developing competent research personnel should take into account: (1) ability to perform assigned research and development tasks; (2) ability to generate proposals; (3) ability to demonstrate originality and a high degree of technical promise in the proposals he generates and the tasks he performs; and (4) ability to provide management with relevant, decision-oriented information as inputs to planning.

SUMMARY

Research and development planning requires a mix of formal, structured planning techniques with informal, ill-structured methods. In the development phases of the R&D process, planning approaches analogous to those used in other parts of the firm are appropriate. Near the research end of the R&D spectrum, however, planning is much less specific, is concerned with the design of an information and organizational environment conducive to productive research efforts, and depends on the participation of the individual researcher in the planning process itself.

Compared with other kinds of business planning, the state of knowledge about planning research and development is very limited. Better understanding of the key features of the R&D process is needed to assure that formal planning techniques are not designed and implemented in ways which are incompatible with process effectiveness. Improvements will come as firms develop a better understanding of the R&D process and its impact on the firm, the distinctions among phases of the R&D process, and the special problems of R&D decision making.

BIBLIOGRAPHY

Bright, J., *Research Development and Technological Innovation*, Richard D. Irwin, Inc., Homewood, Ill., 1964.

Bright, J. (ed.), *Technological Planning at the Corporate Level*, Harvard Business School, Boston, 1962.

Dean, B. V. (ed.), *Operations Research in Research and Development*, John Wiley & Sons, Inc., New York, 1963, pp. 170–188.

Dupre, J. S., and S. A. Lakoff, *Science and the Nation*, Prentice-Hall, Inc., Englewood Cliffs, N.J., 1962.

Miller, R. W., *Schedule, Cost, and Profit Control with PERT*, McGraw-Hill Book Company, New York, 1963.

Orth, C. D., J. C. Bailey, and F. W. Wolek, *Administering Research and Development: The Behavior of Scientists and Engineers in Organizations*, Richard D. Irwin, Inc., Homewood, Ill., 1964.

Price, D. D., *Little Science, Big Science*, Columbia University Press, New York, 1963.

Terleckyj, J. E., *Research and Development: Its Growth and Composition*, National Industrial Conference Board, New York, 1963.

Universities-National Bureau Committee for Economic Research, *The Rate and Direction of Inventive Activity*, Special Conference Series, no. 13, Princeton University Press, Princeton, N.J., 1962.

CHAPTER THREE

Product and Process Development

LAWRENCE W. BASS *Consultant, formerly Vice President, Arthur D. Little, Inc., New York, New York*

Continual improvement of products and processes has become accepted as a key responsibility of good management. This need for persistent upgrading of technology has led to the establishment of organized research and development programs. Because of their importance to the vitality of a company, greater attention is being focused by top management on their planning, execution, economic justification, and implementation. They are becoming increasingly costly, often representing in science-based industries as much as one-half of general administrative expense.

The technical executive responsible for research and development should function as a member of top management. He is the interpreter of technological trends and requirements for the management group. To carry out these responsibilities, he must diagnose the needs of the company for new and improved technology to meet corporate objectives and plans. Unless he is given guidance on the directions in which the business is expected to move, he cannot properly interpret management goals to the technical staff and schedule the use of available skills.

The primary technical resource of a company is the complex of skills of the staff. If they are not distributed among the various activities according to logical priorities, they will fail to provide the needed technology.

CLASSIFICATION OF PRODUCT AND PROCESS PROJECTS

The potential contribution of the total program to the future of the company depends on the probable collective effect of different categories of projects. A helpful guide is to differentiate between defensive work, necessary for the company to maintain position in its present business, and aggressive work, which can lead it into new and attractive areas. In practice, companies spend most of their budgets on the less spectacular but necessary defensive activities, and considerably less than half—sometimes virtually nothing—on aggressive work.

Most businesses have as a primary objective the enhancement of the competitive status of their products. Few companies have process development as a primary goal, but instead look to new and improved processes as a means of obtaining greater economy in manufacturing. Major emphasis in this discussion will be placed on product development, but efficient processes must be developed concurrently if the products are to be profitable.

The following classes of projects will be discussed briefly in terms of their defensive or aggressive character, that is, their potential contribution to the business:

Defensive: product improvement, expansion of present product line, process improvement

Offensive: innovative new products and processes, new product lines for vertical integration or horizontal diversification

The following types may be either defensive or aggressive, depending on the degree of innovation and nature of impact on the business: new uses for present products, utilization of wastes and by-products.

Product Improvement. Product improvement is a universal concern, even in companies which are not technically aggressive. It is undertaken to meet or excel competition, to minimize complaints, and to maintain customer satisfaction. It is strictly defensive, but if product quality is kept high, good marketing skills can expand the business. The activity frequently suffers from lack of imagination, and is often improperly controlled from the point of view of cost of effort in comparison with value to the business.

Expansion of Present Product Line. This is also a key objective of product development. Closely related products can often be developed within a few months at relatively low technical expense and can be more readily handled by manufacturing and marketing; the cost of technical work tends to be less critically evaluated than in the case of longer-range projects. Many companies spend most of their research budgets on such "new products" which have the effect by themselves only of keeping the product line lively, and the management may delude itself into thinking it is supporting aggressive development work.

Process Improvement. Process improvement is a defensive activity to implement ideas for accelerating throughput, increasing yield, reducing waste, using lower-cost raw materials or utilities, consolidating steps, and, in general, improving efficiency of operation. It is necessary and valuable, but because it may be routine, it is often inadequately screened for economic justification. It merges into troubleshooting. It may account for a high percentage of the research and development budget, a situation which often indicates the need for greater technical strength in the manufacturing staff.

New Products. When new products are innovative, they open new areas for satisfying customers' needs in a more satisfactory way, and hence give greater opportunity for expansion of the business. A period of two to five years may be required to develop them from concept to commercialization, and hence the projects are costly; during the course of the work there should be stepwise reviews of technical, economic, and marketing feasibility to prevent waste effort. Such projects involve considerable risk, but because they represent innovation, they offer opportunities for improved profit margins and increased market penetration. They require more depth in market research, economic evaluation, market development, and technical service to customers.

New Processes. When new processes are truly innovative, they enable the company to produce its products on a more favorable cost basis. This advantage may offer a means of diversifying the product line or of entering new areas of business. Such processes may also provide additional income through licensing.

New Product Lines. Entirely new product lines permit the company to enter new businesses. They may represent vertical integration backward toward raw materials or forward into new marketing areas. They may enable horizontal diversification into new types of businesses. Entry is often accelerated by acquisition in preference to the slower course of internal development of all technology, production facilities, and marketing skills.

New product lines involve considerable risk and heavy demands on managerial skills, technical competence, marketing versatility, and financial resources. They offer the advantage of a broader base for the business and for economy by consolidation of operations.

New Use Development for Present Products. This is usually defensive, because it is limited to markets closely related to the present business. At times, it is an aggressive effort directed to creating major new markets, such as the systematic program to promote aluminum as a constructional material, or the entrance of chemical companies into consumer items. Technical efforts need to be closely coordinated with marketing plans to ensure success. Striking examples often are in the nature of interindustry competition.

Utilization of By-products and Wastes. Frequently arising from projects for process improvement are new ways of utilizing by-products and wastes. If the beneficiated products fit the marketing program for the existing product line, the work is defensive and may not be costly or risky. Some projects are very aggressive, such as the creation of the petrochemical industry from waste products of petroleum refineries.

The idea of converting a waste into a salable product has great emotional appeal, and some instances, for example, the manufacture of products from agricultural wastes, have been spectacular successes. The concepts are frequently pitfalls, however. In the aggregate, a great deal of technical effort has been dissipated on unsuccessful projects which were not subjected to incisive scrutiny. Sometimes the work is necessary to abate a nuisance—such as iron and steel pickle liquor, whey, and other undesirable effluents—even when the prospects for economic benefits are not exciting.

CRITERIA FOR PROJECT ANALYSIS

Much greater effort is being devoted to critical technoeconomic analysis of proposed new products and processes at early stages. The major questions being asked are:

Marketing feasibility—is it worth making?

Technical feasibility—can it be made by a practical process?

Economic feasibility—will it pay its way?

A question frequently overlooked is:

Corporate feasibility—is it compatible with company objectives and resources?

Because of the increasing expense of technical work, many companies are using cost versus profitability analyses for screening projects. If rigorous screening procedures are applied too early, they can stifle imagination and innovation. The evaluation procedures must be based on a comprehension of the depth of knowledge available in relation to the criteria that are appropriate. Otherwise, only "surefire" concepts will pass the tests, and opportunities for breakthroughs will be discarded. A common error is failing to recognize an early prototype as a general concept rather than considering it strictly as typifying a product proposed for the market.

Decisions Must Be Based on Managerial Judgment. In the present state of analytical procedures, particularly in the earlier phases of development, firm data cannot be made available to permit evaluation on a purely mathematical basis. Therefore, it is necessary to rely on managerial judgment when evaluating feasibility.

The amount of technical effort parallels the advancing stages of development. Exploratory work to reach a working definition of the product may require a few technical man-months. Small-scale work for product and process development and evaluation may represent a fivefold increase. Commitment to large-scale confirmation of product and process feasibility may expand the expenditure of technical time another five or ten times. But it is only as the knowledge from these successive types of work accumulates that an evaluation in depth becomes meaningful.

There is much literature on economic evaluation procedures used by different companies. These are based on estimates of plant investment and working capital, of production cost, and of projected sales volume and price range on a time scale. The calculations often employ discounted cash flow to provide information for comparing the benefits from this use of corporate funds with alternative uses. Although estimates of cost of plant and operations may appear to be realistic, most companies have had the experience that unforeseen factors reduce the reliability of such estimates. And the sales forecasts are, of course, subject to the uncontrollable factors of the general economic climate and the stresses of competition. Hence, the final decision rests on the judgment of the management in the face of these variables.

PROGRESSIVE STAGES OF DEVELOPMENT

The progress of projects from stage to stage will be traced in terms of the depth of evaluation which is appropriate, the factors which should be taken into consideration, and the corporate functions which are major contributors to the analysis. A summary of the status at these stages is given in Figure 3-1.

The discussion starts with the product or process concept, carries it through successive steps as the scale of investigation increases, and finally reaches the comprehensive review prior to commercialization. The terminology applies to the process industries, such as chemicals, petroleum products, foods, and metallurgical products.

The same series of stages is involved in mechanical-electrical projects, but for this purpose they should in part be redefined as follows: concept; concept evaluation; product definition; experimental model development and testing; prototype design and fabrication; preliminary field test; manufacturing preparation; final field test; and comprehensive review.

It is not necessary or advisable that the stages should follow rigidly the sequence shown in the chart. Judgment should be exercised in deciding when overlapping between two or more phases is warranted. For example, after the product has been defined, it may be logical to work on product development and process development in parallel, as soon as the product definition gives sufficient guidance regarding required process characteristics.

At the end of each stage, a summary of all information accumulated should be prepared. The next stage should then be outlined in terms of objective, program, need for consultative assistance from other functions, nature of conclusions to be drawn, effort and expense required, and target date. This work outline should be approved at the proper level before major activities on the new stage are undertaken.

STAGE	PRODUCT	PROCESS	MARKET	MANAGEMENT INTEREST	RAW MATERIALS	FACILITIES	MANUFACTURING	FINANCIAL	LEGAL & PATENTS
CONCEPT	GENERAL	PROBABLE	POSSIBLE						
CONCEPT EVALUATION	INITIAL PARAMETERS	ROUGH CHECK	ROUGH CHECK	PRODUCT POLICY	ROUGH CHECK			ROUGH CHECK	
PRODUCT DEFINITION	PRELIMINARY	PRELIMINARY EVALUATION	PRELIMINARY ESTIMATE		PRELIMINARY EVALUATION			ORDER OF MAGNITUDE	PRELIMINARY STUDY
PRODUCT DEVELOPMENT	INITIAL FORMULATION	BASIC CHARACTERISTICS	GENERAL CHARACTER	CONFIRMATION	PRELIMINARY SPECIFICATIONS	INITIAL CONCEPT			RECHECK
PROCESS DEVELOPMENT	POSSIBLE MODIFICATION	SEMI-FINAL DESIGN			INITIAL SELECTION	PRELIMINARY ESTIMATE	ROUGH CHECK	PROJECTION	
FIELD EVALUATION	PERFORMANCE REVIEW		SPECIFIC OPPORTUNITIES	RECHECK					
PROCESS CONFIRMATION	POSSIBLE MODIFICATION	FINAL DESIGN			FINAL SELECTION	FINAL FLOW DIAGRAM	CONFIRMATION	SEMI-FINAL ESTIMATE	SEMI-FINAL CONFIRMATION
MARKET CONFIRMATION	FINAL FORMULATION		CONFIRMED OPPORTUNITIES	RECONFIRMATION					
COMPREHENSIVE REVIEW	FINAL SPECIFICATIONS	FINAL SPECIFICATIONS	BEST ESTIMATE		FIRM SPECIFICATION	FIRM SPECIFICATION	FINAL CONFIRMATION	CONFIRMED ESTIMATE	FINAL CONFIRMATION
IMPLEMENTATION				DECISION TO IMPLEMENT					
	CONSULTATION	CONSULTATION	MARKETING MOBILIZATION	COORDINATION	PURCHASING PROGRAM	ENGINEERING & CONSTRUCTION	MANUFACTURING MOBILIZATION	FINANCING	CONTRACTS

FIG. 3-1. *Project status at successive stages.*

Product development, process development, and field evaluation can be conducted at a lower level of expense and are grouped as "evaluation stages." When the project enters the phases of process confirmation and market confirmation, the order of expense rises rapidly, and they are grouped as "confirmation stages." Because of their costliness, it is particularly necessary to evaluate the probability of success at the conclusion of evaluation stages before these larger commitments of effort and cost are begun.

EVALUATION STAGES IN DEVELOPMENT

Project Concept. A project begins when a concept is crystallized for a new product, device, process, or system. The idea may have originated within the development group, or it may have been stimulated by a suggestion from elsewhere in the company, such as long-range research, market research, marketing, or manufacturing. It may have had its origin in an external source, such as customer requests or an item of information in the technical or trade literature.

For preliminary evaluation, the concept should be described in writing, with an explanation of how it could contribute to the business. Some exploratory work in the laboratory or model shop is often necessary to define it in more tangible form. Most companies find it advisable to set a limit on the time to be expended before formal evaluation, because otherwise the effort may get out of hand. The amount of preliminary work may be restricted to the equivalent of one or two technical man-weeks, for example.

Concept Evaluation (Applied Research). Preliminary evaluation is often made by a committee. If the concept has been well described, it can be given a rough analysis for practicality and pertinence to the business of the company. The mortality of ideas at this stage is likely to be very high, perhaps as high as 80 to 90 percent.

Key policies in encouraging innovation are to make sure that the evaluations are objective and that decisions are communicated promptly to individuals making suggestions. Failure to show this consideration leads to low morale and erosion of initiative. If decisions give the appearance of being arbitrary and hasty, there is likelihood that the originator will find subterfuges to keep his idea alive. A written product policy is helpful in making clear why a given concept does not lie within an area of interest to the company.

Product or Process Definition. If the concept passes this initial screening, it still will probably not be defined in sufficient depth to permit thorough examination. It may seem to have general merit, but it may need several weeks or months of study to define it adequately. The decision to invest more time on exploratory work will have to be based primarily on technical feasibility, although it should reflect opinions regarding economics and marketing potential.

This type of activity is often called "applied research." It may be carried out by product development personnel or, in larger organizations, it may be assigned as the responsibility of other groups organized, for example, according to disciplines such as chemistry or physics. "Applied research" is frequently differentiated from "development" on the basis that it is concerned with exploration of possible utility, whereas product and process development projects are the pursuit of specific aspects of application. There can obviously be no sharp differentiation between the two types of work.

Range of Applicability. Investigation of range of applicability of the concept should require a project authorization before this additional exploration is undertaken. The objectives are to define potential commercial utility, to prepare small quantities of materials or preliminary models, to explore the limitations of the idea, and to recommend a program for product and process development.

In cases in which the concept has been sufficiently well worked out in the earlier exploratory stage, it may be moved forward directly into product or process development.

Evaluation. At the end of this stage, evaluation should permit the following conclusions:

The concept justifies belief that the product or process will be commercially useful.

Materials needed for its production or operation are or could be made available in adequate quantities at acceptable cost.

The technological requirements for process appear to be attainable.

A rough cost estimate leads to the belief that the product would be in acceptable range.

The potential market size, probable selling price range, and distribution system are not adverse; the marketing area is in harmony with corporate resources and objectives.

There seems to be no competitive situation in the market which indicates an undesirable degree of risk.

There appear to be no patents, hazards, or regulations that are a bar to a successful venture.

Product Development. A description of product characteristics is made available by the preceding work, and this present stage is concerned with reducing the preliminary definition to finite form for evaluation. Economic and marketing questions do not yet require or warrant investigation in depth because the concept has not yet taken definite shape.

The method of making the product is first examined systematically to reduce it to practical form. Prototype samples or models of the more promising variants are prepared for internal evaluation. They should be as similar as possible to those anticipated from commercial manufacture; this requires representative raw materials in the process industries, or potentially available materials of construction or components in the mechanical-electrical area.

Degree of Innovation. The degree of innovation represented by the product will obviously have a pronounced effect on the program of product development. When the product is an item closely related to the present product line, experience will permit considerable accuracy in evaluating its chances of success. The course of development in such cases can often be compressed into a few weeks or months. Further, because the technology will not vary greatly from existing know-how, and because market testing can be undertaken with more confidence, it is often possible to jump intermediate stages and proceed directly to trial production and marketing. The risk in so doing may be less than the delay and expense of a more cautious approach.

When the product is truly innovative, it is very hazardous to move ahead until systematic evaluation has provided justification. If a new product line is involved, marketing considerations have to be investigated with great care. The distribution system may be very different, and there may be established franchises which make market entry difficult.

Evaluation of Product Performance. This is conducted by existing or improved test methods. The more nearly these are related to actual conditions of use, the more readily the results can be interpreted in terms of market acceptability.

At this early stage, it is well to give initial consideration to packaging and handling problems. If the packaging concept is not framed until the project is nearing final phases, particularly for consumer items subject to deterioration, the necessity for determining compatibility of product and package under conditions of distribution and use can cause unfortunate delays at crucial times.

Evaluation of Products. The evaluation of products which still show promise at the end of this stage should permit the following conclusions with a degree of certainty considerably greater than was possible after product definition:

The product and its variants have been shown by internal tests to have characteristics believed to be suitable for the market.

Use of the preferred small-scale process for making the test samples does not point to major technical or manufacturing difficulties.

There are still no obvious problems concerning availability of raw materials, minimum economic operation, or roadblocks in the form of adverse patents, hazards, or regulations which appear to be too serious to overcome.

Market research, marketing, and management are still favorable to continuation of the project.

Process Development. Perfection of process is usually not undertaken until product development has advanced far enough to warrant a preliminary process flow diagram. A reasonable degree of overlap between the two stages is desirable, so that process expertise may be reflected in the procedures used to make the samples for internal evaluation.

Product development personnel, unless they have broad experience, tend to concentrate on making samples and often fail to take into account the many practical problems involved in a manufacturing operation, such as raw material specifications, materials of construction, machining tolerances, and the like. An early liaison with development engineers helps to orient the preparative work toward a representative prototype.

Development engineers normally work on a larger scale than is used in the product formulation stage. In the process industries, development may be done on large laboratory or "pre-pilot" equipment, often heavily instrumented to aid data collection. These "desk top" units have the advantage of using smaller quantities of material, and the observations are convenient for the development engineer to carry out. Material balances obtained on this scale can be quite accurate, because weights or volumes are susceptible to more precise measurement than in pilot plant work.

First Steps. In process development, the first step is to review the product specifications and the sequence of process steps used in making the samples submitted for internal evaluation. From this information, a revised process flow diagram is prepared. It is critically analyzed from the point of view of tentative raw material specifications, outline of equipment design and construction, sequence and control of operations, and output of finished product and wastes.

Equipment is then assembled for carrying out the operation in a manner that will provide basic information suitable for scale-up to semiworks or commercial size. It should be similar in philosophy of design to the projected manufacturing operation.

Feasibility Check. A systematic check on feasibility is then carried out on this scale. The data should permit approximation of operating cost and plant investment. The process engineer should verify these estimates with other cost analysis groups in the company, such as those in general engineering, accounting, and manufacturing.

The data assembled should include description and layout of plant facilities, estimate of raw material requirements, finished-product yield, requirements for labor and supervision, utilities, storage of raw material and product, quality-control procedures, and in-process control. A revised process diagram should be prepared, showing quantitative flow of materials and specification of major items of equipment, including sizes and materials of construction.

The process development stage may be adequate for determining the feasibility of moving directly into commercial scale when the product and technology are similar to those in which the company is already engaged. But when the product is innovative or the technology is radically different, it is advisable to pilot part or all of the operation.

Samples of products for field evaluation, the stage to be discussed next, are usually prepared by the process development group. They should be as representative as possible of the specifications expected in commercial operation.

Evaluation. At the process development stage, evaluation gives the following information in the case of a successful project:

The process is technically feasible and will yield a product meeting the proposed specifications.

Equipment requirements can be met.

Estimates of plant investment and manufacturing cost indicate that the operation will satisfy the projected production economics.

Tentative quality-control procedures have been established.

If product and process resemble present operations, the project may be judged satisfactory for commercialization insofar as manufacturing aspects are concerned.

If it is decided that further work on a pilot or semicommercial scale is needed, the program required and the cost thereof should be described.

Field Evaluation. The internal evaluation program is usually inadequate to warrant decision regarding the suitability of the product for entry into the market, even on a trial basis. It is therefore customary to institute field tests to confirm the internal conclusions. For industrial products, small-scale trials are often arranged in the laboratories or plants of selected customers. For consumer products, tests are conducted with selected juries of individuals representative of the potential market.

In carrying out such programs, it is essential to obtain objective opinions. Usually the plans are formulated in cooperation with the sales department so that they are not in conflict with company practices and trade relations. For both industrial and consumer products, the programs should keep the amount of product required as small as is consonant with adequate field response.

Industrial Products. For industrial products, it is good practice to choose a small number of customers representing the range of requirements of their industry. Previous experience will aid selection of those who are knowledgeable, objective, and cooperative, and who will most likely be purchasers when marketing begins. It is advisable to give them drafts of technical bulletins describing the functions, tentative specifications, advantages, and directions for use of the products under evaluation.

Consumer Testing. For consumer testing, the juries should be representative of the characteristics of the public sector which is expected to buy the product. Because the opinions they express are subjective, much care has to be given to designing tests to eliminate bias. Blind scoring is commonly used, with one or more comparison samples. The choices should be kept simple. The results are analyzed by statistical procedures to determine significance.

Results of Field Evaluation. The results of this stage should lead to the following conclusions on successful candidate products:

Internal evaluation of the merits is confirmed by field tests.

Comments from the field have been incorporated in a revised estimate of market size and characteristics.

Customer suggestions have been used to improve product specifications.

Comments from users' experience have been incorporated in revised drafts of technical or trade bulletins.

If the product resembles a present product line, it may be ready for market introduction.

If the product is innovative, a test marketing program will probably be advisable.

CONFIRMATION STAGES OF DEVELOPMENT

Process Confirmation. When process development work on a small scale has not yielded all the information necessary for the final process flow diagram, a cost estimation, and economic justification of a commercial plant, part or all of the operation requires piloting. Work on this scale is expensive and should in general be used only to confirm or supplement the results from smaller equipment. It should not be employed for "research" purposes to get information that can be obtained on a reduced scale.

A complete pilot plant for a new process is costly and may represent a surprisingly high percentage of the expense of a small commercial plant. A pilot installation may have additional utility for subsequent work on extensions of the original development project. It is often possible to select certain steps for piloting, with reliance on extrapolation from small scale for the rest of the operation.

Sizing Pilot Equipment. In sizing pilot equipment for innovative processes, a tenfold increase is often felt to be a desirable limit. If the commercial plant is to be very large, this may mean inclusion of an intermediate semiworks plant following the pilot operation.

There is a temptation to use a pilot plant for subcommercial manufacture to supply product for extensive market tests, or for actual sales to secure rapid market entry. Such action may be warranted where timing is critical, but the expense is considerable because pilot plants are usually well below minimum economic size. Computation of cost of operation is often not realistic. If the accounting procedures are on the same basis as those for commercial manufacture, as they should be, the figures will warn against use of pilot facilities beyond their normal purpose.

Evaluation. Evaluation of pilot plant work places the project in the following status:

All steps in the process are technically feasible on a scale adequate to confirm suitability for commercial operation.

All specifications for a commercial plant have been confirmed, including sizing, materials of construction, controlling, and plan for layout, so that if the project moves ahead, information is available on which to conduct detailed design.

The product can be produced within acceptable specifications at the required throughput, and the quality and in-process control programs have been defined.

Information has been accumulated for estimating plant investment with an accuracy (perhaps of 10 to 15 percent) adequate for final economic analysis, unless the project is marginal.

Operating costs have been analyzed with sufficient rigor to permit decision on economic feasibility of commercial manufacturing.

A draft of the operating manual has been prepared.

Information has been assembled on criteria for plant site selection.

Market Confirmation. Field evaluation has provided preliminary information on the utility and acceptability of the product in the trade. The ultimate test is whether customers will buy it. This needs to be firmly established before deciding to manufacture on a commercial scale.

Confirmation of market potential is frequently based on test marketing. This activity is often carried out by the sales department; but in larger companies, a staff group for market development may be set up for the purpose. Their activities should be closely coordinated with sales management. The reason for establishing this special function is that, in the case of an innovative new product, the requirements for stimulating market demand are too involved and time consuming for the regular sales force.

Market development may be entrusted to a member of the sales department who is relieved for the necessary period from other duties to concentrate on this assignment. It may be made the responsibility of the appropriate product manager, a type of marketing specialist being used in many companies. Or it may be set up as a function for a new-products manager or, as mentioned above, a manager of market development, the latter often being a member of the marketing organization, but sometimes located in a corporate development group.

The Market Development Function. This function has as its goal firm establishment of market acceptability. To promote actual sales and purchase contracts, quantities of the product may be needed to fill initial orders. These can be made in the pilot plant or by an extemporized operation in an existing plant. The high cost of making the product on this scale must be kept in mind as a deterrent to expanding commercial development on too wide a scale unless speedy market entry is urgent.

Innovative products which fill a special and immediate need may command an initial premium price which permits intermediate-scale operation without a cost penalty.

For consumer products, test marketing may be carried out in one or more communities through regular retail channels. Introduction of the product is promoted by local advertising, demonstration booths, and other devices.

Evaluation. Evaluation of the market development program establishes the following conclusions:

The product is satisfactory, as demonstrated by test marketing, to confirm customer demand in its present form and at the proposed price.

Projection of the market from these tests permits the estimation of a demand of adequate size and character to justify the venture.

A marketing program has been prepared.

Promotional activities such as trade information and advertising plans are in a stage to permit expansion for full-scale marketing.

COMPREHENSIVE REVIEW PRIOR TO COMMERCIALIZATION

Sound managerial practice for final approval of commercialization requires that all available information should be critically evaluated as a whole so that decision can be based on coordinated analysis of all factors. Neglecting to do this can result in disastrous failure if some major aspect has not been taken into consideration.

The inputs from the major functions should be the following:

Product development should be able to state that no new factors have become apparent which require modification of product specifications.

Process development should confirm the satisfactory state of the process without need for more than minor adjustments during tune-in of plant.

Marketing should confirm satisfactory sales estimates in the face of any new competitive or general economic situations that may have arisen.

Purchasing should confirm the availability of raw materials at suitable quality and price.

Engineering should give approval of plant specifications and estimates of installation costs, including escalation during the time required for construction.

Manufacturing should confirm its satisfaction with the process and the estimate of operating costs.

Finance should present a plan for use of funds in installation, start-up costs, and working capital.

Legal aspects to be confirmed include the patent situation and any matters concerning regulations or hazards affecting commercialization.

IMPLEMENTATION OF THE PROJECT

Decision to go ahead with the project now rests on management. In spite of the documentation on the subjects listed above, the exercise of judgment is necessary. Is this venture still in harmony with corporate objectives and plans? Is this an optimum use of corporate resources in view of alternative courses of action open to the company?

If the decision is favorable, the major activities of commercialization come into play. They should be organized with appropriate timing so that the plant may begin operation on proper schedule and marketing can proceed at an appropriate rate to move the product into the pipelines and on to the customers.

Engineering proceeds with detailed layout and specification of equipment and construction. Engineering contractors are often used for the actual installation.

Manufacturing has to make final selection of plant site, if this has not already been done. The operating manual has to be revised, and the quality-control program has to be laid out. Operating personnel have to be selected and trained for their functions; this may already have been started by giving experience in the pilot plant to those selected as supervisors and foremen.

Marketing has to prepare its final program. The marketing strategy and promotional plans must be readied. Trade contacts should be established in the form of purchase contracts. Dealers, agents, or wholesalers may need to be provided. A training program for salesmen should be planned and implemented. Arrangements for technical service should be confirmed.

Purchasing has to proceed with firm arrangements for obtaining plant equipment and raw materials.

Management must maintain supervision to ensure proper timing, cooperation, and coordination.

COORDINATION OF FUNCTIONAL ACTIVITIES

The trend toward functional specialization, particularly in larger companies, has led to problems in communication which become particularly difficult in creative activities such as product and process development. The individual functions which must make contributions in the progression of a concept to the commercial stage are often carried out by groups of specialists distributed in various parts of the organization. In extreme cases each carries out his assigned task, summarizes his findings, and relinquishes to administrative echelons responsibility for integration into the total solution.

This situation is ameliorated in practice by establishment of formal or informal communication bridges. Informally, individuals at the working level find means of making contact with colleagues in other groups. Formal coordination committees may be set up with representatives of various functions, but they are sometimes dominated by administrators rather than the personnel most familiar with the details of the work.

Solutions to communications problems have somewhat different requirements in the process industries as compared with the mechanical-electrical industries, because of the character of their products. In the process industries, development efforts are normally focused on an end item such as a new insecticide, a new polymeric filament, a new process for preserving foodstuffs, a new lubricant, or a new alloy. The technical objective is homogeneous in that all work of the total program relates to the target product.

In the mechanical-electrical field, however, the end products are usually assemblies of components or subassemblies as in the case of a new automobile, a new television unit, or a new mechanical item for the household. The program tends to be broken down into a heterogeneous pattern of individual components which have to be brought to focus.

Network Coordination. The problems have become particularly acute in cases of complex systems represented by advanced defense technology. To coordinate inputs from several distinct activities which are frequently not in direct communication and to reach a common goal with proper timing, some form of administrative control of planning and scheduling is needed. Network coordination schemes are being used in which major parts of the program are defined, programmed, and evaluated as to technical input required, timing, and probability of technical success, so that allocation of effort may be made more logically. The result has been the evolution of procedures such as critical path methods (CPM) and program evaluation and review techniques (PERT). They separate the planning and scheduling phases and analyze the variables in terms of probability of attaining the end result at the desired time.

MULTIDISCIPLINE TASK FORCES

Another effective scheme for coordinating diffuse technical skills is the use of task forces. This method of operation has been developed over the years to a high degree of success in many organizations.

Instead of assigning separate parts of a problem to individual technical groups and relying on administrative echelons for coordination, a composite group with various backgrounds and expertise is assembled to undertake a task by joint effort. For example, responsibility for the product development phase of a project is assigned to a senior technologist in the development group. As team leader, he must arrange for the necessary technical skills in proper proportion. The brunt of the effort may be borne by men from his group, but to provide a comprehensive answer he will need inputs from other technical disciplines such as the internal evaluation group, development engineering, and market research.

The task-force team is distinct from the formal organization pattern, in that individuals from different administrative groups are brought under the leadership of one man who does not have direct authority over them in the usual sense of the word, but only for the control of their involvement in the specific project. Most of the team will be operating on a part-time basis at the discretion of the team leader, the rest of their time being devoted to other activities, including participation in other task forces. The services of the members of the team are made available with the acquiescence of their respective administrative superiors.

Example of a Task Force. The following example illustrates a task force or project team for the production of a new form of synthetic plastic which has promise as a packaging material for convenience foods. A senior man in the product development group is designated as team leader. He has the responsibility of analyzing the problem and of diagnosing the need for different specialized skills. He prepares a program outline and budget, and sets the target date. He must also arrange with the proposed team members and their supervisors for the amount of time required from them over the life of the project.

He estimates that coordination of the team effort and participation in product definition, refinement of initial process, and preparation of test samples will require half his time for a one-year period. He will need additional help from the product development group to the extent of half time of another senior technologist and the equivalent of two and one-third junior technologists. Internal evaluation of the samples will require services amounting to one and one-half technical man-years from a separate group in the applied research department. Some special test methods will be needed for which he wishes half time of a physicist in still another department.

Certain other types of skills needed to a lesser extent can be provided by other groups on what is equivalent to a consulting basis. The help of a process engineer will be needed, particularly for advice on process and preparing estimates of cost of plant and operation. There should be market research assistance to define performance criteria, to estimate market potential, and to evaluate competition. Because the product will come into contact with foods, toxicological questions must be taken into account to determine what proofs of safety may be required. The package may influence odor or taste, and expert opinion should be obtained from a specialist in flavor evaluation.

The manpower table therefore might take the form of Figure 3-2. From this manpower table, the budget can be prepared. The program and budget are approved, the personnel requirements are confirmed with the individuals, and the project is activated. The team leader oversees all activities and also participates at the technical level. He arranges the reporting schedule and holds review conferences as needed. He supervises the amount of input from the members of the team according to his appraisal of the needs. He may change membership and extent of involvement of the members during the course of the project.

This stage of the project is completed and the results are summarized. The outcome is favorable and decision to proceed further is reached. The original team is disbanded, and new teams are formed for process development and

Personnel	Technical Man-years
Team leadership	
Senior technologist	1/2
Direct participation	
Senior technologist	1/2
Junior technologist A	1
Junior technologist B	2/3
Junior technologist C	2/3
Senior product evaluator	1/2
Junior product evaluator	1
Senior physicist	1/10
Junior physicist	4/10
Consultation	
Process engineer	1/3
Market researcher	1/4
Toxicologist	1/10
Flavor expert	1/20

FIG. 3-2. *Technical manpower for a product development project.*

field evaluation. The new team leaders may be, respectively, the process engineer and the market researcher who participated in the preceding phase. For continuity of background and expertise, they include selected members of the product development team as direct participants or consultants.

Advantages of Task Forces. The use of project teams represents a departure from operation under the rigid lines of a formal organization. Companies frequently use a task force to handle an urgent problem by a crash program, and to do this, carry out much of the procedure just presented. In spite of success in an emergency, they are likely to revert to the formal organization for regular operations.

The major advantages inherent in a task-force system are the following:

1. Professional skills and experience are brought to bear with planned emphasis and timing to reach an optimum solution of the problem.

2. A spirit of joint entrepreneurship is stimulated among the team members, with less influence from a succession of administrative layers.

3. Greater speed in reaching well-rounded conclusions is brought about by coordinating information and opinion from several sources of expertise.

4. Obstacles to success are made apparent at earlier stages.

5. A mechanism is provided for effective transfer of perspective, knowledge, and know-how by providing continuing participation of individuals who were active in earlier stages.

6. By including as consultants individuals who are to be directly involved in later stages, they become identified with the project and are better oriented for subsequent work.

7. Task forces, by encouraging participation of specialists from many functional groups, discourage empire-building tendencies in individual sections.

8. Better utilization is made of technical skills throughout the company.

9. Professional development of technical personnel is stimulated by association with a wider circle of colleagues and by involvement in a broad range of problems.

10. The research and development department becomes a flatter organization, with fewer people sequestered in administrative echelons.

Coordination of Successive Task Forces. A task-force system is particularly advantageous for carrying out a development project in successive stages. It encourages the incorporation of future requirements in the program and the transfer of accumulated knowledge and background into later stages.

FUNCTIONS ⟶

STAGES	APPLIED RESEARCH	PRODUCT DEVELOPMENT	ENGINEERING DEVELOPMENT	MARKET RESEARCH	MANAGEMENT	MARKETING	GENERAL ENGINEERING	PURCHASING	MANUFACTURING	FINANCE	LEGAL
PRODUCT DEFINITION	▩	▨	◪	◪	○	○		○			○
PRODUCT DEVELOPMENT	▨	▩	◪	◪	○			○	○		
PROCESS DEVELOPMENT	○	▨	▩		○		◪	○	○		○
FIELD EVALUATION		◪	○	▩	○		◪				
PROCESS CONFIRMATION			◪	▩	○	○	◪		◪	○	
MARKET CONFIRMATION	○		○	▨	○	◪	◪	○			○
COMPREHENSIVE REVIEW	○	◪	◪	◪	▨	◪	◪	◪	◪		
IMPLEMENTATION	○	○	○	○	▨	◪	◪	◪	◪	◪	○

KEY: TEAM LEADERSHIP AND BRUNT OF ACTIVITY ▩
DIRECT PARTICIPATION IN TECHNICAL WORK ▨
CONSULTATIVE RELATIONSHIP ◪
INFORMATION REQUIREMENT FOR DECISION, ○
COMMENT, OR PREPARATION

FIG. 3-3. *Coordination chart for successive task forces.*

Figure 3-3 illustrates the pattern of involvement of different types of skills in a major project from original concept through commercialization. It designates the functional group which has responsibility for providing a team leader at each stage, and usually a considerable part of the work is done by this group. It shows other functions which will often be needed to provide personnel for active participation. It points out other groups or individuals who can provide consultative help. Finally, it indicates the groups or individuals who should receive information about progress, both to express comments and to make preparation for any actions they need to take.

Obviously, it would not be feasible to expect the succession of project teams at different stages to spring into being spontaneously without some guidance. Hence, it is the responsibility of management to see that the project moves forward. For this purpose, a project coordinator or overseer should be appointed, and he should have the requisite background, breadth, and authority for maintaining an optimum rate of progress.

CONCLUSION

Good management demands continual improvement in product line and technology. Research and development programs are the usual sources of these improvements. The composite technical skills of the organization should be deployed on individual projects in accordance with a master plan for meeting corporate goals.

Product and process development work can be controlled effectively by a project system which recognizes the characteristics of separate stages and different degrees of innovation. These stages provide a series of checkpoints for stepwise evaluation before additional work is undertaken. The evaluation becomes increasingly meaningful as the amount of information accumulates.

Communication between separate functional groups becomes increasingly difficult as organizations expand. Network coordination schemes and multidiscipline task forces are effective aids in planning and scheduling projects.

BIBLIOGRAPHY

Bass, Lawrence W., *The Management of Technical Programs,* Frederick A. Praeger, Inc., New York, 1965.

Heyel, Carl (ed.), *Handbook of Industrial Research Management,* Reinhold Publishing Corporation, New York, 1959.

Hilton, Peter, *Handbook of New Product Development,* Prentice-Hall, Inc., Englewood Cliffs, N.J., 1961.

Lothrop, Warren C., *Management Uses of Research & Development,* Harper & Row Publishers, Incorporated, New York, 1964.

Perry, John H. (ed.), *Chemical Business Handbook,* McGraw-Hill Book Company, New York, 1954.

Roberts, Edward B., *The Dynamics of Research and Development,* Harper & Row, Publishers, Incorporated, New York, 1965.

Stanley, Alexander O., and K. K. White, *Organizing the R&D Function,* American Management Association, Inc., New York, 1965.

Tyler, Chaplin, and C. H. Winter, Jr., *Chemical Engineering Economics,* 4th ed., McGraw-Hill Book Company, New York, 1959.

CHAPTER FOUR

Research Management—
Budgetary and Accounting Controls

RAYMOND VILLERS *Professor, Graduate School of Business Administration, Pace College, and Consultant in Industrial Management, Rautenstrauch and Villers, New York, New York*

Modern industry faces a new challenge. To meet competition, research work is increasingly needed to improve existing products and to develop new products. At the same time, one-man research work has been virtually eliminated. Invention has become the cooperative product of many minds and many talents in large research laboratories.

In recent years, more and more companies have modernized the fundamental aspects of research management and have used well-adjusted procedures for budgetary control and accounting control of R&D expenditures. Their experience has shown that management can reconcile the need for profit making with the need to stimulate the freedom of thinking of the research people.

Not only must research work be effectively coordinated with marketing, manufacturing, and purchasing activities, but the activities of all specialized scientists and engineers must also be effectively coordinated within a research center and among the divisions, so as to make it possible to keep the increasing research expenditures within the financial resources of the company. Also, new functions, such as new-products development, research administration, value analysis, and reliability engineering are needed to bridge the gap between all specialists involved in developing, making, and selling profitable products.

RESEARCH MANAGEMENT

Coordination of Efforts between the Research Center and the Divisions. A duplication of efforts in research work conducted in various divisions and/or at the research center can result in a substantial waste of time and money. On the other hand, competition may step in before the product is ready if the division

5–58

involved fails to recognize quickly that a discovery made at the research center could help to increase its sales volume.

The problem of coordination of efforts within a large company is especially complex for companies which have grown through acquisition of companies having their own research organizations. But, even if this is not the case, special procedures are needed to avoid the waste of time and effort within a divisionalized company. Two points deserve special attention.

1. It is important to clarify the position of the vice president—research who, at corporate level, reviews the research work conducted throughout the company. In too many companies, he can act only as a consultant. It should be his authority and responsibility to avoid duplication of efforts within the company. The experience of many companies has shown that he can act in this position without affecting the independence of the divisional general managers.

2. After effective research work has been completed at the research center, it is important not to waste time in bringing new products on the market.

The case of Company A is very instructive. As is done in most companies, the research center recommends to a division that it take advantage of some accomplishment leading toward new products. But the unusual and very advisable procedure is that the research center's recommendation includes a time limit. After the time limit has passed, if the division has not accepted the offer, the corporate vice president—research takes over automatically, tests the potential market, and reports to top management. The decision is then made either to drop the project, to convince a division to go ahead, to sell to outsiders the patent rights and the benefit of market analysis and development work, or to start a new business in the field by acquisition or the formation of a new division.

At Company A, since this procedure has been in effect, there have been fewer rejections by the divisions of offers made by the corporate research center.

Coordination of Efforts between All Functions Involved. To be profitable to the company, a new product developed by the research function must be made by the manufacturing function at such a cost that the marketing function can sell a sufficient number of units at the price that brings an adequate return on investment. To help attain this ultimate goal, the research people must understand the problems faced by the other functions. But at the same time they must be able to concentrate their thinking on their scientific problems. This is why a special effort must be made to bridge the gap between the functions involved.

Communication between Research and Marketing People. Both functions should be encouraged to make suggestions either for the improvement of existing products or for the development of new products. But they should be helped to understand each other. The research people should not merely be told, as they are in quite a few companies, that they should "meet competition."

After a suggestion of the marketing people has been processed through the appropriate channel, the research people should receive a written memo indicating clearly the technical goal of a specific project to be considered by them.

Communication between Research and Manufacturing People. The geographical location of the research center makes it almost impossible, in most cases, for the research people to know as much as they should about the manufacturing problems.

Time and money will be lost if the research work has to be started again because the need for improvement is detected only when production starts. Even more will be lost if the need for improvement is detected after production has started, when it is found that the equipment available does not make it possible to meet the process specifications without unduly increasing the cost of production and/or the rate of rejects.

An unusual and effective approach is followed at Company B. The system used provides for a "transition period" when a project is transferred from the corporate research center to the R&D laboratory of an operating division. During the transition period both research groups work together. The manufacturing engineers of the operating division, who are familiar with production problems, serve as useful advisers to the research people.

Another approach that has proved to be effective in many companies is to have pilot plant facilities at the research center. The cost of such a pilot plant is tangible, while the resulting savings in cost and time are almost intangible. They are likely, however, to be very substantial.

The use of the pilot plant avoids the loss of time likely to occur when the research people request a test and the plant manager involved answers that production cannot be interrupted abruptly.

The experience of several companies has also indicated that a pilot plant at the research center greatly increases the rate of technical progress. The scientists become acquainted with production problems and can use the facilities immediately to provide a prompt answer to a specific problem. Also, the people in maintenance, quality control, and machine operation who operate the pilot plant can advise the research engineers, because of their personal contacts. As a result, the process specifications delivered to the division's plant are more likely to be effective.

Use of Meetings. Regular periodic meetings can help if they permit an exchange of views among directors of research, sales managers, production managers, and financial executives. In addition, the scientists and engineers should be encouraged to request meetings with other specialists whenever they discover the need for a technical approach different from the one that had been anticipated. At their meetings, the various specialists involved can exchange their views and determine the optimum solution. For instance, a meeting of research engineers, cost estimators, and marketing people will make it possible to evaluate the pros and cons of improving the product, that is, increasing the cost of production and the selling price.

Coordination of Efforts among Scientists and Engineers—Scheduling Methods. In recent years, more and more recognition has been given to the fact that most of the research work, even that involving "basic research," can and should be scheduled. This is not only because research work has to be related to the time element for marketing and financial reasons. It is also because the rate of technical progress has increased so rapidly in recent years that the one-man research work has been virtually eliminated.

Invention today is the cooperative product of specialists such as mechanical engineers, chemists, nuclear physicists, and electronics engineers working as a group. If their activities are not scheduled, the individuals involved may not only lose time but also be prevented from developing new ideas by having to wait too long either for the information they need from another scientist or for the assistance of their technical services at the laboratory where they work.

A prerequisite to the successful use of schedules for research work is a clear understanding of the spirit in which the system will be used. Although the same word, "schedule," is used for plant production or bus transportation, it must be understood that the scheduling of R&D operations differs from other types of scheduling.

Management must avoid a serious misunderstanding by making it clear that

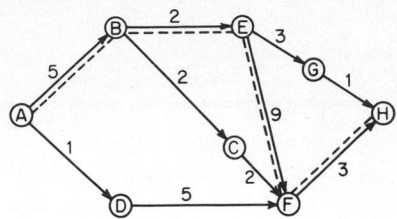

FIG. 4-1. *The PERT network after timing.*

a schedule is not a commitment and that to meet the schedule is only the secondary goal.   The primary goal is to be technically successful.

At the same time, the research people must understand that it is their duty to follow the schedule whenever feasible without affecting their technical performance and to report as soon as possible, but never after the deadline has passed, if they cannot meet the schedule they have accepted at their own discretion.

The time unit should be the week, using a week serial number from 1 to 52 for the whole year.   This provides the flexibility needed by the scientists involved.   When they agree to complete a job within three weeks, starting week 17, it means that they will meet the schedule whether they are ready by Monday or by Friday of week 20.   Some services require only half a day of work, and in such a case, a special memorandum should make it clear in writing that the job has to be completed by Wednesday, 3 P.M., of week 35.   This, however, should be the exception, not the rule.

The PERT network provides the overall picture of a complex project after specific events A, B, C, D, . . . have been selected as milestones and after the time element related to each activity, from one event to the other, has been estimated.   As shown in Figure 4-1, the critical path (the dashed line) can be clearly identified.[1]

The Gantt chart associated with functional decentralization goes into more detail.   It also stimulates the freedom of action of each individual involved in the research work.   It clarifies the position of the project engineer who will work with them without interfering at all with the organizational structure of the research center.   The project engineer, using the form shown in Figure 4-2, has the responsibility of listing all steps to be taken by each scientist or by a department, such as technical service or purchasing.   The names of the scientists and of the supervisors of the departments involved are listed, and the scheduled dates for the start and the completion of their tasks are shown on the form.   But this is done by the project engineer only after his request has been accepted by those whose names are listed.   If they cannot accept his request, they will explain why.   The project engineer will not insist, because he is responsible only for reporting to the adequate level of management that his project conflicts with another one or that outside services are needed.

After the project engineer has completed the schedule, each of the individuals involved should receive a copy of it.   This greatly stimulates their sense of responsibility.   They can see clearly that a delay on the step for which they are responsible will affect many other individuals.   For this reason, they will be encouraged to notify the project engineer as soon as possible that they "will be late," but they will never make the unacceptable mistake of reporting that

[1] For a detailed study, see Robert W. Miller, *Schedule, Cost, and Profit Control with PERT*, McGraw-Hill Book Company, New York, 1964.

STEP NO.	STEP DESIGNATION	RESPONSIBILITY FOR STEP	WEEK NO.								
JOB NO. _____		DISTRIBUTION	PAGE _____ OF _____ PAGES								
PROJECT ENGINEER			DATE ISSUED								
			REVISIONS								

FIG. 4-2. *The Gantt chart, associated with functional decentralization.*

they "were late." The distribution of the schedules also provides for each individual a record of his commitments. It enables him to explain clearly and quickly why he cannot accept a new assignment without being relieved of a previous one. It also calls attention to the possibility of idle time.[2]

There is no conflict between the PERT network and the Gantt chart. The PERT network provides the overall picture and makes it possible to detect the critical path. This is needed for a complex project involving hundreds or thousands of events. In such a case, scheduling should start with the PERT network. It must be recognized, however, that the individuals responsible for the research work should be identified. This can be done by analyzing step by step each activity of the network, using the Gantt chart, and applying the concept of functional decentralization under which each individual is free to accept or refuse a schedule.

If the project is not too complex, it is advisable to start right away with the Gantt chart.

Need for New Functions. Effective communication among all specialists is, of course, a prerequisite to their coordinated effort. But, because of increasing specialization, new functions have been introduced in recent years to narrow the enlarging gap between all functions, especially with regard to R&D operations.[3]

Research Administration. As a new function, research administration should assist the research personnel in budgeting and cost evaluation, handling requests for new projects, and issuing periodic reports. This new function can also operate as liaison between research and all other functions.

If the PERT system is used, research administration should collect the information, prepare the network, and revise it when needed.

The experience of several companies has shown that this new function can also save much time and reduce the risk of duplication of efforts within the company as well as the risk of discovering the obstacle of patent infringement only after research work has been completed. Research administration collects confidential inside information related to research work and is responsible for reading and classifying recent literature related to technical fields of interest

[2] For more details, see R. Villers, *Dynamic Management in Industry,* Prentice-Hall, Inc., Englewood Cliffs, N.J., 1960, chap. 11; and R. Villers, *Research and Development: Planning and Control,* Financial Executives Research Foundation, New York, 1964, chap. 5.

[3] For more details on this subject, see R. Villers, *Research and Development: Planning and Control,* chaps. 9 and 10.

to the company. When working in a specific area, the scientists, at their request, will receive a well-selected list of the books, articles, and papers they should read. They do not have to make the selection and do not run as much risk of not finding the information they need.

New-products Development. This new function should take over the responsibility for market analysis, so as to evaluate the potential market of a product that is not yet ready. This market analysis should not be the duty of those who are concerned, as they should be, with selling current products.

New-products development should also be responsible for model making and test selling and for the orientation of future research work.

Value Analysis. Value analysis is needed as a new function to reduce the cost of producing a new product. To avoid wasting money, the new parts should be standardized or be the same as those already made for other products whenever this does not conflict with the technical requirements of the new product. Also, the material selected should be as inexpensive as possible. Research scientists and engineers should retain control of the final decision, but they need assistance from the value analysis function. They cannot be expected to collect all the information needed or to spend too much time in investigating the material purchase price.[4]

Reliability Engineering. As a specialized new function, reliability engineering reviews the completed research work before production starts, determines the probability of failure of a given design, and relates this probability to the consequence of such a failure. The reliability engineer does not interfere with research work. He acts as a consultant and provides the assistance needed by the scientists.[5]

BUDGETARY CONTROL

Total R&D Expenditures. From an accounting point of view, R&D expenditures are a "current expense." As such, they are deducted from the total sales when the profit for the year is computed even though, as a rule, either a small part of their total, or none, is related to the products sold during that year.

To decide how much money to allocate for next year for research work, management must reconcile the need for profit making now with the need to keep the company profitable in the years to come.

To select the optimum solution, three fundamental factors deserve special attention: return on investment, the stability of the research staff, and the market position of the company.

The return on investment desired, on the basis of high policy decision, is x percent of I. The profit P expected for the coming year should first be computed before the R&D expenditures are deducted. Thus the goal is

$$P - \text{R\&D expenditures} = \frac{x}{100} I$$

This goal can be expected to be reached if

$$\text{R\&D expenditures} = P - \frac{x}{100} I$$

[4] For a detailed study, see L. D. Miles, *Techniques of Value Analysis and Engineering*, McGraw-Hill Book Company, New York, 1961.

[5] For a detailed study, see S. R. Calabro, *Reliability Principles and Practices*, McGraw-Hill Book Company, New York, 1962.

The figure resulting from this computation is no substitute for decision making, but should be available when the other factors are considered.

The stability of the research staff is not an absolutely rigid rule, but it is very desirable. Research people who are laid off may help competitors one day or another by giving them the benefit of their experience. But an even more serious risk is that the talented scientists who have been kept may be lost because they feel insecure and look for another job.

After the above formula has indicated what the R&D expenditures can be without affecting the return on investment, the cost of keeping the research staff should be compared with this figure. If this cost exceeds the desirable maximum for R&D expenditures, its impact on the expected return on investment should be computed and submitted to the board of directors.

Unless the company faces a serious financial problem, the stability of the research staff is more important for the success in the years to come than the strict adherence to the return on investment formula.

The market position of the company can be measured, if the figures are available, by comparing the current share of the total market with what it has been in the past. Other factors related to information about competition may be considered. The decision can then be made to spend more money on research. The money may be allocated for the use of outside services, either because the research needed is very specific or because it does not justify a permanent expansion of the research staff. The impact of such an expansion of research expenditures on the return on investment can be computed at this point. The decision will be made after evaluating the pros and cons of expanding the research work, either by increasing the staff or using outside services.

After these three essential factors have been related to each other, the board of directors will make the optimum decision with regard to the budget for total R&D expenditures.

Budget for Each Division. To reconcile the need for profit making now with the need to be successful in five years is more a challenge for the division general manager than for corporate management.

Research work cannot be successful 100 percent of the time. The x dollars spent on a given project mean a much bigger risk if expressed in percent of the profit of the division than if expressed in percent of the corporate profit. Furthermore, the return on investment is too often considered at corporate level as the rigid standard of measurement of the division general manager's performance.

Analyzing the Budget. An analysis of the budget is advisable to clarify the situation. If a lump sum is allocated for R&D, most of it may be spent for cost reduction. This is why many companies follow the procedure of splitting the budget. The budgets of the divisions can be compared with each other by using a company standard classification and percentage figures. For instance, one division's budget may be:

Basic research	10 percent
New-products development	35 percent
Assistance to manufacturing	30 percent
Assistance to sales	25 percent

Case of Company C. Computing an adjusted return on investment is an unusual but highly advisable approach. When a division of Company C has a big expenditure related to specific research projects, its impact on the return on investment is evaluated and the current performance is considered independently. When the new product is introduced on the market, the profit and loss statement of the division is adjusted by deducting the sales of the new product from the total sales, and the cost of manufacturing and marketing the new product from the total cost.

This adjustment of the return on investment formula clarifies the picture. As proved by the experience of Company C, it encourages the division general managers to request a budget for R&D expenditures that will not only protect the company now but also improve its position in the years to come.

Budget for Each Level of Management. Much of the research expenditure is spent on projects approved by top management. But it is well recognized that part of the total budget should provide free time for the senior scientists who should be allowed to spend about 10 percent of their time conducting research work at their discretion. It is also well recognized that each level of research management should have the privilege of spending some money at its own discretion.

The source of a serious conflict is the splitting within the budgets of the director of research, the department heads, and the section heads. Their budgets should be split so as to allocate some of the money to research work that will most likely bring a profit and some to research work that is merely of great interest to the scientists involved.

A problem is created by the use of the terminology "basic research," "applied research," and "development." Even if there is a joint agreement to adopt one of the many conflicting definitions which have been offered, no clear-cut line can be drawn. There is a zone of transition between these various categories.

Too often there will be a serious disagreement, in complete good faith, between the research people who charge a project as "applied research" and the controller's office where the conclusion is reached that the "basic research" portion of the budget was exceeded because this is how the project should be charged. The answer to this problem is the use of clear-cut definitions.

An interesting fact is that the cost of research is closely related to the time element. As a rule, wages and salaries represent about 75 percent of the total R&D expenditures. This means that money can be allocated periodically for research work that is not scheduled, but that the total cost of a nonscheduled project cannot be estimated.

Some research work is expected to bring a new product or improve an existing one. In such a case, it is reasonable to estimate the expected benefit. But some research work is merely intended to explore new ideas in a specific direction, and no benefit in dollars can be estimated.

It is highly advisable to split the budget for each level of research management in four clear-cut categories:

1. Preproduct-oriented, nonscheduled research
2. Preproduct-oriented, scheduled research
3. Product-oriented, nonscheduled research
4. Product-oriented, scheduled research

Thus, the financially conscious executives can decide how much the company should spend in category 4, which involves less risk, and how much it can afford to spend in the other categories, especially the most risky category 1.

After the decision has been made, there will be no argument. The research people are free to schedule their work or not, and free to conduct some research work without having to indicate what product they expect to develop, as long as they remain within their budget for each of these four clear-cut categories.

Budgeting and Selecting Specific Projects. The clear-cut definitions suggested

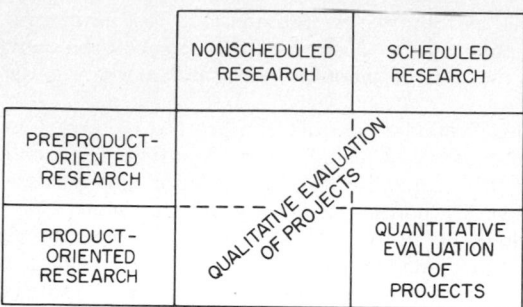

FIG. 4-3. *The borderline between qualitative and quantitative evaluation of projects.*

above will also help clarify the picture for the budgeting and the selection of projects.

As shown in Figure 4-3, a quantitative evaluation should be made only if the research is product-oriented and scheduled, that is, if it is reasonable to estimate both the expected sales volume and the cost of research.

Qualitative Evaluation of Preproduct-oriented and Nonscheduled Projects. No attempt can be made to evaluate in dollars the benefit that can be expected. It should also be recognized that the budget is merely an allocation of money, and cannot be related to specific technical goals inasmuch as the time element, that is, about 75 percent of the expense, is unpredictable.

Qualitative Evaluation of Product-oriented and Nonscheduled Projects. The cost of research in this category is also unpredictable, but a reasonable estimate of the expected benefits can help clarify the situation when the decision is made to allocate money for research. The ultimate goal is not related to the money allocated.

Qualitative Evaluation of Preproduct-oriented and Scheduled Projects. No attempt can be made to evaluate the expected benefit in dollars, but at least the budget can be related to a specific technical goal after a schedule has been prepared by the research people.

Quantitative Evaluation of Product-oriented and Scheduled Projects. The research budget, related to a specific technical goal and the expected expenditures for new equipment or special marketing expenses, can be considered as an investment. A market analysis and an estimate of the cost of production will make it possible to compute the expected return on investment. The amount of return should be related to the probability of success in research work and the probability of marketing success. Periodic reviews of the budget are desirable, because the more research work conducted, the more accurate are the sales volume estimates at various price levels. The estimates of the cost of production can also be expected to be more accurate.[6]

ACCOUNTING CONTROL

Relating the Money Spent to Technical Progress. The controller's office should prepare a periodic financial report showing for each project how much money has been spent during the period considered and on a cumulative basis since the start of the project.

[6] For more details, see R. Villers, *Research and Development: Planning and Control,* chaps. 4 and 9.

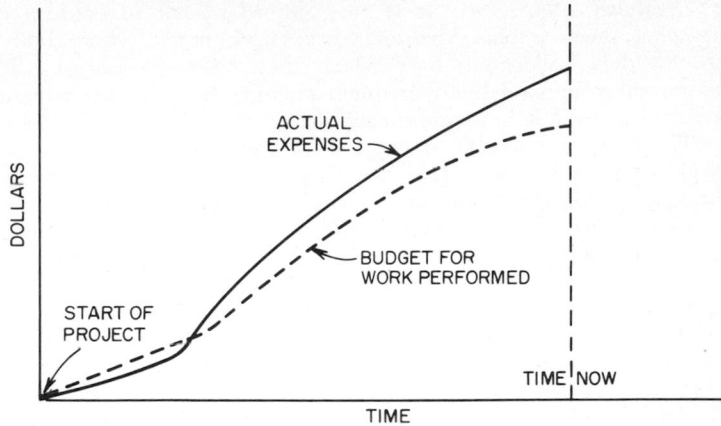

FIG. 4-4. *Actual expenses versus the budget for the work performed on a scheduled project.*

To relate this report to technical progress requires drawing the line between scheduled and nonscheduled projects.

For *scheduled projects,* the controller's office or the research administration function can use the Gantt chart previously described[7] to prepare the graph shown in Figure 4-4. After the research people have indicated which steps have been completed, it is easy to compute the "budget for work performed" and to compare it with the actual expenses.

For *nonscheduled projects,* the actual expenses can be compared with the budget. A periodic technical-progress report should be submitted by the scientists involved, but it is not realistic to try to relate the percentage of money spent to a "percentage of technical progress."

The step-by-step budget is an advisable approach to reduce the impact of the financial uncertainty. The original proposal should include a description of the "long-range objective" and also that of an "immediate objective." When the immediate objective is reached within the budget, or as soon as the money allocated has been spent before the objective is reached, the one who approved the project reviews the situation and decides whether to allocate more money.

The scientists involved should be encouraged to schedule a previously non-scheduled project as soon as they are in a position to do so after reaching one of the "immediate objectives" of the step-by-step budget.

The Need to Adjust the Usual Accounting Procedures. Rigid procedures will discourage talented scientists from cooperating with financial management.

Recording of Time. The research people should be asked to record the time they spend on a specific project or on a trip or at meetings and to record absence because of vacation or sickness. But it is very important not to impose upon them the burden of accounting exactly for forty hours per week. Also, they should not be prevented, because they are overtime exempt, from recording more than forty hours after they have spent a weekend or several nights on a project to which they are devoted.

The need for flexibility can be reconciled with the need for effective control by issuing a weekly report that shows for each department how much time was paid for and how much was accounted for. One hundred percent accuracy should not be expected, but if the variance is excessive, the department manager should review the situation.

[7] See p. 5–61.

Overhead Allocation. It is very important not to confuse the scientists by showing them actual expenses versus the budget where both figures include the overhead allocation over which they have no control. This is especially important where relatively frequent changes in overhead rates introduce an uncontrolled variable in measurement of project performance.

The best approach is to prepare for the scientists involved a financial report that shows only the actual expenses over which they have control versus a budget including only the same kind of expenses.

Use of Actual Wages and Salaries. The wages and salaries of the scientists, engineers, and employees of technical services vary so much even within one department that the use of averages, which of course saves paperwork, often distorts the picture and may seriously discourage the research people. They may feel sure that they met the schedule of a project, but are told that they did not meet the budget. The use of averages may also misinform management if the budget, which was actually exceeded, is met accountingwise.

Capital Expenditures. Scientists cannot issue advance specifications for equipment they will need for testing or model making later on. The approval of their requests for the purchase of such equipment should not be delayed unduly.

It is advisable to ask the board of directors to authorize the various levels of research management to approve capital expenditures within specific limits.

The Need for Long-range Follow-up. Accounting procedures must be adjusted, because as a rule research work must be expected to take more than one fiscal year to reach a specific goal. The sense of responsibility of those who provide the estimates used for decision making will be greatly stimulated if they expect a long-range follow-up. Also, past mistakes should not be considered as "water over the dam"; they should be analyzed, to avoid similar mistakes in the future.

Long-range Follow-up of Budgets for Projects. Expenses should be recorded on a cumulative basis since the start of the project, regardless of the length of time.

The revised budget should be compared with the original one, as well as the actual expenses with the revised budget. Otherwise, the people involved will be tempted to request at first much less than they need and then request revisions frequently enough to meet exactly the last revised budget.

Record of Money Spent on Dropped or Deferred Projects. The one who decides to drop or defer a project often does so only to remain within his budget. But his decision involves a loss of time and money. It may also disturb the scientists who not only have to wait but may be unable to remember their brilliant ideas.

Keeping a record will encourage those who are responsible for decision making to avoid starting too many unsuccessful projects which must be dropped and to avoid deferring or even dropping projects that would most likely bring rewarding results.

Record of Money Spent by Kind of Research. After the decision has been made to split the budget in such categories as product-oriented, preproduct-oriented, scheduled, and nonscheduled research, the actual expenses should be recorded by category. The project serial number should therefore include a digit that will identify the category.

Analysis of Variance of Return on Investment. After a new product is sold on the market, it is important to analyze the variance between the actual and the estimated return on investment, even though the estimates were made a long time ago.

It will stimulate the sense of responsibility of those who make estimates if they know that there will be such a follow-up, especially if, as should be done, their names are kept on record.

CONCLUSION

To avoid the conflict between management mind and scientific mind which has become so evident in recent years,[8] modernized procedures must be introduced for R&D operations.

Effective coordination of efforts is needed between the research center and the divisions and among the research people, marketing people, and manufacturing people.

Also, because research work requires the coordination of efforts of many scientists and engineers, scheduling systems must be provided. This should be done with the clear understanding that they will be used with complete flexibility and that the freedom of each individual will be stimulated by applying the concept of functional decentralization.

The services of new functions such as research administration, new-products development, value analysis, and reliability engineering are needed.

The various R&D budgets prepared for the whole company, the divisions, the research departments, or specific projects must be related to each other. When the decision is made to allocate money for research, full recognition must be given to the fact that the research work must be ultimately profitable but that some flexibility is advisable to stimulate the thinking of the scientists.

Accounting control is required, but the traditional procedures must be adjusted to stimulate the spirit of cooperation of those involved in research work.

BIBLIOGRAPHY

Books

Calabro, S. R., *Reliability Principles and Practices,* McGraw-Hill Book Company, New York, 1962.

Howard, George W., *Common Sense in R&D Management,* Vantage Press, New York, 1955.

Miles, Lawrence D., *Techniques of Value Analysis and Engineering,* McGraw-Hill Book Company, New York, 1961.

Miller, Robert W., *Schedule, Cost, and Profit Control with PERT,* McGraw-Hill Book Company, New York, 1964.

Seiler, Robert E., *Improving the Effectiveness of Research and Development,* McGraw-Hill Book Company, New York, 1965.

Stanley, A. O., and K. K. White, *Organizing the R&D Function,* American Management Association, New York, 1965.

Steele, G., and P. Kircher, *The Crisis We Face,* McGraw-Hill Book Company, New York, 1960.

Villers, Raymond, *Dynamic Management in Industry,* Prentice-Hall, Inc., Englewood Cliffs, N.J., 1960.

Villers, Raymond, *Research and Development: Planning and Control,* Financial Executives Research Foundation, New York, 1964.

Periodicals

Best, R. D., "The Scientific Mind vs. the Management Mind," *Industrial Research,* October, 1963.

Cudd, Herschel H., "A Technique for Improving Research and Development Communications," *Research Management,* Autumn, 1961.

Norden, Peter V., "On the Anatomy of Development" and "SCARDE—A Progress Report and an Invitation to Participate," *IRE Transactions on Engineering Management,* March, 1960, and March, 1961.

[8] See R. D. Best, "The Scientific Mind vs. the Management Mind," *Industrial Research,* October, 1963.

CHAPTER FIVE

Project Management

JOHN STANLEY BAUMGARTNER *Center for Management Sciences, Los Angeles, California, and Lecturer, R&D Management, Graduate School of Business, University of Southern California, Los Angeles, California*

In the early 1950s, the Air Force and large segments of industry were confronted with a problem of tremendous scope: how to develop an ICBM, with all the technical complexities and breakthroughs involved, in half the time usually required for a far simpler weapon system. Normally, responsibility in the government and in industry for development of a major system was fragmented among numerous agencies, departments, and associated functional organizations. If this practice were followed in development of the ICBM, however, the one or two dozen years required for its development would virtually assure its being obsolescent and ineffective by the time it became operational.

The solution lay in "projectizing"—organizing and managing the effort primarily on the basis of its technical, cost, and schedule objectives, rather than on the basis of existing organizations and procedures.

The success of that effort and continuing pressures for technological breakthroughs in space and defense systems, as well as intense competition in industrial and commercial markets, led to widespread application of project management in both industry and the government. In dollar value, the products of project management for government research and development alone exceed $20 billion per year.[1]

Superimposing a project-oriented organization on functional organizations as in Figure 5-1 obviously presents a number of problems in planning, control, and organizational relationships, however. The purpose of this chapter is to capsulize these problem areas and to outline some practical solutions to them.

PLANNING

Most difficulties in project operation, such as schedule slippages, personnel and organization problems, excessive expenditures, and the effects of unexpected

[1] J. S. Baumgartner, *Project Management*, Richard D. Irwin, Inc., Homewood, Ill., 1963.

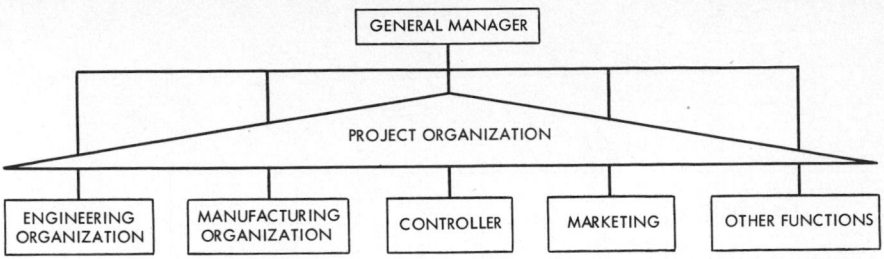

FIG. 5-1. *Superimposed project organization.* (*From* Project Management, *Richard D. Irwin, Inc., Homewood, Ill., 1963.*)

changes, are directly traceable to weaknesses in planning. Personnel and organization problems, for instance, usually stem from not clearly defining relationships between the project and functional organizations and from inadequate orientation on project objectives, the project team, and where the individual fits into the project organization. Time and money problems frequently arise because schedules and budgets are not sufficiently realistic or because they are not maintained vigorously enough.

Planning is particularly important in research and development project management because usually there is no other experience factor to rely on for comparing "actuals" versus previous experience, as there is in manufacturing. The plan itself, in R&D project management, is the standard against which deviations are measured; these deviations in turn indicate where management should take action. Management action in guiding project operations toward time, cost, and technical objectives is therefore highly dependent on a sound, comprehensive, flexible plan.

A "plan for planning" is extremely important in defining what the project plan or plans will consist of, who is responsible for each part of the plan, and due dates for development and revisions of each part. Figure 5-2 outlines one technique for keeping on top of this fundamental activity.

Several far-reaching problem areas merit particular attention in planning.

1. Confusion and loss of project control are often due to faulty work breakdown structure and to confused project/functional administrative practices. The work breakdown structure (project, task, subtask, black box, and so on) must include, for each "piece" of work, a statement of what is to be done; who the responsible manager is; how much time and money are to be allotted for the work; and what technical performance is to be achieved. Allotting a lump sum of funds to a functional department responsible for two or more project tasks virtually ensures loss of project control over these tasks. In large R&D organizations, the project manager may unintentionally contribute to this loss of control by working primarily through functional management rather than through the project organizational structure.

2. Related to the preceding point, and probably the most difficult problem in project management, is the matter of project/functional responsibilities and authority. Who has authority, for instance, over the design engineer in an electronics development department who is working on a communication link for a project? There is no commonly accepted "solution" in defining this relationship, nor is this fact particularly pertinent. What *is* important is that the working arrangement, whatever it may be, must be clearly understood and practiced by the project manager, the department manager, and the engineer himself. In determining this arrangement, physical location, maintaining technical

TYPE OR PURPOSE OF PLANS

PLANNING TASKS	PROJECT OPERATION PLAN	UP-DATE PLANNING	CHANGES IN SCOPE/DIRECTION	TRANSITION PLANNING	CONTINGENCY PLANNING	PROJECT EXPANSION	STOP WORK	ETC
TASK BREAKDOWN AND DEFINITION								
MAKE OR BUY								
SCHEDULING								
BUDGETING			PLANNED DATES					
RELIABILITY AND PERFORMANCE								
ORGANIZATION			FOR STARTING AND COMPLETING EACH					
FACILITIES			PLAN, AND PERSON RESPONSIBLE FOR EACH PLAN					
SUBCONTRACTOR SELECTION								
FISCAL PLANNING								
PERSONNEL								
REPORTING								
TERMINATION								
STOP WORK								
EXPANDING THE CONTRACT BASE								

FIG. 5-2. *Project planning summary.* (*From* Project Management, *Richard D. Irwin, Inc., Homewood, Ill., 1963.*)

proficiency, and responsibility for periodic reviews become important considerations. (In some organizations, such as a propulsion development facility in Texas, the engineer's annual review—and resulting effect on his salary—is made out by both department and project managers.)

3. Both cumulative and rate (of progress, expenditures, manpower application, and the like) plans may be necessary to detect trends requiring management action.

4. Personnel indoctrination and a systematic means of keeping personnel informed warrant thorough and effective planning. The project manager who finds that project operations seem to have bogged down after an early, enthusiastic period has probably overlooked the importance of making his people as effective as possible.

5. Plans must be flexible without being detailed to the extent that they become straitjackets. A straitjacket plan in a rapid-moving project situation invites its being rejected.

As in any kind of planning, the plan is more realistic and more enthusiastically carried out when the "doers" take an effective part in planning.

PROJECT CONTROL

The history of major R&D projects during the decade from the early fifties to the early sixties is replete with examples of costs ballooning to two or three times the proposal estimate and deliveries slipping by as much as two years or more. One reason for these horrible examples was that proposals were unrealistically optimistic. Largely, however, the reason for these excesses was inadequate controls on progress, expenditures, and technical achievement. To the great credit of the Secretary of Defense and the long-term benefit of defense contractors and subcontractors, a series of directed changes in defense procurement in 1963 and 1964, such as evaluation of contractor performance and sharply reduced use of cost-type contracts, resulted in much better project controls. Recognition of control problems and development of interest and techniques in resolving them have permeated industrial and commercial R&D projects as well as government programs.

What are project controls, and what is their purpose? Briefly, the purpose of controls is to show the project manager whether he is "on the beam" as he proceeds toward the technical, time, and cost objectives of the project, and to show him where to take corrective action if there are significant deviations. Controls, to be effective, must lead directly to action by the project or other manager; gathering of data which is merely "nice to know" or which a contractor believes will please his customer, regardless of its utility value, is an extravagance that few competitive organizations can afford.

Management action is highlighted by comparing "actuals" versus plans—actual versus scheduled progress, actual versus budgeted costs, and actual versus planned manpower, for example. On projects which extend over a year or more, it frequently is helpful to have both a cumulative and a rate of expenditure control. For instance, the actual cumulative application (man-months) of electronic design engineers may be within the total manpower budgeted to the current time; but detecting and working out "bugs" may require an increase in manpower at a time when the funding allotment requires a decrease. This divergence is readily apparent when comparing planned *rates* of manpower application, but is more difficult to detect when comparing only *cumulative* application. On a project involving many tasks in-house and out-of-house, controls of this type are useful in pointing out deviations early, when the project manager can take corrective action fairly easily.

Comparison of actuals versus plan for time and cost factors individually is relatively straightforward. PERT (program evaluation and review technique), CPM (critical path method), Gantt (bar) charting, and other techniques provide means of measuring actual versus scheduled *progress*. The company's controller reports on actual *manpower* and *dollar* expenditures which, when compared with work-sheet or customer-approved budgets, provide action indicators for these two factors. The project manager needs to know also, however, whether he is getting satisfactory *achievement* for his money.

A continual comparison of progress versus cost versus technical performance is essential to sound control of project operations. For instance, a project task is not necessarily in financial trouble when actual expenditures exceed the budget, because progress may be correspondingly ahead of schedule. Nor is a missile necessarily over its cost and schedule problems when it arrives at a launch pad on schedule and within budget. If it blows up on the pad, the technical performance factor negates the apparent effectiveness of the administrative controls. Thus it is necessary to integrate these factors—time, cost, and technical performance—to evaluate true status and to detect trends. The question the

TRANSMITTER WORK BREAKDOWN STRUCTURE REQUIREMENTS PLAN

SYSTEM: ZENA — REPORTING ORGANIZATION: XYZ CORP. — CONTRACT NUMBER: 122-36455 — REPORT DATES: 1 JUL - 1 AUG — REPORTS CONTROL SYMBOL

LEVEL/SUMMARY ITEM: 5/TRANSMITTER

CHARACTERISTICS	BREADBOARD		MODEL #1			MODEL #2			PROTOTYPE #1			PROTOTYPE #2			SPECIFICATION / PREDICTION	REMARKS
TEST SEQUENCE NUMBER	1	2	3	4	5	6	7	8	9	10	11	12	13	14		
PEAK OUTPUT POWER	500 KW	500 KW	550 KW	600 KW	600 KW	600 KW	600 KW	600 KW	600 KW	600 KW	600 KW	600 KW	600 KW	600 KW	600 KW ± 5 KW	
FREQUENCY	3,000 MC	3,000 MC	3,000 MC	3,000 MC	3,000 MC	3,000 MC	3,000 MC	3,000 MC	3,000 MC	3,000 MC	3,000 MC	3,000 MC	3,000 MC	3,000 MC	3,000 MC ± 15 MC	
BANDWIDTH	50 MC	50 MC	40 MC	50 MC	50 MC	50 MC	50 MC	50 MC	50 MC	50 MC	50 MC	50 MC	50 MC	50 MC	50 MC ± 1MC	
WEIGHT			450 LB	450 LB	450 LB	375 LB	375 LB	375 LB	300 LB	300 LB	300 LB	300 LB	300 LB	300 LB	300 LB ± 5 LB	
SIZE			$3'\times2'\times2'$	$3'\times2'\times2'$	$3'\times2'\times2'$	$3'\times2'\times2'$	$3'\times2'\times2'$	$3'\times2'\times2'$	$3'\times2'\times2'$	$3'\times2'\times2'$	$3'\times2'\times2'$	$3'\times2'\times2'$	$3'\times2'\times2'$	$3'\times2'\times2'$	$3'\times2'\times2' \pm 1\%$	
OPERATING TEMPERATURE RANGE						20°-120°F	20°-120°F	20°-120°F	20°-120°F	20°-120°F	20°-120°F	20°-120°F	20°-120°F	20°-120°F	-20°F - +120°F	
SHOCK ENDURANCE						≤2G's	≤2G's	≤2G's	≤2G's	≤2G's	≤2G's	≤2G's	≤2G's	≤2G's	≤2G's	
RELIABILITY									300 HR	350 HR	400 HR	400 HR	400 HR	400 HR	MTBF ≤400 HR	
PREVENTIVE MAINTENANCE TIME									4%	3%	≤2%	≤2%	≤2%	≤2%	≤2%	
PREVENTIVE MAINTENANCE COST									$1,200	$1,000	$800	$800	$800	$800	≤$800/YR	
PRODUCIBILITY										$50 K	$40 K	$30 K	$20 K	$20 K	$20K (IN LOTS OF 20)	
TYPE, NAME, AND GRADE			SIGNATURE													

FIG. 5-3. *Technical objective milestones.*

project manager must answer is whether he is getting his money's worth at each point in time; and what the trend is, at each level of effort, if he is getting his money's worth. For a meaningful evaluation, it is apparent that each work package must have its own technical objectives and plan, schedule, and budget, and that the format of reports must enable him to make a comparison among these factors.

Two general techniques are intended to evaluate time-cost status versus the plan. The more prominent of these is PERT/cost, an outgrowth of PERT. Backed by the Department of Defense and NASA, this technique provides the project manager with a mass of data on cost and progress for work packages at several levels (e.g., project, task, subtask, black box). In spite of its official backing, however, the technique has generally been unsatisfactory in practice because of its cost and complexity. Its major weakness as a useful tool is that, even if and when programming and other technical difficulties in the technique are overcome, the massive data confronting the project manager still must somehow be analyzed in terms of what they mean to him. The project manager is in effect told, "Here are all the data you need. You figure out what they mean." As practiced to date, analysis of these data frequently amounts merely to substantiating obvious situations which the project manager had known for some time.

The other general approach in integrating time-cost factors is a comparison of input versus output, a technique successfully used by several major defense companies. Input is generally measured in dollars (actual versus planned), and output is measured in progress versus schedule. The two ratios are compared, and relative progress for the money on each work package is derived. This information indicates to the project manager where he is or is not getting his money's worth, where he should reallocate funds, and what kinds of action to take. Using the status index—a concise numerical indicator of output/input, or efficiency—the project manager can forecast "money's worth" and also evaluate the effectiveness of project planning.

The project manager must also evaluate technical achievement along with progress and cost. Usually technical achievement is compared with scheduled milestones to give a technical performance/schedule comparison. One of the most meaningful and most concise techniques in evaluating planned versus actual technical performance is contained in Army Materiel Command Regulation 11-16, vol. 2. Figure 5-3, from this publication, shows technical achievement in the development of a radio transmitter.

In summary, effective project controls show the project manager where and what kinds of action he should take to meet his project objectives. A comparison of actual progress, costs, manpower, and so on, versus the plan provides basic data for action; but true project control requires consideration of the interactions of time, money, and technical achievement. Only when the project manager knows whether he is getting his money's worth will he be in full control of project operations.

CONFIGURATION MANAGEMENT

The constant flow of engineering changes in a major development project may present a tremendous configuration-control problem. Any one proposed change may go through a number of steps before it is approved. The flow of hundreds of these changes and changes to changes, and accounting for the resulting configuration status, require a control system in themselves.

The need for configuration management is illustrated by the problem of maintaining first-generation ICBM's after they were in place.   In replacing and maintaining subsystems, it was found that almost no two missiles were identical! Further, changes which had been made during development were frequently not documented, so that the configuration of a missile might not be known until it was actually opened up.   A similar problem was detected on a series of high-performance aircraft.

The Air Force subsequently became the leading proponent of configuration management, the procedures by which a system of configuration identification, control, and accounting is established.   Some of the objectives of configuration management are to ensure that:[2]

All end items of equipment in a given series are the same

Delivered items are accurately and completely described by identifying documentation

Changes in end-item (e.g., an aerospace vehicle) configuration are reflected in corresponding changes in supporting tooling, spare parts, training, and the like

All proposed changes are evaluated and acted upon by a configuration control board (CCB)

The specific location and status of each end item is known at all times during the development and production phases

The effect of configuration management is to reduce development time and cost and assure that delivered items are operable on delivery.   The three major aspects of configuration management are as follows.

Configuration Identification.   The technical documentation defining the approved configuration is derived from work statements; analysis of technical requirements; performance, design, and test specifications; inspection of the first-delivered end item against descriptive documentation; and engineering-change proposals and other pertinent documents.

Configuration Control.   Control is exercised by an individual or group, responsible to the project manager, who evaluates and approves or disapproves changes after the configuration "base line" has been established.

Configuration Accounting.   Configuration status of deliverable hardware is compiled and reported by the project manager where required by his customer, as a means of keeping a running record on end-item configuration.

The importance of configuration management is reflected in a trend on some major projects, such as the Air Force's C-5A cargo aircraft, to award a single contract for development, production, and support phases.   The resulting tight configuration control throughout the life cycle is expected to increase the system's operational effectiveness considerably.

THE PROJECT ORGANIZATION

Generally projects involve two or more in-house functional organizations and a number of subcontractors and suppliers who work on project-deliverable items. One can appreciate the challenge confronting the project manager when he realizes that the project manager, in the usual case, depends on these organizations for meeting his project objectives but has no direct authority over them. The project manager must obviously have a high degree of skill in motivating, communicating with, and setting objectives for these elements, which are primarily responsive to someone else.

[2] *Configuration Management,* Air Force Systems Command Manual 375-1.

The following discussion outlines what constitutes the project organization, the relationship between the project manager and these elements, major problem areas and practical solutions to them, and development of the organization into a dynamic, "gung-ho" project team. The project organization considered here is the "partially projectized" type, which is more difficult and much more typical than the "fully projectized" type in which the project manager may be, as he is in some major missile and aircraft projects, a division manager with his own line organization.

Figure 5-4 shows the general relationship between the project and functional organizations. It is in specific areas of approval, coordination, primary responsibility, and information, however, that successful interface of the project and functional operations is determined. Figure 5-5 illustrates a simple, effective technique for defining these key relationships.

On large development projects, the practice of retaining systems work within the project office has evolved as a general principle. Thus, in the flow of work, system analysis and system engineering functions are performed by the project office; detail engineering and prototype fabrication and inspection are a function of engineering research or subcontractor organizations; and system test is a responsibility of the project office. The project office therefore determines the work to be done and determines whether its specifications have been met, although the greatest effort in terms of manpower and dollars is performed by functional and subcontractor organizations.

The In-house Organization. A key question in project management is how to control project operations while cutting across departmental and divisional lines within the project manager's company. The basis for this relationship is a work authorization (WA), which clearly states what is to be accomplished and the level of dollars and manpower allotted by months or other periods of time. The WA must be agreed to, after discussion and negotiation, by both project and functional parties; if agreement cannot be reached (a not unusual situation where stiff competition, tight funding, and a fixed-price contract are involved), the project manager should refer the matter to higher common authority, with his recommendations and basis for them. It is fundamental to planning, control, and the success of the project that disputes involving WA's be resolved *early*, before substantial costs are incurred.

The project manager has a number of tools in addition to the work authorization for gaining the active support of in-house project elements, however.

1. The project manager is, in effect, the customer of in-house project elements; his control of project funds is a powerful "persuasive" lever.

2. In companies which recognize the importance of the project manager's role and appreciate that he needs functional management support, the project manager has a clearly stated charter and position guide which cut through much of the underbrush of confusion and misunderstanding that otherwise tends to arise.

3. A well-planned and continuing employee information program, including an initial orientation of each individual, periodic status reports and presentations, and a "promotion" campaign, is an effective, supplementary tool.

4. Weekly meetings (technical, schedule, and cost) of project and task managers are essential to in-house control.

5. Periodic presentation of project status to company management is necessary, both to keep company management informed and to request assistance if necessary. A major aircraft producer holds project status reviews every Saturday morning; few problems arise which are not soon corrected.

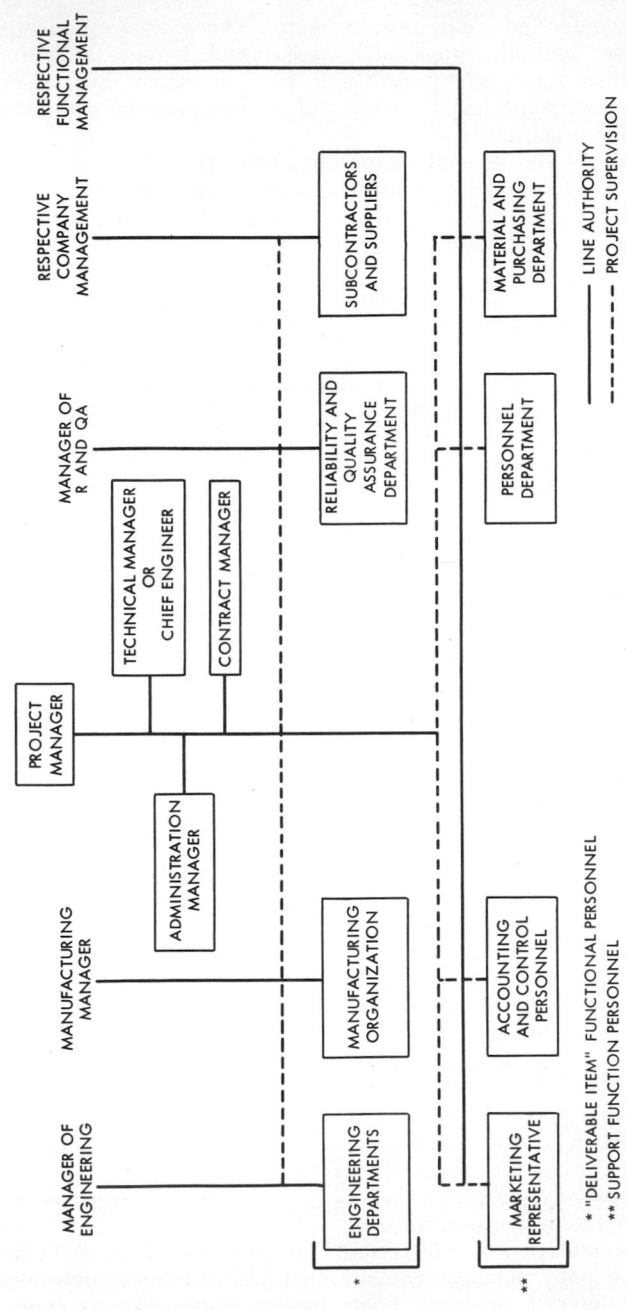

FIG. 5-4. *Project team relationships.* (*From Project Management, Richard D. Irwin, Inc., Homewood, Ill., 1963.*)

* "DELIVERABLE ITEM" FUNCTIONAL PERSONNEL
** SUPPORT FUNCTION PERSONNEL

———— LINE AUTHORITY
- - - - PROJECT SUPERVISION

PROJECT FUNCTIONS

ORGANIZATION	Plans and Controls	System Analysis	System Engineering	Detail Engineering	Prototype Fabrication	Prototype Test	Subcontracts Control	Customer Liaison (Contract)	Customer Liaison (Extra-Contract)	Production	System Test	Etc.—
Company (Division)												
Chief Executive	A				I		I	I		I		
Controller	C				I	I				I		
Manager of R&D		I	C	P,A	P	I				I		
Materiel Director		I			I	C			I	I		
Production Manager		I	I	I	I					P	I	
Marketing Director		I			I		I	P		I		
Director, Product Assurance		I	C		P				C	P		
Etc.—												
Project Manager	A	A	C	I	C	C	A	I	I	C	C	
Controls Manager	P	I	I	I	I		C	C	I	I		
Chief Engineer	I	P	P,A	C	C	I	I	C	I	I		
Subcontracts Manager		I			I		P		I	I		
Manufacturing Representative				I	I				C	I		
Marketing Representative					I		I	C		I		
Contracts Administrator					I		I	P	I	I		
Test & Reliability Manager					A					A		
Etc.—												

FIG. 5-5. *Function/organization responsibilities. P, prime responsibility; C, coordinated with; I, information to; A, approval authority.*

6. An arrangement whereby project engineers are responsible to both functional management (for all purposes other than work contributing directly to project accomplishment) and project management (for work contributing directly to the project) gives the project manager an important administrative control. A developer of propulsion systems effectively uses this dual responsibility concept.

Subcontractor Control. Subcontracts and outside purchases generally account for 50 percent or more of expenditures on development projects. Standard items and subcontract items of lesser dollar amount are procured through the company's purchasing or materiel organization. As to major subcontracts, however, the matter of whether materiel or the project office or engineering has cognizance is often poorly defined but is of prime importance in successful performance on these contracts. One well-known and technically proficient R&D company, for instance, actually has statements of responsibility which are directly contradictory: a materiel directive states that subcontracts responsibility is totally that of materiel, while an engineering directive states that project engineers have this responsibility, where they must subcontract part of their development work. Not surprisingly, the resulting loss of control and the confusion to sub-contractors has caused millions of dollars in overruns and stretch-outs which contributed to two years' delay on one project.

To give proper direction to the subcontractor, the matter of responsibilities must be clearly defined for (1) technical aspects, (2) schedules, (3) cost aspects, and (4) contract administration. It is apparent that a contract administrator (normally assigned to the materiel function) will usually handle matters pertaining to contract administration, and that a project engineer will direct the technical aspects. It is in the areas of responsibility for schedule and cost, and the role of the project office, that confusion often arises. Whether the project engineer or subcontract administrator will monitor and control schedule and cost and whether the project office has a director of subcontracts to whom these people are fully or partially responsible must be clearly defined and must be made crystal clear to the subcontractor. A failure to define these responsibilities invites subcontractor problems.

The mechanics of subcontractor control are generally similar to those of overall project control: a sound *plan* for achieving technical, delivery, and cost objectives; regular *measurements* of achievement and expenditures against the plan; and corrective *action* where deviations appear. The format and periods of plans and reports must be compatible with those required by the project manager's customer, because they are "feeder" information for his project control and progress reports.

Timeliness in taking corrective action is particularly important in subcontracts control, because later the project manager has fewer and fewer opportunities to influence a sub's responsiveness. Greatest control is exercised at the time of source selection; then in order come contract negotiation, post-award conference, and the first two or three months of working with the subcontractor. If by this time the prime has not established a firm leader-follower relationship, he is in for trouble. Later, because of the elapsed time invested in the sub, as well as resources committed, it may be almost impossible to terminate the sub's contract even though he is performing unsatisfactorily.

The Project Team. Collectively, the project office, in-house functional elements working on the project, and the subcontractors comprise the project team. Motivating these diverse organizations to work as a team requires clear objectives, full communications, and full use of available incentives. Fortunately for the project manager, the purposes and objectives of most R&D projects are almost self-evident and are much clearer than those of functional operations. The reasons for high reliability and quality, tight scheduling, and cost and funding limitations are almost immediately apparent to an experienced project team. The nature of this collective undertaking is the basis for developing a strong project team.

The project manager normally uses this common-interest basis to foster a team spirit through such means as:

Constant visual awareness—mockups, pictures, plant newspaper articles, and the like—of the end product

Keeping team members fully and regularly informed about developments, project status, and customer reactions

Advising responsible individuals of particularly good or weak performances, with copies to higher management as appropriate

Regularly scheduled progress, technical, and cost reviews whose purpose is to ferret out problem areas and take early corrective action

Personal visits to work areas

Developing friendly competition between project elements, on bases such as "progress for the money spent"

Making sure that channels of communication are established between project elements

There will be occasions, however, when a balky subcontractor or unresponsive in-house department needs a different approach. The project manager in these instances may have to withhold funds until the problem is resolved, might request higher-management assistance, or, as a last resort, may request action by his customer.

In summary, the project manager has available a number of techniques for controlling in-house and subcontract work toward achievement of project derivatives. It is apparent, however, that *simplicity* of project organization, *clear relations* between project elements, and *full communications* are absolute necessities, rather than merely desirable techniques, in project management. As for authority, it is suggested that the project manager would do well to *assume authority* in those areas where his authority is not defined. Where the choice must be made, project objectives rather than friendship must be the project manager's guide.

FISCAL MANAGEMENT AND COST CONTROL

The history of overruns on R&D-type projects, because of unrealistic proposal estimates, sketchy definition of the work involved, and overengineering, has led to extensive use of fixed-price contracts. This development means that the project manager must manage his dollars far better than he may have in the past. The resulting dollar savings on a national scale are measured in billions.

Fiscal management is concerned with control of funds received for the project and with the project manager's allotment of funds, in turn, to project organizations. This allotment is based on these organizations' work sheets and budgets which formed the basis for contract negotiations with the project manager's customer; but the allotment is usually lower than these estimates, because of the effect of negotiations and because the project manager needs to hold back part of the available funds for contingencies.

Cost control concerns the propriety and amount of costs incurred. For instance, charges may be improperly made against the project manager's project through recording errors or through a functional manager's desire to "cover" assigned personnel even though they did not actually work on the project. In reviewing costs, the project manager's staff should evaluate expenditure reports on the basis of "how does this cost contribute to project objectives?" Regular spot checks will do much to reduce improper "loading" against the project manager's project.

The project manager is dependent on timely reports from his company's controller and from his subcontractors for a comparison of actual versus planned manpower and dollar expenditures. If accounting reports are not timely, accurate, or detailed enough, the project manager himself may have to devise controls which will give him this required visibility.

Unrealistically low estimates—"buying into" a project having a cost-type contract—are less of a problem when R&D projects are on a fixed-price or incentive basis. A number of factors which are more subtle than contract-required manpower, material, and other direct costs may creep into the cost of project operations, however. Some of these are proposals and costing exercises—clearly outside the scope of the contract—which are borne by the project rather than by company overhead or by customer reimbursement. Another is the cost of overtime, which may be incurred on fixed-price contracts as a result of delays caused by the customer. Small, undocumented changes of scope can significantly increase costs.

CUSTOMER RELATIONS AND MARKETING ASPECTS

As a business generalist, the project manager in most R&D organizations must exercise effective liaison with his customer on project matters covered by contract, and also must contact potential customers on matters related to the project but outside the contract.

As trustee to his customers for meeting project objectives, the project manager serves as their focal point in project operations, keeps them fully and frankly informed, provides realistic estimates, and takes whatever actions are needed to meet project objectives.

It is essential to his team's effectiveness, however, that he know well the customer's organization and personnel. The mutual confidence and respect thus developed may reduce or eliminate many problems which otherwise tend to arise. It is particularly important that he stay keenly attuned to the customer's continued requirements for the project. Sometimes the customer's problem, which gave rise to the project, changes or differs from the problem as originally stated by the customer. The project manager needs good rapport to detect basic points such as this as early as possible.

The project manager's contract administrator serves as the day-to-day point of contact with the customer. Correspondence to and from the customer is, on most well-managed projects, routed through him. The reason for this is that unless responsibility for communications is controlled by a knowledgeable contracts individual, engineers and others on the project are likely to accept "suggestions" by their counterparts in the customer's organization as directives. Frequently it later develops, after considerable work on these directives, that a change was neither authorized nor desired by the customer's project manager. Because the work was not contractually covered, however, the performing organization is left holding the bag. The contract administrator serves a valuable function in preventing unrecoverable costs of this type. To do this, however, he must be the main link in communications with the customer.

Project marketing activities take two general paths: maintaining the contract base with the current customer or customers, and expanding the base to additional customers.

A number of factors affect the very existence of a research or development project, such as obsolescence of purpose, technological obsolescence, similarity to another project, and dependency on the outcome of another project (which may be terminated). The project manager's best defense against these possibilities is to stay on the track toward his schedule, cost, and technical performance objectives. An awareness, however, of "outside" factors (such as technological change, similar-purpose projects, changes in customer attitude toward the project) through engineering and marketing channels, as well as through his project team organization, will indicate actions needed to maintain the contract base in an environment of constant change.

Expanding the project base requires active participation by a marketing representative assigned full or part time to the project after it has been under way for some time. For him to become effective, he must be fully briefed and considered a regular part of the project team, and he must prepare a marketing plan (*what* is marketable; to whom; what actions to take, when, and by whom) and report his progress against the plan.

Along with these marketing efforts directed toward actual and prospective customers, the project manager would do well to remember the importance of keeping his own company management "sold" on his project.

DEPROJECTIZING

By its nature and by definition, every project comes to an end. This ending may come about through fulfillment of project objectives or through termination or cancellation of the project. Frequently, on completion of the development phase, project activity phases down as production and operational support phase up. During a long production run, the project team may be partially or fully "deprojectized."

Project completion, termination, and transitions have one major characteristic in common: they require detailed, realistic planning to minimize the effects of dislocation. Where will the people go? When? How can they be made productive as soon as possible in their new positions? How can the costs of deprojectizing be minimized? Will a contract administrator now serve as the focal point for project matters, or can these matters be satisfactorily handled by functional (marketing, control, and production) management? Questions such as these require time and thought by both project and functional management, well before the time comes to phase down. In an environment of constantly changing technology, the time to deprojectize may come with a suddenness which requires *immediate* transfer of personnel, safeguarding of inventory and equipment, and notification of subcontractors to cease work.

The project office, on a reduced scale, may continue to function in the production and support phases, both to give continuity and background and, to a lesser degree than formerly, to provide controls and customer contact. A project office which is closely attuned to the customer's operational requirements can make a great contribution to profit during these phases.

CONCLUSION

The trend toward fixed-price and incentive contracts for R&D projects puts a high premium on sound project management. In controlling the myriad activities toward attainment of his schedule, technical performance, and cost objectives, the project manager "keeps score" on status and problem areas by measuring deviations from a well-conceived operations plan, and takes whatever action is required to assure satisfactory achievement for the money.

Many of the project manager's problems relate to the nature of the project organization, which is partly responsible to him and partly responsible to others. A contractual or semicontractual agreement with these other elements of the team, simplicity of organization, assumption of authority, good communications, and, above all, firm control of funds are all necessary in developing and maintaining an effective project team.

The project manager and contract administrator are focal points of customer contact for changes and other project matters.

As a management generalist, however, the project manager must do more than control operations under contract. He generally has a responsibility for ferreting out new project-related business; he must keep an eye over his shoulder to see whether overtaking technologies and other factors will affect his project; he must keep his company's management informed; and he must help plan and execute the deprojectizing phase.

Because of stiff competition and stringent contracting in R&D work, the project manager is in a key role to please or displease the customer, to return a profit or loss, and to enhance or darken his company's reputation. Part businessman, part scientist or engineer, part lawyer, the project manager is a versatile individual who is not easily found or developed. In every proposal it submits, however, the R&D organization states, in effect, to its owners, its customers, and itself, that it *does* have this kind of individual—and is willing to risk its profit and reputation on him.

BIBLIOGRAPHY

Air Force Systems Command Manuals 375-1 (*Configuration Management*) and 375-5 (*System Engineering Management*), Hqs., Air Force Systems Command, Andrews AFB, Washington, D.C.

Army Materiel Command Regulation 11-16, vol. 2, Hqs., U.S. Army Materiel Command, Washington, D.C.

Baker, Bruce N., and Rene L. Eris, *An Introduction to PERT-CPM*, Richard D. Irwin, Inc., Homewood, Ill., 1964.

Baumgartner, J. S., *Project Management*, Richard D. Irwin, Inc., Homewood, Ill., 1963.

PERT/Cost Systems Design, DOD and NASA Guide, June, 1962.

CHAPTER SIX

Use of Outside Research

PAUL J. LOVEWELL *President, Management & Economics Research Incorporated, Palo Alto, California*

"Outside research" as used here refers to research and development carried out for a company on a contract basis by another organization. Some agencies are in the sole business of doing research for industry and government; others take on contracts as an adjunct to their regular activities. Nonprofit research institutes and commercial research firms exemplify the former category; universities, consultants, "captive" laboratories, trade associations, and professional societies, the latter.

The volume of contracted research with independent laboratories and research institutes was estimated at $2 billion in 1964. The reservoir of competence, experience, and facilities that these organizations represent is so vast that probably every research manager should consider the possibilities of contracting all or part of planned programs. Certainly, outside sources should be considered to help with peak-load research, to furnish otherwise unobtainable expertise, to fill gaps in existing programs, to solve short-range problems, to furnish objective viewpoints, and to provide facilities when intramural capital outlay is not justified.

Although the field for selection is usually necessarily limited by demands for specialized personnel and facilities on a specific project, selection of an appropriate outside facility also depends on the need for confidential handling, on the proprietary nature of the research, on patent considerations, on program size, and on costs. Final choice of a contractor follows the submission of proposals from a few of the most likely prospects. Proposals should be judged primarily on technical competence and availability of facilities.

After a contract has been let, liaison arrangements previously made should be carefully and scrupulously followed both by the industrial sponsor and by the research group. Reports should be submitted as required. The industrial sponsor should not interfere with the course of the research beyond the scope of the contract.

REASONS FOR GOING "OUTSIDE"

The manager who seeks outside research assistance may be prompted by any one of several reasons. Most of these reasons are based ultimately on the capabilities and limitations of his own research operations.

Cost Considerations. If a temporary research program requires substantial capital investment for space and facilities, an outside research program may represent a large saving of funds. Outside research groups can also relieve the pressure of peak-load work within a company.

The small company that has grown to the point that it wishes to establish a research operation has a particularly severe problem. The initial investment for facilities and staff may be so great that it would be more prudent to purchase research "by the piece." The Research Institute of America has suggested a minimum of $125,000 over a five-year period as the smallest internal research operation on which a real return can be expected. It points out that a unit of three or four staff scientists takes $75,000 to $100,000 a year, plus an initial investment in capital equipment. Small companies can avoid part of this high expense by using outside research until an "inside" capability is clearly warranted.

The personnel implications of adding expensive talent to a staff often prompt industrial firms to go outside. Addition of a $25,000-a-year man to a staff, unless he can be kept productively occupied over an extended period of time, lowers professional morale as well as company profits. No responsible management should wish to engage scientific personnel when the company cannot foresee a continuing need for their talents.

Another practical consideration is budgetary control. Research contracts with outside laboratories, although they do not guarantee achieving the desired goal within a stated amount of money, usually provide for a fixed maximum rate of expenditure. This permits close adherence to budgeted costs, for the outside group can change the rate only with client approval.

Other Benefits. Many other reasons are less tangible and therefore harder to assess. When a project seems basically sound but has not been brought to a successful conclusion, outside help should be considered. It may be because the problem is too complex for the company's staff, requires specialized knowledge, has languished for lack of interest on the part of the staff, or needs a fresh approach. Some of these same reasons also will apply to proposed new research that has not yet been undertaken by the company. A fresh viewpoint can give new impetus to a project. Company research staffs, no matter how competent, tend to become oriented in their thinking by the company's products and line of business, whereas an outside consultant or research group will frequently approach a problem from an entirely different angle.

Outside research people are accustomed to dealing with a wide variety of problems for many companies. They have chosen to be consultants or to work in independent laboratories and research institutes because they have an unusual aptitude for analyzing new situations, conceiving a range of possible and even novel approaches, and selecting the approach most likely to succeed. After the problem is understood and the most promising plan of attack developed, this type of person is willing to turn over the detailed execution of the research to someone else. Only rarely is a scientist in a typical company research laboratory placed in a position where he can operate in this manner over a wide range of problems in many different settings.

Research activities within a company are often interrupted because of pressing immediate problems. Though less true in the largest companies, this applies to some extent in almost all companies. Thus, when it is necessary that a project receive undivided attention, it is frequently best to place the work outside.

When diversification is being considered, independent laboratories and consultants can help the firm make the decision to acquire companies, to buy rights to products, or to develop new products. Because the company usually has no experienced personnel in the new areas, an outside laboratory can also aid by initiating research and development programs, training personnel, and gradually relinquishing control to the company as the new activity becomes established.

When there is a difference of opinion within a company about the value of a research program, the potential of a new product, the desirability of adopting a new process, or the usefulness of a patent being offered for sale or license, an independent evaluation by an outside group can provide management with information to help reach the right decision.

If an emergency situation develops, a company may well want to try several approaches simultaneously to improve the probabilities of reaching a solution as quickly as possible. Under these circumstances, it is often desirable to use one or two outside laboratories or consultants, as well as to have the company laboratory work on the problem. This method, although apparently inefficient, may actually yield substantial savings in time.

After a working relationship with an outside group has been established, there are many minor services that most laboratories and consultants can render. Confidential investigations can be made; samples of new materials and new chemicals can be obtained and tested without revealing the company's interest. Literature surveys can be conducted, special tests can be run, unusual equipment can be employed, skilled personnel can be "borrowed," experiments to round out a patent specification can be completed, expert testimony in litigation can be given, and affidavits in support of patent applications can be written. These and numerous other services are available, particularly when there is an already established liaison with an outside laboratory.

Another type of service provided by some outside groups is to keep the company supplied with a steady stream of incidental information both from the "grapevine" and from technical literature not normally consulted by the company's own research staff. This kind of "intelligence service" is directed at the company's broader interests and is not necessarily intimately connected with the project under way. The broad contacts and diversified technical reading of the outside laboratory's staff make this service extremely valuable.

A continuing relationship with one or more outside groups can be a fertile source for new ideas. Even though the ideas may not be related to a client's immediate objectives, the outside group will first present them to continuing clients who might be interested, because consultants and outside laboratories tend to have a greater loyalty to their continuing clients than to new or sporadic clients.

The value of the client relationship increases the longer it exists. The more the outside research group learns about the nature of the client's overall business, the more the research organization is stimulated to come up with ideas of interest to the client.

All these factors should be considered in deciding whether outside facilities might be valuable either for advancing the research program or for effecting savings in research. If any are found to be applicable, or if other special reasons exist, serious consideration should be given to using outside research.

OUTSIDE RESEARCH FACILITIES

After the decision has been made, the search for a suitable and qualified organization must begin. In general, the following types of organizations represent the facilities that should be considered.

Independent Laboratories. Independent laboratories are commercial, profit-making, tax-paying companies whose primary function is to perform consulting and laboratory services for other companies, individuals, and the government. Their number in the United States has been estimated to be as high as 3,000, but many of these restrict their activities solely to testing, analysis, inspection, and sampling. Out of the total, perhaps as many as 1,500 engage in research and development activities. These laboratories are scattered across the country, but they tend to concentrate in industrial centers. The majority are in New York, California, Illinois, Massachusetts, New Jersey, and Pennsylvania.

The research activities of independent organizations are varied, with an emphasis on chemistry, engineering, and physics. They also include metallurgy; biological, agricultural, and medical sciences; geology; economics and social sciences; and other miscellaneous fields. A substantial number offer computer services.

Research Institutes. Of about 100 research institutes in the United States engaged principally in research for industry and government, a dozen are major in terms of staff, facilities, and volume of business. Some have university ties at the top, but all operate independently. Some were originally set up as endowed institutions, and others were founded with industrial support, often to provide technical facilities for a specific area of the country. Through the years, they have individually developed unusual and sometimes unique strengths, e.g., chemistry, economics, engineering, medical sciences, metallurgy, and aeronautics. Most of them use the income from sponsored projects to self-sponsor research in their own fields of interest or to invest in new facilities.

The principal scientific fields of interest to the research institutes are chemistry, physics, and metallurgy. Their activities also include geology, geophysics, and other earth sciences, and medical, agricultural, biological, engineering, economics, and social sciences.

The principal laboratories of this type that accept industrial sponsorship of projects on a confidential basis are Battelle Memorial Institute, Cornell Aeronautical Laboratories, Denver Research Institute, Franklin Institute, IITRI (formerly Armour), Mellon Institute, Midwest Research Institute, Southern Research Institute, Southwest Research Institute, and Stanford Research Institute. There is a growing interest in organizations of this type, and newer ones have been established, including Triangle (North Carolina), Spindletop (Kentucky), North Star (Minnesota), Gulf South (Louisiana), and Midwest Applied Science (Indiana).

Academic Institutions. All technological institutes, most universities, and many colleges and professional schools operate research programs as part of their educational programs. Wherever people are being trained to do research, they must be doing research; therefore, every such institution is a center of research activity.

Traditionally, these research activities have been centered on the idea that there should be no restrictions on the nature of the inquiry. Also, research results customarily are available for publication. Thus, universities have been a major source of important basic and fundamental research. In fact, the term "academic research" has come to mean almost the same thing as "pure," "basic," or "fundamental research." However, the pressures of World War II made many of the schools partially shift their emphasis to much more practical research objectives, thus creating a large number of applied research centers at these institutions.

At the end of the war, the universities had an important decision to make about these activities, and several alternatives were chosen. In those schools where the administrative heads thought that applied research interfered with the basic education function, a policy of refusing further project research was established. In those schools where continued financial support of this sort was considered necessary to maintain the research facilities and to supplement the income of faculty members, project research, both from industry and government, was accepted and, in some cases, sought. A middle ground was found by another group, which separated the applied research projects and set up a research institute (affiliated with the university) to handle them. In some cases, this has amounted to establishing a new independent research institute with its own staff and facilities, but in others, the research institute still utilizes space, facilities, and faculty members of the university.

Industry supports academic institutions in several ways:

1. By contributing to fund drives, either as recognition of the value of the institution in training scientists or to help improve the physical facilities.

2. By granting scholarships or fellowships.

3. By research grants that provide unrestricted support or define only the general area of research interest. This is sometimes used by a company to assure that some research of a fundamental nature is being carried on to advance knowledge in its area of interest. Such arrangements may have other practical advantages. For example, it is possible to maintain liaison with the project during the course of the work and to assess the potential of a graduate research fellow as a possible future employee.

4. By research contracts in which the sponsor sets up some practical research objective, provides the necessary funds, and receives regular reports on the progress of the work. This is similar in many ways to the applied research carried on in independent laboratories and research institutes, but the sponsor usually has less to say about the direction of the work and may have to agree to publication of the results.

Consultants. Consultants, presumably experts in one or more fields, provide services on a retainer, fee-per-job, or per-diem basis. Normally, they act in an advisory capacity and conduct little if any research themselves. They may lecture on a regular basis to the technical staff; come to the research laboratory on a regular schedule for individual conferences with staff members who have problems in their areas of specialization; be called in on a one-time basis to try to give some new ideas to the research staff on a specific problem; or be retained to advise on, or act as liaison with, a research project in outside facilities.

Broadly, five general types of consultants are available to industry:

1. Individuals or groups of individuals who have set themselves up in business as consultants because the challenge of this type of activity is appealing to them and they feel they have the capacity for analyzing problems and proposing the directions to take in seeking solutions.

2. Members of the staff of independent laboratories who make their services available for consultation as well as for directing contract research.

3. Scientific and engineering faculty members of academic institutions, whose arrangements permit them to undertake a limited amount of outside consulting work.

4. Scientists retired from industry. Sometimes arrangements with former employers permit the scientist to consult only with that company or with noncompetitive companies.

5. Engineering consultants whose primary function is plant design. This group can often be valuable at an earlier stage of process development.

Trade Associations. The more than 2,000 national trade associations in this country are nonprofit, cooperative organizations of business competitors who have grouped together to aid themselves and their industry with common business problems. A number of these trade associations have sponsored substantial programs of industrial research and development, with most of the results generally available.

With a few important exceptions (e.g., the National Canners' Association, the Textile Research Institute, the Portland Cement Association), trade associations do not maintain laboratories of their own but sponsor outside research, often in the laboratories of one member. A number of "research institutes" were established to serve specific industries: the Institute of Paper Chemistry, the Institute of Textile Technology, the Institute of Gas Technology, and the Plywood Research Foundation. Another technique often used is cooperative work, with parts of the project conducted in various laboratories. This approach is particularly common when the association is seeking, through its research program, to establish standards, including testing methods, for the industry.

Although, in general, this type of organization is not set up to accept individually sponsored research projects, there are exceptions. It is mentioned here also as a precaution against plunging into an expensive new research program without checking first to see whether some pertinent trade association has already done work in the field.

"Captive" Laboratories. Suppliers of materials and equipment are usually good sources of technical information on the use of their products. When the potential for future business is great enough, suppliers will also often do a limited amount of development work to help find a solution to a problem. Such work will normally be oriented in the direction of making it possible to utilize the supplier's product rather than any other. The amount of work done will be determined by the importance of the problem to the supplier rather than to the customer. Another important factor is that the solution to the problem, if found by the supplier, will then become available to the customer's competitors.

In some cases, company laboratories are available for outside work. Much of this work is done under government contract, but there are laboratories that will accept industrially sponsored projects. Some companies have set up these laboratories as separate corporate entities for legal and financial reasons, but they operate as closely associated affiliates or subsidiaries.

Government Laboratories. Although the laboratories maintained by the United States government are not available to industry for work on specific problems, good research management requires an intimate knowledge of the research under way in these laboratories. Except where national security prevents it, almost all of this research is published and freely available. It is often valuable to know what general areas are under investigation even before the results are published, and this can only be accomplished by personal contact, including correspondence.

From the point of view of potential value to industry, among the most important laboratories in the Federal government, outside of those engaged in strictly national defense problems, are the following: National Institutes of Health; National Bureau of Standards; National Aeronautics and Space Agency; National Science Foundation; the Agricultural Research Service; Forest Products Laboratory; Atomic Energy Commission; Public Health Service; the Agency for International Development; the Federal Aviation Agency; Food and Drug Administration; Bureau of Mines; and the Geological Survey. Information on Federal laboratories engaged in research can be obtained from the National Science Foundation report *Federal Funds for Science*.

Agricultural experiment stations, located at land-grant colleges and state universities, have extensive programs of research on problems relating to agriculture. The results of this research have contributed greatly to the agricultural economy. Facilities are maintained by all fifty states. These stations conduct a wide range of research projects and disseminate information on the development of higher-yield and disease-resistant crops, insecticides and fungicides, soil fertility and conservation, productive soil use, silviculture and forest management, plant and livestock breeding, livestock and dairy problems, and the preservation of foods. Activities are financed largely through state appropriations supplemented by Federal grants. Many of the experiment stations also cooperate with national, regional, state, or local trade associations and receive financial assistance for their research from these associations. A few undertake research projects supported by private companies and individuals, when the subject of the investigation is of public concern and is broad and basic in character.

Land-grant colleges and state universities in forty-four states operate engineering experiment stations in conjunction with their engineering colleges. Fields of research at these experiment stations include aeronautics, ceramics, economics, communication, electronics, farm equipment, flood control, fuels, heating, gas technology, heat transfer, hydraulics, irrigation, metallurgy, power generation and transmission, refrigeration, sanitation, transportation, waste disposal and utilization, weather forecasting, and work simplification. Engineering research in these experiment stations is conducted in cooperation with government agencies, individuals, firms, corporations, and trade associations, as well as by the station alone. Cooperative research is usually conducted under contract or grant.

SELECTION OF AN APPROPRIATE OUTSIDE FACILITY

A careful definition of the research problem and consideration of the ramifications attendant upon its solution are mandatory before an outside facility is selected.

Very often, the nature of the research itself will serve to narrow the field for selection; perhaps only a few groups have the staff and facilities necessary for the work. If the field is fairly broad, inquiries directed to several possible contractors for preliminary statements of interest in the area should yield sufficient information to limit the possibilities. Because the preparation of a good proposal is costly and time consuming, usually only two or three organizations should be asked to submit formal proposals. A potential client who asks for proposals from a long list of bidders may find himself ignored by the better-qualified organizations.

If proprietary information will be generated on the project, the field of contractors usually should be limited to research institutes, commercial laboratories, for-profit research organizations, and consultants. Universities almost always reserve the right to publish results in the scientific literature.

The patent policies of contract organizations differ so much that no detailed treatment is possible here. Questions relative to assigning of patents resulting from sponsored research should be clearly resolved in writing before a formal agreement is reached. In general, however, most of the research institutes and for-profit organizations assign all patents to the client; most universities and cooperative laboratories do not. Company "captive" laboratories have varying practices.

The size of the project may influence the selection of an outside source. Some research buyers contend that short-range efforts—in the $5,000 to $20,000 class—can be handled more efficiently and economically by consultants or smaller organizations. These buyers also believe that research institutes and larger for-profit organizations are best geared to handle projects in the $20,000 to over $1,000,000 range. Regardless of the merit of this view, it is important to be sure that the contractor has the necessary resources, both financial and technical, to meet his commitments.

The Research Proposal. Once the field of possible contractors has been reduced to a small number, the appropriate management and technical personnel of the contracting organization should request formal proposals for the research to be undertaken. Almost always, the proposal is prepared at no expense to the requester; however, before a proposal is formally requested, the company should ascertain whether there will be a charge for the proposal.

The request should delineate the problem as clearly as possible and should indicate, if possible, the projected budget range within which the bidder should stay.

The research proposal usually includes the following parts:

1. An introduction indicating that the potential contractor is familiar with the problem.

2. A statement of objectives, usually couched in the conditional; research results cannot be guaranteed.

3. A statement of scope, which serves to limit the project both in depth and in breadth.

4. A method-of-approach section, primarily aimed at the technical evaluator, outlining the method to be used for solving the problem.

5. A statement of qualifications of the bidding organization, covering facilities and personnel; often biographical statements of key people are attached.

6. The report and meeting schedule.

7. An explanation of patent and publication policies, if applicable.

8. The basis on which the costs are determined, and how invoicing (including any advance payments) will be handled.

9. A time and cost estimate (see below).

10. A statement indicating that proprietary material will be safeguarded, if applicable.

11. The time-limit date for acceptance.

Item 9, the time and cost estimate, is a critical matter. The client should be wary of estimates that are surprisingly low in view of the problem to be solved. It may indicate a lack of understanding or sophistication or even a deliberate effort to obtain a research contract on a price basis with full knowledge that the client, once involved, will find it difficult to refuse additional funding.

The question of how much to spend on a particular project is a vexing one. Most companies have at least crude standards of payout that are applied to both internal and external research. Factors that must be considered include the probable value of the research if successful, the monetary stakes involved, and the probability of success.

A simple cost-benefit analysis is often useful. Most research problems can be studied in varying degrees of depth, ranging from a quick and superficial review of readily available knowledge to a deep analysis by a large number of scientists carried on for years. The research buyer should seek the optimum point in the relationship between cost and benefit.

For example, one might think of the typical research project as following an S curve in the buildup of benefit, while costs progress along a curve that is idealized as a straight line, as shown in Figure 6-1. Early in the project, it is doubtful that any benefits will accrue. After the work has been under way for a time, the benefit curve will rise steeply and intersect the cost curve. We are now in the "payout zone," which can be expected to build up fairly rapidly for a time. Then the benefit curve will begin to flatten out until, at last, costs begin to exceed probable benefits.

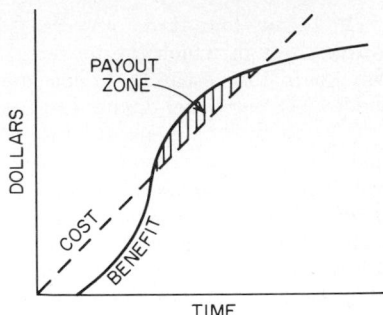

FIG. 6-1. *Cost-benefit of research project. (Courtesy of Paul J. Lovewell and Edward L. Perkins. Copyright 1965. All rights reserved.)*

The problem of the research buyer is to plan the research program so as to halt the project at the point of maximum benefit, and certainly not to continue beyond the "payout zone."

A research proposal should not be judged on its elegance; a four-color presentation, for example, may be indicative of little except a high overhead rate. The document should, however, be literate, well organized, and demonstrate knowledge of the subject.

After the proposal has been reviewed, the management and technical personnel involved may require further explanations, information, or revisions. These can often be resolved by informal discussion with the management and technical people of the proposing group. Occasionally a revised proposal is called for.

In evaluating competitive proposals, competence should be the most significant factor in the decision. "Bargain basement" research is seldom economical in the long run, regardless of the commitment of the research source.

The Research Contract or Agreement. Although the contract form itself may be incorporated in the proposal, be a simple letter of acceptance, or be a separate legal document, the contract should cover the following:

1. The nature of the project, the date for the beginning of work, the duration of the contract, and provisions for extension, cancellation, or termination

2. Agreement by the outside source to refrain from conducting similar work for competitive clients for a specific time

3. A statement indicating where the work will be conducted and defining ownership of equipment purchased for the project

4. The upper limit of the client's liability

5. The basis on which costs are determined

6. Invoice terms

7. Definition of ownership of patent rights

8. Provision for reports

9. Agreements on advertising and publicity

Monitoring the Research. One advantage of outside research is that detailed management attention by the client is not required. However, the client does have an obligation to remain in close touch with the contractor and be satisfied the research is proceeding at a reasonable pace toward the established goal.

Research projects are monitored formally by reports and informally by discussions with the project personnel. Most research contract organizations assign the technical project leader as chief liaison with the client. His efforts are usually most effective if he has a direct line of communication with his counterpart in the sponsoring company.

On larger, long-term projects, it is often desirable to provide a steering committee through which the technical and management personnel from both groups can guide the research. Their meetings serve to keep the client informed and the project personnel oriented to the client's viewpoint.

It sometimes happens, because of unforeseen events or unavoidable difficulties, that the research organization will overrun its contract on time or cost or both. Although such events are bound to occur occasionally even in the best-managed research organizations, the client has every right to a full disclosure of the facts. If it appears that the difficulties were clearly beyond the research group's control, a reasonable settlement should be negotiated regardless of legalities. This applies only if the eventual result is entirely satisfactory to the client.

In general, formal written reports should be kept to a minimum. A requirement that the project leader submit a detailed monthly report will tend to vitiate the research effort and raise project costs. A final, written report nearly always should be required. The final payment for the research work should be delayed until receipt of the final report.

CONCLUSION

Although outside research is, in a sense, competitive with inside research, there is, in fact, a proper and logical role for each. Management's responsibility is to examine its own organization's research needs with an understanding of the particular values (advantages and limitations) of outside research. From this should emerge a formulation that will combine inside and outside research in an optimum way.

The organization which shuns outside research is just as apt to miss important advantages as is the organization that regards outside research as a panacea. The growing importance of outside research, particularly since World War II, is adequate testimony to its effectiveness when intelligently employed.

BIBLIOGRAPHY

DeVos, Henry, *Management Services Handbook*, American Institute of Certified Public Accountants, New York, 1964.

Directory of Membership and Services, Association of Consulting Management Engineers, Inc., New York.

Employment and Compensation of Experts and Consultants, rev. ed., Personnel Management Series, no. 3, U.S. Civil Service Commission, 1964.

How the Management Consulting Profession Serves Business Enterprises, Association of Consulting Management Engineers, Inc., New York, 1959.

Pomeranz, Janet M., and Leonard W. Prestwich, "Meeting the Problems of Very Small Enterprises," Small Business Management Research Reports, Small Business Administration, Washington, D.C., 1962.

Research and Development: A List of Small Business Concerns Interested in Performing Research and Development, Small Business Administration, Washington, D.C., 1963.

Seney, Wilson, *Effective Use of Business Consultants,* Financial Executives Research Foundation, New York, 1963.

Villers, Raymond, *Research and Development: Planning and Control,* Financial Executives Research Foundation, New York, 1964.

Patents

S. BLAKE YATES   *Director of Corporate Licensing, Armour and Company, Chicago, Illinois*

This chapter is intended to provide some practical guidelines to the busy executive on the more important business aspects of patents and other rights. From the manager's viewpoint, the patent laws are rather complex and involved. He does not need a detailed knowledge of patent law, however, but rather a general knowledge of the principal features of patents to communicate effectively with the patent attorney and technical people for the purpose of making a judgment on obtaining, utilizing, and enforcing patents.

Patents provide legal protection to the novel aspects of the results of the research and development activity. They represent an asset that may be more valuable to a company than real property such as land, buildings, and equipment. Therefore, it is prudent business practice to establish objectives, policies, practices, and procedures on obtaining, utilizing, and protecting patents.

PATENT OBJECTIVES AND PROCEDURES

Effective utilization of patents and other rights can be accomplished by maintaining an exclusive position for seventeen years for the patent owner, licensing to others for various considerations, or a combination of these. Because the research and development effort is tailored to the interests and capabilities of the company, the majority of the patents should be susceptible of maximum utilization by the company. If the patent owner cannot utilize his patents to the maximum extent, licensing provides an opportunity to derive income from the investment in the research and development work that led to the patents.

Many firms have established a licensing department for handling both outgoing and incoming licenses. The licensing function is primarily a marketing and negotiating activity. Timely action on licensing is essential, for in this age of rapidly advancing technology, the majority of inventions become obsolete in a matter of a few years.

The licensing program can be started as soon as patent applications have been filed. This activity points up the importance of the patent owner having a well-considered program for enforcing patents. Firms that wish to expand rapidly and diversify their product lines should consider actively searching for patents owned by others that can be developed under license. There are several nonprofit organizations that own patents which are available for licensing. In addition, industrial firms, particularly foreign firms without manufacturing facilities in the United States, represent a source of patents that are available for licensing.

The Patent Committee. Many firms have established a patent committee for handling major decisions on patents and other rights. This committee might consist of a representative from top management as chairman, the research or technical director, and the head of the patent department. The function of the patent committee includes the formulation and implementation of policies, practices, and procedures with respect to the various aspects of patents and other rights. For instance, the following are subjects suitable for consideration by the patent committee: (1) decisions on the type of employee agreement on inventions that is best suited to the needs of the company; (2) awards to inventors; (3) decisions on obtaining United States and, particularly, foreign patents; (4) decisions on contesting or settling Patent Office interferences; (5) decisions on whether to maintain an exclusive position or license; (6) decisions on acquiring licenses under patents owned by others; and (7) enforcement of patents. It is good practice for the patent committee to schedule meetings at regular intervals, say four or six times per year.

Employee Agreement on Patent and Other Rights. It is customary for industry to enter into an agreement with all salaried employees or at least with research and development personnel on patents and other rights. The agreement usually covers the assignment of all inventions relating to the company's business to the employer and also may cover know-how, technical data, confidential information, and trade secrets. The agreement is generally a condition of employment. Such an agreement is in the best interests of both the employer and employee, because it reduces the chances for misunderstandings. A representative specimen agreement on inventions appears as the appendix to this chapter.

Laboratory Notebook Records. Good laboratory notebook records properly dated and witnessed are essential for the legal protection of the results of the research and development activity. Defective or incomplete records of experimental work may result in the failure to obtain a patent in case of a priority contest in the Patent Office or the invalidation of the patent if it becomes the subject of an infringement suit. Nothing short of the type of records that has been found acceptable to the Patent Office and the courts as proof of conception, diligence, and reduction to practice is adequate to protect the employer's investment in research and development.

DECISION TO OBTAIN UNITED STATES PATENTS

Whether or not to obtain a United States patent is a management decision based on recommendations by patent counsel and technical, production, and marketing personnel. It is sound practice to obtain United States patents on all inventions that are patentable and appear to be useful on a commercial scale to the owner or others. The answers to a few simple questions about an invention and the prospective patent will improve the batting average of decisions on obtaining patents. For instance: (1) What are the advantages of the new process, machine, or composition of matter over known methods or products that accomplish the same or similar results? (2) What is the size of the market for the invention? (3) Is it practical or a laboratory curiosity? (4) What would be the probable scope and validity of the prospective patents?

United States patents can be obtained if an application is filed within one year of the first public disclosure or public use of an invention. Public disclosure of an invention usually takes the form of a printed abstract of a paper that is presented at a scientific meeting, publication in a scientific or trade journal, or the cataloging of a thesis in a university or other library. The distribution of technical reports on government-sponsored research may also constitute public disclosure.

Public use means the introduction of an invention into public use. There may be a fine line between public use and experimental use. Therefore, any use of an invention prior to filing a patent application should be done only on the advice of patent counsel.

Timely filing of patent applications cannot be overemphasized. Prompt filing minimizes the chances of the application or recently issued patent becoming involved in expensive and time-consuming Patent Office interference proceedings. The first to file, or the senior party, has an overwhelming advantage, because the burden of proof is on the last to file, or the junior party. It takes an average of about three and one-half years to obtain a United States patent, and a Patent Office interference may delay issuance of the patent for three or four years.

The delay in issuance of the patent and the expense of the interference proceedings can often be reduced by entering into an agreement with the other party covering the settlement of the interference. The terms of settlement agreements vary depending on the circumstances, but the usual practice among manufacturing firms is for each party to grant the other a license. The possibility of reaching a mutually satisfactory agreement with the other party should always be considered. A settlement is often advantageous to both parties.

Foreign Patents. Most industrialized countries are members of the International Convention, which permits their nationals to obtain the benefit of the filing date in their native countries in any convention country by filing within one year of the original filing date. Thus, if an American citizen files a United States patent application prior to public disclosure or public use of the invention, he can obtain the United States filing date in all convention countries by filing in these countries within one year of the United States filing date. Foreign patent applications can be filed any time prior to public disclosure or public use of the invention, but the patent owner cannot take advantage of the United States filing date unless the foreign filing is done within one year of the United States filing.

Foreign patents are relatively expensive to obtain and maintain (taxes and annuities) and should be sought on a selective basis. Consideration of foreign patenting should be limited to the more significant inventions. United States firms usually seek foreign patents to (1) protect foreign manufacturing operations, (2) protect export sales, or (3) create licensing opportunities in foreign countries.

UTILIZATION OF PATENTS

When a decision is made to seek patents, thought should be given to their utilization. In the majority of cases, utilization will take the form of providing an exclusive position for seventeen years for the patent owner. A manufacturer's profit is generally more than can be gained from considerations for licensing.

Occasionally, the research and development activity results in patentable processes, machines, and new compositions of matter that are not susceptible to exploitation or at least exploitation to the fullest extent by the owner. If the patent does not fall within the owner's field of interests and capabilities, licensing provides an opportunity to realize a return on the investment in the experimental work that led to the patent. Licensing should also be considered if the owner is not in a position to exploit the invention to the maximum extent.

There is an increasing recognition in industry of the opportunities for licensing patents, know-how, and technical data. There is also an increasing recognition of the opportunities for locating and utilizing patents owned by others under license. Many firms have established licensing departments which handle both outgoing and incoming licenses. The licensing function is probably more of a marketing and negotiating activity than anything else.

The usual considerations for licensing are: (1) royalties, (2) participation in a joint venture, (3) sharing in the profits of the licensee, (4) rights under patents and know-how owned by others, or (5) a combination of any of these considerations. The licensing program can be started as soon as patent applications are filed. Licenses may include one or more of the following: (1) patents and patent applications, (2) know-how, (3) technical data, (4) technical assistance, and (5) trademarks. A licensing program should be undertaken only after the patent or prospective patent has been subjected to a critical analysis and evaluation by patent counsel from the viewpoint of scope and probable validity. The scope and validity of the patent, as well as economic factors, have a bearing on the terms (royalty rate and base) that will meet the test of the marketplace.

After a decision has been made to license a patent together with any know-how and technical assistance that may be available, the industry, both in the United States and abroad, should be surveyed to locate the best potential licensee(s) The patent owner will want to be assured of the competence of the prospective licensee in the areas of technology, manufacturing, distribution, and sales promotion with respect to the patent in question. A considerable amount of searching may be required to find a licensee that is qualified to commercialize the patent to the maximum extent. Effort spent on a thorough analysis and evaluation of the prospective licensee's qualifications may pay big dividends, because a patent in the wrong hands will reduce or may even nullify the returns to the patent owner.

Another important consideration is whether to license exclusively or nonexclusively. The decision on this will depend on the stage of the development of the invention, the market potential, and the nature of the industry in which the patent falls. If considerable development work will be required to bring the invention to a marketable stage, it may be desirable or even necessary to grant an exclusive license, at least exclusive for a limited period, to provide the necessary incentive to the licensee to do additional development work. There are, of course, situations where licensing broadly on a nonexclusive basis is indicated. For instance, a fully developed improved process that falls in an industry consisting of a large number of processors or fabricators should be licensed to the entire industry.

The terms of the license will depend on a number of factors such as the size of the market, profitability of the product used or sold, and the patent protection. In any event, the owner of patents and other rights is entitled to a share of the benefits that the licensee derives from the use of these rights. A royalty rate that represents a sixth or fifth of the pretax profits of the licensee is not uncommon.   Minimum royalties, performance clauses, and the like should be tailored to the prevailing circumstances.   For a discussion of international licensing arrangements, see Chapter 4 of Section 16.

OBTAINING LICENSES FROM OTHERS

Firms that wish to diversify rapidly and expand their product line may wish to consider an active search for inventions from the outside that can be developed under license.   Industrial firms represent a source of patents, particularly foreign firms that do not have manufacturing facilities in the United States.   There are several nonprofit organizations in the United States, and a few in some foreign countries, that have rather large portfolios of patents that are available for licensing.   Most of these patents emanate from educational institutions.   A few come from government agencies.   The following is a representative list of nonprofit organizations together with some universities that own patents which are available for licensing:

Battelle Development Corporation, Columbus, Ohio
California Institute of Technology, Pasadena, California
Iowa State University Research Foundation, Ames, Iowa
Arthur D. Little, Inc., Cambridge, Massachusetts
National Research Development Corporation, London, England
Ohio State University, Columbus, Ohio
Research Corporation, New York, New York
University of California Board of Patents, Berkeley, California
University of Minnesota, Minneapolis, Minnesota
University Patents, Inc., Chicago, Illinois
Wisconsin Alumni Research Foundation, Madison, Wisconsin

TRADE SECRETS

Opinion on whether to patent in certain circumstances or practice the invention as a trade secret varies quite widely.   It is difficult to generalize in this area in view of the many variable factors.   Probably the safest course to follow is to patent, provided the invention is patentable in a worthwhile sense.   An extremely limited or restricted patent may have less value than a trade secret.

ENFORCEMENT OF PATENTS

All the effort and expense of inventing, innovating, and obtaining patents may go down the drain unless the patent owner is prepared to protect the patent against infringement.   What steps to take in case of suspected infringement is a top management decision.   This is a major decision and requires an analysis and evaluation of all the facts that can be marshalled by general counsel, patent counsel, and technical, production, and marketing personnel. The principal factors to be considered are: (1) probable scope and validity of the patent, (2) damage that may be done to the patent owner's business if patent is not enforced, (3) probable amount of damages that may be recovered if patent is held valid and infringed by the courts, (4) probable cost of infringement suit, and (5) probable willingness of the suspected infringer to take a license. The estimated legal fees may not be the most significant factor in estimating the cost of an infringement suit, because heavy demands may be made on the time of management, the technical staff, and others in the organization. In any event, the decision to sue a suspected infringer is not one to be taken lightly.

Patent Department. Patent counsel usually reports to the vice president for research and development, to general counsel, or to management. Any of the three arrangements is workable, and the manager should select the one that appears to be the most effective for his particular organization. The patent department provides such services as (1) prior art patent and literature searches on proposed research projects, (2) patentability opinions on inventions, (3) preparation, filing, and prosecution of patent applications, (4) infringement opinions, and (5) the preparation of license agreements.

SUMMARY

Patents represent a valuable asset of technically oriented companies spending significant sums on research and development. It is a management responsibility to utilize and protect this asset to the maximum extent possible. A patent committee consisting of a representative of top management as chairman, the research or technical director, and the head of the patent department is recommended for establishing policies and making major decisions on patents and other rights.

Utilization of patents will usually take the form of an exclusive position for the company for seventeen years. In those cases where the patent owner is not in a position to utilize the patents or utilize them to the maximum extent, licensing should be undertaken as soon as patent applications have been filed. This provides an opportunity to realize a return on the investment in the research and development that led to the patent.

Companies that desire to expand rapidly and diversify their product lines should consider an active program for searching for patents, know-how, technical assistance, and the like from the outside that can be developed under license.

APPENDIX

Employee Agreement Relating to Inventions

Executed in Duplicate

Whereas, my employer, _____ Company, hereinafter referred to as the "Company," is engaged in the fabricating, selling, erecting and servicing _____,
_____, _____, _____, _____, and other products and articles, and is directly concerned with research and development work in connection with such products and articles and improvements thereon as well as with machines, apparatus, equipment and processes useful in producing such products and articles and improvements thereon, hereinafter termed the "business" of the Company; and

Whereas, my employment by said Company and the compensation paid to me by it are at least in part dependent upon earnings or profits which may accrue to said corporation through its ownership of or operation under inventions and patents involving or relating to the business of the Company;

Now, Therefore, in consideration of the premises, the compensation paid to me by said Company and the understanding that my employment will not be terminated nor my compensation decreased by said Company except upon _____ notice to me, I hereby covenant and agree that:

1. I will promptly disclose to an officer or official of the Company or to any one designated for that purpose by the Company all inventions and discoveries made by me during the term of my employment and for one year subsequent thereto which relate directly or indirectly to the business of the Company.

2. At the request of said Company and without further compensation to me, but at the expense of said Company, I will do all lawful and necessary acts, sign all patent applications, oaths and assignments and other papers forming a part of or incident to the applying for, obtaining and maintaining of Letters Patent both in the United States of America and countries foreign thereto for any and all such inventions and discoveries which I may make during the period set forth in paragraph 1 and to the transferring to and vesting in said Company of the sole and entire right, title and interest in, to and under such inventions, discoveries, patents and patent applications.

3. I further agree to authorize the Commissioner of Patents in writing, at any time, upon request of said Company, and at said Company's expense, to issue each and every Letters Patent that may result from my inventions or discoveries herein contemplated to said Company as assignee of the entire right, title and interest thereof.

4. If, in connection with any particular invention or discovery which I may make during the period set forth in paragraph 1, I have any doubt as to the applicability of any such invention or discovery to the business of the Company, either present or prospective, I agree to disclose and submit such invention under the provisions hereof, with the understanding that the Company shall have the sole right to determine whether or not any such particular invention or discovery falls within the contemplation of the present agreement, and that if and when the Company subsequently determines that it has no interest in the particular invention or discovery or that the same does not relate directly or indirectly to the Company's business, either present or prospective, then such invention or discovery may be released back or reassigned to me as the case may be.

Signed at _____, this _____ day of _____, 19_____

                                                                              Employee

Witnesses:

_____

Sworn to and subscribed before me this _____ day of _____
19_____

                                                                              Notary Public

(Seal)

SOURCE: A. L. Jacobs, *Patent and Trademark Practice Forms,* Central Book Company, Inc., New York, 1951.

BIBLIOGRAPHY

Berle, A. K., and L. S. de Camp, *Inventions, Patents and Their Management,* D. Van Nostrand Company, Inc., Princeton, N.J., 1959.
Calvert, Robert, *Patent Practice and Management for Inventors and Executives,* Scarsdale Press, Scarsdale, N.Y., 1950.

Eckstrom, L. T., *Licensing in Foreign Operations,* Foreign Operations Service, Inc., Essex, Conn., 1959.

Ellis, R., *Patent Licenses,* 3d ed., Baker, Voorhis and Company, Mount Kisco, N.Y., 1958.

Forman, Howard I., *Patents, Research and Management,* Central Book Company, Inc., New York, 1961.

General Information Concerning Patents, U.S. Government Printing Office, 1959.

Jacobs, A. L., *Patent and Trademark Practice Forms,* Central Book Company, Inc., New York, 1951.

Walker on Patents—Deller's Edition (annual supplements), Baker, Voorhis and Company, Mount Kisco, N.Y., 1937.

CHAPTER EIGHT

Government Research Contracts

DAVID B. SMITH *Professor of Electrical Engineering, The Moore School, University of Pennsylvania, Philadelphia, Pennsylvania*

The Federal government has become the dominant factor in the support of United States research and development and exercises a decisive influence in the direction of much of the R&D undertaken in the United States. A major share of this applied research, development, test, and evaluation is conducted by industry on contract with the government. It is necessary, therefore, for the R&D manager to understand clearly the impact of government activities upon the field of research and development, and the unique character of government contracting.

This chapter deals with the management issues. Should you do R&D business with the government? If so, how does the government conduct its R&D business? How do you go about getting a contract, and what do you do after you get one? Of necessity, this discussion can cover only a few highlights; no one should venture into the intricate and complex area of government contract research and development activity without competent legal, financial, and technical advice.

THE NATURE OF GOVERNMENT R&D

Scope of Federal R&D. Government support of R&D has increased rapidly to the point where, in 1964, about two-thirds of all United States R&D was supported and controlled by government funds. The military budget, through the Department of Defense, provided the large majority of the funding, with the National Aeronautical and Space Administration the next largest source. Many new technical developments and products have come into being as a result of government funding, and a major new industry—the defense industry—has developed to supply the needs of the government, particularly in the area of large systems. The impact of this upon United States industry has been uneven.[1] For example, many new technical products, particularly in the electronics and applied science field, have been largely supported and controlled by the military. In the field of technical components needed for military and government purposes, government-supported programs underwrite part or all of the costs of exploratory development, product engineering, unique production machinery, and major quality and reliability programs. Government hardware purchases then will often specify the use of these particular components. In such cases, a manufacturer who does not successfully compete for the early R&D contracts and continue with the follow-on contracts will find in the production phase that not only will his development costs have been higher, but also his product has to compete with others whose quality has already been established and accepted by prospective customers.

On the other hand, where the component has general industrial use and the government use is similar, the government normally will not support development effort. Thus, for example, government support of chemical R&D, except for unique military requirements such as rocket propulsion, has been relatively low.

The government, of course, issues R&D contracts to supply its own needs. These needs are usually peculiar to some requirement of the government which does not obtain in industry and are largely mission oriented. With the advent of large and complex weapons systems, and the increasing importance of reliability and maintainability, a defense industry has developed whose business is devoted to competing for this type of work. This industry offers many opportunities for subcontractors who are not qualified or do not wish to do business directly with the government. Subcontracting is an excellent way to get started in the defense business, and many prime-system contractors are interested in utilizing the special technical skills of qualified smaller companies.

Management Considerations re Government Business. The government market is a monopsony, that is, the government is the sole buyer dealing with many sellers. In addition, the government is a sovereign power. As a consequence, the government market is not only highly competitive but also highly complex and unique. Government contracts are covered by a rigid set of statutes and regulations which are quite different from those of the industrial market. There are, therefore, many differences between the relationships of a contractor to the government and a seller to a private buyer in ordinary commerce. For example, the information required by the government with respect to costs, personnel practices, and the like; the right of the government to inspect facilities and to determine compliance with other government statutes; and the right to renegotiate profits are unique to this type of business. Accepting a government contract will obligate you to far more than just performing the R&D work specified. Therefore, you should be fully aware of all your obligations before you enter into a contract with the government.

The Armed Services Procurement Regulations. The principal statute covering government contracting is the Armed Services Procurement Act of 1947 which was codified as Chapter 137 of Title 10 U.S. Code in 1956. Under this Act, the Department of Defense published a regulation known as the Armed Services Procurement Regulation (ASPR). This is the basic military procurement document. Other agencies of the government, such as the NASA and AEC, generally

---

[1] Detailed data on funds and performance of United States R&D, including breakdowns by industry (annually since 1956), are available through the National Science Foundation *Reviews of Data on Science Resources*. See, for example, NSF 64-26, vol. 1, no. 1, December, 1964. (Superintendent of Documents, U.S. Government Printing Office, Washington, D.C., 10 cents.)

follow the same basic policies, although there are often significant differences in detail and procedure.

Each of the military services has its own supplemental procedures. These are as follows: Army Procurement Procedure (APP), Air Force Procurement Instruction (AFPI), and Navy Procurement Directive (NPD). These procedures and similar procedures of other agencies delineate in detail the practices to be followed by the government agencies in procurement matters, including the procurement of R&D. The procedures are rigid and inflexible. Because of the wide variety and complexity of government procurement, they are highly involved and complicated. However, they must be followed to the letter.[2]

Government use of R&D is an evolving process. In this dynamic situation, the procurement practices and regulations also are undergoing a continual evolution, reflecting not only evolving technology but also new management practices in the executive branch of government as well as changing public policy reflected by changes in the public laws by the legislative branch. It is not possible in this Handbook to discuss other than some of the broad principles in effect in the early sixties.

The Negotiated Contract. The ASPR provides that although formal advertising with the award to the lowest bidder is the preferred form of public procurement, nevertheless there are many exceptions, including R&D contracts. These are awarded by negotiation. In this process, the government will select that contractor which in its judgment will best serve the overall interests of the government. Price will not be the controlling or even the major criterion.

The rationale for this is that because it is not possible to specify in detail the outcome of an R&D contract, the best interests of the government are served by selecting the contractor most likely to carry out the proposed program successfully. The evaluation criteria used will include estimates of the contractor's technical and management competence, financial capability, past performance, price, and even factors over which the contractor has no control but which affect public policy. The relative importance of these several criteria will vary from program to program. Price will not be a major factor.

Patents and Proprietary Rights. An important factor for the R&D manager to consider is the requirement with respect to proprietary rights. These vary from agency to agency and with changing public policy. As a minimum, the government will require that it be given the equivalent of a free license to use for government purposes any inventions or copyrights made or reduced to practice during the course of the contract. As a maximum, it may require complete ownership. In addition, the government will probably require freedom to use any background inventions. Its general objective is to be in a position such that at the completion of the R&D contract it can proceed to the next phase of development, production, or use with a minimum of limitation upon its freedom to select some other contractor to carry on the next phase of the program.

On the other hand, as a sovereign power, the government cannot be enjoined from using any patent; it can only, with its consent, be sued for damages. In addition, the government has acquired the right to use many thousands of patents. Generally in R&D contracts, the government will include a waiver of liability for patent infringement of adversely held patents, and thus the con-

---

[2] An excellent treatise on government contracting procedures and practice is *Government Prime Contracts and Subcontracts* by Paul R. McDonald, Procurement Associates, P. O. Box 565, Glendora, Calif., 1961. See also *Doing Business with the Federal Government,* General Services Administration, February, 1963, available from the U.S. Government Printing Office.

tractor enjoys considerable patent freedom. At most, he may be held liable for damages for infringement; he cannot be enjoined from using any patented invention.

Military Security. Much of government R&D is classified on the basis of military security. There are several Federal statutes covering this area. Classified work must be carried on in work areas which are adequately guarded to meet security requirements and by personnel who have obtained proper security clearance. As a general rule, it is difficult to intermix classified and nonclassified work, which will introduce some administrative problems in the laboratory and will increase overhead costs. Noncleared personnel obviously cannot enter or work in classified work areas. In addition, classified technical developments cannot be used for commercial purposes until they have become declassified. Technical personnel working upon classified projects cannot publish any technical papers revealing any classified material and in general are subject to the rules of military censorship. Factors such as these reduce the spin-off of results of government research to your broad research program.

Summary of Management Considerations. The relationship between the government and its R&D contractors is a unique one with advantages and disadvantages. In many areas of technology, the influence of the government is so pervasive that the only way to be in the field is to be a government supplier and make the necessary adjustments in your organization and facilities which doing business with the government requires. In the areas where the needs of the government are small or where there is normally a strong industrially supported program, the government influence is much less. In these instances, the disadvantages of undertaking government R&D may outweigh the advantages. Commercial independence may be more important than government support.

THE NATURE OF THE GOVERNMENT MARKET

Assume you have decided that you are interested in a government R&D contract. This contract may be for a small basic or exploratory research effort; it may be for an exploratory or applied research effort seeking to demonstrate the feasibility of a new or improved product prototype; or it may be one of a series of contracts leading to the development of a large system or subsystem. Your primary objective may be research per se; the development of a product you hope to manufacture; or the design, construction, and installation of a large system on a profit basis. The type of contract, method of reimbursement, and procedures of negotiation will vary as markedly as these different types of R&D efforts. However, there are some common principles which should be understood, which apply broadly to all government R&D contracting practice.

Identification of Government Needs. Your first step is to identify some government need or problem to be solved which you believe you can solve to the government's satisfaction better than anyone else. The procedures followed by the military are illustrative of the procedures generally used by government agencies, although there are obviously many differences between agencies and you should be familiar with the practice of the particular agency with which you plan to do business. As in industry, identified new needs come about either because of changes in the operational needs of the services or because of technological advances which make possible new missions. The services may have recognized the need, in which case they will take the initiative in getting it solved, or you may make a technical breakthrough which will generate a need you will then have to sell to them.

The Department of Defense is a tremendous and complex organization. For it to function, it must be highly organized and follow rigid procedures. However, information concerning its practices and procedures is available. Logistic and procurement planning follows the establishment of strategic plans which begin with the joint chiefs of staff. The JCS establish three broad strategic plans.

1. A joint long-range strategic estimate (time frame—seven years and beyond)
2. A joint strategic objectives plan (covering a period four to seven years ahead)
3. A joint strategic capabilities plan (covering the period for the next four years)

These plans are developed in terms of overall policies and take into account likely developments of a very broad nature including technical developments. With these plans as broad objectives, the several services then develop more refined plans to implement them, including plans for specific major systems. R&D planning in detail will be carried out by various laboratories and facilities throughout the country with overall coordination and under broad policies established by the Director of Defense Research and Engineering in the office of the Secretary of Defense. The time frame of reference of such plans follows the JCS three-phase pattern. The areas of activity of the many laboratories are defined. In general, each laboratory is expected not only to keep abreast of the state of its art but also to advance it in those R&D areas of military interest. As these missions or research needs are delineated, the several agencies will send out "requests for proposals" (RFP's) to which prospective contractors respond. In addition, the several agencies will welcome suggestions in the form of unsolicited proposals which are meaningful and contribute to the needs of the government. Such unsolicited proposals are the preferred way to obtain a "sole source" position.

Because of the complexity of the government agencies, planning is a long-time operation. A major new weapons system will go through exhaustive study, and several exploratory development alternatives will be considered before a final program is eventually crystallized. There is no assurance that a contractor who takes part in the early exploratory phases may necessarily have any guaranteed position in bidding the final contract, but he clearly has an advantage. Likewise, even relatively small research efforts aimed at advancing the state of the art will require long and careful consideration before they finally obtain approval and funding. Unless you are quite familiar with the situation and personnel involved before the RFP is released, your chances of successfully competing are quite limited.

Government Marketing. As in industry, government marketing involves:
1. Market research and market planning
2. Identification of your company and product in the mind of the customer
3. Customer contacts (both marketing and technical)
4. Proposal preparation
5. Liaison during contract performance

The government market is very large and complex. Be prepared to spend considerable time and effort in identifying the area in which you can successfully compete, specific agencies you can serve, and the way that agency does business. Fortunately, the government is aware of the complexity of its operations and the need to provide assistance to prospective contractors to help them understand its needs.[3]

[3] A useful primer is *Selling to the Military*, Department of Defense, 1963, available from the U.S. Government Printing Office (35 cents).

Market Identification. The Department of Commerce publishes daily "The Synopsis of U.S. Government Proposed Procurement Sales and Contracts Awards." This synopsis lists all unclassified procurements in excess of $10,000 and unclassified information with respect to some classified procurements. The several agencies of the government also provide information through their public relations offices with respect to their organization, areas of responsibility, and interest. The larger activities maintain bid rooms staffed with personnel whose duty is to provide information to prospective contractors.

The Small Business Administration maintains a number of offices throughout the United States to assist prospective contractors. Personnel of these offices can be quite helpful in making initial contact with the agency. In addition, each agency usually has a small business representative for the same purpose. Each agency maintains a bidders' list. You can get your name on this list by filing an application in the form utilized by the agency. Having your name on the list will not guarantee that you will automatically receive all RFP's, but the agency will make its selection of prospective bidders from this list.

There is a great deal of information available concerning the future plans of the government, but it takes some ingenuity to find it and piece it together. The trade journals, business publications, and technical press all carry significant information. Industry briefings are held from time to time. The budgets for the several agencies are public documents. Contractors with proper clearance, who are willing voluntarily to apply part of their own research resources to feasibility or exploratory studies, can take part in agency programs to develop information for their advanced planning for future needs.

Personal Contacts. In the R&D areas, you will have to have competent engineers and scientists with stature in their field. Such people should develop personal contacts and firsthand knowledge of the agency with whom you wish to do business. First-line government technical leaders are quite willing to discuss their programs with their knowledgeable industry counterparts, but be sure you do not waste their time. You are entitled to the respect due a taxpayer, but if you wish to obtain information, you must also give some in return. Likewise, first-line procurement groups will discuss their needs with knowledgeable industry marketing representatives. Because most R&D procurement requires decisions by both the technical and procurement groups of an agency, you will need both kinds of information. It usually takes an engineer to sell an engineer, but do not let him try to negotiate a contract. That is best done by knowledgeable marketing or business personnel.

It is in the interest of the government to be sure that prospective bidders fully understand the scope of work to be done; therefore, technical negotiations are conducted between the contracting officer and appropriate technical personnel and your technical group. These may be done with individual companies or, in the case of major procurements, through bidders' conferences. An important purpose of these negotiations is to discourage unqualified bidders. The other is to assist in the development of full understanding of the scope of work to be performed.

Although most selling of R&D is accomplished through personal contacts, it is often useful, particularly for smaller companies, to use manufacturers representatives or sales representatives shared with other noncompeting companies to dig out preliminary information. However, if by the time a program gets to the RFP stage both your marketing and your technical people are not thoroughly familiar with it and the agency personnel involved, your chances of being successful are very slim; you simply do not know enough about your customer's needs to be competitive. Be sure also you understand ASPR regulations with respect to fees paid to nonemployees.

THE PROPOSAL

The most important single factor in successful selling to the government is the proposal you make in response to an RFP. The purpose of this proposal is to sell your managerial and technical capabilities to carry out the work required in the best interests of the government and at a reasonable cost. It is the presentation of your capabilities upon which the customer will make the decision to buy or not buy your services. It therefore requires the best efforts not only of your technical but also your financial and management personnel. It must demonstrate that you have a real understanding of the customer's problem and a real interest in it, plus an outstanding technical capability in the specific problem area and the management skill effectively to apply that talent to the solution of the problem. It should stress economy but not to the extent of underestimating the difficulties and uncertainties of the program. It should establish that your company has adequate facilities available for research, development, test, evaluation, and production (if required) and that you have the management capability to apply these resources efficiently to the problem. It should recognize the government's particular interest in reliability, maintainability, and the like, and its somewhat unique needs in this area.[4]

Initial Review of the RFP. Immediately upon receipt of an RFP, it should be logged in at a central clearing house and responsibility for it assigned to some one manager. Only in unique situations will the government accept two different proposals from any one company, even though it be large and consist of many separate, decentralized divisions. It should be screened immediately to determine whether to bid or not bid. This review should consider such items as the following:

1. Are you familiar with the requirement, the technical background, and the needs of the customer? (If there is any question, you should immediately seek clarification from government personnel.)

2. What will be the effect on your operations if you get the contract?

3. Is the proposed work in line with your R&D program and consistent with your long-range objectives?

4. Do you have available the necessary technical personnel and facilities, and is this the most effective way they can be used?

5. Do you have the necessary managerial talent and financial capability to accomplish the requirement?

6. What is your competition and how will success or failure in the proposal contest affect your overall competitive position?

7. Can you meet all the terms of the RFP?

8. Are you familiar with the terms of all applicable military specifications, including those included by reference?

9. Are patent clauses, royalty provisions with respect to proprietory rights, and the like satisfactory?

[4] See *Guidelines for Preparing More Effective Engineering Proposals*, NAVMAT P-4856, March, 1965, and *Guidelines for Developing and Submitting an Unsolicited Proposal to the Navy Department*, NAVMAT P-4201, March, 1965, both available from the Department of the Navy, Office of Naval Material, Washington, D.C. Similar documents are available from the Army and Air Force.

10. Do you understand the financial terms, effect of local, state, and Federal taxes, possibility of special financing, military security and bonding requirements, and insurance requirements?

11. Is government-owned property or material to be used? If so, have you inspected it?

12. Do you understand how your proposal will be evaluated?

13. Have you considered all the risks and advantages?

It is generally desirable to be quite selective in determining which RFP to bid and to concentrate on those which you have a reasonable chance of winning. A good proposal takes time and money. It is not desirable to squander these resources by bidding situations where there is much competition and you do not have some competitive advantages. If you decide not to bid, you should write a letter to the contracting officer explaining why you did not bid. This is necessary to maintain good relations with the agency and to prevent possible loss of future business. Contrary to popular opinion, there is no percentage of proposals you should expect to win. Proposal competition is a game of skill, not of chance.

Proposal Preparation. A major R&D proposal will involve information from technical, financial, manufacturing, and other personnel. It may involve questions of subcontracting or teaming with other contractors. The time available will be short. Therefore this information and these decisions must be developed in parallel, carefully coordinated to avoid internal inconsistencies, and then put together to form an effective selling document. As a minimum, it is desirable to select a proposal director with authority to obtain the necessary information, coordinate the efforts of the different groups, obtain decisions, and develop the final document. In some companies, there are proposal preparation departments established for this purpose.

The immediate task is to determine the final form the proposal is to take and to develop from the RFP a checklist of all the information needed. The proposal may be anything from a simple letter for small research efforts to several volumes of hundreds of pages for major systems. In the latter case, PERT or CPM techniques are often used to manage the proposal effort.

The form and format of the proposal should be determined. The type and quantity of illustrations should be established. The principal issue here is to select that combination of text and illustration which will most effectively get your message across without being extravagant. Remember, the proposal will be evaluated by many people, some of whom may not have the time or inclination to read it in detail, particularly if it is poorly written or poorly illustrated. There should be continuity between text and illustration.

Outline for Each Proposal Area. Each proposal, or principal proposal area of a large proposal, should consist of (1) an executive summary, (2) the body of the proposal, (3) a summary of principal points developed, and (4) appendixes (where necessary).

The readers of the proposal will have a wide variety of interests. Therefore an initial or executive summary is essential. This should state what the proposal is about and how it will be accomplished. It will be read by everyone. It should therefore convince the reader that you understand his problem and that you have an interesting approach to a solution. If you fail to make these two points, the reader is not likely to read further.

The Technical Proposal. The technical proposal should then expand and further delineate these two points. It should provide a convincing analysis of the customer's need. Major problem areas should be identified. Areas in which significant technical advances are required should be separated from those that are within the state of the art. Key assumptions of your analysis should be identified. The relationship between the proposal and the system of which it will be a part should be defined.

The body of the proposal should then explain how you propose to solve the problem and accomplish the results required. Block diagrams, mock-ups, illustrations, and photographs that will facilitate the reader's understanding should be selected from the point of view of the reader. Any areas in which the company has a unique approach should be carefully delineated. Data on performance, parameters, and the like should be presented with tables, charts, and graphs. Mathematical concepts should be explained in words; formulas and equations should be developed in the appendixes. The technical presentation should be in accordance with professional standards.

Technical Proposal Checklist. The following is a checklist of points to be considered in the technical proposal. Not all are applicable to any one proposal, nor is the list complete. It is indicative, however, of the thoroughness with which a proposal should be developed.

1. Program planning charts which indicate checkpoints of technical accomplishment and management review. PERT, PEP, or CPM procedures are usually required for larger R&D systems-type contracts.
2. An identification of major technical problems to be solved and the amount of effort allocated to each. This should also show that you truly understand the customer's problem.
3. A description of novel ideas or new approaches you have developed to solve the customer's problem.
4. A discussion of technical approaches you have explored or will undertake to solve his problem.
5. An outline of alternative approaches and why they were discarded. This and item 4 give you a chance to demonstrate prior independent R&D you have done in this area.
6. Identification of any unrealistic or unreasonable requirements the customer may ask for. The customer may not be aware of all the implications of his request, or you may not be aware of all the surrounding circumstances. In this situation, tread lightly but offer alternative solutions.
7. If you feel you must deviate from the customer's requirement, you should so indicate and justify your deviation. Such deviations should be kept to an absolute minimum.
8. Your proposal, within security limits, should show the relation of this proposal to previous contract efforts with the same or other agencies, both to avoid duplication and to establish your competence.
9. If you intend using proprietory data, this fact should be identified.
10. The company facilities—either in-house or available outside—and who will pay for them should be defined. The extent to which the program will require the use of government facilities should be delineated.
11. You should provide an honest estimate of the likelihood of success of the program.
12. If the proposal is one which will, if successful, lead to manufacture or production of a hardware item or system, then in addition, you should include such items as:
    a. An estimate of maintenance costs and procedures
    b. Identification of any unusual reliability problems or requirements
    c. A demonstration that you have used existing components wherever possible and if not, why not

d. A brief review of how the total program could proceed to a conclusion

e. Your interest in the next phase of development, production, installation, or use

The Management Proposal. The management proposal should delineate the company's experience, personnel, and qualifications in fields similar to the program under consideration. It should include a brief outline of the technical capabilities of the company, management accomplishments, facilities, and the like. A standard company brochure may be used for this purpose. The customer will be more interested in the type of management to be provided for this particular program. Therefore, the specific plan for managing the program, the limits of authority and responsibility of key people, and their position in the company hierarchy should be defined. In a large R&D contract, particularly of a systems nature, it is desirable that the proposed functional organization of the contractor match that of the agency, so there is a simple direct correspondence of functional offices between customer and contractor to provide easy communication between the two. The position of the program and authority of the program director must match the importance of the program in the mind of the agency.

Detailed biographical information should be included for key management and technical personnel. This should consist only of information relevant to the proposal in question. The degree of availability of these people should be stated. Any company regularly doing business with the government should maintain up-to-date files for its principal personnel plus statistical information which will establish the general level and competence of lower-level personnel. If consultants are to be employed, they should be identified and their qualifications given. In general, the management proposal should demonstrate that the company has adequate resources, competent people, and management know-how, and that the proposal has the enthusiastic support of the organization.

The Cost Proposal. Considerable cost information will be required even for simple research contracts. In many cases, cost estimates will be required from a number of different groups within the company for work which cannot be clearly defined. The natural tendency then is to pad the estimate. Therefore, it is quite important to allow sufficient time in the proposal effort to make a careful management review of all cost estimates. Moreover, since these estimates in negotiated contracts may later be subject to audit, it is important to ensure that each estimate is carefully documented in considerable detail by work papers which should be preserved.

Every effort should be made to make these estimates as realistic as possible. The government agencies have become quite sophisticated in their ability to make their own estimates, partly because of the extensive data they require from contractors. They will use this information not only for pricing purposes but also to evaluate the contractor's management acumen and understanding of the problem. An excessively low estimate may indicate lack of technical understanding. An excessively high estimate may indicate a sloppy, poorly done job with the inference that the contract, if awarded, would be done in the same way.

In some instances, you may wish to "buy into" a situation by cost sharing.[5] In other cases, particularly where the R&D has important commercial value, the government may believe its negotiating strength is such that it can require cost sharing. In either case, you should indicate your best cost estimates of

[5] A better business strategy may be to spend the same time and effort on preliminary R&D and proposal effort, and thus avoid "cost sharing."

the total program and then the extent to which you are willing to cost-share, so there is no misunderstanding of your appraisal of the size of the program.

A word of caution is in order on cost sharing. Most companies that regularly do business with the government are allowed to charge a portion of their overall R&D expense to overhead. The portion is identified as independent R&D and must be in the general interest of the government. However, your share of R&D conducted on a cost-sharing basis does not qualify for inclusion as independent R&D. Be sure, then, you understand all the financial implications of cost sharing.

Final Proposal Review. After the several sections of the proposal have been prepared, a detailed final review by senior management and editing is in order. The proposal is your principal selling tool. Review it with that in mind. Is it internally consistent? Does it clearly put your best foot forward—show that you truly understand the customer's need and have a novel and attractive solution for him which is consistent with his ability to pay for it? Does it clearly and succinctly set forth what you will do and why your proposed solution is preferable to all others? Is it easy to read and understand so that the quick reader can readily pick up the main theme and be encouraged to read in more detail? Does it demonstrate substance rather than mere brochuremanship? Is it a good selling document? If it is, be sure you get it delivered to the contracting officer on time.

In negotiated contracts, considerable latitude is permitted the contracting officer in receiving modifications of original proposals. You should, therefore, keep in touch with him after your proposal is filed, and maintain your efforts to improve your position until the die is cast. It is not good practice, however, to submit a poorly prepared proposal in the expectation of being able to fix it later.

PROPOSAL EVALUATION AND CONTRACTOR SELECTION

Procedures and Policy. The government has developed quite sophisticated procedures for evaluating R&D proposals. Some knowledge of these is necessary to prepare your proposal properly and determine whether or not to bid. Within the government, there is a clear distinction between the technical groups who determine the scope of work of the RFP, suggest possible sources, and make the technical evaluation and the procurement groups who have the sole authority to make the final selection and award the contract.

With respect to the evaluation for the award of an R&D contract, ASPR 4-205-4 provides as follows:

(a) Generally, research and development contracts should be awarded to those organizations, including educational organizations, which have the highest competence in the specific field of science or technology involved. However, awards should not be made for research and development capabilities that exceed those needed for the successful performance of the work.

(b) Before determining the technical competence of prospective contractors and concerns that they consider most technically competent, cognizant technical personnel shall consider the following:

(i) The contractor's understanding of the scope of work as shown by the scientific or technical approach proposed.

(ii) Availability and competence of experienced engineering, scientific, or other technical personnel.

(iii) Availability, from any source, of necessary research, test, and production facilities.

(iv) Experience or pertinent novel ideas in the specific branch of science or technology involved.

(v) The contractor's willingness to devote his resources to the proposed work with appropriate diligence.

(c) In determining to whom the contract should be awarded, the Contracting Officer shall consider not only technical competence, but also all other pertinent factors including management capabilities, weighing each factor in accordance with the requirements of the particular procurement.

Evaluation Scoring System. The technical evaluation of your R&D proposal will usually be made on the basis of the following primary criteria, with relative weights of each depending upon the specific case.

1. The quality and responsiveness of the proposal
2. The organization, personnel, and facilities of the bidder
3. The technical approach

Each of these major areas will be subdivided and these subareas further subdivided. Point scores are then assigned to each subfactor and summed. As a minimum, you will have to attain a passing score in each major area to be considered.

These various factors will be selected and evaluated by the government technical personnel for each RFP. An illustrative table of typical principal factors, each of which would be further subdivided in actual practice, is as follows:

A. Quality and responsiveness
   1. Completeness and thoroughness
   2. Grasp of problem
   3. Responsiveness to terms, conditions, time schedule
B. Organization, personnel, and facilities
   1. Quality of proposed organization and management plan
   2. Qualifications of personnel
   3. Facilities
   4. Related experience
   5. Past performance
   6. Follow-on production capability
   7. Geographic location
   8. Security
C. Technical approach
   1. Project planning
   2. Reliability
   3. Maintainability
   4. Producibility and design simplicity
   5. Technical data and documentation
   6. Other specific technical subfactors peculiar to the particular project (usually identified in the RFP)

In some cases, the RFP will identify several phases of a development with a firm proposal required for the first and an estimate for the later phases. In such cases, a technical evaluation will be made for each phase.

Following the above procedure, the technical evaluation panel will then determine which proposals are unsatisfactory and rate the successful ones. This information is then turned over to the contracting officer who will negotiate with several of the successful bidders to establish one or more contracts.

Agency Debriefing. If your proposal does not win, you should prepare a "lost business" report for your guidance in the future. You can be debriefed by the agencies and will be told how they evaluated your proposal and your areas of weakness. You should pay careful attention to their findings even though it is distasteful. They are the customer.

Even if you are successful, it is still a good idea to obtain the agency's evaluation of your proposal so that you can take steps to improve weak areas. The government is quite conscientious in its evaluation, and its candid opinion has considerable management value which you are foolish not to take seriously.

Contract Negotiations. Usually in R&D contracts some type of cost reimbursement contract is employed because of the indeterminate nature of the work scope and "best efforts" nature of the commitment. This may be cost plus fixed fee, cost plus incentive fee, cost sharing, or a combination of these. It is not within the scope of this chapter to discuss the fine art of government contract negotiation. However, certain factors which distinguish it from industrial business should be noted.

1. The contracting officer is the sole responsible government agent authorized to commit the government. Unlike a private buyer, his authority is established by statute. He cannot commit the government for acts beyond his statutory authority.

2. The government will be a hard, shrewd buyer with the benefit of a great deal of staff work to assist in negotiation. Both Congress and the Government Accounting Office will check the agencies to see how well they do. The government, however, will not exercise its sovereign power in negotiations.

3. The term "best interests of the government" is quite broad and includes factors over which you have no control but which will influence whether or not you get a contract. This includes issues as to whether you are in a labor surplus area, small business considerations, industrial mobilization criteria, disposal of facilities, and so on.

4. The government does recognize the value of the profit motive and will expect you to make a profit commensurate with the risk you take. They will encourage contractual provisions which permit you a large profit for excellent performance if you in turn agree to profit reduction for poor performance. The ranges of profits permitted are established by ASPR regulations, and cost-type contracts are usually subject to renegotiation after completion.

5. Larger R&D contracts will require many approvals within the government hierarchy before they are finally authorized. This may extend to the secretary of the particular service or even the Secretary of Defense. You should expect many delays and uncertainties, for you will not have received the award until you have a contract in hand which has been duly authorized, signed, and properly funded. You may sometimes tactfully assist in expediting the process of your proposal, but generally you just have to "sweat it out."

6. Finally, it should be noted that, particularly in the early stages of applied research or exploratory development of a new weapon or weapon system, it is quite probable that the government will enter into contracts with several different contractors with different technical approaches. The idea here is to establish a technical competition and explore alternative approaches before finalizing on a particular one. If you find yourself in such a competition, there is no reason why you cannot change your ideas as your knowledge improves, but be sure you meet your contract commitments for the contract you have.

CONTRACT PERFORMANCE

Some Management Problems. When you finally have your contract in-house, you are then ready to proceed to do the work. You will not be allowed any costs incurred prior to the date of the contract or other contractual authorization such as a letter of intent. If you are ready and able to go ahead of time, this may be tactfully used to speed up delivery of the actual contract, but you proceed at your own risk prior to receipt of the contract. This may cause problems in scheduling your R&D personnel. You should anticipate this and plan your work schedule to provide a reasonable time to build up the work force.

Of course, you will again review your technical proposal and the events which have transpired since you wrote it, as well as the work statement in the contract. You will be expected to do exactly what is called for by the contract—no more and no less.[6] In view of the uncertainty inherent in R&D programs, you should anticipate a number of changes as the work progresses. Both your technical people and those of the government will undoubtedly have many new ideas and will want to modify the scope of work as it develops. A principal management problem will be to keep these changes under control. Document all phone calls and meetings with the customer. Not infrequently, your technical people and those of the government may mutually decide to go off on some tangent. You will not be performing the contract, however, and will be penalized unless the change is formally incorporated in the contract. Only the contracting officer is authorized to make changes, and these must be in writing. Be sure that your technical people do not agree to changes and act on them until they are formally included in the contract.

The Contract Administrator. It is good practice to establish a contract administrator in addition to the program administrator to ensure that all terms and conditions of the contract are fully met and only work authorized by the contract is, in fact, done. A controller-type person is an excellent choice as a contract administrator. You can anticipate some difficulties among the program manager, the marketing people, and the contract administrator. A careful delineation of scope and authority is required for each. The marketing people will naturally favor the customer. The program manager will want to do the best job possible and, perhaps, deviate somewhat from the contract. He may, especially if he is a technical manager, be impatient of nontechnical details and overlook them. The contract administrator is your assurance that each detail of the contract is carried out on time and within budget; that you are not persuaded to do more than you contracted to do; and if something does go wrong, that it is promptly brought to management's attention.

Liaison with the Government. The contract will usually specify some liaison officer to handle details of contract performance, inspection of hardware, and the like. Usually, for companies regularly doing business with the government, one of the services will maintain a resident inspector who will act for all the services. You should be sure you understand the extent and scope of his authority with respect to each contract. Generally, he will be your point of contact for proof of specific contract performance, items delivered, and so on. He will also see that the standard provisions of the contract are fulfilled.

R&D contracts usually provide for monthly or more frequent reports of progress as well as estimates of budget performance. You should plan to monitor progress carefully. If you should find that you have encountered unusual technical difficulties or have budget problems (especially in cost plus fee contracts), these should promptly be brought to the attention of the contracting officer and the issues resolved. It is well always to keep in mind that the complexities of the government are so great that it simply cannot permit any deviation from its procedures. To do so would invite all kinds of trouble.

[6] Good business practice may indicate that you should give the customer a little more than you are required to do.

R&D contracts also usually provide for the assignment of a technical officer to direct the conduct of the investigation. You should plan to keep him fully informed of your progress and problems. You should take the initiative in so doing. Keep in mind, however, that only the contracting officer has the authority to modify the contract. Your technical liaison engineer may be a little sensitive with respect to questions about his authority, but you should tactfully insist upon formal contract modification wherever necessary.

During the course of the contract, you should see to it that meticulous records are kept on all items subject to later audit. These will include hourly time cards for technical personnel, detailed records for all material purchased, and detailed expense accounts for all travel involved. Inevitably, some of your costs will be disallowed by the government auditors, and these items will come right out of your profit. The better your records, the less likely this is to happen.

Follow-on Program. During the course of the program, you should be actively planning for the next phase of the development and utilizing your necessary contacts with the agency's technical personnel to develop a sense of "where do we go from here." The government will welcome thoughtful suggestions on this point even though they may not buy your ideas in their entirety. The chances are that they will discuss freely with you their own thoughts with respect to their future needs and criteria which must be met. This will enable you to prepare follow-on programs or extensions of your existing contract. You both have the common objective of making the most—in the interest of the government—of this particular development.

Finally, you will complete the contract and wrap it up with a final report, and delivery and acceptance of hardware if required; or the government may terminate the contract for its convenience; or you may be unsuccessful. In any case, you will have left some impression of your competence. In larger R&D contracts, the government is developing formal methods of evaluating and recording their impression of your performance. This will be taken into account the next time you make a proposal.

Financial Audit. After the technical work has been completed and delivered, the auditors will move in and your books and records will be minutely scrutinized. If your financial people have been meticulous in their record keeping and your technical personnel have actually followed through on their paper work, your problems in this area will be minimized. Some amount of 20-20 hindsight and second guessing is to be expected at this time. But the better your records, the less of this you will have.

When you have completed the renegotiation program or the statutory period for it has passed, and all the classified work you have done has been declassified, then and only then can you close the books on this particular contract. Hopefully, you will have long since gone off on other follow-on contracts or production programs based upon this particular R&D effort.

SUMMARY

If you decide to seek government R&D business, your first problem is to find a prospective customer to whom your technical and management competence has value. You must become thoroughly familiar with his problems in your area. Good personal contacts with his technical personnel are your preferred method of accomplishing this objective. He will formulate his needs in a "request for proposals" to which you may respond.

Be sure you thoroughly understand the RFP and the competitive situation. Your response is a proposal which is your principal selling document and requires your best efforts. This proposal has at least three basic areas: the technical proposal, the management proposal, and the cost proposal. It should demonstrate clearly that you understand the customer's problem and have an interesting approach to it. The proposal should also be internally consistent, economically and technically sound, and easily understood. The proposal will be evaluated by a panel of people utilizing a numerical scoring system.

If you succeed in this competition, your next step is to negotiate a contract—usually a cost-type contract for R&D—with the contracting officer on the best terms you can get. With the contract in-house, you then perform it, paying meticulous attention to all requirements of the contract, including the extensive paper work and detail requirements. Upon completing the contract and satisfying the technical requirements, your costs and performance will be carefully audited. By then, you should be well along on new contracts which have evolved from your previous association with the agency.

BIBLIOGRAPHY

Doing Business with the Federal Government, General Services Administration, U.S. Government Printing Office, February, 1963.

Guidelines for Developing and Submitting an Unsolicited Proposal to the Navy Department, NAVMAT P-4201, Department of the Navy, Office of Naval Material, March, 1965.

Guidelines for Preparing More Effective Engineering Proposals, NAVMAT P-4856, Department of the Navy, Office of Naval Material, March, 1965.

McDonald, P. R., *Government Prime Contracts and Subcontracts,* Procurement Associates, Glendora, Calif., 1961.

Novick, D., *Program Budgeting: Long Range Planning in the Department of Defense,* Rand Report no. RM3359 ASDC Nn., 1962.

Peck, M. J., and F. M. Scherer, *The Weapons Acquisition Process: An Economic Analysis,* Harvard University Press, Cambridge, 1962.

Research and Development in American Industry, 1962, National Science Foundation, NSF 63-37, U.S. Government Printing Office, January, 1963.

Review of Data on Science Resources, National Science Foundation, NSF 64-26, vol. 1, U.S. Government Printing Office, December, 1964.

Roberts, E. B., "How the U.S. Buys Research," *International Science and Technology,* vol. 33, September, 1964, p. 70.

Selling to the Military, Department of Defense, U.S. Government Printing Office, 1963.

CHAPTER NINE

Evaluating Research and Development Performance

JOHN C. R. KELLY, JR. *General Manager, Advanced Reactors Division, Westinghouse Electric Corporation, Pittsburgh, Pennsylvania*

Universally applicable techniques for evaluating research and development performance do not exist. The spectrum of research from basic to applied and the divergence from specific new products to less specific product and cost improvements make it unwise to attempt to apply any single criterion. However, there is universal agreement that quantitative measurement must be taken and that the best available criteria must be applied to the evaluation of each class of research even if recognition of the uncertainties in the estimation is required. An orderly approach to increasingly profitable research and development must evolve.[1]

Categories of Research Contributions. The contributions by laboratories to profit derive from four definable types of research and development. These types are:

1. Basic research—the investigation of fields of science with no particular product concept or function in mind

2. Applied research—that category of research where the product concept or function is defined when the research is undertaken, but the intent of the research deals with an element of the product, either material or configuration, but not with the product in its entirety

3. Product development—effort which considers the entire product and all of its function and content and the interactions of all of the elements of the product

4. Consultation—providing knowledge from specialists who, because of their researches in specific fields, are able to advise and guide in the solution of specific problems

It is evident that the order of the increasing ease of evaluation is: basic research, applied research, product development. Consultation, by its nature,

[1] A. H. Rubenstein (ed.), *Coordination, Control, and Financing of Industrial Research,* King's Crown Press, New York, 1955.

may be quantitatively evaluated as to its worth in those cases where it contributes spontaneous innovation in the development or improvement of a product, but it is difficult of precise evaluation where it is merely guidance and counsel in some element of design or fabrication of the product. For purposes of exposition, we will discuss applied research and product development in some detail and deal with basic research and consultation only in specific instances.

The Nature of Research Contributions. Contributions from research can be divided into two categories—technical and financial. Technical contributions, which may be quantitatively assessed, are: scientific and engineering papers, specialist articles in trade journals, patent disclosures and applications, patents issued, publicity releases, internal reports and memoranda, and awards for distinguished contribution by individual scientists, groups of scientists, or the laboratory as a whole.[2]

Laboratory dollar values or figures of merit may be assigned to each of these areas of technical contribution, but there is no standard for such values. It is necessary to initiate such an analysis and then carry it through year by year as a means for comparison relative to previous performance and also for goal setting for future performance. Obviously, the value associated with such factors as published information or patented information will vary depending upon the policies of the corporation with which the laboratory is associated.

Shockley[3] advocated the use of papers as a measure of productivity and, therefore, performance of laboratories. This approach has not been adopted other than as a guideline, although basic research current performance may be compared in this way. This measurement can be extended to "patents applied for" or "patents issued," but the identification of factors which influence the performance is largely a matter of judgment. Nevertheless, some use may be made of this type of measurement provided the shortcomings of the techniques are recognized.

The financial contributions of research can be measured directly in dollars in those cases where identification can be made of sales billed by the corporation for products resulting from the work of the laboratory. An estimate may be made of influenced gross sales billed for products and services by the corporation based upon a realistic appraisal of the value of the laboratory contribution to product salability and profitability. This estimate should be made by the marketing executive of the corporation and should take into account the relative contributions of the laboratory and of the division engineers to the ultimate design and content of the product.

In addition, direct income may be derived by the laboratory from sources such as (1) government prime contracts; (2) support contracts carried out as subcontracts from the divisions of the corporation; (3) requisitions for work from the divisions; and, in some instances, (4) actual sale of developmental materials, components, or services. Any license income from patents or engineering agreements should also be considered a quantitative contribution.

Additional financial contributions which cannot be evaluated quantitatively or semiquantitatively relate to the influence on existing and potential customers of the laboratory. The laboratory is used as a showplace to impress upon customers the vital technical content of the product that they may buy. This has an unassessable influence on gross sales billed. The same might also be said of awards and articles in professional and trade journals, but they are

[2] J. W. Hackett, "Proceedings of Industrial Research Institute Study Group Meetings, No. 7, Evaluation of Research," *Research Management*, vol. 5, 1962, pp. 177–192.

[3] W. Shockley, "On the Statistics of Individual Variations of Productivity in Research Laboratories," Operations Research Society of U.S.A., Washington, D.C., 1954.

countable and therefore may be used as a factor in both quantitative and qualitative measurement.

The Relation between Programming of Research and Evaluation of Performance. Research projects should be carefully programmed to take into consideration all elements of risk, including cost of performing the research program, duration of the program as it relates to proper timing of market entry, forecast of expected new gross sales billed or incremental gross sales billed, probability of success both in the research phase and in the marketing phase, and expenditures to be incurred by the corporation after the development is released from the laboratory, that is, the investment of capital funds, engineering, advertising, and marketing costs necessary to introduce the product into the marketplace.

Further consideration must be given to the competitive situation which influences the success of the product. It may be either *offensive,* which would penetrate new market areas with a new product, or *defensive,* which would protect a segment of market currently held by the corporation. The same considerations apply to cost-improvement or product-improvement projects.

During the course of the research and development program, these elements must be under constant surveillance. The size of the market, the growth of the market, the influence of competition, and the influence of competing technologies must be assessed at quarterly intervals. A prerequisite is that the programming be scheduled in such a way as to identify checkpoints in the research and development program at the same intervals. It is then possible by periodic review to identify areas of slippage in financial, technical, or time objectives of the project. This evaluation takes place before the product is ready for transfer to the manufacturing organization. The second step involves evaluation in detail of the financial and time-oriented considerations which are spelled out in another part of this chapter.

Quantitative Measurement of Cost. The following outline summarizes the thinking of a number of writers on the subject of evaluating research and development cost.

1. What was the total expense of the research effort?
   a. Engineering salaries
   b. Engineering overheads
   c. Technician salaries
   d. Technician overheads
   e. Drafting expenses
   f. Model-shop expenses
   g. Original cost of any special equipment not carried in the general engineering overheads
   h. All materials purchased in performance of the project
   i. Consultant fees
   j. Special services such as analytical chemistry, physical testing, electrical testing, underwriters' fees
   k. Patent attorneys' fees and filing costs

Some writers include a proration of the cost of those research projects which have been *concluded without commercialization* during the period of time that the project being evaluated was active in the research laboratory.[4]

Note: The separation of overhead costs in the research laboratory is desirable to highlight the expense of supporting the professional staff in the laboratory.

2. What was the expense of transfer and assimilation by the manufacturing organization? The following listing of division *costs* is to be included *with* overhead:

[4] L. B. Hitchcock, "Selection and Evaluation of Research and Development Projects, Part I," *Research Management,* vol. 6, 1963, pp. 231–244.

   a. Division engineering costs
   b. Division model-shop costs
   c. Division testing and evaluation costs
   d. Consultants' fees (if any)
   e. Capital—new machine tools
   f. Capital—new building
   g. Capital—land
   h. Capital—field warehousing
   i. Marketing and distribution costs
   j. Advertising and sales promotion costs
   k. Warranty allowances and expenses

These costs must be recorded and preserved to be deducted eventually in some fashion from the quantitatively evaluated contributions discussed above. Because of the elapsed time between the establishment of the project and the resulting costs (outflow of cash) and the first sale (inflow of cash), an analysis of this cash flow is advisable.

Cash Flow Analysis. Because economic performance is the criterion for determining the effectiveness of research and development, the analysis must conform to established patterns of business management. It is an accepted practice to utilize cash flow in the evaluation of the effectiveness of any action within the corporation aimed at improvement of profitability. It is therefore possible to utilize a cash flow analysis for determining the performance of research and development. The qualitative elements listed among research contributions may be utilized only as judgment factors in cash flow, but there are definite quantitative measures as defined above. In the research and development and in the production phases of a new or improved product, they may be used for calculation of performance.

Figures 9-1 and 9-2 illustrate the applicability of cash flow analysis to evaluation of research and development performance. Figure 9-1 defines the ideal situation, where the outflow of cash is counterbalanced by the inflow of cash, plus a profitable return over a period of time which is consistent with the corporation's policies for the utilization of its resources. The time scale and the dollar scale are obviously dependent upon the factors identifiable with the product involved. For example, a product must conform to the corporation's standards as they relate to asset turnover and a product lifetime of positive cash flow that will be consistent with the corporation's standards for return on investment over a specified period of time. This may be as short as one year for a high-volume product or as long as fifteen years for a high-technology product.

Good planning requires maintenance of an R&D effort during the lifetime

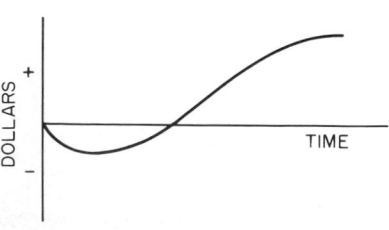

FIG. 9-1. *Cash flow analysis where outflow of cash is counterbalanced by inflow of cash plus a profitable return over a period of time.*

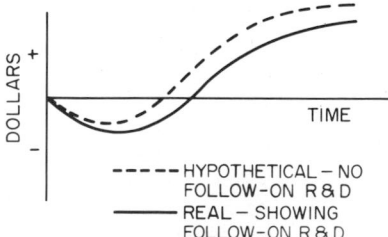

FIG. 9-2. *Cash flow for a high-technology product with and without the maintenance of R&D effort.*

of a high-technology product to remain competitive. This is reflected in Figure 9-2. Within these boundaries, the analysis of research and development performance must, in any evaluation, consider and identify the product and its lifetime, both from a technological and market-acceptance point of view and from the point of view of the ability of the corporation to maintain its market position in that class of product.

Average Profitable Lifetime of a Research Contribution. It is generally true that the average profitable lifetime of a research contribution is three years.

1. A cost reduction may be expected to make a contribution to earnings only for the first year of its introduction. Competitors will quickly copy any cost reduction resulting from a substitution of material or change in design, because infringement of any basic patents held by the innovating corporation will probably not be involved.

2. A product improvement (that is, an improvement in the function performed by the product or in the weight, size, or other characteristics of the product) may be valuable for as long as three years or whatever time competitors require to make an equivalent or advanced improvement. This therefore protects the innovators for that period of time before any decline in increased margin will occur.

3. A new product may be presumed to have a life of from five to seventeen years. If the innovation is a major engineering advance in an area where the certainty of patent protection can never be assured, such as alloy composition, the shorter life is more likely. Where major discovery and therefore monopoly of a new technology may be established, at least as it relates to the principal technological innovation, the seventeen-year life of a patent applies.

These several alternatives may be plotted on the cash flow diagram. They influence only the relationship between the initial investment and the lifetime of the positive cash flow resulting from the innovation. In any analysis of these three areas of contribution, consideration of the predictable or estimated lifetime of the contribution is the most critical variable. It is, at best, hazardous to presume that any cost reduction will exist beyond one year or that any product improvement, in terms of increased function or reliability, will exist after three years. It is most difficult to predict the lifetime of a major technological innovation in the period of time commencing at five years and extending to seventeen years.

In any estimation of costs of research and development as they relate to the negative aspect of cash flow in evaluating research and development performance, those elements of research and development cost devoted to cost reduction must be considered written off within the first year of application in the manufacturing operation. Then, any corporate criterion for return must be applied to this write-off. For example, consider a reduction in cost of $5 in the factory costs of a $100 factory-cost product where the annual production is 100,000 units. This should return $500,000 in gross improvement in margin offset by no more than $50,000 in total cash expended to achieve the cost improvement. The cash expended must include the cost of the research with all overheads and the cost of any new facilities required to achieve the cost reduction at policy rates of amortization. Discount this by the conversion or cash value of any new capital assets acquired to accomplish the cost reduction should its lifetime be as short as the one-year estimate would seem to indicate.

The same reasoning may be applied to a product improvement or major new-product innovation in evaluating the effect of the research and development contribution. But it cannot be ignored as part of the initial cost ratioed to the total benefit achieved from the innovation.

Case History. *Objective.* To develop a new control mechanism for a manufacturing process that would exploit (1) the maximum capability of solid-state devices and (2) the most recent knowledge of mathematical-statistical techniques. The design of the control system for the product should result in maximum saving to the ultimate customer in total manufacturing costs while permitting the originating corporation to design and manufacture a device at a cost which would permit sale to the customer at margins which are commensurate with corporate objectives.

Approach

1. The research program in solid-state technology was related to the application of known devices in new circuitry to accomplish the end result.

2. The cost of development of necessary new solid-state functions was borne by the project only in proportion to the explicit use of the new devices in development of the control system.

3. The mathematical-statistical analysis was, by its nature, far less expensive, involving no laboratory experimentation and no investment in models, but only the periodic testing of the statisticians' prescriptions of the number of variables to be controlled so as to specify the minimum number of variables necessary to control the process required by the customer.

4. The number of customers was identified at the beginning of the program by a corporate market research organization.

5. The extent of the market was defined by that same organization. An estimate was made jointly between the marketing and the manufacturing organization as to the percent of the corporation's participation in the market currently.

6. The estimated increase in market participation and resulting gross sales billed and margin anticipated were also forecast by these two organizations.

The total integrated costing of the project then proceeded as follows: The engineering salaries associated with both the solid-state devices and the mathematical-statistical analysis in the research and development laboratory since inception were $250,000. The overheads on the engineering costs were 100 percent of salaries. The technician salaries were $300,000. The overheads on technician salaries were also 100 percent. Drafting expenses were $100,000 and model-shop expenses for prototype models performing portions, but not all, of the functions were $150,000.

One new piece of equipment was required to make an analog of the potential customer's process; this analog computer, applicable only in model design and development in a very narrow area and not generally useful in the laboratory (therefore not carried in the general overheads), was $75,000.

No special materials other than conventional catalog transistors, diodes, and other component parts totaling $10,000 were required in performance of the project. A consultant, recently retired from one of the corporations in the involved industry, was engaged to consult with the laboratory on the various elements of the process (such as process time, labor costs, and customer end requirements in terms of product performance, reliability, and duty time) at a cost of $10,000. It was necessary to install a module of the control system in an actual plant to obtain information about the performance of this module in the manufacturing environment. This cost was at the request of the customer and was borne jointly by the research laboratory and the customer.

Three patent disclosures were written and two patent applications were filed at a cost of $5,000. In addition, the patent attorneys, recognizing an area of technology that should be protected, recommended filing two other patent applications to protect the total subarea of technology in computer control represented by the research laboratory's initial contribution.

The value of the product was established by performance of the prototype module produced by the research laboratory.   The manufacturing division people then commenced their own engineering evaluation, product design, and engineering related to utilization of the product.   Their total expense was $172,000. They incurred model-shop costs of $140,000 for production of the first prototype complete control system.   The manufacturing division's cost for test and evaluation of this new product in a customer's location was $32,000.   (The rest of the total cost was assumed by the customer.)   The R&D consultant was retained to follow the application of the control system to the customer's requirements, because the customer was not familiar with the control system concept and the manufacturing division was not sufficiently familiar with the customer's needs.   The cost was $5,000.   Having established the value of the new control system, it was decided to invest in new capital facilities primarily for the production of printed circuits which were desirable as modular entities in the control system for easy maintenance and repair of the system in the customer's plant. This cost was $150,000.

An addition to the main plant was required and 40,000 feet of new floor area was added at a total cost of $900,000.   The land for the new building was already part of the original plant's total holdings.   Because the product was designed to meet a specific customer's individual requirements, there was no field warehousing of either component or subcomponent parts.

Marketing and distribution costs were essentially nil, because the marketing force had already been contacting the customer to sell the older technology to perform the same function.   Distribution was not involved, because the marketing contacts were direct with the customer.   Advertising and sales promotion costs were substantial because of the necessity to acquaint the entire customer industry with the new approach to process control, its cost, and its performance advantages.

Warranties were issued as standard one-year terms; warranty-related costs were not significant, for the majority of complaints were about trivial malfunctions of parts rather than total system failure.

At the end of two years, a competitor produced a product performing a function essentially comparable to that of the original new product.   The competitor succeeded in reducing the price and therefore the margin advantage realized by the innovating company—a factor which had not been anticipated in the original cash flow analysis.   This affected the cash flow analysis by 10 percent of total integrated favorable cash flow over the anticipated life of the product which had been, at the original estimate, eight years.   The final ratio of incremental margin integrated over the eight-year period to total dollars invested was 14.5:1.   The realized margins over the total eight-year period, of which four were predicted and four actually realized at the time the estimate was made, ratioed to the research dollars invested, were 156:1.   The return on the total investment then, depending upon whether direct return on investment or depreciated-value return on investment is calculated, was satisfactory in either case by general financial standards.   However, it was clear that an allowance should be made for intrusion of competitive influences in order that the total risk be evaluated earlier in the product lifetime than had originally been estimated.

Case History—Cost Improvement.   The manufacturing division requested that the research and development laboratory explore the possibility of substituting another material or a lower-cost process for the material then being used in the manufacture of a high-volume intermediate-cost product.   The material was a vital functional rather than structural material in performance of the product's total function. Five suppliers were known to produce the functional material involved. There was essentially no competition among them. None of the suppliers had shown any inclination to improve the performance of the material or, alternatively, reduce its cost while maintaining the base performance.

The research laboratory undertook to study the function of the material in the product with the objective of (1) developing a new or improved material for performing the same function at the same or lower cost or (2) developing a new material or improved material for performing an improved function at the same cost. It was recognized at the outset that the corporation producing the end product was not, and was not likely ever to be, a producer of the basic material in question. However, competitive position dictated that the corporation undertake the development of such a material.

The total research costs incurred on the same basis as described above were $750,000. Three fundamental patents were applied for and obtained in a material area that was unlikely to be threatened by competition for a significant period of time. This period of time was estimated by judgment to be ten years. Therefore, the advantage of the research contribution was to be spread over the ten-year period of time.

The manufacturing divisions of the parent corporation were not required to invest any substantial amount in capital equipment. However, the engineering time invested to redesign the current product to utilize the new material, and the manufacturing engineering time required to develop processes for efficient utilization of the new material, involved investments of $150,000.

One of the suppliers had traditionally been a preferred supplier of the corporation. In developing quantity production of the material, the preferred supplier was engaged in a cooperative effort with the producing corporation to develop quantities of the material for initial pilot production and ultimate full-production quantities of product. In this case, the cost of the scale-up development was shared jointly between the originating corporation and the supplying corporation.

Because of the basic nature of the patents, licenses were negotiated with several other corporations which resulted in income to both participating parties in the amount of $2,250,000 over the ten-year period. The estimate was made at the end of the fourth year. A review in the fifth and sixth year showed no significant threat to the technological position held by the originating company and, in the case of the processing technology, by the material supplier.

The result of the innovation of the new material permitted a reduction in size, improvement in performance, and a measurable end-price reduction to the ultimate customer, resulting in improved gross sales billed to the originating corporation of 45 percent. This corporation had, prior to this time, participated in its market in this product area to the extent of 21 percent. The margins on the product changed only to the extent that the gross sales billed increased, because no additional facilities were required to produce the volume of product other than for normally anticipated growth in the market over the ten-year life span of the innovation. Therefore, the research and development laboratory was not credited with normal growth requirements in volume of product, but only with that incremental increase in sales billed attributable to their new-product innovation. They were also credited with royalty income resulting from the licensing of other firms to utilize or to produce the material in question. In this case, the longer term and greater stability of the product position allowed the evaluation of the research and development laboratory contribution to be made over a substantial period of time with less likelihood of sudden deterioration of the forecast as a result of competitive intrusion.

Negative Factors in Evaluation of Research and Development Performance. Two negative areas may be defined in the evaluation of corporate research and development performance. The first of these factors relates to internal attitudes, both financial and emotional. The financial factors that can result in a misleading evaluation of research and development performance are the position of the corporation with respect to its available assets for investment in new facilities, and engineering costs which are inevitably related to the assimilation of a new product or a major product improvement. The research and development laboratory tends, by its nature, to be relatively insulated from economic fluctuations. If the timing of a research and development program planned and implemented five years previously is such as to arrive at a point of exploitation at a low point in the corporation's fortunes, this cannot be quantitatively evaluated as either a positive or negative influence when evaluating the research and development laboratory's performance. In this case, an extension of the original hypothetical analysis of the potential of the product should be conducted, making assumptions as to the ability of the corporation to capitalize on the innovation despite its current transient financial situation.

The second situation that may be a negative influence on the evaluation of research and development performance is one which is inexcusable and should, to the extent possible, be anticipated well before the emergence of a new product or a new concept from the laboratory.

This is specifically applicable in the case of the substitution of a radically new technology for a mature technology to perform the function formerly performed by the mature technology.

An outstanding example of this situation is the substitution of solid-state devices for vacuum tubes in many of the electronic functions performed today. The circuitry associated with the solid-state device and the overall product design criteria which are required by a solid-state device differ by literally orders of magnitude from the vacuum-tube device that the solid-state device replaces.

Vacuum-tube circuit engineers are familiar with the functions performed by the vacuum tube in the circuit and can quickly recognize that the solid-state device performs no different function, for the end desired function must always be the same insofar as the customer is concerned. To the extent that the research laboratory has failed to impress upon the manufacturing division the necessity for developing a confidence in the new technology and has failed to provide personnel and knowledge essential to the development of capability in the new technology, the research laboratory should be assessed for its own failure if the new technology is not effectively utilized in a competitive marketplace by the assimilating division. Research and development must be evaluated not only on the quantitative grounds described above, but also on the qualitative grounds of how effectively it has trained its customer, the manufacturing division, in its new technology well prior to the time of the emergence of that technology from the laboratory and into the division engineering responsibility.

Evaluating Performance on Government Contracts. Most of the criteria used in evaluating the corporation's performance in research and development are equally applicable to work done for government agencies. Technical contributions such as papers, reports, and awards are available to the corporation and its divisions for enhancement of reputation, publicity, and extraction of useful technical content. Useful information is usually available earlier and more completely than if another corporation had the same contract.

For unpatentable information, lead time as a result of any type of research—basic through consulting—may be an important contribution to corporate profit even though difficult to evaluate. Patent rights are negotiable with the government, although there has been a trend from assignment to the corporation toward assignment to the government with perhaps nonexclusive, royalty-free license to the corporation.

Sales billed for products resulting from research funded by the government may be handled in the same way as those resulting from corporately funded research. Because full disclosure may be required, the lifetime of the product may be extremely short, yet a government requirement of multiple sources would cause this to be true even if a product were developed on corporate funds for sale to the government. In estimating share of the market, division by two or three may be advisable.

The most direct, and perhaps smallest, contribution of government-funded research is the fee or profit resulting from contracts. Traditionally, research for the government has been funded at cost plus fixed fee (CPFF) on a best-efforts basis. Some research, particularly of the product development variety, has tended toward cost plus incentive fee (CPIF), fixed-price incentive (FPI), or even firm fixed price (FFP). The Department of Defense has also attempted to evaluate in advance its contractors' performances. The method of weighted guidelines is detailed in Armed Services Procurement Regulation 3-808, effective January 1, 1964. Some examples of profit objectives cited in this ASPR are:

Type of Contract	Profit percent
FFP for contractor-developed military item	19.36
FPI for first missile production, 50-50 sharing, 5 percent ceiling	9.57
FPI for follow-on missile hardware, 70-30 sharing, 20 percent ceiling	6.67
CPFF best efforts for basic research	8.95

In the past, FFP contracts, where accurate cost data were unavailable, have led to unreasonable profits or to disastrous losses. The ASPR is an attempt by the Department of Defense to determine in advance the expected performance, risk, and achievement based on type of contract, difficulty of task, schedule, source of resources, and other factors. From this information, a reasonable expected profit is deduced and applied to the negotiation of a contract.

The source of resources is of particular importance, because although the government may evaluate performance on the basis of profit, the corporation may place greater emphasis on return on investment. It is the nature of the defense industry to produce a low profit and large return on investment due to the use of a large proportion (often 100 percent) of government-owned capital facilities.

In addition, the much-discussed "spin-off" should be considered. Judgment is required in the evaluation of benefits from government work to established or new corporate products developed on corporate research funds. The very size of the government research budget suggests that much new technology has come from and will increasingly continue as a result of government spending in this area. It behooves the progressive corporation not only to take careful account of the effect of contracting for research with the government but to maximize this effect. It also follows that efforts should be made to seek whatever benefits may be available as a result of government-sponsored research and development to which the corporation is not a party.

BIBLIOGRAPHY

Heyel, Carl (ed.), *Handbook of Industrial Research Management*, Reinhold Publishing Corporation, New York, 1959.

Quinn, J. B., *Yardsticks for Industrial Research*, The Ronald Press Company, New York, 1959.

Roberts, E. B., *The Dynamics of Research and Development*, Harper & Row, Publishers, Incorporated, New York, 1964.

Rubenstein, A. H. (ed.), *Coordination, Control, and Financing of Industrial Research*, King's Crown Press, New York, 1955.

MATERIALS MANAGEMENT

CHAPTER ONE

The Materials Management Concept

DONALD E. FARR *President (1960–1966), H. B. Maynard and Company, Incorporated, Pittsburgh, Pennsylvania*

Conceptually, materials management requires a new management philosophy as well as a reorientation of management functions. It is an approach which highlights the flow and the control of material as an integrated function to achieve a maximum return on working capital. Operationally, it becomes a service function parallel in importance to manufacturing, marketing, engineering, and finance, basically established to assist them in their operations.

The results achieved from this concept are a more accurate control of investment; streamlined operations; and better utilization of modern techniques, equipment, and technical specialists.

THE MATERIALS MANAGEMENT CONCEPT

A management concept may be defined as a way of grouping relationships, facts, and ideas pertaining to a management area. The materials management concept is one of these. Its logic is based upon financial facts; its rationale is the need to have authoritative command of the fluid and elusive internal investment in materials, including their storage, movement, and usage. Not only is the total amount of money invested in inventories important, but there are additional annual costs of 24 to 30 percent of the inventory in carrying charges—insurance, storage, movement, obsolescence, and other costs—which have to be met.

In many industries, the *total* cost for material—its storage, movement, and wastage—runs from 50 to 70 percent of the total factory cost of the finished product. It is not unusual for the financial officer to decree an inventory cut which is almost immediately followed by an increase in work in process and, possibly, complaints from the sales staff about lost orders due to nondelivery of material. Why? Because too many unrelated people have independent control over some phase of material cost with no central control exercised short of the president's office.

There are many elements which build up material cost, all necessary but generally quite independent. Purchasing controls are a part of the initial cost of materials; but engineering, who developed the specifications; production planning, who say when and how much they want; and marketing, who project an overall need and supply storage space—all have a strong impact. In addition to these clear-cut elements, there are others that are harder to identify. The why's of the rise and fall of inventory, for example, are complex. They include psychological factors of self-protection as well as the fundamentals of addition and subtraction.

With management committed to research and innovation, it is not to be wondered that fresh thinking developed the idea of reorienting the areas that control material costs so that a tauter control could be held on them as well as the subareas which contribute factors of cost.

Physically and factually, materials management includes the service area where finance, marketing, production, and engineering come together in the manner illustrated by Figure 1-1. Basically, material is specified by engineering, finance pays the bill, production transforms material into products, and marketing sells the end results.

Materials management has an important mission to work among these four areas, keeping movement and availability in balance with needs. It includes planning and scheduling, purchasing, movement of material, and storage.

Areas of Usefulness. Before describing materials management in detail, it seems in order to look at those areas where the concept is useful. The materials management concept is designed to solve problems in the following areas:

Basic material costs
    Material availability
        Location
        Type
    Material-handling costs
        Storage
        Retrieval
        Management
        Rehandling
    Work-in-process inventory
        Location

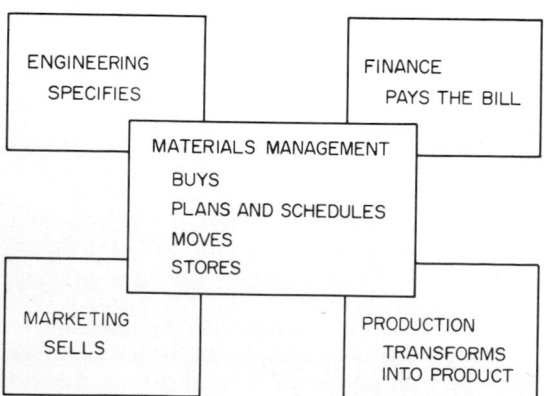

FIG. 1-1. *Relationship of materials management to engineering, production, and finance.*

Amount
Time
Transportation costs
    Raw materials
    Purchased parts
    Deliveries to warehouses and customers
Storage costs
    Space
    Insurance
    Handling
Working capital
    Minimize investment
    Maximize turnover
Marketing service
    Timeliness
    Cost
    Kept promises
Obsolescence
    Raw material
    Parts
    Finished goods

Materials Management as a Service Function. For the materials management concept to be effective, all members of management, including foremen, must have a good understanding of the principles of the division of responsibility and authority under the materials management concept, because the regrouping, simple as it is, has far-reaching implications. A certain amount of regrouping has gone on in industry over the years. Manpower is one element that is increasingly carefully controlled, usually by a vice president of personnel who hires, terminates, and negotiates union contracts, fringe benefits, salary plans, and so on. The financial vice president has strong control over financing, accounting, and policies for budgeting and asset conservation.

The materials management concept gives the technical area the opportunity to concentrate on design, equipment, facilities, quality, and output while the materials department concentrates on having the right material at the right place at the right time at a minimum cost. In this way, the four M's of money, men, machinery, and material are under comprehensive and direct control.

Although each of the four M's has an immediate objective, their common goal is to deliver a top-quality, wanted product to the customer when and where he wants it, at a price that is profitable to both.

Materials management is basically a "supporting" or "service" function. It has an important role to fill. This role must be to serve—not dominate or control—because there is no profit-making end product forthcoming, only service. The rewards for effective materials management must come from customer satisfaction in the end product and from good internal performance in specific areas such as inventory, space usage, and handling costs.

There may even be some merit in calling the materials management function "materials service" to give all concerned the proper connotation of its role. The term "service" is not meant to downgrade the importance of the function but rather to emphasize the support it must give if the company is to be strong.

ORGANIZING FOR MATERIALS MANAGEMENT

The principles of organizing for materials management are not different from those for other areas. Some specifics, however, may be helpful.

First, the mission of the department, or why it is established, must be considered. This should be carefully thought through, taking into consideration the balance of the organization, the type of products manufactured, the availability of qualified people, the characteristics of raw materials, and any other important items which have a bearing on the material area.

As an example, a materials department with full responsibility for materials could have the following *mission:*

To have required materials and products when and where needed at the minimum overall cost.

The *scope* of its activities could be described as follows:

This department will provide services to the company in the location and purchase of needed materials; in storing, moving, and accounting for them; and in planning for their movement through manufacturing, warehousing, and distribution channels to meet the customers' needs as established by marketing. It is responsible to do this in the most economical way, balancing opposing factors to give the best final result.

Within the established mission and scope, it is necessary to develop subareas of responsibility. Before doing this, let us examine Figure 1-2 to see who is responsible at various times for a piece of material from initial design to final delivery.

Most basic policies which determine material management's control of materials come from the other functional areas. Therefore, material policies have to fit into these other functional needs. This can best be accomplished by examining each material-related policy developed by other functions, in the light of alternative material management policies, to find what is best for both. For instance, marketing may have a policy that the end product should be physically available in each major population area not over 300 miles from key markets. Materials

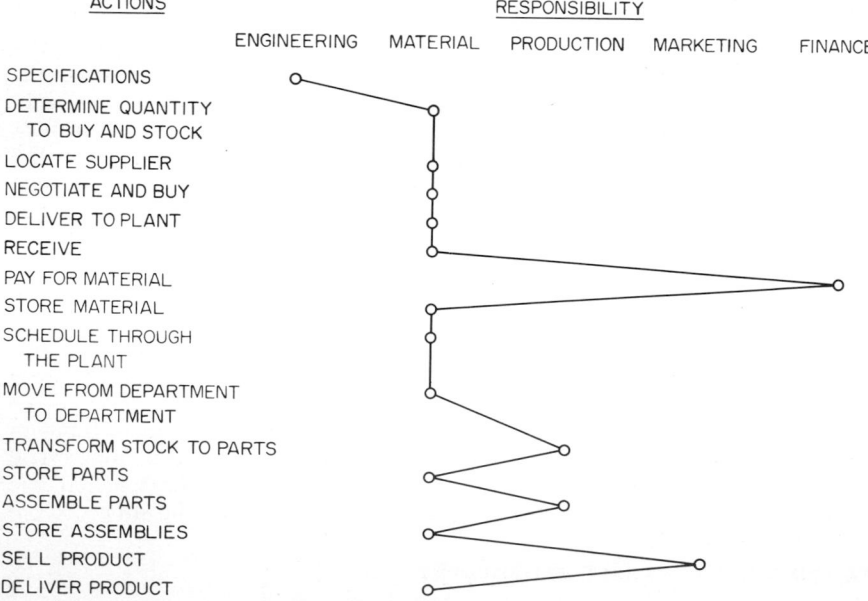

FIG. 1-2. *Functional responsibility for material at various stages.*

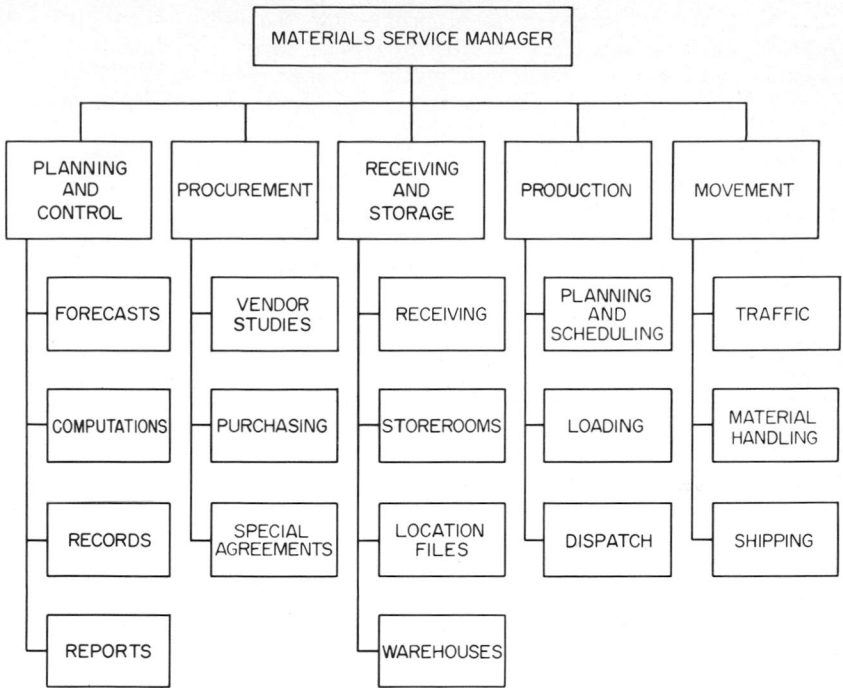

FIG. 1-3. *Typical organization for effective materials management.*

management should assess this policy from the standpoint of service and cost, and price it into varying policies on inventory level and stock points. From this assessment, a new marketing policy as well as a modified inventory policy may evolve.

In another case, finance may have a more or less arbitrary policy that the investment in inventory may not rise to more than, say, 53 percent of the annual sales volume. The effect of this policy on individual segments of inventory should be analyzed to establish an optimum amount and place for each segment. Then finance must be persuaded to alter its policy, if appropriate.

Once basic operating policies are meshed, the development of departments and relationships can be fitted in. In general, the materials management organization is made up of five departments (as shown by Figure 1-3):

Planning and control—is responsible for forecasts of material requirements as well as records and control data

Procurement—locates sources, negotiates price, and has deliveries made

Receiving and storage—accepts and is responsible for quantity and quality received and stores, preserves, and retrieves

Production planning—plans and schedules all activities related to material movement

Material movement—is responsible for equipment, methods, and the internal and external movement of material

The organization structure must be supplemented by interrelationships at the working levels. Figure 1-3, however, shows authority and policy relationships which are quite workable in practice.

It is, of course, necessary to fit people into the organization plan. As this is done, modifications are very often in order. More departments can be manageable, and fewer are practical in specific circumstances.

A Pitfall to Avoid. As in everything else, there are pitfalls to avoid in the use of the materials management concept.

One dangerous pitfall is empire building. It is especially dangerous in materials management because of the wide variety of activities covered and the general lack of good management knowledge in the areas. Materials management is a key spot, also, because any bottlenecks may control overall output. Being aware of this, the wrong person can take advantage of the situation to become extremely powerful in dictating what can or cannot be done. Of course, this same danger is true in finance, marketing, production, or engineering.

Importance of Manager Selection. It is important that the department be headed by a broad-gage individual. He may not have broad experience initially, but he should have the potential ability to see the whole scope of material operations from the tedious record keeping through the mathematical requirements and into the physical movement of material. Where he comes from—purchasing, industrial engineering, production control, accounting, sales, or line—is of less moment than his organizational ability and depth of insight.

Also of importance is the level at which the manager functions. In the plan outlined herein, he should be a vice president on the same level with the vice presidents of engineering, production, marketing, and finance. In modified situations, where only parts of the concept are applied, he should fit in at a level appropriate to that part.

IDENTIFYING THE NEED FOR ADOPTING THE MATERIALS MANAGEMENT CONCEPT

A study of the details of the materials management concept should clarify some of the mysteries of the control of inventory investment and accompanying costs. Further, it should reveal conditions that are presently in existence which may have been overlooked. If, in this analysis, it is found that the scattered control of the elements of material cost is costing money, a change should seriously be considered.

Specific ailments that are often encountered in the scattered control of the elements of material cost are:

High material-cost content of the sales dollar
Large indirect and material-movement costs
Losses in inventory
Inadequate equipment utilization
Lost time in direct labor
Late deliveries
Long manufacturing cycles
High inventory investment
Congestion in manufacturing and/or stores
Chronic shortages

SUMMARY

Many of the isolated problems and hard-to-control costs of business can be traced to scattered control over material and the many different and conflicting ways it can be manipulated to achieve the objectives of the different departments. The materials management concept brings these forces together so that one department can integrate all material-connected activities for best results.

BIBLIOGRAPHY

Ammer, D., "Who Should Be Materials Manager?" *Purchasing*, June 19, 1961.

Conant, B. C., "Centralize Materials Management," *Business Management*, July, 1963.

Deitz, D., and J. Spencer, "M. N. Thomas: A Giant of Material Management," *Material Handling Engineering*, November, 1963.

Farrell, P. V., "Materials Management Gives the Answers," *Purchasing*, Oct. 10, 1960.

"Four Approaches to Materials Management," *Purchasing*, June 17, 1963.

Goubeau, Vincent de P., "Materials Management," in H. B. Maynard (ed.), *Industrial Engineering Handbook*, 2d ed., sec. 7, chap. 6, McGraw-Hill Book Company, New York, 1963.

Hayes, F. A., and C. D. Beers, Jr., "Materials Management: Empire or Profit Builder," *Factory*, April, 1964.

"Managing Materials in a Small Company," *Purchasing*, June 19, 1961.

"Materials Management Pushed," *Iron Age*, July 6, 1961.

"Nobody Neglects Materials Management," *Dun's Review & Modern Industry*, part II, March, 1965.

Van de Water, J., "How Keuffel & Esser Moved Up to Materials Management," *Purchasing*, Nov. 4, 1963.

"What a Material Manager Does," *Purchasing*, June 19, 1961.

CHAPTER TWO

Production Planning and Scheduling

JOHN E. MARTIN   *Arthur Andersen & Co., Chicago, Illinois*

Production planning and scheduling are so closely interrelated in the events preceding production that it is sometimes unnecessary or impractical to distinguish between the two. Both planning and scheduling are directed toward the same objectives—to provide goods for the customer when he wants them and in a manner to minimize *total costs*.

Production planning should precede the completion date of a product or order by a sufficiently long lead time period to enable management to consider alternative courses of action and authorize major commitments for materials, manpower, and plant facilities. Production planning is an area for top management decisions. Senior executives should carefully evaluate various courses of action. They should participate in the development of and accept responsibility for the final authorization of production plans and policies. It should be noted that a sales demand forecast, in most cases, should precede the development of the production plan and supporting schedules. To obtain a clear portrayal of the sales potential when preparing a sales demand forecast, it is best to exclude plant capacity limitations. The production planning phase normally converts a sales *demand* forecast to a master schedule of finished products which incorporates capacity modifications along with planned inventory levels. The master schedule of finished products needed at the end of the production cycle constitutes the authorized starting point for scheduling all the activities which must precede finished goods production.

"Production scheduling" generally refers to the preparation of schedules needed to support the master schedule. These schedules include production schedules prepared by departments and machine centers, and materials procurement schedules. Given an adequately equipped and laid-out plant and facilities with proper processing, sound production scheduling is vital to efficient operation. Scheduling sets the time and pace for all plant material flows and work operations.

Although directly related, production planning activities for most enterprises can be segregated from supporting or detail plant and procurement scheduling;

responsibilities, therefore, can be assigned to separate planning and scheduling groups.

PRODUCTION PLANNING ORGANIZATION

Planning inventory levels and setting rates of change in productive output, which might involve supplementary decisions to increase or decrease capacity, are matters which should be developed in conjunction with a production schedule of finished models that is consistent with expected sales demand.

Staff Assignments. A production planning staff which maintains all related data, statistics, projections, and performance reports can be part of a production control or materials management organization, or it can report to the chief manufacturing, sales, or financial executive, or to the president or executive vice president. The reporting alignment should be decided on the basis of which executive is most likely to provide the planning staff with the most effective direction.

One of the more important services provided by the production planning staff is to develop and evaluate various possible alternatives for production and inventory stock plans. These should be presented in a useful and convenient format which will facilitate review for decision making by the senior executives who will select and authorize the master schedules and inventory stock plans. A production planning staff should not be required, or allowed by default, to exercise final authorization of the production plans and policies. This is a top management responsibility. The production planning staff should then follow up and feed back reports on performance accomplished with respect to such decisions.

Size of the staff is dependent upon the extent, volume, and complexity of the operations. For some companies, these functions can be discharged as a part-time assignment; for others, they may entail a number of specialists working full time under the direction of a production planning supervisor or manager.

Decision Making. Planning committee or board meetings are an effective means for bringing together divisional executives with sometimes divergent viewpoints to study a planning staff's reports and tentatively determine master schedules and inventory investments. These meetings should be regularly scheduled. For most companies, monthly intervals are desirable. Minutes of the meetings should be maintained and should cover individual viewpoints presented, together with the reasons for the major conclusions reached.

The heads of the following divisional activities should usually be represented on the planning committee: sales, finance, materials management, manufacturing, engineering, and planning staff.

The committee should approve sales forecasts and recommend master production schedules, finished goods inventory stock plans, and inventory-control policies.

The directives and policies formulated by the committee should be in the form of *recommendations only* to the chief executive or general manager who is responsible for their final authorization and release. Releases or authorizations for production and purchasing should be approved by the chief executive or general manager after he reviews the committee's recommendations.

SALES DEMAND FORECASTS

Companies making similar products which are sold to a number of customers plan their production in anticipation of sales orders. This is common practice in industries producing appliances, televisions and radios, office equipment, autos and trucks, electrical goods, and many other line assembly-type products. This not only shortens the cycle between the receipt of customer order and delivery, thereby providing better customer service, but it also enables production to be scheduled in lot sizes which can be produced at significantly lower total costs. For these industries, production planning starts with an approved sales demand forecast.

Producers of basic materials such as steel, paper, textile gray goods, petroleum, and chemicals also schedule production according to forecasts of sales demand. Many companies in these industries will endeavor to set schedules annually which will establish a relatively constant rate of production for the ensuing year. Procurement of raw materials also is generally done by contracts related to sales forecasts which extend over a long period such as a year or more.

Schedule of Sales and Inventories by Periods. For some companies, customers' orders, contracts, and stock replenishment orders provide the key information regarding the identity and quantity of end products to be made available for distribution to customers. These sales data must be broken down by calendar periods—days, weeks, months, or quarters—into schedule blocks which list models to be shipped by totals for each period. These shipments must come from finished inventory stocks or from production accomplished between the current planning review date and the planned shipping date.

THE PRODUCTION PLANNING PROCESS

Production planning starts with comparing expected sales demand with inventories currently on hand and estimated to be available for each ensuing schedule period. Once authorized sales demand totals by periods are established, production planning decision making essentially involves determining an acceptable relationship of production output volume to inventory levels. This is illustrated by Figure 2-1.

Production planning can be described graphically by overlaying and fitting a cumulative step chart for production to one for sales and evaluating whether the resultant inventory for each period is satisfactory. It may be described in two stages.

Planned production for each month is overlaid by adding each monthly total to the opening inventory. The open blocks are the resultant inventory levels. For example, level monthly production of twelve units will result in an ending May inventory of five units.

The planning process is completed when the relationship between production rates and inventories is approved by management as satisfactory.

Resolving Conflicting Relationships. The primary consideration in converting a sales forecast to a production plan should be to provide the maximum degree of customer service consistent with plant and material-control operations which will yield the greatest profit. To develop the most profitable production plan, a number of conflicting elements must be evaluated and policies or programs formulated for each to maintain a balanced relationship.

Some of the more important of these conflicting relationships which must be resolved are as follows:

1. The costs and risks of carrying inventories in excess of demand versus the costs and probabilities of shortages.

2. The cost of changing levels of production output with changes in seasonal sales demand versus the risks and costs of carrying inventories in excess of low demand through to periods of high demand.

3. The costs of losing sales because of capacity limitations versus the risk

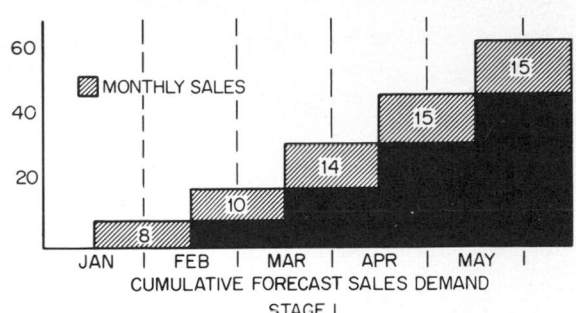

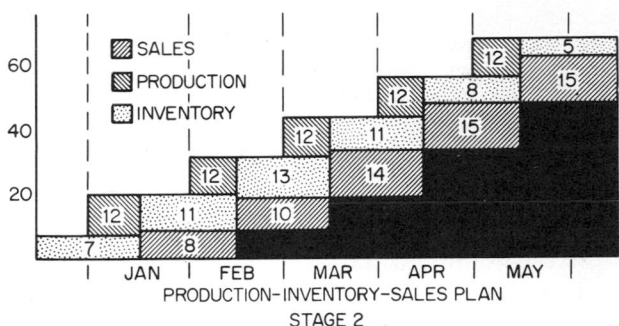

FIG. 2-1. *The production planning process. Stage 1: Prepare a cumulative step graph for the forecast sales. Stage 2: Enter beginning inventory and planned production rates on graph and determine if the resultant inventory is satisfactory.*

of making additional fixed investments in plant and equipment. Capacity is a nebulous concept that can be changed by management decisions regarding overtime, subcontracts, second shifts, make or buy decisions, and the like.

As an initial planning objective, it is generally desirable to project production at current rates of output. The changing of production rates is costly, and it must be determined that there is a change in demand sustained sufficiently far in the future to justify such costs. To minimize the effects on production of short-term offsetting fluctuations in sales, it is desirable to refer to sales forecasts which extend out through periods farther in the future than normally would be required to support procurement and production schedules.

For example, seasonal sales for a watch manufacturer compared with maximum production level conditions are shown in Figure 2-2. Because watches are fine wedding, graduation, and Christmas gifts, sales peaks occur in the middle and at the end of the calendar year. The shaded area represents additional units added to finished goods if production proceeds at a uniform rate throughout the entire year. Costs for changing productive output as sales demand changes can be obtained from studies of past cost experience when production levels were changed. The final decision will compare leveling costs with costs of changing production.

Leveling by producing ahead of normal plant lead times should be directed primarily to those components and assemblies which have the highest labor content

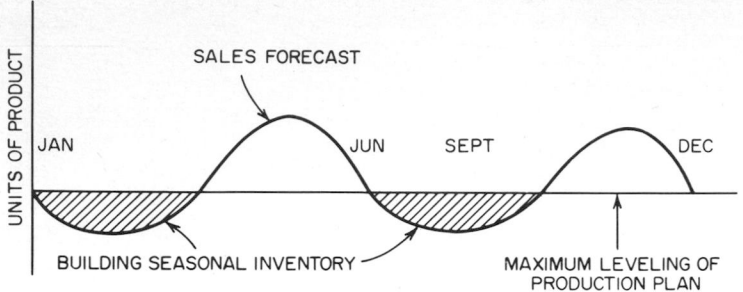

FIG. 2-2. *Chart of seasonal sales with maximum leveling.*

(rather than a total which includes material cost) and which are least subject to sales and engineering obsolescence. Relatively safe ways to level sales requirements are to replenish parts service stocks during off-peaks, persuade customers to provide long-lead orders with deferred shipment, and time new model introduction dates so the distribution pipelines will be filling during off-seasons. It is preferable to produce large sales volume products during off-peak sales periods. This will reserve capacity during selling peaks to produce short-run and specialty items closer to market trends and thereby minimize shortages in this category.

UTILIZATION OF CAPACITY

It should be borne in mind that, for most manufacturing companies, there are significant differences in capacity between departments and machine centers. It is frequently found that perhaps only one or two production centers limit the overall plant capacity. These are the bottleneck groups, and the ones which need special consideration when production is planned. When these limits become severe, action should be taken to increase their potential output so as to achieve a better balance among plant processing centers.

Conversely, it may be found that certain departments consistently have excess capacity with attendant fixed charges above those required to support production levels. Consideration should be given to cutting back these facilities to eliminate fixed charges in overhead expense.

A typical example of scheduled capacity utilization is illustrated in Figure 2-3. Here, the capacities of the punch press and assembly departments appear to be reasonably in line with sales demand requirements, although overtime is indicated for certain periods. The foundry is inadequate to support production, and accordingly, during certain periods some castings must be subcontracted. It would appear that the machine shop may have capacity in excess of requirements, although the standby costs of carrying these facilities might be justified if there is a long-term plan for future expansion of other departments.

It is often desirable to study the effect of various levels of capacity utilization on productive efficiency. Some plants can exceed normal capacity by overtime and the like, but this adds to the cost of production. When capacity utilization drops below 70 or 60 percent in process industries such as paper, refineries, and chemicals, there generally is a significant increase in the unit cost of the product produced. In these instances, it is often preferable to shut down completely and incur the added cost of subsequent start-up so that when the process is operating, it is at an efficient capacity level.

Work Center Loading. In the final planning stage, some procedure must be employed to determine the effect of the master schedules on the major productive work centers.   This can be done in various ways.

If the schedule conforms with current production volumes, it can be assumed that the plant can carry out planned production.   Where there are known bottlenecks, only these need be analyzed to determine their effect on the schedule.

In some instances, it may be desirable to load all machine centers and productive processes.   Four methods that may be employed are described below in order of decreasing complexity.

Detail "Component Process" Load.   This involves identifying the component parts and assemblies required from bills of materials for each model in the schedule and then pulling the process or operation sequence sheet for each manufactured part and assembly.   The time standard for each process must then be multiplied by scheduled units to obtain hours by work centers.   (In certain applications, dollars may be used rather than hours.)   The hours required for all models scheduled are combined by work centers and compared with the available machine and manpower capacity.   This comparison will indicate unbalanced conditions, and the planner can make necessary recommendations for corrective action.

Modern computers have significantly lowered the cost of computing detail machine loads.   Nevertheless, these calculations still are time consuming and involve substantial programming and maintenance of standard time data.   The task of maintaining current standards for all processes needed to produce all models in the schedule is so large for many companies as to be impractical.   Use of shop loading systems also must not presuppose results beyond the practical abilities of the shop processes.   There are many emergency problems of absenteeism, machine breakdowns, defective quality, material shortages, and sudden changes in sales demand which must be provided for and which generally cause actual production to differ from overly detailed production plans.   Detail machine loading, even for bottlenecks or critical equipment, should not be prepared weeks ahead of scheduled work, because it is next to impossible to foresee all emergency problems.   Although there is considerable literature regarding matching "component process" loaded schedules with capacity (mostly from dataprocessing equipment suppliers), it is seldom necessary to carry this out on a detailed basis.

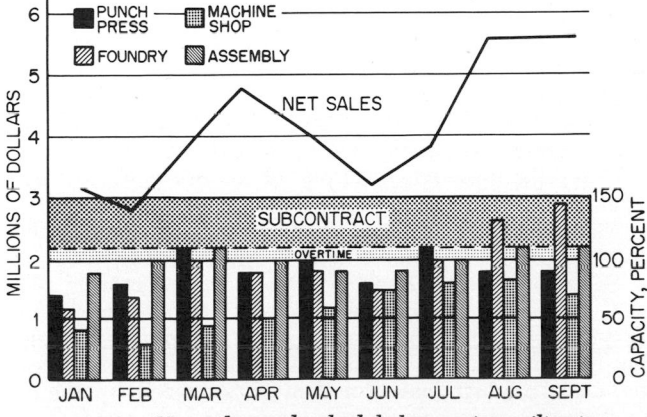

FIG. 2-3.   *Net sales and scheduled capacity utilization.*

Equivalent "Model Work Center" Load. A quicker and less precise, but generally satisfactory, method for balancing schedules to capacity is to prepare in advance a summary of machine hours (including setup) by machine groups, and labor hours by assembly areas or skills for one unit (or ten, or a thousand, depending upon the quantities involved), for each of the major product categories manufactured. This summary is compiled from bills of material and process sheets for one model representative of each product class. It groups the rated standard (or past experience) hours by work centers for the model.

By multiplying, say, the milling machine hours required per model unit by the number of finished units in the master schedule of all models in that product class, the required milling machine hours for that class of products may be obtained. Grouping the milling machine requirements for all product classes will approximate the total milling machine requirements in the planned load for the period. A comparison of this load with the available hours of milling machine capacity will indicate any need for adjusting capacity or schedule. This procedure can be followed for all machine and assembly groups and labor skills. Plans for overtime, hiring and training additional employees, and cutting back manpower can be instituted before the need makes itself evident in the plant.

This computation of an equivalent "model work-center" load involves much less data processing than detail loading and, in many companies, can be performed satisfactorily with desk calculators.

Major Product Assembly Loading. The most common loading method employed by line assembly-type manufacturers and many process-type companies is to determine, by industrial engineering studies and analyses of production data, the standard rates of output by product for the major assembly lines and process centers such as distilling towers, reactors, looms, paper machines, or coating mills. For these industries, production planning schedules specific product or model quantities, their sequence, and work dates for the basic assembly lines or processes according to their predetermined rates of output.

In many companies, final assembly operations require a relatively small amount of labor in comparison with that expended on the major subassembly lines which are common to a number of final products. For these companies, subassembly outputs pace the overall plant activity and should be scheduled by production planning. All other supporting fabricating, subassembly, and final assemblies must conform with the output rates for these basic products. To increase or reduce rates of output of basic products generally involves major process and manning changes. When changes are made, they should usually be significant in terms of output, say, 10 percent or more, to justify the changeover cost.

Loads for fabricating departments and other subassembly and supporting operations are commonly determined in terms of a ratio computed from the planned rate of output for the basic products. For example, a weekly output of 1,000 generators might require 7,000 hours in the armature department and 4,000 commutator department hours. If the generator output is to be increased 10 percent, the productive output of all other supporting departments should be planned to increase proportionately.

Major product loading along the above lines is the system generally used by most companies producing products in quantity.

Sales-dollar Ratio Loading. Many manufacturing plants, including job shops, can establish a reasonably accurate ratio of direct labor or machine hours to cost-of-sales dollars by product or major product categories. These ratios may be broken down by major work centers. The forecast of sales by products or major product lines can then be analyzed by the manning ratios to predict future labor and machine requirements with reasonable accuracy. These loads should be balanced to the planned capacities as described above.

General Consideration. In the planning stage, loads should be balanced to overall capacities in broad time blocks which tend to average out emergency conditions. It is customary not to load to capacity. Predetermined percentages should be left open for maintenance and for handling emergency orders. Where stock replenishment orders are used for some components and the remaining shop orders are generated from the master schedule, sufficient additional allowance must be reserved in the loading to accommodate the stock replenishment orders. The sales division must understand that if their sales exceed forecasts without sufficient lead notification, deliveries must be extended, and conversely, if sales are not met, inventory will be accumulated or emergency reduction in labor will be required.

FINISHED PRODUCTION ORDERS

Master Schedules. A master schedule for production of finished models should project enough periods in advance to provide for authorizing orderly buying and the scheduling of departmental and machine center work loads. Because each issue supersedes all prior schedules, the latest amends earlier schedules issued for the same time period. Master schedules which are reissued monthly for models in repetitive production should provide maximum flexibility for making short-term changes to meet current fluctuations in sales demand. Figure 2-4 illustrates a simplified example of this.

This master schedule projects monthly totals by model for six months. The monthly totals in parentheses are shown primarily as planning guides and as authorizations to procure only certain specified long-lead components, such as special housings or electrical components, to support model production for the quantities shown. This accomplishes the same function as an advance procurement schedule which specifies *component* quantities for procurement rather than models to be produced. The asterisked schedule blocks authorize ordering only those components having procurement leads of two to four months. The other

Model number	Cumulative to date	January	February	March	April	May	June	Cumulative through forecast
M-59	6,500	500 250	1,500 250* 100	2,500*	750* (3,250)	(1,500)	(800)	8,500 12,000* (17,550) 5,150
M-59X	4,800	700	200* 950	450*	50* (500)	(250)	(200)	5,850* (6,800) 11,250
M-40	9,600	50	450* 50	1,850*	150* (2,250)	(950)	(400)	13,700* (17,300) 100
M-45X			50*	250* (100)	(350)	(150)	(0)	400* (1,000)

FIG. 2-4. *Typical master schedule.*

model totals authorize scheduling production work and final procurement of remaining materials to support the schedules. These amend, where applicable, earlier totals shown in previous issues for the same model and month. This procedure minimizes commitments made further in advance than required for each component's order and procurement cycle.

Production Releases. In addition to issuing master schedules for all finished models at periodic intervals, many managements revise these schedules whenever necessary by entering additions and cancellations by means of a document called the "release" or "cancellation." This is used to keep master schedules current; the cumulative net effect of all open releases is shown on the master schedule. A simplified release is illustrated in Figure 2-5.

Stock Replenishment Orders. Rather than authorize production of specific finished models by releases or management-approved orders, some enterprises that carry a wide variety of standard catalog items in finished stock establish predetermined reorder points and order quantities for each item. When reorder points are reached, production orders are written. These orders are consolidated at intervals and scheduled for shop production.

Job Shop and Contract Orders. A true job shop, which produces special-purpose machines and equipment, relates its planning to the contract bids. These estimate the cost and time needed for design, procurement, and production. When an order subsequently is received, the estimate becomes, in effect, the schedule for the job. Frequently, it is found that these shops use major components and subassemblies which have common usage in many of their contracts. To achieve more economical lot production and provide shorter delivery cycles, management-authorized anticipation schedules are released for these common components. It is then necessary only to produce special parts and complete the final assembly after a customer's order is received.

Other Plans and Procurement Schedules. In addition to schedules for finished model production, the following types of plans and schedules frequently are included in the agenda of planning meetings.

January 15, 19--

NO. 134

This is an Authorization to Procure Materials and Produce Models as follows:

	Through April		Through July	
	All Departmental Schedules and Final Purchasing		Long-Lead Purchasing Only	
Model	Month	Cumulative	Month	Cumulative
M-2259	750	8,500	750	10,750
M-2259X	0	5,150	50	5,300
M-3240	300	11,050	150	11,500

J. E. Scott
President

FIG. 2-5. *Typical release authorization.*

PROJECT NO. _____   DATE _____

UNIT NO. _____

SUMMARY	JAN	FEB	MAR	APR	MAY
ENGINEERING					
PRODUCTION PLANNING					
MATERIAL PROCUREMENT					
PRODUCTION					

ENGINEERING DEPARTMENT	JAN	FEB	MAR	APR	MAY
PREPRODUCTION MODEL					
MODEL TESTING					
OTHER MODEL WORK					
PRODUCTION DESIGN					
PRODUCTION TESTING					
PRODUCTION FOLLOW-UP					

PRODUCTION PLANNING	JAN	FEB	MAR	APR	MAY
DETERMINATION OF PART ORIGIN					
OPERATIONS SCHEDULE					
TOOLING					
OPERATION LAYOUT					
PRODUCTION TEST RUN					
PRODUCTION					

MATERIAL PROCUREMENT	JAN	FEB	MAR	APR	MAY
PRODUCTION CONTROL					
VENDOR CONTACT					
BUYING					
EXPEDITING					

FIG. 2-6. *New products schedule.*

1. *Long-term sales and production plans.* These are needed to shape sales, employment, inventory, engineering, and budgetary-control policy. They might project out nine to fifteen months, and in most cases, should be revised quarterly.

2. *New products schedules.* A planning committee should recommend, schedule, and follow up progress of new models for production. The introduction of new models into production should be regulated by planned start and completion dates for engineering design, price estimating, tooling, plant processing requirements, quality-control approval, time standards, and initial production run. An example of a new product schedule is shown in Figure 2-6.

3. *Advance procurement schedules.* Tooling; buying of raw materials, special "made to order" parts, and annual and seasonal contracts; and buying from foreign sources are long-lead activities which frequently exceed lead intervals provided by the authorized master schedules for finished models. This long-lead procurement should be authorized by schedules which specifically identify the inventory classifications or items, quantities, and delivery dates authorized. Commitments for these purchases may have to be made up to six to eight months or more in advance of the "released" schedules.

Inventory-control Policies. Management approval of finished production does not assure that adequate control over major dollar expenditures for production and inventories has been established. It is necessary also to define policies for inventory control, for in their absence it is usually found that junior supervisors and clerks make the decisions governing the company's commitments for labor and material costs. The production planning committee should formulate inventory-control policies for final approval by the general manager or chief executive.

To hold inventory investments within reasonable bounds consistent with efficient operation, it is desirable that management authorize lower and upper inventory limits by classes of purchased materials and in-process production. The lower limit is the protective minimum or safety bank that is authorized to be carried as a relatively fixed investment as protection against variations in demand, breakdowns in material flow, labor stoppages, and temporary quality problems. The maximum inventory limit is determined by adding what constitutes an economic *delivery* lot size to the safety minimum. A shop or purchase order generally should cover the total additional quantity authorized by the released master schedule, but this total should then be broken down and delivery lots scheduled according to the limits established for each classification.

It is best practice to express inventory limits in terms of time to ensure that they conform to seasonal fluctuations and that quantities vary accordingly. For example, a two-week protective minimum policy for a TV speaker might mean a limit of 20,000 in October and 8,000 in April unless this item is covered by a special procurement commitment. Figure 2-7 illustrates the inventory limits that might be established for a TV assembly plant. Procurement and production schedules should conform with the limits outlined in the stated policy. This will assure management that proper controls are being maintained over significant dollar expenditures for production. In addition, the inventory limits policy will be useful for budgeting inventory investments and preparing cash flow forecasts.

The Final Production Plan. The production plan must be balanced to capacities for each period. It should be developed to provide maximum customer service to satisfy expected sales requirements. For periods where sales requirements exceed capacity, management decisions must weigh the risk inherent in building stock earlier than normal in expectation of the seasonal peak against the risk of carrying the inventory over to a new selling period and the possibility of obsolescence.

From master schedules which specify how many finished products are to be built and when, and from stock replenishment orders, schedules for materials

	Protective minimum	Normal inventory	Maximum inventory
Purchased items:			
Wood cabinets...........................	1½ days	2 days	3 days
Kinescope tubes........................	1 day	1½ days	2 days
Foreign procurement.....................	1 month	2 months	4 months
A parts................................	2 days	1 week	2 weeks
B parts................................	1 week	2 weeks	4 weeks
C parts (upper dollar usage limits)...........	2 weeks	3 weeks	2 months
C parts (lower dollar usage limits).............	1 month	3 months	6 months
Assembly banks:			
Chassis, tuners, amplifiers...................	2 days	3 days	1 week
Speakers, cones, cut wire....................	2 weeks	2 weeks	1 month
Power transformers, yokes...................	3 days	1 week	2 weeks
Coil windings, voice coils, plugs, and leads.....	1 day	3 days	1 week

FIG. 2-7. *Typical inventory limits policy for a TV assembly plant.*

and manufacturing components are developed. Materials schedules specify how much material is to be received from vendors related to due dates by lot sizes which provide protective banks ahead of manufacturing requirements. The manufacturing schedule specifies what parts and assemblies must be made by work centers within schedule periods.

PRODUCTION SCHEDULING

Production scheduling is the mechanism which brings to life all productive activities. The scheduling of major assemblies and unusually long-lead procurement items generally is accomplished as part of the production planning process. A detail scheduling group is needed to set the time and pace for all other vendor procurement, plant material flows, and work operations in accordance with the master production plans and inventory-control policies.

Lot Size and Order Frequency. One of the first schedule considerations is to determine order lot sizes and reorder or reschedule frequencies. Assembly line production generally is scheduled according to daily or work shift rates of output. Fabricated parts and intermittently built components usually are scheduled in totals representative of assembly requirements covering a much longer period than a day. Probably the most frequently used schedule block for manufacturing companies is a weekly requirements total, although biweekly and monthly totals are used almost as often. In some cases, particularly for lower-cost parts, quarterly, six-month, and annual requirements may be produced in one schedule lot. One approach to management determination of lot sizes and ordering frequency is by defining inventory limits policies as described above.

Short runs usually involve higher costs because of setups and the lower efficiency of labor. Frequently, possibilities for grouping runs of like items or nearly like items are overlooked. Requirements for common parts should always be grouped within a reasonable period and within limits of a practicable inventory policy. Also, there are machines and some tools which follow progressive steps of adjustment. Schedules should follow the same progression to simplify setup problems.

The theory of economical quantities is to determine an order size which minimizes the total of setup or acquisition costs and inventory carrying costs. The acquisition cost includes the cost of order preparation, the labor involved in setting up tools or other equipment changes, and receiving and inspections costs. Carrying costs are those needed to finance inventories and space-occupancy charges. The smaller the order size, the more frequently the item must be restocked and, of course, the higher the acquisition cost. Conversely, as order sizes increase so do inventory carrying charges. Although it can be proved mathematically that the lowest overall cost occurs where the restocking cost equals the carrying cost, there is considerable flexibility in applying this rule, because the costs generally vary little over a range of plus or minus 20 percent.

ASSEMBLY SCHEDULING

Assembly operations normally are done in separate assembly departments. However, many fabricating departments also may include certain assembly operations, particularly those that involve specialized equipment such as stamping and spot welding. Assembly operations may be classified as those performed in sequence as the work moves sequentially from one operator location to another, and spot assembly where the product is assembled by progressively moving materials and crews to the same location. Line-assembly operations with time

ASSEMBLY LINE SCHEDULE

MONTHS OF	PLANT NO.
OCTOBER NOVEMBER DECEMBER	2

MICROWAVE RELAY

DATE ISSUED: 9-10
LAST RELEASE: 8-2
ISSUED BY: H.A.K

OCTOBER — 22 WORKING DAYS

ASSEMBLY LINE	MODEL OR S-NUMBER	BALANCE TO PRODUCE	2	3	4	5	6-7	9	10	11	12	13-14	16	17	18	19	20-21	23	24	25	26	27-28	30	31	MONTHLY TOTAL
501	9J2	11551	220	220	220	220																			1540
							220	220	220	220	220	220	220	220	220	220	220	220	220	220	220	220	220	3300
502	6H3	34966	500	500	500	500	500	500	500	500	500	500	500	500											6000
	9J0	11551													0	50	70	80	110	120	130	140	140	150	990
	9J2Q	7986																							0

NOVEMBER — 21 WORKING DAYS

ASSEMBLY LINE	MODEL OR S-NUMBER	BALANCE TO PRODUCE	1	3-4	6	7	8	9	10-11	13	14	15	16	17-18	20	21	22	24	27-28	29	30	MONTHLY TOTAL	BALANCE TO PRODUCE
501	9J0	9021																				1540	3221
	9J2Q	4686	220	220	220	220	220	220	220	220	220	220	220	220	220	220						3080	1606
502	6H3	16566																				0	0
	9J0	9021	220	220	220	220	220	220	220	220	220	220	220	220	220	220						4260	3221
	9J2Q	4686																				0	1606

DECEMBER — 16 WORKING DAYS

ASSEMBLY LINE	1	4	5	6	7	8-9	11	12	13	14	15-16	18	19	20	21	22-23	MONTHLY TOTAL
501													X	X	X	X	801
	220	220	220	220	220	220	66						X	X	X	X	1606
502													X	X	X	X	0
	220	220	220	220	220	220							X	X	X	X	2420
													X	X	X	X	0

FIG. 2-8. Assembly line schedule.

allowances for each operator location balanced to the same rate provide greatest labor efficiencies for repetitive assembly work; the line output is paced or rated in terms of hourly and daily totals. Paced line-assembly operations also avoid buildups of banks of materials between operators. These operations frequently can be performed on parts which move continuously on conveyors from operator to operator. At the end of the line, the assembly should be complete and ready for inspection.

Balancing assembly line operations and determining output rates is an industrial engineering task. It is scheduling's responsibility to determine the quantities and sequence of models to be run and to prepare and correlate schedules sufficiently in advance to provide for the orderly flow of component materials to assembly operations.

Learning Curves. When new models are scheduled to start on a line, schedule rates should take into consideration a buildup of in-process parts at the operator positions prior to completion and also should be set in accordance with learning curves derived from past experience. Figure 2-8 illustrates a schedule prepared for a relay. Note that assembly line 502 on October 18 for 9JO shows no scheduled production; this is due to building up in-process parts and training. This assembly schedule shows daily output rates for the next three months, although it is reissued monthly. The purpose is to provide for the orderly scheduling and flow of components for the assembly.

Paced Assembly Lines. Whenever plant processing can be organized so that assemblies can be manufactured on paced lines, considerable improvement in efficiency results. In addition, manufacturing lead times are reduced, and there are reductions in material handling costs and in investment in in-process inventory. Ease of supervision also is improved. Offsetting factors are delays in assembly lines due to material shortages or quality problems that can result in costly idle time; also, frequent changes in model runs result in more costly start-up costs than nonpaced methods.

FABRICATED COMPONENTS SCHEDULING

Scheduling components involves determining the quantity and work sequence to be followed and then ordering each operation to be performed. Work sequences conventionally are obtained from process or operations sheets prepared by industrial engineering, which also usually carry standard or basic time data allowances for each operation. Reproductions of the master operations card with the addition of the variable schedule data, as shown in Figure 2-9, are often used as the shop order.

Scheduling order quantities involves essentially a determination of order priority—the sequence in which the orders will be run on the equipment to provide customer service and minimize changeover costs—start and due dates, and some overall balancing of the order requirements to the available machine center capacity.

Balancing to Capacity. Generally, there are a number of alternative machines in fabricating machine centers which can be selected to perform an operation. Under these conditions, loading the machine center is adequate. Individual machine loading is needed only for bottleneck equipment.

Many manufacturing companies find it unnecessary to balance fabricating order requirements with machine center capacities, providing that, in the production planning process, finished model orders are sequenced and balanced by some method similar to those described above. The term "scheduling to infinite capacity" is often used to describe fabricating scheduling where there is no balanc-

SHEET _1_ OF _1_   PRODUCTION ORDER AND OPERATIONS CARD   PART NO. 30346

| PART NO. 30346 | W.O. NUMBER 5200 | QUANTITY 1500 | LOT | DATE ISSUED 5/15 | DATE REQUIRED 6/25 | AVERAGE RUN 5000 | OPERATIONS RECORD | | | |

DESCRIPTION	SWITCH FRAME				QUANTITY PER C	UNIT COST / TOTAL QUANTITY	STANDARD COST PER C	PREPARED 2/23/53	BY L.Z.	PRINT ISSUE 4
R M NO		DESCRIPTION						REVISED 5/21/56	BY L.Z.	REVISION ISSUE 1
885-5563	14 GA. (.064) 48 × 144 ALUMINUM				.044	.66		MODEL USED ON	3829 BRAZING MACHINE	
	CUT 2304 / SHEET							QUANTITY	1	
88-1528	½ DIA. B1113 CRS				2.9 FT.	44 FT		SUB-ASSEMBLY USED IN	30350	

DELIVER MATERIAL TO DEPT _____ ON _____   TOTAL _____

OPER	DEPT	MACH	DESCRIPTION	SPEED	FEED	TOOLS	LOC	QTY PER HR	SET UP HOURS	HOURS PER C	SET UP PER C TOTAL TIME	LABOR RATE WEEK SCH'D	LABOR COST QTY COMP'T	BURDEN RATE SCRAP	BURDEN COST COMP'T	BY WHOM
2	2	102	SHEAR TO 2¼" STRIPS					278 STRIPS		.02	.3	5/16				
4	4	1631	BLANK OUT PART			BLANKING TOOL	N5	714	1.0	.14	2.1	5/30				
6	4	1631	FORM			FORMING FIXTURE	R8	200	.6	.5	7.5	6/12				
8	10	2114	DRILL HOLE			MILL JIG	P1	200	.5	.5	7.5	6/20				
10	10	2132	TAP			STD	G5	200	.5	.5	7.5	6/22				
12	2	4401	C' DRILL	1100	H	E-1	AA1	41	.99	2.47	37.0	6/25				
			DRILL #9 (.196)	1100	.0025	STD	C3									
			TURN .311 +.000 −.002	1100	.0025	BOX TOOL	F6									
			CUT OFF TO ⁷⁄₆₄ APPROX.	1100	H	⅛" WIDE	BB4									
14			INSPECT													
16			STOCK													

FORM C 808

FIG. 2-9. *Master operations card with variable schedule data included.*

ing of orders to capacity. Instead, a priority numbering system is used to identify the sequence for production on orders released to the shop. This method provides that orders are started and completed to meet sales demand requirements, which, of course, is a primary objective for scheduling.

Schedule Dates to Provide for Vendor and In-plant Leads. Vendor procurement schedules must carry a due date in addition to the required lot quantity. Production work schedules and shop orders prepared for fabricating parts and subassemblies should show a *start* date as well as a *due* date. These dates must be established in relation to the lead intervals for the other components and subassemblies which must be brought together for final assembly.

Figure 2-10 is a simplified lead time chart. This illustrates a final assembly to be started in week 37 of the year and shipped in week 39. If this is to happen, component part 3 should be scheduled to start into production in week 30 for completion in week 34. The four-week interval provided between the start and completion of part 3 should allow time for (1) order preparation, (2) procurement, either from vendors or by manufacturing in the plant, and (3) a safety bank lead to provide a reserve cushion or an expediting interval to ensure that the part is available as of the start date in week 34 of subassembly A.

Scope. Schedule guidance must be given every productive assembly and fabricating operation. The great majority of productive activity should be covered by formally issued assembly schedules or shop orders. There are certain types of operations, however, that can be performed to "as required" decisions made by foremen or dispatchers who initiate operations which are obviously needed to complete an order or schedule. Shearing, plating, and painting are common examples of this type.

Report Exceptions. The study of production facilities usually reveals that once an item is started in production, it may be expected to progress through various levels of fabrication and assembly within certain predetermined ranges of rated output. Schedules should be dispatched with primary attention placed on starting parts on time. If this is done, much of the internal reporting and paper work for transfers can be minimized. Expediting efforts and reports are then based upon the "exception" principle; only delays are reported and followed up. This obviates the need for transmitting a large volume of production count and transfer data to control centers where it must be processed, updated, and analyzed to determine problem areas.

Minimizing Floor Stocks. The release of orders should be regulated so that materials ahead of work stations do not build up excessively. Generally, at the beginning of a day's shift they should not exceed more than 150 percent of the rated daily output for the center. Shops can operate efficiently with considerably less materials ahead of work stations where there is scheduling and effective control over forklift operators and other means for making intraplant material movements. By limiting materials ahead of work stations, shop orders will be completed much more promptly, and in-process inventory investments will be reduced dramatically.

Material Availability. Schedules should not be released to production until material availability has been verified. This can be done analytically in a good record-keeping system by checking perpetual inventories for parts and subassemblies or by comparing cumulative totals of receipts and production of components with the cumulative total of the assembly production. Another method is to issue component stores requisitions far enough in advance of production to permit expediting parts shortages. This method is wasteful of floor space and material handling if materials are moved, and usually exposes materials to unauthorized use. A better plan is to compare requisition totals with materials in the storeroom and count only items which appear to be short. Both these latter methods are expedients pending development of satisfactory record data.

Rework and Scrap. The scheduling of rework and repairs of inspection rejects is often overlooked. There should be a formal means for reporting rejects and expediting their rework. Likewise, a follow-up on the production of parts to

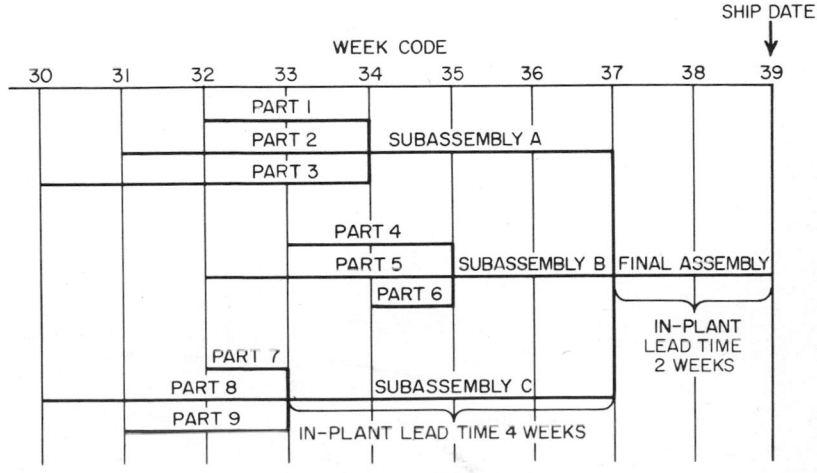

FIG. 2-10. *Lead time chart.*

replace those scrapped is necessary. Often, companies are embarrassed to find that, after they have completed a run and pulled the tooling, there has been an underrun of good parts. This may result in an excess of other matching components if the loss is not made up to complete the original scheduled assembly quantity.

BIBLIOGRAPHY

Biegel, John E., *Production Control: A Quantitative Approach*, Prentice-Hall, Inc., Englewood Cliffs, N.J., 1963.

Greene, James H., *Production Control: Systems and Decisions*, Richard D. Irwin, Inc., Homewood, Ill., 1965.

Holt, Charles C., Franco Modigliani, John F. Muth, and Herbert A. Simon, *Planning Production, Inventories, and Work Force*, Prentice-Hall, Inc., Englewood Cliffs, N.J., 1960.

Hopeman, Richard J., *Production: Concepts, Analysis, Control*, Charles E. Merrill Books, Inc., Columbus, Ohio, 1965.

Maynard, H. B. (ed.), *Industrial Engineering Handbook*, 2d ed., McGraw-Hill Book Company, New York, 1963.

Moore, Franklin G., *Production Control*, McGraw-Hill Book Company, New York, 1959.

Muth, John F., and G. L. Thompson, *Industrial Scheduling*, Prentice-Hall, Inc., Englewood Cliffs, N.J., 1963.

CHAPTER THREE

Purchasing Department Management

E. A. GRUNWALD *Editor-in-Chief,* Purchasing Week, *New York, New York*

The most meaningful label that can be pinned on the industrial purchasing function is "money management."

Although the purchasing agent buys all the commodities, components, and supplies a manufacturing complex chews up (plus their transportation), he does not himself originate the need for them. Nor does he personally use them. Rather, he is the legal representative of the proprietors, acting under the law of agency (whence his title "agent"), who contacts and bargains with vendors. More and more his affinity is for the fiscal side of his company.

This trend becomes even clearer when you consider that his domain, in terms of dollars spent, is by far the largest in an industrial firm. Roughly half a company's sales intake flows back through his hands for new goods and supplies, meaning that in recent years industrial purchasing agents have been dispensing about $200 billion annually.

Indeed, because of the enormity of these amounts, it has become fashionable to refer to purchasing departments not as "cost centers" but as "profit centers." The logic of this paradox is clear when you consider this simple theorem:

Whenever a salesman sells $100 worth of merchandise, he carries about $10 into the profit column.

Whenever a purchasing agent saves $10, he carries *all of it* into the profit column.

Ergo, an intelligent purchasing agent can make just as much profit for his company via a $10 efficiency as a salesman can via a $100 sale.

The major alternatives a purchasing agent uses to gain these efficiencies are:

1. Ordering in mathematically correct lots to hold costs and inventories at a minimum
2. Grouping purchases to earn favorable prices, discounts, and deliveries
3. Selecting materials and particularly vendors by rating systems

Another seeming alternative—purchase of lower-grade merchandise—more and more is considered no alternative whatsoever; in fact, it could be outright suicide. If the inferior goods eventually lead to performance failures, the purchasing agent indirectly could ruin his company's name and all-important market position.

"INVENTORY-LESS" INDUSTRY

Among the major economic phenomena of the 1960s, one of the most spectacular has been the advent of "inventory-less" purchasing—a feat resulting from long experience with and detailed analysis of the so-called cost of possession.

This analysis, loosely stated as a law, says: *The cost of owning high inventories outweighs their insurance value.*

As calculated by such experts as the late consultant F. Albert Hayes, acquisition of more goods than comfortably needed incurs a penalty of 12 to 24 percent per year. Here is how that figure is arrived at:

The needless tie-up of a company's capital in idle merchandise causes a loss equal to 5 or 6 percent of the value of the excess goods.

Obsolescence eats up another 5 to 10 percent.

Space charges consume ¼ percent; handling charges, 1 to 3 percent; insurance, ¼ percent; taxes, ¼ to ½ percent; depreciation, 5 percent; deterioration, 3 percent; and inability to use tied-up capital elsewhere, 4½ to 8 percent.

On the basis of this realization, decision making in purchasing obviously is changing drastically. For example:

It rarely is considered desirable to anticipate price increases by buying large stocks at old prices.

Nor is it wise to amass huge quantities of an item for the sake of a discount—unless the discount is fabulous.

Contrast this reasoning with the old and costly high-inventory philosophy described by Alfred P. Sloan, Jr., in *My Years with General Motors.* On a guess that sales would rise, GM in 1920 boosted its inventory from $137 million to $209 million in ten months. When the rosy sales guess did not materialize, the company was so strapped for cash that it had to borrow $83 million from the banks in one month alone.

Today, all purchasing practice begins with the principle that the best pipeline is a thin, fast one. How carefully this doctrine is observed may be seen in Figure 3-1, depicting fifty months of uninterrupted business boom without any appreciable change in the inventory-sales ratio.

The quick conclusion that can be drawn from "inventory-less" purchasing is that industrial buying is done in smaller, more frequent doses. This is true—but with certain important reservations. More accurately, the trick is turned by a sophisticated gambit: better grouping of purchases.

BETTER GROUPING OF PURCHASES

A moment's figuring will show that any attempt to escape costs of possession merely by ordering in minute quantities leads to a dead end. Suppose a housewife wanted to avoid the nuisance of potato storage by driving to the grocery store every time she needed a pound or two of Idahos. The costs of gasoline soon would outweigh the drawbacks of potato inventory. It is the same for

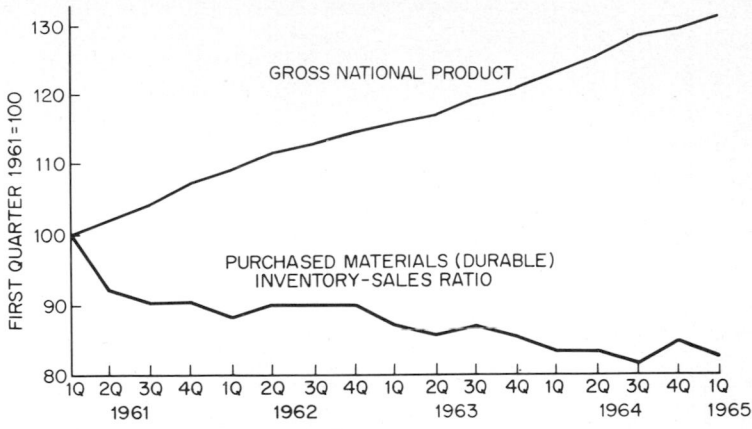

FIG. 3-1. *"Inventory-less" purchasing.* (*Courtesy of U.S. Department of Commerce.*)

purchasing agents: at some point, the costs of ordering (manpower, paper work, and so on) will outweigh inventory costs. Therefore:

The correct amount to buy—or economic order value—is that quantity whose order costs and carrying costs are equal.

The following example of an item with an annual usage of $300 will show how this realization was born:

No. buys per year	Dollar value per buy	Order cost at $2	Average inventory value	Carrying cost at 12 % per year	Total (col. 3 + col. 5)
12	$ 25	$24	$ 12.50	$ 1.50	$25.50
3	100	6	50.00	6.00	12.00
1	300	2	150.00	18.00	20.00

Note that the ultrasmall, frequent buy (twelve times a year) actually is the most inefficient. The best buy (three times a year) has the correct balance between order costs ($6) and inventory carrying charges ($6).

In short, although excess inventory is a cardinal sin, the opposite tack—purchase of uneconomically small quantities—also is costly. The "equilibrium" purchase, or optimum economic order value, is the true goal. It has brought inventories down from old, historic highs, yet it has not fragmented purchases into inefficient bits.

At this point, however, the purchasing agent is playing with quicksilver. By using economic order value, he has solved the problem of excess inventory and uneconomically small purchases, but he simultaneously has created two new problems:

1. Because he is buying in smaller lots, he *loses some quantity discounts.*

2. He *still must issue more orders* than in the days when he bought a huge supply at a single clip.

What makes these considerations particularly nettlesome is that industrial inventories are very lopsided. Numerically, the greatest portion consists of low-value items, usually ordered repetitively. Yet it is in this low-value sector that

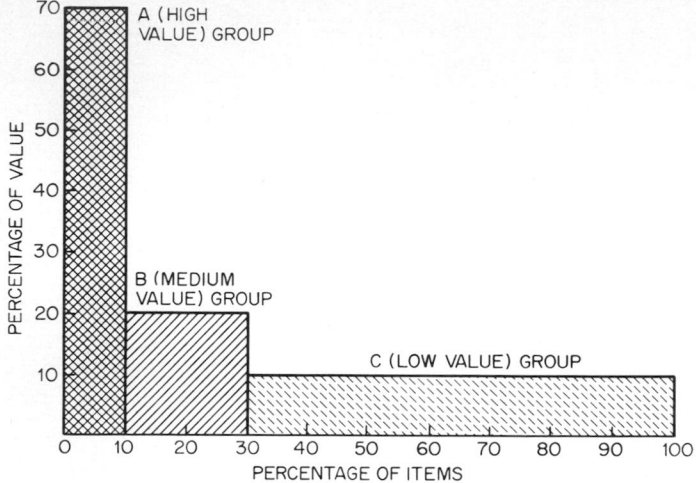

FIG. 3-2. *Composition of manufacturers' inventories.*

the purchasing agent ironically must spend the major part of his time and efforts—unless he can devise an escape from the trap. Figure 3-2 shows what the trap looks like.

The lesson in this diagram is that 70 percent of the items in inventory (the C group) account for a mere 10 percent of total inventory value; whereas—in reverse proportion—10 percent of the items (the A group) comprise 70 percent of the value.

How can the purchasing agent keep his behavior from falling into this skewed mold?   How can he devote more time to the A and B sectors of inventory—the really worthwhile items—and rid himself of the clerical drudgery and costs that the C group demands?

The answer to this question happily also involves the answer to the discount situation.   It is a case of killing two birds with one stone.   In a nutshell, the purchasing agent now puts many C items under long-term-supply contracts (sometimes also called "blanket orders") which (1) cut down the labor and paper work of ordering and (2) earn sizable discounts because they cover a large quantity of goods over a long period of time.

Typically, such a contract specifies:

1. Type or types of items covered by the contract.
2. Length of contract.   Usually this is six months to a year, often with an automatic or semiautomatic renewal (which makes the contract "evergreen").
3. Prices and discounts—both of which are adjustable if there are price or quantity changes during the life of the contract.
4. Delivery times.   These are fixed by economic order value to give maximum benefits to both vendor and purchaser.
5. Terms of payment—generally on a monthly basis so that the buyer ties up the smallest possible amount of his company's cash supply.
6. Shipping points and method of transportation.
7. Ways of altering or negotiating or terminating the contract.

Long-term contracts are used for the purchase of a huge gamut of supplies, ranging from MRO (maintenance-repair-operating) items to many OEM (original equipment manufacture) materials, including certain types of steel.   In other words, the lure of safety and efficiency seemingly inherent in long-term contracts is spreading their use from low-cost "headache" goods to more expensive materials bought less frequently.

Furthermore, the concept of the long-term contract has had important ripples in other areas of purchasing. The logic which led to invention of the contract also has led to:

Use of electronic hookups with long-term suppliers (the data-phone). These instant-order systems, which work on the principle of transmitting coded instructions via phone lines, also automatically eliminate much bookkeeping.

Better nomenclature of inventory. To bulk all identical goods into a blanket contract, the goods obviously must be accurately and identically named.

Better nomenclature, in turn, has made wider use of the computer possible in (1) keeping up-to-the-minute inventory records, (2) compiling performance data, and (3) determining reorder points.

Thus what patently is evolving in the purchasing profession is a combination of mathematical-logical disciplines and electronic data handling whose objectives are speed and lower costs.

In summarizing the steps by which this stage evolved, you would climb this short historical ladder:

Rung No. 1: Realization that buying in large quantities (often by sheer guesswork) endangers a company's cash and profit position.

Rung No. 2: Removal of this danger by purchasing in mathematically correct lots via the economic order value principle.

Rung No. 3: Compensation for loss of discounts and additional paper work inherent in smaller orders by use of the long-term contract, or blanket order.

Rung No. 4: Broadening of the long-term-contract logic to create further economies, often with the help of electronic devices.

SELECTION OF MATERIALS AND VENDORS

Although the purchasing agent's basic role is that of a "money manager," his authority extends far beyond the efficient satisfaction of requisitions. If it did not, the waste in a modern corporation would be enormous, because:

1. There would be little incentive to standardize beyond minimum levels.
2. Information on new products or processes would be disseminated haphazardly at best.
3. Decisions on whether to buy a component from outside sources or manufacture it at home (make or buy alternatives) would be based on sheer guesswork.

Thus the procurement function in the modern corporation has added many overtones of a broad research function. Indeed, "purchasing research" is now part of the standard industrial vocabulary, and "purchasing analyst" has a place on many organization charts. The chore of the analyst is to assemble research on products, prices, processes, transportation, or any other factor that will make the company logistically more efficient.

Two areas in which this probing has dramatic possibilities are value analysis and upstream buying.

Value Analysis. Value analysis is the search for a *more efficient way to fulfill a particular function without loss of quality.* An exaggerated example: Suppose the automotive people decided that the price of the wheels on cars—plus the shafts and gears that turn them—was becoming alarmingly high. A standard response to this proposition would be: "Let's see if we can buy cheaper assemblies." A value analysis response, however, would be: "Maybe we don't need wheels at all. Why can't we float the car on a cushion of air? Let's explore all the alternatives to wheels that we can think of."

The depth probing of value analysis produces best results when it is a team effort. Along with the purchasing department, the design, engineering, production, and sometimes sales divisions should participate.

Usually, though, it is the purchasing department that first spots the need for value analysis, because it has the best overall view of costs. A long-standing practice of the Department of Defense has been to urge procurement officers and purchasing agents to act as watchmen over the requirements in defense contracts so that value analysis will not drift into limbo. In fact, some contracts provide for incentives based on value analysis improvements.

Upstream Buying. Upstream buying involves research on prices and materials for products still in the dream stage. If a company were planning to market, say, a powerful, cordless electric drill for the consumer market, could the device be produced to sell profitably at $30 two years hence? The purchasing department would have to provide the key projections telling the company that (1) the drill can be made to sell profitably at that price, or (2) it cannot be done with present designs, or (3) it may be possible if the designs and the materials were changed slightly, or (4) there is no known way whatsoever to produce such a drill for $30.

Because of the increasingly high premium on innovation, upstream buying has become an important chore of purchasing departments, especially in large, diversified corporations (a notable example is the aerospace industry).

Vendor Selection. Vendor selection, meantime, has grown into a true art—particularly since long-term contracts imply long-term relationships with suppliers. Moreover, the sealed-bid system, accompanied by bid deposits or bonds, is not used nearly so much in industrial purchasing as it is in government or municipal buying. Instead, the industrial purchaser negotiates personally with vendors, hammering out agreements on wide range of considerations including price, delivery, service, research, and rejects.

Therefore, purchasing agents have developed a variety of rating systems to guide themselves (and upgrade vendors). Some are so comprehensive that they can be handled properly only by electronic data systems.

At the top of every rating list stands vendor *reliability*. On this score, the purchasing agent assesses the vendor's financial position, his past performance, and his cooperation when problems develop.

Price history is an equally important matter. A supplier whose prices show an erratic pattern may be an erratic performer in other respects.

Delivery record is vital. A supplier who is tardy in making shipments could cause stock-outs. Also, a supplier with a bad labor record might shut down the buyer's production line—as well as his own—if a strike suddenly broke out.

Research is a criterion rapidly rising to the top. A supplier who can offer technical assistance is providing the buyer with a valuable plus. Furthermore, his alertness will be a guarantee that his goods are up to date.

Other points on which the vendor is evaluated include: How much service does he provide? What does he do about rejects? Will he help with scrap disposal? Does he carry a full line? Does he keep his customers posted on future developments and products?

The concept of vendor rating, of course, implies that the purchasing agent has full authority to select vendors. Is this really true?

The answer is "yes"—with three modifications.

One occurs when the purchasing agent works in tandem with the designers of new products, accepting their brand and vendor lists as the safest way to get the new devices off the ground. Later, however, he may make adjustments and substitutions.

Another consists of the delegation of authority. For example, it hardly would be worth a purchasing agent's time to go through the formal motions of buying minor or emergency items, especially for outlying plants. He therefore delegates authority to a nonpurchasing employee who becomes accountable for the procurement of such goods.

The third—and by far the largest—exception is in the field of "trade relations" (often referred to as "reciprocity"). As the name implies, this means that two companies buy from each other as mutual customers—in other words, A buys from B, because B buys from A. Vendor selection in such cases is highly limited or nonexistent.

The size of the "trade relations" area is unknown. For one thing, its dimensions constantly are shifting. For another, fear that the government may one day look at the practice more severely than in the past—a not unlikely possibility—puts a cloak of caution around the whole matter. Suffice it to say that the purchasing department defers to general management or sales in such situations.

PURCHASING ORGANIZATION

The purchasing profession is a young one. It did not come into existence until industry grew so large and complex that the owners or plant managers no longer could supervise buying personally (though that is still done in small businesses).

In 1965 there were approximately 50,000 industrial purchasing agents. About half were concentrated in 3,000 companies whose sales were in the $5 million-and-up category. As a rule of thumb, the size of a purchasing staff is relatively large if the firm basically is an assembly operation and relatively small if the firm is vertically integrated. Thus General Electric has some 1,200 purchasing agents where Allegheny Ludlum has only about 25.

Within a purchasing department, three or four strata are the norm. The head calls himself purchasing director, vice president in charge of purchasing, or manager of purchases. Under him is a group of agents and/or buyers (if the department consists of more than one person). In large, sophisticated departments, purchasing analysts, expediters, and traffic experts complement the buying staff.

Historically, the purchasing department has been considered an arm of the manufacturing division. But that concept is changing rapidly. Now the purchasing department is more apt to report directly to the president or administrative officer because of its "profit center" characteristics.

Moreover, the trend is toward central purchasing control, especially in policy matters. A case in point is the purchasing setup of U.S. Steel. Whereas the corporation once had a purchasing department for each of its seven operating divisions, plus a Pittsburgh headquarters, in 1965 it had five regional purchasing offices and a much greater emphasis on Pittsburgh, as shown by Figure 3-3.

Worth noting—but as yet not fully assessable—is the materials management concept that some large corporations are adopting. This involves the creation of a special department to handle the total logistics of the company—materials input including purchasing, traffic, inventory, stores, and production scheduling. Proponents say materials management steps up efficiency markedly. Critics

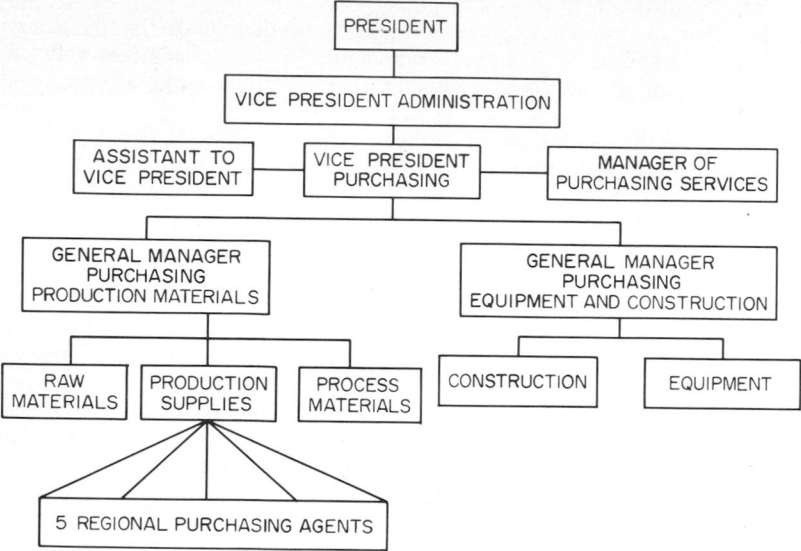

FIG. 3-3.   *Organization of United States Steel Corporation.*

claim it could promote internal strife and misunderstanding.   Whatever the case, the purchasing department figures strongly in such a program, and often the former purchasing director has become the materials manager.

What are the personal characteristics of a purchasing man?   How does he regard himself?

First and foremost, he feels he is a member of a profession which has its own professional association (National Association of Purchasing Agents) and a code of standards that stresses the utmost in ethics and devotion to the task.

His background is most apt to be in business administration or engineering (sometimes also sales).   His average age is in the mid-forties.   His education includes several years of college training (actually, about half of today's purchasing agents have completed college or gone beyond; eventually the entire purchasing population will be college trained, with a strong emphasis on those who have graduate degrees).

Above all, the purchasing profession is not an in-and-out occupation.   The average length of those in service is twelve to fifteen years, a remarkable span for a group so young.

BIBLIOGRAPHY

Aljian, George W. (ed.), *Purchasing Handbook*, 2d ed., McGraw-Hill Book Company, New York, 1966.

England, Wilbur B., *Procurement*, 4th ed., Richard D. Irwin, Inc., Homewood, Ill., 1962.

Farmer, Samuel C., "A Look at Purchasing through the President's Eye," Management Bulletin, no. 33, American Management Association, New York, 1963.

Hayes, F. Albert, and George A. Renard, "Evaluating Purchasing Performance," Research Study, no. 66, American Management Association, New York, 1964.

Lee, Lamar, Jr., and Donald W. Dobler, *Purchasing and Materials Management*, McGraw-Hill Book Company, New York, 1965.

Pooler, Victor H., Jr., *The Purchasing Man and His Job*, American Management Association, New York, 1964.

CHAPTER FOUR

Dynamic Purchasing

SAMUEL C. FARMER *President and Treasurer, Farmer Electrical Supply Division, Seaboard Electrical Supply Co., Inc., Hanover, New Jersey*

In the preceding chapter, the importance of the purchasing function to the overall success of the company was stressed. Some of the purchasing concepts and procedures which have been found effective were discussed. It will now be appropriate to reemphasize some of the points made and to describe in further detail how an aggressive, effective purchasing program can be carried out. The procedures outlined in this chapter, when grouped together into an integrated system, have come to be known as "dynamic purchasing."

Dynamic purchasing is, in ultimate result, the true and effective use of the purchasing function. Its success or failure is measured solely in dollars contributed by the purchasing department directly to net profit.

This concept of purchasing is a necessity for companies where well over 50 percent of the sales dollar must be invested in materials. Actual practice has proved it successful, however, even in companies engaged only in research and development where there are nonrepetitive and low material costs.

Operating under a well-planned and budgeted program, dynamic purchasing requires absolute authority and responsibility over vendors, material, and all matters related to order placement. It may operate either as a profit center or as an integral part of a profit-producing function.

THE BENEFITS OF DYNAMIC PURCHASING

There are a number of benefits which result from the adoption of a dynamic purchasing program. Among the more important are the following.

Measuring Profit Potential. When fully operative, dynamic purchasing is a useful management tool for measuring both profit and profit potential. It defines areas of strength and weakness in determining not just how much money the company makes, but how much it could or should have made.

Departmental Balance. Few companies, despite financial success, achieve equal balance or growth within all divisions or departments. Although one department seldom is held solely responsible for the success or failure of a company, a poorly functioning department can impair the work of others. The sources from which purchasing savings are derived, or the absence of sources, will indicate specific departmental unbalance.

Coordination and Cooperation. Active coordination between departments is a requisite for a well-run company. Making departments get along with one another is one thing; testing or judging the effectiveness of coordination and cooperation is another. Under the dynamic purchasing concept, there exists clear evidence of either cooperation or its lack.

Controlling Cash Flow. When using dynamic purchasing, a company can narrow the gap between significant material expenditures and ultimate customer receipts. In addition, it can avoid or lessen the problems of surplus materials, unnecessary storage costs, obsolete material write-off, and slow inventory turnover.

Eliminating Conflict of Interest. Management no longer needs to worry about payoffs or dishonesty within the material purchase area under the dynamic purchasing method for selecting and evaluating vendors.

Training for General Management. As the concept of dynamic purchasing has grown within industry, the talent exercised by those in purchasing for generating net profit contributions from the material area has proved this department a likely place for general management potential.

ORGANIZING FOR DYNAMIC PURCHASING

Establishing the Function. It is normal to assume there will be a disruption of beliefs, held by other departments concerning purchasing's role in the company, when the dynamic purchasing concept is introduced. For this reason, the purchasing manager must make sure at the beginning that materials continue to be purchased and, above all, that the proper attitude for dynamic purchasing exists, first, within his own department.

He must unalterably hold the conviction that his department's major responsibility is to contribute to net profits. To assure that there is a continuance of purchasing and that dollar savings are achieved, the manager must reorganize his department in the following manner.

Assign Sole Responsibility. Commodity purchases must be split up and given exclusively to each buyer. In assigning specific commodities to a buyer, consideration must be given to factors affecting their purchase, such as a high degree of technical changes subsequent to a requisition, limited vendor sources, and short lead time.

Budget Anticipated Savings. Each buyer must determine the anticipated dollar savings he will realize for each of the commodities assigned him. Whether these savings (expressed as a percentage of annual dollar expenditures for the commodity) are achieved or not ultimately should have an effect upon his promotions, salary increases, or bonuses. Percentage improvements goals, at first, may be set low and even arbitrarily. As data are accumulated and buyers recognize they actually may be in competition with others in another division successfully handling identical commodities, adjustments follow automatically. The existence of an improvement program in a rapidly declining sales market may actually work in reverse order. Experienced buyers appreciate how difficult their task becomes to maintain existing price levels under such conditions, and they welcome a record proving superior performance.

Typed	Item	To be typed
	Purchase order	
	Blanket releases	
	Supplements	
	Inquiries	
	Inquiries for proposals	
	Intercompany orders	
	Purchase order retyped objective	
	Telegrams	
	Letters	
	Form letters	
	Shipping papers	
	Rejection notices	
	Shortage notices	
	Savings reports	
	Memos	
	Masters	
	Follow-ups	
	Reports for expediters	

FIG. 4-1. *Input-output analysis. Note: This form shows work load; it can be used for a stock clerk or errand boy, or to help determine the need for the job (based on what the job consists of); it is used only on a random sampling basis when starting a profit improvement program. No special clerical staff or help is needed to prepare these forms since all data are available daily. (By permission of the American Management Association, Management Bulletin, no. 33.)*

Develop Proper Control Forms. Figures 4-1 through 4-7 show sample forms used in dynamic purchasing. Where necessary, a brief explanation illustrates use within the company.

Restaff and Rebudget. Clerical and routine processing of a purchase order from the requisition to a material receipt can no longer be handled by the buyer. He must become a supervisor over these basic clerical tasks. His time must be spent on the more important tasks such as developing the skills and techniques necessary to generate savings. In effect, he becomes a manager over his commodity areas, judiciously determining every reason—the how, why, what, and where—that dictates the commodity need within the company. As results are documented under the dynamic purchasing program, the addition or curtailment of clerical help necessary to the task will be determined—with results justifying the manpower costs.

Establish a Vendor Rating Program. A consistent method for rating vendors must be based on criteria which include price fluctuations, promptness in delivery, rejected material, and other items vital to the efficient management of the business.

Rating control can be exercised on high-dollar-volume materials, for it is uneconomical to rate everything. Criteria must also be established for selecting new sources and evaluating them against existing sources, enabling the buyer to recognize easily when to shift from one source to another. Merely stating that "three sources exist" is not suitable. The ability and performance of these sources must be known and justified.

The Job of Purchasing Administrator. To one individual, thoroughly experienced in purchasing, must fall all the duties distinct from either the buying

Week ending _____   Buyer A
Requisitions on hand:
  From previous week _____
  Received this week _____
Requisitions carried over to next week:
  Requisitions not on inquiry _____
  Requisitions on inquiry _____
Requisitions processed:
  For blanket _____
  Not requiring purchase orders _____
  For purchase orders _____
Total requisitions carried over/processed: _____
Oldest requisition date:
  Date _____
  Number _____
  Item _____
Supplements issued: _____

FIG. 4-2. *Requisition status report. Note: This report shows input-output; it is used only on a random sampling basis when initiating a profit improvement program. (By permission of the American Management Association, Management Bulletin, no. 33.)*

or the management function.   Normally, this person is given the title of purchasing administrator and is responsible for:

1. Coordination between the purchasing manager and either the buyers or other department heads

2. Establishment of the necessary systems, methods, and procedures used in dynamic purchasing

3. Preparation and leadership of seminars and training sessions devoted to teaching and proving advanced skills and techniques

4. Assistance at all levels to the purchasing manager

HOW DYNAMIC PURCHASING FUNCTIONS

How Savings Are Derived.   After the initial organization and staff development, emphasis is placed on cost improvement.   Buyers must be trained to recognize how savings are made.   Normally, there are four ways:

1. *Negotiation*—by the proper assembling of facts and statistics and the knowledge of how to use them for successful negotiation

2. *Vendor change*—by the initiation of a vendor rating system guiding buyers in the selection of new or additional vendors

3. *Specification change*—by value engineering or value analysis, determining substitute materials or economical specification change

4. *Internal improvements*—by regrouping personnel and collecting information which shows what areas to concentrate on for maximum savings (for example, the ABC's of inventory turnover)

Recording Dollar Savings.   Dollar savings are credited when directly attributable to buyer capability.   No credit is given for quantity discounts, errors in extension, rebates on volume purchases, or improvements generated by others outside of purchasing.

Developing Skills.   Training sessions must be established at frequent intervals to illustrate:

1. The various skills and techniques associated with negotiations, vendor selection, value analysis, and inventory analysis

2. Which method best suits a particular commodity area and the appropriate time to utilize it

SAVINGS THROUGH	YEAR TO DATE	VENDOR CHANGES	NEGOTIATIONS	VALUE ANALYSIS	OTHER	TOTAL	COST REDUCTION REPORTS SUBMITTED
BUYER A							
BUYER B							
BUYER C							

FIG. 4-3. *Individual cost reduction area. Note: This is a monthly report made to the executive (plant manager, works manager, or materials manager) to whom the purchasing department reports. (By permission of the American Management Association, Management Bulletin, no. 33.)*

Enlisting Vendor Support. Vendor support for a cost improvement program can be obtained when the following basic facts are communicated to the vendor:

1. Purchasing alone bears responsibility for vendor selection.

2. Selection criteria are consistent and are applied equally to all vendors, large or small, new or already established.

3. Business is held by vendors on performance, not historical association.

4. Data on each vendor are confidential and a matter of knowledge to purchasing.

5. Articulate excuses "after the fact" will not be tolerated.

EVALUATING DYNAMIC PURCHASING RESULTS

Once in operation, control reports will indicate:

1. *Training needs.* By noting results on Figure 4-3, the manager can determine whether a buyer requires training in an area. For example, if nothing is being accomplished through negotiation, or savings are not within normal ratios (see "Standards and Ratios," page 6-43), the buyer can be given training in prenegotiation techniques, fact gathering, role playing for negotiation, and the like.

LOCATION	TOTAL PERSONNEL	NUMBER OF BUYERS	DOLLARS COMMITTED	NUMBER OF ORDERS PLACED	SALARY COST	TOTAL DEPARTMENT COST	COST IMPROVEMENT	COST PER PURCHASE DOLLARS

FIG. 4-4. *Purchasing activity. Note: This report is also made monthly. Unlike the form in Fig. 4-3, it is completed at the central office, showing a recapitulation of work in the field. (By permission of the American Management Association, Management Bulletin, no. 33.)*

| LOCATION | DOLLARS COMMITTED | HOW SAVINGS AFFECTED | | | | TOTAL SAVINGS | PERCENT SAVINGS TO DOLLARS COMMITTED |
		VENDOR	NEG.	V. A.	OTHERS		
COMPANY A							
COMPANY B							

FIG. 4-5. *Monthly central purchasing office report—purchasing-dollar improvement.* (*By permission of the American Management Association, Management Bulletin, no. 33.*)

2. *Departmental misunderstanding.* A review of purchasing performance will show, according to how savings are derived, whether a company's technical department is cooperating. Lack of cooperation may be due to nothing more than misunderstanding. For example, of two companies or divisions (comparable in type and products handled), one may be twice as successful in achieving savings in the specification change area. The question arises, "Why, or why not the other company?"

3. *Improper use of purchasing.* Figure 4-6 indicates that as many as six divisions can be listed on one control sheet. An unusually high percentage of rush orders in one of these divisions would imply improper production lead time and that purchasing was being used only for expediting. If this were repeated over several months, an explanation would be required.

4. *Excessive zeal by purchasing.* In the event savings result from vendor change only, caution suggests that purchasing may be too aggressive and may be "table thumping" for price cutting. Switching vendors on a price-cutting basis always results in driving away the best vendors. Few will spend the

Location _____   Company A

Personnel	Salary costs	Monthly purchase order date
Purchasing agents Buyers Expediters Stenos Clerks		Purchase orders less than $25 Percent rush: Percent overdue:

Monthly operating report—Cumulative

For month of
                                                                          Cumulative
_____ Dollar value of orders _____
_____ Orders placed _____
_____ Intraplant orders _____
_____ Total all orders _____
_____ Average value of order _____
_____ Total department cost _____
_____ Cost per purchase dollar _____
_____ Monthly cost reduction (estimated) _____
_____ Percent cost reduction to purchase dollar _____

FIG. 4-6. *Purchasing department monthly operating report. Note: Six companies can be grouped and shown on this report.* (*By permission of the American Management Association, Management Bulletin, no. 33.*)

time or money to service an account where there is little opportunity for repeat business.

5. *Excessive inventory buildup.* When monthly material expenditures are known, there is little chance of allowing material costs to exceed gross monthly sales or become excessive. This is particularly true where the purchasing manager has access to sales figures. He can compare actual material purchased against budgeted material estimates that were based on market plans. Any tendency to exceed normal ratios would be detected at once.

PURCHASING'S ROLE IN MANAGEMENT

Three areas affecting the success of the purchasing function are: (1) To whom should purchasing report? (2) What are its major responsibilities? (3) What active participation must purchasing take in areas outside its field? Ultimately, size and type of business are controlling factors. However, practice has indicated the following:

1. *Reports to.* In the optimum environment, purchasing management reports directly to the president. In most instances, this will be true if the greatest portion of the sales dollar is allocated to materials. The actual buying activity, however, normally remains at plant level under the direct control of local management.

2. *Responsible for.* Again in an optimum environment, purchasing would have absolute authority and responsibility for:

   a. Material expenditures and deliveries
   b. Freight costs, inbound and outbound
   c. Raw material inventories
   d. Make or buy decisions
   e. Vendor selection
   f. Budget annual savings

These areas of responsibility demand a thorough understanding of other departmental problems relating either directly or indirectly to materials. Purchasing cannot operate in a vacuum or be an end in itself. In the last analysis, however, whether quality materials are available, economically and in a timely fashion, or whether none of these result, all blame must be borne by purchasing.

3. *Participation outside the department.* If purchasing must bear full blame and responsibility for problems over materials, it is axiomatic that it must know every phase of their use and application. To guarantee there is no chance for oversight, purchasing should have representation on committees or joint programs dealing with:

   a. Research and development

LOCATION	ESTIMATED	ANNUAL

FIG. 4-7. *Purchasing yearly cost improvement. Note: This report is prepared for and shown to the president and the executive vice president on a bar chart form.* (*By permission of the American Management Association, Management Bulletin, no. 33.*)

b. Market planning of new product introduction

c. Production planning and scheduling

d. Product distribution

e. Disposal of obsolete material and equipment

Not only must purchasing participate, it must also contribute. Assuming it has the ability to contribute, by active participation in long-range planning and continuing through the research and engineering stages, it will be able to complete much of its own work long before requests for bids or negotiations are necessary.

TYPICAL PEOPLE PROBLEMS

Any new program will have its initial people problems. They will arise both inside and outside the department. Some of the more typical ones are as follows.

Inside the Department

1. Allegiance to a vendor rather than to the company

2. A desire to remain in the familiar clerical area instead of supervising and managing

3. Concentrating on expediting in contrast to long-range planning

4. A belief that cost improvement is identical to price buying

5. A tendency to shift blame to the vendor for initial failures

6. A desire to be liked rather than respected for performance

Outside the Department

1. A belief that going through purchasing is too time consuming

2. A belief that new ideas from vendors will be screened out and not reach a department

3. A feeling that technical problems cannot be delegated to purchasing (*Note:* They cannot be, nor can they be handled without purchasing. Joint participation is a necessity!)

4. An assumption that specifications and standards can be established after the requisition

5. A belief that purchasing's only responsibility is to buy

NEW TRENDS ASSOCIATED WITH DYNAMIC PURCHASING

Companies considering dynamic purchasing should already be familiar with the following advanced trends. Total ignorance of any of these methods could mean that dynamic purchasing would be too advanced for a company.

1. *Systems contracting*—any method that automatically removes repetition in order placement and receipt, eliminates most of the processing and payment functions, and places responsibility for quality, quantity, and costs on the vendor by prearranged contracts (see Chapter 3 of Section 6)

2. *Purchasing research*—a growing staff function within purchasing, wholly responsible for all factual data on material research and engineering, legal, economic, and political matters related to material

3. *Data-phone systems*—the computerized order placement with sole source, provided there are predetermined and adequate standards with constant repetition per item

4. *Performance evaluation review techniques*—PERT/time or PERT/cost programs used to evaluate either the timeliness or costs of material at various stages of completion in product development or manufacture

5. *The project leader plan*—the cooperative program involving engineering, manufacturing, and purchasing, at the manufacturing-engineering stage, where

responsibility for total performance is given to the department having the major interest in the problem area

STANDARDS AND RATIOS

How Many People. Statistics, readily available from many sources, have proved purchasing personnel represent well under 1½ percent of total company employment. Emphasis must be on the savings derived from annual expenditures, not on people. When these savings are generated, from 300 to 500 percent of departmental costs should be returned in profit contribution.

Percent of Saving. Savings under a cost improvement program are derived:

40–60 percent—from negotiations

15–30 percent—from vendor change

15–30 percent—from specification change

5–10 percent—from internal improvements

Dynamic Purchasing Goals. Standards for purchasing to attain should be:

20 percent of company profits from purchasing

2 percent of annual purchasing expenditures as a profit contribution

300 to 500 percent of purchasing cost as a profit contribution

20 percent of purchases will absorb 80 percent of purchase dollars

50 percent of the sales dollar to be allocated to material

SUMMARY

In conclusion, it must be recognized that dynamic purchasing is an attitude. Demanded initially as an answer to rising material costs, it has now become a necessity for proper company growth and guaranteed net profit.

Quite often the superintendent, at the turn of the century, became the chief executive officer of the company; then later the job was filled from sales and next from finance. In the future, it will not be uncommon to find this position filled by someone with a purchasing background. Skilled in making a profit with the staff and budget given his department, the purchasing manager's activity and his convictions and attitudes parallel the profit goals of the company in a free enterprise system. Then, in truth, it can be said, "It is not how much money or profit the company made, but rather what it should have made!"[1]

BIBLIOGRAPHY

Ammer, Dean S., "Purchasing for Profits," *Harvard Business Review,* May–June, 1961.
Forter, Samuel, "Purchasing Research: The Concept and Its Value," Management Bulletin, no. 17, American Management Association, New York, 1962.
Hayes, F. Albert, and George Renard, "Evaluating Purchasing Performance," Research Study, no. 66, American Management Association, New York, 1964.
"How Good Are Your Purchasing Controls?" *Purchasing Week,* Aug. 29, 1960.
Lee, Lamarr, *Purchasing and Materials Management,* McGraw-Hill Book Company, New York, 1965.
Morse, Leon, "Purchasing: From Rags to Riches," *Dun's Review & Modern Industry,* May, 1963.
Spivack, J., "Measuring Purchasing Performance in Terms of Profit," *Purchasing,* February, 1955.
Zemansky, S. D., "The Purchasing Job: Dimensions and Trends," Management Bulletin, no. 11, American Management Association, New York, 1961.

[1] Lawrence Appley, President, American Management Association.

CHAPTER FIVE

Value Engineering

FRANK J. JOHNSON   *Manager, Value Engineering Department, Lockheed-Georgia Company, Division of Lockheed Aircraft Corporation, Marietta, Georgia*

The Honorable George E. Fouch, Deputy Assistant Secretary of Defense, in a challenging address to value engineers, stated, "Value engineering is not an end in itself . . . it is a means to an end.   Both the value engineers and the manager are seeking the same end, namely, increased efficiency and economy in achieving the desired operational objectives.   Each must be incorporated in the thoughts and actions of the other."   To be effective, value engineering must be part of the daily life of operating management.

Many factors must be considered by management before a decision can be made concerning the establishment of a value program.   There is no standard solution that will satisfy all corporate requirements, and there are as many variables as there are types of companies.   One of the variables having considerable effect on the ultimate decision is the type of industry—whether it is a typical manufacturing plant heavily engaged in fabrication and assembly operations or an industry engaged in a continuous process.

Those companies heavily oriented toward design and manufacture of "hardware" have excellent potential for sizable cost avoidance during the design phase as well as cost reduction resulting from value-analyzing their products and components already in production.

Value engineering, by its very nature, requires that a change be made. Whether the change affects a material, process, or design, it can be expected that the proposal will meet strong resistance along the road to ultimate approval and implementation.   Recognizing the presence of the normal human trait to resist change, we can see that the most important ingredient of a successful value engineering program is complete support from top management.   This support must be tangible and continuous.   An effective method of program control is regularly scheduled review meetings, chaired by top management, to assess the overall performance in each value engineering task area.

DEFINITION OF TERMS

Value engineering is a systematic, creative approach to ensure that the essential function of a product, process, or administrative procedure is provided at a minimum overall cost. For emphasis, the following elements of value engineering are listed:

It is an organized, creative approach to cost reduction.

It places emphasis on function rather than method.

It identifies areas of excessive or unnecessary costs.

It improves the value of the product.

It provides the same or better performance at a lower cost.

It reduces neither quality nor reliability.

Value Engineering Study. A value engineering study is an objective appraisal of all the elements of the design, construction, procurement, installation, and maintenance of equipment, including the specifications, to achieve the necessary functions, maintainability, and reliability at the lowest cost. Value engineering entails a detailed review of product designs and specifications, placing a total dollar value on the costs of production and maintenance and relating these costs to the functional value of each part and assembly. Alternative designs, materials, processes, and methods of fabrication, together with standard products available from specialty suppliers, are explored to find the lowest-cost way to achieve required functions.

Function. Function is that which makes a product work or sell. The function should be defined in two words, a verb and a noun; for example, "support cable." There are two reasons for restricting ourselves to such a definition of function:

The use of two words avoids the possibility of combining functions and attempting to define more than one simple function at a time.

The use of two simple words will assure the achievement of the lowest level of abstraction possible with words; the identification of the function should be as precise as possible.

Primary or Basic Function. The primary or basic function is the most important essential function without the performance of which the product would be virtually worthless.

VALUE ENGINEERING TECHNIQUES

The primary concern in any design is the function. Too often, the subject of cost is pushed into the background and then forgotten. Most of the key value engineering techniques are not new or revolutionary; they are elements of good engineering practice applied in a systematic sequence to achieve maximum value. The following are twenty-one techniques used in value engineering.

1. *Set up the value engineering job plan.* Before starting any job, it is not only helpful but necessary to have a plan of action. The job plan provides such a plan and consists of five phases: (*a*) the information phase, (*b*) the speculation phase, (*c*) the analysis phase, (*d*) the decision phase, and (*e*) the execution phase. These phases will be discussed in greater detail below.

2. *Get all available facts.* As a first step in reducing costs, it is necessary to become completely familiar with the product by factual review. This consists of determining: What is the primary function? What are the secondary func-

tions? Why was it designed this way? How is it made? How much does it cost? What does it weigh? What are the specifications? How many units will be used? What is the lead time for fabrication or procurement of each part? Only after you are armed with all the facts can you approach the problem intelligently.

3. *Get information from the best sources.* To save yourself and others time and trouble, it is imperative that you contact people who can give you the information you need accurately and quickly. For example, contact production engineering for information on metallic and nonmetallic materials, processes, and finishes; manufacturing planning for fabrication methods; material procurement for vendor information and cost estimates of purchased parts; and contract administration for contractual requirements.

4. *Know costs.* To make a complete analysis of any component, it is necessary to know not only the total cost of the component but the breakdown of the total cost. This breakdown will include materials, labor, and overhead. Each operation eliminated will then remove that portion of the cost.

5. *Define each function.* This technique consists of describing the function of each part with a verb and a noun. For example, a diaphragm (*a*) holds pressure, (*b*) seals holes, (*c*) provides reliability, and so on.

6. *Evaluate each function.* After defining each function, set up the relative importance of each function in dollars and cents. Eliminate those functions not essential for adequate use of the component, thus eliminating that portion of the cost. Use the following outline in your evaluation:

What is it?
What does it do?
What does it cost?
What else will do the job?
What does that cost?

Value is measured by comparison. Compare the cost of an item with the costs of other familiar, commonplace products that perform similar functions. It is very easy to say, "We have never done anything like this before, so how can we make a comparison?" Budget limitations have a tendency to force designers to become cost conscious. For comparison purposes, attempt to obtain design data produced by other companies. A number of differences will exist, but a comparison of end-product costs can be made.

7. *Work on specifics, avoid generalities.* This technique can be used effectively with "evaluate each function." You must work on each function individually before attempting to combine them into a single, multifunctioning product. By using this technique, hidden costs can be more easily removed from the overall assembly. Recognize that if a generality exists, it has probably deferred effective action in the past.

8. *Think creatively.* Use as many creative techniques as necessary to get a fresh point of view. One accepted technique has been aptly named "brainstorming." While applying this technique, do not evaluate ideas. Turn the evaluation part of your brain off and become a dreamer. Make short statements to express your ideas. Do not attempt to develop your ideas. Once you have expressed the idea, record it, forget it, and go on to the next idea. Do not limit yourself to the conventional approach. The main purpose is to accumulate as many different approaches to the problem as possible before evaluating any of them.

9. *Blast and create, then refine.* When first attempting to remove costs from a product or process, you will find it helpful to blast away all thought of the

existing concept.   Attempt to remove 50 to 75 percent of the cost, as opposed
to 5 to 10 percent.   Removal of such a large percentage requires that you
use new methods, possibly using a completely different design concept or fabrication procedure, but always without changing the primary function.

As an example, each of the four main wing tanks in the C-130 fuel system
contains an electric booster pump.   To ensure that the booster pump is adequately supplied in all flight attitudes, an electric scavenger pump was provided
to transfer fuel continuously from the opposite side of the tank to the surge
box surrounding the booster pump.   By blasting away the concept of a "pump,"
it was suggested that an eductor, with no moving parts, would accomplish the
transfer of fuel with high reliability.   Bleed air is used as the motivating force.
Additional savings resulted from simplified installation requirements and reduction of functional testing.   Reliability was increased, weight was reduced 16
pounds per plane, maintenance was simplified, and the cost of spares was reduced.   Production and installation costs were reduced $1,000 per airplane,
or more than 85 percent.

Begin to refine only after creating ideas that promise to remove 50 percent
or more of the cost.   In the refining process, it may be necessary to add 10
to 15 percent to ensure that essential secondary requirements are met.   The
net gain should amount to a minimum of 30 percent.   After using this technique,
you will find that it is easier in the long run to go through this procedure
and remove 30 percent of the cost than to refine the present component and
remove 10 percent.

10. *Put a dollar sign on each main idea.*   Prior to launching a thorough
investigation into the whys and wherefores of your ideas, estimate their worth.
Use a dollar sign in setting up a priority on which ideas merit your first and
most serious consideration.   Before evaluating these ideas, try to estimate the
possible dividends in return for your invested time.

The following is an illustration of how a cost breakdown developed in value-
analyzing a filter circuit:

Item	Function	Cost
Diode no. 1	Clips signal	$ 2
Diode no. 2	Clips signal	2
Transistor	Isolates inputs	4
Condenser	Holds charge	3
Filter no. 1	Selects 60 cycles	27
Filter no. 2	Selects 400 cycles	30
Miscellaneous (case, wires, resistors, etc.)	. . . .	15
Total	. . . .	$83

This quickly pointed up the fact that the two filters accounted for more
than two-thirds of the total cost and therefore merited first consideration.   In
this case, it was possible to combine the functions of the two filters into a
single filter that could be produced in the quantity required for $20 each, or
a saving of 65 percent on this item.

11. *Use company specialists and services.*   During the analysis and decision
phases of idea development, be sure to make full use of the many and varied
company services available to you.   Do not hesitate to consult company specialists or service groups.   They are competent and readily available sources of
information.

12. *Use standards.*   Wherever possible use standard components.   The use

of standard hardware reduces cost by increasing competition, eliminating proprietary information or processes, eliminating tooling costs, and ensuring quality products. A little time spent searching for a standard item can pay big dividends.

For example, a design engineer needed a 2-inch lanyard to prevent a push rod from dropping if the nut backed off. The shortest standard lanyard available was 8 inches. He was on the verge of designing a special lanyard when standards engineering suggested using a standard electrical bonding jumper. This suggestion was accepted for an estimated saving of 80 percent, plus the cost of stocking an additional part.

13. *Bring new information into each functional area.* Use specialists when investigating fields unfamiliar to you. A theoretical approach may lead you to previously untried approaches which, when developed, can be great cost savers. Technical breakthroughs and financial breakthroughs usually go hand in hand.

14. *Use industry and vendor specialized knowledge.* Many firms specialize in limited fields. Their ability to stay in business depends on their being well in the forefront of the technology in those fields. Approach appropriate specialty suppliers with your problem—not with a detailed drawing of your solution. Explain the function that must be achieved and ask for recommendations. Frequently, the specialist will suggest solutions which are new to the design engineer and will offer to furnish the hardware at a greatly reduced price as compared with in-plant manufacture of the design engineer's solution. For example, an appliance manufacturer used large quantities of a special screw, threaded for about one-fourth of its length and with the shank undercut between the threads and the head. Made on a screw machine and then undercut, they cost $150 per thousand. When the problem was put before a specialty supplier, he devised a method of using the roll-threading process to remove the metal from the undercut portion. Using this process, he quoted a price of $15 per thousand, a 90 percent saving.

15. *Use specialty processes.* The old tried-and-proved processes are often overused because they require the least investigative work. They also give the least financial return. Using new methods can reduce costs. For example, precision forging is cutting the combined cost of forging and machining. Tape-indexed, three-dimensional machining is replacing forging, machining, welding, heat treating, final contouring, and stress relieving. Precision molding minimizes the high cost of machining, cuts rejection rates, and simplifies assembly procedures.

16. *Use specialty products and materials.* Specialty products are those that are not necessarily covered by a design or blueprint but could be covered by a specification-controlled drawing. A specialty product could be an item which is unlike what you might design, but which would fit the part or assembly and perform the desired function with no sacrifice in quality or reliability, and in most cases at a fraction of the cost of a specially designed part.

17. *Put dollar signs on key tolerances.* Put dollar signs on key tolerances whether they be on dimensions, chemical constituents, weights, or surface variations. It is often difficult during development to relax initial tolerances, because so little is known of their importance to the final assembly.

A careful review of tolerances can lead to worthwhile cost reductions.

18. *Use your own judgment.* Although you should ask the advice of specialists and other designers, do not jump to use the suggestions of others. Use your own judgment. After having come this far in your investigation, you are the expert on this particular project. You have most of the information, and your design sense and your common sense are your greatest aids.

19. *Spend the company's money as you would your own.* Your decisions commit the company's money and our country's money. Spend the company's money exactly the way you would your own. You would be surprised how easy this makes decisions. Many times you will be deciding whether to follow tradition or to do what you know full well is right. Ask yourself, "What would I do if it were my money?" or "If it were my money, would I be willing to pay that much for it?" Applying this criterion can be very effective in eliminating overdesign.

20. *Identify and overcome roadblocks.* Roadblocks are considered to be anything that impedes progress or progressive thinking. They commonly evolve from negative thinking, fear—particularly of personal loss—ignorance, laziness, self-defense, or undesirable habits. Your first hint of danger in confronting one of these roadblocks will be when you hear phrases such as, "We've always done it this way." "Why change it? It works." "It's company policy." When your progress is impeded, clearly define the obstacle. Overcoming the obstacle then becomes the problem. To do this, more facts must be brought to bear.

21. *Use better human relations.* A high percentage of failures can be charged to poor human relations. Convince the people with whom you deal that you are asking, not demanding; suggesting, not criticizing; helping, not hindering; and interested, not bored with them. In this manner, you will not only enlist their voluntary aid but will make contacts that can be useful to both of you in future assignments. It is often difficult to see the other person's point of view and his associated problems. Put yourself in his shoes; take the time to investigate his problems. This makes it easier to understand and live with existing conditions. In a large company, there are bound to be stumbling blocks that must be overcome regardless of the task. But by avoiding personal irritations, the majority of these can be removed. Sell yourself and you have sold your ideas.

METHODOLOGY

The first and perhaps the most important technique of value engineering is the organized approach—the value engineering job plan. If outstanding results are to be achieved in getting better value, and 30, 50, or even 75 percent of the original costs are to be removed, you must have a systematic plan of attack.

The job plan consists of five phases:

The information phase
The speculation phase
The analysis phase
The decision phase
The execution phase

The twenty-one techniques that were just presented are related to one another as well as to the job plan.

The Information Phase. Each problem requires a phase in which all the facts are clearly determined. By securing all the necessary information before attempting to solve problems, you simplify and expedite the solution.

Get complete information concerning costs, inventory, usage, specifications, development history, material, manufacturing methods, and processes. Get drawings, manufacturing operation sheets, and actual samples. Define the primary function and secondary functions. This is a realistic, hard-boiled job. You frequently find that, when all the facts are supposed to be in, they are not! Unless you get more facts than anyone else has accumulated, you miss untold opportunities. You cannot work properly without all the facts, for when you do not have them, you are forced to substitute personal opinions for facts. Many times a problem solves itself when you do get all of the facts.

For making decisions, most successful people agree on these commonsense practices:

Be certain you know what the problem is (define the function).

Collect too much rather than too little information.

Exhaust all possible sources of information.

Separate facts from opinions.

Collect all the facts, not just those that support the conclusion you hoped for. In short, do not "stack" the evidence.

The Speculation Phase. Here is where you put to use your creative ability and the creative approach. Once the problem is defined and you have all the facts, you are ready to find a solution. Try to answer the question, "What else will do the job?"

Blast away old concepts of existing hardware so as to leave your mind free to create many new ideas for achieving essential functions. Make use of the brainstorming method. Exclude negative thoughts. Avoid analysis of ideas at this stage. Record all ideas, then forget them for the time being. To start the ideas flowing, try asking simple, suggestive questions such as:

In what form could this be?

How would I make it in my home workshop?

Should it slide instead of rotate?

What other layout might be better?

What if it were turned upside down?   Inside out?

Record all ideas for achieving the function regardless of specifications, interchangeability, and so on. Many times, good ideas come from trying to develop others that obviously would not work.

Set a target to take out at least one-half of the cost from functional areas and nine-tenths of the cost from some of the components. By so doing, you will be forced into new areas—areas not previously explored. Consequently, you may find it easier to remove 50 to 75 percent of the cost than it would be to remove 5 to 10 percent by conventional cost reduction methods.

The Analysis Phase. In the analysis phase, the primary objective is to analyze and weigh the ideas generated during the speculation phase with regard to cost, function, and feasibility. Establish a dollar value of each idea. Challenge each idea by applying the following tests for value:

Does its use contribute value?

Is its cost proportionate to its usefulness?

Can it or some of its features be eliminated?

Can its required function be achieved in a simpler manner?

Can a usable standard product be found?

Is it made on proper tooling, considering quantities used?

Will another supplier provide it for less?

Is anyone buying it for less?

Refine all ideas that show promise of providing improved value. Evaluate these ideas by comparison. Select for further consideration those ideas that have weathered the storm of evaluation.

It is important to remember that you are not trying to eliminate ideas. You are trying to analyze ideas to see how they can be made to work. A positive approach must be used. It must be understood that ideas emanating from a brainstorming session are not going to spring to life correct in all details. They are concepts only. Do not let an obvious fault hide the merits in a proposal and thus prevent its thorough analysis. With a small modification, it may become a promising idea.

The Decision Phase. In this phase, take the best ideas and plan a program to obtain the information you need to develop these ideas into sound, usable suggestions. You may feel here that you do not have enough knowledge to work on the ideas yourself. This is natural, for no one can ever know everything he needs to know.

What must be done is to recognize the problem and search for the person who can help. There are many specialists in a company, and the services of every specialist in industry are available on request. In drawing help from outside the company, from suppliers or specialists, do not just hand them a drawing and specifications and say, "What can you do with this?" Instead, inform them of the function you want, draw out their ideas on the problem, and give them some latitude to work in. By these means, you can really benefit from their knowledge. They may know of a specialty process, product, or material that can help you. Be sure to determine costs of these ideas.

Now you will see that certain ideas are really beginning to develop and have a future. Each idea should be reviewed with the thought, "Is this really the best idea?" "With this new information could a better job be done?" Now is the time to use your best judgment, select those ideas showing the most promise, and plan your campaign for selling your proposals to management.

The Execution Phase. In this phase, you must sell your idea. You must be prepared to meet and triumph over considerable resistance. People who must make major decisions are a cautious lot, and you must sell your idea to them. To do so, you must present a clear and concise picture of just what it is you are proposing and what your proposal will mean to them, their project, and the company. When making recommendations, always be prepared to give and take. Have an alternate plan ready in the event the primary proposal is rejected. Stress the technical capability of your proposal, and use cost reduction as an incentive.

ORGANIZATION AND STAFFING

Location of the value engineering function within a company is dependent upon the type of industry. With complete backing of top management, location of the function is not as important as the personnel selected to staff the organization. Most companies tend to place the value engineering operation within their engineering branch if the company is heavily design oriented. Process-type industries more than likely will place the value operation within the procurement branch where it is most often called "value analysis." The reasoning behind this approach is based upon the higher percentage of dollar expenditure allocated to the procurement of materials in contrast to the cost of design fabrication and assembly operations.

Selection of the value engineering staff should be based upon the experience and educational background most suitable to the type of industry. The nature of the value engineering task makes certain personality and character traits very important. The job requires extensive personal contact with people in all levels of management and in all areas of the company organization. The ability of the value engineer to deal with these contacts in a positive, constructive manner cannot be overemphasized. The value engineer must possess sufficient initiative to undertake difficult tasks in previewing unexplored areas, and he must be sensitive to the personal views of those with whom he comes in contact. Obviously, he must be articulate in presenting his findings in both oral and written presentations. He must possess a degree of maturity and should not become easily discouraged when his proposals are rebuffed. An engineering degree, or the equivalent in experience, is almost a necessity for value engineers assigned to work on design projects. The formal education requirements are not as stringent in those areas not involving technical design work.

Determining the Ratio. Experience has shown that we can normally expect a 10 to 1 return on value engineering effort. In other words, there should be approximately a $10 net saving for every dollar spent on value engineering investigations. In a design organization, it has been found that a ratio of one value engineer to each thirty technical designers is sufficient to obtain good cost reduction through value engineering efforts.

PROGRAM CONTROL

Value engineering has demonstrated that it can provide substantial cost reductions by taking another look at a company's products and their components. It be approximately a $10 net saving for every dollar spent on value engineering It is generally known that value engineering applied early in the design stage can utilize cost-avoidance techniques to produce even more benefits. This calls for systematic and creative functional analyses during the design, development, and production phases of a program.

Target Costs. An excellent program control is the use of a value engineering target-cost procedure which measures production costs as a function of design and provides a system of program control whereby value engineering personnel continuously monitor the progress of design as it relates to the base configuration. The costs of design deviations from the base configuration are determined and reflected on a target chart of the appropriate item to indicate the under- or over-cost condition. Potential cost increases alert affected management to the problem areas, and prompt action can then be initiated.

Technical Requirement Reviews. Technical engineering requirement reviews should be initiated in the early phases of design and development. These reviews, conducted with the value engineer, serve as the means for identifying the necessary functions, isolating those design requirements necessary to satisfy the functions, and documenting the design-requirement justification. Alternatives for obtaining the functional requirements are determined and evaluated in relation to functional performance lists, subsystem interrelationships, and system cost.

CONCLUSION

Value engineering studies are formal reports utilized to conduct and document functional analyses of design requirements and parameters. They are initiated when multiple approaches are proposed for accomplishing functional requirements. Detailed evaluations of the technical requirements are made and their effect on total system performance determined. Concurrently, the effect on system cost of each alternative is determined and related to the individual technical requirements. Areas of both high cost and high-cost sensitivity are identified and the associated requirement is examined in relation to its contribution to system effectiveness. The requirements identified by these high-cost areas are examined in detail from a cost-effectiveness standpoint. These elements of disproportionate high cost then become the subject of further investigation.

Through this balancing process, the necessary functional requirements are related to design requirements, and the total cost impact of each alternative is minimized.

Verification that functional requirements are satisfied at minimum cost is established by design value reviews prior to final engineering release. Value reviews are composite studies of designs, technical requirements, and specifications which lead to formal approval of designs, specifications, and procurement.

The value engineer makes a continual review from concept to hardware to achieve complete verification of low-cost objectives. He is a member of the design review team. He provides cost-target information of the base-line configuration and generates alternative considerations. The designer is given guidance on the least costly material, production technique, tooling, test, and the cost effect of spares, reliability, and maintainability for the given application. These costs are equated to system productivity. Consideration of these design recommendations is verified by the value engineer's signature on the drawing or specification prior to release.

Value engineering techniques should also be employed in the areas of testing procedures and testing equipment, facilities, tooling, purchasing, packaging, production operations, and information systems. Cost methodology employed in the analyses of design alternatives should be organized to develop a total system cost in terms of acquisition cost plus the operation over a period of years equivalent to the service life of the product. Cost models are used when determining total system cost. After the total system cost has been determined for a particular design consideration, a cost optimization process is employed to determine the best combination of cost measures.

The elements of the value engineering program are separate and identifiable portions of the total tasks associated with the design, development, and production of a system for which value engineering has primary responsibility. These include a target cost and tracking system.

Monitoring elements, on the other hand, are comprised of those tasks which are controlled outside the value engineering organization, but which are implemented and assessed by value engineering review. These include procurement and the value engineering effort of subcontractors, engineering developmental testing, and manufacturing-operations value engineering.

BIBLIOGRAPHY

Fundamentals of Value Analysis, Technocopy, Inc., Morristown, N.J., 1961.

The Journal of Value Engineering (published quarterly), The Society of American Value Engineers, Bethesda, Md.

Miles, L. D., *The Techniques of Value Analysis and Value Engineering,* McGraw-Hill Book Company, New York, 1961.

Proceedings of 1962 Third EIA Conference on Value Engineering, Electronic Industries Association, New York, 1962.

"Value Engineering," U.S. Department of Defense Handbook H-111, Mar. 29, 1963.

Value Engineering, 1959, EIA Conference on Value Engineering, University of Pennsylvania, Oct. 6 and 7, 1959, Engineering Publishers, Elizabeth, N.J., 1959.

Value Engineering, Volume 2, EIA Conference on Value Engineering, Anaheim, Calif., October, 1960, Engineering Publishers, Elizabeth, N.J., 1961.

CHAPTER SIX

Transportation Cost Control

FRANK M. CUSHMAN   *Frank M. Cushman Associates, Sharon, Massachusetts*

Control of transportation cost is a function of top management. It is a policy-making concept—a state of mind of the higher echelons of management.

Transportation cost control is not industrial traffic management, and the two activities are not to be considered synonymous. The former is a forceful decision on the part of top management to maintain transportation cost at the lowest lawful level. The latter consists of the administrative activities of the industrial traffic manager and his department in their efforts to carry out that decision successfully.

The top echelons of management need not be qualified in the skills of industrial traffic management. These skills are highly specialized and properly belong in an intermediate level of management, closely supervised by higher management. However, to carry out its responsibility of establishing the concept of transportation cost control, top management must understand the single, basic, and most important element of transportation cost—*the classification rating of freight.*

In the final analysis, transportation cost eventually relates back to the classification rating of the freight that is being transported. Any increase or reduction in the transportation cost must result from the adjustment of or departure from the classification rating.

Given an intelligent appraisal of the circumstances that create a classification rating, top management will better comprehend its own responsibilities relative to transportation cost control.

TRANSPORTATION AS A FACTOR OF PRODUCTION

Transportation must be recognized as a factor of production much the same as the classic ones—land, labor, and capital goods. Economic productivity springs from the ability of competent management to blend these classic factors effectively. The most important catalyst in this blending process is transportation. Transportation makes the American economy go. In fact, as transportation goes, so goes the American economy.

Industry may stockpile vital materials, train key personnel, select choice plant sites, and make other moves to ensure future progress; but remove transportation from the economy—by weather conditions, strikes, disasters, or other reasons—and all activity grinds to an immediate halt.

Knowledgeable management can achieve greater economic productivity through effective use of lowest-cost transportation commensurate with the most satisfactory service. Viewed as a factor of production, transportation facilities respond exactly the way any other factor of production responds.

Intelligent demand governs production in the American economy. Therefore, if management demands effective and low-cost transportation service, that will be the type of service the transportation industry will produce.

Management's Concept of Transportation. A clear and concise knowledge of the fundamental concepts affecting the intelligent use of the transportation facilities of this country is prerequisite to any competent evaluation by management of its transportation cost pattern. The following basic circumstances, among others, must be understood clearly:

1. Almost any transportation rate or service standard is subject to reasonable adjustment.

2. Definite and known transportation circumstances and conditions underlie transportation rate levels. Professional familiarity with these circumstances and conditions generally can predetermine rate levels acceptable to Federal and state regulatory authorities.

3. Although transportation is subject to Federal and state regulations, *neither level of government controls transportation rates or service,* nor is such control generally contemplated.

4. Intense competition in rates and service exists among the various modes of transportation.

5. Most frequently, *one of the several available modes of transportation* will satisfy *one or more of the transportation requirements of a user,* but *seldom* will one such mode satisfy *all* the needs of any *single* industrial firm.

THE DETERMINATION OF TRANSPORTATION RATE LEVELS

Classification Ratings. The level of transportation rates in dollars and cents per 100 pounds is determined by the classification rating of the freight that is transported.

A classification rating is a category into which a commodity or product is placed for purposes of transportation cost determination. Hundreds of thousands of commodities exist in the commercial and industrial world. These commodities comprise everything we make, use, or sell.

To avoid having as many different transportation rate levels as we have commodities, we place each commodity into one of a limited number of categories. By this method, a huge number of vastly different-appearing goods and products have been organized into a limited number of categories, each category referred to as a "classification rating" and each assigned a number based upon an index of 100.

Classification ratings ranging from 100 down to 50 most commonly apply to commodities as they are transported in less-than-carload or less-than-truckload quantities. Ratings start downward from Class 100 in increments of 7½ points until the level reaches Class 70, setting up ratings as follows:

Class 100
Class 92½
Class 85
Class 77½
Class 70

Below Class 70, the less-than-carload and less-than-truckload ratings drop in increments of 5 points down to Class 50, setting up ratings as follows:

Class 65
Class 60
Class 55
Class 50

Less-than-carload and less-than-truckload classification ratings also may rise above the index of 100. Class 100 functions as a bench mark—a known point of departure—from which point the classification rating levels move up or down depending upon the relationship of the freight in question to all other freight that has been assigned to the Class 100 category. Classification ratings above Class 100 are as follows:

Class 110
Class 125
Class 150
Class 175
Class 200
Class 250
Class 300
Class 400

A Class 85 commodity will take a transportation rate in dollars and cents that is approximately 15 percent below that of a Class 100 commodity. Similarly, a Class 125 commodity will take a transportation rate in dollars and cents approximately 25 percent above that of a Class 100 commodity.

Class 200 rates are double Class 100 rates, and Class 400 rates are quadruple Class 100 rates. Class 50 rates are half of Class 100 rates, and Class 70 rates are approximately 30 percent below Class 100 rates.

The uniform structure of classification ratings, each related on a percentage basis to the index of 100, became effective on May 30, 1952, in the rail transportation industry, replacing the rather heterogeneous and confusing three-way method of classification of freight which preceded it.

Shortly thereafter, the motor transportation industry adopted a uniform *but not necessarily identical* method of classification, also replacing a complicated and confusing three-way method of classification based upon a geographic division of the United States into three major areas.

Classification ratings also fall below Class 50. Ratings in this category are applied to carload and truckload movements of freight exclusively. The two classification ratings immediately below Class 50 are separated by increments of 5 points as follows:

Class 45
Class 40

Classification ratings below Class 40 are separated from one another by increments of 2½ points as follows:

Class 37½

Class 35

Class 32½

Class 30

Class 27½

Class 25

Starting with a top classification rating of Class 400, twenty-five available classification ratings exist, down to Class 25.

Six classification ratings lower than Class 25 exist, all the way down to Class 13, but the use of these extremely low classification ratings is infrequent, and the ratings do not play any major part in the normal transportation cost structure of American industry and commerce.

Significance of Classification Ratings. A classification rating is important, because it represents a category into which thousands of different-appearing commodities have been placed. Despite the differing sizes, shapes, weights, and physical appearances of all of these commodities, they have one characteristic of great significance insofar as transportation is concerned. *Each commodity in that category has been assigned the same classification rating, and each commodity will take the same rate in dollars and cents per hundredweight, when transported by the same carrier between the same two geographic locations.*

Accordingly, the factors that determine the transportation category into which a commodity is placed are highly significant, because they constitute the standards of measurement by which classification ratings are determined originally.

Of equal and frequently greater importance, these same standards of measurement are the ones by which a classification rating for a commodity may be raised or lowered if the classification rating appears to have been determined improperly originally.

Commodities as vastly different from one another as shoes, carpeting, shirts, electric toasters, wool blankets, fountain pens, and desk lamps all find themselves in the same category. These commodities have been assigned a classification rating of 100.

Because each of these commodities on visual appearance is completely different from the others, the "transportation characteristics" by which each has been analyzed to arrive at the Class 100 determination are of great significance.

The Importance of a Classification Rating. The classification rating of freight, and its adjustment if adjustment is necessary, is *the most important single element* in the program of any business firm that seeks to control transportation cost.

If the classification rating of a commodity has been developed correctly, the precise use of that rating together with the proper transportation description applicable to the freight is mandatory. The lowest lawful transportation cost may be secured only by the application of this rating together with the transportation description specifically related thereto.

On the other hand, if the classification rating assigned to a commodity *has not been developed correctly,* the existing rating becomes a point of departure from which a change must be made by some acceptable procedure. That procedure may be one of the following:

1. *Reclassification,* in which the classification rating is altered by a prescribed procedure before the various *carrier classification authorities* or, if necessary,

before the Interstate Commerce Commission.   Alteration of a rating by reclassification *affects the transportation cost of the commodity nationwide.*

2. *Creation of a rating by exception,* in which the rating of a commodity is altered by a prescribed procedure before various *carrier rate-making authorities* or, if necessary, before the Interstate Commerce Commission if the transportation is interstate, or an individual state regulatory board if the transportation is intrastate.   Alteration of a classification rating by the creation of a rating by exception *affects the transportation cost of the commodity on a regional or geographic basis only.*

3. *Creation of a commodity rate,* in which the rating of a commodity is altered by a prescribed procedure before various *carrier rate-making authorities* or, if necessary, before the Interstate Commerce Commission, or an individual state regulatory board, as the case may be.   Alteration of a classification rating by the creation of a commodity rate *affects the transportation cost of a commodity from a specified origin to a specified destination or a group of destinations only.*

Finally, if a shipper of freight should decide to forsake common carrier transportation completely and turn to the use of company-operated vehicles, the existing classification ratings of the freight in question will determine the economic advisability of this decision.

The successful performance of a private carrier operation depends entirely upon the relationship of common carrier transportation cost, determined, of course, by the lowest lawful level of the classification rating, as it compares with the cost of transportation as determined by the full cost of operating a fleet of company vehicles.

Accordingly, whether it be used in a positive or a negative sense, the classification rating of a commodity is the keystone of any transportation cost control program.

DETERMINATION OF CLASSIFICATION RATINGS

Classification ratings are set by the transportation industry.   The rail carriers determine rail classification ratings under the supervision of a group whose collective title is the Uniform Classification Committee.   Motor carrier classification ratings are set by the National Classification Board.

Each group operates under the auspices of the recognized voice of its section of the transportation industry, the Association of American Railroads for the rail carriers and the American Trucking Associations, Inc., for the motor carriers. The activities of the two classification-making groups come within the regulatory provisions of the Interstate Commerce Act, the Federal statute that regulates transportation.

Classification ratings must be just and reasonable in accordance with the provisions of the Interstate Commerce Act.   A rating that has been set too high in relation to the "transportation characteristics" of the particular commodity is unjust and unreasonable from the point of view of the user of transportation. Transportation cost for the user then becomes excessively high.   On the other hand, a rating that has been set too low is unjust and unreasonable from the point of view of the carrier.   Revenue earned by the carrier for the transportation of that commodity is considered inadequate.

A just and reasonable classification rating is one that provides an adequate revenue for the carrier while at the same time providing the lowest lawful cost to the user of transportation.

"Transportation Characteristics" of Freight. In determining a just and reasonable classification rating, one must consider the following transportation characteristics of the freight, regardless of the physical characteristics:

1. Density of the freight when packed for shipment
2. Susceptibility of the freight to damage or loss
3. Intrinsic value of the freight per pound in the event that replacement is required as the result of damage or loss
4. Stowability of the freight in a vehicle
5. Extent to which the freight may damage other freight in the vehicle

Density of Freight. The carriers, as well as the Interstate Commerce Commission, regard density as the most vital factor in classification rating construction. The other four characteristics may be considered secondary factors.

Density of the freight refers to the weight in pounds contained in 1 cubic foot of the freight packed and ready for shipment. Classification ratings vary inversely with the density of the freight. Freight with a higher density—a greater number of pounds per cubic foot—will tend to be related to lower classification ratings. Conversely, freight with a lower density—a lesser number of pounds per cubic foot—will tend to be related to higher classification ratings.

Density is the most vital factor in classification rating because carriers charge for their services on a basis of dollars and cents per 100 pounds of freight hauled.

Because a carrier possesses, at any given time, only a limited number of available cubic feet of space in his truck, trailer, rail car, ship's hold, or aircraft, and because the carrier offers that limited number of cubic feet for sale at a specified number of dollars and cents per hundredweight, the number of hundredweight that may be contained in the limited amount of space is the most vital factor in determining exactly how much the carrier shall charge per hundredweight for the transportation of a given commodity.

Denser commodities permit a greater number of hundredweight for a limited number of available cubic feet; less dense commodities provide a smaller number of hundredweight for the same limited number of available cubic feet.

If the carrier sells his available cubic feet of space at so many dollars and cents per hundredweight, he is forced to obtain more dollars and cents per hundredweight revenue for the freight that takes up more space for its weight— *less* dense freight—than for the freight that takes up less space for its weight— *more* dense freight.

Therefore, the transportation industry customarily assigns higher classification ratings to freight with lower densities and lower classification ratings to freight with higher densities. Some examples follow:

Commodity	*LTL Classification Rating*
Pillows	Class 200
Lead shot	Class 60
Fluorescent lighting fixtures	Class 85
Pillows (compressed not to exceed 3½ inches in thickness in the carton when packed for shipment)	Class 125
Mechanics' hand tools, not powered	Class 70
Books, hardbound	Class 70
Rubber bands	Class 85
Pencil sharpeners	Class 77½
Aluminum kitchen utensils	Class 100

In the initial determination of a classification rating for a commodity, the greatest consideration must be given to density. When one is involved in the adjustment of an existing classification rating either downward or upward, the density of the freight again must be given primary consideration. Should the density factor justify consideration for reclassification, then the other four transportation characteristics may be introduced to determine their influence.

However, if the density factor does not warrant consideration for adjustment in the classification rating, the influence of the remaining four transportation characteristics tends to be only minimally significant. For example, a reduction in freight costs was sought for pencil sharpeners (pencil-sharpening machines). Presented primarily on a basis of density of the freight, the action resulted in a reduction in rating from Class 100 to Class 77½. The annual freight bill in dollars and cents applicable to the transportation of pencil sharpeners was reduced thereby in the amount of 22½ percent.

Secondary Transportation Characteristics. The four secondary transportation characteristics of a commodity each affect the classification rating.

Freight that is more susceptible to damage or loss while being transported will tend to suffer a penalty therefor in the form of a higher classification rating than straight density ordinarily would determine. Conversely, more durable freight presents a more favorable argument for a lower classification rating, particularly if the density factor should be marginal.

Higher intrinsic value of the freight *per pound* of commodity exerts an elevating effect on the classification rating. Lower intrinsic value per pound assists in the possible reduction of the rating.

The intrinsic value per pound of commodity also influences the true importance of the factor of susceptibility to damage or loss. An undesirable pattern of damage or loss may be offset somewhat by a lower intrinsic value per pound of freight.

Because all common carriers are liable for the dollar value of the freight they transport, a built-in factor of insurance must exist somewhere in every rate. This factor is created by the adjustment of the classification rating upward or downward in accordance with the first two secondary transportation characteristics.

Stowability of freight in a vehicle is a negative transportation characteristic. Good stowability is accepted as normal. Accordingly, any adverse stowability features of freight will exert a penalizing effect, either in the form of a higher classification rating or as a barrier to the reduction of an existing rating.

Adverse stowability characteristics include irregularly shaped freight, freight that requires mechanical handling or rigging, and freight that requires preferred placement within the vehicle.

Freight that may damage other freight in the vehicle also exerts negative classification features. Solvents, odorous commodities, permeating powders, and the like tend to carry higher classification ratings because of the possibility of extensive damage to other freight in the vehicle at the time.

CLASSIFICATION DETERMINATION OR ADJUSTMENT

Classification rating determination or adjustment must be initiated before the classification authorities of the two major sections of the transportation industry, rail and motor. Initiation may take place by a carrier on behalf of an interested shipper or receiver of freight, or the interested party himself may initiate the action, supported by one or more carriers.

The latter method is the more desirable, because in the final analysis, the interested shipper or receiver always seeks a reduction. Unfortunately, he must request this reduction from the carriers themselves, through their duly appointed classification authorities.

A simple request that any source of supply of any commodity or service reduce its prices merely for the asking usually meets with little success. In this particular instance, the source of supply is that of transportation service. Because the levels of transportation rates and charges are subject to statutory regulation, further complicating factors creep into the picture.

The vastly redeeming feature of statutory regulation of transportation, however, is the requirement that all classification ratings and rates be just and reasonable. The statute also provides standards of measurement for reasonableness as well as quasi-legal and legal procedures for achieving the standards.

Accordingly, if an existing classification rating is suspect of unreasonableness after competent professional evaluation, an action for adjustment may be brought with reasonable assurance of success, providing the proper procedures have been followed and the evidence on behalf of the adjustment has been presented pertinently and forcefully. The desired objectives must be tied to relevant precedent to substantiate the requested adjustment before the carrier authorities themselves.

The action must be sufficiently substantive so that if the carrier authorities refuse the request, the case may be submitted to the Interstate Commerce Commission for its ruling, because this recourse is available under the provisions of statutory regulation and frequently provides the sole source of relief from unjust and unreasonable classification ratings and transportation rates.

Reclassification versus Quasi-reclassification. Alteration of a classification rating produces a change in transportation cost that is universal in its influence.

The reduction of the classification rating on pencil sharpeners from Class 100 to Class 77½ referred to above affected the transportation rates and charges on pencil sharpeners everywhere in the United States. Regardless of the size of the shipment, the length of the transportation, or the direction of it, the rate per hundredweight applicable to the transportation of pencil sharpeners dropped sharply.

For the most part, the product of the major manufacturers of pencil sharpeners is a standard and uniform one. Accordingly, universal effect upon the transportation cost was a reasonable concept, and reclassification was the proper avenue of approach.

Rating by Exception. Myriad instances exist, however, where products deserve consideration for reduction in classification rating, but the nonstandard transportation characteristics of the freight as it is produced by different manufacturers preclude universality of treatment. Under such circumstances, a partial or quasi-reclassification may be accomplished, awarding a lower rating to the deserving freight and avoiding the same reduction to the less deserving freight. This selective type of reclassification is known as the creation of a "rating by exception."

A rating by exception recognizes, for example, the fact that two tanks or containers of gas (under pressure) may vary sufficiently in transportation characteristics to warrant different ratings for each, even though each is a container of gas. Similarly, the friction and/or electrical tape produced by one manufacturer may possess sufficiently different transportation characteristics from that produced by another manufacturer to warrant different ratings for each, even though each is tape.

Adjustment of classification ratings by exception may be accomplished by the analysis of the same transportation characteristics that affect the classification rating itself. However, the successful achievement of this type of adjustment depends heavily upon the ability of the producer to convince *individual carriers*—trucklines or rail lines—that the freight in question should depart from the classification rating applicable universally and be judged individually on its own merits.

Because of the singular nature of this type of adjustment, the action to secure it is brought regionally before carrier rate-making authorities rather than before the national carrier classification authorities.

The creation of a rating by exception is a twofold beneficial achievement. First, the deserving freight attains lower transportation cost per se. Second, the freight that does not warrant adjustment remains at the higher rating and the higher level of transportation cost, frequently providing a distinct competitive advantage to the former as the result of the adjustment.

For example, a rating of Class 70 was secured for the friction and/or electrical tape of two manufacturers of that commodity, while other manufacturers have continued to bear the burden of a Class 77½ rating for their tape. The advantage of 7½ percent lower transportation rates not only has meant a lower annual freight bill for the two companies, but also has provided a competitive tool whereby they can exploit successfully market areas at a further distance from their plant locations than ever before.

Adjustment of a rating by exception also may serve to remove an unreasonable and unjust difference existing in established classification ratings. For example, the classification rating for beebee guns is a long-standing Class 85. Curiously enough, the classification rating for air rifles is Class 100. One manufacturer of air rifles who suffered a distinct economic disadvantage because of this peculiar relationship sought relief via a reclassification attempt for air rifles. Obtuse technicalities defeated the action. However, a properly devised presentation for a rating by exception before regional carrier rate-making authorities secured a Class 85 exception rating for the manufacturer to all points in the country *from his plant location.*

Two other known and substantial manufacturers of air rifles still bear the burden of a Class 100 rating. Actually, the differential results from a wide difference in the transportation characteristics of the freight rather than any other reason.

The 1-quart cylinder of butane gas that provides fuel for a lantern, heating torch, stove, or refrigerator, and the 2-ounce cylinder of carbon dioxide gas that provides propelling power for a pellet gun or the charge for a soda-water dispenser are both cylinders of gas under pressure, as is the standard tank of oxygen or acetylene gas. Formerly, each bore a Class 70 rating as a cylinder of gas, without regard to transportation characteristics. Properly presented actions before regional carrier rate-making authorities have resulted in Class 60 ratings by exception for the smaller butane and carbon dioxide cylinders, while the larger, conventional cylinders of gas still retain their proper Class 70 classification rating.

Creation of a rating by exception is a highly sophisticated method of transportation cost control as well as an action whose influence is felt broadly throughout the general marketing activities of any manufacturer.

Frequently, its achievement may require fundamental changes in packaging, the use of alternative raw materials, or even redesign of the basic product. However, even obstacles of this nature need not go unchallenged if, as the result of the change, the salability and performance of the product are not impaired while at the same time the transportation cost is reduced substantially. Transportation cost control possibilities that result from the creation of a rating by exception have vast potential.

CREATION OF A COMMODITY RATE

Departure from the classification rating assigned to a commodity frequently may be achieved by the sheer availability of large quantities of freight at any one time from any one shipping point.

This adjustment from the classification rating is known as a *commodity rate*. Volume of freight alone, however, cannot produce the adjustment in rating. Some consideration must be given to the accepted transportation characteristics of the freight, although not nearly as much consideration as when reclassification or creation of a rating by exception may be contemplated.

Commodity rates may be secured quite readily on truckload or carload shipments because of the very existence of the large quantities of freight per se, but they also may be secured on less-than-truckload and less-than-carload shipments if the latter are available in sufficient numbers themselves at any given time.

Commonly referred to as "aggregated shipments," multiple less-than-truckload and less-than-carload shipments may attain the lower rates of regular truckload and carload shipments if they are assembled and shipped in the proper manner.

Once again, basic readjustments in production scheduling and sales commitments may be necessary to secure commodity rate benefits on outbound shipments, and similar readjustments may be required in purchasing activities to attain commodity rates on inbound raw materials.

COMPLETE REJECTION OF THE CLASSIFICATION RATING

A detailed analysis of the classification rating, as well as a careful development of methods whereby one may alter this rating or perhaps depart from it in any of several different ways, provides a basic understanding of why transportation cost is what it is and how possibly it may be altered favorably.

Frequently, however, one must accept the level of transportation cost that results from a classification rating, because that rating is not subject to any of the adjusting features that have been discussed.

An additional possibility exists for the reduction of transportation cost if all of the others described thus far cannot provide relief. A manufacturer may elect to reject the classification rating completely and equip himself with his own trucks for distribution of his product to his customers as well as transportation of his raw materials from their individual sources of supply back to his factory location.

Although by so equipping himself he does in effect reject classification ratings, substituting therefor a known cost of truck operation per mile, nevertheless the lowest level of transportation cost that is set by the classification rating or ratings of his freight must, in the final analysis, be recognized as the highest level of transportation cost that he can incur economically by the use of his own vehicles.

Accordingly, even with the complete rejection of the classification rating and the level of transportation cost that it determines, one still finds himself bound by that classification rating. Should he fail to understand its nature, its function, or the various ways in which it may be adjusted, he may incur grossly excessive transportation cost just by his efforts to reject the classification rating.

SUMMARY

The keystone of transportation cost control is the classification rating. Top management must understand the characteristics of the rating (1) to live with it successfully, if need be; (2) to adjust it in some manner, if possible; or (3) to depart from it completely, if necessary.

Effective policy of a long-range nature in transportation cost control can come only from such an understanding. Armed with the proper awareness of what a classification rating is and how it may be altered, top management may plot a course of transportation cost control that competent, specialized traffic management ability will bring into fruition.

BIBLIOGRAPHY

Colquitt, Joseph C., *The Art and Development of Freight Classification,* National Motor Freight Traffic Association, Inc., Washington, D.C., 1956.

Cushman, Frank M., *Manual of Transportation Law,* The Transportation Press, Dallas, Texas, 1951.

Cushman, Frank M., *Transportation for Management,* Prentice-Hall, Inc., Englewood Cliffs, N.J., 1953.

Friction Tape, Cloth, Rubber and Plastic, Docket SR-10133, Eastern Central Motor Carriers Association, Inc., Akron, Ohio, June 17, 1959.

Gases, Compressed: Petroleum Liquified, NOI (Propane), in disposable steel cylinders of not over one-quart capacity, Docket C-1549-4, Middle Atlantic Conference General Rate Committee, Washington, D.C., Sept. 9, 1959.

Liquified Carbon Dioxide Gas, in disposable steel cylinders not exceeding one-quart capacity, Docket 192-116, Southern Motor Carriers Rate Conference, East-South, Atlanta, Ga., Oct. 1, 1959.

Pencil Sharpening Machines, Docket 106, Subject no. 7, National Classification Board, Washington, D.C., Nov. 15, 1962.

Rifles and/or Air Pistols Powered by Air or Compressed Gas, Docket E3786, Eastern Central Motor Carriers Association, Akron, Ohio, Oct. 21, 1959.

Materials Handling

E. RALPH SIMS, JR. *Principal, E. Ralph Sims, Jr., & Associates, Lancaster, Ohio*

The movement of materials (or "things") is a wasteful and expensive activity. If we had the ability to make anything we need when and where we need it, materials handling would not be a factor in industrial management and economics. However, the worldwide trend toward centralized production, mass marketing, and urban living emphasizes the impact of materials handling, transportation, and storage costs on the economy. Materials handling has been variously defined as an engineering technique, a collection of machinery, a management function, and a science. An objective look at industrial materials handling, however, leads to a different approach. It sees materials handling as a business function.

MATERIALS HANDLING AS A BUSINESS FUNCTION

Industrial Logistics and Material Flow. "Industrial logistics" and "material flow" are terms which describe the movement of materials through the economic system. In considering the full scope of the logistics concept, we note that the levels of movement extend beyond the manufacturing facility in both directions, from the farm and mine, through the wholesaler and retailer to the consumer. All levels must handle, store, control, and transport a large variety of items. The all-inclusive scope of industrial logistics also involves the handling of nonproductive, or nonprofit, items. In a typical foundry, fifty times more handling effort is expended on molds, sand, coke, scrap, and supplies than on the foundry metal. In food packing, the storage cube devoted to containers is significant, and packing materials are a large percentage of the total weight shipped.

Men, Money, Material. The elements of business which have an impact on profits and cost are men, money, and material. Money impact varies with interest cost, cash flow, capital lockup, and cash availability. Men affect the system through productivity, skill, availability, and payroll cost. These two elements can generally be controlled through management decision, policy, and action.

The materials element of business has a double cost impact. Material cost is a function of market requirements and design ingenuity, but materials handling cost is purely a function of management and control. Thus, although materials handling is a control function, controlling the relationship of materials to space and time, it must also be controlled as an active cost factor in business. Material flow is the physical bloodstream of a business; money flow is the control bloodstream of a business; information flow is the nervous system which coordinates business objectives with men, material, and money.

Facilities. Facilities are an expression of material flow and material change. The major elements of facilities design are process technology or material change, process flow or material movement, and process housing or material protection. The interlocking relationship between process technology and material flow can be shown in a glass factory (Figure 7-1) or paper mill (Figure 7-2), where movement and process are one. In each, process technology governs process flow, and handling is integral with process.

Conversely, with a unitized and/or assembled product such as sheet metal (Figure 7-3), process flow is dominated by handling. In most manufacturing operations, plant arrangement is determined by material flow, and each operation is self-contained. The use of pallets, tote boxes, tubs, and the like in a common denominator handling system bridges the gap between optimum flow and optimum process sequence. Variable production rates also introduce a variable material-flow-rate factor.

Material flow and material change cause the introduction of a process factor into facility planning. This is a function of such multiple independent variables as handling characteristics; process steps and equipment; flow rates and economic runs; machine loading and scheduling; in-process, raw, and finished product scheduling banks; seasonal, cyclic, or irregular sales; order and production scheduling factors; vendor delivery and lead times; quality-control requirements; documentation and security; facilities economics; costs; and product shelf life.

In planning new facilities or modifying existing ones, these and other considerations affect decisions concerning:

The structural system—overhead clearances, floor loading, column spacing, door and window sizes and locations, truck and rail dock location and design, security devices, lighting requirements, and heating and air conditioning

Handling equipment—forklifts, powered and nonpowered vehicles, pallets, skids, racks, shelving, cranes, conveyors, storage bins, hoppers, tanks and silos, and highway and railroad vehicles

Office space and equipment—size, location, and sophistication of offices, documentation, procedures, data-processing, and communications requirements

Thus, the whole facility may be considered as a functional, materials handling system which expresses itself in the arrangement, equipment, housing, and control of the process.

Creation, Fabrication, Control. The basic functions of business have, in the past, been stated as engineering or product design, manufacturing or production, sales or marketing, finance or controllership. A new concept has been developing out of the logistics approach to material flow and the integrated data-processing approach to management controls. This approach defines the three major elements of business activity as follows.

Creation. Sales and advertising create demand, engineering and research create product, industrial and plant engineering create facilities.

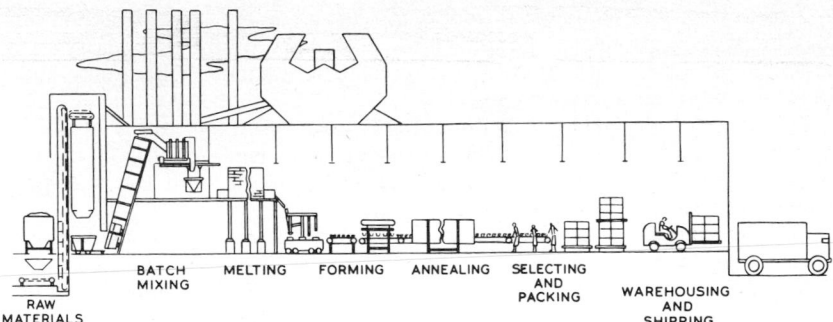

FIG. 7-1. *Process technology and material flow in a glass factory. Continuous-process manufacturing system: bulk-to-unit conversion. Glass making flows in a continuous system from sand to selection-unit handling, from selection to shipping.* (*Copyright E. Ralph Sims, Jr., & Associates, 1966.*)

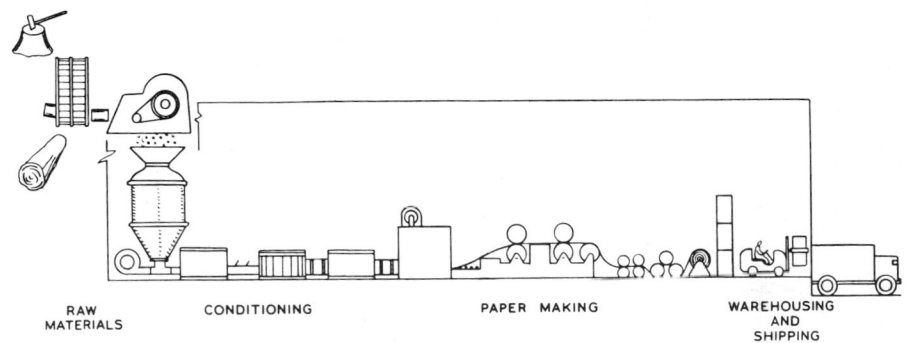

FIG. 7-2. *Process technology and material flow in a paper mill. Continuous-process manufacturing system: unit-to-bulk conversion. Paper making flows from a unitized-raw-material input (logs) through the paper-making machine in a continuous bulk product and through warehousing and shipping in bulk units (rolls).* (*Copyright E. Ralph Sims, Jr., & Associates, 1966.*)

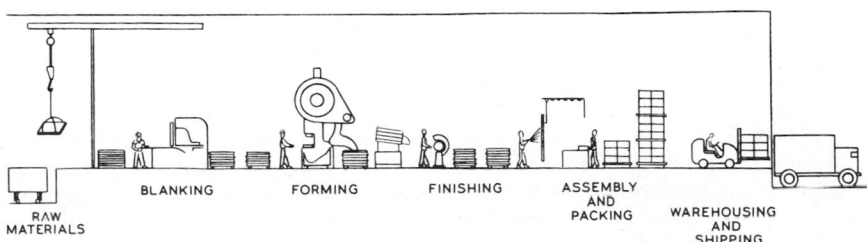

FIG. 7-3. *Process technology and material flow in a sheet-metal operation. Unitized or batch-process manufacturing system: unit-to-unit conversion. Metal processing starts in unit raw materials and moves from operation to operation in unit loads or batches.* (*Copyright E. Ralph Sims, Jr., & Associates, 1966.*)

Fabrication. Raw material processing converts ore to production materials and crops to ingredients. Manufacturing converts production materials and ingredients to parts, and assembly converts parts, packing materials, and paints to salable products and packages.

Control. The president controls the whole business, the sweeper controls the dirt on the floor, the production manager controls material flow, the controller controls money flow, the supervisor controls personnel, and the data-processing manager controls information flow.

Materials Handling—An Element of the Control Activity. This management concept further defines materials handling as the control of material in space and time. Thus, warehousing controls and protects materials, and handling equipment controls and moves materials. *No materials handling activity changes or creates anything. Materials handling is a control function.*

Materials Handling—An Element of Distribution Management. The control concept has hastened the growth of a new management function or position. The distribution manager (sometimes, material manager) has emerged as the coordinating and directing executive in the material flow function (Figure 7-4). This organization concept is often combined with integrated data processing in a composite control function (Figure 7-5). This type of organization gives materials handling the top-level attention it deserves, provides for overall, noncompetitive application of integrated data processing, and permits a controllership audit of cost effectiveness in materials movement.

Thus, the distribution manager controls material flow throughout the logistics system, the controller governs money flow, and these two control activities are coordinated through information flow and data processing which produces unbiased and objective facts for top management action.

Materials Handling—A Physical Manifestation of Cash Flow. Materials in storage or in motion are "locked up," unspendable money. They represent payroll, materials purchases, facilities costs, hidden taxes, insurance, interest, executive cost, general and administrative cost, and the like. Effective materials handling and storage methods accelerate material movement and therefore accelerate cash flow—a major factor in profit performance. Effective inventory management lowers inventory levels and therefore reduces cash "lockup."

Materials Handling—An Element of Cost Control. *Material handling adds nothing but cost. Warehousing adds nothing but damage.*

Handling and storage are not profit-producing activities. They are both *cost* activities! Any move eliminated is a cost eliminated. Merchandise not owned or stored requires no warehousing and generates no warehousing or handling cost. Smooth and effective handling and low inventories are major factors in cost control and profitability.

MATERIALS HANDLING—A TECHNICAL FUNCTION

Facilities Engineering. The planning of a manufacturing or distribution facility has long been recognized as more than a structural or architectural accomplishment. Most modern facilities are planned from "the process out," that is, the layout of the material flow precedes the layout of the buildings. Building specifications must include capability to accommodate optimum flow, maximum "cube utilization" (high stacking), and modern handling and transportation equipment. Because manufacturing objectives vary, it is essential to define them and the management parameters in terms of product class and characteristics; production and sales fluctuations; inventory location, size, mix, and dollar lockup; capital investment limits; inventory limits; product life span, design, and process stability; facility adaptability; and levels of production.

Product Characteristics. The same handling techniques are not appropriate for all products. Differences in product characteristics make consideration of varying handling techniques necessary. Some of the important factors are package strength (stack stability and product protection); fragility and perishability; size and shape; and weight, density, and stability. Other critical characteristics are bulk versus package; flexibility (liquid versus dry, viscosity, air mobility, "dusting," abrasiveness, corrosion); security (fire and explosion, theft, control, vermin, dirt); and odors.

Materials handling methods and equipment selection should be oriented to product characteristics first, and flow or process characteristics second.

Material Movement, Rates, and Routes. There are many alternatives in the selection of equipment. Constant flow over a fixed path might indicate use of conveyor equipment. Cartons and units can move on several types of conveyor, and the size, fragility, unit weight, and load density determine the load capacity of the equipment. Package characteristics, volume, rate, and speed determine the type of equipment and power requirements. Plant layout and structure determine the route.

In the case of wheeled equipment, the pallet is the usual common denominator handling device for homogenizing the system. However, some products are handled better with clamps, special forks, and other devices. The pallet system tends to minimize the effect of poor operators, and except when unitized shipments are a factor, the pallet system is the most economical. Forklifts are versatile and rugged, and wood pallets can make thousands of trips and last many years.

Counting, Control, Routing, and Locating. The control of unit load movements requires a simple dispatch system using move tickets, radio, or "bull horn" communications with drivers. Move tickets identify the load, its source, and its destination; they also record shipments and receipts into and out of the inventory record. "Blind checking" is desirable to assure a good count.

Inventory Characteristics. Inventory characteristics determine storage and warehousing methods. Although product characteristics dominate the selection of handling techniques and flow determines the sophistication of handling methods, these factors have only secondary influence in determining storage techniques.

In general, policing of an order frequency layout develops costs which offset travel savings. Reserve and picking areas should be set up separately to allow two-stage picking (Figure 7-6). Walls are valuable storage tools—never leave one bare. Island patterns give maximum item access. Store by quantity for best space utilization—no fixed item locations (Figure 7-7). Store to maximum cube allowable for floor capacity and item stack strength (Figure 7-8). In reserve areas, aisle space should be minimized to achieve optimum space utilization. A practical aisle width formula for maximum fork truck operation speed and minimum aisle loss is

Width = (forklift manufacturer's aisle recommendation) + (12 inches)

Order Characteristics. Order characteristics determine order-picking areas and methods. In developing order-picking procedures and layouts, the order characteristics (line items per order, pieces per line item, product mix, order volume, and the like) are the basis for planning. In planning order-picking operations, use fixed-location addresses in the pick line, "sample" or representative picking inventories, and high-flow aisles to minimize picking labor and eliminate queue-

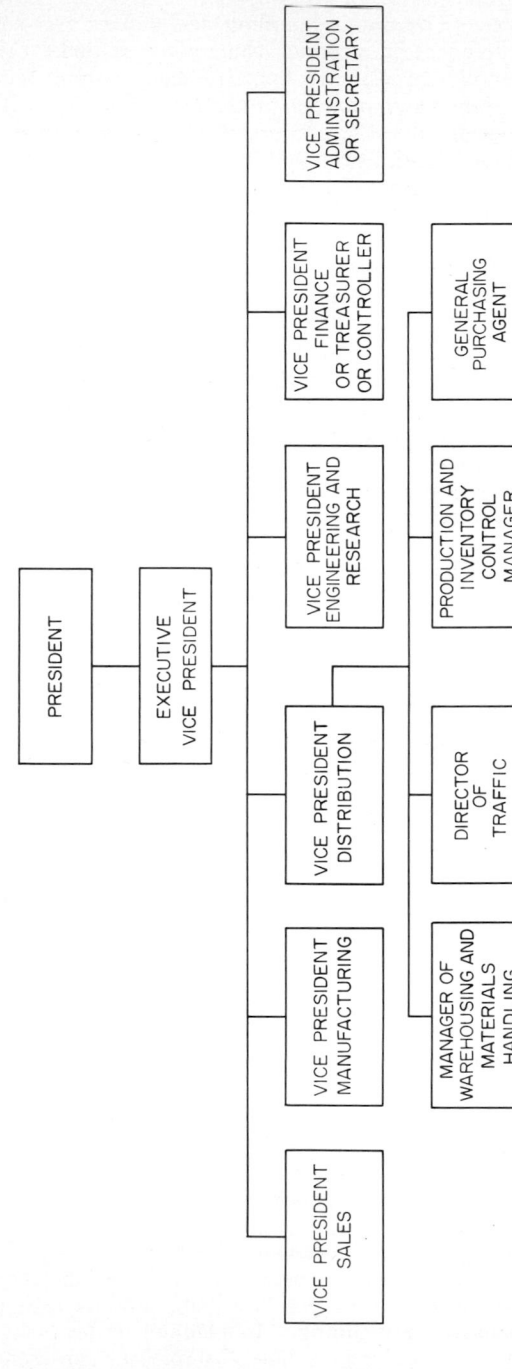

FIG. 7-4. *General outline—material management–oriented organization. In a classical, material management–oriented organization structure, material control (at all levels) is centralized in a "distribution management" function.*

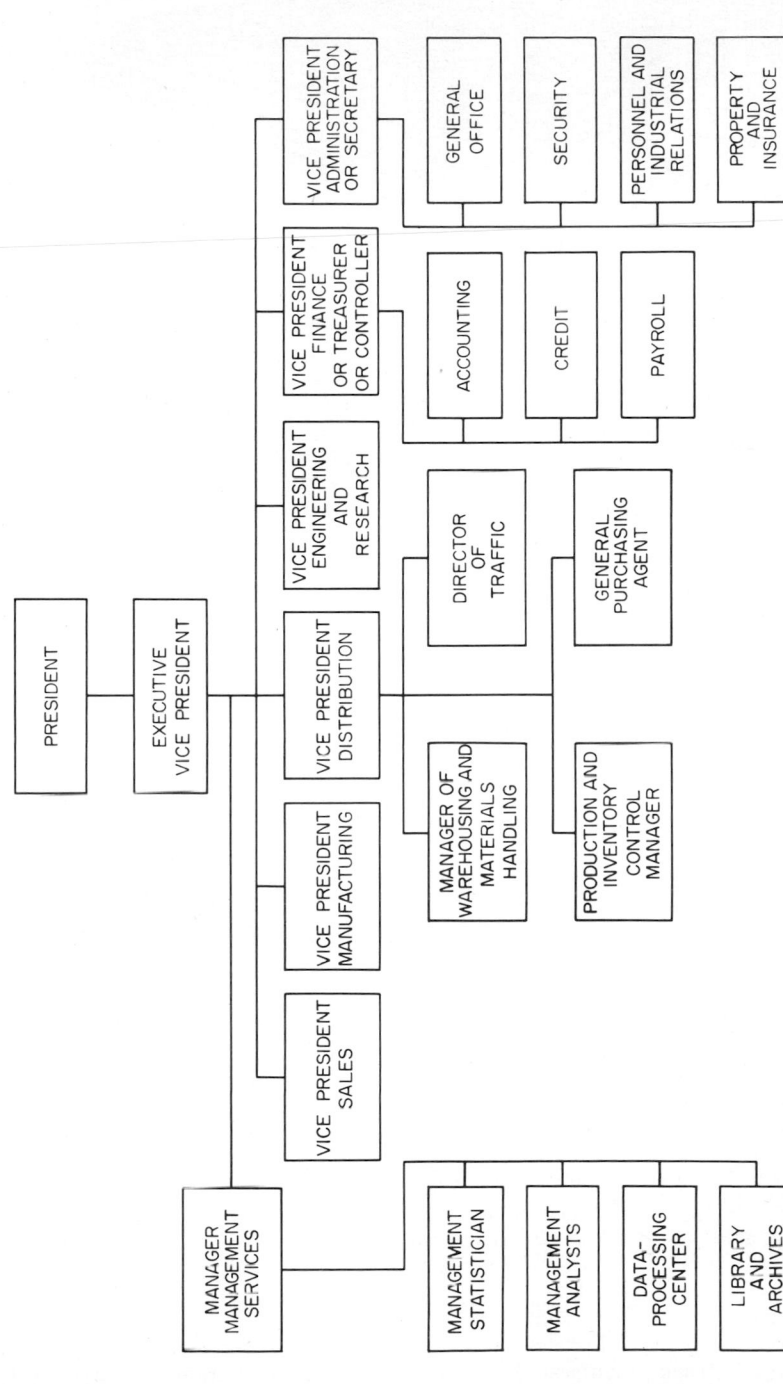

FIG. 7-5. *Staff information center and its relationship to material management–oriented organization. The relationship of data and information services to the material management–oriented organization can be optimized through modern data-processing techniques and a centralized staff "information center" reporting above the function it serves.*

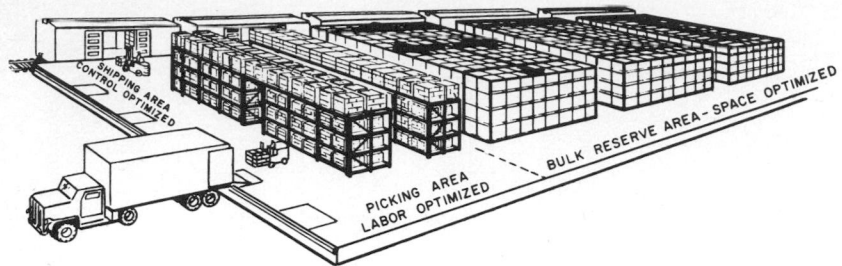

FIG. 7-6. *Reserve and picking areas set up separately to allow two-stage picking. Staged-warehousing concept; block reserve by inventory volume; pick line with stable locations and racks; rail and truck shipping at right angles for joint control of operations.* (*Copyright E. Ralph Sims, Jr., & Associates, 1966.*)

STORAGE BY SEQUENCE

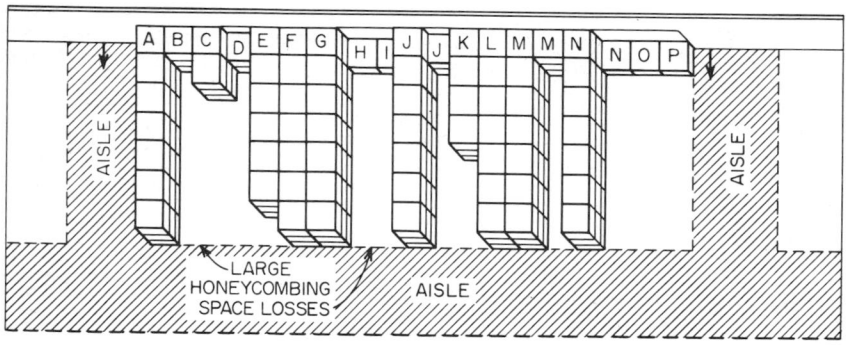

STORAGE BY SPACE

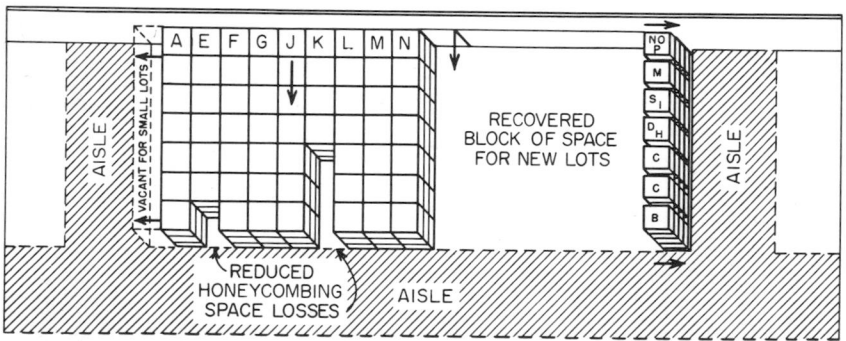

FIG. 7-7. *Storage by sequence and by space with no fixed item locations.*

ing, talking, and jam-ups. A practical aisle width formula to allow passing and pedestrian safety is

$$\text{Width} = (\text{picking vehicle width} \times 2) + (24 \text{ inches})$$

or

$$\text{Width} = (\text{fork truck manufacturer's aisle width recommendation}) + (12 \text{ inches})$$

whichever is greater.

Store in item sequence by product class or by physical characteristics, that is, group by storage technique first (shelves, pallet racks, stacks, bins, racks, and the like), then in item-number sequence. In approaching the order-picking problem, the following checkpoints should be considered. Can the order document be written in warehouse-location sequence to minimize travel and search? Can the orders be released in prerouted carrier groupings to minimize shipping labor? Can a one-writing order–invoice–bill-of-lading set minimize paper work? Can orders be group-picked to minimize travel? Can orders be stage-picked, that is, full pallet lots from reserve, leftovers and less-pallet lots from a pick line? Can the order be picked, packed, labeled, and loaded by one person?

On the inbound side of the stock room or warehouse, an "image" system can simplify location control. A punched card set or a simple snap-out form can be prepared as a part of the documentation of the final operation or in preparing purchasing-receiving document sets. The copies are distributed to inventory control and location control in the warehouse. A photographically reduced 8½- by 11-inch warehouse layout can be marked for supervisory instructions, space reporting, location reporting, and other space-oriented communications.

MATERIALS HANDLING, INFORMATION FLOW, AND MANAGEMENT CONTROLS

Integrated Handling Systems. If you want to know something, "ask the man who is one, not the man who knows one." This cliché emphasizes the simplest technique for defining the common denominators in materials handling or inventory management. A lift truck cannot know or care what is on the pallet—thus the pallet is the common denominator. The conveyor cannot know or care what is in the carton—thus, the carton is the common denominator. The drag line or tractor cannot know or care what is on the warehouse truck—thus, the warehouse truck is the common denominator. The first step in the systems approach to materials handling is to define the common denominators of handling at each stage and identify the interface points between them. These are frequently defined by inventory-control points.

Inventory-control Levels. Inventory-control levels have a direct effect on materials handling operations. The inventory common denominator can be defined

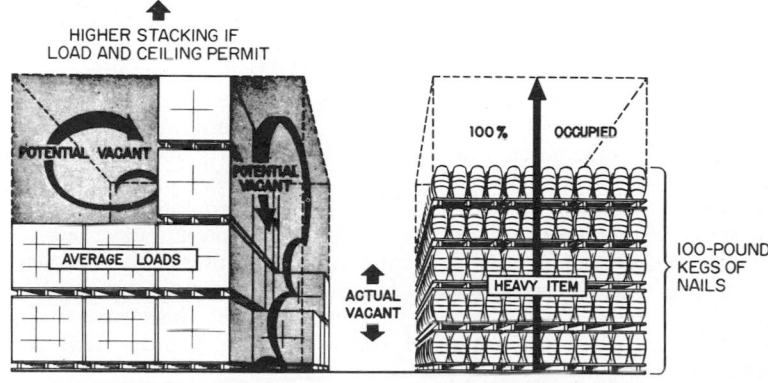

HIGHER STACKING IF
LOAD AND CEILING PERMIT

POTENTIAL VACANT

POTENTIAL VACANT

AVERAGE LOADS

ACTUAL
VACANT

100%   OCCUPIED

HEAVY ITEM

100-POUND
KEGS OF
NAILS

FOR EXAMPLE: FLOOR CAPACITY–500 POUNDS PER SQUARE FOOT.

FIG. 7-8. *Storage to maximum cube allowable for floor capacity and item stack strength.*

by asking the item of inventory what it will be next. For example, the gear blank does not know or care what tooth pattern it will have; it is a gear blank—thus, it is an inventory-control point from which many different tooth patterns can be cut. Its identity will change with the next operation. A carton does not know what it will be next. It does not know or care if it will be in a pallet load, a truckload, a carload, or a stack. It is a carton—and thus the common denominator of both inventory and handling.

An inventory common denominator or control point item is one which can be converted into several different items or handling units. It can also be a handling common denominator.

Production-control Techniques. In defining the common denominator for handling and inventory, the common denominator for control must also be defined. Thus, the relationship between "level by level" inventory control and "level by level" production control is the basis for planning both material moves and storage points.

If production- and inventory-control techniques are tight, less material is required in inventory "banks" and warehouses. If the material is not in the system, it does not have to be handled into and out of storage. If production-control techniques are tight, materials and in-process parts can move between operations without "off-line" travel or storage. If inventory control is tight, raw materials and finished goods can be closely scheduled. "What you don't have, you don't store, and what you don't have, you don't handle."

Integrated Data-processing Systems. An integrated data-processing system can be a materials handling tool. It relates management objectives and decisions to material flow through information control. It has the capability to mix and sort information, time its release, and rearrange it in any appropriate format. Because these systems require people to "talk" to machines as well as people, a mechanically legible language is required. This language permits the data-processing system to instruct and operate handling equipment and to control material movement.

Purchasing Documentation. Purchasing documentation can be a factor in inbound handling costs. The purchasing agent can reduce handling costs by purchasing in production lot quantities, scheduling deliveries, premanufacturing, arranging for parts delivery in kits or subassemblies, selecting proper carriers, and other techniques.

Purchasing documentation can also expedite handling by entering all necessary receiving information on receiving documents as a by-product of purchase order preparation and by assuring that all required documents are in the receiving department before the merchandise arrives. If documentation permits, materials can be picked up once and moved directly to the next point of use.

Paper work should follow or anticipate, not govern, materials flow.

Order documentation affects order-filling cost. Paper-work procedures can reduce handling costs by preposting stock withdrawals to minimize "warehouse refusals" (the search for nonexistent items) and processing of back orders without multiple warehouse handling. Prerouting and grouping of orders for group picking in "carrier" batches avoids rehandling and sorting at the shipping dock. Prerouting of order items in picking-line sequence minimizes order-filler travel, and separation of full-pallet lots from "balance" or short-quantity items permits forklift order filling. Timing of order entry with production schedules often permits direct loading from production onto carriers.

Documentation can also directly control mechanized or automated order-filling equipment through punched cards, punched tape, magnetic tape, magnetic ledger cards, edge-punched cards, and electrical techniques.

Production and Inventory Control.   Data-processing lead time—the proper application of data-processing techniques to speed up information flow—reduces information lead time with the resulting reduction in the inventory or material in the pipeline which supports this lead time.   Production control limits multiple handling and off-line banking of material.   Data processing helps by minimizing in-process inventory, timing moves, and routing materials to avoid unnecessary travel.   Inventory control, by reducing or eliminating on-hand inventory while maintaining available inventory for scheduling production and sales, can often eliminate handling.   For example, if vendors store and deliver on schedule, their inventory is available but not on hand.   It is not stored or handled in the buyer's plant, and by anticipating the buyer's production schedule, the vendor can manufacture for shipment and minimize his own inventory and handling. These and many other techniques are parts of the information system approach to reduced handling and storage costs.

Data Transmission.   Data-processing machines all "read and write" a common language, and the material flow system can be tied together by data transmission between control points.   Data transmission can reduce or eliminate the inventory in the pipeline which is required to cover the communications lead time, thereby eliminating the handling of this material.   Data transmission, radio dispatch of vehicles, and telephone reporting of material movement through a control center help achieve positive and coordinated movements, control feedback, and optimum handling-equipment utilization.

Data processing and data transmission contribute to freight and traffic improvements by permitting preaccumulation and consolidation of shipments for better rates and weights, timing of shipments and receipts to minimize handling and storage, and in-transit inventory control to permit shipment of unsold goods and in-transit sales.

SUMMARY OF MANAGEMENT APPROACH TO MATERIALS HANDLING

The Control Concept of Materials Handling Management.   Materials handling is essentially a control function.   It adds nothing but cost, and its prime service is to control the relationship of materials to space and time.   If we recognize the other control elements of business as parallel functions, then the application of data-processing technology, mechanized or automated materials handling, advanced inventory- and production-control technology, the controllership approach to financial management, work measurement theory, and the mathematical techniques of market management all fit together as a part of a total control concept of material management.

In applying the common denominator approach to materials handling, inventory management, and documentation, it is not uncommon to find that the interfaces (or break points) between each of these areas are compatible with the interfaces of the others.   Thus, through improved precision in one area of control, it is often possible to improve control and reduce costs throughout the whole system.

These factors have resulted in the development of the material or distribution manager concept of organization which tends to apply top management attention to materials handling costs more effectively.   This function, when properly audited by sound controllership and adequately supported by an integrated information system (manual or electronic), can form the basis for handling cost reductions in companies of all sizes.

Because handling adds only cost, it is logical to assume that attention to handling costs can add nothing but profit.

BIBLIOGRAPHY

Apple, James M., *Plant Layout and Materials Handling,* The Ronald Press Company, New York, 1950.

Barker, Curtis H., *Industrial Materials Handling,* Lincoln Extension Institute, Inc., Cleveland, 1950.

Bolz, Harold A., and George E. Hagemann (eds.), *Materials Handling Handbook,* The Ronald Press Company, New York, 1958.

Briggs, Andrew J., *Warehouse Operations Planning and Management,* John Wiley & Sons, Inc., New York, 1960.

Haynes, D. Oliphant, *Materials Handling Applications,* Chilton Company—Book Division, Philadelphia, 1958.

Hoefkens, L. J., *Materials in Works Stores,* Ileffe Company, London, 1954.

Immer, John R., *Materials Handling,* McGraw-Hill Book Company, New York, 1953.

Material Handling Engineering Directory (formerly *Flow Directory*), published every two years by *Material Handling Engineering* Magazine, Cleveland.

CHAPTER EIGHT

Inventory Management and Control

LAUREN F. SARGENT   *H. B. Maynard and Company, Incorporated, Pittsburgh, Pennsylvania*

Management's work consists of establishing objectives and acting to attain them. With few exceptions, management must depend on others to do a large part of the actual work. These statements apply to inventory management and control work. Usually, this work is voluminous, and some of it requires understanding how to use special techniques effectively.

Normally, management's inventory work consists of establishing objectives; setting up an organzation to attain them; providing the required information, data, and facilities; arriving at a mutually agreed-upon plan for attaining these objectives; telling the inventory manager to execute this plan; arriving at a mutually understood way of evaluating the results of the inventory work; and revising the plan when conditions change. In total, this work is as technical as accounting, but it has not been as thoroughly investigated. Hence, management may have to acquire some understanding of inventory control work to be sure that it is properly done. The key concept is: "The inventory investment should be managed as a profit-earning investment. Capital should be invested in inventory only when the expected net rate of return is as high as or higher than that of any optional investment." These simple statements make sense, and they should guide all of the inventory work.

INVENTORY COSTS

The returns on inventory investment come from three sources. They are profits on additional sales gained by having what the customer wants when and where he wants it, savings in stock-out costs, and savings in lot quantity costs.

Stock-out costs are the costs of steps taken to avoid running out of stock, and of quickly obtaining another lot quantity of an item when a stock-out occurs.

The lot quantity costs include all the costs of ordering, preparing to produce, and receiving a lot quantity of an item. Machine setup costs are a typical example of these costs.

As a rule, the annual total of these costs is proportional to the number of orders and is independent of the number of units made or purchased under normal conditions. An increase in the amount of the inventory reduces stock-out and lot quantity costs, but the increase may or may not be profitable.

There also are inventory carrying costs or the costs coming from possessing stocks of items. Each increase in the inventory investment causes an approximately proportional increase in the annual total of these costs which are practically constant per unit of investment. This is not true of the gains from increasing the inventory, which are subject to the law of diminishing returns. When the inventory investment is too small, the net returns from an increase will be high. If the inventory investment is too large, the costs of a further increase will exceed the gains therefrom. Here, a saving can be made by decreasing the amount of this investment.

Table 8-1 shows the gains and losses from increasing the ordering quantity

TABLE 8-1. Gains and Losses Resulting from Increasing the Ordering Quantity

Number of months' supply in the ordering quantity	Number of orders per year	Lot quantity costs per year	Average amount of the related inventory investment	Costs per year of this investment	Total of related inventory costs per year	Gain or loss
1	12	$432.00	$ 112.50	$ 27.00	$459.00	
2	6	216.00	225.00	54.00	270.00	+$189.00
3	4	144.00	337.50	81.00	225.00	+ 45.00
4	3	108.00	450.00	108.00	216.00	+ 9.00
5	2⅖	86.40	562.50	135.00	221.40	− 5.40
6	2	72.00	675.00	162.00	234.00	− 12.60
8	1½	54.00	900.00	216.00	270.00	− 36.00
10	1⅕	42.00	1,125.00	270.00	312.00	− 42.00
12	1	36.00	1,350.00	324.00	360.00	− 48.00
16	¾	27.00	1,800.00	432.00	459.00	− 99.00

of an item. The ordering quantity is stated in terms of month's supply. Thus the number of orders per year is twelve divided by the ordering quantity. The value of a month's supply is assumed to be $225. The rate for carrying inventory is 24 percent. The increase in the inventory investment is assumed to be one-half of the increase in the ordering quantity. The lot quantity costs per order are $36.

In Table 8-1, the lowest inventory costs are found where the annual total of the lot quantity costs equals the annual total of the costs of carrying inventory. In some cases, this relationship can be used to find the amount of the most profitable ordering quantity. In other cases, it gives incorrect answers. The objective here is to show that the law of diminishing returns applies to gains from increasing the amount of the ordering quantity. A brief review of the right-hand column shows these diminishing returns.

This example also illustrates the need for a vocabulary in inventory work. The use of the term "lot quantity costs" saves the use of a short sentence. Having effective communications between management and the inventory manager is one of the requirements for obtaining satisfactory results from inventory work. Special terms for communications in inventory work are as essential as in accounting work.

SIMPLIFYING THE INVENTORY PROBLEMS

The objective of inventory management is to obtain an adequate rate of return on each part of the inventory investment. At best, this presents a difficult problem. Every practical move must be made to simplify it.

One simple and extremely effective move is to include the required net rate of return on the investment in the rate for carrying inventory. This rate of return will be earned when the rate of increase in costs equals the rate of decrease in returns. For example, assume that the actual variable or out-of-pocket costs of carrying inventory are 8⅓ percent, and that management requires a net rate of return of 16⅔ percent on the inventory investment. It wants to make other uses of capital unless it will earn at least this rate of return before taxes. Thus, the rate for carrying inventory for this specific class of items in a specific stock room is 0.08⅓ + 0.16⅔, or 0.25. Management will wish the inventory department to stop investing in these items at the point where the estimated saving from the last dollar invested is 0.25 before taxes. In theory, inventory technicians can find this point. In actual practice, they can only approximate it.

Stock-out Costs. The subject of stock-out costs raises several questions. No one can forecast the cost of the effects of the next stock-out. It may cost the business of an important customer, or it may not cause any serious trouble. The amounts of these costs depend on conditions when the stock-out occurs and how long it lasts. These variables make it a waste of time to seek extreme accuracy in establishing stock-out costs. The policy should be to try to develop a reasonably accurate figure and then use it knowingly. The same idea applies to forecasts. It would be most useful to have accurate forecasts, but a large majority of the forecasts will be inaccurate. The policy should be to make the forecasts as accurate as possible. Then, the amount of cumulative difference between actual and forecasted rates of use that require changing plans should be established. After that, keep records of the amount of this difference and know what to do when it exceeds these limits. These moves will simplify inventory work and aid in managing the inventory investment as a profit-earning investment.

METHODS OF CONTROL

The inventory manager can control the number of locations in which stock is kept and the number of items kept in each location. He can also regulate the amounts of ordering points and ordering quantities and the length of the reserve cycle. Costs and conditions, however, limit his freedom of action in these areas. He can hold the lengths of the in-process and in-transit cycles to a minimum. His decisions in these areas determine the average amount of the inventory investment and the annual total of the inventory costs.

The need for clarity in communications makes it desirable to have a way of referring to this control collectively. The items that are controlled can be called "inventory factors." The regulation of the numbers, amounts, and lengths can be referred to as regulating the magnitudes of the inventory factors."

The objective of inventory work should be to hold the magnitudes of the inventory factors at the level that minimizes the annual total of the inventory costs. This objective stresses the importance of having minimum costs and a satisfactory rate of return on all parts of the inventory investment. It does not consider the amount of the investment or rate of turnover. A high rate of turnover is desirable only when all profitable inventory investments are being made. Not doing this is the equivalent of borrowing money from the inventory at a high rate of interest. Management should control the amount of this investment by stipulating the required rate of return on capital.

The amount of the ordering point or ordering quantity may be less than the indicated or computed economic amount. If so, an additional investment in inventory will earn a higher net rate of return than any known optional investment. If this is not so, the charge for capital in the rate for carrying inventory should be increased until it is so. Then management should make all profitable inventory investments. This provides a logical way of finding an answer to the question, "How large should the inventory investment be?"

Some companies pay a high price for a high rate of turnover. In one case, the findings of a study indicated the annual total of the lot quantity costs of an item exceeded the annual total of the variable costs of the item. In another case, a company was ordering one-fifth of the economic lot quantity of an item. The savings from correcting this condition exceeded $100,000 per year. These companies realized large savings by increasing their inventory investment.

Minimizing the annual total of the inventory costs pays worthwhile dividends and is the logical objective for inventory work. The problem here is to find ways of minimizing these costs; the fact that savings from increases in the inventory investment are subject to the law of diminishing returns provides a basic approach.

The magnitude of the related inventory factor is at the correct level when the savings from the last unit increase equal the costs thereof. If another unit increase is made, the savings will be less than the costs. If the last unit increase had not been made, a profitable investment opportunity would have been lost. The cost of the increase in the investment is the product of the amount of the investment and the rate for carrying inventory. It would also be correct to state that the rate of return on the last unit increase in the investment should equal the rate for carrying inventory. A company has the correct inventory investment when the last unit increase reaches the break-even point. This break-even point is comparatively easy to find.

CLASSIFICATIONS OF STOCK

The stock of an item should not be considered as an undivided total. For inventory management purposes, it is helpful to separate it into the classifications of reserve, turnover, in-process, and in-transit stock. The amount of the reserve stock depends on the amount of the ordering point or the length of the reserve cycle. The actual amount of reserve stock is the in-stock balance at the time of receipt of the next lot quantity of the item. The length of the reserve cycle enters into the amount of the ordering point as follows.

Standard replenishment cycle	4 weeks
Reserve cycle	2 weeks
Established lead time	6 weeks
Forecasted rate of demand per week	80 units
Amount of ordering point	480 units

Attention is called to the fact that the average amount of reserve stock may not be 2×80, or 160 units. There would be some stock on hand part of the time if the lead time were four weeks or the reserve cycle zero weeks. Normally, the actual amount of reserve stock is best left to inventory technicians. Finding the expected average amount of reserve stock is not as simple as it appears to be.[1]

The amount of the ordering quantity also determines the turnover stock. Normally, this is the only part of the stock of an item that turns over. It comes in, is used, and is replenished. When the demands occur in random quantities at random times, the average amount of this stock is approximately one-half of the ordering quantity.

Manufacturing companies usually have substantial amounts of work in process. The average amount of this stock usually is directly proportional to the length of the in-process cycle. When companies ship stock to other plants or warehouses, they may also have substantial amounts of in-transit stock. The average amount of this stock is directly proportional to the length of the in-transit cycle. This cycle begins when the stock becomes unavailable for other use at the point of shipment.

Companies usually have some excess, surplus, held, salvage, and miscellaneous stock. The amounts of these classes of stock should not be large. If one or more of them does become large enough to require individual attention, it usually is comparatively easy to relate its amount to the magnitudes of specific factors.

OBTAINING SATISFACTORY RESULTS FROM INVENTORY WORK

Good results usually come from competently executing well-prepared plans. Executing plans competently requires well-trained, capable people and adequate data, facilities, and systems. In addition, the people must have leadership and an organization plan that permits using these resources effectively. The inventory control department must have a manager, technicians, operators, and clerks.

Management. A manager is a man that causes people to do better work than they think they can do. The manager supplies the support, incentives, and enthusiasm that make this possible. He also trains and develops people, foresees and prevents trouble, and brings in new ideas and concepts. In addition to this, he supports policies and requires meeting high standards of conduct and performance. The inventory control manager must meet the customary requirements for an executive. Beyond this, he must be able to explain and sell new concepts of inventory management to the other divisions of the company.

Inventory Department Personnel. The inventory department requires technical, operating, and clerical personnel. The technicians must have a thorough understanding of the use of formulas to determine the lengths of reserve cycles and the amounts of ordering quantities. They must know the required characteristics of the costs and data used in these formulas. They must be able to make economic analyses of the advantages of having stocks of items. Their work often requires the use of probability mathematics. In some cases, they must be able to recommend changes in design of the product and the facilities for making them that will decrease the annual total of the material costs. Sometimes, they must aid the accountants in setting up systems to gather and process the data used in this work. The systems and procedures people may need their aid and advice in setting up and revising inventory systems and procedures. The inventory technicians require a thorough knowledge of all aspects of inventory work.

The operating people do the day-to-day inventory work—ordering stock, expediting receipt of some items, and retarding the receipt of others. A thorough

[1] An explanation of how to estimate the amount of reserve stock is given in H. B. Maynard (ed.), *Industrial Engineering Handbook*, 2d ed., sec. 7, chap. 5, McGraw-Hill Book Company, New York, 1963.

knowledge of how to operate the inventory system is also an important requirement of their work.   In some cases, these people compute and revise the ordering
points and ordering quantities.   When doing this, they follow the technicians'
instructions.   The inventory control department normally compiles data for use
in the department and throughout the company.   The operating people are
usually responsible for gathering, processing, and distributing these data.

The clerical personnel maintain the records kept within the department, many
of which can be gathered, processed, stored, and distributed by computers if
available.

Information for Inventory Work.   To manage an inventory effectively, it is necessary to have an adequate amount of information that is as nearly correct as
possible.   The inventory technicians need forecasted rates of use, unit costs,
lot quantity costs, stock-out costs, and rates for carrying inventory.   They use
this information to forecast the changes in inventory costs that will come from
a change in the magnitude of one or more inventory factors.

Unit and Lot Quantity Costs.   Normally, there is a large difference between
costs that show how much it costs to make the product and costs for use in
estimating the effects of a change in the magnitude of an inventory factor.   For
example, a 10 percent increase in the amount of a manufacturing ordering quantity may not cause a 10 percent increase in the amount of the inventory investment in material.   This may only transfer the material from raw stock to parts
stock.   The sale of trimmings and cuttings may decrease the investment in
material.   Because of an increased risk of damage and obsolescence, the parts-
stock rate for carrying inventory may be higher than the raw-stock rate.   The
formula for computing the economic length of the reserve cycle uses the value
of the ordering quantity.   This value is used in computing the increase in the
cost of carrying inventory.   The unit cost of the item is used for the same
purpose in the economic ordering quantity formula.   The figures used in these
formulas must give an estimate of the actual change in the inventory investment,
not the cost of making or buying the item.   The economic ordering quantity
formula uses the lot quantity costs per order.   This figure should show the estimated effect of a unit change in the number of orders on the annual total
of the lot quantity costs.

Stock-out Costs.   The estimated cost of the next stock-out is used in the
formula for finding the economic reserve cycle.   This cost should be an estimate
of the effects of a unit change in the number of stock-outs on profits.   This
includes the effects both on profits from sales and on operating costs.

Rates for Carrying Inventory.   The rate for carrying inventory is used in
the formulas for computing the economic length of the reserve cycle and the
economic ordering quantity to estimate the future costs of carrying inventory.
The season influences the costs of carrying inventory in some places.   The cost
of losses from oxidation is higher in warm, wet weather than in cold, dry
weather.   Both hot and cold weather may cause losses.   The rate used in these
formulas should show the expected future, rather than the past, costs.

Forecasted Rates of Demand.   Both formulas require forecasted rates of demand.   There usually are substantial differences between the actual and forecasted rates of demand.   The objective should be to minimize both the individual
and average amounts of these differences.   The pluses should cancel the minuses,
and the amount of each should be held to a minimum.   Sometimes, changing
conditions cause a large percentage of these differences to be in one direction.
For example, the actual demand may exceed the forecasted demand for 75
percent of the items.   This situation results from a substantial unexpected increase in sales.   This requires two kinds of action.   Management should adjust

the planned rate of output in line with the change in the rate of demand.   It should also revise the amounts of the ordering quantities and ordering points.

These moves require analyzing the overall problem carefully.   For example, assume that a company has an unexpected 20 percent increase in sales.   This justifies approximately a 10 percent increase in the amounts of reserve and turnover stock.   The company now has $2,000,000 worth of inventory and wants to increase it to $2,200,000 within two months.   During the next two months, it must produce

Sales.........................	$2,400,000
Increase in inventory............	200,000
Total output....................	2,600,000
Output per month...............	1,300,000
Starting rate of output...........	1,000,000
Increase in rate of output........	300,000 or 30 percent

After producing $1,300,000 worth of product for two months, it plans to cut back to $1,200,000 per month.   A $200,000 increase in demand caused a temporary $300,000 increase in output.   In the same way, a decrease in sales can cause more than a proportional decrease in the rate of output.   Management must try to keep the fluctuations in the rate of output less than those in the rate of demand.   Otherwise, there will be excessive costs for overtime and employee turnover.

Some companies always seem to have their inventory out of phase with changes in the rate of demand.   Their inventory is high when the rate of demand starts to decrease and low when it starts to increase.   They should try to improve the accuracy of their forecasts.   If the probability of doing this is low, they should compare the costs of maintaining a constant amount of reserve stock with the costs of the fluctuations in the rate of demand.   It may cost less to carry an oversupply of reserve stock for a few months than to make large changes in the rate of output.

Stock Rooms and Warehouses.   A company may have the problem of determining when to change the number of stock rooms or warehouses and which items to have at each location.   This is a matter of comparing the amounts of expected gains and costs.   The expected gains are the sum of the profits on the forecasted gains in sales and the savings in transportation costs.   These gains should be decreased by the probable costs of carrying the net increase in the investment and operating the warehouse.   Normally, part of the demand at the new location was already being met at old locations.   If so, the net increase in the inventory investment will be less than the investment in the new location.

Length of the In-process Cycle.   The length of the in-process cycle determines the amounts of in-process and reserve stock in many companies.   This makes the control of the magnitude of this inventory factor rather important.   The method of exercising this control depends on the type of manufacturing.   In a continuous production operation, the length of the in-process cycle depends on plant layout and the coordination of the manufacture of many components. In a batch-type plant, the amount of work ahead of an order has a major influence on the length of the in-process cycle.   This amount can be brought to a minimum by keeping the rate of output slightly larger than the rate of input.   The amount of in-process stock will reach and pass the minimum for existing conditions.   When this happens, there will be a noticeable increase in the amount of time lost waiting for stock.   The rate of input should then be made equal to the rate of output, and every effort should be made to work economically with the existing amount of in-process stock.   This includes moving material between operations promptly and improving the planning and scheduling. It should also include arranging to run two or more operations simultaneously and improving tooling. The findings of studies may reveal places where it will pay to move equipment or purchase new equipment. Management can and should shorten the in-process cycles in many batch-type departments and plants. The results of an analysis of costs will indicate how far to concentrate on decreasing the lengths of these cycles.

A decrease in cycle times decreases the required amount of reserve stock. Management may also be able to state how much will be gained from improved customer service. A company usually realizes substantial gains from holding the length of its in-process cycles at a minimum.

THE INVENTORY PLAN

The objective of an inventory plan is to obtain an adequate rate of return on all parts of the inventory investment. Basically, the plan should be designed to use economic ordering points and ordering quantities and in-process cycles to minimize the annual total of the related inventory costs. This requires spending money for gathering information that otherwise would not be spent. There can be little question about the long-range profitability of such a program. It will, however, cost more than it will save while the program is being started. An effort should be made to hold the length of this period to a minimum. This requires selecting a starting place that offers the largest possible savings and executing a program to realize these savings as quickly as possible. The largest savings can usually be made where the average investment per item is highest. Except when the available information, such as an expected change in design, indicates the advisability of starting in another area, this is the logical place to start. A logical program would include the following.

1. Prepare formula lot quantity costs per order and costs per unit for each item.
2. Establish a rate for carrying inventory for each class of items in the stock room.
3. Prepare forecasted rates of use or demand for each item. These forecasts must be in the same units of measure as the cost per unit.
4. Establish values that will be paid for unit increases in the delivery ratio of each item, or how much will be paid to save one stock-out per hundred orders.

When this information is available, use it to arrive at logical reserve cycles and ordering points. Then compute the cost of the risk of having a stock-out per order. This is the probability of having a stock-out multiplied by one-half the value that will be paid to save one stock-out.

Next, prepare a comparison of the estimated annual costs before and after placing the inventory on an economic basis. These costs should include estimates of the lot quantity costs and the costs of carrying reserve, turnover, and in-process stock. To the extent practical, these estimates should be supported by summaries of the actual number of stock-outs and costs. The comparisons of the number of stock-outs must be for a group of items for a period of time. Normally, the stock-out costs can only come from estimates and analyses of what has happened. The accountants can prepare summaries of the lot quantity and inventory carrying costs. The cost summaries provide an evaluation of the work that has been done. This summary should show individual costs for high-value items, and costs for groups of low-value items.

In many cases, a large part of the inventory investment is concentrated in a comparatively few items, and a large number of items make up a comparatively small part of the investment. Some people speak of an 80:20 rule. This rule states that approximately 80 percent of the value will be in 20 percent of the items and vice versa. Ford Dickey advocates separating items into A, B, and C classifications. Class A items receive careful, detailed attention and control; Class B items, a normal amount of attention and control; and Class C items, a minimum of attention and control. This is a logical approach to inventory management. It can be used in setting up the summary of inventory costs. With the exception of stock-outs, detailed costs would be compiled for Class A items. Class B items would have costs for groups of items. And Class C would receive a minimum amount of attention. An item with unusually high lot quantity costs per order would always require some attention.

CONCLUSION

Inventory management is, to a large extent, control work. The objective is to hold the annual total of the inventory costs at a minimum. These costs include a charge for capital equal to the net highest rate of return that can be obtained from any optional investment. They should also include the profits on any sales lost because of not having adequate stocks of items to meet customers' requirements.

A statement of the amounts of these costs provides management with a basis for establishing an inventory policy and making logical decisions relating to the inventory work. The control of these costs comes from controlling the number of stock rooms and items kept in each stock room, lengths of the reserve and in-process cycles, and the amounts of ordering points and ordering quantities. These values should be held at the point that minimizes the annual total of the inventory costs. The resulting inventory investment will then be the most profitable inventory investment.

BIBLIOGRAPHY

Ammer, Dean S., "It Doesn't Always Pay You to Cut Inventories," *Purchasing*, vol. 51, July 31, 1961, pp. 40–41.

Brown, Robert G., *Smoothing Forecasting and Prediction of Discrete Time Series*, Prentice-Hall, Inc., Englewood Cliffs, N.J., 1963.

Brown, Robert G., *Statistical Forecasting and Inventory Control*, McGraw-Hill Book Company, New York, 1959.

Buchan, Joseph, and Ernest Koenigsberg, *Scientific Inventory Management*, Prentice-Hall, Inc., Englewood Cliffs, N.J., 1963.

Fetter, Robert B., "Discussion of Interaction of EOQ and Reserve Stock," *Proceedings of American Production and Inventory Control Seminar*, Yale University, New Haven, 1959.

Haussmann, Fred, *Operations Research in Production and Inventory Control*, John Wiley & Sons, Inc., New York, 1962.

Heinaman, Stephen T., "Return on Investment Approach to Inventory," *NACA Bulletin*, vol. 36, sec. 1, July, 1955.

Magee, J. F., *Production Planning and Inventory Control*, McGraw-Hill Book Company, New York, 1958.

Raymond, F. E., *Quantity and Economy in Manufacture*, McGraw-Hill Book Company, New York, 1931. (The first book on inventory management; out of print, but available in libraries.)

CHAPTER NINE

Storeskeeping and Warehouse Management

ROBERT W. BOSLER *Senior Consultant, H. B. Maynard and Company, Incorporated, Pittsburgh, Pennsylvania*

Storeskeeping and warehousing are service functions. The storeroom services manufacturing and other plant operations; the warehouse services the market. These services add nothing to the value of the product, but they contribute to its cost. The responsibilities of stores and warehouse management are to receive materials, to protect the materials from damage or unauthorized removal, to issue the materials in the right quantities, at the right time, to the right place, and to provide these services promptly and at the least cost.

The problem in attaining these objectives in many storeroom and warehousing operations is that poorly planned, apparently overcrowded areas are combined with obsolete storage and handling methods, outdated operating policies, and inadequate labor control procedures. The result is a high-cost operation that cannot be tolerated in a competitive economy. The purpose of this chapter is to discuss the major factors that affect the daily cost of the operation and that are controllable on a daily basis by management.

ORGANIZATION

The position of the storeskeeping and warehousing activities in the organization structure varies considerably from company to company depending upon the size of the plant, the type and size product produced, and the cost of raw and finished materials, parts, tools, dies, jigs, and fixtures. A typical organization chart illustrating the relationship of the various stores activities to other departments is shown by Figure 9-1. Although such a plan is representative of good practice for many companies, it is not necessarily the best for all. For instance, in some cases warehousing might report directly to the general manager or to the sales manager. Materials and parts stores may be responsible to the controller because of the value involved in the inventories. Regardless of the organization structure, the responsibility of storeskeeping and warehousing management to operate efficiently does not change.

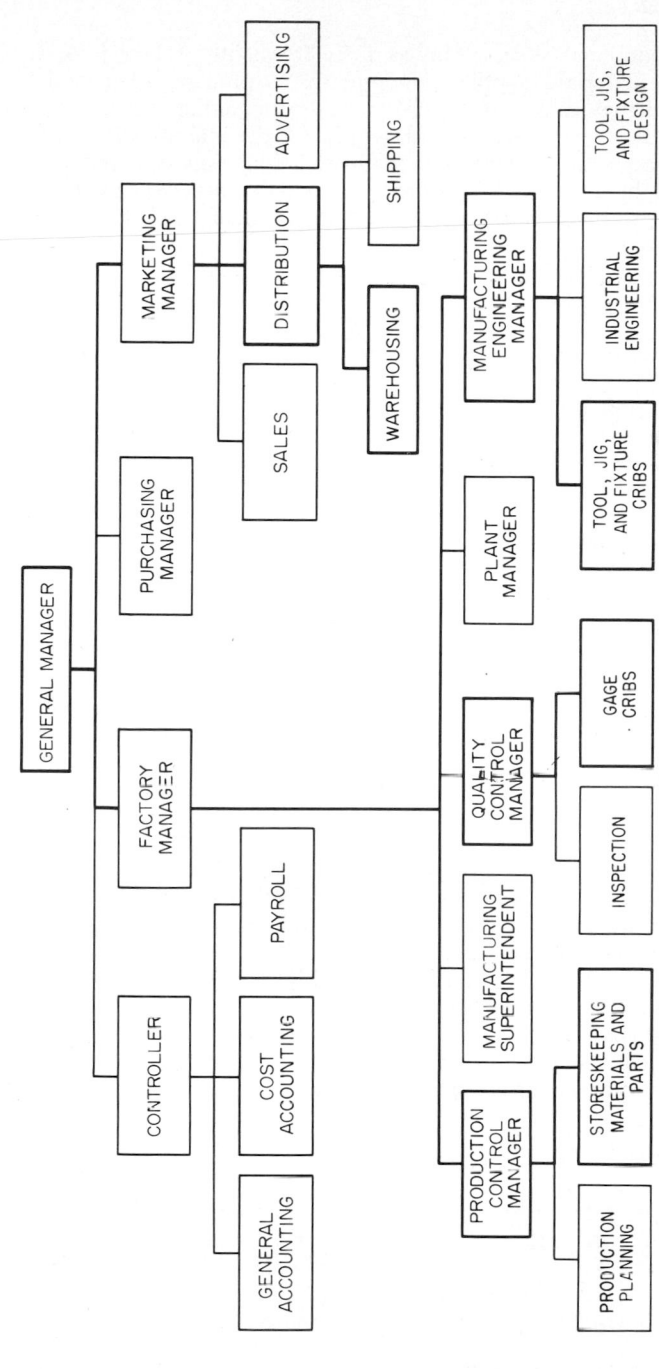

FIG. 9-1. *Organization chart showing typical relationship of storerooms, cribs, and warehouses to other plant activities.*

THE STOREROOM

The storeroom, or "stock room" as it is frequently referred to, is a storage area for raw materials, supplies, and goods in process. The activity permits quantity purchases, makes it possible to take advantage of quantity discounts, and provides an immediate source of supply for the manufacturing activities. In addition, by providing backlog storage for goods in process, it reduces production delays caused by machine breakdown and makes possible a more constant flow of materials to the finished warehouse. The major operations performed in the storeroom are:

1. Receiving raw materials and goods in process
2. Checking receipts
3. Storing
4. Picking
5. Issuing
6. Record keeping
7. Preservation

The degree to which organized storerooms are required depends upon the type of material, its bulk, the turnover rate, the value of the material, and the amount of protection needed to prevent unauthorized removal. Storerooms are classified into five categories according to the type of materials stored.

1. Direct material stores
2. Indirect material stores
3. Tool, die, jig, and fixture cribs
4. Maintenance and janitorial supply cribs
5. Office and clerical supplies

Direct materials purchased in bulk that may be used intermittently are generally stored in protected areas to ensure that adequate inventories are available at all times. Materials in protected stores are issued only on the authority of an approved requisition, production order, or bill of material. Specialized materials used on high-production operations and on standardized products are frequently ordered for delivery according to the production schedule and are delivered directly to the operation area.

Indirect materials such as oils, solvents, and other flammables should be stored in fire-protected areas away from the production operations. Costly tools, gages, and inspection instruments are kept in protected crib areas. Maintenance and janitorial supplies differ considerably from direct and indirect materials and are therefore stored in separate areas that do not occupy potentially valuable manufacturing space.

Office and clerical supplies are usually kept in one central area from which departmental requirements can be drawn as required.

THE WAREHOUSE

The purpose of the warehouse is to store, protect, and release finished goods to the market. In doing this, it also serves manufacturing. It provides an immediate outlet for the production departments and makes it possible to plan and schedule for economic lot sizes to obtain the best utilization of production manpower and equipment. The major operations performed in the warehouse are:

1. Receiving finished goods
2. Storing

3. Checking
4. Picking
5. Issuing for shipment
6. Record keeping

When shipping is included as one of the warehouse functions, there are additional operations:

7. Order consolidating
8. Checking
9. Packing (boxing, crating, parcel posting)
10. Preparation of bills of lading
11. Preservation as required

When large quantities of a standard product, such as refrigerators or household appliances, are made on a continuous basis and distributed on the basis of sales orders, a warehouse or distribution center is almost always needed. Warehousing facilities are not usually needed for job-shop operations where the product is manufactured to order according to the customer's specifications. In this type of manufacturing, the finished product goes directly from manufacturing to shipping for delivery to the customer.

STOREROOM AND WAREHOUSE PLANNING

There are two phases of storeroom and warehouse planning:

1. Original planning—when the areas are set up
2. Maintenance planning—to adjust the areas, facilities, equipment, and procedures according to changing conditions and demands

Planning is therefore a continuing function of management. Changing market demands, seasonal fluctuations, and changing products have an effect on area and space requirements, on the method of handling, and possibly on the control procedures. New developments in storage and handling equipment must be studied to determine the advantage or disadvantage of introducing them into the activity in place of existing equipment.

Storage areas must be planned to make the most effective use of the *space* available, not only the floor area. Ineffective use of storage space, with the exception of warehouse space which may be outside of the plant, and poor location planning can interfere with the flow of materials through the plant, limit the efficiency of the manufacturing activities, and tie up floor area that may be needed for manufacturing at some future time.

Factors of Planning. Each storage area, whether it is for raw materials, goods in process, tools, supplies, or warehousing, must be planned as an individual unit. Consideration must be given to the requirements of the production departments, service departments, accounting department, and the like to develop the plan which is most advantageous to the entire plant. The factors to be considered in storeroom and warehouse planning are much the same. Because there is so much similarity, the word "storage" will be used in the balance of this chapter to mean storeroom or warehouse unless otherwise noted.

In planning a storage area, complete information must be obtained covering:

1. Area and space available for storage and its location
2. Items to be stored in each area—this must be complete and current
3. Storage facilities and handling equipment available and needed

Area Available. The storage area must be thoroughly checked to determine its capacity and limitations. Some of the more important factors to be checked in addition to space availability are:

1. Floor-load capacity
2. Shape and size, including area and dimensions
3. Location in reference to the department it serves—distance from manufacturing area, elevator requirements, and the like

Space Requirements. Space requirements are controlled by the items and volume of items stored and by the method of handling that is used—warehouse trucks, hand trucks, power fork trucks, cranes, and the like. Therefore, a complete listing of all items to be stored should be compiled showing for each:

1. Size and weight of items or container
2. Maximum storage quantity
3. Lot quantities received per receipt
4. Lot quantities issued per requisition or shipping order
5. Transportation distances—receiving and issuing
6. Special handling and storage requirements such as light, temperature, ventilation, bonded storage, and protection from fire

With this information, management can plan the areas, determine the type and quantity of shelves, bins, and racks, and determine the type of material handling equipment needed. The cost of handling the materials with different combinations of storage facilities and equipment can be evaluated. Then the best combination of facilities and equipment can be incorporated into the final plan.

The activity of the items in storage and their controlling characteristics such as size or package weight should be audited periodically to ensure that the requirements have not changed and that the space made available for each item is being effectively utilized.

Handling Equipment. The method of handling materials into and out of storage has considerable effect on the efficiency and cost of the operation. Therefore, a thorough analysis must be made to determine the kind of equipment *most* suitable for handling the materials. Consideration should be given to:

1. The applicability of roller or belt conveyors
2. The applicability of monorail systems
3. The degree to which hand trucks and power forklift trucks can be used
4. The capacity of the equipment in terms of units per hour as compared with the unit demand per hour
5. The equipment cost per unit handled including depreciation and maintenance in comparison with the cost of manual labor per unit

The economics involved in the use of specific types of handling equipment vary according to the volume of materials moved, the care that must be taken not to damage the materials, and the type of package handled. These factors do not remain constant. They may vary between storage areas within the plant, and they will vary as the market demands change. Management should make periodic audits to ensure that insufficient, costly methods are discontinued.

Centralized versus Decentralized Storerooms. There are definite advantages to both centralized and decentralized stores. Which of the two systems should be used depends upon the type of materials stored, their end use, and the degree of protection needed.

Machine shop die storage should be near the machine shop, as should the tool crib and the inspector's gage crib. Materials purchased for use in one department should be convenient to that department. The decision to centralize must be based on the economics involved. Some advantages of both methods are listed below.

Advantages of Decentralized Stores
1. Less transportation time needed to move from stores to the point of use
2. Rush requirements and shortages quickly filled
3. Less waiting time for service
4. Similar or related materials kept together
5. Less interference because of breakdowns of trucks, elevators, and the like

Advantages of Centralized Stores
1. Less supervisory expense
2. Better utilization of storeroom personnel because of the leveling of the work load
3. Less duplication of space for similar items
4. Less total inventory of items that would be stocked in several decentralized storerooms
5. Less total plant space occupied
6. Storeroom records all in one place

Location of Storerooms. The flow of materials from receiving through manufacturing to the shipping dock should be as smooth and uninterrupted as possible. How smooth it is depends upon the layout of the entire plant and the number and size of production material storerooms that are provided. Service and supply materials should never be located so as to interrupt the flow of production.

Storerooms for purchased parts, subassemblies, and goods in process should be located near the point of use but not in the line of flow. Some of the factors that will influence the location of storerooms are:

1. Type of material. Paints, solvents, and flammable materials must be kept in fire-protected areas regardless of where they are used in the plant.

2. Volume of material moved per trip. If material is moved to the production area in truckload quantities, the cost per item is small and the distance moved is relatively unimportant. If the production operator or area material handler gets the materials a few units at a time, travel distance can be a major factor in the labor cost per unit.

3. Materials that require special handling to prevent damage should be transported as little as possible.

The same factors should be given consideration in locating materials within the storage area. Materials requisitioned frequently should be located nearest to the dispensing area. Materials that must be weighed or measured should be as near as possible to the measuring devices to keep the time spent walking and handling at a minimum.

Space Utilization. The method of storing affects the efficiency of the storage area, the degree of service that can be given, and the storage area required. Area is always at a premium. If storerooms must expand because of area requirements, they move into areas that are more valuable for production areas that can be income producing. If warehousing area expands, either it must back up into production areas or additional area must be built or leased. Therefore, it is important that not only the area but the space is used as effectively as possible.

Storage capacity is controlled by the height to which materials can be stacked safely and by the heights of the bins, shelves, and racks. When the area under these conditions becomes inadequate, mezzanine structures can often be provided for the storage of small parts, and additional bins or racks can be installed. This to all intents and purposes doubles the available floor area and uses space otherwise unutilized. The fixed charges per square foot of storage area are reduced considerably.

In areas where pallets of materials are stacked, additional capacity and flexibility can be realized by providing pallet racks that will permit higher stacking. Pallet racks are particularly advantageous when the palletized materials are not strong enough to permit stacking one pallet directly onto another.

Storage Facilities. Materials may be stored in various ways depending upon their size, shape, weight, perishability, and value. In planning the storage of various items, consideration should be given to the advantages and disadvantages of the following "storage aids" as they affect the service and cost of the operation:

1. Floor storage
2. Pallet storage
3. Pallet racks
4. Gravity-feed racks
5. Shelving
6. Cabinets (closed shelving)

Floor storage is usually limited to boxes, cartons, crates, barrels, and the like. In most cases, the stacking is done manually and is comparatively expensive. When large quantities of the same material are stored in this manner, the "first in, first out" method of issuing is usually followed.

Pallet storage is similar to floor storage except that materials are handled on a larger scale by power trucks. With the aid of pallet racks, materials can be stacked higher.

Gravity-feed racks are equipped with rollers or slides on which the materials move progressively to the front of the rack as each unit is removed. They are hand- or hoist-loaded from the back of the rack, depending upon the size and weight of the materials. The racks are designed for specific applications to high-activity materials and are particularly helpful when a large number of small items must be accommodated in a small area.

Shelving is the most flexible type of storage facility. Open shelving can be closed at the ends or backs to separate items. The fronts can be partially closed to make bins. Bin dividers can be installed to accommodate many small items.

Shelves are particularly useful in small-parts storage areas and in tool and maintenance cribs where the volume of parts stored is small.

Cabinets are used when the materials must be protected from dirt and dust and when extra protection from pilfering or unauthorized removal is required.

Automated storage and picking equipment is a major development in material handling. This equipment has proved itself in many installations and should be investigated for use in high-activity warehousing functions. Emphasis is placed on automatic and semiautomatic equipment by the high cost of labor and the competition in many industries. The deterrent to broader use is the initial cost and the length of the payoff period. Nevertheless, the possibility of its use, in all or in part, should be checked against the cost of using the more conventional warehouse storing and picking methods.

LAYOUT OF STORAGE AREAS

The layout arrangement or rearrangement of the storage area can be planned when all information is available concerning the types and quantities of materials to be stored, the space requirements, and the types of storage and handling facilities to be used. With this information collected, the *area and space* required for storing each item and thus for storing all items can be calculated, and the aisle dimensional requirements can be determined according to the type of handling equipment that will be used.

Management Objectives. Management has three objectives in planning the storage layout. They are:

1. To provide quick and efficient service to the production departments and to the market at a minimum cost

2. To provide facilities that can be readily changed or adjusted to compensate for changing conditions

3. To make the most effective use of the areas set aside for storerooms and warehousing

Arrangement of Area. Each storage area must be arranged to provide for the best utilization of the available space. Sufficient area must be provided for aisles, receiving, and clerical record keeping.

Record keeping—desk and table space must be provided in the storerooms for routine record keeping and for inspection or checking of items received.

Receiving area—an area large enough to accommodate materials must be provided as a temporary storage of materials to be checked for quantity, quality, and the like before they can be put into permanent storage.

Aisles—the width of the aisles depends upon the type of traffic. Cribs and storerooms that stock small items, such as tools, gages, stationery supplies, small assembly parts, and the like which are handled manually, require a minimum of aisle space. Areas where pallets and bulk materials are handled by fork trucks require aisles 6 to 10 feet wide to provide room for maneuvering loads into and out of the storage areas. Aisle space can be reduced considerably in some situations, and pallet storage increased, by stacking the pallets at an angle to the aisle.

In general, the main aisles should run the length of the storage area, and the cross aisles or picking aisles should be perpendicular to the main aisle.

Floor and bin layout—in arranging the floor and bin layout, it is best to prepare the general plan first, then to plan the details. There are five steps to follow in planning for the most effective layout.

1. Obtain a dimensioned floor-layout drawing of the area showing obstructions such as columns, permanent partitions, elevator shafts, and stairs.

2. Determine the location of the receiving areas and of the issuing, packing, and shipping areas. Mark these areas off on the floor plan.

3. Determine the sizes of the lots that will be stored, using the item analysis prepared previously.

4. Plan the placement of stock according to its usage. The most active stock should require the least time to handle in picking and issuing and should, therefore, be placed in the storage area nearest the issuing point. The least active material should be at the greatest distance from the point of issue.

5. Plan the assigned spaces to facilitate the most economical handling. The most active items within a material type should be stored at waist to shoulder height. The items with the least activity should be placed in the highest bins. If fork trucks are used in conjunction with pallet racks, the most active items should be at the bottom of the rack to save the time for raising and lowering the forks.

When these steps have been completed, the warehouse or storeroom manager is responsible for implementing the plan. His final step before making any physical changes is to determine the labor cost of the proposed plan to ensure that the anticipated benefits are realistic.

MATERIALS RECORDS

Storage management is responsible for all record keeping concerning the flow of materials through the storage area and for the protection of materials in storage. In brief, the responsibilities are to:

1. Receive materials and count-check them against requisitions, purchase orders, or move tickets.

2. Store materials in the proper location.

3. Enter the quantity received on the inventory records. If inventory records are computerized, the storage manager must see that appropriate information is given to the data-processing center.

4. Make periodic physical count audits to verify the book inventories and take the necessary action to have the records corrected.

5. Make authorized withdrawals, enter the quantity in the inventory record, and adjust the inventory balance. Again, this may be a computerized operation and the manager's responsibility is to transfer the correct information to the data-processing center.

6. Issue materials to authorized personnel for use in production departments or to the shipping department for delivery to the market.

7. Train stock room and warehouse supervisors and personnel.

8. Make periodic checks of material activity to ensure that the layout is conducive to economical operations and good service.

Delegating Responsibility. The manager may delegate some of his responsibilities to foremen and supervisors who in turn may delegate to subforemen or group leaders. This action does not relieve the manager of his responsibility. He is still answerable for the efficiency of the operation, its cost, and the level of service.

Receiving Documents. Storage material receiving documents vary considerably according to their source. However, they can be classified into several groups:

1. Packing slips for purchased materials

2. Bills of lading for purchased materials

3. Receiving department reports for purchased materials

4. Move tickets (as illustrated by Figure 9-2) for goods-in-process stores or finished-goods warehouse

Issuing Documents. Stock should not be removed from the storeroom or the

DELIVER TO UNFINISHED STOCK
PART NO. _____ DATE _____
PART NAME _____ QUANTITY_____
HARDNESS REQ'D. _____ INSPECTED BY_____
FOREMAN'S RELEASE_____ HARD TEST BY_____
REMARKS:_____
_____
_____

FIG. 9-2. *Typical move ticket for goods-in-process stores.* (*Courtesy of the Bendix Corporation, Utica Division, Utica, N.Y.*)

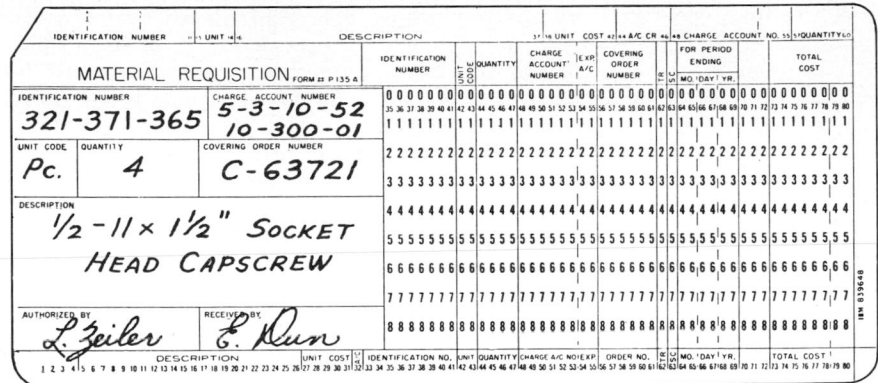

FIG. 9-3. *Material requisition for use with data-processing equipment.* (*Courtesy of Carrier Corporation, Syracuse, N.Y.*)

warehouse without the proper authority. The authority may be:

1. A manufacturing order that stipulates specific materials and quantities
2. Material requisitions
3. Tool requisitions
4. Sales orders

Computerized Control. The trend is toward computerized control of stock movement and inventory. Requisitions that were once prepared on paper and hand-posted to the records are now hard cards and are posted by data-processing equipment. An example is shown in Figure 9-3.

Upon determination of a material requirement, the foreman or material expediter prepares the requisition as illustrated. The requisition is presented to the crib attendant, who picks the material. The recipient then signs the form indicating he has received the material, and the card is set aside in the crib. Once a day, the cards are picked up with similar cards from other crib and storeroom areas and are delivered to data processing.

LABOR CONTROL

Implementing and maintaining a storeroom or warehouse labor control system is a four-step procedure which involves:

1. Setting and maintaining performance standards
2. Reporting work done
3. Preparing labor utilization and cost reports
4. Taking corrective action

The degree to which management can utilize the available labor at an efficient work pace depends on how effectively these four steps are followed.

Performance Standards. Performance standards are used to determine the overall work load, to determine the man-hour requirements at each operation, to measure the work efficiency of the employees as a basis of incentive wage payment, and to evaluate the effectiveness of management.

There are two types of labor performance standards: empirical and measured.

Empirical Standards. Empirical standards are based upon historical records of labor hours or expense as related to shipments, transactions, number of orders, and the like. The records do not indicate the efficiency and skill of the workers during the period which they cover, nor do they show the production time lost because of poor methods and procedures, delays introduced by the workers, improper operation balancing, or even excess personnel. It is impossible to extract from empirical standards the information that management must have to plan and maintain an efficient operation. Empirical standards are perhaps better than none, but care must be taken in using them. They tend to perpetuate rather than eliminate inefficiencies and high costs.

Measured Standards. Accurately measured time standards can be set for every activity performed in the storeroom or warehouse. The degree to which measurement is justified depends upon the number of people involved, the number of transactions, and the potential economies to be realized. Those who have not had experience with work measurement in storeroom and warehouse activities are inclined to believe that the work is so varied that it cannot be measured economically with satisfactory accuracy. This is not the case. Work measurement techniques are available that make it possible to measure the handling activities and the clerical work involved in processing requisitions or orders.

Measured time standards are set on the basis of the work that must be done using the prescribed method of handling each item. Thus, they give an accurate measure of the work load at each operation and make it possible for supervision to preplan and balance the work load to obtain the best labor utilization. They provide the basis for accurately evaluating worker and departmental efficiency.

Operation Balancing. The principal daily responsibility of warehouse and storeroom supervision is to plan for effective utilization of the man-hours available. This is accomplished by balancing the manpower with the work load at each operation. In areas where there are only a few people and they work as a group to perform all operations, there is no balancing problem. In larger activities, however, where groups of employees are assigned to each operation, much time can be lost if the work assignments are not well planned.

The supervisor must determine the work load for each operation and assign his people accordingly. He can get the information he needs for balancing the operations from various sources. In a warehouse, for instance, he can determine the units or types of materials to be received and stored from the manufacturing production schedule. The volume and type of material to be picked, checked, packed, and shipped can be determined from the shipping authorizations, requisitions, and sales orders.

When the supervisor knows what materials and how much of each must be handled, the man-hour requirements can be calculated for each operation. An example of a man-hour–requirement sheet is shown by Figure 9-4. The total standard hours needed for each operation are determined by multiplying the unit time standard by the number of units scheduled. The total is then adjusted to reflect the time needed at the average operating efficiency. The number of people needed is determined by dividing the adjusted time by the normal hours in a work shift.

$$\text{No. of people} = \frac{\text{units} \times \text{time standard}}{\text{efficiency factor} \times \text{hours per shift}}$$

The supervisor is responsible for controlling his labor cost. Therefore, he must know his planned operator and departmental efficiency. These figures are entered at the bottom of the daily man-hours–requirement sheets. In Figure 9-4, the expected operator efficiency is 119 percent. On incentive, the average should be between 115 and 125 percent. The department efficiency is 97 percent. The man-hour–requirement sheet shows the reason for this low efficiency. There are five more people on the payroll than are required to do the work

DAILY MAN-HOUR REQUIREMENT   DATE: *Jan 10*

DEPT: *Warehouse #1*   BY: *H.R.B.*

OPERATION	A WORKERS AVAILABLE ON PAYROLL	B STANDARD HOURS ON SCHEDULE	C OPERATION EFFICIENCY LAST WEEK %	D ADJUSTED HOURS B÷C	E WORKERS NEEDED D÷8 HOURS
RECEIVING	1	18	120	15	2
STORING	6	41	115	36	5
PICKING	13	117	123	95	12
CHECKING	5	33	110	30	4
PACKING	6	36	121	30	4
SHIPPING	4	25	121	21	3
TOTALS	F 35	G 270		H 227	I 30

PLANNED OPERATOR EFFICIENCY = G÷H = 270 ÷ 227 = 119%

PLANNED DEPARTMENT EFFICIENCY = G÷(F x 8 HRS) = 270 ÷ (35 x 8) = 97%

FIG. 9-4. *Man-hour—requirement form used for manpower-requirement determination.*

at the expected 119 percent worker efficiency. The supervisor must find a way to make effective use of the excess personnel. He can:

1. Transfer the personnel to other warehouse or storeroom activities where they may be needed

2. Lend the personnel to other departments within the plant

3. Assign the extra people to miscellaneous operations that must be done in the warehouse but that do not affect the schedule for the day, such as the removal of obsolete or damaged materials, rearrangement of stock on shelves or in bins, and other similar housekeeping operations

Work Reporting. The time each individual spends on each operation and the work accomplished must be reported. The time and production may be reported on a group basis with a group leader or supervisor keeping the records; it may be reported on a daily job sheet by the worker; it may be reported on a separate card for each transaction; or it may be reported by using any combination of these methods.

There is no set procedure for reporting. However, there are three fixed requirements of a reporting system:

1. It must account for all of the time of each worker.

2. It must account for all of the work done.

3. It must require a minimum of the worker's time.

Accurate work reporting is the basis of labor control. It provides the information necessary to determine the efficiency of labor hours used on productive work and the effectiveness of management planning and administration.

Wage Payment Methods. There are two basic types of storeroom and warehouse payment—daywork and incentive. Under daywork, the employee is paid at his base rate for the hours he works, regardless of his productivity. A wage incentive plan encourages increased productivity by providing extra payment for production over a fixed standard. The incentive may be applied on an

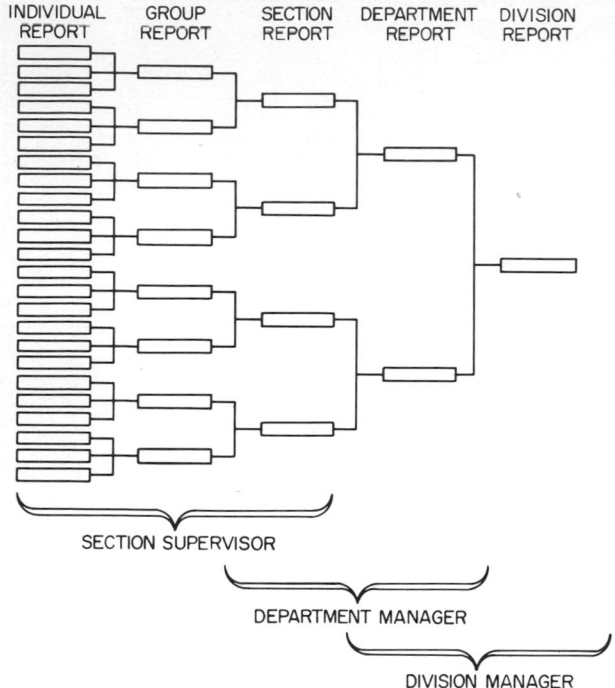

INDIVIDUAL   GROUP   SECTION   DEPARTMENT   DIVISION
REPORT   REPORT   REPORT   REPORT   REPORT

SECTION SUPERVISOR

DEPARTMENT MANAGER

DIVISION MANAGER

FIG. 9-5. *Degree of detail given on labor reports for each level of management.*

individual or group basis. Incentive standards are usually set in terms of time for each operation and are expressed in standard minutes or standard hours. Payment is made on the basis of the standard time earned as follows:

$$\text{Earnings} = \text{hourly rate} \times (\text{units produced} \times \text{standard time})$$

Labor Reports. Storeroom and warehouse labor hours reported on the daily job sheets are summarized and analyzed on the labor report for management to show:

1. Distribution of man-hours worked
   - *a.* Productive hours on measured standards
   - *b.* Productive hours not measured
   - *c.* Total productive hours
   - *d.* Nonproductive and delay hours
   - *e.* Total hours used
2. Analysis of work hours
   - *f.* Standard hours earned
   - *g.* Operator efficiency on standard hours
   - *h.* Nonmeasured hours earned
   - *i.* Total hours earned
   - *j.* Overall (*departmental*) efficiency
3. Control ratios
   - *k.* Nonproductive to total hours available
   - *m.* Standards coverage

The detail of the report varies with the level of management, as illustrated by Figure 9-5, but all labor reports are used to secure labor cost control.

For example, the report for the division or plant manager, shown by Figure 9-6, summarizes the departmental reports and shows the performance of the overall plant operation for the preceding period, usually one week. To provide continuity to the report, the trend of operator and departmental efficiency is shown graphically.

When the manager sees an unfavorable change in overall departmental efficiency, he can find the troublesome department by glancing at the efficiencies shown in column 10. In the example, it is apparent that the storeroom and crib efficiency at 82 percent is far below that of the other departments. This much difference justifies further investigation, and the problem is taken up with the manager of the storeroom and crib department. The report does not show the cause of the trouble; it merely localizes it for questioning.

More detailed reports provide the department manager with information which enables him to:

1. Plan and schedule the work load from day to day
2. Make worker assignments on the basis of area requirements and worker efficiency
3. Balance the work load to provide a smooth, uninterrupted flow of material
4. Pinpoint areas that show a trouble potential so corrective action can be taken immediately
5. Determine if the cost of doing the same or similar work in various areas is different and, if not, why

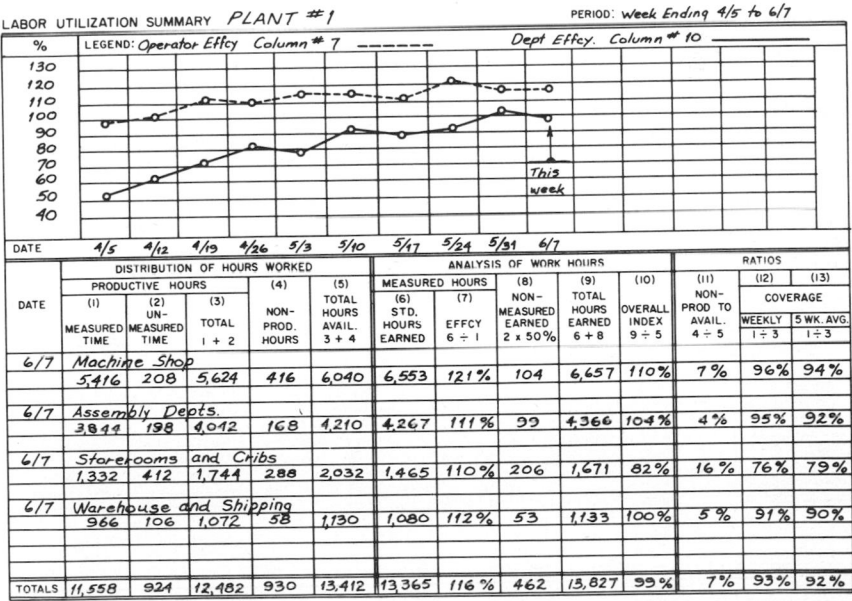

FIG. 9-6. *Weekly labor report for plant manager showing labor utilization and efficiency for each plant function.*

Daily reports in still more detail assist the foreman in:

1. Assigning work to the operators best qualified
2. Balancing his work load
3. Locating trouble areas
4. Determining his manpower requirements

With the exception of the detail given, this report is the same as the department and plant manager reports.

CONCLUSION

The responsibility of the storeroom and warehouse manager is to maintain an efficient, smooth-running, economical operation and give good service to the plant or market. To do this, he must arrange his stock so it is readily available and in good condition, and he must maintain an adequate staff to do the work required at a good pace.

BIBLIOGRAPHY

Bittel, Lester R., *Management by Exception,* McGraw-Hill Book Company, New York, 1964.

Briggs, Andrew J., *Warehouse Operations Planning and Management,* John Wiley & Sons, Inc., New York, 1960.

Eaton, John A., "Blended Automation and Men," *Modern Materials Handling,* November, 1964, pp. 38–42.

McVeigh, E. E., "There's an Angle to Increasing Existing Storage Space," *Flow,* October, 1952.

Muther, Richard, *Systematic Layout Planning,* 3d ed., Industrial Education Institute, Boston, 1962.

"Semiautomatic Warehouse" (editorial), *Factory,* July, 1964, pp. 74–75.

MANUFACTURING MANAGEMENT

CHAPTER ONE

Organizing the Manufacturing Function

W. C. ZINCK *Vice President, Operations, Arbogast & Bastian, Inc., Allentown, Pennsylvania*

What must be done where the material, the machine, and the man meet to make the product so that the cost of goods sold will be competitive? This section, "Manufacturing Management," will outline techniques that have proved successful when properly used to check the efficiency of a present operation, or to set up and manage the production of a new product, or to expand production of an old product. This last provides the golden opportunity to correct past mistakes, to catch up with the proved new techniques, and, with imagination, to take bold steps with developing techniques to the end that the facility will be ahead of its competition until they, too, have their golden opportunities to leapfrog to the front.

The seasoned executive and the imaginative planner must always keep in mind that the same materials, the same machines, and the same skills are available to all at the same prices for equal quantities. Within close limits, the potential direct cost of the material and the direct processing cost of value-adding labor for a similar product can be the same in all plants. The same proved techniques are also available for any manager to set up the support of a production center.

The cost of goods sold varies among plants because the men who control the manufacturing of the product have set up and supported the product-producing centers in such a manner that the overhead applicable to the producing centers varies. It is the application of proved techniques that spells the difference between a low-cost and a high-cost operation. All Andrew Carnegie looked for, he said, as he forged the United States Steel Company, was capable men. This means men who can really follow the dictum of Kettering, "Let the problem be the boss," and see that the right thing is used at the right time in an efficient manner for the correct purpose.

PURPOSE OF THE MANUFACTURING FUNCTION

A successful manufacturing setup requires a clear, coordinated understanding of the part manufacturing plays in the total picture: an understanding of how the other functions—the design of the product; the development of the process; the design of the machines, tools, and apparatus; the procurement and management of the material; and the procurement and training of the production workers—must assist and cooperate with manufacturing. The purpose of the manufacturing function is to make a product that meets the required quality standards with the given tools, materials, and men. Furthermore, there must be a firm acceptance of the fact that when the product has been designed, the facilities specified, the process laid out, the quality standards set, the materials specified, and the machines and tools provided, the cost of goods sold has been fixed, for all practical purposes.

What is left for manufacturing to do is to keep the excess costs to a minimum. For example, when the specifications of the product have been written and the tolerances specified, the work to be done to maintain quality has been fixed. What is left for manufacturing is to keep poor workmanship to a minimum. When the labor contract has been signed and the value-adding operations have been determined, the direct-labor cost has been fixed. What is left for manufacturing is to see that a fair day's effort is received for a fair day's pay, or as one business agent put it, to see that each man works at a "reasonably brisk effort" for a full day, less rest periods. The point is that under modern functional management the major cost-producing factors are not the responsibility of the manufacturing manager. His responsibility is to take what he has been given to do with and use it to make a quality product with the minimum of excess processing costs (idle man and machine time, scrap, rework, and the like) and a low-cost (but not necessarily low-priced) supervisory and staff organization.

The Veto. Because the manufacturing manager has to make do with what he has been given, with all but the value-adding work done by other managers, he must certainly have almost a veto power in accepting what he has to do with. The principle at issue here is fully illustrated by the people assigned to him. Although the manager of human resources (Section 11) interviews, selects, and presents men to the operating foreman, the latter must always have the veto power to accept or reject a man at the end of a reasonable trial period. Otherwise, the foreman has an almost unbeatable alibi for poor workmanship.

The same holds true for other important aspects of manpower, and for material, processes, machines, tools, and apparatus. At any given time, and for the product to be made as efficiently as possible in the future, the maker of the product can demand, if he is to be held fully responsible, that certain things be done in certain ways. Or, at the least, he can demand proof that it is possible to do work at competitive quality and costs with the means provided.

Accounting demands that data be presented to it such and so; selling demands that quality be at a specific level; engineering demands that the design be adaptable to installed facilities. Manufacturing also has its demand. Simply stated, the demand is that what is given to manufacturing to do with to make the products for current sales is given in a form and manner that allows good manufacturing management to add the value with the final result a low cost of goods sold.

A PHILOSOPHY OF MANUFACTURING MANAGEMENT

The basic philosophy of the manager influences greatly the specific application of any principle and its technique. Weaving new techniques into the whole to keep a manufacturing organization efficient is the responsibility of the manager, and a direct reflection of his personality, his motivation, and his creative ability.

Thus, the manufacturing manager will be mindful that any specific technique must be fitted into a going organization with the least friction and change. If a large-scale organization or reorganization is developed, the many manufacturing functions must be ground and polished and fitted together as the manufacturing manager sees it, with due consideration of the personalities, motivations, and creative abilities of the several supervisors who do the actual work.

A principle and its techniques do not stand alone. They have an influence on, and are influenced by, the operating climate at the moment of application. Each manufacturing plant has a distinct atmosphere, a distinct *esprit de corps,* a definite rationale of how things should be done—just as the suggestions in this chapter are a result of the writer's experience and his philosophy of how to run a plant. This philosophy is that the manager is the first assistant to the front-line supervisor. Production, quality, and costs happen only when and where material, machine, and men meet.[1]

The manufacturing manager will be the first assistant to the front-line supervisor to develop him to manage his assigned tasks effectively when the manager does these things, among others:

1. Gives him, in writing, the basic philosophy of management to be followed
2. Allows him his say on a change in policy
3. Permits him to question production schedules
4. Permits him to check production standards
5. Sets definite goals for him to achieve
6. Demands his acceptance of his responsibility for quality
7. Allows him to determine his own disciplinary actions—then sees that he administers them without fear or favor
8. Provides him with opportunities to train himself
9. Forces him to know the capabilities and limitations of his employees, and to assign the work accordingly
10. Demands of him cooperation with, and assistance to, fellow supervisors
11. Prevents him from building his own empire, sufficient unto itself
12. Assigns him tasks that are functions so that he can be held wholly responsible for costs
13. Insists that he operate only from and with written instructions—verbal orders don't go
14. Gives him the respect his position and responsibilities deserve

The wise manufacturing manager places himself in a position to assist his supervisor at the time and place the most good can result—by visiting him on the operating floor, daily, at least.

THE FRONTAL ATTACK ON DIRECT COSTS

The basic step in organizing the manufacturing function is the frontal attack on the direct costs to make the product—that is, plant location, process analysis, and plant layout and design. The location of a plant is a compromise between transportation expenses of raw materials, parts, and supplies into the plant and the transportation expenses of the products sold to the warehouses and dealers; the relative abundance of skilled labor; the going labor rates; the labor climate; the desirability of the community as a place to live; the tax situation; and so forth. Thus, the manufacturing manager must of necessity work closely with the materials manager, the marketing manager, and the manager of human resources. Although facts can be developed for much of the problem, the human

[1] Clem Zinck, "Foremen Who Think Can Trim Your Middle Management Fat," *Factory,* July, 1964, pp. 90–93.

element is a major factor, and the final decision on the location of the plant must be based on broad experience and must result from mature judgment.

The fundamental factors to be considered in organizing to do work efficiently are transportation, delay-storage-idle, and inspection. Aside from new inventions and faster value-adding techniques, every improvement has resulted from an application of a known faster device to reduce transportation, delay-storage-idle, and inspection. The value-adding work is the same whether the parts be made one by one on a standard machine or mass produced on a highly mechanized, or even automatic, single-purpose machine.

For example, a shoe buckle can be made complete on a single-purpose machine with the three sets of tools arranged around a 12-inch dial; or the frame can be made on a blanking press, the tongue on a four-slide, wire-forming machine, and the hand assembly of the frame and tongue and closing the heel of the tongue over the bar of the frame on a bench power press. The value-adding tools are identical and interchangeable with suitable adapters.

Hence, through the techniques of process analysis and plant layout, the manufacturing manager will scrutinize the process and the operation sheets given to him, together with the specifications of the machinery, equipment, and facilities with which to make the product to see that transportation, delay-storage-idle, and inspection have been carefully considered in the design and specifications. Next, he will lay out the process, machines, equipment, and facilities to give the minimum of transportation and delay-storage-idle. Finally, he will build the walls of the building around the process and machinery layout. This is as true for the general-purpose plant as it is for the plant for a specific product in specific quantities. Materials have to be moved, work in process must be stored, stores and stockrooms are needed, and so forth, no matter what the product made or the job-order business sought.

Equipment Management. Maintenance management and equipment replacement analysis have a threefold purpose: (1) to keep machinery, equipment, facilities, and buildings in good operating condition for low excess costs and a uniform quality level; (2) to safeguard the equity of the stockholders; and (3) to keep abreast of competition with new machinery, equipment, and facilities. The manufacturing manager will, therefore, see that maintenance data are submitted in a manner he can use to judge how maintenance is doing its job. He will be sure that the policy and formulas used to figure equipment replacement are as progressive as those of the best companies in the industry. There are tremendous differences in policy and formulas between industries and between plants in the same industry. For example, in one seminar, fourteen different ways were used by representatives of seventeen companies to figure the payout time for a machine replacement.

Quality Control. The manufacturing manager will organize the control of quality and product reliability to give a uniform quality and a satisfactory product performance when he grasps and applies the philosophy expressed by Frank H. Squires, Assistant to the President, Tapp Industries, Los Angeles, California. Squires says, "Actually, 'quality' is not something that can be isolated from the product and controlled. It is the essence of the product—the characteristic for which it is manufactured. The essence or quality of a sword, for example, is its sharpness. . . . Now, a sword without a sharp edge has no salable quality; in fact, it isn't a sword!"[2] To that end, the manufacturing manager will see that the procedures will embody what is necessary of inspection, sam-

[2] Frank H. Squires, "Product Quality: Pretty Good Isn't Good Enough," *Management Review*, October, 1959.

pling, and statistical techniques to maintain at the lowest control cost a quality the customer will buy—with the responsibility for quality resting squarely on the production worker.

The Effective Use of Manpower.　The major contribution that can be made on the cost of a product by the manufacturing manager is to obtain low processing-labor costs by effectively using the knowledge, ability to think and cooperate, and hands of the man himself.　To that end, the manufacturing manager will see that industrial engineering adapts the man to the machine and the material in the most efficient way possible considering the work done.　And where possible, through human engineering, he will have the machine and the material changed to meet the basic requirements for efficient use of the man's senses and physical characteristics.

The manager will insist that in every instance use is made of the *written record*, the foundation of every correct and corrective action, as discovered and presented to management by Frank and Lillian Gilbreth in their paper *Process Charts—The First Steps in Finding the One Best Way to Do Work*, at the annual meeting of the American Society of Mechanical Engineers, December 1921.　The written record takes many forms, besides that of the process chart, but the fundamental principle is constant: "The mere act of investigating sufficiently to make notes . . . invariably results in many ideas and suggestions for improvement. . . ."　When the manager sees that the written record is coupled with the written proposal, the improvement function will be organized effectively.

Although the direct-labor cost is set by the going labor rate, by the time required to do the work with the machines, equipment, tools, jigs, and fixtures supplied to the manufacturing division, and by the assembly work necessitated by the design of the product, there is an area where manufacturing organization has an influence on the effort expended by the worker per unit of time.　The "reasonably brisk effort" may be different in an urban environment than it is in a rural environment; it may vary in different sections of the country and in cities with distinct differences among the ethnic groups that make up the labor force.　However, the manufacturing manager will study his union philosophy on effort, know the mores of his community, and organize the work effort on a sound work measurement technique, based on time study, standard data, or predetermined elemental times, with fair standards open to inspection and thoroughly understood by the workers.

It is the willingness to work that counts.　The measurement of the effort that results from the willingness is the easy part; getting employee understanding and cooperation is the hard part.　Difficult as the choice of the work measurement technique is, the choice of the incentive system to apply is even more so.　Although tradition, mores, and union philosophy are factors to consider in introducing incentive payment, these and, more importantly, the workers' individual temperaments must be judged and evaluated.　In applying an incentive program, there can be no misjudgment without ill effects.　The savings from incentives come only from fringe benefits, after the gross saving in getting "production up to standard" has been attained.　Which system will give the lowest work force in numbers consistent with a uniform quality—a fixed day's task (time incentive), a task and bonus arrangement, a standard-hours system, or a straight piecework system?　The consensus of experience would seem to indicate that what really matters is the validity of the standards, the integrity of their application, and the human touch of the incentive administration.　Name any incentive system, and plants using it with outstanding success can be found.

THE CONTROL OF EXCESS COSTS

It is in labor cost control that the manufacturing manager is really on his own, with only his ability affecting his results. The costs that can be controlled, in the sense that "to control" is "to exercise restraining or directing influence over," are the excess costs of manufacturing, material, direct labor, indirect labor, supplies, and energy (power, light, air, steam, and the like). What the manager does to let the supervisor know what is expected of him, how he is doing, and the help he can expect are the vital things to keep excess costs at a minimum. Questions the manager must consider have been stated by Alex W. Rathe as follows:

1. Do the controls serve
    a. As a guide in planning?
    b. As a traffic signal in operation?
2. Are the controls as simple as possible?
3. Is the scope of the control report identical with the extent of his authority?
4. Have the controls been tailor-made to fit the conditions of his cost centers?
5. Has courtesy been observed? The supporting data of a control should be known by him before his superior sees them.
6. Are there checks and double checks to ensure that negligence does not cause incorrect information?
7. Are management controls available not later than the following day if they are rendered on a twenty-four-hour day, or within a few days if they extend over a four-week or monthly period? Speedy controls serve management; slow ones help historians only![3]

The manufacturing manager can expect the supervisor to do what he alone can do about excess costs at the front line of production only when the manager has met these requirements of responsibility:

1. The supervisor has been told what the cost should be according to a cost standard, a budget, or a similar determination.
2. The supervisor is told promptly what his actual costs are through the medium of an accepted report.
3. The supervisor has regulation over the costs—no requisitions for material, assignment of manpower, or utilization of services or facilities are authorized except by him or his subordinates.

The Vital Few in Cost Control. The manufacturing manager will see that his supervisors understand and use Pareto's curve to control excess costs. In any series of elements to be controlled, a selected small fraction in terms of numbers of elements always accounts for a large fraction in terms of effect. The importance of the vital few lies in the fact that nothing of significance can happen unless it happens to the vital few.

The supervisor is a busy man with his excess costs in production, human relations, and quality. The use of the "vital few" concept will help him keep the total excess costs to a minimum consistent with a wise allocation of his total time on the job day by day. For example, if the supervisor has studied and analyzed his excess costs in material, he knows the vital few that must be controlled to keep the total excess costs to a minimum. When one of the vital few excess costs shows up, the supervisor takes time out immediately to find which one of the vital few causes produced this specific excess cost. Knowing the cause, the supervisor takes the necessary prompt action, whether it is concerned with the quality of the material, the condition of the machine

---

[3] Alex W. Rathe, "How to Set Up Management Controls," Funk & Wagnalls Company, New York, 1948, pp. 61, 62, and 86.

or tool or jig, the skill of the operator, the completeness of information, the accuracy of the specifications, the failure to carry through on an engineering change, or whatever.

A note of caution about the use of the vital-few concept is in order. Be on the alert that one of the trivial many causes has not crept up to become one of the vital few causes and, thus, should be getting prompt attention. The supervisor must be his own detective. He must keep sufficient records of daily happenings by causes to see the trend of each of the vital few causes. If one vital cause is diminishing, and there is no appreciable diminishing of the total excess cost, that is positive proof that one of the trivial many causes has become one of the vital few, and because it has not been given immediate attention, its cost effect has not been lessened. The trend of a total excess cost can be discovered from the cost reports (daily, weekly, or monthly). The trend, or the excess-cost effect of a specific cause of a specific excess cost, must be detected by the supervisor himself from his own record of observations.

A Technique for the Control of Costs. The manufacturing manager himself, no less than his supervisors, must bring the vital excess costs under control. This problem has been faced ever since the first man took over the direction of the first crew to do the first job with their combined efforts. It is a problem common to the president of a company and every executive having any degree of responsibility or authority.

An activity is in need of control when expected results do not always follow specific action. That is, the contradictory factors within an activity must be restrained or directed continuously or periodically if the expected results are to be approached or surpassed. In actual practice, a control is set up when those concerned in an activity agree from sad experience that "something should be done about it."

The technique presented here brings an activity under control through the following basic approach:

1. Assemble all available data on the activity.

2. Study the data and the factors for the activity to find the points which reflect the results of the activity.

3. Secure the acceptance of those points as the basis of control of the activity by all concerned with the activity.

4. Organize a record of all current pertinent data of the activity on a regular, uniform basis.

5. Scrutinize the accumulated data periodically for factors having an adverse effect on the activity, as indicated by the trend of the control points.

6. Then, from experience and consultations, and with full consideration of what the activity is to accomplish, apply restraining and directing influence to eliminate or reduce the adverse factors and thus improve the net results of the activity.

The psychological features of this technique of control are what make it work. The intangible but all-purposeful factor is cooperative acceptance of the restraining or directing influence, because the control points are actual facts, not theoretical standards. The emphasis is placed on doing the best you can about the present situation—trying always to win this ball game, regardless of the score. The principle of this control technique is illustrated in the following example.

It was necessary to increase the personnel of a buffing department. The controlling factor chosen was the rate of improvement of newly hired employees in meeting the standard. Each week the performance records of the new employees were looked over. Those not making a sufficiently rapid rate of progress, in comparison with the new employees as a group, were given special attention to help them improve their effectiveness.

However, it was necessary from time to time to release a trainee because he was not making the grade. One person so released asked, "Why was I fired? Why is the foreman letting me out?"

The reply was, "You fired yourself, Bill. All we have to do is look at the record."

When Bill saw his lack of progress with reference to the other trainees, he was convinced that he had been given a fair chance. He accepted the fact that he just did not have what it takes to be a buffer.

MACHINE UTILIZATION

Aside from the indirect effects on machine utilization that result from the investigation and correction of the vital few causes of excess costs in production and quality, the manufacturing manager's biggest contribution toward making the cost of goods sold competitive must come from the maximum utilization of machine equipment as such. By and large, it is the value-adding work done by a machine that the customer buys, and that direct cost is one that every competitor can meet. It is getting the direct cost with the maximum production per day from all installed machine equipment with the minimum supporting labor and facilities that separates the efficient from the inefficient. To that end, the manufacturing manager will do well to see that the nine basic causes of loss of production on any machine are at a minimum. These losses are:

Machine idle.............................No shop orders to be run
Machine idle.............................Waiting to be set up
Machine idle.............................Being set up
Machine idle.............................Setup completed; waiting for OK
Machine stopped......................Tool adjustment by setup man
Machine stopped......................Waiting for material
Machine stopped......................No operator available
Machine stopped......................Tool repair by toolmaker
Machine stopped......................Machine repair by machinist

One successful control of machine utilization used a chart of utilization as shown in Figure 1-1.[4] The department timekeeper completes a chart for each shift by a personal check of the operating conditions each hour, on the hour. He starts the check at the same machine each hour, and follows the same route in checking each of the twenty-one machines. The activity of each machine is noted by inserting the proper symbols in the spaces reserved for the hour during which the check is made.

As each hour passes, an accurate picture of operating conditions becomes startlingly apparent, even with as rough a check as once an hour. The data literally scream for thought and controlling or corrective action by the foreman, the superintendent, and the manager. What opportunities for better control have shown up? What about the tooling? What about the operating condition of presses? How effectively is the department manned? This is a special application of the written record, with the same result—once all the details are known in proper relation to one another, opportunities for improvement come to mind.

When this writer developed and applied the machine utilization chart

[4] Clem Zinck, "Controls for Coordinating Factory Operations," Funk & Wagnalls Company, New York, pp. 19–24.

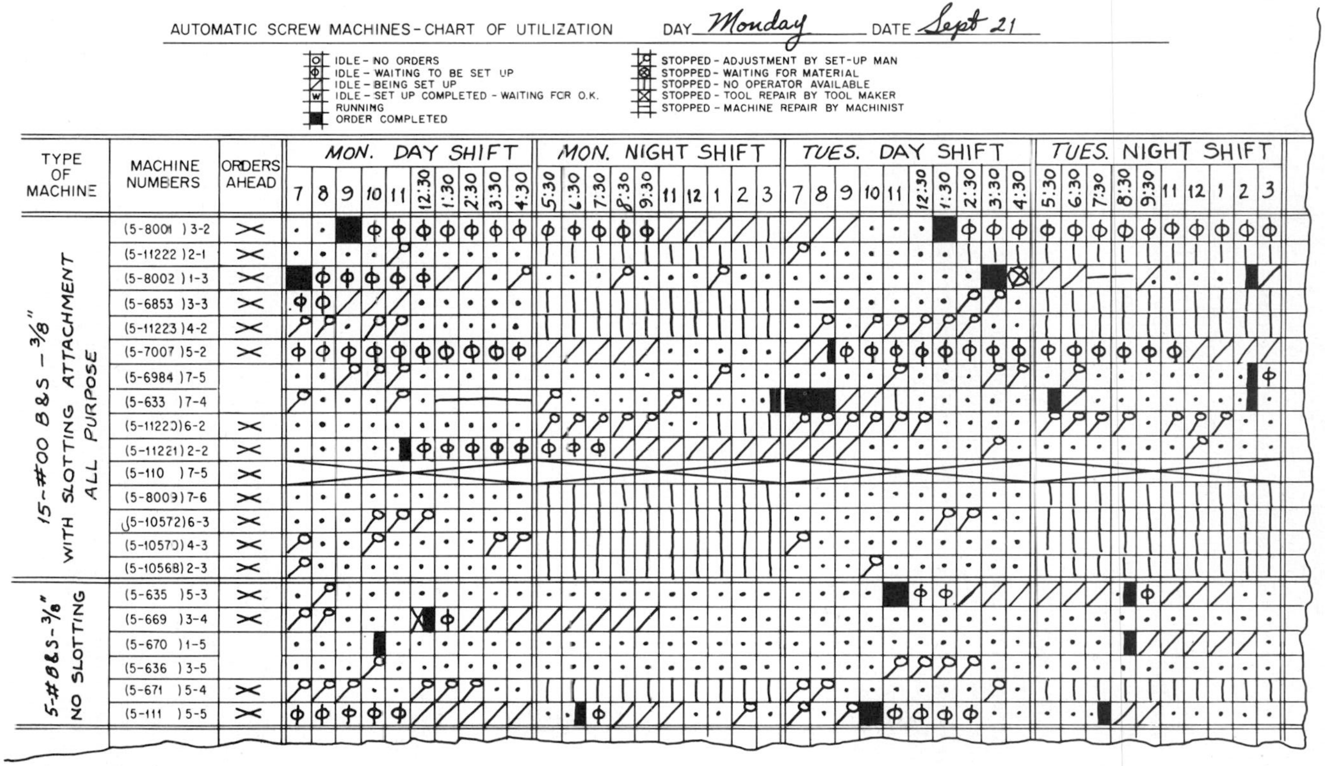

FIG. 1-1. Portion of chart of utilization. Actual chart covers day and night shift for a whole week and the left-hand column lists thirty-two machines.

described above, with pride of authorship he showed it to the president of the company. After a moment's reflection on what one day's chart showed him, the president said, "Mr. Zinck, I now know why I have been forced to provide the plant with two machines to get the theoretical capacity of one. *Do something about this.*" Or again, when the writer took over the management of a recently purchased branch plant and applied the machine utilization chart to the wire-forming department (among others), the foreman said, after a few days, "Me no like the chart." To the reply that the chart was here to stay just because of what it showed up, the foreman said, "If the chart stays, I go." The chart stayed.

SAFETY, WASTE, AND SECURITY

The manufacturing manager will do well to see that his safety program is employee-centered. True, a successful program will save the company money in reduced insurance cost, dispensary costs, employee transfers, loss of production, and so forth, but the program will be successful sooner and have greater cost-reduction returns when it is conducted in such a manner that the employee feels it is mostly for his benefit. After all, he suffers the pain, loses real money, and puts in the boring days of convalescence.

The manufacturing manager will set up waste control, and train himself and all his employees so that the problem of waste is solved in the only way possible—a way of life. Waste opportunities are omnipresent in the use of anything—time, material, supplies, or energy. Waste will be at a minimum when all concerned have the desire not to waste. And that will not come about until every bit of waste observed by a supervisor or a manager is followed up immediately on the spot and the person doing the wasting action is informed of the cost of the waste and the correct thing to do in the future. Not to do that is to condone the waste by failure to act—why worry, the boss doesn't!

The manufacturing manager once again will be employee-centered in organizing for plant security. Here is the age-old penal problem in a mild form. High security can be obtained by tough, police actions at a serious cost of plant morale. Or high security can be earned and obtained by uniform, unbiased treatment of infractions tied in to the education of the employee that plant protection is, after all, protection of his security, immediate and future.

Automation cuts across all the organizational problems of the manufacturing manager. He is forced to automate where he can find ways and means with sufficient payoff to warrant an installation, and he must cooperate with the installation of the other fellow's accepted ideas. To do less is to jeopardize his own job and the security of his company. He must compete or die. At the same time, the manufacturing manager must make the installations of improved equipment with the minimum of disturbance to individual and plant morale—no mean task. His best guides in an automation situation were stated by Louis E. Newman, President, Smithcraft Corporation: (1) It is not enough for managers to be well intentioned—others must recognize their good intentions; (2) tell employees things that they can quickly check for themselves; and (3) give employees a sense of participation in changes affecting them.[5]

The best way to summarize this chapter is to say that Mr. Newman's principles should be the guiding principles of the manufacturing manager as he organizes all phases of the job to make a quality product with the minimum excess costs, using the material, the machines, and the men given to him. The manager must build a smooth organization that puts his basic philosophies into effect,

[5] "Human Values for Management Engineers," *Advanced Management,* July, 1959.

and in doing that, get others to go along with him in the essentials. Others must know and see his intentions, must be able to check the efficacy of what he has told them, must have a sense of participating in his overall planning, and must have an active part in implementing the operating procedures.

The manufacturing manager must be the Andrew Carnegie for his plant—getting good men to handle the functions of plant location, process analysis, and the rest. He must give them their heads to do their jobs their way within broad policies and procedures, guiding and counseling them to better and better individual performances within a coordinated, cooperative effort of manufacturing to do its share of the company's job, while helping the other major company executives to do their jobs equally well.

BIBLIOGRAPHY

Appley, Lawrence A., *Management in Action*, American Management Association, New York, 1956.

Drucker, Peter F., *The Practice of Management*, Harper & Row, Publishers, Incorporated, New York, 1954.

Golden, Clinton S., and Harold J. Ruttenberg, *The Dynamics of Industrial Democracy*, Harper & Row, Publishers, Incorporated, New York, 1942.

Gomberg, William, *A Trade Union Analysis of Time Study*, Science Research Associates, Chicago, Ill., 1948.

Heron, Alexander R., *Why Men Work*, Stanford University Press, Stanford, Calif., 1948.

Heyel, Carl, *Reading Course in Executive Technique*, Funk & Wagnalls Company, New York, 1948.

Juran, J. M., "Universals in Management Planning and Controlling," *Management Review*, November, 1954.

Merrill, Harold F., *Classics in Management*, American Management Association, New York, 1960.

Powell, J. Lewis, "Completed Staff Work: Key to Effective Delegation," *Management Review*, June, 1956.

Schell, Erwin Haskell, *New Strength for New Leadership*, Harper & Row, Publishers, Incorporated, New York, 1942.

Schell, Erwin Haskell, *The Technique of Executive Control*, McGraw-Hill Book Company, New York, 1934.

Viteles, Morris S., *The Science of Work*, W. W. Norton & Company, Inc., New York, 1934.

Yagoda, Louis, "It Takes 3 for Maximum Productivity Improvement," *Advanced Management*, August, 1959.

CHAPTER TWO

Plant Location*

LEONARD C. YASEEN *Chairman, The Fantus Company, New York, New York*

Increased sales, variance in labor costs and productivity, higher freight costs, shifting markets, and the need for more efficient production facilities have been the principal causes for an unprecedented expansion and decentralization of American industry. Unfortunately, most plant location research has been conducted in an atmosphere of guesswork, and decisions are often reached without the application of scientific principles.

Goals can be simply stated: better sales performance and higher profits. But the means to these ends involve increasingly sophisticated concepts. It no longer suffices to deal with marketing problems, for example, on the simple levels of entry into new markets or better coverage of existing ones. The complexities involve depth of penetration, and end-use mix, and even substitution of markets. Unquestionably, technological changes are responsible for much of the rapid increase in plant location activity during recent years. These advances, moreover, have an overriding influence on site selection. New methods of production and new products permit an industry to shift its production points or its markets—or both.

The object of this chapter, therefore, will be to outline a series of suggested steps that are considered accepted practice in determining the best location for a new plant.

RAW MATERIALS AND MARKETS

All manufacturing operations require inbound movement of raw materials and outbound movement of the finished product to the market. Accordingly, it is vital when contemplating new plant location to understand the intricacies of the complex transportation systems which exist.

In plant location study, distance is measured in terms of freight rates. Because the relative costs of assembling raw materials and distributing finished products

* Adapted from *Plant Location* by Leonard C. Yaseen, published by American Research Council, 1956; revised 1960.

will vary from industry to industry, the location pull of raw materials and markets will differ in each problem.   No simplified formula can be provided.   Generally, all other things being equal, an industry will tend to locate at that point where it will possess *the lowest aggregate transportation cost.*

LABOR

The traffic study is a prerequisite for the selection of a broad geographic area.   Once such an area has been determined, specific communities within that area should be explored.   Perhaps the most important single phase of the search will revolve around labor and all its ramifications—cost, availability, stability, and productivity.

It is important that a community have a true and *permanent* labor surplus if it is to receive serious consideration.   The following is a series of steps that are recommended to determine labor availability:

1. Contact the local office of the state employment service.   *Personally* inspect applicants' cards, including age, former position, previous wages, skills, and residence.

2. Determine *qualified* applicants by weeding out applicants who are interested only in domestic, professional, or commercial work; those overage; those eligible for military service; and laborers who may be drawing *temporary* unemployment compensation owing to off-season layoffs.

3. The caliber of available help can often be determined by the number of unfilled jobs.   Hence, compare the number of job openings currently available.

4. Interview present manufacturers to determine what their experiences have been in the community.

5. Examine newspaper want ads over a long period of time to ascertain the skills most in demand.

6. In marginal cases where field investigation and statistical analyses fail to produce conclusive measurement of available resources, it may be necessary to resort to a labor registration.   The purpose of such a registration is actually to solicit applicants for a proposed new plant.

Labor Costs.   Wide variations in wage rates exist among geographic areas, between large cities and small communities, and often between neighboring communities.   Wage scales for unskilled labor and many skilled occupations are traditionally lowest throughout the Southeastern area of the United States. Highest wages appear most often on the Pacific Coast.

Estimates made in 1964 reveal that average family income for all United States families was $7,130 as compared with $7,404 in the West and $5,967 in the South.   In mid-1965, average hourly earnings and average weekly hours for production workers in manufacturing plants approximated the following:

State	Average weekly hours	Average hourly earnings
California.................	39.8	$3.02
Oregon....................	39.7	2.93
Illinois....................	41.2	2.81
New York.................	39.0	2.66
Pennsylvania..............	40.5	2.61
Massachusetts.............	40.1	2.43
Tennessee.................	40.6	2.07
Mississippi................	41.0	1.82
North Carolina............	40.7	1.80

Some economists have advanced the theory that when rural areas become industrialized, wage-rate differentials cease to exist. However, North Carolina's low average hourly rate of $1.80 has been maintained despite the fact that over 290,000 are now employed in the manufacture of textile mill and apparel products alone in that state.

Living Costs. A very important influence on wage rates is the *expenditure standard* of a community. One of the keys to worker satisfaction is the relationship between the contents of his pay envelope and the money he spends to feed, clothe, and house his family.

There is rarely a material difference in the cost of identical-quality food products. There is a tremendous differential, however, in *buying habits* (whether residents are accustomed to buying low-, medium-, or high-quality merchandise). There are huge differences in the *tempo* of spending.

Buying habits can be illustrated by a comparison of food purchases. In 1964, the average family in New York State spent $1,170 in food stores whereas the average family in the state of Tennessee spent $893.

Supporting the intangible variation of expenditure standards and buying tempo are the measurable differences in heating costs, need for winter apparel in colder climes, rentals, community utility and service costs, taxes on the local level, and the like.

Labor Stability. Thorough precautions to assure low production costs are of no avail unless the proposed new plant can operate with continuity and with tranquil labor-management relations. More than one company has been forced out of business because of unreasonable or prohibitive labor demands fostered, in extreme cases, by community-wide antagonisms.

As unions become increasingly stronger, relatively fewer work stoppages are due to the fundamental question of union organization. Wage-increase demands and jurisdictional disputes continue to be important points of conflict, and many stoppages are caused by fringe-benefit demands such as pension and insurance plans.

The question of labor stability must be approached from a positive standpoint. There *are* certain strong indexes of community attitude that should influence its selection. Perhaps the most crucial question that can be asked about a community is, "What is its *past* history?"

POWER

The cost of power as a percentage of total delivered-to-customer costs in most industries is not significant. Hence, the average industrialist will not relocate his plant or establish a branch unit solely because of a power differential. Nevertheless, power costs do constitute a sizable, constantly recurring expense for many industries and should be carefully compared along with adequacy, reliability, and type of service available in the area under consideration.

Most companies considering plant location are prepared to purchase rather than manufacture their own power. The size of the average utility, the diversified load, and particularly the increased efficiency of generating plants have maintained the cost of purchased power at comparatively low levels. If the plant is in operation twenty-four hours a day or a sizable amount of exhaust steam can be used for processing or heating, it may be advisable to generate rather than purchase power. Even so, careful consideration must be given to the capital outlay, cost of failures and repair, and cost of standby service, all of which must be assessed against the total kilowatthour annual bill.

FUEL

Fuel as a locational factor varies in importance from industry to industry. In those processes utilizing fuel as a basic raw material, the plant may be entirely oriented to low-cost supply of the commodity. Substitution of other fuels may be difficult or impossible. Typical examples are the manufacture of coke and coking by-products from bituminous coal and carbon black from natural gas.

Considered along with assembly cost of raw materials and freight rates to markets, fuel has influenced the location of an important segment of heavy industry. For example, the production of 1 ton of pig iron requires the assembly of 1.73 tons of iron ore, 0.41 ton of limestone, and 0.93 ton of coke. Derived from certain grades of bituminous coal, coke is used in the smelting process both as a reducing agent and as a fuel. Orientation to coke sources has accounted for the development of iron and steel making in Pittsburgh and the Mahoning Valley. However, even in this basic industry, changes in pricing policy and shifting markets are reducing the influence of fuel supply on the location of blast furnaces.

Vast differences exist in the quality of coal mined in various areas. Coals found in the central part of the country, for example, are usually of inferior quality to coal found in the Appalachian Highlands, having less fixed carbon and more volatile matter and moisture. Coal in southern Illinois has a much higher carbon content than coal mined just a few hundred miles north. Many manufacturers in comparing the cost of delivered coal fail to assess comparative heating value in terms of Btu's.

It is expected that natural gas will be piped into every important metropolitan area of the United States. The discovery of huge natural-gas reserves in the Gulf Coast and Southwest areas, the improvements made in seamless and welded steel pipe to withstand the high pressure necessary for its transport, and the need of industry for an ideal fuel easily convertible to steam or electric power created a boom. In 1962, 14 trillion cubic feet of gas were produced. Forecasts indicate an average annual increase of 1 million natural-gas customers a year to a total of 45 million in 1970.

WATER

As the population of the nation expands, the demand for water increases. The average United States city requires about 142 gallons per day per capita. Four acres of land are required to support each person in our economy, and, of necessity, over 22 million acres of land in the nation must be irrigated.

New industrial techniques, including the harnessing of atomic power and the production of synthetic fuels, require more and more water. In many industries, the problem of securing usable water at reasonable rates is a pressing one. In fact, water supply is a prerequisite in site selection in steel, paper-pulp, paperboard, wool-scouring, food, and chemical processes.

In the majority of manufacturing operations, public water supplies will prove satisfactory directly from the tap or with minor treatment. The quality of the supply will depend upon the source from which it is derived.

TAXATION

Few industries have relocated their plants solely because of unfavorable state taxes. It is rather the *cumulative* effect of this and other high costs that prompts a manufacturer to consider relocation.

Because of huge budgetary increases, the various states have sought new forms of taxation and have increased existing sales, property, alcoholic beverage, and other taxes. All states have property taxes, but the principal *variation* between states is most apparent in the corporate income tax. As of January 1965, thirteen states assessed no corporation income tax, and thirty-seven other states plus the District of Columbia imposed a tax ranging from 1 to 10.5 percent. Because of differences in application of the income tax and the wide variation in regulations, it is difficult, if not completely misleading, to compare simple tax rates. Some states employ a formula for the apportionment of income, and some do not. Some states permit deduction of Federal income tax, and some do not.

On a statewide basis, the principal source of revenue is the ad valorem or property tax, based on the use or ownership of property and measured by the value of the property. Many states impose some type of real property tax, and some states impose a tax on tangible personal property. Still others assess *intangible* personal property as well, such as money and investments.

The general property tax rate is the total of all school, county, township, and state levies assessed against the property. Because property valuations for assessment purposes are made *on a local level*, municipal or county practices are very important when estimating the total property tax to which a new plant might be subject.

Labor Laws. Virtually all industry is subject to state labor controls, legislation for which may be found in the statutes, codes, and session laws of each state. Because state laws are frequently more stringent and specific, they frequently supersede Federal laws.

The regulation of labor unions, strikes, picketing and boycotting, collective-bargaining agreements, unfair employment practices, anti-injunction laws, and wage and hour laws differ radically from state to state. Interested manufacturers can secure complete digests of state labor legislation from the Department of Labor (or Industrial Commission) of the state capitals. States having labor relations acts include Colorado, Connecticut, Hawaii, Kansas, Massachusetts, Michigan, Minnesota, New York, Oregon, Pennsylvania, Rhode Island, Utah, and Wisconsin. In addition, thirty-five states and Puerto Rico have fair employment practice acts.

A total of thirty-seven states have laws fixing minimum wages. States authorizing administrative minimum wage orders affecting either all or some phases of industry number twenty-six. These states include California, Illinois, Kentucky, Maine, Massachusetts, New Jersey, North Dakota, Oregon, Rhode Island, Washington, and Wisconsin.

Workmen's Compensation Insurance Laws. Workmen's compensation insurance rates are applied against every single dollar the manufacturer expends in payroll. Geographically, there can be a sizable differential to the manufacturer in his annual workmen's compensation insurance bill due to varying state laws. The maximum period for temporary total disability in California is 240 weeks, whereas the worker in the state of New Mexico is entitled to a maximum of 500 weeks. Maximum percentage of wages ranges from 80 percent in Illinois down to 50 percent in Montana and Oregon.

Rates payable on each dollar of payroll can produce sizable differentials depending upon the state under consideration. Iron foundries (classification code no. 3081) are subject to the following rates for each $100 of payroll expended (base rates without giving effect to the individual company's experience benefits):

New Jersey.................. $6.87
Rhode Island................ 5.17
New York................... 4.60
California.................. 3.98
Illinois..................... 3.27
North Carolina............. 2.45
Alabama.................... 1.88
Pennsylvania............... 1.55
Indiana.................... 1.54
Virginia................... 1.49

Unemployment Tax. States vary in their minimums and the employers' actual rate of contribution. State averages range from 0.4 to 4.0 percent.

CLIMATE

It is a proved fact that weather exerts great influence on human efficiency and behavior. More crimes are committed during the hot, humid period between July and August than at any other time of the year. The desire to work and the capacity to produce are affected by weather. Air pressure, humidity, and climatic conditions play a large role in a thousand different industrial processes. Snow, rain, haze, and sunshine all have an effect on both employer and employee, on total costs of doing business, and even on the type of structure necessary to house an industrial operation.

Each area of the United States has a characteristic climate. If certain industrial processes require minimal seasonal differences, the manufacturer would do well to examine southern California. No other section of the country offers so slight a difference between winter and summer temperatures. On the other hand, the Pacific Coast region experiences the greatest degree of fog in the United States.

If a manufacturer requires an area in which he can recruit common labor at competitively low rates, he would consider the cotton belt, whose climate makes it possible to subsist at lower cost than perhaps anywhere else in the country. Heavy winter clothing is unnecessary, heating bills are insignificant, and food crops can be raised at low cost.

Manufacturers utilizing large amounts of floor space in proportion to total number of employees, where maintenance is a factor, will prefer areas where there is no frostline problem and no freeze-and-thaw cycle—thus eliminating continuous pointing up of brickwork, removal of ice and snow, enclosed loading platforms, and the winterizing of trucks and other plant equipment.

In areas where temperatures seldom fall to the freezing level, concerns requiring open storage of drums and other materials can operate with no time lost owing to weather conditions.

FINAL ANALYSIS OF COMMUNITIES

Up to this point in his plant location analysis, the investigator has analyzed his markets; the geographic pull of his necessary raw materials; his labor requirements; the power, fuel, and water costs of various areas; and the effect of various state taxes and laws in his specific operation. He has, through a process of careful elimination, selected a general area within which he must indicate the one outstanding community for his specific manufacturing requirements.

The gathering of *objective* information is fundamental in any important step of this nature. Promotional conversation on the part of civic representatives, no matter how well intended, cannot be substituted for fact. Many questions should be answered before a final decision is reached: What is the true nature of the people of the community? Do they own their own homes? Do they have deeply embedded roots in the city, or is the working force transient and disinterested in the general community good? Have there been many strikes? If so, what were the issues, and what was the reaction of local law-enforcing agencies? How have the tax assessors treated *present* industry? Have zoning boards been sympathetic to the unique problems of industry? Are there hidden but powerful antagonisms and resentment to industry that do not appear on the surface? Is there a traffic problem in the community that has been met with forceful action? Or will employees meet with congestion and delay in getting to and from the proposed plant?

An investigation of the civic administration of the community is important. The form of government, police and fire personnel and equipment, streets and highways, sewers, and, of course, the taxes and budget set up to activate community services all have a bearing on the ultimate safety and protection of a new plant. Cities with a high incidence of crime, abnormal losses from theft and attack against property, or a high ratio of juvenile delinquency should be avoided. Police personnel may be inadequate or civic authorities may be lethargic in combating these abortive influences.

Transportation Facilities. The manufacturer considering decentralization from urban centers must reorient his thinking. He has become accustomed to picking up his telephone and summoning any and all types of transportation service to his plant. In heavily industrialized areas, there is seldom a problem in receiving service. Rather, the only problem is choosing one of the many competitive carriers he wishes to use.

In less industrialized communities, transportation facilities are usually less numerous. It is preferable to locate in a community that is served by more than one major railroad in order to obtain the element of competition, which ensures good service.

For those industries seeking to utilize transit or stop-off privileges for partial loading or unloading en route, it is imperative that responsible carrier representatives be consulted to determine whether or not such privileges will be extended in the community.

For those industries using LCL services, the existence of scheduled merchandise trains is of utmost importance. In this manner, full cars for important key cities will be loaded directly from the local railroad station. Time in transit will be competitive with the most efficient trucking services between the community and these major cities.

It should also be noted that LCL service for small shipments is gradually disappearing in certain areas. Some major railroads are now canceling this service. Future LCL policy of the railroad serving possible industrial sites should be checked.

Becoming more important in the shipping plans of many companies is TOFC (piggyback). Site seekers should find out what plans the railroad offers and whether loading and unloading ramps are nearby.

The existence of motor-truck facilities in the community will tend to reduce time in transit and inbound and outbound movements. Accordingly, those locations should be selected which are trucking gateways if there is much dependence on this type of service. Trucking gateways can be determined readily from various public routing guides. The normal definition of a trucking gateway is as follows: A point at which carriers have pickup facilities including a telephone listed in their company name.

One major caution should be respected. There may be restrictions on the service offered by the carriers in terms of the minimum weight for which they will place a vehicle into the plant. Some carriers insist upon a truckload. Many others have restrictions, such as 10,000 or 5,000 pounds. Those areas served by waterways have distinct competitive advantages. If the industry is of sufficient magnitude so that it can utilize barge loads of inbound commodities or even ship outbound products in this manner, the total annual freight bill can be substantially reduced. The presence of the waterway is another competitive factor in rate making. The industry should be able to negotiate lower rates via all competing types of transportation service because of this situation.

Not to be neglected when investigating water-borne freight facilities, however, is the degree of coordination between water and rail service that can be expected. Those companies presently located near Atlantic port and Gulf port cities have become accustomed to shipping via the intercoastal and coastwise steamships, with corresponding savings compared with overland routes. Removal of the plant facilities to inland communities requires a complete revaluation of the cost of serving markets which were normally reached by use of the lower-cost water service. For example, the differential in rail rates between Ohio points and eastern seaboard cities is frequently insufficient to offset shipping costs from present tidewater locations to West Coast points served via the intercoastal waterways.

Manufacturers are frequently disturbed to find an absence of freight forwarder service in less industrialized areas. This is a natural consequence of the insufficient volume of freight business in and out of the communities to sustain a carloading operation. In other instances, rates from major cities in the manufacturing belt to the smaller communities may be too low to provide a sufficient margin between carload and less-than-carload rates to pay for the costs in assembling and distributing miscellaneous merchandise.

The absence of freight forwarder service is one of those disadvantages of removal to areas with less industrial population. It can be partially overcome by careful review of the company's distribution policy. Pool cars can be consigned to points normally served by forwarder service, and the savings may be of such magnitude that the company will wonder why it has not resorted to such practices in the past. Similarly, local nonprofit pooling associations can be joined which will reduce the total costs on distributing LCL freight.

The investigator should carefully check facilities for parcel post and railway express shipments, as they will undoubtedly differ from those of the present location. Because parcel post regulations are subject to abrupt changes, the existence of other parcel delivery services must also be determined.

The existence of public warehouses can be of utmost importance. There are those inevitable periods in every manufacturing operation when inventories of raw materials or finished products exceed space availability in the plant. During such periods, the manufacturer seeks elbow room in either public space or some short-term lease arrangement. In small communities, the availability of loft space and unused, antiquated industrial structures is limited compared with their availability for storage purposes in urban areas. Unless the manufacturer has local warehouses offering these facilities, he may find it necessary to build such emergency space into his plant at additional cost.

Final Selection of the Community. A proper summation of all the cost factors will provide a dollar-and-cents analysis of the present industrial location and calculated costs at proposed other points of operation. The comparison chart, Figure 2-1, will serve as a guide in comparing the *recurring* annual totals existing in each community.

Basic factors	Present location	City A	City B	City C	City D	City E	City F	City G	City H	City I	City J
Comparison chart											
Total transportation costs:											
Inbound materials..											
Outbound products .											
Total............	$										
Labor:											
Direct production...											
Nonproductive.....											
Total............	$										
Plant overhead:											
Rent or carrying costs, excluding taxes............											
Additional costs due to inefficient layout, lack of siding, etc..............											
Real estate taxes....											
Personal property taxes, etc.........											
Fuel for heating purposes only........											
Total..........	$										
Utilities:											
Power............											
Gas..............											
Water............											
Total............	$										
State factors:											
State taxes........											
Workmen's compensation insurance...											
Total..........	$										
Miscellaneous:											
Other cost factors inherent or peculiar to your present location(s)..........											
Total..........	$										
Grand total.....	$										

FIG. 2-1. *Comparison chart useful for analyzing the theoretical cost factors of several possible plant locations.*

This chart does not take into account the nonrecurring costs of site acquisition, building costs, and the like. Nor does it consider the many intangible factors that deserve great weight and attention, such as community attitudes, labor productivity, background of labor stability, and general surroundings for executives.

Occasionally, superior intangibles together with outstanding community or state cooperation, in the form of bond issuance for new plant construction, tax consideration and financial aid in the building of access roads, and installation of water mains, sewers, and railroad siding as well as free sites, may actually motivate the selection of a location having a less favorable dollar-and-cents advantage. Because every case is different, all interrelated factors must be correctly evaluated to reach a sound conclusion.

SELECTING THE SITE

Probably more mistakes are made because of the temptation offered by a fine site or an attractive building than any other single phase of plant location. An investigation of the specific site is recommended only *after* a community that combines the most favorable economic features has been chosen. Rarely is it necessary to reject a community because of the lack of sites—especially with the definite trend toward peripheral rather than central city operations.

Contrary to general procedure, the first and most important consideration in orienting the proposed plant in the community is the labor pool that is to be employed. Whether the new production facilities are to be near the central district of the city or in one direction or another from the city will depend upon a number of labor-related factors.

Female employees and unskilled male workers usually depend upon local transit systems to reach their place of employment. Where the majority of workers fall into these classifications, the site should be oriented to local bus routes. The amount of the fare, relationship of the site to fare-zone boundaries, and the availability of free transfers will affect recruitment. Although transit authorities are often willing to extend routes to serve a plant offering new riders, careful investigation of the system may reveal blind spots requiring excess transit time and extra fares between the majority of worker residences and the plant site. Also, female labor will be easier to obtain if the plant location offers opportunities for noon-hour shopping.

A factor commonly overlooked is the influence of neighboring industries. Wage rates, radical tendencies, working hours, shift schedules, and even fringe-benefit patterns of manufacturing plants in the immediate neighborhood may have as much effect on the future of the proposed plant as one's own carefully worked out personnel policies.

Generally a site of not less than five times the actual size of the plant is considered the minimum to allow for sidings, loading platforms, truck ingress and egress, parking facilities, storage area, and future expansion. If possible, open land should be available on two or more sides to permit future site expansion.

The adequacy, reliability, and cost of power, water, and gas play an important role in the final selection of the site. If large quantities of water are required for process, orientation to the supply will be a paramount consideration. The underlying aquifers will dictate the amount of groundwater which may be available and the spacing of wells. If surface water is to be utilized, it will be important to calculate the pumping head of the site above the river or stream. The possibility of impounding supplies must be investigated from both a topographical and legal viewpoint.

Barring unusually heavy loads, the local power company will normally extend or improve lines to the site without cost to the industry. City water mains, sewerage lines, and gas mains are less flexible, and their extension may require considerable contribution on the part of the new industry.

It is important for those industries releasing extensive effluent to investigate the local sewage-disposal plant in order to determine whether or not the type of installation is adequate to neutralize the wastes which the plant will release. If streams are to be used for disposal, it is imperative that the industry clear its proposed waste releases with state authorities, perhaps even interstate commissions. Any waste which increases the biological oxygen demand in the stream is certain to meet opposition from state wildlife and game authorities. Discoloration will anger downstream residents.

In an era of uncertainty, it is advisable to minimize the danger of atomic bomb attack by choosing a site at least twenty miles from a vital target, especially if the community has a population over 50,000 and harbors vital war industries. Bridges, airports, railroad marshaling yards, or military installation of any kind are to be avoided.

BIBLIOGRAPHY

Fulton, Maurice, "How Archer-Daniels-Midland Chose Peoria," *Chemical Processing,* January, 1961.

Greenhut, Melvin L., *Plant Location in Theory and Practice,* University of North Carolina Press, Chapel Hill, 1956.

Hoch, L. C., "Intergovernmental Fiscal Competition," *Tax Institute of America,* October, 1965.

Hoch, L. C., and Leonard C. Yaseen, "Is It Over, Over There?" *Dun's Review,* March, 1964.

"Old Factors—New Facets," *Plant Location,* Simmons-Boardman Publishing Corporation, New York, 1965.

Oppel, Edwin I., *A Plant Location Road Map,* American Institute of Banking, New York, May, 1963.

Yaseen, Leonard C., *Plant Location,* American Research Council, Larchmont, N.Y., 1960.

Yaseen, Leonard C., "Plant Location," in H. B. Maynard (ed.), *Industrial Engineering Handbook,* 2d ed., sec. 8, chap. 1, McGraw-Hill Book Company, New York, 1963.

Yaseen, Leonard C., "Techniques of Plant Location," in Carl Heyel (ed.), *Encyclopedia of Management,* Reinhold Publishing Corporation, New York, 1963.

CHAPTER THREE

Process Analysis

BENJAMIN W. NIEBEL *Professor and Head of Department of Industrial Engineering, The Pennsylvania State University, University Park, Pennsylvania*

This chapter presents a method for determining the best way to perform an operation or function, through the analysis of all applicable processes. The method presented involves the tabulation of pertinent parameters in the form of a matrix. Where feasible, probability values are assigned to the important criteria that are under consideration for the evaluation of the processes being considered. Processes with low probability values of needed criteria are discarded from further consideration. Those processes that meet all the criteria established are tested for cost per unit of output in order to determine which process is optimum from the standpoint of functional design, adequate quality, and minimum cost.

DEFINITION AND IMPORTANCE OF PROCESS ANALYSIS

Once the design of any product has been crystallized, it will be necessary to plan the best procedure to produce the product at the quality level desired and in quantities commensurate with demand. Unless the product can be produced at a price that will attract the potential consumer, it is just as much a failure as if the design were incapable of correct function. Thus, process analysis is an important facet of the successful operation of any business or industry. Some kind of product is the output of all businesses, and in a dynamic society, the nature of existing products is continually being changed and new products are being regularly introduced.

With the geometrical increase in technology characteristic of the present era, it is important that process analysis take place not only for determining the best way to produce products that will be made in the future, but also to help assure that the best methods are being utilized in the production of existing products. Thus process analysis may be defined as the systematic procedure of determining the best process or processes for producing a part or performing a service, giving careful consideration to the parameters of quality, quantity, cost, and time of delivery.

Available Processes. In every enterprise, there usually exist several ways to produce a part. For example, to produce twenty-five copies of a form, one could type an original and four copies five times. An alternative would be to type a ditto master and run the twenty-five copies. A similar process would be to use a multilith master or a mimeograph master. Other possibilities include typing an original and obtaining twenty-five copies by means of Verifax or Thermofax or other copying processes. Assuming all these processes were available, it would be the responsibility of someone to plan the process to be used. One process would be superior to the others, based upon the existing parameters.

Similarly there are many ways to produce a ¾-inch hole in a ¼-inch plate. It could be either drilled, drilled and reamed, pierced, broached, electric-discharged, chem-milled, ultrasonically drilled, and so on. One way is the best for a given set of conditions. The process planner has the responsibility of determining the best process to use. It is necessary that he be informed of the available processes within his organization as well as processes that are capable of competing with internal processes that may be located elsewhere.

Outside Processes. Seldom will a manufacturer find it economical to maintain, himself, all competing processes. Usually outside suppliers will provide a source of competitive processes that should be considered during the planning of the process. In considering the outside source, however, the manufacturer must have knowledge of the potential of the processes that the outside supplier has. Effective process analysis will provide this knowledge.

One of the most difficult decisions in process analysis is whether to make a part in the shop or purchase it. Often the supplier's cost is less than the factory cost of the part; in this case, it is generally economical to purchase from the supplier. However, the department may have an overhead charge which has no relation to the manufactured part. If this expense is disregarded, the factory cost may be favorable. Given the same equipment and materials and an overhead charge applicable to the product, the shop should be able to meet competition. Modern process analysis encourages competition between divisions and encourages suppliers to bid in order continually to improve products and reduce costs. Good accounting practice should avoid unrealistic accounting procedures that distort costs and cause unfair competition.

Limited quantities of specialized products such as bearings, machine screws, cotter pins, or lockwire usually can be purchased at less than factory cost. Likewise, it may be more economical to procure specialized processes such as plating and heat treating at a supplier's plant.

DEVELOPMENT OF AN ANALYSIS PROCEDURE

There is no one best process for all applications of a given functional design. Choice of one process over another depends upon many factors which vary from day to day. An economical process may be chosen today, and tomorrow changes in the cost of labor or material, quantity to be manufactured, or equipment available may make it economical to manufacture the part from another material or by a different process. There is intense competition among processes. When the analyst chooses his processes, he must consider the "long-run" economy, or competition will prove his decision wrong. Cast steel versus steel forgings, die castings versus stampings, precision casting versus machining, milling versus broaching, turning versus grinding, welding versus casting—all illustrate such competition. To assist in the making of a decision between two or more processes, a systematic procedure should be followed. Judgment alone will not prove adequate, regardless of one's knowledge of materials and processes. For example, the processes of forging, lost wax, machining, sheet-stock forming, and powder metallurgy all have their proper uses in making gas turbine blades. One analyst can hardly have sufficient experience in all of those processes to prescribe the optimum method, regardless of his mature judgments.

The analyst should be in a position to evaluate possible processes capable of handling the function from the standpoint of the applicable parameters affecting the product. This evaluation should be based on quantitative methods when possible so that decisions will result from objective analysis rather than judgment. When first, second, and possibly third choices have been obtained from objective evaluation, the analyst can consider intangible factors and utilize judgment to specify the process best suited for the design under consideration.

Process Analysis with Few Alternatives. In many instances, the number of alternative ways to perform an operation is limited. There may be but two or three possible ways to accomplish the work. In cases such as this, the use of a right-wrong form (shown in Figure 3-1) will facilitate arriving at the best solution. This form provides for a statement of the general problem at the top. A vertical line then separates the left- and right-hand portions of the form. To the left of this line are placed the positive factors; to the right, the negative factors. The analyst should endeavor to utilize quantitative data for each factor. If a particular process is not capable of maintaining a good surface finish, this fact should be recorded on the right-hand side of the form along with the surface finish that normally is expected. Thus the form should show not just good or bad, but how good or how bad.

After a right-wrong form has been completed, a conclusion should be reached. This conclusion should be either to accept the process for further consideration

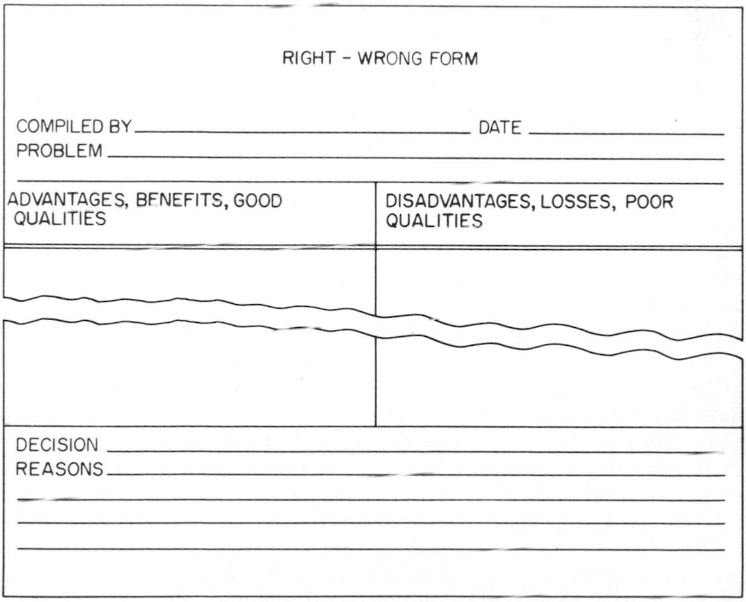
RIGHT – WRONG FORM

COMPILED BY ______ DATE ______
PROBLEM ______

ADVANTAGES, BENEFITS, GOOD QUALITIES	DISADVANTAGES, LOSSES, POOR QUALITIES

DECISION ______
REASONS ______

FIG. 3-1. *Right-wrong form.*

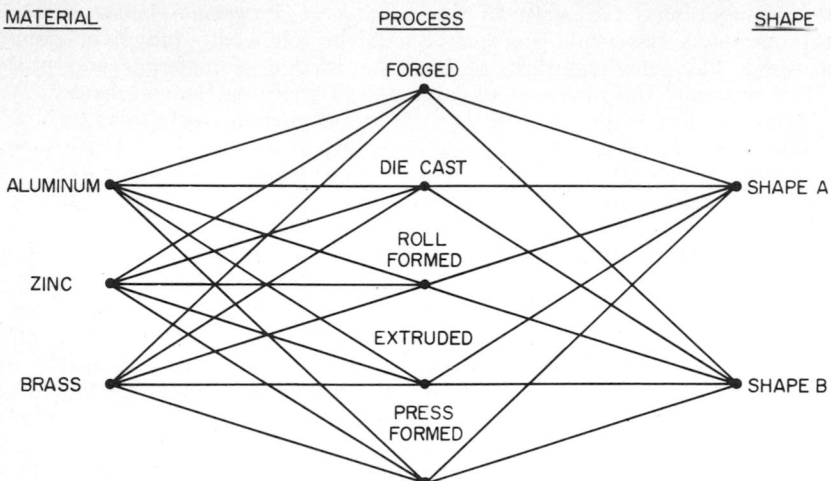

FIG. 3-2. *Alternatives for producing either of two shapes from one of five processes and one of three materials.*

or to reject it.   The reason for the conclusion should be indicated.   One reason, such as cost, may outbalance all others on the form.   The analyst will find this method valuable in selecting processes, materials, and equipment.   A record of the reasons for selection is an aid to writing reports and serves as a check on performance and costs.

Use of Matrices for Tabulating Information.   With the increasing number of manufacturing and business processes becoming available, the problem of selecting the optimum process can be formidable.   Because there may be many possibilities from which to choose, the investigator may have insufficient time to make a detailed analysis of each method prior to getting into production.   And as more technological possibilities are discovered, the number of alternatives increases.   It must be recognized that the addition of one new applicable process will not result in the simple addition of one more alternative.   For example, if a new component can be produced from any of five basic processes (forged, die-cast, roll-formed, extruded, press-formed) and in either of two different geometrical shapes, from any one of three materials (aluminum, zinc, brass), then thirty variations are possible ($5 \times 2 \times 3$).   These alternatives are illustrated in Figure 3-2.   If a fourth material, magnesium, is considered to be a possibility, and assuming it can be produced in the same five ways and in the same two shapes, the number of alternatives increases from 30 to 40 ($5 \times 2 \times 4$).

To tabulate the necessary information related to all available basic processes in workable form, a matrix is recommended.   This permits the tabulation of both the controllable and noncontrollable factors related to a design or situation.   For example, let us assume that we have n applicable processes which we shall refer to as "strategies" and m different design parameters (size, geometry, tolerance level, material, cost) which characterize a specific design.   We can refer to the design parameters as "states of nature."

Each strategy can be identified, that is, $S_1, S_2, \ldots, S_i, \ldots, S_n$.   Likewise each state of nature may be symbolized: $N_1, N_2, \ldots, N_j, \ldots, N_m$.   At the intersection of each row (strategy) and column (state of nature), we can establish an outcome measure which we can identify by O_{ij} ($i = 1, 2, \ldots, n$ and j

$= 1, 2, \ldots, m$). Figure 3-3 illustrates the format of a decision matrix of this sort.

It frequently is convenient to assign probability values to each state of nature tabulated. This can be done from historical data or estimated information. For example, it might be possible to estimate that the probability of a design being produced to a tolerance of 0.0005 is 0.05 and the probability of it being produced to a tolerance of 0.0005 to 0.0007 is 0.15. The P values shown in Figure 3-3 represent the probability values associated with each state of nature. Process analysis can be simplified when the probability of the various states of nature is considered. From an economic or some other criterion standpoint, the size of the decision matrix can be reduced by eliminating from further analysis all states of nature where the probability of occurrence is below some value that is regarded as being significant.

It must be recognized that seldom can an optimum decision be made by consideration of only one "state of nature." Thus, in process analysis, it is usually necessary to consider several states of nature before specifying the most appropriate process to be used for the design under study. States of nature that will have a bearing on most mechanical designs include the general size of the part under study, the geometry of the part, the material being used, the quantity requirements, and the delivery time. Obviously, it is not necessary for the process analyst to consider all states of nature. Only those having a significant effect on the process selection need be considered.

It should be apparent that the decision matrix concept can be extended so as to provide outcomes when states of nature are composed of more than one factor. In such situations, the outcome of the first state of nature and strategy will provide the strategy in the second matrix. The various strategies in the second matrix will be plotted against the second state of nature that is applicable to the design under consideration.

The strategies considered will be all those processes capable of producing the part or performing the function under study. In a typical metal-working

	P_1	P_2	P_3	$\ldots$	$\ldots$	$\ldots$	P_j	$\ldots$	$\ldots$	$\ldots$	P_m
	N_1	N_2	N_3	$\ldots$	$\ldots$	$\ldots$	N_j	$\ldots$	$\ldots$	$\ldots$	N_m
S_1	O_{11}	O_{12}	O_{13}	$\ldots$	$\ldots$	$\ldots$	O_{1j}	$\ldots$	$\ldots$	$\ldots$	O_{1m}
S_2	O_{21}	O_{22}	O_{23}	$\ldots$	$\ldots$	$\ldots$	O_{2j}	$\ldots$	$\ldots$	$\ldots$	O_{2m}
$\ldots$											
$\ldots$											
$\ldots$											
S_i	O_{i1}	O_{i2}	O_{i3}	$\ldots$	$\ldots$	$\ldots$	O_{ij}	$\ldots$	$\ldots$	$\ldots$	O_{im}
$\ldots$											
$\ldots$											
$\ldots$											
S_n	O_{n1}	O_{n2}	O_{n3}	$\ldots$	$\ldots$	$\ldots$	O_{nj}	$\ldots$	$\ldots$	$\ldots$	O_{nm}

FIG. 3-3. *Decision matrix involving n strategies and m states of nature.*

plant, those that will be capable of producing the basic primary design exclusive of secondary operations could include die casting, investment casting, permanent molding, plaster molding, shell molding, drop forging, press forging, cold heading, extruded shapes, impact extrusion, roll-formed shapes, stampings and press-formed parts, powder metals, screw-machine parts, electroformed parts, turret-lathe parts, and rough-machined parts from mill stock.

Outcomes of significance to the analyst will include the adaptability of the process to the state of nature and the cost involved.

EXAMPLE OF PROCESS ANALYSIS

To determine the most favorable basic processes (initial shaping processes) to be used for a broad variety of functional designs, the analyst may establish the following applicable states of nature: size of part, geometry configurations of part, material (ferrous or nonferrous), and minimum quantity required. All other parameters affecting the selection of the basic process are regarded as not being significant and thus will not be considered in the initial process analysis. The strategies involved will be the principal basic processes for shaping metal, as enumerated above.

Since four states of nature are considered significant, four matrices will be developed. The first matrix will plot *size* against the various strategies or available processes. There will be m size classifications. Suppose m equaled five and the five classifications were identified as follows: N_{s1}—weight of each piece is less than 1 ounce (typically more than ten parts can conveniently be held in one hand); N_{s2}—1 to 8 ounces (typically two to ten parts held in one hand); N_{s3}—½ to 12 pounds (one part conveniently held in one hand); N_{s4}—12 to 100 pounds (both hands must be used to control one part); N_{s5}—100 to 200 pounds (two men required to handle one part). Thus all designs produced by this hypothetical business from a size standpoint can be placed in one of five classifications. Outcomes for the intersection of a size classification and a process are identified as either "yes" or "no." For example, the outcome of die casting for size N_{s5} will be "no" since die castings are usually not produced in this size. However, the outcomes for sizes N_{s1}, N_{s2}, N_{s3}, and N_{s4} will all be "yes." If the probability of producing a given size classification can be determined, this information should be added as illustrated in Figure 3-3. In those cases where probability values are considered insignificant, the process can be dropped from further consideration even though the outcome reflected a "yes."

The second matrix developed considers the *geometry configuration*. Perhaps the analyst will be able to identify nine geometries. These classifications may be identified by both verbal and pictorial means to facilitate accurate identification of new designs. These classifications could be identified as follows: N_{g1}—solid or partly hollow rounds involving one or more diameters along one axis. The depth of hollow is not to be more than two-thirds the diameter of the end containing the hollow. N_{g2}—hollow or partly hollow rounds involving one or more outside diameters and one or more inside diameters along one axis. The depth of hollow is more than two-thirds the diameter of the end containing the hollow. N_{g3}—solid or partly hollow shapes other than rounds, such as square, triangular, octagonal, or irregular, involving one or more cross-sectional areas along one axis. The depth of hollow is not more than two-thirds the distance of the major diameter. N_{g4}—hollow or partly hollow solids involving one or more cross-sectional areas along one axis. The depth of hollow is more than two-thirds the major diameter of the hollow. N_{g5}—bowl-shaped concentric geometry. N_{g6}—dish-shaped nonconcentric geometry. N_{g7}—flats with or without configurations.

N_{g8}—flanged geometry. N_{g9}—complex geometry involving two or more of the above configurations.

Here again, outcomes at the intersection of the various processes listed and the nine geometry classifications will be either "yes" or "no." For example, the outcome for the spinning process and the geometry classification N_{g5} (bowl-shaped concentric geometry) will be "yes." Outcomes for all other geometry classifications (N_{g1}, N_{g2}, N_{g3}, N_{g4}, N_{g6}, N_{g7}, N_{g8}, N_{g9}) for the spinning process will be "no."

The third matrix lists *materials* as states of nature. Let us assume that four broad material classes are feasible in our hypothetical plant. These general classes are brass, aluminum, carbon steels, and low-alloy steels. Again, the available processes are the strategies under consideration. As in the case of the first two matrices, the outcome at the intersection of each state of nature and each strategy will be either "yes" or "no." For example, the die-casting strategy at the brass state of nature will indicate a "yes," since brass die castings are feasible. However, at the carbon steels and low-alloy steels states of nature, the outcome will be "no," since the die-casting process is not applicable to ferrous materials.

The fourth and final matrix will have m states of nature related to *quantity*. Let us assume m is equal to seven, with these classifications: $N_{q1} = 10$; $N_{q2} = 100$; $N_{q3} = 300$; $N_{q4} = 700$; $N_{q5} = 1,500$; $N_{q6} = 3,000$; $N_{q7} = 10,000$.

Again, the strategies listed will be the available processes, and the outcomes will be either "yes" or "no." In this case, the quantity state of nature refers to the minimum quantity that is required before it is economical to consider that process. For example, the die-casting process will indicate a "no" for N_{q1}, N_{q2}, N_{q3}, and N_{q4}. N_{q5}, N_{q6}, N_{q7} will reflect a "yes." Here again, probability provides a basis for specifying the outcome. Where the economics of the process reflect low probabilities of utilizing the process on small quantity requirements, the outcome will be "no" and, of course, where high probability values are appropriate, the outcome will be "yes."

To use the matrix procedure as described for the process planning of a new design, the analyst first determines the applicable parameters. These will be an estimate of the size classification, the geometry configuration, the material to be used, and the quantity to be produced.

The first matrix establishes those processes that can produce the design from the standpoint of size. These processes are then reviewed in conjunction with the second matrix to determine which ones will be able to handle the geometry configuration of the design. Those processes that are capable of producing the size classification and geometry configuration under study are then studied in conjunction with the third matrix involved—material.

This procedure is followed with the fourth matrix—minimum-quantity requirements. The result shows those processes that are capable of producing the design based on the established parameters. This listing will invariably be brief since all nonapplicable processes will have been eliminated. In many instances, the procedure outlined will reflect only one process, which will be the one to specify. If more than one process remains to be considered, the analyst will use cost as the principal criterion for his choice. Other criteria, such as current available capacity, expected delivery, and the like, may also be used to assist in the determination of the most favorable process.

Establishing Quantitative Values. To provide a numerical value for the basis of making a process selection, it is feasible to develop decision equations as the outcome for the fourth matrix, rather than "yes" values. These equations replace the "yes" outcomes and are based on expected costs for producing designs of typical difficulty with the material indicated, at the mean quantity level specified.   Thus, the outcome for a given process and a given quantity level reflects four decision equations.   The appropriate equation is used for the material under consideration.   Where a specific material cannot be considered for a given process at a specified quantity level, the outcome will be "no."

The decision equations can be simple or as sophisticated as practical.   Elementary linear equations usually will suffice.   In this case, prevailing labor rates and estimated rates of production for a typical design associated with each strategy provide the basis for predicting direct-labor costs for the quantity required.   Depreciation of capital investment can be based on conventional practice, and an hourly rate to be applied for the number of hours indicated can be determined.   Material costs will be based on current market prices.

With these decision equations established, the analyst will substitute the weight of each piece and the quantity required in the unknown values of the decision equation.   He then solves those equations that are applicable for the parameters established.   The equation that provides the least expected cost will indicate that process worthy of first consideration.

Using the Digital Computer.   Although it is a relatively rapid and simple matter to use the matrix technique in process analysis, considerable planning time can be saved (if much planning needs to be done) by using the digital computer to make the selection.   The format of a FORTRAN formula that may be used is

$$D_t = A_{ijk*}N + B_{ij}$$

where D_t = the value printed in the output (total estimated cost of order through
            primary operation)
     A = the coefficient of N, the number of units to be processed
     i = the size of the part
     j = the process
     k = the material specified
     B_{ij} = the fixed element in the process

The values of A and B will be derived for a specific plant or business.

Where the amount of process planning is not great, the use of matrices as indicated will prove helpful.   In fact, the information on the several matrices frequently can be combined to facilitate the process planning.   Figure 3-4 illustrates how this can be accomplished.   This table reflects information applicable to a given size classification (in this case, metal components less than 1 ounce). Similar tabular information can be summarized for other size components characteristic of the operation of the enterprise.

Once the analyst refers to the correct size-classification data sheet, he then reviews those processes capable of producing the geometry of the part under study.   For example, let us assume the part being analyzed is characteristic of class 4 geometry (see Figure 3-4).   The processes capable of producing this geometry are die casting, investment casting, permanent molding, shell molding, extruded shapes, impact extrusion, roll-formed shapes, powder metals, electroformed parts, and rough-machined parts from mill stock.   If this component were to be made from a ferrous material, we could eliminate the processes of die casting, permanent molding, and plaster molding.   (In Figure 3-4, t refers to nonferrous and s to ferrous.)

Assuming 300 parts were required, it is possible to eliminate shell molding, extruded shapes, impact extrusion, roll-formed shapes, and powder metals from further consideration.

The analyst now considers only those processes remaining to produce the functional design under study.   These are investment casting, electroformed parts, and rough-machined parts from mill stock.   He now solves the decision

Size One—Less than 1 Ounce

Process	Applicable geometry	Applicable materials	Minimum lot size for which process is economical	Decision equation for primary process
Die casting	1, 2, 3, 4, 5, 6, 7, 8, 9	t	20,000	$D_t = .0268N + 515$
Investment casting	1, 2, 3, 4, 5, 6, 7, 8, 9	s, t	300	$D_t = .3205N + 120$ $D_s = .3043N + 120$
Permanent molding	1, 2, 3, 4, 5, 6, 7, 8	t	2,000	$D_t = .1955N + 215$
Plaster molding	1, 2, 3, 4, 5, 6, 7, 8, 9	t	400	$D_t = .2505N + 120$
Shell molding	1, 2, 3, 4, 5, 6, 7, 8, 9	s, t	1,000	$D_t = .1475N + 120$ $D_s = .1313N + 120$
Drop forging	1, 3, 5, 6, 7, 8	s, t	12,000	$D_t = .0542N + 370$ $D_s = .0350N + 370$
Press forging	1, 3, 5, 6, 7, 8	s, t	12,000	$D_t = .0527N + 370$ $D_s = .0338N + 370$
Cold heading	1, 3	s, t	20,000	$D_t = .0233N + 265$ $D_s = .0061N + 265$
Extruded shapes	1, 2, 3, 4, 8	s, t	1,000'	$D_t = .0301N + 140$ $D_s = .0004N + 140$
Impact extrusion	2, 4, 5, 6	s, t	15,000	$D_t = .0323N + 260$ $D_s = .0122N + 260$
Roll-formed shapes	2, 4, 8	s, t	50,000'	$D_t = .0307N + 380$ $D_s = .0077N + 380$
Stampings and press-formed parts	5, 6, 7, 8	s, t	5,000	$D_t = .0342N + 310$ $D_s = .0163N + 310$
Powder metals	1, 2, 3, 4, 5, 6	s, t	5,000	$D_t = .0400N + 210$ $D_s = .0150N + 210$
Screw-machine parts	1, 2, 5	s, t	5,000	$D_t = .0295N + 95$ $D_s = .0081N + 95$
Electroformed parts	3, 4, 6, 9	s, t	100	$D_t = .2124N + 135$ $D_s = .1926N + 135$
Turret-lathe parts	1, 2, 5	s, t	500	$D_t = .0967N + 30$ $D_s = .0735N + 30$
Rough-machine parts from mill stock	1, 2, 3, 4, 5, 6, 7, 8	s, t	10	$D_t = .2017N + 125$ $D_s = .1803N + 125$

FIG. 3-4. *Several matrices combined to facilitate process planning.*

equations for these three processes in order to obtain a minimum D value. The D_s equation is used when ferrous materials are involved and the D_t equation when nonferrous materials are specified. The process giving the smallest value of D will be the process that should be given first consideration. The variable N in the decision equations refers to the number of units to be made.

BIBLIOGRAPHY

Niebel, Benjamin W., *Mechanized Process Selections for Planning New Designs*, American Society of Tool and Manufacturing Engineers Paper no. 737, Detroit, 1965.
Niebel, Benjamin W., and Edward N. Baldwin, *Designing for Production*, Richard D. Irwin, Inc., Homewood, Ill., 1963.
Selector Guide for Primary Forming Processes, AMCP 706, U.S. Army Material Command, Management Engineering Training Agency, Rock Island Arsenal, Rock Island, Ill.
Starr, Martin Kenneth, *Product Design and Decision Theory*, Prentice-Hall, Inc., Englewood Cliffs, N.J., 1963.

CHAPTER FOUR

Plant Layout and Design

RICHARD MUTHER   *Executive Director, Richard Muther & Associates, Inc., Kansas City, Missouri*

Plant layout and design deals with the physical arrangement of factories, plants, warehouses, office and laboratory areas, and commercial establishments. This arrangement involves equipment, the people and their workplaces, the supporting services—utilities, auxiliaries, and communication and control equipment—and the building itself.

Providing these facilities is a responsibility of management. Actual planning of the arrangement and installation of the facilities is generally assigned to some specialist or staff group either within or outside the company. Regardless of where the responsibility lies, modern business and industry are so competitive and specialized that it becomes almost mandatory to have an effective arrangement of equipment, machinery, and buildings to remain profitable. Most well-managed companies recognize both this need and the time required to plan properly to achieve it.

OBJECTIVES OF PLANT LAYOUT

Making a layout plan is not the end result, even of those responsible for the planning. Rather, improved operations, increased output, reduced costs, better service to customers, and convenience and satisfaction for company personnel are likely to be the chief objectives. It is important to target on these real aims; otherwise it becomes easy to drift into the viewpoint that the plan—rather than what the plan can accomplish when properly installed—is the only accomplishment required.

Each planning or rearrangement project will have its own individual objectives, and these will vary with different management viewpoints, operating policies, and the specific considerations surrounding the project. For efficiency in planning layouts and plant designs, it is important that the real objectives be clearly stated early in the planning.

PLANT LAYOUT FUNDAMENTALS

It is probably impossible to achieve all the benefits of a good facility in any one plant. By its very nature, a plant facility involves a multitude of factors and considerations: products, materials, sales volume, people, buildings, services, utilities, and the like. All of these must be blended into a facility that will give the greatest benefits and have the fewest limitations. This is complicated by the short- versus long-time measurement of the benefits and limitations and by the relative importance of each. Essentially, then, a plant facility is a combination of factors or considerations, and its planning rests on a compromise of various isolated benefits and limitations which in turn are modified by time, degree of relative importance, and management attitude or policy.

A manager should aim at certain fundamentals in his facility. These include:

1. Integration—an integration of all pertinent factors affecting the layout
2. Utilization—an effective utilization of machinery, people, and plant space
3. Expansion—easy to expand
4. Flexibility—easy to rearrange
5. Versatility—readily adaptable to changes in product design, sales requirements, and process improvements
6. Regularity—a regular or straight division of areas and relatively even sizes of areas, especially when separated by building walls, floors, main aisles, and the like
7. Closeness—a practical minimum distance for moving materials, supporting services, and people
8. Orderliness—a sequence of logical work flow and clean work areas with suitable equipment for scrap, trash, and wastes
9. Convenience—for all employees, both in day-to-day and periodic operations
10. Satisfaction and safety for all employees

Layout Planning. Basically any layout involves:

1. *Relationships*—closeness desired between various activities or functional areas
2. *Space*—in amount, kind, and shape for each activity or functional area
3. *Adjustment*—of the activity areas into a layout plan

Systematic Layout Planning. One method of dealing with these three fundamental factors is known as "systematic layout planning." SLP is an organized, universally applicable approach to layout planning.[1] It consists of a framework of phases, a pattern of procedures, and a set of conventions.

1. *Framework of phases.* There are four phases through which every layout planning project passes:

I. Location
II. Overall (block) layout
III. Detailed layout
IV. Installation

These phases come in sequence chronologically, and for best results from the layout planner's standpoint, they should overlap. (See Figure 4-1.) The phases recognize the distinction between large projects and small: overall layout involves blocking out departments, buildings, or entire sites, and detailed layout involves the arrangement of specific pieces of machinery and equipment.

SLP follows the philosophy of "planning the whole and then the details." There is a desirable overlap between each phase and the one following it; the

[1] Richard Muther, *Systematic Layout Planning*, Industrial Education Institute, Boston, 1961.

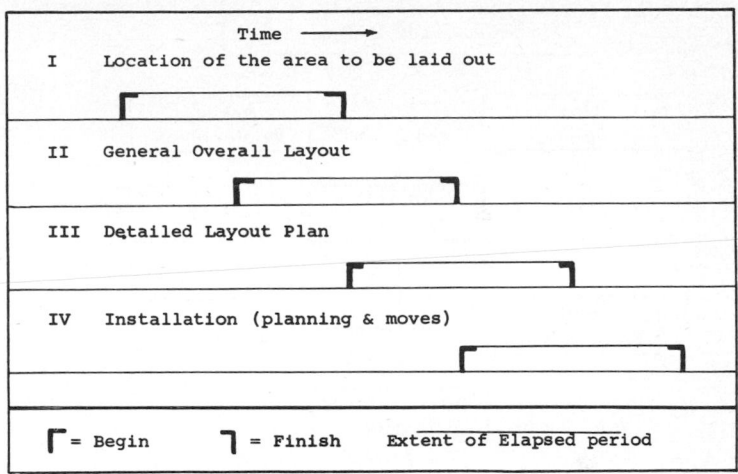

FIG. 4-1. *The four phases of layout planning. Every layout planning project passes through the four phases of layout planning. As shown against the time scale, these phases should generally come in sequence and for best results they should overlap.* (*Courtesy of Richard Muther,* Systematic Layout Planning, *Industrial Education Institute, Boston, 1961.*)

choice of a *location*, for example, will depend in part on what you can do with the *layout* of the facility that will fit into that location.

On large projects, Phase II (overall layout) repeats itself, making Phases II-A and II-B and possibly II-C.

Phase I (location of the area to be laid out) and Phase IV (installation) may or may not be part of the layout planner's responsibility. Phases II and III, on the other hand, are the heart of layout planning.

2. *Pattern of procedures.* The sequence of steps in the full SLP approach calls for a nine-step pattern of procedures. This pattern is used in Phase II (overall block layout) to determine arrangement of buildings, departments, or machine groups. The same pattern repeats itself (in Phase III) in planning the location of each piece of machinery and equipment within each department located in Phase II. As noted above, the phases overlap in practice.

The SLP pattern of procedures is shown in Figure 4-2. It rests directly on our fundamentals of *relationship, space,* and *adjustment.*

Establishing relationships involves three steps: flow of materials, activity relationships, and relationship diagram. It is often logical to establish the relationship between activity areas according to the *flow of materials* through the process (step 1). Of equal importance is step 2, *activity relationships.* Here we establish the closeness desired by supporting-service activities and integrate them with the flow of material. In step 3, we visualize the data established in steps 1 and 2. This takes the form of a *flow diagram,* an *activity-relationship diagram,* or a combination of the two.

Having developed our relationships, we are ready to move to the space portion of our pattern of procedures. Step 4 is the development of our *space requirements.* Seldom, however, are we allowed to have all the space we feel we require. So we have to look at the *space available* (step 5), and balancing the space required against the space available we make a *space-relationship*

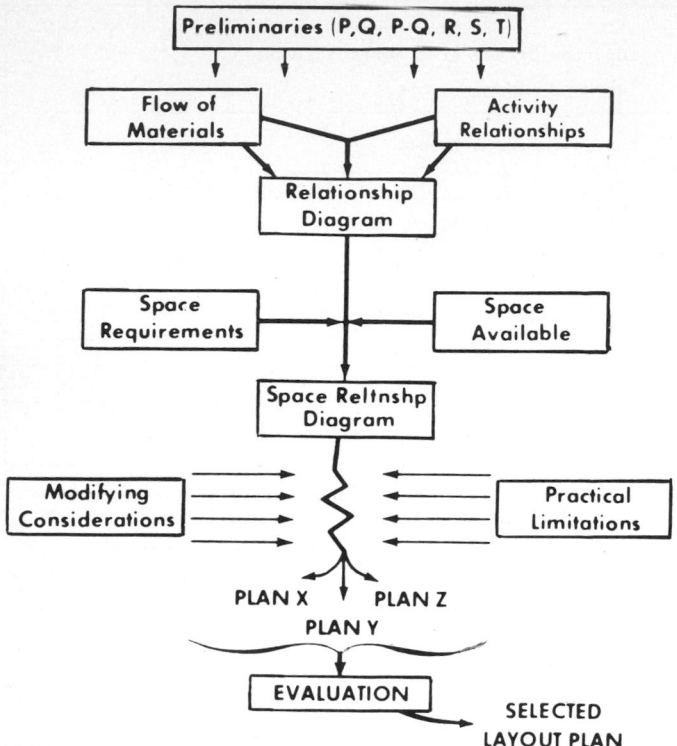

FIG. 4-2. *The pattern of procedures, or steps, for systematic lay-out planning.*

diagram, which is our step 6. In steps 4 and 5, we decided on the allowed space, and by hanging that space on the previously established diagram of relationships (step 3), we have tied together space and relationships.

But the space-relationship diagram still needs adjustment. Adjustment, you recall, is our third basic fundamental. And under adjustment are the *modifying considerations* (step 7) that may cause us to alter our layout. A few of the modifying considerations include the method of handling or transporting materials, storage facilities, utilities, paper-work procedures, and the like. As we adjust our layout based on the modifying considerations, we keep in mind the *practical limitations* (step 8). Practical limitations might be installation costs, existing building features, city codes, safety, and similar restrictions.

The zig-zag line indicates the adjustments—integrating all modifying considerations and practical limitations into our layout—which lead to several logical plans, say plan *X,* plan *Y,* and plan *Z,* or even four or five alternative plans, any one of which will work.

Next, we evaluate our alternative layout plans for both costs and intangibles to get our selected layout plan. This *evaluation* is step 9.

By progressing with this systematic method, and backing up what we do as we go along, we save planning time and management-and-administrative time as well.

An oversimplified pictorial example of SLP in use is shown in Figure 4-3. It illustrates the entire sequence of phases and procedures for a typical project.

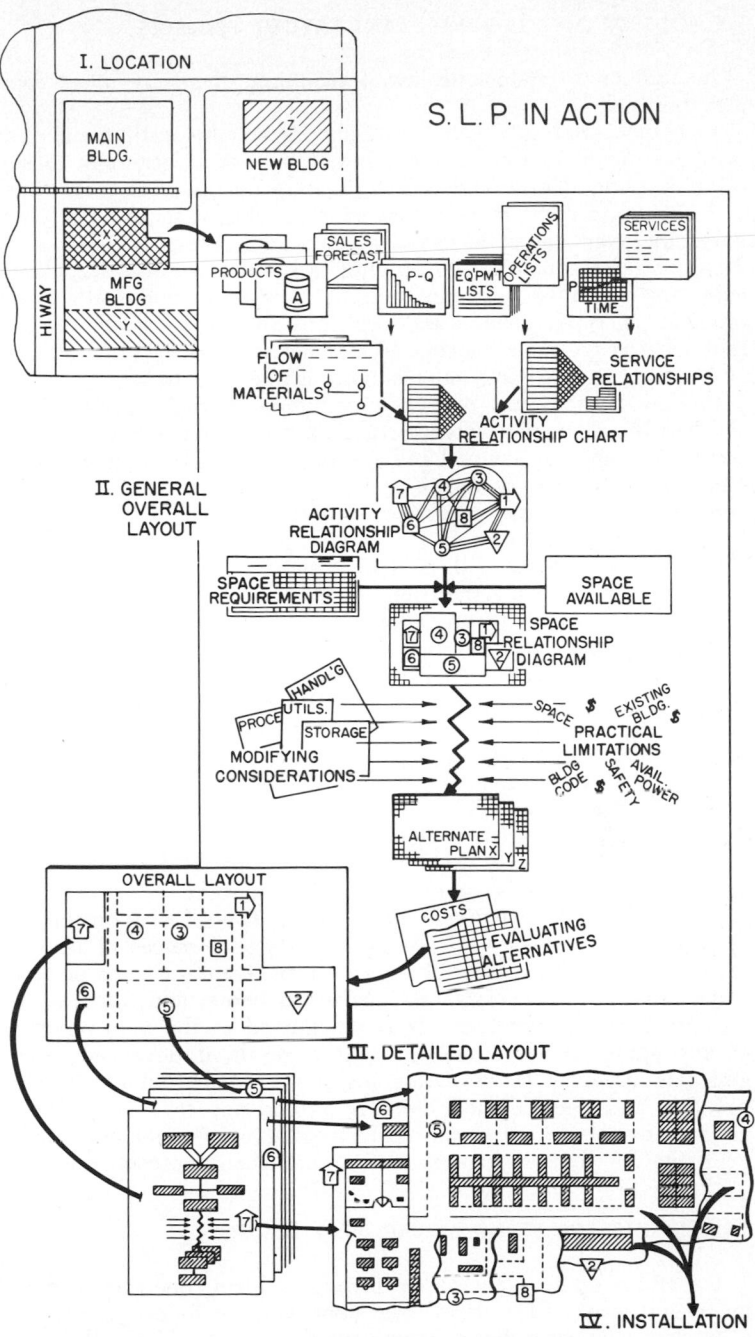

FIG. 4-3. *Illustration showing the phases and pattern of procedures of SLP for a typical project.*

METHODS OF APPROACHING PLANT LAYOUT PROJECTS

In addition to systematic layout planning, there are other approaches which may be used.

1. *Instinct and intuition.* Planning layouts by instinct and intuition is often fast and direct, and saves time; but it is limited generally to situations where there is strong, deep experience and a record of sound decisions in the past.

2. *Find one ready-made.* Magazine articles, visits to other plants, discussions with other company managers at lunch, social events, trade shows, or professional society meetings may lead to "finding" a layout—one that is spoken of enthusiastically and could be "just the thing." New ideas and methods are essential in this day of rapid change and certainly should be sought out; but remember that what is good for someone else is not necessarily suitable for your situation, and without at least some modifications, is likely not to be.

3. *Full participation or "keep everyone happy" approach.* This approach involves the democratic process: get all ideas from everyone, discuss them, and translate them into a visual presentation; then call the group together for comment, make changes, and again solicit agreement of the group. This gives everyone involved a chance to participate and therefore to support the ultimate plan. But this approach draws only on the experience of those solicited; it is usually time consuming; and it does not take advantage of the analytical techniques so important to moving the company forward at the very time it has the opportunity to do something progressive and constructive. Additionally, it tends to put emphasis on discussion and visualization, rather than on problem analysis.

4. *Flow of materials.* Centuries ago, engineers discovered that to move material directly from each operation to the next afforded a logical sequence for control and reduced the cost of handling materials. By analyzing the sequence of necessary moves and arranging the layout accordingly, these benefits are gained. This is the approach most frequently taught in colleges and universities. It is ideal for process-type industries such as oil refineries or flour mills. But this approach is. limited to those situations where there are dominant patterns of materials flow, for it does not fully recognize that relationships other than flow of materials may be equally, or more, important.

5. *Organized systematic methodology.* The SLP approach is a universally applicable methodology. It recognizes the differences of overall versus detail projects, follows a pattern of logical steps, employs a set of meaningful rating codes, symbols, and colors (not discussed here), and forces a systematic documentation of the planning. It is recognized as the most realistically analytical of any approach yet developed. As a result, it develops plans more soundly and gets approvals faster. Learning the approach initially takes time and some training, and once learned there is a tendency to become intrigued with the methodology itself and to substitute mechanics of problem solving for the intelligent analysis and creative synthesis that should accompany the procedures.

ORGANIZING FOR PLANT LAYOUT AND DESIGN

In setting up to plan a new layout or plant, one may organize the project in several ways. The most prevalent way is to assign the responsibility to a trained *staff specialist* or *staff group.* If the individual has extensive prior experience, he should need little help other than a clear statement of what is wanted and the plan-for data on products, quantities, routing (including process), supporting services, and time (and timing). If the individual does not have experience, he should be supported with outside technical knowledge and experience.

Companies not infrequently use a *task force* or *committee*. Although this spreads the participation and presumably focuses on the project the attention of all interested departments, it falls short of expectations more often than not. The looseness and inaction associated with committee projects is offset when a knowledgeable and directive chairman is in charge and when the committee is small, dedicated, and its members individually compatible with each other.

It is possible to let the *manager of the area involved* plan his own layout. After all, he knows most about his operations. The problem is that he is often too close to the problem and too unfamiliar with analytical planning methods. This works most effectively where the manager knows he will be responsible for the long-range operation of the plant and for achieving the budgeted profits or return on investment, and when he is relieved of day-to-day direction and control problems so he can devote full time to the layout planning. Usually, the manager doing his own layout planning is familiar with only his operations, and he misses the big opportunity because of lack of breadth. Moreover, he is likely to be a "doer" rather than a "planner" and therefore short on integrative capacity.

Still another way to organize the project is the use of *outside specialists*. This category includes a variety of management consultants, professional engineers, and architectural construction firms. Properly selected, the specialist can be a real source of aid in factory, office, or laboratory planning. He can handle the entire planning or he can be engaged to guide, assist, and consult with those who are internally responsible. Additionally, an outside specialist can be employed as "added insurance" to audit a layout, or layout alternatives, planned by the firm. If you do go outside, get someone who has broad layout-planning experience rather than insist he thoroughly know your particular industry.

Long-range Plans. The bigger the project, the more important is the need to give sound, long-range plans to your planners. This is especially true when relocating and moving onto a new site. One of the biggest wastes in industry is the failure—when the opportunity presents itself—to make a master site plan, with fully thought-out assignment of its activity areas for future use, its total handling or movement plan, its utilities and auxiliary-services plan, its dedicated areas for buildings and site features, and its communications and coordinative procedures.

For a facility that is supposed to serve a company for, say, the next twenty-five years, current managements are all too prone to wash away their long-range responsibility under the guise of "nobody can know what is going to happen in the future." There is a serious neglect in this area on the part of too many companies. True, we can understand why. Most managers have the opportunity to plan a new site only once in a lifetime. Therefore, it is not surprising that they fail to recognize the long-range implications, and they put the first-needed building in the corner of the new site that is most convenient at the moment.

Shortcomings in Planning. Lack of long-range planning, failure to communicate corporate plans to the layout planners, and hesitancy to start planning sufficiently early are frequent top management faults.[2]

At the same time, the business managers should recognize typical shortcomings

---

[2] This and the next two paragraphs are based on a survey conducted by the Technical Services Division, AMHS, and reported in "Who Lays Out the Plant?" *Modern Materials Handling* Magazine, June, 1963.

on the part of their planners. Most frequently these include: not having the knowledge, ability, and an organized approach to get the planning done quickly and convincingly, and not being as cost-conscious and as realistic or practical as top management and the operating people would like them to be.

One of the most prevalent complaints is time. Planners frequently feel they

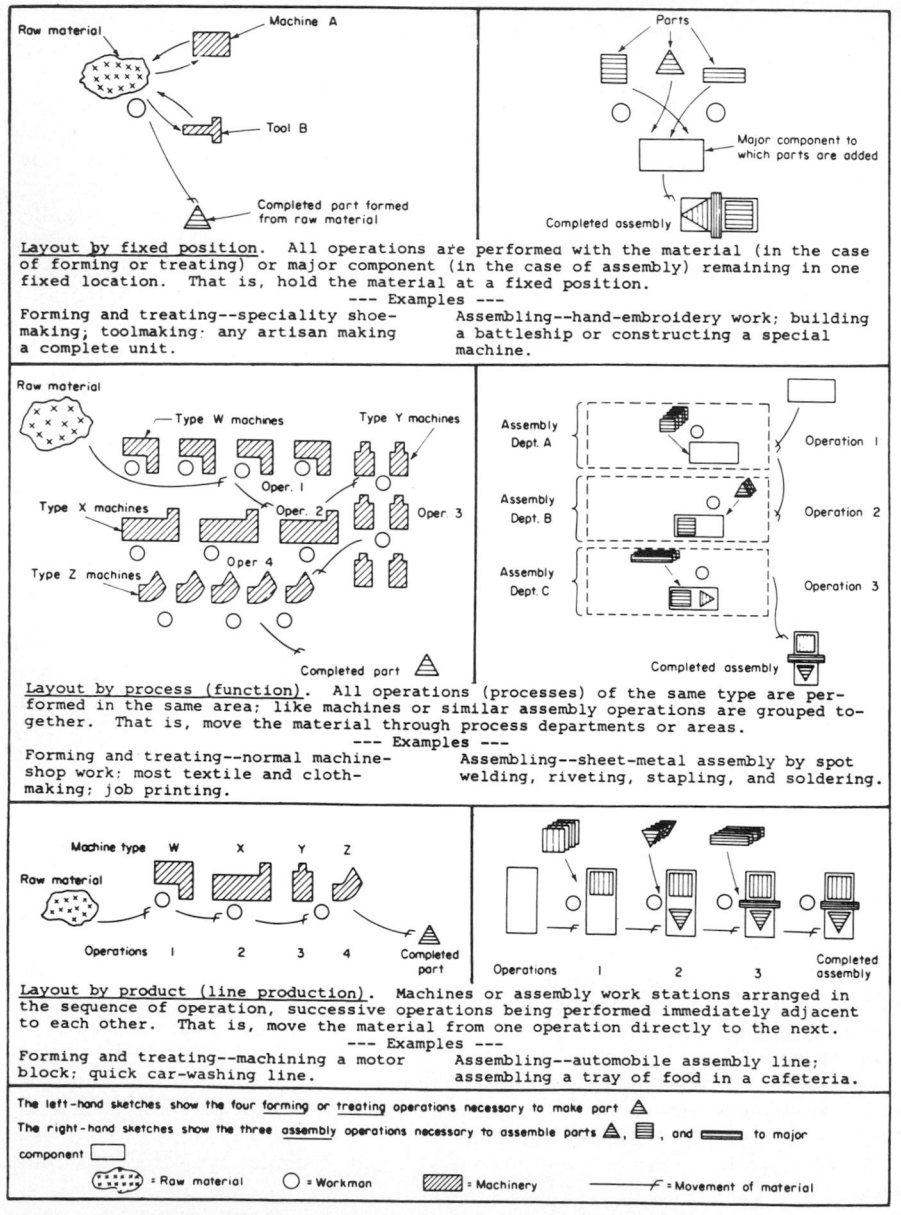

Layout by fixed position. All operations are performed with the material (in the case of forming or treating) or major component (in the case of assembly) remaining in one fixed location. That is, hold the material at a fixed position.

--- Examples ---

Forming and treating--speciality shoe-making; toolmaking: any artisan making a complete unit.

Assembling--hand-embroidery work; building a battleship or constructing a special machine.

Layout by process (function). All operations (processes) of the same type are performed in the same area; like machines or similar assembly operations are grouped together. That is, move the material through process departments or areas.

--- Examples ---

Forming and treating--normal machine-shop work: most textile and cloth-making; job printing.

Assembling--sheet-metal assembly by spot welding, riveting, stapling, and soldering.

Layout by product (line production). Machines or assembly work stations arranged in the sequence of operation, successive operations being performed immediately adjacent to each other. That is, move the material from one operation directly to the next.

--- Examples ---

Forming and treating--machining a motor block; quick car-washing line.

Assembling--automobile assembly line; assembling a tray of food in a cafeteria.

The left-hand sketches show the four forming or treating operations necessary to make part △

The right-hand sketches show the three assembly operations necessary to assemble parts △, ▤ , and ▭ to major component ▭

⬡ = Raw material   ◯ = Workman   ▨ = Machinery   ⟋ = Movement of material

FIG. 4-4. *The classical types of plant layouts.* (*Courtesy of Richard Muther,* Practical Plant Layout, *McGraw-Hill Book Company, New York, 1955.*)

do not have time to do the planning, and managements frequently feel planners take too long.   In reality, this is an outward result; the underlying causes chiefly are those mentioned just above.

TYPES OF LAYOUTS

There are three so-called classical types of layout: fixed position, process (or function), and product (or production line). These are illustrated in **Figure 4-4.**

Fixed position holds the chief material in one place and brings men and machines to it.   This layout is generally most economical when the product or material is physically large and heavy, the quantity of each item is small, and the process is simple.

Process layout, or layout by function, is generally most economical when the process or nature of the operations is relatively complex or costly, the products or materials are diversified or variable, and the quantities of each item are relatively few.

Product layout, or line production, is generally most economical when the quantity is large, the process is fairly simple, and the product or material is relatively standardized, constant, and not too large.

From the above we note that the decision as to type of layout rests chiefly on three elements:

P—Product (or material)

Q—Quantity (or sales volume)

R—Routing (or process or operations)

These three elements determine the flow of materials—a certain P, in a certain Q, moving through a certain R.

Actually, most plants are a combination of these classical types of layout, part of their products being segregated on the basis of their physical characteristics (say size, shape, or metallurgy), and part segregated because of the peculiar processing required (say heat treating or plating), and possibly part divided in terms of fast-moving, standard items versus slow-moving specials.

In other cases, the division may be by special grouping: a particular group of products with a particular grouping of machines which lays out as none of the three classical layouts but, instead, halfway between.   As we would suspect, this type of layout lends itself to conditions where neither P nor Q nor R dominates.

Modern managements look very seriously at the way in which they split or combine their P's, Q's, and R's when a new layout offers them the opportunity. Basically, each of these elements is traditionally under the control of a different department (or division) of the firm.   This means that integration of product design, sales and marketing, and production or process engineering is truly important if we wish to gain major savings in our plant layout.

SPACE REQUIREMENTS

There are at least five ways to establish space requirements.

1. *Calculation.*   Determine the amount of space required for each kind of machine or equipment (including areas for workers, maintenance service, material setdown, and access to aisle); extend this by the number required of each kind of machine; and add in space allowances for aisles and general, or support, areas.

2. *Conversion.*   Determine the amount of space now used for each machine, machine group, or activity area; adjust this to what you should have now to

do the job at present; then convert this by some factor or multiplier to what you will need for the new requirements.

3. *Rough layout.* Prepare a rough detail-layout plan to scale of a proposed or at least possible arrangement. It will in all likelihood not be the final, approved layout, but it will indicate approximate spacing between the activity areas or equipment involved and will allow measuring the rough plan for total area requirements.

4. *Space standards.* In cases where certain types of areas are subject to repetitive layout planning, it is highly practical to develop standard amounts of space. (See also Chapter 1 of Section 14.) This is particularly applicable for office areas or standard, assembly bench layouts. There is danger in using any standard if it is not understood. For example, "300 square feet per car" for parking lots and "75 square feet per draftsman" for engineering offices are good only if we know whether they are gross, net, or somewhere in between. Actually, you can develop your own space standards fairly easily; but be sure to document them so you will know what they mean.

5. *Ratio trend and projection.* There are a number of ratios that can be of value. The first type is "space-to-space ratio." This includes the land-to-building ratios. For example, the ratio of open land to land under-roof may be considered as 3 to 1; if you want 1 acre under-roof with this ratio of land, you will have to obtain 4 acres. Most new plants are established on sites too small for adequate growth, flexibility, parking, green frontage, and out-building services. Ratios of 10 to 1 are considered minimum for new sites by several multiplant manufacturing firms. A minimum ratio of 5 to 1 is frequently suggested for medium-sized plants moving from downtown to the suburbs.

A second type of ratio is the "space-to-function ratio": so many square feet per dollar of inventory, per unit produced, or per employee. A company can build a record of certain meaningful ratios of this kind for several previous periods. From a plot of each ratio against time, a trend of that ratio is noted. This in turn can be projected into the future. Then, by knowing the projected ratio, we can calculate the square feet required for any projected denominator. For example, if 135 gross square feet per office employee is projected, 135 times our five-year-plan figure of 100 office employees means we will want 13,500 square feet of office to meet the five-year plan.

In practice, space requirements are not established quite this simply. In fact, several of the five methods may be employed on the same project. Moreover, space *requirements* must be balanced against space *available.* Here, it may be most helpful to rate each of the activity areas on the relative importance of maintaining its space requirement. The areas rated lowest are squeezed the most when reducing area requirements to a smaller area available. In industrial plants, these areas usually end up being storage, office, and flexible service areas, as compared with production areas or fixed-equipment services.

In any case, it is important to summarize the total plan-for space figures. Space comes in three basic forms: *amount, kind or nature, and shape or configuration.* Most experienced planners want to know early in their projects all three of these aspects of the space with which they are working. As a result, the activity area and features sheet is recommended. Figure 4-5 shows how these data can be recorded.

PLANT DESIGN

There are typical patterns of building arrangement and growth. Those that have proved the most successful over the long pull all have a regularity of

ACTIVITIES AREA & FEATURES SHEET

Plant *Chicago*
Project *472-C3*
By *J.O.Hook* With
Date *7/16* Page *3* of *4*

Activity: **Airlines Food Service** — Total: 2580 ©

No.	Name	Area in Sq. Ft.	"O" Head Clearance (Ft.)	Max. Overhead Supported Load	Max. Floor Loading (PSF/Ft.)	Min. Column Spacing	Water & Drains	Steam	Compressed Air	Foundations or Pits	Fire or Explosion Hazard	Special Ventilation	Special Electrification	Other	Requirements for Shape or Configuration of Area (Space)
A	Office	210	9		100/10	10X	—	—	—	—	—	—	—	—	
B	Food Testing	245	9		100/20	10X	I	—	—	—	—	—	—	—	
C	Wash & Clean-up	280	9	No Overhead Loads	100/20	10X	A	E	—	—	—	I	—	—	
D	Packaging	300	9		100/20	10X	—	—	—	—	—	—	—	—	
E	Pastry/Dessert	320	12		100/20	20X	A	—	—	—	E	—	—	—	Use Existing Hood
F	Hot Food Prep. Salad and Sandwich	240	12		100/20	20X	A	A	—	—	E	—	—	—	Use Existing Hood
G	Raw Food Storage	280	9		100/20	20X	A	—	—	—	—	—	—	—	
H	Ready Food Storage	525	12		100/20	20X	—	—	—	—	—	—	©	—	
J		120	12		100/28	20X	—	—	—	—	—	—	—	—	Rectangular-4½'x27' Hot & Cold Storage Boxes
—	Beverage	50	10		100/20	10X	A	—	—	—	—	1©/	—	—	
11.	Unassigned	10 ©	9		100/-	—	—	—	—	—	—	—	—	—	

Sub-Activities or Areas — rows 1.–15.

Physical Features Required

Relative Importance of Features
A — Absolutely Necessary
E — Especially Important
I — Important
O — Ordinary Importance
- - Not Required

Enter Requirements for Shape or Configuration of Area and Reasons therefore

Notation / References	
a	Does Not Include 360 Sq. Ft. For Rest Rooms
b	Aisle Space To Outside Entrance
c	Need Walk-in Refrigeration
d	Fan Now Being Used

RICHARD MUTHER & ASSOCIATES – 180

No. _____ Activity _____ Sheet *1* of *1*

FIG. 4-5. *Summary recording of area amounts, kind, and shape or configuration. The form is divided into several sections: (a) identity of each activity, (b) area for each activity, (c) physical features pertaining to building structure, (d) features pertaining to auxiliaries or utilities, and (e) any requirements as to the shape or configuration of the areas involved. At the bottom is room for explanation or comments—with letter-code reference to the point needing explanation. (Courtesy of Richard Muther, Systematic Layout Planning, Industrial Education Institute, Boston, 1961.)*

some kind. This regularity can come from equality or consistency in the bay sizes or column spacing, in the overall building dimensions, in the spacing between buildings, or in the blocked-out allocation of space for various types of different activities. Straight, dedicated access ways (roads and main aisles), clearly segregated areas for the increasingly important utility and auxiliary-service activities, and simple rectangular departmental areas are all indications of good planning that lead to regularity.

There are several questions regarding buildings that planners usually must face and answer:

One location or branch locations?
One building or several on one site?
One-story building or multiple floors?
Basement, part basement, or no basement?
Ceiling heights and floor loading?
Module size and/or column spacings?
Degree of permanency wanted?
General type of construction?

As for overall flow patterns, there is generally a choice of:
1. Straight through (in one side and out the other)
2. U-shape (in and out the same side or end)
3. L-shape (in one end and out one side)

Much has been written about the straight-through pattern. It provides a relatively direct and simple flow and allows expansion on both sides with addition(s) of approximately equal amounts of space for each activity.

The U-shape offers the advantage of having incoming and outgoing areas near each other. This usually saves dock space, road paving, and number of doors in the building. It also frequently allows combining receiving and shipping (areas and personnel); puts raw- and finished-goods storage next to each other for occasional convenient exchange of space; and allows moves into production to be combined on the same vehicle as moves out from production, with a resultant reduction in materials handling effort.

The L-shaped pattern frequently is selected in congested areas or where rail lines and/or ship docks dominate one side of a plant. Moreover, the L usually permits a more segregated arrangement of departments and/or product groups, especially likely when there is a mixture of different products and processes in the same plant.

The older a plant becomes, in terms of product life or process life, the more likely it is to depart from one of these three flow patterns and to become a combination. Figure 4-6 shows an example of a combination of L's tied into a long-range expansion plan.

Note, of course, that these patterns hold for total site areas as well as for areas within one building.

Five Components of Plant Facilities. There are five components or physical aspects of an industrial plant:
1. The layout
2. The materials handling methods
3. The communications or controls
4. The utilities and auxiliaries
5. The building itself

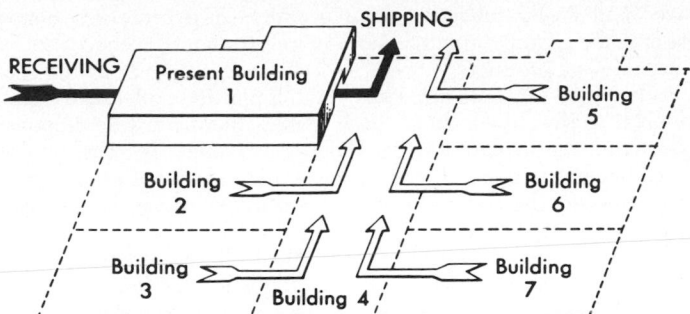

FIG. 4-6. *Plant plans with allowance for future expansion. This plant has plans for the future which will allow it to expand with a minimum of effort to six times its original size.* (*Courtesy of* Factory Management and Maintenance.)

These five components are involved in almost every modern industrial plant. In different plants, of course, different emphasis is placed on each of the five. The important point is that all five must be integrated to have a dynamic, operating plant.

All too often, managers tend to fragment the problem. They may look at layout alone, or isolate the building as a "separate architectural problem." But experience has shown that best results are achieved when each of the five is integrated into a logical whole. In this sense, the layout plan is only one element, or subsystem, of the total plant facility.

DEGREE OF MANAGEMENT INTEREST AND ATTENTION

It is logical that managements should pay attention to plant layout and design in varying degrees. The manager of a cotton gin or a feed mill devotes relatively little attention to this compared with the manufacturer of electrical appliances or automobiles. The extent of this interest depends largely on how continuous a project layout planning is for any company, and this in turn rests on the nature of the conditions involved.

This degree of layout planning continuity can be classified in three ways:

1. Plants requiring *major attention before initial installation* but little or no layout analysis after installation. This condition prevails where the basic methods or processes are expected to remain unchanged during the life of the plant; where installed machinery and equipment—including that used for production, handling, storage, and service—is lasting, very expensive, and very fixed or costly to move; where products and materials are not subject to change for long periods of time; and where plant buildings are less permanent than the process, equipment, and "life" of the products.

2. Plants requiring *periodic or irregular* layout attention. This condition prevails where there are occasional improvements in process or changes in methods; where machinery and equipment is moderately durable, expensive, and fairly difficult to move; where products and materials are occasionally or irregularly changed; and where the plant buildings are about as permanent as the process, equipment, and products.

3. Plants requiring *more or less continuous* attention to layout problems. This condition prevails where there are frequent changes in process and methods—both minor and major; where machinery and equipment is short-lived, inexpen-

sive, and easily moved; where products and materials change frequently; and where the plant buildings are more permanent than the process, equipment, and "life" of products.

Supervision of Facilities Planning. Regardless of the degree of attention and interest as described above, each management must be responsible for supervising its layout and plant-design function. Generally, this involves the following:

1. Specify who is responsible for doing the layout planning.

2. Specify the basic objective and purpose of the layout-planning project (with specific targeted goals).

3. Break down the project into logical phases and steps within phases.

4. Put these phases and steps in sequence; assign a specific person responsible for each; and set a time when each step will be completed.

5. Check the progress at periodic steps, especially during Phases I and II of the project. Certainly management should approve the final decisions made at the end of Phases I, II, and III. (See Figure 4-1.)

6. Make sure planners are not held up for lack of clear data or information from management.

7. Balance forcing accomplishment with getting good results.

8. Do not overlook the opportunity to build morale, improve methods, and sweep away bad practices as a part of the new layout or new plant.

In approving the layout, executives who are asked to approve plans normally look at five things:

1. What does this installation cost? Can we afford it relative to our available funds?

2. What do we stand to gain from this layout? How much will it reduce our basic costs and will it make our work easier, more convenient, and safer?

3. What are the risks in this layout? What could happen to us if certain of the features of the layout went wrong or failed or did not function as planned?

4. How does this layout affect me personally and the group for which I am responsible?

5. How well will this layout or plant function in the long run as well as in the immediate future?

When to Move. It is usually impossible to satisfy everyone when picking a time to make an installation. An attempt can be made to maintain production schedules during the move, or the move can be made on weekends, holidays, vacations, or seasonal lulls when production is normally down. It is frequently advisable to suspend operations and make the move all at once, rather than tangle with everyone during the move.

Once the schedule of moves is set, it is usually better to go ahead than to hold up if something is not quite ready. If we waited until every last detail was completely ready, we might never make the move. And if we tolerate delays, we may find that in the future our installation planners never will meet schedules.

When the move takes place, the layout planner should be on the floor, or at least readily available for consultation with the movers. No matter how well the planning was done, there will be some adjustments or questions at installation time. Therefore, the layout planner must be available to answer questions, interpret plans, inspect for completeness, and secure as early a resumption of production as possible.

Prior to the move, it is well to condition employees for the change. Operating and supporting-service supervisors should be briefed. In some cases, elaborate training of operating people may pay off handsomely, depending in large measure on the relative "newness" of the product, process, and personnel.

BIBLIOGRAPHY

Apple, James M., *Plant Layout and Materials Handling*, The Ronald Press Company, New York, 1950.

Bolz, Harold (ed.), *Materials Handling Handbook*, The Ronald Press Company, New York, 1958.

Briggs, Andrew J., *Warehouse Operations Planning and Management*, John Wiley & Sons, Inc., New York, 1960.

Knill, Bernard I. (ed.), *Material Handling Engineering Directory and Handbook*, Industrial Publishing Corporation, Cleveland, 1963.

Moore, James M., *Plant Layout and Design*, The Macmillan Company, New York, 1962.

Muther, Richard, *Practical Plant Layout*, McGraw-Hill Book Company, New York, 1955.

Muther, Richard, *Systematic Layout Planning*, Industrial Education Institute, Boston, 1961.

Muther, Richard, and J. D. Wheeler, *Simplified Systematic Layout Planning*, Management and Industrial Research Publications, Kansas City, 1962.

Ripen, Kenneth H., *Office Layout Planning*, McGraw-Hill Book Company, New York, 1960.

Yaseen, Leonard C., *Plant Location*, American Research Council, Larchmont, N.Y., 1960.

CHAPTER FIVE

Maintenance Management

SYLVAN L. KAPNER *Manager, Western Division, H. B. Maynard and Company, Incorporated, Los Angeles, California*

Maintaining buildings, equipment, and grounds is an important function of management today. The necessity for adequate maintenance of the facility—whether it be a manufacturing, research and development, service, or administrative facility—is rarely, if ever, questioned. What constitutes adequacy, or the required level of maintenance, however, is often a matter of opinion. Equally important, but seldom questioned, is the degree of effectiveness that the maintenance manager obtains from his maintenance resources. A maintenance budget, or the total amount spent for the maintenance activity, is not a good indicator of either the amount of maintenance service rendered or how effectively the managers of the maintenance activity utilize their resources.

The total amount of maintenance service required, total dollars budgeted or spent for the maintenance activity, and maintenance management effectiveness are interrelated. Whether top management decrees by its actions that the budget shall be the result of need or that the amount of service shall be the result of the moneys available, it nevertheless behooves the maintenance manager to utilize his resources as effectively as possible. The level of maintenance required and the budget established for the maintenance activity are individual matters that vary with the circumstances, conditions, and specific needs of each company. Maintaining a high degree of effectiveness of the maintenance activity follows more or less universal fundamentals, policies, and procedures.

Strictly speaking, most maintenance departments are called upon to perform or contract for considerably more than the term "maintenance" connotes. They often have to erect new buildings or partitions, handle involved rearrangements of equipment, manufacture equipment and parts, design equipment or components, and the like. Because these indirect maintenance functions are usually performed by the same skills and types of labor as the true maintenance functions, however, they can be managed by the same managers using the same techniques and procedures.

Effective maintenance management requires the manager to understand and

I. Maintenance policies
    A. Breakdown versus preventive
    B. Centralized versus assigned
    C. Master rules
    D. Contract maintenance
II. Maintenance organization
    A. Type
    B. Alignment of responsibilities
    C. Levels of supervision
    D. Organization chart and position descriptions
III. Preventive maintenance
    A. Preventive-maintenance routines
    B. Preventive-maintenance records
IV. Work-order system
    A. Preparing
    B. Putting into work
    C. Following up and closing out
V. Planning and scheduling maintenance work
    A. Indirect maintenance
    B. Preventive maintenance
    C. Repair maintenance
VI. Inventory control of parts, materials, and tools
    A. Record keeping
    B. Procuring
    C. Storing
    D. Issuing
    E. Determining and maintaining proper stock levels
VII. Maintenance controls
    A. Developing and applying engineered time standards
    B. Revision of preventive-maintenance routines
    C. Revision of stock control levels
    D. Analysis of maintenance records
VIII. Management information system
    A. Collecting control data
    B. Preparing control reports, graphs, and charts
    C. Interpreting and acting upon control information

FIG. 5-1. *Management functions.*

utilize many of the tools of modern management. This chapter deals with the *managing* of the maintenance activity, employing the management functions shown in Figure 5-1.

MAINTENANCE MANAGEMENT

Maintenance management has as its objective the maintaining of buildings, grounds, and equipment at the optimum level. A good maintenance management system will eliminate the vast majority of breakdowns; it will lengthen, by a considerable degree, the usable life of a piece of equipment; and it will save many dollars through minimizing production operator and equipment downtime. To do this, a considerable amount of *preventive maintenance* is necessary. Therefore, the provision of the proper amount of preventive maintenance is important.

If maintenance management methods have not previously been carefully developed, revising and improving the existing managing philosophies, policies, and procedures following the fundamentals about to be described will usually result in maintenance cost reductions ranging from 15 to 45 percent.

Maintenance Policies. Where *breakdown maintenance* has been the practice, the decision on whether to continue it or to change to preventive maintenance is the first order of business. Not only must plant management understand and agree to put in preventive maintenance as a way of life, but maintenance personnel must understand and agree to it as well. The adoption of preventive maintenance can present problems. The term itself has been used for so long that many who are doing maintenance work believe that they are using preventive maintenance, even though their preventive maintenance may consist of nothing more than a chart showing that certain pieces of equipment are to be lubricated every x hours. This, of course, is far from being the case.

The maintenance manager must therefore win understanding and acceptance of the fact that to have true preventive maintenance it is necessary to establish a comprehensive set of equipment checkpoints and specify the preventive-maintenance operations to be performed according to predetermined frequencies against predetermined schedules. Of course, he must first obtain the backing of higher management.

Breakdown maintenance is, at best, a stopgap measure. It is the fire-fighting approach rather than the fire-prevention approach. Under the breakdown system, repairs are made after breakdowns occur. The breakdowns set the pattern for maintenance requirements. The load placed upon the maintenance organization fluctuates with the number of breakdowns that occur. The result is low overall manpower utilization, high overtime requirements during peak-load periods, and a following rather than a leading type of scheduling system. The emphasis is usually on improving methods of coping with the existing conditions, rather than improving the conditions themselves.

Sound maintenance management cannot possibly embrace the breakdown system.

Although preventive maintenance and engineered time standards are only two of the many functions shown in Figure 5-1, they are the two that will require the most time and effort to develop and install. At the same time, they are the two functions that, once installed and working properly, will produce the greatest savings and other benefits. Therefore, company policies with respect to these two functions should be clearly stated and explained.

Centralized versus Assigned Maintenance. *Centralized maintenance* is exactly what its name implies. All maintenance activities are controlled from a central point, with a great deal of flexibility existing among the maintenance workers. A maintenance man is apt to be assigned almost any repair job within his ability regardless of type of equipment or geographic area in the plant.

Under the *assigned maintenance* approach, each maintenance worker is assigned a certain machine or group of machines. He stays in his area during practically all of his working hours unless he is working in the shop on a part for his machine, and he is personally responsible for the operating condition of his machine.

The decision on which type of approach to recommend depends on the conditions prevalent in the plant. Where the plant is very large and spread out as in a steel mill, where maintenance men are responsible for making highly involved setups such as changing rolls or wires in a paper mill, where equipment is highly specialized in nature requiring intensive training and experience to maintain it, or where the production output is largely due to mammoth and very costly equipment, the assignment of one or more men to look after a specific machine or group of machines is often justified.

Where these conditions are not encountered, centralized maintenance is by far the more preferable. Under centralized maintenance, a greater degree of control is possible with less effort, manpower utilization is higher, maintenance personnel are more flexible, and, generally, total maintenance costs are lower.

Although assigned maintenance does have its place, it should be the exception rather than the rule.

Master Rules. At one time, one of the major firms in the United States adopted eighteen rules for good maintenance management. Subsequently, the United States Navy adopted these same rules. Because they have proved to be sound over the years, they are repeated here as a guide to policy determination.

1. *Set up a responsible organization.* A separate maintenance control group is to be established with overall control of procedures, the conduct of inspections, and analysis of maintenance cost information.

2. *Use a work-order system.* A work-order system is vital to maintenance control. A written work-order procedure requires that every maintenance job be requested on a standard form that becomes the basis for equipment records, job analysis, work scheduling, and work measurement.

3. *Keep equipment records.* An accurate inventory and a permanent record of maintenance work performed are essential.

4. *Analyze and plan jobs.* The importance of an analysis of each repair order should be stressed. A separate planning organization is used which leaves supervisors free for direct supervision and personnel problems.

5. *Make a weekly forecast.* Schedule each week's work by no later than the middle of the previous week. Generally about 75 percent of the work included in the weekly forecast can be performed as specified.

6. *Prepare daily schedules.* Daily schedules for the next day are to be prepared by the supervisors prior to 3 P.M. each day to assure that maintenance men are not required to wait for assignments every morning.

7. *Set up a manpower control.* Manpower control includes a backlog control of manpower requirements that indicates when the crew is too large or too small for the work ahead in each function, area, or shop.

8. *Set up a preventive-maintenance program.* The emphasis should be on doing maintenance work at the best time for all to assure that manpower is continuously busy instead of working in surges.

9. *Use budgetary control.* A maintenance budget is prepared on an annual basis and broken down into monthly subdivisions. The annual budget is fixed; the monthly budget varies to meet changing situations.

10. *Provide material control.* Material control involves the establishment of accurate maximum and minimum amounts for all stores items, material, and replacement parts as well as firm adherence to an established distribution and issue system.

11. *Plan plant shutdowns.* Determine the expected life of various critical components in each equipment group and then plan the shutdown frequency so that overall downtime will be at a minimum.

12. *Set up major overhaul procedures.* Determine the best method for overhaul of any piece of equipment, including a description of the tools, parts, and manpower requirements.

13. *Develop standard practices.* These refer to minor repetitive jobs or shop work.

14. *Use engineered work measurement.* The intent is to evaluate labor performance by recording the amount of actual time taken on a series of jobs and comparing it with standard times established through engineered work measurement.

15. *Improve equipment.* Improvement of equipment is a long-range objective aimed at making maintenance easier by improving design, materials, or manufacture. Standardization of design is also essential.

16. *Train supervisors.* All levels of maintenance supervision should be trained to understand and use maintenance controls. An important part of the training

is to emphasize that maintenance controls have the strong support of management.

17. *Train maintenance men.* Training is essential for new men and for new installations, and when increased effectiveness of experienced maintenance personnel is desired.

18. *Analyze performance and costs.* Analysis of performance and costs consists of continuing self-criticism of the total maintenance effort.

Contract Maintenance. In every maintenance operation, sooner or later a decision has to be made on whether to attempt to maintain a certain type of equipment or to contract it out. Several general rules that will help guide in these decisions are as follows. Consider contracting the maintenance

1. Where specialized skills are required

2. Where specialized equipment is required

3. Where the equipment under consideration is not directly involved with the production of the company's product or service, or where it can easily be circumvented

4. Where the estimated man-hours per year are low

5. Where maintenance can be tied to leasing equipment more economically than purchasing the equipment

ORGANIZATION

Because the total size of most maintenance organizations is relatively small compared with the size of the production departments, the internal organization problems of the maintenance department are often neglected. To a lesser extent, the organization relationship of the head of the maintenance department and his people with the operating or production departments is often hazy.

The strong emphasis on repairing a breakdown with a minimum of delay often causes the maintenance manager to lose control over his personnel. In some instances, maintenance people work directly for production department supervisors, and the head of maintenance has only functional authority over them. Obviously, a coordinated and controlled maintenance activity cannot exist under these conditions.

The relationship of the maintenance manager to the production department supervisors should be clarified if a clean-cut relationship does not exist. Normally, the head of maintenance should report to the works manager or plant manager rather than to one of the lesser production managers such as a facilities manager or the manager of manufacturing engineering.

Within the maintenance organization itself, there must be a fairly clean-cut division of responsibilities and duties. This can usually best be accomplished by establishing a line-and-staff type of organization. The maintenance functions should be separated from the administrative and control functions. This means the creation of a maintenance control section. This permits the separation of staff functions, which are primarily clerical and analytical by nature, from the line maintenance functions, which are primarily supervisory.

Depending upon the size of the organization, the line function may be split or combined. If the size of the organization permits splitting the line function, it should be split on the basis of maintenance categories; that is, (1) buildings, (2) building equipment, (3) manufacturing and processing equipment, and (4) custodial and grounds. The first three may be combined in the smaller organization, the first two in a slightly larger group, and four separations made in the very large organization. The amount and type of maintenance control varies more along these functional lines than it does either by production depart-

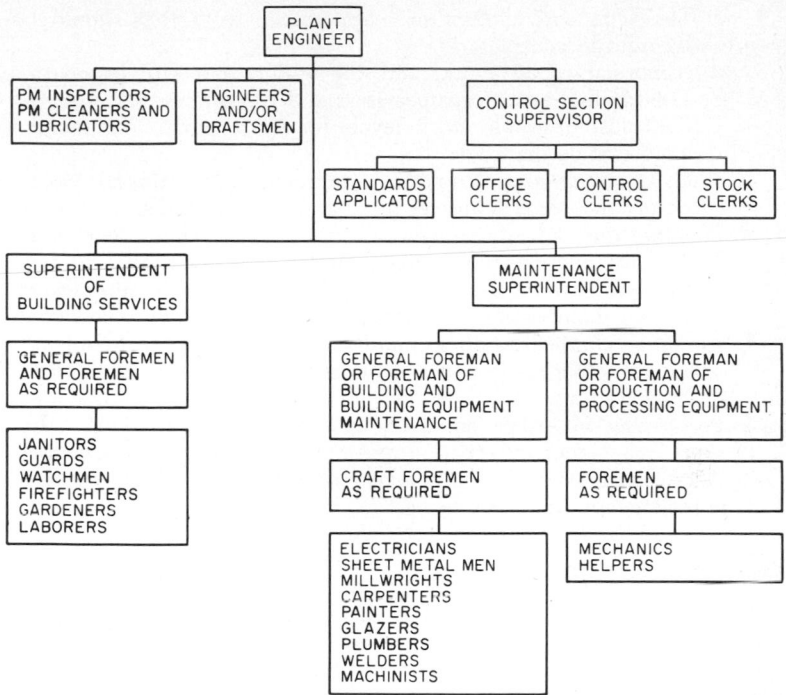

FIG. 5-2. *Functional maintenance organization.*

ment or by craft. A typical functional organization chart is shown in Figure 5-2.

The organization, if it is to function effectively, must be known to all members of the maintenance department and to the other management personnel in the organization. Accordingly, agreement should be reached with top management as to the most desirable organization. Plans should be laid to convert to this organization, using one or more interim organizational plans where necessary. The organization chart and job descriptions should be drawn up and published. The industrial relations department and/or the personnel department should be brought into the project to aid in the organizational phase of maintenance management.

Maintenance Control Section. The purpose of the control section is to provide the necessary control and administration of the maintenance activity. It is the nerve center of the maintenance organization. It is a functional staff group, and its authority stems from the maintenance manager. It exerts functional authority, by acting in the name of the chief, over all other maintenance activities.

The basic functions of the control section are:

1. *Analyzing   and   evaluating   maintenance   management.* Maintenance management is not a static program but recognizes the need to review continually such things as:

   a. The parts of the equipment that need to be inspected, cleaned, lubricated, or replaced, and how often

   b. The modifications that should be made to the equipment, and their costs and benefits *c.* The type and amount of maintenance work that should be performed by outside contractors

    d. Abnormal repair work, and the action that will lessen or eliminate it

    e. The training needs of supervisors and workmen

    f. The most desirable stock levels for spare parts, maintenance tools, and maintenance materials

    Analysis of the control reports, equipment history records, work orders, and inventory records will answer these and like questions.

2. *Planning and scheduling maintenance work.* This is one of the important day-to-day functions of the maintenance control section.

3. *Maintaining maintenance stores.* Without adequate supplies of spare parts, tools, and maintenance materials, serious production delays could result.

4. *Applying engineered time standards.* Fundamental to all adequate management activities is the measurement of results, particularly manpower utilization.

5. Performing all other necessary maintenance paper work. In addition to the management information and control reports, it is necessary to perform office routines such as timekeeping, procurement or requisitioning, and miscellaneous correspondence.

PREVENTIVE MAINTENANCE

Preventive maintenance (PM) is the systematic inspection, cleaning, lubricating, and servicing of equipment. The checkpoints on the equipment, the frequency of attention, and the schedule for performing the PM work should be determined in advance of actual performance.

The objective of PM is to discover incipient malfunctions and to prevent malfunctions and breakdowns. Through PM inspection, many malfunctions can be discovered and corrected before they develop into breakdowns or emergencies. Good maintenance management should reduce the number and intensity of breakdowns to the point where 15 percent or less of the time of the maintenance mechanics is devoted to breakdowns. Before PM is introduced, breakdowns have been found to account for 85 percent or more of the time of the mechanics.

Too often, a PM system is introduced without full consideration of manpower requirements. A net reduction in total maintenance personnel will usually result after the program is fully installed and operating correctly, but because the benefits of PM are long range in nature and do not begin immediately, additional personnel may be required at first. Also, the realignment of duties and responsibilities may require different types of people. Generally, more clerical and fewer mechanical personnel will be required.

PM is based on the scheduling of equipment inspections, cleanings, and lubrications; the written reporting of deficiencies in the equipment; the repair of these deficiencies; and the subsequent recording of the repairs in permanent equipment history records. These records must then be analyzed and evaluated for cause and remedial action. PM also requires estimating, planning, scheduling, and controlling maintenance repair work. An efficient PM system must have built into it controls that will indicate the need for revising the routines and procedures. All these features require a change of organizational responsibilities and duties from those generally found where PM has not previously been used.

Preventive-maintenance Functions. All preventive-maintenance work can be separated into two classifications:

1. Mechanical work
2. Paper work

Both are important to the successful operation of the PM system. Mechanical work consists of the following six PM operations:

1. Inspecting
2. Adjusting
3. Tightening
4. Cleaning
5. Lubricating
6. Routine replacing of parts

PM inspecting is the art and science of discovering and diagnosing incipient failures—a breakdown about to happen. The breakdown may be only a few hours away or, more likely, a few weeks or months away. PM inspection consists in *looking at, feeling, listening to,* or *testing* a predetermined equipment checkpoint. The inspection operation is aimed at finding something wrong rather than finding something right. Some examples are:

Look for frayed or damaged wiring.

Feel motor for overheating.

Listen for noisy bearing.

Test for insufficient or excessive belt tension.

All written PM-inspection operation descriptions should include one or more of the above underlined key words and should always be written in the negative. For example, don't write, "Test for *proper* belt tension; look to see if pulley and shaft are *aligned.*" Write, "Test for *insufficient* or *excessive* belt tension; look for *misaligned* pulley and shaft." Psychologically, most people look for good conditions. When the instruction is written in the negative, the inspector will be more apt to be on the alert for poor conditions.

Although the maintenance department is primarily responsible for performing the six categories of PM listed above, the operating department may also be responsible for performing some of these operations. Generally, operating personnel should not attempt to make repairs or do any PM work that requires special skill or dismantling of the equipment. They should, however, do a certain amount of the inspecting, cleaning, adjusting, and lubricating. Any PM operation requiring tools or equipment in excess of a screwdriver, pliers, and small oilcan should be performed by maintenance personnel. Also, many screwdriver and plier operations, because of skill, time, or safety requirements, should be performed by maintenance personnel. Some examples of PM operations that operating personnel may be expected to do are:

1. Checking equipment for proper operating condition before beginning production operations
2. Certain adjusting, particularly the type requiring frequent adjustment and for which detailed mechanical skill and knowledge are not required
3. Cleaning the equipment at the end of the shift
4. Some oiling, particularly the type that is required often and does not need special equipment or dismantling of the machine, guards, or covers
5. Servicing, such as maintaining proper ink or water levels

PM operations performed by operating personnel should be restricted to those situations where a specific operator can be identified with a specific machine. Wherever operating personnel are expected to perform PM operations, the inspections should be written and posted to both the machine and the operator's job description. The responsibility for preparing these written instructions should rest with the maintenance department and should be approved by operating management.

PM paper work includes PM checklists, PM route sheets, and equipment history records. Additional paper work such as inventory bookkeeping, preparing work orders, and preparing control reports is also necessary.

PM Checklists. Normally, it will be advisable to institute two classes of PM checklists: PM inspection checklists, and PM cleaning and lubrication checklists. The reason is to separate the PM work into the two different skill levels required. Almost all PM operations can be separated into one of two classes:

1. Work requiring *higher* skill and experience levels than the average mechanic has

2. Work requiring *lower* skill and experience levels than the average mechanic has

Most inspection operations require diagnosing incipient malfunctions, that is, finding the cause of trouble before the trouble itself is readily apparent. This type of skill and experience is greater than that required for normal troubleshooting when the trouble has become apparent. Cleaning and lubricating work, on the other hand, normally requires little skill. Given proper training, most mechanics' helpers can do it adequately. Inspecting, cleaning, and lubricating will account for the bulk of the PM work load. Adjusting that requires a high degree of skill can be included in the PM inspection checklists. Most tightening and adjusting that requires little skill can be included in the PM cleaning and lubricating checklists.

Mechanics will not usually do preventive-maintenance work, but will normally perform the necessary repair work uncovered by the PM inspectors.

PLANNING AND SCHEDULING MAINTENANCE WORK

Both short-range and long-range planning and scheduling are necessary for the effective operation of the maintenance management program.

Long-range planning and scheduling consists in establishing preventive-maintenance routines and planned overhauls. It also includes reviewing and analyzing historical information and revising preventive-maintenance routines and planned overhauls.

Short-range scheduling consists in assigning jobs to the maintenance workers on a day-to-day or week-to-week basis. Short-range planning decides how to perform the jobs and also how to coordinate schedules with production needs so that there will be a minimum of conflict with the normal operation of the equipment.

Unless the long-range planning and scheduling is done carefully, the preventive-maintenance routines will not be fully adhered to. Lubrications will be missed; inspections will not be complete; and cleaning will not be performed adequately. In addition, poor utilization of the work force *and* inadequate revisions of schedules to meet changed conditions will result. Control is gained by feeding back information. The longer the program is in operation, provided adequate planning is done, the more accurate will be the preventive-maintenance routines. Accordingly, careful and continuous long-range planning and scheduling is a must.

Short-range planning and scheduling must be performed on a continuing basis. Inadequate short-range planning can lead to interference with the operating needs of the equipment, poor utilization of the mechanic's time, or both. Inadequate planning of how jobs are to be performed will increase equipment downtime and the man-hours required to make the repair.

Scheduling may be performed with punched card tabulating equipment, by

electronic computers, or manually with the aid of scheduling boards.   Normally, the control section will be responsible for scheduling the following:
   1. Inspection route sheets for individual equipment inspectors
   2. Lubrication and cleaning route sheets for maintenance foremen
   3. Repair-work orders for maintenance foremen

ENGINEERED WORK MEASUREMENT

Engineered time standards covering the maintenance work are essential for control purposes, for good planning and scheduling, and for reducing costs.   The development and application of a system of engineered time standards is a professional activity, requiring qualified industrial engineers trained in this area.[1]

CONTROLS AND CONTROL REPORTS

To control is to regulate, that is, to exercise directing and restraining power over an activity.   To control, it is necessary to:
   1. Be aware of conditions and activities
   2. Take corrective action to improve conditions

[1] H. B. Maynard (ed.), *Industrial Engineering Handbook*, 2d ed., sec. 4, chap. 5, McGraw-Hill Book Company, New York, 1963.

SCHEDULED	9	11	15	17	24	23	28	42	52	56	63	70	81
EMERGENCY	48	49	43	45	40	38	35	38	33	21	15	14	15
STANDBY	43	40	42	38	36	39	37	20	15	23	22	16	4

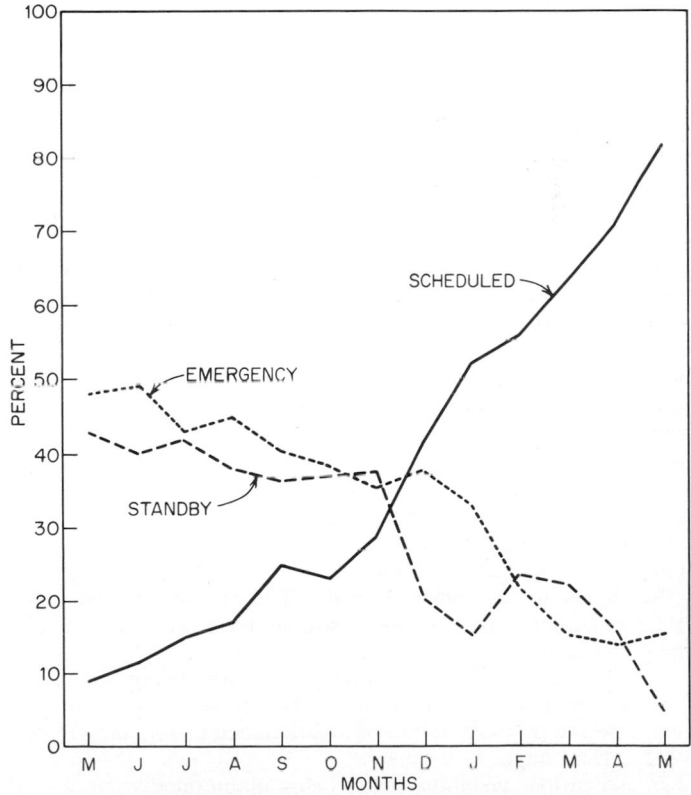

FIG. 5-3.   *Percentage distribution of repair maintenance hours.*

PERCENT

PERFORMANCE PERCENT	44	50	51	62	61	59	54	66	70	74	74	77

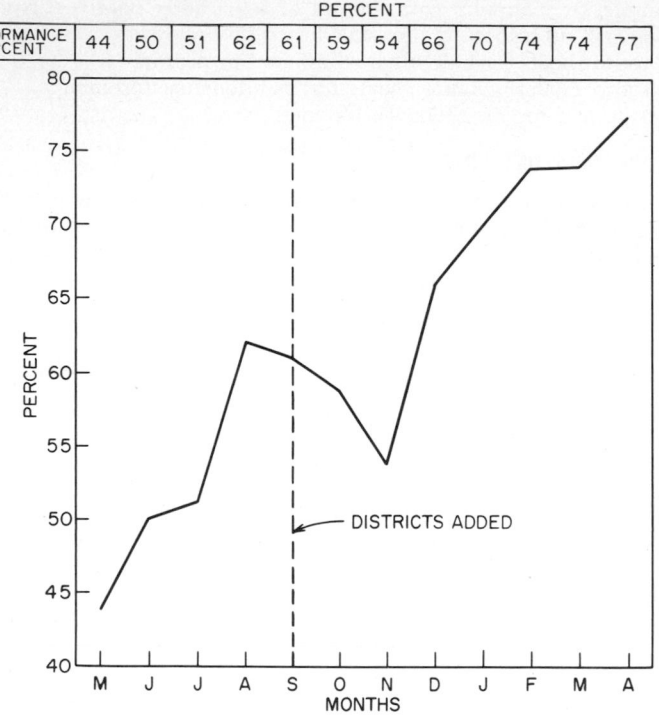

FIG. 5-4. *Performance record of a group of 200 maintenance workers.*

Control requires human action. Graphs and reports do not constitute control, but only the means of control. The "feedback" of information and results, as represented by graphs, reports, and daily contacts with men and equipment, is necessary to achieve control.

The maintenance manager must exercise control over the maintenance organization's activities if he is to accomplish the objectives of the program. This control can be gained in part by his daily contact with the routine work of his office. Visiting the storerooms periodically, spending some time on the work floor each day, visiting the control section office and the shops, and being available to help his key men with their problems will all contribute to keeping him informed of the activities of his group. In plants requiring a fairly large maintenance staff, however, he will not be able to rely on daily contacts to provide him with sufficient control to manage his department properly. To supplement the knowledge gained by daily contacts, a series of control reports and graphs should be used. These constitute the management information system required for good control.

Management Information System. The answers to the following key questions, if obtained on a regular and frequent basis, will help point out the action that must be taken to achieve proper control.

1. How effectively is the maintenance force being utilized?
2. Is repair work being performed on time?
3. Are the proper number of maintenance people employed?
4. Is the budget being met?
5. Are proper inventory levels being maintained?

Some of this information will be developed on a daily basis, some weekly, and some monthly.

How Effectively Is the Maintenance Force Being Utilized?   All repair maintenance work can be separated into three categories:

1. Scheduled repairs
2. Emergency repairs
3. Standby

One of the measures of the effectiveness of the utilization of the maintenance force is the relationship between the amounts of these different types of work. Figure 5-3 is a graph showing the distribution of repair maintenance time. Note that the proportion of scheduled repair time was increased while decreasing the proportion of breakdown and standby time. Included in standby time is the idle time that occurred.

The most important measure of the effectiveness of the maintenance force is the performance level that it achieves. Performance is the quantity of maintenance work produced in terms of *standard* hours divided by the *actual* hours put in. For example, assume that a group of ten carpenters does twenty-two jobs in a week that total 300 *standard* hours of work. If this group worked a total of 400 *actual* hours, its performance for the week would be 75 percent.

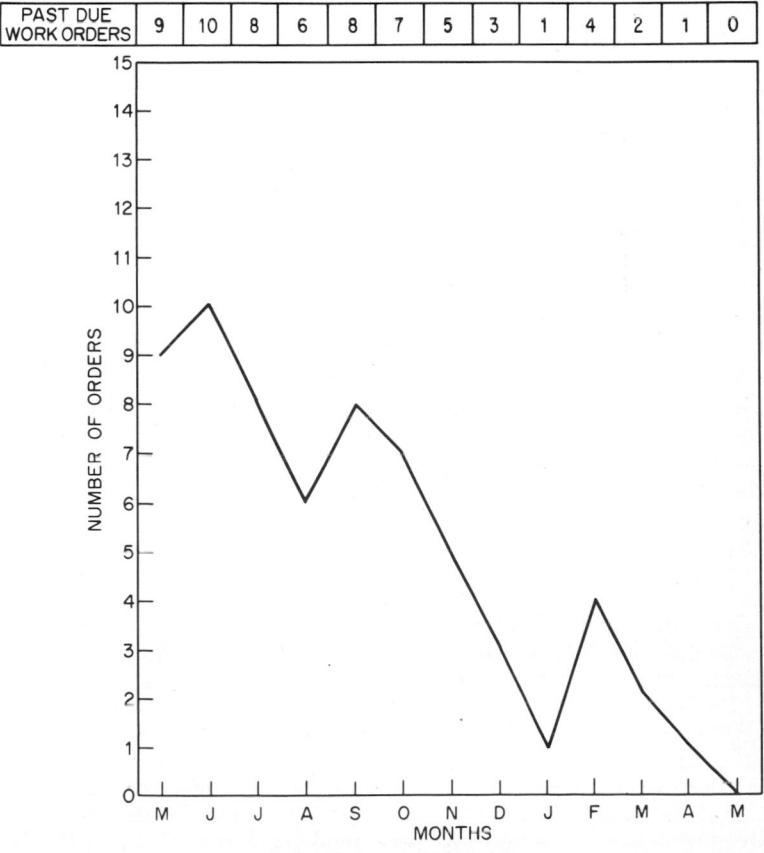

FIG. 5-5.   *Past-due work orders.*

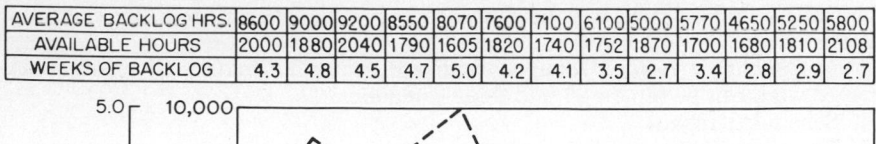

AVERAGE BACKLOG HRS.	8600	9000	9200	8550	8070	7600	7100	6100	5000	5770	4650	5250	5800
AVAILABLE HOURS	2000	1880	2040	1790	1605	1820	1740	1752	1870	1700	1680	1810	2108
WEEKS OF BACKLOG	4.3	4.8	4.5	4.7	5.0	4.2	4.1	3.5	2.7	3.4	2.8	2.9	2.7

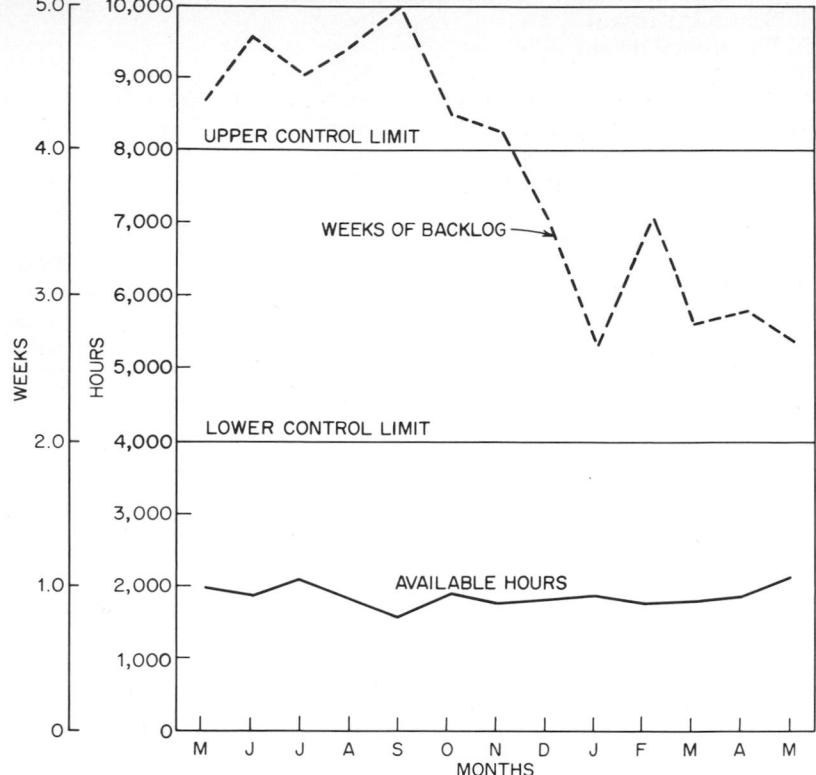

FIG. 5-6. *Backlog of work and hours available (excludes preventive maintenance).*

The standard hours produced for each craft can be added together to ascertain the total production of the maintenance force for each week. Total standard hours divided by the total actual hours worked on the jobs measured will yield the index of performances. These performances are commonly shown as percentages. Figure 5-4 illustrates the actual performance record for a group of approximately two hundred maintenance workers. Note the substantial increase in performance due to the installation of good maintenance management methods.

Is Repair Work Being Performed on Time? Intrinsic to good management over maintenance activities is an accurate and timely knowledge of work that is behind schedule or past due. Having this information will permit the maintenance manager to take corrective action.

Figure 5-5 is a graph showing the daily average number of work orders that were past due each month. This graph clearly shows the trend of past-due work and provides the maintenance manager with an opportunity to judge the continuing performance of this aspect of the department's work.

Are the Proper Number of Maintenance People Employed? Because preventive-maintenance routines are performed on a regular basis, the labor required can be considered to be almost constant. The remaining portion of the time of the maintenance force is available for indirect maintenance and for repairs. A comparison of the man-hours available for scheduled work orders with the backlog of scheduled work orders will indicate whether the maintenance force is understaffed or overstaffed. The backlog hours divided by the available hours will show the weeks of work backlogged. Plotting this curve and then watching its trend will indicate whether additional men will be needed or whether plans should be made to reduce the size of the force.

The graph shown as Figure 5-6 will provide the information required for this control.

Is the Budget Being Met? The budget represents the overall cost of running the maintenance and custodial departments. Figure 5-7 illustrates the type of chart that provides a quick grasp of actual versus budgeted costs.

Are Proper Inventory Levels Being Maintained? Keeping the proper amount of spare parts and maintenance materials on hand is important for effective maintenance. If equipment breaks down, or is in danger of breaking down, the parts must be on hand for immediate repairs.

On the other hand, overstocking can be costly in space, obsolescence, investment, and the like, and should be avoided.

BUDGET	48	48	48	48	48	48	48	48	48	48	48	48	48
EXPENSES	51	51.4	50	50.6	48.4	47.6	51	47.6	47.8	48.2	47.4	47.2	46

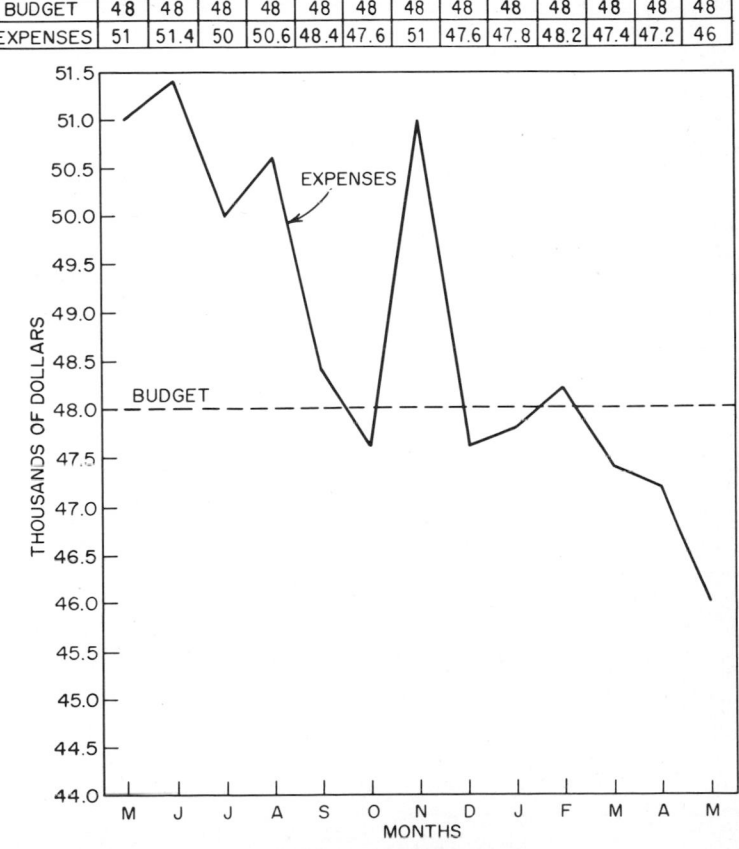

FIG. 5-7. *Expenses and budget.*

A chart can be developed to show the percent of items that are over and under the standard inventory. By watching the trend of this chart, the necessary action can be taken to maintain the desired inventory levels.

CONCLUSION

The development and installation of a controls system as described here is a large undertaking. However, the benefits in terms of savings, increased level of maintenance service, reduced productive-equipment downtime, and the feeling of confidence that comes to a management that knows it has control over its responsibility, make the efforts of installation well worthwhile.

BIBLIOGRAPHY

Carson, Gordon, *Production Handbook,* The Ronald Press Company, New York, 1958.
Hodson, William K., *Control of Maintenance Labor Costs,* Society of Automotive Engineers, New York, 1962.
"Incentives Work Fine in Maintenance," *Factory Management & Maintenance,* 1955.
Maynard, H. B., "Controlling Maintenance Costs," *Iron and Steel Engineer,* 1959.
Maynard, H. B. (ed.), *Industrial Engineering Handbook,* 2d ed., sec. 4, chaps. 4 and 5, McGraw-Hill Book Company, New York, 1963.
Maynard, H. B., and G. J. Stegemerten, "Universal Maintenance Standards," *Factory Management & Maintenance,* 1955.
Morrow, L. C., *Maintenance Engineering Handbook,* McGraw-Hill Book Company, New York, 1957.
"Plant Engineer's Deskbook," *Factory Management & Maintenance,* 1952.
Plant Maintenance & Engineering Techniques (annual series), Clapp & Poliak, Inc., 1950.
Staniar, William, *Plant Engineering Handbook,* 2d ed., McGraw-Hill Book Company, New York, 1963.
Stegemerten, G. J., "Maintenance Incentives That Work," *Factory,* 1960.
Wilcox, Lee, "MTM Applied to the Department of Public Works," *MTM Journal,* 1964.

CHAPTER SIX

Equipment Replacement Analysis

DONALD D. DEMING *Professor, School of Management, Rensselaer Polytechnic Institute, Troy, New York*

ROBERT G. MURDICK *Professor, State University of New York at Albany, Albany, New York*

Companies which do not continually and systematically evaluate prospective investments in equipment and buildings against their current capital investments jeopardize their future existence. Unless they plow back some of their earnings into selective investments, they are merely liquidating their company's capital assets. Ultimately, wear and obsolescence will result in unprofitable operations and inability to compete with firms which achieve superior productivity and quality. To plan and control capital expenditures properly, progressive companies employ the capital budget as a basic management tool. When the capital budget is properly used, it encourages capital-equipment proposals, establishes priorities for the allocation of limited funds, and permits justified changes in allocations during its period of application. Equipment replacement policy provides the company's approach to reviewing equipment proposals.

BASIC APPROACH TO EQUIPMENT REPLACEMENT PLANNING

The basic approach to equipment replacement planning is to create a list of all equipment and plant investment opportunities which offer promise of yielding a profit equal to or greater than current equipment investment yields. This list, when arranged in descending order of rate of return, serves as a valuable guide in directing the most effective distribution of budgeted funds.

At this point, an important question arises: How much money should be budgeted for this type of investment? A newly founded enterprise will frequently plow back most or all of its early profits to improve on and to expand its operating capabilities. Each company must decide for itself and attempt to maintain what it considers the best overall yield to its owners in terms of dividends, competitive position, and growth. The bases for decision making in this area are likely to be complex, involving many interacting forces.

The general approach of creating an ordered list of facility investment opportunities, although sound, is impossible to implement with mathematical precision, for a number of practical reasons. The first and most obvious difficulty results from the fact that today's decisions and commitments will be implemented only at some time in the future. Anticipated earnings will start flowing in at a still later date. This means that the anticipated benefits will be realized only to the extent that forecasts prove accurate or are overrealized. Another problem is that many attractive opportunities are difficult, often impossible, to evaluate in terms of dollar and cents advantages. Consequently, it is not easy to locate them along the scale of relative profitability.

Another difficulty is that nearly all components of an organization make claims on replacement and expansion funds. It is therefore evident that conflicting organization demands must be resolved in favor of strategic considerations to achieve long-run corporate objectives.

Top-level planning first dictates where and how much emphasis is to be applied in different areas. This may well take the form of apportioning funds among various elements of an organization in accordance with overall corporate plans and objectives.

Next comes the problem of apportioning the amounts budgeted in specific areas. Take, as an example, the division of a corporation manufacturing and marketing a family of products, A. Corporate planning might dictate that division A should be operated only on a sustaining basis rather than expanded or contracted. In this circumstance, equipment replacement theory is applied in its most literal sense—maintenance of existing capacity while remaining competitive. If the competitive situation promises to be relatively stable, management's problem will be to apportion budgeted funds in such a manner as to counteract the adverse effects of wear, depletion, and technological inefficiencies relative to competition.

Factors Which Influence the Investment Decision. If division management merely asked departments to submit improvement proposals, it would find that some of the proposals make claims that incremental revenue streams will exceed related incremental costs by calculated amounts, whereas other promising proposals cite nonmonetary advantages. Inasmuch as this situation is almost inevitable, it makes the creation of an ordered list difficult. An example to illustrate this problem is a proposal to install safety devices on all stamping presses. Although estimates of savings that might be expected to result from reducing accidents could be made, no one would claim that this should be the sole criterion or, for that matter, even a very important one in this case. On the other hand, the installation of automatic feed devices for presses might be looked upon as primarily a labor-saving, cost-saving procedure, and would, incidentally, practically eliminate press accidents.

Factors influencing the investment decision which lend themselves to quantitative analysis are:

1. Market analysis and forecasts
2. Alternative uses of capital in terms of yield
    a. Cost of new equipment
    b. Operating costs of old and new equipment
    c. Maintenance costs
    d. Anticipated revenues
3. Taxes
4. Sources of funds—capital structure of the company

   5. Cost of capital
   6. Sources of equipment
      a. Surplus from other plants in the company
      b. New from vendors
      c. Used from vendors
      d. Leasing opportunities versus purchasing
   7. Working capital required for alternative projects
   8. Cash-flow budget
   9. Inflationary price changes
  10. Type of production
      a. Intermittent
      b. Continuous
  11. Timing of decision
  12. Risk and uncertainty of all factors in the future

Justification of Investment Proposals.   Nearly all replacement proposals are justified under one of the following headings:
   1. Reduction in direct production costs
   2. Reduction in costs of "production serving" operations
   3. Improvement in quality of product function or appearance
   4. Improvement in reliability and safety of the product
   5. Improvement in reliability and safety of the equipment
   6. Retardation of deterioration in equipment
   7. Improvement in working conditions, including esthetic values
   8. Improvement in customer service
   9. Improvement in make or buy practices
  10. Expansion of capacity in existing line
  11. Expansion or change of product line

The appropriation request form, Figure 6-1, brings out the justification for the project in a formal way so that a comparison of the relative value of all proposals may easily be made. The important thing to note is that only a few categories truly lend themselves to quantitative analysis. Categories 1, 2, and 9 are likely to be most amenable to computed savings or more correctly the determination of costs of alternatives plus rates of returns on related investments.

The last two categories can be omitted from this chapter's consideration, although the approach is the same as for the replacement problem. It should be stressed, however, that they must be dealt with at the time equipment budgets are considered and rationing of capital takes place.

Finding Candidates for Replacement.   The idea of developing a thoroughgoing, systematic, and technically sound approach to replacement problems is a relatively recent one in industry as a whole. Although the body of literature on economic theory related to replacement problems is rather substantial, very little exists concerning methods used by successful organizations in adapting theory for practical purposes.

Donald F. Istvan conducted a study of "forty-eight of the country's largest firms" to determine who in these companies deal with this vital area of decision making. Concerning the question of how companies seek out ideas for profitable capital expenditures, he says, "All forty-eight indicated that the majority of expenditure proposals originate among the operating personnel, that is, personnel who are not considered members of top management."[1] A study of ninety-one

[1] Donald F. Istvan, *Capital-expenditure Decisions and How They Are Made in Large Corporations*, Indiana Business Report, no. 33, Bureau of Business Research, Bloomington, Ind., 1961, p. 9.

American Air Filter COMPANY, INC.

Project No. _____
Acct. No. _____
Dept. No. _____

PROJECT REQUEST
For Operating Facilities Expenditures

Budget
Number _____

☐ Not in Budget

Time Required for
Completion _____ Wks.

☐ General Purpose
☐ Product _____

PROJECT CLASSIFICATION

Equipment
☐ 1. Replacement
☐ 2. Additional for Volume
☐ 3. Additional for New
    Product
☐ 4. Cost Reduction
☐ 5. Major Overhaul

Tooling
☐ 6. Replacement
☐ 7. Additional for Volume
☐ 8. Additional for New
    Product
☐ 9. Cost Reduction

Administration
☐ 13. Office Equipment &
     Furniture

Physical Plant
☐ 10. New Building
     & Additions
☐ 11. Land
☐ 12. Major Repairs

Engineering
☐ 14. Equipment

Description

Reason for
Project

Is Similar Equipment
Available in AAF?

Reason For
Duplication

Cost
Estimate

	Total	19____	19____
Purchases	_____	_____	_____
Stock Material	_____	_____	_____
Company Labor	_____	_____	_____
Other Expenses	_____	_____	_____
Installed Cost of Project	$ _____	$ _____	$ _____

Service Life of Equipment _____ Yrs.	Next-Year Operating Advantage $ _____	MAPI Urgency Rating _____ %

Program
Summary

Class Budget _____ Quarter Budget _____ Total Budget _____
Class Unallocated _____ Quarter Unallocated _____ Total Unallocated _____

Analysis
Prepared by: _____ Date _____

Recommended
By Dept. Mgr. _____ Date _____

Division Mgr.	Group Mgr.	Mgr. Mgmt. Serv.	Central Controller	General Management
Date _____	Date _____	Date _____	Exp. ☐ Cap. ☐ Date _____	Date _____

Form 1830D – 250 Sets – 3-65 – CP   See PMP-2

FIG. 6-1. *Appropriation request form.*

firms by R. G. Murdick indicated that replacement recommendations are made primarily by middle management.[2]

It appears that a company's approach to capital rationing is a highly individualistic matter. In the absence of generally accepted, clear-cut guidelines, this is probably because of evolutionary development rather than plan.

It appears that management, for the most part, relies on information originating at the operating level largely from operating people. The principal incentive to bring forward promising replacement opportunities is the desire of "operating" managers including foremen and supervisors to prove themselves effective managers and thus merit advancement. Profit-sharing plans tend to sharpen these drives. The practice of budgeting cost improvement can similarly sharpen interest in identifying *and implementing* cost-reduction opportunities.

The availability of effective and well-understood channels for submission of equipment purchase proposals encourages interest and increases practical action in this direction. Forms and manuals, when well designed, make it easy and hence encourage submission of promising ideas—to say nothing of the advantages derived from standardizing methods of analysis and inducing uniform documentation.

Istvan's study indicates that few companies have any difficulty in securing investment suggestions sufficient to exceed available funds. Random methods of search, however, may well fail to turn up the most profitable overall opportunities. A few companies assign the search for opportunities as a functional responsibility to an individual or group. In many situations, this practice can pay rich dividends. In the typical company, the main problem is that of evaluating a variety of proposals and selecting those most promising.

Merging the Equipment Replacement Proposal Lists. The idea of making ordered lists by category of all promising proposals is fine, but in the end, the lists must somehow be merged into a single list so that budgeted funds can be most profitably allocated.

Assume that properly analyzed proposals have been rank-listed under the following headings:

1. Cost reduction
2. Quality improvement
3. Service improvement
4. Safety improvement
5. Environment improvement

There will be a list of numerous proposals under each heading. Cost-reduction proposals start with the proposal showing highest return on the investment over its projected life. Quality-improvement proposals are difficult to express in terms of rate of return, but can be ranked in terms of the volume of sales multiplied by the percent of complaints. An estimate can often be made of the reduction in rate of complaints that will result from a proposal. This, multiplied by sales dollars involved in complaints, will give a relative indication of proposal importance.

Service improvement can be handled similarly using past-due percentage in place of complaint or quality percentage. Safety can be handled on the basis of accident ratios. Environment improvement requires a ranking based largely on the subjective merits of each proposal. Methods for ranking all but the first list must depend largely on their significance to a specific organization.

It is perhaps obvious that records of equipment performance such as downtime, maintenance costs, accidents caused, waste, and scrap are of inestimable value in developing essential data for replacement decision making.

[2] Robert G. Murdick, "Equipment Replacement Practices," *Automation,* November, 1965, p. 121.

Ultimately, five lists will exist side by side. The problem now is to determine which of the five number one candidates is to be first on the merged list. Although this determination must be largely subjective, it is usually not difficult to spot the best one of all. This one is removed from its list and put at the head of the final or merged list. Next, the five lists are again compared. A second-best candidate is selected from the top five and placed below the first identified for the merged list. The first two or three of any one of the original five lists might occupy the first positions on the final list. Ultimately, as the procedure continues, all lists become merged in the final ordered list.

The final list should now be examined. Does it appear reasonably logical? Next, a cumulative subtotal of the ranked investments should be computed. At the point when the subtotal equals funds available, investments for the period under consideration have been selected. As a final review, the following questions should be asked and answered: Does this list make good sense? Is this timing sensible? Are some of the items which were missed more timely and very nearly as desirable? Correlation of the answers to these questions provides the final judgmental check.

To check on the effectiveness of evaluating procedures and to improve an organization's skill, audits of actually realized benefits compared with anticipations should be incorporated as a regular part of the overall replacement procedure.

METHODS OF QUANTITATIVE ANALYSIS

In comparing alternative projects, the manager is concerned only with *differences* in each item which goes to make up the index for evaluation. Thus, it is the *difference* in profit for one alternative over the other, or the *difference* in cash flow for one alternative over the other, or the ratio of such a difference to the *difference* in investment that claims his attention. The term "net" is commonly used to indicate this difference between two sums. Simplified illustrations of the computation of five basic methods of arriving at this follow.

1. *Simple Rate of Return on Investment.* There are a number of variations of this method. The return may be considered as profits before or after taxes or merely operating savings. Return may also be considered as cash return or cash returns before taxes. Investment may be considered net (differential or incremental) investment, gross investment, or average investment. An example is as follows:

	Present machine	Proposed machine
Scrap value today.................	$6,000	
Installed cost.....................	....	$30,000
Scrap value at end of life...........	0	0
Remaining life....................	3 years	6 years
Annual operating costs..............	$24,000	$14,000
Interest rate (cost of capital).........	10%	10%
Income tax rate....................	50%	50%

Net investment = cost of new machine − scrap value of present machine
= 30,000 − 6,000 = 24,000

$$\text{Net straight-line depreciation per year} = \frac{30,000}{6} - \frac{6,000}{3} = 3,000$$

Net operating savings per year = 24,000 − 14,000 = 10,000
Net interest charges per year for capital = 0.10(net investment)
= 0.10(24,000) = 2,400
Net savings = operating savings − depreciation − interest
= 10,000 − 3,000 − 2,400 = 4,600

It should be remembered that all values of terms, including the index of return itself, are based upon the difference between the alternatives. The interest charge represents an "opportunity cost" often neglected by businessmen when it is an implicit cost.

$$\text{Profit return on investment, before taxes} = \frac{\text{savings}}{\text{investment}} = \frac{4,600}{24,000} = 19.2\%$$

$$\text{Profit return on investment, after taxes} = \frac{\text{savings} - 0.50 \text{ savings}}{\text{investment}}$$

$$= \frac{4,600 - 2,300}{24,000} = \frac{2,300}{24,000} = 9.6\%$$

$$\text{Cash-flow return on investment, before taxes} = \frac{\text{savings} + \text{depreciation}}{\text{investment}}$$

$$= \frac{4,600 + 3,000}{24,000} = 31.6\%$$

Cash-flow return on investment, after taxes

$$= \frac{\text{savings} - 0.50 \text{ savings} + \text{depreciation}}{\text{investment}}$$

$$= \frac{2,300 + 3,000}{24,000} = 22\%$$

The relationship between book values, which involve profits, and cash flow as used for economic decision making is illustrated below.

	On books	Cash flow
Net operating savings.........................	·$10,000	$10,000
Less net interest charges.......................	2,400	2,400
	7,600	7,600
Less net depreciation...........................	3,000	
Additional taxable income......................	4,600	
Increase in income tax (50%)................	2,300	2,300
Net additional income after taxes...............	$ 2,300	
Net additional cash benefits after taxes..........		$ 5,300

2. *Total Life Average.* The total-life-average method makes no adjustment for the time of cash receipts and disbursements, but it does take into account the variation in interest over the life of the project. It is an average annual cost over the life of the project. The following example uses the data given above:

	Present machine	Proposed machine
Depreciation........................	$ 6,000	$ 30,000
Operating costs over life..............	72,000	84,000
10% interest on capital...............	1,200*	10,500†
Cost over life.......................	$79,200	$124,500
Life................................	3 years	6 years
Average annual cost.................	$26,400	$ 20,750

* Interest, present machine = $0.10(6,000 + 4,000 + 2,000) = 1,200$
† Interest, proposed machine = $0.10(30,000 + 25,000 + 20,000 + 15,000 + 10,000 + 5,000)$
= 10,500

3. *Payback Period.* The payback period is widely used in industry as a rule of thumb. It is the time required for the earnings or savings to pay back the cost of the investment. Two forms for the same data as used above are:

$$\text{Simple payback} = \frac{\text{investment}}{\text{savings}} = \frac{24,000}{4,600} = 5.2 \text{ years}$$

$$\text{Payback after taxes} = \frac{\text{investment}}{\text{savings} - 0.50 \text{ savings}} = \frac{24,000}{2,300} = 10.4 \text{ years}$$

4. *Discounted Cash Flow.* In the discounted-cash-flow method, the net cash flow for each year is estimated for the lives of the alternative machines. If the machines have different lives, then they must be compared for a period of years which is the least common multiple. For example, if one machine has a life of four years and the other a life of six years, a twelve-year period would be required so that the first would be replaced twice and the second would be replaced once. This would show up in the cash flows for the appropriate years. The *net* cash flow for each year is made up of:

a. Capital costs for the proposed machine and capital costs avoided by not having to rebuild or rework the old machine; new machine salvage received and old machine salvage foregone

b. Net operating savings

c. Net depreciation

d. Net difference in income taxes.

Assume that the net cost of the proposed new machine is $30,500. The question is, what rate of return used to discount the annual cash flows will make the present value of the cash flows equal to the net cost of the project? If this rate is greater than the interest rate (cost of money), it is favorable.

An example in which the cash flows have been found as tabulated shows the trial-and-error approach to finding the rate of return.

End of year	Net cash flow	Today's value at 20%	Today's value at 22%
1	$+15,000	0.8333(15,000) = $12,500	0.8197(15,000) = $12,296
2	+15,000	0.6944(15,000) = 10,416	0.6719(15,000) = 10,079
3	+10,000	0.5787(10,000) = 5,787	0.5507(10,000) = 5,507
4	+ 5,000	0.4823(5,000) = 2,411	0.4514(5,000) = 2,257
		$31,114	$30,139

A rate of return of about 21 percent will make the future stream of net cash receipts, discounted to today's value, equal to today's net investment of $30,500.

5. *Present Worth Method.* The present worth method is simpler than the discounted-cash-flow method and is better grounded theoretically. The net cash flow for each year is calculated as above, but annual values are discounted at the estimated cost of capital. The discount rate is thus in the range of about 5 to 15 percent. The decision is made as follows: If the present worth of net cash flow is greater than the cost of the proposed machine, the evaluation is favorable. If the cost of the proposed machine is greater than the present worth of net cash flow, the evaluation is unfavorable.

6. *MAPI Method.* The Machinery and Allied Products Institute has developed charts which make easy the detailed accumulation of data and the evaluation of a project in terms of an urgency rating. All factors such as salvage,

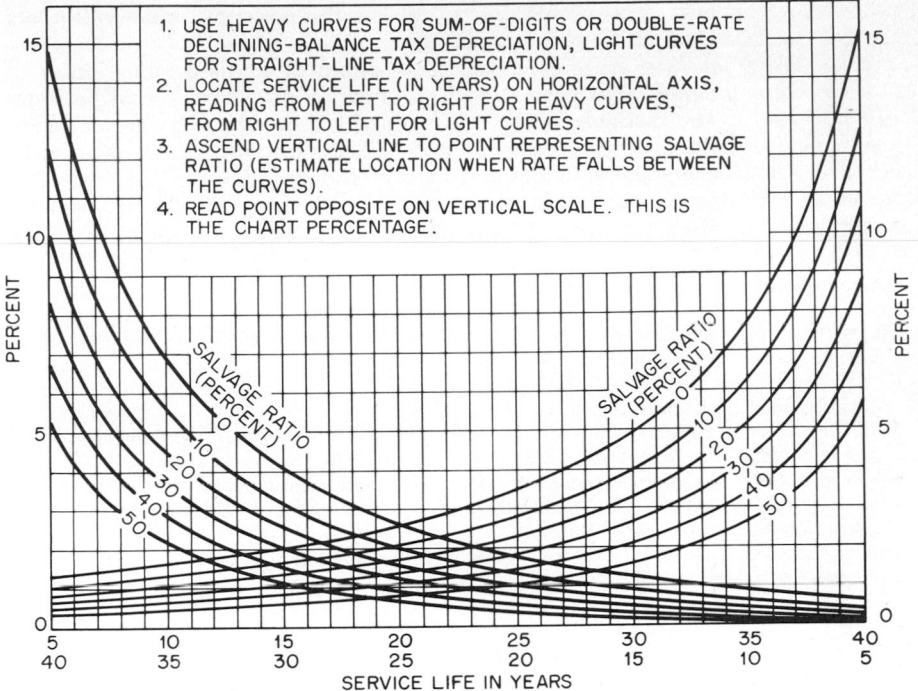

FIG. 6-2. *MAPI chart used for developing urgency ratings.*

depreciation, taxes, and earnings patterns are taken into account. An abbreviated example illustrating the use of one of the charts (Figure 6-2) will indicate the ease of application.

$$\frac{\text{Salvage value}}{\text{Cost}} = 20\%$$

Service life = 6 years
Installed cost = 30,000
Net investment = 24,000
Next year's operating advantage = 10,000
Next year's savings after taxes = 6,000
MAPI chart percentage for project = 6.7%

MAPI urgency rating

$$= \frac{\text{next year's savings after taxes} - \text{MAPI chart percentage} \times \text{installed cost}}{\text{net investment}}$$

$$= \frac{6,000 - 0.067 \times 30,000}{24,000} = \frac{4,000}{24,000} = 16.6\%$$

CONCLUSION

To ensure continuing operating effectiveness, it is important to have a planned approach to equipment replacement planning. Usually there will be no lack of attractive proposals on how the company should spend its limited equipment replacement budget. The problem is to sift out the proposals which will yield the greatest return per dollar of investment.

The making of lists of proposed projects arranged in descending order of rate of return provides management with information on which logical decisions can be based. The methods which can be used for determining rate of return are many (see also Chapter 8 of Section 3). They are touched on only briefly here, for they belong more in the province of the technician. The important point, as far as management is concerned, is that there should be available a planned and orderly procedure for arriving at equipment replacement decisions.

BIBLIOGRAPHY

Bierman, Harold, and Seymour Smidt, *The Capital Budgeting Decision,* The Macmillan Company, New York, 1960.

Hertz, David B., "Risk Analysis in Capital Investment," *Harvard Business Review,* January–February, 1964.

Managing Capital Expenditures, Studies in Business Policy, no. 107, National Industrial Conference Board, New York, 1963.

Schwan, Harry T., "Replacement of Machinery and Equipment," sec. 8, chap. 3, in H. B. Maynard (ed.), *Industrial Engineering Handbook,* 2d ed., McGraw-Hill Book Company, New York, 1963.

Smiley, Lloyd G., "Rate of Return—Toughest Measure of a Manager," *Factory Management and Maintenance,* November, 1958.

CHAPTER SEVEN

Quality Control and Reliability Engineering

L. I. MEDLOCK   *Director of Reliability Control, General Dynamics, Convair Division, San Diego, California*

In a successful manufacturing company, the control of product quality and product reliability must be of vital interest to all managers at all levels. No other factor is more important to a company than the reliability of its products and services. Technological changes, complexities of products, competition within this country and from abroad, high service bills, enormous costs of failures and rejects, and customer dissatisfaction have combined to force a change in attitudes and the application of management techniques for the control of product quality and reliability. These forces make it imperative that each member of a company's team of specialists make use of the basic elements of control established by the quality and reliability program when carrying out his assigned part of the total task. The quality control and reliability program must be a *management team effort* which assures adequate control throughout all functional areas, including the design, development, procurement, manufacturing, packaging, storage, shipping, and customer-use phases.

This chapter treats quality control and reliability as functional activities rather than organizational elements per se. These activities must be tailored to the company and to the kind of product and services being offered. Any business prospers by serving its customers better than its competitors do. The principal concern regarding organization is one of relationship or placement. What gets shipped to the customer is a product of the total organization. Therefore, the person who is responsible for the planning and administration of the quality and reliability activities in a company should report to a member of management high enough in the organizational structure to authorize and enforce the accomplishment of tasks across the entire organization to achieve quality and reliability goals. The quality control and reliability manager is concerned that the proper control functions are performed by the organization, rather than which organizational element actually performs the task.

Each element of a quality control and reliability program is a subject for study within itself. No attempt is made here to deal in depth with these elements. Rather, those elements are discussed that management personnel are most likely to encounter in dealing with the organization and planning of quality control and reliability activities. Readers interested in more detailed information about a specific topic should refer to one of the excellent reference books or papers listed at the end of this chapter.

QUALITY CONTROL AND RELIABILITY PROGRAM MANAGEMENT

Quality Control Background. During the period of the late 1940s through most of the 1950s, it was common practice for quality control specialists to recommend a system of quality control as the solution to most industrial problems. Great emphasis was placed on statistical quality control as a revolutionary means of controlling manufacturing variation. The need for "selling quality control to top management" was a recommended first order of business for quality control managers. Many excellent quality control systems were developed and effectively implemented, but in some instances, management did not take an active interest or provide the motivational support required to make the system work. In other cases, the quality control system was not oriented to the organization's activities or the product. When these conditions existed, the quality control system failed to accomplish desired objectives, and management became disillusioned with quality control. Consequently, the emphasis has shifted from "selling the concept" to making the concept work. Out of this period of evolution have emerged the philosophy and practice of *quality control as a management-inspired function of the total organization.*

Reliability Engineering Background. A similar situation has surrounded the evolution of reliability principles and control techniques and their application as an effective tool for industry. Reliability engineering principles and techniques were first introduced in the early 1950s, and the first reliability programs were applied to electronic equipments and systems. Reliability engineering concepts were limited and untested; specialists working on these new programs placed their primary emphasis on mathematics and the statistical techniques of reliability prediction. After many false starts and through the process of trial and error, meaningful reliability disciplines and control techniques were eventually established and effectively integrated into the operations of many companies. Effective application of reliability engineering techniques in the areas of design review, parts improvement, effects of environment analysis and reliability assurance testing, supported by the proper application of statistical analysis, has made a great contribution to product-reliability improvement on programs where these techniques have been used.

Program Requirements for Reliability and Quality Control. Figure 7-1 lists the elements of a quality control program; Figure 7-2, the elements of a reliability program. Together, these elements combine to form a program of reliability and quality assurance. Reference is made to the integrated program as "reliability control" in some parts of this chapter.

All of these elements are important to the quality control and reliability specialist. The manager is concerned with keeping the proper balance among organizational elements and focusing attention on those elements of control that will assure business success for his company. Quality control and reliability engineering play an important role in the company's integrated program of checks and balances. Planning the inspection program to assure product conformance with requirements and the quality control audit of compliance with procedures are examples of comparing actual performance with the planned objectives.

*Quality management
Quality control procedures
Specification review
Engineering drawing and change control
*Quality control records
*Control of procured and subcontracted supplies
Sampling inspection
Tool gage and test equipment controls
In-process and final inspection

Control of special processes
Acceptance testing
Material storage, handling, packaging, and transportation controls
Control of nonconforming materials
*Corrective action
Quality improvement program
*Quality control audit
Quality cost analysis

* Elements selected for brief discussion in this chapter.

FIG. 7-1. *The elements of a typical quality control program.*

The principles of quality control and reliability functions have a broader application than merely reviewing design criteria and checking the product to the design requirement. Alert management can apply selected quality and reliability techniques to control the output of any element of the business organization. The elements discussed in this chapter are only examples of how the manager can put these functions and the by-products of their work to effective use.

Organizing for the Quality Control and Reliability Program. Design, manufacturing, and use factors are commonly recognized as the three primary influences on product reliability. Quality control has concerned itself with the manufacturing phase, and reliability engineering has concentrated on the design and development phase. There is no clear line of demarcation, however. The technical elements of a quality control program and those of a reliability program tie together and complement one another. They cannot be completely separated by function or responsibility, although they can be separated organizationally if it is advantageous to do so.

The factors influencing a decision to organize quality control and reliability into completely separate organizational elements should be evaluated carefully, for there may be significant cost savings and economy of resources resulting from an integrated quality and reliability organization. Integration ensures better quality and reliability system continuity from design concept to product delivery, and minimizes duplication of tasks by quality control engineering and reliability engineering.

When quality control and reliability functions are combined into one organizational group, they are generally called by such titles as *"reliability control,"*

*1. Reliability program management (planning, direction, review)
2. Reliability requirements analysis
   a. Operations analysis
   b. System mathematical models for alternative design concepts
   c. Statistical methods (apportionment, prediction, assessment)
   d. Human factors consideration
   e. Experience retention
3. Design assurance
   a. Design review
   b. Specification and procedure review
   c. Failure modes and effects analysis (physics of failure)
   d. Environmental analysis

4. Parts selection and application review (standardization and improvement)
*5. Reliability assurance testing (evaluation techniques)
   a. Component qualification status and control
*6. Failure-recurrence control
   a. Failure reporting
   b. Failure analysis
   c. Corrective action
7. Reliability indoctrination and training
*8. Reliability improvement plans
9. Reliability data (success, failure, mistakes, total population, etc.)

* Elements selected for brief discussion in this chapter.

FIG. 7-2. *The elements of a reliability engineering program.*

"reliability assurance," or *"product assurance."* The combined organizational element is a key department, supporting company management in determining, implementing, and auditing the company's reliability program. In addition to reliability engineering, it includes all activities normally associated with the terms "quality control" and "quality assurance."

MANAGEMENT PLANNING FOR THE
QUALITY CONTROL AND RELIABILITY PROGRAM

A properly planned system of quality control lays out in time and event sequence the functions to be performed by the total company organization to control product quality. The quality control system is keyed to the sequential flow of activities—design, development, procurement, production, and delivery. It must be borne in mind, however, that systems and programs in themselves do not control. Management direction, motivation, and follow-up are required to assure success.

It is essential, therefore, that management should influence the planning applied to integrating the elements of the quality control system into the company's overall program. Management planning for the quality control program involves identification of the task elements for control and the assignment of these tasks to responsible organizational elements for accomplishment. Task identification and assignment of responsibility must be followed by the reporting of activities, events, and progress for management evaluation of performance.

Management planning for the integration of the reliability engineering function into the company's operations follows the same concept. Areas of emphasis for reliability engineering will vary based on the product and its intended use. A reliability program plan is built around such a complex set of circumstances that a number of solutions to any one problem may be possible. The best solution is the one which optimizes application of the company's combined capabilities and resources to meet established reliability goals.

Program Phases. The nature of the work necessary to bring a product from the drawing board to the final assembly varies with different products; associated quality and reliability control techniques likewise vary. The relationships among product development and quality control and reliability engineering are most easily described in terms of program phases. For each product development phase, there is a corresponding group of quality and reliability functions, as shown in Figure 7-3.

The total reliability program may be considered to have two "layers," as shown in Figure 7-4. The lower layer consists of the major areas of activity that contribute to the product development process. The upper layer shows quality control and reliability engineering functions as applied to the product develop-

Product Development Phases	*Reliability Program Function*
Predesign	Advance design assurance
Business acquisition	Reliability program planning
Design	Design assurance
Procurement	Supplier quality control
Manufacturing	Manufacturing quality control
Test	Reliability test and demonstration
Product improvement	Quality and reliability improvement
Operational use	Operation assurance

NOTE: These phases and functions overlap in real time, so that all may be in progress to some degree at any one time.

FIG. 7-3. *The reliability program as a function of the product development process.*

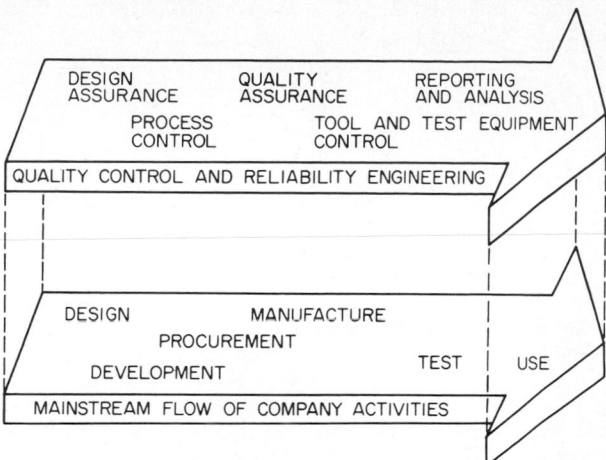

FIG. 7-4. *The reliability control overlay.*

ment process. Note the provision for the reporting and analysis function in the quality control and reliability engineering areas. This provides the feedback function for *management visibility* which is so vital to the execution of a reliability program.

TRADE-OFFS FOR MANAGEMENT DECISION

There are both technical decisions and business decisions involved in managing the quality control and reliability engineering functions. It is important to remember that there are times when the business decisions, for good reason, override the technical decisions, and vice versa. Just as design trade-offs are made at every level of product design to arrive at an optimum selection considering factors such as weight, size, performance, and color, there are trade-offs which affect management decisions concerning the reliability program to be applied to a particular product line. Prime considerations are the intended use of the product and the consequences of failure.

Product reliability, total program costs, and *completion schedules* are the bases for management planning. Reliability is made up of such product attributes as performance, safety, quality, maintainability, producibility, and others. It is possible to achieve any of these elements independently and in varying degrees of acceptance. But to achieve reliability, all of these elements must be controlled, measured, and coordinated as an entity, with a value assigned to ensure end-product reliability.

The RCS Triangle. Reliability (R), costs (C), and schedule (S) form a management trade-off triangle, as shown by Figure 7-5. This illustration considers reliability as the all-inclusive third parameter which, together with cost and schedule, constitutes the management problem. The management actions taken every day on a program can affect this triangle relationship in some way or other.

Basic Program Types. Applications of management trade-offs to three basic types of program are illustrated by Figure 7-6. In Program I, the concurrency concept of product development is illustrated. Because of urgent needs, it is agreed to go into production concurrently with the development test program. A

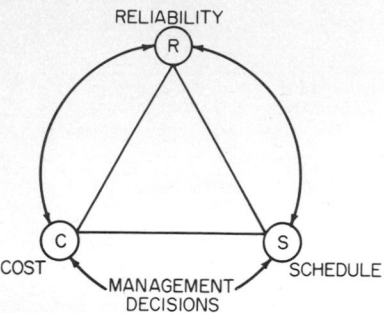

FIG. 7-5. *Management trade-off RCS triangle.*

calculated risk is taken that problems revealed in test can be corrected on the production line by retrofit. Design changes are made as problems are isolated. With enough time, reliability is eventually achieved as the result of corrective action.

In Program II, the austere development program is illustrated. Only limited funds are available. There is no great urgency, but a long-range need is seen. Development is started on an austere budget, taking a calculated risk that the limited state-of-the-art advance will not have adverse effects on areas designed around existing technologies. With the eventual availability of funding and time to make a reliability improvement program effective, reliability is achieved.

In Program III, reliability is the primary consideration, with delivery schedule and early program costs secondary. This type of program calls for the expenditure of more money and time in the development phase to permit extensive reliability controls during the design, manufacturing, and testing phases.

Optimizing the Reliability Program. Based on the management decisions resulting from analysis and evaluation of the trade-offs involved, there is an optimum reliability program for each basic program type. The reliability program is tailored to fit the program type by addition or deletion of quality control and reliability engineering task elements to fit the specific needs.

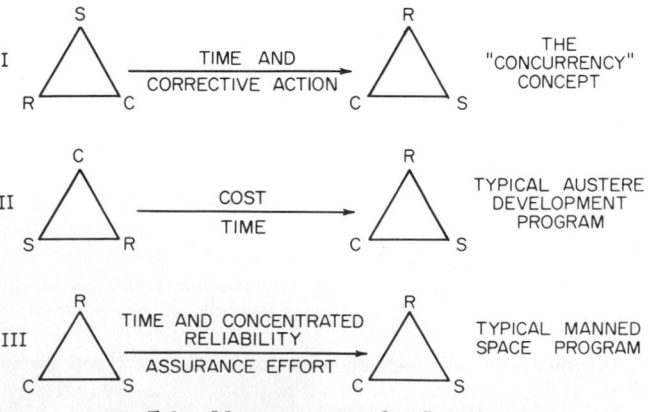

FIG. 7-6. *Management trade-off application.*

The Reliability Program Plan. Quality control and reliability planning for each program or product line should be documented in a program plan. The program plan becomes a handbook of ground rules and operating guidelines for managing the program. The tasks to be performed, references to applicable standard procedures, responsibilities, assignments, work flow charts, and other data pertinent to the execution of the plan should be included. The reliability program plan can become a section within the overall program management plan. A typical reliability program plan might consist of the following six major elements (the same concept and format is applicable to a quality program plan, or a combined quality and reliability program plan).

1. *Reliability program management.* This section states the objectives of the reliability program, reflects top management policy, and defines management and organizational relationships for executing the plan.

2. *Reliability analysis.* From analysis of the operational need and design concept, this section identifies the design assurance disciplines and other special control features to be applied on the program. Control points for application are designated.

3. *Related experience and capabilities.* This section commits personnel (special talents), equipment, and facility resources to the control of special areas identified by reliability analysis.

4. *Task identification.* This section identifies the work to be done. Special functions and new techniques needed for a particular program are described in detail. Quality and reliability functions which are considered standard and are recommended for all programs are merely listed as functions with a reference to the applicable standard procedure.

5. *Task assignment.* This section lists all of the major tasks comprising the program and the group responsible for their accomplishment. It is organized by program phase, responsible group, and task.

6. *Performance control.* This section summarizes the program reporting system to be employed and establishes the major milestones where program objectives will be reviewed and performance will be evaluated.

CONTROL OF PROCURED AND SUBCONTRACTED SUPPLIES

A significant percentage of the raw materials and parts or components used to manufacture any product are purchased from suppliers (vendors). The quality and reliability of the finished product is therefore influenced by the quality of the materials and parts that make up the finished product. Control of the quality of procured material and subcontracted work is of such importance that every system of quality control should place high priority and emphasis on a supplier quality program.

Supplier Quality Program. A supplier quality program is a quality control program applied to procured material and subcontractor products or services. The supplier quality program should be an integrated part of the company's procurement and incoming-material control systems. The program should be involved with those functions of the procurement and material-receiving cycle that must be controlled to achieve the desired quality of procured materials. It must also provide for the supporting functions which assist and complement normal purchasing activities for maintaining communication, working relationship, and technical liaison with suppliers.

Supplier Selection and Control. The supplier quality program shown in flow chart form in Figure 7-7 depicts the flow of activity and information from the supplier selection process through the entire procurement cycle, back to updating

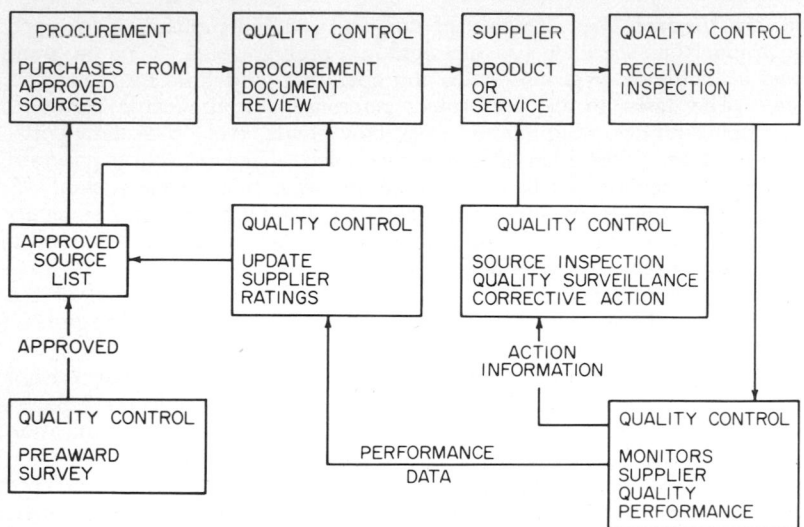

FIG. 7-7. *Supplier selection and control.*

the supplier's performance rating. Some variation of this program should be in effect in any organization that buys goods or services from another company. As a minimum, a program plan might require receiving inspection for shipping damage and correct quantity only. A more comprehensive program plan might require all of the elements of Figure 7-7 expanded for very detailed specific criteria to be met at each step.

The activities depicted in Figure 7-7 are briefly explained in sequential order of the procurement cycle as follows:

Supplier Selection. One of the primary controls over supplier quality is to limit procurement to approved sources.

Preaward Quality Control Evaluation Survey. This survey consists in analyzing the supplier's production and testing facilities, quality control techniques, written procedures, quality records, and management structure to ensure that adequate provisions have been included in their quality control system to prevent reliability degradation during the manufacturing process.

Survey Evaluation and Ratings. Results of the survey are evaluated and summarized by computing a numeric grade and general rating category reflecting each supplier's capability level. Suppliers who meet minimum requirements criteria are added to the approved sources document.

Approved Sources Document. This list becomes an inventory of suppliers who are approved by quality history performance or survey evaluation and is used by buyers when procurement action is initiated. It is also used by the quality control engineer in the audit of purchase orders to see that the orders are placed with approved sources.

Procurement Document Review. Specification of total requirements on the purchase order is essential to supplier performance. Procurement documents are reviewed by quality control engineering to determine that total quality requirements are included on the purchase order.

The flow of information and activities involved in the procurement document review function is illustrated by Figure 7-8.

Supplier Performance Rating. Supplier performance is monitored by source inspection, supplier quality surveillance personnel, and receiving inspection.

Acceptance or rejection of the supplier's product at source or receiving inspection level is the prime criterion for the supplier's performance rating. Capability ratings based on the preaward survey are only an indication of potential quality performance. A supplier rating, updated for actual performance, is more significant.

Procurement Quality Data System. The procurement cycle and the procurement quality system generate information that should be analyzed to measure supplier performance, evaluate internal efficiency, and determine the need for future action. The use of an automated data system to gather and report this information is illustrated by Figure 7-9.

The data system collects and reports the following types of information for use by management and operating departments:

1. Source and receiving inspection scheduled work load
2. Current receiving inspection work load and backlog awaiting inspection
3. Supplier quality performance rating and corrective-action information
4. Procured-material quality level and trends data

Supplier Corrective-action Program. The corrective-action program must be timely and effective, and must demand that deficiencies be corrected. Problem information is furnished to the supplier through the buyer, and corrective action and notification of action taken are requested. (See "Failure-recurrence Control" on page 7-88.)

The flow of information and action involved in requesting corrective action from a supplier is illustrated by Figure 7-10. The supplier reports the action taken back through the purchasing buyer to complete the corrective-action cycle.

Assist to Suppliers. Providing an understanding of program objectives and clarifying the detailed requirements through personal contact and exchange of information and ideas establish the baseline from which a satisfactory working relationship for achieving quality program goals can be maintained. Face-to-face contact to exchange quality requirements information and discuss ideas for meeting these requirements is a helpful technique for preventing or correcting supplier quality problems.

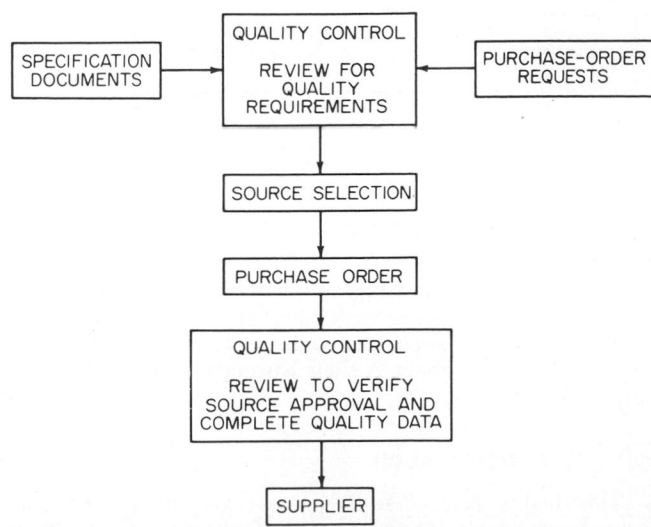

FIG. 7-8. *Procurement document review.*

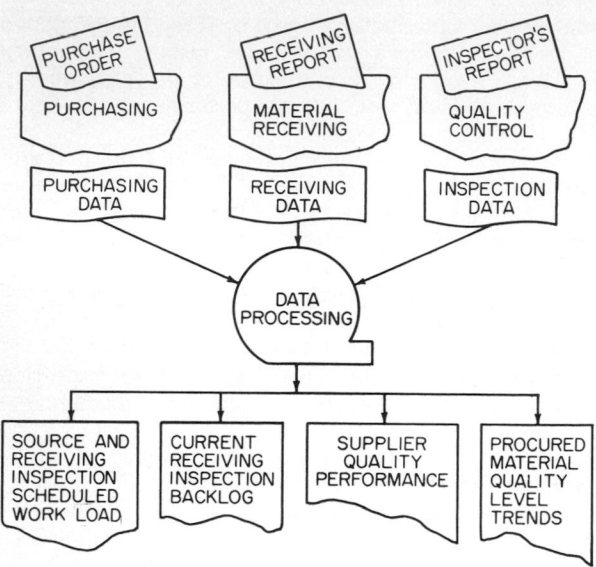

FIG. 7-9. *Typical automated data system for supplier quality program.*

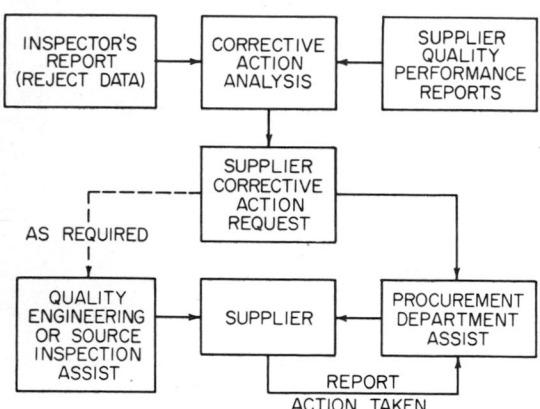

FIG. 7-10. *Request for supplier corrective action.*

In summary, the supplier quality program places emphasis on four important elements:

1. Selecting the most highly qualified suppliers for the type of work involved
2. Providing suppliers with complete requirements information
3. Verifying the suppliers' conformance to requirements
4. Assisting suppliers in their corrective-action efforts to ensure product quality improvement

QUALITY CONTROL AUDIT

The quality control audit process assesses the adequacy of the product and procedures relating to the control of quality. Carefully planned audits of procedures and policies against practices and of the product for conformance to design data provide valuable data that can be used to evaluate organizational performance or verify that the product conforms to requirements. Quality audits should be planned and scheduled on a periodic basis so that all areas to be audited are covered within an established time period. The quality audit program should allow for performing one-time, special quality audits without serious impact on the planned audit schedule. These special audits are an effective means of assuring that procedural compliance or product quality has not deteriorated because of internal changes such as turnover in key personnel, a new process, new or modified equipment, facility relocation, or work area rearrangement.

Performing the Quality Audit. Procedures, specifications, and other documents related to organizational performance for product quality are analyzed to develop a series of significant characteristics for investigation. Utilizing these preplanned audit checklists, periodic audits of randomly selected work areas are performed. The audit is performed by specially trained quality control specialists who have no line responsibilities in the selected work area.

The product audit consists in investigating the manufacturing process by retesting or reinspecting a sample of the product which has been previously accepted.

The procedures audit compares the actual operations against applicable procedures to determine if documents are current and complete and if they are fully understood and are being followed by all personnel.

Audit findings and the auditor's recommendations are then summarized in report form for management information or action as required. If properly administered, the quality audit procedure is a valuable technique to aid in achieving organizational performance and quality goals by indicating to management where action should be taken for improvement. (See also Chapter 6 of Section 10.)

QUALITY CONTROL RECORDS AND RELIABILITY DATA

Traditionally, data from quality control records files have been utilized to provide information to support a feedback control function. The product is compared with the design requirements and established standards by the inspector and the quality control engineer. Information obtained by comparing input requirements with the output is a by-product of their efforts which becomes the basis for evaluating performance and the need for action. Data established or gathered by reliability engineers is maintained and utilized in conjunction with quality control data and records to form the backup to support numerous technical and management decisions.

Quality Control Records and Data. The types of information normally recorded and reported by quality control are:

Source inspection and supplier testing results
Receiving inspection and test results
Manufacturing inspection and test results
Product acceptance reports
Rejection data
Corrective-action history
Failure data
Traceability records

Operating time and operating cycle data
Total quantity (population) information
Component-quality history data
Configuration accounting data
Final acceptance records and historical documentation

Reliability Records and Data. The types of information normally gathered and reported by reliability engineering functions are:

Design review documentation
Reliability analysis records
Reliability assurance test data
Failure analysis reports
Field or service problem reports
Problem closeout reports

Quality history records and associated reliability data are identified and traceable back to the product through an item number, part number, name, serial number, lot number, batch number, and the like. To be of greatest value, records data must be complete, accurate, and available on a timely basis. The results of the quality control and reliability engineer's work are largely dependent upon the completeness and accuracy of the data he is working with. Quality control records and reliability data are typically used to:

Calculate mean time between failures (MTBF)
Provide history of problems or failures
Provide individual-component history records
Provide program status reports
Provide trends data for management review
Provide basis for calculating rework and scrap costs
Detect trouble areas for analysis and correction
Document product status and configuration
Provide customer confidence
Provide records of past experience
Provide permanent legal company records

Reliability Control Data Center. The kinds and quantity of accurate information required to support a reliability control program have grown steadily. Manual recording, gathering, filing, and distribution of quality and reliability records data are an effective method of handling small quantities of such data. If large quantities of data and multiple reports are required, a centralized reliability control data center utilizing an automated data system is recommended. The central data center prevents duplication of clerical help, files, and so on. Automatic data-processing equipment provides a means of storing large quantities of information and the capability for rapid retrieval of almost any data desired. Where the complete record is required, microfilming equipment and microfilm readers and printers become an effective means of record storage and retrieval.

RELIABILITY ASSURANCE TESTING

Determination that parts and component assemblies are qualified as a result of having passed a series of specially designed tests is essential to any successful reliability program. Inadequate emphasis on this important function has often allowed a slow degradation of performance to go undetected and eventually become a serious reliability problem. Typically, a great deal of effort goes into the conduct of test programs, but many problems which are revealed are never thoroughly analyzed and corrected. Time after time when serious failures have occurred in this country's space program, subsequent investigation has revealed that a close analysis of previous testing results would have warned of the potential failure. Every malfunction and observed peculiarity in the behavior of a system is an important warning of potential failure. Steps must be taken to understand the cause and eliminate the possibility of recurrence. This calls for a thorough and continuing evaluation of all test results and subsequent service experience to establish component qualification. The aggressive management of test programs to coordinate and combine the various types of testing into an integrated, meaningful whole is recommended.

Integrated Test Philosophy. Types of tests that can be combined into an integrated test plan to enhance reliability are as follows.

Initial Acceptance Test (IAT). IATs are used to demonstrate a component's ability to perform its specified function in a laboratory static bench test at room temperature. Selected portions of the IAT may be used as receiving inspections tests (IRs). The IAT, or selected portions, may also be used as a proof cycle after environmental tests.

Design Proof Test (DPT). These tests are conducted to demonstrate that equipment of a known design configuration is qualified for its intended use. Successful completion of a DPT is established when a production sample has functioned in accordance with the component specification at established environmental levels, more stringent (one and one-half times design level) than the maximum environmental levels expected in service.

Production Acceptance Test (PAT). PATs are applied at levels of end-use operating environmental stress, simulating actual use requirements as closely as possible in the environmental laboratory. They provide experience data on functional equipments. The PATs are applied as in-line, in-process tests on specimens selected at a sampling frequency dependent upon performance history.

Periodic Revaluation Test (PRT). These tests are conducted at selected design-level environments on types of equipment previously qualified through DPT. Normally, the more adverse environments such as vibration, temperature, acceleration, humidity, and altitude are selected. Items which have shown questionable reliability based on past test histories and field experience, and those items designated as requiring further production verification, are tested.

Stress Limits Test (SLT). These tests are conducted on equipment which has completed DPT and PRT. These tests determine the design safety margin and manufacturing variance at an environmental intensity beyond that for which the equipment was designed. Testing beyond the design intensities also increases the effective sample size for increased statistical confidence.

Extended Time Test (ETT). These tests are conducted on selected components that have completed PAT under simulated flight or ground operational conditions for the determination of realistic mean-time-between-failures (MTBF) data. The ETT demonstrates achieved reliability for each equipment type. A use operation cycle is repeated a sufficient number of times to establish the required reliability with a stated confidence level.

The types of tests described as a function of environmental intensity in the previous paragraphs are shown in Figure 7-11. Note the interrelationship between the individual tests which make up the integrated or unified test program.

Advantages of the Integrated Test Plan. From a program management viewpoint, there are distinct technical and administrative advantages to the integrated

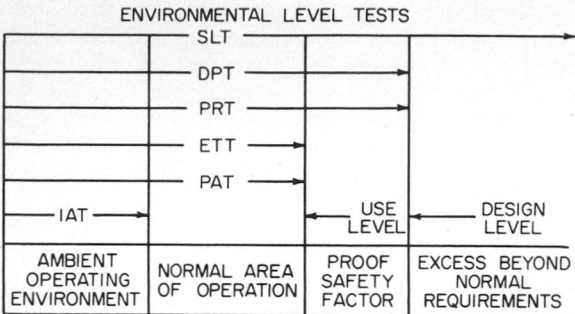

FIG. 7-11. *Tests as a function of environmental intensity.*

(or unified) test program concept. It provides for improved management visibility and control of the overall test program. Through a *central test control* function, tests can be planned, scheduled, and conducted in an orderly manner. The number of component test specimens that must be expended in testing is reduced. The amount of independent test activities is reduced. Fewer facilities and test equipment are required. Administrative tasks are reduced. There is better test program continuity, and less manpower is required. Test data obtained from the program are more meaningful. These combined advantages result in an improved test program at a reduced total cost.

Continuous Verification of Qualification Status. Continued observance of component operating characteristics through subsystem, system, and composite testing and operational use provides valuable information for the reliability engineer in evaluating the adequacy of the component for the application involved. A qualification status report, updated periodically to reflect current status, documents the results of this program for a permanent historical record and for reference by any function that needs the data.

FAILURE-RECURRENCE CONTROL

One of the prime objectives of a quality control and reliability program is to prevent problems, discrepancies, and failures. However, with the best of planning and execution of controls, some problems always occur. When significant problems are discovered, it is important that complete and timely corrective action be taken to minimize further program impact. Failure-recurrence control is a program to identify problems, report them, and assure that they are thoroughly analyzed, with technical follow-up to see that actions are taken to prevent recurrences.

The ability to solve problems and the knowledge that problems exist do not themselves yield solutions to reliability problems. A formal program of corrective action, which is motivated by management emphasis and supported with technical follow-up to assure complete and timely solutions, is necessary to get desired corrective or preventive actions. Every reported problem or failure should be accounted for in detail. Two essential features of the follow-up should be: (1) treat every failure as important and potentially "fixable" whether repetitive or not and (2) do not consider corrective action complete until the change has been incorporated and proof-tested in the product or system.

Problem areas which most frequently result in cause of failure are engineering *design* deficiencies, *procedural* deficiencies, and *manufacturing* variations (or combinations of these). In each of these categories, a different approach or technique may be required to reach a solution to the problem. Therefore, it is important that the corrective-action program include the capability to react to problems wherever they occur and regardless of the cause.

Areas of Activity. The failure-recurrence control plan deals with four distinct areas of activity:

1. The procedure for getting the problem *identified* and *reported*
2. A system to *account for the problem*
    a. Maintain a log of all problems reported
    b. Track the activity and report current status
    c. Maintain historical records including final action taken to close out the problem
3. The capability to determine the *cause of failure* and to determine what needs to be done to correct it and to prevent recurrence
4. The *proper emphasis* to get the recommended action taken

THE FAILURE-REPORTING AND CORRECTIVE-ACTION CYCLE

The flow of information and functions performed in a plan for failure-recurrence control is illustrated by Figure 7-12. In this illustration, the system starts with the receipt of a problem report and the return of the failed product. The problem is recorded in the data center, and distribution of copies is made to the appropriate quality or reliability engineers. The failed product is submitted to failure analysis. Cause of the failure is determined and corrective action is requested from the responsible functions.

Quality control engineers are responsible to close out supplier problems and manufacturing problems. Reliability engineers deal with design, development, and test engineering problems. The responsible agency takes action and advises the quality or reliability engineer. When the action taken is approved by the engineer, problem closure reports are processed back to the data center for permanent record. Copies of the problem closeout are distributed by the data center, and this completes the corrective-action cycle.

Determining the Cause of Failure. A key factor in preventing the recurrence of failures, mistakes, and other problems is to be able to determine what has happened and what the underlying cause was. The cause of failure is often very subtle, elusive, and difficult to prove. Sometimes, as in the case of a fire, the evidence is destroyed. A thorough evaluation of all known facts backed up by simulation and testing of theory is often effective in determining what happened and what caused it to happen. When the failed product is available, failure analysis is a proved technique for establishing the cause of failure.

Failure Analysis Defined. Failure analysis is the documented investigative action to confirm the failure, to establish the mode and cause of failure, to classify the failure as either design or nonconformance to design, and to recommend corrective action. Failure analysis is performed to the degree required to establish ultimate failure cause from which corrective action can be accomplished. This includes dissection and destructive analysis, if necessary. When cause of failure is determined, a failure analysis report is prepared including a recommended corrective action.

From this definition, it might appear that failure analysis is a laboratory function. This is not always the case. A thorough investigation of what happened and the determination of what caused it to happen can often be made at the

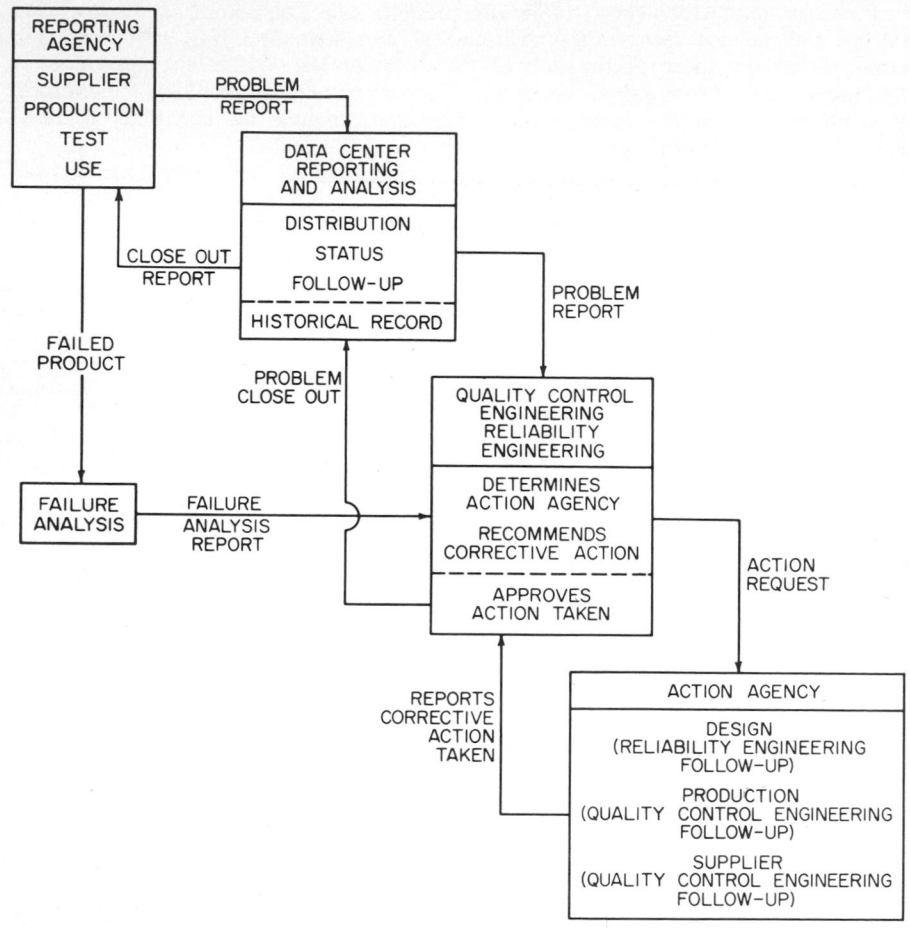

FIG. 7-12.   *Failure-recurrence control.*

point where the failure occurred.   This is referred to as "on the spot" analysis. In other cases, the failed product is returned to the producing department or the supplier for failure analysis investigation.   It is important to document properly how the investigation was conducted and what was found.   The determined cause of failure is the basis for all other action that is taken to correct the situation.   Where other factors permit, a failure analysis laboratory with special equipment and specially trained personnel can do a professional job of finding the causes of failure that cannot be determined in other ways.

Classification of Failures.   Failures are classified as to severity of failure and the effect failure would have on the operating system.   This establishes an order of priority for corrective action.

Critical failure—any failure or performance degradation that normally would cause a safety hazard, program delay, or loss of a prime *use* objective

Major failure—a failure or defect which is not in itself a critical failure, but which might seriously affect the reliability of the system

Minor failure—all failures other than critical or major

Program Reliability Review Board.   Some companies have made significant reliability improvement in their products by establishing a reliability review board.

The reliability review board consists of the program manager and his staff. The board meets periodically (a fixed schedule is recommended) to establish policy and review reliability trends, problems, and reliability program status. The main purpose of the meeting is to emphasize *timely corrective action*. Test histories, failure analysis reports, and other data regarding the cause and significance of the failure being reviewed are presented. Factors such as contractual implications, effects on schedules, consequences of the alternative recommended actions, effectiveness of corrective action taken, and the like are reviewed to provide a basis for making a final decision. Selected representatives from any organizational element that has responsibility for a function or activity relating to the topics being discussed are asked to attend. Transactions of the meetings are documented in minutes which are issued with action items identified to specific individual or organizational elements.

THE RELIABILITY IMPROVEMENT PROGRAM

Reliability improvement programs are often initiated because it is more desirable to improve the existing product so that it will serve a new or different purpose requiring improved performance than it is to develop a totally new product. In other cases, an improvement plan may be required because reliability goals have not been achieved or product performance is marginal. In either case, careful planning of the program is essential. A management-approved *reliability improvement program plan* is recommended. The program plan is organized in a manner similar to the reliability program plan described earlier in this chapter.

Elements of a Reliability Improvement Program Plan. Development of the reliability improvement program should be based on a detailed study of the design and operating experiences with the existing product. From the results of this detailed study, a program can be planned to make maximum use of those parts of the product or system that have demonstrated satisfactory reliability. The improvement program can then be tailored to concentrate on upgrading in other areas where experience indicates the greatest gains in reliability can be made.

The study of the experience with the current product must identify the major contributors to unreliability. These selected items must get priority for improvement over less important problem areas that are to be corrected routinely as part of the improvement program. The need for good experience data emphasizes the necessity of keeping good product records and performance data and making them available on a timely basis.

SUMMARY

The practitioner of quality control and reliability has few opportunities to start over. The need for thoroughness in planning and aggressiveness in managing the plan cannot be overstressed. Reliability and quality assurance engineering is a new and changing field. The quality and reliability program plan requires intelligent application, with continuous review and periodic adjustment to keep it current with other program elements and with the state of the art in the reliability and quality engineering areas.

The importance of complete and accurate quality history records and performance data for use by the quality control or reliability engineer has been stressed. A program of thorough inspection accomplished by technically qualified personnel who have been specially trained and certified to inspect the product and to record the specified data will support the engineer's need.

The functions of quality control and reliability engineering are interrelated and dependent upon one another for efficiency. The exchange of information between them and the combination of their efforts to act on the information will improve performance. Management control to strike the proper balance between the "technical" and the "business" aspects of the quality control and reliability program is important. The manager must constantly guard against "ritualism," "hobby shops," and "paper passing" exercises that ignore the product; and most of all, he must avoid being a "crutch." Once the task is identified and responsibility is assigned to another organizational element, the task of quality control and reliability engineering becomes one of monitoring performance. The reporting, analysis, and follow-up applied to administering the program plan must focus attention on the specific areas where management attention is needed.

BIBLIOGRAPHY

Quality Control

Cowan, A., *Quality Control for the Manager*, The Macmillan Company, New York, 1964.
Feigenbaum, A. V., *Total Quality Control Engineering and Management*, McGraw-Hill Book Company, New York, 1961.
Grant, E. L., *Statistical Quality Control*, 3d ed., McGraw-Hill Book Company, New York, 1964.
Hansen, B. L., *Quality Control: Theory and Applications*, Prentice-Hall, Inc., Englewood Cliffs, N.J., 1963.
Juran, J. M., *Quality Control Handbook*, 2d ed., McGraw-Hill Book Company, New York, 1962.

Reliability Engineering

ARINC Research Corporation, *Reliability Engineering*, Prentice-Hall, Inc., Englewood Cliffs, N.J., 1964.
Bazovsky, I., *Reliability Theory and Practice*, Prentice-Hall, Inc., Englewood Cliffs, N.J., 1961.
Calabro, S. R., *Reliability Principles and Practices*, McGraw-Hill Book Company, New York, 1962.
General Dynamics/Astronautics (a symposium), "Reliability Program," Document Control No. GD/A AFY-64-002, General Dynamics Corporation, November, 1963.
Institute of Radio Engineers, Inc., *Reliability Training Text*, Editorial Department, New York, 1960.
Lloyd, D. K., and M. Lipow, *Reliability: Management, Methods and Mathematics*, Prentice-Hall, Inc., Englewood Cliffs, N.J., 1962.
Society of Automotive Engineers, Subcommittee on Reliability, *Reliability Control in Aerospace Equipment Development*, The Macmillan Company, New York, 1963.

Government Specifications for Quality and Reliability Requirements

(All are published by U.S. Government Printing Office, Washington, D.C.)
MIL-I-45208A, *Inspection System Requirements*.
MIL-Q-9858A, *Quality Control System Requirements*.
MIL-R-27542A (USAF), *Reliability Program Requirements for Aerospace Systems, Subsystems and Equipment*.
NASA Quality Publication NPC 200-2, *Quality Program Provisions for Space System Contractors*.
NASA Quality Publication NPC 200-3, *Inspection System Provisions for Suppliers of Space Materials, Parts, Components and Services*.
NASA Reliability Publication NPC 250-1, *Reliability Program Provisions for Space System Contractors*.

CHAPTER EIGHT

Industrial Engineering

WILLIAM K. HODSON *President, H. B. Maynard and Company, Incorporated, Pittsburgh, Pennsylvania*

The purpose of this chapter is to provide the manager with an understanding of what industrial engineering is and how he can use it to manage an enterprise more effectively.

There has been a tremendous growth in the use of industrial engineers by industry and commerce. In 1964, one engineer out of every seven employed in the United States was working in the area of methods and work simplification. In the decade ending in 1965, membership in the American Institute of Industrial Engineers increased by 84 percent.[1]

During this period of accelerated growth, the role of the industrial engineer expanded rapidly. In the early 1900s, industrial engineers largely confined their attention to manufacturing activities with heavy emphasis on improving methods, establishing time standards, and installing wage-incentive programs. Although many industrial engineers are still engaged in activities closely related to manufacturing, their role, even in this area, has expanded to include not only the traditional functions of methods and standards, but such things as facility layout and planning; production planning; scheduling and inventory-control systems; quality controls; automation; operations research; and others.

More significant, however, industrial engineers are serving many areas of management other than manufacturing. Activities in these areas cover such things as organization planning; long-range planning; compensation plans; product development; distribution methods; warehouse-location studies; standard cost and budget programs; employee training; office systems and procedures; data processing; computer applications for both clerical and process controls; management information systems; and many others. So, although the subject of industrial engineering is included in the section "Manufacturing Management" in this Handbook, it is quite clear that the modern industrial engineering role covers a broader range of activities.

---

[1] "Engineering Manpower in Profile," report from the *National Engineers Register* based on a study conducted by Engineers Joint Council, New York, 1965.

Definition of Industrial Engineering. The scope of the industrial engineering activity cannot be defined in terms of the function of the organization, such as manufacturing, construction, public utility, trade, finance, or insurance. Nor can it be defined in terms of the type of work being performed, that is, manufacturing operations, office operations, plant maintenance, and the like. The formal definition of industrial engineering adopted by the American Institute of Industrial Engineers is:[2]

Industrial engineering is concerned with the design, improvement, and installation of integrated systems of men, materials, and equipment. It draws upon specialized knowledge and skill in the mathematical, physical, and social sciences together with the principles and methods of engineering analysis and design, to specify, predict, and evaluate the results to be obtained from such systems.

Place in Organization. The place of the industrial engineering function in an organization will depend on several factors. If the role of industrial engineering is a broad one covering a number of activity areas of an organization, it will report to a high level—in some cases, to the president; in others, to the vice president of operations. If the services provided by industrial engineering are largely confined to manufacturing operations, then the function will frequently report to a works manager or production superintendent. The guiding principle is this: The industrial engineering function should report to the executive responsible for the activity areas it serves.

Role of Industrial Engineering. Before a manager can determine what areas or activities should be served by industrial engineering or what functions should be carried on by this group, it is essential for him to understand clearly the role of industrial engineering.

Industrial engineering is a service function. Its only role is to assist other groups—either line or staff groups—to carry on their activities more effectively. By its nature, industrial engineering is oriented in the direction of profit improvement. Yet it cannot, by itself, improve profits. It can only do so by helping other departments to improve.

Frequently, improvements involve change, and they also involve controls. Change or innovation does not come easily. There is a common, human tendency to resist changing things that we are used to doing. Introducing change requires great tact, personal skill, and, to an extent, salesmanship. If industrial engineers do not have these potential skills, they will, at best, have limited success. There will be a tendency for people to resist their plans or programs.

Many people do not like to work under controls—controls in the form of budgets, labor performance controls, scrap and rework controls, machine utilization controls, or the myriad of other controls that are an essential part of good management practice. Industrial engineers are closely associated with the development of these controls. Thus, their work is not always welcomed by the departments they serve. As a consequence, the manager to whom the industrial engineering function reports must play a delicate role. He must provide the industrial engineers with support and encouragement for their work. At the same time, he must realize that certain human relations problems may result from their efforts.

The improvements, savings, or profits that result from industrial engineering are rightfully credited to the departments involved. The industrial engineers can take the satisfaction that comes from a job well done. A high degree of teamwork and respect between the managers of line departments and those of service departments, such as industrial engineering, is a good sign of a

[2] Definition adopted by the American Institute of Industrial Engineers, October, 1955.

matured, well-organized, and effective organization. One of the most important jobs of a manager is to develop this teamwork and mutual respect.

THE FUNCTIONS OF INDUSTRIAL ENGINEERING

In the pages that follow, the major functions and activities of industrial engineering will be defined and described. The manager can then weigh and evaluate these functions in relation to his own operation and decide how they can best be used. There are few organizations where industrial engineers perform every function listed. In some organizations, a given function may not be of major importance. In other cases, it may be carried on by groups other than industrial engineering. Each organization must establish the functions to be performed by industrial engineering in a way compatible with the nature of the organization and its organizational structure.

Management Planning. The basic responsibility for management planning rests with the manager of the enterprise. In the past, managers have relied heavily upon their experience, intuition, and basic common sense to plan and direct the efforts of their enterprises. The professional manager of a scientifically managed enterprise, however, relies more and more on an organized team approach to the handling of management problems. This frequently follows the engineering approach to problem solving and, in all cases, requires objective information and a means for analyzing this information to plan and control the enterprise.

Because of his broad understanding of the basic activity areas of management and his engineering approach to management problems, the industrial engineer is frequently used as a staff adviser to top management on problems of management planning. This activity can be subdivided into two main areas—management studies and organization planning.

Management Studies. Included in the management studies classification is a broad category of studies designed to provide the manager of the enterprise with information or recommendations that will permit him to manage more objectively. These studies may include such basic things as the establishment, clarification, or modification of company objectives; or they may include a basic definition of the mission of the organization. Recommendations may be concerned with the most effective allocation of the organization's resources, both human and physical, for the accomplishment of the established objectives. Other recommendations may involve the design of the basic system by which these resources will be utilized. This will include not only the design of the basic system, but also a plan for control of it. This control system measures results and indicates areas of the system that are not producing according to plan.

Organization Planning. By the very nature of his work, the industrial engineer is concerned with many activity areas of management. As a result, he is frequently called upon to conduct an analysis of the organization structure and to assist in planning the most effective form of organization.

Methods and Procedures. This is one of the traditional functions of industrial engineering. It is usually a basic function of all industrial engineering departments. This activity normally includes developing methods, training operators to follow the method, and standardizing material, equipment, and working conditions.

Work Simplification. Work simplification is a technique for finding better ways of performing any type of work. Work simplification applies to every phase of a job—from eliminating waste motions in manual operations to completely rearranging work stations and plant layouts. Work simplification, in its broadest sense, includes process and operation analysis using charts of (1) the flow of materials and paper work in a process and (2) the movement of men in relationship to machines and equipment.

Operation Analysis. Operation analysis encompasses all of the procedures concerned with the design or improvement of production and service operations. Studies of an entire process may be made to determine whether operations or elements can be eliminated, combined, changed in sequence, or improved. An analysis may also be made of the method, motion pattern, materials, and tools and equipment used in an individual operation to determine the "one best way." The main points which should be considered in every operation analyzed are: (1) purpose of the operation or activity; (2) complete survey of all operations performed; (3) inspection requirements or specifications; (4) materials; (5) material handling; (6) setup and tool equipment; (7) possibilities for job improvement; (8) working conditions; and (9) methods.

Motion Study. Motion study is the investigation and measurement of the movements involved in the performance of manual work, their subsequent improvement, and the application of easier and more productive methods. The study of the needs and problems of the operators is the starting point of any motion-study investigation. Its final purpose is to enable the operators to work with minimum effort and maximum efficiency.

Material Handling. Material handling is concerned with the moving, packaging, and storing of materials in any form. Material handling is a broad segment of industrial engineering. It includes problems related to plant layout, storage, mechanical equipment design, automation, management, motion and time study, cost reduction, transportation, traffic distribution, and packaging.

Operator Training. The industrial engineer is vitally concerned with seeing that a new method is properly learned. He, therefore, is frequently responsible for seeing that the operators are properly trained. His responsibility can range from providing a thorough training program to very limited training which may involve just a few words of instruction. When the methods changes have been installed and the training has been given, there is no assurance that the method will always be used in the way it was designed. Therefore, the industrial engineer must follow up periodically to be certain that his method is continuing to be used.

Work Measurement. Work measurement is another traditional function of industrial engineering common to most industrial engineering departments. Work measurement is a procedure for measuring or forecasting the rate of performance of an existing or newly designed operation or activity. More specifically, it involves establishing standards of performance which may be expressed in terms of rate of output, time, quality, and so on. It then compares standards of performance with actual performance. Several techniques of work measurement are in use.

Stopwatch Time Study. Stopwatch time study is a procedure used to determine a standard time for an operation by direct measurement employing the stopwatch as the measuring device. The purposes of time study are (1) to analyze the operations and job conditions for possibilities of improving existing methods; (2) to increase the effectiveness of effort by the use of necessary motions only; (3) to establish and standardize conditions for efficient operation; (4) to establish consistent and equitable standards of performance; (5) to furnish reliable data for use in compiling charts and formulas; and (6) to provide a permanent record of actual conditions associated with the time standard.

Work Sampling. Work sampling is a random sampling method of getting facts about machines and human activities. It is a useful industrial engineering technique for gathering facts inexpensively and accurately about an operation, process, or any other activity—facts which will make it possible to reach decisions to reduce costs, to develop controls, and to improve manpower effectiveness. The work-sampling technique has broad applications in both manufacturing and service endeavors.

Predetermined Motion Times.   Motion-time data systems consisting of predetermined times associated with basic, or fundamental, motions are developed on the basis of two assumptions—first, that all manual work can be divided into basic units, or elements, which are universally descriptive and applicable; and second, that an average time in terms of job variables can be associated with each element.   Some of the more commonly used predetermined motion-time systems are methods-time measurement, work factor, basic motion-time study, and motion-time analysis.

Standard Data.   Standard data consist of an inventory or file of elemental standard times accumulated from time studies or from special studies.   These time values are expressed in terms of job variables.   When it is desired to set a standard on a new job, elemental times are extracted from tables, charts, or graphs and are synthesized in a logical sequence to compute the time required to perform the job.   Variables are generally analyzed and presented by the use of curves or tables.   The kinds of data tables and curves that can be used are unlimited and depend to a large extent on the skill and imagination of the industrial engineer.

Time Formulas.   A time formula is a set of standard data reduced to its simplest form.   The ultimate objective of any formula is to put a set of standard data into such a simple form that anyone knowing the characteristics of the part, the activity, or the job can determine from it the time for the operation.   To accomplish this purpose requires careful analysis by the industrial engineer during the derivation of the formula.

Formulas have an application in the measurement of work in storerooms, janitorial service, shipping and receiving departments, and in any other type of productive or service operation.

Wage and Salary Payment.   Industrial engineers have traditionally been responsible for the design, development, and installation of wage-incentive plans. Their long experience with wages and wage incentives has, in turn, led to their interest in job evaluation, merit rating, and salary administration.

Wage-incentive Plans.   Wage-incentive plans are designed to encourage superior performance through the payment of increased wages for increased productivity.   Accurate work measurement is the basic requirement for the proper application of incentives.

The application of wage incentives is not limited to direct labor.   Wage incentives may be developed also for indirect workers, maintenance workers, and office and supervisory employees.   In fact, the field for application of wage incentives is almost limitless.

Job Evaluation.   Job evaluation is a procedure for measuring the relative worth of jobs through the weighing of the relative importance of certain job characteristics.   Job evaluation plans may be developed for salary and hourly employees not only in manufacturing enterprises, but in any type of organization including commercial, governmental, and nonprofit groups of all kinds.

Merit Rating.   Merit rating is an orderly and systematic way of appraising work performance of individuals in any type of organization.   The development of a merit-rating system includes determining the purposes; establishing job specifications or requirements; determining the characteristics and aspects of work performance to be measured and developing procedures for scoring; developing instructions and training for those doing the rating; designing rating procedures including frequency; and formulating policies relative to the use of ratings to improve employee performance.

Wage and Salary Administration. The industrial engineer is closely concerned with wage and salary administration, because it is his responsibility to develop programs that influence wages, such as wage incentives, job evaluation, and merit rating. The success of wage and salary administration depends, to a large extent, upon the industrial engineering functions of development and proper maintenance of wage-incentive and job-evaluation programs and the development of adequate merit-rating systems.

Control Procedures. The essential elements of scientific management are measurement and control. Without some means of measurement, control is impossible. Measurement, however, to be effective, must be embodied into some form of control procedure.

Planning and Scheduling Procedures. Planning and scheduling is the process of predetermining operations and their completion dates in accordance with delivery dates and of issuing necessary directives, usually by means of special paper-work procedures, so that the production or service required will be achieved within the established quantity, quality, time, and cost limits. Through planning and scheduling, the right combinations of the right operations at the right time and place are determined and directives are issued to the people concerned so that all operations will be properly controlled and coordinated.

The industrial engineer is frequently responsible for the development of planning and scheduling systems best suited to the needs of the organization.

Inventory Control. Inventory control is the process of planning for and maintaining a proper balance among the required kinds and amounts of items and materials so that within the enterprise the optimum combination of the major related costs is attained.

The industrial engineer can devise inventory-control systems and establish procedures and then periodically review and adjust such procedures.

Quality Control. Quality control is the systematic control of the variables which affect the conformance of the end product to established quality standards and specifications. It involves real-time control of quality in addition to after-the-fact inspection and separation of substandard items.

The industrial engineer may (1) participate in establishing the standards and specifications which determine the quality objectives to be measured or evaluated; (2) analyze the economics of where and when in the process control should take place; (3) specify methods of inspection; (4) develop statistical procedures to indicate whether or not quality is under control; and (5) work with supervision to determine and establish corrective action for conditions which indicate that quality is not under control.

Cost Control. The industrial engineer works toward optimizing total cost through the identification, analysis, and control of the major cost components. In a manufacturing enterprise, these costs are manpower, materials, supplies, maintenance, and repair.

He assists in controlling costs of manpower through the techniques explained previously in the paragraphs dealing with methods and procedures, work measurement, and wage and salary payment. He assists in controlling material by conducting special studies primarily directed to more efficient material utilization. He assists in controlling supplies by establishing standard amounts of supplies required. He assists in controlling maintenance and repair costs by establishing preventive-maintenance programs, planning and scheduling procedures, and work-measurement programs.

In the case of indirect costs (those not related specifically to a product), the industrial engineer will establish budgets through the application of methods analysis and measurement to the various items of such cost where justified. In this manner, he will develop "engineered" budgets rather than budgets based solely on historical rates of expenditure.

Standardization and Classification. Standardization has to do with the development of uniform specifications for tools, materials, equipment, and practices. Standards dealing with practices may include such things as drafting-room practices, standard machine-shop practices, a style manual, procedures for paper-work operations, and so on.

Classification is concerned with the development of codes and numbering systems designed to identify and classify such items as parts, materials, products, and the like.

The industrial engineer is frequently charged with the responsibility of designing, developing, and installing standards and classification programs.

Product, Facilities, and Equipment. *Facility Location.* Facility location requires the application of scientific principles in the selection of an area or site most conducive to the purposes for which it is to be used.

The industrial engineer can recommend locations based on an analysis of basic influencing factors including operating costs, transportation costs, utility availability and requirements, tax laws, municipal laws, and the like. Using a manufacturing plant location for illustration purposes, the industrial engineer must analyze such factors as labor laws, skilled-labor requirements, accessibility to raw materials, potential markets, and potential competition. The industrial engineer achieves this analysis through investigation, historical analysis, and survey.

Facility Design and Layout. Facility design and layout aims at the arrangement of work areas and equipment that will provide the most economical operation for the product or service required.

The industrial engineer develops layout plans, in either model or diagram form, to permit analysis of material flow, equipment utilization, material handling, labor requirements, quality-inspection stations, and maintenance and storage requirements. He uses this analysis in developing recommendations for facility design, space requirements, auxiliary equipment, expansion allowance, and material processing.

Equipment and Economic Investigation Studies. Economic investigation studies involve a study of engineering economy. The industrial engineer evaluates equipment replacement, using established interest computation formulas. He makes comparison studies analyzing initial costs, operating costs, and maintenance costs. He considers equipment, product, and market requirements. For certain automation studies, this involves economic and engineering consideration of income taxes, depreciation, accounting apportionments, rate of return on investment, annual operating costs, and the like. Studies involving the alternative of leasing or purchasing plant or equipment fall in this category.

Production-line Techniques. Progressive line production is an arrangement of work areas so that related operations are located immediately adjacent to each other where the material moves continuously and at a uniform rate through a series of balanced operations. This requires the industrial engineer to have a knowledge of the principles of work flow, division of labor, simultaneous operation, fixed routing, and interchangeability. It involves the techniques of timely and uniform transportation, uniform pacing, and progressive line balance. The industrial engineer establishes production objectives consistent with the capabilities of equipment, labor, and material flow.

Product Analysis. Product analysis leads to the determination and specification of products which will be profitable to manufacture and distribute and which will provide human satisfaction. The industrial engineer applies the principles of sound product design from the standpoint of work simplification and economy of production. He normally cooperates with specification and design engineers in the transfer of a product from the blueprint stage to the production line, applying production-line techniques, layout, and other industrial engineering procedures in the conversion.

Tool and Gage Design. Industrial engineers are involved in the development and design of tools and gages from the standpoint of the economical manufacture of products. Because improved or increased productivity is normally an industrial engineering function, the selection, design, and development of proper tools and gages must be consistent with production objectives established by the industrial engineer.

Systems and Procedures. *Systems and Procedures Analysis, Design, and Installation.* Systems analysis is the study of administrative systems in any type of organization. Systems studies can range from a review of the effectiveness of the executive organization to a study of the clerical organization and its procedures for providing flow of control information and reporting of facts and figures.

Development of a new or improved system involves the use of the scientific approach to identify, analyze, and develop solutions to problems of effectiveness of an administrative system. Other tools of industrial engineering are used to improve administrative efficiency. These are work simplification, motion study, work measurement, cost control of manpower, materials, and supplies, workplace layout, and incentive programs.

Forms Design and Control. Forms design is the study of paper forms and the development of the best form for the purpose intended. In forms design, consideration must be given to the favorable mental attitude of the clerical worker using the form, ease of entering and using the data, reduction of tendency for error in clerical work, and paper and printing economy.

Forms control is the continuing study of forms with respect to consolidation of forms requirements of different parts of the organization and the elimination of unnecessary forms.

Records Management. Included in records management is the study of correspondence with respect to simplicity, methods of production, usage, and supplies used; the study of reports with respect to necessity, cost, simplification, possible consolidation with other reports, and distribution; and the establishment of adequate records classification and filing systems including storage and disposal.

Operations Research. The use of sophisticated mathematical and statistical techniques is typical of operations research activities. It should be recognized, however, that these techniques are merely tools and are not operations research in themselves.

Operations research is really an extension of industrial engineering practice to include more of the scientific disciplines and mathematical techniques.

For the purpose of discussion and for illustrative examples, it is simpler to talk about operations research in terms of the typical techniques employed in its use. This is done in the paragraphs that follow.

Linear Programming. Of all the operations research techniques, linear programming has probably been used more than any other to provide solutions to management problems. Linear programming is a mathematical method for selecting the most effective of many possible solutions.

Queuing Theory. This mathematical technique is applicable to problems that are characterized by queues or waiting lines. An example is the problem encountered in determining the number of checkout counters in a supermarket or the number of reservation clerks in an airline reservations office. Another application of this technique is in determining the optimum number of looms to be handled by one loom fixer in a weaving mill.

Monte Carlo Method. This method uses a combination of probability mathematics and the statistics of sampling to solve problems that are too complex to be solved by pure mathematics. It involves setting up a model which can then be used to simulate the results to be expected from a given set of conditions. It has been applied to the problem of classifying freight cars to reduce the amount of time they spend in the sorting yard. It has also been used by an airline to simulate the problems encountered in servicing commercial jet transport planes.

Mathematics and Statistics. In addition to the specific techniques listed above, operations research makes extensive use of basic mathematical and statistical techniques. Probability mathematics and the statistics of sampling, measuring dispersion, and correlation are the procedures most commonly employed.

OTHER ASPECTS OF INDUSTRIAL ENGINEERING

There are a number of activities performed by the industrial engineer that do not lend themselves to classification under any of the general headings previously listed. These activities are largely unrelated, and they are grouped here only for purposes of discussion.

Estimating Procedures. Estimating procedures have to do with forecasting or predicting labor, material, and overhead costs. These procedures are employed when more precise or objective means of measurement are either not available or too time-consuming or costly. Estimating is dependent to a high degree on the experience, qualification, and background of the individual developing the estimate. The subjective nature of most estimating procedures can be substantially reduced by the compilation of statistical data, job costs, and case histories.

Safety. Safety, or accident prevention, is an activity with which the industrial engineer is closely concerned. The design and layout of plant facilities, the specification of machinery and equipment, and the establishment of methods and procedures all have a direct bearing on safety. Because of the interrelationship between safety and methods, work measurement, and plant facilities and design, safety is included in this list of industrial engineering activities.

Suggestion Systems. Suggestion systems are not necessarily a basic activity of the industrial engineering function, but quite frequently, industrial engineers are charged with the responsibility for their operation. Because of the need to evaluate recommendations, suggestion systems are most closely coupled to methods and procedures, work measurement, control procedures, plant facilities and design, and systems and procedures.

Electronic Data-processing Operations. Computers and integrated data-processing equipment are used in many areas of business and government. This equipment is employed to solve problems and to handle the processing of data in virtually all areas of management, including basic research, design engineering, cost accounting, production planning and control, and programming of equipment and processes. As a result, many branches of engineering are concerned with the use and application of this equipment. In addition, certain specialist occupations have evolved such as electronic data programmers and digital computer analysts. Because of the industrial engineer's basic interest, knowledge, and skill in the areas of methods and procedures, control procedures, operations research, and systems and procedures, he is often directly concerned with the installation and operation of electronic data-processing equipment, systems, procedures, and methods.

Labor Negotiations. Labor negotiations are basically the concern of operating managers and industrial relations staff personnel. There is hardly a single activity of the industrial engineer, however, that does not affect labor relations either directly or indirectly. For this reason, the industrial engineer is frequently directly involved in labor negotiations. This is particularly true of any negotiations concerned with work measurement, wage payment, and job evaluation.

SUMMARY

Industrial engineering is strongly results-oriented. It can be utilized by managers in most areas of management to increase profits, improve effectiveness, reduce costs, and promote innovation. It is concerned with management planning; methods and work measurement; wage and salary payment; controls; product facilities and equipment; systems; operations research; and other activities. It may perform any one or all of these activities in an organization. The industrial engineering function should report to the executive responsible for the activity areas it serves.

BIBLIOGRAPHY

"Definition and Description of Industrial Activities," report prepared by the American Institute of Industrial Engineers, Inc., for the Civil Service Commission, Washington 25, D.C., 1959.
"Engineering Manpower in Profile," report from the *National Engineers Register* based on a study conducted by Engineers Joint Council, New York, 1965.
Maynard, H. B. (ed.), *Industrial Engineering Handbook*, 2d ed., McGraw-Hill Book Company, New York, 1963.

CHAPTER NINE

Methods Improvement

WILLIAM ANTIS *Technical Director, Maynard Research Council, Inc., Pittsburgh, Pennsylvania*

DUANE C. GEITGEY *Director of Training Program Development, Maynard Research Council, Inc., Pittsburgh, Pennsylvania*

"Methods improvement" is the term used to describe the various procedures instituted by management when it focuses its attention on increasing the effectiveness of its people to improve the firm's operating efficiency.

Methods improvement at the production level employs techniques developed by industrial engineers. The installation of the program concentrates initially on improving manufacturing processes. The program need not be confined to use in the shop. The interest which is generated in improving plant productivity often forms the foundation for obtaining productivity increases in other areas.

THE NATURE OF METHODS IMPROVEMENT

"Methods improvement" is defined as the procedure used to discover more effective working methods by systematic study.

The productivity of any employee depends upon:

1. The method used in the operation
2. The use of available time
3. The pace or speed of the operator

Research and experience show that *method* has the greatest effect on worker productivity. It is possible for an operator to increase his productivity 13 percent by increasing his effort from an average level to an excessive level. With constant supervision, an operator may double his productive output through using his total available time. But many methods improvements have been made that have increased production two, five, and even ten times. For example, a systematic study of the methods used in performing a bench-assembly operation resulted in a production increase of 370 percent without any money being spent for equipment or tooling.

Methods improvement programs are invariably successful when the participants attain the mental attitude that permits them to view an operation thinking, "Any method can be improved." If a job is not improved as the result of a systematic study, it merely signifies that, at the moment, the analyst was unable to devise a better way of performing it.

ORGANIZING FOR METHODS IMPROVEMENT

A methods improvement program should not be confined to a single functional activity such as the industrial engineering department. Nor will the best results be obtained if this work is left entirely to industrial engineers, methods engineers, time-study engineers, or manufacturing engineers. The complexities of the modern industrial enterprise are so great that the best results cannot be attained unless everyone within the organization works together as a team to improve methods.

The responsibility for the technical work involved in a methods improvement program is generally centered in the industrial engineering department or its equivalent. The members of this department are qualified to make the systematic, detailed study required to uncover all possibilities for improving a

COST REDUCTION REPORT

DWG. NO._____ ITEM. NO._____

PART DESCRIPTION_____

_____

SUMMARY

	MATERIAL COST	DIRECT LABOR COST	OVERHEAD	TOTAL
	DOLLARS	DOLLARS	DOLLARS	DOLLARS
OLD METHOD				
NEW METHOD				
SAVING EACH				
YEARLY ACTIVITY				
TOTAL SAVING				
TOOL & EQUIPMENT COST				

OLD METHOD	NEW METHOD

WORK STATION_____ DEPT._____   WORK STATION _____ DEPT._____

OPERATION	STANDARD TIME	RATE	DIRECT LABOR COST	OPERATION	STANDARD TIME	RATE	DIRECT LABOR COST
	DEC. HRS.		DOLLARS		DEC. HRS.		DOLLARS

DESCRIPTION OF CHANGE:

SUPERINTENDENT_____ FOREMAN_____ METHODS ENGR_____ _____19

FIG. 9-1. *Cost-reduction report.*

method. In making these studies, however, they often come in contact with other members of the organization, particularly the supervisors, inspectors, tool designers, and other key men. If these key men understand the principles of methods improvement, they can lend assistance to the program and much can be accomplished to increase operating effectiveness.

Productivity increases developed through the use of a methods improvement program are not realized until the improved method is actually being followed by the employee. To ensure that the results of the investigation are obtained, it is advisable to put the responsibility for results in the hands of the division or department head. By supplying him with report forms similar to that shown in Figure 9-1, a steady flow of information on results will be forthcoming.

Methods improvement programs are successful when top management participates actively in the total program on a continuing basis. In starting the program, top management must establish the objectives of the program and delegate the authority necessary to direct the attainment of these objectives. The continuing participation includes measuring the results and establishing new objectives.

TRAINING

To be effective, the methods improvement program requires the cooperation of every key member of the organization. One of the main obstacles to cooperation is lack of understanding. It is difficult to cooperate with another man if his aims and objectives are not clearly understood.

An essential part of a methods improvement program is an effective training program in the techniques of methods improvement. The training program can be developed by company personnel, or it can be selected from a number of programs available on the subject. Innovations in methods improvement training include programmed courses which employ self-teaching and eliminate the need for a full-time instructor.

Regardless of the type of training program selected, an effective methods improvement training program should include the following topics:

The approach to work study
Process charts
Operation analysis
Work sampling
Motion study
Workplace layout
Operator training
Work-measurement techniques
Performance controls

Obviously, not all management groups should receive methods improvement training in the same depth.

Analyst Training. The analyst makes the systematic, detailed studies required to uncover all possibilities for methods improvement. Methods engineers or industrial engineers performing the analyst function should receive highly detailed training in methods improvement techniques. This training should include a thorough presentation of all aspects of each item listed in the outline above. For example, the study of process charts should be expanded to include training in the development and use of operation process charts, flow process charts, multicolumn process charts, and multiple activity process charts. Work-sampling training, for example, should include a discussion of the basic principles of work sampling; the procedure for making a work-sampling study, including the determination of accuracy, confidence, and the number of observations; and the preparation and presentation of a complete work-sampling report to management.

Supervisory Training. Supervisors, inspectors, tool designers, and other key men participate actively with the analyst in methods improvement efforts. These men must be trained in methods study techniques to give them the ability to understand these procedures. These men are often in a position to instigate a methods study. By knowing the techniques that are used, they frequently are able to complete and install improved methods. Because they are consulted by the analyst to aid in development or selection of alternative proposals, they need the ability to discuss the problem and its solution. If a supervisor does not understand what the analyst is trying to accomplish, he is likely to look upon methods improvement as a disturbing factor to be tolerated because top management demands it. If, on the other hand, he realizes how vital effective methods are to his own success and the company's success and if he knows how to work with the analyst to develop better methods, his resulting cooperation will add greatly to the accomplishments of the organization.

Supervisory training in methods improvements should include a thorough, but less technical presentation of each of the subjects listed, with greater emphasis on the mechanics of using each technique and less emphasis on the technical principles involved in the technique.

Management Training. Top and middle management personnel, charged with the direction of the methods improvement program, must be trained to the appreciation level in the techniques used.

Management training in methods improvement should consist of an overview of each subject. The purpose of management training is to present the potential advantages of each technique to the manager so that he may recognize possible applications of the technique as they arise. An overview will also provide the understanding necessary for intelligent discussion and evaluation of methods improvement programs carried out by the technical or supervisory groups.

Operator Training. Successful methods improvement training programs must extend beyond the management group. The largest single group that participates in a methods improvement program is the workers doing the job. Although much time and money may be spent by management in developing improved methods, the benefits will not be realized unless the operator is trained to follow these methods. Too often, the advantages of effective methods are lost through failure to follow through with intensive operator training. In addition to operator training on specific methods, it is also advisable to train them in motion study. "Work smarter—not harder" is the theme of such training.

TECHNIQUES OF METHODS STUDY

Questioning Attitude. The key to successful methods study lies in the development of a questioning attitude toward all aspects of any business process. Each step of the process must be questioned, considered, and analyzed. The techniques used in methods study are all based on the application of the questioning attitude. Each technique enables the person seeking methods improvement to apply systematically the questioning attitude to various aspects of the operation or activity under study. Each technique is specifically designed for use in a particular area of potential methods improvement. A person making a methods

○	OPERATION
▷	TRANSPORTATION
□	INSPECTION
D	DELAY
▽	STORAGE

FIG. 9-2.   *Process chart symbols.*

study can vary the depth of the study and the area of concentration by selecting the techniques which are best suited to the type of operation being studied.

Process Charts.   A process chart is a methods improvement tool which graphically presents the events which occur during a series of actions or operations so that they may be easily visualized and analyzed.   These charts conveniently classify the actions which occur into five classifications: operations, transportation, inspections, delays, and storages.

Each of the five activities is identified by the symbols shown by Figure 9-2. The American Society of Mechanical Engineers has established standard definitions for each of the activities listed.

Operation Process Charts.   An operation process chart is a graphic representation of the points at which materials are introduced into the process and of the sequence of inspections and all operations except those involved in material handling.   The advantage of an operation process chart is its simplicity.   It enables the person making the methods study to visualize the relationship between the operations or processes without the sometimes confusing material-handling operations.   Consequently, an operation process chart is particularly effective for illustrating a process to persons who are unfamiliar with the sequence of operations and inspections.   By applying the questioning attitude to the information shown on the operation process chart, the person conducting the methods improvement study can sometimes reduce costs by recommending the combination or elimination of certain of the operations and inspections.

Flow Process Charts.   Flow process charts are similar to operation process charts, but they include information on material handling and storages as well as operations and inspections.   Flow process charts are also an aid for discovering means of combining or eliminating operations.   In addition, however, they are effective for reducing material handling by highlighting excessive travel distances or material storages.   Flow process charts include information such as the time required and the distance moved.   They may be made in either the material type, which presents the process in terms of the events which occur to the material, or the man type, which presents the process in terms of the activities of the man.   The person making a flow process chart applies the questioning attitude to each of the activities shown on the chart.   The systematic questioning of the need for each activity and the search for means of combining or eliminating activities and reducing material-handling distances often result in substantial reductions in the costs of performing the job.

Multiple Activity Charts.   Multiple activity charts, sometimes called "man and machine charts," graphically present the coordinated working and waiting time of two or more men or any combination of men and machines.

The duration of the working or idle time shown on a multiple activity chart is represented by bars drawn to length against a time scale. Multiple activity charts are analyzed to determine the amount and arrangement of nonproductive time to develop a more effective combination by rearranging the work cycle of either the man or the machine or both. In some instances, the cycles of either man or machine can be rearranged so as to include the performance of additional work during the cycle. In fact, it is sometimes possible to eliminate the additional labor time involved in an operation previously performed independently or outside of the machine cycle.

Operation Analysis. Operation analysis is a systematic procedure used to study the factors that affect the method of performing an operation to achieve maximum overall economy. Each part of an operation is considered separately. The operation analysis technique consists in applying the questioning attitude to each of the factors involved in performing the operation. An operation analysis form, Figure 9-3, is used to guide the person making the methods improvement study through the systematic analysis of the operation. The factors examined during the preparation of the operation analysis form include:

1. Purpose of operation
2. Design of part
3. Process analysis
4. Inspection requirements
5. Material
6. Material handling
7. Workplace layout, setup, and tool equipment
8. Common possibilities for job improvement
9. Working conditions
10. Method

As an analyst performs the operation analysis, he questions each of the points listed above to ascertain all of the known facts. He combines these facts with his own knowledge of possible alternatives. From this comparison, he arrives at suggestions for improvement of each facet of the operation. The suggestions for improvement are immediately recorded and are used as the basis for further action. The value of the suggested improvements will depend largely on the ability of the analyst to use his knowledge and experience as a basis for originating more effective procedures. However, a systematic review of each of the points of analysis combined with a searching application of the questioning attitude is likely to produce suggestions for improvement from even a relatively inexperienced analyst. The operation analysis form possesses no mystical powers of its own. The analysis must take place in the mind of the analyst. Methods improvements discovered during the course of the analysis must receive adequate follow-up to ensure their adoption. The use of the form itself ensures only that none of the important factors which should be considered will be overlooked.

Motion Study. All analysis work is done for the purpose of improving the method by which the operation is performed. The various factors which affect method directly or indirectly are considered in detail, and improvements are made wherever possible. As a result, many economies are made which eliminate motions and reduce costs.

Before the study can be considered complete, however, the motions which remain and which appear to be necessary must themselves be studied in considerable detail. It is not enough to say that a part is to be obtained by picking it up from the desk or work station. The location at which it is picked up should be such that the hand can move between it and the point where the material is worked upon with the shortest and easiest motion. The motions

| Date Started _____ Department _____ |
| Dwg. or Spec. _____ Item or Part No. _____ Material _____ |
| Description of Part _____ |
| Operation _____ |
| Yearly Activity _____ Expected Life _____ Yearly Labor Cost Per .0001 Hr. _____ |

DETERMINE AND DESCRIBE	DETAILS OF ANALYSIS	ACTION
1. PURPOSE OF OPERATION _____	Is the operation necessary? Does the operation accomplish the intended result? Can the operation be eliminated by doing a better job on preceding operations? Can the material supplier perform the operation more economically? Can the operation accomplish additional results to simplify succeeding operations?	
2. DESIGN OF PART (Suggest improvements, Make sketches where necessary)	Are all parts necessary? Could standard parts be substituted? Does design permit least costly processing & assembly? What design features do competitors use? Will design allow eventual automation?	

3. PROCESS ANALYSIS (Complete list of all operations performed on part)
 	
No.   Description   Work Sta.   Dept.
1. _____
2. _____
3. _____
4. _____
5. _____
6. _____
7. _____
8. _____
9. _____
10. _____
	Can operation being analyzed
	  be eliminated?
	  be combined with another?
	  be performed during idle period of another?
	Is sequence of operations best possible?
	Should operation be done in another dept. to save cost or handling?	

File Designation

Maynard Research Council
Form No. 103   OPERATION ANALYSIS FORM

FIG. 9-3a.   *Operation analysis form, page 1.*

used for grasping must be worked out so that the fewest possible are employed. If two parts are required, it must be decided whether they are to be grasped and moved together or separately. The best position of the hand and of the material in the hand must be determined so that no time is lost in positioning the material at the place of work.

In short, every motion must be analyzed in detail for the purpose of making it as effective as possible. This, a secondary form of analysis, is known as "motion study."

4. INSPECTION REQUIREMENTS

Tolerances & Specifications_____

Are tolerance, allowance, finish
and other requirements
necessary?
too costly?
suitable to purpose?

Inspection Procedures (Suggest improvements)_____

Should statistical quality
control be used?

Is inspection procedure
effective and efficient?

5. MATERIAL (Suggest better material)

Consider size, suitability,
straightness, and condition.

How can scrap costs be reduced?_____

Can cheaper material be
substituted?

Will tool modifications permit
use of lighter material or
thinner sections?

Would a more expensive
material lower machining
and processing costs?

Processing Materials _____

Is packaging suitable?

6. MATERIAL HANDLING (Suggest improvements)

Brought by _____

Can incoming materials be
delivered directly to the
work station?

Removed by_____

Can signals, such as lights or
bells be used to notify
material handlers that
material is ready to be
moved?

Should crane, gravity
conveyors, totepans, or special
trucks be used?

Handled at work stations by_____

Consider layout with respect to
distance moved.

Are containers correctly
sized?

FIG. 9-3*b*.   *Operation analysis form, page 2.*

"Motion study" may be defined briefly as the study of all movements used for performing an operation to determine the best method for doing it. It consists in dividing work into the most basic elements possible, studying these elements separately and in relation to one another qualitatively and quantitively, and, as a result, determining by synthesis the most efficient method.

A knowledge of the basic divisions of accomplishment and the ability to recognize them are of great assistance in making motion studies. This knowledge and ability permit the analyst to reduce any job whatsoever to terms of basic operations. The next step is to analyze the present method used and the motions employed in order to devise a better method. The better method is in turn analyzed and improved, and the process is continued until no further improvement appears possible.

To establish methods which are truly effective, the analyst should be governed and guided by certain principles which have been established as the result

---

7. WORKPLACE LAYOUT SETUP, AND TOOL EQUIPMENT
(Suggest improvements, making sketches where necessary)

Arrangement of Work Area
Placement of
  Tools
  Materials
  Supplies
How are dwgs. and tools
  secured?
Can set-up be improved?
Trial Pieces.
Machine Adjustments

TOOLS
Suitable?
Provided?
  Ratchet Tools
  Power Tools
  Spl. Purpose Tools
  Jigs, Vises
  Special Clamps
  Fixtures
  Multiple
  Duplicate

---

8. COMMON POSSIBILITIES FOR JOB IMPROVEMENT (Consider the following)

RECOMMENDED ACTION

1. Install gravity delivery chutes.

2. Use drop delivery.

3. Compare methods if more than one operator is working on same job.

4. Provide correct chair for operator.

5. Improve Jigs & Fixtures by providing ejectors, quick-acting clamps, etc.

6. Use foot-operated mechanisms.

7. Arrange for two-handed operation.

8. Arrange tools and parts within normal working area.

9. Change layout to eliminate back-tracking and to permit coupling of machines

10. Utilize all improvements developed for other jobs.

---

9. WORKING CONDITIONS (Suggest improvements)

Light
Heat
Ventilation, Fumes
Drinking Fountains
Wash Rooms
Safety Aspects
Design of Part
Clerical Work Required (to fill
  out time cards, etc.)
Probability of Delays
Probable Mfg. Quantities

FIG. 9-3c.   *Operation analysis form, page 3.*

10. METHOD (Accompany with sketches or process charts if necessary)

a. Before analysis and motion study. ——————————————————

———————————————————————————————————————

———————————————————————————————————————

———————————————————————————————————————

b. After analysis and motion study. ——————————————————

———————————————————————————————————————

———————————————————————————————————————

———————————————————————————————————————

———————————————————————————————————————

Are hand motions symmetrical?

Are parts transferred between hands?

Is a more detailed motion study needed?

Has safety been considered?

Working Posture

Does method follow Laws of Motion Economy?

Are lowest classes of movements used?

RECOMMENDATIONS FOR FURTHER IMPROVEMENTS IF THE ACTIVITY INCREASES:

RECORD OF ACTION TAKEN:

Proposal	Date	Referred To:	Action Taken

COMMENTS: ———————————————————————————

Date Completed ————————————— Analyzed by —————————

FIG. 9-3d. *Operation analysis form, page 4.*

of study and research. These principles are known as the "laws of motion economy." They are five in number and are amplified by eight corollaries.

If an operating method conforms to the laws of motion economy, it is effectively performed. If it does not, it can be improved, although the improvement may not always be practicable.

To make a motion study, the operation is broken down into the basic divisions of accomplishment of which it is composed, inefficiencies are recognized and if possible eliminated, and finally, a new method is devised which conforms as nearly as possible to the laws of motion economy and which makes use of the most effective physical motions.

A motion study may be made briefly by analysis and observation, or it may be made in great detail by means of motion pictures. In practical application, when the principles of motion study are thoroughly understood, the best procedure to follow usually lies between these two extremes.

MTM Analysis. Methods-time measurement, or MTM, is a work-measurement procedure involving the use of predetermined elemental times, which enables the analyst to make a detailed study of method during the development of the time standard for an operation. Methods-time measurement analyzes the basic motions required to perform any manual operation or method, and assigns to each motion a time standard which is determined by the nature of the motion and the conditions under which it is made.

The first step of the MTM procedure is a systematic analysis of the work motions required to perform an operation. After the basic work motions have been determined, the time required for their performance is obtained from data tables which establish the normal time for basic motions under various conditions.

The MTM data tables (Figure 9-4) contain time values established through observation of thousands of industrial operations performed by qualified operators in many geographical areas. Motion pictures of the operations have been analyzed to determine the exact times required to perform each of a group of eight manual movements, nine pedal and trunk movements, and two eye movements. The time for each of the MTM basic motions is determined by the physical conditions involved in the performance of the motion, and the conditions under which the motion is made at the time of the analysis.

The MTM data tables permit the analyst to select the exact conditions under which the observed motion was performed. Time values shown on each table are expressed in terms of time-measurement units or TMUs. Each TMU represents 0.00001 hour. Thus, the analyst can determine the time in hours required to perform an operation by adding the TMUs for each basic motion and multiplying the total by 0.00001 hour.

To simplify recording the individual MTM motions, a system of motion symbols has been established. These symbols reflect the variable factors which affect the motion, thereby enabling a trained analyst immediately to recognize the motion described.

Methods-time measurement can be used effectively for preproduction methods development or for jobs which are already in existence. Before production, it is possible to compare various methods of performing an operation using MTM analysis as a basis of comparison. Thus, a method can be carefully worked out in advance of production. In effect, the methods improvements have been realized before the operation is begun. When the operation is ready for actual use, the method has been fully developed and the cost is at a minimum. The costly operator training period normally associated with a new operation has been minimized because fewer methods changes are required during the early stages of production. As a result, the initial price of the product is lower because of the well-engineered MTM standards.

Methods-time measurement is an equally effective tool for methods improvement on existing operations. The systematic analysis of each basic motion of an existing operation will invariably yield some opportunity for methods improvement. For example, an MTM analysis may call attention to long reaches or moves associated with an existing layout, which can be shortened by a simple rearrangement of the workplace. Although the methods improvement might

MTM CONDENSED DATA CARD

REACH

Inch	A	B	C or D	E	In Motion A	In Motion B
¾ or less	2.0	2.0	2 0	2.0	1.6	1.6
1	2.5	2.5	3.6	2.4	2.3	2.3
2	4.0	4.0	5.9	3.8	3.5	2.7
3	5.3	5.3	7.3	5.3	4.5	3.6
4	6.1	6.4	8.4	6.8	4.9	4.3
5	6.5	7.8	9.4	7.4	5.3	5.0
6	7.0	8.6	10.1	8.0	5.7	5.7
7	7.4	9.3	10.8	8.7	6.1	6.5
8	7.9	10.1	11.5	9.3	6.5	7.2
9	8.3	10.8	12.2	9.9	6.9	7.9
10	8.7	11.5	12.9	10.5	7.3	8.6
12	9.6	12.9	14.2	11.8	8.1	10.1
14	10.5	14.4	15.6	13.0	8.9	11.5
16	11.4	15.8	17.0	14.2	9.7	12.9
18	12.3	17.2	18.4	15.5	10.5	14.4
20	13.1	18.6	19.8	16.7	11.3	15.8
22	14.0	20.1	21.2	18.0	12.1	17.3
24	14.9	21.5	22.5	19.2	12.9	18.8
26	15.8	22.9	23.9	20.4	13.7	20.2
28	16.7	24.4	25.3	21.7	14.5	21.7
30	17.5	25.8	26.7	22.9	15.3	23.2

GRASP

Case	TMU	Limits
1A	2.0	
1B	3.5	
1C1	7.3	D > ½"
1C2	8.7	¼"< D < ½"
1C3	10.8	D<¼"
2	5.6	
3	5.6	
4A	7.3	>1"x1"x1"
4B	9.1	(between)
4C	12.9	< ¼"x¼"x⅛"
5	0	

POSITION

FIT	Sym	Easy	Difficult
1	S	5.6	11.2
	SS	9.1	14.7
	NS	10.4	16.0
2	S	16.2	21.8
	SS	19.7	25.3
	NS	21.0	26.6
3	S	43.0	48.6
	SS	46.5	52.1
	NS	47.8	53.4

MOVE

Inch	A	B	C	B in Motion	Wt. (lb.) Up to	Factor	Constant TMU
¾ or less	2.0	2.0	2.0	1.7			
1	2.5	2.9	3.4	2.3	2.5	1.00	0
2	3.6	4.6	5.2	2.9			
3	4.9	5.7	6.7	3.6			
4	6.1	6.9	8.0	4.3	7.5	1.06	2.2
5	7.3	8.0	9.2	5.0			
					12.5	1.11	3.9
6	8.1	8.9	10.3	5.7			
7	8.9	9.7	11.1	6.5	17.5	1.17	5.6
8	9.7	10.6	11.8	7.2			
9	10.5	11.5	12.7	7.9			
10	11.3	12.2	13.5	8.6	22.5	1.22	7.4
12	12.9	13.4	15.2	10.0			
14	14.4	14.6	16.9	11.4	27.5	1.28	9.1
16	16.0	15.8	18.7	12.8			
18	17.6	17.0	20.4	14.2	32.5	1.33	10.8
20	19.2	18.2	22.1	15.6			
					37.5	1.39	12.5
22	20.8	19.4	23.8	17.0			
24	22.4	20.6	25.5	18.4	42.5	1.44	14.3
26	24.0	21.8	27.3	19.8			
28	25.5	23.1	29.0	21.2			
30	27.1	24.3	30.7	22.7	47.5	1.50	16.0

DISENGAGE

FIT	Easy	Difficult
1	4.0	5.7
2	7.5	11.8
3	22.9	34.7

APPLY PRESSURE

AP 1	16.2
AP 2	10.6

RELEASE

RL 1	2.0
RL 2	0

TURN

TURN	30°	45°	60°	75°	90°	105°	120°	135°	150°	165°	180°
0 — 2 lbs.	2.8	3.5	4.1	4.8	5.4	6.1	6.8	7.4	8.1	8.7	9.4
2.1 — 10 lbs.	4.4	5.5	6.5	7.6	8.5	9.6	10.6	11.6	12.7	13.7	14.8
10.1 — 35 lbs.	8.4	10.5	12.3	14.4	16.2	18.3	20.4	22.2	24.3	26.1	28.2

FIG. 9-4a. *MTM condensed data card—front.*

have been discovered through observation of the existing layout, this type of improvement is often overlooked. An MTM analysis, however, immediately pinpoints the costly motions involved in the operation by assigning a time value to each motion. The analyst, using MTM, can readily see that the lengthy reaches and moves represent a large part of the cost, and he can then concentrate his efforts toward reducing the distances involved.

Thus, MTM is a methods improvement tool that combines the development of effective methods with the standard-setting functions. A well-engineered

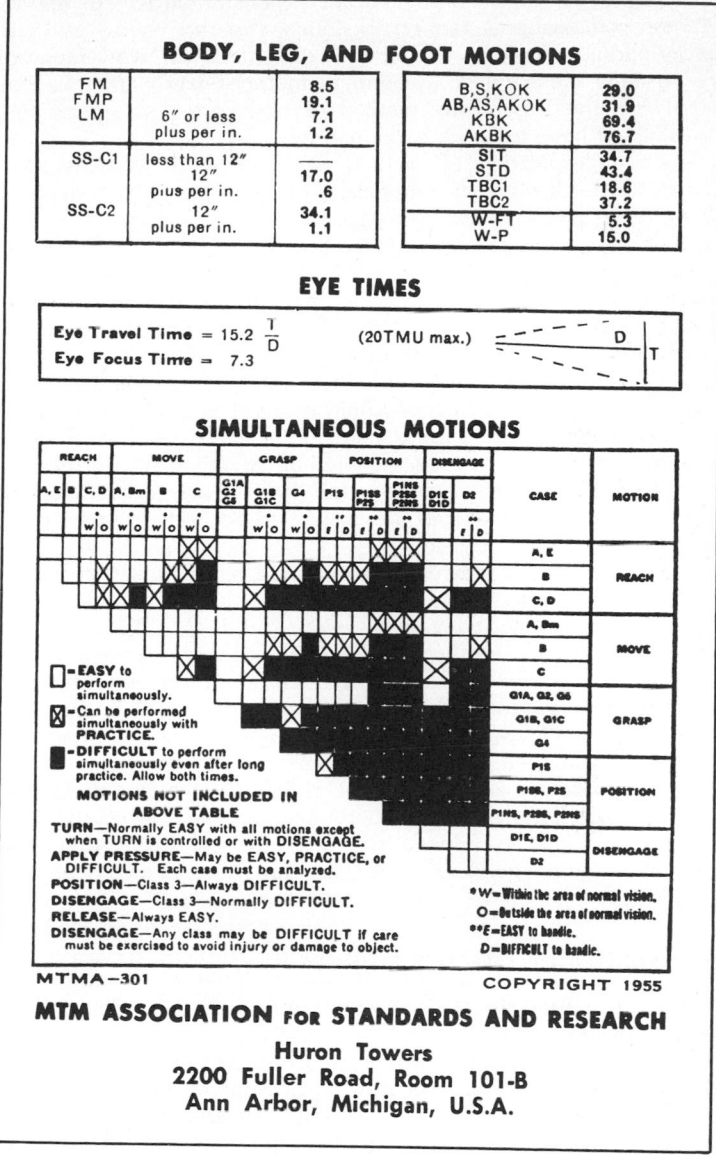

FIG. 9-4b. *MTM condensed data card—back.*

time standard results, which combines the advantages of a thorough methods improvement program and an accurate work-measurement system.

The Relation of Methods Study to Work Measurement. Methods study is an essential part of an effective work-measurement program. In fact, methods study and work measurement are complementary cost-control techniques. Both techniques contribute to the standardization necessary for effective management control.

The standardization of working methods through methods study is an essential prerequisite to the establishment of time standards. If the working methods are not standardized, the responsibility for the choice of methods rests with the individual operator. Under such circumstances, work-measurement standards are virtually meaningless. Thorough methods study prior to work measurement establishes the least costly method of performing an operation and provides a well-defined basis for work measurement.

The standardization of method prior to work measurement is as essential as the standardization of materials, equipment, and working conditions. Unless all of these factors have been standardized, it is impossible to establish an accurate time value for an operation.

Although methods study normally precedes the establishment of a standard on an operation, work measurement itself plays an important part in the selection of the most economical method. The methods analyst is faced with the task of selecting a best method from a number of alternatives. He normally makes this selection by assigning estimated standards to each of the alternatives.

Certain work-measurement techniques such as MTM are particularly well suited for the comparison of various methods. These techniques enable the methods analyst to describe the proposed method in detail, using the work-measurement symbols for the basic elements, and then to assign predetermined time values to each of the elements, thus developing an accurate estimate of the time required to perform the described method.

In addition to methods development and standardization before work measurement, methods study is also an essential part of a continuous program to maintain control over the accuracy of existing standards. Periodic methods audits of existing operations are helpful for pinpointing expensive motion patterns and minimizing the effect of creeping methods changes. Many companies carry out regularly scheduled audits of all operations which represent high labor or material cost. These audit programs, in addition to calling attention to costly variations in method, present an opportunity to develop more effective methods and subsequent work-measurement standards which reflect lower costs.

Thus, the efforts of the methods analyst and the standards analyst must be closely associated to provide the maximum cost-reduction potential. Neither methods study nor work measurement can function effectively as an independent technique.

MAINTENANCE OF EFFECTIVE METHODS

Methods improvement is a continuing activity. The following example is cited to illustrate this fact.

A plant manager, desirous of determining what results could be obtained by the application of a methods improvement program, retained a consultant to guide a group of supervisors through several complete methods studies. In choosing the jobs for study, activity and the life of the job were used as the basis for selection.

The studies were begun, and the first two produced very gratifying results. When the third class of work which had been selected was announced to the group participating in the study, however, they questioned the advisability of spending any time on it. They informed the consultant that about six months prior to his coming the work had been carefully studied. Many improvements had been made, a very efficient setup had been worked out, and it seemed unnecessary to go over the same ground again.

The consultant had not analyzed the work in detail and had no suggestion for improvement in mind at the time. But he pointed out that the fundamental principle underlying all methods study work was that any operation can be improved if studied in sufficient detail with an open mind. He suggested that the work under discussion offered a good opportunity of testing this principle, and at length, on the basis of testing the procedure rather than with the thought that there were known inefficiencies to be corrected, it was agreed to proceed with the study.

The correctness of the principle was quickly demonstrated. The complete process involved nineteen operations, and as each was analyzed in its turn, one improvement after another was made. When the study was completed, an overall improvement of 35 percent had been obtained.

The possibilities for methods improvement are seldom, if ever, fully realized. A continuing program of methods improvement has yet to fail to produce results that far exceed the cost of this continuance. To maintain the benefits of effective methods and to realize the cost savings achieved, it is necessary to overcome the effects of creeping methods changes. This is done through continuing the program and periodically conducting methods audits.

It must be recognized that it is not always easy to teach operators new methods. Because of constant repetition, old methods become habitual, and habits are hard to change. Very often, the easiest and best method will seem harder and slower to an operator than his own method. His production will fall off at first and he will want to return to his own way of doing things. At this point, it is necessary for supervision to insist on the operator following the approved method. Because of the detailed study that went into establishing the method, the analyst is in the best position to audit the method to see that it is being followed. He should be assigned this duty.

AREAS OF APPLICATION

A methods improvement program can produce worthwhile results in any situation where human labor is expended in production or service. Successful applications of the principles involved have been recorded in almost all fields of human endeavor. Any activity subjected to the searching analysis required in using methods improvement techniques will almost always yield cost reductions.

Many managers feel that the area of application for methods improvements is limited to manufacturing operations. This feeling has been engendered by the wide publicity given to the results attained in this field. The same type of intensive study, however, applied to activities in other areas has also resulted in major cost reductions.

Some typical examples are enumerated below.

Direct Labor. A small machine shop instituted a methods improvement program. The improvements that were installed resulted in a 52 percent decrease in standard labor cost. Other benefits in the form of effective operator training and accurate production scheduling were attained. These results were made possible because top management installed a program based on sound principles, continued to take an active part in the program, and established attainable objectives as other objectives were reached.

Indirect Labor. A large appliance manufacturer assigned five analysts to improve the janitorial services in its plants and offices. A methods improvement program resulted in an annual labor savings of $112,000. The methods used by the janitors were improved and standardized; the janitors were trained in using the new methods; and the work assignments were placed on a daily schedule. Cost—less than $20,000.

Office Work. The activities of a credit department of a business were subjected to the searching analysis of a methods improvement program. At the
conclusion of the study and after the employees were trained in the new methods,
a 5 percent larger volume of work was handled by six fewer workers.

Packaging. The wrapping section of a cookware warehouse was processing
171 units per day with twenty-one employees. A methods study directed by
management resulted in having 265 units processed using twenty-two people.
Thus, a 48 percent increase in production was obtained.

Many more examples of the results of methods improvement programs could
be cited. The foregoing, however, are indicative of the benefits that can accrue
when management uses this procedure.

CONCLUSION

Methods improvement is the study of methods following a systematic
approach. It can achieve worthwhile results provided the study is organized,
the practitioners are trained, the techniques are followed, and the improved
methods are installed and maintained.

To be successful, a methods improvement program requires the continuing
participation of top management.

BIBLIOGRAPHY

Barnes, R. M., *Motion and Time Study,* 4th ed., John Wiley & Sons, Inc., New
    York, 1958.
Carroll, Phil, *How to Control Production Costs,* McGraw-Hill Book Company, New
    York, 1953.
Heyel, Carl (ed.), *The Encyclopedia of Management,* Reinhold Publishing Corporation,
    New York, 1963.
Lowry, S. M., H. B. Maynard, and G. J. Stegemerten, *Time and Motion Study,* 3d
    ed., McGraw-Hill Book Company, New York, 1940.
Maynard, H. B. (ed.), *Industrial Engineering Handbook,* 2d ed., sec. 2, chaps. 1–10;
    sec. 5, chap. 3; sec. 10, chaps. 10 and 16, McGraw-Hill Book Company, New
    York, 1963.
Maynard, H. B., G. J. Stegemerten, and J. L. Schwab, *Methods-Time Measurement,*
    McGraw-Hill Book Company, New York, 1948.
Niebel, B. W., *Motion and Time Study,* Richard D. Irwin, Inc., Homewood, Ill.,
    1955.

CHAPTER TEN

Human Factors Engineering*

HUGH M. BOWEN   *Managing Scientist, Laboratory Director, Dunlap and Associates, Inc., Darien, Connecticut*

As technology advances the capabilities of machinery, and as machines and automation in general tend to displace man from his traditional functions, it might be argued that man is becoming a less vital component in manufacturing processes and technological systems. In fact, however, although fewer men may be involved in a process, the role they play is becoming more and more responsible. The advent of automation has furthermore created new functions for men in the form of monitoring and maintenance of machines and control and programming of processes. In many instances, man is not displaced, because he proves to be a less expensive, more available, and often more reliable component than the electronic or mechanical device required to replace him. In other instances, he may not be replaceable at all, for no machine presently conceived could bring to bear the unique constellation of properties that man represents as a resource.

The subject matter of human factors engineering is, broadly, the advantageous use of the human resource in technological (man/machine) processes and systems. The derived advantage is in two directions: first, toward increased effectiveness and achievement of purpose of the man/machine system, and second, to the man himself. Evidence is abundant that unless an individual gains a sense of accomplishment, satisfaction, and, often, progress from his job, he will serve poorly the man/machine system in which he is involved. So, although human factors engineering treats man as a resource in a mechanistic sense (thereby increasing the compatibility of human factors engineering specifications with engineering specifications), it also considers the "human needs" of the individual. It is an essential bridge between those who are concerned with

* The author gratefully acknowledges the assistance of his associates at Dunlap and Associates, Inc.—most particularly Dr. Jack W. Dunlap, President; George Grant, Senior Scientist; and H. E. Blank, Jr., Secretary and Vice President.

personnel and those who are concerned with the design, operation, and improvement of industrial systems.

The presentation in this chapter provides designers and managers of industrial systems an overview of the concepts, techniques, and data of human factors engineering. It describes the field of human factors engineering, indicates the kinds of knowledge and types of work performed by human factors engineers, and offers guidance for managing their inclusion in the design and improvement of industrial systems.

SCOPE OF HUMAN FACTORS ENGINEERING

Human factors engineering is the science and technology of integrating men and machines together so that the man and the man/machine system are effective for the purposes intended. It aims to provide man with tasks which are within his normal ability, but which retain some degree of challenge. He should, ideally, feel consistently a sense of accomplishment from his work and should not be debarred from exercising his powers of judgment to improve his and the system's accomplishments.

The primary focus of human factors engineering work is the interface between men and machines. To promote efficient operation, tasks must be properly allocated between men and machines, demands on the man must be made compatible with his abilities, and work space and environment must be designed to promote his effective operation. The goal is to gain a smooth and accurate flow of information and control from the machine to the man and from the man to the machine. Achievement of this goal will result typically in improved safety, higher quality, lower costs, and, in general, improved productivity and worker satisfaction.

In more specific terms, human factors engineering provides a description of men at work, their properties and capabilities, and also their limitations, deficiencies, and boundary conditions in a work situation. Study of the functional capability of men cannot be pursued without taking into account the environment in which the man is situated and with which he interacts. Thus, human factors engineering studies the influence of both the physical and the social environment on a man's capacity and relates these to the manufacturing process. Cohesion to the practice of human factors engineering is afforded by regarding man as combined with other men and with machines into a system which has various purposes and criteria. The system purposes and criteria impose the requirement for each component's contribution, including man's.

Specialists in human factors engineering are those with training in both psychology and engineering. They may be variously skilled, or require the aid of specialists in such disciplines as physiology, medicine, sociology, and cultural anthropology. Human factors engineers are accustomed to working in multidisciplinary teams with engineers and others responsible for the design or improvement of systems.

Types of Applications. Human factors engineering has a wide range of applications. It can be applied on a "quick fix" basis to correct some specific incompatibility between man and a device. Typical of such applications was the change effected in a micrometer screw gage from the normal circular scale to a numeral readout. The change improved speed and accuracy of reading markedly. At the other extreme, human factors engineering can be applied on an exhaustive basis to the development of a complex man/machine system. Modern aerospace systems, communication systems, nuclear power stations, mining operations, strip steel mills, and post office operations are examples of some of the systems which have received prolonged analysis, research, and development from teams of human factors engineers working hand in hand with the various engineering and other specialties involved in the development or the improvement of the system.

Human factors engineering content also ranges widely. Not only can it be applied to virtually any technological activity in which man interacts with objects, tools, devices, equipment, or systems, but it can be applied to many different aspects of the interaction. It integrates many of the older specialties into a discipline which attempts to treat men at work in a technological society as a whole. Thus, although the focus of human factors engineering tends to remain on the man/machine interface, the discipline extends "toward the machine" in that it deals with the design and functional capability of equipment, with some of the provinces of industrial engineering which determine the functional "throughput" through the man, and with some of the provinces of industrial design which influence the subjective reaction of man to his working situation. The discipline also extends "toward the man" in that it deals with the selection and training of personnel and how selection and training policies may interact with the functions allocated to man and the design of his tasks. It deals also with the social and motivational aspects of man at work, especially in the sense of how to design for an effective working relationship within groups of men and the design of tasks which promote feelings of purpose, achievement, confidence, and satisfaction.

Employing the Human Factors Specialist. Large industrial concerns, particularly those employed on government research and development projects concerned with large systems, normally have a human factors group. Such groups have "line" responsibilities in the development of a system and work as an intermeshed component with all the other disciplines. Although the responsibilities of the human factors group vary depending upon the nature of the system to be developed, they normally include:

Functional allocation—to determine man's functions; strike a balance between man and machine functions with respect to effectiveness, reliability, simplicity, cost, and various specialized factors

Specification of task criteria—to specify what man must do in terms of speed, accuracy, duration, consistency, reliability, and the like, and to develop these criteria to provide engineering design objectives and specifications

Human engineering design—to design or specify all items and factors with respect to equipment, tools, devices, controls, displays, accommodations, environment, and procedures for the purpose of integrating the man with optimum effectiveness

Personnel selection and training—to formulate personnel policies and procedures with respect to the selection of people and their training; as necessary, to develop training course curricula and appropriate training devices

Test and evaluation—to test and evaluate the various designs and procedures and to check on their adequacy for meeting requirements

Although human factors specialists find considerable employment in the development of new systems, they can and do contribute to the modification and improvement of existing systems. The activities may include any or all of the duties outlined above. Modification of a man/machine system may encompass only the simplification of some work activity in the tradition of motion and time studies. It may constitute placing the man in a different functional relationship to a machine. For instance, the old method of assembling components required the operator to process each item on the assembly line as it appeared and then replace it on the line without losing the "cycle." The new method provides a storage of items both on the input and the output sides of the operator. Allowing the operators by this means to set their own pace, the new method serves to increase productivity and lower various indexes of discontent such as time off, absenteeism, and expressed job dissatisfaction.

Other forms of human factors modification of an existing facility may be directed more toward motivational and social benefits. For instance, a control center using a number of persons was found to be committing an unacceptable number of errors and to have low morale and cooperation among the personnel. A major source of difficulty seemed to be the relative isolation of the operators at their various tasks and the oversimplification of tasks. The operators were bored, unchallenged, separated, and felt themselves overpowered by "the system." A series of modifications to the tasks, to the layout of the center, and to the manner in which the team interrelated, both formally and casually, served to remedy the situation.

These examples are typical of how an "in-house" human factors group may serve the interests of a large corporation engaged in various development and manufacturing activities. It is usual, too, to find that the human factors group engages in research within the discipline of human factors.

In-house human factors groups are possible only for relatively large corporations. Consultants and consulting organizations supply the human factors services which are required by smaller corporations or by the various Federal and state departments and agencies which cannot supply all or some of these services from their own resources.

Using Reference Material. The Bibliography at the end of this chapter will serve as a guide to some of the more illuminating and useful literature on human factors engineering. The referenced literature includes considerable data and design guides that will be found useful in assuring the compatibility and effectiveness of equipment, facilities, and human elements of a system. These data range widely, from human dimensions (to apply, for instance, for determining the accessibility and reachability of controls) to attitudinal and motivational factors (to apply in satisfying quality and productivity requirements).

Little of this material has been generated in direct connection with manufacturing systems. Experience, however, has indicated that much of it, although derived from weapon and space-vehicle systems, has a high adaptability to industrial systems that is relatively unexploited. Many human considerations have enough constancy and continuity from one situation to another to afford a general validity to the basic human factors data. There is real need for caution, however, in using published data and for an awareness of its application limitations. Thus in the field of anthropometry (human body dimensions), a machine whose controls have been human-factors-engineered for use by American male operators may be unsuitable for foreign operators, particularly if some females are used, because of markedly different body dimensions. Similarly, switches designed to be "on" when moved up to the right will fit into the stereotyped habits of most people in this country, but not necessarily into those of their counterparts abroad.

APPLICATION OF HUMAN FACTORS ENGINEERING

The application of human factors engineering can range from consultation on some single item or procedure to a full-scale development of the human ingredients in a large man/machine system. There is, therefore, some difficulty in exposition of the theory and practice of the discipline because of this diversity of application. Furthermore, it must be admitted that the subject has not advanced far enough for there to be many theorems which are both explicit and general. Successful human factors engineering depends heavily on the acumen of the human factors specialist and his ability to synthesize the scattered array of rules of thumb, diverse data, theories of varying generality, and data from many different aspects of the subject into a successful solution to a problem at hand.

Techniques and Potentials. There are various general procedural methods in utilizing human factors engineering which will benefit both the man involved and the proficiency of the system under review or development.

Early application of human factors engineering in the development stages of a system is most desirable to realize maximum benefit. It establishes in everyone's mind the fact that proper consideration must be given to the role, functions, tasks, capabilities, and needs of the personnel to be used in the system. Further, by introducing the relevant analytic tools and knowledge about human performance and the conditions which promote it into the broad spectrum of considerations involving total system design or modification, opportunities to improve performance can be perceived and adopted that, later on, might prove unfeasible or too costly.

Fresh perspectives may be obtained on the proper utilization of people in the system for operations and maintenance, or the implication of manned versus automated aspects of the system with respect to reliability, flexibility, costs, and the like, and on the contribution of knowledge about human beings to the total performance of the system. For example, employment of a human factors specialist in the study of a hot-strip steel rolling mill had the consequence (among others) of automating the adjustment of the thickness of the sheet to be rolled by requiring the operator to *preselect* roller screwdown settings rather than make the actual adjustment, which was a major source of error. However, checking on the flatness of the rolled sheet could be performed by the operators easily and accurately, provided they were placed in the right viewing position and the visual environment was engineered to facilitate the visual task.

This example illustrates one solution to the problem of allocation of functions between men and machines. Production and processing systems vary widely in their size, kind, and application of technology. They vary, too, in the extent to which the human can or should be used or excluded. In fact, all systems, when studied in their entirety, always include man, however remotely. The issue in practice is where, who, and how much man should be allocated into the various echelons of a system.

Perhaps the greatest benefit that the use of human factors engineering confers is the deliberate, systematic, and rational consideration of how to use and profit by the human resource. Unless a job enables a man to gain and sustain a sense of self-esteem and competence and provides him with necessary information and action capabilities, he will perform poorly and be an inadequate system component. It is also evident that no system is static. It changes and develops, and man is the initiation of these changes. Men with pride in their jobs will actively seek out beneficial changes and respond to new demands. A responsible, active role in the system is the best assurance that the men concerned will be conscientiously creative in system improvement.

System Development. When a fairly extensive industrial system or manufacturing process is to be established, the cycle of development with the relevant human factors activities employs, in general, the following sequence.[1]

[1] Adapted from "Human Factors Design Standards for the Fleet Ballistic Missile Weapon System," *Design of Systems*, vol. 1, Department of the Navy, Special Projects Office, U.S. Government Printing Office, Washington, D.C., 1963.

PHASES IN SYSTEM DEVELOPMENT CYCLE

Definition of Operational Requirements

End Product. Specification of operational requirements.

System Engineering Activities. Determine purpose, goals, and requirements; identify constraints.

Relevant Human Factors Activities. Establish general personnel policies and determine overall implications of using men in terms of type and number; the operating environment, training needs, and the like, and special factors.

Management Responsibilities for Human Factors Engineering. Provide adequate human factors staff and facilities, and ensure integration of human factors staff into development team; establish chain of command.

Determination of Functional Requirements

End Product. Technical development plan.

System Engineering Activities. Perform gross trade-off studies; define nature and properties of associated hardware and procedures; determine performance, reliability, and maintainability goals; determine flow of action, products, and information; establish operational, maintenance, and support concepts; develop evaluation requirements.

Relevant Human Factors Activities. Contribute to operational and maintenance concepts and maintainability goals; participate in gross trade-off studies; gross assignment of functions between personnel and equipment; gross division of duties among personnel; determine implications for manning and training; determine implications for evaluation.

Management Responsibilities for Human Factors Engineering. Ensure adequate participation of human factors personnel in team and flow of information and concepts within team; assist, as necessary, in the adjudication of issues of men versus machines and the like.

Preliminary Design of System and Subsystems

End Product. System and subsystem specifications.

System Engineering Activities. Evaluate alternative design concepts; determine installation requirements; perform detailed trade-off studies; prepare specifications.

Relevant Human Factors Activities. Analyze information transfer requirements; assign, in detail, functions to personnel and equipment for each alternative design concept; translate information transfer requirements into display, control, and processing requirements for each alternative design concept; evaluate each design concept with respect to human factors (for example, implications for number and type of personnel, training, job aids, man/machine interface design, data-processing requirements, and so on); determine general location of operator and maintenance stations; design, in general, the functional procedures; prepare man/machine portions of subsystem specifications.

Detailed Design of System and Subsystem

End Product. Equipment and component design specifications.

System Engineering Activities. Develop reliability-maintainability analysis, with suitable predictions; determine test and check-out requirements; analyze logistic support requirements; generate evaluation plans and plans of performance, reliability, and maintainability reporting requirements and procedures; establish quality-assurance and equipment-modification programs; define personnel and training requirements; establish technical documentation requirements.

Relevant Human Factors Activities. Translate control and display requirements into hardware requirements; specify location and environment for operator stations; select or design control and display components; design operator panels, consoles, workplaces, and accommodations in general; select and locate communication equipment; specify operating and maintenance procedures for normal and abnormal modes of operation; participate in evaluation planning; determine manning and training requirements in detail.

Fabrication and Testing

End Product. Prototype (or first model) and technical manuals.

System Engineering Activities. Continuously review quality-assurance program results and early performance, reliability, and maintainability reports; define spare parts procurement, inventory, and transportation requirements; implement minor modifications as need arises.

Relevant Human Factors Activities. Evaluate prototype system from human factors standpoint; recommend modifications to design or procedures as deficiencies are perceived; establish training courses; familiarize personnel with system.

Initial Operation

End Product. Completed system, ready for trials.

System Engineering Activities. Analyze installation reports and problems; implement minor modifications as need arises.

Relevant Human Factors Activities. Review installation reports from human factors standpoint; recommend minor design changes; train personnel.

Operational Evaluation

End Product. Test and evaluation reports.

System Engineering Activities. Carry out test and evaluation procedures and analyze results; carry out any modifications required as a consequence of test data; continue review of system performance, reliability, and maintainability.

Relevant Human Factors Activities. Participate in test and evaluation procedures and review data from human factors standpoint; recommend design or procedure changes; determine training adequacy and recommend changes.

MAN'S PROPERTIES AND CAPABILITIES, AND THEIR IMPLICATIONS FOR MAN/MACHINE DESIGN

Man, in most systems, is the most valuable resource. Like any resource, he can be used to advantage, or he can be abused, pushed beyond his limits, and become more a disadvantage than advantage.

Unlike virtually all other components in a technological system, man is inherently variable. Although there are certain basic states of man that can be considered invariant, there are many more instances where man exhibits a basic and fundamental pattern of variance, change, development, flexibility, and adaptability. At the same time, man is a plural being; he is seldom motivated by any single purpose and certainly not for any length of time. He divides his loyalties and allegiances; he can perform many different tasks or the same task in many different ways; he adapts to circumstances by changing his behavior, sometimes constructively and sometimes maladaptively. The sheer complexity of man is baffling and makes one pause when considering the possible truth of any relatively simple description of him. However, it can be shown empirically that man is a lawful being and that true and useful statements can be made about his properties and capabilities, provided one is careful to define that set of circumstances, or that particular subset of behavior, with which one is concerned.

The significance of these very general considerations can be illustrated in the application of a human factors engineering principle. The likelihood of an error in manipulation of a set of controls increases as the number of controls increases and to the degree to which they are undifferentiated by means of location, shape, color coding, and the like. In short, a profusion of controls causes confusion. A simplification or rationalization of the layout of the set of controls does not automatically lead to a reduction of errors. One has to assume that the operator is motivated toward achievement, wishes to reduce errors, and thus will take advantage of the increased man/machine compatibility.

Furthermore, changes in an industrial setting are fraught with difficulties, because any change can be interpreted, in whole or in part, as a threat to job security or to the operator's self-esteem in that he may fail at the new job. These factors can undo the benefits that might be expected from the application of human factors engineering and can lead to faulty conclusions on the part of management. The lesson is that human factors engineering, in the restricted sense of increasing the compatibility across the man/machine interface, will generate its benefits only if the motivational states are such that the operators will take advantage of the new potential.

An illuminating, if paradoxical, example of this relationship occurred in the famous "Hawthorne" studies where a deterioration in working conditions did not stop a continued increase in productivity because of the extremely favorable motivational conditions that were established. An opposite example occurred in the development of a military communication system where the men's tasks were "over" human-engineered so that, although well within nearly anyone's capabilities, they were so dull and monotonous that the men lost interest and many errors and oversights occurred.

The fact that man operates as a whole must always serve to attenuate the generality of statements that refer to some particular function of man, or some particular skill potential, or some advantage to be gained from optimizing in a mechanistic sense the man/machine interface. However, we can also notice that changes in terms of the human factors engineering of equipment or task procedures are relatively easy to make and that the expected benefits are large. A most interesting study[2] showed that proper design of an assembly technology caused the mutually reinforcing benefits of improved morale, job satisfaction, and sense of achievement on the one hand, with increased productivity and lower defect rate on the other. Very similar consequences flow from judicious "job enlargement" policies, where the job is designed to engage more of the man's skill and reduce repetition and monotony.

Comparative Advantages of Men and Machines. Perhaps the most fundamental question in human factors engineering is, what kinds of tasks should a man be required to do and when should he be preferred over machine elements? A general guide for answering this question follows.[3]

[2] T. M. Lodahl, "Patterns of Job Attitudes in Two Assembly Technologies," *Administrative Science Quarterly,* vol. 8, no. 4, 1964.

[3] Adapted from "Human Factors Design Standards for the Fleet Ballistic Missile Weapon System," *op. cit.*

Some Comparative Advantages of Men and Machines in, Typically, an Information-processing Operation

Advantages of Humans	*Advantages of Machines*

Task Element: Sensing

Detecting low levels of energy	Sensitivity to stimuli outside of man's ability
Sensitivity to a wide variety of stimuli	Insensitivity to extraneous factors
Perceiving patterns and generalizing from them	Monitoring of other machines or men
Sensing unusual or unprogrammed outputs	
Detecting signals in a high-noise environment	
Recognizing objects	

Task Element: Processing

Storing and recalling large amounts of information	Responding quickly to control signals
Exercising judgment	Storing and recalling large amounts of data for short periods
Improvising and adopting flexible procedures	Computing ability
Handling low-probability events	Handling highly complex parallel operations
Arriving at new and different solutions to problems	Deductive logical ability
Profiting from experience	
Tracking under a wide variety of situations	
Performing when overloaded	
Reasoning inductively	

Task Element: Actuating

Performing fine manipulations	Performing routine, repetitive, precise tasks
Exercising a variety of response actions	Exerting large amounts of force smoothly and precisely
Taking unprogrammed actions	

This listing is not exhaustive; it concentrates on the types of functions present in some information processing and control operations.

Physical Shape and Properties of Man. Man has a certain physical shape, a certain range of limb movement, a certain ability to exert force, and certain tolerances for environmental conditions such as temperature, noise, and vibration.

With respect to the size and shape of man, one of the best sources of information is "Anthropometry," Chapter 11 in Morgan et al., *Human Engineering Guide to Equipment Design*, McGraw-Hill Book Company, New York, 1963. Data are provided on all significant human dimensions and the ranges of limb movement. For instance, it is pointed out that controls should not be placed farther than 28 inches from the shoulder to be within the reach of virtually everybody without gross changes of body position.

Perhaps one of the most common errors is the "fallacy of the average man." The average man (more strictly, the 50th percentile man) can manipulate a knob at about 30 inches distance without body movement; however, by definition, if a knob were placed at this distance, one-half of the population would have some difficulty in reaching it. It is almost always appropriate to design maximum dimensions with respect to the 1st or 5th percentile man, and minimum dimensions (for example, door height) with respect to the 95th or 99th percentile man. Sometimes, compromises have to be made; if no adjustment devices can be introduced, then it may be appropriate to use the 50th percentile man as a guide for design.

Another area for designing for man's physical properties is the application of force. When cheap power sources are increasingly available, it is sometimes overlooked that man is an effective, inexpensive, and highly adaptable source of power. Often, simplicity and reliability can be increased by judicious use of man's muscles. H. M. Bowen proposed a general guide for designers as follows:[4]

[4] H. M. Bowen, "Rational Design," series of seven articles in *Industrial Design*, 1964.

Preferred Design Values

For long-term work....................... About 0.1 horsepower
For single body movements (assuming good
   coupling of musculature to load).......... About 3.0 horsepower
Push-pull arm load....................... About 30 foot-pounds
Left-right arm load....................... About 20 foot-pounds
Up-down arm load........................ About 20 foot-pounds
Grip load................................ About 30 foot-pounds
Leg load: outward push.................. About 100 foot-pounds seated; ankle flex-
                                    ure only about 20 foot-pounds

As a general rule for designing man-powered devices, allow the hand or foot to exert low static forces and gain power by the motion of the limb.

Chapter 10 of the *Human Engineering Guide to Equipment Design,* mentioned above, covers the effects of environment on human performance. The body has remarkable capabilities of adaptation and habituation to different environments. However, these processes have limits. Deterioration in human performance can set in as a function of temperature, humidity, pressure, oxygen content, noise, vibration, acceleration, atmospheric contaminants, and the like. Often the first effects as the environment begins to depart from normative values are insidious and take the form of impairment of complex function, memory lapses, and defective emotional control; the fine edge of skilled, proficient performance is rubbed off before any dramatic deterioration, obvious to all, sets in.

Man has many specific properties which may be defined and which have implications for the design of the man/machine interface and for the proper utilization of man in an operation. The following lists briefly review some basic guides in the primary categories of information intake (sensing), decision making (information processing), and responding (actuating).[5]

Information Intake: Allocation of Functions to Sensory Modes

Prefer to use:

Vision. For all functions requiring a grasp of spatial relationships; specifically,

Orienting oneself
Scanning multiple displays
Making simultaneous or rapid successive comparisons
Referring to information sources
Gaining fine quantitative information
Judging movements and rates of change
Obtaining "global" impressions

Use vision especially when:

Hearing is difficult because of a noisy environment
Hearing is impaired by air pressure changes

Hearing. Generally, for single-dimension communications and when attention cannot be assured; specifically,

For warning and emergency signals
For short messages requiring immediate attention and action
For displaying the time arrangement of events when they occur close in time
When vision conditions are poor

[5] Bowen, *op. cit.*

Touch. Generally, for objects which have to be found or manipulated by "blind" movements of the hands; specifically,

When vision and hearing cannot be used or when these sense channels are fully occupied

When error-free performance is very important; touch can back up (be redundant to) the other senses

Sense of Movement. Generally, for providing feedback information that the executed motion is appropriate (for example, distinguishing left-right motions and in-out motions)

Decision Making: Precepts for Optimizing Decision Functions

To facilitate decision functions:

Allow the man to take his own time to make a decision within some practical limit (self-paced operation rather than machine-paced operation)

Get the information to the man as early as possible—ahead of the time when he must respond

Avoid having the man idle for long periods of time; keep man in contact with situation

Reduce the amount of information to the man to minimum necessary; avoid irrelevant information; place occasionally used information on an on-demand basis

Reduce the "work" the man has to do by coding display information in a self-evident manner and by designing the display-control relationships so that there is a natural parallelism between the two

Arrange the control layout so that frequently occurring items are located in central easy-to-use positions.

Responding: Selection of Arrangement and Type of Controls

Place controls so that:

They are grouped according to common function or purpose

They occur in sequence (top to bottom, left to right) to parallel activation sequences

Controls that may have to be found by "blind reading" are separated from other controls

Controls are near to (preferably underneath) their associated displays

Use differently shaped and/or sized controls so that:

Possible confusion between controls is minimized

It is possible to identify control without vision

Size is associated with importance of control

Use different mode of operation controls so that:

Possibilities of wrong activation are minimized (for example, toggle switch for on/off, not rotary knob)

Operations are standardized (for example, to right, forward, and up mean on, plus, or increase; to left, backward and down mean off, minus, or decrease)

The control-movement direction is related to an associated display by appearing to "command" the display action (for example, preferably, lever to right, pointer on scale to right)

There are, of course, many other aspects of designing man into the system. Indeed, any instance where man is involved in a process calls for some thought to be given to the manner of his employment. Selection and training procedures (see Chapters 6 and 8 of Section 11) are important considerations to the human factors specialist, as well as to the personnel psychologist or manager. There must be established a compatibility among the people available; the duration, type, and cost of training; and the nature of the tasks allocated.

In the question of personnel selection, a problem of some moment to industry is the employment of older personnel. It has been shown that although, in general, older people tend to work more slowly, cannot do heavy muscular work, need to have their tasks well structured, and take longer to train (and in their training are more dependent on the practice of the actual skills and movements required in the task), they are, nevertheless, characteristically careful, consistent, and dependable workers.

In the question of the relationship between task design and training, it was shown, for instance, that various styles of keyboard and keyboard actuation used in a semiautomatic sorting process led to various combinations of performance levels and training-time requirements. The general relationship emerged that keyboard designs which could lead to the highest levels of ultimate performance required the longest training time. Thus, the selection of the keyboard design had to depend upon consideration of personnel turnover rate, personnel availability, the cost of training, and the cost effectiveness of a unit increment of productivity. A linear program involving these factors can be developed, and management can have the benefit of a rational solution to the problem of selecting, in this case, a keyboard configuration.

TEST AND EVALUATION

Much of the effectiveness of human factors work derives from its attempt to be both thorough and scientific. A typical account of the aims of applying human factors work is given by R. M. Gagne,[6] who pointed out that, because of the comparative imperfection of human factors as an axiomatic science, considerable reliance has to be placed upon empirical methods. When a system is being developed, or is already in existence, the human factors specialist recognizes that improvement will follow the empirical diagnosis of deficiency and that the productivity of the system can only be certified finally by measurement.

In a design development, at some point hardware will become available. It is at this time that the human factors specialist can begin to determine accurately the effectiveness of the human factors design criteria and methods which have been applied in the preceding phases, as well as the effectiveness of the procedures which have been developed for operation and maintenance of the equipment. Tests include the following.[7]

1. Determination of the compatibility between the personnel and equipment: Can the personnel perform the functions which have been assigned to them without undue discomfort to them and with sufficient accuracy and speed to meet operational requirements?

2. Determination of the effectiveness with which human-engineering principles have been applied to the design of the equipment and to the control of the environment. This includes the location, design, and operation of the controls and displays, design of the equipment for maintenance, and the effectiveness with which the environment has been controlled or otherwise compensated for.

3. Determination of the effectiveness of the procedures which have been developed to operate and maintain the equipment; determination of the adequacy of any job aids, handbooks, or instructions that are available at this time.

[6] R. M. Gagne, *Psychological Principles in System Development,* Holt, Rinehart and Winston, Inc., New York, 1962.

[7] A. N. Chambers, *A Systems Approach to Human Factors in the Design of Systems,* Dunlap and Associates, Inc., Darien, Conn., 1963.

4. Evaluation of the design and operation of any training aids and devices that have been mocked up or produced by this time.

5. Preliminary evaluation of the adequacy of the selection and training procedures based on the performance of any personnel who have been selected and trained at this point.

The results of such human factors tests can be used as the basis for immediate redesign if the problems are considered sufficiently serious to warrant redesign, or they can be used as the basis for the improvement of the design of future equipment. In other instances, design problems may be circumvented by modifications to procedures or changes in personnel selection, training, or manning requirements.

Once the system is in operation, further human factors evaluation may be undertaken to accomplish the following.[8]

1. Determination of the compatibility between the system and the user personnel performing as a team, under conditions approximating the operational environment and mission for which the system has been designed.

2. Further determination of the effectiveness of the human engineering aspects of all of the hardware designs and the control of internal environment.

3. Determination of the effectiveness of all the control, operational, and maintenance procedures and their associated handbooks.

4. Evaluation of the effectiveness of the individual and team training and their associated training programs, materials, aids, and devices.

5. Evaluation of the adequacy of the manning structure.

After the system has been in operation for some time, requirements for modification of the system, subsystems, or equipments (through modification of the existing hardware or building new models) can be expected. The reasons for this are as follows.[9]

1. Systems and equipments become obsolete very rapidly, and it is necessary to modify them to prolong their usefulness.

2. Technology advances rapidly, and significant advances may suggest the desirability for modification.

3. Systems, subsystems, and equipments may fail to meet their operational requirements and hence must be redesigned.

4. Operational requirements change with international conditions and national policy.

Depending on the complexity and the extent of the modification requirements, the process may involve any or all of the design and development phases that have been described previously and may vary widely in the level of effort required.

Inevitably, in the evolution of a new system or a modification of an old system, evaluations must be made of its components and overall characteristics. The human factors specialist is brought in here to ensure that the system can be operated, maintained, and controlled by the assigned persons. His further functions at this point are concerned with spotting any design oversights and providing recommendations for modification, if necessary, either immediately or for the future. In proceeding with this work, the human factors engineer typically uses a variety of test procedures and methods, from rating forms to physiological measures. He applies these instruments according to the relevant requirements for such considerations as validity, reliability, objectivity, standardization, and economy. As appropriate, this activity is conducted in the field or experimentally and ranges from direct observation to simulation.

[8] Chambers, *op. cit.*
[9] Chambers, *op. cit.*

MANAGEMENT OF THE HUMAN FACTORS EFFORT

Management's perception of the importance of human factors engineering relates directly to the values that it might obtain from this field of specialization when applied to development or modification of a manufacturing system. As indicated by the foregoing overview of concepts and methodology and the small sample of typical data, the application possibilities range from establishing broad-based goals to specifying minute details. Without demonstrated management interest in human factors engineering at all levels within an organization, any professional effort in this area within any company most likely will prove "too little and too late."

Support of the human factors engineering effort is essential for accomplishing the desirable integration of the activity with all other effort expended on the creation of a new manufacturing system or the modification of an existing one. In planning and budgeting at senior executive levels for the work of the human factors specialists, time scheduling is a vital prerequisite.

This scheduling will be helpful in revealing the areas in which human factors engineering effort is to be applied and the extent of the professional assistance that will be required from time to time as well. Where there is an in-house staff of specialists to perform the work, there may be need to augment their numbers and skills by enlisting the services of outside consultants.

Whether employees, outsiders, or both are engaged for the human factors work, management will be well advised to encourage a proper reception for these professional people. Within the firm, for instance, management can promote an appreciation for the field through sponsorship of seminars and formal training courses. Perhaps more important, adequate authority should be given to human factors engineers so that they can participate effectively in design decision making. Inadequate manning, as well as insufficient influence, can limit the value from human factors engineering effort just as much as failure to provide for it at the very start of work.

Although appreciation for human factors engineering is called for on the part of management and other technicians involved, the human factors specialist also needs to understand requirements for production feasibility (in tooling and quality tolerances), for conforming with industrial and government codes, for accommodating standard replacement parts and components, for recognizing the necessity for using spares or replacements from established inventories, for meeting delivery schedules, and for compromises in view of realistic assessments of available skills, space, and various economic aspects of the total system situation.

If management is willing to consider support for a human factors engineering effort, then it must arrive at answers to such questions as: What scope of effort is necessary to achieve a worthwhile result? Can the company afford the investment? Conversely, can it afford not to make it? If the effort is made, how can it best be provided for by a specialist staff? Once the work is under way or when completed, how can it be properly evaluated?

CONCLUSION

As the human factors specialist has become involved in real systems, sometimes of enormous size and complexity, he has perceived that:

Man acts as a component in the system, and no man or his task are autonomous or can be studied or improved meaningfully except in the context of the supraordinate system in which they are involved.

The utility of man in any technological system is increasingly dependent upon the exercise of man's intelligence and flexibility; thus tasks which men like to do and for which there is little substitute are those tasks in which human skill and judgment are demanded. Often, the most difficult human engineering problems occur when man is underemployed. In these cases, the emphasis is on prohibiting errors of the operator occurring or jeopardizing the system. Although the full utilization of man as a resource offers many problems, the issue of error prohibition falls into the perspective of exploiting the higher abilities of man.

It is dangerous to overlook the fact that the whole man is employed and not just a functional component of the system. The danger is in two forms. In a narrow sense, the overlooking of man's motivations and needs on the job will impair his effectiveness as a functional component in a direct way. A bored or dissatisfied man (for whatever reason) will do a poor job of monitoring himself and his task. In a broader sense, one needs to attend to the involvement of the whole man to maintain the long-term morale and cooperativeness of the personnel in the enterprise.

No technological system can be effective unless it changes and adapts itself to the larger changes taking place in the relevant technology and in the society at large. The initiation and control of change is in the hands of men. The human factors specialist is involved fundamentally in the problem of change.

BIBLIOGRAPHY

Bowen, H. M., "Rational Design," series of seven articles in *Industrial Design*, 1964.

Chambers, A. N., *A Systems Approach to Human Factors in the Design of Systems*, Dunlap and Associates, Inc., Darien, Conn., 1963.

Chapanis, A., *Man-Machine Engineering*, Wadsworth Publishing Co., Inc., Belmont, Calif., 1965.

Gagne, R. M., *Psychological Principles in System Development*, Holt, Rinehart and Winston, Inc., New York, 1962.

Javitz, A. E., *Engineering Psychology and Human Factors in Design*, Electro-Technology, New York, 1961.

Kraft, J. A., "A 1961 Compilation and Brief History of Human Factors Research in Business and Industry," *Human Factors*, vol. 3, no. 4, Pergamon Press, New York, 1961.

Lodahl, T. M., "Patterns of Job Attitudes in Two Assembly Technologies," *Administrative Science Quarterly*, vol. 8, no. 4, 1964.

McCormick, E. J., *Human Factors Engineering*, McGraw-Hill Book Company, New York, 1964.

Morgan, C. T. A., A. Chapanis, J. S. Cook III, and M. W. Lund (eds.), *Human Engineering Guide to Equipment Design*, McGraw-Hill Book Company, New York, 1963.

Ronco, P. G., "A Bibliography and Overview of Human Factors Reference Works," *Human Factors*, vol. 4, no. 6, Pergamon Press, New York, 1963.

Vroom, V. H., *Work and Motivation*, John Wiley & Sons, Inc., New York, 1964.

Woodson, W. E., and D. W. Conover, *Human Engineering Guide for Equipment Designers*, 2d ed., University of California Press, Berkeley, 1964.

CHAPTER ELEVEN

Work Measurement and Incentives

WILLIAM M. AIKEN *Vice President, H. B. Maynard and Company, Incorporated, Pittsburgh, Pennsylvania*

Work measurement and incentives in some form or other are probably about as old as civilization itself. In the industrial world, the first organized development was made in the late 1800s by Frederick W. Taylor, often called the "Father of Scientific Management." Through extensive study, Taylor found that it was feasible to determine better methods for doing work and to measure how much work a man should do in a given period of time.

Following Taylor's original work, a number of other pioneers furthered the development of work measurement and incentives. They refined the time-study procedures and introduced many variations in time-study methods. Concentrating almost entirely on production work, they devised incentive plans for motivating the workers and developed other management control procedures. Their results were often spectacular—so spectacular, in fact, that many charlatans were attracted to the field. Instead of being objective in their work-measurement efforts, their aim was continually to force the workers to greater production. This resulted in the justifiable charge of "speedup," and time study and incentives fell into disrepute in many circles. It took many years for leaders in industrial engineering to overcome the reputation that these unscrupulous individuals created.

Today, work measurement and incentives are well established as valuable management tools. Their application has been extended to almost every kind of endeavor which involves manual work. Their use is *not* to speed up workers, but to provide management with information by which it can control the flow and cost of production in plants and offices. Great strides have been made in the development of new techniques which expedite the work-measurement task and assure the fairness of the productivity requirements made of the workers.

APPROACH TO WORK MEASUREMENT AND INCENTIVES

Frederick W. Taylor long ago developed a formula for maximum production. He stated that the greatest production results when a worker is given a definite task to be done in a definite time and in a definite manner. Although the terminology is somewhat different today, his formula is just as applicable now as it ever was. His definite task involves the assignment of a specific operation to a worker. The definite time is established by time study, a standard data system, or some other recognized means. The definite method involves such things as motion sequences, workplace arrangements, and machine feeds and speeds.

In 1939, H. B. Maynard and G. J. Stegemerten, in defining "methods engineering," covered all of the principal elements involved in the establishment of work measurement and incentives. Their definition was:

Methods engineering is the technique that subjects each operation of a given piece of work to close analysis in order to approach the quickest and best method of performing each necessary operation; it includes the standardization of equipment, methods, and working conditions; it trains the operator to follow the standard method; when all this has been done, and not before, it determines by accurate measurement the number of standard hours in which an operator working with standard performance can do the job; finally, it usually, although not necessarily, devises a plan for compensating labor which encourages the operator to attain or to surpass standard performance.[1]

This definition emphasizes the important steps in the approach to work measurement and incentives.

1. You must establish good methods—eliminating any unnecessary work—on which the work standards will be based.

2. You must provide standard conditions and equipment so that the good method can be followed.

3. You must train the workers thoroughly so that they can follow the proper method.

4. You must use work-measurement techniques which will result in accurate work standards.

5. If you apply wage incentives, you must use a plan that rewards the workers fairly and adequately for meeting or bettering the standards.

THE IMPORTANCE OF WORK MEASUREMENT

An outstanding management authority once stated that:

Measurement + control = scientific management

As this equation points out, measurement provides the means by which management can effectively control the elements of a business. In other words, before you can control something you must first be able to measure it. This applies not only to production, but also to office work, sales, maintenance, engineering, and other functions of a business.

An effective work-measurement program will benefit a company in many ways. Some of the principal means by which benefits are derived are:

1. Methods improvement
2. Performance control
3. Production planning and control
4. Cost control
5. Estimating and pricing
6. Wage incentives

[1] H. B. Maynard and G. J. Stegemerten, *Operation Analysis*, chap. 1, McGraw-Hill Book Company, New York, 1939.

Methods Improvements. One of the most important features of a work-measurement program is the close attention that is paid to methods. It has often been said that there is no such thing as the one best method for doing a job. The "best" method is the best method that a particular analyst or group of analysts can devise today. With a well-planned work-measurement program, however, you can expect that *good* methods will be developed. And in many cases, the *good* method is far superior to the method that existed before the analysis was made. It is not at all unusual for methods improvements achieved in a work-measurement program to increase employee productivity more than 100 percent. In general, gains in productivity resulting from methods improvements are greater than those from any other source.

Methods improvements are a natural product of a work-measurement study. Techniques are employed which question intensively everything about an operation. Operation analysis questions such things as the necessity for and the sequence of the operation, possible combining of operations, materials used, and material-handling methods. Micromotion study and predetermined elemental time systems question the workplace layout, the necessity for the reaches and moves that are made, the positioning of parts, and the feasibility of making it possible for both hands to work at the same time. Inefficient operations and motions are clearly pointed out, so that it is a relatively easy matter to simplify the method and visualize an improvement. Then, with work measurement, the value of the improved method can be evaluated to determine the economies of making a change.

Performance Control. An outstanding use of work measurement is in controlling the productivity of workers. The performance of workers typically ranges from 50 to 60 percent when management has no measure of their productivity. When the work is measured and work standards are provided to the workers and their supervisors, the performance increases significantly. On a measured day-work basis, the performance in a well-controlled operation will range from 80 to 90 percent.

There are several reasons for the substantial increase in performance when work standards are applied. Generally, people work more effectively when they know what is expected of them in the way of a target. Supervisors are able to help their employees when there is a measure to indicate those individuals who are having difficulty in meeting the standards. A poor performance may indicate improper methods, bad material, inadequate tooling, or insufficient training of the operator. When the report shows a poor performance, the foreman can analyze the situation and ascertain the reason for the problem. He will then be in a good position to help the worker correct the problem.

Work measurement is particularly useful in determining manning requirements—especially for production or administrative functions which have widely varying work loads. Without measurement, management can only guess at the correct number of personnel to have available. Consequently, the natural tendency of managements in this position is to overman so that service will always be available when needed. With measurement, management can do a much more objective job of planning personnel requirements to meet forecasted volumes.

Production Planning and Control. In planning and controlling production, there are a number of uses for work measurement. To schedule work intelligently in a factory or an office, the scheduler must know how long a job will take as well as the amount of time that is available in a work center or on a machine. Work measurement provides him with the standard time required to set up and perform an operation. Thus, he can schedule the work for such purposes as quickest delivery, maximum equipment utilization, minimum labor cost, or maximum production.

Work measurement provides the basis for economic-lot-quantity formulas. With these formulas, the planner attempts to optimize costs by achieving the proper balance among setup time, operating time, and inventory investment cost. To do this properly, it is necessary that he have an accurate measure of the time required to set up and perform an operation. The same information, together with additional data, is also useful in planning the amount of inventory that should be carried.

Work measurement is useful in balancing production among work stations on progressive assembly lines. It applies also to balancing production among various production and service centers so that a reasonably constant work flow can be maintained through a shop. It enables management to have a common denominator in defining the capacity of its facility—namely, measured standard hours.

Cost Control. Work measurement is used to establish standard cost-control systems. The measurement determines the cost of standard production hours in a department or a plant. Other departmental costs, such as indirect labor, supplies, and direct labor charged to nonstandard work, are then related to the standard cost. A system of variance reports is developed which compares the actual costs with the standard allowed cost. When the variances reported are unfavorable, management is alerted to the condition so that corrective action can be taken quickly. In a similar way, work measurement is used by many companies to develop manpower budgets which provide management with a good control over labor costs.

Another control involving work measurement is in the determination of standard costs for units of production. The historical records that many companies use point out clearly what their actual costs have been, and if there are any favorable or unfavorable trends in their cost pattern. Standard costs, based on work measurement, however, tell management what their unit costs *should* be. This provides management with a reliable yardstick with which to measure plant performance. When actual unit costs are compared with the standard unit costs, management is in a position to know where costs must be improved, or where changes must be made in the company's price structure or marketing efforts.

Estimating and Pricing. A use of work measurement that is closely allied to unit product costing is in cost estimating and product pricing. One of the most common methods now used for cost estimating is to compare the new product with some similar existing product—and then to use the old estimate for the new product. The problem is that the old estimate was probably made in the same way, and any original error is compounded.

Good estimates are extremely important. If an estimate is too high, chances are good that you will not get the job. If the estimate is too low you may get the job, but lose money on it.

Many companies have developed estimating data for component parts and assemblies that are based on actual historical costs. If the history of the company is such that historical costs compare closely with good standard costs, these data will be excellent. In many cases, however, the historical records do not indicate the real cost capabilities of an organization. Thus, the danger of getting the "tight" estimated jobs and losing the "loose" estimated jobs is still present.

A number of companies use data derived from work measurement for estimating purposes. When the product being estimated involves very large quantities, the estimate must be developed with the same care that a production standard would require—using the most minute measurement data. In many cases, where the product is of a jobbing or low-volume nature, it is often not feasible to use the work-measurement data in their usual detailed form. The data must be consolidated and simplified for easy, quick application.

The accuracy of the estimate has to be consistent with the degree of control that management can exercise over product costs. By using work-measurement data, however, management is reasonably sure that it will get its share of jobs and make money on them.

Wage Incentives. Perhaps the only use of work measurement made by the original time-study men was to establish wage incentives. They demonstrated clearly the motivation that increased earnings have on the productivity of workers. In fact, they did this so often, and without regard to the other motivations of people, that incentives (and work measurement) suffered immensely. There is still a strong feeling in some management and union circles that wage incentives are not worthwhile. On the other hand, many managements and unions endorse wage incentives heartily.

Work measurement provides the basis for practically all wage incentive plans. It has often been said that wage incentives "put a worker in business for himself." Measurement determines the standard rate of production. When an incentive worker produces at a greater-than-standard rate of production, he is paid additional wages in proportion to his rate of production. Thus, his earnings depend to a large extent on his abilities and his own degree of effort.

With a measured daywork plan, workers have shown repeatedly that they will produce at a level of approximately 80 to 90 percent. With a good wage incentive plan, they will produce consistently at a level of 120 to 130 percent. For this they are generally paid a 1 percent bonus for each 1 percent of performance over 100 percent. Thus, the incentive workers have an opportunity to earn substantially more than the going rate of pay for their type of work.

The gain to the company from an incentive plan is the increase in production from the 80–90 percent measured daywork level to 100 percent. Beyond 100 percent, there is no decrease in unit labor cost, because workers receive additional earnings in proportion to their output. There is a gain, however, to the company in the greater utilization of production facilities.

WORK-MEASUREMENT TECHNIQUES

Work measurement was applied originally to production operations. For many years, only production work was studied, and it was studied and restudied many times. A few pioneering companies departed from this pattern and studied work other than direct production work, but it was questionable if the techniques available at the time made it economical to study the irregular nonrepetitive work that makes up most indirect work.

There have, however, been several significant developments in work measurement. Direct production work has been studied so extensively that, in most companies that have had work-measurement programs for some time, there is relatively little more to be gained from studying it again. At the same time, the proportion and numbers of people engaged in indirect work and offices have risen to the point that it is almost mandatory for management to gain better control over these costs. Fortunately, or perhaps because of these changes, new techniques and approaches have been developed which have greatly facilitated the work-measurement job. Where once there was only time study, now there are new systems that have changed the entire work-measurement picture.

There is no one best work-measurement technique. Each of the four major techniques—time study, predetermined elemental times, work sampling, and standard data—have applications where they are best used. The well-equipped industrial engineer should have a thorough working knowledge of all of them. There will be occasions when he will need a combination of all the techniques to complete a work-measurement program.

Time Study. Time study is the oldest of the accepted work-measurement techniques, and is probably the most widely used. There are a number of minor variations among time-study practitioners, such as continuous or snapback watch reading, and speed rating or skill and effort rating. These variations can and do cause some differences in the resulting standards. In general, however, the standards derived by skilled, experienced time-study men should be within ±10 percent accuracy.

Time study requires that the job to be studied be in operation and that a workman who is proficient at this particular operation be on the job. The method for doing the job should have been established by the industrial engineer, usually in conjunction with the foreman. In many cases, however, the method has been developed by the operator himself. Thus, it is often necessary for the time-study man to correct the method that the worker is using before he times the job.

The general procedure that the time-study man follows consists of these steps.

1. Observe the method and correct as needed.
2. Divide the operation into short elements, such as "pick up part," "place part in machine," and so forth.
3. Time the elements with a stopwatch and record the elemental times.
4. Rate the performance of the operator in terms of speed or skill and effort characteristics.
5. Determine and add allowances for delays, personal time, and fatigue.
6. Compute the standard.

The most controversial points in the time-study procedure concern the establishment and recording of the proper method and the performance rating. If the time-study man is not careful to see that a good method is followed, he may arrive at a standard that will be good only until the operator exercises his own ingenuity and finds a better way to do the job. Then, of course, the standard will become loose and will not accurately measure the work.

In rating performance, the time-study man must judge how closely the operator is following the desired method, his skill at the job, and how diligently he is working. Usually, if there is a disagreement between the operator and the time-study man over a standard, it involves the rating that was made of the performance.

On the positive side, time study is a well-accepted technique. If the time-study man is well trained and does his work properly, he will set standards accurately and economically.

Predetermined Elemental Time Systems. Predetermined elemental time systems have had a tremendous impact on work measurement. They have eliminated the use of the stopwatch for practically all work except process times (machining and so forth). They have eliminated performance rating altogether because they do not consider how fast the operator is working, but only the motions that are required to do the job. They focus attention on the method required for an operation so closely that each individual motion can be scrutinized. They have made work measurement a far more objective procedure.

There are a number of predetermined elemental time systems in use, but only a few dominate the field. The first of these, motion-time analysis (MTA), was developed by A. B. Segur in 1924. In the late 1930s, J. H. Quick and W. J. Shea developed the work-factor system. H. B. Maynard, G. J. Stegemerten, and J. L. Schwab completed and authored the widely used methods-time measurement (MTM) system in the late 1940s. Figure 9-4 in Section 7 shows the MTM data card.

These systems, and others like them, have differences in approach and application. Their objectives, however, are common. They are used to analyze work in terms of the basic motions that are necessary to perform it. When the motions have been identified, time values for the motions can be selected from appropriate tables of predetermined elemental time values. In this manner, time standards can be built up synthetically, even before a product is put into operation.

The procedure involved in using a predetermined elemental time system consists of the following general steps.

1. Observe the operation, divide it into elements, and record the basic motions required to do the job.

2. Analyze the motion pattern to eliminate unnecessary motions or to improve the motion pattern.

3. Select the appropriate time values from tables of predetermined elemental times for the recorded necessary motions.

4. Add the recorded time values.

5. Determine and add allowances for delays, personal time, and fatigue.

With a predetermined elemental time system, if the analyst can visualize correctly the method for doing an operation, he can develop the standard before an operation is started. His analysis is then a very effective document for training the operator in the proper method as soon as he is assigned to the job. It is necessary, of course, that the analyst understand the work intimately to visualize the proper method correctly.

When there is a dispute over a time standard set with a predetermined elemental time system, it usually involves the method. Either the operator is not following the proper motion pattern or the analyst has overlooked or misinterpreted some motions while making his analysis. When this occurs, the dispute can be resolved in an objective manner by comparing the recorded motion pattern with the motions that the operator is using.

Predetermined elemental time systems are well accepted as work-measurement techniques. They require more time to learn than time-study procedures, but, when properly used, they do a much more effective job both in methods development and in standards setting. They have made it economical and desirable to measure many classes of work, such as maintenance, offices, warehousing, and jobbing work, which were previously impractical to measure.

Work Sampling. Work sampling is a statistical method of work measurement. The principle of work sampling is that you can observe operators at random intervals, record what they are doing such as busy or idle, and relate the sample to the entire working day or other working period. Originally its use was primarily to determine such things as machine or operator utilization and the amount of delays or other interferences in an operation. It is still used extensively for these purposes.

Work sampling has been used by a few companies with some effectiveness to develop standards. To do this the observer must record not only whether the operator is busy or idle, but also what he is working on. He must also rate the performance of the operator and make at least some rough evaluation of the methods he is using. This information is then related to the number of units that a worker produces in a given time, and a time standard is computed.

The general procedure for using work sampling to determine allowances is as follows.

1. Prepare an observation sheet, detailing the people to be observed, the working classifications (direct, indirect, and so forth), and the idle classifications (personal delay, avoidable delays, unavoidable delays, and so forth).

2. Observe the operators instantaneously at random intervals, classify, and record the observations.

3. Divide the number of observations in the various idle classifications by the total number of observations of working time.

4. Calculate percentage allowances to be applied to time study or predetermined elemental time standards.

The great value of work sampling is that a wealth of information about manufacturing effectiveness can be gathered rapidly and inexpensively. It is probably the best means of gaining an overall evaluation of a plant or an office. It is also probably the most widely used work-measurement technique for determining delay allowances. Its principal shortcoming is that there is generally insufficient emphasis placed on proper methods or on the working effectiveness of the people observed.

Standard Data. Many years ago Frederick Taylor predicted that some day a handbook would be prepared which would list all of the time values needed to measure work. To date this prophecy has not come true. With the advent of MTM and other predetermined elemental time systems, however, great strides have been made toward that end. They have enabled industrial engineers to develop standard data which greatly simplify the work-measurement job for many industries and for many classes of work.

"Standard data" may be defined as a compilation of elemental time data arranged in such a way that their application in calculating a time standard is quick and accurate. Standard data have been used in one form or another for many years to set standards. The reason for this is that with standard data a standard can be set in a few minutes as opposed to several hours with time study. For many years, time study was used to develop standard data. More recently, predetermined elemental times have furthered the cause of standard data considerably. Now there are several levels of data which have greatly reduced the time required to build standard data. For example, from an MTM base, the MTM Association for Standards and Research has developed and issued a broader level of data, known as "general purpose data" (GPD). These data, in turn, have been used to develop a still higher level of data, known as "basic operations data." These data then are used to develop data for specific operations, such as maintenance operations, assembly operations, and machining operations.

The net effect of these standard data developments has been to reduce tremendously the amount of time required to establish data for whole groups of operations. In 1940 it was estimated that two to three months were required to develop sufficient data for a time formula that would cover an operation like painting or the operation of a machine tool. By the 1960s the same development required a week or less. Prospects are that this time will be further reduced as computers are used more and more for standard data applications.

COMPARISON OF WORK-MEASUREMENT TECHNIQUES

Table 11-1 shows a comparison of the four major work-measurement techniques. As the table indicates, each technique has advantages and disadvan-

TABLE 11-1. Comparison of Work-measurement Techniques*

Factor	Time study	Predetermined elemental times	Work sampling	Standard data
Attention to method............	B	A	C	A
Accuracy.....................	B	A	C	B
Consistency..................	B	A	B	A
Record of method.............	B	A	C	A
Speed of measurement..........	B	C	A	A
Time to learn technique........	B	C	A	C
Acceptance of results...........	B	B	B	B

* A = excellent, B = satisfactory, C = fair.

tages. The trend is toward ever greater use of standard data, but all four major work-measurement methods will undoubtedly continue to be used.

THE CASE FOR WAGE INCENTIVES

There is no question of the benefits to be gained from a sound wage incentive installation. Throughout industry, in the United States and abroad, experience has amply demonstrated that wage incentives can increase earnings, raise production, and decrease costs. Yet there are many managements and union leaders who oppose the use of wage incentives. This may be caused by a lack of recognition of the benefits by management and labor. Or it may be a holdover attitude from the years long passed when incentives were badly abused by unscrupulous managers.

When incentives were first applied many years ago, they were the sources of spectacular cost reductions. Unfortunately, the haste to get incentives in and working led to many abuses. Incentives were installed by poorly trained men who neglected to consider even such a basic matter as the method used to do the job. As a result, the incentive workers found many shortcuts, and before long, their incentive earnings far exceeded what management expected. In those days, the corrective action was easy—management simply cut the rates.

Managements, in general, have long since corrected their mistakes and are now extremely careful to be absolutely fair and sound on all phases of wage incentive installation and administration. In doing so, they receive the benefit of increased production from their facilities, and the workers receive substantially greater wages.

When an activity which has been performed on a daywork basis, without standards and without methods study, is placed on incentive—properly, and with due attention to methods improvements—the typical results that a great many companies and their employees have experienced are:

Increase in production, 100 percent

Increase in earnings, 20 to 35 percent

Decrease in cost, 30 to 40 percent

Experience has shown that many wage incentive plans, which may have been properly installed originally, deteriorate over a period of time to the point that they cause serious problems for both management and labor. The fact that plans deteriorate and cause problems has influenced some managements to advocate a measured daywork control, because "incentives are too hard to administer." Advocates of measured daywork plans may be overlooking the point that, for measured daywork plans to operate effectively over a long period of time, they must be administered just as carefully as wage incentive plans. When comparisons are made of measured daywork versus incentives, it is quite often a comparison of well-administered measured daywork with poorly administered wage incentives. If the comparison is made of a well-administered measured daywork plan and a well-administered incentive plan, the advantages will be comparable, *except that the incentive installation will have the additional advantages of greater productivity, lower costs, and greater employee earnings.*

The present state of management knowledge enhances the installation of incentives. Existing work-measurement techniques assure management and labor that the standards are based on good methods, are equitable, and can be maintained economically. The knowledge of incentive administration gained from years of experience provides a clear path for management to follow, first, in installing a sound incentive, and second, in administering it.

TYPES OF INCENTIVE PLANS

Over the years there have been a number of incentive plans developed, installed, and abandoned. Each plan had some special feature which was designed to provide either greater motivation to the workers or greater safeguards to the company if the plan did not work out well. Experience with incentives has practically eliminated all but a few incentive plans which have stood the test of time.

The oldest form of incentive payment and one that still exists in some industries is piecework. Piecework consists of standards which are expressed in money paid per unit of production. As the worker completes units of production, he earns the money value for the units. If he fails to meet the rate, he is paid a guaranteed minimum base rate. This is the easiest type of incentive plan for the worker to understand, and it provides a strong incentive. It is used extensively in the garment industry, in foundries, and in the glass industry. The most serious objection to piecework is that when the hourly base rate changes, there is often a major task involved in calculating new piece rates to conform to the new base rate.

Some of the better-known incentive plans which had a brief flare, but are not in common use today, are as follows.

1. *The Halsey plan* provided that the bonus gained from increased productivity was divided between employee and employer on a set basis—usually 50–50. In other words, if the employee produced at the rate of 160 percent, he got only 30 percent, and the company kept 30 percent.

2. *The Bedeaux plan* also provided for the bonus to be shared. In this case, however, the incentive worker usually got 75 percent of the bonus; the remaining 25 percent was divided among indirect workers and supervisors.

3. *The Haynes plan* provided for the bonus to be shared by the incentive worker, supervision, and the company. Generally, this was 50 percent to the workers, 10 percent to supervision, and 40 percent to the company.

4. *The Rowan plan* was based on a formula which increased bonus amounts at a *decreasing* rate as productivity increased.

5. *The Emerson plan*, contrarily, was based on a formula which increased bonus amounts at an *increasing* rate as productivity increased.

6. *The Gantt plan* provided a sharp increase in employee earnings, approximately 30 percent when the standards were first met. Thereafter, the bonus earnings were at the rate of 1.3 percent for each 1 percent increase in production.

7. *Measured daywork incentive plan* provided that the employee's production rate during a given production period determined what his guaranteed base rate would be for the next production period.

An incentive plan which is widely used is the *standard-hour plan*. It meets the basic criteria of a good incentive plan. It is easy to understand, provides earnings in proportion to production, has a guaranteed base rate, and is economical to administer.

The standard-hour plan requires that time standards be set as accurately as possible. Then, as the worker completes units of production, he earns standard allowed hours. If in a week he earns fifty hours while working forty hours, he is paid for fifty hours at his hourly base rate. If he earns forty hours or less, he is paid for the forty hours that he worked. Thus, as far as the worker is concerned, the plan is easy to understand and provides a strong incentive. It is economical to administer. If the hourly base rate changes, no change is required in the standards—only in the payroll calculation of hours times base rate. The consensus of authorities is that the standard-hour plan is the best incentive plan to install.

ADMINISTRATION OF INCENTIVES

Emphasis must be placed on the need for proper administration of an incentive plan if it is to continue to function satisfactorily. Companies whose incentive plans are well maintained report high productivity, low costs, good morale, high quality, and a good competitive position.

Managements who have had improper incentive administration are quite concerned about rising costs, unreasonable union attitudes, grievances, arbitrations, "pegged" production, and business lost to competitors. Companies in this position did not get there overnight. They got there gradually by improperly or inadequately administering their incentive plans. It is a difficult and costly process for them to correct their situation. It can be done, but it takes time. Once the plan is reestablished on a sound basis, care must be taken to see that incentive administration is sound in the future.

There are several basic rules that management must adhere to if the incentive plan is to be an asset to the company and its employees.

Rule 1. Clearly define incentive policies and commit them to writing. With all the varied forces at work in a company, it is essential to have an agreed-upon, recorded understanding of wage incentive policies. Otherwise, individuals such as the plant manager, whose prime responsibility is production, or the personnel manager, whose main goal is harmony, or the union leader, who wants greater pay for his people, will make some little change that sooner or later can have a mushrooming effect. One authority stated, "Most plans go haywire because, somewhere along the line, management replaces justice with charity." If policies are correct, clear, and in writing, management is much less likely to let this happen, and mistakes can be avoided.

Rule 2. Provide adequate, trained, competent personnel to administer the plan. This applies to the industrial engineers who have the technical task of establishing or correcting standards or investigating potential trouble spots. There is a strong tendency to look on industrial engineering as a source of promotable personnel for other management positions. A certain amount of this is desirable, but not if it strips all of the experienced talent from the incentive administration group.

This rule also applies to the line organization which must make the plan work. The foreman, for example, should cooperate with the industrial engineer and the worker to see that correct standards are developed. It is then up to the foreman to see that the worker follows the right method and that his material is as specified. If the foreman, because of lack of training, has no knowledge of the significance of his actions in giving undeserved extra allowances or in forcing loose standards, he may open the door a tiny crack to a bad incentive situation.

Rule 3. Establish accurate standards based on good methods. The standards, of course, are the heart of the incentive plan. If they are loose, the operator has no trouble in meeting them. He then either restricts his production to keep his earnings down or earns more than his fellow operators for the same applied effort. If the standards are tight, there is insufficient incentive opportunity for the operator, and he will be inclined not to try to beat the standards.

For reasons covered previously in this chapter, it is essential to develop the best possible method before standards are established. This will result in a sounder, more consistent earnings situation and will avoid many future difficulties.

Rule 4. Record the method and adjust standards when methods change. Failure to follow this rule is responsible for wrecking of incentive plans more than any other single factor. Ordinarily, changes in method are more evolutionary than revolutionary. If a change is revolutionary, chances are good that the operation will be restudied and a new standard established. Most changes, however, are small, of the "creeping" variety. Any one of the small changes may have little effect on the plan. Cumulatively, however, they lead to inconsistencies and "runaway" earnings that will eventually destroy the whole incentive structure. Thus, it is essential that management have a record of the method on which the original standard was based and that it adjust the standard as the method is changed. This will require an auditing or reporting procedure that points out changes in methods and the need for standards adjustment. It ties in with Rule 2 in that sufficient trained personnel must be available to perform this vital function.

Rule 5. Cover the work with standards as completely as possible. Complete incentive coverage of a department or a plant will avoid two major problems. First, where incentive and daywork are mixed, it is often difficult to get an accurate check of the time spent on each category. Therefore, time juggling can occur which will weaken the incentive plan materially and raise costs.

Second, when workers become accustomed to incentive earnings, they resist working at the regular guaranteed base rate. This leads to a strong demand for the payment of additional money, such as average hourly earnings, for time spent on jobs not covered by standards. The inevitable result of paying incentive earnings for a nonincentive performance is to weaken the incentive plan—often to the point of destruction.

Rule 6. Train the incentive workers. The operators cannot meet the standard if they do not know the method. Their natural inclination is to bring pressure on management to loosen the standard. If they succeed, and they often do, the standard is relaxed. Sooner or later the operator will begin to find the better method. As he does, the standard will become loose and a difficult situation will be created.

This situation need never exist if proper attention is paid to training. The operators must be trained not only in proper methods, but in the fundamental philosophies of incentive operations. In an area as sensitive as wage payment, it is important that they know the plan thoroughly as it affects them, and understand the reasons for the plan.

Rule 7. Provide the incentive workers with sufficient work and the right tools, materials, and instructions. One of the most discouraging things that can happen to an incentive worker is to work hard, beat the standard, and run out of work so that he loses his bonus. People, in general, will work harder if they can see work piled up ahead of them. This is particularly true of incentive workers.

Every effort must be made to help the incentive worker eliminate delays. If he has to wait for a job, or wait to have materials corrected or tools changed, he will soon lose his desire to try to earn a bonus. When the conditions are correct, however, he will apply himself diligently and produce at an excellent rate.

CONCLUSION

Work measurement and incentives represent only a very small cog in the managing process. Their importance, however, far outweighs their size in the management scheme. They provide the basis for many management plans and controls, and often determine the growth and profitability of an enterprise. The company which has an effective work-measurement program has a great competitive advantage over the company that does not. And the company which has effective work measurement and a good incentive plan has an edge over the company that has only effective work measurement.

BIBLIOGRAPHY

Karger, Delmar W., and Franklin H. Bayha, *Engineered Work Measurement,* The Industrial Press, New York, 1957.
Krick, Edward V., *Methods Engineering Design and Measurement of Work Methods,* John Wiley & Sons, Inc., New York, 1962.
Louden, J. Keith, *Wage Incentives,* John Wiley & Sons, Inc., New York, 1959.
Lowry, Stewart, H. B. Maynard, and G. J. Stegemerten, *Time and Motion Study,* McGraw-Hill Book Company, New York, 1940.
Lytle, Charles Walter, *Wage Incentive Methods, Their Selection, Installation, and Operation,* The Ronald Press Company, New York, 1942.
Maynard, H. B. (ed.), *Industrial Engineering Handbook,* 2d ed., McGraw-Hill Book Company, New York, 1963.
Rotroff, Virgil H., *Work Measurement,* Reinhold Publishing Corporation, New York, 1962.

CHAPTER TWELVE

Labor Cost Control

MITCHELL FEIN   *Professional Engineer, Hillsdale, New Jersey*

Labor cost is a large segment of total costs in every enterprise, and time and effort are required to control it. It is difficult to ascertain how effective management is in controlling costs, because control is relative to how severe the criteria are for measuring performance. If the yardsticks are set leniently, it will appear that performance is more effective than if the standards are set more stringently. Thus, control is effective only when exercised through realistic performance standards.

CONTROL FUNDAMENTALS

Effective labor cost control can be obtained only by competent administration. To comprehend control systems fully, it is essential that there be a clear understanding of the basic concepts.

Control is the act of exercising direction or restraint. An activity is controlled to the extent that it is *efficiently directed toward the attainment of desired objectives.*[1] To be effective, a control system should be goal oriented—designed to achieve specific objectives in definite ways.

Essential to control is the measurement of the difference between the state that exists and the state that is desired. In cost control, this is referred to as a "variance from a predetermined standard." Regulation and measurement of the variance is the primary aim of control.

Control over What? Data for labor cost control report events which have occurred, with records and reports produced *after the fact*. When an employee reports at the conclusion of a job, shift, or a batch of work, whether it be by pencil and paper or into a data-processing input station, this information reports work already done. If the operation continues, it may be possible for management to act positively on the portion not yet done. Obviously, the por-

[1] Russell L. Ackoff, *Scientific Method: Optimizing Applied Research Decisions,* John Wiley & Sons, Inc., New York, 1962, p. 3.

tion of work completed cannot be altered. Even with electronic data-processing systems, the information processing occurs after the fact.

Systems to control labor costs can be designed to influence only *future* operations. The closer management can get to the historical event, the greater will be the opportunity for future control. Conversely, the longer the time gap between the occurrence and the reporting analysis, the less effective will be the control. If an observer were to monitor an operation and make on-the-spot calculations and comparisons with standard, he might make practically instantaneous corrections. However, each change would still be historical. Labor cost control is a technique to control the future by taking a look at the past.

How Control Is Exercised. Labor cost control is exercised by management through decisions that are put into effect in a manner which will affect an activity in a desired direction. Data, labor statistics, and reports are the *basis for decisions, not control.* The essence of labor control is that it stems from decisions put into effect. Too often, management mistakenly assumes that standards and reports will establish control.

DESIGNING THE LABOR COST CONTROL SYSTEM

The ideal systems approach considers the entire business as one system, made up of a number of subsystems, each for a specific purpose. The information system which supplies the needed data and information to all parts of the organization consists of two major elements:

1. Information handling; data gathering, storage, analysis, and reporting
2. Decision making

Labor cost control should be closely integrated with other segments of the total information system so that the labor input data are available for use by all functions. A labor control system designed on this basis will effectively tie in with all other requirements on input and output. A cost control system established independently of other activities often causes wasteful practices and uneconomical collection and handling of data.

Decisions are made by people, and only people can put them into effect to reduce and control costs. It is essential, therefore, that the total information system, of which labor cost control is a part, provide the base from which to make timely and effective decisions.

People Effect on System. The capability of the people and their cooperation in operating the system are vital to its success. This is often more important than the technical design of the system.

In manual record systems, the influence of individuals upon the system can be considerable. It is sometimes mistakenly thought that with data processing, the influence of people is greatly minimized. Every control system, however, depends on people, and no system can be more effective than the people who operate it.

Procedures manuals, position descriptions, and an organization chart showing functional relationships are effective aids in training personnel in systems procedures and in properly relating each organizationally.

ESSENTIALS OF LABOR COST CONTROL

The criteria for effective labor cost control are:
1. Objectives of the control system
2. Definitions of areas to be controlled
3. Definitions of what is to be measured

4. Systematic labor reporting
5. Performance criteria
6. Determination of variances and preparation of performance reports
7. Decisions for applying corrective action to improve performance
8. Organizational responsibility for labor cost control
9. Relationship of labor cost control to general accounting
10. Standard proceduures
11. Periodic review and audit of the control system

Whether the system is small or large, all of these essentials must be included.

Objectives of the Control System. Functions of the system must be clearly defined, with goals precisely detailed. It is not sufficient to state that the system is to provide product cost information and methods of improving productivity; the objectives must be set forth in clear terms. What degree of detail is desired in costs? Are standard costs to be shown separately from variances? Does management wish detailed reasons for variances?

Unless these and other such questions are answered specifically, the cost system may be too elaborate and wasteful, or it may not fulfill management's needs.

Definitions of Areas to Be Controlled. Definitions and limits should be established for the various activities which are to be controlled. This can consist of producing departments, service departments, groups, or individuals; or it can be subdivisions, for example, a battery of similar equipment, a grouping of presses, an individual piece of equipment, or an assembly group; or it can be a large department or an area involving a single person or a single piece of equipment.

Definitions of What Is to Be Measured. A problem in reporting labor cost is usually one of definition: "What is it?" The employees refer to the operation in one way, the supervisor sometimes in another, engineering uses more technical language, and this can confuse accounting. It is necessary that everyone speak a common language in cost reporting.

For direct labor, the most prevalent method of standardizing terminology is through the use of an operations sheet which lists all operations sequentially, shows operation number, department or cost center, time standards, tooling and equipment used, and other pertinent information. Although the operation description is frequently in sketchy form, it is usually sufficient to identify the operation. A typical operations sheet is shown by Figure 12-1.

Indirect labor operations are usually more difficult to define, because these are broader in scope and involve a wide variety of work. Definitions should include an operations title, the number of men involved in the crew, and the measure of the work output. They should also give examples of work which is included and excluded so that the definitions are clear.

With increased mechanization, the ratio of nonproductive to productive labor is steadily increasing. In many plants, the use of the term "nonproductive" is misleading, because maintenance men, skilled technicians, and other such types of labor become an essential part of the production process, often more important than the machine operators. In such cases, more care must be used to identify and define the functions performed.

An effective technique for identifying operations is by the use of an operations code. In practice, this is more reliable than a written description. For data processing, it is essential.

Systematic Labor Reporting. The preparation of input data to the labor control system is perhaps the weakest link in the system. Experience in many plants has shown that the greatest single source of problems is the preparation of faulty input data, resulting from incorrect job numbers, wrong piece counts,

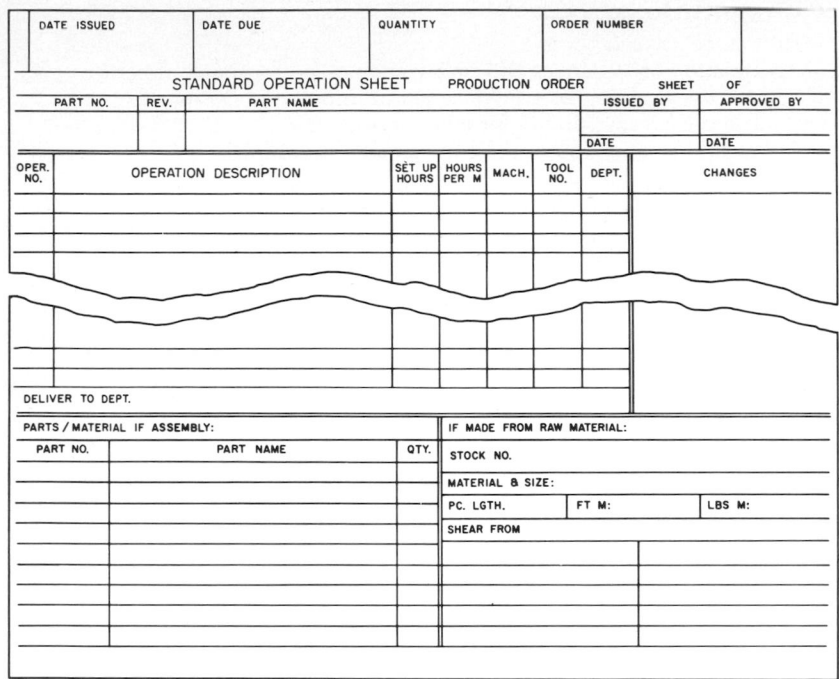

FIG. 12-1.   *Standard operations sheet.*

errors in writing numbers, and various errors caused either by carelessness or by faulty source data.   It is essential that the information available to the employees is in such a form as to minimize errors and be least likely to be mistaken.

In most cases, data are handled in batches.   The working shift is the usual batch time, in which the events for the shift are reported.   In some types of systems, the batch time may be every hour, or four hours, or several days.   The time period depends on the use to which the data will be put and the effect that timeliness has upon decisions and subsequent actions.

Clear-cut procedures should be developed so that the data are processed rapidly with a minimum of delay.   Source data should require practically no interpretation; these should be handled on a routine basis.

A typical daily labor report form is shown by Figure 12-2.   This is handwritten by the operator, timekeeper, or supervisor and becomes the source data for the cost system.   Many variations of the form are possible for specific purposes.

To obviate the need for operators or timekeepers in the plant to prepare labor reports, some plants use intercoms placed throughout the plant and wired to a central point.   When an operator has completed a job, he walks to an intercom and calls in the job information to a clerk who records it on the operator's report.   This technique minimizes plant errors and permits verification at the central station.   Other techniques include the use of mark-sensing tab cards, preprinted job tickets, and various forms to minimize errors in identifying work done in the plant.

There is an increasing trend in data processing to employ data input stations at various locations through the plant to permit the operator to insert his identification badge and a job card into the machine.   These data are communicated

		Clock No.		Date			Start Time		
Name John Doe		475		Nov 12			8:00		
Operation Number	Order No.	Operation	Counter Quant.	Act Quant.	STD	Prod. Time	T. W. Min.	Clock Time	
350	7854	Blank	5400	2700				10:30	
150	8294	Turn	15000	15000				2:30	
55	8371	Grind	1810	1810				4:30	

FIG. 12-2. *Daily labor report form.*

to a central point in the plant where they are reproduced onto punched cards or punched paper tape for later processing.

Cost data are especially adapted to multiple uses, combining such things as daily reports for payroll purposes; cost accumulation by jobs; labor productivity; variance reports; production counts for production control; analysis of downtime by causes for machine analysis; machine utilization for machine-hour rates; labor distribution for budgets; and transfer of labor between departments.

Performance Criteria. Performance measurement is essential to cost control. Without measurement to determine variances, it is not possible to exercise control.

The determination of the accuracy of the yardsticks and the sophistication of the measurement techniques required depend upon the types of operations performed, the total man-hours of labor to be measured, the number of standards required, and other similar factors. Economic considerations should largely determine the effort and expense which can be incurred in setting standards.

Various techniques for measurement can be employed depending on the degree of accuracy required. Where incentives are used, precise time standards can be set by stopwatch time study or by predetermined times. Measurement of indirect labor, clerical work, receiving and shipping, and the like should be based on broad averages. Where sufficient data are available, standards can be established through standard data, the use of work sampling, and other such techniques.

All standards should be fully delineated so that operations will be measured accurately. For example, where a standard requires the operator to get his own materials, make his own setups, and do other such work, this should be listed as part of the standard. Otherwise, in developing department manning, labor budgets, production schedules, and later, in measuring output, errors will occur if the nonproductive labor included in the standard is allowed again.

Budgets are a form of standards, but are usually for groupings of labor categories. Where the product mix is stable, direct labor also can be measured in the aggregate.

An effective method of labor control can be established by continually checking that the labor value of production is equal to the labor input to create that production. This concept has been used in numerous plants, and the author has developed the technique under the descriptive title "Meet the Payroll." Though this technique is the essence of simplicity, it has all the elements necessary for cost control.

The starting point is the establishment of labor cost figures in the aggregate for each product produced. Although nonproductive labor can be included in this technique, it is well to handle it separately from direct labor. The procedure is to compute the labor value of goods produced during a reporting period by multiplying the total of each product produced by the labor standard for the product. This is then compared, either in hours or dollars, with the labor input during the same period. When the manufacturing cycle is longer than the reporting period, a moving average equal in length to the manufacturing cycle should be used.

Where the product is complex and production is performed in stages with subassemblies and parts going into stores, from which these are later pulled for subassembly and to completion, measurement is made of labor value created at the several stages. The labor value of the product going into stores is established as if it were finished product. The labor value of the finished product as it is packed ready for shipping is then established, but with the labor value already included in the first stage excluded. The process is repeated if there are more than two stages.

This concept is a broad-brush approach to labor control and is not designed as a substitute for cost control over departments and specific operations. Although it will not disclose poor performance areas which are averaged into effective areas, it has the advantage of providing an overall picture of the operations. From management's view, if overall costs are in control and meet projections, then at least production management is meeting its cost commitments.

On complex projects, the use of network analysis, such as PERT, CPM, and other such techniques, is helpful not only in scheduling, but in maintaining and analyzing cost expenditures.

Where measurement is of overall activities, an effective technique is the use of ratios, especially where these are carefully designed and clearly delineated. Spencer A. Tucker[2] has taken this relatively simple concept and developed it into a very useful control technique. Masses of numbers sometimes tend to be confusing, especially where lumped figures hide trends and subtle changes. Ratios can highlight meaningful relationships. For example, in a plant measured by time standards, the ratio of earned direct hours on standards to clock direct hours on standards shows the gross productivity ratio of the activity. The ratio of clock hours on incentive to total clock hours worked shows percent incentive coverage. Where incentives are used, these are two very important indexes of vital concern to management and the employees. Ratios can be prepared for downtime costs, excess direct-labor costs, setup costs, maintenance and repairs, supervisory coverage, and numerous other useful indexes.[3]

Ratios can be the bases for standards, with the actual ratio compared with standard to obtain both the index of performance and the cost variance. These can be plotted on graphs and on control charts to provide management with useful control tools. These are overall figures, taking in grouped activities. The lumping of good and poor performance tends to obscure both. However, this is not to diminish the very effective use to which these types of standards

---

[2] Spencer A. Tucker, *Successful Managerial Control by Ratio-Analysis*, McGraw-Hill Book Company, New York, 1961.
[3] *Ibid.*, pp. 34–37.

can be put. The reader is urged to consult Tucker's text for detailed explanations of the varied uses of ratios.

Indexes and percentages should be used with care, because they can sometimes be deceptive. Where percentages are used, the absolute figures involved should also be shown to avoid misconceptions. This is particularly true in checking labor productivity. Where an operator is shown as 30 or 170 percent of standard, if the actual time worked is small, such as 0.25 hour, these figures obviously can be in error from faulty time reporting.

Measuring performance on large-scale projects which cannot be broken down into small components requires special treatment. A method for continuous reporting of direct-labor performance in a commercial research and development laboratory is described in an article in the *National Association of Accountants Bulletin.*[4] The method is similar to evaluating off-standard labor in production. The essential requirements of the control are segregation of the program into definable tasks and responsibilities; establishment of attainable but objective budgets in hours and dollars for each task by area of responsibility; periodic in-process estimates of cost at completion of each task and responsibility; and periodic reporting of budget and actual committed cost to date. The schedule shown by Figure 12-3 is for the laboratory manager. The schedules for the other managers contain the information they need.

The control of costs becomes difficult where learning is a factor, mainly because of the problem of determining the precise effect learning has on costs. In

[4] Forrest L. Heuser, "Direct Labor Control in Research and Development," *National Association of Accountants Bulletin*, October, 1964.

PROGRAM CONTROL AND PRIME COST LEDGER PRO FORMA   PERIOD ENDING AUGUST 23, 1964

JOB NUMBER DASH	SUB DASH	SUB DASH DESCR	ITEM	% ACTUAL TO BUDGET	% ACTUAL TO EAC	TOTAL PROGRAM BUDGET	ACTUAL AND COMMITTED TO DATE	ESTIMATE AT COMPLETION	EAC % BUDG'T	ACTUAL THIS WEEK	ACTUAL THIS MONTH TO DATE	ACTUAL THIS YEAR TO DATE	ACTUAL JOB TOTAL TO DATE	COMMITMENTS PURCHASE ORDERS	COMMITMENTS REQUISITIONS
SCANNER A 666789	1-30		MFG. $	200	83	1,500	3,000	3,600	240	300	1600	2,400	3,000		
			ENGR $	119	91	55,000	64,400	71,800	130	11,450	5,900	52,000	65,400		
			MAT'L $	83	99	10,200	8,500	8,600	84	1,050	2,400	4,300	6,400	2,400	
			TOTAL	115	92	66,700	76,900	84,000	125	2,800	8,600	58,700	74,800	2,400	
SCANNER B 666790	1-30		MFG $	80	89	10,000	8,000	69,000	90	21,000	3,000	5,000	8,000		
			ENGR. $	120	92	50,000	60,000	65,000	130	2,000	6,000	10,000	160,000		
			MAT'L $	150	100	40,000	60,000	60,000	150	21000	10,000	25,000	55,000	3,000	2,000
			TOTAL	128	96	100,000	128,000	134,000	134	5,000	19,000	40,000	123,000	3,000	2,000
JAMMER A 780010	1-10		MFG. $	50	66	8,000	4,000	6,000	75	500	2,000	3,000	4,000		
			ENGR $	60	80	20,000	12,000	15,000	75	1,000	3,000	10,000	12,000		
			MAT'L $	50	63	10,000	5,000	8,000	80	500	1,000	3,000	3,500	1,000	500
			TOTAL	55	72	138,000	21,000	29,000	76		6,000	16,000	19,500	1,000	1500

(1) INDICATES PERFORMANCE AGAINST BUDGET

(2) INDICATES % OF COMPLETION BASED ON ESTIMATE AT COMPLETION ALSO INDICATIVE OF PHYSICAL COMPLETION

IF % TO BUDGET EXCEEDS % TO EAC PROGRAM COST IS EXCESSIVE

IF % TO EAC EXCEEDS % TO BUDGET PROGRAM COST IS BETTER THAN PLAN

INDICATES % OF FAVORABLE OR UNFAVORABLE PERFORMANCE

LABORATORY MANAGER'S CONTROL REPORT

FIG. 12-3. *Laboratory manager's control report.*

such situations, special approaches must be devised to predict the learning factor; otherwise, it can seriously interfere with the true evaluation of labor expenditures.

Articles and text material have been published on learning curves which are easy to follow.[5] Learning curves should be used with caution and be thoroughly tested under actual conditions to assure that the curves properly reflect actual conditions. There is often a tendency to oversimplify the use of these factors.

Determination of Variances and Preparation of Performance Reports. The comparison of actual with standard is the very essence of the labor control system. Without this review, the system merely collects data. Only through a comparison of actual occurrences with standards is it possible to determine the effectiveness of operations and areas which require remedial treatment.

In designing reports, people and purposes must be considered. Will a report go to a department supervisor who needs details, or to a manager who is mainly concerned with overall variances and trends? If decisions are to be made from the report, variances must be calculated and explanations obtained. Without these data, the report is valueless as a control tool.

The input labor data are usually processed into daily productivity reports by individual employee or group. A typical report is shown by Figure 12-4, which is taken from a plant using incentive wage payment. Each line represents a different job or operation; the details show what occurred. This type of report is informative to those who want minute details, for example, supervisors and industrial engineers. Note the last column, which shows the percent productivity as incentive percent. On one job, operator S. Marvin was two minutes below standard, shown as 98 percent. Figure 12-5 is the overall report on the same day for all operators in the department, and it shows only the summary line for each operator. The daily summary for each operator is shown by Figure 12-5, taken from the last line of each operator in Figure 12-4 with the incentive percent added.

In most cases, supervisors prefer to see the entire daily report so that they can check the performance of individual operators, particular machines, certain

[5] Raymond B. Jordan, *How to Use the Learning Curve*, Industrial Education Institute, 1965.

4/20/6

EMPLOYEE NAME	DEPT.	COST CENTER	CLOCK NO.	JOB NO.	MODEL NO.	OP. NO.	REPAIR	TIME WORK	NON PRODUCT	DOWN TIME	BONUS OR MAKE UP	MIN. ON INCENTIVE	INCENTIVE EARNED	TOTAL EARNED	DAILY ACTUAL	INCENTIVE %
S MARVIN	2		013													
	2	B	013	18		001					12	60	72	72	60	120
	2	B	013	18		001					7	30	37	37	30	123
	2	B	013	18		001					19	50	69	69	50	138
	2	B	013	19		001					3	10	13	13	10	130
	2	B	013	19		001					3	35	38	38	35	108
	2	B	013	19		001					16	70	86	86	70	122
	2	B	013	20		001					21	30	51	51	30	170
	2	B	013	18		004					24	90	114	114	90	126
	2	B	013	19		004					2-	105	103	103	105	98
											103	480	583	583	480	
P INFANTE	2		014													
	2	B	014	19		001					10	27	37	37	27	137
	2	B	014	19		001					9	22	31	31	22	140
	2	B	014	17		004					24	50	74	74	50	148
	2	B	014	999		004					9	22	31	31	22	140
	2	B	014	18		004					27	48	75	75	48	156
	2	B	014	18		004					43	105	148	148	105	140
	2	B	014	19		004					3	15	18	18	15	120
	2	B	014	19		004					34	58	92	92	58	158
	2	B	014	19		004					43	75	118	118	75	157
	2	B	014	20		004					22	48	70	70	48	145
	2	50	014			004			10						10	10
									10		224	470	694	704	480	

FIG. 12-4. *Daily analysis of operator productivity.*

4/20/6

EMPLOYEE NAME	DEPT.	CLOCK NO.	JOB NO.	MODEL NO.	OP. NO.	REPAIR	TIME WORK	NON PRODUCT	DOWN TIME	BONUS OR MAKE UP	MIN. ON INCENTIVE	INCENTIVE EARNED	TOTAL EARNED	DAILY ACTUAL	INCENTIVE %
	1	002								85	179	264	565	480	147
	1	003								88–	310	222	392	480	71
	1	004								140	440	580	620	480	131
	1	005											480	480	
	1	006								33	350	383	513	480	109
	2	013								103	480	583	583	480	121
	2	014								224	470	694	704	480	147
	3	022								111–	480	369	369	480	76
	4	026								296	480	776	776	480	161
	4	027								369	480	849	849	480	176
	5	041								91	480	571	571	480	118
	6	046								203	480	683	683	480	142
	6	047								27–	310	283	453	480	91
	6	048								77	480	557	557	480	116
	7	068								304	175	479	784	480	273
	7	069								86–	480	394	394	480	82
	7	070								173	465	638	653	480	137
	8	077								365	479	844	844	479	176
	8	079								27–	480	453	453	480	94
	8	080								246	480	726	726	480	151
	9	089								272	480	752	752	480	156
	9	090								372	480	852	852	480	177
	10	097								150	410	560	630	480	136
	10	098								42–	480	438	438	480	91
	12	106											480	480	
	20	109								144	345	489	623	479	141
	20	110								60	480	540	540	480	112
	20	111								14	275	289	494	480	105
	20	112								127	480	607	607	480	126
	20	113								51	245	296	366	315	120
	20	114								70	170	240	550	400	141
	20	115								95–	305	210	385	480	68
	30	130											270	270	
	40	131											465	465	
	88	888											480	480	
										3493	12128	15621	19901	16408	
										3493	12128	15621	19901	16408	

FIG. 12-5.   *Daily productivity report of incentive operators.*

jobs that are running, or other things in which they are interested. Although an exception report is useful to the supervisor, he needs the detailed report for study when he wishes to check back into the actual situation. The exception report is more useful to higher management levels which do not have the time to check details, but are instead interested in extreme variances and overall figures. A simple technique in preparing management reports is to use the headings of the detail report, but only report subtotals and totals. Anyone desiring further information can refer to the detail report.

When exception reports are reviewed, those processing the analysis and reports should be guided by specific decision rules so that they will have a minimum of decisions to make. For example, where there is an unfavorable or questionable variance, the problem of when to take action arises. The task is simplified if the clerk who prepares the report is directed to highlight all variances where productivity is less than 80 percent and greater than 150 percent of standard, or any other desired figures. This type of decision rule removes the element of judgment, and a clerk mechanically highlights all important variances. Where a computer is used, such decisions are easily programmed.

"How soon do we need the report?" It depends on how long after the occurrence management can wait so that meaningful decisions will be made. Then, what is the cost versus the advantage to be obtained by reducing the time cycle from the occurrence of the event to the preparation of the report? In some instances, the situation warrants fast processing of information. In others, several days' delay may be acceptable. In viewing overall performances or stable production, a week or month may be acceptable. The processing-time cycle should not be shortened just for the sake of timeliness, if the reports may lie on an executive's desk for several days before being used.

Experience in many plants has shown that the percentage of error in the processing of labor input data is usually not significant when compared with the total labor hours reported. An attempt to balance the labor input data against the total time worked can be costly and may not result in useful information. Where a standard cost system is used, the difference between the time reported on the labor time tickets and the total time worked should be charged to a labor reporting variance account.

Labor cost control is mainly concerned with unfavorable variances, where actual exceeds standard. All emphasis should be directed toward pinpointing a variance, determining how it occurred, and devising ways to eliminate it. Labor cost control reports should be as brief and to the point as possible. Complicated and lengthy reports should be avoided.

Decisions for Applying Corrective Action to Improve Performance. The ability to make timely decisions is essential in labor cost control. Putting off decisions beyond the time required to obtain information is probably the worst decision of all. Doing nothing is management by default. Middle management, line foremen, and others who have to act on situations immediately are frustrated by an inability to obtain clear-cut decisions from higher up. Not taking an action when it is required can often create serious restraints. Because this is a decision to do nothing, it is an abdication of management's responsibility.

When investigating variances, it is vital that the cause and effect be clearly separated and understood. This involves the basics of problem solving. For example, the supervisor may claim that his unfavorable variances are the result of poorly motivated workers, improper machine maintenance, inadequate material supply, parts which do not fit together, and so on. These are the supervisor's problems. To the problem solver, however, these are not problems, but symptoms of problems. An obstacle to problem solving is the improper identification of problems and the confusion between problems and symptoms of problems. Symptoms cannot be solved; only problems can be solved. It is therefore essential that management pinpoint the problems and then devise ways of eliminating them.

The time delay between the actual occurrence and the feedback of the data to management should not prevent remedial action. In most manufacturing and office activities, the supervisor should receive a detailed analysis of all work performed in his department ideally by about noon of the day following the activity. This permits him to investigate before the events become ancient history and poor memories prevail. Also, the same job may still be running, and a timely report permits the supervisor to attempt to improve the remainder of the job.

Where employees are on incentive, they welcome management's interest in their productivity because often low productivity or production problems are within control of management. Even on daywork, employees would rather have smooth operations, and they welcome management's investigating production problems.

When management permits substandard production to continue without taking corrective action, the effect is to condone low productivity. With time, the employees come to accept the prevailing level of productivity as normal, making it difficult later to raise the level. The resistance to productivity improvement by the employees sometimes stems from lack of confidence of the employees in management's aims and its ability to manage.

It is often effective to involve operating personnel in the reduction of variances. The people directly on the job frequently have a good understanding of the problems involved, and their cooperation and assistance should be encouraged.

Control depends upon making correct decisions which are put into effect. Management has the responsibility to evaluate operations and make decisions. The success of the entire process rests with management.

Organizational Responsibility for Labor Cost Control. For effective operations, it is important that the organizational responsibility for the functions is properly established. If both control and accounting are established under the controller, it is questionable whether effective control can be established. More satisfactory results will be obtained if the accounting department processes the data and produces the various reports which then go to the operating manager for decisions and execution. Advice and guidance from accounting will be helpful, but the operating manager must make his own decisions. When operating management takes on responsibilities for budgets, product costs, and general manufacturing costs, it must have the authority to analyze the results of its operations, to make its own decisions, and to execute these to obtain the results to which it is committed.

Though operating management sets operations standards and later takes corrective actions, this does not violate sound organizational relations. Having set standards for product costs, budgets, and the like which are accepted by top management as realistic, operating management then has the responsibility to fulfill its commitments. This is a sound policy.

Relationship of Labor Cost Control to General Accounting. A labor cost control system can be established to work effectively even though no attempt is made to produce product costs or to tie the system in with the general books of account. Similarly, a cost-accounting system can prepare costs and financial statements with no attempt made to control the costs. However, effective management will closely relate these functions and conduct both simultaneously.

Budgeting and cost control are vital to the organization. Yet too frequently, management goes through the motions of control when what it is really doing is record keeping, some reporting, and cost accounting. From the operating viewpoint, control is essential to effective operations and profits. Only control can help to reduce costs.

The source data which serve as the basis for control will also provide the input to accounting, when treated according to the accounting rules. The variances which are determined for control purposes should be the same variances used to obtain costs under standard costs. In a direct-cost system, labor control is essential, and the variances generated are used without change in the operating statement.

An interesting approach to the relationship between cost control and accounting was established at the Communications & Electronics Division, Philco Corporation.[6] The system is designed to charge all costs against the destination account. It has the capability to close the books on a cash basis monthly and to control costs within fixed budget periods. This is in contrast to other approaches which utilize two methods of input—one for cost control and the other for closing the financial books. A definition of the system is shown in Figure 12-6. A pictorial view of how the flow of reports and control data function is shown by Figure 12-7.

Standard Procedures. An essential part of systems installation is the preparation of a procedures manual[7] which delineates in detail the various procedures and shows how they relate, how forms and paper work are to be used, and who is

[6] H. Richard Yarp, "An Approach to Cost Control," *National Association of Accountants Bulletin*, September, 1965.

[7] H. John Ross, *How to Make a Procedure Manual*, Office Research Institute, P.O. Box 744, Miami 43, Fla., 1956.

PROGRAM PLANNING

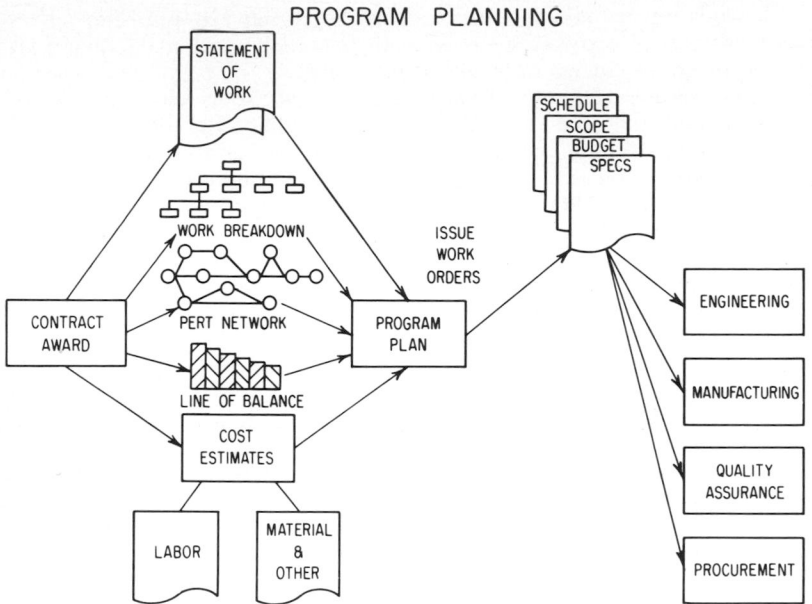

FIG. 12-6. *Definition of a control system developed at Philco Corporation.*

PROGRAM CONTROL

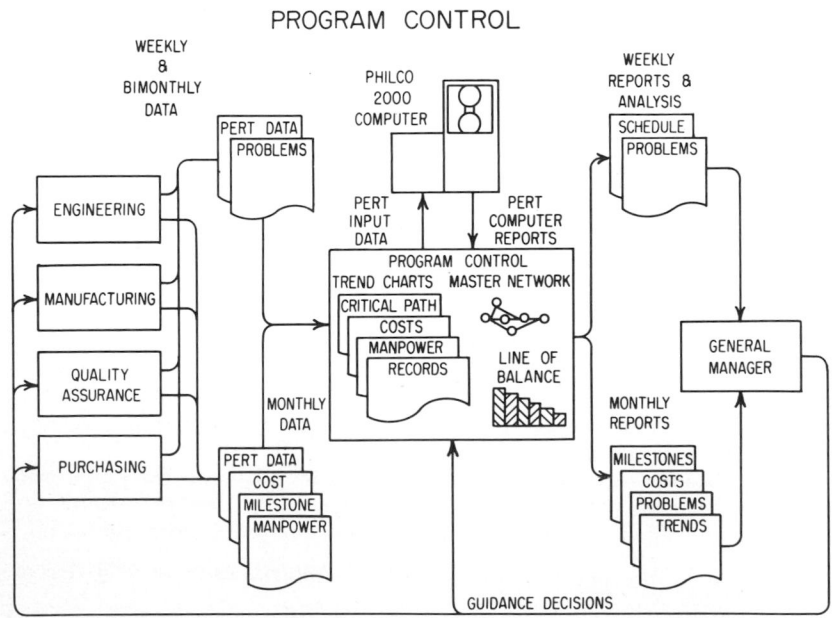

FIG. 12-7. *Flow of reports and control data for system in Figure 12-6.*

to handle the data, carry out the tasks, and so on. The manual is necessary, not only at the initiation of the system to ensure that everyone fully understands the minute details, but also for training new personnel and to assure over a period of time that changes are not made by individuals.

Periodic Review and Audit of the Control System. All systems should be reviewed periodically to check that the original basis for the system has not changed and that the system operates as planned. Small changes which are introduced over a period of time are a serious source of problems. These creeping changes are difficult to detect, and it is only when the system is carefully examined that the changes will be uncovered.

In making the audit, the reviewer must be completely familiar with all aspects of the system so that he can detect unauthorized changes and deviations. The audit should mainly be concerned with the following:

1. Check that the procedures are being followed as specified and that no unauthorized changes have been made.

2. Determine whether persons are following required procedures; corrective coaching may be necessary.

3. Discuss with key people their personal reactions to various aspects of the system to learn shortcomings and areas which can be improved, particularly in the preparation of data and in the analysis of reports.

4. Determine whether the system fulfills the purposes for which it was designed, and that all requirements are met.

5. Make necessary changes to obtain desired performance.

CONCLUSION

The cost control system must be goal oriented, with objectives clearly delineated. Control is obtained by measuring the difference between the state that exists and the state that is desired, and then instituting measures to reduce the variance. Performance standards are essential to control.

Labor cost control is an attempt to control the future by looking at the past. This requires that management have available meaningful information which accurately portrays past occurrences. These must be measured against realistic performance standards to determine variances. Based on evaluation and decision, management can then proceed to influence the course of future events. The closer management can get to the actual occurrence, the greater will be the opportunity for control.

Systems to control costs should be fully integrated with all other systems, particularly those involved with information flow.

BIBLIOGRAPHY

Beyer, Robert, *Profitability Accounting for Planning and Control*, The Ronald Press Company, New York, 1963.

Horngren, Charles T., *Cost Accounting: A Managerial Emphasis*, Prentice-Hall, Inc., Englewood Cliffs, N.J., 1962.

Knox, Frank M., *Integrated Cost Control in the Office*, McGraw-Hill Book Company, New York, 1958.

Tucker, Spencer A., *Successful Managerial Control by Ratio-Analysis*, McGraw-Hill Book Company, New York, 1961.

Welsch, Gwen A., *Budgeting and Profit Planning and Control*, Prentice-Hall, Inc., Englewood Cliffs, N.J., 1963.

Wright, Wilmer, *Direct Standard Costs for Decision Making and Control*, McGraw-Hill Book Company, New York, 1962.

CHAPTER THIRTEEN

Accident Prevention and Safety

RUSSELL DeREAMER   *International Business Machines Corporation, Armonk, New York*

The same management principles and philosophies that are applied to cost, quality, and production must be applied to safety. But an examination of many safety programs reveals that this is not always the case. A production problem is left to line managers for solution. Safety problems are handed to the plant safety committee or the safety department, or posters, safety contests, prizes, or stunts are used in the hope that these gimmicks will in some way stimulate safety awareness and motivate employees to work safely. Special techniques will not work, however, until supervisors and managers have assumed full day-to-day responsibility for safety. Gimmicks may supplement management safety responsibility, but they must not be used in place of it.

Safety must be put on a man-manager basis, because the manager, and not safety personnel or a committee, is in the best position to do something about stopping accidents. The manager has control over men, machines, and working conditions on a daily full-time basis. He is closest to the person most likely to get hurt. He can take direct action. Therefore, where safety has been given a high priority among management activities and supervisors have fully discharged their safety responsibilities, the results have been outstanding in terms of fewer accidents and improved employee and community relations.

Elements of a Safety Program. Experts in the field of industrial safety agree that to achieve good results in accident prevention, the safety program must include seven basic elements:

1. Participation of top management in the safety program
2. A procedure for developing safe working conditions
3. Establishment and enforcement of safety rules
4. Personalized safety training including safety instruction for each job
5. Promotion of employee safety participation
6. Assigned responsibility for administering the safety program
7. Sound method for measuring safety performance

TOP MANAGEMENT PARTICIPATION

After a serious accident in a chemical plant, the company president admitted that "primary responsibility for the accident was failure of line management up to and including the general manager to devote enough time to safety."

Particularly when the safety record is good, it is easy to become complacent and give attention to safety only after a serious accident. To avoid this complacency and to make sure safety receives the day-to-day attention it deserves, positive steps should be taken to keep safety fresh in the minds of all managers.

The following should be standard practice.

1. At every plant and laboratory and at headquarters, top-level managers should hold frequent staff meetings. Examination usually reveals that safety seldom gets on the agenda of these meetings. To avoid this omission, it should be the practice of the general manager or the plant manager to have safety on his staff meeting agenda at least once a month. Companies which follow this procedure usually have the safety manager or safety director, if there is one, present for this portion of the meeting.

Subjects covered should include:

a. A review of planned safety projects

b. A discussion of any significant accidents

c. Injury rates

d. Review of plans for correcting unsafe conditions noted

Following such meetings, members of the staff should hold meetings with managers reporting to them and so on down the line to the first-line manager. By following this practice, information on safety projects, on changes in safety policy or practices, and on significant accidents is relayed from the general manager to the foreman or first-line manager.

2. It is not enough for top-level managers to proclaim their support of the safety program. This support must be demonstrated by positive action.

a. Every serious accident should be investigated immediately by the plant manager or general superintendent.

b. Top-level managers should make periodic safety inspections.

c. Top-level managers should set a good safety example.

The last point means never failing to follow safety rules. This is particularly true in those areas where the use of personal protective equipment such as safety glasses is a requirement. Nothing can do more to destroy a good safety environment than to have the top man walk through an area ignoring a safety rule.

3. If it is a practice to hold periodic meetings of all managers, at least once a year safety should be discussed and should be a major portion of one of these meetings.

DEVELOPMENT OF SAFE WORKING CONDITIONS

In the development of safe working conditions, a principal objective is the elimination of bottlenecks, stresses, strains, and psychological booby traps that interfere with the free flow of work. Supervisors and safety personnel must give attention to many aspects of the work environment, including machine design, machine guarding, personal protective equipment, plant layout, lighting, heating, ventilation, dust and fume removal, and noise reduction.

Although it is not possible to cover all aspects of environmental safety in this chapter, mention of a few good references should be helpful. These include:

Accident Prevention Manual for Industrial Operations, 4th ed., National Safety Council, Chicago, 1959.

American Safety Standards, United States of America Standards Institute, New York.

Fire Protection Handbook, 12th ed., National Fire Protection Association, Boston, 1962.

Noise Control, The Acoustical Society of America, New York, published bimonthly.

Sax, N. Irving, *Dangerous Properties of Industrial Materials,* Reinhold Publishing Corporation, New York, 1957.

Stetka and Brandon, *National Electrical Code Handbook,* McGraw-Hill Book Company, New York, 1966.

Hazard-check Questions. The following questions can be asked when evaluating the safety of any operation.

1. Are there any elements of the operation that might be considered a hazard, such as unguarded pinch points; inadequate clearances; flying particles; dust or fumes; flammable materials; chemicals hazardous to health; conditions likely to cause a trip, slip, or fall; high noise level; crowded work space; poor housekeeping; or poor or distracting lights?

2. Can the hazard be eliminated by the substitution of equipment or material, by a guard, by ventilating equipment, or by isolation?

3. Should the hazard be identified by the use of color, warning signs, or barriers?

4. Should interlocks be used to protect the worker?

5. Does the safety device "fail safe"?

6. Is there a need for standardization?

7. Is there a need for emergency controls? Are controls easily identified and accessible?

8. What unsafe conditions would be created if the proper operating procedure were not followed?

Types of Safety Inspections. Supervisors and department managers should make a safety check of their operations on a day-to-day basis. To maintain a safe plant, however, these daily observations must be supplemented by formalized and regularly scheduled safety inspections including:

1. Plant-wide safety tours conducted by top levels of management

2. Safety inspections of portions of the plant conducted by teams of managers and safety personnel

3. Safety inspections of specific equipment, such as power presses, exhaust hoods, fire equipment, cranes, and hoists, conducted by trained specialists

4. Safety inspections of all new or relocated equipment before it is released to the line manager

To assure that new or relocated equipment is inspected before being placed in use, a "do not operate" tag, as shown in Figure 13-1, can be affixed to the equipment by the crew making the installation.

In addition to the safety inspections made by in-plant people, the safety-inspection services which are available from insurance companies, state health and safety agencies, and safety consultants should be used where practical.

ENFORCEMENT OF SAFETY RULES

It is recognized that safety rules and the observance of such rules are a necessary part of any successful safety program. Yet most supervisors will admit that they seldom take corrective action when safety rules are ignored. Where

NEW OR RELOCATED APPARATUS
DO NOT OPERATE
UNTIL THIS TAG IS REMOVED
BY THE SAFETY ENGINEER

No. 142

FIG. 13-1. *A machine-installation "do not operate" tag.*

this is the case, steps should be taken to correct the situation, because knowledge that corrective action will be taken for failure to follow safety rules is a most effective deterrent to accidents. As a first step, ask these questions:

1. Is there a real need for the safety rule, and do employees understand the need?

2. Have existing safety rules kept pace with changes in conditions?

3. Does the observance of an existing safety rule create an unusual inconvenience or an annoyance that makes it almost human nature for employees to ignore the rule?

4. Are there too many safety rules, or are rules so general and broad that they are meaningless?

Formulating Safety Rules. To be effective, safety rules must be formulated and applied according to the following basic principles.

1. Safety rules should be formulated because of an indicated need, to establish a uniform practice throughout a facility, to correct or control an existing unsafe practice or condition, or to guide employees regarding some specific safety practice.

2. Safety rules should be published and communicated to employees with a full explanation regarding the need for each rule.

3. Safety rules should be specific rather than general, and they should be few in number. Operating procedures and various job instructions such as "always remove the chuck wrench" should not be called "safety rules."

4. Existing safety rules must be followed, and whenever an employee ignores a safety rule, prompt corrective action is required to ensure future conformance.

Corrective Action. It is entirely consistent with the principles of good human relations to stress the need for following safety rules. Corrective action should be taken whenever rules are not observed. In particular, corrective action is essential if a single violation of a rule would place the safety of an individual or the work group in jeopardy. Violations requiring prompt corrective action include:

1. Smoking in a posted "no smoking" area
2. Horseplay

3. Refusal to wear personal protective equipment as required, or refusal to remove ties, jewelry, or other items that might be unsafe on a particular job

4. Unauthorized use of hazardous equipment, machines, or material

5. Deliberately making a safety device inoperative, or operating a machine when it is known the safety device is inoperative

6. Operating a machine or equipment that has been tagged "do not operate"

In the development of a sound safety program, management must concentrate on preventive measures rather than after-the-fact correction. Perhaps the worst mistake that can be made is to take corrective action after an employee is injured rather than at the time of the initial violation. Emphasis must be placed on the violations rather than upon injuries as such. Where supervisors and managers are reasonable but firm on violations and where they are setting a good example by following all the safety rules themselves, a safety consciousness is gradually developed among the entire work force, and the chances for injury are materially reduced.

SAFETY TRAINING

Group or mass training has a place in a complete safety program, but it is far more effective to use a personalized or individual safety-training approach. The advantages of a personalized approach are many. Hazards vary on each job, and because of individual differences, might even vary for employees on the same job. These individual differences can be considered if the safety training is personalized. Personalized safety training permits consideration of the worker's rate of learning, his interests, his natural ability, and his physical limitations. The training can be specific, whereas group training must be general. The key to successful job-safety training is telling the employee what the hazards are and how to avoid them.

Where safety training is carried out on a personalized basis, the first-line supervisor must necessarily do the training. This will take more of his time and require more attention to detail, but the additional effort pays off because of the increased effectiveness of the training method. In launching a personalized safety-training program, the first step is the preparation of a job-safety analysis for each job in the plant. To make the job-safety analysis in an organized manner, a form similar to the one shown in Figure 13-2 is suggested.

In most cases, each supervisor will have to make from five to ten different analyses. Of course, in maintenance and construction work, the variety of jobs will cover a much wider range. Fortunately, these jobs can be grouped by the type of work performed, and a job-safety analysis can be made for each category of work rather than for each job. For example, repair, installation, relocation of equipment, cleaning motors, and unloading cars might be a few of the various categories of maintenance work to be analyzed.

The guide which follows will provide a step-by-step procedure for planning a job-safety analysis, making the analysis, and applying the results.

Supervisor's Guide to Job-safety Analysis

I. Three basic approaches:
  A. Job-safety analysis by machine or equipment.
  B. Job-safety analysis by jobs: assembly, welding, and the like.
  C. Job-safety analysis by occupation: painter, steam fitter, carpenter, and the like.

Job-safety Analysis

Job Description: Three spindle drill press—   Job Location: Bldg. 19-2, Pump section
                Impeller 8406

Key job steps	Tool used	Potential health and injury hazard	Safe practices, apparel, and equipment
Getting material for operation	Tote box	Dropping tote box on foot	Wear safety shoes. Have firm grip on box.
		Back strain from lifting	Stress proper lifting methods.
		Picking up overloaded boxes	Tell employee to get help or lighten load.
Inspecting and setting up drill press	Drill press	Check for defective machines	Do not operate if defective. Attach red or yellow "do not operate" tag.
		Chuck wrench not removed	Always remove chuck wrench immediately after use.
		Making adjustments when machine is running	Always stop spindle before making adjustments.
Drilling	. . . .	Hair, clothing, or jewelry catching on spindle	Wear head covering, snug-fitting clothing. No loose sleeves. Avoid wearing rings, bracelets, or wristwatches.
		Spinning work or fixture	Use proper blocks or clamps to hold work and fixture securely.
		Injury to hands—cuts, etc.	*Never wear gloves.* Use hook, brush, or other tool to remove chips. Use compressed air only when instructed.
		Drill sticks in work	Stop spindle, free drill by hand.
		Flying chips	Wear proper eye protection.
		Pinch points at belts	Always stop press before adjusting belts.
		Broken drills	Do not attempt to force drill, apply pressure.

Signature _____

Date _____   Page _____

FIG. 13-2. *Job-safety analysis form.* (*Courtesy of the General Electric Company.*)

II. Suggestions for making job-safety analysis:
   A. Make a list of all jobs to be analyzed. Set a target date for completion of the jobs listed.
   B. Analyze job while it is being performed and determine key job steps, potential hazards, and safe practices.
   C. Make certain that potential health and injury hazards are described so as to indicate clearly the steps employees must take to avoid them.
   D. Where safe apparel and equipment are designated, give detailed description.
   E. Use checklist on the back of the form as a reminder of things to be considered in making the analysis.

III. Suggested use and follow-up:
  A. Check analysis with employees to see if they can make any additions or corrections.
  B. Have completed analysis checked by superior.
  C. Go over completed analysis with employees presently on the payroll to make certain they understand hazards and means for protecting themselves against them. Always explain "why."
  D. Correct unsafe work habits. Use job-safety analysis as a guide to train all new employees as well as present employees transferred to a new job.
  E. Make analysis available so that employees may refer to it readily; keep a copy of each analysis.
  F. Check employees' performance regularly to make certain that necessary precautions are being taken.
  G. Make analysis of all new operations.

EMPLOYEE SAFETY PARTICIPATION

Employee safety committees are used by many companies as a means of promoting employee participation in the safety program. This approach has weaknesses which should be recognized:

1. Existence of the committee makes it easy for busy supervisors to duck their safety responsibility—safety problems are referred to committee rather than handled by supervisors as they should be.

2. Usually only a small percentage of the work force serves on the committee. Many members are reappointed year after year.

3. The holding of meetings and attendance at them are irregular.

4. Committee members are not qualified to handle the more difficult safety problems, so they tend to deal with the superficial.

5. Action is seldom taken on the recommendations made by the committee, particularly those requiring a large expenditure.

6. Instead of taking prompt action on an unsafe condition, committee members defer action so they will have something to discuss at the next meeting.

Unless production, cost, and quality problems are handled and solved by committees, it does not seem practical or appropriate to handle safety problems by committees. It is recommended that existing safety committees, where ineffective (an examination of a safety committee's minutes of meetings will reveal its effectiveness), be disbanded in an orderly manner. In place of committees, supervisors should hold regular meetings with all of their employees stressing safety. These meetings should be specifically directed at the work the employees are doing and should be held as often as the hazard of the work requires. High-voltage testing, for example, may be sufficiently hazardous to warrant a weekly meeting, whereas a meeting every six months for light-assembly workers might be adequate. These meetings, of course, are in addition to the individual safety contacts all supervisors make on a daily basis.

ADMINISTRATION OF THE SAFETY PROGRAM

To help supervisors discharge their responsibility for accident prevention, functional responsibility for administration of the safety program should be assigned to a single individual. In a small plant, this might be a part-time assignment; and in a large operation, a full-time job. The individual responsible for safety should have a job title consistent with other job titles in the business, such as "safety engineer," "safety consultant," "safety supervisor," or "loss-prevention specialist." If the work to be done is sufficiently technical to call for an engineering background to fulfill the job requirements, then the title "safety engineer" might be preferred. In cases where the individual responsible for safety administration directs the work of other safety specialists and loss-prevention specialists, the title of "safety supervisor," "safety director," or "safety manager" might be used.

Some of the specific responsibilities of safety personnel may be listed as follows:

1. By teaching, counseling, and advising, assist line management to fulfill to the highest degree its responsibility for safety.

2. Provide for periodic safety appraisals to pinpoint unsafe work environments and unsafe practices and processes, and report results of such appraisals with sound recommendations for correction. This includes the responsiblity for appraising all new and relocated equipment and machines and releasing such equipment to the appropriate line supervisor.

3. Promote and maintain a continuing safety-education program which will help create safety awareness at all levels of the organization and which has as a focal point the first-line supervisor's responsibility for safety. Specifically, teach supervisors to develop safe working conditions, to find the cause of all accidents, to use personalized safety training, to promote employee safety participation, and to enforce safety rules.

4. Maintain and interpret accident and injury statistics and accident-cost data.

5. Devise measurements and set standards which provide for an adequate evaluation of accident prevention performance and loss control for each supervisor at each level of management.

6. Provide for the advancement and dissemination of fundamental safety knowledge, conduct safety research, and put existing safety information into usable forms such as safety booklets, data sheets, instruction manuals, and bulletins. Transfer such safety knowledge to the first-line supervisor so it can be used at the place where the action takes place.

7. Maintain liaison with national, state, and local safety councils and take an active part in the activities of such groups.

MEASURING SAFETY PERFORMANCE

Frequency Rates. Disabling-injury frequency rates can be used as a measure of safety performance if managers understand how the rates are computed and what they really mean. Such rates should be used to tell whether the safety record is getting better, worse, or staying about the same. For this reason, it is much more meaningful to compare the frequency rate of a plant with its previous rate rather than with the rate of another plant or company. However, in making this comparison, frequency rates should be regarded as gross measurements—more like pacing off a mile than using a tape measure. Any deviation of the rate of less than 15 percent has little significance, particularly if the rate is low.

In computing frequency rates, the base is the disabling injury, which is described as a work injury that renders an employee unable to work on any one or more days following the date of the accident.

The rate is expressed in terms of the number of disabling injuries per million hours of exposure. For example, a plant of 750 people will work about 1,500,000 man-hours each year. If six disabling injuries are reported during the year, the disabling-injury frequency rate for the plant would be

$$\frac{6 \text{ injuries} \times 1,000,000}{1,500,000 \text{ man-hours}} = 4 = \text{frequency rate}$$

Severity Rates. A severity rate, which is the number of days lost and charged for disabling injuries per million hours of exposure, also may be used. This rate is based on actual calendar days lost because of injuries that keep a person from working, and scheduled days charged for fatalities, amputations, loss of sight, or the like. These charges range from 6,000 days for death or permanent total disability to 35 days for amputation of the tip of a toe.

The method for computing frequency and severity rates is outlined in detail by the United States of America Standards Institute in Standard Z16.1-1954, *The American Standard Method of Recording and Measuring Work Injury Experience.*

Total Injury Rates. In addition to disabling-injury frequency and severity rates, many companies compute the rate of all injuries including anything that requires first-aid attention. This is called a "total injury frequency rate." Where used, total injury frequency rates should be compared against the rate for a previous period—not against the rate of another supervisor, a department, or a plant.

Supervisor's Safety Checklist

	My practice	
	Is adequate	Needs attention
1. I accept safety as just as much a part of my job as production, quality, and cost.		
2. I recognize the relationship among good safety, good housekeeping, and good management.		
3. I give adequate safety instruction to every new employee and to every old employee starting a new job.		
4. I impart to all employees the understanding that the violation of standard safe work practices is just as serious as the violation of any other company rule— I am taking corrective action when safety rules are ignored.		
5. I see that necessary personal protective equipment is provided.		
6. I always set a good safety example myself.		
7. By personal contact and group discussions, I make it possible for each employee to take part in the safety program.		
8. I do not release new or relocated machines or equipment to an employee until I am satisfied that the necessary protective devices have been provided and the employees have received instructions regarding its safe operation.		
9. I investigate and determine the cause of *all* injuries, even the minor cases.		
10. I am constantly watchful for and I take immediate steps to correct unsafe work conditions and unsafe work procedures.		
11. I see that all injuries are reported and promptly treated.		

FIG. 13-3. *Supervisor's safety checklist.*

Supervisor's Checklist. The use of a supervisor's safety checklist as shown by Figure 13-3 provides another approach in the evaluation of safety performance.

In addition to frequency and severity rates and use of the checklist, it is also helpful and meaningful to use the results of a plant safety audit as a safety performance measurement. If numerous unsafe conditions are found, it is obvious that there is insufficient effort being taken to keep the plant safe.

Obviously any one of the measuring techniques mentioned here would not provide enough information to make a judgment concerning the relative safety of a plant or company. Taken together, however, and with a hard look at the causes of accidents, a fairly accurate judgment can be made as to whether safety performance is getting better, staying about the same, or getting worse.

What are the principal causes of accidents? What types of accidents and injuries produce the frequency and severity rates? How do this year's rates compare with last year's? What is the safety behavior of the work force? Do managers take an active part in the safety program? These are the questions that need to be answered to get a fairly accurate measure of safety performance. Use of only frequency and severity rates as *the* measure could be most misleading.

BIBLIOGRAPHY

DeReamer, Russell, *Modern Safety Practices*, John Wiley & Sons, Inc., New York, 1958.
Fawcett, Howard H., and William S. Wood, *Safety and Accident Prevention in Chemical Operations*, John Wiley & Sons, Inc., New York, 1965.
Heinrich, H. W., *Industrial Accident Prevention*, 4th ed., McGraw-Hill Book Company, New York, 1959.

Sources of Safety Information and Educational Materials

American Society of Safety Engineers, 5 North Wabash Avenue, Suite 1705, Chicago.
Industrial Hygiene Foundation of America, 4400 Fifth Avenue, Pittsburgh.
Manufacturing Chemists Association, 1625 I Street, N.W., Washington, D.C.
National Board of Fire Underwriters, 85 John Street, New York 10038.
National Safety Council, 425 North Michigan Avenue, Chicago.
United States of America Standards Institute, 10 East 40th Street, New York.
United States Department of Labor, 14th Street and Constitution Avenue, N.W., Washington, D.C.
United States Public Health Service, 1901 Constitution Avenue, N.W., Washington, D.C.

CHAPTER FOURTEEN

Automation

ANDERSON ASHBURN *Editor*, American Machinist, *New York, New York*

"Automation" is a convenient term to apply to a group of related techniques for making manufacturing operations significantly more automatic. Automation can be applied to mass-production manufacturing, to limited production, and to the process industries.

The most dramatic potential is demonstrated by the application of numerical control to individual machines and the application of computer control to complete manufacturing systems.

"Automation" is a word with a high emotional content. Most employees have a fear of technological unemployment even though there may be no justification for it. Management decisions, concerning both the degree of automation to be installed and the handling of the displaced workers (or even those who only fear they will be displaced), are of critical importance.

DEVELOPMENT OF AUTOMATION

Meaning of the Word. "Automation" is a term applied to a number of related concepts, some of which are new and some of which are not. As applied in manufacturing, however, it generally includes these three related developments:

1. The combination of production operations with handling and control steps to create a link between separate pieces of automatic equipment and form continuous automatic production through a series of operations, an entire line, or a complete plant

2. Automatic control of the variables involved in a machine or plant to produce a product within specified tolerances

3. Information processing and reporting on an automatic basis

The first two areas can be briefly described as "Detroit automation" and "process control." The third is sometimes called "office automation" or "source data automation." (See Chapter 5 of Section 15 for the discussion of this subject.)

There is no generally accepted definition of the term "automation." There is a basic argument between those who feel that it is only a new word for mechanization and those who feel that it involves elements that carry it to a level higher than mechanization. Among those who take the second position, there are different schools of thought as to what elements are required: feedback; the inclusion of electronic elements instead of electrical, mechanical, or hydraulic in the control system; or the employment of computers at some stage in the operation.

For the practical purposes of the business manager, all these arguments can be ignored. "Automation" is a convenient term to apply when things are done in a way that is "significantly more automatic" than the way they were done before. It is so convenient for this purpose that business managers continue to use the term, as do engineers, despite the problems caused by its emotional content.

Background of Automation. As a word, and to some extent as a concept, automation had its origin in Detroit. Del S. Harder, then vice president of manufacturing at the Ford Motor Company, coined the word late in 1946. The next year an automation department was established at Ford. During the next ten years, Ford spent $2.5 billion on the modernization and automation of its facilities, much of it during the period 1951–1954. This period constituted a dramatic turnaround in Ford operations that took it from a money-losing firm that produced a million vehicles in 1946 to a highly profitable firm that produced two million vehicles in 1953. There were other important factors in the Ford performance, but the dramatic accomplishments in manufacturing were avidly studied by manufacturing managements in other industries.

Then, in 1952, John Diebold published a book, *Automation: The Advent of the Automatic Factory*, in which he used the word with a broader meaning.

TECHNIQUES OF AUTOMATION

All automation of manufacturing operations must start with a machine or process that has some form of automatic operating cycle. With this beginning, the first step is to add automatic loading and unloading devices to the machine. Then transfer mechanisms are added to connect the unloading device of one machine with the loading device of the machine performing the next operation in the sequence. When such a system is built up step by step with separate machines and handling devices, it becomes a linked line.

The same job can be done all at once by building the entire sequence of operations into a single machine, called a "transfer machine." Several work stations can be placed compactly around the rotating table of a transfer machine, or the stations can be placed in a straight line. In either case, the work is automatically moved or transferred from station to station through the machine.

The next stage in automation is to apply some system of automatically measuring or inspecting the work at one or more points in the sequence. At this time, it is possible to have the inspection device shut the machine down if work is not going according to the specifications. Or it is possible to go another step and add feedback. With feedback, the results of the measurement operation are fed back to the work station whose operation is being measured, and adjustments are made to bring the work within tolerance. With feedback, the machine does not have to be shut down until the tools have been adjusted to their limit and must be replaced.

Automatic in-process storage units can be added at any point in the system. These maintain banks of parts at various stages in the sequence of operations and make it possible to operate parts of the line (feeding to, or being fed from, the storage units) while a section is shut down for tool replacement or maintenance.

Processing lines for operations such as forging, heat treating, welding, brazing, painting, plating, and assembly can be automated just as lines for machining or pressworking can be. Increasing attention is centering on assembly operations. All automation of processing lines involves a combination of methods for handling individual stages automatically combined with transfer devices to carry the work from stage to stage.

Process Control. An early example of automatic process control is the governor on a steam engine. The petroleum, chemical, and other continuous-process industries are full of operations in which some form of adjustment of valves must be made frequently to maintain the process in equilibrium. Automatic control of such adjustments has in many cases provided better control than was previously available. An operator is usually still required to keep a log of the operations and see that the control system is working correctly.

More recently, the digital computer has been applied to process control. All of the various measurements from different stages in the process are fed continuously to the computer. The computer is programmed to analyze these and calculate what control settings will create optimum conditions, and then transmit instructions to valves, temperature controllers, and other adjustable features in the system. The computer can also be programmed to produce a continuous data log of the operations and calculate and report on the consumption of raw materials and output of finished product.

Although a number of such computer-controlled installations have been made in processing plants, no clear pattern on the economics has emerged.

Not so far advanced is the application of computers to the control of production in manufacturing plants. Many plants use computers for handling much of the routine paper work of production control, but few have applied them to the kind of on-line continuous monitoring of operations that is represented by the computer applications in the continuous-process industries. This does not mean, however, that computer control will not prove economic in some plants.

NUMERICAL CONTROL

Numerical control (NC) is the process of controlling a machine by feeding it instructions in the form of numbers. These instructions can be fed to the control of the machine by holes in a punched tape or card, by magnetized spots in a film of iron oxide, or by setting dials or pushing buttons on a control panel.

In only its first ten years of existence, NC demonstrated that it has immense potential in manufacturing. Following the introduction of the first commercial machines in 1955, the process spread, and by early 1966 it was estimated that nearly 1,800 plants in the United States were using about 7,000 NC machines.

Type of Control. The two basic types of control are the positioning (or point to point) and the contouring (or continuous path). In the simplest positioning systems, the tool and the work are placed in the desired relationship and then the tool is advanced. The route taken to bring the work to this position is not material—it can be a straight line; or it can be by movement first in one axis, then in a second; or it can include extra steps to make the final approach always from the same direction to eliminate any influence from backlash.

An intermediate type of control provides straight-cut milling capability by imposing a rate control on the movements in each axis.

Contouring controls permit the tool to follow a continuously varying path, as in profile milling.

These terms apply to systems operating in either two or three dimensions (two-axis or three-axis). A bit of confusion can arise when a machine with a single operating head is described as a five-axis machine. The fourth and fifth axes are rotation about two of the original three axes. Of course, control systems for machines with two or more independent heads may have even larger numbers of axes controlled.

Basic Advantages. Numerical control tends to bring the advantages of the kind of automation that special automatic machinery makes possible for mass production to the production of only a few parts. Sometimes it will pay to produce a single piece by NC with an automatic program.

With NC, the use of templates, jigs, and fixtures is largely eliminated. The cost of these devices and the storage space they take are both saved. Some form of simple, universal holding device to hold work on the table of the machine is usually all that is needed.

Once programs have been established, there is little setup time, and lead time for production of parts can be reduced. This will permit lot sizes that are closer to needs and reduce inventories of material, parts in process, and finished parts.

Because machine speeds and feeds are planned in advance by trained programmers, they are most likely to be held to the optimum rates. Manual operators working on complex precision work will take extra time to check each setting before cutting, and these delays will get longer as the work invested in a complex part goes up. For both these reasons, machining time is usually reduced with NC.

Because one NC machine can usually replace two or more conventional machines, floor space is reduced.

Because production is more accurate and uniform, closer tolerances may be obtained at no extra cost. This may reduce the cost for inspection, and it may reduce the amount of rejects or rework.

Impact on Management. Perhaps the biggest advantage of NC is the impact it has on all aspects of manufacturing management. Because the initial investment in NC is high and the rate at which it can turn out work is high, it is essential that the machine be kept busy. Because NC is precise and must be fed specific numbers and yet the time it will require for each operation can be known precisely in advance, accurate scheduling becomes both necessary and practical. All the operations of production scheduling, material routing, and inventory control become both more critical and potentially more manageable.

Programming. The first step in any NC operation is that of reducing the operations to be performed to specific steps that are within the capability of the machine, and then writing the instructions in the machine's language. Actually, despite the term "numerical" that is applied to NC, these instructions can include letters and "words."

Simple programming for positioning work is usually done manually by a programmer sitting at a desk, often with the aid of a desk calculator. If the drawings for the part have been dimensioned to zero base lines instead of in the conventional manner, programming is greatly simplified.

Computer assistance is desirable in programming most contouring operations, but it is not necessary for the bulk of NC work. The fact that many companies that have acquired considerable NC and computer experience tend to use the two together is not surprising, but it is still possible to take advantage of the economies of NC for most applications without computer programming.

Much early confusion about NC arose because automation had been generally a mass-production tool. Many managers with small-lot production were slow to realize that NC is primarily for limited quantities and flexibility.

Another source of confusion came from the fact that the early work on NC was sponsored by the United States Air Force. The result was that the most sophisticated types of contouring machines for producing complex aerospace parts were produced before the simpler positioning machines. It may be one of the few cases in which an industry grew from the complex to the simple.

The trend is toward simpler, more reliable, and less expensive control systems. At the same time, more advanced and complex controls have also been developed for those applications that need them.

Applications. Most of the application of NC has been to metal-cutting machine tools. Drilling, boring, milling, and turning machines have been the types most involved. Numerical control has also brought about the development of multi-operation machines, or machining centers, usually capable of doing drilling, boring, and milling work. Efforts to incorporate turning into machining centers have not generally been successful, and the centers are usually confined to operations performed with rotating tools rather than with rotating work.

In addition, punching machines with turret heads were one of the first and most successful NC applications. Many other applications have been found, though they are not as widespread. These include drafting, measuring, inspecting, tube bending, wire wrapping, riveting, and flame cutting. There are also welding, coil winding, and various specialized inspection and assembly machines.

To facilitate the feeding of machining data to a computer and have it produce a tape or other output that will then operate a machine, a number of programming languages have been developed. Some of these are only for point-to-point work; others will handle both contouring and positioning jobs.

Most of the languages are general programs that require an additional step with a "postprocessor" to adapt them to a particular machine and its control. Examples of the most commonly used languages are AUTOSPOT, a three-axis, point-to-point language for medium-size computers; APT, a five-axis, full contouring program requiring a large computer; and ADAPT, a simplified, three-axis contouring language for medium computers.

Computer-assisted programming services for NC machines are available from some computer centers and from some builders of NC machines.

NC Implications. The broadest implications of NC are in what it can do for management. With the sensitive control that it gives to manufacturing operations, combined with the opportunities for computer-assisted design that leads directly to manufacturing tapes, there are new opportunities for management to react quickly to changing market requirements.

IMPACT OF AUTOMATION ON EMPLOYMENT

Almost from the time the word "automation" came into popular use, it began to develop a large emotional content. To many people, "automation" was the word used to describe anything that deprived people of jobs.

In addition to the expected opposition from labor leaders, there were particularly alarming predictions from social scientists, economists, and even some businessmen. During the peak period of attack (from the mid-1950s to the mid-1960s), there were examples and statistics cited in the calls for action that were sometimes based on shaky evidence, to say the least.

In fact, automation seemed to be the favorite scapegoat for the unemployment problems of this period—problems that were basically created by the large number of new workers entering the labor force each year and the failure during much of this time for the economic growth rate to keep pace with this growing labor force.

As an example of how responsible sources could misuse statistics, there is a widely quoted report from the U.S. Labor Department that automation replaces 1.8 million workers a year with machines. This dubious statistic was created by taking the number of civilian workers in the labor force in 1960 (66.7 million) and multiplying it by the average annual gain in productivity (2.8 percent) prevailing at the time. By no definition that has been proposed is it practical to equate automation with all increases in productivity.

The statistical forecasts of the Labor Department were mild, however, compared with some of the forecasts made in an excess of zeal by the real alarmists. These began to turn up in some of the testimonies of witnesses at the various public hearings on automation held by Senate and House committees starting in 1955, but the most ominous were in private studies such as those made by the Center for the Study of Democratic Institutions and the Ad Hoc Committee on the Triple Revolution.

At the other extreme have been those who have asserted with equal firmness that automation created jobs rather than devoured them, and that nobody is ever put out of work by progress.

The Balanced View. Fortunately, a realistic, balanced view of the relation between employment and automation existed all along and is so much in the ascendancy that responsible businessmen and responsible labor leaders are likely to find themselves almost in agreement on the basic principles.

In the balanced view, the real necessity to accept and exploit gains in productivity is matched by a recognition that these gains can create dislocations in employment that must be dealt with. Most of the changes that create major dislocations seem to be new inventions or discoveries, rather than automation as such, but such dislocations are not going to be acceptable to the general public, whatever the reason.

Management Responsibility. The approach of management to automation must begin with a recognition that the fear of technological unemployment is real in most workers. If they believe that changes that are contemplated are likely to eliminate their jobs, they will resist those changes in every possible way.

And if major degrees of automation are undertaken without providing clear and believable explanations of what the effect will be on each worker's job, the worker will probably assume that his job is in jeopardy and resist the changes. This resistance may take the form of individual efforts to negate the increased production of the new system (these efforts, generally more subtle than the wooden sabot dropped into the mechanism, are often suspected as a cause when new, automated equipment fails to operate at the anticipated production levels).

One way to deal with this problem is to include, in the planning for automation, calculations of the immediate effect the automation will have on employment in the plant, make plans for dealing with the displacement that is created, and follow an organized plan to inform the employees of the impact of the program on them.

In some cases, management has decided that it is not practical to modernize an existing plant and has shifted the operations to a different location. Such shifts have taken place with individual plants or, in a few cases, with almost entire industries. If such a move is made without provision for the displaced employees left behind, the chances of a public outcry are large indeed. Even companies that have made extensive efforts to move employees, or to provide funds for training for new jobs, have found themselves the object of efforts to organize boycotts.

Collective Bargaining.   Automation has become a major element in many union negotiations for collective-bargaining agreements.   For some time, it seemed to be an issue for trading purposes, but clauses relating to automation have become a feature of the contracts in a number of industries.   Most of these have taken one of three forms: (1) an agreement to place a sum of money at the disposal of the union, usually based on a royalty on product shipped from the plant, to be used for training displaced employees and to provide for early retirement or for welfare payments to unemployed union members; (2) restrictions on the application of automation in the plant unless the union approves; (3) direct payments to workers of a portion of the savings that are calculated to result from the installation of automation.

There has been little real labor strife over the question of automation, but it has been a factor of increasing importance and is at the root of long and bitter strikes in a few instances.

ECONOMICS OF AUTOMATION

Three major reasons can exist for applying automation to a manufacturing operation: (1) to reduce direct-labor costs, (2) to increase output, and (3) to improve product quality.   The extent to which each of these reasons applies in a given case will greatly influence the economics.   When it is necessary to automate to achieve the required quality, cost is secondary.   In most other cases, cost will be the controlling factor.

In general, the same procedures used to evaluate any equipment replacement can be applied to the decision on how far to automate.   Because of the greater change in methods (and greater cost) that is likely to be involved, the development of realistic evaluations is more difficult than in simple machine-for-machine replacements.

Cost of obsolescence resulting from changes in the product is greatly increased where automation is applied.   This can result in management being locked into a product that has lost its ability to compete or in the write-off of relatively new equipment.   This problem has generally been met in two ways.   One is by trying to anticipate the basic nature that product changes will take and designing the equipment originally so it can be adapted to handle the changes. The other is by making use of standard components or modules (often called "building blocks") in the construction of special equipment.   Surplus lines of equipment can then be broken up and the components used in the construction of new lines.

Work stoppages become a much more serious problem when a plant is heavily automated.   If a simple basic transfer machine performs a hundred operations and difficulty develops at any one point in the line, the entire line has to be shut down while tools are changed or repairs are made.   To deal with this problem, the basic approach has been to break a sequence of operations, a transfer machine, or a linked line into segments and establish banks of parts in process between the segments.

Banking increases the space requirements and the inventory of work in process.   On the other hand, it increases the output efficiency of an automated system.   Some of the most important management decisions involved in automation relate to the decisions on how many parts banks are to be incorporated and what size they should be.

Debugging Automatic Equipment. Debugging is usually a major problem with special automatic equipment. Failure properly to anticipate the time that will be required to debug a new installation is probably the most common reason that new installations fall behind schedule. Debugging is a critical and necessary step, it seems, in the production of all one-of-a-kind manufacturing systems. When a standard machine is placed on the market, it has been through both laboratory and field tests, and those small errors in design and manufacture that seem inevitable in any new mechanical system (bugs, in other words) have generally all been removed. But with special one-of-a-kind systems, the things that have been done wrong or have been overlooked will usually have to be located and corrected over a period of weeks (for complex equipment, it may be months) of debugging. When special equipment is made up largely of standard building-block components, this problem is reduced, but it is not eliminated.

CONCLUSION

Most of the difficulties that arise in applying automation can be avoided if enough time is allowed for careful planning and organization in the early stages of the project.

Equipment and techniques exist for providing any desired degree of automation for almost any manufacturing operation. But some are easy to automate and some are difficult. The basic combination of cost and quality standards will determine the solution for any given situation.

Decisions on the type and extent of automation to be employed in the manufacturing process are among the most critical that management must make. This is because the sums of money involved are often large, the lead time between decision and return on the investment is generally quite long, and the competitive penalties for having either far too little or far too much automation are likely to be severe.

BIBLIOGRAPHY

The Annals of the American Academy of Political and Social Science, special issue, March, 1962.

Bright, James R., *Automation and Management,* Harvard Graduate School of Business Administration, Boston, 1958.

DeGroat, George H., *Metalworking Automation,* McGraw-Hill Book Company, New York, 1962.

Niland, Powell, *Management Problems in the Acquisition of Special Automatic Equipment,* Harvard Graduate School of Business Administration, Boston, 1961.

Terborgh, George, *The Automation Hysteria,* Machinery and Allied Products Institute, Washington, D.C., 1965.

CHAPTER FIFTEEN

Waste Control

PHIL CARROLL   *Professional Engineer, Maplewood, New Jersey*

There are two kinds of waste in manufacturing. One is the type everybody in the organization knows about. Its presence is brought out by various measures of costs and performances. We have work standards, quality limits, and expense budgets, to name a few. The wastes these separate out as variances are thoroughly discussed elsewhere.

The other kind of waste is concealed, in that we do not have commonly used measures for revealing its presence. Some of these important elements of waste will be outlined here.

To a large extent, these wastes exist because of our current state of knowledge. For instance, you often hear someone say, "I wish I had known," or, "Why didn't someone tell me?"

CAUSES OF WASTE

The condition is aggravated by rapidly expanding technologies. Thus, from one point of view, waste is incurred when actual practices lag behind newly discovered methods. In a more practical sense, a definition written in 1921 may serve. It appeared in that remarkable survey entitled *Waste in Industry*[1] as ". . . in the Committee's investigations, industrial waste has been thought of as that part of the material, time, and human effort expended in production represented by the difference between the average attainments on one hand and performances actually attained on the other. . . ."

The report goes on to assay responsibilities after this explanation. "We measure responsibility not by the thing done but by the opportunities which people have had of knowing better or worse."

Certainly, conditions have changed markedly since 1921. Were a similar survey made in the 1960s, probably the percentages would be changed. A

[1] Committee on Elimination of Waste in Industry of the Federated Engineering Societies, McGraw-Hill Book Company, New York, 1921.

Industry studied	Percent responsibility assayed against management	Percent responsibility assayed against labor	Percent responsibility assayed against outside contacts (the public, trade relationships, and other factors)
Men's clothing mfg.	75	16	9
Building industry	65	21	14
Printing	64	28	9
Boot and shoe mfg.	73	11	16
Metal trades	81	9	10
Textile mfg.	50	10	40

fourth column headed "Government" might be added, and the list would be extended to include such important industries as aviation, electronics, transportation, defense, and perhaps even service.

Manager Responsibility. According to the foregoing explanation, managers had opportunities of knowing that wastes existed in their plants. It appears, however, that waste continuations were, in part, blamed on others. Similar comments are heard today. "The union won't let us." "In our industry, that is the practice." "The government requires it." These might be called "pressure factors."

Mixed with these is another influence, or lack of it. Some managers tolerate waste so long as profits are satisfactory. It is more comfortable. Also, "affluence" sets in when business is booming. When profit margins were long, "profit" became a "dirty word" in some circles. The reverse attitude tended to set in when the profit squeeze tightened.

Actions take place in two directions. One is to go after more and more volume. The other is to cut costs. Both are constructive provided the losses do not exceed the gains.

More Volume. Striving for more business is logical. It is the way companies grow. Getting more sales of unprofitable products, however, tends to reduce profits. And there are two wastes involved. Both are concealed in the typical company.

The first is in wrong costs. We apply average overheads to products that are not average. Thus, the further from average a product is, the more incorrect are its costs (see Chapter 2 of Section 10). This is important only in that the comparisons of costs with prices lead to incorrect conclusions about profitabilities.

Managers may spend money for advertising, selling, equipment, and methods to increase volumes of unprofitable sales. Certainly, some of these efforts tend to reduce costs and hence improve profits. Still, the same money and effort spent on other products would be more effective. Therefore, it is a waste when time, effort, and money are used less productively than they should be within a company. The proper control can be had when overhead costs are more correctly assigned to the products that cause them.

Sales Efforts. With the notion that more volume is a cure-all, sales efforts are wasted. Costs may be increased also. Some firms pay commissions for getting volume. Often, these are computed on dollars sold. As a consequence, a salesman will get 95 percent of his commission even when he sells at 95 percent of book or list price. This may be through getting a discount approved. Or as often happens, he sells some form of special product at a standard price.

Behind this is another fallacy, stemming from our concept of standard costs. To use arithmetic, assume a standard cost of $0.90 and a price of $1.00. Our usual deduction is that our profit is $0.10 each. This is not true, as is discussed more fully in Chapter 7 of Section 8. The standard cost is a type of average that conceals an implied quantity. Actually, then, there can be no profit unless more products are sold on an order than that basic quantity. The words "can be" refer to the preceding discussion. The standard cost itself may be incorrect.

Thus, sales efforts are wasted when volume is the sole measure of input. Better control requires more realistic measures of profitability. This in no way is intended to block the sale of "loss leaders" and new products. Presumably, these forms of sales promotions are being controlled.

Cost Reduction. Turning to costs, we usually apply more pressures when profit declines. "Fat is trimmed" in this and that organization, as pointed out in business journals. Middle and top managers look around to see what other folks are doing. Cost-reduction (profit-improvement) programs are instituted. New ways are discovered and utilized.

Thus, wastes are present in varying forms and degrees in most plants. Some types keep going because, as Dr. J. M. Juran explains, ". . . we desensitize ourselves to the existence of the 90 percent (yield). We have, with the best of intentions, learned to live with this bad-smelling mess."[2]

Other kinds of wastes go on because middle managers have been unable to sell the improvements they have learned about or devised. A third class, usually the largest, persists because "opportunities of knowing" have not been grasped. Many managers think performances are reasonably good, because they have not learned about better ways.

Lack of Facts. The big hurdle is lack of facts. As Dr. Ralph Davis once said, "There is no such thing as experience with something that has not been done." For instance, managers say, "It can't be done," or "It's not practical." They may have figures indicating the costs of present methods. But they have few, if any, costs of processing by better ways.

One example is in the general lack of sales forecasts. Failure to look ahead results in great wastes of time and money. Following behind customers means rush orders for materials at higher prices. Often, the right sizes are not available on short notice. So we buy the best substitutes and create waste of materials.

In trying to make up for lost time, we push some orders aside. Inventories are increased and damages occur. Customers start to complain, and salesmen, managers, and vice presidents turn to expediting. Finally, we ship by air express in an effort to ease the stresses.

Most of these extra costs are buried in averages. Consequently, we do not know the actual costs of living without forecasts.

Production Control. The same holds true for production control. We think we have this important function in our organizations. The work done by many such departments, however, often is largely that of "chasing shortages." These efforts result in broken lots, extra setups, and incident increased scrap.

But the major cost is hidden. Again, there are the customer disappointments mentioned earlier. Perhaps some leave us forever. Hence, money is spent to get replacements.

In addition, inventories are increased. Work in process sits around the

[2] J. M. Juran, *Managerial Breakthrough*, McGraw-Hill Book Company, New York, 1964, p. 25.

shop longer for two reasons. Some is backed up by insertions of rush orders in the schedule. More stands waiting in the form of production cushions. We try to keep work ahead to reduce the wait times of people and machines.

Few managers have reported to them the costs of owning these inventories. The chief reason is that we consider the use of our own money (retained earnings) as being "cost free." The usual profit and loss statement does not show the cost equivalent of "lost-opportunity earnings."

Money Cycle. Managers try to control these hidden costs. More and more measure performances in terms of return on invested capital. The factors are seen in the yardstick used by Du Pont.

$$\text{Rate of return} = \frac{\text{profit}}{\text{sales}} \times \frac{\text{sales}}{\text{investment}}$$

In simple words, this expression means making a profit more often.

Or you can look at it another way. In terms of waste control, it is a combination of cost reduction and turnover. The foregoing phases of control affect both. Reducing extra costs increases profit. Cutting delays raises turnover.

How often you make a profit may be seen more clearly if you think of the money cycle. This is the time that money is tied up. It starts when we hand a plane ticket to a salesman to help him get a customer's order. It ends when we deposit the customer's check.

With this viewpoint, take a look at the chart shown in Figure 15-1. The top left variable represents percent of capital invested in inventories. Beneath this range are percents tied up in "fixed" plant and equipment. The chart

PERCENT INVESTED IN SAFETY STOCK				DESIRED ANNUAL TURNOVER							
5	10	15	20	3	4	5	6	7	8	9	10
15		PERCENT		3.8	5.0	6.3	7.5	8.8	10	11	13
20	15	IN "FIXED"		4.0	5.3	6.7	8.0	9.3	11	12	13
25	20	15		4.3	5.7	7.2	8.6	10	11	13	14
30	25	20	15	4.6	6.2	7.7	9.2	11	12	14	15
35	30	25	20	5.0	6.7	8.3	10	12	13	15	17
40	35	30	25	5.5	7.3	9.1	11	13	15	16	18
	40	35	30	6.0	8.0	10	12	REQUIRED			20
		40	35	6.7	8.9	11	13	TURNS			22
			40	7.5	10	13	15	18	20	23	25

FIG. 15-1. *Chart showing that moving inventories must turn over more often as percentages of locked-in capital are increased.*

shows that a given inventory must be turned over more often as we put more money into machinery and shelter for it. The marked example indicates that ten turns of the "working capital" are required to attain six turns overall when 40 (10 safety plus 30 fixed) percent is tied up.

Thus, better forecasting and production scheduling will aid in controlling wastes. These two forms of planning tend to reduce the reported extra costs. Also, they cut down on the many hidden and "cost free" expenses.

Market Research. Another major waste lies in a form of lack of forecasting. It is our tendency to develop revised and new products without serious considerations of customers' needs. Too often, products are designed to incorporate existing capabilities. Frequently, they are overengineered.

Herein are several wastes. The big one is in the lack of attaining anticipated sales. Part of the setup phase of advertising, selling, engineering, and tooling costs, to name a few, are misspent.

If the new product or design competes with others in the line, it reduces quantities sold of the older items. This raises the cost per unit of some overhead expenses.

If we would "sally forth and ask" customers what they need, our failures would be fewer. They now run about 80 percent, according to reports. Losing much of the many different "development" costs of four out of five new designs is a large waste.

Standard Parts. In the same general field is another waste, caused by creativity. This loss is in the engineer's basic desire to apply his skills. He prefers to create a new design rather than use or adapt an existing one.

Two designs, materials, or sizes instead of one doubles almost every overhead cost. On top of these are added expenses caused solely by increased complexity.

Further excess costs arise later if the products require replacement parts. These tend to multiply as time goes on and the original designs are no longer made.

Mixed with this problem of diversity is another waste, usually concealed in average costs. It is caused by incomplete or incorrect specifications. In simple words, the man in the shop makes the piece to fit. He destroys interchangeability. This is bad enough if you will be called upon later to supply repair parts. But it takes several times as long to rework a size as it takes to make it right the first time. Besides, the capital invested per man in the shop is roughly nine times that supporting the engineer in the office.

Such wastes are more prevalent in job shops. The point here, however, is that creativity of this kind tends to make job-shop operations of what might otherwise be mass production. This tends also to prolong "debugging" of all designs. Of course, the control of this type of waste lies in providing more complete and correct blueprints of fewer strictly interchangeable parts.

Paper Wastes. In contradiction to the foregoing, we have too much standardization in our paper-work systems. Generally, we carry out the same procedures for a small order as for a large one. Right here is part of the reason why we fail to make the profit of $0.10 each pointed out earlier.

Taking the *A, B, C* distribution cited frequently, about 65 percent of the sales orders amount to 5 percent of the dollar income. The customer's order is the trunk of our paper-work tree and its branches. The whole tree is more than twice as big as it should be, because we use one system for all our orders.

Some efforts to reduce the losses inherent in small orders show up as adoptions of minimum order quantities or dollars. Such solutions are creditable. However, they are remedies—not cures. The wastes of paper may continue.

The cause to work on is the system. It was devised to control and safeguard the large amounts of money. It may be appropriate for this purpose.

Regardless, the big waste is in applying a system devised to control thousands of dollars to fives and tens. Some companies are changing this notion. Kaiser Aluminum's "blank" checks are one example. Another company is enclosing a coin card in the box with a spare-part order. A third organization reports it cannot afford to charge a customer if he orders $10 worth or less. It makes a present of the items. It is cheaper than sending a bill.

Small Orders. Small orders are inescapable for most companies. They occur when we seek new customers. They happen when new products are introduced. They are created whenever a product is sold that someday will need service parts.

The usual company, then, should have more than one paper-work system. You might think of three. Each would correspond with its proportion of an *A, B, C* sorting. Each system should be devised from the bottom up as a value analyst would go about it.

The system for small orders should be developed from the viewpoint of profitability. First, subtract labor, material, and profit from income. The remainder is all there is to pay for overhead. At this point, decision making begins. In the final analysis, the control of this phase of overhead depends principally upon deciding what you can afford.

Production Flow. Going further with the *A, B, C* approach, it offers a way to reduce another waste. This is by speeding up the main flow of production.

Commonly, our plants are arranged to get high utilization of equipment. All drill presses are in the drill department. All parts that are to be drilled go through that department. As a result, the slow-moving items hold back all the other parts. The *A* products move at about the pace set by the *C* items.

Since roughly 75 percent of the dollars are in the *A* items, they should have a special path. It ought to be arranged to approach continuous operation. Perhaps some special equipment should be used. In any event, stepping up the flow of the *A* items is the easiest way to raise turnover, reduce inventory, and improve deliveries.

Putting the *C* items off by themselves will help also. They can be processed with little or no paper-work system. Besides, when they are the only concern of the supervisor in charge, better service will result. This is vital when some of the *C* orders are for spare parts. It reduces many of the concealed wastes resulting from customer disappointments.

Value Analysis. Many of the foregoing wastes would be uncovered by value analysis. Its basic principle (see Chapter 5 of Section 6) is to define the function to be performed and discover how to do it most economically. When these two conditions are met, in effect, a measure is established. Then, waste becomes the difference between what can be done and what is being done.

Managers need to know these differences. Their basic jobs are to spend money to make money. But they cannot properly make choices among alternatives without having their total costs. When such facts are applied, a managerial form of value analysis is being used.

Generally, these judgments are made after excess costs have come into existence. In most cases, value analysis is another, although very effective, cost-reduction tool. Because it is an analytical method, however, it can and should be utilized to determine economical costs before the extras are built up. That there are excess costs is evident from the remarkable savings made by intensive value engineering.

It follows that these wastes could have been reduced or eliminated at the outset. In summary, then, probably the best waste control is that exercised to prevent excess costs from being created.

Lacking this preventive approach, managers need more and better measures of costs of good, current practices. Mere knowledge of better ways is not enough. It is too easy to say, "Our business is different." It is. But a comparison of costs enables a manager to prove which of several methods is the economical one for his conditions.

CONCLUSION

The wastes discussed in this chapter exist mainly because cost facts are lacking. When these facts are developed, the wastes can be reduced and the measures for control will be determined. Of course, better methods will be learned about tomorrow. But these alter only the yardsticks, because the principle of measurement has been established.

BIBLIOGRAPHY

"ABC Inventory Analysis," *Factory*, July, 1951.
Bittel, Lester R., *Management by Exception*, McGraw-Hill Book Company, New York, 1964.
Carroll, Phil, *Overhead Cost Control*, McGraw-Hill Book Company, New York, 1964.
Carroll, Phil, *Practical Production and Inventory Control*, McGraw-Hill Book Company, New York, 1966.
Carroll, Phil, *Profit Control: How to Plug Profit Leaks*, McGraw-Hill Book Company, New York, 1962.
Cash Flow Analysis for Managerial Control, National Association of Accountants, Research Report, no. 38, Oct. 15, 1961.
Drucker, Peter F., *Managing for Results*, Harper & Row, Publishers, Incorporated, New York, 1964.
Juran, J. M., *Managerial Breakthrough*, McGraw-Hill Book Company, New York, 1964.
MacNiece, E. H., *Production Forecasting, Planning, and Control*, 3d ed., John Wiley & Sons, Inc., New York, 1961.
Schleh, Edward C., *Management by Results*, McGraw-Hill Book Company, New York, 1961.
"Scouting the Trail for Marketers," *Business Week*, Apr. 18, 1964.
Waste in Industry, Committee on Elimination of Waste in Industry of the Federated Engineering Societies, McGraw-Hill Book Company, New York, 1921.

CHAPTER SIXTEEN

Plant Security

SAUL D. ASTOR *President, Management Safeguards, Inc., New York, New York*

The typical manager devotes fifty to seventy hours a week to coping with problems of finance, marketing, and production—making the day-to-day decisions essential to the running of the business. All too often, he finds there is little time or energy left for another management function, equally vital, but, until catastrophe strikes, not so apparently pressing: *plant security*.

Losses from the theft of cash, merchandise, and company secrets are staggering. Informed estimates place the cost of employee dishonesty at upward of $2 billion a year. Once, a million-dollar embezzlement case was rare. In the 1960s, it was fairly commonplace. Increasingly, concerned managements are coming to realize that it is not sufficient to concentrate solely on the task of developing profits and enlarging assets. It is just as important to make sure that every reasonable precaution is taken to safeguard these assets and profits.

CONTROL OF THEFT

By and large, the greatest theft losses suffered by industry are at the hands of dishonest employees. In attempting to install a tight and effective plant security system, it is important to understand the nature of employee dishonesty. The two interacting factors are desire and opportunity. Quite simply, and this is the essence of plant security: remove the opportunity, and the desire is substantially diminished. The old adage is as powerful today as it ever was: The best way to keep a man honest is to remove the temptation.

This can be achieved by (1) making it difficult for the employee to steal and (2) making it clear that if he tries to steal there is a good chance he will be caught and punished.

In general, employees divide into three classifications:

1. The person who is determined to steal and will take every seemingly safe opportunity to do so. This hard-core incorrigible comprises a relatively small percentage of the work force.

2. The person who will not steal under any circumstances. This group, unhappily, may be smaller than most managers would like to believe.

3. The tightrope walker. This employee can be swayed one way or the other. He belongs to what is by far and away the largest group.

It would be wishful thinking to believe that there is a 100 percent cure for the malady of employee dishonesty. But if management is sufficiently concerned about the problem to install a tight, professionally planned security system, it will succeed in keeping that third group honest and in keeping members of the first group off the payroll. Management could do no greater service to its stockholders, to the economy as a whole, to the community, and most particularly to the members of the third group.

In keeping the third group honest, there is no question that good working conditions, fair treatment, and a well-ordered program of training and development are vital contributing factors. But they are no substitute for a system designed effectively to control and detect theft. Case after case proves that even in the best-managed and most paternalistic corporations, employee dishonesty is likely to flourish if adequate measures are not taken to safeguard against it.

Case histories of Management Safeguards, Inc., reveal:

A shipping foreman with nine years' tenure smuggled cases of shoes into his car because employees were permitted to park near the platform.

A trusted porter in a large electronics corporation doubled his income by admitting thieves to the plant after hours. There were no time locks.

A metals company manager supplemented his income by $12,000 a year by labeling top-grade product as "unsalvageable" and selling it at scrap prices. There was no audit of waste percentages.

This list could continue almost indefinitely.

DETECTION METHODS

Devices. There are various detection devices on the market designed to catch dishonest employees in the acts of stealing, making theft plans, or describing theft exploits to others. Some companies install one-way mirrors to observe employees on the job. Others put in one-way TV for the same reason. Some place hidden microphones in rest rooms or around work areas. Although effective in some measure, devices of this type tend to create a furor among trade unions and other organizations whose concern about privacy outweighs their concern for the protection of company assets. Suffice it to say, such concern for privacy is not without its effect on the nation's courts and legislators.

Undercover Detection. Far more effective—and much less obvious—is the prevention and investigation of employee crime by undercover investigators posing as regular employees.

The investigative job is best done on an objective and impersonal basis by an outside organization. The undercover operative placed by a qualified and reputable investigative agency is a skilled and well-trained professional. He knows all the "tricks of the trade." He knows what to look for, where to look, and what steps to take to trip up the hard-core thief. His single function is clear-cut: to investigate and uncover employee dishonesty and to alert management on his findings.

Once the theft is uncovered—and it is in a surprisingly high percentage of companies—the follow-up action proceeds along practical and well-defined lines.

The dishonest employee (or employees—there are often several) is apprehended in the presence of a police officer, usually with the goods on his person or in his home or car. After being informed of his rights, the thief is questioned by a skilled and discreet interrogator. A statement is obtained.

Once this is achieved, full or partial recovery of the company's loss is made or proof of loss is furnished so that insurance claims may be collected.

PLANT ACCESS CONTROL OF PERSONNEL AND VEHICLES

Employee Identification. In a small plant with a small number of employees, access may be satisfactorily controlled on a personal-recognition basis. The larger plant calls for more positive control. Here, to enter, the employee should wear a badge or be required to show an ID card. The badge does not have to be elaborate. But it should be easy to read and difficult to alter. It should include a good photo likeness of the bearer and a clearly visible identification number, along with the signature of an authorizing official.

In large plants, it is desirable for badges to be color-coded, each color authorizing admittance to specified areas or sections only. For the badge system to afford the desired protection, a rigid control must be set up and enforced. Care must be taken when an employee resigns or is terminated, to see that his badge is turned in and invalidated.

Visitor Identification. A visitor should never be permitted to enter a plant without first getting clearance from the guard or receptionist on duty. Normally, the first move will be for the person at the desk to telephone the individual being visited. Then, if the visit is in order, the visitor is asked to sign a plant register, establishing his identity, affiliation, and the person visited. It is then desirable to issue a special visitor's badge or pass. Often, depending on the plant's layout and size, it is useful to issue a color-coded badge denoting the area he is authorized to visit. When the visitor is ready to enter the premises, he should be escorted by a member of the guard force, by the individual being visited, or by a person representing this individual.

Area Control. Steps must also be taken to keep tabs on personnel movement *within* the plant. Restricted areas should be spelled out in writing, and boundaries made clear to employees, visitors, and guards. Employees who leave before the normal quitting time should hand over "early work passes" to the exit guard. Employees or visitors who remain in the plant after hours should be permitted to do so by pass authorization only. And upon leaving, the register should be signed and exit time noted.

Vehicle Control. One of the most common theft methods is to conceal merchandise in vehicles leaving the plant area. Here is a checklist of precautions which will safeguard against such loss:

Keep an extra-close surveillance on vehicles permitted within the plant enclosure. This includes trucks, railroad cars, and employee and visitor automobiles. If possible, locate employee parking facilities outside the plant area.

Employees permitted to park within the plant confines should be issued parking permits. Many companies require employees to sign a statement authorizing a vehicle search at the personnel department's discretion. This serves as a fine psychological deterrent against using vehicles to steal company property.

Require a pass for all trucks entering the plant area, and/or have the guard maintain a log to register the date; time in and out; trucking company name; truck make and license number; truck's origin and plant destination; driver's signature and license number; helper's signature; and signature of the plant employee receiving the shipment. Passes, turned in at departure, should be kept on file in the plant for three months.

Sealed trucks, incoming or outgoing, should be carefully checked to make sure the seal was not tampered with.

SECURITY MEASURES OF PROVED EFFECTIVENESS

There are a great many positive steps a company can take to assure adequate plant protection. A selected sampling of key measures has been compiled and is here presented.

1. Make unannounced, nonroutine spot checks of vulnerable theft areas from time to time. Typical examples: inspections of material slated for the junk heap; car and locker inspections; surprise inventories of tools and materials; inspection of employee lunch boxes, handbags, lockers, and work areas; surprise checks to assure that guards are alert and doing their job. Nonroutine security checks keep employees guessing and guards on their toes. The dishonest employee takes special pride in his skill at beating the system. His strongest ally is his anticipation and dependence upon set patterns of operation. If he knows exactly when the guard will make his rounds, when the supervisor will check his operation, or when the accountant will audit the records, he will be able to plan his theft accordingly.

NOTE: The unannounced spot check is a key tool of the skilled undercover investigator. Part of his job is to test the existing security system to make sure no violations are taking place.

2. Make a periodic premises check to assure that alarms and other protection systems and devices have not been tampered with and are operating as intended.

3. Check perimeter fences for breaks or holes. Check for the possibility of dishonest persons throwing merchandise over fences into overgrown areas for later recovery or transferring merchandise to people or vehicles outside the fence.

4. Deliberately pull invoices and other number-controlled documents from batches and files to determine if their absence is properly noted.

NOTE: It is the experience of undercover investigators who make this test in the regular course of their operation that, in 78 percent of the cases, the absence of the pulled documents is not brought to supervisory attention.

5. Keep the number of plant exits in use to a minimum. Channel employees through a single, supervised point of departure if possible. Keep unused exits locked or adequately controlled by alarms.

6. Restrict the presence of employee packages and personal belongings from work areas. Require package passes for all outgoing parcels, merchandise purchases, and the like. Once the package has been inspected and the pass issued, the package should be sent to the employee's point of departure for his pickup as he leaves the plant.

7. Make sure perimeter fences and internal areas where valuables are stored are adequately covered by alarm protection. Make sure protection devices and systems are up to date.

NOTE: Undercover security checks show many companies to be operating with outdated alarm systems. Many of these systems contain wire connections that are easy to jump. Any alarm more than fifteen years old should be checked and, if necessary, rewired with improved wire and hardware.

8. Make sure that exits, perimeter areas, and high-security sections are well lighted during hours of darkness. Arrange floodlights so that guards or police will be aided in their apprehension of trespassers.

9. Make sure safe combinations are not made available to unauthorized persons. Keep a written record of individuals who have combinations, keys, or access to places where valuable assets or secrets are kept. Make certain that keys are not kept in a place where unauthorized persons have access to them, however briefly.

10. Make sure the hardware used to lock trucks is welded, not bolted, to the vehicle. In many cases, on trucks presumably sealed, the driver merely unbolts the entire unit, removes the merchandise, and then restores the unit.

11. In many companies dock areas are hotbeds of theft. Make sure docks are adequately staffed with guard and supervisory personnel.

NOTE: Undercover investigators pay special attention to guards and supervisors, who, experience shows, are occasionally as prone to dishonesty as others.

12. Provide proper clearance and bonding for all employees entrusted with the handling of cash, valuable assets, and company secrets.

13. Make provisions for close supervision of the accumulation and disposal of scrap materials and trash.

14. Conduct frequent audits of shipping and receiving procedures.

15. Make certain no article of value leaves the premises without a numbered document authorizing its removal. Do not permit privileged employees or executives to violate this rule.

16. Set up the responsibility and division of duties in such a way that no employee ever has full control over any transaction. Good systems and procedures call for the automatic verification of one employee's work by another without an overlapping of effort.

17. Keep to a minimum the accumulation of regular, damaged, or to-be-returned merchandise in shipping and receiving areas or on docks.

18. Make information available on a "must have" basis only. The more individuals exposed to vital facts about formulas, product design, new-product plans, cash on hand, and the like, the greater the risk of theft. Only those who need such information to fulfill their business functions should be permitted access to it. This applies particularly to information concerning the nature of the security system itself and protective techniques used. The more mystery surrounding the plant security setup, the better.

SECURITY PERSONNEL

The Top Man. It is of prime importance that the man selected to head up the security program be knowledgeable regarding plant protection techniques. He should also have a good basic understanding of the law as it applies to security considerations such as apprehension, arrests, interrogation, and company and individual rights.

In addition, the security chief must be the kind of person who commands respect from both his subordinates and other employees. He should inspire confidence, know how to use tact, and be skilled at handling people.

Because the security effort does not directly contribute to profits, there is a tendency on the part of some managements to underrate the job. This is a mistake. The security chief plans and implements the plant protection program. He hires the guard force. He assigns duties, supervises the preparation of written procedures and regulations, plans and either conducts or supervises staff training.

Before filling this key management post, the character, reputation, background, and past record of the applicant should be thoroughly investigated. The security

officer should be physically fit and well groomed.   His bearing and appearance
should provide a fine example for his staff to follow.

The Guard Force.   Because a plant is quantitatively well covered with guards
does not mean it is adequately protected.   The quality of guard personnel is
of utmost importance.   In many companies visited, undercover investigators have
found as much dishonesty among protection personnel as among regular personnel.   The problem of "Who is watching the policeman?" is a serious one indeed.

Case Example.   A nationally known electronics company instituted an investigation of an inventory-shortage problem.   Findings revealed that the company's
guard force was 25 percent *larger* than necessary.   Most of the guards were
near retirement age.   They were primarily employees taken from jobs which
had grown too strenuous for them to handle.   In short, the guard force served
mainly as the company pasture where long-time employees were let out to graze.

Undercover investigators quickly learned that these men resented their assignments.   They regarded guard duty as a comedown in prestige and responsibility.
In addition to low morale, there existed in many cases a chumminess with
regular employees and long-known cronies.   This proved to be a dangerous
combination.   When a massive theft system was uncovered, the guard force
was found to be involved.   They disregarded standard pass procedures.   Some
even helped employees to remove stolen merchandise from the building.

Following the disclosure, the guard force was completely revamped.   Payroll
costs were slashed $32,000 a year.   Quality was substituted for quantity.

Guard Qualifications.   The guard who is treated and regarded as a second-class
citizen is apt to perform like one.   It is also a fact that the majority of guards
who are underpaid are also underqualified.   The degree of plant protection
often matches the quality of guard selection procedures.   The following checklist
will serve as a guide in the selection and handling of security personnel.

1. *Integrity and character.*   Needless to say, the guard's honesty, moral character, and emotional behavior should be beyond reproach.   As theft cases develop, it sometimes becomes necessary for a guard to testify to establish the
company's right to an insurance claim.   In such a situation, the background
and reputation of the person giving testimony take on special significance.

Before a guard applicant is hired, he should be thoroughly investigated.   Local
and state police (and through them, Federal authorities) should be asked to
check his fingerprints and record for possible previous arrests.   The applicant's
neighbors, previous employers, and teachers should also be questioned.   The
objective is to evaluate his working and living habits.   Special attention should
be paid to possible alcohol or drug addiction.   And an effort should be made
to spot irrational emotional tendencies such as uncontrollable anger—a dangerous
attribute for anyone entrusted with a gun.

NOTE: The incidence of alcoholism is high in cases of theft involving a guard
force.   In one company, a guard turned his back for years to the removal
of thousands of dollars worth of merchandise.   His only reward was a bottle
of whiskey each time his eyes conveniently failed him.

2. *Intelligence.*   Extensive formal education is not a key guard requirement,
but innate intelligence and a suspicious nature are.   The qualified guard is mentally alert and responsively observant.   He has the common sense and presence
of mind to act swiftly and decisively when the occasion demands.

3. *Physical fitness.*   A guard's effectiveness is measured largely by his ability
to respond to a situation involving a plant break-in or a criminal's apprehension.
To cope with such emergencies, he must be able to handle himself physically.
Neither his vision nor his hearing should be impaired.

4. *Courtesy and personal appearance.*   The guard who commands respect

serves as an effective dishonesty deterrent.   Respect is considerably heightened by the well-groomed man who conducts himself with dignity and acts courteously. This becomes especially important for the guard who comes into contact with the public.

5. *Age.*   Many security officers will not hire a guard who is under 25 years old.   There are exceptions, of course, to every rule.   But, in general, the man under 25 would find it difficult to command the amount of respect or shoulder the degree of responsibility which the job demands.

The Uniform.   Just as a police officer's uniform adds to the measure of his authority, so does a guard's.   The uniform should be clean, well fitting and well pressed, and smartly worn.   Many companies cut costs by hiring guards of a specified height and build (usually from 5 feet 9 inches to 6 feet tall).   This allows for an interchangeability of uniforms, cutting down on purchase needs.

Guard Supervision.   It is customary for the guard or watchman making his rounds after hours to be equipped with a portable clock.   This controls his time and assures that he is visiting the right places at the right hours.   Here is the way the system works: A key is kept at each location on the guard's round.   As he reaches the point, he inserts the key in the clock.   This records on a tape stored within the tamper-proof clock the time the station was visited. At the end of the shift, the guard turns his clock over to a supervisor for examination.

The central reporting system is another effective way to supervise guard activities.   With this service in force, the guard contacts a headquarters station at predetermined intervals.   The advantage is obvious.   If the guard does not report in when he is supposed to, headquarters immediately checks into the reason.

Many plants are too small to warrant an elaborate guard force or night patrol system.   In such cases, it is often a good idea to arrange with local police, or with a commercial protection agency, for the guard to check in at regular intervals.   If no call is received, an investigation is made to find out why.

NOTE: In a number of cases, it has been found that after-hours theft is perpetrated in collusion *with* the guard.   Often, if a guard is on duty, the tendency is for management caution to relax.   Employees are permitted to work late, whereas otherwise, different arrangements would be made.   It is the feeling among many security managers that unless extra-shift work demands the presence of a guard, it is preferable to have *no guards* on duty.   The reasoning is that the best protection against unlawful entry of an unoccupied building is an effective, up-to-date security system.   Such a building would be safeguarded by a sensitive alarm network which signals an immediate response to a protection control center when a presence on the premises is detected.

LEGAL CONSIDERATIONS

Guards, when appointed, are usually deputized or assigned special police powers and authorized to carry firearms.   It is essential that each member of the guard force understand the legal implications and limitations of such power. Judges and juries are highly sympathetic to complaints of personal-rights violation.   Civil suits stemming from allegations of false arrest, defamation of character, undue force, and the like run high.

State laws vary.   In shaping plant policy, it is wise for the security director to confirm his directives with legal counsel or properly constituted police authorities.   However, the following checklist of legal considerations serves as a useful summary guide to guard rights and restrictions.

1. If the guard is not granted police powers, the only arrest he is authorized to make—except in rare circumstances—is a "citizen's arrest" following the commission of a crime in his presence.

2. The police-authorized guard may make an arrest without warrant if he has reasonable assurance that the suspect committed a felony. Evidence in such cases should be substantial.

3. When an arrest is made, the apprehended person should be told why, and by what authority, he is being taken into custody.

4. A guard is authorized to make an arrest, or assist in an arrest, when he is doing so at the request of a duly constituted peace officer.

5. He may make an arrest without a warrant in the event of a misdemeanor, provided an act of violence is involved or the arrest is necessary to prevent injury, damage, or disturbance.

6. If the guard receives a complaint regarding the commission of a misdemeanor, he may make an arrest if he has good reason to believe that the complaint is valid and that, if he fails to make the arrest, the suspect will get away or will cause additional personal or property damage.

7. If a juvenile is involved in a minor misdemeanor, he should be turned over to his parents or guardian. In case of arrest, his parents should be notified at once.

8. If he requires it, an arrested person should be given medical attention as quickly as possible.

9. If a person is mistakenly taken into custody, he should be freed as soon as the error is noted, and asked to sign a release form. Such signature must be obtained freely, and not coerced. The signed release, judiciously obtained, has served to protect many companies against subsequent legal action which, upon second and more prolonged thought, the employee might have instituted.

10. Force with intent to kill should be used only to *prevent* major crimes such as murder, rape, armed robbery, and kidnapping, or if the use of deadly force is essential to the protection of the guard's own life.

11. The only time an employee should be searched is when the guard is *certain* the employee has stolen goods *on his person*. In such case, the search should be preceded by formal arrest. It is a personal-rights violation to search a person for evidence of stolen goods or to confirm a suspicion that stolen goods *may* be on his person. Suffice it to say that the courts deal harshly with such violations.

12. A suspect may be legally searched if his permission is freely given in advance. If such is the case, it is preferable to obtain a signed waiver statement.

13. Many companies conduct regular or periodic locker, lunch-box, and hand-bag searches to detect and deter theft. Where such searches are used, the company's right to conduct them should be spelled out in writing in the company rules.

14. When it is desirable to search an employee's home in an effort to track down stolen goods, it may be done in either of two ways: (*a*) with the assistance of local police authorities and the possession of a warrant; (*b*) with the written permission of the party under investigation.

Interrogation. The purpose in questioning a suspect is to obtain a signed statement of confession. Interrogation is a delicate art. Often, only a seasoned professional can secure the desired information relating to extent of theft and the involvement of other people.

Case Example. An undercover investigator found proof that a toy company shipping employee had stolen, on two separate occasions, merchandise amounting to $42. The company's inventory shortage was considerable, and a skilled interrogator questioned the man. The interrogation took two hours. It led to the disclosure of an employee theft ring involving nineteen people, outside truckers, and outside warehousemen. The thefts had been taking place over a three-year period, and involved more than a quarter of a million dollars. Recovery in claims and repossessed merchandise was more than half this amount.

In questioning a suspect, extreme tact must be used. The individual must be informed of his rights. He must be given to understand that information is being freely given and that he is allowed to leave at any time. The skilled interrogator knows how to convince the suspect that it is in his best interest to remain and pour out his story.

Each statement made by the suspect should be signed and witnessed. If more than one sheet of paper is required, each sheet should be signed by the confessor. For the proper statement format and text, see Figure 16-1.

PROTECTION EQUIPMENT AND DEVICES

There are innumerable systems, machines, and devices on the market designed to improve and tighten plant security. They range from simple mechanisms costing a few dollars to intricate electronic systems costing thousands. The seasoned security officer is well acquainted with the various types of protective equipment. However, inventions and breakthroughs proliferate rapidly in this business. It is largely a matter of staying abreast of manufacturer's literature and security trade journal articles and advertising to learn what is new and interesting on the market. But the following selected items offer a good sampling of the kind of equipment available. The trick is to tailor the hardware to the specific requirements of the plant in question. Size, location, number of personnel, and type of product and industry are all important considerations.

Master-key System. This is an exceptionally effective protective aid. A master-key setup is best planned and installed with the help and guidance of the lock company. When emergency strikes, the protection officer usually needs swift access to a given area. Minutes could mean the difference between finding a thief on the scene and finding an empty safe. The value of the master-key system is that it provides single-key access to any lock in the plant and thus eliminates key-searching time.

The system also provides for a control key used to remove or insert any lock core in the plant. Cores are interchangeable. Thus if an individual key is lost and security is threatened, swift and effortless installation of a new core is possible, without the expense of a locksmith. The system also includes as many submaster keys as required for specified lock groupings, and a virtually unlimited number of individual keys.

Sequence Lock System. Especially where no perimeter alarm system is in operation, every precaution must be taken to ensure that all exits are locked at night and on weekends. One effective safeguard is the sequence lock system. Under this arrangement, each lock is furnished with two keyholes. A key inserted in the first keyhole releases another key to be used in the next lock, and so on down the line. This arrangement makes it impossible to overlook the locking of any exit.

SECURITY TIP: Any door leading out of the plant should require double-key operation—a separate key to open it on each side.

Emergency Exit Control. It is not enough to equip emergency doors with buzzers that sound while doors are open. The buzzer—or preferably, a piercing alarm signal—should sound while the door is open, but it should be silenced only upon insertion of the proper key. If desired, such alarms may be bypassed

Month, day, year

MAIN STREET MANUFACTURING CO.
Main Street
Anytown, U.S.A.

My name is James Blank and I live at 280 Union Street, New York City.
I have been employed by the Main Street Manufacturing Company for
almost five years.

I started stealing merchandise from the Main Street Manufacturing Company three or four months after I began working for the company. Since
then I have been stealing two or three times a week. The last time I
stole merchandise was last Thursday, when I bought four gidgets from
the company and then added six stolen gidgets to the package. Also, on
Tuesday of last week I stole eight gidgets and on Monday I stole four
gidgets. All of the merchandise I stole I later sold to Sam Brown who
has a gidget store at 628 Hudson Avenue.

In addition, I helped the porter Bob steal by passing full cartons of
stolen gidgets to Mr. White, the freight elevator operator, and I
brought Bob some of the goods from stock that he wanted to steal. I
passed stolen goods to Mr. White for Bob seven or eight times in the last
six months. I believe Bob was selling them to a guy named Herb Black,
who lives in a house next to mine.

Almost all employees have been stealing gidgets from Main Street Manufacturing Company. I have seen the following employees stealing from
the company:

Joseph Hacker	Lilly Mae Torres
Kenny Thorn	Felix Ortez
George Combs	Anna Anthony
Milton Johnson	

I have personally stolen about $24,000 worth of merchandise from Main
Street Manufacturing Company. I am very sorry for stealing all the
merchandise over the past few years and would like to make restitution
to the company.

I make this statement freely. No threats or promises were made to me.
I have read this statement carefully. It is true and correct.

_____

James Blank

Witnessed by:

_____

_____

FIG. 16-1.   *Sample interrogation statement.*

by authorized key-bearing personnel. Alarms may also be set up to signal a
remote security station when a door is opened.

Perimeter Alarm System. This equipment is designed to signal an intruder's
presence to a central control station, a private protection agency, or the police
department.

Internal High-security System. This equipment includes a panel of buttons
(used instead of keys) to open doors electronically. If the intruder, while
experimenting, presses the wrong combination of buttons, the system will go

dead. This may also be hooked up to touch off a signal alerting the police department or a protection agency.

TV Security Setup. TV systems are available which cover an entire plant. With sonic detection included, unexpected sounds may be sensed and expected sounds canceled out. In addition to being visual and sonic, a system may be designed to detect the presence of smoke or a rise in temperature. It may also double as part of the communications network, and be wired to flash signals to remote security stations.

Robbery Surveillance Cameras. These come small and compact, and they are easily concealed. Such cameras may be set up to record activity in or out of vaults and other restricted areas. The springing of an alarm will activate the operating mechanism.

The Polygraph. If used, polygraph or lie-detector tests should be administered with special care and discretion. The equipment is outlawed in some states, and serious opposition to its use has been registered by many unions and civil rights organizations. Says the head security officer of a multiplant manufacturer: "The polygraph is of value as a psychological deterrent, and it serves as an excellent interrogative aid. However, its usefulness is limited by a bad press, negative reactions by many legislators and jurists, and most important, by its adverse effect on employee morale."

BIBLIOGRAPHY

Davis, John R., *Industrial Plant Protection,* Charles C Thomas, Publisher, Springfield, Ill., 1957.

Gocke, B. W., *Practical Plant Protection and Policing,* Charles C Thomas, Publisher, Springfield, Ill., 1957.

Schurman, E. A., *Plant Protection,* Cornell Maritime Press, Inc., Cambridge, Md., 1942.

MARKETING MANAGEMENT

CHAPTER ONE

The Total Marketing Concept

JOHN R. SARGENT   *Partner, Cresap, McCormick and Paget, New York, New York*

The terms "total marketing concept" and "integrated marketing" have come to be used synonymously; yet in actuality, the integration of the marketing function represents a limited though important aspect of implementing the marketing concept. The total marketing concept itself goes far deeper, for it concerns the basic philosophy of the ownership and the managers for running a business.

Adoption of the total marketing concept means that the fundamental strategies of a business and all aspects of both its longer-term and day-to-day management decisions are based on a thorough understanding of the needs and desires of the customers who compose the market. To state this in another way: Under the total marketing concept, the corporate objectives are established and the business managed with the sole purpose of making and selling what the customer wants, in the way he wants it, when and where he wants it, and at a price he is willing to pay.

On the surface, this seems so logical and reasonable (and not particularly earthshaking) that it raises the question of why there has been so much discussion of the total marketing concept as an innovation in the business scene.

DEVELOPMENT OF THE TOTAL MARKETING CONCEPT

A careful look back over the years shows that prior to the early 1950s, very few businesses could in fact be truly designated as marketing or customer oriented. Some were "product" oriented, on the basis of an available raw material or a patented item. A very large number were "production" oriented, on the basis of a particular manufacturing skill. Especially in the early days of United States industry, but also for a major share of the time ever since, the burgeoning economy created markets which were clamoring for products, and the key need was the ability to produce. Of course, it should also be pointed out that, as businesses grew larger, even customer-oriented management found it more and more difficult to maintain personal, direct contact with the customers.

It was not until after World War I that the vast increase in productive power of industry, combined with increased sophistication in managerial techniques, led to greater thought on the part of company managements about what customers really wanted. Despite the Depression, market research as a means for accurately evaluating customer wants and desires began its rapid growth in the 1930s. During this period, the managements of many companies, particularly those in consumer-products fields, gave substantially increased attention to marketing considerations in the overall planning and management of their businesses.

After a temporary halt in this trend during World War II, there was a great resurgence of interest in marketing on the part of top management, once shortages resulting from the war had been satisfied. Early in the 1950s, the total marketing concept began to be discussed as "a way of doing business." The General Electric Company was outspoken in its adoption of the "concept," and is often credited with having originated it. A rapidly increasing number of companies, both large and small, began to integrate their marketing functions under a single executive—whether or not the basic philosophy behind the marketing concept had been accepted at the top management level.

Certainly, this integration of marketing functions represented a significant step forward for the great majority of companies who made the move, but where this was not preceded by the fundamental understanding on the part of ownership and management of the place of marketing and the development of a corporate "philosophy," the full advantages of the total marketing concept were not realized.

To derive maximum benefit from the total marketing concept, then, a company must meet two key requirements:

The proper understanding and attitudes of ownership and management
Integration of the marketing function

OWNERSHIP AND MANAGEMENT UNDERSTANDING AND ATTITUDES

The effective application of the marketing concept starts with a "state of mind" on the part of the owners and managers of a business—taking the customer out of the role of simple sales target and making him the constant focal point for all basic business planning and decision making. As suggested above, too much attention has been given to the mechanics of marketing (for example, functional marketing integration) and not nearly enough to the marketing orientation of the business owners and management.

The leadership of a business stems from the top, so the idea of establishing a dynamic and lasting marketing operation without the complete understanding and collaboration of the owners and the management is usually impossible. Unless, for example, the directors (representing the owners) are marketing oriented, advantageous decisions cannot be made on such fundamentals as the objectives of the business, the guiding policies, capital expenses for facilities, budgets (involving advertising, selling, product development, research, and the like), evaluation of the performance of management, or a myriad of other matters, even including the compensation of top management personnel. Unless company management, in its turn, is marketing oriented, how can it select appropriate personnel and provide leadership to them? How can it determine the proper balance between the marketing function, production, finance, and research and development?

Careful review of the operations of many companies illustrates clearly the essential value of "marketing mindedness" on the part of the owners and top managers; this attitude cannot be "faked" successfully for any length of time. Unless there is a basic understanding and acceptance of marketing principles, decisions will be made that are not consistent with the long-term best interests of the business.

Marketing Orientation at Second and Third Levels. Of great importance are the owners' and the managers' functions in orienting the company's second- and third-line executives on the overall corporate marketing philosophy and the way each major part of the business should work together. Either because there are strong, independent individuals in some divisions and departments, or because of overemphasis on profit centers, some key functions tend to operate as islands within the corporate structure, each with its independent performance goals but without sufficient concern for the profitability of the business as a whole. Production, engineering, financial, and research personnel are not normally marketing oriented. Substantial amounts of management leadership, patience, and direction are required to meld them, along with the head of the marketing function, into a smooth-working team under the total marketing concept.

Essential as it is, achieving "marketing mindedness" in the top echelons of a company where the owners, directors, and management have not had personal experience in, or substantial exposure to, marketing may be a somewhat tedious process (much slower than achieving the organizational integration of marketing functions). Sometimes it is "forced" by competition, with or without the addition or replacement of top-level personnel. Sometimes the chief executive officer comes to recognize the logic and value of the marketing concept and proceeds to reshape the attitudes of his top group.

Unfortunately, the changeover to recognition of the importance of marketing at top levels too often follows the relatively long, slow route of normal executive succession and election of new directors as present directors reach retirement—during which time a company can seriously lose its industry position if its competitors have adopted the marketing concept and put it into practice aggressively.

INTEGRATION OF THE MARKETING FUNCTION

Integration of the marketing function has often been mistaken as the primary, rather than the secondary, element of the total marketing concept. If the concept is understood and accepted by the owners and top management of a business, however, the integration of the marketing function is a logical and necessary step in implementing the concept for maximum success. In Chapter 2 of Section 8, there is a thorough discussion of the various approaches to the organization of marketing. The purpose here is mainly to describe the fundamental principles involved.

"Integration" refers to the combining of all activities related to the effective carrying out of the marketing function under the responsibility and authority of a single executive. Typically, such activities include:

Field sales and sales management

Product service

Sales administration (order handling, and so on)

Marketing personnel (recruiting, sales training)
Marketing research
Advertising and promotion
Product planning

Depending upon the type and size of the business, there may be other activities which properly belong in marketing. For example, some firms have functions such as dealer relations, customer or consumer relations, and distribution planning. In the textile industry, it is not uncommon for production scheduling to be part of the marketing department. In some other businesses, public relations, personnel development, and even long-range planning have been included in marketing's responsibilities, although the advisability of such delegation depends primarily upon the kind of business involved and the type of overall corporate organization employed.

Among the types of activities fully in the marketing area, some can be classed as predominantly "line" and others as "staff." In a number of firms, the line and related activities are grouped under the title "marketing operations" and the staff activities are grouped under the title "marketing services." Marketing operations normally include field sales, product service, sales administration, and marketing personnel; marketing services include market research, advertising and promotion, and product planning. Each company is different, however, and the best organizational arrangement requires "custom" tailoring to the individual company situation.

Where an integrated marketing function is established, very considerable skills are required of the executive selected for this position. It calls for a kind of vision, breadth of managerial skills, and leadership closely related to that of the chief executive. Moreover, in businesses where the "total marketing concept" is accepted, the person in charge of marketing should serve as one of the chief counselors and advisers to the owners and top management executives.

CONCLUSION

Adoption of the total marketing concept can have a fundamental effect on the course of a business. Following are some typical remarks by executives of both large and small companies which have applied the marketing concept on a broad basis.

"Our executives and key personnel have a much better team attitude and understanding of the importance of marketing to our entire business."

"There is broader viewpoint and orientation to customer wants throughout the organization—even on the board of directors."

"We do a better job of making decisions promptly, and we have had fewer costly errors since applying the marketing concept throughout our business."

"Our product and profit planning is vastly improved."

"There is a better balance to our marketing program; we are able to determine the proper roles (and budgets) for selling, advertising and promotion, market research, and even for such things as physical distribution and customer service."

"Among other things, we do a much better internal selling job—which has helped our external marketing stature greatly."

"Adoption of the 'concept' has helped in many ways, but one of the most notable achievements to date has been a tremendous improvement in the way we introduce new products to the market."

"The marketing concept helped our entire executive group understand the need for good planning; we have almost eliminated the kind of snap judgments that cost us a small fortune in the past."

"It forced us to clarify our objectives and policies, and that alone has done wonders for the state of mind and cohesiveness of our organization."

Clearly, then, although the total marketing concept should not be regarded as a panacea for all corporate problems, when applied in conjunction with other good management principles and techniques, it can be a force of great benefit to both the short- and long-term success of a business.

BIBLIOGRAPHY

Borch, Fred J., *The Marketing Philosophy as a Way of Business Life*, Marketing Series, no. 99, American Management Association, New York, 1957.

Changing Structure and Strategy in Marketing, University of Illinois Bulletin, vol. 55, no. 58, 1957.

Jewell, James, *The Marketing Concept*, NAM Current Issues Series, no. 2, May, 1958.

Sargent, J. R., "Imaginative Marketing in the Years Ahead," speech, December, 1952; copies available from Cresap, McCormick and Paget, New York.

Togesen, A. A., *The Switch from a Sales to a Marketing Concept*, Marketing Series, no. 96, American Management Association, New York, 1956.

CHAPTER TWO

Marketing Organization

ARNOLD CORBIN *Professor of Marketing, Graduate School of Business Administration, New York University, New York, New York*

The basic principles and problems of business organization, including structure and planning, are treated in Section 2. This chapter will deal with their application to and within the marketing function. The discussion will be limited to the broader aspects of marketing organization.

The meaning and importance of the total marketing concept are dealt with in Chapter 1 of Section 8. In the treatment of marketing organization in this chapter, it is assumed that a customer-orientation philosophy is essential for maximizing the growth and profit of a business enterprise and that the business will strive to organize its marketing activities in accordance with this philosophy.

IMPLICATIONS OF THE TOTAL MARKETING CONCEPT

The organizational implications of the total marketing concept are fairly clear. Most companies that have adopted this marketing concept have realized the wisdom of an integrated organizational approach to ensure a strong, unified marketing effort. Instead of allowing sales, advertising, and other marketing functions to go their own separate, independent ways, these companies have set up people responsible for coordinating and integrating their efforts, in accordance with predetermined objectives, policies, and plans, to ensure that all marketing activities are conducted with the customer viewpoint uppermost in mind. In large, divisionalized companies, this basic responsibility is exercised by the corporate vice president—marketing. It may also be implemented at lower echelons by marketing managers, product managers, and people with other titles but similar duties. In smaller companies, the marketing director or manager assumes the role of integrating the various marketing functions reporting to him.

Obviously, the organization levels at which the integration occurs, the gamut of functions involved, and the titles of the people concerned will vary with the size of firm, the scope and nature of its product line, and other basic factors. Nevertheless, the underlying principle is fundamental to building a sound marketing organization.

Furthermore, under the total marketing concept, all functions in the business, not just marketing, look to the marketplace for guidance. Therefore, marketing, being the closest to the marketplace, must be so organized in relation to the other major functions, that it can provide the leadership and direction that are implicit in acceptance of the total marketing concept as a way of business life.

FACTORS INFLUENCING MARKETING ORGANIZATION

Proper organization of the marketing function is dependent upon careful analysis and evaluation of a large number of variables, both external and internal.

External Factors. External factors lie outside the company itself, but may exert a strong influence on the type of marketing organization. They fall into three main categories: business environment, markets, and customer requirements and expectations.

Business Environment. The type of environment the firm must operate within influences not only its marketing objectives and strategy, but its organization for implementing them. For example, there can be considerable difference in functional emphasis depending on whether its products are marketed to ultimate household consumers or to business firms. In the former context, the need for preselling in mass markets and the perennial struggle for shelf space in retail stores tend to give advertising and sales promotion organizational prominence. On the other hand, industrial marketing organizations tend to put more emphasis, relatively, on such functions as technical service.

Another environmental factor may be the nature of the particular requirements for success in a particular business—for example, styling and distribution in the automobile industry; cost control and selling a planned mix of products in the steel sheet and rod business; and price, distribution, and product advantages in the replacement tire business. These requirements relate to planning the marketing organization, because they point up the key activities that must be carried on and provide insights into what basic arrangements of activities are most appropriate.

Another environmental influence is the rate of change in the industries being served. If it is high, it may require more frequent corresponding changes in marketing organization than if it is relatively low. The nature and length of channels of distribution and the competitive structure are other environmental variables that must be weighed.

Markets: Size, Scope, Nature, and Location. The nature of a company's markets has a strong impact on the type of marketing organization set up. Thus, when there are relatively few markets, it facilitates a market-oriented structure; when there are a large number of market groups involved, it makes a product-oriented organization more feasible. Markets covering a wide expanse of territory often require some form of geographical organization; more compact markets may not. The number of customers, their frequency of purchase, size of order, degree of service required, and other characteristics are also determinants that shape the ultimate form of the marketing organization.

Customer Requirements and Expectations. The requirements and expectations of the customer may also influence marketing organization. For example, there are certain developments in buying practices that can best be taken advantage of by a market-oriented structure, according to Robert W. Lear, vice

president of marketing, The Carborundum Company.[1] In proof of his point,
he cites the following:

1. Increasing central control of the purchasing function in large companies.

2. Such allied developments as annual contracts, blanket orders, "stockless
purchasing," and price protection coverage

3. Pressures by giant wholesalers, retail chains, and buying syndicates for
special deals and services

4. Unique buying and contracting procedures employed by the government

5. Customers increasingly interested in having the seller's salesmen funnel
back their problems for solution by their suppliers

All these trends, Lear contends, demand a market-oriented approach to
organization.

Internal Factors. Internal factors may be conveniently treated under three
basic groupings: top management philosophy, products, and people.

Top Management Philosophy. Whether good or bad, explicit or implicit,
management's attitudes and value judgments with respect to such concepts as
individual versus group action, paternalism, "by the book" versus "free wheeling,"
and centralization versus decentralization have an important bearing on organizational planning. For example, if management has traditionally held a tight
rein on decision-making authority, it would be hard to follow a decentralization
approach.

Product Policy. The width of the product line is often an organizational
determinant. As product offerings become increasingly diverse, there is a tendency to move away from a straight functional approach to a product-group
approach, or some combination of the two. If company policy dictates increasing
emphasis on new products and entry into new markets, a shift from a purely
functional setup to a more product- and market-oriented organizational structure
may be in order.

People. Manpower considerations are an important factor in organization
planning. As Lazo and Corbin have pointed out,[2] human values are critical;
proper decisions cannot be made without due regard for the people involved—
their type, number, qualifications, capabilities, responsibilities, personalities, attitudes, fears, suspicions, ambitions, and a host of other intangible, but important,
related factors. Any organization must therefore, be tailored, to a degree, to
the people who will have to make it work. On the other hand, one should
not necessarily sacrifice the optimum organizational approach merely because
of the limitations of the people involved. Perhaps the best solution is to accept
a less-than-ideal transitory stage for the present, but work toward the preferable
arrangement as people are developed.

ACTIVITIES TO BE ORGANIZED

The activities and functions to be fitted into the marketing organization will
obviously vary considerably from company to company. Some firms enumerate
as many as forty functional components of the marketing function; others may
slot them into far fewer categories. Much depends upon the size of the company; its product lines, customers, and markets; interpersonal power relationships; stage of evolution toward the marketing concept; and a host of other
factors.

[1] Robert W. Lear, "No Easy Road to Market Orientation," *Harvard Business Review*,
September–October, 1963.

[2] Hector Lazo and Arnold Corbin, *Management in Marketing*, chap. 3, "Organizing
for Marketing," McGraw-Hill Book Company, New York, 1961.

At a very minimum, the marketing organization should embrace such activities as sales, advertising, sales promotion, and marketing research, which is being "broken out" as a separate function in more and more companies.[3] In many firms, including the General Electric Company, product planning is also considered a marketing function, one that works very closely with marketing research. Where it is a factor in maintaining customer goodwill, product service may also be an element in the mix of marketing functions. And under a fully expanded concept of marketing, such additional activities as finished-goods inventory control, production scheduling (General Electric), and even physical distribution may be included.

Each of these functions may, in turn, embrace a number of subfunctions. Thus, the product planning function may involve, for new products, such responsibilities as packaging, designing, scheduling (timing), and related activities.

It is clear that the gamut of marketing functions and subfunctions challenging the organizational planner may be wide and varied. The more activities involved, the more difficult it becomes to integrate them into a smoothly operating organizational entity. It is logical, therefore, to examine next the many alternative forms of organizational structure which may be considered in designing an optimum arrangement.

TYPES OF MARKETING ORGANIZATION

The broad range of factors which influence marketing organization, and the many kinds of marketing functions involved, make it apparent that there is a correspondingly wide variety of forms of organizational structure. Hence, it is rare to find two firms whose organizational arrangements are identical. Even within large divisionalized companies, there may be different patterns among the various divisions.

However varied individual company organizations may be, it is possible to characterize most of them as falling into one or more of the following basic general categories: functional, product, market, geographic, or some combination of these.

Functional. Under the functional arrangement, the basic organizational unit is the marketing function, that is, sales, advertising and sales promotion, marketing research, product planning, and so on (see Figure 2-1). The heads of these functions report to a marketing executive who directs and coordinates their activities. This plan can be used by companies of varying sizes. In a large, divisionalized company, it may find applications not only within the divisions, but at the corporate level as well, as a means of structuring the various marketing services or activities on the staff of the vice president—marketing.

This form of organization, which offers the prime advantage of simplicity, may be found most useful when (1) relatively few products are sold in relatively few markets, (2) specialization by function is considered desirable, and (3) it is desired to centralize authority and responsibility in a single marketing executive. As the business grows, products and markets become more diverse. This, in turn, tends to cause strains on a purely functional organization. For example, problems may arise with regard to proper allocations of selling time, advertising appropriations, and other marketing resources among the wider product line. The time may then be ripe to consider one or more of the more sophisticated types of organization described below.

[3] Henry Bund and James W. Carroll, "The Changing Role of the Marketing Function," *Journal of Marketing*, January, 1957.

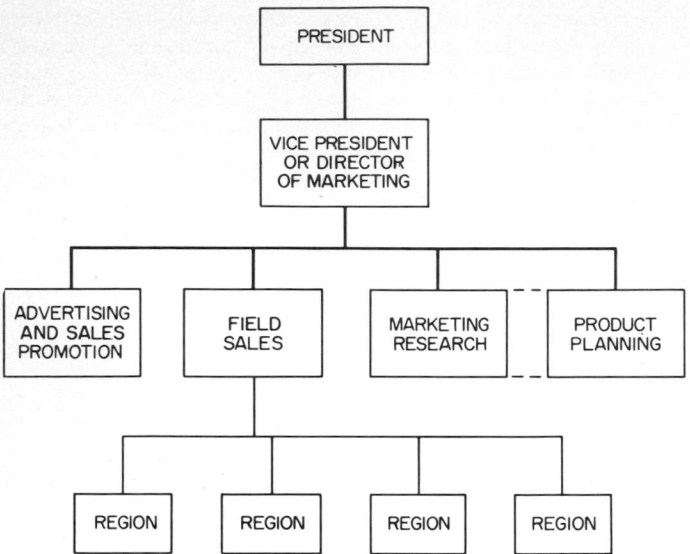

FIG. 2-1. *Simple functional marketing organization.* (*Courtesy of* The Product Manager's Job, *American Management Association, 1964.*)

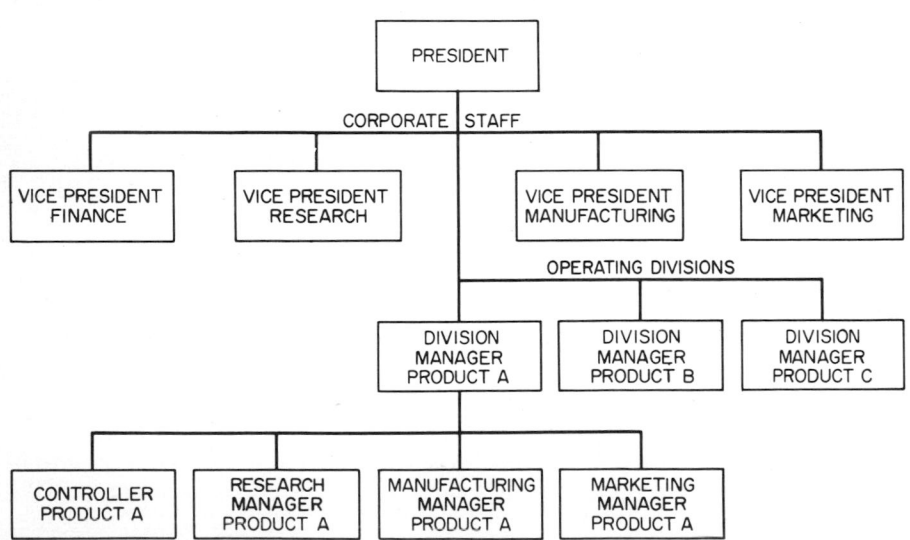

FIG. 2-2. *Separate divisions for complete product specialization.* (*Courtesy of B. Charles Ames,* "*Payoff from Product Management,*" Harvard Business Review, *November–December, 1963.*)

Product. The advantages of specialization become apparent when the product lines of companies expand beyond the point where a simple functional arrangement would be most effective. To be sure that each product receives the attention and support it deserves, management may consider some form of product-line orientation within the marketing organization. Although there are many variations of this type of organization, attention will be focused on four of the most basic patterns: product divisions, product marketing groups, product sales forces, and product managers.

Product Divisions. Under this plan, the company is divisionalized; a separate, self-sustaining unit is organized for each major product or product group, as shown in Figure 2-2. According to B. Charles Ames, of McKinsey & Company, "This is usually the preferred organizational approach when each product group really represents a distinct business which is large enough—or potentially large enough—to support its own production and marketing operations."[4]

Product Marketing Groups. This arrangement sets up separate product marketing units, but keeps manufacturing, research, and finance centralized, as shown in Figure 2-3. "This makes more organizational sense when complete divisionalization is not feasible, but the marketing requirements, for example, advertising, promotion, packaging, and sales, are significantly different for each product."[5]

Product Sales Forces. Instead of separate divisions or marketing groups, the separation under the product sales force plan is confined to sales operations for each product group, with the other marketing functions being performed by functional specialists across the board for all product lines, as shown in Figure 2-4. As under the two preceding plans, manufacturing, research, and finance remain centralized. "This is a more logical approach when separate customer groups must be served, or when the business of each product is too

[4] B. Charles Ames, "Payoff from Product Management," *Harvard Business Review,* November–December, 1963.
[5] *Ibid.*

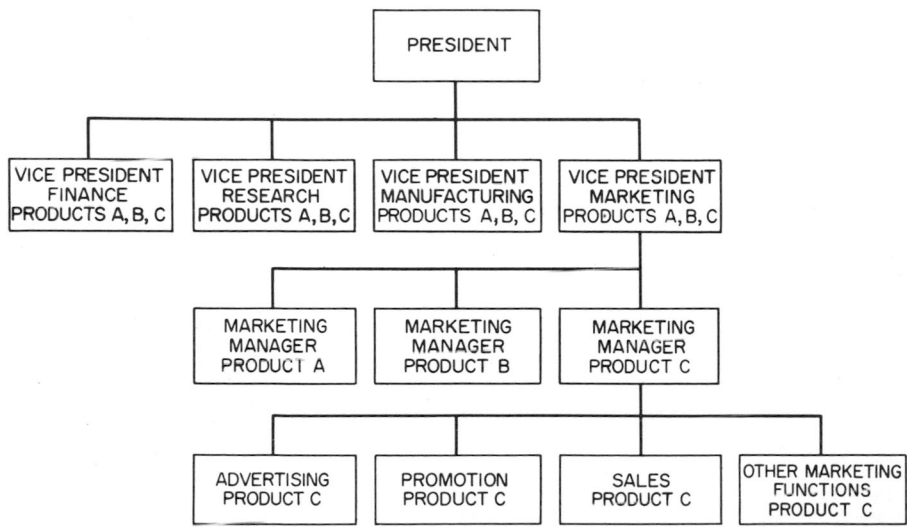

FIG. 2-3. *Separate product marketing groups.* (*Courtesy of B. Charles Ames, "Payoff from Product Management,"* Harvard Business Review, *November–December, 1963.*)

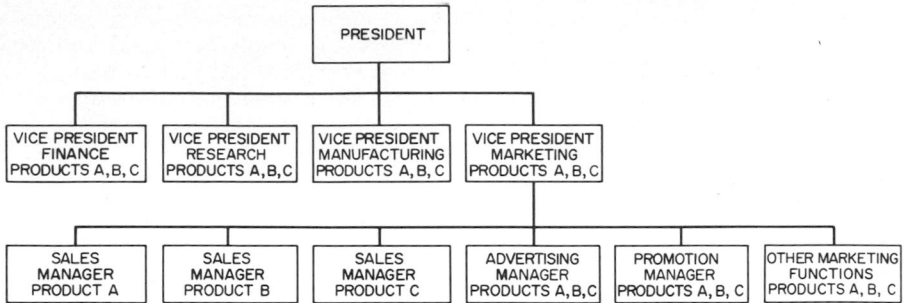

FIG. 2-4. *Separate product sales forces.* (*Courtesy of B. Charles Ames, "Payoff from Product Management," Harvard Business Review, November–December, 1963.*)

small for divisionalization, or when, finally, the only place product specialization is important and practical is in the sales area."[6]

Before discussing the fourth organizational type in this "product" series, product managers, it may be worth noting that, according to Ames, these first three are all valid alternatives to the product manager approach. It is his contention that they are usually easier to use, so that product managers should be set up only when it is not practical, economical, or desirable to employ any of the other three. In his words:

Thus, only in multiproduct companies where physically separated operating divisions, marketing groups, or sales units are not practical, is product management the preferred organizational alternative. In these cases, the product manager provides a means of ensuring individual attention for all major products without separating off any part of the line operations.[7]

Product Managers. In the evolution of modern marketing organization, one of the most interesting and significant developments has been the rapid emergence and acceptance of the product manager concept. The companies that have adopted this concept look upon the product manager as the answer to a long-standing need for a single individual capable of giving undivided attention to the business welfare of a particular product or group of products.

Although there may be a fair degree of agreement among such firms on this basic principle, the number of ways the product management function can be structured within the total organization is almost limitless. It is therefore difficult to illustrate a "typical" product manager organization in chart form. Figure 2-5 should therefore be regarded merely as a conceptual approach which represents the basic structural relationships of the system—a sort of organizational "theme" from which an almost endless number of variations may be developed.

Just as there are many patterns of product management organizational structuring, there is also considerable variation in the nature and scope of responsibilities assigned to the product manager. It is therefore difficult to define the precise role he plays, because it varies so greatly from company to company. And in a sense, it should, because it should be "custom-built" to suit the particular circumstances and needs of each company and each product. Some idea of the wide range of activities and the intricate network of working relationships of product managers in a consumer packaged goods company is shown in Figure 2-6.

[6] *Ibid.*
[7] *Ibid.*

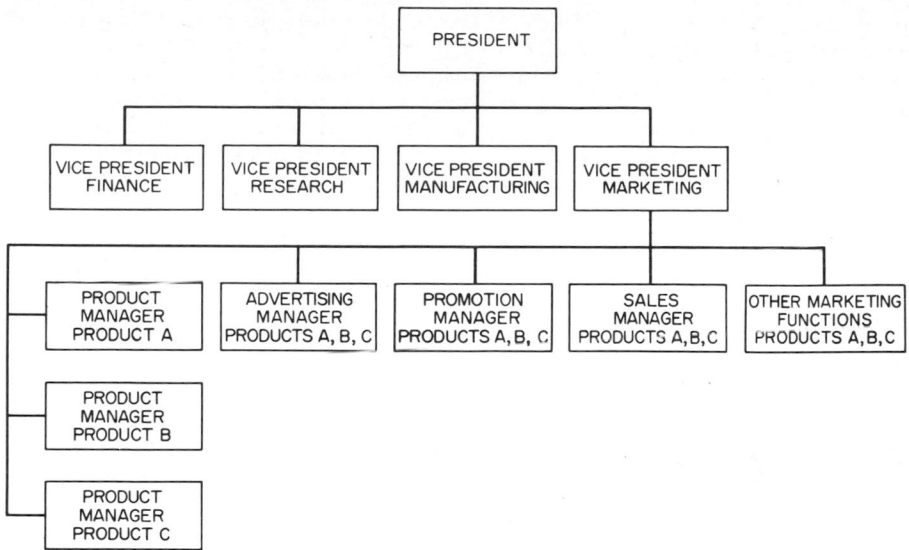

FIG. 2-5. *Product manager organization.* (*Courtesy of B. Charles Ames, "Payoff from Product Management,"* Harvard Business Review, *November–December, 1963.*)

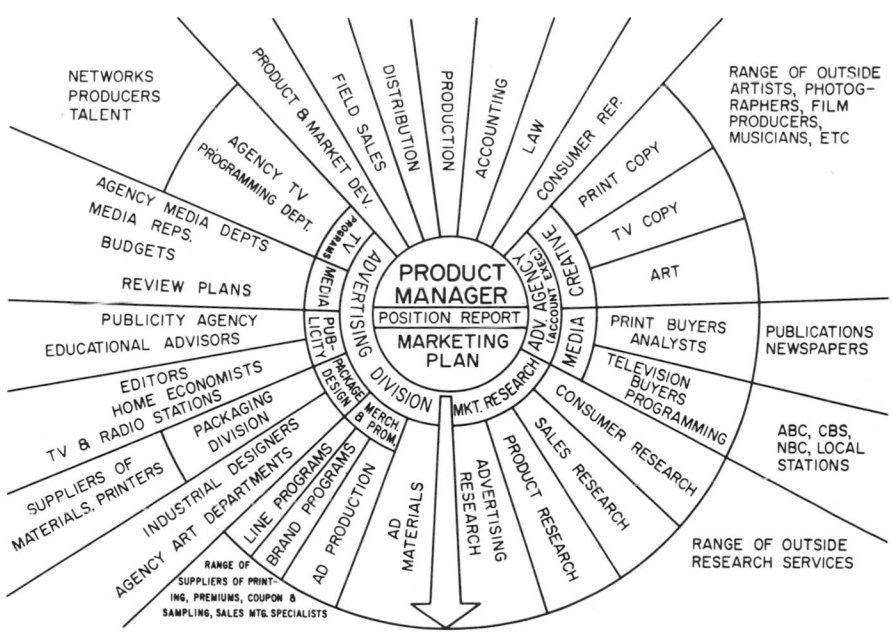

FIG. 2-6. *Sphere of activities and working relationships of Scott Paper Company's product managers.* (*Courtesy of* The Product Manager System, *National Industrial Conference Board, New York, 1965.*)

Despite the growing acceptance of the product manager concept, the product manager still remains a somewhat controversial figure, with considerable differences of opinion existing between executives of those firms who have successfully embraced and employed this organizational approach and their opposite numbers in companies where the concept did not work out well. And ". . . even the strongest proponents of the product manager system acknowledge that finding ways to ensure the most effective use of the position can create some fairly knotty problems."[8]

At the root of the issue lies the disagreement over the degree of authority and responsibility the product manager should possess and exercise. Some of his most enthusiastic proponents regard him as a "little general manager." Less vigorous advocates characterize him as a "passionate persuader."

H. Bruce Palmer, president of the National Industrial Conference Board, has stated the problem quite succinctly:

As planner and coordinator of all major activities related to his assigned product, he has a tough job—and one that remains something of an anomaly. He must generally carry out his mission without having line authority over any of the various company units whose cooperation is essential for the market success of the product.[9]

John W. Enell, director of research of the American Management Association, puts it this way:

Today, the product manager is frequently a high-level planner and coordinator who holds a large share of responsibility for the success of his product or product line.

While he is still regarded as a specialist in the sense that he is an expert on his product and its markets, he has become much more of a generalist than is immediately apparent. The more exuberant advocates of the product manager concept like to speak of him as a "little general manager," but the term can be misleading. He rarely has the authority that such a title implies.[10]

On this key issue of authority and responsibility, Ames makes some good points:

In his relationships with the rest of the organization, the product manager is clearly not a line executive in the classic sense, for he has no line authority. Nor is he staff in the sense of support staff, as are, for example, the market research or advertising managers. The difference is that he does have the unqualified responsibility for seeing that everything related to his product gets done well and on time. His job is to serve as the focal point for planning and coordinating all the activities required for the growth and profitability of his product. . . .

To carry out his role effectively, he must be an expert on all matters relating to his product, both inside and outside the company. He must be able to rely on his superior knowledge, management skills, and sheer persuasiveness to get things planned and accomplished. He has to do this by working through executives who do have line authority. This unique responsibility and these complex relationships with the rest of the management group are what make the product manager an organizational anomaly—and both his responsibility and his set of relationships will be different in every situation.[11]

[8] *The Product Manager System,* Experiences in Marketing Management, no. 8, National Industrial Conference Board, New York, 1965.
[9] *Ibid.*
[10] Gordon H. Evans, *The Product Manager's Job,* Research Study, no. 69, American Management Association, New York, 1964.
[11] Ames, *op. cit.*

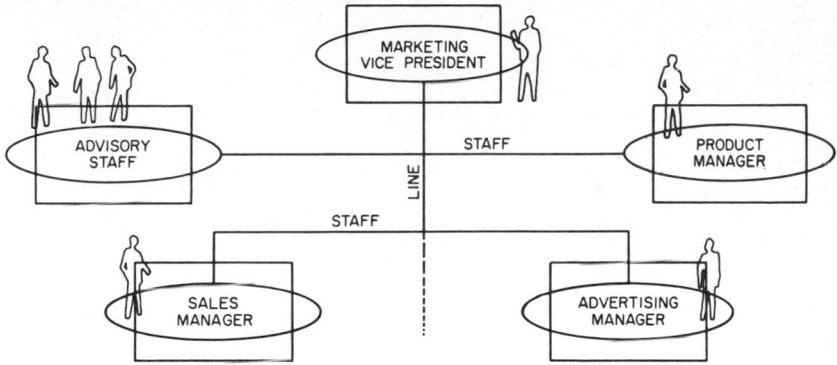

FIG. 2-7. *Two-dimensional organization.* (*Courtesy of David J. Luck and Theodore Nowak, "Product Management—Vision Unfulfilled," Harvard Business Review, May–June, 1965.*)

A key element in facilitating smooth working relationships between the product manager and the heads of the various line functions is the marketing plan. For example, one of his problems is making sure that the field sales force devotes sufficient time and effort to his products. In this context, and assuming a single sales force, he must compete with his fellow product managers for salesmen's time. To ensure optimum allocation of time and effort among all the company's products from the point of view of what is best for the firm as a whole, it is essential that the marketing director review the marketing plans of all the product managers and tailor them so that they allocate company resources optimumly against company objectives. As Sylvester J. Cleary, merchandising manager of the Mennen Company, puts it: ". . . the marketing plan is the core of the product manager's operation."[12]

On this matter of authority commensurate with responsibility, Luck and Nowak feel that for the product manager to be effective, he should be vested with what they call *prescriptive* authority, in contrast to *supervisory* authority. In their words:

The conventional concept of two-dimensional organization admits only vertical (line) and horizontal (staff) relationships. When individuals down the chain of command do not report directly to a product manager, he is depicted as an advisory staff member on a horizontal line. [See Figure 2-7.] The implication is that only the functional managers, such as sales and advertising heads, are vested with decision-making authority.

This view, however, is wholly inconsistent with the concept that a product manager is responsible for the product lines or brands he supervises. It is essential that he have the authority to plan, decide on strategy, and marshal adequate resources to carry out his work. . . .

. . . There are two forms of authority. One is *supervisory* and entails command over personnel. The other is *prescriptive* and involves the power to command resources to implement a program. Prescriptive authority introduces a third dimension into the organization chart. [See Figure 2-8.]

If the product manager is to be effective, he should be vested with prescriptive authority to establish the goals and resources for his products, create distribution and marketing plans, and control his program's execution—subject, of course, to the concurrence of his superiors.[13]

[12] *The Product Manager System, op. cit.*

[13] David J. Luck and Theodore Nowak, "Product Management—Vision Unfulfilled," *Harvard Business Review*, May–June, 1965.

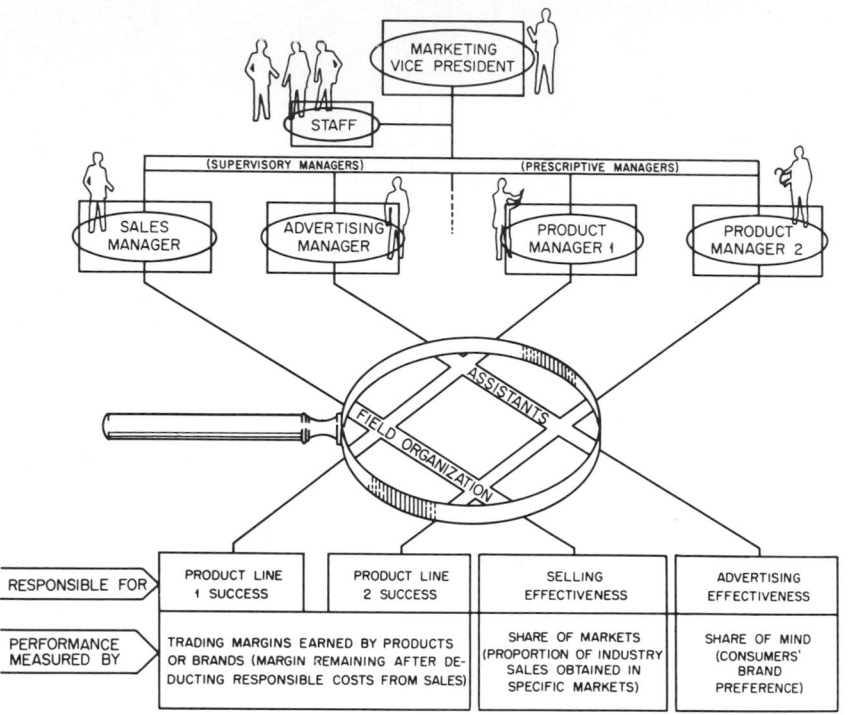

FIG. 2-8. *Three-dimensional organization.* (*Courtesy of David J. Luck and Theodore Nowak, "Product Management—Vision Unfulfilled,"* Harvard Business Review, *May–June, 1965.*)

Market. As companies become increasingly market oriented, there is a tendency to set up organizational units which concentrate on meeting the needs of particular markets, or end-use industries, which purchase many of the company's products. The approach is from the user industry backward, rather than from the product forward. It is generally used when each of these markets is sufficiently differentiated from the others and is potentially large enough to justify special organizational attention, particularly if it requires different marketing strategies, channels of distribution, or technical service. Thus, a manufacturer of consumer goods may be selling his line to retail chains, wholesalers, and institutions. Similarly, a manufacturer of chemicals may be selling the same line of products to several user industries, such as steel, appliances, and automobiles. He might then set up three "industry specialists" or "market managers" to ensure a unified total company marketing effort to take full advantage of the opportunities in each of these markets for all the company's products it may require, regardless of the organizational "home" of each product within the company.

According to Ames, "almost everything that can be said about the product manager applies equally to his organizational first cousin, the market manager.[14] Although the focus of the effort may be different, both are faced with the same organizational problem: getting products to markets without having direct

[14] Ames, *op. cit.*

line authority over the functional heads who must do the actual work of implementing and executing the plans to get the job done.

To Lear, however, it is easier to fit a product manager than a market manager into a product-oriented structure. He cites two possible organizational alternatives when setting up a market manager concept in a multidivisional company: place them within the central, corporate marketing staff, or assign each to the division having the biggest portion of the volume involved, but with supplementary responsibility for serving other divisions too.[15]

Another variant of the market manager approach may be used to implement some forms of "systems selling"—the marketing of a series of related products or processes that make up a single, integrated system or package.

Geographic. This form of organization is most frequently employed when the markets served are widely dispersed and it makes sense to set up separate organizational entities to deal with them as such. Dividing the United States by regions, districts, and territories is a quite common practice among companies marketing nationally, or even regionally. More and more companies have created international divisions or departments, as their businesses have become increasingly "multinational" or "global." On the other hand, purely geographic organizational units are relatively rare: they are usually components of larger organizational entities structured along functional, product, or market lines; and within themselves, they, in turn, may be organized on a functional, product, or market basis, or some combination of these bases.

Combination. This type of organization incorporates a blend of functional, product, and geographic subunits. It is probably the most frequently occurring organizational structure in marketing as product lines and markets served become increasingly complex and diverse.

TRANSITIONAL STEPS TOWARD MARKET ORIENTATION

According to Lear, ". . . few successful companies are yet willing to undergo a full reorganization to achieve complete market orientation, and it usually would not be prudent to do so. A compromise appears to be in order—and this is exactly what most companies are trying to do."[16]

Examples of opportunities for such a gradual "transitional orientation to the marketplace" are many.

Centralized Headquarters. Physically locating all divisional management personnel in the same office encourages managers of different divisions to get together and work out coordinated marketing programs.

Consolidated Field Sales Offices. Consolidated field sales offices encourage joint campaigns, sharing of specialized personnel, and wider-range selling.

Centralized Marketing Staffs. Setting up key marketing functions (advertising, marketing research, and so on) on a centralized basis above the divisional level encourages a coordinated, total-company marketing approach.

Specialized Sales Groups. Specialized sales groups may be set up to sell the products of several divisions to particular market segments. This type of specialized orientation to the market may be by end-use market, by distribution channel, through intermediate distributors, or by geography.

National Accounts Selling. As customers' business operations become increasingly national in scope, companies tend to set up national accounts sales managers who represent all or several divisions and report to the chief marketing executive

[15] Lear, *op. cit.*
[16] Lear, *op. cit.*

or the executive vice president. This is market orientation by individual customer.

Systems Selling. Systems selling encourages market orientation because the "package" often cuts across divisional product lines.

THE CORPORATE VICE PRESIDENT—MARKETING AND HIS STAFF

A comprehensive study by the National Industrial Conference Board of top management organization in divisionalized companies indicates that most of them have large corporate marketing staffs, headed by a vice president who usually reports directly to the president. The purpose of this corporate staff in marketing is:

. . . to extend and expand certain traditional sales and sales support activities, and to give greater emphasis and attention to markets, products, and techniques that go beyond those that might currently exist in the divisions and are beyond the current sales effort. In short, the corporate staff in marketing exists to strengthen and improve the quality and depth of the company's marketing capabilities and potential.[17]

According to the NICB study, the corporate marketing staff units and their types of responsibilities may be classified under five broad categories:

1. *Marketing planning and development,* including marketing research and product planning.

2. *Advertising and promotion* for the company as a whole, and sometimes for the divisions as well. Where the central staff does not actually do the work for the divisions, it usually formulates advertising policies and coordinates and evaluates divisional advertising and promotion.

3. *Customer relations,* which helps divisions do high-level selling to large customers, especially those buying from several divisions.

4. *Executive sales,* which actually sells products of several divisions to specialized customers such as the government, including the military.

5. *Distribution.*

Although these are the most frequently exercised responsibilities of the corporate marketing staff, there are of course major differences in emphasis among companies. Regardless of such variations, however, there is a common thread running through all: ". . . a strong emphasis on overall guidance and coordination of the marketing effort through policy formulation and control. This is one of the major responsibilities of the corporate head of marketing."[18]

The position guides in this Conference Board report reveal additional responsibilities for review and approval of pricing practices, interdivisional sales, government or military sales, product service warranties, and sales compensation program.

As the total marketing concept has become increasingly accepted as a basic business philosophy, many divisionalized companies have construed its organizational implications as demanding the creation of a corporate vice president— marketing and charging the incumbent with responsibility for unifying, integrating, and controlling the total marketing effort as outlined above. However, it is one thing to assign him such a responsibility and quite another for him to implement it successfully through relatively autonomous division general managers who are charged with profit responsibility for their divisions. It sometimes

[17] Harold Stieglitz and Allen R. Janger, *Top Management Organization in Divisionalized Companies,* Studies in Personnel Policy, no. 195, National Industrial Conference Board, New York, 1965.
[18] *Ibid.*

becomes rather difficult for the corporate chief marketing executive to get his ideas accepted by strong-minded, profit-center-oriented division heads, even though the ideas may be in the best interests of the company as a whole.

In a sense, his situation becomes analogous to that of the product manager, who must also try to get his plans implemented by persuading line functional managers to do what he wishes. Although it is fine for the top marketing man and his staff to enunciate corporate marketing policy and to formulate overall marketing plans designed to optimize the company's marketing posture and results, the effort may be an exercise in futility unless he can convince product division management, not only at division headquarters, but also in the field, to operate within the corporate frame of reference. In this sense, his position is somewhat of an organizational anomaly. His success depends greatly on the strength of his interpersonal relationships in dealing with product division management. As a matter of fact, a number of companies have become disillusioned with the concept of a corporate vice president—marketing and have abandoned it after it proved to be unworkable in practice.

It is difficult to say whether the difficulties arise because of the organizational concept itself or the weakness of the incumbents. At any rate, if a company does set up such a position, it is important that the chief marketing executive at the corporate level have at least equal rank and stature with the managers of the operating divisions, and preferably even higher rank because of his "staff" rather than "line" authority. And of course it is essential that he have the complete and unqualified support and backing of the chief executive officer and other members of top management.

PATTERNS OF COMMUNICATION IN MARKETING ORGANIZATION

The types of organization discussed thus far have been essentially formal in nature. Coordination of activities in them is usually achieved through vertical communication between a high-level administrator and heads of the specialized activities which he coordinates. In addition to this vertical method of coordination, there is a second method which, in strong contrast to the first, is based upon a large amount of horizontal communication, particularly by personnel in the specialized areas, through informal organizational channels.

According to Andersen and Cundiff, who conducted some interesting research into this informal communication network,[19] the flow of information through vertical, formal organizational channels consists of statements of policies, plans, budgets, and results. In contrast, the flow of information through horizontal, informal organizational channels occurs through voluntary exchange of copies of correspondence, special-purpose committees, staff meetings, and chance or prearranged executive contacts in offices or at coffee breaks or meals. The contrast between the two types of communication patterns is strikingly demonstrated in Figure 2-9, which was constructed by Professors Andersen and Cundiff. It is clear that the network of horizontal flow of information bears little or no relationship to formal lines of authority, but it "is of major importance in coordinating the marketing activities of the firm." It is also evident that marketing organization planners should bear in mind the necessity for establishing and maintaining clear channels of communication of an informal, horizontal type, as well as the more obvious formal, vertical type.

[19] R. Clifton Andersen and Edward W. Cundiff, "Patterns of Communication in Marketing Organization," *Journal of Marketing*, July, 1965.

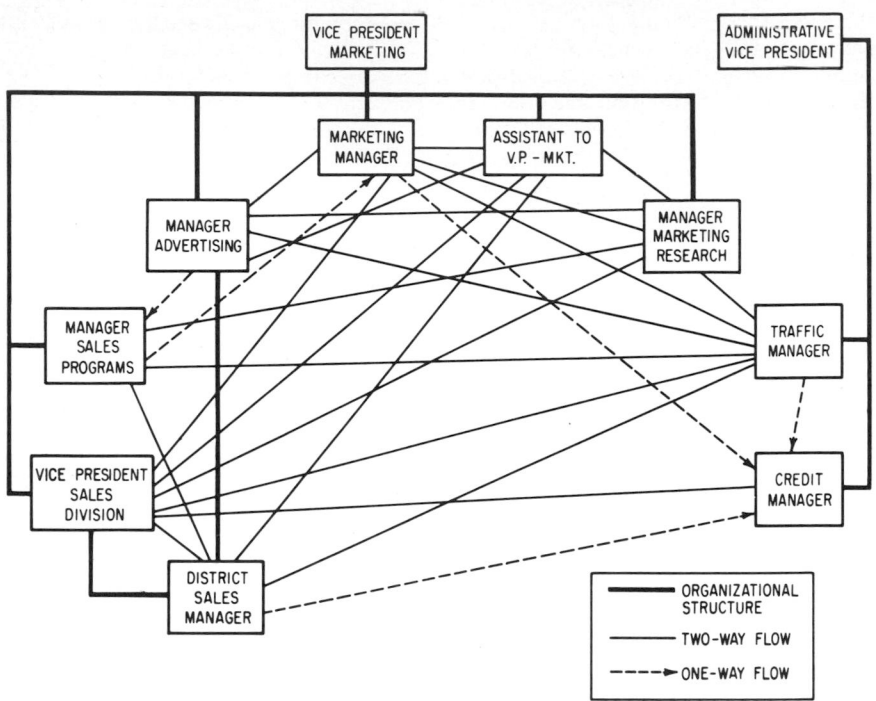

FIG. 2-9. *Flow of communication in Company B.* (*Courtesy of R. Clifton Andersen and Edward W. Cundiff, "Patterns of Communication in Marketing Organization,"* Journal of Marketing, *July, 1965.*)

CONCLUSION

This chapter presents some of the principal factors and problems influencing organization for marketing, as well as the fundamental types of structural patterns themselves. It should be noted that these are, of course, generalizations and that each company has to develop the particular organization best suited to its needs and resources at a particular time. And because changes in the dynamic business environment in which companies operate are occurring at an accelerating rate, it is essential for management to undertake a critical audit of its organization for marketing at regular intervals. The purpose of such a review should be to evaluate its strengths and weaknesses in the light of the ever-changing internal and external conditions with which it must deal, and to uncover opportunities to restructure it and adapt it to meet the new challenges confronting it. The price of good organization is regular evaluation and adaptation to changing conditions and requirements.

BIBLIOGRAPHY

Ames, B. Charles, "Payoff from Product Management," *Harvard Business Review,* November–December, 1963.

Andersen, R. Clifton, and Edward W. Cundiff, "Patterns of Communication in Marketing Organization," *Journal of Marketing,* July, 1965.

Bund, Henry, and James W. Carroll, "The Changing Role of the Marketing Function," *Journal of Marketing,* January, 1957.

DeVoe, Merrill, *How to Tailor Your Sales Organization to Your Markets,* Prentice-Hall, Inc., Englewood Cliffs, N.J., 1964.

Drohan, Thomas E., "How and Why the Product Manager System Works Analyzed by a Director of Marketing," *Advertising Age,* Oct. 26, 1964.

Evans, Gordon H., *The Product Manager's Job,* Research Study, no. 69, American Management Association, New York, 1964.

Lazo, Hector, and Arnold Corbin, "Organizing for Marketing," chap. 3 in *Management in Marketing,* McGraw-Hill Book Company, New York, 1961.

Lear, Robert W., "No Easy Road to Market Orientation," *Harvard Business Review,* September–October, 1963.

Luck, David J., and Theodore Nowak, "Product Management—Vision Unfulfilled," *Harvard Business Review,* May–June, 1965.

"Marketing Organization," sec. 4 in Albert W. Frey (ed.), *Marketing Handbook,* The Ronald Press Company, New York, 1965.

The Product Manager System, Experiences in Marketing Management, no. 8, National Industrial Conference Board, New York, 1965.

Stieglitz, Harold, and Allen R. Janger, *Top Management Organization in Divisionalized Companies,* Studies in Personnel Policy, no. 195, National Industrial Conference Board, New York, 1965.

CHAPTER THREE

Planning the Product Line

D. C. HOOPER   *Director, Marketing Customer Services, Westinghouse Electric Corporation, Pittsburgh, Pennsylvania*

No individual business function can operate successfully by itself.   Recognition of this is found in describing all of the information and interests of such activities as market research, economic analysis, and financial analysis.   Planning the product line is no exception.   Much of the literature describing these activities reads as if the entire business were being run from each function.   This stems from the basic requirement that each function, such as product planning, needs to maintain an active interest in all phases of the business if it is to contribute effectively.

This chapter will be confined to those roles where the function of planning the product line initiates the organization action needed to build a successful product program.

SETTING THE COMPANY'S BROAD OBJECTIVES

A necessary prerequisite to planning the product line is for the chief executive to set the course for his organization by defining its broad objectives.

To maintain a continuing successful business, it is essential for an enterprise to have a clearly defined "reason for being."   Without a soundly conceived purpose, management is in danger of succumbing to strong diversionary pressures, such as short-range profits, attractive-but-unrelated opportunities, and unsound competitive actions.   If it has a clear idea of its basic function or scope, the whole organization can achieve a dedication to a desirable objective.   This purpose must be challenging and constructive if it is to stimulate personnel to their best efforts.   Ideally, a company should provide purpose to its people's lives.

There are many who feel that the only objective of business is profits.   It is difficult, however, to develop a sense of dedication to purely financial objectives.   The late Professor Emeritus Schell at M.I.T. said, "Profits are a reward, not an objective." This does not mean that we must be idealistic, for the highest profits will accrue to those who have chosen a well-defined, desirable objective and have directed the energies of the organization to this purpose.

To define its broad objectives, a company needs to:

1. Identify a market need to be served which falls within its potential capabilities and which capitalizes on its strengths

2. Define it functionally from the point of view of the complete needs of the customer

Examples of Corporate Objectives. Many years ago the Du Pont Company set about to change its war-acquired image as merchants of death and adopted its new objective, which is so concisely described in its slogan: "Better Things for Better Living—Through Chemistry."

Westinghouse has stated its province as "the business of designing, producing, and marketing materials, products, equipment, systems, and services to create, distribute, apply, and utilize controlled power."

Such objectives stated in encompassing terms are not designed to be unduly restrictive to opportunities, but rather to provide a purposefulness to the organization. This simple but difficult process enables the planning activity to get under way. It will be noted that the assignment of planning the product line now must be approached from the point of view of the functional needs of the markets to be served.

EXISTING BUSINESS BASE

Usually, a chief executive who is eager to provide sound guidance in building his company's future must start with an actual set of conditions. He wants to stimulate his organization and encourage initiative, but without damaging the existing business base which must support his new ventures. His first task, under these circumstances, is to make provision for maintaining the virility of his present organization and its continued attention to his going business.

He can accomplish this by identifying within his broad corporate objective specific market areas that should be treated separately. By consolidating under a general manager the marketing function and those product-producing units whose output goes primarily to each market, he is in a position to delegate responsibility in line with his market-oriented concept.

By defining each of these general manager's objectives functionally from the point of view of the customer, he will:

1. Free the organization from its product orientation

2. Place emphasis on how best to meet the assigned market's defined functional needs

The actions will, of themselves, stimulate the existing organization and make its people more alert and flexible in developing products that customers want to buy.

At this point, the chief executive has taken the fundamental actions to provide purpose to his present organization and thus ensure attention to his existing business. As a result of this initial work, he may conclude that the newly assigned goals offer ample opportunity for the profitable growth he is seeking.

New Markets. If the executive concludes that his company is too dependent on mature markets that are faced with limited profit potentials, his product planning program will need to be extended.

In seeking profitable growth in wider fields, he must appraise his financial situation to obtain some concept of the magnitude of investment he can risk.

Because he knows that careful research is necessary to develop and appraise the various alternatives, because the demands of guiding the existing business limit his own time, and because he wants complete objectiveness in this phase of the study, he either retains outside counsel or appoints, in effect, a captive consultant in the field of product planning. He must provide his selected consultant, at least in broad terms, with some idea of the area of his interests. This is probably his most important decision. Just what does he want to make of his company?

He has undoubtedly had brought to his attention a parade of opportunities. The research laboratories are enthusiastic about all of their present projects. The decentralized organization has presented a series of proposals for further extending their assigned charters. He has been approached from outside about potential promising acquisitions. The suggestion system has produced some intriguing ideas.

A selection process based on evaluation of the many possible ventures that by chance come to the executive's attention is essentially an attempt to apply orderliness to a casual occurrence. It may result in establishing their relative worth, but, fundamentally, it does not ensure the best new product.

It is preferable to seek a major market area of potential growth considering the company's strengths and needs. The first examination should cover related or complementary fields where the company can build on its know-how and established reputation. This would include possibilities to extend the business to new industry markets and applications or new geographical areas. It should consider integration, both back to the basic materials and forward to include continuing service of the final product in use.

In addition to these logical areas, the chief executive needs to play his important leadership role of recognizing growing needs of society which have not been adequately served and to which, in his judgment, his organization could potentially contribute.

There was a period in our industrial development when this planning task was almost always approached by analyzing the company's existing skills and facilities and then trying to match the employment of these with market opportunities. This is still a desirable exercise, but too restrictive to be relied upon exclusively.

The urgent requirements for defense brought to the front a more venturesome type of entrepreneur who recognized or accepted a need and then set about to marshal the skills, organization, capital, and facilities to accomplish the defined objective. Applying this same approach to commercial markets can bring a new aggressiveness to industrial operations.

Example of an Approach to Selection of a New Market. An airline executive will not find it difficult to see needs, such as for:

1. Improved safety
2. Providing short hop or feeder service to complement his main-line, high-speed jet traffic
3. Saving time in picking up or delivering passengers or freight in the communities he serves
4. Providing schedules that better meet his customers' travel patterns

Assuming that he believes his outstanding opportunity is to build his air freight business, he is ready to put his consultant to work. Because he wants a broad-gaged, fresh approach to the problem, he asks his consultant to:

1. Look at the total movement of material and goods.
2. Segregate from this universe items that have characteristics that are best served by air transport.
3. Study the economics of the problem from the shipper's point of view.

4. Tabulate the unusual shipping conditions that apply, such as temperature and humidity control.

5. Analyze the entire present path to destination, identifying the elapsed time, cost, and damage experience for each successive stage.

6. Define the magnitude of improvement in time and/or cost needed to divert a significant volume of traffic to a new service.

Hopefully, he will stir his consultant's imagination by making it clear that he is open to innovations in the development of a new functional service. He visualizes the possibility of new air pickup techniques based on carrier experience that bypass the time-consuming local truck congestion. He points out the significant influence time has on both the number of stocking points needed by the customer and the inventory investment in each. By confiding his dreams to his consultant, he contributes to an enthusiastic, knowledgeable approach to the study.

At this stage, the product planner is participating in the creation of a new business venture tailored to the superior performance of an identified needed function. He has not yet involved design, but concentrates on a clear specification of the customer needs to be in a position to offer a valued marketable product or service.

The very process of defining the need, however, will be likely to contribute greatly to the conceptual stage.

This brings out an important characteristic of the product planner. Ideally, he is the catalyst who stimulates and programs the concurrent attention and interests of the many parts of the organization that can help in the process of creating the new business. He maintains a maximum of flexibility and intercommunication during this formative stage and avoids excessive commitment of talent and funds until the risks have been adequately evaluated.

Master Plan. As the potential new-business concept evolves, the product planner must prepare a master plan incorporating the successive steps to be carried out, who is to do the work, the estimated cost, and time allotments. This master plan should include a number of review points to reevaluate the project before authorizing its continuance. PERT or similar techniques should be utilized to manage the balanced progress of the development throughout the organization.

The product planner should draw upon the existing corporate staffs to perform their assigned roles in the project. He should avoid trying personally to function as a market researcher, research design and application engineer, manufacturing engineer, lawyer, merchandiser, and financial analyst. He is essentially functioning as a project manager (see Chapter 5 of Section 5) and must draw upon all of these talents to bring his assigned project to a definite conclusion—namely, either to enter a market or to abandon the project.

This approach to product planning with the objective of entering new markets will result in a purposeful program that makes the research laboratories and all the other subsequent functions more effective in accomplishing the selected objectives.

TECHNIQUES AND PROCEDURES

The preceding description of the broad approaches to planning the product line involves techniques, procedures, and considerations that need to be explored in greater depth.

Defining Customer Needs. This is a key factor in planning a successful product line. For some products, it requires knowing the customer's process sufficiently in depth to be able to design and apply equipment that will improve his operation.

The techniques for defining needs will vary for each product. Where extensive analysis is involved, it may be possible to set up a cooperative study with typical customers, or in some cases, a development contract can be arranged. In less complicated situations, customers will provide the information needed or permit the product engineers to study the product in use.

Successful use has been made of industrial engineering practices such as memo-movies. A manufacturer, by recording the installation process, can uncover deficiencies in product design and installation instructions. In one case, it was found that the contractor was forced to disassemble at the site in order to mount the unit in place. The carefully planned, low-cost, factory-assembly-operation benefits were being dissipated when the field installation operation was reached.

In another case in the construction field, the individual-item packaging of the product incurred the loss of time on the part of the installer and presented him with an annoying waste-disposal problem.

Applying this movie technique to repair calls is an effective way of bringing back vividly to the design engineers a record of their failure to anticipate the problems of the repairman. Showing such movies back at the plant easily brings the attention of a wide variety of talents to the problems from the customer's point of view and thus contributes to the solution of the specific case, plus a continuing awareness of the need for such considerations.

There is an inclination to oversimplify our business problems by utilizing averages excessively in our analytical and planning work. This danger of being misled is present in product planning. In defining customers' needs, it will be necessary to do some type of combining, but it will be helpful to do some stratifying of the data collected to bring out significant differences in needs on which it may be possible to capitalize by developing products with characteristics tailored to specific segments of the market. This has been an obvious approach in many consumer markets, but it can be easily overlooked in the industrial and commercial fields.

Example of Defining a Customer Need. A manufacturer of commercial and industrial lighting equipment might define his objective simply as: "Providing industrial and commercial illumination." When it comes to defining his customers' illumination needs, he is quickly confronted with the necessity of carefully classifying his customers and examining in depth their illumination requirements.

His airport customers will require guidance lighting, safety lighting, flood lighting, space illumination, street lighting, display lighting. The intensity needs will vary; he will need to consider replacement difficulties affecting his design; appearance will be a factor; and there will be regulations that must be met.

Another manufacturer may have three separately operated product divisions which are manufacturing and marketing lighting fixtures, air conditioning, and heating equipment. This company might define its objective as: "Environmental conditioning."

Because this company's three product divisions are serving common customers and because their products are complementary in providing related functions, management recognizes the desirability of coordinating their respective activities. This coordination can be accomplished organizationally or by coordinating committees. A possible move would be to consolidate the marketing and product planning functions. An alternative would be to set up a special systems department responsible for marketing combinations of equipment of the separate product divisions.

The market analysis job for this company is to determine for each class of customer the total environmental conditioning requirements. The engineering design and development task is to come up with products or combinations of products that best satisfy the customer's functional specifications. The illumination level, since it produces heat, will affect heating and cooling requirements to maintain the desired comfort conditions. The equipment, therefore, will need to be balanced as a system to meet effectively the overall requirements. Possibilities of product modifications will become evident when the total function to be provided is examined.

The former lighting equipment division now thinks in terms of developing a lighting fixture that can effectively disperse its heat into the environment. The air-conditioning division can develop heat pumps to match the year-round heating and cooling needs. The need for coordinated application engineering becomes apparent as the customer's total environmental need is accepted as the objective.

In studying the complete needs of the customer, air cleaning and humidity control will become obvious new-product possibilities.

This functional approach from the point of view of the customer also challenges the product planner to raise the question of whether there is an alternative means of satisfying the customer's requirements that is superior to his company's existing product line.

Evaluation. Having selected the objective in terms of functional customer need, it will be necessary to evaluate how well the company's existing offerings match that need compared with competitors' products and services. This should first be done from the point of view of the customer and preferably directly expressed by him. At this stage, we want to know what he actually thinks, not what he should logically be expected to think.

We may be able to prove that our product quality or service is competitive or superior, but if our customer or prospect thinks it is inferior, we have a real problem.

This is market research's job. The product planner should outline the objectives of the research study, which essentially will be to seek the customers' opinion of:

1. How the current offerings satisfy the defined functional needs
2. How the company's product and services compare with competition

Since it may be desirable to collect in the same interview helpful information to be used in either promotion or corrective programs, the product planner should suggest to the market researcher the key features which he thinks influence the buyer. They may cover:

Product characteristics
Service considerations
Economic factors

A service survey designed along these lines is illustrated by Figure 3-1. This objective evaluation approach should be designed to bring out advantages that can be exploited and deficiencies that need to be corrected. Such customer ratings will influence the entire product plan.

Essentially, the same procedure can be followed when a company is considering entering an established field for the first time or when a new product designed to replace an existing product is under consideration.

In developing product recommendations, it is essential to be familiar with the alternatives open to the potential customer. This may mean weighing the

Service Survey Form

Instructions: Place a rating in both columns opposite each service function.
"Meeting customer needs" ratings:

U—Unsatisfactory from customer point of view
S—Reasonably satisfactory in meeting customer needs
O—There is an opportunity to increase volume and price realization by offering unusual service in this area which is closer to customer needs and beyond that offered by all manufacturers

"Compared with best competitive manufacturer" ratings:

P—Poorer
E—About equal
B—Better

Service function	Rating columns	
	Meeting customer needs	Compared with best competitor
Service prior to sale:		
1. Adequacy of catalogs or product information bulletins		
2. Adequacy of price lists	———	———
3. Clarity of price policy	———	———
4. Information on product availability (stock bulletins, delivery estimates)	———	
5. Availability of technical help in specification, design, and application	———	———
6. Proposal service	———	———
7. Handling requests for information	———	———
Service from receipt of order to delivery:		
1. Promptness in processing orders	———	———
2. Communications re status	———	———
3. Delivery time	———	———
4. Reliability of delivery promises	———	———
Service in use:		
1. Adequacy of warranties or guarantees	———	———
2. Promptness in correcting product troubles in warranty	———	———
3. Availability of renewal parts	———	———
4. Availability of help in diagnosing trouble	———	———
5. Adequacy of repair service	———	———
6. Adequacy of product quality	———	———
		Check those you recommend for investigation
Opportunities to improve service by offering:		
1. Longer or more complete warranty or guarantee		———
2. Insurance to cover unexpected failure beyond normal warranty period		
3. Preventive-maintenance contracts		———
4. Continuing-service contracts		———
5. Acceptance of responsibility for meeting defined performance standards		
6. _____		———
7. _____		———
8. _____		———
9. _____		———

FIG. 3-1. *Service survey form.*

Product features	Present model	New design specifications	Competitor			
			A	B	C	D
Functional						
Promotional						
Unit prices...................						
Established unit costs						

FIG. 3-2. *Competitive product rating form.*

features and value of similar products or considering completely different techniques of accomplishing the same function.

In the first area, the product offered may be obviously more rugged, but beyond the requirements of the application. A distinguishing feature must represent a true plus to the customer. For example, the company's electric unit heater may be the best electric heater on the market, but the customer will want to know how it compares with a gas unit.

Benefits can also result from operating tests and complete disassembly of competitive products. Design and manufacturing engineers need to study materials and methods used to uncover opportunities to improve their product or realize savings.

It is desirable to organize and monitor a periodic analysis of competitive products by function, feature, price, and cost. Figure 3-2 shows a form which may be used for this purpose.

A numerical rating system, based on the defined customer need as 100, is suggested to show the relative standing of each manufacturer's product. Unit prices and estimated cost comparisons may be based on typical sizes or styles. The competitive analysis should also consolidate from published financial records, association data, trade magazines, shows, plant visits, directories, technical societies, government statistics, research organizations, field reports, and news clippings a continuing analysis of competition by company, covering their relative sales progress, their strategy in building their business, and an evaluation of their success and the degree to which it stems from their product line.

Product Specifications. Based on the study of customer needs and the evaluation of the company's and its competitors' products, recommendations for the improvement of existing products or proposed products should be prepared and include:

1. The function the product will provide
2. The environmental conditions under which it will be expected to operate
3. Its life expectancy
4. The warranty period that will apply
5. The performance standards it must meet
6. The safety factors needed
7. The selling price needed if it is to be marketed in the quantity planned
8. The corresponding cost target if it is to justify the investment
9. The time schedule needed to meet a competitive threat or to capitalize on an innovation
10. The service features that should be incorporated
11. The standardization and interchangeability desired

12. The promotional features that can be exploited
13. The packaging specifications
14. The product and company identification

PLANNING FOR NEW PRODUCTS

Product planning is a logical place in the organization to place new-product responsibility. Under the recommended concept, this should really be described as responsibility for new customer functions, for the recommended charters of the existing decentralized organization should be broad enough to cover both evolution and innovation in providing their respective defined functions. This leaves only customer functional needs that have not been previously served by the company as the "new product" responsibility of the product planning activity.

In this "new product" capacity, the product planner is usually wise to restrict the number of projects that are marked for thorough exploration. The lesson learned by many companies in this area is the danger of establishing more developments than it has the talent or funds to bring to a decision promptly. If care is not exercised, the research labs will soon be full of one- and two-man teams, each team devoted to its special project and its perpetuation.

It is a sobering exercise to pry out from the record a picture of the company's experience in the new-product field. The product planner would do well to conduct an analytical study and plot expenditure and receipt data as shown by Figure 3-3. A series of such case histories is likely to bring out the fact that developments take longer than most executives realize and that the investment or underwriting period usually exceeds the forecast.

Resolving to keep the number of projects limited to those that can be promptly processed with the available talent and funds will require a selection procedure to screen the many ideas. The flow of suggestions is likely to be copious, and any evaluation procedure designed to be infallible is also likely to be impractical. The product planner can politely acknowledge and file some suggestions on the basis of his personal judgment. In other instances, he should tap the specialized experience of the organization before he decides on those items that should be subject to planned review. To prepare a recommendation to management, he must consider:

1. The extent to which new-product projects already established have committed the available people and budget

2. The promise of candidates for future projects

This second job will need to be approached by progressive analysis. The ideas that remain as potentially feasible after this screening process now justify at least some further investigation before they are discarded, tabled for later consideration, or recommended as development projects. Some programmed preliminary investigation can be conducted simultaneously by drawing on the functional staffs to collect from:

1. Marketing—an estimate of the possibilities, assuming the target performance values are realized

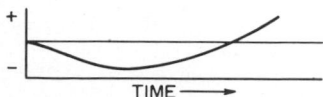

FIG. 3-3. *Accumulated receipts over expenditures.*

2. Research and engineering—a statement of their judgment of the feasibility of developing the items with the defined performance characteristics, together with an approximation of the time, talent, and funds required

3. Manufacturing—an estimate of the facilities that would be needed

4. Legal—a statement of any potential problems that the suggested venture would present

5. Financial—assistance in estimating the investment and return

From this preliminary review, the product planner will be equipped to advise his management on the projects to be selected for intensive study.

The next step is to outline the progressive steps to be taken in the intensive study, assigning responsibility for the commitment of people and money for each step and identifying the checkpoints where it will be determined whether to proceed or abandon. Depending on the importance of the time element, the outline can employ techniques to program concurrent studies in the various complementary areas, or it can be designed to commit a minimum of funds while key feasibility questions are resolved.

Running the program described requires a great deal of flexibility, for the objectives are early decision and effective utilization of important and usually scarce skills.

Marketing Relationships. Either planning the product line must be part of marketing or the product planner must work intimately with this function if the company is truly to attain its desirable objective of being organized to serve customer needs. There follows a discussion of some of the important areas where there is need for a common approach to planning.

Marketing Policies. The product planner should be encouraged to challenge established customs and practices that appear unsound. The following are illustrations of approaches that can have a significant effect on the product line and services offered by his company.

Illustration—Completeness of Line. Many companies have perpetuated a belief that their product lines must include a complete range of sizes, capacities, colors, and prices. In some earlier day, with more limited distribution and service facilities, this completeness of line was important to overall success. Now more companies are taking the position that each item in the line must stand on its own feet.

Illustration—Loss Leaders. This merchandising approach is still being used by some consumer-product manufacturers. Designed to build store traffic to be traded up, it can easily develop into the volume seller and unfortunately live up to its name as a source of loss.

Illustration—Approach to Product Introduction. There are two very diverse approaches to the introduction of a new-product development. One approach adopts the theory that the initial customers should pay the development through prices set to recapture quickly the investment that created it. This is usually followed by either planned or forced price reductions as competitors move in. The other extreme is for a manufacturer, through extensive analysis, to set the price level that will most likely realize the volume needed to support an efficient operation and recover his investment over a larger number of units. The second approach must be based on much more thorough and complete analysis, but offers the advantage of reaching an established market position in less time and tends to discourage imitation.

Illustration—Switching from Development to Cost Reduction. Product development is a continuous process, but frequently a stage is reached where further attempts to attain the next increment of functional efficiency involve an investment disproportionate to the value of the results that can be realized. It may be desirable, at this stage, particularly if the product is advanced in its life cycle, to halt all developments and concentrate on manufacturing and distribution economies.

Marketing Strategy. Planning the product efficiently requires considering how it is to be totally marketed. The locomotive builders who catered to the expressed wishes of the engineers of the individual railroads they were selling to found themselves at a very severe competitive disadvantage when the Electromotive Division of General Motors confronted railroad management with a standardized and, thus, high-value diesel electric unit. It is apparent, therefore, that tailoring the product to the customer's needs requires evaluating those needs from a total point of view. Consulting a customer's repair department may not provide sound advice in the development of a new throw-away unit which would eliminate the customer's repair activity.

Another illustration is the effect that ease of repair or the access to readily available repair service can have on the acceptance of a product. Any item critical to a customer's operation which does not lend itself to spares protection must be provided with service to be successful. Product superiority alone is not enough.

It is important to evaluate the changing needs of the market for advice and help in applying a product. Frequently a product initially will need a specialized technical field organization to assist the customer in understanding how it can be applied effectively. As it gains more general use and becomes familiar to the customer, this specialized help may no longer be needed, and the item can be turned over to distributors, agents, or the company's general sales force.

Shortening this expensive introductory educational phase by providing simple or sectionalized design, clear and descriptive literature, and training courses can be a productive contribution of product planning.

Marketing Effectiveness. The marketing department, in developing plans to advertise, promote, and sell the company's products, is continually seeking features or special values that will make these efforts more productive. As products mature and competition intensifies, active attention to the potential contribution to winning this struggle through product improvement can sometimes overcome the natural tendency to price deterioration. The marketing department can help in evaluating the relative customer appeals of the features or modifications being considered. Again, these must be rated on the basis of what the customer thinks they are worth.

Cooperative Marketing. As functional systems of increasing complexity grow in importance, a company needs to be alert to opportunities to expand its business by adapting its product to complement others. The complex, integrated needs of some defense projects led to project partnerships which brought to bear combined talents and facilities to the solution of a single problem. Similar opportunities exist in the commercial and industrial fields. An engine builder and a boat builder may be able to do better together than they can independently. A motor manufacturer and a pump manufacturer or automotive and trailer manufacturers could consider such possibilities.

This type of cooperative approach to the solution of customer problems may have the additional benefit of avoiding incurring unneeded investment in an industry.

Resale Equipment Manufacturers. Particularly in the components business, there is need for working with the customer while he is in the conceptual or "bread board" stage of developing a new end-use product.

The company's design talent, by cooperating with the customer's development engineers, can assist in the efficient utilization of existing components or can visualize a product modification that will facilitate achieving the customer's objectives. The development engineer will be most effective in this type of work if he has knowledge of the customer's end product, in addition to his component know-how.

Repair and Service. The product planner should haunt the company's repair shops. It is impossible to imagine, without seeing, the conditions under which some products are expected to function. Rotating equipment will be found covered with oil, dirt, stone dust, and chemicals to the point where it is unbelievable that it ever turned over; or lubrication nipples cannot even be found. These operating conditions, however, may be representative, and should, therefore, be anticipated.

Statistics of renewal-part sales, in-warranty repair expense, service calls, and repair expense should be regularly collected and identified to individual products to bring out product deficiencies. Customer complaints, cancellations, and return-goods reports should also be furnished to the man responsible for planning the product line.

It is helpful to enlist the services of product design and development people in the field diagnosis of trouble. The customer's frank expression of his unhappiness will come through clearly under such conditions.

Make or Buy. The purchasing department is in continuous touch with suppliers who can be a productive source of contributions to improving the product line. Manufacturing may fail to be completely objective in this area, but the product planner, with no vested interests except the company's overall welfare, should work closely with purchasing to utilize this possibility to the utmost. Some suppliers will undertake original research and development on their own to achieve defined needs. In other cases, a sponsored development assigned to a supplier may be the fastest or most economical means of achieving an urgent program objective.

PRODUCT DELETION

The elimination of a product or product line is one of the most difficult business problems. There are many natural forces that will resist such action. The responsible organization may be encouraged to update itself, but cannot be expected to eliminate itself. Management feels a responsibility to its people that will be affected and to its customers who have been depending on it for a source of supply and replacement. Pride also may be involved, for there may be a reluctance to admit that the item cannot be made profitable.

Because of these natural forces which will impede corrective action, the product planner should be encouraged to exert pressure to keep before management those products and services that are profit detractors and to suggest programs for their elimination or correction.

The charter form of organization recommended earlier in this chapter should minimize this problem. Because the assignment to each organization unit is to provide a customer-needed function in the best way, each department should be continually striving to update itself, utilizing the whole range of available technologies.

A company may, however, at some point be confronted with a development that makes its product or service obsolete and where the alternative action is beyond its financial or technical capability. Such situations should be minimized by an alert, aggressive, well-managed company. Usually a product progresses through a life cycle which may take it to a peak of profitability from which it experiences gradual erosion as it matures and competition encroaches on its volume. At some stage, an alternative product appears and further threatens its future. Here again, the logical action can depend on what competitive companies do. There could be a substantial continuing replacement market which becomes progressively attractive as competitors abandon the field.

The important management consideration in this area is to make certain that it continually appraises the situation objectively.

SUMMARY

Planning the product line will be most effective if it is done in line with a clear statement of company objectives preferably based on serving a functionally defined customer need.

The responsible product planner must develop a sense of introspection. Although he must be creative and enthusiastic, he will also need to be analytical and objective.

Before he recommends, he must be personally convinced that he has satisfactorily answered the following difficult question: "What is being offered that is so new, different, or valuable that customers content with their existing competitive products and suppliers will abandon these established relationships and buy from us?"

He must develop internal working relationships that enable him to marshal interpreting this knowledge so that it can be employed to the mutual advantage of the customer and his company.

He must develop internal working relationships that enable him to marshal the skills of the organization in the development of a product line that will assure profitable growth.

He must force management's attention to those unpleasant terminal actions that are likely to be put off.

The successful product planner can derive great personal satisfaction from the contributions he makes to his own company's progress by guiding it in the direction of better serving society.

BIBLIOGRAPHY

Alexander, R. S., "The Death and Burial of 'Sick' Products," *Journal of Marketing,* vol. 28, no. 2, April, 1964.

Berg, Thomas L., and Abe Shuchman, *Product Strategy and Management,* Holt, Rinehart and Winston, Inc., New York, 1963.

Gisser, P., "Taking the Chances Out of Product Introductions," *Industrial Marketing,* vol. 50, May, 1965.

Greig, W. Smith, "Quality Competition and Product Development," *Business Topics,* Spring, 1964.

Kotler, Phillip, "Phasing Out Weak Products," *Harvard Business Review,* March, 1965.

Lorsh, Jay W., and Paul R. Lawrence, "Organizing for Product Innovations," *Harvard Business Review,* January, 1965.

Marting, Elizabeth (ed.), *Developing a Product Strategy,* Management Report, no. 39, American Management Association, New York, 1959.

Organizing for Product Development, Management Report, no. 31, American Management Association, New York, 1959.

Scheuble, Phillip A., Jr., "ROI for New-product Policy," *Harvard Business Review,* November, 1964.

Staudt, Thomas A., and Donald A. Taylor, *A Managerial Introduction to Marketing,* chaps. 9–11, Prentice-Hall, Inc., Englewood Cliffs, N.J., 1959.

Tietjen, K. N., *Organizing the Product Planning Function,* American Management Association, New York, 1963.

CHAPTER FOUR

Marketing Research

HARRISON M. RAINIE, JR.   *President, Stewart, Dougall & Associates, Inc.,*
New York, New York

Marketing as a business function is charged with the movement of products and services from the producer to the user. Ability to produce does not guarantee success. Ability to sell at a profit is the critical test. Marketing research is an essential part of the marketing function.

Marketing research is the disciplined collection, array, and evaluation of facts related to the marketing process. Its primary purpose is to solve or forestall marketing problems and thus to increase the efficiency and lower the costs of marketing through the development, selection, and improvement of the best products and marketing methods.

The more progressive companies implement the marketing concept properly. This means that the marketing man is introduced at the beginning rather than at the end of the production cycle. Marketing assumes responsibility for guiding the engineer and the manufacturing man toward products the customer wants at prices he is willing to pay.

It is inherent in the marketing concept that more intimate contact between marketing and production and marketing and finance can serve to reduce isolated thinking and produce managers of greater ability throughout the business. All business functions must look beyond the plant and office walls out into the marketplace for guidance in the planning of their activities. Marketing has become a full partner— and in the more progressive companies, the dominant partner—with production, engineering, and finance in planning for the growth of the entire business. With the implementation of this marketing concept, it is clear that the gathering of accurate, reliable information about the marketplace is essential for planning for profitable growth.

Marketing research is not mysterious. In the discussion that follows, this function is described in terms of how it is done, what kinds of problems it can help solve, where it fits in the organization structure, and how it operates as a department.

NATURE OF MARKETING RESEARCH

Any company selling a product or a service needs information about its market—its customers, prospective customers, and in many cases, the ultimate consumers of its products—to determine what it should produce, to whom it should offer what it produces, and the way in which it should offer its product.

Nearly all companies probably do some kind of marketing research, although it may be very informal. However, it is usually not enough for a manufacturer or service organization to look at its own records and determine what its future course of action should be to achieve profitable growth. There is a need for a disciplined and scientific approach to the gathering and evaluation of the information necessary for making management decisions. There has been considerable discussion as to just how scientific marketing research can be. It is generally accepted that the word "scientific," in relation to marketing research, means basically a systematic and impartial approach to the study of management problems. Marketing researchers draw on other sciences, such as sociology and mathematics, in developing plans for obtaining certain types of information and in analyzing the results of their research activities. How systematic the approach can be depends on the character and scope of the problem that has been presented to the researcher. However, it is essential that the approach to any marketing research project be as systematic and impartial as possible and that the results be evaluated without bias.

There are some basic differences between research in industrial and consumer markets. In industrial markets, purchasing decisions are made in quite a different atmosphere compared with the consumer. Products sold to industry tend to be technical in nature, and even if simple, are subject to technical evaluation by the buyer. In industrial markets, it is necessary that the researcher be able to talk the buyer's own language. In many specialized markets, it is necessary that the researcher be a graduate engineer as well as a marketing man. He must recognize that industrial buying decisions are seldom a single responsibility of one person, and he must be able to select and get to the right people, some of whom are not easily accessible. Finally, he must be experienced in the general practices of business and must be able to interpret as well as observe and inquire.

In the consumer-goods market, marketing research, although it has basically the same objectives, takes different forms. It is necessary to gather information at various levels to assist management in planning for the future. Information can be gathered by interviews conducted in personal visits to the home, by mail, on the street, in stores, on farms, by telephone, or in public groups. Surveys may be made of a neighborhood, a city, a region, or the nation and may cover the public as a whole or be limited to specific types of people.

In both industrial and consumer research, a great deal of information already exists within most companies. Additional information is available from government sources and other outside agencies which can be used in conjunction with information collected directly from the market by the researchers to formulate plans for management.

Functions of Marketing Research. The principal functions of marketing research are describing, evaluating, explaining, predicting, and assisting in making decisions.

Describing includes a description of events or activities that have occurred or are taking place.

Evaluating includes the evaluation of products, sales performance, competition, and the like.

Explaining includes explanation of why certain things have happened or are happening, such as declining sales volume in a certain sales territory or why competition is a leader in a certain product.

Predicting includes prediction of what might, will, or should happen in terms of sales volume, product needs, distribution, pricing, and the like.

Assisting in making decisions implies the requirement that marketing research evaluate its information carefully in an unbiased manner and make actionable recommendations to management.

MARKETING RESEARCH METHODOLOGY

To ensure that the recommendations emanating from marketing research are acceptable and actionable, it is essential that marketing research understand the problem to be researched, establish specific objectives, develop a research plan, choose the proper sample, determine information needs, analyze the information gathered, develop conclusions and recommendations, and prepare a report to management.

Understanding the Problem to Be Researched. If the user of research is to receive full benefit from the researcher, he must define the problem carefully before the researcher can undertake the development of a research plan which will ultimately assist the user in making decisions. The most frequent criticism of research has been that the results were superficial, inconclusive, or not pertinent to the basic problem. Therefore, the definition of the problem to be studied is essential.

Establishing Specific Objectives. The next step is the establishing of specific objectives to be achieved by the research plan. These obviously will relate to the character and scope of the problem to be studied. The problem may be as narrow as what the share of market is in a given area, which may be answered from trade association statistics and company records; or it may be as broad as an extensive study of the marketplace to build a five-year growth plan for the company. In either case, it is mandatory that the objectives of the study be clearly stated and agreed upon between the users and the researchers.

Developing the Research Plan. The development of the research plan itself requires a determination of how to obtain the information required to meet the objectives of the study. This includes all sources of data readily available in printed form within the company and outside the company, such as government statistics, trade association data, and the like. It is essential in planning the research project to determine how much information already exists inside or outside the company. In addition to government and trade sources, there are other outside syndicated services which provide information on a regular basis (such as services for manufacturers of consumer products which measure the movement of goods over retail counters, provide continuing audits of sales by distribution channels, and the like). In most cases, research plans will require study and information gathering in the marketplace.

Choosing the Proper Sample. Having determined what information is required and what already exists, it is next necessary to determine specifically where it will be necessary to go to obtain the remaining information which, in most instances, will be the primary source of explaining, describing, or evaluating a particular situation or problem. One of the critical factors at this stage is the determination of the number of persons that must be contacted, assuming that the critical information must come from the marketplace rather than through published information.

In the field of research on consumer products, the selection of the sample obviously depends on the nature of the problem. There are many texts which explain in detail the procedures for selecting the right number of persons of various types to be interviewed to achieve the objectives of the study. To take a complete census of a large population, or a large number of manufacturing plants, or a large number of retailers can be extremely expensive. In most instances, a complete census is not required, because there are procedures by which the part of the population it is desired to measure can be chosen to be representative of the population as a whole.

Sampling applies to research in both consumer products and industrial products. If a product is sold directly to automobile manufacturers, the sample is not difficult to choose. If a product is sold to electric utilities, a cross section of this industry can be developed readily. If a product is sold through retail outlets, the sample will undoubtedly be larger, but again, it is not difficult to choose, because retail stores are well known and lists are available showing various types and sizes of establishments.

The more complex sampling problems typically occur when the study involves the public at large. Then, carefully designed mathematical techniques must be used to select a representative sample of the population to be measured and to ensure reliability of the data, particularly if projections of quantitative data to the total population are required.

Determining Information Needs. Having designed the sample required to meet the objectives, it is necessary to determine what information is required from each unit or person in the sample. When a large sample is drawn to measure a certain segment of the public at large, a carefully structured questionnaire is usually developed. Because the type of interviewing required is done on a large scale and requires many interviewers in different parts of the country, it is necessary that each interview be conducted in exactly the same manner so that the results can be processed at a later date and put in usable form. The questionnaire is the means of recording the answers to questions that are posed to those persons who will be interviewed. Typically in this situation, no deviation from the questionnaire is permitted. The questions are carefully worded to avoid any bias on the part of individual interviewers in recording the response.

In work in the industrial field, a different approach must be used. To complete a successful industrial interview, it is necessary that the interviewers be persons who understand fully the nature of the problem and are familiar with the industry and its characteristics. Where highly technical products are involved, it may be necessary that the interviewer be a graduate engineer. In any event, the person conducting the interviews must be knowledgeable of general business problems, particularly within the industry which is being studied. This type of interview is carried out in a conversational manner between two businessmen. No formal questionnaires are used, but an interview guide is prepared beforehand which outlines in detail the subject matter to be covered. The actual flow of the interview and the phrasing of the questions are left to the judgment of the interviewer. The interview guides are filled out after the interview has been completed. The outline is the same on each guide to provide for orderly recording of the information so that subsequent analysis can be made of all the interviews successfully completed.

At times, various other techniques of developing information may be applicable. In certain types of work among ultimate consumers, it is possible to obtain information by telephone. The same is true for some industrial projects where the information desired is limited and reasonably straightforward, requiring no detailed technical discussions regarding products or marketing methods.

In some instances, it is possible to obtain information by mail. If the information required is simple and can be structured into a brief questionnaire, the mail technique can be useful for obtaining answers to a limited number of questions. The principal problem with the mail technique, however, is that it is impossible to know who has *not* responded. Thus, the representativeness of those who do respond cannot be determined, and the results are not necessarily projectable to the total group being measured. However, the mail technique is useful for developing preliminary information on limited objectives.

Analyzing the Information Gathered. Having completed the interviewing among whatever population was chosen, the information recorded on either the questionnaires or the interview guides must be analyzed carefully and put into an orderly form. When dealing with large numbers of questionnaires, it is usually necessary to edit these carefully and code them so that they can be processed by data-processing equipment. In this way, large numbers of questionnaires can be processed rapidly and accurately at considerably less cost than if they were done by hand. With the development of sophisticated data-processing equipment, the tabulation of results becomes relatively straightforward.

In many instances, however, where lengthy responses to questions of a qualitative nature are to be analyzed, it may be desirable to do this by hand. In this way, each question can be carefully reviewed and various subdivisions of the question established for analysis purposes.

In most industrial marketing research studies, the information is of such a nature that it usually requires hand tabulation, often by the persons who have done the interviews, particularly on highly technical subjects. This is also true of questions involving policy matters such as distribution, pricing, evaluation of sales effort, or evaluation of engineering effort. In other cases, where the sample has been relatively small, physical tabulation in quantitative terms of the results may not be pertinent. It may, in some cases, be better to analyze and present the results in the form of a case history type of report. In other instances, it may be necessary only to summarize the results of the work, particularly if the problem had been defined rather narrowly and specifically, with a limited number of interviews required to meet the objectives of the study.

Developing Conclusions and Recommendations. Following the tabulation of results or the making of a summary analysis, it will then be necessary to develop specific conclusions and recommendations. Here the researcher is called upon to exercise marketing management judgment. If marketing research is to be practical and useful, it is mandatory that it provide these judgments in the form of actionable recommendations to the users of the research. Without this, the marketing research function does not fulfill its important role in assisting management to plan for profitable growth.

Preparing the Report to Management. All research projects should be presented to the user of the research in the form of a written report. This report should contain a statement of the objectives of the research, its scope, and the approach used. It should set forth the information obtained in factual form and the interpretive analysis of the information in the form of conclusions and recommendations.

PUTTING MARKETING RESEARCH TO WORK

The purpose of marketing research has been described as the solving or forestalling of marketing problems, thus helping to increase the efficiency of the marketing function and the profitability of the enterprise. As a function, it is typically located within the marketing group of the enterprise and should report directly to the top marketing executive of the business. It is this marketing executive's responsibility to be sure that the marketing research organization is staffed with qualified personnel and that it attains the objectives of its function. This is an important responsibility if the total marketing concept is to be truly established in the enterprise, because marketing research can play a central role in achieving the establishment of this concept.

Areas of Activity of Marketing Research. If marketing research is to play this role, it must concern itself with all aspects of the marketing function. Some of its activities will be of a continuing nature, and some will involve special individual projects. At times, it may require the assistance of outside services.

The primary areas of activity, not necessarily in order of importance, include:

1. Products or services
2. Markets
3. Distribution
4. Pricing
5. Sales organization
6. Service
7. Advertising and sales promotion
8. Packaging
9. Brand names
10. Acquisitions

Products or Services. Because of keen competition from both domestic and foreign sources, the development of new or improved products or services becomes a vital part of management planning. In this area, marketing research can make a very important contribution. It should evaluate existing products to determine the extent to which they are fulfilling the needs of customers, and at the same time, look for possible modifications which can provide the basis for gaining competitive advantage. Included in this evaluation of existing products should be careful analysis and constant alertness to competitive product offerings and their impact on the company's market position. The area of new products is particularly important if companies are to build and maintain positions of leadership in their industries. With the substantial investments required to launch new products, failure cannot be tolerated. Thus, marketing research must play an important role in defining product needs. As new products come to the stage of testing, it must supervise carefully their evaluation in terms of their acceptability to customers and make preliminary evaluations of the marketing methods required to make them successful in the marketplace.

Markets. The study of markets is also an important area of activity for marketing research. This includes not only continuing general studies, but specific projects to measure at various points in time competitive practices, market penetration, and the possibility of finding new markets for existing or modified products as they may be developed or as recommendations may be made by marketing research for such development. In this area of studying markets as well as product opportunities, marketing research can make a substantial contribution to planning for growth, because change is important to the lifeblood of most companies.

Distribution. Rather drastic changes are constantly taking place in distribution methods and techniques. Studies should be made and updated frequently to determine the most efficient means of getting a company's product to its customer or ultimate user. Marketing research can make recommendations for changes in distribution methods and techniques to meet the changing needs of the marketplace and the changing needs of those intermediaries within the marketplace who serve their customers. Distribution costs are an important element of these studies of distribution. In a number of industries, the role of the distributor is being seriously questioned. Unless distributors of various types change their methods of operation, services, and costs, they may find themselves out of business. Here, marketing research can help provide the answers as to the best method of distribution and, where appropriate, assist distributors or other types of middlemen to improve the efficiency of their operations for direct benefit to themselves and the companies they represent.

Pricing. Projects in the area of pricing existing products, and new products as they relate to channels of distribution and competitive activities, are also important marketing research activities. Continuing review of competitive pricing is an important activity to help management make pricing decisions. Included in pricing studies should be careful review of discount structure and policies.

Sales Organization. Key areas for marketing research contributions to the sales department include assisting in making sales forecasts, establishing quotas for sales territories, analyzing salesmen's activities, measuring salesmen's effectiveness, and measuring territorial yield. Measuring the effectiveness of competitive sales methods is an important function for marketing research. Research in this area is designed to assist the sales department in carrying out marketing plans.

Advertising and Sales Promotion. Marketing research can be used to measure the effectiveness of advertising, for both the company and its competition. Appraisal can be made of media, copy, and amount of advertising. Another important contribution is its assistance in establishing the objectives of the advertising program.

Service. In most industrial companies and many consumer-goods companies, service can be a very important factor in customer relationships. It should be a part of the responsibility of marketing research to analyze and review periodically the content, facilities, and effectiveness of the service function of the company and its competitors.

Packaging. Packaging should be appraised from two points of view: (1) functional and (2) the merchandising aspects of the packaging. Packaging should be studied for both existing and new products, because particularly in the consumer-goods field, it is becoming an increasingly important consideration, not only in terms of types of materials used and protection of contents, but more importantly from the point of view of appearance on the shelf. The merchandising aspects of packaging are very important in the movement of goods off retail shelves. Effective packaging can often make the difference between the allotment of more shelf space or less.

Brand Names. Brand-name policy should be appraised by marketing research in terms of treatment of the corporate name, product names, division names, and other factors as they relate to the organization structure of the company. It is important that basic policy be established and reviewed by marketing research as the need for new names arises. In addition, marketing research should appraise the strengths and weaknesses of the company's existing brand names compared with competition.

Acquisitions. If the acquisition of another company is the most feasible method of achieving penetration in a new market, broadening a product line, or achieving diversification, marketing research should play an important role in appraising the acquisition. It is a relatively straightforward task for an accountant to check the financial records of the candidate for acquisition and for an engineer to appraise its physical assets. The intangibles which are the most important, however, are the marketing strengths and weaknesses of the candidate, and this is the area in which marketing research can play a significant role.

ORGANIZATION OF THE MARKETING RESEARCH ACTIVITY

The marketing research manager or director should report to the highest marketing executive within the company or specific division which the department serves. He should maintain close liaison with all departmental division heads in the discharge of his assigned responsibilities. His staff, obviously, will be dependent upon the size of the company and the complexity of the marketing operations. In larger companies, it is usually desirable to staff the department with research specialists who can work with various division or department heads. In very large companies, each division may have its own marketing research department. In all cases, it is important for the persons performing marketing research functions to maintain close liaison with the persons requesting research. The recommendations on individual projects should be presented directly to the persons who will use them so that the maximum effectiveness can be achieved in utilizing the results of marketing research.

The research director needs various talents if his department is to be well accepted, have a progressively growing program, and operate harmoniously and efficiently. After a research program or a specific project has been approved and budgeted, it is necessary to determine the demands on the department rather precisely. A number of persons may participate in various stages of the project, and this calls for teamwork and readiness. Because more than one project may be under way at a time, skillful coordination is needed. The director of the department should maintain progress charts to show the progress of each project toward completion.

Planning and coordinating a research department's operations can be a smooth process if the work ahead can be anticipated. In the competitive battle of marketing and with shifting conditions, accurate anticipation may be impossible. Inevitably, executives are confronted with problems requiring decision, whether or not marketing research can provide a factual basis for decision. When a vital job is given to the marketing research director, he may have to tag it "rush" and rearrange other research plans to accommodate it. It is possible, however, to minimize this type of situation if the research director has close working relationships with his marketing colleagues and other departmental groups. The problem is to plan what research shall be done and see that it is effectively accomplished. This means, in many cases, anticipating problems which management may face months ahead so that all possible useful evidence will be ready when the crucial time arrives. The marketing research director who recognizes a need for this liaison with all functions of management can work most projects smoothly into his staff schedules.

One of the most difficult problems for the manager of the marketing research department is to gain acceptance of his function. He must establish and maintain cordial working relationships with the executives served, ascertaining their upcoming problems in research needs, presenting and gaining acceptance of research findings, following up the application of the findings and recommendations, and advising on policy matters. To be able to serve management effectively, he must obtain adequate funds to staff his department properly.

The marketing research manager must do a broad selling job if he is to educate management on the ways in which research can be profitably used. It is not enough to carry out extensive research projects according to the best statistical methods. They must be popularized throughout the company and handled in such a way that they will not cause anyone to believe the marketing research director is seeking disproportionate authority in the business. Acceptance of the findings and recommendations of the marketing research manager will depend largely on his own skill in communications and persuasion. Without these abilities, he may be classified primarily as a technician and consequently will have problems in communicating and selling the value of his function to other operating executives.

Invariably, work-load problems will arise from time to time which will preclude the department from achieving the necessary results within the time specified. Consequently, the use of outside agencies is frequently the answer to the problem. There are many well-qualified marketing research and consulting groups which can be of significant assistance to the marketing research director under these circumstances. When his work load is too heavy or when there is a need for anonymity in carrying out the research project, it is often desirable to use an outside organization. Furthermore, an outside organization can supplement the research director's department in terms of specialized skills or knowledge, particularly when new products, new markets, new distribution methods, or the development of new marketing strategies are involved.

Because companies vary so widely in terms of products, markets, distribution, and the like, it is impractical to generalize on the size of the marketing research department or the budget that should be established. Suffice it to say that marketing research should be a vital tool for management planning. As such, it should have the full support of management.

Impact of the Total Marketing Concept. When management implements the total marketing concept, this has significant bearing on the role of marketing research. Within the total marketing concept, the sale of goods to a customer at a profit is the prime objective of the enterprise, and all planning activities must be centered on the customer and his needs and wants. Thus, it is important for marketing research to study, evaluate, and recommend products and marketing methods which will best satisfy the needs and wants of the customer, be it a housewife or a manufacturer. The most significant impact of the implementation of this concept on the organization structure is that marketing is the focal point for all planning, including manufacturing, engineering, and finance. Thus, the marketing researcher's role is increasingly important in achieving profitable growth as he studies the total demands of the business. This requires, from top management's point of view, a higher degree of sophistication in marketing research and less emphasis on simple day-to-day tasks—not that these are unimportant and should not be performed, but they can be routinized.

CONCLUSION

Marketing research is an increasingly important factor in developing plans for the growth of most companies. Marketing is often the major factor separating the successful from the unsuccessful companies. It is essential that marketing research be ready to meet this challenge. It can only do so within an environment of complete management support. Successful marketing research requires the development of techniques which will permit accurate information gathering, and sensitivity, knowledge, and judgment on the part of marketing research personnel to interpret the information gathered and make actionable recommendations to management. If it remains as a number factory, it will never achieve its potential. Basically, it must help management make fundamental decisions on the present and future course of the business as marketing plays a dominant role in planning ahead for future profitable growth. Change is an accepted fact in business life, but change must be planned for. Thus, marketing research must carry out its function in such a way that it helps management to plan for change.

BIBLIOGRAPHY

Cochran, W. G., *Sampling Techniques,* John Wiley & Sons, Inc., New York, 1953.
Crisp, R. D., *Marketing Research,* McGraw-Hill Book Company, New York, 1957.
Luck, D. J., A. G. Wales, and D. A. Taylor, *Marketing Research,* 2d ed., Prentice-Hall, Inc., Englewood Cliffs, N.J., 1961.
Sampling in Marketing Research, Marketing Research Techniques Series, no. 3, American Marketing Association, Chicago, 1958.
Schreier, Fred T., *Modern Marketing Research,* Wadsworth Publishing Co., Inc., Belmont, Calif., 1963.
A Survey of Marketing Research, American Marketing Association, Chicago, 1963.

CHAPTER FIVE

Planning Marketing Strategy

J. S. SCHIFF   *Dean, Graduate School of Business Administration, Pace College, New York, New York*

The adoption of the marketing concept brought about a heavy emphasis on planning. Before too long, however, it became patently clear that centralized planning for marketing by companies selling a mixture of products to a wide variety of markets was not feasible. What has evolved is a division of the planning responsibility. Corporate planning for both short and long range, embracing all aspects of the enterprise, is now typically a headquarters activity. Planning for marketing has been found to be most practical and effective when it is (1) relatively short range and (2) concerned with a specific product and market.

Most organizations as a result decentralize the function of marketing planning to the marketing staff. The product manager has emerged as the individual charged with the responsibility of producing the annual marketing plan. This document describes in full detail the goals set for a specific product or market and the means for attaining these goals.

The preparation of an annual marketing plan requires a thorough knowledge of the resources of the corporation; its short- and long-range objectives; a customer-oriented point of view; and skill in the technique of planning, as well as analytical ability, imagination, and decisiveness. The contents of the plan will vary from company to company, but it will usually include the following elements.

1. Performance history
2. The current and future situation in the marketplace
3. Statement of general objectives
4. Statement of strategy
5. The marketing mix
   a. Policy elements
   b. Budgetable elements—subplans and schedules
6. Research

7. Financial summary
8. Methods for review and evaluation
9. General summary and rationale

In effect, the corporate marketing plan is the sum of all of the individual annual marketing plans.

This chapter will deal primarily with the subject of marketing strategy, the most critical element of the annual marketing plan. Because of the close relationship between objectives and strategy, a few brief observations on the nature of marketing objectives will precede a broader discussion of strategy.

MARKETING OBJECTIVES

The objectives established for the marketing effort serve as the standard by which the effectiveness of the annual marketing plan is ultimately measured. They can also help to coordinate the activities of the various components of the marketing organization. To function in this fashion, the statement of general objectives in the annual marketing plan must be realistic and specific.

There are numerous, strong advocates of idealistic, unreachable statements of objectives. They see objectives as having a very important motivational value, and hence feel they should be overstated. The validity of this point of view is highly questionable. If objectives are never attained, they cease to be accepted. Furthermore, sound management urges full participation in goal setting, and under these conditions, unrealistic objectives are impractical. On the other hand, realism does not assume timidity. The prudent marketing planner will set objectives which are attainable, but which will also demand maximum, efficient effort on the part of the entire marketing organization.

Specificity in the statement of the objectives will further enhance measurement. Objectives should be expressed in quantifiable terms such as dollars, units, percentages, or time. Furthermore, the objectives should be expressed as results desired rather than as statements of activities to be undertaken. This will reduce the tendency to concentrate on activities for their own sake without adequate regard for the results the activities are to achieve.

One organization used the following as illustrative statements of objectives:

1. To increase return on assets employed from ——————— to ———————
percent.

2. To increase the share of market from ——————— to ———————.

3. To increase consumption of the product nationally by ——————— percent
or a total of ——————— units.

4. To re-create or refurbish the brand's consumer image from one that is
——————— to one that is ——————— as measured by ———————.

5. To change the percentage of sales to consumer, industrial, and government
markets from ——————— to ———————.

Share of Market. The term "share of market" frequently appears in the objectives section of the annual marketing plan, and it was included as item 2 above. It should be pointed out that the term may be misleading, for it suggests that the dimensions of the market are known. It fallaciously assumes that the size of the market is represented by the amount of goods sold to it. All that is actually known is the volume sold; in actuality, the market may be considerably larger. For example, from 1960 to 1965 the volume of automobile sales almost doubled. There is little doubt that during this period of growth the market was considerably larger than the sales volume revealed. Because the term "share of market" has a restricting influence, perhaps it should be replaced by the more accurate term "share of volume" when used in the statement of objectives.

STATEMENT OF STRATEGY

An effective strategy statement in the annual marketing plan articulates the posture to be taken in the marketplace to achieve the marketing objectives. It indicates clearly by whom and in what manner the product is to be perceived. The statement should be carefully thought through and fully developed in the early stages of the preparation of the plan. It can then act as the foundation on which the remainder of the plan is built, thus unifying the thinking of those involved in the planning process. The finished plan, as a result, should contain the concept of the strategy statement as a common thread running throughout the plan. The strategy statement also plays an important role in the execution of the plan. It serves, in this respect, as a guide to action and reduces the extent to which field activities are uncoordinated and proliferated.

Elements of a Strategy Statement. The market for any product in our affluent society is composed of a conglomeration of different clusters or segments that have common characteristics. These segments, be they demographic, social, temperamental, or the like, seem to respond differently to different products, appeals, packaging, prices, and channels of distribution. Efficient marketing forces the astute marketing planner to choose and define the segment of the market with which his product will have the greatest compatibility or congruency. This process of selecting, delineating, and matching is the first step in developing a strategy statement. In many organizations, this procedure is referred to as "positioning" the product.

Not only is the market segmented in a highly complex overlapping pattern, but it is also under a heavy, continuous barrage of communication from a variety of sources, each seeking to induce some specific behavior or action. There is a virtual around-the-clock competition for the eyes and ears of every customer and prospective customer. It is not difficult or unusual for a product to become overwhelmed and engulfed by the noise, tumult, and excitement created by other products. Hence, it is essential that the statement of strategy provide a theme or an idea around which the effort in the marketplace can be polarized to make the product prominent and differentiable.

Of course, skillful segmentation of the market may simplify the problem. Sometimes it may be possible to carve out a piece of the market which has been overlooked and thereby encounter limited competition for the attention of customers. This is usually the exception rather than the rule, and typically it is not a situation which remains unchanged for too long a period of time. It is therefore necessary for the strategy statement to provide a general direction for enhancing the conspicuousness of the product in the marketplace. This aspect of strategy has been called "spotlighting."

POSITIONING

Intelligent positioning involves matching the product with the most compatible segment of the market. A simple approach to segmentation is to divide the market into demographic slices such as age, sex, geographic location, race, occupation, income, or other classifications as provided by readily available sources of statistical data. Matching to one or several of these segments on the basis of the features of the product is a fairly typical practice.

The Polaroid Company decided at one stage in its development to enter the under-$25 camera market. This market had been dominated by Eastman Kodak's Instamatic, with sales of 10 million units. Polaroid's variation of their "Land Camera" was priced at $19.95. It was highly compact, simple to operate, and developed black and white pictures in 10 seconds. After careful research, the question of positioning was resolved with the decision to appeal to the youth market. The product was appropriately named "the Swinger."

Another illustration of demographic segmentation with a rather unusual development is the Gillette Company's experience with their aerosol deodorant, "Right Guard." The product was originally positioned to appeal to the male market, where Gillette has very strong acceptance. With a good deal of effort, and after a period of four years, the product reached 26.2 percent share of sales volume. Research surprisingly revealed that many women were buying the product and, in addition, that a great many male purchasers were sharing the product with their wives. A reevaluation of the marketing strategy with particular emphasis on positioning suggested that the product was perceived as more of a home product to be used by the entire family, rather than something to be confined strictly to the adult male. On the basis of these findings, the product was positioned to appeal to the family unit and to be used by every member of the family. Results were rapid and gratifying.

Another approach to segmentation involves dividing the market by personality types. This technique produces slices of the market which cut across the demographic segments. "Psychographic market segmentation," as it has been referred to, uses original research as the source for the identification of these segments, rather than published data.

In a study of users and nonusers of antacid analgesics, one researcher found that demographic factors provided no real clue to the precise identification of these segments of the market. However, an analysis on the basis of such personality traits as compulsiveness, punitiveness, and permissiveness was much more revealing.

But perhaps demographic and psychographic factors are not as worthwhile a source in resolving the "positioning" question as are the more pragmatic segments suggested by the very nature of the product and its competition. For example, the product of General Foods called "Tang" could have been positioned as a soft drink, snack-accompanying beverage or as a component of the breakfast menu. Research revealed that the average housewife perceived the product as a breakfast-type beverage, and it was positioned accordingly and successfully marketed.

The Du Pont Company faced a similar problem in developing the strategy for Teflon-coated cookware. The original appeal to the public was based on the theme of "greaseless cooking." After an initial flurry of purchases by cholesterol-conscious consumers, sales dropped sharply. A study of 60,000 purchasers and potential purchasers indicated that the "fat free" appeal was actually of minor importance. The research revealed instead that the housewife was more interested in the convenience feature of the product. In short, the Du Pont Company discovered that its initial strategy had positioned the product to appeal to a very small and fickle segment of the market, when in effect, the product was far more congruent with a substantially larger, more stable segment interested in "no-stick cooking with no-scour cleanup." Approximately 40 million Teflon-coated consumer utensils were purchased in 1965 as a result of the change in strategy, and forecasts of 180 million utensils in an average year were predicted.

A manufacturer of diet foods had originally decided that his product was more congruent with the segment of the market that was overweight. Accordingly, all of his efforts were directed at "fat people." Unfortunately, sales were disappointing. Observations of supermarket purchasers showed that overweight women would examine the display of this diet food and then replace the package and leave empty-handed. Further study showed, however, that actual purchasers were slim people—people who wanted to stay thin. The product was repositioned to appeal to the "thin people" market segment instead.

The 3M Company developed an industrial chemical product in 1954 which was used to treat paper for food packaging purposes. Paper treated with this chemical forms a better water and grease barrier, the chemical is economical, and the physical properties of the treated paper are not impaired. Over a period of eight years, the product was promoted directly to paper mills. Sales volume initially was slow and steady and eventually reached a plateau. Little effort, it was observed, was being made by the mills to broaden the demand for the treated paper. Accordingly, the product was repositioned to appeal to the end user. The pet food manufacturers' segment was identified first as the key portion of the market. Sales volume doubled in the space of two years. New specific market segments, such as paper-garbage-bag manufacturers, were then considered.

The consumer market for batteries provides another good illustration of positioning. Total purchases of batteries for flashlights, photography, transistors, radios, and the like amounted to $250 million at retail in 1965. About 90 percent of this volume was shared by the Eveready Division of Union Carbide and the Ray-O-Vac Division of the Electric Storage Battery Company. The Mallory Battery Company, a division of P. R. Mallory and Company, had been concentrating its efforts in the industrial market. A decision was made to enter the consumer market. The critical question facing the company was that of marketing strategy. To answer the "positioning" aspect of the strategy question, a careful analysis was made of the existing segments of the market. It was found that future growth in battery demand was most likely in the radio and photography portions. It was also found that purchasers of transistorized radios, tape recorders, portable television sets, and cameras were becoming much more quality-minded. As a result, it was decided to appeal to that segment of the market that was willing to pay a premium for a battery of higher quality. A line was designed consisting of higher-priced mercury batteries which lose very little power in storage, in comparison with zinc carbon batteries which lose up to 30 percent of their power in a few months.

Identifying New Market Segments. The marketing planner obviously should be constantly studying the reactions of the market to discern the emergence of new significant segments and the decline of others. One source that may portend the emergence of new segments is contained in the input-output tables published by the Office of Business Economics. The data reveal how the output of one industry is consumed or utilized by other industries. Any change in the relationship over a period of time could be extremely significant. For example, a manufacturer of metal containers may find that his industry has a declining consumption by the food industry, but an increasing consumption by the drug industry. Similar variations quickly discerned, validated, and interpreted may help to provide worthwhile clues to the problem of positioning.

For example, observant marketers of consumer products have identified the evolution of a new, rapidly growing, market segment. This cluster of potential buyers is made up of eighteen- to twenty-nine-year olds who live alone or with nonrelatives. This group has been characterized as "not savings-oriented," "optimistic," and "self-indulgent." They have already influenced the design of apartment buildings, furniture, and home furnishings. Interested in food, fun, and getting as much out of life in the short run as possible, and having the wherewithal to gratify their desires, this portion of the market not only can be of immediate commercial value, but also may serve as a spawning ground for some new and as yet unidentified market segments.

SPOTLIGHTING

Although the two elements of strategy, positioning and spotlighting, are of equal importance to the success of the marketing effort, there are some basic differences between them. As illustrated above, the positioning decision usually stems from an analysis of the market and has its roots in research. Spotlighting, which entails making the product conspicuous in the marketplace, involves the use of communications media such as radio, television, newspapers, displays, meetings, and the like.

Typically, spotlighting costs will far exceed the expenditures necessary to determine how to position the product. The selection of the combination of media which will reach the greatest portion of the segment of the market previously designated at the lowest cost is therefore critical. Furthermore an original idea—a theme which is arresting, unique, or distinctive—can multiply the impact of a message many times over and thereby substantially increase the return on the investment in any medium used. This aspect of marketing strategy therefore calls for a thorough understanding of the various media available and their costs, and a good deal of creative thought.

A rather direct means of spotlighting, which is widely used for many products, is the technique of branding. For example, the United Fruit Company retained sole possession of the Chiquita trademark for its bananas. Supported by quality control, labeling, special packaging, and four million dollars of newspaper, magazine, and television advertising annually, United Fruit's aim was to make Chiquita synonymous with banana.

More typical of what is involved in an effective spotlighting decision is illustrated by a product of Chas. Pfizer and Co. called "Visine." A preparation which reduces eye irritation and redness, the product had been known to the medical profession for many years and had been promoted primarily by doctors' recommendations. When the decision was made to promote the product more broadly to the consumer, the questions of media and theme had to be answered. Management decided that the only way to differentiate the product was to get it into the hands of the consumer for trial. Thus the underlying theme was trial before purchase. Instead of using consumer advertising media, a more direct means of communication was used to get this message across. An arrangement was made with the AAA and the Allstate Motor Club to include a bottle of Visine eye drops in the travel kit that is mailed in response to travel inquiries. Sampling in drugstores was introduced during the hay-fever season, and battery-operated display units were installed in these retail outlets. Finally, two million copies of a promotional booklet, "The Little Seeing Book," were distributed at trade conventions, to school systems, in doctors' waiting rooms, and in drugstores.

The Olin Mathieson Chemical Corporation took advantage of two developments to help spotlight its Ecusta Paper Division's Waylite brand. This division sold its products to paper buyers and printing purchasing agents. The two developments which provided the opportunity were an increase in postal rates and the widened acceptance of value analysis by industry. Value analysis, a development in purchasing practice (see Chapter 5 of Section 6), suggests a total cost approach to buying decision making. The price of the item to be purchased is considered as merely one of many inputs. All of the ramifications are weighed by the buyer or purchasing agent cognizant of the technique of value analysis.

In the case of the Waylite brand, the advantages of less weight and bulk were obvious. However, other cost considerations such as in binding, storage, handling, ease of folding, strength, longevity, and printability were usually not stressed by the sales force or considered by the buyer. To spotlight the product for this market segment, value analysis was adopted as the central theme. Communication of the theme involved the use of the sales force, the business press, and direct mail.

A series of three-day seminars was established to train the sales force in value analysis. The seminars ended with specific instructions in the use of a carefully prepared selling kit. This kit contained a prospect list, copies of publicity releases about the use of value analysis in paper purchasing, and details of the advertising and direct mail campaign. The salesmen were also supplied with materials to give to each buyer for the purpose of having him conduct an actual value analysis on the sales call.

The advertising campaign, which used the *Harvard Business Review, Business Week, Purchasing Week,* and *Purchasing Magazine,* offered literature on value analysis with appropriate reference to the Waylite brand. Three separate mailings, expanding on the theme contained in the advertisements, were made to purchasers of printing and paper.

A unique feature was used by one manufacturer as the theme to spotlight the product in an extremely competitive field. Although the General Electric Company had pioneered the electric knife, its marketing position was threatened by the Hamilton Beach Division of Scovill Manufacturing, a later entry for a share of this volume. Unlike the competitor's product, Hamilton's knife had a hole in the handle. This feature differentiated it from competing products and served as the basis for a highly effective marketing campaign. Instead of promoting the benefits of electric knives generally, Hamilton Beach concentrated on the hole in the handle and the resulting ease of grip and distribution of weight of its electric knife.

The company relied primarily on consumer advertising media to get the message across. The twenty-two top appliance-buying markets were barraged with local TV and newspaper supplement advertisements during an October-to-December period. The only promotional activity used was in-store carving demonstrations. Three hundred college boys were hired and trained by the company's home economist. They showed off their newly acquired skill as professional carvers for twenty hours per week over a period of five weeks.

By the end of the campaign in December, all retailers had sold out their inventories with little discounting evident. In an effort to satisfy those buyers whose stocks were depleted early in the period, the company printed up special gift certificates. Of these, 75,000 were purchased as well by late shoppers.

DEVELOPING THE STRATEGY STATEMENT

Ideally, the statement of marketing strategy should be both succinct and meaningful. In the following two case histories, the resolution of the positioning question and the basis for spotlighting the product are described, and strategy statements are illustrated.

The manufacturer of Gainesburgers, a dog food, found that the market could be divided into two segments—those who purchased dry food for their pets and those who bought wet or canned food. Dry food was considered by many to be less nutritious, and wet food was considered inconvenient for the owner. It was decided to position the product between both.   Because Gainesburgers were as nutritious as the wet food, but were odorless and required no refrigeration, it was felt that a new market segment consisting of those dissatisfied with both the existing wet and dry foods could be fashioned.

Spotlighting was to be achieved by presenting the product as a hamburger for the dog.   It was reasoned that this would further differentiate the product from the competition.

Test-market results were extremely disappointing.   Research revealed that the convenience feature was well received.   However, the hamburger theme was completely misconstrued.   Purchasers assumed that the product was a special human-type food rather than a regular dog food.   As a result, it was used as a treat for their pets rather than as a total meal.

On the basis of these data, the product was then repositioned against the canned food competition.   Furthermore, all references to hamburgers were eliminated.   A food which was the equivalent of a canned food, without the accompanying inconvenience, was stressed as the theme.

The strategy statement which ultimately evolved could be expressed as follows: "To present to the segment of the market now purchasing canned dog food, Gainesburgers, as the convenient nutritional equivalent not requiring refrigeration."

The second case history is provided by Yankelovich,[1] who devised an effective strategy for the marketing of Timex watches.   His analysis of the market for watches indicated that demographic classifications were confusing.   For example, the most expensive watches were being bought by people with the highest and the lowest incomes.   In addition, some upper-income consumers bought inexpensive watches which were discarded when they needed costly repairs.

Accordingly, he segmented the market on the basis of value.   One segment of the market consisted of "people who wanted to pay the lowest possible price for any watch that works reasonably well."   They would probably discard the watch and replace it after a period of six months or a year.   He found that this group represented 23 percent of the buyers.

The second segment was composed of those "who valued watches for their long life, good workmanship, good material, and good styling."   This segment was willing to pay for the product features of durability and quality.   It represented 46 percent of the buyers.

The third segment, those "who look not only for useful product features but also for meaningful emotional qualities," purchased a watch for gift purposes, to be given on special occasions.   For these purposes, the brand, styling, a gold case, diamonds, and the like were extremely important.   About 31 percent of the buyers were in this group.

In an effort to decide how to position Timex watches, Yankelovich also carefully studied the marketing practices of the other leading watch manufacturers. He found that, between 1957 and 1962, the competition had selected the third segment of the market, representing 31 percent of the buyers, as their target.   In their efforts to spotlight their products to this segment of the market, the manufacturers tended to equate product quality with the features of shock resistance and waterproofing.   Furthermore, because this segment of the market did the bulk of their purchasing during the Christmas season, the greatest advertising and promotion activity took place during November and December.

At the completion of this careful study of the market, the ideal strategy was clearly evident.   Timex had a new low-priced watch which would have

[1] Daniel Yankelovich, "New Criteria for Market Segmentation," *Harvard Business Review*, March–April, 1964, pp. 84–86.

strong appeal for the first segment. In addition, the company had been able to incorporate the waterproof and shock-resistance features into their watch without affecting the low price. Because these features conveyed the notion of quality, the watch would also appeal to the second segment.

With respect to spotlighting the product, because the two market segments made their purchases year round, Timex decided to advertise throughout the year. As a result, they had little or no competition from other manufacturers for ten months. Because they were trying to reach 69 percent of the buyers, television was used as the key medium. Commercials which were original and dramatic were developed to stress the quality of the Timex watch.

The strategy statement for Timex could read as follows: "To present, on a year-round basis, to those segments of the market who purchase watches for reasons of economy and quality, Timex as an attractive, shock-resistant, waterproof, quality product available at a low price."

CONCLUSION

The annual marketing plan is rapidly becoming the document of critical importance to those involved in the planning of the marketing effort. At the heart of the plan is the statement of marketing strategy. This statement, which indicates how the product is to be positioned and spotlighted, coalesces the thinking of those involved in the full development of the plan and coordinates the activities of those concerned with its execution. An effective statement of strategy seems to emerge out of a combination of reliable research data, original thought, a thorough knowledge of available media, and a pragmatic understanding of the marketplace.

BIBLIOGRAPHY

Alderson, Wroe, *Marketing Behavior and Executive Action*, Richard D. Irwin, Inc., Homewood, Ill., 1957.

Alderson, Wroe, and Paul E. Green, *Planning and Problem Solving in Marketing*, Richard D. Irwin, Inc., Homewood, Ill., 1964.

Gentry, Dwight L., and Donald L. Shawver, *Fundamentals of Managerial Marketing*, Simmons-Boardman Publishing Corporation, New York, 1964.

Klaw, Spencer, "The Soap Wars: A Strategic Analysis," *Fortune*, vol. 68, June, 1963.

Richards, Elizabeth, and Monroe Mendelsohn, *The Marketing Plan in Action*, American Marketing Association, New York, 1964.

Smith, Wendell R., "Product Differentiation and Market Segmentation as Alternative Marketing Strategies," *Journal of Marketing*, vol. 21, no. 1, July, 1965.

Yankelovich, Daniel, "New Criteria for Market Segmentation," *Harvard Business Review*, March–April, 1964.

CHAPTER SIX

Packaging and Branding

WALTER P. MARGULIES *President, Lippincott & Margulies, Inc., New York, New York*

Packaging, as it will be treated in this chapter, is *package design*—the unique combination of colors, graphics, and symbols utilized to distinguish one brand from another of the same product type.

Physical packaging—the general form of a product's container and the material of which it is composed—is important, of course. New materials, new production techniques, and innovations such as the aerosols have helped make packaging one of the most exciting and highly competitive of all industries.

But physical packaging, it must be realized, is governed by factors confronted in common by all competitors in any specific product category. These can include the chemical and structural nature of the specific product to be marketed, the climatic conditions of major geographic areas of marketing, shipping and handling costs from point of product origin to these areas, the cost of supermarket shelf space and the average height of a supermarket shelf, and the competitive profit margin inherent in various available packaging materials such as polyurethane, glass, paperboard, and tinplate. Such factors as these cause all of the more successful corporations engaged in competitively marketing the same type of product to use approximately the same physical packaging shapes and materials.

Thus, when a product comes to the point of package design, it already is encased in the bare bones of a package, in a plain wrapper generally similar to that of its competitors. It is what happens to it from that point on which is of crucial importance to an administrator in a position to expedite the packaging and branding of his corporation's products.

APPROACH TO PACKAGING AND BRANDING

The packaging and branding of a product is a highly complex, highly creative design operation. Its direction and much of its ultimate success depend upon the predesign solution of the marketing problems inherent in the correct positioning of that product.

What constitutes the correct packaging and branding for the product is best attained through the combined efforts of many highly skilled technicians. Along with economists, sociologists, psychologists, and experts in mass communications, the package designer must contribute to a coordinated marketing solution.

The packaging and branding of any product, moreover, should be regarded as an ongoing process—one in which the design, after placement in the market, is periodically checked as to its own efficiency and that of its attendant imagery, and these are altered or "refined" whenever necessary.

In both concept and design, the problems inherent in successful product packaging and branding are resolved by astute marketing solutions, not by graphic solutions alone.

Three Crucial Aspects. There are three crucial aspects which an administrator must be cognizant of if he is to aid his corporation in the most profitable use of packaging and branding. These are (1) how to employ package design, (2) when to employ package design, and (3) how branding can be employed. (Although an integral part of packaging, branding possesses sufficiently specific, complex problems to warrant independent discussion.)

The administrator should become aware of the type of outside design services to retain, how best to utilize them, what information to supply, what responsibilities to delegate, and what results to expect. To be of aid to his corporation in establishing the objectives of a package design program, the administrator should develop a thorough knowledge of the basics of how this program is executed and the marketing situations where it is called for. In terms of attaining these objectives, the administrator will have little direct control over the actual design process. Once it has been set in motion, and until the presentation of the final design, the process is in the hands of the experts retained.

It is possible that the administrator may be called upon to be of assistance in the orientation and evaluation phase to supply pertinent information concerning his unit's duties, responsibilities, and goals as they pertain to the product under consideration. If he is involved with research department administration, he may be called upon to be of assistance in the predesign research phase to supply pertinent corporation or division-executed sales data, or market and motivational research findings.

Evaluations of the results of design programs are customarily made through periodic sales analyses and by market research. These studies concern such factors as changes in use patterns by pertinent demographic segments of the population, or motivational research to determine changes in the brand's consumer-perceived image or personality profile. A thorough knowledge of what research can and cannot do and of the varied techniques available, in terms of their relative value for investigating a specific type of problem, is of value when outside research services are to be employed.

How to Employ Package Design. The administrator should be aware that the path which a package design program takes will be determined by the specifics involved. It is often determined, in fact, by the particular product type to be packaged, the particular corporation involved, and its internal capabilities, patterns of distribution, or relationship with suppliers. Even the type of consumer toward which the product is generally directed must be carefully considered, as well as the activities of the product's competition and any specific problems and opportunities inherent in the industry of which the product's manufacturer is a member.

He should also be aware of what might be called the "ten basic stages" in the creation of successful packaging. If the designer under consideration does not include these basic steps in explaining his program for your company, be sure to ask for an explanation before you hire him.   Failure to do so may place the product or products involved in jeopardy.

Step 1—Orientation and Evaluation.   Led by a design director and augmented by a marketing expert, the assigned staff designers will orient themselves to the product's problems.   This includes learning for themselves how the product is made, advertised, distributed, sold, and used, as well as making a critical design evaluation of present and/or competing packages.

Step 2—Predesign Research.   Execution of this step often depends upon the amount and quality of the data which the corporation itself has amassed.   If existing data are limited, or not available, new marketing studies should be initiated to determine the perceived product characteristics, its packaging requirements, and its present and potential markets.   Although there are exceptions to this rule, it is generally true that without full reckoning of opportunities and problems in the marketplace, the package designer is designing in a vacuum.

Predesign research is particularly valuable for a brand belonging to a product category the members of which are essentially alike in composition and appearance, such as beer, instant coffee, cigarettes, and others where the consumer's image of each brand is its prime sales determiner.   Predesign research can delineate the personality profile of the primary competitors (and of the brand itself, if it is an already established one) as well as being of invaluable assistance in guiding package planning.

Step 3—Marketing Platform.   This document summarizes the direction in which packaging and attendant marketing efforts are to go.   Based upon the results of Steps 1 and 2 and executed by design and marketing experts, it *defines the scope* of the design assignment, *sets the goals* of the program, and *establishes the criteria* against which the final package design will be measured.

Step 4—Design Directive.   Based upon the scope, goals, and criteria set forth in the marketing platform, a directive is drawn up by the design director for internal use by the design staff.   It contains the design director's suggestions for employing the tools of design (color, texture, graphics, and the like) to achieve the goals established in the platform.

From the front-of-the-package illustration to the back-of-the-package copy, the design director makes hundreds of small but very important creative decisions.   Most of the finished package's graphic effectiveness depends upon the skill with which he makes these decisions.   From a multitude of possibilities for the various elements of the package, he selects specific alternatives and then proceeds to translate them into a unique, cohesive whole.

It is in this process that the "mystique" of design operates, for here the design director is dealing almost entirely with symbols.   The various type faces and the colors which he uses are symbols, as are the geometric or abstract representations or the photographs utilized as package illustrations.   They can easily fail to communicate the desired message and thus fail to involve the consumer positively, unless they are used in the "correct" manner and in the "correct" combinations.   They speak a powerful, emotionally audible language to which the consumer strongly reacts, although less than consciously aware that she does so.   It is because their *conscious* interpretation is rarely learned by persons not trained as designers that the design director's choices of individual design components, and the method by which he arrives at these choices, will often seem to "outsiders" to be mysterious, arbitrary, or even somewhat illogical.

Step 5—Internal Approval: The Plans Board Review.   As soon as the design directive has been drawn up, both it and the marketing platform are subjected to critical appraisal.   Some form of the plans review board system is commonly used by all successful industrial design firms.   This system assures the client of top-level supervision of the solution to his problem. The board is composed of specialists in design, marketing, research, advertising, engineering, and production. Kept aware of the problem from the beginning, it meets to review progress to date, interject ideas, suggest possible amendments or changes in design or marketing emphasis, and finally approve the marketing platform and design directive.

Step 6—Creative Design. Following plans board approval, staff designers, working under the supervision of the design director, begin translating the marketing platform into sketches and roughs. As many approaches and combinations of approaches as they can create are developed. Often, hundreds of sketches come out of each of these approaches. Screened by themselves and in concert with the design director, only the very best (perhaps ten or twelve) are selected as exhibiting the best potential.

Step 7—Plans Board Review. These screened selections, or candidate designs, are then presented to the plans board, which measures each against the criteria established in the marketing platform. The number of candidates is usually narrowed down to two or three, representing varying interpretations of the criteria. It is rare, at this point, to find a candidate so obviously superior that a final choice and recommendation can immediately be made.

Step 8—Design Validation. It is a wise precaution, in fact, for the final candidates to be subjected to research studies which will determine the strong and weak points of each and ascertain which one candidate will best function for the product in the marketplace. Here, research may be said to provide a "dress rehearsal" for sales. Practically any reasonably well-designed package looks good on an executive's desk. The problem is to produce one which will stand out and work hard and positively when it is side by side with its competitors in ads and on the market shelves.

Ascertaining the "personality profile" of each design—its perceived socioeconomic status, the price, quality, sex, age, and "typical user" connotations—is usually an intrinsic part of design validation. Designs are also tested as to their "visibility," thus discerning any distortions which may occur in either their visual or psychological interpretation at varying distances and in varying light intensities.

Step 9—Design Refinement and Presentation. As the result of facts disclosed by design validation, the final design may be modified to eliminate any possible "negative" elements or to emphasize its "positives."

Following possible modification, the design is again passed on by the plans review board and is then presented for client approval. This final presentation to the client is made only after the plans review board has determined that the assignment objectives and the design firm's own quality standards have been brought to the optimum level.

The design which will have been produced is one which, with possible minor variations, will be equally effective on all necessary package shapes and sizes and on commonly used forms of physical packaging. The design director, whose task it is to produce the final design, is very aware that boxes and cartons, corrugated shippers, metal cans, and glass containers are still the big four of physical packaging. He is also aware that the market share of metal cans and glass containers is exhibiting a constant, gradual decrease, whereas transparent films, molded plastics, and aerosols are increasing their share of market much faster than are any other packaging materials. Consequently, he will have produced a reasonably flexible design, with its possible future use on any or all of these packaging materials clearly in mind.

Step 10—Production Control. The design director stays with his design through the production stage. Checking such technicalities as color consistency and graphic fidelity, he makes sure that the package which enters the market is the same one which came off the drawing board. Under his supervision, designers prepare permanent color standards against which inks and prints can be checked during the years the design will be in use. Type sizes and styles for use on various sizes of packaging and in advertising also are carefully designated and exemplified.

When to Employ Package Design. Special attention should be given to two basic situations where packaging is of major importance. These are (1) to establish brand effectiveness—that is, as an integral part of the introduction of a new brand or product—and (2) to increase brand effectiveness—that is, to bring about a change in the imagery and resultant sales of an already established brand and thus those of the corporation which produces it. In each of these situations, the package designer must anticipate many requirements which, if neglected, could create major marketing problems.

Establishing Brand Effectiveness. Of all the communications tools which are used to introduce a new brand, packaging's function is one of the most varied and complex. Largely on its own merits, it must work to capture and maintain sales for the new brand. *It is the brand's primary sales tool.*

Through all the consumer advertising, promotion, publicity, and merchandising, the package must perform the introductory role of presenting, acquainting, and convincing. It introduces the brand to the dealer and the customer; at the point of purchase and until the product is actually used, the package is, in effect, both the brand and the product.

In the introduction of a new brand, the package should serve as the focal point for all other promotional communications. Advertising and promotion should be built around it, not vice versa. Any specific advertising campaign is, of necessity, short-lived, as are most display and sales promotional themes. The package, on the other hand, lives a relatively long life and is under constant, often intense, scrutiny by the consumer. In store, in hand, at home, and in use, the package will bear the brunt of identifying the particular brand.

To enable it to so function, a new brand's package must be designed to sell at shelf level, both instantly and on a long-term basis. If it does not possess instant shelf attraction, does not appear convenient to use, does not quickly convey pertinent information, or is not memorable, then the more transient effects of advertising and sales promotion will be lost. The consumer must want to buy the package when it is new and represents a new brand, perhaps even a new product. The package must also be designed so that the consumer will still be attracted by it and will still purchase the brand in a month or six months or a year, when neither the package nor the brand is any longer new.

Within its role in new-brand effectiveness, packaging can also serve as a *link between new and old products in an already established brand line.*

If a company develops a product which is related in form or method of preparation or in general product type to those which it is already marketing, a package may be designed which will be generally similar to the already existing packages of its "old" products. For example, if General Mills were to market a new formula ready-to-mix *hot* cereal, the chances are that its package would be designed to somewhat resemble those General Mills packages already existing in its very extensive "Big G" *cold* cereal line and that it would be branded as a member of the "Big G" line.

In many cases, however, the link from new to old product is no simple matter to execute. For example, what happens when a company known to the consumer for a specific type of product marketed under a distinctive, well-known brand name develops and decides to market an additional, but completely different line of products? By simple duplication of the essential aspects of the current package's format and brand name, packaging can be designed which will link the proposed product line with the established one, and the new product line can ride into market on the good reputation of the established product.

However, unless the new and the established products are quite similar in nature (as in the "Big G" example), such direct linkage can well prove disastrous to both lines. What happens, for instance, if the established product is evaporated milk and the proposed new product line for which the company is in need of packaging happens to be insecticides? If they go to market similar in packaging and alike in brand name, the consumer (because, as market and motivational research has revealed, she is basically emotional, somewhat irrational in her thinking, and naïve concerning other than simple household economics) will inevitably "see" them as both coming from the same factory, perhaps even from the same spigot. And then what happens to the sales of the new *and* the established products?

In cases such as this, packaging clearly becomes a marketing problem. Before design is even contemplated, very important decisions upon which millions of profit dollars each year can ride must be made. These decisions involve exactly how the new product should be "positioned" for consumer acceptance and sales in terms of the structure of the corporation which produces it, the nature and number of its brother and sister brands and products, and ultimately, the needs, desires, and perceptions of the consumer.

Increasing Brand Effectiveness. Although it is no less creative, unique, or complicated, this employment of package design usually involves redesign rather than design "from scratch." Often, only a portion of the design may be radically changed. All dominant colors on all of a brand's similar products may be made uniform, for example, or the packages may be color-keyed to designate product types, or the illustrations of each of the individual packages may be discarded and one key illustration adopted for use across the product line.

There are six basic situations in which package design should be considered to increase brand effectiveness.

1. *To gain new markets.* For example, a heretofore locally marketed brand may be going national. Packaging therefore must be capable of operating effectively in all major competitive markets. If research indicates that it is not, then redesign is in order. Additionally, more and more corporations are engaging in international marketing. In this case, an even more ubiquitously effective package is necessary—one which, with certain language changes, can operate with equal effectiveness in all countries within the area designated for the product's marketing.

2. *When a competitor's package too closely resembles yours.* Redesign is recommended to maintain sales and positive imagery. Also, it is predictable that one of you eventually is going to redesign. If you are first, your brand will capture the profits of consumer excitement which invariably results from new packaging introductions.

3. *When new features or ingredients of definite importance to the consumer are added.* Neither the expense involved nor the risk of consumer confusion warrants package changes for every product formula change which is made. Additionally, consumers by this time are wary of "new" and "improved" product claims. The "newness" therefore must be real, must be obvious, and must be of direct personal importance before the consumer will accept it and before her acceptance warrants package change.

4. *To integrate a hitherto unrelated package into a "family" of product pack-*

ages. Here, all packages of the line may be redesigned, or it may be that design will best serve merely to bring the "maverick" into the line.

5. *When market research reveals that a particular package is an actual deterrent to produce sales.* Here, a corporation should actually be one step ahead of itself. It is when the sales begin to slip that redesign should be effected, rather than when the brand has declined. Not only does it take months to place a new package on the market, but it is more economical to redesign as soon as trouble is apparent. Redesign is often the best way, and sometimes the only way, to bring a brand back to its former sales position.

6. *When there is a major breakthrough in physical packaging materials.* An example is the advent of the economically feasible use of polyurethane for mass-produced packaging. It was quickly discovered, when attempts were made to transfer designs from the product-governed background color of a clear glass bottle to the opaque background of a rigid plastic bottle, that some designs did not operate with their former effectiveness. Similarly, a design geared to a rigid surface is not always capable of presenting itself effectively when subjected to the use-induced distortion of a squeeze bottle or a soft plastic pouch.

It should be borne in mind that a package should never be changed merely for the sake of change. If the package under consideration is a strong sales link—an effective identifier of its brand; is well-integrated with the packages of its corporation's related products; and is considered by consumers to be as modern and as superior in "quality" as it can possibly be, there is no rational reason to change it. Because package design is expensive, very complex, and by no means devoid of risk, it should never be undertaken frivolously.

The frequency with which packaging is redesigned depends a great deal upon the particular industry involved. When Sylvania changed its light bulb packaging, it was the first major redesign program for this product in thirty-six years. At the opposite extreme are companies in some businesses, of which cake mix and detergent producers are two examples, which find it necessary to review their packaging at least once a year and to refine it with almost similar frequency.

How Branding Can Be Employed. Essentially, the major problems in the employment of branding concern the problems of corporate communications.

A corporation brands a product to help sell it; but to sell as profitably as possible, marketing strategy must first ascertain which one of three alternative methods of identification and promotion is best for that particular product: (1) the product alone, (2) the product and the corporation together, or (3) the corporation alone.

There is no general set of rules for these corporate decisions. The following are some of the factors and some of the more pertinent problems, as they bear upon packaging design and implementation, which each corporation must take into account in branding its products.

The Product Alone. It must be ascertained if the individual product, branded with its particular name, the particular "look" which will be designed for it, and the particular reputation which will be carefully constructed for it, will be capable of gaining as much consumer acceptance as possible.

Before such a decision can be reached, the brand's age must be considered. If it is an already established brand whose profits are not equal to its potential, its current image must be studied to find the weak points and steps taken to eradicate or counterbalance them. If it is a new brand, its cost of launching must be borne in mind. Launching a new product is such an expensive undertaking that few corporations can afford to market and promote completely unrelated lines of products. It is more economical to promote a "family" of products, adopting a package design which in some manner resembles those of its established products, and usually employing the already established brand name. However, not all products of a given corporation can logically fit into a "family" (for example, the case cited of the evaporated milk and the insecticides).

If the brand in question is an already established one, it must also be decided whether new packaging should constitute a minor change or a radical departure from its current packaging. There are some brands which, no matter how poorly they may be doing against competition, cannot afford radically new packaging. These are brands the color combinations or style of whose packaging is so firmly entrenched in the consumer's mind that it constitutes the brand's strongest identification franchise. The red and white of Campbell's Soup and the blue and white of Kleenex and Ivory Soap are examples (although these brands are by no means doing poorly). Discerning the degree to which an established brand's packaging may be changed safely is one aspect of predesign research.

The Product and the Corporation Together. It must also be ascertained if the endorsement of the corporation working in concert with the individual branding devices for the product will prove comparatively more profitable. Here, it should be borne in mind that the consumer, even if she wants and is attracted to that which appears entirely new, also wants assurance and a feeling of security as to the quality of what she buys. If the consumer feels that the corporation which markets the new brand is large, stable, and has a reputation for high-quality products, the chances are that she will "see" the new brand as to some degree possessing the superior qualities of its maker, the corporation, and will feel assured by what she "sees."

Corporations as entities generally possess positive, if somewhat nebulous, imagery. Again, because of the high cost of launching a new brand, the tendency is more and more for corporations to capitalize on their generally good reputations by using their names on new products.

Old, established products, too, have their difficulties in capturing their potential share of the market if they must struggle for individual brand acceptance. Campbell Soup, conscious of these competitive risks, included its merger-acquired Swanson, Pepperidge Farm, and Franco-American lines under the Campbell corporate endorsement.

Dual endorsement also aids the corporation. Olin Mathieson Chemical Corporation was diffusing millions of dollars in sales impact through product and divisional advertising (via five agencies) which was completely divorced from promotion of the parent company. Thus, the impact of a multimillion-dollar advertising budget was fractionated and dissipated without producing sales commensurate with expenditure. Olin then came to realize that it could improve its corporate communications and publicize its actual scope of operations comparatively economically if it promoted brand, division, and corporation in the same advertisement. This promotional policy is being adopted by an increasing number of large multidivisional, multibrand corporations.

The Corporation Alone. In deciding whether or not it is most profitable for a product to be marketed with no identifiers other than those of the corporation, the problem is to discern accurately beforehand the breadth of the spectrum of products which the corporation in question can effectively endorse. This process is made particularly complex by the fact that acquisition and merger constitute the major means of corporate growth, with new-product development second.

As a result of acquisition or merger, radical structural changes can occur in each of the corporate entities involved. Each separate corporation involved brings with it its individual brands, often leading to apparently strange or incongruous combinations of product lines. It has been estimated that, throughout the early sixties, corporate mergers occurred at the rate of four per day. As a result of some of them, liquor companies market metals, a gunpowder firm also produces food, a company which began as a group of lobster fishermen produces chemicals, and an automobile manufacturer also markets radios and TV sets.

Through acquisition, merger, or new-product introduction, it may become ineffective or even harmful for a corporation to utilize its name as the vehicle by which to brand its product lines, unless its identity as a corporation is sufficiently broad and encompassing. Johnson's Wax, for example, gives all of its many competing lines of waxes its corporate endorsement; but what would happen if the company decided to branch into the detergent field? (This might seem plausible to the consumer since both detergents and waxes have something to do with cleaning. Predesign research would have to establish just how close a relating link between new and old could safely be made in packaging and branding.)

Kraft, with one of the best "natural" names in the food business, uses this corporate name to brand many of its products; but would the sturdy, homey, "kitchen-crafted" reputation which consumers now associate with Kraft stretch to cover a line of imported delicacy foods? (Kraft would probably have to broaden its own image as a corporation before it could effectively endorse such a line. Predesign research would have to establish just how much the Kraft corporate imagery would have to be broadened and what type of imagery the new packaging and branding would have to connote to implement the imagery.)

It is obvious that, in branding by the corporation alone, a great deal rides on one name and one reputation. Not only is there a danger of the individual product being orphaned in a maze of mergers or lost in a maze of similarly identified products, but there is the danger that one poorly received product can make a real difference in the reputation of the entire corporation.

When the product and the corporation work together in branding and the consumer finds the product to be unsatisfactory, then the product, because it is the smaller, closer, better known of the two entities, takes most of the blame. But, when the corporation alone brands and the product is unsatisfactory, the corporation, in effect, takes double blame. (It is only when the product alone is involved in branding that the corporation remains blameless; but then, of course, it can neither help the product nor have its own image benefit from the product's success.)

The Brand Mark. In the light of orientation and evaluation and the findings of predesign research (Steps 1 and 2 in the creation of packaging), the marketing platform (Step 3) establishes which direction the branding of the product is to take. Now, as part of the packaging program for that product, a graphic interpretation of that branding strategy is designed (Steps 4 and 6). This graphic device is called the "mark." It functions as the brand's key identifier. The mark is usually composed of the word or words to be used as the brand's name and sometimes a symbol which will be made to stand for the outstanding characteristic or characteristics of the brand. Often, a distinctively unique manner of writing the name is utilized, and there is usually a distinctive use of color.

The mark is a shorthand device. It is carefully designed to be the sign by which the brand is identified and recognized down the supermarket aisle, when flipping through a magazine, or on a sign a half-mile up the road. It is carefully designed to trigger the memory so that it, itself, is easily recalled, and as a result of its recall the brand comes back to memory. It is carefully designed to transmit characteristics and qualities of the brand, its product, and, to whatever previously decided-upon degree, the company which markets it.

An example of how a mark is used to identify and promote a product alone is General Mills' use of a red spoon containing the words "Betty Crocker" for its ready-to-prepare foods, most prominently its cake mixes.

Chrysler brands the product and the corporation together, utilizing a mark which signifies the corporation, the Chrysler Pentastar, and the individual automobile brand names—each of which is presented in its own distinctive graphic style.

U.S. Steel brands by means of a corporate identifier alone. All U.S. Steel products are readily identified by their three stylized diamonds, each of a different color, and the unique presentation of USS within a circle.

Regardless of the individual manner of presentation, a mark is consistently employed from year to year, despite model or product changes, the introduction of new product forms, the redesign of package illustration, or changes in background package colors. Once adopted, the mark becomes the one constant identifier. It may be subjected to minor design revisions, to modernize it or to make it more visible at greater speeds, but the design of the mark is changed radically only when it is definitely proved to be weak or when it has become obsolete.

SUMMARY

The packaging and branding of a product are not operations unique of themselves and divorced from other aspects of marketing that product. In both concept and design, the problems inherent in successful packaging and branding are resolved by astute marketing solutions, not by graphic solutions alone.

Packaging and branding should be regarded as salesmen, as identifiers and image carriers, of the product to which they are directly applied and of the corporation which markets that product. Because of the cost of packaging and the time involved in effecting packaging changes, packaging and branding programs should be so designed that their results can both establish the brand in the marketplace and maintain it there as profitably as possible for as long as possible.

Just as the structure of a corporation is fluid and liable to change through acquisition, merger, and the development of new product lines, so too must the marketing strategies for its products be fluid. Therefore, as an integral part of a product's effective marketing, its packaging and branding should be regarded as somewhat less than static. Even though for economic reasons they must be designed for long-term use, they should be subjected to periodic evaluation, and to design refinement or redesign in specific instances where it is to the corporation's distinct financial advantage to do so.

What constitutes the correct packaging and branding for a product is a highly complex problem, and the solution to it is best attained through the combined efforts of many highly skilled technicians. Among the specialists whose skills are needed are economists, experts in the social sciences, and marketing consultants. Package designers are but one type of member on this highly versatile team.

There are three crucial aspects of packaging and branding of which an administrator must be cognizant, if he is to profitably aid his corporation in their use: how to employ package design, when to employ package design, and how branding can be employed. The administrator should develop a thorough knowledge of the basics of packaging and branding and the marketing situations where they are necessary, as discussed at length in this chapter, and be prepared to retain outside expert services for their execution when necessary. He should become aware of the type of services to retain, how best to utilize them, what information to supply them, what responsibilities to delegate, and what results to expect.

BIBLIOGRAPHY

Dun's Review & Modern Industry, New York, annual packaging issue.
Modern Packaging Annual Encyclopedia, McGraw-Hill Book Company, New York.
Packaging Design, New York, annual materials issue.

Recommended Trade Publications

Modern Packaging.
Packaging Design.
Package Engineering.
Food and Drug Packaging.
Advertising Age.
Printers' Ink.
Industrial Design.
Graphics: New York.

CHAPTER SEVEN

Pricing Methods*

SPENCER A. TUCKER *Partner, Martin & Tucker, Little Neck, New York*

Prices are a basic and critical factor in generating the return on capital invested in a business enterprise. Pricing methods and policies contribute directly to the success or failure of a business irrespective of any other single profit activity. Medieval cost-price practices in many otherwise well-managed companies continue to produce inadequate returns on invested capital.

A salable price is not necessarily a company's marked-up cost. Cost-plus pricing methods deny the existence of competition and the effect of market demand. A pricing policy must mesh in the seller's profit objectives with both the marketplace and an estimate of the behavior of competitors and their reactions to price changes. Profits depend on a proper selecting and balancing of prices against the variables of costs, volume, and product mix. Orders and products differ widely in cost, volume, price, profit, and the use of facilities and capital. Orders also differ in specific product made, markets sold, customer classes involved, sales territories, and channels of distribution. Thus, profit is not some single-valued function of time or quantity, but rather is comprised of a number of pooled segments from which a net profit is ultimately expected to develop.

In pricing, management must know the relative profit contribution which each segment makes to total profit to be able to strike a proper balance among prices, product mix, volume, and costs. Pricing is a profit-planning task in which management analyzes the various economic and strategic alternatives and compares them against each other to select the one which appears to be the most advantageous in each situation.

What Pricing Does. Pricing determines significantly the bottom-line figure on the operating statement. Pricing determines what products will and will not be sold, in what volumes, and with what profit. Pricing specifies which equip-

---

* Adapted from *Pricing for Higher Profit: Criteria, Methods, Applications*, by Spencer A. Tucker, published by McGraw-Hill Book Company, New York, 1966.

ment will be operated for how long, what inventory and working capital commitments are required, what cash flow can be expected, where sales efforts should be applied, which markets to approach and penetrate, and ultimately, the return to be expected on invested capital. *Pricing and pricing alone, more than any other single decision-making activity, is responsible for most of the profit differences among similar firms.*

How the order or product is priced will in itself determine the product mix that will be produced. The pricing action will make the product more or less attractive to the buyer. Price is the major factor which determines the buyer's response. And to the extent that costs of the mix produce both profit contributions and favorable responses from buyers, the volume sold will be profitable. The sales revenue then is a mixture of the various prices of the different products or orders, and the resultant profit is a mixture of their profit contributions.

Price Determinants. The major determinants of price are (1) the seller's costs, (2) competitive prices, and (3) market demand. Prices cannot always be based successfully on individual costs, but objective, traceable cost information must be available to measure how much an order will contribute to profits when meeting a "going" price. The seller's costs are specific and identified only with him. Prices, on the other hand, represent the influence of competition in the seller's markets. For the seller arbitrarily to mark up his cost to arrive at a selling price is tantamount to denying the existence of this competition and market demand. Rather than solely determining prices, costs should be used to decide whether to meet or withdraw from a price proposal or to continue to explore the alternatives.

Regardless of any other consideration, the price determines the spread between the seller's cost and the outside market and should be a measure of value to the seller of the output sold. The crucial point is *what kind of cost* the seller must use to make this evaluation and how he develops it. This question is one of the most contentious in the entire cost-pricing area around which much mystery, magic formula, and just plain nonsense still persist.

When cost-plus methods of pricing are used, and the "cost" portion is arbitrarily determined, the resultant price represents a compounding of errors. Indefensible cost allocation acts as a base upon which an illusory price structure is erected that makes no allowance for competition and demand. That kind of profit structure is the result of sales bookings by accident when the seller's offering prices happen to be lower than those of his competitors. To keep the seller in business, these types of repetitive accidents must happen frequently and must combine to net some kind of profit. Obviously, if competitors using similar cost-plus methods have substantially lower costs than the seller, the latter's days in business are numbered.

The Role of Cost in Pricing. It is vital that management know intimately the ingredients and behaviors of its product costs to price most advantageously within the turbulent environment of competition, and the vagaries of market demand and product mix. If a company knows its costs, it can accelerate cost recovery, evaluate proposals to change selling prices, segment the market to gain advantage of the different layers of customer demand, select most profitable business when capacity is limited, determine the price at which to refuse an order, distinguish between volume which adds to the peaks and that which creates bottlenecks, and determine which work to abandon when more attractive opportunities are available.

Even though costs generally do not determine prices, costs for pricing purposes are essential for measuring the profit contribution of the selling transaction. Costs may also be useful for interproduct-line comparisons and rankings. Costs for pricing require estimates of future cost magnitude and behavior and a study of the profit structure of the firm.

COST-PLUS PRICING

Cost-plus pricing is the practice of arriving at a selling price by adding to an estimate of product cost an additional amount of money. This added sum is considered profit and is generally referred to as the "markup on cost." In some cases, the total or "full" product cost is marked up. In other cases, a portion of total cost is used as the base, and the markup is made large enough to cover the balance of cost and a profit.

The derivation of the markup percentage varies from industry to industry and from company to company. Some markups are designed to provide a certain rate of return on sales; others are designed to provide a desired rate of return on invested capital. In some instances, different elements of the product's cost are marked up at different rates to reflect the differences in invested capital in those elements.

Not all methods for arriving at a markup are as rational as this sounds. Many managers set (or attempt to set) prices on the basis of a "fair" profit. This profit percentage, more often than not, amounts to a fixed rate on cost regardless of the ingredients of the product-cost structure, that is, heavy in raw-material content and light in the use of facilities, and vice versa. This "fair" percentage differs from company to company. Where there is no price policy, the amount of the markup tends to be set arbitrarily. The defense rationale offered is that companies want no more than a "fair" profit, even though no one knows how much this should be.

Whether all or a portion of product cost is marked up, the cost-plus pricing method assumes that the price will be attractive to buyers regardless of the prices competitors offer for the same products. If the seller's combination of cost and markup produces higher prices, he will lose volume. If his prices are lower, he will gain volume. But because of the kind of cost used as the base for the latter, the seller has no assurance that this volume will be profitable. Thus cost-plus pricing can be highly illusory.

If cost-plus pricing uses an arbitrary cost base and a flat markup, the pricing problem becomes a compounding of two errors. Because of the widespread use of "full" costs as a pricing base, this method will be discussed in detail.

"Full"-cost Pricing. "Full"-cost pricing is probably the most popular of the cost-plus pricing methods, because it is claimed to be the "fairest" and safest way to price. It is also claimed to be the easiest to explain and justify to customers and others. The method was developed by accountants for use by practical businessmen. The chief concern underlying "full"-cost pricing is that all products must bear their "full" share of costs. The assumption is that if all assigned costs are "covered" by the selling prices, a full recovery of all costs will be achieved.

Costs to be allocated for "sharing" purposes are those which are used in common by more than one facility or product. These costs are generally for services such as management, promotion, and marketing, and for certain other constant costs such as depreciation. The method of allocating these common or constant costs to products is usually done on the basis of the expected future activity of the facilities and/or products.

For example, consider the case of a company that makes one product, and how it would price the product under "full"-cost pricing. Assume that the company's total annual costs are comprised of fixed manufacturing and nonmanufacturing costs of $200,000 per year and a direct (out-of-pocket) manufacturing cost of $2 for each unit of product. The company expects to produce and sell 100,000 units during the coming year. Using the "full"-cost method and a 10 percent markup, the selling price would be calculated as follows.

Direct manufacturing cost, per unit	$2.00
Fixed cost, per unit ($200,000 ÷ 100,000)	2.00
"Full" cost	$4.00
10% markup	0.40
Selling price	$4.40

It is possible for a competitor to project his expected production of units at a higher or lower level, and it is likewise conceivable that a competitor's annual fixed costs could also be different. This could be even if a competitor's direct costs are the same. The result is an intermixture of conjectured forecasts and different cost bases. Thus, what is a unit fixed cost for one manufacturer may be nowhere close to the unit fixed cost of others making the identical product.

The $2 unit fixed cost is an attempt to unitize a period cost, such as depreciation or rent, which is incurred only by the passage of time and not by the volume of units sold. If the guess about future activity is optimistic, the "full" cost will be lower, and the seller's prices may be below market levels even after the arbitrary profit markup.

In the next period, assume that the $4.40 is below competitive levels and sales rise rapidly. The accountant is given a forecasted 40 percent increase in expected sales volume for the next year, and he develops a selling price in the same manner.

Direct manufacturing cost, per unit	$2.00
Fixed cost, per unit ($200,000 ÷ 140,000)	1.43
"Full" cost	$3.43
10% markup	0.34
Selling price	$3.77

When the accountant gives this new price to management, he is telling it in effect to *reduce prices despite the rapid rise in sales.*

The next year new competitors enter the market and start to produce this same product, or there may be a slowdown in general business conditions. In either event, sales for this product drop, and the company forecasts an annual volume of only 60,000 units. The accountant would then price the product as follows:

Direct manufacturing cost, per unit	$2.00
Fixed cost, per unit ($200,000 ÷ 60,000)	3.33
"Full" cost	$5.33
10% markup	0.53
Selling price	$5.86

When the accountant gives this new price to management, he is telling it to raise prices or lose money. The notion of recommending a price increase in the face of additional competitive invasion or in poorer economic times is ludicrous. Yet the "full"-cost method tells management to decrease prices when it is taking business away from competitors and to increase prices when it is losing business to competitors.

Obviously, this example is oversimplified, because only one product is involved. In the multiproduct business, the problem is vastly more complex because of product mix, facility mix, varying facility costs, differing product costs, and the volatile product variations. Basically, however, this method requires any price to recover completely all costs regardless of volume. This forces the period costs which are fixed with time to become unitized to the product as a function of some selected future volume or activity. Thus, regardless of the annual quantity output, the "full" cost of each unit will be made to vary inversely with volume in the hope that the annual costs will be recovered.

Although the arithmetic of this calculation may be logical, the effect is to ignore competitive prices and the company's need to survive.

Assume that the "going" price in poor times for the product is $3.50. Having only the "full"-cost figure available, management would promptly turn down the business that could be obtained at this price. This would deprive the seller of the margin of $1.50 at a time when he needs it most to contribute toward the payment of annual fixed expenses or even toward paying for some of his direct costs such as skilled labor which he may wish to retain regardless of business activity.

The reverse happens with this pricing method in boom times. Then, the "going" price might be $4.50. The unitizing of period costs in this instance makes the customer a willing partner of the seller as the customer ends up with bargain prices.

A REASONED APPROACH TO PRICING

A rational approach for pricing adopts no specific rules, because once rules are set up, they tend to remain in effect when they no longer apply. A rigid pricing method is usually based on a company's own costs and thus makes no allowance for external factors. The rational approach adjusts to changing events and circumstances, without losing sight of the interplay of the internal and external variables.

Effective pricing methods recognize the different behaviors of product cost and separate those costs which are directly identifiable with the product from those costs which are incurred to provide a capacity framework irrespective of volume or the product mix.

It must be understood that in using the phrase "pricing method," there is no implied guarantee of results. If there were such a guarantee, there would only be one pricing method, it would produce the best results, and everyone would use it. No one would be interested in other pricing methods, and it would be a waste of time to present them.

The expression "pricing method" is intended to mean evaluating the economic benefit to the seller of meeting competitive prices in terms of the *tangible* profit contribution of an order, of the return for the use of the seller's facilities, and of the effect of these two on the seller's invested capital. He then has a basis for accepting the "going" price or withdrawing.

The Anatomy of Profit. If a retail operator sold candy bars for 10 cents each, buying them from his supplier for 8 cents each, the difference between these two tangible figures (2 cents) could be called "profit" only if the man incurred no other costs in operating his small enterprise. If this man's annual rental were $1,000, however (and he had no other fixed expenses), then there is really no profit available until enough of the 2-cent pieces are collected within the year to pay for this one fixed cost. Only after 50,000 candy bars are sold (break-even) does any profit develop. The full profit made on the 50,001st bar sold would be 2 cents. And if only 50,001 bars were sold in the year, the total true profit for the year's operations would be just 2 cents.

If the man attempted to establish a "full" cost for candy bars, he would be faced with the task of projecting expected volume and using that figure to unitize his $1,000 rent cost. If he projected annual volume at 100,000 bars, then the unit fixed costs would be $1,000/100,000 or 1 cent each. When this sum is added to his out-of-pocket cost of 8 cents for the cost of the bar itself, he would show a "full" cost of 9 cents. This would imply that each time he sold a bar for 10 cents, a profit of 1 cent would be earned. Obviously this is not correct, because below the 50,000 annual volume level losses are being incurred, and above that level a profit of 2 cents each is being earned.

If the actual annual volume attained is 200,000 bars, the "full" costs would be 8½ cents, but profit per bar would still be 2 cents after 50,000 bars were sold. And if the man should decide to sell his bar at 9 cents (at the 200,000 volume level), a 1-cent profit per bar would be earned above the 50,000 volume point.

This shows that a selling price above "full" cost is not necessarily profitable. Pricing below "full" cost does not necessarily result in a loss. Profits are not made by the sale of an individual unit where there are period fixed expenses to be paid for. Profits under these conditions are made by time period because of the presence of the nonvolume constant costs which are incurred by the passage of time and not by individual sale transactions.

The Relative Contribution Approach to Pricing. The 2-cent piece available from the sale of each candy bar is a *contribution* to the payment of fixed period expenses and ultimately to profits. It is truly a profit only above the break-even point (50,000 bars). Contribution money is the only piece of objective, tangible, and identifiable measurement of the economic value of any selling transaction. This is because it is measured as the difference between two tangible amounts: the selling price (SP) and the out-of-pocket (OOP) cost. No arbitrary element is present in this calculation.

The rate at which contribution money develops in the sales dollar is measured as the percentage which this money bears to the selling price. In the case of the candy bar, it is the percentage 2 cents divided by 10 cents, or 20 percent. This means that for every dollar of candy bars sold, 20 cents is contributed toward the payment of period expenses. This contribution ratio is called the "profit-volume ratio," or more simply, the PV.

Not all sales dollars produce the same PV in multiproduct enterprises. For example, if this small retail operator also sold newspapers for 10 cents and paid his supplier 9 cents for them, the PV for newspapers would be .10. Thus, he would have to sell twice as many sales dollars of newspapers as candy bars to gross the same contribution. If he also sold cigars with a PV of .25 and toys at a PV of .40, it is clear that annual profits would not be a direct function of annual sales. Instead, profits would be the result of the mix of PVs in the product sales. Thus, it would be possible to earn a greater profit on less sales and a smaller profit on more sales, as the product mix swings from a more favorable to a less favorable mix.

Figure 7-1 shows graphically how contributions from each of four products of a manufacturing company are pooled. By exposing the true economic value of each of the four products, management is in a better position to "push" the real contributors and discourage those products which simply have a high price but do little more than swap dollar bills between the supplier and the seller.

Costs which are directly traceable to a job or a product contain no arbitrary elements, such as the arithmetic unitizing of period fixed expenses. Traceable costs are the out-of-pocket costs which are incurred by the production of the order which would not be incurred without the order. The same cannot be

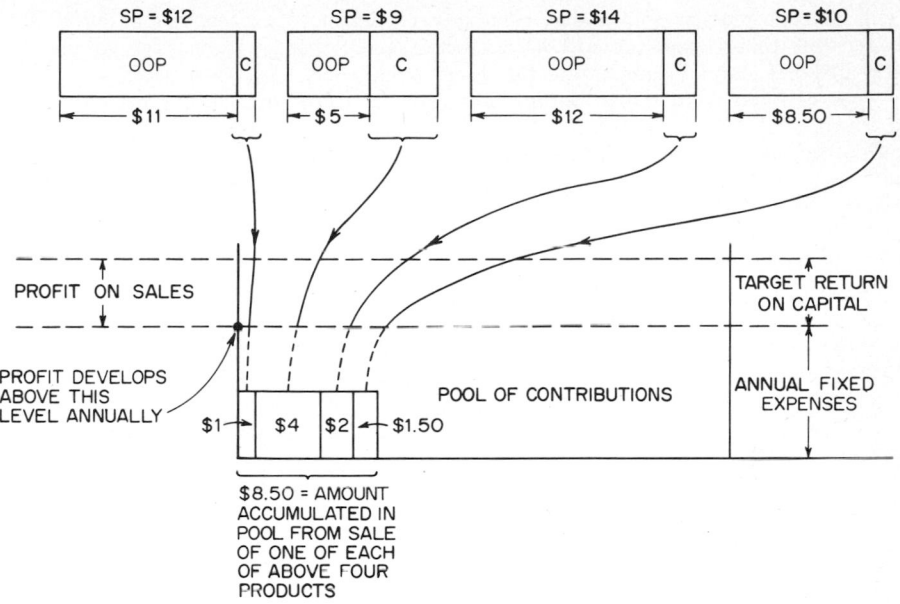

FIG. 7-1. *The contribution pool.*

said for period fixed expenses which are incurred even if there are no orders. General categories of out-of-pocket costs are direct labor, direct material, and direct manufacturing and nonmanufacturing overhead costs. Without a knowledge of out-of-pocket costs, management could inadvertently be pricing its products below this *floor* on prices. In some companies, management believes that volume will compensate for low price. This is not true if the prices fall below the out-of-pocket level.

Pricing for Volume. The following is an example of how the same product may be cost-estimated by four similar competing companies. Each calculates a "full" cost as follows:

	Company A	Company B	Company C	Company D
"Full" cost..........	$12.30	$14.20	$14.20	$16.00

If the "going" price is $14.00, Companies B, C, and D would obviously turn down orders. Company A would believe it could earn a profit of $1.70. This might be the attitude for a normal order quantity.

In an effort to generate volume, however, some of the companies may be tempted to lower their prices and to accept a large order quantity at, say, a $12.00 price. The effect of volume and prices on profits cannot truly be determined until the out-of-pocket costs have been separated from "full" costs. Then the contributions may be measured. Such a separation might show:

	Company A	Company B	Company C	Company D
Out-of-pocket costs..............	$9.20	$7.80	$12.30	$8.80
Contribution at a $12 selling price..	$2.80	$4.20	($.30)	$3.20

This simple analysis shows that Company C produces a cash loss of $0.30 for each unit that it sells at $12.00 regardless of volume. Increasing volume in this instance cannot compensate for price; it can only make losses worse.

Just as each sales dollar per product in a multiproduct firm does not carry the same rate of contribution (PV), neither will one given product necessarily make the same contribution to all of the firms which produce it. The differences in the contributions generated by each of these four companies are, of course, reflections of different out-of-pocket costs. And these differences are the results of the specific operating characteristics of each company with respect to costs of materials, pay rates and productivities of workers, quality factors, delivery costs, and other items which make up the direct overhead charges.

One can see how misleading the "full" costs are by comparing Companies B and C. These costs can be the direct result of how each unitizes its period fixed costs into its product cost. Assuming the same annual fixed cost for each, it shows that Company C reflects a greater measure of optimism than B. In the "full"-cost approach, it is impossible to measure the true profit contribution available by meeting any price, and this could deprive a company of a needed contribution on the one hand, or could mislead a company into booking sales below out-of-pocket cost on the other.

Without a knowledge of its out-of-pocket product costs, management may pursue a policy of selling for the sake of booking revenue dollars instead of generating contribution money. Sometimes, this practice takes the form of desperation pricing to keep facilities busy in the mistaken notion that the more of the capacity that is booked, the more profits will be. Profits, if any, are made by accident and not by plan, and the ironic result is to credit profits to the high activity of facilities. Often, this prompts management to acquire additional facilities which it may attempt to keep just as busy. This, in turn, because of the pricing-for-volume yardstick, can provoke competitive retaliation, driving market prices down to where an entire industry cannot show an adequate return on invested capital.

The Published Price List. In many industries, leading manufacturers may issue a published catalog-type price list. Buyers become acquainted with these established price lists and ask all other companies in the industry to follow suit. Although not all products make the same contribution to all companies which are capable of producing them, it is important to realize that there are contribution variances that exist for the *identical* product by virtue of the order *quantity* differences. Table 7-1 shows what can happen to two similar companies who decide to meet the published prices on one product in varying quantities.

This comparison shows that each company has a different profitable quantity range. Perhaps Company X is a less modern company than Company Y, having slow, older equipment which, however, can be set up in a relatively shorter time. Company Y may be a company using modern, high-speed equipment requiring longer setup times. Company X should not take orders for this particular product much over the 5,000 quantity level, because it starts to incur an out-of-pocket loss somewhere between 5,000 and 10,000 pieces. However, within this low-quantity range, Company Y must incur cash losses because of the costly setups required on their high-speed equipment. From about 10,000 pieces and up, Company Y is able to cash in on its modern facilities.

A published price list usually starts as a reflection of the price leader's costs (usually "full" costs). Over the years, it is modified by buyer reaction and expectations. No established, published price list can ever account for the individual profit-structure differences among different companies. Failure to recognize contribution levels for different quantities can lead to selling below out-of-

TABLE 7-1. Effect of Order Size on Profitability of Two Different Companies

Published price list Product no. 4372		Company X			Company Y		
Order size	Price each	OOP cost each	Contribution each	PV	OOP cost each	Contribution each	PV
1,000	$40.00	$25.00	$15.00	.400	$48.00	($8.00)	(.200)
2,000	30.00	23.00	7.00	.233	35.00	(5.00)	(.167)
5,000	24.00	22.00	2.00	.083	26.00	(2.00)	(.083)
10,000	20.00	21.50	(1.50)	(.075)	19.50	0.50	.025
20,000	18.00	21.25	(3.25)	(.180)	15.00	3.00	.167
50,000	17.00	21.20	(4.20)	(.247)	11.50	5.50	.324
100,000	15.00	21.18	(6.18)	(.412)	9.00	6.00	.400

pocket costs because of the mistaken belief that volume will compensate for a low price. Even though a "full" cost shows a considerably higher figure than a published price for a large volume, the belief still persists that if the quantity is high enough, the company will somehow make money on it.

Contribution Pricing. Product mix means more than the existence of several products made by one firm. The mixture of products and their effect on profits refers also to the different prices at which each is sold; the typical order quantities for each item of the product line; the characteristic PVs of each, at different volumes, as reflected by both the internal out-of-pocket manufacturing costs and the characteristics of the market and territories in which each is sold; the varying use of facilities needed for producing; and the variations in the invested-capital levels of each.

In pricing, management must first measure what contribution is available from meeting a competitive price and then evaluate this against the use of facilities and capital which must be committed to fill the order. At the same time, management must have information on what contributions have been booked to date and what is expected to be generated. It then must stack up these period contributions against the period fixed expenses that have to be covered in the same period. When contributions for a period have equaled the prorated (not allocated) expenses for the same period, the company is at the break-even point for that period. (This is not to imply that management should cost-plus price until the break-even point is reached and then price for contribution above that point. If that practice is followed, the chances are good that the firm may not even reach its break-even point for the operating period.)

The profit formula is a very simple one:

$$\text{Period profit} = \text{period contribution} - \text{period fixed expense}$$

The period contribution is that amount which has been "deposited" in the imaginary contribution pool by different orders booked in that period. To guide management in policing the buildup of that pool and as an aid to future pricing, a Contribution Log is used. An example is shown in Figure 7-2. Also shown are data pertaining to the economical use of facilities, the contribution per facility-hour (CFH), and the target selling prices which provide the desired return on the specific elements of capital invested in each order. These are discussed later in the chapter.

A Contribution Log is a record of pricing transactions during a period. Because entries are made at the time of booking the orders, the data necessarily

Month of _May_   Product Line   _A-22_

| Order No. | Booked SP | Total OOP | Con-tribu-tion | PV | Cumu-lative con-tribu-tion | Facility utilization | | | Target SP | Reve-nue vari-ance |
						Hours	CFH	Cumu-lative CFH		
6706	$ 9,120	$6,170	$2,950	.324	$ 2,950	52	57	$57	$ 8,940	$ 180
6707	5,150	3,080	2,070	.402	5,020	29	71	62	5,970	(820)
6708	4,970	4,230	740	.149	5,760	24	31	55	6,210	(1,240)
6709	10,510	5,860	4,650	.442	10,410	48	97	68	8,190	2,320
6748	8,740	8,020	720	.082	79,818	31	23	49	8,960	(220)
6749	11,360	7,115	4,245	.374	84,063	93	46	48.50	10,980	(380)
6750	7,390	6,112	1,278	.173	85,341	38	34	48	7,210	180

Summary

Total sales booked in month	=	$404,873
Target sales revenue	=	$416,942
Revenue variance	=	$(12,069)
Booked contribution	=	$ 85,341
Average PV	=	.21
Less prorated period expenses*	=	$ 55,000
Pricing profit	=	$30,341
Facility-hours committed	=	1,780
Average CFH	=	$48

* Annual fixed period expenses = $660,000.

FIG. 7-2. _Contribution log._

are estimated rather than actual. As such the Contribution Log reports on the results of pricing and is an advance heralding of profits if actual manufacturing performance is as good as the estimate.

If each entry in this chronological log is coded with other information about the order regarding customer, location, end market, facility, salesman, product line, and the like, contribution data may be sorted according to each of these profit segments. When enough data have been collected and summarized, management can draw inferences about the characteristic PVs of each. Then customers, salesmen, territories, end markets, and the like may be ranked to show management its best sources of profit (contributions).

Besides showing the contribution rankings among the various profit segments of the firm, these data are useful for establishing future prices of these segments by pricing for a target PV.

The formula for accomplishing this is derived as follows:

$$\text{Selling price} = \text{contribution} + \text{OOP}$$

and if

$$PV = \frac{\text{contribution}}{\text{selling price}}$$

then

$$1 - PV = \frac{\text{OOP}}{\text{selling price}}$$

and therefore

$$\text{Selling price} = \frac{\text{OOP}}{1 - PV}$$

If the out-of-pocket cost of an order is $13 for a customer whose "characteristic" PV is .35, management may wish to develop a price which is consistent with that PV.   It can calculate the price from the formula above:

$$\text{Selling price} = \frac{\$13}{1 - .35}$$

$$= \frac{\$13}{.65}$$

$$= \$20$$

As another example, management may feel that to achieve an adequate return for the use of a particular facility, orders which are processed on that facility should yield a minimum PV of .25.   The procedure for calculating this minimum target price is exactly as outlined above. The out-of-pocket cost is divided by 1 minus .25.

When contribution data are known, management can adjust its prices with security to take advantage of market reactions and competitive behaviors.   One economic law which may be applied to pricing is called the "elasticity of demand."

By having some knowledge of how markets will react to price changes, management can price to maximize profits. For example, if a "going" market price for an item is $19, management might decide to raise its price to $22 if it believes that more profit would be available at the resulting lower volume.   Here is what may happen:

	Price	Piece volume	OOP cost each	Contribution each	Gross sales	Total contribution
"Going"...	$19	1,000M	$15	$4	$19,000,000	$4,000,000
Quoted.....	$22	Drops to: 600M	$15	$7	$13,200,000	$4,200,000

A reverse strategy may also be attempted if management believes that a drop in prices could be more than offset by an increase in volume:

	Price	Piece volume	Contribution each	Gross sales	Total contribution
"Going"..........	$19	1,000M	$4	$19,000,000	$4,000,000
Drop to..........	$18	Increases to: 1,400M	$3	$25,200,000	$4,200,000

Naturally, the first strategy is to be preferred because of the company's lower commitments in working capital, storage, collections, and transaction costs.   Most importantly, the higher prices provide more operating latitude and lessen the risk of provoking competitive price retaliation.

Facility Pricing.   Although relative contribution pricing is more realistic than cost-plus pricing because the value of the selling transaction can be objectively measured, it has its limitations and should not be used as the sole criterion of pricing. Contribution pricing shows the expected contribution flow from an order, but it does not take into consideration the amount of facility time which may be required to generate the gross order contribution, nor does it reflect the various investment levels in the different cost elements which enter into the production and sale of the order.

Pricing for gross order contribution which does not consider the amount of facility capacity required to generate it is shallow and can result in several operating difficulties:

1. Booking more capacity than is available in a period
2. Randomly obtaining less annual contribution than would be available with a selective selling of facility time
3. Inability to select best order from among those competing for the same slot of facility time
4. Inability to establish pricing consistency on orders which use the same facilities
5. Inability to maximize profits when at full capacity

In manufacturing, a large portion of the gross national product is devoted to converting raw material (or the finished product of a previous manufacturer) to a finished product. Converting-manufacturing can be characterized in modern profit-planning terms as enterprise which is in the business of selling facility time rather than product, for the converting effort represents the largest element of invested capital on which a return is to be earned.

For example, assume that management books the following two orders to run on the same facility:

	Order A	Order B
Selling price............................	$10,000	$10,000
OOP cost................................	8,000	8,000
Gross order contribution...............	$ 2,000	$ 2,000
PV.....................................	.20	.20

From the relative contribution viewpoint, both orders are equal and make the same contribution to the "pool." If the capacity of the facility is not scarce and management anticipates that excess capacity will always be available throughout the year, management could book both orders and obtain the gross contribution of $4,000. If capacity is limited, however, a further evaluation is required:

	Order A	Order B
Facility-hours required.....................	50	20
Contribution per facility-hour..............	$40	$100

If there are only twenty hours of facility time available, management obviously would want to take Order B. If seventy or more hours are available, it would take both orders. When selective facility booking is practiced, management can avoid booking large segments of capacity merely because the gross order contribution (PV) is high. This could lead to the extending of capacity commitments into periods where more profitable work would be displaced. Preferably, management should select work after evaluating both the PV and the contribution per facility-hour (CFH):

	Order C	Order D
Selling price............................	$5,000	$5,000
OOP cost...............................	4,000	4,500
Gross order contribution.................	$1,000	$ 500
PV.....................................	.20	.10
Facility-hours required....................	30	10
CFH....................................	$33.33	$50

In this case, the lower PV order, Order D, provides a better contribution return per hour than Order C even though its PV and gross contribution are lower. Even if the gross contribution dollars are higher in an order, the return per hour might make it rank below another order of lower PV:

	Order E	Order F
Selling price............................	$19,000	$16,000
OOP cost...............................	15,000	13,000
Gross order contribution.................	$ 4,000	$ 3,000
PV.....................................	.21	.19
Facility-hours required....................	100	60
CFH....................................	$40	$50

Order E has the higher revenue, gross contribution, and PV, but because the facility-hours it requires are disproportionately higher, the contribution return it obtains per hour is not as attractive as that provided by Order F. Order E compared with Order F requires a ⅔ increase in facility time to obtain a ⅓ increase in contribution money. This is not important if excess capacity is available and if the bookings of large-order commitments will not displace more profitable work in the future. Where no consideration is given to the selective selling of facility time, the annual contribution level attained is usually less than what could be attained, because it represents the unplanned cumulative total of all orders booked on a contribution basis.

The CFH approach can be very effective in target pricing to establish an acceptable and consistent return for the use of facilities. For example in the case of Orders A and B, management might wish to accept Order A if it could be priced to yield the same return as Order B. Using the basic pricing formula:

$$\text{Selling price} = \text{contribution} + \text{OOP}$$

and amending it to

$$\text{Selling price} = (\text{facility-hours} \times \text{CFH}) + \text{OOP}$$

and using the CFH of Order B to produce the target selling price of Order A, we have

$$\text{Selling price of A} = (50 \times \$100) + \$8,000$$
$$= \$13,000$$

Pricing for Return on Capital Employed. Measuring gross contributions of booked orders for "go–no-go" pricing decisions is vital for planning profits in a period; cumulative contributions compared with period fixed expenses show the profit trend. Relating gross order contributions against facility time is valuable to show the effectiveness with which the converting facilities are being marketed. Neither of these methods, however, gives consideration to what return on capital is being provided by the selected prices.

Operating a business by aiming for a given profit return on sales revenue is shallow. Until that return is related to the level of invested capital required to generate it, there is no measure of reward for the money used and the risks taken in operating the enterprise. As an exaggerated example, a profit of $100,000 earned on sales revenue of $1,000,000 might seem satisfactory, but if the total capital employed in the business is $10,000,000, the return on total investment is 1 percent (pretax), less than what could be earned in a savings bank or a high-grade security.

By the same token, an order PV of .40 or an order contribution per facility-hour of $150 might seem acceptable in comparison with what other orders are producing. But the question to be answered is whether this represents a fair return on the capital invested.

The ultimate goal in pricing is to establish a selling price for an order or product that produces a desired return on the specific capital invested in that order. Such a selling price is a *target selling price* representing both the seller's specific investment levels and his concept of what a fair return should be. Because this target is an expression of a specific figure and a desire for return, a target price is no guarantee of market acceptance—as is no other formula price. Just as the Contribution Log measures the cumulative period flow of contributions against period expenses, the target selling price provides a yardstick which tells management the trend of its pricing in relation to desired return on capital.

The decision involving meeting a competitive price integrates total order contribution, contribution per facility-hour, and the variance between the "going" price and the target price. Sound pricing involves a balancing among these three variables. Where the company innovates a new product, or where no competitive price bench marks exist for a product, pricing for return on capital is the starting point. Then, the strategic elements such as skimming, penetrating, prestige, and demand pricing factors are added.

Pricing for return on capital is practiced in industry on the basis of "full" costs. This is just as misleading as cost-plus pricing. The procedure merely shifts the base from the return on sales to the return on annual capital employed and applies it to orders on an average basis.

Pricing the Separate Cost Elements for Capital Return. The following method shows how prices are established by separately marking up each major element of identifiable product cost in direct relation to its specific capital investment elements.

Basically, manufactured products contain two major cost elements which can be separated and identified with capital investments. One is raw-material cost; the other is all other direct manufacturing cost. Raw-material cost generally represents a lower investment from the standpoint of risk than the operating facilities do. Raw material turns over faster, is more liquid, and can be discontinued in low periods. Operating-facilities cost consists of elements which cannot be readily adjusted to varying sales levels and represents a long-term investment which cannot be easily discontinued. This is why a dollar's worth of raw-material investment is not expected to earn as much as a dollar's worth of operating-facilities capital.

For example, here are two products which have the *same out-of-pocket cost:*

	Product A	Product B
Material cost.............	$10	$ 5
OOP manufacturing cost....	2	7
Same total OOP cost......	$12	$12

Because both of these products have the same out-of-pocket cost, each will provide the same contribution if they are priced the same. If Product A is priced at $14, the contribution will be $2. But if Product B is priced at $14 because the out-of-pocket cost is the same, this is tantamount to agreeing that the capital invested in Product B is the same as that invested in Product A. Even though Product B contains ½ the material cost of A, the capital invested in Product B will be higher (in most industries), because it has 3½ times the amount of facility cost of Product A. Thus Product B will be under-priced. If Product B is priced at $16 and the same price is applied to Product A, Product A will be overpriced.

When orders are priced with no distinction for the different capital elements, customers are being asked to pay very dearly for a manufacturing service simply because the material cost happens to be so high, as in Product A, or they are receiving partial gifts of the manufacturing service when material happens to comprise a lower portion of total out-of-pocket cost, as in Product B. Where no capital distinction is made, orders loaded mostly with material cost are difficult to sell, whereas highly converted products move fast, but provide a smaller return.

Developing the Markup Factors. Essential for developing separate markups is the projection of an annual profit plan. The profit plan is the foundation of operation in the progressive company and is designed to reflect the planned product mix, the PVs of each that are expected to develop, and the facility times required for each. Although such a plan may be adjusted during the operating year, a first rough projection sets the business ship on the right general heading and provides the markup tools with which to work.

First is the statement of capital and desired return:

```
Total capital employed...................  $2,000,000
Desired return (pretax)..................       15%
Target earnings .........................  $ 300,000
Annual fixed expenses....................  $ 400,000
Target contribution*.....................  $ 700,000
```

* In multiproduct, progressive profit management, the gross revenue approach to budgeting has given way to the use of budgeting annual contribution.

Second, the operating profit plan:

```
Planned sales.......................................  $3,000,000
OOP costs:
    Direct materials........................  $1,200,000
    Direct manufacturing....................   1,100,000
                                                          $2,300,000
Contribution........................................  $  700,000
Less: fixed expenses ...............................     400,000
Planned profit......................................  $  300,000
```

1. *Material Cost Markup.* This markup is obtained by dividing the desired percentage return by the number of turns per year of capital employed for material. Assuming this turnover is three times, the markup on material would be 5 percent.

The selling price of annual material thus would be $1,200,000 \times 1.05$, or $1,260,000.

2. *Manufacturing Cost Markup.* This markup is obtained by subtracting the annual selling price of material from the total sales revenue and dividing by the direct manufacturing cost. Thus

$$\frac{\$3,000,000 - \$1,260,000}{\$1,100,000} \text{ or 58.2 percent}$$

The selling price of direct manufacturing cost thus would be $1,100,000 \times 1.582$, or $1,740,000.

Marking up both elements by their respective factors would produce the planned sales level: $1,260,000 + $1,740,000 = $3,000,000.

Applying these separate markups to the previous two Products A and B, these selling prices result:

Cost element	Cost	$\times$ Markup	= Selling price of element
Product A			
Materials.............................	$10.00	1.050	$10.50
OOP manufacturing.....................	2.00	1.582	3.16
Selling price to provide a 15% return...........................			$13.66
Product B			
Materials	$ 5.00	1.050	$ 5.25
OOP manufacturing.....................	7.00	1.582	11.07
Selling price to provide a 15% return...........................			$16.32

These are the target selling prices which will return to the seller 15 percent return on the specific elements of capital invested in each product.

PV or gross product contribution should not be the sole guide to pricing, as a measurement of contribution shows:

Product A		*Product B*	
Selling price......................	$13.66	Selling price......................	$16.32
OOP cost.........................	12.00	OOP cost.......................	12.00
Contribution....................	$ 1.66	Contribution..................	$ 4.32
PV...............................	.122	PV.............................	.265

Clearly, Product A earns the same return on total capital employed as B at a lower contribution and PV. If Product B sells for $1.00 less, its contribution would be $3.32, but it would not be earning as high a return on capital as A even though its contribution is twice as much as A's. The difference obviously is that the Product A type of transaction turns over mostly material in the sales dollar, whereas Product B is the type of work which enables the manufacturer to merchandise effectively his manufacturing facilities.

CONCLUSION

The profit contributions flowing in from pricing determine company profits. Pricing is the crucial management decision and the most important profit contribution generator in any company. Prices erected on arbitrary cost bases alternately underprice and overprice products in relation to market price levels. Traditional accounting methods cloud rather than highlight the contributions of the different variable profit segments. Traditional cost-estimating and pricing systems distort and obscure the interrelationship of prices, volume, and costs, rather than clarify and expose the profit contributions available from any variable alternative. Effective pricing delivers the maximum profit contribution from the least sales revenue dollars, consistent with the use of productive facilities and invested capital.

Prices are largely determined by customer demand and the community of competition. Realistic pricing methods measure profit contribution in every potential transaction and balance it to facility time and capital to be committed. Profits do not develop from one source, but rather from the contributions of the various profit segments of the company. Sound pricing methods are based on knowing the relative contributions which each segment makes to the overall results. From these data, management can strike the proper balance among prices, volume, costs, facility time, and capital to achieve the greatest return. In this way, management's pricing policy can obtain the maximum profit regardless of the changing product mix, market shifts, or other variables.

BIBLIOGRAPHY

Chamberlain, Neil W., *The Firm: Micro-economic Planning and Action,* McGraw-Hill Book Company, New York, 1962.

Dean, Joel, *Managerial Economics,* Prentice-Hall, Inc., Englewood Cliffs, N.J., 1958.

Tucker, Spencer A., *The Break-even System: A Tool for Profit Planning,* Prentice-Hall, Inc., Englewood Cliffs, N.J., 1963.

Tucker, Spencer A., *Cost-estimating and Pricing with Machine-hour Rates,* Prentice-Hall, Inc., Englewood Cliffs, N.J., 1962.

Tucker, Spencer A., *Pricing for Higher Profit,* McGraw-Hill Book Company, New York, 1966.

Tucker, Spencer A., *Successful Managerial Control by Ratio-analysis,* McGraw-Hill Book Company, New York, 1961.

CHAPTER EIGHT

Advertising

WALTER WEIR   *President, West, Weir & Bartel, Inc., New York, New York*

Of all the tools available to corporate management, advertising is one of the least understood and appreciated. A monthly profit and loss statement or an annual report appears remarkably concrete by comparison, except that the monthly profit and loss statement or the annual report, as any responsible corporate officer can attest, can be made to conceal much more than it reveals. Nevertheless, both *do* contain facts and figures of a concrete nature; otherwise they could not be manipulated. Advertising seems, by contrast, to be virtually ethereal in nature. It isn't.

ADVERTISING—A POWERFUL TOOL OF MANAGEMENT

Actually, advertising—when properly understood—is one of the most powerful tools available to corporate management in its drive and urge to build a profitable business operation; to compete successfully with other, comparable businesses; to attract investors and establish a favorable price for the company's stock as well as a steady turn for that stock on the market; to build employee pride and morale; to attract top personnel; and to facilitate growth through acquisition and merger. Beyond these, there are other areas in which advertising can function effectively for corporate management, but those mentioned will suffice to illustrate the manifold uses of this remarkably efficient, if seemingly impalpable, instrument.

Purpose of Advertising—Controlled Communication. To employ advertising effectively, it is essential—as in the effective employment of any instrument—that the employer understand its purpose, its possibilities, and its limitations. Despite the billions of dollars spent annually on advertising by American business, all too few of the businessmen employing it can clearly state its actual purpose— which is not to build sales or establish brand preference or create a market for the product. Advertising can contribute to these desiderata, but cannot, by itself, bring them about.

Advertising cannot, for example, for very long build sales for an inferior product, a product thinly distributed, or a product overpriced in comparison with competitive products. It cannot establish brand preference for a product that in any way fails to perform satisfactorily for all those induced to buy and use it. And advertising cannot create a market for a product that does not in some way *do* something for people. In fact, the most successful advertising is that which stems directly from the product itself—and some advantage the product has in use.

In short, advertising is essentially *controlled communication about a product.* It is a substitute for sampling. Through the symbols of language, written or spoken, and pictorial presentation, advertising conveys a sense of what a product, or a service or a company, is and can do. It has no other purpose for being, and it can do little else.

Good Advertising Begins with a Good Product. It has been said that advertising adds "value" to a product. It does, in the sense that human beings tend to trust that which is generally known and to suspect that which is unknown or unfamiliar. But if the product itself does not perform to the satisfaction of the purchaser and user, the familiarity established by advertising ceases to be a value and becomes, instead, a detriment, because nothing can so quickly destroy inferior merchandise as to have countless people aware of and acquainted with its inferiority.

Good advertising begins with a good product, and any manufacturer who expects to sell successfully through advertising a product that cannot compete on its own merits is deluding himself. In this respect, because advertising—exactly like a salesman—must, before all else, establish confidence and belief in itself, an advertisement which confesses a fault about a product when the product actually contains a fault or a shortcoming is much more likely to be successful than an advertisement which blatantly proclaims the product as "the best" or "the finest" or "the most outstanding." The manufacturer who uses advertising must see it as representing his company. Exactly as he would not employ a poorly dressed or a loud-mouthed salesman to represent him, neither should he encourage or approve advertising that fails in any way to build respect for and confidence in the product whose features it communicates and for the company behind the product.

Preparatory Steps. Because advertising is part of what has been called the "total marketing mix"—meaning one of a number of factors leading to consumption of the product (including the product itself, its distribution, styling, packaging, pricing, and performance)—it is vital that a manufacturer, before he employs it, determine where his product stands in the marketplace vis-à-vis competitive products, where he would like it to be, all that is going to be required to get it there, approximately how much he will have to spend, and how much he can afford to spend to achieve his goal. This requires a careful assembling of facts that make unmistakably clear the product's present position in the market, the problems it faces, the opportunities presented if, as, and when the problems are solved, and the part advertising—or communication—can play in solving the problems and opening up the opportunities.

Frequently the problems faced involve inadequacies in the product which must be corrected, but which, when corrected, must be demonstrated, through advertising, as having been corrected so that whatever unfavorable attitude exists on the part of the potential consumer toward the product is also corrected.

Insofar as the consumer is concerned, it is important that a manufacturer realize, before advertising, that no product, no matter how universal in use, has a universal market. If only because of its name, any product has a specific market segment to which it appeals and can be sold. An advertiser will find it more economical to communicate with the logical market for his product than to advertise it to all and sundry. This can be determined through market research—which all too many advertisers either are too impatient to employ or consider too costly.

Advertising Research. It is also advisable to use research to determine, before the advertising is ever run, if it communicates its intended message clearly, is interesting, and is believed. Advertising submitted to and proved out by research obviously can be employed with much greater assurance than advertising which is published or aired because someone thinks or hopes it will be effective. One nickel out of every advertising dollar employed to test advertising can substantially improve the investment of the remaining 95 cents, and should prove more productive than a full dollar spent on untested advertising.

Few advertisers reason this way, however. Because any literate person can compose a letter and knows what he likes or dislikes in photography or painting, it becomes all too easy for everyone concerned with advertising to consider his opinion right. But just as no one in his right mind would try to cure himself of an illness by taking medicine he simply *thought* was right, so no profit-minded manufacturer should depend on opinion, particularly uninstructed opinion, if he expects maximum results from the advertising he runs.

Moreover, the people to whom advertising is addressed are not necessarily similar in terms of culture, education, income, or inclination to the person advertising to them. At the same time, the advertiser should not make the mistake of assuming the American public is in any way naïve. In fact, with every year the American consumer becomes more and more sophisticated. He is confronted with so much advertising, day in and night out, that an advertiser is well advised to anticipate a skeptical reception of his advertising message and to take steps to see that what he is going to publish or air is as plausible and believable as it can be made.

To this end, whoever prepares the advertising—and whoever approves it—can greatly improve his chances by thinking of what he creates or approves not as advertising, but instead, as a straightforward and direct communication between himself and the audience he is addressing.

Semantic Pitfalls. Activities, like things, must be named to be used or coped with. A forest, for example, becomes much more interesting when you can name and distinguish the various kinds of trees that comprise it; in fact, anything becomes more interesting when you can attach a name to it. However, as Korzybski, the acknowledged father of general semantics, pointed out, words all too frequently become more real to their user than the thing or the activity they describe. There is a tendency, for example, when you sit down to write or criticize a thing called "an advertisement," to think differently about it from how you would think if you sat down to write or read a letter. Your thinking tends to take the mold of phrases you have come to associate with advertising. Quite likely the principal reason so much advertising in newspapers and magazines or on radio or TV has a false ring is that it began as advertising and not as *one person trying to convey a thought of some kind to another person.*

What is even more limiting is when you sit down to write not just advertising, but a particular kind of advertising—for example, bank advertising. *Now* you begin to think not only in advertising terms, but in bank advertising terms. Nothing could be more stifling to fresh, original, persuasive communication.

The misleading element in most books on advertising is not that what their authors say is personal, but that what they say is assumed to imply that advertising, somehow, is an expertise apart and separate from customary human communication. This is an illusion helped and fostered by the particular jargon that advertising, as a profession, spawns. Because different words are employed to express common, ordinary aims or problems of communication, people concerned with advertising assume it is a form of human communication different from and unlike the conversation of two human beings.

The advertising of products is little different from the conversational coping of human beings attempting to "sell" themselves to other people. Advertising is no more than a substitute for one person talking to another. It is not a mystique. What is effective in terms of persuasion in human conversation will be just as effective in advertising. Honesty. An obvious desire to be helpful, to solve a problem. Eventual proof (when the product is used) that what was promised was realizable through the use of the product.

Even when advertising is not concerned with introducing a new product, it is still concerned with changing an existing habit; and of all things human beings resist strongly, it is change. Advertising must somehow induce the reader or viewer to feel that what he gets is better than what he gives up.

Management Beliefs. There is no business, service, or product that does not have differences that distinguish it from its competitors and that therefore make it more desirable to certain kinds of people. And the controlling factor in the establishment of these differences is management—and what it believes. In arriving at the kind of communication a company should have, nothing is quite so important as getting on paper the beliefs of its management concerning the character of the business it runs and wants to run. The ultimate and continuing success of business communication depends on how accurately the company or its product is translated. If advertising leads *one* person to expect something other than what he ultimately finds, it not only will fail to gain that one customer but will lose the several to whom his disillusionment will be conveyed.

It is generally accepted that a person's manner of address—the way he conducts himself, his language, his voice, his gestures—transmits to the mind and experience of the person to whom he is addressing himself an immediate impression of the kind of human being he appears to be. Most of us—if only because of the press of time—tend to arrive at judgments based on impressions rather than on careful examination and appraisal.

In today's highly competitive marketplace, it is vital to have distinctive and compelling advertising, and advertising becomes most distinctive when it reflects the beliefs of management in the kind of business it wants and is best qualified to run.

CONCLUSION

In the final analysis, that business is built best which attracts the kind of customers and only the kind of customers it can best serve. Every business is qualified by its management's beliefs to serve a particular segment of the total market, and by reflecting its essential character, its advertising can most effectively reach this segment and keep it a long time.

BIBLIOGRAPHY

Ogilvy, David, *Confessions of an Advertising Man*, Atheneum Publishers, New York, 1963.
Reeves, Rosser, *Reality in Advertising*, Alfred A. Knopf, Inc., New York, 1961.
Weir, Walter, *Truth in Advertising and Other Heresies*, McGraw-Hill Book Company, New York, 1963.
Weir, Walter, *On the Writing of Advertising*, McGraw-Hill Book Company, New York, 1960.

CHAPTER NINE

Sales Promotion

CHARLES H. NEWMAN *Independent Marketing Consultant, Chicago, Illinois*

The purpose of this chapter is to provide an overall look at the activities involved in sales promotion. The scope of these activities will be discussed, and some examples of sales promotion planning will be given.

The marketing area has suffered for years, because many of the word forms in general use do not carry with them precise or specific meanings. The term "sales promotion," because it covers such a wide range of activities and is a part of so many different kinds of selling, is one of these imprecise terms. For our purposes, it will be helpful to think of sales promotion as any activity which supplements or improves the effectiveness of personal selling.

Sales aids, letters to the trade, literature, educational material, displays, and trade shows are all examples of sales promotion. The use of these devices varies widely and, of course, changes constantly and may be expanded according to one's own ingenuity. The best sales promotion, however, tends to be thorough rather than spectacular and takes into consideration the communication gaps that always exist between the producer and the consumer.

APPROACH TO SALES PROMOTION

For purposes of classification, the subject of sales promotion may be divided into five different market categories—sales promotion as used in:

1. Industrial selling
2. Selling to wholesalers
3. Selling to retailers
4. Selling to consumers
5. The selling of services

Because the modern technique of selling, as opposed to old methods, requires the seller to consider the buyer's needs, sales promotion directed to the ultimate consumer may begin with the manufacturer and follow the product through

8–88

the channels of distribution. For example, counter displays for the retailer may be packed with merchandise at the factory thereby assuring delivery of the display at the retail level and achieving a low cost of distribution. Therefore, a manufacturer who sells his goods to the wholesaler must nonetheless be aware of the sales problems that will be encountered at the retail level.

It is wise to place the power of sales promotion behind those products or services which are worthwhile to the company and important to those who are involved in the distribution of the product. Otherwise, the effort might be considered frivolous and will not receive cooperation. Too frequently an inordinate amount of sales promotion is directed at a product which intrinsically does not warrant the interest of the trade. The reasoning behind this misconception is that sales promotion in most of its forms is inexpensive compared with advertising and very often can be performed within the company. The penalty for promoting heavily an unworthy product is a loss of prestige with one's own sales organization.

Plan Early. There is a tendency to make no plans for sales promotion until the product begins to show signs of failing in the marketplace. It is always more difficult to revive a failing product than it is to plan adequately in the beginning. Therefore, especially in the case of new products, even though they may seem certain of acceptance, a complete sales promotion job is necessary so that no one element of the distribution system will break down.

Sales promotion is sometimes disguised as price reduction. The forms are well known: promotional models which are not really up to snuff as a product; value coupons worth so much at the time of purchase; premium offers directed at the buying audience; free samples and gifts in return for a product demonstration; and the like. Sometimes these methods are very effective, but they should be recognized as true price reductions and not sales promotion alone.

A company not large enough to support a sales promotion manager will usually combine the sales promotion function with advertising, because the two are closely allied. An even closer alliance exists between merchandising and sales promotion, although the former usually attaches itself to the product rather than to the area of personal selling. The smaller company must rely upon the sales manager for the sales promotion. Depending upon the product, he gives sales promotion whatever time it requires. Almost every time a sales manager writes a letter, he is engaged in some form of sales promotion, and he must remember that both he and his product are judged by the written words coming out of his office. If these words are stilted—couched in business language that smacks of an interoffice memorandum—the readers are likely to be impressed less than if imaginative phrasing and professional makeup are used. He also must be accurate in what he writes, and he must pinpoint the action to be taken.

Be Professional. The use of the printed word or symbol has become quite sophisticated. It is becoming more and more important that printed pieces be well conceived, be printed on good paper, and use photographs or artwork that truly depict the product or the image the company wishes to project. Many professional firms, as well as some printers, are equipped to furnish expert layout and art service, but it is seldom that good and intelligent copy can be purchased along with these services, as is the case in the realm of advertising. Product features, catalog copy, and other writing of this nature should be given extra care and attention, because they are lifted bodily out of manufacturers' literature for use in wholesale catalogs and other printed pieces.

It is all too easy to waste money on printed literature. For example, an annual report produced by a good-sized company was the result of an assignment given to an excellent graphics firm. The cover, featuring an original water color by a prominent artist, was impressive. The type, layout, and artwork were clean and elegant. The content, however, eight pages of imaginary questions from stockholders, answered by the president, was the work of a novice, and the substantial expenditure and the meaningless disclosures surely must have dismayed the management.

If a company does not have adequate talent to produce printed literature of acceptable quality, it should by all means hire this talent. This expenditure is a small one compared with production costs, and it will pay great dividends. Too often a printed piece is rushed to a need in the field with insufficient thought about what it will produce. This thought must come from within the company inspired by the real needs that exist in the field. It is most unrealistic to expect outside firms to produce their own guidelines as well as the work itself. Specific instructions should be a part of every order that is given to an outside firm. When these instructions are clear and accurate, the results will be most rewarding.

Since the early days of the circus and the patent medicine men, sales promotion has had an aura of the carnival about it. Blaring music, colorful streamers, pretty girls, and sky-bound searchlights are not quite as awesome as they were in the early 1900s. Most of these devices, however, still attract crowds, and the only question to be answered is, "Are they customers?" One manufacturer for many years supported a free lunch in a Gay Nineties atmosphere at one of the larger trade shows, only to find that he was entertaining his competitors, his unstable customers, plus a large percentage of freeloaders who enjoyed the entertainment. His good customers were a little hesitant to attend such an elaborate luncheon, lest they be accused of buying the party instead of the product. The Gay Nineties luncheon is now a thing of the past, and in its place is a small luncheon involving the sales manager, the field representative, and an important buyer.

Trade Shows. A word about trade shows is in order: "They ain't what they used to be." At least, that is the usual complaint heard around many trade shows. More specifically, buyers just do not place orders at shows anymore. If this is true, it is true for a very good reason—buyers cannot attend these huge shows, digest all of the competitive information available, and still have time to negotiate for special merchandise. If the factory salesman is doing his job, there are probably few surprises in store for the buyer anyway. In addition to this, the role of the buyer in modern industry and in modern merchandising has been reduced to a specialty of gathering facts about sources of supply and acting upon the recommendation of either a buying committee, a specification group, or a merchandise manager.[1]

On the other hand, trade shows provide an opportunity for buyers to see products and techniques that otherwise might be available to them only on paper. If diligent, they can meet the top management of the companies involved. They can make invaluable contacts with their counterparts in business, and they can seek out new sources of supply.

Similar advantages are available to the seller, and he can, in addition, project a true image of his company if he is so inclined. He can always produce leads and prospects if he has something interesting to offer, and he should not be disappointed if the orders he writes at the show do not underwrite his expenses. A better understanding of the true value of a trade show would

---

[1] This point is made rather clear in E. B. Weiss, *The Vanishing Salesman*, chap. 6, "Giant Retailers—Pygmy Buyers," McGraw-Hill Book Company, New York, 1962.

benefit both buyer and seller alike and would produce a closer liaison in the industry in which they are engaged.

Sales Promotion in Industrial Selling.   The industrial field is usually characterized by a relatively small number of rather important customers, so that the relationship between buyer and seller is unusually close.   The job of sales promotion, therefore, is to produce adequate and descriptive literature which will accurately describe the products or techniques involved.

Because most industrial customers must have confidence in their suppliers, it is most important that up-to-date information should be instantly available in acceptable form.   This is particularly important so that the customers will realize the capabilities of the supplier.   A new technical change, a new process, will sometimes result in the loss of business to a competitor, if the customers are not informed promptly of improvements.   Unless basic patents are involved, there is little danger of disclosing trade secrets by keeping customers informed. Most industrial suppliers hold their customers by how well they do their work and by the service they give rather than by the secret processes they own.

One metal processor has had unusual success by holding sales seminars in the plants of its principal customers or prospects.   This traveling road show, scheduled by appointment, gets an opportunity to show the purchasing agent and the development engineers exactly what the company can do with its metal processing.   This is an authoritative display that packs a punch the salesman himself could never deliver.   In addition, the customer engineers themselves usually learn something about metal processing they did not know before.   After all, metal-fabricated parts must begin with the specifying engineer-designers, and the more they know about your process and your capabilities, the greater the chance of your getting their business.

A manufacturer of fire-fighting equipment has for many years operated a fire-fighting school for its customers.   It should be understood that most fire-fighting equipment is seldom, if ever, used—except in industries such as steel and petroleum.   Consequently, the people charged with the responsibility of fighting fire appreciate the opportunity of tackling a real fire—and you know whose equipment they prefer.

One of the very large manufacturers serving industry in the United States has produced a diary for over thirty years.   This little book, containing useful information, tables, maps, and the like, continues to be in demand throughout industry.   The continuing aspect of this program and the value of the book itself make this sales promotion activity a part of the company's selling program.

The three sales promotion activities described above required a good deal of time and effort to make them effective, but they were in each case a real contribution to the customer, and that is what makes sales promotion effective.

Sales Promotion in Selling to Wholesalers.   Those manufacturers who depend upon the wholesaler as an extension of their own sales forces have learned that they must gear their sales promotion to the needs of the wholesaler and his salesmen.   In this field, sales promotion and sales training are very close indeed.   As a matter of fact, it sometimes takes clever sales promotion to get the wholesaler's attention long enough to supply adequate sales training information.   Many companies have successfully entertained wholesaler's salesmen at group breakfast gatherings to gain attention for a new product or a special offering.   Although the breakfast party itself might be considered sales promotion, certainly there is no faster or easier way of accomplishing sales training.

If the product being promoted is a useful one in the home or otherwise has appeal to the jobber's salesman, it is a worthwhile effort to help him to acquire it.   There is no better sponsor for a product than a satisfied user.

It should be kept in mind, however, that the income of wholesale salesmen depends upon their selling a great variety of different articles, and further, that they cannot jeopardize their relationship with their dealers by forcing goods on them. Sales promotion aimed at stealing all of the salesman's time, or promotion which would disturb the relationship between the salesman and his account, probably is doomed to failure.

The wholesaler's volume depends upon how much the dealer can sell. Therefore, the best sales promotion is planned to help the dealer move his merchandise. Factory salesmen who will work on the dealer's sales floor in demonstrating their own product are killing two birds with one stone. Of course, this is personal selling, but they are lending themselves to a sales promotion effort at the point of sale.

During World War II when the metal shortage was at its worst, the public was forced to buy glass coffee makers, because very few other types were available. The sale of glass, although a bonanza to the wholesaler, created a problem of keeping dealers supplied with spare parts. The glass parts broke easily, and the dealers were in a dilemma as to whether to satisfy their customers with free replacements or to attempt to sell new parts or new units. A sales promotion plan which offered a simple display board showing all of the parts available solved the problem for dealer and wholesaler alike.

Sales Promotion in Selling to Retailers. Probably the best examples of sales promotion for the retailer are various kinds of envelope stuffers which are used either as mailing pieces such as bill inserts or as straight giveaway pieces for those customers who want to know more about the product.

It is quite important to determine in advance the most acceptable size your dealers prefer. It is also important that a place be provided for the dealer's own imprint to appear on any promotional piece. The same thing is true of catalog pages. They not only should carry an accurate description of the product, but should be prepared in the proper size. Dealers usually prefer price lists that carry only the retail price so that confusion does not arise between the dealer's cost and his selling price. If price lists are separate from the catalog (and it is a good idea to make them separate so that in the event of a price change the whole catalog does not have to be reprinted), they should be keyed to the catalog. Rather than use only catalog numbers in the price list, they are easier to handle if small sketches of the product appear opposite the catalog number.

Although there is no substitute for displaying the actual product, sometimes there are so many varieties of models and finishes that a complete line display is impossible. In such cases, the manufacturer can easily supply sample finishes or swatches of material to the dealer. Sometimes these demonstration kits are so expensive that they must be distributed with extreme care, or a small charge must be made to the dealer.

Displays, when they are well done and do not take up too much space, are usually welcomed by the retailer. Most dealers do not expect to pay for manufacturers' displays, so there is an important cost factor involved. Also, many of the largest retailers, particularly department stores, have rules which prohibit them from using any manufacturer's display.

Sales promotion in department stores can be accomplished by selling timely products and ideas for them to promote. Products which can be grouped together logically for selling for holidays or special days fall into this category. Storewide promotions embracing a wide selection of products interest the buying public very much. The manufacturer who concentrates on real promotional ideas and then sees that his product is included is performing a constructive function both for the large retailer and for himself.

Sales Promotion in Selling to Consumers. Selling to customers, of course, is the field that belongs to the retail dealer, the mail-order house, and the house-to-house specialist. All three use sales aids furnished by the manufacturer, but generally speaking they provide their own sales promotion.

Many stores have created a more pleasing shopping environment by decorating their stores, furnishing background music, and creating a generally favorable atmosphere.

Vendors of the house-to-house trade have secured a new kind of entry by the use of well-planned neighborhood parties which provide sponsorship for an otherwise unknown salesman. In other words, "creating the atmosphere" has become an important tool of sales promotion. The discount houses, before they achieved respect, deliberately created a chaos of merchandise that seemed to say, "It's all here at a price, but you've got to dig it out yourself."

Consumers are constantly the target of subtle and sometimes not-so-subtle sales promotion. The 1964–1965 World's Fair in New York might be billed as one giant sales promotion. The ownership of professional athletic teams is usually sales promotion aimed directly at the consumer, and even the organization of plant tours is a means of getting closer to the prospective buyer. In fact, all of this justifies the simple definition of sales promotion as "any activity which supplements or improves the effectiveness of personal selling."[2]

Sales Promotion in Selling Services. Very often sales promotion in promoting the use of a service is modified somewhat by accepted ethical practices. Obviously, independent professional people are extremely limited in what they can do to draw attention to themselves or to the qualities of the services they offer.

There are, however, many forms of sales promotion that are perfectly acceptable in nearly all of the professions. These include participation in community affairs or community projects, active membership in professional organizations, and the authorship of published articles in their specialized field. Speaking engagements should also be included in this category.

When professional people are banded together in groups such as consulting firms, it is often acceptable for them to use sales promotion methods which would be prohibited to the individual.

Generally speaking, modern methods of sales promotion in the service field are aimed at upgrading the quality image of the service offered and guaranteeing that the work performed is satisfactory, all with the purpose of continued service to the customer.

INTEGRATED SALES PROMOTION FOR PROFIT

It should be clear from the foregoing examples that sales promotion, just as all other phases of marketing, should be interrelated and compatible with the entire distribution system of the company. As pointed out earlier, the manufacturer must have the needs of the retailer in mind if he is to satisfy the requirements of the wholesaler. Amazingly enough, the needs of the ultimate consumer are sometimes forgotten in the rush to supply the trade with a "price

[2] For a much broader interpretation of sales promotion, including case histories of many companies and described as the "Principles and Methods for Intensifying Marketing Effort," see Alfred Gross, *Sales Promotion*, 2d ed., The Ronald Press Company, New York, 1961. This book would serve especially well as a textbook for companies interested in conducting courses on this subject.

promotable" item that has no acceptance in the public marketplace. Theodore Levitt has exposed the fallacies of fragmented planning by what he calls the need for "centripetal" marketing.[3] The milk industry certainly had this in mind when they brightened up the public image of bringing milk from farm to market by using gleaming stainless steel tank trucks for this purpose.

It is equally important that sales promotion plans are practical from a profit standpoint. Elaborate promotional plans for marginal profit items which will not support the promotion or cannot be repeated should, of course, be avoided. There are many cases where the "game is not worth the candle." This means that when developing promotional plans, accurate cost figures must be available not only for the promotional expense itself but for the product as well. Sales

[3] Theodore Levitt, *Innovation in Marketing*, McGraw-Hill Book Company, New York, 1962.

HOW TO PLAN SALES PROMOTION REQUIREMENTS

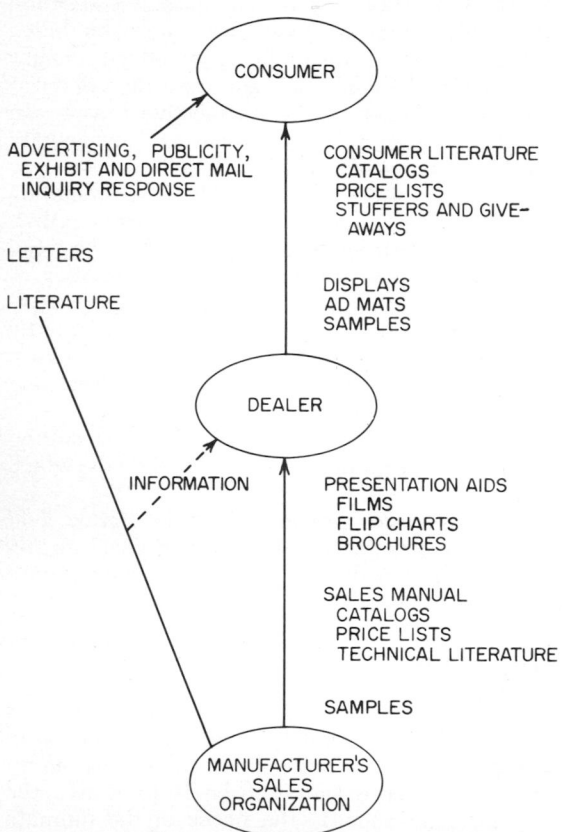

FIG. 9-1. *Literature, sales tools, and printed material required for distribution of a consumer product involving only manufacturer's sales organization and independent dealer selling to the consumer. If additional elements are present in the distribution channel, these same tools may be adapted to meet the requirements.*

promotion should not be attempted without a realistic market appraisal. This often means forecasting sales in advance so that realistic goals and performance standards may be set. This is the best way to avoid disappointments and to ensure profit.

Sales Promotion Budget. Budgets are just as necessary for sales promotion as they are for any other activity of a business, and they cannot be avoided by the plea that ideas, or the need for sales promotion activity, arise on the spur of the moment. Sales promotion must be used as a planned tool of selling and not a device to revive dying products. However, because sales promotion touches nearly every segment of the business, its primary role will always be advisory as a service to those functions which can use it. Therefore, the sales promotion department frequently uses money that has already been allocated to another department, but uses it in a way to integrate with other activities of the company. Letterheads, catalogs, and mailing pieces born of good graphics, good layout, and good content are no more expensive than their poor counterparts. The quality of these standard tools of selling may be reflected by the amount of money needed to staff sales promotion—but essentially the money is going to be spent anyway. The same thing is true for imaginative reception rooms, cheerful store interiors, tastefully painted trucks, or well-cut uniforms—the money has been allocated, but sales promotion can make it a wise and profitable expenditure.

All of this suggests, finally, that sales promotion can be a major force in integrating the sales plan with the company's corporate goals.

Figure 9-1 shows a simple method of planning all of the sales promotion requirements at one time. Planning in advance not only is immensely helpful to the sales organization, but also is economical from a production standpoint and provides the basis for a realistic budget.

CHECKLIST OF TERMS USED IN SALES PROMOTION

Advance Premium. A gift given before the sale, usually in return for a promise to buy later or to become a regular customer.

Bill Enclosure. Small printed pieces that are mailed in the same envelope with the monthly statements.

Broadside. As the name implies, a forceful mailing piece for special occasions, special offers often temporary in nature, and carrying only a brief message.

Brochure. A book bound, stitched, or stapled in semipermanent form carrying a complete presentation. Usually more elaborate than a working catalog and particularly useful in presenting a complete range of skills or services.

Catalog. A complete and current listing of all product information including catalog numbers, descriptions, weights, sizes, colors, and other information necessary to place an order.

Circular. Inexpensive handbills that may be distributed freely.

Convention. The term ordinarily used for industry-wide meetings or association meetings to conduct formal business.

Counter Display. Covers a wide variety and quality of top-of-the-counter displays, usually made to accommodate one or more of the actual product.

Demonstration. A public use of the product, such as making and serving coffee from a coffee maker.

Envelope Stuffers. Small pieces of giveaway literature used either as bill enclosures or for handout pieces.

Fairs. See Webster's Dictionary for the many different kinds of fairs.

Fliers. A seldom-used term for handout literature or special printed announcements usually involving an out-of-the-ordinary promotion.

Free Offers. Free gifts to attract customers in anticipation that a sale of the product will be made.

Giveaways. Items of small value packed together with the merchandise, such as a measuring spoon packed with a can of coffee.

Handbills. Printed pieces usually distributed by hand to passers-by or within a certain marketing area.

Mailing Lists. Classified lists of names of customers or prospects. These may be purchased for almost any purpose.

Open House. An invitation for customers or suppliers to visit one's place of business. Usually food and beverage served with an air of hospitality.

Over-the-wire Streamers. Colorful pennants strung over wire to form a continuous display of pennants. May be hung either inside or outside to create a festival atmosphere.

Pamphlets. Small booklets, not necessarily bound, often used for educational or instructional purposes.

PM or Spiff. A cash bonus paid to the salesclerk for each item sold. A device used by manufacturers, wholesalers, and retailers to focus sales attention on certain products.

Point-of-purchase Display. Displays which help the customer make a selection without help from the salesclerk. Particularly effective for impulse merchandise.

Premium. An article of merchandise used as an extra inducement to buy another product or service.

Reusable Container. A package having continuing value as a product; for example, jellies sold in drinking glasses.

Sampling. Distributing merchandise to the trade or to the public in anticipation that further purchases will result from a free trial.

Self-liquidator. A premium passed along to the consumer at cost in return for the purchase of another product.

Trade Show. An exhibition open only to the trade, not to the public.

Traveling Display. A display constructed so that it can be shipped to many locations, set up, and taken down repeatedly.

Visual Aids. That part of the sales presentation which demonstrates by being seen, such as charts, slides, and the like.

BIBLIOGRAPHY

Aspley, John C. (ed.), *The Sales Promotion Handbook*, 3d ed., The Dartnell Corporation, Chicago, 1962.

Gross, Alfred, *Sales Promotion*, 2d ed., The Ronald Press Company, New York, 1961.

Levitt, Theodore, *Innovation in Marketing*, McGraw-Hill Book Company, New York, 1962.

Simmons, Harry, *Successful Sales Promotion*, Prentice-Hall, Inc., Englewood Cliffs, N.J., 1950.

Turner, H. M., Jr., *Sales Promotion That Gets Results*, McGraw-Hill Book Company, New York, 1959.

Weiss, E. B., *The Vanishing Salesman*, McGraw-Hill Book Company, New York, 1962.

CHAPTER TEN

Distribution Methods and Costs

ROBERT HILLE   *Senior Operations Research Analyst, Management Services, Celanese Corporation of America, New York, New York*

Distribution operates within the marketing system to effect the transfer of ownership of goods from the producer to the consumer. It consists of the agencies and the physical transfers necessary to perform all the activities involved in making the transfer to the ultimate user. Services as well as goods may utilize distribution activities. Principally this is the case where goods are moved, such as in dry-cleaning or repair services.

The role of distribution management is to maximize profit through a favorable combination of service to the customers at a minimum cost. As a result, every element of distribution should be viewed as contributing to the profitability of the company in direct proportion to the degree of success with which these objectives are attained.

A company's distribution system includes not only all of its own distribution facilities and personnel, but also those of the distributors and dealers who sell its products.

THE DISTRIBUTION FUNCTION

The activities of distribution involve the use of distribution facilities—such as warehouses, material-handling equipment, transportation equipment, and stores and fixtures—and the performance of one or more basic distribution functions. These functions are:
1. Movement of ownership
    a. Buying and selling, including advertising, product service, consultation, and training
    b. Risk taking with respect to the ability to sell the goods to the next level of ownership
2. Movement of goods
    a. Transportation
    b. Storage, including material handling
    c. Dividing or assembling

    d. Packing
    e. Grading
3. Marketing management
    a. Credit financing and collections
    b. Market-decision information gathering
    c. Decision making

The above breakdown will be highly useful in distribution analysis and the selection of the best method of reaching the consumer.

Principal Methods of Distribution. There are three basic ways to distribute the product to the user:

1. Direct sales—selling direct to the user by the producer. Examples are: homes, swimming pools, chemicals, and the product of small job shops.
2. Retail outlets—this may take place through:
    a. The producer's branch or store (tires, food products, clothing).
    b. Independent retail stores or retail chain (fashions, sundries, specialty products).
    c. Others, such as direct mail and vending machines. These are not important factors in distribution, although they do market a great variety of products.
3. Through middlemen—these fall into two broad classes:
    a. Wholesalers and jobbers who handle such items as appliances, drugs, and toys.
    b. Manufacturers' agents—these are employed principally to move high-value items such as autos, aircraft, machinery, and components. These middlemen represent the producer and act for him in dealings with the user.

Any one or a combination of these methods may be used by a producer to reach a consumer, depending upon the specific distribution policies he follows. He may sell direct to the retail outlets or he may employ middlemen who, in turn, distribute to retailers. In addition, those middlemen classified as agents may distribute directly to the user while acting as a representative of the producer.

Decisions on which method or methods to use to reach the consumer determine the distribution channel.

Channels of Distribution. Any combination of facilities and functions through which a product passes between the producer's plant and the user may be termed a "channel of distribution." A channel is usually considered to end and another to begin when the form of the goods is changed by some means of manufacture.

Vertical integration refers to the operation under single ownership of two or more stages of distribution. Thus, the manufacturer who owns or operates warehouses and retail outlets is said to be vertically integrated.

Horizontal integration is the ownership of a number of units at the same stage of distribution, as, for example, the wholesaler who owns a number of warehouses or agencies.

A distribution channel can be considered to have two dimensions, *length* and *width.* Length of the channel usually refers to the number of stages through which a product must pass to reach the customer. Width refers to the number of factors at the same stage of distribution. Thus, a wide channel at the retail level would result in placing a producer's drug product in every drugstore in a market.

Channel Length. The shortest trade channel is the one in which the producer sells directly to its consumer. Illustrations of this and other types of channels are presented in Figure 10-1.

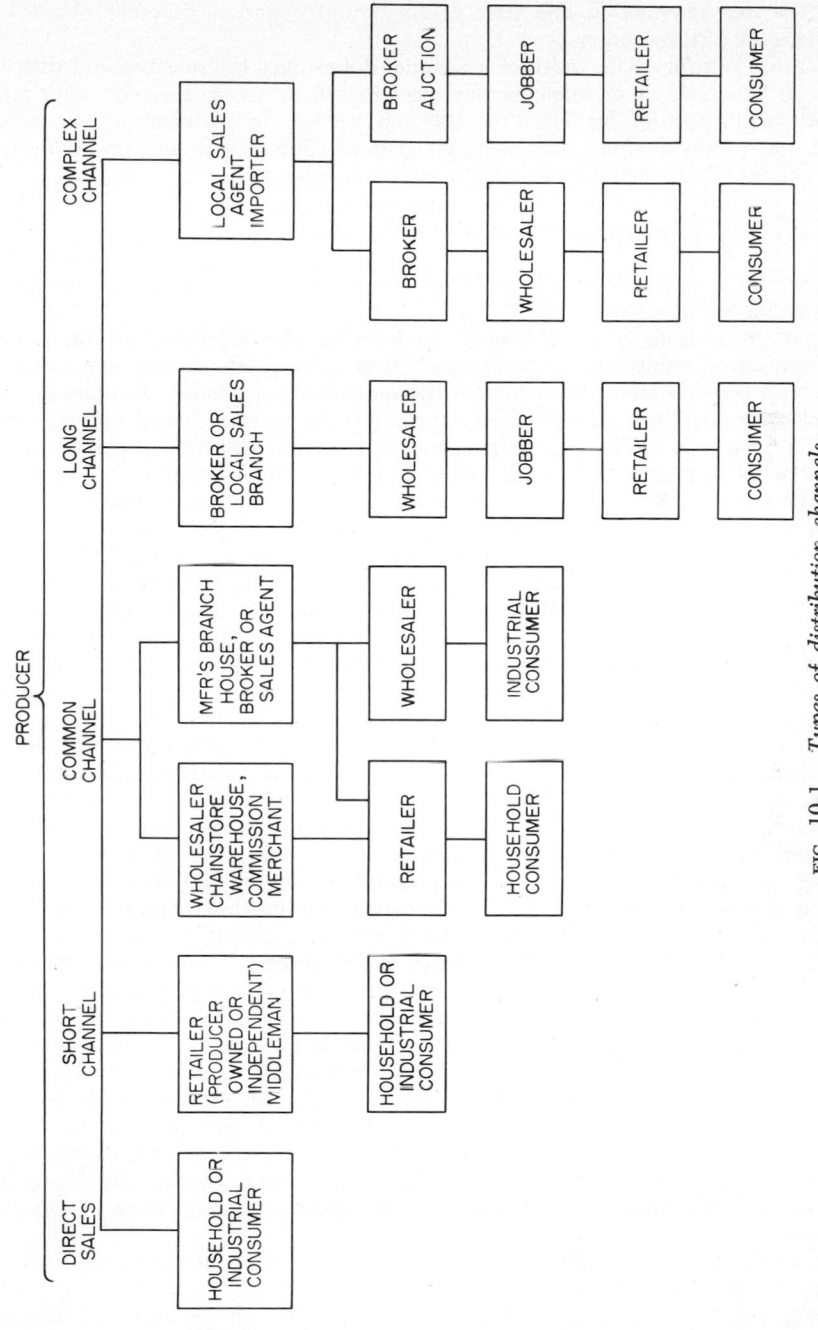

FIG. 10-1. *Types of distribution channels.*

The same manufacturer may utilize a number of channels. He may use one channel for one product and another channel for another product; or he may use one channel in one part of the country and a different channel in another part of the country.

Channel Width. The width of a channel determines the selectivity of distribution. A producer or middleman may elect to sell to a broad market with many outlets or to restrict his effort to selected areas. In distributing to selected areas, the producer must choose outlets that can intensively and profitably conduct selling within those areas.

DISTRIBUTION INSTITUTIONS

Distribution institutions fall into three broad categories: retailers, middlemen, and facilitating agencies.

These institutions were developed to increase the efficiency of distribution. Primarily, they reduce the relationships between the producer and the consumer. They also provide credit financing for the movement of goods. Businesses could not exist in the form that we know them if they were required to reach each consumer directly. The establishment of distribution institutions permits a routinization of decisions and transactions, which results in lower costs. It makes possible the vast array of choices that are open to the modern consumer. Credit financing provides working capital to producers that enables them to carry on their operations and to reduce their risks while goods are being sold. Credit is also often extended to retailers and to customers. The familiar lease arrangement is really little more than a means by which to finance the customer's use of the product.

Distribution through Retail Outlets. A retailer is defined as anyone who sells to the ultimate consumer or user. Those who purchase a product for resale at a profit are not retail customers, but intermediaries. Therefore, any merchant in the distribution chain who sells to the consumer functions as a retailer for that portion of his business, regardless of his prime function or whatever he may call himself. Retail operations may be conducted through various physical means such as stores, offices, assembly-line buildings, and vending machines.

Retail Stores. Retail stores perform the functions of buying, storing, and selling, as well as convenience and promotion. In buying, the retailer must secure goods that are desired by the consumers in the market to which he caters. Producers should sell to retailers who are suited to dealing with the consumer for whom the producer intends his products. The retailer must stock a sufficient amount of merchandise to serve the consumer properly. At the same time, he must achieve a sufficient number of stock turns to minimize his expenses for carrying the inventory. He must strike a balance between turning over this stock too fast and being "out of stock," thereby losing sales, and turning over too slowly, and consequently increasing his expenses and risk. To sell the goods, he must separate and categorize as well as store them. He finances the sale of his goods by the extension of credit to his customers. In addition, he assumes many risks attendant to carrying goods. He must keep hours suited to his trade, and he often delivers goods and packs them to withstand delivery.

Retailers may be classified on the basis of the type of ownership, as well as the characteristics of their operation.

Independent retailers are outlets not owned by the producer. They may or may not be locally owned and operated.

Manufacturers' retail outlets are outlets owned and generally operated by manufacturers. Examples of this type of operation are tire stores, shoe stores, and small specialty jewelry stores.

Both independent retailers and manufacturers' retail outlets may be any of the following types.

A *specialty store* handles a complete assortment in a limited variety of goods within a single line, such as women's apparel or sporting goods. Specialty stores may be departmentalized. They are usually not considered mass merchandisers who maintain large inventories. Therefore, in selling to them, the producer will normally use the services of wholesale middlemen.

Single-line stores carry a single line of goods, such as groceries, meats, drugs, hardware, or furniture. *Department* stores handle a wide variety of lines. A department store is a combination of many departments, each of which is operated under the managership of a person known as the "buyer." Each buyer has as his main function the buying of merchandise sold within his department, and the manufacturer must sell to him. A *supermarket* is a large, departmentalized food store, often carrying other goods in addition to food. Supermarkets are principally *self-service* outlets in which the customer walks into the store and is free to choose any product he wishes with a minimum of assistance by sales personnel. Other stores in this category are drugs and hardware. The manufacturer has the burden of preselling his merchandise, because the self-service outlet will do little other than display it or run local promotional advertisements.

Discount houses are typically volume oriented and sell brand-name merchandise at prices considerably reduced from a well-recognized market price. Discounters may operate within the framework of many of the types of stores mentioned here. A discount operator does not wish to do extensive promotional work, but rather depends upon his and his product's general reputation to draw customers. His high volume and minimum expenses permit him to operate at the lower margins characteristic of discount stores.

A *general store* handles a wide variety of goods without being departmentalized. General stores are usually small and are located in smaller and out-of-the-way communities.

A *chain store* operation is defined by Andrews as having four or more stores under single ownership, or sponsorship.[1] A chain may be local, operating within a city or small region; national, operating throughout the entire country; or international, operating in several countries; or a variation of these. The stores may even be of different types at different locations to conform to the requirements of the local market. Chains may operate entire stores, or they may lease departments in several stores. For example, there are several large chains which operate leased drug departments in department specialty and supermarket stores.

Voluntary chains are associations of independent retailers who have joined together to purchase as a group through a wholesaler to enjoy the advantages of mass purchasing power. Wholesaler-sponsored voluntary chains have also come into being to meet competition from the large chain stores with their integrated purchasing-selling operations.

Nonstore Retailing. *Mail-order* selling is normally carried on through catalog, newspaper, or direct-mail advertising. Uniqueness of the product sold is gen-

---

[1] G. H. Andrews, *Distribution Methods,* International Cooperation Administration, Washington, D.C., 1963.

erally the secret of successful mail-order selling. Consumers generally order by mail because they cannot obtain the product at a local store. The remoteness of some locations often makes it more convenient for people to buy by mail rather than visit local stores. Large mail-order sellers buy direct from manufacturers or even own the factories and combine wholesaling and retailing. Whether it is truly less expensive to sell by mail depends on the return on the advertising expense. Converse, Huegy, and Mitchell[2] have indicated that successful selling by mail depends upon repeat sales to the same customer. This requires selling repeat products such as vitamins or carrying a wide line of products from which to choose.

Vending machines may dispense a great variety of merchandise. However, the problem of selecting products particularly suited to this type of retailing and the selection of locations is every bit as important as choosing what type of product to sell in what stores and at what locations. Expenses for machines are listed as being typically 37 percent of sales, and profit as 3.6 percent of sales.[3]

The principal advantage of personal *door-to-door selling* is that the salesman, once he is inside the door, is able to present the merits of the products directly to the potential consumer. However, there is a great deal of resistance on the part of the consumer to door-to-door selling. As a result, the successful firms in this field are those that have an established reputation, spend a great deal of time training their salesmen, and pay them high commissions. It is, therefore, a high-expense way of selling.

Product leasing is most conveniently handled through direct selling to the customer. A device often used for management control and accounting is to establish a leasing subsidiary through which all agreements of this nature are transacted. A major consideration in this regard is the considerably higher capital outlay required of the producer for inventory and for sales and service organizations than would otherwise be necessary.

Middlemen. "Middleman" is a term that has been derisively employed to connote a useless addition to cost. However, the term is in reality a descriptive one and is used to categorize those agencies performing a specialized service of great value to the efficient distribution of goods and services. They increase the efficiency of marketing by routinization of activities as well as through a reduction of transactions and an increase in the scale of transactions.

Middlemen do not buy or sell directly to household or industrial consumers, but pass goods along to the retail institutions and other wholesale merchants who resell for profit.

Middlemen are grouped into three broad functional categories: manufacturer-owned wholesalers, merchant wholesalers, and agent middlemen. Of the latter two, merchant wholesalers own the goods that they sell or pass along. Agent middlemen do not.

Middlemen provide a wide assortment of services. These services span the whole range of marketing activities and include (1) maintenance of sales force, (2) storage, (3) delivery, (4) financial assistance to the manufacturer, (5) credit to the buyer, (6) sales promotion, (7) product servicing, and (8) collection and dissemination of market information.

Manufacturer-owned Wholesale Establishments. Many producers establish sales offices, branches, and warehouses to lower distribution costs, achieve aggressive promotion of their products, and render better service of the product

[2] Paul D. Converse, Harvey W. Huegy, and Robert V. Mitchell, *Elements of Marketing*, Prentice-Hall, Inc., Englewood Cliffs, N.J., 1958.

[3] *Vending in 1961*, National Automatic Merchandising Association, Chicago.

to the consumer. Any lowering of distribution costs usually occurs because of increased volume or efficiencies rather than the elimination of middlemen profits.

Sales or branch offices do not carry inventory. They are offices from which one or more salesmen operate. Sales offices often include the performance of repair services. They allow a broader coverage of the market and servicing of the trade than direct factory selling to the wholesaler does. They are usually located in close proximity to major markets of the product. Costs of maintaining a local sales office are not large and may be minimized by such devices as the use of a telephone answering service.

Sales branches or branch houses carry inventory and deliver directly to buyers from their stock. The branch has the advantages of a sales office plus that of faster delivery to the customer. The latter is a decided advantage when delivery time is crucial. The higher cost of operating a sales branch may be offset by being able to ship to local areas in carload lots. Credit clearances and collections may also be performed at the branch level rather than in the home office. Controlling local distribution may protect the producer against losing distribution should the wholesaler decide not to carry his product.

Merchant Wholesalers. Merchant wholesalers take title to the goods they carry. Margins in wholesaling are typically small and result in a conservative outlook by most wholesalers. Producers must generally pull their products through the wholesale stage by means of promotional advertising, thereby creating a demand at the retail level. This will force wholesalers to carry the product. A *full-service* merchant wholesaler, found frequently in the hardware, drug, and grocery fields, maintains a sales force which regularly calls on retailers. He owns one or more warehouses in which he carries necessary inventories. He will extend credit to qualified buyers. Under certain circumstances, he will do sales promotion work for the manufacturers. In addition, because the wholesaler pays the manufacturer promptly, the manufacturer obtains funds that he would himself have to finance if he were to fill retail orders at the slow rate encountered at that level. The average full-service merchant wholesaler incurs operating expenses that are 13.4 percent of sales value.[4]

A *rack jobber* is a full-service merchant wholesaler who is normally responsible for specific shelf space within the retail store to which he is assigned. He must count the inventory and maintain an adequate supply of stock. The rack jobber carries only a few lines of merchandise and usually places the merchandise on consignment. In the latter case, he assumes the risk that the merchandise will not sell. Buskirk[5] states that the rack jobber usually passes on 20 to 25 percent of the retail price. In addition, he receives the usual wholesaler's margin of 16⅔ percent. *Cash-and-carry* wholesalers are, as the name implies, engaged in an operation that requires the retailer to come to the warehouse, pay cash, and take away the merchandise. Wholesalers of this type function to provide storage of large quantities and their division into the small units required for retail.

Mail-order wholesalers conduct their business through the mail. The basic disadvantages of this method are slow delivery and high cost. It is not a significant method of wholesaling. *Drop shippers* obtain and forward orders to the manufacturer and have him ship directly to the buyer. The wholesaler himself does no storing and handling. Drop shippers deal in bulky materials

[4] *The Economic Almanac 1964,* National Industrial Conference Board, New York, 1964, p. 324.

[5] Richard H. Buskirk, *Principles of Marketing,* Holt, Rinehart and Winston, Inc., New York, 1961.

and in sales to retailers of carlots of minimum economical truckloads. They also put together assortments of goods such as coal or lumber by representing several producers who each supply their specialties. Drop shippers are also known as "direct-mill shippers," "desk jobbers," or "distributors without a yard."

Truck jobbers or *wagon distributors* have a small warehouse from which they supply their trucks. They sell and deliver at the same time. Truck jobbers are found where the merchandise is highly perishable or where some personal promotion is required. Examples are bread and cake, candy and tobacco, and dairy products. They have a high degree of contact with the retail trade, although their operating expenses are relatively high.

Exporters buy in the domestic market and sell in foreign markets. They sell mainly to foreign importers, wholesale merchants, and industrial users. *Importers* buy in the foreign market and sell in the domestic market. They sell to wholesalers and industrial users as well as to retailers. *Bulk stations* or plants are used to store petroleum and chemical products. *Assemblers* buy farm products, fish, and the like from small producers. They then combine the products in some manner for shipment and resale.

Agent Middlemen. As mentioned above, agent middlemen do not take title to the goods that pass through this stage. Instead, they buy and sell for others. As a result, they are often called "functional wholesalers." They account for about 15 percent of wholesale sales. They are paid either a percentage of the value of the goods that are bought and sold or a fixed fee per unit. The *broker* neither takes title to nor handles the goods that he deals with. Rather, he brings together suppliers and buyers. Brokers usually deal with a single line, such as lumber, sugar, coffee, or frozen foods. When they concentrate on buying, they are called "buying brokers." When they specialize in selling, they are called "selling brokers." Brokers are useful where there are many small suppliers and the market consists of many small buyers. Because each supplier may not be able to afford a sales staff, or if the product is seasonal, a year-round sales staff may not be practical. However, because by nature the broker must be market oriented to be thoroughly familiar with market conditions, his loyalty is to his customer and himself. As a result, manufacturers should not count on him to operate at all times in their best interests. The broker is usually paid by the seller of the merchandise. When he is under direct control of the buyer, he is paid by him.

Sales Agents. A sales or selling agent represents the firm for whom he deals. He usually has the exclusive right to sell the merchandise in a very wide geographic area. The sales agent is normally utilized by small, inadequately financed, production-oriented producers. This allows them to have immediate access to the market without having to build a sales organization. The sales agent often has authority over prices, terms of sale, and other marketing decisions.

One major drawback of the sales agent is that he is customer oriented rather than supplier oriented. As a result, he is very likely to abandon the supplier if a more attractive opportunity comes along, or he may dictate prices on terms of sales that the manufacturer considers unfavorable.

A *manufacturer's agent* is a salesman for a part of the manufacturer's output. He has a limited territory and operates on a straight commission basis. He may or may not maintain an inventory of goods. The manufacturer's agent normally represents several producers concurrently and assembles a line of related but noncompetitive products. The use of manufacturers' agents has the advantage to the manufacturer of his being able to set prices, terms, and policies as stipulated by the sales contract. In addition, should one manufacturer's agent discontinue the line, the distribution of entire production is not lost. Another agent is relatively easy to find. Manufacturers' agents are generally found in the distribution of textiles, machinery, food, automotive accessories, electrical goods, and metals. In the case of both selling agents and manufacturers' agents, it is highly important that the contract obligations be carefully spelled out and in as specific terms as possible.

Export and import agents are agents involved in buying and selling goods in foreign and domestic markets. They include commission houses, export and import brokers, export managers, and manufacturers' export agents.

Purchasing agents and resident buyers are independent middlemen who perform the buying function for one or more principals. Resident buyers tend more to operate for retailers, whereas purchasing agents operate at the wholesale level.

Auctioneers conduct sales to the highest bidder. They are important in the sales of agricultural products and secondhand or used goods.

Facilitating Institutions. Some institutions do not play a role in the legal or physical distribution of products. However, they make it possible to perform the other activities more easily. These facilitating agencies perform a wide variety of specialized services such as research, consulting, advertising, traveling, and testing. They are commonly encountered during distribution analysis and decision making. There are, in addition, trade and industry groups that set standards, conduct trade fairs, grade and classify, and conduct institutional promotion. These activities may substantially aid the distribution of the products of participating manufacturers.

DISTRIBUTION OF SERVICES

Services are described as the performing of a function or activity which does not normally involve buying and selling of goods. Examples are doctors, lawyers, computer assistance, and dry cleaning. In addition, transportation and entertainment are huge industries engaged in the buying and selling of services.

Much the same that has been said previously about the movement of goods applies to services. Retail distribution is analogous to the finding of buyers for local services such as beauty parlors and public utility services.

In many cases, franchise agents and other middlemen are employed to widen distribution and find suitable outlets, handle licensing, and the like. *Financial services* may be conducted directly or through brokers who, in turn, locate outlets for capital on the local level. Services may also be distributed directly to industrial users. The provision of electricity and steam is an example of the latter. In marketing its services, the telephone company employs a large staff of highly trained salesmen who provide counsel to their direct customers in the use of the service.

The distribution of services may be limited to a relatively small geographic area because of regulations, dispersion and dissipation of the product, and the high costs involved in extending distribution. On the other hand, railroads and entertainment profit by the very nature of being able to reach great distances with no inconvenience to the user.

DISTRIBUTION TO INDUSTRIAL USERS

The choice of distribution channels available to suppliers of industrial goods is generally limited. This is because the buyers are few in number and are usually concentrated within geographic areas. As a result of this simplification, costs of distribution are considerably lower than in the field of consumer goods.

This advantage may be offset, however, by the higher degree of technical training required of the salesmen.

Direct selling is most often employed to sell to industrial users. The resulting service and the close touch with production are highly desirable. Because the individual orders are relatively large, it becomes economical to service the accounts with a full-time sales staff. The use of *wholesale middlemen* is the other most popular method of industrial distribution. In this case, the producer may utilize his own or leased warehouse facilities for storage prior to sale. In some cases, such as industrial machinery, for example, the purchasers may, in turn, be sellers to the original producers. Therefore, it may be possible to enter into reciprocal purchasing and selling agreements.

Industrial distributors are usually full-service merchant wholesalers who do not carry products of competing manufacturers. Instead, they represent makers of related but noncompetitive goods. They normally specialize in certain types of industrial goods or machinery.

Mill supply houses are the industrial equivalent of the general line, full-service merchant wholesaler. An example of this type is the automotive-parts supply wholesaler who sells a full line of goods to garages and service stations.

The *commission merchant* maintains facilities for the receipt, handling, conditioning, warehousing, and selling of commodities. When he advances funds to growers and shippers, he may be called a "factor."

PHYSICAL DISTRIBUTION

Physical distribution is concerned with the actual movement of goods and services from the sources to the consumer. The functions involved are *transportation* and *storage*. Frey[6] lists the five common modes of transportation as rail, highway, water, pipeline, and air. In addition, the many forms of communication such as telephone, television, radio, and cable must also be considered.

Transportation. Because transportation constitutes about 50 percent of total marketing costs, it offers good opportunities for significant cost reduction. Careful review and analysis should identify many areas of potential yield. For the purposes of regulation and administration, the modes of transportation are grouped into four categories: common, contract, exempt, and private carriers.

Common carriers are highly regulated. They must publish and make available to the public all their rates and services. They accept responsibility for carrying goods any time, any place.

Contract carriers make themselves available on a selective basis. They may charge different rates to different customers for the same service. They are required to publish the actual rates that they charge their customers.

Exempt carriers are, as a group, basically exempt from government regulations.

Private transportation is the category for firms who transport their own goods without regulation.

The mode of transportation to be used may be considered from two aspects: (1) production and primary distribution facilities established and in being and (2) facilities to be located and constructed in accordance with marketing objectives of the producer. Various combinations of these two conditions may be encountered. The problem of locating facilities is a highly complicated one as compared with consideration of existing facilities. In either case, it is recommended that the transportation problem be viewed from the standpoint of being a part of the total distribution system.

⁶ Albert Wesley Frey (ed.), *Marketing Handbook,* The Ronald Press Company, New York, 1965.

Basic considerations in the choice of a transportation system are:

Speed—permitting better customer service and reduction of inventory requirements through lower bulk stock requirements
Cost—overall to distribution
Capacity—long-term cost implications and limitations on volume

The transportation regulations specify rates for the different ways in which cargo may be carried. Thus, *carload* rates are those for full carload quantities. These are generally lower than for *less-than-carload* (LCL) shipments. There are many other specifications for rates as applied to the movement of goods. They need to be studied in detail to determine the least-cost method of shipping. Speed may be an important advantage not just of the airplane, but of trucks as well. Less-than-carload deliveries may be made in one day by truck. By rail, these deliveries may take from two to ten days. Comparative costs for transportation may not be relevant, because major carriers may specialize in carrying one type of goods. Study must be given to the specific goods and destinations involved.

Storage. In the larger sense usually encountered in examining physical distribution, storage is associated with warehousing, including material handling performed in the warehouse. In reality, storage takes place at any point—at the retailer, in transit, at the producer's facilities, as well as at the warehouse. The cost of carrying inventory is commonly quoted at 17 percent of the average value of inventory. In reality, it may vary widely from this figure, perhaps from 10 to as much as 40 percent.

Innovation. Innovation plays an important part in physical distribution. New techniques and special transportation equipment are constantly being developed and tried to reduce costs or improve service. In some cases, two or more modes of transportation may be combined for point-to-point movement of goods such as in piggyback truck-rail transportation. Other areas of innovation are packaging and containerization.

DISTRIBUTION COST ANALYSIS

In an environment of rapidly changing technology and consumer tastes, it is imperative that producers continually review their methods of distribution, the related costs, and their combined effect on total marketing objectives. The historic approach to distribution cost analysis was to view it as an opportunity to reduce costs. A more up-to-date and beneficial approach is to consider distribution expense as a means of maximizing profits. Taken in this latter context, existing methods may be studied and alternatives sought in terms of their profitability.

Total Marketing System. It is clear that all products of a firm may not pass through the same distribution channel. In addition, the decisions in one area affect all the other areas of corporate activity. Production costs and scheduling, financial limitations, middlemen relationships, and pricing policy all react in one way or another to actions taken in distributing a product. Although the profitability of a product may be negative, this does not mean that a method of distribution or entire distribution of a product need be discarded. On the contrary, the support that a product gives the corporate image and the remainder of the product line of the firm may be the overriding criterion. The cost, however, must be borne by the other profitable lines. Thus, the concept embraced here is one of a total marketing system where every segment of the marketing function affects each of the other segments.

The problem may be stated as one of selecting the optimum *distribution mix*—the proper combination of distribution methods and channels that yields the greatest profits.

In determining the distribution alternatives, the total system concept guides thinking toward three basic considerations—consumer, product, producer.

1. Consumer
    a. The quantity and kinds of customers to whom the products are to be sold
    b. Their location and the territories that need to be covered to reach them
    c. Service requirements of the consumer—giving too much service that will not be used can be costly and as bad as giving too little
    d. The order size—determination of cost and order policy by quantity
2. Product
    a. The products to be sold at a specified price
    b. The nature of the product, its perishability, bulk, fragility, unit value, and the like
    c. The use of the product and the requirements for conversion to some other final product
3. Producer
    a. Location of production facilities
    b. Overall production scheduling—seasons and quantities
    c. Trade agreements and contractual requirements affecting production
    d. Organization and technical capabilities
    e. Relationships to competition and traditional methods of distribution within an industry; dependence of a channel upon the business of a competitor

The profit implications associated with each alternative should be explicitly stated and measured against the following basic corporate criteria.

Corporate Marketing Policy. The distribution decision must be analyzed in the light of corporate image, reputation, overall marketing strategy, and corporate objectives. The support that a product gives to the total product line should be indicated.

Corporate Profitability Criteria. Corporate profit goals should be established. Failure to attain the standards set by management for profitability would suggest continuing the search for more profitable opportunities.

Profit Contribution Analysis. Contribution to profit provides the most effective yardstick by which to measure the profit gain from each transaction. "Contribution" is defined as the difference between sales and all variable costs. Joint costs and standby costs are charged to a common pool of expenses which must be covered by the excess of sales over product costs. As a result, the incremental profit can be measured against corresponding incremental expense.

Profit contribution analysis utilizes two basic information segments:

1. The total potential sales of the company's products as the result of pursuing a particular course of action
2. The distribution expense associated with each of the stages in the channels being considered

Sales Volume Forecasting. A distribution analysis should logically begin by determining the anticipated sales from a course of action. Volume data should be accumulated by user, trade channel, geographic area, and product.

The width of distribution and the degree of geographic concentration of potential customers bear directly upon the length of the channel. A highly concentrated market allows shorter channels to be used. A particular channel may be used to serve many products. Thus, when considering a single product and its distribution, it is extremely important to take into account the current system and the benefits derived from utilizing it. This may then be compared with alternative which may or may not include other products from the current channels. The correlated sales volume should then be estimated.

Costs and expenses should be derived in detail for each of the basic functions of distribution.

Figure 10-2 shows a list of factors that should be considered when collecting costs for analysis. It may be extremely difficult to assign some variable costs that are borne jointly by several products. These are best handled by weighting their share on the basis of sales volume. Where these expenses cover a great variety of goods, they should be charged as total line expenses and not allocated.

It should be kept in mind that costs directly variable for one set of conditions may not be variable for another set. For example, costs that are variable for sales by territory may have to be treated as a joint expense when examining product line or variety profitability.

In comparing alternatives, it will be necessary to estimate many costs. If comparative costs or standards have been established, it will be possible to utilize a yardstick, such as expense per unit sale or margin as a percent of production cost, as an estimate of costs for a particular stage of distribution.

Margin requirements set aside for middlemen should be estimated as being in direct proportion to the amount of work and promotion they must do to

Investment charges
    Interest on static inventory investment
    Interest on goods-in-transit investment
    Investment-opportunity charge
    Insurance cost for static inventory
    Insurance cost for goods in transit
    Inventory-obsolescence charge
    Inventory taxes
Physical-distribution expenses
    Transportation charges—consisting of:
        Raw-materials-to-plant shipping cost
        Plant-to-break-bulk product-transportation cost
        Break-bulk-to-customer delivery cost
        Direct-to-the-job delivery cost
    Product cross-shipment expense
    Loading, unloading, break-bulk cost
    Warehousing commissions
    Agent's bonding cost
    Loss and damage charges
    Physical deterioration and prevention cost
    Packaging cost
Management and administration costs
    Sales expense
    Production/sales overtime expense
    Order-transmission charges
    Order-processing costs—consisting of:
        Prime-order-handling cost
        Back-order cost
    Statistical-services expense
Competitive returns
    Marketing opportunity
    Product-line enhancement
Economy-of-manufacturing enhancement
    Intensification of production investment usage
    Exploitation of outside productive capacity
    Consolidation of production centers

FIG. 10-2. *Cost factors commonly associated with distribution alternatives.*

move the product.   The more successful the promotional effort and associated effort performed by the producer are, the less the margin allowances need be for middlemen.

It is generally of limited use to make an industry comparison of costs.   This is because there are so many combinations of factors that comprise a single cost.   The only valid analysis is to choose figures that are accurate for the detailed components of each alternative.   Should estimates be required, an estimate of their accuracy should be developed which will permit the comparison of projected costs with confidence in the calculations.   A *margin of safety* might be determined as follows:

$$\text{Margin of safety} = \frac{\text{total unit sales} - \text{break-even volume}}{\text{total unit sales}}$$

This percentage results in the proportion by which the sales (or cost) estimate could be wrong without resulting in anything worse than a break-even.

Evaluation of Distribution Alternatives.   Each of the distribution methods under analysis should be measured by the potential contribution to profits accruing to the company while affording a reasonable net profit to the middleman.

Some useful guides to action may be derived from the above analysis to provide a continuing basis for comparison:

1. The contribution made by individual products or group of products
2. The contribution derived from sales to major classes of customers by type and order size
3. The contribution to profits from sales by geographic trading area or trading center
4. The contribution by distribution channel

Once the above data have been collected and the contributions calculated, some simple steps may be taken to begin examination of the distribution system and opportunities for cost reduction as well as increased sales.

1. Rank the items in each of the above groups in order of their unit contribution to profits.   Also prepare a ranking by total contribution.
2. Determine the percentage of the total contribution of whole product line for each item.
3. Indicate the low-contribution items for each of the above.   This will spotlight the uneconomic elements in the distribution system and the costs involved in servicing them.
4. Indicate the high contributors.   In many cases, these may not previously have been explicitly recognized as such.   In addition, those with high unit contribution and low sales present a clear opportunity to increase sales.   This may be accomplished by direct selling effort or reduction of the high markup to increase compensation to middlemen, thereby using their special services to increase sales.

The above will allow the producer to decide the following:

1. Width of distribution.   Should there be a broad coverage with maximum market coverage through large numbers of sales agencies, or should selective coverage be chosen with a limited number of high-quality sales agencies?
2. Length of the channel.   Should sales be made directly to the user through retail outlets, or through middlemen?
3. Optimum location of distribution facilities.   The exact placement of such facilities is normally the subject of a separate in-depth study.   However, a general indication of the need for and the approximate area of location may be

	Method A	Method B
Sales (cases × price).........................	$2,500,000	$2,500,000
Cost of sales................................	1,750,000	1,750,000
Manufacturing profit....	$ 750,000	$ 750,000
Variable distribution costs:		
Transportation out........................	$ 10,000	$ 25,000
Salesmen.................................	15,000	2,000
Distributors and agents...................	1,000	5,000
Advertising..............................	1,000	2,000
Inventory investment.....................	15,000	5,000
Branch office expense.....................	15,000	1,000
Storage of finished goods.................	5,000	2,000
Stationery and supplies...................	1,000	1,000
Traffic and billing........................	2,000	4,000
Total variable charges.......................	$ 65,000	$ 47,000
Profit contribution......................	$ 685,000	$ 703,000
Standby and programmed expense....	200,000	200,000
Operating profit..........................	$ 485,000	$ 503,000
Percent to sales...........................	19.4%	20.2%
Choose Method B.		

FIG. 10-3. *Simplified analysis of distribution alternatives.*

provided by an initial study which shows the incremental costs associated with movement of goods between points.

4. Economic production schedules.   Given the costs associated with warehousing, sales, credit to buyers, and transportation, it is possible to establish breakeven points for the most economic schedule of production by product.

5. New methods of improving distribution programs through analysis of all stages of the physical distribution process.   Warehousing, material-handling

	Product line			
	A	B	C	Total
Sales.........................	$500,000	$300,000	$200,000	$1,000,000
Variable costs...................	350,000	180,000	100,000	630,000
Gross profit contribution.......	$150,000	$120,000	$100,000	$ 370,000
Percent to sales.................	30%	40%	50%	37%
Specific programmed costs........	100,000	36,000	14,000	150,000
Net profit contribution........	$ 50,000	$ 84,000	$ 86,000	$ 220,000
Percent to sales................	10%	28%	43%	22%
General programmed costs........	....	....	....	40,000
Standby costs...................	....	....	....	120,000
Operating profit before taxes....	....	....	....	$ 60,000
Percent to sales.................	....	....	....	6%

FIG. 10-4.   *Analysis of product-line profit contribution.*   (*Adapted from Robert Beyer,* Profitability Accounting for Planning and Control, *The Ronald Press Company, New York, 1963.*)

procedures, packaging, and transportation procedures should be examined for possible improvements, particularly if they represent a high percentage of total cost.

Figures 10-3 and 10-4 illustrate the use of profit contribution analysis in making distribution decisions. Figure 10-3 shows how this technique may be applied to compare different distribution methods for any product or group of products. Figure 10-4 shows a comparison of product-line profitability. Variations in distribution among products are included within the respective profit computations.

BIBLIOGRAPHY

Buskirk, Richard H., *Principles of Marketing*, Holt, Rinehart and Winston, Inc., New York, 1961.

Converse, Paul D., Harvey W. Huegy, and Robert V. Mitchell, *Elements of Marketing*, Prentice-Hall, Inc., Englewood Cliffs, N.J., 1958.

Cutting Costs in Industry: III, Distribution Costs, Studies in Business Policy, no. 41, National Industrial Conference Board, New York, 1950.

Frey, Albert Wesley (ed.), *Marketing Handbook*, The Ronald Press Company, New York, 1965.

Hesket, J. L., R. M. Ivie, and N. A. Glaskowski, *Business Logistics*, The Ronald Press Company, New York, 1964.

Langhoff, Peter, *Models, Measurement and Marketing*, Prentice-Hall, Inc., Englewood Cliffs, N.J., 1965.

Schofield, W. C., "The 'Contribution Margin' Method: How to Make Sharper Sales Decisions," *Business Management*, 1962.

Sevin, Charles H., *How Manufacturers Reduce Their Distribution Costs*, Economic Series, no. 72, Marketing Division, U.S. Department of Commerce, Washington, D.C., 1946.

Sevin, Charles H., *Marketing Productivity Analysis*, McGraw-Hill Book Company, New York, 1965.

Small Orders: Problems and Solutions, Studies in Business Policy, no. 94, National Industrial Conference Board, New York, 1960.

Smith, Charles W., *Targeting Sales Effort*, Columbia University Press, New York, 1958.

Smykay, Edward W., *Physical Distribution Management*, The Macmillan Company, New York, 1961.

CHAPTER ELEVEN

Sales Management

VICTOR P. BUELL   *Vice President, American Radiator & Standard Sanitary Corporation, New York, New York*

The Committee on Definitions of the American Marketing Association defines sales management as: "The planning, direction, and control of the personal selling activities of a business unit, including recruiting, selecting, training, equipping, assigning, routing, supervising, paying, and motivating as these tasks apply to the personal sales force."[1]

The functions of sales management may vary by company according to the organizational alignment. If the company is not organized with a marketing manager in charge of all marketing operations, for example, the sales manager may carry additional marketing functions. In this chapter, however, we assume that the sales manager reports to the marketing manager and that his functions are encompassed by the definition of the American Marketing Association.

Because several of the important jobs of the sales manager are covered in detail in the next four chapters, sales management will be discussed here in the broader sense. Territory alignment, quota setting, regional and branch office management, and selection, training, and compensation of sales personnel will be mentioned in the context of the overall job of sales management, but the reader can refer to succeeding chapters for a more thorough review of these subjects.

Because the job of the sales manager varies according to the product or service being sold and the channels of distribution being used, we will deal in principles that are applicable to all sales management positions. We cover first the role of the sales manager in the modern marketing-oriented organization. Next we show how the sales manager analyzes and defines the sales job that is to be managed. Following this, we explain how the sales manager organizes, plans, controls, and directs the sales operation.

---

[1] Ralph Alexander and the Committee on Definitions, *Marketing Definitions*, American Marketing Association, Chicago, 1960, p. 20.

ROLE OF THE SALES MANAGER

"Promotion" is the term used by marketing authorities to describe the activities that create sales. It includes advertising, sales promotion, publicity, and personal selling.

The marketing manager determines the promotional mix—that is, the amount of effort and money that will be spent for each promotional activity. The mix will vary by type of product sold. In certain types of industrial goods, for example, the major emphasis is on personal selling. In the case of consumer packaged goods such as detergents or hair preparations, on the other hand, the major emphasis is placed on advertising and sales promotion. Most products will require a combination of promotional activities ranging between these examples.

It should be remembered in discussing sales management that personal selling is only one of many activities required to create sales. Sales are maximized when all promotional forces are used in the optimum relationship. It is the job of the marketing manager to determine the promotional mix and to coordinate selling, advertising, sales promotion, and publicity. The sales manager is responsible for the sales activity, but as a part of the marketing team, he should understand the role of the other marketing functions. His plans and the activities of his sales force must be closely integrated with advertising and sales promotion if optimum profitable sales are to be realized.

DEFINING THE SALES JOB

The key to virtually every aspect of sales management is the correct analysis of the personal selling job to be performed. It is the key to the type of salesman required, the training he must have, the size and layout of the territory, the type and amount of supervision, and the organization pattern. And it will affect—to some extent—the sales-compensation plan.

Following is a list of activities that are common to most selling jobs:

1. Locating customers, potential customers, and buying influences and determining their needs and preferences
2. Classifying accounts by potential volume
3. Planning frequency of call by class of account
4. Determining routing of calls on accounts
5. Obtaining interviews with buyers and buying influences
6. Presenting the sales proposition
7. Writing orders or contracts, or making arrangements for orders to be submitted to company
8. Arranging for credit and payment terms (may include collections)
9. Arranging for delivery and service
10. Handling complaints
11. Reporting activities, performance, and market conditions to higher levels of supervision
12. Receiving and digesting information from supervisors and home office
13. Participating in other activities such as trade shows, conventions, meetings, and training courses

These activities vary in their application and emphasis according to the product involved and the market served. And some sales jobs call for special activities not shown in the preceding list. Differences in application can be illustrated by two common types of selling: (1) selling direct to industrial users and (2) selling through intermediate channels of distribution.

A survey made by Sales and Marketing Executives—International, Inc., of its membership showed that members' products were, for the most part, sold directly to the user. The percentage breakdown is shown in the following table:[2]

	Percent
Direct to user	53.3
Direct to retailer	13.6
Through wholesaler—distributor	14.2
Direct to users, wholesalers, retail	12.1
Other and not classified	6.8

Direct Selling. Many industrial products are sold direct to other companies, and shipment is made direct from the supplier's factory or warehouse to the customer's plant. In direct selling, the salesman must perform all key selling functions.

Customers and potential customers must be located, classified, and called on with the necessary frequency. Buyers and buying influences in each account must be identified, their needs and interests determined, and selling propositions made to them. The first sales step in an industrial sale frequently is to get the prospect to test the product and to approve the salesman's company as a source of supply. Orders may be placed by purchasing agents, but the actual decision to buy may be made by the research, engineering, or manufacturing departments, or by higher management levels.

The selling proposition includes not only the quality, performance, utility, and price of the product, but also credit, delivery, and service. These latter considerations may be of greater importance to the customer than the product itself when competitive products are similar in design, quality, and price. Orders may not be written by the salesman, but may be placed directly on the supplier's factory by the customer. The sales job may include handling complaints, following up on delayed shipments, and arranging for changes in specifications to meet customers' needs.

Selling through Intermediate Channels. Whereas selling direct to the using customer requires the salesman to perform nearly all sales functions personally, selling through intermediate channels of distribution—such as wholesalers and retailers—transfers some of the selling function to the intermediate channels. Intermediate channels may be used for either consumer or industrial goods. Most consumer goods go through intermediate channels, however, whereas many industrial goods are sold direct.

Selling through wholesalers or retailers involves two main tasks. The first is to secure market coverage by obtaining the desired quality and quantity of wholesalers—or retailers if wholesalers are not used. The second is to assist the channels of distribution in making sales to the ultimate consumer. Some companies pay attention to only the first of these two tasks. Market-oriented companies, however, consider the second task equally important.

Both tasks may or may not be performed by the same salesman. In selling packaged foods, for example, sales to chain-store headquarters and to cooperative and franchising food distributors may be made by one salesman. In-store merchandising work, such as setting up product displays and point-of-sale promotional material, may be performed by another salesman.

Some companies make the mistake of considering the person or business to whom transfer of title is made—a wholesaler, for example—as the *customer*. In

---

[2] From a study by Sales and Marketing Executives—International, Inc., published in *Sales/Marketing Today*, July, 1965, p. 5.

marketing terms, the customer should always be considered as the end user, whether a consumer or an industrial plant.

Selling to an intermediate channel of distribution is only half the battle. In the final analysis, the size of the company's sales are determined by the amount of product purchased by end users. The sales manager must plan the sales job to ensure that the product moves through, as well as to, intermediate channels of distribution.

Missionary Selling. A third type of personal selling does not include all of the tasks shown in the list above. It has as its purpose the influencing of the ultimate sale, rather than the making of the sale itself. This is called "missionary selling." Prescription drugs, for example, can be sold only on the prescription of a medical doctor. Drug companies, therefore, utilize missionary salesmen to call on doctors to explain the company's products, to distribute samples and literature, and to encourage the doctor to prescribe their products for his patients. When prescriptions are taken to the drug store, the pharmacist must place his order with the wholesaler, and the wholesaler, in turn, with the drug company.

The food salesman referred to earlier, when he does promotional work in the retail food store, is a form of missionary salesman. Although missionary salesmen do not write orders, they exert a definite influence on the placement of orders with their companies.

The qualifications for missionary selling are provided by this description of a Coca-Cola salesman: "Because fountain syrup is sold through 1,000 authorized bottlers, Coca-Cola's salesmen do not actually sell Coke. They really sell service, plus ideas about how the bottler and his dealers can improve sales and profits."[3]

Sales Agents. The sales job may be performed by a company's own salesmen or by manufacturers' representatives (often called "sales agents").

Whereas a company salesman normally sells only his own company's products, the sales agent usually carries product lines for more than one company. There are arguments pro and con for use of company men as opposed to sales agents. As a rule, however, companies will utilize their own men when the potential volume supports the costs, and sales agents when it does not. By selling several products to the same customers or channels of distribution, the agent can produce a satisfactory income for himself in territories that would not support a salesman with only his own company's line to sell.

The purpose of mentioning agents here is not to discuss whether or not they should be used, but to point out that a sales management function must be performed whether company salesmen or sales agents are utilized. Agents, like company salesmen, must be recruited, trained, directed, and motivated. In multiagent organizations, these functions may be performed by the agency head, but the company sales manager must be sure that the functions are performed.

Importance of Defining the Sales Job. The first requirement of successful sales management is to determine who the end customers are, how they can be influenced to buy, and how the product can be made available to them most efficiently and conveniently. The second requirement is to determine what selling tasks must be performed to achieve these objectives.

A third requirement is to establish the salesman's work load. Work load is determined by estimating the time required to handle each class of account, frequency of call, travel and waiting time, and time for ancillary tasks such as reports and service, and adjusting these to the total working hours of each salesman.

[3] Henry Flarsheim, "Which Sales Recruit Is Best for You?" *Sales Management,* Apr. 16, 1965, p. 92.

The fulfillment of these requirements is the process of defining the sales job. Not until the job is defined can the sales manager determine the number and kind of salesmen he needs, determine training needs, lay out territories, structure the organization, or define the support required from other parts of the marketing team.

ORGANIZATION

With the sales job defined, the sales manager is ready to structure his organization. Remember that the definition of the sales job included determining the number, location, and potential of customers and prospects, and the salesman's work load.

A sales organization should be structured from the bottom up. The first step is to decide how many sales territories are needed to achieve the account coverage objectives. The second step is to determine how many salesmen can be supervised by one person. The number will vary by type of sales situation and may vary within the same sales organization. Geography, for example, will be a factor. A sales supervisor on the densely populated East Coast may be able to have the same frequency of contact with twenty men as a supervisor in the Rocky Mountain area with ten men.

Other factors affecting the number of men that can be supervised by one person are the caliber of men utilized, the turnover rate, the amount of training required, the supervisory assistance needed to sell key accounts, and the number of functions assigned the supervisor other than field supervision of his men. Number of salesmen supervised may vary from two to thirty. Eight to ten men per supervisor is common.

Determining Number of Supervisors. The number of supervisors required is found by combining contiguous sales territories into logical groupings considering geography, transportation, and the number of men that can be supervised effectively. If the number of first-line supervisors is too large for direct supervision by the sales manager, then the required number of district or regional managers may be determined by the same procedure.

Although levels of supervision should be kept to a minimum, adequate supervision should not be sacrificed. For some industrial products, or for companies operating regionally rather than nationally, a sales force of a few men may be sufficient to cover the prime accounts, in which case the sales manager will supervise his salesmen directly. On the other hand, many United States companies employ hundreds of salesmen and require three or even four intermediate levels of supervision.

Clerical and order-handling personnel must be provided. If district or regional managers are required to supervise field warehousing and service, they must be provided with the necessary personnel. Depending on the size of his organization and the number and complexity of products carried, the sales manager may need staff assistance of his own, such as product sales specialists, a training director, and a controller.

A bottom-up review of the sales organization should be made periodically by the sales manager. Changing market conditions, growing and changing product lines, changing channels of distribution, and an expanding sales force are all factors that may call for changes in the organization structure.

PLANNING

Good sales management has always involved planning. But with the development of the market-oriented organization, planning has taken on increased significance.   The sales manager not only must develop his own plans but must see that they are integrated with the company's overall marketing plan.

Planning involves a statement of objectives for the period to be covered and a specific plan of action to achieve these objectives.   Planning can be for the short term—periods up to one year—or long term—periods over one year.   Because of space limitations, we will discuss only the short-term plan.   It should be noted, however, that short-term action affects the long term.   Action should be avoided that would hinder achievement of the company's longer-range objectives.

Objectives.   The two major objectives for the sales manager are sales volume and expense budgets.   Although these objectives are established by the marketing manager, the sales manager should have a voice in their determination.   In fact, in many companies the sales manager's forecasts of sales and expenses are an important part of the process of developing sales objectives and budgets. But because sales and expenses are affected by marketing actions other than personal selling, the final objectives must be recommended by the marketing manager and approved by the chief executive.

It is also the marketing manager's job to set sales objectives by product line. But it is the sales manager who recommends how these objectives will be achieved by region and sales territory.   Sales objectives, apportioned by sales area, become sales quotas for regional managers, area supervisors, and salesmen.

Sales objectives are something to be reached or surpassed; expense budgets are regarded as limits which are not to be exceeded.   Sales expenses include such things as compensation for salesmen and supervisory personnel, travel expense, auto rental or depreciation, office rental, secretarial services, supplies, training, samples, presentation materials, meetings, conventions, and customer entertainment.   Profits are improved when the sales manager keeps expense budgets to the minimum needed to attain sales objectives.

Subobjectives.   Volume and expenses are not the only kinds of objectives for the sales operation.   Good planning demands that the sales manager develop a series of subobjectives which are needed to support the prime objectives. These may include such things as staffing, organization, territory, new accounts, share of market, salesmen training, distributor training, dealer training, and new-product introductions.

Objectives, where possible, should be stated in quantitative terms.   Rather than set an objective to "increase the number of Class A accounts," it is more meaningful to set a target of "a net increase of twenty Class A accounts, five each quarter."   The former is a general objective; the latter is a specific objective against which the sales manager can measure his performance as the year progresses.   Furthermore, he can break the total objective into specific quantitative objectives for his supervisors and salesmen.

Preparing Plans.   Effective marketing management requires that plans be submitted in writing.   Writing encourages complete planning and provides a document that can be reviewed by the marketing manager and incorporated into his overall marketing plan.   A written sales plan provides a means of communication that enables all departments of the company which are affected to coordinate their efforts with the actions of the sales department.   Special sales promotions, for example, may require modification of production schedules, increased inventories, short-term borrowing to finance larger inventories and credit, special transportation arrangements, and coordinated advertising and sales promotion programs.   The affected departments of the business are able to operate more efficiently and give better customer service when they know the sales plan.

The sales department plan will spell out how the sales manager expects to achieve sales objectives by time periods—monthly, weekly, or daily. The plan will specify where the volume is to come from—by territory, district, and region. It may even state volume objectives by account.

If the plan calls for a net increase of twenty Class A accounts, for example, it will state the actions to be taken to obtain this increase. It may include a listing of the names and locations of Class A prospects by territory.

Improving the Performance of Below-par Territories. One of the proved means of increasing sales volume is to bring territories with below-average performance up to the company average. If, for example, the company's sales average 10 percent of industry volume, special efforts should be made to increase the share of market in those territories below 10 percent. This calls for analysis of the reasons for the below-par territories. It may be inadequate account coverage, requiring staffing changes or territory realignment. It may be inadequate performance by a salesman, which would call for supervisory assistance, additional training, or replacement of the chronically inefficient salesman. Or the territory performance may be the result of a historically strong position of one or more competitors, in which case extra advertising and sales promotion or special pricing action may be required. The sales plan should include an analysis of the problem and the corrective action that is planned.

Sales plans should include provisions for special sales action when new products are introduced. These, of course, should be coordinated with other marketing plans. New-product introductions may call for an interruption of the normal sales-call pattern until the new product has been introduced to all accounts. If the product is sold through retailers, the plan may call for special in-store promotional activity such as erecting displays.

It is through advance planning that the sales manager has the greatest opportunity to manage the outcome of the period ahead. Some decisions will have to be made during the year to meet unforeseen conditions. But the sales manager who knows in advance what he is going to do to achieve objectives is most likely to reach or exceed them.

CONTROL

Control is the means by which the sales manager keeps informed of progress toward his objectives as the year progresses. A good system of control reports enables the sales manager to know where operations are proceeding according to plan and where they are not. He can then concentrate on those areas that are performing below planned performance objectives.

Essential Control Data. As a very minimum, the sales manager will require regular reports of sales volume by territory or account, sales by product by territory, and expenses by territory. He will also want totals of these data and subtotals by district and region. The sooner these reports can be received after the reporting period, the sooner the sales manager can take corrective actions where needed. In a large organization with several levels of supervision, the sales manager may look only at performance reports by district or region. In such a case, however, his supervisors must have performance reports by territory so that they can spot trouble areas and take—or recommend—corrective action.

The most effective control reports show the objectives—in this case, sales and product quotas and expense budgets—compared with actual performance and any variances from objectives. Such a report permits the sales manager to spot negative variances quickly. It is the negative variances that warrant his immediate attention, as illustrated in Figure 11-1. A look at the columns headed "Variance" tells the sales manager that his total sales are off by 50 for the

Sales Performance Report for May

	Objective		Actual		Variance	
	This month	Year to date	This month	Year to date	This month	Year to date
Total sales...............	200	1,000	150	900	−50	−100
Product class:						
1.....................	100	500	40	350	−60	−150
2.....................	50	250	50	250	None	None
3.....................	50	250	60	300	+10	+50
Expenses...............	10	50	12	48	− 2	+ 2

FIG. 11-1. *Sales performance report.*

month and 100 for the year.   An examination of sales by product class shows that the unfavorable product variance is in product Class 1, but that Class 3 is doing better than plan.   Expenses are up for the month, but have a favorable variance for the year to date.

The sales manager's next step would be to look at similar reports for each region.   From these, he can tell whether Class 1 product sales are running below objective across the country or whether the problem is regional.   If the problem is regional rather than national, the answer must be found in a territory-by-territory examination.   If the problem is national in scope, the answer may be to place greater sales and advertising efforts on Class 1 products, or a pricing adjustment may be necessary.   Or the answer may be to put more marketing effort into product Class 3, which appears to have greater market acceptance than was originally anticipated.

Because the variance for the year to date is greater than the variance for the month, it is apparent the problem is not new.   This report is for May, the fifth month of the company's fiscal year.   If an answer cannot be found soon, production schedules and profit forecasts will have to be adjusted if they have not been already.

Other Performance Information.   Sales by dollars, by product, and by expenses incurred are not the only performance data sales managers should consider. Some companies attempt to measure territory performance by profit.   Profit is the result of sales income, the product sales mix, prices obtained, and expenses. Control reports for this type of operation will reveal variances by total sales, product, price, and sales expense.   If profit is off target, the sales manager knows which factor or factors are causing the trouble.

The control information discussed up to this point should be made available through the company's regular accounting and control report system.   The sales manager may also be able to get additional data from the accounting department, such as a breakdown of sales by account or class of account as compared with objectives.   Other information, such as account call frequency, promotional work, and competitive activity, he may have to obtain from his own sales force.

SUPERVISION AND COORDINATION

When the sales manager has developed and staffed his organization to perform the assigned sales job, developed his plans for achieving objectives, and established a control system to measure performance against plans, he has performed many of his essential management functions. But something is still required to make the organization work. He must coordinate functions within his department and with other departments of the company, he must supervise his organization to see that assigned tasks are carried out, and he must provide leadership.

Of the many qualities that a sales manager must have, the most essential is the ability to lead a large and widespread group of salesmen. He must be able to select good men, train them in product knowledge and sales techniques, provide for their compensation and other forms of motivation, and maintain communications with them. Along with these activities, he must maintain contacts with customers and the industry and develop his own personal skills.

Selection and Training. Even in an established organization, the sales manager is faced with the recurring job of recruiting and selection to upgrade his organization and to fill vacancies created by retirement, separation, and promotion. He may receive assistance from the personnel department and from his field supervisors. But the sales manager must make certain that personnel qualifications are established and that effective recruiting and selection procedures are established and utilized.

A continuing training program must be maintained for both new and experienced supervisors and for both new and older salesmen. Supervisors need to be educated in recruiting, selection, and training procedures; coaching and supervision of salesmen; territory layout; motivation; compensation administration; control methods; reporting procedures; and product knowledge.

New salesmen must receive orientation on their company's products, policies, procedures, and effective selling techniques. Older salesmen require periodic retraining on products and selling techniques and training on new products.

Motivation and Compensation. Motivation of the sales force is a constant concern of sales management. Salesmen work alone and do not receive the close supervision accorded other company personnel. Selling requires initiative, determination, and persistence. Yet, there is a constant temptation for the salesman to avoid unpleasant contacts and to rationalize not putting in a full day's work. For these reasons, the sales manager must utilize motivation techniques that provide incentives for salesmen to perform all facets of the sales job and to put out more than ordinary effort.

One of the most effective motivation tools is incentive compensation by which the salesman is rewarded financially for better-than-average achievement. Figure 11-2 taken from the study by Sales and Marketing Executives—International, Inc., shows that most salesmen are compensated by some means other than straight salary.

It is important that the compensation plan not only reward the man for effective performance, but also cause emphasis to be placed on all key elements of the sales job.

Experience has proved that compensation is not the only motivation for salesmen's achievements. In fact, it is a limiting factor in some cases, because not all men desire the same amount of money. Recognition for achievement is more of a stimulant for many sales people than is monetary reward. For this reason, experienced sales managers use quotas, special contests, and promotion as incentives to better performance in addition to incentive compensation. Regular territory quotas and contest rules must be planned carefully to stimulate as large a number of sales people as possible. But planning for public recognition of the winners is equally important.

Not all men respond to the same stimulants. This is one of the reasons

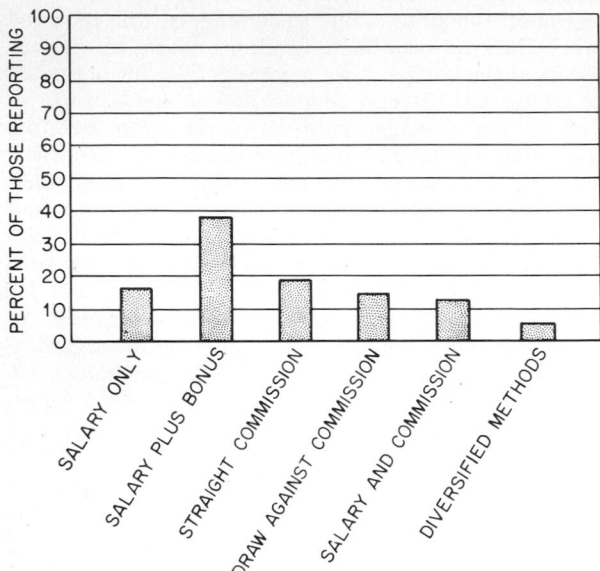

FIG. 11-2. *How salesmen are compensated.* (*From a study by* Sales and Marketing Executives—International, *Inc., published in* Sales/Marketing Today, *July, 1965.*)

that supervision is so essential. Supervisors must know their individual salesmen well enough to recognize what does and does not cause them to perform well.

Communication. Probably the most difficult job in sales management is the job of communication. It is difficult because of the geographic dispersion of the sales force and the levels of supervision through which upward and downward communication must pass.

The salesman maintains the most important contacts that any company has—with customers and channels of distribution. Yet the salesman is often the most poorly informed person in the organization. Sales management, therefore, must maintain an effective communications system. Written bulletins, the most common form of communication, are often supplemented by a company newspaper or magazine. Because salesmen cannot see all accounts at once, bulletins to customers may be used to facilitate communications with accounts.

There seems to be no substitute for regular personal contact with sales people to answer their many questions that do not always get answered through written communications. Many companies find it advantageous to hold at least one general sales convention a year where salesmen can meet, see, and hear company executives as well as meet one another. In addition to the communication value, such meetings help to build *esprit de corps* and promote a feeling of belonging.

In addition to annual sales meetings, many sales managers hold monthly or quarterly meetings with their field supervisors, who, in turn, hold meetings with their salesmen in which they pass on information of importance.

Good sales managers also make as many firsthand field contacts with salesmen as possible. Because in a large organization the sales manager cannot possibly see all salesmen in the field, the chief value of field contacts is the opportunity for the sales manager to learn of salesmen's questions and problems. He can then use other means, such as bulletins and meetings with supervisors, to communicate information to the entire sales force.

Customer and Industry Contacts. One of the major problems of a sales manager is how to handle his many management duties and still retain a firsthand feel of market and industry conditions. There seems to be no effective substitute for discussions with a cross section of customers. Furthermore, important customers expect personal attention from company executives. Yet if the sales manager spends too much time in the field, he neglects his essential assignments of organization, planning, control, and coordination which largely must be performed from the home office.

One of the best means of maintaining contact with the trade and industry is to attend industry and trade shows and conventions. In a few days each year, the sales manager can establish and maintain contacts that would require weeks or months of individual field visits.

Maintaining Management Skills. A sales manager, like any other executive, cannot rest on his laurels. He must devote a portion of his time to reading, study, professional association activity, and even formal schooling.

Sales managers often find it advantageous to participate in associations such as the Sales and Marketing Executives—International, Inc., and to attend the meetings, conferences, and schools which they sponsor. The American Management Association runs seminars for sales executives which are always well attended. Many universities also conduct executive development programs specializing in sales and marketing as well as general management.

The sales manager who will stay on top of his job, or who will prepare for promotion, must continuously improve his skills by both formal and informal means.

CONCLUSION

Personal selling, advertising, and sales promotion are the means companies use to create and close sales. It is the responsibility of the sales manager to develop and manage the organization necessary to carry out the personal selling function. It is the job of the marketing manager to coordinate personal selling, advertising, and sales promotion.

The sales manager recommends sales objectives, develops plans and the organization needed to achieve them, maintains controls to measure performance compared with objectives, and provides supervision and leadership to keep the sales force working toward successful attainment of objectives.

The key to successful sales management is the accurate definition of the sales job. Because this may vary by type of product, markets served, and channels of distribution used, the sales job should be redefined whenever significant changes occur. The sales job to be performed is the base on which all sales management functions are built.

Modern sales management calls for the same skills required of other management positions. But more than most other types of managers, the sales manager must have the ability to lead and motivate a widespread group of people working without close individual supervision.

BIBLIOGRAPHY

Aspley, John C. (ed.), *The Sales Manager's Handbook,* 9th ed., The Dartnell Corporation, Chicago, 1962.

Britt, Steuart H., and Harper W. Boyd, *Marketing Management and Administrative Action*, chaps. 40, 41, 54, 55, and 57, McGraw-Hill Book Company, New York, 1963.

Buell, Victor P., *Marketing Management in Action*, chap. 11, McGraw-Hill Book Company, New York, 1966.

Canfield, Bertrand R., *Sales Administration: Principles and Problems*, 4th ed., Prentice-Hall, Inc., Englewood Cliffs, N.J., 1961.

"Control of Salesmen's Expenses: A Survey of Company Practices," *Management News*, American Management Association, August, 1955.

Field Sales Management, Experiences in Marketing Management, no. 1, National Industrial Conference Board, New York, 1962.

Lazo, Hector, and Arnold Corbin, *Management in Marketing*, chaps. 6, 9, and 10, McGraw-Hill Book Company, New York, 1961.

Maynard, Harold H., and James H. Davis, *Sales Management*, 3d ed., The Ronald Press Company, New York, 1957.

Phelps, Maynard, and J. Howard Westing, *Marketing Management*, part 6, chap. 19, and part 7, chaps. 20–32, Richard D. Irwin, Inc., Homewood, Ill., 1960.

Stanton, William J., and Richard H. Buskirk, *Management of the Sales Force*, rev. ed., Richard D. Irwin, Inc., Homewood, Ill., 1964.

Territory Alignment and Quota Setting

SIDNEY BRUNELL *Vice President, Smithcraft Corporation, Chelsea, Massachusetts*

This chapter covers the techniques and problems of subdividing marketing efforts of a sales organization and setting objectives for sales personnel. Under modern management methods, objectives are set in many areas of a business. Sales objectives are usually the basic planning tool for most other functions in the company. The most common type of sales objective is the sales (volume) quota. Sales objectives can be set on other bases, but whatever the measurement tool is, the attainment of sales objectives calls for a careful balance of work load and costs with sales potential for specific areas.

TERRITORY ALIGNMENT

The starting point in setting up sales territories is to decide how to approach the market—or, looking at it from the customer's viewpoint, how does he *want* to be approached? The answer to this question will be critical to the way sales effort and the work load will be distributed among the sales organization.

The responsibilities for obtaining business can be assigned to a sales force on the basis of geography, customers, products, industries, or some other logical division.

In established industries, the marketing approach may be apparent, but because the method of approaching the market is the basic premise upon which the assignment of sales responsibilities is built, it is worth reexamining the established methods to make sure the existing premise is still valid. This requires an in-depth knowledge of the market; its channels of distribution; the product's position in the market; the competition; and most important, the company's resources.

For example, a national manufacturer of heavy industrial electrical equipment marketed its products by product lines. This meant that each customer would see several salesmen from the same company, each highly proficient in selling a single product line. The manufacturer conducted a market survey to determine if his method of selling was most suited to the customer's needs. He learned that the customers preferred to do business with salesmen who were more intimately familiar with the customer's company and industry than with the manufacturer's product line. From the customer's viewpoint, the salesman who was well versed in the special problems of the customer's industry could offer more service than the salesman who was an expert in his own product.

The manufacturer changed his market approach and reorganized his sales force by industries—with men knowledgeable in depth about the specific industry and/or company they were selling to and with each man selling the entire industrial product line of the manufacturer.

In addition to deciding whether or not to approach the market by geography, product line, customers, or industries, a company has to decide (among other things) whether one class of customers needs more contact than another; whether the market should be covered in depth or "skimmed"; whether to enter regional markets or aim for country-wide distribution; and whether the sales organization should be factory based or field based. With high-speed jet air travel, a company with a limited number of customers comprising its market might find its best approach to the market would be a home office sales organization serving customers' needs from the factory.

Basic Objectives. There are certain basic objectives that should be kept in mind in subdividing the market effort, and these objectives apply whether or not the market is divided by geography, customers, products, or industries. There should be:

1. A clear definition of customer assignment and territorial coverage
2. Territory sizes such that the salesman can provide regular and efficient sales service in the area predefined for coverage
3. A yardstick for measuring the performances of the salesmen objectively

Determining Market Potential. A major step in territory alignment is determining market potential for a particular product in every sales territory.

The ideal would be the names and addresses of the specific people who will (in the future) actually purchase the type of product that a particular industry sells. This would have to include the location and the time of purchase as well.

The next best source of determining market potential is past history plus forecasting of trends in usage, prices, and customers' attitudes to arrive at potential market volume.

If the actual sales history for a product can be obtained on a geographic or customer basis from published information, these data can be used to identify directly market potential on a territory-by-territory basis. However, timely historical data about the sales of a specific product analyzed in sufficient detail to be useful are not easy to find.

Some companies use their own sales histories as a convenient method of developing territory potential. Company sales records, however, are rarely indicative of total demand in each territory and can lead to gross errors in judging salesmen's performance.

For example, Salesman A and Salesman B each sell $250,000 a year in their respective territories. Are their performances equal? It might seem so without market potential figures for each territory. Noncompany data show that the market in Territory A is $1 million and in Territory B $10 million. Salesman A is obtaining 25 percent of the available business and Salesman B is getting 2½ percent of the available business in his territory. Noncompany market potential figures are needed for objective measurement of the two territories.

SOURCES OF MARKET DATA

Much of the available timely market data is in broad categories—populations, buying power, retail sales, wholesale sales, construction awards, and the like. To find market data for specific products, what sources should be turned to? The answer to this question varies from industry to industry and varies between consumer-product and industrial-product marketing. In general, however, the following major types of sources should be considered:

1. Government sources
2. Trade associations
3. Private sources
4. Published data
5. Advertising media
6. Sample surveys

Government Sources. The United States government is a source of a huge amount of useful marketing data not only by products, but by customer type as well. The government spends hundreds of millions of dollars compiling statistics on virtually every product and service sold in this country, and much of these data is available at very nominal cost. A general introduction to the types of statistical information available from the government is provided by a booklet called *Statistical Services of the United States Government* (available from the Superintendent of Documents). It is periodically revised and is helpful in keeping abreast of the many changes which are constantly occurring in the nature, scope, and timing of publication of governmental statistical data.

The government has developed a *Standard Industrial Classification Manual* (SIC numbering system) to provide uniformity in government statistics (available from the Superintendent of Documents). The classification manual covers the whole range of economic activities including agriculture, construction, manufacturing, mining, wholesale and retail trade, services, government, and others.

The statistics provided by SIC detail are particularly valuable in pinpointing industrial markets by size and location of plants. Because industrial markets tend to be highly concentrated, territory coverage and sales potential can be identified by size of plants as well as areas of concentration. SIC data are also valuable in providing details of the total market by product lines, and a manufacturer can use the information to determine his approximate share of the total market for his industry.

Other useful statistical services of the United States government for territory market potential analysis are:

1. Census of business
2. Census of agriculture
3. County and business patterns
4. Analysis tools—county business patterns
5. Construction (monthly publication)

The government will make available to interested companies punched cards of special government data arranged by counties and by trade areas on such items as the number of establishments and volumes of sales for each level of American business—manufacturing, construction, mining, wholesale trade, retail trade, and service trade. These data may be too expensive for an individual company to buy, but trade associations can purchase this information and process it for their members.

Trade Associations. Information useful in developing accurate market potential in some industries has been gathered and published by trade associations and some professional associations. Through the cooperative effort of participating member companies, which often constitute the bulk of the volume of an industry, basic market facts on individual industries and groups of industries are assembled and published. Unfortunately, not all trade associations engage in this type of activity. As a consequence, the availability of data developed by trade associations tends to be somewhat spotty.

All companies in an industry need not be included in a trade association for the association figures to be useful as a territorial measuring tool. What is needed are figures that are representative of the *relative* relationship of the market from one geographic area to another. For example, the National Electrical Manufacturers Association (NEMA) appliance section regularly reports the total sales of household refrigerators by geographical trading areas. A refrigerator manufacturer can match his sales with the total sales reported, territory by territory, and arrive at a market index that tells him how one salesman in his company is doing relative to another. Even if the reported figures are not the total sales of refrigerators throughout the country, they are useful to measure the potential of one territory against another.

Companies that are fortunate enough to belong to such trade associations find that not only do they have a national basis for setting up sales territories, but various trends can be discerned territory by territory and used as a basis for manpower adjustments among territories.

The limiting factor is that companies are almost bound to follow the trade association's territorial breakdown in setting up their own territories. Statistics are compiled and reported on the basis of trade association trading areas. A company whose sales territories differ from the trade association will continually have to adjust its figures. This can be quite costly and subjects the figures to more evaluation than seems necessary. There may be valid reasons why a company cannot follow industry or trade association alignments, but companies should weigh very carefully the values lost in not being able to use ready-made territorial statistics against the values to be gained by an individualized territorial alignment.

Private Sources. In addition to the government and trade associations, there are private statistic-gathering services for specific markets. For example, construction statistics are compiled by the F. W. Dodge Company in considerable detail, and this information is available on a subscription basis.

Published Data. Specialized data on specific industries are compiled by the trade publications covering these fields. One of the most widely used sources for information on market potential is *Sales Management's* "Survey of Buying Power." This is particularly useful in the consumer-product field. The survey is a private publication, but its information is based very largely on data from government sources. It serves to update governmental data on an annual basis.

Of particular significance as sources of marketing data are the business publications which serve every facet of trade and industry. The technical and business periodicals are one of the more important sources of information about the size, location, and characteristics of industrial markets. Each industry has its own trade journals, and the publishers of these periodicals usually maintain detailed data on the specific companies in an industry. They also usually have well-developed market research facilities. Generally, these publications will cooperate in supplying market data about an industry.

Advertising Media. Various types of advertising media—newspapers, magazines, radio and television stations and networks, and the like—have available and often publish a tremendous amount of statistical data applying to the markets they serve. In the case of consumer media, this may apply only to a single local market such as New York or Los Angeles, or to a segment of the national market such as ethnic markets or a group of people who share the same hobby or interests. Most advertising media have data on the characteristics of the audience they serve.

There are published studies of individual industries which can be consulted. These may often be located efficiently by reference to published bibliographies. The American Marketing Association has been especially active in developing and publishing such bibliographies.

Sample Surveys. Often, a company is unable to locate completely reliable and useful data and finds it desirable to undertake a special study of the market for its products. There are services that develop information on different types of consumer products by the use of sampling methods.

CORRELATING MARKET DATA WITH COMPANY SALES

To use available market data, it is necessary to find a broad market category that influences the market activity of the products a company sells and develop a correlation between the general market and the market activity of the company's specific product lines. The resulting relationship is called a "market index." For example, the F. W. Dodge Company, a division of McGraw-Hill Publications, makes available, by subscription, monthly statistics on construction awards on a county-by-county basis for the entire United States. These statistics are broken down by building types, square footage of floor space, and dollar value. Companies whose products are included in the total construction contract award can develop monthly market figures for their products by computing an average usage of their product in the total dollar value or square footage of the award. This can be defined down to types of buildings.

A manufacturer of commercial and industrial lighting fixtures correlated his sales with new construction awards to determine market potential for his products. Because the amount of lighting equipment going into a building varies widely by type of building, he determined the approximate value of lighting per square foot going into various types of buildings. For example, he estimated the available lighting fixture business for his products in new office buildings at 90 cents per square foot and made similar per-square-foot estimates for schools, hospitals, and the like, down to 30 cents a square foot for a factory. This enabled him to convert construction contracts awarded in square feet to dollars of lighting fixture business available.

At this point, however, the manufacturer did not know how long a lag there was between the time a construction contract was awarded and an order placed with him for the lighting fixtures. Also, he did not know whether his portion of the available business varied from month to month, or whether he could get any kind of correlation. He plotted his past performance of net sales billed by months on semilog paper and compared it with a similar plot of construction contract awards in dollars of lighting fixtures. He found that the two quantities followed each other up and down with a high degree of correlation except that they were six months apart. Now he had something he could use—a factor, readily determined, that seemed to lead his actual monthly sales billed by six months.

The accuracy of this factor can be judged from the chart in Figure 12-1. Note that the predicted sales billed for each month was calculated six months in advance of the actual performance.

If consumption or usage data for a specific product are not available in sufficient detail to be useful as a territorial market potential yardstick, it usually is possible to make use of "related factors" which will indicate the size and

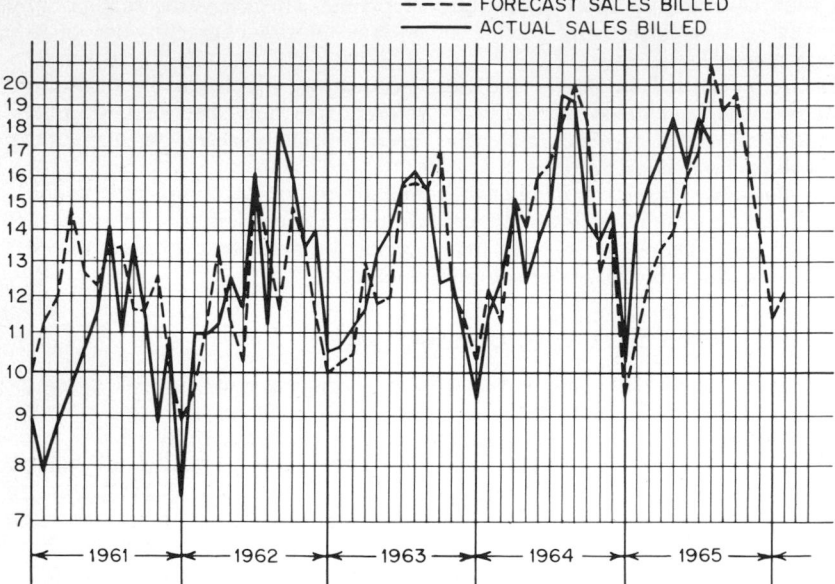

FIG. 12-1. *Correlation of actual sales with forecast developed from construction award statistics.*

the extent of the market. For example, a manufacturer of automotive parts might use automobile registrations as a basis; wired homes might provide the base for a manufacturer of electrical household appliances; manufacturers of industrial products might measure their market potential in terms of factories, shops, or distributors.

GEOGRAPHIC TERRITORY ALIGNMENT

The geographic assignment of sales responsibilities is the most common method of setting up territories, probably because it makes for clear-cut division of responsibilities and is the easiest to administer objectively.

Geographic breakdowns should almost always be used by companies that intend penetrating a large national market in depth. This helps ensure that the entire market is thoroughly covered and that salesmen are given the responsibility for obtaining their full share of the potential business in a territory. Geographic breakdowns should also be used by companies that want to route their salesmen. Routing is sometimes used as a control method by companies selling to retailers where the sales job requires regular and frequent calls and relatively little time is spent with each customer.

Assigning territories by geography starts with a map of the territory, be it international, national, state, city, or local. Many industries have established geographic breakdowns, and sales territories should follow industry practices wherever possible. Trade associations in many industries have established geographic trading areas. For example, the National Electrical Manufacturers Association has established 33 industrial regions and 121 trading areas for distributors and manufacturers of electrical products (see Figure 12-2). There are other published wholesale and consumer trading area studies available. These are maps of the United States on which trading centers are shown together with the boundaries of the trading area served by each.

Whatever the area of the territory, its border should follow well-defined boundaries such as boundaries of states, counties, metropolitan areas, or cities. Much of the market data by public and private sources is given by these subdivisions, and the measurement of salesmen's performance is difficult for areas that do not have established boundary lines.

Where salesmen sell to both wholesalers and retailers, the trading area should try to follow the customary wholesale trading area to avoid the problem of salesmen calling on retail customers serviced by wholesalers from another trading area.

Companies dividing the United States into geographic territories are faced with the problem of how far to go in assigning sales territories, particularly in large metropolitan areas. Wherever possible, division of metropolitan areas should follow county lines. This approach helps establish clear-cut boundaries.

Establishing a Statistical Control Unit. In most sound territory alignment programs, a "control unit" decision is required. That decision is concerned with the selection of the type of geographic unit which is the smallest to which sales allocations are made and for which data are summarized.

For statistical information to be useful for arriving at market potential, it must be supplied in units small enough to pinpoint all of the factors influencing the market in a territory. To the greatest possible extent, the unit should also be self-contained so that it can be moved from one sales territory to another.

There are many different ways to divide the United States into smaller areas for purposes of analysis. Although not all of the following models are used as control units, obviously any of them could be so used:

Unit	Description
4 census regions	Major grouping of census divisions
9 census divisions	Groupings of contiguous states
50 states	Major political units
219 standard metropolitan areas	Metropolitan areas with population of 50,000 or more
229 media communications areas	Areas served by advertising media originating in a central city
509 state economic areas	Relatively homogeneous subdivisions of states, with counties of similar economic and social characteristics
950 ABC city or retail trading zones	City limits, or areas beyond city, whose residents regularly trade in the city zone
3,134 counties	Primary political divisions of states
23,000 census tracts	Small areas into which 180 large metropolitan areas have been divided for census purpose

The largest of these units, the census region, is much too large for any but the grossest sort of market control. And the individual census tract is much too small as a geographic sales control unit.

The most widely used control unit is the county. Much of the statistical data compiled by the United States government is on a county-by-county basis (see *U.S. City and County Data Book*). Also, many private services compiling statistics such as construction statistics use the county as the smallest unit of measurement. Many of the trade associations have developed "retail trading areas" and "wholesale trading areas." Market information is compiled from county data and combined for these trading areas. The establishment of trading areas involves a grouping of several counties into areas that make a natural and homogeneous market.

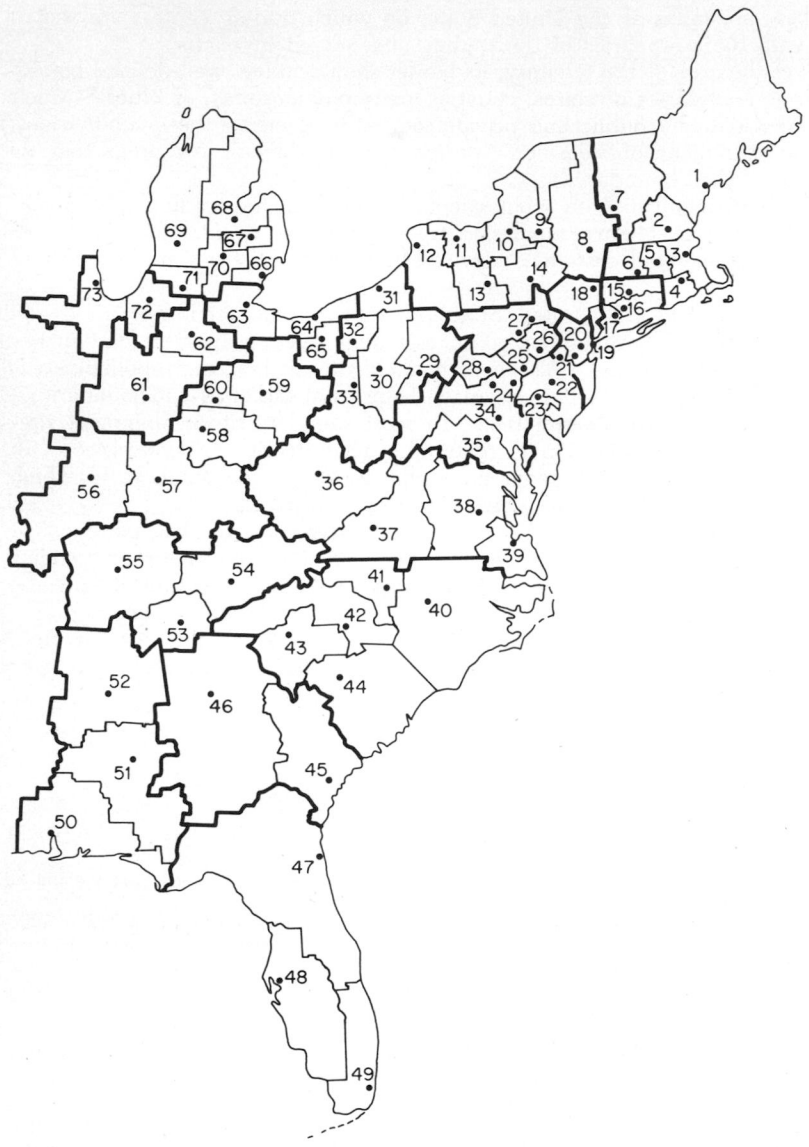

FIG. 12-2.   *NEMA industrial trading area map.*   (*Copyright 1959 by National Electrical Manufacturers Association.*)

1. Portland, Me.	10. Syracuse, N.Y.
2. Manchester, N.H.	11. Rochester, N.Y.
3. Boston, Mass.	12. Buffalo, N.Y.
4. Providence, R.I.	13. Elmira, N.Y.
5. Worcester, Mass.	14. Binghamton, N.Y.
6. Springfield, Mass.	15. Hartford, Conn.
7. Rutland, Vt.	16. New Haven, Conn.
8. Albany, N.Y.	17. Bridgeport, Conn.
9. Utica, N.Y.	18. Poughkeepsie, N.Y.

Distributing the Work Load by Sales Expectancy. Wherever possible, territories should be set up with approximately equal potential sales, or if not possible, enough salesmen should be assigned to the territory to obtain the sales-expectancy objective.

A significant amount of the salesman's time will be spent in traveling. The geography of each territory should be examined in detail and such topographical features as mountains, rivers, and lakes, and such transportation features as superhighways or lack of superhighways, urban traffic problems, and so on should be taken into consideration in determining salesmen's work loads.

The number of salesmen for a particular territory is a matter of judgment, but the territory should be capable of supporting all salesmen doing effective work. If the sales expectancy of a territory is too small to support a full-time salesman and the travel time is such that it cannot be combined with another territory, consideration should be given to part-time salesmen or sales agents—that is, salesmen who will carry the compatible product lines of more than one company selling through the same distribution channels. The theory behind this is that the part-time services of a high-caliber salesman are worth more than the full-time efforts of a poorly paid performer.

Number of Calls. Number of calls can be used as a basic statistic for measuring work load and salesmen costs. There is a relationship between the number of calls made by salesmen and the amount of business obtained. The more calls a man makes, the more opportunities he has to secure an order. Territories should be designed to maximize the number of calls a man can make, taking into consideration the relative importance of each call and the amount of time the salesman is expected to spend on each call. For many products, the amount of time spent on each call is the same whether the customer is a large one or a small one.

19. New York, N.Y.	47. Jacksonville, Fla.
20. Newark–Jersey City, N.J.	48. Tampa, Fla.
21. Trenton, N.J.	49. Miami, Fla.
22. Philadelphia, Pa.	50. Mobile, Ala.
23. Wilmington, Del.	51. Montgomery, Ala.
24. York–Lancaster, Pa.	52. Birmingham, Ala.
25. Reading, Pa.	53. Chattanooga, Tenn.
26. Allentown–Bethlehem, Pa.	54. Knoxville, Tenn.
27. Scranton–Wilkes Barre, Pa.	55. Nashville, Tenn.
28. Harrisburg, Pa.	56. Evansville, Ind.
29. Johnstown, Pa.	57. Louisville, Ky.
30. Pittsburgh, Pa.	58. Cincinnati, Ohio
31. Erie, Pa.	59. Columbus, Ohio
32. Youngstown, Ohio	60. Dayton, Ohio
33. Wheeling, W.Va.	61. Indianapolis, Ind.
34. Baltimore, Md.	62. Fort Wayne, Ind.
35. Washington, D.C.	63. Toledo, Ohio
36. Charleston, W.Va.	64. Cleveland, Ohio
37. Roanoke, Va.	65. Akron, Ohio
38. Richmond, Va.	66. Detroit, Mich.
39. Norfolk, Va.	67. Flint, Mich.
40. Raleigh, N.C.	68. Saginaw, Mich.
41. Greensboro, N.C.	69. Grand Rapids, Mich.
42. Charlotte, N.C.	70. Lansing, Mich.
43. Greenville, S.C.	71. Kalamazoo, Mich.
44. Columbia, S.C.	72. South Bend, Ind.
45. Savannah, Ga.	73. Chicago, Ill.
46. Atlanta, Ga.	

XYZ COMPANY SALESMAN CALL REPORT			
SALESMAN	WEEK ENDING		
INSTRUCTIONS: RECORD EVERY CALL MADE PLUS OFFICE TIME, ILLNESS, VACATIONS		MAIL TO MARKETING MANAGER ON SATURDAY	
CALLS MADE THIS WEEK		SELLING PLAN FOR WEEK AHEAD LIST ACCOUNTS TO BE CALLED ON	
DATE	FIRM CONTACTED AND CITY	DATE	ACCOUNT AND LOCATION

FIG. 12-3. *Salesman's planning guide for calls.*

It is almost axiomatic that salesmen should set up their appointments in advance if they are to avoid spending considerable time waiting in customers' outer offices. It is not always possible to set up appointments in a way that allows for a specific number of calls to be made during a day, but the salesman should be expected to average out at a certain number of calls per day when measured over several days or weeks. Allowances should be made for vacations, holidays, and nonselling time devoted to sales meetings, training, and the like. There will also be a variation in call capacity between urban and rural areas. A planning guide such as the one illustrated by Figure 12-3 can be helpful in getting salesmen to plan their calls in advance. The number of calls made by a salesman will vary widely with the type of business. A rule-of-thumb figure for industrial salesmen is about 750 calls per year. This means a cost of $10 a call for a $7,500 a year salesman or $20 per call for a $15,000 a year salesman. By dividing the total sales and total cost for a territory by the number of calls, managers can determine how effectively a salesman spends his time.

For example, a territory has sales of $150,000 and costs of $15,000 and a total of 750 calls is made in the year. This is $200 of sales and $20 of cost per call.

Another territory has sales of $100,000 and costs of $15,000 and a total of 500 calls is made in the year. This is $200 of sales and $30 of cost per call.

ALIGNMENT BY CUSTOMERS AND POTENTIAL CUSTOMERS

If the company's customers and potential customers are readily ascertainable and these customers make the buying decision, salesmen can be given a specific account on which to call. This becomes a matter of distributing work load among the sales force on an equitable basis, taking into consideration the relative importance of various customers and potential customers, the frequency of calls of each customer, the amount of travel time necessary to cover the assigned accounts, and finally a total work load that is capable of supporting a salesman doing effective work.

In many industries, however, the buying decision is not made by the accounts on the company's books, and salesmen are required to do considerable missionary work in addition to calling on the company's customers. This is particularly true for manufacturers selling to the construction industry.

For example, a manufacturer of electrical products used in new buildings tries to influence the owner or his architect to include his products in the specifications for the building. The architect may hire an engineering firm to engineer the building, and the engineer may determine the specific competitive products that will be used in the project. Most construction projects are bid for by general contractors, who in turn solicit bids from subcontractors for various phases of the project. The materials used by the subcontractor may be purchased directly from the manufacturer or from the manufacturer's distributors.

Many times, the actual project is in one state, the architect in another state, and the engineering in still another. The subcontractor may be home based in still another state.

A manufacturer with this kind of market must assign salesmen work loads by buying influences as well as actual customers, making sure that a salesman earns sales credit for buying influences in his territory where it results in actual sales in other territories. In this situation, close cooperation is required among salesmen, and the competence of all is extremely important to the closing of an order. An objective approach to sales credit division is a necessary part of the job of distributing the work load equitably among the sales force.

One manufacturer in this situation divides sales credit as follows:

50 percent sales credit for obtaining the specification

25 percent sales credit for obtaining the actual order

25 percent sales credit to the territory where the merchandise is shipped

REVISING SALES TERRITORIES

Sales territories are seldom static. Market conditions change, customers move, competitive pressures change, a territory grows too large for the present salesman to service effectively. Territorial setups which at one time were satisfactory become obsolete, and a salesman who once obtained a fair share of the available business in his territory is no longer able to do so.

There is no set timetable to follow in deciding when to revise sales territories, but if the salesman is not getting a fair share of the increasing business in a given territory, his territory should be examined for possible revision.

When it becomes apparent that a revision is necessary, the mechanics used to set up the original territory can be followed for the revision. The human problems, however, are vastly more complicated in the revision, particularly if a territory is to be split up.

A salesman who has spent time in effectively developing a territory establishes close personal friendships with many customers, and splitting a territory can destroy these valuable relationships. One alternative is to let the territory stand, but add manpower to it, with the senior man responsible for the entire territory. This has its drawbacks in that the assignment of accounts is in the hands of the senior man. Unless he has a stake in the performance of the new man, the division of the available business will be on a subjective, not objective, basis. Also, management loses its ability to control individual performance. It is better to have each salesman directly responsible to headquarters or regional managers without intervening territorial control by one salesman.

When it is believed that a territory should be revised or split up, the salesmen concerned should be apprised of the problem before any action is taken. A salesman will view a change in his territory as a threat to his income, and the facts should be thoroughly discussed with him before the final decision is made. Unilateral action in this area can be costly.

SALES QUOTAS

Sales quotas are used *to measure* salesmen's performance and to encourage sales personnel to reach or exceed a predetermined level of performance. The fact that their work is being measured against an objective induces most men to strive for improvement and can produce marked increases in efficiency. The greatest value of a sales quota system to sales management, however, lies in the contribution it can make to measuring salesmen's performance objectively. A sound method of measuring salesmen's performance is an assurance to sales management and to the salesmen that evaluations and benefits will be based on objective measurement and not on personal bias. It also allows sales management to apply the techniques of the leading performers to other men to the betterment of the company's overall sales program.

Uses for Sales Quotas. Quotas for sales personnel can serve three functions— (1) as a measurement tool to compare performance among salesmen; (2) as motivation to spur salesmen to better performance; and (3) as a basis for sales compensation. It is sometimes possible to use the same quota to accomplish all three objectives, but this is not *always* the case. Quotas used as a measurement device should provide a uniform basis for comparing one man's performance with another's, whereas a quota used as motivation may be limited to spurring salesmen to equal or exceed their own past or predetermined performance.

Quotas as a Performance-measurement Tool. Sales quota in dollars is only one of several ways to measure salesmen's performance or to compensate or motivate salesmen. Some of the possible measured activities include sales volume in terms of dollars or units; sales cost as a percentage of sales volume; share of available business in the territory; gross profit contribution; number of calls made; number of new accounts opened; and points earned for selling various products of the company.

Sales quotas, however, are one of the best measuring tools for judging sales performance, provided quotas are set objectively. This requires that the quota be based on the approximate sales expectancy of the territory.

Using Quotas for Objective Measurement. There are certain fundamentals that should be followed when sales quotas are to be used to measure salesmen's performance:

1. Know the approximate total available business (market potential) in each territory.

2. Set *attainable* quotas based on available business in each territory. These objectives should be equal for all territories where the opportunities are equal.

3. Measure performance toward those objectives and identify good and poor performance.

4. Set up a system that rewards good performance and corrects poor performance.

Quotas as Motivation. Sales quotas can also be used to motivate individual salesmen to exceed past or predetermined performance, but this type of quota is more often subjective than objective and is related more to individual salesmen potential than to market potential in a territory. The ideal quota would measure all salesmen on an objective basis and also provide the stimulant to spur individual performance.

Quotas as Part of Sales Compensation. When the company's system for measuring salesmen's performance is tied to compensation, it provides a direct incentive for improvement. However, compensation plans for salesmen sometimes include a quota element either as part of the basic earnings or as an incentive adder that bears little relationship to sales expectancy in a territory. Rather, it is a device to introduce a variable element into compensation so that the salesman can see a relationship between the volume of business he obtains and his compensation. To this extent, it may act as a stimulant to increase his sales volume.

SETTING ATTAINABLE QUOTAS

A basic requirement for using a sales quota as a measuring tool is that the quota be specific, realistic, and attainable and accepted as such by the man being measured. A quota cannot be established on the basis of wishful thinking, but must be derived from a careful analysis of factual information. Also, men perform best when they take part in setting their own sales objectives, or if this is not possible, when they understand and believe in the objectives set for them. Simplicity, fairness, and two-way communication are the basic ingredients in a successful quota plan. If a sales quota is truly accepted—if the man being measured understands how the quota was determined, believes it is fair and realistic, and can measure his own performance and take corrective action to achieve the objective—he then performs by self-control. He acts not because his manager tells him to, but rather because he decides he has to meet his objective.

Setting fair and attainable quotas is not a routine task. Men have varying abilities, and even where market opportunities are equal among territories, market conditions in specific territories can create differences in performance from men of equal ability.

Territory Sales Expectancy. The starting point for setting fair quotas should be the overall performance of the company; that is, the company's sales divided by the total market (product by product, if possible). To expect each territory to perform equal to the average of the company is realistic and is attainable, provided market opportunities and market conditions among territories are equal.

For example, a company is doing $9 million in sales and the total market for its product is $100 million. Its overall penetration is 9 percent. Each territory should then be given a sales expectancy of 9 percent of the total available business in the territory.

At this point, territory adjustments are usually necessary to meet company sales objectives and for factors beyond the salesman's control. Judgment plays an important part in adjusting territory sales expectancy to a sales quota, but when the quota is used as a measuring tool to judge performance among territories, the adjustments should be impersonal and based on factual information.

A comparison of the actual company sales for the territory with expected company average penetration may disclose variation factors that require adjustments in many or all territories. These factors include such things as regional variations in company overall market penetration; number of salesmen in each territory; inexperienced or experienced salesmen; restrictive marketing conditions in specific territories; or abnormal temporary increases in the total market in specific territories because of special projects.

Letting the salesman give reasons why he believes the sales expectancy figure is or is not realistic for his particular territory (where actual performance is below average) is sometimes helpful. The salesman may have factual information about his territory that is not discernible from figures, and by contributing information, he becomes a partner to the quota-setting process.

But comparisons should be made of performance in territories with similar marketing problems to make sure the reasoning is sound and not just an excuse for lack of sales ability. Two common complaints about inability to perform equal to company average performance are "too far from factory" and "too much competition." Comparison of territories in similar situations will either confirm or disprove the allegation.

For example, a New England manufacturer of commercial lighting fixtures determined that his penetration was 5 percent of the available commercial lighting fixture market in the thirty-seven eastern states, and quotas for each territory were set at 5 percent of the available business in each territory. When complaints were received from some salesmen that the quotas were unfair for certain territories because they were too far from the factory, the company made comparisons of adjoining territories equidistant from the factory. For example, in Georgia it was shown that the salesman was getting 6 percent of the market, although next door in Alabama the salesman was getting 1 percent of the available market. For both territories, the products were the same, prices the same, deliveries the same, and major competition was home based in Georgia. The difference in ability of the salesmen in the two territories was apparent from the facts, and the quotas were accepted as fair.

Adjusting Sales Quotas. When all the steps have been taken to arrive at quotas that form a basis for comparing sales performance objectively, a decision has to be made on whether or not the quotas should be further adjusted to encourage the improvement of weak salesmen and/or provide incentives for commission or bonus payments. Making adjustments to quotas for individual performance presents one problem—the quotas are no longer objective measuring devices for comparing performance. A study by the National Industrial Conference Board[1] found that some companies use uniform quotas for measuring performance and individually adjusted ones for spurring salesmen. Sales management uses the unadjusted quota to compare performance, but the double standard can create morale problems when salesmen compare notes. It creates fewer problems when sales management can keep quotas objective and can use other devices to spur weak salesmen or provide incentives for compensation.

MEASURING PROGRESS AND IDENTIFYING PERFORMANCE

There should be a feedback system that periodically tells a salesman his progress toward the sales quota for his territory and also tells him how the other salesmen in the company are progressing toward their goals. This can be done as a percentage of achievement to date for each man and for the company in total, as shown by Figure 12-4. This keeps the salesman aware of the fact that he is being measured. It also shows how his performance compares with that of other salesmen. If he is not keeping pace, he realizes he must take corrective action to improve his performance. This is what is meant by performance by "self-control."

Rewarding Good Performance. To manage salesmen on an objective basis, it is necessary to make a distinction between good and poor performance, preferably by rewarding good performance and correcting or penalizing poor performance. If good and poor performances are treated on an equal basis, there is no incentive to reach targets, no matter how objectively they have been set.

A compensation system should pay the going rates for average performance and give recognition to above-average performance in the form of bonuses, prizes, extra commissions, or increases in salary. Much of the cost of field sales management goes into the improvement of weak territories. Turnover costs, training costs, and missed potential are all heavy sales costs.

A cost-accounting system that accurately allocates all sales costs, including lost market potential on a territorial basis, will disclose that weak territories are generally more costly as a percentage of business obtained than strong territories. Conversely, the strong territories are less costly, and require less super-

[1] *Measuring Salesmen's Performance*, Studies in Business Policy, no. 114, National Industrial Conference Board, New York, 1965.

XYZ CORPORATION SALESMEN'S QUOTA PERFORMANCE TEN MONTHS THROUGH OCTOBER 19__			
TERRITORY RANK	SALESMAN	TERRITORY	PERCENT OF QUOTA SHIPPED TO DATE
1	G	N.Y. CITY	174
2	M	MISSISSIPPI	161
3	P	OREGON	141
4	A	IOWA	133
5	M	CONN.	
		OHIO	22
41	J	ALABAMA	20
42	T	CHICAGO	17
	AVERAGE FOR COMPANY TO DATE 83		

FIG. 12-4. *Statistical report identifying and comparing salesmen's performance.*

vision. Certainly, if there are awards to be given, they are rightly earned by the above-average performer.

Time Period for Measuring Performance. The time period for measuring performance for the purpose of paying awards is generally a year, although, if the performance award is considered part of the basic compensation, it may be paid monthly. A manufacturer of industrial products who supplements his basic compensation plan with bonuses for quota attainment uses a six-month and an annual plan. Salesmen who ship 50 percent of their annual quota before the end of the first six months of the year get 10 percent added to all basic compensation after they cross the 50 percent quota figure. This continues until they reach 100 percent of their annual quota. Salesmen who ship 100 percent of their annual quota before the end of the year get 20 percent added to all their compensation paid after they cross the 100 percent quota figure. This carries to the end of the year.

Correcting Poor Performance. Correcting poor performance requires an identification of the causes on an individual basis and the devising of methods to improve it. When new men are added to the sales force, it takes a period of time before average or above-average performance can be expected. Quotas for these men are generally reduced to start and then increased gradually over a reasonable period of time (usually two to five years) until the full quota becomes the basis for measuring performance.

It should be recognized that any sales quota plan based on company average performance will always have some men above average and some below average. Efforts to improve below-average performance should be concentrated in territories that have the biggest potential gain from improvement—not on a percentage basis, but in actual dollars.

CONCLUSION

One of the primary tasks of marketing management is to increase marketing effectiveness. Intelligent territory alignment based on factual data and properly determined sales quotas are two major management tools to enhance the marketing effort. They are generally indispensable for objective measurement of salesmen's performance, control of sales effort, and overall sales planning.

BIBLIOGRAPHY

Crisp, Richard D., *Sales Planning and Control,* chaps. 4–11, McGraw-Hill Book Company, New York, 1961.

Determination of Sales Territories and Routing of Salesmen, selected bibliography, National Industrial Conference Board, New York.

Lewis, Edwin H., "How to Set Up Sales Territories," *Management Aids for Small Business,* no. 55, Small Business Administration, Washington, D.C., August, 1954.

Measuring Salesmen's Performance, Studies in Business Policy, no. 114, chaps. 2 and 4, National Industrial Conference Board, New York, 1965.

Reynolds, Edward B., "The Field Sales Manager's Responsibility for Planning, Organization, and Control," *The Field Sales Manager,* Report no. 48, American Management Association, New York, 1960, pp. 45–75.

Sales Potentials and Quotas, selected bibliography, National Industrial Conference Board, New York.

Schiff, Michael, and Martin Mellman, *Financial Management of the Marketing Function,* chap. 5, Financial Executives Research Foundation, New York, 1962.

Wedermeyer, Henry, "Planning and Organizing Territorial Coverage," *The Field Sales Manager,* Report no. 48, American Management Association, New York, 1960, pp. 95–111.

CHAPTER THIRTEEN

Regional and Branch Office Management

RICHARD J. MEYERS *General Sales Manager, Moore Business Forms, Inc., Niagara Falls, New York*

The terms "regional," "branch," "district," and "divisional" are used to describe the same functions in different companies. Which term is used to identify a field office generally depends upon how the marketing areas are defined. A common practice is to set up a regional or branch headquarters with six or seven district offices in the same geographic area, all reporting to the central point. Other companies, even in closely parallel types of business, refer to the key field offices as district offices with branch or regional offices subordinated to them. There seems to be no firm rule in this matter.

In addition to sales, these field offices frequently include technical customer assistance such as engineering, mechanical service, or systems aid. They are commonly staffed with specialists in pricing if the company's products are custom-made. Order entry is normally originated at this point.

The distribution channels used by the organization have some bearing on the function of the regional office. If the majority of sales are made through distributors, jobbers, wholesalers, or manufacturers' representatives, the services required of a regional office will differ from those where the great bulk of selling is done through direct sales representatives.

Supporting Services for Branch Regional Sales Offices. On the premise that a field sales manager will be making his most valuable contribution when he is working directly to increase sales in his geographic area through the salesmen reporting to him, some progressive companies relieve him of practically all responsibilities except those directly relating to the selling effort. This is done by setting up a position that might be designated as a "marketing service manager," or "office services manager," reporting to a home office staff man such as a sales controller or general sales office manager.

There are two kinds of service functions in a branch regional sales office:

1. Sales service, which includes those functions that involve dealing with customers, such as making customer proposals, including price quotations.

Also included are all other matters that intimately affect customers, such as:

a. Interpreting customers' purchase orders

b. Preparing order forms supplemented by specification detail and drawings as required for production

c. Expediting orders in process

d. Handling correspondence and complaints

e. Scheduling repairs, and maintaining sold or leased equipment

2. Office services, which include those functions that are clerical in nature and provide the sales office personnel with such services as dictating and transcribing; filing, order typing, and record keeping; cashier's services; mail, telephone, and telegraph; office leases; and clerical recruitment and training services.

The greatest benefits of a position charged with furnishing all the supporting services are usually realized in a regional operation where several district or product managers of equal status operate. It can also be used profitably when the number of salesmen and/or the geographic spread of the territory they cover make so many demands on the regional manager's time that with this added help he can greatly increase sales. The basic consideration should be that it is unsound to "hamstring" a competent field sales manager if certain services can be handled *more* efficiently by a person whose compensation is substantially *less*. By-product benefits can be to give office management the specialized attention warranted by its cost. Sometimes, too, a professional office manager recommends simplification or elimination of records and reports without which sales managers agree they can still operate effectively.

The computer has had a direct bearing on the functions best handled by the field sales office. Credit, billing, inventory control, and a wide range of statistics relating to sales analysis at an individual customer and salesman level, for example, have been transferred to the home office, with the field sales office receiving copies of any needed information.

TYPICAL REGIONAL BRANCH SALES OFFICE ORGANIZATION

Figure 13-1 shows the basic type of organization which will generally apply to an office with no more than ten salesmen covering a geographic area varying from a medium-size city to one or two states in a sparsely populated section. Field customer service normally relates to mechanical or engineering services as differentiated from delivery service of the manufacturing plants. Expediting at the producing units to meet the customers' delivery requirements is usually part of the sales operation.

Figure 13-2 illustrates the concept of segregating all operations not directly related to producing sales and placing them under an administrative manager who may report laterally to the field sales manager, but functionally to a central headquarters.

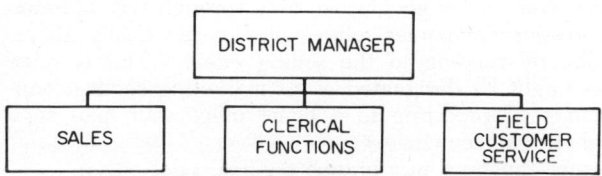

FIG. 13-1. *Organization chart of small branch office.*

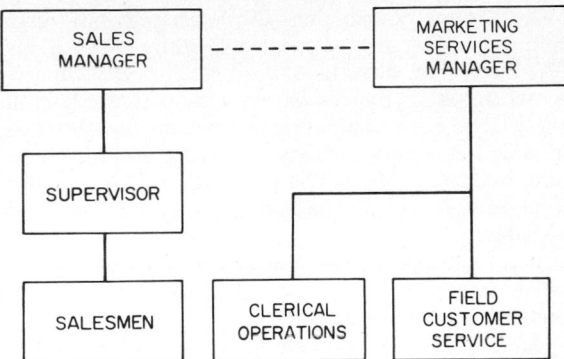

FIG. 13-2. *Branch office organization when sales and service functions are separated.*

When more than one field sales manager—based on product, vocation, or geography—operates from common quarters, it is especially advantageous to coordinate responsibility for all services under an administrative specialist. This concept is illustrated by Figure 13-3.

BRANCH OFFICE MANAGEMENT

Before an additional branch office is established, or in review of present branch office operations, it is fundamental to determine exactly what functions that branch should perform and then tailor the operating structure to accomplish this most efficiently and economically. After this has been done, steps should be taken to clarify the manager's responsibilities and key duties. From the home office viewpoint, some of these may seem so self-evident that they should require no elaboration. However, the manager responsible for directing the company's marketing efforts several hundred miles from the home office—where contacts with top sales management may be limited to one brief visit a year—may not have the same grasp of the company's policies and objectives. Generally, he will show a high degree of willingness to carry them out when he fully understands and is sold on the overall benefits of them. Once this is accomplished, a solid foundation has been set for effective branch office administration.

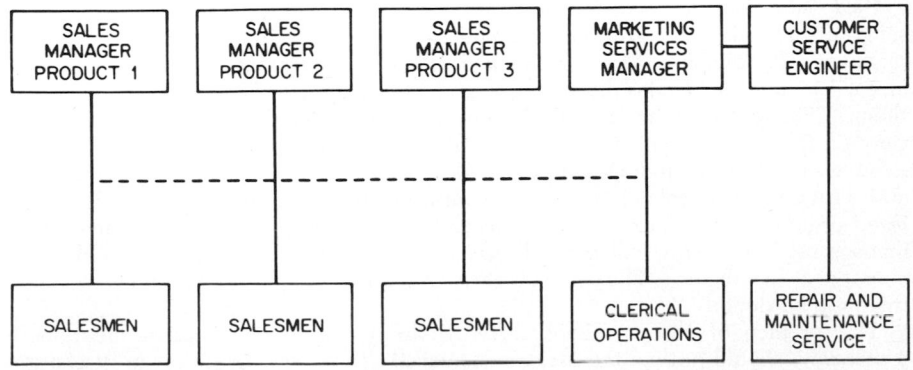

FIG. 13-3. *Organization of branch office with more than one field sales manager.*

Regardless of whether a branch regional office has a provincial-type operation—covering one or more full states with a high percentage of the salesmen not operating directly out of the branch office—or is strictly concentrated in a metropolitan city, the basic function of the field managers should be uniform. It is to direct all marketing operations in the geographic areas over which his jurisdiction extends so as to attain stated objectives within company policies and budgets. He is charged with full responsibility for the execution and follow-through of all marketing programs, with strict accountability for results obtained.

Responsibilities of the Branch Office Manager. With this as a foundation, home office sales management might evolve the major responsibilities of the branch manager along these lines:

1. *Leadership.* Provide effective leadership.

2. *Manpower.* Establish, train, and maintain an adequate supply of manpower which will provide coverage and penetration necessary to attain and exceed the annual volume quota assigned.

3. *Forecasting.* Make monthly, quarterly, and annual forecasts.

4. *Planning.* Develop one-year and five-year plans.

5. *Direction.* Direct the activities of the men for whom he is responsible by working with them in the office and in the field to develop their abilities to the maximum.

6. *Maintain customer contacts.*

7. *Meetings.* Conduct regular sales meetings to improve the performance of the sales force through explanation of new policies, procedures, products, ideas, and sales techniques.

8. *Assignments.* Establish and maintain sound sales assignments and coverage operations.

9. *Growth.* Regularly study all assignments, the geography, available statistics, and manpower, for indications of areas for improvement and expansion.

10. *Reviews.* Conduct periodic reviews to ascertain that maximum procurement of potential volume is being achieved.

11. *Management volume.* Maintain a satisfactory management sales volume.

12. *Relationships.* Maintain all necessary relationships with salesmen, customers, regional managers, and the home office.

13. *Office.* Establish, maintain, and administer adequate quarters and services as a base of operations for the conduct of the business of the district.

14. *Monthly reports.* Prepare monthly reports for the regional managers and the home office.

Field Sales Manager's Handbook. A course of action now being followed by some of the more progressive companies is the development of a field sales manager's handbook. This handbook spells out the duties and responsibilities of each level of field sales management and the policies and procedures governing them. The preparation of a field sales manager's handbook requires thinking through in detail the policies, practices, and procedures that home office management wishes to have followed in the field. It helps clarify management thinking and provides an excellent means of communication among geographically scattered organizational units. The company that is having regional or branch office management problems will be well advised to consider developing a field sales manager's handbook. The rest of this chapter will give suggestions on how this may be done.

The preface of the handbook, after defining the basic function mentioned previously, should outline the major responsibilities. The key duties in discharge of these might then be listed. The following shows how this might be done.

Major Responsibilities

I. Provide effective leadership.
   A. Explain and interpret company policies.
   B. Direct an adequate district sales force supported by an ample, well-trained staff which is properly motivated.
   C. Maintain continuing program of salesman development through scheduled on-the-job training consultations with supervisors and salesmen.
   D. Conduct an annual performance review with supervisors and salesmen to develop the areas in which training assistance for each individual should be directed.
   E. Ensure top-quality salesmanship starting with the personnel recruitment processes and continuing indefinitely with proper training, supervision, and control.
   F. Improve, wherever possible, the company's image.

II. Manpower. Establish, train, and maintain an adequate supply of manpower which will provide the coverage and penetration necessary to attain and exceed the annual volume quota assigned.
   A. Recruit. Be on the alert constantly to recruit good men from all available sources for any additions to the sales force needed to meet stated objectives.
   B. Select. Interview and carefully evaluate the qualifications of all prospective candidates for sales positions in accordance with established selection procedures and man specifications, selecting those who give promise of developing into top-flight sales representatives.
   C. Hire. Hire sales personnel, within budget limitations, subject to approval of the regional manager and in coordination with the industrial relations department.
   D. Train. Train sales personnel in the various sales techniques required to make them successful salesmen. Indoctrination: Make sure the man fully understands all basic training-course material and that he completes each assignment required in it. Explain to him fully the company's plan of selling. Provide, explain purpose of, and demonstrate proper use of all working tools making up his sales kit. Ensure that assignment sheets, block frequency and route schedules, objectives, and quota are properly established.
   E. Correct. Maintain discipline in conformance with company policies and procedures. Dismiss, for cause, any employee, after receiving the counsel and approval of the regional manager.

III. Forecasting.
   A. Submit annual total volume forecast for ensuing year to regional office by end of November, and quarterly forecasts by the end of February, May, August, and November.
   B. Receive and evaluate monthly forecasts of individual salesmen one day after the close of business month preceding the month covered by the forecast. Consolidate into district forecasting procedure and submit immediately to regional manager.
   C. Educate supervisors and key salesmen on importance and benefits of accurate forecasting.
   D. Check performance against forecast on quarterly basis for each man by the end of the month after the preceding quarter.

IV. Planning—one-year and five-year.
   A. Provide regional manager with recommendations, supported by facts on:

       1. Volume

       2. Manpower

       3. Increased supervision

  B. Use management tools (such as town and county sales analyses) and home office assistance from market research and sales control in planning these areas.

  C. Make projections involving expansion of supervision or relocation of district office and include estimated additional cost.

V. Direction. Direct the activities of subordinates by working with them in the office and in the field to develop their abilities to the maximum.

  A. Training and guidance.

       1. On the job (in the office).

         a. Conduct sales presentation kit drills, checking on techniques and conditions of kit.

         b. Spot-check customer cards, prospect registers, and frequency schedules once a week for each man, to ensure strict compliance with the approved coverage plan.

       2. On the job (in the field). Spend at least eight hours a week in the field working with men—working with each man in group, regardless of how experienced he is, a minimum of one day every three months, observing and guiding:

         a. Planning and sales techniques

         b. Work habits

         c. Expanding and upgrading of customer contacts

         d. Condition of working tools—sales kit, work cards, and the like

       3. Watch results and operation by men to detect any weakness and provide close supervision to correct situation, if possible, before it becomes serious. Hold frequent conferences with supervisors to point out their men's weaknesses, and establish methods for correction.

       4. Keep in touch with deals in process through forecasts and close contact with salesmen and supervisors.

       5. Assist in closing orders and determining market prices and levels of competitor prices from available information.

       6. Keep constantly aware of competitive developments and activities.

  B. Attitude and morale.

       1. Seek to ensure that the attitude of the men toward their jobs and the company is a healthy one.

       2. Strive to keep morale at a high level by providing fair and equitable treatment and creating good working conditions within the office.

VI. Maintain customer contacts.

  A. Select customers from the assignments of each salesman in the district for whom it will be desirable to give sales assistance and make goodwill contacts. Selection should be influenced by facts reported on account activity reviews.

  B. Carry out the program of goodwill contacts with a maximum number of major accounts.

  C. Use customer visits as occasions to upgrade contacts in these accounts to executive level.

VII. Meetings. Conduct regular sales meetings to educate and improve the performance of the sales force through explanation of new policies, procedures, products, ideas, and sales techniques.

  A. Prepare and conduct regular month-end meetings for all men, to be certain that all released information is reviewed and understood.

   B. Hold informal meetings with supervisors every two weeks to discuss problems and progress of men under their jurisdiction and to keep the supervisors fully informed of any current developments.

VIII. Assignments. Establish and maintain sound assignments and coverage operations.

   A. Establish assignments which:

    1. Consist of a number of geographic blocks, each having definite geographic boundaries

    2. Are as physically compact and adjacent to each other as possible

    3. Contain only as many blocks as are necessary to provide a territory and have sufficient repeat-business volume to support a reasonable earnings level and sufficient challenge for future growth for the man

    4. Can be adequately covered by the man to whom assigned so that each customer or qualified prospect can be called upon at least once every three months

   B. Constantly review established assignments to bring about compliance with above factors.

IX. Growth. Regularly study all assignments—the geography, available statistics, and manpower—for indications of all possible areas for improvement and expansion.

   A. Recommend changes in sales assignments (promotions, transfers), realignment of territories, and establishment of new districts to the regional manager.

   B. Recommend sales quotas for all salesmen to the regional manager.

   C. Promote improvements in products, methods, procedures, and facilities by month-end reports to the sales development department and to the regional manager; also, by conversation and letters during the month.

X. Reviews. Conduct periodic reviews to ascertain that maximum procurement of potential volume is being achieved.

   A. Conduct reviews of one geographic block in the assignment of each man each week.

   B. Conduct account reviews twice a year for each major account in the district.

   C. Conduct formal salesman-performance reviews annually to have a clear understanding of each man's personal goals and objectives, and prescribe best ways to achieve them. Pinpoint weaknesses and discuss corrective measures. Establish improvement objectives.

   D. Review results of calculated performance achieved versus minimum standards each month with each man, offering suggestions for improvement in areas where needed.

XI. Management volume. Maintain a satisfactory personal sales volume with the accounts specified by the regional manager.

XII. Relationships.

   A. Supervisors and salesmen. Maintain a close contact and confer with all members of the staff. Coordinate efforts through formal sales meetings and informal conversation. Seek and accept functional guidance from them on matters within their respective range of activities.

   B. Internal sales organization. Contact proper department or section for assistance, information, and guidance on any matter necessary for the accomplishment of sales and administrative functions.

   C. Major customers. Call regularly on, and cultivate, key individuals in major accounts.

      D. Community organizations. Participate in worthwhile community affairs and in leading civic organizations and private clubs.

      E. Others. Contact plant personnel and others whose cooperation it is necessary to have.

XIII. Office. Establish, maintain, and administer adequate quarters and services as a base of operations for the conduct of the business of the district.

      A. Maintain an efficient operation of the district office in accordance with prescribed policies and procedures. (NOTE: When the regional and district offices occupy common premises, this is sometimes a regional responsibility.)

      B. Hire capable field office personnel for positions within budget limitations and general policy covering office employees.

      C. Complete periodic reviews and recommend compensation arrangements for administrative personnel.

      D. Authorize all expenditures in operating or capital budgets which have been approved by regional manager and sales control department.

XIV. Monthly reports—to regional manager and home office.

      A. Summarize in monthly reports overall sales activity, including a comparison with previous year.

      B. Include highlights of manpower activity in the district, customer contacts, and any other significant developments relating to general business climate, sales results, or progress against annual objectives. Report outstanding accomplishments for recognition by regional and home office sales management.

Sections on Recommended Practices. A section should be devoted to each major responsibility which spells out the recommended practices in detail for carrying out the key duties under that responsibility. For example, under "Leadership" there could be a detailed discussion of exactly how the field manager should work with his men. This discussion might be organized as follows:

Basic Managerial Responsibility

  I. The manager as the key man
      A. Parent and teacher
      B. Leader
      C. Demonstrate how to operate—in field
      D. Demonstrate how to operate—in the office
          1. Time management
      E. Generator of enthusiasm
 II. Field manager's time spent in field
III. Field supervision
      A. Working with the newer men
      B. Working with experienced salesmen
 IV. Office supervision of salesmen
      A. Indoctrination training
      B. Proper time organization
  V. Sales stimulants
 VI. Handling of complaints with customers to build goodwill

Under "Personal Time Management," the field manager should be given definite guidance as follows:

  I. Allocation of time
      A. Plan and do
 II. Work-plan calendar
      A. Planning and scheduling time
      B. Time per occurrence

    C. Time required
    D. When is time available
    E. Avoid overloading schedule
III. Working your plan
    A. Adherence to schedule
    B. Morning preview
    C. Disposition
    D. Clear the slate

Each managerial responsibility is explored in the same manner.

Using the Field Sales Manager's Handbook. It is highly desirable to launch the handbook in a meeting between home office and field sales management. This is essential to clearly emphasize the concept that the handbook is not intended in any sense to so control operations that executive ability and judgment are no longer necessary. The purpose of the handbook must be clarified as a ready reference on a variety of subjects that confront field managers almost daily. They should be convinced in the presentation and panel discussions which might follow that some operating philosophies can be set forth which serve as a guide in the treatment of people and in conducting the field manager's job.

Stress should be placed on the aspect that frequent reference to the handbook will actually add to management skills and help put the operation of all districts on as uniform a basis as is practical. The field managers should be invited to bring their recommendations directly to the attention of the sales manager if they are convinced there is a better way to handle the aims of any of the subjects covered in the handbook. If this is done, all such suggestions should be considered in the light of their overall application to the entire field management organization. Those adopted should then be published as revisions to the handbook and thereafter be treated as the recommended methods.

CONCLUSION

A handbook is likely to be greeted with varying degrees of enthusiasm by the field managers, depending on their own degree of self-confidence and experience. There is initially a keen interest in reading it from cover to cover avidly in hopes of uncovering some panacea that will help solve all their problems, or at least a sure cure for one of their most perplexing challenges. Obviously, the former hope is never realized and the latter very seldom. A normal reaction then is to file the handbook away and use it only for occasional reference in situations with which the manager has not previously been confronted.

A highly recommended follow-through is to hold a second meeting about a year after the handbook is originally published. In this session, each of the field managerial responsibilities could be divided among the top field and the home office sales executives to present in considerable depth. If advance notice is given that universal participation will be required by those in attendance, it is likely to encourage some research into both the subjects and effective presentation techniques. This has proved greatly beneficial to focus attention on the full scope of the subjects under review. Such a meeting can lead to a high degree of improvement in communicating an understanding and acceptance of company marketing objectives, policies, and procedures.

BIBLIOGRAPHY

Canfield, B. R., *Sales Administration: Principles and Problems*, 4th ed., Prentice-Hall, Inc., Englewood Cliffs, N.J., 1961.

Davis, Robert T., "Sales Management in the Field," *Harvard Business Review,* January–February, 1958.

"Field Organization," sec. 22 in John Cameron Aspley (ed.), *The Sales Manager's Handbook,* 9th ed., The Dartnell Corporation, Chicago, 1962.

Field Sales Management, Experiences in Marketing Management, no. 1, National Industrial Conference Board, New York, 1963.

"Field Sales Management—Weak Link in the Selling Chain?" *ACME Reporter,* no. 1, The Association of Consulting Management Engineers, Inc., New York, 1960.

Newgarden, A. (ed.), *The Field Sales Manager,* American Management Association, New York, 1960.

Operation and Compensation of Field Sales Supervisors, The Dartnell Corporation, Chicago, 1952.

"Sales Supervision—Supervisory Work of Branch Managers," sec. 22 in Paul H. Nystrom (ed.), *Marketing Handbook,* The Ronald Press Company, New York, 1948.

CHAPTER FOURTEEN

Selection and Training of Sales Personnel

BERNARD T. PARKER *President, Tax Research Institute of America, Inc., New York, New York*

Progressive marketing executives are well aware that, assuming certain basic characteristics are present, salesmen can be developed or created—they are not "born." In the development of sales personnel, three areas are considered important:

1. Careful selection
2. Continuous training
3. Effective supervision

Improved selection, training, and supervision are vital ingredients in developing an effective sales force.

The salesman's job has become increasingly complex. Rather than just "selling the product," he is expected to sell the product and assist the buyer to sell it in turn. In addition, he has become an adviser in advertising, sales promotion, credits, and collections. He is required to locate new prospects, handle reports and correspondence, be an expert in planning the use of his time, take care of complaints, and be an all-around goodwill ambassador for the company. Obviously, then, the salesman requires training in a great number of activities to operate at his maximum efficiency.

SELECTION OF SALES PERSONNEL

Careful selection reduces turnover and decreases training time. An additional investment in selecting the right man results in savings of hundreds of training dollars and eliminates having to repeat the selection process if the salesman chosen is not the right man in the first place.

Job Description. Only by knowing what the job requires can an intelligent plan be constructed for selecting and training the right type of individual to perform the job. Therefore, the first step in setting up a careful selection and training program for sales personnel is to prepare a job description. This job description or analysis is the basis for both the selection and training plan.

Man Specifications. A careful study of the salesman's job description and the qualifications of successful producers reveals the characteristics and qualities an applicant must possess to perform the job.

The man specifications constitute a standard or yardstick against which to measure every applicant. Those who do not measure up should be rejected. Those who qualify can be measured one against the other to give a clear picture of which applicant is* most suitable. The chances of finding an ideal applicant are slim. A list of "required" assets along with those "preferred" is shown by Figure 14-1.

Recruiting. Finding applicants requires the use of many different methods to obtain enough applicants so that selection can be exercised. It is essential that a number of well-qualified applicants be looked over for each opening rather than hiring the first man who shows up, which obviously leads to high turnover. There are a number of sources of qualified applicants which need to be used in combination to supply a high enough yield.

One of the most important and most frequently used methods is classified newspaper advertising. A good advertising agency can be extremely helpful in selecting the best paper in each city to reach the right type of audience. Recruiting ads normally are most effective in the classified section, rather than the display section. (The applicant who is seriously contemplating a job change is more inclined to check the classified section, and if the ad is attractive and

Man Specifications

Subject	Required	Preferred	Helpful
Marital status........	None	Married—children; no separation or divorce	Wife not working
Residence...........	Live within the area	Live close to center of area to reduce traveling time	Not boarding with relatives or friends
Car (where necessary).	Have own car in good condition, available for business use	Late model	Under 15,000 miles
Telephone...........	In own home	Private line	
Education...........	High school graduate	College graduate	Additional courses: sales, bus. admin.
Experience..........	Recent two years outside selling; successful in prospecting and closing	Five to ten years sales experience	Successful record— upper 25 % of group
Job stability.........	No more than five jobs in past eight years unless extenuating circumstances exist	No more than two jobs in past eight years	
Unemployment.......	Not out of work more than three months in past three years	Presently employed; not out of work more than one month in past five years	No unemployment
Physical condition....	No chronic ailments or defects	Energetic	Not overweight

FIG. 14-1. *Required, preferred, and helpful assets for sales applicants.*

sizable, experience has shown it will produce better results than ads placed elsewhere in the same newspaper.)

Employment agencies are a prime source, particularly if the company supplies the man specification sheet in advance and also is willing to pay all or part of the agency fee if a qualified applicant is secured.

Referrals of men by present company salesmen should be encouraged. Some companies pay a bonus for a man secured in this way. Referrals from business executives, influential members of the professional community, and internal employees are often productive. Many companies use spot radio announcements, cards, and letters sent to customers at periodic intervals which ask for referrals of well-qualified individuals. The placement directors of colleges and high schools can also be prime sources.

Those doing recruiting should not overlook salesmen calling on them as prospective job applicants. The local chamber of commerce, sales executives club, and fraternal organizations can also provide a source of good applicants. Letters of inquiry from applicants deserve prompt acknowledgment and follow-up by the nearest interviewer.

The Sales Application. What a man has done is the best index to what he will do—basic character and work habits seldom change. Because the application form provides a record of the applicant's employment and personal history, it represents an important tool for determining whether or not the applicant has the required experience and personal characteristics, using the man specifications as the standard.

The data on the application form should be analyzed carefully and any questionable areas circled. These may include omissions, exaggerations, inconsistencies, inaccuracies, and areas in which the applicant fails to meet the basic requirements.

Areas circled may not be cause for immediate rejection. They should be investigated thoroughly during the interview.

Interviews. Interviewing is one of the most important parts of the selection process. Most companies limit the first or exploratory interview to thirty to forty-five minutes. It primarily consists in having the applicant elaborate on his qualifications as stated in the application. If the applicant warrants no further consideration, the selection process is terminated at the end of this interview.

If, on the other hand, the applicant has the basic qualifications, a second interview is scheduled. In cases where tests are to be used, the applicant is often asked to take the test battery before reporting for the second interview. It is customary to give the applicant descriptive brochures about the company and job to look over before he returns for further discussion.

The most important step in the selection process is undoubtedly the depth or comprehensive interview. Wherever possible, it is desirable to have more than one person interview the applicant with the hiring decision based on the pooled judgment of the interviewers. The first step in conducting the depth interview is to examine the application form and record of the previous interview, making notes which will determine what questions should be asked for further clarification.

The interview should be conducted in privacy, away from interruptions, and normally will take as long as two to three hours. In any event, enough time should be scheduled to make sure the interview can be completed without hurrying. Such an interview should cover the following:

1. The applicant's work experience
2. His education and training

3. His physical fitness
4. His emotional maturity and motivation
5. His financial responsibility

The interviewer must be a good listener and have the ability to phrase questions which will elicit the desired information. One of the things that can be used to help the interviewer is a series of questions or a "patterned interview" form.

Reference Checks. It is important to verify as much of the information provided by the application as possible. Many applicants, in their desire to obtain the job, will cover up important information, smooth over gaps in employment, distort previous salaries earned, and generally misrepresent the facts. Sometimes this is done innocently, but often it is done intentionally. Some applicants believe it will be difficult if not impossible for the prospective employer to check the facts of the situation.

Long-distance phone calls can be used to verify the facts by speaking to the applicant's previous immediate supervisors in a matter of minutes for a very nominal cost. Many companies use a telephone reference check such as that shown in Figure 14-2 for this verification process. More information can be obtained about the past performance of the applicant by this method perhaps than by any other.

In addition, most companies use one of the regular agencies to provide a character and credit check. This covers the applicant's personal and business reputation, habits, net worth, and credit standing. Frequently, a credit check will reveal important weaknesses in an applicant—weaknesses that cannot be detected in an interview.

A credit check normally takes one to two weeks, but can be extremely valuable in making sure the right man has been selected. It is therefore important to allow sufficient time before the applicant is put on the payroll for these checks to be concluded.

Physical Examination. The salesman's job is physically and mentally taxing. He works in all types of weather, climbing in and out of vehicles and up and

---

Telephone Reference

Name of applicant	Person contacted	Position

Company   City and state   Telephone number

1. I'd like to verify some of the information given us by Mr. (name), who has applied for employment with our organization. Do you remember him?
2. What were the dates of his employment? From_____19____to_____19____
3. What type of work was he doing for you?_____

4. He says he was earning $_____per_____when he left. Is that right?_____
   If "No," what were his earnings? $_____
5. How much of this was salary? $_____How much was commission or bonus? $_____
6. How was his attendance? Did he lose any time because of drinking, gambling, financial, or domestic problems? Yes_____No_____What?_____

7. How did his sales results compare with others?_____
8. How closely was he supervised?_____
9. What did you personally think of him? Did he get along with other people?_____

10. Why did he leave?_____
11. Would you rehire him? Yes_____No_____If "No," why not?_____

Checked by_____Date_____

FIG. 14-2. *Telephone reference check sheet.*

down stairs carrying heavy briefcases and samples, working long hours, and hurrying to keep schedules.

Fitness is important, and the selection process is incomplete unless a physical examination is given. This is usually available through the company medical department. Where there is no company medical department, arrangements can be made with a local physician. On the other hand, if selection takes place in locations other than at company headquarters, there are organizations providing physical examination services in principal cities.

Recruiting and selecting salesmen is hard, painstaking work; it is particularly so because the manager is operating in an environment which is not customary for him. Although he is normally selling and persuading people to buy, it is necessary for him to refrain from doing this too much when selecting applicants. Selection is half purchasing, half selling. When selecting salesmen, it is necessary to look at every aspect of the "product" with meticulous care, as well as selling the individual on the opportunity. Overemphasis of the latter with sacrifice of the former will lead to poor results.

EFFECTIVE TRAINING OF SALES PERSONNEL

Carefully planned training helps salesmen to achieve effective production in a minimum amount of time. It also reduces selling costs and increases salesmen's earnings. There is a close relationship between effective sales training and salesman turnover. More effective training means less need for close supervision. Salesmen who have been carefully trained are more competent, enthusiastic about their jobs, and anxious to help the buyer, which leads to better customer relations.

To be effective, training must be based on the actual need of the salesman in the field. This can best be determined by examination of the job description, observation of the salesman in the field, and feedback from the field managers on the problems they encounter with salesmen which contribute to ineffective performance.

There are four main areas in which training is needed for success in any type of selling. The main objectives are to improve the salesman's performance by improving his knowledge, work habits, selling skills, and attitude.

The salesman needs knowledge of the product, company, markets, customer, and the sales policies under which he will operate. Most often overemphasized in sales training programs is the first of these—product knowledge. Perhaps most important is the knowledge of the market for the product and the customer's requirements and behavior which, in the final analysis, contribute most heavily to the success of each salesman.

Poor work habits are responsible for the failure of salesmen more than any other aspect of their job performance. The training program should be developed using those work habits which contribute most to superior performance and should include prospecting, planning the day's calls, handling paper work, and techniques of getting in front of enough prospective customers.

Major emphasis in any sales training program should be given to the development of selling skills. The salesman needs substantial help in conducting himself properly in the prospect's place of business, establishing rapport, making effective sales presentations, using the selling tools provided by the company, handling objections, and closing techniques.

Next to the development of selling skills, attitude is probably the most difficult of all to improve. This requires continuous effort over a long period of time to develop pride in the company, confidence in the product, and a feeling of satisfaction in the job. The field manager or immediate supervisor is the individual who must carry most of this burden. The salesman's initial indoctrination in the company and the job, communications with the home office and his manager, prompt attention to customer's complaints, and the knowledge that he can get help when he needs it contribute heavily to high morale. A good boss who is willing to show him how to do the job, listen to his problems, encourage him after failure, and give him recognition when it is due is one of the most important factors contributing to both superior results and right attitude.

METHODS OF TRAINING

Training should be a continuous process. It should start when the salesman joins the company and continue as long as he remains a part of the sales force. Indoctrination training should be given as soon as he starts; he must be given some basic training before he can be expected to do even a minimum job before customers; refresher training should be given at intervals during his career; continuous training by means of sales meetings and on-the-job training from his manager should be a regular affair. Training can also be given by correspondence.

Indoctrination Training. For best results, a salesman should be hired and trained by his immediate supervisor. He should be given his initial training or indoctrination by the supervisor in his own territory. Most companies have found that costs are reduced and results improved when the man has gained some field experience before exposure to any class training at a central location. A sales manual arranged in the sequence with which a man will need to apply the knowledge is an indispensable tool to make the initial training effective. (See also Chapter 13 of Section 8.)

The manager needs to put the man at ease and prepare him for the learning process before setting foot in the field with him. As the training progresses, the manager should take the salesman into the territory and perform the job with the salesman as an observer. Gradually, as the training unfolds, the salesman will become more and more anxious to take over parts of the job. The manager should at all times follow correct training procedure in demonstrating how each part of the job is to be performed, having the salesman practice it with constructive critique (away from the customer's place of business) before allowing the salesman to proceed on his own. After the salesman's confidence has been built up, he should be allowed to handle interviews by himself with or without observation by the manager.

After the manager is satisfied that the salesman has reached a competence level which will enable him to work on his own for a short period of time, the salesman should be allowed to do so. The manager should return at periodic intervals during the initial several weeks to work with the salesman again and to make sure he is forming good habits and is performing the job according to the established successful field procedures. This also gives the salesman ample opportunity to discuss his problems and have his questions answered.

Job Rotation Training. In some cases, it is customary to subject the salesman to centralized training at the beginning of his career with the company by putting him into a job rotation training program where he spends time on each of several jobs at the home office to gain experience. In some companies, he is given time on selected jobs in the factory, in the office, and at the branch level, including experience in the warehouse filling customer orders. This is followed by central sales training classes and working as an understudy to an experienced salesman or field manager.

Training Classes. In some cases, it is not feasible to give the salesman field experience before bringing him to a centralized home office school. This is particularly true if he lacks any previous sales experience or if the product line is complex. Whenever possible, however, class training should be given only after the man has acquired some field experience. This experience gives him an understanding of the problems he will encounter on the job and makes him more receptive to classroom instruction.

From the company standpoint, training classes are more efficient, because one instructor can handle a group of trainees. If held at headquarters, class training provides an opportunity to use experts as faculty and thus get the information across to the trainees in the best, most complete manner. It should not be assumed that the headquarters expert is necessarily skilled in teaching techniques. He should be required to outline each session carefully, use visual aids, and be coached in effective teaching methods.

Class training is particularly effective for giving information on products, the company, the market, and customer behavior. It contributes greatly to the development of the right attitude and can add to an understanding of selling skills. Selling skills and work habits, however, can be mastered only with actual practice in field situations. Role-playing practice in small groups can be helpful in developing selling skills, but work habits primarily need to be developed and supervised by the field manager.

Training is most effective when given in short periods with a rest period at frequent intervals. Normally, a ten-minute break each hour should be observed. The room should be well ventilated and well lighted, with comfortable chairs. In class or group meetings, participation is extremely important and can be achieved by paper-and-pencil tests, role-playing practice, study of actual cases, and discussion with the instructors.[1] Good audio-visual aids such as slides, charts, cutaway models, movies, and tape recordings enhance the learning process.

In more sophisticated sales training programs, short motion pictures of the trainees in action or video tapes produced by closed-circuit television can be employed which can give the trainee additional insight into his performance. When the trainee can see how he actually looks and sounds to others, it motivates him to improve his performance. The opportunity to discuss the results with a competent instructor and receive constructive help and guidance is a must.

On-the-job Training. Sound sales training involves close rapport between the salesman and his field manager. This close contact will identify the misfits who have survived the careful screening of the selection process and will reduce the incompetents before they become too costly to the marketing organization.

In all of his contacts with the salesmen, the field manager should follow the tested training procedure of "prepare, tell, show, practice, and check." This proved method, Figure 14-3, has been used successfully to train salesmen for many years and is indispensable to the manager who desires to get positive results in the minimum of time.

One of the standard tools for on-the-job sales training is the "curb conference" (see Figures 14-4 and 14-5). This simple six-step procedure is also indispensable for improving the salesman's performance. Too many managers spend most of the time criticizing weaknesses instead of showing how to improve

---

[1] For complete list of techniques, see *How to Get Participation in Sales Meetings*, National Society of Sales Training Executives, 600 S. Michigan Avenue, Chicago, Ill.

Steps in Training

1. *Prepare:*
   Put man at ease. Interest him in learning job.
   Learn what he already knows about job.
   Have man observe from position in which job is done.
   Have necessary equipment ready.
2. *Tell:*
   Tell what job is and how to do it.
   Instruct clearly and completely.
   Stress key points.
3. *Show:*
   Show how job is to be done.
   Use materials and sales tools required.
4. *Practice:*
   Test him by having him perform job.
   Repeat until correct work habit is fixed.
5. *Check:*
   Check to see that he does job right.
   Correct errors.
   Verify understanding and acceptance.
   Continue until you know that he knows.
   Follow through.

FIG. 14-3. *On-the-job sales training steps.*

strengths and in the process eliminating the weaknesses. The curb conference offers one of the best methods of doing this smoothly and effectively with each salesman.

Once the salesman is working productively, the field manager needs to check periodically to make sure the tested methods are being used. As one executive puts it, "It isn't what you expect, it's what you inspect that gets done." The manager's responsibility is to inspect each phase of the salesman's performance and retrain him on those parts of the job which require it.

Sales Meetings. Sales meetings at periodic intervals provide an opportunity to enhance still further the salesman's knowledge and skills. Too often sales meetings are confined to imparting factual knowledge about product, sales policy changes, and pricing structure. These meetings should always contain additional training to help the salesman increase his job effectiveness.

Training by Mail. Correspondence training can assist in reinforcing the learning which took place while the salesman was under the supervision of his manager and the training he gained from central schools or sales meetings. These courses can be tailor-made for the individual company or purchased from commercial organizations. Both have their place in a sound training program for the development of trainees and as refresher courses for more experienced men.

It is important that quizzes or tests be given after each lesson or installment and sent back to the trainee with suggestions for improvement. Awards in the form of a small gift and a certificate of achievement as each phase is successfully completed keep interest high and motivate the trainee to complete the course.

Curb Conference Rules

(Explanatory or Corrective Conference)
1. Hold immediately after call or transaction has occurred.
2. Best place is in your office or some quiet place.
3. Make it informal and friendly, but be firm.
4. Cover *one* idea at a time and make sure point is understood before leaving it.
5. Strengthen by constructive criticism—always be sure he understands the correct method.
6. Encourage him to use initiative, but sell standard company procedures.

FIG. 14-4. *Curb conference rules.*

How to Conduct a Curb Conference

1. *Compliment*
   Compliment him on things he did well.
2. *Question*
   Question him to bring realization of need for correction.
3. *Correct*
   Suggest, discuss, or question to bring out correct method.
4. *How and why*
   Ask him to tell you how he will do it next time and why.
5. *Drill*
   Have him drill either orally or physically.
6. *Encourage*
   Build his confidence so he is eager to acquire more skill.

FIG. 14-5.   *How to conduct a curb conference.*

SUMMARY

Effective training is the method by which knowledge, work habits, selling skills, and attitudes can be harnessed to provide the maximum results and the greatest net profit margin.

In the final analysis, no one really trains anyone else—all training or development is essentially self-development. The trainee has to be intellectually curious and motivated to participate in whatever training process is provided for him. If this is properly structured, and he has the right attitude and motivation, he will develop himself to a higher standard of performance on the job. If the structuring is haphazard, or attitude and motivation are lacking on his part, the results will not be as good.

Top management can generate brilliant marketing policies, strategies, and methods of increasing the sale of the company's products, but if these are not transmitted by effective sales training methods, the final results will leave much to be desired. Training is the essence of sales management. It is the key to the problem of transmitting the objectives and the ways and means of achieving them from the top to the bottom of the marketing organization.

BIBLIOGRAPHY

The District Sales Manager, American Management Association, New York, 1957.

Doubman, J. R., *Fundamentals of Sales Management*, F. S. Crofts & Co., New York, 1937.

Gordon, Edward S., *Training Commercial Salesmen*, Small Business Bulletin, no. 56, Small Business Administration, Washington, D.C., 1961.

Haas, Kenneth B., *How to Develop Successful Salesmen*, McGraw-Hill Book Company, New York, 1957.

Hegarty, Edward J., *Making Your Sales Meeting Sell*, McGraw-Hill Book Company, New York, 1955.

Lawyer, Kenneth, *Sales Training for the Smaller Manufacturer*, Small Business Administration, Washington, D.C., 1954.

National Society of Sales Training Executives, *New Handbook of Sales Training*, Prentice-Hall, Inc., Englewood Cliffs, N.J., 1967.

Newgarden, Albert (ed.), *The Field Sales Manager*, American Management Association, New York, 1960.

Nirenberg, Jesse S., *Getting Through to People*, Prentice-Hall, Inc., Englewood Cliffs, N.J., 1963.

Rados, William, *How to Select Better Salesmen*, Prentice-Hall, Inc., Englewood Cliffs, N.J., 1946.

Uris, L., *Developing Your Executive Skills*, McGraw-Hill Book Company, New York, 1955.

CHAPTER FIFTEEN

Compensation of Sales Personnel

JOHN F. CROSBY   *Principal Associate, Cresap, McCormick and Paget, New York, New York*

Compensation of salesmen may seem to be a simple matter; actually it is one of the more difficult tasks a manager must face.   Sometimes the mere suggestion of a special compensation plan for sales personnel provokes questions from management of other functional areas: "Why are salesmen so unique that they warrant special compensation treatment? Why not treat everyone alike?"   Why, then, do we go to the trouble of special programs for salesmen?

The answer to such questions is fundamental.   First, unlike most other employees, the salesman often operates alone, beyond the practical limit of direct supervision.   Control of compensation is one of the devices used to steer his activity along the lines the company desires.   Second, he is the company's constant, and perhaps only, representative in his area.   Adequate compensation is one device to ensure that his representation of the company will be compatible with the image the company wants him to project.   A third, less widely recognized, but valid reason is that selling, despite its aura of glamour, is hard work for the conscientious employee.

Finally, satisfactory compensation of sales personnel is of major importance both to the manager and to the company, because adequate compensation of the proper kind is essential to the development of a loyal employee who will stay with the firm and the job and who will accomplish the sales objectives set for him.   No matter how fine the product may be, the lack of an effective, experienced sales force can be an expensive and almost insurmountable handicap. That the compensation plan for salesmen must be reasonably compatible with the compensation standards for the rest of the organization cannot be disputed. This consideration, however, should not be a barrier to the development of a strong and sensible plan for salesmen.   In competitive markets, such a plan is essential.

BASIC TYPES OF COMPENSATION PLANS

Although the modifications and varieties of compensation plans for sales personnel are virtually infinite, the basic plans may be classified as one of three types: the salary plan, the commission plan, or the combination plan of salary plus a variable increment—commission, bonus, incentive, or whatever it may be called.

Salary Plan. The salary plan is merely an arrangement between the employer and the salesman whereby the employer agrees to pay a defined amount for successive periods—weekly, biweekly, monthly, or even annually—in return for sales work performed.

Advantages. For the employer, the salary plan represents the simplest arrangement, easy to budget and easy to administer. Also, because the salesman's compensation is guaranteed, he will not resist the company's instructions on how to apply his effort whether or not he happens to agree on the wisdom of the course. In short, the employer commitment to a guaranteed salary provides maximum flexibility in managing the sales organization.

From the salesman's point of view, the salary plan has obvious advantages. His income is secure so long as he meets the demands of the employer. The conscientious salesman who sincerely likes to sell has the opportunity to plan a long-range program to build sales, free from financial uncertainty.

Disadvantages. Despite these advantages, straight salary plans have declined in popularity, and for good reason. Most important, salary plans lack any direct incentive. Consequently, should the salesman's personal pride or drive to make good be insufficient to motivate him to accomplish the sales objectives assigned him, the manager has little real control short of the threat of discharge.

The majority of salesmen, too, find the "salary only" concept unacceptable to their temperament. To many salesmen, the attraction of selling is the opportunity to pit their capabilities against other salesmen in the marketplace and to be rewarded according to results. Such salesmen, though willing to accept little if they sell little, expect significant accomplishment to be reflected in immediate monetary reward. This is obviously impractical in a salary plan, because it exposes the company to the risk, after a few successes, of being burdened with an unreasonably high salary structure.

Commission Plan. In its simplest and oldest form, the commission plan is an agreement on the part of the employer to pay the salesman a specific sum for each unit or dollar value of product sold: the so-called straight commission.

Usually, in such a plan, the salesman is entirely on his own. If he is highly successful, he can profit handsomely; if he is unsuccessful, he not only receives no income but can be considerably out of pocket for expenses incurred. Because of its potential severity, the straight commission plan is seldom encountered in an industrial organization, but it forms the basis for compensation in much of the insurance and brokerage industry and for most so-called manufacturer's representatives and similar "outside" organizations that sell for the producer on a contractual arrangement.

Modifications of the Commission Concept. An almost infinite variety of commission modifications can be developed. Two of the more common are discussed below.

1. *Commission against draw.* In recognition that the commission salesman must have current income to provide for his family and meet operating expenses, some plans provide for advancing money to the salesman, to be paid back later from commissions earned. Such payments are commonly termed the "draw," or sales advance. During each draw period, the first commissions earned go to pay the draw, the overage being credited to the salesman.

Draws can be considered money loaned to the salesman and collectible if the salesman should be unsuccessful in offsetting them with commissions earned. When the salesman is unsuccessful, however, despite sincere effort over a reasonable period, the agreement is usually terminated without the company's attempt to collect.

2. *Modified commission scale.* Another way of softening the harshness of the straight commission plan is the use of a modified scale. Under this plan, a commission rate may be set in a series of steps. For example, to relieve the salesman of the burden of the draw as quickly as possible, a relatively high commission may be paid on the first sales in the draw period until the draw is covered; then the rate may drop to lower levels by steps on subsequent sales. Obviously, such a system also protects the employer if sales exceed expectations.

Advantages of Commission Plans. The overriding advantage of the commission plan, both to the employer and to the salesman, is the powerful motivation it provides. Through a commission plan, the salesman's income is controlled primarily by his ability and hustle. The more capable the salesman and the more commission he earns, the more successful the sales program of the employer becomes. Further, since the employer's selling cost is geared directly to sales, costs are low when sales income is least, and sales expenses are at a maximum only when the employer is best able to afford them.

Disadvantages of Commission Plans. The disadvantages of a commission plan to the salesman when sales prospects are poor are obvious. Although the need for income may force him to extra effort in such periods, in the long run the salesman becomes discouraged and seeks a more advantageous situation. Where alternatives exist within the terms of the agreement—for example, where several lines are sold—the obvious answer is to apply effort where prospects are best. Thus, the product line for which strong effort is most needed tends to suffer the most.

A commission plan has additional disadvantages, even under optimum conditions. Most important, the commission plan presents a difficult control situation for the sales manager. The successful commission salesman tends to regard himself as an independent operator. Because his income rests on results, he tends to regard his method of operation as his own affair and to resist any interference. It becomes difficult for the manager even to suggest modifications in the coverage of accounts, or to request attention to tasks that do not produce immediate sales. And it becomes virtually impossible to shift territories or accounts without creating disruption and considerable ill will. Usually, such moves can be made only through offering a guarantee. The plan then is no longer a commission plan. After a few such concessions, the plan soon becomes unbelievably complicated and so involved in personalities that it ceases to be a "plan" at all.

Combination Plans. Combination plans couple a fixed compensation element with a variable element such as a commission or volume bonus. Most plans for the compensation of industrial salesmen fall into this third category, retaining the better features of both salary and commission types.

Forms of Combination Plans. The workings of a combination plan can be simple; for example, an agreement to pay a salary plus additional compensation for every unit or dollar of sales income generated, or for every sale over an agreed-upon quota. Combination plans can be extremely complex, especially where the variable element is governed by a number of less directly measurable factors.

In combination plans, the basic element—the fixed portion—is, in essence, salary. Like any salary, it can be raised periodically; and in many plans, the fixed element is set at different levels or ranges for each stage in a salesman's development or for varying levels of territory and volume responsibility. The variable element can be based upon any number of factors, limited only by the ingenuity of management and the capability of its record-keeping machinery.

1. *Payment on sales volume.* The variable element can be merely some form of commission or bonus on sales. Any sales situation suitable to a commission plan can be handled this way.

2. *Payments on performance evaluation.* Some plans deliberately avoid a direct tie to sales volume (which must be paid whether the sales are developed according to company plans or otherwise), and instead base the variable compensation on such factors as coverage of territory, new accounts serviced, quality of reports, or control of expenses. In theory, such methods attempt to ensure the proficient accomplishment of the day-in, day-out routine of selling that will fully develop territory potential and eventually produce even greater volume increases than the more directly sales-oriented plans.

3. *Combination volume and evaluation plans.* Some of the more complex (and, if well done, most useful) plans combine both the foregoing features; they provide both a bonus or commission on volume and a reward for performance of specific elements of the sales task.

Advantages of Combination Plans. The prevalence of combination plans is itself strong testimony to their acceptance by management and salesmen. Properly handled, they represent an effective compromise between incentive income in return for good performance and protection of the salesman's standard of living if, through no fault of his own, good sales results cannot be achieved. The employer also preserves some flexibility in dealing with his overall sales task. Where necessary, fundamental changes in territory alignment or the assignment of customers can be made, or salesmen can be transferred as needed, without undue penalty to the salesmen and consequent resentment or resignations. In addition, with a thoughtful approach, the employer can choose the variable factors that will motivate the salesman to pursue, largely on his own and without close supervision, a course that will fulfill the longer-range sales objectives of the company.

The particular advantage of combination plans for "team selling" situations is worthy of special note. Direct-acting rewards—volume bonuses or commissions on sales—often fail to reward individuals in proportion to their contributions to "team" accomplishments. With careful preplanning of the variable elements, measures of group accomplishment can often be worked into a combination plan to spread rewards more appropriately.

Disadvantages of Combination Plans. The combination plans are not without disadvantages. Inevitably, they are more complex, and consequently more time consuming to create, harder to administer, and more difficult for salesmen to comprehend fully—and comprehension is a must if the full benefit is to be realized. Because the factors governing the variable element are usually more sophisticated than mere reward for sales over quota, the plan must be reviewed continually to make sure that the factors support the objectives of the sales program.

WHAT AN INCENTIVE PLAN IS

"Incentive plans" are commonly spoken of as if they were a fourth classification beyond the three already discussed. Fundamentally, any compensation plan is an incentive plan—the "incentive" being the paycheck.

Strictly speaking, an incentive plan need not be a volume bonus plan or a commission plan where compensation is geared to sales volume. A salary plan, buttressed by a well-administered performance review program, can qualify as an incentive plan if good performance is a clear route to promotion and higher salary or leads to assignment to better territories. Combination plans where compensation is geared in part to performance evaluation, accomplishment of specific tasks, or faithful execution of nonselling tasks essential to the building of the business can also certainly qualify as incentive plans.

Incentive plans thus are not a breed apart, but merely a characteristic of most of the basic types already discussed. The term "incentive plan," however, is generally applied to those plans in which there is close correlation between additional compensation and performance, with more or less immediate and one-time rewards. Under this more limited definition, salary plans would be disqualified, and only commission or combination plans would be considered true incentive plans.

CONSIDERATIONS IN THE SELECTION OF A PLAN CONCEPT

Seldom is the manager given the opportunity for revision or replacement of a compensation plan until the situation is critical. He is most often handed a red-hot potato which he must somehow handle.

Faced with urgent compensation problems, most managers instinctively attempt either to patch the old plan with provisions that correct the recognized fault or to design a new plan which is primarily aimed at meeting the difficulty. All too often, this is exactly the wrong way to go about the task and a one-way ticket to problems of even greater magnitude. The trouble is that "problems" are frequently only symptoms of far more fundamental compensation malfunctions.

General Approach. Faced with the need to review, overhaul, or replace a compensation plan, the manager is well advised to look beyond the immediate "problem." A four-step approach is suggested:

1. Develop a full understanding of just what the salesman is supposed to be doing—that is, define the salesman's job.

2. Decide to what extent the compensation program can enhance the performance of the salesman's job—in other words, define the objectives of the new plan.

3. Match up the objectives of the plan with the characteristics, advantages, and disadvantages of the kinds of plan that might be selected, and choose the most appropriate alternative.

4. Then, and only then, start the development of the plan itself.

Defining the Selling Job. Although written definitions of all positions in the corporate organization are common, it is a pretty safe bet that the selling job will be the most poorly defined. This is not an accident. The selling job is perhaps the most difficult to define precisely; selling can be a very complex function. A usable definition of the salesman's job, however, in sufficient depth to indicate his full range of responsibility and the relative importance of the various parts, becomes a first order of business. Steps must be taken to develop this understanding.

Realistically, the best way for the manager to develop a full understanding of the salesman's job is to go into the field and review it thoroughly at first hand. Unfortunately, it is usually the professional consultants who will budget sufficient time for this activity. The internal manager tends to bypass it as unnecessary, but very few organization executives are so recently promoted from selling, or so closely involved in sales in their present assignment, that they can afford to do this. Salesmen should be interviewed and given full opportunity to discuss their jobs frankly, including what they think about compensation and how compensation can best be coupled with performance. The views of the sales managers should also be sought, and customer calls should be made both with and without salesmen—to observe the salesmen in action and to learn from the customer what activities should be stressed. The chances of developing a successful and acceptable plan increase in direct proportion to the plan designer's understanding of just what the good salesman can and cannot do within the limits of his assignment. Once this is clearly in focus, the task becomes much simpler.

Determining the Objectives of the Plan. The objectives of a compensation plan must be clearly defined and relatively simple. No plan can be made to serve too many objectives; it may get so complicated that it will actually be less effective than a plan of more limited scope. What should the manager consider when defining the objectives of the sales compensation plan?

First, such objectives should reflect the sales objectives of the company. By way of illustration, if a company's current marketing plan is undertaken to widen market horizons by selling existing products in markets where the company is not now represented, this objective should, as far as possible, be recognized in the compensation plan. Any features in plan design that would automatically dampen the salesmen's efforts in this direction should be rejected.

Second, the objectives of the plan must be legitimate. If, for example, a new plan is to be developed to reduce sales costs at present volumes—and this can be a legitimate objective—plan objectives should not be disguised as something else. If the issue is faced squarely and significant rewards are made available, but only for improved performance standards, reception may not be enthusiastic, but at least it will be based on sound understanding.

Third, the objectives of the plan must be realistic and attainable. If what appears to be a remunerative plan is thwarted by excessively high quotas or similar strategies for effectively reducing payout, the result can be more damaging than no plan at all. If plan rewards are based upon factors salesmen do not control—territory profitability, for example, where the salesmen can do little to influence profitability—the plan will be ineffective. In short, goals must be attainable, and the sales force must be capable of influencing the extent to which they are attained.

As a next step, subordinate characteristics of the plan should be formulated to accord with management's desires. The following are typical examples of features management may wish to have built in:

Reduction of sales costs as a percent of sales when volume increases

Provision to keep out-of-pocket expenses within a defined range as a percent of sales

Heightened sales attention to the performance of nonselling tasks such as reports on competitive activities, development of market information, preparation of sales plans, activity reports, and the like

Somewhat aside, inviting top management to express its individual concepts of desirable goals can serve two purposes for the manager designing the plan. In addition to refining the objectives before development of the plan begins, involving management tends to increase the tolerance and the cooperation the plan receives when it is launched. Although not all suggestions may be appropriate, most of them can be made workable through discussion, and the actual final objectives can be limited to a realistic base on which a useful plan can be built.

Finally, some further, very general objectives—perhaps better termed "criteria"—should be incorporated to ensure a successful plan. For the most part, they are reflections of good common sense. Thus, the plan must be:

Fair to the company and to the salesmen

Equitable and rewarding to all participants in proportion to the value of their contributions to the company

Explainable (plans which are based upon secret year-end calculations, or upon allocation decisions that are kept confidential within management, for example, are handicapped from the start)

As simple as practical in view of the objectives

Matching the Plan to the Company. The manager is now in a position to consider what type of plan and how much incentive are appropriate. The characteristics of the various plan types are summarized in Table 15-1. More than this must be taken into consideration, however. Different sales organizations, even those in the same markets and selling the same products, may not be equally well served by a given plan. Several factors intrude.

Experience and Sophistication of the Sales Organization. As a practical matter, one sales organization may be more ready to accept and benefit from a

TABLE 15-1. Summary of Characteristics of Various Plan Types

Type of plan	Generally most appropriate when	Advantages	Disadvantages
Salary plan.... ...	Sales job is very complex Group effort is required in most sales Sales are of high value but long in maturing Sales are cyclical	Is simple Costs are predictable Promotes stability in the organization Promotes maximum sales control	No direct incentive Most expensive in periods of low sales volume
Commission plan..	Sales volume is the most important measure of sales success Maximum incentive motivation is required Sales success parallels individual effort "Outside" sales organization is used	Offers maximum incentive for volume Is comparatively simple to administer Stabilizes cost-sales ratio Requires minimum capital	Difficult to manage Unpredictable total costs Inflexibility Possible costly "windfalls" Promotes the best interest of the salesman rather than of the company
Combination plan.	Complex selling task is to be rewarded; factors other than volume alone are considered important Incentive element is required	Provides a controlled incentive Combines the best elements of both salary and commission Protects both the salesman and the company Sharpens management involvement in planning and supervision	Complex, difficult to administer Effective only with relatively sophisticated sales organization

complex compensation plan than a second sales organization in the same business. If management has made progressive use of data and reports and has a well-established training program, sales personnel, both management and field, can be expected to be more receptive to a new concept and will more readily grasp its principles and use it effectively. If, on the other hand, management has been informal and previous compensation has been on a simple salary or commission basis, too drastic a departure can be a mistake. In this second type of organization, if a more comprehensive and more complex plan is clearly required, the plan should be implemented in steps, over a span of time, rather than in one major change.

Company Capability to Administer. A plan beyond the capability of the company to administer is almost as disastrous as a plan too advanced for the sales organization. Even though most commission plans are relatively simple, smaller firms with a relatively simple data-processing capability may find it difficult to keep commission accounts up to date and correct. Where commission payments are late or frequently in dispute, much dissatisfaction is generated and the effectiveness of the plan is diminished. Whatever the plan, the company must administer it accurately and promptly if the plan is to be effective.

Availability of Statistical Data. Another frequent problem is the lack of a sound statistical base on which to construct a plan. If good data do not exist, it would be a mistake to devise a plan requiring strong statistical backup. The company should select a more qualitatively based plan instead. If the weakness is in the company's data and not the industry's, a separate program to improve company data could be indicated, but the plan should not be based upon this expectation. To install a new compensation concept, and at the same time develop a statistical base from scratch to support it, is generally not wise.

Application of Incentives. To use or not to use incentives must be decided for each plan on the basis of two questions: Will their use contribute to sales effectiveness? Can they be equitably allocated in the particular situation? If either answer is negative, incentives should probably not be used.

Assuming positive answers, the next question is: How much incentive? Unfortunately, little specific advice can be given on this point, because the specific situation determines the best answer. Incentives must provide only the stimulus appropriate—neither so much that non-incentive-paying activities are neglected, nor so little that they have no effect. In most successful plans, sales incentives range from about 15 to 25 percent of base for good performance, with maximums for truly superior results topping at about 50 percent. Incentives that net the recipient much less than 15 percent in return for good performance will generally not provide very strong motivation. The plan designer must make his own selection of range guided by the salesman's job, the importance of the incentive, company willingness and ability to pay, industry practice, past practice within the company, and (most important) the objectives of the new plan.

DEVELOPMENT OF THE PLAN

Having chosen the type of plan most likely to succeed for the specific organization, the responsible manager is at last ready to begin actual plan design.

Plan Design. Here, a manager is pretty much on his own. The detailed plan should reflect all the requirements and limitations of his company, and therefore must be unique. Although there are thousands of compensation plans, few are more than generally similar. The single plan best suited to the company is an individual creation. Although detailed outlines of plans in actual use are available from numerous sources—the Bibliography at the end of this chapter contains many—the exact design and features of a specific plan depend on the needs of the situation and the ingenuity of the responsible manager designing the plan. Plans in use in his industry, or in organizations selling in a similar manner, will give insight into what may be workable and practical, but the specific features of the plan he designs must be tailored to the personnel of his organization, the selling job, the objectives of the plan, and the capability of his company to administer it and benefit from it.

For this task, the manager is now reasonably well prepared. He can define the appropriate incentive and the way in which his plan should be structured so that it becomes a useful management tool. In general, he should keep in mind the following four principles.

Provide for Change. The most certain single characteristic of a selling situation is that changes can be expected—changes from within and changes in the market. If product changes can be expected with relative frequency, for example, provision must be made to include new products and delete old ones without complete disruption of the compensation plan. Through circumstances beyond the salesman's control, good accounts are going to be lost and good accounts won, often not by all salesmen in proportion. The plan will not be successful if, by its inflexibility, it rewards and penalizes such events unjustly.

Provide for Easy Administration. The manager's responsibility does not stop with the assurance that the data are available or that the administrative requirements of the plan are within company capability. Before the plan can be considered complete, all details must be spelled out. These must include the written procedures for implementation of the plan—provision for instruction of management and salesmen, the necessary forms, the information requirements and their flow, and the authority and responsibility of all participants.

Details that can cause great furor if unresolved can often be handled easily if anticipated in advance. For example, rules must be made in advance to cover such matters as how transfers, terminations, or hirings in midperiod will be handled; how sales credit will be allocated where there are possibilities of split responsibility; how quotas will be established; and so forth.

Provide for Automatic Review. Most plans are reasonably good the day they are installed; the trick is to design a plan that will stay good. This can best be assured by periodic review, detecting problems before they become serious. It is the responsibility of the plan designer to ensure this critical administrative detail. Beyond the procedures for review, it is most important to fix the responsibility for administration of the plan. Build this into the concept, and make certain that this becomes a recognized part of the plan in its final form.

Design for Maximum Benefit. A plan that merely constitutes a mechanism for awarding the spoils may conceivably meet all of the qualifications so far discussed but still short-change the company. A prime value of a good plan is the influence it can exert toward the improvement of sales management. A good plan, by its design, can compel sales management to devote year-round sharpened attention to effective and equitable administration. This somewhat insidious approach—design of a plan that through its administration improves sales management—can pay greater dividends to the company than the mere allocation of sales rewards for which the plan was basically designed.

Testing the Concept. No matter how carefully a plan is thought through, "bugs" will show up when it is first tried. Good common sense suggests that the plan be tested before it is formally introduced.

Testing the Plan on Historical Sales. The simplest method of testing is to go back into previous sales records and synthesize the results of the plan, had it been effective then. If the plan is essentially quantitative, this procedure should provide a fair index of its cost and the way in which rewards would have been distributed. Unfortunately, if the plan calls for management participation and evaluation, this technique will fall short of evaluating the human factor and the problems that may result. For such plans, direct testing is a better technique.

Testing on Current Sales Samples. In some large organizations, it may be possible to apply the plan to selected individuals, or to a small, geographically defined section of the market. Usually, the period can be telescoped so that results can be obtained short of the cycle proposed in the actual plan. In this direct test, the problems in management training, use of forms, and the like, as well as the actual results, can be sampled, and problems identified and corrected.

Testing by Concurrent Run. When a sampling technique is not possible, the present plan and the new plan can be run concurrently for a trial period. Actual compensation should still be based upon the old plan. Results as they would have been on the new plan can then be compared to identify and correct problem areas. This technique is probably the best of the three, because it helps indoctrinate all hands in the new plan in a real situation. It is demanding of management and salesmen's time, however, and on this score may not be fully practical. Salesmen and managers alike tend to deprecate loudly the cost in time of administrative detail.

Installing the Plan. If all previous steps have been faithfully carried through—especially the pretesting—installation should be relatively simple. It is *extremely* important, however, to implement the plan with care. Several precautions will avoid difficulty.

Make Sure of Management Understanding and Support. Before the plan is installed, management must fully understand the plan and support it. This requirement starts with the president, or perhaps the board of directors in a smaller company, and goes down through the person or persons charged with executive responsibility for sales or marketing. To have top management discover features it did not know existed, or did not understand until after installation, can be totally destructive.

Indoctrinate Operating Sales Management. The next step in installation is to acquaint the operating levels of management—sales managers, product sales managers, district managers, and so on—with the details of the plan to be installed, and to explain their responsibilities thoroughly. This presentation also offers a final opportunity for field management to expose potential problems for discussion or to suggest refinements in the concept or administrative provisions.

Introduce the Plan to the Sales Organization Fully and with Care. This is a critical step. A new plan means change, and salesmen are naturally apprehensive of a change that affects their income. If the introduction of the plan to salesmen is slighted and they do not fully understand it, not only will potential benefits be lost, but resistance may be developed and barriers raised which seriously compromise or delay its full effectiveness. The presentations should be carefully prepared. The plan should be presented in a group meeting (or meetings) which, if possible, are personally attended and obviously endorsed by management representatives. Full discussion should be permitted, and explanatory booklets should be distributed for study. Questions arising after the meeting should be handled through the supervisors to whom the salesmen report.

SUMMARY

The manager charged with a sales compensation responsibility should approach it with the awareness that compensation is not a matter to be tinkered with before taking careful thought. His steps in reviewing a plan, or designing a new one, should be methodical and sequential, along the following lines.

Understand the different types of plan generally in use, the reasons for using each, and the general situations in which each is most applicable.

Fully investigate and understand the sales job which the compensation plan is to serve. Before attempting to rectify specific compensation problems, be sure of their source and their relationship to the task assigned the salesman.

Define the objectives of the company sales program, so that the plan can be tailored to the job the company wants to accomplish. Establish the potential role that incentives could appropriately play in the new plan.

Design the new plan, and determine, through test and careful review, that it is workable and effective, and that potential problems and pitfalls have been anticipated.

Install the new plan. Installation is a critical phase. Even if the plan is well conceived and workable, it can fail if top management does not fully understand its role and responsibility, and finally, if the person most affected—the salesman—is not fully aware of all details and has not been given full opportunity to question and understand all provisions.

BIBLIOGRAPHY

Barry, John, "A Guide to Better Methods of Sales Compensation," *Industrial Marketing*, May, 1963.

Barry, John, "How Industrial Salesmen Are Paid," *Industrial Marketing*, March, 1964.

Caswell, W. Cameron, "New Ways to Pay Salesmen," *Sales Management*, Mar. 15, 1963.

Compensation of Salesmen, Practices and Trends, The Dartnell Corporation, Chicago, published annually.

Corcoran, John F., "We Solved the Problem of Paying Industrial Salesmen for Group Effort," *Sales Management*, Jan. 15, 1955.

Day, Cameron, "How Should a Diversified Company Pay Its Salesmen?" *Sales Management*, Feb. 7, 1964.

Dick, Robert F., "Adapting Salesmen's Compensation and Territories to Changing Market Conditions," *Essentials of Successful Sales Management*, Marketing Series, no. 81, American Management Association, New York, 1951.

"How Sales Managers Handle the Split Commission Problem," *Industrial Marketing*, August, 1962.

"How Should Salesmen in Weak Territories Be Paid?" *Industrial Marketing*, September, 1961.

Olson, James C., "Evaluating and Revising Salesmen's Compensation Plans," *Analyzing and Improving Marketing Performance*, part 2, Management Report, no. 32, American Management Association, New York, 1959.

Stanton, William J., and Richard H. Buskirk, *Management of the Sales Force*, Richard D. Irwin, Inc., Homewood, Ill., 1959.

Tosdal, Harry R., and Waller Carson, Jr., *Salesmen's Compensation*, vols. 1 and 2, Harvard Business School, Division of Research, Boston, 1953.

Wilson, C. J., "Common Characteristics of Compensation Plans for Industrial Salesmen," Cresap, McCormick and Paget, New York, 1957.

CHAPTER SIXTEEN

The Government Market

FREDERICK W. HORNBRUCH, JR. *Vice President, Calumet & Hecla, Inc., General Manager, Flexonics Division, Bartlett, Illinois*

The government is a demanding customer. The risks are great—and the rewards can be substantial and far-reaching. Minimizing the pitfalls and obtaining the benefits on a continuous basis requires competent organization. Highly specialized skills in contract interpretation and proposal preparation, pricing and cost control, project and production direction, and attaining quality and reliability levels are fundamental to success. The impact on company operations and profits makes government sales a top management problem.

PROFILE OF THE GOVERNMENT MARKET

The United States government, with its many agencies and their needs, buys every conceivable product and service that the flourishing American economy has to offer. In its role as a customer, the government is demanding. Suppliers to the government may consider this attitude most difficult, but taxpayers should find it quite satisfying to know that public moneys are disbursed, audited, and guarded in a professional manner.

The purposes of government are very different from those of private industry and commerce. First, the basic reasons for the existence of government are to govern, to protect the national interest, and to maintain the prestige and leadership of the United States of America throughout the world. For these reasons, government must be demanding. Second, the government is a purchaser for use—not for resale. Many of the products that it purchases, especially in the fields of defense and aerospace, will be used by people. These products must have a high degree of integrity, and they must function successfully and repetitively. The government goes to great lengths to ensure that the desired degree of reliability is obtained in the products it purchases.

In the light of these demands and the generally known complexities of doing business with the government, why should any individual or any company seek government contracts? A fundamental reason is that patriotic citizens have a duty to serve their government. The productive systems of the United States and of the Soviet Union in their national, ideological, political, and economic aspects tend to engage in both cold and hot wars without letup. American businessmen have a responsibility to supply their government with the most advanced and the very best equipment it needs.

Fortunately, under our economic system it is possible to fulfill this patriotic responsibility and make a profit while doing it. Profit is not prohibited, nor frowned upon, in relation to government contracts. The company that knows its business can make profits in dealing with the government. True, there is a prevailing feeling that profits on government contracts should not be unreasonable and, therefore, legislation by both political parties historically has imposed limitations on profits. Industry generally has not found these limitations too restrictive, but it is absolutely imperative to recognize that special organization and special accounting are required to achieve these profits.

In addition, defense and aerospace plans, reaching far into the future, compel an exploration of technological problems with research into materials and devices well in advance of their use in weapons, systems, and vehicles. A knowledgeable company can participate in solving its problems of the future and in developing products for future markets by performing work for the government. It is axiomatic that the future belongs to the companies that earn it. Working on tomorrow's problems and products today is one way to grasp the leadership for the future.

Government business ranges from simple purchases of standard items to very complex research and development contracts. One way to understand the methods of doing business with the government is to study the most complex situation, knowing that all of the rules apply, but to lesser degrees, in the simpler and more routine cases. Unquestionably, the aerospace-defense market is the largest and the most complicated segment of government business. A company must have thorough and reliable answers to many questions to penetrate this market and perform successfully and profitably under contract. What governmental agencies are involved? How big is this market? What kinds of contracts are awarded? What methods of payment are in effect? What are the special problems to be anticipated and solved? What laws and regulations prevail? How best to organize to meet these conditions effectively?

THE AEROSPACE-DEFENSE MARKET

The aerospace-defense market consists of two basic types of agencies—those concerned directly with defense and the independent agencies possessing broader responsibilities for the national well-being and progress. The defense agencies include the Army, the Navy, the Air Force, and the Defense Supply Agency. The independent agencies are the General Services Administration (GSA), the Atomic Energy Commission (AEC), the Federal Aviation Administration (FAA), and the National Aeronautics and Space Administration (NASA). These agencies represent a combined annual purchasing power of substantial magnitude, as tabulated below for the fiscal year 1966 budgets.

The Aerospace-Defense Market

All Agencies	Billions
Procurement	$11.4
Research and development	6.7
Military construction	1.3
Military assistance	1.2
Atomic energy development	2.5
Space exploration (NASA)	5.3
Total	$28.4

This volume of procurement is awarded to American industry in a variety of ways. In general, the procuring agency determines the method of award. Management, however, to be successful, must understand the fundamental differences among types of awards and the essential requirements of each.

Types of Contracts. Basically, government contracts, especially those of the aerospace-defense agencies, are of two types: fixed price and cost reimbursable. The fixed-price type specifies a firm price for supplies or services and under certain circumstances allows for specific adjustments in price. The cost-reimbursable type provides for payment of contractor's allowable cost in performance to the extent established by the contract. Complete familiarity with the ramifications of these two basic types of contracts is essential for management to make certain that the method of award is workable and that the risks to the company are at a minimum.

Fixed-price Contracts. Firm fixed price provides for a fixed price not adjustable as a result of cost experience in performance. This type places maximum risk and maximum profit incentive on the contractor and is usually used for standard commercial items and military items for which firm prices can be developed.

Fixed price with escalation provides for upward or downward revision with ceilings based on specific contingencies defined by the contract. This type is employed where doubt exists as to the stability of the market or labor conditions for the period of production.

Fixed-price incentive provides for adjustment of profit based on an agreed relationship between incurred cost and target cost. The key is effective cost control and contract performance to maximize the contractor's profit.

Fixed price with prospective price redetermination provides for firm fixed price for initial period of performance and an upward or downward adjustment for the remainder of the performance period. This type is used where it is not possible to establish fair and reasonable prices for the total performance period.

Fixed price with retroactive price determination after completion is used to give weight to management effectiveness and ingenuity of the contractor during performance. This type of contract has very limited application and should be used cautiously.

Cost-reimbursable Contracts. Cost sharing is used for research and development procurements where the contractor agrees to share the cost in anticipation of substantial compensating benefits.

Cost plus incentive fee provides for fee adjustment in accordance with an agreed relationship between incurred cost and target cost. The incentive for maximum profit to the contractor for effective management is the basis for its application.

Cost plus a fixed fee provides for the payment of a fixed fee which does not vary with actual costs. This type provides minimum incentive for cost control and is out of favor as a procurement instrument by defense officials.

Time and materials provides for procurement based on labor hours at specified rates (direct and indirect labor, overhead, and profit) and materials at cost. This type is used when it is not possible to anticipate the extent or duration of the work. It does not encourage effective management control and is used guardedly.

Special Problems for Contractors. Government procurement presents special problems to management. These problems and conditions must be recognized at acceptance of a contract to properly and adequately meet the contractual obligations on a profitable basis. These problems are inherent in every government contract and extend to prime contractors and subcontractors.

Audit of Records. The Comptroller General has access to records pertinent to a contract or subcontract for three years from date of completion of the contract. Under this provision, government audit agencies have the right to audit earnings and costs on fixed-price as well as cost-type contracts.

Cost Breakdowns and Certificate of Current Pricing. In the procurement process, contracting officers have the responsibility to see that prices to the government are fair and reasonable. They have several devices by which they do this, called "cost analysis" and "price analysis." Two methods by which they assure themselves on a price are:

Cost breakdown. This breaks out a price into its components of materials, labor, services, overheads, and profit.

Certificate of current pricing by which the contractor, under penalty of perjury, certifies that he has supplied all current cost information to a contracting office in a price negotiation.

Profit. Profit is always a factor in considering government business.

Profit on fixed-price procurement is not limited by any statute or regulation. However, contracting officers must be satisfied that there is adequate price competition. If in their opinion there is not, they may require cost breakdowns.

Profit on cost-type contracts is subjected to these limitations:

Cost plus fixed fee (CPFF)—7 percent administrative limitations

Research and development (R&D)—10 percent administrative limitations

Architectural and engineering service—6 percent

The weighted-guidelines method of profit determination employed by the Department of Defense seeks to reward the contractor on the basis of judgment of certain factors of his contribution and performance. As a technique, it must be carefully examined and understood.

Inspection. Inspection constitutes a major problem for contractors. The purpose of the system is to see that the items conform to the requirements of the contract, all applicable drawings, specifications, and purchase descriptions. This inspection applies to raw materials, components, intermediate assemblies, and the end products. The inspection process may be many-tiered, as in the case of the Saturn Program, for example, which required:

1. Subcontractor inspection
2. Prime contractor inspection
3. Agency inspection
4. Cognizant service inspection and acceptance

Overhead Rates. At the inception of cost-reimbursable-type contracts, there is an agreement as to preliminary overhead rates to be used for billing purposes. At the end of the contractor's fiscal period, he submits schedules in support of his proposed rates for the period, which are then audited and negotiated. The final settlement is made applicable by amendment to the contract to the period involved. The risk to the contractor is that certain costs may be disallowed in calculating the overhead rates, and this could require a refund.

Government Property. In cost-reimbursable-type contracts, where costs are billed usually monthly, all materials for which billing is submitted, or which are received, become property of the United States government. Thus, the government requires that its property (raw material, purchased parts, completed assemblies, special tools, industrial facilities) be properly recorded, segregated, and controlled by the contractor.

Proprietary Products. The government requires that when it purchases a contractor's standard commercial product it pay a price no higher than that paid by the contractor's other customers.

Proprietary Data. Proprietary data are defined as the contractor's secrets of manufacture, such as his manufacturing methods or processes, treatment, chemical composition of materials, plant layout, and tooling to the extent that such information is not disclosed by inspection and analysis of the product itself. This is an area of great complexity and must be carefully approached prior to any agreement. There is a constant struggle between the government and contractors as to what rights the government purchases when it enters cost-reimbursable-type contracts, especially for research and development. The government takes the position that it purchases all the data generated in the performance of the contract, sometimes including the contractor's background data. Usually, the contractor's position is that the government has rights only to the data developed in the course of performance, and none of the background data.

Government and Customer Residents. Frequently the government and prime contractors want their own personnel on the contractor's premises. The government may assign a resident contracting officer with his own audit, inspection, and administrative staff. A prime contractor may place a resident team, consisting of an engineer, a quality-control man, and a production specialist, to assist with on-the-spot activity. There are plus and minus values to such residency, depending upon the capability, primary interest, and acceptability to the contractor of the people in residence. In general, resident personnel can be very helpful to the contractor.

Federal Statutes and Regulations. In addition to a working knowledge of the types of contracts and the special problems inherent in government procurement, there are important Federal statutes, executive orders, and regulations that must be understood and obeyed. The laws that in 1965 were part of every government contract are as follows.

Armed Services Procurement Act of 1947 brings together in one statute all Department of Defense procurement authority. Under the terms of the Act, Department of Defense issues its Armed Services Procurement Regulations (ASPR), which establish the broad guidelines under which procurements are made. Each service publishes procedures which parallel and supplement the ASPR. They are Army Procurement Procedure (APP), Air Force Procurement Instructions (AFPI), and Navy Procurement Directive (NPD).

In addition, Federal Procurement Regulations (FPR) are the basic procurement policies of the civilian agencies of the government. The Atomic Energy Commission and National Aeronautics and Space Administration have issued detailed instructions which implement the FPR.

Buy American Act prohibits the use of materials and supplies in government-procured items if not produced or manufactured in the United States.

Anti-kickback Act forbids a subcontractor from making payments to a prime contractor or a higher-tier subcontractor to secure a subcontract under certain cost-type contracts with the United States.

Davis-Bacon Act requires that all laborers and mechanics on Federal construction be paid prevailing wages.

Work Hours Act of 1962 provides that wages must be computed on the basis of an eight-hour day, forty-hour week, with payment of overtime for all hours in excess of the basic day and week to certain classes of laborers.

Fair Labor Standards Act of 1938 establishes minimum wages and makes overtime that which is in excess of forty hours per week.

Miller Act requires a payment and performance bond for fixed-price construction in excess of $2,000.

Renegotiation Act of 1951 provides for refunding to the government of excess profits earned on national defense contracts.

Vinson Trammel Act provides for return to the government of all profits in excess of 10 percent of contract price for naval craft, and 12 percent for aircraft.

Walsh-Healy Public Contracts Act establishes minimum wages, overtime, sanitary conditions, and standards for health and safety of employees on Federal supply contracts exceeding $10,000.

Civil Rights Act of 1964 provides for no discrimination because of race, color, religion, sex, or national origin.

ORGANIZATION

Government business is a top management problem of organization, planning, and control.   An effective way in which to organize to obtain government contracts and then to perform to the governmental agency's satisfaction with profit retained by the company is to establish a government contracts department, utilizing the program management concept.   Program management is becoming an increasingly important part of doing business with the government and is a contractual requirement in most major government contracts.

Government Contracts Department.   The organization chart in Figure 16-1 illustrates the three major functions—proposals, contract administration, and program management—of a government contracts department and identifies the important duties to be performed by each functional group.   Under this organizational arrangement, all contracts are processed by the proposals and the contract administration groups, but the activities of the program management group are concentrated on major and highly specialized contracts only.

Program Management.   A significant key to achieving cost, technical, and performance objectives lies in the duties and responsibilities of the program management staff.   (See also Chapter 5 of Section 5.)   The organization chart in Figure 16-2 shows the program manager assisted by a program specialist, a program control engineer, and a program cost analyst.   The program manager supervises and directs the activities of these assistants.   The systems engineering manager, reporting to the director of engineering, and the manufacturing project

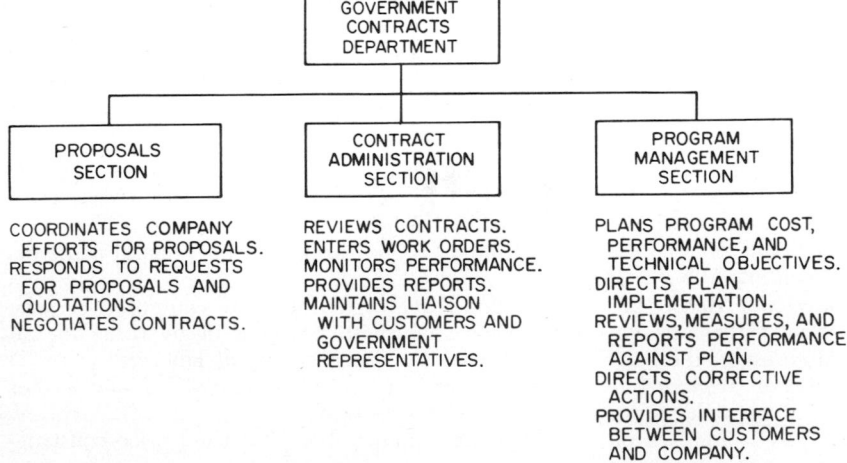

FIG. 16-1.   *Organization of a typical government contracts department.*

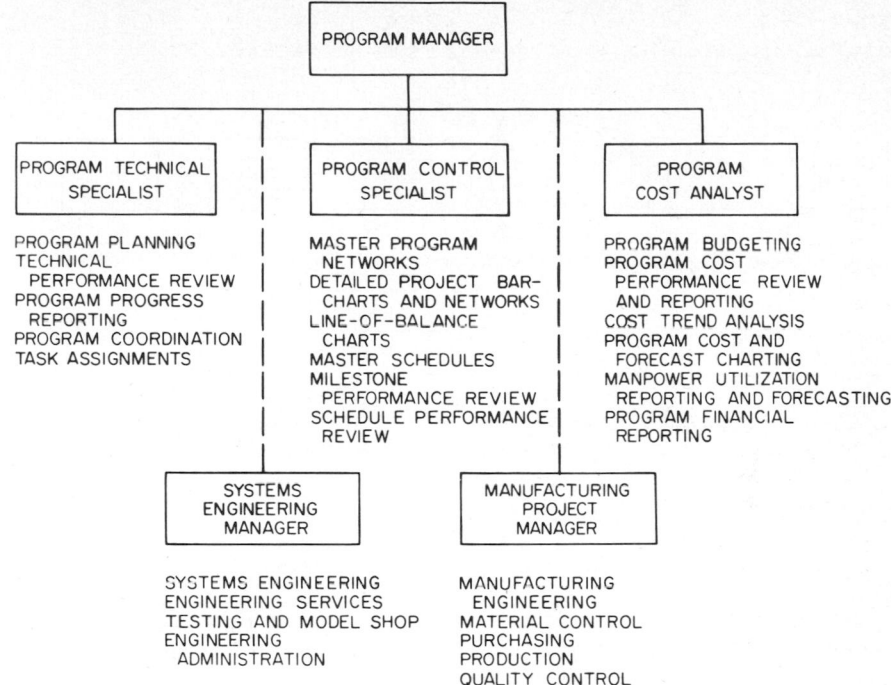

FIG. 16-2. *Organization chart of the program management activity.*

manager, reporting to the director of manufacturing, represent the program manager and are responsible for controlling the programs according to plan within their functional areas. Thus, in effect, the program management team is superimposed on the regular line and staff organization to give detailed attention to every phase of the government contracts under their surveillance. This is a planning and control function. The successful completion of research and development, engineering design, building of prototypes, qualification testing, manufacture of hardware, and acceptance testing is clearly identified and established as the responsibility of the regular line management.

Although it might appear that the start and completion of tasks and the control of costs could be handled simply after the detailed plans and schedules were established, the program management function is able to evaluate trade-off and interface, as well as customer requirements, with much greater speed and effectiveness than normally can be expected by the regular line management and systems centers. In general, this is because of the specialized knowledge needed to understand the ramifications of each major government contract and customer fully, and the total impact of changes and deviations from plan.

Program management can be helpful in recognizing problems well in advance of their effect on the end result of a project. For example, in one situation program management, through constant monitoring of progress, was able to pinpoint that the end date of the project was in serious jeopardy because of minor problems in four unrelated departments. The individual departments were not fully aware of the impact their particular problem area would have on the end result and had not planned for sufficient corrective action. By bringing together top management and the managers of the departments

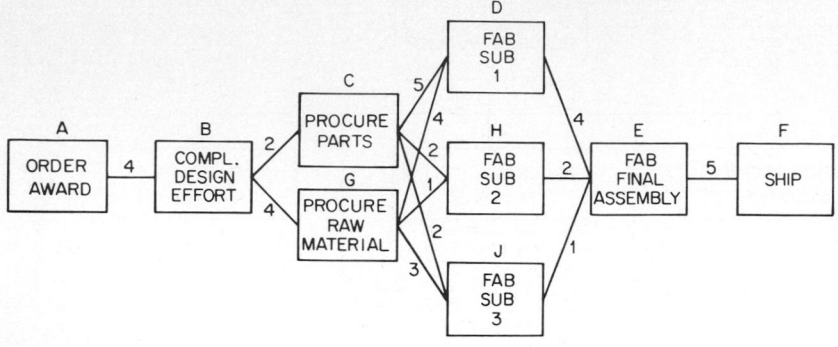

TIME CYCLES

A B C D E F = 20 WEEKS
A B C H E F = 15 WEEKS
A B C J E F = 14 WEEKS
CRITICAL PATH A B G D E F = 21 WEEKS
A B G H E F = 16 WEEKS
A B G J E F = 17 WEEKS

FIG. 16-3. *PERT network. This visual method charts major milestones with time values in the sequence of events. It provides a means for determining the overall completion time and highlights the "critical path" or limiting sequence. (See also Chapter 6 of Section 17.)*

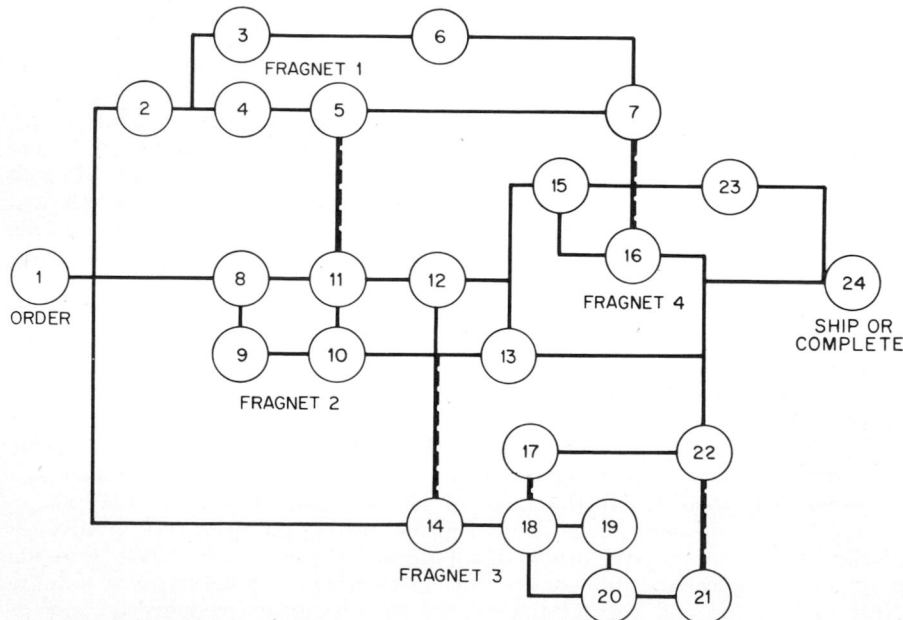

FIG. 16-4. *Program network. A program network, issued at the outset of a contract, graphically relates the work of all involved organizations and provides visibility for critical activity monitoring. No time values are assigned to this type of network. It is revised and reissued only when sequence and restraint between activities are altered. Numbers have no numerical significance, but do define critical events. Dashed lines represent restraints.*

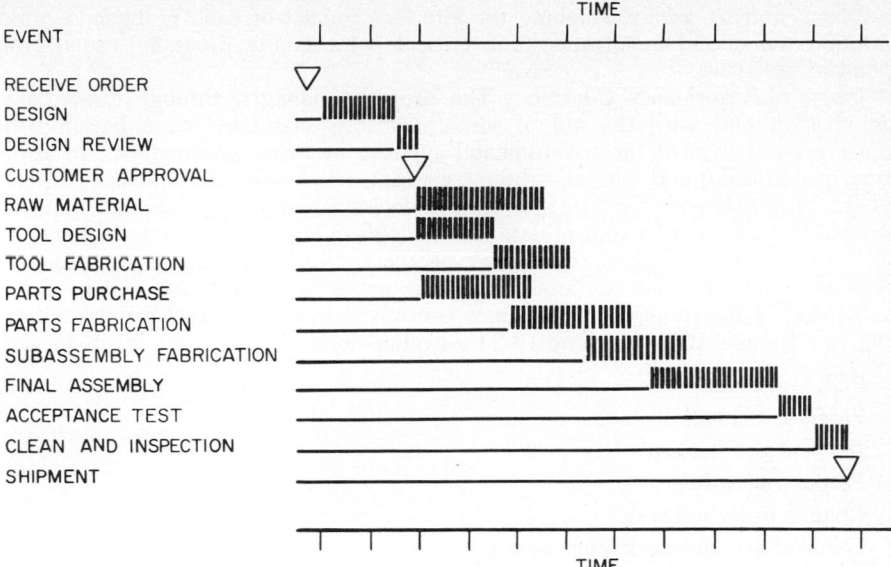

FIG. 16-5. *Bar and event chart. Commonly referred to as a "Gantt chart," this is one of the oldest methods for visual planning and control. Each activity or item is assigned a block of time for its task and is monitored within that segment. The start and completion of each activity is time-related to the other functions to be performed. Program status can be readily evaluated.*

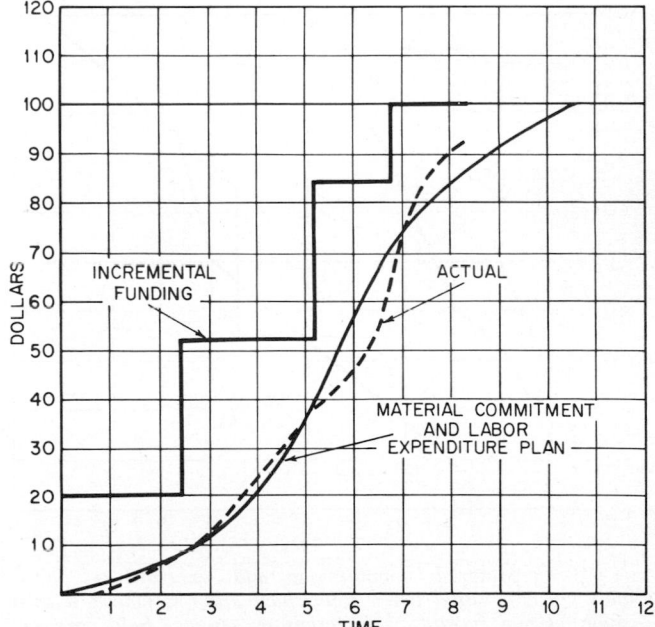

FIG. 16-6. *Cost plan versus funding chart. In incrementally funded contracts, this management tool presents a picture of the expected rates of funding and expenditure with which the actual expenditures are compared. This provides a basis for financial planning and control.*

involved, and by jointly weighing the interface impact of each problem, a rapid solution was found in advance of a critical point in the program—usually the point of no return.

Program Performance Controls. The program manager, through direct communication and with the aid of visual controls, maintains close liaison with the representatives of the governmental agencies or prime contractors. In addition, periodically, and when conditions warrant, he reviews all significant aspects of the programs with top management for decision and appropriate action. The preparation of program control data into simplified, readily understandable charts saves hours of discussion, eliminates needless misunderstandings, and directs management's attention to areas requiring immediate corrective action.

Typical of the program performance controls that may be used are the following (see Figures 16-3, 16-4, and 16-5 for explanations):

PERT network
Program network
Bar and event chart
Program schedule
Change order network
Detailed schedules for engineering
Detailed schedules for production

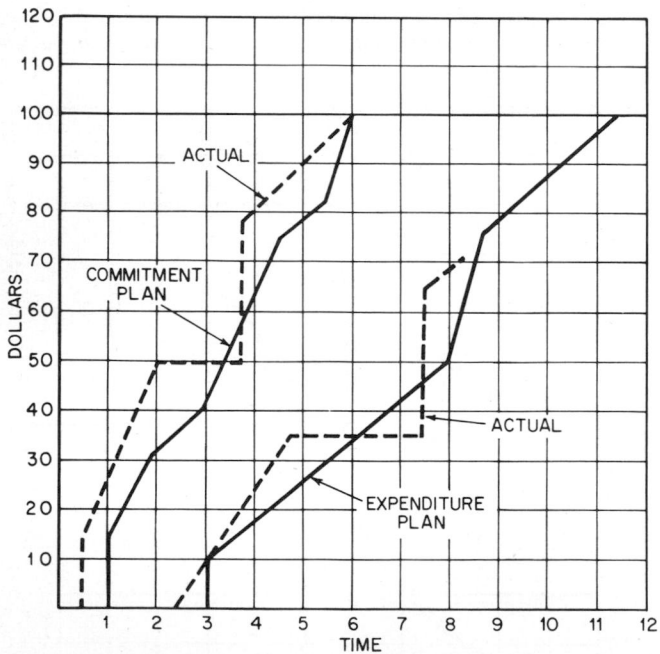

FIG. 16-7. *Material commitment and expenditure chart. Funds are committed when a purchase order is placed with a vendor. Upon receipt of materials or service, funds are expended. This chart establishes a plan for both transactions and provides a basis for funding forecasts and expenditure trend analysis.*

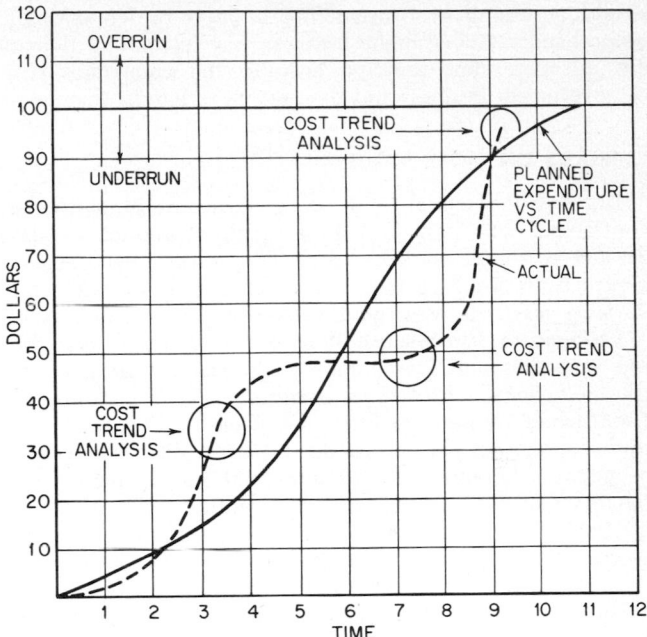

FIG. 16-8. *Cost trend analysis chart. This type of chart allows visibility for comparing planned expenditures with actual costs. It permits analysis on a timely basis of variations from plan. Three points are indicated at which sufficiently significant variations occurred to warrant a detailed analysis of the cost trend.*

Program Financial Controls. Representative program financial controls that should be considered are as follows (see Figures 16-6, 16-7, and 16-8 for explanations):

Program financial forecast
Cost plan versus funding chart
Program budget
Departmental budget and performance reports
Manpower planning and performance tables
Material commitment and expenditure chart
Cost trend analysis chart

Program Management Vital. The program management concept and organization are vital to success in completing complex government contracts profitably and with assurance that the company will be given opportunities to submit proposals for follow-on and additional contracts in the future. Program management, by defining objectives, planning to meet objectives, and controlling within the plan, is valuable in helping management meet technical, performance, quality, and schedule objectives—all within allowable costs. Program management may seem overly complicated and detailed, but government business is complex, and profits are difficult to grasp and to hold. A metal fabricator would not dream of starting up a 100-ton press without first setting it up properly. A contractor would not think of constructing a large bridge without carefully designing it beforehand. Government business has its unique demands, too. The rewards are adequate, but they go only to the companies that study the intricacies of government business and then set up to handle them effectively.

EMPHASIS ON MORE VALUE

Industry in general, and the government in particular, is constantly seeking contractors who can provide a quality product or service of high reliability at low cost and on schedule. The government, especially with development contracts, is firmly committed to the premise that completion on schedule invariably results in costs within forecasts. The emphasis is on more value.

Performance Improvement Programs. Programs may be established for meeting schedules and giving more value by inspiring people to "do the job right the first time." *First-time performance!* These programs can center around the themes of Zero Defects, Do Good Work, Pride, Perfection—all designed to encourage employees to do a better job. These performance improvement programs, although not a contractual requirement, are a significant factor in the evaluation of contractors' capabilities. The Flexonics Division of Calumet & Hecla, Inc., studied the successful programs of other companies in the aerospace-defense market, and with assistance from the government, selected those elements that applied best to its operations. The Flexonics program is a good example of these performance improvement programs, because it was developed by selecting the best of the best. It will be described briefly as a guide to those who may wish to establish a similar program.

Target: Perfection. The Flexonics' Target: Perfection program, FT:P, is a way of life at Flexonics. Expressed in its simplest terms, FT:P is aimed at getting the job—any job, every job—done right the first time, everytime. Flexonics is seeking perfection, and its management believes, urges, in fact insists: "It is a reasonable goal to try to do everything right the first time."

FT:P is a total program involving *all work* by *all employees*, for *all products* to serve *all customers*. It applies to salesmen, engineers, and foremen, as well as to production employees. It covers aerospace, industrial, and commercial work, development and testing, prototypes, and production.

FT:P was announced in a series of employee assemblies and this was followed by a family open house. The open house had escorted tours, displays, refreshments, souvenirs, and brochures telling the families about FT:P. These are two paragraphs from the brochure:

Simple errors made by an assembly worker, a typist, an engineer, and a supervisor are seemingly unrelated. In most cases, they are easily corrected. Most people hardly think twice about them. It could be said that people have grown accustomed to a standard which accepts a few daily mistakes as the price of being human. Unfortunately, if each person at Flexonics makes an "insignificant" mistake each day, the collective result is far from insignificant.

"To err is human"—is it a valid outlook? In personal business, no one is willing to accept a 5% error in his paycheck or in his change at the store. No one expects to get into the wrong car 5% of the time. Why, then, should anyone be willing to settle for making errors in 5%, or even 1%, of his work? FT:P is everyone trying to do the job right the first time . . . everytime.

The facilities are saturated with the FT:P symbol. Employees cannot go 50 feet without seeing FT:P—a constant reminder of the goals being sought. The symbol is the first thing the employees observe coming into the plant and the last thing as they leave. FT:P is on a pennant flying beneath the American flag on the flagpole. It is on gate signs, posters, forms such as interoffice memos, purchase orders, and pay envelopes, and scoreboards.

Pledge to Customers. Following the open house, all employees were asked to sign personal pledges. The personal pledge reads:

Realizing that my work and responsibilities have direct effect on the quality, reliability, delivery, or price of our products, I hereby pledge *to our customers* that I will accept perfection as my personal target and that I will strive for first-time, error-free performance at all times.

In addition, the management staff signed a division pledge. Everyone is committed and dedicated to the success of the Flexonics' Target: Perfection program.

Barrier Identification. A fundamental feature of FT:P is barrier identification. Through the barrier identification procedure, each employee has the opportunity to identify causes of errors and problems—barriers to first-time, error-free performance. It is unnecessary for the employee to offer a solution—just the barrier, which then is investigated. Within ten days the employee receives a report stating the action that will be taken to break the barrier. This is not a suggestion system. A single proposed solution is not being evaluated. The problems are sought, and then it is the responsibility of the functional organization to take appropriate action to solve the problems.

Individual Recognition. Recognition is given from time to time for outstanding individual performances and extraordinary contributions to FT:P. This is done on bulletin boards, through a newsletter, and with other forms of public recognition. The management feels, however, that most important is the self-recognition by the employee and the sense of achievement, the inspiration, and the pride that come from knowing that he or she has contributed importantly to the success of Flexonics.

Scoreboards. The score is kept, also. One thing that makes a ball game exciting is the score. Each employee with a small group of associates has the opportunity to demonstrate "publicly" progress toward the Flexonics' Target: Perfection. Flexonics' employees are assigned to program units, averaging twenty employees per unit, with each unit headed by a unit administrator. Each FT:P unit has a 4- by 4-foot scoreboard for charting improvement in performance as measured by a factor significant to the vital function the group is organized to perform.

These scoreboards are mounted out in full view throughout the plant. Everyone can see the progress that is being made. The scoreboards are plotted weekly or monthly, highlighting a variety of factors, such as pieces rejected, orders delinquent, projects late, customer rejections, vendor rejections, errors made—whatever measurement is most appropriate, most significant for each FT:P unit. Figure 16-9 shows a typical scoreboard.

Organization. The administration of FT:P is carried on by a planning council, headed by the FT:P director, who reports directly to the president. The position is filled by the director of employee and community relations. His staff consists of five FT:P managers, one each from finance, engineering and development, and marketing, and two from manufacturing. Then there are unit administrators reporting directly to the FT:P managers. All of these people are management personnel and administer FT:P in addition to their regular functional responsibilities in the division.

The planning council has a group function to plan the FT:P program, to develop innovations, and to select individuals and units for special recognition. Each member of the planning council also has an individual responsibility to

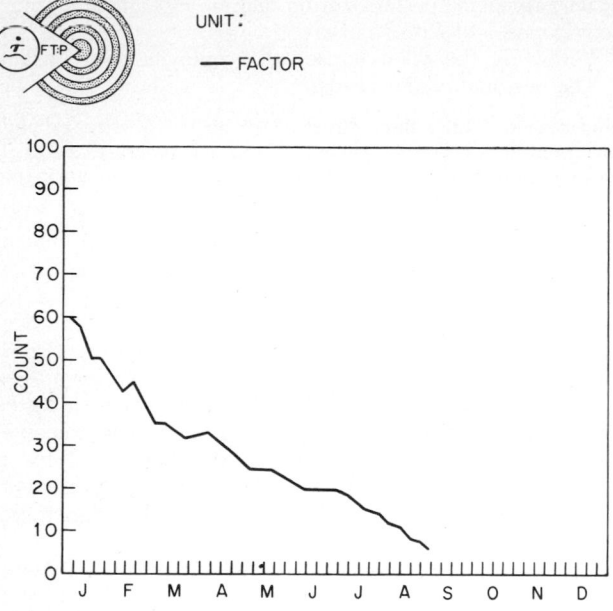

FIG. 16-9. *Typical scoreboard used in the FT:P program.*

maintain effective saturation with the FT:P concept and symbol and to supervise the activities of the FT:P unit administrators. In turn, the unit administrators maintain the scoreboards, make the barrier identification procedure work, and implement innovations to sustain a high degree of employee interest in the program.

Sustaining Employee Interest. The efforts of the planning council and the unit administrators in sustaining the interest of the employees is supplemented in several ways, one of which is employee assemblies. For example, three or four times a year the president meets with the employees to review the progress being made and to spell out plans for the future. At other meetings, customers are invited to speak to the employees. The outside speakers are from both aerospace and commercial companies. A newsletter helps to keep the employees informed and interested. FT:P was announced to the vendors, who responded enthusiastically. The announcement was followed by other enticements and lures designed to bring the vendors into the program in an important way. Internal programs are related to FT:P where there is a logical relationship, such as in training programs and in the work of value-analysis teams. New ideas and innovations are constantly being sought to maintain employee interest at the high level necessary to reach Flexonics' Target: Perfection.

Target: Perfection—A Fundamental Attitude. Flexonics, like most companies, has need for a continuous program for improving quality and reliability, for meeting delivery promises, and for reducing costs. At Flexonics, FT:P is that program, and it is organized to be an important, permanent part of operations. Management expects a lot from FT:P because management expects a lot from the employees. Management has confidence in their natural competence and in their willingness to strive for perfection. The employees know this.

The FT:P program must be administered well, and the organization has been established to do this. However, the success of FT:P has been clearly identified and established as the responsibility of the regular line management. Basically, that success is measured by Flexonics' ability consistently to give the customers more value.

SUMMARY

Continued profitable performance on government contracts requires sound organization staffed with capable, knowledgeable people who are specialists in the many facets of government business. Program management and programs similar to FT:P are important tools which, when used expertly, can facilitate successful penetration of the government market.

BIBLIOGRAPHY

Bloom, William, "Line-of-balance Technique Directs Decision Making," *Aerospace Management,* December, 1961.

Davis, Charles L., "Command Control at Honeywell," *Aerospace Management,* July, 1962.

Defense Industry Bulletin, Director of Community Relations, Office of Assistant Secretary of Defense (Public Affairs), Room 2E 772, The Pentagon, Washington 25, D.C.

Fleming, Quentin W., and Charles W. Ervin, "Management Aids for Program Control," *Aerospace Management,* July, 1962.

Geddes, Phillip, "Centaur: How It Was Put Back on Track," *Aerospace Management,* April, 1964.

Geddes, Phillip, "Customer Closes Loopholes in Program Management," *Aerospace Management,* April, 1964.

Hinckley, Robert H., "The Sub-contractor, Manage or Monitor Him?" *Aerospace Management,* February, 1964.

McDonald, Paul M., "Government Prime Contracts & Sub-contracts Service," Procurement Associates, Inc., Glendora, Calif.

The National Defense Education Institute Publications, Harbridge House, Boston.

Odegaard, Oscar T., "When Planning Contract Production, Add the Financial Dimension," *North American Aviation Bulletin,* June, 1964.

Sobczak, Thomas V., "Basic Networks Can Make or Break Your System," *Aerospace Management,* May, 1962.

Trueger, Paul M., *Accounting Guide for Defense Contracts,* 4th ed., Commerce Clearing House, Inc., Chicago, 1963.

United States Army Missile Command, Redstone Arsenal, Huntsville, Ala., *Zero Defects Kit.*

U.S. Department of Defense, Washington, D.C., *Zero Defects.*

U.S. Government Printing Office, Washington, D.C., *Armed Services Procurement Regulations.*

U.S. Government Printing Office, Washington, D.C., *Atomic Energy Commission Procurement Regulations.*

U.S. Government Printing Office, Washington, D.C., *Federal Procurement Regulations.*

U.S. Government Printing Office, Washington, D.C., *National Aeronautics and Space Administration Procurement Regulations.*

U.S. Government Printing Office, Washington, D.C., *U.S. Government Purchasing, Specifications and Sales Directory.*

The George Washington University Publications, Washington, D.C., *Government Contracts Program.*

CHAPTER SEVENTEEN

Promotional Decision Making

PATRICK J. ROBINSON   *Marketing Science Institute, Philadelphia, Pennsylvania*

Of all the decisions marketing managers must make, questions concerning promotional allocations are the most difficult and troublesome. Some measure of the size and importance of the problem can be gained from the fact that by the mid-1960s some $15 billion were being spent annually for advertising—just one element in the promotional program. Funds are needed for the total promotional "mix" of advertising, personal selling, and sales promotion. Allocation of these funds involves the process of promotional decision making from the time work is begun on planning the program to the final allocation of funds for specific activities and the execution and follow-up phases.

Effective promotional decision-making procedures in the marketing area have not yet been adequately developed. Therefore, this chapter cannot present the kind of "how to do it" information which is typically found in a handbook. It will of necessity largely confine itself to pointing out weaknesses in existing promotional decision-making practices which were identified by a study made in 1964 by the Marketing Science Institute. However, the manager can evaluate the practices currently followed in his own company against those uncovered by the study, and thus identify areas in which improvements can and should be made.

Problems of Determining the Promotional Mix: The Human Element. In decisions involving trade-offs of personal selling, sales promotion, and advertising efforts, consumer-goods companies tend to focus most attention on advertising dollars that are spent, whereas, in contrast, industrially oriented companies appear to focus more on the personal selling function. There is not usually a careful look at the whole cross section illustrated by Figure 17-1. The question is, how should promotional mix expenditures be traded off one against the other? This can be difficult.

For one thing, you may talk to various people with different points of view concerning marketing allocation decisions. Each person's approach will be quite different in terms of what his perception of the problem is and what techniques may seem appropriate to the problem. Furthermore, there exists a difficult communications problem when bringing line management people into direct contact with very theoretical work. The practical operating person tends to be overwhelmed by the complexity of mathematical and behavioral terminology, and rejects analytical representations or models. The management scientist, for his part, frequently throws up his hands at the lack of explicit decision rules or definitive examples as a basis for effective monitoring, control, and prediction.

Figure 17-2 indicates how the three distinct groups bring three different points of view to bear on promotional decision-making problems, and how these groups interact with each other. The double-headed arrows indicate that communication and guidance are potentially two-way activities. The broken arrow connecting "operations and practice" with "basic science" is merely to suggest that this flow appears minimal. Seldom do managers and management scientists enjoy sufficient interaction. All too often, the flow between these groups is slow and uncertain, frequently because of a problem of jargon. Fortunately, however, to a limited degree, the line group benefits from staff support, and staff people benefit from basic research and development.

Adaptive Planning and Control Sequence (APACS). To determine current practices in preparing promotional plans and allocating funds to various activities during the course of the Marketing Science Institute study, intensive interviews were held (over a period of a year and a half) with key personnel in twelve companies and, when necessary, with representatives of the companies' advertising agencies. More than 100 individuals were interviewed, many of them a number of times.

In these discussions, questions and conversations were limited to promotional decisions for distinctly new products, because these decisions were more likely to be made deliberately after a review of a wide range of alternatives. They would be more easily remembered than actions taken on relatively minor variations introduced into established lines. Although each company was found to have its own approach to making marketing decisions, few of the companies had a specific routine or structure that was followed in planning and controlling decision-making activities.

Therefore, to aid in discussing and classifying the promotional decision practices found in the twelve cases, a reference structure (or conceptual model) of the decision process was developed. It is called the "adaptive planning and control sequence," or APACS. The APACS exhibit provides a diagram of the steps that are taken, at least implicitly, from the time a decision is made to promote a product, and the initial statement of the problem, to the eventual evaluation of the decision. The APACS chart illustrates the decision-making

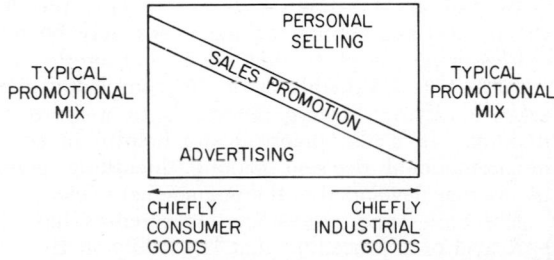

FIG. 17-1. *Promotional mixes for consumer and industrial goods.*

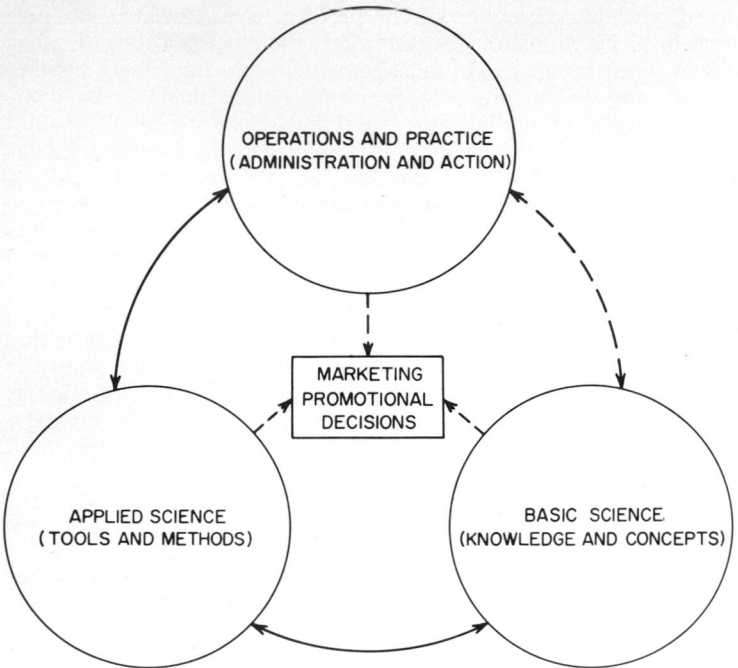

FIG. 17-2. *Illustration of the primary centers of concentration relevant to the promotional allocation process.* (*From Patrick J. Robinson and David J. Luck,* Promotional Decision Making: Practice and Theory, *McGraw-Hill Book Company, New York, 1964.*)

process as a series of eight steps, each with its own descriptive heading and brief explanation. The headings are as follows:

    I. Define problem and set objectives
   II. Appraise overall situation
  III. Determine tasks and identify means
  IV. Identify alternative plans and mixes
   V. Estimate expected results
  VI. Review and decision by management
 VII. Feedback of results and post-audit
VIII. Adapt program if required

In addition to describing these steps, the APACS chart indicates how, in the process of decision making, steps may be retraced or "recycled" when difficulties or new opportunities are encountered. This is illustrated by Figure 17-3.

APACS is a valuable device in comparing and contrasting observed practices and identifying existing deterrents to a more systematic approach to decision making. It is also practical and helpful in considering potential improvements in promotional decision making, including giving perspective to some of the techniques developed in the management sciences.

Executives and professional researchers have found APACS to be a realistic portrayal of a procedure that has utility in their companies' operations. APACS has been adopted as a decision-aiding device by a number of firms. Although it is only a simple, basic tool, subject to further refinement, APACS is of value

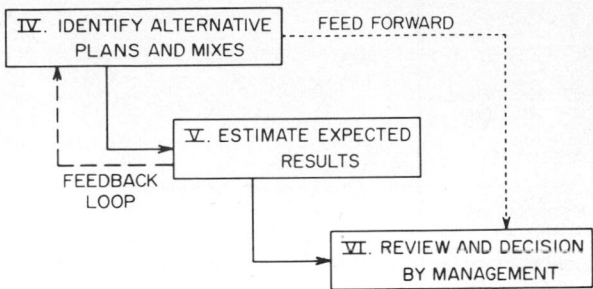

FIG. 17-3. *Example of recycling and adaptive processes.*

in establishing preferred practices and providing adequate records and reviews for company management.

Now, when we look into this promotional decision-making area, one of the things that becomes evident is that the practice of these eight steps can also be matched against theory potentially corresponding to these steps. The trouble is that this theory is loaded with jargon; and much of it is difficult or costly to apply. Each of the jargon words listed in Figure 17-4 includes a whole family of scientific techniques—a few of which may sound familiar. On close examination of the state of the art and practice today, we see that the promise exceeds performance. Much needs to be done. The question is, if you are going to get mileage from these new tools of the management sciences, how do you get it without being overwhelmed in all the detail and jargon? Here again, the problem is one of communication. We are indeed "separated by our common language." There are staff people who are trained in these exotic new methods, and operating people who are actively living these APACS steps. The only question of merit is: What do these people have in common, and how can they get together to exploit the available research and development (R&D) for their own situations? Chapter 5 of Section 1, "The Management Sciences," deals with this important question of recognizing opportunities and exploiting this new form of R&D in business.

General Observations on Typical Practices and Problems of Promotional Administration

1. Frequently, the key product and brand managers are not adequately aware of the objectives and broad strategies of the overall product program which the promotion plan is designed to implement.

2. Personal selling plans are often divorced from the planning of advertising and sales promotion despite their obvious interaction in the marketplace. The few exceptions observed appear chiefly among industrial products.

3. The working planner is customarily expected to prepare only one allocation plan for a product. This is apparently all he has time to do. Alternative marketing or promotional strategies, therefore, do not receive full consideration. Also, the number of alternative promotion tools considered is often limited. Decisions on the funds allocated among alternative promotional methods usually lack objective measures of effectiveness or even reliable sets of guidelines.

4. Lacking alternative strategies, the planner is unprepared to meet contingencies and to adapt the program readily to feedback of its effects, or to adjust to environmental changes.

5. "Negative" planning, to be implemented should expenditures be cut back, is usually missing. The military parallel is called "contingent planning to permit retiring to prepared positions." Unforeseen cutbacks are a frequent occurrence

METHODOLOGICAL CONTRIBUTIONS: (GENERAL CATEGORIES)	I. DEFINE PROBLEM AND SET OBJECTIVES	II. APPRAISE OVERALL SITUATION	III. DETERMINE TASKS AND IDENTIFY MEANS	IV. IDENTIFY ALTERNATIVE PLANS AND MIXES	V. ESTIMATE EXPECTED RESULTS	VI. REVIEW AND DECISION BY MANAGEMENT	VII. FEEDBACK OF RESULTS AND POSTAUDIT	VIII. ADAPT PROGRAM IF REQUIRED	NO. OF CONTRIBUTIONS	
STATISTICAL INFERENCE AND ESTIMATION		X			X		X		3	STATISTICAL INFERENCE AND ESTIMATION
ECONOMETRICS		X			X				2	ECONOMETRICS
EXPERIMENTAL DESIGN					X		X		2	EXPERIMENTAL DESIGN
STOCHASTIC PROCESSES					X				1	STOCHASTIC PROCESSES
ANALYTICAL TECHNIQUES					X	X			2	ANALYTICAL TECHNIQUES
MATHEMATICAL PROGRAMMING					X				1	MATHEMATICAL PROGRAMMING
DECISION AND SEARCH THEORY			X	X	X	X	X		5	DECISION AND SEARCH THEORY
VALUE THEORY	X		X	X	X	X	X	X	7	VALUE THEORY
BEHAVIORAL MODELS	X	X			X	X	X	X	6	BEHAVIORAL MODELS
SIMULATION AND GAMING	X				X	X	X	X	5	SIMULATION AND GAMING
ANALYTICAL PHILOSOPHY			X	X					2	ANALYTICAL PHILOSOPHY
CYBERNETICS AND SERVO THEORY							X	X	2	CYBERNETICS AND SERVO THEORY
NUMBER OF CONTRIBUTIONS	3	3	3	3	10	5	7	4	38	NUMBER OF CONTRIBUTIONS

FIG. 17-4. *Scientific contributions to the adaptive planning and control sequence (APACS).*

and "occupational hazard." Promotional funds are often the first to be reduced when profits are threatened. Sometimes, this is referred to as "cutting out some of the fat."

6. Sales and market-share goals tend to be held constant, regardless of decreases or increases in promotional expenditures. Thus they become unrealistic as guides or directives for planning, or as criteria of promotional effectiveness, or even as a fair basis for application of the judgment of management.

7. Individuals in companies rarely state that they know all they need to know or that they see little need for improvement in decision aids or new tools. However, in these rare cases, it is interesting to note that some of the most successful managers appear to be those who establish a set of guidelines and procedures which they regard as firm and valid, and which they are prepared to pursue resolutely.

8. Some people who earn a reputation as being decisive, self-confident, and successful are individuals who seem to "roll with the punches" and apparently do not tolerate indecision or uncertainty in their operations. They appear to follow the old military axiom that it is better to do something than to do nothing.

9. In many companies, there seems to be a minimum of emphasis on record

keeping. There is a reluctance to worry much about what actually happened in the past as opposed to what was intended. It is argued that such questions are pointless, because there are always extenuating circumstances to explain deviations from plans. It is also argued that it is better to concentrate efforts on the problems at hand than to attempt to improve hindsight.

10. Frequently, senior marketing and general management personnel are not clearly informed of assumptions and conditions underlying lower-echelon decisions, although these decisions influence the spending of millions of dollars on advertising and sales promotion annually. Sometimes, this delegation of authority is not intentional, but is a consequence of gradual relegation and convenience. Furthermore, the programs submitted for management review often lack necessary details for upstream decision making—so details are left to others.

11. Frequently, lower-echelon men are not given the authority to carry out their assignments and responsibilities. Yet they are usually held responsible for results.

12. In many companies, top management seldom asks for support from knowledgeable line and staff groups in arriving at their final decisions. Whatever the reasons, these communications difficulties are a source of confusion and a demoralizing influence.

13. Decisions on the promotional mix are often diffused among a number of decision makers. This inhibits the formation of unified strategy and balanced allocations. Often, last-minute indecision and conflict occur in such promotional programming.

14. Expenditure levels for promoting products are derived typically by working backward rather arbitrarily from sales revenue forecasts. Costs, exclusive of promotion and desired profits, are determined, and the residual funds are made available for promotion. This method is simple and comfortable, but is not likely to arrive at promotion levels which will maximize profits. In spirit, it may appear that this process is similar to critical path planning [for example, the Navy's program evaluation and review technique (PERT) or the PERT/cost method]. However, this casual approach lacks the rigor of the minimization of time or cost which critical path planning methods, often aided by computers, can provide. Quantifying the objective, and then referring all contributory factors to systematic and comprehensive promotional planning procedures, is rarely reported. In those cases where it is found, it may not appear well documented or complete.

15. The allocation of total budgets among the various tasks and tools of promotion is sometimes determined by using unaided intuition alone; or comparing or averaging past patterns of decisions; or working backward mechanically from the "fixed" items to a residual of more flexible items; or relying on the competent judgment and advice of others; or invoking arbitrary "rules of thumb." Some planners try to use a logical decision structure to evaluate a variety of alternative methods and to help screen all available evidence. In some instances, the planner increases his understanding of promotional effectiveness and is guided in modifying particular programs through tests and feedback of promotional effects. Probably, however, this does not apply in most companies.

16. In policy committee meetings, marketing management often presents well-rationalized, but not necessarily well-structured, arguments in favor of various promotional mixes. These presentations may suffer in comparison with the more logical and rational financial and technical proposals presented by other line and staff people. This is particularly true when general management is made up of men who came up through avenues of the corporation other than marketing. They have a different mental "set."

17. Even less prevalent than systematic planning is the practice of looking at prior years' performances through post-audits or reviews intended to enhance the forward planning process. It appears that some people prefer not to be confronted with a quantitative analysis of past performance versus plans, because such confrontations sometimes prove psychologically threatening.

18. The present state of the art in marketing administration is such that cause-and-effect relationships, and other basic insights, are not sufficiently understood to permit knowledgeable forecasts of what to expect from alternative courses of action. Even identifying feasible alternatives can prove difficult. Consequently, after finding one such alternative, further effort is often neglected (this is called "satisficing," that is, taking the first feasible approach).

19. Obtaining detailed sales results or market data without really knowing what to use them for has been cited as an exercise in futility because it confuses issues. High-speed data processing has compounded the confusion by churning out even more meaningless numbers in greater volume, and more quickly. This has been referred to as "merely going inefficient faster."

20. The confusion and lack of adequate insights into cause and effect are analogous to firing a boiler with little knowledge of the kind or amount of fuel to be used. There is no adequate knowledge of what is going on, what to expect next, or how to exercise effective control. The consensus of many executives who have been interviewed or whose views are a matter of record is that there is a great need for more timely information, more deliberate planning, and more effective control procedures. Comments of this sort are made by all levels of management.

21. In MSI's 1964 study, about two-thirds of the product situations studied were reaching sales goals, and one-third were reaching profit goals. These successes may be attributable to the combined impact of advertising messages, to product quality, corporate strength, or effective selling. But it is unlikely that they should be attributed to having just the right level and mix of promotional spending for the task. In any event, no adequate standards were found in use against which to measure performance.

Practical Deterrents to Improved Practice. A number of specific deterrents to more systematic promotional decision making, which may be removed or at least reduced in specific companies, are as follows.

1. There is a high rate of turnover among key marketing management personnel responsible for allocating funds to alternative means of selling and promoting. For example, the average tenure of product and brand managers in the companies interviewed in the MSI project was approximately two years. This provides little time for operating effectively on the basis of experience gained.

2. Many product and brand managers are unable to take advantage of the past experience of other managers, because records of previous promotional programs are not maintained adequately.

3. Some deterrents to improved promotional decision making stem from practices peculiar to a company. In one company, for example, product managers were prevented from having any knowledge of the financial performance of their products. Financial officers in this company believed that if sales managers were aware of the profits being realized on various products they would "quickly spend you into the poorhouse." In another company, the proposal for each element of the promotional mix was prepared by a different individual, without knowledge of what others working on the same product were planning. The separate plans were then combined by a senior executive working under considerable pressure, often without sufficient time or information to coordinate the plans effectively. It was the opinion of this executive that this procedure devel-

oped competition among the individuals to submit the most creative and original plans for their particular elements of the mix, and avoided limiting or "contaminating" their ideas by exposing them to others.

4. Divisions or departments within companies sometimes pursue goals in direct conflict with corporate goals and objectives.   In one company, the sales division shifted sales personnel in a test market from established lines to a new product in an effort to reach 100 percent of the sales goal for the new item.   The quota was not reached, and sales on established products in the test market fell sharply.   Although the procedure was rather clearly in conflict with the company's objective of overall profit, there was no policy statement to deter departments or divisions from actions of this sort, nor any effective sales analysis or marketing information system that would promptly alert senior management to the situation.

5. Management personnel responsible for promotional decisions are sometimes unable to do a better job because they are inhibited by the attitudes and opinions of the senior executives regarding specific products.   In one company, an outdated product was kept alive by special promotions at the expense of a newer product that was showing up very well in repeated market tests.   The older product was the creation of an individual who had since become a senior executive, and it was generally agreed that he would not tolerate suggestions that it be abandoned.   In another instance, a new product was put on the market despite poor test market results because it was a favorite of a corporate official. In another company, a product shown to be highly successful in test marketing was dropped because a key executive believed it might injure sales of another product he felt should not be abandoned.   In another case, a product which had done poorly in market tests was launched "to protect the substantial R&D investment that had been spent in its discovery and development."

6. Problems in communications among line and staff people and so-called practical and theoretical individuals are commonplace.   Differing interests, misunderstandings regarding the responsibilities of others, and the use of unfamiliar technical jargon are some of the things that help create the communications barrier.

7. In some companies, newly appointed personnel responsible for promotional decisions find there is no provision for reviewing the experiences of their predecessors or learning from others in similar positions within the company.   In one instance, a new supervisor was specifically instructed by management to ignore the records and experience of his predecessor despite the fact that he had been quite successful.   The new man was told by senior management that they wanted a "fresh look" at promotional programs, unhampered by prior thinking.   In some companies, a reluctance to admit they needed guidance or advice prevented new managers from seeking help.

8. The lack of specific objectives for products increases the difficulty of selecting the promotional mix.   The failure to have more than one alternative, should difficulties or new opportunities arise, can also create problems.   In many companies, it is not customary to have more than one plan for promotional allocations, although several partial plans are usually developed before selecting the final "mix."   When alternative plans are drawn up, they are seldom given thorough management review and consequently can prove unsuitable if the need arises for an alternative plan.

9. Many steps in planning marketing strategy and preparing operating details require review and rework as in-company revisions occur.   In some instances, these efforts appear to produce improved and refined plans in a series of co-ordinated steps.   In other instances, difficulties arise from the independent re-

vamping by company executives of plans for advertising, sales promotion, personal selling, and tactical pricing. These changes then have to be reconciled at group meetings or by senior management, a costly procedure in both time and effort, and one which seldom appears to produce the best available promotional mix.

10. Forecasting performance and evaluating risks, both widely recognized areas of difficulty among the companies observed, remain two of the decision makers' most perplexing problems. Company executives agree that promotional decisions are usually made on the basis of limited information and under considerable pressures of time. They also state that it is virtually impossible to pinpoint results of specific decisions in the eventual outcome of a product's launch. It is argued that, because the precise test market conditions can never be repeated, there is no opportunity to see how different decisions would have affected the result. This prevents the development of hard and fast rules for the future timing and implementation of promotional decisions.

11. Many companies appear to lack adequate guidelines or written procedures to assist management personnel in appraising the market potential of a new product. For example, listings of "external" factors to be considered, such as competitive activities, customer buying habits, and operating constraints on the one hand, and "internal" factors, such as the ability of the sales force to handle the product's technical service backup, proper channels of distribution, and provision for point of sale or trade promotion of the product on the other, are often incomplete.

12. Many companies do not coordinate efforts with their advertising agencies when formulating promotional plans. Matters in which the agency could have been helpful, such as the development of overall promotional strategy, are often determined by the company without consultation with its agency or agencies. In some instances, advertising agencies are prevented from having information concerning sales, estimated market share, customer lists, and other data which could be most helpful in suggesting appropriate promotional programs. The reason sometimes given is that the advertising agency is subject to change, and information given the agency might eventually find its way into the hands of competitors. In some companies, some key data are even withheld from management personnel responsible for promotional allocation decisions, for security reasons. Although such practices may help to assure secrecy, they can seriously handicap sound promotional judgments.

The Need for Experimentation and Coordination in Promotional Decision Making

1. Inappropriate and poorly designed experiments and field tests are commonly used in determining promotional allocations. As one executive observed, the results of these activities often do little more than confuse the people trying to make promotional decisions. In some companies, only "rules of thumb" and arbitrary guidelines are employed in the decision-making process. Although some of these serve very useful purposes in providing a rationale for decisions, few such practices are put to rigorous tests. They tend to build their strength (and "infallible" image) on the number of years in use.

2. In test marketing and full-scale marketing operations conducted by most companies, there remains a real need for consistent, up-to-date reports on progress and problems in the marketing program. In most companies, provision for accurately recording and analyzing the results of field activities is either superficial or inadequate. A better understanding of current techniques for measuring marketing performance and their use by management in reviewing marketing activities and adopting appropriate action would appear to be of benefit to most companies.

3. When senior management executives review and approve promotional plans, they often act quickly and on the basis of rather limited information. When this happens, much of management's decision-making power is delegated, or inadvertently relegated, to members of middle management and sometimes to junior and clerical personnel. Because these are usually the same people who drafted the promotional plans and took part in the allocation decisions, the plan is not likely to be altered or improved. In one company studied, for example, senior management merely checked to see if the total promotional allocation was within the budget. If so, it was approved without much regard to the manner in which it would be spent.

4. The lack of properly coordinated staff support seriously hampers effective presentations to management in many companies. Poor communications between line and staff personnel are particularly evident in these instances. Line operators frequently do not know what to ask for in the way of data that would be useful in their presentations. On the other hand, staff personnel sometimes accept requests for material and analysis without asking how the information may be used. As a result, the data collected and the techniques employed are often inappropriate. In some companies, staff personnel lack technical competence and experience with methods of obtaining or analyzing useful data.

5. The personal background of senior executives bears a direct relationship to the kinds of proposed plans they are apt to support. Executives with manufacturing and financial backgrounds are likely to be impressed with detailed, analytical studies. Those with marketing and sales backgrounds have been found to be less interested in details and statistics. They tend to favor presentations supported by forceful, appealing arguments.

6. Few instances have been noted of senior management adopting alternative plans to be used if difficulties or unexpected opportunities occur during the marketing period. In one company, it was found that a new product was falling short of its sales goal after several months of test marketing. At the same time, overall profits within the division promoting the new product were below expectations. Although management curtailed the product promotional budget because of the division's financial problems, the sales goal was not reduced. Reluctance to adjust goals and adopt alternative plans was fairly common among the companies taking part in the study. One of the reasons given was, "We don't have the techniques to do it properly." Another view was that it can be a hard cause to fight for without any chance of being a "hero."

7. Few instances are encountered of highly trained specialists doing research in marketing, although there appears to be a growing demand for professional evaluations and factual reporting of findings. In some companies, trainees, men on rotational assignment, and available supernumerary personnel are pressed into service in marketing research, planning, economics, and other staff services. This practice often results in relatively low-level, superficial approaches to important problems. This in turn results in management's reluctance to rely on the data provided by these services.

8. There appear to be two types of people engaged in marketing. Line operators tend to be primarily "practical" in orientation, and staff personnel tend to be "theoretical." The varied interests and responsibilities of line and staff personnel often make it difficult for them to understand and appreciate one another. When a line man finds he cannot understand or obtain help from his staff advisers, he tends to ignore them. When he ignores them, they fail to make any effective contribution toward helping solve his problems and are thus less well equipped and experienced when and if they are called upon.

Conversely, some staff people appear to lack tact and patience, and do not seem to understand management's problems and objectives. They may even believe that the men they serve are inconsistent and irrational. Consequently, the staff men do not put their best efforts into helping solve problems, and their reputations with management falls even lower.

Trends and Opportunities for Better Promotional Decisions

1. Improvement in promotion mixes and expenditure levels poses a substantial challenge. Significant awareness of the problem already exists in management circles. Increasing enlightenment on the issue is being gained through publications, conferences, executive development programs, and the recruitment of increasingly knowledgeable personnel. If these trends continue, many improvements will occur within corporations and advertising agencies.

2. The specific tailoring of decision guides, possibly along the lines of the APACS chart, may help focus attention on responsibilities and operational improvements. Statements of the sequence and nature of each step in the allocation decision process can lead to reconsideration of organizational and working relationships. This should yield increased efficiency and flexibility in making allocations and devising alternative plans.

3. After an appropriate structure of the decision-making process has been identified by a company, forms can be designed for brief notation of the data, assumptions, calculations, and resulting decisions. It may also be feasible to record expected subgoal bench marks for judging feedback from operations.

4. Critical path planning such as the military planning tools—PERT and PERT/cost—may prove helpful in assigning time, personnel, and other resources more effectively. Properly programmed computers may also help in making these decisions.

5. Many of the measurement methods employed to estimate the effectiveness of promotion have been inadequately researched regarding their reliability and the value of what they purport to measure. Comprehensive and cooperative research programs are needed, because the task exceeds the resources of most individual corporations or professional groups.

6. Field experiments or tests of the effects of promotional levels, mixes, and tools are fundamental. A large-scale program of market tests in this problem area appears likely to lead to significant advances.

7. There is a continuing need for more efficiency in research planning, information handling, and the presentation of timely reports to management. One approach may be the preparation of a master plan for the corporation and advertising agency research program. Clear specification of the advertising agency's role will be a part of this development.

8. Increasing research resources and the latitude of the product planner can raise the stature and responsibility of marketing research, while providing needed improvements and guidance in the allocation process.

9. Classifying data and past marketing-plan records and achievements, perhaps using modern storage and retrieval systems, should make them readily available for historical analysis and for more rapid and more reliable pretesting and prediction for alternative plans.

10. Greater efforts should be made to determine how changes in the promotional mix would affect the program. For example, what would happen if advertising were doubled? How would a reduction in the sales force affect sales? It is also increasingly important to coordinate sales and profit goals closely with the promotional program. Inconsistencies and conflicts among the goals can create competitive weakness and problems of morale.

11. The marketing planner should be positioned for complete comprehension

of the entire product strategy and all relevant intelligence. He may be empowered to assemble all of the components of the promotional mix. In time he may produce a near-optimum blend, limited only by knowledge and the techniques available. A corollary to this will probably be the clarification of planners' responsibilities and the results on which they should be judged.

12. There is apt to be increasing emphasis given in studies and management reviews to allocating sales force time and to preevaluating the influence of tactical pricing changes on product salability and promotional yield before they are made. Comprehensive mix planning and delegation of authority to adapt to competitive pressures and market opportunities should result in what one senior marketing executive referred to as "a better track to run on."

13. The knowledge and skills of product planners in allocating funds and efforts and controlling programs will be enhanced. One approach may be through "in-house" seminars (possibly chaired by a qualified outsider at an away-from-work location) for exchange of information, ideas, and experiences—and exposure to more systematic methods. Another approach will include more comprehensive training programs and written materials to guide incoming product or brand managers and others concerned.

14. There seems to be a consensus among a number of experienced marketing managers that too often young men come to jobs from universities or other companies with little business orientation and inadequate training. Sometimes, young men from business schools have a "big picture" background. One might overstate this by saying they are best equipped to relieve the president when he is on vacation! They may not be prepared to sit down at a desk and do relatively mundane, day-to-day assignments to assist a line person to make decisions that seem to center around trivia. They may have little tolerance for this. Many do not have an awareness that this is an essential activity—that someone has to do it and that it is often considered good seasoning. One major company president, for example, stated that there is a real danger of "little" decisions being overlooked down the line. This leads to top management's having to "second guess" and do many of these small things which they, through experience, know must be done.

15. In the view of one chief executive, even a checklist matching tasks and resources would be very helpful in orienting new or promoted employees in his company. Frequently, a man coming out of school does not know, and the company interviewing him may not know, whether he will fit best in line or staff work. Various devices may be helpful in achieving a balanced approach to this problem. These might include easy-to-assimilate written guidelines and historical reviews plus suitable instructional programs designed to orient new people and to develop new skills in new and transferred employees. Universities have become increasingly responsive to the expressed needs of management by supplementing or altering their offerings in night schools, extension programs, and periodic seminars to help the business community at large. The corollary to this is that businesses themselves must be encouraged to explore and exploit the resources which are already at their disposal.

16. Serious communication difficulties were reported in most cases observed. Discussions in companies have indicated the lengths to which certain staff personnel have to go to achieve acceptance of their ideas. One extreme example was that of providing publicity to trade papers concerning industry potentials and trend data, then going to management with the "authoritative" reports and stories which appeared. In one case, these articles had been taken virtually verbatim from staff material which had been previously considered unacceptable. Organizational changes, overcoming language difficulties, and gradual improve-

ment in communications will probably develop to promote more direct and more fruitful integration of line and functional needs with appropriate staff support.

Summing Up Future Implications for the Promotional Decision Maker. At one extreme in business is the practical man in action with his limited reports and basic notions—some jotted on references under his blotter. At the other extreme is the management scientist trying to make an effective (but sometimes naïve) contribution to research in marketing and eventually to the practice of marketing. Between these extremes, there lies the whole gamut of staff services and functional management within ongoing companies. Problems are identified, studies are initiated, tasks are assigned, and almost always, time is of the essence. So shortcuts and compromises occur, because the business must operate. Several crosscurrents underlie promotional mix decision making. Few know how to optimize, fewer feel truly satisfied, and thus "satisficing" (that is, adopting the first and only feasible course of action recognized rather than looking for other feasible alternatives from among which a satisfactory selection is made) often becomes a necessary way of life.

All too frequently, members of line management are not able to employ all of the information and practical insights available to them. Communication remains, of course, at the root of this difficulty. Line personnel are seldom familiar with the language and concepts employed by the more "far out" members of their staff, and generally do not (and often cannot) take time to learn about them. On the other hand, the staff men frequently do not thoroughly understand the problems of management, and thus they may not supply the most appropriate or useful data for operating management. Consequently, the busy operator is often psychologically threatened by, or at least skeptical of, "theory" or textbook answers which he does not understand and may not believe.

It seems likely that the practical marketing man may be some years behind the practical manufacturing or financial man with respect to the state of the art of management under his jurisdiction, as opposed to the state of the science potentially available to him. Clearly, marketing is by its very nature an area of activity which will not lend itself as readily to the systemization one sees in finance or manufacturing.

Demands for more scientific planning and control of promotional efforts will provide a platform of basic information and new insights into decision processes. They will bring systemization into a relatively rudimentary and difficult decision area. This systemization should stimulate individual interest and uncover opportunities in planning and applying research tools and acquiring profitable knowledge of how best to allocate scarce resources and to improve productivity and decision skills in marketing.

BIBLIOGRAPHY

Alderson, Wroe, *Dynamic Marketing Behavior*, Richard D. Irwin, Inc., Homewood, Ill., 1965.

Alderson, Wroe, and Paul Green, *Planning and Problem Solving*, Richard D. Irwin, Inc., Homewood, Ill., 1964.

Bliss, Perry, *Marketing and the Behavioral Sciences, Selective Readings*, Allyn and Bacon, Inc., Englewood Cliffs, N.J., 1963.

Buzzel, Robert D., *Mathematical Models and Marketing Management*, Harvard Business School, Division of Research, Boston, 1964.

Cox, Reavis, Wroe Alderson, and Stanley J. Shapiro (eds.), *Theory in Marketing*, Richard D. Irwin, Inc., Homewood, Ill., 1964.

Howard, John A., *Marketing: Executive and Buyer Behavior,* Columbia University Press, New York, 1963.

Howard, John A., *Marketing Management: Analysis and Planning,* Richard D. Irwin, Inc., Homewood, Ill., 1957.

Langhoff, Peter (ed.), *Models, Measurement and Marketing,* Prentice-Hall, Inc., Englewood Cliffs, N.J., 1965.

Phelps, D. Maynard, and J. Howard Westing, *Marketing Management,* Richard D. Irwin, Inc., Homewood, Ill., 1960.

Robinson, Patrick J., and David J. Luck, *Promotional Decision Making: Practice and Theory,* McGraw-Hill Book Company, New York, 1964.

FINANCIAL MANAGEMENT

CHAPTER ONE

Organizing the Financial Function

GEORGE L. CHAMBERLIN *Controller, Scott Paper Company, Philadelphia, Pennsylvania*

This chapter is directed to organizing factors which have unique importance for the financial function. Illustrations are given of the application of general organizing principles to certain aspects of financial work, but full reference is assumed to Section 2 of this Handbook, "Organization." The standard financial subfunctions and how they can be combined to accommodate businesses of varying size are shown in a chart (Figure 1-1).

Primary emphasis is given to the aspects of organization which are of major importance in attaining the unique objectives of the financial function.

WORK OF THE FINANCIAL FUNCTION

The financial function supplies and maintains the capital or financial resources and provides a system of financial measurement and control for the management of the enterprise. Traditionally, these have been the respective broad objectives of the treasury and the accounting and control functions.

Although the principles which led in the past to structuring this work in separate components under a treasurer and a controller are still valid, there is an increasing trend to the assignment of all financial responsibility to a chief financial officer. The trend represents recognition of the possible economies and increased effectiveness through closer coupling of these two areas in dealing with expanding reporting requirements and in utilizing new information techniques.

GENERAL PRINCIPLES OF ORGANIZATION

Although the financial function is unique and differs in many respects from the other functions in a business, it shares many characteristics in common with them. Thus, basic organizing principles are applicable to finance with equal validity.

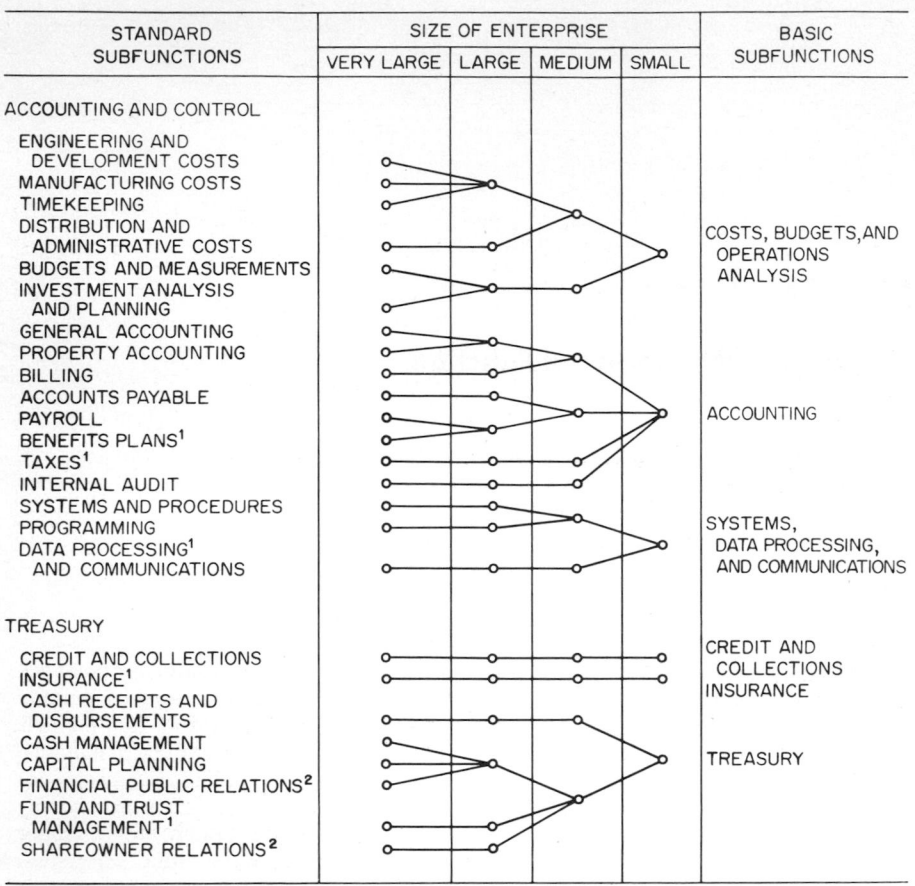

STANDARD SUBFUNCTIONS	SIZE OF ENTERPRISE				BASIC SUBFUNCTIONS
	VERY LARGE	LARGE	MEDIUM	SMALL	

ACCOUNTING AND CONTROL

ENGINEERING AND DEVELOPMENT COSTS
MANUFACTURING COSTS
TIMEKEEPING
DISTRIBUTION AND ADMINISTRATIVE COSTS
BUDGETS AND MEASUREMENTS
INVESTMENT ANALYSIS AND PLANNING

COSTS, BUDGETS, AND OPERATIONS ANALYSIS

GENERAL ACCOUNTING
PROPERTY ACCOUNTING
BILLING
ACCOUNTS PAYABLE
PAYROLL
BENEFITS PLANS[1]
TAXES[1]
INTERNAL AUDIT

ACCOUNTING

SYSTEMS AND PROCEDURES
PROGRAMMING
DATA PROCESSING[1] AND COMMUNICATIONS

SYSTEMS, DATA PROCESSING, AND COMMUNICATIONS

TREASURY

CREDIT AND COLLECTIONS
INSURANCE[1]

CREDIT AND COLLECTIONS INSURANCE

CASH RECEIPTS AND DISBURSEMENTS
CASH MANAGEMENT
CAPITAL PLANNING
FINANCIAL PUBLIC RELATIONS[2]
FUND AND TRUST MANAGEMENT[1]
SHAREOWNER RELATIONS[2]

TREASURY

[1]PART OR ALL OF THE SERVICE IS OFTEN PURCHASED.
[2]USUALLY DEPENDS ON PUBLIC RELATIONS OR ADVERTISING FOR TECHNICAL SUPPORT

FIG. 1-1. *Financial organization subfunctions by size of enterprise.*

The financial function includes two distinctly different kinds of work—direct and indirect. Work such as extending credit, paying out and receiving cash, and buying insurance produces direct results by the action of the work itself. Such work as accounting, cost analysis, data processing, and budget preparation is vital in the management of a business, but the product of the work is reports and measurements which are the basis for action by general management or other functions rather than a direct action itself on the business.

Traditional recognition of the principle of structuring like kinds of work together has resulted in putting the direct work under the treasurer. The measurement and reporting work have customarily been organized under the controller. Even with the trend of combining all financial work under one officer, the advantages of segregating these fundamentally different kinds of work in separate components still pertain.

The general organizing principle of structuring work in components so that they are readily measurable is more easily applied in large enterprises where more subfunctional components are both required and justified. Because the indirect contribution of accounting and control work in itself complicates the measuring process, there is more than ordinary need to determine in advance how the performance of each financial component can be measured to determine how efficiently it performs. In addition to straightforward volume measures such as number of people paid per payroll employee, number of transactions, sales, and asset values, subfunctional components should be designed so that their performance can be compared with discrete sets of work objectives for a year or other appropriate time period.

The general principle of separating long-range and other planning types of work from current operating work suggests that budgeting and cost analysis should not be structured with the work of compiling costs. Similarly, programming should be segregated from data-processing operations.

The application of these general guides to various-sized financial organizations is illustrated in Figure 1-1. Many businesses may require one or more specialized components to fill needs peculiar to their industry.

UNIQUE ORGANIZING REQUIREMENTS

In organizing the financial function, it is important that full recognition be given to certain unique aspects of its responsibilities, relationships, and work demands.

Stewardship Responsibilities. The prime burden of the responsibility to protect the assets of the business is on the financial function. The general principle of "checks and balances," therefore, should be applied in meticulous detail so that there actually is a check and balance in each area where neglect, theft, or natural hazards might cause loss of the company's resources.

Division of work between components or positions so that one person does not have complete, exclusive control of a transaction is the first and most effective line of defense. Bank accounts should be reconciled by someone independent of and preferably removed from the person handling deposits and payments. Payrolls should be distributed by people who have no connection with their preparation. Inventory records should be entirely separated from the people who bill customers or who handle the shipping and receiving functions. These are but a few examples of cases where the work should be divided to provide prompt disclosure of irregularities and errors.

The opportunities for providing safeguards through division of work can be identified by determining if at least two people would be aware of an error in any transaction or the disappearance of any asset. An analysis of the work routines and safeguards for each class of assets will disclose the areas of potential danger. The subdivision of work to provide the safeguard of "checks and balances" sometimes involves additional costs, particularly in small operations. Consequently, the question of the worth of the additional cost is a matter of judgment of the exposure involved.

The organization of a continuing system of internal audit provides a secondary defense against irregularities and errors. To ensure that internal audits are actually made, this work should be assigned to a component or position which is free from responsibility for regular operating work. With the establishment of an independent audit function, some extra costs of subdividing work to provide checks and balances may be avoided with less risk.

Lines of Communications. Many companies have formally established a direct line of communications between the controller or chief financial officer and the board of directors. Similarly, many companies operating with decentralized organizations have established a direct line of communication between divisional controllers who report to division general managers and the corporate controller. These are not lines of command but responsibilities to report significant information outside of the line of command.

It is not a complete solution, and its existence may be a source of problems. It is, however, a useful organizational device to minimize the serious effect of deviations by general management. In addition to the protection afforded the owners, it is even more useful in ensuring full and adequate disclosure before problems reach a crisis stage.

Balanced Work Loads. The traditional peaking of the accounting work load at the end of each accounting period adds to the normal difficulties of combining financial work in positions and components so as to provide an even load.

A detailed analysis of the work flow will provide a basis for balancing work loads. Although careful time scheduling of periodic work can reduce the peaks and valleys, there may also be advantages in combining work that would ordinarily be separated in accordance with other principles of organization. Such compromises are a matter of judgment of the gains and losses involved.

Conformity with Business Structure. Organizing accounting and control work into positions and components which parallel the overall business structure adds importantly to its effectiveness. If basic business responsibilities have been decentralized for product lines or geography, a parallel segregation of the related accounting and control work localizes responsibility and enables the accounting people to become active members of specialized business teams. This principle is equally valid with respect to separate manufacturing locations and the accounting control for the engineering, manufacturing, and marketing functions. The main types of work which should be considered for such special segregation in organizing are the measuring and analysis functions of costs, budgets, and financial planning.

Although initially it may appear that such specialization of the financial function output entails added costs, the productivity gains resulting from teaming accounting and control work with business or other functional components usually offset any apparent added costs.

DECENTRALIZED OPERATIONS

The evidence as to whether the financial function in a decentralized division should report directly to the corporate controller or to the division general manager is not conclusive. General Motors strongly advocates that the responsibility be retained by the corporate controller. General Electric has operated successfully with the financial function reporting to the general manager.

Full decentralization of the financial function along with the rest of the work of a decentralized business avoids many organizational frictions. In addition, it provides a better basis for creating "team spirit" and helps the financial people to identify themselves with the business.

Decentralization in the Future. Advances in data processing and integrated information systems are bringing substantial changes in concepts of decentralized financial organizations. Although it is too early to predict new principles with certainty, it is likely that in the future a substantial portion of the information generation and processing will be done by centralized or "pooled" organizations. A small number of highly skilled financial people in the decentralized organization will specify and interpret financial information.

INFORMATION SYSTEMS AND DATA PROCESSING

With the expanded use of electronic data-processing equipment, the financial function becomes responsible for substantial investment and fixed costs. As a result, the management and operation of information systems is one of the most important jobs in the financial organization.

Because of the substantial gains available in integrated information systems supplying essentially all of the information used in managing the business, some businesses structure this work as a primary function equivalent to engineering, finance, or marketing. This may be a useful expedient to establish the new concept. That same objective, however, is also the continuing goal of the financial function.

In accordance with the general principle of segregating short-term and long-range work, systems planning, programming, and processing of data should be assigned to separate components or positions.

FINANCIAL PUBLIC RELATIONS

The chief executive and the financial vice president or treasurer usually maintain relationships with commercial and investment bankers on a direct, personal basis. Relationships with the financial press, the financial community, and shareowners, however, are most successfully managed with a blend of financial and public relations competence (see Chapters 7 and 8 of Section 12). If a financial public relations position or component is not economically justified, the financial officer will realize important advantages from arranging for experienced public relations services on a part-time basis.

DEVELOPMENT OF NEW TECHNOLOGIES

Provision should be made in the financial organization for development and use of the new tools of analysis and control discussed in Section 17 of this Handbook.

In general, these constitute improved methods of problem identification and solution, and not a new function. Consequently, their application to financial work can be accomplished by staffing the analysis, budget, and systems planning positions with people experienced with these new tools.

It is also important to distinguish between the use of these new tools by the financial and other functions in doing their work and their use for research on the whole business. Research on the business and long-range planning depend importantly on the interest and involvement of general management for successful exploitation and are more appropriately structured as separate *ad hoc* or continuing separate functions.

ANTICIPATORY ORGANIZATION

Anticipating future moves or trends in the business with advance assignment of financial analysis and planning responsibilities enables the business to move much more rapidly. Failure to establish specific financial positions or components until there is a decision to take action usually results in delay until the financial analysis and planning can catch up with the business decision.

CONCLUSION

To ensure fulfillment of important, unique objectives and responsibilities, the financial organization should be structured to:

Provide the "checks and balances" needed to fulfill stewardship responsibilities

Have direct lines of communications to ensure full factual disclosure

Parallel the business structure and encourage participation in decentralized teams

Accelerate the development and use of new information and control techniques

Anticipate and be prepared for new trends and directions in the business

BIBLIOGRAPHY

Anthony, Robert N., *Planning and Control Systems: A Framework for Analysis*, Division of Reports, Graduate School of Business Administration, Harvard University, Cambridge, Mass., 1965.

Curtis, Edward T., *Company Organization of the Finance Function*, Research Report, no. 55, American Management Association, New York, 1962.

Dale, Ernest E., *Planning and Developing the Company Organization Structure*, Research Report, no. 20, American Management Association, New York, 1952.

Division Financial Executives, Studies in Business Policy, no. 101, National Industrial Conference Board, New York, 1961.

Duties of Financial Executives, Studies in Business Policy, no. 56, National Industrial Conference Board, New York, 1952.

Financial Committees, Studies in Business Policy, no. 105, National Industrial Conference Board, New York, 1962.

Heckert, J. B., and J. D. Willson, *Controllership: The Work of the Accounting Executive*, The Ronald Press Company, New York, 1952.

Internal Auditing, Studies in Business Policy, no. 111, National Industrial Conference Board, New York, 1963.

Marting, Elizabeth, and Robert E. Finley, *The Financial Manager's Job*, American Management Association, New York, 1964.

Maynard, H. B. (ed.), *Top Management Handbook*, McGraw-Hill Book Company, New York, 1960.

Professional Management in General Electric, General Electric Company, New York, 1953.

Sloan, Alfred P., Jr., *My Years with General Motors*, Doubleday & Company, Inc., Garden City, N.Y., 1964.

CHAPTER TWO

Financial Planning

EZRA SOLOMON   *Dean Witter Professor of Finance, Graduate School of Business, Stanford University, Stanford, California*

The planning process encompasses the selection of an explicit objective as well as the selection of policies, programs, and procedures which are expressly designed to achieve this objective.

The basic purpose of financial planning is to make sure that capital funds are used wisely. Specifically, financial planning is concerned with providing a systematic answer to three questions:

1. In what form should a company hold its assets? Stated more dynamically: What specific assets should an enterprise acquire?

2. How large should an enterprise be? In a more dynamic sense: What volume of funds should an enterprise commit to expansion in a given year?

3. What should be the composition of a company's liabilities? Translated into the dynamic context: How should funds acquired in a given year be financed?

All three questions are closely interrelated. The total volume of financing will be influenced by the kinds of investment opportunities available as well as by conditions affecting the sources from which financing is derived. Similarly, the cost and availability of funds depend in part on the quantity and quality of investment purposes for which they will be used. In other words, the three questions are really three facets of a single underlying question.

All companies must perforce answer these three questions. This may be done implicitly. It may even be done as a by-product of other decisions. The central task of financial planning, however, is to provide an explicit basis for answering these questions and thereby to provide a conscious design for directing funds into and through a company so as best to achieve the financial goals which the company sets for itself.

STRATEGIC COMPONENTS OF FINANCIAL PLANNING

Many of the component elements of financial planning are covered in detail in other chapters of this Handbook. What follows is an overview of the financial

9–9

planning process and of the following four strategic components into which this process may be subdivided.

1. *Setting Financial Objectives.* As in other types of planning, the starting point of the financial planning process is the explicit formulation of goals and of operating objectives designed to bring about the achievement of these goals.

2. *Planning Ongoing Operations.* This covers a range of issues. At one extreme, there is the fairly routine task of projecting expected cash inflows and outflows over future periods of time for the purpose of making sure that a company has the cash required to meet its obligations as they fall due.

At the other extreme, there is the important problem of asset management which involves the question: Does the performance of existing investments warrant the continuation of funds committed to them? Commonly known as "financial analysis," this topic covers the problem of making sure that available funds are being used in the best possible way. It involves the evaluation of economic performance, most importantly through the analysis of rates of return and asset and turnover ratios.

3. *Capital Budgeting.* This deals with the evaluation of new capital expenditures and the problem of measuring the relative profitability of alternative ways of using funds within the company.

Should a given proposal for the commitment of additional funds be accepted? Not all the decision criteria available for gaging the performance of investment proposals fully succeed in discriminating between the profitable and the nonprofitable. Capital budgeting deals with such criteria and with the problem of determining the cost of capital or the hurdle rate for desirable investment projects.

4. *Optimal Financing Structure.* Arising jointly with the problem of efficient funds usage is the problem of how to finance the assets of the firm. Is there some optimal way of balancing creditor and owner equity? Internal and external financing? Short-run and long-run sources?

FINANCIAL OBJECTIVES

Financial and other plans must serve to further the general objectives of the firm. Statements of overall objectives vary from firm to firm, but for analytical purposes, profit maximization is the one most frequently put forward. Profit maximization, however, is often an infeasible criterion for evaluating the economic efficiency of alternative courses of action. It suffers from three flaws:

1. It is vague. Like most shorthand expressions, it is conveniently brief and familiar but inconveniently loose and hence a source of ambiguity. Which particular definition of profits should be maximized? Short-run or long-run? The rate of profit or the amount? Profits in the sense of total returns to capital? Total returns to stockholders? Returns to common shareholders only? Profits over and above some allowance for the coverage of normal interest and wages on the owners' capital and time? Profits which will be reported by the conventional accounting process, or, profits adjusted to take account of factors which lie outside the purview of this process?

2. A more important objection to profit maximization as a criterion is that it cannot help when the decision must be made between two courses of action which offer benefits that differ with respect to their timing.

3. The third and most important objection is that the profit maximization criterion ignores the quality of the expected benefits. In an uncertain world, neither the amount nor the rate of profitability provides a basis for selection. In addition, a company must take into account the quality of benefits, where "qual-

ity" refers to the degree of certainty with which the benefits can be expected. To do this, a single measure is needed which combines both the quantity and the quality dimensions of benefits expected from each course of financial action. This measure will be a superior basis for guiding decisions and hence will provide a superior basis for stating the operating objective of financial management.

Profit versus Profitability. Rather than profits, a more useful operational concept is what may be called "profitability." This is defined as the ability of an undertaking or of an economic unit to produce or create new wealth. It exists when there is a possibility of using resources to yield economic values higher than the combined values of the inputs required. Profitability is a useful guide to planning: the economic value created by an enterprise is maximized through the use of the optimum volume and combination of resources. The acquisition, management, and disposal of resources are in themselves financial decisions, which therefore must also be resolved with the profitability objective in mind.

How should the concept of profitability be used in actual financial planning? By definition, planning is the process of choosing between alternative courses of action. In financial matters, courses of action involve alternative uses of funds or alternative sources of funds. Each alternative use offers prospective benefits. Each alternative source involves prospective payments. In the former, a present expenditure of funds is expected to yield a stream of future benefits. In the latter, a present receipt of funds is expected to cause a stream of future disbursements. The financial problem is to choose the best of the available alternatives in each of these two main groups of funds transactions.

A theoretically justifiable objective criterion is maximum wealth creation or the maximization of net present worth. The gross present worth of a course of action is equal to the capitalized value of the flow of future expected benefits, discounted at a rate which reflects their certainty or uncertainty. Wealth or net present worth is the difference between gross present worth and the amount of capital investment required to achieve the benefits being discussed.

Wealth creation is, of course, predicated on the continued liquidity of the firm. Assuming that, under all courses of action, the firm's ability to pay its debts promptly is always achieved, the objective of financial planning is to distinguish between acceptable and nonacceptable projects. Any financial action which creates wealth or which has a net present worth above zero is a desirable one and should be undertaken. Any financial action which does not meet this test should be rejected. If two or more desirable courses of action are mutually exclusive (that is, if only one can be undertaken), then the decision should be to do that which creates most wealth or shows the greatest amount of net present worth. In short, the operating objective of financial planning is to maximize wealth or net present worth.

ASSET MANAGEMENT

Financial plans have to cover two important segments of the firm's operations to maximize the net present worth of the firm. First, the funds-use plan must ensure that the existing assets of the firm are being utilized in the best possible way. Second, the plan should provide that additional commitments of funds are made only for profitable projects.

The first segment of the funds-use plan is basically one of continual review of ongoing investments. Existing funds commitments must be evaluated to see if their profitability comes up to expectations—whether existing funds commitments are sufficiently profitable to warrant their maintenance, or whether shifting the funds to some newly available alternative uses will result in a greater net present worth.

Return on Invested Capital. One of the most commonly used yardsticks for evaluating the performance of ongoing investments is the rate of return on invested capital, measured as the ratio of reported income to balance sheet book value. This measure of return on investment is based on accounting data. It is frequently referred to as "book return on investment" or the "financial statement method of computing return on investment."

For analytical purposes, the return on investment can be broken down into two components, (1) the rate of turnover of total assets, and (2) the rate of earnings per dollar of sales. Thus we have

$$\text{Return on investment} = \frac{\text{sales}}{\text{total investments}} \times \frac{\text{earnings}}{\text{sales}}$$

Various versions of this measure are used in practice. Technically, the numerator (income or earnings) is computed net of depreciation and therefore the denominator (investment) should also be computed net of the allowance for depreciation. However, some companies prefer to use gross investment in the denominator. In any event, these are data that are readily available from the financial statements of the firm. Total investment is obtained by adding all working capital items and the fixed assets of the firm. Earnings are calculated from figures on sales and operating and other costs. They are by-products of normal accounting processes, rearranged to provide a convenient framework for a quick review of emerging trends, an overall focus of control, and a point of departure for subsequent and more detailed diagnosis and analysis of specific decisional problems.

All three of these facets of the conventional analysis are relevant for investment and financing decisions.

When combined with a forecast of sales and revenues, a detailed analysis of past and current trends provides the basis for operating and cash flow budgets for the period ahead, generally one year. This gives an estimate of the amount of funds that operations are expected to generate, of the required commitments of funds for increased working capital, and hence of the gross amount of financing available from operations.

The analysis provides a basis for "controlling" investment in the various forms of assets used in ongoing operations and a preliminary test of whether asset usage is being managed effectively. Although the various ratios that can be drawn from the overall framework are not a satisfactory basis for evaluating management performance as such, they serve remarkably well as a device for isolating those operations in which asset usage is not producing commensurate returns. This in turn may lead to investment or disinvestment decisions.

Finally, the information derived from the analysis influences the capital expenditure and financing budget in several ways. It is a basis for estimating the size and quality of future returns from existing operations—which in turn is the basis for estimating a company's cost of capital or its cutoff point for new capital expenditures. It also influences top management's own evaluation of estimates submitted in connection with new investment proposals. Finally, wherever the initial diagnosis leads to further analysis and to reinvestment or abandonment decisions, the associated commitment or release of funds or facilities becomes part of the capital budget for the coming period.

Shortcomings of Return on Invested Capital. Although the book rate of return is the best single indicator of financial performance for a collection of assets, it does suffer from a significant drawback—the observable rate for a division, a company, or an industry may be influenced, sometimes significantly, by factors other than the true underlying profitability of the unit being measured.

Some of the major "extraneous" factors that may affect the accounting rate of return are listed below, together with a notation of the general direction of their effect on the observable rate relative to the true rate of profit being earned.

Cash Flow Pattern. Investment projects which generate cash inflows that rise over time tend to be associated with higher accounting rates of return than investment projects whose cash inflows fall. This is true even if the true rate of profit is the same for both types of projects. The reason is that the value of funds received in the far future is less than the value of funds presently received. If both types of projects have a common true rate, the absolute value of funds flows generated by the first type of project must be greater, and hence reported profits and the accounting rate of return would also be greater.

Age of Investment. Firms with relatively older investments tend to have higher accounting rates of return than firms with relatively new investment projects. Individual investments have a low book rate of return early in life because little of the initial outlay will have been written off. This makes the denominator higher for new investments and hence (for any given earnings figure) produces a lower observable accounting rate of return.

Depreciation Policy. A relatively higher accounting rate of return results from faster write-offs of fixed assets. Assuming a constant pace of new asset acquisitions, reported total profit on all operating investments is independent of how fast depreciation is charged off. This is so because the relatively high depreciation allowances on young projects are balanced out by the low depreciation allowances on old projects. However, a faster write-off policy reduces average book value and hence produces a higher accounting rate of return.

Write-off Policy. When a high fraction of the initial capital outlay is expensed rather than capitalized, the average book value of individual investments is reduced. This will result in increased accounting rate of return for reasons similar to the effects of accelerated depreciation.

Project Life. Investment projects with relatively long lives will lead to relatively higher accounting rates of return. High rates of return on such projects are due to the already mentioned fact that late receipts are less valuable than early receipts, and hence the total absolute amount of cash flows generated by a project increases as productive life is lengthened.

Working Capital Components. Other things being equal, projects with low scrap values and low working capital requirements will result in a relatively higher accounting rate of return than projects with high scrap values and working capital.

Because these factors influence the observable book rate of return, this must be used with care, especially when comparing divisions, companies, and industries which differ with respect to these factors.

CAPITAL BUDGETING

The second major segment of funds-use planning concerns the evaluation of alternative proposals for new investments. Business firms have always faced the problem of evaluating the profitability of new investments in assets. The methods used have ranged from highly subjective intuitive-judgmental approaches to objective quantified approaches. The difference is one of degree rather than of kind: all evaluation of the future requires subjective judgment and even a measure of intuition. But at one extreme, the necessary insights are translated directly into decisions; at the other, they are first developed into explicit estimates of expected measures of profitability which in turn form the basis for decisions.

Apart from subjective qualitative yardsticks, there are four basic approaches to the measurement of investment worth: (1) payback period, (2) book return on book investment, (3) internal rate of return, and (4) contribution to net present worth. Each of these is described briefly below, with a notation of how well the approach succeeds in conforming to the financial objective of maximizing net present worth.

Payback Period. The payback period is the ratio obtained by dividing the original depreciable fixed investment in an asset by gross annual profit expected before any allowance for depreciation. It measures the number of years required for the gross earnings on the project (with no allowance for capital usage) to pay back the original outlay. Also known as the "payoff period" or the "cash recovery period," this is probably the most widely used quantitative measure of investment worth.

The most obvious defect of the payback period is that it does not measure profitability. In other words, it ignores what happens after a project has returned its investment.

The usefulness of the payback method lies not so much in its being a yardstick of profitability as in its being a coarse screening device which will pick off high-profit projects that are so clearly desirable as to require no refined estimates of profitability, or reject quickly those proposals which show such poor promise that they do not warrant further analysis. It is also a useful measure when liquidity, as opposed to profitability, is a dominant short-run consideration—for example, in the rare case of companies which have a high volume of internal investment opportunities but relatively low access to internal or external sources of funds.

Book Rate of Return. Also known as the "accounting method," "level book rate-of-return method," "average book method," or simply as "return on investment," this method of figuring profitability takes the ratio of average annual profits expected from the project (conventionally computed) to book investment in the project.

The method has a host of variants; indeed, one of its shortcomings is that it is an altogether ambiguous concept, particularly with respect to the computation of the denominator of the ratio. Original book investment is sometimes used; sometimes, average book investment; sometimes, a weighted average of period-by-period book investment. It is also ambiguous with respect to the concept of investment itself. In a strict sense, being a book value measure, it should include only capital outlays, including working capital required, but this is frequently broadened to include all expected outlays connected with a project.

Apart from the ambiguities involved, the method fails to take into account the timing of expected earnings or of expected outlays. It therefore provides a correct measure of the rate of return only under fairly specific conditions; that is, when outlays "occur" at a single point of time, when expected benefits flow evenly over the life of the project, and where economic life corresponds to the life assumed for bookkeeping purposes. Without these conditions, the results derived from this approach or from this set of approaches are subject to fairly wide errors.

The Internal Rate of Return. This is the true rate at which an investment is repaid by proceeds from a project. In operational terms, it is that rate at which the incremental cash benefits expected from a project (after taxes, but before an allowance for depreciation) have a discounted present value which is exactly equal to the discounted present value of all incremental outlays required for the project's implementation.

It is conceptually identical to the method, long used by the financial world, for computing the expected yield to maturity of a bond which is purchased for an amount different from its face value. Thus it has also been called the "true yield method," or the "investor's method." Other names given to it are the "discounted cash flow method," the "interest rate of return," and the "scientific method." Economic theory has generally referred to it as the "internal rate of return" or the "marginal efficiency of capital."

Net Present Value. The fourth method of evaluating the profitability of investment proposals involves the direct use of the cost of capital in deriving the contribution to net present worth of the proposed funds use. In using the internal rate of return to evaluate investment projects, the calculated rate of return (r) is compared with the cost of capital (k), and the project is accepted if r is greater than k.

In the present-value method, all cash inflows and outflows are discounted, using k as the discount rate. If the resulting net present value is positive, the project is clearly profitable; but if the net present value is negative, the proposed investment should be rejected.

The third and fourth approaches yield identical results as far as "accept or reject" decisions are concerned. This is so because the net present worth of a project is greater than, equal to, or less than zero if, as, and when r is greater than, equal to, or less than k.

However, for the purpose of ranking and hence selecting from among two or more alternative proposals which are mutually exclusive, the two approaches may yield contradictory results. The relative ranking problem is a common one. For example, two proposals may represent alternative ways of doing the same thing; both are good in an absolute sense, but because only one can be undertaken, the relevant question is which is better.

Conflicting rankings indicated by these last two approaches can be isolated by comparing the relative values of the two projects at some future point of time which lies beyond the terminal date of either project. To do this, an explicit assumption must be made about the rate at which funds produced by each project are reinvested.

The implicit assumption of those who believe the rate-of-return criterion is universally correct is that the appropriate reinvestment rate is the same rate as that earned by a project within its original economic life, that is, its own internal rate. Given this assumption, it is clear that the project which has the higher internal rate of return will also have the higher accumulated terminal value and hence the greater investment worth.

The implicit assumption made by those who believe that the net-present-worth approach is universally correct is that the appropriate reinvestment rate is the cost of capital, k. Given this assumption, the terminal values obtained will always rank the same way as present values.

The question of which method is correct can be resolved only by deciding which assumption is more appropriate. In all but a few exceptional cases, the generally accepted answer is that k is the best available estimate of the reinvestment rate; that is, the extra flow of earnings produced in the early years by a given project will allow the company to invest funds it otherwise would not have had, only at the normal rate k. The logic of this is that the company would invest anyway in all projects offering returns greater than k, and that the special gains available from these do not generally depend on having the extra cash flow offered during earlier years by the project.

Setting the Cutoff Rate. A rational investment policy requires that the new investment budget should include all available uses of funds which promise to create net present worth, that is, which offer returns that have a present worth in excess of the outlays required to achieve them, when both flows are discounted at the company's cost of capital. When two or more courses of action are mutually exclusive, and neither offers special reinvestment opportunities, the one which makes the larger contribution to net present worth represents the correct investment decision.

A central factor in this process is the discount rate to be used in evaluating the net present worth of risky investments. An alternative way of defining this rate is as the cutoff which must be exceeded if a project is to be accepted.

Logically, this rate is equal to a company's cost of capital. Like other providers of productive resources, the owners of capital funds must be compensated for allowing the firm to use their resources. Clearly, minimum compensation for the use of funds would include the pure interest rate which the funds owners would be able to earn on "riskless" securities, namely, government bonds. In addition, funds providers also require a premium to compensate them for assuming risks, such as the risk of losing income and the risk of not recovering the real value of the principal investment, either from inflation or from losses incurred by the firm.

Measuring the expectations of funds providers is not easy, but business has not been able to sidestep the task of setting financial standards. Management has always had to set minimum standards of required performance and to decide the size and composition of capital expenditures. Whether or not these standards were expressed in terms of a cost-of-capital figure as such, management, nevertheless, has had to develop some basis for making these decisions.

What are the bases used by business and how were they derived? Unfortunately, we have little useful documentation on this subject, and explicit documentation is difficult to obtain. There is the usual difficulty caused by the fact that the actual conduct of business decisions may not be adequately reflected by what business spokesmen say they do. In addition, decisions on investment and growth are such broad ones that it is easy and, indeed, irresistible to argue that they are made on the basis of a whole constellation of variables; and this, of course, evades the questions of how specific minimum standards of financial performance are set or what they are. Finally, "high finance" has traditionally been conducted in a citadel close to the top, and the top has always been reticent about stating its own logic explicitly.

Measuring the Cost of Capital. The cost of capital is obtained by measuring the relationship between the amount that can be obtained from selling a security and the future outlays required to support these securities.

The measurement problem is easy for fixed-return types of securities such as bonds and notes. The schedule of periodic payments to the provider of funds is known and so is the maturity date on which the principal amount must be repaid. The net proceeds available to the operating company can also be estimated accurately. From these facts, the effective yield paid to the provider of funds can be measured explicitly as a percent per annum rate. This is the company's before-tax cost of borrowed funds, which can, in turn, be restated on an after-tax basis by using the company's appropriate tax rate.

Although preferred stock dividends are not mandatory, as is true of interest payments on bonds, it is also appropriate to use a similar procedure in computing the cost of capital derived from a preferred stock issue.

Measuring the cost of equity capital obtained from common shareholders requires considerably more estimation. What present shareholders expect to get is the flow of *future* earnings from existing assets, denoted by the symbol E. The value they place on this expectation is given by the market price of the shares, denoted by the symbol M. The ratio E/M provides one acceptable approach to measuring the cost of equity capital.

An alternative approach to measurement which will lead to an identical answer is to measure shareholder expectations in terms of the future flow of cash dividends to them. In this approach, the rate which equates projected future dividends to common shareholders (D_A) to the present market price of common stock (M) measures the cost of equity capital. This rate can be approximated by the value of $D_o/M + g$, where D_o is the current dividend rate and g is the rate at which dividends are expected to grow in the future.

The overall cost of capital which a company should use in planning investment decisions is the weighted average of the individual forms of capital contained in its financial structure. The weights which should be used in this computation are the market values of the component forms of capital.

OPTIMAL FINANCING

The purpose of planning financing is to make sure that the firm obtains capital funds at the minimum available cost.

New issues of debt and equity must be timed to take advantage of varying conditions in the capital markets. This is a problem in financial forecasting. In addition to the forecasting problem, the most important question involved in making optimal financing decisions is to select the extent to which the firm will rely on debt sources of capital.

The use of debt funds offers certain advantages. One advantage is that the nominal cost of debt is lower than the cost of equity funds. A second advantage is that interest payments on debt are deductible for tax purposes whereas dividend payments on equity are not. Because of these factors, an increase in the debt component of total funds tends to lower the average or overall cost of capital.

On the other hand, the use of debt also involves disadvantages. The most important of these is that debt interposes a fixed charge between operating earnings and the amount of income flowing to shareholders. This makes the flow of earnings to shareholders subject to a higher degree of uncertainty. In addition, common shareholders are exposed to a potential loss of their ownership rights in company assets in the event of default. Because of this, an increase in the debt component of total financing increases the cost of equity capital and hence tends to increase the overall cost of capital.

There is no general agreement on the exact way in which these two opposing effects of increasing debt usage operate. The traditional view is that there does exist some optimal mixture of debt and equity for every company or industry at which the company's overall cost of capital is at a minimum. In this view, the judicious use of debt up to the optimal level tends to lower the cost of capital. Increasing the debt ratio beyond the optimal level results in a higher average cost of capital. The level itself is determined by two sets of factors:

1. The sensitivity of company earnings to general economic fluctuations. The more stable earnings are likely to be, the higher the permissible amount of fixed charges.

2. The average practice of other firms in the industry. Financial structures which do not conform to group performance tend to be suspect. These consid-

erations shape bond ratings and credit ratings and thereby set the limit on the use of leverage by any company.

In practice, individual companies within a given industry tend to follow widely different patterns of debt utilization, and the question of debt usage remains an area in which formal analysis and experience have not as yet provided financial planning with firm guidelines.

BIBLIOGRAPHY

Bierman, Harold, Jr., and Seymour Smidt, *The Capital Budgeting Decision,* The Macmillan Company, New York, 1960.

Capital Investment Decisions, reprints from the *Harvard Business Review,* 1964.

Financial Planning for Greater Profits, Management Report, no. 44, American Management Association, New York, 1960.

Solomon, Ezra, *The Theory of Financial Management,* Columbia University Press, New York, 1963.

Weston, J. Fred, *The Scope and Methodology of Finance,* Prentice-Hall, Inc., Englewood Cliffs, N.J., 1966.

CHAPTER THREE

Sources and Costs of Capital Funds

JOEL DEAN   *President, Joel Dean Associates, Inc., and Professor of Business Economics, Columbia University, New York, New York*

Problems of raising capital and rationing it among rivalrous investment projects are common to all business corporations. The long-run profitability of the enterprise hinges on the solution of these two problems. Knowledge of sources and costs of capital is needed for both.

Good management of corporate capital views as quite separate these two problems: (1) sourcing (acquisition) of capital funds and (2) rationing (investment) of that capital. Rationing capital among investment proposals should be on merit (the productivity of capital) independent of source or cost of funds for that particular project. Investable funds of the corporation should be treated as a common pool, not as compartmented puddles. Similarly, the problem of acquiring capital should be solved independently of its rationing and also on the basis of merit (the comparative costs and risks of alternative patterns of sourcing).

The investment of corporate capital is the ultimate responsibility of the company's chief officers. This responsibility is seldom delegated to any great degree, as it commits the company to a largely irrevocable course of development. The sourcing of capital, on the other hand, can be delegated. Rarely do the sources of capital irreversibly determine the direction of corporate development. Once a basic policy as to depth of debt has been established and a prediction made of the amount and timing of needs, acquisition of capital is largely a problem of obtaining the agreed amount of debt and equity capital on the most favorable terms.

The first part of this chapter surveys, for decision-making purposes, the various sources of capital for the corporation; the second part examines ways of estimating the cost of capital obtained from major sources.

SOURCES OF CAPITAL

The supply of capital for corporate investment comes ultimately from the savings of individuals, corporations, and governments. As to immediate sources, the corporation has two choices: use its own savings (internal) or tap the savings of others (external).

Internal Sources. The main internal source of corporate savings is the generation of cash from operations. Corporate saving is the act of not paying out all profits in dividends. This act has an accounting warrant and an economic warrant. The support from accountancy takes the form of depreciation and depletion charges, estimates of the wastage (consumption) of capital accompanying the generation of cash. These charges erect a cultural barrier to payment of dividends which accountants say are not "earned."

The economic warrant for corporate saving is quite different. Stockholders benefit from saving and internal investment of the corporation's after-tax cash generation when the rate of return on the investment is higher than the corporation's cost of capital. This is approximately the opportunity cost of capital to its stockholders, because the corporation usually has the option of buying its own stock. This economic sanction for corporate savings specifies the condition and the amounts that are economically warranted on the basis of the richness of the prospective return of internal investments. In so doing, it makes no distinction (as does the accounting sanction) between plowback of net income and reinvestment of depreciation, viewing gross after-tax cash generation as a single pool of capital, not as separate puddles.

Gross cash earnings generated by operations constitute a common pool of future funds from which dividends will be paid and new investments financed. This pool should have corporate-wide availability for capital expenditures. When each division is restricted to the reinvestment of its depreciation charges regardless of the productivity of its investment proposals, the separability of sourcing and rationing of capital funds is abrogated, and one of the major advantages of the multiproduct firm is destroyed.

Another internal source of capital is disposal of assets. Each trade-in of a truck taps this source. Good capital sourcing should vigilantly ferret out opportunities to dispose of assets whose foregone earnings would in the future produce a rate of return on their disposal value lower than the corporation's combined cost of capital. Such disposals are a neglected source of capital for many corporations.

External Sources—Debt Capital. As external sources there are two ways for a business to get savings from outsiders: borrow (debt capital) or partner (equity capital). Debt capital can be arbitrarily classified as either short-term or long-term.

Short-term Debt. Short-term debt of the business enterprise can be of two sorts. The first is inadvertent borrowing which is a cultural by-product of normal operations. Mostly it is caused by lags between the time a service is performed and the time it is customary to pay for it. The corporation borrows a month's salary from its president. Although inadvertent, this borrowing is seldom avoidable.

The second sort of short-term borrowing is quite deliberate. The main source for most companies is the commercial bank. A *line of credit* is usually established, which sets a maximum amount of borrowing which the company may draw down as its needs dictate.

Other explicit sources of short-term borrowing are: (1) loans from specialized *finance companies,* typically secured by accounts receivable or inventory; (2) *factoring* of accounts receivable, that is, outright sale to a specialist who collects and absorbs bad-debt losses; and (3) sale of *commercial paper,* unsecured promissory notes generally of large corporations, sold publicly through the security markets.

Long-term Debt. Drawing the dividing line arbitrarily at one year, we classify intermediate-term debt capital as long-term. The *term loan* is a typical instrument. Its source may be a commercial bank, an insurance company, or a trust fund. Term loans result from direct (and usually unpublicized) negotiations between borrower and lender. Thus they are privately placed as contrasted with public sale through the money market.

For longest term borrowing, the usual loan contract is a *bond*. It may be placed privately by direct sale to a large financial institution or sold to the public, usually through an investment banker.

Long-term debt can be subclassified in three ways:
1. Nature of security (mortgage versus debenture bonds)
2. Directness of the obligation (direct debt versus off-balance-sheet financing)
3. Degree of participation (pure debt versus contingency debt)

These three bases of classification overlap.

Nature of Security. Borrowings may be secured by pledging specific assets (*mortgage bonds*) or secured only by the corporation's general credit (*debenture bonds*). The basic security for the debt of any corporation is, however, its uncommitted cash generating ability. A bank does not want to run a blast furnace. Sale of a pledged asset is only a resort of desperation. The relevant economic measure of the debt-carrying ability of a corporation is not the balance sheet but the future generation of cash from operations, which can be derived from forecasted income statements.

Directness of Debt. In addition to direct debt, a corporation can borrow indirectly by a variety of devices such as long-term leases, sale-and-lease-backs, oil payments and royalty arrangements, and through-put agreements. Regardless of legal status or accounting treatment, these forms of indirect obligation are the economic equivalent of direct debt. They are contractual obligations to make periodic payments for the use of capital and to repay the principal under specified conditions. These forms of off-balance-sheet borrowing have attractions. They can be (1) tailored precisely to the borrower's needs as to amount and timing, (2) negotiated privately, and (3) left off the balance sheet. The price of these conveniences is usually a slightly higher interest cost.

Participation. Some debt has partnership features. They are common and clear for direct debt (for example, convertibles and income bonds).

Convertible bonds are a cross between debt and equity financing. The bond holder has an option to convert his debt claim into shares of common stock at a predetermined price, which is equivalent to a long-term call on equity.

Income bonds are another hybrid, but a more disconsolate one. They participate only in the downside risk of equity. Interest payments of income bonds are obligatory only if covered by the pretax earnings during that current period.

Quasi-equity features are less clear but nevertheless are present in most indirect debt (for example, lease-backs and oil royalties). Most lease-backs and oil-payment and oil-royalty arrangements give the lender options and residual values that have some attributes of equity.

External Sources—Equity Capital. Equity capital raised externally is of two main sorts: (1) preferred stock, which is a kind of preferential but limited partnership, and (2) common stock, which is full partnership.

Preferred Stock. Dividends of preferred stock come ahead of common but are limited in amount. They are, however, not a contractual obligation and hence are not deductible as an expense for corporate income tax. In liquidation, the par value of the preferred comes ahead of the common though, of course, behind all debt obligations.

The limitations on the partnership of the preferred stock are sometimes relaxed. *Participating preferreds* share with the common stock some prearranged portions of earnings in excess of the minimum dividend. *Cumulative preferreds* get all previously omitted back dividends before any dividends can be paid on the common. *Convertible preferreds* have the option of swapping their limited partnership for the full partnership of common stock at a predetermined price.

Common Stock. Common stock is the economic equivalent of full partnership in the earnings and assets of the corporation. Dividends are discretionary, and common stockholders get only the residual left after other payments. In liquidation also, only amounts remaining after the company meets its obligations to lenders, suppliers, and preferred stockholders will be distributed to common stockholders.

THE COST OF CAPITAL

Saving, which is the ultimate source of capital funds for the corporation, is downright unpleasant. Therefore, we have to be paid to do it. That is the basic reason why it costs the corporation something to get capital.

All resources command a price for their use. Capital is no exception. The financial manager's task is to blend the various capital sources available to him to achieve the lowest long-run cost for his company's total capital requirements. This overall combined cost is the weighted average of the market cost of three main kinds of corporate capital: debt, preferred stock, and common equity. Capital from internal and indirect hard-to-measure sources should be assigned the cost of its alternative direct source. The alternative for lease debt is direct borrowing for an equivalent term. The alternative for internal cash generation, whether labeled "earnings plowback" or "depreciation," is flotation of common stock.

The Cost of Debt Capital. That debt capital has a cost is undebatable. The use of money borrowed from outsiders has a price. This price is established by market forces and is knowable with considerable precision. This price the company must pay.

The price of debt capital fluctuates with changes in supply and demand. At any time, the price differs widely depending on (1) the credit-worthiness of the borrower, (2) the duration and other terms of the loan, (3) the type of lending institution, and (4) the section of the country. The debt-cost range is wide, from 36 percent for trade credit if cash discounts are passed, down to the prime rate. The underlying causes of this wide disparity in the price of debt money are differences in risks and in costs of administration and collection. These two forces sometimes are opposed. For a short loan, the risk is less but the costs of launching and administration are proportionately higher. Other features affect the cost structure of debt capital; for example, privacy has a price. Off-balance-sheet borrowing commands higher prices in the marketplace, and all kinds of corporate private placements cost somewhat more than equivalent public debt.

Market imperfections distort the structure. Ignorance has a price. The astute borrower will try to borrow at the lowest rung of the debt-cost ladder that his credit-worthiness will permit. The competent lender will seek as comfortable a cushion of compensation for his risk differential as knowledge will warrant and competition permit. Thus the twin forces of knowledge and competition continuously eat away at aberrations in the debt-cost structure caused by ignorance, timidity, sloth, and greed, making it come closer to the structure compatible with disparities in risk and in cost of administration and collection.

The true cost of debt capital is often higher than its nominal cost. The disparity is produced by many devices. Discounting (deducting interest in advance) increases true interest rate as does the requirement of minimum balances, because they pare down the amount really available to the lender. Charges for investigation, servicing, and insurance can also raise the effective cost of debt.

The historical outlay cost of debt capital is comparatively easy to measure. It is indicated by the market yield to maturity on the company's debt securities, adjusted for costs of flotation and deflated for corporate income taxes.

The concept of debt cost which is strictly pertinent is a prediction of the long-run average future cost of debt rather than its past cost. But the past is, if averaged over a long period of time, a practical basis for estimating the future. An example of how the debt cost of capital might be estimated by a typical corporation is shown below.

1. Average annual debt outstanding at market value, 1950–1964 $1,000,000
2. Average annual interest payments, 1950–1964.   50,000
3. Average proceeds per $1,000,000 of new-debt flotations.   910,000
4. Average annual interest cost 1950–1964 (line 2 ÷ line 3) 5.49%
5. Estimated future income tax rate. 50.0%
6. Estimated future after-tax cost of debt capital (line 4 × line 5)   2.75%

The Cost of Preferred Stock Capital. Preferred stock differs from debt in that there is no legal compulsion to pay. Dividends can be omitted without subjecting the company to bankruptcy proceedings. The principal, in most cases, never comes due, although the company may have the option to call in the issue. On the other hand, unlike common equity, the preferred stockholder has no claim to the residual profits of the company.

This limitation of the return to dividend payments is the crucial fact in computing the cost to the company of its preferred stock capital. The cost should be estimated in the same manner as debt, with the exception that there is no income tax adjustment (preferred stock dividends are not allowed as a deductible expense). The company's maximum obligation is to pay dividends in the amounts negotiated at the time of issue.

The Cost of Equity Capital. The broad significance of the cost of equity capital needs to be understood if it is to be used intelligently. In a market economy, any resource which is scarce, relative to the demand for it, commands a price—however difficult it may be to measure that price. This is true even though reimbursement for the suppliers of equity capital is a residual, that is, what is left after more tangible costs of operations, including interest on debt, are satisfied. In the long run, equity capital is not a discretionary cost. The fact that the rewards are residual and dividends are discretionary does not, as some think, mean that common stock capital is costless. In the long run, equity capital has a market price which is determined by investors' alternatives. Although owners of equity capital assume the ultimate risk by accepting as their compensation what is left, they have in most companies the option of selling at some price. They will not reinvest or long leave their capital in any corporation which does not offer reasonable prospects of returns as high as those promised by alternative investments.

This residual is called "profit" by accounting convention. Profit is, however, a misnomer disguising the fact that capital is a resource which commands a price for its use. Conventional accounting views equity capital as costless, that is, as a free good. In an economic sense, however, there is no profit to the equity investor unless accounting profits exceed the cost of equity capital. Thus, despite its residual character, the cost of equity capital is a real cost to a business firm. It is what the free enterprise system has dictated and what a market economy has measured as the norm for the price of the use of equity capital in enterprises of this approximate degree of risk.

Over any extended period, meeting the cost of equity capital at the corporate level is a necessity for maintaining the company's financial integrity, fulfilling its obligations to the financial community, and providing a continuously favorable climate for the capital formation that is needed to grow and prosper. To be sure, the earning power of the company at any given point in time is determined by the results of prior, essentially nonreversible business decisions and by the then-current business environment. Hence, current earnings may fall below cost of equity capital. But if they do so for a protracted period, they bring about an offsetting downward pricing of the stock designed to reestablish the balance with the then-anticipated future earnings and dividends.

Looking into the future, the investments made today must be capable of earning enough in the future to cover all costs, including the cost of equity capital, as well as providing for recovery of the capital invested during the economic life of the project. Only thus can the company maintain its financial integrity over the long run. For this reason, the policy of investment selection should establish investment standards which are based on the price it must pay for capital—the combined cost of equity capital and of debt capital—to assure that no investment will be taken on today which will be knowingly incapable of earning the cost of capital in the future.

Measurement. An obvious measurement of what common stockholders expect to receive is their share of the corporation's current earnings. A crude measure of the cost of equity capital, therefore, is the ratio of per share accounting earnings to the then-current price of the stock.

A little reflection indicates that earnings-price ratios are not an adequate measurement of the cost of equity capital. There are four reasons for this: (1) the stockholder buys future earnings, not past earnings; (2) book earnings do not necessarily represent the true economic earnings of the corporation because of inadequacies and variations in accounting practice, especially in regard to allowances for inflation, for technological change, and for the recognition of changes in the value of mineral reserves; (3) earnings per share have no simple relation to earnings growth; growth in earnings is largely the result of retention of earnings and the profitability of reinvestment; and (4) the stockholder cannot get his hands on his share of the earnings.

The problems associated with measuring the price of equity capital by the ratio of current accounting earnings per share to current price of stock can be avoided by casting the analysis in terms of what the investor can get his hands on. The price at which a share of stock is traded represents what the buyer is willing to pay now for a stream of future benefits. At bottom, the stream of future benefits derives from future earnings per share, but the investor has no direct way of getting possession of them. Instead, he gets some combination of future dividends per share and capital appreciation.

If we knew the average expectation of future earnings, we could determine the rate at which they are being implicitly discounted to arrive at today's market price. This rate would be the cost of equity capital. But we cannot measure the investor's expectations of earnings performance. We can only look at past performance. If the time period is sufficiently long and a sufficiently large sample of companies is studied, it is probably a reasonable assumption that expectations, on the average, have been realized, and hence that actual returns can be used to represent expected returns. The argument is that there is no reason to suppose that expectations are subject to a consistent bias relative to outcomes. For any particular company or for any specific period of time, it is doubtful that outcomes would reflect expectations. But for a very long period of time or for a large sample of representative companies, errors of expectation ought roughly to cancel out.

Measuring cost of capital as the discounted cash flow rate of return on an investment in common equity is simple, straightforward, and easily understood as an accurate measure of returns actually received by the investor. At the outset of the analysis time period, our investor pays out a cost of x dollars for the stock. He receives a cash flow of dividends. He liquidates his investment by selling the stock at a price of y dollars at the end of the period. The rate of return which equates the present value of the investor's stream of returns (dividends plus liquidation price) with the purchase price of the stock at the start of the period is an estimate of the cost of equity capital.

The way to calculate the rate of discount that relates the price of the stock to the stream of dividends plus the appreciation of market price is illustrated in Table 3-1. The 1949 market price of ABC stock was $7.71 (adjusted for stock dividends and splits). It reflected the investors' anticipation of increases in earnings and dividends. When we discount the flow of dividends and the market-price appreciation to a present value of $7.71, we find that the actual market yield was 20.2 percent.

A second way to measure the cost of equity capital assumes that net cash flow from a corporation to the financial community as a whole consists only of a stream of dividends (because buying and selling transactions merely redistribute preexisting equity interest among individual investors.) The cost of equity capital, then, is equal to the rate of discount of the future stream of dividends. This is estimated by taking an average dividend yield plus the rate at which dividend is expected to grow (usually approximated by the past growth rate over a protracted period). The method is illustrated for a major oil company in Table 3-2. The average yield, 4.2 percent, is added to the annual growth rate in dividends, 7.9 percent, to produce an estimated cost of equity capital of 12.1 percent.

TABLE 3-1. Company ABC—Measuring Cost of Equity Capital by Discounted Cash Flow (DCF) (1949–1960)

	Year	Cash flow	Present value at 25%	Present value at 20%
Purchase price..........	1949	$7.71	$7.71	$7.71
Dividends..............	1950	nil	nil	nil
Dividends..............	1951	nil	nil	nil
Dividends..............	1952	nil	nil	nil
Dividends..............	1953	nil	nil	nil
Dividends..............	1954	+ 0.79	+ 0.26	+ 0.32
Dividends..............	1955	+ 1.30	+ 0.34	+ 0.44
Dividends..............	1956	+ 1.45	+ 0.30	+ 0.40
Dividends..............	1957	+ 1.52	+ 0.26	+ 0.35
Dividends..............	1958	+ 1.52	+ 0.20	+ 0.29
Dividends..............	1959	+ 1.52	+ 0.16	+ 0.25
Dividends..............	1960	+43.00	+ 3.70	+ 5.79
Net present value.......................			−$2.49 +	+$0.13

DCF return = 20.2% cost of equity capital (not adjusted for flotation costs)

TABLE 3-2.　Company DEF—Measuring Cost of Equity Capital by
Dividend Gradient Method (1958–1965)

Year	Dividend per share	Average price of stock	Dividend yield, %
1958	$0.84	$21.38	4.0
1959	0.97	22.94	4.2
1960	1.00	20.63	4.9
1961	1.12	25.13	4.4
1962	1.15	24.56	4.7
1963	1.27	28.19	4.5
1964	1.33	37.94	3.5
1965	1.55	45.63	3.4

7.9% (annual growth rate) + 4.2% (average yield) = 12.1%
(Cost of equity capital not adjusted for flotation costs)

Return of equity capital, then, is what investors received, measured in terms of either dividends plus growth in market value or dividends adjusted for growth. The return on the stock of a company during a specific time period is not necessarily the same thing as the cost of capital. Cost of capital is, by definition, what investors *require* as revealed by the relationship of (1) the price they are willing to pay for the stock to (2) the *future* economic benefits they anticipate (however hazily) through ownership. However, the rates of return experienced by investors in a group of economically similar common stocks should form a frequency distribution with a concentration around an average value which approximates the investors' required return for any given level of risk. The return actually provided to investors will vary among companies and over time, but should tend to concentrate around what is the investors' requirement.

The cost of capital obtained from internal cash generation is the same as the cost of equity capital except that no adjustment for flotation cost is needed. The cost is the same whether the saving is achieved by capital consumption allowances (depreciation and depletion), which may be viewed as recycling rather than capital formation, or from the reinvestment of net income (earnings plowback).

The Combined Cost of Capital. The company's combined cost of capital will depend on how much of each kind of capital it obtains. The financial manager's task is to blend the numerous sources of capital available to him to obtain the lowest long-run cost of capital to his corporation.

In view of the fact that debt capital is invariably cheaper than common equity, one would expect a very high proportion of debt in the capital structure of most well-managed companies. This, however, is not the case, primarily because as a company's depth of borrowing increases, approaching the theoretical limit of 100 percent debt, the apparent (though not necessarily real) risk of bankruptcy rises. Presumably, lenders will exact higher and higher prices for this increasingly risky debt. Similarly, the hazards of common stockholders increase as debt goes deeper into this danger zone, and they, too, will be expected to require higher rates of return for equity capital (for example, the price of the common stock will fall). Hence, both the cost of debt and the cost of equity can be expected to rise as depth of debt increases. If they rise sharply enough, these higher costs will offset the decline in combined cost of capital which would otherwise result from a greater proportion of debt in the capital structure.

Table 3-3 illustrates part of the effect of capital structure on combined cost of capital. It is limited to the 0 to 50 percent debt range observable in the

TABLE 3-3.   Company HIJ—Combined Cost of Capital (after Tax)
Related to Capital Structure

	Capital structure				
Debt.................	10 %	20 %	30 %	40 %	50 %
Equity...............	90 %	80 %	70 %	60 %	50 %
Cost of debt..........	2.0	2.2	2.4	2.7	3.0
Cost of equity........	11.0	11.0	11.0	11.0	11.0
Combined cost of capital........	10.1 %	9.2 %	8.4 %	7.7 %	7.0 %

petroleum industry. No increase in cost of equity capital is measurable over this range, whereas some increase in cost of debt is. Combined cost declines over this range, but should rise at some point beyond.

This minimum-cost point, where the increasing proportion of debt and the rising price of both debt and equity produce the lowest combined cost, is hard to locate empirically. It is hard because neither borrower nor lender will knowingly risk ruin by supplying the needed data. Locating it is hard also because aversion to risk expresses itself in lending limits and in restrictive covenants rather than in higher interest rates only. The decision as to capital mix, therefore, requires a high order of mature judgment.

SUMMARY

The management of corporate capital can be viewed as two separate functions: the sourcing (acquisition) of capital and the rationing (investment) of that capital. Although investment policy must necessarily remain the responsibility of top management, the sourcing function can be delegated.

The supply of capital for corporate investment comes ultimately from savings: corporate, personal, or government. There are two ways to get capital: save it yourself or tap the savings of others. There are two major ways a corporation saves: (1) sheltering cast generated from operations by means of allowances for capital wastage (depreciation and depletion charges) or (2) holding out on stockholders by paying out dividends that are less than the net income (earnings plowback). There are two ways to get the savings of outsiders: borrow or partner.

The internal sources of capital are retained earnings and depreciation charges less dividends paid to common stockholders. No distinction should be made between retained earnings and depreciation. Each will go into a pool from which dividends will be paid and investments will be made. Capital-expenditure needs above internal cash generations will be financed by new flotations on the capital markets.

Debt capital from external sources can be classified as to duration (short- versus long-term), as to security (mortgage versus debenture bonds), as to participation (pure versus contingency debt), and as to directness (direct versus off-balance-sheet debt). These bases of classification overlap and produce a rich variety of sources of debt capital. External equity capital is of two sorts: preferred stock, whose partnership is limited, and common stock, which is full partnership.

The task of the financial manager is to achieve the lowest long-run cost for his company's total capital requirements. The cost of debt capital is the market yield to maturity of the company's debt securities adjusted for costs of flotation and deflated for corporate income taxes. The cost of preferred stock should be estimated in the same manner, excluding the income tax adjustment. The cost of equity capital is best estimated by measuring the average return to stockholders in many similar companies over a long time period.

BIBLIOGRAPHY

Dean, Joel, *Capital Budgeting*, Columbia University Press, New York, 1951.

Dean, Joel, *Managerial Economics*, Prentice-Hall, Inc., Englewood Cliffs, N.J., 1951.

Dewing, Arthur S., *The Financial Policy of Corporations*, 5th ed., The Ronald Press Company, New York, 1953.

Gordon, Myron J., *The Investment, Financing, and Valuation of the Corporation*, Richard D. Irwin, Inc., Homewood, Ill., 1962.

Hunt, Pearson, Charles M. Williams, and Gordon Donaldson, *Basic Business Finance*, rev. ed., Richard D. Irwin, Inc., Homewood, Ill., 1961.

Lindsay, Robert, and Arnold W. Sametz, *Financial Management: An Analytical Approach*, Richard D. Irwin, Inc., Homewood, Ill., 1963.

Solomon, Ezra (ed.), *The Management of Corporate Capital*, The Free Press of Glencoe, New York, 1959.

CHAPTER FOUR

The Management of Company Cash

S. GEORGE GREENSPAN   *Partner, Adler, Faunce and Leonard, Certified Public Accountants, New York, New York*

Cash has been described as a company asset uniquely valuable to the company having a sufficient amount of it for its operations, but unusually expensive when a company needs to borrow it for continuance. This chapter proposes to show how a company can derive maximum value from its cash funds.

NATURE AND IMPORTANCE OF COMPANY CASH

Cash is money—ready money on hand, in the bank, or in the form of easily convertible notes, certificates, or bills called "cash-like items." It is not accounts receivable, property, prepaid expenses, or inventory. It may well be that these company assets under proper circumstances are capable of being used as or turned into cash, but they are not cash. It takes money to pay suppliers, meet expenses, and provide payroll. Money is what keeps the business going, and for this reason, company cash is the most important asset of any business.

The history of business failures is full of insolvent companies with sizable noncash assets, current or noncurrent, and no cash to operate. Because cash is such a commonly sought-after commodity, it is uncommonly misunderstood, misidentified, and wasted. It is generally believed that a profitable company is necessarily a cash-rich company. Profits are not the equivalent of cash. Included among many insolvent companies are plenty of firms with sizable profits, but unable to pay their debts or meet today's expenses, fit subjects for Chapter XI proceedings, creditor arrangements, and bankruptcy. These promising or profitable companies may have been on the road to substantial growth, diversification, or product development, but did not calculate or wisely plan their cash needs. They mistakenly equated profit growth with generating cash. Overinvestment in fixed assets, poor collections on receivables, bad debts, and unbalanced or obsolete inventories can quickly transform a profitable company

9–29

overtrading on creditors' cash and bank loans into a company with solvency problems.

Generally, large and substantial companies with large cash resources are most careful in managing their cash funds, while smaller companies, which are in need of cash for growth and expansion, fail to manage or poorly manage their cash. Mental knowledge of one's day-to-day cash balances and payments is insufficient. To have the cash facts at "one's fingertips," as many a company manager has remarked, is no answer to the needs of company planning or decision making. Mental controls at best are inaccurate and may be dangerous. Formal cash planning is not complicated, difficult, or costly. Putting the facts to work about (1) cash budgeting, (2) cash analysis, (3) using surplus cash, (4) stretching cash, (5) the use and application of cash, and (6) controlling cash will help one to make correct decisions, operate more profitably, and will guide one to business success.

EXHIBIT A. Welmet Industrial Corporation—Balance Sheet at December 31
(In thousands of dollars)

Item	Actual 196__	Projected 196__	Changes in working capital	
			Increase	Decrease
Assets:				
Cash	$ 257	$ 45		$212
Receivables	365	531	$166	
Inventory	210	360	150	
Prepayments	11	11		
Current assets	$ 843	$ 947		
Fixed assets—net	481	421		
Other assets	17	17		
Total	$1,341	$1,385		
Liabilities:				
Accounts payable	$ 126	$ 110	16	
Expenses payable	51	55		4
Long-term loans, current portion	18	18		
Income tax payable	38	42		4
Current liabilities	$ 233	$ 225	$332	$220
Working capital and changes	610	722		112
Long-term loans, noncurrent	231	213		
Stockholders' equity:				
Capital stock	45	45		
Surplus	832	902		
	$ 877	$ 947		
Total	$1,341	$1,385		

EXHIBIT A-1. Projected Statement of Application of Funds for Year Ended December 31, 196__

Funds provided by:
Net income for year .... $ 70
Adjustments to net income—depreciation 60
                                                                                                    130
Funds applied to:
Reduction of long-term loan 18
Increase in working capital $112

FIG. 4-1. *Year-end balance sheets and projected statement of funds for following year.*

A composite hypothetical example—of the Welmet Industrial Corporation—has been taken from a number of actual businesses and will enable management to become familiar with good company cash management. The following illustrative information about this company is presented in a group (Figs. 4-1 to 4-8), instead of when referred to in the discussion, to facilitate seeing the way the various exhibits fit together.

EXHIBIT B.   Welmet Industrial Corporation—Projected Income Statement
(In thousands of dollars)

Item	Actual 196__	Per- cent	Pro- jected 196__	Per- cent	Per- cent
Net sales—basis..........................	$1,780	100	$1,780		
Sales increment.........................			620	100	
Net sales total..........................			$2,400		100
Material consumption:					
Opening inventory......................	225	13	210		8
Purchases, net.........................	603	34	950		40
	828	47	1,160		48
Closing inventory......................	210	12	360		15
Total material consumed..............	$ 618	35	$ 800		33
Variable costs:					
Direct labor..........................	195	11	* 336		14
Freight and shipping costs.............	32	1	48		2
Commissions..........................	103	6	168		7
Total variable costs..................	$ 948	53	$1,352		56
Marginal income.....................	$ 832	47	$1,048		44
Semivariable costs:					
Manufacturing expenses................	361	20	361		
Increment on increased volume.........			93	15	19
Engineering...........................	32	2	32		
Increment on increased volume.........			6	1	2
	$ 393	22	$ 492		21
	$ 439	25	$ 556		23
Selling and administrative:					
Selling costs..........................	95	5	95		
Increment on increased volume.........			31	5	5
Administrative........................	273	16	273		
Increment on increased volume.........			31	5	12
	$ 368	21	$ 430		17
	$ 71	4	$ 126		6
Other deductions.......................			24		
Other income..........................	(18)	1	(10)		
	89	5	112		6
Taxes.................................	28	2	42		2
Net income............................	$ 61	3	$ 70		4
Comments:					
* Wage increase based on new labor contract					
Average monthly sales..................	$ 148		$ 200		
Expenses percentage to sales:					
Variable costs less materials consumed.........		18			23
Semivariable costs.....................		22			21
Selling and administrative.............		21			17
		61			61

FIG. 4-2.   *Income statement and projected income statement.*

EXHIBIT C. Welmet Industrial Corporation—Projective Income Statement, Year 196__

(In thousands of dollars)

Item	Year 196__	First quarter			Quarters		
		Jan.	Feb.	Mar.	Second	Third	Fourth
Net sales......................	$2,400	$ 180	$ 190	$ 150	$ 600	$ 296	$ 984
Material consumption...........	800	60	63	50	200	98	329
Other variable costs (23%)........	552	42	44	35	137	67	227
Marginal income..............	$1,048	$ 78	$ 83	$ 65	$ 263	$ 131	$ 428
Semivariable costs (21%).........	492	38	39	31	122	59	203
	$ 556	$ 40	$ 44	$ 34	$ 141	$ 72	$ 225
Selling and administrative (17%)..	430	32	34	28	107	53	176
Other income...................	(10)			(2)	(4)	(2)	(2)
Other deductions................	24	2	2	1	6	3	10
Taxes (2%)....................	42	3	4	2	11	6	16
	$ 486	$ 37	$ 40	$ 29	$ 120	$ 60	$ 200
Net income....................	$ 70	$ 3	$ 4	$ 5	$ 21	$ 12	$ 25

Projective Balance Sheet, 196__

	Dec. 31	Jan. 31	Feb. 28	Mar. 31	June 30	Sept. 30	Dec. 31
Assets:							
Cash.........................	$ 257	$ 219	$ 225	$ 231	$ 171	$ 273	$ 45
Receivables...................	365	330	330	281	355	201	531
Inventory.....................	210	222	234	244	281	300	360
Prepayments..................	11	11	11	11	11	11	11
Current assets...............	$ 843	$ 782	$ 800	$ 767	$ 818	$ 785	$ 947
Fixed and other assets..........	498	493	488	483	468	453	438
Total......................	$1,341	$1,275	$1,288	$1,250	$1,286	$1,238	$1,385
Liabilities:							
Accounts payable..............	$ 126	$ 72	$ 75	$ 60	$ 77	$ 37	$ 110
Expenses payable..............	51	36	38	30	39	19	55
Loans payable, current portion...	18	18	18	18	18	18	18
Income taxes payable...........	38	41	45	28	20	26	42
Current liabilities............	$ 233	$ 167	$ 176	$ 136	$ 154	$ 100	$ 225
Loans payable, long-term portion	231	228	228	225	222	216	213
Stockholders' equity:							
Capital stock.................	45	45	45	45	45	45	45
Surplus......................	832	835	839	844	865	877	902
	$ 877	$ 880	$ 884	$ 889	$ 910	$ 922	$ 947
Total......................	$1,341	$1,275	$1,288	$1,250	$1,286	$1,238	$1,385

FIG. 4-3. *Detailed projective income and balance sheet statements.*

EXHIBIT D-1. Welmet Industrial Corporation—Cash Flow Budget, First Half of 196___

(In thousands of dollars)

Schedule	Item		Year 196_	Jan.	Feb.	Mar.	Apr.	May	June
						Receipts and disbursements method			
	Noncontrollable receipts:								
III	Other income, Exhibit B		$ 10			$ 2	$ 2	$ 1	$ 1
	Noncontrollable payments:								
	Taxes, Exhibit B		(38)			(19)			(19)
	Expenses		(1,410)	($122)	($110)	(97)	(108)	(118)	(116)
	Loans		(18)	(3)		(3)		(3)	
			($1,456)	($125)	($110)	($117)	($106)	($120)	($134)
	Controllable funds:								
II	Accounts payable		(966)	(126)	(72)	(75)	(60)	(80)	(80)
IV	Accounts receivable		2,210	213	188	198	148	180	192
	Increase (decrease) cash		(212)	(38)	6	6	(18)	(20)	(22)
	Cash balance, beginning			257	219	225	231	213	193
	Cash balance, end			219	225	231	213	193	171
	Minimum balance required			200	200	200	200	200	200
	Cash gap							7	29
	Cash excess			$ 19	$ 25	$ 31	$ 13		
	Financing—cash gap or excess:								
	1. Investment, short term (days)			15(90)	25(60)	30(30)		(30)(L)	
	2. Short-term bank loan (days maturity)							10(90)	30(60)
	Cash available			$ 4		$ 1	$ 13	$ 3	$ 1

L: liquidated

FIG. 4-4. *Cash flow budget—receipts and disbursements method, first half of year.*

EXHIBIT D-2. Welmet Industrial Corporation—Cash Flow Budget, Second Half of 196—
(In thousands of dollars)

Schedule	Item	Receipts and disbursements method					
		July	Aug.	Sept.	Oct.	Nov.	Dec.
	Noncontrollable receipts:						
	Other income, Exhibit B............	$ 1	$ 1			$ 1	$ 1
	Noncontrollable payments:						
III	Expenses...........................	(75)	(56)	(53)	(183)	(201)	(171)
	Loans..............................	(3)		(3)		(3)	
		($ 77)	($ 55)	($ 56)	($183)	($203)	($170)
	Controllable funds:						
II	Accounts payable...................	(77)	(40)	(40)	(37)	(160)	(119)
IV	Accounts receivable................	191	128	128	112	246	286
	Increase (decrease) cash...........	37	33	32	(108)	(117)	(3)
	Cash balance, beginning............	171	208	241	273	165	48
	Cash balance, end..................	208	241	273	165	48	45
	Minimum balance required...........	200	200	200	200	200	200
	Cash gap...........................				35	152	155
	Cash excess........................	$ 8	$ 41	$ 73			
	Financing—cash gap or excess:						
	1. Investment, short term (days)...		(30)(L)	70(30)	(70)(L)		
	2. Short-term bank loan (days maturity)...				35 (120)	35(90)	35(60)
	3. Short-term bank loan (days maturity)...					65(90)	65(60)
	4. Stretching accounts payable:						
	Defer November (30 days)..........					50(30)	(50)(L)
	Defer November (60 days)..........					32(60)	32(30)
	Defer December (30 days)..........						23(30)
	Cash excess November applied to December.						30(A)
	Cash available.....................	$ 8	$ 11	$ 3		$ 30(A)	

L: liquidated

FIG. 4-5. *Cash flow budget—receipts and disbursements method, second half of year.*

EXHIBIT D-3. Welmet Industrial Corporation—Cash Flow Budget 196___
(In thousands of dollars)

Item	Adjusted net income method					
	First quarter			Quarters		
	Jan.	Feb.	Mar.	Second	Third	Fourth
Net income.............................	$ 5	$ 6	$ 6	$27	$ 15	$ 35
Add: back depreciation.................	5	5	5	15	15	15
Cash generated from income...........	$10	$11	$11	$42	$ 30	$ 50
Current assets, changes (exclusive of cash):						
Cash incr. (decr.) inventory..............	(12)	(12)	(10)	(37)	(19)	(60)
Cash incr. (decr.) receivables.............	33	(2)	48	(80)	151	(340)
Cash increase (decrease)...............	$31	($3)	$49	($75)	$162	($350)
Current liability, changes:						
Cash decr. (incr.) acc. payable...........	54	(3)	15	(17)	40	(73)
Cash decr. (incr.) expense payable........	15	(2)	8	(9)	20	(36)
Cash decr. (incr.) taxes payable..........	(3)	(4)	17	8	(6)	(16)
Cash decrease (increase)...............	$66	($9)	$40	($18)	$ 54	($125)
Net..	(35)	6	9	(57)	108	(225)
Other cash changes:						
Long-term liab. decrease.................	(3)		(3)	(3)	(6)	(3)
Capital expenditures....................						
Product developments...................						
Increase (decrease) cash..............	($38)	$ 6	$ 6	($60)	$102	($228)

FIG. 4-6. *Cash flow budget—adjusted net income method.*

The kind of information illustrated by these figures will assist in running a profitable business.

THE PURPOSE OF CASH PLANNING

Cash planning is used by the firm to:

1. Make sure there is sufficient cash during peaks of high inventory needs and receivable outstandings which is usual in seasonal or cyclical businesses.

2. Meet the maturities of short- and long-term obligations, tax payments, and dividend and interest requirements.

3. Properly plan for capital expenditures—such as buying expensive equipment, relocating, or enlarging the plant.

4. Provide sufficient lead time to enable the company to find and negotiate needed or more favorable financing without pressure.

5. Impress bankers or other creditors with the feasibility and timing of repayments on obligations

6. Properly provide for the strains and problems relating to acquisitions and company integration resulting from the take-over.

7. Allow the company to take advantage of discounts, special purchases, and business opportunities.

8. Invest surplus cash for short or long periods, consistent with company requirements, to get a return on heretofore idle cash funds.

9. Effectively cope with the problems of a tight money market and liquidity.

SCHEDULE I. Welmet Industrial Corporation—Inventory Forecast, Year 196___
(In thousands of dollars)

Item	Factor total		First quarter			Quarters		
			Jan.	Feb.	Mar.	Second	Third	Fourth
Sales forecast.............		$2,400	$180	$190	$150	$600	$296	$984
Beginning inventory........			210	222	234	244	281	300
Less: materials used........	33.3%	$ 800	60	63	50	200	98	329
			$150	$159	$184	$ 44	$183	($ 29)
Add: purchases.............	40%	$ 950	72	75	60	237	117	389
Ending inventory...........			$222	$234	$244	$281	$300	$360

Calculations based on projected statement of income.

SCHEDULE II. Accounts Payable Flow, Year 196___

Accounts payable beginning.		126	72	75	60	77	37
Purchases required.........	$ 950	72	75	60	237	117	389
		$198	$147	$135	$297	$194	$426
Payments on account.......	$ 966	126	72	75	220	157	316
		$ 72	$ 75	$ 60	$ 77	$ 37	$110

Calculations based on projected statement of income, with 30-day payment cycle as normal.

SCHEDULE III. Accruals—Expense Payments, Year 196___

Beginning, accrual.........			51	36	38	30	39	19
Monthly, quarterly expenses.	61%	$1,474	112	117	94	366	179	606
			$163	$153	$132	$396	$218	$625
Ending, accrual............	20%		36	38	30	39	19	55
Expenses incurred.........		$1,470	$127	$115	$102	$357	$199	$570
Less: adjustment for depreciation (noncash).:.......		60	5	5	5	15	15	15
Cash expenses.............		$1,410	$122	$110	$ 97	$342	$184	$555
Average monthly accruals...			$ 40					
Average monthly year sales..			$200					

FIG. 4-7. *Schedules of inventory forecast, accounts payable, and expense payments for projected year.*

What Is the Cash Budget or Flow? The cash budget is an analysis of the flow of cash in a business over a future short or long period of time. It is a forecast of expected cash intake and outlay. It is not an operating statement or an income statement. Income statements are prepared on the accrual basis of accounting, that is, expenses or income are recorded when applicable to the statement period even though these amounts have not been paid or received. Customers are billed and income is recorded, and accounts payable and expenses are entered, yet no cash has passed in either direction. Only by converting an accrual statement into a cash statement can the cash flow from operations be clearly seen.

Cash generated from operations after adjustments that eliminate the differences between opening and closing periods and add back to profit noncash expenses charged to operations like depreciation and amortization of intangibles, such as patents, is only one source of cash input for the company. The cash input of a firm may also be realized from the sale of capital stock, the receipts from long-term debt issues, the disposal of fixed assets, and the like. It is erroneous to label cash flow as being synonymous with net income after taxes plus depreciation. This form of cash input may be drastically lowered by cash output such as property additions and debt retirement. The movement of cash in and out is a total firm activity, embracing income and balance sheet activities.

Short-range and Long-range Cash Budget. It is common practice to prepare short- and long-range cash budgets. The short-range budget covers a year with greater detail for the current period, usually on a monthly basis. At the end of each month, the actual cash movements are placed side by side with the budgeted amounts so that unusual variances can be accounted for. This enables management to maintain a close watch over cash use and availability.

SCHEDULE IV.   Welmet Industrial Corporation—Estimated Receivable Collections, Year 196___
(In thousands of dollars)

Item	Totals	First quarter			Quarters			Deferred collections
		Jan.	Feb.	Mar.	Second	Third	Fourth	
Balance, beginning.........		$365	$330	$330	$281	$355	$ 201	
Sales.....................	$2,400	180	190	150	600	296	984	
		$545	$520	$480	$881	$651	$1,185	
Collections on receivables:								
Prior year balance.......	365	215	100	50				
Current year sales:								
January.............	180		90	54	36			
February............	190			95	95			
March...............	150				135	15		
April................	202				160	40		2
May.................	202				100	100		2
June................	196					165	29	2
July................	101					80	20	1
August..............	101					50	50	1
September...........	94						85	
October.............	404						320	4
November...........	303						150	2
December..........	277							
	$2,400							
Total.............	$2,765	$215	$190	$199	$526	$450	$ 654	$14
Less: adjustments of uncollectibles..............	(24)	(2)	(2)	(1)	(6)	(3)	(10)	
Net collections...........	$2,210	$213	$188	$198	$520	$447	$ 644	
Balance at end...........		$330	$330	$281	$355	$201	$ 531	

Basis for collections:
 50 %   first month after sale   10 %   third month after sale
 30 %   second month after sale   10 %   fourth month after sale
Plus deferred collections: $14 during year

FIG. 4-8.   *Schedule of receivable collections for projected year.*

In small companies, responsibility for a short-range budget is placed with the treasurer or controller. Larger companies maintain a budget director and staff.

The long-range cash budget is usually prepared for a five-year period. It is less accurate and detailed than the short-range forecast. It is used to evaluate the cash effect of long-range plans, new product development, acquisitions, and capital projects. It is indispensable for companies in a dynamic market, growth companies needing long-term funds (stocks, bonds), and companies expanding into new markets, products, and territories.

There are two methods of preparing a cash budget:

1. Receipt and disbursement method, used for short-range purposes (Figures 4-4 and 4-5).

2. Adjusted net income method, usually used for long-range purposes (Figure 4-6).

As explained later in our example, both methods will arrive at the same ending balances as to cash requirements. The receipt and disbursement method is favored for close operations, because it itemizes the expense and receipt figures.

Cash Budget Preparation. A cash budget is no more accurate than the figures it must rely upon in its preparation. These are:

1. A reliable sales forecast—usually furnished by the sales department for the annual period.

2. Accurate information as to credit collection furnished by the credit department after careful analysis of customer accounts, payment patterns, and special arrangements, if any.

3. A good inventory budget which will disclose the various categories of inventory requirements during the period, purchase lead time, and usage. This budget is prepared by the production department.

Other data, such as the operating expenses, financing policies, payments on accounts payable, and capital budget projects, are usually under the control of the company's financial division.

Inaccuracies in budget preparation arise from:

1. Inability to forecast reliably—because of unexpected price movements and too-rapid market changes.

2. Lack of understanding and communication by and between the various divisions preparing underlying budget information.

3. Insufficient attention and experience in adjusting budget figures to changing business conditions.

4. Excessive reliance on historical or untimely data.

5. Failure to relate budget figure to results and make corrections for later periods.

Advanced planning and company education in the importance of company budgeting on the part of the top executives will greatly facilitate interest in and ease of preparation.

Cash budget preparation without control of the actual results is at best only half the job. Control includes:

1. Reviewing and accounting for variances and explaining their significance. This requires discussion and decision, usually at regular meetings with the personnel concerned.

2. Deciding upon bank-loan needs and methods of speeding up cash intake (receivable collections; shipping; and delays in invoicing, shipping, and movement of products).

3. Determining dates for major payments.

4. Weighing the effects of changing company policies and business conditions.

HOW THE WELMET INDUSTRIAL CORPORATION
PREPARES ITS CASH BUDGET

The basis of the cash budget of the hypothetical Welmet Industrial Corporation is the projected sales and income statement for the new year 196__ shown by Figure 4-2. The company expects to increase sales by $620,000, for a total sales of $2,400,000 as against $1,780,000 in the previous year. The income statement is prepared on the basis of this sales increase plus other expense changes (increased labor costs) by the direct cost method (fixed and variable costs are analyzed to find the effect of volume changes on costs). The factors used in preparing the various schedules shown in Figures 4-7 and 4-8 are derived from the income statement, receipt and payment experience of its accounts receivable (four-month collections), and accounts payable (one-month payment).

Schedule I (Figure 4-7), "Inventory Forecast": There is a 33.3 percent material usage factor, and a 40 percent purchase factor to monthly sales as established from Exhibit B (Figure 4-2), "Income Statement."

Schedule II (Figure 4-7), "Accounts Payable Flow": Normal payment is thirty days; purchase amounts are obtained from Schedule I.

Schedule III (Figure 4-7), "Expense Payments and Accruals": Expenses represent 61 percent of sales and indicate monthly expenses incurred. Because the projected income statement is based on accrual accounting, not all expenses incurred are paid in the same month. In addition, noncash expenses must be subtracted to arrive at actual cash monthly payments. Average monthly accruals are obtained by estimating that the monthly expense accruals will average 20 percent of monthly sales.

Schedule IV (Figure 4-8), "Estimated Receivable Collections": A study of collections of accounts receivable based on prior collection experience indicates that the pattern on monthly sales collections is 50, 30, 10, and 10 percent for each subsequent month. The company's aged accounts receivable schedule is a handy form for obtaining these percentage figures. As payments on accounts receivable are obtained, they are recorded in the columns provided for in the schedule of aged accounts receivable.

Exhibits D-1 and D-2 (Figures 4-4 and 4-5) illustrate a twelve-month spread of cash flow. These exhibits were prepared from Schedules I to IV (Figures 4-7 and 4-8), based on the receipt and disbursement method.

Exhibit D-3 (Figure 4-6) illustrates the same cash flow, slightly condensed for space as to the second, third, and fourth quarters, prepared by the adjusted net income method. Provision has been made for cash payments by way of capital expenditures and product development funds should they become a part of Welmet's program.

The essential difference between the two methods—for both methods result in the same ending cash increase or decrease—is that the receipt and disbursement statement deals with absolute figures. The adjusted net income method starts with the cash generated by income. The changes between opening and closing assets or liabilities of the balance sheet as they affect cash are then added or subtracted to arrive at the net increase or decrease in monthly cash. This method is essentially a statement of changes or movements and their effect on cash flow resulting from:

Net income—expenses and income cashwise
Inventory
Receivables
Trade payables

Expenses payable

Other liabilities

Fixed asset changes

Determining Minimum Cash Balance. After the increase or decrease in cash is determined, the resulting ending cash balance is arrived at. At this point, the financial officers of the company must determine how much of a cash balance the company needs as a minimum. The minimum needed can fluctuate from month to month, or remain relatively stable. Many factors dependent upon external circumstances, such as type of industry and rate of cash flow, determine the figure. Internal factors such as the following also enter into the minimum balance:

1. Cash necessary for operating expenses—overhead, labor, and taxes for a stated period. Welmet used a two-month figure.

2. Relationships between receivable and payable cash movements at various months, which are affected by inventory levels and sales cycles.

3. Cash necessary to be kept in banks as compensating balances for services banks render and to facilitate lines of credit when needed. When a number of banks are used, balances need to be adjusted among banks to maintain proper levels. Your bank will be pleased to show you how they analyze your account and determine their cost in servicing your account. From this, you can derive a simple formula for compensating balances for each bank. Obviously, the greater your company deposit, payroll, and check activity, the more it costs your bank to service your account.

4. Cash necessary to maintain a balanced cash ratio to other balance sheet items and sales turnover to ensure good credit references and ratings.

Determining Financing Needs from Cash Flow Budget. The difference between the minimum cash balance required and the actual ending balance determines the cash excess or cash gap. In our illustration (Figures 4-4 and 4-5), the cash excess is invested for periods as short as thirty days. Welmet's cash gap manifests itself in the last quarter of the year, when its seasonal volume exceeds 40 percent of its annual volume and considerable financing is required. This financing is made possible by:

1. A selective deferment of certain payments on accounts payable which carry no purchase discount.

2. Short-term bank borrowings.

It is summarized by the following statement:

Projective Statement of Fourth Quarter Financing, 196___
(In thousands of dollars)

Cash—October 1, 196___		$273
Less minimum balance		200
		$ 73
Cash decrease:		
October	$108	
November	117	
December	3	228
Cash deficit		$155
Deficit financed by:		
Bank short-term borrowings		$100
Accounts payable deferred:		
November	$32	
December	23	55
		$155

Controllable and Noncontrollable Funds—Stretching Cash. The cash flow presented in Exhibits D-1 and D-2 (Figures 4-4 and 4-5) distinguishes between those funds that are noncontrollable and those funds that can be controlled. Funds requiring payments under contractual obligations, such as rent, utilities, labor used, transportation, and debt repayments, are not flexible and must be met promptly if the firm is to operate. Certain forms of income subject to contract are also generally noncontrollable, such as royalties, commissions, and investment income.

Controllable funds are those items which, in the exercise of good management discretion, can hasten cash input or defer cash output. By far the two largest items in this category are accounts receivable and accounts payable. The following management techniques assist in accelerating cash flow:

Accounts Receivable

1. Good credit practices—credit surveillance, customer credit limits, and enforcement of discount practices. Investigate promptly all sales disputes and sales allowances. Do not permit an honest difference or allowance on a minor amount to delay collection of a sizable sum.

2. Prompt deposit of cash once it is received from customers—complexity arises when there are numerous collection points. There may be a number of subsidiaries or divisions throughout the country. Two methods are used to speed up collections. (*a*) Area concentration banking—local banks transfer funds to regional concentration banks by wire transfers, or drafts in the deposit amount, drawn on the local bank and sent to the regional bank where it is credited within a day. (*b*) The lock-box system—the customer mails his remittance to the company at the post office box serviced by the regional bank. The bank picks up collections several times a day, credits the funds to the company, and remits the excess to company headquarters as previously agreed upon.

3. Acceleration of shipping and billing for finished goods. Many companies maintain records reflecting the time intervals to ship, bill, and transport merchandise.

Accounts Payable

1. Try to match payments on large trade bills with the collections on receivables arising from the very merchandise being paid for. This balancing of cash outgo with cash collections on a selective basis can slow down peak drains on cash.

2. Be sure to take advantage of all purchase discounts, even at the expense of borrowing to take purchase discounts. The gain in discounting exceeds the cost of borrowing. Companies can often obtain extra time on their discounts (dating) during peak periods.

3. Watch your mailings of checks to coincide with the due date.

4. Make use of your cash collection float (collections in transit) by committing some of your payments against this float as opposed to using available bank borrowing for payment.

Other Controllable Funds. Expenditures for equipment (replacement or otherwise), product development, relocation, research and development, and plant improvement are usually amenable to some sort of cash deferment. In certain cases, alternative methods of acquiring facilities, even for temporary periods, can ameliorate a difficult cash position. In the long run, these alternative methods may be more costly because of built-in interest factors, sales expense, and commission costs. However, in a situation where there is uncertainty as to the future of a capital undertaking, these extra costs are more than made up when compared with the expenses of disposal and abandonment attendant upon termination of fixed asset ownership. Consider these approaches to lessen cash drain:

1. Determine whether "to buy" is better cashwise than "to make." Review your subcontracting costs—it may be cheaper to make it in your own plant. The criterion to be used is your "out-of-pocket costs," not your general overhead allocations which go on regardless of decision.

2. Analyze cash effect of renting or leasing as opposed to ownership. Renting is more economical when space, equipment, and vehicle usage are characterized by peaks and valleys during the year. Too many firms have enlarged their plants or bought real estate to hold their inventory for seasonal needs, when warehousing would have been far cheaper. The cash drain resulting from plant expansion to meet the needs of temporary increased business is very costly as opposed to subcontracting or leasing.

3. Although royalty payment is a common device to get the use of product development and research quickly and at less cost than it would have taken the company itself to do the developing, too many companies undertake types of research and development that can be better acquired by royalty arrangements.

4. Analyze the cash drain of territorial market penetration—it may be better at this time to use agents or distributors instead of your own fixed-cost salesmen, rented space, and the like. Commission costs dependent upon results may be less of a cash drain than your own sales organization in a particular region.

5. Surplus plant equipment and useless facilities are easily overlooked sources for converting idle assets into cash. Cash may also be obtained by sale and leaseback arrangements of fixed assets, especially real estate.

6. The exercise of certain tax elections and tax-saving methods can substantially defer or reduce cash payments. Here are some of the more widely used techniques:

   a. Expensing research and development costs

   b. Using the completed contract method of accounting for projects beyond a tax year (building, installation, and construction contracts)

   c. Using accelerated methods of depreciation, timing the use of investment credits and bonus depreciation

   d. Electing use of last-in, first-out method of inventory (LIFO), which, in periods of rising prices, will result in less taxable income

   e. Reporting sales of personal property on the installment method, by showing receipts as part cost and part profit

   f. Using the reserve method for bad debts, which permits a deduction even before the debt has become bad

   g. Trading in property as against sale to avoid the tax at ordinary rates on the recapture of depreciation on equipment

   h. Creation of multiple corporations when business reasons so dictate, to avoid the higher surtax rates

   i. Taking advantage of capital gains, particularly in corporate disposals, while avoiding personal-holding-company and accumulated-earnings tax traps

   j. Using stock options and deferred compensation as methods of limiting excessive salaries which are taxed to the recipient at high ordinary income tax rates

Funds Flow Analysis. Fund statements show how or why changes occur in working capital (see Exhibits A and A-1, Figure 4-1). They are also used to show what has happened to the company's cash, in addition to answering such fund questions about the company as what has happened to the profits, why are the current assets down while profit is up, and in reverse, why are current assets up while losses have been sustained, and how was capital equipment expansion accomplished.

Under various titles—"Source and Disposition of Funds," "Source and Use of Cash," "Statement of Application Funds," "Statement of Sources and Uses of Working Capital"—fund statements have become the third statement in annual reports of public companies, after the balance sheet and income statements. Figure 4-9 shows examples of various forms of fund statements. The fund statement (see Exhibit A-1, Figure 4-1) can be rearranged to highlight sources and use of cash within the working capital as follows:

(In thousands of dollars)

```
Cash obtained from:
  Beginning cash balance......................................   $257
  Profit from operations........................   $70
  Depreciation..................................    60
  Increase in expense payable...................     4
  Increase in income tax payable................     4..............    138
                                                                      $395
Cash applied to:
  Increase in receivables.......................  $166
  Increase in inventory.........................   150
  Long-term loan................................    18
  Decrease in accounts payable..................    16..............    350
Ending cash balance.........................................       $ 45
```

It would seem that the preparation of a fund statement merely consists in arranging the differences between beginning of the year and end of the same year balance sheet items. Although the comparative balance sheets provide the information for the report, certain accounts, such as fixed assets and surplus accounts, must be analyzed in detail, as these accounts may represent changes resulting from multiple transactions that affect funds and result in mixed changes:

Surplus—income from operations, dividends paid, and unusual charges and credits

Fixed assets—assets sold, acquired, or abandoned

Book entries, such as write-downs, depreciation, and amortization, do not affect funds and must be eliminated when preparing the funds statement. When depreciation is added back to net income, as shown in Figure 4-9, an expense that does not require working capital is being eliminated.

Fund statements are usually a statement of the funds in the recent past. They can also be prepared on a future basis as a projection from the data prepared as to projective balance sheets and income statements; see Figures 4-1 and 4-3. In this case, they answer the questions concerning what will happen to the funds as a result of projected operations and changes in the projective balance sheet (Figure 4-3). Projective statements are prepared from the figures and schedules used in preparing the cash flow statement.

CASH EXCESS AND EARNING POWER—SHORT-TERM INVESTMENTS

Beyond the cash a company needs for operations and bank balances are the cash funds available for investment. In most companies, this means temporary cash surpluses available for short-term investments up to twelve months. Sometime during this period these excess funds will be needed for seasonal require-

Radio Corporation of America—Year Ended December 31, 196___

Cash funds provided by:		
Operations		
Net profit for year...		$ 82,495
Provisions not requiring cash funds		
Depreciation...	$51,055	
Deferred taxes...	3,109	54,164
Total available from operations................................		136,659
Tax recoveries..		6,821
Stock sales...		11,596
Investment reductions and liability increases........................		5,219
Total cash funds provided.....................................		$160,295
Cash funds used for:		
Repurchase of preferred stock...................................	$64,064	
Cash dividends...	39,294	
Plant and equipment, less $12,379 book value of disposals............	72,549	
Miscellaneous..	10,173	
Investment in Communications Satellite Corp......................	5,000	
Total cash funds used..		$191,080
Decrease in cash funds..		$ 30,785

Continental Copper & Steel Industries—Year Ended June 30, 196___

Funds provided by:	
Net income...	$ 2,488
Depreciation..	1,093
Property disposal, net book value....................................	819
Mortgage receivable...	250
Investment decreases..	179
Other..	428
Total...	$ 5,257
Funds applied to:	
Working capital increase..	$ 3,076
Investment increases..	225
Long-term debt...	653
Plant and equipment..	700
Dividends..	228
Minority interest in consolidated subsidiary............................	308
Other..	67
Total...	$ 5,257

Vibration Mountings & Controls, Inc.—Year Ended March 31, 196___

Source:	
Net income for year..	$ 70
Depreciation and amortization..	13
Sale of common stock..	440
	$ 523
Application:	
Capital additions..	$ 104
Deposits...	13
Increase in working capital..	406
	$ 523

FIG. 4-9. *Examples of forms of fund flow analysis used by public companies (in thousands of dollars).*

ments or taxes, dividends, or capital expenditures. When not so needed, these funds have earning power. The cash flow statement is the basis for anticipating, and planning cash excess amounts and earning realization. Temporary funds are invested usually for periods of 30 to 90 days and when not needed in operations are reinvested for additional periods. These temporary investments are often described as "cash-like investments" because of their safety as to principal and ready convertibility back into cash. A number of different sources for the investment of cash for short-term periods are available. The yields or rates of return on these forms of investment fluctuate and are quoted daily in the financial section of the newspaper. A brief description of the use and merits of the more popular short-term investment securities follows.

Direct Obligations of the U.S. Treasury. These short-term securities include treasury bills, certificates of indebtedness, treasury notes, and tax anticipation securities. They are most liquid, convertible into cash on a day's notice or less. The ninety-one-day treasury bills are most popular—sold at discount and redeemed at par—and are traded in open market and quoted daily. Yield depends upon market and maturity (up to one year). Certificates and notes have longer maturities, up to one year for certificates and from one to five years on notes. Tax anticipation securities are interest-bearing obligations and mature within a few days after quarterly tax payment dates. They can be used for income tax payments on the tax date, while interest accrues to maturity. A free ride of several days' additional interest is obtained to the holder.

Bank Negotiable Time Certificates of Deposit (CD's). These are issued by commercial banks to meet the competition for short-term funds offered by commercial paper, treasury notes, discount bills, and Federal agency issues (Federal Home Loan Bank, Federal Intermediate Credit Bank, Federal Land Bank, Central Bank for Cooperatives, and Federal National Mortgage Association). With no minimum issue amount and of various terms (30 to 89 days; 90 to 179 days; 180 days to 1 year; and 1 year and longer), they pay an attractive rate of interest which depends upon maturity. Easily convertible into cash before maturity in the market, they can also be used as collateral to borrow upon from the bank of issue at a rate at least 2 percent above the certificate rate.

Commercial Paper. This consists of unsecured promissory notes of finance and industrial companies which use this source to raise short-term funds. Prime finance paper is usually sold by dealers or directly by the leading United States commercial finance companies—issued to mature from one to nine months, in many denominations. Prime industrial paper is sold through commercial paper dealers, with flexible denominations and maturity dates, on a discount basis of usually up to 120 days. Although repurchase agreements in case of need are no problem for finance paper, there is no repurchase practice before maturity on the part of industrial companies. Commercial paper rates give the largest return of all forms of generally used temporary investment securities.

CASH CONTROLS

Without proper controls for the collection, custody, and disbursement of cash, the positive accomplishments of good cash planning and utilization would be frustrated by losses arising from errors, fraud, and waste. More important than the need to uncover these losses after their occurrence is the need for prevention or deterrence. Good cash controls remove the possibilities for loose practices by hindering waste, preventing fraud, and promoting efficiency.

No system of controls can detect or foil all frauds. Even if feasible, the cost of doing so may be greater than the savings. In addition, it is not sufficient to install or design a system of cash control and expect it automatically to do the human effort of supervision, review, and revision. Although the attempt, conscious or otherwise, to frustrate controls is well known, constant vigilance can defeat these efforts.

Internal control is one of the most important methods devised to safeguard cash assets. The general requirements for adequate internal cash control consist of the following:

1. No individual should have complete control over all the movements of cash in the firm.
2. Two or more employees, acting independently, should verify the work of each other while carrying on their own work within their clearly understood areas of authority and responsibility.
3. Physical protection of funds by the use of mechanical devices and places of security—registers, safes, locked cages, limited access, receipts, and recording—is indispensable.
4. Separation of the duty of receiving and handling cash from bookkeeping, recording, and depositing is important. The greater the separation of functions consistent with efficiency, the less chance there is for collusion and fraud.
5. The person responsible for each fund must be accountable in writing—daily, weekly, or monthly—for the cash under his control. This written account must be reviewed and audited periodically:
   a. *Cash on hand report* (petty cash): Record of cash movement—receipts, disbursements, and net operating balance—is prepared by custodian. It is checked out by an independent employee, who also performs the physical count.
   b. *Bank accounts:* Balances in books and as reported by the bank must be reconciled by an employee who has nothing to do with receiving or disbursing cash or maintaining the cash records. The bank statements received from the bank go directly to him unopened and remain under his control until the balances are reconciled.
6. Audits. Regular examination of books of account including cash procedures by an independent public accountant should be provided for. The special auditing and accounting techniques of independent confirmation of bank balances, customer and vendor accounts, cutoff procedures, and surprise inspections greatly assist in the prevention and detection of misappropriations.
7. Insurance by way of fidelity bonds, particularly the use of blanket fidelity bonds, which cover on a minimum basis all bondable employees regardless of person or position, supplemented by additional amounts for employees in sensitive areas, is highly recommended. Although fidelity insurance is not a substitute for cash controls, it is an excellent safeguard by spreading the risk.

CONCLUSION

The planned management of company cash is valid for all companies, large and small. When various company plans and operational decisions have been evaluated, cash planning will enable the company to determine, by the use of cash flow analysis, the financial feasibility of the decisions to be made. The employment of even short-term idle funds for investment so as to derive earnings will enhance the profit picture. Cash planning makes management aware of the presence of idle funds. Cash controls are required to prevent and detect cash waste and misappropriation. Cash management serves the company's future by lessening cash crises and enables management to take advantage of business opportunities provided by good buying policies and expansion. Good company cash management enhances the general tone of the company by permitting smoother internal operations and by raising the credit and public image of the company.

BIBLIOGRAPHY

Cash Flow Analysis for Managerial Control, Research Report, no. 38, National Association of Accountants, New York, 1961.

Jaedicke, Robert K., and Robert Sprouse, *Accounting Flows: Income, Funds & Cash, Foundations of Finance Series,* Prentice-Hall, Inc., Englewood Cliffs, N.J., 1965.

Mason, Perry D., *Cash Flow Analysis and the Funds Statement,* Accounting Research Study, no. 2, American Institute of Certified Public Accountants, Inc., New York, 1961.

Pflomm, Norman E., *Managing Company Cash,* Studies in Business Policy, no. 99, National Industrial Conference Board, New York, 1961.

Portfolio for Investment of Temporary Funds, Salomon Brothers & Hutzler, New York, 1965.

CHAPTER FIVE

Financial Ratio Analysis

ROY A. FOULKE   *Formerly Vice President and Director, Dun & Bradstreet, Inc., Bronxville, New York*

The phrase "financial ratio analysis" in business management refers to the interpretation of balance sheets and income statements, more particularly those of industrial and commercial businesses. This interpretation is accomplished by comparing a series of selected dollar items with another series of selected dollar items, and relating the resultant figures (termed "ratios") against standards. Financial ratio analysis had its genesis during the last few years of the nineteenth century when there arose among commercial bankers and mercantile credit specialists the practice of comparing the dollar figure of current assets with the dollar figure of the current debt. Gradually the standard evolved that current assets should be at least twice as large as the current debt.

A study of the ratio of total liabilities to tangible net worth then arose as a supplement to the current ratio. This relationship contrasts the amount of dollars that creditors temporarily have at the risk of a business in the form of its debts with the amount of dollars permanently invested in the business by the owners—that is, the tangible net worth. The standard developed that up to a "one for one" relationship was generally sound. This was the second ratio to come into existence in financial statement analysis. Many others have since come into use.

EXPLANATION OF TERMS

Average Collection Period. The number of days that the total of trade accounts and notes receivables, including assigned accounts and discounted notes, if any, less reserves for bad debts, represents when compared with the annual net credit sales.

Current Assets. Total of cash, accounts and notes receivable for the sale of merchandise less reserves for bad debts, advances on merchandise, inventories less any reserves, listed securities not in excess of market, state and municipal bonds not in excess of market, and United States government securities, direct or guaranteed. In recent years, accountants have added operating supplies, and prepayments for insurance, interest, taxes, advertising services, and similar prepaid items.

Current Debt. Total of all liabilities due within one year from statement date, including current payments on serial notes, mortgages, debentures, or other funded debts. Includes current reserves such as gross reserves for Federal and state income taxes and for contingencies set up for specific purposes, but does not include reserves for depreciation.

Fixed Assets. The sum of the cost or appraised value of land, and the depreciated book value of buildings, leasehold improvements, machinery, tools, equipment, furniture, and fixtures.

Funded Debt. Mortgages, bonds, debentures, serial notes, or other obligations with maturity of more than one year from the statement date.

Inventory. The sum of the dollar value of raw materials, materials in process, and finished merchandise. Retailers, wholesalers, and jobbers have no raw materials or materials in process.

Lower Quartile. The ratio which is three-quarters down a series, when a group of figures are arranged in a graduated series with the strongest ratio at the top and the weakest ratio at the bottom.

Median. The ratio which is halfway down a series when a group of figures are arranged in a graduated series with the strongest ratio at the top and the weakest ratio at the bottom.

Net Profits. Net income after depreciation on buildings, machinery, equipment, furniture, fixtures, and other assets of a fixed nature; after reduction in the value of inventory to cost or market, whichever is lower; after charge-offs for bad debts; after reserves for Federal and state income taxes; and after all miscellaneous reserves and adjustments; but before dividends.

Net Sales. Dollar volume of business transacted over 365 days, net after deductions for returns, allowances, and discounts from gross sales.

Net Working Capital. Excess of the current assets over the current debt as shown in the balance sheet.

Tangible Net Worth. Sum of all outstanding preferred stocks if any, outstanding common stock, surplus, and undivided profits, less any intangible items in the assets such as goodwill, trademarks, patents, copyrights, leaseholds, mailing lists, treasury stock, organization expenses, and underwriting discounts and expenses.

Total Debt. Sum of the current debt and any outstanding funded debts.

Upper Quartile. The ratio which is one-quarter down a series when a group of figures are arranged in a graduated series with the strongest ratio at the top and the weakest ratio at the bottom.

BALANCE SHEET RATIOS

The following eleven ratios are widely used in analyzing the balance sheets of industrial and commercial businesses:
1. Current assets to current debt
2. Current debt to tangible net worth
3. Total debt to tangible net worth
4. Funded debts to net working capital
5. Fixed assets to tangible net worth
6. Net sales to inventory
7. Inventory to net working capital

    8. Average collection period
    9. Net sales to tangible net worth
    10. Net sales to net working capital
    11. Net profits to tangible net worth

Explanations of Eleven Ratios Widely Used in Balance Sheet Analysis. How to arrive at these eleven ratios, their respective significances, and the maxims which may be used as broad guides are discussed in the following paragraphs.[1]

1. *Current Assets to Current Debt.* This ratio tends to indicate the healthy or unhealthy current condition of a business. In the evolution of financial statement analysis, the efficacy of this ratio came to be questioned. When this happened, a second supplemental comparison came into existence—the comparison of the total of cash, marketable securities, and receivables with the current debt. If the current ratio was "two for one" or better, and the total of cash, marketable securities, and receivables equaled or exceeded the current debt, a balance sheet was said to give double assurance of current soundness.

FORMULA. Divide the figure of current assets by the figure of the current debt. Over the years, the practical standard of this ratio has been "two for one" for industrial and commercial businesses.

2. *Current Debt to Tangible Net Worth.* As the tangible net worth serves to guarantee the liquidation of creditor liabilities, the smaller the tangible net worth and the larger the debts, the less security do creditors have. A heavy debt is like high blood pressure—as the pressure goes up, a point is finally reached when the patient cannot survive.

FORMULA. Divide the figure of current assets by the figure of the current net worth. Operating policies should be carefully examined when the current debt exceeds three-quarters of the tangible net worth.

3. *Total Debt to Tangible Net Worth.* Prior to 1900, relatively few businesses except railroads had long-term liabilities. Today many large industrial and commercial corporations have substantial funded obligations, the sizes and types of which depend upon the views of the financial management and the conditions under which the financing arrangements were made.

FORMULA. Divide the figure of total debt by the figure of tangible net worth. Rarely should total liabilities exceed the tangible net worth. When a business has long-term debts, total liabilities may be moderately greater than the current debts of other concerns in the same line of business with no funded debts. This is so because the management has available a longer period in which to make adjustments and plans to solve possible financial problems.

4. *Funded Debts to Net Working Capital.* Net working capital is a key figure in the analysis of balance sheets. Dun & Bradstreet, Inc., computes this figure in its reports, and the manual publishing companies do the same in their publications.

FORMULA. Divide the total of funded debts by the figure of net working capital. Rarely should the aggregate of funded liabilities exceed the net working capital. Where the funded debt is heavier, the relationship is unbalanced. Under such circumstances, the entire tangible net worth is tied up in noncurrent assets and the business must operate from day to day on long-term borrowed funds. In this situation, interest and amortization become a heavy burden.

5. *Fixed Assets to Tangible Net Worth.* The competitive disadvantage of heavy fixed assets is measured by the yearly depreciation charges on that portion of fixed assets which is above the average ratio for its line of business, plus

---

[1] For a more exhaustive treatment of these ratios, see Roy A. Foulke, *Practical Financial Statement Analysis,* 5th ed., chaps. 6–15 and 21, McGraw-Hill Book Company, New York, 1961.

interest charges on borrowed funds, plus any inability to take discounts on purchases because of the consequent low net working capital position.

FORMULA. Divide the figure of fixed assets by the tangible net worth. If fixed assets are excessive, generally net working capital is low or operations are being carried on with funded liabilities. Standards for this ratio vary widely among different divisions of industry and commerce, as will be seen by referring to Table 5-1, but rarely should fixed assets exceed three-quarters of the tangible net worth.

6. *Net Sales to Inventory.* Inventories frequently are the prime cause of business failures. When prices fall, losses are assumed; if both the inventory and the liabilities are heavy, bankruptcy often results. The importance of the inventory increases as the dollar size of the inventory rises in relation to other assets. One method of measuring the relative size of the inventory is the ratio of net sales to inventory.

FORMULA. Divide net sales by the inventory figure in the balance sheet. Even though the five ratios which have been described up to this point vary widely for different divisions of industry and commerce, it has been possible to give general overall standards for them. No maxim can be formulated for this ratio. Standards for each division of manufacturing and trade are essential. These are given for some lines on pages 9-52 and 9-53. Later, sources of standards for other lines will be discussed.

7. *Inventory to Net Working Capital.* The ratio of inventory to net working capital is a supplement to the ratio of net sales to inventory. The relationship between the inventory and the net working capital is between one variable, the inventory, and an item that generally changes moderately from one year to another, the net working capital, so here there exists a relatively fixed base for comparison.

FORMULA. Divide the inventory in the balance sheet by the net working capital. Even though the ratio of net sales to inventory may be in satisfactory relationship, operating policies should be examined where the inventory is greater than the net working capital.

8. *Average Collection Period.* Where no aging of receivables is available, the only measure of the quality of the receivables is a comparison of the average collection period with terms of sale. This gets somewhat complicated where a corporation has many different lines of products with different selling terms.

FORMULA. Divide the annual net credit sales by 365 days to obtain the average credit sales per day. Then divide the total of accounts and notes receivable (plus any assigned accounts and discounted notes) by the average credit sales per day. This gives the average collection period, which may then be compared with the net selling terms. The average collection period should be no more than one-third greater than the net selling terms. With selling terms, for example, of 2 percent discount in 10 days, net 30 days, the average collection period should not exceed 40 days. For concerns selling on the installment basis, the average collection period of the installment accounts, based on the net credit sales after deducting the aggregate down payments, should be no more than one-third greater than one-half of the average selling terms. If the average selling terms are 18 equal monthly installments, for example, one-half of these terms would be 9 months, and one-third greater would give a standard of 12 months.

9. *Net Sales to Tangible Net Worth.* The ratio of net sales to tangible net worth indicates the activity of the invested capital in a business. A high ratio may indicate an excessive volume on a thin margin and the consequent overuse of credit. To overtrade, an excessive use must be made of credit; in that

TABLE 5-1. Fourteen Important Ratios with Interquartile Range for Selected Manufacturing Lines

Line of business	Number of concerns	Interquartile range	Current assets to current debt (Times)	Net profits on net sales (Per cent)	Net profits on tangible net worth (Per cent)	Net profits on net working capital (Per cent)	Net sales to tangible net worth (Times)	Net sales to net working capital (Times)	Collection period (Days)	Net sales to inventory (Times)	Fixed assets to tangible net worth (Per cent)	Current debt to tangible net worth (Per cent)	Total debt to tangible net worth (Per cent)	Inventory to net working capital (Per cent)	Current debt to inventory (Per cent)	Funded debts to net working capital (Per cent)
Airplane parts and accessories	55	Upper quartile	3.08	4.48	17.29	29.23	5.39	7.58	26	11.1	27.7	34.0	56.5	53.8	76.9	24.7
		MEDIAN	2.01	2.64	8.10	14.58	3.88	5.15	43	7.1	49.9	54.9	112.4	74.9	122.0	45.5
		Lower quartile	1.52	1.26	3.46	5.83	2.47	3.98	66	5.3	75.6	105.7	142.9	133.5	215.2	83.0
Automobile parts and accessories	89	Upper quartile	3.91	6.08	20.33	28.09	4.05	6.53	31	9.3	22.5	23.4	45.3	46.8	57.0	5.0
		MEDIAN	2.97	3.63	11.15	16.68	2.96	4.41	42	6.6	32.4	36.3	69.5	71.7	85.5	23.9
		Lower quartile	2.20	2.16	5.94	9.61	2.33	3.43	51	4.7	45.0	57.8	91.7	96.7	114.4	42.9
Bakers	65	Upper quartile	2.92	3.10	13.74	44.07	5.87	28.03	12	35.7	59.8	19.1	31.2	39.0	116.9	18.1
		MEDIAN	1.85	1.89	8.88	26.15	4.65	16.44	16	29.4	71.6	30.5	59.1	63.4	191.3	66.2
		Lower quartile	1.35	0.60	3.45	7.87	3.09	8.74	22	19.3	101.5	46.5	102.2	124.8	269.3	165.1
Chemical, industrial	62	Upper quartile	4.12	7.37	12.26	34.78	3.08	7.36	37	8.9	41.8	18.3	40.7	46.3	55.1	40.8
		MEDIAN	2.91	4.61	9.03	21.98	1.78	3.95	48	5.9	72.4	26.1	67.0	66.1	93.1	89.4
		Lower quartile	1.82	2.67	5.79	8.02	1.32	2.80	62	4.5	99.4	60.3	108.5	95.0	145.2	135.5
Coats and suits, men's and boys'	131	Upper quartile	2.67	1.98	9.48	11.71	7.99	10.61	28	8.7	2.7	48.3	91.3	63.3	68.8	8.3
		MEDIAN	1.89	0.88	5.85	7.23	5.35	5.70	54	5.8	7.7	92.7	140.4	98.9	97.4	23.3
		Lower quartile	1.43	0.41	1.69	1.82	3.38	4.03	90	4.2	18.6	164.0	242.2	164.5	146.6	36.8
Coats and suits, women's	100	Upper quartile	2.31	1.77	14.79	18.50	11.83	13.97	26	25.6	2.9	47.5	56.4	44.1	93.3	9.8
		MEDIAN	1.76	0.65	8.17	9.52	7.75	10.36	36	12.1	6.2	96.4	169.2	90.0	153.7	30.2
		Lower quartile	1.40	0.28	1.59	2.10	4.82	6.31	52	6.4	14.8	177.6	248.9	136.4	239.5	56.9
Construction machinery	78	Upper quartile	3.86	5.32	14.77	23.60	4.21	7.21	39	9.7	22.7	25.9	46.6	59.5	50.2	17.8
		MEDIAN	2.75	2.70	8.08	11.70	2.50	3.93	54	4.9	32.4	42.0	81.4	74.5	79.4	38.4
		Lower quartile	1.89	1.19	3.12	4.37	1.75	2.63	66	3.1	51.0	70.7	136.4	108.8	141.9	88.3
Dresses: silk, rayon, and acetate	129	Upper quartile	2.25	1.71	19.23	22.64	17.13	20.83	29	30.8	3.9	67.8	69.4	41.7	130.7	15.5
		MEDIAN	1.66	0.67	9.28	10.11	11.68	12.95	36	17.3	8.7	132.2	179.2	76.9	190.2	29.4
		Lower quartile	1.38	0.22	2.08	2.70	6.53	8.07	47	10.5	15.6	220.3	269.9	135.6	277.0	48.2
Electrical parts and supplies	63	Upper quartile	4.17	5.61	17.10	30.23	5.00	10.93	29	8.4	26.4	19.7	39.8	61.5	50.0	3.2
		MEDIAN	2.57	2.96	8.78	12.79	3.24	4.47	39	5.6	35.5	43.9	77.1	74.0	87.1	24.6
		Lower quartile	1.60	0.58	1.95	4.55	2.50	3.33	51	4.1	52.3	74.7	106.6	124.0	132.9	49.9
Fruits and vegetables, canners	58	Upper quartile	3.50	5.14	15.52	36.78	5.53	12.76	15	10.6	27.0	21.1	82.5	63.8	50.5	22.0
		MEDIAN	1.95	2.34	8.35	14.54	3.78	7.16	23	5.9	49.4	58.4	111.1	103.5	81.6	49.4
		Lower quartile	1.42	1.33	5.63	8.48	2.60	3.77	39	2.9	62.7	105.7	142.7	215.3	127.6	81.7

Industry	No.		1	2	3	4	5	6	7	8	9	10	11	12	13	14
Furniture............	104	Upper quartile	4.03	3.55	13.26	19.02	6.74	10.35	26	11.5	16.7	24.6	51.9	57.3	60.1	12.3
		MEDIAN	2.15	1.83	6.75	10.43	4.11	6.11	40	7.6	32.8	48.8	93.0	79.3	93.4	38.8
		Lower quartile	1.54	0.53	2.71	4.54	2.63	3.65	55	4.8	54.9	113.1	174.6	139.1	150.0	70.5
Hardware and tools..	108	Upper quartile	4.95	5.64	14.73	26.43	3.37	5.58	34	8.5	21.2	14.2	28.3	56.1	40.5	9.6
		MEDIAN	3.47	3.23	8.97	14.58	2.15	3.63	39	5.1	31.6	25.5	55.8	74.5	61.8	23.5
		Lower quartile	2.42	1.95	3.83	6.39	1.48	2.66	51	3.6	50.3	42.5	98.2	92.5	91.7	51.3
Hosiery.............	57	Upper quartile	4.03	3.55	12.69	21.97	4.11	10.98	23	8.3	29.6	16.9	31.0	75.0	46.3	6.1
		MEDIAN	2.36	1.77	6.52	9.23	2.89	5.50	35	6.7	47.4	34.8	55.6	97.7	71.3	22.9
		Lower quartile	1.82	0.46	1.61	2.09	1.65	2.80	42	3.6	68.0	70.7	101.3	124.4	108.6	69.0
Lumber.............	80	Upper quartile	4.45	5.21	13.21	30.93	4.31	8.12	22	8.8	24.5	19.2	43.0	58.8	52.1	22.2
		MEDIAN	2.24	2.25	8.42	11.80	3.05	5.09	38	6.2	38.4	41.8	78.9	84.9	88.3	39.0
		Lower quartile	1.49	0.90	3.15	3.34	1.93	3.44	55	4.5	68.2	90.3	108.5	130.2	138.4	76.2
Machine shops.......	117	Upper quartile	3.44	6.86	24.94	51.09	4.87	11.71	30	31.9	27.2	20.3	48.8	25.0	90.5	26.2
		MEDIAN	2.17	4.40	15.79	29.30	3.25	7.13	39	14.8	45.9	33.0	77.7	52.9	170.6	56.0
		Lower quartile	1.50	2.06	6.52	16.44	2.28	4.27	54	7.4	81.4	69.0	121.7	91.6	319.2	97.1
Meats and provisions, packers	107	Upper quartile	3.93	1.55	11.82	24.57	12.54	31.02	10	45.5	37.6	20.7	46.8	43.1	59.6	26.7
		MEDIAN	2.51	0.74	7.35	15.50	8.94	20.54	13	30.5	52.9	33.5	70.5	62.9	100.2	50.4
		Lower quartile	1.78	0.36	3.91	7.88	5.78	10.92	16	19.5	77.0	46.9	103.9	88.6	173.1	91.2
Metal stampings....	115	Upper quartile	4.21	5.74	16.36	38.89	4.71	10.17	26	16.4	28.6	15.4	41.6	40.6	61.8	17.6
		MEDIAN	2.53	3.54	10.73	19.60	3.03	5.74	33	9.9	43.5	32.1	68.0	62.0	106.5	48.2
		Lower quartile	1.67	1.33	4.23	8.83	2.10	4.27	39	6.9	71.6	58.5	90.4	108.4	192.0	122.1
Metalworking machinery and equipment	93	Upper quartile	3.73	5.81	15.08	36.90	4.38	8.72	31	21.3	37.1	18.8	42.9	29.8	79.8	20.5
		MEDIAN	2.46	2.98	9.48	17.73	2.53	5.42	41	13.9	55.6	35.7	65.5	52.5	144.3	33.8
		Lower quartile	1.55	1.13	3.04	6.28	1.94	3.24	55	6.2	74.5	66.3	128.6	9.23	294.8	65.6
Overalls and work clothing	66	Upper quartile	3.92	2.96	13.77	16.40	5.89	7.22	27	7.0	9.7	33.5	53.8	65.9	46.6	10.1
		MEDIAN	2.70	1.81	7.96	10.04	4.35	5.23	51	5.9	15.9	51.5	98.3	86.7	71.0	29.8
		Lower quartile	1.79	1.21	4.42	4.71	3.25	3.46	64	4.1	27.0	101.1	168.7	128.4	123.4	48.8
Paints, varnishes and lacquers	132	Upper quartile	4.96	4.81	14.82	21.23	4.23	6.37	32	10.2	21.1	17.7	28.4	42.2	45.9	7.1
		MEDIAN	3.65	2.75	8.11	13.41	3.03	5.30	41	7.5	30.5	24.1	45.3	59.7	74.6	17.7
		Lower quartile	2.59	1.22	4.43	6.41	2.05	3.27	54	5.7	46.3	39.8	85.6	77.5	110.5	39.6
Paper products, converters	50	Upper quartile	4.52	4.24	11.70	23.00	4.46	8.72	27	12.1	26.6	17.0	30.8	41.3	52.4	4.7
		MEDIAN	2.87	2.73	8.52	15.75	3.00	4.99	36	7.6	38.6	33.7	68.4	68.7	83.8	30.7
		Lower quartile	1.67	0.97	3.53	6.70	2.14	3.60	49	5.3	59.0	68.6	120.9	112.7	126.1	69.2
Petroleum refining...	50	Upper quartile	2.83	10.38	11.48	51.81	2.41	6.72	37	10.9	68.4	14.0	24.4	49.8	85.3	32.1
		MEDIAN	2.23	6.92	9.72	35.21	1.38	5.51	48	9.2	87.6	22.3	44.2	69.0	127.2	61.8
		Lower quartile	1.84	3.67	7.02	21.14	0.99	4.28	56	7.1	95.8	36.6	82.9	82.9	180.2	119.3
Structural iron and steel, fabricators	111	Upper quartile	4.03	5.44	16.93	29.14	5.55	10.22	29	12.9	23.3	22.3	70.8	43.6	63.3	17.1
		MEDIAN	2.15	2.61	10.20	13.81	3.85	5.78	47	7.8	38.6	51.7	111.7	71.6	114.3	40.3
		Lower quartile	1.46	1.35	4.73	8.01	2.33	3.48	63	4.9	53.6	98.4	174.3	123.4	191.5	92.5

SOURCE: Dun & Bradstreet, 1963.

process liabilities reach high proportions. A business becomes more and more vulnerable as its liabilities expand.

FORMULA. Divide annual net sales by the tangible net worth. As with the ratio of net sales to inventory, no broad maxim can be given as a guide to the reasonably safe limits of this ratio. As a general rule, if this ratio is more than twice as large as that which is typical (median or average) for a particular division of industry or commerce, one may well feel that overtrading is taking place. The momentum of a concern that is overtrading carries a business forward on its path in the same way that a speeding automobile continues to plunge ahead notwithstanding pressure on its brakes. The faster a business is moving, the more chances there are for vital mistakes and the more difficult it is to change its direction.

10. *Net Sales to Net Working Capital.* It is not unusual for the relationship of net sales to tangible net worth to be in satisfactory proportion but the relationship of net sales to net working capital to be excessive. Such a condition is the concomitant result of a top-heavy investment in fixed or slow assets, leaving a moderate or low net working capital position. Any reasonable volume of net sales on a moderate or low net working capital results in heavy current liabilities in relation to current assets and a consequent low current ratio. For a business to be in healthy condition, both the ratio of net sales to tangible net worth and the ratio of net sales to net working capital must be sound.

FORMULA. Divide annual net sales by the net working capital. Here again no broad maxim can be given as a guide. This ratio tends to be high in those lines of business which handle a large volume of sales per investment on short terms such as meat packers and wholesalers of cigars, cigarettes, and tobacco. The ratio also tends to be high in those lines of trade where the investment in fixed assets is the highest because in these cases the net working capital often is moderate or even low. For standards, reference must be made to the typical ratios in the same or similar divisions of business.

11. *Net Profits to Tangible Net Worth.* There are two widely used measures of net profit for industrial and commercial businesses—a comparison with the tangible net worth and a comparison with the net sales. Both measures are complementary; the net profit on tangible net worth is the guide to the use of funds invested in a business. Those companies that show the highest percentage net profit on tangible net worth, not for a single year but over a sustained period of years, are naturally the most highly regarded.

FORMULA. Divide net profits by the tangible net worth. There is, of course, no standard for this ratio, but it is always interesting to compare a particular ratio with the same ratio for other companies in the same or similar lines of activity.

INCOME STATEMENT RATIOS

Income statements may be divided into sixteen primary items; these items in turn may be classified under the three sections of gross profits, operating profits, and final profit or loss. The sixteen items of primary importance are:

Gross Profit Section
1. Gross sales
2. Returns and allowances
3. Net sales
4. Cost of goods sold
5. Gross margin

Operating Profit Section
6. Administrative and general expenses
7. Selling expenses
8. Provisions for bad debts
9. Operating profit

Final Net Profit or Loss Section
10. Cash discounts earned and given
11. Interest paid
12. Net profit or loss before extraordinary charges
13. Extraordinary charges
14. Federal and state income taxes
15. Net profit or loss
16. Net profit or loss after adjustments for carry-back or carry-forward tax privileges

Several of the above sixteen items, in turn, may be broken down into subdivisions. Selling expenses, for example, may consist of salesmen's salaries, commissions, advertising, overhead of the sales department, and entertainment of customers and prospective customers. On the other hand, several of these sixteen items are often grouped together, so that a condensed income statement may consist of only six or eight items.

In the ratio analysis of income statements, the dollar item of net sales represents 100 percent, and every other item in the statement, whether there are fewer or greater than the sixteen items listed above, is determined as a percentage of net sales. After these percentages are determined, they may be compared with recognized standards to ascertain whether they are high or low. If an adequate volume of sales is being handled (the ratio of net sales to tangible net worth and the ratio of net sales to net working capital provide this information), and if final net profits are low or losses are being taken, then the percentage of some one or several items of expense is too high.

The business executive tends to have greater familiarity with income statement ratios than with balance sheet ratios. If operating losses are being assumed or net profits are shrinking, he is generally able to find some place where expenses may be reduced, perhaps in the advertising department, perhaps by more careful buying to reduce raw material costs, perhaps in salesmen's entertainment expenses, salaries, wages, or even office supplies.

SOURCES OF FINANCIAL RATIOS

There are five direct and indirect sources of financial ratios. By "direct sources" are meant ratios themselves. By "indirect sources" are meant dollar figures from which ratios may readily be computed. These five sources are (1) Dun & Bradstreet, Inc., (2) Robert Morris Associates, (3) the Internal Revenue Service of the U.S. Treasury Department, (4) compilations made jointly by the Federal Trade Commission and the Securities and Exchange Commission, and (5) certain trade associations.

Dun & Bradstreet, Inc. Compiles yearly *Key Business Ratios* for 125 refined lines of business activity. *Balance sheet ratios:* Typical examples for these ratios appear in Table 5-1. In compiling these ratios, Dun & Bradstreet, Inc., computes the individual ratios for each business and then establishes the figure for each ratio representing the upper quartile, median, and lower quartile. *Income statement ratios:* Included in the above computations is the ratio of net profits to net sales. This organization also computes ratios for selected items of expense for 185 lines of business as reported by a representative sample of all corporation

Federal income tax returns. (See second paragraph following.) These annual studies are available at any office of Dun & Bradstreet, Inc., or at its headquarters, 99 Church Street, New York, N.Y. 10007.

Robert Morris Associates. Compiles yearly composite balance sheets and condensed income statements on 183 refined lines of business. *Balance sheet ratios:* Eleven ratios are computed for each line of business. The bases of these ratios are composite figures, so the ratios tend more toward averages than medians. *Income statement ratios:* Six ratios are computed with net sales representing 100 percent. Annual studies can be purchased either in book form entitled *Annual Statement Studies* or by individual single pages covering compilation for a single line of business. The office is located in the Philadelphia Bank Building, Philadelphia, Pa. 19107.

Internal Revenue Service, U. S. Treasury Department. Compiles composite balance sheets and composite income statements based on the Federal income tax returns of all corporations. These are dollar totals. The compilations are by major industrial groupings and not, as in the studies of Dun & Bradstreet, Inc., and Robert Morris Associates, of refined lines of business. *Balance sheet ratios:* From the aggregate dollar figures in the composite balance sheets, one may compute his own ratios. Composite dollar figures tend to be influenced by the figures of large corporations in contrast to interquartile computations where the ratios of each business receive equal weight. *Income statement ratios:* Composite income statements contain twenty-five different items. As with the composite balance sheets, these are dollar totals, and one must compute his own ratios as a percent of net sales, or as the item is termed in these studies, "business receipts." Because of the tremendous compilations, these studies tend to be three or four years old when published. This publication entitled *Statistics of Income, Corporation Income Tax Returns* is sold by the Superintendent of Documents, U.S. Government Printing Office, Washington, D.C. 20402.

Federal Trade Commission and the Securities and Exchange Commission. A more restricted but the most current of all studies is prepared jointly by the Division of Statistics in the Federal Trade Commission and the Office of Statistical Studies in the Securities and Exchange Commission under the title of *Quarterly Financial Reports for Manufacturing Corporations.* These studies are prepared each calendar quarter and provide composite balance sheets and composite income statements for thirty-four major lines and groupings of manufacturers. *Balance sheet ratios:* Contains five balance sheet ratios: (1) current assets to current debt, (2) total of cash and U.S. government securities to current debt, (3) total stockholders' equity to total debt, and (4) and (5) profits, before and after Federal income taxes, to stockholders' equity. Composite balance sheets are (1) in dollars and (2) in percentages with total assets and total liabilities representing 100 percent. Other ratios must be computed. *Income statement ratios:* Contains ratios of profits, before and after Federal income taxes, on annual sales; also ratios of seven items of expense related to annual sales as 100 percent. This publication is sold by the Superintendent of Documents, U.S. Government Printing Office, Washington, D.C. 20402.

Trade Associations. Many trade associations have strong and sustained interests in income statement ratios for their respective trades and industries. They have exhibited less interest in balance sheet ratio studies. Many trade associations make studies year after year. The Mercantile Library of Dun & Bradstreet, Inc., keeps in touch with this activity of trade associations. Among the associations which were active in 1965 in this area are the following:

American Institute of Laundering, South Chicago Street, Joliet, Ill.

American Paper & Pulp Association, 122 East 42nd Street, New York, N.Y.

Kentucky Retail Lumber Dealers Association, Lebanon, Ky.

National Appliance and Radio-TV Dealers Association, 1141 B Merchandise Mart Plaza, Chicago, Ill.

National Association of Retail Clothiers and Furnishers, 1257 Munsey Building, Washington, D.C.

National Automobile Dealers Association, 2000 K Street N.W., Washington, D.C.

National Electrical Contractors Association, Inc., 610 Ring Building, Washington, D.C.

National Institute of Drycleaning, 909 Burlington Avenue, Silver Spring, Md.

National Paper Box Manufacturers Association, Liberty Trust Building, Philadelphia, Pa.

National Retail Furniture Association, 1150 Merchandise Mart Plaza, Chicago, Ill.

National Sporting Goods Association, 23 East Jackson Boulevard, Chicago, Ill.

National Wholesale Druggists Association, 220 East 42nd Street, New York, N.Y.

Ohio Association of Retail Lumber Dealers, 41 Craswell Road, Columbus, Ohio

Shoe Service Institute of America, 222 West Adams Street, Chicago, Ill.

Super Market Institute, 200 East Ontario Street, Chicago, Ill.

If interested in obtaining income statement ratios (often termed "cost of doing business ratios"), be sure to get in touch with specific national or state trade associations to ascertain if they have made any such studies in recent years.

BIBLIOGRAPHY

Annual Statement Studies, Robert Morris Associates, Philadelphia.

Foulke, Roy A., *Practical Financial Statement Analysis,* 5th ed., McGraw-Hill Book Company, New York, 1961.

Key Business Ratios, Dun & Bradstreet, Inc., New York.

Quarterly Financial Reports for Manufacturing Corporations, Federal Trade Commission and the Securities and Exchange Commission, Washington, D.C.

Statistics of Income, Corporation Income Tax Returns, Internal Revenue Service, U.S. Treasury Department, Washington, D.C.

Trade associations for various lines of manufacturing, wholesaling, retailing, and servicing.

CHAPTER SIX

Tax Management

JOHN P. KELSEY *Price Waterhouse & Co., Philadelphia, Pennsylvania*

One of the largest single elements of cost to any corporation is taxes. The forms of corporate taxes, both hidden and apparent, are many. They include the following:

United States government
  Income
  Excise
  Payroll (unemployment and social security)
State, city, or other political subdivisions
  Income and/or franchise
  Personal and real property
  Sales and use
  Payroll (unemployment, social security, workmen's compensation, and the like)
Foreign countries

The layman might think that the major portion of the tax work facing a corporation involves merely the routine function of filling out a return and computing the tax due. This is far from the truth. *Every* tax imposed upon a corporation needs continual interpretation of its specific applicability to the various transactions of the corporation. The field of taxation changes every day as new court decisions and rulings are announced and as laws are changed. Every corporation must be alert to such changes.

ORGANIZATION AND RESPONSIBILITIES OF THE TAX DEPARTMENT

There is no single form of organization that can be prescribed to fit the needs and requirements of every corporate enterprise. The size of the business, its geographical dispersion, the nature, number, and complexity of tax returns which must be filed, and the economics of maintaining a single tax specialist or group of specialists are all factors to be considered in determining the tax organization to be established for a given corporation.

It is axiomatic that every business corporation must have one individual responsible for the control of tax planning, return preparation, filing, and representation of the corporation during governmental audits. The size of the corporate organization will determine whether this individual is the corporate controller, treasurer, or other financial officer, or someone whose full-time duties are manager—tax department. In the larger organizations, the more specific assignments are delegated to a specialized tax manager, whereas in smaller organizations, the tax responsibility generally rests with a senior financial official. The important consideration is that *responsibility must be fixed on one individual* for the conduct and administration of the corporation's tax program.

The functions of the tax department are principally:

1. Tax planning and consultation regarding business decisions
2. Preparation and filing of tax returns
3. Representation during governmental examinations

Without attempting to define specifically the terms "small," "medium," and "large," the following progression of decisions must be considered:

1. Should the tax department be inside the corporate organization, outside the corporate organization, or in both places?

This depends on the degree to which a corporation will utilize the tax services of its outside professional advisers, principally the independent certified public accountant and/or legal counsel. Relative costs and the degree of specialized technical ability required are the prime factors to be considered. As a general rule, small companies will find that a higher degree of specialized talent can be brought to bear on their tax matters at a lower annual cost if they engage independent accountants and/or legal counsel to perform tax planning, return preparation, and representation for government audits. Medium-sized organizations, particularly those with a multiplicity of state and local tax returns and a fairly even spread of tax work over the year, will probably find it desirable to establish their tax departments within the corporate framework and to use the services of outside professionals only for tax planning and for supplemental representation, if required, during governmental examinations. Large organizations are generally better served by retaining the entire tax function within the corporate organization, except perhaps in the area of tax planning. Here, because of his breadth of diversified experience, the outside professional tax adviser is often able to render valuable tax planning services even to those organizations whose internal tax departments have a highly developed specialized technical ability.

2. Should the functions of the tax department be centralized or decentralized?

The answer to the first question will, in some measure, determine the decision on the second. Generally, the tax functions are decentralized to some degree in every corporation. Responsibility for planning, preparation of Federal and state income tax returns, and representation during governmental examinations may lie with the outside professional adviser in small organizations, with the corporation handling the preparation and filing of payroll, property, sales and use tax reports, and state franchise reports.

On the other hand, in a larger corporation, tax planning may be the responsibility of the outside adviser, and all return preparation and representation may be handled within the corporation. Payroll tax returns are more frequently prepared in the payroll department than in the tax department because of their nontechnical nature and the fact that the basic return data are a necessary product of the basic payroll record. Sales and use tax returns may be prepared either by the billing and invoicing section or by the purchasing department. Because of the diverse character of the sales and use taxes levied by the various jurisdictions, however, it is usually preferable that such returns be prepared within the tax department. Personal and real property taxes generally lend themselves to decentralized treatment, particularly in those jurisdictions where local customs as to valuation procedures are not made clear in the taxing statutes or other published information. Experience has indicated that when the home office pays taxes to jurisdictions geographically separated, more favorable tax results can be obtained through local agents, either corporate employees or outside advisers, than is generally possible if such returns are handled within the centralized tax department. Regardless of the degree of decentralization, it should still be the responsibility of the tax department to establish the broad policies for the corporation for all phases of taxation and to satisfy itself that these policies are carried out.

3. To what extent should the company's tax department be divided into specialist groups?

The various types of taxes and taxing jurisdictions which must be dealt with by the tax department tend to force some degree of specialization within the department. Each type of tax requires specialized knowledge of the items includable within the tax base, factors entering into allocation, items specifically exempt, and procedures for assessment, appeal, payment, and refund. The degree of specialization which is desirable is, of course, limited by the needs of the organization, the variety of returns filed, and the number of personnel in the tax department. The most common areas of specialty are Federal income taxes, state income or franchise taxes, and property taxes.

The advantages of specialization are the development of a higher degree of expertise and increased efficiency in handling problems within the area of specialization. The disadvantages are the difficulty of arranging the tax work load in such a fashion that maximum utilization is made of all personnel throughout the year and the difficulty of developing from within the tax group individuals with a broad range of tax knowledge and experience. Many medium-sized and larger corporations are able to overcome these disadvantages through the use of members of the "general accounting or internal auditing staffs" to assist with the work load during peak periods or through a planned rotation program within the tax department, where certain individuals are designated as specialists in specific areas but are also assigned duties in other areas.

THE TAX PLANNING FUNCTION

Tax planning can involve many aspects of a business. It is normally associated instances, is its most important function. In all of its other responsibilities, the tax department is operating in the passive role of reflecting tax liabilities based upon events that have already transpired. Tax planning involves the tax department in a dynamic role of changing or modifying events before their completion to achieve a desirable end result.

Tax planning can involve many aspects of a business. It is normally associated with unusual transactions such as the acquisition or sale of a business. But it may also involve day-to-day transactions related to accounting methods or timing for the realization of income. The tax consequences from ordinary routine business transactions when modified through creative tax planning can result in most significant tax reductions. The planning need not be dramatic to be important. There may be many routine transactions which do not have significant financial impact but which can be changed to result in savings or deferrals in the payment of taxes.

Type of Individual Needed.   For any company to have effective tax planning, it must have individuals who are capable of abstract thinking.   Not all individuals have the ability to envision abstractly the effects of alternative ways of accomplishing something.

An imaginative approach to an unusual business problem such as an acquisition or sale is important.   In this circumstance, the problem is clear and the objectives may be obvious.   Imaginative planning for more routine problems, however, may require a particularly creative individual, because he must first ascertain the existence of a problem and then abstractly determine an objective.

For example, a small company had been using the accrual method of accounting for tax purposes for many years.   When an outside professional tax adviser reviewed the company, he immediately noticed that using the cash basis accounting method rather than the accrual method would result in significant tax deferrals.   To spot such a recommendation, it was necessary that the tax reviewer not have his thinking limited by the accounting method precedents.

It is impossible to determine why some individuals are creative and others are not.   Perhaps only the end result of the operations of a tax department can really indicate the existence or nonexistence of creative tax planning.   If a company has provided the proper environment and has furnished suitable facilities but still does not receive significant results from tax planning, it can only be regretfully concluded that the wrong individuals have been assigned to this function.   It can safely be said that the complexities of the present tax laws and of modern business operations inevitably present tax planning opportunities for any company.

Proper Environment.   The creation of the proper environment to stimulate creative tax thinking is imperative.   One of the vital factors that will result in effective tax planning is management's conviction that it is important.   Management should make it known that such thinking is expected from its tax department.   The tax department should continually have before it the thought that it is expected to devise alternative means of accomplishing business transactions that will result in reducing or deferring taxes.   It is also important that the tax manager be a part of and enter into the major decisions of the corporation.   Absence of opportunities for creative thinking can effectively stifle tax thinking, even for individuals who have the ability to think creatively.

In some instances, management may not be aware that a transaction has tax implications.   This makes it important for the tax manager to be aggressive in reviewing information and communicating with operating personnel so that transactions having tax significance do not go by without tax review.   To accomplish this, a tax manager should:

1. Have access to executive correspondence
2. Review the minutes of the board of directors' meetings
3. Have frequent informal meetings at lunch or on other occasions with key personnel in all corporate departments
4. Make periodic visits to operating plants

There are environmental factors within the tax department itself that will help subordinates think creatively.   Foremost among these is having suitable information at hand through tax services and periodicals to lay the foundation of knowledge from which creative tax thinking must be extrapolated.   Creative tax thinking, like creative thinking in any field of endeavor, can be done only by persons who have adequate knowledge and understanding of the rules of their particular field.   In most instances, there is a direct correlation between the extent of creative tax planning and the extent of understanding of tax laws and rules.

Because taxes affect so many different aspects of a business, it behooves the tax manager to attempt to stimulate tax consciousness on the part of operating personnel. This can be done through informal discussions or by sending tax memoranda to key officials, keeping them informed of new tax developments or telling them of an interesting tax-saving procedure recently adopted by the company.

Importance of Keeping Current. It is important to make adequate tax information available to members of the tax department. Many tax publications are written in a manner to stimulate thinking. Even though the suggestions made by published tax services may not have direct bearing on the problems of a company, the exposure of tax planners to these concepts may serve to stimulate thinking and thereby result in improved tax planning.

There are other means that can be used to stimulate tax thinking. In many industries, there are trade associations whose members meet occasionally to discuss common tax and financial problems. It is important for representatives of the tax department to attend these meetings for the purpose of broadening their outlook on tax problems. It may be even more important for tax planners to attend meetings or discussions that are not directly oriented to their industry. This type of session may present tax concepts or procedures from an entirely unrelated industry that they can use in their own company. In many cases, creative tax planning results when the rules of one part of the tax law are brought to bear upon another seemingly unrelated area.

Proper Time for Planning. Tax planning can be most effective when it is done *before* transactions are consummated. This makes it mandatory that tax management personnel be consulted before the consummation of any unusual transaction, regardless of its significance. In the early stages of planning for a transaction, it is usually quite feasible to arrange the method of accomplishing the end result in a way that will minimize the tax impact. Taxes are determined on the basis of relatively fixed rules which can frequently be complied with in a way that will result in tax savings.

Another aspect of tax planning centers on the compliance function of the tax department. The individuals who prepare and file tax returns should be stimulated to examine them critically, seeking ways of reducing the tax liability. When an individual can see the end result in tax liabilities of a particular method of recording a business transaction, he may be stimulated to rearrange the transaction. This approach tends to emphasize that accomplished transactions should serve as a guide to better methods of handling future transactions.

In some circumstances, it may be possible to recast an accomplished transaction to reduce taxes. This is a less desirable type of tax planning, because the planner must deal with the situation as it has been presented and has no opportunity to change it. Indeed, this type of tax planning may better be categorized as "tax rationalization," because the individual can only rationalize to an end result based upon given facts without having the opportunity to revise the facts. But in any event, a review of completed transactions may at least show how to do things better in the future.

Example. A corporation with several subsidiaries had been operating at a loss and began filing a consolidated Federal income tax return. Because it was a consolidated return, the company became quite careless in allocating expenses among the various subsidiaries. It filed its tax return with a large consolidated loss that resulted in only a minimum refund from the net operating loss carry-back. Upon later review of the return, it was noted that proper expense allocation would result in several of the subsidiaries having net operating losses within the consolidated group and that these losses could be carried back to separate return years for additional refunds. In this case, the review of a completed and filed tax return resulted in significant additional tax refunds.

Independent Consultants. Because tax planning is a highly individualistic skill, it is desirable for a company to receive thinking on its tax problems from more than one source. It is important for a corporation to have adequate tax accounting and legal advice from practitioners who specialize in this area of the law. These independent practitioners bring to a company's tax problems outside experience and a considerable body of professional knowledge. These attributes are difficult to find in an individual whose experience is limited to the tax problems of one company. Thus, the utilization of independent tax practitioners is important to every company of any size.

The independent tax accountant, operating in conjunction with the independent examination of the financial statements of the corporation, can be a particularly important individual for effective tax planning. He is in a position to review the corporation's financial transactions with a view toward minimizing tax liabilities. He should locate tax problems and give recommendations for their solution. Other tax practitioners may be able to render advice only on problems that have already been identified and brought to their attention.

PREPARATION AND TIMELY FILING OF TAX RETURNS

Every tax department should have a "tax calendar" to ensure the on-time filing of all of the corporation's required tax returns. The tax calendar should preferably be in the form of individual cards for each return. These are filed in chronological order and should show, as a minimum, the name of the return, due date, date of extension, and date filed. The proper maintenance of a tax calendar is a must for every corporation.

Accumulating Information for Tax Returns. The tax department does not create the basic financial and accounting data which ultimately result in the computed tax liability shown on the tax return. Such data must be gathered from locations outside the tax department and then accumulated, analyzed, reclassified, adjusted, and finally arrayed in the tax return by the tax department.

The task of gathering the basic information from outside sources is a difficult and complex one for several reasons. In the first place, the problem of return preparation itself is complex, requiring the assembly of a large amount of data. Second, experience has indicated that the accounting records generally do not present the necessary data in the form and classification required for tax return purposes. Third, the diversity in the treatment of data required (particularly in multistate operations) necessitates alternative classifications of the same data. Finally, there is the seemingly ever-present problem of the tax and accounting department work loads. For these reasons, the tax manager should preplan his data requirements carefully as to both the nature and amount of data required and the time when they must be received by his department.

The following general observations regarding data accumulation are applicable to all corporate situations:

1. The tax manager should request all the data that he needs and none that is superfluous.

2. The request should be made in a manner which will clearly indicate the *precise information* desired and the *form* in which it is wanted.

3. The request should be made as far *in advance* of the time when the data are actually required as practical and should clearly state the date required.

Form of Request for Data. For the following reasons, the request for data should be made in the form of carefully designed schedules, each of which requests certain specific data:

1. Well-designed schedules will clearly indicate the precise data required and will ensure its presentation in the form desired.

2. Such schedules will reduce to a minimum the submission of superfluous information.

3. In general, such schedules will allow for preparation of data by lower-salaried personnel, because they remove a significant portion of judgment.

Preparation of Federal and State Income Tax Returns. *Preplanning and Review.* The preparation of the corporation's Federal income tax return is one of the most important functions which the tax department is called upon to perform. In the ideal situation, it is the Federal tax return which embodies not only the operating results of the company for the year but also the tax planning which has been done during the year. Thus, the preparation of the annual tax return actually starts long before the year-end, because events which have transpired during the year, as a result of either company action or outside action, have a direct bearing on the return preparation. Accordingly, the tax manager must review, prior to the preparation of the return, certain specific information to determine the extent to which the return preparation may be affected. This information should include at least the following:

1. New matters in the Internal Revenue Code; regulations, rulings, and tax cases which may have a bearing on the corporation's tax return. This type of information must be reviewed during the course of the year as it becomes available, for it is physically impossible and completely undesirable to defer it to the time of actual return preparation.

2. Changes within the company which may result in tax consequences, such as new methods of selling, changes in places of business, and mergers or acquisitions. The tax manager must be consulted on these changes during the year so that he can develop the most advantageous tax treatment.

3. Revenue agents' examinations during the year which may result in special treatment of certain items on the current period's tax return.

4. The prior years' Federal and state tax returns. The tax manager must refamiliarize himself with awkward presentation problems so that they can be avoided through timely correction in the current year's preparation.

Use of Tax Work-paper Spread Sheet. As noted above, most businesses do not maintain their accounts in accordance with the expense classification system required in the Federal income tax return. As a result, the income and expense accounts, as they appear in the financial records, must be reclassified in accordance with the classifications required on page 1 of the Federal return. The reclassification is most easily accomplished through the use of the tax work-paper spread sheet. There are numerous formats which may be used for a spread sheet, depending primarily upon the number of income and expense accounts involved. The basic arrangement, however, is one in which the income and expense items from the corporation's books are listed vertically with a description and amount column, and the accounting classification from page 1 of the Federal return is arrayed horizontally. Because there are approximately thirty or so classifications of income and expense items on the Federal tax return, the spread sheet can become quite cumbersome. It is generally possible, however, through the use of a simple coding system, to include more than a single tax classification in each column. Several pages are usually required to accommodate the listing of all the accounts from the financial records.

After all the book accounts have been reclassified, the spread sheets should be footed and cross-footed to ensure that the reclassification amounts agree with the totals recorded in the accounts.

Schedule M Items.   Perhaps the single most important schedule in the Federal income tax return is "Schedule M." Its purpose is to reconcile income as shown in the accounts to that reported in the tax return. This schedule covers those items which are treated differently for book and tax purposes. A Schedule M item may affect any income or expense account on the tax return. Accordingly, it is important that such items be included on the tax spread sheet to provide a complete reconciliation of amounts shown on individual lines of the Federal tax return to account classifications shown in the company's books and records.

It is also desirable for the tax manager to retain a permanent file of Schedule M items for his own use and reference and as a continuing control over the amounts and accounts involved. Furthermore, an examining agent can usually be expected to request complete details regarding each difference between book and taxable income. The availability of all pertinent information can be valuable at the time of examination.

Processing and Assembling the Federal Income Tax Return.   After the tax department has prepared the tax spread sheet, including Schedule M items, and reviewed it, together with the supporting data furnished by the accounting department, the processing and assembly of the Federal tax return becomes a fairly routine matter. Depending upon the volume of the data to be included in the return and the number of state income tax returns to be filed, the data from the work sheet may be inserted either directly on the return or on separate schedules to be attached to the return. The use of separate schedules is generally desirable when a number of state income tax returns are to be prepared, because these schedules may be reproduced at minimum cost for use with the state returns. After the Federal return is completed and assembled, it should be checked for mathematical accuracy, internal consistency, and completeness, and subjected to a final review by the tax manager.

Preparation of State Income Tax Returns.   The preparation of state income tax returns must await the completion of the Federal tax return, because Federal taxable income is the starting point for most state tax liabilities. For this reason, and to level the tax work load, it is often desirable to obtain extensions of time for filing state returns. Although this procedure does involve some duplication of work, it is generally preferable to filing state returns on the original due date and subsequently having to amend them because of changes made in the Federal return during its processing.

To as great an extent as possible, schedules prepared for the Federal return should be reproduced for use with the state returns. It is usually possible to adapt page 1 of the Federal return (or the separate schedule prepared in lieu thereof) to individual state uses by merely indicating on the bottom of the schedule (or on a separate schedule) those items of income and expense which are treated differently for Federal and state tax purposes.

The significant additional information required for state returns consists primarily of allocation information. Through proper preplanning by the tax manager in the design of the schedules to be completed by the accounting department, this information can generally be obtained in a readily usable form.

AUDITS OF FEDERAL INCOME TAX RETURNS

Tax returns involving any material amount of money are usually examined by government representatives. Adequate accounting records and documentation of transactions are necessary if favorable tax settlements are to be reached. Such documentation, together with properly prepared and authoritative explanations, may eliminate or substantially reduce costly tax litigation and delays in settlements.

The Role of the Internal Revenue Agent. The Internal Revenue agent is the individual who determines the correctness of the corporation's reportable taxable income. His authority is broad enough to permit him to have access to all records and documents which are pertinent to the discharge of his responsibilities. Most revenue agents have had extensive formal classroom training within the revenue service and have probably participated in periodic refresher or specialty courses at the district or regional level.

Normally, the breadth of an agent's assignments provides him with a broad scope of on-the-job experience over a period of years. On an informal daily basis, he is able to consult with his fellow agents, group supervisor, or technical specialists within his district to utilize their experience on issues with which he is concerned. The agent may be expected to utilize audit guideline programs or checklists and the report of the previous agent's examination for guidance during the conduct of his examination. Agents tend to be more practical and sympathetic toward a taxpayer's position than either informal conferees in the district office or technical advisers at the Appellate Division, especially if provided with adequate written documentation pertinent to the matters at issue.

In general, a taxpayer benefits by settling issues with the field agents rather than taking a protest from them to a higher reviewing authority. The wise tax manager recognizes that the agent is a fellow tax professional and should be respected as such. Above all, the wise tax manager recognizes that if he treats the examination as a personal duel or battle of wits between himself and the agent, antagonism is bound to result which will have adverse effects to his company in the form of either additional assessments or protracted delays in achieving settlement.

Preparing for the Examination. Preparation for an examination of a tax return should begin before the return is prepared and not one or two years, or longer, after the return is filed. Information should be accumulated while it is still fresh in the minds of company personnel who are the source of the data. As a minimum, the following information should be accumulated for possible use by the agent if he so requests:

1. *A copy of the tax work-paper spread sheets* which will greatly simplify the agent's job of reconciling amounts shown on the tax return to figures contained in the accounts. A favorable start to the audit may be achieved if these schedules are offered and available to the agent as soon as he arrives to commence his work.

2. *An analysis and description of each adjustment shown on Schedule M* in greater detail than is shown on the schedule included with the return. The analysis should show exactly which lines on page 1 of the return are affected by the Schedule M items. This analysis may also be furnished to the agent upon his arrival.

3. *A brief memorandum on each significant matter which the tax manager believes is in the category of "questionable" as to deductibility or excludability from income.* This information should be prepared when the decision is made on the treatment to be given in the tax return. The nature and background of the item and citations of authority in support of the treatment given should be indicated.

Additional information may also be assembled. Frequently, before beginning an assignment, an agent will have selected certain specific items for examination and will request that information pertinent thereto be accumulated or scheduled for his use when he arrives. The tax manager should arrange to have the information assembled and given promptly to the agent. The advantage of assembling or scheduling such information by the tax staff (as compared with making the agent dig it out of the basic records) is obvious in that all extraneous matter can be eliminated and the information presented in its best form. The importance of promptness cannot be overemphasized. Delays in furnishing information can raise suspicions in the mind of the agent and can result in a protracted and unwarranted extension of his inquiries.

During the Examination. The tax manager should provide satisfactory working space and equipment for the agent. To relieve the tax manager of unnecessary involvement, a subordinate tax employee may be assigned to provide the agent with such assistance in the area of data accumulation and scheduling of information as he may require. It is generally a good policy for the tax manager to be apprised of all data requested by the agent prior to its release to him. In this way, the tax manager may be kept aware of the course of the examination.

Although the tax manager and the agent will, of course, discuss issues and questions during the course of the examination, the tax manager should, as a general rule, clearly state that, even though he hopes and expects that agreements will be reached on all issues, he will want to evaluate *all* of the proposed adjustments and their effects at one time at the conclusion of the examination before settling individual issues of any magnitude. An exception to this procedure should be made when the tax manager believes that certain issues will not be resolved at the agent level. In this situation, it may be possible to achieve a more acceptable settlement if individual issues are resolved as they are raised. The reason for this is that in unagreed cases, agents generally are reluctant to "compromise" on any individual issue and more likely to protect both themselves and the government by including in their reports all issues which they have raised. If certain issues are resolved during the progress of the examination, the agent, at the conclusion of his work, will generally not reverse himself on an agreement previously reached on a specific "compromise" matter.

Settlement of Issues Raised. To as great an extent as possible, settlements should be effected at the agent level. Issues considered at the informal conference stage or at the Appellate Division are usually subjected to more intensive research by the conferee or adviser who may develop additional cases or authority adverse to the taxpayer's position. In addition, new issues may also be raised at the Appellate level which would require additional information and could result in additional assessments.

In discussing and negotiating the propriety of adjustments proposed by the agent, the tax manager should consider the nature of the adjustment and the possible "precedent" effect thereof. Clearly an adjustment which merely shifts a deduction from one year to the next with no continued future effect costs less than one which establishes a precedent for deferring the deductibility of an item which recurs annually.

CONCLUSION

Every corporation is faced with substantial amounts of taxes imposed by the Federal, state, and city governments. In all their various forms, taxes represent a major element of cost. Each tax needs continual interpretation so that the corporation's total tax bill may be kept to an absolute minimum.

It is imperative that a senior official be charged with the *responsibility* of tax management for the corporation. He may delegate this responsibility to a tax manager within the organization and/or to the company's independent public accountant or legal counsel, but it is nonetheless important that the full responsibility rest with one senior official.

There is no single form of organization that can be prescribed to fit the needs and requirements of every corporate entity. The size of the business, its geographical dispersion, nature and number of tax returns, and the economics of maintaining a single tax specialist or group of specialists are all factors to be considered in determining the specific tax organization to be established.

Regardless of the size and competence of the company's tax department, outside professional tax accountants and attorneys should be consulted as specific problems develop and on a recurring basis to make available to the corporation their wide breadth of experience and professional knowledge.

Probably the most important service to a corporation is the tax planning function which involves the tax department in the dynamic role of changing or modifying events before their completion to achieve a desirable end result. It is imperative that top management of the corporation recognize this fact and create the proper environment to stimulate creative tax thinking.

If history is any criterion, the tax field will continue to grow in complexity and importance, and taxes will continue to have a material bearing on the net earnings of every corporation.

BIBLIOGRAPHY

Barlow, Joel, "A Practicing Attorney Looks at Corporate Tax Management," *The Tax Executive,* vol. 15, no. 3, April, 1963, p. 165.

Company Tax Administration, National Industrial Conference Board, New York, 1954.

Coughlan, Joseph D., "Improving Your Company's Tax Function," *The Tax Executive,* October, 1963.

Doris, L. (ed.), *Corporate Treasurer's and Controller's Encyclopedia,* vol. 4, Prentice-Hall, Inc., Englewood Cliffs, N.J., 1958.

Holland, Vivian W., "Effective Tax Management," *The Tax Executive,* vol. 15, no. 2, January, 1963, p. 99.

McKinsey & Company, Inc., *Organizing for Effective Tax Management,* Tax Executives Institute, Inc., Washington, D.C., 1961.

McLaughlin, Charles, "The Function of Tax Management," *The Tax Executive,* vol. 15, no. 2, January, 1963, p. 106.

Maring, Elizabeth (ed.), *Management and Taxes,* American Management Association, New York, 1956.

Richardson, Mark E., "The Role vs. the Responsibility of the Tax Executive," *The Tax Executive,* vol. 15, no. 2, January, 1963, p. 89.

Vatter, William J., *Management Planning for Corporate Taxes,* Controllership Foundation, Inc., New York, 1951.

Williams, Arnold, *Corporate Tax Management,* Commerce Clearing House, Inc., Chicago, 1964.

CHAPTER SEVEN

Lease versus Sale

R. S. ALEXANDER *Meadow Lakes, Hightstown, New Jersey; Professor Emeritus, Columbia University*

Product leasing is not a new way of doing business. Cottrell and Leonard, makers and lessors of academic caps, gowns, and hoods, began business in 1832. The livery stable of horse and buggy days not only offered the service of caring for the horses and vehicles of others but would lease rigs to horseless citizens who needed transportation. However, until recent years, leasing was a very unusual operation.

The operations of such pioneers as the manufacturers of shoemaking equipment and business machines and the Hertz car-leasing firm probably demonstrated to business management the usefulness of the lease as a means of marketing. These firms also worked out viable techniques of carrying on this kind of business. Since World War II, the use of leasing has been greatly expanded and is constantly being extended to new products and new industries.

There are no reliable figures of the extent to which leasing is used as a substitute for sale. For a long time, most shoemaking machinery has been leased. Probably most data-processing equipment is disposed of in that way. A considerable portion of the total construction equipment is leased to users. Wheels, Inc., reports that in 1963 industry rented about 750,000 autos and trucks for its own use and that about 31 percent of the passenger cars in industry fleets were rented instead of owned. The National Industrial Conference Board reported that between 1958 and 1963, 34 percent of a sample of 220 firms increased the extent to which they held equipment on lease, whereas only 10 percent decreased their holdings on lease. Only 15 percent had rented none of the equipment they used during the period. The practice appears to be much more widespread in the industrial-goods business than in the consumer-goods field. Even a large part of the car-leasing business is done with businessmen.

TYPES OF LEASING ARRANGEMENT

Leasing is carried on under a number of types of arrangement. The following are almost certainly the most common.

By Maker to User. The manufacturers of shoemaking machinery and data-processing equipment usually lease directly to users. This arrangement gives the lessor a large degree of control over the way in which equipment is used and facilitates the rendering of technical and maintenance service. It also vastly increases his capital requirements, because he must finance a heavy investment in machines on lease.

By One User to Another User. For example, many items of construction equipment are expensive in relation to the financial resources of the average contractor. Because much equipment is needed only in one stage of the average job, its use by any one contractor is not constant but irregularly intermittent. Both these difficulties may be overcome to some extent if one contractor buys one type of machine and another owns another type and they lease to each other. A number of firms can participate in such an arrangement.

By a Leasing Company to a User. The scheme just described is somewhat cumbersome and depends on cooperation between firms that often compete with one another. The result has been the emergence of firms that buy machines from the equipment makers and lease them to users. Of course, such arrangements have long existed in the automobile, truck, and truck-tire businesses. *Sales Management* magazine reported that in 1962 there were about one hundred firms engaged in the business of owning and leasing equipment. Some of these are divisions of commercial financing concerns.

By a Finance House to Users. Various types of financial service firms, such as insurance companies, consumer finance houses, and the like which must carry heavy reserves against commitments, have the problem of finding investment opportunities by which such reserves may be held in the form of earning properties instead of sterile cash. A leasing operation is such an opportunity. For example, CIT Corporation, through its subsidiary, the Picker Division, leases X-ray equipment to users. An insurance company may buy oil tankers and lease them to petroleum companies. These arrangements may become complicated. For example, a finance company and a maker or user of equipment may set up a joint-venture subsidiary to buy the equipment and lease it to the user, thus limiting the risks of all parties and changing the maker's or user's contribution from a working capital item to an investment item.

Various modifications or combinations of these arrangements tailored to suit the needs of individual firms have proved useful.

TERMS OF LEASE

The terms of lease vary widely. For example, the period of rental may vary from an hour, a day, or a trip in the case of cars and trucks, to the life of the equipment for tank ships, locomotives, and freight cars. The duration of a lease of industrial equipment used constantly, such as shoemaking machinery or data-processing equipment, is apt to be indefinite with a right of termination by either party after proper notice.

Rentals are usually based on time, per day or per month, or on units of use, such as pairs of shoes processed, miles traveled, or ton-miles carried, or on some combination of these.

The lessor generally undertakes to maintain the equipment in usable condition and reserves the right of access to it for this purpose as well as of recapture in case of default of rentals or misuse. Most leasing firms find it desirable to take the maintenance obligation seriously. For example, one shoe-machinery company maintains a service unit in the plant of one of the big shoemaking concerns. On the other hand, when the purpose of the lease is primarily financial and for a very long period, as with tank ships and railroad equipment, servicing is apt to be done by the user.

The leasing terms for trucks pretty well run the gamut:

Under the *full service* lease, the owner provides everything but the driver. This is usually a long-time affair.

The *short-term* lease is the same as the full service type, except that the period covered is an hour, a day, or a week.

The *trip lease* covers truck and driver, and the charge is based on the load carried and the mileage.

Under the *finance lease,* the owner assumes the ownership and capital risk, and the rest is up to the renter.

Illegal Terms.   Certain terms are illegal or of doubtful legality.

1. It is illegal to charge to a user who rents other equipment used in the same general process a higher rental than that charged for the same machine to a user who rents all his equipment from the supplier.   For example, a maker of a full line of shoemaking equipment cannot charge a higher rental for a machine on which he has a patent to a shoemaker, who rents from another supplier other nonpatented machines, than he does to a user who rents his full line.

2. It is illegal to base the rental for a machine on the user's entire output of the article on which it can be used; the rental can apply only to the part of the total output on which the machine is actually used.

3. The lessor cannot specify that the contract is invalid if the user rents other machines from a competing manufacturer.

4. The lessor cannot legally specify in the contract that the user must buy from him certain supplies or materials sold by the lessor and used in connection with the operation of the equipment.   Nor can he charge a higher rental to nonusers of the materials he makes.

5. It is of doubtful legality to lease equipment without also offering it for sale.   This legal requirement is less certain than the others and probably does not apply to such arrangements as the car- and truck-rental systems and the operations of finance houses.   The fact remains, however, that any exclusively leasing plan of marketing should be submitted to the company attorney before it is put into operation.

All except the last of these restrictions deal with line-forcing schemes, by which the maker of a machine on which he has a monopoly tries to use its lease as a means of forcing the lease or sale of other articles in his line.   They do not always completely prevent his exercise of pressure to influence the purchase of these other items.   For example, it is probably not illegal for him to find it more difficult to maintain the good operating condition of machines that are used to process materials not of his manufacture.   The quality of the service he renders may often speak louder than could the language of a contract. In such cases, the company attorney should probably be aware of what is going on, because the legal pitfalls are many.

THE USER'S VIEWPOINT

Leasing cannot be a useful means of marketing unless both sides enjoy a net benefit from its use.   It is therefore necessary to examine what the maker or owner has to gain and lose by offering his products for lease instead of, or as well as, for sale and the net advantage or disadvantage to the user of renting instead of buying them.   Some of these gain and loss factors are peculiar to individual business situations; others are general. This discussion deals only with the latter, first examining the position of the user.

Financial. Many of the factors involved in the user's decision to buy or to lease are financial. The opportunity to lease equipment cuts down the user's capital requirements. This looks like a clear advantage to the firm that wants to go into a business but lacks the capital to buy the necessary equipment. Many small shoemaking companies and construction companies probably could not be in business if they had to buy all the equipment they need. But this fact also tends to increase competition in the using industry and may make it a less profitable business to be in.

A well-financed firm may find it desirable to lease some of its equipment instead of buying it if the firm has available or can find alternative, more profitable uses for the capital thus released. For example, an oil company may find that by leasing tank ships it can release funds which it can invest in other operations returning a higher rate of net profit than it could enjoy if they were invested in ships. The same thing is true of tank cars used by chemical houses and refrigerator cars needed by meat packers. Relative opportunity cost may be a very important factor in this decision.

A corollary of this principle lies in the fact that by leasing certain equipment necessary to its business, a firm can diminish the dispersion of its managerial manpower over activities, such as transportation, that are incidental to its main business.

By leasing equipment instead of buying it, the user exchanges a debt-servicing charge for an operating expense in his cost structure. All the rental can be charged off as an expense in computing profits on which income tax must be paid. The cost of debt service consists of depreciation on the amount paid for the equipment and interest, actual if it was bought with borrowed money or imputed if funds already in the business were used. Depreciation and interest actually paid are operating expenses, but imputed interest is not. The user with limited funds, therefore, seems to gain a clear advantage by leasing.

But this is subject to a limitation. If the actual useful life of the equipment is longer than the depreciation period allowed by the Bureau of Internal Revenue, the owner-user may be free of depreciation charges and enjoy augmented profits from its use during this excess period while the renter-user pays the same annual rental cost for the machine during its entire useful life.

Mathematical analysis can be useful here, because practically all the factors which influence the financial desirability of renting versus buying can be expressed in dollars. The most important of these factors are:

1. The rate of interest
2. The rate of profit on money used
3. The depreciation rate allowed by the Bureau of Internal Revenue on the equipment
4. The actual useful life of the product—its wear-out time or its estimated date of obsolescence, whichever is shorter
5. The rate at which future dollars should be discounted in terms of current dollars
6. The rate of income tax on profits
7. The annual or per-unit-of-product rental of the machine
8. The percentage of capacity at which the machine is expected to be used

A mathematician can develop a formula including these factors and others peculiar to an individual situation which management can use to choose between renting and buying on the basis of purely financial considerations.

Risks. By renting his equipment, the user avoids the risk of its physical damage and of loss in its value due to obsolescence or failure or decline in the demand for the products it is used to make. This may be very important in an industry in which the technology is highly dynamic. When new products appear very rapidly and new materials and new processes are required to make them, the life of the equipment used is apt to be very short and unpredictable. Sound depreciation rates are difficult to establish.

The renter-user seems to avoid this risk. But in all probability, the rental he pays covers the machinery manufacturer's estimate of it, so in reality the renter-user merely exchanges an uncertain risk for a predictable annual cost. Renting is a sort of insurance against unfavorable change.

Service. When a supplier sells and is paid for an item, he has gotten out of it all the income he can ever expect to get from it. His motive for rendering technical and maintenance service is entirely one of maintaining user goodwill in the hope of selling a replacement at some time in the future. But if he leases the same product, his motivation for service is immediate and continuing, for he cannot expect rental income from it next month unless it is operating satisfactorily. It is hard to measure how much this immediacy of motivation affects the quality of the service rendered. Certainly it has some beneficial effect; several of the firms that depend heavily on leasing as a marketing tool are among the leaders in providing technical use service and maintenance.

But for some industrial users, this may not be an unmixed blessing. To service his equipment, the owner must have access to the user's plant. His servicemen may thus become privy to secret processes and operating know-how which the user would rather not share with his rivals. The secret process is probably rather rare. But tricks of operating know-how are quite common and sometimes afford considerable competitive advantage.

The Psychological Factor. The instinct of ownership is very strong and, for many people, probably constitutes a considerable deterrent to renting. The factor is probably more important in the field of consumers' goods than among industrial users. But the industrial buyer is not immune to human emotions and prejudices. Probably many business executives feel more comfortable and secure when their firms own the equipment they use than when they rent it. This is not an important factor in the user's balancing out of buying versus renting, but it almost certainly has some influence.

THE MAKER'S EVALUATION OF LEASING

As pointed out earlier, leasing can be a useful marketing device only if it is to the advantage of a supplier to offer goods for lease instead of for sale. Let us examine some of the factors which affect this choice.

Total Return. Some manufacturers can get a larger total return from their products by leasing them than by selling them. A certain company offered either to lease or to sell. The sales price of different machines amounted to between fifty and sixty months' rental. Even when costs of maintenance, insurance, taxes, and interest were subtracted from the rental, it was probable that the maker amortized his investment in the machines within six or seven years.

After interest at 6 percent on estimated cost and liberal allowances for maintenance, insurance, and taxes on most of the items leased by another firm were deducted from rentals, its investment in them was amortized within four or five years. Most of these machines had a life expectancy of ten to twelve years. The 1963 *Annual Report* of the United Shoe Machinery Company showed in its financial statement an investment of $51,996,000 in leased machines on which its yearly rentals were $43,631,000. Its cost of leased-machine operations was $14,696,000 and depreciation was $1,662,000. If interest is computed on invested capital at 6 percent, there is another $3,119,800. These figures are not quite as good as they seem, because deferred income must be discounted at a rate which rises with the length of the deferment period.

When the equipment lease is used as a means of promoting the sale of materials or supplies used in operating the equipment, the earnings may be much less favorable—sometimes highly unfavorable. For example, a firm making rivets leased for $500 a year a riveting machine worth $10,000—an amortization period of more than twenty years. The machine was leased to help sell rivets. In another case, some years ago, a company making a doughnut mix leased a doughnut-making machine at a rate that allowed amortization in something over nineteen years. These companies apparently used the lease as a means of marketing other products and probably charged the losses in their leasing operations as a sales expense.

Stabilization of Income. Leasing may be a very effective method of stabilizing both cash inflow and net income over periods of good business and bad business. The following operating figures of the International Business Machines Corporation and the United Shoe Machinery Company during the catastrophic depression years of the early 1930s and the more favorable years immediately before and after the depression illustrate this advantage:

International Business Machines Corp.		United Shoe Machinery Co.	
Year	Net Income (in millions of dollars)	Year	Net Income (in millions of dollars)
1927	4.4	1928	8.5
1929	6.7	1930	9.7
1931	7.4	1932	7.5
1932	6.4	1933	6.0
1934	6.6	1935	8.8
1936	7.6	1937	11.3
1938	8.7	1939	9.5
1939	9.1	1940	9.9
1940	9.4	1941	8.2

During the Great Depression, these firms, which at that time leased much or all of their equipment, suffered some decline in earnings but continued to make profits. This was not true of most machine manufacturers during that period.

A further example of this stabilizing effect may be found in a comparison of the annual cash inflow which the United Shoe Machinery Company enjoyed during a later period from sales of equipment and findings with cash inflow from rentals and royalties, mainly rentals. These figures are shown in the table below:

Year	Net sales (in millions of dollars)	Percentage of fluctuation from previous year	Royalties and rentals (in millions of dollars)	Percentage of fluctuation from previous year
1940	24.9		19.8	
1945	42.8	72	20.7	5
1946	37.5	−12	20.8	0.5
1947	45.7	22	23.2	12
1948	50.6	11	24.4	5
1949	49.1	− 3	24.5	0.4
1950	44.1	−10	24.5	0
1951	55.1	26	27.2	11

The importance of this stabilizing effect may be less than it used to be if, as some observers believe, a way has been found at last to iron out the cyclical fluctuations in business activity.

Variations in Customer Returns. In some cases, the use of the lease makes it possible for the lessor to vary his annual charges among customers roughly according to their ability to pay as indicated by the extent to which they use the article leased. For example, if a contractor uses a piece of construction equipment only a few days, he pays for just that instead of the entire price of the machine. For some of their machines, shoemakers pay a fee per pair of shoes worked on, which may create wide variations in the annual rentals they pay. By thus suiting the charge to the use, the lessor is probably able to increase considerably his total cash inflow from the number of machines he may make or own. Any attempt to vary the sales price among customers in this way would be commercially impractical and illegal.

Increased Capital Needs. By using the lease, a manufacturer increases greatly his needs for working capital over what they would be if he sold outright. When he sells an article and gets paid for it, the cash outflow caused by making and marketing it flows back into the business with a surplus if he has priced it right. But when he leases it, the money he has spent on it remains in his working capital in the form of inventory, and he gets it back in the form of cash only over a long interval in the increments of rental. Not only is his need for capital increased, but its rate of turnover is slowed.

The operating statement of the COMPO Shoe Machinery Company for a typical year showed that it had $2,401,000 invested in its inventory of leased machines from which it received rentals of $1,486,000. It carried an inventory of $907,000 of cements, solvents, and other findings from which it serviced a sales volume of $5,118,000 for the year. The statement of the United Shoe Machinery Company for the same year showed an inventory of leased machines of $52,189,000 from which it received rentals of $27,865,000, and sales of $62,298,000 in machines and findings which it serviced from an inventory worth $22,602,000.

The 1964 *Annual Report* of the Ex-Cell-O Corporation showed that to earn gross annual rentals of $37,094,000 and $32,865,000 in 1964 and 1963, respectively, the company maintained net inventories of machines valued at $50,500,000 and $52,681,000 in those years. If a seller extends credit, outstandings may change the ratios somewhat, but the difference will still be significant. One of the definite drawbacks of the leasing method is the increased need for capital and the slower capital turnover which it engenders.

Service. It is difficult to collect rentals on equipment that is not working properly. This fact suggests two courses of action for the lessor. He will be wise to build his product so that it needs as little maintenance service as possible and is as easy to service as it can be made. He must also build and operate an organization to render fast and efficient maintenance service, with special emphasis on the preventive variety.

If static machinery is involved, the lessor must also be equipped to install or help install it and render technical service in advising the user and perhaps in training his employees in methods of getting the most efficient use from it. The business machine companies have especially emphasized this sort of service. The leasing arrangement probably facilitates the rendering of technical service in many cases because of the close and continuous relations it fosters between lessor and user.

Leasing practically eliminates the pirate-parts problem that bedevils so many manufacturers of mechanical products. Because the lease almost always obligates the lessor to maintain the equipment in operating condition, he controls both the supply of parts and their installation. The pirate-parts producer is squeezed out. Of course, this is less true when the lessor is a third party functioning between the maker and the user.

Cost. It costs money to carry on a leasing operation. The increased capital costs have been mentioned. The cost of repair and maintenance cannot usually be charged directly to the user as is typical in the case of a sale, but is an expense charged against rentals. All kinds of service must usually be more extensive and of higher quality and so more costly. The leasing method requires much more record keeping and paper work than is needed to complete an outright sale. In 1963, United Shoe Machinery Company reported that the cost of its leased machine operations was $14,696,000 on total rentals of $43,631,000, almost 34 percent. The report did not indicate whether this figure included interest, actual or imputed, on money invested in inventory.

Expansion of Market. There is little doubt that the use of the lease method brings about an expansion of the market for the product to which it is applied. There is no overall measure of the amount of this increase. It almost certainly varies widely with different products and in different industries. It enables firms to start in business that could not otherwise raise the capital to do so. In some industries, such as construction, it makes it possible for small concerns to use the most up-to-date equipment for jobs which they would otherwise have to do by hand labor or with makeshift machinery. Many people travel many miles in rented cars who would otherwise stay at home or use public transportation. To expand the market is perhaps the most potent incentive to the use of the lease method of marketing.

FACTORS FAVORING USE OF LEASING

There are certain factors or situations that favor the use of the leasing method of marketing. Let us consider several of the most important of them.

When Use Is Occasional. Generations of college students have patronized the local tailor who had tuxedos for rent. Cottrell and Leonard has for a long time performed a like service with respect to academic dress. In every large city, there are houses prepared to lease theatrical costumes to thespians, professional and amateur. Most of the consumer part of the car-rental business is of this type; the same thing is true of some of the business rentals of automobiles and much of the truck-leasing volume.

A firm which has a less-than-constant need for a piece of equipment can compute with some exactitude the economics of rental versus purchase. The costs of rental and ownership can be estimated fairly accurately and a balance drawn. In making such a computation, the decision maker should be careful to include certain hidden factors, such as imputed interest on money invested and the discounting of future rental payments.

If leasing is a good thing for the user, the maker is usually wise to make it possible to him.

When Equipment Is Expensive. Whenever the buying price of a piece of equipment represents a substantial amount of capital, the prospective user may be expected to give careful consideration to opportunity costs. That is, he will compare the return expected from the purchase and use of the machine with the return promised by the most profitable alternative use to which the capital may be put. This comparison may result in pressure on the maker to participate in arranging some sort of leasing deal, or it may limit the market for the equipment.

In some industries, many using firms could not be in business if they had to raise enough capital to buy their equipment, or they would have to find another, less efficient way of getting the job done. This factor tends to limit the market for the equipment unless its maker offers a leasing arrangement.

When Service Is Very Important. To yield proper results, some equipment requires unusually expert and careful repair and maintenance service or unusual operating techniques. The lease arrangement puts the maker in an advantageous position to see that the machines are kept in good operating condition and to render the technical service necessary for satisfactory results. It thus becomes to the best interest of both maker and user.

When Special Equipment Is Necessary to the Satisfactory Use of Materials. Specially made riveting machines were found necessary to the use of rivets for certain purposes; metal tape could be used for fastening wooden or fiberboard packages only when a stapling machine was supplied; metal containers needed closing machines made for the purpose. To sell the materials, their makers had to supply the processing equipment on lease.

A modification of this situation occurred when the dairy business shifted from the use of glass bottles to paper containers. This required a considerable change in the processing technology and equipment of the dairy industry and an educational program to induce consumers to accept the new containers. The manufacturers of the machines which made and closed the paper containers had to lease the equipment and engage in cooperative advertising campaigns to build a market for their product. The net result was a considerable saving for the dairy industry, infinitely greater convenience for milk consumers, and a highly beneficial effect on the profits of the equipment company.

CONCLUSION

The present strong trend in the direction of leasing is almost certain to result in its being tried in situations for which it is not suited. But it is equally likely to bring to light new situations in which it can be a useful and constructive method of marketing.

BIBLIOGRAPHY

Business Management Record, National Industrial Conference Board, New York, November, 1963.

Griesinger, F. K., "Pros and Cons of Leasing Equipment," *Harvard Business Review,* March–April, 1955.

McNeill, R. B., "The Lease as a Marketing Tool," *Harvard Business Review,* Summer, 1944.

CHAPTER EIGHT

Risk Management

GEORGE M. BETTERLEY *Managing Partner, Betterley Associates, Worcester, Massachusetts*

A successful business depends upon the skillful management of men, money, and materials. But unless these resources are adequately protected against accidental catastrophes, the enterprise may be doomed to failure.

This chapter discusses techniques for determining risks, deciding when and how to buy insurance, and the administrative framework required to give a corporation adequate, economical protection. These and related tasks comprise the risk management function.

DEFINING RISK MANAGEMENT

The term "risk management" has not been in use long enough to have an established definition, in spite of the fact that its basic concepts were first formally recognized in 1930. There has been marked growth, however, in the acceptance of the term to describe the specialized managerial activities of corporate insurance management. Typical of the reluctance to acknowledge the term is the almost 100 percent use by business of the title "insurance manager" rather than "risk manager." (For simplicity, both titles are used interchangeably in this chapter.)

The word "risk" is most troublesome because all management deals with risks. As used here, "risk" will mean uncertainty of loss where the loss is caused by fortuitous, accidental, unexpected circumstances. This is "pure" risk, as opposed to "speculative" risk which may result in loss or gain.

Objectives. The objective of risk management is proper protection of company assets and profitability against loss from pure risk. This is accomplished by systematic analysis of risks and the employment of various techniques aimed at reducing potential loss from these risks.

"Risk management" and "insurance management" are frequently used interchangeably, even though they are not synonymous. The design and administration of a company's insurance program represent major elements in the risk management function, but insurance is still only one device for treating risk. Insurance management is simply a part of risk management.

ESTABLISHING A COMPANY POLICY

A sound risk and insurance management program requires systematic approach, based on an established company policy. Without this, decisions regarding insurance tend to be just a series of loosely jointed responses to recommendations of insurance salesmen, requests by directors, or sudden interest aroused by a catastrophe. Top management needs to lay down certain ground rules to guide the insurance manager or responsible administrative officer. This statement of principles, preferably in writing, should cover at least three points:

1. A statement of strong support for prevention or control of loss as the first consideration in treating risk

2. The amount of financial loss the company is willing to absorb without the benefit of insurance

3. Assignment of responsibility to administer the policy, including (a) authority to select insurance markets and (b) latitude to insure below the assumption level mentioned in no. 2 when tests show this to be economically sound

A well-considered policy statement contributes to good administration by minimizing delay, duplication of effort, inconsistencies, and inevitable higher insurance costs. The following is an example of a relatively concise statement.

Statement of Policy on Corporate Property and Liability Insurance

Recognizing this Company is exposed to various property and liability risks which either may be insured or not insured, in whole or in part, it is our policy with respect to the management of such risks:

To eliminate or modify those conditions and practices, whenever practical, which may cause loss.

To assume as an operating expense losses up to _____ per occurrence. The Corporate Treasurer's Office may elect to insure lower loss levels after giving due consideration to premium savings and the need for insurance company services.

To centralize in the Office of the Corporate Treasurer the authority and responsibility for: (a) administration of insurance programs for all operations in the United States and Canada, including any insurance arranged on a worldwide basis; (b) advisory service to foreign subsidiaries to encourage uniformity in the administration of their local insurance programs.

ADMINISTERING THE POLICY

Responsible Official. Administrative responsibility for insurance is most commonly assigned to the treasurer or principal financial officer. Surveys conducted by various trade and professional associations indicate this is the case with about 50 percent of the respondents. It is also not uncommon to find the controller or perhaps the secretary holding the assignment.

The important consideration is to place the responsibility in a staff function which has both stature and ready access to the kinds of information needed to keep in close touch with changes in property, products, operations, and contracts. Unfortunately insurance is too often assigned solely on the basis of interest, aptitude, or time availability.

Full-time Specialist. There are no standards for determining when a company is large enough to justify employing a full-time risk manager. Gross sales volume is an often-mentioned but misleading yardstick.

For example, a steel company producing $250 million in sales from a single manufacturing location handles its risk management program using an assistant treasurer part time. In contrast, a metal goods manufacturer with half that sales volume produced by twelve plants, in as many states, employs a full-time insurance specialist with one secretary.

The following information is most pertinent to measurement of the work load and thus the need for a full-time specialist:

1. Total number and location of facilities operated by the company
2. Number and degree of autonomy of subsidiaries and divisions
3. Existence of a high frequency of claims and losses
4. Amount of diversification in products and services
5. Amount of risk assumed compared with amount of risk insured
6. Practice with respect to joint administration of employee benefits and general insurance

Centralized Administration. The necessity to view risk for its impact on the total corporation usually dictates that the risk management function be centralized. Further justification for centralization can be found in these reasons:

1. Need for uniformity in the analysis of risks and the selection of proper protection to avoid gaps and overlaps
2. Economies in volume buying of insurance
3. Need for technically competent and experienced personnel
4. Streamlined administration

Decentralized administration is practiced by a limited number of companies. It is especially applicable where a widely diversified and physically separated major division exists within a corporation. A common example of still another form of decenralization is the handling of foreign subsidiaries. Here, distance and uniqueness of problems play an important part in the decision to allow local control. When decentralization is deemed best, it is still wise to retain in the central corporate administrative office the authority for planning and policy control. Branch offices can be used primarily for claims handling, reporting changes in risk, and directed placement of insurance.

Insurance Department Organization. Corporations operating a full-time insurance department face the question of the proper number and type of personnel, as well as that of departmental structure. Unfortunately, there are no pat answers. Only an analysis of the responsibilities and work load in a particular company can determine the optimum size for its insurance department.

The best organizational structure seems to be one which corresponds with types of risks or insurance, for example, property, liability, and employee benefits. In addition, a large department may need to identify such functional areas as claims administration and engineering services. To structure the insurance department along lines which correspond with product divisions or subsidiaries is undesirable because it tends to undermine the analysis of risk from the total corporate viewpoint.

The safety and loss-prevention program is assigned to the insurance department in many companies, but the fact that there are strong arguments favoring its placement elsewhere has restrained the development of a standard practice. If the company's major exposures are to property rather than people, the function may be treated as a plant engineering service. If people hazards are the main concern, the personnel department will inevitably supervise safety. Regardless of where the function is assigned, there must be a close working relationship between the insurance and loss-prevention administrators.

Responsibility for employee benefits follows a similar pattern. If not supervised by industrial relations or personnel, then customarily the program will be administered either by a financial officer or by the insurance manager. In any event, the latter's experience and knowledge certainly should be used in the negotiation of any employee-benefits insurance contracts.

DETERMINING EXPOSURE TO LOSS

The foundation of risk management is risk analysis—the identification and evaluation of risk. What are the risks? What is the measurement of possible loss? Discovering answers to these questions is the most challenging task of the risk management function. Always there is the shadow of concern that some key exposure may be overlooked.

Identification of Risk. A good risk manager needs unusual perception and a real bump of intellectual curiosity: "How is this made? What makes this work? Why do we do it that way? What would happen if . . . ?" As a result, the insurance department is probably the best source of overall information concerning a company and what it is doing.

Checklists as an aid to surveying company risks are available from insurers, trade associations, and other insurance managers. One of the most practical is the *Risk Analysis Questionnaire* developed by the Insurance Division of the American Management Association.[1] At best, any checklist is merely a guide to help each company devise its own system.

The following ten steps are recommended as guideposts for discovering corporate risks:

1. Avoid the pitfall of classifying risks in terms of particular kinds of insurance, for example, fire, boiler, plate glass, contractor's liability, products liability. Think only of the three broad categories of loss: (a) loss or damage to physical property, (b) loss of income, and (c) legal liability for injuries to others. This focuses attention on risks rather than insurance, helps unsnarl the maze of trade jargon, and avoids falling into the trap of buying "traditional" types of insurance.

2. Make actual visits to plants and warehouses. Risk analysis cannot be performed sitting at a desk. There is need for on-the-spot observation of hazardous materials, specialized equipment, bottleneck processes, and unique exposures from water, railroads, filled land, and neighboring buildings.

3. Interview heads of departments and operating divisions regularly to learn their problem areas. Maintain close communication to keep abreast of changes.

4. Educate people processing purchase orders and invoices to be alert for indications of new exposures—rental of outside space, installation of a new boiler, or engagement of engineers to check suspected structural weakness.

5. Establish a routine for reviewing agreements with contractors, suppliers, and lessors to determine extent of hold harmless and other essential provisions.

6. Study inspection reports submitted by fire, boiler, liability, and workmen's compensation insurance companies for clues to a change in their evaluation of risk.

7. Read house organs, news releases, and department bulletins for information on company developments.

8. Learn from the misfortunes of others. The destruction of several thousand rolls of magnetic tape in the 1959 Pentagon fire stirred many private companies to investigate protection of their own computerized data.

9. Be guided more by potential severity than probability in performing risk analysis. This helps overcome the "it has never happened to us before" attitude.

10. Risk analysis is a never-ending process, so repeat these steps over and over again.

Evaluation of Risk. It is one thing to identify risks, another to measure in dollars the possible extent of loss. Both sets of facts are needed to decide upon the proper treatment of the risk.

[1] Originally released to its members in February 1964 by the American Management Association, New York.

Physical Property. With physical property, the governing consideration is the cost of replacing or repairing the damage at current price levels, whether the property belongs to the company or to someone else. Appraisals, new price lists, and contractors' estimates can be used to arrive at total value, but this still leaves for judgment the anticipated extent of probable loss—will it be 50 percent of the building, 90 percent of the inventory, and 70 percent of the equipment? This requires experience and common sense. The risk analyst, in attempting to establish probable maximum loss, must recognize the chance of human error or mechanical failure in the operation of sprinkler systems, safety valves, and other protective devices.

Loss of Income. Evaluating potential loss of income is most difficult. Insurance company forms designed to assist in computing amounts of business-interruption insurance are of limited help in appraising the true exposure. Length of shutdown, amount of income permanently lost, fixed expenses which continue, and extra expenses incurred during the interruption must all be estimated prior to any loss. A variety of other factors must also be considered:

1. Seasonal fluctuation in sales
2. Interdependency of sister plants
3. Possible assistance from competitors
4. Inventories in warehouses and pipelines
5. Spare facilities

Liability Claims. Third-party liability claims pose the biggest problem in estimating potential loss. Unfortunately, a pessimistic but rational outlook is needed. Anticipate the worst! An aircraft equipment manufacturer must judge his products-liability exposure not on the probability of a single plane crash, but rather on the possibility of a mid-air collision between two fully loaded commercial airliners. Fatal automobile accidents are tragically final, but those which leave the victims maimed for life cost a great deal more.

Watch court decisions for indications as to the size of liability claims. There is no exact measurement of maximum liability exposure, so when the time comes to consider insurance amounts, there is some justification for "over-insurance."

ELIMINATING OR REDUCING THE RISK

For each risk that is identified, the question must be asked, "Is there any practical way to eliminate this risk or reduce it so that the loss consequences will no longer be serious?" This should be the first choice before all other methods of treating risk are considered. Conservation of property and lives through risk abatement is far more commendable and invariably more profitable than buying insurance against financial loss.

The following are typical examples of risk abatement measures.

1. Duplicates of vital records (drawings, formulas, accounts receivable, patent and copyright data) stored in a location separated from the original files
2. Development of "backup" production facilities, within and outside of the company
3. Redundancy in critical equipment
4. Leases arranged to relieve either lessor or lessee from responsibility for fire damage to the premises, avoiding duplicate protection by both parties
5. Requirement that independent contractors provide adequate protection for their negligent acts
6. Cash transactions replaced by checks
7. Distribution of property to avoid concentrating high values in a single calamity

The above examples emphasize reduction of risk aimed at minimizing the need for or cost of insurance. Continuous programs of fire protection, personnel safety, and plant security are also essential to the control of risk. These are discussed more specifically in other chapters of this Handbook.

DECIDING TO INSURE OR NOT TO INSURE

Available Tools. The risk manager needs to be systematic in acquiring and sifting the facts necessary to make sound decisions, for at best the question to insure or not to insure is answered largely on the basis of judgment.

The "tools" available to him are several:
1. Full insurance
2. Deductible insurance
3. Excess insurance
4. Self-insurance
5. Captive insurance company
6. Loss charged to operating expense

Obligatory Insurance. Legal and contractual requirements may force a company to buy commercial insurance even though prudent judgment indicates otherwise. Examples of mandatory insurance include workmen's compensation insurance in some states, statutory fiduciary bonds, and insurance required by lending institutions, bond indentures, or leases.

Requirements for Service. The decision to insure a risk is often made based on need of valuable services obtainable from a commercial insurer. Such services include:
1. Periodic inspections of boilers and pressure vessels required by state law
2. Nationwide claims investigation and legal service
3. Engineering studies of hazardous materials and processes
4. Design of fire protection systems
5. Personnel safety inspections and training aids
6. Security checks on new employees

The desire not to become closely involved in third-party claims sometimes motivates the purchase of insurance. In such situations, the buyer is willing to pay a premium for the services of the insurance company as an intermediary in dealing with a claimant who may be an employee, customer, tenant, or benefactor.

Financial Considerations. Probably no one would question the statement that cost is the major factor in deciding whether or not to insure. Yet too many companies apply their insurance dollars unwisely. They spend too much insuring small, frequent losses and not enough to cover the disastrous but infrequent loss.

The following considerations are worth remembering.

1. Generally speaking, insurance underwriters expect to average $2 in premiums for every $1 paid in losses.

2. The larger the insured company, the more its own experience will determine its insurance premiums.

3. Insuring "maintenance" type losses may only place the buyer in a dollar-swapping situation with the insurance company.

4. The same careful analysis which helps a manufacturer decide to "make or buy" a product should go into the decision to insure or not to insure.

5. The use-of-money theory should enter into any cost comparison if the insurance company is going to receive advance premiums and hold reserves against outstanding claims.

6. Premiums paid on insured risks tend to stabilize cash flow compared with fluctuating costs encountered in self-insurance.

Assumption of Risk. In weighing alternate methods of risk treatment, insurance should be the final choice after all other remedies have been eliminated as impractical or impossible. Risk is an inherent part of free enterprise, and every effort should be made, first, to minimize the risk, and second, to treat it as a normal business expense.

By judicious use of deductibles and elimination of insurance on nonseverity exposures such as plate glass, automobile collision, or transportation losses, many companies have successfully reduced their insurance overhead. A valuable by-product of risk assumption is greater awareness at all management levels of the cost of losses and the need to reduce frequency. It is important that the insurance administrator keep a record of *assumed* losses by type and period, such that a comparison can be made at any time with the cost of commercial insurance.

PURCHASING INSURANCE

Types of Carriers. Insurance companies, like people, have personalities. Some are too conservative, others too daring; some are better salesmen than they are underwriters, and vice versa. Their financial status can be checked from reliable rating services, but reputation for good service, fair loss adjustments, and imaginative underwriting must come from the buyer's own experience and the advice of competent outsiders.

The fact that an insurer is a stock, mutual, or reciprocal company does not determine quality. The *management* of a company rather than its corporate structure makes the difference.

Large lines of insurance are frequently written through syndicates, pools, or associations of underwriters. In some cases, the services are performed by the lead underwriter; in others, the association provides central underwriting and adjusting services.

Agents and Brokers. Use of an agent, broker, or a direct-writing company is often a matter of personal preference. The middleman will justify or not justify his commission based on the quality of service rendered. A company is well advised to maintain contacts with all branches of the insurance business, for there may be times when more than one will be required.

A major problem to be judiciously avoided is any attempt to satisfy all insurance friends by parceling out insurance in small units, subdividing large amounts on a single risk, or dividing by subsidiary or plant location. This inevitably will result in gaps or overlaps as well as extra expense.

Competitive Bidding. The use of competitive bidding is growing, although in practice it is really "selective" bidding as opposed to open, advertised bidding required of certain public agencies. Two or more insurance companies are invited to submit proposals on the same risk using identical information on the exposures and details of insurance coverage desired. The insurance manager should avoid "shopping" or unnecessarily creating upheavals in the continuity of his insurance program. And unless all proponents are going to receive equal consideration, they ought not to be put to the trouble and expense of submitting bids. On the other hand, the buyer is justified in periodically subjecting his present carrier to competition to assure management of the equity of the present connection.

Specifications should originate with the buyer (not the agent or broker) and indicate needs, plus protection and service desired. (Historically, most insurance innovations have been in response to buyers' demands.)

Analysis of Coverage. Once an insurance contract has been negotiated and the formal document received, the insured has a real responsibility to examine it in detail to be sure that (1) he understands his obligations as well as the insurer's, (2) the coverage requested has in fact been obtained, and (3) procedures are in effect for keeping the contract up to date.

This chapter cannot discuss in detail the content of various kinds of insurance policies. Numerous books and services are available to assist the insurance administrator.[2] However, it does help to remember that all insurance policies have four essential parts:

1. *Declarations* include names, location, amount, term, and premium. These should be checked for accuracy. Failure properly to name the insured or to designate the correct address has been the basis for more than one lawsuit by an unsatisfied insured.

2. *Insuring agreements* state what is covered. Although usually expressed positively, they do include limitations sometimes more significant than the exclusions. Be sure to clarify any ambiguity.

3. *Exclusions* are a necessary part of any insurance contract, but the type of exclusions and the number of them constitute significant points of comparison between two or more proposals. They are subject to negotiation.

4. *Conditions* include standard clauses required by statute, plus basic provisions common to a species of policy. Usually they can be broadened in favor of the insured, and such amendments may be necessary so that the insurance will do what the buyer intended.

Analysis of Service. Both quantity and quality of service offered by the insurance company should be a key point of comparison in any competitive proposals, and certainly a factor in assessing satisfaction with a carrier once selected. Are plant inspections and visits made regularly, thoroughly, and with conscientious follow-up? Are loss adjusters firm but considerate, well trained, and familiar with the types of loss handled? Are statistical data on premiums and losses readily made available?

Analysis of Cost. Although cost of insurance is important, by no means is the cheapest insurance necessarily the best. In seeking comparative proposals, the insurance buyer must satisfy himself that the low bidder is not merely attempting to "buy" the account, but in fact has realistically appraised the risk and underwritten it in a sound manner.

Many insurance policies are retroactively adjusted to the final premium cost, on the basis either of actual incurred losses or of actual exposures developed during the rating period. The insurance administrator has as much responsibility to verify the accuracy and fairness of these retroactive adjustments as he has the initial proposals.

INSURING FOREIGN RISKS

The same management principles apply whether risks are located in foreign countries or within the United States. The parent company has the same obligation to protect stockholders' assets and earning power. However, a laissez-faire policy is too often allowed to exist with respect to insurance on foreign risks.

[2] For example, *Fire, Casualty, and Surety Bulletins* published monthly by the National Underwriter Company, Kansas City.

Three basic methods prevail for the placement of foreign insurance:

1. Leave placement entirely to local management of the foreign plant or subsidiary.

2. Place entirely from the United States by the parent company.

3. Allow coverage to be arranged by the local management, with excess or "difference in conditions" coverage arranged on a broad worldwide basis from corporate headquarters.

The type of foreign operations, the countries involved, and the parent corporation's philosophy governing subsidiary relationships will affect the foreign risk management program. Locally arranged insurance will be required by the laws of some countries, or public relations may dictate this course of action. On the other hand, many United States corporations choose to control the placement entirely from the United States, using the extensive worldwide market offered by American companies and European underwriters.

As a minimum, the parent corporation should protect its foreign entities under blanket forms of worldwide excess protection to compensate for inadequacies which will exist in numerous local programs. The mobility of personnel, equipment, and products throughout the world makes broad, automatic insurance coverage desirable for serious catastrophes.

SETTLING CLAIMS AND LOSSES

An important fact not to be overlooked is that an insurance policy is a two-party contract. Authored and signed only by the seller, the purchaser nevertheless assumes obligations with his acceptance of the document and payment of the consideration. Some of these obligations are particularly important at the time of loss:

1. Give prompt notice of loss.

2. Take reasonable means to minimize further loss or damage.

3. Do nothing after loss to prejudice recovery against another party.

4. Cooperate fully with the insurance company investigation.

5. Submit as promptly as possible a complete and well-documented claim.

It is the buyer's job to prove (1) a loss was actually sustained and (2) the amount of loss. Doubts and differences of opinion about conditions of settlement should be resolved in the insurance contract before loss occurs. This is why, for example, property insurance on fine arts is written with an agreed amount in advance, because obviously there could be much argument about value *after* loss.

Reporting Losses and Claims. Standard procedures are necessary to assure prompt, complete loss reporting to insurance carriers. Use a simple form to encourage branch locations to notify corporate headquarters of the what, where, when, how, and why of the happening, plus an estimate of the amount of loss.

Branch management can be trained to handle locally the investigation and appraisal of losses other than major property damage. In most cases, however, any incident involving a potential liability claim should be reported to the insurance administrator first, to determine if insurance covers and the manner in which it will be submitted to the insurance company. It is desirable to avoid arousing undue alarm with underwriters who have long memories when it comes time to negotiate renewals.

Nonreporting of Losses and Claims. Some companies do not bother to file property claims below a given amount ($100 to $1,000), even though insured. This avoids administrative expense out of proportion to the loss collection as well as a reputation for high frequency. Others even prefer to settle minor "nuisance" claims directly with injured parties, especially if they are customers, to gain public goodwill and avoid adverse publicity. Obviously, in these situations there must be a prior understanding with the insurance company.

Independent Adjusters. The two best suggestions for successful loss adjustments are: (1) choose insurance carriers with reputations for fair and equitable treatment and (2) earn a reputation for one's own company for fair dealings with the insurance industry. Even when these conditions are met, however, there will be occasions when a company will want to engage the services of an independent adjuster. In such cases, the intent is to save time and worry on large or complicated settlements, rather than to reflect upon the reliability of the insurance company adjuster.

MAINTAINING THE INSURANCE PROGRAM

Allocation of Costs. Loss experience ultimately has its impact on insurance costs. Recognizing this and the need to give departments, divisions, and subsidiaries an incentive to control losses, premiums should be allocated to reflect both experience and volume.

Standards for distributing premium costs to reflect size are already available in the insurance policy itself, for example, property values, employees, payroll, or number of vehicles. Allocating costs to reflect individual experience presents more of a challenge. As general rules, it is suggested: (1) penalties or rewards for experience should apply only where the organizational unit has a capability to control losses and (2) the incentive primarily should recognize *frequency* rather than severity of loss. Large losses should be borne by the corporation as a whole, thus constituting the real "insurance" for the subsidiary or division.

Insurance Manual. Many companies lack even a listing of their insurance portfolio to assist in visualizing the scope of risks insured. A manual need not be elaborate and for a small company may be little more than an insurance register. Preferably, it should include:

1. Statement of the corporate position regarding insurance and the management of risks

2. Brief description of the types of insurance carried

3. List of major risks not insured

4. Procedures for reporting changes in exposure, handling losses, and keeping accounts

Records. Besides customary files for correspondence, inspection reports, property evaluations, and contractors' certificates, three additional records are extremely useful:

1. A tickler file on policy renewals, and due dates for reports needed to maintain the currency of insurance

2. Statistics on loss and premium experience to evaluate results, spot trends, and aid future negotiations

3. Summary of the major points leading to decisions to insure or not to insure important risks

Maintenance of Policies. The untidiness of some company policy files is incredible. Too often it reflects a poorly arranged, inadequate program of protection.

Maintenance of an orderly current file encourages constant reference, analysis, and updating of insurance. If originals are in a vault, keep duplicates handy at the desk. Separate active and inactive policies. Expired contracts, with renewal confirmations attached, should be in the current file until replaced by the new issues. Affix endorsements to policies promptly. Retain with the policies any essential letters of interpretation from underwriters. A suggested schedule for insurance policy retention is three years on property and ten years on liability forms, assuming no outstanding claims.

EVALUATING PERFORMANCE

Management should be kept apprised of how the risk management function is performing. Three techniques are commonly employed to accomplish this:
1. An annual report by the risk manager to top management
2. Analysis of cost trends showing both losses and premiums
3. Periodic audits

Annual Report. In brief form, the annual report should describe major insured and uninsured risks, significant changes effected during the past year, and projects proposed for the coming year. Top management's acceptance of the report would be tantamount to their approving the continued treatment of risk as set forth in the report. On the other hand, the report may trigger a new look by management at its corporate policy on insurance and risk assumption.

Loss and Premium Trends. An annual review of insurance premiums and losses, covering at least a ten-year period, will assist in evaluating a number of points: feasibility of deductibles, elimination of insurance altogether, and equity of rates. For further study, loss statistics should be examined for indications of frequency, severity, and basic causes.

An effort should be made in the case of uninsured risks to cross-check costs of purchased insurance periodically to test the soundness of continued assumption.

Audit. Many companies find it desirable to have their risk protection program periodically audited by an independent firm to obtain objective, experienced analysis. Few companies are equipped to do it themselves without using the very same people who administer their program. Both inside and outside audits are helpful as long as the scope and objectives are well defined.

In addition to formal audits, insurance administrators will find their association with professional groups and other risk managers an excellent means of checking performance. Seminars, conferences, and the informal exchange of ideas between companies have been the educational backbone of the developing risk management field. Leaders in this have been the American Society of Insurance Management, Inc., a national organization with local chapters, whose membership is limited to corporate insurance buyers, and the Insurance Division of the American Management Association. Both provide invaluable assistance through sponsorship of meetings, research studies, and publications. Various trade associations also have their own committees concerned with the management of risks peculiar to their industry.

SUMMARY

The primary purpose of insurance is protection against major financial loss. To accomplish this satisfactorily, a corporate insurance program needs these elements:

A guiding management philosophy on risk

Systematic analysis of risks

Astute handling of insurance contracts

Organization and procedures for competent administration

But this is not enough. If insurance is to be sensibly applied, it must be the last consideration after all reasonable steps have been taken to eliminate risk or absorb risk as a business expense. The orderly approach to discovery and treatment of risk, employing all methods available, is risk management. Sound risk management is necessary and vital to the financial well-being of the corporate enterprise.

BIBLIOGRAPHY

Best's Insurance Reports (Fire and Casualty), Alfred M. Best Company, Inc., Morristown, N.J., annual edition.

Blum, Albert A., *Company Organization of Insurance Management*, Research Study, no. 49, American Management Association, New York, 1961.

Fire, Casualty and Surety Bulletins, National Underwriter Company, Kansas City, monthly service.

Gallagher, Russell B., *Auditing the Corporate Insurance Function*, Research Study, no. 68, American Management Association, New York, 1964.

Goshay, Robert C., *Corporation Self-insurance and Risk Retention Plans*, Richard D. Irwin, Inc., Homewood, Ill., 1964.

The Growing Job of Risk Management, Management Report, no. 70, American Management Association, New York, 1962.

Mehr, Robert I., and Robert A. Hedges, *Risk Management in the Business Enterprise*, Richard D. Irwin, Inc., Homewood, Ill., 1963.

Snider, H. Wayne, *Risk Management*, Richard D. Irwin, Inc., Homewood, Ill., 1964.

CHAPTER NINE

Pension Plans

JAMES KAHN *President, Pension Planning Company, Inc., New York, New York*

Much has been written on the technical aspects of pension planning. This chapter, however, will attempt to deal with some of the fundamental policy questions which management has to consider.

Although the pension movement had its origin many decades ago, its real development has been seen only since about 1935.

There are many important factors which can be credited with the acceleration of this movement. One of the first was the depression of the 1930s, which forced many individuals to turn their attention to the need for retirement programs. From this need, there developed the first social security legislation. Social security established a floor for retirement benefits and gave impetus to an increase in private retirement plans, contrary to the expectations of many individuals at that time.

A second development which had a very marked effect on the pension movement was wage stabilization during World War II. Because there were definite restrictions on wages during that period and pension benefits were not generally subject to the "freeze," many employers instituted pension plans in an effort to attract and hold valuable employees. At the same time, excess profits tax rates made it more attractive for employers to adopt pension programs, because the entire costs of such programs were tax deductible at these high rates.

The Inland Steel Company decision in 1949, when the National Labor Relations Board ruled that pensions are subject to collective bargaining, was another milestone in pension plan history. This decision meant that employers could no longer bypass the unions on the subject of pension plans. The unions in turn took a much greater interest in these programs.

Improvements in social security benefits, higher personal income tax rates, and greater longevity among retired individuals all have operated to create greater interest in more substantial pension benefits. The effect of higher personal tax rates has made it clear to both employer and employee alike that there is a great advantage in deferment of some part of compensation until retirement age. Although this has been generally true principally for higher-compensated individuals, even lower-paid employees have begun to recognize this advantage.

Definition of a Pension Plan. A pension plan is a plan established and maintained by an employer primarily to provide systematically for the payment of definitely determinable benefits to his employees over a period of years, usually for life, after retirement.

WHY EMPLOYERS NEED A PENSION PLAN

Every employer has a pension plan. It is merely a question of what kind of plan. In other words, every company has some kind of policy when either of the following events takes place:

1. An employee becomes superannuated.
2. An employee becomes totally and permanently disabled.

When an employee becomes superannuated or totally and permanently disabled, an employer actually has only four choices:

1. *Dismiss the Employee.* He can discharge the employee and "let the employee take care of himself." It is clear that this policy of management hurts employee morale and will not work. Further, even the improved old-age and survivors insurance benefits under the Social Security Act constitute an inadequate solution.

2. *Hidden Pensions in Payroll.* The second choice of management is to "keep them on the payroll." This involves a steady accumulation of hidden pension costs and fixed overhead in bad business years as well as good ones. This procedure can lead to inefficient and high-cost operations and render the company noncompetitive.

3. *Unfunded Pension Plans.* The third choice of management is a "pay as you go" or unfunded pension plan. The advantage to an employer of such a plan is that it requires the least initial outlay, but this apparent strength is an ultimate weakness, because it is like "a thief that creeps up in the dark." Further, the employees have no protection against reduction or elimination of pensions financed on a pay-as-you-go basis because of adverse future business conditions, changes in management, or the merger, sale, or discontinuance of the business.

4. *Funded Pension Plan.* The fourth choice—to establish a funded pension plan (with pension financing during the years of active service whether by a trusteed securities fund or an insured plan)—has been found to be most satisfactory.

TAX ADVANTAGES OF A FUNDED PENSION PLAN

The tax advantages which flow from a funded tax qualified pension plan apply to (1) the employer, (2) the employees, and (3) the trust.

Deductions for Employer Contributions. The employer is allowed to deduct from his gross income his contributions to the plan within statutory limits. Thus funds which otherwise would be eaten up by taxes become available for the benefit of employees in general. Stockholder officers may directly participate in all benefits under the plan and derive the special tax considerations available under qualified plans.

Employee Tax Benefits. The employee benefits in the following respects.

Deferred Tax Treatment. The employee pays no tax on his employer's contributions and increments of the fund, regardless of whether his rights are forfeitable or nonforfeitable, until the funds are actually distributed or made available to him. These distributions, unless made in one taxable year because of the employee's death or separation from the service of the employer, are taxable under present annuity rules. If the employee contributed to the plan and his own contributions will be recovered within three years, he pays no tax on the amounts received until he recovers his own cost. Thereafter, everything received is taxable in full. If the payments to be received during the first three years will be less than the aggregate of his own contributions, the life-expectancy rule is applicable. In this case, the aggregate of his contributions is divided by his life expectancy. The quotient represents the amount which is excludable annually from taxable income. If, for example, the employee's own contributions total $28,000 and he has a life expectancy of fourteen years, the annual exclusion is $2,000. If his monthly annuity is $300, then $2,000 of the yearly total is excluded as a return of his own contribution, and the balance of $1,600 is included in taxable income. However, at age sixty-five the special credit for retirement income becomes applicable, and another $1,200 is excluded at the first tax bracket.

Long-term Capital Gains Treatment. If the employee's total interest is distributed in one taxable year because of his separation from service or death during employment or after separation from service, such distribution, to the extent it exceeds the employee's own contribution, is taxable as a long-term capital gain. This cuts the taxable amount of such distribution in half, and in no event does the tax thereon exceed 25 percent.

Net Unrealized Appreciation. If the distribution includes securities of the employer corporation, the net unrealized appreciation of these securities, which is attributable to the employee's own contributions or which constitutes part of a distribution in one taxable year because of an employee's separation from service or death either during employment or after separation, is excluded from the currently taxable portion. For example, if the stock has a value of $150 per share but was acquired at a cost of $100, the employee is not taxed on the appreciation of $50. His basis of the stock for subsequent sale, however, is $100. If he dies before selling the stock, his basis is includable for estate tax purposes, but there is no income tax on the appreciation over and above the original basis.

$5,000 Death Benefit Exclusion. The first $5,000 of a death benefit, paid under an exempt pension trust or qualified nontrusteed annuity plan in one taxable year of the distributee, is excludable from taxable income regardless of whether or not the employee has a nonforfeitable right to receive the amount while living.

Estate Tax Exclusion. The value of an annuity or other payment receivable by the beneficiary other than the executor of the deceased employee's estate, under an exempt employees' trust or qualified nontrusteed annuity plan, is excludable from the gross estate of the decedent, except for the portion attributable to his own contribution.

Tax Exempt Trust. The trust which is part of the qualified plan is exempt from tax. It is not taxable on its earnings or on the increments of the fund.

METHODS OF FINANCING A PENSION PLAN

Individual Policies. Many small groups have plans funded through individual insurance policies of various types. An individual contract is issued in the name of each employee covered by the plan. Such contracts are usually in one of three forms—retirement income contracts, annuities, and ordinary life insurance policies. Certain features of the individual policy plans have been found to make them unsuitable for all but very small groups. The employer must pay fixed annual premiums from the time of policy issue until the employee reaches retirement age. Overemphasis is placed on death benefits as opposed to retirement benefits which should be the main purpose of a pension plan. The administrative costs of individual contracts are high compared with costs of group contracts. Putting it another way, when an employer buys an individual contract as part of a pension plan, he is buying "retail" instead of "wholesale."

Ordinary Life Insurance with a Supplemental Fund. This type of plan is a combination of individual insurance policies with a trusteed self-administered plan or an auxiliary fund held by the insurance company. Ordinary life or whole life contracts are used which provide the amount of death benefit under the retirement plan. The insurance coverage is maintained until the employee reaches retirement age. The cash values then are used to provide a part of the pension. The trust or insurance company will also accumulate in an auxiliary fund the additional sums necessary to purchase at retirement the balance of the retirement income benefits of the plan. Upon retirement, enough cash is taken from the trust or auxiliary fund to buy an annuity which, when combined with the annuity obtained from the ordinary life insurance cash value, will provide the total retirement income benefit of the plan.

Group Permanent Contracts. As an alternative to the inflexibility and relatively high costs of individual contracts, the insurance companies offer group permanent contracts to larger employers. A single contract between the employer and the insurance company provides for purchase of life insurance coverage at group rates which, however, unlike group term life insurance, produces a cash value from which part of the pension is ultimately derived. The balance of the pension is provided by purchase of annuities for the employees at group rates. Instead of individual contracts, the insurance company issues certificates to the employees merely outlining the benefits to which they are entitled. Furthermore, group permanent contracts have a certain degree of flexibility in funding, in that premiums may be substantially reduced from time to time if the contract provides for maintenance of the life insurance coverage by payment of the insurance premiums on a group permanent basis.

Compared with individual contracts, group permanent contracts are a less costly and more flexible funding vehicle for pension plans. However, this type of plan has not enjoyed wide acceptance. Most employers find it more advantageous to divorce preretirement death benefits from pension plans completely by entering into group life insurance contracts entirely separate from their pension plans. This enables an employer to provide life insurance protection at the lowest cost. The amount of life insurance can be selected without having to be fixed arbitrarily at some multiple of the expected monthly pension income. The pension plan can then be funded under various types of group contracts with no preretirement insurance coverage.

Deferred Group Annuity Contracts. The deferred group annuity contract is characterized by purchase of units of pension as they accrue each year by payment to the insurance company of single premiums in accordance with rates stipulated in the contract. Once the units are purchased, they are assigned to specific employees and are guaranteed payable for life, after retirement. Two resulting characteristics of the group annuity contract are:

1. The requirement to purchase units of annuity in full as they accrue produces extreme rigidity in cost.

2. The fact that the units of pension are guaranteed for life starting at what, in general, is a date far in the future necessitates an extremely conservative

actuarial basis in constructing the single premium annuity purchase rates, including a loading for expenses and contingencies.

A minimum number of employees is usually required for the issuance of a deferred group annuity contract. If the plan is contributory, the usual requirement is that at least 75 percent of the eligible employees participate. The premium rates and other provisions are generally guaranteed only for the first five years and are subject to change by the insurance company on any anniversary thereafter, although in practice some insurance companies offer additional successive five-year guarantees.

Although deferred group annuity contracts provide security to employees, because as pensions accrue at any point in time they are fully paid for and are guaranteed by the insurance company, such contracts are too inflexible to deal successfully with change in benefits required by collective bargaining or otherwise and by persistent inflation. In addition, the requirement to purchase units of annuity in full as they accrue is too rigid a funding method to fit into the budgetary demands of most corporations in our increasingly competitive economy. Also, turnover among employees results in additional cost, because a 4 or 5 percent charge is usually imposed on released reserves.

Deposit Administration Group Annuity Contracts. Under the deposit administration method of financing, employer contributions paid to the insurance company are held and accumulated at compound interest as a composite undivided fund much like a composite self-administered fund. When an employee retires, the single premium required to purchase his retirement income is drawn from this fund. The rate of interest credited on the fund and the single premium immediate annuity rates applicable at retirement are usually guaranteed for contributions paid during the first five years of the contract, on the same basis as is used under deferred group annuity contracts, although some insurance companies guarantee the interest rates only for a limited number of years.

Contributions required under this plan can be estimated within limits subject to the right of the insurance company to change interest and annuity-rate guarantees on contributions made after five years from the effective date of the contracts. The employer's annual contribution into the deposit administration fund is determined by the benefits to be provided, the cost of annuities at retirement, the expected mortality and the interest rate for the period before retirement, and the age, sex, and earnings of participating employees. Assumed scales of salary increases and expected withdrawal rates may also be taken into consideration. The cost is usually stated as a percentage of payroll. New calculations are made from time to time to reflect changes in the basic data. These calculations require actuarial service.

This type of funding is commonly employed under noncontributory plans when the employer pays the entire cost with no contributions from employees, although it is also used in some plans involving employee contributions. For example, noncontributory past-service pensions financed on a deposit administration basis may be combined with contributory current-service pensions provided on a typical deferred annuity basis; or the employee contributions may be applied to purchase deferred annuities, the balance of the cost being financed by employer contributions made under the deposit administration method.

Immediate Participation Guarantee Contract. A variation of the deposit administration contract is the immediate participation guarantee contract. Its principal feature is to substitute for the usual dividend procedure of the deposit administration contract an arrangement under which the employer obtains the benefit of his own experience, whether favorable or unfavorable, immediately as such experience develops. Under IPG contracts, deposits are made to the fund in accordance with cost estimates, incorporating reasonable assumptions as to mortality, interest, turnover, salary increases, retirement age, expenses, and the like. The deposits are credited with actual interest earnings and debited with actual expenses and benefit payments made each year.

Instead of purchasing guaranteed individual annuities at retirement at rates stipulated in the contract, the fund under this arrangement is charged each year only for the benefit payments made. However, as an employee retires, a portion of the fund is committed to support the insurance company's guarantee of annuities payable to those already retired. An additional amount is committed as each new retirement occurs and the commitment is released for each life at death. The amount committed at any time is based on the rate tables contained in the contract and the age of each retired employee. These rate tables are guaranteed as to retirements occurring during the first five contract years and are subject to change thereafter. Under the IPG contract, expenses chargeable to the contract on an experience basis are withdrawn directly from the fund each year.

Self-administered Trust. As the name suggests, this type of plan is administered by the employer, by a committee appointed by the employer, or by a joint board of trustees for a plan covering the employees of more than one employer through the instrumentality of a trust. The fund is deposited with a trustee for the purpose of investment and payment of benefits to employees under the terms of the plan.

Under the self-administered trust, costs are determined in accordance with accepted actuarial standards and United States Treasury requirements so that contributions made will be fully deductible for tax purposes. The independent consulting actuary retained by the employer calculates such costs each year, taking into account not only the usual salary and personnel changes, but also adjustments for the experience of the previous year. Rather than loading costs for future contingencies, the actuary relies on his annual review, his skillful selection of realistic actuarial assumptions, and the annual experience adjustments to preserve the actuarial soundness of the plan. With regard to the experience adjustments, over a period of time, decreases in costs resulting from favorable experience because of such factors as interest and employee turnover have offset by a wide margin increases in cost traceable to lower-than-expected rates of mortality and salary increases under most trusteed plans. At the very worst, net increases in cost are rarely large and are usually spread over the future working lives of active employees, thereby making the impact on cost minor in any one year.

Pension plans involve the accumulation of reserves over a long span of years, with amounts to be paid out in benefits generally being predictable as to timing and amount. Furthermore, the amounts paid out are relatively small in relation to amounts being contributed by the employer and the total assets held in the fund. Pension funding therefore becomes primarily a matter of achieving the best investment results. It is here that the fully trusteed method has made its greatest contribution.

By investing a substantial portion of the fund in selected common stocks, trustees have been able to build up substantial capital gains. If unrealized, such gains constitute a substantial reserve against future adverse market experience. Or, in certain cases, they have been utilized to a limited degree each year to reduce pension costs. If realized, such gains will either finance improvements in benefits or substantially reduce costs. In any event, the wisdom of substantial equity investments in inflationary times is no longer a matter of serious dispute.

Greater flexibility is usually found in the self-administered type of plan, because the plan is a unilateral document adopted by the employer and can be easily amended subject only to treasury requirements and in some instances collective bargaining agreements. Changes in insurance contracts in contrast are subject also to the underwriting rules and other practices of the insurance company.

Moreover, transfer of assets often required as a result of merging several plans can be made from a trust without the penalties and delays usually inherent in most insurance contracts.

FACTORS AFFECTING PENSION COSTS

Regardless of the funding medium selected, the basic factors of pension costs are the following: rate of pension, retirement age, income return on accumulated funds, mortality, turnover, and salary increases. However, the ultimate cost of pensions is unknown at the time of adoption of a plan. Therefore, estimates are required. A mortality table must be selected and an interest factor must be assumed to produce such an estimate, along with other considerations.

In any event, whatever the basis utilized by the actuary, the actual experience of the group and of the fund will control future costs. The actuary can make such calculations as he deems necessary and sufficient for the purpose of estimating the level cost. His valuation results may be thought of as "educated guesses" based on the information made available to him. The assumptions and methods he uses do not fashion the ultimate cost of the plan; only time does this. Naturally, the employer is very much interested in learning how much an employee benefit program involving pensions is likely to cost. It is primarily for this reason that the actuary is brought into the picture to estimate liabilities and costs. Although the liabilities for pension benefits are not of the sort that are recognized directly on the company's balance sheet (other than by a footnote), the long-range future costs are certainly very real and may get out of hand unless proper recognition is made through some advance provision for funding. This is the area where the actuary is of considerable assistance.

ELIGIBILITY FOR MEMBERSHIP

Who should be eligible to participate in a pension plan represents one of the most important decisions of management. It involves a long-range decision on the solution of employer-employee problems with respect to the attainment of old age and in the event of total disability of any of the employees.

Even where collective bargaining is involved, the employer is generally better off covering all regular employees. Some employers think that because the turnover is too high among, say, their production workers, they cannot afford a pension plan for them. But the very fact of high turnover means low pension costs, if the employer confines the benefits exclusively to those workers (production or otherwise) who stay in service to receive the pension.

Some of the production workers will live and stay with the company. They, too, will be a pension problem. But, if they do not remain with the company, they will not cost the company anything if there are no vested rights prior to normal retirement date. For instance, if an employer has a total of 1,000 salaried and hourly employees but only 25 percent, or 250, become retirees, then he will only have the cost of providing pensions for those 250, provided the plan does not permit employer money to be taken away (that is, vested) by the other 750 who sever employment.

BASIC PROVISIONS OF PENSION PLANS

The question of which benefits to provide and which other provisions should be included in the plan involves a careful evaluation by management and its advisors. Some of the major provisions to be considered are the following:

1. Eligibility requirements for benefits
   a. No restriction
   b. Years of service requirement
   c. Minimum age requirement
   d. Maximum age limitation
2. Contributions
   a. Employee
   b. Employer
3. Benefit formula
   a. Related to earnings
   b. Based on employee contributions
   c. Flat benefit
   d. Integrated with social security
4. Compensation base
   a. Total pay
   b. Base pay
   c. Total commissions for salesmen
   d. Percentage of commissions for salesmen
5. Retirement date
   a. Normal retirement
   b. Early retirement
   c. Deferred retirement
6. Minimum and maximum retirement benefits
7. Vested rights
8. Total and permanent disability benefits
9. Death benefits
   a. Before retirement
   b. After retirement

Although each plan should be "tailor-made" to meet the requirements and budget of each employer, it will probably be best to adopt certain standard provisions initially.

COLLECTIVE BARGAINING ON PENSION PLANS

Pension plans, like other employee benefits, are subject to collective bargaining between management and unions. Therefore, any action management wishes to take in regard to its pension plan involving unionized employees will have to be discussed with the union. In plans subject to collective bargaining, various broad policy questions have arisen.

Separate Plans. It appears, generally, that in most industries an employer has been able to decide whether he wants one plan covering all his regular employees or separate plans for those employees who are members of the collective bargaining unit and those who are not.

Benefits. Frequently, the results of collective bargaining have been to enlarge the existing pension benefits, including higher minimum benefits on age retirement and total and permanent disability, plus the introduction of an earlier retirement age.

Contributory versus Noncontributory Plans. Unions are strongly in favor of pension plans that are financed wholly by the employer, and the great majority of negotiated plans are noncontributory. Of 100 plans studied by the Board of Labor Statistics in 1961, each covering 1,000 or more workers, 81 were found to be noncontributory and only 15 contributory. In the other 4 situations, noncontributory plans existed side by side with optional contributory plans.

Similarly, a study of more than 200 negotiated plans of all sizes made by The Bureau of National Affairs, Inc., in 1961 found five-sixths of them to be noncontributory.

Vesting. Most unions press for more vesting. Prior to 1955, vesting was virtually nonexistent in bargained noncontributory pension plans. Today, many negotiated plans call for vesting after both a minimum age and minimum service requirement, to a deferred benefit beginning at age sixty-five. Many unions press for immediate cash vesting in the form of severance pay—for example, after five years of employment, $50 or $100 per year for each year of service.

Benefits for Persons Already Retired. Although management has traditionally taken the position that the unions have no authority to bargain for persons already retired, nevertheless, the result has often been an increase in pensions already granted. It is interesting to note that in their pension negotiations with the major automobile companies in 1958, the UAW, after gaining increased benefits for those already on the retirement rolls, agreed to waive its rights to bargain for pensioners. The waiver states that UAW will not ask management to discuss changes in the benefits payable to persons previously retired. It further states that management is not obligated to discuss or to make such changes. The union stated at the time that the waiver had to be given because it was not the practice in other major industries to make such adjustments and that help for pensioners in the future would have to come from increased Federal social security benefits.

ADMINISTRATION OF PENSION PLAN

The administration of a pension program can become a substantial burden to a company if proper organization is not worked out from the beginning.

The prime administrative function is the establishment and maintenance of adequate records. These records must be maintained to make available the essential information with respect to each employee under the plan, so as to provide the information required for the periodic valuation, to make available data needed to cover the requirements of governmental agencies, and for union relations.

The area and scope of administration will, of course, vary depending upon whether the plan is self-administered or insured. Where there are insured pension plans, much of the administrative machinery is set up and handled by the insurance company. Where the plan is self-administered, the consulting actuary and the corporate trustee handle most of the administration. In larger companies involving thousands of employees, there is usually an employee benefits department which handles much of the administration in cooperation with either the insurance company and/or the consulting actuary and the trustee. In the case of smaller employers, the administration is generally handled by the outside advisers, namely, the insurance company, consulting actuary, or trustee.

SELLING A PENSION PLAN TO EMPLOYEES

In addition to the fact that the United States Treasury requires that the provisions of qualified pension trusts be communicated to members, the success of an employee benefit program depends on whether these benefits are understood and appreciated by the employees. This cannot be left to chance. A company that invests a substantial sum each year in pensions needs to spend a small amount of extra time, effort, and expense to "merchandise" these benefits so that the company will get full value of the good employee relations that the program stimulates. A real selling job needs to be done. The way to do it is as follows.

Employee Booklet. The booklet is the basic first step in giving employees the necessary information on the benefits they are entitled to under the company's program. Furthermore, Section 1.401-1 (a)(2) of the Internal Revenue Regulations states that "A qualified pension, profit-sharing or stock bonus plan is a definite written program and arrangement which is communicated to the employees and which is established and maintained by an employer." The booklet should be developed in clear, easy-to-read language and should be made attractive to all of the employees through simple illustrations. The booklet should explain the highlights of the plan and contain examples of the benefits, assuming specific earnings and years of service. The employees should also be shown how to figure their own benefits exactly.

The booklet can be a pocket-sized, handy reference for the employee to determine the benefits he would receive or, as some companies prefer, a larger-size booklet for permanent reference at home where the family can check the details of the plan.

Employee Meetings. Small employee group meetings may be held at which the plan is carefully explained on a question-and-answer basis. The meetings should be on company time. A conference leader should be selected to lead the discussion. Visual aids such as charts, slides, and even films are desirable and should be utilized.

Individual Employee Statements. In conjunction with such meetings, each employee should be given an individual statement showing, among other things:

1. The amount of benefit he would obtain from the company's pension plan
2. Social security
3. The total benefit

Each year the employees' individual statement should be brought up to date.

Individual Conference. Each employee should be told the company has arranged for him to have an individual confidential conference in which his personal statement can be reviewed and explained to him so that he will know exactly what benefits he is receiving from the company plan. This should be conducted by a carefully trained representative of the personnel department of the company. If this is not possible, then outside assistance may be arranged. In the case of an insured plan, the insurance company will furnish trained personnel. Where there is a trusteed plan, the consulting actuary will provide this service. Many companies have enlarged their employee statements and include many other benefits which the company provides, such as group insurances, vacation benefits, and the like.

Preretirement Preparation. Conditioning employees who are about to retire is very important. Although retirement, to some degree, may be retarded during any period of labor shortage, many companies are setting up well-thought-out plans for preparing older employees so that they will not resist retirement when the time comes. It is poor employee relations policy to notify an employee just before his normal retirement date that he is to be retired. Old and faithful employees occasionally do not take easily to retirement. It is highly desirable to call prospective retirees into the personnel department (or the president's office in a smaller company) at least one or two years before their retirement dates and prepare them for the leisure time ahead.

Postretirement Projects. A number of companies have made great strides in handling pensioners already on their rolls. It is of considerable value to the company as well as to the retirees to know that a retiree is still a part of the employee family. It may be advisable for the personnel department periodically to check retirees' progress. There are a number of company practices often utilized to achieve this result. These include "old timers' visits," with the retirees invited to visit the company periodically or at least annually. Periodic letters from the president's office also are used.

The effect of these practices on the morale of the currently active employees is always strengthened when they know that the company maintains an interest in the welfare of both the older and the retired employees. This is heightened when they can see and talk to the retirees in person on their periodic visits.

SOURCES OF ADVICE FOR ESTABLISHING A PENSION PLAN

If advice is needed in connection with the establishment of a new pension plan or amendment of an existing pension plan, there are available different sources of assistance including the following.

Consulting Actuaries. Consulting actuaries are needed in the servicing of self-administered retirement plans. In this capacity, they have countless opportunities to study such plans in operation. Many consulting actuaries receive their early training in the actuarial departments of life insurance companies. With this background, they are eminently qualified to give advice in connection with the installation of new plans. Naturally, they must charge fees for services to be rendered. Their fees generally vary in proportion to the amount of work involved. If it is decided to fund a retirement plan by means of an uninsured trust, the actuary will, of course, be available to render the continuing necessary actuarial service after the plan is established.

Trust Companies. Trust companies render trust services for self-administered retirement plans. Most trust companies have not solicited this type of business for as long as have the life insurance companies. However, a number of trust companies are well equipped to give reliable consulting advice. They render this service free in the hope they will be appointed trustee of the plan.

Life Insurance Companies and Life Insurance Agents. Life insurance companies and agents sell, in addition to life insurance, individual and group annuity contracts. Many of them do a large volume of business and are therefore well versed in the technical details of retirement plans as a result of their group annuity business. They do not charge a fee for consulting services, for they expect to underwrite the insurance contracts used as the medium for funding the retirement plan.

Selecting the Right Adviser. In practice, these different sources of advice are not as easily distinguishable as suggested by this brief description. For instance, some insurance brokers operating on a large scale maintain competent actuarial departments and render consulting service. Therefore, they are equipped not only to design a plan but also to service it after installation. This is particularly significant if an employer decides in favor of the trusteed (uninsured) method of funding.

Many individual insurance agents who have wide pension experience make a sincere effort to present cost data and other pertinent information on various funding methods or combinations of methods indicating more of a consulting approach than that of a life insurance salesman.

It would be unfair to single out any of the above sources as being better equipped than another to give constructive advice. Rather than judge them as a class, one should consider their individual qualifications as these become apparent by interview and by reference to other cases in which they have acted as consultants.

Role of Attorney and Accountant. No company should implement a pension plan before getting the advice of both its attorney and accountant. These professionals perform essential guidance in the establishment of a plan. The attorney must participate in the development of the program, because he is the only one qualified to give legal advice.

CONCLUSION

The adoption of a pension plan is a major business decision. Once established, a plan cannot be easily discontinued. Therefore, considerable study by management is necessary, and the utilization of outside professional advisers is essential. Some guides in sound plan design follow.

Generally, a company is best served if it covers all employees under one universal plan.

A funded pension plan should be adopted as opposed to the pay-as-you-go technique. The funding method which offers the greatest flexibility to management should be adopted.

Usually, noncontributory plans are more satisfactory than contributory plans. Where contributions to an overall employee benefit program are necessary for budgetary reasons, it is preferable that they be used for the various group insurances. This may save the employer from 20 to 25 percent, because these contributions are not refunded upon death or severance when applied to group insurance, but are refunded in such cases under a pension plan.

Retirement benefits should produce a level, inclusive of social security, of between 30 and 60 percent of average compensation after thirty years of service.

Early vesting should be avoided to prevent too much employer money from being paid to short-service employees. A reasonable vesting formula might call for vesting after an employee reaches age fifty-five and has completed twenty years of service.

Death benefits before retirement are usually best provided outside the pension plan in the form of group term life insurance. Some form of widow's benefits might be provided inside the plan, say, after an employee reaches age fifty-five and has completed twenty years of service. Eligibility for this death protection should be concurrent with eligibility for early retirement benefits.

Normal retirement age should be sixty-five, although there has been some pressure from unions for lower retirement ages. Compulsory retirement provisions should be avoided, giving management the option of retaining valuable employees on a year-to-year basis after normal retirement date.

BIBLIOGRAPHY

Bernstein, Merton C., *The Future of Private Pension Plans,* The Free Press of Glencoe, New York, 1964.

Biegel, Herman C., *Pensions and Profit Sharing,* 3d ed., Bureau of National Affairs, Washington, D.C., 1964.

Foote, George H., and David J. McLaughlin, "The President's Stake in Pension Planning," *Harvard Business Review,* September–October, 1965.

"Fundamentals of Pension and Profit-sharing Plans," Pension Planning Company, Inc., New York.

Hicks, Ernest L., *Accounting for the Cost of Pension Plans,* American Institute of Certified Public Accountants, Inc., New York, 1965.

Tibbetts, Paul D., "The Competition for Pension Funds in the 1960's," Manufacturers Hanover Trust Company, New York.

CHAPTER TEN

Profit-sharing Plans

J. J. JEHRING   *Director, Center for The Study of Productivity Motivation, Graduate School of Business, University of Wisconsin, Madison, Wisconsin*

In this chapter, we define profit sharing in some depth, outline the various kinds of plans in use in business, and present a brief history of its growth in the United States. The main types of plans in current use are described. Comments are presented on the most important aspects of profit-sharing programs which are likely to concern management, such as formulas, vesting, waiting periods, and employee coverage. The chapter also examines briefly the laws that relate to the practice of profit sharing. The incentive value of such plans is discussed, and the situation regarding plan successes and plan failures is presented.

PURPOSES OF PROFIT SHARING

"Profit sharing," as the term is currently used, refers to a business practice that is made up of a complex of economic, sociological, psychological, political, and moral ideas which have evolved from the actions of businessmen over the past century. In the literature on the subject, profit sharing has been treated on occasion from each of these points of view.

In the field of economics, profit sharing has been looked upon as a method of providing a flexible wage, a means of creating a deferred trust to meet various kinds of employee security, a way of increasing productivity, and a method of improving labor relations.

In the field of sociology, it has been discussed as a superior method of organizing industrial groups to achieve high standards of performance through cooperation. In psychology, it has been described as a method of obtaining ego involvement of individuals and evolving a type of organization under which selfishness becomes merged with unselfishness.

In political science, it has been discussed as an alternative to the welfare state as well as to socialism and communism. It has been made mandatory under the legal structures of a growing number of foreign countries, and the

United States government has endowed certain forms of it with special tax advantages to encourage its use.

In the field of religion, it has been referred to as a desirable moral practice in the Roman Catholic and Protestant as well as the Jewish literature.

All of these points of view can be found at one place or another in the rationale given by various businessmen who have used profit sharing successfully in their enterprises since the turn of the century.

However, two aspects of profit sharing stand out in the thinking of the growing number of businessmen in the United States who are using it successfully:

1. Its ability when used as an incentive to increase productivity
2. The superior means it furnishes of building a retirement trust for employees

Two Definitions of Profit Sharing.   There are several definitions of profit sharing which are pertinent to present practice in the United States.   The Council of Profit Sharing Industries, which is a trade association formed to promote the practice of profit sharing among businesses, currently uses the following definition:

Any procedure under which an employer pays or makes available to all regular employees subject to reasonable eligibility rules, in addition to prevailing rates of pay, special current or deferred sums based upon the profits of the business.

The other definition of special importance is that of the Internal Revenue Code.   This definition is used to describe deferred-payment-type profit-sharing plans which have been singled out by the Federal government for special favorable tax treatments.

A profit sharing plan is a plan established and maintained by an employer to provide for participation in his profits by his employees or their beneficiaries.   The plan must provide a definite predetermined formula for allocating the contributions made to the plan amongst the participants and for distributing the funds accumulated under the plan after a fixed number of years, the attainment of a stated age, or upon prior occurrence of some event such as illness, disability, retirement, death, or severance of employment.[1]

THE HISTORY OF PROFIT SHARING

Historically speaking, the fundamental idea underlying profit sharing is that of incentive and not a method of furnishing funds for retirement.   The concept of sharing profits or gains from enterprise has had a very long history dating back to primitive societies.   In some fishing and agricultural economies, it has had common usage over long periods of time where it was instituted as an incentive to raise productivity.

Profit sharing as practiced in modern business is usually traced to a Frenchman, Le Claire, who was instrumental, during the latter half of the nineteenth century, in spreading the idea among businessmen not only in France but in other countries of the world as well.

Profit Sharing in the United States.   Just prior to the beginning of the twentieth century, profit sharing was started by some American businessmen.   It had a very humble beginning, and records indicate that only a few such plans were placed in operation.   However, an association was formed to interest businessmen in profit sharing.   It was very active, held many meetings, and published a magazine on the subject.   The movement was composed largely of Protestant clergymen and presidents of large church-dominated Eastern universities.   The group could be classified as idealistic in nature and lasted for less than a decade.

[1] Commissioner of Internal Revenue in regulations interpreting Sec. 401a of the 1954 Code.

The second movement for the promotion of profit sharing took place in the earlier decades of the 1900s and was spearheaded by the National Civic Federation. Profit sharing was advanced here largely as a solution to the labor problem. Again, only a relatively few profit-sharing plans were started. The movement lasted only a short time but did publish a book on profit sharing which was reprinted in several editions.

The current interest in profit sharing stems from the favorable report on the subject published by the Vandenberg-Herring Senate Subcommittee (1939). The committee report strongly urged the use of deferred profit sharing by businessmen. Since then, profit sharing has had its greatest growth. The present period is characterized by an approach which can best be described as "realistic" and "practical." The Council of Profit Sharing Industries provides the current leadership.

There are no accurate governmental statistics on the number of profit-sharing plans, the number of employees covered, or the amounts of money involved in the United States. Recent projections by experts who are in a good position to know, however, indicate there were about one hundred thousand profit-sharing plans of all kinds in business in 1964 covering approximately eight million employees.

THE KINDS OF PROFIT SHARING

Basically, there were three kinds of plans in operation in the United States in 1965.

1. Current payment or cash profit sharing. Under this type of plan, the share of profits which is paid to the employee is given to him on a current basis. The most common way of doing this is to pay out the employee's share in a lump sum on an annual basis just after the books are closed for the year. In some cases, the share is paid to the employee either quarterly or semiannually.

2. Deferred profit sharing. The share of the profits which is due to the employee under this type of plan is paid annually into a trust fund and credited to the employee's account. It is held until it is due him under the regulations of the trust. Such funds are usually paid at severance, death, or retirement. Payments to the employees, however, may be called for at other times in the trusts. This type of program provides special favorable tax treatment to the trust fund as well as to the employee when he receives his funds from the trust.

3. Combination profit sharing. This type combines the elements of the deferred and the cash plan into one program. Part of each employee's share is paid to him in cash, usually on an annual basis, and part is placed in trust, invested for him, and held for later distribution.

PROFIT-SHARING PLAN PROVISIONS

Coverage of Profit-sharing Plans. There are, generally speaking, three types of profit-sharing programs for employee coverage:
1. Broad coverage
2. Limited coverage
3. Executive profit sharing

Plans which are classified as broad coverage include those for which all or most employees are eligible for membership, provided they meet the specific requirements set down as to length of service and age.

Limited coverage plans are those which apply only to certain classes of employees such as all supervisory employees or all office employees or all salaried employees.

Many companies have special profit-sharing programs which are limited to a few men at the top of the organization. These are classified as executive profit-sharing plans.

It should be noted that among profit-sharing advocates only broad-coverage profit sharing is considered to embody the true profit-sharing principles.

The Profit-sharing Formula. There is no such thing as a set profit-sharing formula that will serve the requirements of a large number of businesses. With profit sharing, it is usually considered necessary to tailor each specific formula to meet the peculiarities as well as the needs of the enterprise.

The Cash Plan. The formula for a cash profit-sharing plan is often very simple. There are only two sets of laws which must be taken into consideration in drafting a cash profit-sharing program—the wage and hour laws and the labor laws. (See discussion of laws below.)

It is common for cash plans merely to state the percentage of profits to be shared and how they are to be divided among the employees. The percentages of profits shared under cash plans range widely from very low to very high.

The governing factor is generally the ratio of the profits to the payroll of the company; a high ratio usually calls for a lower percentage and a low ratio a higher percentage. The main reason given for installing cash plans is incentive. For this to be effective, a rather substantial amount of money must be forthcoming to each employee. Plans that share token amounts with employees are generally not effective and are often discontinued because they may develop a negative incentive value. Cash plans which accumulate amounts that are in excess of from 5 to 10 percent of the employee's annual salary generally have been considered effective.

The Deferred Plan. The deferred plan is much more complex than the cash plan, and the formulas are more difficult to establish. There are several sets of laws which must be considered in establishing the deferred profit-sharing trust, and the installation and operation of such plans require the services of a qualified attorney. There are a number of things which should be considered in drafting any profit-sharing plan with a deferred element.

The Combination Plan. All that has been stated about the deferred plan and the cash plan applies to the combination plan. This plan can be made up of two separate and distinct profit-sharing plans, one of which calls for a cash payment and another which calls for a deferred payment, or it can be made up of a single formula plan which calls for part of the share to be distributed in cash and part to be placed in a deferred trust.

A type of plan has been approved by the Internal Revenue Service for use in American industry which is essentially a deferred plan that allows each individual employee to decide if he would like to receive up to 50 percent of his annual allocation in cash. The remaining 50 percent must be placed in the deferred trust. This provides a more flexible plan which takes care of the younger employee's need for more cash and the older employee's need for more security.

Contributions. *Defining Profits.* It is necessary in the formula to be specific about what is to make up profits to be shared. As a result, a definition of profits must be established. It is ordinary to have an amount set aside—a percentage of net worth or a certain amount for dividends—before the divisions of profits are made. Designation must be made if profits before or after taxes are to be used. Often provision is made to exclude capital gains or other types of unusual income for the company so that they will not be subject to sharing. Reserves for contingent funds can be estimated and deducted.

Limitations. It is customary to limit the amount shared under deferred plans to 15 percent of the total compensation of all participants, because this is all the law allows for favorable tax treatment.

Sometimes provision is made in the formula to use estimated profits. Specific arrangements are included as to when and how the payments are to be made. Special note must be made in the trust if company stock is to be included as a part of the annual contribution to the trust.

Eligibility. The profit-sharing trust must be drafted, as far as eligibility of employees is concerned, in such a fashion that the requirements of the Internal Revenue Code are met regarding discrimination. Special care must be exercised so that the coverage remains at all times within the requirements of the Code. The rules and regulations regarding employee coverage have become complex over the years, and considerable care must be exercised in applying them. Generally speaking, it is desirable to use the broad-type profit-sharing plan which covers all groups of employees. This not only provides the best incentive approach but is on the firmest grounds with qualification for tax advantages.

Coverage. To achieve adequate coverage, the trust should state specifically what groups are to participate in the program. This could include, for example, all full-time employees or all salaried employees. All employees earning over a certain fixed amount occasionally are covered to integrate the plan with the social security program.

Waiting Periods. It is common under the deferred plan to have at least a one-year waiting period. Legally this can be extended anywhere up to a five-year waiting period but not beyond. The reason for the one-year waiting period is to eliminate that group of employees in which there is the greatest amount of turnover. Longer waiting periods are used to reduce the size of the group in the plan; when this is done, it may result in each participant receiving a larger amount.

Special Problems. There are several special situations which should be provided for. In those companies where the employees are likely to leave for a time, special note must be made as to how they are to be treated in the profit-sharing plan during their leaves. Some of the more common situations in this regard are the approved leave of absence, the leave for military duty, temporary transfer of an employee to a subsidiary, and the return of former employees after a layoff.

A specific mention of the date upon which the employees become eligible for the plan should be included. Arrangements should be made also for those employees who desire to continue to work after the date of their retirement.

Employee Contributions. It is possible under deferred or combination profit-sharing plans to allow the employees to make contributions to the trust funds. These contributions often call for a specific percentage of annual pay and are usually deducted from the payroll. Such contributions are referred to as "mandatory" when they are necessary if the employee is to participate in sharing. If contributions may be made but are not part of the requirement of participating in the plans, they are classified as "voluntary."

If the employees are to be allowed to contribute, it will have to be carefully noted in the trust. There is usually a range of amounts over which the employee can contribute—for example, from 2 to 10 percent of annual salary. Where contributions are a requirement for membership in the plan, special care must be taken to see that enough employees belong to the program so the plan meets the Internal Revenue requirements regarding discrimination.

Allocations to Individuals. The annual company contribution to the trust can be credited to the employee's account in different ways. It is usual to credit it on the basis of the proportion of the employee's annual salary to the salary of all participants. In some cases, special credit is allowed for years of service. If this method is used, a formula may be employed calling for one unit of participation for each $100 of salary plus one unit for each year of service. In plans where employee contributions are mandatory, the distributions are sometimes made on the basis of the amount of the employee's contribution.

The trust must clearly state what is considered to be the employee's compensation for the purposes of figuring the allocations to his account. This in many cases consists only of base salary or straight-time earnings. In other cases, however, it may also include overtime, bonuses, commissions, and other compensation.

To avoid an excessive share going to top executives, it is the practice in some companies to put a ceiling on the amount of the salary that will be used in figuring allocations, such as $10,000 or $20,000.

Vesting. When an employee's rights to the contents of his account become fixed, and he has the right to receive them should he leave the company, he has what is called a "vested right." Vesting must be stated in detail in the trust agreement. It can vary all the way from full immediate up to full vesting at ten years of participation or even beyond.

Full Vesting. Profit-sharing accounts usually vest fully at retirement, death, or permanent disability. Some plans also call for full vesting when a given age is reached, such as age fifty or sixty if it occurs before the stated number of years in the plan is fulfilled. All plans must be drafted so that they vest fully at the termination of the plan.

Partial Vesting. It is very common for plans to be set up to vest a certain percentage each year until full vesting is attained by the employee. Formulas vary, some calling for 10 percent per year for ten years, others for 20 percent per year for five years. Some of the older plans contain vesting beyond ten years. It is an increasing practice to vest at an accelerated pace under profit sharing. More rapid vesting under profit sharing does not cost the company anything extra. More rapid vesting under pension plans, however, adds to the cost of the program.

Allocation of Forfeitures. When a plan has vesting and an employee with less than 100 percent vesting terminates, there is a sum which remains in the trust. This must be reallocated among the remaining members of the trust. It is the common practice to distribute these forfeitures on the same basis that company allocations are made and usually at the same time.

Allocation of Fund Earnings and Appreciation or Depreciation. Because the funds in the trust are invested, there are always earnings, appreciations, or depreciations that must be allocated among the members. These are usually made among the members in accord with their fund balances at the end of the prior allocation date. Allocations are usually made annually, semiannually, or quarterly. In some cases, they are made monthly or at the time of withdrawal by a participant.

Payments to Members. Provision must be made in the trust for methods by which the distribution of the funds in the accounts is to be made to participants. Payments may be made as lump sums upon termination of service; if so, they may be treated by the individuals for tax purposes as a capital gain if received within one year. Payments may be made monthly and extended over a long period of time; up to fifteen years is allowed. The method of payment in a plan may be made at the discretion of an administrative committee or the trustees if the trust so states.

Payments under Special Circumstances. Some profit-sharing trusts provide that employees can make partial withdrawals for certain specified purposes such as meeting an emergency in the family or purchasing housing or providing for family education. It is also possible to design the trust agreement so that the vested portion of an employee's funds can be used for sick benefits or unemployment pay.

Some profit-sharing trusts have provisions whereby participants can make loans from the trust fund. Such loans call for interest and are usually paid off through payroll deductions.

All deferred profit-sharing trusts, to qualify for tax benefits, must be established for the exclusive benefit of the employees and their beneficiaries. Any money once placed according to the formula in the trust by an employer can no longer flow back to that employer.

To qualify for tax advantages, the plan must satisfy the provisions of the Internal Revenue Code. It is possible to draft a plan and submit it to the Internal Revenue Service for approval prior to starting the program. Most companies follow this procedure.

THE TRUSTEES

Deferred profit-sharing plans generally require the creation of a trust and the appointment of trustees for the plan. The laws regulating trusts apply to profit-sharing trusts, and provisions must be made for tenure of office and resignation and removal of trustees. It is possible to appoint individual trustees or a corporate trustee or a combination of the two. The general practice is to appoint several individual trustees plus a corporate trustee who acts as custodian of the funds.

The complete control of the investment portfolio can be placed in the hands of the corporate trustee, but it is more the practice for the individual trustees to retain a veto power over the various investments which are suggested. The trust agreement often spells out the types of investment which the trust is allowed to make. In addition, within this framework the investments must also conform to requirements of Federal and state laws.

Investment in Company Stocks. Some companies have provisions in profit-sharing trusts allowing them to invest a portion of these funds in their own company stock. This is possible provided the investment is cleared with the Internal Revenue Service and meets the standards set up for such practice. Generally, not many of the smaller companies invest profit-sharing trust funds in their own company stock. The preference usually is for a diversified portfolio in stocks and bonds of companies which comprise a cross section of the economy.

The expenses of handling the trust may be paid either by the company or by the trust itself. Often expenses are borne by the company, but sometimes costs are shared between the company and the trust.

It is necessary to keep various records regarding the profit-sharing program. In most cases, the company maintains the necessary records for the plan; sometimes, however, a corporate trustee assumes this responsibility for an appropriate fee.

Administrative Committee. It is practice in a number of deferred profit-sharing trusts to have an administrative committee. Usually this is small, with from three to five members, but in larger companies this committee may be composed of ten or more persons. These committees may be either appointed by the management, elected by the employees, or a combination of both. It is customary to have one or more rank-and-file employees on such a committee. The tenure in office is usually short, because it is considered desirable to rotate the membership. The expenses of these committees are paid either by the company or by the trust. Most often it is borne by the company.

Duties of the Committee. The administrative committee can have a wide range of duties. Ordinarily it deals with the full range of administrative matters regarding the plan. It can decide the status and rights of participants, make decisions regarding loans and withdrawals to employees, furnish information to the trustees of the plan, and be used to make decisions regarding investment of the trust fund.

Advisory Committee. Some profit-sharing plans have an advisory committee which is either appointed by management or elected by the employees or a combination of the two. The purpose of this advisory committee is to consult with the trustees and advise on certain matters. Some companies feel that because the trust is an "employees' trust" it is advisable to give the employees a voice in how their funds are handled. An advisory committee can serve this purpose.

PROFIT SHARING AS AN INCENTIVE

Profit sharing may be classified as a total systems incentive, inasmuch as it is one under which the reward to the individual is not connected directly with his specific contribution but rather is related to the performance of the entire organization as indicated by profits. Other types of total systems incentives are the production-sharing plans and employee stock-ownership plans. In all of these instances, the amount of the reward is related to some measure of the performance of the entire organization, which is then allocated to the individuals on the basis of some measure of their contribution, usually their pay. These types of incentives are completely different from the standard individual incentives, and an entirely different set of principles apply.

Total systems incentives derive their value more from teamwork, cooperation, and efficiency than they do from harder physical work by the individuals. Under the total systems incentive, the important measure of performance is that for the entire group and not that for the individual as it is under piece-rate systems.

Profit sharing's unique contribution as an incentive arises from the fact that it provides the framework for an organizational pattern that has high synergy. This means that because of the way it is organized, a profit-sharing plan is capable of transcending the polarity between individual selfishness and unselfishness. Under such a program, the person who is merely being selfish in creating more profits for himself to share automatically benefits his fellow workers and the stockholders. Likewise, if he decides to be unselfish and tries to benefit his fellow workers by increasing his productivity, the advantage redounds to him. If this realization is made sufficiently clear to the worker, it provides a very high motivation within the enterprise to raise productive efficiency.

To achieve the full incentive potential of profit sharing, it is necessary to utilize organizational and personnel techniques designed to encourage fullest participation of all the employees in achieving company goals. The McCormick Spice Company uses multiple management techniques. The Lincoln Electric Company has an elaborate system of employee consultation on work procedures. Other companies make extensive use of employee committees and elaborate communications programs to keep all the employees informed about the progress of the enterprise. Often it is necessary to make some changes in the organization pattern of the company so this can be accomplished.

Successful profit-sharing programs require superior communication systems between employer and employee. Profit-sharing companies tend to utilize a larger number of employee committees than do other firms. Steps are usually taken which stress labor-management cooperation as opposed to labor-management conflict.

DEFERRED PROFIT SHARING AS A METHOD OF BUILDING A RETIREMENT ESTATE

Deferred profit sharing has a number of unique advantages which it can contribute when it is used as the basis for a retirement program. Among these are the following:

1. There are no fixed commitments. Money must be paid into the trust only when profits are available.

2. In addition to building a retirement estate for the individual, it provides a chance for him to enlarge it through his own actions which result from his contributions to increasing productivity.

3. The program, through investment of part of the trust in stocks and real estate, can have a built-in device to protect the retirement income against inflation.

4. A deferred profit-sharing trust through its investment portfolio allows the individuals to share in the benefits derived from increased productivity in other companies.

5. More rapid vesting under profit sharing does not add to company costs as it does under pension plans.

6. A profit-sharing program has much more flexibility than does the pension plan. Payouts can be made from it to meet a wide variety of employee needs.

7. Under profit sharing, it is easier through the use of vesting to provide for portability, enabling the worker to carry his retirement fund with him and to move more freely in the labor market.

8. Profit sharing usually provides for much larger retirement benefits than pension plans do.

Among some of the disadvantages of the use of deferred profit-sharing plans for retirement programs are the following:

1. It cannot furnish adequate retirement funds for employees who are nearing retirement age when the plan is first installed.

2. Employees may be handicapped if they must withdraw from the trust at a low point in the market and their investments have to be liquidated at lower prices.

SOME LEGAL ASPECTS OF PROFIT-SHARING PLANS

The Internal Revenue Code. The largest body of laws and regulations which apply to profit-sharing plans is those which have grown up as a result of the Internal Revenue Code dealing with the special tax treatment of deferred profit-sharing plans. This area has grown so complex over the years that it is impossible for the average executive to spend the necessary time to be able to deal with it adequately. Thus it is necessary to obtain the services of a lawyer, preferably one who knows this special area of the law.

The main thing to note under the Internal Revenue Code is that the plan should be drafted in such a manner that it qualifies for special tax treatment. The basic criteria for a qualified plan are given as follows in *The Profit Sharing Manual* of the Council of Profit Sharing Industries.

1. The plan must be primarily a deferred compensation plan.

2. It must be part of a permanent arrangement and not a temporary expedient.

3. It must be for the exclusive benefit of the employees.

4. It must cover either a specified percentage of the employees or a nondiscriminatory class of employees.

5. The benefits of and contributions to the employees must not be discriminatory.

6. It must contain a predetermined formula for allocating the profits among the participants.

Fair Labor Standards Act (Wage and Hour Law). Here the problem is how to exclude the contributions under the profit-sharing plans from the employees' regular wage for overtime compensation. There are two ways of doing this:

1. Qualifying the plan as a bona fide profit-sharing plan under the law's definition

2. Qualifying the plan as an irrevocable contribution to a bona fide plan providing old age, retirement, life, accident, or health insurance

Care must be taken to determine that the plan can qualify under either 1 or 2 above. Because the definition in the law of a bona fide profit-sharing plan is more restrictive than that in the Internal Revenue Code, many deferred profit-sharing plans must be qualified under the "benefit plan provision."

Other government areas having special regulations covering profit-sharing plans which must be checked in some cases are:

1. The Renegotiation Act of 1956

2. The Armed Services Procurement Regulation

3. The Security and Exchange Act

Labor Law. Profit sharing has been declared by the National Labor Relations Board as an item that is subject to collective bargaining. There is evidence, however, that in unionized companies with profit sharing little bargaining is carried on by either labor or management on profit sharing. There seems to be a general agreement on the part of both parties to keep this subject off the bargaining table.

It is impossible to treat in any detail the legal requirements of profit sharing within one chapter of this Handbook. The reader should consult the legal reference services on pension and profit-sharing plans of Prentice-Hall, Inc., or Commerce Clearing House to seek answers to specific problems.

PROFIT SHARING AND LABOR UNIONS

Traditionally it has been assumed that unions' attitudes toward profit-sharing plans are antagonistic and that unions try to get rid of profit-sharing plans. In the early days, the statements of union leaders so indicated. Over the years, however, more and more unions at the local level have accepted profit-sharing plans and in many cases have found them to work to the advantage of their membership. In recent years, because of some adverse trends in collective bargaining, a number of national union leaders have suggested in their speeches that various forms of sharing might be a better method for dividing the fruits of the enterprise with labor. As more experience is gained with these plans, the union attitudes toward profit sharing are likely to become more positive in the years ahead than they have been in the past.

DISCONTINUED PROFIT-SHARING PLANS

Although all recent studies made of management attitudes toward profit sharing in companies which have plans indicate that a large majority consider their plans successful, the literature indicates that some profit-sharing plans have been abandoned. Most of the plans which have been dropped apparently were of the current payment or cash type. Evidence indicates that very few deferred-payment-type plans have been discontinued. No doubt one of the reasons for the stability of deferred plans is the fact that because of tax considerations it is not desirable to terminate such arrangements. Cash plans are not subject to this restrictive tax influence.

The reasons most often given for discontinuance of profit-sharing plans are:
1. Reduced earnings or losses in the business
2. Inability to generate large enough profit-sharing payments
3. Pressure from unions for assured rather than contingent pay
4. Lack of employee appreciation

One researcher has indicated that his study of discontinued plans led him to the conclusion that one of the main causes for discontinuance was a lack of knowledge on the part of management as to how to operate a profit-sharing program successfully. With more experience and understanding through education, this situation is likely to be remedied.

Thus it can be said that not all profit-sharing plans have been successful, but that in the majority of cases where the plan was well designed to meet the needs of the enterprise and management understood how to use it, the plans were considered quite successful.

SUMMARY

The practice of profit sharing has become quite widespread in American business. Many of the largest companies in the country have such plans. Among the leading long-term profit-sharing companies are such well-known companies as Procter & Gamble, Sears Roebuck, Johnson Wax, Motorola, Standard Oil of California, Signode Steel, Zenith Radio, Harris Trust & Savings Bank, and Lincoln Electric.

Deferred profit sharing has had a very rapid growth because of the tax benefits which surround the practice. Profit sharing should be considered as an incentive by management. To have it serve as a motivator, certain management practices must be used in conjunction with these plans. Surveys indicate that the great majority of managers feel their profit-sharing plans are successful. Although there have been a number of plans discontinued, these were practically all among the cash-type plans. Because of the success which has been achieved through their use, profit-sharing programs are likely to continue to increase.

BIBLIOGRAPHY

Biegel, Herman C., *Pensions and Profit Sharing*, 3d ed., Bureau of National Affairs, Washington, D.C., 1964.
Meier, Joseph (ed.), *The Profit Sharing Manual*, The Council of Profit Sharing Industries Legal Services, Chicago, 1957.
Metzger, B. M., *Profit Sharing in Perspective*, Profit Sharing Research Foundation, Evanston, Ill., 1964.
Pension and Profit Sharing Plans and Clauses, Commerce Clearing House, Chicago, 1957.

CHAPTER ELEVEN

Buying or Selling a Going Business

DONALD RAPPAPORT   *Price Waterhouse & Co., Philadelphia, Pennsylvania*

Although each management function is important to the overall success of an enterprise, buying or selling a going business is probably the most important decision which a manager has to make. Certainly it is the most important decision he makes with normally little or no prior experience.

The objective of this chapter is to provide guidance by setting forth the elements of a buy or sell decision: investigation, valuation, financing, method of acquisition, tax aspects, Securities and Exchange aspects, and accounting aspects.

Each situation is obviously unique, but experience has shown that typically what hindsight concluded were buy or sell mistakes were not the result of poor judgment based on known facts. The mistakes resulted, instead, from elements of the transaction that were not known at the time the decision was made.

INVESTIGATION

Much information is required prior to undertaking a business acquisition. This information can be gathered by trained people within the acquirer's organization, or the assistance of independent accountants, lawyers, marketing analysts, management consultants, or others can be called on or combined to carry out an appropriate investigation. Set forth below is a brief outline to assist in carrying out an acquisition investigation. Obviously it is an assist only, for there can be no substitute for an experienced investigator performing the work.

I. Determine the rationale for considering the acquisition in as much depth as possible.
  A. Is the purchaser looking for a passive investment?
  B. Is he looking to add his managerial ability or other special ability to the acquired company?
  C. Is there an unusual advantage in an acquisition that combines one company with another so that the combined companies appear to have greater earnings potential than the companies operating separately—for

example, combining raw material supplier, manufacturer, or marketing organization?

   D. Is the seller's reason for sale a satisfactory explanation from the prospective buyer's view?

II. Make a "businessman's" review of the prospective acquisition including the following:

   A. General and administrative.
      1. History of business.
      2. Legal form of organization—major rights, provisions, and restrictions.
      3. Ownership of business. Will any acquired stockholder obtain a major position in combined company?
      4. General policies of corporation.
      5. Organization chart.
      6. Description of management personnel.
      7. Interest of management personnel in continuing after acquisition.
      8. Contracts and patents.

   B. Product.
      1. Description of product.
      2. Competition.
      3. Distribution methods.
      4. New product development.
      5. Pricing policies.
      6. Marketing methods.

   C. Manufacturing.
      1. Process.
      2. Geographical location of plant.
      3. Plant facilities.
      4. Work force.
      5. Efficiency of plant.

   D. Financial.
      1. Obtain financial statements for at least five years.
      2. Determine the reliability of the financial statements.
         a. Audited or unaudited.
         b. Unqualified opinion by CPA or otherwise.
      3. If prospective purchaser is a company, ascertain similarities or differences in accounting principles, practices, and methods. Compare earnings, cash throw-off, net worth, and the like, of the two companies.
      4. Assemble financial data with the view to determining a fair price to pay for the prospective acquisition.
         a. Summarize earnings for last five years, setting out nonrecurring and other extraneous items separately.
         b. Analyze variation between years.
         c. Determine gross profit percentages of major products for recent years, if possible.
         d. Schedule estimated sales and gross profits in total and by product for next two to three years, or longer if longer-range forecasts can be developed.
         e. Determine changes in selling, general, and administrative expenses for the period covered by the sales forecast.
            (1) Pay particular attention to the effect of the acquisition on expenses including:
               (*a*) Depreciation charges if higher values will be assigned to fixed assets as a result of the acquisition.

(b) Amortization of goodwill arising in the acquisition.

(c) Changes in management, manufacturing product lines, or marketing programs.

f. Compute the standard financial ratios for the period under review, and undergone significant or unusual relationships and compare with industry ratios.

(1) Sales to accounts receivable.

(2) Inventory to cost of sales (turnover).

(3) Working capital ratio.

(4) Quick asset ratio.

(5) Earnings as a percentage of sales.

(6) Income taxes to net income.

(7) Earnings, cash throw-off, and sales growth rate.

(8) Earnings stability test.

(9) Earnings and book value per share if stock acquisition.

(10) Cash throw-off.

g. Prepare summary source and application of funds statement for the period under investigation and projected statements for two or three years, or longer if possible.

(1) Again, these should reflect postacquisition changes.

(2) One major obstacle which must be overcome for a useful projection of source and application of funds is an estimate of capital addition requirements.

(3) Attention must also be directed to the maximum and minimum cash position itself during the year, particularly if a bootstrap purchase is contemplated.

h. All major balance sheet accounts should be reviewed with probably the closest attention being directed to the following potential trouble spots:

(1) Accounts receivable.

(a) Past-due customer notes and accounts receivable.

(b) Balances in excess of 10 percent of total receivables.

(c) Adequacy of reserve for bad debts.

(2) Inventories.

(a) Latest review for obsolete stock and action taken thereon— if there are long-term contracts in process, it is of special importance to ensure that costs to complete will not result in material losses not provided for.

(b) Relative balance of materials, especially month's supply of larger-value items.

(c) Physical inventory.

(3) Plant assets.

(a) Differences between book and tax basis of assets.

(b) Latest physical inventory of fixed assets and reconciliation to books.

(4) Investments in unconsolidated, partially owned companies.

(a) Market value, book value, and earnings of such investments with carrying amounts.

(5) Income taxes.

(a) Differences between book and tax income for years under review (at least five) and satisfaction as to reasonableness of differences.

(b) Open tax years and potential areas of controversy.

(6) Contingent liabilities and commitments.
   (a) Contingent liabilities, particularly lawsuits, guarantees on behalf of customers, and service guarantees.
   (b) Major purchase commitments for raw materials, plant expansion, and sales agreements.
   (c) Liabilities under pension plans and profit-sharing plans.
   (d) Lease commitments.

Seller's Viewpoint. From the seller's viewpoint, information should be provided only to serious prospective purchasers. Although a reasonable amount of information may be made available off company premises without a letter of intent, serious consideration should be given to obtaining such a letter before allowing a prospective purchaser to make a detailed on-the-premises investigation.

VALUATION

As the title of this chapter indicates, this discussion is concerned with buying or selling *businesses*, not *assets*. The significance of this distinction is that by the "value" of a business is normally meant its potential for earning income, not the present replacement cost, that is, appraisal value, of the assets.

Generally, the basis for determining the asking or offering price of a business whose present worth is dependent largely on the continuance of the business—as against liquidation of assets—is the present value of the potential for future earnings. The primary problems of valuation, then, are (1) the question of estimating the future earnings of the business and (2) the multiplier to apply to the estimate (price/earnings ratio).

Future Earnings. Consider first the question of estimating future earnings:
1. Are past earnings a guide to earnings potential?
   a. How many years' past earnings should be used in the computation?
   b. Should average earnings for the past period be used or should earnings be weighted?
2. Alternatively, if past earnings are not a guide because anticipated changes will, it is believed, render historical earnings meaningless, an item-by-item sales and costs business forecast is called for.
3. In either 1 or 2 above, if the purchaser is another corporation, adjustments should be made for any cost savings as a result of the combination of the businesses:
   a. In personnel.
   b. In elimination of facilities.

Estimating earnings for buy or sell purposes is no different than estimating earnings for general business purposes except that possibly greater significance is attached to the historical record than to pure projection. And naturally so, when you consider that one party to the transaction is always somewhat remote and therefore more skeptical of projections that depart radically from history which cannot be at least partially verified.

Price/Earnings Ratio. Having established potential earnings, what price should be paid or asked for those earnings? Surprisingly, there is guidance in this area which can be searched out.

In a comprehensive report on buying and selling a small business, prepared for the Small Business Administration by Wichita State University,[1] the authors

---
[1] *Buying and Selling a Small Business,* Wichita State University, Wichita, Kansas, March, 1963.

conclude that the risk factor in small business is high as compared with United States government bonds and excellent corporation stocks, and that normally 20 to 25 percent capitalization of future earnings is appropriate. This means that if a business is expected to earn $25,000 a year pretax, the price should be between $100,000 and $125,000. It is probable that the authors are referring to businesses with, say, less than $1 million in sales.

In McCarthy's *Acquisitions and Mergers,*[2] the author is concerned principally with corporations publicly owned or companies large enough to be publicly owned. He suggests that in cash acquisitions a 10 percent return on investment would be comparable to average return on investment of leading corporations derived from figures presented in the April 1962 monthly letter of the First National City Bank. For acquisitions involving the issuance of capital stock by the acquiring company, McCarthy suggests a general minimum yardstick of not diluting earnings per share by the acquisition. Each of these suggestions is carefully hedged, but they do provide a rough starting place for a valuation.

Secondary Factors. In addition to earnings and the appropriate multiplier, there are secondary factors which should be weighed in determining relative values. No one of the secondary factors is necessarily determinative, but they tend to be cumulative in effect.

Capital Employed in the Business. Capital employed in the business is a factor which cannot be lost sight of completely, because there may be capital invested not required to produce earnings potential, upon which the primary valuation is based. For example, a company has cash and temporary investments of $403,000 and cash surrender value of life insurance of $100,000. Cash required in the business—to pay accounts payable on a discounted basis and to enable some liquidity "comfort"—is estimated at $120,000, leaving $383,000 excess or unemployed capital ($283,000 cash plus $100,000 life insurance). This unemployed capital must be added to the employed capital value derived from earning power to arrive at the total value of a business, because, except for any income earned on temporary investments, unemployed capital is not taken account of in a valuation based on earning power.

Book Value. Occasionally, accounting book values possibly giving effect to replacement costs are a valuation factor, especially if a capitalized earning power valuation results in a figure below book.

Dividend-paying Capacity. Dividend-paying capacity is a factor, for one aim of business is to pay dividends to justify the employment of capital in the business. Thus, a company should have not only earnings potential, but a cash throw-off potential sufficient to produce a return commensurate with the risk.

Profit Sharing, Bonus Arrangements, and Employment Contracts. Profit sharing and bonus arrangements may be factors because the method of compensating the manager-owner in the company to be bought or sold may effectively represent part of the purchase price rather than compensation for services.

Market Price. If the stock of a corporation to be acquired has an established market, this can be used in determining values. Market prices are probably more important where both stocks are actively traded on a national securities exchange and thus where the prices over a period may be considered indicative of relative values.

In this area, prospective long-run sellers might help themselves by establishing market price by means of a small offering.

---

[2] George D. McCarthy, *Acquisitions and Mergers,* The Ronald Press Company, New York, 1963, pp. 82 and 84.

Other Valuation Factors. There are a number of additional factors present that can affect valuation when one company acquires another. Business expansion through acquisitions can result in benefits of combination itself: one and one can make three, and this prospect can be the plus that makes a deal workable. Some other plus factors are (1) managers or researchers who can contribute to both enterprises, (2) more rapid expansion of sales of one enterprise through the stronger marketing organization of the other, (3) improved ability to finance expansion and less expensively because of increased size, (4) increased possibility of utilization of tax loss carry-overs, (5) integration of plant facilities resulting in more efficient production operations.

An Illustration: Valuation of Sellout Service Company

Financial Data
(In thousands of dollars)

	1960	1961	1962	1963	1964
Sales............................	720	1,300	1,410	2,010	2,450
Net profit after taxes...........	60	120	80	160	185

	Dec. 31, 1964
Cash and temporary investments...................	500
Cash surrender value of life insurance...........	100
Cash required in business.........................	95

Valuation. A review of business prospects indicated that past earnings are an objective expression of earnings potential and long-term value. Five years' past earnings, weighted 5-4-3-2-1 with latest year weighted heaviest, would appear to establish a reasonable standard as a measure of long-term earnings potential. The amount is computed as follows.

	Actual	Weighted
1960—weighted 1..........	$ 60	$ 60
1961—weighted 2..........	120	240
1962—weighted 3..........	80	240
1963—weighted 4..........	160	640
1964—weighted 5..........	185	925
Divide by 15...............		$2,105
Long-term earnings potential...........		$140

Further, in the case of Sellout Company, there is a reasonable expectation for an average 5 percent increase in earnings as far as can be seen. This upward-trend factor calls for a more liberal capitalization of earning power than when the future trend appears level. Also, the fact that earnings for the past two years have exceeded the calculated long-term earnings potential must be considered.

A valuation of $2 million, although 14 times the calculated earnings potential of $140,000, is 11 times the current year's earnings, and if the predicted upward trend of 5 percent becomes reality, would be even lower. Thus, a $2 million valuation based only on the primary factor of earnings potential is a figure where buyer and seller could pragmatically meet (although more than an average times earnings because of the upward trend of earnings).

What other factors can influence the valuation of Sellout Company? It is quickly apparent that there are excess cash and temporary investments plus other non-income-producing assets, such as cash surrender value of life insurance, which call for consideration.

There is $505,000 of cash in temporary investments and cash value of life insurance in the business not required to produce earnings potential. Let us assume no other secondary factors need be weighed in our illustration. Then a valuation of $2,505,000 is an acceptable valuation of the business.

Price. In reaching an agreement on *price* as opposed to *value*, however, a number of other factors must be considered. For example:

1. Looking at cash throw-off, the purchaser in a taxable acquisition could pay more than he would in a tax-free acquisition if the valuation is greater than the tax basis of the assets acquired, because of the tax recovery of purchase price paid through reduction in future Federal income taxes resulting from a stepped-up tax basis for the assets acquired. Further, a seller, of course, would ordinarily require a higher price in a taxable deal than in a tax-free deal in view of the tax payable currently.

2. In an acquisition for stock by a company whose stock was evaluated by the public at a high price/earnings ratio, the offer could be more generous than otherwise, because even a generous offer would not dilute earnings per share.

A Limitation. In the illustration presented above, no consideration was given to an additional depreciation expense due to increased amounts assigned to tangible assets because of premium paid over book; nor was any amortization of excess of cost over value of net tangible assets (goodwill) considered.

For Sellout Company, the tangible assets consisted of working capital and rather recently acquired operating equipment, and the excess of purchase price over book was assigned to goodwill. Because the future income of Sellout Company is expected to increase and because the purchased goodwill is essentially the discounted value of future earnings, goodwill per books should in the future tend to be understated rather than overstated and no amortization appears logical. However, there are other situations where goodwill at acquisition does decline in value, is not permanent. In such instances, the estimate of future income over the period of decline should be reduced for valuation purposes by the amount paid for goodwill. The interjection of this calculation, when appropriate, is of vital importance in valuation.

If Buyer and Seller Cannot Agree on Earnings Potential. Where there is a history of unstable earnings, where earnings projections based on past history of rapid growth through following the past trend appear unreasonable, where there are contingencies beyond the control of either party—such as the utilization of tax loss carry-forwards—a purchase price tied to the presently unpredictable future results could be a way out. The purchaser could pay an initial amount with future payments scaled to earnings, the usability of the tax loss, or the contingencies. This method has not been used as frequently perhaps as it should be. For example, let us assume future earnings are uncertain or there is a wide difference between seller's and buyer's estimates. Instead of this kind of difference killing a deal, a simple contingent price formula, say, book value plus 50 percent of future earnings for five years, might be acceptable to both sides.

FINANCING AN ACQUISITION

After the valuation question, the buyer's keenest attention is directed toward ways to finance the acquisition. He has basically three choices in a cash acquisition:
1. Equity capital
2. Debt capital from third parties
3. Debt capital from the seller

Equity Capital. Equity capital can be supplied directly from the resources of the acquirer or his partners, or from the proceeds of a public offering or private placement. The question of how much equity the buyer should invest and how much he should or can borrow has no easy answer. Naturally, the greater the equity base, the greater the possibility of borrowing part of the purchase price.

Debt Capital from Third Parties. Debt capital from third parties is frequently a necessary ingredient to effect a cash acquisition.

Sources of debt capital are:
1. Banks
2. Commercial finance companies or factors
3. Small business administration
4. Insurance companies
5. Local industrial development corporation
6. Small business investment companies
7. Venture capital organization and private investors

The ability to obtain loans from these sources depends upon:
1. The specific assets that can be assigned or pledged as security
2. The cash throw-off available for repayment of the principal of the loan plus interest
3. The earnings potential of the business to be acquired or of the purchaser's present business

Security. The security requirement can be met by the use of personal resources, the acquiring company's resources, or the acquired company's resources. (Where the acquired company's resources are utilized, the financing is termed "bootstrap.")

I. Personal resources.
    A. Life insurance policies.
    B. Stock and bonds.
    C. Mortgages on real property.
II. Business resources.
    A. Accounts receivable as security.
        1. Advance against accounts receivable—usually up to 80 percent either on notification or nonnotification basis.
        2. Accounts receivable factoring involving the outright purchase of accounts receivable by a commercial factor and the assumption of the entire credit risk.
    B. Inventory as security.
        1. Warehouse receipt loans involving specific goods pledged to the lender, held by a warehouseman who issues a receipt—goods held in public or field warehouses.
        2. Inventory loans without taking the step of placing inventory in a bonded warehouse.

    C. Property and equipment as security.
1. Lien agreements, mortgages, or conditional sales contracts on income-producing equipment, both mobile and fixed, of a type easily marketable by the lender.
2. Mortgages on real property.
3. Leasing applicable to land and buildings and to machinery and equipment, the technique being:
    (*a*) To lease rather than purchase certain assets from the seller (bootstrap).
    (*b*) To enter into a sale-leaseback transaction with a third party, the procedure being to sell property owned or acquired in the business acquisition subject to the condition that it be simultaneously leased from the third-party purchaser.
    (*c*) While up to 80 percent financing is obtainable through loans secured by equipment, 100 percent financing may be available on a lease depending on the general credit of the lessee.

Earnings Potential and Cash Throw-off. The ability to repay a loan with interest or to meet lease obligations depends ultimately upon earning power and cash throw-off. Lenders are usually more concerned about the prospective ability to pay off debt than the underlying net worth of the balance sheet, just as purchasers and sellers of businesses are more concerned about potential earnings than asset value.

The lender may look to the debt repayment power of the purchaser's present business, the business to be acquired (bootstrap), or the combined earning power of both (partial bootstrap).

Debt Capital from the Seller. In situations where the purchaser is unable to raise equity or debt capital from his own or third-party resources, the seller may effectuate the deal by consenting to an installment payment of the sales price. This is another form of bootstrap.

In addition to making a deal possible at all, an installment sale is not without other advantages to the seller:
1. Versus payment in full, an installment sale with not more than 30 percent payment in the first year spreads out the tax payment on gain.
2. The seller may receive a high interest return on the unpaid installment, possibly his best investment opportunity.

The principal disadvantage to the seller is his continued assumption of business risks for future installment payments. As security, the seller obtains what liens on assets he can with the knowledge that if the buyer fails to meet his obligations he can take over the business.

Conditions for Successful Bootstrap Purchases
1. No prior debt
2. Ability to stretch payment terms on accounts payable beyond that of the seller
3. Strong working capital position of seller
4. Type of accounts receivable and inventory
5. Substantial cash flow less capital-expenditure requirements
6. Tax benefit from loss carry-backs, tax depreciation in excess of book

METHOD OF ACQUISITION

There are three acquisition choices—purchase stock; purchase assets; some combination of stock and assets or statutory merger, or consolidation. The method used is most frequently dictated by tax or business considerations—the seller being more likely influenced by tax considerations; the buyer, by business considerations and secondarily by Securities and Exchange Commission registration consequences.   Some business considerations are:

1. Assignment of contracts—purchase contracts, sales contracts, noncompete agreements, union contracts, and leases

2. Pension and profit-sharing plans

3. Corporate image

4. Unrecorded liabilities

5. Minority interest

6. Stockholder approval

7. Appraisal rights of dissenting stockholders

Statutory Merger.   A statutory merger means what it says.   It is a creature of the particular jurisdiction and express terms must be complied with.   *De facto* mergers are discussed below.

The dissenting stockholders on both the buyer and seller sides have appraisal rights.   Approval of stockholders of both buyer and seller is required.   Generally, the surviving corporation assumes the obligations of the merged corporations.   But it is most important to review all contracts for provisions that make assignment nonpermissible.

Seller's individual corporate identity is extinguished.

Unrecorded liabilities of buyer and seller have to be met out of the funds of the surviving merged corporation.

Acquisition of Stock

1. Contracts to perform services, leases, pension plans, and union contracts usually carry over.

2. The acquired corporation retains identity.

3. Unrecorded liabilities of seller remain obligations of seller corporation.

4. No overall stockholders' approval is required unless the method of acquisition is for stock, in which case stock exchange requirements may call for approval by acquiring company's stockholders.   Purchaser may be left with outstanding minority interest to cope with.

5. There are no appraisal rights.

Acquisition of Assets

1. Contracts, leases, and the like, may require consent of third parties.

2. Approval is required of seller's stockholders but not buyer's unless authorized shares need to be increased because of above-mentioned stock exchange requirements, or if by statute or by court the transaction is held to be a *de facto* merger.[3]

3. Seller's corporation is lost to buyer.

4. No unrecorded liabilities, including Federal income taxes, are payable by the buyer unless specifically assumed, provided the Bulk Sales Act is complied with.

5. There can be no outstanding minority interest remaining.

6. Dissenting selling stockholders have appraisal rights, not buyer, except possibly when the acquisition is considered by court or statute to be a *de facto* merger.

TAX ASPECTS

Tax aspects frequently play a critical role in deciding the form of a business acquisition.   A business acquisition can be either taxable or tax free—free in

---

[3] Some acquisitions of assets in exchange for stock of the acquiring corporation have been held to be *de facto* mergers, and acquiring stockholders' rights have been the same as in the case of statutory mergers.

the sense that no taxable gain is recognized at the point of sale but is deferred permanently or until a further event with respect to the proceeds occurs.

Taxable versus Tax Free. Whether a transaction is taxable or tax free depends upon the form of the acquisition or the form in which the proceeds are received.

When voting stock only (either common or preferred) is used to acquire substantially all the assets of a business (roughly 90 percent) or for its outstanding stock, when the acquirer will succeed in owning at least 80 percent of the stock, generally the transaction is "tax free." In addition, a tax-free transaction can occur in a statutory merger even with nonvoting stock or, in restricted circumstances, with debentures. The receipt of nonvoting stock can be a problem, because in certain circumstances its eventual sale could result in ordinary income rather than capital gain. Conversely, when all the assets of a business or its stock are sold for cash, nonvoting stock, or debentures, the transaction is generally "taxable."

Generally, it is relatively simple to have a transaction either entirely taxable or entirely tax free. But it is not uncommon to be faced with the proposition of some selling shareholders desiring a taxable transaction while others prefer a tax-free transaction. Several means exist to accomplish this mixed result. The surest is the use of a statutory merger where it is possible to give some selling shareholders cash and the others either voting or nonvoting stock. In this circumstance, those receiving stock will not have a taxable transaction. The Internal Revenue Service will issue an advance ruling in this type of merger as long as no more than 50 percent of the total consideration is payable in cash. Other methods of accomplishing this end may be stock redemptions preceding the tax-free acquisition or stock sales after acquisition. Both of these approaches require careful planning and require expert tax advice.

Seller. In a "tax-free" transaction, the tax to the seller on any gain is deferred until the stock received is sold or disposed of. In a taxable transaction, there is a gain or loss subject to Federal income taxes—at either capital gain or ordinary income rates—measured by the difference between the tax basis of the assets or of the stock sold and the fair market value of the consideration received. Of course, the reporting of any gain could be delayed by making the consideration eligible for the installment-sale provisions of the Internal Revenue Code.

In a taxable sale of assets, there is the further potential of double taxation, at the corporate level and then again in the hands of the seller, unless certain methods are followed. The usual method is to eliminate the corporate tax on assets sold at a gain (including inventory if sold to one person) by adopting a plan of liquidation prior to the sale and completing the liquidation within twelve months. Further, even if double taxation is eliminated, the "depreciation recapture" provisions of the Internal Revenue Code may have an extremely adverse tax consequence. These provisions tax gains on the sale of depreciable property (including buildings in certain circumstances) as ordinary income to the extent of depreciation taken since 1961 (excess of accelerated depreciation over straight line since 1963 for real estate).

Purchaser. The purchaser's basis for the assets or stock acquired remains that of the seller's in a tax-free transaction. Thus, an increment over tax-basis book value paid will never be a tax-deductible item to the purchaser. This can have an important effect on acquisition price negotiations, as has been indicated.

In a taxable transaction when assets are purchased, the purchase price is allocated among the assets purchased pro rata on the basis of fair value. Part of the price may be assignable to goodwill which, although in the strict sense it has tax basis, is nonamortizable for tax purposes and therefore has no useful tax attributes unless the business is sold. In a taxable transaction when stock is purchased at a premium, the basis of the acquired corporation's assets can be increased if it is liquidated into the purchasing corporation within two years of acquisition under Section 334(b)(2) of the Internal Revenue Code. But the depreciation recapture provisions will apply to the liquidating corporation. Liquidation after two years will avoid the recapture, but a stepped-up basis will not be available.

Operating Loss Carry-forwards. If the selling company has an operating loss carry-forward, specific provisions in the Internal Revenue Code limiting availability should be studied. In brief, there are the following significant limitations:

Taxable Acquisition of Stock. Net operating loss carry-over is disallowed if stock ownership changes 50 percent or more and the corporation does not continue to carry on substantially the same trade or business. (The addition of a new business will not necessarily constitute a disqualifying change in business.)

Tax-free Asset Acquisition or Merger. Net operating loss carry-over is reduced if the loss corporation stockholders have less than 20 percent stock interest in resulting combined entity. Loss is reduced by 5 percent for each 1 percent of stock ownership less than 20 percent now owned by the former loss corporation's shareholders.

SECURITIES AND EXCHANGE COMMISSION ASPECTS

The acquisition by one corporation of all, or substantially all, of the assets or stock of another corporation may require the filing of one or more of the following:

1. A registration statement under the Securities Act of 1933
2. A proxy statement pursuant to Regulation X-14 promulgated under Section 14 of the Securities Exchange Act of 1934
3. A Form 8-K under the Securities Exchange Act of 1934

Situations requiring the above filings are briefly summarized below. However, the applicability of these procedures, as well as those of any national securities exchange on which the securities are listed, should be discussed with corporate counsel.

Stock-for-stock Tender Offer. In this situation, the issuance of stock directly to the stockholders of the "acquired" company is likely to be deemed a public offering of securities requiring registration under the Securities Act of 1933, most probably on Form S-1. Although registration is burdensome and expensive, one of its attractions is that the stock may be freely sold thereafter, unless it lodges in control persons of the issuer.

Exemption from registration is usually based on the intrastate offering, the Regulation A offering ($300,000 or less) exemption, and the private offering (to a small, informed, and sophisticated group) exemption. However, reliance on any of these exemptions must be carefully scrutinized in the first instance and closely policed in the execution.

Statutory Merger and Acquisition of Assets (Rule 133). Where approval is required of the acquired company's shareholders to effect the statutory merger or purchase of assets, Rule 133 under the Securities Act of 1933 provides that the transaction does not involve an offer or sale of the acquiring company's stock and that registration is not required. However, because that rule restricts the disposition of such stock by the acquired corporation or its control persons, registration is often effected (having been a negotiated part of the transaction) to permit those persons to resell to the public. This procedure is often followed in situations where proxy solicitation pursuant to Regulation 14 is required to obtain stockholder approval of the merger or acquisition. Listed companies, as well as those over-the-counter companies which must register under the Securities Act amendments of 1964, must comply with the proxy regulations. The SEC's financial statement requirements in "merger proxies" are so similar to those of Form S-1 that little difference exists from the accounting standpoint. In such a case, it is usually very little trouble to place a "wraparound" cover page on the proxy statement giving information as to the offering. The SEC has authorized Form S-14 for this type of situation.

Where, however, no registration is made of stock of the acquiring company held by the acquired company (in the case of an acquisition of assets) or by control persons of the acquired company (in the case of a merger), those parties must continue to hold the stock at the risk of being deemed statutory underwriters upon resale. There is minor relief afforded these persons to the extent they may dispose of a very small percentage of the stock within a defined six-month period.

Form 8-K. Both companies may be required to file a Form 8-K monthly report within ten days after the close of the month of the transaction, whether it be the type discussed in either situation above. In both situations, the acquiring company must report both acquisitions of "significant amount of assets" (as defined) and increases in outstanding securities, and must provide certified financial statements of the acquired company for the last three full years in addition to uncertified interim statements. In a tender-offer situation, the acquired company must report only the change in its control; in the purchase-of-assets situation, the acquired company must report the disposition of a significant amount of assets; and in the merger situation, the acquired company will attempt to obtain SEC approval to terminate its reporting requirements as soon as possible (which, unless the merger is effected primarily in order to escape those requirements, should be forthcoming).

ACCOUNTING ASPECTS

For accounting purposes, the acquisition of one company by another is treated as a "purchase" or a "pooling of interests."

"Purchase" Accounting. In purchase accounting, the assets of the acquired company are recorded at the fair value of such property. In almost all cases, fair value is determined by the amount of cash or securities exchanged for the assets acquired. To the extent that the price paid exceeds that which can be assigned to a specific asset acquired, there is goodwill. Similarly, to the extent that fair value of assets acquired exceeds the price paid therefor, there is a credit item to be recorded in the accounts. Future accounting for the assets acquired will follow generally accepted principles of accounting.

The subsequent accounting for these assets can, and frequently does, result in quite a wide difference between the income reported on the new basis of accounting and the income that would have been reported on the accounting basis in the hands of the previous owner. Depreciation charged for fixed assets can be higher or lower than formerly. Inventory values could be different, and there is the accounting disposition of goodwill or the credit created in establishing the new basis for the assets acquired.

There are two practices in accounting for goodwill. One recognizes that goodwill may not exist permanently and therefore requires amortization over a period of time. The other method calls for no amortization, following the logic that because goodwill represents a price paid for income to be realized in the future, realization of such income would not call for any reduction in the asset value of goodwill, and if the expected income did not materialize, the loss in goodwill value would be unrelated to the period in which the income failed to materialize.

There can be an interesting situation when a so-called bargain purchase is made and the question of disposition of the credit arising from the excess of fair value over price paid is considered when "purchase" accounting is adopted. In such an instance, there may be a credit to income over some period to compensate for the low earning power of the assets acquired which would result in a more advantageous income statement than if pooling accounting were used.

"Pooling" Accounting. When pooling-of-interest accounting is adopted in an acquisition, the new enterprise resulting from the combination is regarded as having always been in existence in the combined state, and the ownership interests of each enterprise are considered to have jointly owned both enterprises. Thus, no new basis for accounting is called for, and there is a combination not only of the business enterprises but of accounting balances and historical data.

"Purchase" versus "Pooling." The classification for accounting purposes of a transaction as a purchase or pooling is not by choice but according to the nature of the combination. The primary requirement that should be weighed in determining whether a particular business combination can be judged a pooling is whether substantially all of the ownership interests in the constituent business become the owners of a single corporation which owns directly, or through subsidiaries, the assets and business of the constituent corporations.

This means, in the simplest form of transaction, that when voting stock is used, a business combination is likely to be treated as a pooling of interests, and where cash or bonds or other nonvoting securities are used, the transaction is likely to be treated as a purchase. There are a number of complex problems and numerous secondary factors which should be weighed in determining whether a particular business combination requires purchase or pooling treatment. Continuity of management is one of considerable importance.

To the manager contemplating a business acquisition, it is obvious that the choice of form of the acquisition will have a significant future effect on earnings that he reports and the balance sheet that he presents. Generally, pooling accounting is more advantageous because a new, usually higher basis of assets is not called for; consequently, future charges against income for amortization and depreciation of the assets acquired over their useful lives will not be increased over those charges that would have resulted if the businesses had not been combined. Of course, if assets were acquired at less than their former book values, the opposite result would be obtained.

It can be seen that the area is extremely complex, and along with the financing tax, SEC, and other aspects of the acquisition, the accounting problems have to be carefully considered before—not after—the transaction is consummated.

SUMMARY

The problems of buying or selling a going business are most complicated. They go to every aspect of the transaction. The problems of investigation, valuation, method of financing, tax, SEC, and accounting are challenges to management which require not only keen business judgment, but technical answers.

There are many questions which management must consider in the most careful way if it is to make the proper decision.

What kind of information must be developed and what kind of questions must be asked in the investigative phases of acquisition consideration?

What kind of factors should be considered in valuing the business?

How can the acquisition be financed so that the maximum leverage on debt capital can be obtained without undue risk?

What method of acquisition is best?

How can the deal be structured to obtain the best tax benefit for both the buyer and the seller?

What are the SEC implications of the proposed form of transaction and can they become too burdensome so that a better approach must be found?

How must the transaction be accounted for—as a "purchase" or "pooling"—and what is the effect upon future financial statements? Should another way be found to make the acquisition and produce better accounting results?

How, in sum, can a manager accomplish a sound purchase or sale of a going business in terms of maximizing the total benefits to both sides of the transaction?

BIBLIOGRAPHY

Buying and Selling a Small Business, Wichita State University, Wichita, Kans., 1963.

Corporate Growth through Merger and Acquisition, American Management Association, New York, 1963.

Link, R. M., *Financial and Legal Aspects of Acquisitions and Mergers,* Blyth & Company, Inc., New York, 1961.

McCarthy, George D., *Acquisitions and Mergers,* The Ronald Press Company, New York, 1963.

Mace, M. L., and G. G. Montgomery, *Management Problems of Corporate Acquisitions,* Graduate School of Business Administration, Harvard University, Boston, 1962.

Mergers and Acquisitions: Planning and Action, Financial Executives Research Foundation, New York, 1963.

Prerau, Sydney (ed.), "How to Buy and Sell a Business," *J. K. Lasser's Business Management Handbook,* McGraw-Hill Book Company, New York, 1960.

Scharf, Charles A., *Techniques for Buying, Selling and Merging Businesses,* Prentice-Hall, Inc., Englewood Cliffs, N.J., 1964.

Pros and Cons of Going Public

THEODORE GOODMAN *Associate, Martin and Tucker, Little Neck, New York*

"Going public" is a process in which a corporation owned by a relatively few individuals makes some of its stock available for purchase by outsiders. These outsiders are the "public." The method by which this stock reaches the public requires the services of an underwriter to distribute the stock to the public. The motivating factors for such action are many: a need for additional working capital; the requirement for expansion capital; a device for resolving personality disputes; a method of planning an estate; a pathway to retirement; diversification of the business; continuity of the business; unshouldering responsibilities; diversification of personal assets; a method of recruiting, retaining, and rewarding key personnel; a device for making acquisitions of other companies; a way of coping with the "unreasonable accumulation" of undistributed surplus; and so on.

The decision to go public is often based on a mixture of these motives. Making the move for just one clear-cut motive invariably brings into play some of the others. That does not mean that the decision "to go" is a good one. Going public is not like selling an interest in your boat or house. Regardless of the number or weight of the "go" motives, the decision also involves certain considerations and costs which must be examined realistically and balanced against the "go" advantages: determining the value of the offered stock, timing of the issue, regulatory disclosures, financial disclosures to stockholders (and competitors), regulatory administrative procedures, high initial cost of filing fees and professional services, communications with stockholders, corporate stockholder relationships, living in a goldfish bowl, and the like.

During an examination of the pros and cons, management may find that the cons outweigh the pros and therefore that alternative routes for solving financial problems should be sought. On the other hand, once a company has become public, it might find that the motives and advantages which originally prompted it to go public no longer exist. In this case, a company sometimes finds that its best course of action because of new motives is to return to a private, nonpublic status, in which case it "de-public-izes."

The purpose of this chapter is to present the major factors in the "go–no-go" decision and alternative solutions.

FACTORS CONTRIBUTING TO INTEREST IN GOING PUBLIC

Corporate managements of small and medium-size companies have increasingly turned to a public distribution of securities to fulfill their financial requirements. Going public has also served the financial and personal requirements of stockholders. Going public, however, is by no means a panacea for solving financial and other problems. Therefore, it is important to examine alternative methods of financing. Foremost in this examination should be the realization that the decision to go public or to seek alternative financing routes is one which must be made on balance, after management and its advisers consider carefully the immediate objectives together with the long-term needs of the corporation.

The growth and development of trade and commerce in the United States, and indeed the world, have made substantial demands for the output of manufacturing and service organizations. Because of changes both in the distribution of national income and in the taxation of income, a great segment of industry has sought funds from absentee public "partners" to meet both the needs of the corporations and the requirements of these "partners." Shares of common stock, representing fractional ownership, are issued and sold to buyers who become stockholders and thereby partners. The obvious attraction to new stockholders is the hope of realizing an appreciation on their investment and/or income return (dividends) on their capital outlays.

The factor that has accelerated interest in the public sharing and distribution of corporate ownership is the increasing affluence of the so-called middle-class layer of the United States population. Smaller corporations consider going public an acceptable route, and more smaller security buyers are active in the various stock markets.

REASONS FOR GOING PUBLIC

The major reasons for a company's interest in going public perhaps can be summarized as follows:
1. To enhance and support growth
2. To enhance the principals' holdings
3. To recruit new managerial talent and hold existing executives
4. To generate prestige and create a public image
5. To cope better with the "unreasonable accumulation" of undistributed surplus
6. To create a marketable security by which advantageous acquisitions may be made

Growth. A major reason for going public is the ability to raise additional equity capital. This should permit a more rapid growth of the company than might otherwise be possible. A growth company will usually have a substantial and ever-growing thirst for capital. To be successful, a proper financial program should be designed to act in a manner similar to a sustained-release vitamin. Additional capital will enable the company to continue its profitable growth; this in turn will add to its capital and retained surplus; this makes the company more attractive to institutional investors who in turn will lend the company long-term moneys which will enable the company to continue its growth—perhaps without further dilution of equity interest.

Additional equity capital expands the credit base of the corporation. This enables the corporation to borrow larger amounts of money for longer periods at more advantageous interest rates. And this borrowing will require fewer restrictions from the lender.

Improving Owners' Capital Position. The owners of a growing business can usually enhance the value of their holdings in the company by going public. Market value in a public offering almost always exceeds book value. If the company continues to expand its growth and profit pattern, it may be expected that demand for its securities will create an opportunity for its owners to sell part or all of their holdings if they wish to create liquidity in their personal financial program. This liquidity allows the owners to diversify their holdings which had been tied up in their company.

The market valuation for estate tax purposes may more readily be ascertained when the company's stock is publicly owned. In addition, if there is pressure to raise cash for the payment of estate taxes, it may be more readily obtainable if there is a ready public market for the stock.

Attracting Management Talent. A rapidly growing company will always have a demand for new, top-caliber management as well as the need to hold onto its incumbent key executives. A publicly owned company usually will have more to offer its executives. The corporation may institute a restricted stock-option plan to allow the executive to participate in the equity ownership of the company and to make him a partner in its growth. The existence of a public market for his company's stock will, at a later date, allow him to sell his stock in the open market if he wishes. The company also benefits, because it need not enter into any buy-back agreements with the executives, as is the case in a privately owned corporation. Such agreements are mandatory to avoid the ownership of private stock by individuals no longer employed by the company.

Improving the Public Image. The trading of a public stock over-the-counter or on a national or regional stock exchange can strengthen the prestige of the company by creating an image uniquely different from other forms of image building. Although a formal public relations effort can focus attention on the company's products, markets, and way of doing business, the stock-exchange listing is a subtle implication that the corporation is solid, its ownership widespread, and its operations government regulated. This in turn may add to its future growth and thereby increase the marketability of its stock.

Avoiding Confiscatory Taxes. Corporations which have "unreasonable accumulations" of surplus are required either to distribute this surplus to stockholders or to be penalized by paying a confiscatory tax. Obviously, the distribution of earnings to stockholders adds to their ordinary income with a resulting increase in their personal tax liability. If the company goes public and continues its expansion, however, it may be possible to escape from this predicament. Going public may enable the corporation to attract additional key personnel, make acquisitions of other companies, pay dividends to the public shareholders, and the like, thereby facilitating the profitable use of its capital and surplus.

Facilitating Acquisitions. Stock in a rapidly growing, publicly owned company may be a valuable tool for its future growth through the acquisitions of other companies. Its stock may be acceptable as the exchange medium for the stock of the other company it seeks to acquire. If its stock has advanced in price from the time of its public offering, it is likely that an acquisition by exchange of stock will be advantageous. The process of public financing to raise equity funds should, without exception, permit management to remain in absolute control of the company and continue to direct its activities and policies.

When public shares are spread broadly among many stockholders, management's control is ensured, even if mathematical control is diluted along the way via merger, acquisitions, or further equity financings.

THE PRICE OF GOING PUBLIC

In the determination of whether to go public, management must assess and evaluate the disadvantages and the advantages in comparison with alternative methods of available financing. There are also the cost factors, which, although they cannot be considered disadvantages, must nonetheless be reckoned with in making the ultimate decision. It is obvious that a decision must emerge on balance from the intertwining effects of all plus and minus factors and cost considerations.

The following are the major considerations which management must weigh and evaluate:

1. Valuation and timing
2. Regulations and disclosures
3. Communications with stockholders
4. Corporate stockholder relationships
5. Fees and costs
6. The goldfish bowl

Valuation and Timing. One of the more difficult management decisions is how much equity must be sold to raise the necessary capital to finance future growth. This problem focuses on the overall valuation of the business. Management must assess and evaluate the probability that the company will be worth more in the future, and that less equity would then have to be sold to satisfy capital requirements. On the other hand, the additional equity capital may be required now to promote the company's growth and expansion. To complicate this matter further, timing enters the picture.

Especially in aggressive companies staffed with younger, dynamic management, the question of valuation is a knotty one. By virtue of motivation and drive, these managements usually project their future performances at high levels and are reluctant to sell their equity at modest valuations. Although financing can be arranged successfully, it requires a unique and creative approach to the problem, because it involves balancing an immediate need for capital against higher future evaluation based on future performance. The entire decision is complicated by the changes, risks, and lost opportunities that may occur during the watch-and-wait period, which are beyond the control of management.

Public financing through the sale of common stock will dilute the equity interests of the present stockholders. To the company that is experiencing rapid growth, this is not welcomed. The decision, however, must be weighed in light of the following factors:

1. The urgency of the need for new money
2. The anticipated result from the use of the new money
3. The availability of capital from other sources
4. The risk of market acceptability at a later date

After the decision is made to go forward with the public offering, there still remain substantial uncertainties beyond the control of management, between the time of the decision and the expected date of the distribution. Such matters as market evaluation of other publicly owned companies in the same industry, monetary conditions, international matters, and the like must enter into the evaluation and ultimate decision.

Time plays an important role in public financing. One must allow a minimum of 9 to 12 weeks to prepare the prospectus for filing with the Securities and

Exchange Commission and perhaps longer before it is finally reviewed and can be effective for the distribution of stock.

Many things may occur from the time of agreement with the underwriter and the start of work on the prospectus to the time the offering is to be effective. For example:

1. Circumstances may change within the company.
2. Domestic economic indicators may change.
3. Foreign affairs may be more complex with resulting effects on the economy.
4. A problem may occur within the industry.

Any one of these factors can affect the price of the stock and even determine if the offering can take place at all.

Regulations and Disclosures.   Publicly owned companies are subject to the jurisdiction and regulations of the Securities and Exchange Commission.   The company may be forced to divulge information heretofore considered confidential. These disclosures could place the company in a vulnerable competitive position, for they become available not only to stockholders but to competition as well. Some of these disclosures may relate to:

1. Salaries, expenses, pensions, and stock options of officers and directors
2. Sales, costs, and profitability of products and services
3. Listing of significant customers and suppliers and terms of contracts
4. Listing of all significant dealings between management and the company

Although the necessity of meeting the SEC requirements may allow stockholders, customers, and suppliers to know the stability of the company and the soundness of management, in many instances the disclosure of these facts could create a competitive disadvantage.

In addition to the requirements to disclose certain vital data, there are additional burdens imposed as a result of being regulated by a governmental agency. Compliance with formal administrative procedures is costly in terms of both time and dollars.

Communications with Stockholders.   Communication between a company and its stockholders is vital.   Because most companies that are about to go public have been closely held, they usually have had little or no reason to establish formal communicating procedures.   Immediately after having its first public offering, the company must institute a detailed program for external reporting to its stockholders.

Stockholder-Corporation Relationships.   It is not uncommon in closely held corporations to find that stockholders have had financial transactions with their corporations.   To be sure, these transactions may have been entered into at arm's length.   They could, however, be the basis for stockholders' suits if a conflict of interest is thought to exist.   Therefore, it is advisable that at the time the company has its first public offering, all stockholder-corporation financial dealings cease.

Fees and Costs.   The cost of an original issue of stock to the public is likely to be high, owing to the substantial amount of initial professional time required of accountants, lawyers, and management consultants to satisfy the requirements of the SEC and the underwriter.

The cost of floating an initial public stock offering for a relatively small company is likely to be higher (based on percentage) than for a large company. This is because the underwriter's risks are likely to be greater and because professional fees and other costs, such as printing, are a larger percentage of the total cost of the smaller issue.

The Goldfish Bowl.   From the first day that a new issue is offered to the public, the company is visually exposed and subject to public viewing.   Among the interested viewers will be union officials, the company's competitors, the company's customers, and the company's suppliers. In some extreme cases, the realization that the public company must now live in the proverbial glass house has put an end to any further consideration of going public.

ALTERNATE METHODS OF FINANCING

Banks. The most direct and usually the lowest-cost method of financing is with a commercial bank. These loans are advanced mainly to well-capitalized, profitable businesses on a secured (collateralized) or an unsecured basis and usually are of short-term duration. Their rules and standards are usually strict. Banks are regulated by state and Federal authorities from whom bank charters are issued. There has been a trend, however, toward flexibility in banking to compete with finance companies which have experienced an unusually rapid expansion.

Commercial Finance Companies. The commercial finance company has a very definite place in the world of finance. Among various methods employed in making working capital available are:

1. Accounts receivable financing or factoring
2. Inventory financing
3. Chattel mortgage financing
4. Equipment lease financing
5. Expansion financing, whether it be for modernization or diversification

The following data illustrate the point that accounts receivable factoring can, in addition to supplying working capital, also improve the company's working-capital ratio:

Cash	$ 20,000		
Accounts receivable	200,000	Accounts payable	$320,000
Inventory	400,000	Net worth	300,000
Total	$620,000	Total	$620,000

If the accounts receivable of $200,000 were sold to a finance company which advanced 90 percent of their value, or $180,000, which was used to reduce accounts payable, the working capital created would also improve the working-capital (current assets to current liabilities) ratio from slightly less than 2 to 1 (above) to better than 3 to 1 as below:

Cash	$ 20,000		
Due from finance company	20,000	Accounts payable	$140,000
Inventory	400,000	Net worth	300,000
Total	$440,000	Total	$440,000

This is an illustration of what can result from the sale or assignment of accounts receivable. It should be apparent that the company's credit standing is improved by this action.

In the above situation, the finance company passes on all credit, performs administrative work in connection with bookkeeping, and collects the accounts receivable. This can save the company costly overhead. Finance-factoring arrangements can benefit a growing business in that there need not be a specific date to repay the obligation as in the case of a loan. This improved balance sheet and credit standing will also permit management to buy in the most advantageous manner at the lowest cost and highest discounts.

Institutional Loans. In appraising its needs for financing, management may conclude that its requirements are for long-term funds which will enable it to plan well into the future. In the case of the acquisition of another company or of developing and introducing new products and machinery, which can require a large initial outlay and "lead time" before a proper flow of cash is generated, it is essential that long-term money be available. This type of long-term money can be had from insurance companies and pension funds, which have substantial amounts of money they wish to invest for long periods of time. Initially, it may be difficult to think of these institutions as "lenders." However, they accumulate vast sums of money that they must put to work. These institutions, therefore, are often willing to make long-term loans to modest-sized organizations.

Since 1950, life insurance companies and pension funds alone have accounted for approximately 75 percent of the total corporate loans outstanding. Because these institutions have an essentially long-term attitude toward investing, they may have little need for marketability of the bond or note, and this skirts the costly requirement of registering the document with the Securities and Exchange Commission.

Small Business Administration. Helping small businesses obtain needed financing on reasonable terms is an important function of the Small Business Administration. Generally the loans are limited to $350,000, interest is not to be more than 6 percent, and duration of loan is not to exceed ten years. The loans must be collateralized and will be granted only to those who qualify as "small business."

Equity is not involved in this type of loan. To those who qualify, an SBA loan, as restrictive as it may be, may be the most inexpensive form of financing. Indeed, it may turn out to be the only source of funds for a company.

Small Business Investment Corporations. Small Business Investment Corporations are licensed by the Small Business Administration. They are organized to finance smaller business through long-term debentures or equity, or a combination of both.

The SBIC provides long-term loans at interest rates of 7 to 12 percent per annum. The SBIC is directly interested in, and has a direct financial stake in, the growth and development of the company. It almost always demands equity when it grants loans.

CONCLUSION

The question of whether or not to "go public" is a most complex issue. It can correctly be resolved only after a thorough examination of facts and objectives by management and its expert advisers. All alternative methods of financing must also be explored.

It is important that advice be sought from an investment banker who has substantial experience in the field and who can act as liaison among all interested parties as the investigation progresses.

Financial creativity and uniqueness are invariably required to meet the financial needs of smaller companies. Stereotyped, conventional formulas probably will not work or at best will produce stopgap results. The investment banker, through the use of ingenuity, should be able to find the best answer to the problem by the concurrent use of a combination of several methods of financing. The first financing must, if continued rapid growth occurs, lead to subsequent successful financings to permit the further expansion of the company.

If handled properly and timed right, public financing can be a valuable financial tool and can result in substantial gains to the rapidly growing company and to its present and future stockholders.

In effect, if management decides to "go public," it must have confidence that the additional equity capital raised will permit continued rapid expansion and profitability of the company. Otherwise, the dilution of equity that results will indeed be a high price to pay.

BIBLIOGRAPHY

Bogen, Jules I., *Financial Handbook,* The Ronald Press Company, New York, 1959.

Corey, E. Raymond, *Direct Placement of Corporate Securities,* Division of Research, Graduate School of Business Administration, Harvard University, Boston, 1951.

Husband, William H., and James C. Dockeray, *Modern Corporation Finance,* Richard D. Irwin, Inc., Homewood, Ill., 1948.

Investment Bankers Association of America, *Fundamentals of Investment Banking,* Prentice-Hall, Inc., Englewood Cliffs, N.J., 1949.

Kahn, Edwin L., Don V. Harris, Jr., Millard F. West, Jr., and Morris L. Forer, *Going Public as a Means of Expansion,* Matthew Bender & Company, New York, 1961.

Lyon, Hastings, *Corporations and Their Financing,* D. C. Heath and Company, Boston, 1938.

Mangold, Maxwell J., *How Public Financing Can Help Your Company Grow,* Pilot Publications, New York, 1959.

Prime, John H., *Investment Analysis,* Prentice-Hall, Inc., Englewood Cliffs, N.J., 1949.

Robinson, Gerald J., *Going Public: Successful Securities Underwriting,* Clark Boardman Company, Ltd., New York, 1961.

Wheat, Francis M., and George A. Blackstone, "Guideposts for a First Public Offering," *Business Lawyer,* no. 539, 1960.

ACCOUNTING AND CONTROL

CHAPTER ONE

General Accounting Practices

HAROLD BIERMAN, JR. *Professor, Graduate School of Business and Public Administration, Cornell University, Ithaca, New York*

To use accounting reports effectively, it is necessary for the manager or analyst to understand that the accountant employs both explicit and implicit rules in deciding how to record financial transactions. These rules are frequently broad guidelines rather than exact specifications; thus we may expect to find several firms recording the same financial transaction in a much different manner. This chapter will review three types of reports presented by the accountant, suggesting their uses and limitations. In addition, some of the components of the reports will be discussed and used as a means of pointing out the types of rules that are applied by the accountant. If the appropriate rules are followed, then the certified public accountant auditing the firm will indicate that the financial report "was prepared in accordance with generally accepted accounting principles." The three reports we shall discuss in this chapter are the balance sheet, the income statement, and the funds statement.

THE BALANCE SHEET

The balance sheet or position statement of a corporation presents a financial picture of the firm at a specific moment of time. The statement that is prepared is very much a result of accounting conventions. A popular form of presentation is to have the assets on one side of a page faced by the sources of assets (the liabilities and the stockholders' equity). Since the sum of the assets is equal to the sum of the asset sources, a popular name of the statement of financial position has been "balance sheet."

Assets. The accountant is very selective in what he considers to be a recordable asset. In general, to be eligible for consideration as an asset, the item must have been purchased. Although intangible assets are recorded in some situations where they have been purchased, an item is more likely to be recorded if the asset can be seen and touched. Unless the item that is purchased is tangible, the likelihood of its being considered an asset is decreased considerably. A corollary of the above insistence on the item being purchased is the fact that the basis of recording the asset is the cost of the asset. However, there are exceptions. For example, in cases where the current market value of inventory is less than cost, we may choose to apply "the lower of cost or market" rule.

We have measurement problems when the cost is difficult to measure (as with determining the cost of a pork chop obtained as one of many products from a pig), when the value of the asset decreases through use (as with an automobile that is used on salty roads), or when the value of the asset increases (as with trees that are growing). In any of these situations, reports prepared by several accountants are apt to differ considerably.

The more frequently encountered assets and the basis that accountants most frequently use in preparing balance sheets are as follows:

Asset Item	*Basis of Recording*
Cash or bank deposits	The face value
Marketable securities (frequently readily marketable governmental securities)	The lower of cost or market
Accounts receivable	Face value less an adjustment for expected uncollectibles
Inventories	The lower of cost or market (but cost may be measured in a variety of ways)
Investments in other firms	The lower of cost or market, or cost, or cost adjusted for the firm's equity in earnings since the acquisition
Plant and equipment	Cost less accumulated depreciation, that is, cost reduced by a measure of the deterioration of the asset
Goodwill and other intangibles	Cost where the goodwill was acquired in the purchase of another firm, but frequently this item is recorded at a nominal amount or not recorded at all

It should be noted that the primary basis of recording each of the above items is objective evidence of the type associated with a purchase invoice. If there is an adjustment from cost, it is generally in a downward direction. This is a result of the accountant's inclination to be conservative.

Any person analyzing the financial affairs of a corporation by inspecting a balance sheet should be aware of the information that is not presented as well as the information that is contained in the report. The following information is frequently not given:

The market value of marketable securities.

The market value of inventories.

The market value of investments in other firms, or the current book value of the investment-type holdings.

The current value of long-lived assets (land, plant, and equipment), obtained in one of several ways—for example, by adjusting for price-level changes using price indexes or by the use of appraisals.

The current value of long-lived assets (land, plant, and equipment), obtained cost. For example, the cost of drilling an oil well does not give an indication of the value of the oil in the ground.

The cost of research and development expenditures. This item is generally treated as an expense of the period in which it is incurred; thus an asset frequently does not appear on the balance sheet.

The cost of training and education of management. This is invariably treated as an expense.

There are reasonable measures for all of the above items, though they are not generally used. However, there are some items that are more difficult to record even if we had the inclination. At what value should we record the value of a top-quality manager or the possession of good location for a store? A chemist may develop a new compound, but we do not yet know how to use it. What is its cost or its value?

Obviously there are some items where the accountant may adhere to the objective measure of cost and present a reasonable measure of value. For example, a ninety-day Federal government note may be recorded at cost, and the fact that the value currently is a bit different from cost plus accrued interest may be ignored. The materiality of the error is small (materiality enters into the treatment of many items).

However, there are other items that either are presented at amounts that are not useful or are not shown on the statement at all. The analyst must be particularly careful in appraising the balance sheet of a firm in an industry that involves natural resources (where factors of value are discovered or grown) or where the firm is engaged in a relatively large amount of research. In these areas, the adherence to cost and a reluctance to record intangible assets is apt to negate much of the usefulness of the financial reports of the financial position.

Note that the term "liquidation value" was not used in this section. Because the accountant assumes a "going concern," the liquidation value is of no relevance, unless the firm is to be liquidated.

Sources of Assets. The asset sources are essentially of two types: liabilities and contributions (explicit or implicit) of stockholders. In general, the measurement problems involving liabilities are much less than those with assets. Usually the liability takes the form of a legal contract, and thus the amounts are reasonably well defined. If the liabilities were all of a short-term value, the measures would be very reliable.

Where the due date of the liability is a long time in the future, however, we have a problem of adjusting for the time value of money via a discounting procedure. It is likely that the book value of the long-term liability, the maturity or face value of the liability, and its current economic value will all be different. Thus the amount shown as the book liability for bonds payable may not be the current economic liability to the firm (it will be only if the current interest rate is the same as the interest rate at the time of issue, and if the security was issued at face value).

A second problem with liabilities involves those liabilities associated with events that are still not completed. For example, a lawsuit may be pending, and the accountant must present a report without the final judgment of the court. In this case, an estimate of the liability may or may not be made by the accountant, and the analyst must be sure that a reasonable estimate is made.

There will frequently appear in the asset sources side of a balance sheet a section containing several "reserve" accounts. These are reserves for this or that, and may have exotic titles such as:

Reserve for self-insurance
Reserve for contingencies
Reserve for possible loss in foreign investments
Reserve for lawsuits

Reserves can be reclassified into subtractions from assets, additions to liabilities, or stockholders' equities. For example, the first three items are stockholders' equity items, and the last is an expected liability. It is unfortunate that the term "reserve" is still used by accountants, with an inevitable attendant confusion. It is particularly confusing since a reserve account of the type we are discussing is not a "reserve" in the sense that most laymen would use the term. No assets have been set aside for a contingency; thus the firm's ability to cope with an unfortunate event is not increased by the bookkeeping entry that gives rise to the account.

There are several liabilities that the accountant does not record. The two most significant are pension liabilities and lease liabilities. Because these amounts may be large, the analyst must be prepared to make necessary adjustments when these obligations exist.

The stockholders' equity section of the balance sheet is divided into several sections. A meaningful split occurs where there are preferred and common stockholders. We shall assume in this discussion that there is only common stock outstanding. The law requires that there be a split between the permanent capital (for example, common stock—par) and the capital available for dividends (for example, retained earnings). For many purposes, an investor is interested in the total sum of the stockholders' equity rather than the breakdown that we have described. On the other hand, creditors may be interested in knowing that the corporation cannot distribute x dollars as dividends because it is permanent capital.

The basic accounting equation (assets are identically equal to asset sources) may be redescribed as: the stockholders' equity is equal to the difference between assets and liabilities. This latter presentation is the basis of a form of statement presentation that shows the financial position not as a balanced array, but rather in a step fashion with liabilities being subtracted from assets to obtain the stockholders' equity. It should be noted that an error in measuring assets or liabilities will also affect the measure of the stockholders' equity.

One of the more interesting measures to a potential stockholder is the measure of book value per share (the total common stockholders' equity divided by the number of shares of common stock outstanding). Unfortunately, this measure is not any better than the accountant's measures of the assets and liabilities; thus it is a somewhat unreliable indicator of value.

THE INCOME STATEMENT

The income statement is considered by many to be the most important financial statement prepared by the accountant. It is the basis of the earnings per share computation (total income of the firm divided by the number of shares).

There are several problems associated with the measurement of income. For example:
1. The timing of the revenue recognition
2. The matching of expenses against the revenue
3. The measurement of expenses
4. The inclusion or exclusion of special nonrecurring items

The accountant does not record revenue until it is realized. In general, this means that a market transaction has taken place that involves the corporation, and the corporation has received in exchange for the asset sold or service rendered either cash, a good accounts receivable, or some other readily measured asset (or decrease in liability).

The matching of expenses against the revenues that they help earn is particularly troublesome in a situation where there are assets being used which have a long life and are expected to earn revenues over several time periods. The decision as to how much of the cost of the asset should be allocated to each time period is a difficult problem. The measurement of the expense becomes even more difficult when there has been a significant change in the general price level that may cause the cost basis of recording the expenses to be less useful than alternative measures (such as adjusting the cost for the change in the price level). To adjust for price-level changes by the use of price indexes is not generally accepted accounting practice.

But even the use of relatively short-lived assets may have its measurement problems. For example, the use of inventory may give rise to an expense. How is the expense to be measured? What assumption should be made as to the flow of costs? The accountant may assume that the last goods purchased are sold first (LIFO) or that the first goods purchased are sold first (FIFO), or rather than make a choice, average the costs. There are also other alternatives, and the choice of cost flow will affect the measure of the asset as well as the measure of the expense and thus the income.

The decision whether or not to include or exclude nonrecurring items from the measurement of income is a troublesome one. If these items are excluded from the income statement, they do not affect the income of this year, nor do they affect the income of any other year. This means that expenses may be understated for a period of years and then the firm may adjust the assets to take note of their decreased value, but not affect the income statement. Each year may show a profit, but the firm suffers an overall loss.

A possible solution to this problem is the so-called "clean surplus" rule. Following this rule, no entry of this type is made directly to retained earnings; instead, all items are run through the income statement. Although this procedure solves one problem, it creates another. The income of this period is affected by items that were caused by the past accounting procedures, and these items may have nothing to do with this accounting period except that the accountant has chosen to recognize them in this period.

It is common practice for the accountant to be consistent in his procedures. Thus, he is not likely to follow one procedure one year and then switch to another procedure in the next year, and in the following year switch back. He may change procedures, but it is not done lightly.

The measurement of income of a corporation is at best an estimate. In some firms, the earning of revenue is an obvious event (for example, a cash sale at the local drugstore), but the revenue-producing event is frequently less obvious with a more complex firm. When is the revenue earned and when should it be recognized by a firm selling magazine subscriptions or by a firm building a ship? If a firm holds readily marketable securities that have increased in value, has a gain been earned? Is it necessary to sell the security? General practice would say that it is necessary to sell the security, but this procedure might enable a management holding a large portfolio of securities to determine its income by judicious choice of the securities that it sells in any time period, rather than by the dividend and market changes of the period.

THE FUNDS STATEMENT

The term "funds statement" is generally applied to a statement of the sources and applications of working capital (that is, current assets less current liabilities). It is sometimes applied to a statement of changes in cash.

If we define "current assets" to include items such as cash, marketable securities, inventories, and other items that are expected to be consumed in the coming twelve months, and if we define current liabilities to be debts coming due in the next twelve months, then the difference is a measure of the liquidity of the firm. The funds statement is a statement showing the causes of the change in this measure of liquidity. Among the sources of working capital are funds generated by operations, the issuance of long-term debt or common stock, and the sale of long-lived assets. Among the uses of working capital would be the retirement of long-term debt or common stock and the purchase of long-lived assets.

One problem in measuring the funds from operations involves the expense deduction for depreciation. Because depreciation expense is accompanied by a decrease in a long-lived asset, it does not use working capital and thus should not be deducted from revenues in computing the funds from operations (as in Method 1 below). If it has been deducted in computing the income, it should be added back to income to compute the funds from operations (as in Method 2).

	Method 1	Method 2
Revenues..................	$100,000	$100,000
Less expenses.............	60,000*	72,000
Funds from operations.......	$ 40,000	$ 28,000
Add: depreciation....................		12,000
Funds from operations.................		$ 40,000

* Excludes $12,000 of depreciation.

Another problem in evaluating working-capital changes occurs when there is a separation of some fraction of marketable securities into a noncurrent classification, because it is thought the securities may be used in the future to acquire long-lived assets. Following this practice, the purchase of the readily marketable securities becomes a use of working capital, but the purchase of plant and equipment does not affect working capital. This practice results in the amount of the reported change in working capital being a result of the somewhat arbitrary decision by management as to how much of the total sum of marketable securities possessed by the firm will be given this special noncurrent classification. Also, when the long-lived assets are purchased, there is a question of how much of the purchase cost should be considered to have been financed by the use of these securities rather than by the use of current assets.

The "cash flow" of a firm (funds from operations) is a useful measure of a change in liquidity, as is the change in working capital. However, these measures are not substitutes for the measure of income. The funds statement supplements the income statement. It does not replace it.

CONSOLIDATED STATEMENTS

It is common practice for the financial reports of corporations to be "consolidated." This means that when a parent company owns a majority of the shares of the subsidiary corporation, the financial affairs of several legal entities are combined into one set of financial statements. This is more desirable than showing the affairs of each corporation separately in many statements. The advantage of this practice is that it simplifies the task of the analyst. Items that could result in double counting are eliminated, and the information is condensed into a form that makes it much more usable.

There are three criteria commonly used to determine whether or not a subsidiary firm is to be included in consolidation:

1. The percentage of ownership
2. The nature of the business
3. The location of the business

If the percentage of ownership is 50 percent or more, if the nature of the business is similar to that of the parent, and if the subsidiary corporation is located in the same country as the parent, the corporation is likely to be consolidated. With a smaller percentage ownership, a different type of business, or a foreign operation, any one of these characteristics might disqualify the firm from the consolidation process. If it is not consolidated, the investment would be recorded at cost or cost plus a proportion of the earnings of the subsidiary. The proportion should be consistent with the percentage of ownership of the parent.

In recent years, the financial subsidiary (a captive financing organization) has increasingly come into popularity. The financial subsidiary finances the purchases by customers of the parent's products. Generally the financial subsidiary will have a capital structure containing a large proportion of debt (more than the parent is likely to have). It is general practice not to consolidate the affairs of the financial subsidiary and the parent, even if the firm may be a 100-percent-owned domestic corporation. The primary argument against consolidation is that the nature of the business of the parent (a manufacturer) and subsidiary (a financial institution) differs.

Another accounting problem arises at the time two corporations merge or one firm acquires a second firm. The event can be handled as an acquisition of assets and assuming of liabilities (a purchase). Or the event can be handled as if the affairs of the corporations flowed together to form a corporation whose financial affairs may be represented as a pooling of the affairs of the two corporations. In this latter situation, the retained earnings of both corporations are carried forward. With a purchase, only the retained earnings of the surviving corporation are carried forward. Following a strict interpretation of the entity concept (that is, the accountant is accounting for the corporate entity), we might start with no retained earnings, because the new corporation is in certain essential ways different from the old corporation. In practice, this latter interpretation is rarely applied.

EVALUATION OF ACCOUNTING PRACTICES

Although there are many valid criticisms that can be made about the current state of accounting practice, there are also many statements of praise that can be made. In general, we know the accounting basis of the financial statements; thus, we are aware of those situations where the information is not very usable, that is, where we cannot use the information as the basis of making decisions. If we are analyzing the financial reports of an oil company, then we know that the long-lived asset measure is likely not to have a reasonable correlation with the value of the oil reserves. We may like to know this latter information that is missing, but at least we are warned, and the informed reader should not be misled. Also, we know that certified financial statements are likely to be honestly prepared. There may be differences of opinion as to how items should be presented, and all firms are not comparable, but at least we know that the figures are not being rigged to suit the arbitrary purposes of management. On the negative side is the type of situation illustrated by the accounting for research and development. A decrease in research and development expenditures will increase the income of the present year, possibly at a cost of the income of future years that might otherwise have benefited from the research.

Thus, the type of income rigging that can take place is a more sophisticated variety that makes use of known loopholes in the accounting practice.   Unfortunately, this type of rigging can have adverse economic effects (the arbitrary cutback in research to improve income of the present year is an example of an adverse economic action).

The analyst or investor who ignores the reports of the accountant because they are not exact is making a grievous error.   At best, reports of the accountant can never be better than a collection of estimates of values and events that are extremely difficult to measure.   But these reports are useful markers.

We live in a world where the future is uncertain and the accountant is reporting events of the past.   However, many useful projections into the future are based on past events.   If we have a firm that in its best year has earned $2 per share, and if there has not been a special event that causes us to think the future history will be drastically different from the past, then to ignore the accountant's measure of $2 and invest in the firm based on a $10 per share earnings does not seem to be reasonable.

We can expect accounting practice to change in the future just as the accounting of the past has changed.   There is room for improvement, but we start from a base that is reasonable and provides much useful information.[1]

BIBLIOGRAPHY

Baxter, W. T., and S. Davidson (eds.), *Studies in Accounting Theory*, Richard D. Irwin, Inc., Homewood, Ill., 1962.

Bierman, Harold, Jr., *Financial and Managerial Accounting*, The Macmillan Company, New York, 1963.

Morrissey, L. E., *Contemporary Accounting Problems*, Prentice-Hall, Inc., Englewood Cliffs, N.J., 1963.

Paton, W. A., *Accounting Theory*, Accounting Studies Press, Chicago, 1962.

Zeff, S. A., and T. F. Keller, *Financial Accounting Theory Issues and Controversies*, McGraw-Hill Book Company, New York, 1964.

[1] The reader who wants to read more on this subject is referred to Paul Grady, *Inventory of Generally Accepted Accounting Principles for Business Enterprises*, Accounting Research Study, no. 7, American Institute of Certified Public Accountants, New York, 1965.

CHAPTER TWO

Cost Accounting

L. J. BENNINGER *Professor, College of Business Administration, University of Florida, Gainesville, Florida*

Cost accounting as presently practiced is essentially a creation of the twentieth century. Although attempts at costing appeared well before Columbus's discovery of America, it was not until after the Industrial Revolution that cost accounting became a discipline of stature worthy of serious study on a professional basis.

Prior to the Industrial Revolution (using 1776 as a reference date), cost accounts consisted for the most part of a simple system of memorandum accounting which compiled the direct-material and direct-labor costs of products manufactured. Although there were instances in this period of cost systems of considerable complexity, these were but random variations of a society where problems of accounting for investment and overhead were negligible.

DEVELOPING NEED FOR IMPROVED COST-ACCOUNTING METHODS

The Industrial Revolution represented essentially a revolution in machine invention making possible our present-day, mass-production industrial society. The production and use of new machine inventions called for the investment of capital on a scale the world had never before seen. The corporate device, as a consequence, became widely used as a method for accumulating capital. The modern corporation brought about a separation of both owners and managers on the one hand and top general management and lower technical management on the other. The industrial corporation called for functional divisions of management, such as manufacturing management, marketing management, and financial management. These specialized managements reported to a top and more general management.

Obviously, a need arose for communication and control between owners and management concerning the use of capital invested as well as communication between top management and lower management concerning the conduct of operations. Communication to stockholders was required regarding the financial condition of the corporation and its operating results, and communication between top management and lower management became necessary with respect to product costs and operating conditions.

The accounting system in existence prior to the Industrial Revolution was designed primarily to answer business problems arising in a trading society. Traditional accounting processes presented periodically information concerning resources and debts, but more particularly information concerning the invoice cost of products purchased and sold and the invoice cost of merchandise remaining on hand in inventory. Basically, the older system of accounts was designed to report historically periodically, as, for example, once a calendar year.

With the advent of the Industrial Revolution, products were not necessarily purchased in one form and sold in the identical form. Instead, materials purchased were given a time-consuming and costly processing, and a complex organization of men and machines was needed to meet production schedules. When applied to industrial situations, the inherited accounting mechanism was found to be inadequate.

Periodic Accounting System for Manufacturing Costs. The first attempts at improvement, building as they did on older methods, left much to be desired. Even when adjusted in an attempt to meet industrial problems, the older system of merchandise accounts provided at best for product costs as illustrated by the following "T" account:

	Manufactured cost of goods sold	

Beginning inventories:
  Materials
  Work in process
  Finished goods
Purchases of raw materials
Direct-labor costs
Indirect manufacturing expenses
	Deduct ending inventories:
	  Materials
	  Work in process
	  Finished goods

In contrast to a thoroughgoing cost-accounting system, this approach is typed as a periodic accounting system for manufacturing costs. Its disadvantages are:

1. Costs cannot be ascertained without the taking of physical inventories.

2. Ascertaining costs applicable to manufactured inventories in an industrial plant having complex and expensive facilities is a dubious process at best. A periodic accounting system for manufacturing costs works reasonably well if there are no inventories of manufactured product or by ignoring them if they do exist.

3. The system does not provide for a determination of the costs of individual products.

4. The system does not attempt to classify costs according to areas of managerial responsibility. Therefore, it has little utility as a control device.

5. A separation of costs into fixed and variable for both products and activities is essential to the making of a great variety of managerial decisions concerning changes in output. This the system does not provide.

Although a periodic accounting system for manufacturing costs has these objections, it continues to be widely used by the smaller manufacturing companies. Where employed, the system is used chiefly to supply information concerning cost of goods sold and inventory costs to be presented in general-purpose financial statements.

OBJECTIVES OF MODERN COST-ACCOUNTING SYSTEMS

In contrast to the limited usefulness of a periodic accounting system for manufacturing costs, modern cost-accounting systems attempt to provide in various degrees as desired by management:

1. Manufacturing costs applicable to individual products
2. Manufacturing cost of a particular complement of goods sold without the necessity of a physical inventory
3. The costing of work-in-process inventories and finished-goods inventories as carried in the stores records and accounts
4. A basis for the control of manufacturing costs
5. Marketing cost analyses on a functional, responsibility, activity, or, in fact, any basis desired by either marketing management or top management
6. A great variety of analyses involving a portion or all of the costs as pertinent to managerial decision making
7. Costs for governmental reporting purposes

"Cost accounting," as employed by today's businesses, may be defined as an area of accounting whereby costs and related data concerning some object of managerial interest are ascertained, such as the cost of a unit of product, the operating cost of a department, plant, or salesman, or costs associated with a particular investment. Its objective is to provide data for financial statements and to facilitate managerial reporting, planning, and control.

Cost Accounting versus Managerial Accounting. Managerial accounting as presently conceived represents a development of the 1960s. It may be interpreted in one of two ways: (1) as a particular classification of accounting knowledge having certain empirical objectives and contained in textbooks and courses of instruction, or (2) as a changed emphasis in both the use and analysis of accounting data. The first interpretation consists of a range of emphases beginning with a nontechnique approach to the use of accounting data to facilitate managerial decision making. It draws upon information commonly developed in general accounting as well as data developed in cost accounting. It gives emphasis to statement and situational analysis, stressing the need for new assemblies of data to meet changing problems.

Managerial accounting courses designed for accounting majors tend to give greater emphasis to data construction and manipulation techniques and to advanced problems of planning and control. Except for a deemphasis of cost-gathering procedures and the inclusion of statement analysis and interpretation, the latter resemble the approach of the better cost-accounting textbooks and courses.

A second interpretation of managerial accounting is simply that of a changed emphasis and approach to all phases of accounting, giving greater attention to the utility of accounting processes to management as contrasted to their service to owners and creditors. This interpretation represents an increased awareness of the value of accounting as an information system and control device. As a consequence, the general conceptual background of financial accounting is in process of modification to suit management's planning and control needs better. Funds statements are receiving renewed interest. Similarly, the areas of cost accounting, governmental accounting, and internal auditing are being given a changed orientation, emphasizing the decision-making needs of the managerial user.

It is interesting to note that controllership studies as an important phase of management accounting antedated processes indicated by both interpretations and have taken on renewed vigor as a consequence of the heightened interest in managerial accounting. Both interpretations presented in the foregoing discussion of the development of managerial accounting remain in force today and represent the processes of change as they bear upon accountancy.

Absorption Cost Accounting. In expediting the cost determination role of cost accounting as applied to manufactured products, reliance has been, for the most part, upon a theory of "full" or "absorption" costing. The cost accountant has sought to obtain through his transforming techniques a cost of manufactured product which, when appearing on financial statements, would parallel the merchant's invoice cost of purchases.

In merchandising, the source of increased wealth is through the process of exchange, that is, placing financial resources in the form of marketable goods and in turn exchanging these goods for increased resources. In manufacturing, increased wealth comes about largely by transforming certain inputs into revenue-producing outputs. The cost accountant tacitly assumes that the costs of inputs can be traced to resulting outputs—products—and that therefore management is provided with cost data needed for a statement of inventory costs and cost of goods sold.

An entire rationale of costing has been established with its structure based upon a foundation of a concept of direct and indirect costs. Direct costs consist of those costs where the sacrifice-benefit relationship to the object of interest (the product in absorption costing) is obvious. Indirect costs, therefore, are those costs whose relationship to the object of interest is not obvious. Indirect manufacturing costs are referred to in a variety of ways and commonly are termed "manufacturing (factory) overhead" or "indirect manufacturing (factory) costs."

Accountants have also recognized that product indirect costs are capable of classification into two groups of costs, one termed "variable" and the other "fixed." Variable costs are those costs which fluctuate in total amount with variations in output. Fixed costs are those costs which tend to remain constant in total amount per stipulated time period, despite variations in output. With regard to product costing problems, fixed costs have generally been construed as indirect in nature.

Up to about 1950, there was little question among accountants as to whether the fixed manufacturing costs were product or period related. A causal relationship between industrial plant and the production of goods was taken for granted, and management insisted upon obtaining product costs which reflected material, labor, and plant-associated costs.

At the beginning of the twentieth century, the problem to be resolved was not whether the fixed manufacturing costs were product related. Instead, the problem was one of the extent of inclusion in product cost of *all* costs outside of the direct-material and direct-labor classifications. The cost accountant at the beginning of the century attempted in a variety of ways to assign indirect costs broadly construed to product, but possibly because of a preoccupation with a single basis of cost assignment, such as direct labor or machine hours, and partly because of the apparent lack of connection between marketing costs and individual products, he settled the matter by a wholesale exclusion of what we would today call "nonmanufacturing costs." Such exclusion was accomplished not because of any thought that the excluded costs failed to benefit product revenues, but primarily because of the difficulty of cost identification and measurement.

The majority viewpoint of accountants today is that fixed manufacturing costs benefit production as do the variable manufacturing costs. Consequently, accountants include both the fixed and variable manufacturing overhead in the computation of the overhead rate. Computation of the variable element of the overhead rate occasions little or no difficulty. Computation of the fixed overhead element, however, gives rise to conceptual problems. Accountants attempt to divide the annual fixed overhead cost by either a quantity representing estimated productive activity or a quantity embodying management's expectations concerning the use of productive capacity. With regard to the latter, accountants attempt to compute a fixed overhead rate per unit of productive output which is representative of fixed costs of output over time. The term "normal overhead rates" is often applied to the results of such computations.

In any case, accountants who advocate including fixed costs in the overhead rate espouse the method of absorption costing. Accountants who are unwilling to assign fixed overhead costs to units of product and who, in theory at least, prefer to treat these as period costs advocate an approach called "direct costing." Although costs may be subdivided into fixed and variable under either absorption costing or direct costing, stress laid upon the variable costs by the direct-costing advocate has led to an increased emphasis in recent years upon the ascertainment of variable costs and their utility to management. (See Chapter 3 of Section 10 for a comprehensive discussion of direct costing.)

COST SYSTEMS

In one sense of the word, it could be rightfully stated that there are as many cost systems as there are organizations using cost accounting. No one system as described by a textbook would be adequate to the needs of a particular business. However, systems in use may be generalized and classified to present the rationale of their operation. Often two or more of the systems generalized in the following discussion may comprise the cost-accounting system of a particular enterprise.

Job Cost System. A job cost system is designed for the purpose of assigning manufacturing costs to product. It is used in those situations where the problem of product costs is uppermost in management's mind. The job cost system represents a happy integration of the older memorandum off-the-cuff system for accounting for material and labor costs, the use of overhead rates, and a concept of cost accounts as an integral portion of the accountant's formal ledger.

The "T" accounts shown below illustrate the tracing of manufacturing costs in a nondepartmentalized system to a summary work-in-process inventory account and cost of goods sold. Supporting the work-in-process account will be a form variously entitled the "job order" or "job cost sheet." For each authorization to produce a stipulated quantity of a particular product, there will be a job (production) order. As work progresses, requisitions drawn on stores in connection with this order will be priced and noted on the order. Similarly, time spent on this order will be accumulated and priced. In job order costing, materials and labor costs obviously related to the order are termed, respectively, "direct-material" and "direct-labor costs." Other manufacturing costs, or indirect manufacturing costs, will be taken to the job order ordinarily by means of a predetermined overhead rate computed in advance of the period's production. In absorption costing, both fixed and variable overhead costs are included in the computation of this rate. In direct costing, only the variable overhead costs are included in the construction of the rate.

An example showing the computation of an overhead rate and a completed but abbreviated job order form follow.

$$\frac{\text{Estimated factory overhead}}{\text{Estimated direct-labor hours}} = \frac{\$50,000}{20,000} = \$2.50 \text{ per DLH}$$

Job Order No. 15

Direct materials (as per requisitions summary)....................	$175.00
Direct labor (as per direct-labor time ticket summary): 150 DLH....	225.00
Manufacturing overhead:	
150 direct-labor hours at $2.50 per direct-labor hour..............	375.00
Total cost of order...	$775.00
Total units of product manufactured...........................	500
Cost of one unit of product....................................	$1.55

Utilization of job cost data in the formal accounts is illustrated by the "T" accounts shown below.

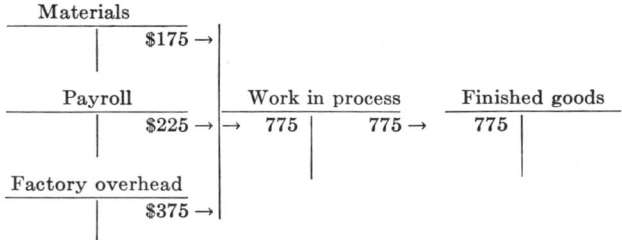

Control Accounts. The work-in-process account illustrated above and used in a job cost system is termed a "control account," because its balance must agree with the sum of the costs shown on individual job orders in process. Periodically, agreement between the balance of the work-in-process account and job orders in process is ascertained. Not shown in the accounts illustrated are actual cost incurrences for materials, labor, and indirect manufacturing costs which would appear on the debit or left side of the applicable accounts. Not indicated also is the transfer of costs from the materials and payroll accounts to the factory overhead account.

The materials account is another control account, for its balance must agree with the sum of inventory costs carried on the individual stores records. Commonly, two overhead accounts are utilized instead of the single account illustrated. In such instance, the factory overhead account becomes a control account and must agree in total with the sum of manufacturing expense shown on individual records, one for each item of expense. A second account, factory overhead applied, would carry the illustrated credit of $375 transferred to the work-in-process account. The factory overhead applied account is often described as a "contra" account to factory overhead. The finished-goods account, like the materials account, is a control account over the individual records of finished-goods items.

The job cost system does well what it is designed to do. It determines factory costs of product where a variety of products are produced. However, it is a costly and time-consuming system to operate and requires the use of numerous business papers. To utilize the system for control purposes, additional documents and accounts bringing together costs by departments or responsibility areas become necessary.

Process Cost System. Where a process cost system is utilized, the problem of product cost determination is not critical. Use of a process cost system assumes no multiplicity of classes of product. Products manufactured are often of the same class: grain processed into different grades of flour, the processing of sugar cane into different types of refined sugar, or bottle manufacture. Thus, the system tends to stress the gathering of costs by areas of responsibility or operations over convenient periods of time, as, for example, the length of time needed to process a run of product, or simply a month of output.

Account ordering under process costing is somewhat along the lines illustrated for the job cost system. However, instead of work-in-process accounts serving as a control over job orders, a work-in-process account is used for each area defined as a process, and interest in the system is centered upon changes over time in the unit costs of elements of expense of a process. Although a process cost report is used supplementary to the process accounts, it is not a subsidiary record in the same sense that a job order is to the work-in-process account of a job cost system. It serves merely to assemble details concerning process operations and to provide a basis for the computation of unit costs of materials, labor, and overhead. A skeletonized description of the accounts and operation of a process cost system is attempted in the "T" accounts portrayed below.

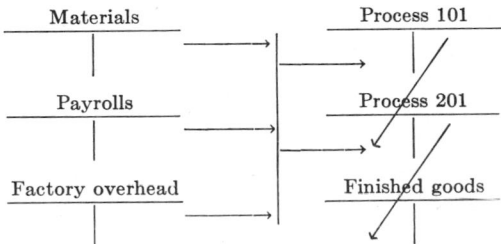

Material requisitions trace materials to consuming processes. Direct-labor time tickets account for process labor usage. Actual factory overhead may be allocated at the close of a time period to process accounts, or a rate or rates may be computed in advance of production as a basis of assignment of fixed factory overhead costs to production and processes. Such a rate avoids the assignment of fixed factory overhead costs to processes on a flat-amount monthly basis; instead, it assigns fixed factory overhead costs to processes in proportion to equivalent output achieved in a particular period.

Process Cost Report. This report gives a detailed summary of costs incurred by processes and is a basis for the computation of factory costs per equivalent unit for the time period under consideration. An outline of the process cost report is shown in Figure 2-1. The 400 incomplete units in process at the close of the period utilized materials in full. Thus, when added to the 600 completed units, a material cost divisor of 1,000 is obtained. Material cost of $1,000 divided by 1,000 equals $1.00 per unit material cost in Process 101. In the case of labor and overhead, the inventory of incomplete units totaled 400, but they had on an average received only 50 percent of required processing; thus, they were the equivalent of 200 completed units with regard to labor and overhead. Adding this 200 to the 600 completed units gives a total equivalent unit divisor for labor and overhead costs of 800. This figure divided into the applicable labor and overhead costs shown on the process cost report, Figure 2-1, results in a labor cost of $3.00 and a factory overhead cost of $2.50 per equivalent unit of production.

Process Cost Report

	Process 101		Process 201	
Prior process cost............................			$3,500	$6.00
Direct materials.............................	$1,000	$1.00		
Direct labor................................	2,400	3.00		
Factory overhead...........................	2,000	2.50		
Total..................................	$5,400	$6.50	etc.	
Units started...............................	1,000			
Units transferred...........................	600			
Units in process, incomplete (½ L & Oh).....	400			
Units accounted for.........................	1,000			
Computation of cost of incomplete inventory:				
Materials.................................	$ 400			
Labor....................................	600			
Factory overhead	500			
Total..................................	$1,500			
Cost transferred............................	3,900			
Total..................................	$5,400			

FIG. 2-1. *Process cost report.*

Unit costs of materials, labor, and overhead shown for Process 101 on the process cost report are utilized at the bottom of the report to obtain both the cost of incompleted inventory remaining on hand in Process 101 and the cost of finished items transferred to Process 201. For purposes of control, these unit costs are compared with unit costs incurred by Process 101 in prior months. Differences in unit costs from month to month are questioned and investigated. Costs assigned to goods transferred out of a process become the basis of transfer journal entries from process to process and from process to finished goods.

In contrast to a job cost system, a process cost system involves considerably less paper work and is therefore less expensive to operate. Its basic function is to provide for a modicum of control over factory costs and to serve as a check on unit product costs. It does this well and also provides data for the operation of the accounting system. Process costing may be refined by more extensive and detailed departmentalization as well as a careful analysis and classification of costs into fixed and variable.

Cost Estimating. It is often necessary or desirable to know what goods will probably cost before they are made. A number of business decisions are capable of resolution as a consequence of advanced cost estimates. Estimates are useful in connection with the pricing of goods made to order, the pricing of potential products, and evaluating the effect on cost of proposed changes in production. Cost estimates may be employed in setting goals toward which to work in controlling costs. Finally, cost-accounting routines may be eased by substituting judicious estimates for product costs gathered repetitively and at great clerical effort and expense. Used for these purposes, estimated costs are in many ways similar to standard costs, to be discussed below.

Cost Estimate Sheet. Cost estimate sheets resemble job order cost sheets in form and are arranged to allow for a listing of the various types of materials to be used for a project, the quantities to be used, and their expected invoice prices. Where necessary, allowances are made for scrap and spoilage as well as for their possible recovery through sales. Similarly, labor operations are listed, with hours required for each operation and the expected hourly wages to be paid.

As in job costing, an overhead rate is applied to the sheet to provide for indirect manufacturing costs. The totals for materials, labor, and overhead costs are added to ascertain the total cost of the project, and this total is, in turn, divided by units to obtain a unit cost of the product to be manufactured. If the estimate is to be used for pricing purposes, total manufacturing cost of the order is increased to allow for selling and administrative cost.

Estimated Cost System. Cost estimates may be used intermittently as desired outside the formal accounting structure. When the estimates are incorporated in the accounts, and accounts themselves carry both actual and estimated costs of manufacturing, the cost system in use may be described as an "estimated cost system." In such a system, cost estimates are used to credit the work-in-process account and as a basis for charging finished goods. Cost of goods sold is debited at estimated cost. The "T" accounts shown below are illustrative of the general nature of an estimated cost system and stress completely its convenience. Other systems could be designed to show a comparison between actual and estimated costs of departmental areas and therefore stress use of the system as a basis for control. Here, departmental accounts on the order of a process cost system would be utilized.

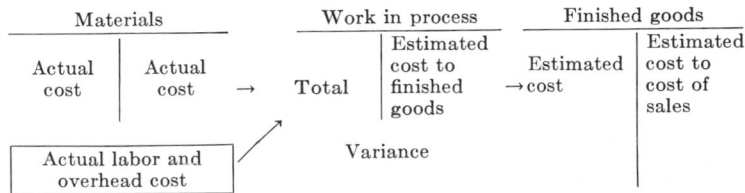

Standard Costing. Standard costs are costs carefully computed before the beginning of operational activities of production, marketing, or finance. They received their initial development in the production area. Well-developed standard manufacturing cost systems are commonly found in the better-managed industrial companies. Procedures followed for determining standard costs include objective processes of calculating, measuring, and weighing the physical constituents of a product, ascertaining the labor and machine time required, and affixing appropriate prices. Although a standard cost system is similar in format to an estimated cost system, standard costs represent what costs should be. Their most important use is to expedite cost control through a comparison with actuals. Estimated costs, on the other hand, are considered for the most part as a convenient substitute for actual costs, and they are incorporated within accounts principally to expedite accounting processes.

Standard Product Cost Card. A standard product cost card is constructed for each product manufactured. It summarizes studies of materials, quantities, operating time allowed, and related costs of materials, labor, and overhead. Data contained on a standard product cost card are shown in Figure 2-2.

Standard product cost cards may be employed independently of the operation of the formal accounting system, but actual cost data will be drawn from that system to achieve control by comparison. Such a utilization of standards is often termed a "statistical standard cost system." Used in conjunction with and closely integrated into the formal accounting system, standard costs provide a basis for control and a convenient substitute for the actual costing of products.

```
                    Standard Product Cost Card
Item name   Safety lever bar                    Item No. X151
Material specification sheet MX151        Lot size quantity 1,000


Materials:
  CC no. 1, opr. no. 3, 10 in. @ $0.05 per in.............  $0.50
Labor:
  CC no. 1, opr. no. 3,  5 min @ $2.40 per DLH.........     0.20
  CC no. 3, opr. no. 4,  4 min @ $1.80 per DLH.........     0.12
Manufacturing overhead:
  CC no. 1, 5 min @ $3.00 per DLH....................      0.25
  CC no. 3, 4 min @ $1.50 per DLH....................      0.10
     Standard cost of one unit........................     $1.17
```

FIG. 2-2.   *Typical standard product cost card.*

Integrated standard cost systems, are used to assign costs to work-in-process inventories as well as to determine cost of goods sold.

Control Use of Standards.   A significant use of a standard cost-accounting system is to expedite control by comparison.   For various areas of supervision and subdivisions of these, material requisitions honored are compared with material allowances, and actual labor and indirect manufacturing costs are compared with standard costs.   Thus, deviations from management's plans as expressed by standard costs are indicated at specific points in operating routines.   A "T" account representing cost center no. 3, operation no. 4, is used to display actual and standard costs:

```
                    Cost center no. 3, operation no. 4
Labor                  $145 | Labor, 1,000 × 12¢            $120
Indirect costs          120 | Indirect costs, 1,000 × 10¢    100
                       ─────                               ─────
                       $265 |                               $220
```

Actual costs of $265 have been incurred by operation no. 4 in cost center no. 3; the standard cost allowed was $220.   A variance of $45 needs to be examined and explained.   This type of comparison is repeated throughout operational accounts in a standard cost system.   Significant operational variances are analyzed into their material, labor, and overhead elements as well as into the quantity and price factors of each element.   Supervisors of areas responsible for variances will be asked to explain them, and plans will be made to bring actual costs in line with standard costs.

Types of Standards.   A major question in constructing standard costs is the degree of tightness of the standards to be employed.   Highly idealistic standards make for the regular appearance of sizable variances.   Variances occur so frequently when tight standards are used that they tend to lose their significance.

Loosely constructed standards, at the other extreme, offer little motivation or incentive.   Their attainment or even their betterment is a common, everyday experience.   In between these two extremes are standards appropriate to the organization's objectives in utilizing standard costs for purposes of control and facilitating accounting operations.

MARKETING COST ACCOUNTING

Marketing cost accounting has tended to be influenced by developments in production cost accounting. At the same time, it stresses uses other than assigning costs to products. Marketing cost accounting stresses:

1. A type of incremental analysis whereby a study is made of what would happen if one factor were removed or added, and the resulting costs saved or increased; for example, the effect of taking a salesman out of one sales district and putting him into another

2. Explorations of the possibility of finding better ways of accomplishing the marketing function; for example, a critical analysis of results attained from present promotional activities compared with results anticipated from the use of prospective promotional techniques

3. Control over various levels of marketing management; for example, the use of a flexible budget in connection with district operations

Standards are utilized in marketing cost accounting as in estimated cost accounting, more as a method of cost assignment than as a device to achieve cost control by comparison. For example, standard costs of packing merchandise for shipment are not constructed to serve as a means of controlling packing costs. A flexible budget is more likely to be used for this purpose. Instead, the standards are constructed as a basis for assigning packing costs to some object of managerial interest, such as a district or sales outlet.

NEW DIRECTIONS IN COST ACCOUNTING

The 1940s represented a period in which cost systems work achieved a high degree of development. Excursions were made in the area of volume variation analysis, and relatively crude studies were made concerning the action of costs with changes in volume.

The 1950s saw the flowering of *direct costing* with its emphasis on the fixed-variable classification of all costs. Here, the least-squares method of analysis was adopted by the cost accountant as a device for separating fixed and variable costs.

In the 1960s, interest in formal cost-accounting-system development declined, and interest in individual problem analysis became heightened. Experience with cost-volume-variation studies has been carried forward into an increasing variety of cost studies of changes in one or more factors of a specific business problem. Among the many problems encompassed by such studies are the following:

1. Computation of minimum order points and economic purchase size in the area of inventory accounting

2. The advisability of investment in a machine, department, or plant

3. Whether machinery should be substituted for hand-labor operations

4. Utilization of idle time of a machine, department, or plant

5. Whether a product should be added to or subtracted from a product line

6. Intercompany transfer price decisions

7. The effect upon income of a change in a salesman's route

8. Product-mix studies

These special study situations could be extended both in scope and in breadth. For example, with respect to the installation of a new machine, what are the profit implications of the move over extended periods of time? Will short-run profits resulting from an excess of added revenues over added costs be outweighed when consideration is given to the need later to replace environmental equipment considered "given" in the short run? Computations made in connection with these decisions often include a discounting of future revenues and the weighting of prospects, utilizing probability techniques. Cost accounting, therefore, enters the decision-making area employing not only concepts of full and direct costs, but also concepts of opportunity costs, relevant costs, discounting, and probability techniques. It has been adapting its problem-solving methods to make use of advanced mathematical techniques and modern data-processing equipment.

BIBLIOGRAPHY

Bennett, Clinton W., *Standard Costs,* Prentice-Hall, Inc., Englewood Cliffs, N.J., 1957.
Dickey, Robert I. (ed.), *Accountants' Cost Handbook,* 2d ed., The Ronald Press Company, New York, 1960.
Grant, Eugene L., and Lawrence F. Bell, *Basic Accounting and Cost Accounting,* 2d ed., McGraw-Hill Book Company, New York, 1963.
Haseman, Wilbur C., *Managerial Uses of Accounting,* Allyn and Bacon, Inc., Englewood Cliffs, N.J., 1963.
Henrici, Stanley B., *Standard Costs for Manufacturing,* 3d ed., McGraw-Hill Book Company, New York, 1960.
Horngren, Charles T., *Cost Accounting,* Prentice-Hall, Inc., Englewood Cliffs, N.J., 1962.
Moore, Carl L., and Robert K. Jaedicke, *Managerial Accounting,* South-Western Publishing Company, Cincinnati, 1963.
Neuner, John J. W., *Cost Accounting,* 6th ed., Richard D. Irwin, Inc., Homewood, Ill., 1962.
Schiff, Michael, and Lawrence J. Benninger, *Cost Accounting,* 2d ed., The Ronald Press Company, New York, 1963.
Shillinglaw, Gordon B., *Cost Accounting,* Richard D. Irwin, Inc., Homewood, Ill., 1961.
Terrill, William A., and Albert W. Patrick, *Cost Accounting for Management,* Holt, Rinehart, and Winston, Inc., New York, 1965.
Thomas, William E., Jr. (ed.), *Readings in Cost Accounting, Budgeting, and Control,* 2d ed., South-Western Publishing Company, Cincinnati, 1960.

CHAPTER THREE

Direct Costing

EDMUND J. McCORMICK *President, McCormick and Company, Yonkers, New York*

This chapter explains the basic principles of direct costing, a powerful analysis tool for all companies, in both manufacturing and service industries. Direct costing enables management to discriminate between costs which vary directly with volume and costs which remain fixed regardless of volume.

The emphasis of the chapter is on informing management of the importance of direct costing in terms of its many and varied uses as a planning and control tool. It is directed at how management should use these tools rather than at the construction of the tools proper.

Direct costing is particularly well suited to computerization, for it is specifically designed to accommodate variances, real or projected, in volume, price, cost, and capacity. It provides investors with a clear picture of the results of operations.

DIRECT COSTING TERMINOLOGY

1. *Variable or direct costs* are those costs which vary with a productive measure; that is, they fluctuate directly with output such as the number of units produced or services performed. These are the specific costs of making or delivering a product or service.

2. *Period costs* are those costs which vary gradually over time periods within normal capacity levels. They are considered the cost of being in business and are not susceptible to short-term control.

3. *Marginal income* is the amount of the sales dollar left after variable costs are covered. It is what remains from sales revenue (after meeting variable costs) to pay period costs and to contribute toward profit if sufficient volume is obtained.

Simply stated then, direct costing employs the following basic elements:

Sales revenue *less* variable costs *equals* marginal income
Marginal income *less* period costs *equals* profit (or loss)

USES IN PROFIT PLANNING AND PRODUCT PROFITABILITY ANALYSIS

Increased profits depend on profit planning. Executives can use the direct costing approach in developing and coordinating the many sales and cost targets that form the overall profit plan. They can apply it to all other areas of the business as well.

A profit plan's basic objective is to reach the return-on-investment target set by top management. The first major step toward it is preparation of the marketing plan. Financial, production, distribution, and service plans all depend on establishing product sales objectives and broad promotional programs.

The Marketing Plan. An effective marketing plan must answer these questions:

What products will sell, and in what volume?
At what prices?
At what promotional costs?

But the answers to these questions are meaningful only if their effects on profit can be determined. Determination of profit contribution answers is one benefit of marginal income accounting[1]—for instance, in discovering which product mix will yield the best profit contribution. Because unit profit contribution—for a particular product—stays constant in the marginal income approach, it is easy to pinpoint the effect of volume swings. The units to be sold are multiplied by the constant rate of contribution.

The resulting figure will be the total contribution to profit for the product. The total contribution to profit from each of a company's products can be compared against the others as a basis for making the best marketing decision.

The following calculations, taken from Figure 3-2, show how marginal income analysis can help determine the best sales mix—and how to achieve it.

Profit Contribution Analysis
(In thousands of dollars)

	Cereals	Baby foods	Dairy products	Detergents	Garden products
Target sales.............	$21,477	$9,237	$10,574	$2,825	$1,564
Variable direct costs......	15,016	5,577	7,264	1,308	872
Profit contribution........	$ 6,461	$3,660	$ 3,310	$1,517	$ 692
Rate...................	30.1%	39.6%	31.3%	53.7%	44.3%

Clearly, cereals make the biggest profit contribution. But detergents, although they lack volume, produce the highest *rate* of profit contribution, 53.7 percent. If management is planning a $250,000 promotion expenditure, detergents offer the most attractive profit opportunity—assuming that there is room for market

[1] "Marginal income control system" is the name of the cost system embracing direct-cost techniques developed by McCormick and Company.

expansion. An increase of only $465,000 in detergent sales would recover the promotion cost. On the other hand, additional sales of $830,000 would be needed to recover the same promotion expenditure on cereals.

Distribution and Sales Costs. Distribution and sales costs, because of their considerable variability, offer an opportunity for marginal income analysis. Cost by sales region can be separated into variable costs (such as commercial travel, automobile, and freight) and period (such as clerical and supervisory office costs). This permits comparison of profit contribution and overhead costs separately by regions. It also may point to opportunities for greater profit contribution in some areas and the need to reduce costs in others.

Product Costs and Profit Contribution. Product costs are building blocks of the profit plan and financial statements. The way the blocks are put together determines the financial structure that emerges.

Direct costing includes as product costs only those costs that change directly with production. The test is whether the cost is affected by some productive measure of activity, such as pounds, units, or machine-hours. If it is so affected, it is variable. If it is affected more by time—that is, if the cost continues regardless of the level of activity—it is period.

By associating only variable costs with a product, management eliminates the information fog caused by volume variance. This variance results under the alternative method of absorption costing whenever actual volume is different from the volume projected in setting unit product costs. When actual volume is higher than projected, product costs appear too high because too much period cost has been absorbed. The reverse happens when the volume falls below the rate projected. Any volume variance—high or low, on any of the company's products—results in inaccurate absorption. This distorts profit contribution and prevents measurement of the effect of changing volume on profits, both by product and overall for the organization.

On the other hand, each product is costed independently of all other products when direct costing is used. A change in one product's volume affects only that product—and the effect on profits can be measured accurately by devices like the break-even chart. With profit contribution based on direct product costs, marketing management can measure what any change in sales levels will do to profit.

Segregating direct product costs furnishes a sensible starting point for pricing decisions. At any figure which equals or exceeds the direct cost for a product, marketing and profit considerations will predominate in determining the optimum selling price.

This presentation has concentrated on direct product costs so far. But the concept of profit contribution can be applied equally effectively to direct selling and distribution costs.

New-product Evaluation. The marginal income approach gives management a realistic basis for evaluating new products. It shows precisely what a proposed new product will *add* to costs, because it focuses on the direct or out-of-pocket costs incurred by the new product. Whenever a company has unused capacity which can be utilized by a new product, direct costs are the only relevant costs to consider. If the product under consideration promises to bring in sales revenue greater than its direct cost, it will make a contribution toward company profitability and should be considered a prospect. The marginal income approach does not confuse the evaluation by burdening the new product with a portion of the company's period costs unless added salaried personnel or other period-type costs are necessary. Any contribution the new product can make toward period costs and net profit will be measured independently of other products. In this way, management can make a sounder judgment as to a product's future value to the company.

The Manufacturing Plan. With sales targets set, the manufacturing plan can be prepared. This contains two cost elements: (1) variable costs relating directly to *product* and (2) volume and period costs relating to *time*. Material and product labor costs rise or fall in relation to production volume. Period costs do not. For example, if two shifts are needed to turn out the product, an extra group of plant guards is needed for the second shift, whether this shift operates at a bare minimum or near capacity.

Some costs are harder to project. For instance, some maintenance charges will be period costs; some will be variable. Better profit planning will result if the variable portion is tied to projected product volume, leaving the period portion untouched.

Service areas can also benefit from marginal income analysis. For example, if the coming year will entail a labor contract reopening, it is important to estimate what negotiations will cost the company. Equally important is the cost effect on products. A straight per-hour increase will add to both period and variable benefit costs according to their present proportions. An increase in retirement benefits or a "sabbatical" vacation, however, as in the steel industry, might increase period costs more heavily.

Profit Plan Chart. A break-even chart makes an excellent test of the financial impact of the profit plan. This shows at a glance the overall marginal income and total profit picture. It also depicts what the profit effect will be for any given volume of sales. And it gets across, in simple, graphic terms, the true significance of achieving volume in sales. The basic break-even chart, illustrated in Figure 3-1, is based on the totals in Figure 3-2. Sales volume is the axis that divides the chart across the center. Below it is period cost, and above it, profits.

The diagonal line in Figure 3-1 represents the marginal income ratio. In this

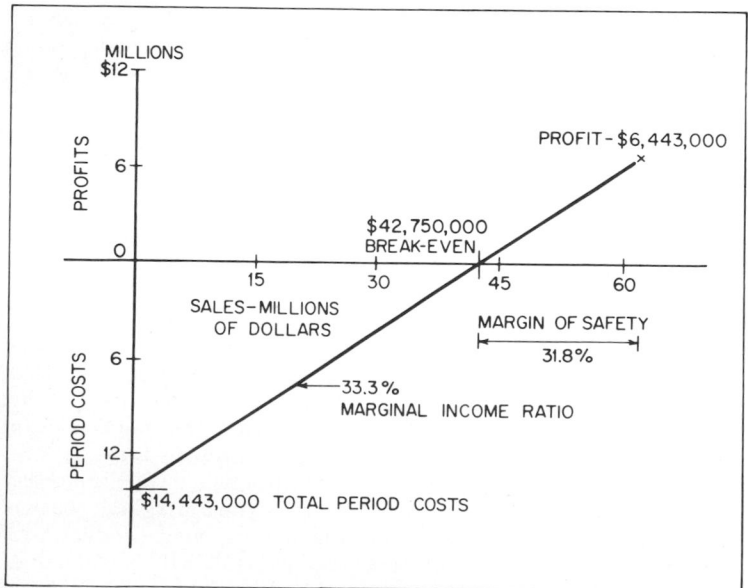

FIG. 3-1. *Consumer Products, Inc., profit plan.*

FIG. 3-2. *Consumer Products, Inc., profit and pricing target analysis.*

		CEREALS	BABY FOODS	DRUG PRODUCTS	DETERGENTS	GARDEN PRODUCTS	OTHER	INVESTMENT DIRECTLY IN PROD.	TOTAL COST
VARIABLE COSTS	Variable Labor & Expense	876,000	405,000	377,000	231,000	206,600	410,600	617,200	617,200
						249,000	668,000	2,806,000	2,806,000
	Variable Packaging & Material or Purchase Cost	14,140,000	5,172,000	6,891,000	1,785,000	852,000	9,504,462	35,889,000	35,889,000
								2,455,462	2,455,462
	Total Variable Cost	15,016,000	5,577,000	7,268,000	2,016,000	1,307,600	10,583,062	41,767,662	41,767,662
PERIOD AND OTHER MERCHANDISE	Unsaleables By Products	230,000	250,000	129,000	–	–	–	609,000	860,000
	Direct Product Per. Cost w/o Depreciation Spread	207,000	78,000	97,000	26,000	35,000	63,500	507,500	2,792,000
	Sales Period Cost							–	2,195,000
	Advert. To Product	600,000	250,000	524,000	206,000	232,000	603,000	2,415,000	2,811,000
	Freight To Product	591,000	239,000	647,000	153,000	89,000	599,000	2,318,000	3,406,000
	ADM Period Cost							–	2,380,000
	Profit Target							–	6,442,771
FACTORS at 22% RETURNS ON INVESTMENT	Equipment	500,000	96,000	318,000	90,000	196,000	439,100	1,639,100	–
	Raw Mat. Inv. (other)	19,100	–	61,800	65,700	1,500	65,600	213,700	–
	Raw Mat. Inventory	792,000	1,056,000	–	–	–	–	1,848,000	–
	Pack Mat. Inventory	45,500	17,400	55,700	18,400	20,500	41,700	199,200	–
	F.G. Inventory	308,000	209,000	110,000	60,000	42,000	261,000	990,000	–
	Total Target Return on Investment to Product	3,292,600	2,195,400	1,942,500	619,100	617,000	2,072,900	10,739,500	20,886,771
TARGET MARGINAL INCOME	Remainder Spread to Product on L&E $	3,167,358	1,464,592	1,363,336	835,360	900,453	2,415,672	10,147,271	–
	Target Sales $	21,476,458	9,236,992	10,573,836	3,470,460	2,825,053	15,071,634	62,654,433	62,654,433
	Actual Sales Value –	23,317,000	7,650,000	13,287,000	3,004,000	2,154,000	11,896,433	62,654,433	62,654,433
	Target M/I at 22% Return	30.1	39.6	31.3	41.9	53.7	28.2	33.3	33.3
	Actual M/I %	35.6	27.1	45.3	32.9	39.3	18.5	33.3	33.3

case, it shows that variable costs amount to two-thirds of the selling price, meaning that one-third of each sale contributes toward profit. Each dollar of sales up to $42,750,000 covers 33⅓ cents of period costs. Beyond that break-even point of $42,750,000, all additional sales generate a net profit of 33⅓ cents on the dollar.

As sales and profits increase, a margin of safety appears. This is the proportion of sales above the break-even point, or the percentage by which sales may drop before profit disappears. It has tremendous value in demonstrating the company's profit vulnerability to price cuts or potential loss of major customers. In the situation illustrated, the margin of safety is nearly $20,000,000, or 31.8 percent.

If the profit plan projects unsatisfactory prospects, the break-even chart will show whether the problem area is in period costs, variable costs, or even in lack of volume.

Return on Investment Analysis. Now the final step can be taken in preparing the overall company profit plan. This type of profit analysis need be made only on an annual or semiannual basis, because it is used for long-range decisions and hence should not be influenced by any short-term fluctuations. The profit analysis calls for developing total costs by product. It entails allocating period costs to the various products on an equitable basis and recognizing return on investment factors. With this information, target prices can be set with confidence and the cost effect on all areas of the business measured. Figure 3-2 shows the master plan created by this analysis process: a total company blueprint for pricing and profits and a gridwork for analyzing any deviations that occur.

This analysis ties together the profit plan objectives by incorporating these basic factors:

1. Total variable costs based on forecast sales permit calculation of product contribution.

2. Period costs such as unsalables are shown by product. Freight and some advertising costs which can be identified with specific products are similarly handled.

3. General period costs become part of an overall distribution.

4. Top management's profit target is included as if it were a cost. By showing it in this way, the analysis will produce a final target return figure for both the company and the individual products.

5. A calculated figure of 22 percent—representing a desired return on investment before tax—is charged on all major investments of the company's funds: inventories and plant. The target rate of return on investment will vary by industry and policy.

6. Unallocated costs are charged to product for planning purposes only, based on variable labor and expense and on a sales factor.

This technique combines the best features of marginal income accounting and absorption costing. It enables management, especially marketing management, to see the financial impact of pricing and promotional plans and to adjust them if the desired return on investment is not going to be achieved.

This dramatizes the high cost of tying up company money. And by spreading the charge to specific products, it encourages the individual managers to make the most efficient use of the company's capital.

USES IN ECONOMIC EVALUATION:
SHORT-TERM AND LONG-RANGE PLANNING

The executive is continually faced with the problem of making many short- and long-range economic evaluations. Changes in marketing conditions and new technologies, coming almost daily, require fast, practical, and dependable analyses to make the correct decisions.

All business problems, even the most complicated, revolve around three fundamental factors: direct costs (activity); period costs (time); investment (assets employed).

Potential Physical Changes. Decisions in the area of potential physical changes involve such factors as equipment, processes and methods, and plant.

Figure 3-3 shows a common evaluation situation—the choice between utilizing an existing plant and investing in a proposed one. The situation calls for consideration of all three fundamentals. Each fundamental tells a different story. Many evaluations could stop at the projected MI figures if sufficient improvements were not indicated for the proposed investment. Period cost figures add another dimension on which decisions can be made. The return on investment is even more revealing. These indexes can be easily projected for the future in terms of elapsed time or of capacity, as shown in Figure 3-3.

This same approach is especially adaptable for evaluating changes in machinery. It also works well for evaluating "make or buy" decisions on a long-term basis. For the short-term decisions, however, where unused capacity exists, direct costs plus a markup for use of specific "investments" will give a reliable answer.

Break-even analysis in conjunction with capacity measures is especially useful for these types of evaluations. For long-range planning, however, ample allowance must be made for possible changes in technology.

Proposed Changes in Expendable Items. The effect of increases or decreases in the elements of direct cost (labor, materials, and direct expense) can be quickly translated into their effects on profit, break-even point, and return on

	PRESENT PLANT	PROPOSED PLANT 1ST YEAR	PROPOSED PLANT 2ND YEAR	PROPOSED PLANT E.T.C.
OPERATING RESULTS				
NET SALES	15,000,000	15,000,000	18,000,000	E.T.C.
— DIRECT COSTS	9,000,000	7,500,000	9,000,000	
MARGINAL INCOME–$	6,000,000	7,500,000	9,000,000	
(%)	40	50	50	
PERIOD COSTS $	5,000,000	4,000,000	4,500,000	
(%)	33.3	26.6	25.0	
NET PROFIT B/TAX $	1,000,000	3,500,000	4,500,000	
%	6.7	23.3	25.0	
INVESTMENT REQUIREMENTS				
CASH	750,000	750,000	900,000	
RECEIVABLES	1,000,000	1,000,000	1,500,000	
INVENTORY	1,500,000	1,500,000	1,800,000	
FIXED ASSETS	3,000,000	19,000,000	17,500,000	
TOTAL	6,250,000	22,250,000	21,700,000	
RETURN ON INVESTMENT				
%	16	15.7	20.7	
BREAKEVEN POINT $	12,500,000	8,000,000	9,000,000	
STATISTICS				
CAPACITY–TO BE UTILIZED	1,500,000	1,500,000	2,000,000	
CAPACITY–TOTAL	1,500,000	3,000,000	3,000,000	

FIG. 3-3. *Economic evaluation of a proposed plant.*

investment—for the overall picture as well as for specific products. Tying these figures into capacity and volume projections will show their long-term effects. The same basic format shown in Figure 3-3 can be used.

It is very useful in assessing the impact of changes in labor costs, material, product design, and material prices. Such changes occur with great frequency; by evaluating their effect on MI, quick decisions can be made and full advantage taken of the opportunity they offer for fast action.

Price Alterations. Altering the price structure, a key executive function, can benefit from the same approach as the one used to evaluate plants in Figure 3-3. The basic principles apply whether a single product or a group of products are to be studied for pricing purposes.

Projected sales revenue of the product reduced by its direct costs shows the potential generation of marginal income. When the period costs directly applicable to the product plus an allocation of general period costs are subtracted from the marginal income, the profit potential of the product can be seen.

At this point, the investment in the product plus its share of general investment must be determined. The percentage of investment return can then be matched with management objectives and compared with projected returns for other products and product groups.

Any revision in the product price can now be directly translated into its effect on:

1. Total sales revenue
2. Marginal income
3. Profits
4. Return on investment

Following this procedure arms management with foreknowledge of the economic results of price changes and helps it make the most advantageous pricing decisions.

Marketing Changes. Revisions in selling and advertising, in market emphasis, and in distribution may involve costs affecting a specific product or a product group. Usually, these costs can be identified with products and the effect on their profitability determined. Appropriate projections for these items can be made, as shown in Figure 3-3. Where specific products are not involved, only the overall effect on key signals, such as break-even point and return on investment, can be calculated.

Administrative Changes. Projected changes in administrative procedures fall into the same category. For instance, the true effect of a computer installation readily shows up when realistic projections are used in the format shown in Figure 3-3.

Cautions. It is rare than *any* significant change can be made in one area without affecting many other areas. Figure 3-3 provides a format designed to trigger key signals. Direct costing provides the individual information needed to activate these signals. Projected changes can be easily forecast. Three rules must be followed to achieve results:

1. The direct costs must be realistic.
2. They must be *controlled* to accomplish projected results.
3. Evaluations should be checked periodically to make sure they are realistic.

DEFINITIVE PROFIT AND LOSS STATEMENTS

The profit and loss statement gives management its most important single control of business. It must be concise, clear, well-defined, and prompt. Statements using the features of marginal income accounting provide the needed

'EARTHLY' CHEMICAL COMPANY

PROFIT & LOSS CONTROL STATEMENT

PERIOD: _____ 1, 1965

− Variance = Unfavorable

	CONSOLIDATED			DIVISION X			DIVISION Y		
	Actual	Budget	Variance	Actual	Budget	Variance	Actual	Budget	Variance
GROSS SALES	$47,100,000	$48,000,000	$-900,000	$28,600,000	$28,800,000	$-200,000	$18,500,000	$19,200,000	$-700,000
LESS: SALES DEDUCTIONS	1,480,000	1,500,000	20,000	888,000	900,000	12,000	592,000	600,000	8,000
NET SALES	45,620,000	46,500,000	-880,000	27,712,000	27,900,000	-188,000	17,908,000	18,600,000	-692,000
LESS: STANDARD VARIABLE MFG. COSTS	22,360,000	22,800,000	440,000	13,579,000	13,700,000	121,000	8,781,000	9,100,000	319,000
STANDARD MFG. MARGINAL INCOME	23,260,000	23,700,000	-440,000	14,133,000	14,200,000	- 67,000	9,127,000	9,500,000	-373,000
M.I. % TO NET SALES	51.0	51.0	0	51.0	51.0	0	51.0	51.0	0
LESS: STANDARD VARIABLE SELLING & DISTRIBUTION COSTS	3,850,000	3,900,000	50,000	2,185,000	2,200,000	15,000	1,660,000	1,700,000	40,000
STANDARD MERCHANDISING M.I.	19,410,000	19,800,000	-390,000	11,948,000	12,000,000	- 52,000	7,467,000	7,800,000	-333,000
STD. MERCHANDISING M.I. %	42.6	42.6		43.1	43.1	0	41.9	41.9	0
LESS: SALES PRICING VARIANCE	- 190,000		- 190,000	- 87,000		- 87,000	-103,000		-103,000
SELLING COST VARIANCE	- 20,000		- 20,000	- 30,000		- 30,000	+ 10,000		+ 10,000
DISTRIBUTION COST VARIANCE	- 30,000		- 30,000	- 30,000		- 30,000	0		0
ACTUAL MERCHANDISING M.I. @	19,170,000	19,800,000	-630,000	11,801,000	12,000,000	-199,000	7,374,000	7,800,000	-426,000
STD. MFG. VARIABLE COSTS ACTUAL MERCHANDISITG M.I. %	42.1	42.6	- 0.5	42.6	43.0	- 0.4	41.1	41.9	- 0.8
LESS: **MANUFACTURING VARIANCES**									
MATERIALS PRICE	+ 10,000		+ 10,000	0		0	+ 10,000		+ 10,000
MATERIALS YIELD & USAGE	- 50,000		- 50,000	- 10,000		- 10,000	- 40,000		- 40,000
LABOR & EXPENSE	- 40,000		- 40,000	- 25,000		- 25,000	- 15,000		- 15,000
ACTUAL MARGINAL INCOME	19,090,000	19,800,000	-710,000	11,766,000	12,000,000	-234,000	7,329,000	7,800,000	-471,000
ACTUAL M.I. %	41.8	42.6	- 0.8	42.5	43.0	- 0.5	40.9	41.9	- 1.0
LESS: **PERIOD COSTS**									
MANUFACTURING	6,900,000	6,800,000	-100,000	4,210,000	4,200,000	- 10,000	2,690,000	2,600,000	- 90,000
SALES & DISTRIBUTION	4,350,000	4,300,000	- 50,000	2,530,000	2,500,000	- 30,000	1,820,000	1,800,000	- 20,000
GENERAL & ADMINISTRATION	2,040,000	2,100,000	+ 60,000	1,220,000	1,260,000	+ 40,000	820,000	840,000	+ 20,000
ADVERTISING	1,350,000	1,340,000	- 10,000	726,000	720,000	- 6,000	624,000	620,000	- 4,000
RESEARCH	2,380,000	2,360,000	- 20,000	1,435,000	1,420,000	- 15,000	945,000	940,000	- 5,000
TOTAL PERIOD COSTS	17,020,000	16,900,000	-120,000	10,121,000	10,100,000	- 21,000	6,899,000	6,800,000	- 99,000
NET PROFIT BEFORE TAX & MISC.	2,070,000	2,900,000	-830,000	1,645,000	1,900,000	-255,000	430,000	1,000,000	-570,000
MISC. INCOME & (EXPENSE)	(280,000)	(300,000)	+ 20,000						
NET PROFIT BEFORE TAX	1,790,000	2,600,000	-810,000						

FIG. 3-4. *A chemical company profit and loss statement on direct costing basis.*

10–31

SINCERITY BANK & TRUST COMPANY	INCOME & EXPENSE CONTROL SUMMARY				PERIOD: 1st QUARTER		
Department	Person Resp.	Gross Income	Direct Expense	Operating Ratio	MARGINAL INCOME		
					Budget	Actual	Variance
BRANCH OFFICES							
AURBURN REGION							
AURBURN	W W	104,281	40,750	39.1	63,098	63,531	+ 433
CONNORSBURG	L M	250,465	·84,708	33.8	163,668	165,757	+ 2,089
DITTLETON	D C	169,217	65,717	38.8	106,641	103,500	– 3,141
FOREVILLE	A B	92,846	38,064	41.0	61,407	54,782	– 6,625
JAMESVILLE	Z J	177,792	69,934	39.3	111,432	107,858	– 3,574
OSTELLER	S J	95,107	35,296	37.1	75,970	59,811	–16,159
MONROE	J W	97,288	37,997	39.1	59,707	59,291	– 416
STEVENS	M N	156,240	51,979	33.3	113,480	104,261	– 9,219
PERRYVILLE REGION							
AVON	A M	315,940	105,621	33.4	195,892	210,319	+14,427
BALL STREET	A S	171,942	108,389	63.0	61,579	63,553	+ 1,974
FOUR CORNERS	N E	53,293	25,939	48.7	27,039	27,354	+ 315
HALLEY CENTER	J J	145,586	46,937	32.2	104,430	98,649	– 5,781
MILTON	P M	148,218	47,549	32.1	102,878	100,669	– 2,209
BASKERVILLE REGION							
COOLEY STREET	T C	33,329	18,357	55.1	17,205	14,972	– 2,233
COMMUNITY CENTER	R D	61,018	22,200	36.4	37,983	38,818	+ 835
GEORGETOWN	H R	122,625	35,334	28.8	86,535	87,291	+ 756
VILLAGE GREEN	G T	918	4,391	478.3	–6,843	–3,473	+ 3,370
TOTAL BRANCHES	T Z	2,196,105	839,162	38.2	1,382,101	1,356,943	–25,158
INCOME DEPARTMENTS							
COMMERCIAL LOAN	C C	206,408	145,333	70.4	22,671	61,075	+38,404
MORTGAGE LOAN	T R	215,471	211,511	98.1	11,112	3,960	– 7,152
INSTALLMENT LOAN	J M	709,455	524,487	73.9	132,145	184,968	+52,823
TRUST	G W	133,800	97,062	72.5	30,877	36,738	+ 5,861
INVESTMENTS	T J	607,384	587,476	96.7	73,367	19,908	–53,459
BANK OWNED PROPERTY	U G	21,472	12,185	56.7	13,937	9,287	– 4,650
TOTAL INCOME DEPTS.	J B	1,893,990	1,578,054	83.3	284,109	315,936	+31,827
TOTALS	W C	4,090,095	2,417,216	59.1	1,666,201	1,672,879	+ 6,678
SERVICE AND					**EXPENSE**		
ADMINISTRATIVE DEPTS.					Budget	Actual	Variance
EXECUTIVE	W C		200,000		165,800	200,000	–34,200
ADVERTISING	L O		50,965		45,294	50,965	– 5,671
CONTROLLER	M A		96,781		109,459	96,781	+12,678
BOOKKEEPING	T S		313,759		314,273	313,759	+10,514
PERSONNEL	L B		12,290		13,139	12,290	+ 849
PURCHASING & PRINTING	D M		24,897		21,231	24,897	– 3,666
LOAN ADMINISTRATION	M R		42,702		46,746	42,702	+ 4,044
TOTAL SERVICE & ADMIN.	J B		741,394		725,942	741,394	–15,452
GRAND TOTALS	W C	4,090,095	3,158,610	77.2	940,259	931,485	+ 8,774
ACCRUAL ADJUSTMENT	W C		35,253			35,253	+35,253
NET INCOME BEFORE TAX	W C	4,090,095	3,193,863	77.8	940,259	896,232	+44,027

FIG. 3-5.   *Example of a profit and loss statement for a bank.*

definiteness and clarity.   Figure 3-4 provides an actual example of a profit and loss statement in a medium-sized chemical company.

The statement is arranged to facilitate quick determination of whether performance is going according to plan and to spotlight any deviations from the profit plan.   Vertically, the statement focuses on performance by major areas of management responsibility: selling and distribution; manufacturing; and staff and administration.   Horizontally, it measures variances in *volume* from the profit plan, both for the company overall and for specific divisions.   This method of analysis can be applied to individual plants, regions, and the like as desired.

The first column, "actual," measures actual results versus the standard for whatever sales level is actually attained.   Management can quickly see where the variances are—by area of responsibility—and what direct effect each variance has on profits.   Such a control statement provides:

1. Rapid focus on exceptions to the profit plan, thus promoting remedial action

2. Control by area of responsibility

3. Management by exception in its truest sense—the form of the statement itself directing attention only to those items where action is needed

Figure 3-5 shows how this powerful form of analysis can be used to guide performance by individual operating units—in this case, the branches and service departments of a bank.   The first and second columns reflect the bank's organization chart.   They list the individual departments and the initials of the person responsible for each one.

The third column shows the *direct* income generated by each unit (except the service and administration departments).   The direct expense column shows what it actually costs to run each department.   The operating ratio is gross income/direct expense and provides an index of operating efficiency for each of the income-producing departments and, in summary, for the bank as a whole.

Gross income less direct expense gives the actual marginal income.   This is the most important column on the control form.   It shows *who* generated the MI, and in conjunction with the "budget" column, provides a "variance" figure which shows *how well* each individual met his target.

The service and administrative departments are evaluated by a comparison of their actual expenses versus the budget.   The bottom-line figure, net income, is the responsibility of the top executive (in this case, the president of the bank).   It gives a direct measure of how well the bank's assets have been put to work.

MARKETING APPLICATIONS: PLANNING AND CONTROL

Marketing has lagged noticeably behind manufacturing and the other functions of business in the ability to predict and control costs.   Until recently, marketing has not assembled the needed cost data or utilized the techniques necessary for sound cost projection and control.

Marketing management has been hampered in its efforts to direct the marketing effort because of inadequate and unreliable information on marketing costs.   Intensified competition and closer scrutiny of the marketing function by top management have spurred efforts to solve the marketing costs problem.

The Prime Importance of Marketing Costs.   Before realistic sales volume budgets and practical marketing action programs can be established, it is essential to determine just what merchandising costs are.

Historical cost data, reported for the total company of for an entire sales branch, are not adequate for planning and control decision making.   Direct costing overcomes this deficiency by providing for timely reporting of cost data in categories that correspond to the types of decisions needed.

For example, management can turn to the relevant categories of period cost for making strategic decisions regarding such questions as how many branch sales offices should be maintained or how much to spend on advertising.   On the other hand, when management is making tactical decisions involving policies on such questions as commission structures, delivery costs and allowances, special discounts, and promotions, it can quickly find the data in the appropriate variable cost accounts.

In addition, direct costing permits association of cost information with specific product-market combinations, thereby simplifying the solution of problems on product mix or direction of the field sales force. It focuses attention upon the profit contribution of each marketing element.

Marketing Cost Standards. The marketing executive can readily control many functions by applying techniques similar to those used in manufacture. Standards can be set for physical distribution—the activities concerned with the storing and moving of products, such as warehousing, order filling, packing and shipping, and the routines for processing inquiries and orders.

But in the other functions that are really the essence of marketing—field selling, advertising, and promotion—both the qualitative and quantitative boundaries of problems are uncertain. Because of these uncertainties, direct cost data, used in combination with probability techniques, provide an improved means for setting cost standards and hence controlling costs.

Consider the complexities in marketing that make new approaches to cost projection and control so essential. Any market is composed of a bundle of highly individualistic demands for goods and services. The strength and extent of these demands fluctuate both in *time* and in relation to the *supply* of competitive products and services. Change is constant in a market: changes in consumer wants and distribution practices, product obsolescence brought about by technological advances, and changes made necessary by the actions of competitors. Some aspects of a market can be measured with reasonable accuracy, but a considerable number cannot. This makes it all the more desirable to use properly organized, reliable cost data where they are available and continually to develop techniques for reducing the residual areas of uncertainty in marketing.

The marketing executive's job is to plan and carry out the sale and movement of an agreed-upon volume of products or services to designated market segments, within a given time and within established cost limits. To execute his planning and control responsibilities most effectively, the marketing executive must have not only timely information on the current nature of the market, but also detailed, timely information on how changing market conditions are affecting the costs of distributing products and services to these markets. Through rapid feedback of market-condition information and direct cost variance analysis data, he can readily detect departures from expected results and make informed decisions to correct out-of-line conditions.

MARKETING APPLICATIONS: ESTIMATING AND PRICING

Under the marginal income approach, *estimating* is the process which provides the bench marks for making pricing decisions. In *pricing*, these bench marks are applied to maximize the sale of those products that will best realize the objectives of the company's profit plan.

As executives concerned with pricing know all too well, pricing policies must be reevaluated continually in response to shifts in competition, demand, and supply. The key to success in pricing lies in rapid and knowledgeable responses to these hectic conditions in the actual marketplace. The marginal income approach provides timely and reliable bench marks for making the successful response.

1. Effective price estimating starts with calculation of standard direct labor and unit expense rates for each product. Then material costs are added in. These "out-of-pocket" costs theoretically would not exist if the product were not being produced.

The resulting figure, the standard direct cost, is the first bench mark. When open plant capacity exists, *any* price set or obtained above the standard direct cost will generate MI to cover period costs and contribute toward a profit. This

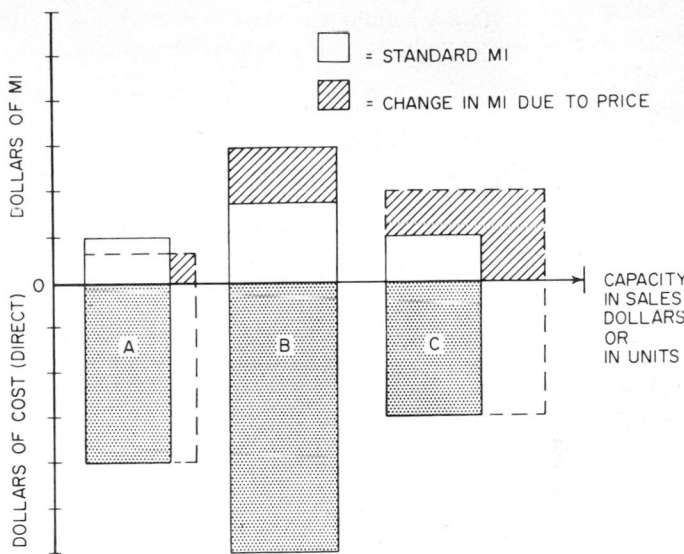

FIG. 3-6. *Price changes and their effect on the generation of marginal income (MI).*

gives a pricing executive a rock-bottom figure; he will not set a price below this standard direct cost under any but the most unusual circumstances.

2. The second step in estimating is the determination of a target selling price. This involves:

  a. Establishing a target net profit—in most cases this is a desired return on investment

  b. Adding this profit target to the period costs for the product—thus showing how much marginal income must be generated

  c. Dividing this total marginal income by expected sales volume—thereby deriving the target selling price per unit which will meet the company's profit objectives

This describes an ideal situation, of course. The pricing executive may have to rework the prices several times to meet the realities of the marketplace. But at least he will be adjusting prices with a full understanding of the effect on profit.

3. When prices are stable or target selling prices have been set for each product, the MI actually generated by each product is a direct measure of its profitability. This measure remains true at any volume. It is a key bench mark in determining product selectivity.

With the knowledge of the MI generated by each product, the pricing executive has a great deal of flexibility in maneuvering both price and volume to obtain optimum results. Figure 3-6 shows how marketing executives can use the MI approach to make the most of changing market conditions.

Product A—Price is reduced, but additional volume increases MI and effectively uses idle plant capacity.

Product B—Changed market condition allows price increase without change in volume.

Product C—Demand permits an increase in both price and volume. If plant is at capacity, sales emphasis should be placed on higher MI-producing products.

These suggest just a few of many possibilities of utilizing capacity most effectively.

Direct costing provides bench marks to measure the effects of actual and projected changes. Here are some of the typical practical questions that it can answer.

1. Pricing: If I reduce the price of brass doorknobs $1 each, how much volume will I need to make up the lost marginal income?

2. Bidding: What is the lowest price I can quote on a job and at least recover my "out-of-pocket" costs?

3. Physical distribution: What additional sales volume is needed to support a new delivery truck?

4. Volume: How much increased volume and MI will I need to cover a $10,000 promotion on men's suits?

SUMMARY

Direct costing or marginal income accounting is basically simple in its principles. It separates costs into natural categories which are a reflection of how each cost will act under operating conditions. These are:

1. Variable costs—costs directly related to an activity measurement, which vary with that measure

2. Period costs—the costs of being in business, which vary more by time periods

This separation of costs permits true determination of product marginal income or profit contribution. Although the installation of a good direct costing system has its technical complications, this is not of direct concern to executives. It is a technician's problem.

Most important, the use of direct costing simplifies the analysis of results and thus clarifies and expedites decision making for all areas of executive management. There is no portion of business or industry which cannot find profitable uses for direct costing.

BIBLIOGRAPHY

"Current Applications of Direct Costing," NAA Research Report, no. 37, January, 1961.

Elliott, Norman J., "Training Management Personnel in Using Cost Reports," *Journal of Accountancy*, vol. 113, June, 1962.

Ferrara, William A., "What Managerial Functions Does Accounting Serve?" *Financial Executive*, vol. 32, July, 1964.

Fess, Philip E., and H. Peter Holzer, "Diverse Functions of Accounting," *Journal of Accountancy*, vol. 118, August, 1964.

McCormick, Edmund J., "Budgetary Control," in H. B. Maynard (ed.), *Industrial Engineering Handbook*, 2d ed., sec. 7, chap. 10, McGraw-Hill Book Company, New York, 1963.

Parker, John R. E., "Give Consideration to Direct Costing for External Reporting," *NAA Bulletin*, vol. 45, sec. 1, October, 1963.

Patrick, A. W., "Direct versus Absorption Costing," *The Controller* (now the *Financial Executive*), vol. 29, April, 1961.

Schlosser, J. H., Jr., "Helping Management Choose between Direct and Absorption Costing," *NAA Bulletin*, vol. 45, sec. 1, November, 1963.

Staehle, R. L., "The Human Side of Cost Control," speech, Financial Executives Conference, June, 1964.

CHAPTER FOUR

Budgeting

STEPHEN LANDEKICH *Editor,* Management Accounting, *National Association of Accountants, New York, New York*

The information contained in the annual financial statements of a business enterprise is generally recognized and used as the basis for the evaluation of its management's performance. Aware of this fact, managements try to envisage financial outcomes. A formalized process of accomplishing this is usually called "budgeting." It enables management to view its decisions and their execution in terms of the ultimate financial results. Applied to all the operations as comprehensive budgeting, it coordinates planning and control in a manner designed to generate performance consistent with desired financial results.

Generally speaking, budgeting has proved its usefulness. The amount of its utility, however, is a function of managerial practice rather than an inherent property of budgeting. This applies particularly to the role of budgeting in engendering company-wide cooperation in striving toward the attainment of planned (budgeted) objectives. In this respect, managerial attitude has a critical impact. Proper attitude is enhanced through comprehension of the basic properties and elements of sound budgeting and through cognizance of the various types of budgets developed in business practice. In deciding on how to organize budgeting and how to apply it as a versatile tool in all stages of the managing process, it is useful to draw on knowledge derived from experience, some of which is exemplified here.

ELEMENTS OF SOUND BUDGETING

Business budgeting (referred to henceforth as "budgeting") is a process of communication and decision making, instrumental in planning and control, which functions through coordination of planning and accounting.

Concept of Budgeting. Budgeting may be, and has been, conceived of as primarily a communication medium. It is clear, however, that the budgeting communication process involves a number of decisions made at various levels of management.   In successful budgeting, these two properties complement each other; they are equally essential.

Purpose of Budgeting.   Budgeting has been developed along with the financial integration of planning and control geared toward profitability as the businessman's way of coping with the increasing complexity of the profit-making process.

Method of Budgeting.   "Budgeting" may be defined as managerial planning and control formulated within the accounting framework.   Coordination of planning and accounting has two focal points: (1) the planning decisions and (2) overall profitability.   In a sense, budgeting is a method of expressing, appraising, and reappraising each in terms of the other.   It enables management to chart the future as a set of feasible outcomes of mutually compatible decisions and to control it through the use of performance information generated by the same process.

Prerequisites.   Numerous management functions are related to budgeting in a twofold manner—their existence is the prerequisite for sound budgeting, and in turn, as the result of sound budgeting, they can be performed more successfully.

The main prerequisite conditions conducive to sound budgeting are:

1. Detailed organizational structure with precisely defined authorities, responsibilities, and lines of communication

2. Comprehensive planning with all the planned operations explicitly determined, though not necessarily in monetary terms

3. Fully developed system of management accounting, including standard costing, break-even analysis, and responsibility and profit contribution accounting

The improvements in these conditions often brought about by budgeting are a valuable side effect, but budgeting itself cannot establish them.   This is a task which goes well beyond the scope of budgeting.   Moreover, budgeting imposed by top management despite the absence of the necessary conditions is likely to be rendered ineffective, perhaps even harmful, as the people subject to such an arbitrary control may be antagonized rather than motivated.

Fundamentals of Budgeting.   Experience has shown that certain characteristics are essential to the effectiveness of budgeting.   W. D. Knight and E. H. Weinwurm list participation, attainability, and flexibility as the characteristics required.[1]

Participation.   In a survey of management planning and control practices, B. H. Sord and G. A. Welsch conclude that "The paramount problem . . . is one of motivating people to participate constructively in the planning and control processes, each according to his ability and position."[2]

A vital factor governing attitudes toward the budget program is the interest displayed by top management in all the phases of the budgeting process.   Provided the proper attitude is engendered throughout the organization, budgeting can substantially contribute to company-wide cooperation, primarily by allowing operating management an active role in preparation and follow-up of their budgets.

Clear instructions, simple procedures, and meaningful reporting at all levels will enhance participation.   On the other hand, as observed by a cost analyst:

Budgets with elaborate procedures . . . create a clique of staff personnel trained in the labyrinths of the system.   The operating personnel form the opinion that this

[1] W. D. Knight and E. H. Weinwurm, *Managerial Budgeting,* The Macmillan Company, New York, 1964, pp. 51–55.
[2] B. H. Sord and G. A. Welsch, *Business Budgeting: A Survey of Management Planning and Control Practices,* Controllership Foundation, Inc., New York, 1958, p. 37.

esoteric instrument has no value other than to harass them. They will institute actions to beat the system, if they are unable to ignore it. When this situation arises, the budget value to the company decreases considerably.[3]

Attainability. Recognizing the fact that a company objective is usually viewed at the level of execution as a personal gage of performance, enlightened managements have adopted a realistic approach designed to foster positive response. Objectives and standards are related to some generally accepted criteria of what constitutes satisfactory performance as stipulated in the budget. Accuracy of the standards and full comprehension of the underlying procedure are believed to be desirable.

There is, however, some disagreement on whether "tight" or "loose" standards are more conducive to efficient performance. The work that has been done by behavioral scientists with respect to the factors affecting performance indicates the significance of relating the budgeted levels to the subjective levels so as to fully utilize the individual's capacity to perform.[4]

Management policies regarding budget variances (deviations from the planned performance) are of special importance. Significant variances, both favorable and unfavorable, should be carefully analyzed. Corrective action, when called for, should then be promptly taken, including a budget adjustment or amendment if necessary. Satisfactory performance, not only conformance to plans, should be considered, so that at no point will the feeling be created that compliance counts more than performance.

Flexibility. Responsiveness by the people is significantly related to the flexibility of the budgeting structure and administration. Flexibility is partly a matter of proper design of the budget and partly an attribute of its implementation.

Built-in flexibility regarding the variable components of the budgetary figures provides for an automatic adjustment to changed conditions. This can be usefully supplemented by standard procedures designed to take care of various minor adjustments. Flexibility may also take the form of multiple budgeting procedures.

In administering the budget program, figures should be interpreted as the best available approximations rather than rigid norms. A margin of acceptable variance introduced into the system facilitates the application of budgeting, for the procedures will not tend to become unduly complex.

TYPES OF BUDGETING

The distinction is usually made between budgeting which covers operations during a certain time interval or period (continuous and periodic budgeting) and that which centers around a certain future operation (project budgeting).

Continuous Budgeting. Continuous budgeting results in a "rolling" budget constantly covering a time interval of the same length; for example, a semiannual budget continually revised by dropping the month just ended and adding the next of the forthcoming months.

Periodic Budgeting. Periodic budgeting refers to a specified time period. The most common is annual budgeting. The annual budget is usually broken down

[3] R. Rhodes, "Company Fracturalization by Budgets," *NAA Bulletin*, October, 1964, p. 62.
[4] Abraham Charnes and Andrew Stedry, "Investigations in the Theory of Multiple-budgeted Goals," in C. P. Bonini, R. K. Jaedicke, and H. M. Wagner (eds.), *Management Controls: New Directions in Basic Research*, McGraw-Hill Book Company, New York, 1964, pp. 186–204.

into semiannual, quarterly, and monthly budgets. In some industries, it is customary to operate on weekly or even daily budgets. Many companies also practice long-range budgeting, which extends over a period of several years. It frequently takes the form of continuous budgeting, revised each year.

Project and Appropriation-type Budgeting. Project budgeting involves considerations relevant to a project rather than a time period. Its typical use is in the analysis and choice among alternative capital expenditures (capital budgeting).

Similar to project budgeting is appropriation-type budgeting which involves allocation of a certain amount of funds in each budget period for a specific activity, such as research, advertising, or the like.

Comprehensive Budgeting. In the literature, the general terms "budgeting," "managerial budgeting," and "profit planning" are often used to denote one type of budgeting—comprehensive budgeting. In comprehensive budgeting, the resulting document, referred to as the "budget," appears in the form of a complete set of budgeted terminal accounting statements, accompanied by supporting schedules. These subsidiary schedules are also commonly called "budgets," and the related process is identified as "budgeting." When both the comprehensive budget and the subsidiary schedules are dealt with, it is preferable to differentiate between them by referring to the former as the budget or master budget and to the latter as subbudgets or, specifically, as sales budget, cash budget, and so on.

Comprehensive budgeting encompasses all the budgeting performed in a company. It is customarily focused on annual budgeting, but also includes project budgeting and long-range budgeting.

The annual budget, often referred to as the "annual profit plan," comprises:

1. Budgeted income statement with the supporting schedules. It shows planned operations and is, therefore, often called the "operating budget."
2. Budgeted balance sheet, frequently accompanied by a budgeted funds statement with supporting schedules. This set shows the anticipated financial position as well as the planned utilization of funds and is, therefore, often called the "financial budget."
3. Supplementary budgets:
   a. Long-range (strategic) budget consists of annual budgets, with supporting analyses, projections, and reports.
   b. Capital budget is a consolidated statement of planned investment into long-lived acquisitions (additions to fixed assets) with supporting schedules.
   c. Variable (flexible) overhead budget is a comprehensive analytical summary of budgeted allowances for overhead costs and related data.
4. Supplementary material, which contains various background information, explanatory data, and analyses pertinent to the understanding and application of the annual budget.
5. Budget reports:
   a. Performance reports are based on comparisons of budgeted and actual operations.
   b. Control reports are based on analysis of discrepancies (variances) between budgeted and recorded figures.

The planned operations may be depicted in two ways: by responsibilities and by activities or programs. The master income statement is, therefore, usually accompanied by a twofold presentation of the operating budget—the responsibility budget and the program budget.

Responsibility Budgeting. Responsibility budgeting is performed in terms of responsibilities for carrying out the planned operations. By distinguishing between controllable and uncontrollable costs at the several levels of management, responsibility budgeting establishes a sound basis for control of performance. The responsibility budget then constitutes a consolidation by functional breakdowns.

Program Budgeting. Program budgeting identifies anticipated costs and revenues by company activities. In a manufacturing firm, the program budget is usually broken down by product lines or products. This arrangement of budgetary figures pinpoints information particularly useful for planning purposes.

Static and Flexible Budgeting. Finally, budgeting may be classified as static (fixed) and flexible (variable), which refers to the distinction between costs that do not vary with fluctuations in activity (fixed costs) and those that do vary as operations expand or contract (variable costs).

In static budgeting, all costs are assumed to be fixed costs. In flexible budgeting, a great deal of painstaking analysis is performed to identify the costs which vary with volume and to establish the pattern of this relationship at various levels of activity. The variable costs are then budgeted so that the budgetary figures correspond to the costs anticipated at various levels of activity.

Static (fixed) budgets are relatively easy to prepare, but they are generally not practicable for the control of variable costs. The budgeted amounts of these costs cease to be relevant for control purposes whenever current activity deviates from its planned level. A static budget is satisfactory provided that (1) the ensuing level of activity is not subject to significant change or (2) total costs remain nearly the same despite changes in the level of activity.

Flexible (variable) budgets refer to both variable costs that vary directly with volume (direct material and direct labor) and those which vary indirectly. In practice, however, flexible budgets usually do not include direct variable costs. Frequently, a flexible budget covers only factory overhead costs.

The budgeted amounts of overhead costs are based on standard rates per unit of activity. An alternative technique is to establish a series of rates for successive ranges of activity on the basis of which the budgeted amounts are then determined. The former would seem more precise and therefore preferable for control purposes. The latter is particularly applicable to variable costs which vary in steps rather than continuously at a uniform rate.

ORGANIZATION FOR BUDGETING

Prior to adoption of a budget program, top management should carefully evaluate its feasibility in terms of managerial needs, suitability of budgeting to meet these needs, and the readiness of the company organization to absorb the budgeting system.

These three basic considerations are closely intertwined. It is important to keep in mind that planning and control, as managerial needs, can be performed and coordinated without budgeting. Budgeting is a superior way of doing it, but not the only way.

Budgeting places planning and control on a different plane, commensurate with that of management accounting. As this provides for an integrated system, it is an advantage. It may also turn into a disadvantage if the conditions for such an integration have not been established, which brings us to the overall company organization as one of the governing factors.

Program of Action. A term often used in practice is "budget program." Indeed, it is useful to think of budgeting as a permanent, company-wide program of action.

To overcome the considerable difficulties likely to be encountered, especially in the beginning, organization for budgeting certainly demands an all-out effort. As a coordinating function which supplements the existing ones, budgeting must necessarily be brought to the point at which it turns into a fruitful activity, or the program will quickly degenerate and perhaps even cease to exist. Hence, organizing for budgeting is a sustaining effort.

Program Responsibility. The responsibility for launching the budget program and establishing initial acceptance throughout the company rests with top management. As Prof. Neil W. Chamberlain put it, "No top management which intended to put a comprehensive plan to work could delegate so important a decision to a staff planning unit, or a controller, or a budget director. To do so would be an admission that the plan was not in fact being taken seriously."[5]

The responsibility for setting up and coordinating the budget program is usually assigned to the corporate controller, or a budget executive who reports to the controller.[6] This responsibility includes the staff functions of designing, analyzing, advice, and assistance, but not any additional line authority with respect to decision making in planning and control. The same applies to budget committees. They serve in an advisory capacity rather than as a directing authority.

"If participation by subordinate levels of management is to be adopted as a company policy, then care should be exercised to assure its fulfillment, and, unless higher management is ready to follow such a policy, subordinates should not be invited to participate."[7]

The approval of the completed budget is also the responsibility of top management. After the budget has been adopted by top management, the budget is usually submitted to the board of directors for final acceptance.

Program Implementation. Implementation of the budget program involves human relations, compatibility of all budgetary information, and the establishment of a communications network. "The importance of human and psychological factors for the success of a budget system can hardly be overestimated. As a veteran budgeteer has put it, budgeting is 75 percent human relations and only 25 percent technical work."[8]

To integrate the flow of budgetary information, all data must be compatible and related to one another in a predetermined systematic manner. In reference to such a budget model built at Esso Research and Engineering Company by use of a computer, E. E. Hoffman writes, "To provide an all-encompassing and therefore extremely flexible form which a computer can readily deal with, the budgeted cost for *each* cost center is expressed in terms of a single equation having 130 elements, i.e., type of expense."[9]

To ensure the needed coordination of *action*, it is also essential to have a communications network through which the budgetary information will be conveyed to all participants in the process of budgeting. The communications

[5] Neil W. Chamberlain, *The Firm: Micro-economic Planning and Action,* McGraw-Hill Book Company, New York, 1962, p. 295.

[6] "Developments in Financial Organization 1915–1965," supplement to *Financial Executive,* September, 1965.

[7] B. H. Sord and G. A. Welsch, *Managerial Planning and Control as Viewed by Lower Levels of Supervision,* University of Texas Press, Austin, Tex., 1964, p. 34.

[8] Knight and Weinwurm, *op. cit.,* pp. 317–318.

[9] E. E. Hoffman, "A Mathematical Model for Budget and Other Computations," *Budgeting,* March, 1965, p. 15.

network includes formal written reports, policies, manuals, and procedural instructions. Other important vehicles are formal and informal conferences, discussions between supervisors and subordinates, and the distribution of excerpts from the budget to the people responsible for the areas involved.

THE BUDGET PROGRAM IN OPERATION

The annual budgeting process may be viewed as a perpetual alternation of two methods and two directions. The methods are analysis (breaking down into simple elements) and synthesis (building up of separate elements, aggregation, consolidation). The directions are (1) from top down and (2) from bottom up, that is, from the general (summary) level to the specific (detail) level and vice versa.

Either of the two methods may be applicable at each level, and the resulting information may be conveyed either upward or downward. By providing at each point for the appropriate method and direction of information flow, a well-designed budgeting system adds still another dimension—lateral coordination of (1) data flow and (2) managerial action.

Building Up the Annual Budget. Budget construction starts at the top level. The general objective(s) is then broken down into divisional objectives which are further resolved down the line until the objectives take the most specific (detail) form. The process of generating data input starts at the bottom level where various elements of costs and revenues are consolidated into the form of budget amounts which are usually related to a unit of physical measurement (direct-labor hour, unit of product, time period). These budget amounts are then successively combined, put together by responsibility and/or product, and finally summarized in the master budget.

Sources of Data. The main sources of data used in building up the annual budget are managerial forecasts and accounting reports. Forecasts provide data on anticipated levels of activity. Accounting reports indicate the financial magnitudes for past and present operations. (See Table 4-1.)

A fully developed system of management accounting includes appropriate analyses to determine the figures for the various levels of activity. If these figures have not been developed, the relevant analyses are performed as part of the budget program.

Budget Coordination. At the detail level, coordination involves uniformity of the physical and accounting units of measurement as applied to diverse elements throughout the company. At each successive summary level, various forecast and financial data are articulated with one another through the coordination provided by the budgeting process, which also relates these data to managerial objectives.

Both the forecast and accounting data may be, and often are, subject to preliminary adaptations needed to establish initial compatibility. A properly designed budgeting coding system, which identifies the data structure at each level of aggregation, greatly facilitates preparation of the data input as well as the subsequent summarization in the various interrelated schedules. Provided that both the forecast and accounting figures are compatible with each other and with the company organization structure—which should be the case if a sound organization for budgeting has been established—the coding structure of the budget model will not require any major changes in available information.

Data Input. In the course of budgeting, the basic data are converted into budget amounts according to management policies and numerous decisions regarding the various goals and alternative ways of attaining them. The budgeting

TABLE 4-1. Formal Profit Planning

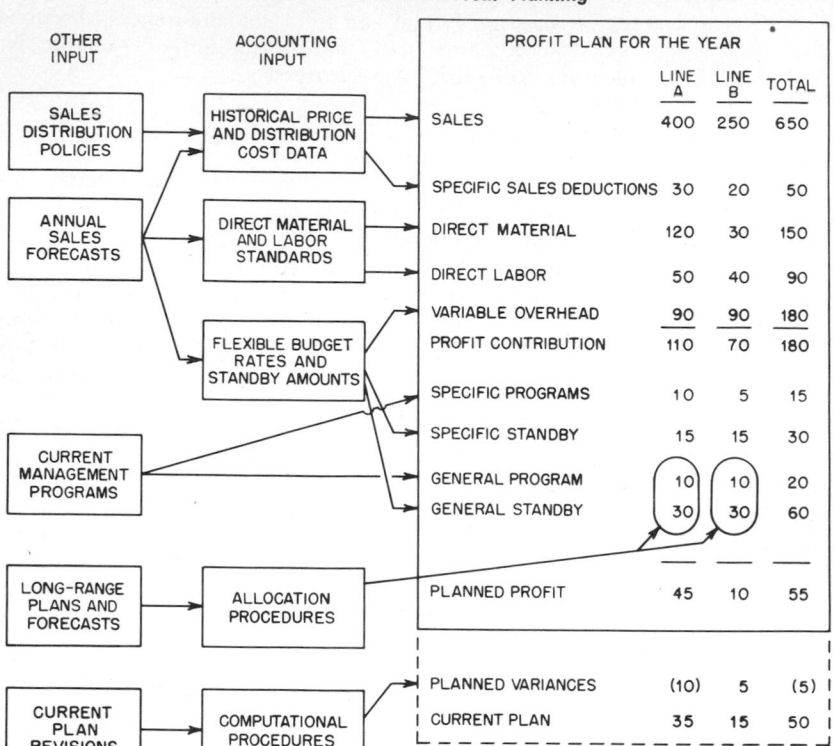

SOURCE: Robert Beyer, *Profitability Accounting for Planning and Control*, The Ronald Press Company, New York, 1963, p. 267.

function integrates this decision-making process at the various levels of aggregation. Budgeting personnel extend all needed technical assistance, but the decisions are made by the managers responsible for the execution of and control over the planned performance.

Even at the lowest level of aggregation, the budget data input is not necessarily identical with the underlying data (standards). When budget amounts differ from standard amounts, say, for direct material and labor costs, because the latter are outdated or established according to a management policy different from that pursued in budgeting, the difference (the expected budget variance) is usually incorporated in the comprehensive budget. This procedure does not preclude the continued use of the standard amounts for control purposes, but it does provide for more realistic planning.

The Basic Procedural Steps. For a manufacturing enterprise, the basic procedural steps in the preparation of an annual budget may be outlined as follows.

1. Sales budget (by markets and products)—the starting point

2. Production and inventory budget—related to the volume and rate of the budgeted sales activity (sales = beginning inventory + production − ending inventory)

3. Materials and labor budgets, for the costs that vary directly with the level of production

4. Manufacturing expense (overhead) budgets—fixed and variable
5. Selling and administrative expense budgets
6. Appropriation-type budgets (advertising, research, and the like)
7. Profit and loss budget (budgeted income statement)
8. Capital additions budget
9. Funds flow budget (sources and uses of funds, budgeted funds statement)
10. Financial position budget (budgeted balance sheet)

The procedural steps and their sequence vary according to the accounting and budgeting techniques employed by individual companies. Thus, in the sequence followed by the computer program illustrated in Figure 4-1, the production budget is completed only after all the relevant variables have been determined.

The Timetable. No matter what the sequence of the procedural steps is, it is imperative that a detailed budget time schedule be prepared to encompass all phases of budget preparation. In large companies, advanced network techniques such as PERT may be used to advantage for this purpose.

At a minimum, the time schedule includes a brief description of each procedural step, identifies the responsibilities, and indicates the due dates.

Follow-up Budgeting. In many ways, follow-up is the most important part of the budget program, for it is instrumental in bringing about the planned performance. The design of the whole program should be centered around it, in the sense that the annual budget should include only those figures that are subject to follow-up budgeting.

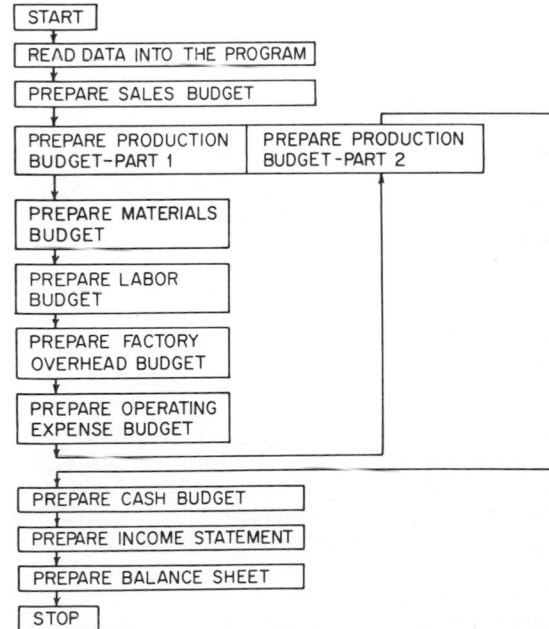

FIG. 4-1. *The budget simulation program flow chart.* (*Courtesy of Richard Mattessich,* Simulation of the Firm through a Budget Computer Program, *Richard D. Irwin, Inc., Homewood, Ill., 1964, p. 13.*)

Follow-up budgeting comprises:

1. Intermediate budgeting
2. Budgetary reporting
3. Performance analysis

Follow-up budgeting serves primarily the purposes of managerial control, whereas the preceding phases of the budget program involve managerial planning.   On the other hand, planning and control within the context of budgeting may be viewed as complementary and often interchangeable functions.   As Prof. Robert W. Anthony observes:

> During the budget year, many activities occur that clearly fit the definition of control, but, simultaneously and as a part of the same process, there may occur an activity called budget revision, which is planning.   In short, planning and control activities are as closely intertwined in the budgeting process that to describe each of them separately is not only difficult, but also pointless—pointless because those concerned with the process usually are involved with and interested in both its planning aspect and its control aspect.[10]

Intermediate Budgeting.   Intermediate budgeting is based on the annual budget and the performance analysis.   It derives from the annual budget the figures related to the successive time periods (quarters, months, weeks) or progressive stages of the budgeted capital additions.   The intermediate budgeting thus establishes a framework for budgetary reporting and performance analysis.   At the same time, it draws on performance analysis for the decisions and procedural steps subsequent to the approval of the annual budget (budget revisions, authorization to spend, and the like).

Budgetary Reporting.   Budgetary reporting accommodates the two-directional flow of information in such a way that it facilitates the relevant managerial functions.   The traditional distinction between reporting for planning purposes and reporting for control purposes is of questionable value.   The appropriate action is a management prerogative, not a matter of reporting.

Comprehensive reporting parallels the budget structure.   Periodic reports are formal statements, issued regularly, which contain a budget versus performance comparison and usually include analytical information on the variances (causes and effects, mutual relationships, trends, possible corrective action, and the like).

The format and the content are often designed to conform to the needs and preferences of the individual executives.   The use of ratios, percentages, and similar measurements can be very effective.   Some reports may refer exclusively to physical units, especially those designed for lower-level executives. The format is sometimes expanded to include cumulative figures (year to date, quarter) in addition to the figures for the period (quarter, month) under review.

In accordance with the principle of "management by exception," comprehensive reporting is supplemented by brief reports which highlight information that warrants management attention.   These flash reports supplement regular reporting, but they may be issued before completion of the full formal reports to assure prompt corrective action.

Computerized information systems can be designed to make required information instantly available.   Speaking of the Chrysler Corporation's plans to link executives' desks to electronic memories, its vice president, E. H. Graham, said,

---

[10] Robert W. Anthony, *Planning and Control Systems: A Framework for Analysis,* Harvard Business School, Division of Research, Boston, 1965, p. 12.

TABLE 4-2.   Summary of the Variance Analysis Procedure

	Standard gross profit	Favorable (unfavorable) variance	Reason
Actual results	$88,265		$(6,638)—Due to unfavorable average selling prices
Volume held constant		$(4,069)	$ 939 —Due to a favorable product mix
			$ 1,630 —Contribution of products not budgeted
Actual units priced and costed at budgeted ASP's and standard cost	$92,334		$(1,933)—Due to selling less units
ASP's and standard cost held constant		$(5,289)	
			$(3,356)—Due to an unfavorable group mix
Budget	$97,623		
		$(9,358)	

SOURCE: Wilbur F. Lube, "The Planning and Control of Standard Gross Profit—One Company's Approach," *Budgeting*, January, 1965, p. 22.

"The time delay inherent in the publishing and delivering of reports will be virtually eliminated."[11]

Performance Analysis. In budgeting practice, performance analysis usually consists of the analysis of variances shown by budgetary reporting. The implicit assumption that the budget figures are correct typifies the attitude which fosters conformance to budget. An alternative, and perhaps more advanced, approach is dynamic in nature; it includes an examination of the detailed reports and regular contacts with operating management to determine whether there are problems which are not reflected in the form of budget variances.

The first step in variance analysis is to isolate those variances that indicate the need for further analysis. Some companies attach more significance to trend analysis as having more meaning than analysis of individual variances. A practicable statistical procedure for determining whether or not to investigate variances is called the "control chart." Reporting on the adoption of this procedure by a division of a large decentralized company, D. J. Amicucci, business policy analyst of IBM, makes the following comment: "The technique has been given a favorable reception and, judging by the expressed interest, it is likely that it will be used by other organizations within the company."[12]

The second step in variance analysis is to resolve the significant variances into their components. Most of the dollar amounts have been computed by multiplying some quantity with its unit price or rate. This suggests that the dollar variance should first be resolved into a quantity (usage, efficiency) variance and a price (rate, spending) variance. The former may be interpreted as a measure of production (sales) efficiency controllable by the factory (sales) manager, while the latter may be the effect of a variety of causes (under certain circumstances, it is controllable by the purchasing department).

These segregations and detailed analyses of each component help identify the causes of each variance. They are then presented to management for appropriate remedial action. The variance analysis procedure is summarized in Table 4-2.

[11] E. H. Graham, "Modern Computer Technology and Management Principles," *Financial Executive*, December, 1965, p. 31.

[12] D. J. Amicucci, "Budget Variance Trend Reports," *NAA Bulletin*, July, 1965, p. 14.

Performance analysis related to program budgeting is considerably facilitated through the use of network planning, scheduling, and control techniques. The critical path method (CPM), for example, provides data in sufficient detail to enable isolation of performance deviations.

THE CAPITAL BUDGET

Sound budgeting practices applicable to comprehensive annual budgeting in general are also valid in capital budgeting. The important distinctions of capital budgeting which necessitate a separate treatment are:

1. The magnitude of each commitment—usually the amounts are relatively large.

2. The risk involved—due to the long time span of the projects.

3. The range of alternatives—much broader than in operation budgeting where the alternatives are limited in both number and degree by existing commitments (fixed costs, contractual obligations, and the like).

4. The impact on future operations—once executed, the capital budgeting decisions are irreversible in the short run (they appear as fixed costs in the forthcoming budget periods).

These characteristics require a special set of policies and procedures to govern (1) proposal screening; (2) capital expenditure review, approval, and control; and (3) project evaluation.

Proposal Screening. The initial point of reference in building up a capital budget is the individual proposal. Many firms have established more or less detailed policies and procedures for proposal submission and its flow through the process of screening. Proposal originators and sponsors are frequently offered staff assistance in complying with the requirements. On the other hand, "contrary to the theories generally advanced, the origination of capital-expenditure proposals receives no special stimulation among the firms studied. Sufficient proposals of merit arise out of the normal manner of doing business."[13]

Capital-budget procedures are usually applied only to proposals concerning the holding and acquisition of plants and equipment. Major changes in the stock of working-capital assets may also involve substantial increase or decrease of the funds needed, but the extension of capital budgeting to cover working-capital assets is relatively rare.[14]

Proposal sponsors may be invited to take part in the proposal screening, not only to supply additional information, but also to participate in the related discussions. Frequently, the procedures call for some form of communication on the current status of the proposals under consideration.

Capital-expenditure Review, Approval, and Control. The annual capital budget is primarily a summary of expenditures scheduled for the budget year. It includes expenditures for previously approved but not completed projects. In addition, the figures for the next budget year may also be shown for information purposes. (See Table 4-3.)

Procedures in proposal screening are usually designed to facilitate their grouping and summarization for review and approval purposes. The proposals are grouped by functional area, organizational unit, project priority, type of asset

[13] Donald F. Istvan, *Capital-expenditure Decisions: How They Are Made in Large Corporations,* Foundation for Economic and Business Studies, Indiana University, Bloomington, 1961, p. 12.

[14] Ezra Solomon, *The Theory of Financial Management,* Columbia University Press, New York, 1963, p. 9.

TABLE 4-3. Capital Additions Budget Summary

For the year ending December 31, 1963

Items	Estimated starting date	Estimated completion date	Estimated cost	Year budgeted for 1963	1964
New building..............	Jan. 1964	Sept. 1964	$120,000		$120,000
Machinery—Dept. 1........	July 1964	Sept. 1964	10,000		10,000
Repair tools..............	Jan. 1963	Jan. 1963	200	$ 200	
Power motor..............	Dec. 1963	Dec. 31, 1963	8,500	8,500	
Total...................			$138,700	$ 8,700	$130,000

Assets funded:
New building... 20,000
Total cash required in 1963 for capital additions.................. $28,700

Depreciation data:
Repair tools—5-year life, no scrap value.
Power motor—10-year life, no scrap value.

SOURCE: Glenn A. Welsch, *Budgeting: Profit Planning and Control*, 2d ed., Prentice-Hall, Inc., Englewood Cliffs, N.J., 1964, p. 72.

involved, the purpose served by projects, or the like.   These classifications occasionally vary for different stages of the capital-budgeting process.

Budget Review and Approval.   Responsibility for coordination of the review and approval decisions in most companies rests with a financial executive.   Budgets are reviewed and approved successively, up the line, except for the projects originated by top management and proposals involving major expenditures which are forwarded directly to top management for review and approval.   These functions are sometimes performed by an advisory committee.

In either case, the ultimate approval of the capital budget is the prerogative of the board of directors.   Its authority for the budget approval may be delegated to a varying degree, especially with respect to the subsequent commitment of the funds.

Appropriation Requests and Approvals.   The approval of the proposed capital budget, in most cases, is only the first major decision-making step; the second step is the authorization to commit the funds required to carry out the approved projects, which is usually given only after a thorough evaluation of each project has been made.   This evaluation follows the approval of the proposed capital budget.

Subsequent to the evaluation, a detailed formal request for the appropriation of funds is submitted to the proper management level.   The authority to appropriate the funds required by a project is often related to the total amount of the investment.   Appropriations for major projects, however defined, are usually the responsibility of top management or a top management committee.

The alternatives considered in capital budgeting may be classified into three groups:

1. Alternative uses of the available funds
2. Alternative projects
3. Alternative means of carrying out an approved project

The alternative uses of funds are given recognition, implicitly or explicitly, in decisions on the overall magnitude of the budget and the basic criteria for project acceptability. On the other hand, most of the capital-budgeting evaluation process deals with the choice among the various projects. Less frequently, this process includes considerations of the alternative means, but it has been increasingly recognized that make-buy-rent, maintain-replace, now-or-later, and other similar decisions may be effectively incorporated into the capital-budgeting process.

The analysis of alternatives lends itself readily to the application of mathematical models,[15] the use of which is facilitated by digital computers.

Capital-expenditure Control. While the projects are in progress, control over capital expenditures is comparable to that exercised over current operations. The budgeted amounts are usually structured to allow for minor discrepancies; or a policy of accepting them, after suitable analysis, is followed in controlling the projects in progress. Supplementary appropriation requests are called for by established procedures whenever the deviations reach a specified amount.

Upon completion of individual projects, a special report is commonly required. In the case of major projects, this report is submitted at some appropriate stage of completion, in addition to the regular periodic reports.

To verify the accuracy of project evaluation and soundness of control over capital expenditures, the control in progress is sometimes supplemented by a follow-up (post-completion) audit. In companies which have no formal auditing program, audits are performed occasionally to provide the data needed for future planning, as a check on past performance, or both.

Project Evaluation. The overall magnitude of the capital-budgeting expenditure is, to a large extent, predetermined by top management policy regarding the requirements to be met by the projects and the amount of funds to be used for this purpose.

Both the acceptability of the projects and the availability of funds may be defined generally for all projects or specifically by category. These decisions thus establish a framework for evaluation, because all commitments are subject to these two basic constraints.

The impact of the constraints on project evaluation varies according to the company situation. If there are only a few proposals and plenty of funds, for example, management may decide not to impose any limitation on the budget size. The evaluation and approval procedures are then designed accordingly, with the emphasis put on the more important constraint.

Capital budgeting is sometimes identified with capital rationing, which implies relative scarcity of the available funds. This assumption, however, may not be valid as a generalization; sources of funds are practically unlimited, provided the projects are sufficiently attractive.

The basic criteria for project acceptability are usually set in terms of profitability (the rate of return on investment), liquidity (the payback period), or both. The lowest acceptable rate of return, called the "cutoff rate," is thus a function of (1) the overall profit rate planned for company operations (the rate-of-return standard) and/or (2) the weighted average cost of the available funds (the cost-of-capital standard), as modified by the other considerations pertinent exclusively to the incremental operations and sources of funds.

In terms of profitability, the evaluation involves an expenditure or revenue comparison for each project over its anticipated economic life. This comparison is often supplemented by an interproject comparison which results in the ranking of comparable projects according to degree of profitability.

[15] H. Martin Weingartner, *Mathematical Programming and the Analysis of Capital Budgeting Problems,* Prentice-Hall, Inc., Englewood Cliffs, N.J., 1964.

In terms of liquidity, the evaluation involves (1) calculation of the time needed for revenues to equate the expenditures and (2) subsequent ranking of the projects according to their respective payback periods. This method, called the "payback method," is a traditional way of taking into account the risk inherent in the expectations of future revenues.

BIBLIOGRAPHY

Dean, Joel, *Capital Budgeting*, Columbia University Press, New York, 1951.

Edge, C. G., *A Practical Manual on the Appraisal of Capital Expenditure*, rev. ed., The Society of Industrial and Cost Accountants of Canada, Hamilton, Canada, 1964.

Hackney, John W., *Control and Management of Capital Projects*, John Wiley & Sons, Inc., New York, 1965.

Heiser, Herman C., *Budgeting*, The Ronald Press Company, New York, 1959.

Knight, W. D., and E. H. Weinwurm, *Managerial Budgeting*, The Macmillan Company, New York, 1964.

Mattessich, Richard, *Simulation of the Firm through a Budget Computer Program*, Richard D. Irwin, Homewood, Ill., 1964.

Pflomm, Norman E., *Managing Capital Expenditures*, National Industrial Conference Board, New York, 1963.

Sord, B. H., and G. A. Welsch, *Business Budgeting: A Survey of Management Planning and Control Practices*, Controllership Foundation, Inc., New York, 1958.

Sord, B. H., and G. A. Welsch, *Managerial Planning and Control as Viewed by Lower Levels of Supervision*, University of Texas Press, Austin, Tex., 1964.

Stedry, Andrew C., *Budget Control and Cost Behavior*, Prentice-Hall, Inc., Englewood Cliffs, N.J., 1960.

Welsch, Glenn A., *Budgeting: Profit Planning and Control*, 2d ed., Prentice-Hall, Inc., Englewood Cliffs, N.J., 1964.

CHAPTER FIVE

Profit-Volume Analysis and Break-even Charts*

LEE H. HILL   *President, Lee H. Hill Consultants, West Palm Beach, Florida; President, Burdett Manufacturing Company, Chicago, Illinois; President, Donnelly Publishing Company, Inc., Tampa, Florida; Chairman, Rogers, Slade and Hill, Inc., New York, New York*

Almost every president of an operating company will vigorously maintain that his company is "different."   And this is true, for it is practically impossible for two companies to have identical operating characteristics.   Even two manufacturing companies having the same operating profit at a given sales level with identical costs of sales and selling and general and administrative expenses may have completely different operating characteristics.

FUNDAMENTALS OF PROFIT-VOLUME ANALYSIS AND BREAK-EVEN CHARTS

Consider the two companies, A and B, whose various elements of cost are tabulated in Figure 5-1.   They have identical sales, costs of sales, selling and general and administrative expenses, and operating profits.   Yet these two companies will respond completely differently to a change in sales volume, if their internal operating characteristics are not the same.

This is shown by Figure 5-2.   When sales increase or decrease $20,000, the operating profit of Company A changes by $10,000, or 50 percent of the change in sales level.   Company B, on the other hand, for the same change in sales shows a profit change of $4,000, or 20 percent of the change in sales level.

If we plot on a graph the values of sales and profit tabulated in Figure 5-2, we develop a visual picture of the two companies which shows that each has quite different operating characteristics (see Figure 5-3).   This graph is known as the "profit-volume chart."   It is a form of break-even chart, because it shows the profit or loss at various sales levels and the sales where profits

---

* Adapted from *Upward in the Black,* by Lee H. Hill, to be published by Prentice-Hall, Inc., Englewood Cliffs, N.J.

Company	A	B
Net sales..................................	$100,000	$100,000
Cost of sales.............................	85,000	85,000
Selling expense...........................	3,000	3,000
General and administrative expense........	2,000	2,000
Total cost............................	$ 90,000	$ 90,000
Operating profit......................	$ 10,000	$ 10,000

FIG. 5-1. *Operating statements of two apparently similar companies.*

start. This level of sales is called the "break-even point." To be valid for all sales levels, the product mix and costs must remain consistent with the change in sales level.

Figure 5-3 shows that Company A and Company B have widely different operating characteristics even though they had identical costs, expenses, and profits at the $100,000 sales level. In the case of Company A, the break-even point is at $80,000; in the case of Company B, it is at $50,000 of sales. In Company A, the loss at zero sales is $40,000; in Company B, it is only $10,000. In Company A, each $100 of increase in sales develops $50 of profit (or less loss); in Company B, only $20 is generated.

Obviously, there is something different about these two companies which brings about these different results. The reason for this is that there are two kinds of cost which affect operating results at differing sales levels.

One kind of cost varies with the level of sales or production—more sales, more cost. In a manufacturing company, the cost of material in the product tends to vary proportionally with the level of sales. The same is true for direct-labor cost, sales commissions, and some overhead costs, such as the cost of power and perishable tools. These costs are called "variable costs," because they *vary* with the production or sales level.

If all costs were variable, we would have profit-volume charts like Figures 5-4, 5-5, and 5-6. In Figure 5-4, the variable costs are less than the sales income, so there would be a profit at any sales level. In Figure 5-5, the variable

	Operating profit	
Net sales	Company A	Company B
0	($40,000)	($10,000)
20,000	(30,000)	(6,000)
40,000	(20,000)	(2,000)
60,000	(10,000)	2,000
80,000	0	6,000
100,000	10,000	10,000
120,000	20,000	14,000

FIG. 5-2. *Profits (or losses) generated at different sales volumes by companies A and B.*

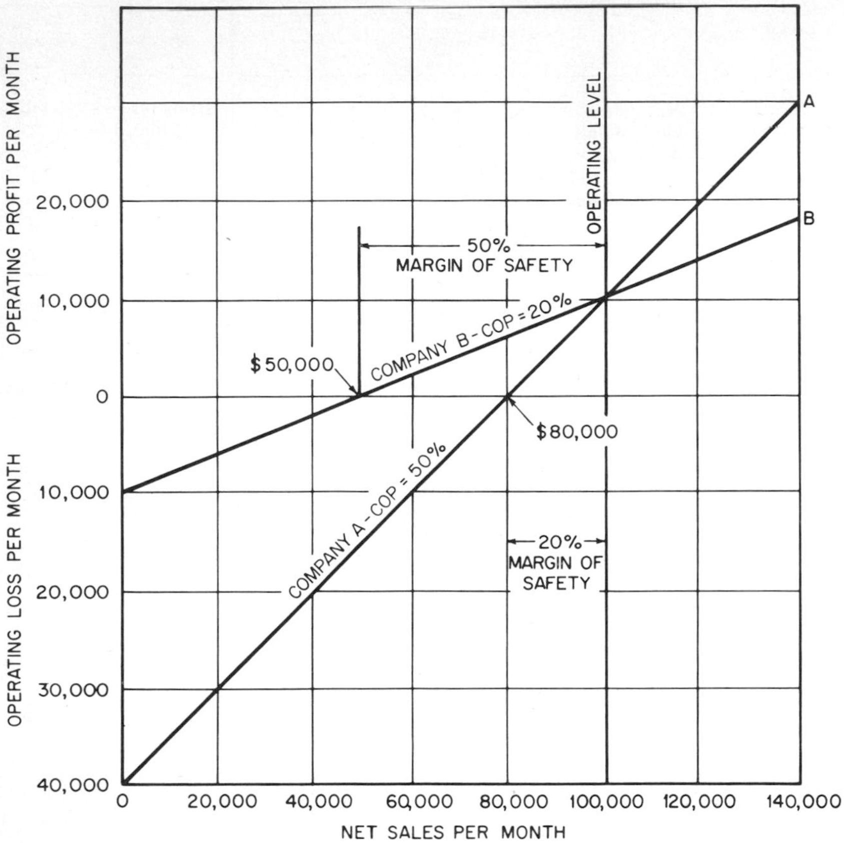

FIG. 5-3. *Profit-volume chart for Companies A and B.*

FIG. 5-4. *Profitable company with no fixed costs.*

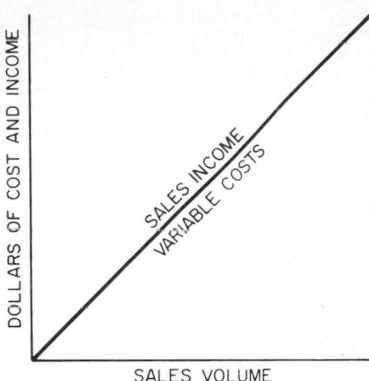

FIG. 5-5. *Break-even company with no fixed costs.*

costs are just equal to the sales income, so there is no profit and no loss at all sales levels. Variable costs in Figure 5-6 are greater than the sales income, so there is a loss at all sales levels.

However, in all businesses, there is another kind of cost, the so-called "fixed cost." Fixed costs are costs which continue for all sales levels within the operating range. These are costs such as rent of the facilities, light and heat, and salaries of administrative and supervisory personnel.

Although these costs are usually called "fixed costs," they are not really fixed, because they can be changed—but changed only at managerial direction. Fixed costs represent the cost of maintaining facilities and personnel to handle a given level of sales regardless of the fluctuation in sales level over a reasonable range. If management finds the sales average to be substantially below the intended sales level, the action to be taken may be to reduce the fixed costs to a lower

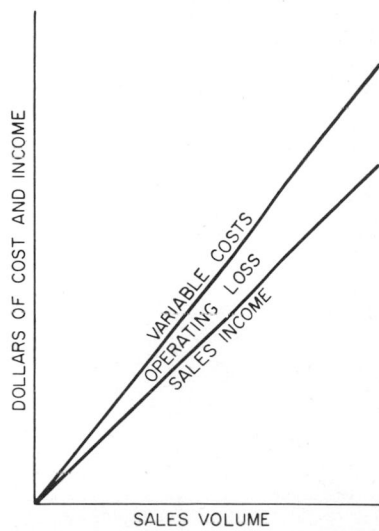

FIG. 5-6. *Unprofitable company with no fixed costs.*

level and thereby provide less facilities and personnel to do business at the new lower operating level.

In the profit-volume chart, Figure 5-3, the loss at zero sales represents the fixed costs, $40,000 in Company A and $10,000 in Company B. The slope of the lines in Figure 5-3 is determined by the amount of variable costs in the two cases.

DETERMINING WHETHER COSTS ARE FIXED OR VARIABLE

There is much confusion over the determination in a given case of whether costs are fixed or variable. Direct labor is usually considered to be a variable cost, but many times it is fixed. Whether or not a cost is fixed or variable depends on company policy and whether the element of cost is controlled by management to be fixed or variable. For example, assume in the case of direct-labor employees that the policy is to lay off such employees when work is slack. If the number of employees is maintained proportional to the amount of work, then the cost is variable. However, suppose the company is afraid of losing these workers to a competitor if they are laid off, and decides to keep them on the payroll even when work is not there for them to do. Now the direct-labor cost is fixed.

The test of whether a cost or component of cost is variable is to ask the question, "Would this element of cost be reduced if the level of sales temporarily dropped a modest amount, say 20 percent?" For example, in the case where there are five clerks in an accounting department and sales drop off in a given month, would the number of clerks be reduced? Usually, the answer would be negative, so the element of expense is not variable, but fixed.

Certain costs may be partially variable and partially fixed. For example, sales expense may include a fixed element, the salaries in the department, and advertising expense. It may have a variable component, such as the salesmen's commissions.

EFFECT OF VARIABLE AND FIXED-COST PROPORTIONS

The ratio of variable cost to sales income and the amount of fixed cost have a major effect on the company's operating characteristics. The difference be-

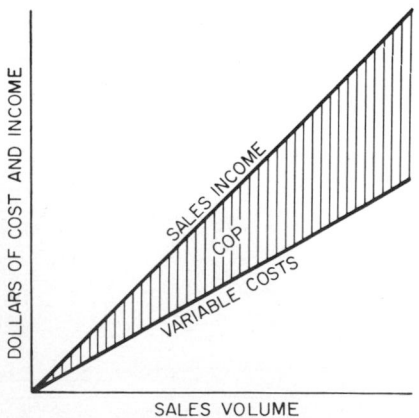

FIG. 5-7. *Contribution to overhead and profit at various sales volumes.*

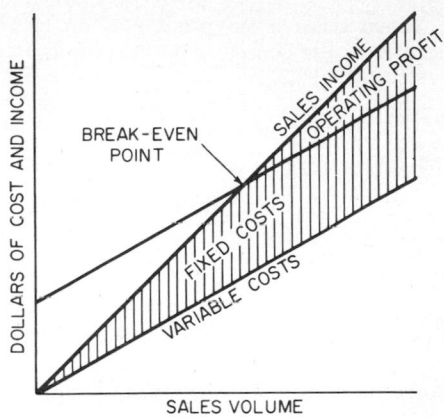

FIG. 5-8. *Figure 5-7 with fixed costs added.*

tween the sales income and the variable costs is the amount available to cover the fixed costs and provide a profit.

For example, Figure 5-7 shows the usual arrangement when the variable costs are less than the sales income.   The difference between the two is called "contribution to overhead and profit" (COP), because this is the amount left over to contribute to fixed overhead.   When enough COP is generated to equal the fixed cost, the break-even point is reached.   Any COP generated above the amount of fixed cost becomes profit.

Figure 5-8 shows graphically the result when the fixed costs are added to the variable costs.   At the break-even point, the COP is shown as equaling the fixed cost.

THE COMPANY PROFIT FORMULA

From these simple definitions, a profit formula for the company can be developed.

By definition, "profit" is the difference between the COP and the fixed cost, so

$$P = COP - F$$

where P = operating profit at a given sales level, S
 COP = contribution to overhead and profit at the given sales level, S
 F = the fixed cost

But
$$COP = \frac{\% \ COP}{100} \times S$$

where % COP is the percentage of COP to sales, so

$$P = \frac{\% \ COP}{100} \times S - F$$

From this equation, we can solve for % COP, and

$$\% \ COP = \frac{F + P}{S} \times 100$$

When there is no profit and no loss, break-even results and $P = 0$. In this case, from the company profit formula

$$P = 0 = \frac{\% \text{ COP}}{100} \times S_{BE} - F$$

where S_{BE} = sales at break-even.

Solving the equation for S_{BE}:

$$S_{BE} = \frac{F}{\% \text{ COP}} \times 100$$

But

$$\% \text{ COP} = \frac{F + P}{S} \times 100$$

Substituting in the previous equation,

$$S_{BE} = \frac{FS}{F + P}$$

where S_{BE} = sales to break-even for a given period of time
F = fixed cost for the same period of time
S = sales at any known level
P = operating profit at the same level as S

While the profit-volume form of break-even chart plots profit or loss against volume of sales, the form illustrated by Figure 5-8 plots costs and expenses and sales income against sales volume. In the case of Figure 5-8, variable costs and expenses have been first plotted against volume of sales and then fixed costs have been added to the variable costs and expenses to give the total costs.

The more useful form of this type of chart is when all of the costs are plotted cumulatively in the order in which they appear in the company's operating statement. Such a chart is shown in Figure 5-9. Here the various elements of cost are plotted in their entirety without splitting them into fixed and variable elements. Such a chart, in addition to showing where the break-even point is, shows the distribution of costs and expenses at any sales level. This gives a picture of the makeup of the company and for that reason is sometimes designated the "company characteristic chart."

In drawing any form of break-even chart, it is important to bear in mind that the fixed costs involved must be considered fixed for the range of operations shown on the chart. Frequently charts are drawn incorrectly by showing changes in fixed cost occurring at a certain point. For example, assume a chart covering a sales-volume range of from zero to $150,000 per month. The fixed costs are based on one-shift operation, but the company contemplates adding a second shift, with additional fixed costs when sales reach $125,000. This added cost is shown with a vertical line at $125,000 to show the addition. This is not correct, because if sales drop back down to, say, $100,000, the fixed cost added by the second shift will not be eliminated. What is needed is *another* break-even chart to show the effect of additional fixed cost incurred by the second shift.

CORRECTING BREAK-EVEN CHARTS WHEN INVENTORY CHANGES

Another very important fact to bear in mind when drawing break-even charts for a manufacturing company is that if there is a change in any overhead com-

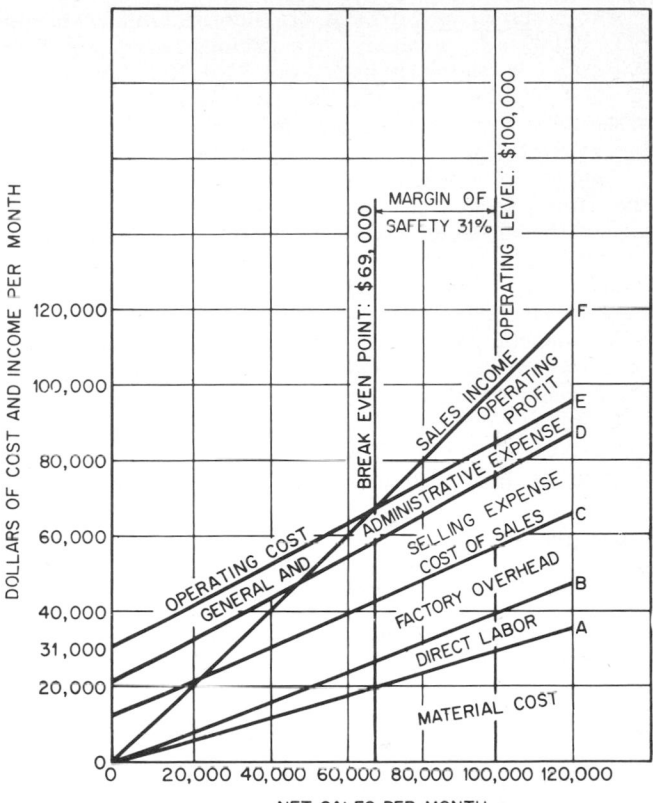

FIG. 5-9. *Company characteristic chart.*

ponent in the inventory during the period, a correction must be made for this. Assume the simple case, where work in process and finished goods in inventory increase by, say, $100,000. If it is the practice to assign a portion of factory overhead to the makeup of the inventory, the reported profit for the period (when the usual absorption accounting system is used) will be increased by the increase in the overhead component in the inventory. This may be as much as 50 percent of the inventory change. All break-even charts are based on no change in inventory. Hence, if there is a change in inventory, correction must be made for this overhead change.

There are two ways to make this correction: (1) determine the difference between overhead in the inventory at the end of the period and that at the beginning of the period or (2) more simply, calculate the operating cost as the cost of material and labor plus *all* the factory overhead incurred during the period, plus all selling and general and administrative expenses during the period.

Making the correction as outlined for use in making break-even charts is not only necessary for making meaningful break-even charts, but essential if operating statements are to be intelligently used. Many apparent discrepancies in operating profit with volume will be cleared up if this correction for inventory change is made.

For example, at $100,000 of sales in January, a company showed a profit of $10,000. In February, the billings were still $100,000, and profit was $20,000. In March, billings were $100,000, but profit was zero. On the face of it, it might be assumed that costs were not under good control. However, costs could have been under perfect control, but inventory changes might explain the whole thing.

Assume, for example, no inventory change in January, so $10,000 represents the "true" profit. In February, assume an increase in inventory of $20,000 with $10,000 representing the overhead part of the increase. This increase in overhead represents overhead costs that were incurred during the period which were capitalized and not charged off as expense during the period. This means that part of the reported operating profit or "book profit" was created by manufacturing goods which were sold and shipped out the door. The other part was created by increasing the inventory to a level higher than that at the beginning of the period.

In March, if the inventory had been reduced by $20,000, the overhead in the reduction of $10,000 would now have been charged to cost of sales, giving a *reduction* of $10,000 in "book profit," or a total "book profit" of zero.

BIBLIOGRAPHY

Bierman, Harold, Jr., *Managerial Accounting*, The Macmillan Company, New York, 1959.

Bierman, Harold, Jr., *Topics in Cost Accounting and Decisions*, McGraw-Hill Book Company, New York, 1963.

Gardner, Fred V., *Profit Management and Control*, McGraw-Hill Book Company, New York, 1955.

Hill, Lee H., *Upward in the Black*, Prentice-Hall, Inc., Englewood Cliffs, N.J., forthcoming.

Tse, John Y. D., *Profit Planning through Volume-Cost Analysis*, The Macmillan Company, New York, 1960.

CHAPTER SIX

Internal Auditing and Control

FRANCIS S. MOLLOY   *Vice President—Operations and Treasurer, United Medical Service, Inc., New York, New York*

Internal auditing can narrowly be described as being concerned with making sure through checks made by its own people that the company's financial and accounting policies, procedures, and controls are being followed. It is in contrast to outside auditing, first in approach, because external auditors perform post-audits almost exclusively, and second in its concern with more than merely the end results of the accounting processes.

This chapter, however, will develop a broader concept of internal auditing more in keeping with progressive management thinking. It will deal with internal auditing and control primarily from an overall managerial viewpoint, illustrating the practicality of expanding the use of a tried and valuable management tool, the audit, to other major aspects of the company's business.

The development of internal quality control of repetitive office operations will be discussed in some detail with appropriate examples given based on applications made at United Medical Service.

PRINCIPAL PURPOSES OF THE INTERNAL AUDITING FUNCTION

The principal purposes of the internal auditing function are:

1. To assist management to determine the results of performance of delegated responsibilities and authority

2. To assist the area supervisor better to discharge his responsibilities of follow-up and control

3. To ascertain if the company's financial and accounting policies, procedures, and controls are being implemented and followed

4. To ascertain if company policies and procedures are being implemented and followed in other major functional areas

5. To recommend corrective action where appropriate

6. To identify instances where company policy has unofficially been modified by practices developed over a period of time by the job incumbents

Objectives of the Internal Auditing Function.   The primary objective of the internal auditing function is to *augment* management's day-to-day follow-up and control of delegated responsibility and authority.   It augments because every company, regardless of size, business, or sophistication, has internal auditing in the broad concept.   Supervision, in the exercise of its managerial responsibilities, is, in effect, doing a type of internal auditing.

This point cannot be overemphasized, because setting up the internal auditing function as the sole method of finding out what is going on in the company means allowing regular line supervision at all levels to abdicate the important responsibilities of follow-up and control.   If this were allowed, a company would have to hire almost as many auditors as it has supervisors, which is a ridiculous prospect.   This prospect, however, serves to point up the fact that internal auditing is not a substitute for the discharge of the managerial responsibilities inherent in any supervisor's job at any level.   It is, rather, an organized approach to supplement day-to-day supervision.

Description of the Internal Auditing Function.   The internal auditing function operates on both a post-audit and a pre-audit basis.   Post-audit serves the useful purpose of reporting what has happened after the fact, identifying errors of omission or commission, and recommending steps for improvement.   The pre-audit is possible as the result of having an internal auditor who can be assigned to assess a process before completion.   It permits detecting significantly unfavorable factors or performance before completion so that corrective action can be taken.   This action will not only reduce costly errors, but eliminate such things as subsequent poor customer relations and increase productive output by reducing the need for costly rework.

Internal auditing can be applied to good advantage in most areas of a business. At United Medical Service, for example, the internal auditing function is concerned not only with the classical accounting functions, but also with the performance of other major activities, such as purchasing, claim reserves, application of renewal rating formulas, overall claim administration and processing, and the like.   It has been expanded to include management audits of organization, current management performance, management succession, and communications.

Organizational Placement.   The internal auditing function is vital and important and should report to someone other than the individual responsible for accounting.   This is based, of course, upon the principle of providing for checks and balances.   The function should be so placed in the organization as to have as much freedom from organizational pressures as possible.   It should report to a person high in the organization with few direct responsibilities for other major functions, so that it can objectively and without hesitation evaluate and report on all major aspects of the company.

ESTABLISHING THE INTERNAL AUDITING FUNCTION

When internal auditing is first introduced, or when a change is made to strengthen and improve the function, management should make clear to all affected employees the purpose of the function and the vital role the internal auditor will play.   The aspect of the assistance it will give the supervisor should be strongly emphasized.   It is axiomatic that for the internal auditor to attain results in the improvement of day-to-day operations, he must receive cooperation from the supervisor and the employees involved.

The internal auditor should become thoroughly familiar with the company's organizational components and their day-to-day operations. He should then establish in manual format the objective and scope of the audit to be made of each major component, including an identification of the statistical sampling formulas to be used, if applicable. The audit plans should then be reviewed by his immediate superior. In addition, a review by the line supervisor is most important to assure that the audit will serve its purpose of identifying the results of performance.

The use of statistical sampling opens many new doors of application to the internal auditor, increasing significantly the productivity and quality level of his work. Its frequent use should therefore be anticipated during the planning stage.

Proper selection of the auditor is important. Previously, the ideal educational background or experience for internal auditing was considered to be accounting. With the expanded scope of internal auditing, however, the candidate should have statistical as well as accounting background.

Providing the Optimum Environment. It is important for management to support the internal auditing function strongly and to see that all supervisors understand and accept its stated purpose and its manner of operation. The auditor will contribute in significant measure to the environment in which he will work. He can either help or seriously hinder the acceptance of the program. His value to the company will be in direct proportion to the degree to which he is accepted and the environment he develops during the performance of his duties. He does not have to be a hale and hearty "swell guy" and try to be all things to all men. But he must be sincere; he must be honest and forthright with the people with whom he comes in contact; he must keep his eye on the objectives and the purposes of his function as well as on the technical tools which he will use in the performance of his job.

There are some supervisors, confident of their performance, who like the idea that somebody will make an independent study and demonstrate to management that they are, in fact, doing a good or outstanding job. Both management and the auditor, however, must recognize that there is an inherent reluctance on the part of the majority to have their performance evaluated and reported. It is important, therefore, to recognize that the development of a good working climate is vital to achieving maximum results from the internal auditing function.

Evaluation and Action. At the conclusion of an audit, the internal auditor will be responsible for submitting a written report identifying the objective and scope of his study, the methods used, and his findings. His findings should not only show the number, percent, or type of errors, but also give recommendations for improvement or at least suggest referring the problem to a specialist area such as methods, personnel, or accounting.

The most effective way to get acceptance of his recommendations is for the auditor to share his findings in draft form with the concerned supervisor. It is important to recognize that the supervisor will always be more technically proficient in his functional responsibilities than the auditor. Thus, preliminary discussion of findings gives the auditor a chance to correct any errors he may have made through misunderstanding, misinformation, or lack of knowledge, because the supervisor will undoubtedly point out these errors to him. Cooperation will also be enhanced if the final report permits the attachment of written comments by the supervisor.

These approaches give the supervisor an opportunity to share in the findings so that he is informed of existing problems before his immediate superior and is able to start corrective action if warranted. He can also identify with the work of the internal auditor and will receive credit for willingness to expose his area to evaluation and to have weaknesses identified, and particularly for willingness, once he knows the situation, to take corrective measures. He will thus demonstrate by his actions a recognition of the concept that the auditor is, in effect, working for him, assisting him with his own functional responsibilities.

The written report should be distributed to the auditor's immediate superior, to the supervisor of the area involved, and to the supervisor's immediate superior. The normal management responsibility for follow-up of the report belongs to the auditor's superior. He should (1) see that the objectives of the audit have been achieved; (2) be sure that recommendations are evaluated and acted upon; (3) see that a timetable for implementation is developed; and (4) plan future studies for the same area to see if circumstances have changed or if other alternatives have developed which would allow for further improvement.

MEASURING THE PERFORMANCE OF THE INTERNAL AUDITOR

Proper measurement of any function must be based upon an accurate job description and preferably on standards of performance. If standards of performance are established, it is relatively easy to measure results, because in the development of the standards what is expected will have been clearly identified.

In the absence of standards of performance, caution should be exercised in implying that the internal auditing function, to be profitable or beneficial to the company, must show significant dollar savings. This is a short-sighted and narrow approach. It is preferable that performance be assessed on the basis of the accuracy of the information submitted by the auditor on the state of affairs in the function which he has audited. If the work is being performed as prescribed, this should be reported. This has the effect of assuring management that its desires are being followed. It also assures the line supervisor that the auditor is there for the purpose of helping him. A supervisor gets deep satisfaction when an independent auditor reports that he is operating in accordance with management's objectives.

Discrepancies, when found, may or may not have a monetary value, but it is logical to assume that the deviations have importance, because they indicate a departure from what has been prescribed for the supervisor to do. Thus the auditor performs a valuable service, not necessarily measurable in terms of money, when indicating deficiencies in performance. For example, there are times when policy is outmoded, but nobody has called this to the attention of management. In some instances, there may be a lack of policy or a policy that is not clear, and identification of this by the auditor is important.

Further, the performance of the auditor can be assessed by the quality of his reports and also by the reactions of the supervisors whose areas he has reviewed. Evaluation of the validity of these reactions can be made by the auditor's superior by observation.

A company that has an internal auditing function or intends to start one should evaluate the tangible and intangible returns on its investment after establishing in writing functional objectives, scope, responsibilities, and duties. If set up properly, it will be readily demonstrated that the internal auditing function pays off.

TRENDS IN INTERNAL AUDITING AND CONTROL

Not only has the application of statistical sampling changed and broadened the concept of internal auditing, but further growth has followed the advent of electronic data-processing machines.   As management learns how to use electronic data-processing equipment better and in a more sophisticated manner, applications of internal auditing will expand to where every aspect of the business may be subjected to the scrutiny of "internal auditing."

A few examples of applications at United Medical Service which can be construed as an extension of internal auditing will help to illustrate this.   After receipt of a claim, the type of service the doctor rendered is coded together with information about the patient such as sex, age, type of coverage, and the like.   A computer is programmed to correlate all the data and "reject" inconsistencies such as a maternity claim for a male patient.   Another example is the identification of impossible repeat services such as an appendectomy reported as performed on the same patient on two different occasions.   The computer is also programmed to reject duplicate claims, that is, more than one claim reporting the same service on the same date for the same patient.

In addition to the use of statistical sampling and electronic data processing, internal controls include the concept of quality audit of paper work.

The business of health insurance requires the processing of millions of individual claims a year.   With this volume and because of the repetition of claims examining in the evaluation of claims, a production and quality control department has been established.   This control is also applied to other functions, such as order processing, purchase requisitions, and the like, where the volume is sufficiently large and the operations repetitive.   The basic tool of this control department is statistical sampling.

Through pre-audit sampling, the quality of the work of the claims examiners is assessed daily on a departmental basis.   The heavy line in Figure 6-1 shows the percentage of error found by the audit.   The audit is based on a statistical

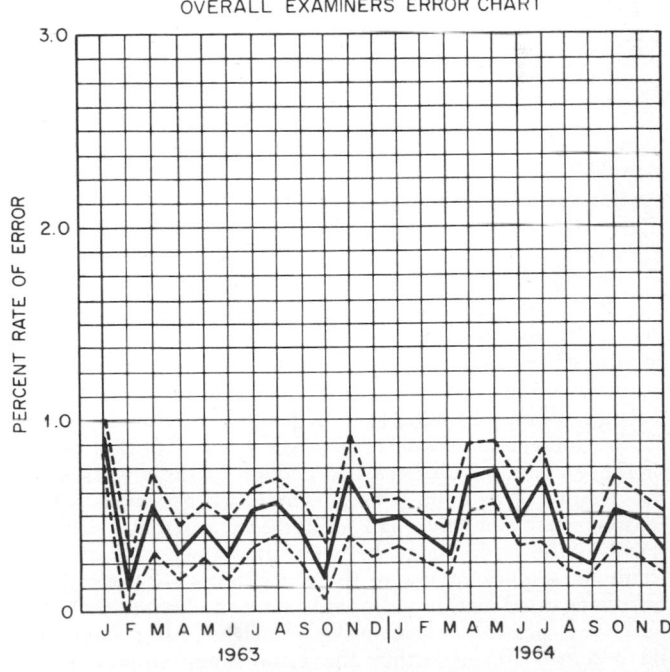

FIG. 6-1. *Departmental chart of examiners' errors.*

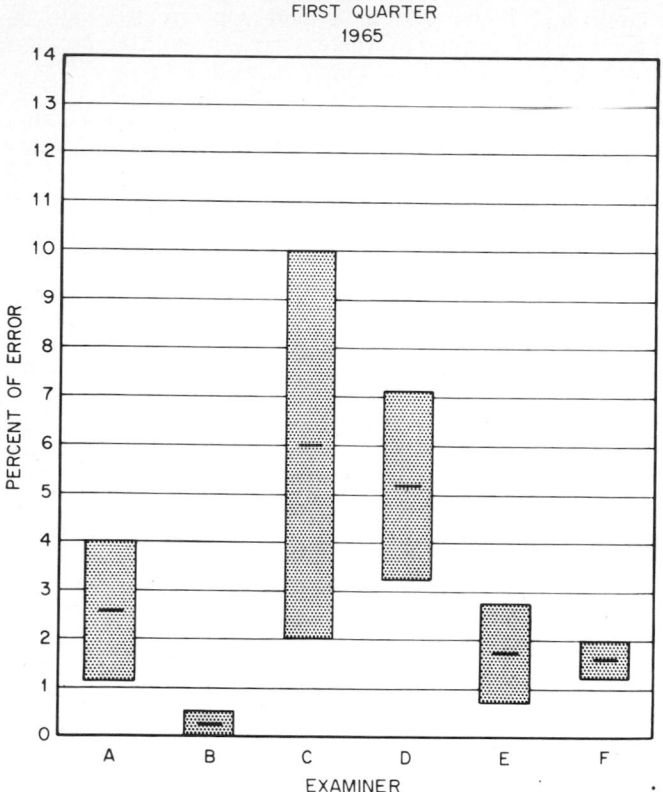

FIG. 6-2. *Percent of errors of individual examiners.*

sample which is developed to provide an 80 percent level of confidence.   The confidence level introduces a range within which the percentage of error falls. Figure 6-1 illustrates how the confidence band is charted.   This serves the purpose of telling the supervisor that while the solid line indicates the percentage of error, it is affected by the fact that the statistical sampling was established on an 80 percent confidence level; therefore, the actual error rate is between the lower dashed line and the upper dashed line, known as the "confidence band."   The higher the percentage of the confidence band, the narrower the range becomes.

High volume permits, as a by-product of the department audit, an evaluation of the individual examiner's work.   Over a period of a calendar quarter, most of the examiners will have had enough of their work sampled to permit charting the results as in Figure 6-2.   There are occasions when individuals, for many reasons, may not have had an audit of adequate sample size.   This will reflect itself in the wide range between the upper and lower confidence levels.   For example, a quick review of the chart shows that examiner C's information should be disregarded because the wide range indicates that the sample size was small and very possibly inconclusive.   On the other hand, examiners B and F can be assumed to be within the error range depicted because of the relatively narrow spacing between the upper and lower levels.

In addition, a written report on individual examiners is sent weekly to the supervisor, giving the specific errors so that where a pattern is indicated, corrective action through training can be taken.

The statistical sampling approach is used to evaluate the quality of correspondence. This has been done for overall area performance and for individual correspondents. The same techniques have also been applied to assessing the quality of telephone contacts with subscribers and physicians based on factual content, tone and approach, courtesy, and willingness to help.

The quality audit of office operations is an additional internal control added to those in more widespread use, such as budgets and work standards. Quality-control techniques are also used to identify peak work performance time as well as let-down periods.

SUMMARY

Management should be interested in broadening the concept of internal auditing from a review of financial or accounting practices to the auditing of performance of other major company functions in relation to policies, systems, and procedures. A broadly based concept of the internal auditing function is that it aids the individual supervisor at all management levels in the performance of his responsibilities of follow-up and control. Management should see that this function is organized with an appropriate job description and standards of performance and that its purposes are fully communicated to the affected supervisors and employees.

The auditor, as an individual, contributes significantly to the success or failure of his function depending upon his approach to the program and to other employees and upon the environment which he establishes. It is helpful if he has statistical as well as accounting education or experience. His formal reports should be submitted after review by the audited area's supervisor to take full advantage of the supervisor's technical knowledge. The reports should also be augmented by inclusion or attachment of additional comments of the supervisor. This provides a complete picture for better understanding by upper-level managers.

Internal controls in office paper work may be broadened by quality audits using statistical sampling. Quality audits are applicable to repetitive, volume-type work such as orders, purchasing requisitions, and the like. Sampling techniques have also been used to identify employee productive peak work periods and valleys in productive effort.

With more management interest in broadened internal audits and internal controls, together with the use of statistical sampling and computers, future applications will be more sophisticated and based on improved techniques. Factors that contribute to more emphasis on internal audits and controls are mounting pressures on costs and profits, company expansion through acquisitions and diversification of products, an increasing number of foreign-based subsidiaries, and improvement in the discharge of management's responsibility to know what is going on in the company as it affects profit performance.

BIBLIOGRAPHY

Arkin, Herbert, and Raymond R. Colton, *Tables for Statisticians*, Barnes & Noble, Inc., New York, 1963.

Blough, Carman G., *Practical Applications of Accounting Standards; A Decade of Comment on Accounting and Auditing Problems*, American Institute of Certified Public Accountants, New York, 1957.

Brink, Victor Z., and James A. Cashin, *Internal Auditing*, 2d ed., The Ronald Press Company, New York, 1958.

Cochran, William G., *Sampling Techniques*, John Wiley & Sons, Inc., New York, 1963.

Jerome, William T., III, "Internal Auditing as an Aid to Management," *Harvard Business Review*, March–April, 1953.

Johnson, Arnold W., *Auditing—Principles and Case Problems*, Holt, Rinehart and Winston, Inc., New York, 1959.

Lenhart, Norman J., and Philip L. Defliese, *Montgomery's Auditing*, 8th ed., The Ronald Press Company, New York, 1957.

Walsh, Francis J., Jr., *Internal Auditing*, National Industrial Conference Board, New York, 1963.

Expense Account Control

S. J. GUADAGNA *Secretary-Treasurer, Pandick Press, Inc., New York, New York*

If business firms had unlimited funds at their disposal, this chapter would not be necessary. The efficient operation of a business requires a complete record of all transactions properly classified and arranged so that the extent of these transactions may be readily analyzed and presented to management in an orderly and organized way. Income and expenses must be grouped in such a manner that management can determine whether it is good policy to reduce one kind of expense or to increase another, and whether one department or facility is profitable and another so bad that it should be abandoned.

Standard Accounting Systems Are No Panacea. Expense account control should not be confused with, nor become embroiled in, the mechanics of double-entry bookkeeping which provides for the recording of transactions as equalizing debits and credits. The debits and credits find their way into individual ledger accounts and culminate in the trial balance—a source for the preparation of financial statements.

Nor should expense account control be confused with "controlling accounts." The latter mechanism is used to reduce the number of accounts in the general ledger. A controlling account is an account which shows in summary in the general ledger an amount that is shown in detail on a subsidiary ledger. In the publishing business, for instance, expenses are sometimes classified as production, editorial, advertising, circulation, and administrative. In each classification, there are frequently many different items. Instead of having a separate account in the general ledger for each one of them, one controlling account may be substituted in the general ledger for each group with a subsidiary ledger maintained for the separate expense accounts within each group. In addition to their use with expense accounts, controlling accounts are used to an even greater degree in connection with real accounts (asset, liability, and capital accounts), such as accounts receivable, accounts payable, inventories, capital stock outstanding, and the like.   Examples of controlling accounts and their counterpart subsidiary ledgers typically used in a cost-accounting system are:

Controlling Account	Subsidiary Ledger
Materials	Stores ledger
Work in process	Work-in-process ledger
Finished parts	Finished-parts ledger
Finished goods	Finished-goods ledger
Indirect cost	Indirect-cost ledger
Selling expense	Selling-expense ledger
Administrative expense	Administrative-expense ledger

WAYS IN WHICH EXPENSE ACCOUNT CONTROL OPERATES

It has been said that expenses are incurred so that profits can be made.   There is a great deal of truth to this, for expense does not exist by itself.   It is always incurred as an investment in results.   And it is the difference between the expense and the result that is the true measure of effectiveness.   The ratio between the two is even more important.

Common versus Distinctive Expenses.   Although there are expenses common to all industries, such as rent, power, and depreciation, different industries incur different expenses and for different reasons.   That is, there are expenses which are distinctive to a specific industry and which therefore require special attention, such as the shaping of metal into sheets or rods in a steel mill.

Classification of Expenses.   It is the function of expense account control to identify and rank expenses properly with reference to the nature of the business and the resulting use for which they are intended.   The various ways in which they may be defined and classified are numerous.   For instance, expenses may be controlled according to the following classifications:

1. Natural characteristics
2. Functional
3. Departmental
4. Process
5. Changes in activity (fixed or variable)
6. Product or part produced

Natural Characteristics.   These refer to the physical aspect of the expense.   Is it material, labor, or supplies?

Functional.   Functional classification relates to how the expense is used.   Is it to be expended for the manufacturing function or for the administrative or selling functions?

Departmental.   Classifications by department are concerned with where the expense is to be incurred and by what facility or cost center.   The management of a printing plant, for example, may want to establish an operating expense control for all printing presses.   To do so, separate accounts can be set up for each type of expense that is general to all press facilities (one account for press blankets, one for press repairs, and so on) or management may prefer a machine-hour rate cost system whereby expenses will be classified according to the production centers responsible for incurring the expenditures.   Classification of expenses by responsibility is important, because it is the basis of control. It is necessary to know where the expense is incurred and who is responsible. Often confusing in the control of expenses is the allocation of service department costs to producing departments.   The allocations are essential for purposes of computing unit costs, but certainly not necessary in the control of expenses. Expenses can be controlled only where they are incurred.   The possible exception to this rule is some repair department costs, which in a sense are controllable by the producing department in that proper preventive maintenance efforts can reduce the number of repairs. Control reports that are generated for which the department manager has responsibility should include only controllable costs. The inclusion of costs which he cannot control acts as a detriment to control.

Process. Process control is applicable to that form of manufacture in which a product is made in production lots that cannot be distinguished from one another. The usual features of process industries are characterized by the following:

1. There is production of identical items with a steady flow through a plant.

2. The finished product of one stage of manufacture constitutes all or part of the raw material for the next stage.

3. It is impractical to distinguish specific production lots, because of the complete identity of the items processed and the steady flow of production.

A good example of this is in the manufacture of bricks and the several stages in their production:

1. *Mixing and drying.* In this division, wet clay is mixed with other ingredients and molded into brick forms. As formed, the wet bricks are placed on racks for transfer to the drying process.

2. *Drying.* In the drying room, excess moisture is removed, and the racks are taken to the burning division.

3. *Burning.* In large ovens, the dried bricks are then baked to the desired degree of hardness.

4. The unit of production in the industry is 1,000 bricks.

The basic control area is the "process." Expenses are gathered for each stage and per "M" costs computed.

Changes in Activity. Expenses can also be classified as to whether they are "fixed" or "variable" depending on how they react to changes in activity. A variable expense is an expense which is proportional to the level of activity under consideration. This expense increases as activity increases, and conversely, decreases as activity decreases; it may or may not be a directly proportionate charge. A fixed expense is constant over the range of projected activity and neither increases nor decreases with volume over the short term. In addition, some expenses can be termed "semivariable" or "semifixed," which denotes that both variable and fixed components are present in the expense. For example, the cost of electricity is incurred on the basis of an energy charge and a demand charge. The demand charge portion is a fixed minimum and is indifferent toward changes in activity, whereas the energy charge portion increases or decreases in direct proportion to activity. Figure 7-1 is a partial chart of accounts separated for fixed and variable expenses. It is arranged under the Dewey decimal system to indicate a further method of identifying expenses under a numerical system.

Product or Part Produced. Before the profitability of a product or part can be determined, it is necessary to gather and allocate all expenses directly identifiable with that product or part. The rate of profitability of the various product lines can lead to decisions relating to both the sales mix and the sales level.

A problem that often arises in classifying expenses by product or part is when a particular expense is associated with more than one product or part. A way out of the dilemma is to label the expense "indirect." But we must know with what we are trying to identify the expense before we rule it as indirect.

Figure 7-2 depicts a method of reporting the profitability of several product lines, highlighting those expenses directly associated with them and subordinating those expenses indirectly associated. In addition, it differentiates between variable and fixed expenses.

Acct. no.	Account name	Fixed	Variable
88.	Operating expense control		
.01	Printing department		
.01	Productive labor		XX
.03	Materials handling		XX
.06	Press supplies		XX
.09	Light and power (energy charge only)		XX
.51	Outside contract maintenance	XX	
.57	Supervision	XX	
.59	Inside maintenance	XX	
.63	Depreciation of equipment	XX	
.09	Warehouse and delivery		
.01	Truck drivers		XX
.02	Warehousemen		XX
.03	Shipping and receiving clerks		XX
.06	Truck operating expense		XX
.52	Supervision	XX	
.56	Depreciation—delivery trucks	XX	
.57	Depreciation—fork trucks	XX	
.58	Depreciation—warehouse	XX	
.11	Selling		
.01	Salesmen's commissions		XX
.02	Brokerage		XX
.03	Traveling		XX
.50	Salesmen's base salaries	XX	
.51	Sales managers' salaries	XX	
.53	Sales office clerks	XX	
.62	Advertising	XX	
.71	Telephone and telegraph	XX	
.12	Administration		
.53	Executive salaries	XX	
.54	Office salaries	XX	
.58	Interest on mortgage	XX	
.69	Protection service	XX	
.78	Insurance	XX	
.91	Dues and subscriptions	XX	

FIG. 7-1. *Partial chart of accounts separated for fixed and variable expense.*

CRITERIA FOR SELECTING THE EXPENSE REPORTING METHOD

No one system can be all things to all people. So it is with expense account control. Different methods of industrial processing require different ways of handling expense reporting. If shellac is being manufactured in a continuous process, obviously an expense account control system which is designed to report expenditures in the production of table radios will fall short of the goals of control for shellac manufacturing.

The following are some criteria for determining which method to use.

Product- or Part-oriented Control. In the manufacture of stock parts, a control different from parts manufacture in job lots or custom produced is required. In the first instance, predetermined economic lot quantities are selected. Batches are uniform, and the major task is to measure the departure of actual costs

XYZ Company Income Statement

	Product A		Product B		Product C		Total all products	
Sales............		$500,000		$800,000		$1,200,000		$2,500,000
Less: Direct variable..........	$200,000		$345,000		$405,000		$950,000	
Indirect variable........	100,000	300,000	160,000	505,000	240,000	645,000	500,000	1,450,000
Excess of sales over variable expenses....		200,000		295,000		555,000		1,050,000
Less: Direct fixed.........	100,000		90,000		250,000		440,000	
Indirect fixed........	50,000	150,000	45,000	135,000	125,000	375,000	220,000	660,000
Net income..........		$ 50,000		$160,000		$ 180,000		$ 390,000

FIG. 7-2.   *Income statement with direct and indirect variable and fixed expenses shown separately.*

XYZ Company Condensed Cost Variance Report

Std. Lot *1,600* Pieces

Department	Quantity, pieces	Actual cost	Standard cost	Cost variance
Cutting............	2,000	$ 180.00	$ 200.00	$ 20.00
Drilling............	1,910	60.00	50.00	(10.00)
Shaping............	1,730	560.00	500.00	(60.00)
Polishing...........	1,670	270.00	300.00	30.00
Plating............	1,610	440.00	400.00	(40.00)
Total............	8,920	$1,510.00	$1,450.00	$(60.00)

FIG. 7-3. *Typical variance report.*

from standard. In the latter case, customer specifications determine the sequence of operations, and any attempt at standard cost is tantamount to second-guessing the market.

Figure 7-3 shows a typical variance report on the complete manufacture of a part.

Considerable attention must be given to the classification of similar types of expenses if control is to be effective. For example, a production facility, say, a drill press, may be classified by the department in which it is located— "drill press department"—or the drill press may be one of several kinds of machines in a department which is capable of completing its own sequence of operations. Obviously, the function rather than the specific type of equipment will determine which method to use.

Process-control Industries. Although expenses are accumulated for each customer order in a job shop, a process-control industry, by contrast, cannot identify materials, labor, and overhead with each order. Each order is part of a continuous process, and the individual order identity is lost. The cost of a completed unit must be computed by dividing total expenses incurred during a period by total units completed.

Process-control methods are used for industries such as brick, cement, chemicals, rubber, steel, textiles, and coal. They are used also in the assembly-type industries which manufacture products like typewriters, automobiles, radios, television, toasters, and refrigerators. So process control is used when products are manufactured under characteristics of continuous processing or under mass-production methods.

A comparison of job-shop and process-control systems with respect to production and expense reporting and cost computation procedures is set forth in Figure 7-4.

Job-shop Industries. In any manufacturing firm, the operations performed on a product usually have to be done in several departments. Each department performs a specific task or process toward the completion of the product. Hence, it is possible to allocate expenses to each order and to compute separately for each the average per unit material, labor, overhead, and total cost. In most situations, this can be done by product line, by departmental classification, or by production center. Any method could be selected, but only one is best for the specific product. Unless examined carefully, deficiencies in one method or the other might not be noticed.

A good illustration of this is a printing plant where the basic sequences of doing work are composition, makeup, proofreading, imposition, presswork, folding, and binding; or artwork, camera work, plate making, presswork, folding, and binding. In a great number of cases, jobs will fall quite readily into one of these patterns, with the determining process dependent on factors of time, machine loading, quality, paper stock, and sometimes even weather.

Let us review the different ways that expenses for a specific printing press, say press G, can be reported.

Product Line. If management's intention is to gather and control expenses attributable to each product produced, the reporting procedure established by the company would probably be to initiate the following key forms to provide source documents:

1. The job cost sheet
2. The materials requisition
3. The labor time ticket

The *job cost sheet* is a form of subsidiary account used to accumulate the material, labor, and overhead charges applicable to each printing order. It describes the various costing points involved in the manufacture of the order, as well as the identifying number assigned and the detailed manufacturing costs applied.

Interlocked with the general ledger, the sum of the incompleted cost sheets at the end of an accounting period will equal the work-in-process account—possibly further separated into three subdivisions: material in process (sum of all the material charges on the cost sheets), labor in process (sum of all labor charges), and overhead in process (sum of overhead applied).

The *materials requisition* is a form used to charge the cost of materials consumed in manufacturing the specific printing order. It indicates the items of materials issued, the cost value of the issued material, and the identification of the order. It also provides for the transfer of costs from the materials-control account to the materials-in-process account in the general ledger.

The *labor time ticket* is the form used to charge the cost sheet with the direct-labor *cost* and *time* applicable to the order produced. It indicates the worker's name, the time worked on the order, the labor rate, and the total labor cost. Similar to the materials requisition, this, too, provides for the transfer of costs in the general ledger, in this case from the accrual payroll account to the labor-in-process account.

Comparison of Reporting and Computation Procedures for Job-shop and Process-control Systems

Particulars	Job shop	Process control
	Manufactures	
	To customer specifications (specific orders)	In anticipation of orders (to stock)
Production is reported by.......	Orders	Departments
Expenses are accumulated by....	Orders	Departments
Total cost is calculated.........	When order is completed	At the end of the period or during the period
Computation of unit costs equals	Total cost of order / Units produced	Departmental expenses / Units completed in the department, for each department involved

FIG. 7-4. *Comparison of job-shop and process-control systems.*

A common method of charging factory overhead to the cost sheets is at an estimated rate per direct-labor hour. This is calculated as follows, when annual manufacturing overhead is budgeted at $500,000 and projected annual activity results in 200,000 direct-labor hours:

$$\text{Estimated factory overhead rate per direct-labor hour} = \frac{\text{estimated manufacturing overhead}}{\text{estimated direct-labor hours}}$$

$$= \frac{\$500,000}{200,000 \text{ hours}} = \$2.50 \text{ per hour}$$

The $2.50 overhead rate would be extended by the number of direct-labor hours applicable to a specific order and charged to its respective cost sheet accordingly.

With respect to the general ledger, the direct-labor time tickets are periodically totaled, the aggregate is extended by the overhead rate, and the result is transferred from the estimated factory overhead account (traditionally termed "factory burden—applied") to the factory overhead-in-process account. This fundamentally completes the interim cycle of charges collected for and identified with a specific printing order.

There is no question that the expense accounts and the reporting techniques are set up to control product line. But without inspecting the system further, the deficiencies it possesses may not show up, such as the distortion that could occur in orders as a result of the overhead rate used which depends so much on actual factory overhead dollars spent and actual direct-labor hours sold. Also, shortcomings could occur with respect to general administrative personnel which, when analyzed, have a direct relationship with the factory order. An example of this would be a production clerk who spends considerable time on planning and laying out how the specific job will be produced. Yet, an even greater inadequacy occurs because facility profitability is obscured. It could not be determined, for instance, what the cost of a thousand impressions would be for printing press G. The cost would be lost as part of the overall cost of the product line. And in printing, the knowledge of the cost of a thousand impressions for a specific press is necessary when an estimate for an order is called for.

Figure 7-5 indicates the flow a production order would follow in a typical printing plant as expenses are accumulated by product line.

Departmental Classification. When control techniques are to be employed departmentally, expenses are collected and charged directly to accounts generally bearing the names of the departments. The accounts are specifically devised

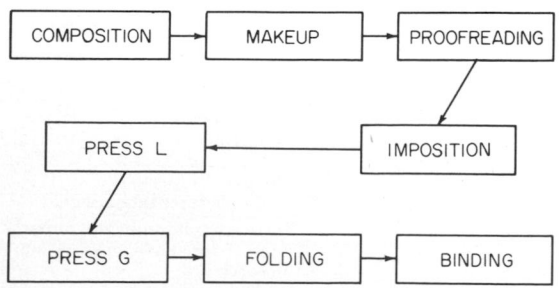

FIG. 7-5. *Plant layout depicting flow of control reporting by product line.*

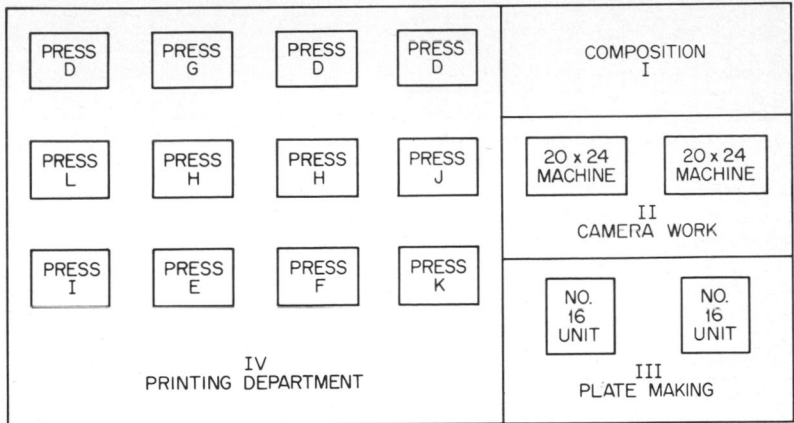

FIG. 7-6. *Partial plant layout depicting control reporting by departments I through IV.*

to record all those expenses incurred on behalf of, or identified with, the several plant departments. Using the printing plant as an illustration, all printing presses would be classified under one account, probably entitled "printing department." Expenses for supplies, repairs, parts, and outside services would be accumulated under the same account regardless of what press facility the expense is incurred for. Consequently, press blankets for a 22 by 34 Harris offset press would be grouped together with press blankets for a 35 by 45 Miehle offset press, and repairs expended for a small job press would be intermingled with repairs expended on behalf of a giant 28 by 41 two-color Miehle letterpress.

Under this method, the average cost per thousand press impressions can be obtained for the printing department as a unit, but because of the intermix of different kinds of printing the data would be ambiguous and therefore could lead to unprofitable decisions. The criteria used here would be the broad similarity of capability and physical location.

Figure 7-6 illustrates the printing department of a printing plant where control is by physical location. Note there are three press type D's, two press type H's, and one type of each of the other presses.

Production Center. Another method of establishing control is to arrange expense accounts by production center. There are several criteria used in setting up production centers in a manufacturing organization, and any standard accounting text will list them. However, it is well to point out that the major criterion is to group the facilities according to how the customer's order will be estimated and priced.

Once production centers are established, an expense account will be opened up for each center, and all costs incurred on behalf of that center will be allocated to it. This, then, provides the basis for a machine-hour rate system. Using the printing plant again as an example, press G will have a budgeted rate developed for that facility alone which can be constructed as either of two types:

    1. An all-inclusive machine-hour absorption cost rate
    2. A two-part machine-hour rate consisting of:
       a. Out-of-pocket cost factors
       b. Full cost factors

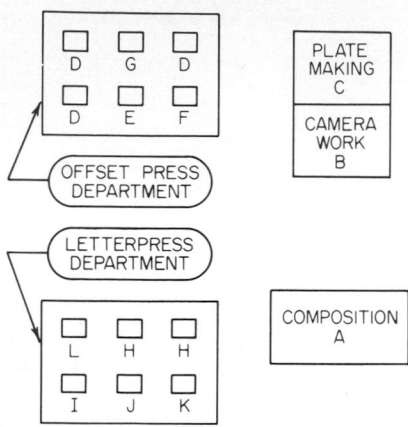

FIG. 7-7. *Partial plant layout depicting control reporting by production centers A through L.*

Naturally, to obtain the latter, the basic account classifications would have to be further separated into variable and nonvariable expense components.

Control by production center (or machine-hour rate) proves to be the most satisfactory method for the printing plant (or any converting operation), because it is limited to one type of printing (one press or one group of similar presses). Press G in Figure 7-7 is not averaged in with all types of printing, nor is it hidden in total product line. More important, this method provides a greater ease in measuring facility profitability.

OTHER APPLICATIONS

A proper set of expense account control data provides a basis for ultimately generating management information reports. Frequently, expense accounts are separated between fixed and variable (direct costing). Proper expense account control helps to determine pricing policies, make-or-buy decisions, justification of acquisition proceedings, interdivisional transfer pricing, expansion determinations, and the like. Many of these decisions require use of incremental data, for example, programming incremental expense for generating incremental business.

As an example of the use to which proper expense account data are put, let us examine how to justify a capital acquisition. It is important in this as well as in other applications to separate expenses which are normally incurred with the passage of time (period, fixed, constant) from those which are incurred with volume (variable, out of pocket, incremental).

Assume that a company's present purchase cost of a part is $1.00 each. It consumes 100,000 pieces per year. To acquire capital equipment to produce these parts itself, the company would have to invest $60,000 of annual fixed expenses. The out-of-pocket costs would be 20 cents each.

To find the break-even quantity, the following formula is used:

$$\text{Break-even quantity} = \frac{\text{annual fixed expenses}}{\text{savings in out-of-pocket costs per piece}}$$

Substituting the given data in the formula, we find

$$\text{Break-even quantity} = \frac{\$60,000}{\$1.00 - 0.20} = 75,000 \text{ pieces}$$

At an annual consumption of 100,000 pieces, the annual profit on this acquisition is

$$(\$100,000 - \$75,000) \times \$0.80 = \$20,000$$

Without proper expense account data which attributes specific costs to specific equipment, this determination could not have been made.

SUMMARY

We have seen that standard accounting systems, of themselves, are no substitute for expense account control and that confusion sometimes exists between expense account control, general ledger controlling accounts, and double-entry bookkeeping.

There are basically two types of manufacturing industries—process control and job shop. The major distinction between the two rests in the fact that in the former, production orders are made in anticipation of customer orders (or stock), and in the latter, production orders are made to definite customer specifications.

The design of an expense account control procedure should be based on the nature of the business and a determination of why expenses are incurred and how they should be measured and controlled. To accomplish this, expenses can be arranged into a variety of classifications, and generally speaking, one best way exists for any given company.

In the age of electronic data processing, the major requirement is accuracy. By the ability to sort data, a system can be made to accomplish almost any desired result. A word of caution, however: EDP is no substitute for an intelligent appraisal of needs and uses and is surely no panacea for preprogram analysis. EDP is as good as the judgment and skills of the individuals doing the thinking. Organize first, then refine. Otherwise, EDP could be an exercise in automating the confusion.

BIBLIOGRAPHY

Bower, Charles E., Jr., "Expense Control Must Focus on Responsibility," *NAA Bulletin*, November, 1964.

Cary, C. R., *Use of Product-line Profit and Loss Statements in the Control of Multiple-line Business*, Financial Management Series, no. 66, American Management Association, New York.

Dean, Joel, *Controls for Capital Expenditures*, Financial Management Series, no. 105, American Management Association, New York.

Dearden, John, *Cost and Budget Analysis*, Prentice-Hall, Inc., Englewood Cliffs, N.J., 1962.

Humfrey, R. D., "Process Control on the Computer," *Management Controls*, vol. 12, no. 7, July, 1965.

Lawrence, W. B., *Cost Accounting*, Prentice-Hall, Inc., Englewood Cliffs, N.J., 1954.

Peck, S. A., "Further Thoughts on the Management Aspect of Accounting Control," *NACA Bulletin*, Jan. 1, 1940.

Specthrie, Samuel W., *Industrial Accounting*, Prentice-Hall, Inc., Englewood Cliffs, N.J., 1959.

Tucker, Spencer A., *Cost Estimating and Pricing with Machine Hour Rates*, Prentice-Hall, Inc., Englewood Cliffs, N.J., 1962.

Tucker, Spencer A., *Successful Managerial Control by Ratio Analysis*, McGraw-Hill Book Company, New York, 1961.

CHAPTER EIGHT

Credit and Collections

STANLEY TULCHIN   *Stanley Tulchin Associates, New York, New York*

It has been said that credit is the lubricant that keeps the wheels of commerce turning. The extension of some form of credit has become such an integral and basic part of our economy that well over 90 percent of all business transactions, on all levels, are conducted on a credit basis.

Although there are many forms of credit, the underlying principles of all of them lie in determining if a promise to pay for goods or services rendered can be accepted as trustworthy, based on the information the one extending the credit has been able to obtain about the one requesting it.

Generally speaking, credit transactions can be broken down into the following two major classifications.

1. *Consumer credit*—deals with consumer purchases of merchandise or services. It is usually in the form of charge accounts, conditional sales contracts, installment sales, and includes consumer loans from various lending institutions to pay for purchases.

2. *Commercial credit*—is used for the purchase of goods, services, and supplies required in the manufacturing process or for purchases of inventory and supplies for the purpose of resale at the wholesale and retail level.

It is primarily with the second category, commercial credit, that this chapter will deal.

To facilitate terminology, we will refer to the credit grantor, who may be a manufacturer, wholesaler, jobber, bank, or commercial finance company or factor, as "creditor" and to the one who receives credit from these sources as the "account."

SOURCES OF CREDIT INFORMATION

To extend credit implies trust. Most trust is based either upon familiarity as a result of one's own prior experience or upon information obtained from other sources who have had experience. Whatever the source, however, getting basic information about the account is the first step in establishing a line of credit. This credit information can be obtained from several sources, the most common of which are:

1. Your own files and ledger cards
2. Credit reporting agencies
3. Other creditors and suppliers
4. Banks
5. Accountants
6. Trade organizations
7. Directly from potential account

Your Own Files and Ledger Cards. A good credit department will maintain accurate and up-to-date credit files. These files should be constantly updated and revised for changes in trend and condition of the account. Copies of all credit correspondence and collection letters should be retained, as well as copies of financial statements, agency reports, newspaper clippings, and all other pertinent data. Because the credit worthiness of an account is not a static, permanent condition, but varies with the rise and fall of the account's financial fortunes, these trends and all information about them should be a permanent part of a credit folder. Included in this category is information covering present indebtedness, prior experience, general manner of payment, high previous credit, and frequency of payment. In the final analysis, one's own experience with an account is one of the major factors to be considered when determining whether or not to extend or continue a line of credit.

Credit Reporting Agencies. Agencies such as Dun & Bradstreet or other specialized industrial agencies are a valuable source of information. They provide reports detailing the history and financial record of the account. It is essential to know the various agencies servicing each industry. Often the services of two or more agencies are required. A credit manager must determine what agencies will best provide him with the necessary information and avail himself of their services.

Other Creditors and Suppliers. It is frequently desirable to obtain experience information directly from other suppliers and vendors. The exchange of information among credit departments is one of the most important sources available to a credit man. It can, in fact, be considered as his stock in trade, for even the most astute credit analyst can base a decision only upon the information he has obtained. Knowing what information *to secure* and *where to obtain it is often the key to a proper credit decision.*

Banks. A great deal of information can be obtained from banks at which the potential account either maintains an account or has had other credit and financial transactions. The credit departments of most banks will cooperate in response to requests for information, and this source should not be overlooked when making a credit investigation. The length of time an account has been with the bank, his average balances, the way in which he has repaid his loans, if any, and other financial information are important details a bank can provide.

Accountants. Accountants are another major source of financial information and should be used as necessary during the course of a credit investigation. An accountant may be contacted either for general financial details or for an explanation and specific comments on details previously obtained. Most accountants will cooperate, recognizing that providing information will serve to the advantage of his client in securing a line of credit.

Trade Organizations. Almost every industry has a trade organization which will provide credit information, based on information supplied by its membership. Membership in the trade organization is often required. These organizations also have interchange groups which are a most valuable and prolific source of information. Joining these groups and participating in their discussions and meetings is an excellent means of not only obtaining information, but meeting other credit managers and keeping in touch with mutual industry problems and practices.

Direct Information from Potential Account. Often, particularly with new accounts or new businesses, it is extremely difficult to obtain sufficient information about a potential account from outside sources. A credit man must then resort directly to the account for information covering financial details, names of other suppliers, the name of the account's bank, the name of his accountant, and the like. Frequently, even after some information has been obtained from other sources, one must refer directly to the account for further explanation or comment and discussions regarding specific problems. Although direct contact with the account is a valuable source of information, one should remember that it is nonobjective. The information thus obtained should be able to be reconciled with other information obtained indirectly from other sources.

Most frequently, several or all of the above sources are used in the course of a credit investigation. The decision as to source of information must be based upon the type of information required and the credit manager's knowledge of where best to obtain it.

CATEGORIES OF CREDIT INFORMATION

The various kinds of information that can be obtained for use in determining a line of credit can be broken down into three main categories.

1. Antecedent information
2. Trade information
3. Financial information

Antecedent Information. The history and background of a business and its principals are revealing. The *integrity* and *honesty* of the account are two of the most important factors to be considered before extending credit. They can reflect not only a sincere desire to meet one's obligations, but also how much a financial statement or other information supplied by the potential account can be relied upon. The finest reference and financial statement are suspect if the account has dishonest intentions or a record of unreliability. Previous business affiliations, prior bankruptcies, records of suits and judgments, and the experience and general background of the principals, all comprise antecedent information and should help form a *complete picture* of the company and its owners. Watch for gaps or omissions in the chronological history of the owners or principals of the account. Ordinarily, the best sources for this type of information are the credit agencies which maintain files and can provide complete antecedent information.

Trade Information. Trade information consists of a record of recent payments to other suppliers that includes high credit, previous amounts owing, terms, amount past due, and general ledger experience. Trade information is often considered by many credit managers as the true test of the credit worthiness of an account. Although there are many reasons for slow payments, they should be considered as a symptom of some defect that must definitely be further investigated. Most accounts would prefer to pay their obligations promptly, and their inability to do so, more often than not, indicates the first sign of weakness. An explanation of the reason for this slowness should be obtained.

Financial Information. Financial information is often the most difficult to obtain and undoubtedly is the most difficult to analyze, because of the many factors that determine the financial strength or weakness of an account. It is impossible to explain in detail, in this chapter, all the complexities of financial statement analysis. (For a more detailed discussion, see Chapter 5 of Section 9.) The ability to understand and analyze the financial statement, however, marks the good credit manager.

In addition to understanding and being familiar with what constitutes a sound or poor financial picture, a credit manager must couple this information with his own thorough knowledge of the industry. What may be a good ratio of "merchandise inventory to sales" in one industry or type of business may be considered a poor ratio in another. In addition, the credit manager must be familiar not only with the general economic conditions in the country, but also with those of the area in which the account is located, as well as the conditions in the industry involved.

There is no absolute rule that can be stated to indicate what is a good or bad financial statement in all cases. Some basic ratios that should be considered and compared with the norm are the following:

1. Working capital
2. Liabilities to net worth
3. Merchandise to sales
4. Sales to net worth
5. Fixed assets to net worth
6. Cash and accounts receivable to liabilities
7. Merchandise to net worth
8. Gross profit to sales
9. Net profit to net worth
10. Net profit to sales

None of these ratios stands by itself; each must be looked upon as part of a composite picture. For example, what may appear as adequate working capital may be offset by the merchandise to sales ratio, indicating that a good part of the working capital is tied up in inventory that is not moving quickly enough. A credit manager, therefore, not only must be familiar with the accepted ratios for his industry and type of business, but must be astute enough to understand the relationships among ratios. A course in accounting, or various courses offered by organizations such as Dun & Bradstreet or the local office of the National Association of Credit Management in financial statement analysis, will serve a credit man to great advantage in learning to understand and analyze these relationships. These are, of course, not the only ratios that a credit manager should be concerned with, but they are the most common ones and will ordinarily provide a sufficient understanding of the financial affairs of the debtor.

Importance of Financial Trends. A credit manager must also take into consideration the trend of an account. A poor current financial statement when compared with an account's prior statement may indicate a definite improvement. Thus, an account showing an upward trend will probably be more worthy of credit than another account submitting the same financial statement, but indicating a downward trend. It is therefore necessary to reconcile *current financial* information with *previous financial* details and tie this in with the history of the company, the trade references obtained, one's own experience with the account, and the general antecedent background as to his integrity.

Other Influencing Factors. The actual decision on whether or not to approve a line of credit and for what amount depends upon more than just the plain, bare facts revealed by the information gathered. Aside from the worthiness of the potential account, there are often other important considerations that a credit manager must weigh. The financial condition and *credit policy of* *his own firm* are of primary importance. A general credit policy must be decided upon by management, and the credit manager must be fully aware of these decisions. Does management wish to carry slow-paying accounts, and if so, to what extent? How much in accounts receivable does management wish to carry and for what length of time? What is the *percentage of bad debt losses* a company can absorb, and what is the largest amount of credit it wishes to expose itself to for any one debtor? All of these questions and more must first be answered before a credit manager can make an intelligent decision.

Also to be considered is the nature of the merchandise or services being sold on open account. Is the item highly desirable and difficult to obtain, and can it be sold to top-rated credit accounts with little or no risk? If so, it may be preferable to deal only with top credit risks and turn down or limit a more marginal account, even though he, too, may be worthy of a line of credit. If the commodity is easily obtained and is highly competitive, or if it is not of a highly marketable nature, the credit manager may decide to approve a marginal account's order in an effort to move merchandise. The time of the year or season is also important.

The general financial condition of the creditor firm and the general economic condition of the industry and of the country as a whole are important factors in determining a line of credit. There is usually a more liberal attitude in so-called good times and a more conservative outlook in depressed times.

The matter of new products or new territories plays an important role. The firm looking to promote a new product or build a new territory will take greater credit risks. The capacity of a firm's manufacturing facilities is a consideration. Quite often, to keep manufacturing facilities working and finished products moving, greater risks must be taken by selling merchandise to accounts that ordinarily are less worthy of a line of credit.

Although each of the above points is not specifically considered by a credit manager for each order he receives, they are all, nevertheless, considered and become part of his experience and training and intuition. These considerations, coupled with general information about the credit seeker, add up to what can be called a "panoramic view" of the potential account and the effect that extending credit will have on the creditor firm. The management decisions involved in keeping the wheels of commerce turning through the judicious extension of credit justify the use of the term "credit executive."

COLLECTIONS

The theme running through any collection program may be best described by the key word "communication." As long as lines of communication are maintained with the account, the opportunity to collect will continue to exist. The prime cause of collection problems is a breakdown in communications. It is almost impossible to collect from the account whom the credit man is not reaching. Contact must constantly be reinforced whether it be by letter, telephone, or personal visit.

It is important that a collection cycle have continuity and be dramatic in its content. Continuity is hampered by the dictated letter. The dictated collection letter will never rank with the great correspondence of history, but it certainly increases the cost of operation. A collection cycle should be predetermined and available for general use. The routine should be "automated." This will reduce the number of accounts which require special attention. The time saved will be available for the largest credits, which always seem to be difficult and worrisome.

When does the account become a debtor in the eyes of the credit manager? Realistically, this change occurs when new merchandise will not be shipped until the old invoices are paid.

Whether or not the account is regarded as a debtor, the lines of communication should always be kept open. Here are a few suggestions that will aid in accomplishing this.

1. The account must feel that he is being treated fairly, but this does not mean that the credit manager should sacrifice firmness when the account is delinquent.

2. All payments should be acknowledged immediately, together with a request for the balance still due. This keeps up communications without waiting for the next monthly statement.

3. The manner in which an account is paid is generally important. Skipped invoices require special attention, for they may indicate a dispute. Immediate inquiry should be made with regard to such invoices. This issue should be isolated as promptly as possible while the evidence is fresh. For example, if delivery is in question, the proof should be established without delay.

4. Partial payment should not be applied to specific invoices, unless the account makes such application in his remittance.

5. In dealing with your accounts, whether by correspondence or conversation, it will be helpful to be direct and specific. This may be illustrated by the use of dates. If a period of time is specified for payment, it is best to mention an exact date. In this connection, as well as in other instances, promises and confirmation from customers should be in writing.

6. It is essential that all correspondence should be directed to an individual's attention, rather than to the "accounts payable" department.

When an account becomes seriously delinquent and dunning is undertaken as a deliberate course of action, a knowledge of the credit file can be critical. The credit information developed when the account was opened will facilitate the collection process. The legal status of the account is of prime importance— that is, whether the account is a corporation, partnership, or sole proprietorship.

When should an account be placed for collection? There is no magic moment for all cases. The decision requires a delicate exercise of discretion, and it should be based upon many factors. An account should be placed for collection when it appears that further communication with the debtor will be unproductive. Collection agencies do not expect to receive an account before the creditor has employed every effort to collect.

The collection agency should be employed as a tool, not as a crutch. A disputed claim will not be improved by placing it with an agency. It will remain disputed, if the dispute is genuine and not merely a sham to avoid payment.

In an expanding economy, credit problems develop and may at times appear to increase. New businesses are constantly trying to get on the band wagon. Many will not make it, although the economy is dynamic and healthy. Fortunately, an overwhelming number of accounts are honest and able to meet their obligations.

CONCLUSION

There is no easy answer to delinquency in credit, but an intelligent approach to collection along the paths charted above should reduce credit problems and permit acceptance, without fear, of the increased volume available in an expanding economy.

BIBLIOGRAPHY

Beckman, Theodore, *Credits and Collections: Management and Theory*, 7th ed., McGraw-Hill Book Company, New York, 1962.

Chapin, Albert F., *Credit and Collection, Principles and Practice*, 7th ed., McGraw-Hill Book Company, New York, 1960.

Ettinger, Richard P., and David Golieb, *Credits and Collections*, 5th ed., Prentice-Hall, Inc., Englewood Cliffs, N.J., 1962.

The Executives Credit & Collections Guide, Executive Reports Corporation, Prentice-Hall, Inc., Englewood Cliffs, N.J., 1965.

Rovelstad, E. A. (ed.), *Credit Manual of Commercial Laws*, National Association of Credit Management, 1965.

Schultz, William J., and Hedwig Reinhardt, *Credit and Collection Management*, 3d ed., Prentice-Hall, Inc., Englewood Cliffs, N.J., 1962.

CHAPTER NINE

The Audit

ALVIN PEDERSON *Partner, Arthur Anderson & Co., Philadelphia, Pennsylvania*

The audit, as discussed in this chapter, pertains to an examination of a company's financial statements by an independent auditor for the purpose of expressing his opinion on them. The audit, in this sense, may be broadly described as the process by which the auditor assures himself of the fairness of the financial statements, their conformity with generally accepted accounting principles, and the consistency with which the accounting principles have been applied from year to year.

The financial statements examined usually comprise the balance sheet at the company's fiscal year-end and the statements of income and retained earnings for the year then ended. Because of the financial community's emphasis on "cash flow," the statement of funds is also covered by the auditor's opinion for an increasing number of companies.

Although the auditor's opinion is usually addressed to a company's board of directors or to its stockholders, it carries a responsibility to all readers of the financial statements—in other words, to the public.

Auditor's Opinion. The independent auditor, through his professional association, the American Institute of Certified Public Accountants, has adopted a standard form of opinion which he uses in most situations where a complete audit has been made. The wording has been changed from time to time over the years. At this writing, it reads as follows:

We have examined the balance sheet of A Company as of December 31, 19—, and the related statements of income and retained earnings for the year then ended. Our examination was made in accordance with generally accepted auditing standards, and accordingly included such tests of the accounting records and such other auditing procedures as we considered necessary in the circumstances.

In our opinion, the accompanying balance sheet and statements of income and retained earnings present fairly the financial position of A Company as of December 31, 19—, and the results of its operations for the year then ended, in conformity with generally accepted accounting principles applied on a basis consistent with that of the preceding year.

The standard auditor's opinion is brief, but says much. It specifically identifies the financial statements covered, it states the basis on which the examination was made—in accordance with generally accepted auditing standards—and it closes with an expression of a three-part opinion. The opinion states that the financial statements (1) present fairly the financial position and results of operations, (2) in conformity with generally accepted accounting principles, and (3) on a basis consistent with that of the preceding year.

Auditing Standards. Various pronouncements have been made over the years by the American Institute of Certified Public Accountants with respect to the responsibilities and duties of the auditor in the examination of financial statements and the way in which opinions regarding these statements should be expressed.

As early as 1917, as a result of a memorandum by the Institute, the Federal Reserve Board published a pamphlet entitled "Uniform Accounting: A Tentative Proposal Submitted by the Federal Reserve Board." In 1918, this pamphlet was reissued under the same sponsorship, with practically no change from the 1917 issue, but with its title changed to "Approved Methods for the Preparation of Balance-sheet Statements." In 1929, the Federal Reserve Board published a revision of the work, which was called "Verification of Financial Statements" and contained the following significant statement:

. . . The extent of the verification will be determined by the condition in each concern. In some cases he [the auditor] may find it necessary to verify a substantial portion or all of the transactions recorded upon the books. In others where the system of internal check is good, tests only may suffice. The responsibility for the extent of the work required must be assumed by the auditor.

In 1936, a further revision was published by the Institute under the title "Examination of Financial Statements by Independent Public Accountants." The sequence of titles is indicative of the trend in thinking from "uniform accounting" to "verification" to "examination." Since that time, of course, the Institute has continued the development of auditing standards and procedures, mainly through the bulletins of its Committee on Auditing Procedure.

In accordance with the concepts outlined above, the Institute has adopted the following classifications of auditing standards: first, personal or general standards which require that "generally recognized normal auditing procedures" be applied with "professional competence by properly trained persons"; second, standards for the conduct of field work; and third, standards of reporting. These standards are quoted below inasmuch as they represent the broad framework within which the usual type of audit examination is conducted.[1]

General Standards
1. The examination is to be performed by a person or persons having adequate technical training and proficiency as an auditor.
2. In all matters relating to the assignment, an independence in mental attitude is to be maintained by the auditor or auditors.
3. Due professional care is to be exercised in the performance of the examination and the preparation of the report.
Standards of Field Work
1. The work is to be adequately planned and assistants, if any, are to be properly supervised.

[1] *Auditing Standards and Procedures*, Statements on Auditing Procedure, no. 33, issued by the Committee on Auditing Procedure of the American Institute of Certified Public Accountants, 1963.

2. There is to be a proper study and evaluation of the existing internal control as a basis for reliance thereon and for the determination of the resultant extent of the tests to which auditing procedures are to be restricted.

3. Sufficient competent evidential matter is to be obtained through inspection, observation, inquiries, and confirmations to afford a reasonable basis for an opinion regarding the financial statements under examination.

Standards of Reporting

1. The report shall state whether the financial statements are presented in accordance with generally accepted principles of accounting.

2. The report shall state whether such principles have been consistently observed in the current period in relation to the preceding period.

3. Informative disclosures in the financial statements are to be regarded as reasonably adequate unless otherwise stated in the report.

4. The report shall either contain an expression of opinion regarding the financial statements, taken as a whole, or an assertion to the effect that an opinion cannot be expressed. When an overall opinion cannot be expressed, the reasons therefor should be stated. In all cases where an auditor's name is associated with financial statements, the report should contain a clear-cut indication of the character of the auditor's examination, if any, and the degree of responsibility he is taking.

Although these auditing standards are subject to the individual interpretation of and the application by the auditor, the use of the terminology "in accordance with generally accepted auditing standards" in the auditor's opinion gives the reader assurance of the quality of the examination on which the opinion is based. It also connotes a limitation on the scope of the examination, inasmuch as generally accepted auditing standards do not prescribe a detailed audit of all transactions.

Many businessmen and others look upon the auditor's function as being performed primarily to disclose defalcations and other irregularities rather than for the purpose of expressing an overall opinion on financial statements. In view of this widespread but erroneous belief, the auditor may include in his arrangement letter with his client a statement to the effect that the examination is to be made in accordance with generally accepted auditing standards and that it will not include a detailed examination of the transactions for any period, such as would normally be required to disclose defalcations or other irregularities.

Auditing Procedures. "And accordingly included such tests of the accounting records and such other auditing procedures as we considered necessary in the circumstances," as used in the auditor's opinion, relates to the mechanics of performing the examination as opposed to the broader standards relating to the quality of the examination.

The principal procedures utilized by an auditor in examining a company's financial statements are:

1. Observation
2. Inspection
3. Confirmation
4. Comparison
5. Analysis
6. Computation
7. Inquiry

These procedures are normally applied on a test basis, by methods and to the extent deemed appropriate in light of the effectiveness of the company's accounting procedures and its system of internal control as discussed in more detail later. It is essential that the auditor have a general knowledge of the company's business, its products, and its operations adequately to comprehend its financial and accounting policies and procedures. This knowledge is also necessary for intelligent planning of the audit. To obtain this knowledge, the auditor must get behind the figures which are, after all, only a reflection of the activities, decisions, and economic events that have taken place with respect to a company. A continuing study of the overall aspects of a company's affairs is essential to the current examination, but beyond that, it is also a vital part of the knowledge that enables the auditor to render constructive service to a company over a period of years.

Observation.   The observations with which the auditor concerns himself primarily are the company's accounting procedures and internal controls, the physical inventories, and property, plant, and equipment.

The observation or review of the accounting procedures and internal controls is probably the one audit procedure with the most influential effect as far as the rest of the audit is concerned. Its primary purpose is to ascertain the effectiveness of the procedures and controls as a basis for establishing the scope of the entire examination. In other words, it determines the appropriate audit procedures to be followed and the extent to which they must be applied to satisfy the auditor. This review involves not only observation and direct inquiries of company personnel, but also a continuing awareness throughout the examination of how the company's accounting procedures and internal controls are actually functioning. The test checking of procedures is discussed further under "inspection."

A reminder of the basic tenets of good internal control would be appropriate here. The essence of an effective system of internal control is the segregation of duties in such a way that the persons who are responsible for the custody of assets and the conduct of operations have no part in the keeping of, and do not have access to, the records which establish accounting control over the assets and the operations. Duties of individuals should be so divided as to minimize the possibility of collusion, perpetration of irregularities, and falsification of the accounts.   The objective is to provide the maximum safeguards practicable in the circumstances, giving due consideration to the risks involved in the cost of maintaining the controls.

We talked earlier of observing physical inventories. One of the objectives in the audit of inventories is to determine that the amounts reflected in the company's books and records are represented by products, materials, and supplies on hand, in transit, in storage, or on consignment. The auditor satisfies this objective by the observation of the physical inventories and the subsequent tracing to the inventory listing of test counts made. The supervision and the actual counting of the physical inventories are the responsibility of the company. The auditor's responsibilities with respect to the physical inventories consist primarily in observing the procedures followed in counting and recording the quantities, and making appropriate tests to determine that the procedures are being properly followed and that an accurate inventory count is being obtained.

The auditor also observes or inspects, again on a test basis, property, plant, and equipment which are carried on a company's balance sheet. If random test observations of property items reflected in unit or other detailed property records check out satisfactorily, then only a limited number of items need be inspected. In the absence of adequate records, however, the auditor usually finds it necessary to inspect most major items and many smaller ones in connection with his first audit. In succeeding years, he confines his inspection tests primarily to additions.

Inspection.   Inspection involves the examination of company records, securities, supporting documents, and the like to determine ownership, apparent authenticity, adequacy of support, agreement of descriptions, quantities, and so on as recorded with supporting documents, proper approvals, propriety of nature of items, and the like.

The inspection procedure is used extensively in test-checking accounting procedures. It is one thing to be told what procedures have been prescribed by management, but another to know how they are actually functioning in day-to-day practice. By test-checking samples of transactions in key areas, the auditor can either satisfy himself with respect to certain accounts or expand the scope of his work until he can satisfy himself.

For example, three significant areas usually test-checked by the auditor are sales, cash disbursements, and payroll. Among other things, the sales test involves the inspection and comparison of the customer order or other sales order data, bill of lading or other shipping document, sales invoice, accounts receivable, and sales journal. The "block vouch" or cash disbursements test involves the inspection and comparison of vendors' invoices, expense reports, receiving reports, purchase orders, canceled checks, voucher register, or other distribution record. The payroll test involves the inspection and comparison of time cards, clock cards, employment and rate authorizations, authorizations for the various payroll withholdings, canceled checks, payroll register, and the like. The size of the "block" or period tested depends upon the company's accounting procedures and internal controls, the volume of transactions, and the extent to which these tests are to be relied upon in limiting other audit work. Sometimes, statistical sampling techniques are used in selecting the items to be tested; however, their use in auditing is still very limited.

Confirmation. Confirmation is probably the most widely known auditing procedure, because it involves parties outside of the company being audited. Confirmation requests, although addressed to the outside party by the company, are selected, controlled, mailed, and received by the auditor. There are basically two types of confirmation requests used—"positive" and "negative." Both types usually show the account balance per the company's books. The "positive" request, however, calls for a direct reply to the auditor, confirming the balance shown on the confirmation or reporting any differences or exceptions; the "negative" request provides that the auditor be notified only in the event the customer, or other outside party, does not agree with the amount shown on the confirmation request. As can readily be seen, "positive" requests provide more affirmative evidence of the authenticity of the accounts covered and therefore are used for large accounts or where internal controls are deficient. "Negative" requests are commonly used in the confirmation of large numbers of small accounts such as department store accounts receivable, and can be in the form of a sticker attached to regular monthly statements to customers.

Direct confirmations with outside parties are also used extensively for verifying bank accounts, notes receivable, consigned inventories, inventories or equipment at outside locations, prepaid insurance and insurance coverage, deposits, securities held in safekeeping, cash surrender value of life insurance, notes and other loans payable, accounts payable, and capital stock outstanding. Too, the auditor is usually furnished directly with a letter from the company's counsel setting forth information on litigation, if any, in which the company is involved, as well as the amount of any unpaid legal fees.

Comparison. The auditor uses the comparison procedure quite extensively in reviewing the current and prior year's account balances, operating statistics, forecasts, budgets, and the like. The objectives in making these comparisons are to disclose and determine reasons for significant variations.

Internal reports on sales volume, profit by product line, plant, or branch, and statistics on manufacturing and marketing unit costs, employment, and the like are examples of data that may be used to explain variations shown by comparisons made by the auditor. He may review and discuss matters with operating and financial personnel to reach informed and reasonable conclusions on the propriety of the accounts and the results of operations. The auditor also uses his general and specific business knowledge and outside industry information in making comparisons.

Among other things, the comparison procedure is helpful to the auditor in ascertaining the accuracy of the third part of his opinion—that accounting principles have been applied on a basis consistent with that of the preceding year.

Analysis. The auditor prepares or obtains analyses of accounts and of accounting and operating data to determine the credibility of descriptions and amounts reflected in the company's financial statements. The analysis procedure is used in many areas of the audit. For example, several analyses are used in connection with the audit of property, plant, and equipment.

An analysis is usually made of the various property, plant, and equipment accounts which shows beginning balances, additions, retirements, transfers, and year-end balances. Where additions to a particular account are significant, a further analysis is prepared showing the more important individual items acquired or constructed. This analysis usually shows the major cost elements of the addition, such as direct purchases, material, labor, and overhead, and is prepared in a manner to facilitate the test checking of selected items to supporting vendors' invoices, payroll records, and overhead allocation computations. The analysis should also show the amount appropriated or approved by the board of directors for the addition so that variations can be investigated. The depreciable lives assigned to property additions are reviewed for reasonableness and for compliance with company policy and income tax requirements. Retirements are analyzed and test-checked to supporting documents for propriety of recording. Analyses and comparisons are also made of repair and maintenance costs to determine that they have been properly expensed in accordance with sound accounting practices and company policy.

An analysis similar to that prepared for property, plant, and equipment is also prepared for the related reserves for depreciation; and individual transactions, where significant, are traced to supporting data.

Analysis techniques are also used in auditing a company's operations, in digging into and finding out why gross profits changed, the effect on net income of various important management policy decisions, and the like. This is a part of what is sometimes referred to as the "business approach" to auditing and can contribute greatly to an auditor's overall conclusions on the fairness of a company's financial statements.

Computation. Computation is the procedure envisioned by many as being the auditor's principal function. Although important, the making or checking of computations requires only a small amount of the auditor's time. Areas in which this procedure is most commonly applied include inventory listings, cost accumulations, depreciation on plant and equipment, various accrued expenses, income taxes, and interest. In many cases, the auditor will make overall computations or computations on bases different from those used by company personnel independently to check account balances and transactions.

Inquiry. Although many of the auditing procedures mentioned above include an element of inquiry, this procedure is of particular significance to the auditor in ferreting out important facts which are not disclosed in the accounts and records, such as commitments, contingent liabilities, or future plans. Commitments may be for additions to property, plant, and equipment; other material assets; or even to buy another company or sell the company being audited. Certain contingent liabilities are disclosed by confirmation work, such as notes discounted with a bank or lawsuits being handled by the company's counsel. There may be others, however, of which the auditor would learn only through specific inquiry of management. A threatened lawsuit, for example, may be significant. Future plans of a company are of particular importance to the auditor inasmuch as they can have a direct effect on the realization of certain assets and may include matters which should properly be disclosed to make the financial statements not misleading. If a company contemplates discontinuing or materially changing a product or a product line, it could raise some serious questions as to the realization of related inventories. It could also raise questions concerning the economic realization of certain property, plant, and equipment.

Audit Objectives. The above auditing procedures, although described separately, overlap extensively in their application. They are applied where and to the extent considered necessary for the auditor to satisfy certain basic audit objectives. For example, with respect to the principal captions in a set of financial statements, the auditor must satisfy himself as to the following.

Cash

1. The cash balances as stated in the balance sheet properly represent cash and cash items on hand, in transit, or in banks.

2. The cash is properly classified in the financial statements and adequate disclosure (by segregation or otherwise) is made of restricted or committed funds and of cash not subject to immediate withdrawal (time deposits, foreign currencies).

Receivables

1. The amounts shown represent bona fide receivables of the company.

2. The receivables are properly classified.

3. Reserves have been provided for losses on uncollectible receivables and for discounts and freight allowable, returns, adjustments, and the like, and whether these reserves are adequate.

4. Any receivables which have been pledged, discounted, assigned, or sold are properly disclosed.

Inventories

1. The quantities properly represent products, materials, and supplies on hand, in transit, in storage, or on consignment that belong to the company.

2. The items are priced in accordance with generally accepted accounting principles consistently applied, at the lower of cost or market.

3. The inventory listings are accurately compiled, extended, footed, and summarized, and the totals are properly recorded in the accounts.

4. Excess, slow-moving, obsolete, and defective items are reduced to net realizable values.

5. Any liens from the pledging or assignment of inventories are appropriately disclosed in the financial statements or footnotes.

6. The ending inventories are determined as to quantities, prices, computations, excess stocks, and the like, on a basis consistent with the inventories at the end of the preceding year.

Investments

1. The physical evidences of the ownership of investments (stock certificates, bonds, notes, mortgage indentures, deeds, joint-venture agreements, insurance policies, and so on) are on hand or held in custody or safekeeping by others for account of the company.

2. The basis on which the investments are stated is in accordance with generally accepted accounting principles, consistently applied.

3. Income from investments has been accounted for properly.

4. Investments and the related income are properly classified and described in the financial statements.

5. Adequate disclosure has been made of the pledging or hypothecation of any investments.

Property, Plant, and Equipment

1. The basis upon which the property accounts are stated is proper, conforms with generally accepted accounting principles, and has been consistently followed with respect to major categories of property which remain in service.

2. The additions during the period under audit are proper capital charges and represent actual physical property installed or constructed; and, conversely, whether material items which should have been capitalized have been charged to maintenance or other expense accounts.

3. The costs and related depreciation reserves applicable to all retirements, abandonments, and property no longer in service, of material amount, have been properly removed from the accounts.

4. Depreciation charged to income during the period is adequate but not excessive, and has been computed on an acceptable basis consistent with that used in prior periods.

5. The balances in depreciation reserve accounts are reasonable, considering the expected useful lives of the property units and possible net salvage values.

6. All significant liens on property are properly reflected or disclosed in the financial statements.

Prepayments, Deferred Charges, and Intangible Assets

1. The balances represent proper charges against future operations and can reasonably be expected to be realized through future operations or otherwise.

2. The additions during the audit period are proper charges to these accounts and represent actual cost.

3. Amortization or write-offs against revenues in the current period and to date are reasonable under the circumstances and have been computed on an acceptable basis consistent with that used in prior periods.

4. The items have been properly classified and disclosed in the financial statements, giving consideration to the relative materiality of the amounts involved.

Liabilities

1. All significant liabilities existing or incurred as of the balance sheet date are reflected in the statements at the proper amounts.

2. Liabilities are properly described and classified.

3. Adequate disclosure is made of:

    a. The pledge or mortgage of assets as collateral against loans or other obligations

    b. Subordination agreements and, where important to an understanding of financial position, guarantees of company obligations by third parties such as officers or stockholders

    c. Significant contingent liabilities, such as pending or threatened litigation, possible assessments of additional taxes, government claims for renegotiation refunds, guarantees of indebtedness of others, and agreements to repurchase receivables that have been sold

    d. Significant commitments such as those for plant acquisitions, long-term leases, unused letters of credit, or unfunded past-service costs on pension plans, or agreements in connection with borrowings to maintain working capital, restrict dividends, or reduce debts

    e. Significant or unusual liabilities incurred after the balance sheet date

Capital Stock and Surplus

1. The amounts shown in the balance sheet as capital stock and surplus are properly classified, described, and stated in accordance with generally accepted

accounting principles and are not in conflict with the requirements of the corporate charter (or articles of incorporation) or with the applicable statutes of the state of incorporation.

2. Transactions in the capital stock and surplus accounts during the audit period (and since inception, in the initial audit) are properly authorized or approved (by the appropriate corporate or legal authority) where necessary and are recorded in the accounts in accordance with generally accepted accounting principles.

3. Adequate disclosure has been made in the financial statements of surplus restrictions, stock subscription rights, stock reservations, stock options, stock repurchase plans, or obligations, and the like, which may be imposed by various authorizations or agreements or by legal requirements of the state of incorporation; also such matters as preferred dividends in arrears, voting rights in event of preferred dividend arrearages, and liquidation preferences.

Revenues, Costs, and Expenses

1. Reported revenues, costs, and expenses are properly applicable to the accounting period under examination.

2. Costs and expenses are properly matched with revenues.

3. Recognition has been given to revenues, costs, and expenses (including losses) which should be so recognized.

4. Appropriate treatment has been given to any material tax reductions or additions resulting from transactions not reflected in the income statement.

5. All material transactions of a nonoperating or extraneous nature have been excluded from net income or otherwise appropriately treated.

6. Revenues, costs, and expenses are appropriately classified and described in the statement of income.

7. The income statement fairly presents the results of operation and was prepared in conformity with generally accepted accounting principles consistently applied.

Generally Accepted Accounting Principles. Repeated references have been made to "generally accepted accounting principles" as used in the auditor's opinion, so perhaps it would be well to comment on the significance of this phrase. The words first came into general use in the early 1930s, but the principles to which they refer have been subject to much discussion and change over the years. Unfortunately, generally accepted accounting principles do not possess the degree of preciseness or finality usually accorded them by most readers of financial statements. Rather, they are a somewhat loosely organized set of principles which have been developed through usage, and many have gained "acceptance" even though there may be sounder alternative principles. The result is that it is possible to have two financial statements covering the same set of facts, each in conformity with generally accepted accounting principles, but with materially different results. There are two schools of thought among professional accountants on this subject. There are those who advocate the formulation of accounting principles on more objective bases with the concurrent elimination of alternative principles to achieve greater uniformity in financial reporting. Others advocate continued flexibility so that individual companies may have some choice in the accounting principles they wish to apply in their own reports.

The auditor usually has a preference as to which generally accepted accounting principle should be applied in a given situation, but he also may discuss the pros and cons of alternative principles. This is desirable so that a company is in a position to decide for itself, on the basis of the facts and the reasoning supporting each acceptable alternative, which of two or more principles should be applied to its financial statements.

The American Institute of Certified Public Accountants has stepped up its efforts in the whole area of accounting principles. An Accounting Principles Board was established in 1959 and a number of research studies on various accounting subjects have been authorized. Several have been completed, including an *Inventory of Generally Accepted Accounting Principles for Business Enterprises* which was published in 1965. This latter accounting research study (no. 7) contains much valuable information on the whole matter of generally accepted accounting principles.

Consistency. Although there are alternative generally accepted accounting principles which can be applied to a situation or a set of facts, a change as between years requires disclosure in the financial statements and in the auditor's opinion. The phrase "applied on a basis consistent with that of the preceding year" in the standard form of opinion assures the reader that differences in financial statements between years are attributable to differences in amounts or facts and not to differences in accounting principles, practices, or methods.

Qualified Opinions. If an auditor is unable to satisfy himself with respect to an important item in the financial statements or a disclosure matter such as a contingent liability, or if he does not agree with something pertaining to the financial statements, then he is obliged to "qualify" his opinion. A qualification may take several forms, depending upon the facts requiring it, but it must be clear and informative to the reader. This whole subject is covered at length in *Auditing Standards and Procedures,* Statements on Auditing Procedure, no. 33, issued by the Committee on Auditing Procedure of the American Institute of Certified Public Accountants in 1963.

Helping the Auditor. An auditor's fees are normally based on regular per diem rates which vary by individuals on the basis of competence and experience. Inasmuch as the auditor must assign adequately qualified personnel to perform an audit, the only element of cost which can be somewhat influenced by the company being audited is the time spent. Good business, therefore, calls for cooperation and assistance from company personnel. Management should cooperate fully with the auditor, and other employees should be instructed to do likewise.

More specifically, cooperation and assistance can be accomplished by making information readily available, by preparing various trial balances, working paper schedules, confirmation letters, and the like required by the auditor, and by coordinating internal audit work with that being done by the outside auditor. A more effective audit can be performed if it is done in at least two visits to the company's premises. Preliminary work, which involves planning, reviewing policies, procedures, and controls, doing detailed tests, and the like, can be done prior to the year-end at a mutually convenient time when neither the auditor nor the company's accounting personnel are working under pressure. This preliminary work can greatly reduce the pressure which usually occurs during final work following the year-end.

Who Needs an Audit? With minor exceptions, publicly held companies are required by the Securities and Exchange Commission to have an annual audit. Some companies may be required to do so by banks, insurance companies, or other creditors. Whether or not an audit is specifically required, it may be good business to have an annual audit, and many companies follow this practice as a matter of course. Because the Securities and Exchange Commission requires audited statements of income for three years in connection with a public stock offering, any company contemplating "going public" must arrange for annual audits. Audited financial statements can also be very helpful in connection with possible acquisition, merger, or sale negotiations. Absentee owners of closely held companies look upon the annual audit as an objective evaluation of the management's stewardship.

Extra Benefits from an Audit. Although the auditor, in connection with an examination of a company's financial statements, is primarily concerned with satisfying himself to the extent necessary to express an opinion on them, he also can be helpful in other ways. During the course of his audit work, he may develop helpful comments and suggestions on business matters generally, on improving the effectiveness and the efficiency of policies, procedures, and controls, and on tax deferment and savings ideas. These comments and suggestions are usually discussed with management, after which they are submitted in memorandum form for future use. Through his educational background, his research and study, and through his experiences in many companies, the auditor is well qualified to be helpful in many areas of a business. The auditor can usually be most helpful and a company can usually receive the most benefit if they maintain frequent contacts throughout the year.

SUMMARY

The audit is an independent examination, by means and to the extent determined by the auditor, of a company's financial statements for the purpose of his rendering an opinion on them. Financial statements are the primary responsibility of the company being reported on, and the auditor's responsibility is a secondary one involving the expression of an independent opinion thereon. The auditor must have substantive support for his opinion for it to be meaningful; therefore, he is required to follow certain prescribed professional standards in performing his examination. An appreciation of these standards, the auditing procedures utilized, and the objectives sought in an audit is helpful in achieving the most constructive results from the auditor-client relationship.

BIBLIOGRAPHY

Auditing Standards and Procedures, Statements on Auditing Procedure, no. 33, American Institute of Certified Public Accountants, New York, 1963.

Blough, Carman G., *Practical Applications of Accounting Standards; A Decade of Comment on Accounting and Auditing Problems,* American Institute of Certified Public Accountants, New York, 1957.

Carey, John L., *The CPA Plans for the Future,* American Institute of Certified Public Accountants, New York, 1965.

Edwards, James Don, *History of Public Accounting in the United States,* Graduate School of Business Administration, Bureau of Business and Economic Research, Michigan State University, East Lansing, 1960.

Grady, Paul, *Inventory of Generally Accepted Accounting Principles for Business Enterprises,* Accounting Research Study, no. 7, American Institute of Certified Public Accountants, New York, 1965.

Holmes, Arthur Wellington, *Basic Auditing Principles,* Richard D. Irwin, Inc., Homewood, Ill., 1957.

Lenhart, Norman J., and Philip L. Defliese, *Montgomery's Auditing,* 8th ed., The Ronald Press Company, New York, 1957.

Mautz, R. K., and Hussein A. Sharaf, *Philosophy of Auditing,* American Accounting Association, Madison, Wis., 1961.

Stetler, Howard F., *Auditing Principles: Objectives, Procedures, Working Papers,* Prentice-Hall, Inc., Englewood Cliffs, N.J., 1956.

Wixon, Rufus (ed.), *Accountants' Handbook,* 4th ed., The Ronald Press Company, New York, 1961.

MANAGEMENT OF HUMAN RESOURCES

CHAPTER ONE

Management and the Behavioral Sciences

ROBERT C. SAMPSON *Sampson Associates, Chicago, Illinois*

If you are concerned with achieving the greatest productivity *over the long pull,* drawing on the ideas of your employees, and securing changes with the minimum of resistance, you should use the behavioral sciences findings and concepts in your managing. *If* you can come to respect the dignity of your subordinates in a genuine, open, trusting fashion, and *if* you work in a system where you are given the same dignity by your superior, you and your people will be on the way to using the findings naturally, informally, and easily.

Applying the behavioral sciences in management is not too involved or difficult if you can let your people achieve their dignity (1) in the work itself, (2) as subordinates, (3) in participating in the decision-making process, and (4) in working together. Your managing becomes essentially that of helping those of your subordinates who *can and will* do the things they can best do. You rely on the internal drive of your people in their motivation to find themselves in work. You base your actions, however, on the way individuals in fact behave, feel, want, and change, not on how you want them to behave or how you think they should behave.

Therefore, you should secure a first-order knowledge of the behavioral sciences so that you come to understand the range of human needs, capacities, and emotions, both normal and neurotic, that you can expect to find in yourself and others. In the stress of working relations, you should have skills in how to evaluate and deal safely with feelings so they will not be harmful to either you or others. You should also have help from competent staff people to assist you in dealing with the ever-increasing tensions of emotionally disturbed people and to integrate and translate the more complex aspects of behavioral sciences findings for you. Whether it is called "emotional" or "mental" health, you can no longer avoid being responsible for the well-being of your people. Unless they stay well, they cannot remain productive, continue to grow, and generate ideas.

Start with the elemental fact that the behavioral sciences in the main are antiauthority oriented because of the misuse and abuse of power. Securing the necessary dignity for the common man in all phases of his life is the *raison d'être* for the behavioral sciences. That the behavioral sciences are peculiarly an American advance should not be surprising. The people who came here were, for the most part, the powerless—the refugees, the outcasts, and the rebels—of other countries. With the recent concern about the work world and the dignity of common man, the behavioral sciences have come finally to one of man's most important needs in life, work, and have also found that the more a subordinate can exercise his powers, the greater will be his satisfactions and productivity.

THE CONTINUING REVOLUTION IN MANAGEMENT

Just as F. W. Taylor and his followers made a breakthrough in management, we are again in a period of a new breakthrough, the behavioral sciences. In this chapter, we shall look briefly at:

1. The continuing revolution in management
2. What the behavioral sciences are
3. What you can put to work
4. Where you can get help

F. W. Taylor started the "scientific management" revolution late in the nineteenth century. His basic contribution, time study, was appropriate to its era. Today we face a diversity of conflicting theories and principles not only in time study but also in "scientific management." At the time of Taylor's death in 1915, the behavioral sciences were more philosophical than scientific disciplines known then and now in the academic world as "social sciences." Almost everyone subscribed to the puritan work ethic that man was expected to work hard without enjoyment, for money.[1] Yet Taylor, when testifying in Congress, had shown his own scientific orientation: "There is another type of scientific investigation which should receive special attention, namely, the accurate study of the motives which influence men."[2]

Unscientific, Pseudoscientific, and Scientific. You should be alert to the differences in the scientific method as opposed to the unscientific and pseudoscientific. They provide guides for your evaluating what you read and hear about management.

Unscientific management is the most common and easiest to identify. Anyone who says in sense, "I say, therefore it is," may be wise and profound. Still, his statements are really personal opinion. Recall how many books and articles on management you have read without footnotes, references to authorities, and findings about people at work.

Pseudoscientific management is the tricky one to spot, for it has the aura of the scientific: a technical vocabulary, lists of principles, a methodology, and authorities. But it is a closed system, resistant to change. It uses one-sided observations, if any, usually on what management is doing. For example, time-study claims generally ignore the effects on and behavior of people, though these have been well documented by William F. Whyte.[3]

Scientific management must be an open, ever-changing system if it is to be genuinely scientific, accepting the behavioral sciences research evidences, experiments, and knowledge about people.

[1] Robert C. Sampson, *Managing the Managers*, McGraw-Hill Book Company, New York, 1965, pp. 110–114.

[2] F. W. Taylor, *Scientific Management*, Harper & Row, Publishers, Incorporated, New York, 1947, p. 26.

[3] William F. Whyte, *Money and Motivation*, Harper & Row, Publishers, Incorporated, New York, 1955.

Two Management Systems. Today there are essentially two basic systems of management: the management engineering system, started by Taylor, and the management behavioral system. The main difference between them is their concept of how people should be managed. Those who cannot fully accept the management behavioral system—and there are many who cannot—try to incorporate "pieces" into the management engineering system. With their unilateral concept of power, they give an ingenious power twist to behavioral sciences ideas. Human relations becomes paternalism. Motivating becomes manipulating. Communications becomes convincing. Counseling becomes appraising. Coaching becomes telling. Leadership becomes bossing. Cooperation becomes conformity. Loyalty becomes personal devotion.

Under the tyranny of techniques, everything must be formalized into a procedure or a practice. People, both managers and workers, are increasingly transformed into things to be controlled, used, and manipulated. Man is forced to respond in unnatural ways as an automaton, not as a whole person, spurred by incentive and stress, euphemistically termed the "carrot-stick motivation." Feelings of frustration, alienation, anxiety, and insecurity become imprisoned within a man, eating away at his interests, values, drives, and emotional health.

The management behavioral system is primarily concerned with the human use of human beings: the giving *of* oneself to the organization and work, rather than giving *up* oneself. A man should never be put in a position of trying to change his behavior to suit another's ideas of what he should be. That is manipulation for conformity and the loss of self-dignity. One should change as the result of becoming more aware of oneself and more accepting of others. The system accepts all of the behavior of people, both formal and informal, in a cooperative but autocratic organization structure with effective utilization of people through their own self-actualization in work. The behavioral sciences findings are so diametrically opposed to present management beliefs that many people view them as heresies. For example, can you accept the fact that you prefer to change the minds of others rather than your own?

Moreover, managers who expect immediate and certain results with detailed how-to steps are doomed to disappointment. There are no pat procedures or tricky techniques. There are no quick and easy solutions. At best, the behavioral sciences deal with the most complex, unstable, inflexible, unpredictable material—people. Predictions in this area, having less certainty than those of the physician or the weather forecaster, are little more than prophecies. The management behavioral system is an open way of life. The particular situation, the people, and their relationships are paramount. The order of everything may well have to be changed, especially a manager's behavior. Changes, at best, are very slow and require experimentation.

Finally, knowledge in the behavioral sciences is exploding to the point that it is now leaving the realm of the manager. Therefore, we cannot expect management people to gain more than a general *first-order* knowledge and skills in the behavioral sciences. Increasingly, managers must be able to draw on competent staff people, behavioral sciences practitioners, who need to acquire a *second-order* knowledge not only for translation and integration of the findings but for assistance in the application of the findings. We must look to behavioral scientists, the academicians and researchers, who possess a *third order* of knowledge, each with his own specialized point of view, vocabulary, and methodology.[4]

[4] That behavioral scientists cannot agree with each other should not be surprising. Dr. Ian Stevenson has traced the resistance of both natural and behavioral scientists to findings of others in "Scientists with Half-closed Minds," *Harper's Magazine,* November, 1958, pp. 66–71.

THE PROPER STUDY OF MAN

The behavioral sciences cover six basic fields: anthropology, political science, economics, sociology, psychiatry, and psychology. In their most elemental sense, the behavioral sciences are concerned with the study of (1) human values, or what people want and need; (2) human behavior, or how they act and why; (3) their institutions, or what people get; and (4) their power structure, or the nature of power and how it is used. The concern about man is based on disciplined methods of systematic inquiry into what people are like as conditioned by their family, school, church, and society, and what happens to them as the result of their adult experiences in institutions such as work, government, and membership in a variety of informal organizations. Replacing common sense, casual observation, philosophy, magic, and religion, the behavioral sciences do not use the same "eternals" of truth and law.

The behavioral sciences all deal with data of essentially the same order—the exercise of man's powers—but the central tendencies of each field are different. Psychiatry and psychology are concerned with the individual as a unique person, his maturation, feelings, motivations, perceptions, behavior, and his problems with himself. Anthropology and sociology focus on the individual as a member of various groups: sociology with organization behavior and anthropology with cultures of both man and his origins. Economics and political science concentrate on the individual as a provider in the behavioral aspects of economics and as a "political animal."

Anthropology. Darwin, a biologist, in 1859 with his *Origin of the Species* shocked our puritanical fundamentalist culture with the theory of the evolution of man. Now there is disagreement among the physical anthropologists on the evolution of man. Evolution may no longer be a straight-line affair, for fossil discoveries in East Africa over the last few years may indicate that there were at least three types of manlike creatures living side by side a million years ago. One of the three types survived to produce modern man.

Through cultural anthropology, we learn that man's significantly human traits are essentially the same for all varieties of man. Although "survival of the fittest" is still a popular concept in business, and unfortunately, within the corporate family, anthropologists appear to agree generally that man does not have to control his alleged innate aggressiveness by imposing on it a cooperative way of life of his own invention. Our racial differences have nothing to do with our cultural differences, which are "socially" rather than genetically inherited. Knowing that the individual is a product of his culture is the first step to a genuine understanding of man:

1. Cultures prove the essential illogical nature of man. Take the paradox of our culture. We stress our spiritual devotion. Yet, we develop the most materialistic culture in the world.

2. The personal drive to achieve is not universal. Some cultures, such as ours, are more achievement oriented than others.

3. There is conflict in cooperation. Primate research suggests that our prehuman ancestors were nonviolent fruit-eating individualists. Apparently, in being forced out of their forest Garden of Eden onto the plains, they organized for mutual survival.

4. That we are evolving culturally at grossly differing rates in this world is well documented by some simple estimates. One-half of the people in the world are growing up illiterate. One-half never have a square meal. Four-fifths never see a physician. Half of the people marry without love.

Political Science. The nature and function of the governing of men and of public administration are two fields in political science. Governing of men may be divided into basic styles, democracy and autocracy. In democracy, the people share in the activities of the state; in an autocracy, the people are ruled by self-appointed kings or dictators. In the push for the dignity of common man in the United States, he was first allowed to vote in the present electoral system in 1824. Women secured this privilege in 1920.

In corporations, membership organizations, and cooperatives, there are both democratic and autocratic management. Democracy is essentially the means for members or owners to exercise their right to control their institutions for their own best ends. The democratic process becomes autocratic when the board directs the top management man to carry out its democratically determined policies.

In management, therefore, we should drop the *democratic mystique*. Employees are not governing themselves; they are working. They cannot practice democracy and elect their manager, because the organization is not being run for their benefit, but for the benefit of some other group.

In public administration, government agencies follow essentially the same practices as business organizations in administration. However, government agencies appear to be no further along than business in the use of the behavioral sciences in management. The Federal government, however, is undoubtedly supporting more behavioral sciences research in management than is industry.

Economics. Economics, with its concern with the financial system, production, and marketing, is also the base of schools of business administration. That business schools are having difficulty in (1) defining their function, (2) offering a synthesis instead of a collection of courses, (3) securing quality faculty, and (4) attracting superior students is well documented elsewhere. To these difficulties we would add (5) accepting and integrating the behavioral sciences in their courses.

That the behavioral sciences are the "inexact sciences" is well illustrated by economics.[5] After years of the economics of scarcity, economists are having a rough time developing new theories to cope with our material abundance. Although our first case of abundance through technology, farming, is now several years old, they cannot agree on a solution to the problem.

Not many economists today accept the idea of an "economic man" who works for money alone. Heilbroner points out that, "Not only is the notion of gain for gain's sake foreign to a large portion of the world's population today, but it has been conspicuous by its absence over most of recorded history."[6]

We should distinguish between the basic forms of government, autocracy and democracy, and the basic forms of business ownership. Private ownership of business is still capitalism. Public ownership of industry is socialism if the move toward state ownership is gradual, communism if the move is through revolution. There is no purely capitalistic economic system, for such things as our public schools and postal service are socialistic endeavors. Today, our welfare state provides for the care not only of people, which many erroneously want to call "socialism," but also of various businesses through subsidy. It is difficult to find an industry that has not been subsidized by the government either directly or indirectly. The increasing interdependence of industry and

[5] Robert L. Heilbroner aptly calls the ten key economists, starting with Adam Smith at about 1775, the "worldly philosophers." See his *The Worldly Philosophers*, Simon and Schuster, Inc., New York, 1953.
[6] *Ibid.*, p. 15.

government is now forcing management and government to work out a new set of relationships. The "arm's length" attitude of business is being replaced by cooperation with government in its enlarged role in our economy and the world. Or, is there a new growth of power among big military, big government, and big business?[7]

Sociology. From the efforts of social reformers, sociology has come to focus on organizational behavior. Sociology is more concerned with the use and abuse of organization power in man's relation to man than any of the other behavioral sciences. Sociology is also the foundation theory for the social worker who counsels with families in helping them to solve their problems. Sociological studies of work started with Roethlisberger and Mayo in the classic Hawthorne experiment of the 1920s, which stressed the importance of membership in small groups and participation in decisions.

Emerson, the poet and philosopher, not only stubbornly pushed for the worth of the individual, but also made the observation that an institution is but the lengthened shadow of the man who heads it. With some modification, sociology has gone on to prove this through professional observation. Today we find that every manager, in some degree, establishes *his own lengthened shadow* for his immediate subordinates.

Sociology also contributes to our understanding of the dimensions of an organization. The informal organization might well be called the feeling or sentient organization, for it is here that a man secures the outlet for his group needs. Individuals form their own associations within the organization power structure.

Psychiatry. Freud made his great breakthrough for psychiatry at about the time of Taylor by demonstrating that man was driven by unconscious forces. Psychoanalytical theory, stemming from medicine, was the first approach to the total personality. Freud is reputed to have said that in the Western culture (anthropology again) man must love and work. Psychiatry is primarily concerned with the treatment of emotional ill health (some call it "mental" ill health) stemming from the "unfinished business" of childhood. People are at the mercy of their dated emotions.

The psychoanalyst, through nondirective counseling, helps a person to resolve his problems by enabling him to make his unconscious material conscious: free association by the individual on the couch for at least 200 hourly sessions. The greatest number of analysts are also physicians. Some are lay persons with or without psychological training. The "nonanalytic" psychiatrists, generally referred to as "psychiatrists," use different forms of therapy, such as shock treatment, drug therapy, hypnosis, and psychotherapy for conscious material.

Freud put quotation marks around the word "normal." Although the normal person has his problems, he is free of mental and physical symptoms of anxiety. Many "normal" people, however, have some neurotic behavior patterns such as smoking, drinking, and gambling. The neurotic person has lost communication with himself and therefore cannot communicate effectively with others.

Psychology. Although psychology is basically the study of the mind, there is no general agreement as to what the mind is, how it works, or how it learns. Still, we have learned much through systematic observation that disproves familiar beliefs about human motivation and behavior. Take your own case. Here are a few psychological facts about you:

You want to achieve—a higher need for you than for the other animals and many Homo sapiens in the world.

---

[7] For a sociologist's version, see C. Wright Mills, *The Power Elite*, Oxford University Press, Fairlawn, N.J., 1956.

You deceive yourself—you tend to avoid the reality of yourself, your existence, your work, and the world.

You hide your real feelings from others—you are afraid to be open with others.

You think that by avoiding conflict with others, it will go away—when all that it does is stay there and fester until you face it and resolve it.

You want easy and quick answers to difficult matters—even though no one has ever been able to produce them.

You tend to set unreasonable goals and standards for yourself and others—and then lose all sense of proportion when you or they fail to measure up.

Psychology has generally been concerned with observation and study of isolated phenomena. Industrial psychology is essentially an "engineering" approach, and clinical psychology, as its name implies, is essentially a "treatment" approach. Industrial psychology, primarily concerned with testing and "measurement" of various human traits, appears to be still suffering from its early but now rejected position: "If you cannot measure it, it is not there." Tests do not cover more than 30 percent of all the known qualities of an individual. They are still in the realm of prophecy, not prediction, about success. When we ask whether the success is related to immediate, intermediate, or long-term job success, we get into muddy waters. Some clinical psychologists evaluate people for management and counsel with them too. This double approach raises an interesting question about how much counseling there is when a person feels that whatever he says may be used in evaluating him for management.

HUMAN USE OF HUMAN BEINGS

Your managing is based on five interdependent processes: (1) managing yourself, (2) organizing and selecting, (3) individual coaching, (4) group coaching, and (5) using staff counsel. In applying the behavioral sciences, you can use much of what is covered in this Handbook, after you have evaluated it, in two ways. First, the technique must be acceptable to your people and adapted to your situation by them in terms of the basic needs of your operations. Second, the technique should lead to increasing the dignity and work satisfaction of the people as well as your own.

Admittedly, any changeover to using the behavioral sciences will be gradual, uncertain, and at times frustrating. You do not have the false security of a program to apply. In your situation, you may well find that the present ways of thinking and working are so deeply entrenched that, as students of anthropology know, they have become rigid cultural patterns. The relationships of the individuals may be so fixed, as students of sociology know, that individuals may perpetuate them against almost any odds. The behavior of individuals may be so molded by personal habit or so compulsive from chronic anxiety, as students of psychiatry know, that individuals must repeat them over and over even though they serve no useful purpose.

Finally, it will be difficult to apply much of the behavioral sciences in your managing (1) if your boss has not given you much freedom and you have little influence with him; (2) if your operations have so much invested in the hardware of production and are so far along on the simplification of jobs that people are used as automatons; and (3) if the system of management in which you find yourself is essentially a management engineering system and you are primarily a pawn who is expected to put pressure on your people to produce.

Your Personal Style. There is no "one best way" to manage. This is the basic lesson of the behavioral sciences research. Each manager organizes and manages according to his way of behaving. Even under the most rigid management rules, individual managers will selectively interpret and adapt to meet their most natural, which in some cases may be neurotic, ways of behaving. The best case in point is the many ways the Office of the President and his White House office have been organized and managed.

There are, however, some guides for your consideration. The key to your managing is planning, with all that it implies, especially your planning for yourself. How do you look at the future? It is axiomatic that you can concentrate effectively on only a few major aspects of all the things you might do. Do you plan your day, or does your day (correspondence and telephone calls) dictate your activities? When your *self-perception* generates feelings of inadequacy and concern as to how others feel, you are bound to have reservations about an open and freewheeling organization. You may well give priority to your own work, keeping needless detail, routine, and controls to be sure things are going right.

However, if you work at your proper level, you will enlarge positions under you which not only take much off your shoulders, but provide enough freedom and responsibility to attract and keep superior people. You should raise your sights above the operations of your unit. As the result of an analysis of the various work episodes of eight management people over a two-week period, Robert Dubin and S. Lee Spray found that verbal face-to-face communications, with a few exceptions, range from one-third to almost two-thirds of their time with subordinates and one-fifth to three-fifths of their "internal time interaction" with peers. The greatest variation in time is with a superior. They stress that with the amount of time that is spent with peers, "there can be absolutely no question of the need for substantial revision in organization theory."[8]

Organizing. The key to organizing is a clear understanding of work. Work is potentially the greatest source for self-realization and self-fulfillment. Job enlargement, about which we have heard so much for many years, is the clue to genuine satisfaction in work. Its best example, which has been reported on by a variety of magazines,[9] is the pioneering approach of Non-Linear Systems, Inc., in San Diego, California. Jobs have been enlarged to the point where a group of six or seven workers and technicians assemble as they decide complex electronic instrumentation and test systems.

After weighing evidence from many sources on how to organize, I can think of only one firm principle which a manager should follow in organizing to suit his personal style: A man should have only one boss. No man can adequately and comfortably serve two masters. One boss also provides for the clear and unequivocal ordering of authority of an organization. Beyond this principle, a manager might use these organization guides:

1. The organization structure should be open and flexible.
2. Administrative units should be self-sufficient.
3. Levels of supervision should be kept to a minimum.
4. Specialized activities should be kept to a minimum.
5. Jobs should be adapted to people.
6. Self-coordination should be built in.
7. Policies should serve only as guides.

---

[8] Robert Dubin and S. Lee Spray, "Executive Behavior and Interaction," *Industrial Relations,* Institute of Industrial Relations, University of California, Berkeley, February, 1964, pp. 99–108.

[9] For example, *Business Week,* Mar. 20, 1965, pp. 93–94.

Managership and Leadership. In both your manager-to-man and manager-to-men relationships, you occupy two basic roles: *managership* and *leadership*. As a manager, it is up to you to reduce stress and undue anxiety to increase productivity and improvement.

Your managership is a continuous evaluating–decision-making process about your people. Think statistically about your subordinates, so that you work with the odds and build on their strengths wherever you can. Out of several people, you should have a few that are outstanding, some that are good doers, some that are middling, and a few that are misfits. Plan so that the outstanding ones can make their greatest contributions. Study your good doers and your middling men. See if a way can be found to help them grow. Once you find that your help does not bring better results, assist them where you can, but do not try to change them. Some middling men need tight supervision or they will produce nothing. A manager will play "father" to others, providing them with emotional and intellectual support. Some will have to be watched and checked to ensure that something constructive is accomplished. When you come to the misfits, the chances are that you, like most managers, cannot take adverse action easily. Still, you should take action quickly and help them get into a job that suits them.

"Coaching," as we use it here, is leadership in the most constructive sense: *helping*. To help requires two attitudes—empathy and caring. Empathy is sensitivity to others in the positive sense, the ability to project imaginatively into another person and momentarily to experience the same feeling he has. When we sympathize with someone, we suffer with him. It is difficult for us to comprehend how a person can care and yet be not sympathetic, but rather empathic—understanding without becoming emotionally involved. For years, physicians, psychiatrists, and social workers have dealt with the emotions of others in crises and still have cared without becoming emotionally involved. They cannot afford to; not only would they not be able to do their jobs, but their emotional structures could not stand it.

There are no tricks in coaching; it is trusting, accepting, and understanding another in terms of his needs and his goals. There is a feeling of power and achievement in coaching. It is, however, a different kind of power feeling than bossing. There is a lot of the dictator in every one of us, and unless a manager looks behind his self-image, he may use coaching to dominate. A manager needs to care about helping others grow to the extent that he is willing to risk changing himself, for helping others also requires that the manager in turn is willing to be helped. Gratitude is not to be expected from responsible adults. The help received creates an obligation which must be discharged by "giving" something to the helper; otherwise, the learner may withdraw from or even resent the helper.

Group Leadership. To build a cohesive, productive, developing, innovating group, you must trust your people enough to share fully with them your management information, your management authority, and your feelings. This is essentially what you do if you practice leadership with one subordinate. In effect, then, you are extending the same conditions to your group. In your managership role, you still set the limits and carry the right to veto. No one should expect you to give these up, for as head of an autocratic operation, there can be no democratic actions. Just as in your working with each man you place on him the onus to take the initiative, so too in your integrating you expect your staff to take the initiative, to be as responsible, with your help, for achieving a cohesive group. There is no other known means for reducing the power struggle among your subordinates or their power struggle with you. Authority does not make leadership.

Ideally, you should help your staff come to accept each other enough in mutual trust and commitment to cooperative effort so that feelings about any matter can be expressed and accepted. The conflict aspect of cooperation must be dealt with if the acceptance aspect is going to succeed. No feeling can successfully be swept under the rug; unresolved conflict will interfere with later attempts at working together. Encouraging people to open up, to express their fear, anxiety, frustration, and anger, means that these matters can be talked over and listened out at the feeling level, rather than ignored, suppressed, smoothed over, or rejected as out of place. If you are going to be of the greatest help to yourself and the group, you must be able to share your own feelings of uncertainty and frustration with your staff. You must open yourself up to them, so that they in turn can open themselves up to you. The opportunity for personal growth in insight, sensitivity, and interpersonal skills may well be one of the greatest rewards not only for the staff, but for you.

As the boss, you cannot see your lengthened power shadow. There are usually wide differences between what you think is happening and what your subordinates perceive. To stay in touch with reality and become more effective in your coaching function (as well as in all your managing functions), you periodically ask the group to give you feedback on your approach—and then you *listen:* How am I carrying out my functions in terms of the needs of the group? What can I do to help the group work together more effectively and efficiently? What can I do to help achieve more improvement in both our work and our personal growth? What should I know to be more sensitive to resources within the group and to individual feelings and needs? Am I being too defensive of myself and my position? How am I using my authority? How can I help expand the total power of the group?

You will be informed not only as to what needs to be done but also as to how you can do your job better. The answers, beyond what any single subordinate dares do, are gradually evolved by the group as each member adds a little to what someone else has said to help you see yourself as they see you. You should not accept everything without question, however. You must finally come to your own understanding of yourself so that you know when you can accept the judgment of your staff and when you must believe your own eyes.

USING RESOURCES

A manager should be able to secure (1) coaching from his superior in work and personal matters, (2) confidential staff counsel in terms of his own personal needs and problems which he feels he cannot discuss with his superior, (3) management development courses, (4) reading, (5) staff counsel in his management planning, and (6) staff counsel on people with problems.

Personal Counsel. You should be able to draw on staff counsel for personal matters and problems beyond the coaching from your superior. Look at it selfishly—every man must take care of himself emotionally. You must be on your own and must finally judge yourself. No one can hold your emotional hand all the time. It is not a question of managing one's time on the job, as so many people point out, but nothing more or less than managing one's life.

A manager should work through his emotional problems and seek the counsel of others for problems on which he needs help. The desire to seek and accept help rests, however, with the person, a recognition of the importance of counseling in his development. Whether counseling is done by a staff counselor, a psychologist, a physician, a psychiatrist, a social worker, or a skilled interviewer, a man needs a skilled listener who is not involved in a continuous or a power relationship with him and who can help him think objectively about himself and his problems.

Development. The man who really wants to learn from management seminars faces special problems. Most of the participants' learning barriers are so high that they accept only what they want to hear. The shared experience can provide zest and interest in cultivating a curious mind.

Table 1-1 gives a rough classification of the levels and dimensions of management development. Sensitivity training is offered at essentially two levels: the sixth and seventh ones. Sensitivity or T-group training tends to emphasize the group aspect of learning individual social behavior at the conscious level. The T-group sessions consist of a small group of individuals who learn from each other rather than from the trainer. The group determines its own learning goals and method of operation. Group psychotherapy, on the other hand, focuses more on a person's developing insight, again with some feedback, as he learns to become more aware of the deeper and less conscious roots and motives of his own intrapersonal conflict.

Although the total effectiveness of sensitivity courses has not been measured, the longer courses should be helpful *if* a person is emotionally ready for and capable of handling this type of experience. We must be careful, however, not to think that sensitivity and insight are synonymous. A person can increase

TABLE 1-1.   Approaches in Management Seminars

Levels of interest	Purpose	Use of group	Use of trainer
Management Engineering System			
First level: *Techniques and principles*	How to control others	None; ask questions	Lecturer
Second level: *"Communication"*	How to persuade others	Personal opinions	Expert
Third level: *"Decision making"*	Solve problems	Suggest solutions	Chairman
Management Behavioral System			
Fourth level: *Cases*	Interpersonal processes	Discussion without solution	"Reflector"
Fifth level: *Motivation and creativity*	Understanding and managing people	Explore people problems	Lecturer and discussion leader
Sixth level: *Personal behavior*	"Social" self and sensitivity to others	Feedback on role behavior	Resource man
Seventh level: *Interpersonal skills*	Group processes and sensitivity to others	Feedback on leader-member behavior	Discussion moderator
Eighth level: *Personal growth*	Insight on self-image and real self	Listen—"reflect"	Counselor

TABLE 1-2. Comparison of Authors' Views

Areas of focus	Sampson, Staff Role in Management	Moore, Conduct of the Corporation	Levinson et al., Men, Management and Mental Health	McGregor, The Human Side of Enterprise	May, Man's Search for Himself	Argyris, Personality and Organization	Levinson, Emotional Health	Likert, New Patterns of Management	Whyte, Money and Motivation	Sampson, Managing the Managers
Organizing	x					x				x
Superior-subordinate			x	x			x		x	x
Superior-subordinates			x					x	x	x
Work itself	x						xx			x
Individual		x	x	x	x	xx	x			x
Group	x	xx	x					xx	x	x
Emotional health						xx	x	xx		x
Staff and line	xx									
Worker			x				x		xx	
Management people	x	xx	x	xx	x		xx	x		x

insight without increasing in sensitivity, and vice versa. Finally, except for some reportedly limited, partial experiments, sensitivity training experiences do not involve the power relationship of the boss-subordinate-work triangle in the sessions.

Reading. · Books about the behavioral sciences are a fruitful source of knowledge. Ten to start with are listed in the Bibliography at the end of this chapter. Table 1-2 shows the different points of view as a guide for reading. These books are *first-order* knowledge, required to practice the application of the behavioral sciences. Remember, too, that not many years ago a man's formal learning, though limited, was enough to last him his lifetime in a stable, almost static environment. With the explosion of knowledge and the ever-increasing pace of change, a manager must stretch his mind with books just to keep abreast.

Management Counseling. Staff counsel by a manager on his managing can be invaluable.[10] Although counseling has been used to cover the appraisal interview by a manager with his subordinate, I suggest that we reserve counseling for the staff man-to-manager relationship and coaching for the manager-to-subordinate relationship. It might be that a more appropriate word would be "consulting," except that we have come to think of this as giving advice, experting, or persuading, which really have no place in counseling.

Staff assistance should be used increasingly in a variety of situations. For example, staff counsel should be used in selecting through tests and evaluations. Rensis Likert[11] recommends the development and use of measures by staff people,

[10] See Robert C. Sampson, *The Staff Role in Management—Its Creative Uses*, Harper & Row, Publishers, Incorporated, New York, 1955.

[11] Rensis Likert, *New Patterns of Management*, McGraw-Hill Book Company, New York, 1961.

along with experimentation by management, to gage the increase in the quality of interpersonal relations looking to increased productivity. Because of the complexity of this approach, he recommends that the measurement phase be experimental, starting out on an almost clinical evaluation basis. Many behavioral sciences counselors use the "clinical" approach to diagnose the kinds of problems with which an organizational unit is faced.

Counsel on People with Problems. Surely it is unreasonable, in the light of the advances in the behavioral sciences, to expect a manager to be the sole judge of a subordinate—or worse, to spot incipient emotional problems and help a person come to an understanding of his need for outside help. Staff counsel should be able to help the manager evaluate a subordinate and skillfully counsel with the subordinate on his receiving professional help.

CONCLUSION

Let us end on a personal note: the evolving dignity of a manager through growth. Every manager must accept the cardinal fact that he lives and works in uncertainty and conflict, beginning with himself. He can become obsolescent at any age, or he can keep up with change by continuing to grow, by learning and by helping others. He should seek to use experimentally the latest ideas from the exploding behavioral sciences in practicing his art—and work not *against* but *for* himself and others, thereby reducing the power struggle.

BIBLIOGRAPHY

Argyris, Chris, *Personality and Organization: The Conflict between System and the Individual,* Harper & Row, Publishers, Incorporated, New York, 1955.

Levinson, Harry, *Emotional Health: In the World of Work,* Harper & Row, Publishers, Incorporated, New York, 1964.

Levinson, Harry, et al., *Men, Management and Mental Health,* Harvard University Press, Cambridge, Mass., 1962.

Likert, Rensis, *New Patterns of Management,* McGraw-Hill Book Company, New York, 1961.

McGregor, Douglas, *The Human Side of Enterprise,* McGraw-Hill Book Company, New York, 1960.

May, Rollo, *Man's Search for Himself,* W. W. Norton & Company, Inc., New York, 1953.

Moore, Wilbert E., *The Conduct of the Corporation,* Random House, Inc., New York, 1962.

Sampson, Robert C., *Managing the Managers—A Realistic Approach to Applying the Behavioral Sciences,* McGraw-Hill Book Company, New York, 1965.

Sampson, Robert C., *The Staff Role in Management—Its Creative Uses,* Harper & Row, Publishers, Incorporated, New York, 1955.

Whyte, W. F., *Money and Motivation,* Harper & Row, Publishers, Incorporated, New York, 1955.

CHAPTER TWO

Organizing the Personnel Administration Function

JOHN W. HANNON *Executive Vice President, Maynard Research Council, Inc., Pittsburgh, Pennsylvania*

Personnel administration deals with the most valuable asset an enterprise has, its *people*. It provides advice, service, and control for the line organization. It is concerned with seeing that the company attracts and hires qualified, imaginative, and competent people. Then, to retain these employees, this activity establishes, for operating executive approval, policies and procedures that will treat the employees well in every respect, including compensation, working conditions, security, and retirement. It is a staff function and as such follows the nautical rule of thumb, "the staff charts the course and the line brings in the ship." This chapter will deal with the general organization of the personnel administration activity, or "industrial relations," as it is known in many companies.

THE PERSONNEL ADMINISTRATION ACTIVITY

The personnel administration activity, in its full concept as practiced currently by the most progressive companies, is relatively new. Only since World War II have many of the functions come into being as separate activities in the corporate structure. In fact, the terminology for describing the head of this activity has not been standardized. A study made by the Industrial Relations Institute which questioned personnel executives found over twenty different titles used to indicate the job of the top man. These included personnel director, vice president—employee relations, personnel and labor relations director, employee relations manager, industrial relations director, and vice president—public and human relations.

Because of the rise in economic standards and the increased sophistication of the total work force from the lowest position in the organization to the chief executive, it has become essential that the personnel functions be carried out in a well-organized, competent way. This can best be done by an effective personnel administration activity.

Personnel administration has been defined as "developing and administering

11–16

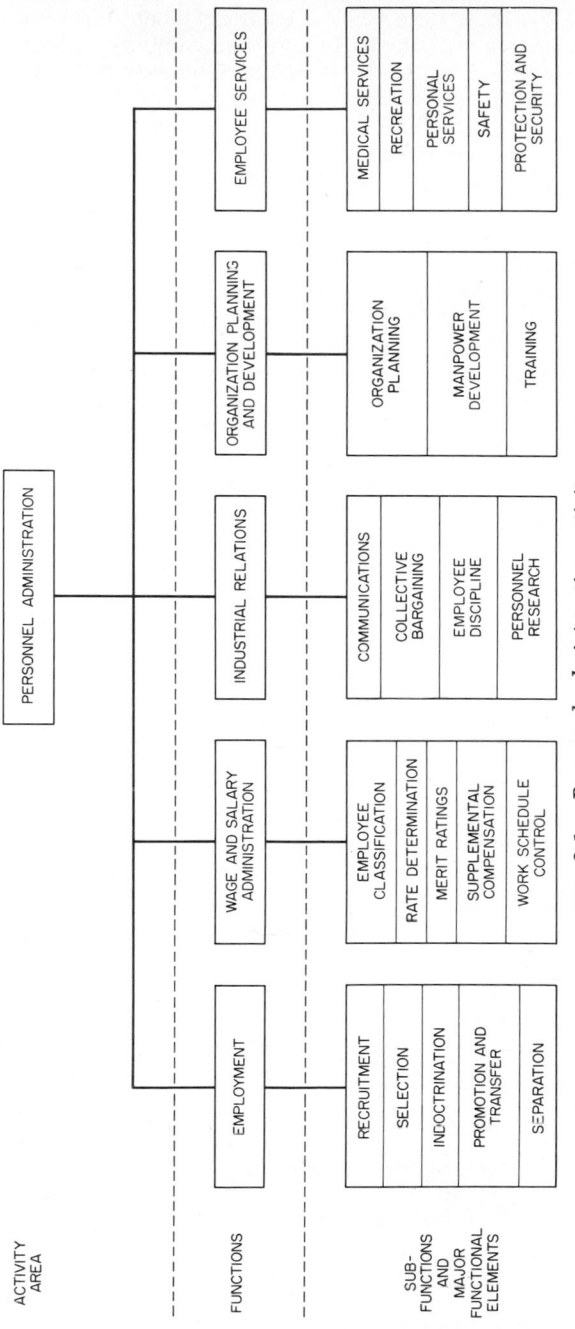

FIG. 2-1. *Personnel administration activity area.*

policies and programs for providing an effective organization structure, qualified employees, equitable treatment, advancement opportunities, job satisfaction, and adequate security."[1]   This is not only a good definition, but an excellent overall objective of the activity pertinent to any company, regardless of its size or character.   The form and shape the personnel administration activity takes, however, differs greatly from company to company, and to be effective, it must be tailored to fit the individual needs of each company.

Functions and Subfunctions of Personnel Administration.   The first step in organizing this activity is to become aware of the many functions and subfunctions which are considered a part of the personnel department.   Figure 2-1 will help in doing this quickly.   This is an activity area chart which was developed by the Association of Consulting Management Engineers (ACME).   It was designed only to show the functions and subfunctions commonly found in the personnel activity area and not as a model organization chart.   Figure 2-1 shows that personnel's major functions fall under five classifications: employment, wage and salary administration, industrial relations, organization planning and development, and employee services.   These, in turn, are divided into subfunctions with their duties and responsibilities clearly and simply stated.   Of course, not all of these functions are of equal importance in every company.   A major classification in one firm may be minor in another.

I. Personnel Administration Activity Area.   Developing and administering policies and programs for providing an effective organization structure, qualified employees, equitable treatment, advancement opportunities, job satisfaction, and adequate job security.
II. Functions, Subfunctions, and Major Functional Elements
    A. Employment.   Insuring that all positions are filled by competent personnel at reasonable cost.
        1. Recruitment.   Searching for and attracting applicants qualified to fill vacant positions.
            a. Analyze job requirements.
            b. Develop job specifications.
            c. Analyze sources of potential employees.
            d. Attract potential employees.
        2. Selection.   Analyzing the qualifications of applicants and deciding upon those who show the most potential.
            a. Interview applicants.
            b. Test applicants.
            c. Investigate references.
            d. Evaluate applicants.
        3. Indoctrination.   Seeing that new employees receive the training and information required to perform their duties effectively.
            a. Orient new employees.
            b. Determine training requirements of new employees.
            c. Follow up performance of new employees.
        4. Promotion and Transfer.   Placing current employees in positions that better utilize their capabilities.
            a. Analyze job specifications.
            b. Analyze employee qualifications.
            c. Test employees.
            d. Evaluate employees.
            e. Determine training requirements of employees.
            f. Follow up performance in new position.
        5. Separation.   Severing connections with employees in a manner most beneficial to them and the company.
            a. Conduct exit interview.
            b. Analyze turnover.
    B. Wage and Salary Administration.   Insuring that employees are fairly and equitably compensated.

[1] *Common Body of Knowledge Required by Professional Management Consultants,* Chart VI, Sub-Committee on the Constituent Elements of Management, Association of Consulting Management Engineers, Inc., New York, September, 1957.

    1. Employee Classification. Assigning officially each employee to a position that is clearly and accurately defined as to its responsibilities and requirements.
    a. Prepare job descriptions.
    b. Assign a proper title to each position.
    c. Audit periodically correctness of job descriptions.
    2. Rate Determination. Setting dollar values on positions that are fair and equitable in relation to other positions in the company and to similar positions in the competitive labor market.
    a. Analyze jobs as described in job descriptions.
    b. Evaluate jobs.
    c. Conduct rate surveys.
    d. Develop rate scales.
    3. Merit Ratings. Appraising objectively the performance of each employee in relation to the duties and responsibilities of his assigned position.
    a. Develop merit rating programs.
    b. Conduct merit rating reviews.
    c. Analyze merit rating results.
    4. Supplemental Compensation. Providing monetary incentives, in addition to basic wages or salaries, to promote initiative and achievement.
    a. Plan and administer profit sharing plans.
    b. Plan and institute stock option plans.
    c. Plan and administer bonus plans.
    d. Plan and institute retirement plans.
    e. Plan and administer incentive plans.
    5. Work Schedule Control. Establishing working hours and periods of absence with and without pay that are fair to employees and company alike.
    a. Plan and administer policies on working hours and absences.
    b. Plan and administer work schedules.
    c. Plan and administer vacation schedules.
C. Industrial Relations. Insuring that the working relationships between management and employees and the job satisfaction of and work opportunities for the company's personnel are developed and maintained in the best interests of the company and its employees.
    1. Communications. Providing the means and climate for developing ideas and exchanging information throughout the company.
    a. Develop channels for presenting information to employees.
    b. Plan and administer suggestion system.
    c. Conduct opinion surveys.
    d. Develop grievance procedures.
    2. Collective Bargaining. Attaining accord with officially recognized and legally established employee organizations in the manner best meeting the interests of the company and its employees.
    a. Negotiate agreements.
    b. Interpret and administer agreements.
    3. Employee Discipline. Developing and maintaining effective work regulations and creating and promoting harmonious working relationships with employees.
    a. Establish rules and regulations for conduct.
    b. Establish and administer disciplinary measures.
    4. Personnel Research. Developing ways and means of improving employee attitudes, conditions of work, employee-management relationships, and the caliber of company personnel.
    a. Analyze personnel techniques and problems.
    b. Recommend improved practices.
D. Organization Planning and Development. Insuring that the company is effectively organized and capably staffed.
    1. Organization Planning. Determining the organization structure and manpower requirements that will most effectively and economically meet company objectives.
    a. Analyze key position requirements.
    b. Analyze organization structure.
    c. Recommend organization changes.
    d. Forecast manpower requirement.
    e. Forecast manpower resources.
    2. Manpower Development. Establishing performance standards for key positions and identifying those areas in which incumbents must grow in order to attain them.
    a. Develop performance standards.
    b. Appraise performance.
    c. Plan individual development programs.

   3. Training.   Developing existing personnel to their full potential for attaining
      established performance standards.
      a. Plan training programs.
      b. Prepare training programs.
      c. Train leaders.
      d. Conduct training programs.
      e. Evaluate training results.
  E. Employee Services.   Maintaining the general welfare of employees on the job and
     assisting them with problems related to their security and personal well-being.
     1. Medical Services.   Preventing diseases and physical ailments and caring for
        diseases, ailments, and injuries incurred by employees on the job.
        a. Develop and administer prevention programs.
        b. Examine employees and job applicants.
        c. Provide medical treatment.
        d. Educate in health matters.
     2. Recreation.   Providing programs and facilities for the enjoyment of employees off
        the job and for making company employment more attractive and satisfying.
        a. Conduct athletic activities.
        b. Conduct social activities.
        c. Provide and direct employee use of recreational facilities.
     3. Personal Services.   Providing services that assist employees in their daily living and
        contribute to their job satisfaction.
        a. Provide insurance counsel or protection.
        b. Provide legal counsel.
        c. Assist with housing and transportation problems.
        d. Operate credit union.
        e. Provide cafeteria and vending machines.
     4. Safety.   Developing and maintaining adequate facilities and procedures for prevent-
        ing on-the-job accidents.
        a. Establish safety rules.
        b. Conduct safety inspections.
        c. Prevent or eliminate hazards.
        d. Educate in safe practices.
        e. Investigate accidents.
     5. Protection and Security.   Taking adequate precautionary methods to safeguard the
        company, its employees, and property from theft, fire, espionage, and similar hazards.
        a. Provide guard or watchman service.
        b. Organize fire fighting service.
        c. Develop and administer security regulations.

Analyzing Personnel Needs.   The amount of time, effort, and honest thought
given to making an initial analysis of personnel needs can in large measure
determine the resulting effectiveness of the personnel administration activity.   It
must be decided which of the functions described in the ACME activity area
chart should be stressed and which are of minor concern.   In determining this,
consideration must be given not only to the size of the company, but to the
number and character of its employees (salaried or hourly, professional or nonprofessional), the type of industry, and even its location.

For example, a company with many union-member employees will have to
stress collective bargaining more heavily than a service organization largely
staffed with professional men and women.   A firm whose manufacturing processes include potentially hazardous materials may find it necessary to have
a larger medical and safety program than others that do not.   If the company
is located in an isolated spot, concern may have to be given to feeding the
employees, whereas a company in a city or town near restaurants and food
services will not have this problem.

Establishing Principles and Charting Organization Structure.   After establishing
the areas of concern of the personnel administration activity, the next move
is to chart the organization structure.   This can best be done by first formulating
a set of principles or objectives which will guide the development of the right
kind of function for the particular company.

The General Electric Company provides an excellent practical example of establishing principles and the resulting organization chart. When General Electric overhauled its organization in the early 1950s, its first step was to define the general principles which, if followed, would assure the most effective personnel activity for the company. It is interesting to note that at that time, GE's general management was prepared to look upon employee relations as a vital new profession and a basic business function on a par with engineering, manufacturing, marketing, and finance, requiring the same degree of talent and effort and having an equal claim to a voice in the day-to-day decision making of a decentralized operating management. This view was accepted in large measure because of the broad new concept of employee and community relations developed in the late 1940s under the leadership of its former vice president, L. R. Boulware. His theme had been "do the right thing voluntarily." Now a new ingredient—communications—was added and conceived of as both a staff and a line responsibility.

GE's concept of corporate relations is summarized under four general principles:
1. Fairness or equity in rewarding each person and each group in accordance with its contribution—a principle most people find agreeable provided they understand it;
2. The responsibility to provide abundant information in a continuous program of communications to the company's customers, shareowners, the financial community, employees, other companies, community neighbors, government representatives, and the public generally;
3. An emphasis on the individual, through policies that respect and promote the personal dignity, independence, aspirations, and potential capacity of every individual associated with the business;
4. Exercising creative leadership in developing, through research and other methods, new and better ways to attract and motivate productive employees.
Union Relations. Once employees have exercised their right to have a union, the Company recognizes its obligation to bargain in good faith with union representatives, whether at the shop level or at the national bargaining table. But the Company's basic obligations still follow in parallel lines to its employees, customers, the community, and its stockholders. If the Company has sincerely tried to "do the right thing" by its employees, and if the employees and the community in which they live are aware that this is so, it follows that at the bargaining table the Company must offer all that it feels is fair and justified. Accordingly, it is General Electric's policy in national negotiations to:
1. Try to reach a determination of what is the right thing to do and encourage union representatives to make their own independent search;
2. Try to explore with union representatives all of the pros and cons of alternative courses of action to determine which course will bring the union and General Electric closest to what is the right thing to do in the soundest way;
3. Try to include in the Company's initial bargaining proposals everything the Company believes to be warranted, holding nothing back deliberately for any "horse-trading" later on;
4. Change the offer whenever additional information from any sources or a significant change of the facts indicates that the Company's initial offer falls short of being right;
5. Try to keep GE employees informed of what the common interests are, so that union officials will have membership support for a fair and just agreement.[2]

Figure 2-2 is the organization structure established by General Electric to meet the principles and objectives described above. Note that GE calls its department "relations services" and that it emphasizes not only employee rela-

[2] *GE Approach to Industrial Relations*, MAPI Study, Machinery and Allied Products Institute, Washington, D.C., 1962, pp. 5-6.

RELATIONS SERVICES

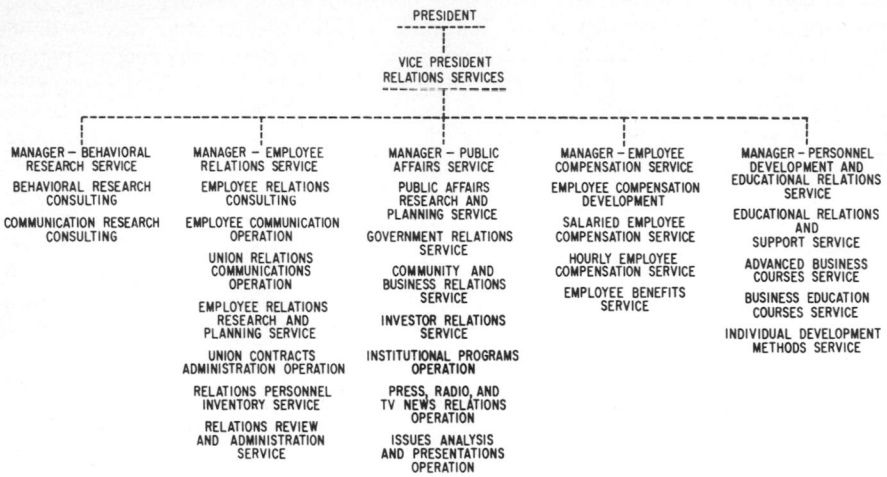

FIG. 2-2. *Relations services functions established by the General Electric Company.* (*Courtesy of* GE Approach to Industrial Relations, *MAPI Study, Machinery and Allied Products Institute, Washington, D.C., 1962, p. 10.*)

tions, but external relations as well. There has been a growing trend in business to charge personnel with "external" or "public" relations, even though in the past public relations was normally a part of marketing. General Electric provides an excellent example of how one company charges its personnel administration activity with responsibility for all "human relations," embracing relations with not only its employees, but the people in the community, its stockholders, the investing public, and the general public. Personnel administration in this case is concerned with all the people problems of the business, and it was specifically organized to meet these particular needs.

Figure 2-3 is another example of how external relations fit in the general personnel administration structure of a large firm. It was developed by the Cummins Engine Company. The chart also shows how the total personnel administration function was staffed, and it is worthy of careful study.

Defining Chain of Command. A valuable by-product in charting the personnel organization is the establishment of a definite chain of command. Of course, this is not necessary in a small firm where the owner or chief executive must double as personnel director with an assistant or secretary aiding him in carrying out these duties. However, it is vital in a large or multiplant company where the personnel activity is much more complicated and requires a larger staff responsible for many varied functions. In this case, it is necessary at the outset to establish and stand behind a defined chain of command. It is recommended that the personnel director report directly to the president. Division personnel managers should report to the division operating managers with functional responsibility to the personnel director at headquarters. The personnel director should have line authority over the other employees of his department, including hiring, transfer, termination, and required disciplinary action within the established personnel policy of the company. Further, he should have authority, subject to the approval of the president, to establish and abolish positions in the department as required to implement the company's personnel policies effectively.

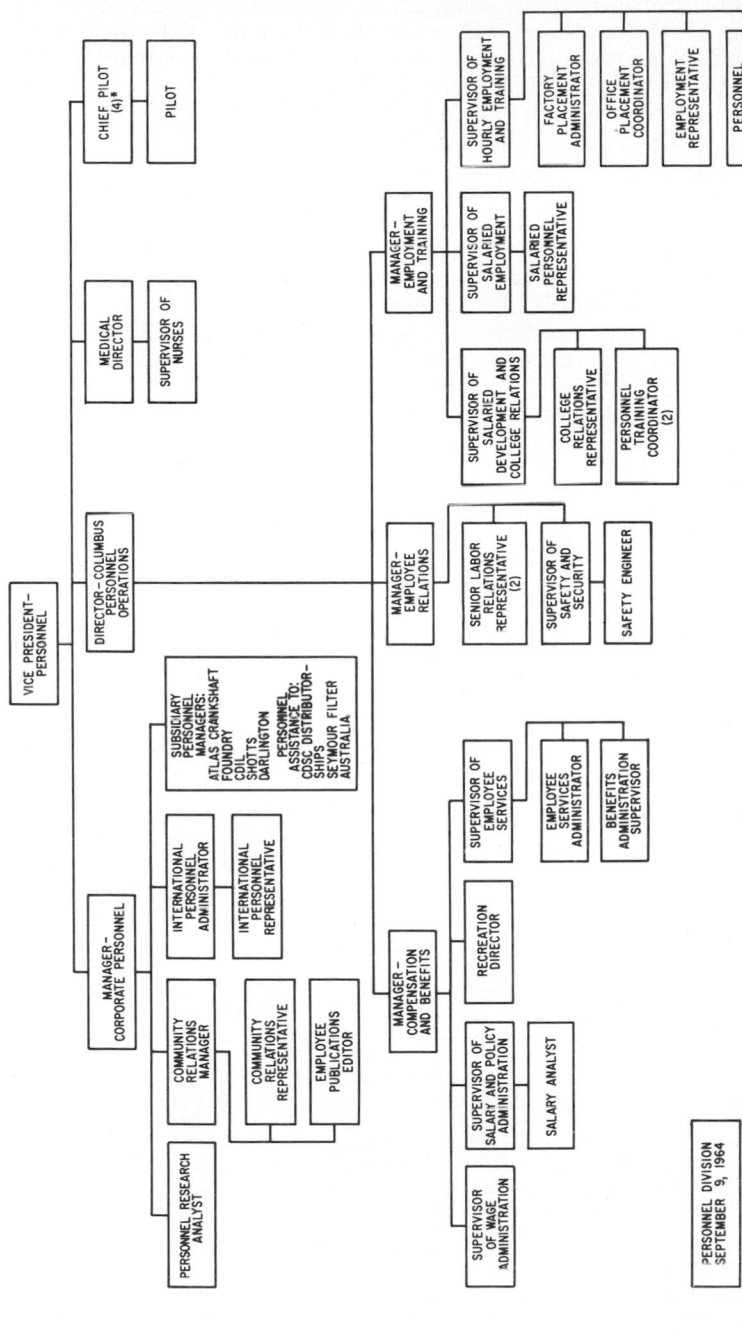

FIG. 2-3. *Personnel administration organization of the Cummins Engine Company. (Courtesy of the Cummins Engine Company. MAPI Study, Machinery and Allied Products Institute, Washington, D.C., 1962, p. 64.)*

Personnel Director and His Staff. The next step in organizing the personnel administration function is defining the job of director of personnel. The most effective personnel managers in any company are the line supervisors who direct the daily efforts of the employees. However, to accomplish the overall objectives of the company most satisfactorily, it is necessary that the personnel director have three things: clear-cut direction in terms of company policies and objectives; a well-organized activity structure to help him carry these out; and a job description which clearly defines in writing his duties and responsibilities so that he knows exactly where he stands in the overall organization of the company.

Position Descriptions. Figure 2-4 is an example of a position description of the top man in the personnel department of a large company. Note that everything is spelled out clearly and simply: purpose of the position; duties; scope of responsibilities; difficulty of execution; and basic requirements and qualifications of the individual. The importance of a concise and complete job description cannot be overstressed. Its value is threefold. First, it tells the personnel director what is expected of him and where his authority begins and ends. Second, it tells the management group exactly what kind of individual is needed to accomplish the goals of the activity and the skills and qualifications he must have. And third, it gives his superior a standard against

POSITION DUTIES

I. Purpose of position
   Direct all industrial relations functions. Functions include: (*A*) labor relations, (*B*) employee relations, (*C*) wage and salary administration, (*D*) plant and industrial security, (*E*) visitor service, and (*F*) medical services.
II. Regular duties
   A. Check following functions which are performed for activity supervised:
      X Plan and schedule work load   X Select and train subordinates
      X Assign work   X Maintain morale of subordinates
      X Recommend budgets   X Review performance of subordinates
      X Control expenditures   X Recommend wage or salary adjustments
      X Report results and unusual situ-
        ations to immediate supervisor
   B. Other regular duties
      1. Labor relations
         a. Conduct labor negotiations and/or communications with unions.
         b. Plan, coordinate, and present management's position on grievances at the plant level and national appeal level. Assist in preparation and presentation of cases at arbitration.
         c. Advise local management on all labor contract and union relations matters.
      2. Employee relations
         a. Take responsibility for proper administration and control of provisions, claims, and expenditures of various employee benefit plans, such as social insurance, pensions, suggestion system, employee purchases, layoff income benefits, medical services, workmen's compensation, and unemployment compensation.
         b. Recommend and coordinate an effective safety program. Assure communication of and compliance with local, state, and Federal safety laws.
         c. Assure utilization of the most effective methods of recruitment, selection, interviewing, testing, hiring, bumping, upgrading, and transferring of employees.
         d. Plant communications coordinator—assure lines of communication to employees are kept open and believable.
         e. Assure communication of and compliance with Executive Orders 10925 and 1114, the Civil Rights Act of 1964, and other applicable laws.
         f. Training—coordinate and/or develop and present local training programs or headquarters-developed training programs to all levels of personnel, from hourly to management staff, including such subjects as contract administration, safety, fair employment practices, operating policies and procedures. Make recommendations and arrange schedules for management development training.

   FIG. 2-4. *Position description of head of personnel department.*

3. Wage and salary administration
   Wage and salary administrator for all levels, from hourly through staff management
   a. Area wage and salary surveys.
   b. Job and position description and evaluation.
   c. Conduct rate reviews.
   d. Coordinate yearly management appraisal and performance evaluations.
   e. Analyze, report, and/or make recommendations regarding local wage and salary administration trends.
4. Plant and industrial security
   Plant security officer:
   a. Responsible for protection of all plant property, equipment, tools, and material by assuring proper utilization of the plant police force, fire-fighting equipment, and alarm systems.
   b. Responsible for communication and enforcement of Department of Defense and Atomic Energy Commission security regulations, recognizing that noncompliance could result in loss of all government contracts to the company. Conduct plant investigations and inspections by DOD, AEC, and FBI representatives.
5. Visitor service
   Establish and maintain strict but courteous visitor service to control visitors for security purposes.
6. Medical services
   Establish and maintain an effective medical department to provide treatment and recording of sickness and injuries. Analyze reports and make recommendations for corrective measures. Assure non-abuse of provided services.

III. Occasional duties or special assignments
   Coordinate local charity and bond-purchase drives and occasional employee affairs, such as picnics, family day, etc.

POSITION ANALYSIS

I. Scope of responsibility
   A. Responsibility for personnel
      1. Line responsibility
         Employees reporting directly to this position

	Total no. of employees reporting through this position
Industrial relations supervisor	6
Confidential secretary	0

      2. Functional personnel responsibility
         a. Recruiting—develop reliable sources and recruit qualified personnel for hourly, salary-clerical, technical and professional positions, and all management positions up to management staff level.
         b. Selection—through developed and proved procedures, determine most qualified personnel available and recommend employment based on findings.
         c. Training—see "Position Duties," IIB2f, above.
         d. Administering salaries—see "Position Duties," IIB3.
   B. Responsibility for physical and financial resources
      1. Expenditures
         a. Control annual expenditure for:
            1. Medical department supplies and equipment
            2. Recruitment services, such as advertising
            3. Educational assistance program
            4. Security investigations
            5. Employee relations services, including communications
            6. Purchase of books, papers, periodicals, and subscriptions
         b. Subcontracting—recommend feasibility and limitations based on labor relations policies and decisions.
         c. Administer and maintain close control on claims and expenditures for:
            1. Workmen's compensation
            2. Unemployment compensation
            3. Layoff income benefits
            4. Suggestion system
            5. Petty cash fund
            6. Social insurance

FIG. 2-4. (*Continued*)

    7. Employee purchase program

    8. Medical services

2. Utilization and protection of physical resources

    a. Utilization—assure recruitment and hiring of most qualified personnel for maximum utilization of machines, tools, equipment, material, and supplies.

    b. Safeguarding of company assets

        1. Responsible for protection of all plant property, equipment, and materials through proper utilization of the plant police force

        2. Responsible, as plant security officer, for required security protection of all classified equipment, material, and paper work

3. Cost reduction and expense control

    a. Wage and salary administration—proper classification of hourly jobs and salary positions.   Combination of jobs or positions where possible.

    b. Minimize negotiating time.

    c. Maintain control of employee benefit plans.

4. Records

Direct the accurate and confidential preparation, maintenance, storage, and disposition of all department records, including:

    a. Employee personal histories

    b. Petty cash fund expenditures

    c. Medical visitations and reports

    d. Insurance claims and expenditures

    e. Unemployment compensation claims and expenditures

    f. Workmen's compensation claims and expenditures

    g. Grievance and arbitration and union negotiation files

    h. Wage and salary administration files

    i. Suggestion system files

    j. Police reports and files

    k. Layoff income benefits claims and expenditures

    l. Employee purchase program

    m. Plant cafeteria

5. Management of money

    a. Financial management

        1. Responsible for proper administration of petty cash fund and airline ticket purchase program

        2. Responsible for negotiation of yearly contract with vending machine and cafeteria concessionaire

    b. Disbursement management

Responsible for recommendations as to settlement of grievances where money or other costs may be involved

II. Difficulty of execution

  A. Problem solving

    1. Investigate and analyze grievances or complaints and therefrom either determine or recommend appropriate management action required to solve the problem or maintain management's position, based on the merits of the case and contract provisions.

    2. Analyze local supplements and therefrom determine, write, acquire headquarters approval, and negotiate appropriate changes.

    3. When a work stoppage is imminent, determine and/or recommend action required by management to handle all possible problems.

    4. Analyze questions by local management regarding industrial relations problems and recommend possible solutions to accomplish desired goals.

    5. When management desires to change a policy, a procedure, or working conditions that will affect employees, plan strategy on how to accomplish the change with minimum adverse affect on employee and/or labor relations.

    6. Determine need for and extent of area wage and salary surveys and, from results, make recommendations on how to maintain competitive rates.

    7. Determine how to most economically protect company property with a minimum of police protection in a community where vandalism is rampant.

    8. From knowledge of security requirements, determine the best method for communicating, investigating, and enforcing established regulations.

    9. Investigate need for training and determine how and when to present developed programs to be most effective.

    10. Analyze and determine solutions to problems on development of recruitment sources, testing procedures, labor turnover, manpower requirements, and other employee relations problems.

FIG. 2-4.   (*Continued*)

B. Decision making
  1. Responsible for final decisions on:*
      a. Contract supplement provisions required
      b. General labor relations problem solutions
      c. General communications to employees
      d. Administration of employment and seniority provision procedures
      e. Hourly and salary job and position descriptions and evaluations
      f. Administration of employee benefits program
      g. Administration of medical department and visitor control services
      h. Administration of vending machines and cafeteria
      i. Coordination and presentation of general training programs
      j. Administration of educational assistance program
      k. General problems regarding the safety program
  2. Responsible for review with top line executives
      a. Management position to be taken on labor problems where work stoppages or large expenditures could result
      b. Specific communications to employees
      c. Management position descriptions and evaluations
      d. Contributions to community organizations
      e. Coordination and presentation of management training and development programs
      f. Administration of plant protection and security regulations
      g. Specific problems regarding the safety program
III. Requirements of the position
  A. Education and experience
    1. High school, college—BSIE or BBA—industry degree
    2. Specialized or technical knowledge and skills
       Specialized training in all industrial relations functions, with specific emphasis on labor relations, time study, safety, wage and salary administration, plant protection, and personnel management
    3. Types of work experience—minimum number of years for each
       Five years experience in various functions, namely:
       Labor relations........................... 1½ years
       Employee relations .... 1½ years
       Wage and salary administration............ 6 months
       Safety.................................... 6 months
       Plant protection......................... 6 months
  B. Skills of persuasion
     Ability to effectively discuss a wide variety of subjects related to all industrial relations functions as an adviser to other management personnel, with force of persuasion to recognize management's positions when dealing with union representatives, and with confidence when dealing with employees and the general public.
  C. Administrative abilities
     Effectively delegate responsibility to subordinates, including such functions as: analyze, plan, organize, effect, control, and follow up.

* NOTE: Several decisions listed as final are actually shared decisions with the line executive, manager of manufacturing, and/or other department managers, but because of specialized knowledge, data, training, and experience, industrial relations recommendations usually coincide with final decisions in the functions listed.

FIG. 2-4   (*Continued*)

which to judge how completely the personnel manager is fulfilling his function in the organization.

Job descriptions should also be written for staff members of the personnel administration activity to indicate the work that is to be carried out by each of them. In actual practice, however, job duty assignments are not rigid, but usually vary with the background and skill of the individual in the job at the time. For instance, a man with the title of "employment manager" may also be in charge of safety, training, recruiting, and grievance handling, if he has had the necessary background in these functions. Therefore, the main concern should be to see that all of the functions of a good personnel administration program are assigned as specific responsibilities to individuals who are qualified to carry them out rather than to attempt to pigeonhole a person in one area simply because his predecessor was so limited.

Also, in assigning personnel job duties, consideration must be given to the time needed to perform these various functions. In this connection, Dale Yoder and Roberta J. Nelson conducted a survey to determine the percentage of the total work time that was devoted to each of seven personnel activities. The results of this survey can be a significant guideline in establishing the work load of the personnel administration department. The statistics shown in Figure 2-5 present the results of the analysis made of a total of 600 questionnaires returned from a possible 1,400 which were sent to men and women who hold employee relations positions in private industry throughout the United States.

Evaluating the Personnel Administration Activity. Not only is it necessary to initiate and organize a comprehensive and well-thought-out program, but personnel practices must constantly be audited to ensure that the original concepts and philosophies are up to date and are being maintained.

An effective audit procedure is shown in Figure 2-6. This employee relations checklist was developed by the Cummins Engine Company for use by its plant managers. This device was designed to focus attention on the elements of a strong industrial relations program which convey the firm's "good faith." The questions are for use in the day-to-day relationships with the employees and

Position	Department administration	Employment and placement	Training	Collective bargaining	Wage and salary administration	Benefits and services	Research
Director of employee relations............	24	19	6	19	10	17	5
Director of personnel, excluding collective bargaining..........	18	27	10	...	14	25	6
Director of labor relations...............	15	10	5	49	7	11	3
Supervisor, employment and placement........	15	40	6	9	12	14	4
Supervisor, training.....	24	10	45	...	...	10	11
Supervisor, wage and salary administration..	31	17	...	...	35	12	5
Supervisor, benefits and services..............	17	17	6	5	6	44	5
Supervisor, personnel research...............	22	5	5	5	10	5	48
Specialist, employment and placement........	12	72	3	...	3	5	5
Specialist, training......	5	5	84	...	...	...	5
Specialist, wage and salary administration....	10	10	...	...	75	...	5
Specialist, benefits and services..............	13	7	...	...	...	75	5
Specialist, personnel research..............	5	15	2	...	...	...	78

FIG. 2-5. *Time budgets of staff jobs in employee relations. Percentage of time devoted in each job to the seven employee relations functions.* (*Courtesy of Dale Yoder and Roberta J. Nelson, "Jobs in Personnel and Employee Relations," The Personnel Man and His Job, American Management Association, New York, 1962, p. 61.*)

Morale

Do you treat all of your employees fairly and without favoritism?   Are you consistent in your actions?

Do you show an interest in your employees?   Do you keep them informed, in advance if possible?

Do you recognize and respect your employees as human beings, ones who hear, see, talk and feel?   Do you acknowledge shortcomings in your management and correct accordingly?

Do you afford an opportunity for your employees to advance before hiring others to fill the job?

Do you attempt to orient new employees?   Do you give your employees a sense of belonging?

Do you regularly and consistently survey the needs of your employees?   Do you provide a forum by which they can be heard without fear of recrimination?

Do you follow up programs which you start?

Do you reduce confusion by proper planning and organization?

Do you exhibit your loyalty to your employees?   Do you exploit your common interests?

Wages

Are your wages and fringe benefits, such as insurance, vacations, and paid holidays, in line with others similarly engaged in your area?   Are you keeping pace?   Do your employees know it?

Are these wages and other benefits fair and reasonable?

Do the same rates apply to all who do the same work?

Do you carefully plot the natural progression of new employees in your overall wage structure?

Grievances

Do your employees need a spokesman?   Do they need to invite a union organizer in to talk for them?

Do you have an effective process for prompt handling of employee complaints, either real or fancied?

Do you keep your office door open—or is this a myth for public consumption only?

Do you follow up your decisions based on complaints to ascertain their effect on morale?

Supervision

Do your supervisors represent you to your employees?   Do they know they speak and act for you—that you are responsible for them?

Do you train your supervisors?   Do you keep your supervisors informed?

Do your supervisors have an ability to teach and to communicate with your employees?   Do they assist employees in understanding their duties and privileges?

Do your supervisors treat all employees fairly and without favoritism?

Do they react properly to criticism?

Do your supervisors promptly and effectively correct problems as they arise?

Do your supervisors nurture and maintain a close relationship between employer and employee?   Do they have the respect of your employees?

Do they understand what they can and cannot do about union activities?

Marginal Employees

Do you carefully select and properly place your new employees?

Do you regularly and consistently weed out marginal employees?

Do you regularly and at frequent intervals dismiss those employees who do not conform to the standard of workmanship required?

Education

Do you give your employees an opportunity to improve their skills?

Do you have communications with your employees regularly to explain company policies, various changes in policies, and plans for the future?

Do you attempt to educate your employees in the profit system?

Do you explain to your employees the necessity of maintaining production schedules, the effect on others when they are not met?

Do you follow up your educational programs so that the employees' newly acquired education can be put to use most effectively?

FIG. 2–6.   *Employee relations checklist.*   (*Courtesy of* The Cummins Engine Company Approach to Industrial Relations, *MAPI Study, Machinery and Allied Products Institute, Washington, D.C., 1965, pp. 28-29.*)

Physical Plant and Working Conditions

Do you have adequate lighting, heating, and ventilation?
Do you require good housekeeping in your plant?
Do you have adequate toilet and cleanup facilities?
Do you have proper provision for first aid?
Does your equipment have proper safety features?
Do you have provision for recreation and/or facilities for eating during lunch hours and break periods?

Fig. 2-6   *(Continued)*

to help the managers show, by action, that the company intends to "deal with its employees on the basis of what is fair in the light of local practices and economic circumstances, regardless of whether or not a union contract exists."[3] Sincere consideration given to each of these questions should enable the firm to establish the kind of personnel activity that will produce an effective work force.

This or a similar audit procedure should be developed so that there is an "ongoing" review of all activities which will feed back information on the effectiveness of plans and procedures that deal with the people in the company. This new information will enable the revision of current practices and organization or the initiation of new.

CONCLUSION

To maintain the personnel administration function as an effective and vital activity, the personnel administration staff must look to the future with a completely open mind and a thirst for new knowledge and concepts. An organization is a dynamic and living complex. By looking back, we can see the tremendous challenge that lies ahead. Since 1935, more basic and dramatic changes took place in the world than in the preceding 300 years. The collapse of time and the unprecedented rate at which change is taking place must be recognized. It has been said that in 1965 we knew four times as much as we knew in 1935 and that by 1980 scientists will have learned as much new knowledge as in all previous history.

All of this unprecedented knowledge acquisition has caused an unequaled increase in the standard of living and the further development of our affluent society. For those concerned with the "people in business," these developments call for an acute awareness of the changing needs of the people for whom they are responsible. For example, one study has shown that where once direct compensation was the most important factor in maintaining employee happiness, job satisfaction requirements have tended to shift to other, nonfinancial needs. First of all, the employee has a strong desire to gain the respect of his fellow workers and the community in which he lives. Further, he seeks the satisfaction of knowing he is really accomplishing something. And the individual selects positions with considerable thought as to whether the firm he is going to be associated with is a pleasant place in which to work.

These nonfinancial goals, coupled with the rapid change in job requirements brought about by the knowledge explosion, require the personnel administration staff to involve itself with continuing education programs for all members of the work force. There will be no place in the personnel field for rigid thinking.

[3] *The Cummins Engine Company Approach to Industrial Relations,* MAPI Study, Machinery and Allied Products Institute, Washington, D.C., 1965, p. 27.

Everyone engaged in personnel work must be constantly alert to the changing environment and must keep abreast of the new findings of social scientists.

BIBLIOGRAPHY

Bethel, Lawrence L., Franklin S. Atwater, George H. E. Smith, and Harvey A. Stackman, Jr., *Industrial Organization and Management,* 4th ed., McGraw-Hill Book Company, New York, 1962.

Common Body of Knowledge Required by Professional Management Consultants, Chart VI, Sub-Committee on the Constituent Elements of Management, Association of Consulting Management Engineers, Inc., New York, September, 1957.

GE Approach to Industrial Relations, MAPI Study, Machinery and Allied Products Institute, Washington, D.C., 1962.

Organization of Personnel Administration, Studies in Personnel Policy, no. 72, National Industrial Conference Board, New York, 1946.

Organizing the Personnel Function Efficiently; Two Company Histories, Personnel Series, no. 158, American Management Association, New York, 1954.

Top Management Organization in Divisionalized Companies, Studies in Personnel Policy, no. 195, National Industrial Conference Board, New York, 1965.

CHAPTER THREE

Industrial Psychology

RICHARD S. GILLMER   *Resident Manager, Humber, Mundie & McClary, Minneapolis, Minnesota*

W. J. HUMBER   *Partner, Humber, Mundie & McClary, Milwaukee, Wisconsin*

Psychology, the science of human behavior, is only 100 years old, but its industrial branch is even younger, dating back to the years of World War I. When that war began for the United States, new recruits would meet at a field bisected by a whitewashed line. Those who could read the daily newspaper were told to move to one side of the line, and those who could not crossed to the opposite side. This and other improvised methods of classifying large masses of men were replaced by the original Army Alpha and Beta Tests, which endeavored to measure intelligence objectively. Nearly four million recruits and officers were classified by these tests, representing one of the earliest applications of scientific psychology to management problems. Also, it was during the same period that military psychologists developed the first performance-appraisal system, a method of rating the effectiveness of officers.

GROWTH OF INDUSTRIAL PSYCHOLOGY

Although it is unfortunate that industrial psychology has been so dependent upon bellicosity for its growth, World War II provided another major impetus. The war effort put heavy demands upon psychology. Many psychologists whose interests had heretofore been primarily academic-scientific became interested in the more practical applications of their discipline. Selection and training programs were established and expanded for all types of military personnel, new tests were developed, principles of human learning were made operational, leadership techniques were explored, and evaluation methods were sharpened.

World War II also brought the advent of engineering psychology, a branch of industrial psychology which attempts to design equipment and the work environment so that they are optimally related to human reaction and perception. The prodigious increase in mechanized equipment and weapons, from airplanes to communication systems, required the psychologist's knowledge of human dimensions to attain the optimum man-machine design.

The growth of industrial psychology since World War II closely parallels the recognition on the part of business leaders that human resources are perhaps the most important element determining the success or failure of a business. At the turn of the century, employees were not central in the concern of the industrialist; he was more interested in the planning of adequate factory buildings, the securing of new energy sources, and the invention of more efficient tools. Since that time, however, management has increasingly recognized that profitability, as a result of effective product development and marketing, production efficiencies, and money management, is achieved through the leadership of knowledgeable and well-motivated people.

The various applications of psychology to people in industry may be considered under the headings of (1) organizational planning, (2) human resources, (3) human engineering, and (4) research.

ORGANIZATIONAL PLANNING

The psychological and economic health of a company is a reflection of the talents and philosophies of those who lead it. For this reason, the industrial psychologist, to be maximally effective in his contribution to the company he serves, endeavors at the beginning of his work with an organization to develop a good working relationship with the executives of the company. He will want to know something of the career history of these men, their philosophy of management, and their hopes and aspirations for the future of the company. Out of this kind of understanding, the psychologist is in a good position to advise, suggest, clarify, and stimulate the decision-making processes. The psychologist at this level of responsibility is seldom, if ever, an operating person. He is a catalyst, an aide to the line and staff officers, a confidant who is free to reinforce or to disagree. He is never in competition with those with whom he works. His commitments are to the values of his own profession. His personal satisfactions evolve out of the achievements realized by those with whom he works.

Working with the men who are responsible for making and carrying out the corporate policies, the psychologist may be helpful in several ways.

1. The psychologist, in the confidence of the consulting relationship, may help clarify and help make more specific and realistic the corporate objectives.

2. The psychologist will be very much interested in the kind of organizational structure management is building to achieve the corporate goals. He knows that people's effectiveness is dependent upon the manner in which the organization system channels their efforts, and he knows that good people can fail in a system which blocks or thwarts their best endeavors. For this reason, the psychologist will feel free to suggest ways in which the organizational plan can be made more meaningful and effective in expediting human talent and interdepartmental communication and cooperation.

3. The psychologist can help the company look clearly and professionally at the talents and potential of those people who have been assigned the responsibility for achieving corporate goals. He will be particularly interested in those executives and department heads who are in a position to influence the behavior and effectiveness of other people. He realizes that people vary not only among themselves, but within themselves, so that one man may be very effective

in one area of the operation, but be frustrated (as well as frustrate others) in a different part of the operation.   He will feel free to suggest environmental changes in operating responsibilities.

4. The psychologist will counsel and work directly with executives and other professional people to guarantee the fulfillment of their corporate obligations and responsibilities.

HUMAN RESOURCES

Psychological knowledge and procedures are applicable and useful in various areas of personnel administration, including such areas as selection, management development, counseling, and motivation.

Selection and Promotion.   When a company hires a new employee or promotes a man into a new job, a prediction is made that the man will behave in certain ways in the new position.   This prediction is made on the basis of several factors, including the employer's past experiences with similar decisions, the past history of the candidate for the job, appropriate reference checks, and with increasing frequency, various psychometric measures which can help improve the objectivity and accuracy of the performance prediction.

It is well known that the best single predictor of future behavior is past• behavior.   Most people tend, unless there are significant intervening variables, to continue into the future the same behavior habits they have relied upon in the past.   Consequently, there is no substitute for a good, clear picture of what a man has done with his past job opportunities.   Psychologists have been helpful in sharpening the objective professional history-taking process, so that those responsible for interviewing and hiring can make a decision based on facts rather than on fiction or wishful thinking.   Carefully selected tests can be helpful in improving still further the objectivity and specificity of the prediction of future employee behavior.   Some people do overcome their past history, and others may fail to live up to past achievements.   Tests help point out such exceptions and highlight those special talents, capacities, aptitudes, and problem areas which might otherwise be obscured in the hiring process.

Employment tests are of several kinds: *achievement* tests, which measure present knowledge and skills; *intelligence* tests, which measure learning ability and mental alertness; tests of *creative ability;* and finally, various measures of *temperament, personality*, and *motivational* traits.   Such tests are available commercially and are standardized on the experiences of various companies in broad job categories.   A more precise and valid procedure recommended by most psychologists is a tailor-made battery of tests based on an evaluation of the unique requirements of a particular job in a specific company.

Executive Evaluation.   Tests are most commonly used in hiring for lower-level jobs where the work is fairly routine and predictable.   Where large numbers of applicants must be processed, tests can save time of both applicant and employer by "screening in" or "screening out" those who should receive special consideration.   Tests often point out special talents or personality needs which might otherwise be lost in the rush of the hiring process.

As a general rule, test batteries are most effective in screening candidates for the less complex and more repetitive jobs such as assemblers, mill hands, sheet-metal workers, loom operators, draftsmen, or typists.   As we go up the occupational ladder, it becomes more difficult to establish a criterion of job success and to find valid predictors.   At the supervisory or executive level, where position requirements are generally quite complex, the usual *group* tests are less likely to play as important a role in selection.   The assessment of executive strength and potential can be made more accurate by the use of certain sophisticated *individual* tests; but more important at this level of responsibility is the assessment of executive strength and potential by a perceptive psychologist who will evaluate the executives' ego strength, creativity, honesty, organizational skills, sagacity, and leadership. Such traits are not easily measured by the usual group tests and can be determined more readily and accurately by a psychologist trained in the use of individual or *clinical* procedures, where the focus of attention is upon the individual rather than upon group norms.

Projective tests such as the Rorschach and Thematic Apperception tests or other non-job-oriented instruments are favored at the supervisory level by professional psychologists. The value in any of these more sophisticated clinical procedures resides not so much in the test as in the skill, experience, and judgment of the psychologist who interprets the meaning and significance of the executive's test behavior as such behavior may be meaningful in a particular job in a specific company.

The Value of Tests in Industry. Employment testing has been held up to criticism in the mass media and in a number of popularized books. Some elements of this criticism are justified; others are not. If we were to arrange the various types of tests on a continuum of most accurate to least accurate, the upper end of the scale would certainly include the tests designed to measure physical characteristics such as eyesight and hearing. Next would come the tests of special abilities and mental skills such as mechanical ability, clerical skill, and general intelligence. Lower down the scale are the instruments designed to measure interests and attitudes. And finally, at the low end of the continuum are the personality measures, tests that attempt to quantify such factors as dominance, sociability, and emotional stability. It is toward this last category, personality measures, that the critics have directed their attention. There is little doubt that these personality measures are the most frequently misused of the tests.

Some management people see all tests as useless or even dangerous; others act as though tests are infallible. In actuality, there is nothing inherently good or bad about tests. As with any tool, it is the degree of skill with which the tests are used that determines the accuracy of the results. The skill of the interpreter is of particular importance with personality measures, and many test publishers refuse to put these instruments into the hands of anyone but a qualified psychologist. On the other hand, all tests are potentially inefficient, and can even compound the problems they are intended to solve if they are not part of a carefully planned and well-administered personnel program.

The arbitrary use of any test for employment screening is at best a speculative affair. The most effective method of reducing the element of risk is through test validation, or in other words, an on-the-job trial of a test's predictive accuracy. Because a test worked in one company for staffing certain types of jobs does not mean that it will work elsewhere for similarly titled positions. Also, the factors that constitute job success are likely to vary from place to place. Therefore, it is more desirable to select a test battery carefully for a specific company and also for a specific job category within that company.

Management Development. The effective selection of people is only one step in the productive development of human resources. People, no matter how carefully chosen, need to be trained, developed, and directed. The most carefully selected people will leave the company or atrophy if the working environment is static. People need and want to be stimulated through *planned experiences* in a healthy milieu.

For example, the writers are acquainted with two foundries operated by the same company, but located ten miles apart. Both foundries live under the same corporate policies, report to the same president, and observe the same selection procedures and employment standards. Each foundry has its own superintendent. In spite of similar personnel standards of selection, the turnover in the one foundry is minimal, but in the other it is excessive. The first foundry develops leaders, some of whom move on to major assignments in the parent company. The other foundry does not produce leaders. The first foundry is characterized by a healthy working environment including planned training, performance reviews, and promotional practices. The other foundry is not characterized by a similar enthusiasm for management development and training. The resulting turnover in the latter plant is a symptom of employee boredom and frustration. Good people do not remain strong unless they are stimulated through programs of growth and expanded responsibility consistent with their own interests and capacities.

For a management development program to be maximally effective, it should be designed to achieve a definite goal or objective, based upon a careful analysis of the present or anticipated needs of the corporation. An essential part of this analysis is a manpower plan. What will the corporate needs in terms of manpower be in five years, in ten years? Are replacements being brought along for those department heads who will be promoted, resign, or retire? Individuals need to be identified who have the potential to benefit from a program of management development.

When the corporate objectives and needs have been defined, the manpower needs specified, and the candidates for management growth identified, definite programs for management development can become operative.

Programs of management development are based on the reasonable assumption that people grow through experiences in tested responsibility. Thus, "the delegation of specific responsibility and authority," "job rotation," and "job enlargement" are phrases meaningful to those responsible for planning growth experiences for potential management people. Such experiences are supplemented by individual and group discussions and training conferences, both within the plant and with the aid of outside resources in the community such as university and college seminars, classes, and specialized instruction. The American Management Association and similar groups offer experiences and instruction in selected areas of knowledge. Psychologists with special experiences and education in sensitivity training offer so-called T-group sessions to executives desirous of gaining insight into themselves and into the nature of their impact on other people. An effective management development program will take advantage of the wide variety of community resources available to supplement the company's own internal training capacities.

The Psychologist's Place in Management Development. The psychologist, either as a consultant to the company or as an employee of the company, functions in a staff relationship to the management development program; except under unusual circumstances, he is not directly responsible for it. Those directly responsible for the effective operation of the program ideally should be those who are responsible for achieving corporate profit objectives. The psychologist functions as a catalyst—a man who helps define problems and suggests ways of solving them, a consultant to those who have the operating responsibility.

In this way, the psychologist can retain his objectivity and not become a part of the power structure of the corporation. His contribution to management at the point of the management development program may be classified as follows. (1) He helps management define its manpower needs to accomplish the corporate objectives. (2) He is equipped, by training and experience, to devise procedures for appraising and training so that potential managers may receive help in objective self-evaluation as well as guidance in how to gain increased self-insight and self-improvement. (3) He helps devise research procedures which will evaluate the changes and improvement achieved by people as a result of the manpower development program. The psychologist will want to find out if the "students" in this continuing program actually change and if these improvements are permanent. Is the cost of the program worthwhile? What happens to the "graduates" of the program? How can the program become even more effective?

Management development takes many forms and can be instituted to accomplish a variety of objectives, both short and long range. It is critical to determine what kind of program best fits each organization and best satisfies specific needs. It is in this careful preparation and evaluation that management development becomes a sound investment in the growth of an organization. The psychologist can help the company set up such a developmental program, and he also will be able to act as a stimulant so that interest in the program does not falter over the years.

Counseling. A logical development of the management training program is the utilization of psychological consultation with individual employees. Whenever possible, psychologists would prefer that management personnel problems be resolved within the regular line structure of the organization—that is, between a man and his supervisor—but this is not always possible. Sometimes an "outside" person who is not directly involved in the line organization can be more neutral and helpful than can the person who is under pressure to achieve daily objectives. At this point, the psychologist can be directly helpful in those situations where the employee, for one reason or another, is not accomplishing his job. In such situations, the psychologist in industry focuses his attention on whatever is blocking the man's development in the company, either the man's own personal failings or, as sometimes is the case, the failure of the organizational structure to support adequately the man's efforts to contribute to the corporate good.

Where the problem lies primarily within the man's own capacities to change or modify his behavior, the psychologist may provide the employee an opportunity, through discussion, to gain greater insights and understanding into his own behavior and motivational needs. The psychologist, using modern principles of learning, holds up a mirror before the employee and allows him to see for himself how he is seen by others. By suggestion, reinforcement, and direction, the psychologist will help the employee modify and redirect his behavior into more productive channels. If the employee's problems are aggravated by something in the job, as sometimes happens, or in the makeup of a particular supervisor, the psychologist may recommend a shift in the employee's responsibilities to another assignment.

Ordinarily, the industrial psychologist avoids developing a prolonged therapeutic relationship with employees whose problems are deeply emotional. When such a situation occurs, the psychologist may recommend the specialized aid of a clinical psychologist or a psychiatrist. Some industrial psychologists are also trained in clinical psychology and may therefore choose to assume more responsibility for therapy.

Counseling may sometimes reveal that the problem is management's rather than the employee's. In such instances, the psychologist, without involving the employee, will need at the appropriate time to call management's attention to an organizational block which would immobilize *any* employee who might serve under the circumstances resulting from such a procedure or policy.

Counseling is, of course, regularly conducted by many management organizations in the form of performance appraisals. Merit or performance reviews provide the most common forms of industrial counseling. The philosophy that "no news is good news" is rapidly being abandoned by thoughtful managements. Fewer executives are clinging to the rationalization that if their subordinates are "good" men, they will make an objective judgment of their own performance and progress. It is unlikely that a subordinate will, or can, evaluate himself and all parts of his work as accurately as can his superior or a group of superiors. It is the supervisor's obligation to communicate his impressions of a man's performance to that man so that self-improvement can be maximized. Most performance reviews are scheduled annually or semiannually and involve both a rating and a face-to-face confrontation during which the superior endeavors to share with the employee or executive his progress or lack of it since the previous appraisal was made. The conference permits a free exchange of information and communication, which hopefully results in better understanding on both sides of the relationship.

Motivation. Since the classic Western Electric–Hawthorne study in 1927, management has become increasingly aware of the important effects of group attitude and climate on work performance. Industrial psychology has learned much about both morale and motivation since that time.

We know that every man has a certain capacity for work or a potential level of proficiency which he is capable of achieving. The extent to which he approaches that level depends upon his motivation. His level of motivation, in turn, is dependent upon his needs and the extent to which the work situation is able to satisfy those needs.

Needs are generally categorized as primary or secondary in character. The primary needs are those which serve some basic physiological or biological function, such as the needs for nourishment and self-preservation. For the great majority of people in our culture, these needs are satisfied to a sufficient degree and consequently are not a major source of motivation in their daily lives.

Secondary needs, on the other hand, are largely social in nature, in that they are dependent upon other people for their satisfaction. Frequently mentioned as belonging to this class are the needs for recognition, status, affiliation, belonging, and self-esteem. Because most people in the North American culture are able to satisfy their primary needs, it is predominantly the secondary or social needs that motivate people in their work as well as in their personal lives.

This whole area of needs, motives, and attitudes is complicated by the fact that researchers have found no simple relationship between morale and productivity. Although motivation is certainly a part of productivity, studies have shown that high morale, as measured by the attitude survey, does not necessarily mean high productivity. Nor does low morale correlate significantly with low productivity. It is possible for a supervisor to create a group working climate where individuals so anesthetize each other with mutual acceptance and woolly good feeling that very little is actually accomplished. High morale is a desirable outcome of good management, but if the goal is high productivity, high morale alone will not accomplish it. Effective management succeeds in creating an atmosphere characterized not only by security and goodwill, but also by a keen awareness of management's expectations of excellent workmanship.

HUMAN ENGINEERING

Human engineering, a form of industrial psychology, has been defined as the adaptation of human tasks and working environment to the sensory, perceptual, mental, and physical attributes of people. This does not represent a new field of endeavor; in fact, the problem of adapting machinery to human characteristics began with the industrial revolution and has continued with increasing complexity ever since.   The discipline of human engineering, however, reflects a shift in emphasis from observation of trial-and-error human experience to the placing of greater reliance upon controlled and systematic research.   Research is carried on in the areas of workplace layout, equipment controls, instrument design, and environmental conditions.

Workplace Layout.   Psychologists have studied workplace layout through such methods as observation, film analysis, and interview.   It has been found that there is an optimum arrangement of work space and equipment position for every situation.   Designing work situations, work areas, tables, chairs, and other equipment with consideration of human dimensions can contribute not only to human comfort and convenience, but also to efficiency.   The problem of fatigue, for example, can be reduced by positioning the individual so that he can comfortably and effectively apply force to the controls and by allowing him to change posture to bring different parts of his body into play.

Equipment Controls.   As a part of a man-machine system, an operator receives information, makes decisions on the basis of this information, and acts upon the decisions.   The design and arrangement of machine controls are an important part of this system.   They can have a direct bearing on the adequacy with which controls are used and therefore can affect the functioning of the complete man-machine system.   In this regard, psychologists work toward making definitive recommendations on the practical size, shape, gearing, and direction of movement of different types of controls to minimize confusion and improve performance.

Instrument Design.   The design of instrumentation is also an important phase of the man-machine system.   Here the human engineer studies the design of graphs, gages, dials, and scales, and attempts to make certain the operator will receive the right type and amount of information as clearly as possible.

The human engineer first determines what information the operator will need, the speed with which it is needed, and the required degree of accuracy.   After establishing these factors, he then must consider to what sense it should be presented: oral, visual, tactual, or perhaps some combination of these.   With this information, he proceeds to the final design of the instrument.

In the study of visual display, for example, such factors as size, shape, and design of letters and numbers are considered.   Human engineers have participated in the design of aircraft instruments, highway signs, industrial gages, and the like.   Their efforts have resulted in advantages in safety, quality assurance, and time saving.

Environmental Conditions.   One final area of concern to the human engineer is the working environment.   Studies have been made of the effects of illumination, noise, humidity, temperature, and ventilation.   Investigations of these factors have had as their purpose the determination of the conditions conducive to optimal production as well as assurance of the workers' safety, comfort, and job satisfaction.

As manufacturing processes become more complex and the machinery more awesome, the job of the human engineer becomes more crucial and challenging. If we are to continue to keep pace with technological progress, we must continue to learn more and more about man's ability to make decisions, monitor tasks, and control complex systems.

RESEARCH

A psychologist is a behavioral scientist, and as such is trained in the methods of rigorous research design.   He approaches problems and opportunities for human betterment with an experimental attitude.   Like any scientist, he challenges the status quo and wonders if things might not be accomplished even better. He suggests hypotheses and sets up experimental designs to test them. He is not willing to accept opinions as final, but wants to evaluate results objectively. He is, in short, endeavoring to apply the experimental, scientific method to human resources in industry. Sometimes the industrial psychologist may be asked to attend to certain specific research problems, but more characteristically he approaches *all* of his problems and opportunities with a research attitude. All of the endeavors heretofore discussed as part of the industrial psychologist's concern would come under the surveillance of his open-minded exploratory methods. He is always, in whatever he may seek to accomplish in the industrial world, a behavioral scientist who will be more critical of his own work than anyone else until such time as he has demonstrated through repeated testing the validity of his efforts.

USE OF PSYCHOLOGICAL CONSULTANT

The increasing attention to the human element in industry has led inevitably to greater contact between business and psychology. Many of the areas which have been discussed require specialized knowledge and training for successful application. In many of the personnel activities, the services of the professional psychologist are of value in the initial planning and development stages. The program may be carried out by others in the organization. In developing a test battery for hourly workers, for example, a psychologist may be called upon to suggest tests, validate them, and establish cutoff scores, but at this point the program may be turned over to the personnel department. Other areas, such as organizational planning, management selection, manpower planning, counseling, and human engineering, may call for the continued attention of the psychologist.

Factors such as the size of the company and its objectives determine whether full or part-time services of a psychologist are advisable. There are advantages in both arrangements. The consultant has the advantage of the objectivity inherent in being an "outsider." He is not involved in the internal operation and has no emotional ties with the employees. He is not predisposed to judge one way or another because of group opinion or past acquaintanceships. On the other hand, for long-range programs of research, training, studies of job satisfaction, or the like, a psychologist who is a member of the organization may be desirable.

Choosing a Psychologist. Before a company engages the services of a psychological consultant, it is important that his qualifications and experience be investigated. It is advisable to query other organizations who are using or who have retained the services of the firm or the individual, just as the references of a managerial candidate would be investigated.

With rare exceptions, all qualified industrial psychologists are members of the American Psychological Association or, if working in Canada, the Canadian Psychological Association. The American Psychological Association publishes an annual directory listing all members, with their educational and work histories. A Ph.D. in the field of psychology from an accredited university is desirable. The APA directory, containing this information, is available in most local libraries.

The majority of states now require certification or licensing of anyone calling himself a psychologist. The best means of checking this point is through the state psychological association, local university, or the Better Business Bureau.

A final point which should be considered in choosing a psychologist is the man's personal characteristics. Are they suitable to the organization and its particular needs? If not, his impact and the potential benefits of the relationship will be diminished. Therefore, as a preliminary step, the key managers in the organization should have an opportunity to meet with the psychologist to estimate the likelihood of their being able to work effectively with him.

During these preliminary meetings, beware of the consultant who makes unusual claims or who guarantees overnight improvement. The American Psychological Association has a strict ethical code prohibiting exaggerated claims. In the first place, the responsible psychologist will not commit himself to cures or likely solutions until he has had time to study the problem. Even then, he will not guarantee absolute success. The well-trained, ethical psychologist knows and is willing to admit the limitations of his science.

Toward a Productive Relationship. The services the consulting psychologist provides for a company depend on a variety of factors, not the least of which are its size, its product or service, the attitude of management toward the psychologist, and the business goals and philosophies of the top executives. Before the psychologist can make a significant contribution, he should be given an opportunity to gain insight into these factors. Every business organization, for example, has a distinct personality or climate which is a reflection of its top management, and the psychologist must come to know this climate if he is to be effective.

Another important factor is the cooperation and support of the significant people in the company. This cooperation and support is necessary not only in the initial stages, but also as a continuing implementation and follow-up of the psychologist's efforts. The psychologist has no line authority, and rightly so. He makes recommendations and suggestions, but the final decisions are the responsibility of management. Thus, in one sense the psychologist is dependent on management, as a source of authority, to implement and take action on his ideas. This obviously suggests that the psychologist is looking not for unequivocal acceptance of all his recommendations, but rather for an environment which provides support and follow-through on those suggestions which are adopted.

Industrial psychology achieves most in those companies where management's expectations are realistic. Given the benefit of management's cooperation and support in working toward a mutually accepted goal, psychologists are able to apply the theories and principles of their profession in a practical, workable way and in a manner which contributes to the organization's goals of profitability.

CONCLUSION

Psychology is the science of human behavior. The industrial psychologist, when invited to serve the business community, endeavors to apply his knowledge of human behavior to its decisions and problems. The areas in which the industrial psychologist has been most helpful include (1) organizational planning; (2) the areas of human resources which involve the selection and promotion of people hired to accomplish specific jobs, the planning of the management development program, the counseling and training of selected employees, motivational studies, and morale surveys; (3) human engineering, which is the application of human tasks and working environment to the sensory, perceptual, mental, and physical attributes of people; and (4) research.

With competition increasing among companies for the markets of the world, one of the areas where a company can still excel over competitors is in the quality of its personnel, including its leadership. Competent psychologists, in cooperation with strong management, can be helpful in bringing this about.

BIBLIOGRAPHY

Albright, L. E., J. R. Glennon, and W. J. Smith, *The Use of Psychological Tests in Industry*, Howard Allen, Inc., Publishers, Cleveland, 1963.

Brammer, M., and H. Shostrom, *Therapeutic Psychology*, Harper & Row, Publishers, Incorporated, New York, 1963.

Cronbach, L. J., *Essentials of Psychological Testing*, 2d ed., Harper & Row, Publishers, Incorporated, New York, 1960.

Fryer, D. H., M. R. Feinbert, and S. S. Zolkind, *Developing People in Industry*, Harper & Row, Publishers, Incorporated, New York, 1956.

Ghiselli, E. E., and C. W. Brown, *Personnel and Industrial Psychology*, 2d ed., McGraw-Hill Book Company, New York, 1962.

Karn, H. W., and Gilmer B. Von Haller (eds.), *Readings in Industrial and Business Psychology*, 2d ed., McGraw-Hill Book Company, New York, 1962.

McCormick, E. J., *Human Engineering*, McGraw-Hill Book Company, New York, 1957.

McGehee, W., and P. W. Thayer, *Training in Business and Industry*, John Wiley & Sons, Inc., New York, 1961.

McGregor, D., *The Human Side of Enterprise*, McGraw-Hill Book Company, New York, 1960.

Mahoney, T. A., T. H. Jerdee, and A. N. Nash, *The Identification of Management Potential*, William C. Brown Company, Publishers, Dubuque, Iowa, 1961.

Merrill, Harwood F., and Elizabeth Marting (eds.), *Developing Executive Skills*, American Management Association, New York, 1958.

Tiffin, J., and E. J. McCormick, *Industrial Psychology*, 4th ed., Prentice-Hall, Inc., Englewood Cliffs, N.J., 1958.

Tyler, Leona, *Work of the Counselor*, Houghton Mifflin Company, Boston, 1963.

Viteles, M. S., *Motivation and Morale in Industry*, W. W. Norton & Company, Inc., New York, 1953.

CHAPTER FOUR

Personnel Administration*

HOWARD M. DIRKS *Vice President—Personnel, Harris-Intertype Corporation, Cleveland, Ohio*

Personnel administration has been defined by Thomas G. Spates, a recognized leader and teacher in the personnel field, as "so organizing and treating people in their work that they will utilize their maximum individual capacities, thereby attaining maximum personal and growth satisfaction, and rendering maximum service to the enterprise of which they are a part." A statement of the purpose of personnel administration, as developed and used by the National Industrial Conference Board, is: "The objective of personnel administration is to help make more effective the administrative leadership of people at their places of work."

Recognized formally as a defined management function only for half a century or so, personnel administration is considered by progressive and successful business organizations to be one of the most important activities of management. Staff responsibility for personnel relations is frequently assigned to a major executive reporting directly to the chief executive officer, with each line executive also charged with maintaining constructive personnel effectiveness in the group he supervises. Principal duties of a staff personnel executive normally include guiding and assisting line management in such activities as manpower planning, employment, compensation, benefits administration, management development, training, union relations, communications, counseling, and employee activities.

In this chapter, the role of personnel administration in business will be examined broadly as a prelude to a more complete discussion of specific personnel activities in the chapters that follow.

* This chapter is an expansion of a statement on "The Function and Scope of Personnel Administration" developed by a group of knowledgeable personnel executives and professors of personnel management. These men, representing leading business and educational institutions, meet periodically to study in depth various aspects of personnel administration. The original version of the statement, which appeared in *Personnel,* a publication of the American Management Association, has been reexamined and updated for this Handbook. Unfortunately, the list of those who contributed is too large to permit personal recognition.

Background of Personnel Administration. *Personnel relations,* or employer-employee relations, have obviously existed for as long as two or more people have been joined together in a common business endeavor. *Personnel administration,* however, as a defined management function, became recognized shortly after the turn of the century. Progress since then, though faltering at times, has been such that personnel administration is now recognized as an essential management activity capable of contributing substantially to the success of any organization. Many specialists in personnel administration have evolved and taken their places in the executive echelon.

The growth and development of the personnel administration function are the results of several factors. First, the number of employees in business organizations has grown substantially, thus increasing the importance of effective manpower management. Size has called for more standardization of employment and compensation procedures and for improved communications. Second, workers have more education and have achieved more responsible places in society. They are more conscious of their rights and continually want to improve their economic lot. Many have joined unions to further these ends, thus creating a whole new activity of union-management relations. Third, and very important, managements realize that dealing with people as individual human beings, recognizing their desire to participate and their ambition to get ahead, is not only ethically and morally right, but good business. Management has learned too that it can provide constructive motivation for employees to do better work by following sound principles of personnel administration.

Finally, and interrelated, a whole series of local, state, and Federal laws has been passed dealing with employee rights, health and safety, compensation, hours, antidiscrimination, benefits, and union-management relationships. These statutes and the complex regulations and interpretations that have followed in their wake have in themselves created a demand for more knowledgeable and more competent personnel administration.

Whatever the reasons for its emergence—and there are many others besides those mentioned—personnel administration is recognized in progressive organizations as a dynamic function, contributing to profits, growth, and the other objectives of the enterprise.

Changing Concepts of Personnel Administration. The personnel function has gone through several stages since it first became recognized as a business activity. The earliest concept was that of a paternalistic welfare program, taking a charitable interest in employees and their families. Then came an emphasis on the employment function, a result of the difficulty of getting people during wartime and the emergence of techniques for selecting people more effectively. Next, during the decade or so starting in the mid-1930s, relationships with unions were the dominant emphasis. Later, there was also the period of following popular techniques and fads mechanically to appear to be up to date. The modern concept of personnel administration as a dynamic management function finally became recognized and is being followed by a sizable number of companies. Many companies, however, are still going through some of the earlier phases, and many thoughtful students feel that sound personnel administration has developed more slowly than other functions of management. The result has been a failure to attract top staff talent in sufficient numbers, and accordingly, the opportunities in the field appear to be limitless for qualified people.

A Word about Terminology. The term "personnel administration," as used in this chapter, covers all facets of the employer-employee relationship. There is much confusion regarding terminology, both in describing the function and in the titles of personnel specialists.

Terms other than "personnel administration" used by various companies include "labor relations," "industrial relations," "human relations," "employee relations," and many more.   No elaborate brief will be presented here for one over the other, but "personnel administration" is intended to connote the modern concept of a strong, dynamic function concerned with developing and utilizing the manpower resources of the business to the optimum extent in achieving the objectives of the business.

The word "administration" also helps to convey the concept that personnel relations is an "activity of all management," rather than the exclusive responsibility of the personnel executive.   This does not mean that the personnel executive's function is a passive one; quite the contrary.   If he is doing a total job, he works closely with the chief executive officer and other executives in establishing personnel policy, in communicating it to the organization, and in developing procedures and programs to ensure results.   His is a creative, administrative, and control function.

It should also be pointed out that personnel administration is concerned with all employees, not just certain groups.   Supervisory, technical, sales, and clerical people are just as much a part of the personnel officer's responsibility as are the so-called blue-collar workers.   Also, he must be familiar with and give counsel and assistance on the people aspects of all kinds of management activities.

Objectives of Personnel Administration.   In our economy, the primary purpose of private business enterprise is the profitable production and distribution of goods and services.   The fulfillment of this primary purpose is contingent upon:

1. The economic need for or usefulness of such goods or services

2. Conditions of employment for all members of the organization which provide for satisfaction in relation to their needs, so that they will desire to work for the success of the enterprise

3. The effective utilization of people and materials in productive work

4. The continuity of the enterprise

All these essential elements may be combined in a statement of purpose as follows: The purpose of business enterprise is the profitable production of goods and services to fill economic needs in such a way as to provide satisfactory returns, both economic and social, to suppliers, owners, and members of the organization, under conditions which provide for the maximum conservation of human and material resources over a continuing period.

The methods adopted by business organizations in fulfilling this primary purpose must, of course, be consistent with the ethical and social values of our society and with the policies and regulations established by legislative action.

The achievement of the purpose of the enterprise involves the coordination of a number of basic functions, such as engineering, sales, manufacturing, finance, and the like.   All these functions are carried out by people.   Therefore, an integral part of each of these functions is the management of people.

The objectives of personnel administration thus are:

To utilize human resources effectively

To establish and maintain productive and self-respecting working relationships among all members of the organization

To bring about maximum individual development of members of the organization

Requirements for Achievement of Objectives.   To achieve these objectives, the following three requirements must be fulfilled.

1. *Obtain capable people.* To obtain capable people, it is necessary first to know what they will be required to do. There should be a plan for the division of the organization's task into functions and positions. There should be a definition of the responsibilities and duties of each position established by that plan and of its relationships with other positions. There should be a determination of the qualifications necessary for the effective performance of each position. After the organization plan has been determined, it is necessary to recruit and select people possessing the desired qualifications (or the potentialities for developing them) and to secure and maintain acceptance of the terms of employment by the selected candidates.

2. *Utilize their efforts effectively.* In order that the organization's purposes may be achieved, each person must know what is expected of him. He should understand the scope of his responsibilities and the policies within the limits of which he must work in fulfilling these responsibilities. He should possess, or be given the opportunity to acquire, the knowledge, skills, authority, "tools," and help necessary for effective performance in his position. His performance should be appraised, and he should be informed periodically of the extent to which he is measuring up to the expected standards.

Effective performance should be rewarded and improvement encouraged. Provision should be made for transfers and retraining where needed to make the most effective use of the individual's capabilities and to facilitate the prompt replacement of the incompetent. To ensure the continuity of an effective organization, this whole process must be dynamic rather than static, providing for the planned development of all capable people within the organization so that their potentialities may be utilized to the fullest extent and so that openings will be adequately filled as they occur.

3. *Maintain willingness to work to achieve the organization's purposes.* Willingness depends upon each individual's expectation that he can satisfy his needs through his work. He must therefore be fairly compensated for his efforts and protected so far as possible against insecurity from illness, accident, old age, and unemployment, and against arbitrary actions by his superiors. He must obtain social satisfaction from his associations on the job. His work should afford opportunities for the development and utilization of his capacities and skills and for recognition of his accomplishments. He should have an opportunity to participate in plans and decisions affecting his job, his economic well-being, and his progress.

Responsibility of Line Organization. Because all the functions of management in a given organization are accomplished through people, the principal responsibility for achieving the objectives of personnel administration is vested in the chief executive. This necessitates the establishment of controlling policy for the organization as a whole and, particularly, attention on the part of the chief executive to the promotion of effective and harmonious day-to-day relationships among his immediate subordinates.

Likewise, the responsibility for carrying out a company's program of personnel administration in any of its organization units must rest with each officer or executive in charge of a key unit. In addition to fulfilling the administrative duties which the program prescribes, he should demonstrate its spirit by his example. He should be the official representative of the company in its relations with his subordinates.

Each manager should, in turn, concern himself with the interest and ability in personnel administration of each of his subordinate managers. He should stimulate this interest and help each to develop this ability. He should continually concern himself with the success of his subordinate managers in carrying out the company's personnel program, should note failures in executing any of the program's features, and should assist in correcting such failures. Though a manager or supervisor may receive counsel and aid from personnel specialists in such endeavors, he cannot avoid ultimate responsibility for the personnel function.

Responsibilities of the Personnel Specialist. Normally an organization of any size can justify the use of a staff executive specializing in personnel administration in addition to other line and staff executives. The functions of the personnel specialist are:

1. To aid line management in the preparation, adoption, and continuing evaluation of a program of personnel administration expressed in terms of definite written company policy.

2. To establish and administer the services that are normally delegated to a personnel department. These include planning for and maintaining a capable working force; carrying out a sound program of salary and wage administration and employee benefits, safety, and health services; coordinating union relations; and other activities described in some detail in succeeding chapters.

3. To develop and coordinate a program of personnel development and training which will provide all members of the organization with information and skills required to do their own jobs, and develop their talents for future and more responsible assignments.

4. To assist management in establishing a relationship among all members of the organization, and between the organization and the community, which is characterized by mutual understanding, confidence, and respect.

5. To assist in developing an effective appraisal system which may be used by management to provide an inventory of current and potential human resources in the organization.

6. To aid management in assuring effective communications throughout the organization.

7. To conduct personnel research which will keep management continually informed so that better decisions and plans can be made and which will add to management knowledge regarding improved motivation and utilization of members of the organization.

8. To develop, as required, a competent and efficient staff to implement the program.

In carrying out these functions, the personnel executive does not have authority to command, except within his own department. In this respect, his authority is parallel to that of any other department or division head in an organization, such as vice president in charge of sales. He does, however, have a major responsibility for strongly influencing the organization to utilize its human resources intelligently and effectively.

Personnel Administration and Collective Bargaining. The basic objectives of personnel administration, and the requirements for attaining them, remain the same whether or not certain groups among the members of the organization belong to labor unions. Some of the specific procedures for reaching the objectives may, of course, be determined by collective bargaining. This does not alter either the objectives or management's obligation to strive to reach them.

The objectives of personnel administration are not in opposition to those objectives of organized labor which are consistent with the successful operation of the private enterprise system. Management can demonstrate the correctness of that fact by its policies and its actions. Actually, the above statement of the objectives of personnel administration is in the best interests of all those to whom management is responsible: owners of the enterprise, the community, consumers of its goods or services, suppliers, and members of the organization itself—including groups who may belong to unions.

Personnel Administration and Management Manpower Planning. Generally, one of the most important aspects of personnel administration is management manpower planning, including management development and organization development. As the economy continues to expand and companies grow in size and complexity, the shortage of able executives becomes increasingly acute. Companies simply have to develop their own managers to survive.

Management manpower planning involves maintaining an accurate inventory of present and potential talent, in both quantity and quality, relating that information to carefully planned future manpower requirements, and taking constructive, timely, and realistic action on discrepancies. Necessary steps will include internal and external development activities, as well as recruiting as required.

Sound management manpower planning, organization development, and management development are manifestations of personnel administration within the management group. Space limitations do not permit an extended discussion of management planning and development, but a listing of some guiding principles developed by General Electric Company, a pioneer and outstanding practitioner in management development, may be helpful. In part, they are:

Managing is a separate and distinct kind of work which is emerging as another profession.

The manager development process is a highly individual matter.

Every man's development in business is *self*-development.

The incumbent line manager at all levels is responsible for encouraging and guiding the development of people who work under his direction.

A man's development is 90 percent the result of his experience in his day-to-day work.

Primary emphasis must be on development in the present assignment, rather than on a promotional ladder.

Effective personnel administration involves following through with line management on the practical application of these principles.

BIBLIOGRAPHY

Blood, Jerome W., et al., *The Personnel Job in a Changing World*, American Management Association, New York, 1964.

Hertzberg, Frederick, Bernard Mausner, and Barbara Snyderman, *The Motivation to Work*, John Wiley & Sons, Inc., New York, 1959.

Pigors, Paul, and Charles A. Myers, *Personnel Administration*, 5th ed., McGraw-Hill Book Company, New York, 1965.

Snider, Paul, *Improving Performance in the Personnel Department*, Special Study, no. 15, Presidents' Professional Association, Hamilton, N.Y., 1963.

Snider, Paul, *A Look at Personnel Administration through the President's Eye*, Special Study, no. 13, Presidents' Professional Association, Hamilton, N.Y., 1963.

Spates, Thomas G., *Human Values Where People Work*, Harper & Row, Publishers, Incorporated, New York, 1960.

Wright, Moorhead, *How Do People Grow in a Business Organization?* (presentation before the 31st NAM Institute on Industrial Relations).

CHAPTER FIVE

Personnel Recruitment

JOSEPH J. FAMULARO *Vice President, Personnel Relations, McGraw-Hill, Inc., New York, New York*

In personnel recruitment, management tries to do far more than merely fill job openings. If not, the formula for personnel recruitment would be simple— just fill the job with any applicant who comes along. However, the act of hiring a man carries with it the presumption that he will stay with the company—that sooner or later his ability to perform his work, his capacity for job growth, and his ability to get along in the group in which he works will become matters of first importance. Because of this, a critical examination of recruitment methods in use should be made, and that is the purpose of this chapter.

ELEMENTS OF A PERSONNEL RECRUITMENT PROGRAM

The function of personnel recruitment is to find sources of manpower to match job requirements and specifications. It is also used as a means for attracting manpower in sufficient numbers to permit adequate selection of a capable and productive work group. Most importantly, recruitment is a *continuing* function.

The basic elements involved in personnel recruitment are:

1. A recruitment policy that describes the intent and objectives of the employer
2. An organization for recruitment, and the delegation of appropriate authority and responsibility for the recruitment function
3. A forecast of manpower requirements
4. The development of manpower sources and various techniques for utilizing these sources
5. A method of evaluating the recruitment program

A Recruitment Policy. To begin a personnel recruitment program, the objectives should be spelled out by developing an adequate and realistic set of recruitment policies. If these policies are implemented by specific procedures, a sound operating framework will result.

Recruitment policy in its broadest sense involves a commitment by the employer to general principles such as, "The company shall obtain the most competent individual for each job"; "All jobs in the company will be filled with the best-qualified person"; or "Present company employees shall be considered first for any job opening in the company."

Some of the more important points in any recruitment policy that should be spelled out include:

1. Promotion from within
2. Employment of:
   a. Relatives of present employees
   b. Older persons
   c. Minors
   d. Members of minority groups
   e. Handicapped individuals
   f. Temporary and part-time employees
3. Centralized or decentralized recruitment
4. School and college relations
5. Community relations
6. Payment or nonpayment of employment agency fees

The following are other items that should be considered in setting recruitment policy and procedure:

1. Promises made during recruitment should not oversell either the company or any job in it. If they do, employees will inevitably become dissatisfied when experience shows them the difference between recruitment talk and employment facts.

2. Recruitment policies and procedures should consider the relevant differences in the kind of employees to be hired.

3. Because the manager and technical type of employee is difficult to find, some firms recruit on the principle that it is impossible to have too much of a good thing. This proves quite untrue of top-caliber employees who become restless if kept too long in subordinate positions where their major capacities remain unused and underdeveloped. High-talent human resources deteriorate if they are hoarded and unused.

4. Applicants for employment should be considered solely on the basis of qualifications. Fair employment practice laws in some states prohibit discrimination on the basis of color, race, or national origin, and the Civil Rights Act of 1964 made this national policy. Farsighted employers have followed this policy voluntarily, and good personnel administration has always required it.

5. Local labor market conditions will affect the attention management gives to recruitment policies and procedures. When there are many job seekers, there is a tendency to pay less attention to screening, interviewing, testing, and placement. When there are many jobs waiting to be filled, recruitment efforts often get a boost. Since World War II, the American labor market has experienced shortages of high-talent manpower. Employers have thus been forced to pay more attention to the kind of effective recruiting and selection that will induce the new employee to remain with the organization.

Recruitment Organization. All employment activity should be centralized if the policies of top management are to be implemented consistently and efficiently in company-wide hiring. Only when personnel requisitions go through one central source and all employment records are kept up to date is there a maximum possibility for efficiency and success in hiring.

If the policy of centralized recruitment is adequately explained by top management, line managers need not feel that, in accepting the services of staff experts, they lose prestige or responsibility. It is easy to explain that the work of the recruitment department (usually a subordinate unit of the personnel division) is a supplement to the judgment of line managers and not a substitute for it. The line manager retains the right to accept or reject an applicant sent to his department by the recruitment people. A line manager can benefit by the assistance of a centralized recruitment effort, because he ordinarily is extremely busy and has neither the time nor the skill to perform the recruitment process himself.

In a small company, of course, the line manager and his supervisors are apt to be charged with the recruitment responsibility in addition to their other duties. In such cases, recruiting procedures are usually informal. Although it may not be economical for the smaller employer to create a specialized recruitment organization, efficient recruitment procedures can nevertheless be adopted.

Organizational specialization for recruitment in the larger company is usual. There is frequently a staff unit attached to the employee relations or personnel division usually called the "employment office" or "recruitment section." This allows specialists an opportunity to concentrate upon the recruitment function, and in this way, they become more efficient in the use of various recruitment techniques.

The recruitment manager, however, is still a staff employee. He receives personnel requisitions from the line; he does not originate them himself. He does not have the final word in the acceptance or rejection of a given applicant; this is customarily the right of the supervisor for whom the applicant will work. But the recruitment manager does have considerable discretion with respect to the sources of manpower. It is he who usually decides which sources will be used and how to go about using them.

Forecasting Manpower Requirements. Replacement requirements at all levels of the work force should be anticipated, and steps to fill them should be planned and scheduled. Orderly replacement is accomplished through the careful and realistic forecasting of needs.

One large organization forecasts manpower needs in the following way. Divisional managers and staff department directors are responsible for making an annual examination of their organizational structures and their adequacy for the work at hand or anticipated changes. This review shows current vacancies and anticipated changes in organization structure. Manpower inventories are developed on a department basis and include detailed statistics on:

1. Anticipated number of replacements required because of:
   a. Resignations
   b. Dismissals
   c. Promotions
   d. Transfers
   e. Retirements
   f. Deaths
   g. Leaves of absence
2. Anticipated number of additions to staff because of growth, reorganization, and so on

Requisitioning Employees. Recruitment activity begins with a personnel requisition. In larger organizations with many different jobs, the requisition should be based on accurate job specifications drawn up by the first-line supervisor in cooperation with a specially trained job analyst. The requisition should be clear-cut regarding the exact demands of the job. It should be definite and realistic regarding what the requisitioner wants. Initial action on a personnel requisition is taken by the supervisor in whose unit manpower needs appear. Although any number of employees may be requisitioned on a single form for

AREA REQUISITION NO.	**REQUISITION FOR EMPLOYEE**	EMPLOYMENT DIVISION REQ. NO.

DATE _____

To: PERSONNEL ADMINISTRATION - EMPLOYMENT DIVISION

LOCATION
OF DEPT. _____

From: DEPT. _____ DIVISION _____   DEPT. NO. _____

POSITION TITLE   POSITION CODE NO.

MALE	FEMALE		PARTICULAR QUALIFICATIONS REQUIRED

EXPERIENCE
YES | NO

[ ] REPLACEMENT   [ ] INCREASE IN QUOTA   [ ] PERMANENT TEMPORARY   [ ] PART TIME   FROM AM PM   TO AM PM   HOURS IN WORK WEEK

REPLACING MR. MRS. MISS	FIRST NAME	MIDDLE NAME	LAST NAME	DATE OF TRANSFER	DATE OF LEAVING

SUPERVISOR _____   OFFICER _____   AREA PERSONNEL

TO BE FILLED OUT BY EMPLOYMENT DIVISION FOR NEW EMPLOYEES ONLY

PAYROLL CODE	DEPT. OR BRANCH NO.	EMPLOYEE NUMBER	LAST NAME	FIRST NAME	M.I.

CERTIFICATE NUMBER	DATE OF BIRTH	ADDRESS (NUMBER & STREET)	SEX	TIME CARD NO.	STATUS
			M	9	TEMPORARY
			F	8	PERMANENT

DATE OF EMPLOY	ADDRESS (CITY AND STATE)	CITIZENSHIP CODE	ADDRESS CODE	MARITAL STATUS	POSITION CODE
				1 SINGLE	
				2 MARRIED	

R. E.	TAX TYPE	AREA CODES PERS. EXEC.	NO. FEDERAL EXEMPTIONS	N.Y. STATE	NO. STATE EXEMPTIONS	SOCIAL SECURITY NO.	PER PAY SALARY INCL. SHIFT DIFF. BI-WEEKLY WEEKLY HOURLY PER DIEM
				8 RES.			
				9 NON RES.			

ANNUAL SALARY INCLUDING SHIFT DIFF.	PER PAY SHIFT DIFF.	SCHEDULED HOURS HOURS TENTHS	PAID BY	WORK COMP. CODE	NEXT REVIEW MONTH YEAR	*IF REEMPLOYED CONT. FROM	DATE RES.
		9	CASH				
		8	DEP.				

TAX DATA	SUBJECT TO	NOT SUBJECT TO	TRANS. CODE	INDI-CATOR	INDICATE REASON IF "NOT SUBJECT TO"	MILITARY STATUS
FEDERAL INCOME TAX WITHHOLDING						CLERICAL T/C 071
FEDERAL SOCIAL SECURITY TAX						
STATE INCOME TAX WITHHOLDING						BUILDING T/C 023
STATE DISABILITY BENEFITS						

EMPLOYMENT DIVISION		PAYROLL DIVISION		COMPUTER CENTER		CHECKING ACCT. NUMBER T/C
AUTHORIZED	POSTED	CODED	PROCESSED	PUNCHED	VERIFIED	

*NOTICE FOR PAYROLL

IF REEMPLOYED AND RECEIVING CONTINUITY OF SERVICE REASSIGN PREVIOUS CERTIFICATE NUMBER, IF ANY. EMPLOYEE BENEFITS DE-PARTMENT WILL ADJUST THE DATE OF EMPLOYMENT FOR CONTINUITY OF SERVICE AFTER THIS DOCUMENT HAS BEEN PROCESSED. IF RE-EMPLOYED DURING CURRENT TAXABLE YEAR REFER TO SPECIAL PROCEDURE NECESSARY FOR ADJUSTING THE TAPE RECORD ACCORDINGLY.

IF THIS REQUISITION IS FILLED BY A TRANSFER - SEE OTHER SIDE

PERS. 64A (REV. 9-61)   PERSONNEL ADMINISTRATION-EMPLOYMENT SECTION COPY

FIG. 5-1. *Employee requisition form—front.*

a particular job, separate requisitions should be made out by the unit desiring workers to fill *different* jobs. Any other procedure invites confusion.

In many cases, however, a company will initiate a personnel requisition for each position to be filled. The more advanced planning and action taken by the requisitioner, the fewer the difficulties the recruiter will meet in filling the requisition. Figures 5-1 and 5-2 show a comprehensive employee requisition form.

A requisition cannot be filled on the spot, nor can an applicant be put to work half an hour after the requisition appears. For most jobs below the executive level, however, long delays will not usually be encountered in filling requisitions except perhaps when the labor market is tight and certain skills are hard to find. The necessity for recruitment as a continuous process becomes evident here. An efficient recruitment section seeks to maintain a supply of applicants necessary for the prompt filling of requisitions for most jobs.

FOR PAYROLL USE ONLY	Due to transfer of _____ from _____			
PAYROLL CODE	to_____ the following data should be changed on your records.			

DEPT. NO.	INTER PAYROLL TRANSFER FROM ONE P/R TYPE TO ANOTHER P/R TYPE				INTRA PAYROLL TRANSFER WITHIN PAYROLL TYPE	
	PAYROLL TYPE	DEPT. NO.	EFFECTIVE DATE		DEPT. NO.	EFFECTIVE DATE
EMPLOYEE NO.				PREVIOUS		
	200	029	031	TRANS. CODE	030	031
				NEW		

EMPLOYMENT DIVISION - COMPLETE THE FOLLOWING DATA WHEN APPLICABLE:

	PERSONNEL AREA CODE
	EXECUTIVE AREA CODE
	TAX TYPE

TEMPORARY	9	PERMANENT	8	} CROSS OUT WHICHEVER IS **NOT** APPLICABLE
CREDIT	8	CASH	9	

FROM	TO	
		POSITION CODE
		PER PAY SALARY INCLUDING SHIFT DIFFERENTIAL
		ANNUAL SALARY INCLUDING SHIFT DIFFERENTIAL
		PER PAY SHIFT DIFFERENTIAL OR OVERSEAS ALLOWANCE
		PER PAY SALARY CHANGE
		REASON FOR SALARY CHANGE
		EFFECTIVE DATE OF SALARY CHANGE
		NEXT REVIEW DATE
		SCHEDULED HOURS - MUST BE SHOWN FOR PART TIME (P/R TYPE 2) AND BLDG. MAINT. (P/R TYPE 5).
		MILITARY STATUS CODE
		CHECKING ACCOUNT NUMBER

SUBJECT	NOT SUBJECT		TAX DATA
			FEDERAL INCOME TAX
			FEDERAL SOCIAL SECURITY
			STATE INCOME TAX
			STATE DISABILITY TAX

POSTED BY	AUTHORIZED BY	DATE

	STRAIGHT TIME HOURLY RATE
	SUB DEPT. CODE
	SAVINGS
	CHRISTMAS CLUB
	BOND DEDUCTION
	BOND INDICATOR
	BOND PURCHASE PRICE
	JOHN STREET

PAYROLL		COMPUTER DIVISION	
CODED	CHECKED	PUNCHED	VERIFIED

FIG. 5-2. *Employee requisition form—back.*

RECRUITMENT ACTIVITY CHECKLIST			Job Title _____ Dept. _____ Date Rec'd _____ Date Filled _____ Time Lapse _____ Interviewer _____ Salary _____					INTERVIEWS				
Source & Date			Resumes Referred	Source & Date	Applicant	Source	P/R	Date	Dept.	Date	Disposition	
House Ads												
Newspaper Ads												
Prof. & Other Mags.												
Employment Agencies												
Assoc. Placement Off.												
Colleges & Univ.												
Other Company Contacts												
Others _____												
Spec. Files _____ ESI _____												
Per. Rel. R & S. 7/62/1000												

FIG. 5-3. *Form for evaluating recruitment program effectiveness.*

Evaluation of the Recruitment Program. Recruitment activity begins before the receipt of approved personnel requisitions, because the recruitment unit takes applications for employment in advance of actual hiring requisitions. Except in periods of tight labor markets, it may be expected that a sufficient number of promising candidates to fill vacancies will be on file in the employment section of the personnel department. This backlog of potential employees is gathered from a variety of sources which will be discussed below. But it is most important to realize that recruitment procedures can be improved only if the personnel administrator carefully studies the correlation among his sources of labor, methods of recruitment, and subsequent job performance. He should be able to answer the question, "From what sources and by what methods have we secured our most satisfactory workers?" This is the crux of personnel recruitment. Some recruiters maintain separate records on a form similar to the one shown in Figure 5-3 for each individual job opening to help them evaluate the success of the action taken on that opening.

RECRUITMENT SOURCES

As the economy continues to expand, more recruitment ingenuity is going to be required in seeking qualified applicants than ever before. It will not be enough to seek applications at the conventional sources that have been the providers in the past. There are newer sources and techniques, often overlooked by many companies, which can provide talented applicants. These sources, along with the conventional ones, should be used.

In-company Recruitment. Often the best employees are in the company. Before looking on the outside, an in-company search should be made. Two main sources are (1) a review of present employees, and (2) referral of applicants by employees.

1. The development and use of a skills inventory will provide the data which may reveal possibilities for transfer and upgrading within the company. An example of an employee skills inventory form used to obtain information on employee experience and training is shown in Figures 5-4 and 5-5. In larger organizations, the information recorded on the form is coded and placed on automated equipment to facilitate the discovery of needed skills quickly. In smaller companies, searches can be made by hand or with the use of hand-sort

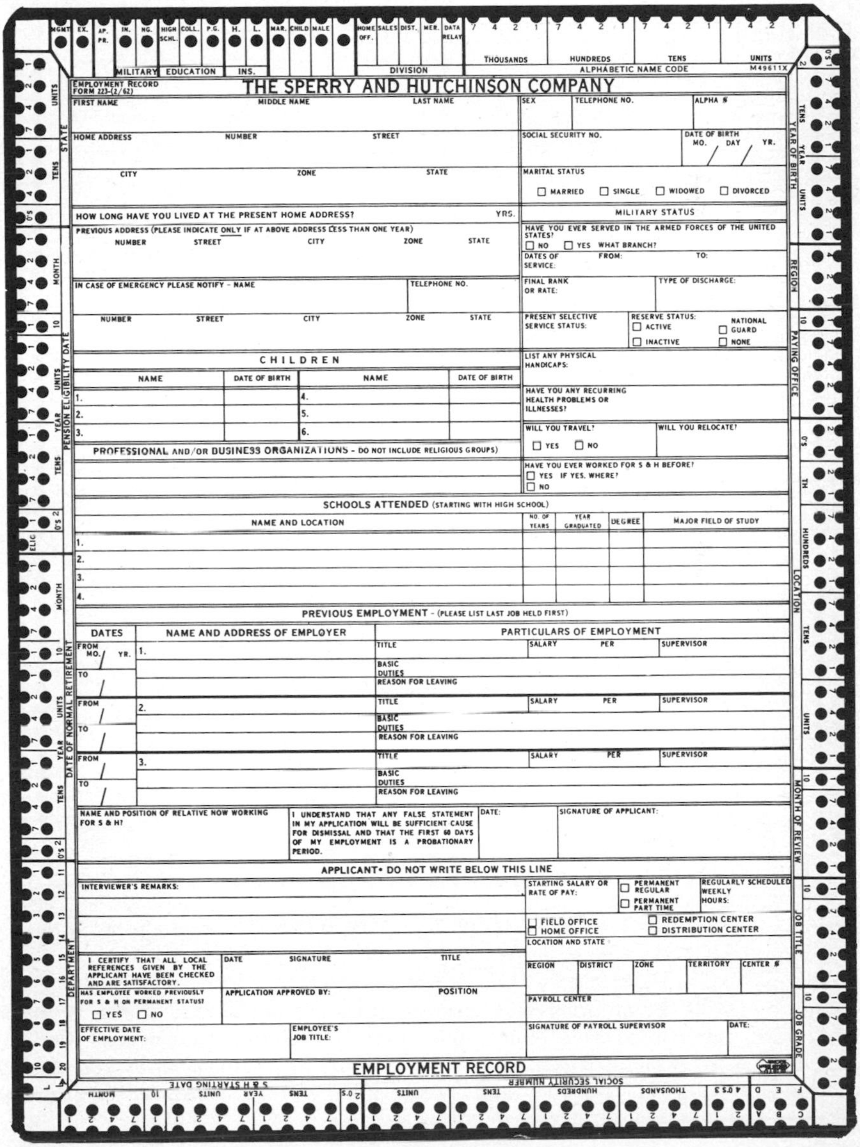

EMPLOYMENT RECORD FORM 223-(2/62)

THE SPERRY AND HUTCHINSON COMPANY

FIRST NAME | MIDDLE NAME | LAST NAME | SEX | TELEPHONE NO. | ALPHA #

HOME ADDRESS | NUMBER | STREET | SOCIAL SECURITY NO. | DATE OF BIRTH MO. / DAY / YR.

CITY | ZONE | STATE | MARITAL STATUS ☐ MARRIED ☐ SINGLE ☐ WIDOWED ☐ DIVORCED

HOW LONG HAVE YOU LIVED AT THE PRESENT HOME ADDRESS? YRS.

MILITARY STATUS

PREVIOUS ADDRESS (PLEASE INDICATE ONLY IF AT ABOVE ADDRESS LESS THAN ONE YEAR) NUMBER | STREET | CITY | ZONE | STATE

HAVE YOU EVER SERVED IN THE ARMED FORCES OF THE UNITED STATES? ☐ NO ☐ YES WHAT BRANCH?

DATES OF SERVICE: FROM: TO:

IN CASE OF EMERGENCY PLEASE NOTIFY - NAME | TELEPHONE NO.

FINAL RANK OR RATE: | TYPE OF DISCHARGE:

NUMBER | STREET | CITY | ZONE | STATE

PRESENT SELECTIVE SERVICE STATUS: | RESERVE STATUS: ☐ ACTIVE ☐ INACTIVE | NATIONAL ☐ GUARD ☐ NONE

CHILDREN

NAME	DATE OF BIRTH	NAME	DATE OF BIRTH
1.		4.	
2.		5.	
3.		6.	

LIST ANY PHYSICAL HANDICAPS:

HAVE YOU ANY RECURRING HEALTH PROBLEMS OR ILLNESSES?

WILL YOU TRAVEL? ☐ YES ☐ NO | WILL YOU RELOCATE?

PROFESSIONAL AND/OR BUSINESS ORGANIZATIONS - DO NOT INCLUDE RELIGIOUS GROUPS)

HAVE YOU EVER WORKED FOR S & H BEFORE? ☐ YES IF YES, WHERE? ☐ NO

SCHOOLS ATTENDED (STARTING WITH HIGH SCHOOL)

NAME AND LOCATION	NO. OF YEARS	YEAR GRADUATED	DEGREE	MAJOR FIELD OF STUDY
1.				
2.				
3.				
4.				

PREVIOUS EMPLOYMENT - (PLEASE LIST LAST JOB HELD FIRST)

DATES	NAME AND ADDRESS OF EMPLOYER	PARTICULARS OF EMPLOYMENT			
FROM MO. / YR. TO /	1.	TITLE / BASIC DUTIES / REASON FOR LEAVING	SALARY	PER	SUPERVISOR
FROM / TO /	2.	TITLE / BASIC DUTIES / REASON FOR LEAVING	SALARY	PER	SUPERVISOR
FROM / TO /	3.	TITLE / BASIC DUTIES / REASON FOR LEAVING	SALARY	PER	SUPERVISOR

NAME AND POSITION OF RELATIVE NOW WORKING FOR S & H?

I UNDERSTAND THAT ANY FALSE STATEMENT IN MY APPLICATION WILL BE SUFFICIENT CAUSE FOR DISMISSAL AND THAT THE FIRST 60 DAYS OF MY EMPLOYMENT IS A PROBATIONARY PERIOD.

DATE: | SIGNATURE OF APPLICANT:

APPLICANT• DO NOT WRITE BELOW THIS LINE

INTERVIEWER'S REMARKS:

STARTING SALARY OR RATE OF PAY: ☐ PERMANENT REGULAR ☐ PERMANENT PART TIME | REGULARLY SCHEDULED WEEKLY HOURS:

☐ FIELD OFFICE ☐ HOME OFFICE ☐ REDEMPTION CENTER ☐ DISTRIBUTION CENTER

LOCATION AND STATE

I CERTIFY THAT ALL LOCAL REFERENCES GIVEN BY THE APPLICANT HAVE BEEN CHECKED AND ARE SATISFACTORY. | DATE | SIGNATURE | TITLE

REGION | DISTRICT | ZONE | TERRITORY | CENTER #

HAS EMPLOYEE WORKED PREVIOUSLY FOR S & H ON PERMANENT STATUS? ☐ YES ☐ NO | APPLICATION APPROVED BY: | POSITION

PAYROLL CENTER

EFFECTIVE DATE OF EMPLOYMENT: | EMPLOYEE'S JOB TITLE: | SIGNATURE OF PAYROLL SUPERVISOR | DATE:

EMPLOYMENT RECORD

MILITARY | EDUCATION | INS. | DIVISION | THOUSANDS | HUNDREDS | TENS | UNITS | ALPHABETIC NAME CODE | M49611X

PENSION ELIGIBILITY DATE | DATE OF NORMAL RETIREMENT | DEPARTMENT | YEAR OF BIRTH | REGION | PAYING OFFICE | LOCATION | MONTH OF REVIEW | JOB TITLE | JOB GRADE | S & H STARTING DATE | SOCIAL SECURITY NUMBER

FIG. 5-4. *Employment record form—front.*

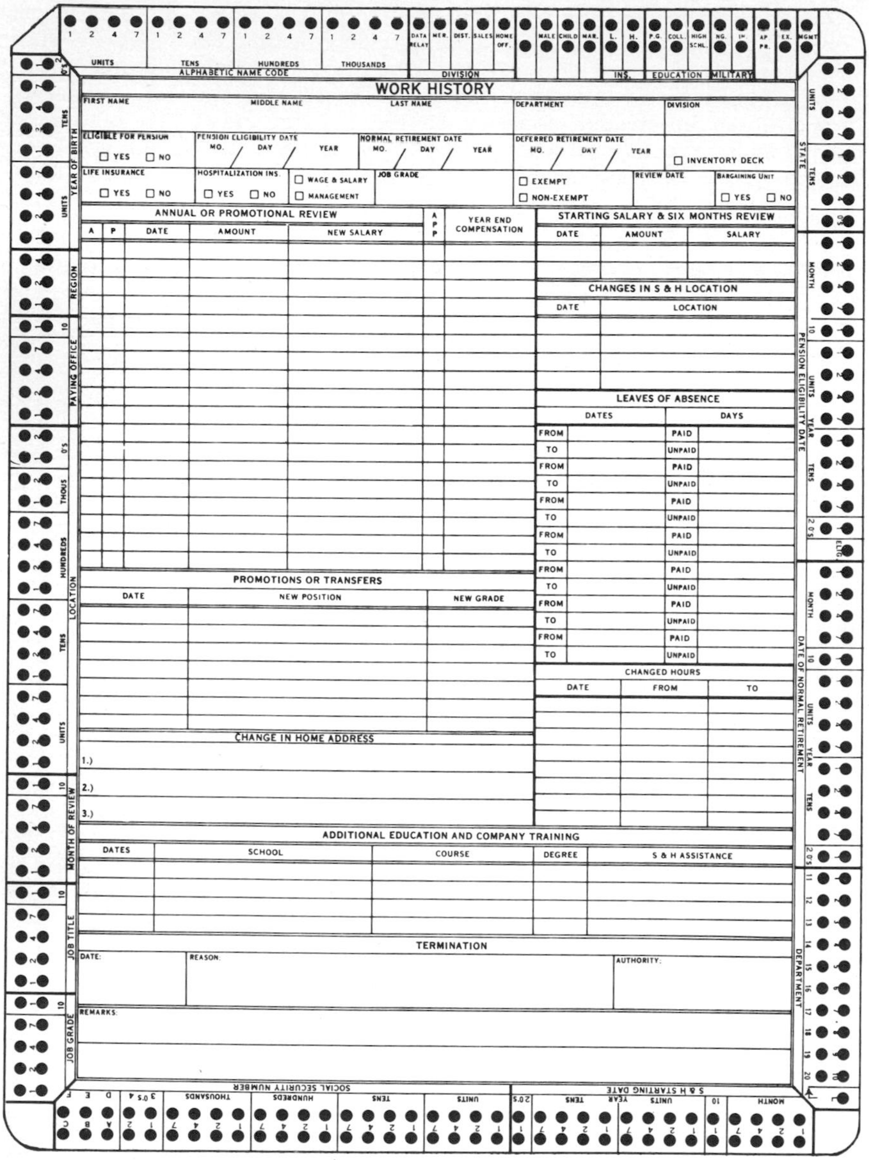

FIG. 5-5. *Employment record form—back.*

systems. Skills inventories will ease recruitment problems, lower recruitment costs, and have a positive effect on employee morale. A company that shows this kind of interest in its employees will be highly thought of by its employees. Action resulting in transfers and promotions will substantiate the company's interest and heighten employee morale.

2. Present employees are excellent sources of suggestions for job applicants. Some companies give cash bonuses or special merchandise prizes when an em-

ployee referral is subsequently hired.   Sales organizations seem to be among the more aggressive and constant users of referrals from employees, although manufacturing concerns also use them heavily.   Recruiting contests among salesmen and contests among various divisions and districts of a company are techniques that will bring forth job applicants.   The advantages of employee referrals are that (1) friends of present employees are prescreened (employees, as a rule, refer people they like being associated with) and (2) recruitment costs are significantly lower.   On the other hand, there are some disadvantages.   Some think that (1) this technique helps develop cliques and that the employee group becomes harder to handle and (2) turning away friends and referrals of employees may not have a positive effect on those employees.   But in general, most companies find that employee referrals get good employee reaction.

Outside Recruitment Sources.   Although many companies fill more-important and higher-rated jobs by promotion from within, there are still numerous positions which have to be filled by using outside recruitment sources.   This is usually true for "entry jobs" and for jobs that require college, technical, or professional backgrounds.   Most companies direct their recruitment efforts outside the company to fill jobs such as junior engineer, accounting trainee, editorial assistant, junior secretary, statistician, legal representative, sales trainee, and the like. There are many outside sources, and a progressive, imaginative, result-getting recruiter will try most of them to determine which are best for his company.

Application by Mail.   Whether or not a company has an employment office, it is sure to receive letters of application through the mail.   Writing to companies is a popular job-finding technique.   The quality and quantity of such applications will usually depend on the size and the reputation of the company.   Using applications which come through the mail can be an effective and inexpensive recruitment source.   Because job seekers will write to more than one company, it is important, from a recruitment point of view, to take fast action.   In other words, if you get a letter of application or a résumé which you think you are likely to use, you should respond to the writer as soon as possible.

One advantage of the letter of application is that the recruiter has a good idea of the applicant's background before interviewing him.   A major disadvantage, however, is that often the applicant will not live up to what he appeared to be "on paper."   If a letter has been personally typed by the job seeker, it should be answered by the company.   Response to mimeographed résumés is generally considered less important.   In any case, however, remember that prompt answers to letters of application will show efficiency on the part of the company, and the favorable impression that is created in the process will be a factor in "selling the applicant" on your company.

Walk-ins.   A walk-in is an applicant who comes to the company premises to make an application for a position whether or not the position has been advertised.   A walk-in has not made an appointment for a job interview.

It is not unusual for large companies to have as many as 20,000 or 30,000 walk-ins a year.   The number of walk-ins will depend somewhat on the labor market conditions, but even this does not affect the number too greatly, although it will affect the kinds of walk-ins.   If there is a shortage of secretaries in the labor market, for example, few or no secretarial applicants will walk in.

A company's reputation is influenced by the way the walk-in is treated when he applies for a position.   Whether or not he is offered a position, he will leave with an opinion of the company which is either unfavorable or favorable. His opinion will be transmitted to other people.   If it is favorable, it will have a positive effect on other job seekers who will come "walking in" to your employment department.   If not, he will tend to keep others away from your door.

It is good recruitment practice to interview each walk-in, even if it is a short interview. If during this preliminary or screening interview the applicant seems promising, a lengthier interview can take place later. If the applicant has a skill that is in demand, it is usually wise to follow up with the longer interview either that day or the next day at the latest. If an applicant is promising and there is no job opening at the time, his application should be filed, which leads us to the next recruitment source.

Application File. Here is the way a major publishing company handles its applications for employment. Applications are issued to all applicants seeking positions. A short form application is completed by each applicant. All completed applications are filed in a central applications file which is maintained by the personnel receptionist. The file is broken down into occupational classifications, by male and female.

All applications prior to filing are coded and identified by the interviewer in the following manner. The interviewer initials the application, adds the occupational code, and adds also a "suspense date." The suspense date indicates the life of the application. Normally, all applications are kept on file for a period of six months, although the interviewer may indicate a longer period if the skill is in short supply. In maintaining the application file, it is important to discard inactive applications on a regular basis.

On the short application form, the interviewer "rates" the applicant in the space provided for this purpose. If an applicant is eventually employed, he must complete a longer application form, which becomes a part of his permanent personnel file. It is good practice to tell the applicant whose application will go into the file how long the company expects to keep it there. If the applicant is seriously interested in the company, he will come back to reapply or perhaps will write the company or may even request at his initial interview that his application be kept on file indefinitely.

When a personnel requisition comes through, the interviewer reviews the application file to see if any applicant has the required qualifications. If an applicant has the necessary qualifications, the interviewer then gets in touch with him and further screening takes place. One disadvantage of the application file is that the longer the application stays in the file, the more remote is the possibility that the better-qualified applicants will still be in the labor market.

Private Employment Agencies. A private employment agency specializes in placing job seekers. The employer has no cost for this kind of placement; the fee is usually paid by the job seeker. However, employer fee-paid jobs are on the rise. In some communities, such as Chicago and Los Angeles, it is general practice for the employer to pay the agency fee.

Employment agencies are a popular recruitment source. Private agencies specializing in given job categories can provide a sizable list of qualified employees in their areas of specialization. For example, in New York City there are employment agencies which deal exclusively with salesmen, secretaries, teachers, domestics, and so on. This specialization gives an employer using the service an opportunity to be somewhat more selective in defining his requirements and gives him a somewhat better chance of finding his specialized employee.

Many applicants who register with private employment agencies are presently employed. (Contrast this with public employment agencies described below.) This gives the recruiter a larger number of people from which to draw—those in the labor market and those currently employed. Many companies rely heavily on private agency placements. In New York City, for example, there are almost 1,000 employment agencies. Many of these have well-trained staff members who are well versed in counseling and placement techniques. A basic limitation of private employment agencies, however, is that they are usually local in scope and are seldom able to canvass available personnel outside their own locality.

Public Employment Offices. Because employees who are covered by unemployment compensation must report to the state public employment office when laid off if they want to become eligible for benefits, this may be the best centralized source of labor. It is unfortunate that such sources are frequently overlooked by employers. If a job placement is made through a public employment service, there is no charge to either the job applicant or the employer. However, it is the feeling of some recruiters that people on the unemployment compensation roles are not as seriously oriented toward job finding as they should be. Because of this, they feel that these job applications will not end up as placements. A recruitment program, however, should not overlook this source.

High School Recruitment. Vocational high schools and private trade schools are an excellent source for apprentices in the skill trades and for young men with technical training. Graduates of business courses in high schools and private business schools are an excellent recruitment source for clerks, typists, stenographers, and junior secretaries. Almost all major firms have recruitment programs in local high schools. Many major insurance companies, for example, rely on high school recruitment to fill their annual quotas for job placements.

College Recruiting. An integral part of any successful recruitment program will include the development and maintenance of college relations, thereby providing the company with a continuous source of college-trained personnel. Before recruiting on the college campus, it is important to determine the number of college recruits required for a given period. Most companies develop college recruitment quotas for the school year. This is usually done by consultation with the various department heads and training directors. The reason for this is to know (1) how many graduates are needed, (2) the kinds of graduates desired, for example, chemical engineers, math majors, and so on, and (3) the number of colleges and universities (and the kind—such as schools of journalism) that must be visited to find the needed graduates.

As a rule, most companies grant the courtesy of an interview to any student who indicates an interest in the company. The recruiter, while he is on the college campus, will make the necessary arrangements to meet and talk with various faculty members regarding the student. Some rating of the student is made by the recruiter at the time he visits the campus. It is customary for recruiters to inform the college student in writing about his employment possibilities.

When a company is interested in a college student, he is usually invited to a "home office interview." This means an interview on company premises. If a candidate must travel a considerable distance to be interviewed, his expenses for the trip are usually borne by the company. The college placement director is kept informed of all home office interviews. If a job offer is made to the college recruit, it is usually made by the requisitioning department.

Recruiters should promote and maintain cooperative relations with college placement offices and faculty members at all times. Most company policies require the recruiter to correspond with colleges and universities within a couple of weeks after their campus visit. The recruiters are asked to encourage college placement officers to visit company premises when it is convenient for them to do so.

There is no question that the student bodies at colleges and universities represent a major source of applicants for key positions in American business and industry. It is not uncommon for some major American firms to visit more than 100 college campuses and to employ as many as 300, 400, or 500 college graduates each year.

Professional Associations. Many companies encourage their supervisory and managerial personnel to become members and participate in the affairs of professional associations. Most professional associations have regular placement services or committees. These committees maintain professional standards, and recruitment at this source ensures the qualifications of applicants. Most recruiters will establish a working relationship with a variety of associations so that they can draw upon their files. Many recruiters place recruitment advertising in professional association journals, magazines, and news bulletins. These prove to be an excellent source of applicants, because the entire audience reached is comprised of qualified professional employees.

Executive Search Specialists. Executive search firms play a significant role in executive recruitment. Their specialists develop a consultant-client relationship with companies seeking to fill executive vacancies. Executive recruiting consultants make a business of cataloging the qualifications of executives from all types of business and industry. They screen candidates, conduct exhaustive reference checks, and present candidates who most closely meet the specifications that have been established by the client company.

An assignment with an executive search firm will be successful only if there is a mutual understanding of the requirements of the job to be filled. A search can be unnecessarily prolonged if the job requirements are not sufficiently understood at the beginning. The client company will sometimes be fuzzy in its concept of the job to be filled and will shift its specifications as the search progresses. This results in added cost and embarrassment when prospective candidates have been interviewed only to be told later that they do not qualify.

When an executive search firm becomes thoroughly familiar with a company's personnel and its operation, there is little chance of misrepresentation or misunderstanding, and the recruiter is in an excellent position to take advantage of a unique service that will relieve him of much frustration in filling managerial vacancies.

These firms do not hesitate to "reach" the men who are successfully employed in other companies and who may have given little thought to a job outside their present firm. There is a third-party aspect to executive recruiting firms that offers another advantage: the opportunity to review qualifications and interview candidates without upsetting customer or competitive relationships. Candidates may be contacted through a third-party route and your company remains anonymous.

Executive search firms charge substantial fees—as much as 25 percent of the first year's salary, plus expenses—but many employers think the results are worth it.

Armed Services. Officers and other military personnel who are ready to retire provide a pool of talent that business and industry should be tapping more and more to fill open positions. Many of these men have an option to retire after twenty years of continuous service, and many enter the civilian job market while they are still relatively young. For example, a person who entered the service at age twenty-two may have the option of retiring at the age of forty-two. At that time, he is still in the prime of life and in a position to establish himself in a new career. If he was an officer, his administrative training and experience in leadership can often be transferred to a managerial position in business with good results. Sometimes a man's technical knowledge of a defense industry puts him in a good position to make a special contribution to a company engaged in space and missile development production.

An excellent recruitment source may be found at separation centers where hundreds of men are being relieved of their military duty. In fact, some centers allow business and industrial representatives to visit them to meet and talk with those being discharged. Other centers provide lists that include name, military rank, specialized training, and the like.

School to Industry. The faculties and staffs of colleges and universities represent sources of candidates for some positions in business and industry. Many competent technicians, supervisors, managers, and executives have gone into teaching; some may be interested in returning to industry. Some teachers and professors, particularly those in the field of business administration, have had a close association with business on consulting assignments. Their experience makes them good candidates for certain jobs. "Pirating" from educational institutions, of course, should not be condoned. There is too much need for good teachers to make this a wise policy.

Temporary Consultants. Consulting assignments offer an advantage to both employer and employee as a trial-run association. As the consultant becomes better acquainted with the company, he is in a good position to know whether he wants to make the change when a position is offered, and the company has an opportunity to evaluate him as a potential executive. On consulting assignments, no commitment about a permanent relationship is required. If and when a mutual interest is developed, a job offer can sometimes be made. If a mutual interest is not developed, no serious damage has been done. If a decision to hire the consultant comes about, the consultant is already familiar with company policies and people. Often, he can adjust quickly to the organization, because he has already been exposed to it. He is also likely to be accepted more readily, because he is known to the people in the company, and he represents proved talent.

Recruitment Brochures. Most companies that recruit develop recruitment literature. This may be as simple as an information sheet similar to that shown by Figure 5-6, or it may be as complex as a multicolored recruitment brochure of forty or fifty pages. In the creation of this literature, the following points should be kept in mind.

1. Length is not important in itself, as long as reader interest in maintained.

2. Company history is not as important as one thinks—it is important, but the applicant is more concerned about what kinds of jobs are available.

3. Case histories provide good material. Many companies have published success stories of graduates they hired several years ago telling what has happened to them in the meantime.

4. The recruitment brochure should be directed to specific audiences. In other words, if you are interested in high school graduates as clerks, do not direct your college recruitment material to this audience.

5. It would be wise to do a special piece on your particular industry—where it has been, where it is now, and its growth possibilities.

6. This literature should be distributed to as many recruitment sources as possible. If you plan to recruit at fifty colleges, be sure that each placement office receives material before your visit. The same is true of high school visits.

7. Recruitment material does not have to be in the form of a leaflet or brochure. Some companies have attractive posters that are placed on school bulletin boards.

Summer Scholarships. Companies that provide summer employment for high school and college students develop good recruitment relations. If the experience of the young worker is a pleasant one, word spreads back to the school. Often, the young worker who spends summers in the company will want to return for a full-time, permanent job.

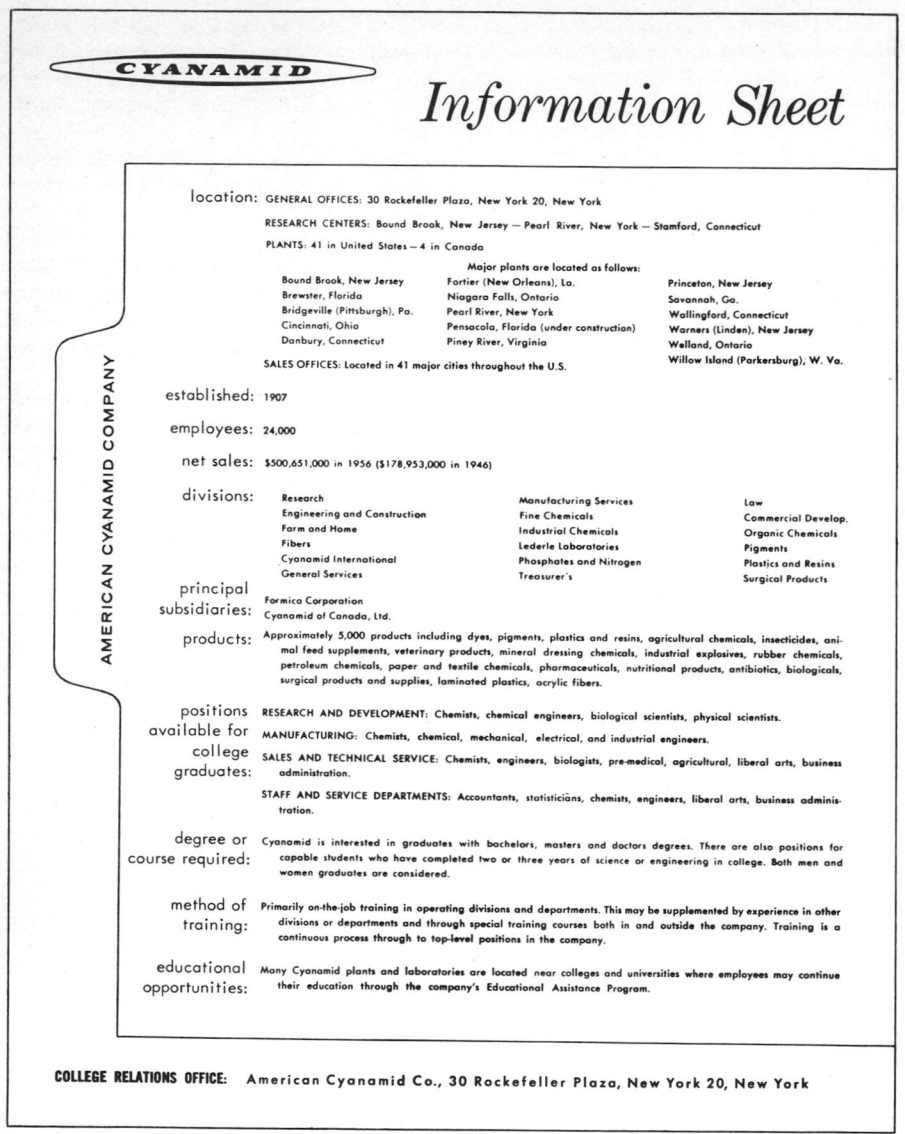

FIG. 5-6. *Recruitment information sheet.*

Special Lectures. Some recruiters will visit schools, groups, societies, and the like to give talks, some of which have nothing to do with employment or a particular company. Subjects for these talks may range from discussing a new industry such as petrochemicals to how best to invest in stocks. Of course, many recruiters discuss subjects more related to the employment function, such as how to handle yourself during a job interview, or what an employer expects from a new employee. The important point here is that good public relations are being established which have a positive effect on recruitment.

Company Films. Many companies have films or sound slides of their company history or on the development of their particular industry. Often, these are loaned to schools, clubs, or societies for public relations purposes, but there is a big recruitment plus in so doing. This is an excellent way to get across the story of your company to students and other people in the community who may be eligible for positions in your company.

Career Days. High schools and colleges sometimes devote one or more days to career expositions or career fairs—where there is a concentration of professional material for purposes of vocational guidance and job placement. Many companies participate in these career days and often have a recruiter stationed at a booth to give out recruitment literature or even to conduct employment interviews. Some private recruitment firms sponsor career centers in major cities across the country. Public halls or hotel ballrooms are used for these career centers, and a participating company pays a fee to be represented.

Trade Shows. There are several ways in which to get a recruitment plus during a trade show. For example, if a newspaper is published during the event, consider inserting recruitment advertising. Or, word-of-mouth comment about a job opening may interest an attendee.

Women Workers. Special appeals can be made to women who once were in the labor market and have since married, raised a family, and now wonder whether or not there is a place for them in the business world. Special advertising or approaches through women's clubs will bring capable women to the employment office. The big advantage in the employment of older women is that they are usually more serious about their work than some of the young high school graduates. Many of these women are college graduates and have many capabilities to bring to the job.

Part-time Jobs. If some jobs are hard to fill on a full-time basis, an employer should consider creating part-time jobs. By employing skilled labor on a part-time basis, he may be able to attract some people who are employed elsewhere.

The Physically Handicapped. Most physically handicapped people are trained in a specialty (either before or since their disability occurred). Many companies have solved a recruitment problem by employing a handicapped individual. For example, one company spent three months trying to find an Addressograph repairman with no luck whatsoever until it had a visit from a Veterans Administration representative. In two days, the job was filled by a man who was deaf and dumb, but extremely skilled in repairing Addressographs. Obviously, this man's disability had almost nothing to do with meeting the job specifications.

Visits to Other Companies. Visits to other companies when they are in the process of closing down or relocating may bring an abundant supply of skilled labor to you. If a firm is relocating and many of their employees do not wish to move, some of the employees will be in the labor market soon. Interviewing arrangements with the personnel director of the relocating firm can be made for you on their premises. The relocating company is usually glad to do this, as it results in good employee relations.

Traveling Recruiters. In a country whose labor force is so mobile, it is almost mandatory to recruit in areas other than the city in which you operate. This is especially true of technical, professional, and managerial employees. A company in Boston which needs engineers will recruit them in Atlanta, Chicago, Detroit, and Los Angeles. In addition to college recruiting trips, an alert recruiter will plan advertising and interviewing dates in other cities.

Recruitment Advertising. The placement of advertisements in city newspapers, magazines, technical journals, trade papers, professional journals, college newspapers, and so on is one of the most frequently used methods of personnel recruiting. There has been much discussion on whether or not recruitment advertising pays; nevertheless, it still is a technique which is employed by almost every recruiter.

Several kinds of ads are used:

1. Classified ad—one that appears in the classified section of a newspaper or magazine.

2. Display ad—one that appears in the display section of a newspaper or magazine. These ads often include artwork or photographs and may run wider than the standard column.

3. Blind ad—either classified or display. Its main feature is that it does not identify the company that is advertising. Usually replies are sent to a box number in care of the newspaper or magazine, which in turn forwards them to the advertiser. Many large firms employ this technique to escape having to answer many, many inquiries.

4. Open ad—one that may be either classified or display, but does show the company name. Companies use this form of ad especially when the company has a good reputation and counts on its "image" as a plus factor in recruiting people.

Advertising can be effective in attracting qualified people if it is employed selectively. Careful consideration should be given to the audience to whom advertising is directed. For example, advertisements in professional and trade publications offer a direct line to specialists in many fields.

Advertisements in high-circulation newspapers reach a wide but less-specialized audience. There is an opportunity, however, to be selective in attracting qualified candidates with display ads in such newspapers as the *New York Times*, the *Chicago Tribune*, and the *Wall Street Journal*.

Once an ad has been placed, there is no control over the number and quality of applicants who respond. A degree of control can be exercised by a sufficiently explicit and definitive statement of qualifications. Although there is likely to be a high percentage of unqualified persons responding, advertisements have the advantage of attracting candidates who might not otherwise come to the attention of a company. In theory, they are supposed to reach any candidate in any field.

Recruitment advertising need not be limited to newspapers and magazines. Some firms have had good experience with radio and television, particularly at the local level. Some colleges have their own radio stations, and this can be a good way to reach students.

There is the danger that a company's recruitment advertising program can be overdone—that in advertising too much, the company is showing signs of desperation in its need for people. One may wonder, "Why are they always looking for people? Can't they keep the ones they have?" It is not an easy task to know where to draw the line as far as recruitment advertising is concerned. If it is carefully planned and executed, however, there is no reason why it should not be one of the good recruitment techniques.

CONCLUSION

Recruitment is a most important function of personnel administration; it is even more important to the whole art and science of management. A plea of "help wanted" in a local grocery store may still have some value for the independent grocer, but today's business dictates that for a company to be successful, it will have to concentrate on a recruitment function. There must be qualified applicants. How else can an efficient work team come about?

BIBLIOGRAPHY

Alleman, R. G., and W. E. Alexander, "Finding and Developing Technical Personnel," *Mechanical Engineering*, vol. 81, April, 1959, pp. 65–68.

Benis, Arthur J., et al., *Executive Recruiting: How Companies Obtain Management Talent, a Special Report for Businessmen Prepared by Students of the Graduate School of Business Administration, Harvard University*, Executive Reports Associates, Lake Forest, Ill., 1960.

"Computer Screens Applicants in Man-Job Matching Process," *Machine Design*, vol. 35, Oct. 10, 1963, pp. 14–15.

Davis, Charles M., "Seven Steps to Executive Recruitment," *Banking*, vol. 54, August, 1961, pp. 49–50.

Farish, P., and M. T. Hoversten, "Ways to Step Up Your Recruiting Power," *Personnel*, vol. 41, May, 1964, pp. 47–53.

Lipsett, Laurence, et al., *Personnel Selection and Recruitment*, Allyn and Bacon, Inc., Englewood Cliffs, N.J., 1964.

Maloney, Paul W., *Management's Talent Search*, American Management Association, New York, 1961.

Mandell, M. M., *The Selection Process*, American Management Association, New York, 1964.

Odiorne, George S., and Arthur S. Hann, *Effective College Recruiting*, Report 13, Bureau of Industrial Relations, University of Michigan, Ann Arbor, 1961.

Recruiting the College Graduate, American Management Association, New York, 1953.

Ricklefs, R., "How Companies Are Using Psychological Tests," *Management Review*, vol. 54, April, 1965, pp. 45–48.

Trice, Harrison M., and William J. Wasmuth, *Effective Hiring in Small Business Organizations*, Bulletin 46, New York State School of Industrial and Labor Relations, New York, July, 1962.

"25 Ways to Better Your Recruiting Skill," *Chemical Engineering*, vol. 68, Sept. 18, 1961, pp. 192ff.

"Use Summer Jobs to Prime Company Recruiting (of College Students)," *Business Management*, vol. 25, January, 1964, pp. 44–46.

CHAPTER SIX

Techniques of Personnel Selection

THEOS A. LANGLIE   *President, Langlie, Goodwillie & Moore, Inc., Stamford, Connecticut*

The manager's concern with techniques of personnel selection is that they be so designed and administered that they provide the bases for effective and economical manning of jobs in the organization.   They must be used in such a manner that results obtained conform to employment policies and comply with legal requirements.

The manager, typically, is not a technician, but he must be prepared to understand selection techniques sufficiently to "audit" the entire employment function.   He must be aware of the extent to which the organization's objectives are being served by this function and the nature, generally, of the science and art of measuring individual differences.   He must be capable of intelligently approving performance criteria and standards.   He should be aware of the importance of the personnel research function and provide essential support to it.

Employment policies must be realistic.   A policy that calls for the employment only of those who have the potential capacity to advance to executive positions would be quite unrealistic.   It would normally lead to a high turnover rate or yield persevering managers without sufficient initiative and imagination.   A policy that calls for employment of all personnel on jobs that require their maximum capacities would, of course, yield a static condition with no real opportunities for successful promotions.   Neither of these policies is realistic.   But then, it is not possible to measure the capacities and personal characteristics of applicants for employment with the precision that such policies imply.

An employment policy that recognizes the limitations of selection techniques, takes into account the significance of averages, variability, and errors of estimate, and attempts to leaven the mass of workers with some proportion of higher-capacitated individuals would appear to be more realistic and constructive.   To determine the effectiveness of employment techniques in relation to such a policy requires an appreciation of some of the fundamental facts and hypotheses about individual differences. The manager should have a working knowledge of these elements.

MEASUREMENT OF INDIVIDUAL DIFFERENCES

The selection of personnel for employment in an operating organization is a most important managerial responsibility. The manager, however, need not and normally should not become directly involved in the technical aspects of the measurement of individual differences. He should, nevertheless, be concerned and reasonably sophisticated about the nature of various techniques of measurement in terms of their reliability and validity and the accuracy of communication about the results obtained by their use.

Without getting involved in technical detail, the manager should have an understanding and appreciation of the following aspects of the problem of measuring individual differences.

1. People differ in essentially all significant measurable characteristics by degree. They do not fall into distinct types, in spite of the use of type names such as "genius," "moron," "introvert," "extrovert," "schizoid," "hypomanic," and the like.

2. Individual differences, typically, may be represented on a continuous scale ranging from "least" to "most," with the bulk of the population clustered rather closely around the average, median, or mode. For purposes of research and communication, scores on a test, ratings on appraisal forms, and judgmental expressions which are reduced to numbers may be expressed in terms of percentiles, standard scores, or other statistical constructs that indicate location on a quantitative scale. Such expressions as "very superior," "superior," "average," "below average," and the like can be used, provided they are defined in terms of the "norm" population and the location in the distribution of scores of the characteristic being described. Figure 6-1 is illustrative of some of the scales used to described these differences.

3. Reliability of measuring techniques means consistency. If the technique

Standard T score.........	30	35	40	45	50	55	60	65	70
Percentile score..........	2	7	16	31	50	69	84	93	98
Stanine scale............	1	2	3	4	5	6	7	8	9
Percent in each group....	4%	7%	12%	17%	20%	17%	12%	7%	4%

Verbal scale (3 to 9 groupings).............	Below standard − ✓ +			Standard − ✓ +			Above standard − ✓ +		

Verbal scale (5 groupings).	Very inferior	Inferior	Average	Superior	Very superior
Percent in each group..	5%	20%	50%	20%	5%

NOTE: In actual use, the distribution of ratings tends to skew in such fashion that there are fewer low ratings and more high ratings. Objective test scores, however, approximate the normal distribution whenever there are no prior selection factors of significant influence.

FIG. 6-1. *Selected scales in common use to illustrate the distribution by degrees of complex human characteristics.*

yields essentially the same results on repeated application, it is highly consistent or reliable. If not, it is relatively unreliable.

4. Validity of measuring techniques means the degree to which the technique or instrument measures what it purports to measure. Obviously, a measuring instrument cannot be valid if it is no more reliable than a throw of the dice. It may, however, be highly reliable but lack validity for a specific purpose.

5. Accurate determinations of validity cannot be obtained in the absence of reasonably reliable and valid criteria, that is, independent measures of that which is being predicted, such as job performance.

6. "Critical scores" may represent the cutoff point for best selection between the optimum and too much of a trait, aptitude, or other characteristic, as well as between the optimum and too little. A person may, for example, be "too bright" for continued satisfactory performance in a job requiring routine application of skills. He must, however, be bright enough to understand instructions. The optimum "brightness" in such situations is a range between the upper and the lower critical or cutoff scores.

7. The measurement and predictive value of personal characteristics is much less reliable and less valid than the measurement and predictive value of the properties of physical materials. Improvement in the reliability and validity of psychological measurements will come about only through the conduct and support of personnel research, to the point where specifications, tolerances, performance standards, and criteria as well as the psychological instruments and techniques of measurement are clearly defined and stabilized. Even then, the social environment in which people work will remain dynamic and more or less unpredictable.

8. Despite inaccuracies inherent in measuring human characteristics and predicting individual performance, the use of systematic techniques with known validities is significantly and substantially more successful than the use of hunches and other methods that are not systematic, validated, or sometimes even describable except in terms of feeling reactions or "intuition."

9. The responsible manager should be prepared to ask, and receive sound answers to, one basic question whenever he seeks to assure himself of the adequacy of the techniques of selection being used in his operating organization. That simple question, which seldom has a simple answer, is, "What is the evidence to support this appraisal (recommendation, classification, judgment, conclusion)?" His personnel experts should be able to provide sound answers, or they should be provided with means and time for the research needed to establish the bases for sound answers.

It is suggested that the responsible manager consider the research requirements for effective quality-control procedures such as specification development, testing, and much that is included under the heading of quality-control engineering, and apply comparable concepts to the quality control of the work force through effective employment and personnel administration policies and procedures. The human organization has frequently been judged to be more valuable than the bricks and mortar and other physical assets of a company. Personnel research budgets, however, generally do not reflect this assessment.

THE TECHNIQUES OF SELECTION

The first essential personnel selection element is the target. What is wanted in a person to fill a job? What are the job requirements?

The manager must be assured that each job is described in sufficient detail so that it can be understood and recognized by the employment technician and by applicants.   In addition to job descriptions, there should be man specifications to describe the qualifications required for successful job performance. These qualifications include the essential mental and physical abilities and characteristics which the employer has found to be necessary and which the employment technician seeks to find and measure in the process of employee selection.

Although standard specifications are often used, it is better to develop man specifications from research within the employing organization itself.   Standard specifications should at least be confirmed and validated.

There are various techniques of personnel selection in use in industry.   They range from the application form to the projective test for psychological analysis and appraisal.

Because the manager should not try to be a technician, these techniques will be described and discussed in relatively general terms.   The selection of specific techniques and their application should be delegated to the technicians.

The Application Form.   Where there is a large volume of job applications, there may be two application forms: one for initial rough screening to determine whether the applicant claims to possess the qualifications (skills, knowledge, and experience) required, and another, more detailed form to be completed by those who have not been eliminated through review of the initial form.

The detailed form, when used for the selection of people for long-term employment and with potential for advancement in the organization, should include questions covering the following areas, except as applicable laws and regulations prohibit their use:

Personal data, such as birth date, sex, marital status, apparent health, and physical handicaps

Family background, such as number of dependents, wife's educational, social, and occupational status, father's, brothers', and sisters' occupations

Community and civic activities

Military service record

Financial status

Educational background, including special courses and training

Employment record, including any periods of unemployment since completion of schooling

The data supplied on detailed application forms can often be interpreted by qualified employment analysts so that tentative and sometimes definite conclusions may be developed about the applicant's stability, reliability, perseverance, and the appropriateness of his educational and occupational experiences for the situation in question.   Such conclusions, unless they lead immediately to rejection of the applicant, must be confirmed by additional evidence stemming from follow-up interviews, reference checks, test results, and other techniques.

It is possible to obtain numerical scores from application forms when systematic research has indicated the validity of such scoring.   This is done by item selection and weighting.   The research techniques used must be sound, with results yielding correlation between scores and subsequent performance in groups other than the original group on which item weighting was established.   The manager must be certain that correct research techniques have been applied before he accepts the validity of such numerical scores.

The Interview.   When the applicant survives the review of his application form, he is usually interviewed.   Despite the unreliability of judgments stemming from interviews, this is an important selection technique. Training of the interviewer in interviewing methods is of great importance.

The interview may follow a structured pattern, similar to the application form. The basic purpose of the interview is to identify behavior patterns that are characteristic of the interviewee. Occurrences and reactions to situations that are repeated in the applicant's experience suggest characteristic reaction patterns.

For example, if job changes occurred almost always because of "supervisors' unfairness and discrimination," there is evidence to suggest that the applicant is overly sensitive or defensive, and that the pattern will be repeated in the future.

It is easy enough, generally, to find and identify various habit patterns in an individual's history if the interviewer stimulates reportings by the applicant and listens more than he talks. Many interviewers are entranced by applicants because they (the interviewers) like what they hear, and what they hear is their own voices expressing their own viewpoints and experiences.

Nondirective interviewing is one of the most fruitful of the interviewing techniques. When applied, it assures that the interviewee talks, usually quite revealingly, about his experience background, feelings, and desires. All interviewers should be well trained in the use of this technique. They still must be able to evaluate the content of what they hear, however, and therein lies the judgmental "error of estimate."

When auditing the interview performance and resulting judgments, the manager should always inquire, "What is the evidence?"

Employment Tests. Employment tests are of many kinds, designed to measure many facets of an individual's characteristics. Whether those used are standardized or tailor-made, their effectiveness should be established through the application of sound research procedures and analysis.

Although no tests are specifically identified in this discussion, they may be classified as follows.

Trade Tests. These tests are designed to measure an applicant's knowledge of, and sometimes skill in, a specific trade such as machinist, carpenter, plumber, and the like. Many of them may be administered in written form or orally.

Achievement Tests. Designed to measure what the applicant can do currently, achievement tests may be applied to such abilities and skills as typing, shorthand, calculating, or any other activity that can be presented in sample or miniature form.

General Mental Ability Tests. These tests are designed to measure learning or problem-solving ability. They provide one of the best measures of potential for growth and may be administered in written, oral, or nonverbal form.

Sometimes a short, simple test of this kind is used for screening purposes, to eliminate applicants who are insufficiently intelligent to be expected to succeed in the lowest levels of jobs. The determination of the validity of these tests for such purposes should be established by research within each organization where they are used.

Aptitude Tests. Aptitude tests are similar to general mental ability tests, except that they are more specialized. Aptitudes may be rather specific, as in mechanical, space perception, mathematics, art, or music, as distinct from general learning ability. Thus there are standardized tests of clerical aptitude, mechanical aptitude, mathematical aptitude, musical aptitude, and others.

Interest Tests. Generally related to occupational activities, interest tests are designed to measure the extent to which an individual's pattern of interests is similar to the interests of experienced people in various lines of work. Such tests seem to have more relevance to vocational guidance activities than to employment selection in the lower ranks of employees. It appears, in general, that a person with above-average mechanical aptitude and intelligence is likely to have interests in common with other mechanically oriented persons. Accordingly, specific vocational interest tests may not add significantly to the data available from aptitude tests.

Personality Tests. These tests are designed to measure such characteristics as emotional stability or maturity and psychoneurotic and psychotic tendencies (in general, the emotional makeup of the subjects). They are reserved, typically, for selection of personnel for executive and professional jobs, although some such tests are used in the selection of sales personnel and to screen out those who may readily become disturbed in pressure situations.

These are the least reliable tests and require a high level of professional skill in their administration and interpretation. Partly because of their nature and the need for skilled judgmental interpretations, there are problems of communication between the professional technician and the manager. Definitive, unmistakable answers to the question, "What is the evidence?" are likely to be esoteric and not fully understood by the nonpsychologically trained manager. The manager accordingly must rely on the competence and integrity of the technician rather than upon his own practical evaluation of evidence-appraisal relationships, except in terms of overall results.

Despite the unreliability of these tests, they serve an important function in personnel selection, not only because of their analytic-descriptive powers, but also because indications provided from their administration open many avenues of exploration in follow-up interview conferences. The manager should see to it that the results of these tests are not accepted at face value unless they are confirmed through skilled, professional interviews following their administration. Even then, of course, there are sizable errors of estimate. These tests, nevertheless, are valuable for employee selection when properly used by skilled professionals.

Reference Checks. Reference checks serve an important function when performed properly. When conducted through the mail, they may provide confirmation about basic facts, such as employment dates, positions held, and sometimes reasons for termination of employment.

When conducted by telephone, it is possible for the skilled inquirer to obtain additional information about the candidate's work, its nature in more detail, areas of difficulty, relations with associates and supervisors, and general effectiveness. All such information must be interpreted in relation to data supplied in the application form and from interviews.

More complete data are obtainable through face-to-face interview contacts with references, preferably with knowledgeable persons not listed by the candidate, but identified through former associates or superiors of the candidate. The time and cost of direct contact for such purposes must be weighed against the importance of the job to be filled. This is a judgment that the manager must make.

Other reference checks in fairly common use are the retail credit investigation and exploration of school and police records. In some instances, a company will conduct the equivalent of an FBI investigation of all employees who are or will be in positions of trust.

THE SELECTION DECISION

There are numerous points in the selection process when decisions must be made. They occur, typically, after each step of the process. Each decision except the last one is a choice between continuing the investigation and analysis and rejecting the applicant. Rejection may take place after reviewing the initial application form or the detailed application form; after the initial or later interview; after each mental test or physical examination; or after the reference checks. Only after the candidate has satisfactorily met all of the specification requirements can there be a sound decision to hire.

Because the selection procedure is a negative selection process, the manager should be assured that there is a minimum of lost time, both for the applicant and for the employer. The sequence of hurdles faced by the candidate should be planned to conserve time and expense. Thus, the simplest and most reliable techniques should come first, and the most complicated ones should come last, within the bounds of practicality.

The manager should also be concerned that the technicians do not become so entranced with their techniques that they lose sight of the whole man under investigation. For example, a properly motivated person can overcome some handicaps by applying more-than-average attention and energy to his task or by developing approaches to the work to be done that may not be standard, but may nevertheless be successful. People do compensate for their weaknesses when motivated to do so.

It is important, however, that limits be established, just as tolerances are established for physical materials. This is an area calling for sound judgment, based on broad perspective stemming from experience, study, and research. The promotion of continuing personnel research by management is needed to increase the adequacy of such judgments.

SUMMARY AND CHECKLIST

The responsibility and primary concern of the manager with respect to the employment function is that it be soundly planned, properly coordinated, and effectively controlled, with objectives and policies that promote the corporate objectives and conform to legal requirements.

This responsibility may be illustrated by the following checklist of questions that the manager should have in mind when auditing the employee selection procedures and techniques:

Are the jobs to be filled described in sufficient detail?

Is there a man specification for each of the jobs?

Are the man specifications sufficiently descriptive of the qualifications required?

Is there valid evidence in documentary form to substantiate the stated qualification requirements by kind and degree?

Is there need for more than one application form, and is the form sufficiently complete without infringing legal limitations?

If the application form is scored by numerical item weighting, has the validity of this technique been substantiated by proper research?

Are the employment interviewers technically qualified for both structured and nondirective interviewing as demonstrated by results obtained?

Are the employment tests used appropriate, reliable, and valid, as determined by continuing research?

Are the "personality tests," including projective tests, administered and interpreted by a professionally qualified person?

Are the physical examinations adequate? Are the results used primarily for placement, and not for rejection unless they are clearly disqualifying in nature?

Are reference checks conducted effectively and appropriately in relation to time and cost?

Is all of the information obtained interpreted in terms of the whole person, with proper balancing of strengths and limitations for each job to be filled—that is, is sound judgment, based on proper techniques and evidence, the foundation of the selection program?

Is there a systematic personnel research program, with adequate management support, for the purpose, among others, of refining and improving the effectiveness of the employee selection function?

BIBLIOGRAPHY

Helmstadter, G. C., *Principles of Psychological Measurement*, Century Psychology Series, Appleton-Century-Crofts, Inc., New York, 1964.

Kahn, Robert L., and Charles F. Cannell, *The Dynamics of Interviewing*, John Wiley & Sons, Inc., New York, 1957.

Mandell, Milton M., *The Selection Process*, American Management Association, New York, 1964.

Wolf, William B., *The Management of Personnel, Part Two*, Wadsworth Publishing Co., Inc., Belmont, Calif., 1961.

Yoder, Dale, "Selection and Placement," chap. 16 in *Personnel Management and Industrial Relations*, 5th ed., Prentice-Hall, Inc., Englewood Cliffs, N.J., 1962.

New-employee Orientation

GRAY L. CARPENTER   *President, Gray L. Carpenter & Associates, Pocono Manor, Pennsylvania*

The indoctrination of new employees takes place in every company. In a sense, it is like public relations—you have no choice as to whether or not you are going to *have* it; your only option is whether or not you are going to *control* it. Just as outsiders will inevitably evolve a mental "image" of a company, so a new employee will inevitably find out what he needs to know to do his job. In both cases, the trick is to influence the results by controlling the information imparted, its sources, and the ways in which it is communicated.

APPROACH TO NEW-EMPLOYEE ORIENTATION

Too often, a new man is simply told to seek out and report to his foreman. Usually, this is at or near the normal start of the work day or shift, when the foreman is feverishly busy; so he quickly marches the newcomer to a work station, tells him to "watch Joe," and hurries away. Unless Joe is unusually empathetic and helpful, the newcomer will find adjustment much harder and longer than it should be. He is bewildered, but afraid to ask too many questions. Joe wants to lunch with his own cronies, and he resents interruptions that cut into his incentive pay. The newcomer has evidence that the foreman and the company are not interested in him. He is embarrassed and disgusted that he cannot even go to the toilet without asking directions, and if he leaves his work station, he cannot find his way back. Everywhere he looks are strange faces, strange surroundings, strange documents, and strange procedures.

The more conscientious he is, the more eager to please, the more he will be upset and frustrated by his ignorance, dependence, and mistakes. As a result, the indifferent or irresponsible newcomers are best able to weather the early confusion, so they stay on. The sensitive, eager-to-contribute men are much more likely to quit, convinced that they are unable or unwilling to master the new job. If Joe happens to be cynical, ill-informed, inept, or disgruntled, the new worker will learn the wrong things first and the right things wrong. In such cases, the new man's very desire to fit in will tend to make him a marginal or troublesome worker.

Similar hazards obtain in the office, too, of course; and women, especially, are self-conscious in a wholly new situation. Each feels uneasy and awkward, so at least some of what she is told does not really register. Result: mistakes, followed perhaps by a scolding or a sarcastic repetition of her instructions.

Frequently overlooked, even in otherwise well-managed companies, is the fact that thoughtful, disciplined orientation is also needed when a man moves into supervision from the rank and file. Moreover, this is as true of the new sales manager or chief engineer as it is of the new shop foreman. In each case, the new supervisor requires more new information, instructions, and re-assurance than does the new employee. Regrettably, these career-milestone needs are often ignored or given perfunctory attention, even in companies that do an adequate job of indoctrinating newcomers to the firm.

In spite of mistakes that have been made in the past, planned, formal orientation procedures have become increasingly common since the 1930s. The details of these programs differ, and a given company usually has somewhat different procedures for different types of workers, amounts of new hiring, and so forth. But generally, the idea is to make the new employee feel welcome and as much at home as possible. If the newcomer finds that others in the company are genuinely interested and helpful, he will be also; he will try to please and to be accepted as a worthwhile member of the group.

More specifically, there are three fundamental things to be accomplished by the orientation: first, to define the terms of employment clearly and exactly; second, to acquaint the new employee with all job requirements; and third, to instill confidence in the company and in the newcomer's own ability to learn the job he was hired for, and his ability to perform it well. It follows from these important functions that new-employee orientation is a line responsibility that must be clearly assigned, understood, and accepted.

Why Have an Orientation Program? Beyond the humanitarian desire to mini-mize the anxiety of a person in a strange environment, and the public relations benefit of a new hire's enthusiastic accounts of his important new job and fine company, there are several very practical reasons for having a sound program for orienting new employees.

For one thing, it can radically reduce employee turnover. By far the greatest turnover occurs early in the relationship. The first few days on the job can easily determine whether or not a new employee stays. He must be encouraged to see himself as able and willing to do well at the job he has accepted. More-over, he must be helped to establish his identity with the new environment, so that he will give the job an honest try, rather than quit after a few distracted and self-conscious efforts. Nearly all newcomers, especially those lacking work achievement elsewhere, are ill at ease and insecure at first. They feel subtly threatened by the many changes and lack confidence in their ability to master their new responsibilities.

Second, the orientation affords an economical and practical means for clearing up the many little details of information that must be exchanged when a new person is added to the payroll. It avoids the necessity of a series of "indoctrina-tion" work interruptions later, which are annoying to supervision and dishearten-ing to the new worker. It enables the company to free the newcomer of un-answered questions, uncertainties, fear, misunderstandings, and ignorance that could affect his performance and morale. In return, it can get accurate informa-tion from him to correct or complete company records.

Third, a carefully conducted orientation will head off employee grievances and disillusionment.   First impressions tend to be lasting, especially in the realm of human relations.   No one responds well to being ignored, or herded about, or regarded as an ambulating payroll number.   Whether the employee's regular attitude will be one of enthusiasm or quiet antagonism is largely determined by the way he is treated during his early adjustment to the company.

Fourth, by clearing the air of tangential questions and misgivings, a formal orientation program will facilitate job training and help the new worker concentrate on learning his new duties, winning coworker acceptance, and improving the performance and *esprit de corps* of his work group.

Fifth, a newcomer with experience elsewhere will arrive with much that must be *unlearned* before he can master the strange new surroundings, routines, expectations, and standards.   Thoughtful orientation can make a real contribution here, and keep the self-confident worker from learning things wrong or learning the wrong things.

Sixth, a proper introduction to the strengths, traditions, and values of the company can nurture drive and creativity in the ambitious newcomer.   (Botched, the orientation can also turn an aggressive new man into an unremarkable, "get by" employee.)

Finally, of course, the first day is the best time to begin to communicate effectively with incoming employees.

PLANNING THE PROGRAM

Good intentions and honest conviction are not enough to assure a successful orientation program.   Small companies and those with relatively static employment situations usually handle the induction of the occasional new employee informally, but these spontaneous efforts are seldom comprehensive, and even more seldom consistent.   Accordingly, even for these firms—and certainly for all companies with regular growth and turnover—a carefully thought-out, disciplined, if not formal, program is recommended.

The formality and techniques of the program can be varied according to the new-hire rate, the nature of the people being brought aboard, and the general level of business activity.   A cannery, say, need not send its hordes of seasonal workers through an elaborate introduction to the company.   (But note: Temporary workers are human, too, and will respond favorably to being adequately informed and appreciated.)

Isolate specific objectives for the program, and draw up checklists as assurance that each newcomer is given a consistent, effective, and thorough orientation. Strive to keep the entire procedure stimulating as well as informative and reassuring.   Work some of the material into vestibule training sessions, where appropriate, and seek other ways of dividing the work load and adding variety. For example, the minimum program should involve the personnel department— preferably the person who interviewed the new hire—and the newcomer's immediate supervisor.   In addition, perhaps the medical, safety, training, and security officials can present relevant information.   Others who might participate range from plant, division, or corporate officers to union stewards and officials.

To avoid gaps and duplication, which might be harmful as well as making a poor impression on the new employee, put together a clear outline of what must be done and covered, by whom, in what order and manner, when, and to what purpose.   Identify the party responsible for each step.

There is a temptation to cover too much in too elaborate a manner.   The orientation sessions in some firms extend for days; and what with lectures, films, tours, and stacks of literature, they end up compounding the bewilderment instead of relieving it. Other programs oblige the newcomer to spend hours wading through administrative red tape, wandering (or being herded) from one department to the next, enduring an absurd succession of handshakes and welcomes . . . each followed by a solemn reading of more rules and regulations. These barrages of data are not only ineffective, but often downright antagonizing.

Do not be afraid to spread things out over a reasonable period of time. Concentrate first on the facts and reassurances the new hire will *need* to get started and to go home enthusiastic about his new situation. Later, material such as overall organization, history, plans, remote operations and fringes, internal mobility, and the like can be added. Small, well-explained pieces of information are better than an overwhelming variety of topics at one sitting.

Bring first-line supervisors and department heads in on planning or overhauling the orientation program. They have a major role to play. Moreover, they know the peculiar problems their charges are having, and what subjects are not being adequately communicated. Their participation also commits them to the program and softens any objections they may harbor about "dancing to somebody else's tune."

Points to Cover. The content of corporate orientation programs varies enormously—as it should. Still, there are certain necessary features, depending in part on the company's objectives. Ironically, one point often not made clear is *where and when to report* for work. Normally, this is explained in the final hiring interview, but people tend to be a little scatterbrained under the stress and anxiety of a strange activity in a strange environment. There is no harm in reiterating these important facts in any event, preferably in writing, complete with a sketched map. Some firms do this in their "welcome" letter to the new hire's home.

The next most important point, perhaps, involves the *terms of employment.* These must be communicated, not just recited. They are easily misunderstood or misinterpreted by the eager, ill-at-ease newcomer; and when this happens, you will never convince him (or his acquaintances) later that he was not duped or the job misrepresented. Some companies ask each new hire to read and sign a written statement of the terms of employment. Specifics should include probation, seniority, required clothing or equipment, training, wages and deductions, shift work, work hours and breaks, travel, patents, off-hours employment, overtime, incentives, timing and form of pay, special allowances, privileges, transfers, work rules and penalties, and so forth.

Explain company policy on *raises and promotions,* and take pains to head off any interpretation of this discussion as promises, unless such are intended. (In this case, put them in writing, date them, and arrange a "call up" on the file, so they will not inadvertently be overlooked.) Detail appropriate standards of measurement and evaluation.

Relevant documents and procedures should be covered adequately: work orders, job tickets, reports, forms, drawings, catalogs, and the like. Explain how, when, and where to make various reports, and how to draw tools and materials. Often, a new man tends to exaggerate his knowledge and experience. He hesitates to ask too many questions, so they should be anticipated. Make sure the newcomers know where and how to seek advice or help, how to register complaints and appeal to higher authority. Provide someone other than a male supervisor to whom female employees can go with certain problems they would be uncomfortable discussing with a man. A mature, intelligent coworker or female supervisor can often fulfill this function informally; but she should be deliberately selected and made known to incoming girls.

Company expectations with regard to quality, productivity, work pace, attendance, tardiness, secrecy, and the like should be clarified early. This is also true for *special conditions* such as safety hazards, temporary inconveniences, sport shirts versus suits, first names, dirt, noise, temperature, extended trips, periodic extra work loads, deadlines, and heavy lifting.

Union activities are a significant factor in some companies, so should be dealt with openly. In fact, union officials and stewards can do much to lubricate the entire indoctrination procedure—introducing new men, explaining contract provisions, grievance procedures, and the like, and in general showing the new man "the ropes" and making him feel welcome and accepted. At minimum, each new hire should be given a copy of the union contract concerning him, and a careful explanation of its provisions.

General company information—history, products, policies, rules and regulations, vacations, and fringes—is commonly gathered into a booklet for distribution to new hires. It is a good idea to emphasize rules bearing on special problems—fighting, say, or abuse of phone and mailing privileges. Special fringes, such as tax help, suggestion awards, savings plans, notaries, and profit sharing, might also be pointed out.

Plant or office facilities should be treated at some point in the orientation program. Whatever you do, it takes new employees a while to feel at home with unfamiliar people; but even in a strange environment, they can quickly feel at home with familiar *things*, such as lockers, washrooms, tools, machines, cafeterias and vending areas, time clocks, supply rooms, and tool cribs. Take advantage of this by pointing out these "old friends" early—they are reassuring. For added impact, have the new employee's badge, tools, supplies, equipment, desk, identification card, special clothing, and so forth ready for him when he reports for work. Assign his locker ahead of time; do not just turn over the first empty one found at the moment. Pin down his work location, too. It is discouraging to "belong" nowhere, to have no "home ground" amidst strange surroundings.

Tools and Techniques. Virtually all companies with formal orientation programs incorporate into them some form of visual aids to add variety, impact, and interest to the presentation. The choice of tools and techniques in a given case depends on at least four variables: first, the company's objectives for the orientation sessions—and by association, the amount and nature of the information being imparted; second, the time available for orienting new employees; third, the number of inductees customarily dealt with; and finally, an important factor, the occupational level of most of the newcomers—unskilled, supervisory, clerical, engineering and technical, sales or management trainees, craftsmen, or whatever. To cope with a broad spectrum of new hires, many companies have taken a modular approach to orientation. All newcomers are given certain fundamental information, and then undergo selected follow-on sessions, depending on their more specific needs. Often, this follow-on indoctrination is provided in connection with vestibule training.

Lectures and Manuals. By far the most popular approach is a combination of one or more orientation lectures and a booklet or manual which is given to the newcomer for examination at his leisure. Firms with substantial hiring activity commonly lecture new employees in rather large groups. Typically, a representative of management "welcomes them aboard," and is followed by a personnel specialist who discusses the company's business, products, history and traditions, reputation and general objectives, policies and practices, and the like. Also covered in some detail are employee benefits, safety and health, plant or office rules, suggestion systems, pensions, vacations, sick leave, probation, performance reviews, pay practices, union relationships, employee newspaper and other communications, and so on.

Two important points must be borne in mind in this connection. First, virtually all the information provided in the orientation lectures is normally included in employee booklets or other literature—often in more useful detail. Second, group lectures are inherently expensive in lost time—especially if several high-level officials are part of the program. Moreover, long lecture sessions tend to get dull, and if a great variety of information is offered at one time, the net effect may be rather blurred and confused. It is surprisingly easy to overdo this sort of thing with the very best of intentions.

On the other hand, group lectures are much more efficient than individual interviews when a significant number of new hires must be dealt with. It is also somewhat reassuring to newcomers to see themselves as part of a rather large group all in the same boat.

Employee booklets containing a summary of benefits, rules, advice, and similar information are frequently used as supplements to, or substitutes for, lecture sessions. The best of these are brief, clearly written—preferably with a cordial, light touch—and intelligently illustrated. Many companies include cartoons, photos, maps, organization charts, diagrams, and other graphic devices. Where no such booklets are offered, it is a good idea to distribute at least a mimeographed sheet or two summarizing the information provided by the interviewers or lecturers.

In either case, it is important to *emphasize salient points* so they will not be overlooked in the general bulk of material. How complete and comprehensive the coverage of the booklet should be will depend on the company's objectives in preparing it and the amount and nature of other material it offers. Note, too, that someone should *check* at some appropriate point to be sure the booklet or manual has in fact been read and understood.

Other Literature. Many companies also distribute other literature as part of their orientation programs. Annual reports, employee newspapers or house organs, selected reading-rack materials, product catalogs, sales and recruiting brochures, safety booklets, anniversary publications, and the like may be offered where appropriate. If the field uses jargon or slang expressions, perhaps a special dictionary will be helpful—especially to new secretaries. Orientation maps are often welcomed. An organization guide, complete with the names, responsibilities, location, and secretaries of managers and officials, can be provided for new office, technical, professional, and management newcomers. (Phone books seldom reveal much about who is the most appropriate contact for what.)

Letter of Welcome. A popular gesture is to mail a letter of welcome to the newcomer's home, perhaps enclosing a few recent issues of the plant or office paper. Should the letter come from a top corporate officer? *Only if it is sincere and believable.* If the man signing the welcome letter mingles regularly with the employees on the newcomer's level, and really knows these people, the letter can have real impact. Otherwise, it may undo other efforts by showing the company's management to be phony or cynical.

Visual Aids. Motion pictures are frequently used for orienting new employees, especially for providing an overview of the operations of large multiplant corporations. Firms too small to justify the expense of having custom movies prepared can get appropriate ones from trade associations, safety and insurance organizations, the giant companies in their industry, commercial film libraries, and so forth. Slides and filmstrips also play prominent roles in the orientation programs of thousands of companies. Normally, sales promotion material and displays—especially models of products—can be very effectively pressed into service.

Guided Tours. Guided tours of company facilities are very common, and in many cases they are effective. They must, however, be carefully thought out and conducted by able, informed, affable, and well-organized guides, or they are likely merely to add to the bewilderment of the newly hired people. Large plants should confine their tours to selected high points, to keep them from becoming marathon performances. They must also be conducted in a logical sequence or pattern. Because of the confusion they might cause, a strong argument can be made against offering general tours to new employees. The sooner newcomers are settled into their jobs, the sooner they regain their self-confidence, identity, and a circle of acquaintances. Moreover, a tour at some later time, after at least some of the facilities are familiar and the newcomers are more relaxed and observant, might be more meaningful.

Programmed Instruction. Programmed instruction is a tool that is more than equal to the task of orienting new employees. It combines in one convenient medium the advantages of lectures, literature, and question-and-answer sessions. With a little imagination, it can also incorporate aspects of motion pictures and filmstrips. Modular programs can be prepared and assembled to suit the needs of an assortment of job categories. Moreover, the company can be sure that emphasis has been placed where it belongs, that everyone who completes the program has mastered the information, and that every newcomer has been given a complete and consistent orientation.

Programs can be now serious, now genial, as appropriate; and material can be added, deleted, or modified easily and economically. Information can be presented via teaching machines or in book form, and may be used repeatedly. Any number of incoming employees may be oriented at one time—there is no need to accumulate new hires until there are enough to justify a formal group lecture. The material to be presented can be divided into convenient segments, with later ones completed by the employee on his own time and at his own convenience. Furthermore, the program is brought to the person, rather than the other way around—a great boon when new employees are widely scattered, as is typically the case with sales trainees.

All these features, coupled with the inherent interest and versatility of the approach, make programmed instruction an effective, efficient, and economical orientation tool. Because of its impersonality, programmed instruction is best combined with a measure of personal contact and counseling, but it can radically reduce the amount of human time and effort required for effective orientation. It also lends itself well to imaginative combination with motion pictures, filmstrips, and other proved visual aids.

The "Sponsor" System. Another technique used by some companies is the "buddy" or "sponsor" system. In a variation of the traditional instruction to "watch Joe; he'll show you the ropes," these companies ask an interested, established employee to act as sponsor of the new hire. Typically, the sponsor shows the newcomer around, introduces him to coworkers, takes him to lunch the first day (on the company), explains such things as smoking rules and how to draw tools, and generally gets him started at the new job. To assure that a thorough and consistent job is done, it is a good idea to prepare a sponsor's checklist of things to cover.

There are arguments against the sponsor system. The sponsor must be wisely chosen, or he may ruin a newcomer by giving him "the lowdown." The sponsor might also antagonize the new worker by making him or her feel mothered. Moreover, the tasks assigned to the sponsor are more legitimately the concern of the new employee's supervisor or manager, who certainly owes the new hire that much interest and attention. Besides, the supervisor is probably more broadly and more accurately informed than a sponsor, and can learn about the newcomer while showing him around.

THE SUPERVISOR'S ROLE

Whatever suggestions, guidance, groundwork, and assistance may be provided by personnel specialists, new-employee orientation remains a line management responsibility. Moreover, no other person has so much influence on the attitude, morale, and performance of a new employee as his immediate supervisor. Accordingly, no matter what else may be involved, the climax of the orientation program is the meeting between the newcomer and his or her supervisor.

In fact, some authorities deplore the staff approach to inducting new people. Staff programs, they contend, tend to get too complex, too elaborate, too formal—and too expensive. New workers soon find that they cannot absorb everything being thrown at them; so, early in the program, they stop trying. The staff men, noting that the program is not proving very effective, react by making it still more elaborate. According to these authorities, line supervisors have two big advantages in conducting orientation sessions. First, they do not have the time (or the desire) to raise the program to a high art. Second, they *do* have time to spread things out over several days, weeks, or longer. Offering a few easily absorbed pieces of information at a time and arranging to provide the facts when they are needed and can be used also helps the supervisor cement his relationship with his new charge.

Whether or not a formal staff program is used, the personnel department typically goes over the general terms of employment and gives the newcomer a fair idea of what is expected of him and what he may expect in return. It remains for the new employee's immediate supervisor to greet the newcomer and fill in the specific department's objectives, role, and resources. To save his valuable time, to head off duplication, and to help him concentrate on his proper contribution, the supervisor should be informed of what the new employee has *already* been told. Many companies handle this by passing along the checklist of things to be covered. This not only assures that the supervisor will do a thorough job, but precludes giving the new employee the impression that the company's communications are disjointed.

Getting the new employee and his supervisor together can be done in various ways. Some companies have the interviewer escort the worker to his department and introduce him to his new boss. More often, the supervisor comes to the personnel department to pick up the newcomer and take him to his workplace. This gives the two men a chance to "break the ice" and perhaps meet a few key people en route. Fortunately, the impersonal practice of having a messenger show the newcomer to his department, or worse, merely giving the new hire a card of introduction and directions to his work area, is disappearing.

However they are introduced, the supervisor must *make the time* available to help his new charge through his adjustment. The newcomer must be greeted warmly—*not* hurriedly—and made to feel welcome and wanted. His questions should be answered carefully, and he should be reassured several times during the breaking-in period. Do not make him wait after he arrives in the department—give him prompt attention; show *immediate* interest in him.

Many supervisors like to go over "what is in the booklet" in their own words, and go on to give the newcomer a good, balanced view of his new job. Safety and quality should be emphasized at this stage—productivity, typically, will follow in time. A tour of the department and some surrounding areas affords a good opportunity to introduce coworkers, storekeepers, setup men, timekeepers, unofficial leaders in the work group, and so forth. Each of these other jobs should be related to the newcomer's job, and his personal contribution to the overall scheme of things should be clarified. Emphasize the orderliness and logic underlying what probably strikes the new employee as a bewildering, perhaps chaotic, situation.

During the tour, the supervisor might point out fire exits, time clocks, lockers, rest areas, and of course, the newcomer's specific work location. Conversation might include such helpful facts as shortcuts to work, where to park, "fringes" such as tool-borrowing privileges, company training and library facilities, the credit union, employee discounts, and so on. It is a good idea to ask if the newcomer is short of cash, too, and if so, the supervisor can arrange an advance (if the relationship is not at least that strong, the person should not have been hired at all).

In all this, the supervisor should bear in mind that his new charge is in an awkward situation and has probably already been exposed to a confusing succession of facts, introductions, tips, and cautions. Consequently, it is important to take advantage of the fact that the newcomer will be around for a while and will need rather frequent contact and reassurance for a time. Information not needed at once can be spread out and presented in small pieces on those occasions when the supervisor "happens by" and stops to see how things are going with the new employee.

Follow-up. The alert supervisor will naturally check the new employee regularly, but on an informal basis, during his first few weeks on the job, to gage his attitude, reassure him, and answer questions. But partly because the supervisor holds the position he does, a good personnel specialist can often uncover doubts and fears more readily. Therefore, it is a good idea to have a specialist—ideally the original interviewer, whom the newcomer already knows and trusts—follow up independently after a month or so.

This can be handled in several ways, according to company preference. The interviewer might drop by the newcomer's workplace, ostensibly on another errand, or he might invite the newcomer to have lunch with him. Some firms feel that a thoughtful, prompt, and straight response can hardly be expected when an interviewer spontaneously asks, "How's it going?" within earshot of the new hire's fellow workers. As a result, they insist that the follow-up interview be planned, scheduled, and conducted in private. Usually, this takes the form of asking the newcomer to report to the personnel office.

In other companies, where supervisors fear that personnel specialists may be interfering with their departments, the supervisors interview the employee, and the specialists then discuss the employee with the supervisor. Commonly, the personnel men interview both the supervisor and the worker himself. Some follow-up with the newcomer's manager or supervisor should certainly take place in *any* event. At minimum, personnel should ask the supervisor to make a written report or fill out a rating form on how well the newcomer is adjusting, his attitude, performance, knowledge, and the like. Checklists are quite useful for this.

However it is done, the object is to get to the new hire *before* he gets discouraged, apathetic, or cynical. Normally, personality clashes, if they are going to occur at all, will show up within a week or two; a simple transfer will often salvage the situation long before the probation period is over.

A final suggestion: One dependable way to show honest interest and make a good impression while gathering valuable information is to mail a follow-up questionnaire to the new employee's home later on, asking for feedback on the effectiveness of the whole orientation program. Important suggestions and improvements may well result.

BIBLIOGRAPHY

Argyris, C., *Integrating the Individual and the Organization,* John Wiley & Sons, Inc., New York, 1964.

Beach, D. S., *Personnel: The Management of People at Work,* The Macmillan Company, New York, 1965.

Calhoon, R. P., *Managing Personnel,* Harper & Row, Publishers, Incorporated, New York, 1963.

Christian, R. W., "Guides to Programmed Learning," *Harvard Business Review,* November–December, 1962.

Ford, G. B., *Building a Winning Employee Team,* American Management Association, New York, 1964.

Hegarty, E. J., *How to Build Job Enthusiasm,* McGraw-Hill Book Company, New York, 1960.

Mee, J. F., *Personnel Handbook,* The Ronald Press Company, New York, 1951.

Pigors, P. J., C. A. Myers, and F. T. Malm, *Management of Human Resources,* McGraw-Hill Book Company, New York, 1964.

Scott, W. D., R. C. Clothier, and W. R. Spriegel, *Personnel Management,* McGraw-Hill Book Company, New York, 1961.

Stone, C. H., and W. E. Kendall, *Effective Personnel Selection Procedures,* Prentice-Hall, Inc., Englewood Cliffs, N.J., 1956.

CHAPTER EIGHT

Training

FRANK E. FISCHER   *Cresap, McCormick and Paget, New York, New York*

This chapter discusses the goals of training and its role in promoting change in individuals and organizations. It describes some of the newer, as well as the traditional, training methods and ends with a discussion of the requisites for an effective training effort.

THE GOALS OF TRAINING

Training, like any other business activity, is expected to help achieve the goals of the enterprise. Training has no value unless it does, in fact, contribute to better performance and thus to the organization's objectives. It may attempt to do this directly through reducing costs, improving quality, and increasing production, or indirectly through improving the skills or attitudes of employees or increasing their knowledge or experience.

In many companies, training is still regarded merely as an "activity" unrelated to the needs of the organization. Increasingly, however, training is coming to be regarded as an essential tool for implementing business strategies. A growing number of managements recognize that they can chiefly hope to find a major and lasting competitive edge, not in the superiority of their plant or products, but in the quality and training of their people. Toward this end, a company must regard training as a management tool for bringing about change in individual behavior and improving organizational effectiveness.

Promoting Change in Individuals. Industrial training has always concentrated on teaching skills to employees. Inexperienced employees have to be taught to operate unfamiliar equipment; new supervisors have to plan and control the work of their units, organize the work of their subordinates, and coach them. Experienced employees have had to be trained to do things differently or better, thus augmenting their repertoire of skills or knowledge.

Industrial training began when the first apprentice was hired or when the first employee was broken into a job. It matured when systematic methods

11–84

were developed for teaching knowledge and skills to the new employee. This happened on the grand scale in the Job Instructor Training Program which was created to train hundreds of thousands of inexperienced workers during World War II. Later, a sophisticated approach to the training of the new employee evolved from the need to man the complex weapons systems developed for the military. In this approach, tasks are carefully analyzed to determine the type of behavior needed in the persons who are to operate the systems and to specify training requirements and standards.

Accelerating technology has forced industry to devote increased attention to the retraining of employees. For example, the Bank of America had to initiate a vast training program for some 2,000 employees who were displaced when the bank converted from manual to electronic bookkeeping. Managers, too, may be threatened with functional obsolescence. Westinghouse Electric Corporation, for example, brings some 1,500 managers to Pittsburgh each year for training intended to update their knowledge and skills.

In addition to the training of new employees and the retraining of experienced ones, companies are concerned with accelerating the process by which employees advance to higher-level responsibilities. Formal management development programs for accomplishing this are described in Chapter 6 of Section 4. Even companies with their own training capability enroll their personnel in courses and seminars offered by universities, associations, and consulting organizations, covering the entire spectrum of management. In addition, organizations like the Port of New York Authority design their training activities to advance the career plans of individuals at various levels of the organization.

Training aimed at individual improvement, whether for beginners or experienced employees, requires an accurate analysis of an individual's aptitudes and performance level and of the requirements of the job he is to perform. It then requires a careful matching of these elements to bridge the gap between present and desired performance.

To be effective, programs for training in individual skills should also take into account the close relationship between training and a company's personnel practices, particularly its selection and placement procedures, promotion policies, and compensation practices. Research has repeatedly demonstrated, for example, the difference in learning among inexperienced employees trained by the same method (see Figure 8-1).

Promoting Change in Organizations. Training practitioners are devoting increasing attention to methods for inducing change in organizations. Without minimizing the need to improve the individual's skills, knowledge, and attitudes, they say that he may not be able to apply this learning effectively, because it is inconsistent with the goals or practices of the organization in which he works.

Trainers have therefore focused on the study of group processes and organizational behavior. They have drawn upon behavioral research and organization theory to help them understand how training can help the organization itself function more effectively. In this concept, training is viewed as a subsystem within the total system of the enterprise. Like planning, organizing, directing, and other functions, training influences the extent to which performance meets overall objectives.

The training subsystem is brought into play when there is likelihood that deficiencies in performance can be met through training. A systematic approach to the changing of organizational behavior through training includes the following steps:

1. An analysis of the organization's operations and of its managing processes

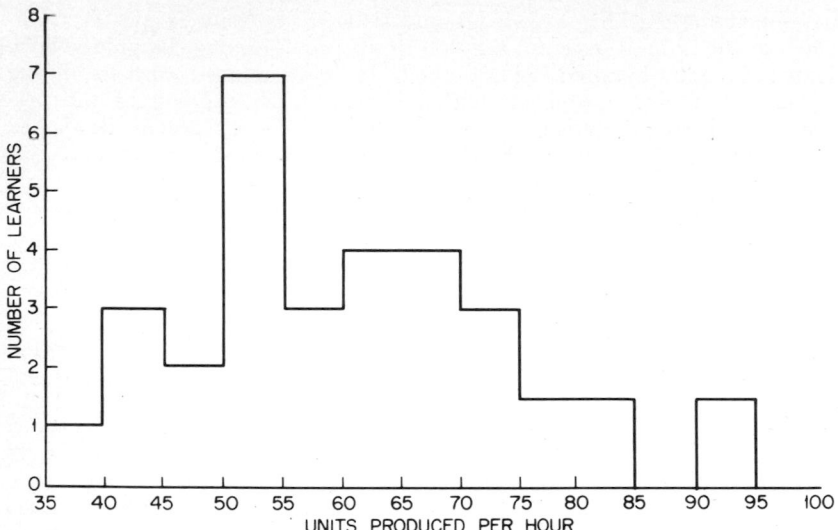

FIG. 8-1. *Individual differences in learning on power sewing machines. Median production during thirteen weeks of training for thirty learners. Range 38–92 (unpublished data). (Courtesy of William McGehee and Paul W. Thayer,* Training in Business and Industry, *John Wiley & Sons, Inc., New York, 1961, p. 5.)*

2. A study of those factors in the organization which significantly influence the behavior of the people working in it

3. An identification of the organization's major problems and requirements

4. A determination of those problems which can be remedied through training

5. A selection of the methods most likely to accomplish the desired improvements

6. Development, execution, and evaluation of the training experience

This approach calls for skills beyond those of the typical training specialist. It requires a person with the ability to perform effectively in diverse ways: as teacher, counselor, and coach; as consultant and problem solver; as planner and researcher. He must be able to design programs of broad scope and a long time span, and to work effectively with all organizational functions and levels. Finally, he must be able to view training not as a series of discrete courses, but as a continuing, long-term activity which can enter at any point of the managing process.

TRAINING METHODS

Training methods and instructional techniques are myriad, along with the ways of classifying them.

Basis for Selection. The choice of a particular training method is governed by the size of the group to be trained and its location; similarities or differences in experience, education, abilities, functions, and organizational levels; the abilities of the trainers; and the cost of the training method compared with the results expected.

The primary consideration, however, is the kind of change the training is intended to bring about. The answer lies not in selecting the "best" technique, but in identifying, adapting, or inventing the one that best fits the situation. The choice of method is strongly influenced by whether the purpose of the training is primarily to (1) increase knowledge, (2) improve skills, or (3) influence attitudes or change behavior. Generally speaking, to impart knowledge, such techniques as lectures, guided discussions, printed matter, films, correspondence courses, case studies, and programmed instruction will be selected. On-the-job training is most commonly resorted to for teaching the skills needed to perform operative and clerical tasks, and problem-solving conferences, case studies, and various kinds of simulation are often used to improve analytical and interpersonal skills. If the aim is to change attitudes or behavior, role playing and sensitivity training are also frequently used. Most of these methods serve more than one purpose; and one not mentioned, coaching, is typically used for all three.

Both experience and research indicate that changes in behavior are rarely brought about by telling people to change or by talking about the change. Rather, participants must have an opportunity to observe their own behavior, its appropriateness, and the kind and direction of change required. This, in turn, requires them to play an active role in the learning process. Most of the newer training methods have been aimed at expanding the role of the trainee through greater participation in the training. The newer methods have also drawn more heavily upon the behavioral sciences to help trainees achieve greater insight into their own actions, their relations with others, and the relationships among groups. Finally, the newer instructional methods attempt to relate the training experience to the problems and activities of the actual organizations of which the trainees are members or with which they work.

Description of Representative Training Methods. Some of the training methods used to improve individual or organizational effectiveness are described below. They include action-oriented as well as more traditional approaches, and methods appropriate to various levels of responsibility and sophistication.

On-the-job Training. On-the-job training is an organized approach to acquiring the knowledge and skills needed to perform a job, using the actual equipment and materials the job requires. It is suited for teaching relatively simple production or clerical operations to new employees. It is also used when job methods are significantly changed or when an employee is transferred to a different job. Properly planned on-the-job training breaks the work to be performed into logical and easily understood units and blends explanation and demonstrations by qualified instructors with opportunities for the learner to practice according to approved methods. It also checks on the trainee's progress against predetermined learning times and provides remedial instruction as required. On-the-job training involves a step-by-step approach similar to the procedure outlined in Figure 8-2.

Apprentice training, like on-the-job training, leans heavily upon guided instruction in the use of tools and equipment, but combines the performance of job tasks with classroom or laboratory training.

Lectures. The lecture is doubtless still the most commonly used method of passing on factual information to large numbers of people. It is applicable for all levels of employees to impart new information or to summarize experiences obtained from other instructional methods. Whether the lecture is presented in person or on film or by television, its ability to influence attitudes or shape behavior is obviously limited. Essentially a one-way communication method, it cannot discriminate among the participants' needs, motivate the participants, or give them a chance to practice what they are taught.

When a group is too large to permit discussion of material covered in the lecture, it is often broken down into small "buzz groups" that wrestle with

PREPARE
1. Skills trainer.
2. Job breakdown.
3. Training—activity timetable.

GET SET
4. Instruct on the job if at all possible.
5. Schedule training to avoid distractions and interruptions.
6. Get the trainee's undivided attention.
7. Find out what the trainee already knows about the job.
8. Explain the *why, when,* and *what* of the job.

INSTRUCT
9. Present job operations step by step, several times if necessary.   Explain and demonstrate at the same time.
10. Give the trainee a chance to perform the operations.   Have him explain and demonstrate at the same time.

CHECK
11. Ask questions as the trainee performs.
12. Correct mistakes as they are made.
13. Require practice until you are sure he knows.
14. Allow the trainee to work a while with close supervision.

FOLLOW-UP
15. Check back to insure continuing performance.
16. Train him to train new men.

FIG. 8-2. *Guidelines for skills training.* (*Courtesy of John H. Proctor and William Thornton,* Training: A Handbook for Line Managers, *American Management Association, New York, 1961, p. 58.*)

questions or problems introduced during the lecture and report back on them to the whole group.

Correspondence Courses. Another instructional technique for the imparting of facts or concepts is the correspondence course. It is particularly suited for training individuals in technical subjects when there is no qualified instructor, when trainees are widely dispersed or few, or when their needs are dissimilar. Unlike the lecture, it requires some activity by the trainee in the form of achievement tests or problem-solving exercises.

Programmed Instruction. A more recent form of self-instruction involves the use of programmed texts, teaching machines, or similar devices. The training principles underlying this method are relatively simple:

The material or information to be learned is given in small steps.

Each step builds upon what has been learned in preceding steps.

The trainee has to do some kind of work at each step, such as selecting the correct answer from among several alternative responses.

The trainee knows or learns the right answer before he proceeds to the next item of information.

Each trainee can proceed at his own rate.

The material gradually becomes more difficult as the trainee proceeds through the text.

Programmed materials require clearly defined objectives and careful sequencing of subject matter. Considerable evidence has accumulated to show that well-written programmed instruction texts may have several advantages over conventional textbooks. They give the trainee more motivation to learn, and they enable him to learn faster and to retain more of what he learns. Figure 8-3 compares the results, in terms of performance and training time, of programs in four companies using both conventional methods and programmed instruction.

Programmed instruction is being increasingly used with employees and supervisors to teach job skills and transmit information. Programmed texts and other self-instructional programs are especially popular in organizations with large numbers of employees to be trained or with employees who must assimilate a great amount of technical information at frequent intervals. Thus, the American Institute of Research prepared a programmed course in the fundamentals of insurance for the Life Insurance Agency Management Association, and Schering Corporation pioneered in programming technical information about a new drug. Hundreds of companies use off-the-shelf programs or programmed material developed by themselves or consultants.

Although most programmed material is presented in textbook form, it can also be put in visual or audio-visual form. Teaching machines and other mechanical or electromechanical devices are also used, though they appear to yield results not noticeably better than those produced by programmed textbooks. Humble Oil and Refining Company, for example, uses a compact reading machine/filmstrip viewer to train service-station attendants in the routines of their job; and the J. C. Penney Company, among others, has had excellent success

IMPROVED PERFORMANCE BY USE OF PROGRAMMED INSTRUCTION

COMPANY	PROGRAM	TRAINEES	AVERAGE PERFORMANCE SCORES		
			CONVENTIONAL INSTRUCTION	PROGRAMMED INSTRUCTION	PER CENT IMPROVEMENT IN PERFORMANCE
IBM	7070 COMPUTER COURSE	HIGH SCHOOL GRADUATES	86.2	95.1	10%
SCHERING	DERMATOLOGY & MYCOLOGY	DRUG RETAILERS	60.1	91.9	53
Du PONT	READING ENGINEERING DRAWINGS	MAINTENANCE MECHANICS, ETC.	81.2	91.2	12
BELL LABORATORIES	BASIC ELECTRICITY	TECHNICIANS	64.9* 47.5†	76.8* 66.4†	18* 40†

*Facts examination.   † Concepts examination.
Source: Basic Systems Inc., 1963.

TRAINING TIME SAVED BY USE OF PROGRAMMED INSTRUCTION

COMPANY	PROGRAM	TRAINEES	TRAINING HOURS PER TRAINEE		
			CONVENTIONAL INSTRUCTION	PROGRAMMED INSTRUCTION	PER CENT TIME REDUCTION
Du PONT	READING ENGINEERING DRAWINGS	MAINTENANCE MECHANICS, ETC.	17	12.8	25%
	ANALOG COMPUTATION	GRADUATE ENGINEERS	40	11.0	72
IBM	7070 COMPUTER COURSE	HIGH SCHOOL GRADUATES	15	11.0	27
SPIEGEL	PACKAGE BILLING	CLERKS	40	26.0	35

FIG. 8-3. *Improved performance by use of programmed instruction. Training time saved by use of programmed instruction.* (*Courtesy of John R. Murphy and Irving A. Goldberg, "Strategies for Using Programmed Instruction,"* Harvard Business Review, *May–June, 1964, pp. 118–119.*)

with "talking manuals" to teach the selling of certain product lines to associates in its hundreds of stores.

The costs of preparing self-instructional programs can be high, and a company should estimate them carefully and evaluate the method against other training techniques before deciding to go ahead.

Coaching. The coaching process is potentially the most direct and effective way for one person to influence the behavior of another. Coaching represents a continuing learning experience in which the individual is given opportunity to perform, is informed of the results he is expected to accomplish, and is counseled on the results he actually achieves. Frequently, the individual being coached is exposed to a series of planned experiences to accelerate his development. He may be given special assignments, perhaps as member of a committee or a task force; he may fill in for the boss or be delegated parts of his responsibilities; his job may be enlarged; or he may be systematically rotated through a series of jobs. When these assignments entail accountability for results, not merely observation of another's work, they can help the trainee perceive the interrelationships of various business functions.

Coaching, as a training technique, is effective at all levels of an organization. It occurs most often and most naturally in the superior-subordinate relationship. Better than any formal program, this relationship provides opportunity for close and continuing shaping of behavior within the work environment. However, the value of the coaching depends upon the coach, specifically on whether he himself possesses the knowledge or skills he is teaching, whether he has correctly identified what his subordinate needs to know or do, and whether he is able or willing to teach this knowledge or skill. The lack of coaching ability among many managers has led to the establishment of more formal training activities to fill the void or to supplement their efforts.

The Conference Method. The conference or discussion group permits a wide range of approaches and applications. Although some conferences are highly directed and include sizable numbers of participants, most of them are limited to groups of ten to fifteen to encourage active participation in the discussions. Research has demonstrated that the conference is a better technique than the lecture for changing group attitudes and behavior and for encouraging participants to think through to their own solutions to problems. Like the lecture, it is suitable for training in many subjects and at all levels. It is a more costly method than the lecture, however, and requires greater sensitivity and skill on the part of the leader.

The Case Method. The case method of instruction, long taught in law schools, was first applied to the teaching of management by the Harvard Graduate School of Business and is now used in virtually every management training program in the country. The case method is the study, analysis, and discussion of concrete business situations. Instead of relying on general principles, the case method draws on real problems in actual companies (with the names, of course, disguised). By dealing with these problems, the trainee learns to relate the situation to the enterprise as a whole and to perceive the interrelationships of people and events.

Cases are of varying length and complexity, because they are used with groups of diverse levels and experience. Though simplified cases are used for employee and foreman training, the case method is most effective at the higher levels, where participants have the breadth of experience necessary for making informed judgments on the technical or human problems of the business.

For maximum benefit, the case method requires careful preparation. Studying the material on his own, the trainee develops his capacity for analysis and his powers of independent judgment. Subsequently, by discussing the case with others, he learns that there is rarely a single or "approved" solution to a problem. From this process of analysis and discussion, insights into management behavior are gradually developed to form practical and viable principles of business management.

Despite these advantages, some have criticized the case method of instruction on several grounds, primarily because it demands too little of the learner and because it tends to equate the ability to verbalize about a problem with the ability to solve it. One of these critics, Dr. Paul Pigors, developed a variant of the case method which he called the "incident process."[1] The incident process briefly narrates a simple event and then requires the group of trainees to search out and relate the facts behind the incident by questioning the case leader. The issue to be decided is isolated and agreed upon, each participant declares his stand, and it is debated in small groups. Unlike the conventional case method in which the leader typically refrains from recounting the actual outcome of the case or from indicating his own solution, the leader in the incident process does both.

Many innovations in training methods have resulted from similar attempts to bridge the gap between the ability to verbalize about management and the ability to practice it. The approaches described in the remainder of this discussion illustrate various attempts to bring about changes in behavior or in actual job performance. Some of the methods employed concentrate on developing the individual's self-understanding; others focus on his ability to deal with his responsibilities.

Sensitivity Training. In the 1940s, the National Training Laboratories (NTL) experimented with sensitivity training, or methods for improving skills in interpersonal relations. More recently, under the name "laboratory training," NTL and its many offshoots aim at improving self-awareness and sensitivity to others, developing leadership and teamwork, and facilitating changes in organizational behavior. Though sensitivity training is applicable to all levels, its chief value is for those having supervisory responsibilites. In sessions normally lasting from one to three weeks, participants meet in small training groups, or T groups, where the subject matter is the participant's own immediate behavior in the group and the effects of this behavior on other members of the group and on the group as a whole. There are also practice exercises for assuming new behavior, and sessions where theories and research findings of behavioral sciences are examined in the light of the group's experiences. Equipped with new insights and improved interpersonal skills, the participants are expected to apply them in dealing with the human problems of their own organizations.

Sensitivity training requires particular sensitivity and skill in the trainer who works with the group. He must assist, and at times guide, the group, but never direct or dominate it. Many otherwise successful training specialists lack the insight into group processes required for this kind of training. Because such training involves honest self-examination and candor in commenting on the actions of other group members, there is always danger of destructive behavior and bruised egos. This, in fact, has happened in some companies which permitted inept or inexperienced trainers to conduct sensitivity sessions among their personnel. To minimize this risk, most companies call in consultants trained in these techniques to lead such sessions. Usually, training groups are made up of diagonal slices of the supervisory organization, but without superiors and

---

[1] Paul Pigors and Faith Pigors, *Case Method in Human Relations: The Incident Process*, McGraw-Hill Book Company, New York, 1961.

direct subordinates in the same groups. Occasionally, a normal work team, such as a department head and his foremen, will form a sensitivity training group, but this requires much trust and confidence within the group, as well as skill on the part of the trainer.

Many other training programs derive from the pioneering work of NTL in sensitivity training. The Kepner-Tregoe programs in problem analysis and decision making have participants "manage" an organization for a given number of days, develop solutions for its problems, and analyze the effectiveness of their decisions and their method of making them. The Managerial Grid program of Dr. Robert Blake[2] begins with an analysis of each participant's leadership style and the dynamics of problem analyses. Subsequently, the grid approach is used by a "team" or normal work group in an organization to deal with the group's actual problems or to improve working relations with other groups. In this type of program, the line between "training" and "operations" grows blurred.

Simulation: Business Games, In-baskets, and Role Playing. In trying to marry management theory and practice, training has developed a number of interesting ways of simulating the business environment. Business games, in-basket exercises, and role playing are among the more successful examples of this effort.

Business games, developed first by the American Management Association in imitation of military games, have been defined as a sort of management wind tunnel. They enable trainees to practice management concepts and techniques in a "training model," representing a vastly simplified facsimile of the business or one of its functions. The essence of the game is the interaction between the trainees, who assume certain roles in the management of the company, and the business environment. The trainees perform tasks and make decisions, the results of which are fed back, often with the aid of a computer, to furnish the basis, in critique sessions, for analyzing what happened and why.

Broadly speaking, there are two types of management games. The first is the general management game, which is designed to provide practice in adapting to an unfamiliar environment, making business decisions under conditions of uncertainty, and developing understanding of basic organizational relationships and management principles. The second type is called a "functional game," which provides practice in dealing with problems or situations found in a specific function—for example, in inventory management or sales planning.

The business game can be thought of as an acted-out case, and it has many of the features and advantages of the case method. Like that method, it is especially suited to training managers, and it tends to broaden the participants' understanding of the management process. A well-designed game also has certain advantages over the case study: it can better furnish insights into organizational behavior; it can promote teamwork among participants; and most important, it teaches at the behavioral rather than the verbal level.

In addition, the business game enables a great many events to be compressed into little time; it permits risk taking without the fears that may accompany it back on the job. And it is a dynamic and challenging exercise. The last has been found to be also a disadvantage; the players may concentrate on "winning" instead of learning, and are often too occupied with beating the computer or their competitors to take the time to analyze why they got the results they did. Another criticism made of the business game is that it distorts reality by grossly oversimplifying it, with the result that participants, on returning to their organizations, find it difficult to apply to their own work the lessons

[2] Robert R. Blake and Jane S. Mouton, *The Managerial Grid,* Gulf Publishing Company, Houston, 1964.

which they learned in the game. For a more complete discussion of the business game, see Chapter 7 of Section 4.

The *in-basket training* technique is a detailed simulation of the materials which a manager might find in his in-basket under certain defined circumstances. The trainee works through the material in an allotted period of time, taking action exactly as he would on the job. For example, he writes letters or memos on stationery which is provided, or he jots comments on an item and reroutes it, makes notes to himself about things to be done, or defers action until a future date. With a realistic simulation and under time pressure, he tends to behave very much as he usually behaves on the job, rather than as he thinks he ought to behave. Following this "working" period, each trainee is asked to recapitulate his actions and the reasons for them, in preparation for a group discussion to follow. This discussion enables the trainee to observe his own on-the-job behavior, and that of others, and to learn from it. With skilled critiquing, he has an opportunity to become aware of, and then possibly to change, his behavior.

Probably the most commonly used technique for providing reality practice is the role play. *Role playing* involves the acting out of situations involving two or more persons—for example, superior and subordinate, salesman and prospect, or members of a task force. Role playing places the participants in simulated circumstances where, under stress, they tend to act as they would in reality. Role plays should never be rehearsed or viewed as demonstrations of good or bad behavior. As with other forms of training simulation, the learning chiefly occurs during the analysis and discussion that take place in the critique sessions.

Although much can be gained from observing role playing, important benefits are obtained from actually playing the roles. The multiple role play is a procedure that makes it possible for large numbers of people to participate instead of only a few, and thus for insights to be obtained into group processes. The multiple role play also makes it possible to compare the outcomes from different groups and to analyze similarities and differences. Sometimes certain training objectives can be achieved by altering one role in half of the groups; in this way, the effect of this one variable on the results can be assessed. There are other variants to the conventional role play, all of which provide opportunity for looking at what people actually do in a situation as opposed to what they say they would do.

Simulation is useful at other than managerial levels, in a somewhat different way. Originally, as in the Link Trainer, it was used to teach technical and motor skills, and it is still used for training in procedures or the solving of technical problems. For example, simulation may be used to train technicians to troubleshoot a television set or to control processes in an oil refinery.

REQUIREMENTS FOR EFFECTIVE TRAINING

The effectiveness of a company's training effort depends upon the extent to which management is committed to support it, the proper assignment of responsibility to line managers and training specialists for the training effort, and the care and skill with which the training is planned, implemented, and evaluated.

Top Management Commitment. Top management can profoundly influence the quality of training in the company by the policies it espouses, the practices it condones, and the extent to which it supports and participates in the training effort. The first requisite is to provide a climate which is conducive to continued learning and growth. Healthy personal development is the product of this climate and of the experiences people are exposed to. Unless training squares with the policies and practices of the company, it can be more frustrating than helpful.

Assignment of Training Responsibilities. Both line managers and training specialists have important roles in and responsibilities for the training activity.

Training is not a personnel program, but a management tool. Each manager, therefore, must accept the development of his people as one of his prime responsibilities, and he should be willing to be appraised on the basis of how well he carries out this responsibility. Although he has much to contribute in planning, conducting, and evaluating the training activity, his greatest contribution is to help his subordinates apply to their jobs what they have learned from training. To do so, he can reach agreement with his men on their responsibilities and specific job goals, measure and discuss the results they get, and provide opportunities and guidance for overcoming their shortcomings and building on their strengths. The manager should also set specific training goals with his men, monitor the results of the training, and make effective use of the company's training staff.

In smaller organizations, the supervisor is usually personally responsible for training his subordinates in acquiring the skills needed to perform their jobs. Because he probably has no training specialist to assist him, if he needs help he will have to call upon another supervisor or personnel representative, or perhaps get help from outside the company. Where there is a training specialist, a manager generally delegates to him the primary responsibility for planning, executing, and appraising the training program.

A Planned Approach. The success of a training program depends on how accurately the needs of the organization are identified and the objectives of the training are specified, whether appropriate training materials and methods are selected, and whether valid techniques are used to measure the program's effectiveness.

Determination of Training Needs and Objectives. Management has a right to expect that its training dollars will be spent on the right people in the right positions and functions, and that they will be used to achieve the proper organizational goals. One investigator found that only one out of thirty organizations surveyed had established training plans in terms of goals to be achieved. Studies have also shown that significant differences may exist between the training needed or desired by management and the training the company's training department provides.

McGehee and Thayer[3] recommend a three-step approach to determining training needs:

1. Organization analysis, which helps determine where training emphasis should be placed within the organization.

2. Operations analysis, which determines what the training should consist of. This requires a study of what a person should be taught if he is to perform his task with maximum effectiveness.

3. Man analysis, which determines who needs to be trained and what skills, knowledge, or attitudes should be augmented or improved.

Many different techniques are used for determining training needs. Some of those identified by the Research Committee of the American Society for Training and Development are:

Interviews and survey questionnaires

Observations

---

[3] William McGehee and Paul W. Thayer, *Training in Business and Industry,* John Wiley & Sons, Inc., New York, 1961.

Group discussions

Performance and other tests

Personnel records

Merit rating and performance appraisals

Job or activity analyses

Production records and other performance results

Long-range business and organization plans

Once the training needs have been identified, the training objectives can be developed. Broadly speaking, they should express the gap that needs to be bridged between present performance and expected performance or, in terms of the educator, between "initial behavior" and the desired "terminal behavior." The more precisely these objectives are stated, the easier it is to develop the training program and the means of evaluating it. Obviously, it is harder to set precise objectives for high-level positions than for clerical or production-type jobs.

Development of the Training Program. Having secured reliable data for identifying training needs and establishing training objectives, the training specialist attempts to meet these needs and objectives by drawing upon his experience in training design and methodology. For technical programs, he may rely for much of the content on personnel who are knowledgeable in those areas, but he himself will be chiefly responsible for shaping the material to training purposes. The trainer begins by drawing up a plan which specifies the training objectives, outlines the scope and subject matter of the program, the training methods to be employed, and the types of participants and instructors who will be involved, and makes provisions for appraising the program's effectiveness. He also develops the training materials and course outlines and may preview the program with management. He may also train those selected to lead the sessions, coordinate the program after it is launched, and assist management in follow-up and reinforcement on the job of what was learned in the program.

Evaluation of Training. A sound training plan includes provision for measuring its effectiveness. Management should be able to tell whether the money spent on training is yielding profitable results, whether better results could be obtained from the same training dollars, or whether organization goals could be better accomplished by some means other than training.

The cost of training is easily determined, but its "profitability"—the benefits resulting from the training—is much harder to measure, particularly for management training programs. Among the more usual techniques for evaluating training are the following.

1. Solicitation of the reactions of participants. Usually this is done by asking them to comment in writing on what they liked about the program, what they disliked, and how they suggest the program be improved. The usefulness of the responses depends on the frankness and perceptiveness of the participants, but at best this technique is more likely to measure the popularity of a program than its effectiveness.

2. Tests to determine whether participants have learned the principles or techniques taught in the program. Pencil-and-paper tests can measure the participants' ability to verbalize what they have learned, but cannot predict that the learning will be applied to the job.

3. Performance tests or observation of behavior on the job. If the tests are valid or the observation is carefully controlled, these techniques can sometimes evaluate the extent to which the learner has acquired new skills and can weigh the benefits against the costs of training him. Most behavioral changes, however,

are difficult to measure, and the changes, if observed, are often difficult to ascribe to training—or to any other single cause.

4. Comparison of results achieved before and after training. This technique, like the preceding one, is most applicable to the evaluation of skill training. Unfortunately, not all training lends itself to the direct and practical kind of measurement applicable to production-type tasks. For example, even if a supervisory course in human relations is followed by a reduction in grievances or rise in output, it cannot be assumed that the training alone was responsible for the improvement.

Despite these limitations, certain training activities can be evaluated with some accuracy. Even where dependable methods have not yet been found, a systematic and conscientious effort to assess the effectiveness of training against its cost is better than guesswork or blind faith.

SUMMARY

Training has come to be regarded as a vital tool of management, capable of making important contributions to the goals of the enterprise. Starting with the identification of the individual's capabilities and needs and the requirements and problems of the organization, training attempts to improve the performance of both by closing the distance between expectations and achievements.

Training is thus defined not as an end in itself, but as a continuing activity, an integral part of the business system. Mindful of its purpose, which is to bring about change in behavior, training is wedded to no particular technique, but adapts or invents the approach that promises best to produce the desired change.

Whether supported by a training staff or not, each manager is responsible for his own training and for fostering the development of his subordinates. This responsibility includes the establishment of training objectives and the measurement of training results.

BIBLIOGRAPHY

Blake, Robert R., and Jane S. Mouton, *The Managerial Grid,* Gulf Publishing Company, Houston, 1964.

Button, W. H., and W. J. Wasmuth, *Employee Training in Small Business Organizations,* New York State School of Industrial and Labor Relations, New York, 1964.

Developing Executive Skills, American Management Association, New York, 1958.

Dolmatch, T. B., et al. (eds.), *Revolution in Training: Programmed Instruction in Industry,* American Management Association, New York, 1962.

Encyclopedia of Supervisory Training, American Management Association, New York, 1961.

Kibbee, J. M., C. J. Kraft, and B. Nanus (eds.), *Management Games,* Reinhold Publishing Corporation, New York, 1962.

Maier, Norman R. F., Allen R. Solem, and Ayesha M. Maier, *Supervisory and Executive Development: A Manual for Role Playing,* John Wiley & Sons, Inc., New York, 1957.

McGehee, William, and Paul W. Thayer, *Training in Business and Industry,* John Wiley & Sons, Inc., New York, 1961.

Pigors, Paul, and Faith Pigors, *Case Method in Human Relations: The Incident Process,* McGraw-Hill Book Company, New York, 1961.

Proctor, John H., and W. M. Thornton, *Training: A Handbook for Line Managers,* American Management Association, New York, 1961.

CHAPTER NINE

Suggestion Systems

A Special Committee of the National Association of Suggestion Systems, Chicago, Illinois

WILLIAM V. KREWATCH   *E. I. du Pont de Nemours & Company, Wilmington, Delaware*

Assisted by

WALLACE H. EGBERT   *Mead Johnson & Company, Evansville, Indiana*

RICHARD J. REBELLINO   *The Timken Roller Bearing Company, Canton, Ohio*

Suggestion programs as a management tool have a firmly established place in business, industry, and government, attested to by references in the annual reports of major companies and government agencies. The gathering from all individuals in the organization of their best thinking on every aspect of the business is in the best interests of the employee, the corporation, and the public. This chapter will briefly cover the fundamental principles and more important considerations found to be advisable in administering a suggestion program.

SUGGESTION SYSTEM REQUIREMENTS

Formal suggestion systems in industry started after 1900. During World War II, the Federal government established a Civilian Award Board which initiated and promoted these programs to obtain maximum participation and assistance from every level of personnel to improve the war effort. Their value was recognized and principles for successful operation determined. In 1942, the National Association of Suggestion Systems was formed as a nonprofit organization to disseminate experience and knowledge in this specialized field.

Use of this technique has spread widely among both industry and government in the United States, Canada, Britain, and Europe. Actual performance statistics from these countries and by individual member companies in the United States are recorded by the National Association of Suggestion Systems, 33 East Congress Parkway, Chicago, Illinois 60604.

Statistics on suggestions for the year 1964 were:

```
Suggestions received per 100 eligible employees................  34
Individuals participating per 100 eligible employees............  24
Suggestions awarded.....................................................  24%
Suggestions awarded per 100 eligible employees...............   8
Average award paid in dollars..............................  41
```

Primary Objectives. When formulating a suggestion plan, clearly defined objectives are necessary; management must decide just what it desires or plans to achieve. These objectives, generally, are: (1) reduce costs; (2) stimulate creative thinking; (3) recognize and reward individuals for their extra contributions; (4) ensure fair consideration and maximum use of ideas submitted; (5) improve employer-employee relations.

Secondary Benefits. The secondary benefits generally recognized by experienced suggestion administrators are: (1) improve competitive position; (2) develop a more favorable employee attitude; (3) emphasize the importance of individual accomplishment; (4) identify individuals with greater potential; (5) provide a two-way communication system; (6) bring to management's attention problems which otherwise might remain unidentified; (7) provide a natural medium for training in creativity and work simplification; and (8) develop a spirit of teamwork between the employee and his supervisor.

Determination of Major Objectives. The initial step in contemplating a suggestion system is a determination by management of the major objectives in order of importance. The program can then be designed to serve these purposes and at the same time be integrated properly with all other plans and policies. Most managements believe that where the savings are sufficient to offset direct costs, employee relations benefits easily justify continued operation.

Another fundamental decision associated with objectives is extending the eligibility of levels of employees upward to include exempt supervisory, professional, and management. Because an award is given for contributions beyond those normally expected from the individual in his position, the extent of normal expectancy must be identified, and ineligible positions determined.

Management Support. More than most industrial programs, a suggestion system must have continuous active management support if it is to be successful and develop its maximum potential.

Typical of such support is a statement made by W. A. Patterson of United Airlines to his supervisors in their booklet "Promoting Employees' Suggestions."

You as a supervisor must accomplish your job through the work of others. Your success or failure depends upon your ability to foster among our employees the spirit of teamwork and the will to work efficiently. This is the way we can provide the best service to our customers. An active suggestion program will help us to achieve these ends; however, no suggestion program will work successfully without your support and cooperation.

When the program in the Federal government was initiated, the following statement was made by President Eisenhower.

The vast complexity of modern government demands a constant search for ways of conducting the public business with increased efficiency and economy. I am firmly convinced that employees of the Federal government can, through their diligence and competence, make further significant contributions to the important task of improving government operations. Wide participation by Federal employees in this task is essential if we are to derive full benefit from the ingenuity and inventiveness that exist in the Federal service. This participation can be obtained only if all levels of management and supervision understand its importance, encourage it, and ensure that it is promptly and properly recognized.

A means for adequately recognizing those employees who contribute to improved government operations was provided by the Government Employees Incentive Awards Act passed by the 83rd Congress. This Act was a part of the Administration's legislative program on personnel management. Under it the Civil Service Commission was given general responsibility for the administration of a government-wide incentive awards program. The Commission has authorized each of you to establish and operate an incentive awards program within broad principles and guidelines. I am relying upon you to provide personal leadership for the incentive awards program in your agency.

I am looking forward to personal participation in the program through the provision in the Act for a Presidential award for employees rendering exceptionally meritorious service. The necessary instructions for submitting recommendations for this award are now being prepared.

DEVELOPING THE SUGGESTION SYSTEM

A well-qualified individual should be selected who will either administer the program or supervise its administration later. He should be given free time, or even full time, over a period of a year or more to research and develop a compatible program. Material on the subject is available from other organizations which operate suggestion systems in the same field of endeavor, or from the National Association of Suggestion Systems, which has available a wealth of experience and know-how. Rules and procedures should be fully and carefully documented. At this point, various levels of management can be brought in to consult and agree on the various program features. Then when the program is initiated, they will be more inclined to support it wholeheartedly.

The basic elements which make up a plan are: (1) primary purpose, (2) statement of ownership of the idea, (3) scope of plan, (4) types of suggestions eligible, (5) types of suggestions ineligible, (6) eligibility of suggesters, (7) when is a suggestion adopted, (8) how to establish the value of an idea, (9) award amount and limitations, (10) how to process suggestions, including those accepted and awarded and those declined, (11) handling a patentable idea, (12) time limit on submission of an idea, (13) how long a suggester has the right to an idea after a decision has been made not to adopt it, and (14) duration of plan with rights of company to terminate or change. All of these points must be determined and clearly stated.

Assignment of Responsibilities. The general flow of a suggestion through the suggestion system is shown by Figure 9-1. Responsibility for the various parts of the suggestion system should be specifically established.

1. An individual should be assigned the direct and full responsibility for administering and operating the system. This system administrator can function best if he is placed in the organization where he is not controlled by a subdivision which he serves, such as manufacturing. Generally, his is a staff assignment under a vice president or head of personnel.

2. The responsibility to be accepted by the line organization should be defined in detail. This will include assigning needed personnel, reviewing and making decisions on suggestions pertaining to their work, determining savings or benefits,

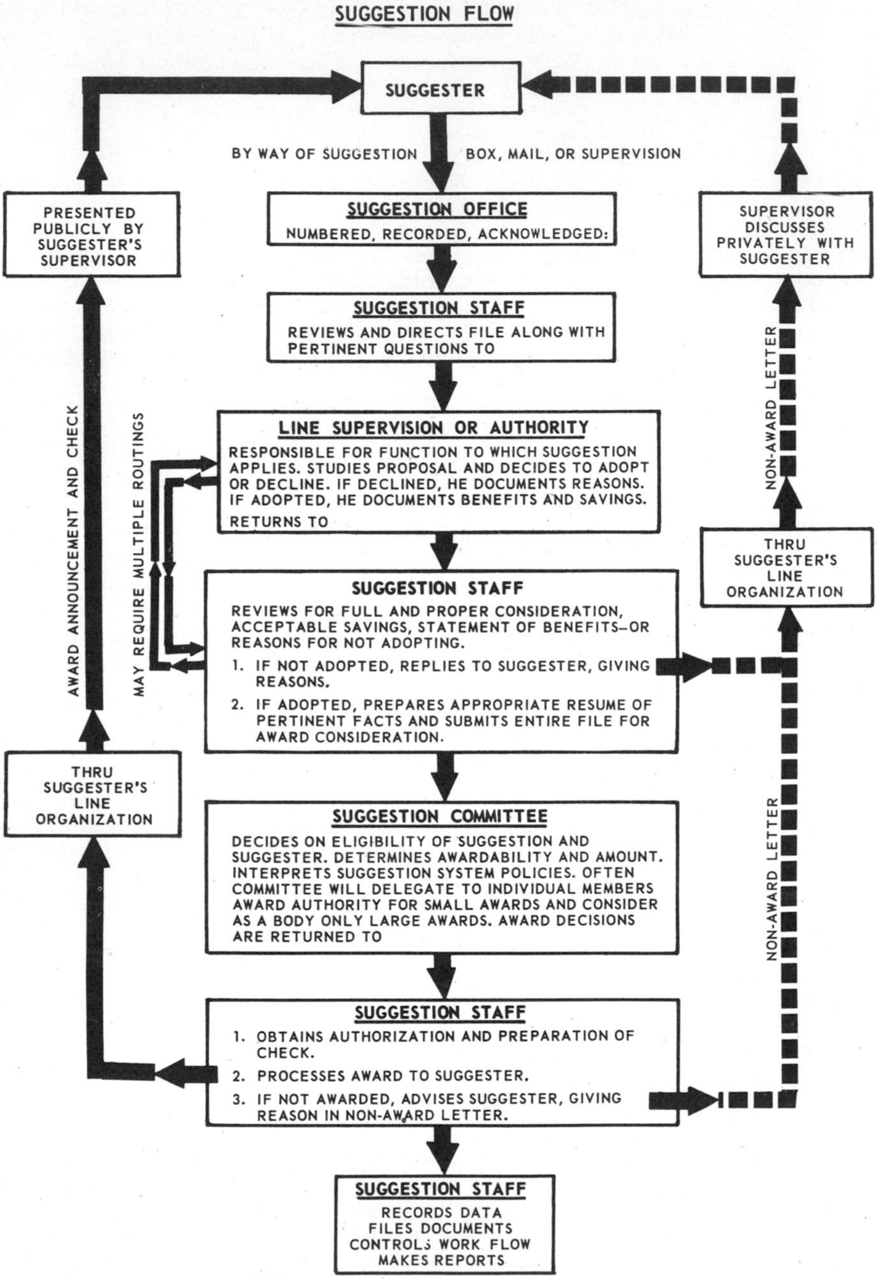

SUGGESTION FLOW

```
                              ┌─────────────────┐
                              │   SUGGESTER     │
                              └─────────────────┘

           BY WAY OF SUGGESTION      BOX, MAIL, OR SUPERVISION
```

| PRESENTED PUBLICLY BY SUGGESTER'S SUPERVISOR | **SUGGESTION OFFICE** NUMBERED, RECORDED, ACKNOWLEDGED: | SUPERVISOR DISCUSSES PRIVATELY WITH SUGGESTER |

SUGGESTION STAFF
REVIEWS AND DIRECTS FILE ALONG WITH PERTINENT QUESTIONS TO

LINE SUPERVISION OR AUTHORITY
RESPONSIBLE FOR FUNCTION TO WHICH SUGGESTION APPLIES. STUDIES PROPOSAL AND DECIDES TO ADOPT OR DECLINE. IF DECLINED, HE DOCUMENTS REASONS. IF ADOPTED, HE DOCUMENTS BENEFITS AND SAVINGS.
RETURNS TO

SUGGESTION STAFF
REVIEWS FOR FULL AND PROPER CONSIDERATION, ACCEPTABLE SAVINGS, STATEMENT OF BENEFITS—OR REASONS FOR NOT ADOPTING.
1. IF NOT ADOPTED, REPLIES TO SUGGESTER, GIVING REASONS.
2. IF ADOPTED, PREPARES APPROPRIATE RESUME OF PERTINENT FACTS AND SUBMITS ENTIRE FILE FOR AWARD CONSIDERATION.

SUGGESTION COMMITTEE
DECIDES ON ELIGIBILITY OF SUGGESTION AND SUGGESTER. DETERMINES AWARDABILITY AND AMOUNT. INTERPRETS SUGGESTION SYSTEM POLICIES. OFTEN COMMITTEE WILL DELEGATE TO INDIVIDUAL MEMBERS AWARD AUTHORITY FOR SMALL AWARDS AND CONSIDER AS A BODY ONLY LARGE AWARDS. AWARD DECISIONS ARE RETURNED TO

SUGGESTION STAFF
1. OBTAINS AUTHORIZATION AND PREPARATION OF CHECK.
2. PROCESSES AWARD TO SUGGESTER.
3. IF NOT AWARDED, ADVISES SUGGESTER, GIVING REASON IN NON-AWARD LETTER.

SUGGESTION STAFF
RECORDS DATA
FILES DOCUMENTS
CONTROLS WORK FLOW
MAKES REPORTS

AWARD ANNOUNCEMENT AND CHECK

MAY REQUIRE MULTIPLE ROUTINGS

NON-AWARD LETTER

THRU SUGGESTER'S LINE ORGANIZATION

THRU SUGGESTER'S LINE ORGANIZATION

NON-AWARD LETTER

FIG. 9-1.   *Flow of a suggestion through the suggestion system.*

controlling suggestion handling, and promoting the submission of suggestions from their employees.

3. Although suggestion committees are used widely, many systems function without committees or use committees only for special suggestion system problems or policy matters. When a suggestion committee is used, it should be appointed with proper organizational representation and with clearly identified limits of authority. Committee members may represent functions or major organizational subdivisions. They may make decisions on adoption, eligibility of idea and individual, amount of award, system rules and procedures, or only some portion of these various responsibilities.

Often, committee members will delegate their authority to one member or to suggestion staff personnel for the small suggestions and those which are commonplace and routine in nature, and give their time only to the lucrative and superior ideas. In many cases, the authority to approve payment of the award is given to management only. Procedures should encourage rapid processing of suggestions with minimum repetitive review and approval.

Introducing the Program. After the administrative details of the program have been agreed upon and the date set for introduction to employees, the actual introduction itself should be carefully programmed starting with the top position and working downward to each employee. At each level of responsibility, the individuals should be given all the information necessary for them to carry out their part of the responsibility and necessary to obtain their acceptance and support of the program. The first-line supervisor must understand the system in sufficient detail to explain its operation to his employees. To do this, a carefully prepared training session is normally advisable. This session should be conducted by either the training section or the suggestion system administrator. An employee's booklet should be developed and given to each employee at this point with the supervisor explaining the program to his employees. Prior to the start-up date, as well as afterward, bulletin boards, house organs, and other promotional media can be used effectively. The suggestion office itself should be completely organized and ready to process promptly suggestions as they are received.

Importance of Supervisory Involvement. The key to a successful program rests with the supervisor. In large organizations, a special booklet can be written for first-line supervision. It should describe in detail the part to be played by the supervisor and point out the reasons why this is important to both the organization and the supervisor himself. A suggestion system should become an integral part of the normal day-to-day operation. Therefore, the supervisor should be included in the original planning and be given direct responsibility for promoting and administering the program in his area. For suggestions applying to his work, this includes making decisions on adoption, establishing the value of an idea, and deciding when and why an idea can or cannot be used. The suggestion system should not bypass or take away any responsibility from the line organization. It is preferable to make the supervisor the key figure in the presentation of awards in his area and give him full recognition for the success of the program. Therefore, he must understand thoroughly all rules and procedures.

Legal Aspects. The suggestion system establishes a contractual obligation in which the employee voluntarily offers an idea for which the company agrees to make payment under specific conditions if it is used. Consequently, if the idea is presented and used, the award is in order even though the employee may resign, be fired, or become deceased. Most companies review the complete plan with their legal department to be sure all legal aspects are considered. Suggestion forms, changes in the plan, and statements to employees such as the suggestion booklet or the supervisory booklet might well be reviewed by the legal department. Also, suggestions should be signed by the suggester even though the plan may choose not to identify him when the file is being processed for adoption or award determination.

Controls, Records, and Reports. The proper and timely consideration of an idea is important to the suggester. Therefore, control procedures must be carefully worked out before the program is initiated.

Suggestion forms should be designed to permit rapid and economical processing and to meet legal considerations. A numbering system can be designed to identify year and month of receipt and subdivision of company from which received, and provide an easy count of receipts. It should provide space for recording present conditions, proposed idea, and a statement of benefits or savings. A short descriptive title is valuable. Space across the top can be used for data identifying the suggester with location, job function, dates, and his supervisor. Signature location is usually at the bottom with a reference to the printed plan on reverse side for legal purposes. Various forms may be used for routing control and comment, savings calculations, award announcements or certificates, recording actions taken on the file for internal processing, follow-up, and other miscellaneous processing needs. Color coding of forms and a distinctive appearance identifying suggestion activity are recommended.

Processing routine involves receiving suggestions, numbering them, coding for duplicate check, titling, recording various data, and then routing for evaluation and decision. Prior to routing, the individual responsible for its processing should be assigned. He reviews the file for deciding the course of action and data needed. Record is made of date and to whom it is routed. Then later, when the file is returned with a decision on adoption and a statement of benefits or savings, it can be analyzed for final decision to award or decline. The data on this final action should be properly recorded.

When a decision is made to decline a suggestion, it is imperative that the suggester understand fully and clearly why. This may be done verbally or by a special letter. Form letters detract from the importance placed by management on employee participation. The contact or letter should encourage additional suggestions. When a file remains open for an extended period, the suggester should be kept informed of its status.

Data recorded for control and statistical reporting may include award; date; amount; savings; follow-up for later savings check for Part II award; type of benefit, such as savings, intangible, safety, or capital reduction; and other desired information.

Reports may be divided between those for supervisory and management information and those for office control. Management generally wants to know the volume of receipts for the various subdivisions, number of eligible personnel, number closed, number and amount of awards, number of different individuals participating, average award, amount of savings, and backlog of open suggestions. For internal control, the suggestion administrator should be interested in knowing how long it takes to complete files, suggestions which are held too long for comment, files lost, those in the office too long, some measure of office personnel efficiency such as unit costs or costs versus annual budget, and data from which formal management reports are made.

If IBM or electronic data-processing equipment is available, it can be used to great advantage if the volume is large—over 1,500 files handled per year. The controls should be such that files can be found at any time and their status identified.

In developing controls, records, and reports, it is well to benefit from the experience of other similar organizations. This type of assistance is available from the National Association of Suggestion Systems.

Promotional Activities. No system can reach its maximum potential without carefully planned and executed promotion. This should be dignified and businesslike, and tailored for the particular type of operation and personnel for which it is to be used. Suggestion boxes where suggestion blanks are readily available are quite standard. Bulletin boards are often associated with these boxes and carry the routine promotional matter.

Special "clubs" which publicize and promote individual or group attainments are effective. Promotional drives of a general nature for special purposes can successfully direct group thinking and competition. Many companies find that a cost-reduction program operated in parallel with the suggestion system is a valuable tool. Training in individual creativity and work simplification effectively complements cost-reduction and suggestion systems.

Delegation of job responsibility and authority down the line will provide employees with greater involvement and personal concern for their assigned duties. The result is broader participation in both direct and associated job functions and an acceptance of increased responsibility for the company's welfare. This, in turn, produces both an attitude and an atmosphere conducive to an increase in suggestions of substantial value.

Regular communications from top management are important. The identification of a suggester of the month and a suggester of the year from the total organization or its major divisions can be recognized at a periodic luncheon or dinner, thus providing additional promotion and publicity. The annual affairs give management an excellent opportunity to review the program and its accomplishments for the past year and point the direction desired for the future. The results of this type of affair can then be released in the house organ.

The annual conference of the National Association of Suggestion Systems always exhibits many promotional programs used by industry and government. This is an excellent source of promotional ideas which have proved successful.

EVALUATING RESULTS

Results and trends should be compared with the objectives established for the program. If a program is properly administered, management can expect continuing improvement year after year over a period of many years. Successful business is never stagnant, but is always changing. New technology, methods, and procedures are always being developed. New and better tools are available; better and less expensive materials are always coming into the market. An alert organization at every level will take maximum advantage of change or will itself bring about change. A formalized system allows management to take advantage of this fact of life.

BIBLIOGRAPHY

Haefele, John W., *Creativity and Innovation*, Reinhold Publishing Corporation, New York, 1962.
National Association of Suggestion Systems, 33 East Congress Parkway, Chicago, Ill., series of Study Reports on different activities employed in administering a suggestion system:
Administration of a Suggestion Plan, 1957
Adoption and Non-adoption Letters, rev. ed., 1965

Anonymous, Partially & Fully Identified Suggestion Plans, 1961
Eligibility of Suggesters, 1959
Evaluating Intangible Suggestions, 1957
Legal Aspects and Implications of Suggestion Plans, 1960
Objectives of a Suggestion System, 1958
Promotion and Publicity for an Effective Incentive Awards Program (U.S. Govt.), 1958
Suggestion Boxes, 1957
Quarterly magazine
Whitwell, W. C., *Suggestion Systems Are Profitable,* Prentice-Hall, Inc., Englewood Cliffs, N.J., 1963.

CHAPTER TEN

Wage and Salary Administration

RANDOLPH S. DRIVER *Manager of Industrial Relations, Atlantic Richfield Company, Philadelphia, Pennsylvania*

Salaries and wages represent a substantial part of total costs in most companies. Although to the economist these are variable costs, to the businessman they are becoming ever-increasing costs in view of the ability of unions to win upward adjustments. Instances of general wage or salary reductions are rare, and where it is necessary to reduce labor costs, this is accomplished more and more through technological change resulting in fewer employees. Notwithstanding this, the control of wage and salary levels is of paramount importance, even though the amount of control which can be exerted may vary among companies and within a company from time to time.

The classical objectives of salary and wage administration have been (1) the control of costs, (2) the establishment of fair and equitable remuneration, (3) the utilization of wages and salaries as an incentive to greater employee productivity, and (4) the maintenance of a satisfactory public relations image. In spite of limitations upon employers in accomplishing these objectives, they are still valid, and in many instances, can be accomplished to a greater extent than may at first seem possible. Federal and state legislation dealing with minimum wages, among other wage and salary matters, requires that conformance to minimum-wage legislation be an additional objective.

Responsibility for Wage and Salary Administration. The responsibility for wage and salary administration usually lies with the board of directors or the chief executive officer, who, in turn, is expected to develop policies and procedures which will accomplish the company's objectives. In smaller companies, the responsibility for administration of these policies and procedures is rarely delegated. In larger companies, however, it must be delegated. Thus the necessity arises for audit and control to be certain that the objectives are attained. Delegation may be to individual executives responsible for subdivisions of the company or to wage and salary committees composed of line and staff executives. Customarily, the delegation is to executives, with committees being established as necessary to interpret policy and act as a control to ensure the desired degree of uniformity.

General Wage and Salary Policy. Various forms of wage and salary policies have been developed, differing according to such factors as the nature of the business and its location. In addition, the wage policy may differ from the salary policy within a given company. Because wages and salaries normally constitute a substantial part of total cost, it is often advisable that the policy recognize competitors' wage and salary levels as well as the level of wages and salaries in a geographical area.

The classical entrepreneurial approach to wage and salary policy has been to recognize that wages and salaries must be at a level which is adequate to attract, retain, and motivate employees competent to perform the tasks assigned to them. It has been alleged that this policy looks upon human labor as a commodity subject to the economic laws of supply and demand and thus fails to recognize human factors, including a desire for a better way of life. As a result of this basic criticism, together with the pressure of organized labor and the impact of Federal and state legislation, many other forms of policy statements have been adopted. Some of the more typical forms of these are described briefly below.

Typical General Wage and Salary Policies. Perhaps the most prevalent general wage and salary policy is one which relates wage and salary levels in a company to those of its competitors, either within its own industry or with those who are competitors for labor in a geographical area. A policy of this sort might read: "The XYZ Company will pay wages and salaries which approximate the average of the companies in its industry." A more limiting form might read: "The XYZ Company will pay wages and salaries which approximate the average of the companies in its industry in its local geographical area." Another variation is to relate the wage and salary levels to companies within the area, regardless of the type of industry.

One of these forms is usually adopted by companies who consider themselves to be "followers" in setting wage and salary levels. Because it makes general wage and salary changes dependent upon the actions of others, it is not a complete policy for a company which is a wage and salary leader.

Another form of wage and salary policy is the formula approach, which recognizes changes in cost of living and productivity as a basis for wage changes. When this type of policy was adopted by General Motors, it was widely copied by other companies. The development of such a policy requires, first, the selection of a rate of productivity increase which in most instances must be assumed, because accurate measurement is not available, and second, the adoption of a relationship between cents per hour of wage increase or decrease and cost-of-living indexes. In many formulas, the companies have accepted the full change in cost of living on a percentage basis, but it may not always be wise to do so. Theoretically at least, there are strong reasons why a company should avoid guaranteeing a standard of living which is no less than the existing one. It must be remembered that the formula approach has not been tested under "runaway" inflation such as has been experienced abroad.

A third form of wage and salary policy is a more generalized statement which might read: "The company intends to pay wages and salaries which will fairly and equitably reward its employees for a fair day's work." A statement of this sort, being unrelated to specific standards, offers maximum flexibility in interpretation, but may not be acceptable to employees who prefer a more tangible form of policy. However, it is important to recognize the need for flexibility in adopting a policy if that policy is to remain unchanged over long periods of time. The degree of flexibility which is adopted must be considered in relation to the objectives of the policy.

Analysis of General Wage and Salary Policies. Although many other forms of general wage and salary policies exist, they tend to be variations of the three examples just discussed. It is obvious that the advantages of one are the disadvantages of another. It is this that has led many businessmen and academicians to conclude that no fully satisfactory statement of wage and salary policy currently exists. Hazard went so far as to conclude that the only pragmatic wage and salary policy was one of expediency because of the pressures of organized labor.[1] This gloomy conclusion may understate the value of a forthright policy.

A general wage and salary policy can have real value as a basis for collective bargaining, because it is only when the leaders of organized labor and the employees are aware of the company's point of view that there can be any hope of developing accommodation to it. It is not unusual to find a company which has convinced its employees that its policy on wages and salaries is fair and realistic. To do so, however, a company must adhere to its policy as consistently as possible.

A general wage and salary policy is also an advantage in recruiting new employees and in retaining old employees in times of labor shortage. To accomplish this, it must be publicized. The policy that is adopted, therefore, must be selected carefully to make certain that conformance to it is attainable.

The ability of the company to pay must be a prime, underlying factor in the choice of any policy governing wages and salaries. Ability to pay, as a basis for collective bargaining, is in disfavor, in part because of the necessity of supporting the company's position with detailed financial information. No company, however, can afford to fail to consider its ability to continue to pay in accordance with any statement of policy it may make.

In addition to the general wage and salary policy, additional policies are needed to cover specific wage and salary considerations such as promotion. These will be discussed below. However, it should be recognized that traditional salary and wage administration is based upon payment for the job rather than payment for the individual. Thus, rates are established which are applicable to any individual who might be assigned to a job. Although this practice is customarily followed with hourly rated and lower-level salaried jobs, its weaknesses have resulted in a developing tendency to pay higher-level salaried employees, managers, and executives to a greater extent as individuals, with less emphasis upon the job that they perform. This is not to say, however, that higher-level job duties should not be evaluated and aligned in accordance with their importance and worth.

Methods of Payment. Traditional methods of payment include the following.

1. Hourly rates. In some cases, these may take the form of a prescribed number of cents per hour. In other cases, they may be in the form of a range of rates, such as from $2.50 to $3.50, with several steps in between. The rates within this range which are paid to employees usually are based on length of service, but occasionally may be based on meritorious performance or a combination of service and merit.

---

[1] Leland Hazard, "Wage Theory: A Management View," in George W. Taylor and Frank C. Pierson (eds.) *New Concepts in Wage Determination*, McGraw-Hill Book Company, New York, 1957, pp. 32–50.

2. Salaries.   There may be a fixed salary for a position, such as $150 a week. More normally, however, salaries are in the form of a range with intermediate steps.   Salaries are usually established on the basis of meritorious performance, but occasionally on the basis of service.

3. Piece rates.   These are typical in some industries, but have limited application in industry in general.

4. Commissions.   These form the basis of payment in some marketing occupations.

5. Wage incentives.   These are, or should be, based on time study and industrial engineering concepts.

The choice of the appropriate method of payment is dictated by a number of factors, including traditional considerations in the area or industry, the practicality of the measurement of production or sales, and pressures of organized labor.

A number of years ago, it was fairly common to consider that salaries were paid for periods of work such as a week or month, and that hours of work were not a factor.   Salaried employees received certain fringe benefits not available to hourly employees.   Hourly employees were paid only for the hours worked.   They might work less than a full day or less than a full week.   Over the years, hourly employees were accorded various overtime and other premium-pay provisions which at first were generally not available to salaried people.

After the Great Depression, the distinction between the two methods of payment became less and less easy to determine.   Certain salaried employees were paid overtime because of legislative requirements, and hourly employees rarely worked less than a full work week because of union pressure.   Fringe benefits tended to become more uniform, but not necessarily the same in every respect.   Thus, by the middle 1960s, assignment to hourly rate or salary became more nearly a matter of tradition than anything else.   Some companies, the Gillette Company being an example, transferred many or all hourly workers to salary status and reported beneficial results as measured by production and the level of morale of employees.

The use of piece rates is limited by the relatively few instances where this form of payment is practical.   The use of incentive based on industrial engineering concepts requires considerable skill to establish satisfactory standards for certain occupations and to adjust or "tighten" existing standards.   Robert H. Roy discusses the problems inherent in this type of payment in an article entitled, "Do Wage Incentives Reduce Costs?"[2]

Commission payments are generally limited to salesmen.   They may be the sole basis of compensation for certain kinds of salesmen or may be combined with a salary to produce a desired level of total compensation.   Sales managers differ in their opinions of the value of commissions as incentives, but probably more favor commissions than oppose them.   Little or no completely objective evidence is available on their incentive value.

In summary, except for unusual circumstances where objective measurements of production are available, most employees are paid on either an hourly rate or a salary basis, with the assignment to one or the other being largely a matter of tradition.   Thus, blue-collar workers are generally paid on an hourly rate and white-collar workers on a salaried basis.

Administration of General Wage and Salary Increases.   Problems arise in connection with the application of general increases to wage scales or salary schedules. The following are common:

[2] Robert H. Roy, "Do Wage Incentives Reduce Costs?" *Industrial & Labor Relations Review*, vol. 5, no. 2, January, 1952.

1. The internal relationship among rates is altered.   In the following chapter, which covers the subject of job evaluation, the development of a wage structure is discussed which provides differentials among jobs which are sufficiently attractive to encourage employees to develop themselves for promotion.   These differentials are also necessary to maintain morale within the group.   General wage increases, when granted in cents per hour, tend to reduce these differentials when measured as a percentage of a rate and thus "flatten" the wage curve.   On the other hand, general wage increases in percentage form tend to maintain differentials when measured as a percentage of rate and to increase them in cents per hour.   Thus, they make the wage curve "steeper."

Since the early 1940s, industrial unions have usually negotiated cents per hour increases.   A continuing practice of this sort can sharply reduce the slope of a wage curve.   Accordingly, it has been necessary for some companies to make special increases in rates for higher-skilled jobs, such as craftsmen, to restore differentials.

The slope of the wage curve should be a matter of concern to management. Although there is no ideal slope, most managers tend to feel that a steeper wage curve with larger differentials among jobs is a greater source of incentive and is therefore preferable.

2. Whether general increases will or will not be extended to clerical and other nonmanagement salaried personnel subsequent to negotiations with hourly rated personnel must be decided.   The predominant practice appears to be to give the increases to nonrepresented personnel for reasons of equity.   The increases may be granted in the same form as those granted hourly personnel or in a different form, such as percentage versus cents per hour.   In many instances, however, the net effect is to destroy the alignment of a company's rates with comparable rates in the labor market.

3. Most general increases are considered to have relatively little or no incentive value.   Further, when extended to management personnel in the form of a general increase, the effect may be to convince managers that they are beholden to the union for the increase.   To maximize the incentive value and to distinguish between union employees and management, some companies have discontinued general increases for management and substituted yearly salary budgets of sufficient magnitude to cover forecasted changes in the general economy and to recognize meritorious performance.   These companies announce to management employees that general increases will not be applied to them, but that their salaries will be considered each year and adjusted on the basis of merit.

Reactions among management personnel to this practice vary.   Higher-level managers seem to understand and accept it better than lower-level managers. Some companies which use this approach have made distinctions between the two groups by continuing to grant general increases to the lower-level group.

Administration of Merit Increases.   Merit increases are usually given to salaried employees when there is a range of rates established for each job.   The increases may be in accordance with a predetermined table of step rates, may be a prescribed percentage amount such as 5 percent, or may be an unspecified amount. Normally, increases are granted on a periodic basis with provision for special increases to meet unusual circumstances.

Generally, merit increases are granted for improved performance.   The rationale of merit increases is that the minimum or lowest rate in the range is an adequate rate for those who are new to the job or whose performance is marginal.   The highest rate of the range is reserved for those whose performance is considered truly outstanding.   Administration is complicated by the absence of objective performance standards for most jobs.   Although all will agree that such standards should exist, it would be a herculean task for a company to establish them for all jobs, and particularly for higher-level, salaried jobs for which objective methods of measurement do not generally exist. In addition, the appraisal of an individual's performance is largely subjective. In the final analysis, it must generally be made by the immediate supervisor. Although his ability to appraise can be improved through training and the use of formalized merit-rating techniques, in most instances the appraisal is primarily a matter of judgment and subject to all the weaknesses inherent in this type of evaluation.

There is no complete solution to these problems. They can be partially solved by establishing performance standards where practical and by supervisory training and the development of adequate merit-rating techniques. Because they cannot be completely solved, however, companies have often resorted to other control mechanisms.

One objective of these control mechanisms is to stabilize costs at a desired level; for example, at the average of the salary range. Thus a company might require each organizational unit to make certain that the average of the actual salaries paid to employees does not exceed the average salary of the range of the jobs. Unless some such mechanism is used, companies which are not expanding or which do not experience high turnover find that as a result of leniency in granting salary merit increases, most of the employees in the group eventually receive the top rate or a rate close to the top rate. Thus, instead of salaries averaging at the midpoint of the range, the distribution is skewed toward the top, and the company's cost may exceed the planned amount.

A budgetary control approach, in which organizational units are granted, for merit-increase purposes, only enough funds to bring their salaries to the midpoint of the range, works reasonably well in large and fluid departments. In static, nonexpanding situations, however, the result is that few, if any, increases are granted, and employee dissatisfaction arises. If the budgetary approach is to be used, it requires extensive training of supervision and forthright communication with employees about the reasons for it and the reasonableness of it.

A variation of the budget approach is to require a predetermined distribution of salaries. Such a distribution might be the so-called normal or Gaussian curve. Under this procedure, within each department relatively few employees would be paid the top rate. A few more would be paid less than the average rate, but most would receive approximately the average rate. This procedure is justified on the basis that within any large group this is the type of performance variation that might be expected. As with the previous control procedure, it too can breed employee dissatisfaction unless thoroughly explained.

Another control is the utilization of a salary committee to approve the increases recommended by managers. The salary committee is charged with the responsibility for investigating recommendations, questioning those which appear to be not in conformance with the policy of the company, rejecting increases recommended by overly lenient managers, and requesting managers who may be unduly strict to reexamine their recommendations. The objectives are not only cost control, but consistency within the company. Success depends upon the support the salary committee receives from top management and the energy and integrity of the salary committee in actively pursuing its responsibilities in a most difficult area.

Administration of Wages and Salaries in Promotion and Demotion. Wage and salary increases are usually granted in instances of promotion, and decreases are made in instances of demotion. Certain commonly accepted practices have developed in applying this aspect of the principle of paying the employee the rate for the job which he performs. Wage earners are normally paid the rate of the jobs to which they are either temporarily or permanently promoted, even if the promotion occurs during the working day and is of short duration. Thus, an employee could receive several different wage rates for the same day because of varying job assignments. The effect of this practice is to complicate the administrative burden of first-line supervision, who are the primary control mechanism, and of the payroll department. The practices are so widespread, however, that it is the exceptional company which makes adjustments only when temporary promotions are of a day's or a week's duration. Substantially all companies immediately adjust rates in case of permanent promotion.

In the event of permanent demotions, it is traditional to reduce wage rates immediately. There is a growing tendency in some industries, however, to defer the reduction for periods of time ranging from a few weeks to a few months, the extent being generally related to the length of service of the employee. The rationale of this procedure is to "cushion the shock" and permit a period of readjustment, recognizing that employees may have financial commitments based on existing wage rates.

Permanently promoted, salaried employees normally receive a salary increase effective as of the date of promotion, but not in the case of temporary short-term promotions. In most instances, the salary ranges overlap to such an extent that an employee temporarily performing a job a grade or two higher than his permanent job still receives a salary within the range of the higher grade. Longer-term temporary promotions, lasting a month or more, usually warrant an immediate salary increase.

As with wage earners, most salaried employees' salaries are reduced immediately in cases of demotion. The practice of deferring the effective date of the decrease is more widespread among salaried employees than it is with wage earners.

When decreases are made, some companies reduce the employee's salary to the top of the range of the new job to which he is assigned if his previous salary exceeded this. Others reduce the employee to a position in the salary range of the new job corresponding to that which he held in the range for his former job. The latter procedure avoids skewing the salaries of employees toward the top of the range if there is a widespread necessity for demotion. It is further justified by the fact that the demoted employee's performance may be no better on the lower job than it was on the higher. The former procedure is justified by the overlap in salary grades and by the desire to minimize the salary reduction for employees who are demoted for other than disciplinary reasons.

Companies whose salary scales include predetermined step rates normally make promotional or demotional adjustments in accordance with the step rates. Those whose ranges do not include step rates generally adopt a normal promotional increase, such as 5 percent, but provide for larger or smaller increases in the event of unusual circumstances. Most companies grant a promotional increase at least to the minimum of the range if there is no overlap between an employee's former salary range and the salary range of his new job.

"Take-home" Pay. In addition to base rates and salaries, employee compensation includes payments from several other sources.

1. Statutory overtime payments, such as the Federal requirement to pay rate and one-half for hours over forty and the requirement to pay time and one-half for hours over eight under the Walsh-Healey Act governing companies with government contracts.

2. Incentive and bonus payments, made either under an existing formalized plan or in the form of lump sums usually related to the profitability of the company.

3. Premium payments generally negotiated with unions for hourly rated employees, based on the fact that the working conditions or the work required is usually onerous.

4. Special emoluments, such as lunches, work clothing, transportation, and the like, paid for by the company.

In the final analysis, the "take-home" pay for each employee, regardless of its source, is what is important to him. It is also important to the company, for it represents true cost. Those responsible for salary administration should have the responsibility for making sure that "take-home" pay, as well as base wages and salaries, is in line with general wage and salary policies.

BIBLIOGRAPHY

Backman, I., *Wage Determination: An Analysis of Wage Criteria,* D. Van Nostrand Company, Inc., Princeton, N.J., 1959.

Belcher, David W., *Wage and Salary Administration,* 2d ed., Prentice-Hall, Inc., Englewood Cliffs, N.J., 1962.

Gilmour, Robert W., *Industrial Wage and Salary Control,* John Wiley & Sons, Inc., New York, 1956.

Jacques, Elliott, *Equitable Payment: A General Theory of Work, Differential Payment, and Individual Progress,* John Wiley & Sons, Inc., New York, 1961.

Michael, Lionel B., *Wage and Salary Fundamentals and Procedures,* McGraw-Hill Book Company, New York, 1950.

"Objective Measures for Pay Differentials," *Harvard Business Review,* January–February, 1962.

Roy, Robert H., "Do Wage Incentives Reduce Costs?" *Industrial & Labor Relations Review,* vol. 5, no. 2, January, 1952.

Taylor, George W., and Frank C. Pierson (eds.), *New Concepts in Wage Determination,* McGraw-Hill Book Company, New York, 1957.

Weintraub, Sidney, *Some Aspects of Wage Theory and Policy,* Chilton Company—Book Division, Philadelphia, 1963.

CHAPTER ELEVEN

Job Evaluation

BRUCE A. LENTZ *Chief Engineer, Century Furniture Company, Century Chair Company, Hickory, North Carolina*

Industry needs a way to determine an employee's worth to the company. A good wage-payment system provides equitable wage-rate relationships and helps minimize employee discontent. Job evaluation, a part of any good compensation plan, is the systematic and orderly procedure for establishing a correct value relationship between all production or clerical jobs within a plant or company.

The four major areas which account for job differences are skill, effort, responsibility, and working conditions. Basically, the purpose of job evaluation is to help management attract, motivate, and keep good workers by properly compensating them for work done.

PLANNING A JOB EVALUATION PROGRAM

Top Management Support. No job evaluation program, however well planned, developed, and installed, will be successful unless it has the active support and participation of top management. A rubber-stamp approval is not sufficient. Management must understand the purpose of job evaluation and how it functions. Job evaluation—no matter how simple—also requires the training and participation of operating management.

Consultants or Company Personnel. Who will do the job? There are three alternatives:

1. Engage a management consulting firm with a staff specializing in job evaluation to do the complete program.

2. Assign the job to a qualified employee and give him special training, or hire an experienced and qualified job evaluation man as a full-time employee to handle the program and maintain it.

3. Engage a management consulting firm to supervise and direct company personnel in the development and installation of the program.

Probably the easiest, but most expensive, method is the first. Outside consultants will be impartial, complete the job in a specified time, and provide a technically sound plan. There are some disadvantages, also. Company personnel get little or no training or experience in job evaluation and feel no responsibility for the program's success or failure. Maintenance of the program is difficult without experienced personnel.

When company employees handle the program, they are a part of the project and will support it. Personnel receive training and experience and can explain it on a firsthand basis. The disadvantages are that after initial interest and momentum, the program tends to get bogged down in the details required. Other work will be considered more important, and the program can easily be sidetracked. Further, serious problems can be expected in the technical phases of the work if no one has had actual job evaluation experience. Job evaluation, if it is to be done successfully, requires professional competence and a thorough understanding of its principles and techniques.

The third method uses a consultant to supervise and direct the program using company personnel. This method tends to combine the good points of the other two methods, eliminating most of the disadvantages.

INSTALLING A JOB EVALUATION PLAN

There are five steps necessary to develop, install, and maintain a job evaluation program.

1. Preparing job descriptions. A good understanding of any job is necessary for proper evaluation.

2. Selecting and preparing a job evaluation plan and manual. A selection of the important characteristics or factors, the value of these factors, and written instructions for evaluating.

3. Evaluating and classifying the jobs. Applying the manual equitably and grouping jobs into classifications for wage payment.

4. Installing the job evaluation program. Explaining it to employees and putting it into operation.

5. Maintaining the program. Job evaluation cannot continue without updating for new jobs and job changes.

JOB DESCRIPTIONS

Good job descriptions are necessary for any job evaluation program to achieve its objectives. A job description is a written record of the duties, responsibilities, and conditions of the job. It provides the rater or evaluating committee with all important information about the job which should be considered. Job descriptions may serve other purposes. Properly prepared, they can be used as a guide in hiring, transfer, and promotion and as an aid in methods improvement, estimating costs, and the like. Descriptions should be prepared by a trained, qualified person. Supervisory personnel can be used, but usually this is not satisfactory. When a number of people from different departments or areas prepare descriptions, the degree of detail is not the same, and varying styles of writing make descriptions misleading and comparisons difficult. It is important to remember that a job evaluation program can be only as good as the job descriptions which are used.

The correct procedure for preparing any job description is as follows:

1. Prepare a list of all jobs to be covered by the job evaluation.
2. Make a preliminary announcement of the program.
3. Talk with the department head and/or supervisor.
4. Interview the job occupant.

5. Prepare a written job description.

6. Review the job description with the supervisor to ensure that all relevant information has been included.

7. If advisable, review it with the department head and job occupant.

8. Prepare the job description in its final form.

List Jobs to Be Evaluated. This sounds simple, but requires some analysis. Often a company has similar or identical jobs in the same or different departments. These jobs may have two or more different titles. A preliminary survey is needed to determine which jobs are to be included in the program and to combine similar jobs under a single job title whenever possible. For example, is an expediter, shipping clerk, or receiving clerk to be included in the hourly production group or the office group? A separate job description should be prepared for each job on the list.

Preliminary Announcement of Program. Be sure that management, union officials, and the workers themselves have been notified of the program and are generally prepared for cooperating with those seeking information, before interviews with supervisors and job occupants begin. Very often, employees and supervisors will be interested in how they might be affected by the preparation of job descriptions. Fears should be allayed where possible. Emphasize that no one will suffer a reduction in pay as a result of the program.

Interviews with Plant Supervision. After clearance with top management, the program of writing job descriptions should be started by interviewing department heads and front-line supervisors. This step will be concerned with generally orienting the person preparing the descriptions with the department. Various administrative problems and policies such as any existing union-management agreements on job contents or possible sources of disagreement, over- or under-qualified employees, or changes that will be likely to occur in the near or distant future also should be discussed.

When talking with front-line supervisors, discuss each job in detail, including any verbal agreements with the union or job occupant as to job content. At all times, let the supervisor know that he is responsible for the final job description and its accuracy. Make detailed notes and check on any plant rules which may relate to the job.

Interview with Job Occupant. After clearing with the department head and immediate supervisor, interview the job occupant. Frame questions to avoid putting words into the occupant's mouth or suggesting preconceived ideas. The interviewer should listen most of the time and ask only a few questions to start discussion or clear up any points not fully understood.

The interview should preferably take place at or near the occupant's place of work with only the interviewer and the job occupant present. Observe the worker actually performing the work where possible. Where this is not practical, accompany him through his work area and observe his machinery, equipment, tools, and working conditions. Continue listening, observing, and asking questions until a complete mental picture of job duties is obtained. Take detailed notes during the interview or else some point will be left out.

Review of Job Descriptions. Job descriptions are written in rough draft form and reviewed with the supervisor and job occupant to assure accuracy before final typing. A sample description is shown by Figure 11-1. At this stage, it is important to point out to the supervisor any areas that might lead to confusion or misunderstanding at a later date. Ensure that he has every opportunity to discuss the content of the descriptions. Although it is the supervisor's responsibility to approve the descriptions, it is the responsibility of the person preparing the descriptions to make sure they are not approved just because

Job Description

Job No. *4-11*

Department	Maintenance	Plant Title	Repair machinist
Plant	Main plant	Date	November 23, 1965

Primary function

Set up and operate machine tools, and adjust and repair machines and mechanical equipment required for plant maintenance and operation.

Tools and equipment

Standard machine tools such as lathes, drill press, milling machine, hydraulic press, shaper, planer, etc., and hand tools and precision measuring instruments such as wrenches, drills, taps, micrometers, calipers, etc.

Materials

Various metals such as mild and stainless steels, brass, bronze, cast iron, and copper.

Source of supervision

Maintenance foreman.

Direction exercised

Works alone or directs helpers or other workmen as required.

*Working procedure**

Receives instructions, blueprints, sketches, and trouble reports.

Plans work, makes sketches as required, and selects tools and methods to be used in the overhaul, inspection, repair, replacement, and maintenance of all pumps, compressors, cranes, scales, and other mechanical equipment.

Sets up, adjusts, and operates all types of machine tools to make or repair metal parts' required tolerances, fits, and finishes.

Uses precision measuring instruments, shop formula, and machinist hand tools in determining tapers, dimensions, etc.

Makes tools and devices for use in maintenance and production operations.

Grinds and sharpens cutting tools.

Works in shop or plant as required.

Keeps workplace, equipment, and work clean and orderly.

* These duties will not be considered as a detailed description of all work requirements that may be a part of this job.

FIG. 11.1.   *Rough draft of a job description for repair machinist.*

they are well typed and read smoothly. The final description should be signed by the department head and/or plant manager to show that he approves it.

SELECTING A JOB EVALUATION PLAN

In selecting a job evaluation plan, the first decision is to determine whether to use a nonquantitative or quantitative type of evaluation. There are two systems for each type. The nonquantitative systems are ranking and grading. They compare the job as a whole with other jobs or different levels or grades of jobs. The quantitative systems, factor comparison and point, are basically analytical in that they require each job to be broken into elements. The first compares one job with another, factor by factor; the latter relates each factor to a defined quantitative scale.

Ranking Method.   There are five steps in the ranking method.

1. Preparation of job descriptions.

2. Selection of raters and key jobs. Persons doing the rating should be familiar with all jobs. Ten to twenty jobs should be selected which include all major departments and functions.

3. Ranking of key jobs. Key jobs should be ranked in relation to each other in a single list.

4. Ranking of all jobs. All jobs should be ranked in a single list; first, in relation to key jobs, and then, where of similar types, in relation to each other.

5. Preparation of job classifications from the rating. The total ranking should be divided into an appropriate number of groups or classifications, usually eight

to twelve. All jobs within a single group or classification would receive the same wage rate or range of rates.

Grading Method. The grading method also consists of five steps:

1. Preparation of job descriptions.

2. Preparation of grade descriptions. These are definitions which are designed to identify different levels or grades of jobs. They form the basis of the classification structure. Once grade levels have been established and defined, each job can be assigned to the appropriate grade level on the basis of complexity of duties, nonsupervisory responsibilities, and supervisory responsibilities. Usually eight to twelve grades are created.

3. Selection of graders and key jobs. Persons doing the grading should be familiar with all jobs. Ten to twenty key jobs should be selected which include all major departments and functions, and cover all grade levels.

4. Grading of key jobs. Key jobs should be assigned to the appropriate grade level and their relationship to each other studied. This relationship should support the grade definitions.

5. Classification of all jobs. Jobs should be classified by grade definition, and all jobs in the same grade should receive the same wage rate or range of rates.

Analysis of Ranking and Grading Systems. Ranking and grading have about the same advantages and limitations, although the latter is a little more refined. Both are of limited application and effectiveness. The major advantage of the two nonquantitative systems is that they can be done quickly and inexpensively. The limitations are:

1. Raters must be thoroughly familiar with all jobs.

2. Raters are subject to an unconscious bias for or against jobs, especially if wage rates or job relationships are known.

3. There is no written record of how or why a job received a particular rank or grade.

4. One rater may rate in terms of job knowledge required, although another thinks in terms of responsibilities or working conditions.

In short, the two nonquantitative evaluation systems do not provide a sound or satisfactory basis for a good job evaluation program of any size. Anyone with a company of any size who is interested enough to choose a job evaluation plan will undoubtedly prefer either the factor comparison or point system.

Factor Comparison Method. This method requires the selection of five to seven factors that are a part of all jobs in the plant or company. Common factors are:

Skill	Supervisory responsibilities
Experience	Supervision received
Mental effort	Education
Physical effort	Responsibility—material and/or equipment
Working conditions	Safety

This method has the following steps.

1. Prepare job descriptions.

2. Select the factors to be used.

3. Select the raters and key jobs. These are fifteen to twenty jobs varying in wages from the lowest to the highest rates where the duties are clearly defined and the wage rates are considered correct.

4. Assign each factor a value dependent on its relative importance in the operation. Two or more factors may have the same value.

5. Rate key jobs factor by factor. All key jobs are placed above or below other key jobs in each factor.

6. Assign monetary values to each factor of every key job. Again, this should reflect a range from the lowest to the highest values.

7. Rate all jobs. Place each job, factor by factor, by relating it to the key jobs in the factors. Assign monetary values accordingly.

This method becomes more difficult with each additional factor. Additional factors require more juggling of ranks and amounts of money. There is no established ceiling for any factor. A new job can be rated higher than any previous job rated in one or more factors.

Advantages and Disadvantages of the Factor Comparison Method

Advantages

1. Excellent descriptions of factor comparison systems are available.
2. With five to seven factors, there is little overlap between factors, which tends to simplify job of evaluation.
3. Evaluation scale is expressed in cents per hour, which shows not only relative position of each, but monetary values.
4. There is a job-to-job comparison.
5. This system is relatively easy to use.

Disadvantages

1. Requires fifteen to twenty key jobs, from lowest to highest wage rates, with well-defined duties and accepted wage rates.
2. Cents per hour is not a constant figure, but will fluctuate in inflation and depression periods.
3. When content of key jobs changes, it can affect the entire scale.
4. Requires extra time and cost to develop and install.

Point System. The point system selects characteristics or factors considered to have a bearing on all jobs in the program. These fall into four areas: skill, effort, responsibility, and working conditions. Typical factors are experience, education, responsibility for materials, safety, and working conditions. Each factor is divided into degrees or levels, and a point value is assigned for each level. A definition is prepared for each level, and each job is then compared against each factor. The sum of the point values assigned to each factor gives the total point value for the job, which can be compared or related to all other jobs.

Developing a Point Rating Plan. There are six steps in developing a point rating plan.

1. Preparation of job descriptions.
2. Selection of factors which relate to all jobs. Eight to twelve factors are most desirable. Factors must have the following conditions:
   a. Must be ratable
   b. Must be judged to be important
   c. Must not overlap in meaning
   d. Must meet both employer and worker standards
   e. Must be universal in application or be applicable to the type of jobs for which the system was constructed
3. Determination of weight of factor. Assign a percentage value to each factor. The total percentage of all factors is 100.
4. Definition of factors. A general definition describes the scope and elements to consider in evaluating the factor.
5. Division of each factor into levels, and definition of each level. Levels should meet the following conditions:
   a. Use only enough levels in a factor to differentiate among all jobs being rated.
   b. Make selection so that some jobs fall in each level.
   c. Define each level clearly with examples in terms which the worker can understand.
   d. Avoid the use of ambiguous terms. Such terms as "intelligence,"

"character," or "sociability" should be avoided unless sufficiently defined to eliminate any chance of misinterpretation.

    e. Write definitions of levels in objective terms.

6. Determination of relative values of levels within factors. Factors can be divided into point values by arithmetic- or geometric-type progressions. Values are easier to understand when whole numbers are used.

Advantages and Disadvantages of the Point System

Advantages	*Disadvantages*
1. Agreement among raters on same job is usually very close.	1. It is difficult to determine factor levels within factors and assign point values.
2. Definitions are written in terms applicable to the type of job being evaluated.	2. It is difficult to explain to supervisors and employees.
3. Factors are rated by points, which makes it possible to be consistent in assigning monetary values to total job points.	3. Extra time and cost are required to develop and install.
4. Prejudice and bias and human judgment are minimized.	4. Considerable clerical work is necessary.
5. The system is difficult to "manipulate."	
6. There is more accuracy and consistency in the wage structure than with other methods.	

In summary, if you are not an expert in doing job evaluation, the point system usually will give a more satisfactory result. It usually offers the best evaluation system to management.

PREPARATION OF THE JOB EVALUATION MANUAL

Once the job evaluation plan—ranking, grading, factor comparison, or point system—has been established, it is necessary to prepare a manual. The job evaluation manual is the basis for an evaluation program. Once prepared, reviewed, and approved, it remains constant throughout the entire program and provides for smooth continuity of wage administration in the future. Job content may change, the wage structure may be adjusted from time to time, but the manual terminology and use must be constant.

If a consulting firm is retained to assist with the job evaluation program, it will in all probability be able to provide a suitable manual with a minimum of new preparatory work.

Ranking and Grading. For the first two categories, manual preparation is a rather simple procedure. Merely outline the method to be followed, with sufficient instructions for the person or persons who are going to do the ranking or grading. Instructions should include grade definitions, how to select key jobs, how to classify rated or graded jobs, and a provision for a periodic review, usually annually, of the program.

Factor Comparison and Point System. The factor comparison and point systems are more complex and require more attention in the preparation of the manual. The manual serves as the instruction book for all persons associated with the job evaluation program.

The manual should be so written that the newest employee can, within a reasonable length of time, understand the function of the job evaluation program.

Maintenance of Program. Many manuals fail to establish a procedure to update and review the evaluation program. This is important because the contents of jobs change and jobs are added or eliminated from year to year. Do not regard job evaluation as a one-time proposition.

This section of the manual should establish a procedure for reviewing all job descriptions periodically, probably annually or biennially. Changes creep into any job over a period of time. Jobs with significant overall changes in content should be reevaluated, but only for those factors affected by the change. For example, working conditions normally would not change if the job were still performed in the same location. New jobs and individual jobs whose content has changed should be reviewed when requested by plant management or union.

EVALUATING AND CLASSIFYING THE JOBS

A committee should be used to evaluate all jobs. It should consist of from four to six members. A typical five-man committee consists of a permanent chairman, usually the one heading up the program; two permanent members, one from management and one from the union; and two temporary members from the department being evaluated at the time, usually the foreman and the departmental steward.

The job evaluation committee should meet first to review the manual factor by factor and to clear up any misunderstandings on definitions or examples. Only after all jobs have been evaluated will they be classified. In some cases, as in the steel industry, the classification is predetermined. However, in most cases, management does not know the distribution of evaluated jobs in advance.

Evaluation Meetings. At the beginning of each meeting, the committee will determine the number of jobs to be evaluated during the session. Job evaluation is an impersonal and objective procedure. The *job* is measured, *not* the individual filling the job. It is best to avoid mentioning any worker by name during these meetings.

During the session, all jobs will be evaluated for the same factor before proceeding to the next factor. In this way, attention is focused on the factor and its relationship to the job rather than on the overall importance of the job itself. This minimizes the possibility of anyone subconsciously trying to build up points for individual jobs. Each committee member should have a work sheet of some type on which to record his evaluation privately. An example is shown by Figure 11-2. After everyone has assigned a point value to the same factor for each job, the values are compared. Whenever one or more committee members disagree, and normally differences will be slight, the committee will continue to discuss the factor in question until everyone is in agreement. Total points will not be computed until the evaluating session is complete. No committee meeting should end until the evaluation is complete for all jobs under consideration.

The committee should designate a secretary who records all evaluations. The secretary should keep a chart similar to the work sheet in Figure 11-2, on which all evaluations are recorded for reference by the committee during discussions of a factor.

Classifying the Jobs. The total evaluated points for each job are plotted on a scatter chart. Often this chart is divided by department, section, or plant. The next step is to decide the number of wage classifications required. This will usually run from nine to fourteen, with the higher-skilled industries requiring more classifications. Next, determine the difference between the minimum and maximum point value for all evaluated jobs. This "spread" will then be divided into job classifications.

The division may be made by:

1. Assigning the same range for each job class, for example, 10 points, as 0–10, 11–20, 21–30, and so on.

2. Assigning increasing ranges to each job class, for example, 10, 15, 20 points, to give ranges of 0–10, 11–25, 26–45, and so on.

JOB EVALUATION RATING SUMMARY

Department	Job Title														
Plant No.															
Date															
Job Number															
Eff. Date of Eval.															
Descrip. Rev. No. Factors	Code No. Pts.	Code No. Pts.	Code No. Pts.	Code No. Pts.	Code No. Pts.	Code No. Pts.	Code No. Pts.	Code No. Pts.	Code No. Pts.	Code No. Pts.	Code No. Pts.	Code No. Pts.	Code No. Pts.	Code No. Pts.	Code No. Pts.
Skill 1 Knowledge															
Skill 2 Training & Exp.															
Skill 3 Mental Skill															
Skill 4 Manual Skill															
Responsibility 5 Mat'l. & Process															
Responsibility 6 Tools & Equip.															
Responsibility 7 Work of Others															
Responsibility 8 Safety of Others															
Effort 9 Physical Demand															
Effort 10 Mental or Visual Att.															
Cond. 11 Surroundings															
Cond. 12 Hazards															
Total Points															
Rate Group															

FIG. 11-2. *Job evaluation rating summary.*

3. Assigning values by visual observation of scatter chart without regard to job titles.

After the classification has been made, review each job and its relation to other jobs in the same category. For instance, an assistant boiler operator and a boiler operator should not fall in the same class.

INSTALLING THE JOB EVALUATION PROGRAM

Employees should be convinced, if possible, of the fairness of the basic principles of job evaluation. Normally, they should be informed of the program when it begins and should realize the following:

1. Job evaluation will not solve *all* wage problems.

2. The job evaluation program will be understandable; it is not an "experiment."

3. No individual will suffer any loss of wages as a result of the program.

4. The program does not take any rights or privileges away from the foremen or supervisors.

5. The job evaluation committee is competent.

Company magazine articles, letters to employees, bulletin board announcements, and general meetings are some of the ways of informing employees and answering any questions.

The actual mechanics of reclassifying all jobs can be handled by the personnel department. At the time of installation, job classification lists should be available for supervisors and employees.

Red Circle Rates. There are always a few employees whose present wage rate will be higher than the new wage rate which the job evaluation program establishes. This is called a "red circle" job or rate. Most companies *do not* reduce the wage rate of workers on this kind of job, but all new people starting this job are paid the new or lower rate. Be certain the workers understand this. When future wage increases are made, red circle employees receive either no increase or a reduced increase until they are at the proper rate or until they transfer to another job.

Low Wage Rates. Employees whose wages are below the new wage rates are usually handled in one of two ways.

1. They receive an immediate wage increase to the new rate.
2. They receive scheduled increases over a one- to two-year period to eliminate the difference.

MAINTAINING THE PROGRAM

No job evaluation program will operate properly without periodic reviews and adjustments. Jobs do change and many job evaluation programs have failed because management failed to recognize this fact. A good job evaluation maintenance program requires:

1. A permanent job evaluation committee, usually headed by the personnel director or chief industrial engineer.
2. A periodic review, usually every one or two years, of all job descriptions.
3. A monthly or quarterly meeting of the permanent committee to review old jobs as requested by plant management and to evaluate jobs newly created. Do not allow wage rates to be established for jobs which have not been evaluated.

CONCLUSION

The main purpose of job evaluation is to determine the relative worth of the jobs in a company. The success of any plan depends on:

1. Full approval and support of top management
2. A carefully established job evaluation plan
3. Union acceptance where applicable
4. Adequate administrative control during and after installation

Remember, the most technically perfect plan will not survive unless as much attention is given to its maintenance as to its development and installation.

BIBLIOGRAPHY

Baker, Helen, and J. M. True, *The Operation of Job Evaluation Plans,* Industrial Relations Section, Department of Economics and Social Institutions, Princeton University Press, Princeton, N.J., 1947.
Evans, Gordon H., *Managerial Job Descriptions in Manufacturing,* Research Study, no. 65, American Management Association, New York, 1964.
Halrington, Carl C., *Job Evaluation and Wage Incentives,* Conover-Mast Publications, Inc., New York, 1949.
Lanham, Elizabeth, *Job Evaluation,* McGraw-Hill Book Company, New York, 1955.
Lytle, Charles W., *Job Evaluation Methods,* 2d ed., The Ronald Press Company, New York, 1954.
Otis, Jay, and Richard H. Leukart, *Job Evaluation, A Sound Basis for Wage Administration,* Prentice-Hall, Inc., Englewood Cliffs, N.J., 1954.
Patton, John A., C. L. Littlefield, and Stanley Allen Self, *Job Evaluation Text and Cases,* 3d ed., Richard D. Irwin, Inc., Homewood, Ill., 1964.

CHAPTER TWELVE

Salary Evaluation

H. DWIGHT MEADER *Manager, Business Effectiveness Consulting Service, General Electric Company, New York, New York*

The elements of salary administration are (1) job descriptions, (2) salary evaluation, (3) salary structures, and (4) performance appraisal. This chapter is concerned with the salary evaluation process.

The objective of a salary evaluation system is to provide a means for establishing an equitable salary range for each position, considering both what other employers pay in the marketplace for similar jobs and the relative value of the job in relation to all other jobs in the organization. The end purpose of salary evaluation is to place the position in the proper salary range of the salary structure.

Information will be furnished concerning various salary evaluation methods which might be used, the types of compensable factors employed, and practices for converting factor values into salary ranges.

JOB DESCRIPTIONS

The salary evaluation process begins with the preparation of written job descriptions for each position to be evaluated. A job description is an important element in providing an employee and his manager with a common understanding of the work to be done and in determining exactly what the work elements are which will be evaluated.

Good job descriptions can be useful to managers and subordinates:

To provide a basis for job evaluation

To check on soundness of the organization structure

To aid in assigning of functions to positions

To establish a framework for manager-subordinate agreement of specific work assignments, objectives to be accomplished, and limits of authority and responsibility

To specify the factors to be used in measuring the individual's accountability for performance

In the case of nonexempt clerical jobs, the description may be quite simple. Frequently the information is summarized as follows:
1. Job title
2. Department and location
3. Supervisor
4. Description of duties
5. Training and experience required
6. Mechanical skills required
7. Mental skills required
8. Degree of supervision received
9. Responsibility
10. Working conditions

For exempt salaried positions, the job description may be expressed in the following form:
1. Position title
2. Responsible to
3. Organizational component
4. Broad function
5. Principal responsibilities and relationships
6. Authority and reservations of decision making
7. Measures of accountability

Format of Exempt Job Descriptions.   The content of the job description sections for exempt employees is as follows.

Broad Function.   This section states briefly the position's basic objectives and responsibilities.   It should make clear the primary purpose of the position and those features that distinguish this position from others.

Principal Responsibilities and Relationships.   This section lists the significant specific responsibilities assigned to the position.   These will constitute the objectives of the position against which standards of performance can be established. The major relationships that are important both up and down within the line of authority and at all levels outside the line of authority are detailed.   Relationships should be defined in such a way as to encourage rather than hinder individual initiative in accomplishing the objectives of the position.

Authority and Reservations of Decision Making.   The position should be given authority to do what is required to accomplish the responsibilities of the position. Where authority is withheld, the limitations should be carefully expressed and referenced to company policies and instructions.   The scope of authority defines an important relationship between the subordinate and his manager, and the superior should realize that withholding the delegation of authority requires the responsibilities of the position to be tailored accordingly.

Measures of Accountability.   The accountability section of the job description states the standards to be used in measuring the performance of the individual. These standards should relate to the responsibilities and authority previously defined.   There should be mutual agreement between the subordinate and his manager that the standards will fairly measure the success or failure in accomplishing the position objectives.

SALARY JOB EVALUATION METHODS

Purposes and Steps.   Salary evaluation provides a means for measuring job values and for relating such measurements to appropriate salary levels.   An important purpose is to determine the relative level of ability needed to perform the work assigned to the position, meeting planned performance standards.

Regardless of the method used, the broad steps are:

1. Jobs are classified and grouped into grades or levels according to developed criteria.

2. The classifications or groupings of jobs are related to a salary scale or structure to determine levels of salary compensation.

Summary of Methods of Salary Job Evaluation. A wide variety of salary job evaluation plans have been developed. The methods employed can be summarized as follows.

Method	*Description*
Ranking	Jobs are ranked from low to high according to their complexity or value to the company.
Classification	Jobs are sorted into categories. Then each job is compared with class or category specifications determined in advance. It is a ranking system on a category basis rather than a job basis.
Point rating	A number of factors common to positions to be evaluated are selected. Each factor is assigned degrees, ranging from low to high. Each degree is assigned point values in advance. Each job is analyzed, factor by factor; points representing the degrees selected are assigned to the job.
Factor comparison	Jobs are compared on a number of factors common to each job, taken one at a time. Jobs are compared with other jobs rather than against a scale of defined degrees.
Specialized	These are modifications of the above methods that use criteria such as sales, profitability, number of employees, and the like.

Salary Job Ranking Method. The simplest method of salary job evaluation is to rank each job in relation to other jobs from low to high, according to some criterion such as difficulty or complexity. Frequently, the evaluator establishes a base or entry level in a job series, then determines the most difficult or important job in the series and ranks the jobs in between, based upon judgment. Or, the evaluator may merely compare two jobs, one against the other, and determine which is the more important or difficult. Then another job is compared with the first two, and the process is repeated until all jobs are ranked from low to high. It is common to find secretarial jobs evaluated according to the organization levels of their bosses. Other secretarial positions in the organization may then be related to such evaluations. One of the disadvantages in the ranking method is that differences among some jobs may be minor, whereas differences among other jobs may be quite large. These variations in differences should be properly reflected in relating the rankings to salary scales.

Classification Method. The classification method is similar to the job ranking technique. Both systems arrange jobs in sequence according to difficulty or importance to the company. In the classification method, specific specifications are established in advance for each type of job category. A job category contains positions that are similar to each other, as, for example, draftsmen or stenographic jobs.

Each job is then compared with the predetermined specifications for a job category and the position is assigned to that job classification where it best fits. An example of a class specification follows. These specifications for a secretarial position indicate the distinguishing characteristics of the class. They were developed by the Technical Military Planning Operation (TEMPO) of the General Electric Company as a part of their salary administration plan for nonexempt salaried employees.

Secretary 1

Function. Under direction, to perform work involving to some extent the taking and transcribing of stenographic notes; to perform complex clerical work of administrative detail involved in servicing a supervisory, administrative, or executive superior.

Examples of Duties and Responsibilities. Prepares letters, bulletins, and lists from marginal notes, oral or written directions, or on own initiative; transcribes from dictating machines; compiles information from general instructions for nonroutine detailed reports; establishes and maintains varied files and card indexes; sets up format as required for the presentation of reports and other materials; provides information to others relative to functions of the specific office in which the position exists; conducts interviews to obtain information and to provide information; recommends improvements in office procedures; reads, and to some extent interprets, technical information; has continuing responsibility on own initiative for making appointments and other detailed arrangements for superior and other persons; has responsibility for initiating and ensuring the proper and timely completion of specific projects or processes involving contacts with new employees and persons outside the TEMPO organization; independently maintains lists and files required for accomplishing specific purposes; checks financial and statistical data; prepares and proofreads financial reports and other documents.

Distinguishing Characteristics

Dictation: Factors pertaining to shorthand speed are not considered highly significant in allocation to this class. Rather, other characteristics listed below are of more importance. However, where shorthand speeds of 120 words per minute are specifically required by the nature of the position, allocation should be made to this class rather than to a lower one.

Scope: Positions in this class have responsibilities for handling administrative detail.

Initiative and analytical requirements: Work assignments are unformalized and made on a broad, undetailed basis by the superior. Procedures, priorities, and methods of work are independently chosen by the employee. The employee devises formats and independently arranges and evaluates diversified material. Work requires the employee independently to secure more information than is generally given with the assignment, involving the selection and application of subtechnical or subadministrative concepts and procedures. Employees may make modifications of work methods to facilitate a more efficient operation.

Contact responsibilities: Frequent contacts may be made, both within and outside the organization, where definite skill is required in obtaining information. The employee is called upon to provide information or answer inquiries which involve interpretation of policies and procedures, and the employee is required to exercise substantial discretion in determining whether or not certain information may be properly given out.

Supervision received: Supervision is not usually available for immediate review of many tasks performed. Work is seldom supervised in progress.

Supervision exercised: Employees do not have any responsibility for the direction of the work of others, except that they may be called upon to assist in the training of new employees.

Qualifications Guide

Knowledge of: Modern office methods and practices; filing systems, receptionist and telephone techniques; standard business forms; letter writing; proofreading; report writing; office-machine operation.

Ability to: Use good judgment in recognizing scope of authority; understand and apply general instructions to specific situations; prepare and maintain accurate and complete records and reports; type at a speed of 50 words per minute; take dictation at a speed of 110 words per minute, and transcribe it at 30 words per minute; perform types and levels of duties as described above.

Experience: Three years of responsible clerical and stenographic experience.

Education: Equivalent to graduation from high school, supplemented by college or business school training.

Although it is frequently stated that the classification method is less analytical than the point rating or factor comparison system, it does have advantages. It is relatively easy to use. It can be readily understood by employees. It particularly lends itself to the more routine jobs where differences among them can be objectively determined. On the other hand, if the specifications for each class are too broadly stated, they may not differentiate properly among different skills.

Point Rating Method. The point rating and factor comparison methods are much alike. They both separate a job into basic factors and measure each factor as an entity. In the point rating system, a number of factors that are common to all positions being evaluated are selected. Obviously, the factors should be chosen with care. Examples of factors and subfactors frequently used are the following.

	Number of *Degrees Defined*
Factors and Subfactors	
1. Training	
a. Education	2
b. Depth of knowledge	5
c. Experience	7
2. Analytical	
a. Problem solving	6
b. Guidance	5
3. Creativity	7
4. Decisions	
a. Scope	6
b. Differentiation	5
5. Communications	
a. Skill	6
b. Scope	6
6. Planning of activities	5
7. Managing people	6

A number of points and degrees are assigned to each factor. The number of points and degrees should represent the number of discernible differences found in the factor as related to the kind of positions being evaluated. For example, a major factor might be training, which in turn is divided into the subfactors of education, depth of knowledge, and experience. These subfactors might have a number of degrees assigned to them, such as education, two degrees; depth of knowledge, five degrees; and experience, seven degrees.

The definitions and assigned points establish a standard to be used when evaluating each factor of a position. Each position is analyzed factor by factor, and the degree that each factor is a requirement of the position is determined. Points corresponding to the degrees selected are allocated to the position. The points assigned to all factors are added to obtain the total point score of the position. This score, then, determines the relative value of the job as compared with other positions.

Number of Factors. The number of factors selected should be based upon the need to distinguish differences among the jobs to be evaluated. In an analysis of the point rating plans in use in the General Electric Company, the average number of factors employed is six and the maximum number is nine. These factors are frequently divided into subfactors. The General Electric study showed the maximum number of subfactors is twenty-two, the minimum is zero, and the average of those plans using subfactors is slightly more than eleven.

A study of the factors used in point rating (and factor comparison) plans in General Electric indicates that they can be classified into two broad groups:
1. Job responsibility factors
2. Personal qualification factors
These groups can be further subdivided as shown in Figure 12-1.

Factors
1. Job responsibilities
   Subfactors
       For people
       For money and other assets
       For policy and methods
       For relationships
       For programs, projects, and operations
       For application of knowledge
2. Personal qualifications
   Subfactors
       What incumbent needs to know
       Personal characteristics
       Ability required to apply knowledge and skills

FIG. 12-1. *Classification of factors and subfactors used in point rating plans at the General Electric Company.*

Factors can be determined by a study of those used by others outside the company or by an analysis of the job requirements within the company.

After the factors have been selected, the relative weight of each characteristic must be determined. There is no fixed method for assigning weights for any factor used in a point rating plan. One company may decide that the factor "supervision" has a weight of 10 percent, whereas another company may decide the weight should be 40 percent. However determined, the weightings represent a judgment decision of the relative importance of the factors to the company.

A major advantage of the point rating method is the use of stable rating scales that may be used over a considerable period of time. The use of defined factors makes it possible for the evaluator to use uniform criteria in evaluating jobs. A major disadvantage of this method is the difficulty of developing acceptable degree definitions. The definitions must be so stated that they have the same meaning for all evaluators. If the definition of one factor overlaps another factor, the final evaluation may reflect such overlap. Because point values are assigned to each degree, they must be carefully determined and tested.

Factor Comparison Method. Although the factor comparison method is quite similar to the point rating method, there is a major difference. In the factor comparison method, there are no defined degrees for the factors selected for the jobs. Positions are compared, one with another, on the selected factors common to all jobs. The comparison is based on each factor, taken one at a time. For example, assume that the factor being considered is "creativity." The evaluators will rank all jobs with respect to this factor, from those which require the most creativity to those which require the least creativity. The evaluators will then rank all jobs with respect to the second factor and so on until separate rankings have been determined for all of the factors being used.

The factors commonly used in the factor comparison method are shown in Figure 12-2.

A number of key positions are selected which are representative of the range of positions being evaluated. Each of these is ranked on each factor, and values are allocated to such bench-mark positions. The values may be expressed in points or in percentage terms.

The selection of the key positions is very important, because they become the foundation of the comparison scale. The number of bench-mark jobs selected should be representative of the entire range of positions to be evaluated. Generally, ten to twenty-five jobs are adequate for this purpose.

The factor comparison evaluation method is easier to develop than point rating

Job responsibility factors
    Supervision and administrative responsibility
    Money and assets (profits, property)
    Programs, projects, operations, products
Personal qualification factors
    Knowledge
    Planning
    Decisions and recommendations
    Creativity and ingenuity
    Judgment and initiative

FIG. 12-2. *Classification of factors and sub-factors used in factor comparison plans.*

plans. It avoids the difficulties of determining degree definitions. Positions are compared with each other to establish relative value, and the method provides a systematic means for evaluating differentials in positions. A major disadvantage is the fact that the job content of selected bench-mark positions may change over time. It is possible that some key positions may be discontinued. Thus, the yardsticks used in this method may be changing. Another difficulty is the need for evaluators to understand the work content of all the bench-mark positions if they are to compare other positions with them successfully.

Factor Weighting in Point Rating and Factor Comparison Methods. Determination of factor weights is usually based upon the relative importance of the degrees of the factors to a particular business. The evaluators first agree on a ranking of the factors based upon their importance, and second, assign a percentage value to each factor based upon its relative importance. Having decided what the total points of the plan should be, the evaluators can determine the maximum points to be assigned to each factor.

Factor weights may also be determined statistically. This can be accomplished by using a sample of key positions which have been evaluated on each factor of the plan and which have had their salary grades determined by some independent means, such as judgment of a separate group of evaluators or by market comparisons. Using the method of least squares, a regression equation can be calculated. The regression coefficients in the equation are proportional to the weights that need to be applied to the factors to have the evaluations (based upon the plan) coincide with the salary grades which were determined independently.

Determining the Value of Factors. A factor is useful only if it helps to measure differences in value among different positions. Consequently, factors should be examined to discover if they serve their end purpose. A means of doing this is to determine their predictive value. The predictive value of a factor (that is, the correlation between degrees assigned and salary grades) is a function of both the number of degrees actually used in a factor and how the assigned degrees are distributed among positions at different salary grades. A factor which can be used to evaluate positions over a range of a number of salary grades into two or three degrees generally has a lower predictive value than a factor which evaluates into five, seven, or more degrees. Also, a factor which has the same degree assigned to positions in widely different salary grades will have a lower predictive value.

A means for examining the predictive value of factors is to plot the degrees used in evaluation against the salary grades of those positions. The scatter of points can then be observed about the regression line. A regression line is the line which best fits the data plotted. It can be drawn by inspection or calculated by the method of least squares. Figure 12-3 indicates two examples of such plots. Factor *A* is a better predictive factor than factor *B*. In

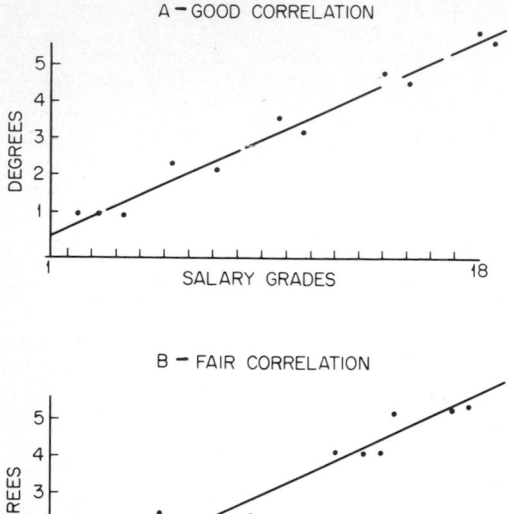

FIG. 12-3. *Predictive value of factors.*

instances where there is a much wider scatter than is shown for *B* in Figure 12-3, the use of such a factor should be questioned.

Conversion Scales. There is need to determine how to convert the total points assigned to each position to salary grades. In point rating plans, the factor degrees must be first converted to points. Typical forms of conversion scales for degrees to points are shown in Figure 12-4.

The conversion of degrees to points may be either linear or nonlinear. An example of linear or arithmetic scale is shown in *A*. If the scale used is nonlinear, it may follow a geometric progression, as is indicated in *B*. In this case, there is a constant percentage increase in points with degrees. Or, the nonlinear scale may follow a progression as shown by curve *C*, where the percentage increase in points between degrees is variable, generally increasing.

The conversion of total points to salary grades usually is associated with the means used for conversion of degrees to points in point rating plans. Examples are shown in Figure 12-5.

Associated with the linear conversion shown in *A* of Figure 12-4 is a nonlinear conversion of total points to salary grades shown in *D* of Figure 12-5. Related

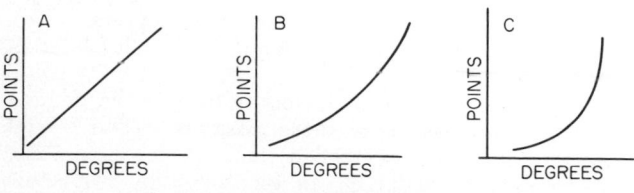

FIG. 12-4. *Conversion scale—degrees to points.*

to the nonlinear conversions of degrees to points indicated by B and C of Figure 12-4 are the nonlinear conversions of total points to salary grades shown by E and F of Figure 12-5. It is also possible, however, to obtain a linear relationship similar to that shown by A.

Salary Grades. The means of fitting salary job evaluations to salary grades is related to the design of the salary structure itself—which is not a matter for discussion in this chapter. Knowing the number of points assigned to benchmark jobs and the market prices for such jobs, it is possible to assign a dollar value to the points. However, to assign dollar values to all jobs in proportion to the assigned points is impractical, because it would create too many grades and would become an administrative nightmare. Consequently, positions are grouped into salary grades.

The salary grades can have fixed percentage differentials between their values or they can have increasing percentage differentials between grades. The method used in assigning points to grades, therefore, should take into account the design of the salary structure. The principal task is to determine cutoff points so that all jobs within a certain number of evaluation points, say, from 350 to 400 points, will be grouped into the same salary grade.

A common method is to analyze the results of salary evaluation to determine where logical cutoff points exist based upon internal relationships. A progression between such groupings can be determined statistically (or by determining a line of best fit by plotting points against dollars). Once more the results can be checked for reasonableness of internal relationships. Usually, selected jobs from among the various groupings are also checked with similar positions in other companies to determine how the relationships compare with those existing in the market. When it is felt that the relationships between cutoff points are proper, all jobs which have points within the cutoff points are assigned to the salary grade.

Specialized Job Evaluation Methods. *Internal Relationship Method.* This is a version of the ranking method. An important difference is that it is assumed that management positions, in a hierarchy of jobs, should have reasonable relationships one to another. These relationships are usually determined by a combination of company policy and comparison with market price data. The relationship approach can be applied to a function, to an operating component, or to an entire company.

An example of management relationships is shown in Figure 12-6, where there are four levels of supervision between the department head and workers. It has been assumed that first-level supervisors should receive compensation of 135 percent of that paid to those being supervised. Thus, if those being supervised receive $100 a week, the salaries of first-level supervisors would be $135 a week, and so on up the job hierarchy to the department head. Job evaluations can be determined accordingly. An objective is to maintain orderly

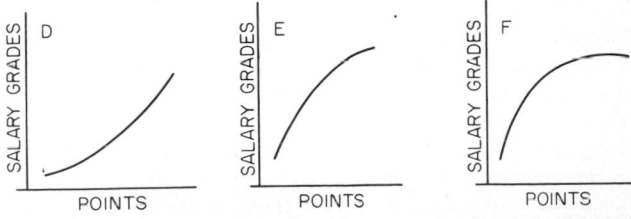

FIG. 12-5. *Conversion scales—total points to salary grades.*

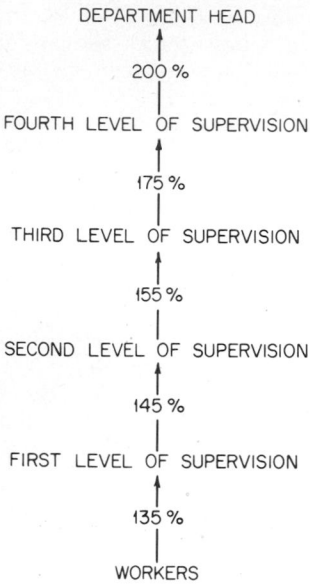

FIG. 12-6. *An example of internal relationships.*

differentials between supervisory positions. Based upon the matrix supplied by these differentials, other jobs can be ranked with respect to them. Also, ranking comparisons can be made with jobs on a horizontal basis in other functions or in other departments. Usually, a close check is maintained on market prices so that the relationships can be adjusted as required.

Use of Size Data. Job evaluations for operating heads of divisions or departments, or for chief executive officers, are frequently established by using data that indicate the relative magnitude of responsibility and accountability of the position as compared with other, similar positions. It is assumed that the job contents of chief executive officer positions, for example, are generally the same and that the important variables are size indicators of accountability.

Examples of size measurements used are sales billed, net profits, contributed value, number of employees, and net worth.

In evaluating chief executive officer positions using this approach, a list of other chief executive positions is prepared. These are generally positions in similar industries, representative in size, or viewed as competitive in other ways. The compensations (salary plus bonus) paid to such positions are secured from proxy statements, by exchange, or for publicly held corporations from Security Exchange Commission files. The compensation data are then plotted against the size indicator selected. Double logarithmic chart paper is used for this purpose. A regression line or line of best fit is determined for the data plotted.

An example, using sales billed as the size indicator, is shown in Figure 12-7. Knowing the amount of sales billed related to the position being evaluated (point *B*), one can determine the amount of compensation indicated by the trend line (point *A*) that is associated with such sales volume.

The same process can be repeated for other size indicators, such as net profits, and the correlation between them determined. The amount of compensation indicated by this method can then be related to the salary structure to determine

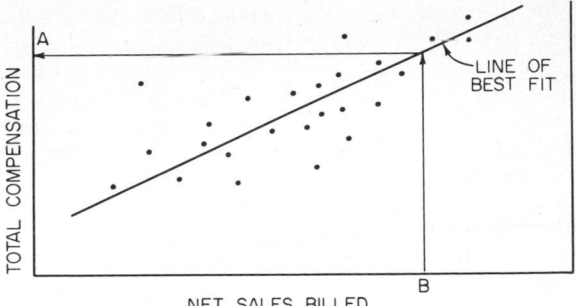

FIG. 12-7. *Compensation for chief executive officer positions compared with sales billed. Note: Plotted on double logarithmic chart paper.*

the grade the job should be evaluated into. Because total compensation (salary plus bonus) is used in this approach, care will be needed to adjust for the bonus involved in determining the proper salary grade.

Career Method. In a real sense, this is not a method of job evaluation, but it has considerable use as a means for determining salaries of professional employees. Rather than attempting to evaluate professional jobs, this approach assumes that following graduation, professional employees will increase their contributions as a result of experience. It is argued that nonsupervisory professional employees are individual contributors whose roles are largely creative and whose assignments are related to their personal abilities. Under these circumstances, it is said that it is extremely difficult to define and evaluate the work of such employees.

This approach develops salary curves, which relate salary to years since graduation. An illustration of the curves is shown in Figure 12-8. The curves are determined by a combination of company policy and surveys of actual salaries of professional employees as related to the years since the degree was obtained. The survey data are generally collected separately by discipline and by type of degree. Because it is recognized that abilities of professional employees

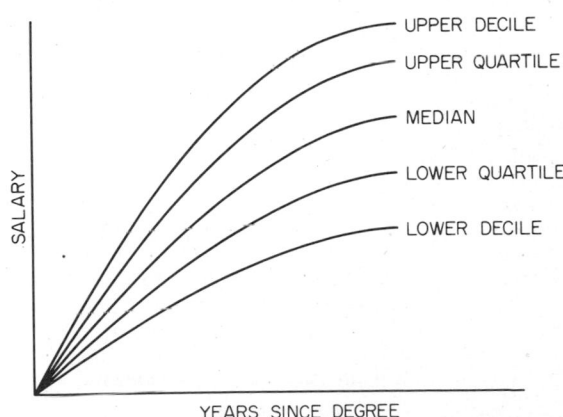

FIG. 12-8. *Example of career salary curves for professional employees.*

with the same years of experience following graduation will vary, several curves are produced for each year since degree, as shown by Figure 12-8.

The curves are generally drawn representing a distribution of salaries of those professional employees who will fall in the upper decile, upper quartile, median, lower quartile, and lower decile. Survey data are collected in the same manner.

After a company has determined the slopes of curves most appropriate for its use, a supervisor determines the level of performance for his employees, that is, upper decile, upper quartile, and so on, and then determines the proper salary rates by following the appropriate curve to the years since degree that is correct for a particular employee.

SUMMARY

Salary job evaluation plans are useful management tools to determine the relative value of positions. It is necessary to determine what a company wants to pay for and how to measure it.

There are a variety of different salary job evaluation methods available. A company should select that method or combination of methods that best fits its needs. Whatever salary job evaluation method is selected, it should not be allowed to become routinized. There is need to:

Keep all aspects of the plan up to date.

Realize that job contents will change and reevaluations will be required.

Use well-trained job evaluators.

Check the developments taking place in job evaluation techniques outside the company.

Obtain understanding and acceptance of employees to whom the plan applies.

Realize that job evaluation is not scientific, but is based upon judgment.

Compare job values with what others outside the company are paying and be flexible to changes in market prices.

Secure the understanding, attention, and support of managers at all levels.

BIBLIOGRAPHY

The AMA Handbook of the Wage and Salary Administration, American Management Association, New York, 1950.

Bexson, J. D., "A System for Job Ranking," *Personnel Management and Methods,* March, 1964.

Doulton, Joan, and David Hay, *Managerial and Professional Staff Grading,* George Allen & Unwin, Ltd., London, 1962.

Evaluating Managerial Positions, Studies in Personnel Policy, no. 122, National Industrial Conference Board, New York, October, 1951.

"Guide in Writing Position Descriptions," Office of Personnel, U.S. Department of State, Washington, D.C., 1963.

Kulberg, Ralph A., "Relating Maturity Curve Data to Job Level and Performance," *Personnel,* March–April, 1964.

Langsner, Adolph, and Herbert C. Zollitsch, *Wage and Salary Administration,* South-Western Publishing Company, Cincinnati, 1961.

Lovejoy, L. C., *Wage and Salary Administration,* The Ronald Press Company, New York, 1959.

Lytle, C. W., *Job Evaluation Methods,* 2d ed., The Ronald Press Company, New York, 1954.

Marlucci, Nicholas L. A., "Compensating First-line Supervisors in Factory and Office,"

Highlights for the Executive, National Industrial Conference Board, New York, October, 1960.

"Maturity Curves and Salary Administration," *Management Record,* National Industrial Conference Board, New York, January, 1962.

Patton, Arch, *Men, Money and Motivation,* McGraw-Hill Book Company, New York, 1961.

Patton, John A., C. L. Littlefield, and Stanley A. Self, *Job Evaluation Text and Cases,* 3d ed., Richard D. Irwin, Inc., Homewood, Ill., 1964.

Roberts, David R., *Executive Compensation,* The Free Press of Glencoe, New York, 1959.

Schwitter, Joseph P., and David W. Davis, "Analyzing Jobs for Job Evaluation with Work Sampling," *Personnel Journal,* May, 1965.

Sibson, R. E., *Wages and Salaries,* American Management Association, New York, 1960.

Smyth, Richard C., *Financial Incentives for Management,* McGraw-Hill Book Company, New York, 1960.

CHAPTER THIRTEEN

Wage and Salary Rate Surveys

DONALD KIRCHHOFFER *Manager, Wage and Salary Administration, Radio Corporation of America, Camden, New Jersey*

One of the major questions which must be answered in most difficult and important compensation policy matters is, "What do others do?" The purpose of this chapter is to describe in the simplest terms how a firm can plan for a survey to determine the wage and/or salary rates of other firms, how to gather the data, how to analyze it, and how to apply the information obtained from the survey. This chapter will also describe the reasons for making a survey, and when and under what conditions it is appropriate and practical to "find out what others are doing."

THE REASONS FOR CONDUCTING A SURVEY

Before discussion of the "when" and "how" of wage and salary surveys, we should briefly review the "why."

Competition. The pay policies and levels of a firm must not be appreciably higher than those paid by competitors in the marketplace, for the product or the firm costs will then be too high. The degree of cost disadvantage will depend upon the amount of labor costs of the product. On the other hand, if the wages and salaries paid are significantly below those paid in the geographical area of the firm's plant or office, the firm will not be able to attract the quality of personnel required. Thus, in making the policy decision relating to pay, management must tread the line between paying high enough wages and salaries to attract personnel of the required abilities and adversely affecting the price of the product or service. Such decisions cannot be intelligently made unless the pay practices of other firms are known.

Morale or Attitude. Studies have shown that individual employee's attitudes about pay are affected as much by the level of pay outside the company as by the pay of the employee's fellow workers. This is particularly true of middle and top management and engineers. This means that a firm might think that it is "getting away with" paying below the market to its managers or its engineer-

ing force because there is no one leaving for higher wages, while the morale
and the productivity of the employees are costing more than the salary "savings."
The evidence is fairly clear that a pay level significantly below the going rate
will not save money. Turnover, poor morale, and low productivity will more
than offset any apparent savings.

On the other hand, the payment of wages and salaries significantly above
the going rate does not result in high morale and increased productivity.[1]

It must be clearly understood that the above discussion is about general wage
levels, not individual pay. The high or low pay of an individual will not affect
a firm's competitive position, and individual high rates can increase productivity
and morale. The determination of individual rates is covered in Chapter 10
of Section 11. Although the results of a survey may assist in making individual
pay determinations, many other factors not covered in this chapter must be
considered.

USES OF SURVEYS

A wage and salary survey can be an important aid in deciding compensation
matters, but management must be careful not to attempt to use surveys as
a substitute for management policy judgment. Many basic compensation decisions cannot be made intelligently without the help of a survey, and many
firms avoid difficult decisions by conducting surveys. No survey should be conducted without a specific purpose in mind before it is planned. To assist in
determining whether or not a survey is called for and can contribute to intelligent
management policy, a review of the major uses of surveys is in order.

Negotiations. A wage or salary survey is necessary before a company starts
negotiations with a labor union. Company representatives should not sit down
to negotiate a labor agreement without intimate knowledge of the wages paid
in the immediate area, in the industry the firm is part of, and in firms in which
the same union represents the employees.

The company representatives must have accurate survey data for negotiations
(1) to assist in determining the wage position of the company and (2) to
justify this position to the union committee. It must be understood that the
term "wage and salary survey" includes all major pay matters, such as insurance,
holidays, vacations, pensions, overtime, and other conditions of employment.

The company negotiating committee must have a position and a reason for
the position on every matter of pay in its negotiation with the union. One
of the best arguments is what others in the area and industry do. The survey
is the only way to build these arguments.

New Plants and Offices. The establishment of a plant or office in a location
new to the firm also requires knowledge of the wage and salary practices in
the new location. Although many large, well-managed firms use uniform pay
schedules throughout the United States, most do not. It is not appropriate
to pursue here the arguments for and against uniform pay throughout the United
States. It should be noted, however, that the firms that have uniform pay
scales are large, national manufacturing concerns which can afford to operate
contrary to wage patterns that exist in the community. This policy is not recommended for the smaller company. And even if the decision is to follow the
pay pattern used elsewhere in the company, the firm should survey the area
practice to determine where its policy is at variance from the community pattern.

It should be noted here that the data obtained from a survey can modify

[1] Frederick Herzberg, Bernard Mausner, and Barbara Snyderman, *The Motivation to Work*, John Wiley & Sons, Inc., New York, 1959.

the decision on the relative position of occupations in the pay structure as established by job evaluation.   (See Chapter 11 of Section 11.)

If it is found that the order of occupations established by job evaluation is different from the order in which the occupations are paid in the community, careful attention must be given to which order to follow.   No matter how good and how scientific the job evaluation plan is, it should not be followed blindly if the survey of pay in the community shows that the relative pay positions of the occupations in the community are different.   All that one has to do is look at the community wage surveys of the Bureau of Labor Statistics of two different cities to know that this can happen.[2]

There are other reasons for knowing the pay practices in the area before a new plant or office is opened.   The most important one, pointed out above, is that the firm must establish wages high enough to attract qualified employees.   This cannot be done unless the pay for the occupation is known.

Another caution is appropriate here.   Some firms have assumed that they could obtain wage and salary information from local employment agencies or state employment officers.   Information from these sources can often be misleading.   For example, the state employment office could, in all good faith, give the firm the starting rate for office clerks or assemblers, although the average rates and the maximum rates may be considerably higher.   There is no shortcut to getting the correct information.

Employee Relations Problems.   When employee relations problems are evident, a survey is often one of the studies that should be made to determine the cause of the problem.   A pay inequity may be at the root of such employee relations problems as turnover, absenteeism, low productivity, or excessive grievances.   The pay problem may be as simple as one occupation being out of line, or as complex as the whole pay policy and level being out of line.   A survey of practice in the area is the only way to find out.

PLANNING THE SURVEY

As in all management matters, planning and preparation are vital to the success of a survey.   This is more true in wage and salary surveys than in most other personnel activities.   More time, money, and paper are wasted in unnecessary, poorly planned surveys than one likes to admit.   Proper preparation and the following of a few rules can avoid much of the waste.

Necessity of the Survey.   The first bit of planning is to ask the question, "Is this survey necessary?"   This appears too elementary, but the fact is many surveys are not necessary.   They do not help the management make a decision.

The second obvious question to ask is, "Is the required information already available elsewhere?"   Have other firms in the area recently conducted a similar survey?   Does the chamber of commerce, manufacturers' association, personnel association, bank, or local or state government already have the information?[3]

Purpose of the Survey.   After it has been determined that a survey is necessary and that the information is not available from any other source, the objective of the survey must be defined clearly.   One way to think this through is to assume three or four different results from the survey.   For example, there

---

[2] *Occupational Wage Surveys*, U.S. Bureau of Labor Statistics, Washington, D.C., annual publication.

[3] Tolles and Raimon, *Sources of Wage Information: Employer Association*, Cornell Studies in Industrial and Labor Relations, Ithaca, N.Y., 1952; and Bower, Brown, and Simpson, "Sources of Wage and Salary Data," *Industrial and Labor Relations Review*, vol. 13, no. 3, 1960.

is an alleged problem on the salary rates of four secretaries whose average salary is $125 per week. It is decided that a survey must be made. Before the survey is conducted, sit down and decide what action will be taken if the survey reveals that the average rate of secretaries is $150 per week? $85 per week? $135 per week? $115 per week? If no action would be taken under any of these circumstances, then there is not much point in conducting a survey.

One of the best ways to be sure that the survey is well planned and will produce meaningful results is to plan and design the report of the results of the survey first. Lay out the complete final report of the survey before gathering the data. Then it is reasonably certain that you will get all the information you need the first time, that you will not get unnecessary information, and that the data obtained will be useful in making the required decisions.

In the secretarial problem above, it might be found when designing the final report that, because of differences in rates based on experience, you must find out the rate ranges of the secretaries in the survey area. On the other hand, there is no need to survey such matters as starting times, hours of work, vacation, and holidays, because these policies will not be changed, regardless of the results of the survey.

Occupations to Be Surveyed. In the secretarial problem mentioned above, there is no difficulty in determining the occupations to be surveyed—one specific occupation is being investigated. In cases where the area of investigation is wider, however—as when the purpose of the survey is to prepare for negotiations, to determine the adequacy of the total wage structure, or to set up a new wage structure—the selection of occupations to be covered is an important and difficult matter.

Before determining which specific occupations are to be surveyed, it is helpful to break down the total work force into smaller groups and then to make the selection of occupations within the groups. There are many ways to categorize the groups of employees in the work force, but the following is often adequate:

Nonexempt:
  Unskilled
  Semiskilled
  Skilled
  Clerical
  Technical

Exempt:
  Administrative
  Professional
  Engineering
  Sales
  Middle management
  Top management

Although these categories overlap, there is a fairly precise and general understanding among personnel and financial people on the meaning of these terms.

Before discussing the selection of occupations among any of these groups of occupations, there are two general rules that can be followed. For an occupation to be included in a survey, it should be *universal* and *representative*.

Universal. This means that there must be a general understanding of the duties and responsibilities of the occupation, and the occupation must be used in most firms. Continuing with the clerical area as an example, if after investigating the secretarial problem we find the problem is more widespread, and we must survey the clerical wages in the area, what occupations meet the requirement of being universal? Although there are wide variations in the levels of secretaries, it is a commonly understood occupation. So is a file clerk, accounting clerk, key-punch operator, typist, and several others. But clerks operating unusual machines such as varitypers or unique jobs in an organization such as payroll clerk-cashier combinations should not be included in the survey. There will not be enough people doing this special kind of work to give a large enough sample, and it is possible that the pay of such occupations will not follow the general pay patterns.

This does not mean that the rate of a varitypist or other specialist cannot be surveyed. It can. But it should be a special survey, and it will have to cover many more firms to get enough cases to be meaningful. For this reason, it should not be included in a survey of the clerical field.

Representative. It is unnecessary and burdensome to survey all the occupations in a firm. And it is doubtful if a firm whose cooperation is needed would be willing to spend the time involved in such an undertaking. A sample of occupations must, therefore, be selected. The sample must represent all levels of skills, responsibilities, and pay. In the clerical group, this would range from the lowest-paid mail boy and typist to the highest-level, nonexempt accounting clerk. If the survey is in preparation for negotiation with a union representing the production and maintenance employees, the entry production occupation through the toolmaker must be covered. The number of occupations selected must tread the line between enough to obtain a significant sample of the employees in both the surveying and surveyed firms and not so many as to discourage participation in the survey. It must be realized that not all firms will have all occupations, so the number of occupations selected must allow for this.

These rules apply to all the groups of occupations listed above, but a special note must be made on the higher-paid occupational groups. It is obvious that the two standards of universality and representation are difficult, if not impossible, to apply to top-level executive and professional occupations. Thus there are special problems when surveying high-level management and engineering occupations.

Engineers. Because the duties of individual engineers are determined largely by education, experience, and ability, it is difficult to find occupations which meet the requirements of universality and representation. Therefore, it is the practice of most firms to gather data on *all* engineers in a firm. The data obtained include the age and/or the date of the bachelor's degree. The data are then plotted, salary being a vertical axis and age or year of degree the horizontal. A curve drawn through the mean or median salary of each year provides a simple, accurate method of comparing relative pay levels.

The Bureau of Labor Statistics[4] does not follow this method, but gathers its data on the basis of occupational classification. The Engineering Manpower Commission of the Engineers Joint Council[5] annually publishes a survey based on year of first degree as described above. Any firm contemplating conducting a survey of engineering salaries should review both of these carefully before embarking on the project. The author recommends the "experience" or "maturity" method over the classification method.

Management and Executives. Many of the same problems of surveying comparable occupations exist in the higher-level occupations. No two companies

[4] *National Survey of Professional, Administrative, Technical and Clerical Pay,* U.S Bureau of Labor Statistics, Washington, D.C., annual publication.

[5] *Professional Income of Engineers,* Engineering Manpower Commission of Engineers Joint Council, 345 E. 47th St., New York 10017, annual publication.

assign top-level management responsibilities in the same way. Added to this are the problems of the many methods of paying executives (deferred compensation, stock options, incentive bonuses, and the like). Although the principles outlined in this chapter apply to the surveying of executive occupations, the practical problems encountered are numerous. There are frequent articles published in the business magazines on levels of executive pay,[6] and the American Management Association has an Executive Compensation Service which should be investigated. The undertaking of a management or executive compensation survey is a major one, involving much preparation and planning that is beyond the scope of this chapter.

Establishments to Be Surveyed. In determining the firms to be surveyed, the first decision to be made is whether to survey the *industry* or the *area*. Except in the largest metropolitan districts, both cannot be done at once. To be thorough, both should be done, particularly the production jobs when setting up a new plant or preparing for negotiations.

In either case, the criteria for surveying another firm should be size, proximity, competition for employees, similarity of work performed, and, obviously, willingness to exchange wage information. The textbooks provide many criteria on the selection of firms to be surveyed,[7] but a basic knowledge of the industry and the community and a commonsense selection of firms which meet the simple criteria listed above will result in an adequate survey.

Fringes. In planning the survey, one of the most important decisions to be made is whether the survey is going to be limited to wage and salary rates. If it is determined that information is to be gathered on fringe benefits, the survey becomes much more complicated. The wide variations and the effect of fringes on wage levels make the collection of fringe benefit data necessary if a complete job is to be done. Before making the decision about including an analysis of fringe benefits in the survey, the Bureau of Labor Statistics[8] and the Chamber of Commerce[9] studies of fringe benefits should be reviewed. They may provide enough information to remove the need in the survey. If fringes must be surveyed, this review will help determine what should be surveyed and provide a good description and definition of fringes.

Security. In planning the survey, a decision must be made about the confidentiality of the information gathered. Again, the standards vary. Some companies will not participate in a survey unless the report lists all the participants and each firm's individual data. The reason is a feeling that all participants should have all the data, not just the company that conducts the survey. The other extreme is the company which will participate only if all data are combined and individual company information is not even reported. The middle ground is the reporting of individual company data identifying the company by code rather than name. Some surveys then provide a method by which participating companies may exchange codes.

The important thing is that a policy should be determined and rigidly adhered to. If individual data are to be reported, but not identified (the most common method), the individual codes must not be revealed.

[6] See annual articles by Arch Patton in *Harvard Business Review.*

[7] For a more detailed description of the whole process of wage and salary surveys, see David Belcher, *Wage and Salary Administration,* 2d ed., Prentice-Hall, Inc., Englewood Cliffs, N.J., 1962; and E. Lanham, *Job Evaluation,* McGraw-Hill Book Company, New York, 1955.

[8] *Supplementary Compensation Practices for Manufacturing, Production and Related Worker and Composition of Payroll in 1962,* U.S. Bureau of Labor Statistics Bulletin 1428, April, 1965.

[9] *Fringe Benefits, 1965,* U.S. Chamber of Commerce, Washington, D.C.

GATHERING THE SURVEY DATA

If all the factors discussed above have been considered, and the suggestions followed, the gathering of the data should be fairly simple. There are only a few more points that should be made.

Forms. Regardless of the type of survey, the methods used, and the data to be gathered, forms must be designed to gather the data. A well-planned survey, carefully thought out in advance, will demand its own specially designed forms.

Methods to Be Followed. There are three ways to gather the wage data: mail, personal visit, and telephone. The advantages of each are fairly obvious, and each type is acceptable under appropriate circumstances.

Information to Be Gathered. On production and clerical occupations, the usual data gathered are:

1. "Book" minimum
2. "Book" maximum
3. Actual minimum
4. Actual maximum
5. Average, by occupation

The book rates are the structure or policy minimums and maximums. The actual are those rates being paid to individuals at the time of the survey. With these figures and the average by occupation, all necessary analyses of the wage structure can be made. In many cases, these five can be reduced.

The survey should be made as simple as possible to reduce the burden on the cooperating firms. If the book rates will suffice, do not request the actual. This will reduce greatly the amount of work of the participating company.

Comparability. The most difficult decision and that which determines the value of the survey is what occupations can be compared. Few if any jobs are exactly similar. Therefore, the surveyor must determine if the surveyed occupation is similar *enough* to be considered at the same pay level. This is a matter of judgment, and the reliability of the survey will depend upon the competence of the two analysts comparing occupations.

The textbooks refer to the practice of going through the evaluation of the surveyed companies' occupations to assure that the same levels of occupation are being compared. This is time consuming and places a burden on the co-operating companies. Such methods are not much used in practice.

Short, precise job descriptions are a necessary tool to assist in determining the comparability of surveyed occupations. These descriptions should be written to describe the level of duties and need not contain the detailed duties performed that are often included in job descriptions.

Incentive Rates. Where production incentives exist, the average earned rate must be obtained. The book rate is often meaningless.

Fringes. If the survey is to cover fringe benefits, it is much simpler to gather data on the benefit rather than the cost to the company of the benefit.

ANALYSIS OF THE DATA

The matter of the analysis of the survey data is a complicated and important one. Statistical analysis is discussed in several books.[10] Two more simple methods which will meet the needs of most surveyors can be covered briefly.

[10] For example, George W. Snedecer, *Statistical Methods*, The Iowa State College Press, Ames, Iowa; and Herbert Arkin and Raymond R. Colton, *Statistical Methods*, College Outline Series, Barnes & Noble, Inc., New York.

The Bureau of Labor Statistics method of showing the distribution of paid rates by occupation is a very good one. It requires that each individual rate be gathered. The form used by BLS in addition to the median, mean, and middle range reports the number of employees receiving pay in 10-cent increments.

If individual rates are not gathered, a listing of the occupations surveyed, from low to high, as follows, is recommended.

| Occupation | No. surveyed | Average book | | Average actual | | |
		Minimum	Maximum	Minimum	Maximum	Average
Janitor						
Assembler						

This summary form can be expanded and each firm's data reported by occupation. The combinations, variations, and order of presenting the data are almost limitless and should be made to suit the purpose of the survey.

Many technical considerations are involved in what statistical techniques should be used: mean versus median, weighted versus unweighted, and the like. Again, common sense and simplicity are recommended. Sophisticated techniques are very seldom necessary.

USE OF THE SURVEY

The wage rate survey is one of the factors used in making wage determinations. Generally it is in an indirect way. Few firms use any direct statistical techniques to apply the results of a survey to the company wage structure. The literature does not reveal any. General increases and changes in the levels of individuals and groups of occupations are the usual changes made as the result of a survey.

CHAPTER FOURTEEN

Employee Merit Rating

GEORGE P. RUDERMAN *Consultant, Exempt Employee Compensation, General Electric Company, New York, New York*

Many of the functions that managers perform in attaining their personnel and business objectives can be enhanced by effective use of employee merit ratings. As used in this chapter, an "employee merit rating" is part of a formal systematic technique under which an employee or an employee's performance is judged against some set of measurement standards. These standards may be qualitative, quantitative, relative, or purely judgmental.

This chapter will cover these questions about employee merit rating:

1. Why have employee merit ratings? What can they contribute to helping the manager manage?

2. What format should be used for rating? What should be rated?

3. Who should do the rating? How frequently should they rate?

4. How should raters be trained?

5. What should be done with the rating results? How should they be used by the manager with the employee, for documentation, and for the various purposes rating can serve?

6. What can be done to check on how well a merit rating program is operating?

PURPOSES OF MERIT RATING

The basic purposes of having employee merit rating programs from management's standpoint are (1) to improve the effectiveness of employees' performances on their current jobs and (2) to help in the administration of personnel functions such as wage and salary administration, promotions, transfers or termination of service, and manpower development. To the degree these personnel functions are helped, ratings play a role in making the best use of employees, getting them on the right jobs, and rewarding them fairly, all of which can add to the motivational impact on employees to increase their contributions.

In addition, management may be well served by the documentation provided by merit ratings as backup to personnel actions it may take. Rating information can aid in resolving grievances stemming from removals, demotions, transfers, and the like.

From the employee's standpoint, a merit rating program can help him learn how well he is doing and get clarification as to what is expected of him. These are valuable inputs to help him improve his contributions. When the merit rating is used as part of a wage or salary program or for identifying promotable personnel, the employee knows that at least he is being considered for an increase or for another position.

Particularly in the case of a new employee or one on a new job, a merit rating program provides a framework for a discussion during which a manager can define the basic requirements of the job and how progress or performance is "measuring up."

A case made against merit ratings for blue-collar workers is that they are not justified or necessary because the large majority of these workers demonstrate their abilities and produce results against the quantity and quality standards established for their shop work. Many believe that these blue-collar workers accept being judged against these objective criteria, but balk at being judged on a subjective basis. Also, some managers do not advocate using merit ratings where union relations considerations mitigate against a formal documented program.

In deciding whether to have a formal merit rating program, it should be borne in mind that the benefits of merit rating can never be yielded by a procedure itself. They will result only when the procedure is supported by a consistent and fair application of judgment and managerial acumen by the reviewing manager.

MERIT RATING FORMATS

There are many formats that can be used in rating employees, but basically they are of the three main types discussed below.

Relative Ratings. This type of format is used to measure an employee or his performance against others. It is generally the simplest type in design and in ease of administration. In one approach, the rater lists a group of employees in rank order of merit. This may be in one overall evaluation or in a series of rankings, one for each of a set of selected qualities such as dependability, productivity, and the like, with some weighting then made of the series of rankings to arrive at an overall evaluation. The ranking can serve as the basis for selecting employees for promotion, determining which employees would be first to be considered for transfer to other kinds of work, or identifying those who should be separated from employment. When employees are ranked in order of merit, the population considered should be as homogeneous as possible. For example, a ranking could be made of all cost-accounting clerks or all maintenance men. Other populations that might be grouped for ranking are those in a particular pay grade, seniority classification, or a given work classification. If policy or contract calls for promotion or layoff on the basis of merit or a combination of merit and seniority, these groupings of populations for merit rating ranking may be desirable.

A variation of relative ranking is the forced distribution. In this method, the rater must identify those employees who are his upper decile performers (that is, he must rate 10 percent of his employees in this category) and his next 15 percent, middle 50 percent, next 15 percent, and lowest 10 percent performers. Of course, he needs to have enough employees to have the distribution be meaningful.

Another technique that has been used to get comparative ratings among groups of employees is based upon paired comparison. The rater selects the better of two employees, making sufficient comparisons of pairs of employees so that a statistically derived overall ranking can be calculated.

Individual Measurement against General Job or Personal Factors. This is a common format in which the appraiser rates the employee against a given set of factors. The simplest application is a listing of factors which the rater checks to show whether the employee is judged to be acceptable or not acceptable. For example, a factor could be stated as:

Versatility—adjustment to changing conditions with little difficulty, requiring only normal instruction time.

Acceptable _____ or Not acceptable _____

A more comprehensive rating scale is often used. Ratings for each factor can be made over a range of levels, typically four to six. As examples, some scales are:

1	A	Excellent	Outstanding
2	B	Good	Superior
3	C	Fair	Satisfactory
4	D	Poor	Acceptable
5			Unacceptable

The ratings for each factor can be combined on a weighted or unweighted basis into an overall rating. An example of this type of rating is shown as Figure 14-1.

Another type of merit rating format for measuring individuals against general job or personal factors goes one step beyond the previously described format and defines for each factor exactly what is meant for each rating level. Figure 14-2 is illustrative of this type of format.

Ranking methods give the rater little to review with the employee except how shaky or solid his chances compared with others may be for various personnel actions, such as promotion or transfer. However, the individual measurements against general or personal factors do provide the rater the opportunity to discuss the ratings with the employee and to cover specifically the reasons for his ratings on various factors.

Prescribed ratings may be used as the basis for giving or denying an increase in pay or as a basis for demotion or removal.

Individual Measurement against Specific Work Assignments or Work Plans. Dissatisfaction with the individual measurement against personal or general factors[1] has led to another approach by which the individual is measured against the work of his job.[2] This method has been particularly advocated for professional, administrative, and executive employees. The feeling is that merit plans based on trait rating and the use of general factors are limiting and provide a weak counseling tool for the manager. The feeling stems from the fact that personality and character are difficult to measure effectively, that they are even more difficult

---

[1] Douglas McGregor, "An Uneasy Look at Performance Appraisal," *Harvard Business Review*, May–June, 1957, p. 89.

[2] Alva F. Kindall and James Gatza, "Positive Program for Performance Appraisal," *Harvard Business Review*, November–December, 1963, p. 153.

PERFORMANCE REVIEW – HOURLY EMPLOYEES

NAME _____ COMPONENT _____ DATE _____

PAY NO. _____ MANAGER _____

CLASSIFICATION _____ JOB RATE _____ PD. RATE _____

CURRENT STATUS (Check one)	ON SCHEDULED OR IN-GRADE PROGRESSION _____
	AT JOB RATE _____

FACTORS FOR REVIEW	UNSATIS-FACTORY	NEEDS IMPROVE-MENT	SATIS-FACTORY	SUPE-RIOR	SUPPORTING COMMENT
1. KNOWLEDGE The knowledge and information applied with respect to total job requirements.					
2. PRODUCTIVITY The amount of acceptable work produced. (i.e. as compared with standards, schedules.)					
3. QUALITY The accuracy and acceptability of work produced with respect to established standards.					
4. DEPENDABILITY Adherence to plant rules, consider absences, lateness working during schedule etc.					
5. RESPONSIBILITY The care exercised in the use of materials, tools and equipment.					
6. SAFETY The observance of safety practices and good housekeeping requirements.					
7. COOPERATION Works effectively with others and willingness to accept assignments.					
8. JUDGMENT The reasoning and thought exercised in carrying out work assignments.					

OVERALL REVIEW	RECOMMENDED ACTION
_____ SUPERIOR (PERF. OR PROGRESS) _____ SATISFACTORY (PERF. OR PROGRESS) _____ NEEDS IMPROVEMENT _____ UNSATISFACTORY	_____ INCREASE-SCHEDULED STEP _____ INCREASE IN-GRADE STEP _____ INCREASE MERIT STEP _____ RE-REVIEW DATE _____ _____ REMOVAL _____ OTHER (EXPLAIN)

REVIEWED WITH EMPLOYEE_____ MANAGER'S SIGNATURE _____
NOTE: EMPLOYEE MUST BE GIVEN A COPY OF REVIEW.

FIG. 14-1. *Performance review form for hourly employees.*

	1	2	3	4	5	Value / Weight
Skill and knowledge	☐ Has and applies adequate skill and knowledge to same phases of the job. Needs further skill and training.	☐ Has and applies satisfactory skill and knowledge to most, but not all, parts of his job.	☐ Frequently, but not always, shows satisfactory application of skill and knowledge to all phases of his job.	☐ Is entirely satisfactory in the application of skill and knowledge in all phases of his job.	☐ Has and consistently applies above-average skill and knowledge to all phases of his job.	5%
Quality of work	☐ Adequate quality somewhat irregular. Meets minimum standards moderately.	☐ Work generally meets minimum standards. Occasionally needs checking.	☐ Frequently, but not always, produces work of adequate quality.	☐ Constantly produces work of an entirely satisfactory quality.	☐ Always produces work of unusually high quality.	5%
Quantity	☐ Frequently below requirements. Needs further experience.	☐ Irregular in meeting minimum requirements.	☐ Generally, but not always, meets requirements.	☐ Consistently meets requirements.	☐ Consistently exceeds requirements.	5%
Versatility	☐ Generally slow to adjust to changing conditions. Requires repeated instructions.	☐ Somewhat slow to adjust to changing conditions. Requires detailed and complete instructions.	☐ Adjusts satisfactorily to changing conditions—but with somewhat more than normal instruction time.	☐ Adjusts in an entirely satisfactory manner with little difficulty. Normal instruction time required.	☐ Displays unusual versatility. Adjusts to changing conditions easily and quickly.	1%
Dependability	☐ Dependability irregular. Requires frequent follow-up and direction.	☐ Somewhat dependable. Requires more than normal direction and follow-up.	☐ Fairly dependable. Needs only occasional follow-up.	☐ Uniformly dependable—is entirely satisfactory.	☐ Displays an unusually high degree of dependability.	1%

FIG. 14-2. *Performance review form with definitions.*

	1	2	3	4	5	Value / Weight
Cooperation	☐ Cooperation irregular. Has some difficulty in getting along with others.	☐ Somewhat cooperative. Shows a reluctance to fully cooperate with others.	☐ Frequently cooperative. Works reasonably well with others.	☐ Always cooperates readily. Is entirely satisfactory.	☐ Is exceptionally good team worker. Goes out of his way to co-operate.	1%
Safety and good housekeeping	☐ Somewhat inattentive to good safety and housekeeping rules.	☐ Observes safety and good housekeeping practices, but needs to be cautioned regularly.	☐ Usually follows safety rules and precautions. Needs to be occasionally reminded of safety and good housekeeping practices.	☐ Always follows safety rules and precautions. Keeps workplace in good order. Is entirely satisfactory.	☐ Is outstanding in observing and adapting safety rules and precautions. Work area exceptionally neat and orderly.	1%
Absence and tardiness	☐ Excessive absence, tardiness record.	☐ Tardiness and absence record less than satisfactory.	☐ Tardiness and absence record generally satisfactory.	☐ Tardiness and absence record entirely satisfactory.	☐ Nearly perfect attendance record. Invariably punctual.	1%

FIG. 14-2. *Performance review form with definitions.* (Cont.)

MEASURES OF ACCOUNTABILITY		DEGREES OF PERFORMANCE						

APPPRAISAL OF PERFORMANCE ON MEASURES OF ACCOUNTABILITY

INCLUDED IN THE POSITION GUIDE

Employee ....   Date of this Appraisal ....

MEASURES OF ACCOUNTABILITY (Please fill in number of Measure of Accountability being appraised and, if desired, abbreviated statement of actual factor)		DEGREES OF PERFORMANCE						COMMENTS IN SUPPORT DEGREE OF PERFORMANCE INDICATED
NUMBER	ACCOUNTABILITY FACTOR	INADEQUATE	MINIMUM ACCEPTABLE	GOOD	VERY GOOD	SUPERIOR	OUTSTANDING	
Composite*								

* Represents the over-all rating of employee's performance with respect to the Measures of Accountability included in his Position Guide; in this composite rating, consider the relative importance of each Measure of Accountability as it pertains to the position involved.

FIG. 14-3.   *Form used for appraisal of performance on measures of accountability.*

to change, and that, in addition, most employees reject the idea that the change is necessary or even desirable for them.

The simplest format for this type of merit rating (against work assignments) is designed for appraising each individual against a list of the responsibilities and accountabilities which appear in his position guide or position description. Figure 14-3 shows such a format.

A more comprehensive approach has been developed to focus on the results an individual achieves on specifically assigned work projects. This merit rating framework is intended to help a manager establish a relationship so that each employee will:

Know what is expected of him.   Jointly, man and manager establish a work plan consisting of specific projects or activities, and criteria for measuring expected results.

Have the opportunity to perform effectively.   The manager gives the man authority and freedom to carry out work and assists in identifying and in eliminating or reducing any obstacles affecting good performance.

Know how well he is doing.   The manager objectively reviews and appraises work results.   He gives reassurance and praise when earned and constructive criticism when appropriate.

Receive assistance and suggestions as needed.   The manager provides guidance and help as needed and in a manner which will enable the man to solve similar future problems on his own.

Work plan			Performance summary and appraisal		
Projects and activities to be carried out	Relative impor- tance	Results expected and criteria for comparing actual results with planned goals	Status of projects and activities: what has been accomplished, what remains to be accomplished	Additional data to support appraisal of per- formance and implications for future performance	Appraisal

Overall performance

FIG. 14-4. *Form used for rating performance by results achieved on specific assignments.*

A format for such a merit rating is shown by Figure 14-4. Note that specificity can be built in, because the actual work projects can be indicated in the work plans, and their priority is identified in advance as are the criteria which the results are to be measured against.

The individual merit rating based on work assignments or work goals is aimed at helping individuals improve their performance on the job, forming the basis for managerial determination of proper pay as a reward and as a vehicle to guide the individual and manager in the occupational development of the employee.

THE RATER

It is possible for rating to be done by one or a combination of the following:
1. The immediate manager
2. Other managers familiar with the employee's work
3. A higher-level manager
4. An industrial relations staff specialist
5. The employee's peers
6. The employee himself
7. The employee's subordinates

In most cases, the individual's immediate manager is in the best position to know the employee and his work. Because the manager generally is also responsible for recommendation or approval of personnel actions which may depend upon the merit ratings, it is usually desirable to have him be a party to the merit rating. A further reason is that in a majority of instances, the immediate manager is responsible for feedback of the merit rating to the employee. Research has indicated that the best job of rating is done by the level of supervision closest to those being rated.[3]

In the design of rating programs, it is frequently recognized that there may be drawbacks to placing the entire burden on one manager. Such considerations as the tendency for raters to differ in their standards and thus to be "tough" or "easy" appraisers, or a need to have a check on managers to protect employees from ratings that reflect innocent or purposeful bias on the part of raters, have led to having a manager's ratings either reviewed by others or supplemented by other ratings.

A higher-level manager than the individual's immediate manager may also be required in the merit rating system either to review all ratings or to make them himself. The review is intended to help in achieving reasonable consistency between the raters and to eliminate any gross misratings.

Frequently, staff industrial relations specialists are included in the merit rating process. They serve as advisers to the managers who are doing the rating. These specialists probe and question each manager as he goes through the ratings for individuals, forcing the manager to think about how much evidence he actually has on which to make appraisal judgments and how the ratee stands up in comparison with other employees being rated. The specialists can point out and counsel in instances where managers have a tendency to rate with a central tendency or to have ratings bunched at the high end or the low end of the rating scale.

Employees' peers are sometimes asked to participate in the rating process. There is some belief that a group of employees can identify its outstanding performers and poorest performers more reliably than managers who are not part of the group. Further, when the peer group has a role to play in the rating process, there may be more acceptance of the outcomes of ratings (pay raises, promotions, and so on) than when the ratings are done by managers.

Particularly with respect to merit ratings for the purpose of improving individual performance, there may be value in having the individual himself do the appraisal. In some cases, managers who have made a rating ask the employee to prepare for a rating review session by also filling out a rating sheet. The employee and manager then compare the ratings they have made and focus discussion on the reasons for any significant differences of ratings.

Another self-appraisal use involves ratings made against work plans. Here the individual is put in the role of briefing the manager on the progress he is making. This places the individual in a self-determining or "take charge" role. It gives him the chance to give his opinion of his achievement on his various goals and his thoughts on how he should modify his plans or adapt his working methods to accomplish more. The manager can build on these thoughts by adding his own experience or the perspective he may have from his different vantage point in the organization. The use of subordinate-prepared ratings may produce more productive and constructive discussion between the subordinate and his manager. They may tend to result in better upward flow of information, force the employee to do systematic thinking about his job and his performance, and clarify differences of opinion regarding job requirements and job performance.

Ratings by subordinates find their chief usefulness in the selection process for promotions. For example, consider a plant where the management hierarchy consists of a plant manager, several superintendents, a group of assistant superintendents, and foremen. The assistant superintendents, from their perspective

[3] Dean K. Whitla and John E. Tirrell, "The Validity of Ratings of Several Levels of Supervisors," *Personnel Psychology*, vol. 6, no. 4, Winter, 1953, p. 461.

of having worked for the several superintendents, could be asked their ratings as to which superintendent would make the best plant manager. Their ratings might agree or differ from that of the plant manager, who would be rating his superintendents to determine which should succeed him, but these ratings will add another dimension to help in the final selection.

FREQUENCY OF RATING

Many rating programs are designed so that each employee is rated annually. Although this may be an acceptable rule of thumb for the frequency of ratings, there are some additional considerations.

1. The frequency of rating must fit the purposes for which ratings are being made. If the ratings are part of a selection process that is reviewed by top management semiannually, for example, then ratings are also required semiannually.

2. For new employees or those on new jobs, more frequent ratings may be required than for other employees.

3. Learning experiments show that when feedback is delayed in time much of the impetus to learning is lost. So feedback should not always be "saved" for an annual appraisal, but should be given quickly.

4. In the case of an unsatisfactory rating, the next rating is generally advanced in time so that quick appraisal can be made of whether the employee has improved.

TRAINING OF RATERS

Studies have shown that managers can be trained and helped to improve their ability to rate and discuss ratings with employees.[4] It has been demonstrated that managers with training have been more successful in merit rating than managers who have not been given a training course.

For example, one training program used in industry was designed as a series of five 3-hour meetings for managers who had direct responsibility for making formal performance ratings. The first session was devoted to examining why managers do merit rating, gaining acceptance of the format being used, familiarizing participants with the format, and developing a common understanding of the application and meaning of the rating scale. The second session consisted of a group discussion of ratings based on reading and problem assignments of cases. In the next meeting, the importance of day-to-day coaching between formal rating sessions was explored and means developed to improve informal coaching practices. A fourth meeting was held just prior to actual ratings and rating reviews with employees. Using a role-playing technique, the participants practiced rating reviews to give them skill and confidence in using and discussing merit ratings. Finally, after actual discussions with their employees, the managers reconvened to review experiences in conducting formal appraisal discussions and to discuss and practice ways of overcoming difficulties encountered in actual reviews.

USE OF RATING RESULTS

A general guide is to make the rating results available only to those who absolutely need the information for counseling or administrative purposes. The confidential nature of merit ratings should be protected.

[4] C. G. Moon and Theodore Hariton, "Evaluating an Appraisal and Feedback Training Program," *Personnel*, November–December, 1958.

The use of the rating results is largely determined by the purpose for which they are intended.

Wage and Salary Administration. Under pay systems in which an increase or a level of pay is directly related to a given performance rating, the use of the rating is determined by the system. For example, if the system calls for a 2 percent increase in pay each six months if performance has been satisfactory, the rating of satisfactory by the rater is usually forwarded to the personnel and accounting departments who record and process the pay increase. Likewise, a nonsatisfactory rating will hold up the pending pay increase. A satisfactory rating under such a system should be discussed with the employee. For unsatisfactory ratings, the employee should know where improvement is needed. Employee awareness of a shortcoming may be half the battle.

There are also pay systems where the merit rating affects pay only indirectly, as in the case of a merit pay program under which the manager sets an individual's salary within a salary range. Here the merit rating should be documented and supplemented with reasons for setting the salary at a particular point within the salary range. Generally, the employee should be given an explanation of how the manager set his salary where he did. To the extent the merit rating entered into the decision, the employee should be given feedback on his rating.

Future Potential. Ratings of future potential are usually made to help management inventory its manpower assets. They are used as an input to build up personnel inventories. They normally are not used in counseling or individual development and hence are not discussed with the employee.

Other Personnel Actions: Layoff or Transfer. The use of merit ratings for these types of personnel actions is to serve as documented backup data. Thus, the ratings are generally kept on file in the personnel component and reported to the employee where such reports are required. For example, an employee might be notified that his rating has been unsatisfactory and that if the subsequent rating is also unsatisfactory he will be subject to removal.

Performance Improvement. Feedback to an employee of performance rating or appraisal as a means of helping him improve is frequently cited as the prime reason for ratings. If an employee knows where he stands, what his shortcomings are, what he has done well, and how he can improve, he may be helped and motivated to increase his contributions. Some of the guides for feedback sessions with employees are:

1. Be prepared; bring all available facts to the session; structure the approach to the particular individual.

2. Schedule the review in advance so that the employee is ready with questions, points for discussion, or his list of accomplishments.

3. Establish a friendly atmosphere; conduct the review in private (or with union steward present if employee desires).

4. Explain the purpose of the review; discuss the rating. If the format includes several factors, discuss the rating for each one separately; review ratings covering both strengths and weaknesses.

5. Listen, so employee has the opportunity to comment. Be open-minded as he brings additional facts to bear; be willing to add to or amend the rating as additional information is brought out.

6. Be positive and constructive; attempt to arrive at conclusions about a future program for improvement that satisfy both parties to the fullest possible extent.

7. Conclude on a positive note; summarize the review; go over the plan for future as agreed upon; reassure the employee.

Conducting Effective Performance Reviews. Some recent research has brought out these results about the review process:[5]

Criticism has a negative effect on achievement of goals.

Praise has little effect one way or the other.

Performance improves most when specific goals are established.

Defensiveness resulting from critical appraisal produces inferior performance.

Coaching should be a day-to-day, not a once-a-year, activity.

Mutual goal setting, not criticism, improves performance.

Interviews designed primarily to improve a man's performance should not at the same time weigh his salary or promotion in the balance.

Participation by the employee in the goal-setting procedure helps produce favorable results.

The conclusions of the authors were that:

Comprehensive annual performance appraisals are of questionable value.

Coaching should be a day-to-day, not a once-a-year, activity.

Goal setting, not criticism, should be used to improve performance.

Separate appraisals should be held for different purposes.

EVALUATING THE RATING PROGRAM

There are several inputs that can be helpful in evaluating the effectiveness of the merit rating program.

The most basic measure is a statistical analysis of the frequency with which appraisals have been completed. Generally, the accounting department or personnel department can provide a periodic tally showing how many employees were scheduled for a merit rating during a given period and how many actually had a rating as evidenced by the filing of appropriate records.

Another source of data to measure a merit rating program is the employee attitude survey. Some questions which employees might be asked to respond to are:

How well do people know where they stand in the eyes of their managers?

Did your manager discuss your last merit rating with you?

How much opportunity did you have to express your opinion when your managers reviewed your rating?

When was the last rating made for you?

How well do people know what specific factors are used in making merit ratings?

A distribution of the ratings made by each manager or rater is another means of evaluating the merit rating program. If there are some managers who rate all employees at the high end, low end, or middle of the rating spectrum, a check should be made to be sure the ratings are being equitably handled.

SUMMARY

Merit ratings can be a useful technique for managers in working with their employees. Although there are many formats that can be used, the choice of a format depends largely on the intended purpose of the merit ratings. The main purposes are (1) to improve an individual's performance and (2) for

[5] Herbert H. Meyer, Emmanuel Kay, and John R. P. French, Jr., "Split Roles in Performance Appraisal," *Harvard Business Review*, January–February, 1965, p. 123.

various personnel actions such as wage and salary administration, promotions, and layoffs. There is evidence that training in merit rating and particularly in feedback to employees is a must for those who do merit rating. Generally, the immediate manager should do the merit rating, although others may supplement and review the immediate manager's ratings. Annual merit ratings are the rule. More frequent ratings, however, and particularly more frequent coaching of employees seem to be desirable as means of helping employees improve their performance.

In most cases, feedback of merit ratings is a vital element in the rating program. Especially for professional and administrative personnel, the trend, supported by research, is in the direction of appraisals of performance based on the work responsibilities or, more pertinently, on the agreed-upon specific work plans the manager and the individual have worked out in advance.

BIBLIOGRAPHY

Heyel, Carl, *Appraising Executive Performance*, American Management Association, New York, 1958.

Kellogg, Marion S., *What to Do about Performance Appraisal*, American Management Association, New York, 1965.

CHAPTER FIFTEEN

Wage Systems

H. B. LAWSON *Principal, H. B. Maynard and Company, Incorporated, Pittsburgh, Pennsylvania*

Preceding chapters have described methods of establishing and administering wage rates for industrial jobs. The managers of industrial organizations are also concerned with receiving a fair return for the wages paid to their workers. Success in receiving a fair day's work is determined in part by the type of wage system used and how well that system is administered.

As early as 1880, some of the pioneers in the scientific management movement recognized that productivity could be increased if workers were offered financial incentives to produce. As the work of Frederick W. Taylor and Frank B. Gilbreth made the standardization and measurement of shop work a practical management tool, management became interested in introducing wage-incentive plans. Many plans installed during the 1920s have operated well ever since. On the other hand, many plans have failed to accomplish their objectives and have been abandoned. The usual reason given for abandoning wage incentives is that it was difficult to maintain them. It has been found that difficulties in maintaining most wage systems are caused by lack of management understanding of the proper administration necessary to make them work.

A wage system is not a technique used by one management function. It is a system which is operated by the entire manufacturing organization to provide a control over the use of the labor resources necessary to produce products. Its administration is the responsibility of top management.

The purpose of this chapter is to provide an insight into the complexities of wage systems and an awareness of the interlocking and coordinating efforts necessary to administer a wage system.

DAYWORK WAGE SYSTEMS

A daywork wage system is one in which the worker's earnings are not dependent upon output. The worker is paid hourly wages for time on the job.

This is the most common type of wage system, particularly in smaller organizations, in many process-controlled industries, and for the majority of indirect operations. Hourly rates for the workers can be established in several ways. These are described in Chapters 10, 11, 13, 14, and 18 of Section 11.

Unmeasured Daywork. Minimum management effort is required to administer unmeasured daywork systems. The worker's output is not measured. Thus, no records are maintained for the purpose of evaluating the worker's productivity. This lack of information concerning production results in minimum management control over output.

Measured Daywork. The method of wage payment under a measured daywork system is similar to that under an unmeasured daywork system. The worker is paid an hourly sum for each hour at work. Wages are not determined directly by output. The significant difference between the two systems is that with the measured daywork plan, management determines a rate of output which the worker is expected to produce in return for his wages.

A well-designed and well-administered measured daywork system contains the same degree of control that is necessary in wage-incentive systems. Although measured daywork systems do not provide for wage payment based on output, it is desirable to establish accurate and consistent time standards and to provide timely control procedures for the use of foremen who are trained to use the system for maintaining an acceptable level of productivity.

Worker performance under daywork plans varies considerably in different companies. With unmeasured daywork plans, performance may be as low as 25 to 30 percent of standard with performances of 50 to 70 percent most commonly encountered. Under the measured daywork system, a well-managed shop may increase production to as high as 80 to 85 percent of standard or even more.

Under the daywork system of wage payment, the worker has minimum motivation to produce. The main impetus to maintaining acceptable production levels rests with the foreman. Under a wage-incentive system, the worker has incentive to produce as much as possible, because his production level determines his earnings. It is essential that the foreman maintain constant surveillance over his operations when the daywork system is used. Generally, workers not working under incentive plans will accept job conditions that satisfy their foremen. Material shortages, nonstandard material conditions, machine malfunctions, and other delays that hold back production are consistently reported by workers when these affect their earnings. This seldom happens in most daywork situations.

Merit rating plans are often used in daywork plants to encourage the workers to produce at higher performance levels. Usually, worker output is one of the factors considered in merit rating plans. Because it is only one of many factors, it usually does not offer much inducement to increased effort on a day-to-day basis.

WAGE-INCENTIVE SYSTEMS

The American Society of Mechanical Engineers defines a wage-incentive plan as: "A method of payment which directly relates earnings to production. A system which enables workmen to increase their earnings by maintaining or exceeding an established standard of performance."

The only difference between a well-administered measured daywork system and a wage-incentive system is that the worker is paid additionally for production which exceeds the established standards of performance. A properly installed wage-incentive plan offers benefits to both the employer and the employee. It results in increased production per man-hour and, therefore, lower unit costs for the employer. The employee benefits by having an opportunity to increase his earnings.

The amount of increased production potential and additional earnings opportunities will vary from plant to plant because of many factors. The plan's design, the manner in which it is installed, how well it is administered, and the manner in which it is maintained all will affect its operation. It is generally accepted, however, that the majority of operators working on incentive with well-engineered standards can produce at a rate in excess of 120 percent of standard. Comparing this with the expected rate of production for workers producing under unmeasured daywork systems, it may be seen that productivity is, in most cases, doubled.

These increases result from several factors. Some will come from increased effort by the worker. Most, however, are the result of steadier application to the job, better planning to avoid delays, and following correct methods.

Requirements for Successful Use of Incentive Payment. The operation of a wage-incentive system is the concern of many functions in management. It is not the job of the industrial engineer alone to see that it is operated properly. Many well-designed and properly installed plans deteriorate because management is not alert to the many pitfalls which can destroy the effectiveness of the plan.

Top Management Support. Top management must support the installation and maintenance of any incentive system. There are innumerable cases where lack of management support has caused incentive plans to fail. The administration of the wage-incentive system is subject to pressures from many divergent forces within an industrial organization. Production supervisors, industrial engineers, controllers, industrial relations personnel, and the workers all are affected by the system's administration. Their special concerns with their primary functions have significant effects upon their views of the operation of the plan.

It is essential, therefore, that clear management policies and procedures be established at the plan's inception and rigidly adhered to on a continuing basis. These policies and procedures should be committed to writing and understood by all who are affected.

Supervisory Understanding and Cooperation. When wage incentives are introduced, the supervisor's role changes. Under a daywork system, he is concerned with finding ways to motivate the workers to produce. The initiative for determining that delays or nonstandard conditions exist rests with the foreman. With a wage-incentive plan, the worker motivation to produce is provided by the opportunity to increase earnings. The worker, therefore, will place pressure on the foreman to eliminate production delays. The foreman will be urged by the worker to see that the proper material is on hand, that machines are operating properly, that the workers are instructed in the proper methods, and that more work is available as each worker finishes his job.

Supervisors must be trained in all facets of wage-incentive administration. They must understand the need to standardize and teach operators proper methods. They must know the details of the task which the time standard covers. They must see that correct time and production reports are made by the workers. They must use performance analysis data to investigate abnormal performances and out-of-line, nonstandard conditions. They must report new jobs and changed methods and conditions to the people responsible for standards maintenance.

When a change is made from a daywork system to a wage-incentive system, converting the supervisors' attitudes and methods of operating is a difficult task.

Strong management leadership is required, and comprehensive supervisory retraining is needed. Management must not only educate the supervisors in the new practices, but also see that the new practices are carried out. After the wage-incentive system takes hold and the supervisors become proficient in its administration, their work becomes easier, because they have procedures which permit them to manage their operations better.

Good Methods and Standards. Accurate and consistent standards based upon standardized methods are the chief requisites of a good incentive plan. Chapters 9, 11, and 12 of Section 7 describe the establishment and administration of methods and standards. The importance of these to the successful use of wage incentives cannot be overstated. Weaknesses in the areas of methods and standards are major causes for wage-incentive failures.

When incentives first were introduced in industry, standards were often established without preliminary methods analysis. Often, estimates or past performance records were used for setting standards. The workers, stimulated by bonus-earnings opportunities, usually were able to introduce their own methods improvements. These resulted in earnings in excess of management expectations. In many cases, managers arbitrarily cut the rates to reduce earnings opportunities. This, in turn, created labor unrest and suspicion of management's administration of the incentive plan. As a result, workers learned to peg their production at a rate beyond which they suspected management would cut rates.

Rate-cutting practices are no longer prevalent in industry. Most incentive plans include a feature which guarantees that standards will remain in effect unless methods, material, equipment, or quality requirements change. This guarantees the worker that his earnings will be consistent with his application of effort to the job. It also guarantees the company that standards will not get out of line because of operator-introduced methods improvements.

Creeping Methods Changes. It is relatively easy for both the worker and the company to recognize major methods changes which result from technological improvements or major workplace changes. Often, however, methods changes are minor and have only a minor effect upon standard times for performing operations. These minor improvements are most difficult to recognize as they occur. They accumulate over periods of time and ultimately result in significant looseness in standards. These "creeping methods changes" are responsible for destroying the effectiveness of wage-incentive plans more than any other factor.

To prevent creeping methods changes, it is necessary that methods be studied, standardized, and recorded in detail. Continual attention must be given to methods by both line supervisors and the people responsible for maintaining the standards. When minor methods changes are found which result in changes in time standards amounting to less than 5 percent, they should be recorded. When the cumulative total of the changes amounts to 5 percent or more of the established time standard, a new standard should be issued.

Changes in methods, conditions, materials, or quality requirements that result in tightening of the standards often occur. These generally are automatically called to management's attention, because operators usually will report anything that affects earnings.

The Industrial Engineering Staff. The degree of accuracy and consistency in developing and applying standards is directly related to the competency of the industrial engineering staff. It is necessary to provide sufficient talent to perform the methods and standards function on a continuing basis. An incompetent or insufficient industrial engineering staff results in poor standards coverage and insufficient attention to methods. Low coverage weakens the effectiveness of the incentive plan in two ways. First, a large amount of daywork mixed with incentive work makes it difficult to control time reporting and results in time juggling. Second, workers accustomed to incentive earnings expect to maintain a high level of take-home pay. When abnormal amounts of daywork time occur, the workers pressure for average earnings to be paid so that their take-home pay will not be reduced. This defeats the purpose of the incentive plan, for it results in paying incentive rates for nonincentive work.

Employee Understanding and Acceptance. The installation of a wage-incentive plan for workers who have been working under a daywork system affects the two most important objectives of their jobs—the amount of money earned and the amount of work they produce. Working conditions, promotional opportunities, fringe benefits, working hours, rest periods, and the like, are overshadowed by these two factors. Because a wage-incentive plan changes these, its acceptance by the participants is of prime importance.

There is always a natural resistance to change, particularly if the purpose and details of the change are not clearly understood. Therefore, it is necessary that workers understand how new systems will work and are sold on the benefits they will receive. The most meaningful selling point for workers is that they will have an opportunity to earn more money. On the other hand, they must be assured that management is not introducing a "speedup" plan which will require them to produce at unreasonable performances.

In the design of the wage-incentive system, one characteristic is that the plan must be easy to understand. It should be possible for the worker to be able to calculate his own earnings. If he does not know how to determine his pay, his motivation to produce is weakened. Also, a complicated plan is difficult to explain and, therefore, difficult to sell to both supervisors and workers.

The major burden of getting employee acceptance lies with the foreman. When wage incentives are first introduced in a plant, many poor working conditions usually have to be corrected. It is the supervisor's responsibility to provide working conditions that will enable the workers to perform at incentive performance. He must provide work for each worker, so that lost time between jobs is eliminated. He must make sure that material, tools, equipment, and conditions are the same as when the standard was established. He must train the workers in the methods upon which the standards are based. He must assign operators to work for which they are suited. He must promptly investigate complaints about standards and, when necessary, request industrial engineering assistance. He must make sure that proper reports of downtime and nonstandard work are made when they occur.

Proper System Maintenance. After a wage-incentive system is designed and installed, it must be maintained to be effective. The problem of creeping methods changes has already been mentioned as a major maintenance problem. There are many others about which management must be aware.

As new personnel enter the organization or are moved to new functions, they must be trained in their responsibilities in connection with the incentive plan. Newly appointed supervisors must learn their responsibilities. New industrial engineers must be trained in the work measurement and analysis techniques which are used to establish and maintain the methods and standards programs. New operators, or operators moved to new jobs, must be trained in the methods for those operations.

Count control, production reporting, performance analysis, and incentive-earnings reports must be established and used by the supervisors and industrial engineers. These reports are the records which indicate when weak spots are occurring. Fall-down and abnormal-performance reports are symptomatic indicators of inaccurate standards, incorrect time or production reports, or nonstandard conditions. Their timely investigation on a continuing basis helps to prevent deterioration of the wage-incentive plan.

Types of Incentive Payment Formulas. There are three general types of wage-incentive curves commonly used.

One for One. In plans of this type, a 1 percent increase in wages is paid for each 1 percent increase in productivity over standard performance. When the one-for-one plan is used, unit labor costs decrease as performance increases up to standard. Thereafter, unit labor costs are constant, for beyond 100 percent performance, the same amount per piece is paid to the worker.

This type of plan is perhaps the most common. It is easy to understand and economical to administer, because unit costs and earnings are easily calculated. It offers a good incentive to produce.

Increasing Bonus as Performance Increases. This type of plan normally is installed to provide a strong incentive to meet or better standard. There are many variations of plans which offer increased earnings as performance increases. Some plans offer a higher base rate after performance reaches a predetermined level. The make-out level may be lower than 100 percent of standard in some cases.

Decreasing Bonus as Performance Increases. Many incentive plans installed during the days when standards were estimated, or at least not established accurately, were designed to limit earnings. These paid the worker only a percentage of the gains resulting from increased productivity. Others offered high incentives at certain performance levels by steps or differential wage rates and decreasing incentive as output increased. Unless such a step is installed, this type of plan does not usually offer sufficient motivation for the worker to produce at or above standard.

Bonus Shared by Supervisors and Workers. Some plans permit supervisors and indirect workers to participate in the bonus earned by the incentive workers. Most of these were installed at a time when the measurement of indirect work was almost unheard of.

A classic plan of this type is the Bedaux plan, in which the incentive worker is paid 0.75 percent for each 1 percent increase in productivity above standard. The remaining 0.25 percent is pooled and paid out to the supervisors and indirect workers.

Typical Wage-incentive Plans. When a wage-incentive plan is selected, five key points should be considered.

1. Present pay
2. Present output
3. Proposed standard output
4. Expected output
5. Expected pay level on incentive

The relationship of these points will determine how employees will react to the plan and the resultant benefits that management will receive from its operation. There are a large number of standard plans and features that can be incorporated in new installations. Some of the older plans were introduced with certain control and time-study features, and these are usually still identified as integral features of the plans. The design of an incentive plan, however, can be accomplished by using the best features of several to satisfy the conditions in a particular organization.

The following paragraphs describe some specific incentive plans to illustrate the three types of wage-incentive plans.

Piecework and 100 Percent Premium Plan. Although piecework, as such, is seldom used because of minimum-wage laws, it was the forerunner of most of the present wage-incentive plans. Under a true piecework system, the worker is paid a fixed amount of money for each unit of production.   In the early days, this was not related to an hourly wage rate.   Many existing wage-incentive plans still are referred to as "piecework systems."   However, almost all are incentive plans where the time to produce units of production is estimated, calculated from past performance records, or derived from time study or standard data.   The time units are converted to monetary terms by multiplying the time unit by the hourly wage rate.

The "100 percent premium plan" is the name given to a piecework system when the production rate is expressed in time (minutes or hours, usually), rather than money.   Therefore, the 100 percent premium plan with a guaranteed hourly rate base is a true one-for-one incentive plan.   Its advantages are that it is easy to understand, is economical to administer, and offers a strong incentive (under appropriate conditions).

Gantt Task and Bonus Plan.   The Gantt task and bonus plan offers a strong incentive to meet or exceed standard performance by paying a bonus at 100 percent performance plus 1 percent for each 1 percent increase in production over standard.   The original plan was designed with a low guaranteed base rate and a 33⅓ percent increase in earnings at make-out and 1 percent increase in pay per each 1 percent increase in production thereafter.   Modified versions of this plan were based upon guaranteed base rates that were comparable to going rates and the increase at make-out was reduced to 10 percent.

The Gantt task and bonus plan is relatively easy to understand.   It is somewhat difficult to administer because of the base rate differential.   However, it offers a strong incentive to meet and exceed standard.

Halsey Premium Plan.   The Halsey premium plan is an example of a plan initially designed for applications where standard times were estimated and were somewhat loose.

At performances above the 100 percent level, the savings from increases in productivity are shared by the worker and the company.   Less than 1 percent bonus is paid to the worker for each 1 percent increase above standard.   The worker's share of the bonus above 100 percent varies from company to company. However, in most cases it is 0.5 percent or 0.6 percent for each 1 percent increase in production over 100 percent performance.

The Halsey premium plan's major disadvantage is that it offers only a moderate incentive to meet and exceed the standard.   It is relatively easy to understand and economical to administer.

Methods of Calculating Incentive Earnings.   The methods used to calculate incentive earnings have a significant influence upon the effectiveness of the plan and the amount of administrative effort required.

Individual.   Maximum motivation to produce is generated in a wage-incentive plan that relates individual performance to earnings.   For that reason, maximum results in terms of increased productivity can be expected when wage incentives are applied on an individual basis.   Each worker, theoretically at least, is in business for himself.   He will strive to produce as much as possible, because his earnings will increase proportionately.   Individual incentives also enable supervision to analyze the performance of each worker and take corrective action to help the individual improve his earnings.   Experience has shown, over and over again, that the most direct incentive is the most effective.

Group System.   The group system of incentive payment offers definite advantages in many cases.   One of the disadvantages of individual incentive plans is that each man is interested only in his own production and earnings.   There is a natural reluctance to help new men or to perform any extra work for which incentive earnings are not paid.

The group system has been developed to overcome some of these problems and to provide incentive-earnings opportunities when working on progressive assembly lines and on operations where it is difficult to measure each individual's contribution to the total task.

In the group system of wage payment, each man shares in the earnings of the group in proportion to the amount of time he works in the group.

In forming groups for wage-incentive purposes, best results are obtained if the group size is limited. Cooperation and fellowship are better in smaller groups. As group size increases, the individual begins to lose sight of his contribution, and motivation to produce decreases.

Generally, groups are formed only on similar types of work. Nothing is gained if a machine operator in one department is grouped with an assembler in another whose work has no effect upon his machining operations.

There are distinct advantages in using the group system of wage payment.

1. Better cooperation is obtained among operators.
2. Less supervision is required.
3. New men are trained by experienced men.
4. Nonproductive labor is reduced.
5. More accurate costs prevail.
6. Relationship between operators and staff departments is simplified.
7. Costing routine is simplified.
8. Timekeeping is simplified.
9. Quality of product is improved.
10. Checking is simplified.
11. Men work more conscientiously.
12. Wages are fairly distributed.
13. Wages do not fluctuate greatly.
14. Operators are assured of a steady flow of work.
15. Operator gets work for which he is best fitted.
16. System of promotion is provided.
17. Working environment is made more pleasant.

The disadvantages are:

1. It is difficult to care for incomplete jobs.
2. There is no check on time allowances on individual jobs.
3. There is no check on individual efficiency.
4. It is sometimes hard to find the right man for group leader.

Incentive Payment Periods. The period selected as the basis for the payment of incentive earnings has an important bearing on the administrative task. The usual periods used are the job, the day, and the pay period.

When the job basis is selected, the time taken and time allowed for each job worked on are calculated, and incentive earnings are paid at the rate earned for each job. This is the most costly method of payment to administer, because operators working on several jobs each day will have varying performances and rates of earnings. The clerical task of computing earnings is therefore most costly.

Another problem with the job basis is that the short time intervals invite time juggling and distorted performance levels. When standards are established, they include allowances for minor delays, personal time, and the like. These are averages of incidents that occur over periods of time. It is possible that an operator working on an operation will encounter little or no delay time. His performance will be inflated on that operation. Later, he may be on another job where his delays will pyramid over a two- or three-hour period. The result may be a fall-down for which management must pay the guaranteed base rate.

The day basis is somewhat better than the job basis. The same objections apply, however. Time juggling, increased clerical work, and peaking of delay times occur when incentive payments are made on a day basis. The day basis also introduces the problem of accounting for incompleted jobs at the end of the day.

The pay period basis is the most practical method of calculating incentive pay. The temptation to misreport time spent on individual jobs is eliminated. Delay and personal time averages out over periods of a week or longer. Clerical work is reduced. Finally, the problem of accounting for incomplete jobs is minimized.

CONCLUSION

The administration of a wage system is a top management responsibility, because it affects many functions of management and requires considerable coordination among these functions.

The complexity of a wage system requires that it be properly designed, installed, and administered. It is not a procedure that can be installed and forgotten. Because of the dynamic nature of a manufacturing organization, it must be maintained continuously.

BIBLIOGRAPHY

Carroll, Phil, *Better Wage Incentives*, McGraw-Hill Book Company, New York, 1957.
Gilmore, Robert W., *Industrial Wage and Salary Control*, John Wiley & Sons, Inc., New York, 1956.
Ireson, W. G., and E. L. Grant, *Handbook of Industrial Engineering and Management*, Prentice-Hall, Inc., Englewood Cliffs, N.J., 1955.
Louden, J. Keith, and J. Wayne Deegan, *Wage Incentives*, 2d ed., John Wiley & Sons, Inc., New York, 1959.
Lytle, Charles W., *Wage Incentive Methods*, rev. ed., The Ronald Press Company, New York, 1942.
Maynard, H. B., *Industrial Engineering Handbook*, 2d ed., McGraw-Hill Book Company, New York, 1963.

CHAPTER SIXTEEN

Fringe Benefits

ROBERT E. LEVINSON   *Vice President and General Manager, The Steelcraft Manufacturing Company, Cincinnati, Ohio*

From 1955 to 1965, fringe benefits rose almost twice as fast as wages, according to the Federal Reserve Bank. The average worker in 1965 got more than 25 percent in extras tagged to his base pay. That is 2,000 percent more than in 1930.

The mushrooming cost of fringe benefits is creasing a growing number of employer brows, according to *U.S. News & World Report.* This gives the manager a narrow tightrope to walk in his twin role as donor of the largesse and keeper of the till. On the one hand, he is responsible for buying the best protection for his people, for maintaining an effective work force, and for keeping his company competitive. On the other, he must keep the lid on spiraling costs. This poses some definite obligations. Not only must he look hard at the current fringe picture, but he must also keep up with trends. He must know what each benefit costs and what it does for the employee and the company. Too often the purpose of a benefit is obscured. There are times when a stated goal can be achieved as well with one benefit as with another. The informed personnel man is qualified to recommend to his management the most economical benefit available. Only by keeping his finger on the total pulse can the manager exercise reasonable control and have some measure of assurance that his company is getting a fair return for its money.

The ultimate goal, of course, is to draw maximum value for both the employee and the company out of every benefit dollar spent. Obvious though it may seem, it is well to pose the question: Why does a company give fringe benefits? Needless to say, the moral issue is not the only one involved. Still, a company is obliged to obtain for its people the greatest measure of protection, convenience, and comfort that the benefit dollar can purchase.

At the same time, the manager must keep in mind that, properly applied, the employee extra is a powerful recruiting tool and one way to keep good workers happily and productively rooted.

FRINGE BENEFITS

Exactly what is a fringe benefit? There is wide controversy as to what constitutes an extra and what does not. In 1965, the average employee's slice of the benefit pie as reported by the U.S. Chamber of Commerce came to 25.6 percent of payroll. This adds up to 68.8 cents per payroll hour, or $1,431 a year. But in deference to the dissenters, the Chamber also cites a 30.7 percent and a 38.2 percent figure arrived at by more liberal schools of thought. The most liberal insists that holiday *premium* pay, shift differentials, production bonuses, and the like are valid extras. Opponents do not agree. Other bones of contention include overtime payments, suggestion awards, supplementary unemployment benefits, and workmen's compensation.

Fringe benefits vary from company to company. They range from such basics as vacations and holidays to far-out extras such as art instruction offered free to aspiring Rembrandts, skin diving lessons, and beer breaks. One expert on the subject cited by the Administrative Management Society lists a variety of 127 benefits in existence, with a projection of 200 by 1970. And this excludes the wild and rare ones.

Definition of Fringe Benefit. Fringe benefit definitions are equally diverse. But one that will serve as well as most is: a fringe benefit is any and every labor cost added to regular wages paid for time worked.

Selection of Benefits. The one good way to help ensure that maximum value is derived from benefit dollars spent is to take care that the benefits offered are those which are most important to the employee. This does not always coincide with what the manager feels *should* be most important to the employee. In recognition of this need, there is a growing trend to individualize employee benefits as much as possible. The idea is to structure sufficient flexibility into the plan to permit the employee to exercise a certain amount of selectivity on his own. The concept makes sense to many managers.

The company's retirement plan, for example, may have little meaning to the 20-year-old, but it could be the most important benefit of all to the mature employee. Conversely, a liberal tuition reimbursement program might be extremely attractive to the ambitious youngster, but of little consequence to an employee in his fifties or sixties.

It is thus useful for the administering manager to keep abreast of employee preferences, as well as such factors as age, economic climate, and the like, which cause preferences to change. A study conducted by Mark R. Greene of the University of Oregon pointed up this need. The study used responses to a questionnaire based on a 10 percent sample drawn at random from about 15,000 production workers in the Portland area. Findings showed a number of discrepancies between employee preferences and employer offerings. Table 16-1, drawn from the Oregon study, bears this out.

The right benefit can be a powerful motivator. On occasion, an employee will even settle for a meaningful benefit in lieu of higher wages. A worker in one company with attractive recreational facilities was offered a better job elsewhere at a higher rate of pay. He turned it down. "Give up the country club?" he exclaimed. "I wouldn't think of it."

TYPES OF BENEFITS

A complete description of all benefits would take months of research and require volumes to record. A listing of the principal extras, however, along with a discussion of key points, is worthwhile. It will give the reader a good

TABLE 16-1.   Employee Preferences for Selected Employee Benefits

Benefits	Employee rank	Percent of employees in 111 firms indicating benefit was of great importance	Percent of total firms providing benefit
Insurance benefits:			
Hospitalization insurance.....................	1	79.6	93.2
Doctor bill insurance.........................	2	73.9	94.4
Major medical................................	3	64.8	45.7
Retirement plan (other than social security)......	4	63.5	70.4
Disability income............................	5	61.3	53.7
Accidental death and dismemberment...........	6	58.8	53.1
Group life insurance..........................	7	55.9	70.4
Noninsurance benefits:			
Paid vacation................................	1	87.0	81.5
Paid holidays................................	2	81.0	98.1
Paid sick leave...............................	3	54.1	25.9
Profit-sharing plan...........................	4	42.2	15.4
Credit unions................................	5	38.7	24.1
Paid rest periods, lunch......................	6	38.2	71.0
Other paid leaves............................	7	38.0	46.9
Free medical exams...........................	8	31.0	30.2
Layoff allowances, SUB.......................	9	28.0	11.1
Stock options	10	20.6	8.6
Merchandise discounts........................	11	18.0	55.6

insight into the scope of fringe benefits.   To make the benefits easier to consider and digest, they have been broken down into six main groups:

1. Government-required insurance benefits
2. Employee comfort and protection
3. Employee security
4. Employee pleasure and recreation
5. Employee financial extras
6. Other employee benefits

Government-required Insurance Benefits.   The insurance benefits required by state or Federal law are fairly well known and understood.   They include the following.

Old Age, Survivor's, and Disability Insurance (Social Security).   This takes in the Medicare package funded by increased taxes shared by the employer and employee.   The social security deduction will rise from its 1965 rate of 3.625 percent to 5.65 percent by 1987.

Unemployment Compensation.   Unemployment insurance rates are governed largely by work-force stability.   It may thus be argued that with an improved benefit program, morale goes up and turnover declines, and the insurance rate declines.   The rub, of course, is that the theory only works if the benefit program is improved selectively and in a way that is meaningful to employees.   Only then can a manager hope to use the program as a tool for favorably influencing employee attitudes.

State Disability Insurance.   Says *Modern Office Procedures:* "One-third of your present employees will be either totally or partially disabled before the age of 65."   State disability coverage is, in most cases, minimal.   This spurs insufficiently recuperated workers to return to the job prematurely, often against the doctor's advice. The potential danger of this is obvious: it heightens the accident hazard, lowers efficiency, and, in some cases, jeopardizes the safety of other workers. For these reasons, it may be worthwhile to consider supplementing state disability insurance with private coverage. This should lower the number of compensation claims. Doctor and clerical costs are also reduced. The insurance company administers the plan and uses its own doctors to determine the worker's fitness for returning to the job. And when a worker is disabled, the company need worry only about the wages of his replacement.

Workman's Compensation. Workman's compensation to protect the employee against occupational hazards has long been required by law. It is designed to offset loss of income resulting from disabling accidents and work-connected illness.

Employee Comfort and Protection. In most industries, a company's insurance program has a strong bearing on its recruitment efforts, its ability to keep good employees, and its success at maintaining a reasonably high level of productivity. One conclusion drawn from the University of Oregon study is that a company with a low rate of employee turnover stands about twice the chance of having a program of good insurance benefits as a company with high turnover. Important benefits in the "comfort and protection" category include:

Group hospitalization	Salary continuation plans
Major medical plans	Dental insurance
Group life insurance	Home nursing care
Group accident insurance	Optical insurance
Travel insurance	Psychiatric care
Death allowance	Weather allowance
Supplementary disability insurance	Sick pay

Statistics released in the Administrative Management Society's 1965–1966 salary survey are of particular interest to managers who administer benefit plans. The study covered 600,172 clerical workers in 8,486 American and Canadian companies. Some of the highlights relating to insurance benefits are shown by Table 16-2.

Even if the employee pays for the total insurance himself, he is still receiving a benefit, because he is permitted to take advantage of the lower group rate arranged for by the company. As the AMS figures reveal, most companies pay all or part of the cost. But there is much to be said for the contributory plan. Says one expert: "There's nothing like giving the worker a vested interest

TABLE 16-2. Allocation of Insurance Benefit Costs

Insurance benefit	Percent of companies providing benefit	Percent of companies paying full premium cost	Percent of companies sharing premium cost with employees	Percent of companies where employee pays full premium cost
Group life insurance..............	89	45	55	
Health insurance.................	97	41	50	9
Medical surgical insurance........	96	41	50	9

in his benefit. It causes him to view what he gets in an entirely different light than if he were getting it for free."

Employee Security. Pension benefits take on ever-increasing importance at labor-management bargaining tables across the nation. Settlement of more than one contract has hinged, for example, on the palatability of a retirement plan.

Of special importance to the manager is a consideration of the long-range effects of each fringe benefit on labor costs. A pension plan, for example, has to be funded. The company's contribution depends on the ages and number of employees covered. Once the actuary calculates the amount, it becomes a fixed yearly cost, variable according to the annual inventory of insured workers.

In considering pensions, or for that matter any fringe benefits, too many companies fail to plan far enough ahead. As a company develops and grows, its complexion changes. New skills are needed, and different categories of personnel. It is not enough to consider only the employees on hand when the benefit is introduced, or even those projected five years thereafter. Once a benefit is built into a program, it is difficult to take it out without causing serious morale repercussions. Before implementing a benefit, it makes good sense to consider what its impact will be twenty years later.

Another point to consider in planning a benefit program is the desirability of providing a plan that will continue insurance coverage for retired employees. This is a particularly attractive feature for many workers, and one that is offered by a number of companies.

The pension plan is one of the most popular ways to provide security for workers. It is best set up in collaboration with competent legal and insurance advisers. Under most plans, the company takes a predetermined amount of its annual earnings as an income tax deduction. This money is shuttled to the pension fund. Management of the fund is controlled by a set of clearly defined corporate rules, permitting investment in specified types of securities. It is thus possible to appreciate a well-managed fund to the point where the company's annual contribution may be reduced or even eliminated entirely.

Pensions and retirement plans are, of course, widely used to encourage valued employees to stay with the company. But one pitfall should be of special concern to the benefits manager. Some plans are powerful motivators indeed— so much so that they cause people to cling to their jobs although they are desperately anxious to make a change. These employees are apt to feel trapped. They become bitter and nonproductive. In such cases, the plan is self-defeating. A generous plan may have an obvious and positive bearing on the reduction of employee turnover, but it offers no guarantee that this reduction is always desirable. In short, even the best pension plan is no adequate substitute for a strong program which produces able supervisors, develops employees, and stimulates job interest and satisfaction.

Employee Pleasure and Recreation. This category of benefits, perhaps more than any other, is responsible for rising fringe costs. The biggest amount goes for vacations, holidays, and rest periods. Here are the major items that contribute to an easier, more pleasant, and more relaxed life for the majority of American employees:

Vacations	Personal time off
Holidays	Wash-up time
Rest periods	Recreation programs
Sabbaticals	Lounge or cafeteria facilities

One of the most substantial and certainly the most popular of all benefits is the paid vacation. Every employee should have at least a week off sometime during the year, however urgent his services may be. This is often essential to his good health and well-being. He returns to work renewed and refreshed. More than one company has come to realize that the policy of paying an employee for vacation time not taken is self-defeating.

This is particularly true of managers and supervisors. Getting away from his job for a week or two gives a man a new perspective. And it gives his boss instructive insights into the operation. It helps in furnishing answers to these key questions: Does the department or function run smoothly in the supervisor's absence? Is he playing the role of indispensable man, keeping his knowledge locked up? Or is he conscientiously developing subordinates—training them to pinch-hit for him in his absence?

Also growing is the practice of giving employees a freer hand in selecting their preferred vacation time. The trend is to go along with vacations split between summer and winter, or to accommodate people who prefer to take one week in a lump and the balance of their vacation in Fridays or Mondays.

Holidays. In general, companies in Europe, Canada, and our neighbors to the south grant more holidays than we do. Twenty-seven percent of the American companies responding to the AMS clerical salary survey grant six paid holidays. But, says the survey, the policy of granting seven paid holidays is gaining in popularity. And reports show that some union contracts provide for eight or more.

It is good business and good employee relations for a company to spell out in writing the conditions under which an employee is eligible for holiday pay. Must he be on the job at least thirty days? Must he work a specified time before and after a holiday? These questions must be carefully considered and a clear-cut policy must be established and communicated to all employees. The specific day off should also be made clear well in advance. In most cases, if the holiday falls on a weekend, the paid day off is either Friday or Monday. Another area of consideration is the employee who is required to work on a paid holiday. For example, if Saturday work calls for pay at the time-and-a-half rate, the employee who works on a Saturday that is also a paid holiday would normally be entitled to two-and-a-half times his contractual wages for time put in on this day.

The Rest Period. The rest period is a deceptively expensive fringe benefit. It should be carefully considered in accounting for indirect labor costs. The question which often comes up is whether to establish a single rest period for all employees of a company or department or to arrange for staggered rest periods. Where a continuous production facility—such as an assembly line—is in operation, there may be no choice but to declare a one-time period for the whole crew. But where the situation permits, staggered breaks, if properly supervised, are usually more efficient and economical.

In one company, the taking of extended breaks became a serious discipline problem. Periodic campaigns were launched to tighten up on the procedure. But when the clamp-down wore off, old habits were resumed. Finally, a manager had an idea. Employees were presented with the option of foregoing the afternoon break and getting instead a half day off once a month. Most of the workers jumped at the offer, and the company benefited substantially.

Sabbaticals. A fringe benefit that has advantages to both the company and the employee involved is the granting of paid sabbaticals to executive or middle management personnel. These individuals are "loaned" to the community to head up worthwhile programs or to chair civic betterment committees. This is good public and community relations. It helps build the corporate image. It fosters the enthusiastic cooperation of local officials. At the same time, it provides managers with excellent organizational experience, gives them a broader perspective on the functions and responsibilities of a corporation, and in general helps to develop them along desired lines.

Recreation. The well-planned recreational facility can be a powerful and meaningful employee relations tool. It gives workers a chance to relax together and strengthen rapport. Rank-and-file workers get to meet their superiors and workers from other departments socially and to know them better. Often, teamwork attitudes developed on the bowling lanes or the ball field are automatically carried forward to the job. A good program also serves to develop unsuspected talents and personality traits of potential value to the company.

In spite of their merit, however, company-sponsored recreational activities can easily mushroom out of proportion. One company's employees organized a baseball team on their own. They then appealed to the plant manager for financial support. Uniforms and other expensive equipment were furnished. For a while, enthusiasm ran high. Then the team joined an industrial league. After being badly beaten in five straight games, the fervor declined. Bickering broke out among the players, and the team dissolved. If anything, the long-range effect of the venture was negative.

One good way to provide a strong recreational program is to make it self-supporting. In one large company, the "country club" was voted by more than half the employees as the most popular noninsurance benefit. The club was more than 75 percent self-supporting. For a small membership fee, the employees played golf (without waiting), bowled, and played billiards and pool. To help defray operating costs, they ran occasional dances. At specified times, outsiders were permitted to use facilities at standard rates.

Employee Financial Benefits. The push for more time off, more conveniences, and increased insurance protection has taken no edge off the appeal of increased financial extras. This holds true even though the extra is often in the form of "futures." Some of the more popular financial benefits offered by American companies are:

Profit-sharing plan	Severance pay
Stock purchase program	Service awards
Bonuses and awards	Credit union
Purchase allowances	Company loans
Low-cost meals	Free parking
Paid lunch periods	Extra-shift differential
Low-cost housing	Work clothes and laundering
Free transportation	Travel pay

Profit Sharing. One company president fixes its sharp upswing in profits at the month that its profit-sharing plan was started. The plan was designed to replace the annual bonus system that had been in existence for years. "In the past," says this executive, "employees merely partook of the fruits of profit. Now they participate in the creation."

Depending on the plan's objective, profit sharing may take a variety of forms: (1) outright cash payment at Christmastime; (2) cash payment at the end of the fiscal year; (3) stock offered at a reduced price; or (4) deferred plan, with funds set aside for the future.

The deferred plan is one of the most popular. It offers advantages to employer and employee. Like the pension, it helps to satisfy the employee's need for security and so reduces turnover. It gives the worker a chance to build up his net worth without adding to his current tax burden. When he is taxed, it is at the capital gains rate. And from the employer's standpoint, he, too, can cash in on a tax advantage by expensing the profit-plan deduction. It should be stressed, however, that the constantly changing tax situation could have a marked effect on the profit plan. In setting up and maintaining such an arrangement, it is wise to work with legal and financial counsel.

Executive Sweets. Executive benefits and executive compensation are closely interwoven. The subject covers a variety of plans. Profit sharing is one. There are also stock option and purchase plans, pension and retirement plans, insurance plans, and many more. One important objective, of course, is to defer income to the executive's later and less-productive years and thus cut down on the current tax liability. Here again is a program to be considered in consultation with qualified legal and financial advisers.

Another benefit of special concern to the executive—though not always admittedly so—is the so-called status symbol. One company's top-producing advertising director resigned unexpectedly. The reason came out later. He had felt that, compared with those of his peers, his office was too small and shabbily furnished. This led him to believe he was not part of the "inner circle." A similar case occurred in another company where a research chief quit in a huff when denied a company car. The financial consideration was not an issue, a subordinate confided later. It was a question of status. Others got cars; why not he? In his eyes, the fact that some of his associates had more job-related justification for a car did not diminish his assumed "loss of face."

Bonuses, Gifts, Awards. The practice of handing out merchandise gifts should be carefully evaluated. One company gave all its workers Christmas turkeys at the end of a year when profits were high. The gesture did more to undermine, than improve, morale. Says one industrial relations manager: "In my view, giving away anything less than a $25 savings bond to office people or supervisors at Christmastime is worse than giving nothing at all." In some major corporations where morale is notably high, the practice is to give nothing at all.

The cash bonus, although considered by some experts to be less effective than incentive or profit-sharing awards, is still superior to the merchandise gift in many cases. One simple way to arrive at bonus amounts is by the point system. An employee is credited with one point for each month of service. He is credited another point for each $10 pay increment. The company then establishes a dollar value for a single bonus point. Next, by mathematically calculating the earned service of all employees along with their income, it is a simple matter to determine the total bonus dollars to be awarded and to calculate each employee's share. A system of this type eliminates the tiresome and sensitive problem of arriving at individual bonuses each year.

An important incentive tool, and for some companies a prime source of money-making ideas, is the suggestion system. Improperly managed, however, a suggestion system can cause more problems than it solves. More than one system has been known to backfire because of employee disgruntlement when management failed to respond enthusiastically to a proposed idea to make a fast million.

The key to effective idea stimulation lies in a good communications effort. The program should be well publicized. Winners should receive recognition from top management, preferably the president. And most important in the suggestion program is the follow-up procedure. If an idea is rejected, the employee should be told why in clear and logical terms. Management, and line supervisors in particular, should express appreciation for all ideas, good or bad. And, accepted or not, follow-up notification should be as quick as possible. It is particularly frustrating and demoralizing for an employee to take the time and trouble to work up an idea and muster the courage to present it, only to see it die a slow and unaccountable death in committee.

Service Awards. The service recognition program can play an important role in the stimulation of employee loyalty and "family" pride. The usual practice is for the long-term worker to receive a service pin together with a cash or other tangible award as he reaches appropriate milestones in his career. An annual ceremony is generally arranged for this purpose. A growing trend is to increase gradually the amount of the award as each milestone is achieved. In one company, employees get a $50 bond after five years of service. This builds to $300 by the time the thirty-year mark is reached.

Other Employee Benefits. This category is a catchall for benefits ranging from tuition reimbursement to a variety of counseling services such as retirement advice and insurance help. Before World War II, in most companies, the number of such extras could have been counted on the fingers of one hand. Twenty years later, they were commonplace. The following list, although incomplete, will provide a fairly representative sampling:

Educational aid	Rack booklet program
Military leave allowance	Savings bond plan
Company-paid subscriptions	Open house
Company car	Free flu shots
Voting time	Free counseling
Medical supplies	Jury duty
Medical exams	Grievance and negotiating time
Meetings (not job-related)	

Education. Educational aid quite justifiably heads the list. It is cited by personnel executives as one of the most powerful recruiting and development tools. A special Administrative Management Society study of the educational policies of 448 firms shows most tuition refund plans to be liberal. Of the 448 firms, 410 provide this benefit, often by outright payment of tuition costs. In many cases, books and materials are also paid for. But there is one important proviso. Only 23 of the 410 companies stated that the course taken need have no relationship to the employee's job.

When is the cash actually paid? Usually *after* the course is completed. And some companies will pay only if a passing grade is obtained.

Open House. Many companies set aside a day from time to time to bring the family into the plant to observe where and how "Pop"—or in some cases, "Mom"—works. In addition to being an employee fringe benefit, the open house is also a useful public relations and employee relations tool. It enables the family and the community to identify more closely with the company. It instills greater job pride in employees. "And," says one practical-minded marketing executive, "in some instances it helps to boost sales."

The well-planned open house affair is a warm and festive occasion, often accompanied by refreshments and small gifts for the visitors. Some companies schedule the open house at Christmastime, in combination with, or in lieu of, the Christmas party.

ADMINISTERING THE BENEFIT PROGRAM

Cost Considerations and Mergers. One effective way to evaluate fringe benefits is to assign a percentage of payroll value to each extra. This makes it fairly simple to compare one benefit with another. Expanding the concept, when companies are merged, it is easy to compare the benefits of the parent company with the ones granted by the acquired firm.

Needless to say, when a merger is consummated, the fringe benefit cost becomes a vital factor. More than one merger deal has fallen through because of it. In general, the trend is toward uniformity. There is much to be said for bringing the extras of the acquired firm up to the standard of those offered by the larger company. This becomes especially desirable if it is likely that employees will move from one company to the other.

The main goal in revising an acquired company's benefit program is to maintain its competitive position. Thus, as a general practice, any obvious reduction of extras could prove to be false economy. In fact, as one company learned, not only should benefits in general be held to previous levels or made better, but particular care should be paid to specific benefits. This company acquired a smaller firm. To make the program uniform, the benefits of the acquired company were revised upward by more than 10 percent. Incongruously, however, the vacation allowance turned out to be slightly less favorable. The ill will created as a result served in large measure to offset the effect of the gains.

It is also significant to note that although uniformity of benefits is often desirable, this is not always the case. One large company, in making an acquisition, was on the verge of following its policy of standardization. But in this case, the acquisition was in a new and unrelated field. Closer study showed that the industry practice in the new field was to grant much lower benefits than the parent company's field. It was decided that increasing the acquired company's benefits out of proportion with the rest of the industry would result in a considerable expense with no proportionate return. The uniformity rule was broken in this case, and thousands of dollars were saved. Industry benefit fluctuations warrant the manager's thoughful consideration. The U.S. Chamber of Commerce reports that they vary from an average of 20.2 percent in the textile industry to 32.9 percent for banks, finance, and trust companies.

The Need to Publicize Benefits. One company's chief officer went along with a proposal to broaden the scope of the pension program. But he did so grudgingly, with this comment: "The average employee dips into the benefit grab bag without a second thought. He doesn't have the least idea what is being done for him." This pretty well sums up a wide segment of executive sentiment. Benefit programs impose a staggering burden on most companies. Employee misunderstandings and indifference only add salt to the wound.

This holds especially true for older firms where negative attitudes are more deep-rooted, according to the University of Oregon study. And the Management Information Center in Deerfield, Illinois, points out that 78 percent of organized companies claim that unions get most of the credit for company-paid extras. This puts the employer, the MIC survey states, in the unhappy position of spending a lot of money in behalf of its unions. Yet, only one-third of the companies appear to be doing anything about it.

What can a company do about it? It can publicize its benefits program, for one thing. The publicity effort should keep two objectives in mind: (1) make sure employees understand what they are getting and why; (2) make sure they are kept informed of who is paying the bill. The importance of these objectives is stressed by the comment of one company's personnel vice president:

It's amazing how many people aren't even aware that certain benefits exist. Others are fuzzy about some of the most significant and costly benefits offered. Major medical insurance, pensions, and disability coverage are good examples. Some employees don't know the employer pays for unemployment insurance. Some believe that the granting of vacation, holidays, and even rest periods, is a legal requirement.

Robert E. Sibson, a New York consultant, in urging companies to make a continuing effort on all fronts to get across the benefits story, suggests this triple-barreled approach:
1. Use the payroll check stub to its full potential.
2. Include the benefits story repeatedly in company literature.
3. Equip line supervisors to carry the message.

No document is more closely scrutinized than the paycheck. At virtually no additional cost, the check stub can be made to double as a powerful communications tool. It should include, in addition to a figure spelling out each deduction, the purpose of the benefit and who is paying for it.

The booklet explaining the company's benefits program in fast-moving and easy-to-read language is another highly effective way to increase benefits awareness and appreciation among employees. The following techniques of distribution serve to broaden and sharpen the effect of this useful communications medium:
1. Booklets should be mailed to the home where exposure is expanded to the whole family.
2. Benefit information should be updated annually or every eighteen months, and a new mailing sent out.
3. A benefits booklet should be given to each new employee when he is hired.
4. Foremen and supervisors should have a supply of booklets in a convenient place so they are available if employees ask for them and as a reference source when questions arise.

Newsletters, posters, and the company publication are also helpful in putting across the benefits story. And according to *The Conference Board Record,* it is a story employees want to have told. A recent survey showed that 85 percent of the workers interviewed desired more information about their benefits. The story should be told over and over again. Otherwise, it is soon forgotten.

The most effective of all communicators is the line supervisor. Special pains should be taken to make sure, first, that all supervisors have a complete understanding of all benefits, and insurance-type extras in particular. Second, supervisors should be encouraged to keep employees informed, both at regular meetings and at informal exchanges. Third, the climate should be such that rank-and-file workers are encouraged to come to their supervisors with benefit questions and problems.

CONCLUSION

There is one unfortunate truism tied to fringes. It involves the law of diminishing returns, and it is applicable even where the best communications program with the most expertly administered setup is in force. The problem is that as each benefit is more broadly used and more widely accepted as "standard operating procedure," the degree of employee appreciation fades. An employee may be grateful for a three-week vacation, because he knows he is not automatically entitled to a three-week vacation. But he is not likely to appreciate a vacation per se, because just about everyone gets some kind of vacation. The same holds true for holidays, sick leave, rest periods, and all other fringes.

BIBLIOGRAPHY

Allen, Donna, *Fringe Benefits: Wages or Social Obligation?* Cornell University Press, Ithaca, N.Y., 1964.

Annual Clerical Salary Survey (U.S. and Canada), 1965–66, Administrative Management Society, Willow Grove, Pa.

Backman, Jules, *Wage Determination: An Analysis of Wage Criteria,* D. Van Nostrand Company, Inc., Princeton, N.J., 1959.

Belcher, D. W., *Wage and Salary Administration,* 2d ed., Prentice-Hall, Inc., Englewood Cliffs, N.J., 1962.

Fringe Benefits, U.S. Chamber of Commerce, Washington, D.C., biennial report.

Greene, Mark R., *The Role of Employee Benefit Structures in Manufacturing Industry,* School of Business Administration, University of Oregon, Eugene, 1964.

CHAPTER SEVENTEEN

Supervisory Compensation

ROBERT E. SIBSON   *President, Sibson & Company, Inc., New York, New York*

The first rule of sound supervisory compensation is to recognize that supervisors are also employees. This means that they are concerned about equitable pay in relation to others in the company; they seek pay which is competitive with respect to those doing comparable work in other companies; and they expect reasonable pay progress. This, in turn, means that sound principles of compensation must be applied to supervisors as well as to any other group of employees within the company.

Supervisory duties differ in some significant ways from the duties of management, professional, administrative, sales, technical, office, or factory positions. The nature of their duties, the conditions under which work must be accomplished, and the climate surrounding the work comprise the basic reasons that some special compensation methods and techniques need to be applied to supervisory positions.

This chapter presents some special methods and practices. The presentation of these, however, should not cloud the fact that the essential principles and proper practices of salary administration are the real key to sound compensation for supervisors as well as for any other group of employees.

THE SUPERVISORY GROUP

The key to special methods and practices of compensation for any group is to be found in the nature of the job. Therefore, it is first necessary to define the supervisory group and identify positions and persons covered.

The Supervisory Group Defined. As used here, "supervisors" are basically those who supervise nonsupervisory employees. Specifically, the supervisory group is characterized by the following:

They are one, or at the most two, organization levels removed from nonsupervisory employees.

They must have considerable administrative and operational knowledge of, and an involvement in, the work of nonsupervisory persons, even though they may seldom or never do the same work.

They generally have at least 3 and no more than 100 total subordinates.

They have genuine supervisory authority in the traditional "hire or fire" sense, rather than functioning merely as group leaders.

They generally do not have total accountability for an operation. For example, the factory supervisor typically does not have responsibility for methods of work or for work standards.

Careful definition of the supervisory group is more than an interesting academic exercise. It is the practical first step for a company in building a sound personnel program for supervisory persons, including a sound supervisory compensation program.

Types of Supervisors. To complicate matters, there are at least three types of supervisors in many companies. Compensation practices, as well as personnel administration generally, must reflect or at least accommodate all three types of supervisors where they exist. For convenience, we will call them supervisory types X, Y, and Z.

The X supervisor is the classic type whose activities almost exclusively involve work assignment, scheduling, training, correcting, and generally controlling the work of nonsupervisory employees. He is the qualified, experienced supervisor who has usually come up through the ranks or has had work experience comparable to the type of operation he is now supervising. He is well versed in the mechanics and techniques of the operation. Those who fill the supervisor X mold, however, have about reached their business zenith and are not likely to receive significant promotions in the future.

The Y supervisor is the exact opposite of X. Y supervisors generally fill the same type of position as X supervisors. The difference is in their personal background. Generally Y is the bright young man who is getting supervisory experience and broadening for future management responsibilities. In all probability, he has never performed any of the operations which he supervises. Furthermore, he will probably not be in the position very long, but is passing through on his way to bigger and better jobs.

The Z supervisor is a person who is primarily a technician and secondarily a supervisor. Most of his time is spent doing things himself, and his first value is as a professional. Those supervised are either other professionals over whom he exercises essentially administrative guidance and control, or technicians who assist him in performing his own professional work.

Supervisory Types and Pay Practices. The X supervisor is paid primarily for the performance of his subordinates. His salary is administered within a range which is related to the scope of operations which he supervises. The Y supervisor, however, is paid primarily for personal worth and long-term potential. He might actually be paid far in excess of the maximum of the position he now holds. The Z supervisor's responsibilities must certainly be considered in his overall compensation, but the primary focus must be on his professional capabilities and his professional accomplishments.

There was a time when 99 percent of all supervisory positions would tend to fit the X model. In the modern business environment, however, there are probably more Y- and Z-type supervisors than X types. Furthermore, the trend is for more and more supervisors in the Y and Z mold and for those who still fit the X category to assume more and more of the characteristics of the

Y or the Z model.   Unfortunately, most thinking and practices in compensation fit only the X supervisor.

FACTORS AFFECTING SUPERVISORY PAY LEVELS

The second step in developing a sound supervisory compensation program is to identify the major factors which affect supervisory pay levels.   These factors will vary from company to company by type of operation and, to some extent, by geographic locations.   The general factors outlined here must, therefore, be viewed from the individual company situation and modified where appropriate.

X Supervisory Pay Levels.   Administrative and market forces affect, to some extent, the pay of all supervisory positions.   In supervisor X positions, however, administrative decisions generally have far more impact than market forces.

Market forces are generally not very strong, because the "market" for X supervisors is so often the supervised, or those with technical and operational knowledge in the immediate geographic area, or supervisors from other company locations.   The absence of strong market pressures plus the intermediate position of supervisory jobs between the management and the nonmanagement groups makes the administrative factors such as job evaluation, merit pay practices, and internal pay comparisons the dominant determinants of pay levels for supervisor X positions.

The easiest and most practical internal pay comparison for supervisory X positions is the relationship of pay between the supervisor and his subordinates. Inadequate differentials between a supervisor and his highest-paid subordinates cause obvious inequities—obvious to the supervisor as well as to the company. Inequities may also create one of those absurd situations where a candidate cannot afford to take a "promotion" to a supervisory position.

Two general rules apply to supervisor-subordinate base pay relationship:

1. Under job evaluation, the supervisor pay grades should be at least two levels higher than the highest-rated subordinate position.   In practice, there is usually a 3 to 5 pay grade difference.

2. The supervisor's base pay should be at least 15 percent higher than the earnings (excluding overtime, but including shift differentials and incentive earnings) of the three highest-paid subordinate positions.

Various studies indicate that base pay differentials between the supervisor and the three highest-paid subordinates average closer to 25 percent.   Like most averages, however, the actual differentials vary from a minus figure to over 100 percent.

For model X supervisors, there are also some gross pay guides.   As a general rule:

1. The supervisor's gross pay should be no less than 10 percent more than the three highest-paid subordinates.

2. The gross pay should be no less than 25 percent more than the average gross pay of all subordinates.

3. The gross pay of the supervisor should be no more than 75 percent over the gross pay of all immediate subordinates.

There are other factors which affect supervisory pay levels to a lesser degree than those already indicated.   Geographic differentials exist to some degree, because many supervisors are at an income level where community living costs must be taken into consideration.   The economic characteristics of the industry will also have some impact.   The better-paid supervisor on this basis tends

TABLE 17-1. Average Annual Salary Increase Percent*

Type of position	Age bracket		
	Under 30	30 to 45	Over 45
Supervisor Y...............	10 %	15 %	Not applicable
Supervisor X...............	5	4	3 %
Middle management.........	15	10	5
Professional................	12	8	5

* Includes pay increases for any and all purposes and reflects averages of widely varying amounts, including those not receiving any increase at all.

to be in industries where labor costs are a low percentage of total costs. Whether "merited" or not, age and length of service also have a measurable effect upon supervisory pay levels.

Y Supervisory Pay Levels. By the nature of model Y supervisory positions, the primary determinants of pay are related more to the individual than to the position. Studies are not available which would give a factual basis for indicating the primary determinants of pay levels for supervisory Y types. However, observation of the practices of a number of companies, as well as logic, would tend to indicate that the primary determinant of pay levels for such supervisors is the pay level and pay progress of their contemporaries both within the company and in other organizations. Companies make considerable investment in such supervisors, so it is a first objective to keep their progress, in terms of both job challenge and income, attractive enough so that they are satisfied. In fact, some companies consciously overpay Y supervisors to protect their investment. Some large companies have actually formalized this practice into what they call "advanced compensation practices," which, for the bright young man just starting his career, is what deferred compensation is for the top executive nearing retirement.

Pay progress of Y-type supervisors is quite rapid. The data given in Table 17-1[1] provide a general guide and are contrasted with typical pay progress of supervisor X and other types of positions.

Z Supervisory Pay Levels. In supervisory Z positions, market forces play the dominant role. The market is neither a geographic nor a competitor company market, but rather a professional or a functional field-of-activity market. As a result, although companies attempt, with some success, to administer the salaries of supervisory Z employees (as well as nonsupervisory professional persons), they must recognize that the market forces are dominant. This means in practice that broad-based surveys, such as those of the Executive Compensation Service of the American Management Association, or special professional surveys must be referred to frequently to determine the proper level of pay for Z supervisory positions.

[1] This table and other data included in this chapter are based on accumulated statistics in client assignments of Sibson & Company, Inc., and surveys conducted in connection with these assignments. Because of the confidential nature of the data, they cannot be broken down on a company, industry, or occupational basis. It is strongly recommended that the data be used for information purposes only, or as a broad guide. *The author is not recommending use of these data but is merely reporting what happens.*

JOB EVALUATION METHODS

Administrative forces thus have some impact upon all supervisory positions and have particular importance with respect to the X model supervisors. Because of this, administrative methods such as job evaluation must not only embody excellent techniques, but also be characterized by excellence in administration.

Job Descriptions. Probably 90 percent of all supervisory positions (except those in quite small companies) are covered by some form of position descriptions. In most cases, position descriptions have been used by companies for many years.

Unfortunately, the position descriptions used for supervisory positions are seldom completely adequate for supervisory X-type positions and are usually inadequate in important respects for other supervisory positions. The basic reason for this is that the position description writing has not been geared to the nature of the position which it attempts to describe. Frequently, for instance, the description form and format are merely the same as used for production or office positions and do not contain some of the information necessary to truly understand and therefore measure the relative value of supervisory positions.

There are two basic rules which should apply to the writing of any position description, and these apply to supervisory positions as well. The first rule is that the description should be written primarily for the purpose of communicating to the supervisors and other interested persons the scope and nature of the responsibilities assigned. The second is that they be clearly written. The basic requirement of position description writing is clear, direct English. One of the best position description manuals ever written is *Elements of Style* by William Strunk, Jr., and E. B. White.[2]

In addition to an outlining of responsibilities, however, there are certain areas of information which must be identified and described in supervisor X positions to understand the positions and correctly assess relative job value. These areas include:

Scope data, such as number of persons supervised, value of accountable resources or assets, number of transactions, budgets, confidential data, and any other indicators which are pertinent to the specific job

Importance of various duties, and possibly their relationship to the goals and objectives of the business

Latitude of action, or the authority to act

Relationships with others inside or outside the company, including frequency, level, and nature of contacts

Climate, which includes those intangibles such as rate of technological change, whether an activity is being developed or maintained, and conditions of the job which are unique

Goals and objectives of the job, including any specific targets, standards, or expectations

Supervisor Y positions can be similarly described and analyzed. The incumbent's pay, however, may not be related to that job. In supervisor Z positions, the outline of some duties must be described in a generic fashion, rather than functionally.[3]

[2] William Strunk, Jr., and E. B. White, *Elements of Style,* The Macmillan Company, New York, 1959.

[3] R. E. Sibson, *Wages and Salaries,* chap. 7, American Management Association, New York, 1960, pp. 168–169.

Job Evaluation Plans. With regard to job evaluation programs, covering supervisory positions, it should first be noted that it is seldom desirable to have a special evaluation system exclusively for supervisory employees. Second, it is obviously necessary that the usual standards of a sound job evaluation system should cover supervisory persons as well as any other group.[4]

The plan which is applied to supervisory positions should first be geared to the system or systems used to measure management, administrative, and professional positions, rather than the system or systems used to measure the relative value of positions in the nonexempt groups. The plan should also serve to make distinctions among supervisory positions as well as among supervisory and other positions.

So far as supervisory positions are concerned, the job evaluation plan need not be complex. No more than six factors are necessary to measure the relative worth of supervisory positions, for instance, and no more than five degrees within any of these factors will cover the scope of relative value under each factor for supervisory positions.

Salary Structure. Probably 90 percent of all supervisory positions (except those in very small companies) are classified into a pay range, with a minimum and a maximum pay value established for each pay range. There are no special characteristics of pay structures which apply to supervisory positions. Rather, the basic principles of sound structure which apply to positions of comparable pay levels are equally applicable to the supervisory position. As a general rule, for instance, the progression from one pay grade to another should be no less than 8 percent and no more than 12 percent; and the spread within a range from minimum to maximum should be no less than 30 percent and generally no more than 40 percent.

SALARY INCREASES

Almost all companies report some form of merit increase program for supervisory employees, although how much the increases really reflect merit and how much of a program is really involved is questionable.

Size of Pay Increases. Pay increases for supervisor X positions are more closely related in terms of amount, form, and procedure with the pay increase program for nonsupervisory employees than for management, professional, and administrative employees.

Merit increases for supervisor X employees from 1960 to 1965, for instance, averaged a little over 4 percent. Probably little more than 1 percent of this was based on improvements in performance.

This figure is very close to the amount granted to nonsupervisory employees and is about half the amount granted in the same companies to management, executive, administrative, and professional employees during the five-year period.

Frequency of Increases. Approximately 80 percent of all supervisory employees receive increases each year. Table 17-2 provides a general guide with respect to actual practice, contrasted with practice for other types of positions. The company which seeks to inject more performance motivation into supervisory compensation should aim at a distribution more like that actually reported for other exempt groups.

Distribution of Increases. In practice, about 80 percent of the increases for supervisors were the same, or about the same. Among the companies studied,

---

[4] All job evaluation plans should be tailored to the individual company, be geared to the marketplace, serve as a guide to management decisions, and be understood by those affected by the plan.

TABLE 17-2.   Frequency of Merit Pay Increases*

Type of position	Percent of cases where frequency was:				
	Less than 6 months	6 months to 1 year	About 1 year	1 to 2 years	Over 2 years
Supervisor X..................	Nil	5	80	10	5
Supervisor Y..................	10	25	65	Nil	Nil
Supervisor Z..................	5	15	70	10	Nil
Professional..................	5	15	70	10	Nil
Middle management............	Nil	5	50	30	15
Nonexempt....................	10	15	60	10	5

* Rounded to 5 percent; "average" is for each group.

this was about the same distribution of increases as for nonsupervisory employees. About one-fourth of all companies grant general increases to supervisory employees. The amount of the general increase is typically very close to the amount of general increase granted to the employees they supervise. As shown in Table 17-3, even in companies that do not officially grant general increases to supervisors, there is relatively little differentiation in the percent increases granted to most supervisor X employees.

Even in those companies that have merit increase programs for supervisors, the amount of any general increase granted to supervisory employees is considered when merit increases are given. The increase of the supervised generally becomes the floor for supervisory increase. This, of course, is necessary to preserve the pay relationships between supervisors and those supervised.

Pay Increase Practices. With respect to administrative procedures for reviewing and controlling increases granted to supervisory employees, the practices in most companies are more closely related to practices for the nonsupervisory employees than to those for management and professional people. One study, for instance, indicated that about three-fourths of the companies studied set definite minimums and maximums of merit increases which could be granted to supervisory employees. These minimums and maximums were a relatively

TABLE 17-3.   Patterns of Distribution of Merit Pay Increases*

Type of position	Over 20% more than A†	To 20% more than A	About A	To 20% less than A	Over 20% less than A
Supervisor X..................	5	5	80	5	5
Supervisor Y..................	15	10	50	15	10
Supervisor Z..................	10	20	40	20	10
Professional..................	10	20	40	20	10
Middle management............	15	15	4	15	15
Nonexempt....................	5	5	80	5	5

* Rounded to 5%; "average" is for each group.
† A is average increase for all supervisors in the group.

small range. This is in sharp contrast to the more typical practice of salary administration for management and professional employees.

These are the basic and summary facts of salary practices for supervisory persons. They are not recommendations, but rather a reporting of what happens generally. Like most average statistics, they certainly do not indicate universal practice. Specific practices in individual companies vary a great deal. Also, experiences with a number of companies indicate that all too often the actual practices reflect tradition and what is considered necessary, rather than management policy or objectives.

MERIT PAY ADMINISTRATION

Many top management groups seek to inject more incentive into pay practices by gearing increases to differences in performance. They recognize that the absence of true performance considerations in pay decisions reduces the incentive for supervisors to perform to the best of their abilities. They also recognize that to the extent that supervisors are treated the same as nonsupervisory persons, the supervisor will tend to think and act less like a manager and identify himself more and more with the supervised. Studies conducted to determine the means of injecting more merit differentiations into supervisory compensation, and to bring supervisory compensation practice more in line with policies and practices for management and professional persons, indicate that there are certain basic conditions which must exist before any meaningful progress can be made.

The first requirement is that the supervisory jobs be so organized that significant responsibility and decision-making authority are built into the position. In other words, the positions must be more management oriented before management salary practices can reasonably be applied. Also, unless this is done, the resulting evaluation level will not be sufficient to permit meaningful differentiations based upon performance or anything else.

Having built a more substantive management position, the second requirement is to staff the position with persons who can assume such responsibilities and to make sure that the incumbents have sufficient training to do this job well.

The third basic requirement is that methods of observing and measuring performance be established.

Once these three basic requirements have been met, it is then possible to establish supervisory positions at pay levels which make meaningful differentiations based upon performance possible, without creating pay relationship problems with those supervised. Only then can a true merit program be put into effect for supervisors.

OVERTIME COMPENSATION FOR SUPERVISORS

The question of overtime compensation for supervisors is one of the most difficult and most constantly recurring problems in the area of supervisory compensation. In companies where the work force supervised is required to work more than casual or intermittent overtime, it is a very practical problem. The extra compensation received by the work force can result in inequitable gross pay relationships between the supervisor and the supervised unless the supervisor also receives some extra compensation. In companies where the supervisor, by the nature of operations, must be at work essentially the same amount of time as those he supervises, there is also the problem of expecting the supervisor to come to work without being paid.

Faced with this problem, there are a number of alternative solutions. No one of these alternatives is ideal for all company situations. We can only outline here the alternatives and suggest some of the advantages and disadvantages of each.

No Overtime Pay. One alternative is to do nothing. Probably one-third of all companies do not, in any way, pay overtime or extra compensation for supervisors for overtime work. In a survey of company practices, companies which pay nothing to supervisors for overtime work listed the following reasons for such a policy:

Concern about administrative or other types of problems which they think would result

Belief that there are other values in the supervisory positions and that these other values, such as status, adequately compensate supervisors

Concern that the payment of overtime compensation for supervisors might, in fact, motivate supervisors to work themselves and their departments longer hours merely to gain the extra compensation

Supervisors' acceptance of the resulting situation

The fact that little overtime is worked by nonsupervisory persons, and thus, there is no problem

Although few like to say it, some companies do not pay extra compensation for supervisors because this will save them some payroll costs. Undoubtedly this results in significant payroll savings where sizable amounts of overtime are worked. Whether or not these savings are real, however, is another matter. Cost savings must be measured not only in dollars spent, but in values received. If supervisory morale and working effectiveness are adversely affected by pay inequities, savings in payroll dollars may be more than offset by ineffective operations.

Premium Pay. At the opposite extreme of company practices, some companies pay supervisory personnel overtime on the same basis as nonsupervisory persons. Although an expensive solution, this course certainly does preserve the pay differentials between the supervisor and those supervised.

However, premium pay for supervisors tends to transfer the problem to a different level. If an office supervisor, for instance, is paid overtime compensation on the same basis as those he supervises, it will, indeed, solve the pay inequity relationships between the office supervisor and his subordinates, but it will create a new inequity between the office supervisor and his supervisor. Such overtime compensation practices for supervisors may also discourage supervisors' efforts to reduce or minimize overtime work. Finally, premium pay plans can have a negative effect upon supervisors' attitudes.

Modified Premium Pay Policy. An increasing number of companies are following a middle course with respect to overtime payments for supervisory personnel. The actual practices inherent in this middle course can vary quite widely.

One example which illustrates the middle course states:

1. A normal amount of intermittent overtime is a part of the supervisor's job. Therefore, supervisors will not receive overtime compensation for hours worked during any given work week up to and including forty-four hours per week.

2. Supervisors will receive extra compensation equal to straight-time pay for all hours worked in excess of forty-four hours per week when such work is scheduled for their departments.

An alternative to such a provision is to relate the rate of overtime pay or

TABLE 17-4. Overtime Pay Provisions for Supervisory Persons*

Pay grade	Salary ranges	Overtime premium rate
8..........................	$6,000–8,000	1.5
9..........................	6,600–8,900	1.5
10..........................	7,250–9,800	1.25
11..........................	8,000–10,800	1.0
12..........................	8,800–11,900	0.75
13..........................	9,700–13,100	0.5
14..........................	10,700–14,500	0.25
15 and above............		0

* Policy covered all positions in these pay ranges.

extra compensation to the pay level of the supervisor.   An example of a provision which embodies this approach is illustrated in Table 17-4.

BONUS PAYMENTS FOR SUPERVISORS

About one-fourth of the companies which do not pay overtime compensation to supervisors do pay some type of bonus.   Very few companies pay both bonus and overtime.

About half of the companies with bonuses for supervisors include them in either the overall management profit-sharing plan or a profit-sharing plan designed for all employees.   For supervisors, the yield from such bonus plans is quite small, averaging between 5 and 10 percent of annual compensation. Some companies view this as a literal sharing of profits with supervisory as well as other employees.   Others, however, consider that this in some way compensates supervisors for extra hours of work on the theory that profits will be good in years in which extra hours are worked.

The difficulty, of course, with any profit-based plan is that profits are not necessarily directly related to hours worked.   Also, such plans probably have little incentive value to the supervisors, because it is difficult for the individual supervisor to see any significant and tangible relationship between his own performance and overall company profitability.

Only about 2 percent of all companies studied give supervisors some type of incentive bonus directly related to their achievements.   The reason for this low percent of utilization of bonus plans specifically geared to the supervisory job is not any lack of enthusiasm for such a concept.   The difficulties are practical.   They involve, first, identifying the factors which should determine bonus or incentive compensation for supervisors, and second, measuring these criteria.

Where they do exist, there are basically two types of bonus plans.   The first is based upon budget or cost data and rewards supervisors for controlling or reducing costs.   The difficulty here, of course, is to establish meaningful and equitable budget data in the first place.   It would, for instance, create a severe inequity if supervisors who already had achieved lower levels of cost were penalized by the introduction of such a plan.   The second type is a special awards plan.   Special or extraordinary achievements are identified, and a committee determines an appropriate cash reward for them.   The difficulty with such plans is that they sometimes focus attention on achieving the demonstrable and the extraordinary at the expense of the important day-to-day jobs.   Also, of course, it poses the difficult problem of judging what is extraordinary and fixing a value on these results.

IMPORTANCE OF EXCELLENCE IN ADMINISTRATION OF SUPERVISORY COMPENSATION

Excellence in administration of supervisory compensation is important for supervisors, as well as other employees, because they expect equitable treatment and reasonable salary progress. It is important for a second reason. Supervisory personnel, of course, play a dual role in the company; compensation practices are important both because they are supervisors and because they are employees.

The care, thoughtfulness, and equity with which their own salaries are administered must certainly have an influence on how carefully and equitably supervisors administer the salaries of their subordinates. In addition, the method and excellence with which salary actions which affect them personally are explained to them by their supervisors must have an effect upon the nature and excellence of the communications which they carry on with their subordinates.

Thus, the way in which the supervisor administers salaries for subordinates and communicates salary policies and practices to subordinates must be affected, at least to some degree, by the manner in which the salary program is administered for him and communicated to him. It is for this reason that the excellence of supervisory compensation has a twofold importance.

BIBLIOGRAPHY

Marlucci, Nicholas L. A., "Compensating First-line Supervisors in Factory and Office," *Highlights for the Executive,* National Industrial Conference Board, New York, October, 1960.

O'Brien, John, "Bonus and Incentive Plans for Supervisors," *Management Record,* January, 1956.

Selby, J. L. A., "The Next Five Years in Supervisory Incentives," *Personnel—Management and Methods,* July, 1962.

Sibson, R. E., *Wages and Salaries,* American Management Association, New York, 1960.

Supervisory Management Compensation Report, 11th ed., American Management Association, New York, 1966.

Survey of Supervisory Personnel Salaries, Commerce & Industry Association of New York, June, 1960.

CHAPTER EIGHTEEN

Labor Relations:
Collective Bargaining, Arbitration, and Mediation

C. W. UFFORD *Vice President—Industrial Relations, The Warner &*
Swasey Company, Cleveland, Ohio

Labor relations, as dealt with in this chapter, is the management function
of dealing with the *organized* aspects of the affairs of those employees who
are covered by collective bargaining agreements. Terminology varies. For example, the function of labor relations is called "industrial relations" by many
employers. Conversely, the term "personnel administration" normally applies
to the handling of the affairs of *all* employees, including those affairs of organized
employees which are not controlled by contract provisions or collective bargaining
procedures.

Labor relations also includes management's dealings with the efforts of unions
to organize its employees. These activities are governed not by contract provisions, but by labor laws and regulations: Federal, state, and sometimes local.

Labor relations, for all its importance, difficulty, and cost, is a specialized
part of the broad field of "management of human resources," the subject of
this section of the Handbook. It deals with the roughly 20 percent of United
States employees who are organized in unions. Yet the labor relations laws,
regulations, practices, and agencies which have developed go far to set the
patterns and standards which strongly influence the handling of most United
States employees, whether unionized or not.

Labor relations developments often force improved policies, standards, and
procedures. Many labor relations specialists believe that the same attention
applied to employee affairs prior to unionization often would have prevented
the unionization—a good or bad situation depending upon the point of view.

Equally good policies and standards must be applied to nonorganized employees or these employees will usually conclude that organization would benefit
them. This fact is frequently overlooked by management with the result that
salaried and professional employees sometimes organize to achieve benefits which
they believe will be better than those they enjoy.

A realistic awareness by management of the costs and complexities of handling formalized labor relations affairs should alert management to the value of paying more attention to the other chapters of this section as a means of avoiding or minimizing the problems discussed here.

LEGAL BACKGROUND FOR MODERN LABOR RELATIONS

The period since about 1930 has seen most of the development of Federal labor laws (with its state and local counterparts), the agencies which administer them, and unions as we know them today. The National Labor Relations Act (Wagner Act), the Labor Management Relations Act (Taft-Hartley Act), and the Labor-Management Reporting and Disclosure Act of 1959 (Landrum-Griffin Act) are the principal legislations that should be understood by any manager or student of labor relations.

Collectively, labor laws have established the right of employees to organize into unions for mutual protection; the right of unions representing a majority of employees in a group to bargain collectively with employers for all employees in that group; unfair labor practices banned to employers and to unions; a National Labor Relations Board to enforce the laws; state and some local counterparts to the laws and agencies; and the Federal Mediation and Conciliation Service.

Ever-changing laws and practices affect your business. The National Labor Relations Board issues regulations and decisions, courts decide specific cases, and arbitrators build up a mass of decisions resulting in a substantial body of law and regulations. Union and management attitudes and practices change (mostly for the better) as the experience of all concerned increases. You must accept the fact that these laws, regulations, agencies, precedents, and practices do exist, that they may become a real concern to a business at any time, and that, when they do, the actions taken by management may cause or prevent costly mistakes, often with far-reaching results which are sometimes impossible to undo.

Need for Professional Help. You will need professional help to handle this complex and fluid field of law, decision, and maneuver as it applies to your business. Whether this help is in the form of internal staff specialists or outside professional counsel or both, it should be thoroughly experienced in the fields of collective bargaining and labor law. The company's general counsel may or may not qualify. If you retain outside counsel, he should have the same high reputation and character the company would require in any other field of law or negotiation.

Beware of self-styled "labor relations experts" who may be former union business agents, company personnel men, or government agents who claim the ability to perform miracles through "inside channels" into the labor union involved or through "under the table deals." There may be such people who are as good as they claim, and there may be specific situations where "under the table deals" can solve a labor relations problem. But this approach to labor relations is littered with big bills for disappointing results and sometimes with charges of unfair labor practice against the company.

UNION REPRESENTATION ELECTIONS

Management's first awareness that it is involved in a union organizing campaign may be a notice from the National Labor Relations Board (NLRB) or from the union involved. Management is told of the union claim that a majority of the employees in a group or unit have designated the union as their exclusive collective bargaining agent.   You may discover that supervision has been aware of furtive activity, circulation of cards among the employees involved, and strange behavior of certain employees (who have been asking for trouble), but that it has not reported or acted upon this activity.

Management must control its reactions, especially if employee organization is a new experience.   Management and supervision must not go off half-cocked, become angry, threaten the employees, butter up the employees, ask strange questions, make promises, or grant unusual concessions.   Management is "under notice," and unusual actions may result in trouble.   Normal conduct and alert awareness are important.   Threats and promises are illegal and can produce charges of unfair labor practice.   Anger, however righteous, can raise real issues for the union to use against management.   Unusual concessions can be ruled an unfair labor practice, can be wasted, or can be claimed by the union as examples of its power.   ("See, brothers, just the presence of the union shows up management for what it is.   When we get in, we will *really* get things changed for you. . . .")

The basis for a union's claim for an NLRB election consists of cards signed by at least 30 per cent of the employees in the collective bargaining unit the union wishes to represent.   The National Labor Relations Board will check the cards against an alphabetical list, secured from the company, of the names of employees in the bargaining unit at issue.   Invalid cards will be rejected.   If the valid cards do not represent at least 30 percent of the unit, the NLRB will throw out the union's claim.   However, the union normally will present cards from more than 30 percent of the employees to take care of such contingencies.

Signed cards do not always establish the employees' desire to be represented by the union.   They may be only an effort by employees to get a union organizer off their backs.   The employees may have faced threats or implied threats.   These, of course, are illegal, but it is usually hard to do much about them.

Alternative Management Actions.   There are several courses of action open to management.   It can:

Accept the card count and the bargaining unit as sought and agree to recognize and negotiate with the union.   There is, however, no compulsion to do this if the employer has a good-faith doubt of the union's majority.

Agree to an election by secret ballot supervised by the National Labor Relations Board.   An election has the advantage of determining the actual desire of those employees *who vote* in the election.

Challenge the appropriateness of the collective bargaining unit as claimed by the union.   There is much regulation by the NLRB on this subject.   For example, "all production and maintenance employees" would be an appropriate group under NLRB regulations, but the same group plus "engineers and draftsmen" normally would not be considered an appropriate unit.   The NLRB will not normally sanction a faulty collective bargaining unit, but often there is room for a difference of opinion which must be settled with the NLRB and the union.

Refuse to consent to an election if it has reason to believe an election is not appropriate.   A hearing by the NLRB will follow to determine whether an election should be held, and if so, in what manner it should be held.

Preparing for the Election.   A preelection conference is usually held at the local NLRB office between the Board, the union, and the company.   Its purpose is to seek agreement upon the holding of an election and upon the time, place, and manner of the election.

Union Preparations. Preelection campaigning by the union will normally continue up to the day of the election. The campaign may include leaflets, union meetings, radio or television and newspaper advertising, and much word-of-mouth effort depending upon the size, vigor, and resources of the union. The union will usually attack any statements made by management when it can be done to the union's advantage. Occasionally, union campaigns will include threats or implied threats toward employees who do not favor the union. These methods are illegal but, when encountered, are usually difficult to stop.

Company Preparations. Preelection campaigning by the company usually includes a drive to get out the vote, because the representation issue is settled by a *majority of those who vote at the election.* The strongly pro-union and anti-union votes will be cast in any event. It is the moderate and undecided employees who need to be encouraged to vote and who often swing the election.

The company can inform its employees in the proposed bargaining unit about the election, the parties involved, and the time, place, and manner of the election. The company can state its views about the union and about the issues involved. It can give the employees information refuting the union's claims. This can be done verbally or by written notice, by letters to the home, or by public news media. The company can always answer specific questions by the employee. Except in the last twenty-four hours before an election, it can call meetings of the employees on company time to express its views. In most cases, the company can refuse to grant time for similar meetings by the union, but there are some exceptions. This should be checked with counsel.

The company cannot threaten or promise what it will do if the union is or is not voted in. It *cannot* safely "corner" employees individually or in small groups or otherwise talk to them under conditions which create pressure or threat. It cannot hold meetings on company time during the twenty-four-hour "quiet period" preceding the election, although it can answer specific questions during that period.

Physical Arrangements. Physical arrangements for the election will include a place or places provided by the company for the election and facilities for secret balloting free from supervisory or other pressures. The company must post the required notices regarding the election as agreed upon with the Board. These notices contain a sample ballot showing the choices to be voted upon. Care should be exercised to keep employees from marking choices on the notices, a frequent prank. The importance of such care was shown by a representation contest between two unions in the equipment industry in the Midwest. One union won the election. The loser challenged the election on the basis of marked notices. The Board supported the challenge and held a new election. The challenging union won, and a year or more of strife ensued, to be lived with by the company and all concerned.

Conduct of the Election. At each polling place, the NLRB will have a representative of the Board and an equal number of observers selected by the union and the company. A company observer must be a nonsupervisory employee and should be one who can identify those employees who are authorized to vote. Neither the company nor the union may be represented at the polling place by anyone other than the observers.

Challenged Votes. An observer may challenge a vote if he believes the person is not on the agreed list, if there is such a list, or if he believes him not to be included in the categories authorized to vote. Sometimes a union observer will challenge a vote for some other reason, for example, "This man works in the bargaining unit, but he is a nephew of the superintendent." Matters of this sort probably were discussed and settled in the preelection conference with the Board and the union, but such challenges occasionally occur anyway. If the employee is not challenged, he casts his secret ballot and leaves the polling place.

Challenged votes are set aside. If the total vote cast for one choice or another is great enough so that the number of challenged votes would not affect the election, the challenged votes are not counted. If the majority is small enough so that the challenged votes could affect the results, then a hearing will be held by the NLRB, usually within a few days, to hear arguments by the company and the union and to decide whether the challenges should be sustained.

Improper conduct by any party may also be the subject of a complaint upon which the NLRB will rule.

Ballot Count. Ballots are counted immediately after the polls close. Normally only the Board representative touches the ballots. Each party's observers tally the other party's ballots. Ballots are checked for clarity of intent. Each observer certifies the tally. Both company and union officials may observe the counting of the ballots. Except where challenged votes can alter the election or where the entire election is challenged for some reason, the results are certified within a few days.

It takes a majority of those voting to establish the union as collective bargaining agent. A tie vote does not do so. If there are three or more choices on the ballot and there is no clear majority, the two choices with the most votes are placed in a runoff election conducted in the same manner at a later date.

There cannot be another election for a period of twelve months after a valid election.

If the union wins, the victory does not automatically give the union or the employees any new rights, privileges, or benefits except the right to bargain collectively with the employer. It is the resulting agreement which gives the union and the employees any gains which may be agreed upon with the employer. In spite of claims which may have been made by the union during the organizing campaign, the employer does not have to accept the union's dictates or the provisions of what may be claimed as "the union's standard contract." The union probably has many contracts, most of which vary in numerous important provisions. Except as agreed in the contract, stewards achieve no automatic right to roam the plant, "sass" the foreman, or loaf on the job. Although the union acquires the right to bargain with the company, it also acquires the obligation to bargain in good faith. The company is obligated to bargain with the union in good faith.

THE LABOR AGREEMENT

The union's attitude in approaching negotiations will vary with circumstances. It may present:

Extreme demands, many of which are pure "feelers" or "padding" which may be only ideas expressed at random in a membership meeting.

A "boiler-plate contract" which the union committee claims is "the only thing they will sign." With some exceptions, this is pure hokum, as research into the contracts the union *has* signed will show.

A mild approach to feel out the situation. This is likely where the vote was close and the union does not want to split its membership.

A lead from strength if the union's majority was great.   Under these conditions a bargaining committee may be "full of zip and no control," acting with little judgment and often with no experience.

The company's attitude in approaching negotiations may vary from experienced poise to anger or fear.   Under the stress of emotions, inexperienced management may pound the table and refuse to settle anything, or it may concede to demands which it will later regret because of their interference with operations or established policy.   A calm, professional approach by the company is much to be preferred.   Such an approach usually has a stabilizing influence on the union committee.   A professional approach presupposes that a careful analysis of the condition and needs of the business has been made and sound ideas developed concerning the contract provisions necessary to enable the company to operate successfully.

Keeping Supervision Informed during Negotiations.   Supervision should be kept informed about all significant points of the negotiation; otherwise the union committee will understand the resulting contract and its sidelights better than supervision.   This situation may cause "the boss" to lose position and control. One multiplant company always has supervisors sit in on the negotiating sessions as observers on a rotating basis, reporting back to the other supervisors.   This provides excellent training for supervision in handling its responsibilities under the contract.   This policy has particular value, because it lets the operating people guide the company's negotiators in the practical implications of the contract language being arrived at.   This knowledge can prevent costly mistakes. Likewise, such participation keeps supervision thinking, learning, evaluating, and sharing responsibility; otherwise, it may give only lip service to the contract procedures with unnecessary grievances as the costly and disruptive result.

A word of caution on the use of supervisors as observers: No one bargaining session is typical of the whole negotiation.   One session may be calm, another angry, another windy, another productive.   The company view and the union view on any issue may change in the light of developments on other issues.   The final picture will not be clear until the last words have been written and signed.

Scope of Labor Agreements.   The scope of labor agreements varies.   Some are brief, limited almost to a letter of intent by both parties in which very little procedure or detail is spelled out.   Other agreements go into infinite detail trying to anticipate and provide for every contingency.   Experienced counsel should be followed under the specific circumstances.   In general, however, a moderate course is advisable, producing an agreement which lays out the broad principles of each item agreed to and includes modest detail on important procedural areas.

Typical Sections.   Typical sections included in labor agreements and some suggestions as to content include the following:

Intent, recognition, and representation is the section which recognizes the union as the exclusive collective bargaining agent for the employees in the bargaining unit.   It describes the bargaining unit in terms of the jobs or broad categories of jobs both included and excluded.   Normally this is the same language as was used in setting up the bargaining unit by the NLRB for election purposes.

Membership requirements: Is this a "union shop" contract requiring all employees to join and remain members of the union?   Is it an "open shop" where employees need not join or remain in the union if they do not wish?   Is it a "maintenance of membership" contract under which all employees who join the union must continue to pay dues and remain in good standing?   (Closed shop contracts are illegal. A "closed shop" means that an employee must be a member of the union in good standing before he can be employed by the company.) Is there an escape clause permitting an employee to drop out of the union at specified intervals?

Wage rates and methods describes wages and procedures such as job evaluation plans, handling of rate changes in transfers, upgrading and downgrading, incentive plans, and the degree to which the union may participate in such plans and procedures.

Management rights is an area in which both law and practice have changed. In theory, at least, management retains all rights which are not specifically limited by contract provisions. The NLRB, the courts, and some arbitrators have ruled in varying ways on this subject and continue to do so. Some companies try to protect their rights by a detailed list of retained rights. Convincing as this approach sounds, it can be attacked by pointing to "rights" not enumerated. In any event, the company *must* reserve the rights required to manage the business effectively over the years. The company must realize, however, that any such contract provisions must be bargained with the union.

Hours and overtime normally covers workweek and workday starting times, basis for computing overtime, rest periods or coffee breaks (if any), washup time, and the like. Specific attention is usually paid to provisions for continuous operations such as powerhouse.

Shift differential states the premiums paid for different shifts and the application of the premium for overtime and irregular shifts.

Seniority is one of the most vital sections of the agreement. Seniority must be defined carefully and its application to operating conditions evaluated and clearly described. This section usually includes a definition of probationary period and contains provisions for retention or loss of seniority in layoffs and leaves of absence. It frequently includes provisions for posting of job openings and the method to be followed by employees in bidding for the jobs, as well as the conditions governing the company in selecting the person for the opening.

Report and call-in pay provides the basis of payment when an employee comes in as scheduled and finds no work or is called in to perform only a small amount of work when he is not otherwise scheduled.

Bereavement pay covers days off, if any, with pay, to attend a funeral in the family as defined. This may or may not vary when a weekend or holiday is involved or when the funeral occurs during a paid vacation period.

Holiday pay specifies the paid holidays, how much pay is granted, the qualifications to be met to receive holiday pay, the rate of pay an employee receives if required to work during the holiday, and whether or not holiday pay is given for holidays falling during vacations or during a layoff or leave of absence.

Vacations specifies the vacation allowances in time and/or pay in relation to length of service and the requirements to qualify for vacation pay. This section may provide that the company may "buy off" some or all vacation and give vacation pay in lieu of time off. It may set forth limits as to the time of year in which vacation can be taken and may specify the accumulation of vacation from year to year, if any.

Grievance procedure defines what subjects are grievable, whether the problem must be taken to the supervisor informally first, what the grievance procedure is in successive steps, and the time allowed for each step. It deals with the final disposition of the grievance by arbitration, by strike, or otherwise. It should specify whether or not stewards are paid for grievance time and the degree to which they may leave their jobs to "service" the employees on grievance matters.

Safety and health deals with working conditions, safety equipment, safety committees (if any), and the conditions, if any, under which production work can be shut down for safety purposes and by whom.

Apprentice programs covers the nature and purpose of apprentice programs, the rates of pay for successive periods of apprenticeship, what, if any, participation the union has in apprentice affairs, and the limits on the number, location, and use of apprentices.

Employee benefits specifies insurance coverages, pension programs, and basis of employee contribution, if any. This is a section of great interest to employees and one which should be clearly spelled out to "merchandise" the costly benefit program.

Provisions for time off with or without pay may be included for such purposes as jury duty, court appearances, military leave, public services, and union duties.

Strikes and lockouts deals with the handling of wildcats, walkouts, slowdowns, and the like. This section specifies when a strike can occur legally under the agreement and the union's responsibility for an illegal strike. It provides for disciplinary action the company may take against the union or employees for illegal strike actions.

Effect of agreement—amendments settles the degree to which the agreement disposes of items not discussed in negotiations and the manner in which the contract may be amended.

Use of bulletin boards by the union is usually specified, setting forth whether the union has its own bulletin boards or whether it may use the company boards, with or without approval, and for what type of material.

Term of the contract must be specified. Is the contract for a one-year period or longer? Sometimes changes in wage rates or other subjects are agreed upon to become effective on certain dates during the term of the contract. These are called "automatic" or "built-in" increases. Or the contract in general may continue for a period longer than one year, but with provision for reopening at specified times for negotiation of wage rates only, or of certain other items. The contract language must make clear whether the union may strike during the reopener on the specific subjects.

Negotiation Strategies. Some basic considerations in conducting negotiations are the following:

Nothing should be finally agreed to by the company during negotiations until everything is agreed to. The union has the same privilege.

Although both parties are required by law to bargain in good faith, neither party is required by law to concede to the other.

The company is foolish to agree to provisions not clearly thought out or which it cannot live with. Sometimes negotiators avoid thinking issues through by agreeing that certain matters will be decided at the time of occurrence by "mutual agreement between the company and the union." This may seem wiser (or easier) than trying to settle the matter during negotiations, but it leaves open the question of what happens if agreement *is not reached.*

The union usually notifies the Federal Mediation and Conciliation Service that a negotiation is in process. Usually the Service contacts the employer to offer its services.

Severe pressure builds on both sides. The union usually threatens strikes with increasing seriousness, and management must prepare against that event.

The company may communicate an offer to the employees. However, the company must not put the union bargaining committee in an untenable position by communicating its offer to the membership before the committee has heard it or has had a chance to consider it. Such actions can only result in angry reaction, possibly upsetting any chance of endorsement of the company's offer by the committee, or in an unfair labor practice charge before the NLRB.

The company often must educate the union committee, especially a new committee, on the meaning of the company's offer and the reason the company takes the position it does. Of particular help may be written summaries of the ground covered in negotiations, the offers made by the company, the issues agreed to, and the issues which are not yet agreed to. This information helps the committee understand the complex issues and convey that understanding to the employees. Similar summaries are equally valuable for keeping supervision informed.

The union committee (and sometimes the business agent) may be limited in the knowledge required to evaluate complex situations of the business as management habitually must do, and it may not have the office facilities to duplicate material which management takes for granted. Under these conditions, management can help itself by helping the union.

The Moment of Truth. The time arrives in negotiations when it is clear that agreement will or will not be reached by the offer and the attitudes which have been laid on the table. At that moment, it is evident that there will be a strike unless one side or the other compromises.

Both sides are worried, possibly scared, yet each realizes that there may be some element of bluff in the position of the other. Normally both sides want to settle. Some very small concession may tip the psychological balance.

Conversely, the company, by taking a final firm stand, may give the union committee the opportunity to go to the membership and say, "We have pushed the company as far as it will be pushed. This is it!" This firmness may produce a settlement.

Management must recognize the "professional viewpoints" involved in the negotiation. A strong sense of professional pride or political need is felt by the union committee, the business agent, the company negotiators, the company legal counsel, and the conciliator if one is involved. Sometimes a wise manager can detect a roadblock comprised of these conflicting psychological needs and can guide the professionals out of the conflict.

Signing the Contract. A contract must be prepared for signature when agreement is reached. The company is frequently asked to do this preparation job, particularly if the union's resources are limited. The company must adhere to the letter and spirit of the agreement reached across the table, some of which may never have been put into final draft. It may be tempted to sneak in a point by slanting a word or emphasis, but this can be an expensive mistake, because the confidence of both the union and the membership in management is at stake.

The agreement may be signed by the plant manager, a corporate officer, the company negotiator, the company counsel, or a combination of these. It should be signed by each of the members of the bargaining committee, by the local business agent, and by the international representative of the union. This makes all union parties actual signatories.

STRIKES

The status of a strike is very important. A strike may be classified as a "legal," "illegal," "economic," or "unfair labor practice" strike. The difference between one category of strike and another may be based on very minor or debatable actions or conditions. If a strike seems imminent, the company's position should be evaluated by competent counsel in the light of circumstances. It would be unwise to attempt to state even general rules here.

The basic requirement in negotiation is that both parties are obligated to bargain in good faith, and this obligation is not met until the parties have bargained to an impasse. To fail to do so may result in an unfair labor practice strike. The importance of avoiding this situation is indicated by the fact that, although in an "economic strike" striking employees *may be permanently replaced* by new employees, in an "unfair labor practice strike" strikers are entitled to their jobs back, even though they may have been replaced by new employees.

Management Actions. Management must be firm and realistic in strikes. It must protect and utilize its legal and contractual rights in strikes, or it will prove to the union and to the membership that strike pressure is an effective way to get more concessions. Firm stands must be realistic. An ill-considered, tough stand by management may be reversed by that same management when the final awareness of the cost of the strike becomes clear in terms of lost production, broken promises to customers, effect on the year's profits, and the reaction of stockholders and directors. Such a backing down can destroy management's bargaining position and prejudice the company's position with the union for many years. An experienced company negotiator, counsel, or plant manager will prepare the hierarchy's thinking about a strike along very realistic lines, so that he does not have the corporate rug pulled from under his carefully prepared position.

The first few days of a strike are critical. They are likely to be enthusiastic, determined, and violent. Keeping a plant or office open during these days can be a difficult assignment. Employee attitudes are unsettled. Law enforcement authorities may be reluctant to move into a violent new situation, and in small communities, they may not be equipped by experience or manpower to do so.

Some things to be done by the company include the following:

Decide whether to let the strike simmer a few days, in which case do not encourage your employees to break the picket lines when little help may be available.

Secure the necessary court injunctions to give the company legal access to its property.

Convey to law enforcement officials the company's position and start them doing whatever they are willing and able to do. Their performance will vary with their resources, the attitude of the community, the reputation of the company, and the union background and sympathy of the officials involved.

Insist upon right of access to the plant for officials and salaried employees, if there is work for them to do; for passage for raw material and finished goods; and at an appropriate time, for access to the plant by employees who want to work.

Control threats and violence as much as possible. Such actions may not be restricted to the company gates. Employees, their wives, and their children may be threatened at home, at school, or on the highway. Such actions will have a serious influence on employees' attitudes, yet it is usually impossible for the company and law enforcement authorities to protect every employee and his family wherever they may be.

Inform suitable news media of the company's position and keep them informed.

Send letters to the employees' homes about the company's position, its plans, and its instructions.

Maintaining Perspective. Keep the parties in focus. Most strikers are basically "loyal to the company," regardless of their attitude toward the strike. They will be happy when the strike is over. Most of the employees will be manning the plant again. The company and its supervisors will do well to keep emotions about the employees under control.

All parties usually recognize that the company owns the plant and has many rights. Even so, management must sell, fight, insist, and bargain to retain its rights with the same vigor, wisdom, and calmness with which it must sell its product.

The union is likely to be a factor in the business for a long time, whether management likes the idea or not. More benefit will be gained by facing this fact than by bemoaning it.

In a strike, each side is under great pressure. Neither the employees nor the management are usually of one mind. The situation is usually fluid. Calm judgment must prevail.

The company usually should stand firm on a well-considered offer. To give in on more than details will certainly convince the employees that they can get "more" by keeping the pressure on until the company stops giving in.

A strike may have long-range value to all concerned if it settles a serious controversy. A plant in the machinery industry suffered a six-month strike some years ago which was almost ruinous to all concerned. The employees finally broke the strike on the basis of the standing economic offer. Both the company and the union learned that management *must* run the plant and also that it *must run it well enough* so that its actions will be hard to criticize. Relations in this plant have been unusually harmonious since the strike.

Conversely, some good companies never seem to settle their controversies, but have stoppages as a way of life. One respected and successful company in the office-machine field spends large amounts of executive time on collective bargaining and suffers stoppages year after year. These two extremes attest that there is more than one way to deal with collective bargaining problems.

ARBITRATION

Arbitration, if included in the agreement, is the final stage in grievance procedures. Some such final and binding step in problem solving is needed if the parties are to sign a contract guaranteeing that there will be no strikes and no lockouts.

A typical contract provision providing for arbitration in one plant in the construction-equipment industry reads in part as follows:

If the grievance is not settled within three working days after the above meeting, to carry the matter further, the Union must in writing to the Plant Manager request arbitration within 15 working days of such meeting. The arbitrator shall be selected by mutual agreement between the Company and the Union, provided that, if an arbitrator cannot be selected by mutual agreement within 10 working days, the Company and the Union shall jointly in writing request the Federal Mediation and Conciliation Service to submit a panel of five prospective arbitrators. Within 5 working days after receipt of the list of names, the parties shall meet. Each party shall strike off two names alternately. The remaining name shall be the arbitrator. His decision shall be final and binding on the company, the union, and the employees involved. . . . The company and the union shall each pay half of the arbitrator's fees and expenses.

The American Arbitration Association will also supply panels of arbitrators. Many arbitrators appear on both AAA and Conciliation Service panels.

There are divergent views about the use of arbitration. Some contracts do not provide for its use, relying upon negotiation to settle all issues with strikes as the end process. Among companies and unions which utilize arbitration as a final step in the grievance process, some will utilize arbitration on a large percentage of problems, whereas other company-union combinations will resort to it only on rare occasions. The cost of arbitration undoubtedly is a factor in these latter cases. Basically, however, the difference is one of philosophy of the parties in settling conflicts between them. One multiplant company, for example, dealing with various unions in several industries, averages about one arbitration per year and has never lost an arbitration. Management believes this record is based on a willingness on the company's part to settle early any case where the company is not on solid ground and to *prepare to win* any arbitration where it is on solid ground. Conversely, another major company arbitrated an identical issue in every one of its numerous plants and lost every time to the same union. This certainly illustrates the need for a company to develop its own philosophy regarding arbitration.

Arbitration Procedures. Arrangements for the arbitration are made by joint letter directed to the selected arbitrator describing briefly the nature of the problem to be decided and asking the arbitrator for dates on which he can be available at a mutually satisfactory place. It is advisable to send the arbitrator a statement of the contract provision under which the arbitration is being conducted.

The union's case may be presented by a local officer, a business agent, an international representative, or an attorney assigned by the union. The capability may range from inexperienced confusion to professional competence. The company may be represented by its own labor relations people, its company attorney, special counsel, or a combination to put a "winning team" into the process.

Three basic questions need to be settled.

1. *Shall the testimony be given under oath?* Recommended answer: "Yes!" The oath dignifies the procedure and makes most witnesses more aware of the importance of truthful testimony.

2. *Shall a reporter take a transcript* of the proceedings? Recommended answer: "Yes!" It dignifies the proceedings, helps keep the witnesses closer to the truth, gives the arbitrator a complete record, and helps hold the arbitrator to the contract provisions. It gives the company a record of the problems and attitudes revealed in the arbitration for use in improving its operating and labor relations practices.

Either party may engage a reporter and pay the entire cost, or both parties may use the same reporter, sharing the cost.

3. *Shall briefs be permitted* after the hearing and before the decision? Recommended answer: "Yes!" The brief allows each party to summarize its position and its arguments after hearing the total testimony presented. Either party can point out departures from fact and can highlight key issues and points which it believes are binding upon the arbitrator.

Limits on the Arbitration. The contract clause which provides for arbitration should limit the scope of the proceedings and the authority of the arbitrator. Some of these limitations are as follows.

The arbitrator's "decision shall be final and binding on the company, the union, and the employees involved."

"The arbitrator shall not have authority to change the contract in any respect." This limitation is extremely important to the company and must be maintained by every possible means. Unions sometimes urge departures from the contract provisions as practical ways to achieve their idea of justice. Such new ideas are subjects for the bargaining table, not the arbitration procedure.

"Both parties shall have the opportunity to present all relevant evidence on the subject to the arbitrator and be permitted to cross-examine the other party's witnesses within bounds of established practice of local Federal courts." Arbitrations normally are orderly procedures. Sometimes the parties may not know the practice in local Federal courts. The provision is a good one to have, however, to pull the proceeding back to order if it becomes slack or disorderly.

Timetable. The timetable for arbitrations will vary with the volume and complexity of material presented and with the work load of the arbitrator (a factor in selecting the arbitrator in the first place). Generally, however,

A transcript will be available within about three to five days.

Post-hearing briefs should be submitted to the arbitrator within fifteen days (allowing the counsel to use the transcript in preparing the brief).

The arbitrator's decision should be submitted to the parties within forty to sixty days after the hearing unless arrangements are made for more rapid adjudication.

MEDIATION

The Federal Mediation and Conciliation Service is a small, independent agency of the government headed by a director who reports directly to the President. Considerable emphasis is placed, as it should be, on the independent status of the Service. The mission of the Service is clearly that of an impartial agency.

The Role of the Conciliator. The Service, working out of regional offices, supplies a conciliator whose role is to enter deadlocks or crises in negotiations to get the parties to reach new compromises and settlements. The Service can mediate and conciliate, but it cannot compel agreement.

The Service enters the picture at the request of either party. Usually an agent of the Service calls the parties early in the negotiation process to offer its facilities at any point where they can be helpful. It usually offers its services again as the deadline approaches. Unions or managements may call in the Service when they feel they have gone as far as they can in the negotiation through their own resources.

The Mediation Process. The mediation process varies in detail with each negotiation, but it follows a simple basic pattern. The mediator:

Calls both sides to the offices of the Conciliation Service or meets with them at the employer's plant or office.

Introduces himself to both parties jointly and has them review the general issues for him.

Meets separately with each party to identify the real issues.

Alternates between the parties to develop fresh points of view, make trades, and break roadblocks.

As the deadline approaches, simplifies the remaining issues and faces each party with the seriousness of a strike compared with the value of some final concession, possibly only a face-saving fragment. When suitable, he may urge management to stand firm to convince the union that this is the time to settle.

May suggest a step which both parties can accept by blaming it on him and so reach agreement.

Value of the Mediation and Conciliation Process. This writer has never encountered a mediator who was grossly partial to either side. The ability of the individual conciliator, however, varies from great to limited.   In either case, the conciliation procedure may be of value in reanalyzing and resolving the issues.   In some cases, mediators have made outstanding contributions toward settlements with great benefit to both parties.

CONCLUSION

The point of view taken throughout this chapter has been that of the small- to middle-size business.   Obviously, the greatest number of businesses fall in these categories, and these are the businesses which have limited specialized staff.

Each part of the subject matter covered in this chapter has been a mere sketch of the laws, regulations, policies, and procedures involved to serve as a checklist for the manager or student of business administration.   A few fragments of philosophy have been included as guides on what to do and how far to go under the widely varied conditions which are likely to be encountered.

Labor relations, with its subsidiary fields of collective bargaining, arbitration, and mediation, is the product of the entry of unionism into the American business scene.   Unions, and hence labor relations, are solidly established by law, regulation, and practice.   The collective bargaining relationship of American business with these unions has set the tone and many of the standards in the broad field of business' dealings with all its employees.

The field of labor relations is complex and constantly changing, so the manager or student will need special counsel and much study to understand and deal effectively with its ramifications in:

Campaigns to organize employees
Collective bargaining elections
Negotiating labor agreements
Handling strikes
Utilizing arbitration
Mediation and conciliation

The total knowledge and judgment required can be gained only from long and extensive experience.   A manager must rely heavily on counsel and the specialized staff personnel available to him.   Yet, it may well be the manager who must make the final decision on whether to stand or yield, strike or settle, not only in the light of the labor relations events, but also in relation to the broader business considerations of customer requirements, profits, and the long-range health of the business.   Making these key decisions certainly involves knowledge, judgment, and courage not exceeded by the requirements of any other function of the business.   Management should be prepared accordingly.

BIBLIOGRAPHY

Summaries Directed to the Layman

Guidebook of Labor Relations, Commerce Clearing House, Inc., Chicago.
Labor Guide, Prentice-Hall, Inc., Englewood Cliffs, N.J.
Labor Policies and Practices, U.S. Bureau of National Affairs, Washington, D.C.

More Complete Services

Labor Law Reporter, Commerce Clearing House, Inc., Chicago.
Labor Relations Reporter, U.S. Bureau of National Affairs, Washington, D.C.
Labor Relations Service, Prentice-Hall, Inc., Englewood Cliffs, N.J.

CHAPTER NINETEEN

Employee Health Problems

J. S. FELTON, M.D. *Professor of Occupational Health, School of Medicine, University of California, Los Angeles, California*

Health problems, derived from both physical and emotional causes, arise among employed groups, and are either initiated by the basic genetic fabric of which the worker is woven or precipitated by the pressures of the group living in which he has found himself. Individual employees may demonstrate any of a variety of health impairments, and a certain low number of these difficulties, constantly present, is to be expected. When this expected level is exceeded, the problems which have been endemic become epidemic, and they will demand close managerial scrutiny.

Health problems may involve individual work behavior patterns, or they may spread to groups, suddenly increasing the rates of such measures of industrial effectiveness as absenteeism, turnover, medical service visitation, or injuries from job-related accidents. A discussion of health in an office or plant population cannot be structured solely from medical or clinical data, because of the close interrelationship of physical or emotional solidarity and job performance. Each affects the other, and a unilateral study will disclose part of the template only. It is necessary that the medical support of the enterprise be sensitively attuned to the possible effects of weakly glued physical or personality structure, and, obversely, that it be aware that disordered behavior, individual or group, indicates investigation of the total health of the worker or workers.

PRIMARY HEALTH PROBLEMS

The strength of a company's human resources is first among the many materials and intangible commodities intruded into the manufacturing, service, research, or distributive process. In the totality of men, machines, materials, money, management, methods, minutes, and modules of space, men occupy the position of primacy. A breakdown in the effectiveness of the worker can stultify the functions of all the other components. The relationship of health to successful industry is the core of the present residency training programs for physicians in occupational medicine. The theme central to the instruction is that from a study of clinical signs and symptoms the perceptive plant physician can identify not only the physical cause of the difficulty, if one exists, but also the group behavioral or environmental stress etiology of the disorder. The occupational health physician views this as his most valuable offering to management personnel.

Absenteeism. If one were to ask, "What is the health status of your plant?" the medical director of the company would be hard pressed to design a reply. One measure is the extent of the employee's actual participation in the mission of the organization. If he is self-invested in his job, he comes to work. If he is unmotivated, he withdraws from the work scene and remains home.

A thirty-seven-year-old plant manager, rapidly risen through executive ranks, was visiting the plant medical department. He had a respiratory infection and a fever of 102.5°F, and was informed by the physician that he must go home. He ruminated as follows:

You know, it's a funny thing. When I worked for the X Company as an assistant chemical engineer, I would wake in the morning with a slightly scratchy throat, I'd call in and say I was ill, and remain in bed. Now, I'm arguing with you about going home when I'm sick. What a difference a job really makes!

Most diagnostic listings of medical causes of absenteeism place respiratory diseases as the most frequent cause. Yet, when many of these employees are interviewed, their relationship to the job, to the supervisor, or to the company is frail, there is no real identification with the mission, and there is no sense of purpose or commitment in what they do. From this emotional set comes a medical sequence of reported, recorded, possibly investigated, and excused absence, presumably with illness as the origin. Most workers lose between four and ten days yearly from alleged or genuine illness. When the figure rises above this, the absenteeism is considered above average and excessive.

There are both managerial and medical inputs in this situation, diagnostically and therapeutically. Because the period away is termed "illness absence," the responsibility for corrective action usually is assigned to the medical department. Yet, any inquiry or repair comes after the fact, when determination of actual illness is not possible. The health service can identify the absence repeaters and work individually with them on the problem, but from an overview, it is managerial administrative toughness that is most effective in reducing high rates of absenteeism.

Action: Medical investigation, and medical action for those repeatedly, genuinely ill. Administrative action for those absent excessively without a solid medical rationale.

Alcoholism. It has been estimated that in each industrial or commercial enterprise 1½ to 2 new chronic alcoholics per 1,000 employees will be identified each year. Each company, irrespective of the opinion of its management and regardless of the location of the plant, the type of organization, or the sex or age ratios of its workers, has a certain number of employees who are problem drinkers. (The present estimate is 1 out of every 50 employees.) These are persons who no longer can drink socially, but who, once they have taken one drink, continue on to the point of blackout. They cannot control their drinking, and their condition is one which has attendant occupational, physical, emotional, social, family, and economic problems.

Chronic alcoholism has been redefined as a disease, but acceptance of this concept outside the medical profession is slow in its growth. This new view has encouraged the admission of alcoholic patients to general hospitals and has stimulated a large body of research in academic centers. That the problem is one of considerable dimension is given testimony by the estimated total of five million men and women in the United States who are afflicted; of significance to management is the fact that at least two million of these are employed. Each alcoholic loses about twenty-two, and sometimes more, days per year from work. Further, he loses two more days than his coworkers from illnesses *other* than alcoholism, has twice as many accidents, and loses twelve years of his life span when compared with the nonalcoholic.

The problem in the work scene is that supervisors tend to protect the alcoholic, and his absences are not reported or are given another etiology. Group peers, at first, will do some of his work for him, but after a prolonged period of this, they resent the increased burden and do not enjoy the reputation given the group because of the decrement in effectiveness brought about by the partially contributing problem drinker. Morale suffers, and group cohesiveness begins to melt.

A forty-four-year-old pipefitter in a research establishment reported to the medical department because of recurrent gastrointestinal upsets. On soliciting the history, the physician learned that the worker was a chronic alcoholic, but recovered. He had been an attorney, and in 1941 enlisted in the Army to avoid disbarment proceedings because of repeated drunkenness. On discharge from the service, he did not return to his profession, but learned a craft, once again altering his life.

The alcoholic is a good employee, voluble, frequently perfectionistic, and often cultured in the arts. The loss incurred in having him on the payroll is from his days away, and not in the early stages from the quality of his work while present or from any drinking on the job. Sooner or later, because of change in capability, he will be unable to undertake precision work and will have to be reassigned to much more gross tasks or be relieved from creative functions requiring clarity in thinking.

To salvage the worth of alcoholic employees in whom many years have been invested by the company—most are between thirty-five and fifty years of age—and to preclude further loss for the organization, certain actions may be undertaken. First, the company must have a declared policy, written or understood. With little organizational change, the policy brings about certain programmatic undertakings, all based on the disease concept of alcoholism. Supervisors should be oriented to the whole problem of alcoholism, including a briefing on the nature of the illness, its symptoms, stages in the progression of the disease, and on the manner in which they can detect and handle it among the employees in their groups. Meetings, group discussions, the showing of films, and the use of printed materials are the bases for the orientation. Supervisors newly aware of techniques in identification will refer their workers whom they identify as alcoholics to the medical department, and these workers, in turn, will be referred to those sources in the community skilled in caring for the chronic drinker.

Most effective, however, in the recognition and recovery effort is having in the company a member of Alcoholics Anonymous (AA), who will make himself known to the medical department and can be called upon for assistance when the alcoholic employee has expressed his interest in help. If such a person is not known to the medical department, a local AA group can be called and word will be sent to one of the employees.

Frequently, there are no facilities in a community to which alcoholic workers can be sent. In many communities, there are special alcoholism clinics, physicians who have interested themselves in the disease, and social agencies in welfare or rehabilitation, in addition to AA. If none exists, several industries might combine their efforts and support in establishing a clinic at a university medical center or hospital which will offer a multiprofessional team to work with referred workers. The disciplines represented are medicine (clinician and psychiatrist), social work, psychology, nursing, and occasionally, sociology. In a large number of cities, there are Alcoholism Councils, affiliated with the National Council on Alcoholism, New York, which serve as information centers. Many companies have employed special alcoholism counselors (usually recovered alcoholics themselves) to develop a program.

Often, the company policy will have built into it a step that calls for termination of the alcoholic if all attempts at recovery have failed.

Action: Develop a company policy regarding the illness of chronic alcoholism. Establish a referral system through the medical department. Maintain close relationships with effective community agencies concerned with alcoholism.

Accidental Injuries. In spite of consistent in-plant programs of accident prevention and the installation of the maximal number of safety devices, a seemingly unchanging number of accidents occur among employed persons, resulting in injury or death. The ratio of job-incurred injuries to nonoccupational illnesses as causal agents of lost time has changed, admittedly, since the enactment of the first workmen's compensation insurance legislation. Somewhat less than 10 percent of the days lost from work are chargeable to work-related injury or illness, but the injuries which are sustained are serious and result in permanent partial or permanent total disability. The fatalities are shattering to families and are costly. Concomitants of many of these injuries are claims requiring hearings before industrial accident board referees, which prolong settlement and retard rehabilitation through litigious delays and the complexities of legal calendars.

Whereas the nonindustrially ill experience short-term conditions, those disabled by injury undergo prolonged periods of recovery necessitating time away from work and alternative placement until completely recovered. In some firms out of step with current thinking, the injured employee finds himself discharged.

To meet this supposedly unresolvable dilemma, medical and safety departments expend much personnel effort and time. Yet, these attempts at correction follow old patterns. Accidents are credited to "carelessness," and the physical environment is restudied and resurveyed for flaws or omissions. Significantly missing, however, is a studied concentration on the accident sustainee, the worker who gets hurt. Disregarding research findings which point to accident causes within, and not outside, the individual, the safety officers have failed to adopt known epidemiologic investigative methods and have not incorporated the psychologist or his skills in tracking the emotional causes of accident repetition.

A twenty-six-year-old, muscular, ex-athlete carpenter expressed to the medical director his wish to join a professional football team being organized in a nearby city. Because of his long history of repeated traumata in his craft—once, he slipped on a ladder, catching his arm over a bottom rung, which injured the large nerves under his arm—the personnel director was warned that if this man were to play football, he would be injured. The team met for practice, and on the first scrimmage, this man dislocated his shoulder and was out the entire season.

Findings have pointed to the need of consideration of off-the-job injuries; and in revisions of the method of computing injury rates, there has been inclusion of data derived from disabling events occurring away from work. This emphasizes further the concept of holistic medicine, in which the total man is reviewed in the relationship of his behavior strengths and deficits to his work output.

Health-impairing experiences off the job lead to loss of work time and temporary partial disability. In the case of vehicular accidents, there may be prolonged disablement or even fatalities which, apart from their emotionally and socially disruptive impact, cause drains on the group's health and accident insurance plans.

In substance, the medical department, along with representatives of management, labor, and the safety analysis group, should conduct investigations of the accidental injuries sustained by workers, both at work and away. But this is not sufficient unless professional skills from the behavioral sciences are utilized to understand the causes of the events resulting in injury to the personnel. True epidemiologic reviews are needed to identify specific significant factors manifesting a positive correlation with the injuring process. Only with a complete inclusion of the physical, environmental, and personality information can the company's injury experience be understood and can the rates be lowered.

Action: Investigate all accidental injuries sustained by employees, taking into account both on- and off-the-job events, and account for all the factors—physical, behavioral, and environmental—etiologically related to the temporary or permanent loss of human resources. Take managerial action in the form of corrective procedures, the action being dictated by the epidemiologic findings.

Occupational Diseases. Although becoming fewer in number because of occupational hygiene control measures, there are still certain illnesses arising directly from contact with work materials or the job environment. The traditional cases of lead, radium, and mercury poisoning are becoming minimal, apart from the unanticipated work process or the premature introduction of new materials whose toxicity is yet to be evaluated. Diseases arising out of and in the course of employment still present problems in diagnosis and litigation.

Because it is a company's traditional role as the defendant to oppose through counsel all claims filed against it under workmen's compensation law, rather specious arguments will be offered in the defense. Recognizing the reality of numerous claims based on unfounded allegations, there will be the frank clinical case of occupational poisoning from inhalation, ingestion, or absorption of a toxic chemical or from contact with one of the hazardous forms of physical energy. To fight the claim is foolish when medical evidence and expert opinions develop a documented cause-and-effect relationship. What can be done to minimize the number of occupational diseases?

First, there must be industrial hygiene studies and understanding of all the noxious substances, including raw materials, intermediates, and even finished products, when necessary, to evaluate the extent of worker exposure. Implicit in this kind of study are identification of the materials, analysis of their composition if unknown, and a direct measurement of the amounts which have been dispersed into the workroom air or a quantitative determination of the exposure levels through analytic chemical or physical procedures conducted on air samples.

Second, and in parallel with the environmental mensuration, is constant medical surveillance of the workers in contact. This is executed through repeated health examinations and laboratory measurement of the body burden carried by the exposees by means of bioassay studies of the blood, urine, feces, or, infrequently, tissue. By comparing work-site air levels with clinical findings, a measure of the amount of absorption of a hazardous substance is obtained.

Intoxication is to be differentiated from absorption; in the latter, the body has taken in certain quantities of the work elements and retained them, but the level is insufficient to cause clinical illness. If there has been any tissue injury resulting from their presence, the body's reparative processes have been able to meet the chemical or physical insult and restore the tissues to normal functional effectiveness.

Most important, however, from a medical *and* a managerial point of view is the treatment accorded the employee who presents himself as ill following a potentially deleterious work contact. The philosophy which should permeate every medical attention is expressed simply as: "Do everything possible." By conducting all the indicated examinations, laboratory tests, and X-ray studies, and by getting the needed consultative assistance, the company is protected, the physician is protected, and the employee patient is protected, these not necessarily in order of priority.

A forty-one-year-old, asthenic woman tool-crib attendant worked over 125 feet from an area where a jet plane was undergoing modification. She alleged poisoning, particularly liver damage, by trichlorethylene, a solvent used in considerable quantity in cleaning metal surfaces within the aircraft. A simulated operational setup permitted measurements of ventilation within the building and the level of solvent vapor at various radii from the work epicenter. No vapor was encountered in the tool-crib air, and a persistent seeking of past medical data on the woman revealed a condition of gallstones with a one-time blockage of the common bile duct. Through the mechanism of compromise and release, the claim was settled for $3,000.

The worker who alleges occupational disease deserves the same diagnostic services as the employee genuinely made ill by exposure to toxic workstuffs. Every clinical or consultative measure should be taken to prove or disprove the allegation. The final decision as to the presence of disease or liability of the company can then be made on a firm foundation.

In most legal difficulties involving malpractice, it is frequently the omission of diagnostic or therapeutic measures, rather than the commission of erroneous ones, that leads to suits.

Action: Study the work environment to identify the presence of, use of, and extent of exposure to toxic raw materials, intermediates, or finished products. Conduct frequent procedures in medical surveillance to determine the possible absorption by, or intoxication of, the worker following such exposure. For each employee alleging occupational disease, do everything necessary to establish or disclaim the presence of work-generated illness.

PLACEMENT AND RETENTION

Although at first blush placement and retention may appear to be problems of the department of industrial relations, they are ones which often come to the attention of the medical department. Frequently, an employee dissatisfied with his job and unwilling to relate the true reason for his feelings will state that he is leaving the company because of health reasons.

During World War II, when the "job freeze" was an established policy, a forty-five-year-old millwright wished to move from California to Arizona "for his health." He claimed that he had developed sinusitis owing to the fog and dampness of the bay area. Examination revealed no evidence of sinus disease. Inquiry directed toward other reasons elicited the information that he really did not want to leave the community, but he could no longer tolerate his foreman, who had been unable to adjust to the need for greater supervisory skills during the exigencies of wartime and for a mixture of workers different from those he was accustomed to directing. A review with the personnel director resulted in a local job transfer, and a valued worker was retained.

Even though worker mobility has increased and families anticipate frequent moves, it rarely is dictated by medical necessity. Considered and thoughtful investigation and counseling by concerned medical personnel can keep down a high loss rate and the costs of worker replacement.

Careful selection of job candidates can be highly effective in the retention of workers. This does not imply a rigid system of physical standards for acceptance or rejection of applicants. It does mean that for a useful and efficient method of placement, it is necessary to know the physical and environmental demands of each job, developed and supplied usually by personnel analysts. With the data derived from a complete medical[1] examination, and in many instances a personality appraisal plus laboratory and X-ray diagnostic studies, the candidate's physical and emotional capacities to undertake the job he is applying for are determined. When these are matched against the requirements of the job and they prove to fit, the applicant can be placed in the position with considerable confidence. This procedure also permits the employment of the physically limited person.

Although the candidate's many qualifications are reviewed as part of the initial interview—his training, experience, intelligence, occupational history, aptitudes, and possibly dexterity—and his health status is measured, the elements that frequently remain without appraisal are his motivation and work characteristics or habits. Unfortunately, it is only by a prolonged trial of work that one can judge if an employee is functioning below or above his skills. A deviation in either direction will lead to inefficiency and poor utilization of work time.

A twenty-eight-year-old design engineer moved to a southern state after a lifetime of the competitive pace of education and work in New York City. He made many visits to the plant dispensary for a variety of complaints. These were not comparable to the psychosomatic manifestations of any underlying disorder, but seemed to indicate that medical department visitation was a way of passing time. On questioning, it was learned that he really did not have enough to do at work. His department head was requested that he be given twelve hours of work to complete in eight. The employee undertook this with considerable enthusiasm and made few future visits to the dispensary.

The candidate for work, following examination, is classified by the examining physician according to a four-point scale:

1. Physically (or medically) qualified for any position
2. Physically (or medically) qualified for any position, but has minor remediable defects
3. Physically (or medically) qualified for modified or restricted work only[2]
4. Not physically (or medically) qualified for job applied for

Infrequently, another classification may be inserted to cover the employee who has a serious constitutional disorder such as diabetes which requires no limitations at work.

A system of this type makes useless the classification scheme of "may do heavy work," or "moderately heavy work," or "light work." These statements employ adjectival modifiers which mean vastly different things to different

[1] The term "medical" is used in preference to "physical," for "medical" can cover a broader health status determination. It can be argued legitimately by unions or nit-picking job candidates that personality testing cannot be performed as part of a physical examination.
[2] Restrictions, for example, not to work at heights (ladders, narrow balconies, catwalks, or roofs), are listed.

viewers and perceivers. To a weight lifter, pushing 300 pounds fifty minutes out of every hour might actually be light work, whereas to an underweight physicist, carrying a dozen books might be exceedingly demanding.

Also to be relegated to a position of obsolescence is the system of rigid physical standards. A clerk applies for a job and his blood pressure is found to be 150/90. As the standard calls for rejection of anyone with a tension over 130/80, the clerk is told he cannot be employed. On the same day a Nobel laureate in molecular biology is to be added to the plant's personnel, and his pressure is recorded at 185/95. Is he rejected? Of course not. The standard is overlooked and he is accepted, after some kind of peculiar waiver formality is gone through to retain the sanctity of the standards.

In brief, careful placement will provide, as nearly as possible, a working force which fits its jobs, and will not subject the company to costly high labor turnover.

Action: By matching a job applicant's physical and emotional capacities against the demands of the job, sound placement can be effected, with a minimum of worker turnover. Request medical investigation of all employees seeking termination on the basis of impaired health.

CHRONIC DISEASES AND THE AGING EMPLOYEE

Americans are living longer, and with the increase in longevity comes greater opportunity for the degenerative diseases to appear and create certain dysfunction for the worker. Cancer, arthritis, cardiovascular disease, respiratory disorders, peptic ulceration, and certain kidney changes are concomitants of the aging process, and in certain instances, these are the results of wear and tear on the body. Associated with physical changes, there may be some alteration in mental capacity, or there may develop frank neuropsychiatric changes.

When the senescent process appears and proves totally, or nearly totally, disabling, most organizations have disability retirement schemes which will permit the ailing worker to leave and still have a good pension. The situation is odd, in that many workers with severe levels of impairment are able to work each day, turning in highly competent performances and losing a negligible amount of time from work, usually from the same acute conditions to which most of the physically intact are equally subject.

Many of the chronic conditions are responses to stress, and the physical symptoms wax and wane in proportion to the intensity of the stress or the person's ability to absorb or tolerate it.

A thirty-six-year-old welder had an acute rheumatoid arthritis of one ankle joint, so that it was red, tender, hot, and swollen. This precluded weight bearing, but with the redesign of a chair he was able to weld while in the sitting position. With steroid medication, the symptoms and signs subsided remarkably for a period of several weeks. A wildcat strike, called without the union's sanction, involved his craft, and on the second day of enforced idleness his ankle returned to its original morbid size and associated painfulness. Subsidence of the difficulty came long after his return to work.

Among other diseases of a chronic nature which are present in the earlier years, but have some of the same characteristics of duration, are diabetes, the convulsive disorders (the epilepsies), and multiple sclerosis. Skin diseases, such as psoriasis, may have their more serious complications, but present a cosmetic defect rather than a generally disabling condition.

The presence of these disorders in a plant population requires constant medical monitoring to determine the extent of progress or regression and the ability of the employee still to carry out his work tasks on the job in which he was placed initially. It might be necessary to place restrictions on the worker or modify the work assignment. Infrequently, a job reclassification will be necessary, or even part-time work or retirement.

There must be close liaison between the medical director and the worker's private physician so that the latter will be familiar with the job's physical demands, and so that both practitioners will be able to work toward the goal of the patient's comfort with full understanding of his motivations, drives, ability or willingness to follow a therapeutic regimen, and psychic need for productive, meaningful work.

A point to be stressed in connection with the chronic diseases is that work rarely makes the pathologic state worse and actually improves the employee's total well-being. Enforced disability retirement places suddenly on the worker a feeling of utter uselessness compounded by a disease to which he now directs more attention than is needed. Work is rehabilitative, supporting, emotionally nutritional, and absolutely mandatory for most who grow up under the Protestant ethic.[3] This was demonstrated further in the Watts riots, where, in spite of public assistance, there were still demands for jobs because of the pervasive need for self-actualization.

The degenerative diseases will disable certain workers, but with understanding surveillance by the industrial physician, compliance by the worker with the therapeutic regimen prescribed by the family physician, and insightful supervision by management, the afflicted employee will be able to perform effectively.

Action: Constant medical appraisal of the status of chronic disease among workers so affected. Orientation of managerial personnel to the changing work skills of the aging employee. Retention of the aging or chronically ill worker for as long a work life as is compatible with the company's mission and the employee's health.

RETIREMENT

The descent from a pinnacle can be a slow, tortuous, anguished trip to a point deep in the valley's trough where one becomes small, insignificant, and almost invisible. The movement away from the top is always carried out reluctantly, for the successful one dislikes being replaced. The news photograph of the late Presidents Hoover and Roosevelt taken during the processional to Roosevelt's inauguration showed a sad incumbent, with an expression in great contrast to the smiling, outgoing glow of the one newly elected.

But retirement comes to all except a small number of self-employed who can continue in their work until a terminal illness cuts short a productive life. How to make this cessation from work a rewarding experience, and not a vacuum in time, is a challenge met successfully by few retirees.

A sixty-five-year-old retired vice president of a manufacturing concern moved to the Pacific Coast to be near his daughter and grandchildren. He has undertaken little in the way of activity, so that shopping at the supermarket has become an anticipated relief from boredom. He chats with the preschoolers in the neighborhood, turns on the sprinkler system for the lawn, and exchanges infrequent social "do's." From a busy, demanding existence, he has come to psychically empty days, with no satisfying resources to draw upon.

It is not unusual to hear of the early death of retirees, even though their

---

[3] "The idleness of the mendicant was both a sin against God and a social evil; the enterprise of the thriving tradesman was at once a Christian virtue and a benefit to the community." R. H. Tawney, *Religion and the Rise of Capitalism*, New American Library, New York, 1954 (originally published 1926), p. 101.

health had been good during the working years. As work is so central to our needs, emotionally as well as economically, some planning must be done to avert the sudden loss of fulfilling experiences. For many who have habits of learning, productive hobbies, or approaches to art, music, writing, or even editing, the years which are now suddenly freed for creativity are exciting and stimulating. For those whose lives have been bereft of these kinds of enrichments, retirement is found to be dull, difficult, and dreary.

Both industrial management and medicine can work effectively together in developing a preretirement counseling program which should go on stream long before the day the sixty-five-year-old leaves the company. The personnel director can devise readily the program content for a discussion of investments, taxes, retirement villages, and the like, but the medical components should have a specific emphasis which, oddly enough, need be oriented only briefly to somatic illness or care.

Significant positioning should be given the emotional health aspects of the post-work life, and certain time should be devoted to the development of appropriate and reasonable health attitudes. A checklist somewhat related to the following items might aid in designing the medical discussion.

1. *Determinants of the full life*
   Continuous mental exercise.
   Skills in relating to people.
2. *Physical health*
   Skin and use of cosmetics.
   Heart—need for activity.
   Arthritis—warmth.
   Obesity—diet and activity.
   Chest diseases—smoking and emphysema.
   Vision—corrective lenses, cataracts.
   Hearing—hearing aids.
   Dental health.
   Bowel habit.
   Accidental injuries.
   Personal hygiene and grooming.
3. *Health attitudes*
   Do not bore people with discussions of health and medical problems.
   Do not take dozens of medicines or health foods.
   Accomplish corrective surgery, preventive medical reviews, and needed dental work *before* retirement when still on maximal income.
4. *Emotional health*
   Be busy with community organizations, church, or committees.
   Try writing, painting.
   Renurture old hobbies.
   Experiment with crafts, gardening, and cooking.
   Stay out of children's family situations.
   Live in the present—"think young."
   Understand contemporary slanguage.
   Avoid "now when I was young. . . ."
   Do not deprecate change.
   Help with youngsters—everything from babysitting to bike repair.
   Undertake continuing education—extension or night classes.
   Do not change suddenly, for example, from city dweller to chicken raiser.
5. *Essence of retirement*
   Relate well.

Direct thinking toward others.

Maintain good emotional health.

The spirit of personal growth in retirement has been expressed well by Gitelson:

To die with one's boots on is the keynote of the mental hygiene of old age. Never to know that one is through, never to feel superfluous, never to lack significance, never to be without an outlet for the creative urge, never to be without a word in the affairs of men—these are the other notes.

Action: Initiate an effective preretirement counseling program with strong medical content, emphasizing emotional rather than physical health.

MENTAL HEALTH

Inclusive in all the topics so far considered is the general subject of mental or emotional health. With the demands made by the industrial culture, old and poorly healed personality fractures may rebreak to cause disorder behavior on the job. A simple interpretation of the factors involved may be offered in the following.

Predisposing Factors. Work, by itself, does not bring on or cause emotional disruptions. There must be a long-standing culture medium on which a behavioral problem can grow, and this is the personality—molded, shaped, and polished long before the employee's work life has been started. This was given evidence by the American troops in World War II. Some underwent serious psychiatric disturbances during training while at the military installations in the United States. Others went through the heartbreaking rigors of combat, undergoing shattering experiences, but were able to handle the situations as they came along without "cracking." There must be predisposing factors for a problem in interpersonal relations or response to stress to blossom in adult life.

Precipitating Factors. An incident or series of incidents at work can trigger off an emotional difficulty or rekindle an old psychic flame which has not been burning brightly. A sudden stress, a situation redolent of an unhappy experience in one's youth (remembered or forgotten), can create a devastating loss of work effectiveness, but there must be something stored in the memory cores to be retrievable by the experience.

Perpetuating Factors. When the stress or unpleasing situation persists without relief or corrective therapeutic action, the emotional difficulty remains and may worsen. The lack of supervisory or medical identification of a problem will permit a personality deficit to grow to unbelievable heights of maladjustment.

A thirty-three-year-old chemist had consulted several dermatologists because of an eruption involving both hands. A wide variety of medications and physical treatments failed to change the skin disorder. The condition necessitated one full hour's time of an occupational health nurse in the plant medical department each morning while she changed the dressing and rebandaged each finger and each hand. It was believed by the staff that the skin was manifesting an underlying emotional problem, and it was suggested that this kind of causation be sought. Reluctantly, the employee agreed to testing and interviewing. The background came to light when it was learned that the skin "broke out" just at the time that a peer had been appointed to the suddenly vacated supervisor's position. The employee had always unconsciously identified this fellow worker with his brother, with whom he had had a remarkably difficult relationship throughout his life. As he resynthesized his life while under professional care, he became aware of the cause-and-effect correlation, and the dermatitis disappeared.

Predisposing factors: Longstanding difficulty with sibling

Precipitating factor: Promotion of peer

Perpetuating factors: Retention of situational stress and lack of appropriate therapy

A program of mental health must be initiated by the medical department and must be supported by management to identify and correct these manifestations of impaired personality structuring:

Chronic absenteeism

Diminished work output

Lowered efficiency

Sabotage of supervision

Excessive reliance on supervision

Creation of poor examples of work behavior

Withholding of constructive ideas

Increased turnover

Increased number of rejects or amount of scrap material

Increased number of accidental injuries

Increased number of, and lengthened, rest periods

Increased number of infectious complaints

Increased dispensary visitation

Development of psychophysiologic responses to stress, such as: headache, "fatigue," "ulcer," "nervousness," sudden weight gain, sudden weight loss, allergy, and insomnia

Inability to travel

Tardiness

Premature arrival at work or undue extension of work day

Various means of rectification can be instituted to minimize these manifestations of disorganized behavior. Of the greatest worth in any effort directed toward human conservation, as mentioned, is the unquestioned agreement by management that the activity is sound, needed, and worthwhile.

Without detailing the undertaking, there are certain components to be built into a mental health program:

1. Preplacement testing. This might consist of a formal battery of psychological tests or an interview by a mental health specialist (psychiatrist, psychologist, or both). Testing, without an interview, is to be decried as insufficient and possibly misleading.

2. Interpretive observation of dispensary visitors. The employee who presents evidence of reaction to stress should have his symptoms interpreted in this light and in relation to the job; the difficulties described by the employee should be investigated physically, but their emotional planking should not be missed.

3. Orientation of supervisors to behavioral change.

4. Group discussions among employed groups. Such an activity will bring problem areas to light and permit resolution by the group discussion method.

5. Pertinent articles in company house organ.

6. Familiarization of management with the numbers and kinds of conditions encountered by the medical department, without identification of the persons involved.

7. Active counseling program within the medical department. This may take the form of "emotional first aid" or brief therapy by a professional counselor.

8. Referral to community mental health sources of care.

9. Environmental modification. Through conferences with supervisors, modifications can be made in the work milieu to lessen the strength of stress impinged upon the employee.

Mental health was defined some years ago, in a practical sense, by Dr. George H. Preston as ". . . the ability of one human being to live with other humans in whatever situation he may be placed without having to sacrifice his own happiness or to destroy that of those around him."

Action: Establishment of a program of mental health which will provide recognition of the behavioral problems, reassurance of the affected employees, and referral of those in greater need of care to professional sources.

MEDICAL PROGRAMMING

Fully Developed Multiservice Program. Unelaborated, so far, has been the structuring of the medical department or its program to reverse some of the ill health trends reviewed above. Yardsticks are shakily premised, at best, but it has been the consensus among many in occupational health that a plant of 1,200 persons requires one full-time physician; and then, possibly, one can add a physician for each increment of 2,000 employees. Organizations with employees at greater health-hazard risk may require more professional staff persons, and companies with great numbers of women employees, engaged in office work or sales, may need fewer.

This kind of program is the fully developed multiservice program, implying medical direction at all times. Nonphysician personnel will include occupational health nurses, an occupational or industrial hygienist, medical and X-ray technologists, medical records librarians, clerks, and, if needed, such further persons as custodians, a health information specialist, a health physicist, an ophthalmic dispenser, a sanitarian, or a statistician.

Occupational nursing coverage may be provided on other than day shifts and over weekends; there may be satellite dispensaries peripheral to the central medical department, or there may be mobile units for dispersion to outlying facilities. If the company manufactures toxic chemicals, a toxicology laboratory may be included as part of its medical facility. A complete in-plant program will usually have its policies and procedures collected in an operating departmental manual which will include guiding principles for occupational nurses.

Partial In-plant Medical Program. Although a *partial* in-plant medical program may be in operation for a full work shift, a physician will be in attendance for only a portion of this period. His time will be divided between his private practice and the occupational medical practice which he carries on at the plant medical department. In his absence, the occupational nurse will be in charge of the dispensary, or dispensaries, and other persons in the department will function in accordance with written guiding principles.

When there is only a partial program, there will rarely be additional personnel beyond other nurses or a clerk. Although first-aid attendants are to be found in many industries in the United States, the employment of such persons is to be condemned, for there is no organized system of training, examination, registration, or licensing; and although positions of this type are described in some of the governmental personnel classification systems, the use of such personnel should be discouraged. The addition of workers of this kind as full-time members of an occupational medical program bespeaks ignorance on the part of management or the persistence of a practice long rendered obsolescent by the contemporary availability of skilled nurses for program assignments.

Out-plant Medical Program. Implicit in the out-plant medical program is that it is executed almost exclusively in the office of the private physician who serves in consultative capacity to an organization. Rarely does he visit the company for whom he has this responsibility, because prospective employees are referred to his office for physical appraisal, as are workers who have been injured. This type of program is strictly expediential. It is conducted as "occupational medicine," when in actuality it is one of traumatic surgery and rather routinely performed physical examinations—with little knowledge of the work environment or job demands built into the examination or treatment situation. For intelligent medical guidance to management, visits must be made to the plant's operating area so that the examination and treatment procedures can be carried out with logical goals and objectives.

Other measures frequently cited for partial medical coverage call for two hours of physician time per week for the first 100 employees, and one additional hour for each additional 100 workers. One full-time nurse can be completely occupied with a plant population of 200 to 400; below the 200 level, a part-time visitation service would suffice.

Program Costs. Costs of medical program operation vary with plant location, completeness of service, existence of potential occupational health hazards, philosophy of management, and methods of cost accounting. In a representative number of companies, surveys have shown a median cost of $21 per employee per year. As the company size increases, the per-employee cost drops. For example, companies under 500 averaged $32.52; those of 5,000 to 10,000 employees, $28.57; for concerns of 10,000 to 50,000 workers, the cost was $24.72; and it was $14.22 in organizations of 100,000 persons or over.

A cost of $25 per capita per year will provide a reasonably good program, although in companies with special hazards, an annual expenditure of $50 would not be unreasonable.

BIBLIOGRAPHY

Brown, Mary Louise, *Occupational Health Nursing,* Springer Publishing Co., Inc., New York, 1956.

Collisson, N. H., "Preventive Medicine in Industry," *Public Health Reports,* vol. 79, November, 1964, pp. 948–952.

Felton, J. S., "Illness Absence Recording—Accurate or Inaccurate?" *Archives of Environmental Health,* vol. 5, November, 1962, pp. 495–504.

Felton, J. S., "Organization and Operation of an Occupational Health Program," *Journal of Occupational Medicine,* vol. 6, January, 1964, pp. 26–68; *ibid.,* vol. 6, February, 1964, pp. 93–103; *ibid.,* vol. 6, March, 1964, pp. 132–151. (Available as a single publication from the Industrial Medical Association, 55 E. Washington St., Chicago, Ill. 60602.)

Gafafer, W. M. (ed.), *Occupational Diseases—A Guide to Their Recognition,* Public Health Service Publication, no. 1097, U.S. Department of Health, Education, and Welfare, Washington, D.C., 1964.

Klem, Margaret C., and Margaret F. McKiever, *Small Plant Health and Medical Programs,* Public Health Service Publication, no. 215, U.S. Department of Health, Education, and Welfare, Washington, D.C., 1958.

Levinson, H., *Emotional Health: In the World of Work,* Harper & Row, Publishers, Incorporated, New York, 1964.

Levinson, H., et al., *Men, Management, and Mental Health,* Harvard University Press, Cambridge, Mass., 1962.

Maisel, A. Q. (ed.), *The Health of People Who Work,* The National Health Council, New York, 1960.

Manual on Alcoholism, American Medical Association, Chicago, 1962.

Shepard, W. P., *The Physician in Industry,* McGraw-Hill Book Company, New York, 1961.

Siegel, G. S., *Periodic Health Examinations—Abstracts from the Literature,* Public Health Service Publication, no. 1010, U.S. Department of Health, Education, and Welfare, Washington, D.C., 1963.

CHAPTER TWENTY

Employee Services

SAMUEL L. H. BURK   *Boyden Associates, Inc., New York, New York*

The employee services discussed in this chapter have demonstrated their practical value in increasing productivity of human resources while avoiding complications arising from possible limitations on individual freedom of choice, labor union representation, and the growth of public as against private company ownership. The services provided by employers for their employees can be generally defined—with some danger of oversimplification—in terms of the following distinguishing characteristics.

1. The cost of providing them is borne, in whole or in greater part, by the employer.

2. They are not related to individual salaries or wages, organizational status, length of service, present or future direct financial benefit to the employee, hours worked, or the basic individual "contract of employment."

3. They have a measurable or otherwise rationally demonstrable effect upon conservation of human resources and hence contribute to company profits and growth.

The more commonly provided services falling within this definition are medical services, recreation, safety, miscellaneous personal services, and protection and security. Although the majority of these activities fall logically within the general area of "personnel administration activity," individual company needs may dictate actual organizational assignment to other functional areas. The matter of organizational placement will be discussed, as deemed appropriate, as the services are described.

MEDICAL SERVICES

Medical services should be planned and administered with the advice and counsel of a professionally trained and licensed physician, preferably certified in industrial medicine. In larger companies, it is common practice to employ a full-time medical director who serves at corporate headquarters. In smaller

11–218

companies, an industrial physician is more often employed on a part-time, retainer basis. Generally speaking, the same considerations that govern the choice between employment of "house" counsel and that of "outside" legal counsel should guide decisions on medical counsel. At least equal care must be accorded to defining objectives, position content, and human qualifications required, and to selection of an appropriate individual as in the case of any high-level corporate executive, or professional, independent adviser.

Objective. The objective of the medical function is the maintenance of high degrees of employee physical and mental health at all levels of the organization. Achievement of this objective requires a knowledge of potential job-related health hazards. It also requires an up-to-date knowledge of statutes, governmental regulations, and the medical aspects of court decisions determining employer responsibility for the maintenance of safe and healthful working conditions. In addition, it necessitates the selection of an individual with sensitivity to the established rules of ethical medical practice as they apply to the relationships among a man's personal physician, the employer's medical director, and the employer.

Authority and Responsibility. The medical function should be a part of the councils of top management. This can be readily accomplished without undue stress on either the chief executive's limited time or the medical director's professional dignity by having the medical function report, organizationally, to the vice president in charge of the corporate personnel administration function. This assumes, of course, that the medical director will be assigned authority commensurate with his responsibility.

The medical director should be permitted, within the limits of overall company policy and his budget, to organize his activity as his judgment dictates and to staff his subordinate positions with individuals of his choice.

Duties. The duties assigned to the company medical organization should include:

1. Determination of minimum physical standards for employment, *especially* in jobs or positions placing unusual physical or mental demands on the incumbents thereof

2. Designation of positions in which handicapped persons may be employed

3. The conduct (or outside assignment) of preemployment physical examinations and periodic employee examinations, including interpretation of results of both types

4. The initial treatment of injuries or illnesses occurring while at work, and the determination of the recommended course of treatment thereafter

5. Investigation and analysis of physical and mental causes of absenteeism, and the making of recommendations for reduction or elimination of the causes that stem from the employment situation

6. Counseling with employees and their superiors on alleviation of medical causes of decreased individual productivity—as ethical limitations permit

7. Conduct of interim physical examinations upon return to work after serious injuries or illnesses, and certification of the employee's fitness to return to his duties

8. Determination by plant medical inspection trips or otherwise of health hazards at the workplace, and the making of recommendations for their elimination or alleviation

9. Participation in the deliberations of at least the top-level safety committee

10. Testifying, as the company medical representative when required, at workmen's compensation hearings

11. Making physical examinations at the time of employee termination, certi-

fying to the state of the employee's health at that time—especially in companies with occupational disease hazards

12. Making regular or random inspections of operations that require product or process sanitation precautions

13. Assisting in training employees in first aid and in developing adequate programs for keeping first-aid groups up to required strength

14. Making periodic inspections of the effectiveness of first-aid training

Records and Controls. Records of all examinations, treatments, referrals, medical counseling, and other activities should be maintained. These records should be the basis for periodic reports that summarize total services rendered, types of services, and dispositions made or actions taken. Such "control" reports should contain data on frequency by types of action, but more importantly, they should indicate necessary preventive measures and ways of improving the medical service.

Individual employee medical history records should be maintained in separate, locked, confidential files in the medical department. They should not be included in the individual employee history files, nor should they be made available to anyone without the permission of the medical director. Even when made available, interpretation of the records should not be left to those lacking medical training. Nothing is more dangerous than diagnosis, prognosis, therapy, or other action based on laymen's translations of medical terminology.

RECREATION

The extent and kind of recreational facilities that should be provided for employees have long been a source of disagreement among executives. With the possible exceptions of "company housing" and "the company store," recreation provided, financed, or guided by the company can lead to charges of "paternalism" more than any other employee service. This is particularly true when the company locations are in, or reasonably close to, urban or suburban locations.

In cases where the local areas provide a number of recreational opportunities, duplication by the company is of highly doubtful value to either employees or company owners. In more remote localities, however, it may be essential to the personnel effort to supply at least a minimum of the kinds of facilities that will satisfy the majority of the employees. Because of a general increase in available leisure time, a high percentage of the working population has developed a taste for both indoor and outdoor personal and spectator activities ranging from individual cultural pursuits to attendance at amateur and professional contests.

Objectives. It is obvious that the employer cannot satisfy the recreational needs of every individual. Moreover, any actual or apparent attempt by the employer to pressure individuals into company-selected activities will defeat the purposes for which the facilities are provided. On the other hand, if the following statements are true, the provision of recreational facilities may well be justified.

1. There are no facilities (or quite inadequate facilities) within a reasonable distance for the types of activities required by an appreciably large segment of the plant or office employees.

2. Provision of an appropriate facility is essential to attracting and holding good employees.

3. Recreational facilities can be expected to help foster a feeling of common interest among employees.

4. The facilities can provide a common point at which managers and subordi-

nates can meet and get to know each other in situations not connected with the day-to-day work.

5. The facilities will provide favorable opportunities for employees in different departments to get to know each other better.

6. The facilities and their related activities will contribute to the achievement of higher-level individual satisfactions such as personal recognition, need for competitive achievement, a sense of belonging, enjoyable off-hour activity, and the like that are not provided by the job itself.

There are some reasons frequently used to justify recreational expenditures that have little or no validity. Typical of these are the following:

1. The company should "lead the parade" among area employers in providing recreation facilities in the community.

2. The employer has a "social obligation" to see that his employees are provided with wholesome recreation.

3. The employer is a better judge of what makes for wholesome recreation than is the individual employee.

4. Good, healthy, after-work exercise in which many can partake makes for a healthier work force (and takes employees' minds off inequities in the job situation).

5. Provision of after-hour amusement will help to keep labor unions out.

Authority and Responsibility. When employer-provided recreational facilities can be validly justified, it is highly desirable to secure employee participation in both the guidance of the activities and partial contribution to the costs. Company-sponsored recreation is generally looked on more favorably when employees share at least equally in "managing" it and do not feel that it is a charitable gift from a benevolent despot.

In smaller companies, the personnel manager may act as chairman of a "recreation committee" on which representatives of each major organization unit serve on a rotating basis. In larger companies, a suitably qualified assistant of the personnel manager may chair the committee. Only in the very large companies will the job of the recreation director be a full-time position, and in only highly exceptional cases will he require any staff other than secretarial assistance.

Costs. The cost of providing facilities, at least initially, may be appreciable. Costs of administering the recreational activities should be small. Costs of facilities maintenance will vary in accordance with the nature of each facility. Wherever practicable, the cost of supplying equipment should be borne, at least in part, by participating employees. For example, in the case of an intramural softball league, team members might supply their own gloves, and the employer might supply bats, balls, and uniforms.

It is quite common to have nominal monthly or annual dues paid into an "employees' recreation association." In the case of spectator activities, admission is often charged with the understanding that any "profits" will be turned over to the association. All employees, especially the committee members, should know that the company must budget its costs and that it looks to the association for the same kind of forward planning.

Records and Controls. A financial and statistical report should be made at appropriate intervals, by either the recreation director or the chairman of the recreation committee, to both top management and the employees. The report should set forth at least the following items.

1. Amount budgeted by the company for the year and for the period to date

2. Amount spent over or under the company budget

3. Amount remaining in the company budget for the remainder of the year

4. Similar data as in 1, 2, and 3 on the association contributions
5. Totals of company and association figures
6. The number of employees enrolled in each regularly scheduled activity
7. The number of times each activity took place in the period
8. The number of employees actively participating each time and the total number for the period
9. Total spectator participation and income, if any, therefrom
10. A statement from the association treasurer on income, expenditures, and balance on hand in the treasury

Both management and employees will benefit from this information. It should be obvious at the end of each report period what activities have been most popular and also most "profitable." The reports thus serve as guides to management and the employee committee members in preparing the next year's budget, in deciding recreation policy, and in laying future plans.

Industry Opinion and Information. Management opinion seems to demonstrate conclusively the validity of the following assumptions with respect to recreational services for employees.

1. There is, in every company among the employee group, interest in organizing some group activity in the recreational field—and the potential leadership required to direct that activity.

2. The most successful programs have been initiated on a small scale on the basis of known employee interest.

3. The family as well as the employee should be considered in selecting and planning activities.

4. Activities are best planned with the groups involved.

It should be noted that there are local, industry, and national associations from which specialized advice on employee recreation services can be secured. The personnel director should know the names, nature, and membership of such groups.

SAFETY

Provision for safe and healthy working conditions ranks high among the manager's social, ethical, statutory, and economic responsibilities to his employees and to his company's owners. The responsibility for developing and maintaining safe working habits starts with the individual employee at his workplace. The responsibility for providing equipment that is safe to operate, facilities that minimize or remove accident and disease hazards, communications programs for employee indoctrination in accident and sickness prevention, frequent inspection, and prompt remedial action lies with every member of management. The degree of responsibility increases geometrically up through the organization pyramid.

Objective. The attempt to eliminate waste of human resources caused by time lost because of industrial accident or illness should be never-ending. The cost in terms of human suffering places a social and moral demand on all management people. Realization of the truth of this caused the safety function to be among the earliest of employee services to be given specialized attention. In fact, many modern personnel departments started as and grew out of the plant safety units.

Duties. There are at least six essential activities involved in achieving the objectives of the safety function:

1. Educating all employees in *safe* working habits and practices and instilling "safety consciousness."

2. Conducting frequent, systematic, and thorough safety inspections and immediately following through to assure that all hazards uncovered are reduced or eliminated.

3. Checking engineering plans and installations and operation manuals from the safety viewpoint, preparing and publishing required safety instructions for new equipment and processes, and revising them as necessary on the basis of post-installation operating experience.

4. Investigating *every* accident or occurrence of occupational disease to determine its cause and to recommend appropriate action to prevent recurrence.

5. Establishing, publishing, and keeping up to date a complete set of safety rules and regulations.

6. Maintaining, publishing, and interpreting complete industrial accident and illness records.

Organization and Planning.   Maintenance of essential safety activities requires both managerial and employee participation. This can best be accomplished by establishing a network of safety committees corresponding to the various organization levels of the company.   For example, in a multidivisional, multiplant organization, there might be:

A corporate-level safety committee

A safety committee for each product or geographical division

A safety committee for each plant or major sales location

Departmental safety subcommittees under each plant or sales-location safety committee

To keep the number of members of any one committee to a practical minimum (perhaps five to eight people at any one time) and to provide for maximum participation, a committee's chairman should generally be a line management representative.   A personnel department representative might act as "permanent" secretary and perhaps also be the "local staff" representative of the corporate safety director.   Thus, with a committee of eight, there would be a chairman, a secretary, and six members, two of whom might be replaced each year by two new appointees.

A successful safety director, at any level in the organization, should have the following qualifications, varied only by the needs and knowledge required by each level or locality:

A thorough knowledge of what makes operating equipment, facilities, and operating practices safe, currently unsafe, or potentially dangerous

The ability to "sell" safety and safe practices

Knowledge of the processes, materials, facilities, and equipment involved

Skill in conference leadership

Personal popularity among and acceptance by workers and members of management

The size of the staff of the corporate safety director will vary in accordance with company size, geographic decentralization, and the inherent hazards of the industry.   The safety director should make personal visits to each location once a year, if possible.   He should be provided with enough experienced and capable assistants to make it possible for some representative of the corporate safety group to spend several days at each major location at least twice a year. Certainly at least one member of the corporate safety unit should be on hand as promptly as possible in the case of any major catastrophe, regardless of whether the cause is company-connected or stems from extraneous causes such as natural forces.

For a more detailed discussion of the safety function, see Chapter 13 of Section 7, "Accident Prevention and Safety."

MISCELLANEOUS PERSONAL SERVICES

There are a great many helpful personal services which can be provided by the employer if circumstances warrant. Location is again a chief factor in determining the need. Listed below are the more commonly provided services that (1) can often be justified by companies located in typical industrial and commercial areas and (2) might be justified only when employees cannot find in the location adequate outside, local means for satisfying their personal needs.

Typical of services falling in the first category are:

Eating facilities

Assistance, through company-approved realtors, in finding houses when employees are moved into the locality, and financing settlement on the new home before the old one can be sold

Parking facilities

Vocational and educational counseling

Counsel on retirement plans and on social security costs, benefits, procedures, and the like

In the second or "doubtful" category might be found:

Company operation of an employee "thrift" or "savings plan"

Provision of company-owned, employee housing

Provision of banking facilities

Provision for property, personal liability, and other general insurance coverages

Plans for employee purchase of company stock on an installment payment, "average-cost-of-stock" basis

Services such as package wrapping, shipping, and mailing

Medical services for members of the employees' families (or for the employee himself outside of the place of employment)

Investment counsel

Food Services.   Employee eating facilities are probably the most common personal service provided. This is almost mandatory when the place of work is located in an area in which suitable luncheon or midshift food services are not readily available off the premises.

Types of meals offered, the times of meal serving, and kinds of service will also vary by location and by company philosophy on its obligations to its employees. In the relatively few cases in which the employer requires employees to stay in the office building or plant during luncheon period (usually providing free meals for this reason), the minimum requirement would be to make anything available from a full course "dinner" to a soup, sandwich, dessert, and beverage selection. Usually such services are provided in attractive surroundings which include a "recreation room" for use between the end of the meal and the close of the lunch hour.

Employers who do not require employees to stay on the premises at meal time frequently provide attractive dining rooms, cafeterias, or vending-machine centers in which food is prepared and served at or below cost.   These companies believe that the costs are justified by reducing the abuse of the time allotted for the lunch hour and by greater efficiency resulting from eating a nourishing lunch or midshift meal.   Although the attractiveness of being able to obtain a relatively inexpensive meal is great, most workers prefer to make their own choice each day, rather than be committed to eating always in the same place and with the same people.   They may come to believe that provision of even the best food in the finest in-plant surroundings, *if they have no other choice,* is an "invasion of their individual freedom of choice."   When employee-customer demand fluctuates from day to day because a varying number of employees choose to "eat out," difficulties in meal planning will almost invariably increase the company's costs.

For these and other reasons, most companies contract for catering services from large "industrial feeding" companies that are professionals in this field.   The caterers buy supplies in large quantities, know how to plan for customer fluctuations, and can interpret customer and food-choice statistics.   They relieve the manager of the additional burden of running a restaurant as well as his regular business.   It may be desirable and profitable, however, for larger companies to employ a trained dietitian to oversee and work with the caterer.

Coffee Breaks.   The coffee break has, since World War II, become a common practice that has made the provision of beverage and "snack" services almost obligatory.   Because the time periods are short compared with the lunch "hour," employee use of outside facilities for the coffee break is generally impractical. When companies have cafeterias or lunchrooms, time spent at the coffee break can be suitably controlled.   Otherwise, mobile food units can be used in large plants, vending-machine centers can be set up, or "snack bars" established at strategic locations.   A combination of these can be arranged to meet any specific requirements.

The use of vending machines for employee feeding deserves special mention. These machines are usually provided and serviced by outside contractors.   In return for space and utilities, the contractor rebates a portion of his profits on the machines to the company.   These devices, when well serviced and when tasty, quality products are used, enjoy great employee patronage.   They can be set up as single hot or cold beverage dispensers or combined in machine centers in which everything from soup to fresh fruit is automatically dispensed. They may be located so that no one has to go far from his workplace for his lunch or coffee break.   Many companies encourage the use of the machines by turning over their share of the profits to an employee fund.

Other Services.   The justification for providing any one of a host of other possible employee personal services can be based on one generally accepted principle: "The employee who has unsolved personal problems or worries is not usually a good performer."   Some of these problems arise directly out of the work situation.   Perhaps most of them, however, stem from causes outside of the job or are only indirectly job-connected.   The manager will find it profitable to alleviate the problems in the first category when he can do so without materially reducing company profitability, creating inequities for other employees, interfering with individual freedom of choice, or opening his company or its agents to charges of unethical, unprofessional, immoral, or criminal practices.

Controls.   Minor services, which in themselves appear to be justified, can add up to appreciable total expenditures of time and money.   It is advisable to make periodic checks on the individual and total costs of such miscellaneous personal services and to apply the rule of reason in keeping their costs in line with their value.

PROTECTION AND SECURITY

The objectives of protection and security activities are twofold. The first purpose is to provide protection for the company against theft, pilferage, sabotage, and unauthorized disclosures of secret or otherwise "classified" information. The second purpose is to control or reduce the losses arising from such actions, from human carelessness, and from the effects of the forces of nature. Thus, it is apparent that there can well be some question as to the inclusion of these responsibilities under the heading of "employee services."

It must be conceded that the primary purpose of protection and security is the protection of company property of whatever kind; of information or other "property" for which the company is held responsible; or against damage to the persons or property of others that may be legally attributed to company negligence. From the protection and security viewpoint, the fact that employees may be hurt or penalized, directly or indirectly, is of secondary importance. From this limited viewpoint, the question of including this function under "employee services" can be justified only by the fact of its close relationship to the "manpower" function in general.

Responsibilities and Authority. The safety and the medical functions have been defined above. They are concerned primarily with the protection of the employee against the hazards of employment and with the alleviation of the results of exposure to these hazards. The function of protection and security is one primarily of "policing" and fire fighting and is clothed with *enforcement authority* over all individuals within or outside of the company who threaten company security. The function might be likened to a governmental department of public safety. Both the safety and medical functions are clothed with the "authority of ideas" (as against the authority of law) and might be compared with a governmental department of health and welfare.

Organization. It might logically be concluded from the above that the safety and medical functions protect employees against hazards at work, whereas the protection and security function protects the owners of the company against damage to property. From this conclusion, we may go one step further and say that in cases in which hazards apply to both areas, both have jurisdiction *insofar as their respective primary functions are concerned.* Thus, part of the organizational problem resolves itself into defining the separate functions and not drawing fine lines of distinction.

The major organizational question is whether the protection and security function should report to the line manager or to the personnel manager. Equally valid and persuasive arguments can be made for both points of view. In this writer's opinion, because the "line" functions have primary responsibility for the planning, construction, maintenance, and use of property of all kinds, including the performance of people who use the property, the protection and security function should report to line management. Should there arise any question of hazards applying to both functional areas, they may be resolved by the coordinating executive to whom both the line and the staff executives report.

Internal Organization and Staffing. In most plants, protection and security forces are internally organized, "ranked," and uniformed in a manner similar to military practice. In some sensitive or dangerous situations, part of the force may wear civilian clothes for the conduct of "undercover" assignments.

The uniformed police and fire force practice has at least two very cogent arguments in its favor. First, it affords a kind of discipline that is not afforded by nonuniformed, civilian-type practices. Second, uniforms and insignia of rank provide readily discernible identification of authority and responsibility levels in setting up and carrying out emergency procedures and in enforcing protection and security regulations.

Use of Outside Contractors versus Company Employees. In many plants in which there are appreciable security risks or fire and other hazards, outside contractors are employed to supply plant guard and watchman services. In most cases, this involves an apparent higher cost to the company. Companies believe that the higher cost can be justified for several reasons.

1. The contractor's employees take orders only from and are responsible only to the contractor. Thus they are free from influences of the prestige or status of company executives.

2. Qualified contractors are more expert and effective in recruiting, selecting, training, and supervising the required personnel.

3. The contractor assumes all of the employer responsibilities for his employees.

4. If unionized, the contractor's employees have union loyalties distinct and separate from those of company-unionized employees.

5. The company is not required to bargain with a smaller unionized group.

6. The contractor usually posts a bond to cover losses resulting from negligence or malfeasance of his employees.

Should the company decide to employ and administer its own protection and security force, the matter of selecting a qualified leader becomes quite important. There are two essential requirements. The right man should have successfully demonstrated, through prior employment, his willingness and capacity for exercising the kind of authority required for immediately decisive action. Furthermore, his past performance should have indicated that he has an unusually high level of emotional stability, particularly when under pressure or in emergency situations.

It may be appropriate to employ an individual who has held a relatively high rank in a municipal fire or police department or perhaps an officer's commission in the armed forces. He should have the physical stamina and ability to carry on for relatively long periods under pressure. In many situations, it will be highly desirable that he be willing to live quite near the plant. He certainly should be willing to be "on call" at all times.

Regulations. The stringency of protection and security measures will depend to a large extent on the nature of the business; the secrecy required by the company and its customers, licensers, or prime contractors; the hazards involved in processes and operations; the amount of money that the owners are willing to pay for protection of their property; the value of all forms of property; and the desired degree of calculated risk the company is willing to take. There are some basic requirements for even a minimal protection and security program, among which can be listed the following:

1. Strangers should be checked in and out of the plant and plant offices, and employees should be provided with means of identification.

2. Areas involving special hazards or housing in restricted operations should be clearly marked with respect to who is entitled to be in the area, precautions to be taken by anyone in the area, and any special rules of conduct to be observed.

3. Both employees and outsiders should be subjected to close scrutiny when entering or leaving areas containing classified documents or valuable materials, documents, or products.

4. Care should be taken to check new employees for security clearances where required, in strict accordance with the appropriate classification agency's procedures.

5. All especially valuable materials and confidential documents should be secured by locks, safes, fireproof or fire-resistant cabinets, special enclosures, limited-access rules, and similar precautions.

6. Fire, the forces of nature, theft, or sabotage should be guarded against by alarm systems, sprinklers, and other appropriate automatic devices.

7. Operations involving use of explosives should be housed in separate buildings in areas with natural or artificial barriers for the protection of neighboring buildings.

8. Volunteer employee fire-fighting units should be set up for the purpose of containing smaller local fires until the plant or municipal units can reach the scene.

Chapter 16 of Section 7 contains a more detailed discussion of plant protection practices and procedures.

Justification and Controls. All fires or explosions, evidences of attempted or actual forcible entry, suspicious loiterers, and the like, should be reported by the protection and security forces. Actions taken or recommended should be reported daily by the head of this function, who should also investigate, report on, and make recommendations concerning strengthening security and protection by means of new or improved devices.

Plant and office protection and security cannot be considered by management as a "frill" to be adopted in good times and dropped when profits fall, or even as a nuisance to be endured as well as possible. In many companies, the loss from theft and pilferage alone can be many times more than the cost of guarding against it. Protection and security against sabotage, fire, explosion, or the effects of natural forces require no special pleading. Few, if any, shareholders will question the reasonable and logical expense of safeguarding corporate assets, but many would forcefully criticize the management that does not take needed precautionary measures.

CONCLUSION

Employee services, properly selected and appropriately administered, are profitable because they make an appreciable contribution to obtaining, holding, and motivating desirable employees. They cannot be used as substitutes for sound management, but they can enhance the ability of managers to make the most productive use of the skills and capacities of well-recruited, selected, trained, compensated, and motivated subordinates.

BIBLIOGRAPHY

Anderson, August J., *Industrial Recreation*, McGraw-Hill Book Company, New York, 1955.

Belli, Melvin M., *Ready for the Plaintiff: A Story of Personal Injury Law*, Holt, Rinehart and Winston, Inc., New York, 1957.

Blake, Roland Patton, *Industrial Safety*, Prentice-Hall, Inc., Englewood Cliffs, N.J., 1963.

Correlated Activities in an Employee Health Program, Metropolitan Life Insurance Company, New York, 1962.

Crosby, Ralph J., "Long Range Planning for Safety," *The Growing Job of Risk Management*, Management Report, no. 70, American Management Association, New York, 1962.

Dahl, J. O., *Restaurant Management*, Harper & Row, Publishers, Incorporated, New York, 1944.

Fleming, A. J., and C. A. D'Alonzo, *Modern Occupational Medicine*, Lea and Febiger, Philadelphia, 1960.

Flippo, Edwin B., *Principles of Personnel Management*, McGraw-Hill Book Company, New York, 1961.

Gocke, B. W., *Practical Plant Protection and Policing for the Security of Business and Industry*, Charles C. Thomas, Publisher, Springfield, Ill., 1957.

Handbook of Accident Prevention for Business and Industry, National Safety Council, Chicago, 1953.

Hayt, Emanuel, *Law of Hospital, Physician and Patient*, Hospital Textbook Co., New York, 1952.

Selleck, Henry B., with Alfred H. Whittaker, *Occupational Health in America*, Wayne State University Press, Detroit, 1962.

Simonds, Rollin H., and John W. Grimaldi, *Safety Management: Accident Cost and Control*, Richard D. Irwin, Homewood, Ill., 1963.

CHAPTER TWENTY-ONE

Employee Communications

ROBERT NEWCOMB   *Partner, Newcomb & Sammons, Chicago, Illinois*

MARG SAMMONS   *Partner, Newcomb & Sammons, Chicago, Illinois*

The art of communicating with employees has not flowered under the warm and indulgent gaze of management—it has been rammed into the executive consciousness by circumstances too painful to ignore.

For many years, employee communication was entrusted principally to informal and not too informative conversations between the employer and employee or to employee magazines which were essentially reports of the activities of employees, a sort of social potpourri. There was little to be found concerning a company's operations, its policies, or its problems. The infrequent editorial messages of management were either largely innocuous success essays or other aimless rhetorical excursions into generalities. It added up to very little.

With the growing awareness of the importance of communications, however, the employee publication experienced rather drastic changes with respect to both physical appearance and content. As surveys of employee readership came to corporate attention, the true viewpoint of employee readers—and their families—commenced to find the light. Employees, it developed, were indeed interested in the comings and goings of employees, but they were also interested in those factors which influenced their livelihood. Management found that employees were concerned about the serious matters that involve job stability. Management began to perceive that, in the struggle for men's opinions as characterized by the bargaining table sessions, employees wanted to know what *management* thought about controversial issues. It had been assumed that the union viewpoint was the only viewpoint that interested employees; managements began to discover that this was not necessarily so.

The results of these findings are to be seen in modern employee communications. The typical management discusses with considerable forthrightness the state of the business, the menaces of competition, the urgency of quality, the need for profit. The messages of management have taken on a new, clearer tone; the boss has begun to "speak up."

TYPES OF EMPLOYEE PUBLICATIONS

When you talk communications, think *plural.* The label no longer applies to the single, simple, highly occasional "house organ." Instead, in the progressive company, it covers such printed devices as the factual and informative newsletter for employees; the highlight newsletter report or "tip sheet" for supervision; the internal-external magazine for image building, inside and out; the up-to-the-minute bulletin board; the instructive and readable indoctrination handbook; the annual report for employees, tailored to fit an employee's wish to know; the executive letter into the home; the invitingly streamlined and simplified booklets on benefits; the persuasive recruitment manual; the "fact card" for the employee's wallet or handbag; and the so-called welcome pamphlet for the open-house visitor.

For many years, of course, the employee magazine was the principal agency of management communication to employees. Gradually it began to yield to the tabloid newspaper format, which is simpler and generally less costly to produce. No dependable statistics appear to be available, but the two formats are probably about equal in popularity among industry publishers.

Magazines and newspapers of industry are infinitely better designed than they once were. There is more reader sensitiveness on the part of editorial staffs to the tastes of the reading public. After all, employees read the professionally created publications too, and have some appreciation of what makes a publication attractive.

The most significant turn of the tide is in the audience approach of the company publication. The vast majority of employee magazines and newspapers have been—and still are—monthlies. Companies are finding new audience possibilities in the employee publication, however; if broadened somewhat in its editorial "slant," it can become an effective ambassador outside as well as inside the plant gates. Thus the so-called internal-external magazine has been born.

This internal-external is simply a publication for multiple audiences—employees and those outside the company. Most of the companies which have invaded this broader field of publishing issue their internal-externals on a quarterly rather than a monthly basis. Most are attractively, professionally designed. Most reach out to influential audiences such as stockholders, customers, and sometimes prospects; opinion leaders in the industry and within the plant communities; and schools and libraries. (See also Chapter 5 of Section 12.) Some publications are edited, consciously or unconsciously, as though they were directed essentially at company employees with an invitation extended to these other readers to scan the contents over employees' shoulders.

This procedure would appear to reduce the impact of direct communication, because the internal-external in a sense shares audiences. Companies which have embarked on this newer type of publication program, however, generally rearrange their internal publication structures so that no actual weakening of communication occurs. For example, a multiplant company may merge its monthly magazine into a quarterly internal-external magazine, but meanwhile introduce a simple biweekly or monthly tabloid newspaper. Or it may decide that more local-level communication is needed and accordingly introduce a series of local newsletters, edited and produced at the individual plants. Quite often a company will accelerate its internal bulletin board program, thus utilizing a fast, inexpensive means of communication.

PUBLICATION CHECKS AND BALANCES

An employee publication—as part of the company's total communications effort—needs its checks and balances. If it becomes the exclusive responsibility of a single department with no particular involvement on the part of other departments, then it obviously tends to become the single department's mouthpiece. To ensure the publication's reasonable balance, the single department should buttress itself with the experience and counsel of other department representatives.

One oil company set up a publication advisory process which was supervised by the director of public relations, who reported directly to the company president. The director, however, was counseled by a committee which represented major areas of the company's activity—sales, manufacturing, industrial relations, and research and development. Article ideas for the company magazine were developed at least six months in advance by the editor and his staff and submitted to the committee for review and approval. If there were valid objections to any subject proposed, it was either scrapped or temporarily shelved. When the meeting was concluded, the public relations director and the editor who reported to him had a clear set of signals. They knew precisely what material to develop for publication, and they had the assurance of the approval of the subject by the department or departments involved. One of the major roadblocks in employee communication generally is the difficulty of securing executive approvals of material; this procedure whittled down approval time to the point where deadlines could be realistically met.

In this company, as in many others, employee communications is a top-level responsibility. Something as delicate as communicating with employees, the management feels, can no longer be safely entrusted to someone down the line hamstrung by policy. Decisions in employee communications must be made quickly and emphatically, the experienced and successful managements appear to feel, or there is little sense in attempting to communicate at all.

Checklist for Publication Content. Rather than move aimlessly into the subject possibilities of employee publication preparation, companies prefer to take an occasional look at the bench marks. The following are five general subject areas, and under each is a list of suggested topics.

To provide information for employees: Company products and their uses; plant operations; sales operations; benefits plans; production; research and development; divisions and departments, how they operate; plans and programs of management; history of the company and of the industry; changes of personnel, promotion from within; company problems; policy; competition; customers; important news as it occurs.

To enlist employee cooperation: Prevent waste and scrap; increase productivity; stimulate efficiency; reduce costs; curtail personnel turnover; encourage better communication between management and employees; correct rumors; assist in bringing in new, desirable personnel; reduce resistance to change; stimulate political action and participation in civic affairs.

To educate employees: In matters of health; safety and accident prevention; good public relations; industry, company, and general economics; automation; social change; good citizenship; importance of the industry and the company to the national economy.

To provide inspiration for employees in respect to: Pride in the job; pride in the company; teamwork; customer goodwill; community goodwill; employee goodwill; annuitants' goodwill; employee morale; confidence in and loyalty to management initiative and "drive"; the importance of the individual.

To entertain the employee reader: With articles of high human interest; personality sketches about individuals in the company; "hobby" stories; news and features on sports and recreation.

It is a profitable practice for a management to review, at the end of each year, what it has accomplished within the period. Such a list as this provides some guidelines.

THE NEWSLETTER IN COMMUNICATIONS

For high-speed, low-budget communication, many managements use the newsletter. This is the most convenient form of communication in print. Newsletter audiences are as wide and varied as the publisher chooses. Among the possible internal audiences are employees (shop, office, or both); managerial-level employees (this involves the so-called confidential letter to upper-range officialdom); the supervisory group; and such special groups as technical staffs. The product may be carpentered to specific requirements; actually this is not difficult to do if certain ground rules are respected.

Any concern can produce a newsletter, but not every concern produces an effective one. For clues to creating and maintaining an effective newsletter, examine these common characteristics of the more effective letters:

They appear to enjoy the solid and continuing support of top management. They show no signs of having been neglected after a few issues.

They are issued regularly. The newsletter without a regular, scheduled deadline will ultimately be without influence.

They are simply designed. Quite often they are printed internally on plant equipment. Hence they cost little; they do not overawe the employee.

The content is forthright, which means that editorial restrictions are few.

The approval system for copy is simple. Publishing schedules are not missed simply because some subaltern wanted his finger in the pie.

They cover the ground. Management knows what areas to cover, because it has taken the trouble to discover *what employees want to know.* Often this has proved to be precisely what management wants most to tell them.

What Employees Wish to Know. In this connection, not long ago before introducing a newsletter program a multiplant company decided that it would first check to determine (1) if employees were actually interested in such a medium and (2) if they were, what sort of information they would want the newsletter to convey.

More than 1,000 employees voiced their opinions in face-to-face interviews. From these direct interrogations came the answers to management's questions: (1) yes, employees definitely wanted a newsletter at the individual plants and (2) they had specific suggestions to make with respect to content.

This company built its entire plant-level communications program around the suggestions made by the interviewed employees. Here are the recommendations the employees made for newsletter topics, in the order of their preference:

1. *The outlook.* What is the status of future business so far as the management can see it? How do things look for a man who has his security tied up with the company?

2. *Product information.* What is new in our product line? What improvements are we making on existing products?

3. *Construction and expansion.* Does it look as though we are growing? Are we expanding nationally? How will national expansion involve us locally?

4. *Problems of the company.* Are these affecting us in any way? If so, is there anything the individual employee can do to help improve the situation?

5. *Competition.* Specifically, who are the competitors? How are they doing? Is there any possibility of being advised, from issue to issue of the newsletter, where we stand in relation to competition?

6. *Customers.* What happens to our products when they go out the door? Who are the customers, and are there end uses of our products we do not know anything about?

To these, the interviewed employees added others: how sales are made, and the relationship between sales and production; company officials (at the headquarters level); promotions and transfers; departmental operations (so a man could show his wife what work he performed in the shop); questions and answers (where a man could write in a question and get a straight reply); new equipment coming into the plant; research and development; and, of course, the personal comings and goings of employees at the plant—service anniversaries, hobbies, sports events, benefits information, and the like.

The list of possible contents for a newsletter is limitless. In one list of more than 100 topic areas a company developed, ranging from "Advancement—who has been promoted lately?" to "Waste—how can we help reduce it?" the company found enough editorial fodder to keep it and its employee readers nourished for years.

Authorship and Approvals. In the larger company with a public relations or publications department, the authorship of a newsletter is clearly fixed. Without such departments, however, a company must turn to other service departments (probably personnel first of all) to find the editor. The job is actually neither onerous nor time consuming, provided it is properly set up. It is important, however, that management give the project its full, active endorsement and that the editor establish specific, reliable news sources so that he may develop his material quickly and efficiently by interview. If a top official is to approve copy (and he should), then arrange it so that all copy comes to him *approved at the source,* a final approval for policy being all that is needed.

If the president—or the plant general manager—is to draft an editorial regularly, he too should respect the deadline. A delay in the executive message means a delay of the issue, and delays can be costly.

The most effective newsletters, and the best received, are those which are informally, even conversationally written. Sentences are short and uninvolved. Copy is directed at the reader—it is "you" copy or "we" copy. It is written within the framework of the employee's own experience, in terms he understands. The editor writes neither up to his audience nor down to it. This, of course, takes some skill.

Newsletters—most of which are mailed to employees' homes—are looked upon as an established, continuous link of communication with employees, if used as they should be. They are of particular value when labor difficulties are brewing. For a management to leap into print with a new, unexplained newsletter during labor difficulties may invite suspicion; it certainly will not necessarily invite cooperation.

The Supervisory Newsletter. A comparison piece to the employee newsletter is the newsletter built especially for supervisors. It came into being when the oral communication processes between the company and supervision, and between supervisors and their own people, began to wear down. Management recognized that some form of printed support was necessary. Thus the supervisory newsletter was born as a form of assurance that the maxim, "The supervisor is the key man of management," has substance.

Some supervisory letters cover essentially production matters, but many others recognize the broader purposes of the medium: (1) to keep supervisors assured that they are members of the management "team"; (2) to make more effective the role of the supervisor as a communications link between company and employee; (3) to encourage company-employee cooperation; and (4) to build or maintain a good image of supervision in the eyes of employees.

The companies which appropriately respect the continuity of communications recognize that management information begins at upper levels of management, moves to supervision, then to the union committee if the concern is organized, then orally by supervision to employees with the information simultaneously printed and posted on the bulletin boards. That, ideally, is the flow. Too often the supervisor finds himself bypassed as a result of management's haste to reach the press; the news is frequently garbled in the plant, and the rumor mill has its field day. A sound program of supervisory communication via newsletter—plus good newsletter and bulletin coverage to employees—will avoid much of that distress.

If the company wishes to introduce a supervisory newsletter, bring up the topic at a supervisory meeting. Ask supervisors to jot down—anonymously if they prefer—the topics they think most need discussion in such a bulletin. The responses should keep the editor supplied with ideas for many, many issues.

THE BULLETIN BOARD

In the argot of the inexperienced, the plant bulletin board is a catch-basin for outdated notices, and that is all it will ever be. This cynical view is on the decline. There are mounting evidences that bulletin boards—in shops and offices around the country—are being treated with new managerial respect. Why? Because, probably next to the grapevine, it is the fastest communications medium in the plant.

Bulletin boards are not solely a shop medium, either. Advertising agencies, insurance companies, banks, and department stores use them widely, and each year more effectively. Management on the whole has begun to view the bulletin board as a point of employer-employee contact—not once a day, but several times a day. If your company is building an employee communications program, by all means see to it that bulletin boards are not overlooked.

The technicalities of construction and layout are not important here. It is important only that whatever boards you use be clean, efficiently located, and well arranged. Color helps, obviously; so do lighting and glass; so does an attentive interest to the material that is posted on the boards themselves.

This is an up-to-the-minute medium of communication—the flash-news device, the "special extra!" spot. Since speed is one of the essentials of good communication, make sure your bulletin board handlers have everything ready for quick reproduction. One company which prepares a daily newsletter bulletin starts its assembly at seven o'clock in the morning, has it posted on 103 boards by nine. Another company publishes a large picture newspaper, prints it overnight, and has it displayed on the boards in time for the first shift, telling the men today what happened as late as yesterday. Do not ignore the medium; *use it.*

Bulletin Board Uses.   The novitiate asks: Use it for what?

First, for spot news announcements; the fast-breaking developments you need to rush to the people—such items as plant visitors prior to arrival; accidents; deaths; developments in negotiations; changes of work schedules; promotions and appointments; status of production; service anniversaries, preferably within the week they occur, or if possible on the same day; names (and if possible, pictures) of new employees the day they begin work; any special events of immediate interest; production jobs going through the plant that day.   One company posts weather reports, another road conditions.

Additionally, the bulletin board is your place to feature—prominently and dramatically—the developments in your plant, company, or industry that *interest and concern employees*.   To suggest a few: new customers and what they are buying from you; new construction or new equipment, announced prior to start or installation—possibly what it costs and in what ways it may affect employment in the plant; changes in personnel—promotions, new appointments; company expansion—acquisitions or mergers; company plans; competition—who the competitors are, what they are making; end products applications—what happens to the product when it goes out your door; financial news; reprints of advertisements.

It might be noted that material posted on bulletin boards and material used in newsletters appear to overlap in certain areas.   They do, deliberately.   The newsletter is a *home* medium, an external tool of communication, with a broad audience.   The bulletin board is a *plant* medium, with a restricted, quick-impression, on-the-run audience.   To do the job right, tell your story over again.

The bulletin board, industrial experimenters with boards have found, serves educational purposes.   It may be used to present graphically the status of business and the influences that move it up or down; developments in research; the basics of business economics.   In short, it is a teaching tool.

THE EMPLOYEE ANNUAL REPORT

The employee annual report can be an important addition to the management communications cabinet.   The report to employees, an acknowledgment by management of employee interest in company welfare, once took the form of a condensed version of the stockholder report, published in a few pages in the employee magazine or newspaper.   As employee interest heightened, as more employees became shareholders in the business, as the whole management concept of partnership mellowed, the employee report assumed an independent format.   Many are published as employee annual report booklets, separate and distinct from the company magazines.   In certain companies, the practice is to recognize the common interest of stockholder and employee and thus to merge the two reports into one.

Employee-report publishers tend to think first in terms of oral presentations of the financial year, to be documented later with written or printed material. One company stages an annual "jobholders' meeting" at which a panel of company officials makes brief summaries of the year, department by department. The meeting is then opened up for discussion and questioning.   Later the foremen meet with their own departmental people to clear up any doubtful points, the foremen having all been briefed prior to the conference.   Employees are given a copy of the employee report to take home and digest.   In another company, officials make an annual circuit of the plant communities, carrying the story of the year with them for presentation on a face-to-face basis to employees and their families at the local school auditorium or armory.   They supplement their "story" with visual aids such as films and the printed employee report, and throw open the meeting for questions at the end.

The printed employee report in most companies is normally a review of the company year combined with a simplified version of the statistical report (under such headings as "We took in," "We spent," "This amount was divided as follows," "Balance retained for use in the business"). It is a booklet which, if attractively prepared, is geared to a fairly long life on an employee's living room table. It becomes a reference book and often a "conversation piece" with friends and neighbors.

Characteristics of an Effective Employee Annual Report. The more experienced compiler of employee reports, sensitive to the interests and preferences of employee readers, normally keeps such pointers as the following in mind.

He avoids "accounting language." Facts are localized in a way that appeals to the person who works in the plant. The "pro" editor explains difficult terms; his copy is full of examples. He uses simple, easy-to-grasp graphs and dollar charts. He knows that the "gimmick" type of employee report lived only a short time; too often the "offbeat" technique left the employee annoyed and skeptical. Hence the good report is simple, straightforward, and unaffected.

He includes the employee *family* in his listening audience. He recognizes that the wife and children have a major stake in the employee's job.

Before he begins work on his report, he probes for the informational vacuums. Through informal shop and office interviews, he learns what employees want to know about a business year, and he puts his emphasis there. If he feels that profit—or the lack of it—is misunderstood, he uses his report to explain it. If employee benefits are simply being taken for granted, he amplifies and interprets. He senses the opportunity to bring employer and employee more closely together in a relationship of common interest, and he grasps it.

He starts his project *early*. He collects his background information, photos, and graphs month by month. By the time the publication deadline looms, he has little to do but to insert the final figures from the shareholder report.

A note of caution is in order. If the company issues both a stockholder report and an employee report, make the stockholder report *available* to employees. Do not give out the stockholder report without an employee request— he will appreciate it more if he must ask for it, and he will be more apt to read it after he gets it.

Not all concerns are interested in publishing an employee report. The privately owned concern rarely issues such a report; those which are closely held generally refrain from it. A company can accomplish much in its own behalf, however—without producing a report—if it publishes instead an "annual review." In a year-end review, the management can discuss the state of the business, the prospects, research and development, and other topics of interest and concern to employees without exposing the company's books.

The employee report, potentially at least, is a great welding medium. It can and does unite employer and employee. It is an open acknowledgment that the employee also has a stake in the company's future, and it invites him to share in building it.

THE EMPLOYEE HANDBOOK

Among the tools of employee communications, there is probably no medium actually older than the "rules and regulations" booklet. In the early days of industry, rules were posted on bulletin boards (and many still are), but today most concerns assemble their rules and regulations information in booklet form so that each employee may have his own copy for reference.

The physical size of the employee handbook or indoctrination manual—which today includes the rules and regulations—has not changed particularly. (Management continues to believe that employees carry them around in pockets or handbags, which they do not.) The design of the book, however, has been altered and frequently brightened. The text of these manuals has been softened to eliminate the often strident, imperious language. It is no longer the "ABC Co. Rules and Regulations"; it is more apt to be "Welcome to ABC!" In the more modern manuals, the type is easier to read than in the older prototypes. Illustrations—even humorous illustrations—are now quite common.

Handbook Contents and Distribution. Whether the manual is to be developed for a multiplant company with 50,000 employees or a small plant with 150, the approach is fundamentally the same. Keep in mind that this is essentially a book of welcome to the new employee, designed to make him feel at home and to point out to him the rules by which your company lives. The knowledgeable manual compiler will break his manual into parts: first, the introduction, history, and general information about the company or plant and its products; second, company or plant practices and the specific rules, or as some concerns prefer to put it, the "standards of conduct."

In the opening section, the compiler should consider using a message of greeting from the top official (in the single plant, generally the president; in the plant of a multiplant operation, normally the plant manager). Follow with a brief—very brief—history of the company; a report of physical operations; a detailed listing and illustrations of end products. (Some companies, where practical, include a floor plan, and others an organization chart with photos, even at the risk of a major personnel shift within the life span of the manual.) In the second section, the compiler uses pictures and descriptions of services—personnel, first aid, and safety; then the rules and regulations.

Rules and regulations copy can be both overlong and deadly. It is good policy to phrase the rule both temperately and logically. If there is a sound reason for a no-smoking rule, for example, state it.

An employee manual is a "sell" book. Its aim is to welcome the new employee, certainly, but also to affirm a company's interest in and concern about those already on the payroll. The manual broadly edited has value as a recruitment manual; if you use it for such purposes, by all means talk length of service and promotion from within. (If you cannot, perhaps some company rule needs regulating.) If the manual is built with external audiences in mind, the rules and regulations section applicable solely to employees may be omitted from the externally distributed copies. Do not make the mistake of viewing an employee manual as a medium of limited internal value. It has persuasive powers far beyond the plant gates, if you so create it.

The title of the employee manual is of great importance. The cold, formal title will repel; the warm, informal title will invite. It is important, too, to consider the front cover in terms of its appeal to the employee, new and old alike. Look at your own present employee manual; would *you*, as an employee, be encouraged to pick it up?

How long should the employee manual "last"? What is its "life"? There is no accurate answer. Obviously, when the text material is obsolete or shows signs of it, it is time for a change. The average manual life is influenced also by the rate of personnel turnover. As a target, figure on a life span of three to five years for a manual.   At the end of three years, look it over with an eye to the need for change.

Distribution of a handbook is a problem in some companies.   Some mail it to the home, with a covering letter from a plant official, a few days after the new employee has been hired.   Others require personnel department interviewers to pass out copies to individual employees as they are signed in.   The best method, in the minds of most, is to hold a brief, face-to-face indoctrination session, where a personnel department representative explains the booklet, hands it out to the new employees, and immediately checks their ability to use the manual as a reference.   A point to remember about the value of proper handbook introduction is that the better a new employee understands the manual, the fewer questions he will need to submit to supervisors.   The good manual, properly presented, is a strong, time-saving supervisory assist.

The multiplant publisher frequently faces problems with his manual's production: Benefit X, let us say, applies to Plant A, but not to Plant B; Plant Y has a cafeteria, but Plant Z does not; a rule that applies to six company plants does not apply to a seventh.   In such instances, the company will be well advised to produce a manual with general pages *common to all plants* and to include an insert specifically localized to the individual plant.

CONCLUSION

The communications devices described above are considered the *major* devices of employer-employee communication; each should be supported, of course, by strong and consistent *oral* communication.   A communications program may be further strengthened by the introduction, as needed, of such devices as the executive letter to the home; the recruitment manual; the "fact card"; and others referred to above.

In building or refining a communications program, a management often is confronted with questions.   Here are a few, together with capsuled answers:

Q *How do we determine publication costs in advance?*

A Costs vary from city to city, from company to company, and from printer to printer.   We suggest you first determine what publications you want and need, then ask for competitive bids from suppliers.

Q *With what communications tools should a company with a modest budget begin a program?*

A Try a simple monthly newsletter first, backstopped by an up-to-the-minute bulletin board program.

Q *What should we look for in a company publication editor?*

A Technical competence, of course.   More important, however, you should evaluate his interest in mingling with his audience, his ability to present the management "story" in a manner understandable to employees, and his skill in serving as a two-way communications agency so that he can reflect what is on the minds of his readers.   He should have broad experience in communications, rather than experience limited simply to "house organ" editing.   He should have less immediate interest in stepping up the corporate ladder than in making the job he has important.

Q *How can we determine whether our communications efforts are "on the beam"?*

A Check them periodically, through either internal or external survey.   Face-to-face interviews obviously reveal the most, but even simple, internally conducted postcard samplings can indicate strength and weakness. The point is: Make sure you check it.

BIBLIOGRAPHY

Dooher, M. Joseph, and Vivienne Marquis, *Effective Communication on the Job*, American Management Association, New York, 1956.

Dover, C. J., *Effective Communication in Company Publications*, U.S. Bureau of National Affairs, Washington, D.C., 1959.

Dover, C. J., *Management Communication on Controversial Issues*, U.S. Bureau of National Affairs, Washington, D.C., 1965.

Merrihue, Willard V., *Managing by Communications*, McGraw-Hill Book Company, New York, 1960.

Newcomb, Robert, and Marg Sammons, *Employee Communication in Action*, Harper & Row, Publishers, Incorporated, New York, 1961.

Newcomb, Robert, and Marg Sammons, *Speak Up, Management!* Funk & Wagnalls Company, New York, 1954.

Reddick, DeWitt C., and Alfred A. Crowell, *Industrial Editing*, Matthew Bender & Co., Inc., New York, 1962.

Scholz, William, *Communication in the Business Organization*, Prentice-Hall, Inc., Englewood Cliffs, N.J., 1962.

CHAPTER TWENTY-TWO

Attitude Surveys

DOUGLAS WILLIAMS *Chairman, Douglas Williams Associates, Inc., New York, New York*

What is morale? In the military, the definition of "morale" is the "will to fight."

In industry, it could be—and should be—the "will to work."

In the minds of many, however, the term "employee morale" has come to signify something different. "Job satisfaction" is a phrase used interchangeably with "morale"; and "job satisfaction" often seems to have a connotation of happiness, of contentment. Contentment in a work situation does not suggest a high degree of work effort. Indeed, the implication of passivity is clear.

When the matter of improving employee morale—or job satisfaction—is considered, there are those who advocate a "social worker" approach. Their orientation seems to be how to make things easier or more enjoyable for the employee, rather than how to increase productivity through more effective employee performance.

Real Purpose of Attitude Surveys. It is easy to place attitude surveys into this social worker context, so let us clarify the definition of "attitude surveys" as a management tool which helps an organization to be more successful by ensuring the best possible contribution to the company's objectives from the employee body.

More specifically, the purpose of employee attitude (or morale) research is to help management understand how best to:

Motivate people to work
Enable them to work most effectively

Enabling involves matters such as providing training; ensuring a smooth work flow, availability of parts, and effective physical working conditions; making sure all employees understand how their jobs relate to the work of other departments; and seeing that they are informed about company plans.

This basic purpose of attitude surveys underscores the belief that most employees want to turn in a good job performance. The more a person feels his work is useful and necessary and that what he does is important in the company's scheme of things, the more genuine job satisfaction he will have.

Another Aspect of Attitude Surveys. An important corollary value of an attitude survey is the opportunity it extends to employees to participate in the project. Management demonstrates its interest in the opinions and ideas of the people, and the problems and experiences they have in doing their job.

Employees appreciate being able to express their criticisms with complete candor. "Participation" is a word which is positive in nature, and attitude surveys, therefore, have a positive aspect.

Too often they are regarded as a channel for airing complaints. But a survey can produce useful employee ideas regarding improving customer service or increasing product quality.

This is not to imply that employee dissatisfaction revealed in a survey is *ipso facto* negative in nature. In one survey, the manufacturing vice president was concerned because the younger foremen in his supervisory group were so critical of certain problems in the plant. The fact that these men were alert enough to see the dangers in such problems, and interested enough to express their objections, testified to their value to the organization. If they had been bland in their interviews, he would have had real cause for concern.

Final Note Regarding Fundamental Purpose. One of the most difficult problems of management is achieving a healthy state of communications, a free, steady stream of information throughout the company—operating information, organizational information, social information.

On the communications front, an upward flow—from bottom to top—is usually the route where most blockages and most distortions occur. An attitude survey is a means of seeing that employee attitudes do get up the line. The information gathered this way has not been filtered. It is authentic.

PRELIMINARY STATEMENT REGARDING SURVEY METHODS

The matter of survey techniques is discussed below. Because of a common misconception which exists, however, it is necessary to bring out one point regarding methods early. This guards against the false assumption that employee attitude research equates with a questionnaire study; that if a survey is done, the technique used is a questionnaire with checklist questions—and only a questionnaire. There have been many magazine articles devoted to criticizing attitude surveys, assuming them to be "poll type" in nature and describing the inadequacies which can be characteristic of questionnaires. Such authors, it is apparent, are not trying to manipulate their readers by an unfair presentation of the facts. They are just unfamiliar with how surveys can be done in an optimum fashion.

Personal interviews, usually conducted on a comparatively unstructured basis, should almost invariably be an essential part of the attitude survey process. Sometimes this is the only method utilized. Interviews, of course, are conducted on a basis of anonymity assured to the respondent.

Interviews should be carried out by highly qualified people who are at the consultant level. People doing this kind of interviewing need to have a sensitive understanding of human behavior and a sophisticated familiarity with the realities of corporate life in the factory, office, laboratory, and selling areas. They must have an appreciation of matters such as: When employees do not believe management pronouncements, why don't they? What change takes place in an hourly worker when he is promoted to foreman—probably with little or no advance training? Is the truth told in performance appraisals? And so on.

If a survey is to have real value to management, the findings depend, at least in part, on the kinds of insight and the depth of understanding which are singularly the product of personal interviews. If a questionnaire is to be administered, it should be tailored to the particular group. The questions should be constructed on the basis of what was learned in the personal interviews.

The following example demonstrates how important the personal interview approach can be to a down-to-earth understanding of the morale climate of an organization.

In this particular case, one aspect of the findings can be summarized as follows. A plant manager, harsh and vindictive in the extreme, had been replaced by a new man. His successor comported himself at the other end of the scale. He was permissive in the extreme. He listened patiently to the hourly men's complaints, usually accepting their version of problems on the floor. Then he would criticize the foremen for not being fair with their men or for being unnecessarily tough with them.

The foremen began to refrain from insisting on proper work standards, for fear of not being supported by higher management. They even ceased to jump into emergency situations by stopping machinery which was producing faulty work; they were afraid they would be censured for taking over the duties of hourly employees.

The foremen deeply resented their emasculation, and made this clearly evident in their treatment of hourly paid men. The latter retaliated against this "treatment as inferiors" by carrying even more complaints to the plant manager. Production fell off. The attitude climate was miserable. Truly, a vicious circle was in full orbit.

Perception of a problem like this cannot come out of a questionnaire of formal, categorized answers. Nor do employees fill out "freehand" questions in their own words to such an extent that an analyst can obtain this depth of understanding.

It is necessary for a task force of interviewers to probe and ask questions, to follow up clues, to build one question on another in the same interview, and to use the learning from one interview in following sessions to develop the kind of understanding reflected in the foregoing evaluation.

SPECIFIC REASONS FOR DOING ATTITUDE SURVEYS

Do Not Delay. The kinds of situations in which attitude surveys can be singularly useful are countless and ever-recurring. There is, however, one underlying principle regarding the timing of these studies which can be stated at the outset: Do not wait too long. Do not wait until the trouble has worked in deep and is really festering.

A classic example is for the management of a plant in which the employees do not belong to a union to wait until an organizing drive is under way before deciding an attitude survey would help their understanding of the situation. Another illustration is a company with a union, having suffered a bad strike, considering a survey to throw light on why a continuingly bitter spirit in the employee group seems to prevail.

In both cases, surveys should have been conducted at much earlier points in time. When employees go out on strike, they often have deep sources of resentment against the management. These are not necessarily clearly evident in the ostensible issues. Not infrequently, the management does not "read" the temper of the people correctly, because it is not tuned in on what is really on employees' minds.

The purpose of an attitude survey is to develop this kind of information objectively, accurately, and insightfully.

Periodic Attitude Surveys. One way to look at attitude surveys is as a periodic physical examination. Individuals who uncover problems of health at an early enough stage find they can be handled on the basis of mild medication, diet, or exercise rather than radical surgery.

"An ounce of prevention is worth a pound of cure" also applies to corporate health.

Surveys are most effective, too, if they are timely and are aimed at specific situations or at problems the organization needs to lick. A responsive action program is the very purpose of an attitude survey. When a survey comes to grips with a specific opportunity to improve or a specific problem to cure, management is likely to be more keenly interested in the findings, to be in a frame of mind to learn from the results, and to move forward with follow-up action steps.

Sometimes it is an advantage for an organization to employ a rather open, even general, line of questioning in its first survey. This ensures bringing out those matters (both problems and opportunities) that are on employees' minds. Many of these opinions, ideas, and experiences might be partly, or totally, unknown to management.

Once this basic morale inventory is established, attitude surveys can be used as a continuing tool to aid management on the many specific problems either constantly present, such as communications, or newly arising, such as increased automation.

Examples of Specific Reasons for Surveys. *Communications.* The communications problem exists in every company. There is no organization which does not make mistakes or have misses on this score.

Some managements are notably more successful than others in establishing a healthy climate for communications. People feel freer to speak up to those above them. Operating specifications do reach their mark, and on time. Adequate advance notice of changes is given. Company policies are communicated down the line.

When a better job is done on these and related items in the communications picture, productivity is increased—and vital factors such as interdepartmental relationships are kept on a more even keel.

One of the best ways for a company to check on the effectiveness of its communications and to devise ways to improve what it is doing is through an employee attitude survey.

Training. The caliber of training is another element which varies tremendously from company to company.

This applies to training of employees at the hourly paid and clerical level and at the supervisory and key-person level, and to developmental programs for the management ranks.

Before training programs are devised and put into effect, a great deal of really pertinent information can be garnered via the survey technique as to what kinds of training people need and in what ways they do not feel properly prepared for their responsibilities. After the programs have been completed, an evaluation can be made of their effectiveness—again through an inquiry among the employees.

Often a "before and after approach" has been employed with good results.

Employees are queried before the training experience regarding their knowledge and ability, and then afterward to determine the impact of the program. This technique has been used to evaluate programs lasting as short a time as a day for hourly paid people (on subjects such as an understanding of the work done in related departments); it is also used on executive development programs that take several months to complete. The results of such studies develop insights that can lead to far-reaching improvements in both the content and method of training programs.

The survey technique can be simple. For instance, if a training film is being produced, it can be shown to small groups of employees while it is still in a rough state—easy to follow on the screen, but still subject to changes. They can then be interviewed as to their reactions, to determine the clarity of the message, consistency of understanding of what is portrayed, and the like.

Customer Service. Surveying employees on their ideas regarding *improving customer service* has been referred to above, but it is such an important concept it should be mentioned again. Obviously, this approach has great merit for companies dealing directly with the public—airlines, retail establishments, public utilities, and so on.

Sometimes a survey done simultaneously among the organization's customers as well, with respect to their attitudes toward the quality of service, adds to the value of the study among each group.

Plant Performance. If a plant's *product quality* starts to fall off, if *productivity* starts to decrease, if employee *turnover* starts going up, any of these developments might signal the need for an attitude survey.

Innovation. Attitude surveys can sometimes be most useful when they are done in *concert with an innovation* or change that is being made. For instance, let us assume a company is introducing a new standards system, involving a new wage-incentive plan. A program of interviewing among the machine workers, their supervisors, and the standards men in the engineering department can uncover problems before they become deep-seated and can point up where improved communications are needed.

The same applies to an installation of electronic data-processing equipment. How do the professional people providing the EDP service see their role in relation to the rest of the organization? What is the level of understanding in the operating departments regarding the help they can get from EDP? Do they regard it as interference or a threat to their status? Problems such as these are easier to handle when management is aware of them in their emerging state—before they become full bloom.

Segmented Surveys. Often, a survey can have singular utility when carried out in just one segment of the organization. For instance, the professional people in the research division of a corporation are a group with distinct characteristics. Their motivations, their frustrations, and their sense of reward are on a different end of the scale from those of assembly-line operators. A company's ultimate success can be largely dependent on the contribution to its technology made by these scientists and engineers. It is essential for top management to have a realistic appreciation of what "makes these men tick" to ensure that the company obtains their top efforts.

A sales force out in the field, which does not have full contact with headquarters, can get to feel like orphans. Management may not be getting the benefit of the salesmen's reactions to sales policies and their customers' reactions to product quality, delivery, and servicing of their accounts.

As a final example, an internal survey can be carried out at the top of the corporate pyramid to determine the clarity and consistency of understanding this group has of corporate goals. Are they "on board" with respect to fundamental company policies? Has the intent of the very top management, with respect to corporate objectives, gotten through to these men responsible for executing them? A company can increase the strength of its operations manyfold by ensuring a clarity in the company's goals at the top. This is essential to the management's having a "sense of mission."

SURVEY METHODS

The importance of the personal interview, conducted anonymously, was emphasized above. Interviews must be done by mature, skilled people who are able to establish rapport and encourage the respondent to talk freely. They must be able to recognize clues which need following up and to discern what is most significant in what the respondent is describing.

Such interviews usually have to be carried out by personnel from an independent agency, not by members of the corporation itself. Employees are not likely to speak up fully and frankly about their frustrations and motivations, about company programs and policies, or about working problems to someone in the same organization who might be in a position sometime to endanger their status in the company.

In an interview, the employee is usually first asked to bring up what is on his mind. This is because he may make a contribution to the survey findings by volunteering some ideas or by having a viewpoint of a situation which is unknown to the management or the interviewer. Thus it is usually wise not to channel the subject matter too quickly. As the session progresses, the interviewer can introduce topics of particular interest to management.

The interview should be probing and exploratory in nature. The employee is asked to go into the "why" of his attitudes. Sometimes such reasons are as important as the actual pro or con of his viewpoint. And it is helpful, too, to get specific examples from his work experiences. The specificity that can be produced by these personal interviews is one of their most important characteristics.

Even if a questionnaire contains quite a few "freehand" questions in which people are asked to express their opinions in their own words, the answers are not as complete, as thorough, or as explicit as those obtained in a two-way verbal session. Nor can the intensity or the flavor of attitudes be conveyed via the questionnaire technique, as it can through a personal interview.

Everyone knows that *communications* in a company are important. But a true appreciation of the significance of communications can be heightened immeasurably by the results gained from interviews. In these, it is possible to trace how employees actually are prevented from carrying out a task, or completing it effectively, because of poor information. Just as important, one can see in its real proportions how employees feel left out and are made to feel unimportant and "not on the team" if superiors up the line do not bother to communicate with them.

Everyone knows that a wage-incentive system can be the source of extreme aggravation in a plant. A program of interviews can produce findings, supplemented by a host of specific illustrations, which the respondents have vigorously expressed.

Machine operators give their viewpoint of methods changes and new rates; machine breakdowns and "average time" pay; reliability of supply of parts; speed and adequacy of repair of machine; and the like.

Then foremen give their version. They may reveal a lack of understanding of the system, accompanied by a lack of sympathy for it —which has an unmistakable effect on the worker.

Interviews with mechanics and those supplying material for the machines will probably further attest to the problems created by the state of their relationships with the machine operator.

The sessions with the "time-study engineers" will reveal how sensitive they are to the level of understanding of the system the employees have.

After such a series of interviews, a perspective can be developed which cannot be evolved in any other way.

Sampling. Unless the unit to be surveyed is very small (under 100), personal interviews are usually carried out on a sampling basis in the interests of economy and time. A carefully drawn sample will produce, for all practical purposes, all the information a census would.

The size of the sample is not determined on any kind of "percentage of the whole" basis. For one thing, the complexity of the organizational structure is relevant; also relevant are such matters as the number of shifts. A sample must be representative of all the different departments, types of work, and kinds of employees. Therefore, it is built up cell by cell rather than based on the population as a whole.

Actually, the sample size is a matter of judgment based on experience, coupled with the current experience of the particular survey. This means that when the interviews among any group of employees become repetitive and are not producing new information, no more are necessary.

It usually makes sense to pick the smallest sample that might suffice. If, after completing interviews with this number, the survey team thinks it needs more—from some particular segment, such as supervisors, the engineering department, or operators in some assembly room—then additional interviews can be scheduled. This procedure guards against covering an unnecessarily large cross section.

Usually, a heavier sample is drawn at the top of an organizational pyramid; somewhat lighter across the middle (in general, the supervisory level); and lightest at the bottom among the hourly paid people in the factory and clerical employees in the office. Of course, the largest number of people, in absolute terms, would be in this nonmanagement grouping.

In a unit of 500 employees, a sample might well be made up of 100 people, composed as follows:

Management level (all or nearly all)	10
Supervisory and technical (about one out of two)	25
Nonsupervisory	65
	100

If the unit had a population of 1,000, the number of interviews would not double. The sample would probably be about 150. If the organizational structure were complex, however, the sample might have to be larger.

Within any organizational segment (such as level of personnel, department, or shift), those in the sample are selected on an every-nth basis. Thus, if a department had 50 people and 10 were to be interviewed, every fifth name would be pulled from a roster arranged, for instance, in alphabetical order or according to clock number.

The sample should then be visually inspected to be sure that the approximate proportions of seniority, type of job, sex, and the like are represented. This guards against some vagary having had an unwitting effect on the way the roster lists employees or the way names are checked off. If bias is discovered, modifications in the sample are made according to some objective procedure.

Personal Interviews. Depending on the purpose of the survey and the size and complexity of the organization, the personal interview technique may represent the total research design.

Or there may be a need for quantitative results. The organization may be large enough that it is necessary to have the assurance of exact percentages. (It might not be economical to carry out an adequate number of personal interviews.) It could be very important to be able to categorize the results according to department, level of job, type of work, level and/or kind of compensation, sex, seniority, or the like. In such a case, a questionnaire is, of course, essential.

Group Interviews. If it is known ahead of time that there is going to be a questionnaire, it sometimes makes sense to arrange some of the interviews on a group basis. This means small groups of two or three people at a time, or at the most, four. The groups should probably be homogeneous—not a mixture of men and women, widely varying seniority levels, or supervisory and nonsupervisory levels.

Group interviews are less satisfactory than those with one individual, because respondents may be less inclined to speak up frankly in front of their colleagues. A full range of problems, however, can at least be delineated as having importance—so that such interviews help the determination of what subjects the questionnaire should cover.

The group interviews do have one actual advantage: discussion is stimulated. What one person says motivates someone else to say something that might not otherwise have occurred to him.

A primary point is that in scheduling some group interviews, a greater coverage of employees can be gained, in less time and accordingly with less cost. Of course, not all of the interviews should be on a group basis. There should be enough individual interviews to ensure getting the kind of information produced when the interviewer is alone with a respondent.

The Questionnaire. Usually a questionnaire is filled out by a census of the employees in the organization. Only if the population of a unit were in the many thousands would it make sense to go through the process of having the questionnaire answered by a sample. Tabulation expenses represent only a minor portion of the cost. There is also an advantage when all employees have a feeling of participating in the survey.

When a questionnaire is used, it should be custom-made for the particular survey. The questions should be prepared for that particular organization, with its particular employees, at that particular time.

The interviews previously conducted have defined the problems. The questionnaire measures these problems. The questions have to be based on and aimed at what was learned in the interviews.

A questionnaire unaccompanied by personal interviews—and lacking this tailored aspect—can easily pass over significant findings or indeed the most important problems.

The questionnaire stage of a survey can be carried out by the company's own personnel. The questionnaires are, of course, not signed, and the factor of anonymity does not have the same kind of sensitivity as would be the case if members of the company staff were doing personal interviews.

Some Examples of Questionnaire Items. Some questions are completely "freehand" in nature:

"What do you think are this company's strongest points—the most favorable things about it?"

"What do you think are this company's weakest points—the ways in which it has the most need for improvement?"

A dozen or so lines would be left for the answer in each case.

Some questions ask explicitly for reason why:

Do you feel that your pay is comparable with other jobs *in your department* requiring the same amount of skill?

Yes.. ( )

No... ( )

Don't know... ( )

What is the reason for your answer?_____

_____

_____

Some questions encourage additional comments:

How fair do you feel the work standards are for incentive-paid jobs in the XYZ Company?

I don't know enough about incentive-paid jobs here to answer................ ( )

All or nearly all of the incentive standards are as fair as they can make them.... ( )

Most of the incentive standards are as fair as they can make them .... ( )

Not many of the incentive standards are fair................................. ( )

Few or none of the incentive standards are fair.............................. ( )

Please write your comments on the incentive system here:_____

_____

_____

_____

_____

Some questions permit the employee to make a different answer, if he so desires, than the formal categories provided:

In some companies the pace of work is hard and fast to the point where the people feel unreasonably overworked. In other companies, the way the place is managed is so "loose" that there is too little expectation of what should be accomplished, so that some people "get away" with a lot. How would you rate the situation *in your department?*

Too much is expected—more than a reasonable amount...................... ( )

Too little is expected—less than a reasonable amount....................... ( )

Just about what is reasonable is expected.................................. ( )

Some other answer (*please explain below*)................................. ( )

_____

_____

_____

_____

Some questions are quite general (and can be used to make comparisons with other companies):

If you had it to do over again, would you choose this company as a place to work?

Yes.. ( )

No... ( )

Can't decide.. ( )

If a friend of yours were looking for a job, would you recommend this company as a good place to work?

Yes... ( )
No.. ( )
Don't know... ( )

Sometimes a series of questions is aimed at the same general point:

Now, here are some questions on your immediate superior—the *supervisor* or *manager* you report to directly.

In your opinion, which of the answers below best describes how your superior handles each of the following?

	Very good	Fairly good	Not so good	Not good at all	Can't decide
Planning and organizing the work so it goes efficiently..................................	( )	( )	( )	( )	( )
Giving you clear and complete instructions.......	( )	( )	( )	( )	( )

Etc.

About a dozen such questions would be asked in a series like the above.
Questions can be aimed at the top management as well as at immediate supervision:

The next few questions are about the top management of the XYZ Company—the ten or fifteen men who have the top positions of responsibility.

Please mark with an X one answer for each question, to show whether you feel *top management cares enough* about each thing or whether they should care more.

	Top men should care more	Top men care too much	Top men care about enough	Don't know
Producing high-quality products.............	( )	( )	( )	( )
Safety for the employees.	( )	( )	( )	( )

Etc.

Some questions are specialized according to the type of employee:

First please answer if your own work is on the incentive wage system.
My work is on the incentive wage system now ....( )
My work is not on the incentive wage system now, but it has been in the past ..( )
I have never worked on the incentive wage system ....( )
Now, here is a question on how you feel about the incentive wage system.
Is the system, as it is intended to work, a good idea?
Yes ....( )
No ....( )
Don't know ....( )

Etc.

How clearly do you feel you understand your responsibilities—what is expected of you as a supervisor?
Very clearly ....( )
Fairly clearly ....( )
Not so clearly ....( )
Not clearly at all ....( )

How do you feel about the amount of authority you are given to carry out your responsibilities, schedule the work, etc?

Have all I need ....(   )
Could use a little more ....(   )
Could use a lot more ....(   )
Not sure how much I have ....(   )

Etc.

Questions can be highly specific:

Which of the following practices regarding salary increases for office people do you prefer?

After plant employees receive a pay increase negotiated between the company and the union, office employees should be given a *general* raise—in which the pay of all office people is increased by about the same amount as was true of the plant employees ....(   )

Office employees' pay raises should be based on merit. This would mean that the same total amount of money would be available for salary increases, but those who were judged to be the most deserving would receive larger raises than others, and some could receive none at all ....(   )

Neither of the above ....(   )

I would prefer _____

_____

_____

_____

_____

Modifications in Survey Methods. There are modifications to the approach that has been described which are very important.

In the foregoing discussion on survey methods, it has been assumed that the organization has been undertaking a survey for the first time. Once a company has had experience with attitude surveys, however, it can work out a programmed approach. A series of standardized questions can be devised for its own organizational groupings and circumstances. These can be administered periodically to different units within the corporation. When the results from certain batteries of questions suggest problems or difficulties, personal interviews can dig into the reasons for such "departures from par."

STEPS IN CONDUCTING A SURVEY

Almost invariably, the intended objectives of the survey should be expressed in writing so that management and the survey team have a completely consistent perception of the survey's intent.

Announcement of the Survey. First, the survey—its purpose and how it is going to be conducted—should be reviewed personally with management. Unless completely infeasible, these personal reviews should be continued down through the supervisory level. If this cannot be done, the supervisory group should be informed about the survey by letter, before the nonsupervisory employees reporting to them learn of it.

The purpose of this approach, of course, is to enable higher management and supervisors to answer questions their subordinates may ask about the project. And naturally, this procedure puts people in a frame of mind to support the survey.

The final announcement step is to send a letter describing the survey to all employees. In an organization represented by a union, it is usually appropriate to discuss the survey in advance with the union officials.

Sampling. This procedure was adequately described in the discussion of survey methods. One additional point: In announcing the survey, tell employees how the sampling was done, to avoid the feeling that bias played a part.

Scheduling of Interviews. Interviews are usually scheduled in a sequence starting at the top of the organizational pyramid and proceeding downward to the bottom. One reason for this is that the survey team gets valuable ideas toward the top about the kind of information it will be most helpful to develop from the employees down the line.

Typically, interviews are scheduled to last one hour. Depending on the subject matter and the group, they can be longer or shorter. If, in an interview, an individual has a lot more to say than time allows, he should be rescheduled. Unless some unusual circumstances are present, an interviewer should not try to conduct more than half a dozen interviews during a normal workday.

Interviews should be held on company property and company time. Employees on shift should be interviewed on their shift, not asked to make a special trip in for the convenience of the survey team.

Employees should be notified only a day or a half a day in advance that they are going to be interviewed. This makes for a desirable degree of naturalness in the interview, as contrasted with what could amount to overpreparation—a lack of spontaneity.

Facilities for interviewing need not be plush, but they must be completely private and comfortable. Smoking should be allowed.

Interviewers should take notes. Trying to remember after the session all that an employee said is not a practical procedure. Notes taken in the first person, in the employee's own words, are usually most effective. Practiced interviewers can take notes with amazing speed. On those few occasions when note taking makes the respondent nervous, however, the interviewer will have to be content with writing up the interview after the session.

Preparation of Questionnaire. As in the case of interviewing, questionnaire preparation requires the talents and experience of highly qualified people. Questions must be phrased in a way that is neutral, but still with bite and significance. Do not ask for answers on a dual topic—"How do you feel about wages and working conditions?" If too many biographical questions are asked (department, job, level of seniority, pay classification, and so on), the employee will become suspicious that he will be identified. It takes experience to become sensitized to matters like these. Also, it takes experience to know how to word questions so they are clear to the employee without "talking down" to him.

Even the most experienced questionnaire writers should pretest questions on a small portion of the employees before final approval of the questionnaire. This ensures clarity of the questions—that they are not ambiguous and have the same meaning for all people. Also, the pretest stage serves to indicate how long it will take for the questionnaire to be answered. This period is usually set for an hour. A questionnaire necessitating sixty minutes for the slowest person can usually be filled out by the fastest in close to half an hour.

Administration of the Questionnaire. As in the case of the interviews, the questionnaire should be administered, if at all possible, on company property and company time. A cafeteria, a large conference room, or a portion of an office or plant furnished with chairs or tables are all suitable. Again, smoking should be allowed.

A proctor should hand out questionnaires, answer questions, and emphasize (as also written on the face sheet of the questionnaire) that the survey is anonymous.

If employees are so widely scattered geographically, in small groupings or even singly, that mailing completed questionnaires back to the survey team headquarters is the only practical means of administration, naturally this procedure must be followed. This method, of course, lacks the advantages of control that apply when employees are together for the purpose of answering the questionnaire.

ANALYSIS OF RESULTS

The procedures involved in the analysis of personal interviews and questionnaire results are quite technical and involved. They can be referred to only in a very brief and general way here.

Handling of Interview Results. The important point regarding the analysis of interview results is that it should start during the interviews. In most surveys, the field work will be carried out by a task force of from two to five interviewers. These interviewers should confer twice a day if possible, but certainly at least once a day. Then if any individual is uncovering findings of which the others are unaware, he can pass on this information. These conferences are also the beginning of an appreciation of the survey's important findings and themes.

By the time the interviewers sit down with their interview transcriptions when the field work is finished, they should have already discussed the results enough to be well on the road to carrying out the analytical process.

Handling of Questionnaire Results. Even small batches of questionnaires—in the few hundreds—are most speedily, economically, and effectively tabulated by computer programming. The computer can print out percentaged results so that the need for lengthy and tedious statistical typing is done away with. At the time of preparing the questionnaire, it is important that it be precoded, with answer categories numbered according to a sequence that conforms with the computer system (for instance, an eighty-column key-punch card).

In an overall discussion of attitude surveys, it is feasible to refer to only a couple of the most general aspects of questionnaire analysis. One is that it is often the comparison among different organizational segments that brings out the real significance of the questionnaire results—rather than the percentage totals. Consider, for instance, the following question:

There are different ways of thinking about the basis for paying people for their work. In the case where two people are doing the same kind of job and one person has more ability and turns in a better performance, some people say: "Pay the better performer more." Other people hold that, in industry, people in the same job category should each receive the same pay. Which of these two ideas do you think works out best in practice?

The results are:

	Nonsupervisory personnel	
	Lab	Plant
Better performance should receive more pay	66%	31%
In practice, it's best to pay men in the same job the same pay	29	60
No opinion	5	9

Sometimes differences are less dramatic, but nevertheless significant:

How hard are you expected to work at XYZ?

	Nonmanagement/Office		
	Total	Men	Women
Much too hard............................	5%	6%	5%
Somewhat too hard........................	17	16	17
About right..............................	68	61	70
Not hard enough to suit me...............	7	15	5
Undecided...............................	3	2	3

The fact that this proportion of the men in an office say that not enough is expected of them is indeed a morale-sapping situation.

Sometimes a cross tabulation of the results between two attitude questions can be very revealing. For instance, take these two questions:

Is XYZ a place where you have a desire to do a good day's work?
Always 46%
Usually 33
Seldom 15
Don't know 6
Does the makeup of your job allow you to carry out the best effort—to make the best contribution—you are capable of?
Yes, my job is okay in that respect 45%
No, my job is below my capacity 37
Problem just the opposite; my job demands too much of me 18

When the answers to the second question are analyzed according to the first question, it can be seen that those who "always" have a desire to do a good day's work also believe the makeup of their job allows them to make the best contribution.

Have desire to do good day's work	Makeup of job allows best effort		
	Yes	No	Opposite
Always....................	66%	8%	
Usually...................	26	18	16%
Seldom, never.............	4	58	50
Don't know...............	4	16	34
Total...................	100%	100%	100%

A document of percentaged tabulations can represent a formidable piece of reading. This is particularly true when questions have four or five answer categories and breakdowns according to several organizational segments are shown for each question. Often, a procedure which calculates index numbers—which give one score for a question—makes it much easier to peruse the results quickly. In the following example, the numbers at the top of each column are the indexes.

Everything considered, how do you feel about XYZ as a place to work?

	Management		Nonmanagement	
	Office	Plant	Office	Plant
	82	90	76	71
The best place to work I know.........	30%	62%	18%	25%
Better than most places...............	55	32	54	35
About the same as most places........	11	3	21	24
Not as good as most places...........	....	3	2	12
Can't decide........................	4	....	5	4

Finally, regarding the analysis of results, the survey responses should be compared with all the objective data available. If absenteeism and turnover are high in some parts of the plant, what light do the attitudes in these areas throw on the problem? What about attitudes where there is an increasing ratio of grievances and a decreasing rate of submissions to the suggestion system? If quality is falling off in some departments, what do the survey results show in those same places? And so on.

REPORTING THE RESULTS, FOLLOW-UP ACTION

Reporting should be regarded as a phase in the project, not solely as a written document. The best procedure is for the survey director first to discuss the results with management. This enables a better understanding of the findings and what to do about them than does reading a written document only. After the written document has been submitted, there should be a program of "playing back" the results to the employees.

Report of Findings and Recommendations for Action. A report is often divided into an objective portrayal of the results, an evaluation of what is most significant about them, and recommendations for action.

With respect to recommendations, one of the most important functions of those responsible for the reporting is to determine which few courses of action are *key*—which will do the most to bring about improvements in the problem areas uncovered by the survey.

For instance, an emphasis on improving communications—ensuring that employees can bring problems and ideas upward and seeing that information about company plans is transferred downward—could have a far-reaching influence into many matters affecting morale. Improving training is another example. This could open up opportunities for job advancement and transfer which could cure many underlying problems adversely affecting basic attitudes. Or a systematic, highly visible attempt to improve physical working conditions could convince employees that management was interested in their well-being.

The reason for stressing this skill in selecting a few key courses of action is that a common error is to prescribe an ambitious action program composed of so many different parts that it falls of its own weight. The program of action must be optimum. Its scope should permit the most mileage, but be realistic enough so that the organization can absorb it into its operational activities.

Playback of Results. One of the most effective steps in a survey is the "playback" of results to the employees. Unless the population surveyed is just too large to make it feasible, this is best done in groups called together for the purpose. Otherwise, of course, it must be done through the written word. Hopefully, the groups should be small enough in size so that a two-way discussion will ensue.

One technique is to use an easel or slides to illustrate the survey findings. This graphic portrayal—the easel pages or slides can often be in the form of humorous drawings—lends a liveliness to the presentation which heightens its appeal immeasurably.

The person who should give the presentation varies with the circumstances. In some cases, it is best done by a member of the organization's management—for instance, the plant manager. Sometimes it is better if the director of the survey team does it. On occasion, a combination of two such people is effective.

This playback process represents a major asset. Employees appreciate it. They have cooperated in expressing their attitudes to make the survey success-ful. Now, turnabout is fair play, so management shares the results with them. These playback sessions become a real morale booster. It imparts a sense of teamwork when the organization as a whole takes a look at itself in open meetings.

Action Program. The reason for undertaking the survey in the first place is to provide a basis for action. Additionally, management must bear in mind that if follow-up action is not taken, the employees will become cynical and the project could boomerang. The central point, however, is a positive one. The actual steps in the action program will produce concrete improvements in the company's operations, stemming from an improved morale climate.

Despite, or perhaps because of, the fact that much of the action is coming to grips with intangibles such as people's attitudes and the matter of relationships, the program should be systematic. For example:

Responsibility for the overall action program should be assigned to an indi-vidual. Other people, and perhaps committees, can report their accomplishments to him.

The program should be in writing. This includes a schedule for carrying it out.

There should be a built-in means of evaluating progress in carrying out the schedule and the effectiveness with which commitments are being met. This will necessitate meetings and written reports to higher management.

As various steps in the program are carried out, they can be reported to the or-ganization as a whole. In this way, employee appreciation for the survey can be extended long after the completion of the study itself.

Time Involved in a Survey. The time involved in a survey is subject to con-trol. The number of members of a task force can be varied. The steps in the survey can be carried out with varying degrees of speed, depending on the needs of the situation. Under any circumstances, a survey is usually most effec-tive when carried out with dispatch.

Assume that, in a company of 2,000 employees, a survey team of four has been assigned to the project. The study technique involves interviews with a sample of 150 and a questionnaire to be prepared and administered to all. A comfortable time estimate would be that management can expect a verbal report within six weeks from the beginning of the interview phase. The written report can be submitted within two weeks after this, and playback sessions with the employees can be carried out within another couple of weeks.

CONCLUSION

Esprit de corps is a factor which varies widely from company to company. Indeed, it can vary widely among different divisions in the same company.

Employee morale is inextricably interwoven with an organization's success. In the final analysis, increased productivity, improved quality, and lowered costs depend on the caliber of the work effort put forth by the employees.

Surveying employee attitudes is an eminently practical, down-to-earth approach to point the way toward improving an organization's morale. What can be done to motivate employees to work harder and better? How can people be encouraged to express their ideas regarding better ways of doing things? How can relationships among departments be improved so that work in process is coordinated more effectively? What kinds of information and training need to be developed so that people can contribute closer to the top of their potential?

Attitude surveys are a singular source of providing answers to these questions— answers that are obtained objectively and tuned in to the realities, on a current basis, of how employees actually feel.

The question really is not *whether* management should use these surveys. The question is *when* these surveys should be used, and what methods should be used, for management to derive the greatest benefit from them.

BIBLIOGRAPHY

Brown, J. A. C., "Attitudes and Opinion Surveys," *The Social Psychology of Industry,* chap. 6, Penguin Books, Inc., Baltimore, 1954.

Fleishman, E. A., "The Measurement of Leadership Attitudes in Industry," *Journal of Applied Psychology,* vol. 37, 1953, pp. 153–158.

Green, Bert F., "Attitude Measurement," in Gardner Lindzey (ed.), *Handbook of Social Psychology,* vol. 1, Addison-Wesley Publishing Company, Inc., Cambridge, Mass., 1954, pp. 335–369.

Habbe, Stephen, *Following Up Attitude Survey Findings,* Studies in Personnel Policy, no. 181, National Industrial Conference Board, New York, 1951.

Kahn, Robert L., and Charles F. Cannell, *The Dynamics of Interviewing,* John Wiley & Sons, Inc., New York, 1957.

Merton, Robert K., and Patricia L. Kendall, "The Focused Interview," *American Journal of Sociology,* vol. 51, no. 6, May, 1946, pp. 541–557.

Peterfreund, Stanley, "Communications in Action," *Bell Telephone Magazine,* Summer, 1963.

Raube, S. Avery, *Experience with Employee Attitude Surveys,* Studies in Personnel Policy, no. 115, National Industrial Conference Board, New York, 1951.

Stouffer, Samuel A., Edward A. Suchman, Leland C. DeVinney, Shirley A. Star, and Robin M. Williams, Jr., *The American Soldier: Studies in Social Psychology in World War II,* vols. 1–4, Princeton University Press, Princeton, N.J., 1949.

Wakeley, J. H., "One Way to Get Meaningful Results from Attitude Surveys," *Personnel,* vol. 41, November, 1964, pp. 43–47.

Williams, Douglas, "Program Your Approach to Attitude Surveys through Frequent Spot Questionnaires," *Employee Relations Bulletin,* Report no. 923, Oct. 7, 1964.

Williams, Douglas, "Six Policies Increase Will to Work," *Nation's Business,* November, 1958.

MANAGING EXTERNAL RELATIONS

CHAPTER ONE

Planning and Organizing the Public Relations Program

RICHARD R. CONARROE *Conarroe Associates, Inc., New York, New York*

Public relations is no different from any other valid management tool in that, when applied with intelligent planning, it will produce predictable results.

Often, the right kind of public relations action is the fastest, most practical way to solve certain management problems. Sometimes public relations can economically replace techniques such as advertising. More often, public relations effort is strengthened when it is linked with equally well-planned actions in advertising, sales promotion, employee relations, and so on.

Many companies find they can get along well without a formal public relations program. All they need to do is provide for handling the routine functions such as answering questions from the press. At the opposite extreme, some companies spend vast sums of money on public relations for no better reason than that they think they should.

Despite these two extremes, the trend is clear: In steadily increasing numbers, companies of all sizes and types are using planned public relations to accomplish key company goals.

PUBLIC RELATIONS AND COMPANY GOALS

Consider this sampling of some specific company goals public relations is used to reach:

Attract sales inquiries
Reinforce customer loyalty
Attract better distributors
Provide salesmen with selling aids
Attract investor attention
Attract merger partners or smooth the way for an acquisition
Attract better employees

Dissolve or block union problems

Minimize competitor advantages while you are catching up

Open a new market

Launch a new product

Reward key people, as well as rank-and-file workers, with recognition

Bring about favorable, or avoid unfavorable, legislation

The Picture Others Have of You. In addition to specifics like those above, there is the matter of "corporate image"—that nebulous, often misused, but nonetheless necessary idea that should not be omitted in any public relations plan. Corporate image is the picture people have of your company. Public relations can create or strengthen that picture, or change it.

For example, suppose that through past management lethargy, a company has come to be thought of in its trade as inflexible, slow moving, or unable to handle challenging assignments. Top management in such a company has its choice. It can delude itself into believing that the company reputation is intact among the people who really count. It can sit back and wait for suitable opportunities to reveal that this negative impression of the company is not accurate. Or it can take an aggressive, planned action to correct the misconception as quickly as possible so as to clear away a roadblock that is probably decreasing the effectiveness of the sales force and the advertising program, the ability of the company to attract top-caliber personnel, and so on. One well-planned public relations action might be all that is needed to turn the company's reputation around. This action might, for example, take the form of a very carefully written article published in a trade or business magazine, followed up with a distribution of reprints to the people the company wants to influence.

What Public Relations Is Not. Of course, positive facts must exist before a company can make a favorable case for itself. This brings up a key point that is frequently ignored or misunderstood. Public relations is essentially a means of communication. In some cases, public relations can be used to create facts and ideas, but mainly, its part of the management job is to convey—accurately and favorably—the facts and ideas that already exist.

Few professional public relations men, if they are experienced and ethical, will undertake to execute a public relations program when the facts to work with are weak or nonexistent. Sometimes the public relations man's first job is to counsel the company on how to get the house in order so that a public relations program will produce meaningful results.

For public relations to be effective, there can be no confusing it with press agentry.

Furthermore, as public relations men are fond of saying, public relations must not be confused with publicity. Publicity is a specific part of public relations— the job of getting your company's name in the newspaper—but the entire function of public relations encompasses much more.

What Public Relations Is. What is public relations then? How can it best be defined?

Ask three associates to give you their definitions of public relations. Odds are you will get three halting, uncertain answers, all different, each dealing with a different phase of public relations rather than the field as a whole. At least two of the three will probably be highly theoretical, not down to earth and practical.

But public relations *is* down to earth and practical. At least, it can be when it is applied with good planning. Thus, a good starting point in planning a public relations program is to establish a clear definition of this function in your mind. For example:

Public relations is the action of amplifying what you say about yourself through existing facilities of communication.

An even simpler definition:

Public relations means educating people in favor of your company.

The biggest problem in planning a public relations program lies in the fact that public relations encompasses a whole universe of varied activities, ranging from the simple distribution of news releases to the most imaginative kinds of promotion schemes. It is this unlimited nature of the beast—with its unlimited possibilities—that sometimes causes its failure. Even a big public relations budget will produce relatively few results if time and money are sprinkled in all different directions.

To paraphrase a Bible story, an abysmal quantity of public relations money is poured into sandy places, disappearing quickly without a gurgle, never to be seen again, because no worthwhile results will ever grow there. More of it is splashed into rocky places where the results that do grow are scraggly and short-lived. But wise companies ration their public relations money into only fertile ground where they know it will produce a bountiful harvest.

The first real step in planning a public relations program, therefore, should be to establish the limiting confines of the work to be done. To succeed, the public relations program must be disciplined, confined, narrowed down, aimed, channeled, steered, focused.

FOUR STEPS TO PUBLIC RELATIONS RESULTS

Once this is understood, planning a public relations program need vary little from the procedure followed in planning other kinds of management activity. Here is a four-step procedure that has been used time and again in planning public relations programs. Experience proves that when a program is organized on this four-step framework, favorable results, measured in terms of high return on invested dollars, are virtually predictable.

1. *Set Specific Goals, Not General Goals.* If your goal is merely to create a better corporate image, most of your public relations budget will probably be wasted. But if your goal is to double sales of Product A, to attract a higher grade of distributors, to get certain other companies to think of your company as a good merger partner, or something equally specific, then you have taken the first step toward public relations success.

For example, when one company was planning a public relations program, a meeting was called of all department heads. The personnel manager said he thought public relations should be used to show the company as a good community citizen and as a good place to work. The sales manager thought the public relations program should be aimed at making the company's products better known. The production manager thought the effort should be aimed internally, toward employees, to try to balance or overbalance the union's efforts to influence their thinking. The financial officer had still other ideas; he thought public relations should be used to stimulate investor interest in the company and to establish the company as having a better-than-average growth record and better management than any other company in its field.

A public relations program aimed with equal vigor at all of these worthy objectives would have been weak and wasteful. The president of the company knew it. He decided to accept part of the financial officer's suggestion—to concentrate on the company's good management and growth record—and make all of the other goals subordinate to this main one. The company's public relations counselor advised the president that reaching this main goal would indirectly and at least in part accomplish some of the other objectives, with little or no additional work.

2. *Make a Plan of Action Aimed Directly at Your Goal or Goals.* Limit your plan to those actions that (*a*) you know you can afford and (*b*) will move you toward the specific goals you have set.

Be sure your plan includes several alternative actions. Success in public relations usually depends on selling your ideas to someone else. Sometimes, for reasons beyond your control, the right person just will not buy your ideas, and if you try to keep on selling him, you merely waste your time and his, and perhaps antagonize an important contact who could be helpful to you later.

In public relations, when you do not succeed with one action, rather than try to force the idea to work, it is generally wiser to shift to an alternative action that will produce equal or at least similar results.

But here is a vital point: Make sure your plan of action spells out clearly what combination of alternative actions will be considered to constitute public relations success.

One company in the optical field built a public relations program designed specifically to make known a new process that had the potential greatly to improve a widely used product. One planned action was to get news of this new development reported in a mass-circulation magazine where it would be read by three important groups: the general public who buy the product, optometrists who sell it, and businessmen and engineers who might see the process as a solution to certain production or processing problems.

The action failed. No major national publication would use the story. Editors said it was too technical.

The public relations manager had foreseen these objections. Without wasting further time, he shifted to the alternative actions he had planned in advance. He sent carefully written news releases and illustrations of the new process to all publications in the optical, plastics, and medical fields. Editors of many of these publications featured the story, recognizing the interest it contained for their far more select readers. After these stories had appeared, the public relations manager wrote a brief news story quoting favorable things said about the new process by one of the respected optical journals. This news release was sent to a special list of widely read publications and syndicated news services that devote special columns or features to new products. The story was widely used.

Thus the company reached its public relations goal by an alternative route. It would have been faster, less costly, and more dramatic to have the story in a big national magazine in the first place, and even though he failed, the public relations man was justified in trying for this "long shot" before shifting to his alternative action. In fact, he never gave up on the first approach. He continued to accumulate more facts and figures, plus case examples and other supporting material, against the day when some news angle or other change would make it possible for him to win the interest of the publications he had sought in the first place.

3. *Measure Your Results against Your Plan at Regular Intervals.* A strong, well-planned public relations program can become a weak, unplanned program if it is not appraised regularly. Experience proves that a formal appraisal should be built into the program at least every six months—more frequently in many cases.

In appraising the program, look at both your successes and failures. Where the effort and money invested were productive, determine why, and how things could have been better. Where the effort and money invested were *not* productive, determine why again.

Do not think in terms of the general good that may have been done for the company by the public relations effort. Instead, analyze the program strictly in terms of the goals you set, the actions you planned, and the criteria you established of what would constitute public relations success. That is really what counts. The rest is a by-product.

There is a lesson to be learned from one young public relations man who fell into a trap. He confused public relations activity with public relations results. It is a trap that even some experienced public relations men fall into sometimes.

In this case, the public relations man was giving an appraisal report to the company president. The president listened patiently as the young public relations manager enumerated news releases he had sent out over the past six months, the speeches and articles he had written, the brochures he had revised, the letters from stockholders he had answered, the people his assistant had toured through the plant, and so on.

When he had wound up his report, the public relations man sat back with a grin of satisfaction and waited to be complimented by the president. Instead, the president opened a folder on his desk and read from the initial public relations plan: "The primary goal . . . during the first year will be to attract qualified distributors in locations where our products are not now sold."

Then the president looked up at the public relations man and said, "Tell me, what have these activities of yours contributed to this objective?"

The public relations man was left without much of an answer.

4. *Based on Appraisal and Analysis, Alter Your Goals, Your Plan, Your Actions.* Probe the validity of your public relations goals, and the validity of your public relations plan. Sharpen the goals and alter the plan as necessary, and continue the cycle over and over again.

In the case cited above, the president made it devastatingly clear that the assortment of activities of which the public relations man was so proud had little relationship to the stated objective of the public relations plan. The actions for the next six months were revised drastically to bring them into line with the specific goal. Then, eighteen months later, when imaginative, precisely aimed public relations effort had helped the company expand its distribution into the desired new markets, the decision was made to redirect public relations effort for the following year toward a new primary goal—this time it was to lay some groundwork for the company to move into a different but related product area through a company acquisition or merger. This change in emphasis called for an entirely new plan and an entirely new set of public relations actions.

By keeping its public relations program flexible and on target through regular appraisal, this company continues to profit from the time and money—and planning—it invests in this important management function.

GETTING OPTIMUM RESULTS

There are many good rules to follow in getting optimum results from a planned public relations program. Here are just a few:

Focus on the Pivotal Jobs First. Try for multiple results from a single action if possible.

For example, a company selling a service wanted to be better known in several industries. The initial plan was to by-line several articles for various trade publications reaching these industries. Then it was decided to invest the same time in one definitive article, good enough for a major business magazine reaching all industries. The plan worked. In fact, because the article's quality was obvious, several trade journals later reprinted it. Thus, for this company, one piece of good work produced multiple returns.

Give People What They Want, Not Just What You Want. A company sent out a news release, reporting some facts the president felt people should know. Result: zero. Why? Because the news was presented from the company's point of view, not the public's.

All public relations—and especially publicity—depends on winning not only attention but cooperation from two completely self-interested parties: (1) the editor or other intermediary who votes on whether to use your material and (2) the people who decide whether or not your material is of enough concern to them to give their time to. Satisfying one or the other is not enough; your material must appeal to and be appropriate and good enough for both.

Have a Point of Distinction. Rosser Reeves, the advertising man, said every product has a "unique selling proposition" and that all advertising should focus on it. The same applies to public relations: Every company has a distinctive quality, and all public relations effort should focus on it. In the final analysis, it is only a company's point of difference that makes its news or other publicity material worth anything at all.

Go Far Enough Fast Enough—Then Stop. A company in the South had a story to tell about a year of unusual growth. The public relations man was sent to New York to try to get some national publicity. When he returned after three days, the president asked, "Where are the clippings?"

"I have no clippings," he replied, "but I made some wonderful contacts. I think we can get a wire service story. Several investment letters are interested. A couple of business magazines may do features. They all want special material. I'll have to get it to them fast."

"What assurance do we have they will use it?" the president asked, and then answered his own question. "None, really. We'd better not put in any more time on something that may not pay off. Maybe later we can do some work on these things."

This is an example of an all-too-common mistake: wasting all of the public relations effort by turning off the power too soon.

Some public relations men, to protect themselves, tell their bosses or clients, "Don't expect to see any results from my work for several months." This is usually an overstatement. But the fact is that public relations results seldom, if ever, accrue overnight. Quitting too soon is as wasteful as continuing to race after you have crossed the finish line.

Shortcut Oblique Action with Direct Action. Sometimes the smallest direct public relations action produces the biggest results. Consider the following example.

A small company in Illinois was planning a unique meeting for its distributors. Press releases were being written for the trade papers. Then the president said, "Maybe a magazine like *Time* would be interested in this." Other managers pooh-poohed the idea. "We're too small for *Time;* we have no contacts there," they said. The president thought it was worth a telephone call. He looked up the number of *Time*'s publisher, phoned him in New York, described the meeting. The publisher expressed interest, asked for a letter giving details. When the meeting took place, a *Time* reporter was there to cover it.

It would be nice to say that a story appeared in *Time* the next week. It did not. But the presence of a *Time* correspondent gave the meeting a lot of extra importance in the minds of the distributors who attended it.

There is a great deal of roundabout action taken in the name of public relations. But direct action is usually faster, costs less, and gets more results.

Never Substitute Words for Ideas and Honesty. "Undersell, never oversell" is the watchword of professional public relations men. A financial consultant had been interviewed by a series of important editors. Each time, he answered questions with candor, sometimes admitting weaknesses in his own service and his field as a whole. Later one of his associates advised him to be a little less candid, a little more glib with the press.

"If I have to make up facts to get my picture in the paper," he replied, "it isn't worth it."

The man's honesty paid off. The editors, appreciating his straight answers, have continued to call him for quotes and give him mentions over a period of years.

Some executives treat press people like second-class citizens. Other executives treat them with too much solicitousness. Either can be self-defeating. The best advice: Treat the press like people. That way you just cannot go wrong.

Tricks Are Not Worth the Trouble. Imagination is one of the most important ingredients in good business public relations. But too much may backfire. Imaginative ideas should be executed with dignity and simplicity. If you want public relations results, stay away from press agentry.

Of course, there is an exception to prove every rule. An overly imaginative publicity man for a hearing-aid company arranged for a wire service to distribute a photo of a deaf little dog wearing a hearing aid contributed by his company. Hundreds of newspapers published the photo and lauded the hearing-aid company, much to the delight of animal lovers everywhere. Then the whole thing was revealed as a hoax and a stunt to get publicity. When the humiliated public relations man apologized to the wire services, the photographer who had made the picture replied, "Don't be silly; I won a contest with that picture."

Do Not Overlook the Economy of Specialists. Special public relations jobs call for specialists who can do the work better, faster, and thus at lower cost than it could otherwise be accomplished.

A sea captain will use a pilot to get his ship in and out of New York harbor even though he has a lifetime of experience at sea.

In most specialized fields of work, the use of qualified specialists has proved a lot less risky than the do-it-yourself approach. Especially when a public relations job's success depends on speed and knowing who to talk to, using specialists usually makes sense.

CONCLUSION

Public relations is the job of educating people in favor of your company. Planning is the key to success. With planning, public relations can be an adaptable and economical management tool. Without planning, public relations effort may merely waste time and money.

To get good results with public relations at low cost, adhere closely to these vital principles:

Plan your public relations goals.

Plan specific actions to meet these goals.

Measure results against the plan at regular intervals.

Alter the program as soon as your analysis shows you can improve either goals or actions.

BIBLIOGRAPHY

Baus, Herbert M., *Publicity in Action,* Harper & Row, Publishers, Incorporated, New York, 1954.

Bristol, Lee, Jr. (ed.), *Developing the Corporate Image,* Charles Scribner's Sons, New York, 1960.

Cutlip, Scott M., and Allen H. Center, *Effective Public Relations,* 3d ed., Prentice-Hall, Inc., Englewood Cliffs, N.J., 1964.

Lesly, Philip (ed.), *Public Relations Handbook,* 2d ed., Prentice-Hall, Inc., Englewood Cliffs, N.J., 1962.

Marston, John, *The Nature of Public Relations,* McGraw-Hill Book Company, New York, 1963.

Samstag, Nicholas, *Persuasion for Profit,* University of Oklahoma Press, Norman, Okla., 1958.

CHAPTER TWO

The Tools and Techniques of Public Relations

ARTHUR W. PEARCE *Director of Public Relations, The Warner Brothers Company, Bridgeport, Connecticut*

Contrary to popular impression, there is little or no "black magic" about public relations or its tools and techniques. The stunts and hocus-pocus associated with Hollywood-style publicity have little, if any, place in public relations as it is used to serve practical business objectives.

Every company and hence every manager is concerned to a greater or lesser degree with a variety of groups of people that are important to the enterprise. These groups will include (1) the community where the business operates, (2) present and prospective employees, (3) customers, (4) suppliers, (5) stockholders, (6) the financial community, and (7) the general public.

These groups can importantly affect the success of the enterprise, and they will inevitably form impressions and judgments about the business and its management. It is clearly important that these impressions and judgments be constructive, accurate, and favorable to the extent possible.

Public relations in the basic sense is the effective use of communications—most often the printed or spoken word—to achieve the most favorable impression or image for the enterprise with some or all of these groups or publics.

There are tricks in the trade, and there is a definite place for professional skills, but from the manager's point of view, the essential elements of successful public relations can be summarized as follows.

1. The tools of public relations are basically informative and newsworthy material about the company and/or its people and the channels of communications through which this can be brought to the attention of the public.

2. The techniques of public relations largely involve determining what is newsworthy at what time and to what audience, and the ways to serve and utilize various channels of communication. This includes both established channels of communication and channels created by the company for special purposes.

WHAT MAKES NEWS?

In some ways, the most difficult challenge for the manager in the area of public relations is the trick of putting himself in the other person's shoes. What frequently seems of extreme importance to him may or may not be of equal importance to those outside the confines of the business operation. It is also obvious that what may be of genuine interest to the community where the business operates may or may not be of interest or value to the public elsewhere.

In general, however, the following areas can be expected to generate newsworthy material.

Company Action. Major expansion steps, acquisitions of other companies, a major installation of new equipment, and similar company developments will be of definite interest to the community, to the trade, and frequently to the financial community and the general public if the company is relatively large. The areas of company action will frequently include steps that are of major community interest such as corporate gifts, an open house in connection with a new plant, efforts to improve community facilities for recreation, and the like.

Company Plans. What is going to happen in the future will generally be of interest, and in this sense, a company's future plans will make solid material for projecting the company image. These would include plans to enter new markets, plans to increase employment, or projections of the company's future in terms of sales and earnings. (The area of future sales and earnings is distinctly newsworthy but should be handled with professional caution. See Chapter 7 of Section 12, "Relations with the Financial Community.")

People. It is axiomatic that people are most interested in what happens to other people, and it follows that personnel changes and promotions make news. The extent of the news interest varies directly in relation to the importance of the position and the size and importance of the company. Relatively minor personnel additions or promotions will be news in the plant community and almost always for the local press in the man's hometown. In the case of relatively large companies, top executive promotions or additions will certainly have interest to the financial community and may well have national interest.

Products. The company's products can be the basis for newsworthy material in both the trade and the general press depending, of course, on the nature of the product. The new automobile models from Detroit, for example, have wide public interest and will be heavily reported in general newspapers and magazines as well as in the industry's trade press. By contrast, an improved lubricant for electric motors will be of definite interest to manufacturers but of limited news value to the public.

Feature Material. While hard news involves specific plans, actions, or personnel changes, there are opportunities to project the company's story with feature stories. These may include the company's history, company philosophy or policies, if they would be useful to others in business, and general feature stories about company personnel dealing with accomplishment or based on pure human interest. Generally, feature stories take special planning and placement.

GENERAL CHANNELS OF COMMUNICATION

In the program to project a favorable impression of the company, the manager is fortunate in having working partners in the field of communications. These include the editors of the local, national, and trade press, and the news editors in radio and occasionally television. They have a parallel interest in presenting accurate and newsworthy information to the audience they serve. Here again, the scope of the interest will be determined to a large extent by the size of the company and the importance of the action, plan, or personnel change.

Local Press and Radio. The manager can expect the newspapers and radio stations in his community to have an active interest in the company and its developments. Properly handled, they can be counted on to give attention to important company action or developments and can also be expected to print or broadcast relatively minor developments that would not be of interest outside the community.

The Trade Press. The second most useful channel of communications for most companies will be the trade press. Nearly every business or industry is served by one or more newspapers or magazines that deal directly with the field of its operations. They can be expected to print a wide range of company news, much of which would not be of general interest, such as minor product changes, interim sales trends or market developments, new techniques or methods, and similar subjects.

The Financial Press. Most companies of substantial size and all companies publicly owned or whose securities are listed on the stock exchanges are concerned with placing their news stories in the financial press. In fact, it is a requirement of the major stock exchanges that companies report significant news—both good and bad—as widely as possible. These channels usually include the *Wall Street Journal,* one or more of the major New York City daily newspapers, and the major wire services. In general, these publications are receptive and will print significant news in summary form for the average company. The corporate giants, of course, such as General Motors and U.S. Steel, will be extensively reported not only in financial centers but throughout the nation.

News Magazines. The weekly news magazines, such as *Time, Newsweek,* and *Business Week,* are important channels for news stemming from the major companies and for high-interest news from smaller business operations. Developing news stories or features in these outlets usually requires a close knowledge of what the editors are interested in and well-developed contacts with the editorial staff.

General Magazines. Magazines with large national distribution are not normally interested in what we have described as basic company news. Certain service groups, however, such as the women's fashion magazines or those appealing especially to the home owner, are extremely valuable outlets for product reports. Generally speaking, this field of communications requires highly specialized contact work.

SERVING THE COMMUNICATIONS CHANNELS

The form and manner used to serve the various channels of communication described above will importantly determine results. These are the techniques or, if you like, some of the ground rules of effective public relations.

The Press Release. By far the most widely used public relations technique is what is known as the "press release." This should be a straightforward statement of the news story; it usually quotes a company official—most often the president—and its length will be determined by the importance and newsworthy facts of the story. It should be dated as of the date of sending and carry a release date or be noted "for immediate release." In releases having to do with earnings reports or major company developments, it is usually wise and possible to include a certain amount of background about the company and the comments or opinion of the company spokesman on the significance of the news and the prospects for the future.

In the case of personnel changes, it is not wise to include company propaganda of any sort, especially in releases sent to the large national newspapers. They will be interested only in the bare facts unless it is an extremely large company and a major personnel change. Community newspapers, on the other hand, will usually be interested in biographical material on the individual—residence, size of family, civic connections, and the like.

As a rule of thumb, it is not wise to distribute press releases of minor news interest beyond the local or trade press areas. The editors on the big newspapers are flooded with competing news stories and develop a natural coolness toward the company that bombards them with insignificant news. In cases where the news is important and its appearance is of great importance to the company, it may be wise to follow the press release with a courteous telephone call to the editor. Handled properly, he will appreciate the reminder and avoid the inadvertent mistake of omitting legitimate news.

A frequently overlooked news channel is the local area radio station. Be sure to include its news department on the mailing list for the press releases.

It is important to time press releases for the convenience of the editors involved. It is also obviously important to give equal treatment as far as possible. In communities where there are both morning and afternoon papers, it is frequently good business to alternate release dates, giving the morning paper the news break one time and favoring the afternoon paper on another occasion.

Mechanics of the Press Release. Whereas the content of a press release will determine its value as news, the form is important in making it easy for the editor to use. The following are some useful rules to keep in mind.

1. The name of the company, the address, and the name and telephone number of the person sending the release should obviously be included, usually in the upper left-hand corner of the page.

2. Instructions for the date of release should appear in the upper right-hand corner. For example, if the story is to be released immediately, the instruction should read "For Immediate Release," or if it is to be released in a few days, it should read "For Release (day and date)." (See Figure 2-1.)

3. Copy should be double- or triple-spaced and typed on one side of the paper. Ample margins on both sides will allow for copydesk marking.

4. Newspaper copy should be written in a simple, straightforward style. No attempt should be made to color the story to impress the reader, and editorial comment or personal opinion should be avoided.

5. In the use of names, the first name, middle initial, and last name of the person should be given, with his title, if any. In sending a story to someone's hometown paper, his address and some background material may be used.

6. If the release runs more than one page, write "more" on the bottom of each page. The story should be concluded with one of the following marks: "# # #," "****," or "30." If possible, each page should end at the end of a paragraph.

The Telephone. A telephone call to the editor is a useful tool in laying the groundwork for a news story to come. It can also serve in an emergency in place of a mimeographed release. If, for example, the board of directors increases the dividend in a late afternoon meeting and the news must be reported in the morning papers, the telephone may be the only way to contact the news desk before the morning editions go to press. In the case of an earnings report, however, where several comparative figures are included, the experienced editor will be reluctant to take the information on the telephone for fear of making an error. In such cases, the best method is to call first and then confirm the figures by wire where such facilities are available.

325 LAFAYETTE STREET, BRIDGEPORT, CONNECTICUT 06602

News From: The Warner Brothers Company

WARNER SLIMWEAR / WARNER LINGERIE / HATHAWAY SHIRTS / LADY HATHAWAY SHIRTS / PURITAN SPORTSWEAR / HARBOR ROAD SWIMWEAR / WARNER PACKAGING

Arthur W. Pearce
Public Relations
203-367-8661

August 2, 1965

FOR IMMEDIATE RELEASE

WARNER BROTHERS POSTS

19% EARNINGS GAIN

Record sales and earnings for a first half of the year
are reported by The Warner Brothers Company, diversified producer of apparel and packaging.

Sales for the six months ended July 3 amounted to $43,339,958,
a 12 per cent gain over the previous year's $38,768,728. Net
earnings increased 19 per cent to $1,837,939, as compared to
$1,541,717. Net earnings per share of common stock amounted to
$1.43 compared to $1.16 in the first half of 1964.

In reporting the figures, John W. Field, president of this
Bridgeport-based company, said that all major divisions had
contributed to this year's gain with especially strong showings
by the company's menswear divisions -- Puritan Sportswear and
C. F. Hathaway. He also noted a satisfactory gain in Warner's
position in the lingerie field.

Looking to the balance of the year, Mr. Field said that
fall bookings were ahead of last year and that barring a serious
disturbance in the economy, the company expected to continue its
progress in sales and earnings for the year as a whole.

* * *

FIG. 2-1. *Typical press release.*

Press Conferences. In cases where the news is of considerable importance and the news treatment would be improved by providing an opportunity for further questions, the manager may want to consider holding a press conference. This form of releasing news is particularly appropriate for announcing a major acquisition or for unveiling an important new product or development. It provides a good opportunity to prepare detailed and background material in advance and can be expected to result in a substantially longer story on the company. This technique, however, should be used sparingly and only in cases of significant developments. Once bitten, the newspaper man will be twice shy of invitations to a press conference that does not warrant his time and trouble.

The Executive Interview. Closely related to the press conference but more specialized in nature and purpose is the executive interview. In this case, a principal company spokesman arranges to meet with an appropriate editor or reporter. This is particularly valuable where the company seeks to become better known in the financial and investment community. If the company and/or the executive has newsworthy trends to report, the interview will usually result in an exclusive feature report of substantial size.

Technical Articles. Special articles in the technical or professional press provide opportunities to report directly on company accomplishment or to further the company reputation through the standing of the individual doing the article. In this growing era of specialization in management, most companies will have research scientists, engineers, marketing and accounting specialists, and the like, whose developments, method improvements, and points of view make acceptable material for the appropriate magazine or journal. Papers prepared for delivery to technical associations and societies often form the basis for such articles.

Speeches. Talks by executives of a company serve the dual purpose of reporting directly to people and usually generating news for publication. Such opportunities will range from appearances before business groups and civic groups in a community to being on the program of regional and national business gatherings. The business manager who has something to say and who develops the knack of good delivery will find many opportunities to present his company directly and indirectly in a progressive and favorable light.

Photography. Appropriate photographs are a desirable tool in effective public relations. Personnel changes and promotions should be accompanied by head shots of the individual to the community and trade press and to the national press if of sufficient importance (certain publications, such as the *Wall Street Journal*, carry no pictures and releases to them should not include pictures).

In many cases, a good photograph and caption will be more effective and more welcome than a news story. These might include an employee being retired and congratulated by the president, a local government official opening a new plant, company products in a novel or unusual situation, and the like. The smaller community newspapers are usually intensely interested in colorful or human-interest photographs.

SPECIAL COMMUNICATION CHANNELS

Although effective public relations relies largely on existing channels of communication, most companies today supplement this program with a variety of direct-reporting devices.

Financial Reports. The annual report to stockholders has become a major communications channel for many companies. It serves to present the company effectively not only to stockholders but also to the investment community, and it can be effectively and properly sent to business leaders, public officials, and others. (See Chapter 7 of Section 12.) Some companies also have developed their interim reports to stockholders to reach these various groups more frequently. The interim report traditionally carries a short message from the president and summary financial results, but there are also opportunities to tell the basic company story through photographs of the company's products or doings.

Fact Sheets. Many companies prepare and distribute relatively inexpensive fact sheets to report company progress or to provide background material for special audiences. These are particularly useful in satisfying the needs of the security analysts and others who want more detailed information than is normally provided in the regular financial report.

The House Organ. Many companies today use one or more varieties of company publication in their public relations programs. Large companies, such as Standard Oil of New Jersey, Du Pont, and the big auto companies, publish handsome and well-edited magazines for public distribution. It is also a trend for more companies to use a newspaper or magazine for both internal and external communications. As employee publications have become more sophisticated—dealing more with policy and hard company news and less with personal notices—they are of greater interest to the outside world. At Warner Brothers, we have found this to be particularly true with security analysts and investment counselors who like to keep well-informed on company developments.

Institutional Advertising. Paid advertising can be a valuable public relations tool, but should be carefully planned. People are generally not impressed by the advertising which says, in effect, "Look how good we are." More effective is association with or sponsorship of a worthy cause, a public service message, or reporting dramatic technical accomplishment in a modest and interesting manner. A now famous example of good institutional advertising is the New Year's advertisement by a whiskey company urging that "the one for the road" be coffee.

There are a number of specific instances in which paid advertising can probably be used to convey important information. These will include the following: (1) Paid advertisements may be used to notify employees of changes in work schedules and similar information that must reach the audience quickly. (2) Special announcements to a community that a company will be establishing a plant may be made through paid advertising. Similar announcements are sometimes used to thank a community for its welcome. (3) A change in the company name will frequently require a broad advertising campaign to educate the public and especially the financial community. (4) It is frequently desirable to explain the reasons for interruption in service in the case of a utility company or the background of issues in a strike or work stoppage. In all these cases, of course, great care should be taken to report facts objectively and fairly. (5) Some companies report regularly to their communities on their activities. General Electric, for instance, publishes progress reports as advertisements, thus assuring that the complete story will reach the public at the right time.

Industrial Films. A highly specialized but very effective public relations tool is the company film. Good commercial pictures will be welcomed by service groups, women's clubs, consumer groups, schools, and to some extent, the movie theaters themselves.

To be effective, a commercial film must strive just as hard to please the audience as does a Hollywood feature. This obviously involves creative talent and highly specialized professional experience. The average cost of a black and white industrial picture produced by a qualified producer is about $15,000. A quickie can be made for less than $5,000. Some companies budget $150,000 or more per picture.

FOLLOW-UP AND EVALUATION

As with other areas of business operation, the modern manager will be concerned with measuring the success of the company's public relations program. In this connection, some of the yardsticks are obvious and provide a clue on the success of the effort.

The volume of newspaper clippings and magazine stories, although not necessarily conclusive, is a clear indication of success as far as the media are concerned. Informal conversation with members of different groups of interest to the company will also provide some indication of the image which the company has projected and the extent to which the company's message is getting through.

In an effort to refine the accuracy of these evaluations, many companies have turned to questionnaires or opinion surveys taken by professional organizations. Surveys can be made at relatively low cost among easily identified groups such as employees, stockholders, or the community, and will provide both an indication of what the company needs to do to improve its position and a progress report on the success of the company's public relations program. In some cases, such as a survey of stockholders, the company can make its own survey by mail with reasonably accurate results. In other cases, such as gaging the opinion of the community, the manager will turn to professional research organizations, which will use accurate sampling techniques and can interpret the results for future company planning action.

A FAVORABLE PUBLIC RELATIONS CLIMATE

We have outlined some of the more important and useful tools and techniques of public relations. It should be kept in mind, however, that they cannot be used effectively unless the company and its management have a positive attitude and philosophy about public relations. Some of the essential environmental factors include the following.

1. The manager must recognize that he and his company do operate in the "goldfish bowl" of community and public interest. He has both the opportunity and the responsibility to keep people informed.

2. Honesty and accuracy are essential in all communications. Misleading statements, exaggerations, and efforts to "duck" a story will soon destroy the confidence of those who handle news, and will seriously limit the opportunity to present the company's story.

3. Public relations is a day-to-day affair at all points of company contact. The reception accorded a visiting salesman or the attention received from the company switchboard is vitally important in building a long-range image. The same is true of the careful and courteous handling of letters from outsiders, whether they be complaints from customers, inquiries from stockholders, or requests from students and others for information.

CONCLUSION

In this chapter, we have tried to indicate that public relations today is an important part of the success of a business and very much the concern of the manager. We have also tried to point out that it does not concern itself primarily with publicity, but rather with the intelligent conveyance of many kinds of news about the company and its people.

Most companies today seek professional assistance in their public relations program in terms either of their own staff department or of outside counseling services. The skilled professional, however, can be only an extension of the manager's attitude toward public relations. In the final analysis, it is the management that determines the success of the public relations program.

BIBLIOGRAPHY

Bernays, Edward L., *Crystallizing Public Opinion*, rev. ed., Liveright Publishing Corporation, New York, 1961.

Brink, Edward L., and William T. Kelley, *The Management of Promotion*, Prentice-Hall, Inc., Englewood Cliffs, N.J., 1963.

Canfield, Bertrand R., *Public Relations: Principles, Cases and Problems*, Richard D. Irwin, Inc., Homewood, Ill., 1960.

Cutlip, Scott M., and Allen H. Center, *Effective Public Relations*, 3d ed., Prentice-Hall, Inc., Englewood Cliffs, N.J., 1964.

Lesly, Philip (ed.), *Public Relations Handbook*, 2d ed., Prentice-Hall, Inc., Englewood Cliffs, N.J., 1962.

Marston, John, *The Nature of Public Relations*, McGraw-Hill Book Company, New York, 1963.

Report of Special Studies of the Securities Market, "Broker-Dealers, Investment Advisors and Their Customers—Activities and Responsibilities," chap. 3, and "Obligations of Issuers of Publicly Held Securities, Part C: Corporate Publicity and Public Relations," chap. 9, House Document 95, 88th Cong., U.S. Government Printing Office, 1963.

Stephenson, Howard (ed.), *Handbook of Public Relations*, McGraw-Hill Book Company, New York, 1960.

CHAPTER THREE

Creating and Promoting the Corporate Image

EDWIN C. MEAD   *Partner, Mead-Ross Associates, Hanover, New Hampshire*

ROBERT T. ROSS   *Partner, Mead-Ross Associates, Hanover, New Hampshire*

One often hears the expression by management: "We don't have a corporate image." Nothing could be further from the truth. Everything has an image of some kind. It may not be a good one, or it may not amount to much—but there is one. And in the case of the corporation, it is likely there are several images, depending on whom you happen to be talking to.

Management undoubtedly has *its* image of the company. Employees always have a pretty strong image (possibly different from management's); and then there are dealers, jobbers, distributors, suppliers, stockholders, and certainly customers or clients.

So, before worrying about creating and promoting a corporate image, it might be well to determine exactly what management intends to do about the one it has.

THE CORPORATE IMAGE

Before proceeding, let us consider the word "image" that has been thrust on the business world as a result of intense competition. Because products are so much alike, in both quality and price, the buying public has been forced to rely on the more intangible aspects of a company and its products or services. "Brand personalities" plus attitudes toward the company by its various publics have a decided influence on sales and profits.

Image Defined. A corporate image is the sum total of attitudes and opinions toward the company and its products. "Reputation" is another way of saying the same thing. Thus, creation or at least recognition of the corporate reputation is necessarily the first phase of any public relations program.

It is no secret that many public relations programs end in partial or complete failure even though conscientious practitioners have worked diligently and skillfully to carry them out. All too often, the lack of success is due to insufficient research and planning based first and foremost on the determination, recognition—and correction, if necessary—of the corporate image.

Fostering a Good Image. Business failure itself is an everyday occurrence in our country. Since 1945, both the number of failures and the failure rate have increased. Lack of working capital, extreme competition, production technique changes, style and fad changes, and other reasons have been cited as causes of business failure, with lack of working capital heading the list. Yet, the best product, the most attractive plant, and the biggest potential market become liabilities, not assets, under poor management. Excluding personal attributes, poor management often is characterized by the failure of management to determine the corporate character and mission (image), and then to conduct (consciously or unconsciously) a public relations program to foster that image.

A good image may be one of conservatism or progressivism, of sophistication or friendliness, of practicality or creativity. "Good" images come in many different shapes and sizes.

Which should be chosen? An electronics company may decide to convey technical sophistication and reliability. An insurance firm may lean more toward a conservative but friendly corporate personality. Depending on the company's product or service, some types of images will be more suitable than others.

Why Bother? It is not unusual for management to ask, "Why bother?" Why bother about the corporate image—the attitudes and opinions of others? The reason is simple—yet, in our society, often not given adequate consideration. It is just that *people* have been, and will remain, more important than machines or other *things*. Social scientists and social psychologists learned this long ago, but many business executives learn this simple truth the hard way—generally at the expense of their pocketbooks.

Often the benefits of a strong corporate image become obvious to the Monday-morning quarterback, but not so obvious when the signals are called on Saturday. There are tangible benefits, both internal and external; yet the idea of improving the impression or image of a business firm can lead to the danger of ignoring the importance of what already exists.

We have said that sales and profits are the obvious items affected by the corporate image, but there are many others. A good product helps form the corporate image, and that image significantly influences the ability of a company to attract good executives as well as assembly-line workers and to hold on to workers already employed. Also, a good reputation or image of a business opens doors to its salesmen that might otherwise remain closed; and a good corporate image helps gain retailer cooperation, influence shareholders to pay good prices for company stock, and interest prospective stockholders in the business. There are other advantages: obtaining capital on favorable terms, avoiding trouble within the trade, and avoiding trouble within the company-located community.

Perhaps, then, it becomes easier to recognize that the main function of public relations is image development; and because it is, public relations *must* be a function of management.

The firms that are conservative in their thinking and content to maintain a good reputation among established customers with a product outstanding ten or more years ago are a vanishing breed in today's competitive and aggressive business picture. Yet it has been proved that even these firms, when management recognizes the importance of a continuing, progressive corporate image sustained and promoted by adequate budgets for public relations and institutional advertising (providing its policies and practices are acceptable to its publics), can continue operations in the black.

Source of an Image. Even before a firm opens its doors for business, opinions and attitudes about that company begin to form among management, staff, and employees, and very quickly shape themselves into an initial corporate image. But, unless that image is immediately conveyed to others as they are exposed to the company through its products and personnel, the corporate reputation may give way to stronger and perhaps less favorable images from the outside.

Once a company is established and can be said to have a favorable image, it is not enough to rest on the old laurels. There are too many competitors with comparable products (if not, there soon will be) noisily clamoring for attention in mass media, loudly projecting their own image and keeping an eye on yours, waiting to drive their own wedge into any crack that appears in that image.

Creating an Image. The important first step, then, in launching a corporate image, or in launching a public relations program to correct or project that image, is the development of the company's (management's) mission and character in the world—including desired social, ethical, and moral standards, essential parts in fulfilling that mission.

It is not enough merely to discuss these elements of a corporate image. The organization's broad objectives must be itemized and clearly defined on paper—as well as the manner in which they will be pursued. Once this is done, there must be an honest evaluation of the company's current image or images; then management must determine and evaluate the image that is being projected, what factors determine the image, and the underlying depth or meaning of emotion associated with these factors.

MEASURING THE EXISTING IMAGE

The task of auditing the company image(s), in the extraordinarily complex and competitive business world, is no off-the-top-of-the-head job. The manager can attempt it himself, or he can hire a professional public relations director or outside counsel to do the job. In either case, the future of the company for a period of time will be based on the results. We say "for a period of time" because management should never assume the company image, once determined, will not change. It does, in fact, undergo continual change.

The Communications Audit. First of all, a *communications audit* will provide proper preliminary research and give logical direction to public relations planning based on the determination of the company image.

Basic phases of the communications audit include: (1) determination of what, and how effective, the company's communications activities have been to date; (2) establishment of a set of communications goals directly related to overall organization objectives; and (3) preparation of an objective picture of the organization's posture as seen by its major audience groups or publics, such as employees, customers, and stockholders.

It is interesting to learn, as outside counsel, how little management may sometimes know about the company it operates. It may well be knowledgeable about the mechanics of marketing, production, sales, advertising, and profits, but have little knowledge of the relationship between them and the corporate image—and even less knowledge of the effect of its actions on the various publics.

Conducting the Audit. Complete familiarization is the first step in conducting a communications audit. It is necessary to get to know the company—not just its day-to-day problems in the various departments and markets, but the relationship and direction of members of the management staff, production-line employees, products and services, sales methods, marketing areas, communication activities, and the various publics—and to see what correlation there is between each of these and corporate and public relations objectives.

Then define and rank in order of importance the primary and secondary audience groups—customers, stockholders, employees, suppliers, industry competitors, and such—and set down your own impressions of each and the image you *think* they might have of the company—not from your swivel chair, but from their shoes. Comparison later with their true image of the corporation may be very revealing.

Next, study and analyze every type of company communication, verbal as well as written. In the visual area, you will need copies of sales literature, news releases, trade articles, speeches, corporate brochures, financial reports and statements, advertisements, and typical correspondence. Less obvious visual material to be studied includes such things as company trademarks, signs, buildings and grounds, packaging, forms and invoices, company trucks and cars, and the company name. In the verbal area, check the manner in which the telephone is answered—not just at the switchboard, but by secretaries, supervisors, management, and in fact everyone having telephone contact with the company's various publics. Observe the receptionist's handling of visitors. Review any tapes of speeches or radio-TV appearances.

With this information, you can now begin to design questionnaires to be directed to the various publics in a sincere and honest effort to determine the corporate image.

Because content and form of the questionnaires are vital to the success of the communications audit, you may decide, at this point, to enlist the aid of a competent opinion research firm. In any case, base the questionnaires on the information already gathered. Include questions the answers to which will either confirm or contradict your own suppositions about attitudes. And include questions, too, that will indicate whether or not the image that management has or would like to convey is, in fact, realistic and shared by others.

Generally, the simplest and most practical method of getting meaningful returns—although certainly neither the most scientific nor recommended over experienced opinion research—is to mail questionnaires to a given percentage of each audience group, analyze the returns to see that they follow a consistent pattern, and then double-check the results by a small number of personal, in-depth interviews based on the same questionnaires.

Once the returns have been tabulated, you will find it fairly easy to form a reasonably accurate picture of how well the desired corporate image and stated objectives mesh with the existing attitudes of its publics. You will be able to spot areas of success, progress, and failure (the latter sometimes indicating impractical objectives). And frequently you will spot additional objectives for consideration in future planning.

If you have done a good job, you will have in your hands accurate information on the firm's current corporate image or images, *plus* logical and convincing direction for a public relations program in gear with that image.

EVALUATING AND ALTERING THE EXISTING IMAGE

If the results of your communications audit and your image analysis jibe with the desired and chosen image, well and good. We can only advise that you, your staff, and your employees live it and communicate it in *every way*.

Assuming your honest evaluation of the company's reputation has shown you what image the company currently is projecting, plus the factors and emotions affecting that image, you now should have either an undesirable image, a neutral image, or a desirable image.

If you have uncovered an undesirable image, there is little doubt that management has, until now at least, poorly judged the attitudes of its various publics.

The "nothing" or neutral image, most would feel, indicates (1) a complacent attitude by management toward its image and the public in general; (2) an "if it was good enough then, it's good enough now" attitude; or (3) purely and simply the fact that management is old and tired.

If nothing more, we would expect a desirable image to reflect a sincerity from the respondents that may not picture the best image in the world, but does strongly indicate interest. In addition, however, a desirable image should show that the company gives good value, has and respects a high level of ethical standards, and, through a two-way communication relationship with its employees and others, shows a desire for public approbation. Such an image, too, reflects company ability to draw people to it and its products or services.

When it comes to weighing the amount of emotional involvement in the replies to the communications audit, the important thing to establish is whether the respondent was actually talking about your company or may have it confused with a competitor. There is no need to fear this possibility where company and product are clearly superior or inferior to the competitor—only when the respondent has a "good" image of both. This comparative factor makes the measurement of emotion a critical factor when one good image is appraised against another.

At this point, it is not unusual at all to find yourself with, say, a fairly strong positive image with one or more disturbing counter or negative images. In planning the next step—the determination of a course of action or basic groundwork for a public relations program—this could present problems. So let us assume, first, that there is only one image that shows up, but that it is undesirable.

The Negative Image. It should be obvious that a company with a basically undesirable image requires immediate action from management toward changing to more realistic corporate practices and policies. This is the actual point where so many public relations programs are doomed to failure before they start. A public relations program designed and carried out to answer some whim or correct some blunder of management, with little or no regard for whether that program opposes corporate policies and practices, is headed in the wrong direction. And, most decidedly, it should be recognized also that no amount of communications or other public relations techniques will reverse a company's image unless there are, first, basic policy changes by management. It has been shown time and again that no company is going to live a lie for long by fostering a false image.

Nothing stands still in this world. Everything is undergoing change of some sort, and a business firm is no exception. There still are those managements who would like to keep things the way they are. And "things" may actually *appear* to be the same as they were twenty years ago, but one day management wakes up to find out differently. The business is the same, many of the old employees are still around, the market has not changed much, and other things are pretty much as they always were. But the one thing that can always be expected to change is the competition. Suddenly the old market is not big enough to pay the new wage scales. Suddenly someone across the country has come out with a vastly improved version of the old product. And suddenly (or is it eventually?) management is trying to figure out just when the steady decline and deterioration first started. A company has to go down—or grow and expand. It will not stand still for long.

The Neutral Image. A management that turns up a neutral image of itself better decide immediately which way it intends to go, too. The neutral or so-called nonexistent image really is a misnomer. The fact is there are so many diverse and weak images held by the various publics of the company, from employees to customers, that the hodge-podge leads to nowhere.

We presume, if your communications audit turns up this sort of image, that you will want to do something constructive about it. The place to begin, as usual, is with basic changes in policies and practices. In some instances, this seems a bitter pill to swallow, and attempts to sell such ideas to some old-line managements may meet with considerable resistance.

The Positive Image. For the management that uncovers or confirms a positive or desirable image of the company, the future can be both challenging and exciting, because now it can safely begin discovering and using the vast new technologies of communications.

This is not to say, however, that anything goes or that everything will work. It still remains to determine the correct course of action, a course that will promote, not help destroy, that positive image.

As a course of action gradually is developed, management must continually remind itself that the public is not a homogeneous mass. Depending, of course, on the type and variety of the company's products or services, management will want to refer once again to that "order of importance" of its various publics; but this time it must consider also their ethnic, economic, sociological, and geographic backgrounds and influence. Obviously an image that one particular public considers good may well be considered bad by another. The group management wants most to influence will determine which one it may be forced to ignore or at least pay less attention to. The object of a course of action is to appeal favorably to the largest possible number of the company's publics.

This need not present undue difficulties. Actually, you will find a basic program can be designed which can be varied as needed to appeal to the largest number of people; and, by and large, you will notice you have an excellent testing ground within your own corporate family, for right there are probably represented the variety of likes, dislikes, and desires you will find outside the corporate home.

The Dual Image. Returning for a moment to the management whose communications audit has turned up a positive image that is countered by a negative image (and we include one or more of either), there must be two courses of action established. One, as above, will be to promote the positive image, and the second to begin trying to change the negative attitude(s). As always, however, the latter must not be attempted before the basic policies and practices of management that caused the negative image in the first place are changed. Be careful in planning these two courses of action. One affects the other, and they should become a single public relations program.

We cannot overemphasize the fact that public relations programs do not perform miracles. Some managements are prone to believe public relations is the panacea for their own shortcomings; this, of course, is not so.

MEASURING RESULTS

Measuring the results of a communications program that has been designed either to correct popular misconceptions about the corporation or effectively to advance a positive image of the firm is a fairly simple process, but it should never be hurried.

If your homework was done well in setting up management policies, designing and conducting the communications audit, and interpreting the results, your public relations course of action should, when measured, not only show results but turn up additional benefits.

Time is the controlling factor. Assuming the audit was done conscientiously and that management's "imagined" image of itself colored neither the audit nor the results, at least a full year should go by before any attempt is made to measure the results.

Then, repeat the audit and evaluation undertaken initially, in exactly the same form. The results of the second audit can be plotted against the first, and the net difference will be the measure of progress toward your objectives. This comparison also should spot trouble areas, change in audience attitudes, and responsiveness to specific communications techniques. But, one word of caution: Do not automatically assume that either the image first turned up or your audit is wrong if there are no appreciable results. Chances are your first try at specific communications techniques may have left something to be desired. There are many techniques and many ways of applying them. Look for improvement in this area first. You are now deep into the area best done by the public relations professional. He may not have all the answers, but his education and experience should save time, money, and mistakes in the long run.

PLANNING THE COURSE OF ACTION

Communication techniques must be matched to the objectives of management, with the overall program designed to bring the ideal and the existing to a common meeting ground. Therefore, a public relations program to be fully successful must be based on sound, achievable goals, established through a careful communications audit that reflects the policies and practices of management.

Well before a course of action is discussed and the basis for a sound public relations program is laid, management must become acquainted fully with the function of public relations. True corporate public relations is such a far cry from the concept that some managers have of the field that, even at this point in the image-building venture, the effort could grind to a halt or, at the very least, prove completely ineffective, unless management takes the time to make this acquaintance.

As indicated throughout this chapter, the corporate image is the sum total of all attitudes toward the company. A public relations program designed to sustain or improve those attitudes must not only be concerned with all these attitudes, but must involve itself in the public relations aspects of every function and department of the corporation. Any manager who holds to the view that public relations should concern itself solely with publicity and sales promotion might just as well let the corporate image fall where it may.

How to Use a Public Relations Director. If the corporation employs its own director of public relations, no matter what sort of identification is given him and his department, the director should be part of the program of image building from the start and should be treated as part of management at the policy-making level.

For management to make all the decisions and do all the planning and then toss the ball to the public relations director to activate the program is inefficient use of the specialized skills and talents he is anxious to use in your behalf.

It is not enough simply to take him into your confidence. You must open doors for him and make his task clear to other members of management, department heads, and supervisors, informing them that you expect each to give him all possible cooperation. See that he gets all the facts and figures he needs, and indicate in every way that he is working with you and that his work has your blessing.

The public relations director, on the other hand, has the responsibility of conducting himself properly. Your blessing does not give him permission to barge into departments demanding this, that, or the other thing, or to disrupt daily routines. Personal conversations, meetings, and other methods of research can be worked out tactfully with those concerned. The result must leave a positive impression of the director and the function of public relations in the company.

In other chapters of this section, the elements, planning, and organization of a public relations program are discussed in detail, but it is extremely important that the top executive officer and other key management executives recognize that corporate image communications (that is, the public relations program) is both an art and a science. It is an art in the sense that communications should do more than merely pass along information, because communications should represent a blend of skills and judgment—influencing by inspiring, motivating, or changing thought patterns. It is a science in the sense that the communications must be controlled by and oriented to management's objectives, reaching the right people in the right way at the right time.

BIBLIOGRAPHY

Berni, Alan, "Evaluating Visual Identity," *PR Reporter, Tips & Tactics,* Mar. 16, 1964.

Bill, Harold V., "A Company Gets Its Portrait Painted," *Public Relations Journal,* July, 1960.

Bristol, Lee H., *Developing the Corporate Image,* Charles Scribner's Sons, New York, 1960.

Finn, David, *How to Create a Company Personality,* Ruder & Finn, New York.

Gaynor, Paul, "Projecting the Corporate Image," *PR Reporter, Tips & Tactics,* May 23, 1964.

Mead-Ross Associates, "How to Conduct a Communications Audit," *PR Reporter, Tips & Tactics,* Jan. 6, 1964.

Prerau, Sidney (ed.), *J. K. Lasser's Business Management Handbook,* 2d ed., McGraw-Hill Book Company, New York, 1960.

Riley, John W., Jr. (ed.), *The Corporation and Its Publics,* John Wiley & Sons, Inc., New York, 1963.

CHAPTER FOUR

Corporate Giving

ALLEN D. MARSHALL *President and Chief Executive, United Student Aid Funds, Inc., New York, New York*

Philanthropy by business corporations has been an increasing activity over the years. The United States Treasury Department reported that contributions by corporations in 1962 amounted to $595 million. These contributions are a major support of many charitable and educational institutions, as the community leaders who raise funds for hospitals, libraries, colleges, and community chests can testify. At the same time, this well-motivated activity can be a most troublesome one for the average business executive who is accustomed to think in terms of the profitability of each activity with which he is concerned.

This chapter will describe some guidelines and objectives for corporate giving, show how they are being applied, and point out pitfalls which should be avoided. Of course, the first and most important guideline is the definite assignment of responsibility for the function.

PURPOSE OF CORPORATE GIVING

It is not easy to state in simple terms the purpose of corporate giving. One excellent statement is found in the preface to a book by Richard Eells.[1] "The wider frame of reference for corporate giving is an urgent necessity, however, for entirely different reasons than those which might interest the tax collector. Foremost among these reasons is the vital importance to private business enterprise of strengthening and preserving all the private sectors that sustain a constitutional pattern of society."

More concretely, a corporation gives to charitable, philanthropic, and social-betterment organizations to benefit employees, shareowners, and their families; to make the local community a better place in which to live and work; and

[1] Richard Eells, *Corporate Giving in a Free Society*, Harper & Row, Publishers, Incorporated, New York, 1956.

12–28

to promote the national welfare. It gives to educational institutions to augment the national resources of trained personnel, particularly in the areas of interest of the corporation and in the communities in which it operates. Over and beyond these objectives, a wise program of corporate giving can enhance a corporation's reputation among community and educational leaders.

Effect on Corporate Profitability. The first effect of a program of corporate giving is to reduce the corporation's profits by a percentage of the gift which depends on the income tax rate. The same thing can be said, however, for any expenditure for labor, equipment, or research and development. In the long range, a sound program of corporate giving can have a favorable effect on corporate profitability, although a contribution, to be tax deductible, must have a much broader objective than to promote the business interests of the donor.

CORPORATE GIVING POLICIES

Policy decisions in corporate giving involve not only objectives, but also procedures. This chapter can do no more than merely point out the areas in which the decisions should be made, with some of the considerations concerning each, and give a few examples of successful operating procedures.

Giving Mechanism. First of all, should the corporation create a tax-exempt foundation through which to channel contributions? The answer will involve study by financial and tax experts and the public and employee relations executives of the company.

A foundation supported by corporate giving during profitable years can level out contributions to community enterprises during bad and good years. Unexpected windfalls—such as securities which have appreciated in value and other surplus properties—can provide the foundation with funds which can then be spread in gifts over longer periods of time. A foundation's personnel can provide technical advice and act as a buffer between corporate officers and fund raisers. Foundations, however, may be more trouble in administration than they are worth. Corporations whose principal customer is the Defense Department may have problems with contributions to such foundations.

How Much and to Whom. How much should the corporation give annually, in total and to specific worthy enterprises? Given a profitable enterprise, this is a basic question, for there are always worthy causes which can use any amount of money.

The appropriate size of an annual budget is determined by such factors as profitability of the enterprise, needs of the community, opportunity to build goodwill for the corporation and its products, the need to build the community as a desirable place to live and work, and the desirability of providing opportunities for a continuing education for employees and their families.

Basically there are two approaches. One is to gather together the recommendations of managers about all requests for contributions and then fit them to the appropriate total in much the same manner that annual appropriations for plant and equipment are considered.

Another approach to the total annual budget is one used by some companies in the insurance industry. This states the maximum to be given as x dollars per million of admitted assets for operating fund contributions and y dollars per million of admitted assets for capital contributions.

The annual budget of a corporation for contributions rarely exceeds the allowable deduction for income tax purposes, but the tax expert should advise on the Internal Revenue Service regulations which change from time to time. One publication gives the 1960 data from the IRS for 1,140,575 corporations whose contributions amounted to 1.1 percent of their net profits.

A general observation is that only the top manager can and should make the decision on the total budget and the amount to be given to individual recipients. Professional fund raisers and community leaders should be listened to and their arguments should be analyzed carefully, but in the end, it is usually the chief executive who must make the final decision. For example, a contribution to a local community chest of $50 per employee for a chemical company may be no more generous in terms of profit per employee than a $10 contribution per employee for a job-shop operation in heavy machinery.

A corporation must also look forward to the capital fund drives of the institutions in its community. Its annual budget should provide not only for gifts for operating budgets, but also for gifts for capital building funds, requests for which come with increasing regularity as the demand grows for more facilities for colleges, hospitals, and character-building organizations for the young.

Some corporations make gifts to selected colleges, students, teachers, and others in the form of scholarships, fellowships, contributions to annual operating budgets, and the like. These are all worthy objectives and bring credit to the donor. It should be borne in mind, however, that for every happy recipient there are usually many who applied and were refused. It is possible to minimize ill will by having third parties make the selection. For example, the corporation outlines the rules and furnishes the money. Then the college picks the recipients of the scholarships, a committee of academicians picks the fellowship winners, or a group of prominent citizens picks the colleges to which grants are made. Selection by employee alumni is illustrated by the matching-gift program in which many companies match the gifts of their employees to their alma maters.

Advantages of Written Policies. It is well to have a written corporate policy in giving. This enables the busy executive quickly to review and answer many of the requests received.

The National Industrial Conference Board in its publication *Company Contributions Primer* outlines the advantages of a written policy as follows:

Companies with written contributions policies report the following advantages:
A written policy expedites control and administration of company contributions.
A written policy makes for a consistent pattern of giving.
A written policy facilitates decentralized giving in corporations with multiple plants.

In the educational area, a policy can range from giving only to institutions of higher learning in plant communities, where employees can take advantage of the facilities, to a broad program such as one national corporation with an expert staff has which includes such things as annual awards to leading, nonaccredited colleges to help them obtain accreditation.

Guidelines for Giving. Though no one pattern of giving suits all corporations, a few guidelines are generally applicable.

There are several areas which most corporations, in policy statements or otherwise, specifically exclude from their programs for legal or other reasons. Examples are:

Contributions to political parties or candidates
Organizations on the Attorney General's list of subversive organizations
Labor unions
Religious and sectarian organizations

Usually, a wide area of discretion is left to local management for small contributions to organizations in the plant community with the only control being company policy and an annual budget.

Under special circumstances, especially in connection with appeals from educational institutions, it may be sound policy to give only to the capital fund drives of those institutions in which company officers and other executives have a personal interest. Such specialized giving programs are not common, however, partly because they are difficult to administer.

Regardless of company policy, or perhaps in consonance with it, many companies find it advisable to be generous with organizations whose fund-raising drives are headed by important customers.

Investigation and Review. Important information concerning organizations requesting gifts may be obtained from outside reporting agencies—better business bureaus, credit-rating organizations, and the like. These reports are of limited usefulness, however, and they usually should be supplemented by additional and thorough investigation where substantial gifts are being considered, even though the recipient may have a generally favorable reputation.

A wise procedure is to find some employee in a responsible position who is sufficiently interested in the work of the prospective recipient to be willing to follow its activities and report, at least annually, to the corporate officer responsible for contributions.

Sometimes corporations are tempted to dictate the activities of the institutions to which they make grants. This is a serious and perhaps fatal error. Much of the goodwill gained by the gift is lost, and the donor wastes valuable time, energy, and skill in unfamiliar areas.

Policy Changes. A stated policy is helpful. But one which is never reviewed, never changed, and to which no exceptions are made can in a few years be as outdated as the products of a manufacturer who has no research or application engineering. New institutions will come into being to fill new needs. Old institutions will have completed their work or will have become completely tax supported. Even with a sound policy, the alert executive concerned with corporate giving should always be receptive to the sound new idea.

As a matter of fact, a few corporations and a number of foundations, as a matter of policy, look for causes which lack popular appeal and organizations which need funds to demonstrate that they can make a real contribution to the community and thus command support from others.

A final word of caution: The need has been indicated to consult the financial expert, the lawyer, and the tax expert as well as the public and employee relations expert. This is again emphasized, but only for the purpose of pointing out that a major objective of corporate giving is the creation of goodwill. Procedures which irritate recipients should not be allowed. Every program, whether for home building or education, may create much goodwill when the loan is made, but this may be offset by the ill will which results when the recipient is pressed to repay. An audit of the results of a corporate giving program is a much more difficult and sophisticated procedure than the financial audit of even a complex corporate enterprise.

CONCLUSION

Corporate giving is a big business. It can be a major headache to the executive who feels he should be devoting his time to other things. However, with sound policies, a reasonable annual budget, and a recognition of the need for periodic policy changes, corporate giving can be a goodwill builder and a major factor in improving the community in which the corporation operates.

BIBLIOGRAPHY

Andrews, F. Emerson, *Corporation Giving*, Russell Sage Foundation, New York, 1952.

Andrews, F. Emerson, *Philanthropic Giving*, Russell Sage Foundation, New York, 1950.

Carter, Richard, *The Gentle Legions*, Doubleday & Company, Inc., Garden City, N.Y., 1961.

Company-Sponsored Foundations, Studies in Business Policy, no. 73, National Industrial Conference Board, New York, 1955.

Corporation Support of Higher Education, Council for Financial Aid to Education, Washington, D.C., 1965.

Eells, Richard, *Corporate Giving in a Free Society*, Harper & Row, Publishers, Incorporated, New York, 1956.

Giving U.S.A.—Annual, American Association of Fund Raising Counsel, Inc., New York, 1964.

Mason, Edward S., *The Corporation in Modern Society*, Harvard University Press, Cambridge, 1959.

The Performing Arts: Problems and Prospects, Rockefeller Brothers Fund, Inc., New York, 1965.

Ruml, Beardsley, and Theodore Geiger, *The Manual of Corporate Giving*, National Planning Association, Washington, D.C., 1952.

Shapiro, Leo J., *Company Giving*, Survey Press, Chicago, 1960.

Watson, John H., III, *Industry Aid to Education*, Studies in Public Affairs, no. 1, National Industrial Conference Board, New York, 1965.

CHAPTER FIVE

Community Relations

WILLARD V. MERRIHUE   *General Electric Company, New York, New York*

Just what is the management function known as "community relations"? What is its purpose? Why is it important? How does it pay its way? What are the elements of a successful community relations program? How do you know if it is successful? What are the criteria for success?

These and other considerations of concern to the chief executive of a business will be discussed in this chapter, along with a brief history of the function; a code of company conduct in a community; the most effective methods of communicating with key segments of the community; how to organize, staff, and measure the function; and the mature concept of community relations being practiced by sophisticated business enterprises.

Let us begin by stating what the more perceptive managers of industry, institutions, and other business enterprises already know: It is impossible to operate an establishment satisfactorily and to grow for any extended period of time without the continuing understanding, respect, and approval of the community in which it is located.

This climate of understanding, respect, and approval must first be deserved and then assiduously and continually cultivated. The management function responsible for this critical piece of work is known as "community relations."

A DEFINITION AND SOME GOALS

Community relations is the management function which identifies and interprets community interests and attitudes, relates company policies and practices to these local interests and attitudes (within feasible economic parameters), initiates programs of action to earn for the company the respect and confidence of the community, and actively shapes conditions of mutual advantage to the community and to the business.

It may be easier to conceptualize community relations if we think of it as public relations practiced at the local-plant–community level. Unlike the corporate public relations director of a large multiplant or multioffice enterprise, the local community relations manager or representative can geographically circumscribe his audience and precisely zero in on the specific publics of interest to him.

The community relations goals of the more enlightened companies are likely to comprise some or all of the following:

Building public understanding of the business and of the private enterprise system

Working to make the community a better place in which to live, work, and raise a family

Contributing with other civic leaders to the solution of basic community problems

Helping the community, county, and regional leadership meet the specific needs of the company—skilled labor, vocational training, pure water, good air, rail and trucking service, and the like

Taking an active interest in local and state political affairs

Working with other groups to improve the local and state business climate

HISTORY OF THE EVOLUTION OF COMMUNITY RELATIONS

The management function of community relations has grown to its present importance and sophistication and receives the personal attention of top operating executives because of the radical changes in the public's expectations of business since World War I.

Early community relations efforts by business were largely built on a generally paternalistic or even philosophic recognition that industry had some responsibility "to do good works" at a time when civic social responsibility was undeveloped. Welfare and social needs were met by the churches and the business leaders who helped by aiding social agencies to develop. Business leaders were willing to see tax dollars go into good civic work—but all this was a kind of largess for the poor. Business leaders reacted to the social demands of the time, but it was considered bad taste to advertise their contributions. These things were thought to be understood and appreciated.

Meanwhile, other forces were at work to claim credit for progress. What business leaders did in the community was assumed locally to be merely "good public relations." These business leaders found that they not only did not get credit but were assumed to have unlimited resources to do for communities what they were not willing to do for themselves. This was also a period of social reform in which industry was increasingly pointed to as the breeder of social ills. As the unions became stronger and their political power greater, a subtle but profound change of viewpoint came about—namely, that industry must be forced to pay a bill for damages rendered. This led to the development of workmen's compensation, unemployment compensation, and social security.

In the aftermath of World War II came the great strike wave and the rude awakening for many business leaders, large and small, enlightened or otherwise, that community populations had little love or respect for them. In many cases, these leaders were shocked to see their community friends, lawyers, doctors, and pastors marching in picket lines in support of strikers—a disillusioning and bitter experience which caused the soul searching leading up to the development of a more sophisticated and perceptive community relations function.

The subsequent self-evaluation led to one conclusion. It is not enough for an employer to *deserve* good treatment from the community by virtue of his conduct as a good employer and corporate neighbor. He must, additionally, convince the community through communication that he is deserving and should be given the benefit of the doubt in times of crisis, when he needs community support.

The chief executive who wishes to put community relations to work to increase the profitability of his business must first develop a policy which will optimize the success of the function.

Four Essentials for Success.   Analysis of the most successful community relations functions reveals this simple, sensible, down-to-earth pattern of conduct and communication:

1. Do right inside the plant or offices.

2. Keep telling the employees what you are doing to give them the best jobs you know how to provide.

3. Do right in the community.

4. Keep telling the community what you are doing to deserve their approval and cooperation.

The "do right in plant" course of conduct is the bedrock foundation of all successful community relations programs. It is wasteful to spend a nickel on community relations if your employee relations are sour. Your best ambassadors are your employees and their families.

Recently a company which had been carrying on a most intensive and constructive community relations activity called in a group of social scientists to measure the results of its work. To its surprise it found that, despite its expenditures in mass communication, the favorable attitudes toward the company had been largely shaped by word-of-mouth selling by satisfied employees.

Experienced managers know that good employee relations are the prerequisite of good community relations. But good employee relations are not enough. Employees need the reassurance of their families and other groups that their faith in their employer is well founded.

A CODE OF COMMUNITY CONDUCT

The business enterprise which sets out to earn the respect and approval of the community must live right by these criteria. It must be, in fact:

1. A good employer of local labor, so planning and running the business that it achieves maximum stabilization of employment

2. A friendly, hospitable employer, granting *all* applicants for employment a fair, tactful, courteous interview and applying the same rules of courtesy to visitors as to guests in one's house

3. A good housekeeper, maintaining a clean plant in neat surroundings and with a systematic plan for abatement of offensive smoke, noise, odors, or waste products

4. A buyer of goods and services locally, to the maximum degree that is prudent

5. A good taxpayer, demanding justice but no bargains

6. A generous but not paternalistic contributor to local charities and capital fund drives

7. A good corporate citizen, actively participating to achieve good government, good schools, good churches, and the like, and taking an active role in helping achieve a better community

8. A company which encourages all its employees to assume their individual citizenship responsibilities, including active participation in a political party of their choice

But even such an enlightened code of community conduct is not enough. Experience proves that an action program of this type will fail to achieve a widespread, favorable reputation for the sponsor and resulting community cooperation when needed, unless the various aspects of the program are communicated continually and skillfully.

COMMUNICATING TO THE COMMUNITY

One company with a national reputation for successful community relations recommends to the managers of each of its major installations the following communication techniques and public relations ideas that have been found most effective in merchandising a local plant's good neighbor policies.

1. *Develop a mailing list of civic-thought leaders* and all identifiable members of the local power structure. Use this list to distribute any information that will enhance understanding of the company's enlightened employee and community relations policies such as attractive features of pay and benefit plans, employment stabilization planning, and expansion or contraction of jobs. Use the list also to explain the company's point of view during union contract negotiations or in periods of unsettled labor relations, walkouts, or strikes.

2. *Build and maintain good relations with the local press, radio, and TV.* Of prime importance to a successful community relations program is an understanding of the needs and unique problems of these mass conveyors of news and information to the local publics. No trouble should be spared to see that representatives of these media get, to the maximum degree practical, what they want when they want it. Of great aid to local editors is a list of home telephone numbers of a number of designated company spokesmen to aid the reporters in checking material after the plant is closed for the day.

Plant managers should be taught that the words "no comment" are rarely to be used and often represent a priceless opportunity missed. The pompous, hollow cliché, "A company spokesman stated . . ." should be taboo. If you are authorized to speak for the company, let the reporters use your name. Names make news!

3. *Invest in some local newspaper advertising.* The wise employer will supplement the news coverage accorded him (*when his releases are newsworthy*) with occasional paid advertisements in the local newspapers.

Some of the more progressive employers publish an annual report to their community neighbors in the form of a full-page newspaper advertisement. Titled with some such headlines as "Here's What the Kay-Ess Company and Its 1,200 Employees Meant to the Community Last Year," it presents a sectionalized, illustrated story on annual payroll, charitable contributions, civic activities, research, new products, and the like. This is a dramatic and highly effective method of merchandising the "live right in the community" course of conduct.

Other suitable subjects for newspaper advertisements are explanations of new union contract settlements, invitations to open houses, wholesome effects on employees and community of the company's benefit programs, advance notification and economic reasons for impending layoffs, recruitment of employees, appeal to community for support in labor disputes, threatened strikes, secondary boycotts, illegal picketing, company policies, and progress as an "equal opportunities" employer.

Note: The far-sighted employer never waits until he is in trouble to initiate the use of any of these communication media in the community. He should expect little audience attention to, or interest in, any medium unless he has used it naturally in normal times.

4. *Utilize local radio time and TV* where local rates are reasonable. In many communities, local radio time is so relatively inexpensive that it provides a most attractive institutional medium of communication. Many plant managers buy fifteen minutes of radio time to use while their workers are driving to work. These workers seldom have time to read a morning paper and are grateful for local and national news, weather, and sports, as well as company news interspersed between musical recordings. However, such a medium should not be used as pure entertainment or as an employee benefit. It should be used as another very effective device to communicate the goodness of the jobs and other desirable social products flowing from the employer to the employees, their families, and neighbors listening in.

Many companies also use radio programs at other intervals in the day or evening. Some companies make an excellent investment in local good will by sponsoring all home games of the local baseball team. Other employers sponsor religious programs on Sunday, to the great gratitude of the local clergy and thousands of neighbors.

Local television is being increasingly used by the larger companies to win greater understanding and approval of their local business units. The rates of many local TV stations are not at all unreasonable, and the high audience impact of this medium makes it well worth consideration. In some cities, a group of employers will cooperatively sponsor a program with each employer being given a certain evening to tell his particular story—a sensible method of spreading the cost.

5. *Operate a speakers' bureau.* The speakers' bureau returns a double dividend to the progressive user. It provides a deeply appreciated service to the scores of civic groups in every town that are eager for speakers but cannot afford honoraria, and it is an excellent self-development and training device for employees.

The employer invites employees to volunteer for the bureau and to pick out one or more subjects which may deal with the employees' vocations or avocations. A brochure listing the speakers and subjects is prepared and distributed to all civic groups. The community relations man schedules the speakers as a part-time assignment. The bureau, although featuring talks of general entertainment and educational value, should also include talks on various aspects of company policies, benefits, corporate conduct, human relations, and business economics.

Some companies supplement their speakers' bureau with a film library. A catalog of films describing company products, their manufacture and use, engineering and research, employee recreation, human relations, opportunities for advancement, company history, and basic economics is distributed to civic organizations, schools, and church groups, and the films are loaned gratis on request. Appropriate films from other sources are also made available. This is unusually effective with many groups!

6. *Consider an "open house" and guided plant tours.* Any family knows the friendliness and better understanding resulting from holding a periodic "open house" for neighbors and friends. Employers in increasing numbers are finding that these dividends accrue to their enterprise on a community-wide basis when the plant is thrown open for inspection by the entire community or by specialized groups.

The open house must be carefully planned and publicized far in advance of the date. Such problems as routes of the plant tour, training of tour guides, placement of interpretive signs on important machinery and processes, the serving of light refreshments, the choice of souvenirs, if any, balloons or caps for children, baby-sitters, and safety measures all deserve detailed planning, delegation, and follow-through.

The event should not only entertain, but also thoughtfully educate, and should advance the broad community relations objectives of the company.

Many plants that manufacture products of special public interest have set up facilities for daily guided tours. By careful planning, they see that these tours win new customers for the firm's economic products and create a new awareness of the beneficial social products of the enterprise, as well as satisfy the innate curiosity of families as to where dad, mother, or brother works.

7. *Interpret the business to specific community groups.* The skilled community relations practitioner tailors his communication to the specialized interests of specific local publics. Let us observe the operation of such a program with a typical local group—the educators, for example.

The starting point is a sincere interest in the problems and aspirations of this group and an earnest desire to be helpful from *their* point of view. Both employers and employees should actively support all worthy efforts to improve the educational facilities of the community and the quality, compensation, and status of the teachers. Managers and other employees should be encouraged to affiliate with and be actively constructive in school boards and PTA's. Many communities sponsor "education-business" days in which businessmen personally visit the schools to observe the quality of the faculty, the facilities, and the curriculum, and to obtain a firsthand knowledge of the school problems. Employers should vigorously participate in these events.

The employer who makes this initial investment in understanding and empathy for this important community public is then in a position to solicit this group's interest and understanding of *his* problems and goals.

He can put the educators on his mailing list to receive his employee publication; he can mail, periodically, pamphlets which create a fuller understanding of his goals and accomplishments; he can solicit eager cooperation in the development of better and more adequate vocational training. Periodically, he can invite the teachers in a group to a plant visitation where they can observe firsthand his working conditions and the huge investment required to provide a job for a single employee. He can explain his benefit plans, his need for special skills in local graduates, and the need for and the role of adequate profits.

He can do this job as an individual employer or he can participate in a group employer effort common in many communities, which is known as "business-education" day. In this practice, the educators are divided into groups, each group being assigned to a specific employer's plant. Solo or cooperatively, a prime requisite in planning is to provide ample opportunity for the frankest questioning by the educators.

A successful community relations program will embrace just such careful individual treatment of the clergy, physicians, dentists, lawyers, merchants, local government officials, and any other groups whose understanding, approval, and support for the local enterprise are sought.

EMPLOYMENT OFFICES AND RECEPTION CENTERS

The foregoing seven broad methods of communicating a local plant's good-employer, good-neighbor policies have been repeatedly tested and proved most effective. It should be cautioned that much of this effort will be wasted if the community's physical contacts with the plant leave a bad taste. Two of the most important ingredients of a successful community relations program are attractive, competently manned employment offices and visitor and vendor reception centers. A shabby, uncomfortable employment office, staffed with brusque, autocratic help, can undo all previously described attempts to develop good community relations. Every applicant for employment, whether or not accepted, should be treated with dignity and courtesy. He should be processed speedily and interviewed in a friendly, tactful manner, especially if not accepted. Even if he is not a prospective customer for the product, he is likely to have influence in some local group, and he votes his approval or aversions at the polls.

Equally important is the first impression of the main reception center or "waiting room," where visitors, customers, and vendors register for plant visitations or official business.

In putting one's house in order as a prelude to initiating a community relations program, look to the employment office and the very important reception center *first*.

EMPLOYEE PARTICIPATION IN COMMUNITY AFFAIRS

The utmost encouragement should be given to all employees to participate in civic activities. The top officers or managers should set the example through their own participation; through issuance of a clear, positive policy; and through procedural implementation which permits reasonable absence for short periods during working hours to perform useful civic work. By actively participating in community organizations, employees help build a better home town, help create widespread understanding and favorable attitudes for their company, and contribute to their own self-development.

Some employers maintain a card index system to stimulate civic participation. The name and department of each employee active in a civic group are filed centrally. This enables the community relations representative to keep the employee's supervisor informed so that he may encourage the man or woman in specific terms.

The presentation of awards or managers' dinners to employees active in the community and publicizing their contributions in the plant or office or corporation house organ are other effective incentives.

The National Industrial Conference Board (NICB) found the following through a survey of employee participation in community affairs:

Eighty-five percent of the 213 responding companies granted time off with pay to employees who participate in worthy community activities. Approximately 75 percent permit the use of secretarial help, and most offer other forms of assistance, such as use of company meeting rooms or duplicating equipment.

Quite a few companies, though, find it necessary to restrict the classes of employees they help in community work, and some restrict the types of community project for which they supply assistance to participating employees.

Granting Time Off. The NICB survey further found the following:

A very effective way to encourage participation in community affairs by a broad section of employees is to permit the use of business time in these activities. As a rule, those companies that grant time off for community service do so liberally, and many set no specific restrictions. However, management does rely on employees to exercise good judgment. As one top executive puts it: "By the nature of their jobs some employees have more time for civic activities than others. We expect them to use their own good judgment. The company allows reasonable time from the job to perform civic functions but tries to make certain this time is necessary and not abused." A watchful hand on the controls by management can make sure that possible abuses are nipped in the bud.

STAFFING THE COMMUNITY RELATIONS FUNCTION

There are no norms or standards for staffing the community relations function and no "customary" reporting position in the organization. The number of functional specialists engaged in this work and their reporting levels vary markedly among companies of similar assets, sales, product mix, and presumably, similar problems. This may be because the practice of formalized community relations is only about half as old as the broader field of industrial relations and public relations of which it is often a subcomponent.

A survey of some well-kown companies carrying on manufacturing in numerous communities here and abroad revealed no definite pattern nor, indeed, any uniform emphasis on the problem. Some example follow.

Automobile Manufacturers. There is intense emphasis, from president down, with responsibility meticulously delegated at corporate and field levels. At headquarters, a manager of a community relations department reports directly to the vice president of civic and governmental affairs. This department consists of five specialists. In the field, the responsibility is delegated to one of six regional civic- and governmental-affairs managers. These men work through community relations committees in each company location. The committees are composed of the top management of each of the company facilities in the community—assembly or parts plant if there is one, parts depot, subsidiaries, nonautomotive components, division sales offices, service organizations, and so on. There are more than sixty of these committees, each headed by a locally elected chairman and each presenting a united corporate voice on community matters and working to earn a favorable corporate image. In addition, two of the "big three" automobile manufacturers carry on community relations programs in nonplant cities through dealer committees. The chairmen are selected by a panel of their peers and serve for two years.

Steel Manufacturer. One of the largest, this company produces steel in a number of United States communities. At only their largest plant, however, is there a community relations manager. He reports to the superintendent. At all other plants, this function is the responsibility of the local superintendent, who calls on one of twelve regional district directors of public relations in case of serious local problems. These regional public relations men report to the corporate vice president of public relations at headquarters. This would indicate that community relations is viewed as a fire-fighting function rather than a continuous building of a local image.

Chemical Manufacturer. This company has six large plants (over 2,000 employees) and many smaller plants with 250 or fewer on the payroll. In the larger plants, the function is performed by a full-time manager of community relations. He usually has an assistant, for he normally is responsible also for in-plant communication as well as press relations in the community. In the smaller plants, community relations is a part-time function of the industrial relations manager where there is one, otherwise of the plant manager.

At headquarters in this company, community relations is the responsibility of one man and several assistants who report to the director of corporate relations rather than to the director of industrial relations.

Electrical Company. This company, which is noted for its pioneering work in, and emphasis on, community relations, utilizes a full-time community relations manager in all plants of 750 to 1,000 or more employees; this manager reports always to the manager of employee, union, and community relations.   In plants of less than this working population, the function is a part-time but heavily emphasized and appraised job of the industrial relations manager or plant manager where the plant is too small to support much overhead.

Quite often the community relations manager will be assigned the quite complementary task of in-plant communication.

At headquarters, this company maintains a manager of community relations positioned in the public relations department.   He is assisted by a field man who travels the circuit, advising and teaching and informally appraising the field discharge of the function.

This company also maintains eight regional public relations managers who, among many other duties, are expected to look after community relations in important nonplant cities in their regions.

Pulp and Paper Company.   In each of five large plants, a full-time community relations manager reports to the plant superintendent or to a division vice president where the latter is located in a plant city.   At headquarters, a director of community relations reports to the vice president of public relations.

Electronics Company.   The community relations function is highly centralized, with no functional specialists in the field.   At headquarters, a manager of community relations, reporting to the vice president of public relations, advises and assists local division and plant managers on projects to be initiated; prepares community relations advertisements, publications, and exhibits for use in the plant community; and visits the plants to give direct assistance on open houses, community exhibits, and the like.

MEASURING THE COMMUNITY RELATIONS FUNCTION

Presumably a local employer can live right both inside the plant and in the community, and can communicate his intentions and his actions, and still be misunderstood.   How does he know where he is failing or how his neighbors regard him, short of overt hostility, when he needs their cooperation?

Answers to the following questions provide a form of measurement.

1. Do the best of the local high school or vocational school graduates eagerly seek jobs with us?

2. Do local graduates of colleges tend to come home to seek employment with us?

3. Do the reporters of the communication media respect us, or do they frequently pillory the company and its officials?

4. Do our employees "talk up" our company as a good place to work and encourage their families' members and friends to seek employment with us?

5. Are city and county government officials helpful when a new access road or land for expansion is needed, or do they consider it good politics to be overtly hostile and to harass us with restrictive ordinances?

6. Are local tax assessment and policies fair to the enterprise?

7. Can we be sure of impartial enforcement of local laws and ordinances if our plant is struck or plagued with picketing?

8. If we are a public corporation, do our neighbors invest some of their savings in our stock?

9. If we produce consumer goods or services, do our local sales markedly exceed regional, state, or national sales?

Community Attitude Surveys.   There is another increasingly popular method of evaluating progress in attainment of established community relations goals.   It is the periodic opinion survey to determine community awareness of the company and its attitudes toward the local enterprise.

It cannot be emphasized too strongly that the community attitude survey is not only a gage for measuring results but also an essential step in planning the community relations program. Just as the employer utilizes market research experts to study the needs and preferences of his market before planning any new product, so should he utilize a reputable polling firm to appraise the attitudes of the community before planning his initial community relations program.

For either of these two usages, the first step in the process is to select the neighbors to be polled on a scientific, random-sampling basis. The polling is done through personally conducted depth interviews. If expense is a serious factor, however, quite satisfactory results may be obtained by a mail questionnaire which has previously been tested through limited use in personal interviews.

Many companies publicize the survey in the local press in advance of the starting date, and a complete report of the findings is featured in the same medium. The survey results are likewise communicated to the employees through in-plant media.

The questions asked should be tailored to suit the requirements of the company, but in general, consideration should be given to the following categories: (1) the adequacy of the company's wages and salaries; (2) awareness of the company's individual benefit plans and how they compare with those of other local employers; (3) extent and relative generosity of company and employee contributions to local charities; (4) extent and quality of company and employee participation in civic activities; (5) knowledge and acceptance of products or services produced; (6) community's appraisal of quality of products or services; (7) steadiness of work; (8) quality of labor relations; (9) quality of working conditions; (10) sources of most accurate information concerning company; and (11) solicitation of spontaneous comments.

Employers who have acquired requisite skills through experience in community polling can personally conduct such surveys periodically to measure trends. An interesting variation of this "do it yourself" technique is the use of local teachers as the interviewers during summer vacation. This results in a valuable by-product, inasmuch as this important segment of the local public acquires a firsthand knowledge of the function and policies of a local business enterprise.

In essence, the community survey is a planned effort to discover how much your neighbors know about you, how they feel about you, and in what ways they would prefer to have you act differently. It provides a partial basis for your remedial program and a partial bench mark for measuring your community relations performance.

A NEW CONCEPT OF COMMUNITY RELATIONS

In no country in the world other than the United States do employers and employees give so generously and effectively of their time and money to improve their communities. Unfortunately, this invaluable contribution is all too often taken for granted by a community which progressively makes it more difficult for these same employers to grow and be profitable. That is why employers must continue to communicate what they are doing and must in addition educate the community on the "care and feeding" of good, profitable employers—with particular emphasis on the maintenance of a favorable local climate for business. The community must make it possible for desirable employers to prosper and grow. It usually will want to attract new employers as well.

All too often community relations is a unilateral outpouring of time and money on the part of an employer—a one-way street, a defensive posture of winning friends and hoping for the best when and if the employer needs understanding and support.

Hard-headed employers know that their first obligation to their employees, stockholders, and community neighbors is to make a profit so that they can continue to provide jobs or create additional jobs through growth financed by profit. This means they must develop an awareness in their local communities and states of the two-way nature of the employer-community relationship with the employer striving constantly to provide expanding numbers of steadier jobs in addition to being a responsible citizen, and the community, in turn, striving to maintain an equitable business climate in which deserving employers can prosper and grow.

The business climate of a community is an amalgam of political, social, and economic factors which enhance or sap a community's good health. It is a composite of competitive labor costs; harmonious labor relations; a nondiscriminatory tax structure; good local government; a prudent level of government expenditures; adequate housing, schools, and cultural facilities; fair treatment of business by the press, clergy, and thought leaders; impartial, no-nonsense law enforcement; and a community with spirit, belief in itself, and a progressive, unselfish power structure.

Improving the Local Business Climate. Thoughtful employers periodically audit the business climate of their plant cities and states and report their findings to city fathers, governors, private utilities such as the power and telephone companies, merchants, realtors, local railroads, trucking and airline officials, and all who have an economic stake in the robust health of a community's or state's employers. These economic partners know only too well that the quickest and least expensive way to create more employment locally is to help existing employers remain profitable and expand locally.

The local plant manager has an ongoing obligation to keep city fathers, civic leaders, employees, and labor leaders cognizant of the local and state business climate—to point out the dire consequences of an eroding business climate, to point out what elements need to be remedied, and to show the community what it must do to foster continued profitability and expansion of existing plants and to attract newcomers.

This two-way, *quid pro quo* concept is the distinguishing feature of the mature manager's practice of community relations.

BIBLIOGRAPHY

"Company Social Responsibility—Too Much or Not Enough?" *The Conference Board Record,* National Industrial Conference Board, New York, April, 1964, pp. 7–17.

"Employee Participation in Community Affairs," *Management Record,* National Industrial Conference Board, New York, October, 1963, pp. 8–15.

Hodges, Wayne, *Company and Community,* Harper & Row, Publishers, Incorporated, New York, 1958.

Jones, Thomas R., "Top Management's Responsibility to the Community," in H. B. Maynard (ed.), *Top Management Handbook,* McGraw-Hill Book Company, New York, 1960, pp. 1114–1143.

McCarty, J. T., *Community Relations for Business,* BNA, Inc., Washington, D.C., 1956.

CHAPTER SIX

Government Relations

LUIS J. A. VILLALON   *President, Communications Associates, Inc., Westport, Connecticut*

To the average businessman, the words "government relations" will inevitably summon up visions of the dapper professional lobbyist pursuing his reputedly devious, but more often routine, efforts to persuade a reluctant legislature to pass laws favorable to a given company or industry—or to block legislation proposed by well-meaning but not too well-informed "reformers." This chapter, however, is not about lobbying, because very few owners or managers of businesses will find themselves involved in this activity. Lobbying *is* carried on by industry, as it is carried on by every other interest group in the country; but it is primarily the concern of only the biggest corporations and, indeed, of very special categories of these, and of the trade associations which normally represent smaller companies in a given field. Accordingly, this entirely legitimate activity—and a necessary one in a world of conflicting interests—is touched upon here only as a generally unusual aspect of business-government relationships that the average executive must deal with.

Nor does this chapter deal with the matter of selling to government or otherwise conducting normal business relationships with it. This is discussed in other chapters (for example, Chapter 16 of Section 8). There is, however, no question that a high level of general communication with government will help in the customer relationship. Walter Wheeler's enlightened concept of business-government relations was extremely useful in building Pitney-Bowes into the largest purveyor of postage meters in the world; you do not purvey postage meters without some degree of communication with government.

NEED FOR MAINTAINING GOOD GOVERNMENT RELATIONS

In the world of "big government," all but the smallest companies have multiple relations with government—their local government, as well as the state and Federal administrations. In areas of selfish interest, a company must be concerned with problems of zoning, traffic, taxes, public transportation, housing, roads, and the like. It must also keep a weather eye out for adverse legislation that would set up regulations inimical to its competitive position, on either the local, state, or national level. Adverse zoning can keep a company from a logical and necessary expansion. Congested traffic can, in effect, chop half an hour or more off the workday of each employee. A loss of public transportation can mean a loss of a considerable percentage of the work force. Poor housing can mean a more difficult recruitment problem. The unwillingness to establish a road to a particular freight depot or some other necessary location can inhibit a company's progress. Any executive will recognize some of these specific problems.

In the broader sense, one does not have to be an idealist to realize that a modern company must assume the obligations of corporate citizenship just as broadly as an alert individual assumes his. Practically speaking, a company's ability to attract competent and skilled personnel depends significantly upon its environment—specifically, the schools, recreation, services, and other advantages or disadvantages that a town or city offers—and that environment depends on the quality of the town or city government. It becomes the business of a company that wants to continue to live happily in a given community to help establish and maintain as high a level of competence as possible.

Relations at Federal, State, and Local Levels. As all executives come to realize—many with sorrow and annoyance—conducting a modern business requires dealings with government, in varying degrees, at all three levels: Federal, state, and local. The Federal government, as regulator, purchaser, taxer, and economic determinant, has what amounts to a life-and-death importance to many industries and companies. However, in the areas of this chapter's concern, most individual companies deal with Uncle Sam nationally largely through the medium of trade associations or other industry combinations. The average individual company's primary and usually most pressing communications problem with government is at the state and local levels, particularly the latter. Accordingly, this chapter is primarily concerned with these two "governments" that most often affect an average, middle-sized business.

The word "average" is used to exclude the special kinds of companies that have unusual and often particularly difficult relations with government. These would include a railroad that depends upon government aid to maintain commuter service, a public utility which is heavily regulated, a semimonopoly which receives special attention from government, and other companies whose activities directly affect the public interest. The same rules for communicating apply in these cases, but their use is more intense and they are supplemented by special techniques that are too detailed to be treated here.

COMMUNICATING WITH GOVERNMENT REPRESENTATIVES

Traditionally, the average businessman has not been very successful in communicating with representatives of government. Anyone who was in Washington during World War II could not help but observe the monumental frustrations of the American business executive when he came up against the civil servant, military man, or other representative of a world not his own. The business-trained executive was impatient with red tape of a shade significantly different from the variety that he knew so well in his own company. He did not like all the complicated rules which, although set up for the benefit of the taxpayer, did not apply at a time when things had to be done quickly. He soon found that government-office politics and business-office politics are two different things. He never could get used to the fact that government has the public looking over its shoulder to a degree much greater than exists in private industry. In a nutshell, the American businessman did not understand this field of action, and, even more important, he did not understand the kind of creatures that inhabit it.

The first key, therefore, to intelligent and effective relations with government is to understand and recognize the kind of people who are in government. They fall into two general categories—the elected officials and the civil servants, often designated more crisply, respectively, as the politicians and the bureaucrats.

Elected Officials. Practically all elected officials of government, whether they be governors, mayors, legislators, or councilmen, have to be politicians. If they were not politicians, they would not get elected. Being politicians, their first objective is to get, and stay, elected—or, even better, to get elected to a higher and more desirable post. They tend to be ambitious, just as corporate executives tend to be ambitious; they are merely climbing another kind of ladder. Their "profit" motive is usually a different one. Most corporate executives consider income as the most important symbol of success; most politicians consider the powers of office and the plaudits of the crowd as their symbols, although, admittedly, a few combine both symbols effectively.

Most political leaders see "industry" as (1) rich (a good source of contributions); (2) powerful (because American folklore says it is); (3) vaguely unpopular with the rest of the citizens (as a result of labor conflicts, consumer complaints, and the like); and (4) naïve (because politicians do not normally understand businessmen's methods and motives any more than businessmen understand the politicians'). Until they are told, political leaders usually fail to recognize that a company has to live in the fierce business of battling its competition, that it creates wealth for the community through its purchases and its employment, and that it normally exists to provide a badly needed service of one kind or another. A principal communications problem of business is to correct this distorted image.

This generally distorted image makes it advisable to start literally at the beginning when discussing a corporate problem with a mayor or a legislator. You cannot assume that he knows anything much about business, about the method of conducting business, or about the particular problems that affect a business decision. Even at the risk of repeating the obvious, it is well to outline all this before getting to the specific problem about which you are concerned. For instance, the chief executive of a community will be considerably more understanding about a zoning difficulty if it has previously been explained that the company employs a certain number of people in the community, wants to employ more, is unable to expand without additional space, and is unable to stay in the community or to compete effectively with its competition unless it can expand. Too often, a simple request that sounds perfectly logical to the company making it is considered merely asking a favor until the background is made clear.

The average public official is neither *for* business nor *against* it. He will usually go along with a reasonable request, if no large and identifiable voting group is opposed. When there is loud and vigorous opposition to a specific project—such as a zoning waiver or a needed new road—a company has a tough time getting its way unless it can demonstrate that most of the community favors its position. In other words, in difficult cases, to sell a politician, you must first sell his constituents. Accordingly, communication with government is really part and parcel of communication with the community itself. Because government is nothing more nor less than the crystallization of the community, this should not be too surprising.

Once one understands the politician's special motivations, it is possible to deal with him pretty much on a businessman-to-businessman basis. His "profit" is pretty much personal credit. He wants to take the bows for whatever progress is made. Once this is understood, the negotiations can usually proceed.

An executive dealing with government, particularly at the local level, will note that there is really very little difference between Republicans and Democrats. Social philosophies have very little to do with local governments.

Reform-motivated Officials. The foregoing has described the characteristics of the vast majority of elected public officials—the ambitious, pragmatic, voter-sensitive men who, by and large, make our laws and run our governments. There is, however, another type that is showing up more and more in legislative halls and important positions in municipal government. The old-fashioned politician refers to him scathingly as a "do-gooder." Actually, he is usually a man whose only motivation for political activity is to accomplish what is, in his lights, "best" for the community. Depending on how practical his lights are, he can accomplish an enormous amount of good or fumble around to an almost impossible degree. In approaching him, a strong case of community benefit must be presented. He is often less than interested in practical considerations. If he happens to think that a business advantage is coincident with a benefit to the community, there will be little problem in communicating with him effectively; if not, however, there is hardly any use talking. Frankly, it is often easier to get along with the professional politician whose motives are closer to earth and more easily definable.

Civil Servants. The civil servants are largely those who "work for" the elected officials. Most of these government workers have tenure and varied degrees of professional status; few governments depend importantly on the spoils system, except in a few relatively unimportant categories of employment. These, then, are career workers in the field of government, much as are those who devote their working life to a private company.

Professional Civil Servants. As far as the matter of business relationship is concerned, these civil servants fall into two categories. The first, and most important, is the "professional." He is one of an increasing new breed of individuals who have been specifically educated in one or another field of public service. He may be a trained assessor, or a planner, or a controller, or a town manager. He may be skilled in one of the specialized areas of state government. In any event, he is an academically ordained expert, and takes great pride in his profession—very much as a company's most skilled technical men take pride in theirs. He is also usually a little defensive about his particular profession, because he is not quite sure whether the public knows that it exists. Generally speaking, this rising class of government professionals, in taking the mechanics of government out of the hands of amateurs, is accomplishing a healthy revolution in the quality of government that will benefit industry and the rest of the community.

These frequently underpaid professional administrators—both of laws and of men—tend to be expert in their special field, honest to a fault, a bit on the pedantic side, but entirely dedicated to their chosen job of serving and improving a given community. They sometimes seem less than completely "practical" from the strictly business point of view, much as technical and engineering personnel within a company sometimes appear to have that same trait. They can, however, be highly objective and, as such, can be reasoned with. It makes good sense to involve your own technical men in the discussions; they usually talk the same language. These public professionals do not respond well to patronizing, and the strong-arm technique has nothing but a negative effect. In the long run, a company will find them far easier to deal with over a period of time than the local amateurs that they are likely to have replaced.

Government Clerks. Perhaps the most irritating category of government worker, with whom the busy executive must necessarily communicate from time to time, is that multitudinous band of clerks who take care of all the details. These administrative understrappers are quite often underpaid, have been selected with more regard for politics than for competence, consider themselves overworked, and are slaves of inadequate systems. Though not as bad as their counterparts in some other countries, they do tend to assume a degree of importance that they would not be permitted in a well-run business establishment. The business-government relationship is one of the few in which a $50,000-a-year executive quite often has to deal with a $5,000-a-year clerk who, as it happens, has a good deal more power than the executive has in a specific area of immediate importance. However irritating the specific encounter may be, it does no good to get impatient; this part of bureaucracy is a system that cannot be beaten. Flattery and courtesy will tend to get you somewhere considerably faster than any other technique.

TECHNIQUES FOR BUILDING GOOD GOVERNMENT RELATIONS

In the business of communications, knowing the characteristics of your audience is about half the battle; the rest involves the techniques of reaching them. In one sense, "reaching" government is a relatively simple matter. After all, they usually reside in designated public buildings, and there is seldom any difficulty in getting an appointment. Reaching them effectively, however, takes a little more than that. The following dozen suggestions, culled from the experience of many companies that have successfully done business with government over the years, will help any executive in any business maintain good relations with the governments with which he has to deal and create a favorable climate for the solution of any problems that his company may have with its locality, its state, or, indeed, in even broader fields.

1. *Establish continuous communication with government at all levels.* Confining communication with your government to the time when you want something is about as sensible as expecting emergency service from a supplier from whom you buy nothing through the year. There are many easy and natural ways to keep in touch with public officials and other important government figures. One is the informal luncheon date. Most executives would be surprised to find out how flattered the town's mayor or the local legislator or even the congressman would be to be asked to lunch on an entirely casual basis; after all, it is their business to talk to significant people in the community and a leading business executive is certainly one of them. Additionally, various other plant executives might well make it their business to invite their "opposite numbers" in government to lunch sometime during the year—for instance, the personnel man might talk to the planner who is concerned with housing and transportation, or the controller might make it his business to get acquainted with the assessor. The pattern of luncheon opportunities depends importantly on the particular personnel in a given company, and even upon their personal friendships, but it always works with a little thought.

Many companies see to it that their annual report is sent to all important government officials in areas in which they have plants. They send it not as a cold document, which is likely to be tossed aside, but with a personal letter from the president of the company. The letter, at least, is likely to be read; it should, in itself, contain the substance of the report and any particular messages that seem appropriate at the moment.

Letters to legislators and elected officials of communities need not be confined to annual-report time. There are other times during the year when the company has something significant to impart; officials and legislators like to get such information firsthand, rather than read it in the papers. Many companies hold an annual "open house" for government figures, or some other event such as a collective luncheon or a display of some sort; this can sometimes be combined with a community affair via a special showing or other "VIP" treatment.

Sometimes the smallest things are most important. All legislators and municipal officials are plagued by complaints. They very seldom hear any favorable comment. One of the soundest ways to make a lasting impression is to drop a note to one of them when you are particularly pleased with something that he has done—whether it particularly affects your company or not. A good sales department knows all about these techniques—they are called "customer cultivation." They work just as effectively when applied to public servants.

2. *Identify the movers and shakers.* Any good politician knows that information is the heart of his business. Accurate information is also the key to successful business relations with government. In every community or other governmental unit, there are a number of men, in and out of government, who are in a position to make things happen. It is useful to know who they are when the time comes to get something done. The same is true in a legislature. All such bodies are dominated by a dozen or so "leaders," and some of these do not have titles to fit their influence. All these prime movers should be cultivated not only for influence but for advice as needed. They are universally knowledgeable, and if they were not shrewdly intelligent they would not be where they are in the political spectrum.

3. *Make it your business to know what is going on locally and in your state.* In a large city, a company sometimes has to rely on the chamber of commerce and similar organizations to keep it informed on the course of policy and legislation. However, unless this assignment is given to someone in the company— whether a lawyer or a public relations man—the useful chamber of commerce bulletins and other material are quite likely to go unread in the pressure of business. In a smaller community, there is no reason why individuals in the company cannot be assigned specific areas of a town's government upon which to stay informed.

All this may sound a bit afield from the normal business of buying or selling or manufacturing or whatever. However, more than one company has awakened, after years of complete unawareness of governmental processes in its community, either to find a badly deteriorated town which no longer is a decent site for its operations or to discover with a shock that legislation has been passed that makes the company's existence in the community extremely difficult.

4. *Encourage your officials and employees to participate in local government and politics.* Many companies seem to feel that political participation on the part of their employees is a positive disadvantage to the company image, and they actually discourage their officials' getting mixed up in any outside work of a political nature, especially the kind that takes any time away from their presumed total devotion to business. This policy is disadvantageous from two points of view. In the first place, how can industry expect its side of the case to be represented in the give and take of governmental discussion if those who know it best are forbidden to participate? No other group that might

be thought of as competitive takes this point of view. Second, the individual company has a great deal to gain by allowing its interested personnel to assume strategic posts in the local political and governmental structure. Many towns below the rank of full city are partly governed by volunteer, or almost volunteer, part-time boards and commissions. The part-time officials who occupy these posts wield very considerable influence and, if they do a good job, their participation reflects definable credit on the company for which they work. Political organizations are always run by volunteers, and there is always room for the energetic partisan to achieve a position of influence. Here, again, the company can benefit directly and indirectly.

5. *Fit your key officials and employees into the geographical pattern of the area in which you operate.* In other words, know where your key people live and be ready to take advantage of their services in the neighborhoods and communities where they are informed and are known. They form useful listening posts for the company, should a matter arise of company concern in a particular location. They also can serve as excellent corporate missionaries if they are, themselves, reasonably informed as to company policy and objectives. In the last analysis, their support can be conveniently marshaled if a controversy arises which requires public interest and participation.

6. *Let your governments know that you count.* Make sure that your community relations program includes information about the wealth your company creates, the employees it hires, and the purchases it makes locally. Devise ways and means to see that this information is transmitted on a regular basis to your representatives on the state and national level, and to the officials and legislators of the town in which you operate.

7. *Maintain an entree with local political leaders of both parties.* Sometimes, for obvious reasons, this is best done through two different executives. Try to see that both parties receive some contributions from key officials in your company, but there is no need to see that they are equal. Obviously, it is impossible to ask a man to contribute to a party that he does not belong to or respect. There are two good corporate reasons for this relationship with politics. In the first place, a corporation—as a citizen—has a real stake in the continuance of a two-party system which depends on two reasonably financed entities. Closer to home, there is no doubt that it is often easier to get things done faster through politics than through the routine avenues of government.

8. *Use salesmanship.* When you have something to sell to a local board or commission or a council, put on the same kind of presentation that you would make if you were going after a new customer. Presentations should be full, complete, and detailed—but never fancy. Use local people, if you can, to talk to a given local government. In matters of zoning or other problems that affect neighboring residential communities, presell just as much as you can; send corporate representatives around to talk to neighbors and explain what you are trying to do before they read about this "invasion" in the newspaper. In matters of zoning and plant expansion, be particularly careful of your associates. Very often, the developer or real estate agent, through lack of tact, puts the company in an impossible position from which it never recovers.

9. *Supply advance notice of your major moves that affect the community, wherever possible.* Local political and governmental officials much prefer to hear about important changes that are to take place in their town—and, indeed, in their state—before they read it in the newspapers. It is well worth the time to make sure that they are informed before the publicity breaks.

10. *Use your trade association intelligently.* Most companies belong to trade associations routinely and seldom make use of all the help and information

that is available.   The trade association is usually a source of more information than is credited.   It is particularly helpful in keeping up with governmental activities on the national level that will affect your industry or your company.

Few companies bother to tell the trade association what *they* want.   Even a medium-sized company is in a position to influence the policies of both the trade association and the services that it supplies, particularly because most companies do not bother to communicate with it at all.   The average trade association can be an extremely useful adjunct in a company's dealings with the various levels of government.

11. *Offer active cooperation on school, housing, and other community problems that are of interest to you.*   Often, a large company can accomplish more in this area than can government itself.   Consider dedicating unused land to recreational projects.   Look into the possibility of scholarships for the local school system.   If you have a great many employees, make sure that a mechanism is set up that will enable you to take fullest advantage of housing opportunities in the community.   Approach the town planner with ideas that will ease the flow of traffic in your area.   In other words, make a habit of doing some of the thinking for the community.   Very often, it will fall into a vacuum and be accepted gratefully.

12. *If you get into a community scrap over a problem that seems important enough to fight about, remember your natural allies.*   Your employees' unions can be enlisted in any manner that does not affect your own negotiations over wages and working conditions.   Customers are interested, as are suppliers.   And, incidentally, if a proper program of government and community relations has been carried on over past months, the community itself is quite likely to rally to your side.   In any event, give it a chance.   Remember, the easiest way to convince a politician of your point of view is to convince his constituents first.

Lobbying.   If a continuous relationship with government at the several levels is developed along the lines suggested by these dozen points, there will seldom be any need for "lobbying" in the usual sense.   In essence, the company will be doing its own continuous lobbying by telling its story on a year-in, year-out basis to the very targets of the skillful lobbyist.   When the right background has been built up over the months and years, the top executive of the concern can himself accomplish just about as much as the skilled lobbyist, by a few personal phone calls, letters, and luncheons.

There is a legitimate field for the professional lobbyist—but when one gets into it, it is far better to find an expert and stick to him.   The "lobbyist" may be either a lawyer or a public relations man; he makes a business of the intricate matter of cultivating and influencing legislators and government officials.   Some of them are extremely competent, and the profession is a perfectly legitimate one in a day in which government can have such a sweeping effect on the operations of an industry or a company.   Lobbyists are, however, only as good as the support the company can bring to them.   They must be constantly reinforced with "campaign" material, and the more skilled help they get from the home office in supporting the position to be sold, the more constructively they can work.

CONCLUSION

Perhaps the greatest mistake the business executive can make is to consider government as his natural enemy—or, at best, a confounded nuisance.   The average "government," whether executive or legislative, is not antagonistic to business; it merely suffers from industry's own inability to tell its story effectively. Once that story has been clearly told—and told continuously—business is quite likely to get a fair shake.

Furthermore, government can, in many ways, be a constructive servant of industry. It has powers that industry often needs to accomplish objectives that are desirable both to a company and to the general public. It supplies services and information that can be extremely useful to industries and to individual companies. After all, you—and your company—pay for government. You might as well use it!

BIBLIOGRAPHY

Bernays, Edward L., *Propaganda,* Liveright Publishing Corporation, New York, 1928.

Cutlip, Scott M., and Allen H. Center, *Effective Public Relations,* 3d ed., Prentice Hall, Inc., Englewood Cliffs, N.J., 1963.

Danielian, N. R., *AT&T: The Story of Industrial Conquest,* Vanguard Press, Inc., New York, 1939.

Fitzgerald, Stephen E., *Communicating Ideas to the Public,* Funk & Wagnalls Company, New York, 1950.

Griswold, Glenn, and Denny Griswold, *Your Public Relations,* Funk & Wagnalls Company, New York, 1948.

Kelley, Stanley, Jr., *Professional Public Relations and Political Power,* Johns Hopkins Press, Baltimore, 1956.

Key, V. O., *Politics, Parties, and Pressure Groups,* 5th ed., Thomas Y. Crowell Company, New York, 1964.

Long, Norton E., "Public Relations of the Bell System," *Public Opinion Quarterly,* October, 1937.

Villalon, Luis J. A., *Management Men and Their Methods,* Funk & Wagnalls Company, New York, 1949.

CHAPTER SEVEN

Relations with the Financial Community

OSCAR M. BEVERIDGE *President, Beveridge Organization, Inc., Chicago, Illinois*

The capital needs of American business have grown relentlessly. The annual demand for funds by nonfinancial institutions rose from $20 billion in 1940 to $44 billion in 1950. In 1964, it amounted to more than $50 billion.

In the past, it was relatively easy for business to obtain from institutional investors and wealthy individuals those sums that could not be generated internally. There was little reason to be concerned with a larger audience, for the bulk of America's wage earners possessed little discretionary income until the 1950s.

After the middle of the century, the situation became far different. The increasing affluence of the public was reflected in the dynamic rise of stock ownership. In 1965, there were more than 20 million stockholders, and the New York Stock Exchange projected a total of 35 million by 1980. Figure 7-1 shows this graphically.

Thus, corporate managements have had to recognize that the opinion held about fund-seeking corporations by institutional and individual investors and the financial press is of vital importance to the financial success of the enterprise.

BENEFITS RESULTING FROM A SOUND FINANCIAL PUBLIC RELATIONS PROGRAM

A sound, continuing financial public relations program offers six main advantages, as *Corporate Relations,* a report of the New York Society of Security Analysts, Inc., points out:

1. The stock of a company well known to the financial community will normally sell at a higher price-earnings ratio than will that of a lesser-known company of equal worth. A high price-earnings ratio facilitates financing on the most favorable basis, makes it possible to accomplish acquisitions for stock with less dilution, and renders the company less vulnerable to a raid.

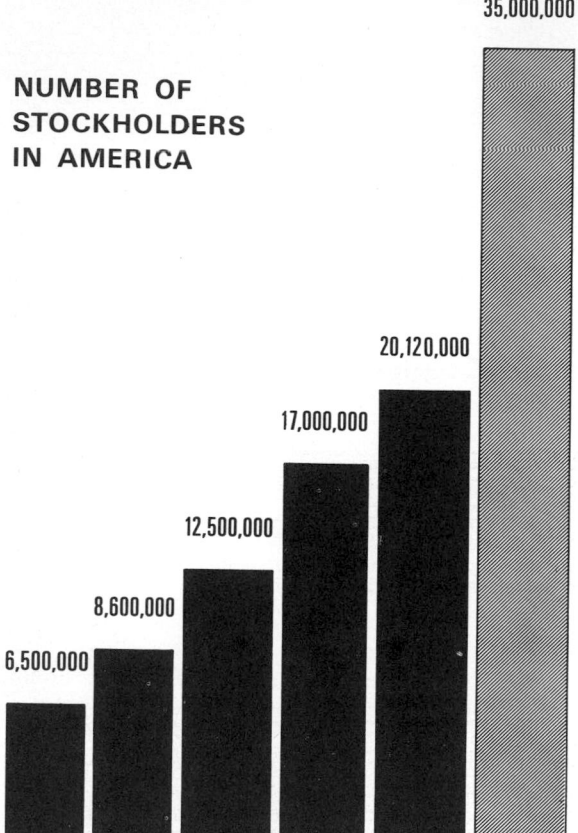

NUMBER OF STOCKHOLDERS IN AMERICA

35,000,000

20,120,000

17,000,000

12,500,000

8,600,000

6,500,000

1952   1956   1959   1962   1965   1980

SOURCE: Census of Shareholders; Projection from N.Y.S.E.

FIG. 7-1. *Growth of number of stockholders in United States of America.*

2. A company conducting a well-planned and well-executed financial public relations program will avoid stock gyrations that result from factors such as short-term good or bad news which will have no lasting effect.

3. The company knowledgeable in the ways of good financial public relations usually has more stockholders. They may be the most loyal customer group, not only buying goods themselves but, as unofficial and welcome additions to their companies' sales forces, encouraging purchases among friends and acquaintances.

4. Well-informed stockholders generally return signed proxies, resulting in a higher percentage of votes recorded.

5. A company in constant touch with analysts normally prepares better annual reports because it knows beforehand the questions which need answering. Weaknesses pointed out by analysts can be avoided in the following year's presentation.

6. The company which has a sound financial public relations program is usually considered a superior investment.

FINANCIAL PUBLIC RELATIONS DEFINED

What is financial public relations? It may be defined as the relationship of a corporation with all of the audiences important to its financial success. Involved are an evaluation of the attitudes of members of the financial community and the planning and execution of a program designed to strengthen favorable attitudes and change unfavorable ones.

Financial public relations is sometimes regarded as being synonymous with stockholder relations. Informed managements, however, recognize the necessity of maintaining effective contact with a far wider range of audiences. Of concern, in addition to stockholders and prospective stockholders, are security analysts; investment counselors; the financial press; statistical services; managers of investment company, pension, and endowment funds; bank trust and investment departments; other trustees; insurance companies; officers, partners, and registered representatives of investment banking and brokerage firms; the company's own employees; financial vice presidents and treasurers of other corporations; and students and teachers of business in colleges and universities. Of these diverse groups, the most important are generally acknowledged to be stockholders, financial analysts, and the financial press.

To implement their financial public relations programs, managements are turning increasingly to executives, whether from within or outside the corporation, with specialized experience in the financial public relations area. Nevertheless, if the highest possible return is to be obtained from the expenditure of the public relations dollar, it remains incumbent upon management to be sufficiently conversant with this specialized function to be able to employ the proper personnel, to direct it, and to evaluate the results obtained.

STAFFING FOR FINANCIAL PUBLIC RELATIONS

The qualifications necessary for a financial public relations man embrace those needed by the general practitioner, and several others as well.

To be the voice of management in communicating with the various audiences important to the financial situation of the corporation, the financial public relations man must think in both management's terms and those of the targets. He must appreciate the profit system, but beyond this he must comprehend the highly technical jargon of the world of finance and be able to interpret it in terms meaningful to a wide swath of audiences ranging from the neophyte investor to the most sophisticated investment analyst. In addition to finance, he must be familiar with accounting and statistics.

The most important attribute a financial public relations man can have is the capacity to think public relations problems through in the light of overall management objectives. He should have company objectives and policies in writing so that he can construct a program whose projects will be of importance to the corporation.

He should be given sufficient authority to permit him to deal effectively with those in other departments, such as financial, accounting, and legal, whom he will sometimes advise and from whom he will sometimes seek advice.

His opinions should be sought by management as to the financial public relations consequences of policies in the making. And he should be permitted to guide the timing and manner of presentation of company statements directed to any financial public.

Growth in Use of Consultants. Especially since financial public relations has mushroomed to major importance, a growing number of firms have elected to hire outside consultants to conduct their programs, or to work with inside specialists. There are two major reasons for this development.

First, the stiff combination of requirements for a qualified financial public relations practitioner means the demand vastly exceeds the supply. Outside consultants can spread their specialized talents over several companies.

Second, even if competent financial public relations personnel are available, the use of consultants permits the size of staff to be kept to a minimum.

RELATIONS WITH STOCKHOLDERS

Certainly there is no target more important to a corporation than its owners. Any company would be well advised to survey this group to determine who they are, why they purchased their shares, who influenced their decision, and most importantly, what they think of the company.

The respect with which the public regards a corporation affects demand for the firm's products or services; acceptance of company objectives and policies; relations with communities, employees, suppliers, and the press; and the sale of new common shares to potential stockholders.

The opinion of present stockholders, because of the prevalence of "rights" offerings, is of immediate financial consequence. A loyal stockholder group is the major factor in obtaining new equity financing with a minimum of trouble and expense.

If stockholders wish, they can vote to turn down stock options or profit sharing, or even dispose of management.

Although companies have no difficulty in recognizing the unhappiness of stockholders, evidenced in correspondence, remarks at annual meetings, or the price of the stock, too often executives are stymied as to the cause. In too many cases, the reason is the withholding of information, either by inadvertence or by deliberate action.

Full Disclosure Vital. A company's foremost responsibility is to communicate fully any information that can have a bearing on the owners' investment.

Many corporations show favoritism toward security analysts in their dissemination of news, bypassing the media of communication valuable in carrying the corporate message to the stockholding public. Vital information should be given to stockholders promptly and not as an afterthought. News affecting the value of a company's stock should not be held up in order to obtain better press coverage. Prompt treatment of such news has been requested by the major exchanges and should be accorded the same handling by over-the-counter firms.

Interim reports and news resulting from directors' meetings should be distributed promptly and as widely as possible. Board meetings should be held early enough in the day to permit release of news in time to afford maximum press coverage.

Letters of Welcome and Regret. There is a trend toward a letter of welcome from the president to each new shareholder. Such a letter should be changed periodically to avoid repetition to investors who have sold a stock and repurchased it. Autotyping may be used in the interest of speed and lower processing costs.

In addition to making the shareholder feel that he is recognized as important by management, the letter of welcome serves other useful purposes. "If you owned the Yankees, would you root for the White Sox?" asks the Denver U.S. National Bank of its holders. Of course, corporate efforts to enlist support of stockholders as users and boosters of products are not limited to the welcoming letter. Oil companies have sent credit card applications with dividend checks, and a hotel chain sends "room dividends" along with dividend payments, which entitle recipients to discounts at stated times.

The letter of welcome also confirms that a buyer's purchase has been completed and is in good order, down to the listing of his correct name and address on the corporate records.

The letter of regret should be similarly regarded as an effort to make and keep friends, even though they be ex-stockholders. They may be back some day.

Stockholder Visits Revealing. A few companies, including American Telephone, Western Union, and the Chesapeake & Ohio, send management representatives to visit stockholders, not only to afford holders an opportunity to air "beefs" in private and obtain honest answers to their criticisms, but to demonstrate that management is concerned with stockholder opinion.

It is uneconomic, of course, for management to send its own people across the country to survey stockholders. Most publicly held concerns have holders in several dozen states and to visit even 5 percent of them would mean an astronomical expense. But one or two calls by management personnel each trip as they travel about the country will amount to an impressive total over a period of time.

Annual Meeting Requires Planning. Although it presents a number of problems and requires careful planning, the annual meeting is worth the effort, because it is one of the few—and certainly the most important—of the opportunities for face-to-face encounter between management and owners. "Even if stockholders ask silly questions," declares the head of a major rubber company, "the annual meeting is their one day in court. They deserve to be taken seriously."

General Mills has held regional meetings in various parts of the country for its thousands of stockholders since 1939. Says a company spokesman of the regional meetings:

We believe they not only broaden communication with our owners, but also serve as a springboard for reaching important members of the financial community. About 25 to 35 percent of stockholders residing in the meeting cities attend, and we have been well satisfied with representation from the financial press and investment analysts.

Moving the meeting site helps to bring out stockholders. Westinghouse found it was attracting the same crowd year after year in Pittsburgh. Then it moved the meeting to Philadelphia; Bloomfield, New Jersey; Sunnyvale, California; and other locations. When it returned to Pittsburgh, a substantially higher number of holders was attracted.

The entire meeting should be transcribed or recorded in some fashion, either by a stenotypist or by a tape recorder, for several reasons. In the first place, any subsequent dispute as to what was actually said at the meeting can be resolved. Second, the transcript forms a valuable aid in preparing the annual meeting report. Third, it can be useful in helping management prepare for the next year's meeting.

Summary of Meeting Recommended. An annual meeting report should be utilized to make available to other holders as much information which might affect the price of the stock as was obtained by those present at the annual meeting. Even for those in attendance, it serves as an authoritative review of what transpired.

Such a report need not be elaborate in presentation or lengthy in content. It should, however, cover all important points and be mailed within a day or two after the meeting.

Some companies find it worthwhile to send stockholders newsletters or other communiques between annual and quarterly reports. A public relations executive of Standard Oil Company (Indiana) reports that special letters are sent to holders from time to time:

. . . when time or space requirements preclude use of the same material in periodic publications. They are simply prepared when a situation demands explanation quickly, and they receive the same close attention that our management accords other stockholder communications. Over the years, these letters have covered such topics as a new dividend policy, a major refinery fire, and the company's position on the natural gas issue.

All stockholder correspondence received by any company should be answered promptly and appropriately, preferably by the president. However, it is acceptable for him to refer the missive to a department with the request that it be handled by a senior member.

RELATIONS WITH SECURITY ANALYSTS

In 1965, the Financial Analysts Federation had approximately 10,000 members in forty chapters from coast to coast. The New York Society alone had nearly 4,000 members who held about 250 weekday meetings annually. So anxious were corporate managements to present their stories that programs were scheduled six months to a year in advance.

It is the task of the analyst to gather information, both quantitative and qualitative, for use in comparing similar firms. Next, he must determine the type and extent of risk inherent in the securities of each company. Finally, he is responsible for advising investors as to the price at which the securities he has examined constitute an attractive buy. Primarily, his concern is with earning power, which provides safety for bonds and ratification for purchase of common stock.

Competent Communicators Required. How can companies work most effectively with analysts? An executive of one of the most highly regarded firms in the investment advisory field has said that the analyst does not expect to gather information exclusively from the top corporate officer. But whoever fills the role of communicator—treasurer, secretary, public relations director, controller, advertising manager, or sales manager—should know what he is talking about and have the authority to speak for the company. Furthermore, the communicator should be in touch with the analysts on a regular basis, not just at times when corporate fortunes are at a zenith.

Both favorable and unfavorable developments should be discussed by managements in their contacts with analysts. A president who is having problems, but is willing to discuss at least some aspects of them and give indications as to how he plans to tackle them, tends to gain a substantial amount of sympathy and cooperation from analysts with whom he talks. He gains a plus for frankness and determination, assets that are remembered as the picture begins to change for the better for the company.

Truthfulness is, of course, paramount. "In rare cases," reports a Wall Street electronics man, "your faith is really shattered. You run into a company which lies about its plans or about what its earnings are likely to be. Believe me, they get a name that's hard to overcome."

Many companies send copies of financial news releases to an analyst mailing list. Such dissemination of information is likely to mean fewer telephone calls from the financial community to busy members of top management.

Overexposure Is Detrimental. Overexposure is likely to hurt a company's relations with analysts. Says the Wall Street electronics analyst:

Do you know that I get two or three press releases a *day* from some companies? These same outfits make speeches when they don't have anything new to say.

An analyst is really interested only in earnings. Whatever questions he has boil down to this. Anything that might have an impact on earnings should be brought to the analyst's attention in written communications from the company. But trivia? Well, just don't bother us with that.

"Puff" copy is another pet peeve of the professional financial community. "My main objection to corporate reporting," declares an economist at one of the nation's leading investment counseling firms, "is the tendency to make news sound spectacular." As a case in point, he cites a release concerning a company which, after thirty-three years, declared an initial dividend of 5 cents a share. According to a news release from the firm, the reason for the action was "the company's tremendous growth over the period." Says the investment counselor, "We laughed and laughed."

Analysts confess they must not only be adept at reading, understanding, and drawing conclusions from figures, but they must also master the art of evaluating management and the overall force that is a company.

How is a firm's executive team to be analyzed, beyond drawing conclusions from growth in earnings, profit margins, and return on equity? Either through reputation or personal appraisal. As the director of research for a leading brokerage firm says:

Only in getting to know management can an analyst attempt an evaluation of the prospects and possibilities of a company and the prospective longer-term value of that specific company's securities. In our profession, you train yourself to look, to look at, to look around, and even to look through.

Face-to-Face Contact. There is no point in waiting to be invited to appear before a securities group, for competition is too keen. Rather, the public relations department or counsel of the interested company should contact program chairmen to make the chief executive's availability known. In the case of smaller, lesser-known concerns, the best offering is usually on a standby basis, whereby the officer may be called upon with scant notice to fill in for another performer who is forced to cancel.

To gain maximum mileage from an appearance, the company's public relations representative makes certain that all members of the group—attending or not— receive copies of the remarks made, and he furnishes the text and/or an abstract to the press for release at the time the address is made. Normally, stockholders receive copies as well.

Analysts appreciate managements which make an effort to develop imaginative presentations. One executive whose company produces semiconductors made a hit because he brought a number of the then-new products with him and magnified the tiny objects on a screen. Another official wasted no time wading through history, products, markets, financial records, and other data. He distributed this information in writing, concentrating his entire talk on answers to the ten questions most frequently asked him in the previous year by members of the analyst fraternity.

Companies desirous of reaching analysts, account representatives and principals of brokerage firms, and others in the professional financial community may do so by holding a series of small luncheon meetings. Such conclaves should be set up on a regular basis, so that interested persons may follow the progress of a company over a period of time.

Wisdom of Forecasts Questionable. There is divided opinion among analysts about the advisability of forecasts by management. The personal view of the investment advisory firm representative is that managements should present the facts as they see them but that they should avoid forecasting definite levels of earnings. If they are right, they will get very little credit and this can soon be forgotten. But if they are wrong, the forecast can haunt them for a lengthy period.

There was a time when few, if any, corporations would break down their sales figures to show volume and profit by divisions or types of products. More recently, the analysts note, this kind of information is available from more companies, but it remains generally difficult to get.

If data are considered vital to an accurate evaluation of a company, the analysts will dig them up somewhere. Says one researcher, "It's amazing what you can piece together by reading the trade papers." Or, the analysts will turn to commercial bankers, investment bankers, the company's customers or competition, or departing or recently departed executives for information. The resulting information may not be accurate. A company should take a long, hard look at the pros and cons before refusing information which analysts say they need.

RELATIONS WITH THE FINANCIAL PRESS

For a financial public relations program to succeed, a company's public relations representatives must maintain effective contact with news media, including daily and weekly newspapers, TV, radio, business and financial magazines, trade books reporting financial news, market letters, investment advisory services, and statistical services.

The criticism leveled by members of the media against news releases from public relations people generally falls into one of these areas: (1) the material is not applicable to the medium to which it is offered; (2) the writing is poor; (3) the timing is poor; (4) pertinent material is omitted; (5) the story is slanted too much in the employer's or client's favor.

If a corporation has a financial news story, it should make every effort to get it distributed as widely as possible, with equal treatment for all. All media are inundated with material. As one example, the typical business and financial department of a large metropolitan daily receives up to 10,000 releases a week. Seldom does a paper use as much as 5 percent of this material. However, a well-written news release containing newsworthy material is always welcomed.

A press conference should be called only when a story is spot news, when it is of major import, and where there is a distinct likelihood that new angles can be developed by questioning. Any reporter who attends a conference must obtain a real story, or he and his editor will feel cheated. The time of the conference should be decided with the deadlines of the media in mind, and a location convenient for the press should be selected. A press kit should be prepared in advance for distribution at the meeting, and the conclave should be convened promptly.

Feature Treatment Often Appropriate. If an organization has a story to tell which is not of such a pressing nature that it requires or rates either a general release or a press conference, feature treatment may be employed. In such an event, the story is offered on an exclusive basis to a single outlet. Often, simply by changing the "angle" of his approach, the public relations man may derive several worthwhile features from the same basic story line.

Size of circulation should not be the chief concern in outlet selection. Rather, the quality of audience reached by each publication or program must rank as the first consideration.

In all contacts with media, on features as well as news, a corporation's representatives should be concerned with establishing and maintaining a reputation for prompt service, the fullest possible cooperation, and accurate information. Newsmen avoid, whenever possible, contact with companies which are not ready to supply information upon request, or which try to dictate how stories should be written.   The newsman is always in control of how any story will eventually come out.   It is up to the public relations man to service the press so efficiently and effectively that the newsman will get the story he wants without getting a story the public relations man and his company do not want printed.

HOW MANAGEMENT CAN EVALUATE EFFORTS

Every organization has public relations duties to perform and public relations decisions to make.   In the absence of specialized assistance, most of the important work in this area will, of necessity, have to be handled by members of management itself.

Therefore, the skillful operation of a well-organized financial public relations program staffed by specialists is profitable to a company in two ways: (1) it will result in a substantial saving in executive time, which can be translated into concrete dollar savings, and (2) it will result in improved communications with the various publics whose beliefs and actions have a profound impact on the financial affairs of the corporation.

Many managements, accustomed to dealing with specific products and profits resulting from their manufacture and sale, attempt to use the yardsticks with which they are familiar in measuring their return on expenditures for public relations.   They do not succeed because such standard gages cannot determine with any degree of accuracy the effectiveness of a program that deals primarily with influencing opinion.

Thus rebuffed, all too many managers resign themselves to depending on the volume of such tangible items as clippings from newspapers and magazines to judge the impact of their public relations efforts.   This procedure accords to publicity far greater importance than it deserves as only one portion of a concerted program, and downgrades all other aspects.

But it is not necessary for management to accept the adequacy of financial public relations programs solely on faith.   And it is well that this is so, for in the last analysis, no program will be any better or any worse than management permits it to be.

Some specific ways by which managements can measure the results of their financial public relations efforts, provided they recognize that most objectives can be achieved only over a long period of time, are as follows.

1. When proxies are called for, response from stockholders should be substantially greater than it was formerly.

2. Stock turnover should be reduced.   It is also evident that, as large blocks of stock are liquidated or new shares are issued, there should be a significant increase in the number of stockholders.

3. Provision of full information on a consistent basis should result in a decrease in inquiries, and particularly critical comments, from stockholders.   There is also likely to be some increase in helpful suggestions as well as in support for public causes management espouses.   Annual meetings should be livelier and better attended than formerly.

4. There should be a somewhat increased volume of activity in the stock, whether listed or unlisted.   The resulting enhancement of marketability will, in turn, increase investor acceptance.

5. The price-earnings ratio of the stock should be in line relative to other concerns in the same industry.

6. Questioning of management by analysts should be confined to specific inquiries in depth, since general questions will have been answered through a regular flow of information.

7. There should be an increase in the number of brokerage house research reports on the company.

8. Media should show an increased acceptance and usage of financial news concerning the company.

9. It should be easier to sell new shares less expensively to those presently owning shares.

10. Underwriting fees in connection with sales of additional shares should be at a minimum.

11. Banks should evidence increased willingness to make loans and provide extra services.

12. A greater number of top-quality executive personnel should be attracted to the company.

13. A better selection of workers should be available at lower levels, and a larger percentage of employees should become stockholders.

14. Labor relations should be more satisfactory than they were formerly.

15. The ranks of customers should be swelled with the addition of enthusiastic and perhaps vocal stockholders.

16. Commercial and industrial customers, as well as suppliers, should evidence a higher regard for the company.

A financial public relations program, particularly in conjunction with a broader, overall public relations effort, is budgetable. Costs can and should be controlled. However, the budget should be determined by someone knowledgeable in the field and not by a financial officer applying arbitrary standards.

Regular surveys of the opinions of stockholders, analysts, and other important financial publics will serve to demonstrate with more precision how effectively the allocated funds are being used.

SUMMARY

What the financial community thinks about a corporation can be crucial for its growth. Progressive management must be concerned with the relationship of the company to all of the audiences important to its financial success. A good relationship can be a formidable asset. To achieve it, management must recognize the significance of financial public relations, understand its dimensions, and know how to design, staff, and evaluate a comprehensive financial public relations program.

BIBLIOGRAPHY

Anderson, Corliss D., *What the Financial Analyst Wants to Know,* Financial Analysts Federation, Auburndale, Mass., 1962.

Beveridge, Oscar M., *Financial Public Relations,* McGraw-Hill Book Company, New York, 1963.

Blood, Jerome W. (ed.), *Investor Relations: The Company and Its Owners,* American Management Association, New York, 1963.

Chatlos, W. B., "The Danger of Getting Things Done in Wall St.," *Public Relations Journal,* May, 1963.

Cross, B. C., "Common Sense of Public Relations Society of America's Financial Code," *Public Relations Journal,* April, 1964.

Fox, H. W., and G. C. Thompson, "Care and Feeding of Stockholders," *Business Week,* Mar. 24, 1962.

Fox, H. W., and G. C. Thompson, "Courting the Stockholder," *Conference Board Business Record,* April, 1962.

Hall, R. C., "Basic Guide to Financial Public Relations," *Industrial Marketing,* April, 1962.

Hettinger, Herman S., *Financial Public Relations,* Harper & Row, Publishers, Incorporated, New York, 1954.

Saxon, O. G., "Industry and the Financial Community," *Management Review,* February, 1961.

Saxon, O. G., "Making Money Talk," *Chemical Week,* June 24, 1961.

CHAPTER EIGHT

Company Financial Reports

PHILIP BOYER *Philip Boyer Organization, Inc., New York, New York*

Most publicly held companies in the United States could satisfy the annual report requirements of the Securities and Exchange Commission, and the exchanges on which their securities are traded, by publishing, at the close of a given fiscal year, a balance sheet, a statement of income and surplus, plus a letter testifying to the accuracy of these statements by a firm of independent auditors.

In most cases, this information could be set down quite comfortably on one or two sheets of paper measuring 8½ by 11 inches, printed in one color, at a cost of a fraction of a penny per copy.

Fortunately for stockholders, security analysts, and other audiences to whom the annual report is addressed, modern corporate management takes a very different view of this document. In it they set down—in terms understandable to the financial neophyte as well as to the sophisticated investor—not only details of the company's financial record for the past year in comparison with former years, but also management's own assessment of its performance and its prospects. They use the annual report to project the personality of the company, to explain developments which may affect the stockholders' investment, and to portray, in words and pictures, activities about which they feel the stockholder should be informed.

In the material which follows, an outline is presented, in sequence, of some of the procedures which have proved effective in preparing annual reports.

WHO IS IN CHARGE?

More than any other document, the annual report expresses top management policy. It follows that the individual or committee responsible for the annual report should be intimately concerned with policy or have immediate access to policy makers. Some chief executives like to have a hand in every phase of planning and preparing the annual report, which, after all, is an accounting

SUGGESTED ANNUAL REPORT
ORGANIZATION CHART

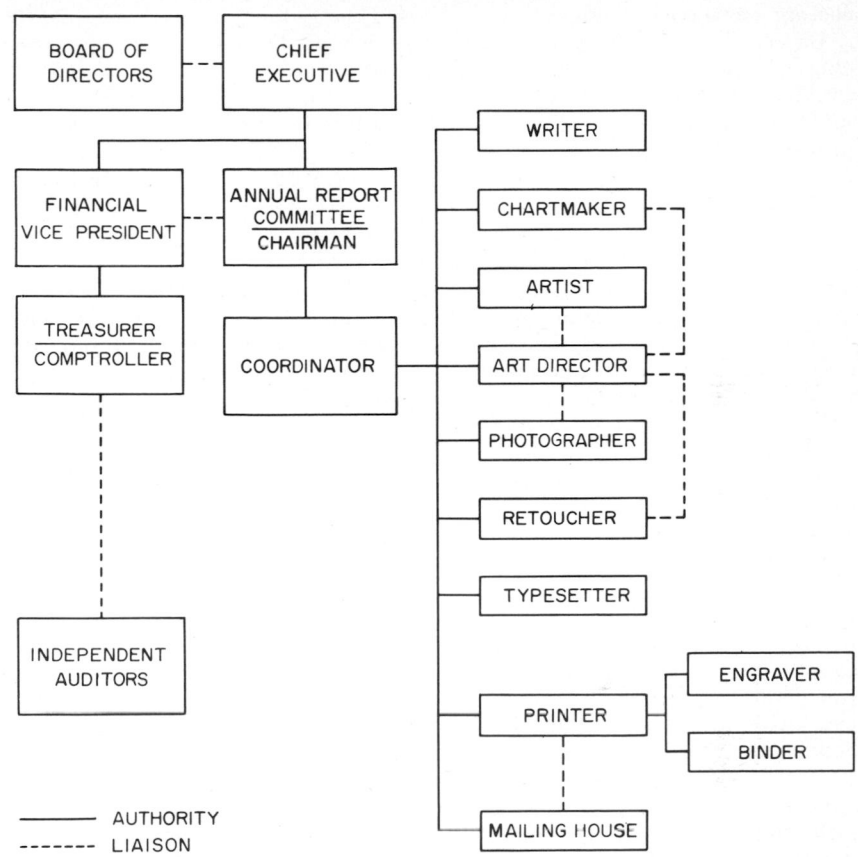

FIG. 8-1. *Typical organization for annual report preparation.*

of their stewardship. Other chief executives prefer to delegate the job to a committee, frequently headed by the financial vice president.

Only the very largest corporations are equipped to plan and prepare an annual report within their own organization. The range of skills required for the job is large. Consequently, the individual or committee charged with the report usually appoints a coordinator to pull the job together. He may be the public relations director or the advertising manager of the corporation. Or he may be the account executive of an advertising agency or of a firm of publications specialists. The organization chart, Figure 8-1, suggests one way that responsibility for the annual report might be set up.

HOW TO GET STARTED

The annual report committee and the coordinator have a number of basic questions to resolve before actual work on the report can begin. It cannot be emphasized too strongly that this planning be begun early. For a corporation with a fiscal year which ends December 31, the first week in July is none too soon. By this time, preliminary figures for the first six months will be in hand, and management will have a pretty good idea of how the year is shaping.

There are four basic subjects which management should explore with the coordinator about this time.

Theme. What developments does the company want to tell its audiences about? The answer could run the gamut of American business activity. It could concern new products, new plants, important research advances, marketing, or a manufacturing breakthrough—obviously presented in such a way as to provide no aid or comfort to competitors.

Budget. At this stage, it is virtually impossible to budget the project except in very general terms, but the amount spent for the annual report of the previous year may prove a valuable guide. Later on, when a rough dummy is in hand and the quantity and method of mailing have been decided, the cost of the completed project can be estimated within very narrow limits. One rule of thumb is that for a medium-sized company (annual sales of $25 to $200 million), a first-class report usually splits into 50 percent for preparation (copy, design, illustrations, retouching) and 50 percent for production (mechanicals, type, press-work, engravings, binding). But the coordinator should have some kind of dollar figure in mind to guide him in preparing a rough dummy.

Schedule. The way to start making a schedule is to determine a practicable date on which the stockholders should receive their report, and then work back from that date. The New York Stock Exchange requires that annual financial statements be published and submitted to stockholders at least fifteen days in advance of their annual meeting but no later than three months after the close of the company's fiscal year. Whether or not a company is listed on the New York Stock Exchange, the obvious desirability of reporting financial results to the stockholder as early as possible makes these rules good ones to adhere to. In the case of companies with a fiscal year ending December 31, there is an additional factor in favor of early publication. The majority of companies use this fiscal year, and the earlier the report can be issued, the more attention it will command. Assuming that all other preliminary work has been completed, the issue date of the report will usually depend on when the accounting department and the company's auditors can release final figures.

Distribution. First, who gets the annual report? Almost every company has a different distribution policy. The report should reach, within reason, every audience whose good opinion is valued by management. The stockholder, obviously, is at the top of the list. Other important audiences are security analysts, the financial press, employees, customers and suppliers, business schools, and libraries. Because of the comparatively low cost of printing additional quantities of the report while it is on the press, distribution—and consequently the print order—should usually be on the generous side. The annual report can also prove a highly useful document for welcoming new stockholders and for answering requests for information about the company.

Along with determination of quantity, the committee should also consider the method of mailing. Bulk rate is obviously the cheapest and slowest, third class comes next, and first-class mail is the fastest and most expensive. Another question to be decided is whether the report is to be mailed in an envelope or as a self-mailer.

WHAT SHOULD THE REPORT CONTAIN?

There is no established pattern for an annual report. It can be tailored in an almost infinite number of ways to reflect the specific personality of the individual company and its activities during the year just passed.

The minimum essentials, as indicated above, are a balance sheet, a statement of income and surplus, and the certificate of a firm of independent auditors. Beyond this, the content of the report represents an interesting challenge to corporate imagination. The elements selected for the report, the order in which they are arranged, and the way each one is presented is strictly up to management. The list below describes some of these elements, with observations on current practice in handling them.

Covers. The front cover design should almost certainly include the name of the company, its corporate symbol or trademark, and the words "Annual Report 19____." In addition, the front cover should express the personality of the company and the theme of the report. The design of the cover should be simple rather than "busy." A single picture or drawing can usually do the job far better than many illustrations. Consideration should be given to extending the front cover illustration or design to the outside back cover as a "wraparound."

Title Page. This usually repeats the elements found on the front cover (name of company, "Annual Report 19____," and corporate symbol or trademark). It also may contain a notice of the annual meeting and a table of contents.

Table of Contents. Reports of modest size frequently dispense with a table of contents; with larger publications it is almost a "must." The table of contents should appear very early in the book: on the title page, on the inside front cover, or on the cover itself. The headings should be kept very short. Whether or not a table of contents is included, the pages of the report should be numbered.

Company Directory. This should include:

List of directors (A useful practice is to identify the principal business affiliation of "outside" directors. Directors may be listed alphabetically with the board chairman heading the list, or in the order of their election to the board.)

List of officers, with their titles (Here again, it is good practice to list officers holding the same title in alphabetical order.)

Important committees—finance, executive, etc. (List separately, or use footnotes, with asterisks opposite names in directors' and officers' listings.)

Subsidiaries (Names, addresses, chief executives.)

Transfer agent (Name and address.)

Registrar (Name and address.)

General counsel (Name and address.)

Auditors (Name and address.)

Address of corporate headquarters

Financial Highlights. This is the one page of the report that will be read by almost every stockholder. He should be able to grasp the results at a glance. It is good practice to compare the past year's results with those of the preceding year, emphasizing current data by means of screens, color, or some other design device. The number of items should be kept to a minimum. Short, capsule copy may be useful for interpreting figures

President's Letter. This can be handled in a variety of ways, ranging from a single-page letter to a lengthy, illustrated narrative covering many pages and reviewing the year's developments in detail. Whatever its form, the responsibility for writing it should be determined very early, and its language should be clear, simple, and down-to-earth. This is the place for the chief executive to appraise his company's performance, tell how it is doing at the moment and what its prospects are for the future. It is also the place to record important personnel changes. When unfavorable developments arise, they should be faced squarely, not glossed over. Charts, graphs, and tables summarizing sales, earnings, dividends paid, and fixed assets over a period of years are often very useful to supplement the text. Facsimile signatures of the chairman and/or the president lend credibility, but unless they are unusually legible, they had better be supplemented by printing the executive's name in type.

Theme Article. In addition to the overall review of the year's operations, management often may desire to inform the stockholder about one or more specific developments such as an important acquisition. This can be accomplished very effectively through use of the picture story in which illustrations and text are integrated as they are in news magazines.

Financial Section. This is strictly the province of the financial vice president, his treasurer, his comptroller, and the company's auditors. This section is bound to contain in some form a balance sheet, a statement of income and surplus, any necessary notes, and a letter from the auditors. Additional statements, to give a more complete picture of the company, will be included at the discretion of the financial experts. For instance, corporations are increasingly including statements describing source and application of funds (cash flow). Design and typography can play a big part in making the financial pages clear, inviting, and readable.

PRELIMINARY PAGE ALLOCATION

When the elements which will compose the annual report have been settled, the next step is for the coordinator to make a preliminary page allocation. This is done by estimating the space for text and illustrations that will be required for each element and fitting them into a format which has a multiple of four pages. The breakdown might look something like that shown in Figure 8-2.

Obviously, this is a job which cannot be done overnight. For example, the "review of operations" section will probably require consultation with several top management officials before the topics to be treated, the way to illustrate them, and the space they will occupy can be tentatively decided on.

By the same token, before space can be allotted to a picture story, the subject will have to be intensively researched. From this research, a copy outline and a shooting script can be developed. It is then a fairly simple matter to determine the number of pages required. The space which will be allotted to the financial section will depend on the specific statements and the length of the notes which the financial people want to include. This, in turn, will require consultation with the treasurer, the comptroller, and possibly the auditors.

Once the page allocation is set up, the coordinator can start working with his art director to produce a rough dummy of the report. A word here about the importance of the art director: He will play a vital role in the preparation and production of the report. He will be responsible for the "look" of the publication—including the relationship between text and illustrations, the typography, and the selection and use of colors. In addition, his advice will be invaluable on such matters as the selection and supervision of artists, photographers, and chart makers who may be required; on the paper stock which will be specified; and on almost every matter which concerns the appearance of the finished report. Further, as a part of his training, the art director is thoroughly familiar with the various printing processes as well as the most economical methods for using them to achieve a desired effect.

PREPARING THE ROUGH DUMMY

The following are some of the considerations which must be kept in mind by the coordinator and the art director as they prepare the rough dummy.

SAMPLE PAGE ALLOCATION

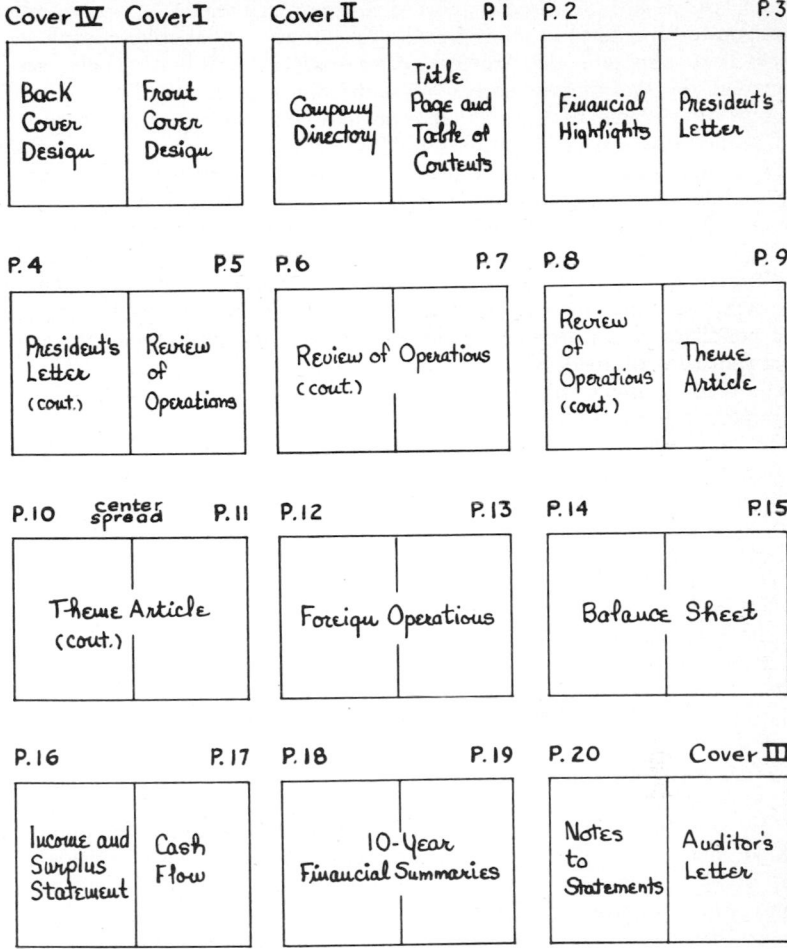

FIG. 8-2. *Example of preliminary page allocation.*

Color. Black and white is less expensive than two colors, which is less expensive than four colors. One color in addition to black can do wonders to enliven a report. A skillful art director can achieve a multicolor effect with two colors through the use of screens. Stay away from red as the second color, particularly if the year has not been a good one. Today most large corporations are using four or more colors in their reports. There is no substitute for four colors for showing consumer products, for portrait photographs, and for making an illustration look like real life, but four-color process should not be used unless there is a real reason for doing so. Besides being relatively expensive, four-color subjects take longer to engrave and to print. In addition to the four process colors (red, yellow, blue, and black), the art director may specify one or two additional flat colors to obtain the effects he wants.

Illustrations. With the layout sheet as a guide, the coordinator should review every element, starting with the front cover, with a view to effective illustration.

On the front cover, what single drawing or photograph can best illustrate the theme? Should there be a photograph or a drawing of the president, the chairman, the board of directors, or of a top management group to illustrate the corporate directory or the president's letter? What photograph or drawings will best illustrate the "review of operations"? What specific shots will be needed for the picture story? Are the illustrations available or will some or all of them have to be created especially for the report? These are some of the questions the coordinator should work out in preparing his rough dummy. Experience has shown that illustrations prepared especially for a report are usually more effective than material obtained from other sources. Almost invariably, it is also found that drawings and photographs prepared specifically for the report later find a host of other important advertising and promotional uses.

Typography. In planning a rough dummy, the art director should establish a type style for the report, including type faces for body text, several sizes of headlines, and captions. A well-designed and legible type face can contribute substantially to readership and comprehension of the report. The art director will bear in mind that the bulk of stockholders are middle-aged or older and consequently prefer to read large type.

It is extremely useful to settle on a type face as early as possible in the annual report preparation process. If for any reason the type style used in the previous year's report seems unsatisfactory, the art director can have set in a number of faces sample pages containing both text and figures. With these in hand, the determination can usually be made quite easily.

Once the face has been decided upon, copy can be written to fit the space allotted to it, eliminating rewriting and resetting which can be costly in terms of both time and money.

Paper Stock. At this stage, it is good practice to select the stock which will be used for the report and its envelope. Most printers or paper houses are happy to supply blank dummies of papers which the art director considers appropriate for the job.

The dummies not only give the feel of the report but also can be used to approximate the weight—and consequently the cost—of the eventual mailing.

By and large, coated papers provide better reproduction for photographs than other stocks. If the report is twenty-four pages or more, consideration should be given to having the covers heavier than the inside pages. The art director may want to consider using a colored stock for his cover.

By the end of the third quarter, the coordinator should be able to present to management a rough dummy through which, page by page, they can visualize what the finished report will look like in terms of content, illustration, and color. A number of alternative cover designs may be shown.

At the same time, the coordinator should submit his type specimens and the paper stock he proposes for both the report and the envelope, as well as his recommendations on distribution.

SAMPLE PRODUCTION SCHEDULE

The coordinator should also present at this stage a detailed schedule for producing the report. In preparing the schedule, he should work closely with all individuals and organizations who will be concerned with the report, and specifically with the printer, to make sure the due dates are realistic. He should keep in mind the holidays which fall in February and March. A sample production schedule is shown below.

This schedule is designed for the comfortable production of a report of twenty pages or more, illustrated throughout by charts, photographs, and drawings, with several subjects in full color, to be printed in offset lithography, and to be in the hands of stockholders before the end of March.

Rough dummy submitted to management	September 30
Rough dummy approved by management	October 15
Comprehensive dummy with original drawings and photographs, plus bids from competitive printers based on dummy, submitted to management	December 1
Comprehensive dummy approved by management; printer selected and authorized to order paper for report and envelopes	December 15
Four-color subjects to engraver	January 4
First proofs of all text not requiring year-end figures	January 15
First proofs of all remaining text except financial section	January 22
First proofs of four-color subjects received from engraver (If major corrections required, allow seven working days to make revised proofs.)	January 26
First proofs of financial statements, notes, and auditors' letter	February 2
Charts completed and checked	February 3
OK of financial section proof from comptroller and auditor	February 5
Paste-up dummy approved by management	February 8
Mechanicals, charts, and illustrations released to printer	February 10
Blueprint submitted by printer	February 15
Final OK of blueprint	February 18
Report and envelopes on press	February 23
Envelopes to mailing house for addressing	March 1
Printed sheets to bindery	March 8
Binding completed; first copies to management	March 15
Mailing to stockholders completed	March 22

Finally, the coordinator will submit a budget, based on the dummy, covering preparation, production, and mailing. The major items in this budget are:

Art direction	Mechanicals
Copywriting	Photostats
Art (including charts)	Engraving and printing
Photography	Binding
Retouching	Addressing and mailing
Lettering	Postage
Type	Coordination

In approving such a budget, management should make sure the coordinator understands it will be satisfied with nothing less than professional publication standards in the finished product. This means that design, photography, art, and copy must all be first class. It also requires high-quality performance from the typesetter, the engraver, the printer, and the binder. Incidentally, there is no substitute for an intelligent, reliable printer in producing an annual report.

An annual report in which there are no last-minute changes is very rare. Careful adherence to a schedule can minimize such changes which almost inevitably result in costly overtime. But some provision for overtime should be included in any sensible annual report budget. By using this overtime allowance for preliminary work, such as chart making, typesetting, and making mechanicals, much more costly overtime on the presses and in the bindery may often be avoided.

COMPREHENSIVE DUMMY

After management has approved the rough dummy and the material which accompanies it, the coordinator can proceed with preparation of a comprehensive photostatic dummy. There are many ways of producing such a dummy; the method outlined below has worked well.

The first step is to secure the actual illustrations which were sketched in the rough dummy. These may already be in existence, or they may have to be created by artists and photographers who will work under the coordinator's direction.

With the illustrations in hand and an indication from the coordinator of how much copy each section will require, the art director can make a precise layout of the individual pages of the report. This includes sizing each illustration, pasting a photostat of it in position, lettering headlines, and indicating other areas which will be occupied by type by means of horizontal, parallel black lines. The spaces allotted to text are specified, to the character, in accordance with the approved type style and size. Copy for text blocks and captions can then be written to fit, leaving blanks to be filled in later where final figures are not yet available.

The pages are then assembled and bound into a book. It is well to make several copies of this comprehensive dummy to obtain quotations simultaneously from competitive printers, to facilitate communication between the coordinator and management, and as a guide for writers, the retouchers, and the printer who gets the job.

The comprehensive dummy, supplemented by data which specify size, paper stock, type, nature of illustrations, printing process, quantity, date wanted, and data on delivery, is used to obtain quotations from competitive printers and mailing houses. When these bids are in hand, the dummy is ready for management's approval.

When the comprehensive dummy has been approved, the coordinator uses standard publication techniques to translate it into the finished report—under management's overall direction—in accordance with the established schedule. These operations involve copywriting and editing, retouching, proofreading, making and checking engravings, preparing mechanicals, presswork, and binding.

PASTE-UP DUMMY

Before the report goes on press, it is useful for the coordinator to submit to management a final dummy in which all elements of the report are assembled exactly as they will be printed. This paste-up dummy will include proofs of all color and black-and-white illustrations, and of all type, with every color break indicated.

In addition, as soon as figures for the financial section are released, the statements should be set in type and submitted not only to the comptroller's office but to the auditors. Some companies like to have their auditors check the entire report as a safety measure.

FINAL CHECKLIST

Even the most critical proofreaders have been known to let errors slip by. Strangely enough, these slips usually occur in areas which have been scrupulously examined by scores of trained eyes. In checking the final dummy, management would therefore do well to give special attention to the following questions.

1. Are the names of the company, of its subsidiaries, and of its officers spelled correctly?

2. Do all page references within the report agree?

3. When figures are repeated (as in financial highlights, charts, the president's letter, financial statements), do they tally?

4. Are all registered and trademarked names correctly indicated?

5. Does the report contain "Printed in U.S.A."? If it is to be exported, it must indicate the country of origin.

6. Does the coordinator have releases signed by all individuals who can be identified in photographs?

OTHER STOCKHOLDER PUBLICATIONS

In addition to the annual report, most corporations publish quarterly statements which often serve as enclosures for dividend checks. It is desirable for the overall appearance of these statements to conform with that of the annual report, as well as of other stockholder publications, such as reports of annual meetings, in respect to design, illustration, type style, and use of color. Such a family resemblance will help greatly to establish the personality of the company in the stockholder's mind. In addition to presenting financial information, quarterly statements can be used to inform the stockholders about important developments such as new products and new plants.

CONCLUSION

As is evident from the foregoing material, the preparation of a worthwhile annual report is far from a simple undertaking. It requires imagination, energy, time, professional competence in many fields, and money. But, as the managements of many of America's most distinguished corporations will agree, the informed stockholder is a good stockholder. The annual report is the most effective information medium which corporate management has at its disposal.

BIBLIOGRAPHY

Beveridge, Oscar M., *Financial Public Relations,* McGraw-Hill Book Company, New York, 1962.

Bristol, Lee H. (ed.), *Developing the Corporate Image,* chap. 19, "The Image via Annual Reports and Other Publications," Charles Scribner's Sons, New York, 1960.

Engel, Louis, *How to Buy Stocks,* 3d rev. ed., Bantam Books, Inc., New York, 1962.

Goldstein, Bernard J., *Annual Report Guide,* Oxford Paper Company, New York, 1963.

Low, Janet K., *The Investor's Dictionary,* Simon and Schuster, Inc., New York, 1964.

Modern Business Research Bureaus, Inc., *The Annual Report: A Document of Modern Business,* vol. 1, Detroit, 1959.

S. D. Warren Company, *The Annual Report,* Boston, 1961.

SECRETARIAL AND LEGAL ACTIVITIES

CHAPTER ONE

Legal Forms of Business Organization

THOMAS J. PURCELL, Esq. *Attorney, Pittsburgh, Pennsylvania*

The classic legal forms for carrying on a business are the individual proprietor-ship, the partnership, and the corporation. In addition, the trust has been used as a business form together with combinations of all of these forms working under contract with one another. Each of these forms can expand its influence by the use of franchise or license agreements for the conduct of some part of its business or to market a particular product which has been developed.

The formation of a business may begin and exist by a contract between the persons who will own it, or the business may depend for its existence on a statute of the legal jurisdiction of its creation. For this reason, although called by the same name, the specific attributes of a legal form can vary from state to state. Also, since both the partnership and the corporation can be subject to agreements between the owners or partners, many variations of the classic forms have been created. The type of business to be carried on, together with a consideration of the liability to third persons, capital requirements, possible expansion, and efficiency of management all have influenced not only the choice of form but its particular adaptations.

For these reasons, this chapter will not attempt to bare every bone of the legal skeleton of each possible form, but rather will portray to the reader the general legal outline of the classic forms, together with the most significant points of contact which these forms and some lesser used forms have with the businessman so that he can consult with his advisers with some background knowledge.

THE PROPRIETORSHIP

Probably the oldest of the forms for carrying on a business, if indeed it can be technically called a form, is the sole proprietorship. No legal means is prescribed for beginning such a business other than the licensing or registration of the business according to the laws of the particular jurisdiction in which it is to be conducted. If the business is to be carried on under a trade or fictitious name, most jurisdictions require notice and registration. No contracts are needed, for the individual is responsible to himself and his creditors. From the moment he begins his business, he assumes personal liability for its conduct. There is no separation of business and personal assets. A business debt can be enforced by the creditor against all assets owned by the proprietor.

In many jurisdictions, it is possible for a husband and wife to own property as tenants by the entireties so that the creditors of either one are barred from execution against the joint property during the lifetime of both. This form of property ownership is often used as a method of protecting personal assets. The proprietor can employ numbers of employees who are his agents while acting in the scope of their employment. Because the legal organization consists of only one person, there is technically no organization for the government of the business.

Professions such as law and medicine, which are denied the corporate form of operation, are conducted as proprietorships or partnerships, because the ethics of the profession and the law require personal responsibility. In those professions which can be conducted in corporate form, the licensing laws of the state generally require some pledge of the individual for personal responsibility even though the form of business does not.

The individual proprietorship ceases with the death of the owner unless the owner has made provisions in his will or by a contract prior to death for the purchase of the business. For probate court purposes, though, the business is terminated with the death, and the individual assets of the business must be inventoried by the personal representative of the decedent. For tax purposes, also, even in the event of a contract for the continuance of the business, the business terminates with the death of the owner.

THE PARTNERSHIP

A partnership is an association of two or more persons to carry on as co-owners a business for profit. This definition is contained in the Uniform Partnership Act which has been adopted by a majority of the states. The term of existence of the partnership may be at will or for an agreed-upon length of time. The basis of the association of partners is a contract which may be oral or written. The terms of the agreement will control matters among the partners themselves; however, the operation of the partnership as it affects third parties may be controlled by court decisions or legislation such as the Uniform Partnership Act or some special legislation of the jurisdiction in which the business is to be conducted.

In a sense, the partnership is a concept rather than a form, a concept the incidents of which will finally be determined by the local law of the jurisdiction in which the business is conducted. The broad outline of the relationship, however, is generally agreed upon.

The word "persons" in the above definition can mean individuals, other partnerships, corporations, or other associations. Such persons must co-own the business, not just the profits or property of the business. Ownership of property jointly will not of itself establish a partnership. A contract for profit sharing will not create a partnership, although the receipt of a share of business profits may be evidence of a partnership. The partners must be responsible for the profits and losses of the business.

Because a partnership is created by contract, the parties must have the legal ability to make such an agreement. Minors, except in rare instances of emancipation, will not have such capacity. Likewise, a mentally incompetent person does not have capacity. With the removal by many states of the legal prohibition on married women, it is possible for a married woman in these jurisdictions to be a partner. Many states have laws which will not allow a licensed professional to practice his profession as a partner of an unlicensed practitioner. In these states, there is no prohibition for both to join in a business not related to the licensed profession. The partnership agreement may be entered into for any lawful purpose, even a single transaction.

The Partner Relationship. The relationship of the partners to each other is a fiduciary relationship. Each partner is an agent of the partnership and can legally bind all partners by his acts or deeds in the course of the partnership business. The governing document of the partnership is the *Agreement* or *Articles of Partnership*.

Between the partners, this agreement can have a very broad scope. It can, among other things, provide for different shares for partners as to profits and losses; continuation of the business in the event of the death of a partner; management of the firm; and any other matter upon which the parties, between themselves, shall agree.

The Uniform Partnership Act provides in part that, subject to any agreement between them, the parties shall share equally in the profits and losses; be indemnified by the partnership for payments made and personal liabilities reasonably incurred in the ordinary course of business; have equal rights in management; have unanimous consent of the partners on new members; and settle differences arising in the ordinary course of business by majority rule. If the partnership agreement does not otherwise provide, the books of the firm are to be kept at the principal office.

Because of the fiduciary relationship, each partner must account to the others for any benefit and hold as trustee any profits derived by him. Incident to this same relationship, each partner has the right to an account of partnership affairs.

Where a partnership is created for a fixed term or a specific undertaking and is continued beyond such term or undertaking, the rights and duties of the partners remain the same for such extended period.

Partnership Property. The interest in the partnership owned by each partner is an interest in personal property. Even real estate loses its character in the partner relationship and becomes part of the partnership interest. As to matters of liens and judgments regarding creditors and third parties, real property still retains its character as real property. Legislation in the state of operation of the business may also determine the measure of formality necessary to transfer partnership property and the incidents of ownership of such property between the parties. The Uniform Partnership Act, for example, lists the property right of a partner as a combination of (1) his rights in specific partnership property, (2) his interest in the partnership, and (3) his right to participate in management. This Act defines a partner's right in specific property as a tenancy in partnership and states the legal incidents of this tenancy as follows: such property may only be held for partnership purposes; is not assignable except in connection with the assignment of the rights of all partners in the property; is not subject to attachment or execution except on a claim against the partnership; vests in the surviving partners on the death of a partner; and is not subject to dower, courtesy, or allowances to widows, heirs, or next of kin.

Relationship to Third Parties. Between the partners, partnership status is a matter of intent. Each partner is an agent of the partnership in the course of its business, and the act of a partner in the ordinary course of the business will bind the partnership even if, in fact, such partner has no authority, unless those dealing with the partnership have knowledge of the fact of his lack of authority.

As to third parties, however, even a nonpartner may be held to be a partner by construction of law if the partnership benefits from a representation by words or conduct by such party or others with such party's consent that he is a partner. Also, an attempt to create a corporation which is defective may result, as to third parties, in a partnership of the incorporators.

Acts of the partners not in the ordinary course of the partnership business imply notice to third parties to inquire about authority. The Uniform Partnership Act states that unless a partner is authorized by the other partners or they have abandoned the business, a partner alone, or less than all of the partners together, has no authority to assign the partnership property in trust for creditors; dispose of the goodwill of the business; do any act which would make it impossible to carry on the ordinary business; confess a judgment; or submit a partnership claim or liability to arbitration or reference.

One partner cannot bind the firm as guarantor or surety for a third person without the assent or ratification of the other partners, because this act is generally not in the ordinary course of business. The same applies to borrowing or lending money unless the scope of the partnership business, such as trading or manufacturing, would imply such acts to be ordinary. The partnership will be held liable for misconduct of a partner in the ordinary course of business but not for negligent acts committed individually and separate from the business unless the partnership adopts these acts.

Often, a partner will have an interest in more than one partnership, and if this fact is known, third parties must exercise care to ascertain which firm the partner is acting for and the scope of his authority.

The partners are jointly and severally liable for the debts of the partnership according to the Uniform Partnership Act. At common law, partnership property was first liable and then the individual property of the partner. Partners who join a going firm may be liable for debts incurred prior to the time of their admittance. In some states, this liability is restricted to their share of partnership property.

Management and Operation. One of the rights of a partner as co-owner of the business is to share in the management of the firm. By agreement, such management may be given to a managing partner or it may be implied from his conduct. In the absence of such authority in one partner, the majority vote controls the decisions of the firm.

When a partnership uses an assumed or fictitious name, a registration will generally be required in the jurisdiction of operation. Such registration will indicate the partners' names and addresses. Failure to register can subject the partners to fines and can prohibit the use of the courts of that jurisdiction for the enforcement of their claims until such registration is made.

The Limited Partnership. When a partnership consists of general partners and, in addition, special partners who contribute cash or property to the partnership but not services, it is called a "limited partnership." The special partners are known as "limited partners." So long as these limited partners do not take part in the management of the business, their liability will be limited to the amount of their investment in the partnership. Such a partnership must have one or more general partners as members who manage the firm and conduct the business. The general partners remain liable to third parties personally and beyond their investment in the firm. A limited partner who takes part in the management becomes a general partner as to third parties.

The limited partnership is created by contract, but state requirements to establish the relationship of the different kinds of partners are more formal. A certificate or declaration must be filed stating the name and character of the business, the term of the partnership, and the obligations of the limited partners. This certificate will be signed by all partners. The Uniform Partnership Act provides for partnerships with such limited partners and the information, in detail, to be filed in those jurisdictions which have adopted the Act.

Unlike the interest of the general partner, the limited partner's interest may be assignable. Such an assignee may further become a limited partner if all other partners consent. If they do not, then the assignee is only entitled to receive his share of the profits and may be refused the right to demand an account from the other partners.

Taxation of Partnerships. Partnerships, being associations rather than separate entities, generally have the tax consequences of doing business placed on the partners themselves. The United States Federal income tax is the responsibility individually of the partners at the rates due by individuals. The partnership itself serves only as a reporting medium. For some technical tax situations, such as the basis of partnership property, the partnership is regarded as an entity rather than an association. The Federal tax concept of a partnership is much broader than the legal definition discussed in this chapter. Such organizations as joint ventures, investment pools, and associations not treated as corporations are taxed as partnerships. Partnerships which by the agreement operate more like corporations because of centralized management and assignable interests will be treated as corporations for Federal tax purposes.

The separate states can tax a partnership doing business within their boundaries. In those states which levy an income tax, a partner residing in another state may be liable for a tax on his share of the partnership income produced in the state levying the tax.

THE TRUST

Possessing some of the characteristics of the limited partnership and the corporation, although legally quite different from both, the trust has been used as a form of doing business. A trust exists when the legal title to property is in one person and the beneficial or equitable estate is in another. The business trust is created by contract called the "trust instrument," which provides for the management of the business, and certificates which are issued to the beneficiaries who are then similar to stockholders of a corporation.

Some states have held the beneficiaries liable as partners if their rights are such as to allow them to participate in management. Most jurisdictions now regulate such forms, and the original advantage of escaping corporate restrictions has been lost. A business trust may be treated as a corporation for tax purposes.

PROFESSIONAL ASSOCIATIONS

A majority of states have enacted legislation which provides for the conduct of a profession as an association. These statutes relate to those professions such as law, medicine, and accounting which have long been denied the use of the corporate form. Most of these statutes provide for a centralized management of professionals within the same profession and for the issuance of stock, the transfer of which is restricted to others of the same profession. The insulation from liability, as is present in the business corporation, is not available to the professional associate stockholder.

THE CORPORATION

The corporation is the legal form most widely used for conducting the medium-to large-size business. Its characteristics suit the expanding business and allow a stability of organization which is necessary to attract large investments. The corporation is a separate entity, an artificial person created by law. The death of its managers or stockholders does not affect its legal life. Ownership in the corporation is evidenced generally by stock certificates which can be bought and sold. It has centralized management operating through a board of directors who are elected by the stockholders with whom the board occupies a fiduciary or trust relationship. The stockholder's liability is limited to his investment in the stock of the corporation.

Formation. Upon request from the incorporators, the state will grant a charter which creates this fictitious legal person. The charter contains all of the corporation's authority to act. Generally, before the charter is granted, the incorporators and future stockholders subscribe for stock. Upon the grant of the charter, the subscribers become stockholders. Some states require that evidence be submitted that the corporation has a minimum amount of capital paid in before it may begin business. Each state has its own requirements and procedures for obtaining the charter, and the requirements must be complied with to create a *de jure* corporation or legally sufficient person. The request for the charter will also set forth the purpose for which the corporation is to be formed; the term for which it will exist, which may be perpetual; and the name under which it will exist, together with the address from which it will conduct business. The corporate name cannot be similar to names of other corporations operating in the same community. The request for a charter is generally required to be advertised to effect notice to the community.

Corporate Powers. A corporation has no powers outside those conferred on it by the charter or statutes of the state of its creation and such implied power as may be necessary to exercise these expressed powers. Generally the corporation has power to sue and be sued; have a corporate seal; own, lease, sell, and mortgage real and personal property; borrow; invest; and do all things incident to the approved purpose of the corporation. If the corporation acts outside its granted powers, it is said to have committed an *ultra vires* act, for which it may be liable to its shareholders and third parties.

Management. Internally, the affairs of the corporation are guided by the bylaws which are adopted by its shareholders. In some states, the directors may be given power to change the bylaws, but this is usually subject ultimately to the authority of the shareholders. The bylaws serve as regulations within the corporation and will not affect its dealing with third parties unless such parties have actual knowledge of the bylaws. The business and affairs of every corporation are managed by a board of directors who are elected by the shareholders in accordance with the bylaws. The number of directors will vary according to the laws of the state of creation and the bylaws. Generally, the minimum term of office of a director will be prescribed by statute. This term is usually one year. A director may, however, be removed by the shareholders prior to the end of the minimum term for failure to perform his function. Vacancies may be filled by the remaining directors until the next election.

The directors elect the officers of the corporation—the president, secretary, treasurer, and such other assistant officers as may be necessary. The president and secretary cannot be the same person. The treasurer, in some states, may be a natural person or a corporation. All officers, if natural persons, are required to be of legal age. The officers and directors, who may be the same persons, stand in a fiduciary or trust relationship to the corporation.

Shareholders. The shareholders are the owners of the corporation. In a small corporation, they may also be the directors and officers. At the annual meeting of the corporation and at such other times as the bylaws may prescribe, they meet and vote on the business of the corporation which requires their approval. At the annual meeting, they elect the directors of the corporation. The notice required to be given for these meetings is contained in the bylaws. If the stock of the corporation is actively traded, the directors must fix a time to determine the shareholders of record, for both meeting purposes and dividend purposes. In some states, the shareholder is allowed to vote cumulatively, that is, multiply his votes by the number of directors to be elected and cast the entire number for one candidate. Where a corporation has provided for preemptive rights, new issues of stock must first be offered to the shareholders before sold to others. In certain situations, if a shareholder dissents, he may require a redemption of his shares by the corporation. Shares of stock owned by the shareholder are personal property.

Stock of the Corporation. A corporation can issue, if the charter permits, many kinds of stock with such voting rights, dividend preferences, and conditions as may be allowed by the law under which it is formed. Common stock of a corporation carries with it the right to vote for the directors of the corporation. It has become popular in some jurisdictions to issue common stock which does not carry the right to vote, or Common B stock, in situations where the type of business requires that managers have some special ability, such as personal service corporations. Preferred stock does not have the right to vote but may, by the conditions of its issuance, be given this right in certain situations. For instance, such a condition might be the nonpayment of a dividend for a specified period of time. The preferred stock may carry a preference as to the payment of dividends, or a preference as to payment on liquidation, or both. It may also carry the right to have cumulative dividends paid, that is, dividends which are due annually and, if not paid, accumulate from year to year as obligations of the corporation. These dividends are fixed in amount, and if the corporation has more profits than it needs to satisfy such dividends, then it may pay dividends to the common stockholders. Corporations are restricted as to the source of dividends. In some jurisdictions, dividends can be paid only out of earned surplus.

It is possible that the corporation may be formed to include bonds or notes in its capital structure. The holders of such documents are not stockholders but, rather, creditors unless the bonds, as part of the condition of issuance, are convertible into stock. Even then, until such an option is exercised, the holder cannot vote. For tax purposes, the bonds or notes of the corporation may be called a form of preferred stock so that the interest payable may be treated as a dividend. Although this problem does not usually concern state law or the granting of the charter, it certainly must be considered prior to incorporation.

The issuance of stock may further be subject to a state regulatory body which is similar to the Securities and Exchange Commission in Washington, D. C. Most states require registration if stock of the corporation will be sold within the borders of the state. If the sales of stock are to be made without regard to state boundaries and if the sales are broad enough, a registration may be required with the Securities and Exchange Commission in Washington.

Operation in Other States. Because the corporation's existence is specified by the state, the boundary of its existence is likewise confined to the state which has granted the charter. Each state has a law which defines the creation of the corporation and the rules under which it will be allowed to exist. Each state also has a procedure under which "foreign corporations," those created in other states, may be allowed to do business within its boundaries. It will be necessary for a corporation to qualify with each state in which it will conduct some kind of permanent business. Each state also has its own definition of "doing business," and a "foreign corporation" can subject itself to penalties for the conduct of unlicensed business. Such penalties include fines and the prohibition of using the local courts to enforce its legal rights. Every state has the right to tax any corporation doing business within its borders when the corporation has attained local business significance and is not wholly engaged in interstate commerce.

Sometimes, the kind of business done in one state is not permitted the use of the corporate form in others. An engineering corporation may be required to carry on its operations in some other form in a state other than the state of its creation because the new state will not permit a corporation to do engineering. Also, each state has its own list of corporate names in use which will not be available to the foreign corporation seeking to do business there.

Taxation of Corporations. For Federal tax purposes, the corporation is taxed as a separate legal person. This tax is not at the graduated rates paid by individuals but at a flat percentage of net income. The shareholders are taxed separately from the corporation. Many groups of associations doing business are treated as corporations for Federal tax purposes. Partnerships, trusts, and other profit associations, if they have the incidents of centralized management, continuity of existence, and transferable interests, will be treated as corporations. Each state of operation has the right to tax the corporation for business done on a recurring or permanent basis within its boundaries. Taxes paid to the states by the corporation are deductible by the corporation in the computation of its Federal tax.

CONCLUSION

The nature and extent of the business to be carried on will determine the best legal form to be used. The exposure of the owners to liability because of the character of the business may be minimized or eliminated by the proper choice of form. The extension of the business into other states or countries will complicate its operation, be more expensive, and so will influence the pattern of its legal contacts. Just as each state may define each form with a shade of legal difference, the variance is much more pronounced the farther we go from the law we know, such as to an operation in a foreign country.

BIBLIOGRAPHY

Cavitch, Zolman, *Business Organizations*, Matthew Bender & Co., Inc., New York, 1963.
Corporation Law Guide, Commerce Clearing House, Inc., Chicago, 1961.
Fletcher, William Meade, *Cyclopedia of the Law of Private Corporations*, rev. ed., Callaghan & Company, Chicago, 1963.
Hornstein, George D., *Corporation Law and Practice*, West Publishing Company, St. Paul, Minn., 1959.
Model Business Corporation Act, research project of the American Bar Foundation, West Publishing Company, St. Paul, Minn., 1960.
Prentice-Hall Corporation Volumes, Englewood Cliffs, N.J., 1965.
Rohrich, Chester, *Organizing Corporate and Other Business Enterprises*, 3d ed., Matthew Bender & Co., Inc., New York, 1958.
Rowley, Reed, *Rowley on Partnership*, 2d ed., The Bobbs-Merrill Company, Inc., Indianapolis, 1960.

CHAPTER TWO

Role of the Corporate Secretary

JAMES L. VINCENT *Secretary and Treasurer, Anaconda Wire and Cable Company, New York, New York*

The corporate secretary, as an executive officer of the corporation, occupies a fiduciary or quasi-fiduciary relationship to the corporation and its stockholders. He acts as the liaison between the board of directors and the stockholders and between the board and other company officials.

A corporation must act through its officers or agents. Usually, the officers are enumerated in the corporation's charter or bylaws. The statutes in most states expressly provide for a president, a secretary, and a treasurer or similar officers, and such other officers and agents as shall be chosen in the manner provided for in the bylaws. A person cannot be an officer if no such officer is provided for in the corporation's articles of incorporation or bylaws or specifically required by statute.

CORPORATE DIRECTORS AND OFFICERS

It is practically a universal rule that the secretary is elected or appointed by the board of directors. However, there are occasional variations where the clerk (an office roughly corresponding to that of secretary) is required to be elected by the stockholders. The same person may hold several offices unless expressly prohibited from doing so. Generally, the offices of president and secretary cannot be held by the same person.

The tenure of office of directors and officers is generally fixed by statute or by the corporation's bylaws.

The officers have such authority as is conferred upon them by statute, articles of incorporation, bylaws, stockholders, or the board of directors, or the authority implied from the powers conferred or incident or inherent thereto. Sometimes, the corporation's charter expressly provides that the board of directors shall prescribe the duties and powers of the secretary.

Duties of the Corporate Secretary. The services performed by the corporate secretary ordinarily fall into four general areas—stockholders, directors, committees, and administrative duties.

In the absence of provisions to the contrary, the secretary is traditionally responsible for the keeping of minutes of stockholders', directors', and executive committee meetings.   It is generally his duty to make and keep the corporate books and records, except such financial records as may more properly come within the treasurer's or comptroller's function, and to make proper entries of votes, proceedings, and resolutions of the stockholders and directors, and of all other matters required to be entered on the records.   He has custody of the corporate seal and is responsible for the attestation of corporate documents and the certification of extracts from the bylaws, minutes, or other corporate documents in his care.   The minute book, if properly kept, is prima facie evidence of what occurred at the meeting.

Depending upon the duties conducted by his office, the secretary attends the meetings of stockholders, the board of directors, and various committees; schedules the meetings; gives notice and prepares the minutes of the meetings; drafts appropriate resolutions; prepares or reviews papers presented for execution; handles notification of action taken at the meeting; corresponds with stockholders, transfer agents, stock exchanges, brokerage houses, and the Securities and Exchange Commission; publishes any action taken with respect to dividends; handles stock transfers; files or records documents as required; and testifies in court when required in connection with the books and records of the corporation.

The secretary issues all corporate stock certificates, or they are issued under his supervision and control.   He has control of the stock certificate book, stock transfer book, and stock ledger.

The secretary should be an authority on the corporation's charter, bylaws, and minutes. He should be familiar with corporate procedure and corporate and other laws which affect his duties as secretary.   Unless the corporation has legal counsel to handle all legal matters, the secretary generally advises and guides the corporation regarding the retention of counsel.

He should guide and help the presiding officer in the conduct of meetings.

A copy of all reports prepared by the secretary as a part of his official acts should be kept in the secretary's file.

In many corporations with subsidiaries and affiliates, the corporate secretary of the parent company occupies a similar office and performs similar duties for the affiliated companies.

ARTICLES OF INCORPORATION

The articles of incorporation are the certificate filed in conformity with a general corporation law setting forth the rules and conditions upon which the corporation is founded.   The powers of a corporation are created and determined by the statutes under which it was organized and the terms of its certificate of incorporation.

In some jurisdictions, the certificate may specify the number of directors necessary to constitute a quorum, and the number of shares, or the number of shares of any class, having voting power necessary to constitute a quorum.

STOCKHOLDERS

The corporate power vested in stockholders is vested in them as a collective body and not as individuals.   They do not have power to act as or for the corporation, except at a properly conducted meeting.   Management of the corporate affairs is generally handled by the directors.

Stockholders may transact any ordinary business which may come before a general meeting, but they cannot transact unusual business unless notice, specifying the subject matter, was given to all stockholders or unless all stockholders entitled to vote are present and do not object.

STOCKHOLDERS' MEETINGS

The laws of some jurisdictions call for the holding of a first meeting at which directors are elected and bylaws adopted. Most states outline the procedure to be followed in adopting bylaws. General practice is to hold a meeting on consent and waiver of notice. The waiver should be signed by all the incorporators.

Most statutes require that there shall be at least an annual meeting of stockholders. All such meetings should be held regularly as scheduled.

Notice. Written notice of the time and place should be given by the secretary of all meetings, including the annual meeting, and he should arrange for publication when required.

Notice should specify the record date for voting and the purpose of the meeting, including the election of directors and any other matters which will be brought before the meeting. If a vote is to be taken by classes of stock, the notice should so state. The subject of giving notice with respect to stockholders' meetings is generally regulated by statute. Notice of an adjourned meeting is expressly dispensed with in some jurisdictions.

Notice of Special Meeting. Notice of special meeting must be given to every stockholder entitled to vote at the meeting and must state the purpose for which called. After the first meeting, notice need not be in any particular form, unless required by charter or bylaw. In some jurisdictions, notice may be waived in writing by a stockholder.

Time and Place. Some statutes require that stockholders' meetings be held at a specified place. Where the statute does not so prescribe, the corporation should prescribe the time and place in its articles of incorporation or bylaws.

Proxies. Statutory provisions concerning voting by proxy vary from state to state. In the absence of charter or bylaw provisions, the proxy may be in any form. Under the Securities Exchange Act of 1934, proxies solicited from stockholders of any security registered on any national exchange must be in accordance with rules and regulations of the Securities and Exchange Commission.

Proxies may be either general or limited. A general proxy can vote on all ordinary business matters. A limited proxy is limited to a specific subject only. The proxy may be for a specific meeting or for all meetings. It may cover all shares standing in the name of the stockholder or only a specific number of shares.

When more than one proxy has been executed, the latest one executed is deemed to have revoked all previous ones. The proxy generally includes a power of substitution and may name two or more persons as proxies who may act jointly or severally.

When proxies are slow in being returned, the secretary should send a letter to the stockholder requesting return of the proxy, to assure a quorum being present at the meeting.

Quorum

A quorum must be present before any business can be transacted at a stockholders' meeting. In the absence of any provision in the general laws, the charter of the corporation, or its bylaws governing the determination of a quorum, it has been held that any number of stockholders or members present at a duly called meeting constitute a quorum, even though they might not represent a majority of the outstanding stock or a majority in number of stockholders or members.[1]

The statutes, articles of incorporation, or bylaws usually prescribe the number of stockholders required to constitute a quorum, and a valid meeting cannot be held unless the quorum specified is present.

Voting. Generally, directors are elected by plurality vote unless a greater percentage is mandatory. Each stockholder of record is generally entitled to one vote per share. The bylaws may require that voting for directors shall be by ballot.

Cumulative Voting. Under ordinary voting, directors are elected by a plurality of votes cast, and holders of 50 percent plus one voting share can elect the entire board. Under cumulative voting, each stockholder is entitled to cast, for each share held by him, as many votes as there are directors to be elected. Thus, if ten directors are to be elected, each share will have ten votes, all of which may be cast for a single candidate or distributed among two or more candidates.

Minutes. It is the duty of the secretary to keep complete and accurate records of the proceedings of all stockholders' meetings, showing the date, place, and time when held. They should follow the general order of the proceedings and show the manner of call or notice and whether it was a regular or special meeting. The minutes should show how many shares of each class voted. Motions made should be seconded and the minutes should so indicate. The affidavit of mailing of notice of the meeting, the inspector's oath, reports, and other official documents of the meeting should be filed by the secretary in the appropriate place with the minute book.

Secretary's Preparation. The secretary should do as much preliminary work before the meeting as possible. The amount of preparation necessary will depend upon the size and scope of the meeting and the duties, if any, performed by an outside service organization. Statutes often prescribe the minimum requirements. The following may be used as a guide:

1. Resolution of directors (if required) fixing the time and place of the meeting, the date for closing the stock transfer book, or record date for determining stockholders entitled to notice of and to vote at the meeting
2. Preparing form of notice
3. Preparing form of proxy
4. Clearing proxy material with SEC if necessary
5. Preparation of annual report
6. Preparing letter and other enclosure material
7. Mailing of notice, proxy material, annual report, and so on
8. Publication of notice if required
9. Sending proper material to stock exchanges if necessary
10. Advising transfer agent of procedure he is to follow
11. Preparing stockholder's list for the meeting
12. Tabulating the returned proxies
13. Preparing the ballots
14. Selecting nominees for inspectors of election
15. Preparation of slate and motion for nomination of directors
16. Selection of person to make the nomination of directors
17. Checking that all directors meet qualification requirements
18. Preparation of space and equipment for meeting

[1] 19 AM Jur 2d Corporations § 620.

19. Arranging for recording or shorthand reporters as required
20. Arranging for ushers at the meeting
21. Handling of the press and press releases

Material to Be Taken to Meeting by Secretary

1. Copy of corporation law of state in which corporation is incorporated
2. Copy of certificate of incorporation with amendments
3. Copy of bylaws with amendments
4. Minutes of last stockholders' meeting and minutes of interim directors' meeting where their acts are to be formally ratified and approved by stockholders
5. Certified alphabetical list of stockholders entitled to vote with number of shares, by each class of stock, for each stockholder
6. Returned proxies arranged in alphabetical order
7. Copies of notice of meeting and other material mailed
8. Affidavit of secretary or transfer agent of mailing notice
9. Affidavit of publisher of publication if necessary
10. Substitute proxies
11. Supply of proxies, annual reports, and the like
12. Oath of office of judges or inspectors or tellers of election
13. Ballots for the election of directors
14. Prepared copies of proposed resolutions to be adopted

Order of Business. In the absence of charter or bylaw provisions, the conduct of the stockholders' meeting is controlled largely by custom and common practice. In the absence of charter or bylaw limitations, any business may be brought before the annual meeting of stockholders. However, no business may be transacted other than that specified in the call or notice of a special meeting of stockholders.

Inspectors or Judges of Election. The statutes in some jurisdictions provide for inspectors and outline their duties. Unless otherwise provided, inspectors or judges of election may be appointed by the board of directors, and if not so appointed, they may be appointed by the chairman of the meeting. No candidate for office should be named as an inspector. Certificates made by the inspectors are prima facie evidence of the facts stated in the certificate.

ANNUAL REPORT

The corporation's annual report is one of the most important reports issued to its stockholders. The modern practice is to have the annual report printed and mailed to the stockholders with the notice of the annual meeting and proxy material. It is generally the secretary's duty to supervise the printing and distribution of the annual report to stockholders (see also Chapter 8 of Section 12) and to spread it properly upon the minutes.

The statutes in some jurisdictions require corporations to file annual reports, and failure to do so imposes a personal liability upon the directors and officers. Generally the secretary of state or other public officials provide forms for proper corporate reporting.

DIRECTORS

The general authority to manage corporate affairs is vested in the directors or trustees of the corporation, not individually, but as a board. Directors occupy a fiduciary relationship to the corporation and its stockholders. Liability insurance covering directors and officers is written by some insurance companies. In every state will be found statutes governing corporations and their agents. The secretary should file all statutory reports required relating to the election of directors.

Except where provisions are made for a staggered board, directors are generally elected to hold office until the next annual meeting and until their successor has been elected and qualified.

The statutes or articles of incorporation may prescribe the qualifications of its directors, such as the requirement that directors be stockholders.

DIRECTORS' MEETINGS

The *first* meeting of the directors is a most important one and the secretary should prepare a detailed agenda for the meeting. If the meeting is held without a formal call, a written waiver of notice should be signed by all the directors.

Regular meetings are those provided for by the bylaws or otherwise held at a fixed time. When the time and place are fixed by statute or by the articles of incorporation or bylaws, the meeting must be held at this time and place.

Special meetings are those called by officers of the corporation authorized to issue such call. A special meeting must be called in the manner prescribed. If all of the directors are present and raise no objection, the validity of the meeting is not affected by failure to give notice.

Notice. Generally, no notice is required for regular meetings, the time and place being fixed by the charter, bylaw, or board resolution.

Special meetings generally require notice designating the time, place, and purpose and must be personally served, if practicable, upon every director. When the length of notice to be given has not been prescribed, a reasonable notice is ordinarily required.

When no form of notice is prescribed, any form that will advise the directors of the time, place, and purpose of the meeting is generally sufficient. As a general rule, no notice need be given of an adjourned meeting. The secretary should send notices of all meetings, even though a notice may not be required.

Generally, a *waiver of notice* of the meeting may properly be executed before the meeting, but not subsequent thereto. However, some statutes provide that such a waiver may be signed before or after the time stated therein or after the action has been taken.

Place. In the absence of charter or bylaw provision, directors may select the place for holding their meetings, either within or without the state of incorporation.

Quorum. The general rule is, in the absence of charter or bylaw provision to the contrary, a majority of the authorized number of directors constitutes a quorum, and this number is not affected by any vacancies on the board. The statutes in some states permit the stockholders to fix a quorum at less or more than the majority of the board. Directors who are disqualified from voting because of personal interest cannot be included in determining a quorum.

Voting. Directors must be personally present at meetings to vote. They cannot vote by proxy.

Agenda. The secretary should prepare an agenda for the meeting, in accordance with an established uniform order of business, and furnish the directors with copies of all reports and of special resolutions to be acted upon.

Minutes. It is the duty of the secretary to keep full and accurate minutes of all meetings of directors and to see that they are properly entered in the minute book. This is important in case of litigation or when making application for the listing of its stock on a public stock exchange. The minutes are prima facie evidence of what they purport to show as to the business transacted at the meeting.

Generally, the discussions that take place are not a part of the minutes, except when a member specifically requests that his views be spread upon the record. If a director did not vote upon a particular transaction because he was personally interested, the minutes should so show. The minutes should show the names of any directors voting against the action taken.

Some secretaries limit the minutes of directors' meetings to a record of the resolutions and motions upon which action was taken. Resolutions should be drafted in sufficient detail to show clearly the scope of the board's action. The person who acted as secretary of the meeting is the proper person to write up and sign the minutes of the meeting.

In the case of adjourned meetings, some secretaries do not close the minutes of the first meeting until the adjourned meeting is finished. However, it is preferable that each meeting be considered a separate meeting and the minutes written accordingly. The heading of the adjourned meeting should properly show that it was an adjourned meeting.

When the execution of a formal document is to be approved by the board, the instrument should be presented to the entire board for consideration.

Certified copies of resolutions and excerpts from the minutes should be signed by the secretary and the corporate seal affixed.

The secretary should furnish a copy of any minutes to be approved to directors or committee members prior to the meeting to conserve the time required for reading at the meeting. The minutes should show that a copy of the minutes was sent to each member and that, on motion, reading was dispensed with.

The secretary should keep carefully prepared *indexes* of the minutes and maintain a file of resolutions by subject matter. A brief caption in the margin of the minutes opposite each resolution or item will save time in searching for a specific subject.

A *uniform format* should be used when copying the minutes in a minute book. The minutes of each meeting should commence on a new page, appropriately headed with the name of the meeting, date, place, and time of the meeting. The following information is almost always included:

1. Whether the meeting is regular or special, a copy of the notice or waiver of notice being filed with the minutes
2. Names of directors present and those absent
3. Whether or not a quorum was present
4. Names of other persons present
5. Names of the chairman and the secretary of the meeting
6. Adjournments taken; also the time when the meeting was reconvened
7. Approval of the minutes of the last meeting, either after reading or on motion to dispense with reading
8. Report of current operations and other matters
9. Report of committee action
10. Adjournment

A director who dissents from any vote or resolution is entitled to have his opposing vote recorded in the minutes.

BYLAWS

The bylaws provide the rules and regulations, subject to charter provisions, enacted by a corporation for the operation of its affairs. They set forth the rights and powers of the stockholders, directors, and officers.

Generally, the bylaws should cover the following:

1. Stockholders' meetings, the time, place, and required notice of annual and special meetings of stockholders, voting, and quorum

2. Election, number, classes, qualifications, and tenure of directors; filling of vacancies; time and place of regular and special meetings; notice of meetings and quorum requirements; committees

3. Officers and their duties; term of office, qualification, bonds if any

4. Form of share certificate, signature, lost certificates, registration

5. Procedure relevant to the transfer of shares

6. Corporate seal

7. Fiscal year

8. Indemnity of directors and officers (where appropriate under the statutes)

9. Any other matters peculiar to the corporation

10. Procedure for amendment

COMMITTEES

Because of the variety and complexity of doing business, the committee system is necessary in the operation of larger corporations. The bylaws may authorize the designation of committees subject to charter limitations. The board of directors generally appoints an executive committee of its members to act for and exercise the power of the board when the board is not in session. In addition to the executive committee, many larger corporations appoint finance, salary, pension, auditing, and similar committees to conduct the business of the corporation in particular matters.

The proceedings of committees should be formal and recorded by the keeping of minutes which, with reports of the committee, will keep the board of directors fully informed of the work of the committee.

BOOKS AND RECORDS

The proper custodian of the official books and records of a corporation is its secretary or clerk. In the absence of statutory regulations giving the custody and control of the books and records to the secretary, the stockholders or directors may prescribe the person who shall have custody of them. Generally, statutes prescribe what and where books and records must be kept. Rules for the filing of records for public inspection are generally prescribed by the various departments, boards, and commissions.

Minute Book. The original, photostatic, or a conformed copy of the certificate of incorporation and the official receipts showing the filing, the payment of fees, taxes, publication, and the like and a copy of the bylaws should be filed in the minute book. Any amendments should likewise be filed. Statutory provisions as to the revising of bylaws are found in certain states.

If a bound minute book is used, the original set of bylaws is sometimes pasted into the minute book. If a loose-leaf book is used, the bylaws should be inserted at the proper place in the minute book. If the original set of bylaws is not inserted in the minute book, it should be permanently preserved by the secretary and a copy, certified by the secretary, inserted in the minute book.

The majority of secretaries keep minutes of meetings in special loose-leaf binders. Some binders are equipped with special locks, the key to which is kept by the secretary, so that sheets cannot be withdrawn or inserted without his approval.   Pages are generally numbered and sometimes each page is signed by the secretary.

In smaller corporations, the minute book may contain the minutes of stockholders', directors', and committee meetings.   In larger companies, however, it is usually more convenient to keep each set of minutes in a separate book.

Generally, all corporate documents pertaining to the incorporation of the company and all of those required to be filed or recorded should be filed by the secretary.   Likewise, the authority of admission to do business in foreign jurisdictions, deeds, mortgages, proxies, inspectors' oaths and certificates, ballots, affidavits or mailing of notices, publication, waivers, resolutions, contracts, canceled stock certificates, and other formal documents should be preserved by the secretary.

Indexing.   The secretary should develop a method of keeping a record of and filing all documents in his custody and of producing the document itself with a minimum of delay.   A document register should be maintained showing the title of each document and giving a short description of it.

Some secretaries keep the document register in numerical order, numbering each document in consecutive order and filing it by number.   The register is cross-indexed so that the document may be found with a minimum amount of information.   Any document removed from the files should be signed for personally by an authorized official entitled to such file and the "out card" or "receipt" filed in place of the document removed.

If the documents are numerous, a separate register may be maintained for various types of documents such as leases, patents, trademarks, license agreements, real estate, and labor contracts.

Inspection.   The right of inspection of corporate books and records, or at least certain specified books, is generally fixed by statute or by the articles of incorporation or bylaws.   In most jurisdictions, there are statutory provisions securing to stockholders the right to inspect the books and records, including the bylaws, at a proper and reasonable time and for a proper purpose.   Statutes sometimes impose upon the corporation, or upon the officer denying the right of inspection, penalties for refusal to allow inspection.

Stock Records.   Complete and accurate records of stock ownership are essential.   Most states have specific provisions respecting the keeping of stock records and their availability for inspection by stockholders.

A separate *stock certificate book* should be kept for each class of stock.   If the secretary keeps the stock record in a stock certificate book which has a stub to correspond with that of the issued certificate, the stub should bear the name and address of the stockholder, the date and number of the certificate, the number of shares, and whether it is the original issue or a transfer from a former owner to the present owner.   If it is a transfer, the number and date of the certificate surrendered should be entered on the stub of the new certificate.   The surrendered stock certificate should be properly canceled and pasted to the corresponding stub in the stock certificate book.

The New York Clearing House Association has adopted uniform procedures for the use of abbreviations in registering stock and addressing stockholders.

When the stock certificate is delivered, the secretary should obtain a receipt bearing the signature of the person in whose name the stock is issued.   If delivery is made by mail, the certificate should be sent by registered mail and a return receipt requested.

Record of Subsidiary Companies.   A copy of the articles of incorporation, bylaws, minutes, resolutions, and other important documents of subsidiary companies should be maintained in the secretary's office of the parent corporation.

TRANSFER AGENT

If the corporation has a transfer agent, usually the issuance, transfer, and the detail of keeping a stock ledger are handled by him. The extent of the transfer agent's work and liability depends upon the agreement between him and the corporation. Generally, a transfer agent is authorized to sign and impress the corporate seal on the corporation's stock certificates issued by him and to maintain the stock books and stockholder's ledger containing the names and addresses of all stockholders. The secretary should receive a daily record from the transfer agent of all stock transfers made by him.

If, however, the company does not employ a transfer agent, the secretary is responsible for the proper issuance and transfer of corporate stock and the maintenance of proper stock books, ledgers, and records.

REGISTRAR

A registrar maintains a record of all stock certificates issued and surrendered showing the name of the transferor and transferee. He maintains a record to assure that there is no overissue of the securities. He passes upon the correctness of all certificates issued. If correctly issued, he countersigns them. The national stock exchanges require that securities listed by them be issued through a transfer agent and registrar

OFFICERS

The officers are the agents of a corporation and their authority is substantially the same as that applicable to agents generally. They derive their powers from the statutes, the corporation's articles of incorporation, bylaws, and resolutions of the board of directors. Most states generally require at least a president, a secretary, a treasurer, and also a resident agent upon whom service of process can be made. When there is no statutory requirement, the articles of incorporation or bylaws generally provide for the number of corporate officers and directors. Directors and officers are often the same persons.

Officers are usually elected or appointed by the board of directors. Many states have statutory provisions governing the election of officers.

Statutes sometimes prescribe restrictions as to the qualifications of corporate officers for particular offices. If not required by statutes, the articles of incorporation or bylaws often prescribe the requirements.

Generally, the term of office is fixed by statute, by the articles of incorporation, or by its bylaws.

Ordinarily, corporate officers are not required to give bond. However, the directors have power to require a bond for the faithful performance of the officer's duties. When bonds are required, the secretary should arrange for such bonds. They should be filed with the secretary and proper reference to them made in the minutes.

Taking an oath of office is sometimes required by statute or by the articles of incorporation or bylaws.

When an officer resigns, the secretary should insert the resignation in the minute book with the minutes of the meeting at which the resignation was presented or acted upon.

CORPORATE STOCK

Statutes in many jurisdictions prescribe the general form and contents of corporate stock certificates. Some jurisdictions require that the designation, class, preferences and rights, and limits of restrictions be set forth or summarized on the stock certificate. Others permit a choice of showing this information on the certificate or agreeing to furnish it to any stockholder upon request.

Stock Transfer. The essentials for the transfer of stock are (1) a change in ownership, (2) proper endorsement, either on the certificate itself or by a separate instrument, (3) surrender of the certificate for cancellation, and (4) issuance of a new certificate to the transferee.

A stock certificate assigned in blank may be passed from transferor to transferee any number of times without change of the assignment. If the name of the transferee is inserted, the certificate must be surrendered and a new certificate issued in the name of the transferee before it may again be transferred. If the certificate is delivered without endorsement, but is accompanied by an assignment, it has the same effect as an endorsement upon the certificate itself and must be surrendered for the issuance of a new certificate in the name of the transferee.

A corporation is responsible for any fraud or error committed by its officers or agents in the issuance or transferring of its stock. To prevent the possibility of liability or forged assignment, the secretary or transfer agent should demand a guarantee of the signature of the transferor. If the transferor is a corporation, a certified copy of the resolution authorizing the execution by the officer who assigned the certificate should be required. Likewise, proof of the authority should be demanded when the assignment is made by an executor, trustee, and the like.

Erasures should not be made on stock certificates. If an error is made, the certificate should be canceled and a new certificate issued.

Before the secretary or transfer agent reissues a replacement certificate to cover one lost or destroyed, he should require appropriate bond of indemnity.

Transfer of shares on the books of the corporation is necessary for the transferee to exercise his rights as a stockholder.

Closing of Transfer Books. In order for the secretary or transfer agent to prepare a list of stockholders entitled to receive notice of and to vote at meetings, some corporations close the stock book for a certain period before the meeting. Generally, if the closing of the transfer book is not specifically covered by statute, it is covered by the corporation's bylaws. A more convenient procedure is to establish, by resolution, a record date for stockholders entitled to receive notice of and to vote at the meeting. The notice of the annual meeting usually sets forth the period during which the transfer books are closed.

Usually, transfer books are not closed preparatory to the payment of a dividend. Instead, the resolution declaring a dividend establishes the date on which stockholders of record shall be entitled to receive the dividend.

Dividends. In corporations where the stockholders' record is kept by the secretary, the secretary prepares a list of stockholders of record and number of shares held by each as of the record date. This list is usually transmitted to the treasurer, who prepares the dividend checks. The dividend checks are then usually mailed by the secretary. If the corporation employs a transfer agent, he may also act as dividend disbursing agent.

When a dividend is declared, the secretary handles the news release of the declaration and notifies the stock exchanges, if the stock is listed on the exchange, and the dividend disbursing agent.   The secretary prepares and delivers to the disbursing agent any notice and other material to be mailed with the dividend checks.

Ordinarily, dividends are paid to the registered stockholders.   When stockholders direct the dividend to be paid or mailed to someone other than themselves, the stock ledger is so marked and the dividend paid accordingly.   The secretary or disbursing agent should promptly follow up all dividend checks which have not cleared after a fixed period of time.

REGISTERED AGENT

The statutes in the state in which the corporation is incorporated and in foreign jurisdictions in which the corporation is qualified generally require the appointment of an agent upon whom process against the corporation may be served.   Many state statutes provide that service of process may be made upon the secretary of the state involved instead of upon the registered agent of the corporation.   To assure prompt notice of service of process, it is advisable to appoint one of the service companies as agent for such service, rather than an individual.   However, in many corporations, the "corporate" secretary of the corporation acts as agent for such service.

OTHER CONCERNS OF THE SECRETARY

Corporate Seal.   The power of an officer to affix the corporate seal to an instrument is generally conferred by the charter or bylaws.   Statutes in most states require stock certificates to be signed by designated officers and sealed with the corporate seal.   Statutes in many jurisdictions provide that signatures of officers and the seal may be facsimiles, engraved or printed, when the stock certificates are signed by a transfer agent or registrar.

An impression of the seal adopted by the corporation should appear in the minute book where it was adopted.

Resolutions.   The proper framing of resolutions is most important and should generally be drafted prior to the meeting and a copy made available to each director of committee member at the meeting.

The resolution, although it may consist of more than one clause, should cover only one subject.   This simplifies the preparation of certified copies covering a specific matter.

Public and Investor Relations.   With a high percentage of corporate stock held in the names of brokers, banks, and trust funds, it is important that the secretary follow an active program to keep all stockholders informed about the company, its financial condition, and its policies and programs.

Securities and Exchange Commission.   Federal regulation of public interstate sales and the sale of securities listed on the national security exchanges are governed by the Securities Act of 1933 and the Securities Exchange Act of 1934.

State regulations governing the sale of securities are generally covered by the state "blue sky" laws.

Secretary's Calendar.   The secretary should maintain a calendar, similar to that shown by Figure 2-1, of various meetings and actions to be done such as the mailing of notices, holding of meetings, and filing of reports.   Whether the calendar includes subsidiary companies or a separate calendar is maintained for each company depends upon the preference of the secretary.

Meetings	No-tice	Time	Place	Remarks
January:				
7 Notice of executive committee meeting				
14 Notice of directors' meeting				
18 Executive committee meeting	X	9:30	Board room	Annual budget
26 Directors' meeting	X	10:30	Board room	Regular
February:				
4 Notice of executive committee meeting				
14 Notice of directors' meeting				
15 Executive committee meeting	X	9:30	Board room	Regular
23 Directors' meeting	X	10:30	Board room	Regular—approval of annual report
23 Notice to transfer agent re record date for annual meeting				
25 Preliminary copy of notice and proxy statement to SEC				
March:				
4 Notice of executive committee meeting				
8 Definitive copies of notice of annual meeting and proxy material to SEC				
11 Notice of directors' meeting				
15 Executive committee meeting	X	9:30	Board room	Regular
23 Directors' meeting	X	10:30	Board room	Regular
29 Mailing of annual report, notice of annual meeting, and proxy material				
31 Affidavit of mailing of annual report, notice of annual meeting, proxy, etc., by transfer agent				
April:				
8 Notice of executive committee meeting				
12 Final agenda for annual meeting				
15 Notice of directors' meeting				
19 Executive committee meeting	X	9:30	Board room	Regular
25 Annual stockholders' meeting	X	11:00	Convention hall	
27 Directors' meeting	X	10:30	Board room	Organizational

FIG. 2-1. *Typical secretary's calendar.*

CONCLUSION

The secretary should maintain, at all times, close contact with the corporation's operations so that the activities of his office may be closely correlated with those of other officers in the conduct of the business and its relations with stockholders, governmental agencies, and other outside parties. It is of the utmost importance that the myriad duties of his office be handled with meticulous detail to afford the maximum protection of the corporation's legal position, assure conformance with applicable laws and regulations, and minimize litigation.

BIBLIOGRAPHY

American Jurisprudence (Corporations), 2d ed. (with current supplements), The Lawyers Cooperative Publishing Company, Rochester, N.Y.

Company Manual, New York Stock Exchange, New York.

Corporation Law Guide; Federal Securities Law Reports; Blue Sky Law Reports; Stock Exchange Guides, Commerce Clearing House, Inc., Chicago.

The Corporation Manual (Statutory Provisions Relating to Domestic Business Corporations), United States Corporation Company, New York, 1965.

Fletcher Cyclopedia of Corporations (permanent edition with current supplements), Callaghan & Company, Chicago.

General Rules and Regulations under the Securities Act of 1933, and Securities Exchange Act of 1934, U.S. Securities and Exchange Commission, Washington, D.C.

Modern Legal Forms (with current supplements), Vernon Law Book Company, Kansas City, Mo., and West Publishing Company, St. Paul, Minn.

Nichols Cyclopedia of Legal Forms—Annotated, Callaghan & Company, Chicago.

CHAPTER THREE

Legal Responsibilities of Businessmen

ROBERT N. CORLEY *Associate Professor of Business Law, Department of Industrial Administration, University of Illinois, Urbana, Illinois*

Even a cursory examination of the legal responsibilities of businessmen is not possible in less than several volumes. Businessmen are subject to laws promulgated at all levels of government. Every businessman in the United States is subject to and has the responsibility for complying with all of the statutes enacted by the Congress of the United States as interpreted by the courts. In addition, every businessman is responsible for complying with all of the laws of his own state which may pertain to him and the laws of his county or parish, township, city, town, or village as well as the multitude of smaller legislative bodies such as park districts, health districts, drainage districts, and sanitary districts. Therefore, for a businessman to meet his legal responsibilities, it is necessary for him to recognize the various sources of law which affect his business.

MAJOR SOURCES OF THE LAW

The major sources of the law are generally considered to be the Constitution of the United States and the constitutions of the various states, the statutes enacted by the various legislative bodies, and the judicial decisions of the courts or the so-called common law. In addition to these traditional sources of law, there has developed a body of law sometimes referred to as "administrative law," which is frequently the most important source of law insofar as the legal responsibilities of businessmen are concerned.

The statutes of the various states cover almost an endless variety of topics and are subject to change in every legislative session. State statutory matters include such a variety of items as commercial law, taxation, employment, competition, and practically every other aspect of business operations. In many of these areas, there are also Federal statutes. It is noted that the statutes of various states vary substantially, and therefore the businessman is cautioned to consult his attorney on any particular question.

Statutes are by their very nature general and are frequently ambiguous; therefore, it becomes necessary to have judicial interpretation of statutes to ascertain their exact meaning. In areas which are not covered by statutes, the law is developed by judicial decision in accordance with the concept of *stare decisis*, which in effect states that every rule of law used to decide a legal question becomes a precedent for future decisions. The concept of *stare decisis*, which has given us the common law, means that every state has its own body of precedent, thus preventing any national uniformity of legal principles. This fact compounds the extreme difficulty of stating the legal responsibilities of businessmen with any degree of accuracy and also dictates the need for individual counsel on legal problems in each individual businessman's local community.

Administrative Law. Administrative law as a source of ascertaining the legal responsibilities of businessmen is often considered to be the product of a "fourth branch" of government. Administrative agencies possess the characteristics of each of the other branches of government. They are created by a delegation of the legislative function by legislative bodies to an agency. The delegation allows administrative agencies to make rules and regulations which are, in effect, laws to carry out the general policy stated by the legislature. The legislative policy and delegation are frequently quite broad and authorize an agency to make such rules, for example, as may be in the "public interest" in a certain field.

The agencies also perform executive functions such as investigating compliance with their rules or the need for new rules, prosecuting violators of the rules, or serving in an advisory capacity. The quasi-judicial functions of administrative agencies are well known by most people and include the determination of liability for workmen's compensation, the determination of rates of public utilities, or decisions concerned with unfair labor practices. An examination of the Federal agencies such as the Federal Communications Commission, Federal Trade Commission, National Labor Relations Board, Interstate Commerce Commission, and Securities and Exchange Commission indicates the tremendous scope of activities of these agencies at the Federal level. Every state has its own commerce commission, industrial commission, and other administrative agencies which make rules and regulations affecting business at the state level. Zoning boards are an example of administrative agencies at the local level. The scope of activities of these agencies illustrates that administrative agencies materially affect day-to-day business operations.

Therefore, it can be seen that the legal responsibilities of businessmen are to comply with the thousands of statutes, judicial decisions, and administrative regulations and decisions which are concerned with their activities. Although it is not feasible to discuss any of these in detail, the following discussion is an attempt to give an idea of the general concepts found in the basic areas of law which deal with private relations with others, such as contracts, torts, and employment. The material contained herein should not be accepted as the law in any particular area because independent study and research are required to determine the actual responsibility of businessmen in any particular factual situation in each state.

CONTRACTS

In analyzing the legal responsibilities of businessmen, it is readily apparent that a major area of this responsibility is in the field of contracts. Each businessman must realize the significance in our legal system of valid and enforceable contracts and of the remedies available to a party who has been a victim of a breach of contract. The following is a *general* outline of the basic elements of a contract.

Valid Contracts. A contract or agreement is generally considered to consist of a definite offer by one party which is accepted by the other for which consideration is given by each party to the other, assuming that both parties are competent (possess the legal capacity) to enter into the contract and that it is for a legal purpose. There are technical legal rules concerning the duration of an offer which involve such matters as rejections, revocations, and the lapse of an offer, each of which is generally concerned with problems of time and the effectiveness of communications which have been sent in the mail or by telegram or by some other method. These rules vary from state to state, and questions as to the existence and nonexistence of a contract based on communications should be referred to an attorney for advice.

The concept of consideration or mutuality indicates that each party must be bound to the agreement and must receive something of value before there is an enforceable contract. Many documents purport to be contracts, but on close scrutiny and examination it often appears that one party or the other has not actually agreed to do anything, in which case the law holds that there is not a binding contract because of no consideration. Another problem area involving consideration concerns the discharge of debts through part payment and by using such notations as "paid in full" on the check used in payment. As a general rule, part payment will not discharge an undisputed debt even though it is marked "paid in full," but part payment which is accepted with such notation will operate to discharge a disputed debt. The businessman is cautioned to note the significance of this distinction in accepting payments on account.

Another question concerned with the law of consideration deals with the modification of contracts. Generally, a modification is not binding without additional consideration; but in states which have adopted the Uniform Commercial Code, a promise by one party to do something different than originally agreed upon is binding without additional consideration from the other party in cases involving sales of personal property.

Voidable Contracts. Contractual liability may be avoided and the responsibility previously incurred ignored under certain circumstances. Such contracts are said to be "voidable," and the legal remedy of rescission is available in these situations. Perhaps the most important of these is where there has been fraud or misrepresentation. It should be noted that fraud consists of an intentional misstatement of fact (rather than opinion) which is justifiably relied upon by the victim of the fraud. The usual "puffing" in a sales contract is not fraud. In addition to avoiding a contract induced by fraud, the victim may sue for dollar damages in a tort action of deceit.

Another important ground for avoiding a contract is lack of legal capacity to enter into a contract. This allows minors, insane persons, and even intoxicated persons to disaffirm contracts. It is imperative that every businessman recognize that a minor can disaffirm a contract any time during his minority and for a reasonable time after reaching majority merely by returning so much of what he received as he has left. A minor has liability only for necessities actually received, and therefore any businessman who sells something other than food, clothing, or other necessity to a minor should do so only upon the realization that the minor can disaffirm the contract and obtain his money back. Of course, if the amount of money involved is relatively small, the expenses of litigation will, as a practical matter, deter the minor from suit for his consideration.

Oral and Written Contracts. As a general rule, a contract is enforceable whether it is oral or in writing. There are certain obvious advantages to a written contract such as ease of proving its terms, but it must be recognized that oral agreements are for the most part enforceable in court. The Statute of Frauds which has been enacted in most states does, however, require that there be written evidence of certain types of agreements before they are enforceable in court. These generally refer to contracts involving real estate, contracts which cannot be performed within one year of the date of making, contracts by which one person promises to pay the debt of another, and contracts involving the sale of personal property worth over $500. These statutes vary from state to state, and again the businessman is cautioned to consult his attorney on the question of enforceability of an oral contract in any specific case.

Many contracts are declared to be illegal by statute, and still others are declared by the court to be illegal as being contrary to public policy. Examples of the former are gambling contracts and contracts which charge an illegal or usurious rate of interest. Examples of the latter are agreements which disclaim liability for negligence and agreements not to compete where the time or area of the restraint is unreasonable. To illustrate the latter, if an employer provides in a contract that a salesman will not compete in an unreasonable area or for an unreasonable time upon termination of his employment, such a term of the contract is said to be illegal.

Breaches of Contract. A party who breaches a contract is, of course, subject to a suit of dollar damages. The measure of damages is the amount of money it takes to put the innocent party in as good a position as he would have been in if the breach had not occurred. This concept of making a person "whole" includes only those damages which reasonably could be expected to result from the breach. The fact that actual dollar damages are frequently not substantial because of the availability of similar products or the like has resulted in few lawsuits as compared with the total number of breaches of contract which actually occur.

Businessmen are responsible not only for contracts which they have entered into, but also for contracts entered into by their agents if the agent possesses actual or apparent authority to enter into the agreement. "Apparent authority" refers to something which the principal has done which leads the other party to believe that the agent possesses authority. The burden is on the party dealing with an agent to establish the agent's authority. A principal who is not bound by a contract because the agent does not possess the requisite authority may nevertheless become bound if he chooses to ratify the agreement, that is, subsequently approve it in some way.

From the foregoing, it can be said that businessmen have the responsibility of performing in accordance with the terms of all valid and enforceable contracts. There are, however, many legal questions to be resolved not only in the creation of a contract, but in their construction, enforceability, and legality. All of these matters require the advice of counsel.

TORTS

Another important area of responsibility of businessmen is concerned with the law of torts. A tort has been defined as a wrong or wrongful act upon the person or property of another as distinguished from a contractual wrong. Although the law of torts encompasses such intentional wrongs as libel, slander, malicious prosecution, trespass, and assault, the most important wrong which results in liability for businessmen occurs in that area of the law concerned with negligence.   There are literally hundreds of thousands of lawsuits brought annually on a theory of negligence arising from automobile collisions and personal injuries suffered by customers on the premises of a business.   Each person has a duty to conduct himself and his business in such a manner as not to injure another person intentionally, and in addition, he has a duty to exercise reasonable care and caution for the safety of others and their property.   Failure to exercise this reasonable care and caution is generally referred to as "negligence," for which liability results for all damages of which the negligence is the proximate cause.

The businessman is responsible not only for his own torts, but also for the torts of his agents and servants if these torts are committed by the agent or servant during the course of his employment.   This concept of vicarious liability requires proper risk management and spreading the risk by purchasing insurance to cover all activities by employees of the firm.   (See also Chapter 8 of Section 9.)

Businessmen have a liability for products, which was originally considered to be a part of the law of torts but is today frequently considered to be a part of the law of contracts.   This liability, frequently referred to as "product liability based on breach of warranty," is created by statute in most states and arises from the warranty of a seller of goods that they are of merchantable quality and reasonably fit for their intended purpose.   There are other warranties which arise in special situations and also impose liability to the businessman who fails to meet his responsibility in this respect.   Every businessman should assume that he has the full responsibility for the products that he sells and that he has a liability to anyone who may suffer an injury from the use of the product.   The trend of the law in this area is toward strict liability for the manufacturer or seller of goods, irrespective of fault.   Possession of adequate liability insurance is thus the responsibility of every businessman.

TAXATION

One of the major responsibilities of businesses is to pay the several taxes and fees and file the necessary reports required by various governmental bodies. Federal taxation in addition to the income tax consists of social security taxes, generally referred to as FICA, and the unemployment compensation tax.   In addition, there are Federal excise taxes which are applicable to certain products and certain types of transactions.   Employers are required to withhold income tax on their employees and to file quarterly reports as well as annual reports on these amounts.   Withholding taxes in excess of $100 per month are required to be deposited monthly for which Federal depository receipts are obtained.

State taxation of businesses creates many difficult legal questions, particularly insofar as interstate businesses are concerned.   Businesses are required to pay general property taxes which are an ad valorem tax computed by multiplying the tax rate by the assessed valuation of the property as equalized throughout the taxing state.   Although each state has its own procedures for the levying of the general property tax, there is a valuation problem in all cases, because the valuations are based on the discretion and judgment of a tax assessor.   The businessman should keep track of his valuations as compared with other tax papers to avoid excess taxation.

In addition to general property taxes, many states also levy a state income tax.   For a business which has earnings in several states, the income is apportioned by various formulas to prevent multiple taxation of the same income. Interstate commerce is required to pay its fair share of the state's tax burden.

Each state may have its own formula for apportionment, and the businessman is required to keep the records prescribed by each state.

Many states impose a sales tax and a use tax as a major means of revenue. The sales tax is a flat percentage of sales of property within the state, and the use tax is an adjunct to it to prevent evasion by purchasing property in other states and bringing it back to the state of domicile. The courts have held that a business in one state can be required to collect the sales tax and/or use tax of another state when it knows that the goods are to be shipped into the taxing state.

In addition to the foregoing taxes, states also levy various license taxes for certain types of businesses, unemployment compensation, and other corporate taxes such as the franchise tax and a capital stock tax. The multiplicity of these taxes requires the services of a competent accountant as well as the frequent assistance of an attorney.

It is important to note in connection with the unemployment compensation tax that it is paid to both the Federal and state governments and that a business which has few or little claims filed by its former employees will receive a reduction in the tax based on its "experience" factor.

EMPLOYMENT

There are many Federal statutes which determine the legal responsibilities of businessmen to their employees. The National Labor Relations Act of 1935 (Wagner Act) as amended in 1947 (Taft-Hartley Act) determines the responsibility of business and labor in the field of collective bargaining and labor relations. This subject is discussed in Section 11.

Fair Labor Standards Act. The Fair Labor Standards Act is concerned with wages, hours, and working conditions for persons engaged in work in interstate or foreign commerce or in work which substantially affects interstate commerce or foreign commerce. The Act generally is applicable to:

1. Employees engaged in interstate or foreign commerce, including workers in the telephone, telegraph, radio, television, and transportation industries; those who build, maintain, and repair highways, railroads, and airfields, or service vehicles or equipment used in interstate commerce; employees in distributing industries such as wholesaling who handle goods moving in interstate commerce, as well as workers who order, receive, or keep records of such goods; clerical and other workers who regularly use the mails, telephone, or telegraph for interstate communication; and employees of businesses such as banks, insurance companies, and advertising agencies who regularly utilize the channels of interstate communication.

2. Employees engaged in the production of goods for interstate or foreign commerce, including those who work in manufacturing, processing, and distributing establishments and in mines, oil fields, and quarries that produce goods for interstate or foreign commerce. This means everyone, including office, management, sales, and shipping personnel and maintenance, custodial, and protective employees, whether they are employed by the producer or an intermediary. Employees may be covered even if their firm does not ship its goods directly in such commerce. The goods may leave the state through another firm.

3. All other employees employed in an enterprise if:
   a. There are, in the activities of the enterprise, employees engaged in inter-

state or foreign commerce or in the production of goods for interstate or foreign commerce, including employees handling, selling, or otherwise working on goods that have been moved in or produced for such commerce by any person.

   b. Such enterprise is one which:

      (1) Has one or more retail or service establishments and an annual gross sales volume of $1 million or more, and procures at least $250,000 annually of goods for resale that move or have moved across state lines, or

      (2) Is engaged in the business of construction or reconstruction and has an annual gross volume of $350,000 or more from such business, or

      (3) Is a gasoline service establishment which has an annual gross sales volume of $250,000 or more, or

      (4) Is engaged in urban or interurban transit operations and has an annual gross sales volume of $1 million or more, or

      (5) Is an establishment of any other such enterprise, where the establishment has some employees engaged in interstate or foreign commerce or in the production of goods for such commerce, and the enterprise has an annual gross sales volume of $1 million or more.

Exemptions. Some employees who would otherwise be entitled to the benefits of the Act are excluded from the minimum wage or overtime provisions, or both, by specific exemptions. These exemptions apply only in those cases where their terms and conditions are specifically met. Employers should check carefully the terms and conditions of any exemption which they seek to use.

Exemptions from the minimum wage and the overtime provisions include the following:

1. Executive, administrative, and professional employees and outside salesmen, as defined in regulations of the Secretary

2. Employees of retail or service establishments which are primarily engaged in selling automobiles, trucks, or farm implements; and employees of any of the following which are retail or service establishments that make most of their sales within the state:

    a. Hotels, motels, restaurants, motion picture theaters, seasonal amusement and recreational establishments, hospitals and nursing homes, schools for handicapped or gifted children

    b. Other retail or service establishments which have less than $250,000 in annual sales exclusive of specified taxes, or

    c. If the enterprise of which they are a part has less than $1 million in gross annual sales exclusive of specified taxes or procures less than $250,000 annually in goods for resale that move or have moved across state lines

3. Employees of retail or service establishments who are employed primarily in connection with certain food or beverage service

4. Employees of certain laundries and dry-cleaning establishments, of certain small newspapers, and of urban and interurban transit systems which have less than $1 million in annual gross sales; switchboard operators of telephone companies which have fewer than 750 telephones; employees of taxicab companies; seamen employed on vessels other than American vessels; fishermen; farm workers and employees engaged in certain operations relating to specified agricultural or horticultural commodities; and employees engaged in small forestry and logging operations

Exemptions from only the overtime requirements include the following:

1. Employees of railroads, pipelines, carriers by air, and urban and interurban transit systems, seamen on American vessels, certain employees of motor carriers, and local delivery drivers paid on a trip-rate basis or other delivery payment plan

2. Employees engaged in certain operations on specified agricultural or horticultural commodities or in certain dairy product operations

3. Employees employed in canning, processing, storing, marketing, and distributing fisheries' products

4. Employees of gasoline service stations, and certain higher-paid commission employees of retail or service establishments

5. Announcers, news editors, and chief engineers of certain nonmetropolitan broadcasting stations; and employees of certain wholesale or bulk petroleum distributors whose annual gross sales (exclusive of certain taxes) are not more than $1 million

Important Provisions. The Fair Labor Standards Act contained in 1965 the following provisions affecting employees covered by the Act:

1. A minimum wage of $1.25 an hour must be paid to every employee.

2. Covered employees must be paid time-and-one-half for any hours over forty in one week.

3. The employees of one sex must not be paid wages at rates lower than are paid employees of the other sex for equal work on jobs requiring equal skill, effort, and responsibility which are performed under similar working conditions.

4. Child labor provisions establish sixteen as the basic minimum age for employment in nonhazardous occupations and eighteen as the minimum age in occupations declared to be hazardous, a list of which is available from the Department of Labor. Children fourteen and fifteen may be employed outside of school hours, but children under fourteen may not be employed.

5. The statute authorizes criminal prosecution for violations and also has procedures for collecting back wages with the assistance of the Secretary of Labor in such suits.

WORKMEN'S COMPENSATION

A major legal responsibility of business is to protect its workers from the hazards of occupational diseases, accidental injuries, and deaths which may arise out of and in the course of their employment. Every state has a statute to cover these risks, generally referred to as "workmen's compensation," for providing payment to employees, usually in stated amounts based on their earnings and size of family. The statutes, in addition to providing a death benefit, usually require the payment of a weekly sum for temporary total disability and often include a pension for permanent total disability. The purpose of these statutes is to allocate to employers the risk of loss to their employees for work-connected sickness, injury, or death. In recent years, the scope of these statutes has been expanded by judicial decision to include such injuries as broken legs received while playing softball during a lunch hour and heart attacks suffered after returning home from work. The decision of whether or not the accident or injury arose out of and in the course of employment is left to the administrative agency for determination in the first instance, and the decision of the agency will not be reversed if there is substantial evidence on the record as a whole to support the agency's finding. Every business must either have adequate funds to pay these claims or carry appropriate workmen's compensation coverage.

CIVIL RIGHTS

The Federal Civil Rights Act of 1964 and similar statutes enacted by several of the states imposed an obligation on business not to discriminate against employees or customers on the basis of race, color, religion, sex, or national origin. The following aspects of the Civil Rights Act concerning employment must be recognized by all businessmen covered by the Act:

1. The Act prevents discrimination in hiring, firing, wages, terms, conditions of employment, and facilities.

2. Objections of other employees are not an excuse for noncompliance.

3. Color cannot be a job qualification.

4. Help-wanted ads must not contain unlawful restrictions.

5. Professionally developed tests may be used so long as they are not intended to discriminate.

6. Photographs may not be required of job applicants.

7. It is unlawful to discriminate against persons who are "civil rights" advocates.

8. Employers can hire and promote on a merit basis, but should be able to prove the merit.

9. The employment statute covers employers and unions with 100 or more employees or members to start with and ultimately goes down to 25.

The public accommodation provisions of the Civil Rights Bill prevent discrimination in the following businesses:

1. Hotels, motels, and other places offering lodging to transient guests. However, facilities which are actually occupied by the proprietor and which offer no more than five rooms for rent are excepted.

2. Restaurants, lunch counters, soda fountains, and other facilities engaged mainly in the business of selling food to be eaten on the premises. Specifically included in this category are eating places located within retail stores.

3. Theaters, sports arenas, and other public places of exhibition or amusement.

4. Establishments which either are located within or contain a business listed above and hold themselves out as serving the patrons of such business. For example, a retail establishment which contains a public lunchroom or lunch counter has all other facilities covered. Similarly, all business facilities located within a hotel and intended for use of its guests are required to give nondiscriminatory service.

CONCLUSION

It becomes obvious from the foregoing discussion that it is impossible as a practical matter to enumerate the legal responsibilities of businessmen in any detail. A businessman should become as familiar as possible with laws of his own state and with the Federal statutes applicable to his business. It is advisable for a businessman to have an attorney to whom he can refer even routine questions where doubt exists as to the legal effect of a certain factual situation. In addition to the required services of an attorney, most businessmen will require the services of an accountant to assist them in the multitude of tax problems confronting them.

A major portion of the legal responsibility of business is to comply with the rulings and regulations of the various administrative agencies at both the Federal and state levels. It should be kept in mind that the decisions of these agencies are not reversible by the court unless there is no substantial basis for the decision of the agency. Businessmen must comply with all requests and demands of these agencies, and this is particularly true in the field of civil rights.

The law has been described as a seamless web which, in fact, touches every activity of society. Every person is presumed to know the law and to comply with it. A reasonably satisfactory effort in this regard can be made by business only with the assistance of competent counsel.

BIBLIOGRAPHY

Bowen, Howard P., *Social Responsibility of the Businessman,* Harper & Row, Publishers, Incorporated, New York, 1953.

Dale, Ernest, *The Great Organizers,* McGraw-Hill Book Company, New York, 1960.

Greenwood, William T. (ed.), *Issues in Business and Society,* Houghton Mifflin Company, Boston, 1964.

Hale, Robert L., *Economic Liberty in a Democracy,* Columbia University Press, New York, 1952.

McGuire, Joseph, *Business and Society,* McGraw-Hill Book Company, New York, 1963.

Merrill, H. F. (ed.), *Responsibilities of Business Leadership,* Harvard University Press, Cambridge, Mass., 1948.

Selekman, Benjamin, and Sylvia Selekman, *Power and Morality in a Business Society,* McGraw-Hill Book Company, New York, 1963.

Towle, Joseph W. (ed.), *Ethics and Standards in American Business,* Houghton Mifflin Company, Boston, 1964.

CHAPTER FOUR

Antitrust and Fair Trade Legislation

E. NOBLES LOWE   *Vice President and General Counsel, West Virginia Pulp and Paper Company, New York, New York*

J. WILLIAM ROBINSON   *Secretary and Assistant General Counsel, West Virginia Pulp and Paper Company, New York, New York*

There is a common aphorism that all any businessman wants is a fair advantage over his competitor. The antitrust and trade regulation laws do not forbid this; they only insist that the fair advantage be obtained by fair means. It is not fair to obtain that advantage by conspiracy or collusion with competitors, by unethical actions, by abuse of power even though legally obtained, or by unreasonable external growth by acquisition.

A businessman also wants the right to select his customers and to deal with them and the public at arm's length. The antitrust laws concede this right, insisting only that his selection be based on his individual decision, that he not discriminate between competing customers, and that he not mislead or deal unfairly with his customers or the public.

ANTITRUST LEGISLATION

The common law is the foundation of the Federal antitrust or trade regulation laws. Legislative actions commencing at the end of the nineteenth century accelerated and directed the growth of the common law toward prohibition of deliberate commercial injury resulting from unsavory business practices such as conspiracy, coercion, and the elimination of competitors.

The growth of the impersonal corporate entity and the expansion of markets made possible by improved transportation fostered rapid economic growth during the post-Civil War era. It also resulted in increased concentration of economic power. To control the antisocial effects of monopolistic power and its abuse, the first of the Federal antitrust laws was enacted in 1890. The goal of this legislation is the protection of free enterprise by fostering market rivalry and free access to the marketplace. These laws have constantly expanded.

Federal Legislation. The *Sherman Act* of 1890 sets forth two simply worded but far-reaching substantive propositions. Section 1 declares "every contract, combination . . . or conspiracy in restraint of trade or commerce . . . to be illegal." By logic and court interpretations, the restriction is not against "every" restraint but only "unreasonable" restraints. Section 2 declares illegal monopolization, attempts to monopolize, and combinations and conspiracies to monopolize.

The *Clayton Act* of 1914 supplements the general prohibitions of the Sherman Act by outlawing specific distribution practices and structural arrangements which Congress felt were incipient steps toward monopolization. Section 2 of the Act, as amended by the *Robinson-Patman Act* of 1936, prohibits discrimination in prices where there may be adverse competitive effects. Section 3 outlaws a wide assortment of tying and exclusive-dealing arrangements. Section 7, as amended by the *Celler-Kefauver Act* of 1950, prohibits stock and asset acquisitions, whether horizontal, vertical, or conglomerate in nature, where the effect may be substantially to lessen competition. Section 8 prohibits interlocking directorates of competing companies meeting fairly minimal standards of size.

The *Federal Trade Commission Act*, enacted in 1914, created the Commission as a separate antitrust enforcement agency. Under Section 5, the Commission is given broad authority to move against all "unfair methods of competition" and, by amendment in 1938, against all "unfair or deceptive acts or practices."

Supplementary Legislation. The Sherman, Clayton, and Federal Trade Commission Acts are the fundamental Federal antitrust and trade regulation laws. They are supplemented by a large number of special acts. Some give limited exemptions to certain practices, such as Fair Trade legislation and the Webb-Pomerene Export Association Act. Others give limited exemptions to special groups such as labor unions and agricultural and horticultural cooperatives. Special rules apply to industries coming under the supervision of other governmental agencies, such as the transportation, radio and television, shipping, and banking industries. In most of these areas, the trend of the enforcement agencies is to limit the scope of the exemptions narrowly.

In addition, there are a number of related regulatory statutes, such as the flammable fabrics and textile, fur, and wool products labeling acts administered by the Federal Trade Commission.

State Antitrust Legislation. A stiffening of enforcement has made state antitrust laws a matter of increasing significance. Although the major impact of the state laws is to extend all or part of the antitrust principles to transactions in intrastate, as distinguished from interstate, commerce, they can and have been used against interstate transactions, particularly where sales to state or local governmental bodies are involved. The businessman whose activities come within either of these categories should certainly get acquainted with his state's laws.

Civil and Criminal Acts. Violations of Sections 1 and 2 of the Sherman Act are both criminal and civil offenses. Criminal and civil proceedings are often brought at the same time based on the same set of facts. The only other criminal antitrust law is Section 3 of the Robinson-Patman Act, which declares illegal certain predatory acts of price discrimination. All the other antitrust laws are enforced by civil proceedings.

Antitrust Enforcement Agencies. Only the Department of Justice can institute criminal proceedings. On the other hand, only the Federal Trade Commission enforces Section 5 of the Federal Trade Commission Act. Civil proceedings for violation of the other major antitrust laws may be brought by either of the enforcing agencies. Overlapping of investigations and cases is avoided in part by cooperation between the two enforcing agencies. In addition, the Federal Trade Commission has assumed the primary role in enforcement of the Robinson-Patman Act.

Private Remedies. One of the most effective tools for enforcing the antitrust laws is the authority given private persons to sue for treble damages, to petition for injunctive relief, and to defend contract and patent infringement actions by alleging an antitrust violation. The large successful treble-damage actions brought against the electrical equipment industry publicized this statutory procedure widely. The prevalence of private actions and the probability of a continuing increase in the number of such actions should be sufficient additional incentive to businessmen to induce them to install effective compliance programs.

PRICING

Price Fixing

Horizontal Agreements. Any agreement or conspiracy among competitors to fix prices or to do any acts which would have the effect, directly or indirectly, of fixing prices is a per se violation of Section 1 of the Sherman Act. This means that the courts have determined that such agreements or conspiracies are conclusively presumed to be unreasonable; it is not necessary to show any injury. No excuse or justification will be heard.

The courts will not listen to arguments that the pricing agreement was entered into to stop "ruinous competition," to assure all competitors a fair price, to help small and defenseless competitors, to assure the public a "reasonable" price, or as the result of the coercion and threats of larger competitors.

An agreement setting the base or list price of a product or service is obviously illegal, whether it seeks to stabilize, raise, or lower prices. Fringe activities which affect price in any way are likewise illegal. Thus, the Sherman Act prohibits agreements fixing uniform credit rules, uniform freight equalization arrangements, agreements to discontinue quantity discounts, agreements not to give trading stamps or premiums to customers, and agreements not to advertise price prominently so as to attract customers. An agreement setting quality specifications for the purpose of price stability can also be a violation of the Sherman Act.

In short, the courts have held that any act which has the purpose or effect of stabilizing prices is illegal. In a landmark decision, the United States Supreme Court held that an agreement among a group of major oil companies in the 1930s to purchase surplus gasoline from independent refineries had a material and illegal influence on the market price by maintaining a floor under the market.

Vertical Agreements. It is likewise illegal under Section 1 of the Sherman Act for a manufacturer or distributor to establish, with or without the express agreement of his customer, the price at which the customer will resell the product, unless he can bring the transaction within the narrow limitation of resale-price maintenance under the "fair trade" exemption discussed below. The general policy of the enforcement agencies, largely adopted by the courts, is that once a producer has sold his product, he no longer should be permitted to exercise any control over it, particularly in the area of resale pricing.

A seller may issue suggested resale prices and has the right to select and cut off his distributors. The trend of the cases is, however, such as to make these rights less and less meaningful. Any attempt at policing the resale policies of distributors or threatening a violator with withdrawal of a distributorship is highly questionable.

Suggested Resale Prices. As pointed out above, a seller may not fix the price at which his product is resold by his customer unless he has brought himself within the narrow limitations of fair trade legislation. If he does not, or cannot, bring himself within such legislation, he may still suggest resale prices to his customers. Emphasis must be placed on "suggest." If he goes further and polices his customer's pricing practices and threatens, directly or indirectly, to cut him off unless he conforms to such prices, he is inviting a charge of violation of Section 1 of the Sherman Act.

Consignment Sales. For many years, most lawyers believed that a seller was able to exert control over the price at which his goods are sold by delivering them to his distributor on a consignment basis. Title to the goods is in the seller, and as the owner he may determine the price at which his goods are sold. Now there are doubts as to the legality of the use of consignment sales for this purpose. Certainly, a seller is courting trouble by changing his normal sales policy to one of consignment sales on a temporary basis to bring pricing under control. A seller should not place all the burdens of ownership on the buyer, such as full risk of loss, and expect the courts to accept his control of resale prices.

Consignment selling serves a useful purpose and is probably legal in many circumstances, but it should be adopted or continued as a practice only after careful legal review.

Common Sales Agency. The use of a common sales agency for competing products is subject to question. It can certainly furnish circumstantial evidence of price fixing where there are uniform prices.

Price Uniformity

Every businessman has the right to set his own price for the product he sells. If his prices are reasonable and competitive, he will receive a share of the total business, provided his quality and service are equal to those of his competitors and his salesmen are effective. Individual decision in pricing is the very heart of the free enterprise system. It is also a major concern of the Federal antitrust laws.

There is certainly adequate justification for the statement that price uniformity is as much evidence of competition as it is of a conspiracy among competitors to fix prices. This is particularly true of many commodities and nonspecialty products. It is less true of specially manufactured goods and products where quality and services are likely to vary.

A seller of a standard product must be prepared to meet his competitors' prices or he may lose customers. In a period of shortage, it is natural for him to try to obtain the maximum profit permitted by the marketplace.

Price uniformity is no more than *circumstantial evidence.* Standing alone, price uniformity and the related business phenomena of price leadership and conscious parallelism are meaningless. However, if there is evidence of open or covert meetings with competitors, extended exchange of price information, particularly future pricing plans, or any evidence indicating an agreement or conspiracy, then price uniformity becomes important evidence, difficult to justify as pure coincidence or the natural effect of competition.

Price Intelligence. Information about competitors' prices is, of course, a basic tool of the businessman. Without it he is incapable of acting rationally in setting his current pricing policy. This important information should be obtained in a manner that avoids suspicion of conspiracy with a competitor. In a wide variety of circumstances, exchanges of price information between competitors, either directly or through the medium of trade associations, have been attacked by enforcement agencies as price-fixing arrangements.

Resale-price Maintenance

Eroding prices during the 1930s helped bring about the enactment in 1937 of the Miller-Tydings Act which permitted state fair trade legislation. Fair trade legislation purports to protect the manufacturer's goodwill embodied in trademarks and trade names from impairment by price cutting and loss-leader sales. An essential feature of these laws was a "nonsigner" provision by which all resellers are bound to follow the manufacturer's price set by contract with any one reseller. After the United States Supreme Court held that the Miller-Tydings Act did not bind nonsigning resellers, Congress passed the McGuire Act of 1952 expressly covering "nonsigner" enforcement.

Fair trade legislation is directly counter to the anti-price-fixing philosophy of the Sherman Act, because vertical price fixing is a per se violation. It is not surprising that fair trading has been under constant court attack. As a result, the courts of twenty-four states have held the basic state statutes unconstitutional, particularly as to "nonsigner" provisions.

In the seventeen states upholding such legislation, fair trading has been faced with other difficulties. Generally, the laws have been narrowly construed. They may not be used by a seller who competes with his customers (for example, a manufacturer who sells both direct and through distributors) or in the absence of open and free competition. A seller seeking to use the laws must comply carefully with all statutory requirements.

Because fair trading is not sanctioned in a majority of states, a fair trading program for a nationally distributed item creates additional problems. It is a natural step to combine fair trading with a suggested resale-price program in the non-fair-trade states. Such a dual program must be carefully controlled so as not to violate the Sherman Act's prohibition against vertical price fixing. The strong enforcement policies required in the fair trade states involving policing of prices, dealer "education" programs, and cutting off of price cutters create a business pattern which, if used in the non-fair-trade states, may result in a Sherman Act violation.

Price Discrimination

The Robinson-Patman Price Discrimination Act of 1936 resulted from an investigation into the growth and marketing practices of chain stores. The thrust of Section 2 of the 1914 Clayton Act, before it was amended by the Robinson-Patman Act, was to protect a local manufacturer or wholesaler against predatory geographical price discrimination by his more broadly based competitor. The Robinson-Patman Act substantially broadened the scope of the law and placed emphasis on the protection of the smaller customers by outlawing unwarranted price concessions by manufacturers or wholesalers to larger customers. It was designed also to protect manufacturers and wholesalers from oppressive buying practices of a large buyer.

There is a general feeling among some businessmen that the law is unfair and ineffectual. There is evidence that it is honored more in its breach than its observance in some areas. However, the great number of investigations and cases initiated by the Federal Trade Commission and especially the constantly increasing threat of treble-damage actions by customers and competitors make a policy of compliance with the law a prudent business policy as well as a legal requirement.

Elements of Price Discrimination Violation. Section 2(a) of the amended Clayton Act (the Robinson-Patman Act) sets forth the essential elements which must be present for discrimination in price to be illegal.

First, there must be a difference in price, either direct or indirect, between two or more purchasers at about the same time. A different base or list price is the most obvious form of price discrimination, but indirect differentials are equally prohibited. These may include direct price reductions in the form of special discounts, refunds, rebates, commissions, allowances, credits, or payments of any kind. Free goods, intentional overdeliveries not billed, and credits based on unjustified refunds can also be a price differential.

Second, at least one of the sales involved must be in interstate commerce. Although not applicable to foreign sales, the law applies to sales for use, consumption, or resale in United States territories and the District of Columbia.

Third, the sales must involve commodities of like grade and quality. The legal tests for determining whether commodities are of like grade and quality are difficult to apply to many products. If the products are significantly different physically or include materially different components, there is no violation. Minor differences in sizes or substituted components would not make the products "unlike." Under some circumstances, tailor-made products produced on the same machinery with minor variations may not be justification for a price differential. The difference between the price of private brands sold by a manufacturer at a lower price, not cost justified, and the price of his higher-advertised brand has been held unjustified. The law is inapplicable to services.

Finally, the discrimination must cause an adverse competitive effect at either the seller or buyer levels of competition. The usual seller-level complaint is based on predatory geographic price discrimination aimed at the destruction of a local competitor.

The more common case involves the buyer level of competition. An essential element is that the purchasers involved in the price discrimination be in direct competition. There is no violation if the same product is sold at different prices to purchasers who use the product in different industries or for different purposes. There also is no violation if the different purchasers do not compete by reason of the fact they carry on a different marketing function, for example, super jobber, distributor, retailer, or consumer. Functional discounts are permissible. However, to the extent that the purchaser carries out a dual function, it may be necessary to sell him the same product at different prices based on his different functions.

Defenses and Justification. The Robinson-Patman Act sets forth certain specific defenses. Furthermore, there are certain practices which permit differences in prices without violating the law.

Cost Savings. Cost savings is a defense to a price discrimination case. It is, however, of somewhat limited availability as a practical matter.

Section 2(a) states that price differentials are justifiable if they are limited to differentials which make only due allowance for differences in cost of manufacture, sale, or delivery provided the differences result from the differing methods or quantities in which the commodities are sold or delivered. Incremental cost savings are not acceptable as the measure of cost in any particular sale.

The general attitude of the Federal Trade Commission toward cost-savings defenses has been one of skepticism. To be of value as a defense, a cost study should be made prior to the granting of the discriminatory price. It should be based on acceptable accounting principles and preferably prepared by independent experts. Customer classifications must be reasonable, and any savings must be made specifically and clearly available to all customers within each class.

Meeting Competition. Section 2(b) permits a seller to defend a price discrimination by showing that his lower price was made in good faith to meet an equally low price of a competitor.

Despite the clear statutory language and the acceptance of the defense by the courts, the Federal Trade Commission has been most reluctant to accept this essential defense. The Commission has indicated a willingness to accept the defense provided it can be shown that the business decision has truly been made in good faith to meet a competitive situation. "The standard of good faith is simply the standard of the prudent businessman responding fairly to what he reasonably believes is a situation of competitive necessity."

A seller may meet or partially meet a competitor's price, determined on the basis of net delivered cost to the buyer, but he may not knowingly beat it. Because the exact price is often difficult to determine (checking directly with the competitor raises Sherman Act problems), a seller often acts at his peril in meeting competitive prices. Good faith is the test; but in determining whether the test has been met, the seller should make a careful, honest self-appraisal of the facts and the available proof. Self-delusion and business myopia are not defenses.

A price can be met only for substantially the same quantity for the same period. Open-ended competitive pricing is permissible but should be periodically checked to determine if the competitive offer is still in effect and must be rechecked in the event of any significant market development such as a general price change.

Records of Competitive-pricing Information. Good records are of extreme importance, both for business use and as a possible legal defense. Reports of each competitive-pricing situation met by the salesman in the marketplace are of great value to the manager in making his pricing decisions and may be essential evidence in support of a meeting-competition defense. In a situation where the purchasing agent gives little or no competitive-pricing information other than that he has a lower offer, the cumulative knowledge gained from sales reports may permit the seller, in good faith, to assume that his competitor's lower offer is the same as made to other purchasers. Some companies have adopted competitive-pricing forms to record these data.

An effort should be made to obtain the best evidence available. At times, purchasing agents will give detailed information of the competitive price, including all discounts, the seller's name, quantity, and duration of the offer. Copies of the offer or invoices are most helpful. More often, the only evidence may be in the form of salesmen's reports. It should be recognized that the Commission and courts tend to question the accuracy of such reports when standing alone. Many times, a buyer will cooperate with his supplier by acknowledging the competitive price in writing or by accepting without objection statements in a contract, by separate letter, or by appropriate stamps on order acknowledgments or invoices, to the effect that the stated price meets a competitive price.

Changing Conditions. A seller may have special lower prices from time to time in response to changing market conditions or changes in the marketability of his product, such as perishability, obsolescence of seasonal goods, court-directed distress sales, or "going out of business" sales.

Charitable Institution Sales. The sales of supplies to schools, churches, hospitals, and charitable institutions not operated for profit are specifically exempted from the operation of the Act.

Government Sales. Sales to Federal and state governments are also exempted, although some states can be expected to take a different approach if the price to them is higher. Sales of products for use in the manufacture of other goods to be sold to government agencies can legally be made at a lower price, provided all customers bidding or capable of bidding on the government contract are aware of the availability of the lower price.

Two-package Offers. If a seller offers his product at two prices based on different conditions, such as short- versus long-term credit charges, or immediate versus delayed delivery, a buyer, aware of the two packages, has no valid complaint if he purchases at the higher price.

End-use Pricing. As mentioned above, an essential element of illegal price discrimination at the buyer level of competition is an adverse effect on competition. If the buyers use the product for different purposes, there can be no such adverse effect, because they do not compete. A buyer of a component for use in manufacturing a refrigerator is not adversely affected by his supplier's sale of the identical product to a manufacturer of a computer. A seller could remove himself from Robinson-Patman Act concern by selling his products to only one company in each industry he supplies.

Quality-line Pricing. The Act applies only to discriminatory sales of commodities "of like grade and quality." If there is a significant difference in quality there may be differences in prices, without regard to cost savings involved. This may not be abused by selling the large customer a higher-grade quality at a price lower than that to his smaller competitors, or by use of different trade names for essentially the same product.

Sales at Unreasonably Low Prices. Many states have enacted legislation of varying effectiveness prohibiting loss-leader sales and sales below cost. Section 3 of the Robinson-Patman Act, the criminal section of the Act, declares illegal sales at unreasonably low prices "for the purpose of destroying competition or eliminating a competitor." A sale at an "unreasonably low price" has been judicially interpreted as a sale below cost. Although "cost" is difficult to determine, it appears that the courts will place less emphasis on its definition than on the predatory intent of the seller. Few cases have been brought under this section, but there has been at least one criminal conviction under this section.

Price Systems

At one time, the Federal Trade Commission questioned the legality of delivered pricing, taking the position that a price was illegally discriminatory if the "mill net" to the seller was different. The abandonment of the "mill net theory" has allowed the seller to adopt at his option either single price f.o.b. mill pricing or single price delivered pricing. Zone pricing or its variant, maximum-freight-absorption pricing, is also permissible, provided the zones are not arbitrarily determined to favor the large customer and there is a relation of transportation costs to the zone differentials.

Transfer Pricing. In vertically integrated companies, it is common to refer to the price at which a product is "sold" by a manufacturer to one of its corporate divisions. What occurs is a transfer of the goods at a cost arbitrarily determined by the common management. The use of the term "sold" merely creates a spurious basis for a claim of price discrimination by a nonintegrated customer of the manufacturer and is best avoided. A company does not "sell" a product to itself, and unless the seller is under a specific court order to the contrary, such a transfer price cannot support a claim of price discrimination.

Sales to subsidiaries, even when the subsidiaries are wholly owned, are true sales because different entities are involved. They may create a legal problem if made at a lower price than is charged other buyers. The safest practice is to have all such sales made at list price.

New-product and Test Pricing. When introducing a new product, a seller may experiment in his pricing and is free to choose his price without fear of the antitrust laws unless he has some predatory purpose. Test pricing of presently marketed products raises some problems under the Price Discrimination Act. Generally, however, test pricing in a separate market area for a limited period, free of predatory purpose, would not be a violation of the Act.

Deceptive Pricing

The Federal Trade Commission may proceed against deceptive pricing under its broad power to attack unfair methods of competition and unfair and deceptive acts under Section 5 of the Federal Trade Commission Act. Its purposes are to protect not only competitors but customers and the public generally.

For example, it is deceptive to promote a product as being sold at a price below "list" or "suggested" prices when, in fact, there has been no substantial number of sales at such prices. Similarly, preticketing a product at a price which dealers regularly sell below may be deceptive. Control of such situations, in the absence of an effective, legal fair trading program, involves the danger of violating the vertical price-fixing prohibitions of the Sherman Act.

The Federal Trade Commission has issued several guides and trade-practice rules on deceptive pricing, bait advertising, the use of the term "free," and similar practices relating to pricing. These guides and rules may be obtained from the Commission.

ANTICOMPETITIVE AGREEMENTS

Agreements among competitors not to compete in particular product lines or in particular territories or for particular customers are illegal per se under the Sherman Act. A limited exception to this per se rule exists where a seller of a business agrees as a condition of such sale to restrict his competitive activity in a limited territory for a limited time. Such an agreement may be reasonable and necessary to protect the buyer's investment.

A manufacturer or distributor may assign areas of primary marketing responsibility to his distributors or retailers, but, except under unusual circumstances, the assignment of rigid territorial and customer restrictions is illegal. No justification exists under the law for distributors and retailers to agree upon such restrictions among themselves.

Production Controls. Agreements to limit production are illegal per se. Their obvious purpose and effect are to stabilize, if not directly fix, prices.

Group Boycotts. It is not proper for competitors to boycott suppliers or customers. An agreement not to purchase from a particular supplier, or an agreement among retailers not to handle a particular manufacturer's goods or to sell to a particular distributor or retail outlet, is illegal. The law intends each businessman to make his business decisions individually.

TRADE ASSOCIATIONS

Trade associations serve many legitimate and useful purposes in industry. Membership in a trade association can be of major importance to the individual company. But the decision to join or remain in a trade association should be made only after careful consideration of the nature of the association and the potential impact of the antitrust laws.

Section 1 of the Sherman Act is violated when there is a combination or agreement among competitors to do any act which unreasonably restrains trade or commerce. A trade association is a voluntary combination of competitors which addresses itself to the common problems of its members and formulates and takes common action to protect their interests. The only missing element of violation of the law is the unreasonableness—as seen through the eyes of the law, not the businessman—of the agreement reached or action taken.

To the antitrust enforcement agencies, a trade association, by its very nature, is a suspect organization and subject to careful scrutiny at all times. In many of the criminal and civil proceedings based on illegal combinations and conspiracies, it has been alleged that trade associations were used, directly or indirectly, as an instrument for conspiracy.

Moreover, membership in even the most carefully supervised association involves hazards. Although the formal meetings may be controlled, it is difficult to control "rump" meetings and the general business chatter that inevitably takes place at social gatherings or on the golf course during the days set aside for annual or other meetings.

Illegal Activities. An association gives no immunity to its members to enter into any agreement or plan to fix, maintain, or stabilize prices; to allocate territories; to restrict production; to boycott offending members, distributors, or customers; or to do any other act which unreasonably restrains trade. To the contrary, the opportunity afforded for such agreements through a gathering of competitors is an area of prime suspicion.

Legal Activities. A program normally considered legal may be illegal when viewed in the context of all the surrounding facts. There are, however, some programs which normally involve minimum risks.

Trade associations are often the major spokesmen for industry views on the vast array of government activities which affect business. They also often afford a quick and effective means of cooperation with the government. Employee relations, including exchange of some information and industry-wide bargaining, is another common association activity. Associations may also be useful forums for common problems in the fields of air and water pollution, transportation, taxation, safety and health, research, industry advertising and promotion, and employee training programs.

Programs Requiring Careful Supervision. *Statistical Information.* The collection and distribution of statistical information of various types is a common and often useful activity of associations. Current and accurate business intelligence can have the very positive effect of enhancing competition. This is not true of a program which, by design or natural development, is intended (or can be interpreted as so intended in the light of circumstantial evidence) to fix or maintain prices or limit production.

It is safer for statistical programs to include general but not detailed information such as information as to individual companies. The information disseminated should be generally available to governmental agencies and all interested persons, including nonmembers and customers. There should be no interpretation of the data or recommendations of any kind.

Product Standardization and Uniform Specifications. Government agencies, particularly the defense agencies, have instigated many programs of product standardization and uniformity in product specifications. Many trade associations carry on active programs in this area. If justifiable for technical, safety, health, or other reasons beneficial to the public generally, they run little chance of violating the law. If one of the results of the standardization or uniformity is to stabilize prices or adversely affect competition, the program may run afoul of Section 1 of the Sherman Act or Section 5 of the Federal Trade Commission Act.

Policing Unfair Activities. Any indication of a boycott of competitors or distributors who violate association standards should be carefully avoided.

Checklist for Membership. It is prudent for any organization to make a careful business and legal review before joining any association. There should be a similar review periodically to test the association activities against the changes in the antitrust laws and the changing needs of the company in the light of the association's programs.

Every review should include a careful examination of the incorporation documents and bylaws of the association and the minutes of meetings. There should be a specific requirement that a lawyer knowledgeable in the antitrust field should be in constant attendance at all meetings with strong instructions to intervene instantly if any statement or act creates any risk of an appearance of an antitrust violation. No counsel should be retained who allows himself to be excluded from any meeting or condones "rump" meetings. If association counsel is not present, a member's representatives should be advised to leave the meeting with the fact and the reason stated clearly in the minutes.

Membership should be on an open and nondiscriminatory basis. The association should be administered by a highly professional and ethical staff.

Counsel should clear in advance all agendas and meeting programs and all reports and all speeches by association officers and members. Counsel should regularly stress the importance of compliance with the antitrust laws. Repetition in this area at effective intervals is essential.

Associations which meet more often than legitimate association activities demand should be suspect to any member or prospective member. There should be a demand for complete justification of a proliferation of local sections of an association with their own frequent meetings.

A company would be well advised to have its representation limited in number and restricted to those who are aware of the antitrust pitfalls. Representatives should be instructed to avoid "rump" sessions and any discussions, formal or informal, relating to sensitive antitrust areas. The minutes of all meetings and the nature of the association programs should be regularly reviewed by company counsel.

CUSTOMER RELATIONSHIPS

A seller has broad scope in the selection of his customers, but not without limits.

A seller must carry on his discussions with a prospective distributor concerning resale pricing carefully so as not to be subject to a charge of vertical price fixing, which is illegal unless it complies with fair trade laws. He may discuss his suggested resale-pricing policy, but he should avoid exacting any condition of compliance with that policy.

A seller may choose not to supply a customer for any reason, but he may not do so as part of a concerted agreement with a competitor or another customer.

It is still true that a manufacturer may cut off a distributor for poor performance, poor credit, and similar legitimate business purposes. Under the present state of the law, the use of customer reports of price cutting, price policing and tracing of price cutters, or a requirement that dealers sell only to "accredited" (or conforming) retailers may be sufficient evidence of vertical price fixing.

Territorial and Customer Restrictions. Protected territories and reserved customer lists involve substantial antitrust risks. With protected territories of questionable legality, manufacturers should rely on the assignment of areas of primary marketing responsibility. Although this accepts some territory crossing as normal, failure to concentrate on and develop the assigned territory can be used as a basis for cutting off the offending outlet.

Greater leeway is available in the case of patented articles, but the developing policies of the enforcement agencies and the trend in the law to limitations on patents indicate need for caution.

Some recent cases have raised questions as to the availability of agency and consignment sales systems as an alternate means of exerting marketing controls.

There are indications that territorial and customer restrictions will receive greater consideration if imposed by a failing company or one subject to strong, aggressive competition or if used by a small company entering a new market. The difficulty is that if the company using these exceptions becomes successful, a change in marketing approach will have to be made.

Product Restrictions.   Section 3 of the Clayton Act is aimed at specific marketing practices which either may substantially lessen competition or tend to create a monopoly.   In the usual case, a violation of this section is found only after full analysis of the product and geographic markets.   Any vertical marketing agreement affects commerce to some extent, but only those with a significant adverse effect are illegal.

Exclusive-dealing Agreements.   Contracts requiring customers to deal only in the supplier's products are illegal if the effect is to foreclose the supplier's competitors from a substantial share of the market.   A dominant supplier may not exact long-term exclusive-dealing contracts with a substantial number of distributors to such an extent that competition may be adversely affected.

Tying Sales.   Agreements conditioning the sale or lease of one product on the purchase of another are extremely questionable.   The situation usually arises where one of the products is insulated from competition by a patent or copyright, contains unique attributes, or is in short supply.   An owner of a patented machine may not condition its lease on the purchase of material to be used in connection with the machine.   A variant of this practice is "full-line forcing" under which the purchaser is required to take the full line of products manufactured by the seller if he wishes to take any.

Requirements and Output Contracts.   Such contracts may be questionable if they are of such size or significance as to foreclose or threaten foreclosure of competition in a substantial share of the market.   Factors considered are the relevant strength of the competitors, the duration of the contracts, the volume of the market involved, and the potential effect.   A rule of thumb has been that one-year contracts of even substantial size are legal, with the chances of illegality increasing as the contract term increases.

Special Customer Treatment

Promotional Allowances and Services.   In addition to prohibiting price discrimination, the Robinson-Patman Act declares it unlawful for a seller to discriminate among customers in granting advertising or promotional allowances or in furnishing merchandising services and facilities.   Any promotional or service program must be carefully tailored if it is to meet the exacting tests imposed by the Federal Trade Commission.

There is an affirmative duty on the part of the seller to notify all customers, preferably in writing, of the availability of the program; he cannot advise some and wait to be asked by others.   The program must be tailored to meet the needs of all customers.   A program will fail if it is completely unsuitable for some customers unless reasonable alternative plans are made available.   A program restricted to television advertising would be impracticable for the small retailer-customer.   These customers should be afforded an alternative such as local newspaper advertising or handbills.   The program must be made available to all on proportionately equal terms—to each according to his worth.   Normally this requirement will be satisfied if based on percentage of sales or dollars for a specified number of units.

Brokerage Payments.   The Robinson-Patman Act specifically prohibits the payment by a seller of brokerage or an allowance in lieu of brokerage to either the buyer directly or to any broker acting on behalf of the buyer or subject to his control.   Brokerage payments are proper only if the broker is an independent agent working for or receiving his compensation only from the person engaging him.   Brokers who are captives of buyers may not be paid commissions by the seller.   The prohibition applies to both the buyer and seller.

PATENTS

Patent Monopolies.   The Federal patent laws grant an inventor a limited monopoly under which he has the right to exclude all others from making, using, or selling his invention for the term of the patent grant.   The concept of patents runs contrary to the general policies of the Sherman and Clayton Acts adopted to prevent monopolies and unreasonable restraints on trade.   In a period of strong antitrust enforcement policies, it is not surprising that the patent monopoly has been subjected to increasing restrictions.

Accumulation of Patents.   A patentee may accumulate patents without limitation by his own research and development programs.   Acquisition of dominant patents in a particular market by purchase or exclusive-licensing arrangements with the intent to monopolize that market is illegal.   Grant-back provisions in license agreements, once common, are of extremely doubtful legality.   Patent pooling or cross-licensing arrangements may be illegal as having the effect of unreasonably restraining trade.   They will not have such effect if made available on reasonable terms to all others interested in participating.

Patent Licensing.   A patentee may share his monopoly with licensees and collect royalties from them.   He does not, however, have unrestrained control over his licensees and may not condition his license with unreasonable restraints.

Pricing.   So long as the patent owner retains the exclusive right to sell his patented product, he is free to determine its price.   However, he may not dictate its resale price.   Nor may he fix the price at which a licensee of a patented machine may sell unpatented products manufactured on that machine. There are legal authorities for the proposition that a patentee may fix the price at which a licensee sells a patented product, but reliance on such authorities would be unwise without first clearing with legal counsel.

Restrictive Provisions.   The inclusion of restrictive provisions in licenses—for example, exclusivity, production controls, territorial, customer, and end-use restrictions, and agreements not to contest validity of the licensed patent—should be carefully reviewed by patent and antitrust counsel.

Extension of Patents.   It is a violation of the antitrust laws to tie in the sale of an unpatented product with that of a patented product.   It is likewise illegal to require payments of royalties under a license to continue after the patent has expired, forcing a licensee to take a full package of patents, regardless of his needs or desires, or requiring him to pay full royalty rates for only a portion of the patents offered for licensing in an unreasonable extension of the patent monopoly.

PURCHASING

Buyers fare no better under Section 1 of the Sherman Act than sellers.   It is illegal for buyers to combine, conspire, or agree among themselves as to the price at which they will purchase a product.

Inducing Lower Prices.   Although the Robinson-Patman Act is primarily aimed at the sellers' activities, it also applies to buyers who knowingly induce or receive a discrimination in price.   There have been relatively few cases brought against buyers, but there have been indications that the Federal Trade Commission is examining buying practices of large buyers more carefully.   A purchasing agent who deliberately misinforms or misleads a seller as to an alleged lower competitive price is vulnerable to a charge of inducing an illegal discriminatory price.

Inducing Discriminatory Promotional Allowances and Services.   The Federal Trade Commission has successfully prosecuted several proceedings against large retail outlets, alleging illegal demand for special allowances and services from suppliers.   In a few instances, proceedings against sellers have been discontinued by the Commission for the announced reason of investigating the buyers' practices.

Reciprocity.   Sometimes referred to as "trade relations," reciprocity ranges from a mutual sale and purchase of products based on any set of facts ranging from outright resort to coercion by one of the parties, through a voluntary arrangement based on the idea of mutual backscratching.

Coercive reciprocity has long been held an unfair method of competition under Section 5 of the Federal Trade Commission Act.   Certain reciprocity practices have been held to be unreasonable restraints under Section 1 of the Sherman Act and as evidence of monopolization under Section 2 of the Sherman Act and of the illegality of mergers under Section 7 of the Clayton Act.

The line between the legal and illegal cannot be definitely drawn.   Coercive reciprocity based on a threat of withdrawal of substantial patronage unless the buyer's products are purchased is illegal.   The use of the practice, particularly by a company in a monopoly or dominant position in an industry, should be carefully controlled and limited.

FOREIGN ACTIVITIES

The Robinson-Patman Act and the Clayton Act's prohibitions against tying and requirements contracts do not apply to sales to customers in foreign countries, but they do apply to transactions with persons in United States possessions and territories.   It is doubtful that the Federal Trade Commission Act applies to "commerce with foreign nations," but Section 5 of the Act has been applied to foreign activities of a United States citizen found injurious to exports by his United States competitors.   Section 7 of the Clayton Act has not been applied to a merger with, or acquisition of, a foreign business, but it may be applicable to an acquisition resulting in substantial lessening of competition in the United States.

The Sherman Act prohibits monopolies and conspiracies in restraint of "trade or commerce among the several states or with foreign nations."   This language defines jurisdiction and indicates the markets in which antitrust problems will be analyzed.   Some writers restrict the application of the law to matters clearly affecting exports and imports, but this may not be the law.   To be safe, "trade and commerce" should be considered as including all forms of commercial activity abroad if there may be a direct or substantial effect upon the trade and commerce between this country and foreign nations.

The United States Supreme Court has invalidated a contract made abroad by a United States company with a foreign company under our antitrust laws. Even though the contract was carried out abroad to a substantial extent, the Court found an illegal restrictive effect on our foreign commerce.

Although there are relatively few cases, it is clear that some acts must be avoided in international trade even though there may be competitive handicaps in dealing with foreign businessmen. Among the precluded acts are allocation of markets, allotment of customers, stabilizing of prices, regulating production, or agreeing not to do business with others.

Some foreign countries and the European Common Market Treaty have laws or regulations comparable in some respects to our antitrust laws. Enforcement by other jurisdictions, however, has not approached the enforcement in this country.

An exemption from the Sherman Act is provided by the Webb-Pomerene Act of 1958. This Act provides for the establishment of export associations that may fix prices of products for export within the narrow confines of the Act. Associations created under the law are few in number and are subject to close control by the Federal Trade Commission and the Department of Justice.

A Webb-Pomerene export association may require its competing member (which may not include a foreign competitor) to agree to sell at fixed prices for export or to sell only through the association for sale abroad. It may also establish some limitations and restrictions on distributors in foreign countries to prohibit the sale by such distributors of products of nonmembers of the association.

CORPORATE GROWTH

Monopolization. A monopoly obtained by legal and ethical business practices, such as by building the better mousetrap, is not per se illegal. Product or geographic market dominance obtained by predatory business practices with an intent to monopolize is illegal. A competitor may not justify his market dominance if he has engaged in ruthless competitive activities such as discriminatory pricing policies intended to destroy competitors, wholesale acquisition or suppression of competitors and patents, or coercive reciprocity practices.

Acquisitions and Mergers. Section 7 of the Clayton Act declares it illegal for a corporation to merge with or acquire the stock or assets of another corporation where, in any line of commerce in any section of the country, the effect may be to lessen competition substantially. Mergers and acquisitions are generally classified as horizontal (involving competitors), vertical (involving a supplier or customer), or conglomerate (involving diversification or product-line or market extension). Each may be illegal under Section 7 if the requisite adverse competitive effect is found.

Basic to the determination of legality are the product and geographical markets, including submarkets. Some additional factors to be considered are the relative sizes of the merging companies, both in gross and by market shares, the merger histories of the industry and the corporations involved, the extent markets may be foreclosed to others, the intent of the parties, the ease of entry into the market, and reciprocity potentials.

Horizontal mergers or acquisitions, unless of insignificant size or involving a failing company, are most vulnerable.

Joint Enterprises. A joint enterprise, involving product and geographic markets in which joining companies have substantial competitive positions, may be found unlawful. Joint enterprises that involve competitors seeking to develop new products or new geographic markets, or noncompetitors wishing to join in an enterprise related to their present business, may be illegal if the opportunity for potential competition is thereby eliminated.

ANTITRUST COMPLIANCE PROGRAM

Every company would be well advised to institute an antitrust compliance program. The sophistication of the program should be the subject of careful consideration by management and counsel.

A compliance program may range from occasional policy reminders for selected managerial and sales personnel of general antitrust principles and company policy to regular educational programs, detailed antitrust audits by counsel, and formal internal control procedures. The choice of any program will depend on a number of factors such as the size of the company; its market position; the nature of the business—manufacturer, distributor, or retailer; the nature of the marketing problems; and the existence of a history of antitrust investigations or proceedings in the industry or against the company. A compliance program is essential if a company is operating under an outstanding court decree or commission order.

Basic to any program is the attitude of top management. Without the complete support and sympathetic understanding of the antitrust laws by management, no compliance program—no matter how sophisticated—will succeed. This support must be reiterated often and demonstrated in many ways constantly and consistently so that other employees accept compliance with the laws as a major company policy. Lip service only is never effective.

CONCLUSION

The antitrust laws were designed to keep free enterprise alive and healthy. There have been, and will continue to be, many criticisms of specific provisions of the laws and the policies of enforcement as being contradictory to other basic provisions or anticompetitive. It is alleged that in some instances the law protects a competitor instead of competition.

The many complicated realities of the marketplace and the balancing of equities necessary to maintain free enterprise in a constantly changing economy will inevitably create problems. It is recommended that every businessman acquire a general knowledge of the laws and a good acquaintance with those portions that affect his day-to-day business.

Any set of laws regulating such a complicated activity as business must of necessity be difficult to understand and apply. A lawyer will be needed to help with most of the antitrust problems. The laws are designed for the overall long-range benefit of the business community. The manager should know enough about them to comply and to ask for legal advice when needed.

BIBLIOGRAPHY

Van Cise, Jerrold G., *The Federal Antitrust Laws*, American Enterprise Institute for Public Policy Research, Washington, D.C., July, 1965.

SECTION FOURTEEN

OFFICE ADMINISTRATION

CHAPTER ONE

Office Planning, Layout, and Facilities

RICHARD L. FORSTER *Vice President and Director of Planning, Frederic R. Harris, Inc., New York, New York*

Planning for the physical facilities which are to house the business is an accepted practice of modern management. As with other staff functions, however, the place of the planning function in the organization structure varies, as does the designation by which it is called. Generally, if it is specifically identified, it will be known as "facilities planning," and as such may include planning for plants and other properties as well as for offices. This chapter will be confined to office planning, layout, and facilities, but the terms "office planning" and "facilities planning" will be used interchangeably.

Office planning is both a management and a technical function. Because it involves providing the physical facilities in which the specialized activities of the specific business are to be performed, each planning program will have its own unique problems and approaches. Nevertheless, there are certain basic techniques upon which all planning must be based. This chapter will treat with the application of those techniques.

Planning is an integral part of the building process, as well as a useful tool for efficient office administration. Carrying out a planning program therefore requires a considerable understanding both of business practices and procedures and of building construction. This chapter presupposes such familiarity on the part of the reader; where it does not exist, reference is suggested to handbooks or other publications covering the specific subjects on which more detailed explanation is required.

This chapter will cover first a brief discussion of the approach to planning, then an explanation of some specialized techniques which are basic to planning and the data gathering for it, and finally an outline of a comprehensive program for planning a new office building project. It is recognized that many readers will be denied the luxury of "beginning at the beginning" as this outline suggests. However, the basic elements which must be included in any planning project are included in this program. To make an adaptation, it will be necessary only to eliminate the items which are not pertinent and thus construct a working outline for the specific project.

APPROACH TO PLANNING

Office planning and the layout and facilities which result from it are the foundation necessary for a continuing program of effective space administration which has as its objective providing and maintaining facilities which are useful and correct for the organization throughout the term of occupancy of the premises. Without the proper job of planning, attainment of such an objective is difficult if not impossible, and is always unnecessarily expensive. There is seldom much difference in first costs in providing the right amount of space in the right places with the right kind of facilities, if plans are made to build them correctly in the first place. Once built, however, the costs of demolition and disruption must be added to the higher costs of patching, painting, and cleanup around existing installations which also must be protected against damage.

Failure to provide space of the optimum effectiveness is also poor economy from an operations standpoint. Inefficiencies caused by poorly planned space—excessive walking distances, awkward communications, disturbances from over-crowding, poor lighting in critical areas, bad noise control or ventilation, to mention just a few—cost far more than the original planning which would have prevented them. These inefficiencies are not one-time costs. They recur every day the space is used, every time the operation they affect is repeated. Thus it may be said that the cost of planning is inescapable—either by positive action where the benefits may be enjoyed and the costs recaptured through improved operations, or by default where the penalty is exacted and the price paid in unnecessary operating costs which cannot be recaptured.

Office planning is a staff function which must cut impartially across all departmental lines. Decisions regarding the use and treatment of space must not only have company-wide consistency, but must also consider both short-term and long-term company objectives and plans. Such decisions can only be a reflection of management policy. A prime requisite for an effective planning program is top management guidance and support, implemented with clearly defined company objectives.

The planner finds himself in a difficult role in the technical side of office planning. He is the coordinating link between the organization and the various engineering and technical specialists. In his plans, he must develop the potential areas of application and the basic requirements for the installation. Then he must participate in the final judgments as to what and how much will be provided.

The planner can be neither as proficient as the engineer or technician nor as knowledgeable about operations as the departmental personnel charged with responsibility for a function. Nor should he try to be. But, by knowing what is available, and by introducing the appropriate outside expert into the situation at the proper time, he is assured of a correct start. Then by following developments and continually measuring them against the broader company objectives, by applying cost-benefit analyses to results to be secured, and by checking amortization of installation costs against the programmed space occupancy, he has definite criteria upon which to base the program and to support recommendations for expenditures.

A final word of caution: Advances in technology, new processes, and new equipment are regularly being announced in every field. The planner can hardly hope to keep abreast of all of them—or to know of the things being worked on but not yet announced. The specter of providing an office which is up to date today and out of date next year confronts the planner who attempts to rely on his own knowledge to the exclusion of outside advice. Reliance on outside sources is not a weakness in the planner; it is a guarantee of strength.

TECHNIQUES OF THE PLANNER

In contrast to the foregoing, there are basic techniques which are the sole responsibility of the planner. Because the information to be developed through the use of them provides the base upon which the entire program rests, it is not possible to overstress the importance of understanding both the techniques and the philosophies underlying them.

Space Requirements. The first fundamental to remember in accumulating space requirements is that although office buildings are for people, it is the equipment which the people use that determines the amount of space that must be provided. This is why the question "How many square feet per person should be provided?" provides such meaningless answers. The clerk who uses a desk and a posture chair is automatically taken care of when space is provided for the equipment. So also is the senior clerk who may need a desk, a table, a side chair, and a two-drawer file; or the supervisor with his small functional office. Obviously, it is the "mix" which establishes the average, and the mix will vary by size of company, type of business, or any of a host of other reasons.

It is also important to recognize that the kind and amount of equipment which should be provided are those which will contribute most to helping the employee perform his job. This is one of the ways to maximize the return on the payroll dollar. As long as stock equipment items are used, it will be found that total workplace costs are usually well below 10 percent of just one year's salary of the employee using it. The objective of the planner should be neither to give nor to deny, but rather to provide that which the function indicates is needed to do the job—no less, and certainly no more.

The above is not meant to suggest a detailed workplace analysis for each position. This is more appropriately the function of the systems and procedures specialist. Besides, there usually is not time for such detailed analysis when a major space-planning program is under way. Provision of space for standard equipment—desks, tables, side chairs, files, bookcases, and the like, with adequate clearances and access aisles—will provide the basic space in which subsequent refinements can be made as and when they can be justified.

It will be helpful in accumulating requirements data if a chart such as that shown in part by Figure 1-1 is prepared to show various workplace arrangements. The alphabetical key provides a convenient identification to use during the survey. The arithmetic can be better performed at a desk, with an adding machine close at hand.

There is no mystery or difficulty in accumulating space requirements for the organization as it exists at the time of the study. The thing always to remember is that present requirements are not the amount of space which is presently being occupied, but rather the amount of space which is needed for the equipment which people should have, without crowding and with adequate access and aisle space. Of all the mistakes made in planning, this one probably occurs the most frequently, is the most serious, and is the least excusable.

Space Requirements Form. All that the right answer requires is time, manpower, and a logical system for recording the data which is accumulated. A form which provides such a system of recording is shown by Figure 1-2. Every

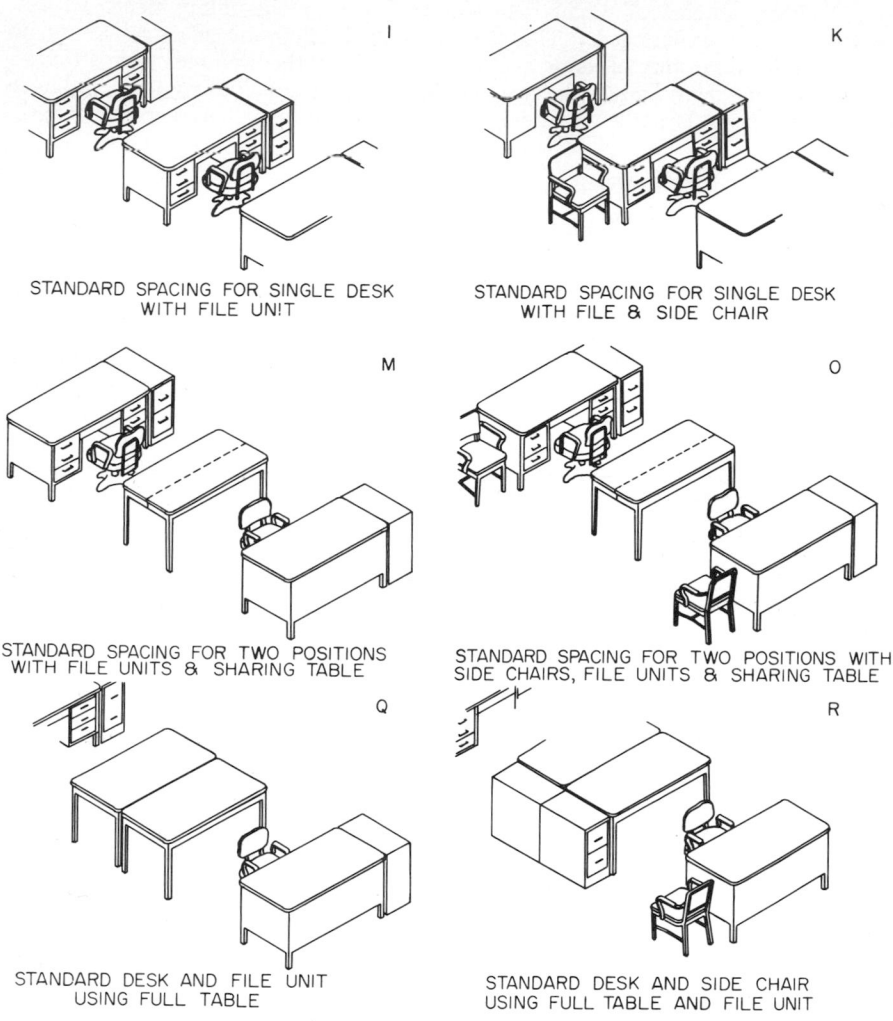

STANDARD SPACING FOR SINGLE DESK
WITH FILE UNIT

STANDARD SPACING FOR SINGLE DESK
WITH FILE & SIDE CHAIR

STANDARD SPACING FOR TWO POSITIONS
WITH FILE UNITS & SHARING TABLE

STANDARD SPACING FOR TWO POSITIONS WITH
SIDE CHAIRS, FILE UNITS & SHARING TABLE

STANDARD DESK AND FILE UNIT
USING FULL TABLE

STANDARD DESK AND SIDE CHAIR
USING FULL TABLE AND FILE UNIT

FIG. 1-1. *Some typical office arrangements, showing alphabetical key for convenience in entering on space requirements form.*

approved employee position must be accounted for on the form. The term "approved employee" is very important. Every organization has turnover, and on any given day there are employees who are getting ready to leave, others who will not report for a week or two. The number of positions in each department, section, and subsection should be ascertained before space requirements are taken. Then, as a safeguard, the supervisor in charge should approve both the number of positions, the arrangements, and the space allocations after the study has been completed.

The planner, or one of his staff, should always make the survey and complete the forms. It is not a satisfactory practice to leave the form with the department head to be completed and picked up later. In altogether too many instances, the form will reflect what now exists, not what should be there. Improved

SPACE REQUIREMENTS

CLIENT		
DEPARTMENT/DIVISION	SECTION	UNIT
PREPARED BY — DATE	APPROVED BY — DATE	

LINE NO.	FUNCTIONAL TITLE	EMPLOYEE'S NAME (INDICATE IF VACANCY EXISTS)	FUNC. REL.	PERSONNEL WORK AREA: KEY	PERSONNEL WORK AREA: SQ. FT. 1	EQUIPMENT: ITEM	EQUIPMENT: UNIT SIZE: HEIGHT	UNIT SIZE: WIDTH 2	UNIT SIZE: DEPTH 3	UNIT FLOOR AREA (2X3) 4	UNIT WORK SQ.FT. AREA 5	TOTAL UNIT SQ. FT. AREA (4+5) 6	NO. OF UNITS 7	TOTAL SQ. FT. (6X7) 8	OTHER AREAS: CONF. CONT. 9	OTHER AREAS: 10	OTHER AREAS: 11	GRAND TOTAL 1+8+9 +10+11	ADDITIONAL REQUIRED AT FIRST PROJECTION	ADDITIONAL REQUIRED AT SECOND PROJECTION	LINE NO.
1																					1
2																					2
3																					3
4																					4
5																					5
6																					6
21																					21
22																					22
23																					23
24																					24
		TOTALS																			

TOTAL EMPLOYEES	THIS PAGE M	THIS PAGE F	THIS SECTION M	THIS SECTION F	CUMULATIVE M	CUMULATIVE F
1. NOW ON PAYROLL						
2. ADD. NOW REQUIRED						
3. ADD. REQ. AT FIRST PROJ.						
4. ADD. REQ. AT SECOND PROJ.						
TOTALS						

TOTALS			
THIS PAGE			
THIS SECTION			
CUMULATIVE			

FIG. 1-2. *Suggested form for accumulating space requirements.*

working conditions are taken for granted, and it is assumed that all deficiencies will somehow be corrected when move-in time comes. The result will be that the department just will not fit in the space which has been allocated—and it is the planner's fault, and his problem.

Providing for Expansion. There are many ways of providing for growth, and any one of them has a chance of at least "being in the ball park," provided the expansion space is in addition to the correct "present requirements" figure. Obviously, growth is more orderly in some companies than in others. In companies with volatile business swings, it becomes pointless to make detailed projections when a simple percentage allowance would stand the same chance of being correct. The justification for analytical studies can usually be determined by looking at business volumes and payrolls over the five most recent years. If a reasonably orderly growth pattern is indicated, there is a technique for projecting future requirements that the planner will find most useful.

The key to making space projections is to relate growth in requirements to a percentage of change from the present—never by periods of years. A five-year forecast means one thing to the optimist, quite a different one to the pessimist. On the other hand, a 10 percent increase in work load, as and when it occurs, is a definite thing which is not subject to differences in interpretation.

What is required is to determine work volumes by departments and sections at the existing level of business activity. Care must be taken to express work load in terms of the work which the department actually performs. Dollars of sales volume do not represent work load. Orders processed, bills of lading checked, customers served, bills issued, and other such specific work items are meaningful and can be translated into numbers of employees required for varying volumes. Starting with the basic growth index which the company as a whole uses, derivative load indexes will need to be established for the various departments and sections of the organization. Correlation with periods in the past few years will serve as a validity check for the indexes which are thus established.

With the work load indicators established for the existing level of activity, the basic index can be changed to reflect company goals or reasonable expectations of growth—expressed in terms of percent of the present. One, two, or even three projection levels can be established, and the work loads calculated for the organization at those levels. These are then translated into employees to be added, which in turn means increased space requirements. Then, and only then, should years be added to growth stages—and these will merely represent the goals toward which the company is aiming. The matching of the target years to the growth percentages may and probably will change, for no one possesses the key to the future. To the planner, this is unimportant—he can revise his space availability every year, and he will always know where he stands.

The form for accumulating space requirements contains columns for adding projection information. Because space is required by specific categories of employees with differing equipment needs, expansion requirements should be shown by the addition of specific positions with their appropriate space arrangements. Use of the form makes it easy to follow this practice.

A typical summary of space projections as they might appear on a consolidated work sheet is shown by Figure 1-3. Not shown, but obviously required, are the detailed backup tabulations for the positions in each of the departments listed.

Layouts. Much has been written about the art of preparing layouts, and for that reason it is not repeated here. What is important to remember is

Summary of Home Office Space and Personnel Allocations Now Existing and Required at Various Levels of Business Growth

Division	Space (net usable in square feet)						
	Presently		Percentage difference	First projection required	Percentage difference (over presently required)	Second projection required	Percentage difference (over presently required)
	Occupied	Required					
Operations.............	64,011	105,910	65.4	107,088	1.1	118,674	12.1
Security research........	11,938	14,128	18.3	16,460	16.5	17,349	22.9
Administrative..........	10,514	15,902	51.2	17,113	7.6	17,682	11.2
Sales.................	10,490	10,822	3.2	11,478	6.1	12,487	15.4
Commodity............	3,071	3,548	15.5	3,647	2.8	3,647	2.8
Underwriting...........	4,871	5,740	17.8	6,391	11.3	6,391	11.3
Management/executive..	4,794	5,740	19.7	5,965	3.9	5,965	3.9
Home office/foreign.....	4,296	4,993	16.2	5,902	18.2	6,481	29.8
Nondepartmental.......	2,256	5,591	147.8	5,921	5.9	6,331	13.2
Subtotal.............	116,241	172,374	48.3	179,965	4.4	195,007	13.1
Utility................	28,484	58,510	....	60,666	3.7	64,241	9.8
Total...............	144,725	230,884	59.5	240,631	4.2	259,248	12.3

Division	Personnel						
	Presently		Percentage difference	First projection required	Percentage difference (over presently required)	Second projection required	Percentage difference (over presently required)
	On payroll	Required					
Operations.............	1,577	1,727	9.5	1,872	8.4	2,126	23.1
Security research........	177	191	7.9	240	25.7	260	36.1
Administrative..........	91	98	7.7	117	19.4	127	29.6
Sales.................	147	153	4.1	167	9.2	192	25.5
Commodity............	35	38	8.6	39	2.6	39	2.6
Underwriting...........	37	37	0.0	43	16.2	43	16.2
Management/executive..	23	25	8.6	30	20.0	30	20.0
Home office/foreign.....	68	78	14.7	96	23.1	109	39.7
Nondepartmental.......	1	1	0.0	1	0.0	1	0.0
Subtotal.............							
Utility							
Total...............	2,156	2,348	8.9	2,605	10.9	2,927	24.7

NOTE: "Presently occupied" is the net space now occupied, excluding such utility and waste areas as main corridors, columns, elevators, elevator lobbies, escalators, stairs, janitor closets, lavatories, and the like.

FIG. 1–3. *A typical consolidated summary of space projections.*

that there are a number of layouts to be prepared—not just one. First is the "block layout," which shows only total areas for organizational components (departments, sections, or subsections), private offices, and fixed installations such as telephone rooms, machine rooms, toilets, lounges, reception areas, cafeterias, and the like. No detail is shown; hence, a scale of ⅟₁₆ inch equals 1 foot is most convenient to work with at this point, because the objective is to show total allocations and relationships.

The second layout is the working one in which equipment placement and arrangements will be studied. It is also the one which will be used for discussion with departments, and which management will ultimately approve. A scale of ¼ inch equals 1 foot is most satisfactory at this point because this is the scale familiar to most people, and it is the largest which it is practicable to use.

Succeeding drawings will be for the purpose of transmitting information to the professionals and technicians designing and building the space. A scale of ⅛ inch equals 1 foot is most commonly used at this point because of the more convenient-size drawing which results.

It should not be necessary to point out that all layouts should be drawn accurately to scale. It will not be possible to show dimensions in any but the most critical areas or the drawing will be hopelessly cluttered with numbers. Lines and distances between lines will therefore be scaled, and the building will be constructed from them. This is a part of the reason for the difference in scales used—at ⅟₁₆ inch equals 1 foot, a carelessly angled pencil can mean an error of a full foot. An experienced draftsman is often a good investment in preparing layout drawings.

OUTLINE OF A PROGRAM FOR AN OFFICE BUILDING PROJECT

The purpose of the following outline is to present a comprehensive list of items which will have to be considered at some time or other between the time that a major change in office facilities is first contemplated and the day the company moves into the new facility. The items are presented without designation of the parties responsible for various phases of the work. Projects of lesser magnitude than this outline contemplates can be prepared by eliminating the items which are not pertinent.

Generally, a project of this type falls into three major steps.
1. Establishment of a course of action
2. Facilities planning
3. Design

The subdivision of effort into these three stages permits the program to develop logically and progressively, and enables it to be completely developed and evaluated before the company is required to make any major contractual commitments.

Establishment of a Course of Action. Prior to the start of any specific planning, define the need, scope, and most effective means of achieving an agreed-upon plan. This will include the following:
1. Review the company's present organization, policies, and operating practices, and consider changes which may be desirable or possible in connection with any relocation of headquarters operations.
2. Determine the company's headquarters office requirement in terms of kind and amounts of space and facilities. At this stage, go into only as much detail as necessary to define the nature and scope of a possible new office

building project to permit management decisions on the operating and economic feasibility of the program.

Facilities Planning. If the first step indicates that a new headquarters office building is in the best interests of the company, facilities planning becomes concerned with the development of the most effective plan for providing the new facilities. This involves the following.

1. *Review present operations*

    a. Make a detailed physical survey of all areas now occupied by activities to be accounted for in the planning. Confine examinations to operations within existing systems which may affect space requirements. If necessary, set up coordinated studies to evaluate the effectiveness of existing procedures and systems. Prepare up-to-date drawings of the company's present space indicating the location of all departments, functions, individuals by name and job title, furniture, and equipment.

    b. Observe and record personnel activity, and review with department heads the proper flow of work within their units, the interrelationship between units and individuals, and the requirements to carry on present levels of activity without regard to existing conditions.

    c. If observed personnel activity does not appear to agree with prescribed procedures, it may be necessary to conduct a detailed traffic survey to record the actual contact between components (in-person visits, interoffice mail, and telephone) to define actual working relationships which will need to be either provided for in a new facility or modified by the company.

    d. Evaluate and compile all data gathered in the survey and tabulate for reference use. The information gathered in the survey will:

        (1) Be the basis for establishing the functional needs and the workspace requirements of each employee.

        (2) Ensure that all necessary functions have been considered and that no functions will be planned for if they are found to be unnecessary as a result of consolidation or improved arrangements.

        (3) Provide a basis for determining requirements not only for operating at the present level of business activity, but also for future levels of activity as projected by the company.

        (4) Provide a basis for determining the effect of consolidating at a single location clerical and office functions which may presently be located in widely scattered areas.

        (5) Determine whether any functions now located in the present building should possibly be located elsewhere.

2. *Basic workplace arrangements*

    a. Develop workplace arrangements for each position on the basis of a functional analysis of assigned tasks rather than on the basis of present arrangements. Consider the applicability of new and advanced design in office furniture and equipment. Evaluate the adequacy of existing furniture and equipment and, where necessary, indicate the need for different and additional equipment.

    b. Develop standard arrangements to provide optimum facilities for all work units. Specify basic workplace arrangements for private and general offices, conference areas, equipment areas, and the like.

    c. To achieve flexibility in the arrangement of functions, translate requirements for the various work positions into standard space allowances developed on a modular basis which can be adapted to the column and window spacing of the premises to be occupied.

3. *Determine present space requirements*
   a. Tabulate by organizational component all personnel, equipment, and facilities required for the proper performance of the company's work at the present level of business activity. Consider job vacancies; allow for planned changes in organization or procedures which may not yet have been instituted in anticipation of the present plans to move.
   b. On the basis of space allowances established in 2 above, determine the space required to accommodate each organization component.
4. *Determine future space requirements.* On the basis of information developed for present levels of business activity, project future space requirements of the operation to be accommodated for anticipated growth stages of company activity.
   a. Where possible, establish applicable "yardsticks" for determining the probable effect of changes in the company's activities upon space requirements. This may involve some statistical analyses of company operations to establish correlations and relationships in various phases of company growth which will serve as patterns from which future growth may be projected.
   b. Apply "yardsticks" of company growth established above to all activities by growth stages from the present level to the anticipated maximum to be considered in the planning program.
   c. Arrange all information developed for the projection of future requirements in tabular or graphic form whereby it can serve as reference material for the present planning program, as well as a valuable reference for future use by management.
   d. Consider the probability of changes in organization or operating practices and adjust projections accordingly.
5. *Develop functional relationships.* Analyze the working relationships within and among departments. Where necessary, prepare flow diagrams to illustrate significant operations affecting space.
   a. Determine the proper locations of departments based on functional effectiveness, rather than individual preference, prestige, or special influence.
   b. Discover any unusual situations which might require special space arrangements.
   c. Determine whether any presently maintained relationship will be modified by the application of new or advanced devices or technology; for example, facsimile transmission, high-speed reference devices, or closed-circuit television.
6. *Develop ideal grouping of components.* Develop a theoretically perfect arrangement of components, with only general regard to architectural limitations, to establish a functional ideal. Compromises may have to be made to arrange the various departments within the physical limits of the premises to be occupied.
7. *Prepare performance or end-product specifications.* This is to be prepared for all items bearing upon the effective utilization of the premises, including but not limited to the following:
   a. Illumination and color,
   b. Electrical power—supply and distribution,
   c. Communications,
   d. Heating, ventilating, and air conditioning,
   e. Sound conditioning,

    f. Walls, partitions, and other space dividers,
    g. Floor covering,
    h. Toilets and plumbing,
    i. Surface treatment,
    j. Vertical transport,
    k. Food service,
    l. Building services,
   m. Parking,
   n. Access, and
   o. Emergency.
  In the planning stage, these specifications should be broad and indicate only the conditions or effect to be created in the various areas within the premises. For example, under illumination, the quality and intensity of lighting required for the performance of a function will be specified rather than a type of fixture.

 8. Arrange all data developed in the planning stage into a statement of the company's requirements suitable for use by an architect.

 9. Evaluate available locations and sites with respect to their capacity to meet the company's requirements.

 10. Prepare preliminary time and cost estimates based on data developed in the planning stage.

 Design. The design stage of the program will be concerned with translating the statement of requirements developed in the planning stage into a set of plans and specifications from which a building tailor-made to the company's requirements can be constructed. This will generally involve the following steps.

 1. *Select architect, engineers, and other outside specialists*
   a. Establish criteria for selection.
   b. List those to be considered.
   c. Evaluate qualifications.
   d. Select.

 2. *Establish procedures*
   a. Define working relationships and scope of responsibility of all parties associated with the project.
   b. Establish procedures for the transmission and exchange of information, including required controls and records.
   c. Establish a performance schedule indicating time requirements and target dates for various phases of the work. This schedule will be tentative at first and will become more definitive as the full scope of the work evolves and the capacity of various groups becomes known.
   d. Establish a program of report sessions to keep the company informed on progress of the work, to ensure complete and free exchange of thinking, and to ascertain that data developed as a basis for design are complete and accurate.
   e. Maintain planning consultation and review of work throughout the design and implementation stages to ensure that decisions developed in the planning stage are completely and accurately carried out.

 3. *Prepare preliminary building plans.* On the basis of data developed in the planning stage, prepare preliminary plans of the building showing:
   a. General conformation of the building;
   b. Relation of the building to the site;
   c. General arrangement of the interior of the building; and

d. Provision for accommodating the company's growth requirements either through recapture of space leased to others during initial occupancy or through additional construction.

4. *Analyze the premises to be occupied.* On the basis of preliminary building design:

   a. Determine the best adaptability of different areas to fit the requirements of the various functions.

   b. Establish dimensions for typical private offices of various sizes which can be most effectively fitted to the building's column and window spacing. Determine most effective basic grouping of general office areas for typical building bays. Apply this information to the standard space allocation established for basic workplace arrangements.

   c. Determine which floors and locations within the building are best suited for special areas such as the executive offices, board rooms, and other areas requiring special decorative treatments, and also for the fixed or costly-to-move functions such as telephone equipment, automatic data processing, kitchens, and dining rooms.

   d. Determine optimum basic arrangement of aisles, corridors, and service areas. Consider the need for flexibility and interchangeability of areas to accommodate changing requirements throughout the period of occupancy.

5. *Prepare a long-range occupancy schedule of the premises.* This will permit an orderly expansion of the company's operations. Consider the following:

   a. The initial arrangement of space with provision for growth into reserve areas.

   b. The arrangement for future stages showing expansion into optioned or recaptured space and the corresponding shift of departments and functions.

   c. Fixed functions and facilities which may limit flexibility, such as the communications center, executive offices, cafeteria, heavy equipment areas, mechanical conveyors, and so on.

   d. The relative advantage of expanding functions horizontally versus vertically within one building.

   e. Arrangement of space to be made available for rental to others during the initial occupancy; or alternatively, the arrangement of space to be made available through additional construction.

   f. Interim moves of departments in the course of rearrangement.

6. *Prepare preliminary interior layouts.* Immediately following, and in some areas concurrently with, preliminary building design and the establishment of the building occupancy schedule, prepare area block layouts (1/16 inch equals 1 foot) for each growth stage to be considered, showing:

   a. The location and outline of the area to be occupied by each organizational component;

   b. The general location within each area of private offices and other enclosed areas;

   c. The number of persons and square feet of space allocated to each component; and

   d. The basic aisle and corridors pattern.

7. *Make necessary revisions.* On the basis of analysis, long-range occupancy, and preliminary layouts (3, 4, and 5 above), revise preliminary building plans, as necessary, until an overall building program is approved by the company.

8. *Prepare final building plans.* On the basis of preliminary plans approved by the company, prepare final architectural and engineering plans and specifications necessary for the construction and finishing of the building and grounds, but not the interior areas of the building which are to be occupied by the company.

9. *Prepare final interior layouts*

   a. Upon approval of preliminary interior layouts prepared in 6 above, prepare final interior layouts of all areas to be occupied by the company. These should be ¼-inch scale, and should be approved by the affected departments and by management, before proceeding with succeeding steps.

   b. Upon approval of the layouts, prepare final layout drawings (⅛-inch scale) for the move-in growth stage, showing:

   (1) Location of all departments, functions, and individuals;

   (2) Furniture, machines, equipment, files, storage areas, vaults, dumbwaiters, conveyors, chutes, closets, and wardrobes;

   (3) Electrical and telephone outlets, lighting;

   (4) Fixed and movable walls, partitions, and other space dividers;

   (5) Private lavatories, water closets, water coolers; and

   (6) Information pertinent to the effective performance of operations.

10. *Prepare interior plans.* Prepare working drawings and specifications and other related information necessary for the construction and furnishing of the premises in accordance with decisions established in the planning stage and in accordance with approved interior layouts. The drawings are to provide the following information:

    a. Interior construction. Description and location, with plans, elevations, and details as required, of:

    (1) Walls and partitions, fixed or movable, of masonry, wood, metal, or other materials;

    (2) Doors and other openings;

    (3) Carpentry and cabinet work; and

    (4) Special facilities.

    b. Structural. Show the changes to the basic structure of the building necessary to accommodate any unusual loadings or requirements. Include such items as additional reinforcings to accommodate heavy equipment and the telephone room and other areas requiring unusually heavy machines or equipment.

    Show all structural changes required to accommodate special stairways, vertical conveyors, and the like.

    c. Electrical. Show the location and description of underfloor duct work for both high tension (110 volts) and low tension (communications) plus location of all floor outlets for same.

    Show wall and base outlets, special electric circuits (if required), and boxes and cabinets for telephone relays, connection strips, and the like.

    d. Communication (telephone and intercom)

    (1) Location of all instruments;

    (2) Name and line number of each user;

    (3) Wiring plans and bridges; and

    (4) Layout of communication equipment rooms.

    e. Ceiling

    (1) Detailed lighting layouts, locating and specifying lighting equipment required to achieve established design levels of illumination and the necessary switch controls;

   (2) Location of air-conditioning grills, registers, and diffusers plus air volumes required to maintain design conditions; and

   (3) Ceiling finish, indicating location and description of plastered, acoustical, and special ceiling treatment.

f. Mechanical

   (1) Plumbing fixtures and associated roughing for facilities such as water coolers, lavatories, water closets, kitchen equipment, darkroom equipment, first aid room, and other special areas;

   (2) Materials handling facilities such as dumbwaiters, hoists, chutes, conveyors, and pneumatic tube systems;

   (3) Blowers and exhaust equipment other than standard air-conditioning equipment; and

   (4) Kitchen, darkroom, and laboratory equipment.

g. Furniture and furnishings

   (1) Location and description of all furniture, office equipment, and machines, indicating which is new and which is to be transferred from present location;

   (2) Names and job titles of personnel;

   (3) Location code numbers;

   (4) Location and description of carpet and/or special floor coverings;

   (5) Window draperies; and

   (6) Special materials for furnishings.

h. Schedule of finishes. Specify material, color, and type of finish of all walls, floors, ceilings, and other surfaces.

i. Schedule of doors and hardware

j. Specifications. As necessary to supplement information outlined above.

k. Interior design of special areas

   (1) Executive offices,

   (2) Board room,

   (3) Auditorium (if any),

   (4) Executive dining room,

   (5) Cafeteria (if any),

   (6) Reception areas,

   (7) Lobbies, and

   (8) Others.

Develop basic layouts of above areas according to functional requirements.

Prepare preliminary sketches and renderings for submission to management.

Prepare final design drawings of special areas: plans, elevations, and details; color schemes; material and fabric samples; and detail drawings of special furniture and equipment.

The program described will result in a completely developed plan for a new headquarters office building. The company, at this point, can evaluate the total plan and make its final determination without having incurred any contractual commitments other than for services incident to the development of the plan and the securing of options for properties it might be considering.

CONCLUSION

Planning for the office and the facilities which will make the office an effective place in which the functions of the business can be carried out is a complex undertaking. It involves competence as a planner, an understanding of the business, and a knowledge of building construction. The information the design team—architect, engineers, technicians—will require to produce the optimum facility must be thoroughly understood by the office planner. Knowing how to develop that information, the techniques to use, and how to organize and transmit it is the essence of the planning process. The planner is responsible for the basic information upon which all succeeding action is based. The degree, therefore, to which he performs a professional, accurate, and complete planning job is the measure of the effectiveness of the space which he has planned.

BIBLIOGRAPHY

Archer, Fred C., et al., *General Office Practice*, McGraw-Hill Book Company, New York, 1958.

Barish, Norman N., *Systems Analysis for Effective Administration*, chap. 6, Funk & Wagnalls Company, New York, 1951.

Carr, J. Gordon, "Considerations in Modern Office Planning and Design," *The Changing Dimensions of Office Management*, Report no. 41, American Management Association, New York, 1960.

Forster, Richard L., "Space Administration and Planning," *The Changing Scope of Office Management*, Bulletin no. 49, American Management Association, New York, 1964.

Hood, Malcolm F., "Programming for a New Office Building," *Experiences in Improving Office Administration*, Office Management Series no. 137, American Management Association, New York, 1954.

"The Integrated Office—A Handbook for Management on Remodeling, Relocating, Building," *Management Methods*, Sept. 15, 1955.

Maze, C. L., *Office Management*, chaps. 11, 12, and 13, The Ronald Press Company, New York, 1947.

"Office Layout: The Conquest of Inner Space," *Supervisory Management*, October, 1962.

Radley, G. S., "The Space Planner and the Records Manager," *Records Management Journal*, Summer, 1964.

Ripnen, Kenneth H., *Office Building and Office Layout Planning*, McGraw-Hill Book Company, New York, 1960.

"Where to Put the New Machines to Avoid a Roomful of Problems," *Administrative Management*, April, 1962.

CHAPTER TWO

Organizing and Staffing the Office

C. SPENCER EVERHARDT *Controller, Administrative Management Society, Willow Grove, Pennsylvania*

Earlier chapters of this Handbook were concerned with defining the principles of organization, describing various types of organizational structures, and discussing how to plan and lay out the physical facilities. Armed with this knowledge, we will approach the subject matter of this chapter from two positions. First, how do we go about organizing and staffing an entirely new office? Second, how do we reorganize an existing office?

THE NEW OFFICE

As in any management situation, you must first identify and articulate the problem before you can arrive at the answer or answers. When preparing to establish a new office, you should ask yourself such questions as:

What is the work to be performed?
What special skills are required?
How many people will be needed?
How do you get the people?
What are the job relationships?
What kinds of equipment will be needed?
How much space will be required?
How much money do you have to work with?

What Is the Work to Be Performed? Each office will have a personality of its own. This personality will be a reflection of the purposes for which the office exists. The manufacturing office will have a profile that differs from the sales office. The accounting office will have a different orientation than the research and development office. In organizing a new office, you must first determine the prime reason for the existence of that office and then add the

14–18

necessary ingredients to bring about an efficient operating entity that achieves predetermined results.

Although offices will differ from one another in prime responsibility, many activities are carried out that are common to all office structures. Some of these activities are:

1. Processing incoming mail
2. Processing outgoing mail
3. Dictation
4. Transcription
5. Typing
6. Printing
7. Copying
8. Filing
9. Records retrieval
10. Records disposal
11. Communications

What Special Skills Are Required?   Obviously, if you are establishing a law office, you will wish to staff it with people who have had legal training. In addition to this basic requirement, you might look for people who have had professional legal experience in your industry or with one or more of your product lines. The same rationale applies to every office. You must staff it with people who possess the necessary training and experience to make the office achieve its objectives. Information relative to the skill requirements for various office jobs may be obtained from organizations such as Industrial Psychology, Inc., New York City.

How Many People Will Be Needed?   C. Northcote Parkinson, in his now famous Parkinson's law, states: "Work expands to fit the organization that is developed to perform it and there is a tendency for each unit within an organization to try to build up its importance by expanding the number of its personnel." Where a job is machine controlled, it is not too difficult to determine the personnel requirements. In the office area, however, the problem becomes an increasingly difficult one. Chapter 6 of Section 14 deals with work standards and work measurement. It will give you some insight into the methods of determining production standards which relate to personnel requirements. If you are establishing a small office with limited funds, the chances are you will not resort to sophisticated methods to determine people requirements, but nevertheless it will be your responsibility to decide how many people you will need.

One thing to keep in mind is the use of outside organizations to supplement your manpower requirements until such time as you feel you can justify hiring for these positions on a full-time basis. Whether you are thinking of a part-time bookkeeper or an attorney on a retainer basis, many times this is the most efficient method of getting a small office under way. Keep in mind also that peak work loads will occur. Can you cover this situation by shifting personnel from one job or department to another? Can it be covered by hiring temporary or part-time help?

How Do You Get the People?   Studies have been made indicating that to get one qualified worker for an office job, twenty to twenty-five candidates must be screened. Getting the right people involves recruiting and screening all applicants. Recruiting can be achieved by using one or a combination of the following:

1. Newspaper advertising
2. Employment agencies
3. Referrals by present employees
4. Unsolicited applications

If you are setting up a new office, item 3 will not be applicable. If the new office is a branch operation of a going concern, you should consider the possibility of staffing the key positions from within the organization. Section 11 of this Handbook provides a detailed account of the intricacies involved in getting the right people.

What Are the Job Relationships? Assuming that you know how many people you will need and the means you will use to get these people, you must now determine how various jobs will mesh into the overall organizational structure. From a practical point of view, it makes sense to attempt to group like or related special skills or even to group according to the type of equipment used. Grouping according to these common denominators results in better supervision and control, better utilization of equipment, reduction of considerable duplications of effort, better space utilization, and a significant savings in operating expense. Consider such things as what it would cost to operate with a centralized typing or filing function versus having these functions decentralized. Carry this concept out with every activity that will be performed in your office. You are now in a position to "departmentalize" your organization chart. You have determined where and with whom the different members of your staff will work.

What Kinds of Equipment Will Be Needed? Let us refer to the activities listed earlier and relate these activities to equipment possibilities.

Processing Incoming and Outgoing Mail. Depending upon the volume, mail processing can range from having one person designated to "hand-process" the mail to a highly automated mail-room operation. The degree to which you mechanize or automate will relate to the specific realities of your own office. To get an idea of what is realistic and practical for your organization, it may be helpful to consult with several outside organizations that have volume requirements similar to yours to see how and what they are doing and the results achieved. Also, talks with the manufacturers of the various makes of mail-room equipment will give an idea of what is available and the costs involved.

Dictation and Transcription. Even in the smallest office, the use of dictating and transcribing equipment is highly advisable. Basically, there are two methods of recording the dictated word. One method is by cutting a groove in the recording medium (such as a record or belt); the other method is by magnetically imprinting the spoken word on the recording medium (same principle as in the home tape recorder). Some dictating units can also serve as transcribing units whereby one machine will serve the dictator and the transcriber. In many instances, however, the purchase of a separate transcribing unit is the most efficient answer.

One of the "sacred cows" that is slowly being slaughtered by a scientific approach to office management is the "one-for-one" concept whereby a girl (transcriber, typist) is assigned to a specific man (dictator, supervisor). Many large companies have established a centralized transcription department or "pool" and have realized a considerable increase in production with fewer people.

The first thing to do in setting up the centralized transcription department is to designate a qualified person as the supervisor. All work should be funneled through her, and it is her direct responsibility to see that the work is processed in as smooth and uninterrupted a manner as possible. Even if all dictators have individual dictating machines, it will not be necessary to have a like number of transcribing machines in the transcription department, for the simple reason that one girl will be doing the transcription for several dictators.

Another variation in the dictating-transcribing activity is the use of remote dictating units that feed directly to one or more centrally located transcribing units. This approach can result in considerable savings over purchasing individual dictating units. One word of caution: There will be times when one or more dictators will not be able to dictate because the central transcribing units are already in use.

Typing. The same factors which were just mentioned with regard to dictating-transcribing activities also hold true for typing work. If you can centralize the activities, you should experience more productivity at a lower cost.

A very important consideration is whether to purchase manual or electric typewriters. Each has certain advantages. The main attraction of the manual typewriter is that it is considerably less expensive to purchase than the electric, and that it is a "hardier" machine and will require less maintenance and experience less "downtime." On the other hand, the electric is faster, less fatiguing, and produces more attractive copy than the manual. The electric will produce better carbon copies and also will produce quality copy for photo-offset reproduction.

Printing and Copying. There was a time when printing and copying were easily identified and separated. With increased sophistication of "copying" equipment, the distinction is not as sharp or as easily recognizable. Printing and copying run the gamut from mimeographing to producing a highly professional printing job on an offset press or on the newer models of copying equipment. Again, the degree of sophistication of your operation should be directly related to your needs and how much you have to spend. There are a multitude of copiers available that involve different processes and varying degrees of copy quality at a wide range of cost. Determine first of all what your requirements are; then proceed with caution. The fact that copies can be so easily created has led to many instances of abuse and misuse of the equipment and has resulted in the proliferation of unnecessary copies.

Filing, Records Retrieval, and Records Disposal. With the advent of "total management information systems" whereby all aspects of company activities are interrelated, it becomes necessary to view the filing, retrieval, and disposal of records as being related and integrated to one another. For the small office, "filing" can be as simple as merely placing a copy of a letter in a file drawer in some predetermined sequence so that it can be located again at some future time. "Retrieval" will be the act of manually removing the item from the file. "Disposal" will be the physical destruction of the item.

As with every other activity, these activities can be mechanized or automated to conform to the requirements and available money of the particular company. The computer has provided the means by which a mass of information can be stored, retrieved, and related with a speed and precision that is impossible through manual or mechanical processes. The closer you get to a "total information system," the closer you get to the centralization of these functions. Do not underestimate the part that records creation, filing, retrieval, and disposal play in your total administrative cost picture. Considerable sums of money can be saved through the establishment of a sound records management program. Chapter 5 of Section 14 discusses this further.

Internal Communications. Among internal communication facilities are:

Internal messenger service
Pneumatic tubes or conveyors
Internal telephone system
Internal public address systems
Closed-circuit TV

The two most important considerations in determining the internal communications system or systems that will be most appropriate for your organization are speed and cost. How important is speed of transmission and how much can you justify spending for the installation and maintenance of your communication structure?

With regard to the items listed above, pneumatic tubes or conveyors are expensive installations but may well be justified by the increased speed attained. The internal telephone system is probably the most common communications device listed. The telephone company has numerous variations in internal communications equipment that will merit your investigation.

Internal public address systems can be relatively inexpensive and can be used for background music when not actually being used for public addresses. Closed-circuit TV is coming into more prominence. An example of this is the closed-circuit TV receivers used by the airlines to show the status of scheduled flights. The video phone will become an actuality, and this will add further to communication possibilities. One word of caution: It is easy to become entranced by all the buttons and gadgets that are available for internal communications systems. Question each and every instrument, button, or gadget that you are paying for. Compute the annual cost of these items. Then determine if you are spending the money wisely.

External Communications. External communications systems include the following.

1. Tie-lines or Foreign Exchange Lines. This enables you to reduce your costs for toll charges if your volume of toll calls is high enough. The rule of thumb is that a tie-line or leased circuit is justifiable if the total cost of toll calls between two points is 150 percent of what the cost would be for the tie-line.

2. WATS (Wide Area Telephone Service). This service entitles you to unlimited calls within specified areas for a flat monthly rate.

3. Telpack. This is primarily a point-to-point service that enables you to transmit telephone and teletype messages as well as facsimile and data information.

4. PBX. This is the familiar telephone switchboard installation. The operator routes incoming calls. However, outgoing calls may be made without going through the switchboard.

5. Centrex. This system provides PBX stations with the following capabilities: (*a*) Direct Inward Dialing (DID)—outsiders can call direct to any telephone in your office without going through the switchboard. (*b*) Direct Outward Dialing (DOD)—outside calls can be placed without going through the PBX operator. (*c*) Intercom—calls can be made to other telephone stations within the organization without going through the PBX operator. (*d*) Night Connections—with the regular PBX board, the operator must plug in cords for specific stations to receive calls at night; with Centrex, each station can dial in or out at any time without the assistance of the switchboard attendant.

Another rule of thumb is that DID service will cost about 40 percent more than a conventional PBX system.

6. Card Dialer. To operate the card dialer, you insert a prepunched card into a special slot in the telephone instrument, lift the receiver, push the start bar, and the number is automatically dialed. You have a file of punched cards for those telephone numbers you call most frequently.

7. Dataphone. The Dataphone system can be used for data transmission between offices or plants, or can be used by customers to order directly from suppliers. Additional information on the Dataphone system may be obtained from the telephone company.

Desks, Chairs, and File Cabinets. In addition to the equipment already mentioned, you must consider items such as desks, chairs, and filing cabinets. There are many different types of equipment available from numerous manufacturers. You must consider the specific function or activity to be served by this type of equipment and then try to determine the best buy for your needs.

Buyers Laboratory. One source to use for guidance in equipment decisions is the Buyers Laboratory, Inc., New York City. This is an independent testing laboratory specializing in the testing of the major office equipment lines. The results of their tests are available in report form on an annual subscription or per report basis.

Leasing Arrangements. It is possible to acquire your equipment needs without having to make a large capital outlay. Almost every major equipment manufacturer will arrange a lease or lease/purchase agreement whereby you can rent the equipment at a fixed monthly rate. If you are interested, they will give you an option to purchase at some future time and give you credit against the sale price for some portion of your rental payments. (See Chapter 7 of Section 9.) Bear in mind that you will eventually pay more on a lease arrangement than on a straight purchase. One of the advantages of leasing is that you are not as vulnerable to equipment obsolescence through technological changes in equipment design and capabilities.

Standardization. If you standardize your equipment, you will find you have greater operating flexibility. If your transcribing load is heavy, you can spread the work among several girls if dictating and transcribing units match. Standardization also eliminates the need for retraining when employees are transferred from one location to another. With standardization, you deal with one company on the servicing of the equipment and therefore have less confusion and possibly receive better service.

Service Contracts. There are two schools of thought on whether or not it pays to have annual maintenance contracts on equipment. Some take the position that you will save money by having your equipment serviced on a "per call" basis, which could be true. Keep in mind, however, that with a service contract which provides for periodic inspections and service, you are buying "preventive" maintenance that could result in fewer breakdowns and longer equipment life. You might consider keeping an actual service record on your equipment and compare what the cost would have been on a per call versus a contract basis and then make your determination. Another point to consider is that as your equipment gets older, it will in all likelihood require more service.

How Much Space Will Be Required? Although this question is pertinent to this chapter, it has been fully covered by the preceding chapter, "Office Planning, Layout, and Facilities."

How Much Money Do You Have to Work with? It would be easier to organize and staff a new office if you were handed a blank check at the time you were given the assignment. Unfortunately, it does not work that way. You will have a specified sum of money with which you will have to do the job. Chances are you will not be able to do everything in the way that you might wish. You will have to make concessions and start out with those items that are most urgent and most "affordable" with the thought that you will add to or improve on them as time and funds permit.

REORGANIZING AN EXISTING OFFICE

All of the points relative to organizing a new office apply to reorganizing an existing office. The one major difference is that with the reorganization you are faced with a people problem. Regardless of how honorable your intentions may be, you are suspect from the very start when you begin to introduce changes. You cannot effectively bring about the reorganization unless you have top management support, and also the support of the people involved.

Your best approach to gaining the cooperation and confidence of the people concerned is to be as tactfully straightforward as you can. If you are not, the people will see through you anyway. Your attitude in approaching the task of reorganization should be one of helping everyone in the office to do a more effective job in as efficient a manner as possible. Talk with the people who are doing the work. Find out what they are doing, why they are doing it, and how they are doing it. Determine what is being done that should not be done. Determine how something should be done differently and more effectively. Determine what should be done that is not being done at all.

There are different techniques by which you can record and relate this information. These techniques are described in Chapter 6 of Section 14. When your studies have been completed, submit your findings and recommendations to top management. When they are approved, proceed with the installation of your plan. There is no such thing as "the perfect way" or "the best way," so even after your reorganization has been completed, maintain a constant watch for further refinements and improvements.

THE THIRD PROFIT

The Administrative Management Society has stressed the "third profit philosophy." Management has long recognized the first profit, which is the profit from the manufacturing operation, and the second profit, which is the profit from the sales efforts of the organization. In addition to these, AMS calls attention to the third profit, or profit from administration. As an example: If your company is realizing a 5 percent profit on gross sales, then a $1,000 reduction in administrative cost is comparable to a $20,000 increase in gross sales. Keep this in mind when going through the processes of organizing, reorganizing, or administering the office activity.

CONCLUSION

This chapter has covered the principal areas of consideration in organizing or reorganizing and staffing an office. This is a difficult task, to say the least, but can prove most rewarding to the person responsible, to the people involved, and to the company itself. Only through thorough and systematic diagnosis can the proper corrective measures be prescribed to maintain the life of a company and to assure a continuing maturity and competitive position.

BIBLIOGRAPHY

"Can Your Company Use Closed-circuit Television?" *Business Management,* September, 1964.
"A Cost Analysis of Teleprinter Communication," *Business Management,* December, 1964.
Day, Donald J., "Common Sense Work Measurement," *AMS Systems Management Bulletins,* August, 1965.
"How the Telephone Consultant Works with a Client," *The Office,* May, 1965.
Levin, Jules, "An Appraisal of Centrex Telephone Service," *The Office,* September, 1964.
Percival, James H., "The Dictation and Stenographic Area of Communications," *Noma Management Quarterlies,* March, 1962.

Rekart, John L., "Methods Improvement Program," *AMS Systems Management Bulletins*, August, 1965.

Report on Service Contracts, Buyers Laboratory, Inc., New York, 1964.

Scharback, Ronald, "Centrex: A New Concept in Telephone Service," *Noma Mangement Quarterlies*, January, 1964.

Shiff, Robert A., "Rx for Retrieval," *AMS Systems Management Bulletins*, August, 1965.

Wacker, Alvin T., "Communicating Cost Control," *Noma Management Quarterlies*, March, 1962.

Weill, Peter R., "Equipment for Your Mailroom," *Administrative Management*, September, 1964.

"What Business Spends for Its Phone Service," *Administrative Management*, June, 1964.

CHAPTER THREE

Administrative Management in the Office

WALTER A. KLEINSCHROD   *Editor,* Administrative Management, *Vice President and Editorial Director, Geyer-McAllister Publications, New York, New York*

Unlike the plant, which, simply stated, makes what the company sells, or the sales department, which sells what the company makes, the office, home base of the administrative management function, has no single, clear-cut relationship with the whole organization. Rather, it maintains relationships on at least six levels, all of which touch activities in every part of the firm.

It is important to understand the full range of the operations carried out through the office. Without this, the responsibilities in this area remain ill-defined—a weak foundation for any management endeavor.

This chapter will present an outline definition of this unique relationship between office and organization, and will discuss in detail, from a management viewpoint, factors affecting the choice and operation of various office machines, supplies, and services.

DEFINING THE FUNCTIONS OF THE OFFICE

Most administrative management people have a fairly good understanding of what the modern office does, of what their responsibilities are, and of how the one helps carry out the other. Why is it, however, that too often they have difficulty putting this understanding into words?

One reason, of course, is that the office-based administrative responsibilities are so ramified and broad. They *are* an assortment. They reach into all sectors of the company. They are *management* responsibilities at a high level—an abstraction to begin with. Still, the main lines of their interactivities can be drawn.

First, the office is the locus of company policy—the place in which it is formed and from whence it is executed.

Second, the office is the information hub of the company. It is the intelligence center for coordinating vital activities. Here is "memory"—on papers, cards, tapes, and microfilm; in letters, reports, files, and ledgers. Here is calculating and data-processing ability.

The office is, third, the company's paper-work go-between with customers, vendors, and others outside the organization. It bills, collects, pays, and corresponds.

Fourth, it is overseer of the office furniture, machines, and supplies for all or most of the firm—buying, leasing, maintaining, and replacing them.

Fifth, it is the center of the personnel function, supplying people for the work force and setting standards of performance and compensation.

Finally, the office is the provider of other, special services—offering to all divisions, in one degree or another, methods analyses, internal communications systems, copying and duplicating facilities, mass feeding facilities, environmental controls, and much more.

In small firms, these levels may overlap as one man's responsibility. In larger firms, they separate into functional units—the billing department, personnel, reproduction services, and so forth—under one overall administrative executive. In either case, for managers, the administration of office operations transcends "office management" as that term, now falling from good usage, was once conceived. Modern office functions are far more tightly interlocked with other company operations. And responsibility for them continues to grow higher, broader, and more influential.

OFFICE MACHINES AND EQUIPMENT

The office runs on paper. The function of most office machines is to do something useful with that paper: type on it, copy on it, punch coded holes in it, fold it, mail it, or shred it. In determining which machines an office should have, one of the first considerations will be to fit its capacity for work to systems needs at *optimum* cost.

The "right" machine in any situation most often embodies trade-offs of many factors. One side of the trade is usually cost. The other side may be versatility of performance (the machine does many jobs—but are they necessary jobs?), or quality of output (essential?), or speed (how necessary?). If the answer to any of these parenthetical questions is "yes," by all means pay the price to equip the office with the needed capability. High-quality output may be a "must" for example, if a firm deals mainly with blue-chip clientele. But if the output of, say, the copying machine is used mainly for in-house reference, the most expensive unit on the market will probably not be needed.

Other things to consider, besides performance capabilities, include ease of maintenance, the advisability of a service contract, whether to lease the equipment or buy it, and how fast it depreciates.

Maintenance and Servicing. However well designed an office machine may be—and most of them *do* work well—it is going to need servicing eventually. There are five generally recognized methods: (1) a service contract with the manufacturer of the equipment; (2) a service contract with independent servicemen; (3) the use of one's own company servicemen; (4) use of manufacturers' servicemen on a per call basis with no contract; and (5) use of independent servicemen on a per call basis with no contract. Managers' choices among these five are usually governed by in-house cost studies of one kind or another, compounded by one of two prevalent opinions, the first of which holds that service contracts usually "pay," the other contending that they usually do not.

One well-publicized study of nearly 500 organizations, with more than 250,000 desk-top office machines among them, concluded that contract costs for servicing these machines were "about twice what the cost would be for servicing . . . on a per call basis or by internal repair departments." According to this study, service contracts on electric typewriters averaged $34 a year per machine. The cost of per call service averaged $18 a year.

The only trouble with findings such as these is that they deal only with *immediate* costs that show. They do not take account of *secondary* costs which often lie hidden. There is, for example, the "hidden" cost of processing an invoice and writing a check. It comes to slightly more than $6 per occurrence based on national averages—a one-time expense with an annual contract, a four-time expense if the machine breaks down that often in a year. Then there is the "hidden" cost of downtime—something that cannot be avoided regardless of the type of servicing, but an expense that *preventive maintenance,* a feature of every service contract, could curtail. Periodic inspections, if carefully done, can reduce machine breakdowns to maybe one a year, possibly none. Without a contract, the tendency is to wait until something has gone "way wrong." Then the machine may be out of commission for days. Is the loss of productivity worth the no-contract "economy"? Machine servicing is clearly a matter for constant review; there is no "final" answer. There are individual *right* answers, though. Each manager must find them for *his* firm.

Accounting Machines. Accounting machines perform the basic functions of accounts receivable, accounts payable, and payroll. The ways in which these jobs are accomplished vary with the sophistication of the machine. In addition to the three basic accounting functions, accounting machines can also be used for inventory control, banking operations, complex sales analyses, the recording of data, and kindred tasks. The number of such jobs a particular machine will handle and the degree of automation it provides depend again on the level of sophistication. Some of the nomenclature is apt to change, too, from one level to another.

For very small organizations, a simple *bookkeeping* machine may be all that is needed. Some machines of this type offer several advantages in addition to their low cost: automatic totals, subtotals, tabulation, and open carriages. Other mechanical desk-top units include *receipting* and *computing-billing* machines. With the latter, it is possible to type, compute, and total an invoice quickly. But the real innovations have come in machines based on *tab card* and *computer* technology. Some of them actually are small computers. They supply many businesses—even smaller ones—with faster and more accurate accounting than ever before.

Addressing Machines. The name "addressing machine" has become something of a misnomer for, in addition to addressing, these machines can also aid in billing, collecting, paying, ordering, shipping, and controlling inventory. In short, any situation in which repetitive writing is involved may be an area where addressing machines can be used. Three basic methods used in addressing are *metal-plate, stencil,* and *chemical transfer.* In addition, addressing can be accomplished by means of computer printout or automatic typewriters with paper tape or other input.

Metal-plate units use thin, single or multiple metal plates on which characters have been "punched up" by special embossing machines. Among this system's advantages: carbon lists are easily produced, the inking by ribbon is a relatively clean arrangement, and plates may be notched by category for selective control over mailings.

Stencil systems use tough, cardboard-rimmed address units which work on a mimeograph principle. Some of them, such as larger mimeograph stencils, can be "cut" on a typewriter. Other advantages: they are lightweight, easy to handle (the difference in weight between a tray of metal plates and cardboard stencils is often considerable); their operation is quiet; they can be color-coded for quick identification.

Chemical transfer systems apply the principles of spirit duplication or hectography to "master" address cards. These cards take many forms, including data-processable tab cards. Being flat, the cards store compactly, and it is possible to add typed or written information to their surface.

Most manually operated machines address as fast as a secretary can insert a mailing piece and pull the imprint lever. With many models, the plates, cards, or stencils are ejected automatically and restacked in proper order. But it would be misleading to infer that size is an accurate measure of the complexity or speed of an addressing machine. Rates of 3,000 impressions an hour are not unusual with several relatively small desk-top units. Beyond a certain point, however, larger, heavier-duty equipment must be employed.

Copiers and Duplicators. There is no sharp line dividing copiers and duplicators. Generally speaking, however, copiers are geared to reproduce original documents in quantities of from one to about fifteen. Duplicators are for longer runs. Generally speaking, too, the processes upon which their reproductive abilities are based differ, although new units combining the best features of both the copier and the duplicator are available.

Copiers can be classified in several ways: *wet or dry,* depending on whether or not liquid chemicals must be used (and sometimes, if they are used, on the presence or absence of dampness in a fresh copy); *one-step or two-step,* depending on how many times papers must be run through the unit; *flatbed or rotary,* depending on whether original material is exposed on a flat glass plate or conveyed into and out of the machine on rollers. Cost factors vary. Some machines are purchased outright along with their supplies. Others are leased, the user paying the manufacturer a monthly amount based on the number of copies produced.

Because copiers differ so widely in their inner workings, it is important to reconcile their strengths and weaknesses in terms of office needs. What is right for one office may be totally out of place in the office across the street. In choosing, four questions should be asked:

1. *What Kind of Documents Will Be Copied?* Flexible copy—or rigid? Remember that rotary units cannot accommodate thick originals or solid objects. Color? Some processes reproduce some hues better than others. Photos and halftones? All machines copy them, but fidelity varies. Opaque and double-sided originals? Machines of the diazo process will not reproduce these.

2. *How Many Copies?* The different processes offer different user optimums. Some are the answer to single-copy needs; others are best for multiple copies.

3. *How Good the Copy Quality?* Must it always be so high that no one can tell the copy from the original? If factors of legibility and prestige are paramount, the answer may well be "yes." However, the answer might also lean toward less glamour and more economy if, in the main, the copies are merely interoffice transients, looked at and discarded.

4. *How Much Will It Cost?* Not just the cost of hardware rental or purchase—that is easy to figure. What about supplies? And the hidden costs of maintenance, downtime, and operator inconvenience? They are not so easy to figure, but are no less important for all that.

Many of these same criteria also apply to duplicators.

Of the three main duplicating processes—*spirit, stencil,* and *offset*—spirit is generally considered the simplest, fastest way to produce runs up to 500 copies.

Quality of reproduction, however, is usually well below that of the other two processes. But spirit has many important office uses, including forms production and internal memoranda. Spirit duplicators cannot reproduce photographs, but can produce multicolored copies with one run through the machine. Such work is prepared by typing or drawing on the same master with differently colored carbons.

Stencil is probably the most inclusive process in terms of use. If a firm has just one duplicator, chances are it is a stencil machine. Often called a "mimeograph," it utilizes the familiar fibrous-tissue stencils which hold back ink except where cut by typewriter key or stylus. Stencil machines can reproduce photos with fair fidelity. Runs of between 1,000 and 3,000 copies are common; special stencils can extend that volume to around 5,000.

Offset duplicators, although often used for short runs, are designed to accommodate volume work of high quality. They are an in-office adaptation of the offset lithography presses used by large commercial printers. Three types of masters are available: *paper,* for runs up to 2,000 copies; *plastic,* for runs to 5,000; and *metal,* to 25,000. Skilled operators often can manage to extend their runs beyond the stated figures.

Dictating Machines. There are many types of dictating machines. Choice will depend, here again, on a leveling out of price and systems need. Some dictating machines are better suited for recording over long periods of time, for conferences, and for phone conversations. Others are designed for the executive who dictates one or two letters at a time. Some are portable and battery operated. Others work on electric current. Some work both ways. Weights range from less than 2 pounds to more than 20.

Some machines are for dictation only. A separate unit then must be used to transcribe, or "play back." Many machines, however, permit both dictation and transcription. These usually also allow the user to back up and hear the last few moments of his dictation.

In terms of recording media, all dictating equipment can be grouped under two main classifications—*embossed* and *magnetic.* Essentially, the embossed kinds are like phonograph records, though their wavy grooves may wind around plastic belts as well as around circular discs. The magnetic kinds are essentially tape recorders adapted for office use.

There are advantages and disadvantages with each type. Although both are durable, tapes may snap, and discs and belts may crease. Embossed recordings cannot be erased, which eliminates the error-correcting advantage of the magnetics—a "detriment" until it is considered that nothing can be erased inadvertently. Discs afford longer recording time than belts; tapes allow longer time still. Discs sometimes have a tendency to pick up high background noises. Nevertheless, it is impossible to say that one type or the other is better overall. Choice of a machine, or a system of machines, remains an individual matter, based on the requirements and preferences of one's own office. If the office is a large one, the possibility of remote dictation, by telephone, to a bank of dictating machines located in a transcription pool should be investigated.

Mail-room Equipment. Even the smallest firm has a mail department, whether or not it is so labeled. In the "one girl" firm, the secretary usually has the chore of collecting, inserting, stamping, and dispatching the mail. A scale is probably her only piece of mail equipment. The postage scale, in fact, is probably the most ubiquitous piece of office equipment except for the typewriter.

Scales are of three types: *pendulum, beam,* and *spring.* Although beam scales enable weighing mail with constant precision, most scales found in the mail room are of the pendulum variety. Fast and easy to use, they are accurate enough for most applications. Spring scales are best used where mail volume is light. Most handle up to 20 ounces by ½-ounce gradations; some go as high as 70 pounds. Generally speaking, they are the least accurate of the three types.

A mail department with only a scale, however, could hardly be said to operate at maximum efficiency. Whatever its size, its management could probably improve procedures with a postal meter.

Meters generally consist of two parts: a *mailing machine* and the actual *meter,* a detachable unit licensed for use by the Post Office Department. Meters range from desk-top devices to large, automated systems which, in addition to meter stamping, also collate, insert, seal, count, and stack. There are many reasons for meters: they save time and effort, speed mail through the post office, stop stamp losses, date parcel post (something not done at the post office), and add prestige to mailings.

The well-managed mail room might also include sorting tables, sorting racks, paper sorters, mail carts, envelope openers, sealers, label wetters, stapling machines, counting and numbering machines, imprinters, mailbag racks, and, of course, mailbags.

Typewriters. The aristocrats of typewriters do far more than "just type." They are versatile instruments capable of producing binary codes or punched paper tape for computer input, or of activating auxiliary "slaves." Some produce straight right-hand as well as left-hand margins. Some have interchangeable type faces. If an office does not require all this sophistication, there are still plenty of workaday models to choose from.

Regardless of systems needs, a decision to be made in selecting typewriters is whether they shall be *manual* or *electric.* Ever since electric typewriters became a fact of office life, managers have argued over which kind is better. There are good things to be said for both.

Manuals have the obvious advantage of price—about half that of electrics. Repairs and downtime are apt to be less with a manual, too. Manuals are not "tied down" to electrical outlets; they can be placed anywhere.

Electrics, however, inherently possess more features and speed than do manuals. A typist's production is less likely to fall off after several hours' work with an electric, because less keystroke effort is required. The same factor allows for greater speed within a given interval. Certain built-in features of electrics add to this speed: a shorter keystroke, repeat keys, and the electric carriage return.

If a firm does a lot of repetitive typing, it should investigate the benefits of automatic typewriters—machines activated by tape or punched cards. They clack away at speeds of 100 to 150 words per minute with accuracy, a feat no human could perform except in isolated spurts.

Office Furniture. Efficiency should be the main criterion in selecting office furniture. The best of the basic chairs, desks, tables, files, and other units will provide that efficiency by (1) saving space, (2) reducing the movements of users, thus increasing productivity, and (3) improving psychological conditions by providing pleasing surroundings.

Some furniture manufacturers have established design departments to aid in structuring a more efficient office. Design help is also available from many office equipment dealers.

The first choice faced in selecting furniture is between *metal* and *wood.* Broadly, the choice will depend on factors such as the purpose for which the furniture will be used, the present condition of the office, and, of course, personal preference. But more specifically, each material has its own advantages.

Metal, for example, is extremely durable, being capable of standing up to hard usage.   A second plus is flexibility, which allows great interchangeability of units (modularity), also possible with some wood lines.   Another advantage is metal's resistance to fire.

Wood, on the other hand, is usually easier to transport and repair.   Wood, it should be noted, will last more than a lifetime if properly used.   Although it is a matter of taste, many people feel that wood furniture is more aesthetically pleasing than other types.   This is why metal manufacturers frequently surface desk tops with plastic laminates or linoleums which resemble wood.

OFFICE SUPPLIES

There are literally thousands of supplies available for the well-equipped office, as can be seen by browsing through any large commercial stationery store.   Space will permit only a general discussion here of three widely used office commodities: *ribbons, paper,* and a special application of paper, *forms.*

Office Machine Ribbons.   Once a fairly standard item demanding little attention, the office machine ribbon has taken on many new forms and characteristics.   In addition to the familiar fabric ribbons, special film ribbons are available.   And even the fabric types have undergone marked changes.

Fabric ribbons, usually of cotton, silk, or nylon, are ideal for general office typing and for most office machines in which long life and hard use are important considerations.   Many of the fabrics render lint-free, even-toned performance. There is a wide color range.   Some are specially inked for blueprinting, tab card imprinting, transfer posting, photostat work, thermographic copy-machine reproduction, and so on.

The polyethylene or Mylar-based film ribbons produce sharp impressions with minimum "feathering," well suited to prestige correspondence and all but essential for offset reproduction and copy for optical scanning.   Most film ribbons are "single release"; that is, they can be used only once.   However, some film types are available which are reusable.

Paper.   So many office procedures depend on paper in so many forms that generalizations about it can be dangerous.   Broadly speaking, paper must accommodate handwriting or printing or the chemistry of copying, singly or in combination.   Sometimes its use life is short—a memo.   Sometimes permanence is paramount—the minutes of incorporation.   Factors of weight, translucency, color, prestige—and inevitably cost—enter in.

Much general-purpose office paper is known as "bond" paper.   This is one of those terms that everyone uses, but not everyone can define.   To Merriam-Webster it is "a kind of firm, uncalendered paper."   But it is also a "grade" of paper, which becomes involved in another paper word, "weight."   When we speak of 20-pound stock, we mean that a *ream*—or 500 sheets—of a particular *grade* of paper weighs 20 pounds.   There are at least seven grades of paper, ranging from *bond, book,* and *cover* through three grades of *bristol* to *tag.*   Each grade has a "base weight" determined by its special "base dimension."   Thus, the base dimension of all bond is 17 by 22 inches; the base of book is 25 by 38; the base of tag 24 by 36.   It takes a ream at these particular dimensions to determine the poundage of papers within each grade.   In practical terms, this means that weight alone may not be a sure guide to paper thickness; it is necessary to know the paper's grade as well.

There is no clear price policy or method of purchase that applies generally to all paper companies.   Some of them sell directly to the user.   Others sell indirectly through office supply dealers or paper merchants.   Again, some of these sources hold rigorously to the quoted list prices. Some discount freely, and under pressure can be persuaded to shave yet another few cents per thousand off the price of their competitors.

Even at list price, however, most companies offer unit savings on quantity orders. Naturally, the largest order is not necessarily the most advantageous. Much of what is saved through quantity discounts can easily be dissipated by the cost of storing a heavy paper inventory. With chemically treated copy paper, more costly still could be the waste incurred from holding supplies beyond their "shelf life" expectancy. This holds true for developer fluid, toner, and other copier supplies, as well as for paper.

One arrangement used by some administrative managers is to allow their local office products dealer to act as a kind of auxiliary supply room for them. A sizable paper order—a year's supply, say—is placed with a dealer, and arrangements are made for him to deliver small portions of it at regular intervals. Thus he handles storage, and fresh stock is always available.

Forms. Someone once said that forms are the tracks of printed papers on which business systems run. Poetic but essentially true: forms keep operations moving in a given direction. They are instruments of control.

Basically, all business forms are printed pieces of paper with convenient spaces in which to enter information to be transmitted to other persons. The most familiar kinds of forms are those printed on single sheets of paper. Sometimes known as "cut" forms, they are often furnished in pads, which makes their distribution easier and minimizes waste. Some 90 percent of all forms made are cut forms. They are usually designed by the user and printed by a local printer, or bought ready-made from a stationery dealer carrying "stock" forms. Several copies of such a form may be prepared in one writing by the use of carbon paper, becoming, in effect, a "set" of forms.

Specialty forms have been developed to overcome the problem of handling separate forms and separate sheets of carbon when multicopies are required. Generally speaking, specialty forms are custom designed, patented by their manufacturer, and obtainable only through him or his authorized dealers. Often, they operate only on special equipment. The more common types of specialty forms include:

1. Fanfold continuous forms. These are suited to systems requiring large quantities of forms and are relatively inexpensive to make.

2. Single stub sets. Featuring interleaved snap-out carbons, these save clerical cost by minimizing setup time on machines. The stub may be on any of the four sides.

3. Register forms. For handwritten entries, these are common on retail counters and have found their way to such places as loading docks and public libraries.

4. Tab card forms. Used as input in data-processing systems, this form can originate as a single card, a set of cards, or as one part of a continuous form.

CLERICAL OPERATIONS

It is sometimes fashionable to speak of office operations as a "paper-work pipeline" analogous to the production line in a factory. Where office work is standardized and repetitive as in the plant, the analogy holds up fairly well. But most office work is not that standard—too many exceptions and matters of judgment enter in—and here the comparison falls down.

Any discussion of clerical operations must recognize this duality of the subject: on the one hand is work conducive to measurement against a standard; on the other, work in which "ability to think" is paramount. Some clerical phase of the accounts payable function might be an example of the former. Secretarial work is a good example of the latter.

Routine Work. To schedule and control routine work effectively, a manager should know (1) how much work an employee is capable of producing, that is, a *work standard;* (2) the status of work in the department on as timely a basis as possible—*backlog;* (3) how much work is received into the department—*volume;* and (4) what employees are doing in relation to the schedules—*performance.*

Thus the first step is to identify activities capable of standardized control and to establish the unit of work, or unit of measure, against which performance may be judged.

The unit of measure can be a definite line item—a document or batch of documents—which can be correlated to, and be indicative of, the time required to process the unit. It should be kept as simple as possible to minimize record keeping and simplify control, yet reflect as complete an operation as practical. In accounts payable, for example, the work unit might cover four steps: *matching* a supplier's invoice with the receiving report and purchase order; *stapling* them together; *posting* date received, quantity, unit cost, and so on; and *stamping* and coding the invoice. Remember, however, that the greater the number of steps that are combined, the greater the chance for performance variation to occur.

Three forms can help gather these and other data: an *activity log,* listing each employee, his activity, units assigned, and the times he starts and finishes his unit of work; a *backlog report,* an inventory of the work at hand, showing each job (billing, for example), its standard, the number of units, and the hours it should take; and a *performance report,* which again names the activity, lists man-hours (actual and standard) and the favorable or unfavorable variance between them, and the number of units processed.

It cannot be overemphasized that once such a system is implemented, it should be perpetuated. Maintained on a continuing basis, it can aid greatly in determining (1) how many people are needed to perform specific functions, (2) how to cope with peak and valley work loads, and (3) how to evaluate the performance of individual workers. But if not maintained for the "long pull," all the time, effort, and expense of initiating it will be of no avail.

Incentives. Performance standards suggest incentives—the idea that work above a standard should be compensated for with rewards of some kind, usually bonuses. The experience of many companies has shown, however, that it takes more than money to make incentives succeed. It takes a business environment with characteristics that include the following.

1. *Fair but Tough-minded Management.* Any incentive plan, regardless of its type, requires management time and willingness to judge individual contributions and to identify outstanding and below-average performance. Unless management makes these judgments, there cannot be a strong performance-reward relationship. There will be no outstanding reward for outstanding performance, nor will poor performance be penalized. Instead of an atmosphere of "planned uncertainty," there is an aura of guarantee.

2. *Environment Favoring Result-based Performance Evaluation.* Some industries are, by nature, more conducive to this than others. Yet, whatever the industry, it is management leadership that sets the tone or the atmosphere internally. If individuals are to be held accountable for results and rewarded accordingly, management must define individual responsibilities as clearly and as precisely as possible.

3. *Rewards of Reasonable Size.* What is "reasonable size"? It depends on many things—the level of fixed income, the impact of uncontrollable external influences and internal organizational or procedural limitations, and so on. General guidelines are available, but optimum reward sizes should be individually tailored to the specific jobs of each company.

Answering "Do They Think?" Many clerical jobs, especially in the secretarial area, depend less on routine productive ability than on the ability to think, judge, and take initiative.

These attributes are too subjective to quantify. Some companies, however, do test for them in a simple if roundabout way. They give secretarial job applicants a "typing" test that is actually a test in thinking. The test contains errors of fact and logic as well as spelling errors. The questions it answers, without ever putting them into words, are: Will the applicant notice the glaring discrepancies? Will she do something about them? Will she at least *ask?*

OFFICE SECURITY

No one knows how much is lost to American business every day through dishonesty, but law enforcement agencies and private security-service firms agree it is prodigious. Losses of this type take many forms—the loss of business secrets to the *espionage* efforts of competitors; the loss of funds to *embezzlers;* the loss of property to *burglars;* or the loss of a carelessly placed purse to a *sneak-thief* delivery boy.

Losses of the espionage variety are too involved to dwell on here. Suffice it that discarded "secret" papers should be destroyed by incineration, shredding, or other means—under supervision. Employees should be educated to the importance of security through posters, house organ articles, and directives. The importance of not discussing classified information with "innocent" strangers should be stressed.

Good accounting and auditing procedures are the antidotes to embezzlement.

The antidotes to burglaries and desk-side thefts begin with the development of "security-mindedness" and embrace such specifics as reception room procedures and a knowledge of vaults and safes.

Security-mindedness. Security-mindedness is part attitude and part sensitivity—an *attitude,* to be shared by all in the company from president to mail boy, that regards security measures as commonplace prudence; and a *sensitivity* to places and practices in the office that spell potential trouble. This sensitivity develops through experience; some call this "learning to think like a crook." It means being aware of, and making personnel aware of, danger points such as:

Coffee Breaks. Two-thirty in the afternoon, when many desks are vacant, is the favorite time for office crime; 10 A.M. ranks second.

Closets. Those that open onto "blind" corridors—outside the line of sight of any work station—are particularly vulnerable. Keep these closets securely locked.

Stairwells. Particularly in buildings with light interfloor traffic, stairwells offer a haven to sex offenders and a path of escape for thieves.

Draftsmen's Departments. Their small, costly, precision equipment makes them vulnerable. Such items should be put away after use. Be particularly watchful during lunch breaks.

Ways of buttoning down office security include:

Indoctrination. Periodically brief the staff in methods of curtailing office losses.

Receptionists. The good "greeter" is a major defense against loss. Tactfully, she checks persons arriving and leaving, especially those carrying parcels. She asks to see an authorization slip of anyone removing office equipment.

Warnings. Signs pointing out that an area is "protected" are psychological deterrents. The would-be thief does not know which of many protection devices are being used. He cannot be sure if "protection" means a weekly walk-through inspection or closed-circuit TV already trained on him.

Building Service Discipline. For example, custodians should not be allowed to prop open self-locking doors for "convenience sake." Locked exits should lock.

Safes and Vaults. In this area, theft losses and fire losses must be discussed together, if only to clear up some common misconceptions. Many people believe that money or other valuable items placed in a safe are "safe" from burglary. More than likely, however, the protection the equipment is providing is against fire loss, not theft. The difference is in the terminology and the construction. Generally speaking (and recognizing certain exceptions), *safes* protect important records from fire damage; *vaults* or *money chests* protect belongings from theft.

OTHER ADMINISTRATIVE TOPICS

The reader is referred to the monthly magazine *Administrative Management* for articles on many subjects other than those discussed in this chapter. Topics covered in *AM* fall into the general areas of office equipment, office environment, systems improvement, personnel, self-management, overall management, and book reviews. Yearly indexes, covering hundreds of article listings, are available without charge from the publication. Requests should be addressed to Reprint Department, *Administrative Management,* 212 Fifth Avenue, New York 10010.

BIBLIOGRAPHY

Bauman, J. R., "Seven Ways to Contribute to Profits," *Administrative Management,* May, 1965.

Close, Guy C., Jr., *Work Improvement,* John Wiley & Sons, Inc., New York, 1960.

Frank, George, "Threat of Management Obsolescence," *Administrative Management,* December, 1964.

Gager, Arthur H., *Practical Office Timesavers,* McGraw-Hill Book Company, New York, 1957.

Grillo, Elmer V., *Control Techniques for Office Efficiency,* McGraw-Hill Book Company, New York, 1963.

Heyel, Carl, *The Supervisor's Basic Management Guide,* McGraw-Hill Book Company, New York, 1965.

Jehring, J. J., and Donald D. Illig, "How Clerical Incentive Plans Work," *Administrative Management,* September, 1964.

Kleinschrod, Walter A., "The Crossfire on Middle Management," *Administrative Management,* September, 1964.

Kleinschrod, Walter A., "Three Facets of the Changing Office," *Administrative Management,* January, 1965.

Levin, Jules, "Setting Up an Effective Internal Policy Program," *Administrative Management,* October, 1964.

Newman, William H., *Administrative Action,* Prentice-Hall, Inc., Englewood Cliffs, N.J., 1963.

Poschmann, Andrew W., "How to Establish an Effective Company Procedures Manual," *Administrative Management,* January, 1965.

Robichaud, Beryl, *Selecting, Planning and Managing Office Space,* McGraw-Hill Book Company, New York, 1958.

Walsh, L. J., and J. R. Birkhofer, "Scheduling and Controlling Work," *Administrative Management,* January, 1964.

CHAPTER FOUR

Forms Control

FRANK M. KNOX *President, Frank M. Knox Company, Inc., New York, New York*

Office and plant forms are the raw materials and, in many cases, the sole tools for the performance of clerical and administrative functions. The central of office and plant forms is an absolute necessity if management wants to reduce and control the indirect expense of doing business.

OBSTACLES TO FORMS CONTROL

Most executives agree that forms should be controlled, but few companies take any meaningful steps to accomplish this. The reasons for this failure to act are several. The most important reasons are:

1. Management has too many other seemingly more important things to think about.

2. Management equates forms control with systems and procedures control. It thinks that a study of the major systems and procedures of the company automatically brings about forms control as a by-product, and it depends on the systems and procedures staff to accomplish the objective.

3. The systems and procedures staff is primarily engaged in two areas: first, the "fire alarm" area of taking care of immediate, critical problems arising in the day-to-day paper-work operations of the business, and second, the installation of advanced electronic data processing systems, probably with a computer. Because the fire-alarm situation cannot possibly achieve forms control and because 75 percent of all forms will never be affected by a computer or electronic data processing system, the systems and procedures department simply does not reach the problem of forms control.

4. The majority of all forms have relatively small usage, and many of them are produced in the using departments on office duplicating machines. Neither management nor the systems and procedures staff even knows of their existence.

5. There is a misconception of what forms control is. Too many in management think of it as consisting in having the stationery stock room or the purchas-

ing department ask questions about each form before it is reprinted or in not having the form reprinted without the office manager's approval. Neither of these amounts to forms control. There is no adequate management force behind such action, and again these units never see the forms which are produced wholly within the using departments.

6. Some managements ignore the fact that the cost of using forms in the paper-work operations of the company amounts to twenty or thirty times the cost of buying or producing the forms. They do not accept forms control as being important enough to command their attention.

THE BASIC NATURE OF THE FORMS PROBLEM

The forms problem is inextricably interwoven with the overall paper-work and data-processing problem of business, but it has certain unique aspects apart from that overall problem. Much of the forms problem is centered in the fact that most forms are used in quite small quantities and, form by form, do not appear on the surface to be of sufficient importance to command the attention of management.

Automated data-processing equipment uses carbon-interleaved, continuous forms in very large quantities. Other major forms, such as the purchase order, invoice, and work order, are usually in carbon-interleaved unit sets and used in large quantities. These forms are well known to management and command the large majority of all attention ever given to forms.

Forms salesmen concentrate their attention on these large-usage forms, and some of these salesmen are qualified to give valuable design assistance. In some cases, this assistance is given reluctantly, because the salesman knows that the purchasing department will probably get competitive bids on the first rerun of the form, and he will probably lose it to some other printer who did not help design it in the first place.

But such forms, important as they are, are the smallest part of the forms control problem. They are already under control to a great degree. Qualified machine men watch the designs of machine forms carefully. The forms just will not work unless they do. Furthermore, such forms create a relatively small amount of clerical expense. The clerks, stenographers, secretaries, supervisors, and other paper-work people work on the myriad of small-usage, flat forms which are not carbon interleaved, are not bought from the specialty forms houses, do not receive the benefit of salesmen assistance, are not used mainly on machines, are produced on office duplicating machines more often than purchased from commercial printers, and are relatively unknown to either general management or the systems and procedures staff.

Where Forms Come from. The head of a department, who is charged with the responsibility for operating his department, conceives the need for a monthly or weekly or daily report on certain aspects of the work. Or he feels that he should report at regular intervals on his work to a higher level of management. Or he wants to keep track of certain things that go on in his department. So he makes up a form.

Forms of this type are not going to be used in annual quantities of more than a few hundred or, at most, a few thousand. To purchase such a form means an expenditure of relatively few dollars and, rather than bother with a purchase requisition and purchase order, the department head has them run off on the duplicating machine in his own department or in the company reproduction unit where there is little or no management control. No money is spent, at least not visibly, no red tape has to be combated, and he gets his forms quickly and puts them to use.

But someone has to write data on them; someone has to route them elsewhere; someone has to file them or otherwise dispose of them; presumably someone has to read them and use the data; and for every dollar that went into the production of the form, visibly or invisibly, twenty or thirty dollars of time is devoted to their use.

This is repeated time and again, not only in that department but in all the other departments and plants of the company until there are literally hundreds, if not thousands, of uncontrolled forms in use in the company. Some call them "bootleg" forms, although such a term is more of a reflection on management's failure to control forms than on the local production of them.

Management could remain in blissful ignorance of this situation if it were not for the fact of budgets. Management has to formulate and live by a budget, and one of the troublesome items in that budget is the growing clerical and administrative expense. The clerical payroll never seems to get smaller; instead it gets larger year by year. It gets larger because it takes people to fill out and use those forms.

Periodically the word gets out for everyone to cut his office payroll by 10 percent; for a while this is done, but a year or so later the payroll is larger than ever. This clerical payroll is the only aspect of the use of forms that management sees, but the payroll is just far enough removed from the pieces of paper that the true cause-and-effect relationship is lost, and the problem is seldom, if ever, seen or effectively acted upon.

Surveys show that as many as three-fourths of all forms are used in annual quantities of less than a thousand each. These include the office-duplicated forms which are born as described above. Few of them are well designed; few have been carefully scrutinized as to actual necessity; few, if any, were compared with forms in other departments or plants to see if they duplicated each other; many carry no identifying form number for control purposes; and few have been built into procedures flow charts.

A survey of eighteen companies, including all sizes and kinds in different parts of the country, showed a total of 52,677 different forms being used. Of this number, 48,783, or 92.6 percent, were of the flat, small-usage, common garden variety of forms as described above. Only 3,894, or 7.4 percent, were of the carbon-interleaved, continuous or unit-set variety. Unfortunately, this 7 percent commands about 95 percent of all the control attention given to the forms. The result is an uncontrolled increase in the clerical and general paper-work expense in the company, and no one ever seems to relate cause and effect sufficiently to do anything meaningful about it.

THE OBJECTIVES OF FORMS CONTROL

The objectives of forms control are:

1. To reduce the total number of forms in the organization to the practical minimum consonant with the operating requirements of the company

2. To prevent the inception of new forms when others already exist for the same purpose

3. To consolidate similar forms already in existence when they duplicate each other for the same function

4. To improve the design of forms for greater clerical efficiency and administrative use

5. To provide a source for all paper used in a given procedure

6. To establish standards of design for the most economical production or purchase of forms

7. To provide work-load studies for determination of make or buy decisions on internal reproduction of forms and the operation of a captive printing plant

8. To provide a basis for proper and economical storage and distribution of forms throughout the organization

9. To establish the control on a permanent basis to prevent the recurrence of the problem and the subsequent need for repeating the program

Forms Control Files.   If forms are going to be controlled, there must be some means by which they can be made available to those who have to do the controlling.   Nothing can be more frustrating than collecting together a mass of a thousand or more forms which are so disorganized that no one can put his hands on what he is looking for without having to search through the entire pile.

Obviously, what is needed is a means of classifying the forms into forms control files to organize them so they can be identified and found quickly.   That does not sound difficult.   But it is difficult, as anyone who has tried it has quickly found out.

There are several deterrents to a quick and easy method of classifying forms for control purposes.   The first is the large number of forms which bear no form number and, in all too many cases, bear no title or descriptive heading. The problem of filing these forms poses difficulties all along the line, because they are difficult to file even numerically, let alone by any functional means.

Another deterrent is the fact that a single file will not do all the things that are necessary for effective control.   Numerical filing is effective if you merely want to find a form, providing, of course, the form has a number to begin with.   But a numerical file keeps apart different but functionally related forms instead of bringing them together so that they can be studied and consolidated.

Effective forms control requires two distinctly separate but related files, a numerical file and a functional index.

The Numerical File.   This file is just what its name indicates.   It is a file in which all forms are filed numerically so that any given form can be found for reference purposes.   It is a historical file in that it contains the record of the individual form.   It is permanent for the life of the individual form.

The numerical file should contain a sample of every form in use in the organization regardless of where or how it is produced, whether it is permanent or temporary, or whether it is used in quantities of just a few hundred or many thousands annually.   This poses the question of the so-called bootleg forms which remain hidden from the average form control program.   But, unless the company is merely sweeping the forms problem under the rug, the locally produced, unnumbered, and so-called temporary forms must be ferreted out and included in the control files.

Those forms which contain no identifying number must be given a temporary number until such time as they are assigned a formal number in the control program.

When the form is studied, a standard number can be assigned and the temporary number discarded, providing, of course, the form has not been completely eliminated.

The numerical file folder should show on its face every organizational unit which uses that form.   This information could, of course, be kept in some other place, but experience shows that it is much more efficient to have it on the face of the numerical file folder so that those working on the form can have instant knowledge of the users of the form. Opposite each user's name should appear the average annual usage. This is not intended to replace essential inventory data but merely to provide a guide to the forms control staff of the forms that are the most important from a usage standpoint.

The numerical file should contain all the historical data on each form. This should include correspondence, specifications, samples of revisions, record of approvals, and the like. A few working samples of the form may well be included, although it should not be made a source of working copies for the users.

The Functional Index. The really critical problem in forms control is the classification of the forms to bring together all forms doing the same thing. Several different departments or plants may have several different forms doing the same thing; keeping track of personnel, for instance. Undoubtedly there is a standard form for employee records, but nevertheless many managers and supervisors will have their own peculiar version of the same thing for use in their own unit.

No control can possibly be effective unless such duplications and overlappings are brought together for study. To do this, the forms must be collected—and if this is done with any degree of completeness, the volume of paper coming in will provide the first shock to management and the staff undertaking the study. There will be many more forms than anyone thought existed. It is not at all unusual to find double the number of forms of which there is a record in any central point.

Several samples of each form will have been collected. One of these will be laid aside for the building of the functional index, and the others will go into the numerical file. It is at this point that the problem of unnumbered forms becomes serious. Some units will take a numbered form which is intended to be standard throughout the organization and make their own local version of it on their own duplicating equipment, with or without minor changes. No number will be put on the local version, and the control staff will be hard put to remember whether or not that same form has appeared previously as a numbered form.

When the company's forms number in the thousands—and it does not take a very big company to have several thousand forms—memory does not serve throughout the entire classification in the control files. The result will be that the same form, or minor versions of the same form, will be located at several places in the numerical file, and the duplication can only be revealed in the functional index.

Forms Classification. This brings up the problem of forms classification. Obviously, a departmental classification will not serve, although this is almost always the first approach tried. If two separate departments have different versions of the same form, the departmental classification will keep them apart instead of bringing them together.

The next approach ordinarily tried is to put all forms of the same type together, that is to say, all forms with the same title or name. This brings all bills of lading, all invoices, all checks, all premium notices, all statement forms, and so on together in as many classifications. This is fine except for one thing—more than half of the forms will not fall under any such common title or name. The bootleg forms created in the departments and produced locally will, for the most part, fail such a classification. This leaves a great many forms unclassified, and these are the very forms which call for the greatest degree of control.

The answer is to classify the form by its subject, its operation or condition, and its function. These terms need definition, and in defining them many areas of gray are encountered. Different people will classify the same form by different definitions of these terms, and each will have some basis for his method.

A typical example is the well-known payroll record which contains a list of employees, the time they worked, their rate of pay, their gross earnings, the deductions, the net pay, and possibly a check number.

One person would say the subject was "payroll," another would use "earnings," another might choose "deductions," another might want to use "time," but the fact of the matter is that a payroll record is a record of the payment of cash and should be filed under the subject "cash," under the operation "payment of," and under the function "to record." The fact that the payment of cash was for the purpose of meeting a payroll is a procedural matter insofar as this particular form is concerned.

Here we see a source of great difficulty. If it is a systems and procedures man doing the classification, he will be unavoidably tempted to look down the procedural road to the subsequent or related operations and mix them into the classification. Because the file is a forms control device and because it will probably be operated and used by other than an experienced systems and procedures man, the classification must be determined only by what is apparent on the face of the form itself and not on some related but somewhat removed procedural operation.

An actual example was a request-for-appropriation form. This is a request for cash and should be filed under "cash," "appropriation of," "to request," but the man setting up the index insisted upon using the subject "project" and ended up by wanting to use "capital asset," both of which are legitimate forms subjects. If the money were appropriated, and if the project were ever finished, it would probably become a capital asset, but there was nothing on the face of the form to dictate that classification. If the money were not appropriated, the project and the capital asset would never even exist.

Figure 4-1 shows one page of a recap of a completed functional index and relates many forms to their applicable classification factors. Table 4-1 shows a few commonly used forms with the classification factors by which they would be filed in the functional index.

In the following list are the names of some well-known forms and the applicable subject, operation or condition, and function for an adequate classification in the index. A moment's reflection will show the logic of this method of forms classification. Consider just what these forms do and see how the subjects, operations, and functions fit. For instance:

A "bank check" orders a bank to pay out cash to someone.

A "monthly statement" notifies the customer of the status of his account with the company.

A "personnel record" records the status of the employment of the individual employee.

An "inventory report" reports the status of materials and supplies or other more specific material. It should be noted that the "perpetual inventory record" varies in that it does not report but merely records the status of the material, so only the function will be different for the two forms.

A "bill of lading" acknowledges the receipt by the common carrier of a shipment of some kind.

So it is with all forms. If the purpose of the form can be put into a simple sentence, it will almost automatically reflect the subject, operation or condition, and the function involved in the use of the form. It is equally important to

FUNCTIONAL INDEX SPREAD SHEET
FMK-36

Page 4

FILE NO.	SUBJECT / OPERATION OR CONDITION	TO ACKNOWLEDGE 1	TO AGREE 2	TO APPLY 3	TO AUTHORIZE 4	TO CANCEL 5	TO CERTIFY 6	TO CLAIM 7	TO ESTIMATE 8	TO FOLLOW-UP 9	TO IDENTIFY 10	TO INSTRUCT 11	TO NOTIFY 12	TO ORDER 13	TO RECORD 14	TO REPORT 15	TO REQUEST 16	TO ROUTE 17	TO SCHEDULE 18	TOTAL
30.0	Estimate														1	1				2
31.0	Event												1							1
32.0	Food														2	2				4
33.0	Forms														2	1				3
.1	Information About															1				1
34.0	Formula												2							2
.1	Adjustment/Correction Of														1					1
.2	Issuance Of				1															1
35.0	Freight														2					2
.1	Payment Of												6							6
36.0	Fire Drill																4			4
37.0	Grievance															4				4
38.0	Housing																			
.1	Availability Of														1					1
39.0	Income														1					1
40.0	Injury-Illness																			
41.0	Injury														8	37				45
42.0	Insurance															1				1
43.0	Invoice																6			6
.1	Receipt Of												1							1
.2	Status Of															1				1
.3	Transmittal Of												4							4
44.0	Job														2					2
.1	Analysis Of															1				1
.2	Rating Of															5				5
.3	Requirements Of															1				1
.4	Safety Of															2				2
.5	Status Of															6				6
45.0	Labor							1								5				6
.1	Cost Of														2					2
.2	Distribution Of														3					3
.3	Status Of														5	5				10
46.0	Land and Buildings																			
.1	Inspection Of												32							32
.2	Safety Of												3							3
.3	Status Of															1				1

FIG. 4-1. *Functional index spread sheet.*

note that this terminology is common to all phases of the entire paper-work processing area. Even in the programming of a computer, certainly in the charting of a procedure, the pieces of paper still relate to these same subjects, operations, and functions. Thus the classification in the functional index serves the entire paper-work area and not just the area of forms control in itself.

Two of the most fruitful results from a correctly constructed functional index are seen in the following actual examples.

TABLE 4-1.   Classification of Typical Commonly Used Forms

The form	Subject	Operation	Function
Bank check................	Cash	Payment of	To order
Statement..................	Account receivable	Status of	To notify
Personnel record............	Employment	Status of	To record
Inventory report............	Supplies	Status of	To report
Insurance claim.............	Loss	Compensation for	To claim
Invoice....................	Merchandise	Sale of	To notify
Bill of lading...............	Shipment	Receipt of	To acknowledge
Medical report..............	Employee	Examination of	To report
Laboratory report...........	Material	Analysis of	To report
Payroll record..............	Cash	Payment of	To record
Watchman's record..........	Premises	Inspection of	To report
Work order.................	Work	Performance of	To order
Accident report.............	Property*	Damage to	To report
Pass......................	Person	Passage of	To authorize
Bond.....................	Person	Insurance of	To agree
Cash receipt................	Cash	Receipt of	To acknowledge
Demurrage form.............	Equipment	Status of	To report
Expense report.............	Travel*	Cost of	To report
Insurance policy............	Person*	Insurance ot	To agree
Premium notice.............	Account receivable	Status of	To notify
Loss (insurance)............	Cash	Payment of	To record
Manifest...................	Shipment*	Status of	To certify
Passport...................	Person	Passage of	To authorize
Hat check..................	Property	Ownership of	To certify

* These forms could relate to another subject as well as the one indicated.

1. *Procedures studies* were uncovered in one company's paper work through the functional index which brought together all forms doing the same thing. Here are samples of what was found:

20 different forms for recording and reporting customer sales in district sales offices

32 different forms to report the inspection of land, buildings, and equipment

5 different forms for reporting departmental expenses

50 different forms for reporting, in all locations, employee attendance

5 different forms to notify concerning job ratings

22 different forms for reporting plant medical and safety activities

9 different forms to report the local scheduling of production

13 different forms for handling temporary changes of rates for reassigned employees

These were only a few of the data-processing situations where local personnel acted without the benefit of standard procedures. The result was not only inefficiency in the local area but considerable confusion in headquarters, particularly in those cases where the reports had to be sent in for recapitulation or control, such as in the scheduling of production.

This, it should be noted, was not a giant company but a medium-sized one with several plants and a number of district offices.

2. *Management reports* were shown to be a bigger-than-realized problem in another major industrial company where there were a systems and procedures

department, a computer installation, and generally well-organized controls. However, when the company's 6,000 forms (management previously had thought there were about 3,500 forms) were organized in the functional index and all report forms were identified, it was found that no fewer than 2,774 forms reported some kind of information to someone else in the organization.

Experience shows that from one-third to one-half of all forms serve the function of reporting. This company was no different, but management was shocked when the facts were brought to light. A subsequent study of these report forms brought the following results:

642 report forms (23.1 percent) were totally eliminated as being unnecessary.

321 report forms (11.6 percent) were kept under study for procedure or management requirement analyses.

294 report forms (10.6 percent) were redesigned and improved for more efficient use.

107 report forms (3.9 percent) were reduced in the number of copies made and distributed.

1,410 or 50.8 percent of the report forms were kept without change.

Such a result as this could never have been brought about if the forms control program had not classified all of the forms in the company as to subject, operation, and function. "To report" is one of the essential functions, and all 2,774 forms falling in that category were properly related to their specific subjects and operations, thus making a real study of reports possible.

Many of the reports that were kept without change were those which were intimately known to management and which were the product of carefully studied tabulating and computer operations. They included the reports on finances, sales, production, payroll, inventory, and other areas in which the vital management decisions had to be made. These forms were the only reports of which management was previously aware at the corporate level.

To build such an index is not a quick or simple job, but there is little likelihood that forms will ever be controlled unless a classification is made and the index built. An extremely important factor is the changing of personnel in the forms control program. Given time for a certain amount of trial-and-error experimentation, an index can be built by any intelligent person with considerable analytical ability. When it is completed, however, and when that person goes to another job or possibly another company, the subsequent forms control operator will have untold difficulty finding forms unless there has been a record made of the classification used. This means the compiling of a dictionary of terminology and this is almost as big a job as building the index in the first place. The author has never seen a case where a really usable record of classification terminology has been made by the analyst on the job. Without a record, the index quickly becomes almost useless and a graveyard of expensive effort when new people cannot find forms in it. At best, it discourages rather than encourages further efforts at forms control.[1]

THE STAFF-LINE RELATIONSHIPS IN FORMS CONTROL

More forms control programs fail because management does not establish workable staff-line relationships than for any other reason. Line management

[1] For detailed intructions for the building of a functional index, see Frank M. Knox, *The Knox Standard Guide to Design and Control of Business Forms*, 2d ed., McGraw-Hill Book Company, New York, 1965.

has both the authority and the responsibility for the performance of its work, and if the department does not function, it is the line management which suffers.

In the face of this fact, it is entirely reasonable that line managers should be responsible for their own paper work, and if they want a form to do something, they should have it.

On the other hand, top management must meet the bill for the general administrative expense of the whole company, and here is where the cost of paper work becomes a real problem. Therefore, forms control must be based on the requirements of both the line and staff. It is the failure to coordinate these requirements that is the reason for most of the forms control failures.

Since paper work and forms are usually no more than a nuisance to line management and appear to be far removed from its primary responsibility for making a profit, it is no wonder that little or no attention is paid to them by line management. When top or central management starts to instigate forms and paper-work control on the corporate level, it runs directly into the fact of line authority which cannot be abrogated to establish a staff control.

The answer is found in three steps by management: first, the establishment and promulgation of a policy for the control and reduction of paper-work expense; second, establishment of a staff to accept and discharge the primary responsibility for the program; and third, establishment of a joint responsibility in the line organization for the program's success.

The Policy Statement. There should be a statement by top management that there is to be a control program and this should be issued to all interested parties, which means the entire line organization. This policy should not be issued until the program is carefully worked out and the authorities and responsibilities defined. Once this is done, the policy statement can be issued.

Establishment of a Staff. There should be a staff at corporate headquarters which should bear the primary responsibility for the program. But it must be made abundantly clear that this staff has *no authority* over the forms and paper work; that must remain with the line organization.

The Staff-Line Relationship. A great deal of forms control will never happen unless it is done by the line units. The operating departments need the paper to perform their functions, and they create the forms. Here a close distinction must be made between the authorship of a form and the design of the form. It is the responsibility of the line unit to *author* the form, that is, decide on the words and information that are to appear on the form. Except for corporate-wide procedures, no one else can do this.

On the other hand, seldom does anyone in the line department have the technical knowledge of form designing to produce the maximum of clerical and administrative efficiency. Therefore, the central staff must have someone qualified to take the "authored" form and translate it into an efficient *design*.

This requires the application of two kinds of standards of design: functional and physical.

Functional standards are those which apply to entering data on the forms; reading and using the data after they have been entered; minimizing the possibility of error in clerical operations; and creating a satisfactory mental attitude on the part of the people who have to work on or use the forms.

Physical standards are those which apply to the production of the form; the size and kind of paper stock; the printing or reproduction of the form by the correct process; the establishment of adequate and correct specifications for its production; the correct preparation of the composition which must be done before it is printed; and the type faces to be used.

The central staff must have the knowledge and ability to use these standards, but the design, after it has been drawn, must be returned to the line unit for final approval. No form should be sent to the printer or reproduction department without the written approval of the using department.

This requires that the line organizations must assign specific persons to discharge the responsibility for the forms control program in their areas. These persons become the authorized contact for the central staff. They provide a bridge between the staff and the line, and the whole becomes the organizational framework within which the program will work.

Failure to establish this staff-line relationship defeats more forms control programs than any other single factor.

SUMMARY

Forms control means the control of *all* forms in the company, not just the big, important forms that are used on machines or in connection with electronic data processing. It means control over all the paper which creates clerical and administrative expense in the company.

It must include all forms that are created and produced within the various departments and plants, whether or not they are ever sent outside that department. It must include all office-duplicated forms as well as those purchased from commercial printers.

The emphasis of forms control must be directed mainly to the clerical and administrative use of forms rather than the production or purchase of forms, because twenty or thirty dollars of expense are consumed in the use of the form for every dollar spent producing the form.

Forms control must be backed by company policy. Management must provide for the correct staff-line relationships with adequate definitions of authorities and responsibilities for the creation and use of forms. The central staff, probably part of the systems and procedures unit, must be aware that they have no direct authority over forms but must accept and discharge a primary responsibility for the forms control program. At the same time, management must be sure that the line organization accepts and discharges a joint responsibility for the program with a large measure of direct responsibility for the forms which may be created and used solely within their particular department or plant.

The authorship of forms must fall within the prerogatives of the line manager. The design, however—for economy and efficiency in procurement and use—must be under the control of trained personnel in the central staff.

Provision must be made for the mechanical operations of composition and typesetting so that the production of the form by the printer will not defeat the design standards built into the form for clerical and administrative efficiency.

The control files must be built in such a way that they will uncover duplication and prevent the origination of forms when one or more already exist for the purpose. Techniques of classifying the forms in the functional index must be made a matter of record so that the index will not fall into disuse with personnel changes due to the inability of new personnel to find forms in the file.

Above all, the program must be a permanent one and not a temporary palliative.

BIBLIOGRAPHY

Knox, Frank M., *The Knox Standard Guide to Design and Control of Business Forms*, 2d ed., McGraw-Hill Book Company, New York, 1965.

CHAPTER FIVE

Records Management

C. A. CAMERON   *Partner, Leahy-Cameron Associates, New York, New York*

An ocean of paper so vast as to stagger the imagination threatens to engulf American business and government. Fifteen hundred trillion pieces of paper are on file in the nation's offices and storerooms. Two million file clerks are kept busy servicing them. And the ocean keeps swelling at the rate of 62 million file drawers each year. In 1965 the annual dollar loss from *unnecessary* paper work alone was rapidly approaching the billion-dollar mark. The loss incurred by the failure of vital information to get through when it is needed for key business decisions is far greater.

A two-way control is urgently needed. First, measures must be taken to stop the production and retention of useless paper. Second, specific procedures must be organized and spelled out to identify the most efficient and economical ways to file, store, and access those documents which are found to be paying their way.

Giant strides have been taken along these lines in recent years. Significant records management breakthroughs have resulted in savings of millions of dollars in slashed labor costs, released filing and storage facilities, and precious floor space. The purpose of this chapter is to disseminate this information to practicing managers and students of management.

SCOPE OF THE PROBLEM

The creation and retention of records vary from company to company. But it will help the manager draw a sharper bead on his target if he gets a general picture of what the nation's files contain and the costs involved. Studies in hundreds of companies reveal the following:

Of the nation's papers, 35 percent could be destroyed today and not be missed. This would produce an annual saving of $500 million, or $20 per cubic foot.

Another 20 percent is equally useless. But these papers are interfiled with useful records. It would cost more to weed out the useless papers than to retain them.

Of the remaining papers, 95 percent are useful for five years or less. About 50 percent of this bulk can be kept in low-cost storage rather than office space. *Only 1 percent must be kept permanently.*

It costs an average of 4 cents to index and file a paper—$640 for a single four-drawer cabinet.

It is with these factors that the records management specialist is concerned. The effective control program has four main objectives: (1) fewer and better office files, (2) regular schedules for retirement and destruction of records, (3) preservation of historical documents, and (4) protection of vital records against enemy attack and natural hazards.

THE DRIVE FOR FEWER AND BETTER RECORDS

Functions of the Control Program. It is the responsibility of the company's records manager or consulting specialist to identify the functions bearing on the program objective. These fall quite naturally into the following three main categories.

Production Controls Affecting Quantity and Quality of Records
1. Improvement of office organization and procedures
2. Paper-work simplification through:
   a. Correspondence improvement
   b. Reports control
   c. Forms control
   d. Control of internal office instructions and directives
   e. Better machine utilization in duplicating, storing, and retrieving data

Files Organization and Maintenance
3. Design of filing systems
4. Training in filing methods and techniques
5. Equipment control; setting standards for procurement and use of filing equipment and supplies
6. Operation of files: indexing, filing, reference

Disposition of Records
7. Schedules to retire and dispose of records
8. Designing and servicing low-cost housing centers for retired records
9. Retiring semiactive records; destroying dead records
10. Determining feasibility of microfilming records
11. Identifying and preserving papers of historical value
12. Protecting vital records

RECORDS MANAGEMENT PERSONNEL

Top management support is essential to an effective records management program. Traditionally, overall records responsibility is in the lap of the top financial executive or corporate secretary, who often is a vice president as well. In smaller companies the man at the helm may be the office manager, systems manager, or even the chief clerk.

The true architect of the program, however, is the records manager. He plans and organizes the system. He sees to it that subordinate personnel execute the system as planned. How many people does he need on his staff? This depends on the volume of office-held records. The following table, developed from experience in companies and government agencies of varying sizes, may be helpful in planning staff requirements after the initial program phase is completed.

Cubic Feet of Records	Staff Requirement
Up to 25,000	1
25,000 to 75,000	2
75,000 to 150,000	3
150,000 to 250,000	4

No army is better than its general. What are the qualifications of the ideal records manager? Briefly, he is astute enough to avoid "empire building" by using staff facilities to their utmost. He is also a skilled persuader, because the wholehearted cooperation of managers and supervisors, secretaries and clerks, is essential to the success of any records management program.

The records management pro is a clear thinker, and is analytical by nature. He is also an idea man, always after that "better way," and a good idea salesman. Finally, he knows departmental functions, and appreciates the information problems relating to these functions.

GETTING STARTED

Because most companies are indiscriminate paper savers, their files must be inventoried and appraised before an effective records retention schedule can be set up. Whether or not an outside consulting firm helps with this task, certain prerequisites are important.

First, the man tapped for the job must have top management's blessing and backup. He must then develop a chart of file locations, distinguishing between those held in the office and those in storage. To budget and control the project, the total time estimate should be prepared on a "walk through" basis. This rough census is accomplished by starting with the first file cabinet in sight and counting the total number of drawers in offices, plants, and storerooms. This will turn up enough information to give the experienced pro a good working idea of the volume and age of records. The usual yardstick is 1.5 cubic feet to a letter-size file drawer; 2 cubic feet to a legal-size file. The census taker may open an occasional drawer to check the age of the papers, or he can get this information from the file custodian.

Finally, the identity of the person with primary records responsibility in each department must be determined. This individual will ultimately approve or disapprove the recommendations made by the records manager.

When inventorying files, the records specialist starts with office-held, not storage-held, records. For one thing, office records are more diversified; for another, office space and equipment are more costly.

In making his inventory, the skilled records man is after at least six pieces of information: (1) volume of records in cubic feet, (2) class of records by descriptive title, (3) age of records, (4) manner of organization, (5) extent of duplication, especially between files, and (6) average number of references per month.

During the inventory, and in cooperation with the department heads, each class of records is appraised for the length of time it should be held for administrative needs. This gives the records manager the raw data he needs to develop a comprehensive records retention schedule.

THE RECORDS RETENTION SCHEDULE

The records retention schedule is a timetable governing the retirement and destruction of *all* company records. Each file, listed by department and class title, shows (1) how long it is kept in the office before destruction or transfer to storage and (2) the length of time in storage before destruction. Except for historical records, which, presumably, are kept permanently, length of retention hinges mainly on legal and auditing requirements. Retention refers to *official* files only; duplicate files can be destroyed at any time. The only way to distinguish a duplicate file is by a "yes" answer to the question: If the duplicate file is destroyed, will the *official* file take its place?

Legal Requirements. Certain records are needed to protect the company against legal action or prove compliance with the law. As there is no statute of limitation on criminal prosecution, it is risky to destroy documents that might protect the company against criminal action. Also no problem are those records whose length of retention is spelled out by Federal or state law.

How long to keep many other records, however, can be a brow-knitting question. Often legal counsel must be sought. It also helps to refer to the retention schedules of other companies. Setting up a schedule can be a painstaking task. But the payoff in savings of labor, time, space, and facilities makes the job well worth the effort.

Audit Requirements. More and more, retentions for internal audit requirements are superseded by Federal and state rulings. Still, the controller or chief auditor is a valuable consultant when preparing a retention schedule.

Once completed, the schedule should be reviewed and approved by financial management, the company attorney, and the various executives who exercise administrative authority over individual departments.

THE MODERN CENTER FOR INACTIVE RECORDS

More and more organizations are relying on the modern records center to store and service inactive records. In most cases, records center storage is cheaper than microfilming. Here is why. Center space and equipment are relatively inexpensive. The latest storage and accessing techniques assure the most efficient use of manpower and space. The records retention schedule triggers document transfers to the center.

It is often cheaper to build a center than move. Some companies relocate records three or more times during a 10-year period. Records researchers find that a local move involving commercial movers and company porters costs $1.50 for a standard file drawer (1.5 cubic feet of records).

An example of a well-run center is the one at General Electric Company's Hanford Works at Richland, Washington. The building and equipment cost $131,000. But the center has taken over the storage job of 28,666 file drawers costing more than a half-million dollars. Add to this an estimated annual saving of $43,000 to $172,000 worth of released office space (at $1 to $4 per square foot).

The Hanford center was built in 1950. Even more efficient are those centers constructed recently from plans developed as a result of twenty-five years of records management research and experience. The Leahy Archives at Chicago; the Grumman Aircraft Engineering Center at Bethpage, Long Island; and the New Hampshire Archives and Records Center at Concord, New Hampshire, are prototypes of up-to-date centers. These buildings were designed with special emphasis on protection, accessibility of records, and maximum space utilization.

Each building will house two-and-a-half times as many records per square foot as the Hanford Works Center.

THE NETWORK SYSTEM OF OFFICE FILING

A controlled network of file stations will serve to improve record-keeping efficiency by eliminating duplicate files and upgrading service. The network idea embraces a chain of centrally controlled file stations. Three general types of stations are involved: (1) *The official station.* This may be a *central* station shared by several offices, or a *local* station servicing a single office. The official station is often the only station where a class of records is documented. Or it is the one where the class is documented best. (2) *The independent station.* This is a duplicate file maintained for business convenience. (3) *The limbo station.* This houses records referenced too infrequently to be kept in prime office space, but not inactive enough for relegation to a records center. The limbo station is usually kept in less-valuable office space.

The connecting link between stations is called the "central locator index." Reference to this index will pinpoint the location of any document that is not kept at hand.

Planning the Network. Generally speaking, records control is the unwanted orphan of managerial functions. In many companies, the responsibility is palmed off to the point where the person who finally winds up with the onerous task of trying to create order out of chaos resents the assignment as a lowering of status. Yet good organization and planning are the only key to effective records control. The occasional "cleanup," inspired out of desperation, is rarely a suitable solution. It is apt to be costly, repetitive, and of short duration. The planning and development of a network control are a job for an expert. Each of the following critical phases calls for analytical talents and seasoned judgment:

Studies to pin down the extent and nature of reference interest in all classes of records

Designation of the various types of file stations

Determination of the feasibility of central filing

Relocation of stations for better service

Development of the central locator index

Establishment of controls and written procedures to keep the network system running smoothly and efficiently

The efficiently operated network system is geared exclusively to the service of its "customers." For this reason, the selection and location of official file stations are of key importance. The main determining factor is usage. To appraise this factor the skilled recordsman asks himself four searching questions: (1) How often is the file consulted? (2) Who consults it? (3) Why? (4) Is the file duplicated elsewhere? A form designed to answer these questions is shown in Figure 5-1.

A harrowing problem that perennially plagues the records manager is the one of duplication. The question is: How can the same records be made accessible to a number of scattered offices without turning out multiple copies and maintaining the same files in a variety of locations? Much has been said about the wastefulness of duplication. Yet it is often the lesser of two evils. The cost of running a duplicate file may be much less than the cost of delaying business transactions because of inaccessible records. Still, there is no reason

FILE STATION ANALYSIS		NAME OF CUSTODIAN	
FROM	TO	CLASS TITLE OF RECORDS	
STATION LOCATION		FILE SYSTEM	

PART I. PERSONS REQUESTING REFERENCE SERVICE. (FOR USE BY FILE CUSTODIAN)

NAME	SECTION	NAME	SECTION
		☐ CONTINUED ON SEPARATE PAGE	

PART II. ANALYSIS AND APPRAISAL. (FOR USE BY ANALYST)

ARE COPIES OF DOCUMENTS KEPT IN THIS STATION ACCESSIBLE ELSEWHERE?   ☐ YES   ☐ NO

IF SO, WHERE?

HOW MANY REFERENCES WERE MADE FOR ACTION PURPOSES?_____ HOW MANY FOR INFORMATION?_____

INDICATIONS ARE   ☐ OFFICIAL FILE STATION   ☐ INDEPENDENT FILE STATION

    ☐ CENTRAL   ☐ NONESSENTIAL STATION

    ☐ LOCAL

FIG. 5-1. *File station analysis form.*

why a company should invest so heavily in duplicate-file insurance. A better insurance, at a smaller investment, is available. The answer lies in the well-cultivated network of file stations, controlled to provide quick reference service whenever and wherever needed in the company.

THE FILING SYSTEM

The ultimate in professional records management is called the "pro-file," distinguished by *simplicity, efficiency,* and *usefulness.* The pro-file is easily loaded and unloaded. It is referenced often enough to earn its keep. It is relatively free of unwanted papers. It proves its value by running smoothly and economically. Here are some key pointers in attempting to achieve this objective:

Always use a name arrangement if you can. If names are few and volume large, a subject breakdown will serve to restrict the area of search. One time *not* to use names is when some of the papers in the file cannot be associated with name headings.

Numerical filing benefits include ease of checking for missing, serially numbered documents and ease of referencing prenumbered paper such as invoices. Numbers may be associated with dates to simplify retirement and disposal.

Date sequence is often the easiest, but laziest, way to set up a file. With few exceptions, such as tickler files for action follow-up, current information files, or papers within folders, the date arrangement is of small help in finding records.

Subject files, adaptable to less than 15 percent of modern business records, constitute a major managerial headache. The hope is that electronics will soon solve this problem. But with or without electronics, the solution lies in better classification and indexing. To deal with subject filing in detail would require more space than is here available. But the following classification tips will help for a starter: (1) Keep topics short—just long enough to get the idea across. (2) For primary subjects, select key words descriptive of the entire subject. (3) In dividing subjects, be guided by the number of papers involved. (4) Keep an up-to-date classification outline with primary subjects defined.

Filing Case No. 1. *Problem:* A company's employment application file consisted mainly of job inquiry letters. Referencing was made most often by applicant name, and three times out of ten by class of employment. The personnel head, in view of company plans to expand to new areas, felt a geographical file would be useful.

Solution: One alphabetical file in order by applicant name was set up; group (not individual name) folders for alphabetical divisions; papers filed in date order within the folders; disposal made annually. Since only 15 percent of all applicants were eligible candidates, job classification filing was not justified. Instead eligible names were posted to a roster index. Guided by the principle that no file should be set up for a short-term or indefinite period, the personnel chief was convinced that a geographical file was not practical.

Filing Case No. 2. *Problem:* An insurance company had been running a central correspondence file for thirty years, complete with tons of musty papers, mountains of index cards, eye-shaded clerks, and terrifying silence. Probing this underground sanctum, a records specialist unearthed hoards of worthless documents serviced by a crew of hollow-eyed clerks. Thirty years of custom was behind the waste. Each department mindlessly funneled its papers underground.

Solution: The central file was discontinued. Each department now keeps its own file by correspondents' names. Disposal is annual. Hundreds of cabinets and thousands of feet of space were released. A network control keeps duplication to a minimum.

Filing Case No. 3. *Problem:* A French-speaking Canadian lad was saddled with the task of filing purchase order copies for his American employer. One day he decided to pose a question to a visiting, high-level executive. Why, Pierre wanted to know, was all of this work necessary when an identical file was maintained in the receiving department across the hall?

Solution: Today, where sixty cabinets of purchase orders stood, are storage bins filled with component parts. Pierre? He is now company chauffeur for the executive staff.

THE FILE STATION—KEY OPERATING POINTERS

Names. A person's surname should be alphabetized first; for example, file "Henry Adams" under "Adams Henry." Follow suit with company names; for example, "John Jones Company" under "Jones John Company." The well-known company, such as Marshall Field, is an exception—file this as is. Do not treat classification words such as "hotel" or "university" as primary units; for example, file "Hotel Astor" under "Astor Hotel." File papers of United States government organizations first by "United States government," then by agency name, then by department. File numbers as they are spelled; for example, "23 Club" as "Twenty-three Club."

Sorting. If a mechanical sorter is not used, table sort 2,000 or less papers by breaking them down into four, five, or six alphabetical groupings. After the first letter is sorted, follow suit on the subsequent ones until the desired sequence is obtained. When manually sorting numbered papers, the breakdown may be from left to right, or right to left—but always from 0 to 9.

Classification. When classifying, always consider the paper first in its relation to a primary classification. Then narrow it down to its most fitting subhead in the classification outline. Do not force classifications. The paper worth filing should have a well-defined niche. If the niche is elusive, it may mean the wrong file station was used—or that the classification outline needs revision or expansion. Mark papers uniformly as a subject filing guide, preferably in the upper right corner.

Filing. When vertical files are used, the insertion and reference of papers are made easier by keeping more active records in upper cabinet drawers. In loose filing, do not take folders from the file drawer. Simply drop the paper in front of the folder. Stick to the prescribed filing setup. If filing is in date order, run sequence from the back of the folder to the front, with the most recent papers in front. For best space utilization and operating ease, keep file drawers four-fifths filled.

Referencing. The cross-reference sheet describes a record and tells how it is filed. A single-sheet document can usually be duplicated on a copier for less than the cost of preparing a cross-reference sheet. Provide ample table space at the file station to permit callers to examine papers. This will cut down on unnecessary removal. With the low-cost copiers available, it is often cheaper to duplicate a one- or two-page document than to loan it out. Some records call for more control than others. If a follow-up system is established to recover overdue papers, control should be rigidly enforced. Otherwise, the system should be abandoned. A standard form for requesting records (studies show) is usually not used often enough to justify its printing.

Disposal. Periodic retirement or destruction of records in large blocks is no problem for the qualified custodian. But paper-by-paper disposal is time consuming and inefficient. Continuous weeding is more effective than periodic cleanup spurts. This is done by a rapid spot examination any time a folder is removed from the file.

COORDINATE INDEXING

The technical and scientific information explosion has spawned a monstrous retrieval problem. Conventional indexing is slow, clumsy, and inadequate to the task of finding the right papers, and *all* the right papers, buried in today's massive collections. Documents vary considerably. One will deal with a new kind of aircraft; another with a tiny instrument part. Yet both documents may be related. The retrieval problem is essentially one of coordination. And the solution for many companies and government agencies lies in the coordinate-indexing concept. Coordinate indexing, once set up manually, is easily adaptable to machine processing. Here, in simple terms, is how the system works.

First, a deck of cards is created. Each card contains a key word, or "uniterm" as it is called in the trade. Each uniterm, as the word implies, identifies a single word or term. The uniterm card is divided into ten vertical columns numbered 0 to 9 from left to right. The cards are filed in alphabetical order according to the uniterm description on top.

Under this system all documents are numbered, and they are filed in numerical order. Here is how the indexer represents the documents on the uniterm cards. If the document deals with aircraft, he would select the "aircraft" card and enter the document number in the column corresponding with the terminal digit (units position) of the number. Document number 32 would be in column 2, number 788 in column 8, and number 1071 in column 1.

NYLON

0	1	2	3	4	5	6	7	8	9
170	181	122	373	84	5	106	77	218	719
250	361	352	403	744	105	726	227	318	999
310	511	982	723	804	935	776	307	778	1039
770	1141	1502	1183	934	1165		377	1018	1089
	1391		1613	1114			417		1989
				1724			987		2019
				1984			1007		
							1117		

FABRIC

0	1	2	3	4	5	6	7	8	9
30	171	232	313	14	225	666	327	308	219
90	361	292	523	304	385	726	887	318	349
170	781	312	723	674	715	978		478	579
830		452	1173	854	935			578	
1010		682	1203	1004	1005	1058		838	
		742		1894				1568	
		1402							

SHRINKAGE

0	1	2	3	4	5	6	7	8	9
10	361	2	33	334	665	16	7	118	1009
120	421	102	183	484	185	76	187	228	1129
280	571	572	263	504	815	126	917	318	
	601	812	723	724		196	1457		
	1241	1322	1023	914		406			
			1463	1074		726			
				1314		1116			

FIG. 5-2. *Coordinate index cards.*

In searching for documents, cards with uniterms descriptive of the documents sought are pulled and scanned for matching numbers. For example, a chemist wants information about the shrinkage of nylon fabric. Three uniterms—*shrinkage, nylon,* and *fabric*—are involved in the search. A scan of the uniterm card for shrinkage shows several numbers (documents filed) on this subject. The uniterm card for nylon is now checked for any duplication of the numbers appearing on the shrinkage card. These duplicated numbers represent documents on both nylon and shrinkage.

Finally, the card for fabric is checked to see how many of the duplicated numbers (nylon and shrinkage) are repeated here. Any numbers appearing on *all three* cards pertain to documents relating to the specific subject, shrinkage of nylon fabric. It is then a simple matter to pull the specified documents by number from the file. Figure 5-2 illustrates this procedure. As can be seen, by arranging the numbers according to their terminal digits on the cards, the search is narrowed considerably.

In practice, the system is highly effective. It is also fraught with problems. Does "wolf" stand for a surname or the animal? Do "index" and "card" mean an index card or a card index? Provisions must be made to distinguish between various categories of information. The more complex the search requirement and the more voluminous the file, the greater the depth of indexing and the degree of differentiation.

BUSINESS ARCHIVES

T. R. Shellenberg, former director of archival management for the National Archives of the United States, defines "archives" as: "Those records of any public or private institution which are adjudged worthy of permanent preservation for reference and research projects and which have been deposited or which have been selected for deposit in an archival institution." There are two broad classes of business records generally considered worthy of permanent retention: (1) those that *must* be kept as continuing evidence of corporate and individual rights; (2) those that *may* shed light of historical interest on the organization, functioning, and accomplishments of the company.

In addition to the goal of releasing high-rental space and expensive facilities, old and valuable documents should be removed from the office to protect them against deterioration. Special restorative or preservative methods are sometimes required. This is no task for an amateur. Prized documents should be turned over to a specialist for skilled handling.

CONCLUSION

Perhaps the greatest service the professional recordsman can render his employer or client is to help hew down as much of the paper-work jungle as he can. This formidable growth consists mainly of correspondence, forms, reports, internal communications, and technical bulletins. Basically, the problem is one of *too many copies and too many words.* The byword of *Modern Archives Principles and Techniques* by T. R. Shellenberg, the topnotch records manager, is "Why?" Every document and every copy made should be able to respond to this test with a practical, cost-justified answer. Any paper that cannot respond is a profit drainer and should be dumped, its further production ceased.

The truly talented recordsman is a proponent of brevity, a trimmer of excesses, a combiner of forms. In a sense, he is the corporate dietitian. He keeps the vital functioning body of information well exercised and in tiptop condition. And he knows that the best way to do this is to keep the fat from forming.

BIBLIOGRAPHY

Bourne, C. P., *Methods of Information Handling,* John Wiley & Sons, Inc., New York, 1963.

Case Studies in Records Retention and Control, Controllership Foundation, Inc., New York, 1957.

"A Guide to U.S. Federal Requirements," *Corporate Records Retention,* vol. 1, Controllership Foundation, Inc., New York, 1958.

Leahy, Emmett, and Christopher A. Cameron, *Modern Records Management: A Basic Guide to Records Control, Filing, and Information Retrieval,* McGraw-Hill Book Company, New York, 1965.

Odell, Margaret K., and E. P. Strong, *Records Management and Filing Operations,* McGraw-Hill Book Company, New York, 1947.

Retention and Preservation of Records with Destruction Schedules, 6th ed., Record Controls, Inc., Chicago, 1961.

CHAPTER SIX

Office Work Measurement

WILLIAM M. AIKEN *Vice President, H. B. Maynard and Company, Incorporated, Pittsburgh, Pennsylvania*

JOHN F. LEWIS *Controller, H. B. Maynard and Company, Incorporated, Pittsburgh, Pennsylvania*

Work measurement applied to office work is not new. Indeed, one very prominent insurance company not only has applied time study to clerical work for some forty years, but has paid incentive on the work as well. In general, however, only since about 1950 has work measurement in offices gained much prominence, probably because of the large increases in clerical activity.

Office work measurement has some features which distinguish it from other areas where work measurement has been applied extensively. The benefits, however, parallel very closely the benefits that have been realized from many, many work measurement installations. Clerical cost reductions ranging between 15 and 30 percent are the rule when work measurement controls are applied to office work.

This chapter points out the approaches which have been successful in measuring and controlling office work. It describes the manner in which management should use office work measurement and the results that they will attain.

THE NEED FOR OFFICE WORK MEASUREMENT

Office work has seemed to enjoy a privileged status with management for many years. Although attention was focused repeatedly on shop labor costs for reduction and control, office work ran along without much fuss or particular attention. In the years following World War II, skyrocketing office costs forced management to look at them seriously. What they saw were areas of tremendous cost-reduction potential.

Various approaches have been used effectively by management to reduce office costs. Many innovations have improved the capability of office machines.

Data processing has automatized many clerical jobs. Systems and procedures analysts have streamlined and eliminated other jobs.

Work measurement has played an increasingly important role in decreasing and controlling office costs. Alone, and in conjunction with other cost-reduction approaches, it has been valuable to management. Its principal uses have been to:

1. Reduce and control costs. The typical uncontrolled office operation is normally 50 to 60 percent effective. With measurement and control, this performance can be raised to the level of 85 to 90 percent without incentives—over 100 percent with incentives. Managers can expect a reduction in the clerical force of from 15 to 30 percent, with 20 percent being a good "rule of thumb" saving. The control procedures enable management to maintain the performance at the acceptable level of 85 to 90 percent by adjusting manpower for various seasonal or cyclical needs.

2. Improve methods. Invariably a work measurement program leads to methods improvements. The close scrutiny that work analysts must give to the work cannot help but point out many possibilities for improvement.

3. Provide correct costing for office services. The value of this information is that management can compare the cost of a report or procedure with the benefits it provides. For banks and insurance companies, this information helps to determine the prices for their services.

4. Strengthen systems and procedures work. One of the difficulties in systems and procedures work is that the analyst often cannot predetermine the degree of improvement, if any, from a new or changed procedure. With work measurement, he can prove the value of a new or changed procedure before any installation is actually made.

5. Evaluate equipment needs. Managements often install new equipment without accurately predetermining the anticipated gain. Many times new equipment is justified by comparing an uncontrolled condition with a highly mechanized situation. If work measurement controls were established first, there would be many cases where new equipment could not be economically justified. In other cases, work measurement would clearly establish the desirability of new equipment.

6. Train clerical workers. The detailed analysis required for work measurement provides an excellent instrument for training employees on new jobs. The performance records are useful also for the selection of employees for promotions or changed positions. Of all the uses of office work measurement, probably the most important ones are to establish proper manning in the office and to improve the effectiveness of the workers and the supervisors.

Establishing Proper Manning. One of the main reasons why clerical personnel work at 50 or 60 percent performance before controls are applied is either overmanning or lack of work. This results in a tendency to stretch out work to fill the hours. Work measurement points out clearly to the office supervisor how many clerks he needs for various work loads. He should man his office accordingly. Instead of routinely manning for peak loads, he should man for a normal load, and use overtime and temporary help to handle the peaks. As the overall work load increases or decreases, he can use the measurement to adjust the size of the work force as needed.

Many companies use work measurement to screen requests for additional office help. This is helpful even in offices with as few as three clerical people. Although it may not be practical to have work standards and performance reports as a routine matter for as small an office as this, it is entirely practical to measure the work load before authorizing the hiring of an additional clerk.

Improving Performance. In addition to indicating that a work force may be excessive, poor performance can indicate other things to the supervisor. If a worker is having difficulty meeting standards, it may be because he is experiencing excessive delays. The supervisor can work with the individual to eliminate these delays. One popular method for doing this is to assign the worker only one or two hours' work at a time—with instructions to report back at a stated time when the work should be completed. Another method is to make an extensive study with the clerk to identify and eliminate the causes for delay.

Poor performance may also indicate that the worker is not following the proper method. The standards are based on good methods that the average office worker can follow. If the clerk is not trained to follow the right method, he will naturally lose time and be unable to meet the standard. The office supervisor must work with the individual to be sure that he uses good methods.

Evaluating Supervisors. The performance reports measure not only the effectiveness of the individual clerks, but also the ability of the supervisor to manage his personnel effectively. Higher management is not particularly interested in the productivity of an individual clerk, but it is quite concerned about the output of a department or an office. The control reports that higher management receives show the performance of each department. This information is valuable to management for evaluating and guiding supervisors and for recognizing the management ability of supervisory personnel when promotional opportunities exist.

PREPARING FOR THE WORK MEASUREMENT PROGRAM

There is little question that a work measurement program will benefit a company. But it must be well organized and properly introduced into an organization for the benefits to be realized.

Need for Top Management Support. Management, in undertaking an office work measurement program, should realize that the program may not always be met with enthusiasm by everyone in the organization. The office supervisors and their immediate superiors are, in the abstract, in favor of economies, and desire to hold down the company's expenses. At the start of the program, they may give it their vocal support. Later, however, the program may indicate the need for some changes or economies in their own groups. At that point, if not before, many supervisors can find a multitude of reasons to prove that the program does not apply to their work or possibly that it is unsound. Thus, it is important that the program be introduced with the full support of top management. It must also have top management support during the early stages when changes must be made. If not, the program can flounder from inertia to resistance. Eventually, it may even be discarded as impractical or not suited to the conditions of the company.

A good way of securing top management support—particularly during the early and critical stages of installation—is to have the program under jurisdiction of a steering committee. This committee need not be very active, but should inaugurate the program, follow it up, and give support if and when it runs into any resistance.

The steering committee should be made up of key managers from different departments. This permits the program to cut across departmental lines. Thus, it is not a program that the controller, for example, is forcing on the sales department or the plant, nor a program that the industrial engineers are forcing on the accounting department. Members need not be at the top management level, but they should have the backing of top management when needed. On the other hand, they should be high enough in the organization that they can realize the overall benefit of changes and not be blinded by weaknesses in their own personal administration.

Areas Selected for Study.   There is a wide difference in the susceptibility to measurement and control of different kinds of work.   Thus, before spending much time to analyze any office for measurement, the analyst should estimate how long it should take to measure the work and what tangible gains may be expected from the measurement.

This judgment is based on three factors:

1. Number of different tasks done in the office
2. The number of clerk hours devoted to a given task
3. The work count or volume of each task

As a general rule, if an office has fewer than four clerks, chances are that there will be such a wide variety of tasks that the activity is probably not worth measuring.   By "task," we refer to an operation that can be counted.   For example, a task might be preparing invoices or paying bills.   If the office prepares 1,000 invoices a week, the task of billing should be susceptible to measurement; if it prepares 100 a week it probably is susceptible; but if it prepares only 10 a week it may not be worth analyzing.

In addition to the volume, the analyst should note the clerical hours devoted to any given task.   If our example of 1,000 invoices a week occupies the full time of ten clerks, the analyst should spend considerable time studying the operation, perhaps several weeks.   When he is finished, he will have brought a large number of clerical hours under control.   At the other extreme, a filing operation, in which a clerk files 1,000 documents a week, may require only an hour a day.   The analyst cannot afford to spend much time on this operation.

It is important that the program be started in the area, or areas, most susceptible to measurement and control.   This will demonstrate the potential gain from the program at an early stage and will be helpful in overcoming resistance. Once it has been proved in one or two areas that the company can use office work measurement to advantage, the program will proceed through the other areas with greater dispatch.

Introducing the Program.   There are several groups of people to be considered when the program is introduced.

1. The analysts selected to do the work
2. The office supervisors affected
3. The clerical personnel whose work will be analyzed

Selecting the Analysts.   There are three predominant qualifications needed for people doing this type of work:

1. An interest in doing the work
2. Above-average intelligence or ability
3. Practical experience

Practical experience may consist of an industrial engineering background, systems and procedures work, or regular office work.   Generally, industrial engineers are the best qualified.   They may not be too familiar with office work, but they understand the value of measuring work as such.   Although systems men understand office procedure, they often are not familiar with the concept of measurement and control, and consequently may be uncertain of its value to the company.   Many times, good results are obtained by selecting regular office workers who have the interest and ability.   They know how office work is done and can help greatly to sell the program.

Discussions with Supervisor. Before any actual work is done in the office, the office supervisor should be informed of the program. He must have a good understanding of it if he is expected to cooperate during the program. He must also be in a position to explain and help to sell the program to the clerical people reporting to him. The primary objective of the program is to give the supervisor information that will enable him to do a better job. This point cannot be emphasized too strongly when the program is first discussed with the supervisor.

Discussions with Clerical Personnel. Last, but far from least, the clerks whose work will be analyzed should be informed of the program before it begins, and before any rumors spread about its purpose. It is difficult for the clerical people to see how the program will benefit them before it starts. A main point that should be stressed is that the measurement will help management to recognize good performance. It is *not* a "speed-up," but will point out areas where the supervisors can be helpful to the workers. If at all possible, assurance must be given that the program will not result in the discharge of any employee. Attrition is by far the best means of reducing the size of any work force.

OFFICE WORK MEASUREMENT TECHNIQUES

There are four principal techniques used to measure clerical work, each having advantages and disadvantages.

Work Sampling. Work sampling consists of a number of random observations of clerical work. The observations are divided into categories of productive work and nonproductive work. The study extends over a period of time so that the results are truly representative of the work that the clerks do. With this information, the analyst can determine how much time was devoted to each task. When this is related to a count of the work done during the period, the analyst can determine standards for the work.

Historical Data. This is the most elementary measurement technique. It requires the analyst to review time and production records to see how much time was taken to do various tasks. From this, he establishes a time allowance for a worker to complete an operation.

In some cases, the historical data are factored arbitrarily so that the resulting standard calls for more production than the clerks formerly turned out.

Time Study. Time study has been used to measure office work for many years. It requires that the operation be set up and an operator trained to follow the prescribed method. The analyst divides the operation into short elements and times the operator doing the elements. A rating factor is applied to the recorded times to adjust them according to the ability of the worker. The total of the elemental allowed times then gives the standard for the operation.

Predetermined Standard Data. This technique requires the analyst to study each task to see exactly what is required to do it. The task is recognized as consisting of different motion patterns. The time for each required motion pattern can be developed from basic predetermined motion-time systems, such as Methods-Time Measurement, or it can be developed from elemental standard data built up for clerical work. The time for an operation is the sum of the elemental allowed times assigned to the required motion patterns. This technique provides excellent standards based on good methods and has been widely used for office work measurement.

Table 6-1 shows a summary of the advantages and disadvantages of the four measurement techniques.

TABLE 6-1.   Comparison of Office Work Measurement Techniques

Factor	Work sampling	Historical data	Time study	Predetermined standard data
Skill of analysts	Low	Low	Average	High
Time to install..........	Low–average	Low	High	Average
Administrative cost.......	Average	Average	Average	Average
Savings potential........	Low	Low	Average	High
Methods improvement potential..............	Low	Low	Average	High
Accuracy of standards....	Low	Low	Average	High
Applicability to:				
High volume...........	High	High	High	High
Low volume............	Average	Low	Average	Average
Employee acceptance.....	Average	Average	Low–average	Average
Supervisory acceptance...	Average–high	Average–high	Low–average	Average–high
Flexibility (as changes occur).................	Low	Low	Average	High

THE WORK MEASUREMENT PROCEDURE

The purpose of work measurement is to determine how long it should take to perform a given quantity of office work. When the operation involves very large quantities of the same document, the analyst is careful to arrive at an accurate standard. In general office work, however, the analyst does not attempt to determine exactly how long a particular item or task will take. He recognizes that rarely are two items exactly alike and that one invoice, for example, may take twice as long to prepare as another invoice. Thus, he tries to determine how long it should take to handle an average item.

The general steps of the office work measurement procedure using time study or predetermined standard data are shown in Figure 6-1.

Determine Principal Operations. Before the analyst begins to study any operation, he must know generally the relative importance of each task. This helps him to determine the amount of time that his measurement will control, as well as the amount of time that he can afford to spend on his analysis. To make these determinations, he prepares a task list.

The task list, as the name implies, lists the major operations or duties that a given clerical group and the individual workers perform. Together with the office workers and the supervisors, the analyst estimates the amount of time devoted to each task. The time may be expressed in hours per day, week, or month, or as a percentage of the total time available. From this, the analyst plans his time so that he can concentrate on the block of work that will yield the greatest return.

At a later stage, the task list may have additional value. As the work of the analyst proceeds, there is usually a reduction called for in the number of clerical hours assigned to a given task. There is frequently a tendency for tasks, other than the original ones, to "creep in" so that there is a reluctance to reduce the total assigned hours. A review of the task list will point out how the office work has "swollen" to nullify the savings needlessly.

Analyze Principal Operations for Elimination or Improvement. When the analyst measures the operations, he frequently finds that the methods can be improved. In some cases, he finds after he has put considerable time into the study that some operations are not necessary at all and can be eliminated. In order not to waste his time on unnecessary work measurement, he should review the operations first so that the unnecessary operations can be eliminated before he spends much time on them.

To make this preliminary analysis, he can use flow process charts which show the work flow of an entire procedure. This gives him a visual representation of all the operations involved so that duplication and overlapping become apparent.

The analyst can also apply operation analysis to the various operations. This technique, which can be applied very quickly, questions many things about the operation, such as: "Is the operation necessary?" "Can it be combined with other operations to avoid handling and duplication?" "Can it be divided so that specialization of skills will reduce costs?" "Is the report used for the

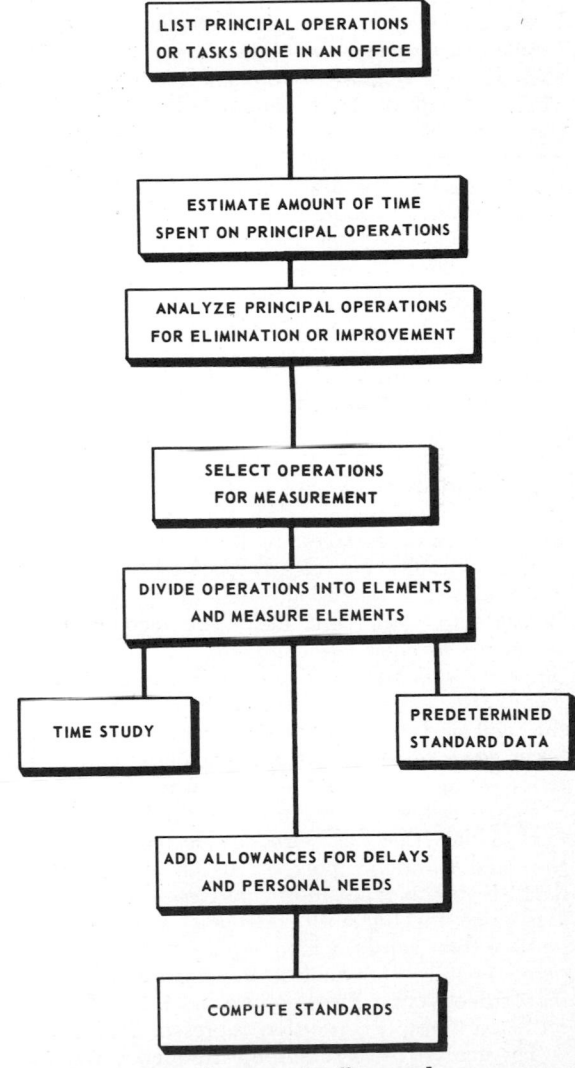

FIG. 6-1. *General steps of office work measurement procedure.*

purpose for which it was intended?" and "Can better materials (forms, carbons, and so forth) be used to reduce the time required?"

Obviously, the analyst must use discretion in determining the amount of time he will spend trying to improve the operation. If the operation requires only 20 clerical hours a week, his analysis will be cursory and informal. If the operation requires 200 hours a week, his study will be made in detail. He must be careful, however, that he does not become embroiled in systems and procedures work which can extend over some length of time. A good rule of thumb for him to use is that if the change he proposes can be recommended, accepted, and acted on within a day, he will base his measurement on the changed method. Experience has shown that if a change takes more than a day to install, it generally can take a lot more than one day. Thus, if the change will require more than a day to install, the analyst will recommend it, but base his measurement on existing methods.

Select Operations for Measurement. From the task list and his analysis of the principal operations, the analyst will select the tasks that he will measure. Practically all clerical operations lend themselves to measurement. Secretarial duties and attendance-type operations do not. Most of the principal operations will be studied in detail using time study or predetermined standard data. Some of the principal operations which are rather intangible and all of the minor miscellaneous operations—the so-called thousand and one things—are not economical to measure in detail. These can be controlled by developing an allowance for them to be applied to the time values for the major operations, or a lump-sum amount of time can be allocated to a clerk or to an office to take care of them. In establishing this allowance or allocation of time, the analyst must take care that unnecessary time-filling chores have not expanded to use up time saved from improved operations.

Measure the Work. The analyst first determines what the operation is. He looks at the finished product or result of the operation, as well as the source data or information that comes to the clerk. Then he observes the method that the operator is employing so that he can divide the operation into elements. At this time, he discusses with the clerk just how each part of the job is done so that he has a complete understanding of it.

The elements are clearly defined steps that the operator goes through in completing the operation, such as "pick up form and place in typewriter" or "select card from card file." The element may take from several seconds to a minute or more to complete. If the analyst is using time study, he then times the operation for several cycles and records the time taken for each element. He applies a rating factor to the recorded times to adjust them for the skill and effort of the operator while the study was being made. Quite often when he reviews the elements he can detect short cuts and improvements in the operator's method or in the workplace arrangement.

If the analyst is using predetermined standard data, he selects the appropriate time values from data tables. He records the code for the motion pattern and the time value for part or all of the element. This is done in much more detail than the time-study time recordings. Where a time study might provide one value for the entire element, predetermined standard data might call for perhaps ten values which equal in total the element time. This much finer detail enables the analyst to examine the element for wasted motions much more effectively. Furthermore, no rating factor is required to adjust the predetermined times, because they represent average skill and effort.

The analyst must determine frequency factors for each of the elements. For example, a clerk may go to a desk and pick up a batch of twenty invoices and return to her workplace. That would be one element that occurs once every twenty invoices. Next, she might, among other things, check the prices and extensions on each invoice. This would be an element that is allowed once for every invoice. In a similar way, the analyst determines how often each element will be performed for a unit of production. He then multiplies the elemental value by the frequency. The basic time value for the operation is the total of the factored elemental times. This is the time that the average clerk would require to do the operation if she worked at it steadily and without interruption.

Add Allowances. Office workers, of course, do not work without interruption. In general, they usually have more interruptions than factory workers. In addition to the personal time they must have, there are other delays such as phone calls for information, exceptions that must be checked, or urgent special tasks that are assigned.

The analyst must make allowances for all of the interferences. He generally does this by developing an allowance that incorporates time for personal needs, time for delays, and time for minor miscellaneous duties that are too small or irregular for detailed study. Work sampling is often used to make this determination.

The allowance, which can range from 15 to as high as 30 percent, is added to the basic time values. It compensates for time lost by the clerical workers from the performance of major operations during the working period.

CONTROL PROCEDURES

As the standards are developed for the office operations, steps must be taken to establish the control procedures and reports in which the standards will be used. This involves time and production reporting by the clerks, and various performance reports for the office supervisors and higher levels of management. It is essential that the control procedures be well prepared and accurately followed. Otherwise, the standards will be of little value in controlling costs.

Figure 6-2 shows a list of some of the operations performed in the payroll section of the hypothetical XYZ Company. This section consists of six clerks, one of whom is a leader or working supervisor. Their function is to work with the time and production reports from the shop, compute incentive and daywork earnings, and prepare the pay checks. Each line in Figure 6-2 shows the number assigned to the clerical task, a brief description of the task, the

Task number	Description	Work unit	Time
1	Check daily time and production	Time card day	0.011
2	Check weekly time cards	Time card week	0.007
	Post to pay records:		
3	Incentive employee	Time card day	0.014
4	Nonincentive employee	Time card week	0.008
5	Balance hours—weekly	Department	0.250
	Compute pay and write check:		
6	Incentive employee	Pay check	0.081
7	Nonincentive employee	Pay check	0.023
8	Make addition to payroll	Name of employee	0.320
12	Trip to collect cards and production (etc.)	Daily trip	1.400
25	Supervision, handling inquiries	Day	4.000

FIG. 6-2. *XYZ Company payroll section—standard operations.*

Name _Ann Brown_	Department or section _Payroll_	Week ending _August 20_

Hours							
Assignment	Mon	Tues	Wed	Thur	Fri	Sat	Total hours
Standard work...............	6	8	8	8	4	...	34
Nonstandard work............	2	...	...	...	...	...	2
Absent......................	...	...	...	...	4	...	4
Total hours................	8	8	8	8	8	...	40

Production									
Task number	Task	Std	Mon	Tues	Wed	Thur	Fri	Sat	Total units	Earned hours
1	Check cards	0.011	150	...	250	270	130	...	800	8.8
12	Collect cards	1.400	1	1	1	1	1	...	5	7.0
3	Post daily	0.014	60	...	100	80	60	...	300	4.2
6	Pay checks	0.081	10	50	...	...	...	...	60	4.9
5	Balance	0.250	...	2	...	...	...	...	2	0.5

Total earned hours.. 25.4

FIG. 6-3.   _XYZ Company—weekly report of hours and production._

work unit that is counted, and the allowed time for each task. For example, Task 1 consists in checking the time and production reports collected each day for workers on incentive. There may be more than one production count from a given worker, but the analyst has determined that the work unit for this task is the number of time cards and has set his standards accordingly. By measuring the work, the analyst has set a standard of 0.011 hour per time card, which means that a clerk should check the time cards for 100 employees in 1.1 hours. Actually, because the standard includes allowances for time lost during the day, she should complete her work on 100 cards in less than 1 hour if there are no interruptions.

Tasks 1 through 12 are the regular work of the section. One of the tasks (12) is a daily trip through the plant to collect the cards. With an average number of delays, this requires 1.4 hours.

During his study, the analyst found that half of the working supervisor's time is spent doing routine operations. The other half is spent handling questions from the other clerks or personnel outside the section and handling special projects. For these nonroutine matters, the analyst allows 4.0 hours per day and numbers the task 25 so that it will be handled differently than the routine tasks.

Figure 6-3 shows a typical weekly report form used by the XYZ Company, filled out by one of the six clerks in the payroll section. The form has two parts—the upper part showing how Ann Brown's hours were spent during the week, the lower part showing what she did. In this example, she reported that she worked 34 hours on tasks for which there are standards, and 2 hours on a special project. In the production portion of the form, she listed the task number, name, and the number of units completed.

The clerk records for each day her hours and work counts, and totals the work counts at the end of the week. In some offices, the clerk also extends the work counts and the standards to arrive at the earned hours for the week. Then the supervisor needs only to check the computations and verify the counts. During the first few weeks of the installation, the analyst works closely with the supervisors in checking results, but he turns this duty over to the supervisor as quickly as possible.

During the week of August 20, Ann Brown earned a total of 25.4 standard hours. She worked a total of 36 hours, but only 34 hours were worked against standard. Thus, her performance was 25.4 standard hours divided by 34 hours on standard, or 75 percent. This, of course, is not a very satisfactory performance. Either she must be provided with more work, or the supervisor will have to work with her to help her improve her performance.

The other five people in the payroll section have turned in similar reports from which the supervisor computes the earned hours and effectiveness for each person. He then consolidates them into a summary report that shows the performance of each person in the section. This takes the supervisor approximately 1 hour a week and is considered to be part of the 4 hours per day he is allowed for supervision.

The summary report, shown by Figure 6-4 as the "performance report," indicates that the performance of the payroll section for the week was 70 percent. This recognizes the 20 hours for the week that the supervisor is allowed for his supervisory tasks. The report shows clearly that three people in the section have unsatisfactory performances which the supervisor must help to improve. The most immediate improvement apparently would be to reduce the size of the payroll section by one person. This would then provide the section 164 hours to produce the 142.6 standard hours of work. If this could be accomplished the performance would rise to nearly 86 percent.

Similar performance reports are prepared for the other offices which have clerical functions. Copies are sent to the immediate superior of the office supervisor and to a central point—generally the controller's office. There they are combined into a consolidated report, such as shown by Figure 6-5. With the information in this report, responsible higher management is in a position to

			Actual hours			
Name	Perf. %	Earned hours	Standard	Non-standard	Absent	Total
Green (supervisor).........	98	39.2	40	...	...	40
Brown...................	75	25.4	34	2	4	40
White...................	56	18.0	32	8	...	40
Black...................	77	23.0	30	10	...	40
Gray....................	50	14.0	28	8	4	40
Silver..................	58	23.0	40	...	...	40
Total.................	70	142.6	204	28	8	240

FIG. 6-4. *XYZ Company—performance report, payroll section, week ending August 20.*

Office	Number of employees	This week			Last month	Three-month average	Date initiated in office
		Perf. %	Earned hours	Actual hours			
Payroll................	6	70	143	204	67	. . .	6/30
Accounts payable.......	6	75	168	224	72	71	3/21
Accounts receivable.....	8	51	142	280	. . .	. . .	8/13
Order/billing...........	24	80	696	872	72	69	4/23
Data processing........	7	82	197	240	81	80	2/15
General office..........	12	49	216	440	. . .	. . .	8/6
Total...............	63	69	1,562	2,260			

FIG. 6-5. *XYZ Company office control program—consolidated performance report, week ending August 20.*

compare and evaluate the performances in all the offices. They can then assist the office supervisors whose performances are lagging.

During the program's early stages, the consolidated report is of particular value to the steering committee of the program. It shows in a concise manner the progress of the entire program and where the committee and the analysts should be concentrating to make the program successful. Initially, the report is prepared on a weekly basis so that rapid action can be taken. When the performances reach the acceptable level of 85 to 90 percent, the program no longer needs the close attention of top management. Then the reports can be prepared on a monthly or longer basis so that higher management can see merely that the offices are operating effectively.

CONCLUSION

Although it is considered to be an innovation by many managements, office work measurement has proved itself to be of great value many, many times. For any company which has not made a thorough study of its office costs, a well-designed and well-executed work measurement program will save a great deal of money. The emphasis, however, must be on the words "well-designed and well-executed." If the program is not set up properly, it may save only a fraction of its full potential, or, indeed, it may save nothing. It will be a worthwhile program and pay rich rewards if management ensures that the program is properly installed.

BIBLIOGRAPHY

Aiken, W. M., and J. F. Lewis, "Office Cost Control," in H. B. Maynard (ed.), *Industrial Engineering Handbook*, 2d ed., sec. 10, chap. 3, McGraw-Hill Book Company, New York, 1963.
Gordon, Colver (ed.), *A Guide to Office Clerical Time Standards*, Systems and Procedures Association, Detroit, 1960.
Karger, D. W., and F. H. Bayha, *Engineered Work Measurement*, The Industrial Press, New York, 1957.
Loeber, Anita P., "Work Measurement in the Office," in Carl Heyel (ed.), *The Encyclopedia of Management*, Reinhold Publishing Corporation, New York, 1963.
Maynard, H. B., W. M. Aiken, and J. F. Lewis, *Practical Control of Office Costs*, Management Publishing Corp., Greenwich, 1960.

SYSTEMS AND DATA PROCESSING

CHAPTER ONE

The Total Systems Concept

HERMAN A. AFFEL, JR. *President, Standard Computers Incorporated, Philadelphia, Pennsylvania*

A new term has been added to the lexicon of business management: "total systems." As commonly used, it refers to a reasonably large, computer-based, information-handling system, which supplies the information needs of the entire corporation. To accomplish this, the functional operations of a corporation—production, engineering, marketing, purchasing, and so on—are dealt with as related parts of a single system rather than as separate independent operations.

Although the implementation of integrated business information systems on the scale made possible by the computer is relatively new, the concept of all the operations of a business being related parts of a single system, which underlies the implementation, is an old one. In fact, the concept has been implemented to a greater or lesser degree by every successful business organization in existence. The difference between past and present implementation of the total systems concept is one of degree and can be attributed to several developments. One development has been the growing complexity of business operations, which has given impetus to the application of a formalized scientific methodology for structuring highly complex entities, such as a business corporation. This methodology is called "systems engineering," and it is based upon the recognition of information as the common element that ties together the numerous and diverse parts of a complex entity. Another contributing development has been the general-purpose electronic digital computer. This machine's ability to perform highly complex manipulations on vast amounts of detailed information makes it possible to put together systems that are functionally superior to anything we could previously imagine.

The benefits of a total system, when it is properly implemented, can be described most succinctly as improved cost effectiveness at every operational and managerial level. But successful implementation is not a simple task. It requires a logical rigor to a depth of detail that is normally characteristic only of the scientific and engineering communities, and it must be learned by business management. The effective implementation of a total information system also requires a new corporate staff function, which must use types of technical people new to this level of the corporate hierarchy. Then, too, a set of severe problems involving the motivations and relations of the current managers may have to be resolved before a total system can be fully implemented. And finally, our business technology is not yet far enough advanced in a pragmatic sense to achieve a theoretically ideal system.

For these reasons, a total information system cannot be implemented in one fell swoop. But there is no valid reason why almost every company cannot make a beginning now. The problems to be overcome are not insurmountable, and the benefits to be gained, even from a considerably less-than-perfect system, are significant.

WHAT IS A TOTAL SYSTEM?

A "system" is by definition "a set of organized operations to satisfy a definable user requirement." By definition, then, every corporation is a system. This is not to say that there are not large differences in the effectiveness of the various business systems in existence. But all of them are complete systems in the sense that they have user requirements, established by management for the stockholders, and a prescribed set of operations. The elements in a business system are the people and machines that perform the operations and the procedures that define the operations.

From the viewpoint of the systems engineer, this collection of people, machines, and procedures is organized around and controlled by the flow of information. Looking at a business corporation in sufficient detail shows that there are basic data common to all the functional parts of the system, and that, in fact, these common data tie together all the functional parts into a single entity.

DEVELOPING NEED FOR THE TOTAL SYSTEM

Until recent years, it was impossible to deal with the information at the level of detail where the various operations of the corporation were truly integrated parts of a single system. The volume of information that has to be handled and the complexity of the manipulations that have to be performed on the information to reach this level of detail would have required, in precomputer days, such large numbers of clerical help as to be impractical.

Consequently, it was necessary to divide the corporate information flow into functional areas: engineering, production, marketing, accounting, purchasing, and so on. Integration of these areas existed only at the top management levels. Naturally, all of the elements (people, machines, and procedures) of the corporate system were organized the same way.

This does not mean that in the past corporations were never viewed as total systems. Able professional top management people always viewed them in that manner—most notably Alfred P. Sloan, Jr., who, looking at General Motors as a total system, put together one of the most effective business mechanisms in the world. But, lacking anything more exotic by way of information-handling equipment than hand calculators and typewriters, his integration of the total system could not then reach the lower levels with full effect.

The total systems concept talked about and practiced today is considerably more pervasive than anything we have seen in the past. This is because there have been three major developments that have given us both the reasons and the tools to work with the corporate information flow at the level of detail where the individual functional areas can be efficiently integrated.

As society has grown bigger and technologically more sophisticated, it has also grown more complex. Communications and transportation have speeded up and increased the interactions among people. Science and engineering have enabled us to do more complicated things and, more importantly, change our environment more rapidly than ever before.

All this means that business now is a vastly more complicated operation than it was at the turn of the century and must respond more rapidly to its external environment.

The antidote to this growing complexity has been the development of a formalized methodology for logically ordering chaotically complex operations. This methodology, which is still more of an art than a science in complex cases, is called "systems engineering." It is based upon recognition of information as being the prime common element that ties together and provides the basis for controlling the numerous and diverse parts of a complex entity, such as a corporation.

The other development that played a key role in bringing about total information system possibilities was the general-purpose electronic digital computer. This machine's ability to store, recall, and perform incredibly complex manipulations upon huge stores of data has made it possible to get down to the level of detail where the full integration of diverse functional operations becomes possible. With the computer, it is no longer necessary to assemble thousands upon thousands of clerical workers to perform simple data-processing tasks. Not only is electronic data processing fast but, more importantly, it has a virtually error-proof memory which can be enormous and permanent.

INTEGRATION AT DETAILED OPERATIONAL LEVELS

The combination of these two tools—systems engineering and the general-purpose electronic digital computer—has made it possible to build information systems that permit a corporation to be run as a single, integrated entity at the detailed operational levels, rather than as a collection of individual functional units integrated only at the highest levels of management. In a realistic sense, this is what is really meant by the term "total system." We do not really mean the corporate entity itself, which obviously is nothing new; we do mean a controlling information system that supplies the information needs of the entire corporation on an integrated basis.

A slightly less abstract view of the total information system can be established by categorizing corporate information and data handling into three basic types: external detail, historical records and reports, and control.

External Detail. This type of data and data handling involves routine changes in the form of the internal data that must be communicated to the outside world. Paychecks and invoices fall into this category, which is essentially a process for putting data into a specific, traditional form.

Historical Records and Reports. This category consists of data that provide the corporation with a record of what happened. Included are such things as the normal accounting figures, labor distribution, personnel records, inventory figures, sales statistics, and the like. These are running records, continually updated from such source documents as time cards, shipping statements, receiving slips, and purchase orders.

Control. The most important function of the system is not the production of historical records but the production of information comparing performance with predictions. This is the difference or feedback information that provides the basis for management control. All effective control requires an estimate of the future—an extrapolation of the past that becomes the managers' view of what the future reasonably should be. Such estimates include operating budgets, sales forecasts, resource allocations (manpower and dollars), inventory levels, cash-flow demands, and return on investment. A complete system includes provisions for putting these estimates in a form that permits comparison with the historical data and for generating reports that identify for management significant high or low deviations in performance as measured against forecasts.

A total information system handles the full range of data operations required to meet these information needs of a corporation—data collection, transformation, display, and measurement of performance against forecasts. In addition to reporting upon last month's successes or failures, it provides management with both the information and information-manipulating ability to carry out nondestructive tests of alternative courses of action.

IMPROVED COST EFFECTIVENESS

The only proper and compelling reason for designing and implementing a total information system is to increase the cost effectiveness of all operations within a corporation. This can be accomplished through a total information system because, as previously explained, a corporation is by definition a system comprised of various functional units which are related to each other by a common information base.

Before the advent of the electronic digital computer, the data in a corporation could not be treated as a common, corporate resource because of the volume and complexity of the data manipulation. Each functional activity or department in the corporation set up its own system for collecting, manipulating, analyzing, and reporting information. Each of these systems had its own particular methodology and information formats.

The problem was that the same information was being independently collected, manipulated, and reported at several different points within the organization, adding up to a substantial duplication of time, money, and effort. Under this arrangement of handling information on a departmentalized basis, it was not unusual to find the engineering department and the controller's department both running independent cost-accounting operations on the same projects. Each of the departments would collect information from a common source—engineering time cards—but would then manipulate the information according to its own systems and report the results in its own specialized terminology.

One of the ways in which a total information system improves the cost effectiveness of a corporation is by eliminating this type of duplication. Information is collected once, at the point of origin, and entered into the system, where it is manipulated at one pass for all departments concerned. The methodology of the manipulations is standardized to provide a more consistent basis for decisions. Terminology is standardized to reduce the degree of confusion in interdepartmental communication. The result is fewer man-hours spent on handling information, which, although it is essential for control, is a nonproductive activity.

The other way in which a total information system increases cost effectiveness is by making better information available. By "better" we mean more timely, more detailed, and more accurate. This makes possible a much higher degree of internal coordination and improves the corporation's ability to react to the outside world.

This benefit of the total system is best demonstrated by an example, such as the activity of processing a customer order. When handled on an independent, departmental basis, this activity requires a long cycle of paper work involving numerous departments—sales, production, inventory control, purchasing, billing, and shipping. The paper work is frequently done sequentially, each department using the information on the order to perform its particular operation and then passing the information on in another form to the next department in the chain. Each department also traditionally maintains its own separate files. The time lag inherent in sequential, departmental manipulation and communication of the information on the order makes this cycle a long one.

A total information system reduces the cycle sharply. When the order is entered into the system, the information is manipulated at computer speeds to supply each department that will be affected by the filling of the order with the information pertinent to that department. Sales records are updated, inventory records and production schedules are adjusted, records of materials needed for production are changed, the order is added to the shipping schedule, and an invoice is prepared.

The system really is doing the same things that were being done in the chain of departmentalized systems, but it is doing them on an integrated basis for all the departments. The paper mill in each department is eliminated or at least drastically reduced. The filling of the order is not held up by sequential processing and communication from department to department. Each department involved has a more accurate picture of its operations, because it is getting pertinent information faster. Inventory is more tightly controlled and probably can be reduced as a result. Production is able to respond faster to orders. Schedules are more realistic. Deliveries are speeded up. The company meets a higher percentage of its delivery commitment. Money turnover is increased.

Effect upon Management Decision Making. Integration of the corporate information system down to this level of detail also has a considerable effect upon management decision making. Management at all levels has at its command a store of information that shows the state of the corporation. The picture of the corporation provided by the information is sufficiently detailed to permit a penetrating look into any given combinations of departments and is timely enough for managers to correct undesirable situations. In addition, the information is in one place and in a form that is common to all corporate operations.

This common data store provides a better base for making decisions than has ever before been available. Without it, detailed analyses of operations were restricted by the time-consuming and expensive process of collecting information from multiple sources, interpreting it, and putting it into some common workable form. Even then, the value of the information was doubtful, because the original data were arrived at by a variety of different means and very likely were not current enough to use as a basis for short-term operating decisions. With the common data store provided by a total system, management has basic information of sufficient quality and in sufficient detail to perform scientific analysis, which can isolate trends, identify strengths and weaknesses, and define problems. The data can also be used in mathematical models and computer simulations to test the effect of alternative courses of action before a policy commitment is made.

A LOGICAL DESIGN METHODOLOGY

Designing a total information system for a going concern is, of course, primarily a process of updating, upgrading, and integrating the existing departmental systems. No one really has the opportunity to start from scratch.

The process starts with a formal description of the existing information flow. The material for this description is gathered by finding out from department heads what information they use, what they do with it, and what information they pass on to other parts of the organization. The description is put into the form of a flow diagram, which shows each department as a "black box" and defines the information that goes into each black box, the manipulations that are performed on it, and the information that comes out of each box. The flow diagram also contains some measure of the cost of the information manipulations performed in each box.

The second step in the design of the system is a user-needs study. This starts with the chief executive and encompasses everyone in the line of managerial responsibility. The purpose of this study is to find out what kinds of information the managers feel they want or need to perform more efficiently and effectively, and to determine the relative importance of each information tool. These needs have to be defined in some detail. For example, if a manager wants manufacturing costs, it must be determined whether he wants them by product line or manufacturing facility and whether the costs should be shown as direct labor and overhead or as the total cost per unit.

This part of the design process is both critical and difficult. It is critical because the system cannot be designed to provide information that is more useful unless the manager can define what is more useful. It is difficult because people tend to let their experience get in the way of their imagination; they are more likely to limit their requests to what they think is possible rather than what they think is desirable. If in the 1890s a survey had been conducted to find out what kind of improvements people would like in transportation, most people undoubtedly would have asked for two horses rather than one. Few would have had the imagination to ask for a horseless carriage.

To counteract this tendency, managers must be given a reasonably accurate idea of the kinds of information manipulations that can be performed by electronic data-processing equipment and the kinds of information packages this equipment can create. Every attempt must be made to encourage the managers to slip out of the restrictions of experience and use imagination in making requests for new kinds of information tools.

The needs of all the managers are then analyzed, and a system is designed in rough, functional-diagram form to satisfy all these needs. A preliminary step in this stage is a reduction of all the user needs to a common denominator by going through and defining the needs in some sort of standard terminology. In many cases, two different departments will use different terminology to express a common data need. The reduction strips away the ambiguities created by specialized terminology and reduces the possibility of unnecessary duplication.

At this level of system design, rough estimates are also generated of the cost of each operation in the system. This is done to provide management with a reasonably realistic and balanced picture of the proposed system—better information tools on the one hand and the cost of each of these tools on the other.

The next phase is the inevitable one of making trade-offs. Faced with a proposed system that will be all things to all managers but also will cost several times more than anyone's wildest dreams, management must start trading information for dollars. This is why the managers are asked to rank their requests according to relative importance during the user-needs phase of the study.

Usually, there are several trade-off sessions alternated with revised system designs. This process leads to a consensus of what is an optimum system in terms of effectiveness per dollar. A plan for implementation is then devised and carried out.

TYPICAL DESIGN AND IMPLEMENTATION DIFFICULTIES

This is the methodology of systems engineering—a relatively simple and reasonably logical series of steps that may be extremely difficult to implement. Some of the difficulties are obvious to anyone who thinks about the problem. One of the obvious pitfalls lies in the area of system implementation. Implementation must be carried out in an orderly, evolutionary fashion to make sure that none of the critical functions of the organization goes undone because the old way of doing it has been discontinued before the new system is ready to pick up the function. This calls for rather careful planning.

The less obvious difficulties in implementing this systems engineering methodology are even more formidable, because they heavily involve people.

First, there is the problem of placing the responsibility for the design, implementation, and operation of the total information system in the existing organizational structure. This is a critically important decision, one that more often than not dooms the entire undertaking. Responsibility for the information system should be a top corporate staff function; the person responsible should report directly to the chief executive of the corporation.

There are two reasons why this is so essential. One is that the job cannot be done unless the man who is responsible for doing it has adequate authority. When someone goes wandering around a corporation asking managers to explain in detail what they do, how they do it, and what they need to do it better, a degree of suspicion is generated regarding the motivations behind the questions. These suspicions can never be completely dispelled, but the situation can be kept within manageable bounds if the systems people are cloaked in the authority and objectivity of a corporate staff position.

The other reason is that anyone who is part of the system has difficulty in making objective decisions. Operating managers are a part of the system and, therefore, are frequently subject to the pitfalls of the relatively narrow viewpoints and biased judgments of specialists. This accounts for many of the difficulties experienced by companies that have put the responsibility for the information system into the controller's department. A very good case can be made for placing the responsibility here, but the decision should be made only after carefully weighing the factors mitigating against success. The major mitigating factor is that, although the controller's department is largely devoted to the process of manipulating data, the data are of a specialized nature. General accounting is the primary function of most controller offices, and they concern themselves mostly with the data relating to this function. Few of them are concerned or knowledgeable in the importance of patterns and statistics, for example.

The selection of a man to run the information system operation presents another problem. This man must be capable of being an effective liaison between two completely different and only recently related worlds, the world of business management and the technical world of computer programmers, mathematicians, systems analysts, and computer engineers. Experience has shown that this position is best filled by someone who is more management oriented than engineering oriented. Generally, he should have an extensive management science background. He must have enough practical knowledge of management to help the managers define their needs and to know what is and is not realistic in terms of integrating these needs. On the other hand, he must know enough about the various aspects of information technology to translate these needs for his technical staff, to relate problems to solutions, to have a feel for the relative merits of various alternative technical solutions to a problem, and to understand the implications of given technical decisions.

The reason the man responsible for the system function should be more of a professional manager than a professional technician brings us to the most severe problem in designing a total information system. The problem really has two parts to it. One part concerns the mechanics of business operations, and the other part concerns the horrendous detail in which the electronic data processors must be instructed in order to get them to perform the simplest operations.

The harsh truth is that the mechanics of business are not thoroughly understood, particularly when you get out of the area of simple clerical functions and into the areas of decision making. This does not mean that managers do not know what they are doing. By and large, they perform in an excellent manner. But the precision required for the purposes of systems engineering is based upon a logical and analytical viewpoint that is characteristic of only the scientific and engineering fields. It is particularly difficult to apply to business operations which are so complex that they are made up of a large variety of specialties. No one person can hope to understand, in complete logical detail, more than one of these specialties. What is more, each specialty has its own jargon and point of view. Add to that the inherent lack of precision in our common language as a communications medium and the fact that hard-core engineering of systems is performed by mathematicians, analysts, and programmers who have little or no understanding of business, and some idea is gained of the difficulty of the translation job that must be done by a person responsible for the systems function.

As mentioned above, the highly detailed set of instructions, called the "computer program," which must be provided to the computer for it to perform the simplest operation complicates the problem still more. Programming is not a science, but rather a series of logical techniques whose effective application to a programming problem requires a special type of ability and experience. Not everyone can be a programmer, regardless of training, and a good programmer needs experience. All of this adds up to the simple fact that good programmers are, and will be for a long time, in short supply and expensive. The better the definition of the job the system is to perform, the easier and less expensive the programming task. Unless sophisticated computer applications can be defined in a highly precise manner, the cost of programming often can be high enough to make the application economically unfeasible.

FUNDAMENTALS OF BUSINESS AUTOMATION

The general-purpose digital computer is not really a functional descendant of earlier business data-processing equipment, namely, punched card machines. Unfortunately, business management has been somewhat slow in recognizing and understanding the relationship between the two types of machines. As a result, the computer has been thought of in business more as a giant high-speed calculator than as a data processor which involves considerably more than mere calculation.

The reason for this misunderstanding of the computer's role in business is not hard to find. Technologically, the computer does not have its origins in the punched card equipment that preceded it; it did not naturally evolve as a series of technical improvements on punched card machines. Rather, it sprang almost full grown from the scientific world, which devised it to work on problems whose solution required extraordinary amounts of computation. What the scientists needed and what they devised was an internally programmed, high-speed calculator, and this is what was handed down to business. This heritage is still visible in advertisements that describe the computer in terms of how many calculations it can perform a second. And this heritage is responsible for a considerable amount of expensive misuse of the computer in business systems.

A computer system, despite its descriptive name, is and should be considered by a corporation as substantially more than a computer. Certainly, its utility as a business-management tool is not based upon its computational ability. In fact, the computational requirements of business management are relatively trivial, except in some special applications such as distribution analysis by linear programming.

The business utility of the computer lies in its use, in conjunction with input devices, output devices, and mechanized files, as an electronic data-processing system. This processing system can maintain in itself all the data needed, and all the methods used, for performing the required computations. It can, upon demand, rearrange, summarize, and correlate the facts related to a business operation and present them in any form required. It can do this very nearly without error (the undetectable error rate is in the range of one in a billion). Available equipment allows rapid access to any set of information, down to a single item in a file, and the item can be provided in printed form or even displayed on a televisionlike tube.

If the system is properly designed, with appropriate file structures and programming aids, management can get what it wants by talking to one man. Very few people are needed to run the system. Multitudes of clerks do not have to be hired, trained, and supervised to produce a series of reports or process special forms.

Electronic data-processing equipment, therefore, should be viewed by business management as:

An enormous, structured, viable file, with

One or more data-processing units capable of extracting and manipulating the information in the file, and

Input and output devices capable of accepting the written word, or data from another mechanized source, and displaying the data as required

As good as it all sounds and as well as it all works, there are still some problems to be solved.

One problem is that really complete EDP systems come in what might be described as the "large economy size." As with many other devices, there is a considerable cost saving per unit of memory, per unit of computation, and per unit of data manipulated as the system gets bigger. Thus, the economics appear to favor centralization of equipment within a large corporation or, for smaller companies, through an independent data-processing service company.

A second problem is the one of input equipment. Our ability to design large files and to get to the information very rapidly is well developed and improving. Our ability to process the data after retrieving them is on the verge of fantastic in terms of both speed and accuracy. And our ability to put the results of the processing into usable form has reached the point where the machine can generate a list, compose a report in prose, draw graphs, and produce three-dimensional shapes in either hard (printed) or soft (displayed) form. But the development of input equipment has not kept pace with these other areas.

The most common method of putting information into machines is still punched cards which require a sizable clerical operation. In only a comparatively few special cases have we managed to devise equipment, for use at the point where the information is generated, that can mechanically and painlessly put the information into machine-processible form.

The strength of the currently available EDP equipment lies in its ability to memorize enormous masses of data and endless sets of procedures for handling the data. Its major weakness, despite various arguments to the contrary, from a business-utility point of view is that the equipment does not think; it does not relate data to experience except upon specific and detailed instructions. It can be used to take over many types of clerical operations, but it is not capable of completely eliminating clerks, and it certainly poses no threat to management.

The degree of utility that any one corporation can get out of EDP equipment is directly related to how realistically the corporation views it. If the corporation realizes that the equipment is capable of doing no more than manipulating information according to specific instructions and if management does what it must do formally to define its needs, the EDP equipment will be the means for substantially improving the cost effectiveness of the corporation. It cannot do any more than that, but it certainly should do no less.

BIBLIOGRAPHY

Data Processing Series, vol. 6, Data Processing Management Association, 1963.
Total Systems, American Data Processing, Inc., Detroit, 1962.

CHAPTER TWO

Concepts and Trends in Data Processing

ALBERT KUSHNER *Partner, Cresap, McCormick and Paget, New York, New York*

The electronic computer is a logical next step in the development of equipment to integrate the performance of data-processing functions. The use of magnetic tape and of direct-access devices eliminates the size limitations of punched cards, and permits significant improvements in systems design and processing speeds. However, the requirements for batch and sequential processing to make effective use of tape, compared with the decreasing cost of direct-access equipment, make the latter increasingly important.

When a company decides to investigate the possible use of a computer, three key elements require consideration: the need for study of the individual firm; the need for an integrated systems approach to the problem; and finally, the need for top management attention in organizing the study, during the study, in evaluating the study results, during conversion, and after conversion.

Trends in electronic data processing toward increased capabilities at lower costs are affecting both systems concepts and equipment utilization.

THE NATURE OF DATA PROCESSING

"Data processing" is the general term applied to the procedures for handling the inevitable paper work required to produce and distribute goods and services.

For many years, only manual methods and simple office machines were available for these purposes. Then the punched card machines found their way into the field, and since the early 1950s the magic word "electronics" has been added to the businessman's vocabulary.

Definitions. To clarify the subject, let us define immediately a few of the relevant terms: "data processing," "integration," "automation," "electronics," and finally, "electronic data processing."

"Data processing" refers to the performance of certain clerical functions upon a selected body of information. Four basic clerical functions are involved, whether they are performed manually (that is, by persons) or mechanically (by machines). These functions are *input,* or the introduction of raw data into the system; *manipulation,* or the arrangement of data into a desired pattern; *computation,* through which arithmetic operations are performed on the data; and *output,* or the presentation of the results of manipulation and computation in the required form. These functions, together with the controls exercised over them, constitute a data-processing system.

When data-processing functions are combined into a system, we find that the system can be improved through "integration." An integrated data-processing system is one designed as a whole, which permits the data, once recorded, to be used for whatever purpose is required, as often as necessary, without manual copying. An integrated system may be manual, mechanized, or a combination of both. For example, the use of carbon paper between multiple copies of an order form is an elementary example of manual integration; the use of punched cards and punched tapes represents mechanical integration; and the computer provides electronic integration.

"Automation" refers to a substitution of machine labor for human labor. Either manual or intellectual labor may be automated, and the range of potential applications covers a wide field of activities in the factory and in the office. The use of adding machines, bookkeeping machines, tabulating equipment, and computers represents automation of data-processing functions.

The term "electronics" is far too frequently misused. Electronic equipment is any equipment which uses vacuum tubes or their equivalent—and hence the flow of electrons—to help operate the machine.

The use of electronic equipment to perform integrated data processing has been accorded the name "electronic data processing," and the equipment so used is commonly called a "computer" or an "electronic data-processing unit."

Reasons for Management Interest. Managers are interested in these data-processing devices because the devices have four capabilities of vital importance. They have the potential for fulfilling data-processing requirements with substantial *savings* in personnel. Greater reporting *accuracy* is possible with computers than is feasible manually or with punched card machines. Data can be made available and reports can be prepared at *speeds* far in excess of any hitherto thought possible. Moreover, along with savings in personnel, greater accuracy, and increased speeds, the computers can digest more data and provide more *analyses* than it is practical to produce by any other means.

STAGES OF MECHANIZATION

There have been three major stages in the mechanization of the data-processing functions: the use of mechanical aids which merely assist the human operator, the use of devices which actually perform the functions, and the integration of these devices into a system.

Provision of Mechanical Aids. Some devices are merely mechanical aids in an essentially manual system. The edge-punched key-sort cards expedite various sorting operations. The notches in charge plates classify customers and assist in producing output. Sorting racks assist in both sorting and collating operations. Counters and slide rules assist in accumulation and calculation.

Mechanization of Performance. The second stage is mechanization of the actual performance of clerical functions. This may mean the performance of a single function or the combination of two or more functions in a single machine.

Some machines perform a single data-processing function. For example, a document sorter will drop various paper documents into bins assigned by an operator, who presses the appropriate keys on the keyboard of the machine. The rotary calculator does only one thing—it performs the computation function. The typewriter is a good example of a device which mechanizes output.

Some machines handle several data-processing functions. The Addressograph, for example, will select appropriate plates for printing and produce the output. A bookkeeping machine mechanizes some of the manipulation, computation, and output functions, as do window-posting machines and cash registers. The adding machine will compute and then print its results.

Integration. The next step after combination of several functions into a single machine was the development of integrated machine systems. The first approach to integration was the punched card tabulating system. Here, the system is built around the punched card as the basic element, and all machine operation is dependent upon the information punched into these cards as holes. Once created, the cards provide for automatic input, manipulation, computation, and output.

Another approach to integration is represented by the punched tape system. With tape, the various office machines can be integrated into a continuous data-processing system. The tape can be produced as a by-product of bookkeeping machines, typewriters, cash registers, and adding machines, among other devices. This tape can then serve as an automatic input to a typewriter, or can be automatically converted to punched cards on a tape-to-card converter, thus serving to mechanize the input function for a punched card system.

Punched cards and punched tapes are steps toward the full integration of data-processing functions. However, the integrating medium, whether cards or tape, must still be handled by people as well as machines. To the extent that communication among the various data-processing elements of the system can be mechanized, processing speeds will increase and the possibility of human error will be lessened. By providing electrical interconnection among the various processing units, the electronic computer has reached this goal.

The basic computer system consists of three major parts: an *input* device, through which the data enter the system; the *processor*, which handles the functions of manipulation and computation; and finally, the *output* device, which produces the permanent record. Once the data are entered into the system, the computer handles all the other functions automatically. The electronic computer is thus the logical next step in development of an integrated data-processing system.

STORAGE MEDIA

A computer is capable of performing internal operations in millionths and even billionths of seconds. The data with which it works can enter the computer from data-storage media, such as punched cards, magnetic tape, or direct-access devices. When it handles cards, the central processor in effect spends valuable time waiting for the relatively slow punched card equipment to read in data or punch out the results of internal processing.

Magnetic Tape. Magnetic tape equipments eliminate this major disadvantage of punched cards. Data magnetically recorded on a strip of plastic tape can be fed into the computer at extremely high rates of speed which are more nearly equal to the internal speed of the central processor.

A practical example of the operation of a magnetic tape file is illustrated in Figure 2-1. A major chemical company maintains records of sales, accounts receivable, and inventory on magnetic tape. These tapes are kept current and are used to prepare customer invoices as well as analyses and reports.

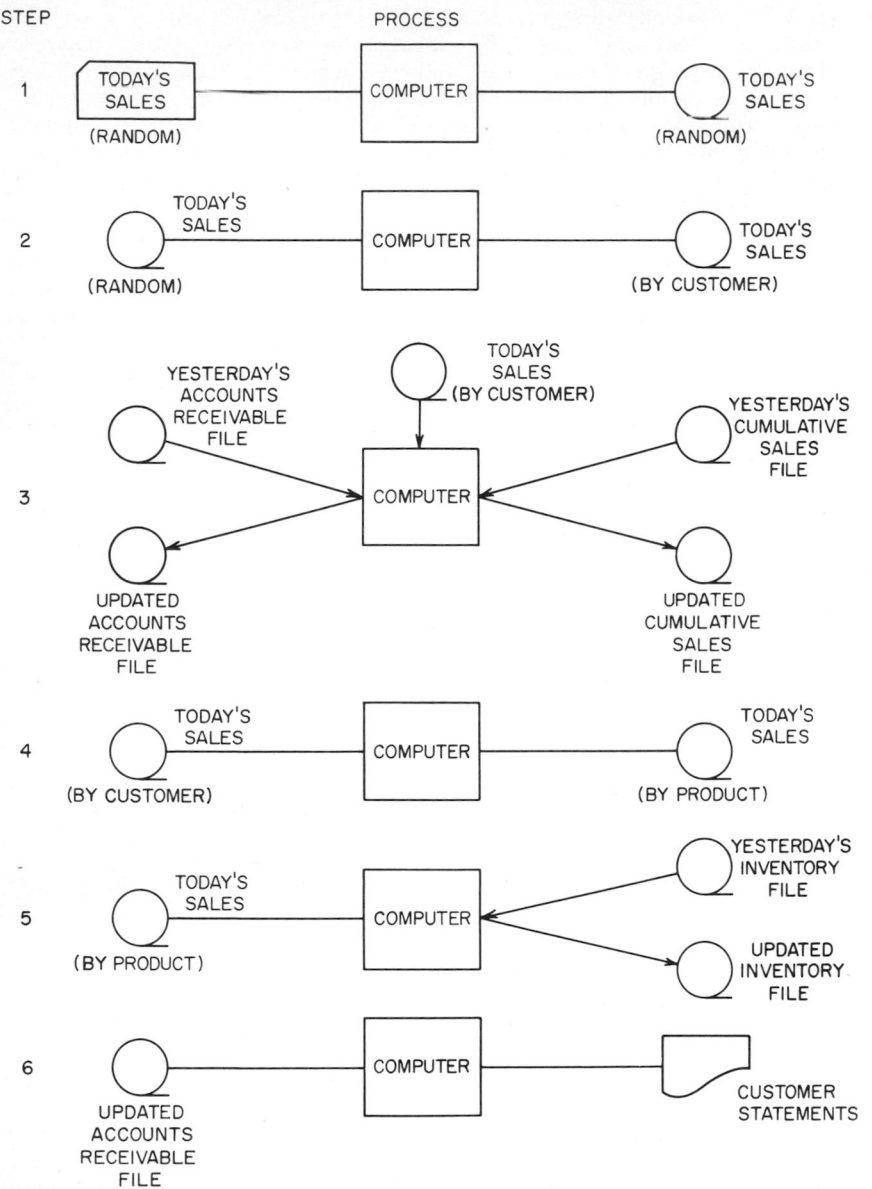

FIG. 2-1.   *Example of use of magnetic tape files.*

The first step in the process is to punch cards from data provided on invoices and other documents, and then convert these data from punched holes in a card to magnetic spots on a tape. The "today's sales" tape is then sorted into sequence by customer.

As the third step, "today's sales" are posted to the cumulative sales file for each customer and to the accounts receivable records during a single computer run. Each of the files, as well as "today's sales" transactions, is arranged in customer-number sequence (that is, a customer number identifies each tape record, and the records are arranged in ascending customer-number sequence).

As part of the record updating operation, the computer examines every record for possible activity, comparing the customer number on the "file" tape with the customer number in the next entry on the "today's sales" tape. If the two agree, the computer updates the record and writes it on the new tape. If the customer numbers disagree, indicating no activity, the unchanged sales and accounts receivable records are transferred to the new tapes. In addition to examining records for possible activity in terms of new transactions, the computer can also examine codes within the record itself for possible internal activity. For example, a code in an accounts receivable record could tell the computer to prepare a dunning notice if payment had not been received by a specified date.

The same "today's sales" tape is used in another computer run to update the inventory records. However, the "today's sales" tape must first be sorted into product-number sequence for this run, because the inventory records are maintained in that sequence.

At billing time, the accounts receivable tape is run to print statements to be mailed to customers; at the same time, any desired sales analysis reports are printed from the sales file.

Magnetic tape EDP systems are utilized in a wide variety of applications. This simplified application illustrates only a few of the many ways in practically every industry in which magnetic tape can serve as the principal file storage and input/output medium.

Characteristics of Magnetic Tape Systems. This simplified example also illustrates two characteristics common to nearly all magnetic tape applications: batch processing and sequential processing.

In batch processing, transactions are accumulated and grouped in batches before they are run into the EDP system to update various files. For example, in the illustration of the maintenance runs for the sales and accounts receivable files, the "today's sales" data would be coming in singly or in small groups throughout the day, but the file maintenance runs would be scheduled for the end of the day when all of the day's transactions could be accumulated and batched. It would not be economical to set up runs for small groups of transactions as they occurred. Because the system is used most efficiently when the maximum number of transactions can be entered at one time, grouping the input data in relatively large batches is a characteristic of almost any system employing magnetic tape as the primary input/output and file storage medium.

The second common characteristic of tape systems is sequential processing. If tape files are to be processed against one another by the computer, the records must be identified by a common number or data field, and ideally the files should be organized in the same record identification sequence. The processing of each record, then, is from the beginning of the file to the end, or from the lowest-numbered record to the highest-numbered. For example, in the illustration, the "today's sales" tape, the sales file, and the accounts receivable file were all arranged in ascending customer-number sequence, and the comparison within the computer to determine whether a customer record showed activity was based on the customer number which identified each record in each of the tape files. To update the inventory file, it was necessary to sort the "today's sales" tape from customer-number sequence into product-number sequence. Because sequential processing is common to all electronic data-processing systems employing magnetic tape as peripheral equipment, tape sorting constitutes a significant part of the activity in such installations.

These two common characteristics of magnetic tape systems—the batching of input transactions and sequential processing—are also limitations. Hours and even days may sometimes elapse between batches, and the batching limitation means that the tape files can be only as current as the last batch of transactions entered into the system.

The second limitation becomes serious when it is necessary to retrieve a single record, or a piece of information, from the files. Because magnetic tape processing is sequential, access to any record on a tape requires that all preceding records be moved past a reading mechanism before a desired record can be located. The computer must search through a long series of records to locate the desired piece of information. Access is thus time consuming and represents inefficient use of the computer's time.

Direct-access Devices. Direct-access equipment, also called "random-access equipment," is designed to alleviate these problems. The storage media used in random-access devices include magnetic drums, discs, tape strips, and cards. In computer systems employing these media, a record can be directly located in the file without passing all the records in sequence. Transactions affecting the contents of the file are fed to the computer at random, as they occur. The computer locates the corresponding record in storage and adjusts the master record accordingly. Transactions are not batched, and they need not be sorted before processing.

Figure 2-2 illustrates how a direct-access system might handle the same application illustrated for tape in Figure 2-1. Here, the cards punched from invoices can be entered into the computer at random. Because direct-access devices provide almost equal speed of access to any record in the file, and because all files are always accessible, transactions can be entered into the system at any time—that is, it is unnecessary to batch them. This single input can update rapidly an accounts receivable file, a cumulative sales file, and an inventory file, whatever their sequences.

The second step of Figure 2-2 illustrates a valuable operating characteristic of direct-access storage equipment—its ability to handle random inquiries about the status of a record on file. For example, in an application involving the

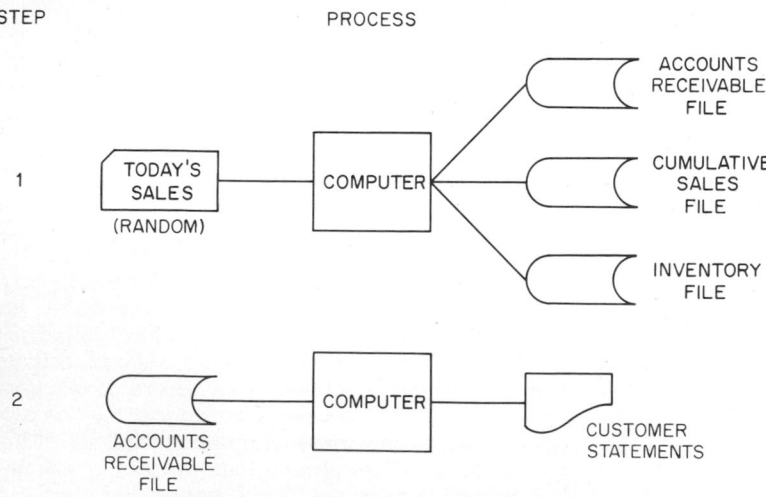

FIG. 2-2. *Example of use of direct-access files.*

maintenance of accounts receivable records on disc files, interrogation units can be employed to handle random inquiries. Should the status of a customer's account be required, the account number is keyed into the inquiry unit and relayed to the computer. This causes the computer to locate the record, extract it from the file, and print or otherwise display a copy of the record—all in a fraction of a second.

These characteristics combine to provide a significant advantage: multiple files can be maintained in a random-access system in different sequences, and all of these files can be updated with a single entry. With magnetic tape, on the other hand, the input data would have to be re-sorted for entry to each file.

Unfortunately, the random-access devices have disadvantages as well. In nearly all such devices, each record is assigned a fixed numerical code to identify its location. As a result, part numbers or account numbers must be translated to the fixed numerical code—or the numbering of parts or accounts must be redesigned to conform exactly to the random-access location codes.

Another general disadvantage of random-access devices is that they erase previous data when updating file information. If anything happens to a file, a reconstruction procedure must be undertaken because the previously recorded data have been lost. Therefore, periodic listings of the file contents on magnetic tape or some other medium are necessary, either for file reconstruction or for periodic audits of the system.

KEY ELEMENTS FOR CONSIDERATION IN THE APPLICATION OF EDP

When the decision is made to investigate the possible role of electronic computers in a specific business or application, three key elements require consideration: the need for a study of the individual firm, the need for an integrated systems approach to the problem, and the need for top management interest.

Need for Individual Study. There is no universal electronic computer system, just as there is no single accounts receivable or accounts payable system, suited to all companies. The volume of work, the extent to which data processing is centralized, the potential savings, and the background and habits of management and personnel are some of the many factors that vary from company to company, even within the same industry. The variability of these factors makes each installation an individual problem.

Integrated Systems Approach. Any computer study involves more than a simple analysis of isolated functions. To make such equipment really pay off, an integrated systems approach is usually necessary. Such an approach views the whole company as an integrated operation, working toward common goals which have been specified by management. The manufacturing, sales, personnel, and various control and accounting activities are looked upon not as separate operations but rather as parts of a single overall operation.

From a data-processing viewpoint, the objective is to achieve a balanced flow of accurate and timely information throughout the company according to the needs of the different departments and as economically as possible. The basic data required to direct the company's entire activities must be determined, the flow of these data must be established, and the data must be integrated into a system that will avoid manual copying once the data have been entered.

Through the integrated systems approach, substantial benefits which are not otherwise available can be achieved from electronic data-processing equipment. This does not mean that no benefits can be obtained from the piecemeal approach or that the entire system must be installed at once. It does mean, however, that the full potential of a computer cannot be realized until the system is integrated.

Top Management Interest. It has become clearly evident that there is a direct relationship between the quantity and quality of top management interest in a computer project and its success. Because this interest must be expressed through active involvement in all aspects of computer-related systems, it is worth-while to spell out the responsibilities of top management during each phase of the installation of a computer.

MANAGEMENT RESPONSIBILITIES

Organizing the Study. Top management has three important responsibilities to discharge before an EDP study is even undertaken.

1. Establish the objectives of the study—that is, define the basic goal for the program and set down the policies that are to be adhered to in attempting to reach that goal.

2. Develop an organization capable of making a sound feasibility investigation.

3. Win employee support for the program.

The success of an electronic data-processing system is usually measured against two general standards—its ability to lower data-processing costs and its ability to provide the information required to operate and control the business in a more timely and complete manner, and with greater accuracy, than previously was possible. The first of these standards implies expense reductions through the elimination of personnel or equipment, and the second implies increased volume and profits through better knowledge of the business. Either usually means that a substantial portion of the company and its employees will be affected in some way by the computer program. Therefore, top management's first responsibility is to participate actively in the formulation of the overall objectives of the study. Systems and equipment decisions can be significantly affected by these objectives.

After top management has formulated the basic objectives and the overall policies pertaining to the computer study, the responsibility for detailed planning and implementation of the study is assigned to others. The management of an EDP project should be entrusted to a person with some depth of experience in data processing who also shows evidence of real leadership capabilities. The leadership shown by the study manager—or the lack of it—will have a pronounced effect upon success or failure. It makes little difference whether the manager has been selected because of his experience as manager of a punched card installation, or as a computer programmer, systems analyst, accountant, or controller. Certainly, familiarity with business procedures and a good working knowledge of data processing are important to his success. But the overriding characteristic (often found lacking) should be that elusive quality of leadership.

Antagonism or reluctance on the part of employees, especially those with supervisory responsibilities, can seriously impede an EDP program. Unless middle management—department heads and their assistants—believes in the study and actively participates in it, it is almost impossible to obtain the cooperation of rank-and-file employees, and their resistance to change will present serious problems.

Guiding the Study. An important provision in any computer study is that at least one member of top management must retain continuous responsibility for interpreting policy and making the key decisions necessary for the progress of the program. This in turn means that the interpreter of policy should have certain specific qualifications.

1. He should be high enough in management to be objective about the specialized interests of accounting, sales, production, engineering, and other departments concerned.

2. He should have a thorough knowledge of the company's objectives and policies.

3. He should have a broad understanding of the company's overall systems and their interrelationships. (If he lacks this understanding, he should choose an assistant who has it.)

4. He should have the authority and the ability to make decisions on his own.

5. He should have the ability to "sell" his decisions to the persons affected and to obtain cooperation in carrying them out.

6. He should be sufficiently free from other management burdens to give adequate attention to the data-processing project.

Of these qualifications, the ability and authority to make decisions with a minimum of delay have proved to be of particular importance. If the policy interpreter lacks these, the committees or individuals assigned responsibility for various phases of the program may encounter repeated delays. Furthermore, the need under such circumstances to refer requests for decisions to higher authority has occasionally encouraged "politicking": those affected, lacking an arbiter for their differences, try to sell their viewpoints to top executives who have only a limited knowledge of the overall computer program.

Evaluating the Study Results. Management's next major area of responsibility is to provide the necessary time and attention for thoroughly evaluating the findings and recommendations of the study team. Management must measure its study team's proposal in some way, whether directly in terms of lowered costs or indirectly in terms of improved information and control. If cost reduction is the objective of a computer application, the anticipated savings should be clearly and carefully developed. If improved control is the justification, the improvements should be identified and realistically compared with the increased costs involved. The same criteria should be used in evaluating these proposals as are used to evaluate any request for substantial funds:

Is this venture feasible?

What will we gain from it?

What will it cost?

Are the benefits worth the cost?

Could we do the same job as well, or less expensively, another way?

Conversion. Once management has approved the results of the feasibility study and authorized the computer installation, conversion begins. This phase of the work takes a great deal of time; thinking is no longer in terms of weeks or months, but rather man-years. Detailed programs must be prepared; personnel must be trained and oriented for new jobs and new responsibilities; computer operations must be started; and finally, the old routine must be dropped.

And, having selected the system and decided upon conversion, a company finds that its real difficulties are just beginning. Any conversion from manual to mechanized data processing brings with it numerous problems that must be solved, worked around, or lived with. An electronic data-processing system introduces a myriad of such problems; many directly affect company personnel, and many require system changes.

Systems changes arise because efficient utilization of a computer almost always demands a system substantially different from that which is appropriate to a manual or partially mechanized approach. The difference arises because the computer can process data from start to finish and make logical decisions with a minimum of manual interference. The systems changes entailed may be relatively minor, or they may necessitate a comprehensive review of major company policies.

Postconversion. After the computer is installed, it is management's responsibility to provide continuing guidance to the EDP effort. An electronic computer is an expensive, powerful resource which cannot be ignored or forgotten after the initial applications have been put into effect. It normally takes several years to reach the payoff point, and the EDP function should be dynamic. New applications require the same systems design and conversion effort as the initial ones and should be just as carefully controlled and monitored by management. Moreover, management must establish and communicate priorities for new or revised applications, for once the EDP function is understood and accepted by all parts of the company, the demands for data processing service often are much greater than can be economically supplied.

A most important function of management is to require a periodic comparison of the results of actual operations with systems proposals. Progress can be measured effectively through an annual report on the EDP function which, for each system installed, compares actual with proposed changes in each of the following areas:

1. Decrease in personnel, or absorption of increased volume of work without clerical additions

2. Improved timing and content of reports and records, or use of special new reports in making important management decisions

3. Specific cost savings, such as those that result from reductions in working-capital requirements

The review program should ensure that the primary objectives of the various applications are being continuously met. Periodic postinstallation reviews will confirm or deny the economical application of the computer to various segments of the business and will help avoid the costly continuation of an application which has outlived its usefulness.

TRENDS IN DATA PROCESSING

One distinguishing feature of the data-processing field is phenomenal growth; another is rapid technological obsolescence. Both the commercially available equipment and its economics have changed considerably since computers first came into general use.

Components. Perhaps the most easily recognized changes have taken place in the components that have become generally available. First of all, input devices have multiplied. Punched card readers have been joined by input devices that permit automatic optical reading and magnetic reading of both coded and English-language data.

To the earlier punched card and printed outputs have been added punched paper, human voice, graphic display, and visual display output devices.

Storage devices, originally confined to magnetic tapes and drums, have been augmented by magnetic core, disc, card, and tape-strip files.

The central processor has changed from a large vacuum-tube device, with sonic delay-line, cathode-ray tube, or magnetic drum memory, to smaller, more reliable, transistorized devices with high-speed core memory.

Characteristics. The characteristics of many familiar and well-established components have also changed appreciably. To the development of off-line printing capabilities have been added the abilities to print on multiple adding-machine tapes and on magnetically coded ledger cards.

Some computers can read magnetic tape in one direction only, so that a section of tape that has passed must be rewound to be read. Others can read while the tape is going in either direction, an ability which is particularly useful in sorting and filing operations. Some computers can write on the tape they are reading, thus reducing the time it takes to maintain low-activity files.

Direct-access memory has gone from a device of fixed size to demountable devices that give to direct-access equipment the storage capabilities of tapes.

Speed. The speeds of the equipment have increased substantially. Internal speeds that were first spoken of in milliseconds (thousandths of a second), and then microseconds (millionths of a second), are now timed in nanoseconds (billionths of a second).

A great improvement has been the development of ways to balance the speeds of the central processor with those of the slower input/output components through buffering, simultaneous processing, priority processing, and multiple programming. Buffers are simply additional memories, which permit the central processor to release information at a fast speed and then hold it while waiting for the output unit, or to store input information in readiness for a later processing step. Simultaneous-processing capabilities permit the simultaneous operation of several components; for example, while a card is being read, output can be printed. Some central processors have the circuitry needed to respond to input, output, or other signals according to an assigned priority. For example, when an input or output device has completed an operation, it can signal the central processor to interrupt its current program and transfer to another program designed specifically to handle the input or output processing. If signals from two separate input or output devices compete for the central processor's attention, the central processor will first connect the device with the highest assigned priority; after the central processor has served this device, it will serve any others signaling suitable priorities, and then will return to the original program at the point where it was interrupted. Multiple-programming capabilities permit a computer to process two or more completely independent programs simultaneously.

Combined Capabilities. Many installations use two sizes of computers to make more effective use of the central processor. The smaller computer performs media conversion, printing, and some computation—all intended to save the time of the larger, faster, more expensive computer for work better suited to it.

Another development along these lines is on-line computer coupling. There is a trend toward connecting smaller computers with larger computers to perform such functions as editing and control. Several manufacturers have a high-speed transfer device that permits direct coupling of the core storages of two systems. In these configurations, one complete computer handles all input/output and buffering, while the second (higher speed) processor compiles, assembles, and executes programs. Communications and the exchange of information between the systems are under program control.

Other changes have increased the versatility of equipment. There is a tendency, where a combined work load exists, to select a single computer to handle both business and scientific applications. For example, the computer can be used as a character-oriented, business data processor in one mode, and as a fixed-word, scientific computer in another mode.

Compatibility. A significant equipment development is the introduction of compatibility within computer families and between manufacturers. In its simplest form, this involves input/output compatibility, so that different computers can read from the same input media or write in the same mode on output media. It also extends to program compatibility—that is, the ability to accept and perform the same program with little or no modification.

Input Mechanization. The input for a data-processing system typically comes from a variety of sources—for example, from employee time cards, orders and invoices, and sales transactions. The transcription of manually recorded data into a machine-readable form is slow, inefficient, costly, and subject to error. The goal in mechanizing input is to record the data just once, in a way that will ensure maximum accuracy, and in a form that will be suitable for all subsequent processing. The techniques and equipment used to achieve the automated collection of data can be considered in two categories: "source" data mechanization and "turnaround" data mechanization.

Devices for "source" data mechanization collect information at its point of origin—the factory floor, the warehouse, or the sales counter—and prepare it in a form suitable for entry into a data-processing system. (See also Chapter 5 of Section 15.) These devices may produce their own output in the form of tapes or cards, or they may transmit the information directly to a central unit that collects it from many units and prepares it for processing.

A second basic category of input mechanization is called "turnaround" data mechanization. There are some applications in which the document that provides input data is created by the ultimate user but leaves his control and returns at a later time with additional data. Examples of such documents include retail garment tags, bank checks, and utility bills.

Data Communication. Rapid communication is an increasingly integral part of many business data-processing operations. Rather than wait for the relatively slow mails to convey data between locations, companies turn to other means of communication. There are at least three circumstances in which automated data communications should be considered. The first of these is when the information has a "time value." The second is when a firm is considering sharing its computer installation because surplus processing time is available; for example, several groups of engineers in a company can share the use of a single computer by using automated communication facilities. Finally, automated data communications should be considered when there is an opportunity to improve customer service, perhaps by reducing order-processing time and shipping customers' orders sooner.

There are three elements to a data communications network: the circuit or network through which the data travel; data sets for converting recorded information for transmission over telephone lines; and the business machine terminal unit. Circuits and equipment that vary widely in speed are available to business for both data and voice transmission. Telegraph transmission is the slowest method, operating at 6 to 10 characters per second. Voice-grade circuits are needed for the transmission of data contained in punched cards or paper tape; these lines are capable of transmitting data at rates between 125 and 300 characters per second. Facsimile transmissions, and rapid transmissions of data between such media as magnetic tape or computer core memories, require high-speed lines which transmit between 5,000 and 10,000 characters per second.

Economics. The costs of equipment have dropped significantly. Rental of a medium-size computer in 1956, for example, was twice that asked in 1965 for an equivalent second-generation computer with the same kinds and number of components. At the same time, both the card-reading speed and the printing speed of the older computer are only 25 percent of that of the newer computer, and the add time is three times faster on the newer computer.

Real Time. The growing use of direct-access equipment has permitted development of computer applications in "real time." Because records can be updated at the time events occur and can be interrogated at will, the computer can be a source of genuinely current information.

New Types of Applications. The increase in the number of EDP applications has been even more dramatic than the increase in the number of computers. The newer applications include resource allocation, production planning, inventory control, sales forecasting, and materials distribution and flow.

As individual systems such as payroll, accounting, and inventory are converted to a computer, it is soon realized that they are interrelated—the output from one becomes the input to another—and that they represent parts of a company's total operation. This raises the question, "Why not construct a system interrelating the entire operation of the company?" This concept, often called the "total systems" approach (see Chapter 1 of Section 15), visualizes all functions of a business as parts of a continuous, integrated process or system, but also takes into consideration the fact that it is no monolithic affair but made up of numerous interlocking subsystems.

A fundamental element in the computer's contribution is its usefulness in manipulating large, complex mathematical models according to operations research techniques. The techniques of the management sciences have been available for many years, but their full potential could not be realized before the advent of high-speed computers. Solving even small linear programming problems manually is tedious at best, and rapidly becomes uneconomical as the number of variables involved increases.

The usefulness of computers in measuring results is well recognized. They can also give help in planning and in adjusting plans. Two particularly promising areas are forecasting and system simulation. Business forecasting involves the prediction of many factors, only some of which can be controlled by the company. Product sales, especially, are heavily affected by external factors. Yet accurate sales forecasts are a highly desirable goal. Because the company's entire resources of men, money, materials, and machinery are committed on this basis, no company can afford a serious error.

An example of the use of EDP in sales forecasting is the system developed by RCA, for which an accuracy within 2 percent is claimed. In this approach, the computer not only investigates the correlation possibilities of a given set of indices, but also selects and weighs the most significant factors.

First, the computer is fed statistics on a period of sales that is considered typical (for its own needs, RCA chose a six-year period). The computer then is fed a selected series of historical economic or demographic indices, such as gross national product or population. The computer statistically tests the data and selects those indices which most closely resemble the historical sales pattern of the company. The resultant model is used to project sales into the next year.

By withholding one year's known sales from the original input, it is possible to examine how well they would have been forecast by the model. If this comparison shows a deviation, the model maker has several options—he can submit a new set of indices, change the present set by some transformation, provide different combinations of indices, or make any number of other modifications. The data are then recycled through the computer, and the ensuing output tested in the same way. Management continues to refine the model step by step until it feels it has a true reflection of the marketplace.

Thus, management supplies the judgment, the economic indicators, and the pattern of historical sales. The computer performs the routine but complex statistical analyses.

A second area of planning in which the computer has demonstrated its value is the development of budgeting models and the simulation of the business system to determine the "most profitable course" for a business.

This area represents a highly sophisticated computer application, because the construction of a budgeting model requires translating a traditional budgeting system into algebraic terms. One experimental model, when fully spelled out, consists of several hundred simultaneous equations. It uses sixty-five symbols with four subscripts and two superscripts. Although this particular model is in the experimental stage as this is written, it has already provided valuable insights into the relationships among budgetary elements, based on the simulation of a large number of different conditions.

CONCLUSION

EDP has made major contributions in the area of clerical cost reduction. However, the results in this area are as yet far from optimum; costs can be further reduced, and returns greatly increased. On the other hand, although there is room for improvement in the past and present applications of EDP, its most important contribution is to multiply, many times over, our abilities to perform quickly and economically functions associated with key elements of planning and control, namely:

Analyzing known facts and conditions

Predicting unknown facts and conditions by extrapolating those that are known

Comparing the planned operation with actual performance

Evaluating plans in terms of current performance

Providing continuous information about operations

BIBLIOGRAPHY

Glossary of Data Processing and Communication Terms, 2d ed., Honeywell Electronic Data Processing, Wellesley Hills, Mass., 1965.

Gregory, Robert H., and Richard L. Van Horn, *Automatic Data Processing Systems,* Wadsworth Publishing Company, Inc., Belmont, Calif., 1960.

Gregory, Robert H., and Richard L. Van Horn, *Business Data Processing and Programming,* Wadsworth Publishing Company, Inc., Belmont, Calif., 1963.

Johnson, R. A., R. E. Kast, and J. E. Rosenzweig, *The Theory and Management of Systems,* McGraw-Hill Book Company, New York, 1963.

Laden, H. R., and T. R. Gildersleeve, *Systems Design for Computer Applications,* John Wiley & Sons, Inc., New York, 1963.

Wainright, Martin E., Jr., *Electronic Data Processing, An Introduction,* Richard D. Irwin, Inc., Homewood, Ill., 1961.

CHAPTER THREE

Punched Card Equipment and General Office Mechanization

JOHN R. CROWLEY *Manager, Administrative Services, International Bank for Reconstruction and Development, Washington, D.C.*

This chapter is concerned with examining the various ways and means of mechanizing the processing of business data, particularly through the use of punched cards and punched card (tabulating) equipment, to minimize clerical and administrative costs and provide more accurate, timely, and useful management information.

The emphasis will be less on the physical characteristics of punched card equipment—because this information is constantly changing and is available from the two leading American manufacturers (International Business Machines Corporation and the UNIVAC Division of Sperry Rand Corporation)—and more on the nature of data processing, the nature and reasons for punched card data processing, the methods of appraising punched card applications, and the methods of establishing, controlling, and evaluating such applications.

THE NATURE OF BUSINESS DATA AND BUSINESS DATA PROCESSING

"Data processing" has been defined as "the clerical routine involved in the preparation of a firm's operating records, accounting records, and management reports."

Types of Business Data.   Generally, business data can be classified according to seven principal functional areas of business operations:

1. *Accounting data:*
    Charts of accounts
    Journals
    Ledgers
    Financial statements, trial balances, profit and loss statements, balance sheets

2. *Sales data:*
Order acknowledgment, processing, invoicing
Sales accounting, sales and market analysis
Accounts receivable
Cash receiving and credit control

3. *Purchasing data:*
Requisitions, purchase orders, receiving
Purchase and expense distribution
Accounts payable
Cash-paying procedure
Vendor analysis

4. *Production data:*
Scheduling
Production control
Inventory control
Cost accounting
Plant and equipment control

5. *Payroll data:*
Employment
Timekeeping
Payroll processing
Salary and labor-cost distribution

6. *Engineering data:*
Engineering plans and specifications
Bills of materials
Engineering change notices

7. *Personnel data:*
Employee history records
Wage and salary analysis
Turnover analysis
Tardiness and absentee records

Characteristics of Business Data. Business data have certain characteristics that give a clue to the possibilities of mechanization.

1. A substantial amount of business data is constant in nature and is used repetitively many times, in normal business transactions.

A customer places repeat business. A salesman makes a number of sales. Orders are placed repetitively with the same vendor.

2. Business transactions tend to interact on one another, and data created in one transaction may affect other transactions.

Thus, an order from a customer not only results in a shipment (involving the manufacturing process); but relieves inventory (the inventory-control function); then produces an invoice (billing function), which in turn can be analyzed for sales and market data; creates an accounts receivable record, involving credit problems; and concludes with the receipt of cash.

3. Finally, no matter what the area of business, no matter what the operation, relatively few different functions are involved in processing data. They are:

Recording
Classifying
Sorting
Calculating
Summarizing

Early Mechanization Efforts. Prior to World War II, with the exception of the military and the government, improvements in data processing were largely concerned with simplifying the *method* of handling the five basic functions of data processing or attempting to combine one or more functions into one operation. This, then, was largely an era of simplification and mechanization. An adding machine, for example, could not only add or subtract a group of figures (*calculating*), but also *record* such data for future use, for checking, or for controlling, and total (*summarize*) such data. A bookkeeping machine could record data, segregating it by debits, credits, and totals (*classifying*), *calculate* the effect of such transactions, and finally, *summarize* the totals. The accounting Addressograph, in addition to *classifying* and *recording*, could also accumulate limited amounts of numerical information for accounting purposes. A microfilm card could *record* and *classify* information, and if combined with a key-sort principle, could *sort* such information.

Although such efforts tended to speed up clerical processing and minimize errors, essentially they did not change the traditional system or organization for processing data. A bookkeeping machine could supplant or improve upon manual methods and still leave surrounding routines essentially the same. Most such mechanical aids were limited by the speed, skill, and knowledge of an individual manually providing the basic input data. Finally, there was no common medium by which data could be manipulated through the various data-processing functions.

The Advent of the Punched Card and Punched Card Systems. Although they had been used for statistical purposes for some time, punched cards were not generally used for routine processing of paper work prior to World War II, and even during the war their use was greatest among large defense industries and the government. It was only in the postwar period that their use became widespread in business. By 1966, expenditures for punched card equipment and electronic data-processing equipment—much of which uses punched cards as one of the basic input media—amounted to billions of dollars.

THE NATURE OF PUNCHED CARD DATA PROCESSING

In a punched card system of processing data, basic source data are converted into a common medium—the punched card. The holes in the card can represent alphabetical characters and numerical figures and certain special characters. When processed through the various electromechanical pieces of punched card equipment, the punched hole can do the following things:

1. It will add itself to something else.
2. It will subtract itself from something else.
3. It will multiply itself by something else.
4. It will divide itself by something else.
5. It will list itself.
6. It will reproduce itself.
7. It will classify itself.
8. It will select itself.
9. It will print on a card.
10. It will produce an automatic balance forward.
11. It will file itself.
12. It will post itself.
13. It can be punched from a pencil mark on the card.
14. It will cause a total to be printed.
15. It will compare itself with something else.

16. It will cause a form to feed to a predetermined position, or to be ejected automatically, or to space from one position to another.

The Advantages of Punched Card Systems. Essentially, punched card systems satisfied a number of basic needs with respect to the processing of data.

1. They provided a medium (the punched card) for effectively and economically storing constant data.

2. They provided a unit medium (the punched card) which was standard and could be processed through a wide variety of equipment to produce variable reports and records. In such processing, they could perform all the five basic functions of data processing—classifying, sorting, calculating, summarizing, and recording.

3. They provided electromechanical equipment of a wide variety of speed and costs—whose speed and effectiveness were largely a function of the machine, not the person who operated it.

4. They provided speeds far in excess of what could be achieved in manual or manual/mechanical processing.

5. They provided a flexible system for processing data that could, relatively inexpensively, be modified in light of changing conditions or requirements.

THE PUNCHED CARD

The punched card is a unit record of approximately 7⅜ by 3¼ inches in size. The two main types of punched cards in widest use are made by the International Business Machines Corporation and the UNIVAC Division of Sperry Rand Corporation—the two largest manufacturers of tabulating equipment. Neither of the two types of cards is compatible with the other. IBM cards can be used only with IBM machines or machines (including computers of other manufacturers) designed to accept them. The same is true of Remington Rand (UNIVAC) cards.

The IBM card is distinguishable by its rectangular holes and its eighty-column format. The card is divided into eighty vertical columns, or "card columns." These are numbered 1 to 80 from the left side of the card to the right. Each column is divided into twelve punching positions called "rows" which are designated from the top to the bottom of the card by 12, 11 (sometimes referred to as X), and 0 through 9. Each column of the card is generally used to accommodate a digit, a letter, or a special character. A hole punched in the 0 to 9 column represents numerical digits. Alphabetical characters and special characters are represented by a combination of 1 to 9 punches and a punch in the 12, 11, or 0 columns. Cards are available in square-edge or rounded-corner cuts.

On the Remington Rand card, data are recorded in the form of round holes punched in forty-five columns. These columns are divided horizontally into two areas of six punching positions per column, so that there is a total of ninety columns in the card. Numerical and alphabetical punches each require two holes per digit or character.

Items of information are recorded on a card in groups of consecutive columns called "fields." A field in an IBM card may consist of one column to eighty columns of information, depending upon the length of the particular item of information to be recorded in it. Field length is determined by the maximum length of information which will be entered into the field. For example, if a company had 2,500 employees with the prospect of never having more than 9,999 employees, an employee reference card would be designed with four columns of the card allotted to the employee number. Machine processing requires a consistent arrangement of data in cards used in the same job. Thus, if in a payroll system columns 17 to 21 were allotted to an employee serial number, normally no other data would be punched in these positions. Actually, this is no different from most handwritten documents, where standard arrangements prevail.

Basic Types of Cards. Generally, punched cards used in tabulating systems are of four types:

1. *Transcript cards* are cards punched from information previously recorded on another document (for example, a sales analysis card showing customer, item of sale, and dollar amount punched from a sales invoice).

2. *Dual cards* are punched from information recorded on the card itself, that is, the card serves a dual purpose as source document (for example, a customer payment card that may be punched with amount of payment upon return from the customer).

3. *Mark-sensed cards* are automatically punched from special graphic-pencil marks in significant positions on the face of the card (frequently used by meter readers, who mark-sense reading values on previously punched customer cards).

4. *Summary cards* are automatically punched with totals resulting from accumulated results in accounting machines or calculating punches.

In addition to the detail, master, and summary cards used in normal internal business data processing, many specially designed cards have come into use—checks, vouchers, statements with or without stubs attached (such as telephone bills), and even addressing stencils.

PUNCHED CARD EQUIPMENT

Punched card (tabulating) equipment provides the means by which punched cards perform the basic processing functions of *recording, classifying, sorting, calculating*, and *summarizing*.

The equipment and processes by which this is accomplished in a punched card system can be classified as follows.

Recording Systems or Processes. The function of recording consists in creating holes in a punched card as a basis for processing through subsequent operations. Processes include:

Card Punching. This is a basic method of converting source data into punched cards. Using a manually operated key-punch machine with a typewriter keyboard and a ten-key numerical keyboard, an operator reads the source document, and by depressing keys, converts the information into punched holes. The machine feeds, positions, and ejects the card automatically. The punch is located by a predetermined format visible to the operator. Key punches can be equipped with mechanisms to interpret automatically the punched information at the top of the card directly above the hole being punched.

Duplicating. Repetitive information is punched automatically from a master card into a group of succeeding detail cards. This is a function of the key-punch machine. Duplicating is controlled by a program card which designates fields into which repetitive data are to be punched automatically. Thus, an employee number punched into an employee card could be punched automatically into all subsequent detail cards.

Card Verifying. Card verifying is a means of checking the accuracy of the original key punching. With IBM equipment, a second operator verifies the original punching by depressing the keys of a verifier (a different machine from the key punch) while reading the source data. The machine compares the key depressed with the hole already punched in the card. A difference causes the machine to stop, indicating a discrepancy between the two operations. A notch is cut in the upper right edge of the card if the key-punch and verify operations agree. If these operations do not agree, a notch is cut directly above the column in question.

With UNIVAC (more commonly known as Remington Rand equipment), the key punch itself, with a certain lever set, does the verifying. If the punchings agree, a slightly oblong hole is created. A round hole signifies disagreement. Another machine is available through which cards may be run to detect round holes. If such errors are found, a colored card may be dropped on top of the error card to notify the operator.

Gang Punching. Here, punched information from a master card is copied automatically into one or more detail cards following it. The process is useful in producing a number of cards of the same type, such as punching a customer number into a set of detail cards indicating individual items ordered by that customer.

Reproducing. This is the process of punching information from one set of punch cards automatically into another set. Both decks are fed into the machine, and the originals are duplicated, one by one. Thus, in taking an inventory, a plant number or a department-location number could be punched into all cards indicating details of equipment located within the plant or department. Special machines perform reproducing operations.

Mark-sensed Punching. The card can be punched automatically by means of electrically conductive marks made on the card with a pencil. Thus, original facts may be recorded anywhere—in the field, plant, or office, by workmen, timekeepers, or field workers—and these facts can be translated into punched card forms.

Ticket Converting. There are special machines which can convert holes punched into a small card or stub into punched holes in a regulation-size card suitable for processing. These are used in mechanizing inventory control and on various forms of credit stub forms.

Tape-to-Card Converting. Here, holes punched into paper tape by the so-called common language machines may be converted to regulation punched cards for future punched card processing. Thus, when an invoice is prepared on a typewriter with a tape punch, the tape may be converted to individual punched cards for each item sold, and an analysis of such sales may be performed on punched card equipment.

Data Transceiving. Here, punched card data may be transmitted over special telephone, telegraph, or private wire lines, using special equipment, to be received in punched card form at a receiving location. This method is useful in transmitting sales, payroll, or inventory data from plants to a central location.

Typewriter Card Punching. The preparation of a punched card as a by-product of typing a record or report is possible by means of a cable connection between a typewriter and a punching unit.

Interpreting. The process of translating punched holes into printed information on a card so that it can be visibly read can be done on a special interpreter or a printing key punch.

Classifying Systems or Processes. Classifying or sorting consists in arranging punched cards in an order or sequence for processing through other machines for report preparation. Processes include:

Sorting. This is the process of grouping cards in numerical or alphabetical sequence according to any classification punched on them. To group cards by account, for example, they are sorted into account sequence. This makes possible summarization by card by account. Sorting is done one column at a time. Thus, an account with a four-digit numerical identification may require four sorts. Alphabetical punching requires two sorts per column. Sorting speeds may range from 200 to 2,000 cards per minute.

Selecting. The function of selecting consists in pulling from a mass of data certain items that require special attention. Selection of cards is accomplished automatically by either a sorter or a collator. Thus, if a deck of cards contains a number of master cards and a number of detail cards and the master cards are to be selected and returned to file, this may be done in the selection process.

Merging. Merging is the combining of two sets of cards into one set of cards of a given sequence. Both files of cards must be in the same sequence before they are merged. This function makes possible automatic filing of new cards into an existing file of cards. This is done on equipment known as a "collator."

Matching. This is a checking function used to check the agreement between two sets of cards. Groups of cards in one file are compared with similar groups in a second file. Unmatched cards or groups of cards in either file may be selected or separated from the file. This is accomplished by the collator.

Calculating Systems or Processes. Calculating is the computing of a result by multiplication, division, addition, or subtraction. Any combination of these calculations can be performed, often in one run. Factors to be calculated may be read from each card, or a series of cards, emitted by a device within the machine, or may be developed by the accumulation of a series of calculations. One or several results are punched in each card or in a trailer card which follows a group of cards carrying the factors. Special machines are used for this purpose.

Summarizing Systems or Processes. Summarizing is a function performed by specialized equipment which can print in legible form the information punched into cards and which can accumulate data from successive cards and from groups of cards and print out totals of selected groups or reports. It is the medium for producing all punched card records and reports. Processes include:

Detailed Printing. Information from each card is printed as the card processes through the machines. The function is used to prepare reports that show complete detail about each transaction. During the operation, the machine can add, subtract, cross-add, or cross-subtract, and print many combinations of totals. Speeds can be from 50 to 150 times per minute on conventional punched card equipment.

Group Printing. The accounting machine function that summarizes groups of cards and prints the totals on a report is group printing. Totals may involve adding, subtracting, or cross-footing. Information read from punched cards is entered into counter units, and at the end of each group, the totals are read out of the counters and printed on the report. This function is used in preparing all types of reports requiring summarized totals.

Summary Punching. Summary punching is the automatic conversion into punched card form of information developed in the subsequent summarizing processes. It serves to summarize data, carry balance figures forward, and eliminate detail and volume.

PUNCHED CARD APPLICATIONS

Punched card applications in business include a wide assortment of systems and segments of systems. Some of the typical applications include:

 1. Employee payroll
 2. Labor distribution
 3. Employee records
 4. Material accounting and control
 5. Accounts payable
 6. Billing
 7. Accounts receivable
 8. Sales accounting
 9. Production control
10. Inventory control
11. General accounting
12. Cost accounting
13. Capital asset accounting
14. Maintenance scheduling
15. Budgetary accounting
16. Dividend accounting
17. Engineering records
18. Waste and reject analysis
19. Sales and market analysis
20. Vendor analysis

Obviously, punched card systems, applications, and methods will vary by industry and by individual business application. Punched card equipment manufacturers have generalized data on typical applications within each area. Although this information is helpful to illustrate given approaches and sample forms, any system developed must meet your particular application and your particular requirements. There is no easy way to punched card systems design. *Any system must be designed specifically for your needs—your requirements.*

DETERMINING THE FEASIBILITY OF PUNCHED CARD APPLICATIONS

Basically, management should consider the possibilities of punched card applications under these conditions:

1. If its present system is not providing *adequate* management information
2. If its present system is not providing *timely* management information
3. If the present system is unable to handle current work loads without excessive overtime
4. If the present system appears too costly, or if costs are increasing

These are generalities, but they do provide a key to problems with the present system. Whether or not a punched card system is the answer is another question. Some keys to the possibility of a successful punched card application are contained within some of the principles which follow.

Keys to Potential Punched Card Applications

1. Is there a large amount of constant data copied from form to form in a particular system? A simple sheet listing vertically all items appearing on various documents of a system and listing horizontally all documents on which such data appear may provide an indication of the potential inherent in capturing the data originally in punched card form for subsequent processing.

2. Is a majority of the data in a given system contained in the original source document (the sales order, the purchase requisition, the inventory record) and reused throughout the system in other documents? (In one study of the purchasing routine of a large manufacturing company involving the use of six different forms, of 8.5 million alphabetical and numerical characters copied throughout

the system, over 4 million were contained in the original document.) Obviously, if such data could be captured in a compatible form, they could be used to produce other documents.

3. Does the system use a large amount of constant data that could be referred to and used again and again throughout the system? If so, and if these data were in a form mutually compatible with other elements of the system, it would be advantageous to convert to such a medium.

4. Is there a large amount of sorting, calculating, or printing that could be done better automatically than manually?

The Cost and Feasibility Factor. Although such questions provide the "hint" to punched card application feasibility, they do not provide the hard answer about the capability and timeliness of punched card equipment to produce results at a satisfactory cost. This necessitates a basic study of the present manual and mechanical system compared with a potential punched card system. This study should include the following:

1. Preparing a statement of present job
   a. Summary of objectives and procedures
   b. Cost estimate of present job
2. Listing improvements and objectives of proposed punched card system
3. Documenting present work flow
4. Preparing detailed statement of proposed job
   a. Input and output required
   b. Files required
   c. Special reports and exceptions
5. Establishing and verifying input and output volumes
   a. Peak loads and "averages"
6. Determining "due in" and "due out" schedule
7. Evaluating amount of calculation
8. Selecting manufacturer
9. Working with manufacturer to:
   a. Lay out *major* logic of data flow within system
   b. Estimate operating times
   c. Determine equipment requirements
   d. Determine personnel requirements
   e. Determine proposed operating costs
10. Comparing operating costs, schedules, and anticipated advantages of proposed punched card system

PUNCHED CARD SYSTEMS DEVELOPMENT

Punched card systems development is substantially different from evaluating the feasibility of a punched card system. The latter instance calls for a broad brush to outline and evaluate the basic potential of a punched card application. The former calls for a fine brush to define, determine, classify, and specify the *exact* requirements of the punched card system. The user must keep in mind a basic systems rule—"the higher the degree of mechanization, essentially the less flexibility exists, and the more exact specifications must be." Computer experts express this more succinctly with the phrase "GIGO"—"garbage in, garbage out." With respect to punched card applications, this applies to all phases of the application—card design, report design, work flow, work control, scheduling, balancing, and checking.

Essentially, punched card systems development should include:
1. Establishing a general flow chart of the proposed system
2. Reviewing source document information
3. Designing specific input, master, and record card forms
4. Designing specific record and report forms
5. Determining specific work volumes
6. Establishing timing and scheduling requirements through punched card equipment based on generalized work flow
8. Establishing necessary controls
9. Determining overall equipment and personnel requirements
10. Providing necessary physical layout of punched card equipment
11. Developing final detailed procedures for input sections, punched card operators, and machine operators
12. Training necessary personnel
13. Arranging for timing of cutover to punched card system

SPECIAL PROBLEMS IN PUNCHED CARD SYSTEMS DESIGN

Like computer systems, punched card systems present special problems not usually associated with manual or mechanical systems design.

It has been said by knowledgeable systems designers that "the most flexible systems tool is a man (or woman) with a pencil and intelligence. Here one has the greatest computer memory (the brain); the greatest calculator (the mind); the finest decision maker (human intelligence); the most flexible output (the pencil)." With such a tool, instructions can be deleted, added to, changed, and the process still goes on. This is not so always with computers or, to a lesser degree, with punched card applications. Instructions must be specific. Forms must be standard. Reports must follow systems design. These limitations provide the special problems and challenges in punched card systems design.

Some specific problems are:

1. Input forms must be legible and arranged in a sequence to permit productive and accurate key punching.

2. Input cards must be designed in such a form that they can be effectively used throughout the systems process.

3. Wherever possible, data should be reduced to numerical codes. Alphabetical designations and descriptions are difficult and costly to process.

4. Coding presents a special problem. Codes must be developed to provide for maximum expansion and minimum processing time.

5. Wherever possible, prepunched information should be used to minimize key punching and improve accuracy. (*Of all punched card equipment, key punches and key verifiers are the only ones that require one person per machine.*)

6. Equipment setup time and physical card-handling time must be considered in estimating punched card systems time. Unlike a computer system, a punched card system involves a sequence of specific processing operations through a series of machines. This sequence of operations may require manual movement of cards from machine to machine, establishing intermediate controls to make sure all cards are accounted for, and setting up machines to process different jobs or applications.

7. Special care must be taken to establish control totals on input documents, and the original punched card input must be carefully balanced against these controls to prevent inaccuracies throughout the entire processing.

8. It may not be possible to accommodate all data relative to a transaction on one card; several cards appropriately coded, may be required.

EVALUATION AND IMPROVEMENT OF PUNCHED CARD OPERATIONS

Often, existing punched card systems installations can be substantially improved if a determined effort is made to evaluate them systematically and if an open mind is kept with respect to the possibilities of making improvements.

Evaluation should include:
1. Recording basic operating data
2. Classifying and summarizing data
3. Establishing comparative production and cost records
4. Observing trends

Improvements can be made in:
1. Quality, effectiveness, and cost of reports
2. Procedures
3. Machine utilization
4. Operations

Recording Basic Operating Data. Certain basic operating data should be recorded for any punched card job:
1. Job name or number
2. Operator name or number
3. Machine name or number
4. Date and time job is started
5. Date and time job is completed
6. Elapsed time
7. Volume of work handled

Such data may be obtained from job tickets, machine tickets, operation records, operator reports, and operation tickets.

In addition, data should be kept on operating costs (salaries, machine rental, supplies, overhead), errors made, card volumes, and key-punch production.

Classifying and Summarizing Operating Data. Basic data can be classified or summarized manually, or in larger applications, through the use of punched cards. Typical summaries might include:
1. *Machine utilization and performance summary* showing for each machine in the installation:
   a. Actual time in operation
   b. Available time
   c. Idle time
   d. Percent of time utilized
   e. Standard time (if available)
   f. Performance as a percent of standard
2. *Job performance summary* showing for each job:
   a. Actual time required
   b. Standard time
   c. Performance as a percent of standard
3. *Key-punch error summary* showing key-punch machines:
   a. Number of documents received
   b. Number of cards key-punched
   c. Number of errors
   d. Percent of errors
4. *Cost of operations summary* showing by month cost of operations in total and divided between salaries, machine charges, supplies, and overhead

Establishing Comparative Production and Cost Records. From recorded basic data and summary records, certain comparative records of production and costs can be developed.

Production comparisons might include:

$$\text{Cards handled per machine operator} \quad \frac{\text{Cards processed}}{\text{No. of operators}}$$

$$\text{Cards punched per operator} \quad \frac{\text{Cards punched}}{\text{No. of KP operators}}$$

$$\text{Cards per man-hour} \quad \frac{\text{Cards processed}}{\text{Total man-hours}}$$

$$\text{Cards per machine-hour} \quad \frac{\text{Cards processed}}{\text{Total machine-hours}}$$

Cost comparisons might include:

$$\text{Cost per machine-hour} \quad \frac{\text{Total cost}}{\text{Actual machine-hours}}$$

$$\text{Cards processed per dollar cost} \quad \frac{\text{No. of cards processed}}{\text{Total cost}}$$

$$\text{Cost per document} \quad \frac{\text{Total cost}}{\text{Documents processed}}$$

$$\text{Cost per report} \quad \frac{\text{Total cost}}{\text{Reports processed}}$$

$$\text{Cost for one job} \quad \text{Total cost} \times \frac{\text{actual machine time on job}}{\text{total machine time}}$$

Observing Trends. Basic operating data and comparative production and cost records observed over a period of time may reveal significant trends that point the way to problem areas where improvement may be possible.

A drop in key-punch production may reveal problems in training of operators, poor morale, lack of incentive, poor card design, or bad input documents.

A rise in idle time over a period of months should indicate that too much equipment is available.

A rise in cost per report may indicate improper system, too many reruns, lack of training, or lack of understanding of a job.

This information and these trends, plus personal observation and study, may reveal opportunities for improvements.

Improvements of Reports. Periodically, the reports produced on a punched card installation should be reviewed to determine if they are necessary, if they are satisfactory to the users, if they could be improved upon, and if they are timely enough. Frequently, quotas, standards, and budget figures can be introduced with a small amount of effort. For comparisons in time, previously punched cards can be added to produce comparisons between "same month last year," "last month," and "year to date." Comparisons may be made automatically to show net difference, percent of standard, and percent of totals.

Frequently, timeliness is important to the user and to the punched card installation. Earlier cutoffs of input data may ensure that reports are issued at a time when they can be most effectively acted upon. Reporting time may be changed to alleviate a bad peak-load situation.

Improvement of Procedures. Supervisors of punched card installations must be kept aware of changing management requirements for reports and records. Frequently, sheer inertia will result in records and reports being produced far beyond the period of usefulness. The detailed requirements of reports can change. Changes in volume of input data may show that the originally designed system is entirely inadequate for the new requirements.

Control procedures should be investigated to determine if they provide too little or too much control.

Improvements of Machine Usage. Basic operating records may indicate under-utilization of expensive punched card equipment. Unusual downtime may eat up productive time. Improvement in machine usage may involve improved scheduling to reduce standby time, machine conflicts, and peak loads.

Improvements of Operations. Flow of work through the installation should be charted and observed. Idle time of operators and machines should be checked. Excessive card handling may reveal system deficiencies. Idle operators may indicate "waiting for work" situations as a result of poor scheduling. Repeated reruns may indicate lack of training or lack of understanding of a job.

Peaks and valleys of work volumes should be checked and, where possible, schedules revised to smooth out work flow.

Priorities should be established for various jobs.

SPECIAL MANAGEMENT CONSIDERATIONS

Installation of a punched card system presents certain problems that are different from those usually associated with the installation of manual or mechanical systems.

Costs. Normally, the investment in a punched card system in terms of personnel, equipment, training time, and space is considerably larger than that in a comparable mechanical or manual system. A very small system consisting of a key punch, verifier, collator, sorter, accounting machine, reproducer, and interpreter, with three operators, will cost approximately $2,500 per month to operate.

In the early stages of conversion to such a system, utilization is normally small and offsetting benefits negligible. Frequently, parallel runs are required for a period of time in which both manual and punched card costs are involved.

Personnel. Skilled and experienced operators are at a premium. Existing employees can be trained through manufacturers' schools, but initial productivity is limited. In addition to operators, systems and management skills are required in an effective installation.

Organization. Installation of a punched card system will necessitate certain organization changes. Personnel on previous mechanical or manual systems may have to be transferred. Controls and frequently organizational responsibilities are considerably changed. Frequently, employees resent the systems change.

Procedures. Forms and records are different. Procedures must be more standardized. Exception routines, easily handled in manual systems, become costly and frequently impossible to achieve effectively. Schedules may need to be more rigidly adhered to. Documentation in terms of written procedures and instructions frequently increases. Systems design is time consuming and costly. Many management decisions must be made about what is to be included in or eliminated from a report, what controls should be established, what records or reports should be changed, and what additional data are required.

Management Solutions.   To prevent some of these problems and alleviate others, management must do certain things.   It must:

1. Establish objectives for the program.

2. Take an active part in planning the scope of the program, the approach to be taken, the feasibility study, the conversion timetable, and the type and sequence of applications to be installed.

3. Recognize the organizational problems involved and take steps to minimize any adverse effects.

4. Insist on and provide for adequate time and staff to complete systems study.

5. Be prepared to make decisions about information requirements for the system.

6. Select high-caliber personnel to run the system and provide them with adequate training.

7. Allow for adequate parallel operations and recognize that, initially, start-up costs may be high.

8. After a "shakedown" period, insist on an evaluation of the program as compared with objectives.

SUMMARY

Punched card systems can provide an effective and economical method of mechanizing the processing of business data where such data are constant in nature, are used repetitively throughout the business system, and can be captured in punched card form early in the systems process, and where a large amount of sorting, calculating, and printing is done.   They are especially effective where it is necessary to sort out and accumulate large amounts of clerical data.

Punched card applications are unique and must be designed to meet the specific requirements of each business.   Care must be taken to develop exact specifications for all phases of the application—card design, report design, work flow, work control, scheduling, balancing, and checking.   Inaccurate or incomplete specifications or systems design results in costly or unworkable applications.

Punched card operations should be carefully evaluated.   Comparative production and cost records should be developed for all phases of operations.   Trends should be observed.   Specific improvement programs should be established.

Finally, management must take an active part in establishing the objectives of the punched card system, in planning the system, in demanding reasonable performance, and in evaluating results against objectives.

BIBLIOGRAPHY

Gillespie, Cecil, *Accounting Systems: Procedures and Methods,* Prentice-Hall, Inc., Englewood Cliffs, N.J., 1951.

Johnson, Eldred A., *Accounting Systems in Modern Business,* McGraw-Hill Book Company, New York, 1957.

Lazzaro, Victor (ed.), *Systems and Procedures—A Handbook for Business and Industry,* Prentice-Hall, Inc., Englewood Cliffs, N.J., 1959.

McGill, Donald A. C., *Punched Cards: Data Processing for Profit Improvement,* McGraw-Hill Book Company, New York, 1962.

CHAPTER FOUR

Electronic Computer Applications

DAVID V. SAVIDGE   *UNIVAC Division of Sperry Rand Corporation, Blue Bell, Pennsylvania*

Electronic computers are tools used in the management of data, which includes recording data about business transactions as well as taking care of the data and having them available for reproduction or analysis. The same data are grouped and regrouped many times to manage a business. This chapter will outline some general guidelines for identifying useful work for electronic computers. It will also identify sources of information on the details of specific applications.

ELECTRONIC COMPUTERS AS TOOLS

One advantage electronic computers have over other tools is that they always do the same thing the same way with a minimum of human intervention. Another advantage lies in their speed. After the work is laid out for it, one computer can get two numbers from specific cells, add them together, and store the total in another cell 2,880,000,000 times in one 8-hour day. If one person could record 2,000 such numbers in one day, the output of 2,880,000 people would keep one electronic computer busy doing this simple operation.

More than 15,000 electronic computers were doing useful work in the United States in 1965. Not all of them have the speed mentioned above. Users of electronic computers have found that they can learn more about their businesses by recording more information about transactions and analyzing it in many new ways. The speed of the computer is so great that the answers are available in time to be meaningful.

A third advantage lies in the ability of electronic computers to communicate with each other. One transcription of the record of a transaction is all that is needed to place data under the control of a network of computers. Not all of the work performed on the data needs to be accomplished at one time.

After a business has developed a system to manage the data about current transactions, the electronic computer can perform any analysis which anyone considers significant from the historical data available. The computer is fast enough to permit the businessman to test the effects of different courses of action and different external conditions and then select the best course of action. In this instance, the electronic computer is used to help manage the business rather than just manage the data.

Criteria for Use of Electronic Computers. One of two criteria must be met to make the application of electronic computers practical—complexity or volume. The amount of detail recorded about transactions is related to the variety of analyses desired. If we were only concerned with the total number of men and the total number of women in the population, the management of census data would be simple. As it happens, we also want to know the distribution by sex, age group, and geographical area. The number of units or cells for analysis increases as the product of the individual elements increases. For 2 sex groups, 15 age groups, and 3,000 geographical areas, we would have 90,000 units for analysis. This requires some form of electronic computer. The frequency with which such analyses are required determines the power of the equipment to be used. The application of electronic computer systems becomes practical when either the number of different units for analysis is great or the number of times an individual piece of information is reproduced is high.

As a general rule, whenever there are more than 10,000 units for analysis, some form of electronic computer can have a practical application. This can be represented by 100 customers each capable of buying 100 different things. It can also mean buying and processing 10,000 different items. The power of the computing system must be increased as the number of cells increases if the results are to be published on any regular schedule. Similarly, if the results shown in 10,000 cells are to be published at very frequent intervals (less than one day) or on demand, the power of the computing system must be increased.

KINDS OF DATA TO BE MANAGED

Data about the transactions of a business are necessary to manage the business. We define a "transaction" as any event or act which involves the expenditure of labor or material, a change in the value or condition of any asset or liability, or a contract to do so. Every transaction involves the elements of a time, a place, a motive, an action, some value, and at least two of the following:

1. Data about persons
   a. From whom the business buys things or services
   b. To whom the business sells things or services
2. Data about things
   a. Bought from others
   b. Sold to others
   c. Processed by the business
   d. Consumed by the business
   e. Produced by the business
3. Data about services
   a. Bought from others
   b. Sold to others
   c. Performed by the business for the business

Given any statement describing one event, whenever any of the above items change, we have another event or transaction. From the viewpoint of a data-processing system, there needs to be some identifying symbol or number to represent the combination of elements which make up a transaction. If a transaction number is used as an abbreviation, it is not necessary to repeat all the information about the transaction every time it is referenced. In some businesses, the identity of some elements of a transaction is unimportant unless something else happens. The identity of a retail buyer is not significant in a cash sale. When an article is returned for refund, the requirement to present a cash-register receipt which identifies the seller, the date, and the amount is all that is needed. There is no proof that the person requesting the refund actually made the purchase. From the viewpoint of the store, the identity of the purchaser for cash is of interest only if the cash accepted turns out to be counterfeit at some later time.

Establishing the Information Retrieval Trail. The determination of what is a practical unit or kind of recording depends on the kind of application. A time clock can record time in units of one one-hundredth of an hour. This is reasonable for payroll applications covering hourly employees if hundredths are used in the multiplier. Hundredths of an hour are not required for recording the presence of a salaried employee or an hourly employee under some wage contracts. Even though particular applications do not require time to be recorded in very small units, time should be recorded in the smallest possible unit available at some minimum cost. If the initial record of a transaction is stored in machine-intelligible form, any subsequent grouping on the basis of time can be done in any larger unit. On the other hand, if the initial record is not machine-intelligible, the transcription to machine-intelligible form may perform an arbitrary grouping such as eliminating the hundredths or tenths of hours. This is often desirable to reduce the number of digits transcribed. All data should be recorded in that detail which is available for some minimum cost.

Transaction Number. When any part of the detail of an initial record of a transaction is not carried forward through all analyses and summaries, it is necessary to maintain an information retrieval trail. This is accomplished by always carrying the transaction number—a serial designation which is unique. This number is listed as the detail supporting every analysis or summary. By this means, it is possible to trace back to the initial record. It is then possible to analyze the characteristics of any of the other elements of the transaction which may have been deleted in intermediate transcriptions. The common denominator is the transaction number or identifier. As long as it is listed in machine-intelligible form in every analysis or summary, the complete details of selected transactions can be retrieved if required.

Seldom is it necessary to reanalyze the entire universe of data. It is often desirable, however, to examine further those transactions which have some common combination of characteristics. The transaction number provides the information retrieval trail. This is the same as the accountant's audit trail. If the transaction number identifies the chain and the sequence within the chain, as well as the relative time of occurrence, the amount of recording per transaction can be minimized.

Master File. Some installations find it economical to maintain a master file or record on each account. Where this is done, one can recopy all the unchanged data as well as the changed data every time a transaction is posted. The master file is always up to date. The alternative approach is to accumulate changes or transactions in a sorted sequence and answer inquiries by referencing both the master file and the accumulated transactions.

With an electronic computer, a historical record of any account may be constructed whenever it is desired. It is not necessary to maintain all the detail of all transactions affecting one account in one file. With continuous storage media such as tape, recirculating devices, magnetic drums or discs, or a bank of magnetic cores, it is possible to locate data by position or address. Thus, the effect of a historical record may be achieved although one is not created until it is needed. The latter approach requires minimum copying of data.

Data Banks. An information retrieval trail can lead to a data bank or file. Some of the existing data banks which can be purchased contain economic data about places (U.S. Bureau of the Census), firms (Dun & Bradstreet), and people (credit bureaus). If a business has access to files containing information relating to persons, places, or things with which it deals, it is only necessary to store, in its own files, a cross-reference to the other files. This is in contrast to filing all the information in one place. The price a business can pay to store information in one medium or another depends on the uses it wishes to make of the information. The more frequently one needs to refer to something, the more one can pay for rapid access to it.

Managing Data about Time. Time can be measured in very small units approaching zero time. Such fine detail is of little value in managing a business. In murder investigations, the hour and the minute of a transaction become important. Investigations of fraud, however, are seldom concerned with more than the relative time within one day that a transaction took place. Such references are concerned with the transaction before and the one afterward. The identification of the day of the month is of little interest after that day has passed and any record of the transactions has been validated.

Data about time present some of the problems that can be found with any of the other elements of transactions:

1. They can be identified in greater detail than may be considered desirable or even necessary at the time the system is installed—hundredths of an hour for the start of a job, for example.

2. They are used as an index to maintain records: for example, a cash-register tape shows a sequence of transactions; an accounting journal lists transactions in sequence by time; a customer's account lists the changes in his net liability over time.

3. They are used as an index for analyses and summaries: for example, year-to-date information; last-twelve-month data; moving averages; seasonal studies.

4. When used as an index, the more detailed portions lose significance with successive summaries until a level of historical significance is reached: for example, minute to hour to day to pay period; pay period to quarter to year; day to month to limit (accounts receivable); day to period to end of job (costs).

5. When a level of historical significance is reached, it is imperative that the data be retained in a form which a machine can understand (machine-intelligible form) to permit the businessman to use an electronic computer to manage his business; the type of correlations which are required will change.

6. Sampling and statistical techniques can be used to select detail not included in the original summaries: for example, finding the ages of workers who check in early or leave late; determining the average purchases by persons living in different geographic areas during a specific season.

7. Date as well as time of day can be represented in many ways: for example, day of month, month, year; month, day, year; year, month, day; day of week, week, year; year, day of year; and so on. Numbers, names, or abbreviations may be used for the month or day of the week. In identifying a particular time, we must identify the larger units of which this time is a part.

Data about time are related to the other elements of transactions. The time of each individual transaction should be recorded in as small a unit of time as is practical. At least a relative time is known at the time a transaction is executed. The serial numbers of preprinted forms provide relative time.

Time clocks provide absolute time expressed in terms of some unit. The time of occurrence, if recorded, becomes an element of the transaction. If it is not recorded at that time, it may be deduced by implication and recorded at a later time when it achieves significance.

Managing Data about Places. A "place" can be defined as a point in space. A "point" is defined as an indivisible part of a whole. This provides a unit with zero dimensions. In this respect, place is like time. It can be identified in smaller units than are normally required in business. The grouping of small units into larger units is far more complex for places than for time. Groupings of places are generally according to geopolitical subdivisions. The boundaries of these subdivisions change. They are also subject to change in identifications or names. The information retrieval trail for places must provide the cross-referencing needed to cover changes in name as well as grouping.

Some abbreviations for geographic groupings are available—Post Office ZIP codes, telephone area and exchange numbers, census tract designations, and the Association of American Railroads' shipping points. These groupings by themselves will seldom satisfy the complete needs of a business. A shipper, for example, wants to know all of his customers who lie along a particular truck route. A group of ZIP codes or telephone numbers will only give those locations which could not qualify. As a general rule, location or place codes will only identify a place or group it with contiguous places. It is necessary to store other information about each place for the system to be effective. This is sometimes called a "data bank." The research required to get useful information about each place will generally prove worthwhile. It needs to be stored only once. With electronic computers, these additional characteristics can be retrieved for every possible requirement.

The general rule is that if any information retrieval trail is maintained, it should only be necessary to store any characteristics about any place one time. Some of the characteristics about places which have been found useful are:

1. Transportation routes going to or through the place
2. Distances on those routes to the nearest other places referenced by the system
3. Time to transport goods to the other places
4. Cost to transport goods to the other places
5. Power facilities available
6. Water availability
7. Structures available by type and size
8. Population size and characteristics
9. Mean temperatures and rainfall
10. Economic data

A cross-reference to such data must be included in the plan for the total system. It is not necessary to research all this information before the system is installed. The important consideration is to provide a place for cross-referencing, so that when a particular subject becomes of interest, the findings of the investigation can be stored in machine-intelligible form and indexed to the identifiers for the places involved. This maintains the information retrieval trail. The objective is to avoid performing the same research twice.

Managing Data about Motives. Every transaction takes place for some purpose or motive. The motive for a sales transaction is to convert assets into cash to buy more assets to make more profit. The fact that a profit may or may not be made on an individual sale is not an element of the sales transaction. The profit is assumed at the time the article is priced. The acts of marking up, marking down, or pricing are transactions just as much as the act of selling.

They change the value of the asset. The sale changes the negotiable condition of the asset.

The motives for ordering, buying, or spending are often not so easy to discern. The chain of reasoning for spending is longer than to buy more assets to make more sales to make more profit, except when this is all one does. The list of motives which is used by any business as the basis for analyzing transactions will vary according to the type of business and the volume of transactions. The volume of transactions determines the level of detail required. As a general rule, the level of detail should be so low as to result in no more than one page if all of the transactions for one period under one motive are listed together. Thus, the longer the period for review, the lower the level should be. Otherwise, the list becomes too long.

The major consideration when organizing a classification scheme for motives is that every transaction takes place so that some other transaction can occur. It must be possible to indicate this dependency by means of a tree diagram similar to that shown in Figure 4-1. The results or outputs of one transaction become inputs to the next one in the chain. The ultimate motive for a commercial concern must be to make a profit. Educational institutions have "teach people" at the end of their tree. Unless all transactions can logically be placed somewhere within such a tree, it will not be possible to use an electronic computer as an effective tool in the management of the business. The tree shows the cause and effect relationships of all transactions. It shows the relationship of the horseshoe nail to the nation.

The objective in managing data about motives is to provide sufficient detail in the initial record of a transaction so that any kind of analysis can be made when required. The detail should make it possible to associate every transaction with the one which was necessary prior to it and with the one which depended on it for inputs. This will permit any higher-level grouping or analysis which may be required, whether this is within one input/output chain or across such chains.

The difficulty arises when procuring things or services which can be used in more than one chain. Note the caption "to hire people" in Figure 4-1. The purpose to be served by a particular hiring action will not be known at the time the personnel office is established. Burden rates are often applied to the amounts expended for direct labor or material only because this has been the simplest method. With an electronic computer, one can develop more realistic distribution methods so that job or object costs can reflect the actual conditions. It is not necessary to develop a complete scheme to make direct charges of all expenditures prior to the installation of an electronic computer. The system should be sufficiently flexible to permit the conversion of indirect costs to direct costs as rapidly as realistic bases for allocation are developed. The speed of the electronic computer makes it possible to distribute expenses on the basis of:

1. Elapsed time—down to the minute
2. Man-hours of a particular skill
3. Counts of work units or output
4. Space occupied over time
5. Machinery or tools utilized over time
6. Machinery or tools utilized over work units or outputs
7. Power consumption

These are only suggestions. The businessman who knows the relationship of his expenses can have a data-processing system to express that relationship.

Most businesses are subject to some regulation concerning record keeping.

Regulatory bodies have prescribed charts of accounts which may not satisfy all of the internal requirements of a business. An electronic computer has the speed to satisfy the regulatory requirement as well as to meet the operating needs of the business whenever the two do not coincide.

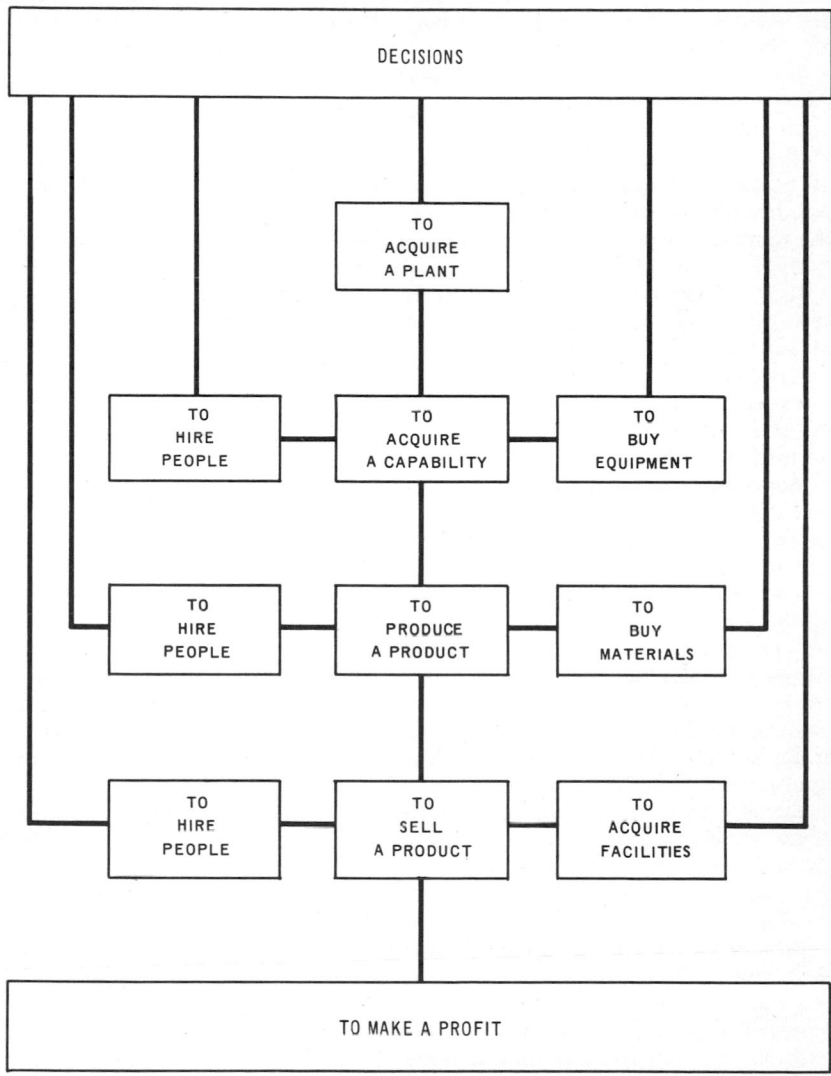

FIG. 4-1. *Chains of motives.*

Managing Data about Actions. Business buys and sells. Before, between, and after these two actions, many other actions take place. Every transaction has as one of its elements a thing acted upon. This may be a material thing or some intangible thing such as a value. In all cases, the thing or things acted upon are inputs to the transaction. They were outputs of a prior transaction. In turn, each transaction or event produces one or more outputs which become inputs to another transaction. The operation on the inputs to produce output is called an "action."

In the same manner as motives can be expressed in general or specific terms, so also can actions. The words used to identify actions will vary among industries, among localities, and among different points in time. These words change as technological improvements occur. Historical data concerning actions are always subject to interpretation.

An analysis of transactions by kinds of actions is sometimes useful to compare the cost or effectiveness of different methods. This type of study cannot be made by the electronic computer unless the action is identified in the record of the transaction. The identification can be expressed or implied. A member of a particular craft union working in a particular department is assumed to be performing his usual task or action unless an exception is noted. Under the normal case, the motive can also be assumed. Care must be taken to record every exception fully. The information retrieval trail must be unambiguous.

It is seldom necessary to analyze all transactions for an extended period by kind of action. Quicker and simpler analyses by product will give an indication of improvement or impairment. The analysis by kind of action will help to determine the cause of the change. Thus, the kind of action is seldom explicitly recorded for every transaction if the information retrieval trail permits picking it up for analysis when it is needed. The important consideration is that it be available when needed.

Managing Data about Values. Values are the measurements of time or space and the counts of things and money. Although we insist on accuracy in any calculations involving these values, most businesses are rather lax in the initial measurement or count of something and the recording of that value. There is always a limit to the amount one can afford to pay to assure accurate input values. In one case, the individual making the initial record cannot profit from any error he may make. Here the amount one can pay for protection is an estimate of possible losses from errors which are detrimental to the business. In the case where the individual making the initial record can profit from a misrecording, the limit is much higher. Banks, as well as dealers in volatile, mobile, or high-valued merchandise, have developed checks which reduce the exposure from misrecording to a minimum.

Errors which can result in profit to the person committing the error are reduced when an electronic computer is used. This is due, in part, to the fact that less human intervention is possible after the initial recording. From then on, the data are in machine-intelligible form which renders them less intelligible to man.

Because an electronic computer performs arithmetic operations in accordance with rules which are built into the hardware, input values must always be presented in the form which the particular computer can use. Data are represented by a stream of bits. The presence or absence of a bit in a particular position or at a particular time denotes data. Every stream has a starting position or time. Most streams are subdivided into groups of bit positions for ease of handling. The size of a group affects the design of the hardware. If no arithmetic operations are performed on the data, it is only necessary to be sure the size of the group of bits in the input data coincides with the size used by the computer. Data fed into an electronic computer for the purpose of performing arithmetic must conform not only to the size of the group or "byte" used by the computer but also to the code used for a byte. An example of this is indicated by the following table:

Binary values	Decimal values	
	Binary coded decimal	Excess-3
0000	0	Nondecimal
0001	1	Nondecimal
0010	2	Nondecimal
0011	3	0
0100	4	1
0101	5	2
0110	6	3
0111	7	4
1000	8	5
1001	9	6
1010	Nondecimal	7
1011	Nondecimal	8
1100	Nondecimal	9

Any two numbers to be added together must be fed into the adder in the code which was designed into the computer.

Decimal Point. Another aspect of values which requires attention is the decimal point. Within most computers, this never appears; it is assumed. Thus, anyone dealing with arithmetic operations must plot the position of the decimal point in every result value. Most computers have some provision to take care of such things as arithmetic overflow (a result larger than the space provided) and improper division (division by zero or an improperly positioned divisor). The rules of arithmetic built into an electronic computer must be learned by the people contemplating using it. Some computers have built-in "floating-point arithmetic," where every value has with it a scaling factor which tells the location of the decimal point to the left or to the right of the value. This is useful to express either very large or very small values. It has the disadvantage that some significant digits may be dropped if results generate too many digits in iterative processes.

Plus or Minus Sign. The sign of a value also requires attention. Although there are only two possible conditions, plus or minus, most decimal computers—those that are built to perform decimal arithmetic—use as many bits for the sign as for any other character. Some, including binary computers—those that are capable of performing binary arithmetic—only use one bit position for the sign with 0 denoting either plus or minus and 1 denoting the other. A computer of the latter class must make some special provision when it tries to print the sign, because few printers will print only zeros and ones. Some of the early computers did this, but very few are still in operation.

Managing Data about Persons. One of the most difficult classes of data to manage is data about persons. Human beings change their:

1. Addresses
2. Physical characteristics
3. Names
4. Occupations
5. Possessions
6. Marital status

Legal entities can also change everything except their marital status, but they must comply with certain formalities to change their address of registration, name, or occupation. Human beings are required to change only name or marital status in a formal manner. The human being who conducts a business in his own name is more readily identifiable than one who does not trade in goods or services.

Because of all of the changes to data about persons which are possible over a period of time, it has been found desirable to assign an identifying number to the concept of an individual person. At different times, this number means a different combination of the six items listed above. Each worker in a covered occupation is assigned a Social Security Number. If the person enters military service, he receives a serial number. Every credit card he receives has another unique number. If he becomes an employer and liable to withhold taxes, he receives an Employer Identification Number. If he has been rated by Dun & Bradstreet, he may be assigned a D-U-N-S number (Data Universal Numbering System).

Each of these numbers has been assigned for the purpose of establishing an information retrieval trail within a given aspect of the life of the individual. Some of the data banks developed are not accessible to anyone but the agency accumulating the data and the individual. Other data banks, particularly those relating to credit information, can be accessed for a price. The most useful data banks are those which can provide historical data on the individual rather than just a snapshot.

The numbers mentioned above are only a sample. As many different numbers for one person as are known should be accessible through the information retrieval trail. This is accomplished by adopting some identifier, which may be different from the one used for sorting within the data-processing system, as the cross-reference key to lead to the other identifiers which can lead to other data banks. A reasonable cross-reference number for human beings can be the Social Security Number. Persons without Social Security Numbers can be assigned ten-digit numbers for many years to come. Similarly, an Employer Identification (EI) number can serve for legal entities which do not have Social Security Numbers. In some systems, the D-U-N-S number may be preferred because its definition is different from that of the EI number. The American Bankers Association has a number to identify stock issues. The current definition of each system should be studied before adopting one number or the other as the cross-reference key.

Managing Data about Things. Very few of the characteristics of things change over time. Persons can be identified by using one common pattern to show the physical and other characteristics, but every different kind of thing requires a different pattern or set of descriptors to identify it.

A further complexity is created by the fact that more than one physical item will generally fit a particular description. Thus, it becomes necessary to attach a serial designation to identify a specific physical item. Because of these conditions and the effort required to put an identifying tag on every piece, descriptive documents which are intelligible to human beings are required if human beings handle the merchandise. Such documents will often contain detailed information, such as storage location, shipper, carrier, and so on, which loses significance as time passes. Great care must be exercised in converting to machine-intelligible form the data most probably needed in the future. This is an area where the cost of retaining some information in machine-intelligible form must be evaluated over time against any losses which could be sustained due to the lack of it and the cost to reconstruct it when needed. The information retrieval trail can lead to paper documents as well as computer files.

Each business generally establishes its own numbering system for things. This is because records pertaining to things are generally arranged according to the item number assigned, and very few businesses want the same identical grouping. The groupings used by Sears, Roebuck and Company are not the same as those used by Montgomery Ward & Company.

A Federal Stock Number System has been developed by the Federal government under the control of the Defense Logistics Services Center, Defense Supply Agency, Battle Creek, Michigan. The Federal Stock Number consists of three parts—a four-digit supply commodity class, a three-digit commodity code, and a four-digit serial number. These numbers are assigned by DSA on the basis of information supplied in accordance with description patterns established by DSA for different classes of property. The American Standards Association adopts standard specifications and, in turn, from the activity of the Sectional Committee on Computers and Information Processing, ASA X3, approves some standard codes for such specifications and names. In addition, most trade associations, such as the Engineers' Joint Council, develop catalogs or lists with accepted terminology and nomenclature for their trade.

These systems can prove useful in setting up a scheme for an individual business. Where a business does have an item identification system in use prior to the installation of an electronic computer, it is imperative that all ambiguities be eliminated from that system before the installation is completed. A computer is only aware of the data under its control at any one time.

Managing Data about Services. When bought or sold, services are often treated in the same manner as things which are bought or sold. When services are performed by the business for the business, the identification rules are dictated by the chart of accounts. Labor spent in carpentry or building maintenance can be allocated to chains of motives as described above. The importance of ascribing a motive to every expenditure of labor or material is explained under "Design of the System," below.

REPRESENTATION OF DATA

Every electronic computer is designed around some specific character set. The internal set may differ from the set of characters accepted by an input device such as a card reader or displayed by an output device such as a printer. If the conversion from one set to another is not accomplished by hardware, computer programs can be prepared to convert any single set to any other single set. The internal character set for a binary computer consists of only two characters, 0 and 1. For input and output functions, these internal characters can be grouped together. The number of internal characters included as a group for an input or output character depends on pure hardware considerations.

An example of this is the 5-level Teletype code which uses a separate code as a shift to print more than 31 different characters. If only 31 characters are involved, the 5-level code is sufficient. Every time 31 is exceeded, two 5-level groups are required. It is more economical to go to a 6-level code with 64 characters if 20 percent or more of the characters are beyond the range of a set of 32 characters. It is significant that very few electronic computers are being built with a character set smaller than 64.

The 7-level American Standard Code for Information Interchange (ASCII) uses a set of 128 characters or symbols. This, in turn, can become part of a set requiring 8 levels for 256 characters. Hardware to operate on an 8-bit character may be more economical than hardware to operate on a 7-bit character. Decimal arithmetic is performed on only 4 bit groups. Thus, two decimal digits can be stored in one 8-bit character or byte. If one-fourth or more of the data is decimal, an 8-bit character has advantages over a 7-bit character. Most statistical studies show that about 15 percent of the data in a business application is purely numerical. Thus, there may be an economic justification for selecting 8 bits in preference to 7 in the design of a system. This is especially true if 25 percent of the systems will be used in a scientific environment.

STORAGE OF DATA

Data in an electronic computer system must be protected and also must be accessible to properly authorized individuals. This is the normal records management function. Because an electronic computer system does not provide the neat physical boundaries of file-drawer-divider-folder-record, mapping and indexing schemes assume greater importance. Storage in an electronic computer system is divided into logical units or cells which may or may not be physically identifiable. The contents of each unit or cell must be known to the person using the system. The type of code in which the data are stored, the kind of information represented by the data, the beginning or ending cells in which the data are found, and the length of the data must be known if the data are to have any meaning to the electronic computer.

The identification of the cell is dictated by the addressing structure of the electronic computer. A certain number of bits is considered to be a unit for a particular storage medium (drum, disc, core, or the like). Each unit is assigned a discrete number or address which identifies it. Bits within, starting from, or ending at some address will be processed every time the electronic computer executes an instruction.

Different storage media will require different lengths of time to find a particular address. Media which do not rely on physical movement, such as magnetic cores, plating, or electrical delay lines, can be accessed faster than media which rely on rotation, such as drums or discs. If the drum or disc has movable sensing heads, where there are fewer heads than there are tracks of recording, additional time is required to position the head physically over the track to be sensed. If the motion of the medium or head is not rotational, the length of time is directly proportional to the total distance one or the other must move. This is the situation with tape or any other continuous medium. The range in access times within an individual system is very large, from nanoseconds to seconds, or a billion to one.

The success or failure of an application will often depend on the extent to which the following rules are applied.

1. Data fields should conform in size to the unit accessed by the addressing scheme of the electronic computer used.

2. Record lengths should provide simple mapping and indexing throughout the storage system.

3. Hierarchies of storage should be organized to require the minimum delay on the part of the arithmetic or processing unit waiting for data.

4. Memory accesses to any one unit of one medium should be overlapped with accesses to other units and media as well as overlapped with computing.

CONTROL OF THE COMPUTING SYSTEM

The requirements just outlined indicate that the organization of the data and the design of the electronic computer used are closely related. The designer of the electronic computer tries to foresee the requirements of the data to be processed. In turn, the person using the computer tries to fit his data to the equipment he has selected. Another group of designers (programmers) assists in accomplishing the adaptation of the electronic computer to the data-processing problem. Programmers are consulted during the design of the hardware, but are later called upon to accomplish the objectives of exploiting the capability of the hardware and making the equipment easy to use. This is generally done by the manufacturer, assisted, or at least prodded, by customers trying to get jobs done.

Exploiting the Capability of the Hardware. In the category of exploiting the capability of the hardware are programs such as:

1. Input/output subroutines—groups of instructions tailored to the hardware to start, stop, test, and control the input and output gear (tapes, readers, punches, printers, and the like).

2. Sorts and merges—programs which rely heavily on the input/output subroutines and their interaction.

3. Contingency routines—subroutines and also programs which are executed under abnormal conditions to diagnose the situation and either restore normal operation or report the diagnosis to the operator.

4. Operating routines—special-purpose routines which match work waiting to be done with hardware available to do work. These routines can interrupt lower priority work on a temporary basis and restore it when the higher priority work is accomplished. They can also measure the time used by one program and interrupt it if the time exceeds some predetermined limit. These routines keep the hardware busy doing useful work, assigning maintenance diagnostic routines if there is nothing else to be done.

Making the Equipment Easy to Use. In the category of making the equipment easy to use are programs such as:

1. General-purpose source language processors—programs which accept statements of a procedure in a language and form which require translation to the instruction code of the electronic computer. Generally speaking, one such statement will result in one or more computer instructions. Such a language will also contain terms which relate to the allocation of storage and peripheral devices. The language permits the programmer to use a tag or name for either data or instructions and perform operations on tags without knowing their addresses. The processor will supply the addresses. In this group are general-purpose assemblers and compilers such as COBOL. Each manufacturer provides at least one for each computer.

2. Special-purpose source language processors—programs similar to the general-purpose processors, but more limited in their application. FORTRAN and ALGOL are examples of this group for the field of mathematics.

3. General-purpose generators—programs which accept parameters as input and either produce a program to use at a later time or execute the program immediately. In this group are report generators and editing routines.

4. Special-purpose application programs—programs which are hybrids combining procedure statements with parameters for functions such as:
   a. Numerical control of machine tools
   b. Linear programming
   c. PERT/cost and critical path method
   d. Matrix manipulation
   e. Statistical packages
   f. Inventory control

This group is the means by which knowledge in the field of data processing is put to fullest use. Trade associations, computing organizations, and manufacturers generally have access to the available programs. Each program will normally require some modification before it can be used in an individual business, but the framework will be useful.

DESIGN OF THE SYSTEM

Every event or action which takes place in the conduct of an enterprise can be arrayed within a network which shows the relationships of the inputs and outputs of every action. Although the PERT (Program Evaluation and Review Technique) system was developed to control construction projects, network diagrams were used to indicate the relationship of steps in a process before electronic computers were built. Thus, the application of the network to the description of what happens within a business and to the design of a data-processing system is a logical step.

To use a network to describe what happens within a business, it is necessary to delimit the definition of a "transaction" as involving either time or money in a manageable amount. This permits the chart to be at a practical level of detail to suit the circumstances within the enterprise at any time. This type of analysis of what is done must be accomplished whether one is contemplating the acquisition of an electronic computer or whether he has one in use. It provides the details within each chain of motives, and thus can be used to develop the chart of accounts.

The processing of data which is the record of the successive occurrence of the events in the network must also be reflected as a network. It is only if both the work performed and the data flow are treated as networks that the full capability of the electronic computer can be realized. This cannot be accomplished overnight. The following series of steps is recommended.

1. Develop a network chart or listing for the events of that part of the enterprise which you wish to control first.

2. Develop the corollary network for the processing of the data for the part covered in step 1.

3. Fit the data-processing work you are now doing into the data-processing network in step 2.

4. Expand the data-processing work in step 3 to help manage that part of the enterprise.

5. Return to step 1 for another part.

CONCLUSION

The foregoing gives general rules and caveats which can be applied to every data-processing problem. Data processing consists of three types of operations—arithmetic, logical, and transfer. These operations are combined for the functions of recording, storing, analyzing, summarizing, and reproducing the data needed to manage an enterprise.

Differences between kinds of enterprises and between enterprises of the same kind require different sequences of the functions and of the operations within the functions. Thus it is important to adopt and adhere to a conventional form of network representation. This provides the road map between a decision and its end effect.

The standardization efforts discussed above facilitate the comprehension of network charts. The principle of top-down analysis can be applied starting with a chart similar to that in Figure 4-1. Each block on such a chart can be broken down by another chart. This process can be repeated, level by level, until a chart gives the instructions to a person to do work. Each level of management can thus be given a set of charts at the appropriate level of detail to help him carry out his responsibilities.

An electronic computer can process data at any level of detail desired. Thus, it can provide management control on the data-processing system as well as on the enterprise which that system is intended to control.

BIBLIOGRAPHY

Burke, Kenneth, *Grammar of Motives,* Prentice-Hall, Inc., Englewood Cliffs, N.J., 1945.

Gore, William J., *Administrative Decision Making,* John Wiley & Sons, Inc., New York, 1964.

Reynolds, Charles O., *Work Simplification for Everyone,* Pyramid Publications, Inc., New York, 1962.

Schlaifer, Robert, *Introduction to Statistics for Business Decisions,* McGraw-Hill Book Company, New York, 1961.

Shaffer, L. R., J. R. Ritter, and W. L. Meyer, *The Critical Path Method,* McGraw-Hill Book Company, New York, 1961.

Stilian, Gabriel N., et al., *PERT,* Report no. 74, American Management Association, New York, 1962.

Stires, David M., and Raymond B. Wenig, *PERT/COST,* Industrial Engineering Institute, Boston, 1964.

Vazsonyi, Andrew, *Scientific Programming in Business and Industry,* John Wiley & Sons, Inc., New York, 1958.

See also publications of the Association for Computing Machinery, the Data Processing Management Association, and the Systems and Procedures Association.

CHAPTER FIVE

Source Data Automation

NORMAN STATLAND *Director of Systems Development, Automatic Data Processing, Inc., New York, New York*

Source data automation (SDA) means capturing information in machine-processible form as soon as possible after it is generated. Approximately 90 percent of the information fed into computers for processing or analysis is converted into machine-processible form from handwritten documents. This means that information gathered in the plant, in the shop, in the outlying office, and at countless other data origin points is handled at least twice—once when it is manually recorded and again when it is transcribed from manual documents to machine-legible media. Every time data are manually handled after their generation, time and money are wasted and the opportunity to introduce errors is increased.

Many times, gathering source data directly in machine language is seen by management as either too complex for clerical people to understand or too expensive in terms of increased equipment costs. For this reason, heavy manual operations still exist in such divisional operations as timekeeping, production reporting, warehouse operations, bill-of-lading writing, sales-order writing, trade transactions within the brokerage business, and almost any other point of entry into a business data-processing system. To clear away some of this confusion and to indicate that source data automation can be used economically within most business organizations, this chapter will attempt to demonstrate how different equipment can be used at varying levels of SDA.

Within this chapter, key punching is not considered as a means of source data automation, because use of a key punch to create a machine-processible medium—the punched card—is the prime example of what SDA will change. The most typical means of creating a source document, such as a sales order, involves manual preparation of the form, followed by clerical handling of the order before it becomes the document from which the punched card is prepared at the key-punch machine.

This chapter will cover the various types of devices and procedural concepts that can be used to implement source data automation under varying environ-

TABLE 5-1. Comparison of Manual Input Transaction Recorders

Input device	Usage	Transaction recording unit	Cost per unit,* dollars
Key punching	(Or any form of key-stroke operation such as Friden Flexowriter)	Key punch (026)	3,475
		Typing key punch (826)	4,850
Partially punched cards	Complete the punching manually with stylus (IBM Porta-Punch)	Porta-Punch	5.50
Mark-sensed punched cards or data sheets	Complete the recording of source data with manual entry of variable data (primarily limited to numeric data) with a pencil mark	Mark-Sense Attachment to 519 Summary Punch	5,000
		Optical Mark Reader (1231)	26,500
Optical character recognition	For reading turnaround documents created by the data-processing system and documents imprinted at retail sales outlets	Optical Character Reader to read paper tape rolls	75,000
		Optical Document Reader	125,000
Magnetic ink character recognition	For reading specially encoded fields of checks and other multiple-user documents (e.g., coupons)	Magnetic Ink Character Reader	110,000
By-product data creation	Used to record sales transaction data (cash register, bookkeeping, or adding machine coupled to a paper tape punch)	Cash Register with paper tape output	1,600
Prepunched tags	Used in retail chains for product identification and sales data to be converted to punched card input (Dennison and Kimball tags)	Cummins Tag Reader	20,000
Document imprinter	Records data in punched card and/or one or two lines of document data for entry into optical character reader (manufactured by Farrington, Universal Time Punch, Inc., Addressograph-Multigraph, etc.)	Document Imprinter	150
Add punch	Records data in either punched paper tape or punched card media and also provides control totals as well as detailed listing (e.g., Friden and NCR equipment)	Add Punch with paper tape output	1,900
		Add Punch with punched card output	4,000
		Add Punch with optical font imprinted on adding machine roll	500
Magnetic tape recorders	Records data on magnetic tape for direct input to computer (e.g., UGC and Digitronics equipment)	Magnetic Tape Source Recorder with hard-copy output	1,600
Off-line transaction recorders	Used to record factory-generated data (Friden Collectadata 30 or IBM 357 systems with badge readers and variable data entry positions)	Off-line Transaction Recorders	1,900 per station + 2,000 for control unit
On-line transaction recorders	Used to key in factory- or warehouse-generated data via wire cable connection to a computer (IBM 1050, IBM 1092)	On-line Transaction Recorders	2,930 per station + 5,790 for control unit

TABLE 5-1.   Comparison of Manual Input Transaction Recorders *(Continued)*

Input device	Usage	Transaction recording unit	Cost per unit,* dollars
Data cartridges	Used with IBM 1030 data collection system for remote preparation of variable data	Data Cartridges	5.50
On-line consoles	For both input and output via common carrier communication trunks (IBM 1030 data collection system or more advanced use of cathode-ray tube displays and light-pen indicators)	On-line Display Console	1,450

* These cost figures represent average costs for typical units rather than individual costs for specific units.

mental conditions. A survey of the data-capture devices available in 1965 is shown in Table 5-1. The sequence of items is related only to the order in which the various units are treated in this chapter. Included in the table are certain features and common uses of each type of equipment. These guidelines are primarily intended to provide the reader with a means of translating his data-capturing requirements to a group or single type of equipment.

Source data automation's most promising equipment seems to be optical character recognition devices and magnetic tape source data recorders. Both of these units provide the shortest path from point of data origin to entry into the computer (see Figure 5-1). The shortest path between these points should be the least costly, for only one handling of input data is necessary. To this end, the production of machine-processible input data as the by-product of necessary posting, sales-recording, or message-generation procedure is a good step toward source data automation.

KEY PUNCH—THE CHALLENGE TO SOURCE DATA AUTOMATION

The most frequently used piece of equipment for creating machine-legible input data is the standard IBM key punch, which until 1964 had not been revised for many years. It is estimated that there were approximately 250,000 of the 024 or 026 key-punch units in use throughout the United States in 1965. (The 026 is the same as the 024 but offers a printing facility so that the character is printed or interpreted at the top of the column punched.)

The unit includes a punched program-control card contained in the program unit that controls skipping, duplication, data field definition, alphabetic-numeric shifting, and (model 26 only) print suppression and left-zero print. Optional features include alternate program control selection, variable card length feed, high-speed data field skip, and self-checking number. The model 29 card punch, announced in 1964, provides the same features plus facility for a 64-character expanded keyboard (eliminating the need for two-stroke punching of special characters) and left-zero insertion.

Key-punch equipment has been basic in source data capturing, because over 70 percent of the computer installations operating in the United States have grown to computer users from tabulating-machine users; thus, the entire orientation has been to use punched cards as input. As costs and volumes of transactions rise, these users are looking to SDA for relief from the burden of economically and accurately capturing large volumes of input data.

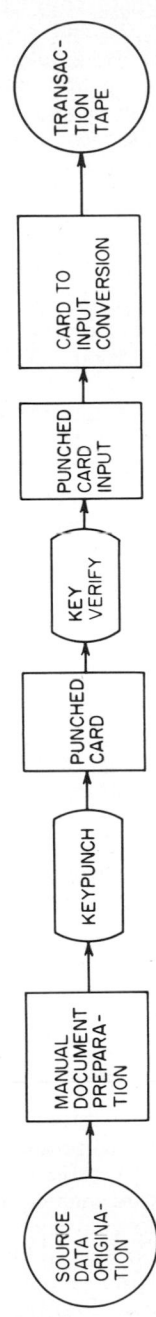

CONVENTIONAL DATA-CAPTURE PROCEDURE

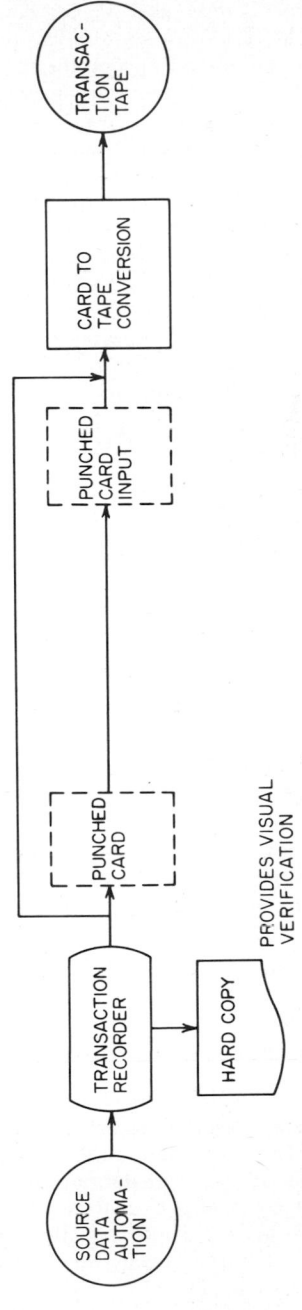

SOURCE DATA AUTOMATION

FIG. 5-1. *Comparison of conventional data-capture procedure with source data automation.*

Variations on the key-punch unit are:

1. The IBM 826, which simultaneously provides a hard copy and a punched card (sometimes known as a "typing key punch")

2. The IBM Porta-Punch, which permits the user to employ a stylus-like instrument to punch out preperforated rectangles (up to 960 since the eighty columns each have twelve rows to represent 0 through 9 and two zone rows known as X and Y) from a punched card encased in a special holder designed to permit punching a limited number of input cards as the user moves about.

Still another means of getting around the key-punch problem, when using punched card input, has been mark sensing, in which data are entered directly on the punched card by making marks with special (heavy carbon content) lead pencils in coded areas of the card and then processing the card through a card reproducer to produce a fully machine-legible document. Mark sensing has been most successful where a relatively small number of columns is marked by a small group of people working under close supervision. These conditions permit extensive control of imprint quality.

Another development in mark reading permits use of data sheets with pre-printed marking positions (up to 1,000 positions on one 8½- by 11-inch sheet) to be read through a 1231 Optical Mark Page reader directly into a computer. Data to be read can be placed on data sheets with ordinary No. 2 pencils or by a high-speed printer. Data words and segments can be grouped into various combinations to form fields for recording the source data. In a way, mark reading provides for extension of key stroking to multiple-data-recording personnel without requiring the use of a key punch. Furthermore, control over imprinting need not be as stringent as in earlier mark sensing, because the new reader is not as sensitive to stray markings.

One reason for attempting to circumvent the key-punching problem is the increasingly high cost of operators and the problems in supervising and controlling the accuracy of a key-punching operation of any size. The accepted figure for key-stroke production in the industry is an average of 7,500 key strokes per hour. There are many variations from this typical production figure, depending upon whether the source document is relatively legible and whether uniformly formatted documents with left-to-right arrangement of information of alphabetics versus numerics are to be punched, as well as the number of characters per card. Nevertheless, the figure of 7,500 character strokes per girl-hour is a reasonable basis for estimation and comparison purposes.

OPTICAL SCANNING

The most promising means of replacing key punching as the major means of producing computer input data has been the use of optically read printed material.

Characters that can be read optically can be imprinted through use of document imprinters, cash registers, add punches, high-speed printers, or electric typewriters. Each of these input devices provides for creation of a machine-legible input at the point of data origin. The predominant technique for reading characters has been stroke analysis of the characters to convert the input data to electrical signals. These signals are received by a special-purpose digital computer with a wired recognition program. The program searches for various strokes or bars of a character, and records what it finds. From a "truth table" or matrix stored in the special-purpose computer, the electronic decision is made as to whether or not the combination of strokes is a recognizable character. If a character is recognized, it is stored and then transmitted to the output mechanism (most frequently computer storage or magnetic tape). If a character cannot be recognized, automatic reread circuits may be employed or the document is rejected. The key to effective operation of a character-sensing unit, whether it be magnetic or optical, is the unit's ability to cope with quality variations in the printing.

The Economics of Optical Character-sensing Equipment. A rule of thumb has been developed that any installation preparing 10,000 documents per day for input to the electronic data-processing system is a potential prospect for optical character-recognition equipment. Since normal key-stroke production is somewhere around 7,500 characters or 125 cards per girl-hour, and one can expect to obtain about seven hours of productive labor per day, anyone using eight to twelve key-punch operators could be a candidate for an optical character-recognition device. It is interesting to note that when the volume approaches 30,000 documents per day, optical scanners may cost significantly less than key-punch devices to operate.

In comparing optical scanning equipment with conventional key-stroke methods of obtaining large-volume inputs to a computer system, a formula has been developed which includes the following parameters:

1. *Machine Rental Cost.* Key-punch machine, $60 per month. Optical scanning equipment, $2,000 per month (obtained by dividing median purchase cost of $80,000 by arbitrary figure of 40, which is approximately that used by most machine manufacturers in deriving their rental price from the purchase price).

2. *Operator's Salary.* $350 per month. Estimate three-fourths of one operator's time per optical scanning device.

3. *Production Rate.* Estimate rate of key punching is 7,500 key strokes per hour. Nominal optical scanning rate is 400 to 600 characters per second, but a lower figure of 200 characters per second should be used for estimates, because the effective speed is determined by the speed of the output device.

Let F be the number of characters produced per dollar. Then

$$F = \frac{c}{a + b} = \frac{\text{total characters produced}}{\text{cost of equipment} + \text{operator's salary}}$$

$$F = \frac{200 \, \text{char/sec} \times 3{,}600 \, \text{sec} \times 7 \, \text{hr} \times 20 \, \text{days}}{2{,}000 + 350} = 42{,}893 \text{ characters per dollar using optical scanning equipment}$$

$$F = \frac{7{,}500 \, \text{char/hr} \times 7 \, \text{hr} \times 20 \, \text{days}}{60 + 350} = 2{,}561 \text{ characters per dollar using conventional key-punch equipment}$$

The result is a ratio larger than 17 to 1 in favor of the character-recognition equipment when compared with straight key punching without verification. Whatever changes are made to the somewhat arbitrary numbers used in calculating F for optical scanning equipment should only increase the ratio. Also, there is no attempt to introduce accuracy as a factor; this is another point to be added to the character-recognition side of the balance sheet. This potential saving in input preparation may be partially offset by increased document-writing costs (that is, special type fonts, credit-card imprinters, or the like), but these are minor considering the overall dollars.

Optical character recognition has also promoted use of turnaround or reentry documents to a state where consumer acceptance is high enough to make their use economically practical. Reentry documents are prepared by the data-processing system, sent to the customer, and then returned to provide reentry of machine-processible data. Because customers can also read the same data that the machine reads, they are more likely to accept the concept of turnaround documents and send the document back to the point of origin for reentry.

The computer system can only reflect the accuracy of the input data. A commonly used paraphrase is seen in the acronym GIGO, which is literally interpreted to mean "garbage in, garbage out." Over the course of computer history, there has been a continual demand for input equipment to keep pace with the progress of increased central-processor speed. Faster machines can consume more data than it is economically feasible to prepare by key punching, and the costs of controlling accuracy mount as labor costs rise.

BY-PRODUCT DATA RECORDERS

The second level of equipment for capturing source data in machine-processible form is the recording of the transaction in machine language, as a by-product of a necessary manual operation. At this level of use, one finds bookkeeping/accounting machines for order writing, billing, accounts receivable, or any type of combined data-entry and posting operation using ledger cards or magnetic strip ledger cards (to store previous transaction data in machine-legible media).

Bookkeeping/accounting machines generally function as independent, manually operated units. The degree of automation in these machines varies considerably. The simplest are manually operated, much like adding machines. More complex units permit mechanical "programming" (arrangement of bars to define fields), automatic tabulation, automatic form feed, and in some of the later models, automatic data entry by means of magnetically encoded strips on ledger cards.

This class of equipment is used for payroll, inventory control, accounts payable, billing, accounts receivable, cash control, and other purposes. It is also widely used in banks for posting and proving accounts, and in large hotels for integrating and totaling customer charges.

Examples of this equipment are the IBM 6400 accounting machine, IBM 632 calculating typewriter, SCM Typetronic, the Friden Computyper, the Burroughs Sensimatic line, the Burroughs E2100 and E1100 models, and the NCR Sensitronic equipment, as well as some other items within their respective equipment lines that can be coupled to an auxiliary device to produce a machine-legible record (that is, punched paper tape or punched card) as the transaction is simultaneously posted through keyboard entry and a hard-copy record is produced. Generally, the limited number of totals (accumulators), small storage capacity, and lack of programming flexibility require that the transaction be entered into a data processor if any significant degree of data analysis is to be performed.

More specialized versions of this type of equipment can be seen in the Friden Flexowriter, Dura Mach 10, and Teletype Corporation equipment such as Model 19, Model 28, and Models 33 and 35 Data Sets. Each of these equipments can be used with other equipment but can be adapted for specific production of a machine-legible output—primarily a punched paper tape, although card punches can be coupled through special equipment attachments. Hard-copy output is also produced at the same time. The differences between this equipment and that described in the preceding paragraph lie primarily in the absence of any arithmetic capabilities in the Flexowriter and Teletype equipments.

CASH REGISTERS AS TRANSACTION RECORDERS

Another kind of by-product data recorder is illustrated by cash registers that are connected to paper tape or punched card punches. As the sale is rung up, the clerk records the department number and other product identification as well as the dollar amount via the register keyboard. Both are punched into the paper tape or punched card, which is collected and carried to the data-processing center at the end of each day to provide input data for sales analysis and stock control. Incorporation of the customer's account number into the paper tape record of each transaction would enable billing from the same input. The obvious advantage of this is that source data are captured in machine-readable form as a by-product of a normal cash-register operation. Disadvantages are the cost of the paper tape punch to be attached to each cash register (approximately $900 extra), the frequency of clerical errors in entering department and other identification numbers, and the number of tape rolls that must be collected and spliced for efficient computer processing. Another problem in selling these more expensive cash registers (as sold by both Monroe-Sweda and National Cash Register) is that in older department stores and other retail outlets the present number of cash registers represents a significant capital investment.

There has been a trend to utilize character imprinters as part of the cash-register system and to read into the computer system the tape produced (that is, a tally roll tape) via an optical character reader. The cost of modifying the cash register to produce an optical font that can be scanned by an optical reader is approximately $500, and the optical character reader necessary for the computer-center use costs approximately $75,000. Optically readable document imprinting represents a possible avenue for widespread acceptance of source data recording equipment, because the source data generating unit is inexpensive and only relatively minor changes in present operations are necessary.

TRANSACTION RECORDERS

Transaction recording units are devices that can record pertinent data about a transaction in machine-readable form at the time the transaction occurs. The objective of such devices is to collect data accurately and quickly in a form suitable for processing on a computer or tabulating equipment, thus eliminating the need for key punching. Transaction recorders can be very useful in conventional batch-type data-processing systems, and they are virtually mandatory in on-line systems.

The techniques used in transaction recording range from very simple to highly sophisticated. One of the simplest techniques—prepunched and preprinted tags such as the Dennison or Kimball tags—has been widely used by retail outlets. When an item is sold, the sales clerk is instructed to tear off one section of the tag (which normally contains the item identification and price) and deposit it in a box near the cash register. These tags are collected periodically, carried to the data-processing center, and converted to punched cards for use in sales analysis and inventory-control applications. Although the method is simple and inexpensive, it generally involves a high error rate because clerks frequently neglect to tear off and deposit the required tickets. Furthermore, the prepunched tags are difficult to modify for exceptions. The prepunched-tag method is useful for sales analysis to indicate the fast-moving and slow-moving items, but has generally been found inadequate for accurate inventory control.

Many organizations employ simple manual data imprinters which record machine-readable-form information that is taken from embossed cards (for example, credit cards) and manually set levers or slides. Imprinters for this purpose are produced by Addressograph-Multigraph, Dashew Business Machines, and Farrington Electronics (approximate cost ranges from $75 to $175), and are most frequently used by gasoline service stations and other retail credit operations using embossed credit cards.   Usually the coded information is read by an optical character (or bar code) reader to produce a punched card or magnetic tape output for use as input to the computer system.   Like the prepunched tags, the data imprinters are simple and relatively inexpensive; they can also be used to capture a record at the source.   The record contains certain relevant information about each transaction and requires transportation of the recorded data to the processing center.   The input is generally suitable only for billing and sales analyses by territory, because only the customer's name, identification number, and amount of transaction are currently imprinted.   The reject rate has been found to be relatively high because of poor-quality imprinting.   Advanced versions of these imprinting devices are electrically powered and can provide accumulators for development of batch control totals.

Another device for recording point-of-sale transactions is the add punch (manufactured by NCR and Friden), which costs just under $2,000.   The add punch provides a numeric keyboard for recording input data.   The device has the option of using an incremental recording (one character at a time) or a block recording of the entire transaction.   Block recording provides for use of visual error checking and correction prior to actual recording of the data.   Output is in the form of either punched tape or punched cards.   The advantage of the add punch is that it provides a built-in means of adding controls totals.

PUNCHED PAPER TAPE VERSUS PUNCHED CARDS

The secondary issue of producing either paper tape or punched cards is best decided on the basis of the handling costs associated with each medium.   The costs of the paper tape and punched card are approximately the same, but the card reader is considerably more expensive (approximately $15,000) than the paper tape reader (approximately $1,500).   Paper tapes cost about $2.25 per thousand-foot roll.   A character density of 10 characters per inch is equal to 120,000 characters per roll.   Because punched cards cost $1.05 per thousand, the equivalent number of characters, using an average of 60 characters per card, would occupy 2,000 cards at an almost equivalent cost of $2.10.

The biggest disadvantage in using paper tape as opposed to punched cards is that paper tapes remain unreadable by humans for all practical purposes. Punched cards, on the other hand, can be interpreted when punched to make them into a visible, separable document.   Punched cards can also be used for off-line sorting and editing on readily available punched card equipment (available at low rentals).   In commercial use, there seems to be a decided trend to use punched cards rather than paper tape.   Paper tape has traditionally been a by-product of another operation because it is somewhat less expensive to couple a paper tape punch (cost of coupler and punch is only $1,200 to $1,500) and an accounting machine or adding machine than it is to do the same for a card punch (cost of coupler is approximately $1,200 plus $2,150 for card punch).

MAGNETIC TAPE RECORDERS

An adaptation of an older concept, the recording of data directly on magnetic tape at the point of origin, has been developed by UGC Instruments, Inc.   The SODA (Source Oriented Data Acquisition) product allows the user to record data at extremely low information densities (approximately equivalent to those used in home tape recorders) by punching up to 10 digits on an adding machine coupled to a tape recording unit, or by use of a battery-powered portable magnetic recorder that can record up to 960 words of 10 characters each on a 60-foot reel of $\frac{1}{4}$-inch-wide magnetic tape. The battery-powered unit provides 10 position dials that are set by the operator prior to block recording of the entire transaction.

The use of a magnetic tape source data recorder provides the most direct means of getting input data from the point of origin to the computer. Therefore, this input medium offers great potential for source data automation.

TRANSMITTING DATA COLLECTION SYSTEMS

The highest level of transaction recorders and the ones that will be of maximum value to most large manufacturing companies are the transmitting data collection systems used extensively for employee-attendance recording, production control, labor distribution, inventory control, and a variety of other applications. Such systems generally consist of:

Input units which accept and transmit fixed data from prepunched cards or badges and variable data from dial, lever, or slide settings or keyboards

Output units which record the transmitted data on punched tape or cards, or control its direct entry into a computer system

Cables or communications facilities to transmit the data from the input units to the output units, which may be located in the same plant or many miles apart

Transmitting data collection systems can be classified as "on-line" systems, which feed data directly into a computer, or "off-line" systems, which produce punched or printed transaction records that will generally be processed later by a computer.

A typical transaction message in a production control and labor distribution application might consist of employee number (read from the employee's badge); job number (read from a prepunched card traveling with the job); machine operation number, transaction code, and quantity completed (entered by the employee via manually operated dials or levers); input station number (transmitted automatically); and time and date (added automatically at the central recording unit).

Companies currently producing transmitting data collection systems include Control Data (180 and Transactor line), Digitronics (521), Friden (Collectadata 30), General Electric (3100), IBM (357 and 1030), and RCA (EDGE).

One of the unique features of transmitting data collection systems can be found in the IBM 1030 system, an in-plant network specifically designed for manufacturing control where data cartridges are used to enter variable data. Input to this system consists of a reader which can interpret fixed information from cards and/or badges, and variable data from slides or data cartridges. The data cartridge is a pocket-sized unit with twelve positions (slides) of numerical data entry. An advantage of the data cartridge is that it permits the worker to set up the variable information at his work station. This eliminates intermediate transcription with the subsequent possibility of transcription error. The data cartridge, set up away from the 1030 reader, also enables the worker to complete his transaction rapidly and thus reduces queues at the reader unit.

The output from this system can be directed to either a card punch or a computer. When the 1030 is used with the computer on-line, it is possible to have the computer actually print the man's next assignment on a job printer located on the factory floor (that is, dynamic dispatching).

Another device used in on-line operations is the IBM 1050 data terminal which uses a common carrier data set as a transmission medium. In insurance applications, for example, the system is used to transmit policy, payment, and coverage data, thus providing better and faster service on claims. In the railroad industry, it handles railroad car accounting for better utilization of rolling stock. For trucking concerns, the 1050 provides data for input to centralized freight billing and accounting. In general manufacturing, its use allows a customer to do invoicing, accounts receivable, sales statistics, and inventory control at a central location while preserving the advantages of decentralized warehouses and sales locations at reduced unit cost for paper-work operations.

Another somewhat unique data recording device is the IBM 1092 programmed keyboard terminal, a matrix-type keyboard which uses interchangeable plastic overlays with actual industry terms to identify the keys. Changing the keyboard overlays customizes it to satisfy many industry requirements—enabling a nurse in a hospital to enter patient data, a truck driver in a petroleum bulk plant to enter data on the products he delivers, or an automobile dealer to order a car with all the features requested by his customer.

With this unit, a plastic overlay fits directly on the keyboard, indicating to the operator the specific information represented by each of as many as 160 keys. On the keyboard of a conventional data transmission terminal, each key represents a specific letter, number, or symbol. On the 1092, though, an individual key can be made to represent detailed facts such as the type or color of an inventory item, the item, the body style of an automobile, or the type of medicine, dosage, and frequency of dosage to be administered to patients. When a key is pressed, the computer processes the fact represented by first identifying the overlay in use and then calling into action the appropriate program instructions.

FACTORS TO CONSIDER IN IMPLEMENTING SDA SYSTEMS

The recording of source data in a common machine-legible language to be carried throughout the data-processing system requires adherence to the following principles.

1. Input data should be captured at the point of origin. Where feasible, data for more than one processing need will be captured at the same station to provide single-transaction recording. The principle espouses the concept that carrying unused data through some segments of the processing is less costly than capturing data repetitively at isolated points.

2. A single source medium—punched paper tape, punched cards, magnetic tape, or optically readable tape—should be used for all input transactions. This will avoid problems in data handling and input batch control.

3. All potential applications should be carefully considered. Dual systems will create continual problems and additional expense. For example, an integrated data collection system in a production plant can be used for attendance reporting, inventory control, parts and material requisitioning, shipping, purchasing, billing, inspection, and numerous other functions—all in addition to the primary functions of production control and labor distribution. Complications will arise from material substitutions, returns, damaged items, obsolete parts, inaccurate counts, unplanned requisitions, or reworks. Provisions should be made to handle all such complications without deviating from the cardinal design principle: Send *all* messages relating to a particular application through the

mechanized system. Do not plan to mechanize only the high-volume transactions and handle the exceptions manually.

4. Message lengths should be minimized to reduce data entry and data transmission times. In determining capacity of individual input stations, one must add the time required to enter the necessary cards, badges, and/or variable data. The service time, in turn, determines the maximum number of input stations that will be necessary to handle peak loads. Closely related to system capacity is the question of where to locate the input stations. One must consider the maximum distance an employee should have to walk to get to an input station, the maximum waiting times that can be tolerated, and the costs of walking to the station and waiting to use it as compared with the costs of additional input stations and transmission lines.

5. Training must be given to each employee who will be using a transaction recorder. To ensure acceptance of the mechanized system by the employees, they must be thoroughly briefed in advance. The briefing should explain why the system is needed, how it will operate, and how it will affect each employee. Several data collection installations have failed because the need for preinstallation training and indoctrination was ignored, leading to a strongly rebellious attitude among the workers.

CONCLUSION

Advantages of recording source data in machine-legible form at the point of origin include:

1. Increased accuracy of data entry, that is, the removal of the opportunity for human operators engaged in the transcribing operation to insert errors of transposition or to commit errors of omission or combinations of the two.

2. Reduced number of points for data capture and lower equipment and operator costs for data capture using single-source recording stations to supply data for use throughout the data-processing system.

3. The capturing of additional information at a single point has a small effect on work-load operations, because there is only a small incremental cost for capturing additional data beyond the cost of capturing the basic data that must be part of any input transaction record. This, in turn, means reduced number of points of data origin and reduced span of control over data entry operations leading to improved error control, and elimination of duplicate labor for manual entry of data.

It is actually sometimes more difficult to convince top management of the need for SDA to feed the computer system effectively than it is to convince management of the savings inherent in an electronic computer system. There are at least two significant reasons for this. First, top management is not often conscious of the exact flow of data within the processing system, but rather is more concerned with whether individual pieces of equipment can be economically justified by a reduction in the clerical labor force. SDA equipment and the accompanying set of procedures that must be written to govern the operation represent tools within the system that can be scattered throughout the firm, and in most cases, merely mechanize what had been a completely manual operation. Thus, SDA lacks the glamour of large computer installations and does not receive as much management attention, although it can in some cases generate substantial savings that approach those projected for computer facilities during their entire first or second year of operation.

The second reason why opportunities for SDA go without successful implementation is that those within the organization who are primarily machine oriented are usually concentrated in the data-processing department. Many times, one puts the cart before the horse, so to speak, and pays primary attention to the computer applications and their data flow design, leaving the area of input to the computer system as a last-ditch effort which receives only minor attention in the total implementation phase. One might say that SDA is the poor man's automation, but it is a very essential cog in the advanced utilization of data-processing equipment.

In large organizations, the use of transmitting data collection systems will substantially reduce key-punch work loads from production reporting, payroll and labor distribution, and materials control applications. Similarly, mark reading of order forms can be expected to reduce the key-punch work load resulting from order-processing, billing, and related applications, and the use of turnaround documents can provide the input to accounts receivable applications.

In smaller, less-structured organizations, data imprinters or by-product transaction recorders can be employed to capture data at the point of origin and thus reduce or eliminate the need for key punching. The economic advantages and improved speed of operations in either case can best be summarized by the comparative diagram shown in Figure 5-1.

BIBLIOGRAPHY

Brett, J. J., "Breaking the Input Bottleneck," *Computers and Data Processing*, vol. 1, no. 6, June, 1964.

Canning, Richard, "New Developments in Optical Scanning," *EDP Analyzer*, vol. 3, no. 8, August, 1965.

Eckenbach, Raymond, "Source Data Automation," *Business Automation*, vol. 12, no. 7, July, 1965, pp. 40–42.

Neuschel, Richard F., *Management by System*, McGraw-Hill Book Company, New York, 1960.

"Optical Character Recognition Devices," *AUERBACH Standard EDP Reports*, vol. 1, November, 1962.

Statland, N., and J. Hillegass, "A Survey of Computer Input-Output Equipment," *Data Processing Yearbook*, American Data Processing, Detroit, 1963, pp. 39–46.

CHAPTER SIX

Managing the Computer Center

MELVIN POSIN *Manager, Industry Sales, Electronic Data Processing Division, Radio Corporation of America, Camden, New Jersey*

Management of the computer center has undergone an evolutionary change. As recently as 1956, computers were all too frequently installed because of a vague feeling that somehow they were necessary to the future of the company. Justification was either on a direct economic basis—replacement of clerical personnel—or because of some hoped-for intangible benefit to be derived—and that to be determined by experimentation after the computer was in. Because of the interest generated in this new "toy" by upper management—for indeed, in many instances, this was what it was regarded as—more effort was often devoted to designing the viewing area than to the basic layout of the machine room. Equipment was placed to provide spectator convenience rather than the most suitable arrangement for work flow. Because so much effort was experimental in nature, only limited attempts to apply normal management principles were made. Expense budgets were more frequently exceeded than met, schedules of implementation were constantly missed, and the application of individual work standards and measurement of performance against these standards were virtually nonexistent. In short, whether by nature or design, there was very little true "management" applied to the computer center.

Time and an increasingly competitive business environment had a tendency to cure this. The computer became accepted as a necessary and functioning business tool, and to a great extent, it was treated as any other business tool. Management no longer viewed it as an interesting experiment, but as an important factor contributing to management's success and one whose performance and contribution could be measured. This required the computer center manager to apply to himself and to his organization the same standards of organization, control, and financial and performance responsibility that are applied to any operating segment of a business.

For some time, there has been an industry-wide trend toward increasing decentralization. In conjunction with this, because of the huge volumes of remotely generated data needed to control the business effectively and because of the inability to gain rapid access to these data, there has also been the parallel movement of decentralizing management control by placing an increasing amount of responsibility and authority on remote locations. With the advent of larger and less expensive computers capable of simultaneous multiple tasks, however, together with improved and less expensive data communication facilities, a tendency to recentralize management control has resulted. This in turn places greater responsibility on the computer center as the center increases its scope and sphere of influence within an organization's framework.

The basic fundamentals of any management function—planning, organizing, and controlling—are equally applicable to the management of the computer center. If these elements are adequately covered, proper and adequate management will result. The purpose of this chapter will be to examine these elements individually as they apply to the operation of the computer center.

PLANNING THE COMPUTER CENTER

To plan for the computer center, certain fundamental questions must be answered long before the physical and operational plans are developed. For example, just where does the center fit within the corporate organizational structure? Is its primary use to be as a tool of the financial department? How many hours a day will be utilized by the production facility for scheduling, inventory control, or other related manufacturing operations? Is the equipment being acquired primarily for the use of the engineering department? Or is the intent to establish a centralized facility to serve all functions equally, with priorities based upon the relative importance of each job to the company as a whole?

Studies of these questions can occupy the efforts of many people. For this discussion, we will assume a centralized facility supporting all company efforts, with the computer center manager a member of an operating committee formed of department heads (or their representatives) of all using departments. Final adjudication of disputes as to planned usage will be the responsibility of a member of the top management team not specifically concerned with a limited segment of the business.

Feasibility Study. Assuming the initial phase of the planning effort has been accomplished, the next step is a "feasibility study." Many questions must be explored at this stage. What applications are to be scheduled for implementation and in what sequence? What is the economic worth (either tangible or intangible) to the company of automating certain functions, and what will be the result and cost of so doing? Although no attempt is made here to define this segment of the planning function in detail, it can be said that this phase is all-important, for it justifies the need for the center. It also establishes the goals of the center—both operational and financial—and hence the responsibilities of its management.

Equipment Selection. When the individual applications to be performed are well defined, the next step is the selection of appropriate equipment. Usually, with the aid of equipment manufacturers, appropriate equipment components can be selected, and approximate performance times can be established to determine the adequacy of the selected system to do the total job. Additional factors to be considered at this point are: Can the selected system start small (small and economical enough, for example, to handle the initial applications) and yet have the capability of being expanded to encompass the total planned requirements? Does it have the capability of being expanded into other application areas heretofore not considered, or by growing with the company over the expected life of the equipment? How can this growth be most economically accommodated? For example, reprogramming costs to take advantage of increased capacities are generally lower if the initial system contains a large internal memory and slow-speed peripherals (with increased capacity obtained by the substitution of higher-speed and more peripheral devices), than if the initial system has a smaller memory system and higher-speed peripherals initially. Adequate planning for system growth, in terms of cost of that growth to the company, is a function of the manager, even if the costs are not incurred by his department.

Personnel Requirements. As in any operation with a high ratio of equipment costs to personnel costs, the greater the usage, the lower the unit product cost. Hence, it appears economically desirable to load the computer to the greatest extent possible (multiple shifts). In planning for this, however, the manager must not overlook certain basic factors which could preclude achieving his planned production goals. Computer equipment, to provide sustained, trouble-free operation, must periodically undergo preventive maintenance, usually scheduled for several hours daily. Establishing work schedules that preclude this maintenance can easily result in longer downtime periods for malfunction repair. In addition, equipment will occasionally fail, requiring emergency maintenance time. Operators will periodically err, requiring rerun time. Finally, no programs are static. Changing business conditions, management philosophies, and techniques will require modification or rewriting of existing programs even if no new applications are scheduled. This will require time to be set aside for further program debugging and systems testing. All of these items must be considered in determining the personnel required to operate the system.

Installation Schedule. When a system has been selected, a schedule for its installation should be developed. Here again, appropriate planning can provide significant economic benefits. Most equipment manufacturers will allocate time on one of their machines for program debugging and systems testing. Adequate time should be allowed prior to installation to permit preparation of programs and files so as to minimize the time between installation and "on-air" of initial applications.

Computer Center Layout. In preparing the floor plan of the computer center, it would be well to consider this as a production-type operation. Equipment should be located to provide an optimum work-flow arrangement. A computer system will operate only as fast as raw data are made available to it, as fast as tapes can be changed, and as fast as its output can be carted off and distributed. These operations take people. Hence equipment layout should be in accordance with achieving maximum productivity from them. Machines always run at "clock" rates—people do not.

In spite of limitations such as maximum cable lengths between interconnected units, the desirability of placing the console operator where he will be able to observe the functioning of certain equipments, and the unwillingness entirely to sacrifice "viewability," it is still possible to arrange both the equipment and the adjacent servicing areas to provide for easy access and egress of operating personnel with their materials. Card and tape storage areas, for example, should be located conveniently to their respective user units, printers should be close to paper supplies and paper-handling devices, and so on. Failure to do this will result in longer standby periods when changes are necessary or in the use of aisle space for intermediate storage which, in turn, places obstacles in the way of efficient operation. The application of well-known layout techniques in the relative positioning of interdependent production-type equipments can help to provide maximum machine-use efficiency.

Testing the Plans. If each of the following questions is considered during the feasibility study and the installation planning period, there is little probability that any significant area will be overlooked.

1. Have the objectives (either quantitative or qualitative) been clearly defined?

2. Are all necessary and related elements included?

3. Are all the specific activities to be performed, and their sequence, indicated?

4. Are there beginning and end points in time for each activity?

5. Are all elements of cost included?

6. Have formal criteria been established for evaluating progress?

7. Are alternative courses provided for, and are there checkpoints to allow for periodic replanning?

8. Has the plan been adequately communicated to others?

ORGANIZING THE COMPUTER CENTER

There are two basic approaches underlying the organizational structure of a computer operation. The first of these is to consider the center essentially as a pure machine production facility, with the responsibility for systems design, programming, and the like lying outside the area of responsibility of its manager. Centers providing support to engineering and scientific activities are generally set up in this fashion, as are centers established by large corporations to service numerous operating divisions having highly diverse requirements. The second is the center which provides a complete service to the user department, including systems design, programming, and subsequent operations. In addition, combinations of these appear where, for example, an organization will centralize all activities for its business data processing but permit the engineering department to provide its own specialized efforts.

Much can be said for the first structure, because it places the responsibilities for the implementation of a given application and for its use thereafter directly upon the group currently performing that function. The second approach requires educating a "disinterested" group. This disinterested group, however, not being familiar with the historical development of the manual or punched card system which is being superseded, is more apt to attempt to redefine objectives in the light of current business requirements and to make greater use of the computer's capability and capacity for servicing the company's basic needs.

Because of the more extensive use of the second approach, and because as industry moves more closely to totally integrated business systems this organizational structure takes on greater importance, the discussion which follows will be focused on the requirements for this type of organizational structure and its two major functions—systems design and programming, and operations.

Systems Design and Programming. The systems design and programming activity divides itself naturally into a systems design group and a programming group. The systems design group must have two differing orientations. On one hand, it must understand the goals and needs of the business, the desires and capabilities of its people (from what the president wants to see in a report to the probability that a key-punch operator will strike a desired key), the interrelation of various departmental activities within that business, and the operating requirements of each of them. It must also have a thorough understanding of the equipment it is working with, and its capabilities, capacities, and limitations, so that it may translate business requirements to efficient operating systems.

The systems design function is complex. Management information systems, with their "data base" consolidating and reducing file requirements, necessitate an understanding in depth of the relationships of previously autonomous departmental activities. In addition, providing the ability for management to inquire directly into that file through a remote interrogation unit, or for a clerk on a remote on-line input device to enter or change data in that base, necessitates sophisticated machine control procedures to guard the integrity of the data.

It is important to recognize that the systems design effort is quite different from historical "systems and procedures" concepts. Forms design and data movement procedures are a small part of the activity, and a high degree of professionalism is required.

This raises problems. The systems designer is, in a sense, a developer, or engineer of systems. As an engineer is wont to do, he can easily spend ten minutes developing an invention and two years perfecting it. There is no "perfect" or "ideal" system. Extensive effort beyond developing a system that meets the business requirements and environments within the framework of machine capability is, to a great extent, an unprofitable effort. Hence, it is important to develop, within reasonable limits, a time framework within which to operate, and to establish a point at which a system design is complete and documented for the programmer's use without further engineering "tinkering."

Adequate documentation is a must. Communication between the analyst and the programmer should be well defined. Errors based upon misinterpretation or misunderstanding can be extremely costly and time consuming.

Programming. Programming, or the translation of the system diagram to machine-operable codes, once considered almost a mystic art, has become practically a science. This results from the manufacturers of equipment providing an increasing array of aids such as language systems, specialized subroutines, operating and executive systems, and others to assist the programmer in achieving good machine efficiency with reasonable standardization and without Herculean efforts.

There are significant managerial decisions that should be made prior to expending any effort on programming. The selection of a programming language, and its use thereafter, can have significant long-term implications. Does the selection of a particular language limit the possibility of the future acquisition of another manufacturer's system, or force the user to remain within one line of equipment of his present supplier? Is the language suitable to the major areas to be programmed? With the increasing need to retain flexibility as the movement toward total systems gains momentum, selection of programming languages which preclude equipment growth and changes can place severe financial burdens on the future.

It is also important that basic programming specifications be established. Such commonly used procedures as tape labeling should be standardized. Unless this is done, each programmer will select his own technique or approach, resulting in unnecessary confusion and providing an area of future difficulty when equipment changes are considered.

Programming specifications should also include documentation requirements, both for the initial program and for subsequent changes. Programs are relatively complex assemblies, and unless a current blueprint is available, they cannot be maintained by anyone other than the original designer.

Computer use is dynamic. Hence, even if no new areas of application are considered, it is well to plan that at least 10 percent of the original programming effort will be required to maintain and update existing programs to meet even simple user changes in requirements.

Operations. The operations area of the computer center also subdivides itself into two distinct categories—machine operations and data control. The former area concerns itself with the physical operation of the equipment, while the latter is concerned with the preparation of input data, the control of machine records, and the distribution of output data.

In the machine operations area, it should be recognized that there are various levels of ability required of operating personnel. If all personnel are at the same training and capability level, then the machine room is either under-equipped or overequipped. As in any production operation utilizing mechanical equipment, the degree of sophistication of the machine determines the level of training and capability of its operator. Simple devices such as tape stations, card readers and punches, and printers obviously do not require the same level of technological competency as, for example, the computer console, whose operator may have to determine whether a particular situation is the result of bad data, a program error, or a machine malfunction.

An adequate number of personnel should always be provided. In most installations, the cost of equipment is well in excess of the manning bill. Staffing should be sufficient to keep the equipment running efficiently. Frequently, large sums are expended in upgrading machine systems to achieve greater capacity, when a careful analysis would have shown that a more modest expenditure for personnel would have achieved the same result by more efficient utilization of existing capacity.

Assuming an adequately staffed operation, the next most significant factor is the establishment of well-defined operating procedures, job priorities, and schedules. It is not uncommon to see a machine room in complete chaos for the initial half hour in the morning because the computer is hanging up for some reason, and to discover subsequently that this was because someone had omitted to put in the day's date at the console (perhaps a requisite of the program to be run, but not an assigned operating procedure). We are dealing with a series of interrelated, highly complex machines which are operated by people. Jobs and procedures must be well defined, priorities established, and schedules laid out to assure an efficient and orderly work flow. This is also important from the standpoint of establishing the requirements imposed by the computer operation on the second group concerned with the overall operations aspect—the data control activity.

The functions of the data control group may be subdivided into three basic categories—the preparation of new input data, the maintenance and availability of historical files (either magnetic tape or card) for further processing requirements, and the auditing and distribution of output.

Data preparation, in machine-readable format, has long been a subject of much discussion covering techniques to ensure accuracy, provide audit trails, and evaluate performance. The field has become increasingly complex with the advent of far-flung communication systems providing direct computer access for raw data. New control procedures are in a constant state of development to meet this challenge. In evaluating a specific situation, however, if several fundamentals are always considered, many pitfalls can be avoided. These fundamentals are:

1. Have these data been validated in any way through verification, control totals, or by the data content itself? If not, what machine verification can be made? If neither, what effect does this have on the output, and does a normal error rate produce usable results?

2. Is there an audit trail provided? Assuming errors can be detected, can we return to the raw data and either enter the correct information or make an appropriate correction?

3. Will the data arrive at the proper time to be effectively utilized by the equipment?

The structuring of the data preparation organization will be determined largely by the most effective means of achieving "yes" answers to the above questions.

The maintenance of historical files for further processing is primarily a library function and is determined by the system design requirements. The operating requirement placed on this activity is to have available, when required by machine and job scheduling, the appropriate files at the appropriate locations. In addition, backup files must be maintained so that in the event of machine malfunction, programming problems, or human error resulting in file destruction, adequate material is available to reconstruct the destroyed file.

The final function of the data control group, that of auditing and distributing output, is no less significant than any of their other tasks. As in any operation, no matter how carefully planned and implemented, final evaluation must be based on the use of the end result. Is it what we desired to produce, and did we get it into the hands of the user when he wanted or needed it?

The more mundane tasks of such operations as decollating, bursting, and mailing need not be gone into here, other than to state that they must be considered in establishing overall time and performance objectives. What is frequently overlooked, however, is the auditing function. This might be as simple as merely noting the alignment of the printed data on a form, or the checking of the preprinted starting and ending bill or invoice numbers, or as complex as the visual inspection in detail of the reasonableness of the data. Auditing procedures, dependent upon the nature and ease of their application and the significance of errors, should be planned for in the systems design phase and implemented by the data control function.

CONTROLLING THE COMPUTER CENTER

Control is essentially the action exercised by management to assure meeting the desired results. Having established a plan and organized to meet its requirements, management must continually evaluate performance against objectives, ascertain variances, investigate their causes, and adjust either the plan or the objectives accordingly. This is the control function in its simplest terms.

In the earlier days of computer installations, management had little or no experience in the control area. The parameters necessary for accurate planning were not available, nor were the yardsticks for measuring performance. Variances were probably more frequently created by poor planning than by poor performance. Objectives were reached by revising plans rather than by taking other suitable actions, and all too frequently, they were never attained.

This era, however, passed. Parameters are available which assist in establishing accurate and realistic plans. Checkpoints can be established so that performance can be evaluated at sufficiently frequent intervals to permit corrective action. Yardsticks are available to measure the same areas as for any business operation—productivity, quality, and cost.

When planning for a given area of application, the following factors should be considered:

1. The time and costs required to develop the system and program it
2. The method, time cycle, and cost of converting from the existing system, including file conversion
3. Methods of input data preparation, including accuracy controls and costs
4. Machine running times, with allowances for setup time, operator errors, machine malfunctions, and rerun times

In the analysis and programming areas, frequent checkpoints should be set up to determine progress and adherence to time schedules, costs, and machine running times. This can be done rather easily because almost any system divides itself naturally into a sequence of individual programs. Checkpoints can be established at the conclusion of each portion of the system design, of the flow charting, and of the individual program completion. Documentation should be simultaneously examined to assure its adequacy in supporting the next step forward. Individual programs should be debugged as completely as possible before succeeding programs are developed. Adequate test data (both good and bad) should be scheduled and made available sufficiently in advance to permit this.

Because conversion from one system to another is considered a one-time event, its cost, time cycle, and methods employed, if not overlooked, are frequently only casually considered. Yet the net effects can be significant. For example, significant errors in a file conversion can lead to perpetual problems in the usefulness of desired outputs, excessive machine-time requirements, and continuing expensive correction procedures. Conversion should be well planned and carefully controlled if end objectives are to be met.

For example, in the area of conversion from manually maintained records to a machine-readable file, frequently a great deal of manual editing is required prior to any key-punching operation if the desired accuracy of the resulting file is to be achieved. This is a costly and time-consuming, yet necessary, process. Not only must it be adequately planned, but close control must be maintained if the types of problems indicated above are to be avoided. Checkpoints should be established, with segments of the file edited, key-punched, and then run against operating programs to check whether existing procedures fall within the time schedule, costs, and accuracy limits established by plan.

In the same manner, all aspects of system change, such as modification of operating procedures, introduction of new forms, methods of data preparation, and the like, should be sequentially tested, monitored, and controlled so that at system cutover time, each phase of the new operation has been thoroughly tested.

This is particularly important if adequate future control is to be maintained. No system can be any better than the data provided to it. Hence, adequate continuing control over the quality of the input data is imperative. There are many techniques available to provide this—key-punch verification, batch totaling (either actual or hash totals), machine verification or limit checking, and the like. Each provides an inherent accuracy level at a determinable cost, and the appropriate method should be selected within the system requirements. The control exercised over this function becomes increasingly important as provision of remote terminals permitting direct-entry access to the computer center increases.

Controls exercised within the machine-room operation itself should start initially at the gross level, but should be constantly refined to permit monitoring and identifying the possibility of further improvement in operations. Running job times (including setup) should be established, and performance measured against these. In planning, provision should be made for problems encountered because of machine malfunction, operator errors, and rerun times resulting from these. Accurate records should be maintained, so that variances can be pinpointed and appropriate action taken. Many installations maintain such job records in the computer itself and produce periodic reports for performance evaluation.

Control of files is an additional significant factor. Tape libraries with their attendant controls must be established, not only to provide a means of locating and providing the appropriate tape files when required, but also to control formerly used tapes to assure their availability for recovery procedures should a current tape be inadvertently damaged or destroyed.

The areas of controls in the computer center serve the same purpose as for any business operation, measuring performance (adherence to time schedules, productivity, and so on), quality (accuracy, usefulness of output), and related costs. The computer center is utilized to generate control information for other segments of a business operation. It should have the same techniques applied to itself.

SUMMARY

The computer center has become a fairly commonplace functioning unit of the business world; the romance and mysticism formerly associated with it no longer exist. It is now a measurable operating tool of management. As such, it must meet the same criteria that are applied to any business function. Complete and comprehensive planning is possible; organization structures have been developed to assure efficient and economic utilization; and controls can be exercised to assure meeting predetermined objectives.

CHAPTER SEVEN

Using the Data-processing Service Center

JOSEPH H. REDDING *H. B. Maynard and Company, Incorporated, Pittsburgh, Pennsylvania*

Do you have a good computer application but feel your company is too small to acquire a staff to operate its own computer?

Do you have peak loads that are exceeding your present computer capacity, but are not enough to justify your acquiring a bigger computer to handle all your needs?

Does your computer work load tend to force you to a third shift which you cannot readily staff?

Is your engineering function having trouble getting the service it requires on computer applications because of heavy accounting demands on your computer?

Do you have a special problem, say linear programming, that your own computer department says it cannot handle?

Do you have a computer application with a good payoff potential that your programming group says it cannot get to for a year?

Do you have a technical problem that you are sure someone else has solved, and would you like to save yourself the cost of new program development?

If you find yourself in any of these situations, you are probably in need of assistance from a computer service center. If you take a hard-headed, profit-and-loss look at your computer needs and the cost of alternative ways of satisfying them, the service center will often be your best approach.

This chapter will discuss briefly:

1. The modern computer service center
2. Where you can procure computer services
3. How service centers can help you

THE MODERN COMPUTER SERVICE CENTER

In working with a service center, it is well to understand how they operate so you can use them most effectively. Service centers generally make their money by renting a computer.   The service center, like any business, is normally sustained and made profitable by several large, often accounting-type applications.   If you can provide a service center with such an application, you should get a reasonable price and first-class service.   You do not have to be a real big user to get service.   Most centers operate around the clock.   They perform the large-volume work on the evening shifts and leave the day shift open for smaller users.   So almost any problem can be gotten through the center in one day.

The economies of computer operations are usually such that half of a firm's operating costs are in equipment rental and half in staff to support the equipment.   Equipment rental is virtually the same for a one- or a three-shift operation.   Extra-shift rentals vary from 0 to 20 percent of prime-shift rates.   So it is almost mandatory that these firms operate around the clock to get the maximum return on their investment.

Many of a service center's jobs are done for businesses which do not have computer departments.   Thus, it is essential for the center to have a competent programming staff.   This means that the user can get a full range of data-processing services—and can often get programming help alone when a center's programming group is not fully utilized.

The full range of services also includes key punching, which is another service that can often be purchased by itself if the key-punching force is lightly loaded. You must remember, though, that programming and key-punching services are maintained primarily to assure full utilization of the center's computer.   If you try to buy either of these services alone, you usually cannot expect your work to be given a high priority.

At a computer center, programming is an overhead item, and centers strive to get the maximum revenue from their programming expenditures.   If one program can serve several customers, the operation will be less costly for the center.   Often a customer can realize part of these savings.

If you have a problem which is shared by others in your area, you can often get a computer center to program it without cost to you, if you give them proprietary rights to the program once it is developed.

Finally, it is the general nature of computer programs that the larger the job, the less time is required per unit processed.   There are economies of scale. Centers generally try to avoid billing on the basis of computer time used; they prefer to have a price tied to a flat fee per unit processed.   Usually, the fee includes a percentage which goes to pay off the costs of developing the program.

You will often gain by paying for program development separately and paying for computer time as required.   Unfortunately, you can also lose under this arrangement.   You may end up with a very inefficient computer program that will require an excessive amount of computer time.   Unless you are in a position to know whether or not your program is efficient, you are better off operating under a prearranged fixed unit price per transaction processed.   Under this type of contract, programs are generally quite efficient, because all machine time saved becomes available for other revenue-producing work.

WHERE YOU CAN PROCURE COMPUTER SERVICES

Five main places to look for computer service are as follows.

1. *Private Service Centers.*   These are generally small businesses formed by people who have worked in the computer field.   They have one medium-scale, general-purpose computer and do normal programming for business applications. There are a few of these private centers that are quite large with a number

of branch centers in major cities. The large centers can provide a full range of data-processing services.

2. *Computer Manufacturer Service Centers.* Most computer manufacturers operate at least one service center to display their wares—many operate a national network of these centers in major cities. These centers exist largely to help sell computers and are not for computer service alone. The extent of services that can be obtained from them will probably be better if you are a good prospect for that computer. These centers, however, can be expected to be fairly competitive with privately run centers.

3. *Commercial Banks.* Many large banks have invested heavily in computers. They have jumped into the computer service business, seeking a better return on this investment. They have leaned on their close tie-in to many companies' financial affairs to develop a clientele. They are for the most part providing standard accounting services—the main one, naturally, being preparation of payrolls along with the appropriate tax forms at year-end. To try to hold programming costs to a reasonable level, many banks have developed standard accounting packages. Banks will require the user to change his forms to their standard forms. The inconvenience of this change will be more than compensated for by the lower cost of the computer services. Because the bank can use a standard program, its operation will be more reliable; this is an advantage for both the user and the bank.

4. *Large Corporations Which Are Big Data-processing Users.* Most large aircraft companies and many large manufacturing corporations, like the banks, are looking for a better return on their computing investment. Corporate policies among this group are quite variable. Some big users will not let *anyone* else use their equipment. Some will permit outside use on an occasional basis. Others encourage, and even solicit, outside work.

The value of these big organizations lies in special computer applications (linear programming, information retrieval, engineering design) rather than in the standard accounting applications. These companies have the cream of the country's computer specialists. They work on problems that most small companies can only dream about. They do not normally market their proprietary developments, but they will use their talent to develop similar applications for others. Also, they have the biggest computers and can take on problems from the simplest to the most complex.

If you have a somewhat unusual computer problem, it will pay you to investigate this source, even if it means going to another city for the service.

5. *Miscellaneous.* There are several other minor factors in the service center business. These sources, though small in number, will probably grow in predominance as time goes by.

First, there are a small number of cooperative service centers formed by several companies with common problems. For example, a group of four midwestern banks formed such a captive service center to perform their accounting. Balanced against possible administrative problems are economies of common programming and in computer rental (the bigger the computer you get, the lower the unit cost of each computation).

Second, a firm of public accountants opened a service bureau to perform general accounting for their clients. Like the banks, these centers play upon their special expertise in accounting and financial matters to build their clientele.

HOW SERVICE CENTERS CAN HELP YOU

Most service centers can provide a full range of accounting services—from payroll to total accounting. Further, they can assist in a wide range of special problems for which computers are especially helpful, such as engineering design. They can also make it possible to use any of the computer techniques developed by either manufacturers (to help sell computers) or computer-user organizations (to help themselves).

In the accounting area, payroll, billing, accounts receivable, purchase orders, accounts payable, and inventory accounting are typical of the applications available. Sales analyses are another major service area. Some companies, mainly in the retail distribution area, have turned over the bulk, perhaps 90 percent, of their accounting work to service centers. The applications are mainly in the area of billing and accounts receivable. Other businesses in various areas (brokerage houses, city planning commissions) have turned over their computing or accounting chores to service bureaus to permit themselves to devote their full time to their main line of business.

In the special application area, engineering design is most predominant. Computers are widely used in structural design of bridges, beams, and utility towers; they are used to design motors, transformers, piping systems, and airplanes.

There is a type of service available which is especially useful for engineers. This goes under the name of "time sharing," or "multiprogramming." The service lets a customer use a piece of a big central computer by way of a small input/output station located on the customer's site. The customer's station is connected to the central computer by regular leased telephone lines. It is possible today to use several large scientific computers from anywhere in the country (although not with equal economy because of varying telephone rates).

This concept is not limited to engineering applications. At least one eastern firm is marketing a "time shared" computer for standard accounting applications in the wholesale and retail fields.

Computers can be employed profitably for solving any complex problem where there are a number of optional courses to evaluate. They have been used to plan new highways, to lay out a railroad hump yard, to locate branch warehouses, to route truck shipments, and to fill out income tax returns.

There are several programs designed to compute and maintain work standards in large companies. Most of these applications, if already developed, are proprietary with the developer. They may generally be rented from the developer at a price including his development costs. It is still less expensive to use someone else's work rather than to develop your own unless you expect considerable use of the program.

Last among applications are the standard nonproprietary program packages developed by manufacturers and user organizations. These cover a wide range of applications including:

Basic mathematical and statistical calculations such as curve fitting and regression analysis

Management techniques such as PERT, critical path scheduling, and linear programming

Information retrieval techniques such as KWIC (Key Word in Context) indexing

Data-handling routines for sorting and merging

Management-oriented packages for inventory control

How to Realize Maximum Benefits from a Service Center. Your selection of and method of working with a service center will vary slightly if you have a one-time problem as opposed to day-to-day accounting or other processing requirements. For accounting or other day-to-day work, you will want reliable, timely, and accurate results at the most favorable price. For convenience and timeliness, you will want a local firm to do your work. Chances are that you will have to rely on them for help in systems design, so you will also want them to have reasonable capabilities in this area.

As with any outside service, you will get better results if you give the service center a detailed specification of what you want to accomplish. This will include the nature of the reports you desire, specifications of the source documents that will provide the data for the reports, the volume of source documents to be handled, and the frequency of reporting, check writing, and so forth. The key element of processing cost that you can control or vary is the report frequency. Because this is also a major determinant of cost, you should ask for cost estimates based on several reporting frequencies.

Naturally, you cannot expect to make detailed specifications yourself. But if you make a general outline of the job you want done, the service center representatives can help you refine it into final specifications.

It is imperative that you contact several service centers when you set out to get a job done. Prices and capabilities can vary considerably, and the only way to see this is by getting several estimates. The larger centers are usually more expensive and have more extensive capabilities. Yet most jobs do not require these capabilities. Most of the smaller centers have at least a few people of exceptional ability and can often do just as good a job as the larger ones.

Accurate results will require tight control of input data accuracy. Whether you start your own data-processing department or go to a service center, you will find it essential to tighten your control of input data accuracy. The service center should tell you in detail what will be expected of you in the preparation and transmittal of source data. They should also tell you how data errors will be corrected, once found. There is a basic principle in data processing called Murphy's law: "If anything can go wrong, it will."

Reliable results will require that you prepare for Murphy's law. The service center should also be prepared. They should have firm arrangements to use other similar computing equipment in your area if their equipment should fail. You should satisfy yourself that they have these arrangements.

For one-time jobs other than accounting jobs, your approach will be different in two respects. First, it is unnecessary to use a local service. In fact, unless you are in a very large city, it will probably be undesirable, because it is less likely that you will find either the size computer or the capable programming staff to implement your plans.

Second, the need for tight data controls is considerably less. Any data problems can be ironed out by your representative as they occur. In these one-time situations, it costs more to anticipate all these potential problems than it does to solve them as they arise.

CONCLUSION

Data-processing service centers are a major factor in the data-processing field. They are used by large and small companies just like any other contract service such as management consultants, production subcontractors, contract maintenance personnel, and the like. For the big company, they provide the "extra hand" that is often needed in exceptionally busy times. They allow smaller companies a chance to reap the advantages of electronic data processing without the heavy capital cost and lengthy training period required if they establish their own computer department. And because they are continuously developing unique new computer applications, they offer the possibility of special new services to users of all sizes.

BIBLIOGRAPHY

"Choosing a Service Bureau," *Computers and Automation,* December, 1964.

"Choosing and Using an Outside EDP Center," *Administrative Management,* January, 1965.

"Computers for Everybody," *Dun's Review & Modern Industry,* December, 1961.

"A CPA's Experience with Punched Tape and a Service Bureau," *Journal of Accountancy,* September, 1961.

A Directory of Data Processing Service Centers, Association of Data Processing Service Organizations, Inc., Abington, Pa., 1964 (annual supplements).

"How a Jobber Uses Computers," *National Petroleum News,* January, 1964.

"New Computer Services for Small and Medium Sized Companies," *Computers and Automation,* March, 1961.

"Profits or Headaches from Computer Services," *Banking,* October, 1963.

"Rise of the Service Center," *Dun's Review & Modern Industry,* September, 1964.

"Roster of EDP Service Centers," *Computers and Automation,* September, 1965.

"What Service Centers Offer in Data Processing," *Office,* February, 1962.

MANAGEMENT OF INTERNATIONAL OPERATIONS

CHAPTER ONE

Organizing for International Operations

ALEXANDER O. STANLEY *Associate Director, International Marketing Institute, Cambridge, Massachusetts*

Management has multiple choices in positioning its products in global markets, and the choices are not mutually exclusive. It can develop an export or import capability:

Through the use of service organizations performing total or special functions

By dividing the responsibilities among its existing corporate or company divisions (the horizontal approach)

By creating a separate corporate or company division in which all international functions are centered (the vertical approach)

By joining United States or foreign cooperatives or syndicates

And it can develop a foreign-based international marketing position:

Through total, partial, or limited investments in foreign-based production or distributive facilities, sometimes in United States or foreign tax havens

Through licensing, leasing, or other oblique-type arrangements

By providing management or technical know-how to fully or quasi-foreign government owned or controlled enterprises

Or to overseas projects underwritten by the U.S. Agency for International Development (AID) or other United States agencies

Or to projects sponsored or financed by supranational institutions such as the United Nations (UN), the General Agreement on Tariffs and Trade (GATT), the World Bank (IBRD), the International Finance Corporation (IFC), the International Development Association (IDA), the Inter-American Development Bank (IADB), and other equivalent organizations

Or to private projects on a company-to-company basis or through consortia

It is in their variety that these organizational patterns assure American management of effective organizational models within which to fit their products in the different markets and segments of markets. But in the main, the organizational problem is not so much a matter of selecting an "ideal" system as it is of making use of those combinations of systems which will accommodate the pace and phase of the individual firm's marketing span.

APPROACH TO OVERSEAS OPERATIONS

The orthodox evolution has been that of penetrating overseas markets through use of an escalating technique, that is, first via export brokers; then combination export managers; then built-in export divisions or separate international (United States–based) corporations; then foreign licensees; then foreign-based subsidiaries wholly, partly, or jointly owned. The quick-penetrating technique, however, seems to find favor with more and more management groups, whatever their capital positions. It is commonplace to see announcements of joint ventures or licensing agreements covering products, old and new, that have never been marketed or even market-tested. abroad. And it is also commonplace to find that the United States licensor or company investor involved has never before operated abroad, in any form, in any overseas market.

Contrast this with the parochial and cynical attitude that dominated the United States business scene in the first half of the twentieth century—"You don't sell your shirts abroad, you lose them." Intrigued by the continuing sales and profit potential in the common-market blocs now on the European, Latin American, and African economic scenes, American business, both the big and not so big, has made a turnabout in its policy. It is swiftly moving to open competitive bridgeheads in markets abroad, in both the single and the bloc variety.

What are the organizational choices, the most effective patterns that build up marketing power overseas? *Perhaps the strongest index is the degree of marketing risk assumed by the organizational module involved.* Put another way, the more remote the control of marketing decisions by the parent manufacturer, the greater the risk of competitive attrition, except in the case of subsidiary adits. As entrepreneurial groups interpose, marketing control diminishes. Measured against this index of marketing risk, it is possible to evaluate each of the modules in its totality and its parts, so that an eclectic approach to organizational structures becomes feasible. In fact, the organizational charts of hundreds of companies examined by the author reinforce this point. Companies are apt to have a management mix including combination export managers, licensees, overseas sales branches, and other variations within the framework of a formally structured export or international division.

The operational and marketing objectives of each company influence considerably which type of functional apparatus is used, but this is also modified by the pace and the point in time of the individual firm's aspirations. The combinations of modules are arithmetically large. But practical limits are imposed by such factors as capital and credit power, by caveats in United States and foreign legal codes, and always, of course, by tax considerations at home and abroad. Against this backdrop, sometimes murky, sometimes distorted, but always intriguing because of its huge dimensions, management can actually operate quite comfortably, whether its marketing needs are simple or complex.

THE INTERNAL ORGANIZATIONAL VARIATIONS

In organizing its functions internally, the international operations management has two basic choices, either the horizontal or the vertical approach. Here again, these can be commingled in their parts, but for purposes of this discussion, each is schematically and basically separated. Managements are prone to follow the horizontal approach in the opening phase (see Figure 1-1 and read horizontally). This consists in spreading the international work load among all the management disciplines with perhaps special emphasis in the areas of production, financial, legal, marketing, and sales functions. Initially, and presupposing that the activity is limited to export and/or import, the typical pattern is to let each of the executives involved gain his experience empirically, drawing in outside specialists on a by-the-project or by-the-problem basis. This is especially so in the case of financial and legal divisions. Here the kinds of problems encountered are too complex and the decisions too critical to permit any other than the best available professional information to be sought for and applied.

As the level of export operations rises, companies either shift the work load and responsibilities to a self-contained export division or encourage division administrators to create executive assistant posts, at least in the heavy work-load

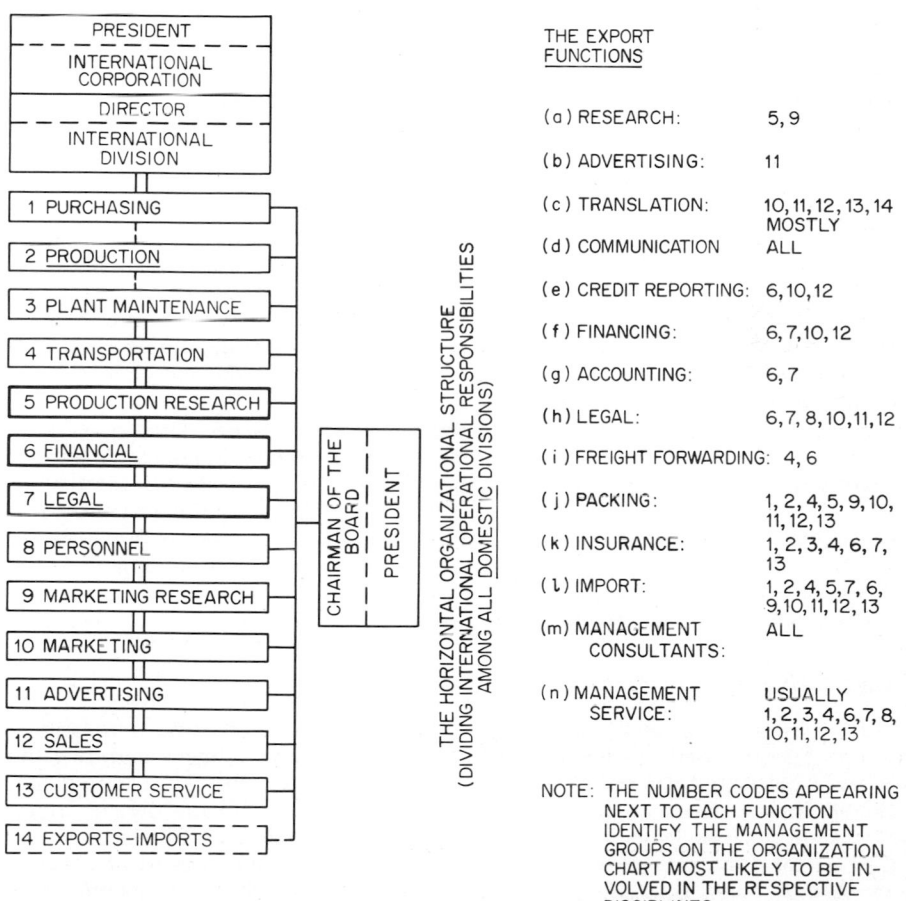

THE VERTICAL ORGANIZATIONAL STRUCTURE
(A SELF-CONTAINED ENTITY)

PRESIDENT
INTERNATIONAL CORPORATION
DIRECTOR
INTERNATIONAL DIVISION

1 PURCHASING
2 PRODUCTION
3 PLANT MAINTENANCE
4 TRANSPORTATION
5 PRODUCTION RESEARCH
6 FINANCIAL
7 LEGAL
8 PERSONNEL
9 MARKETING RESEARCH
10 MARKETING
11 ADVERTISING
12 SALES
13 CUSTOMER SERVICE
14 EXPORTS-IMPORTS

CHAIRMAN OF THE BOARD
PRESIDENT

THE HORIZONTAL ORGANIZATIONAL STRUCTURE
(DIVIDING INTERNATIONAL OPERATIONAL RESPONSIBILITIES AMONG ALL DOMESTIC DIVISIONS)

THE EXPORT FUNCTIONS

(a) RESEARCH: 5, 9

(b) ADVERTISING: 11

(c) TRANSLATION: 10, 11, 12, 13, 14 MOSTLY

(d) COMMUNICATION ALL

(e) CREDIT REPORTING: 6, 10, 12

(f) FINANCING: 6, 7, 10, 12

(g) ACCOUNTING: 6, 7

(h) LEGAL: 6, 7, 8, 10, 11, 12

(i) FREIGHT FORWARDING: 4, 6

(j) PACKING: 1, 2, 4, 5, 9, 10, 11, 12, 13

(k) INSURANCE: 1, 2, 3, 4, 6, 7, 13

(l) IMPORT: 1, 2, 4, 5, 7, 6, 9, 10, 11, 12, 13

(m) MANAGEMENT CONSULTANTS: ALL

(n) MANAGEMENT SERVICE: USUALLY 1, 2, 3, 4, 6, 7, 8, 10, 11, 12, 13

NOTE: THE NUMBER CODES APPEARING NEXT TO EACH FUNCTION IDENTIFY THE MANAGEMENT GROUPS ON THE ORGANIZATION CHART MOST LIKELY TO BE INVOLVED IN THE RESPECTIVE DISCIPLINES.

FIG. 1-1. *The vertical organizational structure. The horizontal organizational structure.* (*Copyright applied for by Alexander O. Stanley.*)

areas. In any event, the export responsibility is centered in one individual, whether his title is vice president, international export manager, or export director. In the main, he functions as coordinator, whatever his job title.

When the scale of activity or degree of operational sophistication requires overseas-based units, the centralizing process takes place, similar to that described in the preceding paragraph. Contrariwise, if the company focus is on imports, the tendency is to keep this as a parafunction within existing domestic divisions, usually under the direct control of the purchasing division. This is so because fewer divisions are directly concerned with import operations than with export. The central point here is that imports are buying activities involving less functional coordination, whereas export, as a selling function, involves the full management spectrum.

Overall, the eventual drift is toward a separate corporate structure of the vertical variety to house the overseas subsidiary or affiliate units because of operational and (sometimes) tax conveniences. At that point, a decentralizing process begins with management and marketing decisions left more and more to the dictates of subsidiary managers. Sometimes they work in concert with large-scale regional administrators or committees operating from bases outside the United States. The parent corporation spells out the broad policy lines, but its administrative practices and operational controls are usually limited to three management disciplines: financial, legal, and product research (technical).

As the international involvements become elaborate, the day-by-day needs require more consistent application of the management disciplines oriented to the overseas picture. So the vertical approach creating the separate international division or corporate subsidiary becomes imperative (see Figure 1-1 and read vertically). Within this framework, first the key divisions and eventually all the staff and line divisions are organized to assume full responsibility for the international side of operations. Here they function as an extension of their domestic division counterparts, but with separate identity and autonomy. Direct links between the international and domestic units, when they exist, are of the liaison type and not necessarily between equivalent functions. Indeed, they tend to cut across functional lines, with respect to both the rank and the file, on the organization chart.

Because the basic export or international functions are not discrete and each impinges on others to some degree, the need for liaison is critical. More so than in domestic practice, the international administrator is first a coordinator, then a line executive, and finally a policy maker. The range of responsibilities is closely akin to a marketing executive who roams the entire executive lineup in assembling the resources in men and methods, to develop the strongest market image of the firm's product groups. In the large sense, the international divisions add a third dimension to the total corporate picture.

THE INTERNATIONAL SUBSIDIARY CORPORATION

Until passage of the 1962 Revenue Act, United States firms were able to set up foreign-based operations under a United States investment incentive that allowed protracted deferral of United States tax payouts. But the rush of United States firms to secure a European common-market base and the rash of United States subsidiaries in some forty tax havens abroad had their repercussions. A new set of United States tax laws was devised. Ostensibly aimed at checking the United States gold and dollar drain, the 1962 Revenue Act, in its applicable sections and the subsequent interpretations of these, cut out or cut down many of the immediate tax pauses. Definitive guidelines remain elusive, for it is less the changes and more the interpretations by the Internal Revenue Service (IRS) that are reshaping the tax retention features. Based on the changes in the Act itself, here are the major points that can affect the United States tax calendar of overseas subsidiaries:

Tax-exposed Income

If the United States parent company owns more than 50 percent of the voting power *and*

If the foreign subsidiary operates mostly as a sales outlet for goods produced outside its country of incorporation and sold for use outside that country, *and* the goods are either bought from or sold to or on behalf of an affiliated company and/or if it is a holding company with substantial investment-type income such as dividends, interest, rents, royalties, and gains on sale of securities.

If it has substantial income from services performed on behalf of affiliated companies in a country not of its incorporation.

Tax-deferred Income

If the foreign subsidiary is engaged in local manufacturing or production.

If it sells goods produced by the United States parent in the country of incorporation.

If "tax-exposed income" is less than 30 percent of total gross income. If between 30 percent and 70 percent, actual percentage is tax exposed. If over 70 percent, entire gross income will result in tax-exposed net income.

If investment-type income is received from an affiliated company organized and operating in the same country.

If investment income is received from and reinvested in less-developed countries.

If creation of the foreign subsidiary does not effectively reduce tax on income.

It must be repeated that none of the foregoing points can be regarded as fixing an absolute line of demarcation between the paying- and the deferring-tax subsidiary types. Newer interpretations are relieving or creating new tax situations, so that currency in legal and accounting expertise is a prime requirement *before* the fact of investing abroad.

Marketing Advantages. From the operational side, foreign-based subsidiaries enjoy some distinct marketing advantages. They can:

Create a national image for their product and bypass, to a large degree, the natural and artificial restraints imposed by public or government pressures.

Establish a solid production and distribution base within a common-market bloc, not only to take advantage of immediate trade and tariff *preferments* but also to accommodate long-term growth.

Shorten reaction time to shifts in customer desires and needs, and stay alerted to competitive maneuvers in the local marketplace.

Sometimes generate higher profit margins because of lower labor, materials, management, capital, and tax inputs.

Sometimes provide a more competitive price position.

Improve delivery schedules and sometimes cut overall transit costs.

Provide access to local financing of equity capital and short-term working funds, and sometimes tap the local version of export credit insurance, if available and if needed.

Obtain investment cover in certain of the less-developed countries (LDCs) through the U.S. Agency for International Development (AID).

Take advantage of tax "holiday" or preferment situations offered by some countries. These can include tax exemption or abatement, high depreciation rates, and accelerated amortization write-offs.

Extend the life of "obsolescent" equipment by transferring it to overseas areas where smaller production runs or less-sophisticated equipment are still viable. This "salvaging" can also be applied to patents.

Maximize the benefits of the R&D function, usually through cross-fertilization. Also, the rapid growth of R&D abroad in recent years makes it imperative to monitor research there.

Expand contacts with and service to United States industrial customers by serving their locally (foreign) established subsidiaries.

Corporate and Company Forms of Overseas Subsidiaries. The variety of corporate and company forms that are available to accommodate overseas subsidiaries are as numerous as the markets themselves. Aside from the distinctions that arise from the commercial code, which differs in the different countries, the popular groups fall into these four large patterns:

1. Public limited-liability companies, similar to our publicly held corporations.

2. Private or proprietary limited-liability companies, roughly equivalent to our closed or private corporations.

3. Silent or limited partnerships, with or without capital stock issues. In this type of partnership, the total assets of general partners are exposed to liability and those of silent partners are limited to their investment in the specific enterprise.

4. Proprietorships, which are less popular for investment situations. Overseas branches of United States firms can sometimes fall in this category. Least desirable because of direct exposure to the jurisdiction of foreign governments, branches tend to be used more for test situations, especially because they are easy to "collapse" and their losses are immediately chargeable against parent current income.

THE WESTERN HEMISPHERE TRADE CORPORATION (WHTC)

Primarily a tax-oriented United States corporate structure, the WHTC was designed to induce both United States and foreign business to extend operations to all areas of the Western Hemisphere outside the perimeters of the United States. On the tax books since 1942, the WHTC offers in effect these two-step corporate tax formulas to firms that qualify:

The WHTC effective rate*	15.58 % on the first $35,294 of net income
The standard United States corporate rate	22.0 % on the first $25,000 of net income
The WHTC effective rate*	34.0 % on all net income in excess of $35,294 of net income
The standard United States corporate rate	48.0 % on all net income in excess of $25,000 of net income

    * Based on the formula given in IRS Section 922.

To get this 14 percent tax differential, some tight operational requirements are set:

At least 95 percent of gross income must have come from sources outside the United States

All its business must be done within the Western Hemisphere

At least 90 percent of gross income must derive from the conduct of a trade or business

All foregoing conditions must have been in effect for three consecutive fiscal years or from incorporation of the WHTC if that was a shorter period

Intercompany dealings between a WHTC and its United States parent firm (if one is involved) must be at arm's length so that parent profits are not switched to the WHC under the ruse of reduced charges for goods and services

To meet the 95 percent foreign-source-income rule, title to goods sold must be passed outside the United States

Almost all purchases must be made within the Western Hemisphere

Qualifying for the WHTC tax differential is at best arduous, requiring both legal and accounting expertise, but the reward lies in a stronger profit and competitive position.

The approximate fourteen-point tax differential also can shorten the period of capital recovery in subsidiary risk ventures undertaken within the defined WHTC boundaries.

THE EXTERNAL ORGANIZATIONAL VARIATIONS

Whether it is to initiate or implement any one or a combination of functions required of international programming, United States management can tap a host of service organizations. Sometimes the services are free of charge (as promotional measures), but usually the best professional assistance is on fee, by-the-project or by-the-year basis. The order of the services list given in Figure 1-1 is random, without any qualitative implications. As to the all-encompassing types of organizations, the more popular versions are reviewed below, ranging from the simpler to the more sophisticated and finally to the more specialized distributive channels.

Export Brokers or Commission Houses. Acting ordinarily as entrepreneurs, this group, whatever its label, reaps its fees from buyer or seller commissions and discounts. There are some large, well-established houses which have strong contacts in specific regions and with specific industry or consumer groups. Such firms function through overseas-based sales agents or distributors (wholesaler importers) and can provide a full range of marketing services and marketing continuity. But the more effective they are, the more they tend to be heavily committed in the number of products and accounts carried, limiting their availability to newcomers as an export markets channel. This is especially so when there are competitive conflicts of interest.

A much larger number of much smaller firms, usually based in port areas, can be tapped, but here the marketing spectrum is blurred. These sometimes one-man enterprises tend to do little marketing as such and are involved more with matching overseas orders to United States suppliers. They can be freight forwarders, even packers or free-lance brokers, or they can be buying agents for overseas companies where it is family connection rather than functional ability that counts. As casual order placers, they can make exporting a relatively painless activity for the United States manufacturer, because they take over all the shipping detail and ordinarily pay in cash or in discountable commercial paper. But they hide many of the marketing essentials from the United States producer, such as where the goods go, at what price, under what guarantees, and under what trademarks. In fact, they obscure the full marketing mix. It is because of this system that numerous United States firms are "push-button" exporters, some not even aware that the goods they sell domestically are earmarked for overseas customers. If the risk is small, so are the results.

Import Merchants, Commission Houses, Brokers, Wholesalers. Whatever the label used, the scope and the *modus operandi* of these groups are much the same as those of their export counterparts. The distributive function is, of course, reversed, because suppliers from abroad are linked with United States industrial and commercial public consumers. But essentially, the same mechanics and much the same techniques are observed.

The Combination Export Management Firm (CEM). Headed by a single executive or a group with some or considerable expertise in selling abroad, the CEM provides a more controlled approach to overseas marketing. CEMs tend to specialize in product groups or in market groups, but usually can provide some degree of selling effectiveness in any overseas area. That degree depends primarily on the size of the domestic staff, the quality of the CEM overseas sales outlets, and the earnings spread offered by the CEM contract.

The strong point in the CEM is that the manufacturer's management can exercise considerable marketing judgment, because all overseas policy is cleared through it, especially in the sensitive areas of prices, credit terms, and service agreements. In fact, the CEM pattern is one of functioning as the export division of the manufacturer, though outside its organizational framework. CEMs, for example, use the client's letterhead, promotional and instructional material, and so on, although all export inquiry is eventually routed to and through the CEM. The weak point in the CEM structure is one of numbers—numbers of clients, numbers of products, numbers of markets and miles between markets, and the numbers of responsibilities. All or any of these can impose a top-heavy work load if the capital base is narrow and the staff structure thin.

For managements with little or no export exposure, the CEM can provide a quick means of getting into markets overseas at small immediate expense in management time and money. For products that have restricted potential because of natural artificial inhibitors in any and all markets, the CEM can provide a seeding or holding type of marketing. This is done sometimes by putting together a family-of-products package, thus maximizing sales efforts and spreading operation costs. For high-export-volume products and markets, the CEM can sometimes extend its tenure by giving clients more sophisticated services: licensing production and sales, generating R&D facilities, and anticipating significant market shifts. But in the more typical situation, the CEM term of contract with its average client is inverse to the degree of its export success.

Overseas Management Service Organizations. Designed for tax havens, this type of organization offers a full spectrum of management services, usually in the LDC areas. It can attend to all formalities of setting up a going enterprise such as finding plant and office space, hiring and managing staff, keeping books, observing all legalities required by the commercial code, and even finding candidates for or sitting as delegates on the board of directors, required in the case of some overseas subsidiaries. As a means of creating "suitcase corporations" (tax-haven devices), it has worked quite well, but as a substitute for direct management control and involvement, its effectiveness is moot.

The Webb Pomerene Trade Association (WPTA). An export sales cooperative, this syndicated approach to selling abroad is partly anti-antitrust. Authorized by the United States law in 1918, the WPTA actually permits firms within the same industry to band together; agree on prices, terms, and sales policies; use common sales channels; allocate orders; and in fact, break many of the strictures fixed for United States business by the Sherman Antitrust Act. But there are limits. The WPTA may not in any way restrict trade within the United States or restrain export sales of its domestic competitors. And it may not artificially rig prices within the United States. It must keep the administrating agency, the Federal Trade Commission (FTC), informed of its composition and keep its books open for FTC inspection. Whatever the administrative responsibilities, the permissive functional aspects are interesting. The WPTA may:

1. Act as a central selling agency for all its members, ranging from order taking to shipping the goods abroad

2. Consolidate export operations in an existing export department of one member company or consolidate only some export sales functions within the WPTA; also it may use member company agents abroad to get business; also it may combine procedures (1) and (2)

3. Buy its members' products and resell them abroad on commonly agreed terms

On paper, the WPTA holds out these many advantages:

Its total association overhead can be less than the sum of its member parts. This is particularly helpful to smaller business.

The high costs of penetrating new markets are divided into smaller, less onerous shares.

Large orders, especially when contraseasonal or of an emergency nature, are easier to fill.

Pooled shipments can improve delivery schedules and sometimes secure reduced ocean-freight rates.

Standards adopted in practices and products can reduce customer claims and build customer relations.

Prices, terms, and policies can remain flexible, because the agreed-to indexes in these areas of agreement are considered minimum. In some cases, members are free to quote their own prices and are required only to report changes in price patterns to the WPTA.

Export quotas may be distributed among members to spread the export load evenly and sometimes shorten production peaks and valleys.

Prices and terms agreements can create an orderly market for the overseas buyer and stabilize advance buying.

Long-term contracts can be more easily secured, because the pooled supply source reduces questions about delivery performance.

Credit and market changes can be reported faster, more accurately, and less expensively.

A larger, more permanent field sales staff can be supported overseas because of larger income actuals and potentials.

Joint trade names and trademarks can be registered (when necessary) and policed less expensively in more countries.

The combined sales power can build up to a stronger competitive posture vis-à-vis foreign suppliers.

There are, of course, the curbs and levelers on practices, policies, and profits usually identified with the cooperative type of ventures. On balance, the WPTA is worth scanning by management, whatever the extent of previous export exposure and whatever the scale of objectives.

The Manufacturers' Export Cooperative Department. Still in the experimental stages, the United States–based cooperative type falls between the CEM, which tends to be overcrowded with products, and the WPTA, which tends to be overscrutinized by the FTC. Ordinarily, the evolution of this type of cooperative results from export operations becoming too large for a company to maintain a part-time program but too small to justify the expense load of a fully staffed export unit. Operating on a selective basis and usually drawing on "neighboring" (local or regional) manufacturing plants as candidates, the central exporter firm in a sense "sells" its expertise on a share-of-the-cost basis.

As a temporary vehicle, this cooperative device offers some interesting inducements to management groups in the earn-while-you-learn pattern. But the marketing focus is too diffused and the profit motivation too fragmented to sustain for any one firm an effective export program of strong potential.

The International Licensee. Because they suggest quick access to established production and distribution facilities and because they imply a limited and flexible management commitment, licensing agreements have been a popular vehicle in "going international." But there are these critical factors:

Royalties are usually subject to foreign government approval, especially among the LDC group. Because they tend to siphon exchange reserves, royalties are usually pinched to marginal minimums for the United States or other foreign licensor.

Product, process, or marketing know-how is difficult to restrict and to recover in the event of contract termination. Licensors sometimes get a paltry return while they are, in effect, installing their future competitors.

Unless stock options are available to the United States licensor under the agreement, there is no marketing continuity. Here again, it is important to pin down foreign government approval.

Selecting the right licensee involves a close scrutiny of character, technical know-how and management/marketing capacity, and the capital/credit position, in about that order. These points, rather than the detail of contract clauses, can spell the difference between licensing agreements and disagreements.[1]

As a basic approach, it might be well to use the permissive (optional) rather than the prohibitive (restraining or coercive) approach to licensing. And if there are licensing contracts in force, these should be reexamined for antitrust sensitivity, not only with respect to the United States but also with respect to the EEC regulations in this area.

Contract Manufacturing and Distribution. The availability of idle or "downtime" in men and machinery, on either a protracted seasonal or short-term basis, opens still another approach to management for overseas operations. This applies both to production and to distribution facilities, in some cases with United States–owned subsidiaries and in other instances with those of (foreign) nationals who have the technical and marketing know-how. Here patent protection is usually a prerequisite, and even know-how can be guarded by effective agreements.

The Overseas-based Distributor. In a more direct penetration, export managements use the overseas-based distributor, usually a wholesaler or local importer, as the sales funnel. Here the marketing involvement tends to be long term and total on both sides.

The manufacturer supplies stock on a cash, credit, or consignment basis. The distributor, given exclusive selling/service rights in a specific marketing area,

---

[1] Some critical, practical, and legal guidelines for drawing licensing contracts will be found in Alexander O. Stanley, *Handbook of International Marketing*, McGraw-Hill Book Company, New York, 1963, pp. 447–461.

accepts the local marketing and credit risk. He usually buys the merchandise for his own account, maintaining stock on hand. If necessary, he installs and services the articles sold.

There are these advantages in working through distributors:

1. The distributor buys in large quantity, making it possible to effect savings in cost of bank drafts, special invoicing, marketing, and shipping. The credit risk, if any is involved, is concentrated rather than diffused.

2. Because he is committed to the sale of the goods to recover his investment, the distributor has every incentive to push sales aggressively.

But there are also some problems for the manufacturing principal:

1. There is little or no contact with the local retailing or manufacturing buyers of the product.

2. There is limited or no control over local marketing and credit policies, and no supervision over selection of accounts.

3. There is limited or no control over local price schedules, discounts, and related policies and practices.

4. Although the distributor usually shares in the expense of local advertising campaigns, he ordinarily selects the media and has a loud voice in determining the budgetary appropriation.

5. The principal's trademark or company name may be subordinated to that of the distributor. Thus, if the relationship should be severed, there is the possible loss of an established market for some time, especially if the distributor should switch over to a competitive product.

6. The "sales quotient" (size of the sales staff employed divided into the number of product lines carried), although ostensibly good, may conceal the fact that a few high-yield product lines are churned while others are left to languish. Sales efforts tend to follow the line of least resistance and thrive on the fattest profit-margin accounts. Consumer shifts of interest to "glamour" products can also have repercussions on attitudes of distributors, responding to pressures at the retail level.

7. Because commitments are usually larger, they are usually longer. This can cause difficulties in realigning sales territories to meet competitive challenges or to capture an equitable share of new market potentials. New roads, new industries, new population clusters, and, of course, new common markets can affect sales patterns and call for territorial splits or shifts that may be opposed by existing distributors.

8. Although the distributor's capital base may be relatively substantial, it is the liquidity, the turnover rate, and the composition of inventory in terms of the "products quotient" (number of product lines carried divided into the inventory) that determine whether the working-capital range is adequate in terms of any one principal's program. If the product's quotient shows high diffusion, it spells narrow inventory capacity for individual product types and sizes, with a consequent backlash on demand fulfillment and delivery schedules.

As a general guide, commodities which lend themselves best to bulk shipments and which require the maintenance of large stocks in foreign markets, for both supply and service, are usually handled through distributors. But distributors also prevail at the other end of the market spectrum where the sales area is too small, geographically or for export coverage. In brief, large-scale or concentrated operations tend to be channeled through distributors; small-scale, scattered operations tend toward the sales agents' group.

The Overseas-based Sales Agent. The sales agent or representative is an individual or concern, usually of national origin, operating in an overseas territory or sometimes a whole market, appointed by a United States or foreign company to obtain orders on a commission or occasionally a salary basis. The manufac-turer/supplier checks and assumes all marketing and credit risks, because the agent carries no inventory. Normally, the sales agent contacts the local outlets and files his orders directly with his manufacturing principal. Depending on the product involved, such outlets would be either retailers or local manufacturers or users buying raw materials, supplies, equipment, and so on. Shipments are usually made directly to the buyer. On shipments involving credit, the agent ordinarily collects his commission after the bill of goods is paid. He assumes no credit responsibility, and his activities are substantially those of a salesman.

There is this large advantage to the principal in working through an agent:

1. Direct contact with local outlets

There are also these secondary advantages to the principal:

2. Direct control of sales policies, prices, and the types of accounts selected

3. Immediate market intelligence on the competitive position in respect to price, product design, quality, and so on, because of this direct contact with local outlets

4. Unilateral control of the advertising budget

5. The opportunity to establish the company trademark and company name firmly in the local market, retaining identity here no matter how often agents are changed

But there is an offset in these disadvantages:

1. The need to handle many small or moderate-sized direct shipments with the attendant expense of paper work and a complexity of credit problems that arise from checking many accounts. Balancing this is the fact that the credit risk is spread over many accounts rather than concentrated in few.

2. The need for the agent to make frequent call-backs, thus tending to process frequent and small reorders, limiting his range and number of productive calls in the workday. Also, his typical retailer customer, operating from a small capital base with many lines, cannot maintain a strong position in any one product line, so he tends to carry representative rather than complete stocks. This re-duces, for the individual product, the point-of-sale space availability and exposure time. The problem is compounded if transportation links are extended in dis-tance and time to the more remote areas.

3. The tendency of agents to carry many, and sometimes too many, related although noncompetitive lines to get more blocks of orders per call. And be-cause they have only a small stake involved—their time—and live by commissions, agents tend to put the greatest effort in the lines encountering the least sales resistance.

The Agents' Agent. Still in an experimental stage, a new approach to the selection and control of local agents and distributors is under way in France, Morocco, Israel, and Mexico. The concept is to funnel new product lines through one local organization which recommends and then monitors the agent or distributor who is finally appointed. The agents' agent is responsible to the individual exporting manufacturer or group of manufacturers and receives a flat fee annual retainer or small percentage from the principal. Ideally, he should assume the role of referee between the local representative and the manufacturer to resolve all manner of marketing conflicts.

The Overseas Traveling Representative. The maverick of the sales staff, the traveling representative (TR), may be a free-lance, per diem, or per contract representative or consultant, intermittently covering regions or handling specific assignments. Then again, he may be on the permanent payroll. Factory trained, the TR can be an extension of the overseas field force, which he contacts inter-mittently to (1) update sales personnel on new products, new methods, and new programs; or (2) train foreign service personnel on improvements in mechanical or technical procedures, which can range from the proper installation of heavy equipment down to replacing the burnt-out tube or troublesome element in some household gadget; or (3) advise executive personnel in a broad spectrum of policy and operational revisions. Sometimes he is responsible for all three.

The TR may be the export manager or director of exports or even a vice president drawn from the executive staff, or then again he may be a specialist in sales, service, or management functions with prescribed duties and limited authority. The trend has been toward the use of specialists, sending these into areas where the scale of operations supports the expense. More and more, the export executive in modern management relies on organizational controls and indicators to point up the trouble spots.

The Overseas-based Retail Systems. Faster, more frequent, and convenient communication and transportation links; bigger markets; expanded purchasing power; accessibility to and improved processing of trade and consumer lists and directories; freer currency convertibility, all are factors behind what may well become a strong trend in the future—the direct channeling of sales to retail and consumer levels from central depots or factory bases. Here is a capsule review of the key retail systems.

Department stores, chain stores, cooperatives and buying combines, supermarkets, large and moderate-sized independent retailers purchasing independently or as a block, resident or roving buying agents (usually employees) acting for one or a group of companies, all are a part of the growing complex of retailers who bypass middlemen in more and more supply areas in the mechanics of buying. Large-sized purchases make these accounts desirable but also connote competitive pricing. In some cases, these are carried as commissionless house accounts under supervision of the sales executive. In other cases, the initiative for buying (and the attendant expense) stems from the purchaser, whose staff searches out the supply sources for the new, the better-designed, or the better-priced products.

Improved mailing lists, the spate of colorful Sunday supplements and consumer magazines published or circulated abroad, the spread of TV as an advertising medium, spreading stability in exchange rates, and the relative ease of making payment by international (and local) postal money order have created the machinery for generating direct consumer sales and order taking by mail. Still experimental, still beset with numerous question marks, this system is worth examining, especially for the low-priced mailable and novelty items. It is a matter both of indoctrination and of investigation. Some possible approaches involve setting up a supply depot and mail drop in centrally located points abroad to process orders. Receipts can be deposited in local banks and easily converted into dollar deposits for future exchange or remittance. The program can be developed in a central point within a single market, a common market, or bloc of markets.

Direct-selling companies that handle appliances, housewares, cosmetics, toiletries, floor waxes and brushes, and clothing are now reaching out to knock on the doors of overseas customers. One United States company producing household supplies now has door-to-door canvassers in the Western Hemisphere and has recently gone into the EEC. Another reports that it has 10,000 overseas salesmen calling on customers in Latin America, Great Britain, and West Germany to sell a wide range of its cosmetics and toiletries which are priced from $0.50 to $20.00.

PX stores overseas are still another huge and effective outlet not only to move goods in volume but especially to introduce made-in-U.S.A. products into the sophisticated, exotic markets of the world.

Purchasing agents based in the United States and sometimes in key cities abroad act for single or multiple buying groups abroad, not only in the retail area but also for the extractives industries. These may be of United States, foreign, or mixed ownership.

Government purchasing agents based in the United States and key cities abroad act for their respective governments in buying military and nonmilitary commodities as well. They can act for state-owned industries including mining, tobacco, beverage groups, and a host of other government-dominated enterprises.

Visiting buyers/sellers from overseas, although here today and gone tomorrow, can point the way to unique opportunities for market expansion overseas as well as new-product acquisitions on the domestic scene.

Trade centers, trade missions, fixed and mobile fairs, and sample showcases are still another cluster of sales channels used by both the export division and the overseas-based United States subsidiary. Sometimes permanent, more often temporary, they are a means of product display and introduction. They are especially popular among overseas businessmen as a means of creating sales contacts and acquiring sales agencies. Some counterparts or variations of these sales outlets are found on the United States scene, usually in the large port areas, but they are aimed at generating more import than export interest.

Equipment-leasing Organizations. There are leasing organizations that provide industrial, commercial, and consumer equipment and service on a rental basis. Where they exist, the leasing organization can create fast contacts and strong marketing links in overseas areas, particularly for original equipment manufacturers (OEM), especially where the equipment is of advanced type and/or in higher price brackets. But the commercial code is one to watch here as to its provisions on the right to recover the equipment and the right to recover damages in the event of default.

Consortia. A popular vehicle for large-scale investments in industry, especially the extractives group, the consortium is either a meld of several foreign companies in a jointly owned local venture or a mix of foreign and national companies and sometimes even government entities.

The International Group. Appearing on the international horizon is the multinational company or, to use a more descriptive term, the "nonnational corporate enterprise." Pressures imposed on LDC governments by local groups to resist and reduce the grip of foreign-owned enterprises on the economic machinery of the individual states have caused organizational and policy reshuffling in some overseas-based units. Sometimes blunting, sometimes diverting the direction of this pressure, has been the competition for industry and infrastructure investments exerted by a growing list of the have-nots, looking for infusions of fresh capital to generate (or sometimes regenerate) a broad economic base. Common markets, too, have encouraged a less nationally identifiable type of company. And finally, the lateral spread of companies into completely unrelated product groups through mergers and acquisitions has made household names mavericks in the national and global marketplaces.

In the press to move forward, the more sophisticated managements have gone either the alphabet-abbreviation route or the "group" route which, in that order, either obscure the function or disguise the national character of the new empire-enterprise. In the case of the alphabet-abbreviation technique, United

States firms have taken a leaf from the corporate nomenclature of European and Latin American firms, whereas the "group" additive to the corporate style probably stems from the insurance community. At any rate, the latter is more indicative of status and conveys a more supranational mien to the international corporate image.

Whatever the method or the intent, much of the trend toward statelessness is first influenced by tax considerations and then the many more-immediate marketing considerations. This is pointed up by Prof. William S. Barnes in his *Harvard Business Review* article "Guides to International Operations": [2]

In the internal administrative policy of many companies, there is an increasing multinationalization of executive responsibility. In other words, the present trend is away from the national base and foreign subsidiary approach in favor of an overall multinational administration. No single country can accept responsibility for regulating the behavior of these large multinational businesses, since they have no home and no nationality. Such huge multibased enterprises often befuddle local authorities in spite of the conscientious efforts made to adhere to local regulations.

In addition, national taxation policies have been affected by the difference between the multinational corporation as it is developing today and the old international company with a firm base in one country and permanent establishments abroad. For instance, the League of Nations was very active, between the First and Second World Wars, in developing treaties to avoid the double taxation of international profits. Today the problem is in reverse, and treaties are being signed by governments principally in order to avoid the loss of revenue from multinational corporations which have so arranged their business as to be outside any government's tax jurisdiction. The recent changes in the United States income tax also reflect growing concern that businesses are getting away with no taxes paid to any country as the result of their multinational character.

BIBLIOGRAPHY

Bryson, George D., *Profits from Abroad*, McGraw-Hill Book Company, New York, 1963.

Fairweather, John, *Management of International Operations*, McGraw-Hill Book Company, New York, 1960.

Robinson, Richard D., *International Business Policy*, Holt, Rinehart and Winston, Inc., New York, 1964.

Seghers, Paul D. (ed.), "What to Do about Proposed Section 482 Adjustments and Relief under Rev. Proc. 64–54," *Proceedings*, Institute on U.S. Taxation of Foreign Income, Inc., New York.

Stanley, Alexander O., "How to Export, Import, and Invest Overseas," *Handbook of International Marketing*, McGraw-Hill Book Company, New York, 1963.

Stanley, Alexander O., *Organizing for International Operations*, American Marketing Association, Inc., New York, 1960.

Stieglitz, Harold, *Organization Structures of International Companies*, Studies in Personnel Policy, no. 198, National Industrial Conference Board, New York, 1965.

Surrey, Walter S., and Crawford Shaw (eds.), *A Lawyer's Guide to International Business Transactions*, The American Law Institute, Philadelphia, 1963.

[2] *Harvard Business Review*, November–December, 1965.

CHAPTER TWO

Selling in Foreign Markets

FRANK MEISSNER *Marketing Manager, Latin American Group, W. R. Grace & Co., New York, New York*

Aside from improving our competitive position in foreign markets by insuring cost and price stability, vigorous efforts are required to increase exports by bargaining down foreign tariffs and nontariff barriers to trade, providing better insurance for credit risks run by exporters, pressing for the removal of discriminatory ocean-freight rate differentials, *stepping up trade promotion activities* of the Department of Commerce and by exploring ways in which corporate tax payments could be rebated to exporters.[1]

So said the 1965 *Joint Economic Report* of the United States Congress in recommending export expansion as one of the country's official policies.

It is the objective of this chapter to

1. Explain the reason for the emphasis on "stepping up trade promotion" and

2. Show how an American entrepreneur can get into this profitable export business.

THE IMPORTANCE OF EXPORTS

In the five-year period 1960–1964, United States exports increased from $19.5 to $25.3 billion, or by about 30 percent. About one-fourth of the export volume consisted of agricultural commodities.

Imports increased from $14.7 to $18.6 billion, or by 27 percent. This means that the United States had an annual balance-of-trade surplus of about $5 billion, with an all-time high of $6.7 billion reached in 1964. This surplus was more than being gobbled up by economic and military aid commitments, flow of United States private investment funds abroad, and American tourists visiting foreign countries. As a result, there has been a chronic balance-of-payments deficit of something like $3 to $4 billion annually. (See Table 2-1.)

[1] *Joint Economic Report*, 89th Cong., 1st Sess., Mar. 17, 1965, p. 73.

TABLE 2-1. Balance of Payments, United States, 1956–1964

(In billions of dollars)

Year	Trade		Investment		Travel		Defense		Foreign aid†	Balance of payments
	Export	Import	Inflow	Outflow	Inflow	Outflow	U.S. sales abroad*	U.S. expenditures		
1956	17.4	12.8	0.65	3.07	0.71	1.28	0.16	2.95	4.30	−0.9
1957	19.4	13.3	0.49	3.58	0.79	1.37	0.38	3.22	4.03	+0.5
1958	16.3	13.0	0.02	2.94	0.83	1.46	0.30	3.43	3.90	−3.5
1959	16.3	15.3	0.86	2.38	0.85	1.61	0.30	3.11	3.61	−4.2
1960	19.5	14.7	0.34	3.89	0.88	1.73	0.34	3.05	3.43	−3.9
1961	19.9	14.5	0.62	4.18	0.89	1.74	0.40	2.95	3.32	−3.1
1962	20.6	16.2	0.16	3.43	0.88	1.89	0.66	3.08	3.46	−3.6
1963	22.1	17.0	0.30	4.46	0.93	2.09	0.66	2.93	3.40	−3.3
1964	25.3	18.6	0.23	6.46	1.10	2.22	0.76	2.82	3.44	−3.1

* Sales of military equipment to other countries.
† Foreign aid, military, and economic grants only.
SOURCE: U.S. Department of Commerce.

What are some of the constructive ways out of this dilemma? Export expansion, says the United States Congress.

THE BLUTRADE APPROACH TO EXPORT EXPANSION

The major difficulty which any export promoter has to overcome is psychological: American entrepreneurs are not export minded. Of the roughly 330,000 manufacturing establishments, only about 15,000, or 4.5 percent, are actively engaged in some aspect of international marketing. The vast majority of United States manufacturing and trading firms have, therefore, no direct contact whatsoever with foreign markets.

The majority of managers are therefore laymen as far as export is concerned. However, they should and can learn from successful exporters in their own country. This experience sharing can be systematically arranged via the community-wide Business-Labor-University Teams for Research and Assistance in Development of Exports, or BLUTRADE for short.

The first BLUTRADE project was developed in Worcester, Massachusetts, by the staff of the International Marketing Institute (IMI) in Cambridge, Massachusetts.[2]

BLUTRADE is based on two major premises. First, virtually thousands of American businessmen and agencies offer free advice and counsel in an effort to help fellow entrepreneurs increase exports. Among them are members of the U.S. Department of Commerce, National and Regional Export Expansion Councils, Chambers of Commerce, bankers, world trade centers, insurance and transportation companies, sales and marketing executive clubs, and university personnel. In contrast, the number of advice seekers runs in hundreds. The

[2] IMI is a nonprofit entity engaged in promoting good marketing practice around the world. Since 1960, it has held annual six-week summer seminars at the Harvard Business School, followed by eight-week tours of enterprises across the United States. By 1965, more than 500 executives and senior civil servants from abroad had participated in activities of IMI.

TABLE 2-2. Exportability Coefficient: Product Attributes

Any plus mark in the following nine questions indicates exportability; minuses indicate progressively lower-than-average export capacity.

The typical Worcester exporter answered these questions almost invariably with "yes." A respondent who reports two or less "no's" in the comparison section should be in a stronger exporting position than the average Worcester exporter. Three or more "no's" indicate likelihood that you would have greater-than-average difficulty exporting your products.

Attribute	Yes	No	Your score
1. A product which enjoys growing demand in United States markets has good chances of being exported successfully. Although many foreign markets are behind the United States in sophistication and development (certain products whose markets here are declining still have excellent markets overseas), the better long-range prospects are enjoyed by products whose United States markets are still growing. Is the demand for my product growing?	0	(−60)	
2. A "Made in U.S.A." label has plus value in international trade because overseas users or consumers have strong preference for American-made goods, stronger often than American producers realize. Is my product able to carry a "Made in U.S.A." label?	(For discussion only)		
3. "Superior quality" refers to ability to do a task better rather than to quality or uniqueness. Major reasons for strong United States product preference abroad are: the products last longer, run smoother, are freer from breakdowns, cost less to operate, or are easier to repair. Is my product superior in its field?	0	(−74)	
4. The wider a market for a product in the United States, the easier it is to establish substantial export outlets. Even more important, the management of a company which is able to deal with the problems of national marketing can easily overcome the problems of export marketing. Local-minded firms are not equipped *administratively to consider exporting.* Does your product have national distribution in the United States?	0	(−88)	
5. We take it for granted that the American manufacturer makes his product after a considerable study of what consumers expect. This consumer-oriented approach to product design is not yet as prevalent in other areas of the world. We assume that the American who is willing to fit his product to the needs of his overseas customers has an advantage in international trade. Has your product been designed after a study of the potential user or customer?	0	(−74)	
6. Products whose various characteristics can be fitted to a variety of different needs indicate consumer orientation. Are various design and functional characteristics of your product easily adaptable to change?	0	(−54)	

TABLE 2-2.   Exportability Coefficient: Product Attributes (*Continued*)

Attribute	Yes	No	Your score
7. American manufacturers often have a competitive advantage because of their marketing knowledge and skill. At present, there is an option as to whether they want to use these skills in helping push sales abroad. Within a few years, it will no longer be so. American firms will find it necessary to market their products aggressively or find European partners who will do that for them. Are you willing and able to accompany your product with the skill to demonstrate, sell, install, and service your commodities?	0	(−60)	
8. Experience shows "foreign" businessmen have as good a record of meeting their obligations as their American counterparts. An American businessman who does not believe this may not be successful in export marketing. Do you trust foreigners?		(For discussion only)	
9. Developing countries are often faced with acute shortage of foreign currency. Import controls are usually established to keep out many commodities. Products "essential" to provide food, shelter, and clothing, or to national economic development have, therefore, priority in markets through the world. Such products can make their way across tariff barriers. Can your product be designated as "essential"?	0	(−48)	
Total score..			

Add 120 to total score.

Instructions: Circle appropriate answer, and carry indicated number to the "your score" column.

export expansion drive does not need more administering or assistance; it needs more customers willing to give international trade a good try.

Second, practically all United States products are basically exportable; some more than others. Yet, few books on overseas marketing adequately explain criteria to be used in determining exportability of a product. BLUTRADE seminars have developed the following clue.

"Companies that do not export, do not want to export; companies that do some exporting, want to do more. It is our task to help nonexporters break this (indifference) barrier."[3]

Cosponsored by several important organizations (National Association of Manufacturers, American Express Company, American Institute of Marine Underwriters, Port of New York Authority, Time-Life International), BLUTRADE export promotion programs are available in many communities within the United States.

Establishing an Exportability Coefficient.   An interested would-be exporter might start with assessing the degree of exportability of his existing product line.   A two-part questionnaire has been designed for that purpose.   In the first part, you answer nine questions which help *compare* your product and attitudes with those of manufacturers who are successful exporters.   (See Table 2-2.)   The

[3] E. J. Enright and Alexander O. Stanley, *BLUTRADE Export Expansion,* International Marketing Institute, Cambridge, Mass., 1965, p. 14.

ten questions in the second part provide some indication about the ability of your product to compete in world markets.   (See Table 2-3.)

Both tables start with an overall explanation of purpose.   Each subsection has two parts: a reason why the topic is an important indicator of exportability, and a formulation of a specific question you need to answer.

The indicated bench-mark scores are based on results of a 1964 survey of 236 firms in Worcester, Massachusetts.

Making the First Contact.   Once the product and exportability analysis legwork has been done—whether by yourself or with BLUTRADE or other help—you are ready to start searching for customers.

There are many ways in which a neophyte can round up some prospects: telephone, visit, write, advertise, travel, and, of course, use the Trade Contact Survey of the U.S. Department of Commerce.   Telephone and visits are best used locally.

By Letter.   Many successful export experiences have begun with writing a "letter to a stranger" offering some product or service.

To save needless correspondence later and to make it easier for the receiver to reach some sort of decision, the opening letter should include an adequate description of the firm: date established, capitalization, picture of plant, customers whose names might be known abroad, interest in agents, distributors of direct sales, willingness to support sales with credit terms, and catalog sheets without commission or discount offers.   If possible, a Dun & Bradstreet credit-rating report should be filed abroad.

The letter should be written in the language familiar to the addressee, or in the language of his preference.   Port cities have translating services available in most languages.   Translation is an indicator of sincere desire to do business, rather than a mere "fishing" letter which is not worth answering.

The first letter contact between parties in different countries is not likely to produce immediate sales—just as the first call or the first direct-mail piece to an American manufacturer seldom results in an immediate order.   The initial letter is to be considered a sales contact which puts the exporter in personal touch with a potential buyer.

By Advertising.   Numerous American companies advertise in magazines and directories that circulate throughout the world.   The *Standard Rate and Data Service* contains an international section of about thirty pages that includes a list of some United States magazines with a foreign circulation.   Each profile contains details on the trade covered, circulation figures, and readership data. Advertising in such a medium can be used not only to contact customers, but to interest agents and distributors in handling the offered product.   Trademarks and trade names must be guarded *before* advertising.   In some countries, prior *registration* is the only protection against pirating or patent infringement.

One of the most specialized media is the *International Yellow Pages,*[4] which carries some 540,000 listings of importers and exporters indicating country of operation and address (town, street, telephone).   The commodity information is printed in English, French, Spanish, and German.

By Personal Contact.   If export is to be a significant activity of your company, there is no substitute for the direct contact afforded by *travel*.   It is one of the simplest and strongest means to get to know the plus and minus factors of one's marketing partners, whether at home or abroad.   Then too, there is the added advantage of personally marketing one's goods, especially when the qualities of a product are not self-evident or familiar.

[4] International Yellow Pages, Inc., 1151 Midtown Tower, Rochester, New York, 1,700 pages, circulation 36,000.

TABLE 2-3. Exportability Coefficient: Potential to Compete

Ideally, the average score on this series of questions should be close to zero. But here again, the *higher the plus result*, the *stronger* the "exportential"; and, of course, the *larger the minus score* the *lower* the export capability.

Six "yes's" and four "no's" may be considered a good line of reference. A respondent with fewer "no's" would to that extent be better than average in export capability. In contrast, answers containing five or more "no's" would not appear to be as well positioned toward exporting.

Product attribute	Yes	No	Your score
1. Assume that if your product does not have a United States price advantage, it does not have a price advantage in world markets either. It would probably have to sell on performance excellence or other nonprice advantage. Does your product have a competitive price advantage in the United States market?	0	(−2)	
2. There is a connection between manufacturing characteristics (which make a product difficult to imitate) and exportability (such various elements of product quality as design, quality of material used, and the extensive use of skilled labor). Does the manufacture of your product require extensive use of skilled labor?	0	(−12)	
3. Exportability of a product increases if high American wages can be offset by high labor productivity. Is the labor used highly productive, thus constituting a relatively low proportion of your total production cost?	0	(−24)	
4. In developing countries—where labor is normally in plentiful supply but money is scarce—commodities which help save capital goods are most welcome. Does your product result in any saving of capital goods?	(+36)	0	
5. In contrast, labor-saving goods are welcome in overemployment countries such as West Germany, but not in areas of underemployment such as Turkey. Does use of your product save labor?	(+32)	0	
6. Methods of manufacture or ingredients may well give the product unique export advantages or disadvantages. In the following five questions, some of the attributes of differentiation are referred to. Is your product free of any ingredients which would preclude exports to certain areas of the world?	0	(−26)	
7. Does the making of your product depend on application of peculiar skills?	0	(−8)	
8. Does the quality of your product result from use of an unusual process?	(+26)	0	
9. Does your product have a wide range of adaptability and flexibility of operation?	(+2)	0	
10. Are exporting costs a relatively small percentage of the selling price of your product?	0	(−38)	
Total number of...			
Total score...			

Instructions: Circle appropriate answer and carry indicated number to the "your score" column.

Before doing market *riding*, the prospective exporter should do a lot of market *reading* and planning so as not to jet himself out of business by hasty, poorly laid out itineraries. Plenty of lead time is needed to establish comfortable visiting schedules. Perhaps a reverse travel technique is best—arrange to have overseas contacts visit your own plant.

Better yet, any American manufacturer wishing to find an agent or a distributor in any specific place in the Free World can request that the U.S. Department of Commerce make a *Trade Contact Survey*. For as little as $50, commercial attachés at United States diplomatic posts will personally contact a number of potential customers and report back on businessmen who show specific interest.

RESEARCHING EXPORT MARKETS

Once an entrepreneur has tasted the sweet fruit of profitable exporting, he may wish to continue in it permanently. A decision of this sort should be guided by systematically gathered knowledge. Such intelligence is produced by marketing research.

The scientific methodology behind researching export markets is exactly the same as the approach used in researching domestic markets. Over the years, a tremendous wealth of marketing research experience has been accumulated in America. A careful application of this know-how to researching markets abroad can potentially provide American exporters with a competitive advantage over some of the more tradition-bound local competitors in different countries. Practically every successful exporter has developed his own formula or philosophy of doing and using marketing research.

The approaches range from extremely informal speculations and annotations on backs of envelopes to highly structured systems and charts. Many of these experiences have been written up and published. A list which provides references to some of this valuable work appears below.

No matter what product or service is involved, the export research job will have to focus on providing information on different aspects of the supply and demand situation plus the balancing mechanism, called "price."

Sources of Intelligence. Knowledge is power. The executive interested in export has easy access to a steadily growing volume of books, manuals, texts, cases, directories, statistical compilations, bibliographies, periodicals, and consulting services.

A few of the outstanding publications that will be useful to an export beginner follow. Some of these, plus a number of other valuable publications, are also discussed in Chapter 9 of Section 16.

Books. The McGraw-Hill Handbook Series leads the field. Thus, Alexander O. Stanley's *Handbook of International Marketing* (1963, 680 pages) puts at the executive's fingertips principles, practices, data, forms, and formulas usable in converting paper research into powerful tools for analyzing and developing marketing opportunities on a broad scale as well as on a market-by-market basis. Stanley's handbook presents a behind-the-scenes look at how companies are structured overseas, how they function, and how they get products to markets at low cost and on time.

It details the financing facilities for short-term credit or equity-capital needs, the United States government's export credit insurance program, trademarks, licenses, trade names, patents, copyrights, and other intangible but vital business assets.

The volume also contains an analysis of recent tax, credit, and trade-expansion legislation; discusses how common markets operate, where they exist, and how they can affect the immediate and future patterns of trade and investment; spells out the growing necessity of imports as a means of improving the product mix of United States companies to increase profit margins; and reviews in depth where and how to get specific government help.

Similar publications are Watson Dunn's *International Handbook of Advertising* (1964) and Karl E. Ettinger's *International Handbook of Management* (1965, 671 pages). To these handbooks, one can add the following text and case books and the U.N. bibliography.

Robert D. Stuart, *Penetrating the International Market*, American Management Association, New York, 1965, 176 pages.

John Fayerweather, *International Marketing*, Prentice-Hall, Inc., Englewood Cliffs, N.J., 1965, 120 pages.

Franklin R. Root, *Strategic Planning for Export Marketing*, Einar Hauck, Copenhagen, 1964, 146 pages.

Robert Bartels, *Comparative Marketing*, Richard D. Irwin, Inc., Homewood, Ill., 1963, 317 pages.

John S. Ewing and Frank Meissner, *International Business Management*, Wadsworth Publishing Company, Belmont, Calif., 1964, 560 pages.

David S. R. Leighton, *International Marketing: Text and Cases*, McGraw-Hill Book Company, New York, 1965, 675 pages.

Bibliography of Industrial and Distributive Trade Statistics, Statistical Series M, 36, United Nations, New York, 1965, provides annotated lists of statistical surveys and data pertaining to wholesaling, retailing, and such related services as production, sales, consumption, employment, structure of trade, inventories, fixed assets, and capital costs.

Periodicals. The best sources of information on periodical literature are *Check-list of Reports and Publications on International Operations*, the *Export Market Guides* (U.S. Department of Commerce), and such directories as *Combination Export Managers* (U.S. AID, Department of State); *Export Packers* (Port of New York Authority); *Stores of the World* (Newman Books, 68 Welbeck Street, London W1); and *Business Publication Rates and Data* (5201 Old Orchard Road, Skokie, Ill.), which features a monthly section on international trade with about 115 publications under some forty groupings.

In October 1965, the National Association of Credit Management (44 East 23d Street, New York 10010) started publishing a *Digest of Commercial Laws of the World*. It parallels the *U.S. Credit Manual of Commercial Laws*, which has been issued annually since 1908. Some fifty-six countries are included. For ease of comparison, each country chapter is laid out uniformly including such topics as contracts, agencies and representations, recognition of foreign judgments, executions, arbitrations, attachment, liens, assignments, and bankruptcy and composition.

Among the monthly publications one can refer to are *American Exporter* (in English and Spanish, 386 Park Avenue South, New York 10016); *Bureau of the Census Report FT 410* (U.S. Department of Commerce, Washington, D.C. 20233); *International Advertiser* (Hotel Roosevelt, 45th Street and Madison Avenue, New York 10017); and *International Trade Review* (Dun & Bradstreet, 99 Church Street, New York 10008).

Among the weeklies are *Business Abroad and Export Trade* (Thomas Ashwell and Co., 99 Church Street, New York 10007) and *International Commerce* (U.S. Department of Commerce)—an absolute must.

On a daily basis, one might refer to the "Foreign Buyers" column in the *Journal of Commerce*.

Worldcasts (Economic Index & Surveys, Inc., Colonnade Building, Cleveland, Ohio) contains over 15,000 foreign country forecasts from official government plans, newspapers, journals, bank letters, international agencies, and special studies. All the material is abstracted and systematically arranged by country and product. Composite forecasts through 1975—for population, GNP, major materials, energy sources, and key products—are presented for all major foreign countries.

The International Marketing and Management Group (4300 Prudential Tower, Boston) assists companies and trade organizations with counsel on marketing analysis and programming; mergers, acquisitions, joint ventures, and licensing; training of management, marketing, and sales personnel; and promotional support.

Business International Inc. (757 Third Avenue, New York 10017) provides the most comprehensive publishing and professional consulting service available in the United States.

The *publishing* activities consist of seven different types of reports: *Business International, Business Europe, Research Reports, ILT Service, Management Monographs, Round-Table Briefing Papers,* and *Latin American Business.*

1. The weekly *Business International* consists of six sections:
   a. *Case studies*—showing how individual firms solve problems of international organization, finance, export, taxation, personnel, and marketing.
   b. *Business outlooks*—on dozens of countries, aimed at helping find new export markets, forecast sales, time investments, judge credit risks, and check distributor performance.
   c. *New opportunities and dangers*—up-to-the-minute reports on currency controls, exchange allocations, trade agreements, tax treaties, and import regulations.
   d. *Investing and licensing conditions*—analysis of changing foreign laws affecting taxes, labor, foreign ownership, transfer of earnings and repatriation of capital, use of foreign-based companies, financing, and local incentives.
   e. *New sources of capital*—review of sources of funds for export sales, investments, and overseas corporate expansion.
   f. *Political and economic changes*—focus on developments in the European and Latin American common markets and free trade associations, plus vital political and market forecasts on a country-by-country basis.

2 and 3. *Business Europe* and *Latin American Business* are weeklies aimed specifically at firms doing business in Europe and in Latin America.

4. Periodically, BI publishes *Research Reports* on business prospects in a specific country and on successful development of key functions of international management.

5. Since October 1965, BI has issued a loose-leaf monthly *ILT Service* (*Investing, Licensing, and Trading Conditions in 50 Countries*).

6. In addition, BI issues occasional *Management Monographs,* which are brief action reports based on corporate experience with solving such specific problems as establishment of sales companies abroad, setting up a world-wide distributor network, after-sales servicing, and improving foreign distributor performance.

7. Since 1965, roundtables with cabinet ministers, presidents, or prime ministers have been held in Brazil, Italy, Argentina, Colombia, the Soviet Union, Japan, the United Kingdom, India, Spain, Mexico, Canada, the United States,

and with the officials and ministers of the EEC, LAFTA, and EFTA. For each roundtable, a *Briefing Paper* is published.

CONCLUSION

The balance of payments deficit will be with us for many years to come. The United States government will therefore continuously strive to encourage United States businessmen to expand their exports. Something like a rate of increase of 10 percent annually has been set as a goal.

To achieve this objective, the frame of mind of the majority of business executives in this country must be gradually changed: today they are "domestically oriented"; tomorrow they will need to consider the entire world to be their oyster.

This chapter has suggested some initial steps that will help bring about this reorientation.

CHAPTER THREE

Manufacturing Abroad

WICKHAM SKINNER *Associate Professor of Business Administration, Graduate School of Business Administration, Harvard University, Boston, Massachusetts*

Companies manufacturing abroad must deal not only with the problems inherent in domestic manufacturing, but with additional issues arising from the facts of international existence. The purpose of this chapter is to delineate these management problems and to explain their significance. Suggestions for dealing with these challenges in a variety of international settings are addressed to managers located at the overseas plants as well as to those at the corporate headquarters.

PROBLEMS INVOLVED IN INTERNATIONAL MANUFACTURING MANAGEMENT

International manufacturing management differs from the strictly domestic because three sets of problems are encountered when a corporation with headquarters in one nation owns[1] and operates a production facility in another nation. These are:

1. Problems which arise from operating in an environment differing from that of the corporation's home base

2. Problems which stem from delegating management functions to foreign nationals

3. Problems which result because the ownership and headquarters are in a different country from the plant

Environmental Differences. Differences in economic, political, and cultural environments force a management to decide whether to handle manufacturing functions—production control, procurement, labor relations, and the like—in the company's accustomed ways or attempt to adapt to the different environment. A company must decide which of its management tools, techniques,

---

[1] Ownership may be 100 percent or partial.

and attitudes are useful abroad and how much of its know-how to leave at home.

For example, a company transplanted an apparently successful incentive-wage plan to its ten international plants. In most locations, the plan appeared to work satisfactorily, but in several plants it was viewed as unfair. Labor trouble resulted. Another company with excellent domestic worker-company relationships offered its overseas plants neither a wage system nor advice on the conduct of labor relations, because they felt that "labor relations is a local problem and should be left to local people." These two companies took the opposite extreme positions on the issue of adapting to foreign conditions.

Neither company was wise to attempt to solve the dilemma of adaptation to a strange environment by a "yes" or "no" policy, for the particular circumstances at each location have a bearing. As a starting point, it is generally safe advice neither to transplant a production management system in its entirety nor to assume that there is little from headquarters or domestic plants that is applicable abroad. A flexible, situational point of view is required.

This point of view is difficult to acquire and exercise. The managers involved must possess an unusual personal skill and have a keen sense of perception relative to economic, political, and cultural environments which differ from their own. Special training and considerable experience are usually required to develop sound judgment in international manufacturing.

Delegating Management Functions to Foreign Nationals. The second set of problems arises from the necessity of delegating management responsibilities to men whose culture, education, and business training are generally different from those of managers in the parent company. National pressures for reducing the number of "foreign" managers sent overseas from the parent corporation are universal. Hence, staffing an overseas plant with experienced expatriate managers, seasoned and trained by the company itself, is seldom possible. In any case, worker supervision, with its impact on productivity, morale, and labor relations, must be performed by local nationals. Similarly, procurement and production control management at all but the very top levels are necessarily handled by local managers. Development of foreign national managers often progresses slowly. Surprisingly few companies have recognized the high costs of mediocre manufacturing performance that result from slow middle-management development.

A handful of corporate managers must develop and work with the indigenous management cadre. This requires coaching ability on the part of those overseas managers. It also offers opportunities to speed the process of management development by using headquarters or regional staff to assist in the improvement of men, policies, and practices.

Foreign Ownership. The third source of problems arises from foreign ownership. The international corporation has objectives and policies which make up its total strategy for growth and competition. The local plant must fit into this strategy and conduct its operations in a way that will benefit the corporation as a whole. But the local plant must also shape its policies and practices to be congruent with the needs of the nation in which it is located. This is a fact which is frequently repugnant to corporate managers who resent government interference, but it is a fact which cannot be avoided. For example, the nation may insist that the plant manufacture 90 percent or more of its needs, whereas the international corporation may wish to consolidate the sourcing of certain items in one location to gain economies of scale. International manufacturing requires the constant reconciliation of these points of view.

Geographical decentralization across international boundaries also introduces problems of organization, control, and communication between headquarters and branch plants.   Policy and corporate know-how must be transferred across political and cultural interfaces so that the corporation and its plants benefit from each other, cooperate, and prosper.

Overseas manufacturing problems center around who determines manufacturing policy, how control is obtained, and the headquarters services needed abroad.

Circumstances which are peculiar to the locality, nation, or culture must be taken into consideration at the corporate policy level.   Hence, manufacturing policy questions (such as whether the plant should expand, diversify, make a larger fraction of its total product, and the like) can rarely be answered unilaterally by the corporate headquarters.   For example:

> An American corporation turned down a capital appropriation requested by its subsidiary in India for a major diversification because the forecasted return on investment was less favorable than alternative uses of the corporation's funds.   The company's Indian management argued that once India's capacity for the commodity was adequate, the government would not permit other companies to invest in competitive facilities.   Nevertheless, the headquarters rejected the appropriation, a competitor built the plant, and the United States company has been blocked for many years from a major diversification which would have improved its competitive position.

ENVIRONMENTAL PROBLEMS IN MANUFACTURING ABROAD

It goes without saying that a company manufacturing abroad operates in a different environment than it does at home.   It is not so immediately evident, however, to what extent the foreign environment actually affects plant operations or requires managers to modify domestic production management practices.   The effects of the environment are often subtle and far reaching.

A manufacturing plant may be viewed as a system.   The system is composed of *workers* and *equipment* carrying out a *process* of transforming *materials* into a marketable *product*.   The ingredients of the system are guided and coordinated by a set of *policies and rules* designed to optimize productivity and profit.   When one part of the system changes, therefore, adjustments may be necessary in other parts of the system to keep it in balance.

The environment in which the production system operates affects costs, availability of materials and equipment, skills and attitudes of workers and managers, acceptable quality, and price of product, to mention several broad categories.   Therefore, a production system must be designed for its environment.

A specific example of how the foreign environment may invalidate a transferred production system is furnished by the manufacturer of an electrical-mechanical product in the Middle East.

> Equipment and tooling had been largely imported from Europe.   After six months of barely profitable operations, cost analyses indicated that the two primary factors in the company's poor showing were the high cost of local financing and inventory losses.   The equipment and tooling were designed for relatively long runs, which resulted in high average inventories of parts.   Because local capital was scarce, interest rates were about 2 percent per month (approximately four times greater than the United States rates and three times greater than those of Europe), which made a carrying cost of 24 percent per year.   In addition, poor material handling, storage, and record-keeping systems were causing an abnormally high loss and damage of parts in inventory.   Hence, the total carrying cost of inventory was nearly three times that in Europe.   And because the annual usage requirement was about one-fifth of that experienced in Europe, the net result

was an economic order quantity of about one-fourth of that for which the process tooling and equipment were established.

Thus, a change in interest rates and skills in materials handling and inventory control—both of which are environmental factors—caused a domino effect throughout the production system. To reduce inventories and lower costs, shorter runs were necessary. Engine lathes, for example, would have been more appropriate than turret lathes, which required different skills and training on the part of workers, setup men, and supervisors. Quality was adversely affected by shorter runs, loads on equipment increased, and production scheduling became more crucial. The managers faced the necessity of making wholesale changes in the entire system to make it more profitable and competitive.

If environmental differences are understood in advance, many of them can be taken into account and the production system designed to be appropriate to the circumstances.

Adjusting to Environmental Differences. Of course, manufacturing abroad often involves adjusting to environmental changes which, even though identified in advance, are apt to seem volatile and difficult to predict to foreigners. The starting point is a thorough analysis of the environment. For this purpose, a listing (Figure 3-1) of major environmental factors and some of their primary and secondary effects may be useful. The effects of these environmental factors may be many and the particular effects shown on Figure 3-1 are merely examples.

The cultural system is more difficult for most administrators to delineate than the economic, political, or technological environment, because values, beliefs, and philosophic assumptions are intangible. They are nevertheless as real as more easily measured differences such as interest rates or foreign-exchange controls, and failure to take the culture into account has typically resulted in baffled managers and antagonistic foreign nationals.

It is desirable for the overseas manager to be interested in cultural anthropology.[2] Although expertise is not necessary, it is fundamental to view a given set of values and beliefs as neither "right" nor "wrong" but rather as a result of people's responses to their environment and history. Some of the more essential elements of culture systems are shown in Figure 3-2, again with random examples of possible responses and the components of the production system which they may affect.

Finally, the expatriate firm must be especially concerned with the establishment of precedents and with public, government, and labor relations, because it is a guest whose continuation depends on the host government.

The complexities and difficulties of establishing and successfully managing foreign manufacturing plants should now be clear. The managers involved must (intuitively or explicitly) redesign their domestic production system so that it is appropriate to the economic, political, technological, and social facts of the adopted environment. When this is not done carefully, the unrealistic mismatching of equipment, policies, and organization results in excessive cost, lost production, antagonized government officials and workers, and constant fire-fighting by harried executives.

This is a stern warning. Yet the task of matching the system to the environment is one of great complexity. Even with the present tools and techniques of analyzing environments and synthesizing production systems, managers are seldom fully equipped and equal to the task. Imperfection, trial and error,

---

[2] Cultural anthropology is the study of man relative to the characteristic features of the behavior of a group of people who share the same environment and traditions.

Environmental factor	Some primary effects	Which in turn may affect
Economic:		
Cost of:		
Interest	Inventory, choice of equipment	Scheduling, labor skills, supervision
Materials and supplies	Procurement organization	Make or buy decisions
Labor	Equipment decisions	Training, wage system
Equipment	Technological strategy	Capital versus labor intensity, number of shifts, tooling
Taxes	Net profit	Return on investment
Utilities	Plant location	Choice of process
Local availability of:		
Foreign exchange	Ability to import	Make or buy, scheduling
Capital	Ability to borrow	Inventory policy
Workers	Selection, training	Labor relations
Subcontractors	Investment requirements	Technical skills required
Materials and supplies	Plant location	Equipment, maintenance
Technological level:		
Skills and knowledge of labor	Equipment and process	Training, supervision, maintenance organization
Supervision	Worker productivity	Labor relations
Engineers	Technical independence of overseas plant	Costs, quality, reliability of process
Middle management	Numbers and skills of expatriates needed	Needs for headquarters-staff services
Communications services	Customer, distributor, and vendor relations	Plant location, local offices
Vendors' skills	Quality, delivery	Amount and type of vendor assistance needed
Utilities	Reliability of service	Standby equipment
Transportation	Warehousing, inventory requirements	Planning, forecasting
Equipment, spare-parts availability	Plant downtime	Planning, inventory
Marketing situation:		
Purchasing power	Size of market	Scale of plant
Competitive prices	Operating margins	Cost-control system
Distribution channels	Delivery requirements, customer-service requirements	Scheduling, inventory controls
Political:		
Laws pertaining to foreign investment	Taxes, incentives, risk	Start-up process
Governmental attitudes toward foreign industry	Government cooperation with company	Middle-management organization
Permits, licenses, paper work	Need for men trained to handle government liaison	Lead times, schedules
Government regulation of:		
Manufactured content	Equipment needs	Costs and capital (required)
Prices	Operating margins	Manufacturing strategy
Working conditions and fringe benefits	Labor costs	Equipment strategy
Foreign exchange	Make or import	Increased local flexibility
Quality	Reduced freedom to change product specifications	Quality controls
Government involvement in company relationships	Labor relations	Increased concern with precedent
Employment of foreigners	Management development	Headquarters assistance

FIG. 3-1.   *The effects of an environment upon a production system.*

Environmental factor	Some primary effects	Which in turn may affect
Process and equipment.....	Use of secondhand or local equipment	Maintenance
Plant location.............	Labor supply, transportation	Choice of process
Expansion................	Expansion timing may not be ideal	Excess capacity or limited capacity
Profit repatriation.........	Financial policy	Modify objectives of local plant
Competition..............	Umbrella over prices	Dependence on government
Distribution..............	Channels established by government	Finished-goods stocks
Suppliers.................	Government monopolies	Quality and delivery from vendors
Political strength of economic interest groups, unions, farmers, business	Political climate re taxes, regulation, unions, importing	Procurement, labor relations
Social:		
Educational levels...........	Selection	Training
Urban/agricultural populations..................	Continuity of employment	Dollars invested in training
Population mobility.........	Plant location	Housing needs
Attitudes toward business....	Quality of managers available	Headquarters assistance
Union strength..............	Supervisory techniques	Grievance procedures
Position of minorities........	Interpersonal relations	Hiring practices
Democratic institutions......	Worker attitudes	Supervisory practices

FIG. 3-1.   *The effects of an environment upon a production system.*   (*Continued*)

and numerous failures are inevitable in even the most carefully thought out international manufacturing enterprise.   But the impossibility of a perfect matching of system and environment should not imply that efforts in that direction are wasted.

Guidelines for Environmental Adaptation.   Analysis of the experiences of many companies suggests the following guidelines for achieving congruence of a firm's production system with a foreign environment:

1. Describe the environment in as precise and explicit terms as possible, using the outlines in Figures 3-1 and 3-2 as a checklist.   The facts may be collected and assembled from a wide variety of sources: historical and anthropological literature about the country or area, discussions with personnel from other companies, marketing and staff personnel in the foreign country, government sources of both the United States and the foreign country, and legal representative overseas.

These data should be assembled and analyzed, preferably under the direction of the manager who is or will be responsible for the overseas operation.

2. Contrast the environmental conditions with conditions at another location where a company production plant is operating.   The latter plant should be one whose operation is both familiar and generally considered to be successful. Identify differences, using specific data and examples to highlight the differences.

3. Identify those foreign conditions which are essentially static or persisting and those which are in the process of or likely to be subject to change.

4. Identify and describe the company's technological requirements and basic policy constraints which must be considered as "givens," not subject to significant latitude or management choice.   These facts can be considered as a company environment which it takes wherever it goes.   They include minimum specifica-

Differences in these cultural factors	. . . affect a people's values and habits relating to	For example, the local employee might feel that	. . . and this would affect approaches in these (and other) areas of manufacturing management
I. Assumptions....	Time	Time is not measured in minutes, but in days and years.	Production control, scheduling, purchasing
	One's proper purpose in life	The only purpose which makes sense is to enjoy each day.	Management development
	The future	The future is not in man's hands.	Short- and long-range planning
	This life versus the hereafter	Life and death are completely ordained and predetermined.	Safety program
	Duty, responsibility	Your job is completed when you give an order to a subordinate.	Executive techniques of delegation and follow-up
II. Personal beliefs and aspirations	Right and wrong	I give the boss inventory counts which please him.	Inventory-control system
	Sources of pride	A college degree places one higher in society for life.	Selection of supervisors
	Sources of fear and concern	A man laid off finds it hard to get a job regardless of the cause of layoff.	Layoff policy
	Extent of one's hopes	Without the right education and social class, advancement is limited.	Incentives, motivation
	The individual versus society	The individual's own needs must be subordinated to the whole group.	Labor relations
III. Interpersonal...	The source of authority	My men don't like the new process. It won't work.	Quality control
	Care or empathy for others	I'd rather give my salary raise to my foreman than have to tell him he is not to receive one.	Merit reviews
	Importance of family obligations	I had to stay home because my father was sick.	Absenteeism
	Objects of loyalty	Friendship is more important than business.	Work-group relationships
	Tolerance for personal differences	If you don't agree with your boss, he will be insulted.	The decision-making process

FIG. 3-2. *The cultural system as it affects production management.* (*From* **C.** *Wickham Skinner, "Management of International Production,"* Harvard Business Review, *September–October, 1964.*)

Differences in these cultural factors	. . . affect a people's values and habits relating to	For example, the local employee might feel that	. . . and this would affect approaches in these (and other) areas of manufacturing management
IV. Social structure..	Interclass mobility	I'd refuse to work for a man who has no trade school certificate.	Promotion from within
	Class or caste systems	Men with my standing don't move heavy objects such as typewriters.	Job descriptions—flexibility of job assignment.
	Urban-village-farm origins	The company must take the place of the village in caring for its people.	Fringe-benefit programs
	Determinants of status	Elderly people have wisdom. They deserve the most important jobs on big machines.	Equipment selection

FIG. 3-2.   *The cultural system as it affects production management.*   (*Continued*)

tions on materials and products, identification of segments of the process which cannot be subcontracted or which require critical company control and know-how, proprietary information, and key policies relating to products, ownership, quality, and finance which the company considers inviolable.

5. Design the production system.   This is, of course, the most difficult step, because it requires synthesizing a practical and concrete plan from a combination of dozens of facts and variables.   A critical question is where to start and in what order to consider the different parts of the plan.   The decision sequence should lead from markets and strategy to product to process, thus making the most basic and critical decisions first.   The production system can then be built around the process.   When the process is determined, the equipment, organization, work force, procurement, control and planning systems, and the like can all be designed around that process.   The key environmental forces—marketing, economic, political, and social—affect all the production system decisions; hence, each decision must be checked not only for internal congruence with the rest of the system but for external congruence with each environmental factor.

A conceptual scheme for this analysis is shown in Figure 3-3.   The approach shown may be followed in the original design of a production system or in the reappraisal of an overseas manufacturing operation.   Eight sets of decisions are shown, taken in order from top to bottom.   In general, the arrows indicate a logical flow of thought and decisions—those on the same line can be worked out as a set, in parallel, and decisions on a lower line should typically follow all those on higher lines.

The simplicity of this format is not intended to suggest that the process itself is simple or that there are short cuts which can guarantee good results. Instead, the diagram's purpose is to indicate an orderly approach to a problem of considerable complexity.

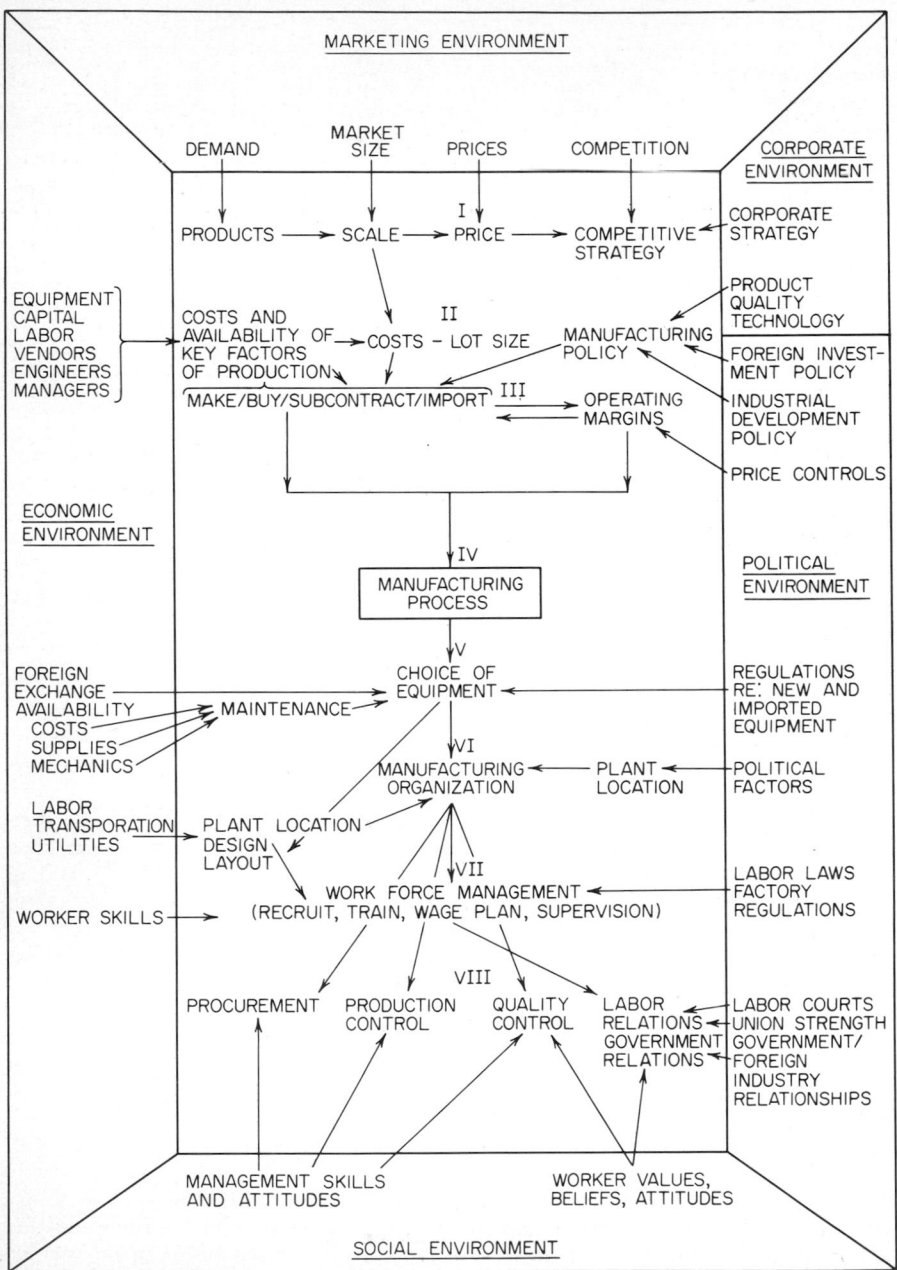

FIG. 3-3.   *Sequences and environmental influences in production system design for an international manufacturing plant.* (*Used by permission from the Division of Research, Harvard Business School.*)

Typical Problems Encountered. This discussion of the impact of foreign environments on manufacturing concludes with a short description of some typical problems encountered in several key management areas of international production operations, together with some lessons from experience.

Equipment and Process Decisions. The most common mistake in choosing equipment and processes is to copy them from another plant, typically a domestic plant. In so doing, the company ignores a different cost mix, and often a different product specification, lot size, maintenance capability, scale of production, and labor and supervisory training demands as well.

Such mistakes often come about because of one or more of three contributing causes:

1. Original equipment decisions are usually made at headquarters by engineers who are not always familiar enough with the environment abroad to specify appropriate facilities.

2. Production managers consider equipment decisions "technical" and delegate them to engineers without realizing that equipment and process decisions largely determine the makeup of the entire production system and thereby involve far more than technical aspects. Designing from a distance, engineers sometimes tend to "play it safe," overspecify, and apply the same equipment they have used elsewhere instead of flexibly adapting the process to the new environment.

3. Overseas manufacturing plants are frequently understaffed in industrial engineering talent. Reequipment and process improvement are apt to be done "by the book" instead of tailored to fit the environment.

For example, at a plant in eastern Europe a superintendent ordered a new piece of equipment which he felt would make savings. It was approved by the headquarters because it had been used in other locations. When asked how long it would take to pay for itself, the superintendent said, "Oh, I'm sure that it will pay for itself very soon." On-the-scene analysis indicated that the machine could not possibly pay for itself in less than eight years.

Inadequate industrial engineering is most frequent where labor rates are low. But capable industrial engineering is needed even where labor is cheap to increase productivity from relatively expensive equipment and to develop economic processes which are appropriate to the requirements of the plant's total environment.

Manufacturing Organization. In different environments, different parts of the organization become more or less critical. Organizational structure can place emphasis where it is needed. For example, assigning a key function as a full-time activity of one manager who reports to the top executive gives it attention and raises its status. But it is expensive to give each function its own executive, and similarly, every function cannot report to the top. Hence, organizations must be designed to fit the situation.

One environment may place a premium on effective management of the maintenance function. For example, if spare parts are limited in supply, skilled mechanics are rare, and the economics or technology requires the use of closely linked equipment, when one machine fails a large part of the plant has to shut down. Tire plants in India, for example, are dependent on capable maintenance management.

Frequently, organizations are not adapted to environments abroad but are transplanted as they are from one country to another. Many companies tend to use the same basic organization world-wide. Other companies let the head man at each location set up his own organization, but often this does not result in an organization which fits the environment, for the executive organizes the plant in accordance with his own previous experience and biases.

Work-force Management.   Many companies have found that the initial recruiting, selecting, training, compensating, and supervising of workers in a foreign country are simpler than expected.   Surprisingly, the problems often seem to magnify after the first several years, particularly in the process of improving productivity and quality levels through training and first-line supervision.

It has been proved repeatedly in many types of manufacturing, from Brazil to France to India, that workers can be taught how to operate highly complex machinery with adequate proficiency in three to six months.   But adjustment to the discipline, time demands, and necessity for cooperation essential to daily industrial life has frequently proved more difficult and time consuming than learning manual skills.

Appraising worker morale and productivity through the filter of a strange culture via indigenous supervisors is a further challenge.   It is difficult for managers abroad to know what is going on.

Yet productivity must increase to meet growing competition and narrowing operating margins.   This requires developing more advanced skills in the work force and more effective supervisors.   The harried expatriate and his inexperienced middle management often need trained assistance from headquarters.

Overseas managers generally receive little help from the home office in handling this type of problem.   Headquarters can hamper the process by exerting too much control over specific personnel policies and practices, while simultaneously offering inadequate transfer of knowledge and experience from one location to another.

There are many indications in foreign manufacturing plants that hard-earned expertise developed over many years could be useful abroad.   Too often, work-force management is perceived as a "local problem" and principles of respect for the individual, improved communications, and employee participation are not transferred overseas.

Labor Relations.   A well-developed sense of perspective is a prime requisite for effective labor relations abroad because company-worker relationships appear to grow and evolve through stages which are difficult to recognize amidst the current situation, although clearly discernible over the years.   The stages are influenced by a wide variety of factors:

   a. Cultural attitudes and beliefs of workers and managers

   b. The political environment for labor unions

   c. Structure of labor and industrial laws affecting workers, wages, bargaining, grievances, health, and safety

   d. Precedents established in country, area, and factory

   e. Company policies and practices in work-force management, especially wages, grievance handling, supervision, and training

The author's study of many plants in eight countries suggests that an overseas plant's labor relations tend to pass through five stages over a period of time:

Stage	*General Characteristics*
1. Family style................	Company strong and organized relative to workers. A paternal management deals with employees as individuals.
2. Skirmishing................	Protests from workers. Grievances, union organizing, immature worker organization.
3. Open battle................	Both sides take ideological positions. Strikes, sabotage, use of power by company and workers.
4. Postwar..................	Acceptance of workers' and management's rights. Relationships structured with clear procedures and precedents.
5. Industrial peace...........	Recognition of mutual interests. Strong, mature leadership.

The length and intensity of each stage depend on the factors listed above, and in particular on *e*, the company's labor practices. In some plants, for example, it has been possible to bypass the open-battle period.

Managers in stage 1 often do not realize that as workers become accustomed to factory life some form of industrial protest[3] is almost inevitable, and they fail to prepare for it. They see labor relations as a "snap," with labor docile and unions weak. They are disappointed and antagonistic when workers later become "ungrateful" and "union-minded."

In periods of skirmishing or strife, managers with a sense of perspective can recognize that more peaceful relationships can be developed as labor organizations mature and both company and workers accept each other's "rights" as natural and normal, and as adequate and satisfying procedures are worked out for handling grievances and negotiations.

Controls of Production. Many companies assume that abroad, where the scale of operation is often small and the costs of labor are relatively low, the careful control of costs, quality, and inventories is "frosting" and largely unnecessary. Frequently, therefore, controls of production are loose and excessively informal by United States standards.

In reality, overseas environments actually require exceptional competence in the control of production. Newly trained workers who lack a sense of product quality and mechanical intuition may make quality control especially difficult. Limited capacity of relatively expensive equipment, price controls, the necessity of using local materials, and increasing competition often add up to a requirement for better cost controls. High interest rates, long lead times, limited local capital, and lack of adequate quantitative orientation on the part of inventory clerks and production-control supervisors require close attention to inventory control in many overseas locations.

Production controls, by their very nature, must be largely delegated to lower and middle management whose skill in handling a myriad of details largely determines the effectiveness of the system. Further, a surprisingly high degree of sophistication is required to develop special systems for economic conditions differing from those of the United States. Transplanting domestic systems will usually not suffice. For this reason, headquarters and overseas staff assistance is especially needed to develop systems, approaches, and lower- and middle-management skills. Here is another area where a "local problem" cannot be delegated solely to local people.

Procurement. Procurement problems are commonplace and often highly troublesome abroad. Even in Europe, vendors frequently fail to satisfy the needs of foreign manufacturing plants. The problems generally center around reliability of delivery promises and quality standards.

Sometimes the problems are culturally derived. The vendor's notions of adequate quality and the importance of time differ from those of his customer. Or the problem may be one of adapting to specifications which are unfamiliar. Frequently, there is inadequate competition, and the vendors simply do not have sufficient incentive.

Procurement, for these reasons, is often a management area which calls for more attention and expertise than is necessary in a domestic operation. Development of vendors may take years of special attention by an experienced and expert team. This is expensive, but nationalistic laws very often require local purchasing. Top management must recognize that procurement problems have

[3] See Clark Kerr, John T. Dunlop, Frederick H. Harbison, and Charles A. Myers, *Industrialism and Industrial Man,* Harvard University Press, Cambridge, Mass., 1960.

been one of the most frequent causes of major failures and problems in overseas manufacturing.

PROBLEMS WHICH STEM FROM DELEGATING MANAGEMENT FUNCTIONS TO FOREIGN NATIONALS

Inherent in manufacturing abroad is the necessity of entrusting much of the management of the plant to foreign nationals. Daily decisions in production scheduling and control, procurement, and supervision of the work force must be made by foreign nationals regardless of their experience and capabilities. In domestic branch plants, new lower and middle managers can be supported and closely supervised by an ample number of more experienced men from the parent corporation. Abroad, because of cost, distance, and nationalistic pressures, it is usually not possible to cover the plant with enough headquarters expatriates for sufficient years to train a competent local team.

The central problem is inexperience—inexperience in manufacturing in general, in the particular industry, and with the specific company. No one nationality has a monopoly on effective management of manufacturing plants any more than only one nationality can efficiently run a turret lathe or assemble electronics components. But there are ingredients in the experience of a competent manufacturing manager which take time to acquire and assimilate.

Some of these ingredients are present when a trained and experienced manager goes to work for a different company, but even he requires time to learn the particular customs, policies, and ways of his new firm. If the new company is a foreign-based firm, the amount to learn is generally much greater.

Similarly, the requirements for new learning are enlarged if the manager's experience has been in another industry, and further expanded if he must adapt to industry from a prior post in government, military, or other nonfactory occupation. If the candidates are from a non-Western culture, the requirements are greatest of all, because certain elements of Western culture—particularly its emphasis on time and personal responsibility—are usually assumed in the management of an international firm. Pictorially the adaptation requirements are shown in Figure 3-4, with each adaptation building on those below it.

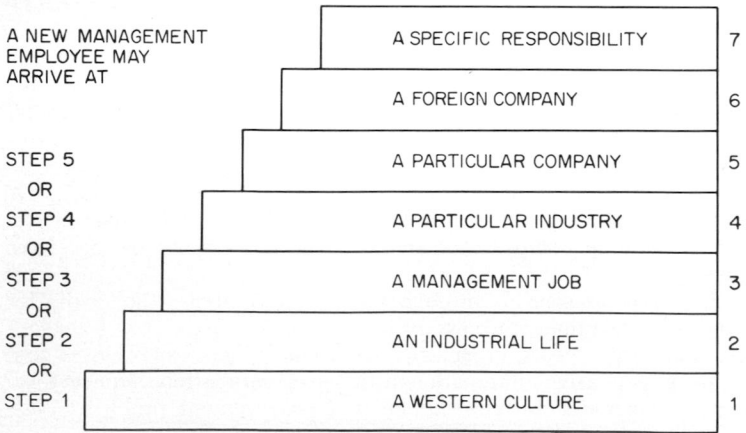

A NEW MANAGEMENT EMPLOYEE MAY ARRIVE AT	A SPECIFIC RESPONSIBILITY	7
	A FOREIGN COMPANY	6
STEP 5 OR	A PARTICULAR COMPANY	5
STEP 4 OR	A PARTICULAR INDUSTRY	4
STEP 3 OR	A MANAGEMENT JOB	3
STEP 2 OR	AN INDUSTRIAL LIFE	2
STEP 1	A WESTERN CULTURE	1

FIG. 3-4. *Seven steps in a foreign manager's adaptation to his job in a United States foreign-based company.*

With all these adjustments to be made by foreign national managers, it is no wonder that expatriate production managers are typically disappointed over the performance of their subordinates. Foreign managers are often criticized by headquarters and expatriates for one or more of the following attributes:

1. Being idealistic and impractical
2. Magnifying their position, status, and responsibility out of proportion to reality
3. Working too little
4. Failing to follow through and take responsibility
5. Carelessness about time
6. Technical incompetence
7. Showing poor judgment
8. Paternalism in their personnel practices

Many of these criticisms are imprecise labels open to various interpretations and meanings. Many represent the frustrated complaints of expatriates who have been unable to communicate satisfactorily with their subordinates or counterparts, do not understand their behavior, and therefore condemn their performance. Such criticisms are natural, but they are also unfortunate because although frequently justified, they accomplish little but building resentment and mutual dissatisfaction. Hence, it is not surprising to find foreign nationals equally critical of United States managers.

Understanding and Developing Foreign National Managers. To move beyond mutual criticism, managers of foreign manufacturing need special skills and insights in selecting, managing, and developing their foreign national managers. Specifically, the expatriate manager has four problems:

1. Determining how effective his foreign managers are going to be
2. Minimizing production problems and failures during the learning period
3. Maximizing the development rate of the foreign managers
4. Dealing with his own frustrations and difficulties during the maturing period of his managers

Neither the approach of "when in Rome, do as the Romans do"—adapting to the foreigner, respecting his methods of managing, delegating fully—nor the approach of "this is an American company; they must learn to do things our way" is an effective way of dealing with these four problems. Instead, it is more practical to think about the problem in a different frame of reference.

Several ingredients appear essential in developing workable ways of handling these four problems. Basically, they all depend upon the manager improving his understanding of foreign managers. This is a complex task which calls upon many disciplines: anthropology, psychology, political science, economics, and organizational behavior. The critical ingredients are:

1. To recognize, identify, and isolate how particular foreign managers, as individuals, behave and work
2. To determine which deviations from conventional or expected company, industry, and managerial behavior are actually important and which are merely surprising or annoying
3. To develop specific ways of dealing with important shortcomings and differences on the part of foreign managers

The first calls for some specific approaches to analyzing individuals' behavior. The managerial grid[4] is one good approach. A questionnaire[5] developed by

[4] See Robert R. Blake and Jane S. Mouton, *The Managerial Grid*, Gulf Publishing Company, Houston, Tex., 1964.
[5] Mason Haire, Edwin E. Chiselli, and Lyman W. Porter, "Cultural Patterns in the Role of the Manager," *Industrial Relations*, vol. 2, no. 2, February, 1963.

Mason Haire and associates is another example of a useful tool. This analytical pattern examines managers' beliefs and values: (1) leadership beliefs, (2) beliefs about the manager's role, (3) motivations and needs, and (4) the degree of satisfaction of these motivations or needs achieved by the managers. Finally, a study of managers in terms of Figure 3-2 can also lead to useful insights.

The common element in these approaches is that the expatriate (or head-quarters executive) attempts to understand his managers instead of criticizing. Group discussions and training sessions are used by some companies to help develop the skills of understanding in their managers.

Evaluating the effects of the differences in managers is the second ingredient. This, too, is difficult. But much is accomplished by the attitude of questioning and searching rather than condemning.

Culturally derived differences between expatriates and foreign national managers are not all bad; many expatriates tend to criticize foreign managers for any divergencies from their own conventional behavior. Differences in dress, in religion, and in beliefs about the future, optimism, democracy, and the uniqueness of each individual are relatively immaterial to managerial performance, although they may be annoying and disturbing. By and large, these differences are because of lack of Westernization (step 1 in Figure 3-4). For example, the fatalistic manager who does not believe that his own energy can bring about change may need close and persistent supervision but, properly led, he can become efficient at carrying out assigned tasks.

Differences due to lack of industrialization (step 2 in Figure 3-4) are more serious, yet somewhat more susceptible to change. Industrial life has imperatives of time, cooperation, self-discipline, and consistent application of effort and attention to details which are not demanded by nonindustrial occupations—farm, government, education, or military. These imperatives are built into the very nature of manufacturing. A manager new to industrial life in any country has much to learn and many old habits and outlooks to change.

A third important area of analysis is the amount of pertinent industrial management experience a manager has had (steps 3 and 4 in Figure 3-4). Experience in a copper mill may be scarcely applicable to a job in a food processing plant. But new skills and knowledge may be transferred in due course with application and training.

In summary, the "foreign" differences which matter are more apt to be inadequate industrial experience and disciplines and less apt to be lack of Westernization, even though the latter characteristics may be more difficult to change and more readily apparent. To help a manager develop, his superior must carefully attempt to identify his deviations from truly important habits, attitudes, and beliefs. This approach is more likely to net results than labeling him "impractical" or "irresponsible."

Development of Coaching Relationships. The final ingredient necessary for dealing better with foreign managers is the development of coaching relationships to replace superior-subordinate relationships. It is becoming a cliché to state that the expatriate must be a teacher and a coach, but the practice of listening (as a good teacher would) is an administrative technique which is useful not only for developing managers but in communicating acceptable and accepting attitudes to them.

The process of coaching and teaching involves the expatriate in many details, and it provides information which can help him prevent mistakes while training a foreign manager. It is not a "let him sink or swim" process, but one in which the expatriate involves himself in all aspects of the job, observing, listening, and explaining.

It should be clear now that members of the headquarters staff can and should be very useful in the early years of any new foreign plant. Their role, too, must be in coaching and training, becoming involved in all manner of local operating problems and details. This violates the rule that a staff manager should stay out of details, a rule which is often invalid overseas where a plant has managers who simultaneously have many steps to climb in their adaptation process.

PROBLEMS DERIVED FROM THE FACT THAT OWNERS AND PLANT ARE IN DIFFERENT COUNTRIES

There are two kinds of problems which arise because the owners and plant are in different countries. The first has to do with the compatibility between the international corporation and the host government and conditions in the foreign country. The second deals with problems of administration at a distance across international barriers.

Relations with Foreign Governments. Problems often erupt because the plant's policies and operations may not serve the international corporation and the foreign nation equally well. For example, the foreign government may require the use of local materials which are expensive or off-grade and which increase costs to the point where the firm cannot compete in the nearby export market.

Something must give in these conflicts. Sometimes governments can be persuaded, but more often, the international corporation must adapt. A number of United States firms have pulled out of countries rather than accede to apparently unreasonable government demands. This has usually proved to be short-sighted. In the long run, the country's markets remain and grow, and the government is forced to moderate unwise economic policies.

Analysis of corporate experience abroad suggests two critical conditions which should be met before a company decides to invest in a manufacturing plant abroad:

1. The company's needs and plans for the plant should be congruent with the long-range requirements of the host nation.

2. The company's anticipated investment and returns should be realistic in terms of the competitive conditions existing or forthcoming in the industry in the host country.

The first condition involves these manufacturing considerations:

a. Products and markets served

b. Plant location

c. Equipment and processes

d. Make versus buy; local versus import

e. Labor relations—personnel policies

f. Use of expatriates

g. Local financing of work in process

The second condition is concerned with the corporation's realistic assessment of the competitive situation in the local industry. In particular, the company should carefully examine the operating margins available and projected, that is, the difference between prices and costs of materials, labor, and manufacturing equipment. This spread must be adequate to cover marketing and administrative costs and profit. Its breadth is a good clue to the possibility of successful competition. It will reveal the emphasis necessary on each *part* of the production system if it is to be viable.

In seeking compatibility between corporate strategy and local conditions, it has proved valuable to recognize as realities foreign government objectives and competitive conditions which are difficult to change.   Usually, the international corporation must do the adapting.   The expatriate company operates in the spotlight of the foreign nation's public opinion and government attention.   The role of a "foreign investor" is fraught with delicate relationships.   Sensitive nationalistic feelings often create political and public relations pressures.

Administering the International Manufacturing Corporation.   There is nothing new about managing geographically decentralized organizations across international boundaries.   Roman emperors, world-wide religious orders, colonial systems, and the British Admiralty faced these problems hundreds of years ago.   In commerce, the East India, Hudson Bay Trading, and the Balfour-Guthrie Companies operated profitably long before the post-World War II flood of United States investments abroad.   These enterprises faced the same task as modern international corporations: achieving effective operating controls and policy direction from remote headquarters.   In overseas manufacturing, this broad problem boils down to three key issues:

1. The nature of home-office control
2. The nature of home-office support
3. The nature and type of the communications between the home office and overseas plants

Although the issue of home-office control is usually debated in terms of "centralization" versus "decentralization," this dichotomy is rarely meaningful in conducting international manufacturing operations.   Situations differ in terms of key variables in manufacturing, the nature of the environment, and the developed abilities of local executives.   Appropriate controls and influence from headquarters are entirely different from one plant to another.   It is a mistake, therefore, to attempt "a philosophy" or take a position on how much or what type of controls "our company" should exert.   But unfortunately, many companies do attempt to apply one universal approach to this facet of international management.

In contrast, it appears more sensible to examine each situation in terms of critical variables: the competitive situation, the aspects of manufacturing most vital to success (procurement, work-force productivity, equipment maintenance, and the like), and the strengths of the overseas management relative to the task.   The inputs needed from headquarters are those necessary to fill the gap between tasks required and skills available abroad.

In tailoring headquarters administration to the needs at each foreign plant, it is necessary to establish where and how decisions should be made, ranging from broad policy and planning to specific operating decisions.   The "where" and "how" affect the amount of headquarters control.   But the concept of "headquarters control" is too vague to be very useful.   More precise terms are needed.

In fact "headquarters control" can be divided into two key facets: *involvement* and *command*.   A headquarters can be highly involved but exert only minimum command over a foreign plant if it keeps in close contact with progress and problems abroad and if its charter allows it to offer advice which the local plant is free to accept or reject.   No one combination of involvement and command is "right" for all situations.   Figure 3-5 describes and graphically represents the range of possible combinations of involvement and command.   This matrix is not intended to be definitive but to demonstrate the possibility of different headquarters-plant relationships in each functional area of manufacturing.   A company should explicitly decide what combination is best for each functional manufacturing area—manufacturing policy, procurement, work-force management, equipment and process, labor relations, and controls of production.   These decisions should be reviewed annually to ensure that the chosen point in the matrix for each area (and the entire set of administrative practices which follows from each matrix point) is in keeping with the actual situation.

Degrees of command

Degrees of involvement	A. Observe and advise if requested. Approve capital budgets.	B. Observe and offer unilateral advice. Approve capital budgets.	C. Command per B plus approve annual budgets on capital and operating expenditures.	D. Command per C plus require policy plans and decisions to be submitted for advance approval.	E. Command per C plus require approval of any deviations from budget and any changes in operations or procedures.
I. No headquarters involvement. Reporting is only on broad overall basis and infrequent.					
II. Involvement in general policy, objectives, strategy, long-term planning. Receives frequent information on overall results.					
III. Involvement per II plus more detailed reports on results. Participate in short-range planning. Participation in general approaches for achieving aims, i.e., organization, general systems.					
IV. Involvement per III plus participates in procedures, specific approaches, and local controls. Reports more detailed and frequent.					
V. Involvement per IV plus regular deep involvement in specific operating decisions, schedules, manpower, expenses. Constant information required.					

FIG. 3-5. *Selecting the appropriate degrees of headquarters involvement and command.*

CONCLUSION

The quality of the job performed by the headquarters staff is a critical ingredient to success in manufacturing abroad. In many cases, it is the single most vital requisite to improved production performance overseas.

This conclusion grows out of analysis of the experiences of international firms in handling the three principal sets of problems discussed in this chapter. The environmentally derived problems are moderated by tailoring the production system in its original design and subsequent adjustments to the total environment. This is a demanding task calling for situational thinking and many skills. Managers assigned to overseas plants can play a major role in this task, but they need the specialized support and unbiased analytical outlook of a trained headquarters staff.

In each functional area discussed (procurement, work-force management, and so on), the overseas plants typically need more headquarters assistance. Leaving "local problems to local personnel" has often been a mistake, for foreign managers generally can benefit from accumulated know-how relating to operating problems and systems. The expatriate manager is seldom able to transmit this experience in more than one or two areas.

For the same reason, problems arising from the necessity of delegating management functions to inexperienced foreign nationals can be mitigated by the use of a headquarters staff to assist the overseas management in the massive coaching and training job often needed.

Problems in administering the international manufacturing firm center around achieving compatibility between corporation and foreign nation while competing successfully. Developing the overseas company's plans and competitive strategy so that they are congruent with the needs of the firm as a whole and its host country requires a breadth of viewpoint which a home-office staff can develop by repeated experience throughout the world.

The control issue is clarified by separating control into two ingredients—involvement and command. The thrust of this discussion is that headquarters should emphasize more involvement and less command. In fact, a headquarters actually controls overseas plant managers very little. Attempts at control are normally resented and confuse the assignment of responsibility. Thus, less command is more realistic and appropriate when accompanied by more responsible involvement.

The complexity of managing foreign operations demands broad training, insights, and experience. Men need to be particularly competent and mature to be effective either as expatriates or in headquarters manufacturing positions. To succeed in international business, a company must be willing to assign a full share of its best talent to manage its manufacturing.

BIBLIOGRAPHY

Abegglen, J. C., *The Japanese Factory,* The Free Press of Glencoe, New York, 1958.

Barlow, E. R., *Management of Foreign Manufacturing Subsidiaries,* Harvard Business School, Boston, 1953.

Brooks, T. R., "Labor, the 'X' Factor Abroad," *Dun's Review & Modern Industry,* May, 1962.

Drucker, Peter, "Modern Technology and Ancient Jobs," *Technology and Culture,* vol. 4, no. 3, 1963.

Fenn, D., *Management Guide to Overseas Operations.* McGraw-Hill Book Company, New York, 1957.

Kerr, Clark, John T. Dunlop, Frederick H. Harbison, and Charles A. Myers, *Industrialism and Industrial Man*, Harvard University Press, Cambridge, Mass., 1960.

Lambert, Richard D., *Workers, Factories, and Social Change in India*, Princeton University Press, Princeton, N.J., 1963.

Levine, S. B., *Industrial Relations in Postwar Japan*, University of Illinois Press, Urbana, 1958.

Management of Industrial Enterprises in Underdeveloped Countries, UN Department of Economic and Social Affairs, New York, 1958.

Savage, Charles H., Jr., *Social Reorganization in a Factory in the Andes*, Monograph no. 7, Society for Applied Anthropology, Ithaca, N.Y., 1964.

Skinner, C. W., "Management of International Production," *Harvard Business Review*, September–October, 1964.

Skinner, C. W., *Production Management in U.S. Manufacturing Subsidiaries in Turkey*, doctoral thesis, Harvard Business School, Boston, 1961.

Skinner, C. W., "A Test Case in Turkey," *California Management Review*, Spring, 1964.

Skinner, C. W., "Wanted: Frontier Managers," *Dicta*, Virginia Law School, Charlottesville, April, 1960.

U.S. Business Performance Abroad (series including Sears in Mexico, Firestone in Liberia, Stauvac in Indonesia, Grace in Peru, and others), National Planning Association, Washington, D.C.

Willner, Ann R., "A Case Study of a Javanese Factory," *Human Organization*, Summer, 1963.

CHAPTER FOUR

International Licensing Arrangements

EUGENE M. LANG   *President, Resources and Facilities Corporation, New York, New York*

Licensing has become an increasingly important tool of international trade. In part, it has been used to overcome export barriers such as tariffs, import quotas, and the lack of "hard currency" purchasing power. However, licensing has also become a preferred technique for solidly penetrating foreign markets and for meeting local competitors on more equal terms. Smaller manufacturers in particular have been attracted by the fact that licensing tends to minimize the commitment of capital and executive personnel in achieving overseas objectives.

THE LICENSING CONCEPT

In essence, licensing represents a simple concept: one party (the licensor) grants to another party (the licensee) certain rights to manufacture and sell a product (or to use a process) under specified patents, trademarks, technical "know-how," or any combination of these proprietary values. In return, the licensor receives various considerations from the licensee. Special conditions adapt the relationship to the individual circumstances and objectives of the parties. These grants and considerations, together with conditions related to the mechanics of their fulfillment, are embodied in the instrument of licensing—the license agreement.

License Agreement Terms. License rights can be granted exclusively for a specified territory, nonexclusively to more than one licensee, or exclusively for one territory and nonexclusively for others. An exclusive licensee may be given the right to sublicense others, generally or under specified circumstances.

The licensor may further agree to furnish engineering, manufacturing, and marketing services, and quality-control assistance. The latter is particularly significant if the license includes the right to use the licensor's trademark. The licensor may also undertake to furnish special product designs and equipment or personnel.

The scope, content, and duration of a license agreement are influenced by characteristics of the individual product. These characteristics include the range of product application and sales potential in the licensed territory, the strength of patent protection, the cost of furnishing technical data, the value of technical know-how, the cost of initiating production, and the prospects for rapid market acceptance. Rights under a license are granted for a stipulated period of time—five years, ten years, the life of patents, and the like—with renewal and cancellation clauses.

In return for the rights and services he provides, the licensor receives a royalty, usually based on sales or output of the licensee. To stimulate adequate effort by the licensee, a minimum annual royalty may be required. Royalties may be supplemented by an initial cash payment, perhaps as a fee for engineering and other services. In addition to cash considerations, the licensor may receive full or partial rights to improvements, patentable or not, which the licensee may develop. He also may receive rights to existing patents or products of the licensee.

Supplementing the basic exchange of considerations, a license agreement should spell out the mechanics for fulfilling commitments and for handling contingencies. These mechanics cover items such as royalty payment procedure, maintenance of records, method of giving notice or exchanging data, cancellation conditions, resolution of differences, patent litigation, and rights of inspection. The areas of responsibility and obligation of both parties should be clearly demarcated so far as language permits.

Frequently, a licensee may prefer to give equity participation in lieu of all or part of cash engineering fees and royalties. Likewise, a licensor may prefer equity participation, particularly if the know-how aspects of a license relationship cannot be supported by valuable trademarks and patents. Under this circumstance, equity in the foreign operation may be the best way to establish a secure long-term interest. It may even be advantageous to enlarge such equity by a supplemental capital contribution or by using future royalties to pay for additional shares.

When a company takes an equity position with foreign associates, the undertaking becomes a joint venture in which elements of a license may or may not be retained. It is often felt that the most satisfactory relationship combines the growth aspects of equity participation with the surer income of licensing.

Reasons for Licensing. The adoption of licensing as an avenue to world markets must be carefully weighed. Many companies turn to licensing only when they see little prospect of developing or maintaining a satisfactory volume of export sales, and/or because they are unable or unwilling to set up overseas manufacture of their own.

To license, however, merely because or when other export techniques seem deficient is not wise. The implications and commitments of a license relationship can be far too important. On the other hand, even if export or investment alternatives seem favorable, licensing may often provide distinctive advantages. For example, licensing may be a means to maintain an existing relation with important customers, to obtain access to new products or development capabilities, to acquire sales and service outlets for unlicensed products, or to obtain tax advantages or other benefits that a particular local situation may offer.

The desirability of licensing is affected by the circumstances of each company (size, capital availability, ownership); of each product (complexity, patentability, exportability); and of each market (size, competition, governmental regulations). Moreover, the world market is so broad and complex that the adoption of licensing to develop one market does not preclude alternative export forms in other areas.

PREPARATION FOR LICENSING

Before embarking on a licensing program, a company should take three important preparatory steps: establish executive direction, appraise licensable values, and determine licensing objectives.

Executive Direction. A licensing program should be planned and carried out under the authority of a qualified executive.   So far as possible, qualifications should include knowledge of foreign markets, languages, business practices, and regulations, as well as specific product knowledge.   Experience in international trade and negotiations, coupled with an ability to work well with people of other nationalities and business environments, is also desirable.   License relationships, more than most company-to-company associations, tend to be influenced and nourished by the quality of personal contact.

Determining Licensable Values. Licensable values—product and proprietary— must be objectively appraised.   Product must be considered in terms of its sales and profit potential in territories where manufacture is contemplated.   This potential focuses, in varying degrees, on factors such as basic market statistics, the nature of local competition, availability of raw materials, industrial or consumer standards that must be met, and the cost of setting up manufacture.   It varies with each market and with the facilities and experience that prospective licensees may provide.

The profit potential of a product in a given market is significantly governed by the extent to which it is or can be protected by patents, trademarks, and know-how.   Thus, proprietary values—the strength of patent claims, the status of trademark recognition, the ability to control secrecy of manufacturing knowhow—must be realistically assessed.

Licensing Objectives. Objectives to be sought from licensing must be considered.   A prospective licensor should develop a reasonably defined idea of the benefits he seeks and what he is able and willing to offer for them.   Such benefits can be cash income (short term or long term), technical exchange, creation of export potential for product components, overseas product sources, or tax and special personal advantages.

It should also be anticipated that licensing objectives may change in nature or emphasis as the conditions and opportunities become apparent during the course of negotiation.   Accordingly, licensing should be approached with reasonable open-mindedness so that the "give and take" of negotiation can permit the most equitable and profitable mating of advantages that licensor and licensee can exchange.

Gathering Needed Information. The problem of obtaining and evaluating foreign market information can be formidable.   As a starting point, the U.S. Department of Commerce is recommended, both for the general data it continuously assembles and for the facilities it provides, to obtain specific information in relation to individual licensing projects.   Harnessed to this are the local fact-finding capabilities of American embassies and consulates.

Banks, credit agencies, international airlines and shipping companies, trade associations, and chambers of commerce can also be useful sources of information.   Many countries maintain trade-promotion offices in the United States.

Published professional services can provide essential background data concerning taxes, legal details, and special political or regulatory problems that may apply in given countries.   Supplementing these sources are many professional people and agencies, in the United States and abroad, who can carry out factfinding surveys, furnish valuable guidance in assembling and evaluating information, and deal specifically with the specialized aspects of negotiating and establishing license relationships.

During the fact-finding process, a prospective licensor, armed with information from these sources, should visit the markets where he intends to license. He should have some "feel" of these territories and of the operating situations of possible licensees in relation to his product, its manufacture, and its sale.

PLANNING THE LICENSE RELATIONSHIP

The negotiation of any license relationship raises questions that require special precaution and prudent consideration. Some of the more general questions are commented upon below.

What Shall We Ask for a License? A prospective licensor must place a "price" on his license. This price can variably consist of an initial payment (perhaps for blueprints or technical services), a royalty, and an annual minimum royalty guarantee. It may also require the licensee to purchase certain parts or additives from the licensor.

The figures and percentages must yield sufficient income to make it worthwhile for the licensor to grant the license, while permitting the licensee to profit from its exploitation.

Depending on the product and technology, initial payments can range from zero to hundreds of thousands of dollars. Occasionally, an initial payment can be, wholly or in part, a prepayment of royalties for a specified period of time.

The royalty rate is governed by the nature of the product, its profitability, and competitive factors. Royalty rates can range from ¼ to 1 percent of net sales of products produced by a particular process, to 15 percent for complex apparatus having limited sales possibilities. Royalties can also be assessed on the basis of units of production, different product applications, or markets served. They can be assessed on a sliding scale based on volume, time period, or a combination of both.

A minimum royalty is primarily intended to assure that the licensee will actively exploit his franchise. Thus, its size and conditions vary with the circumstances of the contracting parties. The minimum royalty may be an absolute requirement or may merely confer on the licensor a right to cancel if the minimum payment is not made. It may go into effect only after a reasonable time has elapsed to permit the licensee to start production. It may increase from year to year over the life of the agreement.

Many companies are reluctant to accept minimum royalty obligations, and in some cases, it may be desirable to respect this attitude. In any event, a minimum royalty normally represents but a fraction of sales and resulting royalties that licensor and licensee may reasonably anticipate.

The financial details of an agreement can also be affected by nonfinancial considerations. For example, the licensor may receive, as a license consideration, some product or development whose value exceeds any monetary benefit. Thus, the company willing to pay the highest cash price need not be the best choice for licensee. A product may be more important to a small company with less immediate capacity to pay than to a large company for whom a greater obligation is less burdensome. In the long run, the "hungry" licensee may well be a better and more profitable licensee.

How Can We Protect Our Know-how? A prospective licensor often hesitates to disclose know-how related to product manufacture and design, especially if patent protection is limited or nonexistent. Will it be properly guarded by the licensee? Will it be misapplied or misappropriated? Can it be recaptured if the license terminates?

These concerns, although valid, are frequently exaggerated. There is a tendency to overrate the inherent secrecy of know-how. A license may provide only an economical shortcut to experience that can be otherwise obtained or developed. Similarly, the licensee, just as the licensor, is motivated to protect his market position by safeguarding valuable know-how.

Protective Provisions. A licensor, however, can and should build appropriate provisions into a license agreement that will help protect his know-how interests. These provisions may include the following:

1. The agreement can spell out the licensee's responsibility for maintaining the secrecy of know-how, his procedure for guarding it, and the manner and extent of disclosure to employees. The location and concealment of manufacturing facilities and processes can be specified in detail.

2. The licensor's obligation to transmit know-how can terminate one or two years prior to the actual expiration of the license agreement. Thus, a licensee, when the agreement expires, would not have the latest improvements and know-how of the licensor.

3. The licensor may restrict certain areas of know-how from disclosure under the agreement. For example, he may require that the licensee obtain proprietary additives, components, or subassemblies from him.

4. Premature or improper disclosure by the licensee of secret data can give the licensor grounds for exacting specified penalties, for claiming a bond that may have been fixed, or for terminating the license agreement.

5. The licensee may be enjoined, in the event of license termination, from continuing the manufacture of the licensed products, or similar products, for a specified number of years.

6. The licensee may be required to market the licensed products under the licensor's trademark so that, while exploiting the licensor's know-how, the licensee is also building up a proprietary goodwill over which the licensor can keep absolute control.

7. The licensor must have the right to visit all phases of the licensed operations. In this connection, good licensee contact is very important, because the protection of know-how, as with other phases of a license relationship, is facilitated by the continued goodwill and cooperation of the parties.

How Can We Be Sure that a Licensee Will Live Up to His Agreement? The administration of a license agreement imposes no extraordinary difficulty if the contract has been prepared so that the intent of the parties, their respective obligations and manner of fulfillment, and the procedure for resolving differences are all spelled out with sufficient clarity.

Problems of contract administration normally arise because some contractual provision has proved to be seriously inequitable, unworkable, poorly translated, or inadequately expressed. Also, they may come about because of a situation not covered by the agreement.

The avoidance of administrative difficulties starts with the quality of the original agreement. The licensor should obtain competent legal guidance with respect to contractual form, content, and language.

Contractual Provisions Governing License Administration. Although most differences between licensor and licensee are worked out by discussion, license administration is usually implemented by the following contractual provisions.

1. The licensee must be obliged to maintain books and records which the licensor may reasonably require so that the fulfillment of licensee obligations can be effectively controlled. The licensor must have the right, at specified intervals, to audit these records and make extracts thereof.

2. The licensor should have the right to visit and inspect all facilities of the licensee which relate to the production of the licensed products. This right can be extended to require product samples at no charge for purposes of testing

to be sure that the standards of the licensor are being maintained. It can also tie in with the obligation of licensees to disclose developments and improvements related to the licensed products or their manufacture.

3. The licensee must be obliged regularly to report operating results and any other activities covered by the agreement. The licensor can secure the services of an overseas agent or professional representative to expedite reporting.

4. The licensor should have clear cancellation rights if the licensee defaults in fulfilling any conditions of the agreement. Cancellation clauses should define precisely the actions that the licensee must take or refrain from taking when cancellation becomes effective. The procedure for cancellation should be spelled out, allowing the licensee a reasonable opportunity to cure any default.

5. The procedure for dealing with questions of default or differences between the parties should be set forth in the agreement. The procedure can be through regular legal processes, usually through the local courts, or by binding arbitration. Most countries have legal and arbitration procedures that afford reasonable protection and redress. It should be noted that arbitration is not always the most expeditious manner for settling differences. The choice of an arbitration agency varies, and the parties have a choice as to where and under whose auspices the arbitration is to be conducted.

By Licensing Now, Are We Giving Up Better Opportunities to Establish Ourselves in Foreign Markets? A license relationship obviously involves commitments that, for their duration, preclude conflicting actions or associations. An agreement, however, can provide for varying degrees of flexibility and future options.

Apart from its duration, a license can be restricted in the scope of product and/or territories covered. The licensor can retain the right to sell independently in the licensed markets under his own trademark. He may have the right to exclude new or improved products from the license. He may have the right to terminate or assign the agreement on specified notice or conditions.

Should he wish to provide for the possibility of acquiring equity in overseas manufacturing, the licensor can often build this option into the license agreement. Moreover, a licensed activity in one market still may permit the development of other activities through a wholly owned subsidiary, joint venture, or export.

IMPORTANT LICENSE AGREEMENT PROVISIONS

There are many fringe considerations that derive from the particular circumstances of each license and its parties. There are some basic subjects that deserve special comment.

Patents. Patent rights are usually one of the prime values offered by a license. In most cases, licensing is prefaced by establishing a patent base, or by determining the base that can, in the light of individual circumstances, be established. For this purpose, the services of patent counsel are usually necessary.

Many parties fail initially to realize that patents offer protection only in the country of issue. Thus, a United States patent protects only in the American market. Foreign protection must be separately sought in each country as desired. For full priority protection in most countries, a patent application must be filed within one year after the date of filing in the country of original application.

Patent laws vary among countries with respect to application procedure, patent structure, and interpretation. Also, dates and time limits can be crucial in obtaining patent coverage. Patent coverage, even in only the major industrial countries, can become costly, and professional guidance can help control patent expenditures in relation to anticipated patent values and the income potential that they may create.   (See also Chapter 7 of Section 5.)

Except under special circumstances, licensed patents should remain the licensor's property, even though the licensee may be obliged to assume all or part of the cost of obtaining them or of keeping them in force.   (In most countries, annuities must be paid to keep a patent in force.)   The licensee should be required to mark the licensed products, their containers, and catalogs to satisfy applicable patent laws with respect to notice, patent ownership, and the fact of license rights.

The agreement should also spell out the rights and obligations of the parties with respect to new patents that may be obtained or that become obtainable.   It must cover "grantback" rights of the licensor, obligations to apply for new patents, and the ownership thereof.   The licensee may also be required, at least for the duration of his license, to concede the validity of the patents under which he is licensed and to refrain from any opposition to the granting of new patents to the licensor.

It may also be desirable to restrict the licensee's right to apply for a patent in a particular area of technology, unless the licensor consents, for two reasons. First, a licensee's premature disclosure may preclude the possibility of stronger or more basic patent protection by the licensor as a result of his research. Second, it may be preferable to keep certain developments secret rather than have them published as patents.

Trademarks.   The right to use a registered trademark can be a most important part of a license relationship.   For the licensee, it can facilitate sales promotion. For the licensor, it provides a local proprietary position that should become more valuable as time goes by.   Particularly if a license is not anchored to strong patents (or there may be no patents at all—just know-how), the right to use a trademark can be a vital tool whereby a licensor can protect his interest in the license.   It can prevent unauthorized parties from trading improperly on goodwill and brand identification.   Thus, prospective licensors should register their trademarks in their principal foreign markets.   These registrations must be separately made in each classification of goods on which they are to be applied.   Once made, they are valid for terms of ten years or more, and their lives can usually be indefinitely prolonged by prescribed renewal routines. Trademark laws and practice vary among countries, and competent counsel should be retained to assure suitable and effective registration.

Licensors must be cautious of the form in which rights to use their trademarks are conferred.   In some countries, trademarks can be licensed as part of an agreement covering patents and/or know-how.   In others, a separate document is required or preferred.   However, even if trademark rights can properly be combined with patent and know-how rights in one license agreement, it may be desirable for tax, technical, or security reasons to deal with trademarks separately.

Trademark laws may specify certain forms and procedures that must be followed to preserve the proprietary value of a trademark, even after registration. Therefore, agreements under which trademark use is permitted should prescribe the manner of such use.   The trademark owner should have the right to inspect all catalogs, advertising material, labels, and products on which the trademark is applied.   Failure of the trademark user to follow marking specifications (or immediately to correct any improper usage upon notice thereof) should be grounds for canceling the trademark and/or license agreement involved.

Agreements conferring trademark rights should provide that trademarks remain the property of the licensor. The licensee should be enjoined from using the mark in any way that might impair its proprietary value to the owner. This may require that the licensee meet product design and quality standards that the licensor must have the unequivocal right to prescribe, police, and enforce.

Infringement Actions. A licensor is often requested by his licensee to assume a contractual obligation to act against any third party who allegedly infringes a licensed patent or trademark. Similarly, the licensor may be asked to defend or hold the licensee harmless if the latter, by exercising his licensed rights, incurs infringement liability to a third party.

These requests must be weighed in relation to the burdens that they can involve. Infringement actions can be costly, and obligatory pursuit of every suspected transgression can be a severe burden. On the other hand, unless there are collateral factors, a licensee may object to paying royalties on a patent which a competitor is using freely.

The wisdom of prosecuting infringement, alleged or proved, may depend on a variety of commercial, technical, and legal factors as evaluated by the licensor and licensee. Therefore, infringement provisions of a license agreement often permit the parties to exercise individual judgment and option. Especially if the license is exclusive, infringement actions can probably best be dealt with by a cooperative procedure, contractually defined.

Except for special situations, a licensor should not warrant the validity of his patents or assume an unqualified obligation to attack alleged infringers. Rather, before a license agreement is signed, the licensee should have the opportunity to study the patents and estimate their strength.

On the other hand, a licensor would normally accept a more affirmative obligation to defend his licensee or to hold him harmless if the latter, by exploiting his license, were accused of infringing a patent of a third party. A licensee may properly be entitled to assume that, by exploiting his license, he will not be violating the rights of another.

Government Validation. In most foreign countries, license agreements require official approval in some form before they become effective or before payments may be remitted under them. The procedures for obtaining validation vary greatly in severity and duration. In some countries, it is obtainable as a routine formality. In others, agreements are carefully scrutinized by one or more official agencies such as ministries of industry, economics, or trade or the central bank.

Validation authorities usually analyze agreements in terms of foreign-exchange obligations they may create, the contribution that the licensed technology may make to local industry, export potential of licensed products, and the protection of local industry against new competition. They tend to examine, with particular care, items such as royalty rates, minimum royalty obligations, duration of agreement, equipment and materials that must be imported to support the licensed operation, strength of local patent protection, extent of export territories and potential granted by the license, and the local need for the technology involved.

Countries that are most severe in validation requirements are often specially influenced by protectionist and "foreign exchange" payment considerations. Ministry officials frequently seek to reduce royalty rates, to eliminate minimum royalty commitments, and to provide for broader export privileges. Indeed, a foreign company may accept license terms and expect its government to require reduced payment and other obligations as conditions of validation.

Accordingly, when negotiating an agreement, a licensor should ascertain local validation requirements and procedures, and the administrative yardsticks by which local authorities are guided. The licensor may be required to supply facts and analyses, occasionally in what may seem needless and vexatious detail.

Much time can elapse during the validating process and the license renegotiations that may be involved.

The onus of securing license validation is usually assumed by the licensee. By informal consultation with authorities concerned during the course of license negotiation, he may have paved the way for prompt validation. The licensor, however, should retain the right, directly or through professional representation, to take the initiative or to collaborate with the licensee in seeking official approval. The licensor should also be able to terminate an agreement if it cannot be made operative with official sanction within a stipulated period of time.

Apart from validation, some countries provide for the possibility of, or may require registration or formal recording of, license agreements. The necessity or desirability of doing so should be checked.

Antitrust Considerations. Because license agreements confer stipulated and usually restricted rights to manufacture, use, and sell, they should be reviewed in relation to applicable antitrust and "restrictive business practices" laws. Such laws exist not only in the United States but, with varying content and vigor, in many foreign countries. In this connection, it should be noted that United States antitrust restrictions may affect overseas as well as domestic operations of American companies. Also noteworthy are the antitrust provisions established by the Treaty of Rome for the European Common Market.

Antitrust and "restrictive business practices" laws are subjects for special professional study. License provisions most prone to scrutiny in relation thereto are those which refer to exclusivity of rights granted, territorial rights and limitations, patent and know-how "grantback" clauses, prices and pricing, and supplier and supply restrictions.

The construction of antitrust laws is complex and highly subjective. Beyond some basic textbook taboos, the impact of antitrust regulations on individual situations is not exact or predictable. Thus, expert opinion of a contemplated agreement is often indecisive and the licensor may be obliged to make an "on balance" businessman's decision with respect to the inclusion or scope of specific provisions.

Taxation. License agreements and their structure, content, and language should be negotiated with due regard for the domestic and foreign taxes to which they are subject. Royalties are variously subject to income, turnover, and royalty taxes. License values may be subject to capital taxes. Engineering fees may be subject to tax at source or only in the United States. Royalties of United States licensors which are blocked abroad may still be currently subject to domestic income tax. Noncash considerations, including equities received in exchange for know-how or technical services, may be subject to income or capital-gains taxes.

The foreign tax obligation of United States companies on license income often is governed by provisions of so-called bilateral tax treaties between the United States and foreign countries. Such treaties may call for reciprocal exemption of certain types of tax. They may permit foreign levies to be credited against United States tax obligations to avoid a double tax on the same income.

Foreign licensees are usually required to withhold local taxes due on license remittances. However, the licensee may be required, by agreement, to absorb certain taxes as an additional license cost. By negotiation with governmental authorities or by following specified procedures, the licensee may be able to gain a reduction or exemption from specific taxes.

The impact of taxes on a license can depend greatly on the amount and manner in which licensee obligations are identified and paid. For example, in some countries, engineering fees may be taxed at a lower rate than royalties.

Taxes on royalties may be exempt up to a given percentage or amount. Payments in the form of equity participation may escape certain taxes. Under proper conditions, it may be possible to have know-how considerations received by American licensors taxed in the United States as capital gain rather than income. Under appropriate conditions, even royalty income may be treated as capital gain.

It is therefore important that a licensor study or receive competent professional advice on the tax regulations that apply, under various forms and definitions of a license relationship, both in the United States and in the country where the license is to be granted. (See also Chapter 8 of Section 16.)

Remittances. Most United States companies want their license income paid in United States dollars or other hard currency. This can be well assured if the license agreement specifies the currency in which payments are to be made, the conversion rate to be applied, and the remittance procedure to be followed.

To the foreign licensee, it makes no difference whether his payments are in dollars or in local currency, so long as dollars may be remitted legally and without suffering adverse conversion premiums. In countries requiring official license validation, the fact of such validation provides strong presumption that currency and remittance provisions, as approved, will be followed. The same presumption applies, without official sanction, in countries where license agreements are not subject to official scrutiny and where currencies are freely convertible.

Despite contractual provisions, however, licensees and foreign validating authorities may retain the right to suspend or limit dollar remittances if government regulations make such remittances illegal or in the event of national financial crisis. Occasionally, where licenses impose a minimum royalty, dollar remittances may be restricted to royalties actually earned. It should also be noted that for many less stable countries it may be possible to ensure dollar remittances through a United States government agency.

In providing for currency conversion, the license may specify use of the rate of the International Monetary Fund, or of the local central bank, or of a similarly recognized agency, as of the due date of each payment. The licensee should be required to follow the licensor's remittance instructions so long as they do not violate local currency regulations.

Technical Data. A license agreement should state, as precisely as possible, the types of technical information and support that a licensor is to provide. For given products, he may be obliged to furnish all design details and formulas, tooling drawings and possibly certain tools themselves, blueprints, standard sheets, handbooks, service manuals, and the like. He may be obliged continuously to furnish technical details of product changes and improvements in manufacturing methods.

The licensee usually has the right, within reasonable limits, to send his engineers to the licensor's factories for training and consultation. Also, the licensee, generally at his cost, can often require the licensor to send qualified technical personnel to assist in starting up the licensed operation abroad.

Frequently, technical data submitted by the licensor must be translated into the licensee's language. Product specifications may require conversion, adaptation, and even redesign to meet foreign standards, measurements, or market preferences. Most licensors are not able or prepared to undertake this task, and the licensee, by agreement, normally accepts this burden. Nevertheless, the licensor should furnish guidance and may even insist on examining and approving technical changes and adaptations before they may be used by the licensee.

Caution should be observed in establishing obligations to furnish technical details of product developments and improvements. Although a licensee may object if he fails to receive such information promptly, he can also suffer much harm if a new design or manufacturing process is prematurely disclosed and then proves defective. For this reason, some licensors agree to supply new data only after they decide that such data can be prudently released.

AGREEMENT FORM AND CONTENT

Conventional contract forms used in the United States are substantially satisfactory as licensing instruments in most countries. Because, however, there can be local variations in contract law or usages, a license agreement should be scrutinized by counsel knowledgeable in the law of the country in which it is to be exploited. In any event, the agreement should specify the system of contract law that is to be applied in resolving differences between the parties.

A typical license agreement consists of a suitable preamble (the "whereas" clauses) and an appropriate sequence of paragraphs which can be entitled as follows:

Definition of Terms (define terms such as "licensed products," "know-how," "net selling price," and the like); Scope of License (details of license and sublicense rights granted); Technical Data and Assistance (technical help to be supplied by the licensor); Sales Data and Assistance; Patent Data (items such as concession of patent validity, patent maintenance responsibility, and new patent applications); Trademarks and Marking Data (instructions for use and protection of trademark, for marking products and catalogs); Royalties and Payments (royalty and other payment details and procedures); Records and Reporting (obligations to maintain proper records and licensor audit rights); Duration of Agreement (life of agreement and renewal provisions); Termination of Agreement (conditions and procedures of cancellation and related obligations of parties); Arbitration (procedure for resolving differences between parties); Notice (procedure for parties to give each other notice); Waivers (license obligations waived only by written agreement); Third-party Infringement (action to be taken by parties in case of possible patent or trademark infringement); Secret Data (obligations of licensee to guard confidential data and know-how); Visitation Rights (rights and obligations of parties to visit and inspect each other's operations); Official Validation (provisions relative to obtaining license validation).

CONCLUSION

There can be other contract provisions that individual circumstances and objectives of each license relationship may suggest. It is important that a license agreement accomplish the intent of the parties and integrate their respective interests to yield the greatest mutual advantage. The more effectively this is accomplished, the greater is the likelihood of a profitable and durable license association.

BIBLIOGRAPHY

Cardinale, Joseph S., *Manual on the Foreign License and Technical Assistance Agreement,* Thomas Ashwell & Company, Inc., New York, 1958.
Eckstrom, Lawrence J., *Licensing in Foreign Operations,* Foreign Operations Service, Inc., Essex, Conn., 1958.

Ladas, Stephen P., "Foreign Licensing of Industrial Property," *1961 Proceedings of Wisconsin's Seventh Annual Corporate Lawyers' Institute*, Madison, Wis., 1962, pp. 85–117.

"Licensing—Technology for Hire," *American Exporter Industrial Magazine*, February, 1958.

Lovell, Enid, *Foreign Licensing Agreements*, 2 vols., National Industrial Conference Board, New York, 1958 and 1959.

Pollzien, Gotz M., and George B. Bronfen (eds.), *International Licensing Agreements*, The Bobbs-Merrill Company, Inc., Indianapolis, 1965.

CHAPTER FIVE

Importing

WILLIAM GUY CHATER *Bronxville, New York*

Practically every industry in the United States requires the use of some for-eign-produced material to turn out a finished product. The American steel industry, for example, in addition to ever-increasing imports of basic iron ore, uses about forty separate materials from as many, or more, different foreign countries. The increasing importance of aluminum and stainless steel products widens our dependence on imported basic metals. Some of the many foodstuffs for which we are dependent on foreign sources for all or most of our needs are coffee, tea, cocoa, and sugar, as well as drugs, fibers, and oils. We also require fissionable materials for the production of atomic energy.

Many types of finished goods requiring special craftsmanship or specialized production methods also find extensive markets in the United States and help maintain the high level of production and living standards we enjoy. Further-more, only by maintaining and increasing our volume of imports can we provide the necessary foreign exchange to the rest of the world, with which they can finance our expanding export trade by actual financial trade balances instead of "foreign aid" at the taxpayer's expense.

Detailed statistics of our import trade are carefully compiled by the U.S. Department of Commerce. The items imported, listed by value, amount, and foreign source, can be readily secured from the Bureau of the Census, Foreign Trade Division. A careful study of such statistics is a required preliminary for any person or firm contemplating activity in the importing field.

UNITED STATES IMPORTS

About 40 percent of our import volume embraces crude or raw materials and foodstuffs not produced in the United States or produced only in insufficient volume. Important examples are ores, crude petroleum, industrial diamonds, hides, spices, certain foodstuffs, and fishery products, as well as specialized grades of tobacco, cotton, wool, and so on, imported to blend with or supplement our own production.

Another 20 percent of our imports are in the semimanufactured class, not generally produced locally or produced only for a higher cost. These include some of the basic coal-tar products, fertilizers, industrial chemicals, and fish and vegetable oils.

All of these imports are for specialized trade requirements. They are usually marketed in substantial quantities for use by large industries. Many are traded on the commodity exchanges; others represent important investments abroad by United States corporations which control all details from the time the product is produced abroad to actual delivery in the United States, including financing, shipping, insuring, and other details.

The remaining 40 percent of our imports consists mainly of finished products or components used in many different products, both staples and specialties. They originate in practically every part of the world and ultimately reach all parts of the United States.

FINDING IMPORT SOURCES

Once the product to be imported has been decided upon, there are many factors that must be considered to secure the quality or grade wanted at the most satisfactory price. To avoid costly later losses, it may be practical at first to experiment in a limited way by purchasing from import merchants or commission houses in the United States who represent important foreign sources and have stocks on hand for early delivery. There are also resident import brokers or agents of foreign shippers who can supply samples, quote prices, and give other required details. It is usually not difficult to get trade references on such houses, and information from their other customers about the merchandise supplied by their principals. It must always be borne in mind that direct importing is a long-range project and ample time must be allowed for delivery. In many cases, a trial or experimental order, even if a little more costly, will prove to be well worthwhile in preventing costly mistakes resulting from the inevitable unforeseen circumstances that so often crop up to aggravate those who engage in foreign-trade operations.

Buying and Importing Direct. Most importers operating on a large scale find it to their advantage to obtain all or the larger part of their needs through direct contact with producers, merchants, and other suppliers in the countries where the merchandise originates. Direct purchasing is of increasing importance, especially to department stores, mail-order houses, and specialty shops. Many operate their own buying branches in the more important areas where their sources exist. Where a large and steady volume of import business is carried on, an import department is maintained in buying headquarters in the United States to coordinate purchases and to take care of import details such as financing, customs clearance, and warehousing and distribution activities.

To locate and negotiate with foreign sources of supply, there are a number of established aids that are available.

1. Most foreign governments maintain commercial offices in the United States. These offices are only too glad to furnish lists of sources in their countries. Many are located in New York, but all can be reached by writing to the embassy of the country, in Washington, D.C., where the letter will be referred to the proper commercial attaché.

2. The larger banks, with offices or correspondents abroad, can supply source information, usually with a report on the financial status of the source. It must be remembered, however, that financial information in most foreign countries is not divulged with the same completeness that we are accustomed to locally, and allowance must be made accordingly.

3. Overseas airlines, such as Pan-American World Airways and TWA, and the United States offices of foreign airlines operating to the United States are interested in increasing their business volume. They can supply names of sources in the countries where they have agencies or offices.

4. Dun & Bradstreet have extensive overseas operations and can frequently be of service. Their reports can be depended upon to give more complete financial details, but, of course, there is a charge for them.

5. The U.S. Department of Commerce, Bureau of International Commerce, has extensive reports from its offices abroad. These can be consulted at its headquarters in Washington, D.C., or at field offices maintained in forty-two cities throughout the country. It should be remembered, however, that their primary objective is the encouragement of our export trade. Import information is, therefore, subordinated accordingly.

6. Other methods of securing names of potential suppliers include enlisting the aid of local state and port authorities with offices abroad and studying trade magazines and periodicals published in foreign countries. A personal trip by a company official with the time and means to locate sources in the countries of origin is highly desirable if the cost is warranted.

COSTING IMPORTED MERCHANDISE

A condensed import product analysis form is shown by Figure 5-1. Other items of cost in addition to those shown on the form, with special application depending on the nature of the product, might include development expenses, finding fees, extraordinary overhead expenses, advertising, and the like. If these

Date_____

Product_____
Description and/or specifications_____
Packing details_____
Supplier_____ Sample no._____ Delivery_____
Unit purchase/sale_____ Unit weight_____ Unit cube_____
Ocean-freight class_____ Rate_____ U.S. customs para._____
  1. FOB foreign seaport
  2. Cost and freight
  3. U.S. duty (—— % FOB value)
  4. *a.* Ins., cust. entry, L/C expense
     b. Wharfage and handling (if applicable)
     c. Other expenses incidental to landing
  5. Ex dock cost (total lines 2 through 4)
  6. *a.* Cartage to warehouse
     b. Warehouse handling and storage (mos.)
  7. Ex warehouse cost (total lines 5 and 6)
  8. *a.* Freight allowance (if applicable)
     b. Cash discount (if applicable)
     c. Dating/anticipation expenses (if applicable)
  9. Desired margin (—— % ex dock cost)
10. *a.* Selling price, ex dock (lines 5 plus 8 and 9)
     b. Selling price, ex warehouse (lines 7 through 9)
11. *a.* Selling price, competitive domestic product
     b. Selling price, competitive imported product
12. Differentials: *a.* Our cost versus market
             b. Our price versus market
Estimated annual volume_____ units $_____ customers_____
Probable market movement_____
Other special considerations_____
Decision: (Yes) (No) If yes, how many?_____ When?_____
Other comments_____

FIG. 5-1. *Condensed import product analysis form.*

items exist, they must be included in cost computations to ensure realization of the profit required to warrant carrying on the business.

Customary Trade Terms. For a more complete listing and definition of the usual terms of the importing trade—such as FOB, CIF, and the like—reference should be made to the *Revised American Foreign Trade Definitions—1941*, adopted July 30, 1941, by a joint committee representing the Chamber of Commerce of the United States, the National Council of American Importers, Inc., and the National Foreign Trade Council, Inc. The terms used in this chapter are based on these definitions.

The FOB Point. The FOB point establishes the place and time where liability for loss or damage passes from the seller to the buyer. It is extremely important that all purchase orders specify exactly what is intended between the parties involved. Generally speaking, it is to the advantage of the importer to require that the merchandise be sold in proper condition for export shipment, including all necessary packing, and actually placed on board the carrier that is destined for the port of arrival in the United States. When this cannot be done, the importer should have his representative—a resident buying office or freight forwarder, for example—take care of shipment from the foreign interior point where title passes, and arrange for shipment via the loading port of export. This can be costly, however, and hence the desirability of arranging for the seller to take care of these details.

Cost and Freight Pricing. This is the purchasing method preferred by most import trades. The foreign seller quotes a price including the cost of transportation to the named port of destination.

The seller must

1. Provide and pay for transportation to named point of destination
2. Pay export taxes or other fees or charges levied because of exportation
3. Obtain and dispatch promptly to buyer, or his agent, clean bill of lading to named point of destination
4. Where "received for shipment" ocean bill of lading may be tendered, be responsible for any loss or damage, or both, until the goods have been delivered into the custody of the ocean carrier
5. Where "on board" ocean bill of lading is required, be responsible for any loss or damage, or both, until the goods have been delivered on board the vessel (IMPORTANT NOTE: "On board" bills of lading should be specified wherever possible. This is the only way to assure definite ocean shipment within the time specified.)
6. Provide, at the buyer's request and expense, certificates of origin, customs invoices, or other documents in the country of origin or of shipment, or of both, which the buyer may require for importation of goods into country of destination, and where necessary, for their passage in transit through another country

The buyer must

1. Accept the documents when presented
2. Receive goods upon arrival and handle and pay for all subsequent movement of the goods, including taking delivery from the vessel in accordance with bill of lading clauses and terms; pay all costs of landing, including any duties, taxes, and other expenses at named point of destination
3. Provide and pay for insurance (see below)
4. Be responsible for loss of or damage to goods, or both, from time and place at which seller's obligations under 4 or 5 above have ceased
5. Pay the costs of documents mentioned in 6 above (NOTE: The term "cost and freight" is usually abbreviated "C&F." This should not be confused with

the French language "CAF" for "cost, assurance, fret." The proper French designation is "C et F.")

Ocean-freight Costs. Even if the foreign shipper pays or is responsible for ocean freight, its cost should be known to the importer, because duty is paid on the foreign value and the freight expenses can be deducted from the invoice for dutiable purposes.

Because their cubic capacity is limited by the size of their vessels, ocean carriers follow the practice of charging freight based either on the actual weight of the merchandise or on its cubic measurement, whichever is to their advantage. Importers must watch carefully the practices in the trade in which they are operating. The standard British practice, also used in countries of origin accustomed to these terms, is to use a ton of 2,240 pounds weight, or a 40 cubic foot measurement. From areas where the metric system is used, however, freight may be assessed on the metric ton of 2,204.6 pounds weight, or per cubic meter (35.314 cubic feet). And in the United States and some other countries, the so-called short ton of 2,000 pounds may be the basis for calculating freight on heavy merchandise weighing more than a ton per 40 cubic feet.

The necessity of keeping cubic measurements to a minimum requires careful consideration in advance. Wherever possible, goods should be nested, compressed, or otherwise packed with this in mind, or shipment can be made "knocked down" for final assembly after arrival. For instance, bamboo lawn rakes are frequently shipped with the heads in one package and the handles in another, at a considerable saving in the total size of the shipping packages.

In established trades, the shipping companies operating regular services have published tariff rates which can be referred to for calculating transportation costs. These are often called "conference" rates. Regular users of the lines are expected to sign contracts calling for exclusive use of the conference vessels or be penalized by being charged higher rates. However, there are frequently tramp or "nonconference" services that can be used at substantial savings. These alternatives should be carefully explored when freight expense is an important factor. Generally, the shipper abroad is in a better position to know what opportunities exist for savings, and this will be reflected in more advantageous "cost and freight" quotations.

INSURING MERCHANDISE

In international commerce, the importer must constantly be aware of prices, competition, market changes, and supply and demand. The slightest miscalculation can mean the difference between financial success and failure. It can be readily appreciated therefore that no importer can afford to run the risk of losses or damage beyond his control such as marine casualties, loss or damage by rough handling or pilferage, war risks, or other potential causes that can be neither foreseen nor avoided. Even if he decides to run such risks for his own account, any bank or other participant in financing the business will require that adequate insurance be provided.

Marine insurance is customarily placed through an insurance broker, and selection of a firm well versed in the trade will make it much easier to decide upon the risks to be covered, the right policy to be written, and the proper insurance company to be used. Selection of an American insurance company makes it easier to settle claims quickly and without the possibility of loss should foreign currencies fluctuate in value.

By far the greater volume of marine insurance is now written under what are known as "open policies." Such insurance contracts remain in force until canceled and provide protection for merchandise which may have been shipped at the buyer's risk long before he has knowledge of it. This automatic protection applies, within the limits of the specific policy, from the time the shipment leaves the warehouse abroad and continues during the complete transit until it is delivered at the named destination. The policyholder warrants that shipments will be declared as soon as practicable, but unintentional failure will not void the insurance, because the goods are "held covered," subject to policy conditions. If necessary, the broker will arrange for a certificate of insurance to be issued, certifying that the merchandise is covered by the underlying open policy.

How Much to Insure. An example of the insurable value in an open policy would be "valued, premium included, at the amount of invoice, plus prepaid or guaranteed freight, plus all other charges in the invoice, plus 15 percent." This simple clause permits all parties to compute the insured value easily. The additional 15 percent advance reimburses the importer for his profit and expenses even though the merchandise is lost, or provides a possible reserve for extra expense should it be necessary to replace the goods at a premium to meet sales obligations.

"All Risk" Insurance. Most open policies are issued under this general broad coverage. Although it would seem to cover all possible loss or damage to the goods, it is, however, not as broad as sometimes imagined. It is designed to protect against all physical loss or damage from any external cause, but it does not cover what might be termed "inherent vice" from conditions existing before shipment such as improperly cured hides, foodstuffs not properly dried or otherwise prepared, or conditions that might develop from the very nature of the article covered.

Special mention should be made in the policy of losses that might arise and should be protected against. Breakdown of refrigeration machinery, which would damage frozen foods, and loss by breakage of glass or china articles are examples. A broker who is familiar with the assured's needs and the cover available in the market will be able to give invaluable advice from both a cost and a coverage standpoint. In many cases where normal conditions might result in some loss or damage under even usual circumstances, a franchise of approximately 3 percent is written into the policy, and claims are paid only when the loss is greater than this deductible amount. *Warehouse to warehouse* insurance protection is the most desirable form, and should be written into the policy wherever possible. The importer is then protected from the time the merchandise is packed and leaves its point of origin until final delivery in the same packing at the store or warehouse of destination. There may be a number of carriers involved, by rail, truck, and the like, as well as the risks while in warehouse or on dock at either shipping or arrival port, but warehouse to warehouse insurance covers all such risks, and makes collection of loss easier, even if it cannot be determined just where the loss occurred or who is primarily liable.

War risks and possible loss or damage from strikes, riots, and civil commotions are not covered by "all risk" insurance unless specially provided for. They are an essential part of the importer's insurance needs and should be either covered by a separate policy or added by a special clause in the open-cargo policy. The war policy covers only against such risks as outlined in detail in about a dozen rather specific paragraphs which should be read carefully for complete understanding. In general, delay or loss of market is excluded, as is loss or expense arising from government actions or seizure, embargoes, or seizure under quarantine or customs regulations. A war-risk policy cannot be canceled on shipments upon which insurance has already been attached, but is subject to cancellation on forty-eight hours notice by either party in the case of unshipped goods. Usually the policy can be reinstated, but at possibly higher rates depending on current or expected developments affecting the risk. When world or domestic uncertainties exist, it is only prudent to carry such insurance on all overseas shipments.

In Case of Loss. Should merchandise be lost at sea or arrive in a damaged condition, it is the obligation of the insured to give immediate notice to his insurance company and also to file preliminary notice of loss to the carrier, usually with advice that formal claim will be filed as soon as the extent of the loss can be determined. The importer is, in effect, the agent for his insurance company and must take every possible step to minimize the loss. This might require prompt cooperage of leaking containers, repacking or manipulation to sort the good merchandise from the damaged portion, or the like. Normal costs for this work can be included in the insurance claim and will be recognized by the insurers, as this work was done to keep their loss to a minimum.

The insurance company expects to secure all, or partial, reimbursement for claims paid by in turn establishing a claim with the carrier found responsible for the loss or damage, subject, of course, to bill-of-lading terms applying, which might reduce liability to a nominal sum per package. The importer must transfer his rights for claims against a carrier when his insurance claim is paid, and cooperate in any way required in case of need to press the insurance company's case. To determine the amount of the loss and the proper responsibility for reimbursement, a firm of "average (or loss) adjusters" is usually called in. Their decision must be accepted as final unless the aggrieved party considers it to his interest to take the case to court or to a board of arbitration.

General Average. Even though the merchandise arrives in perfect condition, an insurance claim may arise when a vessel in time of danger must incur unexpected costs for the common good. For instance, in case of stranding, the cost of towage or other salvage operations will be assessed against both the vessel and the cargo. In such cases, because the total costs and the pro rata share of expenses cannot be determined immediately on arrival, it is customary to release the merchandise against a deposit or a bond to pay the amount when it has been computed. An importer with an open policy can arrange for his insurance company to take care of this without cost, and the insurance company will pay the amount due at a later date. This is one of the prime perils insured against under all marine policies. For additional definitions of the terms in general use in marine insurance, such as FPA, WA, and the like, and the basic fundamentals of the policy, most larger marine insurance companies have booklets or pamphlets which will be supplied on request.

Air Shipments. Open policies of insurance are also issued for import shipments by air and by international parcel post. The rates are very reasonable because the time in transit is reduced and there is less possibility of damage in handling, loading, and unloading.

Increased Value in Transit. Frequently goods are sold while en route, and the new buyer may find that the current market value is greater than that declared at time of original shipment. In such cases, insurance companies will revalue their insurance protection or issue additional policies, always provided that no known loss or damage has occurred prior to the time such insurance is underwritten.

If merchandise continues its passage to final destination after it has been declared in the customs house, and duties have been collected or are due under bond, this should be also covered by insurance, the cost being very nominal.

FINANCING IMPORT PURCHASES

Because rates of interest to finance commercial transactions are generally higher abroad than in the United States, it is to the importer's advantage to place his foreign seller or shipper in a position to collect the value of the goods as quickly as possible. Otherwise, the foreign source must necessarily include the cost of interest on capital invested in the cost of the goods and ask a correspondingly higher price. (An exception is where the shipper can secure a low-interest loan from his government, granted to stimulate export sales, in which case, of course, advantage should be taken of such concessions.) It is customary, therefore, for the United States importer to arrange bank financing from the time the goods are shipped until they are sold to, and paid for by, his domestic customer. Even though his financial capital may be adequate to carry the investment without recourse to bank borrowing, the use of a bank with a foreign trade department is generally advisable to facilitate the documentary detail that exists in each import shipment.

The Import Letter of Credit. The import letter of credit is the method used to meet the seller's desire to obtain cash promptly upon shipment and at the same time to safeguard the buyer's desire that all documents be in order to facilitate customs entry and carrier delivery on arrival. An importer arranging with his bank for such a credit in favor of the foreign shipper does so by first securing a "line" of credit, which is to some extent similar to that used in other types of domestic borrowing. When arrangements have been completed, his bank will establish a letter of credit in favor of the foreign shipper through its branch or correspondent bank in or near the city of the beneficiary. (See also Chapter 6 of Section 16.)

This irrevocable obligation of the United States bank to honor drafts drawn and negotiated in accordance with its terms enables the beneficiary to arrange for shipment, with the assurance that he will receive the value of the credit provided its terms are complied with. When he has made the shipment, the documents are attached to a draft and submitted with the letter of credit to a bank in the city of the shipper. That bank examines the documents carefully and, if they are found in order, negotiates the draft, paying the shipper the equivalent in local currency and endorsing on the back of the letter of credit the amount involved. The letter of credit can then be used again until the total face amount is exhausted.

The foreign bank sends the draft and documents, either direct or through its American correspondent, to the bank that issued the letter of credit, where they are again carefully examined to see that they conform to its terms. If there are discrepancies, the bank will confer with the importer. In some cases, if the discrepancies are of a minor nature, they may be waived. Otherwise, the acceptance or payment may be refused. If the documents are in order, a sight draft is paid on presentation and charged to the account of the importer. If the letter of credit provides for later payment, usually at 30, 60, or up to 180 days' sight, the bank accepts the draft for payment when due. This "banker's acceptance" is then readily negotiable by the shipper or his correspondent in the United States. Because the importer will want the documents at once to secure immediate possession of the goods on arrival, it is customary for his bank to release them to him without immediate payment, provided a "trust receipt" is signed under which title to the goods remains with the bank. The importer agrees to hold at the disposal of the bank either the goods or, if they are sold, the proceeds. In any event, the importer must pay the obligation not later than one business day prior to maturity of the corresponding acceptance under the letter of credit.

A bank's commission charge for the issuance of import letters of credit is moderate, depending upon the tenor of the drafts to be drawn and the currency used. In most cases, it will be under 1 percent of the value of the invoice. If further financing is required after arrival and payment of the foreign shipper's draft, it can usually be arranged under the customary trade terms granted on loans in the domestic market.

Foreign Exchange. When goods are purchased in foreign currency, the burden of the risk, if exchange values fluctuate before final payment in United States currency, falls on the importer. He can minimize this by contracting with a bank maintaining a foreign department to sell him foreign currency for future delivery at a fixed rate. This forward contract, somewhat similar to "hedging" in domestic commodity markets, can be arranged at the time of purchase or at any time prior to the date of payment of the foreign shipper's invoice or draft.

UNITED STATES CUSTOMS FORMALITIES

All merchandise arriving in the United States must be declared to the customs house at the nearest port of entry (there are approximately 287 such ports) by the master of the vessel, the aircraft carrier, or the rail or truck carrier on which the goods are loaded. The customs officers are thus made familiar with what articles are arriving. When the importer makes entry for his merchandise, it is checked against the manifests of the arriving carriers. Imported merchandise not entered through customs within five days after its arrival is sent by the collector of customs to a bonded warehouse to be held as unclaimed. If it remains unclaimed at the end of one year, the merchandise is sold. (NOTE: The term "bonded" as applied to a warehouse or carrier denotes that a surety bond has been filed with the Secretary of the Treasury to pay duty on any merchandise that may be lost or damaged while in the possession of the carrier or warehouse. The bond does not protect the owner of the goods in any way.)

The customs service does not notify the consignee or importer of the arrival of his shipment. This is usually done by the carrier of the goods. The importer should make sure that the foreign shipper records on the shipping papers the complete name and address of the party to be notified on arrival to avoid delay and extra expense should the goods be stored as unclaimed.

On its arrival, the importer may make the following disposition of his merchandise.

1. He may enter the goods for consumption, either paying duty as provided in the tariff act or clearing them free of duty if so classified.

2. The goods may be placed in a bonded warehouse for payment of duty at a later date, and in partial quantities as desired, or for export free of duty. Final disposition must be made within three years after arrival.

3. Goods may be transferred "in bond" to another customs port for entry there, as provided above. This usually applies when an importer located at an interior point of entry desires to take care of customs details near his place of business.

4. An immediate export entry can be filed, under which the goods will not be examined by the customs officers, and liability for possible duties ends when the customs officer at the place of export certifies that the goods have been loaded and shipped abroad.

5. Arrangements can be made for transfer, without customs examination, to one of the six foreign-trade zones, where later action can be taken in accordance with the importer's requirements.

When transacting business with the customs house, an importer will find it greatly to his advantage to use the services of a licensed customs house broker, who can take care of all details of entry, bonds, and the like for a fee which will be approximately $10 to $25 for an ordinary shipment without unusual complications.

The Customs Invoice. A special customs invoice must be prepared by the seller or shipper for each shipment dutiable at a rate based on its value, if the purchase price exceeds $500. This is known as Customs Form 5515. Supplies may be obtained free of charge from United States consular offices. Besides giving full details of the merchandise, including marks and numbers, description, grades, quality and quantities, and purchase price, the invoice must also show the currency of purchase, itemize all rebates, drawbacks, or other bounties allowed upon the exportation of the merchandise, and give the price for home consumption if this differs from the export selling price.

Rates of Duty. A handbook listing all United States import duties, including supplements to date, can be secured from the Superintendent of Documents[1] or inspected at any of the field offices of the U.S. Department of Commerce. Although rates and classification in 1965 were still basically those of the Tariff Act of 1930, there have been numerous changes based upon reciprocal trade agreements with many foreign countries. Under our "most favored nation" treaties, when a tariff reduction is agreed upon with any of these treaty countries, the same advantage automatically applies to all others. The exceptions are the so-called Iron Curtain areas, which do not subscribe to GATT (the General Agreement on Tariffs and Trade). Imports from Russia, Red China, and countries generally under their sphere of influence pay higher rates of duty. This should be clearly determined before making import commitments, by conference with customs officers at the proposed port of entry if necessary.

Value for Duty Payment. Two principal methods are used for determining the value upon which rates of duty for dutiable merchandise apply. A reference to the customs tariff or consultation with customs officers is necessary to determine in which class the imported merchandise belongs. In general, the value is either the export or the home market value. (It should be noted that for customs purposes, the value upon which duty is paid is that applying at the *time of export,* generally the date on which the steamer sails or when the merchandise actually leaves the country of origin. It would be quite possible, therefore, that three or more importers of similar merchandise arriving at the same time might have perfectly proper invoices, but at different values. One importer might have purchased, or contracted for purchase, at an earlier date when prices were lower; another might have a long-term contract for an average cost over a period of months; and still another might have paid a premium for quick dispatch. The customs appraiser must take all of these facts into consideration and arrive at a single price on which duty will be collected. To avoid later additional duties, and perhaps penalties, the importer should have his customs broker confer with the customs officers before making customs entry.)

The export value is the market value or price at which imported goods are freely offered for sale *for exportation* to the United States in the principal markets of the country of exportation in the usual wholesale quantities and in the ordinary course of trade to all who wish to purchase.

[1] U.S. Government Printing Office, Washington 25, D.C. Price $5.00 domestic or $6.25 for foreign mailing.

The foreign value, used for all articles in a special list compiled by the Treasury Department and known as TD 54521, is defined as the market value or price at which the imported goods are freely offered for sale *for home consumption,* under the same conditions. Under this section, appraisement is accomplished at either foreign or export value, whichever is higher.

Conversion of Currency. For customs dutiable purposes, the value, if in foreign currency, is converted into United States dollars based on the New York market buying rate for the currency involved, as determined and certified by the Federal Reserve Bank of New York. The rate applying is that for the date when the vessel carrying the merchandise left the last foreign port in that country or the date of exportation if by other means of transportation. The importer, however, may have covered his foreign-exchange commitments at another date, and therefore the duty may be based upon a figure other than his actual cost in this case as well.

Final Determination of Duty Due. At time of entry, an estimated amount is deposited with the customs to cover the duty, and a bond is usually given, duly signed by the importer or his customs broker acting by power of attorney on his behalf, and by a surety company or other surety accepted by the collector of customs. This permits immediate delivery of the merchandise to the importer after the estimated duty payment has been made. The customs appraiser will then examine the goods, or a reasonable sample from the shipment, to verify both the classification for duty and the entered value. After his report is filed, the customs entry is "liquidated," and the final definite amount of duty determined. If additional duty is due, demand for payment is made. In case the deposit made at time of arrival is in excess, a refund is made. As this final liquidation may take months, even years, the importer is never absolutely sure of his liability for some time after arrival, and frequently after the goods have been sold and delivered to a third party. The importer's customs broker should notify him whenever there seems a likelihood that additional duties will be due so that he can set up a reserve for this contingency when calculating his estimated delivered cost of the merchandise.

Miscellaneous Import Requirements. In addition to providing for payment of any duties that may later be found to apply to the importation, the surety bond given when the goods are released to the importer permits the collector of customs to demand redelivery into his custody if any other import requirements are found not to have been met after examination of the goods. The principal legal regulations to be complied with include the following.

Marking with Country of Origin. Imported merchandise must be legibly marked in a conspicuous place and in a manner to indicate to the ultimate purchaser in the United States the English name of the country of origin. The packages and inner containers, if any, must also be so marked. There are certain exceptions where this cannot be done without damaging the material or articles, but in such cases, this should be discussed with customs before contracting for the importation.

Trademarks, Trade Names, Patents, Copyrights. Anyone holding legitimate rights under these or similar laws can prevent any unauthorized importations that might infringe upon their rights. An importer must be guided accordingly.

Pure Food and Drug Regulations. The importation of food, beverages, drugs, and cosmetics is governed by the provisions of the Federal Food, Drug, and Cosmetic Act, and all provisions as they apply to articles of domestic production must be complied with on imports as well.

Other prohibited import items, or those where special restrictions exist, include obscene, immoral, and seditious matter; narcotic drugs and derivatives; alcoholic beverages destined to a state where prohibition laws apply; arms, ammunition, and implements of war as designated in the United States Munitions List; counterfeit coins, currency, and stamps; Communist political propaganda; unlicensed goods from mainland China or North Korea; wool, fur, textile, and fabric products restricted by the various labeling acts administered by the Federal Trade Commission, unless they meet such requirements; wild or game animals, birds, fish, reptiles, and so on, subject to quarantine or other regulations of the Department of the Interior, Bureau of Sport Fisheries and Wildlife; dogs, cats, and pets except as permitted by the U.S. Public Health Service; livestock, meat products, food, vegetables, plants, and insects subject to Department of Agriculture regulations; and products of convict or forced labor.

Import Quotas. Certain products can only be imported in limited quantities, an indirect form of customs protective tariffs. These quotas are of two types—tariff rate and absolute. Tariff-rate quotas provide for the entry of a specified quantity of the product at a reduced rate during a given period. Excess quantities pay a higher rate of duty. They apply to cattle, certain dairy products, certain fishery products, potatoes, and stainless steel cutlery.

Absolute quotas are quantitative, and no more than the amount specified may be permitted entry during a quota period. Principal items involved are butter substitutes, certain grades of raw cotton, peanuts (except peanut butter), wheat, and lead and zinc ores.

Foreign-trade Zones. These areas—located in 1965 in New York; New Orleans; San Francisco; Seattle; Toledo, Ohio; and Mayaguez, Puerto Rico—facilitate the handling of merchandise without compliance with customs regulations. Goods can be reexported or transshipped as desired, and also graded, sorted, or otherwise manipulated, including intermixing with American products. They may be exhibited for sale, but only in wholesale lots, no retail trade being permitted. When brought into customs territory from the zone, they become subject to all existing customs laws and regulations. There is no limitation on the length of time goods may remain in the zone. Some of the advantages are that if an importer is not certain that goods comply with all regulations, such as marking with country of origin, compliance with pure food laws, or the like, he may transfer them to the zone for examination or manipulation to comply with the laws, and then enter them for consumption when ready. Or he can enter only that part that has been sorted out, exporting the balance without customs examination. Or goods can be combined with domestic ingredients, and the product exported without the payment of duty on the imported portion. Other advantages may apply to products of a specialized nature.

Drawback of Duty. Up to 99 percent of duties paid on imported merchandise may be claimed when the goods are combined with domestic products and then exported. For instance, when jams made of domestic fruit and imported sugar are exported, the manufacturer may claim for drawback a refund of 99 percent of the duties paid on the sugar used. The process requires careful maintenance of records and notification to the customs before export, so that the actual shipment can be verified by the customs inspector at the point of exportation. It is usually best to employ a customs house broker who specializes in this phase of customs operations.

DELIVERY TO DOMESTIC DESTINATIONS

When customs formalities have been completed and a delivery permit received from the carrier showing that freight and other charges have been paid, and when proof of ownership has been satisfied by surrender of the endorsed bill of lading if consigned to the shipper's order, the importer can take delivery and arrange for shipment to his warehouse or to an inland destination. Merchandise moving in railroad carload quantities will in most ports be loaded without charge by the rail carriers, either by placing cars on the dock or by transferring the goods to cars on their tracks by lighters owned by them. This "lighterage free" operation is an important advantage in ports such as New York, where unloading docks are located over a very wide area in the harbor.

If goods are picked up by truck, either for local transfer or for over-the-road movement to interior points, it will frequently be found that rates applying are somewhat higher than for purely domestic movement because of delays and higher costs of loading the merchandise on the carrier. In many areas, union "loaders" have a monopoly on this operation, and charge for the loading operation, whether it is performed by them or not.

CONCLUSION

Imported goods have now entered the domestic stream of merchandise movement. Further details, such as selling, advertising, distribution, and the like, are handled generally in a way similar to that of handling merchandise made in the United States, as outlined in other chapters in this Handbook.

BIBLIOGRAPHY

"Buyers' Guide to Marine Cargo Insurance," The Atlantic Mutual Insurance Company, New York.

Custom House Guide, Import Publications, Inc., New York, published yearly.

Directory of New York Importers, Commerce and Industry Association of New York, published every two years.

"Export and Import Procedures," Morgan Guaranty Trust Company, New York.

Exporting to the United States, Treasury Department, Bureau of Customs, U.S. Government Printing Office, Washington, D.C.

"Financing Imports and Exports," Chemical Bank New York Trust Company, New York, 1965.

Foreign Commerce Handbook, 14th ed., Chamber of Commerce of the United States, Washington, D.C., 1960.

Guide to Foreign Information Services, Chamber of Commerce of the United States, Washington, D.C., 1961.

International Commerce, Department of Commerce, U.S. Government Printing Office, Washington, D.C., published weekly.

An Introduction to Doing Import and Export Business, Chamber of Commerce of the United States, Foreign Commerce Department, Washington, D.C.

"Marine Insurance," Insurance Company of North America, Philadelphia.

"Practical Aspects of Commercial Letters of Credit," Irving Trust Company, New York.

CHAPTER SIX

Financing International Trade

SYLVESTER F. MAJESTIC *Vice President, Chemical Bank New York Trust Company, New York, New York*

EXPORT TERMS

To understand financing imports and exports better, it may be helpful to draw comparisons between domestic and export terms of sale.

Open-account terms are well known to every businessman. Although open-account sales are made to both domestic and foreign concerns, there are considerably fewer of them in export transactions than in domestic trade. In the United States, many sales are COD, but in international trade the equivalent is sight draft–documents against payment (S/D–D/P). This means that when the buyer pays a sight draft he receives the shipping documents which are necessary to obtain the merchandise.

Most businessmen are acquainted with trade acceptances. The export-import equivalent is a bill of exchange or time draft. Drafts may be drawn at thirty, sixty, or ninety days sight, or date, with shipping documents released to the buyer only after he has accepted the draft calling for payment a specified number of days in the future.

There is a certain amount of consignment selling domestically, but very little of this occurs in international trade. On the other hand, letters of credit, which are used only occasionally in the United States, are very popular in overseas transactions.

One of the problems in export trade is that buyers often look for longer terms than are extended to domestic customers. The reason is easy to see—it takes longer for the merchandise to reach the foreign market, so that if buyers abroad are to be on the same basis as domestic customers, they should be given more time. Usually, goods will be shipped by ocean vessel, but the draft and documents which give title to the merchandise go by airmail. It can hardly be expected that buyers in the United States will pay for goods before they are received, so why should buyers abroad be treated differently? As a matter of fact, it has become the custom in certain areas not to pay a sight draft or accept a time draft until arrival of the carrying vessel; magnanimously, many exporters give instructions to their banks not to present the drafts until the carrying vessel arrives. These, then, become known as "arrival drafts."

FINANCING

Many people look upon financing as being primarily a banking function. But financing (or extending credit) can be and is done by others. As a matter of fact, it can be done by (1) the buyer, (2) the buyer and his bank, (3) the seller, (4) the seller and his bank or a specialized financing firm, or (5) one of the government agencies set up for that purpose.

The Buyer. The buyer finances (1) when he pays in advance for the merchandise or (2) to the extent to which he makes an advance deposit. It should be noted that in some countries importers are required by government regulations to deposit a certain percentage of the purchase price before an import permit is granted.

The Seller. The seller finances exports when he ships his merchandise without immediate payment, as, for instance, when the sale is on a sight draft–documents against payment basis, with the draft and documents given to a bank for collection. The seller finances for a longer period when time drafts are concerned.

Bank Financing and Factoring. A form of bank financing that has become quite customary with those concerns doing a regular export business is advances against export bills. However, many manufacturers who are not fully conversant with this type of financing are inclined to look upon it in the same way as they do domestic accounts receivable financing. The reasoning is easy enough to see, particularly when the majority of accountants classify all types of receivables as "accounts receivable."

There is a big difference in receivables, as any person inclined to study the situation will soon realize. Domestic accounts receivable financing is considered a matter of course with certain industries, such as the textile industry where the mills set up their own selling or commission agents and are more concerned with production and sales than passing on credit, making collections, and financing.

Accordingly, factoring has long been a customary way of life for the textile industry. Through factoring, the mill is able to concentrate on production and sales, leaving the credit judgment and collection of the account to the factor. This eliminates both a credit department and a collection department for the mill. Accounts are guaranteed by the factor, and when the mill needs funds, the factor is prepared to supply whatever may be required.

Insofar as most banks are concerned, domestic accounts receivable financing is regarded somewhat in the nature of a "work-out" situation. This would be where the borrower, having exhausted what credit facilities may be available on his own note and not being able to meet whatever loan requirements may have been established between the borrower and the bank, finds it necessary to make some kind of arrangement with the bank to work out his problem. The bank then will consider lending against an assignment of the borrower's receivables on either a notify or nonnotification basis.

Many concerns have a distinct aversion toward factors, usually without reason except for possible higher costs than bank financing. Also, most concerns feel that receivable financing represents a "hocking" of the company's accounts and is a borrowing of last resort.

Advances against Foreign Collections. Having these things in mind, the ordinary concern regards it unthinkable to obtain advances against its export bills. It is not realized that banks that have engaged in this business for many years look upon this as a very desirable and interesting form of lending. In the first place, such loans are covered by transactions which are fully understandable to the bank inasmuch as documentary evidence is supplied. Here, from the papers submitted, the bank is able to determine what merchandise is involved and who the foreign buyer may be, and by reason of having title documents, considers itself in a secured position. When the foreign collection is liquidated (paid in local currency by the foreign buyer, which funds are then converted into United States dollars and remitted to the bank in the United States), the payment automatically retires the loan to that extent.

Advances against foreign collections may be on either a "global" or an "individual" basis. On an individual basis, each loan is liquidated automatically when funds are received from abroad. On a global basis, the borrowing exporter undertakes to maintain a "pool" of current export collection items against which loans are taken from time to time. Under this arrangement, the customer borrows as his needs arise, and he pays back when he again is in funds. The bank's only requirement on this basis is that there be a sufficient margin of good current foreign collections in the "pool" at all times.

Usually, advances against foreign collections are on a basis of 80 percent of the invoice value, whereas on a global basis, the borrower perhaps would be required to maintain a pool of no less than 125 percent of export bills against borrowings. The margin of protection required by the bank would depend on the borrower's financial position, type of product, buyer abroad, country involved, extent of profit, and the like.

At one time, banks discounted export customers' foreign-collection drafts, but when foreign-exchange shortages developed in various countries, making it almost impossible to estimate when dollars would be received in payment, banks changed to advances against customers' documentary export bills. For such financing, however, the bills of lading must be negotiable—usually to shippers' "order"; "straight" bills of lading (consigned directly to the buyer abroad) are not negotiable, and, as they therefore are not title documents, do not lend themselves to bank financing.

LETTERS OF CREDIT

Letters of credit for hundreds of years have filled the needs of importers and exporters, having originated with the Lombard merchants of Italy. Ever since, buyers and sellers have regarded letters of credit as a guarantee of performance and payment. The buyer, through his bank, in effect tells the seller that if the latter performs as set forth in the letter of credit, he (the seller) will be assured of payment by a bank.

Ordinarily, a seller may feel that in dealing with a new customer he should be paid in advance, with credit extended only after good credit checkings and satisfactory experience. On the other hand, if the buyer should pay for the merchandise before it is shipped, there is no assurance that the seller will perform. Both buyer and seller, however, are prepared to go through with the transaction if a bank assures the seller that, if he performs as specified in the letter of credit, he will be paid. At the same time, the bank assures the buyer no payment will be made until there is evidence that the seller has performed as agreed upon.

Pitfalls to Avoid. Does this mean that the buyer has a guarantee from a bank that the merchandise will be delivered when and exactly as ordered? The answer must be "no," because *banks pay only against documents*. In other words, if the papers presented to a United States confirming bank are exactly as called for in an irrevocable letter of credit opened by a foreign correspondent bank, the United States bank will pay. However, if the seller is unscrupulous, he may ship a crate of stones instead of machinery but mark the crate (and all shipping documents) to indicate it is machinery. Also, if the letter of credit calls for automobile tires, an unsavory seller might ship used (possibly useless) tires but mark his documents as though they were brand new tires.

If a bank cannot assure the buyer that merchandise is not in strict conformity with the sales contract, how can the buyer know that he is getting what he ordered? To assure himself on this point, the buyer may stipulate that an inspection certificate be submitted by a recognized inspection company attesting to the fact that a sampling of the shipment indicates the merchandise is in conformity with the purchase contract. These inspections may be for only a portion of the shipment or they may be for the full amount.

Many shippers are somewhat careless when it comes to letters of credit. As long as they receive an advice on a bank's letterhead (or on impressive water-marked paper), some exporters feel they have "money in the bank." Nothing could be further from the truth, because any one or more of several things could happen to prevent the shipper from being paid. There may be strikes at the manufacturing plant, or there may be strikes by the trucking company, the railroad, the longshoremen, the steamship unions, or anyone else, making it impossible for the beneficiary under a letter of credit to obtain an on-board bill of lading as called for in the letter of credit. There may be machinery breakdowns, making it impossible to fulfill production schedules. There may be changes in models, so that even though a later and better product may be shipped, the bank would not pay because it would be different from that called for in the letter of credit. A description of the merchandise in the letter of credit may be "black on white," whereas the actual merchandise may be "white on black." It could be the old question of whether a zebra is a white animal with black stripes or a black animal with white stripes. As far as the paying bank is concerned, if the letter of credit calls for black on white, it had better be black-on-white merchandise.

Another pitfall is in the matter of consular invoices. It is perfectly proper and, as a matter of fact, a requirement of many foreign governments that the local consul legalize shipments for customs and other purposes. Suppose a letter of credit requires a consular invoice and the consul's office is closed when the shipper calls to have his invoices consularized. If the office will not reopen before the scheduled vessel sails and the letter of credit expires, the shipper will not be able to produce a consular invoice as required within the validity of the letter of credit and will not be paid by the bank. On the other hand, a consul may refuse to legalize a shipment and is not required to give the shipper any reason for his action.

A *checklist* should include the following whenever a letter of credit is received:

1. Does the description of the merchandise agree with the purchase or sales contract?

2. Does the quantity agree with the purchase or sales contract?

3. Does the unit price (if so indicated) agree with the sales or purchase contract?

4. Does the shipping date agree with the purchase or sales contract?

5. Will the plant be able to produce and deliver the merchandise specified within sufficient time to permit shipment to be made in conformity with the letter of credit?

6. Has shipping space been booked so that the required bill of lading can be obtained in time before the credit expires?

7. Has any provision been made for extra time required by changeovers, production failures, transportation problems, and the like?

8. If the sale has been made on an FOB port of shipment basis, does the letter of credit provide for freight and other shipping expenses?

9. If terms are FOB plant, does the credit provide for cost of transportation to the shipping port and does it include ocean freight?

10. If an insurance policy is required, have arrangements been made with your insurance broker to furnish this rather than the usual insurance certificate?

11. Will you provide the full amount of insurance that may be called for in the letter of credit?

12. If no insurance is indicated, are you insuring for your own protection up to the time you are paid under the letter of credit?

When the letter of credit calls for a specified number of units at an overall price, you will not be paid if you ship over the quantity indicated in the credit even though you invoice within the letter of credit amount. Of course, if you over-invoice, your documents also will be turned down by the bank. And if the letter of credit does not permit partial shipments, you will not be paid if you ship less than the amount indicated in the credit.

Types of Letters of Credit. For most people, to paraphrase Gertrude Stein, a letter of credit is a letter of credit is a letter of credit. This is not so, because there are many kinds of letters of credit—for instance, irrevocable, advised (unconfirmed), confirmed, sight, time, deferred, guarantee, standby, red clause, revocable, and travelers.

Irrevocable. An irrevocable letter of credit is one where the issuing bank undertakes to pay the shipper (beneficiary) if and when the shipper submits all the documents specified in the letter of credit and within the amount and time indicated. Having given its undertaking, the bank will not make any changes (amendments) in the letter of credit unless both the buyer and the seller are in agreement.

Advised or Unconfirmed. An advised (or unconfirmed) letter of credit may be an irrevocable letter of credit issued by a bank abroad which is forwarded to the seller by a United States correspondent bank either in its original form or on the stationery of the United States bank. Such a letter of credit is irrevocable insofar as the foreign bank is concerned, but the United States bank assumes no responsibility for its payment, even though the letter of credit may call for drafts to be drawn on the United States bank.

Confirmed. A confirmed letter of credit is one where the United States bank obligates itself to pay if all documents are presented within the validity of the credit and exactly as called for.

Sight. A sight letter of credit is one that calls for drafts to be drawn at sight, accompanied by the documents specified in the letter of credit.

Time. A time letter of credit will call for drafts to be drawn on the confirming or advising bank at so many days sight. In other words, instead of being paid immediately as with sight letters of credit, if all documents are found to be in order, the United States bank "accepts" the draft drawn by the shipper (beneficiary) payable 30, 60, 90, 120, 150, or 180 days after the draft has been accepted (when it becomes known as a "bankers' acceptance").

There is a ready market for bankers' acceptances. Investors, particularly foreign banks, wanting to put their short-term funds to good use make active use of bankers' acceptances. Acceptance brokers in the major cities supply the market by buying bankers' acceptances from the banks and selling them in blocks to satisfy the particular investor. Bankers' acceptances are sold on a "discount" basis. This is somewhat of a misnomer because the "discount" is not earned by the accepting bank. Actually, the "discount" represents interest in advance which is taken by the buyer of the bankers' acceptances and ordinarily is paid by the beneficiary of the letter of credit unless it has been agreed between the buyer and seller that the "discount" is for the buyer's account. A quotation of 5⅞ to 5¾ percent "discount" for 30- to 90-day bankers' acceptances means that the seller of a bankers' acceptance would receive the face amount of the acceptance, less the "discount" at the rate of 5⅞ percent per annum from the date of sale of the acceptance to its maturity. The 5¾ percent relates to the per annum return on the bankers' acceptances purchased by the investor. The ⅛ percent spread represents the acceptance broker's fee for his services.

Deferred. In another category is the deferred-payment letter of credit. Inasmuch as the Federal Reserve Bank does not consider as eligible for rediscount bankers' acceptances that have more than 180 days outstanding to maturity, banks are reluctant to create acceptances running beyond 180 days. On the other hand, there are many instances where terms in excess of this are mutually agreeable to the buyer and seller as well as the foreign bank. For instance, there may be a sale of machinery amounting to $200,000 of which 10 percent (or $20,000) would be paid as an advance deposit on signing the contract, with a letter of credit opened for the $180,000 balance, payable in three semi-annual installments beginning one year after shipment. Accordingly, the beneficiary (seller) would draw a sight draft for one-third ($60,000) of the letter of credit a year from bill of lading date, another sight draft for $60,000 six months later, and the third and final sight draft for $60,000 two years from the time the goods were shipped. Although the three drafts would be presented after the shipping date specified in the letter of credit, the credit will always provide for these deferred payments. The beneficiary, however, would not have bankers' acceptances, as would be the case with a time letter of credit.

Letters of credit have been opened on occasions which combine all three of the preceding; that is, upon shipment the beneficiary would draw two drafts, one for a given amount at sight and the other for a certain percentage at perhaps 180 days sight, the balance being payable by the drawing of sight drafts one year, one and one-half years, and two years from bill of lading date.

Letter of Guarantee. In certain countries (for example, Ecuador) where commercial banks have been prohibited from opening letters of credit, it will be found that they issue a similar instrument, in some instances known as a "letter of guarantee." This letter of guarantee is similar in every respect to a letter of credit.

In the Far East, a form of letter of credit in use is known as an "authority to purchase." The difference between the two types of financing is that the United States bank, under an authority to purchase, is authorized by the opening bank abroad to purchase draft(s) drawn on the buyer by the shipper. Such authorities to purchase may be confirmed or unconfirmed and may contain instructions for the drafts to be drawn either with recourse or without recourse to the beneficiary.

Another type of credit instrument similar to the authority to purchase just mentioned is known as an "authority to pay." Under an authority to pay, the United States bank is authorized by the foreign opening bank to pay drafts drawn by the beneficiary (seller) on the foreign bank. Such authorities to pay also may be confirmed or unconfirmed, similar to letters of credit.

Guarantee. A guarantee letter of credit may be opened for one of various reasons. It may be to take care of a situation where a parent company in the United States wishes to guarantee the obligations of a subsidiary in a foreign country to a local bank. In such instance, the letter of credit would indicate that if the foreign subsidiary fails to repay its loan to the local bank, the latter would be authorized to draw at sight on the opening bank in the United States for the dollar equivalent of such loan.

Standby. When a bank abroad opens a letter of credit for the purpose of guaranteeing the obligations of an American subsidiary or affiliate, it opens a standby letter of credit. This type of letter of credit enables the United States lender, as the beneficiary, to call upon the foreign bank for payment in the event the borrower fails to pay its obligations as agreed upon. Standby letters of credit have been opened by banks abroad, not only in favor of banks, but also in favor of United States shippers to guarantee payment of drafts drawn by the United States supplier on the foreign buyer if, for one reason or another, United States dollars are not promptly remitted in payment of such sight or time drafts.

Red Clause. From time to time, United States companies will want to assist foreign buying agents or others by enabling such agents to obtain prior advances from local banks in order to make purchases of various commodities and prepare them for export. Eventually, ocean documents covering such shipments are presented to the local bank, at which time the latter pays the agent the amount of the invoice less whatever loan(s) may have been made against the merchandise. This is known as a "red clause" letter of credit, and in effect is a guarantee of payment for advances made by banks abroad.

Revocable. As its name implies (and contrasting with irrevocable letters of credit previously described), a revocable letter of credit may be canceled at any time by the opener (buyer) or the bank. Because of this risk, revocable letters of credit are used only under special circumstances. If an exporter selling readily disposable merchandise feels the amount ordered is in excess of what he (the exporter) deems prudent to ship on regular terms, he may be willing to accept a revocable letter of credit which, in effect, gives him a bank guarantee up to the time of shipment. If the credit should be canceled, it would be expected that the merchandise could readily be sold elsewhere without loss.

Travelers. A traveler's letter of credit (also known as a circular letter of credit) may be used to finance international trade in certain situations. An art collector, for instance, may decide to take a trip to Europe and combine business with pleasure by making on-the-spot purchases if anything should appeal to him. A traveler's letter of credit will not only provide funds for his personal needs but, in addition, will enable him to purchase such works of art as may appeal to him at the time.

Foreign-currency Letter of Credit. Letters of credit usually are opened calling for payment in United States dollars, but on occasions, United States importers will be required to open letters of credit in the currency of the foreign shipper. There is no particular difference in the operation of such a foreign-currency letter of credit except, of course, that the drafts will be drawn in a foreign currency by the shipper and presented for payment at a bank abroad instead of the United States bank. In the case of foreign-currency letters of credit, it usually is suggested that the United States importer cover himself against any foreign-exchange risk by entering into a forward (or future) exchange contract with the bank.

Amendments. As mentioned earlier in this discussion, an irrevocable letter of credit cannot be changed or amended without the full knowledge and consent of all parties to the transaction. These changes are made in the form of amendments to the original letter of credit, and if accepted by the beneficiary, form an integral part of the original letter of credit. If such changes or amendments are not satisfactory to the beneficiary, he is required to make this fact known to the United States confirming or advising bank immediately and to inform the buyer abroad. Under no circumstances can the beneficiary of a letter of credit avail himself of one or two amendments without obligating himself for all amendments made at a given time. In other words, if a letter of credit is amended extending the shipping date by a month and also calling for a reduction in price, the beneficiary cannot avail himself of the extended shipping date without also agreeing to the change in price.

United States banks, in opening letters of credit, are governed by "Uniform Customs and Practice for Commercial Documentary Credits," International Chamber of Commerce, brochure no. 22 (rev. 1962).

Discrepancies. In the event documents presented are not strictly in conformity with the letter of credit, the confirming or advising bank will return the documents noting the discrepancy or discrepancies. In certain instances, if these discrepancies cannot be easily corrected, the bank may be willing to accept a guarantee from the beneficiary for the discrepancies. This is a credit judgment to be made by the United States paying bank. In the event the purchaser should refuse permission for the opening bank abroad to make payment because of stated discrepancies, the bank here will call upon the beneficiary to return whatever payments may have been made by the United States bank. In a declining market particularly, a buyer may well use any excuse not to authorize payment. Therefore, the suggestion is given that the beneficiary under a letter of credit should be well satisfied with the credit standing of the one to whom he is selling because a guarantee for discrepancies, in effect, cancels out whatever benefits there are in the letter of credit.

In the case of an *import letter of credit,* where documents have not arrived but where the importer urgently needs the merchandise, the importer's bank which opened the credit may be requested to issue a *steamship guarantee* so that the importer may be able to obtain the merchandise from the steamship company and clear the goods through customs. Under a steamship guarantee, the bank obligates itself to indemnify the steamship company in the event the latter should be faced with a loss as a consequence of the missing bills of lading being presented by an innocent third party. In turn, the bank issuing such guarantees requires that its customers give an equivalent undertaking to the bank. This therefore means that having already received the merchandise, the importer can raise no questions should there be any discrepancy in the documents, because the opening bank under such circumstances is required to make payment of such drafts and documents as may be presented under the letter of credit, regardless of discrepancies.

Transferable Letter of Credit. A transferable letter of credit (previously known as an "assignable letter of credit") permits the original beneficiary to assign any portion of the letter of credit to his supplier. The beneficiary under such circumstances will approach the opening bank to effect a transfer which may be for the full shipment or possibly only a portion of it. In other words, there may be more than one supplier and more than one transfer, but unless specifically authorized in the letter of credit, the confirming or advising bank cannot permit a supplier to transfer to a third party. One problem with transferable letters of credit is that documentation must be identical with the original letter of credit. In other words, if the original credit calls for on-board, freight-prepaid ocean bills of lading, the transferred credit will call for the same papers. If the original credit calls for consular invoice (and most letters of credit do), the transferred credit will require a consular invoice.

Inasmuch as the transferred letter of credit possibly would name an inland supplier as the new beneficiary and the latter invariably would insist on payment against railroad bills of lading, truck or dock receipt, it can be seen that he would not be satisfied with a transferred letter of credit. On the other hand, the exporter (beneficiary) would not want his supplier to know the name of his buyer, and vice versa. What most banks permit is a substitution of the supplier's invoice for that of the original beneficiary. Because the original beneficiary (the exporter) has a profit in the transaction, the transferred letter of credit would be for a lesser amount than the original. Also, because a certain amount of time would be required to prepare documents for ocean shipment as undoubtedly would be called for in the original letter of credit, the transferred letter of credit would have an earlier shipping and expiration date. To be effective, a transferred letter of credit might stipulate ocean documents but without a consular invoice. It is not likely that a foreign buyer or the foreign-exchange authorities in the buyer's country would permit the opening of a letter of credit against other than on-board bills of lading.

Financing Import Letters of Credit. In the case of letters of credit covering imports into the United States, the extent to which a bank will extend such facilities will depend upon the financial position of the importer and conceivably the type of merchandise involved. If the bank is not too satisfied with either, it may require cash collateral to the extent that it wishes to be secured in the event the buyer-customer should refuse or be unable to make payment when documents are presented (we repeat, when documents are presented, *not* when the merchandise arrives). In the same manner that a bank judges the extension of credit on its own note or against other collateral, a bank will come to a decision with regard to the amount of letters of credit it wishes to have outstanding at any one time for the particular importer.

If sight import letters of credit are involved, the bank must be certain that when the documents arrive there will be sufficient credit balance in the customer's current account to cover such payment. In many instances, however, the importer requires additional financing, in which event the bank may be satisfied to release the documents after they have been carefully checked and approved for payment. Banks formerly had their customers sign trust receipts by which title to the goods was retained by the importer's bank, but since the advent of the Uniform Commercial Code in many of the states, banks are protected by the signing of security agreements and the filing of financing statements in the proper locations. In this manner, banks enable their customers to clear shipment through customs, process the merchandise, place the goods in the warehouse or on the customer's shelves, and sell to the customer's buyers with the bank not being paid until after the importer-borrower is paid by his customers.

With respect to *financing against export letters of credit,* it should be understood that in and of themselves letters of credit are not collateral in the same sense as stock exchange securities or other easily negotiable securities. If a bank should make an advance against shipping documents to be submitted at a later date, an unscrupulous exporter might conceivably present his documents directly to another bank and receive payment through that bank without paying off the loan at the bank where he borrowed the funds.

With regard to export letters of credit where the beneficiary needs financing and documentation permits its operation, a bank may be willing to issue a *back-to-back letter of credit.* In a back-to-back letter of credit, the bank would do almost exactly the same as in the case of a transferable letter of credit. In other words, documentation must be identical except for earlier shipping and expiration dates and a lesser amount to pay. The risk on the part of the bank in the case of a back-to-back letter of credit, where the original letter of credit is opened by the same bank, is nominal. If the original letter of credit is opened by one bank and the back-to-back letter of credit by another, the second bank is taking the risk that its interpretation of the documents (which must be identical) may be different from that of the bank which opened the original letter of credit.

Bridged Letters of Credit. Another method of financing export letters of credit is by the opening of bridged letters of credit. In this instance, the documentation in the second credit would be different from that of the original credit. For instance, the original credit might call for on-board bills of lading and a consular invoice. The bridged letter of credit, however, may stipulate railroad bills of lading to enable the manufacturer to receive payment as soon as he has put the merchandise on a railroad car. The risk taken by the bank in opening a bridged letter of credit is that from the time it makes payment to the second beneficiary (supplier) until the original beneficiary (exporter) can complete the documentation required under his letter of credit, circumstances beyond his control, such as strikes, may arise and make it impossible for the bank opening the bridged letter of credit to be paid under the original letter of credit. Because this is an added exposure, banks look closely into the credit of the customer requesting such facilities.

Assignment of Proceeds. In the event the beneficiary of an export letter of credit does not consider it practical to open a back-to-back letter of credit or a bridged letter of credit, or his bank is not prepared to extend such facilities, it sometimes is possible for a bank to arrange for an assignment of proceeds. On this basis, the bank will advise the exporter's supplier that the exporter is the beneficiary under a particular letter of credit, without naming the amount. The supplier is advised that after the exporter presents all the documents required under the letter of credit and payment is made by the opening bank, the supplier will be paid the amount of its invoice.

Authority to Negotiate. Somewhat similar to a letter of credit, but quite different in many respects, is the authority to negotiate, which is used primarily in the Republic of South Africa. Whereas every letter of credit must have an expiration date, invariably is in United States dollars, and is irrevocable (usually confirmed), an authority to negotiate has no expiration date, is subject to cancellation at any time, is in a foreign currency, and is revolving so that as payments are made abroad, the amount available by the exporter automatically is reinstated. Also, when a bank negotiates drafts on this basis, it is with recourse to the shipper. In other words, if the item is unpaid at the other end, the shipper must reimburse the United States bank in the foreign currency. This means that the exporter has an additional risk, that of foreign-exchange fluctuations, which, however, can be covered by means of a forward-exchange contract.

The question might arise as to why any exporter should accept an authority to negotiate. The exporter must supply his own answer to this, based upon his knowledge and experience of and with the buyer. If the exporter is satisfied to ship on a draft basis, he is in a considerably better position with regard to an authority to negotiate, because the financing is provided by his buyer so that the exporter is able to consider this above and beyond the regular credit facilities available from his own bank.

FOREIGN EXCHANGE

"Foreign exchange" is defined as the conversion of freely usable funds of one country into freely usable funds of another country; the rate at which such conversion is made is known as the "foreign-exchange quotation." Inasmuch as each transaction is a matter of "trading" between the buyer or seller of the foreign currency involved and his bank, the rate quoted applies only to that particular moment. The quotation for the next transaction may well be somewhat different.

Foreign exchange is divided into "spot" and "forward," the latter also being known as "future" transactions. Where the transaction calls for the immediate delivery or sale of foreign funds, it is a "spot" deal. But where it is desired to protect the purchase or sale of the foreign funds for delivery at a later date, a "futures" contract is arranged with the bank. This would occur, for instance, if it is intended to pay for a purchase of French perfume in francs, 90 days hence; the cost in United States dollars thus is established immediately for the purpose of obtaining orders from the trade. Or, if it is desired to quote the buyer in England in pounds sterling on a particular order for shipment 90 days hence, it is possible, by entering into a "futures" contract, to fix the sale price immediately.

Most United States concerns buy or sell abroad in United States dollars, but competition often makes it necessary to consider doing business in other currencies.

FACTORS AND FOREIGN FINANCE COMPANIES

Formerly, factors and foreign finance companies were not particularly interested in international financing. Now, however, several large organizations have become active in this type of business. As a rule, they will finance without recourse.

Usually, exporters who use factors or foreign finance companies have not been able to obtain all the credit from their banks that they feel they need. Because of added risks which may be involved, the cost of such financing invariably is somewhat higher than at the banks. These companies, however, provide various services which banks are not able to give, and when all is said and done, it should be appreciated that factors and foreign finance companies serve a very useful purpose.

EDGE ACT CORPORATIONS

Similar in many respects to foreign finance companies are Edge Act corporations, named after Senator Walter Edge of New Jersey, who sponsored a bill in Congress in 1919 to broaden the base for international financing and investing. Provisions of the law are contained in Regulation K of the Federal Reserve Act (amended September 1, 1963), which permits the establishment of international banking and financial corporations under Federal Reserve supervision to enable Edge Act corporations to assist United States exporters and importers in particular—and United States commerce, industry, and agriculture in general—by means of financing international trade.

Sufficiently broad powers have been given to enable them to compete effectively with similar foreign-owned organizations through branches, agencies, and correspondents or through direct and indirect ownership in foreign-chartered companies engaged in banking, or other international or foreign corporations. Activities in the United States are restricted to operations clearly related to international business.

Edge Act corporations offer facilities similar to foreign finance companies in the form of nonrecourse export financing, but in addition may do a general banking business and may assist United States concerns abroad through loans to, and equity financing of, foreign subsidiaries and/or affiliates.

GOVERNMENT FINANCING ORGANIZATIONS

There have been many occasions when government agencies have been of assistance in financing exports. First and foremost is the Export-Import Bank of Washington (whose stock is entirely owned by the United States Treasury), which has done an outstanding job in behalf of United States exporters. Many exports involving letters of credit never indicate on the surface that the Export-Import Bank is in the picture. This is the case in connection with project financing by the Export-Import Bank where letters of credit in favor of United States manufacturers and exporters are opened by foreign banks in behalf of some department of a foreign government or some company located abroad and where such credits are confirmed by a United States bank in the usual manner.

Another branch of the United States government that has been helpful in financing our exports is the Agency for International Development (AID). Exporters usually know when AID is in the picture because of the special documentation that is required.

Still another arm of the United States government is the Commodity Credit Corporation (CCC), but quite likely few regular exporters have transactions involving the CCC.

International organizations which assist our exporters in one way or another, but not necessarily by direct financing, are the International Monetary Fund, the International Bank for Reconstruction and Development, the International Finance Corporation, the International Development Association, and the Inter-American Development Bank.

FOREIGN CREDIT INFORMATION

Obtaining credit information—so essential to credit executives—is a problem to many where foreign buyers are concerned. Credit investigating has become a fine art in the United States. Businessmen coming to the United States from abroad for the first time are amazed at the free interchange of experience among competitors. They just cannot understand it. On the other hand, banks, manufacturers, and trading organizations in other parts of the world may belong to the same consortium or group. With this in mind, it can be understood why it often is difficult to get the information wanted.

When inquiring of a bank on a name abroad, complete particulars should be given as to the inquirer's own experience, the amount involved, and terms. Then, when a reply is received, it should be considered in relation to the specific questions raised when the checking was requested.

Financial Statements. Another problem is financial statements. In this country, we are accustomed to giving and requiring audited balance sheets. This is not quite the custom in other parts of the world. In most countries, credit is very tight or almost nonexistent. Further, there may be no stock exchange to speak of where one can invest, or if there is, the country may have gone through so much inflation and/or devaluation of its currency that the only thing which has not lost its value (and therefore constitutes a good investment) is real estate. Another consideration is that because of high taxes, balance sheets may not always reflect the current value of a particular asset. Registered (or authorized) capital ordinarily has little or no meaning, and frequently paid-in capital is limited for the reasons just cited.

A good, close, personal relationship with the principals probably is the best means of determining a foreign firm's true net worth.

EXPORT CREDIT INSURANCE

It is a rare occasion when any discussion on financing exports does not, at some point, bring up the question of export credit insurance. Because of this, it is appropriate to refer briefly to the activities of the Foreign Credit Insurance Association (FCIA). This organization, which started operations in February 1962, is composed of some seventy-five of the leading private insurance companies and the Export-Import Bank of Washington.

Working through the exporter's own insurance agent or broker, FCIA provides short-term (up to 180 days) and medium-term (181 days to 5 years) insurance in a comprehensive policy covering both the commercial credit risk and the political and transfer risk on sales to overseas buyers. For those who desire political and transfer risk only—the commercial risk then being taken by the exporter—FCIA is prepared to write appropriate policies.

Under its comprehensive short-term policy, FCIA requires all export sales to be declared monthly, unless the shipper has elected to exclude letter-of-credit transactions and/or sales to Canada. (Naturally, sales on the basis of cash in advance need not be reported.) Under certain circumstances, FCIA may be willing to negotiate a policy to exclude specific buyers (possibly customers of one or more of a manufacturer's several product divisions, and in some cases, sales to certain countries) if the remaining overseas buyers provide a reasonable and acceptable spread of risk.

A "discretionary" limit is given each policyholding exporter, which enables him to extend credit to any of his buyers, up to the amount named, without referring to FCIA for approval. In such instances, the exporter is expected to have on file current credit reports, justifying the credit granted, from any two of the following: domestic or foreign credit mercantile reporting organizations; domestic or foreign banks; or the U.S. Department of Commerce (through their *World Trade Directory* reports); or one mercantile credit report and a three-year favorable current-ledger experience.

Where shipments over the fixed discretionary limit are concerned, the exporter must apply to FCIA for a "special buyer limit." Shipments are covered to the extent of 90 percent of invoice value insofar as the commercial risk is concerned and 95 percent for the political and transfer risk; in other words, the exporter is co-insurer for 10 percent and 5 percent, respectively.

Insurance on medium-term sales is on a case-to-case basis; the exporter is not required to insure all shipments (as is the case with short-term shipments). If such sales are to be repetitive, however, the exporter may obtain policies to cover. This type of transaction invariably covers capital goods (rather than consumer merchandise), and the insurance coverage includes interest on the unpaid balance at a rate of not more than 6 percent per annum. This insurance is for 90 percent of both the credit and political and transfer risks, although in certain markets the percentage may be less.

FCIA also provides contract (preshipment) coverage on both short-term and medium-term sales which is designed to cover the exporter from the time an order is accepted (instead of only after shipment) against insolvency or government regulations making delivery impossible.

Other types of coverage include overseas technical and engineering services, consignment sales, leasing, and products exhibited at trade fairs abroad.

CONCLUSION

This discussion has related primarily to financing United States imports and exports. However, large American banks which have well-established international divisions also finance foreign correspondent banks and others, covering not only shipments into and out of the United States but also transactions between two or more other countries. Such financing takes the form of opening letters of credit, as described above, reimbursement credits, creating bankers' acceptances, foreign-exchange transactions, and advances against items in transit, the latter representing payments out of a foreign correspondent bank's account with a United States bank before offsetting credit items are received, even though these transactions may have been effected at the same time by the correspondent bank abroad.

BIBLIOGRAPHY

"Financing Imports and Exports," Chemical Bank New York Trust Company, New York, 1965.

"Financing International Operations," American Management Association, New York, 1965.

"Guide for New World Traders," Department of Commerce, U.S. Government Printing Office, Washington, D.C.

"Guide to Export Credit Insurance," Foreign Credit Insurance Association, New York, 1966.

MacDonald, Philip, *Practical Exporting and Importing*, 2d ed., The Ronald Press Company, New York, 1959.

Madeheim, Huxley, *International Business—Articles and Essays*, Holt, Rinehart and Winston, Inc., New York, 1963.

Sanchez, J. Rodriguez, *Foreign Credits and Collections*, Prentice-Hall, Inc., Englewood Cliffs, N.J., 1947.

"Selling around the World," Department of Commerce, U.S. Government Printing Office, Washington, D.C., July, 1964.

Shaterian, William, *Export-Import Banking*, 2d ed., The Ronald Press Company, New York, 1956.

Stanley, Alexander O., *Handbook of International Marketing*, McGraw-Hill Book Company, New York, 1963.

"The Whys and Hows of Exporting for Manufacturers," State of New York, Department of Commerce.

"World Trade Is Banking's Business," The American Bankers Association, New York.

CHAPTER SEVEN

Personnel Administration in Foreign Operations

JAMES E. BOYCE *Associates for International Research, Inc., Cambridge, Massachusetts*

Foreign operations as an integral part of American business are, with certain exceptions, largely a product of the post-World War II era. Although the patterns of personnel administration owe a debt to the practice of the colonial companies of Western Europe, there have developed a number of characteristic ways of dealing with the foreign service employees of American companies. This is particularly true with regard to compensation practices, which are remarkably little varied either by industry or by the size of the foreign operation in terms of numbers of employees.

Although a fairly standard body of American practice exists in personnel administration, it is continually changing. Very few companies retain the policies established in the immediate postwar era. In fact, many, perhaps most, companies have found it necessary to make substantial changes in their personnel practices every few years.

These rapid changes are the personnel administration reflection of the overall evolution of American foreign operations. Foreign operations were initially viewed by many companies as another department or branch of their essentially United States business. There has been, however, a gradual evolution toward an international concept in which the company views itself not as a United States firm with a foreign operation, but as an international organization with the largest part of its business in the United States.

In the early phases of large-scale foreign operations, the primary concern of personnel administrators was with the United States employees sent abroad. This is still an important area, but its importance is increasingly shared with the problems of other nationalities of foreign service employees, the so-called "third-country nationals," and with the interrelationship between policies with regard to these foreign service, or "expatriate," employees and the local national managerial employees.

To an increasing extent, the international corporation tends to divide its employees into an international management group, including local national management, on the one hand, and the various other national employee groups, on the other.   Thus, there are four groups of employees of concern to the personnel administrator in foreign operations: the United States foreign service employees, the third-country nationals, the local managers, and the other local employees.

Typically, the personnel administrator of an international operation is primarily concerned with the managerial groups, the administration of the local employees being left largely to the management of the local foreign subsidiary.   Because much of personnel administration in foreign operations is patterned after and similar to that of domestic operations, this chapter considers only the problems peculiar to foreign operations.

SELECTION OF FOREIGN SERVICE EMPLOYEES

Recruiting and selecting employees for foreign service is at best a difficult and time-consuming task.   The difficulty lies primarily in lack of specific guidelines.   Although some research has been done on problems of adapting to a foreign culture, little of this work is in a form directly useful to the personnel administrator.   The methods by which the employee is evaluated in the domestic company have to be supplemented by an evaluation of the potential effectiveness of the employee in a foreign environment.   Because this foreignness factor may seem vague, management—particularly management new to foreign operations— may consider the problem of the employee's ability to adapt to the foreign environment as much less significant than the technical or managerial qualifications by which he is judged in the domestic organization.   Thus, the personnel administrator who is sensitive to this problem may find himself in a position of sometimes resisting management's choice of foreign service personnel.

Guides to Selection.   Unfortunately, there are no standard tests whose results provide much help to the administrator in his selection task.   There are, however, certain guides which can be suggested.

The Employee Must Be Considered in His Family Context.   The company is sending the employee abroad with his wife and children.   Many administrators feel that the wife is the key to a successful foreign adaptation.   Certainly it is extremely risky to ignore the wife in the selection process.   This is not the place to discuss the role of the American wife in business either here or abroad. However, it should be noted that the wife and husband face quite different problems in adapting abroad, and that, in general, the problems faced by the wife are the more difficult.   For the husband, the work situation is generally familiar, and he is surrounded by employees who understand that situation and who can communicate with him in his own language.   The wife, on the other hand, is faced with setting up housekeeping in an environment which is relatively more foreign than the one her husband faces.   Many of the labor-saving devices missing in the foreign home are replaced by domestic help frequently not English-speaking and not acquainted with the norms of American living in such matters as cleanliness, eating habits, and dozens of similar things. Where full-time domestic help is the standard, such as in much of Latin America and the Far East, the wife may feel her role in the family is partially supplanted.   Frequently the husband finds his foreign assignment both challenging and time consuming.   The wife, on the other hand, may find herself with little to do.   Alcoholism is a not infrequent problem with American wives abroad, and a seriously disrupted or broken home is too often the result of the failure of the wife to adapt successfully.

Children, with the exception of those in their teens, seem to present less of a problem than wives.   For the teen-age boy abroad, many of the activities normal to life in America are not available. For example, he will not be able to find part-time or summer work, for a variety of reasons. Furthermore, work he would normally do about the home may be preempted by servants. His problems, like those of the wife, may stem from too much idle time for which there are too few outlets. The teen-age girl may have similar problems although they are generally less acute. For both the boys and the girls, there are the social and dating problems as they grow older. Concern over such matters, coupled with worry lest the foreign education the teen-ager is receiving will not prepare him for college in the United States, makes the teen-age child a frequent cause of concern for his foreign service parents, and not infrequently the reason for requesting the father's reassignment back home.

The Employee and His Family Must Be Stable and Adaptable. The best bet is clearly a family which has shown itself able to move from one place and fit into another. Although the change to a foreign country is much more abrupt than any change within the United States, a family which has moved in the past will find the move abroad easier than one which has not.

If there is any indication of problems between the employee and his wife or with the children, he should definitely be turned down for foreign assignment. Too often, the hope that things will work out has led to a disruption in the foreign subsidiary, a damaged career for the employee, and a severely strained or wrecked home.

Motivations for Accepting Foreign Assignment. Aside from a feel for the stability and adaptability of the employee and his family—assisted if possible by professional psychological or psychiatric help—the best tool available to the administrator is a yardstick based on his evaluation of the motives of the employee in accepting the foreign assignment. Acceptable motives would include a realistic appraisal of better opportunities abroad; most unacceptable motives revolve around an attempt on the employee's part to escape from a problem either of a work or of a personal nature. Nearly equally unacceptable are those employees with an overly romanticized view of foreign travel and living.

Volunteers versus Draftees. Obviously, the best choice is the employee who wishes to go abroad and who has some idea of what he will find there. Almost invariably, those employees who have accepted foreign work as part of their career plan are more successful than those who have been drafted into foreign service.

The prototype of the successful foreign service employee is thus a man young enough to accept the challenge of foreign life with a young, stable, and closely knit family who have lived in more than one location and who are familiar with life in a cosmopolitan urban environment. The worst choice is the small-town couple who have never left home and whose children are in their teens.

ORIENTATION OF FOREIGN SERVICE EMPLOYEES

When the employee has been selected for foreign service, he, his wife, and possibly even his children should receive an orientation to familiarize them with the post to which they are assigned and to foreign living in general. Many of the personnel problems encountered in sending a family abroad for the first time, or even to a new foreign post, result from a disparity between their expectations and the reality they find. The orientation program should be designed to reduce this gap and to help the family make its adjustment to foreign living as smoothly as possible.

The personnel administrator in foreign operations should develop an orientation program for his foreign service employees. This is particularly important for families going abroad for the first time. A number of companies have made the course given by the Business Council for International Understanding (BCIU) a central part of their program.

For the personnel administrator who wishes to develop his own orientation course, the following suggestions will be helpful.

Orientation in Foreign Cultures. Unless the employee and his wife have, by virtue of their academic background or experience, a familiarity with different cultures, the orientation course should acquaint them with the concept of cultural relativity. Even an elementary understanding of the idea that men in different cultures react differently to similar circumstances, and what is held of value in one culture may be of much less significance in another, can be very useful to the foreign service employee. The most dangerous point of view to take into foreign operations is the parochial one which holds that one's values, attitudes, and ways of doing things are not only best, but also *morally* right. Thus, the foreigner acting normally and properly within his own context may appear dishonest, unscrupulous, or even immoral when viewed in American cultural terms.

The understanding of foreign cultures is, of course, the business of anthropology. Unfortunately, most anthropological writings are not of the sort to be directly relevant to the problems of the American businessman and his family adjusting to overseas life. There are exceptions. Among them are Edward Hall's *The Silent Language* and the oft-reprinted speech of Kalevro Oberg on cultural shock. Somewhat more academic, but clearly written and easily read (and available in pocketbook form) is Clyde Kluckholm's *Mirror for Man*.

The preparation of a bibliography and making such materials available to the employee and his wife are a start. If possible, it should be supplemented by lectures and discussions of the materials. Because many personnel administrators do not feel competent to give such lectures, it is often necessary to look outside the company for a speaker. The obvious choice is a professor at a convenient college or university who can be useful in the orientation program—provided he can keep his remarks on the desired practical level of understanding.

The need for preparation in cultural relativity varies, of course, with the foreign area to which the employee is being transferred. Obviously, it is much more necessary when the employee is being assigned to Asia, the Middle East, or Africa than it is when he is being assigned to Europe or even Latin America. Even for employees assigned to Europe, however, it has proved helpful. At the least, the employee and his family will appreciate their employer's recognition of the problems involved in moving into a foreign culture.

Information on the Place of Assignment. Although the employee and his wife may be interested in the general orientation to differing cultural values abroad, their real concern will be in learning of the specifics of the place to which they are assigned. What sort of housing and shopping and recreational facilities will be available, and what should they take with them?

To provide this type of informaton, many companies rely on orientation manuals describing the foreign city and its facilities. These manuals vary from substantial volumes to a few mimeographed pages. In any case, they are worth the effort of preparation. Materials may come from a variety of sources. Travel guides will provide some information, as will the personal experience of the personnel administrator. One frequently overlooked but excellent source is the *post reports* prepared by each American embassy abroad and on file in the U.S. Department of State for the orientation of United States foreign service employees.

Perhaps the best source of information, particularly for the wife, is contact with others who have served in the foreign location.   Some administrators make a point of asking returning wives to assist them in orienting the families of new foreign service families, and thus keep on tap a supply of usually very helpful assistants for their programs.

Language Training.   No part of an orientation program is as important as language training.   This is recognized by most companies that send employees abroad.   Some companies rely on instruction after the employee and his family reach the foreign location.   A frequent arrangement is to pay tutoring costs either on the employee's own time or on the company's.   Other companies, with concentrations of employees, have regular language courses.   The former arrangement, which leaves language learning up to the employee, seldom produces the desired results.   This seems to be the result of frequently poor instruction on the part of a local tutor coupled with the typically heavy job demands on the employee during his first months on the new job.   It is probably better to provide at least the beginnings of language instruction before the employee leaves the United States.

Fortunately, instruction in speaking foreign languages has received considerable attention in the United States beginning with the famous Army courses of World War II.   Modern instruction techniques, usually relying on tape recorders, have accelerated and simplified a learning process typically quite difficult for adults, particularly Americans who normally have had no previous exposure to a foreign language.   However, even the mechanical techniques and the emphasis on developing a speaking, as opposed to the traditional reading, ability do not produce magical results.   A few weeks' exposure in one of the many schools specializing in language training may give the employee and his wife a basic familiarity and lead to their feeling somewhat more at ease in their new foreign environment.   However, it takes months of hard work to acquire any real competence in even the relatively simple-to-learn languages of Western Europe.

For those companies desiring to acquire their own language "laboratories" for taped instruction, several firms specialize in such installations.   However useful such taped instruction may be, it is probably not worth the investment unless it can be combined with live teachers.

COMPENSATION FOR FOREIGN SERVICE EMPLOYEES

Perhaps the most difficult aspect of personnel administration in foreign operations concerns compensation systems for foreign service employees.   American business has developed an approach to this problem which is remarkably consistent both among industries and among large and small foreign operators.

Extra Compensation for Overseas Service.   For compensation purposes, American companies, almost without exception, view foreign service as an extension of domestic service.   Thus, the salary paid in the employee's home country for a given position is also considered appropriate as the basis for the employee's compensation wherever he is assigned.   To this base salary are normally added two types of supplements: a bonus or premium for foreign service and various adjustments to compensate the employee for higher living or tax costs in his country of assignment.   Using a domestic base salary and adjusting it to fit the foreign situation clearly makes the employee more flexible in his assignments.   No matter where he is sent abroad, he retains his domestic base salary.   On repatriation to his home country, he returns to his base salary.

Although it is the usual, and probably the best, basis for a foreign service compensation system, the concept is sometimes applied so rigidly that one loses sight of the fact that one is staffing a foreign job and not one in the domestic organization.   The comment frequently heard that the foreign job involves more than its home country counterpart is another way of saying that the foreignness factor in the overseas position is not considered in the domestic job evaluation. Frequently, the foreign job involves more independent responsibility if only because of distance from the home base.   Staffing is often less adequate in overseas subsidiaries, resulting in a heavier work load on the foreign employee than he would have at home.   Finally, there is the intangible of representing the parent company in a foreign context.   It has been suggested that an effective evaluation of this foreignness factor would put overseas compensation and particularly the bonus or premium element of this compensation on a more rational basis.

The Overseas Bonus or Premium.   The payment of a regular overseas bonus or premium is partly a tradition.   The practice seems to have been begun as compensation for hardship areas abroad.   Stemming from colonial business practices of Western European companies, the custom was adopted by the American oil companies well before World War II.   After the war, as American business began to expand abroad, this pattern of foreign service premiums was copied by other companies without regard to the hardship element which was probably the original motivation for such payments.   Thus, in a survey of 121 companies employing Americans abroad conducted in 1965, 102 companies, or 84 percent, indicated that they paid such a bonus.

Equally traditional is the manner of computing the foreign service premium. With only random exceptions, companies paying a premium calculate it as a fixed percentage of the base salary.   Although some companies apply a monetary limit, most companies merely apply the premium percentage to the base salary without limit.

With the oil companies, the traditional premium was 25 percent of base salary. On a world-wide basis, 15 or 20 percent has become more nearly standard.   Furthermore, there is evidence of a gradual return to the hardship concept which evidently accounted for the original foreign service bonuses.   Now many companies distinguish between Europe, where premiums of 10 to 15 percent are fairly standard, and hardship areas with 25 percent or higher premiums.   Some companies have eliminated the premium completely in recent years, substituting a hardship allowance in some areas.

The personnel administrator who recognizes a need for an added incentive to attract, motivate, and retain personnel in overseas service may be able to devise systems superior to the percentage-premium approach.   However, he is apt to find the weight of tradition, as expressed in competitors' and other companies and as articulated by his foreign service employees, a difficult obstacle to overcome.

Clearly, the future trend is toward declining premiums, particularly in the advanced countries.   A personnel administrator establishing a new system would be well advised to include within the system provision for varying the premium percentage (probably downward) in the future.

Allowances for Higher Living Costs Abroad.   The most complex part of the overseas compensation package involves the determination of the proper allowances to compensate the foreign service employee for higher living and tax costs abroad.   It may surprise the uninitiated, accustomed to thinking of the United States as a country with a high standard and high cost of living, to discover that most companies regard living abroad as more expensive than living in the United States and compensate their employees accordingly.   The notable exception is the Latin American countries aside from Venezuela.   This uniformity of view reflects the equally uniform use of the Department of State index of foreign living costs as a measure for determining appropriate allowances. Because this index does not consider either housing or educational costs, the usual cost-of-living allowance package consists of three components: a cost-of-living allowance (excluding housing and education), a housing allowance, and an educational allowance.

Cost-of-living Allowance. Again following a pattern originated by the oil companies, most American firms use the Department of State index as the measure of cost differences for purposes of establishing cost-of-living allowances. Unfortunately, this index is designed and maintained specifically for the purposes of the Department of State in determining living-cost adjustments for government personnel abroad. Well fitted to its intended purpose, it is not a particularly good measure of living costs for American businessmen. From an operational standpoint, its strongest point is its use by a majority of American firms in overseas operations; its weakest point is the lack of confidence which many managements and foreign service employees have in its accuracy. These concerns are amplified by the fact that the index is updated only annually regardless of changes within the foreign country, and these updatings are frequently several months out of date when published. As a result, there is a need for cost measures better fitted to the requirements of American business which are more responsive to changes in foreign living costs. This need is beginning to be filled by private consulting groups.

An examination of the makeup of the Department of State index and its typical application by American companies supports the lack of confidence with which it is sometimes regarded. Briefly, the index uses as its measuring base point a salary lower than that usually paid a businessman abroad, and at this point uses some weights which are not realistic in terms of living patterns of American businessmen abroad. The result is a tendency for the index to be high in Europe and low in Latin America from the standpoint of the business user.

These inaccuracies are amplified by the manner in which the index is normally applied by businesses. To determine a cost-of-living allowance at a given salary, the index is multiplied by a "spendable income." This spendable income is the statistical expenditure in the United States for current consumption. In determining an allowance in this fashion, the assumption is implicitly made that expenditures abroad increase with income the same as they do in the United States. Both logic and research studies support the view that expenditures would tend to increase less rapidly overseas, with the isolated oil or mining camp as the ultimate example of a nearly flat consumption expenditure curve.[1] Applied in this fashion, the resulting allowances tend to be too high for the upper incomes and may be too low for the lower incomes.

Housing Allowance. Most companies provide a housing allowance for their foreign service employees. The normal practice is to pay the foreign cost, within some limit, to the extent that this cost exceeds the statistical housing cost in the United States. There are various methods used to determine the foreign housing costs, ranging from using the actual rent which the employee is paying to setting a limit based on the housing-allowance figures published by the Department of State. To determine the assumed United States housing cost, the most frequent method uses a flat percentage of salary, generally 15 percent, as the average United States housing cost. Actually, as statistics will show, this figure is somewhat high except at low levels, and the percentage declines with increasing income. A United States housing curve derived from a statistical source

[1] See J. E. Boyce, "Determining Cost-of-living Allowances for Overseas Personnel," *Personnel,* January–February, 1961.

such as Bureau of Labor Statistics' *Urban United States 1960–61: Consumer Expenditures and Income* is preferable, from the standpoints of both accuracy and reasonableness.

Education Allowances. To offset the cost of private education for the children of foreign service employees, most companies make a practice of reimbursing the employee for the actual cost, or the actual cost within a fixed limit, of the education of his children abroad.

Fortunately, the problem of schooling for American children abroad has produced American schools in nearly every foreign city in which American business operates. Normally partially staffed with American teachers and using American teaching materials, these schools generally are academically adequate, but frequently lack the range of extracurricular activities associated with a large public school in the United States.

Allowances for Income Differentials. In addition to allowances to compensate the employee for higher living costs abroad, an increasing number of companies make provision for "income tax equalization." Tax equalization, a form of guaranteeing the employee his home-country after-tax salary wherever he is assigned, is generally accomplished by deducting an assumed home-country tax and paying his foreign tax obligations.

For United States employees, the assumed home-country tax (normally called the "hypothetical tax") is usually computed using standard deductions although often with a higher limit than the $1,000 provided in the tax law. Some companies use United States statistical tax figures computed from the data compiled by the Internal Revenue Service on actual taxes paid. Clearly more reasonable as the basis for the hypothetical tax, the deductions in these statistical taxes run from 14 to 16 percent rather than the 10 percent with a $1,000 limit provided in the law.

The payment of the actual foreign tax bill of the employee presents three types of problems: (1) it involves the employer more intimately in the affairs of the employee than many employers feel is desirable, (2) it may involve paying tax on extra-company income, and (3) to provide proper control, it involves some sort of audit of the tax bills or tax returns. To counter these problems, it has been suggested that the employee be paid a tax allowance based on comparing the hypothetical United States tax with a foreign tax computed on a similar basis. This idea has few adherents, primarily because of disparities between the tax laws of some countries as written and the application of these laws in fact. It seems likely, however, that the awkwardness of present tax-equalization schemes will move more companies in the direction of a tax allowance based on a comparison of estimated or hypothetical taxes in the employee's home country and country of assignment.

The "Balance Sheet" Approach. Because the various living and tax cost adjustments are not all necessarily positive, some companies combine all these elements algebraically to produce a single adjustment figure. A 1965 survey showed 34 of a sample of 121 companies, or 28 percent, using the balance sheet approach at that time.

Problems of "Split Compensation." The capstone to the complex structure of foreign service compensation is the problem of split compensation, or dividing the compensation paid the foreign service employee between the United States and his country of assignment. Dividing compensation in this manner probably stems from the desire of the employee to retain any funds not needed for current expenses as dollars in the United States. It has become a problem both in the equalization of personal income taxes for the employee and in determining what portion of the employee's salary should be carried as a business expense for corporate tax purposes both in the United States parent organization and in the foreign subsidiary.

The problem is that the division which has been traditionally used in many companies of approximately 70 percent of the salary paid abroad and 30 percent retained in the United States does not coincide with a reasonable charge for corporate tax purposes for either the subsidiary or the parent organization. Furthermore, the 70 percent paid abroad, usually shown as "local income" on the subsidiary's books, is not in most cases the legally taxable income in the foreign country for the employee. This problem has become more acute as both the United States Internal Revenue Service and the tax departments of foreign governments examine ever more carefully the relationship between compensation payments for foreign service staff and the personal and corporate taxes related to these payments.

"THIRD-COUNTRY NATIONALS"

Many companies employ foreign nationals as foreign service employees assigned to countries other than their own. These third-country nationals are usually British or North European. The rationale for the use of such personnel is generally their greater familiarity with foreign environments and languages, their greater willingness to live abroad in many cases, or merely their availability. A number of such persons were employed in the early 1950s when opportunities abroad with American companies were superior to those then available within Europe. Many third-country nationals are persons who have risen within the ranks of the subsidiary in their home country and who are sent on to larger responsibilities abroad. Whatever their source, they pose problems to the personnel administrator in foreign operations, particularly with regard to compensation.

The usual approach is to treat these foreign service employees in the same manner as the Americans, applying the same type of adjustments to salary. The problem is how to make these adjustments. Does one use the American foreign service premium percentage or some other? How does one measure cost differences between the home country and the country of assignment in the absence of any measure such as the Department of State index? The answer for many companies has been to bring these employees onto the United States payroll and provide the same allowances as would be paid an American of similar salary. The problem with this approach is that the disparity in salary that exists between the United States and the home countries of the third-country nationals is carried into the foreign service group. As a result, two men may be performing the same task at different salaries, purely because of their national origin.

LOCAL NATIONAL MANAGERIAL EMPLOYEES

The continuing expansion of American business abroad has brought increasing numbers of the national employees of subsidiary operations into managerial positions. A frequently expressed objective of American companies is to replace most, if not all, of their foreign service employees with local nationals in their foreign operations. Thus, these managers are rapidly becoming an important part of the managerial group with whom the international personnel administrator must deal.

As the local managers rise in importance, the personnel administrator is faced with a growing problem of consistency in treatment between the foreign service employees and their local managerial counterparts. The problem may become acute in companies professing the desire to convert from American companies to international ones. The problem is, of course, primarily one of compensation.

Although the local manager may be fairly treated from a standpoint of salary scales within his own economy, any serious difference between these scales and the compensation for his foreign service counterparts is bound to raise difficulties. On this question, many companies have taken the same path they have followed with third-country nationals, that of providing American salaries to top local management. In fact, these salaries are sometimes equal to the American salaries paid the foreign service employees of similar responsibility, and thus higher than a comparable United States base salary. Although such policies produce a desired consistency between the local and foreign service managerial groups, they are not satisfactory in that the local salary is no longer directly related to the operation in which the local manager is participating and whose fortune should be the ultimate determining factor in this compensation.

MANAGERIAL COMPENSATION FOR THE SUPRANATIONAL CORPORATION

It should be clear from the above description of the problems of interrelating the compensation of the foreign service groups with the local managers that, in terms of managerial compensation systems, the truly international company has yet to be achieved.

Although there is no body of corporate practice in the development of such international compensation systems, there have been experiments which may be indicative of future trends. Most such experiments take as their starting point the desirability of freeing managerial compensation from the bondage of the national economics of the countries in which the various segments of the organization function. This bondage is seen primarily in terms of differences in economic levels leading to differences in the real value of compensation, in income taxes, and in pension and social benefits.

The solution to the problem involves, first, establishing international standards for salary evaluation. As difficult as this is, it is less of a problem than providing compensation commensurate with the salary standards once set. To do this involves determining a standard and constant unit of value in which to express these salaries. This unit is probably best stated in terms of purchasing power. A system built on this principle would provide equal purchasing power for a given salary level, although the gross compensation, in local currency terms, would vary with internal tax rates and internal purchasing power. In such a system, the manager of a given salary level would receive the same compensation value in purchasing-power terms wherever assigned.

The difficulty with this approach is that although it equalizes value received with contribution provided, the value received and the cost to the company are not the same. However, the gain from consistent treatment of managers on an international basis, regardless of national origin or place of employment, may well outweigh the disadvantages of having to relate contributon to value received by the employee rather than to the cost to the employer of the services.

OTHER POLICIES FOR FOREIGN SERVICE EMPLOYEES

The principal problem areas in personnel administration of foreign operations have been covered above. Mention should be made, however, of other policies which are characteristic of the treatment of foreign service employees by American firms.

Home Leave.   Again following European practice, American firms nearly uniformly provide home leave for their employees.   At one time, these leaves were frequently three months or longer occurring after each three or so years of service.   With air transportation, home leaves have been reduced to a month or two each second year.   The tendency seems to be toward eliminating such leaves entirely and eventually putting the foreign service employee on the vacation plan of his home country.

It is usual to pay transportation to and from the home country, normally at economy-class air rates.

Travel for College-age Children.   Most companies pay the transportation expenses for college-age children to visit their parents abroad once each year.

Emergency Leave.   It is also a usual practice to provide leave and transportation expenses for husband or wife in the event of the death of a person in their immediate family.

Shipment of Household Effects.   Most companies ship household effects abroad as they do in the United States.   Growing appreciation of the high costs abroad has led to limitations on the amount shipped in some companies and to providing cash payments in lieu of shipping effects in others.

Automobiles.   Automobiles provide a continual difficulty in the administration of foreign service personnel, particularly in those locations where importation is difficult or impossible.   In some locations in South America, it is practically impossible to import a car and very expensive to buy one locally.   In these cases, many companies have resorted to policies of paying a portion of the cost of local purchase of a car.   It is normally provided that the depreciated value of this portion is recovered by the company on sale of the automobile.   Administrators contemplating such policies should be aware of the liabilities the company assumes in acquiring such partial, though indirect, ownership of the car.

BIBLIOGRAPHY

Boyce, James E., "Determining Cost-of-living Allowances for Overseas Personnel," *Personnel*, January–February, 1961.

Compensating American Managers Abroad, American Management Association, New York, 1958.

Dustan, Jane, *Training American Businessmen for Work Abroad*, Council for International Progress in Management, New York, 1961.

Dustan, Jane, *Training Managers Abroad*, Council for International Progress in Management, New York, 1960.

Henry, Edwin R., and Hollis W. Peter, "Steps to Better Selection and Training for Overseas Jobs," *Personnel*, January–February, 1962.

Jannis, C. Paul, *Salaries, Allowances, and Fringe Benefits for Americans Abroad*, American Management Association, New York, 1958.

Management Policies Concerning U.S. Personnel Stationed Abroad, National Foreign Trade Council, New York, 1957.

Oxley, G. M., "The Personnel Manager for International Operations," *Personnel*, November–December, 1961.

"Personnel Policies for Americans Overseas," *Management Record*, June, 1953.

"Recruiting, Selecting and Developing Personnel for Foreign Operations," *Management Record*, July–August, 1959.

Standardized Regulations (*Government Civilians, Foreign Areas*), Department of State, U.S. Government Printing Office, Washington, D.C., 1961.

"Worldwide Profit-sharing Plans Help U.S. Firms Attract, Keep Capable Managers," *Business International*, Mar. 17, 1961.

CHAPTER EIGHT

Taxation of International Operations

HENRY J. GUMPEL *Price Waterhouse & Co., New York, New York*

We speak of international taxation if a transaction—a sale, a licensing agreement, a transfer by reason of death, or the like—transgresses the frontiers of a particular country, with the result that the same income, property, or transfer is or may become subject to tax in more than one jurisdiction. It then becomes necessary to find an accommodation among the various tax systems concerned to prevent burdensome or confiscatory double taxation which acts as a serious deterrent to international commerce. This accommodation can be accomplished through unilateral statutory rules or international tax conventions.

Apart from the prevention of double taxation, which is a matter of concern to all industrialized nations, a country may wish either to encourage or to discourage foreign investments by its nationals, or investments by foreigners in its area, through special tax devices, depending on its economic outlook and needs. Although the applicable rules are described for convenience as the law of international taxation, they are rules of national as distinguished from international law. There is no body of international or constitutional law which limits the freedom of a country to tax its nationals with respect to foreign-source income or property located abroad, or to tax foreigners on income from sources in its area or property located there. Such limitations on the taxing power of a country exist only to the extent that a country accepts them voluntarily in relation to another country under a bilateral tax treaty.

PATTERNS OF INTERNATIONAL TAXATION

There is an almost infinite variety in the rules of the various countries which deal with foreign or international tax matters, that is, those that have a foreign element concerning the person of the taxpayer, the source of income, or the situs of property or a transaction.

Some countries still adhere, at least in theory, to the territorial system of income taxation under which nationals and foreigners alike are taxed only on income from sources in that particular country. The practical difficulties of determining the source of income and the applicable deductions under this system of taxation are obvious, and it is neither applied in a similar manner by the various countries which claim to observe it, nor followed consistently by any one of these countries.

Most countries tax their residents on foreign as well as domestic income and limit the taxation of nonresidents to income which is derived from sources in their area. Within this general framework, however, the differences in the definition of terms are so great that the rules of no two countries are more than superficially alike. Residence of an individual may be defined in terms of domicile or some lesser connection with the home country, or different degrees of residence may be distinguished in order to apply certain rules of taxation or to make them inapplicable. A very limited number of countries, including the United States, still use citizenship in addition to residence as an alternative criterion through which full tax liability of an individual is established. Residence of a corporation or other taxable entity may be based on the place where it is organized or registered, the place where its effective management and control are located, the place where its principal business establishment is situated, or any combination of these factors.

Although most countries recognize the fact of double taxation and employ certain devices to prevent or to mitigate it, the forms which this accommodation takes are very different. To name only the prinicpal methods, the double taxation of the same income both at the taxpayer's domicile and in the country of source may be prevented or mitigated by the country of domicile through excluding the foreign-source income from the tax base, applying lower rates of tax to foreign-source income, limiting taxation to such foreign income as is actually remitted to the home country, or permitting the taxpayer to claim the foreign tax as a deduction from income or as an offset against the tax of the home country. The latter form of relief (the foreign tax credit) is the principal unilateral measure through which the United States seeks to prevent or alleviate double taxation.

UNITED STATES LAWS AFFECTING FOREIGN BUSINESS OPERATIONS OF UNITED STATES ENTERPRISES

The following discussion is limited to the rules of United States tax law which affect foreign business operations by United States enterprises. No attempt can be made, within the scope of this chapter, to deal with foreign rules of taxation or, other than in summary form, the integration of United States and foreign tax law under international tax treaties.

The discussion is based upon the laws, regulations, and practices which were in effect in mid-1965. It must be recognized that tax laws are continually changing, so that although much of what is said may be expected to apply for some time to come, tax planning should always be checked against the latest laws, regulations, and practices before the plans are actually put into effect.

United States Jurisdictional Rule. United States citizens, resident alien individuals, and domestic corporations are subject to United States tax with respect to domestic-source income as well as foreign-source income. In general, only income which is realized by the taxpayer according to the accounting method followed by him (cash receipts and disbursements method or accrual method) is taxable. Certain extensions of this rule with respect to undistributed income of foreign personal holding companies and certain income of controlled foreign corporations are discussed below.

Nonresident alien individuals and foreign corporations are taxable only with respect to United States–source income. The rules of taxation which apply to nonresident alien individuals vary according to the nature and amount of the income and the length of time the alien is present in the United States. Foreign corporations are also subject to different rules of taxation depending on whether or not they are engaged in business in the United States. Significant changes in the United States tax treatment of foreign individuals, corporations, and estates were introduced by a Treasury bill (HR 13103) submitted to Congress of Mar. 8, 1965, and designed to promote foreign investment in the United States.

Definition of Terms. *Resident and Nonresident Alien Individuals.* Whether or not an alien individual who is physically present in the United States is a resident for Federal income tax purposes is a question which is decided according to all the circumstances of the case and, in particular, the taxpayer's intention regarding the length and nature of his stay. Although an alien, because of his foreign citizenship, is presumed to be a nonresident [Reg. Section 1.871-4(b)], every alien who is not a mere "transient or sojourner" is held to be resident for Federal income tax purposes [Reg. Section 1.871-2(b)]. An alien who lives in the United States and who has no definite intention regarding his stay is a resident, but one who comes to the United States for a definite purpose that can be promptly accomplished is not. If the purpose of the visit may require an extended stay, however, and the alien makes his home temporarily in the United States to accomplish this purpose, he becomes a resident for tax purposes even though he intends at all times to return to his home country.

The type of visa issued to the alien is another factor which will be considered in determining his status as a resident or nonresident. In general, an individual who enters the United States on the basis of an immigration visa is a resident from the time he arrives; conversely, an alien whose stay is limited to a definite period under the immigration laws (foreign visitor or trainee) will not be considered as resident for tax purposes in the absence of extraordinary circumstances [Reg. Section 1.871(b)].

Domestic and Foreign Corporations. Under United States law, the status of a corporation as resident or nonresident is determined solely by the place of incorporation. The seat of control and management or the location of the principal business establishment is of no consequence. Consequently, domestic corporations are all corporations which are created or organized in the United States or under the laws of the United States or one of its states or territories [Code Section 7701(a)(4), Reg. Section 301.7701-5]. Every other corporation is a foreign corporation [Code Section 7701 (a)(5)].

Resident and Nonresident Foreign Corporations. A corporation which is engaged in trade or business in the United States is termed a "resident foreign corporation." The phrase "engaged in trade or business" has been interpreted to include any activity for profit that is exercised in a somewhat sustained manner. A resident foreign corporation is, in general, subject to United States tax according to the same rules and at the same rates as a domestic corporation, except that it is taxable only with respect to income from United States sources. A foreign corporation that is not engaged in trade or business in the United States is described as a "nonresident foreign corporation." A nonresident foreign corporation is subject to United States tax only with respect to certain fixed or determinable income from United States sources, and it is in general not taxed on capital gains realized in the United States.

THE SOURCE RULES

In the case of nonresident alien individuals and foreign corporations, liability for United States tax depends on the proper characterization of income according to its source, because these taxpayers are taxable only with respect to income from United States sources. The characterization of income according to its geographical source is hardly of lesser importance to domestic taxpayers who engage in foreign transactions of one kind or another. The source rules determine the exemption of foreign-earned income of United States citizens working abroad (Code Section 911) and that of individual residents of Puerto Rico who are not subject to United States tax on their Puerto Rican–source income (Code Section 933). They determine whether a United States corporation qualifies as a Western Hemisphere trade corporation and is entitled to the preferential tax rates available to such corporations (Code Sections 921, 922), or whether it can claim exemption of its foreign-source income as a possessions corporation (Code Section 931). The source rules are further important in connection with the attribution, to United States shareholders, of certain undistributed income of controlled foreign corporations, as described below. Above all, these rules determine the extent to which a United States taxpayer can claim foreign income taxes as an offset against United States tax.

The Source Rules in Detail. The United States source rules are included in Code Sections 861–864 and the regulations thereunder. They are briefly summarized below.

Income from Sources within the United States (Code Section 861)

Interest. All interest on obligations of the United States or a political subdivision thereof and interest owed ˙by debtors who are residents of the United States, except interest on bank deposits paid to persons who are not engaged in a business in the United States, or paid by a resident alien individual, a resident foreign corporation, or a domestic corporation if less than 20 percent of the payer's gross income is derived from sources in the United States.

Dividends. All dividends distributed by a domestic corporation, unless less than 20 percent of its gross income is derived from United States sources, or the payer of the dividend is a possessions corporation (Section 931). Dividends paid by a foreign corporation which derives at least 50 percent of its gross income from sources in the United States are treated as income from the United States in the proportion which the corporation's United States–source income bears to its total gross income.

Compensation for Services. Compensation for personal services performed in the United States, except for certain service compensation of aliens who are temporarily present in the United States.

Rentals and Royalties. Rentals and royalties from property located in the United States or any interest in such property, including compensation for the use, or the privilege of using in the United States, patents, copyrights, secret processes and formulas, goodwill, trademarks, franchises, and similar properties.

Sale of Real Property. Gain from the sale of real property situated in the United States.

Sale of Personal Property. Gain from the *purchase* of personal property outside the United States and the *sale* thereof within the United States. A sale is deemed to be made at the place where the seller transfers all his rights, title, and interest to the property to the buyer, unless the passage of title is arranged in a particular manner for tax avoidance purposes.

Income from Sources without the United States (Code Section 862)

Interest.   Any interest not from United States sources.

Dividends.   Any dividends not from United States sources.

Compensation for Services.   Compensation for services performed outside the United States.

Rentals and Royalties.   Rentals and royalties from property located outside the United States, or for the use, or the privilege of using outside the United States, patents, copyrights, secret processes and formulas, goodwill, trademarks, franchises, and similar properties.

Sale of Real Property.   Gain from the sale of real property situated outside the United States.

Sale of Personal Property.   Gain from the *purchase* of personal property in the United States and the *sale* thereof outside the United States.

Income from Sources Partly within and Partly without the United States [Code Secion 863(b)]

Income of certain types is considered to be derived in part from United States sources and in part from foreign sources.   The income tax regulations include detailed source rules with respect to these categories of income.   In general, this classification includes income from transportation services that are rendered partly within and partly without the United States, income from the sale of personal property produced in the United States and sold abroad, and income from the sale of personal property which is produced abroad and sold in the United States.

STATUTORY RELIEF FOR CERTAIN FOREIGN-SOURCE INCOME

The following describes the special statutory rules through which the United States grants certain tax preferences for foreign-source income or relief from its own tax to prevent double taxation.

Foreign-earned Income of United States Citizens.   Section 911 of the Internal Revenue Code grants a limited exemption from United States tax for foreign-earned income of United States citizens.   The exemption applies to earned income such as salaries, wages, commissions, and other compensation for personal services, except for compensation paid by the United States or any of its agencies.   The exemption does not apply to unearned income from domestic or foreign sources, including dividends, interest, rentals, royalties, or other income from capital.   Although foreign-earned income may be exempt as described below, it must be reported on a special form filed with the taxpayer's return.

A United States citizen can claim the exemption for foreign-earned income under one of two conditions:

1. If he has been a bona fide resident of a foreign country or countries for an uninterrupted period which includes at least one full taxable year (calendar year);

2. If he was physically present in a foreign country or countries for at least 510 days (17 months) during any consecutive period of 18 months.

The amount of the exemption is limited to $20,000 a year, except that individuals qualifying under no. 1, above, can claim an annual exemption of $25,000 after completing three full years of foreign residence.   The exemptions are prorated for fractional parts of a year, and the exemption under no. 2, above, is reduced for working days spent in the United States.

Western Hemisphere Trade Corporations.   A Western Hemisphere trade corporation (WHTC) is a domestic corporation all of whose business, except for incidental (insignificant) purchases, is done in the Western Hemisphere. Further conditions for qualification are that 95 percent of the corporation's gross income must be from foreign sources and that 90 percent of its gross income must be derived from the active conduct of a trade or business (Code Section 921). The term "Western Hemisphere" covers, in general, all countries in North, Central, and South America (including the United States), with certain exceptions (Bermuda).

A WHTC can claim a percentage of its taxable income as a special deduction. For 1965 and subsequent years, this percentage is 14/48 or 29.167 percent. In effect, the maximum tax rate applying to a WHTC is approximately 34 percent, compared with a regular maximum corporate rate of 48 percent. On taxable income of $100,000, a WHTC would pay a Federal income tax of $27,500, compared with a tax of $41,500 for an ordinary corporation.

WHTC's cannot be used for manufacturing operations in the United States (because of the requirement that 95 percent of gross income must be from foreign sources) or for holding-company functions (because of the requirement that 90 percent of gross income must be from active business operations). They are widely used, however, to serve as trading vehicles for exports to Latin American countries. In the usual case, a WHTC is organized as a subsidiary of a United States manufacturing corporation. Care must be taken in these cases to ensure that the full manufacturing profit remains taxable to the parent company and that the trading profit assigned to the WHTC is determined in a manner which will not give rise to a reallocation of income by the Internal Revenue Service under the provisions of Section 482 of the Internal Revenue Code.

Income from United States Possessions.   United States citizens and domestic corporations deriving certain income from possessions of the United States are entitled to exclude such income, and other income from foreign sources, for purposes of United States taxation, provided that certain conditions are complied with (Code Section 931). Specifically, at least 80 percent of the taxpayer's gross income must be from sources within a possession, and at least 50 percent of such income must be derived from the active conduct of a trade or business within a possession. However, all items of income that are received in the United States remain subject to United States tax regardless of the geographical source of the income. This rule, however, only applies to direct receipts of income, and a possessions corporation will not destroy its status as such by placing its funds in a bank account in the United States.

As a result of these rules, a qualifying possessions corporation—for example, a manufacturing or trading subsidiary of a United States corporation all of whose business is carried on in Puerto Rico—can claim full exemption from United States tax. The corporation is, of course, subject to tax in the country of operation. As a domestic corporation, a possessions corporation has a significant advantage over a foreign corporation in that it can be liquidated tax-free under Section 332 of the Code without an advance ruling by the Commissioner of Internal Revenue (Code Section 367), whereas a liquidating distribution made by a foreign corporation out of post-1962 profits is generally taxable at ordinary income tax rates (Code Section 1248).

The term "possession" includes the Panama Canal Zone, Guam, American Samoa, Wake Island, and the Midway Islands, but does not include the American

Virgin Islands. For the purposes of the provisions discussed here, Puerto Rico is considered a possession with respect to domestic corporations but not with respect to individual United States citizens or residents.

The Foreign Tax Credit. Under the United States tax system, the foreign tax credit is the principal unilateral device for preventing or mitigating the international double taxation of the same income. The mechanism of the foreign tax credit is also used on the United States side for preventing double taxation in relation to countries with which the United States has concluded a tax treaty.

Crediting a foreign income tax means that the foreign tax is used as an offset against the United States tax. If the rate of the United States tax is higher than that of the foreign tax, only the balance of tax remaining after applying the credit is payable to the United States. In this case, the aggregate effective rate of the United States tax and the foreign tax equals the United States tax rate; conversely, the foreign rate will determine the aggregate rate of tax where the foreign tax rate is higher than the United States rate.

In lieu of claiming the foreign tax credit, a United States taxpayer can use foreign income taxes as a deduction from income. This deduction is usually far less effective than the credit against the United States tax, and it is used only where it is not possible to credit the foreign tax, as in the case of operating losses.

Taxpayers Entitled to the Foreign Tax Credit. There are two types of foreign tax credit—the "direct" credit and the "indirect," or "deemed paid," credit. These terms are explained below. The direct foreign tax credit can be claimed by all United States taxpayers, that is, United States citizens, domestic corporations, and (on the basis of reciprocity) resident alien individuals. The deemed-paid foreign tax credit, on the other hand, can be claimed only by a domestic corporation which receives a dividend from a foreign corporation in which it holds a certain stock investment, as explained below.

Creditable Foreign Taxes. The foreign tax credit can be claimed for foreign income taxes including excess profits and war profits taxes. It also can be claimed for foreign taxes that are imposed in lieu of a general income tax. The term "in lieu" is specifically defined in the income tax regulations (Reg. Section 1.903-1). Whether a foreign tax qualifies as an income tax or similar tax is decided according to United States concepts. Another requirement is that the foreign tax must be imposed on income which is foreign-source income by United States standards.

Types of Foreign Tax Credits. *Direct Credit.* The direct foreign tax credit can be claimed for foreign income taxes that are directly imposed on the United States taxpayer. Examples of such taxes are foreign withholding taxes on dividends, interest, royalties, or service fees, and foreign income taxes that are payable in connection with direct business operations abroad.

Deemed-paid Credit. The deemed-paid foreign tax credit can be claimed for foreign income taxes paid by a foreign corporation that is at least 10 percent owned by a United States corporation, and for income taxes paid by a second-tier foreign subsidiary that is at least 50 percent owned by the first-tier foreign subsidiary. The credit can be claimed for foreign income taxes that are attributable to dividends distributed to the United States corporation by the first-tier foreign subsidiary or through the latter by a second-tier foreign subsidiary.

Computation of Deemed-paid Credit. Different rules apply, for purposes of computing the foreign tax credit, to dividends received from foreign corporations which qualify as "less developed country corporations" and those which do not so qualify. Dividends received by a United States corporation from a subsidiary that is not a less developed country corporation must be "grossed up"; that is, the amount of the distribution must be increased by the foreign tax that is attributable thereto. Dividends received from a less developed country corporation are not grossed up. If there is a chain of foreign subsidiaries (a foreign subsidiary and a sub-subsidiary, and so on), the status of the first-tier subsidiary as a developed or less developed country corporation decides whether grossing-up is required. The credit is computed according to the following formula:

Less developed country corporation

$$\text{Foreign tax credit} = \text{foreign tax} \times \frac{\text{dividends}}{\text{profits before income tax}}$$

Developed country corporation

$$\text{Foreign tax credit} = \text{foreign tax} \times \frac{\text{dividends}}{\text{accumulated earnings and profits (profits after foreign income tax)}}$$

Limitations on Foreign Tax Credit. The Internal Revenue Code places certain limitations on the amount of foreign tax credit that can be claimed, to prevent excess foreign tax credits being availed of to reduce United States tax on domestic-source income. These limitations are known as the "per-country" limitation and the "overall" limitation.

Per-country Limitation. Under the per-country limitation, the amount of foreign tax that can be claimed as a credit may not exceed the same proportion of United States tax against which the credit is taken that taxable income from sources in each foreign country bears to entire taxable income. This limitation can be expressed by the following formula with respect to income from each foreign country:

$$\text{Limitation} = \text{United States tax on total taxable income}$$
$$\times \frac{\text{taxable income from country } X}{\text{total taxable income from domestic and foreign sources}}$$

The credit cannot exceed the amount of foreign tax actually paid, if this amount is less than that of the statutory limitation.

The per-country limitation treats income received from each foreign country as a separate unit and limits the credit to the amount of United States tax that is attributable to income from that country. Accordingly, if the effective tax rate of the foreign country exceeds the effective United States rate, the credit is limited to the amount of United States tax and the excess of foreign tax is not available as a credit.

Overall Limitation. Under the overall limitation on the foreign tax credit, all income from foreign sources and all foreign taxes paid on such income are aggregated. In effect, all foreign-source income is treated as if it were derived from one foreign country, and all foreign taxes are treated as if they were paid to that country. This limitation may be expressed by the following formula:

$$\text{Limitation} = \text{United States tax on total taxable income}$$
$$\times \frac{\text{taxable income from all foreign countries}}{\text{total taxable income from domestic and foreign sources}}$$

The use of the overall limitation will be more advantageous than that of the per-country limitation for any year in which the effective tax rate in some foreign countries from which income is derived is higher, and the effective tax rate in other foreign countries is lower, than the United States rate. On the other hand, the use of the overall limitation will be less advantageous than that of the per-country limitation if the taxpayer, during the same taxable year, sustains losses in one or more foreign countries and derives income from others.

To use the overall limitation on the foreign tax credit, the taxpayer must make a specific election. Once made, the election is binding for all future years unless the Commissioner of Internal Revenue consents to a revocation.

Carry-overs and Carry-backs. In general, an unused foreign tax credit of a particular year can be carried back to the preceding two years and forward to the following five years. However, an unused credit originating in a taxable year for which the per-country limitation is in effect cannot be carried to a year for which the overall limitation has been elected, and vice versa. Where the taxpayer has carry-overs of unused credits from per-country limitation years or where there are substantial losses from operations in certain foreign countries, it will in general be advantageous not to elect the overall limitation until the credit carry-overs or loss carry-overs are absorbed. Apart from these two situations, the use of the overall limitation will generally result in the greater tax benefit.

EXTENSION OF UNITED STATES TAX JURISDICTION

As a general rule, United States citizens, residents, and corporations are taxed on foreign-source income at the time such income is realized. If operations abroad are carried on through a foreign corporation, realization of income occurs at the time when the income of the foreign corporation is distributed to the domestic shareholders as a dividend. Until such time, United States tax on the foreign income is deferred. The paragraphs below summarize the provisions of United States tax law under which the principle of deferral is set aside and United States shareholders are taxed directly on undistributed income of certain foreign corporations.

Foreign Personal Holding Companies. A foreign personal holding company (Code Sections 551–558) is a foreign corporation which has certain characteristics regarding income and stock ownership. With respect to income, the rule is that 60 percent of the corporation's gross income during the first year in which it qualifies as a foreign personal holding company (50 percent in later taxable years) consist of passive investment income such as dividends, interest, royalties, annuities, or gains from the sale of securities or certain commodities transactions. Rentals and income from personal service contracts are also included in foreign personal holding company income under certain conditions. With respect to stock ownership, the rule is that more than 50 percent in value of the corporation's outstanding stock be owned directly or indirectly by five or fewer individuals who are citizens or residents of the United States. The "five or fewer individuals" rule is greatly expanded through far-reaching attribution provisions under which stock held by a corporation, partnership, estate, or trust is considered as being owned by the shareholders, partners, or beneficiaries, and an individual is deemed to own the stock held by his partners or certain members of his family. In a surprisingly large number of cases, an analysis of the shareholdings in large American corporations reveals that more than one-half of the stock is owned by five or fewer groups of individuals who are treated as one person under the attribution rules, and great care must be taken by the tax planner to avoid application of the foreign personal holding company provisions with respect to foreign subsidiaries of such corporations.

If a foreign corporation meets the statutory definition of a foreign personal holding company, its "undistributed foreign personal holding company income" is taxed to the United States shareholders as if such income had been distributed to them as a dividend. The income which is so attributed is reduced by United States and foreign income taxes imposed on the corporation and certain other items. In effect, the deferral of United States tax is removed and the shareholders are taxed as if the foreign corporation had made current distributions of its entire investment income to them.

Controlled Foreign Corporations. To curb certain abuses that had become apparent, the Revenue Act of 1962 introduced stringent provisions under which United States shareholders are currently taxed on certain undistributed income of controlled foreign corporations. The new provisions are included in Subpart F of the Internal Revenue Code (Sections 951–964). These provisions, and the regulations thereunder, are extensive as well as extremely complex, and only the barest outline thereof can be given here.

The attribution rules under Subpart F apply to profits derived by a controlled foreign corporation from certain third-country operations. They are aimed at foreign corporations organized in so-called "tax-haven" countries, that is, countries which either have no income tax or do not tax their corporations, or tax them only lightly, on foreign-source income. Subsidiaries organized in tax-haven countries were able to engage in selling, licensing, or servicing operations in third countries in a manner which did not give rise to taxation in the country of operations under either its local law or the provisions of a tax treaty with the tax-haven country; where taxation in the country of operation could not be avoided, as in the case of manufacturing, the affiliate in the tax-haven country would organize a local subsidiary and act as a holding company. In summary, the advantages of incorporation in a tax-haven country, combined with deferral of United States tax for the undistributed profits of foreign subsidiaries, made it possible to accumulate profits abroad or to invest such profits in other foreign operations without repatriation and reduction by United States tax. These possibilities were severely curtailed by the 1962 law. In addition, the new provisions also impose tax on investments by controlled foreign corporations in United States property. The latter rules, although of broad application, are aimed primarily at "disguised dividends," that is, investments by foreign subsidiaries in the United States which have the effect of a dividend (such as a long-term loan to the parent) or which utilize earnings that might otherwise have been repatriated in the form of a dividend.

Control. For purposes of the Subpart F provisions, a foreign corporation is a controlled foreign corporation if more than 50 percent of its voting stock is owned by United States persons (United States citizens or residents, domestic corporations, partnerships, estates, or trusts). In determining control, only shareholders who own at least 10 percent of the corporation's voting stock are counted, and only those shareholders are taxed on the undistributed income of the foreign corporation.

Categories of Income Subject to Attribution. The types of income of a controlled foreign corporation that are taxed directly to the United States shareholders are summarized here in outline form.

   I. Subpart F income (Code Sections 951, 952)
      A. Income from insurance of United States risks (Code Sections 952, 953)
      B. Foreign base company income (Code Section 954)
         1. Foreign personal holding company income [Code Section 954(c)]
         2. Foreign base company sales income [Code Section 954(d)]
         3. Foreign base company services income [Code Section 954(e)]
  II. Previously excluded Subpart F income withdrawn from investment in less developed countries (Code Section 955)
 III. Increase in earnings invested in United States property (Code Section 956)

The various elements of "foreign base company income," the major category of income of a controlled foreign corporation subject to attribution, are briefly summarized below.

Foreign Base Company Income. *Foreign Personal Holding Company Income.* Foreign personal holding company income of a controlled foreign corporation includes, in general, the types of income that were discussed above in connection with the foreign personal holding company provisions of the Code. Income of this kind which is not in the nature of passive investment income, such as rentals or royalties derived in the active conduct of a trade or business, or dividends, interest, and gains from securities transactions derived in the conduct of a banking or financial business, is not attributed to the United States shareholders, always provided that these items of income are received from unrelated parties. Dividends or interest which a controlled foreign corporation receives from a related corporation that is incorporated in the same foreign country, and rentals or royalties received from a related person for the use of property in the controlled foreign corporation's country of incorporation, are also excluded from the application of the Subpart F provisions.

Foreign Base Company Sales Income. Foreign base company sales income is income from the sale of personal property that is produced outside the controlled foreign corporation's country of incorporation and sold for use outside that country, provided that either the seller or the buyer of the property is "related" to the controlled foreign corporation, for example, the parent company or an affiliated corporation. Sales income is not subject to attribution under Subpart F if the controlled foreign corporation converts the products bought by it or adds substantial value to the products.

Foreign Base Company Services Income. Foreign base company services income is income from commercial, industrial, technical, or other services which a controlled foreign corporation renders for or on behalf of a "related person" (parent company, sister subsidiary, or the like) and performs outside its country of incorporation.

Relief Provisions. The two major relief provisions through which the attribution, to the United States shareholders, of undistributed income of a controlled foreign corporation can be prevented are the minimum distribution provisions which apply to all Subpart F income and the 30 percent rule whose application is limited to foreign base company income. Other relief provisions of more limited application are briefly referred to below. Where application of the Subpart F provisions cannot be avoided, United States shareholders can claim the foreign tax credit for foreign taxes on income of a controlled foreign corporation that is attributed to them.

Minimum Distribution Provisions. A United States corporation can prevent being taxed on undistributed Subpart F income of a controlled foreign corporation by having the latter make actual dividend distributions in an amount sufficient to result in an aggregate foreign and United States tax rate which is not substantially lower than the United States rate [Code Sections 951 (a)(1)(A), 963]. The required minimum distribution, in terms of a percentage of the earnings and profits of the controlled foreign corporation, is determined in the inverse ratio of the effective foreign tax rate, and varies between 83 percent (where the effective foreign tax rate is less than 9 percent) and zero (where the effective foreign tax rate is 43 percent or higher). The minimum distribution election can be made for single directly owned foreign subsidiaries or for "chains" or "groups" of foreign subsidiaries. In the latter two instances, certain operating losses of one or more subsidiaries can be offset against profits of other subsidiaries. No minimum distribution is required where the foreign group has a net deficit on a consolidated basis.

Thirty Percent Rule. Foreign base company income of a controlled foreign corporation is not attributable to the United States shareholders if such income amounts to less than 30 percent of the controlled foreign corporation's total gross income for the year. On the other hand, the entire net income of the controlled foreign corporation will be attributed to the United States shareholders if foreign base company income amounts to more than 70 percent of the controlled foreign corporation's gross income [Code Section 954(b)(3)].

Other Relief Provisions. The Internal Revenue Code provides for limited exceptions from the application of the Subpart F provisions for qualifying investments in less developed countries, to encourage United States investment in these areas, and for certain income of "export trade corporations," to promote exports of American goods.

Investments in Less Developed Countries. Subpart F income of a controlled foreign corporation is not generally exempt from the attribution rules if such income is derived from investments in less developed countries. Section 954(b)(1) of the Code merely provides for an exclusion from the attribution rule for dividends, interest, and capital gains from "qualifying investments in less developed countries" to the extent that this income is utilized for other qualifying investments in such countries. Subpart F income of a controlled foreign corporation that was previously excluded from the application of the attribution rules becomes immediately taxable to the United States shareholders if it is withdrawn from qualifying investments in less developed countries.

Export Trade Corporations. Subpart G of the Internal Revenue Code (Sections 970–972) deals with controlled foreign corporations that qualify as export trade corporations. An export trade corporation is a controlled foreign corporation engaged in the export of American products. Subpart F income of such a corporation will not be attributed to the United States shareholders if the corporation meets certain extremely rigid requirements. In view of these requirements, export trade corporations are of rather limited usefulness.

Disposition of Stock of Controlled Foreign Corporations. Section 1248 of the Code, which supplements the provisions of Subpart F, deals with gain upon the sale or exchange of stock of a controlled foreign corporation, and distributions in liquidation made by such corporations.

Prior to the Revenue Act of 1962, such gains were taxable to the United States shareholders at capital gain rates, thus permitting realization of the accumulated earnings of a foreign corporation at a very low tax cost. This treatment still applies if the controlled foreign corporation qualifies as a less developed country corporation and if its stock had been held by the United States shareholder for at least 10 years. If the foreign corporation does not qualify as a less developed country corporation, the gain realized upon its liquidation, or the sale or exchange of its stock, is taxed at ordinary income tax rates to the extent of the earnings and profits of the controlled foreign corporation accumulated in taxable years beginning after Dec. 31, 1962. Section 1248 applies to United States shareholders owning 10 percent or more of the voting stock of the foreign corporation.

TAX TREATIES

Tax treaties are international agreements for the prevention or mitigation of double taxation. Most treaties further provide for the exchange of fiscal information and mutual assistance by the two governments concerned. In addition to income tax conventions which are the subject matter of this chapter, there are treaties dealing with estate and gift taxation or more limited areas such as profits from the operation of ships or aircraft. There were, in 1965, at least 200 tax conventions. The United States was at that time a party to 23 tax treaties, and additional treaties or revisions of older conventions were in various stages of completion.

Most of the United States treaties are with industrialized nations, and these treaties follow a definite pattern. The draft conventions with less developed countries (Israel, Philippines, and Thailand) show variations from this pattern because of the special situation of these countries—in particular, their urgent need for revenue and the absence of a mutual flow of investment between them and the United States.

The method by which double taxation of the same income is prevented under the treaties usually follows the internal law of the contracting countries. The principal device used by the United States, and certain other countries, is the foreign tax credit. European countries usually follow the "exclusion" method under which foreign income, or certain foreign income, is excluded from the tax base in various ways. Although these mechanisms are part of the local law of the countries and therefore apply even in the absence of a tax treaty, they have proved inadequate in many situations. Consequently, all developed countries have found it necessary to supplement their unilateral measures with bilateral tax treaties. With respect to business income ("industrial or commercial profits") derived by an enterprise of one of the treaty countries from sources in the other country, the treaties usually provide that the country of source shall not tax such income unless it is derived through a fixed place of business ("permanent establishment") maintained in its area by the foreign enterprise. Through this device, the tax jurisdiction of the source country is preserved where the foreign enterprise displays a substantial and sustained business activity in its territory and it is removed where the transactions of the foreign enterprise are limited to exporting or the purchase of goods or mere preliminary or auxiliary activities such as advertising, delivery, or the mere storage of goods.

The treaties usually reduce the rates of the withholding taxes on payments to foreigners such as dividends, royalties, interest, or service fees, and in some instances eliminate these taxes entirely. The value of these treaty provisions, and the comparative inadequacy of unilateral relief measures such as the foreign tax credit, become apparent upon a comparison of the effective tax rates of the contracting countries and the differences in their source rules. Because withholding taxes are almost always levied on gross income, a withholding rate on royalties of 25 or 30 percent (the United States rate) may be the equivalent of a rate of 50 or 60 percent on net income after cost and expenses are considered and thus be higher than the United States rate of 48 percent on net income. As a result, the foreign withholding tax cannot be fully absorbed by the credit against the United States tax unless the foreign country reduces its rate.

In addition, differing concepts of source in the two countries will often result in severe double taxation unless relief is available under a treaty. For example, the foreign country may tax services rendered to one of its nationals by an American enterprise because the services are utilized in that country or paid for by one of its enterprises, even though they are not performed in its area; conversely, the United States, under its source rules, will not consider the compensation as foreign-source income and thus will not allow the application of the foreign tax credit, because the services are not rendered abroad. Similar instances of double taxation arise where the foreign country defines the place of a sale as the place where the order is accepted, while the United States relies on the title passage rule, or where the two countries have different concepts regarding the proper allocation of profits between a parent company in one of the countries and a subsidiary in the other. In these instances and others, the treaties attempt to find an accommodation between the conflicting tax claims of the two countries concerned.

Tax treaties are one of the most important tools in international tax planning, and treaties among foreign countries may be as important in this respect as those concluded by the United States. To illustrate the point, assume that a United States corporation has a subsidiary in the Netherlands which in turn owns the shares of an Italian corporation. The Italian withholding tax on dividends (normally 30 percent) is waived under the tax treaty between Italy and the Netherlands. The Netherlands, on the other hand, does not tax its corporations on dividends received from a foreign corporation, provided that at least 25 percent of its share capital is owned by the Netherlands corporation. As a result, the Italian dividends are exempt from both Italian and Netherlands tax and can, subject to the Subpart F provisions of the Internal Revenue Code, be reinvested in other ventures. If the dividends are redistributed to the United States parent, they will be subject to Netherlands withholding tax at the rate of 15 percent or 5 percent under the revised tax treaty between that country and the United States.

SELECTING THE FORM AND METHOD OF INTERNATIONAL OPERATIONS

The foregoing survey describes the principles of United States tax law which are of particular significance in the planning of international operations. The choice of the form in which such operations should be conducted, and the most advantageous method of conducting them, will vary from case to case according to the nature of the business, its operational objectives and requirements, the foreign markets concerned, the supply of materials and labor in the foreign area, tax incentives that may be extended by the foreign government, and numerous other considerations. Basically there are only three possible forms of organization—branch, domestic subsidiary, and foreign subsidiary. However, the branch may be that of the parent, of a domestic subsidiary, or of a foreign subsidiary; the domestic subsidiary may be a Western Hemisphere trade corporation, a possessions corporation, or an ordinary corporation without special tax attributes; and finally, the foreign subsidiary may be organized in any one of the various forms provided by the laws of the foreign country involved, and it may conduct operations in that country or in other areas. In general, the use of a branch of a United States corporation will be helpful during the initial stage of a foreign venture, if operating losses are expected during that period.

Foreign and international operations of United States enterprises are closely reviewed by the Office of International Operations (OIO), a special branch of the Internal Revenue Service. The Service has power under the authority of Section 482 of the Code to reallocate income and deductions between domestic and foreign enterprises under common control, and it has used this power extensively to adjust intercompany prices, to disallow deductions to an American corporation where, in its opinion, the expense should be borne by a foreign affiliate, and to impute income to the United States corporation where a charge should have been made to the foreign subsidiary. Consequently, the area covered by Section 482 of the Code will have to be given careful consideration in any tax planning for foreign operations.

BIBLIOGRAPHY

Bittker, B. I., and L. F. Ebb, *Taxation of Foreign Income,* Cases and Materials (preliminary edition), International Legal Studies, Stanford Law School, Stanford, Calif., 1960.

Common Market Reporter, 2 vols., Commerce Clearing House, Inc., Chicago.

Heller, J., and K. M. Kauffman, *Tax Incentives for Industry in Less Developed Countries,* Harvard University Law School, Cambridge, Mass., 1963.

Nortcliffe, E. B., *Common Market Fiscal Systems,* Sweet and Maxwell, London, 1960.

Owens, E. A., *The Foreign Tax Credit,* Harvard Law School International Program in Taxation, Cambridge, Mass., 1961.

Price Waterhouse & Co., *Information Guides on Doing Business Abroad* (a collection of pamphlets on. the business and tax structure of about forty-five countries, revised annually), New York.

Price Waterhouse & Co., *Tax Guide for U.S. Corporations Doing Business Abroad,* New York, December, 1965.

Price Waterhouse & Co., *U.S. Citizens Abroad,* New York, December, 1965.

Roberts, S. I., and W. C. Warren, *U.S. Income Taxation of Foreign Corporations and Nonresident Aliens,* Practising Law Institute, New York, 1966.

Stanley, A. O., *Organizing for International Operations,* American Management Association, Research Study, no. 41, New York, 1960.

Treumann, W., "Recent Internal Revenue Service Audits of Foreign Operations," *Taxes,* vol. 40, October, 1962, pp. 788–804.

Wilson, Robert A. (ed.), *Proceedings of the Institute on Private Investments Abroad,* 5 vols., Matthew Bender & Co., Inc., New York, 1959–1963.

World Tax Series, Harvard Law School International Program in Taxation, Little, Brown and Company, Boston, to 1962; Commerce Clearing House, Inc., Chicago, from 1963.

CHAPTER NINE

Export-Trade Aids

ERNEST J. ENRIGHT *Director of Research, International Marketing Institute, Cambridge, Massachusetts*

The American manufacturer who would make the most of the continuing opportunities to increase his sales and profits by expanding his export sales volume has a wide variety of advice, assistance, and direct aid available to him on request. The export-trade-aid climate is so favorable that this situation can be described as a strong "buyer's market" for anyone who seeks export expertise. And most of this help can be available to the manufacturer at his own office if he does not wish to leave his desk.

The American manufacturer must take the aid initiative, because as in other countries, the American export expansion program is restricted by law and lack of powerful industry associations from being highly channelized or centralized. Even the U.S. Department of Commerce, which is the heaviest contributor to successful export promotions, is considerably limited in its activities. American industry has not developed a strong central voice or action center, nor have the associations that serve it.

The will to increase exports is found in all sectors of American business, and so the call to export expansion is many-voiced. The trade aids offered are of all types and from many sources, as varied as the offering organizations. The national export expansion coordinator, operating literally without budget of money and men, has through his regional volunteer committees done much to unify and thus multiply the benefits of these aids.

Despite such efforts, the trade aids are substantially diffused and must be sought out by the manufacturer. It is the purpose of this chapter, therefore, to identify the dominant types of trade aids and to propose ways in which the exporting manufacturer may avail himself of these with a minimum of time and effort. These principal types are described below.

Many manufacturers, although already making use of these aids, are not making optimum use because they neither know all that is available nor inquire properly to find out. As a first step in understanding the specific nature of the assistance available, the export-interested executive should, if he has not already done so, visit his local Department of Commerce Field Office and ask for a drawer-by-drawer tour of its information files.

ADVICE ON EXPORTABILITY

Comparative studies of exporting and nonexporting manufacturers show that a most serious hurdle to be overcome by the manufacturer new to exporting is his lack of conviction that overseas buyers want his product—he has no measure of its exportability. The managerial roadblock created by this lack of confidence is mainly responsible for the statistic that some 95 percent of America's 330,000 manufacturers confine their sales activities to domestic markets.

Export Assets of American Firms. A few pertinent generalities may be of some help in evaluating basic possibilities of selling overseas:

In most ways, especially in a quality sense, the American market is the most competitive in the world. Success at home in this sophisticated business atmosphere is a good indicator of probable success abroad.

The more broadly (or extensively) a product is sold throughout the American market, the greater are the chances of finding adequate markets abroad.

Quality of product, defined in the sense that the product does its task better—with more efficiency, more adaptability, and fewer repairs—sells most American products abroad despite their higher prices.

The American product offering (in lieu of or in addition to quality) differentiation or favorable price can also find good overseas markets. Americans are world specialists in product differentiation, and American goods are not nearly as "out-priced" in world markets as many nonexporters believe.

Other major assets of the smaller American exporter include managerial ability to sell at long distances from the factory, long experience in selling through agents and/or distributors, willingness to provide distributors with marketing help, and managerial flexibility to handle overseas relationships effectively.

The small American exporter is not physically different from his far more numerous nonexporting American competitors.

In sum, the most numerous group of American exporters (the smaller-sized producer) is made up of quality-conscious, adaptable, flexibly managed companies.

Foreign Competition. The presently nonexporting manufacturer may realize the made-in-U.S.A. export value of such generalities, but will hasten to point out that many foreign manufacturers—British, French, German, Japanese, and Italian—also qualify abroad and may be much nearer the larger foreign market. To reassure him, some additional observations may be pertinent:

In a great many cases, the American firm can offer faster and more satisfactory delivery and supply service despite the longer distances involved.

The American firm is often more ready to offer marketing aids and technical and repair services.

The overall performance reputation of made-in-U.S.A. goods is a valuable export plus.

Domestic Competitors. More specifically and as a quick check on exportability, each manufacturer is advised to find out what his competition is doing already in foreign markets. Receipt of news that a competing firm is successfully selling abroad is good news in that it indicates that new markets are available, but it is bad news because:

1. The competitor has gained an edge in volume, product, and market knowledge abroad.

2. The competitor has overseas contacts that may provide him with new ideas and product developments which will enable him to strengthen his domestic market position.

Classification Numbers. Finally, an executive who has any measurable interest in exporting can begin profitably by doing the small amount of desk research needed to find the classification numbers that would identify his product in foreign trade. He should choose the appropriate numbers from each of the following classification systems:

Standard Industrial Classification (SIC). Developed by the Bureau of the Census for classifying United States industry according to the primary materials, these classification numbers are used only indirectly for foreign-trade purposes.

Schedule B Classification System. Developed by the Bureau of International Commerce to classify American goods in international trade, this numbering system was completely changed on Jan. 1, 1965, to conform fairly closely to the United Nations' system mentioned below.

Standard International Trade Classification (SITC). This system was developed by the United Nations and is recommended for use by all countries to facilitate accumulation of comparable world-trade statistics.

The appropriate classification numbers can be found in special manuals, but these source volumes may not be located in a place convenient for the manufacturer. Given an adequate description of the product to be classified, the local freight forwarder or the Commerce Field Office will seek out the classification number. However, it is advised, when the manufacturer has the chance, that he personally check the classification number that has been given him by someone else. Anyone who has worked on these classifications can see the many opportunities for inappropriate selection. It could be the wrong one because the product description given was inadequate, and if wrong, could be a disadvantage in several important ways. With the proper classification number, the manufacturer can examine foreign-trade statistics for himself to find out whether his product has had an adequate overseas market, and he can spot the location of such markets.

PINPOINTING LOCATION AND SIZE OF MARKETS

The exercise of watching the location and growth or change of domestic markets is a research effort that most well-managed firms make on a continuing basis. Such exercise should include a similar scan of overseas markets, but seldom does.

The interested nonexporting producer would like to know where in the world he can sell his product. Certainly he will be interested initially to learn the names of those overseas markets for his product that import the highest volume, reasoning that he might try to sell in those markets with a proved demand. He should become aware, however, of secondary, less developed markets, because they may provide adequate volume with less competitive pressures.

The exporter, frequent or infrequent, is well advised to watch these figures to assure himself that his distribution is adequately extensive (Is he covering a reasonable number of markets?) and that his distribution is adequately intensive (Is he, directly or through his representative, getting his proper share in the several markets?).

Sources of International Statistics. Almost complete international statistics can be found in three major sources:

U.S. Department of Commerce. Bureau of the Census Report FT 410, "United States Exports of Domestic and Foreign Merchandise," is published monthly and annually by the U.S. Department of Commerce and contains complete, accurate, and timely information on the quantity and value of export sales of United States goods. Analyses of these figures are very useful:

1. To show where *American* producers have been most successful in selling each class of goods
2. To suggest reasons why some markets are better than others
3. To show roughly by differences in unit value of exports which markets are using the bigger, heavier, or higher-priced units

Whatever the figures being examined, the user is advised to scan the export figures for at least the past three years. Such a scan can show or at least indicate whether:

1. A particular year's export volume was normal
2. A product has a wide or narrow world market
3. Developed or developing countries offer the best market
4. Transportation costs are a significant factor
5. The overall market is changing in size, and if so, in which direction
6. The market is steady or volatile

Statistics from Supranational Organizations. Figures published by the United Nations (UN) and by the Organization for Economic Cooperation and Development (OECD) can help fill the major analytical gaps left by a study of only United States trade volumes. These UN figures are not as current, but they are used by the knowledgeable to trace the relative trade success of firms from the United Kingdom, Germany, Italy, Japan, and others, to estimate the size of the world market, and to measure the United States share of such markets and determine whether this share is increasing. Possible reasons for the comparative United States performance may be inferred. A basis is thus found for a decision about whether the specific manufacturer would prefer to reach for markets now dominated by American or British or Japanese or German competitors.

Individual-country Statistics. Once a manufacturer develops a strong interest in a country, he should seek out the latest foreign-trade bulletins for that country. Reference to the specific bulletins will serve as a double check on other figures assembled, and in many instances, the commodity breakdowns are more narrow and more specific. Some caution should be observed in the use of trade statistics from many of the recently established countries whose compilation methods are the subjects of many stories. Fortunately, the accuracy of data from the developing nations is increasing every year.

Although the cautious use of trade statistics can be very valuable, these sources are not often on hand for study. Tight budgetary limitations make it impossible, except through outside generosity, for the Department of Commerce Field Offices to stock books other than those of government origin. The libraries of local universities are not completely tuned to the specifics of export marketing and seldom have an adequate collection of such sources. In the United States, the two most complete libraries of trade statistics are in the UN building in New York City and in the Department of Commerce building in Washington, D.C. Neither of these is very conveniently located. If regular sources fail, try telephoning the international research director of the nearest large firm; he may have what you need.

TRADE CONTACTS: PUBLISHED SOURCES

The busy, time-pressed American manager, when he discovers the location of interesting overseas markets, is not inclined to investigate such markets intensively, nor is he willing to accumulate a file full of papers concerning these opportunities. He prefers to take the shortest path to export action—an investigative path that will provide him with the names of potential agents, distributors, and clients.

The American exporter need never be without an adequate list of foreign contacts. In general, published sources of names are found in directories, special lists, and trade leads. The Bibliography at the end of this chapter contains many references to these sources.

Directories. Directories of many types can be found in abundance. The truth of this statement is evidenced by the annual publication of the loose-leaf directory of *Trade Directories of the World.* These volumes of business names and addresses are printed to serve the many segments of business and industry and are available under a number of covers such as: telephone and yellow pages; regional and national exporters, importers, and manufacturers; manufacturers using telex; store buyers; transporters and packers; and so on. One of the easiest tasks of overseas marketing is that of finding rows of interesting names. The corollary task of choosing among them is more difficult.

For this reason, specialized lists are more useful because they contain additional information that makes name selection easier. The lists published by the international rating services give, in addition to the firm name, mention of the product line handled, relative size, general credit rating, and whether the firm is a manufacturer, wholesaler, or retailer. Lists of foreign business visitors that are published in current magazines and newspapers enable the busy American executive to arrange to meet the foreign buyer who comes to our shores. A most useful compilation is the collection of *Trade Lists* by industry and country published by the U.S. Department of Commerce. These list the names of potential importers, distributors, and dealers and include some reference to each company's size, market coverage, width of line, and size of sales force. For $2 each, these lists are the best bargain in valuable lists of names.

Trade Leads. Some American exporters have used "trade leads" to develop a list of overseas contacts. Trading requests coming from foreign importers and buyers stream in to American banks, export service associations, and state and Federal commerce departments. These requests ask for contacts with American sellers (or buyers) of specific merchandise. A long-standing complaint of the impatient exporter is that such leads are too often "old" or have already been satisfied by a more alert exporter. Some knowledgeable Americans collect the names from all legitimate-appearing leads in the hope of getting a chance to fill the next order.

Legitimate-appearing trade leads, in contrast to the "fishing expedition" type, are those that give the receiver the conviction the inquiry is serious and honest. Such leads contain appropriate requests for specific merchandise, are businesslike in appearance, and provide the reader with some means of judging the business capacity of the sender. The best-known source of trade leads is the weekly section of *International Commerce;* and because the United States overseas commercial attaché runs a check of most companies which submit these leads, an adequate amount of background material is available upon request.

CHECKING ON FOREIGN CONTACTS

As soon as the would-be exporter finds the name of a promising overseas contact, his first question is concerned with the contact's payment record, followed by questions as to financial, marketing, and other managerial abilities. Fairly complete information on all these points is available from professional sources. The exporter need not stir from his desk, but the collection of this material will cost a modest sum.

The least substantial but most up-to-the-minute search may be made through your banker who uses the services of his overseas correspondents. The "bank check" is used, therefore, as a double check on other information; it is not a fruitful primary source.

Services such as those made available by the Foreign Credit Interchange Bureau provide a payments history of the individual concerned—the type and size of credit extended, payments, and a rating of the credit risk. A report of the *Dun & Bradstreet International* type is very valuable for background material that would be useful for making a judgment about the financial health and organization of the company concerned.

Similar to Dun & Bradstreet reports but a little more descriptive of the operational side of the foreign firms are the U.S. Department of Commerce's *World Trade Directory* reports (WTDs). Selling for only $2 each, the WTD may contain information detailed to include the number and location of offices and branches, number of salesmen, lines carried, foreign companies represented, and share of company sales from products of each country represented.

A desk analysis of an overseas company with the use of two or more of these reports should provide the executive with the basis for sound judgment on whether the subject is a good prospect as either a customer or distributor. Although such evaluation is not a perfect substitute for a personal meeting, this exercise should be carried out before personal interviews to save valuable overseas time.

TRADE CONTACTS: PERSONALIZED BUSINESS SERVICES

Export Service Organizations. An outstanding and meritorious feature of trade aid is the personalized marketing contact offer. This type of offer is made by the large export service organizations which have offices abroad, including banks, freight forwarders, and air and sea transportation companies. These companies volunteer, at no charge, to use their overseas-based operations personnel to make marketing contacts or seek answers to manufacturers' requests. The service works in this way: The American executive makes his marketing request known to the local agency of the offering company. This request is forwarded to company personnel in the overseas area designated, who, because they have a specific knowledge of the business community, can make discreet inquiries, contacts, and market checks. To service one such request may take up to three months. Among the organizations offering this type of service are Pan American World Airways, American Express Company, Committee for American Steamship Lines (CASL), British Overseas Airways (BOAC), and Air France.

Through these and other service contacts, the American manufacturer is in a buyer's market for export assistance, and if he knows how to ask, he can utilize the personal contact services of a large number of knowledgeable overseas businessmen. Most frequent users of these services are the biggest American exporters who take every advantage to reach markets where their own organization is not sufficient.

Trade Contact Survey. If, however, the executive prefers not to accept such free services with their implied commitments to hire company services if the export order is landed, personal overseas contacts will be made by United States commercial officials abroad for a fee of $50, and there are no business strings tied to this offer. This service is known as the "trade contact survey." Other personal contacts abroad may be handled by an ever-growing list of consulting firms and advertising and research agencies.

Whatever the channel used to make personal contacts, the American manufacturer may be well advised to let others make the initial calls, report on market conditions, locate areas of interest, and set up appointments and visits where a favorable reception is indicated. A great deal of wasted motion and money will be avoided.

Trade Missions. The trade mission in its many variants is an internationally famous means of getting a personalized contact abroad. This method entails no significant cost or effort to the individual, who submits a business proposal carried overseas by a mission member. Trade missions are sponsored by the Federal and state governments, industry associations, and regional trade centers; and although trade missions are of varying effectiveness, use of the appropriate trade mission will cost virtually nothing. It can offer, moreover, excellent chances of direct personalized contact. The profit odds are all on the side of the participating manufacturer.

Agents or Distributors. A different type of personalized contact for overseas information about dealers is an informal but often rewarding one. Many exporters get personalized contacts in many countries by asking their present satisfactory agents or distributors for good names in noncompeting territories. Other exporters compare distribution notes with manufacturer-exporters of complementary (noncompeting) products and may agree to share their overseas agents with each other.

FINDING MARKETING KNOWLEDGE

The larger-sized American exporter has his own overseas marketing system and gets much of his knowledge directly. The typical smaller-sized exporter cannot invade an overseas market directly from the home office or through branches, but must find and use an agent/distributor who has an adequate knowledge of the markets concerned. The overseas agent/distributor is expected to use his localized knowledge to sell the product. The American's chief problem is finding an effective, cooperative representative.

It is true that specific knowledge of overseas markets is much more scarce in published sources than lists of names and financial and economic analyses. The fact searcher will be rewarded, though, if he takes a few pains to look; the marketing facts added by such a search will be of help to the exporter in finding an agent and in providing his agent with appropriate marketing assistance.

Earlier, mention was made of the marketing request service offered by the export-aid institutions, such as American Express. In addition, some marketing studies are available from United States magazines with international circulations, such as *Time, Life,* and *Reader's Digest.* In some instances, the industry trade associations have published studies, notably in the machine tool industry. Articles on overseas marketing are beginning to appear more regularly in professional marketing magazines.

The U.S. Department of Commerce provides two sources that have been insufficiently publicized. First, the Department of Commerce commissions a market research study before spending its time and effort on a specific industry exhibit at any of its six trade centers. Abstracts of each research project are available at the Field Offices. Also available are copies of dispatches from United States commercial attachés abroad. A listing of the monthly marketing dispatches is available from the Field Offices. Larger companies make extensive use of these reports; the smaller ones should. This information is free, as the dispatches are loaned upon request.

Detailed information of specific markets may be extracted from a cluster of *Trade List* and *World Trade Directory* reports (WTDs). A word is needed about how to use these reports to extract a picture of the marketing pattern. From the U.S. Department of Commerce, buy WTDs (at $2 each) of all the distributors of your type of product in a particular area (city, state, or country), scan the reports, and extract the array of marketing facts available. A strong, usable marketing pattern will be the result.

KEEPING UP TO DATE

The task of keeping informed on changes and events in overseas markets is not difficult, because so many specialized sources are readily available. If a graphic representation of the progress of overseas markets is your forte, the monthly statistical (foreign-trade) publications of the United States and other countries will provide the coordinates for plotting.

The schedule for coming international marketing events, notes of changes in markets and laws, and the listing of export opportunities are available (1) in the regular issues of *International Commerce* (the United States), *Foreign Trade* (Canada), and *Board of Trade Journal* (the United Kingdom); (2) in the monthly reports of the more important banks in your area; (3) in the periodic revisions of the major published services such as the *Gallatin Annual* and *Exporter's Encyclopedia;* and (4) in the minutes of professional service societies such as the Foreign Credit Interchange Bureau.

The National Export Expansion program has stimulated a great deal of interest in training for export activities. An interested manufacturer should check with the local branches of the international trade clubs and/or the chamber of commerce to get the schedules of coming export programs and seminars. The back inside page of the weekly *International Commerce* lists such meetings for the coming month. In 1964, these pages carried notices of some 600 to 800 instructional meetings in export marketing.

TECHNICAL AIDS

A major drawback to greater American export participation is the unwillingness of the smaller American company to add export marketing personnel, and executive time is at a real premium. Chapter 1 of Section 16 covers the subject somewhat of the extent to which the services of export technicians can be used as an effective substitute for adding staff personnel.

Generally, the manufacturer is mostly uninformed about the many types of help and the specific nature of the help he can get locally. Ideally, each manufacturer should be trained to locate the sources of assistance before the needs arise. Locate the nearby sources of publicized information; of translation services; of handling, packing, and transportation assistance; of overseas financial credit and insurance advice; and of overseas marketing, customs, and tariff counseling. Such aid sources can be found through the local "international clubs," regional trade centers, field offices and cooperating offices of state and Federal departments of commerce, the Small Business Administration, chambers of commerce, and state manufacturers' associations.

After the location of these sources, it is equally important to know how to approach them for assistance. The exporting manufacturer is advised not to tell his source of help what he wants done; rather, he should describe the problem and ask his source what alternatives are available to him. He will be surprised at the number and variety of aids available.

An interesting and valuable tool for the manufacturer is a clear knowledge that the functional lines between freight forwarder, international banker, insurance broker, and transportation agency are breaking down. If the required service is not available or is reluctantly given by one of these trade technicians, the others will supply what is needed. The manufacturer-exporter should ask for any help he needs and ask about any point that is uncertain. The assistance is available around the corner or on the other end of the telephone. As a corollary dictum: *Never spend the time and money to go overseas until the homework is completed.*

GETTING THE PRODUCT EXHIBITED OVERSEAS

American goods that are shown, exhibited, or demonstrated overseas where buyers live are much easier to sell. The U.S. Department of Commerce has long taken the lead in getting made-in-U.S.A. products overseas where they can be more effectively marketed. Commerce efforts have been increasingly successful in a hard-hitting sales sense with the recent adoption of the following practices at trade fairs and United States trade centers: market research before promotion; vertical or narrow products to be exhibited; company representation to negotiate sales or distributor contracts; and special invitations to potential buyers.

In some cases, the American manufacturer may display his goods at United States–sponsored pavilions in international fairs or at one of the six permanent United States trade centers to sell these goods directly to foreign buyers. More often, the smaller United States exporter expects to market his products through overseas agents and distributors. In such cases, the manufacturer will use his exhibit efforts to find and sign the best representatives in the market. With United States government subsidies of various kinds, the out-of-pocket costs to the participants are very low. If the busy executive cannot spare the time to accompany his display overseas, a United States commercial attaché will find a local stand-in for $50.

The private sector has been active on a more limited scale in getting products overseas by means of "mobile fairs." In several instances, exhibits of United States goods have been moved to various foreign ports by ship, and the Hartford Chamber of Commerce chartered an airplane for a similar purpose. Other proposals include a trade-fair ship, trains, and trucks. The best bargains in overseas exhibits, however, are the traditional international trade fairs and the United States trade center exhibits.

CONCLUSION

This discussion of the various types of assistance available to the exporter will have been to some businessmen an introduction, to others a review. In either case, it is hoped that the businessman will commence or increase export operations, informed through the full use of the assistance programs of government and private organizations. Indeed, he will realize that exporting as a marketing field offers unique advantages in enabling him to draw upon the skills and resources of highly trained specialists at very little cost.

BIBLIOGRAPHY

Advice on Exportability

Commodity Indexes for the Standard International Trade Classification (rev. ed.), 2 vols., Publishing Service, United Nations, New York, 1963. Vol. 1, $5; vol. 2, $4.50. The official UN numerical classification system covering all commodities in international trade.

Schedule B: Statistical Classification of Domestic and Foreign Commodities Exported from the United States (rev. ed.), Department of Commerce, Jan. 1, 1965 (and supplements). Includes a numerical and alphabetical product index revised to specific or broad SITC numbers and classes. Also contains Schedule C: classification of country designations for statistical runoffs.*†

Pinpointing Location and Size of Markets

Bureau of the Census Report FT 410, "United States Exports of Domestic and Foreign Merchandise" (monthly and annually). Analysis by value and quantity of United States exports by commodity and by country of destination. Also, *FT 125* (monthly and annually). Details imports into the United States by commodity and country of origin.*†

Commodity Trade Statistics, Publishing Service, United Nations, New York; annual subscription, $10. UN series D of imports and exports of the various countries.

Market Share Reports: 1962–1964, The Clearinghouse for Federal Scientific and Technical Information, Code 41012, Springfield, Va. 22151. $1 per commodity volume; country analyses range from $1.60 to $4.60 depending upon number of pages. Two series of 1182 studies covering 48 leading world import markets for manufactured goods. Data reported in dollars, commodities in SITC groupings.

OECD—Statistical Bulletins A, B, and C (quarterly and annually), McGraw-Hill Book Company, New York, Series A, $8; Series B, $10; Series C, $10. Series C is most useful. Foreign trade statistics on each of the European and North American countries showing origin and destination of foreign trade by product and by country.

World Trade Annual—1963; 1964, 4 vols., Walker & Company, New York. Costs up to $100 for full annual set. Reports global movement of 1,312 commodities in world trade identified by SITC numbers.

Trade Contacts: Published Sources

AID Procurement Information Bulletin, Agency for International Development, Department of State. Information in this bulletin includes country for which AID is destined, commodities to be purchased, contract period, terminal delivery dates, and dollar appropriation.*

Directory of Combination Export Managers, Agency for International Development, Department of State; $1.*

Directory of Export Packers, The Port of New York Authority, Port Promotion Division, 111 Eighth Avenue, New York 10011; free upon request.

Dun & Bradstreet International Market Guides, International Division, Dun & Bradstreet, Inc., 6 St. James Avenue, Boston, published annually. Lists 91,000 enterprises in Middle America; 88,000 in South America; and in a separate publication, 225,000 firms in continental Europe. Details capital and credit standing of each firm, gives trade classification and contains other data useful in a marketing scan city-by-city and country-by-country.

"Foreign Buyers," *Journal of Commerce* (daily column). Lists names and addresses of foreign companies importing commodities as shown.

The International Yellow Pages, International Yellow Pages, Inc., 1151 Midtown Tower, Rochester, New York; $14.95.

West African Directory, Thomas Skinner & Co., Ltd., 111 Broadway, New York 10006, published annually; $14.

Checking on Foreign Contacts

Foreign Credit Interchange Bureau Reports, The Foreign Credit Interchange Bureau, 44 East 23d Street, New York 10010.

Trade Lists, Bureau of International Commerce, Department of Commerce; $1. Lists of foreign firms by commodity handled and for each country.*†

World Trade Directory (WTD), Bureau of International Commerce, Room 6059B, U.S. Department of Commerce, Washington, D.C. 20230; $2 each. Reports containing financial and business background information for each company reviewed.

Trade Contacts: Personalized Business Services

Five Steps to Success in Overseas Markets, American Express Export Marketing Service, New York. A guide for management seeking new or expanded markets abroad.

Pan Am's Worldwide Marketing Service, Pan American World Airways, 28–19 Bridge Plaza North, Long Island City, New York 11101, or local Pan American Airways offices.

Top-Trade Opportunity Program, Air France sales offices. Service to exporters.

Trade Contact Survey, Bureau of International Commerce, Department of Commerce. U.S. commercial attachés abroad will seek out personally candidates for sales agency or distributor connections on individual company requests. Fee is $50 per country search.*†

Finding Marketing Knowledge

Advertising Age, 630 Third Avenue, New York 10017 (annual review, usually in March). Contains profiles of more than 400 advertising agencies in all parts of the world.

Bartels, Robert, *Comparative Marketing—Wholesaling in 15 Countries,* Richard D. Irwin, Inc., Homewood, Ill., 1963.

European Common Market and Britain, a marketing survey sponsored by *Reader's Digest;* complimentary.

Export Market Guides, Bureau of International Commerce, Department of Commerce. Excellent summaries of marketing research made abroad in connection with exhibitions at U.S. trade centers.*†

Sales Promotion in Europe, Intam Ltd., Romano House, 399–401 Strand, London W.C. 2, England.

Survey among Distributors and Agents in Latin America, conducted for Time-Life International by Erdos and Morgan, Inc., New York, 1965. Readership survey among executive and managerial people in Latin America.

Survey of Foreign Machine Tool Markets, National Machine Tool Builders Association, 2139 Wisconsin Avenue, Washington D.C. 20007.

Keeping Up To Date

Board of Trade Journal, H.M. Stationery Office, 423 Oxford St., London W. 1, annual subscription, 3 pounds 18 shillings. British counterpart of U.S. *International Commerce* and an excellent source of most recent events and conditions in international trade.

Checklist for International Operations, Department of Commerce; free. Checklist of overseas business reports and publications.*†

Foreign Trade, Queen's Printer, Government Printing Bureau, Ottawa, Canada; $7 per year. Contains excellent articles on markets abroad. As useful in the United States as in Canada.

The Gallatin Annual of International Business, Copley International, New York. Replaces files full of numerous statistical and topical documents on international business.

Information Guides for Doing Business outside the U.S., Price Waterhouse & Co., 60 Broad St., New York 10004. A series on business conditions in countries in which Price Waterhouse has offices.

International Advertiser (monthly), International Advertising Association, 475 Fifth Avenue, New York 10017; $15 per year. Magazine for international marketing executives.

International Commerce, $16. Latest news on economics, government articles, trade opportunities and leads, new books, and export activities calendar. **A must for all.***

Investing, Licensing & Trading Conditions in 50 Countries, Business International, 757 Third Avenue, New York 10017.

Overseas Business Reports, World Trade Information Series, Department of Commerce, published intermittently. By country—economic, operational, statistical reports on conditions in all the world markets.*†

Technical Aids

Exporter's Encyclopedia, Exporter's Encyclopedia, Inc., New York, published annually (supplementary bulletins). Full and authentic information relative to shipments for every country in the world.

FCIB Monthly Round-Table Conference Minutes, Foreign Credit Interchange Bureau, 44 East 23d Street, New York 10010.

The Pan Am Guide to Business Customs in Europe, Pan American World Airways, New York. Tells how to plan your itinerary, make appointments, shake hands; tells about business cards, business dress, business titles, business hours, lunch-time business, selling yourself, closing an agreement, wining and dining, tipping, and Pan Am's marketing service.

Tariffs & Trade, 10 East 40th Street, New York 10016, or 1097 National Press Building, Washington, D.C. 20004.

* U.S. Government Printing Office, Washington, D.C. 20402.
† Also available from all U.S. Department of Commerce field offices.

TOOLS AND TECHNIQUES OF
MANAGEMENT DECISION MAKING AND CONTROL

CHAPTER ONE

Management Information Systems

ROBERT A. SHIFF   *President, Naremco Services, Inc., New York, New York; Chairman of the Board, National Records Management Council, New York, New York*

An effective management information system is a system of communications designed to keep all levels of management completely informed on all developments in the enterprise which affect them.   Its purpose is to provide effective working tools for management personnel so that the best possible action can be taken at the right time with respect to the functions and operations for which they are responsible.

A management information system must be part of and closely linked with the total information flow through the organization—but the emphasis is on *information for decision making*, rather than on the detailed systems and procedures for authorizations, instructions, record keeping, follow-up, and control. Information for decision making is usually served up in the form of reports on the results of past actions and on conditions and trends which are presumed to have a bearing on future actions.

Traditionally, management reports have been end products of existing accounting and data-processing systems.   There has been growing recognition, however, of the fact that the conventional types of accounting and control reports supplied to foremen, department heads, top executives, and board members are often far from satisfactory in content, format, and timing for intelligent decision making—and that, indeed, many reports presumably for this purpose are largely ignored or given only cursory examination.

ROLE OF THE COMPUTER IN MANAGEMENT INFORMATION SYSTEMS

The advent of the electronic computer and collateral developments in high-speed communication networks have actually aggravated the problem of providing meaningful information while at the same time offering glittering vistas of "real time" control.   At the output end of computers, carbon-interleaved multicopy reports spew from high-speed printers capable of producing millions of characters per hour. Kenneth P. Morse, president of Standard Register Company, has stated that "the rate of obsolescence of paper systems is remarkably higher than the machinery for which they form the input and output. Too many print-outs in too great detail are being distributed to people who can't digest them."

Since their introduction, computers for business data processing have attained impressive capabilities for the analysis of huge quantities of information and have thus opened up whole new dimensions in the management of large corporations. At the outset, however, it should be stressed that they remain merely a tool—admittedly a highly sophisticated tool—in any management information system. The conceptual approach to developing such a system is quite independent of the availability of a computer. It is related to the *information needs* at any level of management and can be brought to a high degree of effectiveness in any department or business office, no matter what its size or equipment resources. Indeed, even a vaunted "real time information system" may, at some levels of operation, depend upon no more than a telephone or a simple intercom.

Some Basic Concepts. It will be useful to set the stage by elaborating briefly upon some basic concepts inherent in our opening statements of definition and purpose.

First, as to "information" itself, a sharp distinction must be made between *data* and *information.* Data are any raw facts known or available. Information means data that have been processed, that are *up to date, accurate, timely, germane,* and *set in the proper perspective* to the issue at hand. A decision maker wants information, not data. Reports are useful to him only for their information content.

Second, an efficient management information system must, for specified classes of recipients, guard against *too much, too little, or the wrong kind of information.* Every effort must be made to avoid an intolerable burden of processed data from which users are required to extract meaningful information. Thus to Dean's[1] four C's of management information—that it be correlated, consistent, current, and complete—we can properly add a fifth: that it be concise.

Third, the information must, for each level of management concerned, highlight *significant variables* and indicate *out-of-line conditions,* so that effective action can be taken in time. Only when information is summarized and pinpointed in this fashion can the principle of "management by exception" be applied. This is the principle of concentrating on trouble spots without having to review mountains of information on operations that are going according to plan. The correlative information format becomes increasingly important as reports are directed to higher rungs on the management ladder.

Fourth, the information must be *tailor-made to the needs of specific levels of management.* A foreman of a production department may need hour-by-hour (or more frequent) information about individual units going through his department. A department head may need less-immediate information regarding machine loading. The division head may need longer-range information on how the division's capabilities are presently occupied and booked. At the corporate level, a vice president may need broad information on how the various divisions reporting to him are performing. There are obviously vast differences in require-

[1] Neal J. Dean, "A Management Information Service for Finance," in *Control through Information—A Report on Management Information Systems,* Management Bulletin, no. 24, American Management Association, New York, 1963.

ments for immediacy and detail and the time frame within which corrective action must be taken.

In general, the literature on management organization and planning, an example being Dearden,[2] distinguishes between the following levels of management functions which govern the types of management information needs:

1. *Strategic planning*, consisting of (a) determining corporate policies and objectives; (b) deciding on changes in them; and (c) stipulating the resources to be devoted to attaining these objectives

2. *Management control*, consisting of (a) breaking the strategic plans down into logical subdivisions; (b) authorizing the funds to carry out the subdivisions of the plan; (c) assigning to specific individuals the responsibility for carrying out each subdivision; and (d) following up to see that the assignments are carried out satisfactorily

3. *Operational control*, consisting of (a) determining the specific personnel, equipment, and material necessary to accomplish the subdivisions of the plan; (b) making specific assignments for the work; and (c) keeping close supervisory contact, comparing current results with plans and taking corrective action as required

As Dearden points out, for practical purposes strategic planning may be thought of as deciding on long-range plans and objectives; management control as supervising and evaluating operational personnel; and operational control as carrying out the day-to-day operations of the business. It can readily be seen that from the same master file of information, a management information system must provide for a selective sifting and refining of information as it flows upward—meaningful and necessary "information" at one level being but the "raw data" for successive higher levels.

Relation of the Management Information System to Other Information Flows. The management information system—by definition, the decision-making system—will not be created in a vacuum. It will rest upon and be an adjunct to other phases of information processing within the organization. In general, its effectiveness will depend upon the completeness and sophistication of these underlying and adjunct information systems. They are listed and discussed briefly here for clarification, since the issue is often confused in papers and articles which embrace most if not all of them in the term "management information system" without distinction between "administrative data processing" and "management information processing."

Administrative Processing. This comprises the systems and procedures for carrying on the day-by-day operations of the business, and must be independently designed with that end in view. The analyst developing the management information system draws upon by-products of administration processing for management decision-making information, and may ask for extensions of processing in certain areas to provide him with the decision-making information he needs; or he may set up additional systems of source-data gathering.

With the computer, it is possible to concentrate all transaction information into one or a few master files and, through "integrated data processing," to capture in "machine language" more and more information at the source of transactions for direct input into the central computer memory with a minimum of fallible human intervention. What is usually meant by "total information processing" is the trend in smaller as well as larger companies toward a single, central, master computer-memory file of *all* information needed for administrative

[2] John Dearden, "Can Management Information Be Automated?" *Harvard Business Review*, March–April, 1964.

processing—a development made possible by large-scale increases in computational and data-storage capability of computers.

Thus, it is possible to have elaborate and highly effective "total" *administrative data-processing* systems without correspondingly sophisticated *management information* systems. Indeed, the former and not the latter are what many national corporate computer networks actually are. (And, by the same token, a company may have an effective "total" management information system with no elaborate and far-flung computer system.)

An important by-product result of computerized data-processing systems, whether "total" or various degrees of "integrated," has been the maintenance of files of data covering all transactions of the business in consistent and comparable form, thereby improving the consistency and quality of information available for management decision-making needs. As of, roughly, 1964, computers became available with practically unlimited capacities of central direct-access computer system memories together with "time sharing" features. This makes possible the storage of vast quantities of information for decision making *independent* of transaction data, accessible and manipulatable without interfering with transaction processing.

Information Storage and Retrieval. Although there are some who contend that information storage and retrieval are part of a management information system, this is actually a quite independent activity, and the management information system may be only one, and not even the major, user of information available from it.

A company's records and documents fall into two broad categories—transaction documents and reference documents. The former comprise over 75 percent of the total records load of any company, but transaction files can readily be arranged alphabetically or numerically, and present no special indexing problems for retrieval. In computerized systems, many of these records form only backup files, once their data have been captured on cards or tape.

Reference documents are reports, research data, marketing information, books and brochures, and the like. Although in bulk they comprise the smaller percentage of filed information, they represent by far the greater problem in terms of prompt and comprehensive information retrieval.

Reference document files have always presented retrieval problems, because of the many subjects of which a single document or report may treat. Traditional multiple cross-indexing cards proliferate almost endlessly for even a passable attempt at anticipating possible lookup approaches, and 1,000 reports or documents may easily give rise to 10,000 index cards.

A powerful technique to overcome these handicaps, and one which lends itself to simple manual retrieval methods as well as to punched card or computerized search, is the so-called inverted indexing method (also referred to as "concept coordination"), and the management information system designer will do well to familiarize himself with it.[3] In inverted indexing, the flexibility and control are all in the indexing. The documents themselves are given a distinctive address number and are simply filed by number. The "inversion" consists in turning the whole idea of indexing around. For retrieval purposes, instead of cataloging the documents themselves, the information that is indexed is a limited number of appropriate *basic concepts*, or descriptors, predetermined with a view to known and probable lookup approaches. In a manual system, a card is set up for each descriptor, and this card contains the addresses of

---

[3] Robert A. Shiff, "Rx for Information Retrieval," Administrative Management Society, Willow Grove, Pa., 1965.

all documents containing information on that concept, no matter what the document's main subject or title is. (In a completely automated system, the descriptors could be in a computer's memory.) Because many of the same basic concepts are treated in numerous documents, the number of descriptor cards in an inverted index will be only a fraction of the total number of documents in the file. (See also Chapter 5 of Section 14.)

DEVELOPING A MANAGEMENT INFORMATION SYSTEM

It can be seen that the management information system must be structured within the total information flow of a company—not of itself necessarily calling for highly expensive or "exotic" computation, print-out, and display equipment, but taking full advantage of existing systems and hardware installed for administrative processing. It would be unlikely that a computer system would be installed for management information purposes alone. The availability of modern computer systems and information-processing networks, however, together with new input/output devices, has stepped up by several orders of magnitude what *can be done* in management information processing. The important thing is to put the computer into proper context by first doing a thorough job of determining the *information needs* at all levels of the enterprise and then making use of whatever degree of automation is called for and can be made available.

At the lower operating levels, the analysis is usually straightforward, because the tangibles of, say, the order-billing cycle, work-in-process control, and the like, are readily determinable. Reports can readily be made explicit in terms of pieces, dates, and so on, and conventional follow-up procedures established. The information-reporting requirements will, in fact, almost automatically develop out of the procedural routines set up for handling the flow of work. Clear-cut limits—such as order points, purchase quantities, back-order tolerances, or due dates—can be established, and suitable danger signals and exception reporting can be inaugurated. Many types of corrective action can be triggered, with no human decision making involved beyond the establishment of the original rules.

As one moves up the management ladder, the "thinking through" job becomes much more difficult than finding the hardware to process and transmit the information required. It will be found that most higher levels of management are disappointingly inarticulate in defining their basic operational objectives and the type and urgency of the information they need for the kinds of decisions for which they are responsible. Indeed, the root problem still is that higher levels of management find difficulty in analyzing and putting into words for the systems analyst their own decision-making process. Affel[4] has underscored the problem as follows:

The harsh truth is that the mechanics of management are not thoroughly understood, particularly when you get out of the area of simple clerical functions and into the areas of decision making. They are not even understood thoroughly enough to provide the relatively general guidelines the system designer needs, let alone a computer programmer who must translate the mechanics into detailed instructions. . . . I do not mean to imply that managers do not know what they are doing. They do know and by and large perform in an excellent manner. The kind of precision I am talking about is hard to come by. It is particularly difficult to come by in business, which is a complex operation.

[4] Herman A. Affel, Jr., "Presentation on Cybernetics in Business" (unpublished paper), Auerbach Corporation, Philadelphia, 1965.

Development Guidelines.   In developing a management reporting system, failure to articulate needs is not the only problem.   Resistance to change, the presumed prestige value in getting certain reports, and the reluctance to release information or to have results too explicitly reported to higher echelons all serve to throw barriers in the way of the analyst.   The following eight guidelines will be helpful in any systematic approach to the problem.

1. Determine objectively and with a minimum of controversy *what* information is needed by *whom,* and with what *frequency.*   With respect to information requests by higher levels of management, be sure there is an awareness of the costs of procuring it on a regular basis, if it is not readily available from existing routines.   With respect to *all* levels, determine the need for urgency— and whether "real time" (or approaches to it) is worth the cost or is even desirable.

2. Organize this information to facilitate the design of the reporting system without being overwhelmed by the sheer volume of data.

3. Separate essential from nonessential data without sacrificing control information.   Determine "significant variables" and implement the "management by exception" principle.

4. Stress *information,* not *pieces of paper.*   Information may be transmitted more quickly, at less expense, and more conveniently through a variety of voice and display media that may already be available.   (Do people need "information copies" of documents whose essential information may, for example, be readily accessible in computer memory or by simply picking up a phone or using an intercom?)

5. Structure paper reports into the routine record-keeping system to achieve simple, integrated paper work.

6. Establish "birth control" for development of new information reports—tying in with the routine records control system which may already be established.

7. Gain acceptance of the reports before installing them as standard procedure.

8. Establish a system for checking up on use of reports and on possible needs for modification of the reporting system.

Where to Start.   The conventional approach to revision of the management reporting system involves a laborious flow charting of all the paper-work channels of a company, a painstaking collection of all forms and regular reports used, and then a time-consuming matching of forms and reports to the charted paper-work flow.   Only after this entire process is completed do simplification and consolidation of forms and reports, and subsequent reduction of the number of reports, take place.

This conventional "paper-work reduction" approach starts at the bottom with the basic clerical worker, as the analyst studies what he does and what he produces, traces the results of his work to the next step, and so on.

Based on consulting experience in all types of industries, it is the writer's conviction that for management information system development, the approach should be completely reversed.   It should begin at the top level first, and from that point work down to the bottom.

All information filters from the bottom clerical level, where original source data are first generated, on up to the executive suite.   Ideally, it goes through a series of interpretation, refinement, and consolidation at intermediate levels. Experience, however, testifies to the fact that, regrettably, significant consolidation does not take place at intermediate levels.   Instead, basic information is passed up the line, and each level adds on comparisons, interpretations, and different emphases.   This being so, the best way to reduce the management paper-work burden, and to make as meaningful as possible any reporting that remains, is to make sure that every bit of superfluous information or undigested data is eliminated at the top management level, then every bit at the level below that, and so on.

A case in point: A vice president in charge of sales requires certain basic categories of information concerning orders, inventory, sales expenses, sales forecasts, and the like. These need not all be submitted at the same time. They should be organized to reach him at periodic intervals as needed for him to keep informed, make decisions, and take action. The information must be fresh (current), and if he needs it daily, round figures or close estimates will suffice to reach him on time. If he has to wait until the second week of the following month, he may find that six weeks have gone by without the corrective action needed on a serious problem. Flash reports can be generated to communicate significant information or deviations from normal activity between regular periodic reports.

Thus, the approach recommended is an analysis of all executive jobs to see precisely what information each one needs. Assume a vice president needs five basic operating facts for his day-to-day work. All operating information coming across his desk that is not concerned solely with those five basic requirements should be eliminated, and the reports he does receive on those categories should contain only the essentials he needs for his decisions. He should, of course, have knowledge of where any additional information he may need can be obtained.

The next step is to move on to the level directly beneath the top, where information coming up from subordinate levels should be consolidated for the top level. Here everything that is superfluous for top management must be screened out. Moreover, reports of interest to the sales vice president, but of no concern to the corporate secretary, are eliminated from the secretary's list. Continuing in the same vein, we can determine the streams of information the executives at the second level actually need. The process of elimination is followed through each succeeding level down the hierarchy.

Modus Operandi. *The "Instrument Panel" Concept.* It is not in the province of the analyst to dictate to higher levels of management the information they require for their decision making. However, he can definitely be of help, and his suggestions will usually be welcomed. In this connection, the "instrument panel" concept as elaborated by Rathe, Schaffir,[5] and others will provide a useful guide.

Consider a motorist on a routine trip. He is not concerned with the detailed technical performance of his car. He knows that if he keeps tab on only a handful of basic criteria, he will reach his destination smoothly, without trouble. Thus:

1. Is there enough gas?
2. Is the battery charging?
3. Is the motor overheating?
4. Is the oil pressure adequate?
5. What is the speed?

The instrument panel on the dashboard gives him just that information, and no more. The driver is not interested in the exact temperature of his motor, but only in whether it is close to a predetermined critical point. He stops occasionally to check his oil, water, and tire pressure, and he may even bring his

[5] Walter B. Schaffir, "Developing a Management Control 'Instrument Panel'; A Practical Approach," American Management Association Systems and Procedures Seminar, American Management Association, New York, 1963.

car in for a more thorough checkup every 10,000 miles—but he does all these things systematically, without worrying about all of them all of the time.

The analogy to management information systems planning is obvious. At every level of management, there are rarely more than a dozen factors which are crucial for control and must receive constant attention. Certain others have to be reviewed less frequently—the equivalent of the occasional oil check and the detailed 10,000-mile checkup.

The specific factors will, of course, vary for every level and for every type of job. Detailed analysis and discussion of information needs with every responsible executive should lead to agreement on them and to the minimum amount of routine reports required at his level. Like the automobile dashboard, these routine reports should not be required to tell everything about everything. They should provide warning signals and raise pertinent questions. The information system should provide for detailed information only in the event of trouble.

Information-need Analysis. The analyst will not make much progress if at each stage of the information requirements study he asks the person concerned, "Do you really need all this information you have been receiving?" The normal tendency of an executive or department head thus queried is to assert that every bit of data received is absolutely essential.

A more productive approach is to ask each executive, "What do you do with this information?" with respect to each report he is receiving. He cannot answer without thinking, as he can when asked whether he needs the information. And once he thinks about it, he will usually admit, with respect to nonessential information, that he can do without it. As a matter of fact, he will not have much choice, because it is difficult to invent a valid use for information which is in fact not used at all.

Once the analysis of the use of reports *now being* received at all levels has been made, the next step is to determine the existing reports which *should be* received. Three basic charts will be of value.

The Functional Responsibility Profile (Figure 1-1). On this chart, basic functions are listed in relation to managerial positions. Codes denote whether a particular position initiates, reviews, or approves a particular function.

The Information Distribution Chart (Figure 1-2). This shows current reports in relation to the same positions, indicating whether the information items in them are received and used, received and not used, or needed but not received.

When the second chart is compared with the first, a quick picture is obtained of which reports certain executives are not receiving even though they require

Function	Pres.	Exec. V.P.	Div. mgr.	Dept. head	Sec. head
Function 1.......	...	A	R	I	
Function 2.......	A	R	R	I	
Function 3.......	A	I			
etc.					

I: initiates; R: reviews; A: approves.
NOTE: For example, typical functions include sales analysis, production scheduling, operating costs, and budgets.

FIG. 1-1. *Functional responsibility profile.*

Information	Pres.	Exec. V.P.	Div. mgr.	Dept. head	Sec. head
Report 1					
Info item a	X	✓	✓	✓	
Info item b	✓	✓	✓	X	
Info item c	X	X	X	✓	
etc.					
Report 2					
Info item d	...	✓	X	✓	X
Info item e	...	✓	✓	✓	X
etc.					

X means information is received; ✓ means information is received and needed.

NOTE: For example, typical information items include total orders received, complete orders shipped, partial orders shipped, orders in process, back orders, and returns.

FIG. 1-2. *Information distribution chart.*

them for the functions for which they are responsible, and which reports they are getting for which they have no real need.

The Item Repetition Chart (Figure 1-3). This chart provides details useful in redesigning a reporting system. It shows the extent to which the same basic information items are used by different functions and the frequency with which the information is required to be issued and summarized.

Information	Report Periodically				Summarize Periodically				Summarize Selectively			
	M	Q	SA	A	M	Q	SA	A	M	Q	SA	A
Function 1												
Info item a....	X				X				X			
Info item b....		X										
Info item c....												
etc.												
Function 2												
Info item d....		X										X
Same as b.....			X				X					
Same as c.....		X										
etc.												
Function 3												
Info item e....	X				X				X			
Same as a.....	X						X					
Same as d.....		X										
etc.												

M: monthly; Q: quarterly; SA: semiannually; A: annually.

FIG. 1-3. *Item repetition chart.*

These charts develop a rational use of reports already in existence. In addition, the analyst must determine, on the basis of the review of information needs, how existing reports should be modified and what, if any, information should be developed which is not now available. Following are checkpoints to use as a guide.

1. Is this information part of a previously agreed-upon plan, such as a sales forecast or a budget? If so, will it have to be repeated in every report cycle, or will it be sufficient to report only deviation from plan?

2. Is management at this level prepared to take action on the basis of this information?

3. Is this information placed in proper perspective with other information bearing on the function in question at this responsibility level? Would the information be more meaningful if combined with another item—for example, one item shown as a percentage of another?

4. Is it necessary to show actual magnitudes, or rounded figures, or simply whether a critical point has been exceeded or is being approached?

5. Will graphic presentation be more effective for the particular recipients than actual figures? Would graphs be easier to keep up to date?

6. What is the time lag in producing this information? Can meaningful action still be taken? If not, how would the information suffer if the time lag were cut?

7. How long does it take for this item of information to change significantly? In view of this, what should be the frequency of reporting?

8. Are the *significant variables* clearly pinpointed?

Information Dissemination. Once the type and frequency of management information have been decided upon, serious consideration should be given to the mode of dissemination, with a view to further reduction in paper work. The only time anyone must have written (printed) records in his possession is when he is dealing with complex or detailed information. Information which he needs only incidentally, or to which he refers only infrequently, need not be in his possession at all, as long as he knows where and how to get it when he needs it.

It is common practice to dial a phone number to get the exact time, the latest weather report, baseball scores, directory information, and the like. This same principle can be followed in management information systems. About 1964, such direct inquiry began to come into use in computer systems. But even without computers, many categories of information should be obtainable from central information departments by phone or intercom, with response by actual voice or by recording—for example, the latest information on sales, inventory, market projections, budget variances, and the like. Mailed dictating-machine tapes or disks are another possibility. For example, Kaiser Aluminum and Chemical Sales, Inc., has all its branch offices submit periodic sales statistics and reports in this fashion.

Thus, a final checkpoint to be added should be:

9. Can the paper medium of reporting be replaced by a faster, simpler method?

COMPUTERIZED INFORMATION SYSTEMS AND "MANAGEMENT INFORMATION ROOMS"

The impact of computers on management information systems has already been cited. Technological developments, including important breakthroughs which became commercially available in 1965, make a close approach to truly "total" information systems possible.   As a result, most of the large corporations are actively planning new corporate-wide information systems, and a number have already been able to make highly elaborate systems operative.   The significant computer developments in existence or being discussed by 1965 may briefly be recapitulated as follows:

1. New "software" which makes it easier for noncomputer technicians to communicate with the central processors—the so-called "machine independent" languages in which many computer commands closely approximate everyday English

2. Mass, random-access computer memory systems of practically unlimited capacity, making possible the "total" master files already mentioned

3. New and even "exotic" terminal devices, making possible direct inquiry into a computer, with output in the form of visual displays, audio response, or nearly instantaneous hard copy

4. Advanced communications switching and data transmission, coupled with "third generation" computers distinguished by time-sharing capabilities which have the effect of handling many inquiries simultaneously—together making possible "real time" systems[6] that give immediate responses in the form of up-to-the-minute information

All of this adds up to two important new capabilities:

1. Any corporation, no matter how far-flung its operations, can have completely centralized files, with any degree of "on line" access and "real time" information desired.   Sales, inventory, and other information can be updated in the computer as the transactions occur, instead of the formerly necessary "batch processing" method of updating files, say, once a day or even once a week.   And the large central computers can be readily interrogated from remote points.

2. Technically (depending upon the investment in hardware), any level of management can be in as close touch as it desires with any phase of operations with which it is concerned—in "real time" if it wishes—by means of cathode-ray-tube displays or even computer-manufactured voice response.   Or the computer can be "brought to the board room" or to specially designed "management information rooms."

"Management information rooms" promise to have a profound effect on top management decision making and control.[7]   The idea has been widely applied to military command-control centers.   Its application is growing for *business* command control in the sense of electronically operated and computer-oriented displays—"war rooms" where managements can view detailed information about all company operations, together with projections of trends.   Du Pont has long had its famous chart room, but the new element is the flexibility of the up-to-the-minute displays, the variety of the forms of displays used, and the computer systems and communications networks which permit top management to react in real time in the military sense.

In their most sophisticated form, modern rooms of this sort combine all of the latest audio and visual techniques, including motion pictures, slides, tape recordings, TV and radio, and on-line cathode-ray displays or audio response from computers.   Extremely important is the inclusion of facilities for random access to past records, selected as desired by lectern pushbuttons from either tape recordings or computer memory.   Closed-circuit television and other advanced information devices can link major field offices with the home office

[6] According to military definition, "real time is that type of system whose inputs can influence outputs within a time when the change is still significant."

[7] Carl Heyel, "Management Information, 1965," in "Report on the Office," Supplement to *Dun's Review & Modern Industry*, September, 1965.

for executive conferences. Thus, home-office sales executives, for example, may sit down in an information room at one o'clock on Monday afternoons to discuss their plans for the week. At the same time, other executives in their own offices all over the country can join in at the flick of a switch. Links with the central electronic computer will permit executives to summon any information they may need and have it flashed on the conference room screen and across the country over closed-circuit television.

BIBLIOGRAPHY

Affel, Herman A., Jr., "Presentation on Cybernetics in Business" (unpublished paper), Auerbach Corporation, Philadelphia, 1965.

Dean, Neal J., "A Management Information Service for Finance," in *Control through Information—A Report on Management Information Systems,* Management Bulletin, no. 24, American Management Association, New York, 1963.

Dearden, John, "Can Management Information Be Automated?" *Harvard Business Review,* March–April, 1964.

Heyel, Carl, "Management Information, 1965," in "Report on the Office," Supplement to *Dun's Review & Modern Industry,* September, 1965.

Schaffir, Walter B., "Developing a Management Control 'Instrument Panel': A Practical Approach," American Management Association Systems and Procedures Seminar, American Management Association, New York, 1963.

Shiff, Robert A., "Rx for Information Retrieval," Administrative Management Society, Willow Grove, Pa., 1965.

Shiff, Robert A., and Alan G. Negus, "Information Please," *Administrative Management,* June–August, 1964.

CHAPTER TWO

Operations Research and Related Developments

JAMES A. PARSONS   *Management Science Services Group Leader, Lederle Laboratories, Division of American Cyanamid Company, Pearl River, New York*

The decision problems confronting modern industrial, governmental, and institutional managements are ever increasing in their complexity and far-reaching scope. To maintain the present success of an enterprise, protect its competitive standing, and guard against costly mistakes, timely and accurate decisions are needed. For this reason, it is of the utmost importance for management to have sound, factual frameworks for its decision-making process.

Operations research, or, as it is sometimes called, "operations analysis" or "management science," offers to management a collection of techniques which can be of tremendous value in establishing its decision-making frameworks. It has been applied to such diverse problems as the allocation of advertising budgets for maximum expected return, the assigning of salesmen to the right market areas, the scheduling of production for minimum costs, the selection of investment portfolios, the establishing of equitable bonus systems, and urban planning and area redevelopment.

What are the essential characteristics of operations research? What can it do for the executive or manager? What are its limitations? How should management organize it and administer it? These are some of the questions this chapter will attempt to answer.

Management Planning, Control, and Decision Making. An executive or manager devotes a major part of his time and attention to making decisions. A decision can be classified by whether it concerns something of a short-term or of a long-term nature. What style, size, or color product to manufacture this year, how much inventory to accumulate in anticipation of a holiday season, and what piece of equipment to use for the manufacture of a specific product are examples of short-term decisions. Some examples of long-term decisions are: how much capital outlay should be provided for plant and equipment needs, what new market areas should be entered, or how required financing should be obtained.

Usually short-term decisions which are frequently made are ones of control, whereas seldom-made long-term decisions are more of the planning type.

Plans are merely the means by which policies are implemented. Management has become more and more preoccupied with planning. With special emphasis on such basic areas as finance, new production, distribution, and personnel, plans are made more frequently and further ahead in time. To ensure that plans are properly carried out, effective control systems must be established. For plans pertaining to such areas as plant development, production capabilities, and sales or R&D projects, controls must be devised for inventory, expenditures, costs, quality, and efficiency.

At the crux of all planning and control problems lies the process of management decision making. The problem is defined; the alternative solutions, with their expected consequences, are developed; a choice of the solution that best fits the circumstances is made; and this solution is converted into the necessary action.

The Role of Operations Research. Operations research is an arm of management and is never a substitute for the executive or manager. Its role is to present a comprehensive analysis of the tangible elements of a problem, thus providing a factual basis for the support and guidance of management in its decision making. It frees the decision maker's time and attention from the necessity of considering all the facets of the problem, thereby allowing these to be devoted to those areas where his intuition, experience, and judgment are of critical importance.

The inclusion of the effects of such factors as the moral and ethical standards of doing business; responsibilities toward employees, stockholders, the community, and the nation; and human satisfaction will always be the responsibility of management.

THE NATURE OF OPERATIONS RESEARCH

Operations research received its name and identity during World War II. At the beginning of the war, Britain's military management called upon teams of scientists for assistance in solving some of its most difficult strategical and tactical problems. The best use and deployment of defensive radar systems, the best allocation of aircraft to bombing missions, and possible methods for improving bombing accuracy are a few examples of the problems studied by these teams.

After the war, Britain was faced with the necessity of rebuilding major segments of its industrial facilities. At the same time, certain industries were being nationalized. These conditions gave rise to managerial problems, which stimulated the application of operations research to peacetime industrial problems. Before long, most of the major British industries maintained their own operations research groups; examples are the United Steel Companies group, the National Coal Board, and the British Iron and Steel Research Association.

The United States military organization followed Britain's lead and installed operations research in its own ranks. It has continued to use it since the end of the war, and an operations research group is active in each of its branches; for example, Operations Evaluation Group (Navy), the Operations Analysis Group and the RAND Corporation (Air Force), and the Operations Research Office (Army).

It was not until 1950, however, that American industry began to take operations research seriously. This interest was partially stimulated by the new managerial problems generated by the push toward automation. Since that time, the activity has rapidly grown in acceptance, to a point where most of the larger industries report sizable, well-established operations research groups.

A Working Definition of Operations Research. We may define "operations research" as the application of the basic ideas of science, analysis, logic, and good judgment to the study of the quantitatively treatable aspects of problems that arise when decisions have to be made involving operations.

What is meant by an "operation" is any sequence of actions which is required to achieve a desired result. An assembly line is an operation, as is the process of receiving, sorting, and distributing mail. Operations are parts of a larger entity, called a "system," and the systems with which operations research is concerned are purposeful ones, within which decisions are made and objectives pursued. What we normally think of as an "organization," whether industrial, military, or commercial, is such a system.

Models in General. A model is a simplified representation of the system, or operation, under study. The particular form of a model depends on the use it is to serve. If physical or geometrical relationships are to be studied, then the model may be a blueprint, a photograph, or a physical scale model. Flow charts, graphs, and organization charts are examples of models.

Very often, the model is given in symbolic terms. For example the area, A, of a triangle may be represented in terms of the triangle's height, h, and its base length, b. This model is $A = \frac{1}{2}b \cdot h$. Here, we have an example of a mathematical model which relates the area of any triangle to its base length and height. It is called a "mathematical model," because it is an abstraction of the system into mathematical symbols.

A model is built for the simple reason that it is easier to study and manipulate than the system which it represents.

Operations Research and the Model. The construction of models is the best-known facet of the operations research methodology. It is safe to say that operations research cannot be performed without it.

To understand better the connection between operations research and model building, we must first consider what is commonly called the "scientific method." This is a logical sequence of steps followed in any scientific research, as well as in operations research. It consists of the steps of observation, forming of theories, testing, and control.

Some form of experimentation is always needed when applying the scientific method. A chemist determines the composition of a substance by performing a systematic sequence of experiments on it; an aeronautical engineer builds scale models and experiments with them in wind tunnels. The operations researcher, however, usually cannot experiment with the problem he is studying. He cannot bring the competitive marketplace or the production line into a laboratory and perform experiments on it. To fill this need for experimentation, the operations researcher constructs a likeness of the process he is studying in the form of a model and performs experiments on this. In constructing the model, a theory is developed to explain the observed characteristics of the process, and by manipulating the model—that is, experimenting with it—the theory is interpreted and tested against reality.

As an example of an operations research model, we will construct what is commonly called the "economic production-quantity model." Consider a certain item which is produced on a specific piece of equipment. Suppose the yearly demand for this item is 1,000 pieces. We could produce this item by setting up the equipment and running the total 1,000 pieces off at one time. By doing so, we only have to set up and take down the equipment once; our average inventory, over the year, will be 500 items. If we produced the 1,000 items in two production runs of 500 items each, then our average inventory would drop to 250 items, but we would have to set up and take down the equipment twice. Thus, it is seen that as we decrease the number of items produced at any one run, we lower the average inventory, but increase the number of setups and takedowns. Because there are costs associated with carrying inventory and with the setting up and taking down of the equipment, to produce this item in the most economical way these two costs must be balanced against each other. This is done by selecting that production quantity which will minimize the sum of these two costs. For this purpose, the economic production-quantity model was developed.

We begin the construction of the model by noting that if D is the yearly demand for the item and Q is its production quantity, then we will have to make (D/Q) production runs per year to meet the yearly demand. If S is the cost of a setup and a takedown, then our yearly preparation costs will be $(D/Q) \cdot S$. The yearly average inventory will be $\frac{1}{2}Q$; thus, if I is the cost of carrying one item in inventory for one year, our average annual inventory carrying cost will be $(\frac{1}{2}I \cdot Q)$. We denote the sum of these two costs by T, and it is this sum which we wish to minimize. The model for this operation is $T = (D/Q) \cdot S + \frac{1}{2}I \cdot Q$, which is a mathematical model.

A graphical model (Figure 2-1) can also be used to represent this operation. In the figure, Line 1 describes the inventory carrying cost $\frac{1}{2}IQ$; Line 2, the setup and takedown costs $(D/Q)S$; and Line 3, the sum of Lines 1 and 2, which represents T as it is related to Q.

The model we have constructed is actually a model type, and is not restricted to production quantities. It has been used to determine economic purchase order quantities, to size maintenance repair crews, and to control the flow of water from reservoirs.

The operations research model offers certain benefits to management. A greater understanding of the problem is gained from the model; the sensitivity between the variables of the problem can be evaluated through the use of the model; the model provides a quantitative basis for the selection among alternative courses of action; and, once a solution to the problem is proposed, the model serves as a means for evaluating this proposal.

Other Characteristics of Operations Research. Along with model building, other basic characteristics of operations research can be summarized. These are (1) the whole problem approach; (2) the use of interdisciplinary teams; and (3) the wide diversification of solution techniques.

The Whole Problem Approach. This philosophy is most clearly expressed by the term "optimize" rather than "suboptimize," or by the phrase "improve total company performance" rather than "improve departmental performance."

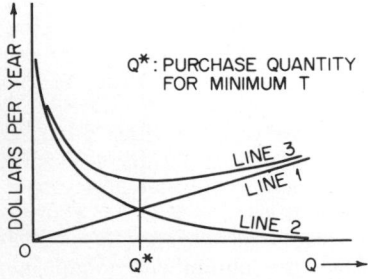

FIG. 2-1. *Economic purchase-quantity graphical model.*

Under this directorate, operations research stresses the conceptualization of the whole enterprise as a system, rather than just a given problem area. For example, in a study concerned with the warehousing of finished stock, this approach would attempt to incorporate into the problem statement such factors as the methods of distribution, the location and capacity of production centers, and forecasts of market trends.

Although every area of planning is affected by, and has effects on, every other plan or area of the enterprise, this whole problem approach is usually never carried out to its fullest extent.   Problems are just too big and interrelations too numerous to allow it.   Furthermore, the process of expanding the problem statement may terminate before all relevant factors are included because either available time and money are limited, the expansion process has reached the limits of control of the sponsor of the study, or further research does not promise enough justification to continue.

The Use of Interdisciplinary Teams.   Because of the demands for scientists in the technological aspects of war, the first military operations research teams were built up by acquisition rather than by selection.   Thus, the members of these teams came from a variety of scientific fields.   Yet, such interdisciplinary teams, whose members had no previous knowledge or experience with the military subject matter, were extremely effective in problem solving.   This was due to the fact that a collection of experts from different fields of specialization, each with a variety of technical skills and experiences, increased the problem-solving ability of the "team mind."

The complexity of today's managerial problems makes the use of the mixed team most desirable.   This is especially true at the initial stages of a study, because it is at this point that the important facets of the problem must be uncovered and the approaches to it selected.   These phases need more knowledge and experience than one individual can be expected to possess.

The Wide Diversification of Solution Techniques.   As a general proposition, operations research applies all forms of human knowledge to the solution of whole problems.   For this reason, the tools and techniques which it uses are extremely diverse.   "Anything goes" in the study as long as it leads to a better understanding of the problem or allows a more complete solution to be developed.   The specific technique used does not necessarily have to be a highly sophisticated one; many successful studies have involved only the intelligent use of simple arithmetic and sound logic.

Some of the techniques which are closely identified with operations research are linear programming, waiting-line theory, sequencing theory, replacement theory, game theory, decision theory, and simulation methods.

THE PHASES OF AN OPERATIONS RESEARCH STUDY

The phases of an operations research study will, to a large degree, be dictated by the problem and the individual researcher.   There are, however, certain general phases which are usually included in any study.   These are (1) formulating the problem; (2) constructing the model; (3) testing the model; (4) solving the model; (5) controlling the model and its solution; and (6) implementing the results.   These phases constitute an integrated whole, where each phase modifies every other phase.   For example, the sophistication of the model will be greatly influenced by the availability and knowledge of computational methods, for there is little point in posing a problem for which a solution cannot be found.

Formulating the Problem.   In this phase, a general examination of the environment of the problem is carried out.   The jargon to be used in describing the problem is established and the people and things that are associated with the problem are identified.   The decision maker's objectives, the values he places on these, and the alternative courses of action open to him are all determined.

One course of action is chosen over another because of its greater merit in achieving objectives.   For this reason, it is necessary to develop some means of relating the objectives to the alternative courses of action.   An effectiveness scale is developed for this purpose.   Each course of action has associated with it a measure of its effectiveness in achieving the objective.   This measure of effectiveness positions this particular course of action somewhere on the effectiveness scale.   Some scales are dimensionless, where, for example, their divisions measure the probability of an out-of-stock condition, the probability of a machine breakdown, or the probability of intercepting an enemy missile.   More often, effectiveness scales have dimensions, such as dollars of net profit, return on investment, percent share of the market, or accidents per year.

Once the courses of action are related to the effectiveness scale, a rule for selecting the best course from all those possible must be decided upon; a criterion of choice is needed.   This criterion may be to maximize effectiveness, as maximize net profit, expected return on investment, or market share; or it may be to minimize ineffectiveness, as minimize costs, production time, or scrap losses.

Also in this phase, a broad appraisal of the costs and returns of a successful study is made.   Estimates of the required time and effort, as well as a plan of approach, are developed.   This information is useful in determining whether or not the study is worthwhile, and if so, in what scope and in what depth.

Constructing the Model.   Within the area of responsibility delegated to a manager, there are certain factors which he controls.   These are called "controlled variables."   Some examples are the purchase quantity of supplies, the capital allocated to a department for its yearly budget, and the work assignments of personnel.   Other factors, called "uncontrolled variables," are present in the system; over these, the decision maker exerts no control.   Customer demand, competition's sales effort, political and economic conditions, and the strategical and tactical methods used by an opposing army are examples.   Furthermore, the freedom of the decision maker is usually limited by such things as budgets, procedures, rules, manpower, materials, and equipment availabilities.   These controlled and uncontrolled variables, as well as all pertinent restrictions, are included in the model if their presence is necessary properly to relate the courses of action to the effectiveness scale.   All models of operations research follow this same pattern, that is, they fuse the actions to the effectiveness scale by means of a relationship which involves all pertinent variables and restrictions.

In Table 2-1, some examples of decision problems with their variables, restrictions, effectiveness scales, and criteria of choice are presented.

Testing the Model.   The model must be tested before it can be used as a basis for decisions.   Its ability to predict future events is probably its most important feature.   Appropriate data are collected and analyzed to test the model.   Based on the testing results, the necessary modifications and refinements of the model are developed.

Often, some form of experimentation is used in this phase.   To evaluate the rate at which market share decayed when no advertising was used, one operations research study selected a test market area and suspended all advertising there for a period of a year.   With the data thus collected, the decay rate was evaluated.

TABLE 2-1. Examples of Problems and Possible Model Characteristics

Decision problem	Effectiveness scale	Controlled variable	Uncontrolled variable	Restrictions	Criterion of choice
			Possible characteristics of the model		
Determine economic production quantities	Annual cost	Production quantity	Customer demand	Limited setup hours, or warehouse floor space	Minimize costs
Assign salesmen to markets	Expected market share	Number of salesmen per area	Competition's sales force and its distribution	Number of available salesmen	Maximize expected market share
Stocking antimissile missiles	Probability of intercepting an enemy missile	Types and number of missiles	Number and types of enemy missiles	Budgets, area limitations, or time	Maximize probability of interception
Investment of capital	Return on investment	Types and number of stocks and bonds invested	Economic, political, and world conditions	Available capital, company policies	Maximize expected return
Allocating advertising budgets	Market share or exposure of products	Types of media and timing	Market conditions, competitor's effort	Size of budget	Maximize market share
Schedule preventive maintenance on equipment	Cost of downtime plus cost of PM program	Time between replacements	Times of failures and seriousness of failures	Manpower, budget, and parts limitations	Minimize total costs
Schedule production of many jobs through a production process	Total production time or costs of setups	Sequence of jobs, machines used, amount of overtime	Delays in material deliveries, equipment breakdowns, and equipment rush jobs	Equipment capacities, available manpower, and due dates	Minimize time to complete all jobs or minimize total costs

Solving the Model. Available techniques can be used in this phase if they are appropriate, but a problem should never be warped to fit an available technique. Completely new techniques are often required, and these must be developed by the researcher. Operations research is not a cookbook procedure.

In many studies, some form of simulation—which is essentially a sequence of trial and error steps—may be needed to develop a solution. Simulation almost always gives usable results and is especially useful when the problem escapes standard analytical approaches.

In many cases, the solution to a problem will be presented as a decision rule. These rules relate the "best" value of the controlled variable to the uncontrolled variables. In our purchase-quantity model, we can develop the decision rule which relates the minimum cost production quantity to customer demand. This decision rule is

$$Q = \sqrt{\frac{2 \cdot D \cdot S}{I}}$$

Because models cannot consider all the complexities of reality, the decision rules developed from them should be used as guides and not necessarily as dictates.

Management stands to benefit from an operations research study, even if a complete solution to the problem cannot be developed. A greater problem understanding, a meaningful problem statement, an isolation of the critical controlled and uncontrolled variables, a usable and meaningful effectiveness scale, and a mechanism for gathering and processing information are some of the benefits.

Implementing Results. The study is wasted unless the decisions which it produces are correctly implemented. Many good studies have died at this stage. Who does what? When does he do it? With what does he do it? These types of questions must be answered. The conversion of the solution into practical operating procedures, and the necessary explaining and training that go with it, must be supplied by the operations researcher. Furthermore, the impact which the new system will have on the human element must be considered, and preparations must be made in anticipation of this.

This phase is the most vital part of any operations research study, for it is the success at this stage which management will use as a yardstick to measure the worth of the entire study, as well as the applicability of operations research in general. Management must insist on a detailed, coordinated plan of implementation as part of the project's output. This plan should include the milestones to be used in the phasing out of obsolete and redundant systems.

An inventory study, the results of which showed that a substantial reduction in inventories could be expected, serves as an example of a study whose benefits were almost lost at the implementation phase. For when the new rules, developed by the study, were installed, peak inventories built up. The reason for this was that all items with too low an inventory level under the new rules were immediately ordered brought up to the desired levels, but no compensating effect was present for those items with too high an inventory level under the new rules. Thus, inventories peaked. The study should have provided for this by recommending that the items be changed a few at a time rather than all at once.

APPLICATIONS OF OPERATIONS RESEARCH

Operations research has been applied to problems in the military, the government, and in almost all types of business and industry. In particular, it has found application in the aircraft, automobile, banking and investment, chemical, electronic and computer, merchandising, petroleum, pharmaceutical, textiles, and transportation institutions.

The General Scope of Applications. The scope of operations research covers the decision-making problems involved in organizational planning and control problems.

When applied on the level of management where policies are made, such as the level where capital budgeting and financial decisions are made, operations research aids the executive in an advisory capacity. On the operational or tactical levels, where production, personnel, purchasing, inventory, and administrative decisions are made, it provides management with a means for handling and processing information. Because there are always interlocking aspects of decisions, a study may extend horizontally across the organization chart, involving production, marketing, and administration departments, as well as vertically through the different levels of management. Furthermore, it can extend from the short range to the long range in time considerations.

Specific Areas of Application. Some of the specific problems to which operations research has been applied are:

1. Selecting the building site for a plant, scheduling and controlling its development, and designing its layout

2. Locating points of distribution and warehousing, and determining best distribution methods

3. Locating within the plant, and controlling the movements of, required production materials and finished-goods inventories

4. Forecasting manpower, production capacities, and capital requirements, and developing plans for their acquisition

5. Selecting pricing, advertising, and bidding strategies

6. Designing accounting and auditing procedures

7. Developing capital-investment plans, and portfolio selection

8. Estimating credit and investment risks

9. Selecting research and development projects, and allocating budgets, facilities, and personnel to them

10. Controlling large-scale development and construction projects

11. Studying personnel recruiting procedures, absenteeism, accident rates, and labor turnover

12. Scheduling medical examinations

13. Developing quantity discount schedules

Recurring Decision Situations. Certain types of decision situations arise over and over again in operations research studies. Each type has stimulated the development of specific techniques and models designed to handle the decision problems associated with it. We discuss seven such categories, but emphasize that in any study several of them will usually be involved simultaneously rather than just one.

The Waiting-line Situation. Frequently, decision situations arise in a process involving the arrival of units or customers which require service at one or more service facilities. Ships arriving at berths to be unloaded, mechanics arriving at tool cribs for tools, aircraft arriving at airfields to be landed, and vehicles arriving at toll booths all serve as examples of such a situation.

Along with periods of time during which customers wait for service in a waiting line, there will be other times when the service facility stands idle, waiting for customers. There are costs associated with each type of waiting, and the decision problem is to minimize the sum of these costs.

The Sequencing Situation. Sequencing theory is concerned with the doctrines followed in selecting the next customer from the waiting line to be serviced. The rule used may be first come, first served; a system of priorities; quickest jobs first; or a purely random selection. This theory has been used to approach such problems as sequencing of production jobs through a process and general routing problems. Such objectives as minimizing costs or processing time, maximizing profit or equipment utilization, or meeting due dates have been used.

PERT and other critical path methods have been successfully applied to the controlling of new-product introduction, major construction and development projects, and research programs. Here, unique activities, which are performed only once, are sequenced. Some of the activities must be completed before others can begin, and there is a path of activities, the critical path, which dominates the time and cost of the entire project.

The Inventory Situation. An inventory is an idle resource of any kind—production materials, finished goods, men, machines, money—provided that such resource has some economic value. For a decision situation to exist, we must have two types of costs involved. As the amount of inventory increases, one cost should increase while the other decreases. For finished products, the inventory carrying costs increase, while the costs of shortages decrease, as the amount of inventory increases.

The decision problem is usually concerned with controlling the quantity of inventory acquired per order and the frequency of acquisition, but it can also be concerned with the location and nature of the inventories.

The Competitive Situation. In a competitive situation, one individual's decisions are affected by the decisions of one or more other individuals. This situation most naturally arises where there are conflicts of interest involved, such as in marketing sales, military conflict, or contract bidding.

The theory of games and statistical decision theory are most closely associated with this situation, as well as a type of simulation called "gaming." In gaming, real data and circumstances are simulated, or played out, as games. A specific type of gaming, military gaming, has long been used to train officers and men for combat.

The Search Situation. The first search model was developed during World War II to solve decision problems connected with air patrols and their search for enemy submarines. Advertising agencies search for customers; personnel departments search for good potential executives; the retrieval of information is a search; auditing is a search procedure, as are most accounting operations; and exploration problems are searches.

The decision problems are related to how much coverage a search area should receive and what type of coverage should be used.

The Allocation Situation. Many important decisions involve the allocation of scarce resources such as men, time, money, equipment, and materials to the various activities which have need for them. The objective of the allocation might be to minimize costs or total processing time, or to maximize profit, equipment utilizations, or returns on investments.

Seldom are there sufficient resources available to perform each of the activities in the best possible way. To work within these limitations, some of the activities will be done in a less-than-best way, and some may not be done at all. The limitations encountered may be of the resource-availability type, or they may take the form of a company policy, such as a limitation on the rate of hiring or laying off of personnel, a restriction on types of investments, or a ceiling on inventory levels.

The Replacement Situation. Replacement situations can be classified into two general types. The first is concerned with equipment which deteriorates with use or becomes obsolete in the light of technological innovations. Most heavy equipment is of this type. The decision problem is that of determining the optimum point in time, or in cumulative usage, to replace the equipment, as well as the selection of the equipment with which the replacement should be made. These decisions are made to minimize the cost of the new equipment, maintenance costs of the old equipment, and the opportunity costs involved. A good replacement policy helps control the borrowing and spending of capital used for replacements.

The second type of replacement situation is one which is concerned with equipment which does not necessarily experience any degradation with use, but which suddenly and permanently fails. Light bulbs, electronic circuits in missiles, and component parts of larger pieces of equipment serve as examples. The decision problem is to determine which items should be replaced, and with what frequency, so that the sum of the cost of the replacements and the costs due to equipment failures is minimized.

INSTALLING OPERATIONS RESEARCH INTO THE ORGANIZATION

Once management has decided upon using operations research, there remain the questions concerning its installation into the organization. In this area, there is no one procedure which applies equally well to all types of organizations, but there are some guidelines which may be helpful.

Locating the Operations Research Group. The final position and level of the company's structure which the operations research activity should hold must be determined in the light of the particular circumstances in each individual case. If the group is to work on problems which will cut across divisional boundaries, then it should report to top management directly. For here, it is paramount that the group knows the goals of top management and obtains a corporate view of the organization. When first introducing operations research, it is probably better to have the group report to a level of management other than the very top, perhaps to the head of production, planning, or finance. But, in any case, it must be allowed to develop and grow into a more prominent position as it proves its worth.

Maximizing Benefits from the Operations Research Group. If the full effectiveness of the group is to be obtained, there are certain necessities which must be provided: The group should be on a staff level, and not restricted to a specific and limited operating area; it must have free access to company information as it needs it; it should report to that level of management which is responsible for the functions, departments, or divisions which are involved in its studies; and a yardstick must be readily available with which a project's success or failure can be measured. Profit improvement and cost reduction have been used as yardsticks, but a better measure is the effectiveness of implementation of the study's results.

Most of the obstacles which impede the successful implementation of a study are in the basic areas of communication and management participation. Results of the study must be effectively communicated to operating management if they are to be understood and fully accepted. Equally important is the active participation in the study by management. Top management as well as operating management supplies to the study guidance, technical know-how, and such external information as political, economic, and competitive factors.

Staffing the Operations Research Group. The operations research group can be staffed in three ways: by using external consultants, by staffing from within the organization, or by a combination of these.

External Staffing. If the solution to a problem is urgently needed, the quickest way of obtaining it is by using outside consultants. External consultants bring in fresh viewpoints, supply a wide variety of experiences, and do not permanently commit the company to a group or department.

The greatest disadvantage of using only external staffs is that once they leave the company all the valuable knowledge and experience gained in the study leave with them.

Before final selection of a consultant, several should be presented with the problem to establish a basis for comparison. Furthermore, whenever possible, the consultant's previous clients should be contacted for their evaluation of him.

Fees paid to consulting staffs will depend upon the size of the staff, the problem's complexity, and the length of time needed for the study. A fair rule of thumb is a fee of from $250 to $300 per day per consultant, for a fairly complex problem.

Internal Staffing. The establishment of a permanent internal staff is more practical for medium-sized or large-sized companies than it is for smaller ones. Most companies with internal staffs report a gross annual sales of over $30 million. However, the small business can carry out operations research by supporting a graduate student in operations research who agrees to work on the company's problem as his thesis subject, or by retaining one man who can be used in operations research studies as well as in other activities.

Internal operations research groups can be staffed either by recruiting experienced operations researchers from the outside or by training men already in the organization.

When recruiting experienced researchers, it is best to allow a year's lead time and expect to pay between $15,000 and $20,000 per year. This would be for someone with five to ten years' experience and one who is qualified to head an operations research group. The opinion of a competent operations researcher on the qualifications of the applicant is recommended if the company is just getting started with operations research. This assistance may be obtained from a consulting firm or from an academic institution.

When staffing solely from within the organization, it is best to start the group with a competent scientist or engineer. Sufficient time must be made available for his education and training in the operations research techniques. Involved in this will be visits to firms with established groups, attendance at seminars and classes at nearby institutions, and the reading of the current literature on the subject.

Initially, it is best to keep the size of the group to about two or three members. Additional members are added as the need arises. The additions should be made not only to meet increasing demands on the group, but also to supplement the specialties of its existing members. A survey of many companies, of different sizes and in different fields, reports that the size of a permanent group ranges from three to twenty people. Engineers account for 42.3 percent of the group's members, mathematicians for 15.6, statisticians for 11.4, and scientists for 18.4 percent. The remaining percentage is accounted for by a variety of categories, such as social scientists, accountants, psychologists, and biologists.

An internal staff becomes more efficient and less costly as it carries out more and more studies. It allows for closer contact and deeper acquaintance with management's objectives, policies, and needs than is possible with external staffs.

Combined Effort in Staffing. This is probably the best approach for starting the operations research activity. The consulting group initiates the work and provides assistance in getting the internal staff started and training its members. After a period of a year, it should be expected that the internal staff can assume project responsibility, and after two years the group should be able to handle most projects without assistance.

Equipping the Operations Research Group. The needs of the activity in equipment and facilities are modest. The following is a basic list.

1. Adequate office space, with one or two researchers per office, is necessary. Each office should have ample blackboard space and the usual office furniture. Free access to a conference room is highly recommended.

2. A basic library of textbooks, reference books, and current journals should be provided. A basic library will cost from $200 to $500, with a yearly cost for journal subscriptions of about $100 to $200.

3. An automatic desk calculator, of the electronic type, should be supplied to every three to five team members.

4. Access to an electronic computer should be given to the group. This computer time may be rented from service agencies or other companies if the parent company's facilities are not adequate.

Organizing for Study. Most of the success of an operations research study depends upon the way things are organized for it. Provisions should be made for drawing on the experience and judgment of management and for easy communication between management and the operations research group. One method of organizing for a study—which has accounted for success in both the analysis and implementation stages—is the formation of what is called a "task force." The task force is a temporary group to last the duration of the study, and it is formed once a project is definitely accepted for study. At this stage, the membership and size of the task force will be determined, but essentially should include one or more researchers from the operations research group, together with technical representatives from the departments whose work comes into the picture. In this way, technical and political knowledge are pooled, and each department is represented in the study and is involved in the development of the outcomes.

The task force should report to a steering committee composed of managers of those functions of the company most vitally connected with, and affected by, the study. Meetings should be held every two to four weeks, where reports on progress and future plans are given.

The task force and steering committee may meet with a top management committee every six to ten weeks. This top management committee would normally include a representative from each major function of the company and may be a regularly functioning committee of the organization.

When studies are properly organized, the task force can be effectively guided during the course of the study, thus preventing any last-minute realizations that important factors were overlooked. In addition, the potentials of operations research are exposed to more people, and the time-consuming job of preparing lengthy written reports is reduced to a minimum.

Selecting Projects for the Operations Research Group. On the basis of short-term payoffs from the first projects, management may decide the future of operations research in the company. Thus, considerable care and effort must be devoted to the selection of the first projects.

Management should map out several general problem areas of possible projects and present these to the operations research group. Such things as the size of the problem, the money involved, the currentness of the problem, and the comparative expense of the operations research approach to the more conventional approaches should be considered by management. The operations research group should comment on the aspects of the problems which are amenable to study, point out which problem statements are clearest, and give estimates of procedures and the likelihood of success. One important type of information which the team must supply to management is what simplifications and assumptions will have to be made to handle the problem. This is often a point which is overlooked and one which may disappoint management when final solutions are presented.

As a general rule, the characteristics of a suitable problem for the operations research approach are: an opportunity exists to decide among alternative courses of action; the process under study lends itself to quantitative study and measurement; the necessary data are available or designs can be made by which they can be obtained; and there are, readily available, ways to evaluate the results of the study.

There is one caution concerning future projects of the operations research group. There will be a tendency to use the team to solve present crisis problems. A certain amount of this activity should be expected, but the group should be allowed to refuse such problems if they become excessive. The most effective use of operations research will be on projects which will prevent future crises from arising, these being of wide scope and of long range.

RELATED DEVELOPMENTS

Systems Engineering. Systems engineering, like operations research, studies complex man-machine systems, uses multidiscipline teams, employs the scientific method, and stresses the whole system rather than the component approach. However, it is concerned with the decision-making situation as it is related to choices of equipment systems. Thus, the difference between systems engineering and operations research is one of approach. The former is primarily interested in making equipment changes, whereas the latter is concerned more with making procedural changes. In other words, systems engineering makes improvements in the performance of an organization by making changes in its content, whereas operations research makes changes in its control.

Behavioral Science. Operations research models generally do not include the psychological and the social variables of a problem. These are undeniable variables of the system, and awareness of them is extremely important, especially at the implementation stages. These behavioral variables are not easily characterized and do not lend themselves to manipulation as readily as those variables which are normally found in operations research models. The inclusion into operations research models of the effects of such things as status relationships, manager-worker attitudes toward each other, and other psychological and social factors will come as the behavioral scientist involves himself more in operations research.

Human Engineering. Consideration of human factors in the design of equipment has come to be known as "human engineering," "biomechanics," or "ergonomics." What color should control buttons be to ensure that the proper one is pushed? What type of lighting is best in a certain work area? How do temperature and changes in temperature affect the output of a machine operator? These are the types of problems which the human engineer studies. Like the systems engineer, he looks at the organizational content, and more specifically at the relationship between the human element and the equipment. He strives to develop ways of modifying equipment used by people, actual operations, or work environments to match human capacities and limitations. In this way, human productivity, accuracy, and reliability can be increased.

Computer Technology. We can classify business data processing into two parts: the housekeeping part, such as payroll, billing, and the like; and the data-producing part, where data are produced for the purpose of decision making and management control.   As computer systems become larger and capable of higher speeds, data can be handled in greater quantities, broken down in a more detailed fashion, and produced more quickly or more frequently.   This increased detail and speed of reporting greatly aid management control and allow for the routinization of many lower-level decisions.

High-speed computing equipment is not absolutely essential for an operations research study.   Very useful results have been obtained with mathematical techniques, without a computer.   But computers can solve formulas, develop data, and offer greater exploration of data to determine existing relationships.   For these reasons, more complex problems, with many factors and interrelationships between them, can be solved.   Often, a technique of the operations researcher becomes feasible only on a high-speed computer, such as large linear programming applications and almost every simulation.

The growth in scientific programming languages, such as FORTRAN, has made the computer easily accessible to the operations researcher.   Along with these normal programming languages, there are a growing number of simulation languages specifically designed to allow systems simulations; GPSS, SIMSCRIPT, SIMPAC, and ESP are examples.   These languages have been used to simulate manufacturing, advertising, and administrative processes.

BIBLIOGRAPHY

Ackoff, R. L., and P. Rivett, *A Manager's Guide to Operations Research,* John Wiley & Sons, Inc., New York, 1963.

Bowman, E. H., and R. B. Fetter, *Analysis for Production Management,* Richard D. Irwin, Inc., Homewood, Ill., 1961.

Bursk, E. C., and J. F. Chapman, *New Decision-making Tools for Managers,* Harvard University Press, Cambridge, Mass., 1963.

Enrick, N. L., *Management Operations Research,* Holt, Rinehart, and Winston, Inc., New York, 1965.

Flagle, C. D., W. H. Huggins, and R. H. Roy, *Operations Research and Systems Engineering,* The Johns Hopkins Press, Baltimore, 1960.

Hertz, D. B., and R. T. Eddison, *Progress in Operations Research,* vol. 2, John Wiley & Sons, Inc., New York, 1964.

CHAPTER THREE

Probability and Statistics for Business Decisions

PATRICK J. ROBINSON *Marketing Science Institute, Philadelphia, Pennsylvania*

For some business administrators, "probability" is a word that the weatherman uses when he says there is a 40 percent probability of rain. For others, probability has something to do with probable errors in business forecasts. The word "statistics," on the other hand, may conjure up images of tables of numbers and reams of historical data, recorded and manipulated by people called "sales analysts," "bookkeepers," or "statistical clerks."

This chapter is designed to do two things: (1) define probability and statistics for those who are not familiar with them in the business sense, and show how they can be helpful; and (2) support and possibly add to the information that some businessmen may already have about these important concepts.

It does not pretend to summarize all that there is to know about probability and statistics. Rather, it is an overview of these subjects written for those who are management, rather than research, oriented.

It is not a "how to do it" manual; the subject is too broad for that. What this chapter does attempt is to present some examples of proved, although often untapped, resources which can help decision makers. Now then, what should probability and statistics really mean to the businessman?

THE DEVELOPING FIELD OF STATISTICS

In the first place, the subject of statistics is a field of scientific endeavor that is central to the "scientific method" (see Chapter 5 of Section 1) in the proper design of experiments and the drawing of valid inferences about events in sampling from a given population or so-called universe.

The astonishing thing to an interested neophyte in statistics is the extraordinary sophistication and resolving power provided by available techniques. These techniques permit one to process data systematically and to sense what is meaningful among vast quantities of information; all this with seemingly uncanny consistency.

17–30

Many of the techniques employed by professional statisticians have come into their own only since the advent of the modern electronic computer and the arrival of the management scientist on the business scene. Some powerful statistical tools were known previously in theory, but could not be applied in practice. Some of these were too ponderous and unwieldy for routine manual manipulation, even when aided by desk calculators and punched card data-processing equipment. They took too long, cost too much, and ran the risk of too much human error in the maze of arithmetic required. Other techniques were not so much ponderous as they were conceptually sophisticated. Although they may have been elegantly straightforward in application, they required a level of mathematical insight and expertise in measurement beyond the competence or experience of most staff personnel.

By 1960, things had begun to change, and we were "in a different ball game." Most of this "impractical" theory had been brought within the economic grasp of people with significant problems to solve. Not only is statistical method the best way to handle many complex problems involving measurements, but generally it is the least costly, most reliable, and fastest feasible approach. Sometimes it is the only feasible way of coping with information, short of ignoring it.

Unfortunately, statistical method has been a mixed blessing. Mere availability of practical potential has not led automatically to practical applications. Communication barriers have kept apart the business administrators with significant problems and the business researchers with promising problem-solving statistical techniques. Of course, there are noteworthy exceptions in certain companies and in some industries or specialized phases of business where there have been important successes.

For several decades, agriculture and biology have benefited greatly by successful applications. These fields pioneered many applications and helped evolve many techniques. In industry, statistical quality control has been with us since before World War II. The pioneering work in statistical sampling for defectives in Western Electric's production of telephone components led the way. Subsequently, hundreds of companies exploited the cost savings and greatly improved quality control made possible for mass-produced goods through the proper sampling of output. Nevertheless, even with substantial successes over the past several decades, many companies still fail to utilize (and some may not even know of) statistical sampling and rigorous quality-control techniques.

The accounting profession provides another example of our apparent inability to "farm as well as we know how." Just as standard cost systems are seldom properly engineered, many opportunities are missed for auditing and using statistical sampling (at substantially reduced cost and with improved reliability) instead of taking a complete census of items.

A third illustration of old-fashioned practice versus new-style theory is in the area of forecasting sales and business conditions. There is really only one truism concerning forecasts, and that is: They are going to be wrong! The only question of merit is: By how much? What does an error of 10 percent matter? Is this close enough for practical purposes? When does a difference make a difference, and how may one anticipate the probable range of error to make allowances for over- and underestimating? Mathematical statistics may help.

We are all familiar with the use of an arithmetic mean or simple average. But how many of us stop to think how much a single number fails to reveal about the data being averaged?

Clearly, an average income of $5,000 among a group ranging from a low of $4,500 to a high of $5,500 may exhibit important differences from another group averaging $5,000 but with a much wider range from $2,500 to $15,000. It is the *range* that is often as important to decisions as the average itself. And how about grouping or clustering? There may, in our illustration, be a majority of people clustered in the extreme low and high ends of the range with very few in the middle. We can all think of similar well-concealing averages that tend to disarm and confuse the user by obscuring key characteristics such as the way the population is distributed about its arithmetic mean. Whether we speak of production figures, market facts, financial data, or business indicators, staff professionals and line operators alike must recognize that naïve belief in "the facts" may lead to costly mistakes and unnecessary misunderstandings in management.

Methodological Scope and Content of Probability and Statistics. To explain how probability and statistics may help you with your business decisions, let us begin by listing some of the fundamental principles and available techniques with which you should become familiar. This list is followed by a brief description of each item in turn. Remember, our purpose is to create an awareness of some of the key insights and range of equipment at the disposal of professionally qualified mathematical statisticians. This awareness should help you to identify possible opportunities from an operating point of view and to be more responsive to suggestions and possibly more tolerant of the technical jargon of specialized consultants. Some readers may wish to gain some personal facility also, in which case short courses (for example, two-week intensive summer sessions), offered by a number of leading business and industrial schools, may be taken. Furthermore, texts, such as those suggested in the Bibliography at the end of this chapter, may provide a satisfactory basis for self-instruction.

The topics that we shall touch on in this chapter include:

1. Permutations, combinations, and elementary probability
2. Frequency distributions
3. Averages and central tendencies
4. Measures of dispersion
5. The normal, binomial, and Poisson distributions
6. Statistical inference
7. Statistical sampling
8. The chi-square (χ^2) test
9. Comparisons of means using the t test
10. The method of least squares, correlation, and regression
11. Time-series analysis
12. Statistical confidence limits
13. Analysis of variance and covariance
14. Statistical control charts
15. The design of experiments
16. Subjective probability and Bayesian statistics

Using this list as a general guide, we will take each topic in turn and develop a short, unsophisticated, layman's description of what each means and, where appropriate, illustrate how it operates or at least suggest its practical potential.

PERMUTATIONS, COMBINATIONS, AND ELEMENTARY PROBABILITY

Let us first deal with permutations and combinations in some detail and then move on more quickly through the other topics. This initial illustration may serve to indicate the depth and care required when dealing with even the simplest concepts.

Permutations and Combinations. "Permutations" and "combinations" refer to the number of feasible arrangements of some items being considered.   To illustrate: If we have the letters A, B, and C marked on three separate cards, and we select any two of the cards at random (that is, by pure chance selection), there are six possible sequences of letters or *permutations* (AB, BA, AC, CA, BC, CB).   If we ignore order, however, there are only three pairs or *combinations* (A and B, A and C, B and C).   We see from this trivial illustration that if the *order* of selecting the items makes AB different from BA, there are more arrangements (permutations) than if we consider AB and BA as essentially identical (combinations).   So it is with larger numbers of items and more complex arrangements.

Of course, more complex cases become quite involved and lengthy.   They require the use of formulas which can handle the necessary computations efficiently and rigorously.   Let us illustrate the general-purpose formulas using the simple three-card illustration.   Even though simple, the explanation and execution of these examples will still require several minutes reading—and some contemplation of the logic at work.

In the case of permutations, we have the general mathematical statement: $_nP_r = n!/(n - r)!$.   As with any formula, this one can be translated into plain English (although not all such translations are easy to comprehend).   The left-hand side of this formula merely states that "P," the number of permutations or different arrangements of "n" things, is to be considered "r" at a time.   In our example, we had $n = 3$ things (A, B, C) taken $r = 2$ at a time (AB, BA, and so on).   This completes the translation of $_nP_r$.   On the right-hand side of the equality sign, we can again interpret the equation.   First, the letter "n" followed by an exclamation mark means that we multiply (n) times ($n - 1$) times ($n - 2$) and so on, until the last item in the series is 1.   In this case, we have $3 \times 2 \times 1$.   Similarly, $(n - r)!$ in our simple example is $(3 - 2)! = 1!$.   By definition, this is merely 1.   (Incidentally, 0! is also taken by convention as equal to 1; this avoids computational difficulties when $n - r$.)   So now we see that the equation $_nP_r = n!/(n - r)!$ boils down in our example to

$$_nP_r = \frac{3 \times 2 \times 1}{1} = 6 \text{ permutations}$$

This agrees with the answer of 6 that we "spelled out" earlier by enumerating all the sequences of A, B, and C taken two at a time.   Now for combinations of A, B, and C (without regard to order) we have a slightly different general equation:

$$_nC_r = \frac{n!}{(n - r)!r!}$$

(As a matter of interest, this also equals $_nP_r/r!$.)   The following useful additional relationship can sometimes save time: $_nC_r = {}_nC_{n-r}$.   In our illustration we have

$$_3C_2 = \frac{3!}{(3 - 2)!2!}$$
$$= \frac{3 \times 2 \times 1}{1 \times 2 \times 1}$$
$$= 3 \text{ combinations of 3 things taken 2 at a time}$$

We know that $_nC_{n-r} = {_nC_r}$ and so $_3C_1$ should also equal 3 and it does, with

$$\frac{3!}{(3-1)!1!} = \frac{3 \times 2 \times 1}{2 \times 1 \times 1}$$

$$= 3 \text{ combinations}$$

Of course, the real value of the foregoing equations is in simplifying much more complex problems involving large numbers.

Elementary Probability. Having illustrated permutations and combinations (both informally and formally), we proceed now to the subject of elementary probability. Consider, first, several simple examples which are intuitively clear. Then we may proceed to less obvious and more involved applications.

In using the term "probability" in a technical sense, we refer to two extremes and a range in between. At one extreme, we say that an absolutely impossible event has a probability of zero. At the other, an absolutely certain event is said to have a probability of one. An event with some likelihood of occurrence between these extremes is expressed as a decimal fraction between zero and one. For example, an event with 50-50 odds, or equal likelihood of occurring or not occurring, is said to have a probability of $p = 0.5$. If the probabilities can be specified in advance (for example, the likelihood of tossing a coin's head or tail), we speak of "a priori" probability (before the fact). If, however, we measure probability by observing occurrences, we have empirical probability (after the fact or "posteriori"), and

$$p = \frac{\text{number of occurrences of event}}{\text{total number of trials}}$$

An illustration of a random (nonsystematic and purely by chance) pattern of occurrence would be the falling of raindrops on an area of pavement. The rain falls in a haphazard or random manner and the pavement becomes uniformly wet as the scattering pattern of drops gradually covers the entire area observed. Generally, there is no apparent clustering or special preference for any part of the area of pavement.

If one draws a graph of the occurrence of the numbers generated by repeated rolls of a single die, the uniform height of the bars is referred to as a "rectangular or equal-likelihood distribution." For example, in sixty rolls we would expect (a priori) the results shown by Figure 3-1. Each bar in this chart represents ten occurrences of the value indicated. Of course, if you try this experiment, you will only approximate (posteriori) this uniform frequency of occurrence of ten showings of each value. The reason for obtaining only an approximately even scattering is not hard to see, for it is obvious that there is a degree of uncertainty associated with tossing the die, although there is an equal chance of any single face showing. If we kept repeating our sixty-roll experiment

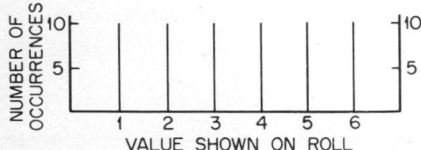

FIG. 3-1. *Occurrence of numbers generated by repeated rolls of a single die.*

and averaging the results, we would, over the very long run, achieve a close approximation of this uniform pattern—although never *exactly* equal numbers of occurrences. In fact, the likelihood of all six sets of occurrences being the same in number gets less as the number of rolls increases.

Now let us consider a pair of dice. We add the values on the face of each die so that a 7 results from a 3 and 4, or a 4 and 3, or 5 and 2, or a 2 and 5, and so on. It is obvious that there are more permutations of outcomes (six in fact) that yield a 7 than there are for a 2 or a 12, for each of which there is only one arrangement possible. If the values are now plotted for sixty rolls, a different pattern will emerge than the rectangular pattern considered previously. Clearly, each single die has an equal (1/6) probability of showing any one side. Whether we roll one die twice in succession or a pair of dice together, the number showing on each is quite independent of the other. Yet, because 7 may occur in six ways, we know that it will be the most frequent number achieved over the long run.

The probability of the simultaneous occurrence of two independent events is the product of the separate probabilities. For example, what is the probability of "snake-eyes" (two 1's) showing? Because the probability of a 1 on a single die is 1/6, the probability of the joint occurrence of a 1 on each of a pair of dice is $1/6 \times 1/6 = 1/36$. The same probability would apply for "boxcars" (two 6's). For a 7, however, there are more ways (by enumeration we obtained six permutations: $1 + 6, 6 + 1, 2 + 5, 5 + 2, 3 + 4, 4 + 3$) which yield this result. Each of these arrangements has a $1/6 \times 1/6$ or 1/36 probability of occurring each time the dice are rolled. This means that a priori 6/36 or 1/6 of the time we should expect to roll a 7. In fact, we may perform this experiment and again closely approximate our expectations.

The bar chart, Figure 3-2, is referred to as a "discrete frequency distribution diagram." Its bell shape conforms to what is known as the "binomial distribution." (This is a mathematical description which will be referred to later. It has certain special properties which are helpful in describing results and in making predictions.) This is a so-called *discrete*, as opposed to *continuous*, distribution because only discrete values such as 2, 3, 4 can occur in the given range.

Naturally, if you roll a pair of honest dice 36 times, most likely you will arrive only approximately at the distribution of occurrences illustrated in the foregoing histogram. The histogram was constructed a priori (before the fact), based on our conclusions on what to expect on the logic of the ways in which the dice could fall.

A further illustration of a tendency for one particular value to show up more frequently than another can be arrived at by taking six honest coins and tossing them simultaneously. With a pair of dice, we know that the number 7 will

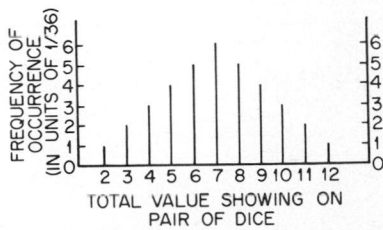

FIG. 3-2. *Discrete frequency distribution diagram or probability bar chart.*

show most frequently in the long run. If we now consider which sides are apt to show among the six coins tossed, several things are intuitively clear. In tossing six coins a considerable number of times, experience with tossing a single coin would suggest that if heads show up half the time, then among six coins we would anticipate seeing three heads on the average. Clearly, each of the six coins would have a $p = 0.5$ chance of falling with a head showing. It may not be intuitively obvious that for six coins falling we have an expectancy of showing all heads of $1/2 \times 1/2 \times 1/2 \times 1/2 \times 1/2 \times 1/2$ or $(1/2)^6$, which is $1/64$. Similarly, if we considered the chance of getting all tails, we would again obtain $1/64$.

If the six coins were six different colors, we could keep track of what each coin was showing on each toss. We can visualize that there are many possible permutations of six coins which could yield a total of exactly three heads. There are, in fact, $6/64$, or 6 out of 64, chances of showing only one head; $15/64$ chances of showing two heads; and $20/64$ chances of showing three heads. It is possible to enumerate all possibilities in a so-called sample-space tabulation as in Figure 3-3.

Of course, enumeration (for even this simple illustration) would be a tedious and undesirable way to compute expected frequencies of occurrence. As might be expected, there are formulas which handle this problem with ease. We will touch on this problem again in connection with the binomial distribution. However, because your curiosity may be aroused, the formula for this problem is expressed $(p + q)^n$, where p is the probability or expected frequency of one outcome (here tossing a head); q is the other expected frequency (tossing a tail); and n is simply the number of coins or whatever we are using. For a coin, $p = 1/2$ and $q = 1/2$.

Incidentally, if we were tossing dice and wondering how many sixes we should expect to see, we could set $p = 1/6$ and $q = 5/6$ (that is, the expected frequency of seeing a six on a die versus seeing a non-six). Of course, n would merely designate the number of dice being thrown together. With our simple coin illustration, we would have $(p + q)^6$, and by using something called "algebraic expansion," we would convert this to: $q^6 + 6q^5p + 15q^4p^2 + q^3p^3 + 15q^2p^4 + 6qp^5 + p^6$. This looks difficult, but there is a very neat shortcut that

Case no.	Coin 1	Coin 2	Coin 3	Coin 4	Coin 5	Coin 6	Total heads showing
1	H	H	H	H	H	H	6
2	H	H	H	H	H	T	5
3	H	H	H	H	T	H	5
.							
.	And so on for 64 cases with all possible permutations.						
.							
62	T	H	T	T	T	T	1
63	H	T	T	T	T	T	1
64	T	T	T	T	T	T	0

FIG. 3-3. *Sample-space tabulation.*

easily reduces $(p + q)^n$ to an expanded equation in a minute or two. Then all that remains is to substitute the suitable frequency values for p and q in the expanded equation (remember, in our coin illustration both p and $q = 1/2$). So q^6 is simply $(1/2)^6$, which we saw previously is 1/64, and so on to yield $1/64 + 6/64 + 15/64 + 20/64 + 15/64 + 6/64 + 1/64$. These expected frequencies correspond to the probabilities of our observing one, two, three, four, five, or six heads.

Notice how much more there is to even simple coin tossing than a surface examination might suggest to the casual observer. Note, especially, how involved calculating probabilities becomes. We have the tools available, however, to make the task relatively easy.

Most importantly, one may appreciate that just as a small-scale problem is made easy by such computational aids, so may very large and complex problems be rendered manageable (particularly when electronic computers can handle the tedious arithmetic). In a continuous distribution, an infinite number of "in-between" fractional values are also possible (such as measurements of people's heights).

Let us consider the subject of measuring heights and plotting these data. It is clear that, in theory at least, the number of possible variations in height, even for boys in a five- to six-foot range, is infinite. Of course, this assumes that we count even infinitesimal differences as being separate. Clearly, if we measured boys only to the nearest inch, then we would have only twelve height classes in a one-foot range. If we measured to the nearest tenth of an inch, there would be ten times as many possible groupings. Naturally, for any given sample of boys, we need not find some boys falling into every height category. Consequently, if we are grouping such information, it is customary to plan each category not to lump or aggregate too many subjects (for example, one category for each foot of height difference) versus too few.

Furthermore, we may plot our chart either as a bar chart (grouping data in a probability histogram) or as a line chart (or frequency polygon). Figure 3-4 shows the results of measuring the heights of eighty boys to the nearest inch. Their arithmetic mean height is 68.5 inches. Both the histogram and the frequency polygon are plotted. Note that the latter line graph is constructed by joining the midpoints at the top of each bar in the histogram. In addition to frequency of occurrence, a scale showing proportion is given. This proportion measure relates the heights to the total area plotted (which is one square unit), and the diagrams are said to be "frequency distributions" of the plotted measurements.

Another useful way of thinking about these data involves plotting a cumula-

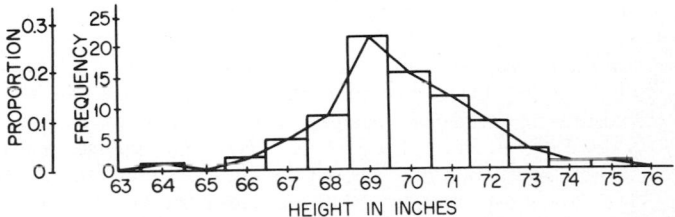

FIG. 3-4. *Histogram and frequency polygon resulting from measuring the heights of eighty boys.* (*Courtesy of Wilfrid J. Dixon and Frank J. Massey, Jr.*, Introduction to Statistical Analysis, 2d ed., McGraw-Hill Book Company, New York, 1957, p. 8.)

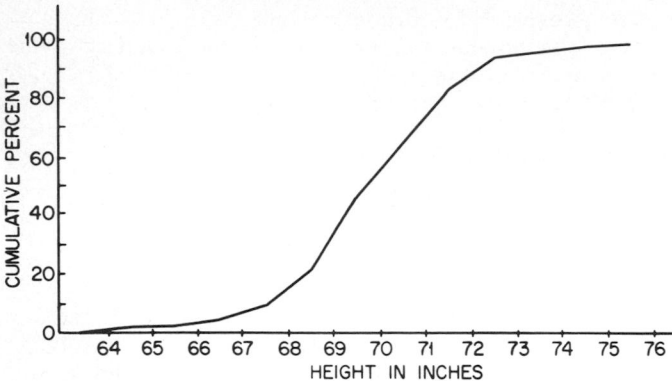

FIG. 3-5. *Data from Figure 3-4 plotted cumulatively.* (*Courtesy of Wilfred J. Dixon and Frank J. Massey, Jr.,* Introduction to Statistical Analysis, *2d ed., McGraw-Hill Book Company, New York, 1957, p. 11.*)

tive-distribution polygon. This is easiest to explain by showing the foregoing data on the eighty boys plotted cumulatively as in Figure 3-5. Using this graph is simple and versatile. For example, if we read horizontally across to the curve at a level of 10 percent and then drop a line vertically to the bottom of the chart, we read 67.5 inches. This tells us that 10 percent of the boys are less than 67.5 inches tall. Similarly, reading across from 80 percent we find that our vertical dropped from the curve intercepts the horizontal axis (the abscissa) at about 71.5 inches. This tells us that 80 percent of the boys are less than 71.5 inches tall. And so on.

Another use for such a chart is to enter at the bottom with a height such as 70 inches and then read up to the curve and across to the vertical axis (the ordinate), where we read 59 percent. This tells us that a boy of 70 inches is in the 59th percentile rank. Incidentally, the median occurs at the 50th percentile. Percentiles are often used in speaking of personality and aptitude rankings and also for school grades to indicate relative standings.

The Addition Theorem. Another useful general principle or "law" of chance is called the "addition theorem." This states that if an event may occur in several different ways, then the probability of the event occurring should be stated as the sum of the probabilities of each of the different ways.

Perhaps this seems obvious, but it is important to "spell it out" along with other less obvious principles. If there is a possibility of two mutually exclusive events A or B occurring, then the probability of one or the other happening is stated as $P(A + B) = P(A) + P(B)$. This can be generalized for any number of mutually exclusive alternatives. For example, if there are five mountain climbers trying to scale a mountain and only one can reach the top first, the probability of someone reaching the top first is $P(A + B + C + D + E) = P(A) + P(B) + P(C) + P(D) + P(E)$. Of course, *this need not total 1;* because in a situation like this, all the climbers may fail to reach the mountain top.

Now, we must recognize that certain joint occurrences (hence not mutually exclusive) may occur (such as ties in a race). If we wish to state the probability of A or B winning, we must allow for the possibility of both events happening together. Thus we have from the complete statement of the addition theorem: $P(A + B) = P(A) + P(B) - P(AB)$. This equation may be read as follows:

"The probability of event A or B occurring equals the probability of event A alone or not plus the probability of event B alone or not, minus the probability of their joint occurrence." Think about this before reading on. It may be clear, but it is not as obvious as our first illustration, which did not provide for both events occuring together.

This form of the addition theorem, which takes into account events which may or may not be mutually exclusive, can also be generalized—but it becomes more involved. For example, with three possible outcomes A, B, or C, we have

$$P(A + B + C) = P(A) + P(B) + P(C) - P(AB) - P(AC) - P(BC) + P(ABC)$$

A special form of graphical logic (set theory, such as is taught in so-called modern mathematics) can help illustrate what is involved here in the *Venn diagram* shown by Figure 3-6. We are interested only in the net areas labeled A, B, and C. We wish to exclude the areas representing the joint occurrence of two or three events. The preceding equation accomplishes this selection of the total of the mutually exclusive occurrences, after removing the joint possibilities represented by the areas of overlap of the three circles.

Clearly, if the circles do not overlap, the addition theorem reduces to its simple form, which was stated previously, for mutually exclusive events (that is, the combined terms in the longer equation merely become zero). However, if events are not mutually exclusive, then the longer version must be employed. For example, if we wished to compute the probability of rolling 6 *at least once* with two rolls of a single die, the equation could be stated: The probability of a 6 on the first roll $P(A) = 1/6$, plus the probability of a 6 on the second roll $P(B) = 1/6$, minus the probability of a 6 on each roll $P(AB) = 1/6 \times 1/6$. Hence

$$P(A + B) = P(A) + P(B) - P(AB)$$
$$= 1/6 + 1/6 - 1/36$$
$$= 11/36$$

In using the addition theorem, we have focused attention on mutually exclusive "either/or" (but not both) types of events. In the Venn diagram, we discarded the areas of overlap. We now turn our attention to the areas of overlap representing simultaneous occurrences or sequential occurrences of two or more events.

The Multiplication Theorem. Consider two events, A and B. The probability of their joint occurrence $P(AB)$ equals the probability of A's occurrence $P(A)$

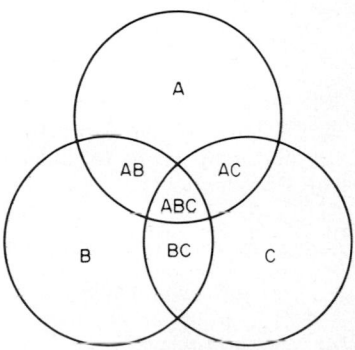

FIG. 3-6. *Venn diagram.*

times the probability of B's occurrence given that A has occurred $P(B|A)$. In short, $P(AB) = P(A)P(B|A)$. This equation can be generalized for more events, but it becomes somewhat involved.

In the case of independent events, the equation simplifies. Thus, the probability of B occurring, given that A already has occurred, is the same as the probability of B occurring irrespective of what happens to A. In equation form, this is expressed as $P(B|A) = P(B)$ and $P(AB) = P(A)P(B)$. The multiplication theorem can be generalized most readily in this latter case of independent events for reasons that should be intuitively clear, because only a simple series of multiplication is needed.

We can illustrate the multiplication theorem quite simply by considering the probability of drawing a spade from a 52-card deck followed by another spade. If we draw our first card, the probability of a spade is 13/52. It follows that our second draw has a different probability of being a spade, namely, 12/51. According to the multiplication theorem:

$$P(S_1S_2) = P(S_1)P(S_2/S_1)$$

so
$$P(S_1S_2) = 13/52 \times 12/51$$
$$= 1/17$$

as the probability of drawing two spades in succession from a 52-card deck.

The foregoing assumed that we drew two cards in succession from the deck *without replacement*. Consequently, the removal of the first spade affected the probability of drawing a second. However, if we *replaced* our first card in the deck before our second draw, then each draw would have a 13/52 probability of yielding a spade. The simpler (independent) interpretation of the formula would apply and

$$P(S_1S_2) = P(S_1)P(S_2)$$

so
$$P(S_1S_2) = 13/52 \times 13/52$$
$$= 1/16$$

as the probability of drawing two spades in succession from a 52-card deck, assuming replacement of the first card drawn before drawing the second.

The implications of these trivial illustrations are quite profound in connection with statistical sampling theory. In sampling from a human population, we usually operate *without replacement*. Thus, whether we are drawing a winner at a raffle or wish to interview customers respecting their buying habits, it is customary not to give anyone selected an opportunity to be selected again during the drawing of the same sample.

Because the populations being sampled in business (whether people, bills of lading, items in inventory, or factory output) are usually comparatively large, differences between samplings with and without replacement become insignificantly small. From a practical point of view, this permits us to use the simpler formulas that apply to independent events (even though the events are not truly independent).

AVERAGES AND CENTRAL TENDENCIES

There are several types of averages available to provide a "typical" representation of a group or population. It is often useful to compare the average value for one group with the corresponding average for another. Which average to use depends on the use intended and the type of data being represented.

The Arithmetic Mean.   The arithmetic mean is the most common type of average, and it is often referred to as the "average" or the "mean." The less ambiguous term is the latter when speaking with people who have more than just a nodding acquaintance with business statistics.

The formula for the mean represents the sum of observations divided by the number of observations. In mathematical shorthand, this is stated: The mean "X bar" equals the sum of the items $X_1, X_2, X_3, \ldots, X_n$ divided by the number of items, n. Thus:

$$\bar{X} = \frac{X_1 + X_2 + X_n}{n} \quad \text{or} \quad \frac{\sum_{i=1}^{i=n} X_i}{n}$$

The symbol Σ is the Greek capital letter sigma and means "summation of"; in this case, the summation of X_i (read "X subscript i") from $i = 1$ to $i = n$.

For example, if we had the numbers 10, 12, 14, 14, 16, 22, 22, 26 to average in this manner, we would have the mean

$$\bar{X} = \frac{10 + 12 + 14 + 14 + 16 + 22 + 22 + 26}{8} = \frac{136}{8} = 17$$

If we speak of a "weighted average," we refer to a form of arithmetic average in which certain values occur more than once. Rather than repeat such numbers, we use all the values and multiply each by its frequency of occurrence. Thus, the formula is a modification of the standard one for the weighted arithmetic mean:

$$\bar{X} = \frac{\sum_{i=1}^{n} f_i X_i}{\sum_{i=1}^{n} f_i}$$

where f subscript i stands for the frequency of occurrence of each X_i.

The Geometric Mean.   The geometric mean is encountered in engineering applications or elsewhere when using averaging rates of increase or decrease of a statistical population. It is computed as the nth root of the product of the n observations, thus:

$$\bar{X}_g = \sqrt[n]{X_1 \times X_2 \times \cdots X_n}$$

A useful alternative method of calculation avoids most of the "messy" calculation:

$$\log \bar{X}_g = \frac{\log X_1 + \log X_2 + \cdots \log X_n}{n}$$

Incidentally, the arithmetic mean will give inappropriate answers for this class of problem. This may be illustrated simply. Consider the numbers 100, 50, 100, 50, 100. The ratios (or rates of changes) for these numbers are 1/2, 2, 1/2, 2. The geometric mean is

$$\sqrt[4]{1/2 \times 2 \times 1/2 \times 2} \text{ or } \sqrt[4]{1}$$

which equals 1. This says that the average ratio of increase (or decrease) is 1. This agrees with the fact that the overall change is 0 (we started with

100 and are back to 100). However, the arithmetic mean of the ratio would be

$$\frac{1/2 + 2 + 1/2 + 2}{4} = \frac{5}{4} = 1.25$$

Clearly, if we multiply our starting value of 100 by 1.25, we will not obtain 100, which is what the proper average rate of increase should yield.

The Harmonic Mean. This method of averaging data is approximate for combining ratios such as costs per unit of output or miles per hour of speed. It is computed as the reciprocal of the mean of the reciprocals of the values. Thus:

$$\text{Harmonic mean} = \frac{n}{\sum\limits_{i=1}^{n} \frac{1}{X_i}}$$

where n = the number of items being combined and X_i is the value of the item. For example, if a truck averaged 10 mph for one mile, 20 mph for a second mile, and 30 mph for a third mile, the average speed over the 3 miles is *not* $(10 + 20 + 30)/3 = $ mph. Consider these facts: The truck require 1/10 hour for the first mile, 1/20 hour for the second mile, and 1/30 hour for the third mile. So the 3 miles require $1/10 + 1/20 + 1/30$, or $6/60 + 3/60 + 2/60$, or 11/60 hour (so, in 60/60 hours = $3 \times 60/11 = 16\frac{4}{11}$ miles). But if the 3 miles were calculated as traveled at an average speed of 20 mph, the total time would be $1/20 + 1/20 + 1/20$, or 3/20, or 9/60 hour, clearly a different answer than our step-by-step analysis shows to be correct. The arithmetic average fails to weigh properly the 10 mph slow travel time versus the faster time.

In contrast, our harmonic mean formula yields

$$\frac{3}{1/10 + 1/20 + 1/30} = \frac{3}{11/60} = \frac{60}{11} \times \frac{3}{1} = \frac{180}{11} = 16\frac{4}{11} \text{ mph}$$

This corresponds to our painstakingly computed value above.

The Median. The median is a much more common average and merely consists of the middle observation of all our observations when they are arranged in rank order of magnitude. For example, if we had 2, 5, 7, 6, 9, 8, 5, we could arrange these in rank order to obtain 2, 5, 5, 6, 7, 8, 9. The median

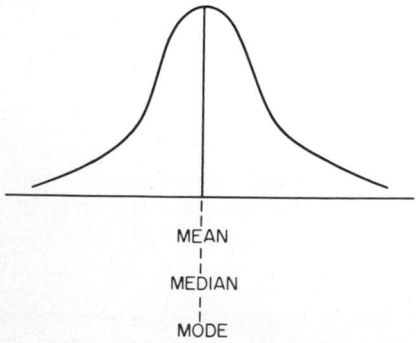

MEAN

MEDIAN

MODE

FIG. 3-7. *Symmetrical frequency distribution curve.*

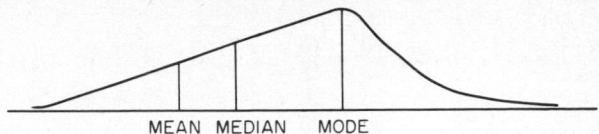

MEAN MEDIAN   MODE

FIG. 3-8. *Frequency distribution curve skewed to left.*

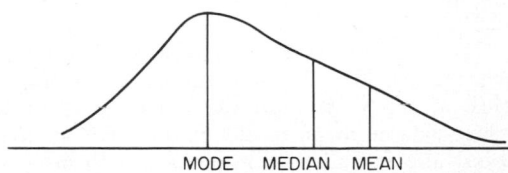

MODE   MEDIAN   MEAN

FIG. 3-9. *Frequency distribution curve skewed to right.*

in this series of seven numbers would be the middle or fourth one, which is 6.

The Mode. The mode is the most common value taken from the most frequently occurring or clustering of numbers. In the foregoing illustration, 5 is the mode of the series of seven numbers.

Skewness. "Skewness" is a word for the distortion to the right (positively skewed) or left (negatively skewed) of the normally symmetrical frequency distribution curve. This statement can be clarified best diagrammatically as in Figures 3-7, 3-8, and 3-9. These are all examples of unimodal frequency distributions.

A bimodal distribution has two humps (like some camels), and as one may appreciate intuitively, there is no typical average for the distribution. Actually, there are two modes, and the mean and the median may fall anywhere, not necessarily between the modes, in a bimodal density curve.

MEASURES OF DISPERSION

Having considered averages as single values intended to express something representative of the whole population which they represent, we can appreciate some of the obvious shortcomings inherent in this attempt. The "well-concealing average" is clearly a poor substitute for a graph or table of values for the whole distribution. Yet, we cannot afford to prepare and examine such detail every time we consider a group of numbers. We would be much better off to accept a single value, such as the arithmetic mean, and some measure of dispersion or variation about the mean to convey what we need to know.

Clearly, the three distributions illustrated by Figure 3-10 cannot alone be represented by just a mean value (it is the same for each), because we cannot differentiate among the variations in population diversity.

One possibility would be to calculate a mean value and also a mean absolute deviation about that value. For example, if we had the numbers 12, 15, 18, 25, 30, they would sum to 100 and have a mean of 100/5 = 20. The individual differences of these five values from this mean are (without regard to a deviation being plus or minus, but rather just a variation to the right or left of the measure of central tendency):

$$20 - 12 = 8$$
$$20 - 15 = 5$$
$$20 - 18 = 2$$
$$25 - 20 = 5$$
$$30 - 20 = 10$$

$$5\,\overline{|30}\ = 6 \text{ mean absolute deviation}$$

With this approach, we could now represent our five-item population (and it could equally well be 5,000 items) by only two numbers: the mean = 20 and the average deviation = 6.

The number 20 tells us where the center of the population is located, and the number 6 tells us that, on the average, the items in this population lie plus or minus 6 from the mean value of 20. Of course, another group of items with a mean of 20 might have an average deviation of 2, and this we could also visualize and compare with other distributions more objectively than with only their mean values.

However, this is still not good enough. A much better measure is available than mean deviation. It is called the "standard deviation" and has some very special properties of great practical significance.

Calculating the standard deviation requires us first to determine the mean for the data being used and then to determine the deviation of each item of data in turn from that mean (as we demonstrated with the average deviation). Then there is a departure from the earlier procedure. Each individual departure is squared (multiplied by itself), and the sum of all the squares so obtained is divided by n to obtain the mean squared deviation. Then we take the square

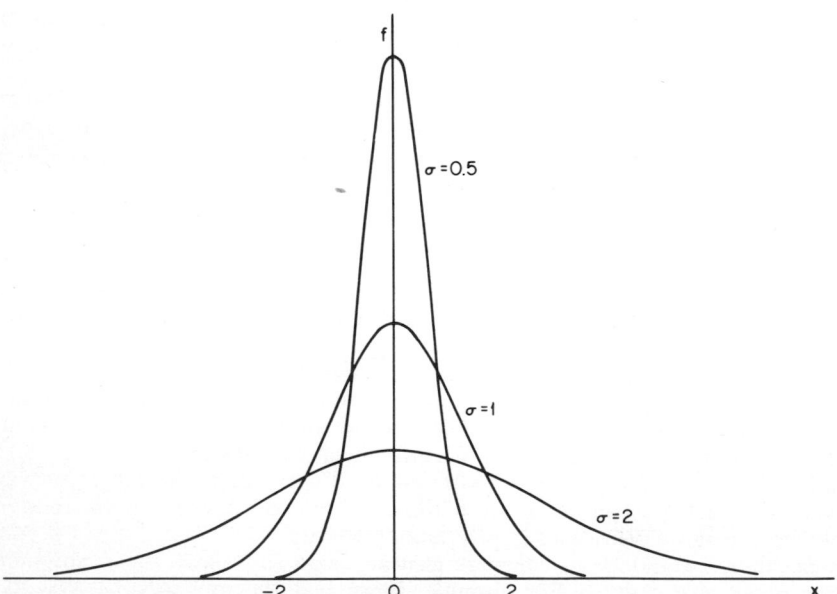

FIG. 3-10. *Normal distributions with fixed* μ *($\mu = 0$) and selected values of* σ. *(Courtesy of George P. Wadsworth and Joseph G. Bryan,* Introduction to Probability and Random Variables, *McGraw-Hill Book Company, New York, 1960, p. 106.)*

root of this value.   In equation form:

$$\text{The standard deviation} = \sqrt{\frac{\Sigma(X - \bar{X})^2}{n}}$$

As a matter of convention, the symbol used for the standard deviation of a population is the lowercase Greek letter sigma (σ); if it is the standard deviation only for a sample drawn from a larger population, the lowercase letter s is used.   Correspondingly, the mean value of a population is generally noted as the Greek letter mu (μ), and for a sample, the symbol is usually the lowercase x with a bar on top ($\bar{x}$).

Each time that we draw a sample of observations from any universe or population, we can determine the mean, denoted by $\bar{x}$, and a variance (standard deviation squared), denoted by s^2.   "Variance" in the statistical sense must not be confused with the accountant's use of the same word for an entirely different concept of income and expense deviations from accounting standards.   If we continue to draw different samples from a single universe, we can expect to obtain a somewhat different $\bar{x}$ and s^2 for each sample.   Of course, if we drew a sample representing a 100 percent census, then this $\bar{x}$ would be a special case.   It would be the mean, μ (mu) for this whole population, and similarly the s^2 would be the σ^2 (sigma squared) for the whole population.   However, because our samples are usually much smaller than 100 percent, we could not expect to obtain this result.

If we assume that our samples are drawn at random (that is, completely by chance and *not* by some judgmental quota which is almost certain to introduce some statistical bias), it can be shown that the average of all the $\bar{x}$ values from our samples will approach the true value of μ for the universe being sampled. In short, the mean value of all possible $\bar{x}$'s will always equal μ, and this is a very powerful tool, as we shall see.   However, the average of the s^2 values of the samples will depend upon the size of the sample in relation to the size of the population being sampled.   This relationship is also important, because it permits an estimate to be made of σ from s.

When simple random sampling is employed for a number of samples drawn from a given universe, the standard $\sigma_{\bar{x}}$ of the sampling distribution of $\bar{x}$ (that is, the variability of the $\bar{x}$'s of the samples) is always given by this relationship:

$$\sigma_{\bar{x}} = \sqrt{\frac{N - n}{N - 1}} \; \frac{\sigma_x}{\sqrt{n}}$$

where N is the population size
$\quad$ n is the sample size
$\quad$ σ_x is the population standard deviation
$\quad$ $\sigma_{\bar{x}}$ is the standard error of the mean

For so-called infinite populations (which need only be relatively large when compared with the sample size—generally when the sample is 5 percent or less of the population), this formula simplifies to

$$\sigma_{\bar{x}} = \frac{\sigma_x}{\sqrt{n}}$$

The finite correction factor $\sqrt{N - n/N - 1}$ approaches unity for populations which greatly exceed the sample size.

THE NORMAL, BINOMIAL, AND POISSON DISTRIBUTIONS

The Normal Distribution. The normal distribution is the most common (and in many respects the most useful) frequency distribution encountered in statistics. It appears to be one favored by nature in many occurrences. The normal distribution has a number of desirable characteristics that permit us to employ it to great advantage in many applications.

Some of the special properties of normal distribution are illustrated in Figure 3-11, in which areas under the curve are divided and labeled with one, two, and three standard deviations on either side of the mean, with the corresponding approximate percentage areas shown. Because we are dealing generally with samples of things in statistics, we might illustrate Figure 3-11 by assuming our arithmetic mean $\bar{x} = 100$ and our standard deviation $s = 10$. This tells us that the sample mean is 100 and that the measure of deviation or scatter about this mean states that roughly two-thirds (68 percent) of the numbers in the sample fall into the range $\bar{x} \pm s$ or 100 ± 10 (that is, between 90 and 110). It further implies that about 19/20 (95 percent) of all the items in the sample fall into the range $\bar{x} \pm 2s$ or 100 ± 20 (that is, between 80 and 120). Similarly, almost 100 percent of the sample data are included in the range $\bar{x} \pm 3s$ or 100 ± 30 (between 70 and 130).

If the standard deviation had been smaller, say, $s = 2$, and the mean was the same, then we would have much narrower numerical ranges at one, two, and three standard deviations (100 ± 2; 100 ± 4; and 100 ± 6).

Central Limit Theorem. There is one exceedingly important discovery in sampling that was demonstrated experimentally after World War I. It is the basis for the central limit theorem. Figures 3-12 and 3-13 are largely self-explanatory for they clearly portray what happens when a series of random samples are drawn from a population, and these individual $\bar{x}$ values fall into a normally distributed scatter *despite the shape of the population or universe distribution*.

This is not at all obvious intuitively. In fact, it may remain counterintuitive

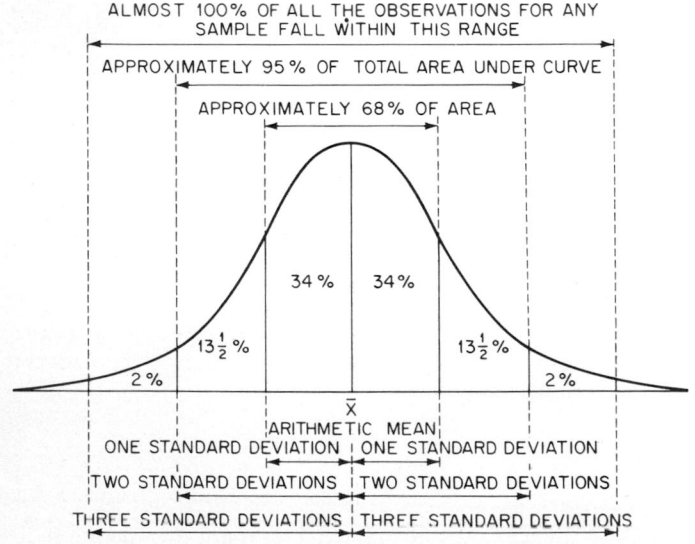

FIG. 3-11. *The curve of normal distribution.*

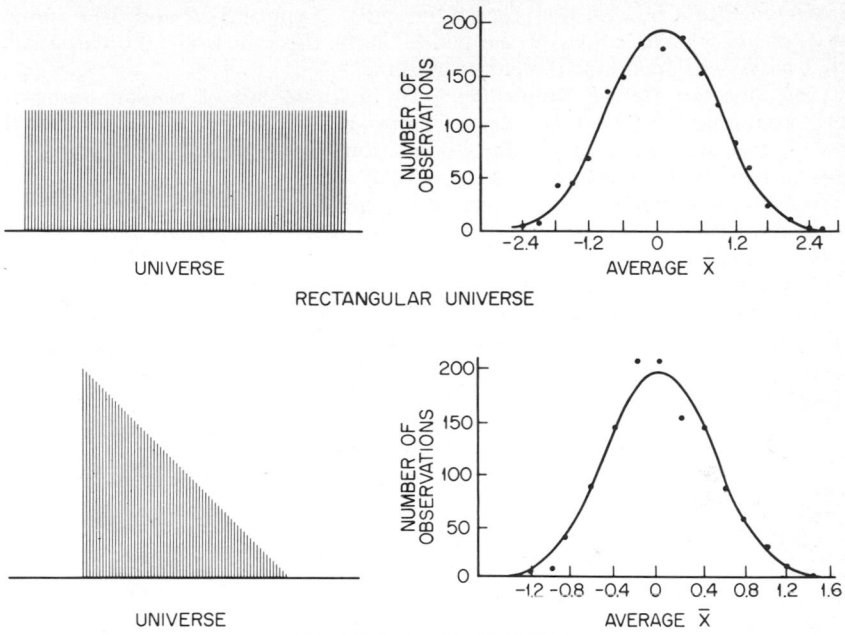

FIG. 3-12. *Shewhart's experimental distributions of $\bar{X}$ based on 1,000 random samples of four observations each, from rectangular and right triangular universes.* (*Courtesy of W. A. Shewhart,* Economic Control of Quality of Manufactured Product, *D. Van Nostrand Company, Inc., New York, 1931, p. 182. Reprinted by permission.*)

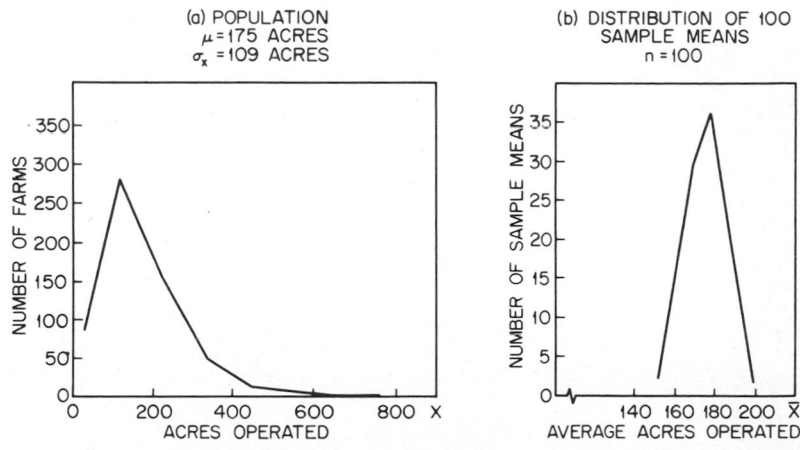

FIG. 3-13. *Distribution of population of 556 farms in Seneca County by total acreage operated per farm in 1948, and distribution of 100 sample means from the population.* (*Courtesy of John Neter and William Wasserman,* Fundamental Statistics for Business and Economics, *2d ed., Allyn and Bacon, Inc., Boston, 1961, p. 354. Reprinted by permission.*)

even when one reasons the process through. Figures 3-12 and 3-13 summarize two major demonstrations of the central limit theorem using the empirical data that were developed in two separate studies.

The Standard Normal Distribution. To facilitate use of random samples and our knowledge of the properties of normal distributions, a very useful device is the standard normal probability distribution.

Consider bales of cotton weighing, on the average, 520 pounds with a standard deviation of 11 pounds. Suppose we wish to state the probability that one bale of cotton will weigh between 512 and 525.5 pounds. Then we see the desired probability as shown by the shaded area in Figure 3-14. Note that under the poundage scale (X), we have another scale calibrated in standard deviations from the mean. This z scale is very convenient in use. It always has a mean value of 0 and a standard deviation of 1. When the shaded area under the curve is to be evaluated, we merely use a standard formula and a corresponding table of values. The formula is

$$z = \frac{X - U}{\sigma_{\bar{X}}}$$

Only one table of numbers, Table 3-1, is required to compute areas for all normal distributions. The total area under the curve is always 1, and the shaded area is the decimal fraction indicated in the body of the table corresponding to the z value taken to the second decimal place.

In our bale of cotton illustration, we would compute the shaded area in two steps as follows:

$$z = \frac{512 - 520}{11}$$

$$= \frac{-8}{11}$$

$$= -0.73$$

From the z table, this area to the left of the mean is 0.2673.

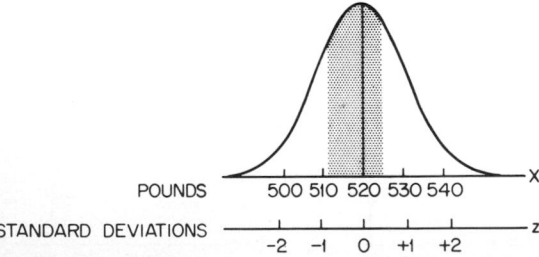

POUNDS   500 510 520 530 540

STANDARD DEVIATIONS   -2   -1   0   +1   +2

FIG. 3-14. *Shaded area showing probability of one bale of cotton weighing between 512 and 525.5 pounds. (Courtesy of John Neter and William Wasserman,* Fundamental Statistics for Business and Economics, *2d ed., Allyn and Bacon, Inc., Boston, 1961, p. 299. Reprinted by permission.)*

TABLE 3-1.   Areas from Mean to Distances z from Mean for Normal Probability Distribution

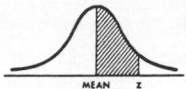

z	.00	.01	.02	.03	.04	.05	.06	.07	.08	.09
0.0	.0000	.0040	.0080	.0120	.0160	.0199	.0239	.0279	.0319	.0359
0.1	.0398	.0438	.0478	.0517	.0557	.0596	.0636	.0675	.0714	.0753
0.2	.0793	.0832	.0871	.0910	.0948	.0987	.1026	.1064	.1103	.1141
0.3	.1179	.1217	.1255	.1293	.1331	.1368	.1406	.1443	.1480	.1517
0.4	.1554	.1591	.1628	.1664	.1700	.1736	.1772	.1808	.1844	.1879
0.5	.1915	.1950	.1985	.2019	.2054	.2088	.2123	.2157	.2190	.2224
0.6	.2257	.2291	.2324	.2357	.2389	.2422	.2454	.2486	.2518	.2549
0.7	.2580	.2612	.2642	.2673	.2704	.2734	.2764	.2794	.2823	.2852
0.8	.2881	.2910	.2939	.2967	.2995	.3023	.3051	.3078	.3106	.3133
0.9	.3159	.3186	.3212	.3238	.3264	.3289	.3315	.3340	.3365	.3389
1.0	.3413	.3438	.3461	.3485	.3508	.3531	.3554	.3577	.3599	.3621
1.1	.3643	.3665	.3686	.3708	.3729	.3749	.3770	.3790	.3810	.3830
1.2	.3849	.3869	.3888	.3907	.3925	.3944	.3962	.3980	.3997	.4015
1.3	.4032	.4049	.4066	.4082	.4099	.4115	.4131	.4147	.4162	.4177
1.4	.4192	.4207	.4222	.4236	.4251	.4265	.4279	.4292	.4306	.4319
1.5	.4332	.4345	.4357	.4370	.4382	.4394	.4406	.4418	.4429	.4441
1.6	.4452	.4463	.4474	.4484	.4495	.4505	.4515	.4525	.4535	.4545
1.7	.4554	.4564	.4573	.4582	.4591	.4599	.4608	.4616	.4625	.4633
1.8	.4641	.4649	.4656	.4664	.4671	.4678	.4686	.4693	.4699	.4706
1.9	.4713	.4719	.4726	.4732	.4738	.4744	.4750	.4756	.4761	.4767
2.0	.4772	.4778	.4783	.4788	.4793	.4798	.4803	.4808	.4812	.4817
2.1	.4821	.4826	.4830	.4834	.4838	.4842	.4846	.4850	.4854	.4857
2.2	.4861	.4864	.4868	.4871	.4875	.4878	.4881	.4884	.4887	.4890
2.3	.4893	.4896	.4898	.4901	.4904	.4906	.4909	.4911	.4913	.4916
2.4	.4918	.4920	.4922	.4925	.4927	.4929	.4931	.4932	.4934	.4936
2.5	.4938	.4940	.4941	.4943	.4945	.4946	.4948	.4949	.4951	.4952
2.6	.4953	.4955	.4956	.4957	.4959	.4960	.4961	.4962	.4963	.4964
2.7	.4965	.4966	.4967	.4968	.4969	.4970	.4971	.4972	.4973	.4974
2.8	.4974	.4975	.4976	.4977	.4977	.4978	.4979	.4979	.4980	.4981
2.9	.4981	.4982	.4982	.4983	.4984	.4984	.4985	.4985	.4986	.4986
3.0	.49865	.4987	.4987	.4988	.4988	.4989	.4989	.4989	.4990	.4990
4.0	.4999683									

Illustration: For $z = 1.93$, shaded area is .4732 out of total area of 1.

SOURCE: John Neter and William Wasserman, *Fundamental Statistics for Business and Economics*, 2d ed., Allyn and Bacon, Inc., Boston, 1961, p. 809.   Reprinted by permission.

Similarly, for the area to the right of the mean:

$$z = \frac{525.5}{11} - \frac{520}{11} = \frac{5.5}{11} = 0.50$$

and again from the table, this z value corresponds to an area of 0.1915.

The combined areas $0.2673 + 0.1915 = 0.4588$ (or more approximately if we desire only two-significant-figure accuracy, 0.46). This area is the probability we are seeking—namely, 46 percent. In other words, we have a chance of

0.46 of picking a random sample bale of cotton in the range of 512 to 525.5 pounds.

Other uses for the z table include starting with the desired probability (sometimes referred to as the "confidence interval") and working the problem backward to determine what range of values to include (centered on the population mean). In this example, if we wanted to know what range of weight of bale to sample 95 percent of the time, this would correspond to plus or minus z values of 1.96 on either side of the 520-pound mean. Because one standard deviation was given as 11 pounds, this represents 11 × 1.96 or 21.6 pounds. Thus, we would expect nineteen times out of twenty (95 percent of the time) to select bales in the range 520 ± 21.6 pounds (that is, between 498.4 and 541.6 pounds).

The Coefficient of Variation (V).   Sometimes the standard deviation or SD (denoted by σ) is ill-suited to comparing the dispersions of two sets of data we wish to compare. It may be that the units in which one set of data are expressed are different from those of another, or it may be that the magnitude of the numbers is greater in one than in another.

Whatever the reason for doubting the suitability of comparing sigmas, a straightforward method of bringing them into comparable terms is as follows:

$$V = \frac{\sigma}{\bar{x}} \text{ or } \frac{100\sigma}{\bar{x}} \text{ percent}$$

Suppose, for example, that we wished to compare the exceptional performance of an employee from one group with the exceptional performance of an employee from another group. One might be in production, the other in sales. Perhaps we have an efficiency measure (or batting average) for each group, but the basis for each is quite different.

Let us say that the man in production has a performance of 330 in a group with an average of 280 and a standard deviation (SD) of 40. Let us presume that the salesman has a score of 600 in a group with a mean of 540 and an SD of 60. Clearly, the man from production was exceptional to this extent:

$$\frac{330 - 280}{40} = 1.25 \text{ SD's above his peer group's mean}$$

The man from sales was

$$\frac{600 - 540}{60} = 1.00 \text{ SD above his group's mean}$$

(and so was the less exceptional relative to his peer group).

Using the formula for V in this illustration, we may contrast the two peer groups. The production group had $V = 40/280 = 1/7$, versus the sales group: $V = 60/540 = 1/9$. Because 1/7 is greater than 1/9, we say that the higher relative dispersion in the production group showed greater variability about its performance mean than that for the sales group.

Normal Deviate.   Related to preparing objective standards of comparison is computation of values of z and values of V using the z table. However, when dealing with small samples of $N = 30$ or less, the standard deviation (SD) of the sample is no longer reliable as an approximation of the population being sampled. A t table is used instead of a z table. For samples with N in excess of 30, the so-called "student" t distribution approaches the normal distribution. The use of the z table introduces an index called the "number of degrees of freedom."

Do not be misled by the apparent simplicity of this phrase. It is one of many extremely rigorous expressions used in mathematical statistics for a purpose which is not what the surface appearance might suggest (other examples include "average," "combinations," "state of nature," "correlation," "analysis of variance," "marginal probability," "hypothesis testing," "expected value," "statistical control chart," and "argument").

The Binomial Distribution. This is a particularly useful frequency distribution which is applicable to events or phenomena which can be classified dichotomously. For example, we may say that the outcome of an event is judged to be a success or a failure, or is a win versus a loss, or productive versus nonproductive, by specifying these two alternative categories.

It is customary to designate the probability of one outcome by p and the other outcome by q (which is, of course, $1 - p$ if these two alternatives represent "mutually exclusive and exhaustive outcomes"). By convention, the lowercase letters such as "p" and "q" are used for parameter values in a probability equation, and uppercase "P" refers to the specific probability of any unique occurrence.

The binomial probability distribution applies if each trial or test in a succession is independent of the outcomes of previous trials and if the probability p is constant from trial to trial.

For example, consider a situation in which the probability of receiving a damaged shipment $P(A)$ of certain goods is constant and equal to $p = 0.1$, and the complementary chance of no damage $P(B)$ in shipment is $q = 0.9$. It follows that in a random sample of two shipments, the probability of finding damage in both is $p \times p$, or $p^2 = 0.1 \times 0.1$, which is 0.10 [remember that, with statistical independence, $P(A \text{ and } B) = P(A)P(B)$]. Likewise, the probability of sampling three shipments and finding the one undamaged and the next two damaged $P(B, A, A)$ is given by $q \times p \times p = q(p)^2 = 0.9 \times 0.01 = 0.009$. In similar fashion, $P(A, B, A) = 0.009$ and also $P(A, A, B) = 0.009$. Each *permutation* has the same probability of occurrence. The probability of the *combination* of two damaged shipments and one undamaged shipment (without regard to order) in a sequence of three shipments is the sum of these three permutations or $P = 0.027$.

In practice, many more involved situations arise for which permutations or combinations of possible outcomes may be important. For our purpose, we will not dwell on these here except to note several useful characteristics.

Binomial probability distributions are not symmetrical (in contrast to our normal distribution) except when $p = 0.5$. An illustration that summarizes the simple case of finding possible damaged shipments with a sample of only $n = 3$ is shown by Figure 3-15. However, despite this frequency distribution being skewed to the right (that is, the "tail" off to the right), if we continued drawing samples from the population, the sampling distribution would become increas-

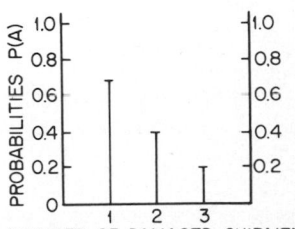

FIG. 3-15. *Binomial probability distribution for damaged shipments* (with p = 0.1 and n = 3).

ingly symmetrical (as in the case of the central limit theorem discussed previously.)

The mean value of any binomial distribution is given by $\mu = np$. For our simple illustration, $\mu = 3 \times 0.1 = 0.3$ damaged shipment, and the corresponding standard deviation is given by

$$\sigma_x = \sqrt{npq}$$

(where x refers to the outcomes to which p applies). x is given as a damaged shipment, and so

$$\sigma_x = \sqrt{(3)(0.1)(0.9)} = \sqrt{0.27} = 0.52 \text{ damaged shipment}$$

Summing up this illustration, with small samples of three shipments at a time drawn from a population for which $p = 0.1$, we should expect an average of 0.3 damaged shipment plus or minus 0.52 shipment about two-thirds of the time, or 0.3 ± 1.04 nineteen times out of twenty. Needless to say, for many practical purposes such imprecision in expected measurements would be intolerable, and therefore much larger samples would have to be drawn to reduce the variance $(\sigma_x{}^2)$.

In many instances, a desirable procedure is to calculate the proportion of damaged shipments rather than the absolute number. This sample proportion may be denoted by $\bar{p}$ (read "p bar") and $\bar{p} = x/n$. In our example, the number damaged x could be 0, 1, 2, or 3, and $n = 3$. So $\bar{p}$ could be 0, 1/3, 2/3, or 3/3.

Two other simple formulas now apply for distribution of sample proportion:

$$\sigma_{\bar{p}} = \sqrt{\frac{pq}{n}} \text{ and } \mu = p$$

In our illustration:

$$\mu = p = 0.1 \qquad \text{and} \qquad \sigma_{\bar{p}} = \sqrt{\frac{(0.1)(0.9)}{3}} = \sqrt{0.03} = 0.17$$

This states that we can expect one-tenth damaged plus or minus 0.17 two-thirds of the time (or 0.1 damaged $\pm$ 0.34 with 95 percent confidence). This is another statement of the inexact situation encountered previously, and we would probably opt for larger samples in practice.

Poisson Probability Distribution. This distribution often applies very well when we have a large number of independent events with only a small and constant probability of a certain outcome. Examples of such operations would be the arrival of trucks at a large terminal, customers at a checkout desk, the number of telephone calls or computer communications received per minute at a particular time of day, or the number of machines in a large factory which are out of service on any one day.

Before we can use the Poisson distribution, we need to gather evidence as to the mean (μ) by empirical observation. Once we have μ, we can obtain the standard deviation very easily because

$$\sigma_x = \sqrt{\mu}$$

Poisson tables covering a wide range of values of μ are available to assist in quickly determining the probability of any desired number of occurrences of the "rare" event in question. Certain problems in inventory control and the formation of queues or waiting lines at facilities are aided by the appropriate application of the Poisson distribution.

CORRELATION AND REGRESSION

One of the seemingly simple, "commonplace" terms encountered in statistics is "correlation." Many of us use the word "correlate" in everyday conversation to mean that something ties in with something else. We may admonish an associate to "correlate" this with that—almost in the sense of coordinate or perhaps combine. Not so the statistician. He means something much more specific and potentially much more useful.

Consider some measure such as production which we know to be related (or more specifically, co-related) with orders. If we say that increases in orders lead to production increases, then we are speaking of a cause-and-effect relationship. We may label orders as the "independent variable," x, and production as the "dependent variable," y.

The next step might be to plot an order curve period by period (so-called times-series analysis) and also a corresponding production curve. If both lines run closely together, we can see that they are related. However, this is a crude method at best. A superior approach is to plot y and x on a simple scatter diagram. Each point represents a pair of statistics for a period's orders and a period's production. If a best-fitting line is drawn through these points, we can utilize this line of relationship to consider how good the fit is in "explaining" past "correlation." Hopefully, it will also be of value in predicting what production to match with any anticipated level of future orders.

Such "scattergrams" might result in various possible outcomes. In the case of Figure 3-16a, we say there is no correlation between x and y. For b, there is a positive correlation; and for c there is a negative correlation. (Even though we might not expect, in our illustration, an increase in orders to yield a decrease in production, nevertheless, it could occur under certain conditions.)

If you have not dealt with scatter diagrams before, you may wonder how a line is best fitted through the scattering of points. Clearly, one may do an "eyeball correlation" by using a transparent straightedge or a stretched thread to fit a line which appears to best "satisfy" the plotted points. However, this is a subjective method (slightly different for each person doing it), whereas we have an objective (and hence uniform) method available.

The objective method is called the "method of least squares." Just as one may fit a line (straight or curved) to the points by eye, so the method of least squares can fit a straight or curved line to the plotted data. A straight line is called a "curve" of degree one (a linear equation). A curve of the second degree is a quadratic function (a parabola having a squared term in the equation).

Consider the simple case of a straight line fitted to a number of plotted points as illustrated by Figure 3-17. It is intuitively obvious that if every point in this diagram fell exactly on the straight line we would have a perfect correlation of y on x. Thus, if we knew that a certain value of x was going to occur, we could

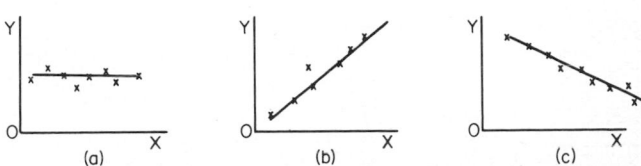

FIG. 3-16. *"Scattergrams" showing correlation between* x *and* y.

read y from the graph (or from the equation $y = a + bx$ after substituting the numerical values found for a and b).

Note, also, that if we did not recognize this dependence of y on x, we could only look at all the y values alone. From these, we could obtain the mean value of y from $\Sigma Y/n$ and also compute the standard deviation and variance as discussed previously. Thus, we could state from this analysis of the past behavior of y what we might expect in terms of stating the range within which y would seem apt to fall (in terms of its mean value and one or more standard deviations on either side).

Yet, when we detect a significant relationship between x and y, we can produce a much more reliable prediction of what y is apt to be, not merely in terms of y's own past data, but taking into account x's influence on y as a consequence or result of a known x value. In the case of perfect correlation, if we know what x will be (say, the fixed height of an object above the moon's surface), we can state precisely what will be the corresponding value of y (say, the velocity of impact of the body if permitted to fall to the surface).

In Figure 3-17, you will notice a bell-shaped curve drawn parallel to the y-axis. This is indicated as illustrating the scatter of points about the $a + bx$ line of relationship. If there is no scatter, then obviously the bell-shaped curve disappears. If there is scatter, then there is a measure of dispersion that can be computed which is called the "coefficient of correlation" (and an analogous one called the "regression coefficient" denoted by r). There is also a name given to r^2 ("coefficient of determination"), and this is a ratio of explained variance to total variance around the dependent variable mean.

In the case of perfect correlation, $r = 1$ and $r^2 = 1$. In the case of no correlation (with the best-fitting line parallel to the x axis), $r = 0$ and $r^2 = 0$. Various degrees of correlation have values between 0 and 1, and r's are designated as positive or negative depending on whether the y values increase or decrease with increases in the x values. Of course, r^2 is always positive (because the square of any negative number is, by algebraic convention, positive).

More complex situations occur if the best-fitting line is curvilinear (such as a parabola $y = a + bx + cx^2$). Again, a least-squares line can produce the mathematically best-fitting line. And again the coefficients of correlation and determination are an indication of the goodness of fit of the line to the data.

Aside from complication coming from higher-order curvature (quadratics, cubics, and so on), an even more important source of complexity arises with multiple correlation or multiple regression in which y may be dependent not just on one factor, x, but on many factors, $x_1, x_2, \ldots x_n$. We then have partial co-

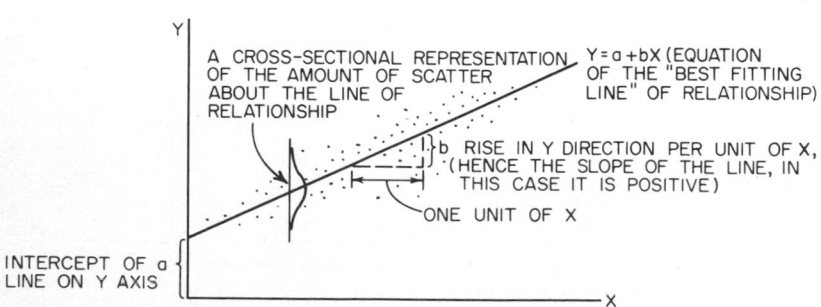

FIG. 3-17. *Straight line fitted to a number of points.*

efficients of correlation which appear to explain the deviations in y. No matter how many such independent x variables there are, their sum total coefficients of correlation may be thought of as never exceeding 1. Usually, two or three such independent variables will be shown to account for most of the variation, and bringing in other variables will eventually prove of little help in predicting y. In fact, the addition of still more factors will eventually disappear in the random "noise."

Although it is possible to do graphical multiple correlation analysis, it is awkward and time consuming, particularly with the ready availability of "canned" computer programs which can be used inexpensively and readily to process even very involved masses of data. In effect, one puts into the program data covering all suspected causes of variation and then runs the program and obtains a complete diagnosis of the apparent significance of x as an influence on y, of x^2 as an influence on y, and sometimes also of x^3 on y, and so on. It is also customary to obtain more complex (interactive or synergistic) relationships, such as the combined influence of x_1 and x_2 together on y, and x_1 and x_3 together on y, and other such combinations. Naturally, one has to draw the line somewhere, because there are costs associated with increasing computations for various permutations or combinations and powers of independent variables being tested. Good research and management judgments can be pooled to consider the more appealing possibilities and to proceed "stepwise" in determining how far to go.

As to the technical distinction between the terms "correlation" and "regression," correlation involves determining the apparent strength of interrelationship among variables. Regression is customarily concerned with predicting the behavior of one variable on the basis of predictions of one or more others.

CLASSICAL HYPOTHESIS TESTING AND STATISTICAL INFERENCE

Natural laws and theories such as those formulated by physicists and other scientists are, in fact, only hypotheses or explained regularities in observed behavior. These observed "truths" are used to predict what to expect under given circumstances. From time to time, exceptions are noted that tend to "disprove" notions that had been previously accepted as "proved." For example, although Newton's "law" of gravitation may still serve for certain purposes, it is well known that Einstein's insights are more appropriate for interstellar mechanics involving heavenly phenomena and their gravitational interactions.

Essentially, the proof of anything rests in testing it. If the testing suggests that a hypothesis "works," then it is customary to use it as a working hypothesis, rule of thumb, theory, or even as a law until it fails or is supplanted by something better. If tests show a hypothesis to be defective, it is rejected, and the search for a better hypothesis may be resumed.

The question of merit in hypothesis testing is, "When do we have sufficient evidence to accept or reject a hypothesis?" This is a question which can be answered quite objectively by the systematic gathering and evaluation of evidence. Unfortunately, in most business (and laboratory) situations, operators and scientists alike are unaware, or inadequately informed, of what "the rules of evidence" are for unambiguously formulating and accepting versus rejecting hypotheses.

Consequently, many business evaluations, and even laboratory tests and experiments, are wasted or improperly appraised owing to lack of familiarity with statistical tools. This uninformed approach to assessing results and testing hypotheses can be risky and misleading. Although a sample of "one" is representative if we are dealing with a completely homogeneous universe, any other kind of universe has to be sampled with care following appropriate guiding principles if it is to be properly represented.

The Null and the Alternative Hypotheses.   Classical statisticians generally adopt the position that hypothesis testing concerns selecting one of two "falsifiable" hypotheses which are two carefully worded statements intended to be mutually exclusive (that is, they cannot both be true together) and exhaustive (that is, there are no other alternatives available).   One or the other of these two statements must be demonstrated to be false (hence, it is rejected); the other is presumed true (hence, accepted) in simple hypothesis testing.

In addition to assuming only two hypotheses, one of which is tested against the other, convention dictates that the hypothesis under "test" is called the "null" hypothesis, and the alternative is called the "alternate" hypothesis.   In statistical testing of the null hypothesis, the object of the exercise is to accumulate a sufficient weight of evidence to be able to state with stated statistical reliability the likelihood that either the null hypothesis is rejected (and the alternative hypothesis accepted) or the null hypothesis is supported.

You may well ask, "So what?"   What do you do once a hypothesis is selected?   This is a very relevant (even though at times seemingly irreverent) question.   Clearly, the time to ask this question is *before* conducting tests or experiments (which may be time consuming and costly).   One should always ask, before the hypothesis testing, "Is this trip really necessary?"   What nourishment (in a practical or operational sense) can we derive from knowing that one of the hypotheses is probably correct?   If the answer is merely, "It would be nice to know," then chances are we should reconsider the worth of the test.

Perhaps there is obvious importance attached to the answer.   If we can say the outcome of the test will indicate something that we should (or equally important, something that we should not) do, then we should consider the costs associated with testing in the light of the importance or value of having the hypothesis test results as a guide to decisions.

It may be intuitively obvious that hypothesis testing entails some risk of error in possibly rejecting a true null hypothesis, or, conversely, accepting a false one.   In the case of erroneously rejecting a true null hypothesis, it is conventional to term this a "Type I error" (or error of the first kind).   The error resulting from accepting a false null hypothesis is referred to as a "Type II error" (or error of the second kind).

It is customary to arrange any test so that the possible error having the greatest penalty and gravest implications will be a Type I error.   For example, if we were evaluating the design of an airframe or of a bridge structure, we would formulate a null hypothesis such as "the structure is unsafe" (and the corresponding alternative hypothesis would be "the structure is safe").   Clearly, a Type I error must be guarded against with every reasonable precaution, because lives are at stake.   A Type II error could be costly, but not nearly so serious.   At worst, we would discard, or needlessly alter, our structural design.

When the means of two samples are compared, there can be serious difficulty in stating whether, in fact, the difference between these means is statistically significant or whether it is more likely that chance variations or other reasons may account for their separation.   It is intuitively evident that two such samples, if drawn from the same population, can have standard deviations on either side of their means such that there is a substantial overlapping of their frequency distribution curves.   If two different populations have been sampled, it is even possible for the statistic with the higher value for its sample mean to have come from a universe with a mean lower than the other owing to sampling errors resulting in this anomalous crossover. Clearly, the closer together that two sample statistics appear, the greater is the likelihood that no significant difference exists between them.

To assist in evaluating differences between sample means, various formulas are available. In the case of two samples drawn from the same population, they will have sample means of $\bar{x}_1$ (read "x one bar") and $\bar{x}_2$. If a large number of pairs of samples were drawn from this same population and their mean differences taken, these differences could be plotted and would form a normal distribution with a true mean difference of zero (that is, the sample means would tend to average out at the universe mean). The standard deviation of the distribution of the differences between means of samples (N_1 and N_2) is given by

$$\sigma_D = \sqrt{\sigma_{x_1}{}^2 + \sigma_{x_2}{}^2} = \sqrt{\frac{\sigma_1{}^2}{N_1} + \frac{\sigma_2{}^2}{N_2}}$$

It is usual to use this formula to test the null hypothesis that the difference between the sample means is *not* significant (due only to chance variation). Consequently, statistical confidence limits are computed in accordance with the z table (or for samples of 30 or less, the t table). As an illustration, let us consider some performance measures for an operating division on a sample of $N_1 = 32$. The value of this measure is a sample mean of $\bar{x}_1 = 103$ with an SD of $\sigma_1 = 10$. This same measure is also applied to another division, and a sample of, say, $N_2 = 64$ is drawn with a mean of $\bar{x}_2 = 95$ and an SD of $\sigma_2 = 12$. The question of whether a significant difference exists between the two sample means is resolved as follows (using the z table, because for both samples $N > 30$):

$$z = \frac{\bar{x}_1 - \bar{x}_2}{\sigma_D}$$

$$= \frac{103 - 95}{\sqrt{\frac{(10)^2}{32} + \frac{(12)^2}{64}}} = \frac{8}{\sqrt{5.38}} = 3.45$$

This value exceeds the critical value of $z = 1.96$ at the 5 percent ($\alpha = 0.05$) level of confidence, so we *reject* the null hypothesis and state that there is a significant performance difference in favor of the first division sampled.

STATISTICAL CONTROL CHARTS

A natural extension of comparing sample means in pairs is to compare samples in a continuing sequence as they are drawn from a population over which we wish to maintain control.

The pioneering work in this field was done in the statistical quality control of production. The same principles apply to sales performance statistics, accounting controls, and other measures which can be calibrated objectively. There are many references available on this subject, and Figures 3-18a and b are taken from a good one. In both a and b, the horizontal axis (or abscissa) is calibrated in time units (here, in days) to indicate when the samples are drawn. However, the vertical axis (or ordinate) differs. In Figure 3-18a, the assumed (or desired) mean (μ) of the population is drawn as a solid line. Individual sample means ($\bar{x}$) are plotted as points. The broken upper and lower boundaries are established as control limits (usually at two or three SD above and below the

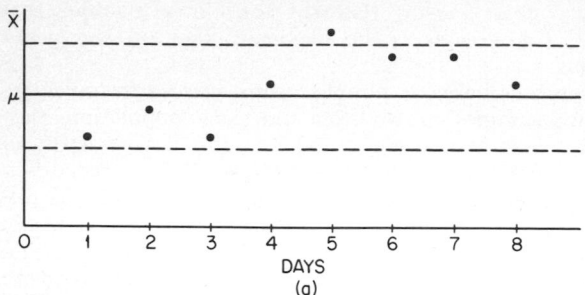

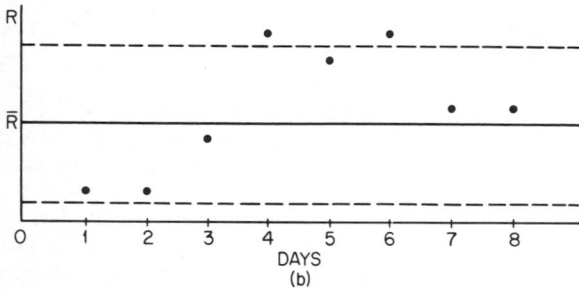

FIG. 3-18. *Statistical control charts.* (*Courtesy of Wilfrid J. Dixon and Frank J. Massey, Jr.,* Introduction to Statistical Analysis, *2d ed., McGraw-Hill Book Company, New York, 1957, p. 131. Reprinted by permission.*)

mean line). For a normal distribution of means, the 5 percent risk level would be given by $\mu \pm (1.96\sigma/\sqrt{n})$. Sometimes one, two, and three sigma limits are drawn in and early indications of trends noted (for example, six points in a row on the same side of the mean line, or two in a row beyond the one-sigma boundary).

Figure 3-18*b* is merely a useful variation that has some practical advantages of easy use. It focuses on dispersion measured by sample range, R, instead of standard deviation, s. For small samples, this is satisfactory. However, setting up such procedures should be done by an experienced statistician or statistical quality-control specialist.

ANALYSIS OF VARIANCE AND COVARIANCE

In going from relatively simple comparisons of two means to more involved comparisons, it is necessary to compare variances (σ^2) for dispersion among the means and also within the classifications.

This is just as complicated as it sounds, and although the methodology employed is well known to specialists, it is not suitable for a "cookbook" treatment by giving a few formulas. Large-scale computer programs are readily available which permit a competent statistician to process even very involved "data banks" with comparative ease.

In general, the technique helps users to discriminate between causality and mere chance. This is similar in concept to the use of the so-called chi-square (χ^2) test of significance. This is a statistical method of screening data to compare observed versus theoretical frequencies of occurrence. The chi-square technique indicates whether or not the actual differences observed are greater than could be expected through chance variations alone. Critical values of χ^2 are specified for desired probability levels after allowing for a parameter called the "number of degrees of freedom." This is again a relatively sophisticated notion that is best handled by competent professionals and can only be explained satisfactorily at some length (and on the assumption of some basic knowledge of statistical method).

Statistical Decision Rules. Many examples of statistical decision rules are available in the literature which draw upon the mathematical statistics of hypothesis testing. Decision rules are usually described in terms of "power curves" or "operating characteristic (OC) curves." These show the appropriate conditional probability of rejecting the null and alternative hypotheses respectively.

It would involve too much detailed discussion and presentation of the "arguments" (lines of reasoning) required for us to deal with this topic adequately here. However, Figure 3-19 should be indicative of what is entailed. The curves to the left of the critical dividing line (separating Type I and Type II errors) are the relevant portions of power curves, and the curves on the right are the corresponding portions of the OC curves. Any complementary pair of these curves (for example, the lowest on the left and the highest on the right, and so on) covers all possibilities of errors of both types.

In Figure 3-19, note that $n = 100$ indicates that management is prepared to absorb the cost of a sample of size 100. Here we see various levels of α risk stated from $\alpha = 0.01$ to $\alpha = 0.5$. An α risk of 5 percent ($\alpha = 0.05$) is quite common (just as in statistical quality control it is usual to concentrate on a two-

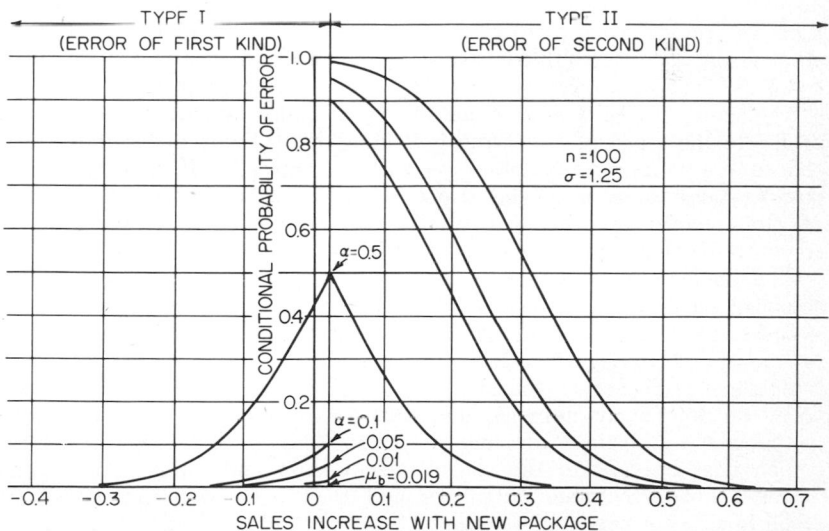

FIG. 3-19. *Operating characteristic curves.* (*Courtesy of Robert Schlaifer, Probability and Statistics for Business Decisions: An Introduction to Managerial Economics under Uncertainty,* McGraw-Hill Book Company, New York, 1959, *p. 619.*)

sigma band of confidence on either side of the mean to capture "out of control" points 95 percent of the time).

In this chart with fixed sample size, the four small curves on the left side of the graph show the maximum conditional probability of a Type I error along the vertical scale (ranging from 1 percent for the lowest curve to 50 percent for the highest as specified by the four α values. The corresponding probabilities of a Type II error rise to the complementary levels of 99, 95, 90, and 50 percent).

A little care in examining this diagram will reveal "how it works" and some of its implications. To illustrate, consider the following:

1. The null hypothesis here illustrated states that the mean value of a sales increase resulting from a specific new package design does not exceed 0.019 (that is, that the mean is really less than or equal to 0.019).

2. Suppose that the null hypothesis is really true ($\mu \leq 0.019$). Now, what risk of rejecting this hypothesis and committing a Type I error are we prepared to run?

3. Clearly, the penalty costs of a Type I versus a Type II error should be reflected in selecting our decision-rule alpha level. The left side of the diagram shows that if our sample average yields a sales *decrease* of as much as 0.30, there is only a slight chance (even with the "risky" $\alpha = 0.50$ curve) that we will draw the wrong inference. If, however, our alpha level is set at 0.01, we are not apt to make a Type I error, because almost all negative values of sales increase fall outside the error curve for our sample of $n = 100$. Of course, if we used a larger sample of $n = 500$, then even less variability would occur in the chart, and all the curves would stand in a narrower range on either side of the dividing line μ_b.

4. We note that a Type II error (the curves on the right-hand side of the diagram) is more apt to occur with small values of alpha. In effect, in classical hypothesis testing, one "trades off" the risk of making a Type I error versus the risk of a Type II error. If either error were apt to be equally regrettable, then we could select $\alpha = 0.5$ and so undertake an equal risk of one or the other errors occurring (this is sometimes recommended in statistical quality control of production, but rarely in standard hypothesis testing).

5. Clearly, if the value of an observed sample mean falls far to the left or far to the right of the critical dividing line of our decision rule, then the chance of a wrong interpretation is greatly diminished. If, for example, a strong positive sales increase in the region of 0.7 were observed, then the chances of our committing even a Type II error would virtually vanish, even with an $\alpha = 0.01$ which implies a $(1 - \alpha)$ of 0.99.

6. Summing up, the classical theory of hypothesis testing provides a rigorous objective set of quantitative guidelines which can be useful in testing statistical hypotheses. To the extent that these statistically stated hypotheses conform to operationally relevant hypotheses such as an administrator formulates, there is practical relevance to the approach. Furthermore, the scientific method depends on objectively designed and tested experiments in which representative sampling and statistical inference play a vital role. However, this classical approach does not exploit the considerable insight and information contained in people's subjective . value judgments and their subjective probability estimates (their hunches or personalistic odds).

It remains for modern statistical decision theory to provide a means of taking into account people's "best guesses" as well as considering the relative cost versus value of acquiring additional information, and also how to employ systematically this information in modifying prior perceptions.

As a first step beyond the best that the purely classical hypothesis testing has to offer, we may consider the so-called "opportunity loss" functions associated with errors.

Clearly, from a practical standpoint, it is not sufficient to consider merely the probability of making a Type I or II error given certain conditions. It is equally important to take into account the penalty costs or "regrets" associated with each type of error. For example, let us assume that a Type I error has an opportunity loss (for example, lost opportunity profit) of 10,000 and we are using an $\alpha = 5$ percent. Correspondingly, we have a zero penalty if we make the correct decision (and for this we have a 95 percent chance). Consequently, the expected penalty cost is \$500 (5% × \$10,000 + 95% × \$0). We are likely to anticipate a substantial positive value for our decision, because a correct selection will undoubtedly have profits (or savings) associated with it.

In establishing a decision rule which goes beyond merely accepting or rejecting the null hypothesis H_0, we can set up a revised version of the previous chart that explicitly reflects the expected terminal (final) monetary consequences of a decision over the entire range of uncertainty. Figure 3-20 illustrates the same problem as before, but with expected dollar losses (expected "regret") in place of simply conditional probability of error. Although it is true that this illustration may not lend itself to casual scrutiny—and again this is not the place to go into details—nevertheless it is intended to suggest that here

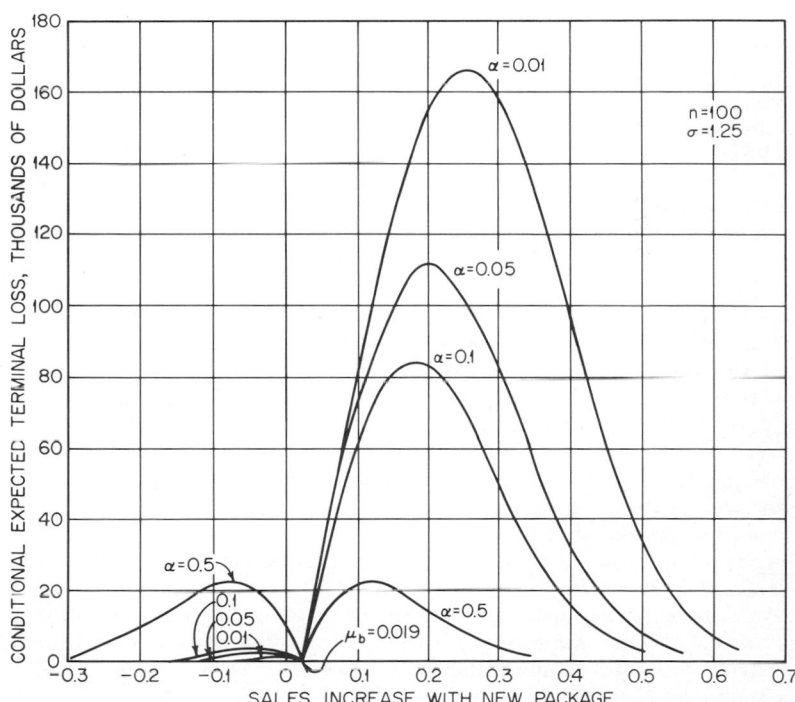

FIG. 3-20. *Problem charted in Figure 3-19 showing expected dollar losses.* (*Courtesy of Robert Schlaifer*, Probability and Statistics for Business Decisions: An Introduction to Managerial Economics under Uncertainty, *McGraw-Hill Book Company, New York, 1959, p. 628.*)

is a modern statistical technique with potential for progressive business administration. True, one needs a professional to prepare and help apply such a technique, but often the potential has to be first suggested before the professionals can be invited to "show me!"

EXPECTED VALUE AND STATISTICAL DECISION THEORY

Along this line of objectively aiding decision makers, one approach is to maximize expected values (EV); the other is to minimize expected regret. There are various formal approaches available, including the use of so-called game theory (method of least regret, or minimax—minimize the maximum expected regret penalty). Again this brief overview of such a vast subject area cannot hope to do more than indicate the range and potential utility of such approaches.

Among the more exciting and most powerful of modern statistical tools for aiding management decisions are sequential and adaptive planning models. The subject of statistical decision theory is usually considered to be synonymous with Bayesian statistics. This class of analysis takes account of an impressive array of considerations and can produce decision aids of utmost discrimination tailored to the individual manager's prior experiences and subjective value judgments, yet responsive to additional information (and the cost versus utility of same).

As an example of evaluating the cost versus utility of information, it is customary to compute the expected value of perfect information (EVPI) as a useful guide to any information buyer as to the maximum possible value of having absolute certainty about any future "state of nature" in any case being studied. Clearly, this upper bound is a theoretical limit, because perfect information is seldom, if ever, available. However, there is below this theoretical limit another value that is of practical interest, called the expected value of sample information (EVSI). This takes account explicitly of the cost of obtaining additional information. The EVSI indicates what residual benefit may accrue to the user once having obtained this information versus not having obtained it at all (and having to take a terminal act based on only the information previously available).

A discussion of expected value and utility theory can be very helpful in considering means of quantifying businessmen's subjective responses to uncertainty (an unknown distribution of possible outcomes) and risk (a "known" probability distribution of possible outcomes).[1]

It can be shown that when we are unable or unwilling to assign an expected monetary value to the various possible consequences of alternative acts, we may approach this problem using the notions of utility (the economist sometimes refers to arbitrary units of utility measure called "utiles"). The probability of "winning," π (pi), and the potential value of a win (versus any penalty associated with a loss) can be recast in terms of a "reference lottery." This sounds like heresy—but it is really an exceptionally successful way of objectivizing our judgments by providing a realistic counterpart to which we apply our real-world inclinations.

Unfortunately, understanding this point of view requires careful thought (and discussion) of the implications and consequences—plus a willingness to try a few test cases and compare their outcomes with your previous style of making decisions, and their consequences. However, the following quotation from

---

[1] A comprehensive treatment of this subject is presented in Chapter 2 of Robert Schlaifer's book, *Introduction to Statistics for Business Decisions*, McGraw-Hill Book Company, New York, 1961.

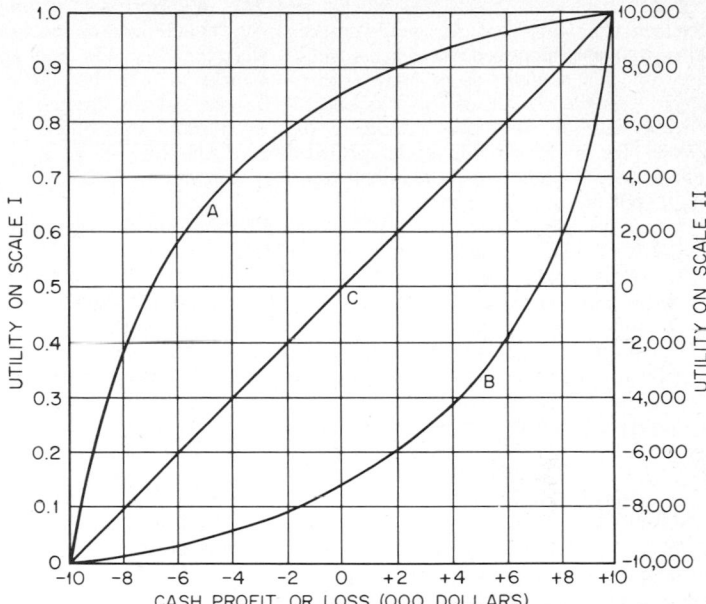

FIG. 3-21. *Utilities of various cash consequences for three different businessmen. (Courtesy of Robert Schlaifer,* Introduction to Statistics for Business Decisions, *McGraw-Hill Book Company, New York, 1961, p. 42.)*

Schlaifer's Chapter 2 may prove beneficial, and should lead to further exploration and application by the interested reader.

Differing Attitudes toward Risk. In Figure 3-21 we reproduce with the label A the utility curve of the businessman whose preferences in risky situations we have been examining thus far, and we also show utility curves which we might have obtained from two *other* businessmen with quite *different* preferences in risky situations. Utility as we have defined it above is to be read from the *left*-hand vertical scale in this figure; the use of the *right*-hand scale will be explained later on.

From the curves in Figure 3-21 we now read off and show in the table below the amount of cash which each of the three men would be willing to pay for tickets in reference lotteries with three different probabilities of winning rather than losing $10,000. The differing evaluations of the various lotteries can then be explained as follows.

Cash Values of Reference Lotteries
for Three Different Businessmen

Probability of $10,000 profit π	Cash equivalent for		
	A	B	C
¾	−3,000	+9,000	+5,000
½	−7,000	+7,000	0
¼	−9,000	+3,000	−5,000

Because a loss of $10,000 would put Mr. A's business in an extremely critical position, he feels that he would rather pay $3,000 out of pocket than run a risk of a $10,000 loss even though he thinks that there is only one chance in four that this loss will actually occur against three chances in four that there will be a $10,000 profit. As the chance of the loss becomes larger and the chance of the profit smaller, Mr. A naturally becomes willing to pay even more to avoid the risk: he will pay $7,000 for a release when the probability of the loss is ½, and when it is ¾ he will even pay $9,000 certain rather than run the risk of losing the extra $1,000 which might put him in bankruptcy.

Mr. B has attitudes diametrically opposed to those of the very cautious and conservative Mr. A; he represents the player of long shots, the man who feels that even a large loss could not make things much worse than they are now whereas a large profit would very substantially improve his whole situation. This attitude is more commonly found among players of numbers pools and the like than it is among business executives, but it is perhaps worth pointing out that even the extremely conservative Mr. A might take this attitude if his misfortunes continued to the point where he would not be able to meet his next payroll unless something extremely fortunate happened between now and Friday. Whatever his motives, Mr. B wants an additional $10,000 so badly that he would consider a $\pi = \frac{1}{4}$ chance of making it to be worth as much to him as $3,000 cash certain even though this chance was accompanied by a ¾ chance of taking a $10,000 loss; by the time $\pi = \frac{3}{4}$ and $(1 - \pi)$ is only ¼, he would not sell his chance at $10,000 for less than $9,000.

The attitudes of Mr. C will serve as a kind of standard of comparison. Mr. C represents a businessman well supplied with working capital who believes in self-insurance against moderate risks, considers $10,000 to be in fact a very moderate risk, and is therefore willing to use expected monetary value as his guide to action in any problem where the stakes do not exceed plus or minus $10,000. When the chances of a $10,000 profit and a $10,000 loss are equal, Mr. C does not care whether he takes the gamble or not. When the probability of winning is ¾, he would be willing, but not eager, to trade the gamble for its expected monetary value of $5,000; if the probabilities of winning and losing were reversed, he would be willing, but not eager, to pay $5,000 to avoid the gamble.

The Interpretation of Utility. In a certain sense analysis of a problem in terms of conditional and expected utilities rather than in terms of reference lotteries enables us to gain a better feeling for the reasons behind a given person's preferences, but unless we are very careful this feeling will do our real understanding more harm than good.

Nonparametric Methods. There is an entire class of statistical techniques that have special utility when we are dealing with data that cannot be quantified readily, but may be scaled or ranked in order of relative magnitude and indicated as positive or negative in character. These include nonparametric techniques which permit easier collection of data for which distributions are not known, because absolute measures can be dispensed with and relative measures for observations such as "better" or "worse" are sufficient. For small samples, this approach can be particularly helpful and superior to classical techniques (rather than using special small-sample-size techniques such as Chebyshev's inequality).

Occasionally, unusually deviant or atypical items of data which cannot be rejected as spurious must be included (such points are sometimes called "sports," because they lie outside the extremities of clusters of the other available data). These can be handled satisfactorily using techniques such as rank correlation to utilize all the data yet to minimize distortion which sports or outliers might otherwise introduce.

In any event, the cost versus potential value of gathering data must be considered, and many good references are available on this subject. Of course, the nonparametric approach also permits handling otherwise qualitative information, quite apart from its usefulness in handling small quantitative samples.

BAYESIAN DECISION THEORY

As an example of modern statistical decision theory, it is often helpful to prepare a "tree diagram" illustrating the branching alternative paths confronting the decision maker.   Probabilities and "payoffs" are indicated for each branch, and the entire network of lines can be interpreted in sensible terms.   Figure 3-22 shows a decision tree.

In this instance, the problem is whether we should purchase a survey containing information about the state of affairs that may prevail in the future or make a decision on the basis of information currently available to us.   The decision involves two possible terminal acts: A_1 (opening a new sales territory) and A_2 (not opening the new sales territory).   The upper branch illustrates our strategy under currently available information.   The future states of affairs are indicated by S_1 and S_2, standing for high state of demand (S_1) and low demand (S_2).   If we were to decide to open the new territory (A_1) and demand turns out high (S_1), our payoff, calculated from other data, is $5 million.   This decision-state combination is represented by the topmost path through the decision tree.   On the other hand, if demand turns out low (S_2), we have calculated that we would lose $2 million.   Our existing, or "prior," appraisal of the likelihood of these two states is 0.4 and 0.6, indicated on the branches following S_1 and S_2 respectively.   Of course, if we do not open the sales territory (act A_2), we incur no incremental costs, and the branches following this act so indicate.   The expected "value" or return from act A_1 is 0.4($5 million) + 0.6(−$2 million),

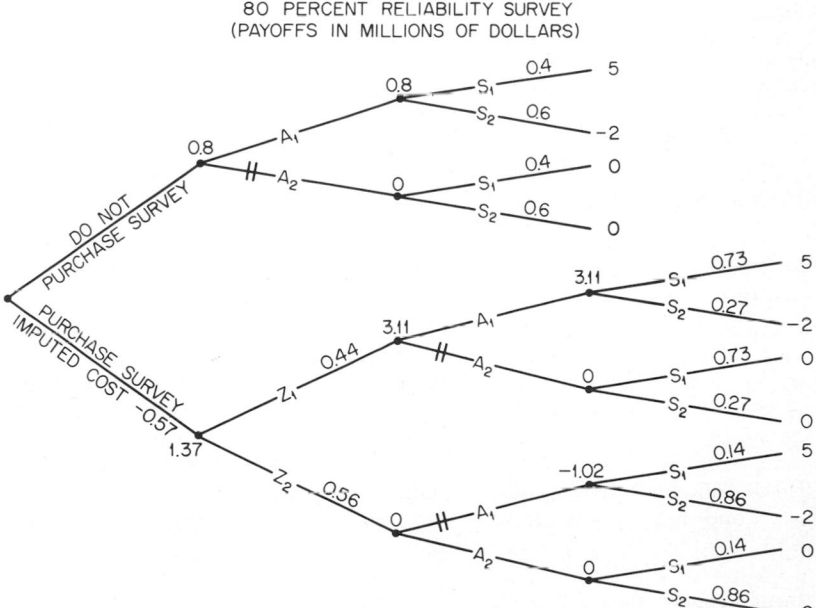

DECISION TREE–SALES REGION PROBLEM
80 PERCENT RELIABILITY SURVEY
(PAYOFFS IN MILLIONS OF DOLLARS)

FIG. 3-22.   *Decision tree.   The decision maker's view of alternatives presented statistically with costs of survey information and marketing payoffs.   (Courtesy of Wroe Alderson and Paul E. Green,* Planning and Problem Solving in Marketing, *Richard D. Irwin, Inc., Homewood, Ill., 1964, p. 123.)*

which equals \$0.8 million, shown at the initial junction of the "do not purchase survey" possibility.

The alternative route—to purchase a survey that is 80 percent reliable in its prediction of the true state of affairs and then make our decision when the survey outcome is known—can now be traced. The route Z_1 stands for the survey result indicating that state S_1 (high demand) exists, which would lead us to open the territory (act A_1). The likelihood of our taking this route is 0.44. This follows from the survey accuracy of 80 percent when S_1 is true and the error of 20 percent when S_2 is true (0.8×0.4 plus $0.2 \times 0.6 = 0.32 + 0.12 = 0.44$). The chance of S_1 being the true state when Z_1 is the survey indication is $0.32/0.44 = 0.73$, which is shown in the upper branch along the sequence $Z_1 \rightarrow A_1 \rightarrow S_1$. Similarly, the chance that S_2 (low demand) is the true state when the survey indicates otherwise is $0.12/0.44 = 0.27$, shown on the $Z_1 \rightarrow A_1 \rightarrow S_2$ decision branch. The value of this route is $0.73(\$5 \text{ million}) + 0.27(-\$2 \text{ million})$, or \$3.11 million. But the chance is 0.56 that the survey will indicate a low state of demand, causing us to decide not to open the sales territory. This alternative involves no cost subsequent to the survey, as is indicated along the $Z_2 \rightarrow A_2$ branch. The "blocked-off" $Z_2 \rightarrow A_1$ branch would not be taken, but is shown for completeness of the logical possibilities involved. The value of the entire "purchase survey" alternative is then $0.44(\$3.11 \text{ million}) + 0.56(\$0.0 \text{ million})$, which equals the \$1.37 million shown at the first junction of this branch. Acting after taking the survey will have an expected return \$0.57 million greater than acting on the basis of just the information available now. If an 80 percent reliable survey can be purchased for any amount less than this, it is a superior alternative to deciding now. This capability of providing an advance assessment of the value of information is the great payoff of Bayesian statistics for business administrators.

A further extension of Bayesian statistics of potential value to policy and planning administrators concerned with government responsibilities is presented by Prof. Morris Hamburg, of the Wharton School of Finance and Commerce of the University of Pennsylvania, in *Proceedings of the 12th International Meeting of the Institute of Management Sciences*, September 1965. His paper is entitled "Statistical Decision Theory and Benefit-Cost Analysis for Preferredness of Choice among Alternative Projects."

CONCLUSION

In this chapter, there has been space enough to present only a brief overview of classical and modern statistical methodology. The interested reader will discover, however, much additional reference material in countless business journal articles and in textbooks on the subject. A few of these references are recommended in the following Bibliography. In addition, you might plan to attend one of the many seminars specifically designed for the busy executive, or you could enroll in a university short course in statistical decision theory. It should also be stressed that qualified technical and research people within your own firm (and appropriate outside consultants) can prove particularly helpful to you.

BIBLIOGRAPHY

Alderson, Wroe, and Paul E. Green, *Planning and Problem Solving in Marketing*, Richard D. Irwin, Inc., Homewood, Ill., 1964.

Arkin, H., and R. R. Colton, *Statistical Methods*, 4th rev. ed., Barnes & Noble, Inc., New York, 1955.

Burington, R. S., and Donald C. May, Jr., *Handbook of Probability and Statistics,* McGraw-Hill Book Company, New York, 1953.

Dixon, Wilfrid J., and Frank J. Massey, Jr., *Introduction to Statistical Analysis,* 2d ed., McGraw-Hill Book Company, New York, 1957.

Hoel, Paul G., *Introduction to Mathematical Statistics,* John Wiley & Sons, Inc., New York, 1947.

Kemeny, J. G., J. L. Snell, G. L. Thompson, and A. Schleifer, Jr., *Finite Mathematics with Business Applications,* Prentice-Hall, Inc., Englewood Cliffs, N.J., 1962.

Levin, R. I., and C. A. Kirkpatrick, *Quantitative Approaches to Management,* McGraw-Hill Book Company, New York, 1965.

Mood, A. M., and F. A. Graybill, *Introduction to the Theory of Statistics,* McGraw-Hill Book Company, New York, 1963.

Moroney, M. J., *Facts from Figures,* Pelican Books, Baltimore, 1963.

Neter, J., and W. Wasserman, *Fundamental Statistics for Business and Economics,* 2d ed., Allyn and Bacon, Inc., Boston, 1961.

Schlaifer, R., *Introduction to Statistics for Business Decisions,* McGraw-Hill Book Company, New York, 1961.

Schlaifer, R., *Probability and Statistics for Business Decisions,* McGraw-Hill Book Company, New York, 1959.

Wadsworth, G. P., and J. G. Bryan, *Introduction to Probability and Random Variables,* McGraw-Hill Book Company, New York, 1960.

CHAPTER FOUR

Monte Carlo and Waiting-line Techniques

WILLIAM R. VOGEL   *Chief, Management Research Division, Directorate of Management Systems and Data Automation, Headquarters, United States Army Materiel Command, Washington, D.C.*

This chapter will briefly discuss the management significance of queuing or waiting-line theory and the application of Monte Carlo methods to these problems.

QUEUING THEORY OR WAITING-LINE PROBLEMS

Queuing theory or waiting-line problems are characterized by "arrival times," "servicing times" (or "processing times") per channel, the number of channels, and the resulting "waiting times." A common situation involving queuing analysis occurs when people are waiting in line at commercial tellers' windows in a bank with a specified number of windows or channels. The arrival of people will follow some pattern and therefore the probability of a person arriving will follow some probability distribution. The time it takes to service a customer varies from one customer to another, but over a long period of time follows some frequency distribution of service times (that is, a given percentage of service transactions will take less than one minute, between one and two minutes, and so on). Thus, given a specified number of windows (channels), we are concerned with two probability distributions: (1) the probability of an arrival in a specified time period and (2) the probability that a service time will lie in a specified interval of time.

One way of looking at the queuing theory problem is to ask: For a given distribution of arrivals, a given distribution of service times, and a given number of tellers or channels, how long does the customer have to wait? The answer to this question may be given in terms of the *average* waiting time or in terms of the distribution of waiting times generated by the arrival time and service time distributions (that is, what percentage of the customers will wait less than one minute, between one and two minutes, and so on).

Another question might be: What happens to the waiting time distribution of customers if more channels (tellers at windows) or less channels are employed? Finally, the question arises: What are the cost-effectiveness trade-offs involved? What is the cost increase or decrease to the bank by decreasing or increasing the number of tellers and therefore increasing or decreasing the wating time? The queuing theory analysis will provide a *basis* for answering this question, but other considerations must be evaluated, such as: What happens to the number of customers as the average waiting time per customer increases? What is the value of the customer to the bank?

Examples of Queuing Theory Situations.   Some other examples of queuing theory situations are:

1. Machines waiting to be serviced by maintenance men.   This involves the distribution of machine breakdown times (arrivals), the distribution of repair times (service times), and the number of channels (maintenance men).

2. What is the optimum number of loading docks for a truck fleet loading at a specified warehouse?   The distribution of arrivals here is that of the trucks arriving to be loaded or unloaded.   The distribution of service times is that of loading or unloading a truck.   The number of channels is the number of loading docks, which in this case is what we wish to solve for.

3. How many waiters should be hired for each shift in a restaurant?   The distribution of arrivals is that of the patrons of the restaurant.   The distribution of service times is that of waiting on a customer.   The number of channels is the number of waiters available.

Graphic Portrayal.   Queuing theory problems involving decisions as to the optimum number of channels to minimize "costs" can be portrayed graphically in much the same manner as the economic order quantity situation in inventory control.   In the latter case, one relates the "cost of procurement" and the "cost of holding" to determine which combination will produce minimum total cost.   In the queuing theory counterpart, we relate the cost of idle capacity (underutilized channels) against the cost of waiting (economic loss because of waiting) and determine the number of channels which will result in a minimum for the sum of these costs.   This is illustrated by Figure 4-1.

Complexities.   The situations mentioned above are illustrative of the queuing theory situation.   In a given problem, however, many considerations other than

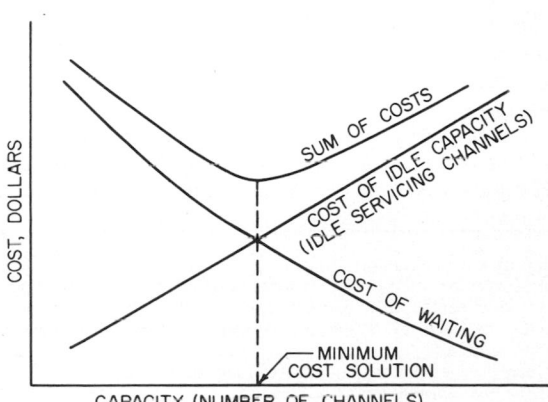

FIG. 4-1. *Graphic portrayal of a queuing theory problem.*

the basic ones discussed will have an impact on the formulation and methodology used in the solution.   The manner in which the units become part of the waiting line is one such consideration.   The statistical distribution of arrivals is no doubt of quite a different form in the machine breakdown case (where it tends to be randomly and uniformly distributed over time) as compared with the restaurant case, where the arrival rate of customers is usually quite different at different hours of the day.

Queue discipline is another complicating factor.   The simplest case is where the arrivals are serviced on a first-come, first-served basis.   However, in many applications this is not a reasonable policy.   For example, in the machine break-down situation, if one maintenance man must choose which one of two machines to repair first, the extent of repair required and the effect of machine down-time on production and profit are usually much more important than the order of their breakdown.

Methodology.   The mathematical methods of solving queuing theory problems are largely statistical in nature and presume a level of knowledge of statistics beyond the scope of this discussion.   Excellent illustrations indicating the mathematical formulation and solution to these problems can be found in the texts listed in the Bibliography at the end of this chapter.

MONTE CARLO METHOD OF SOLVING QUEUING THEORY PROBLEMS

"Monte Carlo methods" is a general term referring to the methods of simulated random sampling from a probability distribution which is assumed to represent the distribution of the variable of interest.

Monte Carlo methods of solving queuing theory problems amount to taking a series of samples from the assumed distribution of arrivals and the assumed distribution of service times.   The composition of each sample, when we wish to determine the optimum (minimum cost) number of channels, is made up of one random observation from the distribution of arrival times and one observation from the distribution of service times associated with a given number of channels.   By taking repeated samples, we can then describe the distribution of waiting time associated with a given number of channels.   By associating estimates of the economic loss because of waiting time and the cost of operating a channel, we can determine the "minimum cost" number of channels.

There are many variations of the sampling procedures used.   For example, the distribution of arrival times may be expressed analytically if either logic or experience dictates the mathematical form of the distribution, or it may be described in terms of a table or frequency histogram with no simple, known analytic form.

As an illustration of Monte Carlo technique, let us consider the bank teller problem during a two-hour Friday evening period.   Assume the following statistics have been collected based on repeated simulated sampling from history:

	1	2	3
Number of tellers on duty	1	2	3
Average arrival rate of customers per five–minute interval	1	1	1
Average service rate per five–minute interval	$1\frac{1}{4}$	$1\frac{3}{8}$	$2\frac{1}{2}$
Average (estimated or sampled) number of customers lost because of waiting	15	3	1
Cost (loss of profit) because of lost customers	$45	$ 9	$ 3
Cost of channels (bank tellers)	$10	$20	$30
Total cost	$55	$29	$33

Thus, in this oversimplified example, we would choose two bank tellers as the optimum solution. The "cost (loss of profit) because of lost customers" may not include the loss due to customers who close their accounts and go elsewhere. This indicates the need for management's awareness of the assumptions and factors included or neglected in the analysis.

CONCLUSION

Queuing theory and Monte Carlo applications are valuable tools of analysis. Their importance to management is sometimes hidden in the details of computation and the necessary precise formulations of mathematics and statistics. The value of these techniques is twofold. First, and most apparent, they are tools which provide answers to some of management's perplexing questions. Second, and perhaps more important, they force a clear statement of the problem. They show clearly what considerations *are* taken into account and what the trade-offs are in making managerial decisions. They involve thought processes which may be new to many managers and thus add to his perspective. They share with the other techniques of operations research a contribution to the discipline of managerial thinking.

BIBLIOGRAPHY

Enrick, Norbert L., *Management Operations Research*, Holt, Rinehart and Winston, Inc., New York, 1965.
McCloskey, Joseph F., and J. Coppinger, *Operations Research for Management*, vol. 2, The Johns Hopkins Press, Baltimore, 1956.
Sasieni, Maurice, A. Yaspan, and L. Freedman, *Operations Research—Methods and Problems*, John Wiley & Sons, Inc., New York, 1959.
Staff of U.S. Army Management Engineering Training Agency, *Queuing*, unpublished text material.

CHAPTER FIVE

Linear Programming

STANLEY ZIONTS *Program Specialist to the Ministry of Steel and Mines, Government of India, The Ford Foundation, Calcutta, India*

Linear programming is one of the most used techniques of management science, and there are a number of reasons for this. First, linear programming is one of the oldest techniques. The simplex method, a solution method for solving linear programming problems, was developed in the 1940s by Prof. G. B. Dantzig and has been utilized by military and industrial users almost since its inception. Second, the method is rather flexible, and it can be used to solve many different problems.

Finally, linear programming is of such a nature that general-purpose computer programs for solving linear programming problems of a given size can be prepared, and in fact, many excellent computer programs have been prepared.

The approach in this chapter is as follows:

1. To define the general problem solved by linear programming methods
2. To discuss the interpretation of the solution to the problem
3. To review the method of solution
4. To discuss the kind of problem that can be solved utilizing linear programming methods
5. To consider certain types of linear programming problems for which special (generally efficient) solution methods exist
6. To consider a much more general case of related problems—that is, integer programming problems

In describing linear programming methods, it has been necessary to use a few mathematical expressions. One does not have to be a mathematician, however, or even fully understand these expressions to understand what linear programming is, in general how it works, and, most importantly, its value to management for solving certain kinds of problems.

THE LINEAR PROGRAMMING PROBLEM

Linear programming can be used when a problem can be described by a linear function to be either maximized or minimized subject to linear equalities

17–72

and/or inequalities.[1] In other words, the problem must be expressed in the following form (some or all of the inequality signs may be reversed or replaced by equalities):

Maximize (or minimize) $c_1 x_1 + \cdots + c_n x_n$
subject to: $a_{11} x_1 + \cdots + a_{1n} x_n \leq b_1$
                          $a_{21} x_1 + \cdots + a_{2n} x_n \leq b_2$

$$a_{m1} x_1 + \cdots + a_{mn} x_n \leq b_m$$
$$x_1, x_2, \cdots, x_n \geq 0$$

The a's, b's, and c's are known constants that describe the problem, and the x's are variables that are determined in the problem's solution. The array of coefficients a_{ij} is referred to as the "matrix of coefficients"; the array of coefficients c_j is referred to as the "objective function vector"; and the array of coefficients b_i is referred to as the "requirements or stipulations vector." The notation used for the subscripts is such that a_{ij} is the numerical coefficient[2] of x_j in equation i, c_j is the numerical coefficient of x_j in the objective function, and b_i is the constant term of the equation or inequality in row i. Having stated the general form of a linear programming problem, we now turn to the consideration of a specific type of linear programming problem.

The Allocation Problem of Linear Programming. One linear programming problem is concerned with allocating scarce resources to competing activities. This type of problem is known as an "allocation problem," and is, in fact, intended to allocate the resources under consideration to maximize some measure of effectiveness.

Consider an example of an allocation problem. Suppose a processing machine (Machine 1) has 24 hours of processing time available per day. Suppose further that a product (Product 1) requires 1 hour of machine time per unit produced, and that a second product (Product 2) requires 2 hours of Machine 1 time per unit produced. The inequality

$$x_1 + 2x_2 \leq 24 \qquad\qquad (1)$$

represents the limitation of Machine 1 capacity where x_1 is the number of units of Product 1 produced and x_2 is the number of units of Product 2 produced. [The inequality expression (1) is read "x sub 1 plus $2x$ sub 2 is equal to or less than 24." It means that the amounts made of Products 1 and 2 cannot exceed the capacity of Machine 1.] We also require that the number of units of each product produced be nonnegative. In other words, we require that

$$x_1 \geq 0, \ x_2 \geq 0 \qquad\qquad (2)$$

Consider now the combined set of inequalities (1) and (2). The three inequalities admit many possible solution points that satisfy the constraints, namely, any solution corresponding to a pair of values for x_1 and x_2 that satisfy relationships (1) and (2). These include, for example, the solutions: $x_1 = 12$, $x_2 = 0$; $x_1 = 1.9$, $x_2 = 7.4$; $x_1 = 10.5$, $x_2 = 2.7$; and $x_1 = 0$, $x_2 = 12$. Suppose a second machine has a capacity of 18 hours per day, and Product 1 requires 1.5 hours of

[1] A comprehensive bibliography of actual problems solved using linear programming may be found in S. I. Gass, *Linear Programming, Methods and Applications*, 2d ed., McGraw-Hill Book Company, New York, 1964.

[2] "a_{ij}" is a general notation representing a constant which multiplies a variable in the ith row and jth column.

Machine 2 time per unit produced, and Product 2 requires 1 hour of Machine 2 time per unit produced.   This may be described using inequalities as

$$1.5x_1 + x_2 \leq 18 \tag{3}$$

Finally, suppose that a packaging unit is required for Product 1 whereby 11 units, at most, of Product 1 can be packaged per day.   (Product 2 does not require packaging.)   This can be described as

$$x_1 \leq 11 \tag{4}$$

The general linear programming problem is defined in terms of linear inequalities such as (1), (2), (3), and (4) with, in general, inequalities of either direction as well as equalities.   Returning to the example, the manager of the plant is concerned with maximizing the operating profits of the plant.   Suppose that the unit profits are \$4 for Product 1 and \$3 for Product 2.   The goal, therefore, is to:

Maximize $\qquad\qquad 4x_1 + 3x_2$ $\qquad\qquad\qquad\qquad$ (5)

(In general, the goal may be to maximize or minimize depending on the nature of the problem, but there can be only one goal per problem.)   The linear programming problem to be solved here is one of allocating scarce resources (machine capacities) to competing activities (producing different products), namely to:

Maximize $\qquad\qquad\qquad 4x_1 + 3x_2$
subject to: $\qquad\qquad\qquad x_1 + 2x_2 \leq 24$
$\qquad\qquad\qquad\qquad 1.5x_1 + \ x_2 \leq 18$ $\qquad\qquad$ (6)
$\qquad\qquad\qquad\qquad x_1 \qquad\quad \leq 11$
$\qquad\qquad\qquad\qquad x_1,\, x_2 \geq \ 0$

We shall, for the moment, ignore the method of solution and assume that by trial and error, or by some other means, the optimal solution can be found. The solution thereby obtained is to produce 6 units of Product 1 and 9 units of Product 2.   The profit generated by this solution is \$51 per day.   (Although the example problem has a unique optimal solution, many problems have a number of optimal solutions, all having the same profit.   No solution, of course, can have a greater profit than the optimal solution.)

The Pricing Problem of Linear Programming.   Consider a second linear programming problem, a pricing problem.   This type of problem is concerned with determining prices at which to value scarce resources.   To illustrate, we continue with the above example.   Suppose now, instead of choosing to operate the plant, we consider leasing it to another party.   Because the only assets to lease are the hours on the processing machines and the capacity of the packaging unit, it is desirable to know what rental rates can be charged per hour used or per unit produced—as appropriate—on each machine.   Designate as y_1 the rent per hour that is charged for Machine 1, as y_2 the rent per hour that is charged for Machine 2, and as y_3 the rent per unit packaged on the Product 1 packaging machine.   Because there are 24 hours of Machine 1 time available per day, 18 hours of Machine 2 time available per day, and a capability of packaging 11 units of Product 1, the total daily rental is

$$24y_1 + 18y_2 + 11y_3$$

Obviously, the party renting the plant desires to have this daily rental as low as possible.   The owner of the plant, of course, has certain alternatives (namely, production of Products 1 and 2), and the rental received for the plant should be economically attractive relative to these alternatives. To reflect these alternatives, we first require that these prices be zero or greater, because any resource rented at a negative price could more profitably be left idle. Accordingly, y_1, y_2, $y_3 \geq 0$. Second, because 1 unit of Machine 1 time together with 1.5 units of Machine 2 time and 1 unit of Product 1 packaging capacity can be employed to produce a unit of Product 1 and thereby generate a profit of $4, we require that the rental prices chosen be at least as profitable as the alternative of production. In other words, given the alternative of production, the following inequality should be fulfilled:

$$y_1 + 1.5y_2 + y_3 \geq 4$$

Similarly, 2 units of Machine 1 time and 1 unit of Machine 2 time can be employed to produce a unit of Product 2 and thereby generate a profit of $3 per unit. Hence, the following inequality should also be satisfied:

$$2y_1 + y_2 \geq 3$$

There are no further restrictions; therefore we may now formulate a second linear programming problem, a pricing problem:

Minimize $\qquad 24y_1 + 18y_2 + 11y_3$
subject to: $\qquad\quad y_1 + 1.5y_2 + y_3 \geq 4$
$\qquad\qquad\quad 2y_1 + \quad y_2 \qquad\quad \geq 3$
$\qquad\qquad\qquad\quad y_1, y_2, y_3 \geq 0$

The solution to this problem is a set of prices that minimize the total daily rental of the plant subject to the alternative of utilizing the plant as a production facility. As in the case of the allocation problem, assume the optimal solution is found by trial and error or by some other means. The optimal prices are $y_1 = \$0.25$, $y_2 = \$2.50$, and $y_3 = \$0.00$. The corresponding daily rental is $51.00 per day. Note that this is the same as the maximum profit attainable in operating the plant on a given day. This is no coincidence! The two linear programming problems are intimately related, and if, and only if, one problem has a finite solution, then so does the other. These two problems are so closely related that one is commonly referred to as the "dual problem" of the other. In fact, when either problem is solved using standard methods for solving linear programming problems, the solution to the other is obtained as a by-product.[3]

Consider again the meaning of the prices that were solved for above. As stated above, the optimal prices are those that minimize the daily rental and provide assurance that the alternative of utilizing the plant as a production facility is not more favorable than leasing it to another party. In other words, at these prices, the plant owners should be indifferent as to whether they should lease or operate the plant. Given higher rental prices, of course, the owners would prefer to lease the plant. In other words, these prices can be viewed as minimum prices that the owners should be willing to accept if they are to lease the plant profitably.

The prices have another meaning, as well: these "optimal" prices are the maximum prices that the plant owners should be willing to pay to rent some

[3] A more thorough treatment of the duality relationship of linear programming problems is beyond the scope of this chapter, but may be found in texts listed in the Bibliography. At a minimum, however, we point out the symmetrical relationship between the statement of the pricing problem and the allocation problem presented earlier.

additional capacity on machines identical to the ones they own, from some other party. In the same vein, these prices can be interpreted as the marginal value of additional capacity, because, for example, the plant owners would be willing to add some number of additional Machine 1 hours if the "average cost per hour" were less than $0.25.

Establishing an "average cost per hour" for additional capacity is seldom a precise calculation, because of the uncertainties of future demand for the products produced, the time value of money, and the fixed capital outlay that must be made to expand the capacity. Rough estimates of such costs can be made, however. These estimates can then be compared as ratios to the problem solution's prices. Ratios that are significantly less than 1 indicate that increasing the amount of that resource may be an economically wise alternative and that the possibility of increasing capacity should be investigated further. Further studies should always be made, because the prices are relevant only over some range (which may be large or small depending on the structure of the problem), and the demand for the products produced may be unusually high in the current period for which the linear programming problem is being solved. Some of these studies can be made, as we shall point out below, utilizing linear programming.

The prices are valid only over some range. In other words, holding everything else in the problem constant, the marginal value of a resource (such as hours on Machine 1) would remain constant as the availability of the resource was increased, and then—once the upper limit of its range of validity was reached—the value would drop. The reason for this is that the availability of some other resource becomes limiting once enough of the first resource is made available.

In a similar manner, as the availability of a resource decreases, the value of that resource increases. As an example, consider the value of Product 1 packaging capacity. In the optimal solution, the value of the capacity is zero, because it is not all being utilized. If the capacity were to be decreased to less than 6 units, holding everything else constant, then the value of additional capacity would jump to some positive value. Detailed studies evaluating the relative merit of altering capacity or altering objective function coefficients can be made using linear programming methods. (In some instances, studies can conveniently be made for altering coefficients in the matrix, but this is not always practical.) Normally, such studies are tailor-made to each problem. The technique used to make the studies is known as "parametric linear programming," and is a variation of ordinary linear programming. The studies thereby conducted are appropriately referred to as "parametric studies."

SOLVING THE LINEAR PROGRAMMING PROBLEM

In the preceding discussion, the method for solving linear programming problems was ignored. Before proceeding to a discussion of the simplex method (the method normally used to solve linear programming problems), it is worthwhile to consider a method for graphically solving problems consisting of not more than two variables. In principle, problems having more variables could be solved in a similar way also, but in fact it is not practical to use the method for such problems. The procedure is as follows:

1. Graph the constraints and indicate the area in which the constraints are satisfied (that is, the region in which feasible solutions are found).

2. Draw one line of constant profit that goes through the region in which feasible solutions are found.

3. Draw parallel lines corresponding to lines of equal profit higher than the original. Find such a line having the highest profit that has at least one feasible solution point on it.

4. Such a point (or points) corresponds to an optimal feasible solution(s), and the values of the variables may be read from the graph.

We shall illustrate this method for the allocation problem considered earlier [expression (6), page 17-74]. Following the steps given above, it can be seen that Figure 5-1 is a graph of the constraint set. The set of feasible solutions is outlined with a bold line. The line of equal profit $4x_1 + 3x_2 = 12$ is indicated. Parallel to it are shown the dotted lines of equal profit $4x_1 + 3x_2 = 24$, $4x_1 + 3x_2 = 36$, $4x_1 + 3x_2 = 48$, and $4x_1 + 3x_2 = 51$. Note that any line of equal profit greater than 51 would not intersect the feasible solution space. Therefore, we select a feasible point on the line $4x_1 + 3x_2 = 51$ (in the present example, there is only one such point), and determine an optimal solution from the graph. As can be seen from Figure 5-1, the optimal solution is $x_1 = 6$, $x_2 = 9$.

The Simplex Method. Most real linear programming problems are solved using the simplex method or a variation. This method solves a linear programming problem by first converting inequalities to equalities by defining variables that denote the amount by which a constraint is in excess. For example, in equation (1) in the above example, the variable x_3 denoting the excess (or idle) machine hours on Machine 1 would be added in this manner:

$$x_1 + 2x_2 + x_3 = 24$$

Once all constraints are converted to equalities in this manner, a number of variables are set equal to zero, so that the remaining set of equations is a set of simultaneous equations having a unique solution. Such a solution can easily be found (or made up) for all problems. (For the example problem, such a solution is to set x_1 and x_2 to zero.) Next, one variable originally set equal to zero is exchanged with one variable not originally set equal to zero, and the new set of simultaneous equations is solved. The latter step is utilized a number of times and in such a way that evidence is ultimately generated indicating either that an optimal solution is at hand or that no feasible solution to the problem can be found.

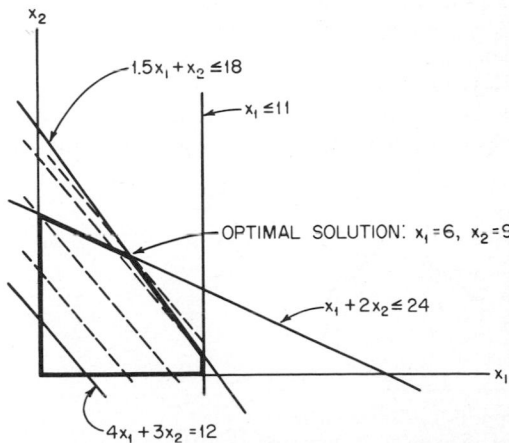

x_2

1.5x_1 + x_2 ≤ 18

x_1 ≤ 11

OPTIMAL SOLUTION: x_1 = 6, x_2 = 9

x_1 + 2x_2 ≤ 24

x_1

4x_1 + 3x_2 = 12

FIG. 5-1. *Graphic method of optimization.*

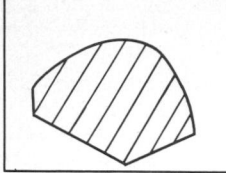
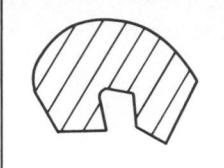
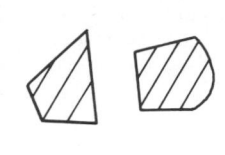

A CONVEX SET   A NONCONVEX SET   A NONCONVEX SET

FIG. 5-2. *Graphs of nonlinear and nonconvex areas representing nonlinear restrictions.*

There are a number of simplifications that are employed in actual computations for the simplex method, but the underlying approach is that which has just been outlined. Other methods significantly different from the simplex method have been proposed, but few, if any, have been used to solve problems on a practical basis.

Formulating and Solving a Linear Programming Problem. We now turn to the problem of practically formulating and solving a linear programming problem. Essentially, there are the following steps.

1. Determine whether the problem can be adequately formulated in linear programming terms: (*a*) Is the function to be maximized (or minimized) linear? (*b*) Are the constraints linear? (*c*) If there are any nonlinearities, can they be represented adequately by linearizations? That is, can the nonlinear relationships of the problem be adequately represented by convex linear approximations? By "convex," we mean that the geometry of the constraint set is such that a straight line connecting any two points of the set will be entirely in the set. Consider the constraint set graphs in Figure 5-2 where the cross-hatched area is the feasible region. The first depicts a nonlinear region that is convex, and the second and third graphs depict nonconvex regions. To illustrate how a nonlinear convex set can be approximated by a number of linear constraints, see Figure 5-3, in which the convex set of Figure 5-2 is approximated.

2. If the problem can be solved using linear programming methods, prepare a rough version of the model. Write out the necessary types of constraints, estimating the number of each type required for problem formulation. Indicate which are necessary for each type of resource or restriction and define the appropriate variables. Often, there are alternative ways of formulating a problem, and it is usually worthwhile to investigate the possibilities at this stage. Normally, the model having the fewest constraints is the one selected, but in some instances a problem formulation having slightly more constraints than the minimum may be chosen if its structure is considerably simpler or if the absolute

FIG. 5-3. *The convex set of Figure 5-2 approximated by straight lines.*

magnitude of all of the coefficients is considerably closer to unity than that of the formulation having the minimum number of constraints. There are even some instances where a seemingly inefficient linear programming formulation leads to solution by special methods much more efficient than the simplex method for solving problems that can be so formulated. Some of these special methods will be discussed below.

3. Gather the data required and set up the linear program matrix. For large problems, it is often most convenient to store the raw data in a computer in organized files and then to use a computer program to construct the problem coefficients directly. For small problems, the matrix can be written out manually and examined before being put into the computer. At this stage, a dimensional analysis of all of the constraints is sometimes made to point out errors in the formulation.

4. Solve the problem for a base case whose solution is already known and validate the model. By solving the problem first in this manner, errors in formulation or transcription are found by obtaining either no feasible solution or a ridiculous solution. If this cannot be done, some known way of operating with the real system that the model represents should be checked in the formulated model to assure that the known solution satisfies the model's constraints.

5. Solve the problem. Sometimes errors in formulation are discovered even at this point. Once the problem is solved correctly, perform a sensitivity analysis on the solution to determine how sensitive the optimality of the solution is to minor changes or to errors in the objective function coefficients or the stipulations vector entries. Examine these to determine how sensitive the solution is to changes in these data.

6. Perform parametric studies as required to investigate the alteration of the stipulations vector entries and the objective function coefficients either as a result of highly sensitive parameters or as the effect of capital expenditures or certain other changes.

Solving Linear Programming Problems on Digital Computers. It is well to digress here and briefly discuss the role of the digital computer relative to linear programming. The simplex method, as well as all of the methods, yet to be discussed has been programmed for digital computers, and relatively large problems can be solved on many computers.[4] Current capabilities of a large computer are such that problems having as many as 2,000 constraints with a much larger number of variables can be solved. Techniques for solving by computer even larger problems possessing certain structures are available, and some of these techniques will be discussed below.

Although it is possible that problems will be formulated that are reasonably solvable manually, such problems are quite rare. Hence, in general, it is assumed that linear programming problems are solved with a computer rather than manually.

METHODS THAT SOLVE SPECIAL LINEAR PROGRAMMING PROBLEMS

A Network Flow Technique: The Out-of-kilter Method. Many problems that can be formulated as linear programming problems can be formulated in special ways and thereby be solved by special methods. Some of the methods involve problems whose formulation can be made as network flows. We shall consider

---

[4] See S. I. Gass, *Linear Programming, Methods and Applications*, 2d ed., McGraw-Hill Book Company, New York, 1964, for a list of some computer codes available for solving linear programming problems.

a method that solves such problems. The problem representation consists of network nodes and paths between the nodes. Each path (or more precisely, arc) has a fixed maximum flow as well as some specified minimum flow, and a cost per unit flow. The problem is to determine the minimum cost flow that balances the flow at each node, that is, the minimum cost flow in which the total flow into each node is equal to the total flow out of each node. A method simpler and more efficient than the simplex method for solving this problem is the "out-of-kilter method" of Ford and Fulkerson.[5] Though the method is not as widely used as the simplex method, it appears to be fast and effective for solving linear programming problems that can be formulated as network flow problems.

To make this more concrete, consider the following example. Suppose a shipping line having a fleet of interchangeable vessels has the following shipments to make in a season:

30 loads from port A to port B
20 loads from port C to port D
15 loads from port A to port E
5 loads from port E to port C

A schedule of trip times in days is given below:

From	To	Time	From	To	Time	From	To	Time
A	B	15	B	E	20	D	C	10
A	C	20	C	A	20	D	E	15
A	D	5	C	B	10	E	A	5
A	E	5	C	D	10	E	B	20
B	A	15	C	E	15	E	C	15
B	C	10	D	A	5	E	D	15
B	D	20	D	B	20			

We desire to determine the schedule of shipments that minimizes the total time spent hauling no cargo. To do this, it is only necessary to add to the above two schedules any limitation on the number of trips that can be made via each link. In the above example, any nonnegative number of trips is acceptable for the empty trips, whereas the specified number of trips is required exactly for the loaded trips. The function to be minimized is the sum of the times given above for the empty trips multiplied by the appropriate number of such empty trips. Thus, we see that this problem can be formulated as an out-of-kilter problem. Such problems can be solved very rapidly with a computer. Though it may not be obvious to the reader how much simpler the out-of-kilter approach is than the ordinary linear programming formulation, it may be of interest to the reader to formulate the shipping problem as a linear programming problem, and then compare the amount of linear programming data with the data contained in the above two tables. The latter data are all that are needed to solve the out-of-kilter problem. We should point out that an implicit assumption has been made in the above formulation: it has been assumed that there are a sufficient number of ships to fulfill the total demand for the loaded trips. If this were not the case, then a slightly more complex model framework would be required to formulate and solve the problem.

[5] L. R. Ford and D. R. Fulkerson, *Flows in Networks*, Princeton University Press, Princeton, N.J., 1962.

The Transportation Method. Another linear programming problem that can be formulated and solved by a more expedient means than the simplex method is the transportation problem of linear programming. This problem (which can also be formulated as a network problem and solved with the out-of-kilter method) requires that the problem be cast as a problem consisting of a number of source points each having a limited supply of a commodity and a number of destination points each having a fixed demand for the commodity. Associated with each source-destination pair is a cost of transporting the commodity from the source to the respective destination. The problem is to satisfy all the demands at the destinations by shipping from the various sources so that the total shipping cost is minimized. Variations of the problem that do not equate the total supply and total demand can also be formulated as transportation problems.

Linear Programming Problems with Integer Solutions. Before concluding, it is worthwhile to consider one additional category of linear programming problems: those in which some (or all) of the variables must have integer values $(0, 1, 2, 3, . . .)$ in an optimal solution. Such problems are known as "integer linear programming problems," or more generally, "integer programming problems." The solutions to such problems can be very useful, as we shall see shortly.

Integer linear programming problems can be solved with ordinary linear programming solution methods, but there is no assurance that the answers will be integer, as required. If the solution with ordinary linear programming methods is conveniently integer, then, of course, the problem is solved. In general, however, special methods are required to assure that the answers will be integer. A partial list of the methods available for solving integer linear programming problems is found in the Bibliography at the end of this chapter. Although some of the methods available have solved certain problems reasonably fast, no method can be prescribed, in advance of solution, that can solve any given class of problems in a "reasonable" amount of time in all cases. However, since research in solution methods is progressing and more effective methods have been and are being developed, and since the integer framework appears to be potentially powerful, it is well to consider some of the ways in which integer variables in linear programming problems can be employed.

In addition to the obvious uses of integer variables to assure an integral number of some commodity in an optimal solution—as, for example, that the number of barges leased by a company be integer—there are other uses. These include the representation of various nonlinearities, including ones that are nonconvex, as well as the representation of certain logic requirements that an optimal solution must possess. Consider, as an example of a nonconvex representation, a process for which a fixed cost c_f must be incurred if a factory is to operate at all. Assuming the variable cost per unit produced is c_p, a set of equations that represents this condition is as follows:

$$\text{Total cost} = \begin{cases} 0 \text{ if } x_p = 0 \\ c_f + c_p x_p \text{ if } x_p > 0 \end{cases}$$

A graph of cost c versus production x_p corresponding to this set of equations is given in Figure 5-4. To represent this using integer variables, we require that

$$x_p \leq k_c \delta$$
$$\delta \leq 1$$

where k_c is the capacity of the plant and δ is an integer variable. To the objective function (assumed to be a minimization function), the terms $c_f \delta + c_p x_p$ are

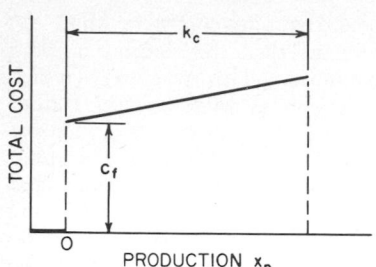

FIG. 5-4. *A cost function with a fixed-cost component.*

added. Only by virtue of the fact that δ is required to be integer is the proper representation assured.

To illustrate that integer variables can be used to assure the fulfillment of certain logical conditions, consider a firm that has two possible alternative projects in which it may invest. The two projects are mutually exclusive; that is, undertaking either one of the projects excludes undertaking the other project. By representing the undertaking of one project as x_p and the undertaking of the other project as x_q, and indicating that a project is adopted if its value is 1 (and not adopted if its value is 0), the addition of the constraint

$$x_p + x_q \leq 1$$

as well as the requirement that x_p and x_q be integer, provides that, at most, one of the pair will be included in an optimal feasible investment program.

CONCLUSION

In this chapter, we have presented the linear programming problem in its basic form. We have discussed the two problems of linear programming—the allocation problem and the pricing problem—and their interrelation and have indicated the kinds of problems that are amenable to linear programming formulations and solutions methods. In addition, special techniques capable of solving certain linear programming problems have been described. The latter include the out-of-kilter network balancing method and the transportation method. Finally, we discussed briefly a different but closely related set of problems— those of integer programming—in whose framework a much more general set of problems can be structured. As yet, however, many problems formulated in the integer programming framework cannot be solved in a reasonable length of time.

The purpose of this chapter has been to present an introduction to linear programming and related topics without getting too involved with mathematical details. We have also tried to provide some awareness for the kinds of problems linear programming methods can and cannot solve.

BIBLIOGRAPHY

Charnes, A., and W. W. Cooper, *Management Models and Industrial Applications of Linear Programming,* John Wiley & Sons, Inc., New York, 1961.

Dantzig, G. B., *Linear Programming and Extensions,* Princeton University Press, Princeton, N.J., 1963.

Ford, L. R., and D. R. Fulkerson, *Flows in Networks,* Princeton University Press, Princeton, N.J., 1962.

Gass, S. I., *Linear Programming, Methods and Applications,* 2d ed., McGraw-Hill Book Company, New York, 1964.

Gomory, R. E., "All-integer Integer Programming Algorithm," in J. F. Muth and G. L. Thompson (eds.), *Industrial Scheduling,* Prentice-Hall, Inc., Englewood Cliffs, N.J., 1963.

Hadley, G., *Nonlinear and Dynamic Programming,* Addison-Wesley Publishing Company, Inc., Reading, Mass., 1964.

Llewellyn, R. W., *Linear Programming,* Holt, Rinehart and Winston, Inc., New York, 1964.

Vajda, S., *Mathematical Programming,* Addison-Wesley Publishing Company, Inc., Reading, Mass., 1961.

CHAPTER SIX

PERT, CPM, and Other Network Techniques*

ROBERT W. MILLER *Vice President, United Research, Inc., Washington, D.C.*

Both PERT and CPM, which are used primarily for special-purpose or "one-time-through" projects, arrived on the industrial scene at about the same time as essentially independent developments. Because the basic work on CPM was done in 1957 and on PERT in 1958, we shall introduce the subject of CPM first.

CPM, or the critical path method, was developed by Morgan R. Walker of the Engineering Services Division of DuPont and James E. Kelley, who was at that time with Remington Rand. Walker and Kelley were concerned with the problem of improving scheduling techniques for such projects as the building of a pilot model plant and the shutdown of a plant for overhaul and maintenance. After considering the premise that all activities of such projects must be executed in a well-defined sequence, they came up with the arrow diagram as the most logical representation of the interrelationships among jobs for any project. Their arrow diagram and method of calculating the longest or critical path through it are the same as the PERT network and critical path calculation. However, Kelley and Walker used a single-time estimate, and did not go into the problem of uncertainty of time duration for individual jobs.

Because CPM and PERT were independent developments, the notations of the systems are quite different, as can be seen in Table 6-1. Another important difference is that Kelley went on at an early stage to develop a mathematical method for handling the problem of expediting a project for minimum cost. This special use of the network technique in relation to cost will be described later in this chapter.

During the period of the early development of the networking technique,

---

*Excerpted from R. W. Miller, *Schedule, Cost and Profit Control with PERT,* McGraw-Hill, Inc., New York, 1963. Used by permission.

TABLE 6-1. PERT versus CPM Notation

PERT	CPM
Network	Arrow diagram
Event	Node
Activity	Job
Activity expected or scheduled time	Duration
Slack (primary)	Total float
Slack (secondary)	Free float
T_E	Earliest start
T_L	Latest start

Kelley,[1] Fulkerson,[2] and Clark[3] did most of the underlying mathematical work, and their referenced papers are basic in this field.

PERT was developed in the Navy's Special Projects Office because of the recognition of Admiral W. F. Raborn that something better was needed in the form of an integrated planning and control system for the FBM (Fleet Ballistic Missile) program, commonly known as the "Polaris Weapons System." With his support, a research team was established in 1958 to work on a project designated as "PERT," or "Program Evaluation Research Task." By the time of the first internal Navy report on the subject, "PERT" had become "Program Evaluation and Review Technique." D. G. Malcolm, J. H. Roseboom, C. E. Clark, and W. Fazar, all of the original Navy-sponsored research team, were the authors of the first publicly published paper on PERT.[4] Because of the complexity and size of the Polaris program, this original research team decided to restrict the initial application of PERT to the time area, which, as it turned out, was a very wise decision.

Since these original contributions to the development and application of the network technique, the amount of literature on CPM and PERT and the number of network systems derived from them have increased at an exponential rate. Any complete bibliography on PERT and CPM would number entries in excess of a thousand.

BASIC PERT

Now let us turn to the methodology of PERT/TIME, or as it now is referred to, "basic or original PERT." From this point on in this chapter, the fundamentals of network technique common to both PERT and CPM will be discussed using PERT notation, except where there is a deviation in technique between the two systems.

Figure 6-1 shows a small sample network, which is taken from a larger operating network actually used in industry (in this case, the electronics industry). This sample network is representative of the lowest level of detail found in operating networks for industry development programs. This is the level at which the development and design work is actually carried out, and the activities on the network represent the "inherent" or "intrinsic" size of tasks (that is,

[1] J. E. Kelley, "Critical Path Planning and Scheduling; Mathematical Basis," *Operations Research*, vol. 9, no. 3, May–June, 1961, pp. 296–321.

[2] D. Fulkerson, "A Network Flow Computation for Project Cost Curves," *Management Sciences*, vol. 7, 1961, pp. 167–178.

[3] C. Clark, "The Optimum Allocation of Resources among Activities of a Network," *Journal of Industrial Engineering*, vol. 12, January–February, 1961, pp. 11–17.

[4] D. G. Malcolm, J. H. Roseboom, C. E. Clark, and W. Fazar, "Application of a Technique for Research and Development Program Evaluation," *Operations Research*, vol. 7, no. 5, September–October, 1959, pp. 646–670.

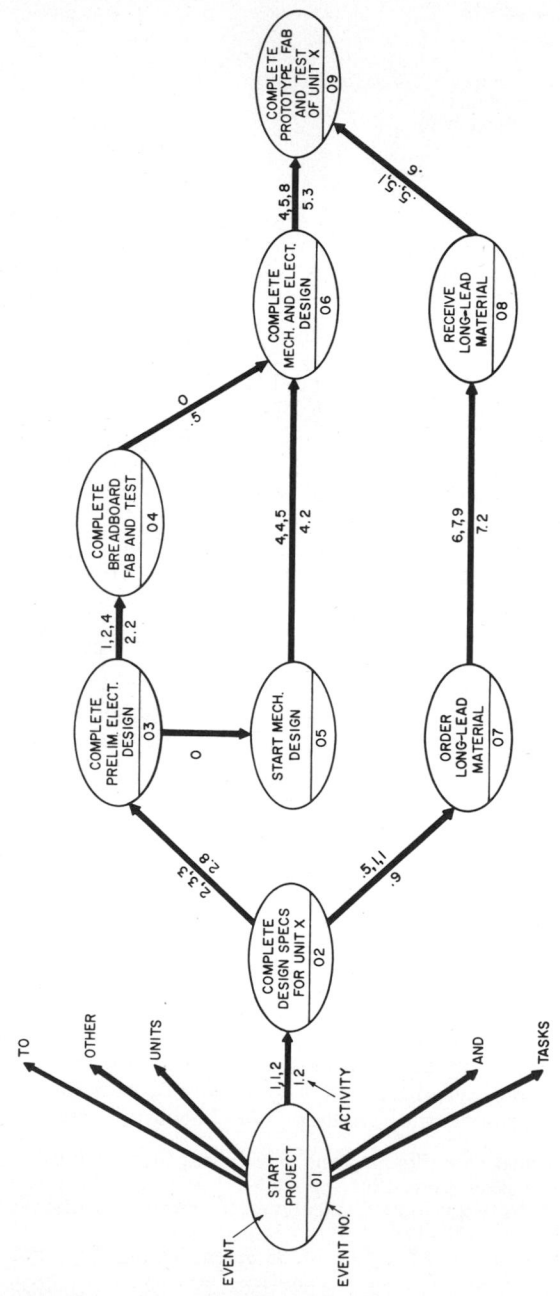

FIG. 6-1. *Small sample network.*

in terms of weeks in this work). The network therefore also represents the amount of detail required by operating-level supervision, if not by higher management. (Another restriction on level of detail will be described below under "Network Ground Rules.")

Events. The ellipses on the network (they can be circles or squares) are called "events." Events are defined as being highly identifiable points in time, as they must be for a network to have any real meaning. For instance, Event 01, Start Project, would represent the receipt of formal authorization paper to start a project; Event 02, Complete Design Specification, would represent the completion of an approved specification in accordance with an established format and procedure; Event 08, Receive Long-Lead Material, would represent the receipt and acceptance of the last item of long-lead material needed to build a prototype. Finally, Event 09, Complete Prototype Test, would mean completion and acceptance of prototype test results, again on the basis of established or approved specifications.

Event 01 is called the "starting event" and 09 the "terminating" or "ending event" for this particular network as it stands. If the network in Figure 6-1 is considered to be a subnetwork, or part of a larger network, Event 09 might be called a "milestone event." If this network is considered to be one of a group of networks, Event 09 might be called an "interface event"; in this case, the event would occur in another network with the same description and event number. In Figure 6-1, all events are connected by paths leading to the terminating event.

Activities. Events are used in connection with the definition of an activity on a PERT network. The arrow between any two events on a network is called an "activity"; in an "event-oriented" network such as Figure 6-1, an activity is defined by its *predecessor* and *successor event numbers*. An activity represents elapsed time, usually stated in seven-day calendar weeks with an assumed five-day, forty-hour workweek. Activities carrying a time estimate which is not zero also represent the expenditure of resources, usually in terms of manpower and material, although there are special situations which do not exactly fit this definition (for example, Waiting for Approval). Activities which involve an expenditure of resources are sometimes called "real activities." There is one type of activity which does not represent an expenditure of resources; this is the so-called "dummy" or "zero-time" activity. An example of a dummy activity is shown between Events 03 and 05 in Figure 6-1. This dummy activity is used to indicate a constraint not requiring resources; in this particular network, it indicates that Mechanical Design work can start immediately after completion of Preliminary Electrical Design, but not until then.

Like events, activities should be well defined or understood to be useful in PERT applications. This is more difficult than might generally be imagined. In the actual construction of a PERT network, in its early phases there is a tendency to be "event-oriented"; this has also been true in the history of PERT implementation. To achieve good activity definition, rework of "first-pass" or early event-oriented networks is sometimes necessary. This problem becomes particularly important in the application of PERT to resources or cost; in fact, for a PERT/COST application to be at all valid, the network must be worked up to a point where it is thoroughly "activity-oriented." In CPM, activity orientation is emphasized.

Network Ground Rules. There are a number of important ground rules connected with the handling of events and activities on a network. These ground rules must be followed to maintain the correct topology of the network. In addition, they have an important impact on the quality and depth of planning required to construct a network.

Ground Rule 1.   Each activity must have a predecessor and successor event. Similarly, each event must have a preceding and succeeding activity, with the exception of starting and terminating events.   However, an event may have more than one preceding and succeeding activity.

Ground Rule 2.   No activity may start until its predecessor event is completed.   In turn, no event may be considered complete until all activities leading into it have been completed.   This is the key topological ground rule of the networking technique.   It is the one that requires clear event and activity definition and, in addition, a depth of analysis to uncover and portray on the network the real restraints of a program, which is not found in Gantt's bar chart technique.

Ground Rule 3.   Referring to the matter of looping, this rule simply states that no given event can be followed by an activity path which leads back to that same event.   An example of this is shown in Figure 6-2.   In complex networks, and particularly those worked on by a number of different individuals or organizations, this kind of situation can happen, and most PERT computer programs have built-in diagnostic routines to isolate such loops.

Time Estimates.   After all events and activities have been identified and drawn up in accordance with the ground rules, elapsed-time estimates are made for each activity.   As has been stated, these elapsed-time estimates are generally made in terms of a seven-day calendar week, assuming a five-day, forty-hour workweek.   At this stage of network development, the effects of holidays and vacations are generally excluded.   These are taken into account later in the calendar scheduling process.

In the CPM technique, only a single elapsed-time estimate is made.   With this approach, the problem of uncertainty in time estimates is disregarded, although sufficient "buried padding" may be included in the estimate to account for uncertainty.   The single-time estimate works very well in such applications as construction projects, where standards exist for individual activities, or where there is a large amount of prior history on comparable activities.

In development-oriented projects, there are also a good many "conventional" activities where there is no significant amount of time uncertainty.   The single-time approach can be used to advantage in these cases.   However, there are

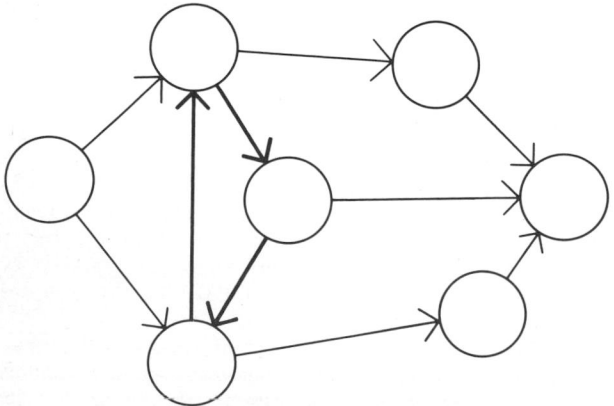

FIG. 6-2.   *Illustration of looping.*

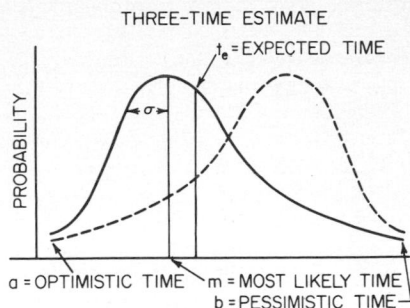

FIG. 6-3. *Illustration of beta distribution.*

also a good many activities, typically in the early phases of development engineering and in all testing phases, where a significant amount of time uncertainty comes to the fore during the estimating process, that is, where no standards or comparable history exists. It was this very important problem that the original PERT research team was attempting to handle when it introduced the three-time estimating concept, which accounts for the statement that PERT is designed for programs where there are no established standards.

In the three-time approach, estimates are made of the *optimistic, most likely, and pessimistic elapsed times* for an individual activity, using a known or assumed level of availability or resources. Interpretation of the meaning of the terms "optimistic," "most likely," and "pessimistic" has varied somewhat since their introduction in original PERT. The definitions which, in the opinion of the author, represent a useful consensus are as follows:

1. *Optimistic:* An estimate of the minimum time an activity will take—a result which can be obtained only if unusual good luck is experienced and everything "goes right the first time."

2. *Most likely:* An estimate of the normal time an activity will take—a result which would occur most frequently if the same activity could be repeated independently a number of times.

3. *Pessimistic:* An estimate of the maximum time an activity will take—a result which can occur only if unusually bad luck is experienced. It should reflect the possibility of initial failure and fresh start, but should not be influenced by such factors as "catastrophic events"—strikes, fires, power failures, and so on—unless these are inherent risks in the activity.

Once the three-time estimates are obtained, they are thought to be connected in the form of a unimodal probability distribution, with m, the most likely time, being the modal or most frequent value, as is shown in Figure 6-3. Because a, the optimistic time, and b, the pessimistic time, may vary in their relationship to m, this distribution can be skewed to the left or right, as is seen also in Figure 6-3. It was because the beta distribution seemed to fit these general properties that it was chosen by the original PERT research team as the model for determining the *mean or expected time, t_e,* and *standard deviation, σ,* associated with the three-time estimates. After an analysis which involved an assumption of the relationships between range and standard deviation, and an approximation with respect to the relationship between the mean and the mode in the beta distribution, the PERT research team came up with the fololwing general formulas for t_e and σ:

$$t_e = \frac{a + 4m + b}{6}$$

$$\sigma = \frac{b - a}{6}$$

$$\sigma^2 = \left(\frac{b - a}{6}\right)^2$$

For the benefit of those readers not acquainted with statistics, t_e, the mean or expected time, represents a point in Figure 6-3 where the area under the probability curve is divided equally, or in half. In addition, σ, the standard deviation, or its squared version, σ^2, *variance*, represents a measure of the dispersion or spread of the curve. Another way of looking at these concepts is that t_e represents the point where there is a 50-50 chance that the actual completion date will be earlier or later than t_e. The amount by which the actual date is likely to be earlier or later than t_e will be greater with a higher value of σ.

Cumulative Expected Time—T_E. We now turn to some concepts needed for calculating the critical path (or paths) through a network, another important contribution of the PERT technique. Turning back to Figure 6-1, it will be noted that there are three-time estimates, given in weeks, above each activity arrow. The figures underneath the arrow are the calculated expected times, t_e. We now introduce the concept of T_E, *the cumulative expected time* for an event, which represents the sum of all individual t_e's along the path leading to that event. In calculating T_E, the longest path leading into any one event is the determining factor; the resulting T_E value then represents the earliest time that event can be completed.

This can be verified from Figure 6-4, which represents Figure 6-1 with individual T_E calculations above each event. Leading into Event 06, Complete Mechanical and Electrical Design, there are two possible paths, one with a T_E value of 4.0 + 4.2, or 8.2 (from Start Mechanical Design), and the other with a T_E value of 6.2 + 0.0, or 6.2 (from Complete Breadboard Fabrication and Test). The T_E of 8.2, being the larger of the two figures and representing the longest path leading into Event 06, is the dominant one. The same situation exists at the final Event 09, where the reader can verify that the correct T_E is 13.5, coming in from Event 06, rather than 9.9, coming in from Event 08, Receive Long-Lead Material. After calculating the T_E's for every event, which involves starting at the beginning of the network and examining all paths leading into any one event, the so-called forward pass through the network has been completed.

Latest Allowable Time—T_L. In PERT terminology, we can now "anchor" the network on 13.5 weeks and make the "backward pass" through the network. This is done to calculate T_L, *the latest allowable time for an event*. T_L represents the latest allowable time that an event can be completed and still not disturb the completion time of the terminating event of the network. The reader may verify on Figure 6-4, where T_L figures are shown below each event, that the method of calculating T_L is just the reverse of the method of calculating T_E. At Event 03, Complete Preliminary Electrical Design, the longest backward path from terminal Event 09 leads through Events 06 and 05 and produces a T_L equal to 13.5 − 5.3 − 4.2 − 0, or 4.0 weeks. The other path leading back to Event 03 is through Events 06 and 04 and is equal to 13.5 − 5.3 − 0 − 2.2, or 6.0. It will be noted the smaller figure, 4.0 weeks, is then chosen for T_L,

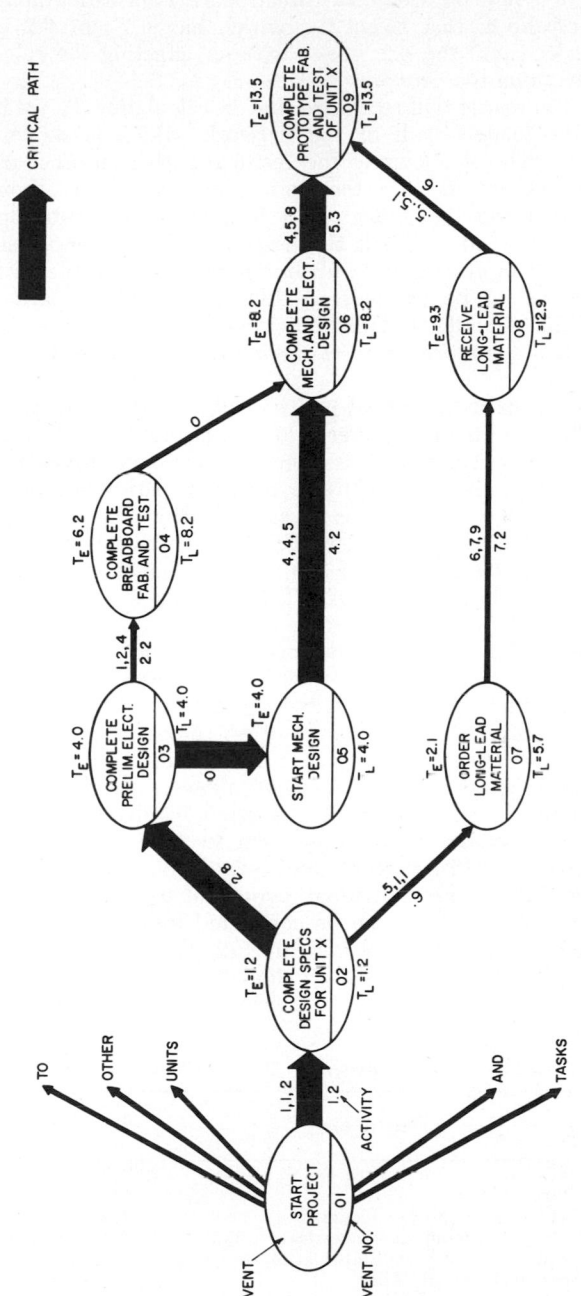

CRITICAL PATH

EVENT

EVENT NO.

ACTIVITY

START
PROJECT
01

TO

OTHER

UNITS

AND

TASKS

1,1,2
1.2

COMPLETE
DESIGN SPECS
FOR UNIT X
02
T_E=1.2
T_L=1.2

2,8

.5,1,1
.9

COMPLETE
PRELIM. ELECT.
DESIGN
03
T_E=4.0
T_L=4.0

1,2,4
2.2

0

START MECH.
DESIGN
05
T_E=4.0
T_L=4.0

ORDER
LONG-LEAD
MATERIAL
07
T_E=2.1
T_L=5.7

COMPLETE
BREADBOARD
FAB. AND TEST
04
T_E=6.2
T_L=8.2

0

4,4,5
4.2

6,7,9
7.2

COMPLETE
MECH. AND ELECT.
DESIGN
06
T_E=8.2
T_L=8.2

RECEIVE
LONG-LEAD
MATERIAL
08
T_E=9.3
T_L=12.9

4,5,8
5.3

3,5,1
.9

COMPLETE
PROTOTYPE FAB.
AND TEST
OF UNIT X
09
T_E=13.5
T_L=13.5

FIG. 6-4.   Network of Figure 6-1 with T_E and T_L calculations shown.

because it represents the longest backward path. Finally, it will be noted that the value of T_L for Event 04, Complete Breadboard Fabrication and Test, is 8.2; the significance of this is that Event 04, which has a T_E of 6.2 weeks, could be delayed 2 weeks (until the 8.2 week) without affecting the calculated T_E of the terminating event on the network.

Critical Path. The reader will recognize that in calculating T_E we have actually traced through the longest path of the network, which is shown as a heavy line in Figure 6-4. This is known as the "critical path"; all other paths through this network are shorter and are therefore "subcritical." It should be clear that if any activity along the critical path is delayed, the entire program will be correspondingly delayed. This is the basis for the very important predictive feature of PERT and represents its contribution to the principle of management by exception. It should be emphasized that if the critical path is shortened for any reason, the subcritical paths may become equal to it and therefore critical. Again, if a subcritical path is delayed, it may emerge as the critical path.

There may be one or more critical paths in any given network, that is, paths with T_E values that are the same or very close to each other. In PERT analysis, particularly on larger programs, it is therefore common to examine the first two to six critical and subcritical paths, or all those paths that have a T_E value within several months of each other. One trend which should be watched in the management of a program under PERT control is the tendency to neglect subcritical paths, or let them slide. If this trend is allowed to go on indefinitely, all paths will tend to become critical. This process is known as "tightening up the network."

The development of a valid network—one where the configuration of events and activities is correct, the activity times are estimated on a realistic basis, and a meaningful critical path(s) results—represents a very significant accomplishment in most programs. The result often comes as a surprise to people who have judged the critical areas of a program on an intuitive basis. The achievement of such a critical path analysis allows management to "begin to manage by exception," based upon PERT as the tool involved.

Slack—Positive and Negative. We now turn to the subject of *slack*, another important feature of the PERT technique. Table 6-2 shows the T_E, T_L, and *positive slack* figures for the individual events of Figure 6-4. The slack of an event is equal to $T_L - T_E$, as can be confirmed in Table 6-2. By definition, the slack for any event along the critical path is equal to zero. Thus the critical path itself is said to have slack value of zero, and all subcritical paths

TABLE 6-2. Calculation of Slack for Figure 6-4

Event no.	Description	T_E	T_L	Slack
01	Start project	0	0	0
02	Complete design specifications	1.2	1.2	0
03	Complete preliminary electrical design	4.0	4.0	0
04	Complete breadboard fabrication and test	6.2	8.2	+2.0
05	Start mechanical design	4.0	4.0	0
06	Complete mechanical and electrical design	8.2	8.2	0
07	Order long-lead material	2.1	5.7	+3.6
08	Receive all material	9.3	12.9	+3.6
09	Complete prototype fabrication and test	13.5	13.5	0

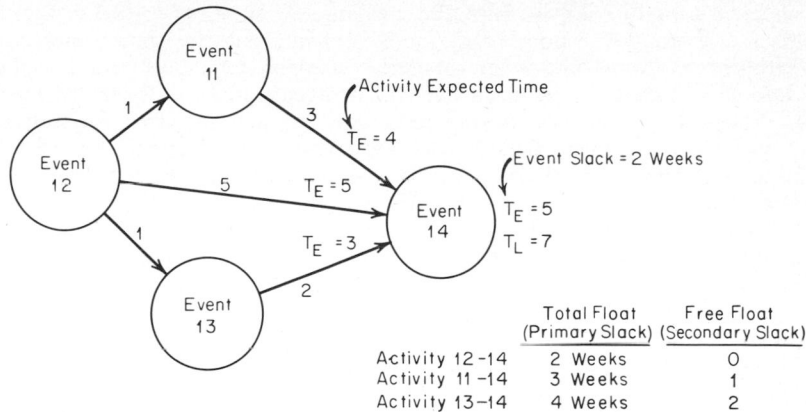

FIG. 6-5. *Activity slack and float.*

have their individual positive slack values. The slack value of a series path is another way of expressing its criticality in the network.

When a *scheduled objective date,* or T_S, is introduced for the terminating event, then the network is "anchored" on T_S, and T_L is set equal to T_S. If T_S is earlier than the calculated T_E for the critical path, then we have the case of *negative slack,* that is, the critical path is late with respect to T_S by an amount equal to $T_S - T_E$. It should be emphasized that negative slack can exist only in the case where a scheduled objective date T_S has been established which is earlier than T_E. A T_S date may be established for other events than the terminating event; in this case, we have the possibility of more than one T_S restriction creating negative slack.

So far, we have discussed slack only with respect to an event or path. *Activity slack* has a somewhat different definition and significance. The slack value of an activity is equal to the T_L (or T_S) of its successor event, minus the activity's individual expected time, expressed in terms of weeks. The special significance of this can be seen in Figure 6-5, which shows a portion of a network taken from a larger network. The slack of Activity 12–14 is 2 weeks, the same as its successor event slack, since this is the longest activity leading into Event 14. The slack value for Activity 11–14, however, is equal to 3 weeks, and for Activity 13–14, 4 weeks, since both these activities are shorter, or have a smaller T_E, than Activity 12–14.

Thus, a number of activities leading into the same successor event can have different activity slack values as long as they have different individual activity T_E values.

It should be clear by now that the concept of positive slack, whether thought of for an event, activity, or path, represents the "degree of freedom" with which an event, activity, or path can be moved without delaying the end result of a program. Areas in the network with a high degree of positive slack do not generally require direct management attention. However, if the critical path is in a negative slack condition, it may be necessary to consider transferring manpower or dollars from the areas of positive slack to the critical path to bring the program back on schedule.

Float and Secondary Slack. Before further discussing the utilization of slack, it is important to discuss one more refinement of the concept of activity slack which is widely used in the CPM technique. In CPM, activity slack is called "float"; there are a number of kinds of float, but we shall concern ourselves with the two most important categories, namely, *total float* and *free float*. The difference between total float and free float can best be illustrated by reference to Figure 6-5. As was mentioned earlier, the activity slack for Activity 12–14 is equal to 2 weeks, that is, the activity can be delayed 2 weeks before it becomes later than the T_L of its successor event (Event 14). If we are interested in the impact of this activity on the T_E of Event 14, however, it is clear that it cannot be moved at all. Thus, Activity 12–14 is said to have a total float of 2 weeks and a free float of 0 week. Activity 11–14, however, has a total float of 3 weeks and a free float of 1 week; it can be delayed 1 week without interfering with the T_E of its successor event. Similarly, Activity 13–14 has a total float of 4 weeks and a free float of 2 weeks. The concept of total float versus free float has been introduced into PERT under the terms "primary slack" and "secondary slack."

Another way of understanding the concept of free float, or secondary slack, is that it represents the amount of time an activity can be delayed from its earliest start time to the point where it interferes with the earliest start time of its succeeding activity. It is particularly important to keep these concepts in mind during the scheduling process. That is why the CPM approach emphasizes such information as the "earliest start" and "earliest finish," "latest start" and "latest finish" states for individual activities.

Probability Aspects of PERT. We now come to an aspect of PERT which has been somewhat controversial ever since its inception in original PERT. This is the concept of the probability of accomplishing a scheduled objective date, T_S. It will be recalled that T_S is generally determined from an overall schedule-phasing approach and is introduced into the situation as an objective date. It may also be an arbitrary date which a high government official or top industrial manager has set as a "challenging goal." If, after conducting a PERT analysis, we come up with a T_E which is later than T_S, we can talk about the probability of meeting such an objective date.

The statistical argument for this calculation is as follows. Though the distribution of possible completion times for each activity on the critical path may vary (that is, can be skewed from left to right), the distribution of possible completion times around T_E for the termination event approximates the normal, or bell-shaped, distribution. This assumption follows the central limit theorem, when there are a large number of activities on the critical path (for example,

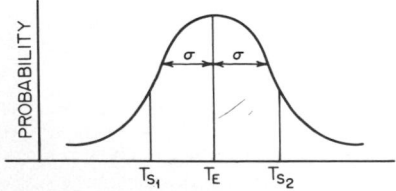

$$T_E = \Sigma t_{e_1} + t_{e_2} + \cdots t_{e_n}$$
$$\sigma^2(T_E) = \Sigma \sigma^2(t_{e_1}) + \sigma^2(t_{e_2}) + \cdots + \sigma^2(t_{e_n})$$
$$T_{S_1} = \text{scheduled time (earlier than } T_E)$$
$$T_{S_2} = \text{scheduled time (later than } T_E)$$

FIG. 6-6. *Probability of meeting a scheduled objective date,* T_S.

more than ten) and their individual distributions are random. This probability situation is portrayed in Figure 6-6, where a terminating event is shown with its cumulative expected time (T_E) and variance (σ^2). In addition, there are shown two possible scheduled objective dates, T_{S1} and T_{S2}. In this situation, the probability of achieving a T_S is defined as the ratio of the area under the curve to the left of T_S to the area under the entire curve. The value of this probability is found most quickly by expressing the difference between T_S and T_E in units of σ, or

$$\frac{T_S - T_E}{\sigma}$$

and entering the result into a normal probability distribution table. This final result will yield a value for the probability of accomplishing T_S. Thus:

$$\frac{T_{S1} - T_E}{\sigma} = -1.2\sigma \qquad \text{Probability (accomplishment of } T_{S1}) = 0.12$$

$$\frac{T_{S2} - T_E}{\sigma} = +1.2\sigma \qquad \text{Probability (accomplishment of } T_{S2}) = 0.88$$

The use of this probability figure by personnel who do not understand the underlying statistical assumptions and significance can be very misleading. For example, it is possible to have a low probability figure in a case when activity times are estimated to be quite certain and therefore the cumulative variance figure is quite small. This will yield a low probability figure in a situation where the expected date is less than a month behind the scheduled date. In general, it is the magnitude of the difference between T_S and T_E, expressed in terms of months or weeks, which is of greater interest to the decision maker than the PERT probability figure. Another way of saying this is that the decision maker will be interested in the amount of projected negative slack.

Replanning. Now that the fundamentals of basic PERT/TIME have been covered, the reader unfamiliar with the technique may well ask, "What happens if the T_E and T_S for a terminating event are far apart, and there exists a figure which shows a high degree of negative slack, or low probabilities of accomplishment, or positive slack?"

In the opinion of the author, the answer to this question also constitutes one of the fundamental features of the PERT technique, although it is not often understood or treated as such. A negative slack condition obtained after completion of a first-pass network and PERT analysis is by no means unusual; it is the rule, not the exception.

The answer to this apparent dilemma of PERT lies in *replanning* the network. There are three basic ground rules which can be legitimately applied to the replanning of a network to meet a T_S objective. A fourth, if somewhat obvious, ground rule is that time estimates along the critical path cannot merely be adjusted to meet the T_S date. Experience has shown that if a PERT network is developed with the proper approach and to a low enough level of detail, the first estimates made of activity times are as good as any and should not arbitrarily be adjusted to meet a scheduled date.

The three basic ground rules for replanning the critical path areas of a network are as follows:

1. Change series activities to parallel. This is the "concurrency" approach which may involve a "risk trade-off" which has to be evaluated by the manager.

2. Apply additional resources to susceptible activities (overtime, better people, and the like). In some cases, such as in common drafting and shop areas,

it is fairly easy to transfer additional personnel from positive slack activities. In other cases, where personnel cannot be easily transferred, or are not available, new personnel and/or funds will have to be obtained.

3. Delete activities (change scope of work; for example, delete part of an environmental test). Though generally not as easy, this approach can and has been used where time is of paramount importance.

It should be emphasized that these ground rules must be applied to specific activities in an explicit manner. A generalized approach to replanning is not considered acceptable in PERT. When a network has been replanned in accordance with these rules so that it meets, or comes as close as possible to meeting, the scheduled date T_S, the application of "basic" or "fundamental" PERT/TIME planning and analysis has been completed.

Scheduling. When the basic process of replanning has been accomplished, the conversion of the network to a final calendar schedule plan is carried out. Calendar scheduling involves consideration of such factors as total manpower loading and availability, funding limitations, vacation periods and holidays, and any other special organization rules affecting scheduling. Thus, a mechanical approach to final calendar scheduling is generally not possible, although several computer routines are available to assist in the loading area when manpower data are associated with the network, as in PERT/COST. In the case where a number of "one-time-through" projects are being undertaken within a given organization, priority ground rules will clearly have to be established to complete final calendar scheduling.

Updating. In most PERT applications, the network schedule is updated every two weeks or month. This process generally involves direct inquiry by a PERT analyst into the status of old events scheduled to be started or completed during the prior period. Updating does not generally involve all activities of the network, but is likely to produce new critical path and slack data. Thus, the formal process of analysis, replanning, and scheduling is started over again and continues to recycle until the end of the program. The amount of effort involved in the updating process will be a function of the quality of the original plan and the uncertainties in the program.

Use of PERT/TIME in Production. The applicability of PERT to production operations is a subject of continuing discussion and investigation. The fact that PERT is not useful in such situations as continuous assembly-line production appears obvious. Even here, however, one must be careful to distinguish between the flow or process charts used in planning the production cycle and a PERT network. Though the two may seem very similar, the former system is used for the determination of such factors as cycle times and line balancing, whereas the PERT technique, at least as it is generally defined, is oriented toward critical path analysis of a "one-time-through" project.

It is also important to emphasize that there are areas of production where PERT planning and control techniques are very much applicable. One area involves the preliminary manufacturing phases of production prototype or pilot model construction and the buildup of tooling and facilities for large-scale production. Still another area involves the actual fabrication, assembly, and test of initial production units, generally of a large, complex nature, which are still "high on the learning curve." Individual networks for these phases of production can often be quite useful; after these phases, established production-control techniques are generally more applicable.

Other Uses—Long-range Planning. Just as PERT can be applied with a certain flexibility of approach to the production phase, so can it be applied to the early conceptual or feasibility investigation stages of a program. Thus, it is possible to use the network approach in the early stages of long-range planning or in initial efforts leading up to the formal definition of a program. This type of application rarely contains much critical path significance, however, because the end goals of this early planning effort have not been, or cannot be, clearly defined. In this situation, interim goals may be established, such as a "go–no-go" decision for a commercial new-product venture, after preliminary marketing investigations have been completed. In long-range applications of this kind, there may be a series of networks, each terminating in a go–no-go ending event. Early planning networks of this type usually represent the dependency relationships among the various elements of the organization which must participate in initial planning and conceptual efforts. The network can be "calendar time scheduled" or not, depending on the urgency which is believed to exist concerning completion of the early planning effort.

BASIC PERT/COST

One of the first differences between PERT/TIME and PERT/COST is that in the PERT/COST application, the networking of the program must be very complete. Generally speaking, all activities which generate a direct cost to the program must be indicated on the network. This is a very different approach from earlier applications of PERT/TIME where only major elements of the program thought to have an effect on schedule outcome were generally PERTed. It is clear that if we wish to develop the cost of a program in association with networks, we would like to talk about the total cost of the program, not a figure with some unknown percentage of the program costs missing.

Work Breakdown Structure. To provide a framework for *complete networking*, the Work Breakdown Structure was formally introduced as the first item of analysis in carrying out basic PERT/COST. Figure 6-7 is an illustration of a Work Breakdown Structure for a larger program.

In connection with programs such as the one illustrated in Figure 6-7, there has been considerable controversy on the subject of at what level the Work Breakdown Structure should become "functionally" or organizationally structured versus "product structured." Suffice it to say that one of the main objectives of PERT/COST, and in fact one of its new features, is to establish a time and cost correlation for tasks which are product-oriented phenomena. As will be seen, functionally oriented budget and cost information is available from the PERT/COST system, but as a derivative, not as a prime feature. It should be pointed out that portions of the Work Breakdown Structure can be structured on a functional basis where task orientation is not significant, such as in the case of program management or systems engineering.

As can be seen in Figure 6-7, it is generally necessary to develop the Work Breakdown Structure through a number of levels, that is, five or more levels on a major development program, before an End Item level is reached against which meaningful PERT/TIME networks can be developed. After a thorough PERT/TIME analysis has been carried out covering all the End Item Subdivisions, including such final network areas as system integration and test, the next step is to establish Cost Work Packages which are associated with the networks.

Cost Work Packages. Work Packages constitute the basic units in PERT/COST for cost planning and control. They represent a breakout of End Items into elements of work whose beginning and ending points may be directly related to network events.

A Work Package is defined as the unit of work required to complete a specific

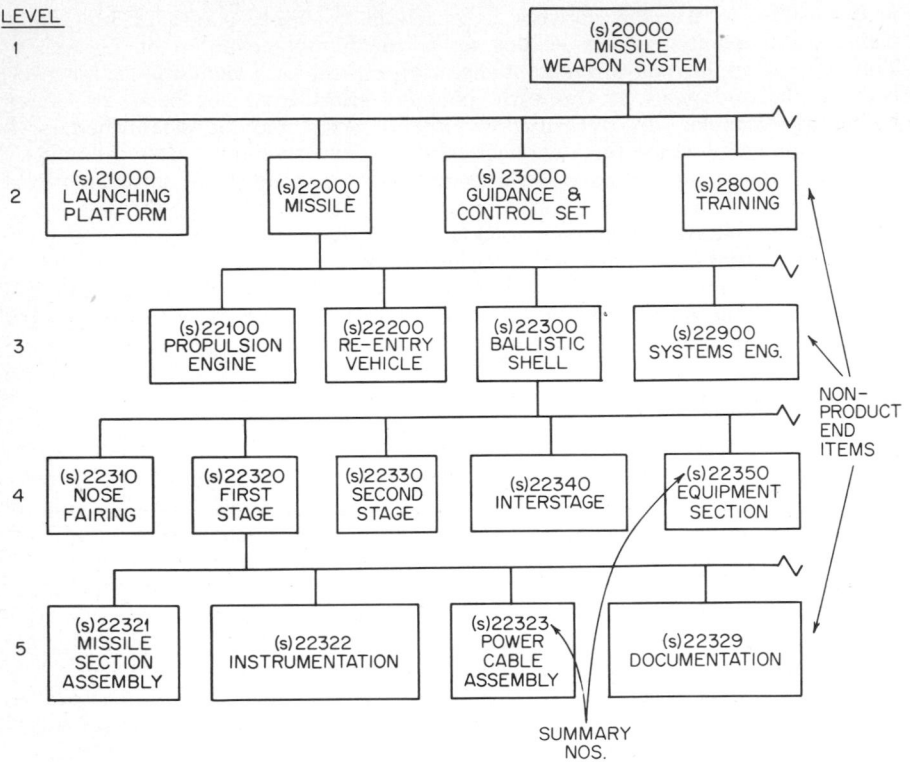

FIG. 6-7.   *Illustration of work breakdown structure.*

job or process such as a report, a design, a document, a piece of hardware, or a service, and will usually contain a number of activities on the network.   The content of a Work Package may be limited to the work which can be performed by a single operating unit in an organization or may require the contributing services of several operating units.   The overall responsibility for the work content of a Work Package should be assigned to a single organization or responsible individual.

A useful guide to the size of Work Packages is that they cover a time span of not more than three months and that they represent no more than a $100,000 expenditure.   In this way, the time span and amount of investment between positive reports to management may be limited.

This guide is by no means rigid.   Small projects may require considerably smaller Work Packages for proper control.   On large projects, on the other hand, the subdivision of work to such a level of detail could conceivably result in excessive fragmentation of homogeneous tasks.   In such instances, the above guidelines may be applied only to those portions of the total job where complex technical problems are anticipated and where, therefore, overruns and slippages are most likely to occur.

Charge numbers are assigned at the Work Package level so that costs may be summarized and analyzed in a variety of ways.   The End Item must be identified so that costs may be summarized up through the Work Breakdown Structure.   Contributing and responsible organizations should be identified for analysis along organizational lines. Function and subfunction identification allows for summarization and analysis by functional categories. Other identification (for example, contract or type of funds) may be included as required.

PERT/COST Computer Requirements. With the development of the Work Breakdown Structure and time networks, plus the establishment of Work Packages (including cost estimates), the initial steps of PERT/COST implementation have been completed. Generally speaking, some sort of data-processing equipment is required for the handling of PERT/COST just as it is for any detailed cost-accounting system. If just PERT/TIME is being used, however, a computer will not be necessary to calculate critical path and slack data for networks under 100 events. For a limited PERT/COST application, a minimum data-processing equipment configuration may be sufficient, but to produce the full spectrum of output reports specified in the Department of Defense PERT/COST system, a medium- to large-scale machine is usually required.

PERT/COST Outputs. There are a number of outputs from the Department of Defense PERT/COST system. Perhaps the most significant of these is the Management Summary Report shown in Figure 6-8.

This is the top program-management-oriented report of the basic PERT/COST system. It typically covers a subsystem, or second-level item, on the Work Breakdown Structure, and all the third-level items underneath the subsystem. Costs are displayed on a "Work Performed to Date" and "Totals at Completion" basis It should be noted that under the "Work Performed to Date" heading, the first column is labeled "Value," meaning value of work performed. This is not the original planned budget through the current calendar date, but rather represents a special computation relating to the planned budgets of all completed Work Packages and those which are still in process. The figure in the Value column is obtained by adding the originally planned budgets for all completed Work Packages and the planned budgets for all Work Packages in process, multiplied by the ratio of Actual-to-Date to Revised-Forecast-at-Completion for each of these Work Packages in process. The accuracy of this calculation is therefore a function of the length of Work Packages; the shorter the Work Package, generally speaking, the greater the accuracy of forecast at completion.

The purpose of the Value figure is to provide a consistent basis for comparing budget with actual in the case of Work Packages which have had effort expended on them. Its introduction assumes there may be Work Packages which were not started in accordance with the original schedule plan owing to changes in network schedules at the detailed level. This concept requires a complete explanation for personnel who will be using it. On the right-hand side of the Management Summary Report, we see schedule data on a comparable basis to cost data, which of course fulfills one of the main objectives of the PERT/COST system. These schedule data are shown on a reduced calendar-time scale with two columns devoted to a prior year, the next twenty-four columns to two years by months, and the last four columns representing a single year each.

Other outputs of the Department of Defense PERT/COST system include such reports as a Project Status Report, Organization Status Report, Financial Plan and Status Report, Manpower Loading Report, and so on.

Cost of PERT/COST. An area of concern to management is the cost of implementing PERT/COST. As in the case of PERT/TIME, more detail is involved than is generally found in most industrial job cost-accounting systems. (It should be emphasized again that this is not always the case.) The cost of implementing PERT/COST is certainly greater than that of implementing PERT/TIME; it is thought to be in the range of 1 to 5 percent of total project cost, as compared with PERT/TIME alone, which is in the range of 0.5 to 1 percent. It should be

REPORTING ORGN. | **CONTRACT NO.** | **REPORT DATES**

ABC – MISSILE AND GHE
LEVEL/SUMMARY ITEM: 3/BALLISTIC SHELL 22300 — XYZ – A & S DIVN 22300 — 33(600)28369A — TERM (SPAN): TOTAL PROGRAM / CUT OFF DATE: 30 MAR 63 / RELEASE DATE: 10 APR 63

COST OF WORK $(000)

ITEM	WORK PERFORMED TO DATE VALUE	ACTUAL COST	(OVERRUN) UNDERRUN	TOTALS AT COMPLETION PLANNED COST	LATEST REVISED EST	PROJECTED (OVERRUN) UNDERRUN	MOST CRIT SLACK (WKS)	COMPL DATE	REMARKS
BALLISTIC SHELL LEV 3 22300	19,600	20,500	(900) (.05)	35,200	39,650	(4,450) (.13)	0.0	10 DEC 64 / 31 DEC 63 / 31 DEC 63	SEE PROBLEM ANALYSIS REPORT ITEMS 1-3
NOSE FAIRING LEV 4 22310	27	25	2 .07	175	175		8.6	10 DEC 64 / 10 JUN 63 / 10 AUG 63	ITEM 6
FIRST STAGE LEV 4 22320	6,700	6,400	300 .04	9,200	9,700	(500) (.05)	0.0	30 APR 64 / 31 DEC 63 / 31 DEC 63	ITEMS 9-12
SECOND STAGE LEV 4 22330	1,645	1,650	(5)	3,500	3,570	(70) (.02)	0.0	15 JUN 64 / 31 DEC 63 / 31 DEC 63	ITEM 15

SCHEDULE

S – SCHED COMPL DATE -- TOTAL
A – ACTUAL COMPL DATE -- ITEM
E – EARLIEST COMPL DATE -- CRITICAL
L – LATEST COMPL DATE -- ITEM

P YR | 1963 JFM AMJJASOND | 1964 JFMAMJJASOND | 5 6 7 8 | L YR

TIME NOW

FIG. 6-8. *PERT/COST management summary report.*

pointed out that these figures may represent learning-curve costs because extensive experience with PERT/COST has not yet been obtained. In addition, these costs should not be considered as incremental or additive, for clearly a great deal of effort was put into costing systems and estimating methods in prior approaches. The major gains that are being sought from the implementation of PERT/COST are very significant improvements in both original cost estimating and cost control during the execution phase of the program.

OTHER PERT/COST TECHNIQUES

There are several variations of the PERT/COST technique. One of the more commonly known is termed "time-cost optimization or augmentation," the model of which was originally developed in connection with CPM.[5] Figure 6-9 illustrates the principle involved, using a small network for illustrative purposes.

The lower path of the small network in Figure 6-9 is the critical path, with an initial value of seventeen weeks. For every activity on this network, let us now assume we can obtain a set of "normal" and "crash" time and cost data as shown in the table of Figure 6-9. To speed up this program for a minimum cost, we will first want to shorten those critical path activities which give us the most time acceleration for the least cost. In other words, we will operate on the critical path activities which have the smallest cost-time slopes. After the first operation, or iteration, we will proceed to the activity with the next smallest cost-time slope.

After two iterations, both paths on the network are of the same length and are therefore equally critical. We must now work simultaneously on both paths

[5] J. E. Kelley and M. R. Walker, "Critical Path Planning and Scheduling," *1959 Proceedings of the Eastern Joint Computer Conference,* Spartan Books, Washington, D.C., pp. 164–167.

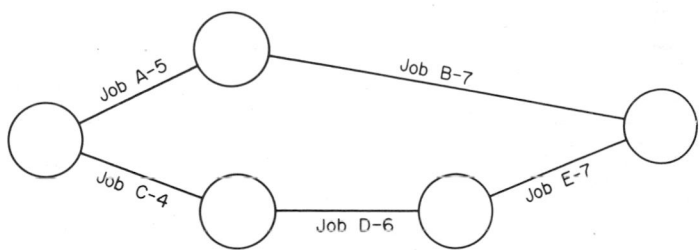

	Normal		Crash		Cost slope	First iteration		Second iteration		Third iteration	
	Time	Cost	Time	Cost	Dollars/week						
Job A	5	$ 8K	3	$ 9.2K	$600					+ $ 600	
Job B	7	10K	4	12.1K	700					+ $ 500	
Job C	4	6K	3	6.5K	500					−1 + $1100	
Job D	6	10K	4	10.8K	400			−2 + $800			
Job E	7	12K	4	12.9K	300	−3 + $900					
	17 weeks	$46K		$51.5K		14	$46.9K	12	$47.7K	11	$48.8

FIG. 6-9. *Time-cost augmentation.*

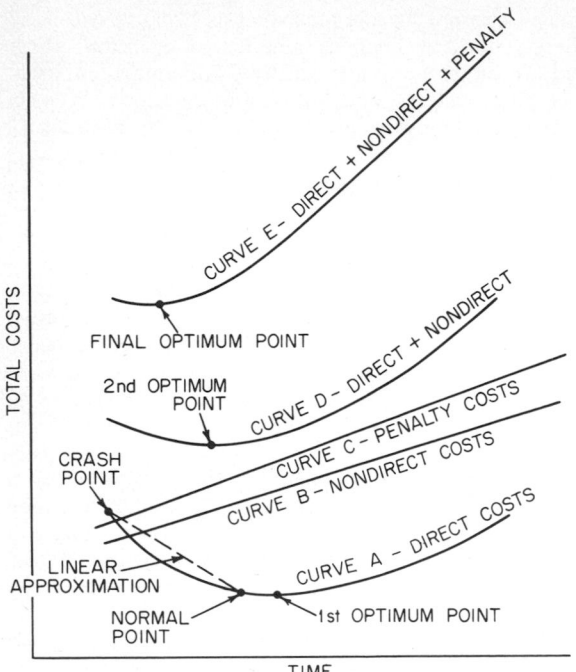

FIG. 6-10. *Time-cost relationships.*

to achieve any further reduction in the schedule. Here again, the principle is to accelerate activities with the lowest cost-time slopes. The final result is shown in the table of Figure 6-9, where, after three iterations, the project can be improved from seventeen to eleven weeks. It will be noted that cost of the program on a "normal" basis was $46,000 and that after three iterations an optimized acceleration cost of $48,800 was achieved. This is in contrast to the total potential cost of $51,500 shown in Figure 6-9. With this model, we have achieved maximum program acceleration for minimum cost. Although there is argument about the validity of such a model, generally in terms of the assumption of linearity between "normal" and "crash" time-cost points, the real problem of using this time-cost technique is the difficulty of obtaining good data for input to the model.

In addition, we have so far discussed the use of *direct costs* in this model, that is, costs which vary directly with time, as shown in Figure 6-10.[6] Curve A shows these direct costs and an "optimum point" which may or may not coincide with the "normal point." If applied *overhead or nondirect costs* are now brought into the picture, as shown in curve B, the optimum time-cost point shifts significantly. This new result is shown in Figure 6-10 as the second optimum point, which lies on a curve representing the addition of both curves A and B.

If one more cost concept is brought into the model, the optimum point again shifts. This is the concept of a *penalty cost*, shown as curve C. This cost

[6] R. W. Miller, "How to Plan and Control with PERT," *Harvard Business Review,* March–April, 1962, p. 101.

might represent the loss of profits resulting from lack of production in a plant which was not completed at the earliest possible time or which was down for maintenance and overhaul. It might also represent the loss in value of a product which did proceed through development, production, and marketing at the earliest possible time relative to competing products. If such a penalty-cost curve can actually be developed, as it sometimes can in the case of "outage" costs during plant overhaul, the result of adding curve C to curves A and B will shift the final optimum point as shown in Figure 6-10.

BIBLIOGRAPHY

Clark, C., "The Optimum Allocation of Resources among Activities of a Network," *Journal of Industrial Engineering,* vol. 12, January–February, 1961, pp. 11–17.

Fulkerson, D., "A Network Flow Computation for Project Cost Curves," *Management Sciences,* vol. 7, 1961, pp. 167–178.

Kelley, J. E., "Critical Path Planning and Scheduling; Mathematical Basis," *Operations Research,* vol. 9, no. 3, May–June, 1961, pp. 296–321.

Kelley, J. E., and M. R. Walker, "Critical Path Planning and Scheduling," *1959 Proceedings of the Eastern Joint Computer Conference,* Spartan Books, Washington, D.C., pp. 164–167.

Malcolm, D. G., J. H. Roseboom, C. E. Clark, and W. Fazar, "Application of a Technique for Research and Development Program Evaluation," *Operations Research,* vol. 7, no. 5, September–October, 1959, pp. 646–670.

Miller, R. W., "How to Plan and Control with PERT," *Harvard Business Review,* March–April, 1962, p. 101.

CHAPTER SEVEN

Computer Simulation

KALMAN J. COHEN   *Professor of Economics and Industrial Administration, Graduate School of Industrial Administration, Carnegie Institute of Technology, Pittsburgh, Pennsylvania*

Of all the technological innovations that have been developed since the end of World War II, none has had a more profound and pervasive impact upon business management than the electronic digital computer. Although in its early days the computer was utilized only by the scientific research and engineering departments of business firms, it gradually became recognized that the computer could also be used profitably to perform many routine data-processing functions. Indeed, it has gradually become recognized that the ultimate potential of the computer in industry is not to replace clerks or to process checks more quickly, but rather to help executives do a better job of planning and decision making.

The purpose of this chapter is to survey one very powerful use of the computer—the technique known as "simulation"—as an aid in management planning and decision making. Definitions of "simulation" and some important related terms are provided. Then a brief but broad survey of some representative management applications of computer simulation is given. This is followed by a discussion of some statistical considerations in simulation. Finally, the summary provides an assessment of the future role of simulation techniques in management.

SIMULATION[1]

Scientists and engineers, in studying the behavior of complex systems, frequently utilize a type of intellectual construct known as a "model." A formal model of a complex system is an abstract representation of the real system,

[1] The material in this part of Chapter 7 has been adapted from Kalman J. Cohen, "Two Approaches to Computer Simulation," *Journal of the Academy of Management,* vol. 4, no. 1, April, 1961, pp. 43–49.

which is rigorously defined by a set of explicitly stated assumptions. Any model must necessarily be a simplification of the corresponding real system. To prevent the model from being "oversimplified," however, it is necessary to determine in advance the types of applications for which the model is intended. This enables the model builder to focus attention on those areas which require considerable amounts of realistic detail and treat in summary fashion other areas where greater abstractions are permitted.

One particular type of formal model is a simulation model. The explicit assumptions that characterize a simulation model are intended to describe the dynamic processes which determine the behavior of the complex system under study. To simulate a complex system is to carry out in sequence the dynamic processes which are specified by a simulation model's explicit assumptions. This procedure can provide a considerable amount of useful information about the corresponding real system, provided the simulation model is properly formulated relative to the types of questions it is intended to answer.

There are three broad classes of simulation models: physical, analog, and mathematical. A physical simulation model can be regarded as a miniaturized reconstruction of the corresponding real system. Scale model airplanes in wind tunnels, scale model ships in flood basins, military maneuvers in peacetime, and pilot production plants for new industrial processes are typical examples of physical simulation models. Although there are a few types of management applications for which physical simulation models are extremely useful, such models generally are more expensive to construct and more awkward to manipulate than either analog or mathematical simulation models.

The components of an analog simulation model are interconnected in ways that are analogous to the corresponding components' interrelations in the real system. A mechanical analog of a production and distribution system, an electronic analog of an oil pipeline network, and a hydraulic analog of the circular flow of money in an economic system serve as typical examples of analog simulation models that are of some interest to management.

Mathematical simulation models are composed entirely of abstract symbols. A set of mathematical relations is used in a mathematical simulation model to characterize the dynamic processes present in the real dynamic system; to simulate such a model, some computational device is used to trace numerically the implications of these mathematical relations.

Computer Models. A mathematical model that is intended to be simulated on an electronic digital computer is referred to as a "computer model." This type of model is the most widely used and versatile type of simulation model. Because any mathematical model, no matter how large and how complex, in principle can be simulated by an appropriate electronic digital computer, the potential applicability of computer models is limitless. In practice, however, the comprehensiveness of computer models is limited by economic considerations; even the largest and fastest electronic computer does not possess unlimited storage capacity and negligible operating speeds, and the costs of computer time often are substantial. Nonetheless, to a greater extent than is true of other types of simulation models, computer models have demonstrated their usefulness for studying the behavior of complex systems in such diverse areas as management, engineering, the physical sciences, the social sciences, and the military.

Computer models often have many advantages in comparison with other types of simulation or nonsimulation models. Foremost among these is the relative ease with which they can be made to embody considerable amounts of realistic detail, which often means great complexity as well. Adding complexity to non computer models not only will increase the expense and difficulty in deriving the implications of the model, but will often lead to models which, even in principle, cannot be made to yield any conclusions.

Computer models possess four other important advantages. First, because modern electronic digital computers operate at extremely high speeds, it is usually much faster to derive interesting consequences from computer models than from other types of simulation models. Second, because electronic digital computers are extremely accurate, it is not very likely that arithmetical or other simple errors will occur and cause erroneous inferences to be drawn from the model. Third, the results from a computer model are completely reproducible; a given computer program, using the same parameter values and data input, can be run any number of times, and it will always produce precisely the same output. Finally, it is easier to provide a modular character to computer models than to other types of simulation models. This means that one can often first develop and study several component submodels before integrating them into a complete simulation model.

When comparing computer models with conventional mathematical models, it is necessary to consider the extent to which the different types of models describe the corresponding real system. When it is possible directly to solve a formal mathematical model, this provides considerably more information about the corresponding system's behavior than would be provided by using simulation procedures on the same model. Furthermore, it is usually less expensive, when possible, to solve a mathematical model directly, rather than to trace its solution numerically using simulation procedures. It is often the case, however, that a direct mathematical solution cannot be obtained for a computer model. The researcher, in this situation, then must decide whether to use computer simulation techniques to obtain "less general" and "more expensive" results on a complex, realistic, and meaningful model or, in contrast, to simplify the model until he can solve it mathematically and obtain "more general" and "less expensive" results for a simple, unrealistic, and possibly inapplicable model.

Increasingly, in many management areas, the practical answer to this question is turning out to favor computer simulation models, because extremely large amounts of relevant and realistic detail can be incorporated in them. This trend toward the use of computer models should accelerate as management scientists gain more experience and greater ability in working effectively with computer simulation techniques and as electronic digital computers become larger, faster, less expenisve, and more widespread.

REPRESENTATIVE MANAGEMENT APPLICATIONS OF SIMULATION

A representative sample follows of ways in which computer simulation techniques have been employed as an aid in management planning and decision making. Space limitations prevent extensive treatment of any of these cases; the interested reader can find in the Bibliography at the end of this chapter more complete descriptions of these applications and extensive discussions of the procedures that are involved in formulating, programming, or simulating a computer model. The specific examples discussed here have been chosen to suggest some of the diverse methodological ways in which simulation methods can be used in business and industry.

Inventory-control System. Computer simulation was used in developing a system for determining the optimal amounts of inventories for approximately 15,000 items at thirty-six branches of Thompson Products' replacement division.[2] The

[2] Kalman J. Cohen, "Determining the 'Best Possible' Inventory Levels," *Industrial Quality Control*, vol. 15, no. 4, October, 1958, pp. 4–10.

computer model that was found to be appropriate represented sales demand each week for any item as an independently distributed Poisson variable, and replenishment cycle time as a serially correlated, normally distributed random variable. In the inventory system being used, a copy of the sales slip for each part sold in any branch was immediately sent to Cleveland, where the central warehouse invoiced the customer. The Cleveland central warehouse batched all the sales slips from a branch for an entire week and then prepared a replenishment shipment to restore the inventories of all items at a branch, replacing each part that was sold during the week on a one-for-one basis.

A first necessary step in determining the optimal levels for branch inventories was determining the relationship between the level of inventory for a given part at a branch and the lost sales that would be experienced on the item. Monte Carlo simulation procedures were used to enable an electronic computer to "reconstruct" the histories of branch warehouse operations to determine the average levels of lost sales that would result for given inventory levels. An economic model of the relationships among selling prices, costs, sales demand, and the lost sales–inventory level relationships was then developed to determine the optimal inventory levels.

The inventory-control study also involved developing procedures for forecasting item-by-item sales demand at each branch warehouse. Procedures for testing and then implementing the inventory-control system also had to be considered. In particular, the implementation procedures paid important attention to the role of managerial discretion, and it was not intended that the computer would automatically and in all cases establish inventory levels. Information was provided by the inventory-control system to indicate the extent to which out-of-pocket profits would be foregone in the short run by modifying the suggested inventory levels to pursue some long-run management objectives that were not explicitly incorporated in the model.

The use of a computer model in developing and implementing this inventory-control system is fairly typical. Simulation was only one part, although a very important part, of the entire process. Other types of management science techniques were also utilized in this particular study.

Bank Teller Window Schedules. The value of computer models as an aid in developing schedules for bank tellers was first indicated in some research conducted by NABAC (the Association for Bank Audit, Control and Operation). This procedure was subsequently utilized at a great many banks, following the pioneering application efforts of the First National Bank of Minneapolis.[3] In carefully made, empirical studies of customer arrivals and servicing times in various banking offices, it was found to be impossible to make accurate and precise predictions of such events. It proved to be feasible, however, to develop probability distributions that portrayed the uncertainties inherent in customer arrivals, types of transactions, and servicing times. When appropriately simple forms of probability distributions are adequate to describe these characteristics of a real bank, and when comparatively simple queuing disciplines are assumed to describe the behavior of individuals in determining which of several alternative queues to join and when to shift from one queue to another, then the resulting mathematical model can be analytically solved to indicate the average waiting time per customer and the average length of waiting line that will result from specific teller schedules. In more general cases, however, the result-

[3] Richard A. Byerly, "The Use of Mathematical Models in the Analysis and Improvement of Bank Operations," chap. 21 in Kalman J. Cohen and Frederick S. Hammer (eds.), *Analytical Methods in Banking*, Richard D. Irwin, Inc., Homewood, Ill.. 1966.

ing mathematical model is not analytically solvable, and the only feasible procedure then is to fall back on Monte Carlo computer simulation techniques.

Adopting the scheduling procedures implied by such models has led to both improved customer service and reduced teller costs for many banks.   This results from the fact that these banks were previously operating their teller window facilities in an inefficient manner, so that as a result of the computer simulation study, it was simultaneously possible to obtain both improvements in customer service and reductions in teller costs.   Once the results of the model have been applied at a bank, however, management cannot expect further simultaneous improvements along both dimensions.   At some stage, management has to use its own judgment to determine the extent to which increases in customer waiting time and length of waiting line are justified to obtain further teller savings.   Even here, the results of this type of computer simulation are especially valuable, for they indicate in precise quantitative terms the exact nature of the trade-offs that are involved.

Risk Analysis Simulation.   Risk analysis simulation is an approach to capital budgeting which has been operational in a number of major industrial firms.[4]   Although it is a technique readily transferable to many problem areas in banking (specifically, to situations in which a decision is required about a major commitment of funds, the returns on which are fraught with uncertainty), one application focused on its applicability to branch bank location decisions.[5]   In this context, risk analysis simulation was used as a procedure for quantifying and measuring the extent to which uncertainty is present in the determination of the rate of return anticipated from the establishment of a proposed branch bank.

The profitability of a future branch bank can be regarded as depending upon such factors as the market potential of the area it services, the share of this potential market actually tapped by the bank, the total amounts of the bank's deposits and its mix between demand and time deposits, the earnings yields realized and the expense ratios incurred by these deposits, the deposit growth rates that will materialize, and the magnitude of the initially required investment.   Until recently, the most sophisticated analysis of future branch profitability that bankers would make involved obtaining one "best possible estimate" for each of these critical factors and then employing the resulting numbers to compute the rate of return that was to be anticipated if the branch were actually opened.   This distribution is implicit in the estimates of the many critical factors upon which the branch's profitability depends, when these estimates are themselves realistically regarded as probability distributions rather than as "best possible" single values.   Once the distribution of the anticipated rate of return is obtained, meaningful probability statements can be made concerning such important questions as the chance of loss, the range of likely outcomes, and the like.   Accordingly, a more comprehensive understanding of a proposed branch's risk can be obtained, and the quality of branch bank location decisions can be improved.

Simulation to Test the Usefulness of Analytical Techniques.   Another interesting managerial application of computer simulation is its use to test the extent to which an analytical technique will prove profitable in practice.   This has been

[4] David B. Hertz, "Risk Analysis in Capital Investment," *Harvard Business Review,* January–February, 1964, pp. 95–106.   Reprinted as chap. 23 in Cohen and Hammer, *op. cit.*

[5] Kalman J. Cohen, "Risk Analysis and Branch Bank Location Decisions," *Banking: Journal of the American Bankers Association,* vol. 58, no. 8, February, 1966, pp. 53–56.

done with great effectiveness in two management science studies of analytical techniques applicable to consumer installment loans.

In a project that was conducted for the Universal Finance Company of Los Angeles, it was found that statistical techniques were useful in developing numerical credit-scoring systems for installment loan applications.[6]   In a numerical credit-scoring system, points are assigned to each item on a loan application form, the particular number of points depending upon the specific answers given to the questions asked in the application.   A weighted sum of the points received by an application is computed, and the application is then accepted or rejected for a loan depending upon whether this weighted sum is above or below some critical level.   Whether a numerical credit-scoring system proves useful in practice depends, among other things, on the validity of the weights used for each factor.

In the development of a numerical credit-scoring system for the Universal Finance Company, several different statistical techniques were employed to determine the relative weights assigned to the various questions on the application form.   To determine whether any of the resulting scoring systems could be useful, a simulation test was conducted in which each of several potential scoring systems was applied to a fresh sample (that is, a set of data not used in developing any of the weighting systems) of consumer installment loans that previously had been made.   The simulation results indicated, for different possible cutoff scores, the numbers of good and bad loans that would have been eliminated from the sample.   This type of simulation proved to be invaluable not only in enabling management to determine the best set of weights and a cutoff score, but more broadly in showing that the analytical technique in fact had great promise for increasing profits in actual operation.

Because both numerical credit-scoring systems and the intuitive judgments more commonly employed in deciding whether to grant installment loans will inevitably make some errors and extend some loans to people who turn out to be poor credit risks, a problem faced by consumer lending institutions is determining the most profitable way to try to collect a defaulted loan.   An analytical model for this purpose was developed in a study performed for the Bank of America.[7]   This technique employed a quantitative statistical model for determining the cutoff point beyond which continued attempts to obtain collections from a defaulted loan would be more expensive than the expected benefits from future efforts.   Before the model was implemented, a computer simulation study was conducted to determine the results that could be expected from actually adopting these procedures.   The simulation test showed that a potential increase in net profits from defaulted loan collection activities of approximately 33 percent was obtainable.   These results gave management confidence in the new analytical technique, and it was successfully made part of standard operating procedures at the Bank of America.

Simulation as an Aid in Management Training.   The final important managerial application to be considered here is its use as part of a training program for either current or future managers.   The types of simulation models that are employed in this context are more commonly known as "business games."   The interested reader is referred to the following sources for an extended discussion

---

[6] James H. Myers and Edward W. Forgy, "The Development of Numerical Credit Evaluation Systems," *Journal of the American Statistical Association*, vol. 58, no. 303, September, 1963, pp. 799–806.   Reprinted as chap. 6 in Cohen and Hammer, *op. cit.*

[7] Morton Mitchner and Raymond P. Peterson, "An Operations Research Study of the Collection of Defaulted Loans," *Operations Research*, vol. 5, no. 4, August, 1957, pp. 522–545.   Reprinted as chap. 8 in Cohen and Hammer, *op. cit.*

of this topic: Chapter 7 of Section 4 of this Handbook; Kalman J. Cohen, William R. Dill, Alfred A. Kuehn, and Peter R. Winters, *The Carnegie Tech Management Game: An Experiment in Business Education,* Richard D. Irwin, Inc., Homewood, Ill., 1964; and Kalman J. Cohen and Eric Rhenman, "The Role of Management Games in Education and Research," *Management Science,* vol. 7, no. 2, January, 1961.

STATISTICAL CONSIDERATIONS IN SIMULATION

In the past, most management applications of simulation techniques have focused more upon the substantive business issues involved than on some of the statistical issues that should be considered in simulations. Some of these statistical considerations will be briefly indicated: techniques for estimating model parameters, procedures for validating the simulation model, and methods for exploring the model's dynamic properties.

Computer models usually contain large numbers of parameters which must be given specific numeric values before actual simulation runs occur. It is first necessary to recognize that there must be made explicit some criterion of "good" parameters. In particular, this means that some norm must be established by which it is possible to state unambiguously that one set of parameter values is better or worse than a second, alternative set of parameter values. Also involved is some type of search and evaluation procedure for determining which alternative conceivable sets of parameter values should be examined in an attempt to find the best set. Often, standard statistical methods, such as multiple regression analysis or simultaneous-equation econometric estimation techniques, may be used for estimating parameters in simulation models. At other times, direct search procedures such as gradient methods or response function fitting techniques might be required. Many times, especially in connection with simulations intended to solve management decision problems, some type of optimizing algorithm, for example, linear programming, may be used to set parameter values in certain portions of the model. Heuristics from actual business practice may also be used to determine parameter settings in decision-oriented simulation models.

Once all the parameters have been specified in a simulation model, the model is ready to be run. All too often, that is all that is done in actual management applications. It would be much better methodology to attempt to validate the simulation model to determine whether it has a satisfactory degree of correspondence to the real system being modeled. Because a simulation model is used as a basis for predicting the changes that will occur in a real system if it is modified in particular ways, for this type of inductive inference to be valid it is necessary that the simulation model reproduce reasonably well the relevant properties of the real system. There is no way to be confident that this is the case without careful statistical comparisons of the output generated by the simulation model with observed data on the corresponding system.

In validating a simulation model which involves probability distributions as some components, it is generally possible to adopt a probability theory framework for determining correct statistical validation procedures.[8] Some difficulties may

---

[8] Murray A. Geisler, "The Sizes of Simulation Samples Required to Compute Certain Inventory Characteristics with Stated Precision and Confidence," *Management Science,* vol. 10, no. 2, January, 1964, pp. 261–286; and Murray A. Geisler, "A Test of a Statistical Method for Computing Selected Inventory Model Characteristics by Simulation," *Management Science,* vol. 10, no. 4, July, 1964, pp. 709–715.

be introduced into this process by the fact that any simulation model generally produces a wide variety of outputs, and there may not be the same degree of interest in validating them all. Thus, some choices as to which output variables to focus on in the validation process, as well as how and when to aggregate them either temporally or across units, are required. The various outputs from the simulation model may be compared with real world data along many different dimensions: for example, one can make these comparisons in terms of average values of variables, extreme value or other measures of variability of the variables, correlation coefficients, time-series measures, and structural characteristics of the multidimensional outputs as revealed through coefficient estimates from econometric models or principal components analysis.[9]

Once a model has been adequately formulated, its parameters estimated, and the model itself satisfactorily validated, it is generally desirable to devote several simulation runs to exploring the model's dynamic and structural properties. "Dynamic properties" refers to stability considerations, the existence and nature of equilibrium positions, and the responses of the model to various types of artificial forcing functions. In addition to the model's dynamic responses to contrived or artificial forcing functions, one is often interested in determining its responses to exogenous data inputs from the real world. Simulation procedures also can be used to determine the structural properties of the model and the effects of parameter and model changes on structural properties. Also of interest is an attempt to try to generalize from the results of several simulation runs to determine general properties of the model, rather than merely finding out that for specific inputs particular output series will result; that is, repeated simulation runs to explore the properties of the model can be viewed as an attempt inductively to determine general properties of the model's behavior. Finally, when the model is intended to be used as an aid to managerial planning or decision making, part of the process of exploring the model is generally devoted to trying to find ways of improving the model to produce better results in the corresponding real system.

SUMMARY

The survey of representative business applications of computer simulation provided in this chapter has revealed many different ways in which this technique has been useful as an aid in management planning and decision making. The actual case studies reviewed here are intended to be merely illustrative, rather than to be a complete enumeration. Even those few that have been considered, however, indicate that substantial contributions to improvement in management practices can result from judicious application of the simulation methodology.

Computer simulation represents an unparalleled vehicle by means of which we can formulate extremely detailed and highly precise models of business behavior, test the empirical validity of these models, experimentally manipulate the models in ways which would usually be infeasible in real firms, predict the future behavior of existing or redesigned firms, and train people to behave more effectively in business environments. It is clear that many important applications of scientific and quantitative techniques to business planning and decision problems will involve the use of simulation models.

[9] Kalman J. Cohen and Richard M. Cyert, "Computer Models in Dynamic Economics," *Quarterly Journal of Economics*, vol. 75, no. 1, February, 1961, pp. 112–127.

BIBLIOGRAPHY

Beshers, James M. (ed.), *Computer Models in the Analysis of Large-scale Social Systems,* Joint Center for Urban Studies of the Massachusetts Institute of Technology and Harvard University, Cambridge, Mass., 1965.

Conway, R. W., B. M. Johnson, and W. L. Maxwell, "Some Problems of Digital Simulation," *Management Science,* vol. 6, no. 1, October, 1959.

Forrester, Jay W., *Industrial Dynamics,* The M.I.T. Press, Cambridge, Mass., and John Wiley & Sons, Inc., New York, 1961.

Hull, T. E., and A. R. Dobell, "Random Number Generators," *SIAM Review,* vol. 4, no. 3, July, 1962.

Krasnow, Howard S., and Reino Merikallio, "The Past, Present, and Future of General Simulation Languages," *Management Science,* vol. 11, no. 2, November, 1964.

McMillan, Claude, and Richard F. Gonzalez, *Systems Analysis: A Computer Approach to Decision Models,* Richard D. Irwin, Inc., Homewood, Ill., 1965.

Naylor, Thomas H., Joseph L. Balintfy, Donald S. Burdick, and Kong Chu, *Computer Simulation Techniques,* John Wiley & Sons, New York, 1966.

Orcutt, Guy H., Martin Greenberger, John Korbell, and Alice M. Rivlin, *Micro-analysis of Socioeconomic Systems: A Simulation Study,* Harper & Row, Publishers, Incorporated, New York, 1961.

Teichroew, Daniel, and John Francis Lubin, "Computer Simulation—Discussion of the Technique and Comparison of Languages," *Communications of ACM,* vol. 9, no. 10, October, 1966.